THE GREAT SYNAXARISTES OF THE ORTHODOX CHURCH

May

THE GREAT SYNAXARISTES OF THE ORTHODOX CHURCH

May

Translated from the Greek

Holy Apostles Convent
Buena Vista, Colorado

Dormition Skete
Buena Vista, Colorado

Printed in the United States of America

All Saints

Printed with the blessing of the Holy Synod of Bishops
of the Genuine Orthodox Church of America

Library of Congress Control Number: 2006935461
ISBN-13: 978-0-944359-28-0   ISBN-10: 0-944359-28-0
First Edition, October 2006
Second Edition, December 2010
Third Edition, September 2020

Iconography and Art Design: Courtesy of Dormition Skete, Buena Vista, Colorado

TABLE OF CONTENTS FOR THE MAY SYNAXARISTES

MAY 13

MAY 14

MAY 15

MAY 16

MAY 17

MAY 24

MAY 25

MAY 26

MAY 27

MAY 28

MAY 29

MAY 30

MAY 31

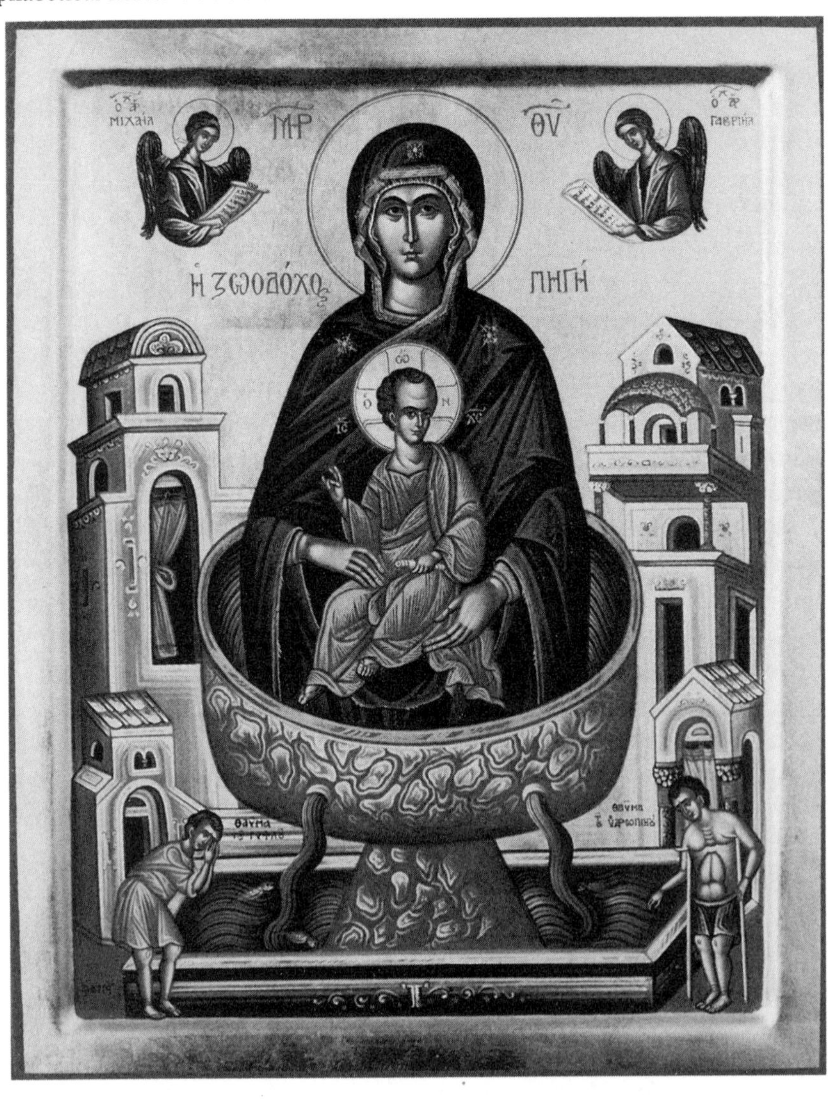

On the 1st of May, the holy Church commemorates the holy Prophet JEREMIAS (Jeremiah).

Prophet Jeremias

Jeremias, the wondrous prophet of the Lord, was sanctified from his mother's womb, as God says of him: "And the word of the Lord came to him (Prophet Jeremias), saying, **'Before I formed thee in the belly, I knew thee; and before thou camest forth from the womb, I sanctified thee; I appointed thee a prophet to the nations** [Jer. 1:4, 5]**.'"**

The prophet's book opens, saying, **"The word of God which came to Jeremias the son of Chelcias, of the priests, who dwelt in Anathoth in the land of Benjamin** [Jer. 1:1]**."** The prophet received a popular name in biblical times, meaning "may the Lord lift up" or "the Lord exalts" (Heb. *yerim-yahu*).

Jeremias was born in about 646 B.C. and hailed from Anathoth, situated 2½ miles northeast of Jerusalem over the shoulder of Scopas, which was a town in Benjamin assigned to the Levites [Jos. 21:18; 1 Chr. 6:80]. According to Alexander Mavrokordatos, in his *Judaica*, Jeremias was a scion of the priestly tribe of Levi and the son of Hilkiah. The prophet lived during the reigns of Josias (Josiah, 640-609 B.C.), Joachaz (Jehoahaz, 609), Joakim (Jehoiakim, 609-598), Jechonias (Joachim or Jehoichin, 598), and Sedekias (Zedekiah, 597-586).

In accordance with the Lord's command, Jeremias was unmarried: **"Thou shalt not take a wife, and there shall be no son born to thee nor daughter in this place** [Jer. 16:2]**."** Blessed Jerome (ca. 342-420) remarks, "He had been sanctified in his mother's womb [Jer. 1:5], and now he was forbidden to take a wife because the captivity was near. Nebuchadnezzar (Nabuchodonosor) is hard at hand; the lion is bestirring himself from his lair. What good will marriage be to me if it is to end in slavery to the haughtiest of kings? What good will little ones be to me if their lot is to be what the prophet sadly describes, **'The tongue of the suckling child cleaves to the roof it its mouth for thirst; the little children ask for bread, and there is none to**

break it to them [Lam. 4:4]**.'"**[1] Saint Chrysostom (ca. 347-407) also says that such evils as never occurred under heaven happened in Israel.[2] What evils were these? **"The hands of tenderhearted women have sodden [boiled] their own children; they became meat for them in the destruction of the daughter of My people** [Lam. 4:10]**."**

Jeremias began his forty year prophetic ministry in 626, from the thirteenth year of Josias to 586 B.C. There are three stages in his ministry, including: (1) the time when Juda was threatened by Assyria and Egypt (727-605 B.C.); (2) when he proclaimed God's judgment of the besieging of Juda by Babylon (605 to 586 B.C.); and, (3) when he ministered after the fall of Juda (586-ca. 580 B.C.). He preached in Jerusalem until the fall of Juda in 586. Afterward, he labored among the survivors in Juda, and much later among those Jews who sought refuge in Egypt [Jer. chaps. 50, 51 LXX; 43-44 KJV].

This grace-filled prophet laments, **"Who will give water to my head, and a fountain of tears to my eyes** [Jer. 9:1]**?"** He was conspicuously marked by his pathos and sympathy with the wretched, as will be heard in both of his books, entitled Jeremias and Lamentations, especially when relating his profound sorrow for his fellow citizens and country that had fallen so miserably.

He was a contemporary of Prophets Sophonias, Abbakoum, Daniel, and Ezekiel. He is placed second among the Four Major Prophets. His book is narrated in fifty-two chapters and his Lamentations in five chapters.

The Greek Septuagint (LXX) and Hebrew Massoretic texts vary in length and arrangement to a greater extent than any other book of the Old Testament. The Septuagint is approximately 2,700 words shorter than the Hebrew. Among the Judaean scrolls there are some fragments which attest to the shorter text. The Greek is nearer to the original text.

The following order may be observed for chapters and verses:[3]

---

[1] Blessed Jerome, "Letter XXII," *The Principal Works of Saint Jerome: The Letters of Jerome,* The Nicene and Post-Nicene Fathers Series, 2nd Ser., Vol. VI, p. 30. [Henceforth, the Series' name will be abbreviated as Nicene, 2nd, with the volume number preceding the page number by a colon.]

[2] Saint John Chrysostom, *Discourses Against Judaizing Christians*, The Fathers of the Church Series, Vol. 68, pp. 8, 119. [Henceforth, the Series' name will be abbreviated as FC, with the volume number preceding the page number by a colon.]

[3] Table showing the order of several chapters and verses in Jeremias, as they appear in the Hebrew and Septuagint respectively, was taken from, *The Septuagint Version of the Old Testament and Apocrypha* (London, UK: Samuel Bagster & Sons Ltd.), p. 971.

In subsequent Scriptural passages, we shall list both cites for the reader's ease and information. In most cases, however, the Septuagint listing is quoted and cited first.

CHAPTERS OF THE HEBREW, VULGATE, & ENGLISH v.	*THE LXX*
25 to v. 14	25 to v. 14.
25 from v. 14 to end	32.
26	33.
27 to v. 19	34.
27 from v. 19 to end	wanting.
28	35.
29	36.
30	37.
31	38.
32	39.
33 to v. 14	40.
33 from v. 14 to end	wanting.
34	41.
35	42.
36	43.
37	44.
38	45.
39 the first 3 verses, and 5 last	46.
39 from v. 3 to 14	wanting.
40	47.
41	48.
42	49.
43	50.
44	51 to v. 31.
45	51 from v. 31 to the end.
46	26.
47	29 first 7 verses.
48 to v. 45	31.
48 from v. 45 to the end	wanting.
49 first 5 verses	30 first 5 verses.
49 from v. 7 to 23	29 from v. 7 to the end.
49 from v. 23 to 28	30 5 last verses.
49 from v. 28 to 34	30 the last 6 verses following v. 5.
49 from v. 34 to the end	25 from v. 13 to the end.
50	27.
51	28.
52	52.

The prophecies concerning the nations, given in chapters 46-51 in the King James Version, are inserted in the Greek text beginning at Chapter 25:14. Even the order within these messages is different. In addition to these variations, there are also some verses in the Greek text that are missing either in whole or in part. We know that the Prophet Baruch,[4] who served as a scribe, recorded Prophet Jeremias' messages.

Prophet Jeremias prophesied among the captive Jews transported to Babylon; and he foretold their freedom. He also prophesied against nations and cities, including Egypt, Philistia, Moab, Ammon, Edom, Damascus, Kedar and Hazor, Elam, and Babylon.

This ever-memorable prophet endured insults, hardships, and bore chains and imprisonment by contemporary false prophets. Almost as a solitary during this tragic period of his nation's history, he exposed immoralities, superficial reforms, and fanatical reliance in the temple structure. When he spoke of the coming destruction of the temple, he incurred the insults and abuse of temple priests [Jer. 20:2]. He was even in danger of his life from his own townsmen [Jer. 11:21], the priests and false prophets of the temple [Jer. 33:8, 9 LXX; 26:8, 9 KJV], the wayward and erratic king, and also the military [Jer. 45:4 LXX; 38:4 KJV].

Nonetheless, he received homage from some of his people. There was also the Ethiopian slave, Abdemelech, who was stirred to help the man of God when the latter was cast into prison [Jer. 45:7 LXX; 38:7 KJV]. The Chaldeans treated Jeremias with consideration, after they released him from the manacles [Jer. 47:1-5 LXX; 40:1-5 KJV]. The Egyptians revered him as a prophet, while he was among them, and long after his repose.

He yearned to flee the discord amid his people and lodge in the wilderness [Jer. 9:2]. He grieved that he was born as some man of strife, at variance with the whole earth [Jer. 15:10]. He cursed the day of his birth [Jer. 20:14], and was pressed to utter that he would by no means **"name the name of the Lord"** and to speak in His name, **"but it was a burning fire flaming in my bone, and I am utterly weakened on all sides, and cannot bear up** [Jer. 20:9]**."**

In Orthodox iconography, the prophet is characterized as being elderly, small in bodily size, and having a beard wide at the top and narrow at the tip.

A History of the Prophet's Message and Actions

When the prophet began to preach, the godly Josias (640-609 B.C.) commenced his reforms to purge the land of idolatry. Jeremias also spoke among this recalcitrant people, urging them to make a genuine repentant return to the Lord. The prophet never departed from his message regarding either the pending destruction of Juda and Jerusalem by a nation from the north or the coming captivity and deportation [Jer. 4:5-9; 6:22-26].

---

[4] Prophet Baruch is commemorated by the holy Church on the 28th of September.

1. The Prophet's Symbolic Actions.

"To speak after the manner of men," says Saint Chrysostom, "means to use human examples....This use of human examples frequently occurs in types also, as when the prophet takes a girdle [Jer. 13:1-9], and goes down to the potter's house [Jer. 18:1-6]."[5] We also have two other early symbolic signs using a broken earthen bottle and a cup of unmixed wine.

A. The Linen Girdle:

"Thus saith the Lord, 'Go and procure for thyself a linen girdle, and put it about thy loins, and let it not be put in water.' So I (Jeremias) procured the girdle according to the word of the Lord, and put it about my loins. And the word of the Lord came to me, saying, 'Take the girdle that is upon thy loins, and arise, and go to the Euphrates, and hide it there in a hole of the rock.' So I went, and hid it by the Euphrates, as the Lord commanded me. And it came to pass after many days, that the Lord said to me, 'Arise, go to the Euphrates, and take thence the girdle, which I commanded thee to hide there.' So I went to the river Euphrates, and dug, and took the girdle out of the place where I had buried it: and behold, it was rotten, utterly good for nothing [Jer. 13:1-7]**."**

"The prophet," says Blessed Jerome, "is sent from Jerusalem to the Euphrates, a river in Mesopotamia (250 miles away), and leaves his girdle to be marred in the Chaldean camp, among the Assyrians hostile to his people [Jer. 13:6,7]."[6]

"And the word of the Lord came to me, saying, 'Thus saith the Lord: "Thus will I mar the pride of Juda, and the pride of Jerusalem; even this great pride of the men that will not hearken to My words, and have gone after strange gods, to serve them and to worship them; and they shall be as this girdle, which can be used for nothing [Jer. 13:8-10]**."'"** Blessed Jerome asks: "Would you know that the saints are as a girdle and the vestment of God? God Himself says to Jeremias: **'For as a girdle cleaves about the loins of a man, so have I caused to cleave to Myself the house of Israel, and the whole house of Juda; that they might be to Me a famous people, and a praise, and a glory: but they did not hearken to Me** [Jer. 13:11]**.'** God's people are as close to Him as a man's clothing is to his body. But because this loincloth, this splendor in which the Lord had been robed, was cast off on the other side of the Pharat, and laid aside in the cleft of a rock and there rotted [Jer. 13:4-12], and was taken into captivity by the Assyrians, what does the Lord do? He is not naked; He cannot be without a loincloth; He cannot be

---

[5] Saint Chrysostom, *Homilies on Galatians*, Ch. III, The Nicene and Post-Nicene Fathers, 1st Ser., XIII:27, 28. [Henceforth, the Series' name will be abbreviated as Nicene, 1st, with the volume number preceding the page number by a colon.]

[6] Blessed Jerome, "Letter XL," Nicene, 2nd Ser., VI:54.

without a covering. Because the first people had been lost, He makes Himself a garment of the Gentiles."[7]

B. The Prophet Goes to the Potter's House [Jer. 18]:

"The word that came from the Lord to Jeremias, saying, 'Arise, and go down to the potter's house, and there thou shalt hear My words.' So I went down to the potter's house, and behold, he was making a vessel on the stones. And the vessel which he was making with his hands fell: so he made it again into another vessel, as it seemed good to him to make it. And the word of the Lord came to me saying, [Jer. 18:1-5].

"'Shall I not be able, O house of Israel, to do to you as this potter? Behold, as the clay of the potter are ye in My hands [Jer. 18:6].'" Saint Paulinus of Nola (353/354-431) explains, "Only the craftsman is master of his own trade, and only the potter has dominion over his clay [cf. Jer. 18:6]. The Lord of all, He Who had made all men, deigned to descend to our world and to take us up in His body; so that with the same skill or power with which He had made us, He could form us anew."[8]

C. The Sign of the Broken Earthen Bottle:

"Then said the Lord to me, 'Go and get an earthen bottle, the work of the potter, and thou shalt bring some of the elders of the people, and of the priests; and thou shalt go forth to the burial-place of the sons of their children, which is at the entrance of the gate of Charsith; and do thou read all these words which I shall speak to thee [Jer. 19:1, 2]....

"'Therefore, behold, the days come,' saith the Lord, 'when this place shall no more be called, "The fall and burial-place of the son of Ennom," but "The burial-place of slaughter" [Jer. 19:6].'" The scene of guilt was chosen as the scene of divine retribution against Israel. In the very place where they looked for help from their idols, that was to be the scene of their own slaughter. The Valley of Hinnom ("Ennom" LXX or also known as "Topheth" KJV) was where the most abominable form of idolatry was practised. Topheth was the center of sacrifices, that is, human sacrifices, to Molech [4 Kgs. (2 Kgs.) 23:10].

"And thou shalt break the bottle in the sight of the men that go forth with thee, and thou shalt say, 'Thus saith the Lord, "Thus will I break in pieces this people, and this city, even as an earthen vessel is broken in pieces which cannot be mended again [Jer. 19:10, 11].'""

---

[7] Idem, "Hom. 26 on Psalm 98(99)1," *1-59 On The Psalms, Vol. 1*, FC, 48:204, 205.

[8] Saint Paulinus, "Letter 12," *Letters of Saint Paulinus of Nola: Letters 1-22, Vol. 1*, Ancient Christian Writers Series, No. 35, p. 107. [Henceforth, the Series' name will be abbreviated as ACW, with the volume number preceding the page number by a colon.]

"Give heed," says Saint Chrysostom, "for earthen vessels when crushed do not permit refashioning, on account of the hardness which was gained by them from the fire. But the fact is that the vessels of the potter are not earthen, but of clay; therefore, also, when they have been distorted, they can easily, by the skill of the artificer, be brought again to a second shape. Thus, when God speaks of an irremediable calamity, He does not say 'vessels of the potter,' but an 'earthen vessel.' Thus in the instance when the prophet wished to teach the Jews that the Lord would deliver up the city to an irremediable calamity, He bade Jeremias take an earthen wine-vessel, and crush it before all the people. But when He wishes to hold out good hopes to them, he brings the prophet to a pottery, and does not show him an earthen vessel, but shows him a vessel of clay, which was in the hands of the potter. When the vessel fell to the ground, the prophet says: 'So he made another vessel, as it seemed good to him to make it. And the word of the Lord came to me, saying, "Shall I not be able, O house of Israel, to do to you as this potter? Behold, as the clay of the potter are ye in My hands [cf. Jer. 18:4, 5]."' It is possible, therefore, for God not only to restore those who are made of clay, through the laver of regeneration, but also to bring back again to their original state, on their careful repentance, those who have received the power of the Spirit even if they have lapsed."[9]

D. The Cup of Unmixed Wine, Judgment Upon the Nations:

"Thus said the Lord God of Israel: 'Take the cup of this unmixed wine from Mine hand, and thou shalt cause all the nations to drink, to whom I send thee. And they shall drink, and vomit, and be mad, because of the sword which I send among them [Jer. 32:15, 16 LXX; 25:15, 16 KJV].'"

Blessed Jerome writes regarding the cup of punishment that is unto healing: "Jeremias received this same cup of foaming wine from the hand of the Lord in order to give drink to Jerusalem and to all the nations round about; and upon drinking of it, they are convulsed and fall to the ground and, with broken pride, lie prostrate unto repentance."[10]

2. King Joakim (Jehoiakim).

With Josias' son, Joakim (609 B.C.), Jeremias also had a public ministry, as demonstrated by his temple address [Jer. chaps. 7 and 33 LXX]. The prophet continued to pray for his people, though the Lord forbade him. Now during the fourth year that Joakim was king of Juda, Jeremias was commanded by God to take a roll of a book, and write upon it all the words which God spoke to him against Jerusalem and Juda and the nations.

[9] Saint Chrysostom, "First Instruction," § 4, *Instructions to Catechumens*, Nicene, 1st Ser., IX:162.

[10] Saint Jerome, "Hom. 60 Psalm 10(11)," *60-96 On The Psalms, Vol. 2*, FC, 57:13.

"Perhaps," said the Lord, **"the house of Juda will hear all the evils which I purpose to do to them, and they may turn from their evil way; and so I will be merciful to their iniquities and sins** [Jer. 43:2, 3 LXX; 36:2, 3 KJV]**."**

So Jeremias called for Baruch, his secretary, and dictated the messages the Lord gave him; and he transcribed the messages on the scroll. Now Jeremias was in prison and unable to enter the temple. He commanded Baruch to go and read the roll, on the fast day, in the ears of the people at the temple. Baruch did all according to Jeremias' command. Present at the reading executed by Baruch was a certain scribe, who later reported to other scribes and the princes what was written in the roll. They called for Baruch who then read it before them, at which point they decided that the king ought to hear him too. The king was apprised of the matter, and he sent Judin to fetch the roll. Judin then read it in the ears of all the princes that stood around the king. Now it was winter and the king sat in his house where there was a fire on the hearth just before him. **"And it came to pass when Judin had read three or four leaves, he cut them off with a penknife, and cast them into the fire that was on the hearth, until the whole roll was consumed in the fire that was on the hearth. And the king and his servants that heard all these words sought not the Lord, and rent not their garments** [Jer. 43:23, 24 LXX; 36:23, 24 KJV]**."** The king then commanded his son to take Baruch and Jeremias, but they were hidden.

The word of the Lord then came to Jeremias: **"Again take thou another roll, and write all the words that were on the roll, which king Joakim has burnt. And thou shalt say, 'Thus saith the Lord: "Thou hast burnt this roll, saying, 'Why hast thou written therein, saying, "The king of Babylon shall certainly come in, and destroy this land, and man and cattle shall fail from off it** [Jer. 43:27-29 LXX; 36:27-29 KJV]**."'"'"** The Lord then said this about Joakim: His descendants shall not sit on David's throne; and when he dies, his body will be cast out in the heat of the day and left in the frost by night. I will visit him, his family, and his servants [Jer. 43:30, 31 LXX; 36:30, 31 KJV].

Jeremias took another scroll and gave it to Baruch. As Jeremias spoke, Baruch wrote on the scroll. **"And there were yet more words added to it like the former** [Jer. 43:32 LXX; 36:32 KJV]**."**

Saint Chrysostom acknowledges that some of the prophets' writings have been lost: "For many of the prophetic writings have been lost; and this fact may one see from the history of the Chronicles [2 Chr. 9:29]. For being negligent, and continually falling into ungodliness, some they suffered to perish and others they themselves burnt up and cut to pieces. The latter event Jeremias relates [Jer. 43:20-32 LXX]. He who composed the fourth book of Kings [4

Kgs. (2 Kgs.) 22:8 ff.] says that after a long time the book of Deuteronomy was hardly found, for it was buried somewhere and lost. But if, when there was no barbarian there, they so betrayed their books, much more when the barbarians had overrun them."[11]

In the fourth year of Joakim's reign [Jer. 25:1], or in the third year according to Babylonian computation [Dan. 1:1], Nebuchadnezzar of Babylon first invaded Juda. Battling for world supremacy, he defeated Pharaoh Neco of Egypt at the Battle of Carchemish (605 B.C.) With the routing of the Egyptians, Jeremias advised his people that it was contrary to God's will to resist the Babylonian king. As a result of this admonition, his message was unpopular among the people. Joakim is characterized as one of Juda's most notorious kings. The Babylonians had made Joakim their vassal and exiled a number of Jewish nobles [4 Kgs. (2 Kgs.) 24:1], including holy Daniel [Dan. 1:1].

Joakim cared nothing for the worship of the true God; and was not troubled by abusing his fellow man. He is characterized in this passage, as follows: **"He builds his house not with justice, and his upper chambers not with judgment. He works by means of his neighbor for nothing and will by no means give him his recompense** [Jer. 22:13]**."** He held back wages, promoted idolatry, and had a hideous record of social injustice in his realm; for he did not judge **"the cause of the afflicted, nor the cause of the poor** [Jer. 22:16]**."**

In 598/597 B.C., Joakim revolted unsuccessfully against Babylon, which compounded the problems of his people. As a result, "the Lord sent against him the bands of the Chaldeans, and the bands of Syria, and the bands of Moab, and the bands of the children of Ammon, and sent them into the land of Juda to prevail against it [4 Kgs. (2 Kgs.) 24:2]." The king, finally, at Jerusalem, died in the eleventh year (598 B.C.) of his unholy rule, as the prophet predicted: **"They shall not bewail him, saying, 'Ah brother!' Neither shall they at all weep for him, saying, 'Alas, Lord!' He shall be buried with the burial of an ass; he shall be dragged roughly along and cast outside the gate of Jerusalem** [Jer. 22:18, 19]**."** During Joakim's reign, the king destroyed the prophet's written prophecies, persecuted him, and imprisoned him under the most appalling conditions [Jer. 45:7-12 LXX; 38:7-12 KJV].

3. The Prophet Conceals the Ark of the Covenant [2 Macc. 1, 2].

It is written that before the burning of the temple of Jerusalem by Nabuzardan (Nebuzaradan), who was the chief magus of Nebuchadnezzar, Prophet Jeremias took the ark of the law and the holy things in the ark. The

[11] Saint Chrysostom, *Homilies on the Gospel of Matthew*, Nicene, 1st Ser., X:58, 59.

prophet took care that they should be placed under a rock in a cave, saying to those standing by, "The Lord traveled from Sinai to the heaven and again He desires to come to Sinai with power and to bestow upon you, believing in Him, a sign of His presence: that all the nations shall worship the Wood."

It is also said that he uttered, "This ark and the tablets therein shall no one bring out of the earth, except Aaron; and no one shall open it—not a priest nor a prophet—save Moses the elect of God. At the universal resurrection, the ark will be the first to be raised up. Since it appeared from out of the earth, God desires to lay it on Mount Sinai. All the saints desire to assemble to it, that is, as many that persevere to come unto the Lord and who flee from the enemy—the devil—who desires to slay them."[12] Then on the top side of the rock which received the ark, Jeremias wrote with his finger the dread and fearful name of God. The letters took form as if they were inscribed with a carving tool and iron. Straightway, a shining and bright cloud overshadowed that name and no one could learn that place; nor was it possible that any should be able to read the name of God from that day.

This rock is in the wilderness where the ark was first constructed by Beseleel, between two mountains wherein is also found the precious relics of Moses and Aaron. Therefore, during the night, light appears, as a cloud, in that place, according to the ancient type, just as the cloud appeared to the Israelites during the night and illuminated them.[13]

It is written in the Second Book of the Maccabees: "When our fathers were led into Persia, the priests that were then devout took the fire of the altar privily, and hid it in an hollow place of a pit without water, where they kept it sure, so that the place was unknown to all men. Now after many years, when it pleased God, Nehemias, being sent from the king of Persia, did send of the posterity of those priests, the ones who had hidden it, to the fire. But when they told us they found no fire, but thick water, he then commanded them to draw it up and to bring it. And when the sacrifices were laid on, Nehemias commanded the priests to sprinkle the wood and the things laid thereupon with the water. When this was done, and the time came that the sun shone, which afore was hid in the cloud, there was a great fire kindled, so that every man marvelled [2 Macc. 1:18-22].

"It is also found in the records that Jeremias the prophet commanded those, the ones who were carried away, to take of the fire as it hath been

---

[12] Prophet Jeremias, May 1st, *The Great Synaxaristes of the Orthodox Church*, 5th ed., Vol. V (Athens, GR: Archim. Matthew Langes, Pub., 1977), p. 14; "The Lives of the Prophets," *The Old Testament Pseudepigrapha*, Vol. 2, ed. by James H. Charlesworth (NY: Doubleday, 1985), p. 388.

[13] *The Great Synaxaristes of the Orthodox Church* (in Greek), pp. 14, 15; taken from the apocryphal book, entitled *Paraleipomena of Jeremias*.

signified. And it is also found how that the prophet, having given them the law, charged them not to forget the commandments of the Lord; and that they should not err in their minds when they see images of silver and gold, with their ornaments. And with such speeches exhorted he them, that the law should not depart from their hearts [2 Macc. 2:1-3].

"It is also contained in the same writing that the prophet, being warned of God, commanded the tabernacle and the ark to go with him, as he went forth into the mountain where Moses climbed up and saw the inheritance of God. And when Jeremias came thither, he found an hollow cave, wherein he laid the tabernacle, and the ark, and the altar of incense; and so he stopped the door [2 Macc. 2:4, 5].

"And some of those that followed him came to mark the way, but they could not find it, which when Jeremias perceived, he blamed them, saying, 'As for that place, it shall be unknown until the time that God should gather His people again together and receive them unto mercy. Then shall the Lord show them these things; and the glory of the Lord shall appear, and the cloud also, as it was shown under Moses, and as when Solomon desired that the place might be honorably sanctified [2 Macc. 2:6-8].'"

The *Great Synaxaristes* (in Greek) identifies the place as Mount Nabav or Nebo, where Moses reposed. It is written that certain ones say that, after the discoveries made by Nehemias, they were "reported in the writings and commentaries of Nehemias. It is also recorded how Nehemias founded a library, gathering together the acts of the kings, of the prophets, and of David, as well as the epistles of the kings concerning the holy gifts [2 Macc. 2:13]."

4. King Jechonias (also known as, Conias or Joachim or Jehoichin).

Joakim was succeeded by his wicked son Jechonias, whom Prophet Jeremias also strenuously denounced [Jer. 22:24-30]. As a result of his father Joakim's revolt against the Babylonians, the son capitulated [4 Kgs. (2 Kgs.) 24:12]. He was exiled to Babylon with many of Juda's upper class, including the Prophet Ezekiel [Ez. 1:2]. The temple was also plundered [4 Kgs. (2 Kgs.) 24:10-16]. Jechonias was a prisoner of the Babylonians for thirty-seven years. He was released from prison by Evialmarodec (Evil-Merodach), son of Nebuchadnezzar. The Babylonian king then changed Jechonias' prison garb and permitted him to eat bread continually before him all the days of his life [4 Kgs. (2 Kgs.) 25:27-30].

"In his case," remarks Saint Hippolytos (ca. 170-ca. 236), "is fulfilled the prophecy of Jeremias, saying, **'As I live,' saith the Lord, 'though Jechonias son of Joakim king of Juda were indeed the seal upon My right hand, thence would I pluck thee; and I will deliver thee into the hands of them that seek thy life, before whom thou art afraid, into the hands of the Chaldeans. And I will cast forth thee, and thy mother that bore thee, into**

Prophet Jeremias

a land where thou wast not born; and there ye shall die. But they shall by no means return to the land which they long for in their souls. Jechonias is dishonored as a good-for-nothing vessel; for he is thrown out and cast forth into a land which he knew not [Jer. 22:24-28].' Thus, the captivity in Babylon befell them after the exodus from Egypt. Most of the people were then transported, and the city was made desolate, and the sanctuary was destroyed, that the word of the Lord might be fulfilled which He spoke by the mouth of the Prophet Jeremias, saying, **'All the land shall be a desolation; and they shall serve among the nations seventy years** [Jer. 25:11].'"[14]

As for this man Jechonias, hear the word of the Lord: **"Write ye this man** (Jechonias) **an outcast: for there shall none of his seed at all grow up to sit on the throne of David, or as a prince yet in Juda** [Jer. 22:28]." Saint Basil the Great (ca. 330-379) records, "On the destruction of Jerusalem by Nebuchadnezzar, the kingdom had been destroyed. There was no longer a hereditary succession of reigns as before....And none of Jechonias' descendants attained to this dignity. Much later, during the return of the captivity with Salathiel and Zorobabel, the government rested to a greater degree with the people, and the sovereignty afterward transferred to the priesthood, on account of the intermingling of the priestly and royal tribes."[15]

Jechonias had seven sons [1 Chr. 3:17], but none succeeded him on the throne. In the Gospel of Saint Matthew, Jesus' genealogy includes Jechonias [Mt. 1:11], but this only shows who the legal father was—not the natural one. The Evangelist Luke traces our incarnate Lord's parental line through Nathan [Lk. 3:31], a son of David, not through Solomon. Zorobabel, a grandson of Jechonias, was governor in Juda (520 B.C.), but he never ruled as king, nor did any other descendent of his. Jechonias' uncle, Sedekias (Zedekiah), reigned

---

[14] Saint Hippolytus, *The Extant Works and Fragments of Hippolytus: Fragments From Commentaries*, Fathers of the Third Century, The Ante-Nicene Fathers Series, Vol. V, pp. 177, 178. [Henceforth, the Series' name will be abbreviated as Ante-Nicene, with the volume number preceding the page number by a colon.]

[15] Saint Basil, "Letter CCXXXVI," Nicene, 2nd Ser., VIII:277.

after him but died before him. Thus Jechonias was the last of the Judaean kings.

"Nevertheless," says Saint Basil, "the tribe of Juda did not fail, until He, for Whom it was foreordained, came. But even He did not sit upon the material throne. The kingdom of Judaea was transferred to Herod, the son of Antipater the Askalonite, and his sons who divided Judaea into four principalities, when Pilate (A.D. 26-36) was procurator and Tiberius (A.D. 14-37) was master of the Roman Empire. It is the indestructible kingdom which Jeremias calls the throne of David on which the Lord sat. Jesus is the expectation of the nations [Gen. 49:10] and not of the smallest division in the world."[16]

Blessed Jerome warns, "It is our sins which make the barbarians strong....Miserable must those Israelites have been compared with whom Nebuchadnezzar was called God's servant [Jer. 27:6, KJV only]. Unhappy, too, are we who are so displeasing to God that He uses the fury of the barbarians to execute His wrath against us."[17]

5. King Sedekias (Zedekiah).

King Sedekias, Jechonias' paternal uncle, who reigned from 597 to 586 B.C., was weak and unsure of himself before his nobles. It was Nebuchadnezzar who set him on the Judaean throne. This puppet-king of the Babylonians, who had sworn fealty in the name of the God of Israel, was opposed by his pro-Egyptian nobles and officials.

Now Paschor, a priest, was appointed chief of the house of the Lord. He heard Jeremias prophesying in the temple courtyard, and smote him. He then cast the prophet into the dungeon, the one by the gate of the upper house that was set apart, which was by the temple. When Paschor removed him from the dungeon, the prophet said, **"The Lord has not called thy name Paschor, but Deportation. For thus saith the Lord, 'Behold, I will give thee up to captivity with all thy friends. And they shall fall by the sword of their enemies; and thine eyes shall see it. And I will give thee and all Juda into the hands of the king of Babylon; and they shall carry them captives, and cut them in pieces with swords....And thou shalt die in Babylon. And there thou and all thy friends shall be buried, to whom thou hast prophesied lies** [Jer. 20:1-6].'"

The prophet bore many trials in his ministry, suffering affliction, dishonor, and evil report. He then utters, **"Thou hast deceived me, O Lord, and I was deceived. Thou hast been strong, and hast prevailed: I am become a laughingstock, I am continually mocked every day** [Jer. 20:7]." Saint Chrysostom explains: "There is also a good deceit; such as many have been deceived by, which one ought not even to call a deceit at all. For this

[16] Ibid.

[17] Blessed Jerome, "Letter LX," Nicene, 2nd Ser., VI:130.

reason Jeremias remarks, **'O Lord, Thou hast deceived me, and I was deceived'**; for such as this one ought not to call a deceit at all. For Jacob also deceived his father [Gen. 27:19-24]; however, that was not a deceit but an œconomy."[18]

"Jeremias," continues Saint Chrysostom, "having borne many temptations, gave in upon these. And when he was reproached, he said, **'The word of the Lord is become a reproach to me and a mockery all my days. Then I said, "I will by no means name the name of the Lord, and I will no more at all speak in His name. But it was as burning fire flaming in my bones; and I am utterly weakened on all sides, and cannot bear up** [Jer. 20:9]**."'**"[19]

Saint Ambrose (ca. 339-397) tells us, "When Prophet Jeremias speaks of the burning fire flaming in his bones, he signifies his receiving the Holy Spirit; for fire was a type of the Holy Spirit."[20]

Saint Isaac the Syrian (d. ca. 700), speaking of delightful hope, says the prophet spoke thus because "hope excites the natural longing in the soul and gives them this cup to drink and makes them drunk."[21]

The prophet continues, **"I have heard the reproach of many gathering round, saying, 'Conspire ye, and let us conspire together against him, even all his friends: watch his intentions, if perhaps he shall be deceived, and we shall prevail against him, and we shall be avenged on him** [Jer. 20:10]**.'"** But the prophet rallies again, and says, **"The Lord was with me as a mighty man of war: therefore they persecuted me, but could not perceive anything against me; they were greatly confounded, for they perceived not their disgrace which shall never be forgotten. O Lord, Who dost prove just deeds and dost understand the reins and hearts, let me see Thy vengeance upon them: for to Thee have I revealed my cause** [Jer. 20:11, 12]**."**

During the fourth year of King Sedekias' reign, Ananias the false prophet spoke to Jeremias when they were both in the temple. In front of the priests and all the people, Ananias claimed to speak in the name of the Lord. He took the yokes from the neck of Jeremias, and broke them in pieces before all the people. He then said, **"I have broken the yoke of the king of Babylon** [Jer. 35:2 LXX; 28:2 KJV]**."** Ananias also presumed to say in the Lord's name that all the vessels of the house of the Lord would be returned to the temple, together with Jechonias and all the captivity. Prophet Jeremias said before the people and the priests that stood by in the temple, **"May the Lord indeed do**

---

[18] Saint Chrysostom, "Hom. VI," *Colossians*, Nicene, 1st Ser., XIII:284.

[19] Idem, "Hom. XII," *Second Corinthians*, Nicene, 1st Ser., XII:338.

[20] Saint Ambrose, *Duties of the Clergy.-Book III*, Nicene, 2nd Ser., X:84.

[21] Saint Isaac the Syrian, "Treatise LXXIV," *Mystical Treatises by Isaac of Nineveh*, translated from Bedjan's Syriac text, by Arent Jan Wensinck, Volume Two, p. 344.

thus....Nevertheless, the prophets that were before me and before you of old also prophesied...concerning war. As for the prophet that has prophesied for peace, when the word has come to pass, they shall know the prophet whom the Lord has sent them in truth [Jer. 35:8, 9 LXX; 28:8,9 KJV]." Then, observing the broken yokes, Jeremias uttered this word of the Lord: **"Thus saith the Lord, 'Thou hast broken the yokes of wood, but I will make instead of them yokes of iron.' For thus said the Lord, 'I have put a yoke of iron on the neck of all the nations, that they may serve the king of Babylon** [Jer. 35:13, 14 LXX; 28:13, 14 KJV].'" Jeremias then said to Ananias that "the Lord hath not sent thee," and that "thou hast caused the people to trust in unrighteousness." Therefore, **"Thus said the Lord, 'Behold, I will cast thee off from the face of the earth: this year thou shalt die.' And so he died in the seventh month** [Jer. 35:15-17 LXX; 28:15-17 KJV]."

Blessed Jerome observes that "Jeremias announced the captivity and was stoned by the people. Ananias, the son of Azzur, for the present, broke the bars of wood but was preparing bars of iron for the future [Jer. 35:13 LXX; 28:13 KJV]. False prophets always promise pleasant things, and they please for a time. Truth is bitter; and they who preach it are filled with bitterness."[22]

The replacement of yokes of iron for the lighter burden of yokes of wood was dealt them. This is because when the lighter affliction was not freely accepted, a graver affliction was allowed to follow. False prophets, such as Ananias, who advocated the casting off the lighter yoke of the deportation, were made to take up the far heavier yoke laid upon them by Nebuchadnezzar. It would have been better for them to have humbled and subjected themselves under God's healing treatment of their disease rather than obstinately refusing the remedy.

"Behold," utters the prophet, **"thus saith the Lord, 'I have set before you the way of life, and the way of death. He that remains in the city shall die by the sword, and by famine; but he that goes over to the Chaldeans that have besieged you, shall live, and his life shall be to him for a spoil, and he shall live. For I have set My face against this city...**[Jer. 21:8-10].'"

6. The Sign of Two Baskets of Figs [Jer. 24:1, 5-10].

After Nebuchadnezzar took Jechonias and the captives to Babylon, Prophet Jeremias writes: **"The Lord showed me two baskets of figs, lying in front of the temple of the Lord. The one basket was full of very good figs, as the early figs; and the other basket was full of very bad figs, which could not be eaten, for their badness** [Jer. 24:1]." The Lord gave the interpretation to the prophet, saying, **"As these good figs, so will I acknowledge the Jews**

[22] Blessed Jerome, *The Principal Works of Saint Jerome: Against Jovianus.-Book II* Nicene, 2nd Ser., VI:415.

that have been carried away captive....And I will fix Mine eyes upon them for good, and I will restore them into this land for good [Jer. 24:5, 6]." The Lord also promised to give them a heart to know Him, and that they shall be to Him a people.

But as for the bad and inedible figs, He said, "**So will I deliver Sedekias king of Juda, and his nobles, and the remnant of Jerusalem, them that are left in this land, and the dwellers of Egypt. And I will cause them to be dispersed into all the kingdoms of the earth, and they shall be for a reproach, and a proverb, and an object of hatred, and a curse, in every place whither I have driven them out. And I will send against them famine, and pestilence, and the sword, until they are consumed from off the land which I gave them** [Jer. 24:8-10]."

The two baskets of figs are not an offering brought to God as first-fruits or tithes. These fruits symbolize the people who appear before God. The very good figs represent the captives now in Chaldea. They included the Prophets Daniel, Ezekiel, and the holy Three Children. The bad figs, those who prided themselves as being preferred to those taken away to Babylon, included the rebellious and stubborn Jews who stayed with King Sedekias.

God looked with favor upon the exiles and indicated that the chastening effect of bondage would be worked to their good. The bad figs were those who challenged the judgment of God and the message of the prophet. If they had yielded and surrendered to their due and just captivity, it could have healed them of their madness for idols. Opposing the will of God and the prophet only brought about their destruction.

Concerning the captivity, the prophet gave them this word from the Lord: "**Build ye houses, and inhabit them, and plant gardens, and eat the fruits thereof; and take ye wives, and beget sons and daughters; and take wives for your sons, and give your daughters to husbands, and be multiplied, and be not diminished. And seek the peace of the land into which I have carried you captive, and ye shall pray to the Lord for the people: for in its peace ye shall have peace....Let not the false prophets that are among you persuade you;...I sent them not. When seventy years shall be on the point of being accomplished at Babylon, I will visit you, and will confirm My words to you, to bring back your people to this place** [Jer. 36:5-10 LXX; 29:5-10 KJV]."

7. The Prophet is Imprisoned.

King Sedekias maintained a close relationship with the Prophet Jeremias and listened to him, but vacillated when it came to protecting Jeremias from the destructive designs of his strong-willed nobles and princes who mistreated the prophet. "**It came to pass, when the host of the Chaldeans had gone up from Jerusalem for fear of the host of Pharaoh, that Jeremias**

went forth from Jerusalem to go into the land of Benjamin, to buy thence a property in the midst of the people. And he was in the gate of Benjamin, and there was a man with whom he lodged, Saruia the son of Selemias, the son of Ananias; and he caught Jeremias, saying, 'Thou art fleeing to the Chaldeans.' And he said, 'It is false; I do not flee to the Chaldeans.' But he hearkened not to him; and Saruia caught Jeremias, and brought him to the princes. And the princes were very angry with Jeremias, and smote him, and sent him into the house of Jonathan the scribe: for they had made this a prison. So Jeremias came into the dungeon and into the cells, and he remained there many days. Then Sedekias sent, and called him; and the king asked him secretly, saying, 'Is there a word from the Lord?' And he said, 'There is: thou shalt be delivered into the hands of the king of Babylon [Jer. 44:11-17 LXX; 37:11-17 KJV]**.'"** Sedekias was vexed that his city should be given into the hands of the king of Babylon. He kept Jeremias in prison, and gave him a loaf a day out of the palace bakery until the bread failed from the city. So Jeremias continued in the court of the prison, and uttered, **"Thus saith the Lord: 'He that remains in this city shall die by the sword, and by the famine; but he that goes out to the Chaldeans shall live, and his soul shall be given him for a found treasure, and he shall live.' For thus saith the Lord: 'This city shall certainly be delivered into the hands of the host of the king of Babylon, and they shall take it** [Jer. 45:2, 3 LXX; 38:2, 3 KJV]**.'"**

Even as the prophet was imprisoned, the host of the king of Babylon had made a rampart against Jerusalem. But in the meantime, Anameel, Jeremias' cousin, came to the prison. He asked Jeremias to buy his field in Anathoth of Benjamin. The prophet understood that this was from God, and he weighed him seventeen shekels of silver and bought the land. In the prison, the purchase was written in a book and seals with the testimony of witnesses, and given to Baruch who was instructed to keep it in an earthen vessel for many days. Jeremias then uttered, **"Thus saith the Lord, 'There shall yet be bought fields and houses and vineyards in this land** [Jer. 39:15 LXX; 32:15 KJV]**.'"** For God said to the prophet that **"as I have brought upon this people all these great evils, so will I bring upon them all the good things which I pronounced upon them. There shall yet be fields bought in this land; for I will turn their captivity** [Jer. 39:42-44 LXX; 32:42-44 KJV]**."** Saint Chrysostom, commenting upon the prophet's imprisonment, writes: "The righteous, when they are in tribulations and in bonds, are then especially more energetic; for to suffer anything for Christ's sake is the sweetest of all consolation."[23]

[23] Saint Chrysostom, "Hom. VIII," *Ephesians*, Nicene, 1st Ser., XIII:94.

Some of the officers heard what Jeremias prophesied, and they complained to the king. "Let that man, we pray thee, be slain; for he weakens the hands not only of the fighting men that are left in the city but also of all the people." Unable to resist them, Sedekias said, "Behold, he is in your hands." They took Jeremias and cast him into the dungeon of the king's son, which was in the court of the prison. And they let him down into the pit, where there was no water but mire [cf. Jer. 45:1-6 LXX; 38:1-6 KJV].

The Ethiopian eunuch, Abdemelech, who was in the king's household, learned that Jeremias was set inside a deep and muddy pit. He went before the king, and said, "Thou hast done evil in what thou hast done to slay this man with hunger; for there is no more bread in the city." Sedekias then said, "Take with thee thirty men, and bring Jeremias out of the dungeon before he dies." Abdemelech took the men and went into the underground part of the palace, and took from there some old rags and ropes. He then threw down the rags to Jeremias, saying, "Put these under the ropes." The prophet did so, and they drew him out with the ropes, but he remained in the court of the prison [cf. Jer. 45:7-12 LXX; 38:7-13 KJV].

Sedekias then said to the prophet, "I will ask thee a question, and I pray thee hide nothing from me." Jeremias replied, "If I tell thee, wilt thou not certainly put me to death? And if I give thee counsel, thou wilt not at all hearken to me." But the king swore that he would not deliver him up to his men. Jeremias then told Sedekias to give himself up to the captains of the king of Babylon, in order to save himself and his household, and to prevent the city from being burned. If he refused, he would not escape and the city would be burned with fire [cf. Jer. 45:14-18 LXX; 38:14-18 KJV]. Sedekias, however, disclosed his fear that the Chaldeans would deliver him up to the Jews who had gone over to them, and they would mock him. Jeremias assured him that the Chaldeans would not do this; and again he urged him to listen. "Let no man know these words," said the king, "and thou shalt not die. If the princes hear that I have spoken to thee, tell them that thou didst bring supplication before me that thou not be sent back to the prison to die." The princes indeed came to interrogate Jeremias, but he told them according to all those words which the king commanded him. They kept their peace, and Jeremias remained in the prison until the time when Jerusalem was taken [cf. Jer. 45:26-28 LXX; 38:26-28 KJV].

8. The City is Besieged.

In the fourth year of Sedekias' reign, the king plotted rebellion against Babylon. He made a confederacy with the kings of Edom, Moab, Ammon, Tyre, and Sidon [Jer. 34:3-11 LXX; 27:3-11 KJV]. The prophet denounced the scheme which ultimately was brought to nought. In the ninth year of his reign (588 B.C.), Sedekias conspired with Pharaoh Hophra (Apries) against

Nebuchadnezzar. Babylon retaliated by invading Juda. The city fell in the summer of 586 B.C.[24] During the siege, the prophet continued to press Sedekias to surrender.[25]

Saint Hippolytos comments on Sedekias' reign: "After making agreement with Nebuchadnezzar by oath and treaty, he revolted against him. Sedekias then went over to Pharaoh, king of Egypt. And in the tenth year of Nebuchadnezzar, the latter came against him from the land of the Chaldeans. He surrounded Jerusalem with a stockade and completely shut it up. In this way the larger number of them perished by famine, while others perished by the sword or were taken prisoners. The city was burned with fire, and the temple and the wall were destroyed. The army of the Chaldeans then seized all the treasure that was found in the house of the Lord, and all the vessels of gold and silver, and all the brass. Nabuzardan, chief of the slaughterers (that is, the chief cook), carried them to Babylon. Then the army of the Chaldeans pursued Sedekias himself, as he fled by night along with seven hundred men. But the Chaldeans surprised him in Jericho, and brought him to the king of Babylon at Reblatha. And the king, in wrath, pronounced judgment upon Sedekias, because he had violated the oath of the Lord, and the agreement he had made with him. He slew Sedekias' sons before his face, and then he put out Sedekias' eyes. He then cast him into chains of iron, and carried him to Babylon; and there he remained grinding at the mill until the day of his death. And when he died, they took his body and cast it behind the wall of Nineve."[26]

Saint Chrysostom recounts the siege, saying, "Nebuchadnezzar and all his host came against Jerusalem. They pitched against it and built a wall against it round about....And there was no bread for the people to eat, and the city was broken up [cf. 4 Kgs. (2 Kgs.) 25:1-4]. God, indeed, at once from the first day, might have delivered them up into the hands of their enemies, but He permitted that they should first be wasted for the space of three years and experience a most distressing siege; to the end that, during this interval, being humbled by the terror of the forces without or the famine that oppressed the city within, they might compel the king, however unwillingly, to submit to the barbarian, and some alleviation might be obtained for the sin committed.

"But when God did not prevail with the king by this address—for Sedekias remained in his sin and transgression—God delivered up the city, displaying at once His own clemency and the ingratitude of that king. And entering in with the utmost ease, it is written that those with the captain of the guard 'burnt the house of the Lord, and the king's house, and the houses of Jerusalem—even every great house; and they overthrew the walls of Jerusalem

[24] 4 Kgs. (2 Kgs.) 24:20-25:7; 2 Chr. 36:16; Jer. 46:1-3 LXX.

[25] Jer. 21:1-10; 41:1-5; 44:3-10, 16, 17; 45:14-23.

[26] Saint Hippolytus, *The Extant Works and Fragments of Hippolytus*, loc. cit.

[cf. 4 Kgs. (2 Kgs.) 25:9, 10].' And everywhere there was the fire of the barbarian.

"'And the captain of the guard carried away the rest of the people that were left in the city, and the fugitives that fell away to the king of Babylon [cf. Jer. 39:9 KJV only].' And 'the Chaldeans broke up the pillars of brass that were in the house of the Lord, and the bases and the brazen sea. They took away the pots, flesh-hooks, bowls, censers, and all the vessels of brass. They also laid hold of the firepans, and all the golden and silver bowls. Moreover, Nabuzardan took away the two pillars, and the bases, and the sea which Solomon had made in the house of the Lord. And they took away Seraias the chief priest, and Sophonias the second priest, and the three keepers of the door. And out of the city they took a eunuch who was over the men of war, and five men that were in the king's presence, and the secretary of the commander-in-chief, and threescore men. And Nabuzardan took them and brought them to the king of Babylon, and he smote them [cf. 4 Kgs. (2 Kgs.) 25:13-20].'"[27]

In the eleventh year of Sedekias' reign, Nebuchadnezzar appointed Godolias as governor of Juda. In the meantime, Nabuzardan, the captain of the guard, removed Jeremias' manacles from his hands and released him, giving him leave to depart Rama. Nabuzardan said to him, "The Lord thy God has pronounced all these evils upon this place, and the Lord has done it, because ye sinned against Him, and hearkened not to His voice." The captain then gave the prophet two options, saying, "If it seems good to thee to go with me to Babylon, I will set my eyes upon thee. But if not, depart. Go to Godolias, whom the king of Babylon has appointed governor over Juda, and dwell with him in the midst of the people of Juda, to whatsoever place seems good." Nabuzardan then gave him presents and let him go. Jeremias departed and went to Godolias, and dwelt with those people left in the land [cf. Jer. 47:1-6 LXX; 40:1-6 KJV].

Blessed Jerome observes that "when all were captured, and even the vessels of the temple were plundered by the king of Babylon, Jeremias alone was liberated by the enemy. He knew not the insults of captivity, and was supported by the conquerors. And Nebuchadnezzar, though he gave Nabuzardan no charge concerning the Holy of Holies, did give him charge concerning Jeremias. For that is the true temple of God, and that is the Holy of Holies, which is consecrated to the Lord by pure virginity."[28]

Saint Gregory the Great (ca. 540-604) points out that "Nabuzardan, the chief of the cooks, throws down the walls of Jerusalem, because, when the

---

[27] Saint Chrysostom, "Hom. XIX," *Homilies on the Statues*, Nicene, 1st Ser., IX:478, 469.

[28] Blessed Jerome, *Against Jovianus.-Book I*, Nicene, 2nd Ser., VI:371.

belly is distended with gluttony, the virtues of the soul are destroyed through lechery."[29]

Now this Godolias had but a short rule, and was assassinated by Ishmael, of the seed royal [Jer. 48:2 LXX; 41:2 KJV]. Fearing reprisals, the survivors were bent on fleeing into Egypt. The remnant of the Jews at Mizpah, against the prophet's pleas, chose to find refuge from the Babylonians in Egypt [Jer. 50:4 LXX; 43:4 KJV].

9. Flight Into Egypt.

Juda now went in search of Egypt, but was only to be overwhelmed by the Assyrians. "By 'Egypt,'" expounds Saint Dorotheos of Gaza (early 6th C.), "the fathers understand the bodily inclination to be at rest, which teaches us to set our minds on pleasure and soft living. By 'Assyrians,' they understand passionate engrossing thoughts which trouble and confuse the mind and fill it with unclean images; and, furthermore, such thoughts carry the unwilling mind forcefully toward sinful acts. If, therefore, a man willingly gives himself up to bodily pleasures, he will of necessity be led unwillingly by the Assyrians and forced to serve Nebuchadnezzar. Knowing this, the prophet was troubled and kept saying to them, 'Do not go down to Egypt. What are you doing, miserable wretches? Humble yourselves, bow your shoulders and work for yourselves under the king of Babylon and go on occupying the land of your fathers.' And again he encouraged them, saying, 'Do not be afraid before his face, for we have God with us, to deliver us out of his hands [cf. Jer. 49:11 LXX; 42:11 KJV].'

"Then he prophesied all the affliction that would come upon them if they disobeyed God. For he said, 'If you go to Egypt, you shall be in a wilderness at the mercy of everyone for abuse and cursing.' But they replied, 'We do not want to occupy this land. But we do want to go down to Egypt, where we shall not see anymore war or hear the sound of the trumpet; and we shall not hunger for bread.' And they went down and willingly became Pharaoh's slaves. But soon they were taken forcefully by the Assyrians and made their unwilling slaves.

"Fix your attention on what I have said. If a man humbles himself before God and bears the yoke of his trial and affliction with thanksgiving, and puts up a little fight, the help of God will deliver him. But if he flees labor and goes after bodily pleasures, then he is necessarily led into the land of the Egyptians and, without wishing it, becomes their slave. The prophet then says to the people, 'Pray for the life of Nebuchadnezzar, because his life is your salvation [cf. Bar. 1:11, 12].' Nebuchadnezzar stands for someone who neither

---

[29] Saint Gregory the Great, *The Book of Pastoral Rule*, Ch. XIX, Nicene, 2nd Ser., XII:43.

underrates the value of the affliction that comes to him from temptation nor kicks against it, but he bears it humbly as something due to him."[30]

Prophet Jeremias told them that they shall perish by sword and famine, for the Lord said, **"As My wrath has dropped upon the inhabitants of Jerusalem, so shall My wrath drop upon you, when ye have entered into Egypt. And ye shall be a desolation, and under the power of others, and a curse and a reproach. And ye shall no more see this place** [Jer. 49:18 LXX; 42:18 KJV]**."** The men shouted, **"It is false, the Lord has not sent thee** [Jer. 50:2 LXX; 43:2 KJV]**."** And they refused to hearken. The leaders then took all the remnant of Juda—men, women, and children—and went into Egypt. Prophet Jeremias was taken also to Taphnas of Egypt [Jer. 50:7 LXX; 43:7 KJV], which in the Greek tongue was named Dafnas (Daphnae or Tell Dafana), in lower Egypt, the Delta.[31] He was also accompanied by the Prophet Baruch, his disciple and faithful amanuensis. In Egypt, the prophet predicted Nebuchadnezzar's conquest of that land [Jer. 50:8-13 LXX; 43:8-13 KJV] and he prophesied against the remnant in Egypt [Jer. 50:11 LXX; 43:11 KJV].

"And the word of the Lord came to Jeremias in Taphnas, saying, 'Take thee great stones, and hide them in the entrance, at the gate of the house of Pharaoh in Taphnas, in the sight of the men of Juda. And thou shalt say, "Thus hath the Lord spoken: 'Behold, I will send, and will bring Nebuchadnezzar king of Babylon, and he shall place his throne upon these stones which thou hast hidden; and he shall lift up weapons against them. And he shall enter in, and smite the land of Egypt, delivering some for death to death, and some for captivity to captivity, and some for the sword to the sword. And he shall kindle a fire in the houses of their gods, and shall burn them; and he shall carry them away captives. And he shall search the land of Egypt, as a shepherd searches his garment; and he shall go forth in peace. And he shall break to pieces the pillars of Heliopolis that are in On, and shall burn their houses with fire [Jer. 50:8-13 LXX; 43:8-13 KJV]**.'"'"**

This prophecy, based on the prophet's symbolic action, indicates that the stones shall form the basis for the throne, which the king of Babylon will set up in front of the palace of the king of Egypt at Taphnas. Pharaoh's dominion shall crumble, but the throne which Nebuchadnezzar shall set up rests

---

[30] Saint Dorotheos of Gaza, *Discourses and Sayings*, No. 33, Cistercian Studies Series, pp. 195, 196.

[31] 30°52′N 32°10′E. Saint Hippolytus (ca. 170-ca. 236), Bishop of Rome, also makes mention that the prophet was carried with the remnant that was left after the deportation of the people to Babylon, to Egypt, and dwelt in Taphnas (Taphnae). He confirms that while prophesying there, the latter was stoned to death by the people. See Saint Hippolytus, *The Extant Works and Fragments of Hippolytus*, Ante-Nicene, V:191.

on large stones, betokening his mighty and durable rule. With his entry, each shall receive their appointed lot. Nebuchadnezzar will torch the Egyptians' temples and carry off their idols. Moreover, as effortlessly as a shepherd in a field wraps himself in his cloak, so shall Nebuchadnezzar easily take hold of Egypt. And he shall throw it about him as one would a light garment, that he may thus be dressed, as it were, with the booty, and leave the land without being thwarted as victor.[32]

The Stoning of the Prophet Jeremias

10. The Martyrdom of Prophet Jeremias.

Saint Chrysostom relates that when the Judaeans had resorted to Egypt, God allowed them. "Nevertheless, it was not required of them to desert to irreligion as well as to Egypt [Jer. 51:8 LXX; 44:8 KJV]. We hear: 'The word came to Jeremias for all the Jews dwelling in the land of Egypt, and for those settled in Magdolo and in Taphnas, and in the land of Pathura, saying, "Why do ye provoke Me with the works of your hands, to burn incense to other gods in the land of Egypt?...Have ye forgotten the sins of your fathers [cf. Jer. 51:1, 7-9 LXX; 44:1, 7-9 KJV]?"'

"Seeing that they would not comply, God sent the prophet along with them, so that they might not after all suffer total wreck. For since they did not follow the Lord when He called, the Lord followed them to discipline them. He did so in order to hinder their being hurried further into vice—even as does a father who, full of affection for a child that takes all treatment in the same peevish way, conducts him about everywhere with himself and follows him about. This was the reason why He sent not Jeremias only into Egypt, but also

[32] The demolition of the famous temple of the Sun at Heliopolis at On is another indication of Egypt's submission to the power of Nebuchadnezzar. House of the Sun is the Hebrew rendering of the Egyptian *Pe-râ*, the name of the city called On [Gen. 41:45]. It lays northeast of Cairo, near the modern village of Matarieh. It was renowned for its grandiose temple dedicated to Râ, their sun-god. Though the Egyptian king is not identified by Jeremias here, according to his message elsewhere [Jer. 51:30 LXX; 44:30 KJV], it is Pharaoh Uaphres (Hophra). C. F. Keil and F. Delitzsch, *Commentary on the Old Testament, Jeremiah, Lamentations*, 1st ed., Vol. 8, p. 165.

Ezekiel into Babylon; and they did not refuse to go. For when they found their Master loved the people exceedingly, they continued themselves to do so likewise....For it was for the people of the Jews that Jeremias has composed Lamentations in writing. And when the general of the Persians had given Jeremias liberty to dwell securely and with perfect freedom, wherever he pleased, what did he instead prefer? Jeremias preferred, above dwelling at home, the affliction of the people and their hard durance in a strange land."[33]

A large group of Judaeans, at one time, who were living in southern Egypt, met together. There were among them multitudes of women who were burning incense to other gods, and their husbands knew it [Jer. 51:15 LXX; 44:15 KJV]. All these people spoke to Jeremias, saying, **"As for the word which thou hast spoken to us in the name of the Lord, we will not hearken to thee. For we will surely perform every word that shall proceed out of our mouth, to burn incense to the queen of heaven, and to pour drink-offerings to her, as we and our fathers have done, and our kings and princes, in the cities of Juda, and in the streets of Jerusalem** [Jer. 51:16, 17 LXX; 44:16, 17 KJV]**."** They told Jeremias that at that time they had plenty of food and prospered. However, now that they have stopped making sacrifices to the queen goddess and pouring out drink offerings to her, they have been brought low and consumed by famine and the sword [Jer. 51:16-19 LXX; 44:16-19 KJV].

The prophet asked the people, "Did not the Lord remember the incense which ye burned?...And the Lord could no longer bear you, because of the wickedness of your doings, and because of your abominations which ye wrought? And so your land became a desolation and a waste, and a curse, as at this day, because of your burning incense, and because of the things wherein ye sinned against the Lord. And ye have not hearkened to the voice of the Lord, and have not walked in His ordinances, and in His law, and in His testimonies; and so these evils have come upon you [cf. Jer. 51:20-23 LXX; 44:20-23 KJV]."

"The inspired prophets," writes Saint Chrysostom, "foretold what would happen to the Jews, so that they would ascribe none of the events to idols, but would believe that both punishments and blessings always come from God: the punishment came for their sins, and the blessings because of God's love and kindness."[34]

Jeremias urged them not to rely on the support and might of the Egyptians, but to trust in the loving-kindness of God toward man. Now the prophet continued to prophesy in that place for four years, until he was stoned by the people of Israel who fled into Egypt seeking refuge. Dying as a result,

---

[33] Saint Chrysostom, "Hom. XIV," *Romans*, Nicene, 1st Ser., XI:448.

[34] Idem, "Discourse V," *Discourses Against Judaizing Christians*, FC, 68:111.

he was buried in an area of the palace of Pharaoh, because the Egyptians reverenced him.

The world in Jeremias' day was in upheaval, which included five epochal events: (1) the dissolution of the Assyrian Empire after the death of Ashurbanipal (669-ca. 630 B.C.); (2) the fall of the empire (612 B.C.); (3) the emergence of the Babylonian Empire under the Chaldeans; (4) the demise of Egypt (Assyria's confederate) by the Chaldeans and Medes at Carchemish (605 B.C.); and, (5) the fall of Jerusalem with the destruction of Solomon's Temple (587 B.C.).

Egypt Remembers the Prophet

Now Egypt glorified and honored Prophet Jeremias, because they were recipients of benefits through him. By his prayer, the prophet slew asps which were destroying them. Moreover, he also slew the wild creatures which were found inside the waters of Egypt. There were, in particular, those beasts called *efoth* by the Egyptians, but the Greeks named them crocodiles.

While in Egypt, the prophet spoke to the priests of that place foretelling a sign: in the future, the idols of Egypt shall be shaken and cast to the ground by the Child, the one Savior, Who would be born of the Virgin inside a manger. The pagan priests, far from scoffing at these words, believed the prophet. They, on account of this, deified the Virgin and the Infant lying within the manger, and worshipped Him. Later, when King Ptolemy inquired of the Egyptians wherefore they had this custom, they answered, "This mystery was an ancestral tradition that was handed down to our fathers from a righteous prophet." Then they added, "We patiently await for the fulfillment of these words."[35]

According to *The Great Synaxaristes* (in Greek), Alexander the Great (d. 323 B.C.) visited the tomb of Jeremias. Learning more about the Hebrew prophet's life, Alexander esteemed him and translated his relics from that spot in Egypt to his self-built city of Alexandria. The relics, however, were not kept intact in one place, but spread about to all the boundaries of that city. On account of this, verily, all the asps were driven out. However, Alexander, in the meantime, brought in from the Greek city of Argos of Pelasgikon in Thessaly another kind of serpent called argolas. It was his intention that upon transferring the Thessalian serpents to the rivers of Egypt that they would slay the indigenous asps. Notwithstanding, the relics of Prophet Jeremias not only slew the indigenous asps but also the imported Thessalian ones.

---

[35] *The Great Synaxaristes* (in Greek), pp. 11-16. The *Synaxarion of Constantinople* and the imperial *Menologion* of the 11th C., also have Jeremias announce to the Egyptian priests the fall of their idols and the birth of the Savior in the manger. F. Halkin, *Saints moines d'Orient* (London, 1973) in *The Oxford Dictionary of Byzantium*, Alexander P. Kazhdan, editor-in-chief (NY, NY: Oxford University Press, 1991), s.v. "Jeremiah."

Later, many Christians took recourse to the prophet's tomb and received healing from him; in fact, dust from his tomb was taken as an antidote against snake bites.

The Christ-like Sufferings of the Prophet

When compared to our Lord Jesus Christ, one cannot fail to notice how many similarities exist between our incarnate Lord Jesus and Prophet Jeremias. So striking are some of the parallels that when Jesus asked His disciples, "Whom do the people say that I the Son of Man am?" they said, "Some say John the Baptist, and other Elias, and others Jeremias or one of the prophets [Mt. 16:13, 14]." The historical setting, where Jerusalem is about to fall and the temple destroyed, coincides. They both lived during a time when their brethren were immersed in a religion of formalism. Both had a message for their brethren and for the world. Both used figures and types in their messages. Both came from a high tradition. Jeremias from a priest-prophetic background, and the incarnate Christ from the Davidic line and priestly line (from his maternal grandmother Anna).

Both Jesus and Jeremias condemned the commercialism of temple worship: **"Is My house, whereon My name is called, a den of robbers in your eyes** [Jer. 7:11]**?"** And Jesus said unto them, "It hath been written, 'My house shall be called a house of prayer'; but ye made it a den of robbers [Mt. 21:13]." Both were accused of political treason, and were tried, prosecuted, and imprisoned. Both foretold the destruction of the temple: **"Therefore I also will do to the house whereon My name is called, wherein ye trust...**[Jer. 7:14]**."** And Jesus, answering, said unto one of His disciples, "Seest thou these great buildings? By no means shall a stone be left upon a stone which surely shall not be put down [Mk. 13:2]." Two great pending catastrophes would destroy Jerusalem: both Nebuchadnezzar and Titus' destruction of Jerusalem and its temple.

Both Jeremias and Jesus wept over Jerusalem: **"Who will give water to my head, and a fountain of tears to my eyes? Then would I weep for this my people day and night, even for the slain of the daughter of my people** [Jer. 9:1]**."** And when Jesus was come near, "He saw the city and wept over it [Lk. 19:41]."

Both condemned the religious leaders of their day. Both were rejected by their kin: **"For even thy brethren and the house of thy father, even these have dealt treacherously with thee** [Jer. 12:6]**."** And Jesus "came to His own, and His own received Him not [Jn. 1:11]." Both were tenderhearted and loved Israel. Both knew ostracism: **"Woe is me, my mother! Thou hast brought me forth as some man of strife, and at variance with the whole earth** [Jer. 15:10]**."** And, **"From this time on, many out of His disciples went away to the things left behind, and no longer walked about with Him.**

Then said Jesus to the twelve, 'Ye do not also wish to go away, do ye [Jn. 6:66, 67]**?'"**

The Prophet's Calling [Jer. 1]

1. The Prophet is Known Before Birth.

"And the word of the Lord came to him, saying, 'Before I formed thee in the belly, I knew thee; and before thou camest forth from the womb, I sanctified thee; I appointed thee a prophet to the nations [Jer. 1:4, 5]**.'"**

Saint Irenaeos (ca. 130-ca. 200), Bishop of Lyons, identifies "the Logos of God" as He Who "forms us in the womb."[36] Saint Ambrose contends that this verse "proves that men were in being before they were born....What testimony can we have stronger than the case of this great prophet, who was sanctified before he was born and was known before he was shaped?"[37]

In another exegetical work, Saint Ambrose applies this passage to the two begettings of Christ: His divine generation before all worlds, being begotten of the Father before all ages, and that one according to the flesh; in other words, that according to the divinity and that according to the flesh. "The virgin womb of Mary, which brought forth for us the Lord Jesus, the Father speaks of through the Prophet Jeremias: **'Before I formed Thee in the womb, I knew Thee; before Thou wast born I dedicated Thee** [Jer. 1:5]**.'** Therefore the prophet showed that there was a twofold nature in Christ, the latter from a virgin, but in such a way that Christ was not deprived of His divinity when He was born from a virgin and was in a body."[38]

2. The Prophet Acknowledges His Inability.

"And I said, 'O Being, Master, Lord (ὁ Ὢν, Δέσποτα, Κύριε), **behold, I know not how to speak, for I am a child** [Jer. 1:6]**.'"** Note how the prophet addresses the Deity with the name given in answer to Moses' question, "They will ask me, 'What is His name?' What shall I say to them?" And God spoke to Moses, saying, "I am the Being....Thus shalt thou say to the children of Israel, 'The Being has sent me to you [Ex. 3:14, 15].'"

Considering the prophet's readiness to the divine calling, Saint Gregory the Theologian (ca. 329/330-ca. 390), Patriarch of Constantinople (380-381), says, "Jeremias was afraid of his youth [Jer. 1:6], and did not venture to prophesy until he had received from God a promise and power beyond his years."[39]

---

[36] Saint Irenaeus (Irenaeos), *Irenaeus Against Heresies*, Ch. XV, Ante-Nicene, I:543.

[37] Saint Ambrose, *Of the Christian Faith-Book.-IV*, Nicene, 2nd Ser., X:277.

[38] Idem, *Seven Exegetical Works: The Patriarchs*, FC, 65:268, 269.

[39] Saint Gregory Nazianzen (the Theologian), "Oration 3," *Orations*, Nicene, 2nd Ser., VII:227.

"Therefore, you see," says Saint Chrysostom, "they (the prophets) had power either to speak or to refrain from speaking. For they were not bound by necessity, but were honored with a privilege. For this cause,...Jeremias excused himself [Jer. 1:6]. And God thrusts them not on by compulsion, but advising, exhorting, threatening, but not darkening their mind; for to cause distraction and madness and great darkness is the proper work of a demon. But it is God's work to illuminate and with consideration to teach things needful."[40]

Saint Gregory the Great writes: "It does not behoove anyone to contradict what Jeremias and Daniel, as boys, perceived by the Spirit of prophecy."[41] He describes the prophet's fear and refusal. "Jeremias humbly pleads that he should not be sent, saying, 'Ah, Lord God! Behold I cannot speak: for I am a child [cf. Jer. 1:6].'...Jeremias longed to cleave sedulously to the love of his Creator through a contemplative life, and remonstrated against being sent to preach. He did not wish to lose the gains of silent contemplation....Therefore, since it is very difficult for any to be sure that he has been cleansed, it is safer to decline the office of preaching—though it should not be declined pertinaciously against the supernal Will."[42] His continuing desire for solitude is borne out even later when he utters, **"Who would give me a most distant lodge in the wilderness, that I might leave my people and depart from them** [Jer. 9:2]?" He, daily, renounced the present world, and said as much: **"I have not been weary of following Thee, nor have I desired the day of man; Thou knowest** [Jer. 17:16]."

3. The Prophet's Work.

"Behold, I have appointed thee this day over nations and over kingdoms, to root out, and to pull down, and to destroy, and to rebuild, and to plant [Jer. 1:10]."

"Unless the Prophet Jeremias," says Saint Gregory the Great, "first destroyed wrong things, he could not profitably build right things; unless he plucked out of the hearts of his hearers the thorns of vain love, he would certainly plant to no purpose the words of holy preaching."[43]

4. The Parable of the Almond Tree, the Prophet's Preaching.

"And the word of the Lord came to me, saying, 'What seest thou?' And I said, 'A rod of an almond tree.' And the Lord said to me, 'Thou hast well seen: for I have watched over My words to perform them [Jer. 1:11, 12].'"

---

[40] Saint Chrysostom, "Hom. XXIX," *First Corinthians*, Nicene, 1st Ser., XII:170.

[41] Saint Gregory the Great (the Dialogist), "Hom. II," *The Homilies of Saint Gregory the Great On the Book of the Prophet Ezekiel*, p. 23.

[42] Idem, *Pastoral Rule*, Ch. VII, Nicene, 2nd Ser., XII:5.

[43] Ibid., Ch. XXXIV, Nicene, 2nd Ser., XII:66, 67.

The rod of the almond tree is a confirmatory token. Its significance is this: The prophet is asked what he sees; after responding, he is given a divine word. "I am watching My word, to carry it out." It is necessary to understand the Hebrew word play which cannot be conveyed in the translation. In response to the initial question, Jeremias says he sees a *shaqed* (almond); God responds that He is *shoqed* (watching). Thus, the word play intimates that the tree and the divine watching are interrelated. This is an indication of the swift fulfillment of His word, much like the almond bough with its bright pink blossoms flowering in January and bearing fruit in March. Its green leaves are the token of an early spring, rising out of winter. The name of the tree means "the wakeful tree" or "the watcher" or the tree "that hastens to awake," since it precedes other trees out of their winter's sleep.[44]

Saint Ambrose makes this point: "So the prophet is bidden to take an almond rod, because the fruit of this tree is bitter in its rind, hard in its shell, and inside it is pleasant, that after its likeness the prophet should not fear to proclaim harsh things. Likewise also the priest; for his teaching, though for a time it may seem bitter to some—and like Aaron's rod be long laid up in the ears of dissemblers—yet after a time, when it is thought to have dried up, it blossoms."[45]

5. A Caldron of Fire, Judgment upon Iniquity.

"And the word of the Lord came to me a second time, saying, 'What seest thou?' And I said, 'A caldron on the fire: and the face of it from the north.' And the Lord said to me, 'From the north shall flame forth evils upon all the inhabitants of the land. For, behold, I call together all the kingdoms of the earth from the north,' saith the Lord, 'and they shall come, and shall set each one his throne at the entrance of the gates of Jerusalem, and against all the walls round about her, and against all the cities of Juda. And I will speak to them in judgment, concerning all their iniquity, forasmuch as they have forsaken Me, and sacrificed to strange gods, and worshipped the works of their own hand [Jer. 1:13-16]**.'"** The seething pot has its face turned from the north, and is at the point of emptying out its scalding contents toward the south, that is Juda. Blessed Jerome says, "The devil is, as it were, the Lord's torturer. They who do not walk to God in justice are given over to the devil.... What this means is this: I give sinners over to the devil so that tortured by him they may be converted to Me. Jeremias says of this: **'What seest thou?' And I said, 'A caldron on the fire** [Jer.

[44] C. F. Keil and F. Delitzsch, *Commentary*, 8:42, 43; Craigie, Kelley, and Drinkard, *Jeremiah 1-25*, Word Biblical Commentary (Waco, TX: Word Books, Pub., 1991), p. 16; and Dr. Herbert Lockyer, *All the Parables of the Bible* (Grand Rapids, MI: Zondervan Publishing House, n.d.), 26:53.

[45] Saint Ambrose, "Letter XLI," Nicene, 2nd Ser., X:445, 446.

1:13].'...Great mercy, a great mystery! Pieces of meat are put into a caldron that the heart of man may be melted and he may learn that it is the Lord."[46]

6. The Prophet is Made Strong.

"**Behold, I have made thee this day as a strong city, and as a brazen wall, strong against all the kings of Juda, and the princes thereof, and the people of the land** [Jer. 1:18]."

Though all the world is at war with him, Prophet Jeremias would be made as a brazen wall. Blessed Jerome says, "The Lord says this to the prophets,...to the end that they should not be afraid of the insults of the people, but should by the sternness of their looks decompose the effrontery of those who sneered at them."[47] The prophet is also told later, "**'They shall fight against thee; but they shall by no means prevail against thee; because I am with thee, to deliver thee,' saith the Lord** [Jer. 1:19]."

Saint Chrysostom then applies these words to the Father speaking of the Son. "And though Jeremias would be as a brazen pillar, and as a wall to one nation only, this Man (Jesus) would be in every part of the world."[48]

Prophet Jeremias' Messages of Warning to His People

Prophet Jeremias loved his people deeply in spite of their sins, and has been called "the weeping prophet." The Prophet "Jeremias," says Saint Ambrose, "knew that penitence was a great remedy, which he, in his Lamentations, took up for Jerusalem."[49] "**Mine eyes shall pour down torrents of water, for the destruction of the daughter of my people** [Lam. 3:48]."

The prophet says, "**I am pained in my bowels, my bowels, and the sensitive powers of my heart** [Jer. 4:19]." Saint Gregory the Great says, "Truly, in holy Writ, 'belly' is sometimes written instead of 'mind,' as it is also said through Jeremias [Jer. 4:19]. But because he spoke of his spiritual and not his physical belly, he added, 'The senses of my heart are troubled within me.' Nor did it pertain to the salvation of the people if the prophet were to proclaim that his physical belly pained him. But he felt pain in his belly who perceived affliction of the mind."[50]

The prophet's announcements contained warnings against idolatry and Israel's infidelities with many lovers, yet God is willing to have His prediction of judgment fail if they should return to Him.

---

[46] Saint Jerome, "Hom. 34, Psalm 107(108)," *1-59 On The Psalms, Vol. 1*, FC, 48:250, 251.

[47] Idem, "Letter LXVI," Nicene, 2nd Ser., VI:136, 137.

[48] Saint Chrysostom, "Hom. LIV," *Matthew*, Nicene, 1st Ser., X:334.

[49] Saint Ambrose, *Concerning Repentance, Book II*, Ch. VI, Nicene, 2nd Ser., X:351.

[50] Saint Gregory the Great, "Hom. X," *On the Book of the Prophet Ezekiel*, p. 111.

1. Against Idolatry [Jer. 2:9-13].

A. Prophet Jeremias chides his people who have changed their glory:

"Therefore I will yet plead with you, and will plead with your children's children. For go to the isles of the Chettians, and see; and send to Kedar, and observe accurately, and see if such things have been done [Jer. 2:9, 10].

"See if the nations will change their gods, though they are not gods: but My people have changed their glory, for that from which they shall not be profited [Jer. 2:11]."

Saint Chrysostom says he means this: "Those who worship idols and serve demons are so unshaken in their errors that they choose not to abandon them nor desert them for the truth. But you, who worship the true God, have cast aside the religion of your fathers and have gone over to strange ways of worship. You did not show the same firmness in regard to the truth that the idolaters did in regard to their error...He did not say, 'You have changed your God,' for God does not change. But he did say, 'You have changed your glory. You did no harm to Me,' says God, 'because no harm has come to Me, but you did dishonor yourselves. You did not make My glory less, but you did diminish your own.'"[51]

Continuing, Saint Chrysostom says, "For since you are not persuaded out of the Scriptures, I am compelled to shame you by them that are without."[52] For, "Kedar was a nomad tribe of the Syrian desert. Kittim refers to a Phoenician colony in Cyprus. The two names represent east and west."[53] In fact, "He even sends us oftentimes to the irrational creatures: 'Go to the ant, thou sluggard, and emulate her ways,' and 'go forth to the bee [Prov. 6:6-8].'"[54]

Moreover, "Everywhere," says Saint Chrysostom, "God condescends. And what wonder? For He permitted opinions erroneous, and unworthy of Himself, to prevail, as that...He delighted in sacrifices, which is far from His nature. He utters words at variance with His declarations of Himself, and many such things. For He nowhere considers His own dignity, but always what will be profitable to us. And if a father considers not his own dignity, but talks lispingly with his children and calls their meat and drink not by their Greek names, but by some childish and barbarous words, much more does God. Even in reproving He condescends, as when He speaks by the prophet, 'Hath a

---

[51] Saint John Chrysostom, "Discourse IV," *Against Judaizing Christians*, FC, 68:79, 80.

[52] Idem, "Hom. XVII," *Matthew*, Nicene, 1st Ser., X:122.

[53] Idem, *Against Judaizing Christians*, FC, 68:79, note 24.

[54] Idem, "Hom. XVII," *Matthew*, Nicene, 1st Ser., X: loc. cit.

nation changed their gods [cf. Jer. 2:11]?' And in every part of Scripture there are instances of His condescension both in words and actions."[55]

B. "'The heaven is amazed at this, and is very exceedingly horror-struck,' saith the Lord [Jer. 2:12]."

Saint Basil says this verse "describes astonishment in heaven at the tidings of the unholy deeds of the people."[56]

C. "For My people have committed two faults, and evils [Jer. 2:13]."

The two faults or "double sin [Jer. 2:13]," according to Saint Dionysios the Areopagite (1st C.), are "first by not knowing how we offend and, secondly, by justifying ourselves on our own account and by thinking we see what in fact we do not see. Heaven is amazed at this [Jer. 2:12]."[57]

2. Outside Worship.

"They have forsaken Me, the fountain of water of life, and hewn out for themselves broken cisterns, which will not be able to hold water [Jer. 2:13]."

A. Baptism Abroad:

Saint Irenaeos alerts those outside of the Church, saying, "For where the Church is, there is the Spirit of God; and where the Spirit of God is, there is the Church, and every kind of grace; and the Spirit is truth. Those, therefore, who do not partake of Him, are neither nourished into life from the Mother's breasts nor do they enjoy that most limpid fountain which issues from the body of Christ; but they dig for themselves broken cisterns [Jer. 2:13] out of earthly trenches, and drink putrid water out of the mire, fleeing from the faith of the Church lest they should be convicted, and rejecting the Spirit that they may not be instructed."[58]

Saint Cyprian (d. 258), Bishop of Carthage, applies this passage to holy Baptism, and warns, "No one can be baptized abroad outside the Church, since there is one Baptism appointed in the holy Church. And it is written in the words of the Lord: **'They have forsaken Me, the fountain of water of life, and hewn out for themselves broken cisterns, which will not be able to hold water** [Jer. 2:13].'"[59]

B. Empty Idols:

Saint Aphrahat (early 4th C.) identifies the broken cisterns as the idols, and remarks, "They forsook Him, and worshipped idols, as Jeremias said

---

[55] Idem, "Hom. III," *Titus*, Nicene, 1st Ser., XIII:529.

[56] Saint Basil, *On the Spirit*, Ch. XIII, Nicene, 2nd Ser., VIII:19.

[57] Pseudo-Dionysius, "Letter 8," *The Complete Works: The Letters*, trans. by C. Luibheid with P. Rorem (New York, NY: Paulist Press, 1987), p. 276.

[58] Saint Irenaeus, *Against Heresies*, Bk. III, Ch. XXIV(1), Ante-Nicene, I:458.

[59] Saint Cyprian, "Epistle LXIX," *The Epistles of Cyprian*, Ante-Nicene, V: 375, 376.

concerning them [Jer. 2:10-13]. For the broken cisterns are the fear of images and idols."[60]

3. Against Apostasy and Rebelliousness [Jer. 2:20, 21, 27, 30; 5:3].

A. The Yoke of Idolatry:

"For of old thou hast broken thy yoke, and plucked asunder thy bands; and thou hast said, 'I will not serve Thee; but going upon every high hill, and under every shady tree, there will I indulge my fornication [Jer. 2:20].**'"**

Saint Chrysostom reminds us of our Savior's words, "'Take up My yoke upon you and learn from Me, for I am meek and humble in heart; and ye shall find rest to your souls. For My yoke is good and My burden is light [Mt. 11:29, 30].' Nonetheless," he says, "they failed to take up the yoke because of the stiffness of their necks. And not only did they fail to take it up but also they broke it and destroyed it. For Jeremias said, 'Long ago you broke your yoke and burst your bonds [cf. Jer. 2:20].'"[61]

B. A Bitter Vine of Evil:

"Yet I planted thee a fruitful vine, entirely of the right sort: how art thou a strange vine turned to bitterness [Jer. 2:21]**."**

Saint Kyril of Jerusalem (ca. 315-386) says, "The planting was good, but the fruit of set purpose was evil. Therefore, the planter is blameless, but the vine shall be burnt with fire since it was planted for good but its product was evil with malice aforethought."[62]

C. Their Denial and Impenitence [Jer. 2:27, 30; 5:3].

So enamored were they with their idol madness that the prophet utters, **"They said to a stock, 'Thou art my father,' and to a stone, 'Thou hast begotten me'; and they have turned their backs to Me, and not their faces; yet in the time of their afflictions they will say, 'Arise, and save us** [Jer.2:27].**'"** Blessed Jerome writes: "He means they would not turn toward God in penitence; but in the hardness of their hearts turned their backs upon Him to insult Him."[63]

"In vain have I smitten your children; ye have not received correction [Jer. 2:30].**"** And, elsewhere, he laments, **"O Lord, Thou hast scourged them, but they have not grieved; Thou hast consumed them, but they would not receive correction. They have made their faces harder than a rock; and they would not return** [Jer. 5:3].**"** Saint Cyprian reflects

---

[60] Saint Aphrahat, "Demonstration XXI—Of Persecution," *Select Demonstrations*, Nicene, 2nd Ser., XIII:395.

[61] Saint John Chrysostom, "Discourse I," *Against Judaizing Christians*, FC, 68:7.

[62] Saint Cyril (Kyril) of Jerusalem, "Catechesis II," *The Works of Saint Cyril of Jerusalem, Vol. 1*, FC, 61:96.

[63] Blessed Jerome, "Letter CXXII," Nicene, 2nd Ser., VI:226.

sorrowfully, "Lo, stripes are inflicted from God, and there is no fear of God. Lo, blows and scourges from above are not wanting, and there is no trembling, no fear. What if even no such rebuke as that interfered in human affairs? How much greater still would be the audacity in men, if it were secure in the impunity of their crimes!"[64]

Saint John Cassian (ca. 360-435), in a conference with Abbot Theodore, speaks of the trials of the incorrigible. "The Lord thus laments that to no purpose has He applied this salutary cleansing by fire to those who are hardened in their sins, in the person of Jerusalem crusted all over with the rust of her sins."[65]

Saint Aphrahat enumerates for us the tribulations of Israel: "They were made to serve in Egypt for two hundred and twenty-five years. And the Canaanites made Israel serve in the days of Barak and Deborah. The Moabites ruled over them in the days of Ehud, the Ammonites in the days of Jephthah, the Philistines in the days of Samson, and also in the days of Eli and of Samuel the prophet, the Edomites in the days of Ahab, and the Assyrians in the days of Hezekias. The king of Babylon uprooted them from their place and dispersed them. And after being tried and persecuted much, they did not amend. So God said to them: **'In vain have I smitten your children; ye have not received correction** [Jer. 2:30]**.'**"[66]

4. Their Impudence and God's Long-Suffering [Jer. 3:1, 3, 6-8, 20]**.**

A. "'Thou hast gone awhoring with many shepherds, and hast returned to Me,' saith the Lord [Jer. 3:1]**."**

Saint Gregory the Great writes, "Gather how great is our wickedness if we return not, even after transgression, seeing that, when transgressing, we are spared with so great pity. Or what pardon is there for the wicked from Him Who even after our sin ceases not to call us?"[67]

"Thou hadst a whore's face; thou didst become shameless toward all [Jer. 3:3]**."** Saint Gregory the Great says, "Here the Lord openly upbraids the impudent people of the Jews."[68]

B. "And the Lord said to me in the days of Josias the king, 'Hast thou seen what things the house of Israel had done to Me? They have gone on every high mountain, and under every shady tree, and have committed fornication there [Jer. 3:6]**.**

---

[64] Saint Cyprian, "Treatise V," *The Treatises of Cyprian*, Ante-Nicene, V:459.

[65] Saint John Cassian, "Conference of Abbot Theodore," Ch. XI, *The Works of John Cassian: Conferences and Institutes*, Nicene, 2nd Ser., XI:358.

[66] Saint Aphrahat, "Demonstration XXI—Of Persecution," § 7, Nicene, 2nd Ser., XIII: loc. cit.

[67] Saint Gregory the Great, *Pastoral Rule*, Ch. XXVIII, Nicene, 2nd Ser., XII:58, 59.

[68] Ibid., Ch. VII, Nicene, 2nd Ser., XIII:28.

"'And I said after she had committed all these acts of fornication, "Turn again to Me." Yet she returned not. And faithless Juda saw her faithlessness [Jer. 3:7].

"'And I saw that for all the sins of which she was convicted, wherein the house of Israel committed adultery, and I put her away, and gave into her hands a bill of divorcement, yet faithless Juda feared not, but went, and herself also committed fornication [Jer. 3:8]....

"'But as a wife acts treacherously against her husband, so has the house of Israel dealt treacherously against Me,' saith the Lord [Jer. 3:20]."

"She," writes Saint Chrysostom, "is a woman beloved, but who had despised Him that loved her. She is now on the point of being punished, and yet He pleads, **'Turn again to Me** [Jer. 3:7].'"[69] Elsewhere he counsels, "The evils we have once perpetrated cannot provoke Him so much as our being unwilling to make any change in the future. For to sin may be a merely human failing, but to continue in the same sin ceases to be human and becomes altogether devilish."[70]

Saint Gregory the Great writes: "The people of Israel deserted almighty God, refusing to return, and accepted the bill of divorce....But her sister, Juda, since she too saw the people of Israel sent away in their passions, herself also kindled with the impurity of fornication. Because she saw the adulteress flourish in her perversity, she herself did not fear to commit worse sins and to withdraw from her union with the Lord, as from the marriage bed of her lawful husband. Thus, it is needful that we consider each and every sinner the more wretched when we see them abandoned in their sin without scourge."[71]

5. How I Find You, I Shall Judge You [Jer. 18:7-10, 22:10].

A. "If I should pronounce a decree upon a nation, or upon a kingdom, to cut them off, and to destroy them, and that nation should turn from all their sins, then will I repent of the evils which I purposed to do to them. And if I should pronounce a decree upon a nation and kingdom, to rebuild and to plant it, and they do evil before Me, so as not to hearken to My voice, then will I repent of the good which I spoke of, to do it to them [Jer. 18:7-10]."

"For God even preferred that His own prediction should fall to the ground, so that the city should not fall," declares Saint Chrysostom.[72] Continuing elsewhere, he adds, "For in order that neither at the denunciations

---

[69] Saint Chrysostom, "Hom. LXXIV," *Matthew*, Nicene, 1st Ser., X:447.
[70] Idem, *Letters to the Fallen Theodore*, Nicene, 1st Ser., IX:106.
[71] Saint Gregory the Great, "Hom. XII," *On the Book of the Prophet Ezekiel*, pp. 148, 149.
[72] Saint Chrysostom, *Concerning the Statues*, Nicene, 1st Ser., IX:376, 377.

of punishment any men should despair, and become more hardened, nor by the promises of good things be rendered causelessly more remiss, He remedies both these evils."[73]

B. "Weep not for the dead, nor lament for him; weep bitterly for him that goes away; for he shall return no more, nor see his native land [Jer. 22:10]**."**

Blessed Jerome says that "the prophet laments over his impenitent people....Weep rather for those who, by reason of their crimes and sins, go away from the Church. Though they suffer condemnation for their faults, yet shall they no more return to it. It is in this sense that the prophet speaks to ministers of the Church, calling them its walls and towers, and saying to each in turn, **'Ye walls of Sion, pour down tears like torrents day and night** [Lam. 2:18]**.'** In this way it is prophetically implied that you will fulfill the apostolic precept: 'Be rejoicing with those who rejoice, and be weeping with those who weep [Rom. 12:15].'"[74]

6. The False Prophets [Jer. 23:16, 17, 30, 32]**.**

A. "Thus saith the Lord Almighty, 'Hearken not to the words of the prophets: for they frame a vain vision for themselves; they speak from their own heart, and not from the mouth of the Lord. They say to them that reject the word of the Lord, "There shall be peace to you"; and to all that walk after their own lusts, and to every one that walks in the error of his heart, they have said, "No evil shall come upon thee [Jer. 23:16, 17]**."'"**

The prophet reproves the false prophets who were lulling the people into a false security. Saint Cyprian, Bishop of Carthage, writes: "Whatever is established by human madness, so that the divine plan is violated, is adulterous, impious, and sacrilegious. Withdraw far, flee, from the contagion of men of this kind and avoid their speech as cancer and pestilence."[75]

B. "'Behold, I am therefore against the prophets,' saith the Lord God, 'that steal My words every one from his neighbor [Jer. 23:30]**....**

"'Therefore, behold, I am against the prophets that prophesy false dreams, and have not told them truly, and have caused My people to err by their lies, and by their errors; yet I sent them not, and commanded them not; therefore, they shall not profit this people at all [Jer. 23:32]**.'"**

Saint Cyprian admonishes: "For he who steals from evangelical truth the words and deeds of our Lord, and does not do what the Lord did, both corrupts and adulterates the divine teaching as it is written in Jeremias."[76]

---

[73] Idem, "Hom. LXIV," *Matthew*, Nicene, 1st Ser., X:392.

[74] Blessed Jerome, "Letter CXXII," Nicene, 2nd Ser., VI:226.

[75] Saint Cyprian, "Letter 43," *Letters 1-81*, FC, 51:109.

[76] Idem, "Letter 63," FC, 51:214.

By the same token, Saint John Chrysostom forewarns those who would take scriptural passages out of context, saying, "Not only should a text not be taken out of context but also it should actually be proposed in its entirety, with nothing added; for many people bandy about passages from the Scriptures, drawing out distorted interpretations."[77]

The Message of True Circumcision

[Jer. 4:4; 6:10; 9:25, 26]

Prophet Jeremias then speaks to his people about circumcision. The first circumcision of the flesh shall be made void, and the second circumcision of the Spirit is promised. **"Circumcise yourselves to God, and circumcise your hardness of heart, ye men of Juda, and inhabitants of Jerusalem, lest My wrath go forth as fire, and burn, and there be none to quench it, because of the evil of your pursuits** [Jer. 4:4]**."** "The circumcision of the body," says Saint Chrysostom, "is no longer superior....Thus, Jeremias rightly brought forward, **'For ye shall circumcise the foreskins of your hearts** [Jer. 4:4]**.'**...Now if you must seek circumcision, Paul says that you will find it among us 'who worship God in spirit [Phil. 3:3],' that is, who worship spiritually."[78]

Saint Kyril of Jerusalem says, "By the likeness of our faith,...we become the adopted sons of Abraham; and consequent upon our faith, like him, we receive the spiritual seal being circumcised by the Holy Spirit through the laver of Baptism. This is not in the foreskin of the body, but in the heart, according to the words of Jeremias [Jer. 4:4] and according to the apostle: 'In Whom also ye were circumcised with a circumcision made without hands, in the putting off of the body of the sins of the flesh in the circumcision of the Christ, having been buried with Him in the Baptism, in which also ye were raised with Him through faith in the energy of God, Who raised Him from the dead [Col. 2: 11, 12].'"[79]

"To whom shall I speak, and testify, that he may hearken? Behold, thine ears are uncircumcised, and they shall not be able to hear: behold, the word of the Lord is become to them a reproach, they will not at all desire it [Jer. 6:10]**."** Saint Chrysostom says, "So deaf are all men become even to the very instruction of virtue, and thence are they filled with an abundance of evils."[80]

"'Behold, the days come,' saith the Lord, 'when I will visit upon all the circumcised their uncircumcision; on Egypt, and on Idumea, and on

---

[77] Saint John Chrysostom, "Homily on Jeremiah 10.23," *Old Testament Homilies*, p. 11.

[78] Idem, "Hom. X," *Philippians*, Nicene, 1st Ser., XIII:230.

[79] Saint Cyril of Jerusalem, "Catechesis V," FC, 61:142, 143.

[80] Saint Chrysostom, "Hom. XXIII," *First Corinthians*, Nicene, 1st Ser., XII:135.

Edom, and on the children of Ammon, and on the children of Moab, and on everyone that shaves his face round about, even them that dwell in the wilderness; for all the Gentiles are uncircumcised in flesh, and all the house of Israel are uncircumcised in their hearts [Jer. 9:25, 26]**.'"**

The Martyrdom of the Prophet Jeremias

"Do you see," Saint Justin Martyr (ca. 100-ca. 165) asks Trypho the Jew, "how God does not mean this circumcision which is given for a sign? For it is of no use to the Egyptians, or the sons of Moab, or the sons of Edom. But though a man be a Scythian or a Persian, if he has the knowledge of God and of His Christ, and keeps the everlasting decrees, he is circumcised with the good and useful circumcision, and is a friend of God; and God rejoices in his gifts and offerings."[81]

The Temple and Sacrifices

[Jer. 7:4; 11, 21-24; 11:15; 12:9; 16:9; Lam 4:1]

1. Dependency on the Temple.

"Trust not in yourselves with lying words, for they shall not profit you at all, saying, 'It is the temple of the Lord, the temple of the Lord [Jer. 7:4]**.'"**

"The Jews," states Saint Chrysostom, "greatly prided themselves on the temple and the tabernacle. They, therefore, said, 'The temple of the Lord, the temple of the Lord, the temple of the Lord [cf. Jer. 7:4].' For nowhere else in the earth was such a temple constructed as this, either for costliness, or beauty, or anything else. For God Who ordained it, commanded that it should be made with great magnificence, because they also were more attracted and urged on by material things. For it had bricks of gold in the walls; and any one who wishes may learn this in the Third Book of Kings,...and how many talents of gold were then expended."[82]

In a discourse, Saint Chrysostom asks, "Do you wish to learn that, together with the sacrifices and the musical instruments and the festivals and

---

[81] Saint Justin Martyr, *Dialogue with Trypho*, Ch. XXVIII, Ante-Nicene, I:208.

[82] Saint Chrysostom, "Hom. XVII," *Hebrews*, Nicene, 1st Ser., XIV:446.

the incense, God also rejects the temple because of those who enter it? He showed this mostly by His deeds, when He gave it over to barbarian hands, and later when He utterly destroyed it. But even before its destruction, through His prophet, He shouted aloud and said, 'Put not your trust in deceitful words, for it will not help you when you say, "This is the temple of the Lord [cf. Jer. 7:4]!"' What the prophet says is that the temple does not make holy those who gather there, but those who gather there make the temple holy. If the temple did not help at a time when the cherubim and the ark were there, much less will it help now that all those things are gone, now that God's rejection is complete, now that there is greater ground for enmity."[83]

2. A Den of Robbers.

"'Is My house, whereon My name is called, a den of robbers in your eyes? And, behold, I have seen it,' saith the Lord [Jer. 7:11]**."**

Speaking of the magnificence of this temple, Saint Chrysostom tells us that "the fashioning was not the work of human art, but proceeded from the wisdom of God, where the walls were on every side resplendent with much gold, and where, in surpassing excellence, costliness of material and perfection of art met together, and demonstrated that there was no other temple like this upon the earth! Yea rather, not only the perfection of art but also the wisdom of God assisted in that building. For Solomon had learned all, not intuitively and from himself but from God. And having received the design of it from the heavens, he then marked it out and erected it. Nevertheless, this temple, thus beautiful and marvellous and sacred, when those who used it were corrupted, was so dishonored, despised, and profaned that even before the captivity it was called **'a den of robbers, a cave of hyenas** [Jer. 7:11]'; and afterward it was delivered over to hands that were barbarous, polluted, and profane!"[84]

3. God Did Not Command Offerings.

"Thus saith the Lord, 'Gather your whole-burnt offerings with your meat-offerings, and eat flesh. For I spoke not to your fathers, and commanded them not in the day wherein I brought them up out of the land of Egypt, concerning whole-burnt-offerings and sacrifice. But I commanded them this thing, saying, "Hear ye My voice, and I will be to you a God, and ye shall be to Me a people: and walk ye in all My ways, which I shall command you, that it may be well with you." But they hearkened not to Me, and their ear gave no heed, but they walked in the imaginations of their evil heart, and went backward, and not forward [Jer. 7:21-24]**.'"**

Saint Irenaeos reiterates: "God points out that it was not for this that He led them out of Egypt, that they might offer sacrifice to Him, but that,

[83] Idem, "Discourse I," *Against Judaizing Christians*, FC, 68:28.
[84] Idem, "Hom. XVII," *Homilies on the Statues*, Nicene, 1st Ser., IX:456.

forgetting the idolatry of the Egyptians, they might be able to hear the voice of the Lord, which was to them salvation and glory."[85]

4. Flesh Offerings for Wickedness.

"Why has My beloved wrought abomination in My house? Will prayers and holy offerings (flesh) take away thy wickedness from thee, or shalt thou escape by these things [Jer. 11:15]?"

Saint Irenaeos repeats that "the fat and the fat flesh shall not take away from thee thy transgressions. 'This is the fast which I have chosen,' saith the Lord. 'Loose every band of wickedness, dissolve the connections of violent agreements, give rest to those that are shaken, and cancel every unjust document. Deal thy bread to the hungry willingly, and lead into thy house the roofless stranger. If thou hast seen the naked, cover him; and thou shalt not despise those of thine own flesh and blood.'"[86]

Saint Basil says, "Indeed, not everyone's gift is acceptable to God but only his who brings it with a pure heart. For Scripture says, 'Vows paid out of the hire of a harlot are not pure [Prov. 19:13],' and Jeremias says, **'Will prayers and holy offerings (flesh) take away thy wickedness from thee, or shalt thou escape by these things** [Jer. 11:15]?'"[87]

5. A Hyena's Cave.

"Is not My inheritance to Me a hyena's cave...[Jer. 12:9]?"

Blessed Jerome informs us that "the hyena is a beast that devours blood, that is lured by bodies, and that always wanders in the night, never in the day. Its only pleasure is in the cadavers of the dead and in dogs. It wants to kill those who guard the house. They say, too, that by nature the hyena has a backbone all in one piece and, therefore, it cannot bend. If it wants to turn around, it must turn its whole body; it cannot twist itself about as other animals do. So you see, this is a creature that is always in the darkness—never turning, never converting. This is all said, however, in application to the priests of the Jews. You can easily lead the ordinary Jew to repentance, but not one of the priests nor the teachers; for they are always attracted by the corpses of the dead—of those whom they may seduce."[88]

6. A Corrupted Priesthood.

"How will the gold be tarnished, and the fine silver changed! The sacred stones have been poured forth at the top of all the streets [Lam. 4:1]."

Saint Gregory the Great speaks of those priests before the destruction of the temple who were overseers of souls, but were engaged in the very

---

[85] Saint Irenaeus, *Against Heresies*, Bk. IV, Ch. XVI, Ante-Nicene, I:483.

[86] Ibid., Bk. IV, Ch. XV, Ante-Nicene, I:543.

[87] Saint Basil, "Hom. 13 on Psalm 28," *Exegetic Homilies*, FC, 46:194.

[88] Saint Jerome, "Hom. 83," *60-96 On The Psalms, Vol. 2*, FC, 57:182, 183.

earthly cares for which it is their duty to reprehend others. Thus he interprets here: "For what is expressed by gold, which surpasses all other metals, but the excellency of holiness?...What are signified by the stones of the sanctuary, but persons in sacred orders?...And truly these stones of the sanctuary lie scattered through the streets, when persons in sacred orders, given up to the latitude of their own pleasures, cleave to earthly businesses. It is also to be observed that they are said to be scattered, not in the streets, but in the top of the streets. This is so because even when they are engaged in earthly matters, they desire to appear topmost, so as to occupy the broad ways in their enjoyment of delight."[89]

7. The End of the Synagogue [Jer. 16:9].

The prophet foretells the end of the temple ritual and the Synagogue herself, saying, **"Thus saith the Lord God of Israel, 'Behold, I will make to cease out of this place before your eyes, and in your days, the voice of joy, and voice of gladness, the voice of the bridegroom, and the voice of the bride** [Jer. 16:9]**.'"** Saint Cyprian comments on this verse, saying "that Christ is the Bridegroom, having the Church as His Bride from which spiritual children were to be born."[90]

Pray Not for this People

[Jer. 7:16; 11:14; 15:1]

What are these people doing? **"Their children gather wood, and their fathers kindle a fire, and their women knead dough, to make cakes to the host of heaven; and they have poured out drink-offerings to strange gods, that they might provoke Me to anger** [Jer. 7:18]**."** This deity so zealously worshipped by the people, known as the queen of heaven, is only so-called by the Prophet Jeremias. The goddess is also referred to elsewhere [Jer. 51:18 LXX; 44:18 KJV]. Her worship was zealously pursued, and she was adored as the bestower of earthly possessions. This worship was combined with that of the stars, the host of heaven, which was cultivated under Manasses [4 Kgs. (2 Kgs.) 21:5]. It may be presumed that the queen of heaven was one of the deities who came to western Asia with the Assyrians, and that she corresponds to the Assyrian-Persian Tanais and Artemis, who in the course of time took the place once occupied by the closely related Phoenician Astarte. She was originally a deification of the moon, the Assyrian Selene and Virgo coelestis, who, as supreme female deity, was the companion to Baal-Moloch as sun-god. Evidently, they made some kind of sacrificial cakes that were kindled on the altar together with a libation or drink-offering.[91]

---

[89] Saint Gregory the Great, *Pastoral Rule*, Ch. VII, Nicene, 2nd Ser., XII:17, 18.

[90] Saint Cyprian, "Testimonies," § 19, *The Treatises of Cyprian*, Ante-Nicene, V:523.

[91] C. F. Keil and F. Delitzsch, *Commentary*, 8:160.

"Therefore, thus saith the Lord, 'Behold, I bring evils upon this people, out of which they shall not be able to come forth; and they shall presently cry to Me, but I will not hearken to them [Jer. 11:11]**.'"** Saint John Cassian, in a conference with Abbot Theodore, examines this verse, saying, "God allows these things to happen with an eye to their good, thus, these sorrows and losses with which they shall for the present be chastened for their soul's health 'shall also at length drive them to return and hasten back to Me, Whom in their prosperity they scorn.'"[92]

"And thou, pray not for this people, and intercede not for them in supplication and prayer: for I will not hear in the day in which they call upon Me, in the day of their affliction [Jer. 11:14]**."**

Saint Chrysostom writes: "That reconciliation might not become an occasion for listlessness, thus to Jeremias He also said, **'Pray not for this people, for I will not hear thee** [Jer. 11:14]**,'** not as wishing to stop his praying (for He earnestly longs for our salvation), but to terrify them. And this the prophet also seeing did not cease praying. And, indeed, it was not through a wish to have him turn from prayer, but to shame them."[93] Continuing, Saint Chrysostom says that the prophet forewarns us: "Do you not hear what God said to Jeremias about the Jews? **'Pray thou not for this people, and intercede not for them to be pitied, yea, pray not, and approach Me not for them: for I will not hearken** [Jer. 7:16]**.'** And, **'Though Moses and Samuel stood before My face, My soul could not be toward them. Dismiss this people, and let them go forth** [Jer. 15:1]**.'** That is how far some sins go beyond forgiveness and how incapable of defense they are. Therefore, let us not draw down such anger on ourselves."[94]

Saint Chrysostom makes the point that God is wont to defend Himself before the visitation of their well-deserved sufferings, as He did to Abraham, Lot, Noah, and Ezekiel. Thus He says to Jeremias, **"Seest thou not what they do in the cities of Juda, and in the streets of Jerusalem** [Jer. 7:17]**?"**[95] On this account He says to Jeremias, **"Though Moses and Samuel stood before My face** [Jer. 15:1]**."** Indeed Moses was their first lawgiver, who delivered them from so many dangers; and Samuel was dedicated from his earliest youth. "Knowing these things, let us neither despise the prayers of the saints nor throw everything upon them. Let us not, on the one hand, be indolent and live

---

[92] Saint John Cassian, "Conference of Abbot Theodore," Ch. VI, Nicene, 2nd Ser., XI:354.
[93] Saint Chrysostom, "Hom. XIV," *Romans*, Nicene, 1st Ser., XI:448.
[94] Idem, "Discourse VIII," *Against Judaizing Christians*, FC, 68:229.
[95] Idem, "Hom. XLIII," *Matthew*, Nicene, 1st Ser., X:274.

carelessly, nor, on the other hand, deprive ourselves of a great advantage."[96] Elsewhere, he advises, "Let us not then be looking open-mouthed toward others. For it is true, the prayers of the saints have the greatest power—on the condition, however, of our repentance and amendment."[97]

Saint Ambrose supports that the intercessor be worthy: "Rightly, then, it is said, 'Who shall entreat?' It implies that it must be such a one as Moses to offer himself for those that sin, or such as Jeremias, who, though the Lord said, **'Pray not for this people** [Jer. 7:16]**,'** yet he did pray and did obtain forgiveness for them. For at the intercession of the prophet and the entreaty of so great a seer, the Lord was moved. Jerusalem repented and said, 'O Lord Almighty, God of Israel, the soul in anguish, the troubled spirit, crieth unto thee, "Hear, O Lord, and have mercy...[Bar. 3:1, 2]."' And the Lord bids them lay aside the garments of mourning, and to cease the groans of repentance, saying, 'Put off, O Jerusalem, the garment of thy mourning and affliction, and put on the comeliness of the glory that cometh from God forever [Bar. 5:1].'"[98]

Against the Heathen

[Jer. 10:1, 2, 11]

"Hear ye the word of the Lord, which He has spoken to you, O house of Israel. Thus saith the Lord, 'Learn ye not the ways of the heathen...[Jer. 10:1, 2]**.'"**

Saint Cyprian also affirms that "the believer ought not to live as those of the nations....One ought to separate himself from the Gentiles lest he should be a companion of their sin, and become a partaker of their penalty, as we read in the Apocalypse: 'And I heard another voice from heaven, saying, "Come out of her, My people, in order that ye might not be partakers in her sins and that ye might not receive of her plagues [Rev. 18:4]."'"[99]

"Thus shall ye say to them, 'Let the gods which have not made heaven and earth perish from off the earth, and from under this sky [Jer. 10:11]**.'"**

Saint Irenaeos explains: "The Scripture terms them gods which are not gods; it does not declare them as gods in every sense, but with a certain addition and signification, by which they are shown to be no gods at all....For from the fact of Jeremias having subjoined their destruction, he shows them to be no gods at all."[100]

---

[96] Idem, "Hom. 1," *First Thessalonians*, Nicene, 1st Ser., XIII:327.
[97] Idem, "Hom. V," *Matthew*, Nicene, 1st Ser., X:34.
[98] Saint Ambrose, *Concerning Repentance, Book I*, Ch. IX, Nicene, 2nd Ser., X:336.
[99] Saint Cyprian, "Testimonies," § 36, *Treatises*, Ante-Nicene, V:544.
[100] Saint Irenaeus, *Against Heresies*, Bk. III, Ch. VI, Ante-Nicene, I:419.

According to Blessed Jerome, "This one section of Jeremias was written in the Chaldee language."[101] This is the only verse in the book in Aramaic. Though some interpreters believed this verse to be an interpolation or gloss of some copyist, it enabled the pagan idolaters to read the judgment of God in the language of the day.[102]

The Prophetic Messages of Prophet Jeremias

1. The Incarnation of Jesus Christ.

"The heart is deep beyond all things, and He is Man, and who can know Him [Jer. 17:9]**?"**

Saint Irenaeos extracts this verse as a proof of the manhood of Christ: **"He is a Man, and who can know Him** [Jer. 17:9]**?"** He asserts this may be used to "exhibit the union of the Logos of God with His own workmanship. It declares that the Logos should become flesh, and the Son of God man;...and having become what we also are, He (nevertheless) is the mighty God, and possesses a generation that cannot be declared."[103] He then responds to the question, **"Who can know Him** [Jer. 17:9]**?"** He answers: "He to whom the Father Who is in the heavens has revealed Him [cf. Mt. 16:17], knows Him, so that he understands that He Who 'was not begotten either by the will of the flesh or by the will of man [cf. Jn. 1:13],' is the Son of Man; this is Christ, the Son of the living God."[104]

Saint Cyprian says the prophet here declares "that Christ is both Man and God, compounded of both natures, that He should be a Mediator between us and the Father."[105]

According to Saint Ambrose, when the apostle says, "Because of the impossibility of the law, in that it was weak through the flesh, God sent His own Son in the likeness of the flesh of sin—and in regard to sin, condemned sin in the flesh—in order that the ordinance of the law might be fulfilled in us, who walk not according to the flesh, but according to the spirit [Rom. 8:3,4]," he reminds us that "he did not say 'in the likeness of flesh,' for Christ took on Himself the reality not the likeness of flesh, nor does He say 'in the likeness of sin,' for He did no sin, but was made sin for us. Yet He came 'in the likeness of the flesh of sin'—the likeness, because it is written: **'He is Man, and who shall know Him** [Jer. 17:9]**?'** He was man in the flesh, according to His human nature, that He might be recognized. But in power He was above man, that He might not be recognized. So He has our flesh, but has not the failing of this

---

[101] Blessed Jerome, *Prefaces*, Nicene, 2nd Ser., VI:493.

[102] *The Expositors Bible Commentary*, Vol. 6, Frank E. Gaebelein, Gen. Ed. (Grand Rapids, MI: Zondervan Publishing House, 1986), p. 449.

[103] Saint Irenaeus, *Against Heresies*, Bk. IV, Ch. XXXII, Ante-Nicene, I:509.

[104] Ibid., Bk. III, Ch. XIX, Ante-Nicene, I:449.

[105] Saint Cyprian, "Testimonies," § 10, *Treatises*, Ante-Nicene, V: 519.

flesh. For He was not begotten, as is every man, by intercourse between male and female, but born of the Holy Spirit and of the Virgin. He received a stainless body, which not only no sins polluted but also which neither the generation nor the conception had been stained by any admixture of defilement."[106]

We, therefore, chant, *Having cleansed thy radiant heart with the Spirit, O glorious Jeremias, great prophet and martyr, thou didst receive from on high the gift of prophecy and didst cry aloud among the lands, "Behold our God! There is none other to compare with Him, Who hath appeared, incarnate, on the earth!"*[107]

2. The Righteous Branch, Christ.

"'Behold, the days come,' saith the Lord, 'when I will raise up to David a righteous branch [Gk. *anatole*; Heb. *tzeh-magh*], **and a King shall reign and understand, and shall execute judgment and righteousness on the earth** [Jer. 23:5].'" The Greek *anatole* literally means rising, east. The Hebrew *tzeh-magh* means sprout or shoot. Saint Leo the Great (d. 461), writes: "David's Lord was made David's Son, and from the fruit of the promised branch [Jer. 23:5] sprang One without fault, the twofold nature coming into one Person, that by one and the same conception and birth might spring our Lord Jesus Christ, in Whom was present both true divinity for the performance of mighty works and true manhood for the endurance of sufferings."[108]

3. The Hypostasis of the Lord.

"For Who has stood in the substance of the Lord (Ὅτι τίς ἔστη ἐν ὑποστήματι Κυρίου), **and seen His Logos** [Jer. 23:18]?"

Saint Hippolytos says that "the Logos of God alone is visible, while the word of man is audible. When he speaks of seeing the Logos, I must believe that this visible Logos has been sent. And there was none other sent by the Logos. And that He was sent Peter testifies when he says to the centurion Cornelius: 'He sent to the sons of Israel the Logos Himself preaching the Gospel—peace through Jesus Christ—this One is Lord of all [cf. Acts 10:36].' If, then, the Logos is sent by Jesus Christ, the will of the Father is Jesus Christ."[109]

Saint Ambrose, in his work, *Of the Christian Faith*, refutes the Arians, inasmuch as "they assert the Son to be of another substance (ἑτεροούσιος, *etero-ousios*). The reason they avoid using the word hypostasis or substance is that they will not confess Christ to be the true Son of God. So how," he asks, "can the Arians deny the substance of God? How can they suppose that the

---

[106] Saint Ambrose, *Concerning Repentance, Book I*, Ch. III, Nicene, 2nd Ser., X:331.
[107] May 1st, Prophet Jeremias, Kontakion, Mode Three.
[108] Saint Leo the Great, "Sermon XXVIII," ¶ III, Nicene, 2nd Ser., XII:142.
[109] Saint Hippolytus, *Against the Heresy of One Noetus*, Ante-Nicene, V:228.

word 'substance' which is found in many places of Scripture ought to be debarred from use, when they themselves do assert that the Son is of another substance, thus plainly admitting substance in God? It is not the term itself, then, but its force and consequences that they shun, because they will not confess the Son of God to be true God (by nature, not adoption). For though the process of the divine generation cannot be comprehended in human language, still the fathers judged that their faith might be fitly distinguished by the use of such a term, as against that of *etero-ousios*, following the authority of the prophet, who said: **'Who hath stood in the *substantia*** (ὑπόστασις, **hypostasis) of the Lord, and seen His Logos** [Jer. 23:18]**?'** Arians, therefore, admit the term 'substance' when it is used so as to square with their blasphemy; contrariwise, when it is adopted in accordance with the pious devotion of the faithful, they reject and dispute it. What other reason can there be for their unwillingness to have the Sun spoken of as *homoousios* (ὁμοούσιος), of the same essence with the Father, but that they are unwilling to confess Him to be the true Son of God?"[110]

4. The Woman.

"The Lord hath created a new thing in the earth, a woman shall compass a Man [Jer. 31:22 KJV and Hebrew text]**."**

Though the Septuagint does not render this verse in the Greek, neither in this chapter nor in chapter 38, we have included it herein, since Blessed Jerome refers to it, remarking, "Concerning her (the Virgin Mary), we read of a great miracle in the same prophecy—that a woman should compass a Man, and that the Father of all things should be contained in a virgin's womb."[111]

Thus, at the Feast of the Forefeast of the Nativity, we chant, *Showing forth the advent of Christ in the flesh, Jeremias cried aloud, "God hath appeared on earth, incarnate; and He hath found every path of knowledge, being born of His Mother in Bethlehem."*[112]

5. The Massacre of the 14,000 Innocents.

"A voice was heard in Rama, of lamentation, and of weeping, and wailing; Rachel would not cease weeping for her children because they are not [Jer. 38:15 LXX; 31:15 KJV]**."**

Saint Andrew of Crete (ca. 660-740) chants: *When Jesus was born in Bethlehem of Judaea, the dominion of the Jews was abolished. Let the infants slaughtered for Christ leap up, and let Judaea lament. For a voice was heard in Rama: Rachel, weeping, bewaileth for her children, as it is written, for the all-iniquitous Herod in slaying babes fulfilled the Scriptures* [Jer. 38:15 LXX;

---

[110] Saint Ambrose, *Of the Christian Faith.-Book III*, Nicene, 2nd Ser., X:259, 260.

[111] Blessed Jerome, *Against Jovianus.-Book I*, Nicene, 2nd Ser., VI:370.

[112] December 20th, Feast of the Forefeast of the Nativity, Canon at Compline of the Forefeast, Ode Seven, Mode Two.

31:15 KJV], *filling Judaea with innocent blood and staining the earth red with their blood. But the Church of the nations is mystically purified thereby and is arrayed in beauty. The Truth is come! God Who hath been born of the Virgin hath appeared to those who sit in a shadow* [Is. 9:2], *that He may save us all.*[113]

Speaking of the slaughter of the innocents by Herod [Mt. 2:16-18], Saint Chrysostom writes: "Thus having filled the hearer with horror by relating these things—for the slaughter was so violent and unjust, and extremely cruel and lawless—he comforts us again by saying, 'Not from God's wanting power to prevent it did all this take place, nor from any ignorance of His, but when He both knew it, and foretold it'; this was done loudly by His prophet [Jer. 38:15 LXX]. Be then neither troubled nor despond, looking unto His unspeakable providence, which one may most clearly see, alike by what He works and by what He permits."[114]

The ungodly king seized the multitude of infants and transformed them into martyrs; for he knew not that they, being citizens of the kingdom on high, would expose his madness unto the ages.[115]

Saint Ambrose writes: "Rachel died in childbirth [Gen. 35:16-19] because, even then, as the patriarch's wife, she saw Herod's wrath which spared not the tenderest years. Likewise, in Ephratha she gave birth to that Benjamin of surpassing beauty, the last in the order of mystery, namely, Paul, who was no small grief to his Mother (the Church) before his birth, for he persecuted her children (the Christians). She died and was buried there, that we, dying and being buried with Christ, may rise in the Church."[116] He also comments that "Rachel wept for her babes that were washed with her tears and offered to Christ."[117]

A hymn also confirms this of Rachel that she foresaw in the spirit the massacre of the infants. *Rachel was without consolation, beholding the unjust slaughter and timeless death; and she wept for them while suffering in her womb; but now she rejoiceth, beholding them in the bosom of Abraham.*[118]

The Venerable Bede adds, "According to the oracle of Jeremias, **'A voice was heard in Rama** [Jer. 38:15],**'** that is, 'on high,' **'of lamentation, and of weeping, and wailing** [cf. Jer. 38:15 LXX; 31:15 KJV]**.'**...The fact that Rachel is said to have bewailed her children and wished not to be consoled,

---

[113] December 29th, 14,000 Infants Slain in Bethlehem, Vespers Aposticha Doxastikon, Mode Plagal Four.

[114] Saint Chrysostom, "Hom. IX," *Matthew*, Nicene, 1st Ser., X:57.

[115] December 29th, Vespers Sticheron, Mode Four.

[116] Saint Ambrose, "Letter 45, Ambrose to the Priest Horontianus (dated ca. 387)," *Letters*, FC, 26:235.

[117] Ibid., "Letter 50," FC, 26:269.

[118] December 29th, Vespers Sticheron, Mode Four.

because they are not, signifies that the Church bewails the removal of the saints from this world, but she does not wish to be consoled in such a way that those who have been victorious over the world by death should return once again to bear with her the strife of the world; for surely they should no longer be called back into the world from whose hardships they have once escaped to Christ for their crowning. Now figuratively speaking, Rachel, which means 'sheep' or 'seeing God,' stands for the Church who, with her whole attention, keeps watch so that she may deserve to see God. And she is that hundredth sheep whom the good Shepherd goes out to seek on earth, having left behind the ninety-nine sheep of the angelic virtues in heaven; and when He finds her, He puts her on His shoulders and carries her back to the flock.

"However, according to the literal sense, the question arises how it may be said that Rachel bewailed her children, since the tribe of Juda, which contained Bethlehem, sprang not from Rachel, but from her sister Leah. The answer is easily come by in this case, because the children were slaughtered not only in Bethlehem but also in all its regions. The tribe of Benjamin, which sprang from Rachel, was neighbor to the tribe of Juda. Hence, we should rightly believe that the area where this most cruel slaughter occurred also included no small number of children of the stock of Benjamin, and Rachel bewailed these descendants with her voice raised on high.

"It can also be understood in another way: Rachel was buried close to Bethlehem, just as the inscription of her tomb, which remains until today to the west of the city beyond the road which leads to Hebron, bears witness; therefore, in the manner of prophetic speech, she is properly said to have done those things which were done in that place, since the place itself was distinguished by her body and her name."[119]

6. The Mystery of the Passion and the Cross.

"O Lord, teach me, and I shall know: then I saw their practises. But I, as an innocent lamb led to the slaughter, knew not. Against me they devised an evil device, saying, 'Come and let us put wood in his bread, and let us utterly destroy him from off the land of the living, and let his name not be remembered any more.' O Lord, that judgest righteously, trying the reins and hearts, let me see Thy vengeance taken upon them, for to Thee I have declared my cause [Jer. 11:18-20]**."**

Saint Justin Martyr claims that certain passages have been removed by the Jews from Esdras and Jeremias. They have cut out Jer. 11:19; for the Lord is speaking through His prophet of His crucifixion. "And since this passage from the sayings of Jeremias is still written in some copies (of the Scriptures) in the synagogues of the Jews—for it is only a short time since they were cut

---

[119] The Venerable Bede, *Homilies on the Gospels*, Bk. I, "Homily 1.10," Cistercian Studies Series: No. 110, pp. 97, 98.

out—and since from these words it is demonstrated that the Jews deliberated about the Christ Himself to crucify and put Him to death, He Himself is both declared to be led as a sheep to the slaughter, as was predicted by Esaias, and is here represented as a harmless lamb. But being in a difficulty about them they give themselves over to blasphemy. And again, from the sayings of the same Jeremias these have been cut out, 'The Lord God remembered His dead people of Israel who lay in the graves; and He descended to preach to them His own salvation.' This is wanting in our Scriptures: It is cited by Saint Irenaeos, under the name of Esaias, and under that of Jeremias."[120]

Commenting upon these verses, Saint Cyprian states both that "Christ is called a sheep and a lamb Who was to be slain, and that such words concern the mystery of the Passion."[121] Elsewhere, he believes that this prophecy was also a reference that "the Jews would fasten Christ to the wood of the Cross."[122]

Saint Kyril of Jerusalem, speaking of Christ's prescience and voluntary Passion declares, "Someone will say, 'Show me from a prophet where the wood of the Cross is spoken of in Scriptures. You are inventing sophistries, unless you produce testimony from a prophet, I am not convinced.' Hearken to Jeremias and be convinced, 'I was as a meek lamb that is carried to be a victim; did I not know it [cf. Jer. 11:19]?' (For read it thus as a question, as I have put it.) For He Who said, 'Ye know that after two days the passover taketh place, and the Son of Man is to be delivered up to be crucified [Mt. 26:2],' did He not know?...What sort of lamb was He? Let John the Baptist interpret, when he says, 'Behold the Lamb of God Who taketh away the sin of the world [Jn. 1:29]!' They devised a wicked counsel against Me, saying (was it that He Who knew the counsels did not know their issue? And what did they say?): **'Come let us put wood in His bread** [Jer. 11:19]**.'** (If the Lord shall count you worthy, hereafter you shall learn that His body, according to the Gospel, bore the figure of bread.) 'Come, and let us put wood in His bread, and cut Him off from the land of the living.' (Life is not cut off; why do you toil to no purpose?) **'And let His name not be remembered any more** [Jer. 11:19]**.'** Your counsel is vain; for, before the sun, His name abides in the Church."[123]

---

[120] Saint Justin Martyr, *Dialogue with Trypho*, Ch. LXXII, Ante-Nicene, I:234, 235 [On page 235, note 1: Saint Irenaeus, iii.20 and iv.22 under Jeremias—Maranus].

[121] Saint Cyprian, "Testimonies," § 15, *Treatises*, Ante-Nicene, V:521.

[122] Ibid., "Testimonies," § 20, *Treatises*, Ante-Nicene, V:524.

[123] Saint Cyril of Jerusalem, "Catechesis XIII," ¶ 19, *The Works of Saint Cyril of Jerusalem: Vol. 2*, FC, 64:17.

Saint Ambrose affirms that the Son speaks here "of the mystery of His coming incarnation—for it is blasphemy to suppose that the words are spoken concerning the Father."[124]

Saint Theodore the Stoudite (759-826) chants, *The wood which the prophet of lamentation saw placed in Thy bread* [Jer. 11:19]*—Thy Cross, O merciful Lord—we do venerate.*[125] Also from the *Triodion*, we chant, *Let us honor this holy Wood which, as the prophet said of old, was put into the bread of Christ by the Israelites who crucified Him.*[126] And from the divine office of the prophet, we hear: *As a mystery, thou didst recount beforehand the death of the Deliverer, O divinely eloquent one; for the iniquitous assembly of the Jews lifted Christ upon the Tree as a lamb, the Author of life, the Benefactor of all creation.*[127]

7. The Crucifixion at Noon.

"She that bore seven is spent; her soul has fainted under trouble; her sun is gone down while it is yet noon; she is ashamed and disgraced. I will give the remnant of them to the sword before their enemies [Jer. 15:9]**."**

Saint Irenaeos points out that both the Prophets Jeremias and Amos [8:9,10] are here speaking of the time of the Lord's crucifixion. They "plainly announced that obscuration of the sun which at the time of His crucifixion took place from the sixth hour onward; and that after this event, those days which were their festival according to the law, and their songs, should be changed into grief and lamentation when they were handed over to the Gentiles."[128]

Saint Cyprian relates that this verse was a prophecy "that at midday in His Passion there would be darkness [cf. Mt. 27:45]."[129]

Saint Ephraim the Syrian (ca. 306-383) interprets this passage in this way: He makes reference to the parable where it is spoken that a spirit departed and wandered about waterless places, but found no resting place, and thus returned to its former place with seven of its companions [cf. Mt. 12:43-45]. "These seven evil spirits entered and took up residence among this people (the Jews), according to the number of the days of the week, and did away with all its religious observance. The seven spirits dwelling in this people were those concerning whom Jeremias said, 'She lamented and gave birth to seven [cf. Jer. 15:9].' Her womb was swollen, for Israel bore a calf in the desert [cf. Ex.

---

[124] Saint Ambrose, *Of the Christian Faith.—Book IV*, Nicene, 2nd Ser., X:283, 284.

[125] *Triodion*, Sunday of the Cross, Orthros Canon, Ode Six, Mode One.

[126] *Triodion*, Wednesday in the Fourth Week, Orthros Canon, Ode Eight (Second Three-Canticled Canon), Mode One.

[127] May 1st, Prophet Jeremias, Orthros Canon, Ode Six, Mode Plagal Four.

[128] Saint Irenaeus, *Against Heresies*, Bk. IV, Ch. XXXIII, Ante-Nicene, I:510.

[129] Saint Cyprian, "Testimonies," § 23, *Treatises*, Ante-Nicene, V:525.

32:1-35], the two calves of Jeroboam [cf. 3 Kgs. (1 Kgs.) 12:26-32], and the four-faced image of Manasses [cf. 2 Chr. 33:7, Peshitta]. 'The sun set [cf. Jer. 15:9],' because they were dwelling in darkness, without the light of prophecy."[130]

8. Christ is Laid in a Tomb.

"Therefore, I awaked, and beheld; and My sleep was sweet to Me [Jer. 38:26 LXX; 31:26 KJV]**."**

"The death," says Saint Ambrose, "that was freely chosen by Christ could not have held sorrow; for in it was the future joy of all men and the refreshment of all. Concerning it the Scripture says, **'I awaked, and beheld; and My sleep was sweet to Me.'** Good is the sleep that has made the hungry not to hunger and the thirsty not to thirst, and has prepared for them the pleasant savor of the mysteries. How then was Christ's soul troubled when He made the souls of others not to fear? He was sad, then, even unto death, until grace should be fulfilled."[131]

9. The Holy Sepulcher.

"The fowlers chased Me as a sparrow, all Mine enemies destroyed My life in a pit without cause, and laid a stone upon Me [Lam. 3:53]**."** Saint Kyril of Jerusalem, referring to the holy sepulcher of our Lord Jesus Christ, asks, "Tell us exactly, O prophets, about His tomb also, where it lies, and where we shall look for it. But they answer, 'Look to the solid rock which you have hewn, and seek the Lord...[Is. 51:1]'; look and see. You have in the Gospels, 'in a rock-hewn tomb [cf. Lk. 23:53].' What next? What kind of door has the sepulcher? Again a prophet says, 'They have ended My life in the pit, and they have laid a stone over Me [cf. Lam. 3:53].' I, Who am 'the chief cornerstone, chosen, precious [1 Pe. 2:6; Is. 28:16],' lie for a while within a stone, I, Who am 'a stone of stumbling [1 Pe. 2:8],' to the Jews, but of salvation to them that believe. The Tree of Life, then, was planted in the earth, to bring blessing for the earth, which had been cursed, and to bring release for the dead."[132]

10. The Spirit and Christ the Lord [Lam. 4:20].

"The Spirit before our face, Christ the Lord (Πνεῦμα προσώπου ἡμῶν Χριστὸς Κύριος)**, was taken in their destructive snares, of Whom we said, 'In His shadow we shall live among the nations** [Lam. 4:20]**.'"**

Pnevma is understood by Saint Justin as "breath," while the other fathers interpret it to mean the Spirit.

---

[130] *Saint Ephrem's Commentary on Tatian's Diatessaron*, Journal of Semitic Studies Supplement 2, pp. 178, 179.

[131] Saint Ambrose, *Seven Exegetical Works: The Prayer of Job and David*, FC, 65:397.

[132] Saint Cyril of Jerusalem, "Catechesis XIII," ¶ 35, *The Works of Saint Cyril of Jerusalem: Vol. 2*, FC, 64:28.

Saint Justin Martyr, speaking about symbols of the Cross, observes: "The human form differs from that of the irrational animals in nothing else than in its being erect and having the hands extended, and having on the face extending from the forehead what is called the nose, through which there is respiration for the living creature. And this shows no other form than that of the cross. And so it was said by the prophet: 'The breath before our face, the Lord Christ [cf. Lam. 4:20].'"[133]

Saint Irenaeos cites this verse as proof that the one and the same God, the Creator of heaven and earth, is He Whom the prophets foretold, and Who was declared by the Gospel. "He is indeed Savior, as being the Son and Logos of God, but salutary since (He is) Spirit; for he says, 'The Spirit of our countenance, Christ the Lord [cf. Lam. 4:20]'; and He has become our salvation, taking flesh, for 'the Logos was made flesh, and dwelt among us [Jn. 1:14].'"[134]

Saint Basil, in his discourse against those who assert that the Holy Spirit ought not to be glorified, propounds that "to a certain extent an intelligent apprehension at the sublimity of His nature and of His unapproachable power may be arrived at by looking at the meaning of His title, and at the magnitude of His operations, and by His good gifts bestowed on us or rather on all creation. He is called Spirit, as 'God is Spirit [Jn. 4:24],' and **'the Spirit before our face, Christ the Lord** [Lam. 4:20]**.'** He is called holy, as the Father is holy, and the Son is holy, for to the creature holiness was brought in from without, but to the Spirit holiness is the fulfillment of nature; and it is for this reason that He is described not as being sanctified, but as sanctifying. He is called good, as the Father is good, and He Who was begotten of the Good is good, and to the Spirit His goodness is essence. He is called upright, as the Lord is upright, in that He is Himself truth, and is Himself righteousness, having no divergence nor leaning to one side or to the other, on account of the immutability of His substance. He is called Paraclete, as the Only-begotten, as He Himself says, 'I will ask the Father, and He shall give you another Paraclete [Jn. 14:16].' Thus names are borne by the Spirit in common with the Father and the Son, and He gets these titles from His natural and close relationship. Again, He is called governing [Ps. 50:12], Spirit of truth, and Spirit of wisdom [Is. 11:2]."[135]

Saint Gregory of Nyssa (ca. 335-ca. 395), touching upon the views held by the Church on the Holy Spirit, maintains that the Father, the Son, and the Holy Spirit are not three Gods, but one God. Saint Gregory, in his writings

---

[133] Saint Justin Martyr, *Dialogue with Trypho: The First Apology*, Ch. LV, Ante-Nicene, I:181.

[134] Saint Irenaeus, *Against Heresies*, Bk. III, Ch. X, Ante-Nicene, I:424.

[135] Saint Basil, *On the Spirit*, Ch. XIX, Nicene, 2nd Ser., VIII:30.

against Evnomios, criticizes him from refraining to say, "Holy Spirit." For, "Evnomios did not wish by this name to acknowledge the majesty of His glory, and His complete union with the Father and the Son....The appellation of 'Spirit,' and that of 'Holy,' are by the Scriptures equally applied to the Father and the Son; for 'God is Spirit [Jn. 4:24],' and 'the anointed Lord (Christ) is the Spirit before our face [cf. Lam. 4:20],' and 'holy is the Lord our God [Ps. 98:10],' and 'one is Holy, one is Lord Jesus Christ'" [Response to the words of the priest, after the elevation, and at the breaking, of the Lamb, in the Greek Liturgies]. Saint Gregory then quips that Evnomios avoids using these terms, "lest there should be bred in the minds of his readers some Orthodox conception of the Holy Spirit, such as would naturally arise in them from His sharing His glorious appellation with the Father and the Son!"[136]

"What we eat," explains Saint Ambrose, "and what we drink, the Holy Spirit expresses: 'O taste and see that the Lord is good; blessed is the man that hopeth in Him [Ps. 33:8].' Christ is that sacrament, because the body is Christ's. So the food is not corporeal but spiritual. Therefore the apostle also says of its type, 'Our fathers ate the spiritual food and drank the spiritual drink [cf. 1 Cor. 10:1-4]'; for the body of God is a spiritual body; the body of Christ is the body of the divine Spirit, for the Spirit is Christ, as we read, **'The Spirit before our face, Christ the Lord** [Lam. 4:20]**.'**"[137]

Elsewhere, Saint Ambrose repeats, "But what wonder, since both the Father and the Son are said to be Spirit? Of this indeed we shall speak more fully when we begin to speak of the unity of the name....The Father is also called Spirit, as the Lord said in the Gospel: 'For God is Spirit [Jn. 4:24]'; and Christ is called a Spirit, for Jeremias said, **'The Spirit before our face, Christ the Lord** [Lam. 4:20]**.'**"[138]

"He came," asserts Saint Kyril of Jerusalem, "of His own free choice to His Passion, rejoicing in His noble deed, smiling at the crown, cheered by the salvation of men. He was not ashamed of the Cross, for it saved the world. It was no ordinary man who suffered, but God in man's nature, striving for the reward of His patience. The Jews, of course, ever ready to object and slow to believe, deny this....The Persians believe, but not the Hebrews. The people whose study is the Scriptures reject what they study. They answer, 'Does the Lord then suffer? And did the hands of men prevail over His sovereignty?' Read the Lamentations, for in them Jeremias, lamenting you, has written what is worth a lament. He saw your ruin; he beheld your downfall. He bewailed the

136 Saint Gregory of Nyssa, *Against Eunomius, Book II*, § 14, Nicene, 2nd Ser., V:128.
137 Saint Ambrose, *Theological and Dogmatic Works: The Mysteries*, FC, 44:27.
138 Ibid., *The Holy Spirit*, FC, 44:73, 74.

Jerusalem that then was, for that which now is shall not be bewailed.[139] For that Jerusalem crucified Christ, but that which is now worships Him. Therefore, lamenting he says, 'The Spirit before our face, Christ the Lord is taken in our sins.' Do I invent what I say? You see he bears witness to the Christ seized by men. What follows? Tell me, O prophet. But he says, 'Of Whom we said, under His shadow we shall live among the nations [cf. Lam. 4:20].' He indicates that the grace of life will no longer abide in Israel, but among the nations."[140]

11. The People of God.

A. "'In that day,' said the Lord, 'I will break the yoke off their neck, and will burst their bonds; and they shall no longer serve strangers, but they shall serve the Lord their God; and I will raise up to them David their King [Jer. 37:8, 9 LXX; 30:8, 9 KJV]**.'"**

Saint Cyprian says "that the old yoke would be made void, and a new yoke would be given."[141] The people of God shall break off the yoke of the evil one and burst the bonds of the passions and no longer serve strangers, that is, the vices. They shall serve God Who shall raise up David their King, that is Jesus of his lineage.

"Why then," asks Saint Chrysostom, "has he made mention of David? The man was in the mouths of all. For not only Jeremias but also Ezekiel ('And I will raise up one Shepherd over them, and He shall tend them, even My servant David, and He shall be their shepherd; and I the Lord will be to them a God, and David a Prince in the midst of them; I the Lord have spoken it [Ez. 34:23, 24]'), and Hosea ('And afterward shall the children of Israel return, and shall seek the Lord their God, and David their King; and shall be amazed at the Lord and at His goodness in the latter days [Hos. 3:5]') speak of David as coming and rising again. They mean not him that was dead, but them who were emulating his virtue....For great was the glory of the man, both with God and with men."[142]

B. "They went forth with weeping, and I will bring them back with consolation, causing them to lodge by the channels of water in a straight way, and they shall not err in it [Jer. 38:9 LXX; 31:9 KJV]**."**

---

[139] The translator notes that by "the Jerusalem that then was" the saint means the Jerusalem captured and destroyed by Titus and reduced to further ruin by Hadrian. The boundaries of the later Jerusalem did not coincide with those of the old city. See Saint Cyril of Jerusalem, "Catechesis XIII," *The Works of Saint Cyril of Jerusalem: Vol. 2*, FC, 64:9, note 29.

[140] Saint Cyril of Jerusalem, "Catechesis XIII," ¶¶ 6, 7, *The Works of Saint Cyril of Jerusalem: Vol. 2*, FC, 64:8, 9.

[141] Saint Cyprian, "Testimonies," § 12, *Treatises*, Ante-Nicene, V:511.

[142] Saint Chrysostom, "Hom. II," *Matthew*, Nicene, 1st Ser., X:11.

We left the garden of delight weeping, but now find consolation being brought back through holy Baptism and "the water of tears and the weeping of repentance," says Saint Ambrose.[143]

C. "For the Lord has ransomed Jacob, He has rescued him out of the hand of them that were stronger than he [Jer. 38:11 LXX; 31:11 KJV]**."**

Saint Irenaeos states: "When Jesus spoke of the devil as strong, it is not absolutely so, but as in comparison with us; but it is God Who obtains and retains possession. 'How is anyone able to enter into the house of the strong one and plunder his vessels, unless he should first bind the strong one? And then he will plunder his house [Mt. 12:29].'"[144]

12. The Old Sacrifice.

"Wherefore do ye bring Me frankincense from Saba, and cinnamon from a land afar off? Your whole-burnt offerings are not acceptable, and your sacrifices have not been pleasant to Me [Jer. 6:20]**."**

Saint Paul writes: "I beseech you therefore, brethren, by the mercies of God, to present your bodies a living sacrifice, holy, well pleasing to God, your rational worship [Rom. 12:1]." Saint Chrysostom declares: "As great a difference as there is between Aaron and Christ, so great should it be between us and the Jews. For see, we have our Victim on high, our Priest on high, our Sacrifice on high. Let us bring such sacrifices as can be offered on that altar, no longer sheep and oxen, no longer blood and fat. All these things have been done away; and there has been brought in, in their stead, 'the rational worship.' But what is 'the reasonable service'? The offerings made through the soul, those made through the spirit....These sacrifices one may see in the Old Testament also, shadowed out beforehand....**'To what purpose do ye bring the incense from Sheba** [Jer. 6:20]**?'**...Thou seest also that already from the first that the one class have given place, and these have come in their stead."[145]

13. The New Covenant.

A. "'Behold, the days come,' saith the Lord, 'when I will make a new covenant with the house of Israel, and with the house of Juda: not according to the covenant which I made with their fathers in the day when I took hold of their hand to bring them out of the land of Egypt; for they abode not in My covenant, and I disregarded them,' saith the Lord [Jer. 38:31, 32 LXX; 31:31, 32 KJV]**."**

Saint Justin Martyr remarks, "The Prophet Jeremias speaks of a new covenant. If, therefore, God predicted that He would make a new covenant, and this for a light to the nations, and we see and are convinced that, through the name of the crucified Jesus Christ, men have turned to God, leaving behind

[143] Saint Ambrose, *The Prayer of Job and David*, FC, 65:395.

[144] Saint Irenaeus, *Against Heresies*, Bk. III, Ch. VIII, Ante-Nicene, I:421.

[145] Saint Chrysostom, "Hom. XII," *Hebrews*, Nicene, 1st Ser., XIV:420.

them idolatry and other sinful practises, and have kept the Faith and have practised piety even unto death, then everyone can clearly see from these deeds and the accompanying powerful miracles that He is indeed the new law, the new covenant, and the expectation of those who, from every nation, have awaited the blessings of God. We have been led to God through this crucified Christ, and we are the true spiritual Israel, and the descendants of Juda, Jacob, and Isaac. We are the descendants of Abraham, who, though uncircumcised, was approved and blessed by God because of his faith and was called the father of many nations."[146]

Saint Irenaeos adds this is not the covenant made with their fathers in Mount Horeb. "But one and the same household produced both covenants, the Logos of God, our Lord Jesus Christ, Who spoke with both Abraham and Moses, and Who has restored us anew to liberty and has multiplied that grace which is from Himself."[147]

Blessed Jerome says the prophet speaks in this verse "concerning the future kingdom."[148]

B. "'For this is My covenant which I will make with the house of Israel; after those days,' saith the Lord, 'I will surely put My laws into their mind, and write them on their hearts; and I will be to them as God, and they shall be to Me for a people [Jer. 38:33 LXX; 31:33 KJV]**.'"**

Saint Chrysostom teaches us that "God is made manifest, both by His words and by His doings, since, to Noah, Abraham and his offspring, and to Job, and Moses too, He discoursed not by writings, but Himself by Himself, finding their mind pure. But after the whole people of the Hebrews had fallen into the very pit of wickedness, then and thereafter was a written word, and tablets, and the admonition which is given by these. And this one may perceive was the case not only of the saints in the Old Testament only but also of those in the New. For neither to the apostles did God give anything in writing, but instead of written words He promised that He would give them the grace of the Spirit: for 'that One,' saith our Lord, 'shall teach you all things, and shall remind you of what I said to you [Jn. 14:26].' And that thou mayest learn that this was far better, hear what He saith by the prophet: 'I will make a new covenant with you, putting my laws into their mind, and in their heart I will write them,' and, 'they shall be all taught of God [cf. Is. 54:13; Jn. 6:45; Heb. 8:8-11].' And Paul too, pointing out the same superiority, said, that they had

[146] Saint Justin Martyr, *Dialogue with Trypho*, Ch. XI, FC, 6:164, 165.

[147] Saint Irenaeus, *Against Heresies*, Bk. IV, Ch. IX, Ante-Nicene, I:543.

[148] Blessed Jerome, *Against Jovianus.-Book II*, Nicene, 2nd Ser., VI:409.

received a law not in tablets of stone, but in fleshy tablets of the heart [2 Cor. 3:3]."[149]

Christ wrote through the prophets; for "He put His laws into their minds and He wrote them upon their hearts [Jer. 38:33 LXX; 31:33 KJV]," so all might be "taught of God [Is. 54: 13]." But he said to His disciples: "The Paraclete, the Holy Spirit, Whom the Father will send in My name, that One shall teach you all things, and shall remind you of what I said to you [Jn. 14:25, 26]"; and, "whenever...the Spirit of the truth, should come, He will guide you into all the truth [Jn. 16:13]." Saint Isaac remarks that "He will show man the holy power, which surrounds him at all times; that power is the Comforter."[150]

Prophet Jeremias

C. "And they shall not at all teach every one his fellow citizen, and every one his brother, saying 'Know the Lord'; for all shall know Me, from the least of them to the greatest of them. For I will be merciful to their iniquities, and their sins I will remember no more [Jer. 38:34 LXX; 31:34 KJV]**."**

Saint Chrysostom explains that by this phrase the prophet is "showing the rapidity of the change and the facility with which they would embrace Christ's teaching."[151]

"And I will make with them an everlasting covenant, which I will by no means turn away from them; and I will put My fear into their heart, that they may not depart from Me [Jer. 39:40 LXX; 32:40 KJV]**."**

14. The Holy Apostles.

"'Behold, I am sending many fishers,' saith the Lord, 'and they shall fish them; and after those I am sending many hunters, and they shall hunt them upon every mountain, and upon every hill, and out of the holes of rocks [Jer. 16:16]**.'"**

Saint Ephraim the Syrian comments: "There came to Him fishers of fish, and they became fishers of people; as it is written: 'Behold, I am sending

---

[149] Saint Chrysostom, "Hom. I," *Matthew*, Nicene, 1st Ser., X:1.

[150] Saint Isaac the Syrian, "Treatise LI," *Mystical Treatises by Isaac of Nineveh*, translated from Bedjan's Syriac text, by Arent Jan Wensinck, Volume Two, p. 252.

[151] Saint John Chrysostom, *Demonstration Against the Pagans*, FC, 73:230.

forth hunters. And they will hunt them from every mountain and from every high place [cf. Jer. 16:16].' But, if He had sent forth wise men, people would have said that they had either persuaded them to take hold of them or led them astray to grasp hold of them. If He had sent forth rich men, again people would have said that they had stirred them up by either feeding them or bribing them, and so gained authority over them. If He had sent forth powerful men, again people would have said that they had either stunned them by their force or constrained them by their violence. But the apostles possessed none of these things. Through the example of Simon, He helped them all understand. He was timid, because he was frightened at the voice of a young servant girl [cf. Mt. 26:69-72]. He was poor because he was not able to pay his own tax—a half stater [cf. Mt. 17:27], and he said, 'Silver and gold have I none [Acts 3:6].' He was unwise, for when he denied our Lord he did not know how to take flight astutely. These fishermen went forth then and were victorious over the strong, the rich, and the wise. This was a great miracle, for, although weak, they attracted the strong not by force but by their teaching. Although poor, they taught the rich; and although unlearned, they made the wise and clever their disciples. The wisdom of the world yielded place to that wisdom which is itself the wisdom of wisdoms."[152]

Saint Basil tells us that "everyone of us, indeed, whoever is instructed in the holy Scripture is the administrator of some one of those gifts which, according to the Gospel, have been apportioned to us. In this great household of the Church not only are there vessels of every kind—gold, silver, wooden, and earthen [2 Tim. 2:20]—but also a great variety of pursuits. The house of God, which is the Church of the living God [1 Tim. 3:15], has hunters, travelers, architects, builders, farmers, shepherds, athletes, soldiers. To all of these this short admonition will be appropriate, for it will produce in each proficiency in action and energy of will. You are a hunter sent forth by the Lord, Who says, **'I am sending many hunters, and they shall hunt them upon every mountain** [Jer. 16:16].' Take good care, therefore, that your prey does not elude you, so that, having captured them with the word of truth, you may bring back to the Savior those who have been made wild and savage by iniquity."[153]

Blessed Jerome says, "Without any doubt, it is the Lord Who contrives snares for sinners themselves. He does so in order to entrap those who abuse their freedom and to compel them to tread the right path under His bridle, thereby making it possible for them to advance through Him, Who says: 'I am the way [Jn. 14:6].' Therefore, in Jeremias, we read that the Lord sends fishermen and hunters [Jer. 16:16] to spread nets for the lost fish tossed about

[152] *Saint Ephrem's Commentary on Tatian's Diatessaron*, p. 94.
[153] Saint Basil, *Ascetical Works: Give Heed to Thyself*, FC, 9:437, 438.

in whirlpools, and to hunt down unto salvation the beasts that rove through mountains and hills."[154]

15. The Nations Shall Hear [Jer. 6:18].

Saint Irenaeos writes: "For inasmuch as the former have rejected the Son of God, and cast Him out of the vineyard when they slew Him, God has justly rejected them, and given to the Gentiles outside the vineyard the fruits of its cultivation. This is in accordance with what Jeremias says: **'The Lord has reprobated and rejected the generation that does these things. For the children of Juda have wrought evil before Me** [Jer. 7:29, 30].' And again in like manner does Jeremias speak, **'I have set watchmen over you, saying, "Hear ye the sound of the trumpet." But they said, "We will not hear it." Therefore have the nations heard, and they that feed their flocks** [Jer. 6:17, 18].' It is, therefore, one and the same Father Who planted the vineyard, Who led forth the people, Who sent the prophets, Who sent His own Son, and Who gave the vineyard to those other husbandmen that render the fruits in their season."[155]

16. Islands, the Churches.

"Hear the words of the Lord, ye nations, and proclaim them to the islands afar off...[Jer. 38:10 LXX; 31:10 KJV]."

Saint Irenaeos says, "The promises were not announced to the prophets and fathers alone, but to the Churches united to these from the nations, whom also the Spirit terms 'the islands' (both because they are established in the midst of turbulence, suffer the storm of blasphemies, exist as a refuge from those who love the height of heaven, and strive to avoid Bythus, that is, the depth of error)."[156]

17. The Ethiopian, A Figure of the Nations [Jer. 45 LXX; 38 KJV].

Saint Ambrose says, "The people of the Jews despised the word of prophecy and plunged Jeremias into a dungeon. And not one of the Jews was found to bring the prophet forth, except an Ethiopian, Abdemelech (Ebed-Melech), as Scripture testifies [Jer. 45:11, 12 LXX; 38:11, 12 KJV]. In this account there is a very beautiful figure, for we, namely, sinners of the Gentiles, formerly black with sins, and once fruitless, have brought forth from the depth the words of prophecy which the Jews had thrust, as it were, into the mire of their minds and of their flesh. And so it is written: 'Ethiopia shall hasten to stretch out her hand unto God [Ps. 67:32].' In this a figure of Holy Church is signified, which says in the Canticle of Canticles: 'I am black, but beautiful, O ye daughters of Jerusalem [Song 1:5]'; black through sin, beautiful through

---

[154] Saint Jerome, "Hom. 60 on Psalm 10(11)," *60-96 On The Psalms, Vol. 2*, FC, 57:11.

[155] Saint Irenaeus, *Against Heresies*, Bk. IV, Ch. XXXVI, Ante-Nicene, I:515.

[156] Ibid., Bk. V, Ch. XXXIV, Ante-Nicene, I:564.

grace; black through normal condition, beautiful through redemption; or surely black by the dust of their exercise. So she is black, while there is fighting; she is beautiful, while she is crowned with the decorations of her victory. And well is the prophet raised with cords and rags out of the dungeon, for the faithful writer said: 'Cords have fallen to me in the mightiest places [Ps. 15:6].'

"And well is it said 'with rags,' for the Lord Himself, when those who had first been invited to the wedding made excuses, sent to the ends of the highways, that as many as might be found might be invited to the wedding [cf. Mt. 22:9, 10]. So with these rags He raised the words of prophecy from the mire."[157]

Saint Ephraim adds: "Jeremias, though sanctified in the womb, they...cast him into the pit. Holy was the prophet in his befoulment, for clean was his heart though he was in the mire."[158]

Expounding upon the status of eunuchs, Blessed Jerome writes: "There are eunuchs, who thinking themselves dry trees because of their impotence, have a place prepared in heaven for sons and daughters [Is. 56:3, 4]. Their type is Abdemelech the eunuch in Jeremias [Jer. 45:7 LXX; 38:7 KJV], and the eunuch (named Djan Darada) of Candace (named Quarsemot) [Acts 8:27], who on account of the strength of his faith gained the name of a 'man.'"[159]

18. The Prophet Warns Against False Baptisms [Jer. 15:18].

Saint Cyprian, in an epistle regarding the so-called baptisms of heretics, maintains: "Widely different is the faith with Marcion and, moreover, with the other heretics; nay, with them there is nothing but perfidy, and blasphemy, and contention, which is hostile to holiness and truth. How then can one who is baptized among them obtain remission of sins and the grace of the divine mercy by his faith, when he has not the truth of the faith itself?...This matter of profane and adulterous baptism, Jeremias the prophet plainly rebukes, saying, **'Why do they that grieve me prevail against me? My wound is severe; whence shall I be healed? It is indeed become to me as deceitful water, that has no faithfulness** (as to healing) [Jer. 15:18]**.'** The Holy Spirit speaks, by the mouth of the prophet, regarding deceitful water which has no faithfulness. What is this deceitful and faithless water? Certainly that which falsely assumes the resemblance of Baptism, and frustrates the grace of faith by a shadowy pretense. But if, according to a perverted faith, one could be baptized without, and obtain remission of sins, according to the same faith he could also attain the Holy Spirit; and there is no need that hands should be laid on him when he comes, that he might obtain the Holy Spirit, and be sealed.

---

[157] Saint Ambrose, *The Holy Spirit*, FC, 44:135, 136.

[158] Saint Ephraim, "Hymns for the Feast of the Epiphany," *Hymns and Homilies*, Nicene, 2nd Ser., XIII:277.

[159] Blessed Jerome, *Against Jovianus.-Book I*, Nicene, 2nd Ser., VI:356.

He could either obtain both privileges (Baptism and the Holy Spirit) outside the Church, on account of his faith, or receive neither."[160]

Saint Ambrose tells us also that "there is in some even a deceitful water [cf. Jer. 15:18]; the baptism of unbelievers does not heal, does not cleanse, but pollutes."[161]

19. Antichrist [Jer. 8:16; 17:11].

A. "We shall hear the neighing of his swift horses out of Dan. The whole land quaked at the sound of the neighing of his horses; and he shall come, and devour the land and the fullness of it—the city, and them that dwell in it [Jer. 8:16]**."**

Saint Irenaeos, speaking of the Antichrist, cites the prophet's verse, bringing to our attention the following: "Jeremias does not merely point out his sudden coming, but even indicates the tribe from which he shall come (that is, Dan). This, too, is the reason that this tribe is not reckoned in the Apocalypse along with those which are saved [Rev. 7:5-7]."[162]

Saint Hippolytos, forewarning us of the coming Antichrist, says, "In reality, it is out of the tribe of Dan, then, that tyrant and king, that dread judge, that son of the devil, is foreordained to spring and arise....Jeremias also speaks to this effect: **'We shall hear the neighing of his swift horses out of Dan: the whole land quaked at the sound of the neighing of his horses** [Jer. 8:16]**.'**...These things are said of no one else but that tyrant, and shameless one, and adversary of God."[163]

B. "Prophet Jeremias," discloses Saint Hippolytos, "speaks of Antichrist in this passage in a parable: **'The partridge utters her voice, she gathers eggs which she did not lay; so is a man gaining his wealth unjustly; in the midst of his days his riches shall leave him, and at his latter end he will be a fool** [Jer. 17:11]**.'** For he will call together all the people to himself, out of every country of the dispersion, making them his own, as though they were his own children, and promising to restore their country, and establish again their kingdom and nation, in order that he may be worshipped by them as God." Then Saint Hippolytos goes on to describe how Antichrist will collect his whole kingdom "from the rising of the sun even to its setting: they whom he summons and they whom he does not summon shall march with him. He shall make the sea white with the sails of his ships, and the plain black with the

---

160 Saint Cyprian, "Epistle LXXII," Ante-Nicene, V:381.

161 Saint Ambrose, *The Mysteries*, FC, 44:13.

162 Saint Irenaeus, *Against Heresies*, Bk. V, Ch. XXX, Ante-Nicene, I:559.

163 Saint Hippolytus, *Treatise on Christ and Antichrist*, Ante-Nicene, V:207.

shields of his armaments. And whosoever will oppose him in war shall fall by the sword."[164]

Saint Gregory of Nyssa, in the same vein however, refers this to the enemy of humanity, the evil one, and writes: "Since by the wiles of him that sowed in us the tares of disobedience, our nature no longer preserved in itself the impress of the Father's image, but was transformed into the foul likeness of sin; for this cause it was engrafted by virtue of similarity of will into the evil family of the father of sin. Thus, the good and true God and Father was no longer the God and Father of him who had been thus outlawed by his own depravity, but instead of Him Who was by nature God, those were honored who, as the apostle says, 'were not gods by nature [cf. Gal. 4:8]'; and in place of the Father, he was deemed father who is falsely so called, as the Prophet Jeremias says in his dark saying, 'The partridge called, she gathered together what she hatched not [Jer. 17:11].'"[165]

20. The End of the Days.

"And the Lord's wrath shall return no more, until He should accomplish it, and until He should establish it, according to the purpose of His heart: at the end of the days (ἐπ' ἐσχάτου τῶν ἡμερῶν) **they shall understand it** [Jer. 23:20]**."**

Christ is the treasure hid in Scriptures, according to Saint Irenaeos. "Jeremias also says, 'In the last days they shall understand these things [Jer. 23:20].' Every prophecy, before its fulfillment, is to men full of enigmas and ambiguities. But when the time has arrived, and the prediction has come to pass, then the prophecy has a clear and certain exposition. For this reason, when at this present time the law is read to the Jews, it is like a fable. For they do not possess the explanation of all things pertaining to the Son's advent, which took place in human nature. When it is read by Christians, it is a treasure, hid in a field, but brought to light by Christ's Cross. When it is explained, it both enriches the understanding and shows forth God's wisdom, declaring His dispensations with regard to us, and forms the kingdom of Christ beforehand. It preaches by anticipation the inheritance of the holy Jerusalem. It proclaims beforehand that he who loves God shall arrive at such excellency as even to see God and hear His word; and from the hearing shall he be glorified to such an extent that others cannot behold the glory of his countenance."[166]

Saint Cyprian affirms that "the Jews would not understand the holy Scriptures, but that they would be intelligible in the last times."[167]

---

[164] Ibid., Ante-Nicene, V:207, 215.

[165] Saint Gregory of Nyssa, *Against Eunomius*, Bk. XII, Nicene, 2nd Ser., V:241.

[166] Saint Irenaeus, *Against Heresies*, Ch. XXVI, Ante-Nicene, I:496, 497.

[167] Saint Cyprian, "Testimonies," § 4, *Treatises*, Ante-Nicene, V:509.

Spiritual Counsels

1. Consider Another's Salvation.

"If thou wilt bring forth the precious from the worthless, thou shalt be as My mouth: and they shall return to thee; but thou shalt not return to them [Jer. 15:19]**."**

Saint Chrysostom writes: "Consider to what a dignity he exalts himself who esteems his brother's salvation as of great importance. Such a man is imitating God, as far as lies within the power of man. And God says so through His prophet [Jer. 15:19]. What He says is that he who is eager to save a brother who has fallen into careless ways, he who hastens to snatch his brother from the jaws of the devil, that man imitates Me as far as lies in human power. What could equal that? This is greater than all good deeds; it is the peak of all virtue."[168] Continuing, he says, "And though thou mayest not persuade today, tomorrow thou shalt persuade. And though thou mayest never persuade, thou shalt have thine own reward in full. And though thou mayest persuade not all, a few out of many thou mayest, since neither did the apostles persuade all men but still they discoursed with all; and for all they have their reward. For not according to the result of the things that are well done, but according to the intention of the doers is God wont to assign the crowns. Though thou shouldest pay down but two farthings, He receiveth them; and what He did in the case of the widow [Mk. 12:42], the same will He do also in the case of those who teach."[169]

2. Trust in God [Jer. 17:5].

Saint Cyprian, in a treatise concerning those who had lapsed, repeats: "Let no one cheat himself, let no one deceive himself. The Lord alone can have mercy. He alone can bestow pardon for sins which have been committed against Himself, for it was He Who bore our sins, Who sorrowed for us, Whom God delivered up for our sins. Man cannot be greater than God, nor can a servant remit or forego by his indulgence what has been committed by a greater crime against the Lord lest to the person lapsed this be moreover added to his sin—if he be ignorant that it is declared, **'Cursed is the man who trusts in man, and will lean his arm of flesh upon him, while his heart departs from the Lord** [Jer. 17:5]**.'** The Lord must be besought."[170]

Saint Basil says, "Now by the words, 'who trusts in man,' the Scripture forbids a man to place his hope in another; and by the words, 'makes flesh his arm,' it forbids him to trust in himself. Either course is termed a defection from the Lord. Further, in adding the final issue of both—**'He shall**

---

[168] Saint John Chrysostom, "The Sixth Instruction," *Baptismal Instructions*, ACW, 31:100, 101.

[169] Idem, "Hom. III," *First Corinthians*, Nicene, 1st Ser., XII:15.

[170] Saint Cyprian, "Treatise III, On the Lapsed," § 17, *Treatises*, Ante-Nicene, V:442.

be as the wild tamarisk in the desert. He shall not see when good shall come; but he shall dwell in barren places, and in the wilderness, in a salt land which is not inhabited [Jer. 17:6]'—the Scripture declares that for anyone to place his trust either in himself or in anyone else is to alienate oneself from the Lord."[171] Speaking of the tamarisk, he comments, "It has a double life; it is an aquatic plant, and yet it covers the desert. Thus, Jeremias compares it to the worst of characters—the double character [Jer. 17:6]."[172]

The Venerable Bede (ca. 673-735) adds, "It is an unfruitful and low-growing tree, very bitter to the taste, and in a word utterly unworthy of human cultivation; therefore it grows in the desert. A person who turns away from fear and love of God, who hopes for a kingdom and riches from human beings, is rightly compared to this kind of tree."[173]

3. Keep a True Sabbath.

"'And it shall come to pass, if ye will hearken to Me,' saith the Lord, 'to carry in no burdens through the gates of this city on the sabbath days, and to sanctify the sabbath days, so as to do no work upon it [Jer. 17:24]**....'"**

Saint Gregory the Great reminds us that the Lord and Redeemer did many works on sabbath days. Thus how does this apply to us now? "For this which is said by the Prophet Jeremias [Jer. 17:24] could be held to as long as it was lawful for the law to be observed according to the letter; but after the grace of almighty God, our Lord Jesus Christ has appeared and the commandments of the law, which were spoken of figuratively, cannot be kept according to the letter. For if one says that thus the sabbath is to be kept, he must needs say that carnal sacrifices are to be offered; he must say too that the commandment about the circumcision of the body is still to be retained.

"We therefore accept spiritually, and hold spiritually, this which is written about the sabbath. For the sabbath means rest. But we have the true Sabbath in our Redeemer Himself, the Lord Jesus Christ. And whosoever acknowledges the light of faith in Him, if he draws the sins of concupiscence through his eyes into his soul, he introduces burdens through the gates on the sabbath day. We introduce then no burden through the gates on the sabbath day, if we draw no weights of sin through the bodily senses to the soul."[174]

4. "Cursed is the man that does the works of the Lord carelessly, keeping back his sword from blood [Jer. 31:10 LXX; 48:10 KJV]**."**

---

[171] Saint Basil, *Ascetical Works: The Long Rules*, FC, 9:318.

[172] Idem, "Hom. V," *The Hexaemeron*, Nicene, 2nd Ser., VIII:81.

[173] The Venerable Bede, *Homilies on the Gospels*, Bk. II, "Homily 11.25," Cistercian Studies Series: No. 111, p. 258.

[174] Saint Gregory the Great, "Epistle I," Bk. XIII, *Selected Epistles of Gregory the Great, Books IX-XIV*, Nicene, 2nd Ser., XIII:92.

Saint Basil the Great counsels us: "Do not allow another to do the work that is rightly yours, so that the reward as well may not be taken from you and given to another, and he be enriched with your wealth while you are put to shame. Perform the duties of your ministry decently and with care as if you were serving Christ, for **'Cursed,'** says the prophet, **'is the man that does the works of the Lord carelessly** [Jer. 31:10]**.'**"[175]

Saint Gregory the Great warns, "Let them see, then, in how great guilt they are involved who, knowing the sores of souls, neglect to cure them by the lancing of words. Whence also it is well said through the prophet, 'Cursed is he who keepeth back his sword from blood [cf. Jer. 31:10].' For to keep back the sword from blood is to hold back the word of preaching from the slaying of the carnal life; of which sword it is said again, 'My sword shall devour flesh [Deut. 32:42].'"[176]

As the most sympathetic of the prophets, O all-blessed and God-inspired Jeremias, deem us worthy of compassion who are in desperation over our many passions. But since thou hast become a mediator of the revelation of secret things and divine illumination, by thy mediation make peaceful the much-troubled tempest of our lives.

On the 1st of May, the holy Church commemorates the holy Hieromartyr VATAS of Persia.

Vatas (Batas), the holy martyr, hailed from Persia. His ancestral religion was the Christian Faith. When he came to be thirty years of age, he heard the Lord speaking in the Gospel these words: "If anyone come to Me, and hate not his own father, and mother, and wife, and children, and brothers, and sisters, and still, his own life also, he cannot be My disciple [Lk. 14:26]." Vatas, at this utterance, became filled with the Holy Spirit and thus acknowledged the godly requirement. He, thereupon, forsook all of the transient things of this world, repairing to a monastery where he became a monk. He preferred the strict and laborious life of the monks. He surpassed all the brethren in abstinence, vigilance, and continence. He in no wise would give entry to the door of his senses, which could usher in the death of the soul. Much rather, by keeping the senses under surveillance and exercising attention over them and his heart, he came to yearn for a martyric end.

Therefore, when the Persian idolaters instigated a persecution against the Christians, the brethren of his monastery decided to depart and give place to anger. This is in accordance with the words of our Lord Who said, "Whenever they persecute you in this city, flee ye to another [Mt. 10:23]." On the one hand, all the monks of the brotherhood were resolved to leave; but, on

---

175 Saint Basil, *Ascetical Works: On Renunciation of the World*, FC, 9:29.

176 Saint Gregory the Great, *Pastoral Rule*, Ch. XXV, Nicene, 2nd Ser., XII:53.

the other hand, Father Vatas stood alone and did not wish to flee. With the opportunity to contest for martyrdom came the fervent longing to compete.

At length, after Vatas had spent some thirty years in asceticism, he was apprehended by the fire worshippers. They brought him to Yasdeech, who was the brother of Varsanava. The latter was the ruler and authority in a place called Vitzios. Father Vatas was commanded to pay homage to the sun in the sky. Seeing that he was in no way persuaded to comply, but that he rather proclaimed himself a Christian, he was handed over to the rack masters. They tied him by his two hands and then stretched him by means of ten soldiers tugging at his limbs. The joints of Vatas' shoulders were utterly wrenched and displaced. Following this torture, they administered a thrashing using thick staves. Afterward, they bound him by his genitals, from which twenty soldiers dragged him along the ground. Since the valiant monk persevered and remained loyal to the Faith of Christ, the idolaters placed a pile of many heavy rocks on his abdomen. Next, they drew their knives and cut away his shoulder blades and the area below his breasts. After having survived all this maiming and mutilation, they finally beheaded him. Thus, the ever-memorable Vatas received the crown of martyrdom.

On the 1st of May, the holy Church commemorates the holy Martyr PHILOSOPHOS of Alexandria.[177]

Philosophos, the great martyr of Christ, was perfected in martyrdom at Alexandria, the Egyptian city of his birth. According to Anthony, the great one among the ascetics, Philosophos achieved martyrdom in the following way.

In Alexandria, there was a most beautiful garden. It was filled with many pleasant things. Now the pagan tyrant of that time had ordered that a comfortable and adorned couch be set in this garden. The holy Philosophos, a Christian, was forcibly set upon this couch with fettered hands and feet. A

---

[177] What is known about Saint Philosophos is taken from the *Paradise of the Fathers*. In the *Synaxaristes* of the Monastery of Dionysiou, of the new coenobium, Saint Philosophos is named Justin. Philosophos bears the name of "philosopher." What has Saint John Chrysostom to say about the philosopher? He writes in his commentary on the Epistle to the Ephesians: "For what, tell me, is the duty of a philosopher? Is it not to despise both riches and glory? Is it not to be above both envy and every other passion?...Such is the true philosopher, such is that wealth of which we spoke. He has nothing, and has all things: he has all things, and has nothing." ["Homily XXI."]

It should also be noted that the Martyr Niketas in the time of the Decian Persecution (249-251) was also placed upon a bed, bound, and incited to be drawn into sensual desire by a harlot. In order to avoid this sin, Niketas bit off his own tongue with his teeth and spat it into the harlot's face. His name Niketas in the Greek language suggests that he triumphed over this temptation. This account was recorded by Nikephoros. [See *Politikon Theatron*, Ch. 8.]

certain harlot was brought to him. She stood over the saint, attempting not only to entice him with indecent words but also to have him commit a shameful act. She embraced him with her defiled hands and kissed him ardently. The valiant contestant of Christ, even though he was bound, found a way to escape the harlot's arms which enveloped him like a noose.

At first, Philosophos closed his eyes lest he should gaze upon her. Then he bit down hard with his teeth into his tongue. The unbearable pangs made the senses of his body less responsive to pleasure. The wound filled his mouth with blood, which he spat into the face and on the clothes of the harlot. When she saw his blood streaming forth, she staggered backward in shock and revulsion. In this manner, therefore, the magnanimous one struggled against, and vanquished, his senses. He kept himself passionless by the grace of Christ. After this triumph, his head was struck off. He then departed into the heavens, bearing his crown, and received everlasting and unutterable joy.

Saint Philosophos

On the 1st of May, the holy Church commemorates our venerable Mother ISIDORA of Egypt, the Fool for Christ.[178]

Isidora, our holy mother (amma), was a nun at a convent in Tabennisi on the right bank of the Nile, north of Thebes. The great river proved a natural boundary between the convents and monasteries, with the monks on the left bank. Monks did not cross the river to enter the convents, except for priests and deacons—and then only by invitation on Sundays. Mother Isidora lived during the fourth century. She may have been born in Egypt. There is no way to confirm the place or year. The year of her repose is given as 365. Our holy mother's convent had four hundred nuns. It was considered a large community.

---

[178] The Life of Saint Isidora was recorded by Palladius in *The Lausiac History*, under § 34, entitled "The Nun Who Feigned Madness." Palladius wrote ca. 417, after spending twelve years visiting the holy monastics of Egypt. See the English translation of R. T. Meyer's *Palladius: The Lausiac History* in Ancient Christian Writers, No. 34 (NY, NY/Ramsey, NJ: Newman Press).

Saint Isidora

From the time that the maiden Isidora entered this life of chastity and self-denial, she pretended to be a fool for Christ. She, therefore, appeared to all in the sisterhood as one mad and even demon possessed. But Isidora was mindful of the words of Saint Paul who said that "we are fools for Christ's sake [1 Cor. 4:10]."

Saint Paul also wrote and advised the Corinthians, saying, "Let no one be deceiving himself. If anyone among you think himself to be wise in this age, let him become foolish, in order that he might become wise [1 Cor. 3:18]." Such persons, who are fools for the sake of Christ, are a spectacle both to angels and men. While they appear as fools for Christ's sake, others are deemed wise in Christ. They appear weak, while others are strong. They are dishonored, while others are held in honor. They suffer hunger, thirst, nakedness, blows, and no place to rest. They toil with their own hands. They endure being reviled and persecuted, while they bless their persecutors and bear up. Others speak evilly of such persons, while the fools beseech and repay evil with good. Indeed, as the apostle said, such persons have become as the filth of the world, the off-scouring of all. Saint Paul wrote these words with regard to what the apostles have endured, not that he wished to shame the Corinthians but that he might admonish them paternally as beloved children.

So it was with Amma Isidora in the coenobium. She was one of the sisterhood, but lived apart from the others in the following manner. While the other nuns covered their heads with cowls, she dressed her head in a rag. She went about barefooted, being of service to her sisters. No one ever observed her to sit down at table with the rest of the community. In fact, no one ever saw her chew or eat. After the communal meal, she would partake of the crumbs left behind on the table. She took upon herself all the menial service of the convent or tasks that the others found irksome or disagreeable. Thus, she could be seen scouring pots and scrubbing and cleaning. Other nuns, seeing her lowliness, came to despise her. Although they accepted and enjoyed all of her selfless ministrations, still they mistreated her with insults, curses, and even blows. Isidora neither grumbled nor complained. She was not angry in her heart nor remembered wrongs. She continually kept her mind on Jesus and turned the other cheek. As time went by, the other nuns kept using her as the convent broom and community sponge.

In the meantime there dwelt a famous anchorite, Abba Piteroum, at Porphyrites situated between the Nile and the Red Sea. This mount was known at that time as the abode of hermits. One day, an angel of the Lord appeared to Piteroum and declared, "Thou hast a high opinion of thyself, abba. Thou deemest thyself pious and ascetical for living in this stark wilderness. Wouldest thou see another more pious than thyself, and what is more, a woman? Well then, go to the convent at Tabennisi. Thou shalt discover a nun who wears a rag around her head. She is thy superior. Know this: though she is buffeted by the crowd, she has never taken her mind or heart from God. But thou dwellest here in isolation and seest no one. And though thou goest about nowhere, yet in thy mind's eye thou hast traversed city after city."

Abashed at the words of the angel, Abba Piteroum left his mountain retreat and went to see the prefects. He requested permission to visit the convent at Tabennisi. The authorities agreed only because he was advanced in age and was held in great repute by all for his sobriety and sanctity. Piteroum crossed over to the right bank and was allowed entry into the convent. He requested of the abbess that the nuns assemble. He looked hither and thither, but he saw no nun with a rag tied around her head. He turned to the superioress and asked, "Is there anyone else? Have all been mustered?" The sisters remarked, "We are all here, holy father." He said, "Nay, one is absent." At first, they were puzzled by his insistence until it was remembered that Isidora was in the kitchen. The sisters said, "We have one nun who is in the kitchen. But there is no need to bother with her, as she is an imbecile." Abba Piteroum then said, "Bring her to me that I may see her." They went to call her out, but no answer came from the kitchen. Either Amma Isidora heard he had come or God revealed to her the reason for his arrival. Since she did not respond by either appearing or answering their shouts, they went in after her. Finding her in the kitchen, they said, "Abba Piteroum has asked to see thee. Make haste and come with us, for he is a holy man of renown." Seeing that she made no move to leave the kitchen, they took hold of her forcibly and dragged her into the reception area.

When Abba Piteroum caught sight of the nun with the rag around her head, he at once made a full prostration before her feet and said, "Bless me, holy amma!" Mother Isidora then prostrated herself and said, "Bless me, milord!" All members of the sisterhood were astonished at this spectacle. Attempting to intervene, they said, "Abba, take no insults. She is touched in the head. Pay no heed to her." Abba Piteroum then addressed the sisterhood and said, "You are the ones who are touched in the head. This woman is a spiritual mother. She is amma to you and to me as well. Verily, I pray that I may be accounted as worthy as she on the day of judgment."

Hearing this pronouncement, all the nuns made a prostration to Piteroum. Many public confessions soon followed. With eyes misted over or blinded with tears, one by one, each nun acknowledged how she sinned against Isidora. One admitted, "I poured the leftovers of my plate on her." Another acknowledged, "I struck her with my fists." Another said, "I hit her on the nose and caused it to bleed." And others disclosed how they cast insults and curses in her face. Thus, salvation came to that house on that day. Abba Piteroum prayed for the repentant nuns and the sisterhood. He departed much edified and returned to his philosophical retreat in the desert.

As for the convent at Tabennisi, Mother Isidora became the object of much deference and honor. All extolled her for several days, until she could no longer endure the burden of their constant apologies and praises. She, therefore, found it necessary to take herself away. She departed secretly and disappeared from sight in order to continue her ascetical struggles unencumbered. Nobody discovered where she went. No one learned how or when she reposed.

By this account, we see that the wisdom of this world is foolishness with God. "For it hath been written: 'He taketh the wise in their own craftiness [cf. Job 5:13]'; and again, 'The Lord knoweth the reasonings of the wise, that they are vain [Ps. 93(94):11; 1 Cor. 3:19, 20].'"

Saint John Chrysostom speaks about such fools, writing: "This is the meaning of fools for Christ's sake. For whosoever suffers wrong and avenges not himself, nor is vexed, is reckoned a fool by the heathen who dishonor such a one as weak."[179] In fact, such fools are grateful to their persecutors.[180] Saint Paul wrote these exhortations lest any Christian should be puffed up against another. "For who," he asks, "maketh thee to differ? And what hast thou that thou didst not receive [1 Cor. 4:7]?" The apostle, thereupon, urges us to keep striving to become imitators of him [1 Cor. 4:16].

On the 1st of May, the holy Church commemorates the holy Martyr SAVVAS, who was hanged from a fig tree.

On the 1st of May, the holy Church celebrates the CONSECRATION OF THE NEW CHURCH, when the patriarch entered the palace and then went forth in a procession to the New Church where he conducted the Liturgy.

---

[179] Saint John Chrysostom, "Homily 13," *First Corinthians*, *P.G.* 61:110 (col. 108).
[180] Ibid., *P.G.* 61:110 (cols. 108, 109).

On the 1st of May, the holy Church commemorates our holy father among the saints, PANARETOS, Archbishop of Paphos in Cyprus.[181]

Panaretos, our holy father among the saints and far-famed archbishop of Paphos of Cyprus,[182] is whom we celebrate today. He flourished during the eighteenth century on the famous island of Cyprus.

Now we know that honey is produced in the bees' honey sacs collected from the nectar of flowers blooming on trees, shrubs, plants, and herbs. Honey is then stored in the beehive or nest in a honeycomb, constructed of beeswax secreted by the worker bees. The beeswax is obtained, after removal of the honey by drainage or extraction, by melting the honeycomb. Both the honey and the beeswax of the bee become useful for all. From this similitude with the bee, we see how it was with today's saint. For when virtue is born in our hearts and we cultivate it, then it comes to light and gives light. As a result, this virtue not only is useful to those who possess it but also is a light to those who do not have it.

This quest for virtue is not exclusive to desert ascetics and monks of the coenobium, for whom this attainment ought to be their chief and general goal. With some effort on their part, they certainly will advance. The same holds true for kings and patriarchs and bishops, who have so many concerns and responsibilities with regard to the people, cities, and dioceses. Indeed, not only those in such positions of authority take up this pursuit but also many from among the lay folk have shown themselves pleasing to God. Moreover, it can be demonstrated that the undertaking of virtue and moral excellence was not

---

[181] The Life of Saint Panaretos, as presented in *The Great Synaxaristes* (in Greek), was composed during the early 19th C., not long after the saint's repose in 1791. Much of it was composed by the Greek compilers from divine offices to the saint. It is a pity that there is such a scarcity of biographical information concerning the saint's youth and life before his consecration to the episcopacy. *The Collection of the Lives of the Saints of Cyprus*, published in 1988, includes the Life of Saint Panaretos and furnishes us with a few other details.

[182] Paphos is situated at the western end of Cyprus. Since Salamis was in the east, the Apostle Paul passed through the isle from Salamis to Paphos [Acts 13:6-13]. Paphos was also the name of two ancient cities that were the precursors of the modern town. Old Paphos, where there was a temple to Aphrodite, was located at modern Pirgos (Kouklia); New Paphos, which had superseded Old Paphos by Roman times, was ten miles (sixteen kilometers) farther west. New Paphos and Ktima together form modern Paphos. Old Paphos was settled by Greek colonists in the Mycenaean period. New Paphos, which had been the port town of Old Paphos, became the administrative capital of the whole island in Ptolemaic and Roman times. The city was attacked and destroyed by Muslim raiders in A.D. 960. *Encyclopaedia Britannica Deluxe Edition 2004 CD-ROM*, s.v." Paphos."

only the pursuit of some in former eras. Even in these latter times, it has been shown that it is possible to cultivate virtue though one is in the midst of the world or is just a simple and private individual.

What else is virtue other than the keeping of the divine commandments, the exercise of good works, and the turning away from evil deeds? Who can doubt that without such works it is not possible for one—and not only monks—to be justified before God? Who can doubt that God asks these things from laymen, too, while from monastics He asks more? On account of this, monks, and indeed even all the clergy who are found in this life, have an obligation to do and render more than those abiding in the world. Priests and spiritual shepherds ought to maintain themselves as a good example for the laity, according to that which has been written: "Let your light shine before men [Mt. 5:16]."

The Gospel exhortations were known and were being followed by the blessed Panaretos, though he was living and going about in the world. But he did not have the spirit of the world and had escaped its pollutions.[183] When he was among men, he was gladly executing the duties of a Christian layman, that is, keeping the divine commandments, turning away from evil, and laboring to be rich in good deeds. But afterward, as a clergyman and, indeed, a hierarch and shepherd of the people named for Christ, the thrice-happy one continued struggling in the great task of virtue as if he were in the middle of the deepest wilderness and not in the midst of the city.

In another source, we are told the following: he was born ca. 1710, in the region of Mesaoria, southeast of Nicosia (Lefkosia), where he also grew up. During his lifetime, he was in the midst of a difficult period on account of Ottoman rule. The oppressive suffering and slavery of the Orthodox under the Muslims defy description. He was the scion of pious parents who were people of some, or at least sufficient, means. When the lad Panaretos came of age, he was sent to Lefkosia[184] to attend the Orthodox school in the city. After he completed his studies, he returned to his village.[185]

---

[183] Cf. 1 Cor. 2:12; 2 Pe. 2:20.

[184] Nicosia or Lefkosia is the capital of the Republic of Cyprus. It lies along the Pedieos River, in the center of the Mesaoria Plain between the Kyrenia Mountains (north) and the Troodos range (south). The city is also the archiepiscopal seat of the autocephalous (having the right to elect its own archbishop and bishops) Church of Cyprus. Nicosia came successively under the control of the Byzantines (330–1191), the Lusignan kings (1192–1489), the Venetians (1489–1571), the Turks (1571–1878), and the British (1878–1960).

[185] This paragraph is taken from *The Collection*, op. cit.

Due to his unfeigned love for the angelic life, Panaretos abandoned home, family, and all the rest, in order to obtain the pearl of great price.[186] He first repaired to the Monastery of Saint Anastasios, situated below his village. The monastery, at that time, was in a state of deterioration. As for the young Panaretos, he was bent on applying all his soul, heart, mind, and strength in cultivating the good seed of piety which already was planted in his early youth. In the monastery, he exercised patience and stability. He labored at humility and prayer, so that he ascended the ladder of the virtues. Reading from the sacred Scriptures and the writings of the fathers were part of his daily activity. Somewhat later, he was appointed for a time to the responsible position of exarch of the holy Archdiocese of Cyprus. Though unwilling, he was obliged to accept the position. He had no wish of distinction. He also served admirably for a short time as abbot at the Monastery of Saint Neophytos. Later on, he was superior for many years at the Monastery of the Theotokos at Pamoriotissa.[187]

"It is my desire," confesses the Greek biographer, "to narrate this thrice-blessed man's life and God-inspired achievements. My first reason for taking up my pen is because this holy bloom, named Panaretos, sprouted in our Orthodox Church in these last times of dessication and drought. No, he was not sanctified by a martyr's end, as have many of the spiritual athletes due to the oppressive yoke of the godless Hagarenes. In these latter years, the new-martyrs abided steadfast in their Orthodox Faith and, thereby, enriched the Church of Christ. As for our holy Father Panaretos, instead of martyrdom, he undertook ascetical struggles. In this present generation, such a course of conduct is rare indeed. My second reason for compiling this biography is this. Although Father Panaretos is already numbered among the saints and hierarchs, still there are but a few who honor him as is meet—as a saint. But this may also be due to the fact that the book containing his life is not easily found.[188] Most people, nonetheless, are ignorant that there is a saint with such a name. They indifferently consider that the appellation of the holy Panaretos is not a proper name. Much rather, they imagine it is some form of address used by monks. Why? The answer is by reason of the good connotation in the meaning of Panaretos, which in Greek literally means 'all-virtuous.' Other names also have been misconstrued similarly. Having then begun with a prologue for his life, I shall now endeavor to commence his biography."

Our father among the saints, Panaretos, had his name from his works and his works from his name. For having practised every virtue, he was fittingly glorified by God. Concerning his way of life and pursuits, before his ascent to the episcopal dignity, we have little or no testimony. This scantiness

---

[186] Cf. Mt. 13:46.

[187] This paragraph is taken from *The Collection*.

[188] The name of this book is *Ὅρμος Σωτήριος*.

of information is owing to the blessed man's own desire to keep his virtue concealed.[189] It will be exhibited later on that no one knew of his labors and contests, despite the fact that he struggled above man's nature. He, evidently, was not the sort of person to raise anyone's curiosity. We, nonetheless, can draw conclusions about his earlier way of life, although it is mostly couched in silence. For, if throughout the tenure of his episcopacy, he was struggling ascetically in the midst of the world, that is, in the episcopal house, certainly when he was a private citizen, hidden from the eyes of others, he made gains in secret. But now, as bishop, when there were other clergy always present, concelebrating with him, as well as attendants, according to the order and custom of hierarchs, and ecclesiastical rules and forms, he was even more keen to keep secret the treasure of his asceticism. In fact, both attendants and clerics did not perceive very much at all about their chief shepherd other than his total modesty of spirit. Therefore, precisely because Panaretos gave this appearance to the eyes of the world, divine providence settled on him as hierarch. For in the eyes of God, Panaretos was pure and well pleasing. Panaretos, secretly and diligently, exercised himself in acquiring sagacity and every virtue. He, consequently, was elected hierarch and installed on the episcopal throne of the city of Paphos in Cyprus, becoming by this elevation the catholic successor and close match of Lazarus the four-days-dead.[190] The elevation to the episcopacy took place on the 14th day of January, in the year 1767. The consecration took place in the holy Church of the Theotokos Phaneromene.

Immediately upon the ascent to the episcopal throne, all the servants and attendants of the metropolis, as well as the clergy, loved and esteemed the saint as a good and worthy prelate, saying to one another, "Glory to our holy God because He has granted us a hierarch who is humble, meek, temperate, patient, unaffected, and a lover of quiet!" They certainly did not, however, as we said, perceive the lofty sanctity that dwelt within him. This was due to his extreme humble-mindedness. Panaretos' acquisition of the virtues was kept secret. But as he approached the blessed end of his earthly sojourn, his holiness

---

[189] In the year 1764, the Turkish rebel named Kalil, with some two thousand troops under him, attempted to besiege Lefkosia. The insurgent demanded that the Turkish authorities surrender themselves to him. In the meantime, Kalil laid waste to surrounding villages and cities. Father Panaretos, as a tonic for all, set about building churches. This labor not only afforded him consolation but it also blunted the festering bitterness of the persecuted Cypriots. Both the clergy and the people came together some three years later to elect a new metropolitan to the city of Paphos. The unanimous and considered choice was Panaretos. The outpourings of the beleaguered people settled on such a one as their shepherd. The saint could not impeach their purpose. [*The Collection of the Lives of the Saints of Cyprus*, op. cit.]

[190] Jn. 11:17, 39.

came to be revealed not only prior to his death but also afterward. It was the time prior to his repose that his acquaintances finally became cognizant of his sanctity. Although it was ever before them, yet only now had they become discriminating. Only now had they become sensible of the loss they were about to incur in his death. Everything concerning him, therefore, that remained in the memory of his acquaintances was made manifest after the saint's repose. They wrote down their remembrances and brought them to life. From this, we may understand that Panaretos' disciples wrote down only the things that they themselves had witnessed, since they were unfamiliar with the events of his early life. We, being also satisfied with these alone, will relate all that we have found to glorify God in Trinity.

Thus, when the divine Panaretos ascended the summit of the high priesthood, it is no exaggeration that he hid his holiness even from those of his own household. All that appeared to the eyes of bystanders were his meekness, humility, scrupulous care for his flock, sympathy, and, of course, the manner in which he was teaching the rational flock of Christ. We should mention his diet and some of his habits of which it was not possible to escape complete notice. His food was extremely frugal—just a simple repast. He ate once a day, after Vespers. There were no varied or savory dishes among his table service. The excuse he gave for such abstemiousness was a stomach complaint of some indisposition. After his supper, he would enter his bedchamber and shut the door, feigning that he was taking his ease. When some of the household attendants peered through a tiny opening in the door, they observed him standing upright in an attitude of prayer. He carried on in this manner throughout the night. He alone would make his bed. He did not wish any to take notice that he had neither a soft mattress nor a pillow. Whenever a friend would come and pay him a visit, he was the epitome of graciousness. He even allowed the impression that the ways of his residence were luxurious and dainty. He was especially cautious whenever he needed to remove his shirt. He wished that none should see him naked. We shall divulge the reason later for his eagerness to maintain privacy, for it is a matter left to the occasion.

Metropolitan Panaretos, during the twenty-three years that he served as a hierarch, always deemed himself the lowly servant of the people of Christ. He ever brought to mind the Savior's words: "For even the Son of Man came not to be served, but to serve, and to give His life a ransom for many [Mk. 10:45; cf. Mt. 20:28]." Panaretos, also, was the good shepherd, ever prepared to lay down his life for his flock.[191] He became all things to all men that he might save some[192] by making their hearts steadfast with longing for salvation. As a bishop, he engaged in building projects. Many churches were either built

---

[191] Cf. Jn. 10:11.

[192] Cf. 1 Cor. 9:22.

or renovated during his tenure, as for example in the villages of Nikokleia, Arminou, Galataria, Alektora, Lemona, and other places, as well as other sites in western Cyprus, together with his former sacred Monastery of Saint Anastasios.[193]

Now during the celebration of the divine Liturgy, his thoughts were collected. He was pensive and tearful. This was due to his great reverence of the mystagogy. Since we have said that the early and middle years of his life have not been committed to paper, we need to recount at least two miracles. They were wrought toward the end of his life. It was from these miracles that his virtue and holiness were ultimately uncovered. Indeed, if his own disciples had not seen them with their own eyes, they would not have revered him as a saint. The idea never impinged on their minds. They were remarkably obtuse and showed no great powers of discernment. Hearken that you may be persuaded concerning the truth of that which has been spoken about these wonderworkings.

A certain senior priest in a village of the Saint Panaretos' diocese was vanquished by the passion of being sordidly greedy for gain. He so oppressed those in his parish that they, not having any other recourse, sought refuge with the saint. Weeping, they asked him to settle the matter between the priest and themselves. After the saint had heard their complaints, he summoned the priest. He disclosed the allegations made against him. The bishop then delivered his own reproof and admonitions. The priest, however, replied to the saint, "The accusations are nought but slander." The saint, then, believed the priest and dismissed him in peace. Returning home, the priest did not cease his evil practises. The inhabitants, seeing that he conducted himself in the same manner, went forth again to the saintly hierarch. For a second time, they denounced the priest's behavior. When the saint again called forth the priest, the latter maintained what he said earlier. The saint, thereupon, sternly rebuked the priest. Panaretos then sent him forth to his home. That priest, however, did not leave off his avarice but went on to commit worse deeds.

The Christians came again and told the saint all that had taken place. Grieved at the priest's hardness of heart, the ill-used Panaretos summoned him for the third time and delivered a strict reproof. But the priest, fearing neither God nor man, showed no deference to the saint. The negligent one, immediately, spat forth strange and dangerous oaths in order to justify himself, invoking the all-holy name of Jesus Christ. The priest's character, thus illustrated, caused the holy Panaretos to feel very troubled at the impropriety of such behavior. Shuddering at the priest's lack of fear, the saint, filled with holy fear, said to him, "May thy mouth be blocked that it not swear falsely!"

---

[193] This paragraph is from *The Collection*.

And—O the wonder!—from that moment, the priest became dumb and was unable to speak. But the saint, being humble-minded, kept saying, "I, the unworthy one, did not do this, but the fearful name of our Lord Jesus Christ has chastened him." The humbled priest, ashamed at what he had suffered, went out from that place. He remained dumb for a long period. Then, afterward, he fell gravely ill and was in danger of dying. The smitten priest, dreading the righteous judgment of God, which indeed had come upon him while he was yet alive, was sorrowful beyond measure. With fear, he was then resolved to write the holy Panaretos. He besought the saint's condescension, begging the bishop to come to him for the purpose of making his confession and receiving his forgiveness.

The saint, seeing the priest in a state of repentance, hastened to him with joy and eagerness. As he drew nigh to the bed of the afflicted priest, who was breathing his last, the bishop said, "Take courage, child, for since thou hast repented, thou shalt find mercy with God." The remorseful priest, with tears streaming from his eyes, was able, only by means of gestures, to communicate with the saint. He was imploring the saint to pray to God to loose his tongue, so that he could be free to confess his sins to the saint. The saint, moved with compassion, shut the door. Standing in prayer, he supplicated God for the priest. Lo, the miracle! As the saint blessed him, the priest was straightway loosed from the bond. The repentant priest, confessing his sins with great lamentation, sought forgiveness. The saint consoled him and said, "Take courage, my child, for thou art marching toward death; and the Lord will be gracious to thee." And so it came to pass, according to the saint's utterance. This miracle is testified to by many, above all by the then Metropolitan of Thessalonike, Gerasimos, who was then spending some time in Cyprus. Hear now the second miracle.

When he had thus passed his earthly sojourn in a God-pleasing fashion, the saint also arrived at the end of his life. Foreseeing that he was about to depart from this present world, he began to prepare his grave and to dig it with his own hands. He, afterward, sewed the garments of white cloth that he would wear to the grave. When he had finished this preparation, he succumbed to a slight illness. He then told his disciples, "The hour of my death is nearing, O children, and may the Lord expiate me!" His disciples, however, were thinking that he was raving and talking nonsense. The only thing that caused them uncertainty was an alteration in his routine: although he regularly made his confession every Saturday, yet that week he had not. Hence, they had a slight suspicion and waited to see what would be the outcome. The saint, worn out by his sickness, toward evening, said to his *protosynkellos*,[194] "Tomorrow, in the

[194] The *protosynkellos* was the fellow boarder and confidant of a patriarch or bishop.

(continued...)

morning, do thou take along an extra mule and go down to the shore. Thither thou shalt see a ship that has on board lord Parthenios, the former Bishop of Karpathos.[195] Relate to him that I beseech him to take the trouble to come to confess me." The *protosynkellos*, however, behaving ill, went out and recounted to those present what his elder said, adding, "He is babbling out of senility and on account of his sickness. For how could he know that the holy Bishop of Karpathos is on our shore, since neither news nor epistle concerning him has come to us? Nor has he any reason to come to our city." So reasoning, the odd-tempered *protosynkellos* acted negligently in regard to the elder's command.

The saint, however, had foreseen these things. He did not nourish a resentful temper, for he continued to imitate the Master Christ's love for men. As soon as he arose from sleep, immediately, he said again to the *protosynkellos*, "Bestir thyself! Why dost thou hesitate and attend not to that which I have bidden thee? The holy Bishop of Karpathos is arriving by ship down at the beach. Run along and tarry not!" Then the *protosynkellos*, wondering at the saint's words, forthwith went down to the shore as commanded. Straightway, from the place where he stood, he espied a ship sailing with a fair wind. He waited until the ship arrived and docked in the harbor. Not much time passed before the captain disembarked onto dry land. The *protosynkellos* approached him and asked, "Dost thou have a hierarch aboard the vessel?" The captain, for his own reasons was beset with suspicions at this question, initially concealed the truth. But later, when he was sure that the inquiry was not asked toward fulfilling some evil design, he replied, "I have on board the former Bishop of Karpathos; but because of a contrary wind, which found us evening last, we were driven off course. We were compelled to come down here to Cyprus."

Then the *protosynkellos* boarded the ship with the captain. The moment he set eyes on the Bishop of Karpathos, he marvelled greatly at his holy elder's gift of clairvoyance. The *protosynkellos* approached the hierarch and told him all that had occurred. "A mule awaits thee, *despota*," said the *protosynkellos*, "so that we may go up together to the city of Paphos." The Bishop of Karpathos disembarked, marvelling at what had been said. Rejoicing and

---

[194](...continued)
The title was limited at that time to priests and deacons. The *protosynkellos* came to be viewed by some as the successor designate of the reigning bishop.

[195] Karpathos (Italian, Scarpanto) is an island of the Dodekanese group in the Aegean Sea, Greece. The island was closely bound with Rhodes in antiquity and the Middle Ages. Karpathos was under Venetian rule from 1306 to about 1540, when it fell to the Turks. In 1912 it passed to Italy, but after World War II it was awarded to Greece. The islanders' Greek dialect, containing ancient Doric as well as modern Italian words, resembles that of Rhodes and Cyprus. *Encyclopaedia Britannica*, s.v. "Karpathos."

glorifying God, they both mounted the mules and departed for the cathedral and to Saint Panaretos, Metropolitan of Paphos. When the Bishop of Karpathos entered Panaretos' residence, the metropolitan rose up from his sickbed and received him with joy. Panaretos observed that the visiting bishop was eminently suitable. For Panaretos desired time to prepare for death, which must at no long period ensue. After they had exchanged a holy kiss, Saint Panaretos remarked, "God has sent thee here to us lowly men, O brother, since I am suffering and my life is nearing its end. I beseech thee to remain here so that I, the sinner, may make my confession to thee and, if it be thy will, may partake of the immaculate Mysteries. Take the trouble then to serve the Liturgy, so that thou mayest also bless my Christians."

The former Bishop of Karpathos, hearing the saint's words, fell in with his plans gladly. He deemed it his happiness to be of such service, though he believed it a melancholy task to perform. Nevertheless, he promised to fulfill all that was asked of him. Indeed, on the following day, Metropolitan Parthenios, former Bishop of Karpathos, served the Liturgy and blessed the congregation. Saint Panaretos, also, received the immaculate Mysteries. Though weak and infirm, the saint himself also blessed his own flock after the communion of the immaculate Mysteries. He also asked forgiveness from the faithful. Following the service, he again spoke to the Bishop of Karpathos, commenting, "Brother, since the wind is contrary and thou canst not set sail, I beseech thee to remain here till tomorrow. By doing so, thou shalt be on hand to give burial to my body." The visiting bishop, looking grave, gave his nod of approval. Panaretos, with resoluteness, continued and said pointedly, "Now it is also needful that I should implore thee for another favor: I also ask thee not to change my clothes, since I am already dressed in what is needed for burial. In the same state as I am found, sew me up in a sack and cast me into the hole that I have prepared." So then did the saint give his last express orders. On the morrow, while praying to God and making supplication for his flock, Panaretos surrendered his holy soul into the hands of the holy God, in the year of our Lord 1791, in the month of May.

Bishop Parthenios, thereupon, announced to the *protosynkellos* the holy father's last wish, saying, "I am commissioned to express the holy metropolitan's wishes regarding his burial. Forasmuch as the dead man is dressed in the white graveclothes he prepared for himself, let us, in accordance with his command, not wrap him in a shroud. Let us place him, as he is, in the grave, in accordance with his original request." These words, however, put the *protosynkellos* out of countenance. He gainsaid him and spoke as a privileged confidant of the deceased, saying, "I must protest. How can I not fittingly bury my holy elder, my benefactor, especially since he is the prelate of this place? Besides, the saint, only because he was humble-minded, spoke in this fashion, whereas I am obliged to dispatch my duty by him. Nay, I will not overturn established custom." In view of his declaration, the visiting bishop, thinking the *protosynkellos*' scruples probably did him credit, checked himself. He did not make too strenuous an objection. He did not wish a confrontation. He thought it best to show some delicacy, for he could not prevent him. Thus, the *protosynkellos*, having asserted his claim, commenced taking up those things that needed to be done.

As they were undressing the holy relic, as is the custom, the whole company came to be filled with astonishment. They discovered a chain wrapped around the saint's naked body. The spectacle was full of wonder. Panaretos had worn it in such a way that it formed a cross in front and in back, reaching to his loins. With the passage of much time, it had nearly sunk into his flesh. Seeing it, all that were present marvelled exceedingly at the saint's hidden labors and great virtue by which he attracted divine grace. He had, all along, been contending in an aged body as do young men. Panaretos set himself apart for painful labors, being enlightened by the thought of suffering and mortifying the flesh.

The former Bishop of Karpathos and the *protosynkellos*, with profound reverence, unwound the chain and dressed him again. They conducted his funeral, burying him with great reverence and glorifying God as was meet. The stunned mourners, coming to themselves, finally understood the reason that the saint shunned being undressed for interment. True to his character, he wished, even after death, to conceal his secret contests. After these events had come to pass, Saint Panaretos was straightway glorified by God by means of this miracle we are about to tell lest it should remain unknown to posterity.

A certain pauper, being a paralytic, was lying down in the church's courtyard. He had been fed by the saint from the alms of the Christians. He, seeing the saint's relics being carried into the church and escorted to the grave, lamented. With tears, he wailed on account of being deprived of his father and benefactor. He began dragging himself along, as fast as he could. He approached the holy relics, asking the saint for his help. And—behold the wonder!—as soon as he touched the sacred bier, he was completely healed. His limbs, previously deprived of their normal function, appeared and moved with no trace of his former palsy. When the Archbishop of Cyprus[196] learned of this,

---

[196] The tenure of Archbishop Chrysanthos of Cyprus was from 1767 to 1810.

The conquest of 1571 of the island by the Ottoman Turks not only liberated the Orthodox Church from centuries of control by the Latin hierarchy but also its previous tradition of independence was reasserted under a revived archbishopric. The Roman Catholic Church of the Crusader and Venetian rulers was expelled. Its buildings were confiscated and converted into mosques, or were sold to the Orthodox Church.

(continued...)

he came and kissed the saint's tomb. He took the chain with him and transferred it to his archiepiscopal residence. By reason of this chain, there gathered multitudes of ailing sufferers to the archbishop. The petitioners kissed the chain with reverence, thereby receiving healing of every malady.

These incidents concerning Saint Panaretos are universally testified to by all the Cypriots, who have their boast in him. A description of these events was also recorded afterward by the Archbishop of Cyprus, the report of which was dispatched to the most holy Patriarch Gerasimos of Constantinople who was then on the throne.[197] They were also attested to by many others, especially around the year 1793. It was at that time that the former Bishop of Karpathos, as we have said, heard Saint Panaretos' confession. He went to Constantinople to testify to everyone regarding the wondrous virtues and the miracles performed by the man of God; and since Bishop Parthenios had seen these wonderworkings with his own eyes, he dissolved in tears when he related them.

After these things had occurred and the saint had become famous everywhere, certain men thought to steal his holy relics. Then, at night, the saint appeared, simultaneously, to the sleeping *protosynkellos*, prior, and other brothers of the monastery, warning them that thieves were afoot. All were stirred from sleep and began telling one another the reason they had awakened. Going in haste to investigate the truth of this unusual coincidence, they found the door shut and all in peace. But then suddenly, they dashed in the direction of the saint's tomb. Looking there also, they observed, in fact, that some thieves were digging up the saint's tomb and had nearly reached the casket.

---

[196](...continued)
Some Papists chose exile, while others converted either to Islam or to Orthodoxy. Thereafter, some thirty thousand Muslim Turks were settled on the island amongst a population of perhaps 150,000 Greek-Cypriots. This proportion, around 1:5, is still true today.

In the 16th and 17th C., the actual governor of Cyprus, though he commanded a small garrison of 3,000 troops, was relatively powerless. He held authority for a brief period and was principally concerned with recouping the purchase of his office with the minimum of fuss and with the most profit. He was only able to do this through the aghas (community leaders) of the Turkish community and the bishops of the Greeks.

The archbishop grew particularly influential, and in 1660 became recognized as the official representative of the Greek Cypriots, with the rights of direct access to the sultan's palace in Istanbul. In 1754, the archbishop was made responsible for the collection of taxes and later gained the right to appoint the *dragoman* of the *serai*, who was the head of the civil service. By the early 19th C., the archbishop had almost become of greater consequence than the governor.

[197] Patriarch Gerasimos III of Constantinople served from 1794 to 1797. Prior to him was Patriarch Neophytos VII from 1789 to 1794, and again from 1798 to 1801.

When the thieves saw the brotherhood, they quickly fled. The would-be despoilers were never identified.

By reason of this attempt, the monks, conferring with one another regarding what measures ought to be taken, judged it best not to transfer the holy relics from thence, that is, until some legitimate and correct site could be found. For they wished to post a guard around the tomb, made up of men from among themselves and the authorities. Having so decided, they appointed guards who, out of fear and reverence, but more so because of the boundless miracles worked by the saint, securely guarded the tomb.

Behold, then, how even in these present times, Saint Panaretos has shone forth brilliantly by means of his great virtue before God! The holy hierarch, indeed, verified the efficacious intercession of the ancient saints. By his own deeds, he confirmed the wonders and miracles of old. He also manifested in himself the kinship with God apportioned to every man dedicated to the Orthodox Faith and virtuous conduct. Behold how he is still conspicuously glorified by God and by man, with everlasting and incorruptible glory, teaching us the way of salvation by his own example! And even after his repose, he is showing us that the servants of God have never failed from the Eastern Orthodox Church of Christ. It is her confession which the gates of Hades shall not prevail against, according to the unerring mouth of our Lord Jesus Christ,[198] to Whom is due all glory, honor, and veneration, to the ages of the ages. Amen.

Epilogue

Saint Panaretos also encouraged and supported Archimandrite Cyprian of the Archdiocese of Cyprus to write the history of the island of Cyprus. In 1783, with great danger to his life, the holy Panaretos, advanced in years, traveled to Constantinople in the company of three other Cypriot hierarchs, Archbishop Crispus, Bishop Meletios of Kition (Larnaca), and Bishop Sophronios of Serenia.[199]

---

[198] Cf. Mt. 16:18.

[199] The bishops in Saint Panaretos' party are mentioned in *The Collection*.

Even though tradition claims that the evangelization of Cyprus came about through the missionary work of the Apostles Paul and Barnabas, there is no data on the Cypriot ecclesiastical hierarchy before 325. Thus, in the list of the Archbishops of the Autocephalous Greek Cypriot Orthodox Church, its foundation begins with Saint Barnabas in A.D. 45 and then jumps to Gelasios in 325. It is certainly one of the oldest autocephalous, or ecclesiastically independent, churches of the Eastern Orthodox communion. Its independence was first recognized by the Third Œcumenical Synod of Ephesus (431). During Crusader occupation it never lost this distinction. Under the feudal French dynasty of the Lusignans (1191–1489) and the Venetians (1489–1571), the efforts of the Latin bishops to submit the Orthodox Church of Cyprus to the pope's

(continued...)

This journey was fraught with perils and difficulties—where their purpose was to solicit a private audience and petition the Sublime Porte to remove Mutsukil Hadjibachi. This Islamic tyrant of Cyprus ruled for eight years, showing himself to be an unrelenting foe of the Christians. Panaretos maintained the initiative, but we do not know the outcome of this mission. Whether it proved effective or not, the very fact that he undertook such a dangerous mission with such strength of purpose underscores his unfeigned love for the Christians in his charge. Even though his prospects were blighted from the start, he persevered. Thus, instead of pandering to his own needs, he chose to pass through the fire for his flock. The only privilege he claimed for himself was to be of service to the Church, even if it meant being publicly set down by the Muslims when he complained of their abuses. He was peculiarly free of satisfying himself, but was ever mindful of the apostolic utterance: "Who is weak, and I am not weak? Who is made to stumble, and I am not set on fire [cf. 2 Cor. 11:29]?" His fame remained inextinguishable. He was a hierarch who mixed ascetic and civic virtue. Thus, by using my forefinger to give listeners a taste of the sweetness of the honey made by Saint Panaretos, who was all-virtuous in both name and deed, we bring this account to its termination, begging to receive the Cypriot hierarch's blessing as well.

On the 1st of May, the holy Church commemorates New-martyr AKAKIOS, as well as the SYNAXIS of the New-Martyrs EFTHYMIOS, IGNATIOS, and AKAKIOS the Hagiorites as celebrated today according to the Skete of the Honorable Forerunner.[200]

---

[199](...continued)
authority proved unsuccessful. Until the Turkish conquest of the island in 1571, under the realm of Selim II, the Greek bishops were often submitted to the authority of the Latin archbishop and forced to serve as auxiliaries of their Latin colleagues.

The highest ecclesiastical authority lay with the synod, composed of the Archbishop of Nicosia and the three other bishops of the island—Paphos, Kition, and Kyrenia—who were, and still are, elected by both clergy and laity, each of the four bishoprics being divided into several parishes. *Encyclopaedia Britannica*, s.v. "Cyprus, Church of."

[200] The common celebration of these three venerable new-martyrs is commemorated today, the 1st of May. Both Saints Efthymios (commemorated the 22nd of March) and Ignatios (commemorated the 8th of October) have their own day of commemoration. The reason for their individual commemorations, apart from Akakios, is because they were slain earlier, in 1814, whereas Akakios suffered martyrdom soon thereafter. Their synaxis is celebrated today because all three new-martyrs had been members of the Athonite Skete of the Honorable Forerunner (Skete of the Prodromite), which is under

(continued...)

Akakios, the righteous new-martyr, in holy Baptism was named Athanasios. He hailed from a certain village of Macedonia, called Neochori, which was near Thessalonike. He was the scion of pious parentage. Since his folks were poor and unable to provide for the necessities of life, they migrated to the city of Serres.[201] Athanasios was the eldest of the siblings. When he was nine years of age, Athanasios' parents had him apprenticed to a certain cobbler. It was their intent that the lad learn a trade while young, but momentous consequences followed. The cobbler, taking the lad under his roof, proved to be a harsh man who pitilessly and savagely applied the rod.

Athanasios, being unable to endure the violence, wished to be released from this tyranny. He fell, unfortunately, into servitude to the noetic tyrant, the devil. The adversary, as a crooked serpent, attempted to trip up Athanasios' heels on the very day of the saving Passion, that is, Great Friday. On this day, the man-slaying devil incited the cobbler to administer a fierce thrashing. This youth, wearied and enfeebled from the abuse, wept. Although in much pain from his wounds, still he managed to flee when it was evening. Wicked Satan, therefore, found the opportune moment to supplant the child's Faith in the following manner.

Before the gates of their house, there happened, by way of satanic energy, to be sitting two Ishmaelite women. They observed Athanasios crying, at which sight they supposedly felt compassion. They took the boy by the hand and brought him into their house of perdition. After plying him with many consolatory words, or rather venomous ones, those accursed women not only offered the hungry child bread but also urged him to deny the Savior Christ and

---

[200](...continued)
Iveron Monastery. All three, also, endured martyrdom in Constantinople within about a year's time. They were spiritual children of that most reverend spiritual father, Nikephoros, also of the Skete of the Forerunner (Prodromos). They were obedient to Elder Akakios, also, a fellow Prodromite. Saint Efthymios, who was slain by the sword on Palm Sunday, was from Demetsana of the Peloponnesos. Saint Ignatios, who was hanged, hailed from Eskee Zagora (the Bulgarian city of Stara Zagora). Saint Akakios, who was slain by the sword, was from Neochori of Thessalonike. The sacred and reverent relics of the three new-martyrs are treasured at both the Skete of Iveron and the Kalyvee of Saint Nicholas of the church of the same name. The unabridged hagiographies, written in the vernacular, and divine offices for the saints were composed by the most reverend Onouphrios of Iveron. The somewhat abridged version of the martyrdom of Saint Akakios was authored most eloquently by the ever-memorable Metropolitan Meletios of Caesarea. All editions were published by Akakios the Prodromite at Athens in 1862. From these versions, the martyrdom of Saint Akakios was extracted and reproduced in *The Great Synaxaristes* (in Greek).

[201] Serres prefecture, located in east northeastern Greek Macedonia, is the capital.

accept their loathsome religion of the deceiver Mohammed. Gradually, the women's affectation of concern and solicitude staked a claim on his affections. Thinking that all other prospects were blighted, he could not thank them too profoundly. Athanasios, still feeling burdened and oppressed from the mistreatment he suffered under the pitiless cobbler, began thinking that he finally found deliverance. He wished to put the cobbler behind him. The women perceived his disordered feelings and applied their old and interminable arguments in favor of Islam. The foolish boy, by reason of the words cleverly spoken by the Turkish women, agreed to give his oath. As for those profane women driven mad by Islam, they were filled with unholy joy hearing his word of consent given unguardedly. Without further ado, those miscreants led him to the treasury which was then under the governance of Yousouf Bey, that is, the ruler Sir Yousouf.

The interview was far from displeasing to the ruler. When he was informed by those roguish women that the youth consented to pronounce an oath, he was filled with abundant joy. He thanked the women for drawing such a prize and bringing the lad forward. He then took along Athanasios to his home. That same evening, which was Great Friday of Holy Week, the youth professed Mohammed. He renounced the Faith of the Christ and drank from the turbid waters of impiety. Then, according to Mohammedan tradition, he underwent the procedure for circumcision. Thus, the former slave of Christ became the slave of Satan. He stepped upon the Cross and shouted aloud the impious Islamic confession, showing forth one finger. This action was thought by those antichrists to be a refutation of the trihypostic Trinity as believed by the Orthodox. All these sorry events occurred to the ignorance of both the cobbler and Athanasios' parents.

Saint Akakios

As for that son of perdition, the treasurer, he began addressing Athanasios with a Muslim name. He also adopted the youth and meted out no ill-treatment. In fact, both he and his wife cherished a deep love for him. The wife, since she harbored a special affection and sympathy for the lad, entrusted the affairs of the whole house to Athanasios. She was wont to give him money to purchase candles and offer sacrifice to the demons of the imam, who was the prayer leader at the mosque. Though the youth was walking in the dark and associating with the ungodly, yet he did not buy candles as directed. Instead, he was spending the money on ring-biscuits, pies, and flat cakes. He would then eat them secretly outside of the house. Upon his return home, he was wont to tell her that he made the offering for candles; thus was he both scorning the tenets of his religion and being mocked by Satan. The youth lived and dwelt among the irreverent for nine years, that is, the equal amount of time that he had lived nine years of his early childhood in godly reverence. He finally reached his eighteenth year. The all-good God, Who desires not the death of the sinner but desires that he should return and live,[202] foreknows the end of each and provides beforehand for those being saved. He dispensed in His œconomy the good return of the young man. In the following wonderful manner, He plucked him out of the gullet of the noetic beast.

The mistress of the house, his adopted mother, was licentious and intemperate. With the passage of time, as Athanasios grew older, that foul woman's tender feeling for her adopted son was changed into a shameful and satanic fancy for him. She was unable to constrain her amorous desires, so she declared her attachment and passionate love for him. She used the same ploys as the Egyptian temptress, the wife of Petephres,[203] who made indecent advances toward that pillar of prudence, Joseph the all-comely one. But blessed be our God! For even as God then showed forth the chaste and moral Joseph as triumphator and trophy-bearer, so He invisibly strengthened this young man. God also established him as victor over that vixen, who was madly seeking to commit adultery with him. The blessed one refused her addresses and in no way would be polluted by her. He accurately reckoned that any such alliance was reprehensible and shabby. When the defiled woman saw that the young man was unwilling to lie with her and fulfill her wicked desire, her love converted to hatred against him. Even as the inconstant and fickle wife of Petephres was filled with wrath, when spurned by Joseph, the vindictive and ill-balanced Turkish woman, also, as the Egyptian temptress, calumniated the blameless young man to her husband. She shrieked that he had brought the Greek into the house and that now the ungrateful youth had mocked them by trying to force his attentions upon her. When the treasurer heard all the words of her accusation, he wished neither to punish the young man nor to exhibit harshness against him. Whether he was guided by God or understood the impropriety of her behavior and that she was slandering his beloved adopted son, he resolved quickly to drive him forth from the house. Yousouf Bey told Athanasios that he was free to go whithersoever he should like.

Athanasios, since he was released from his bondage by the providence of God, gave heartfelt thanks to the Redeemer and Savior Christ. Straightway,

---

[202] Cf. Ez. 18:23.

[203] The infatuation of Petephres or Potiphar's wife is recorded in Gen. 39:7 ff.

without further ado, he took the road to his much-desired parents who were then found in Thessalonike. Years ago, when they were informed of the distressing news of their son's abjuration, they left the neighborhood of Serres. When, beyond all expectation, they caught sight of their son, they were filled with inexpressible happiness. Their joy knew no bounds when they heard from his own mouth that he truly abandoned the bloodstained religion of the Hagarenes. He admitted that he had accepted Islam in ignorance. "I was a juvenile and tricked. I also had been much-tried by the hardness of that undiscerning cobbler." Thus, not only the family rejoiced exceedingly over the good conversion of Athanasios but also the angels in the heavens, according to the word of the Lord: "Thus, I say to you, joy ariseth in the presence of the angels of God over one sinner who repenteth [Lk. 15:10]."

After Athanasios spent some days in his home, his mother said to him, "My child, most beloved Athanasios, know that for thee to abide here with us is advantageous neither for us nor for thee. Should the Hagarenes of this place learn of thy background, both we and thee would be in grave peril. Hearken to my counsel, my boy, and betake thyself to the Holy Mountain. There thou shalt find the harbor of the salvation of sinners. With my blessings, go and make a round of visits. Make thy confession to the spiritual fathers. Thereafter, when thou hast been chrismated, cleanse thyself with fitting repentance. Learn that even as thou didst repudiate the Faith before the unregenerate, as thou oughtest not to have done, in this manner also it is necessary that thou shouldest again confess our Lord Jesus Christ and submit to death for His love's sake." That pious and God-loving mother did not place natural affection for the firstfruits of her womb before her son's salvation. Much rather, that solicitous mother intended to prepare her beloved son for martyrdom. She sought not to spare his body for Christ's love, so that both body and soul might enjoy everlasting life.

Upon hearing his mother's admonitions, that goodly son, Athanasios, as one with understanding and discretion, was exceedingly glad. Then, without further delay, since he was furnished with his mother's blessing as a provision for the journey, he departed for the Holy Mountain. With the help of God, he came to the sacred Monastery of Hilandar, dedicated to the Feast of the Entrance of the Virgin into the Temple. Hilandar, closed in by low and thickly wooded hills, lies on the northeast side of the peninsula and is the most northerly of the monasteries. The founders of the monastery were the saintly twelfth-century Serbian ruler Stefan I Nemanja (Saint Symeon the Myrrh-gusher) and his son Rastko (Saint Sava).[204] Athanasios sojourned there for some time. On account of the advice of the fathers of the monastery, he went forth

[204] Saint Symeon is commemorated by the holy Church on the 13th of February. Saint Sava is commemorated on the 14th of January.

to the Skete of the sacred Coenobium of Xenophontos[205] where the spiritual Father Nicholas was abiding. Athanasios made his confession before the Priest Nicholas, who then read the appointed expiatory prayers of the Church. Athanasios was anointed with holy Myron (Chrism) and sent away again to Hilandar.

After the passage of one year, Athanasios left the skete and went to the revered Monastery of Iveron, dedicated to the Feast of the Dormition. It is situated above an inlet on the northeast side of the Athonite peninsula. When Athanasios arrived, the fathers had just finished frescoing the Chapel of the Archangels (1812), which was situated to the side of the inner narthex of the *katholikon*. He sojourned at Iveron for six months, serving one of the senior fathers. It was there that he learned of the contests of two righteous martyrs, Saints Efthymios and Ignatios, who suffered martyrdom in 1814. Those two martyric fathers had struggled first in asceticism at the sacred Skete of the Honorable Forerunner, which lies above Iveron. They had been spiritual children of the spiritual father and Elder Nikephoros. In the latter's *kalyvee* or small hermitage, there was a chapel to these new-martyrs. The martyric relics of Saint Ignatios, after having been translated from Constantinople, were also interred within. Hearing these accounts, the heart of Athanasios was inflamed with emulation of these venerable new-martyrs. He, thereupon, went directly to see that spiritual father who had trained Efthymios and Ignatios. But that Athanasios' plan might not become known to anyone in the monastery and provoke agitation among the brethren, he went straight to the Monastery of Hilandar. From there, after ten days, he turned back to the Skete of the Honorable Forerunner where, also, he was welcomed by the aforementioned Father Nikephoros.

Athanasios made his confession before this spiritual father. He disclosed his yearning to follow the same path of a martyric contest as the venerable Martyrs Efthymios and Ignatios. Father Nikephoros did not conceal from the young man the inescapable difficulties and the labors to which he would be subjected in order to obtain that most longed-for martyric end. Nikephoros, perceiving the blessed young man's ardor and persistence, consented to receive him into his *kalyvee*. He placed Athanasios under the supervision of the first father of the brotherhood, the most righteous Elder Akakios. This elder also had been with the martyrs who previously contested.

---

[205] Xenophontos, dedicated to Saint George, was established in the 10th C. It is built on a low hill close to the sea. When Saint Akakios was there, the new *katholikon* (1809-1819) and bell-tower (1814) were being built. To Xenophontos belongs the Skete of the Annunciation, which lies about an hour's walk to the east, on a green mountainside with a view toward the Singitic Gulf. At that time, it followed the idiorrhythmic way of life.

When the Elder Akakios had taken Athanasios under his wing, he guided him with care and diligence in ascetical struggles. Athanasios kept striving uninterruptedly, eagerly, and tirelessly, both day and night, whether he was engaged in fasting or all-night standing or unceasing prayer.

Nevertheless, after thirty-five days, the evil one prompted cowardice in the would-be martyr. He exceedingly harassed the contestant and overcame him. Athanasios, without divulging his warfare or purpose to the Elder Akakios, took flight by night. He did not premeditate where he might go. He just kept walking in the dark on a road going northwesterly that led to Karyes, the small town that is the capital of the Athonite monastic state. In the deep of night he wandered about, going up and through a forest until the office of Orthros. At that hour, he distinguished the outline of the sacred Monastery of Koutloumousiou. The monastery, dedicated to the Feast of the Transfiguration, lay close to Karyes. It was situated on a sweeping slope of thick trees and bushes. It was still dark, when Athanasios passed the night at that monastery. The following morning, which happened to be the eve of the Feast of the Nativity of the Lord, Athanasios mingled with the others celebrating the festal occasion. It was, however, a bittersweet festival for the routed athlete for Christ. Afterward, Athanasios departed and traveled south to the southwest side of the peninsula, to Simonopetra, dedicated to Christ's Nativity. This seven-storied monastery was founded in the middle of the fourteenth century by Saint Simon.[206] The monastery had recently returned to the coenobitic life (1801). After the feast, Athanasios approached the hegumen of Simonopetra and requested admission. He was denied acceptance on the basis of his beardless countenance.

But Athanasios kept insisting. He also told the abbot that he knew the trade of a cobbler, so that the elder finally relented. Athanasios was there only a few days when trouble arose. His beardless face among grown men became the cause of offense and scandal to some of the brethren, since they insisted his admittance was contrary to long-established monastic rule. Thus, the abbot was enjoined to ask him to remove himself. Before Athanasios' expulsion, he beheld in his sleep a certain venerable elder who bade him leave from that place. "Return to thy spiritual father," said he, "and resume thy struggles in which thou wast earlier engaged." Athanasios asked him, "Who art thou?" The holy elder replied, "I am known as Simon the Myrrh-gusher and the builder of Simonopetra." The sacred elder, who had reposed more than three hundred and sixty-five years earlier, exhorted him further. Athanasios was not inclined to listen to the divine visitor, for he felt he had already disgraced himself by reason of his conduct. He said to himself, "How can I return to the Prodromite

[206] Saint Simon the Myrrh-streamer is commemorated by the holy Church on the 28th of December.

Skete and my spiritual father? I am too ashamed of myself, after running away in the middle of the night!" So what did he do in order to avoid any mortifying conference? Athanasios went northward, repairing again to Hilandar. But the senior fathers were unwilling to accept him inside the monastery. "When thou wast last here," said the fathers, "thou didst take thyself away in a clandestine manner." Despair was written broad across the face of the forlorn Athanasios, to which the senior fathers felt pity and yielded. They said to the young man, "Well then, thou art assigned to remain outside the monastery in the vineyard. And, as a penance, thou shalt dig alone in that vineyard."

A few days after Athanasios was laboring at that obedience in the vineyard, one of the notable fathers of Hilandar fell ill. The same father had the notion to dispatch Athanasios to Karyes, where he could fetch medical supplies. But Athanasios, not so amenable and dejected in spirit, would not obey. The elder then remarked, "The way that thou art conducting thyself, thou art neither a Turk nor a Christian." This sharp rebuke smote the heart of Athanasios, so that he said within himself, "Let me do that which is right and go thither whence I wrongly fled." He understood that he had allowed himself to brood too long. He recovered his hopes. He was now ready for imputations. Thus, after the passing of forty days, from the time that Athanasios departed from his spiritual father, Nikephoros, he returned to him. It was evening. When Father Nikephoros saw him, he said, "Where wast thou? And how hast thou come hither again?" The blessed Athanasios, with tears welling up in his eyes, said, "I have sinned, father, against heaven and before thee.[207] I left because I was deceived and misled by the devil; but I will not leave henceforth." The spiritual father spoke sternly and said, "I no longer will accept thee. Rather, go thy way to some monastery. Once there, weep for thy sins; and it is possible that God will save thee through thy repentance and tears." Athanasios, hearing these hard words, fell before the elder's feet and kissed them. Blinded and choked with tears, he began saying, "Receive me, father! By the tender mercies of God and the help of the Theotokos and thy prayers and those of the newly martyred venerable athletes Efthymios and Ignatios, I hope that thou mayest also rejoice over me, the sinner."

Then the hallowed Nikephoros had compassion upon him and said to him, "Behold, child, I do receive thee, but it is fitting that thou obeyest whatsoever I should command thee." After Nikephoros spoke these words, he called forth the Elder Akakios to his side and said, "Place him under thy supervision and take care for him, even as thou hadst formerly coached the holy Efthymios and Ignatios. Guide him in the spiritual exercises." Father Akakios took along Athanasios and brought him inside a special dwelling. He

---

[207] Lk. 15:18.

determined for the young man astringent medicines: greater exertions than the first round, that is, Athanasios was to redouble his efforts in fasting and making full prostrations. He, therefore, endeavored to deserve their trust. He performed more than three thousand and five hundred prostrations in one twenty-four-hour period. The number of prayer ropes that he recited was without number. His feats, surpassing his former ones, were carried out with much humility and love. For his sincere compunction, God granted him the gift of tears. Thus, in the space of a few days, Athanasios' eyes were as fountains of tears. Since he accelerated his ascetical labors with the application of unfeigned fervor, he implored that he might be garbed in the Angelic Schema. Perceiving Athanasios' advancement in virtue, together with his stability and constancy in warding off opposing thoughts and temptations, his spiritual father consented. Athanasios was vouchsafed the tonsure on the fourth Sunday of the Great Fast.[208] Instead of Athanasios, his name was changed to Akakios.

It is worthwhile to narrate the prophecy which he spoke to his overseer and trainer, the Elder Akakios. This is in regard to a query put to the newly tonsured Akakios by the elder, when he asked, "Where wilt thou have thy remains taken and interred after thou undergoest a martyric death in Constantinople?" The young Akakios then inquired, "Tell me, how many days remain until the Feast of the Ascension?" Elder Akakios replied, "Forty." Then the young Akakios began counting on his fingers. He then looked up at the elder and said, "After about thirty days shall I be here." The elder, with some hesitation, remarked, "Yes, certainly thou shalt come." The young Akakios then added, "If I do not come, then may God not deem me worthy of martyrdom." Then the young Akakios showed the elder where he would be buried, that is, before the icon of the most holy Theotokos.

Spiritual Father Nikephoros and the brethren around him, noticing the good signs wrought by Father Akakios' asceticism, concluded absolutely that the time came for Father Akakios to tread the path of martyrdom. They decided to send him to Constantinople. He was to be accompanied by the Elder Gregory, who was the same companion to the two previous contestants: the righteous Efthymios and Ignatios.

A ship was found, therefore, at Kalee Agra. They boarded the vessel and set sail on the 10th day of April. Inasmuch as the wind was favorable, they sailed as though they were being piloted by a divine angel. While they progressed, Father Akakios' escort, the Elder Gregory, foresaw that the voyage would take thirteen days until they reached Constantinople. The elder, guided by God, made provision and arranged for the following necessity which he knew would prosper and complete this God-pleasing endeavor. Perceiving that

[208] The Sunday of the commemoration of Saint John Klimakos, author of the *Ladder*.

the ship's captain was a man possessed with a Christian disposition, and that the crew members were pious and considerate to monks, he secretly explained to them the affairs of Father Akakios. He, therefore, confided in them what the young monk was planning to do. The captain, filled with divine zeal, made this promise to the Elder Gregory: "With the help of God, when Akakios completes the struggle of the contest, I will purchase his martyric body from the executioner, doing whatever I can, and then convey him again to the Holy Mountain whence he came." When they assented to these arrangements it was the 23rd day of April, the day when the holy and Great-martyr George is celebrated, a festal day radiantly kept by all the pious.

From those days, with God's help and providence, the martyric course of the venerable Martyr Akakios commenced. It was on this day, while the sun was setting, that the ship docked at Galata, a promontory on the north side of the Golden Horn facing Constantinople. Throughout that night, Elder Gregory and Father Akakios kept vigilant in prayer on the ship's deck. With all their hearts, they offered up to the Lord hymns that He might accept the sacrifice as a sweet smelling savor. The following day, the 24th day of April, which was Monday, they disembarked from the ship as soon as the sun arose. Together with the ship's captain, they went to a grocery of a certain Orthodox Christian, formerly of Caesarea, who was an acquaintance of Father Gregory. As soon as the grocer beheld them, he welcomed them with exceeding gladness and lavished upon them friendly hospitality. The captain then returned to his vessel. As for the blessed men of God, they remained hidden away in that shop. No one knew of their arrival. The evening of the following day had passed when the Elder Gregory revealed to the grocer both their purpose and goal.

Akakios, consumed with divine love, was no longer able to restrain himself. He kept troubling the Elder Gregory by asking permission to appear before the Muslim authorities. The elder simply said, "Have patience until the will of God should be made manifest." Then, during the following Thursday,[209] the 27th day of April,[210] he gave his promise to Akakios that he would give him

---

[209] April 27/May 9 was a Thursday in the year 1816.

[210] The blessed Akakios penned the following epistle to his spiritual father and elder, Nikephoros.

"Constantinople, the 27th of April, 1816.

"I venerate and kiss the holy right hand of my most reverend spiritual father.

"My present humble epistle regards nought else but to seek thy blessing and to acquaint thee with our favorable arrival. By the grace of God and thy holy prayers, we came directly into the queen of cities on the 25th day of April. I hope in the grace of God, and in thy fervent entreaty to the Lord and those of my spiritual brothers, to receive an end to this matter of ours. I greet my brethren and very much beseech them

(continued...)

the permission for that which he so desired. Thus, he might go forth to martyrdom that coming Saturday. Akakios, filled with joy, sent up glorifications and entreaties to the most sweet Jesus Christ. On the morning of that Saturday, consequently, Elder Gregory took Akakios and brought him to the sacred Church of the Theotokos at Galata. During the divine Liturgy, by the hands of the priest, Father Akakios communed the immaculate Mysteries. After the dismissal, they departed the church and made their way straight to the ship which brought them to Galata. The ship's captain was waiting for them. They asked him, "Hast thou prepared the garments, which we asked to have readied?" The captain then presented to them the clothing of some Turkish seaman who had been in his employ. The captain, together with the elder, attired Akakios in that clothing. They began thinking to send someone to accompany Akakios, so that the athlete of Christ could appear at the higher court of the vizier.

While they were considering these things and were wondering how to bring about what they wished to accomplish, Akakios' fervor was mounting. But Akakios was also beginning to anguish over the delay. Then one of those found there, the brother of the captain, of his own accord gave this response: "I know the way and I am ready to guide my most beloved Akakios to the vestibule of the vizier." Straightway, he took Akakios by the hand and said to him, "Come, let us be off!" They boarded a boat. They set sail toward the gate by the garden, that is, Baze Kapi as it is known in Turkish. Upon arriving, they went forth and walked for a distance.

---

[210](...continued)

not to forget me. Whenever thou shouldest hear of my end, I ask thou givest thanks to our Lord Jesus Christ and to the most holy Theotokos. I also ask that thou sendest up doxologies for the whole week, with joy and gladness of soul. For the labors and toils by which thou wast put to the test, to this very day in my behalf, I am not capable of giving thee thanks. Only the heavenly King can reward thee with a fitting recompense in the kingdom of the heavens. May the Lord vouchsafe us all that we may dwell together with Him in the kingdom!

"Similarly, for as many who have and still are contributing and helping in this work, may they also receive a reward from my heavenly King! I salute and venerate reverently all the holy fathers of our Skete, especially my teacher, Elder Onouphrios, and my fellow brethren, Elders Akakios, Iakovos, and Kallinikos. I also send my greetings to the teacher Gabriel. I send my respects and prostration to the Priest Agathangelos, whose right hand I kiss. I, moreover, send my veneration and prostration to the Priest Dositheos and his elder, as well as his synodia. I salute our neighbor and Elder Michael, along with his synodia. I am writing these things in an abbreviated manner, my elder and spiritual father. Tomorrow, then, is Friday, the 28th of April, at which time I shall take the path of the contest; and may thy prayer and blessing empower me! So be it. The least one, Akakios, Monk."

The blessed Akakios, rejoicing, made haste to enjoy the martyric end for which he yearned. He, in fact, even ran ahead of his guide, so that the captain's brother remarked, "Behold, thou runnest a course for which thou hast desired, O Akakios! Behold, the hour of thy martyrdom has come! And, in a little while, with God, thou shalt bring to an end the struggle of thy contest and achieve a martyric close, for which may the Lord be well-pleased to guide thee and strengthen thee!" As they walked and talked together, they drew near to the courthouse. Then the guide said to Akakios, "Do thou, O slave of God, also remember me, the sinner, after the severance of thy holy head, whensoever thou shouldest be set forth bearing a crown at the fearful judgment seat of the Master Christ."

Akakios, hearing these words, kneeled before his guide's feet and cried out with a great voice, "It was I who denied Jesus Christ, the Son of God, before men; and, furthermore, I bear the abominable sign of the circumcision. How then shall I dare to make entreaty for thy salvation? And can I, who am utterly bereft of grace and unworthy of compassion, supplicate the Christ and seek from Him grace and mercy?" This and similar things did Akakios blurt out, sighing and drenching the ground beneath him with tears. He gave no account to the crowds that were passing by on that street. He, thereupon, was appearing to all passersby as an object of wonder. The guide then stretched forth his hand and helped him up from the ground, weeping and sighing, and brought him before the outside gate of the courthouse. The guide then said to Father Akakios: "This is the palace and the higher court of the Ottomans. It is here then, when thou hast presented thyself, that thou shalt profess the good and saving confession. And it is here that the decision will be given for thy voluntary death for the sake of Christ's love. For it is He Whom thou hast preferred to this present transient life, so that thou mightest enjoy eternal beatitude. Do thou, therefore, without fear, enter into the contest of thy martyrdom." Akakios, then, entered into the judgment hall, while his guide made haste to depart that place lest he should be recognized.

With courage and inexpressible joy, the divine Akakios entered the vestibule. He first met the vizier's chief gatekeeper, who also was called letter-carrier by the Ottomans. The gatekeeper addressed Akakios and said, "Who art thou? And what is thy business here?" The valiant Akakios intrepidly answered, "I am an Orthodox Christian and originated from Thessalonike. When I was a child, nine years of age, I was tricked by you Muslims and foolishly denied my Christ and God. I then subjected myself to the antichrist devil and worshipped him and his forerunner, Mohammed, and received the defiled seal of the circumcision. After the passage of nine years, I meditated on past events and came to recognize the deception into which I had tumbled. By that time I had come to be well informed of your profane traditions and superstitions, as well as the fallaciousness of thy misleading and erring religion. I, therefore, returned with my whole heart to my ancestral and holy Faith handed down by my fathers. I acknowledge that my Lord Jesus Christ is true God. I, also, confess and believe in the all-holy and coessential and trihypostatic Trinity: in Father, Son, and Holy Spirit, Three Persons but Divinity one in essence and undivided. I believe in one God, the only God, Maker of heaven and earth and those creations that are seen and those that are noetic. I recant all the error and the ungodliness of the Hagarenes. And I confess and proclaim, clearly and openly, that I am an Orthodox Christian and the offspring of Orthodox parents. I admit that I was baptized in the name of the Father and of the Son and of the Holy Spirit, the coessential and undivided Trinity."

Akakios, speaking these words with an uplifted voice, took hold of his borrowed turban, which he purposely wore upon his head, and cast it to the ground. He trampled and spat upon it. He also mocked the mindless error of their religion. The gatekeeper, upon hearing these unexpected aspersions, became angry. He lunged at Akakios and began raining blows down upon him in a pitiless manner. Since this took place at an hour when court was not in session and no cases were presented to the vizier, the gatekeeper seized some chains and bound the martyr's feet, for which Akakios offered no resistance. The gatekeeper then shut away Akakios in the prison for the rest of that day. The gatekeeper, during the night, with others who were of the first circles and dignitaries, went to the martyr's cell. Those Muslims began speaking blandishments. They employed gentle words. They uttered promises without number, offering splendid gifts befitting their ranks and stations. But they were gifts which those senseless ones thought would please a man of Akakios' young years. Hence, they were looking to deceive him and trip up his heels. In like manner, all the Hagarenes in the courthouse were harrying him: some found the occupation to be amusing; whereas others, taking the matter seriously, were wearing themselves away. They were utilizing every means at their disposal to extinguish the young man's piety and convert him. They lectured him, attempting to quench his divine desire and love; for it was their aim to cast him down headlong again into the pit of perdition, that is, the erring and hateful religion of Mohammed!

The martyr kept silent, except for his continual invocation, in a clear voice, of that sweetest name of our Lord Jesus Christ. He also was making the sign of the precious and life-giving Cross over his entire body. He abided steadfast and immovable as an anvil. When the blackguards understood that their flatteries did not succeed with Akakios, they threatened him. They started smiting him with rods. They also tyrannized him by mercilessly applying other torments. The martyr, as though another were suffering, endured the tortures manfully and was even joyful. His countenance appeared radiant and grace-filled. As for his martyric body, it remained unharmed. There were no traces of wounds, despite the diverse chastisements of blows and strokes. They kept him in confinement until Sunday to the fourth hour or ten o'clock in the morning. At that hour, the prison officers released him from the bonds of the chains. They next brought him before the great governor who questioned the detainee, asking, "What became of thee that thou shouldest reject our true faith, which thou hadst embraced voluntarily? Thou art young, handsome, intelligent, and capable of recognizing the truth of our religion. So why hast thou forsaken it? We can conclude by thy conspicuous characteristics and the modest aspects of thy countenance that thou art a prudent and sensible man." Now these dissembling words were spoken by the governor in order to hoodwink Akakios.

Despite their flattery and fawning, the undaunted Akakios, responding to their duplicity and claptrap, said, "When I was nine years old I was duped. I disavowed the Orthodox and true Faith of my Christ. But following the passage of another nine years, I came to my senses. I became cognizant that one alone is the true and unerring Faith: that of the Orthodox Christians. For this reason, also, I betook myself to Constantinople, so that I should confess, before thee and all thine attendants standing by, Jesus Christ the crucified. He was born of the Theotokos and Ever-virgin Mary. He is the Son and Logos of God. Now the Only-begotten of the Father,[211] Who was with the Father, was manifested to us[212] and became perfect Man. He is in the Father and the Father is in Him.[213] He is, in every season and hour, glorified and worshipped, together with the Father, by angels and men both in heaven and on earth. I came to profess these things, as well as to receive ten thousand punishments. By the shedding of my blood and death, I shall wash away from my much-laboring body the uncleanness of denial. I shall be freed from the abominable circumcision of my foreskin and, thus, remain free of condemnation. For as thou hast commented earlier, I have a natural sagacity to know the true and only God, Jesus the Christ. I, therefore, with a sure knowledge and a bold voice, confess and proclaim Him to be omnipotent God. I profess Him, so that in the life to come I may depart, without condemnation, for His kingdom."

As the martyr made his stirring and brilliant confession, the governor was sitting upon his high throne. Although he heard the words and felt the blood in his temples rise, still he feigned an untrammeled countenance. He did not betray the least anger, on account of his habitual preservation of his assumed air of magnificence and haughtiness. He fancied himself grandeur

[211] Cf. Jn. 1:14.
[212] Cf. 1 Jn. 1:2.
[213] Cf. Jn. 14:11.

personified. He gave express orders that Akakios be escorted to the appointed judge of the city. He charged the bailiffs, those assigned to this office, to treat Akakios as one condemned. He commanded the bailiffs that once they received the writ with Akakios' death sentence, they were to hand him over to the executioner for beheading, without fail, the very next day. Consequently, in this manner, were things decided by the governor against the martyr. The venerable Elder Gregory, preconceiving these events, besought many Christians to investigate and learn any details, whatever information they could gather in regard to Akakios. Hence, when they had learned all the things that we have already narrated above, those Christians came from the city over to Galata. This was Sunday evening. They found Elder Gregory and related everything to him. From the elder's excessive joy, he became divinely inspired and ecstatic in spirit, so that he thanked the Lord with his whole soul for these good tidings.

That same night, Elder Gregory was ruminating upon Akakios. He kept going over in his mind the tribulations and dangers which Akakios must have been experiencing. He, thereupon, adjudged it to be a blessing if he could find a way to send the martyr a portion of the heavenly bread, the all-holy body and the immaculate blood of our Savior Jesus Christ, so he might commune before the end. He was, therefore, resolved to call upon the brother of the ship's captain—Akakios' previous guide to the courthouse. He would beseech him to undertake, once more, another mission. In the morning, therefore, Elder Gregory proceeded toward the sacred Church of the Theotokos. He begged the priest to give him a portion of the life-creating body of the Christ, for which he was found worthy of the request. Elder Gregory, thereupon, reverently received the holy body of the Lord that was enclosed in an *artophorion* or pyx, the tabernacle or vessel holding the reserved Mysteries or Sacrament. The elder then called forth that Christ-loving man and, with warm entreaties, persuaded him to bear the Mysteries to the prison. The captain's brother, though he feared to carry and convey the Holies, yet he realized the gravity of the martyr's situation. He, therefore, obeyed and took the *artophorion* from Father Gregory's hands that he might offer it to the holy Akakios. He entered a ship and set sail, going toward the prison. When he arrived, by the good will of God, he entered the prison without the least hindrance. This is because the assigned guards, who numbered more than forty, coming from various regiments (*tagmata*), were eating breakfast at that moment in the mess hall. On account of this, not one of them noticed the ship captain's brother entering into the prison.

The captain's brother, however, since he was unfamiliar with the layout of the prison, entered the outer prison chamber. In that section were jailed those who were debtors that could not repay their creditors. Looking about hither and thither, he kept hoping to see the saint. He did not know that the condemned were kept in another section. Not before long he was in doubt what he should do. Behold, how the providence of God was at work! The servant boy of the grocer had permission to enter the prison thrice daily, that he might transport supplies of water. This was the same Caesarean grocer who had offered the fathers hospitality earlier. The grocer's servant went over and asked the brother of the ship's captain, "What seekest thou, friend, that thou shouldest come to this place?" He answered, "Perhaps thou hast heard that they have brought someone here who was desiring to undergo martyrdom?" The boy replied, "Yea, surely. Is he the one whom thou dost wish to meet? Come with me so thou mayest see him from the window." The boy then showed him Akakios, who was fettered to one corner of his cell. He was bound with four chains, while his feet were in wooden stocks. The boy remarked, "The vizier commanded that he be kept in prison in this manner. I know that no one else, except myself, is permitted to enter into his cell. On this account, if thou wouldest say something to him, tell me and I will relate every word."

The captain's brother clearly saw that he was unable to do anything alone. He handed over the *artophorion* to the boy, whom he recognized to be an Orthodox Christian. The captain's brother then began uncovering the whole truth to the boy. He then said, "Do say this to Akakios. Tell him that the Elder Gregory, his spiritual father, sent forth to him the life-bestowing treasure and supplicates God fervently in his behalf that He strengthen him." The boy, taking the *artophorion*, entered into the prison cell where the martyr was incarcerated. He approached the martyr and placed the *artophorion* in his hands, at the same time conveying to him the exhortations of the elder. This message, charging him to remain firm and valiant in his resolve, comforted Akakios in every way.

The blessed Martyr Akakios, although he was shackled and his feet were secured in wooden stocks and his hands were bound tight, still, as much as he was able, managed to open the *artophorion*. Upon beholding the heavenly and divine Lamb, he reverently offered veneration, and partook of the Mysteries. With all his soul, he sent up a doxology of thanksgiving to God the dispenser. Akakios then said to the lad, "I pray that all that is good and saving come to thee. I implore thee to relate to my spiritual father all that is happening to me. Relate to him that, for the love of Christ, I am being vouchsafed that end for which I had so greatly longed." When the lad exited the prison cell, he met again with the captain's brother and handed back the *artophorion*. He also recounted all that the martyr instructed him to say. The captain's brother was exceedingly glad because God hearkened to the elder's supplication. The captain's brother then decided to depart from that place quickly, so that he might apprise the elder that he had fulfilled the command.

But what do you suppose happened to the goodly courier, the captain's brother? Hearken. As we mentioned earlier, when that Christ-loving man entered into the prison, he passed by unnoticed by any of the guards. This, too, was a benefaction of divine providence, so that the martyr might be vouchsafed the divine Communion. Now the captain's brother wished to exit the prison posthaste. He had just gone a few steps, when the guards saw him. They had already finished their meal and were at their stations. They rushed at him, striking him with wooden staves and clubs. With their feet, they kicked him heartlessly. They kept shouting at him in their barbaric tongue, demanding an answer: "Infidel, how darest thou penetrate the prison? How didst thou slip in unseen by us?" The captain's brother answered ambiguously. But according to the divine will, he was delivered from that perilous encounter. As for the *artophorion*, it went unobserved by the guards. After he passed into the street and had distanced himself somewhat from the prison, he could feel that his whole body had sustained wounds from the staves. At one point, he stood in the midst of that street. He began considering those tests which he had suffered. At the same time, he was starting to feel the sharpest pains throughout his body. He then reckoned to himself that, despite all, he was delivered from deadly blows and dangers.

Nevertheless, even though he found himself in a bad situation, yet his fear, trembling, and agitation of his heart were calmed when he brought to mind the inimitable tortures and the afflictions of the martyr. He did not deem his own sufferings worthy of comparison with those of Akakios. While he was yet turning over in his mind what manner of end the holy martyr might receive, his reverie was suddenly interrupted. A multitude of Hagarenes were converging. They were taking along the divine Akakios, as one condemned. They dragged and shoved him. Akakios' hands were tied behind his back, as his torturers took hold of him. They were moving quickly and hurling insults at the martyr, roaring all the while like lions. They kept spitting in his holy face and thrashing him with rods. These occurrences were witnessed by the captain's brother, who thought to follow after them.

The captain's brother then acted on that prompting and followed them from a distance until they brought the saint to the execution site, called Daktyloporta (Parmak-Kapi). It was situated on the third hill of the seven-hilled city of Constantinople. In the meantime, the blessed Akakios had still not yet been informed by his persecutors that they were at the very spot where he would receive the longed-for end. Then Akakios suddenly heard the executioner thunder aloud, "Kneel, unbeliever!" Straightway, the holy martyr of Christ, without any trembling, bravely bent his knees and head. He then raised his voice and said to the executioner, "Strike with the sword manfully, and cut my neck! Take no pity whatsoever!" While the athlete was saying this, the executioner wielded the sword and struck at his neck, thus severing the martyr's holy head. Concurrently, ranks of angels took up the sacred soul and led Akakios up on high to the everlasting abodes. As many Orthodox Christians who were vouchsafed to be standing by at the martyric death of the saint, they beheld with their own eyes those things which came to pass. They kept marvelling and glorifying the Lord Who strengthened and crowned the venerable Martyr Akakios.

They narrated that the righteous Martyr Akakios, to the very last moment when his head was struck off, appeared neither sullen, nor sad of countenance, nor fearful. He neither ate nor drank from the hour he emerged from the ship until the beheading, other than partaking of the holy Communion of the immaculate Mysteries. He was counted worthy to partake of them twice, as we mentioned earlier. He finished his martyric course on the 1st day of the month of May, in the year 1816,[214] on a Monday at the fifth hour[215] of the day.

After all these events came to pass and were recounted to the Elder Gregory by the above mentioned Christ-loving brother of the ship's captain, who had accompanied the martyr and faced danger with him, the elder gave glory with all his soul to God Who had empowered and animated His righteous martyr. The elder, therefore, undertook the concern of buying up the martyric relics. With diligence, therefore, he urged the Christ-loving shopkeepers and dealers of Galata to take up this God-pleasing task. They readily pursued the sponsorship of this soul-benefitting proposal. After ten thousand struggles and exertions, they paid a considerable sum—eight hundred piasters—to the greedy Turks. Finally, on the third day after the martyrdom, since according to custom the corpses had to remain three days at the execution site, they received permission to take the holy body of the martyr and transfer it as far as to

---

[214] *The Great Synaxaristes* (in Greek) records the year 1815, while *The Athonite Patericon* (in Russian), Vol. 1 (January-June), pp. 393-410 (Moscow-Efimov Press, 1897), records 1816. After further inquiry, it was discovered that Pascha in 1815 occurred on Sunday, April 18/30, and that the Feast of the Ascension took place on Thursday, May 27/June 8. [Note that the Julian Calendar date precedes the Gregorian date, at which time there was a 12-day difference.] In the year 1816, Pascha occurred on April 9/21, and the Feast of the Ascension on May 18/30. As a result of these findings and the information that the 1st of May, the day of the saint's martyrdom, was a Monday, his repose could only have occurred in 1816, not 1815. The year 1816 is further confirmed by the new-martyr's own prophecy. He had told his elder that his relics would return to the Skete some thirty days after Pascha. We are told that the ship's captain returned the relics on the 9th of May. Again, when Pascha took place on the 9th of April, in the year 1816, thirty days later would have been the 9th of May.

[215] *The Athonite Patericon* records "the sixth hour at noon," instead of 11:00 o'clock in the morning.

Kontoskalio, where many Christians had gathered that they might escort the sacred relics to the Princes' Islands.[216]

However, before arrival there, Elder Gregory informed the captain, with whom he had entered into an agreement to convey the sacred relics of the martyr to Prinkipo of the Princes' Islands. (In fact, the captain. who harbored a sincere love for the new-martyr, agreed to tarry to Akakios' end and then transport the new-martyr's relics back to Mount Athos with the Elder Gregory.) As it happened, the Elder Gregory arrived on the island first before the others. Six hired boats were waiting for him. The elder boarded one of them. He then requested of the bearers of the martyric relics that they deposit the saint on the same boat with him. This came to pass. Elder Gregory embraced and kissed the holy relics of his much-desired spiritual child and friend. He wept hot tears profusely, so that he drenched the relics. The elder then said aloud, "Thou hast conquered the man-slaying devil, O godly-minded Akakios!" He then turned and charged the oarsmen to undertake their rowing as quickly as they were able.

When they had rowed as many of those who had permission to board all the other boats, they followed the boat which ferried the martyric body. They, therefore, sailed to the isle of Prinkipo of the Princes' Islands. When they had rounded the promontory, near the headland, they espied a cockboat that was waiting for them which belonged to the ship that had brought the Elder Gregory and the holy Martyr Akakios from the Holy Mountain to Constantinople. When they arrived, they put on shore the holy relics where they had prepared in advance a chest, a reliquary. Into this they laid the much-tried sacred body of the martyr. Immediately, they transferred the reliquary to the ship and cast off, with the seamen rowing as vigorously as they could. At the fifth hour of the night, they drew near to the ship which was readying to sail but had been waiting for the others. When all boarded the ship, they sent up a doxology of thanksgiving to God Who energized these mysterious and extraordinary happenings. While they were sending up praise to the Lord, the ship was shaken by a mighty wind blowing from the north. The ship's captain, observing that the time and weather were favorable, lifted his voice and said openly to all those present, "Christ did show His mercy out of love for His slave Akakios, who, for the sake of the Lord's all-holy name, endured death; and even now, by the present conditions, I am informed that we ought to depart."

Then those who had come on board to venerate the saint departed by means of the cockboat. The captain then ordered his crew to loose the ropes

[216] The Princes' Islands were nine islands in the Sea of Marmara. The largest are Prote, Antigone, Chalke, and Prinkipo. The smaller ones include Plate, Oreia, Pita, Niandros, and Terebinthos.

and weigh anchor. This was achieved without delay and they got under way. They put to sea with the hand of the Lord guiding them and granting them a favorable voyage. They brought the ship to anchor at the Holy Mountain on the 9th of May, putting into the port near Kalee Agra by the shore of the Monastery of Iveron, where the holy spring of the Theotokos Portaitissa is situated. From thence, they brought the holy relics to the monastery's Skete of the Honorable Forerunner, and translated them to the Kalyvee of Saint Nicholas where Saint Akakios formerly engaged in his ascetical struggles.

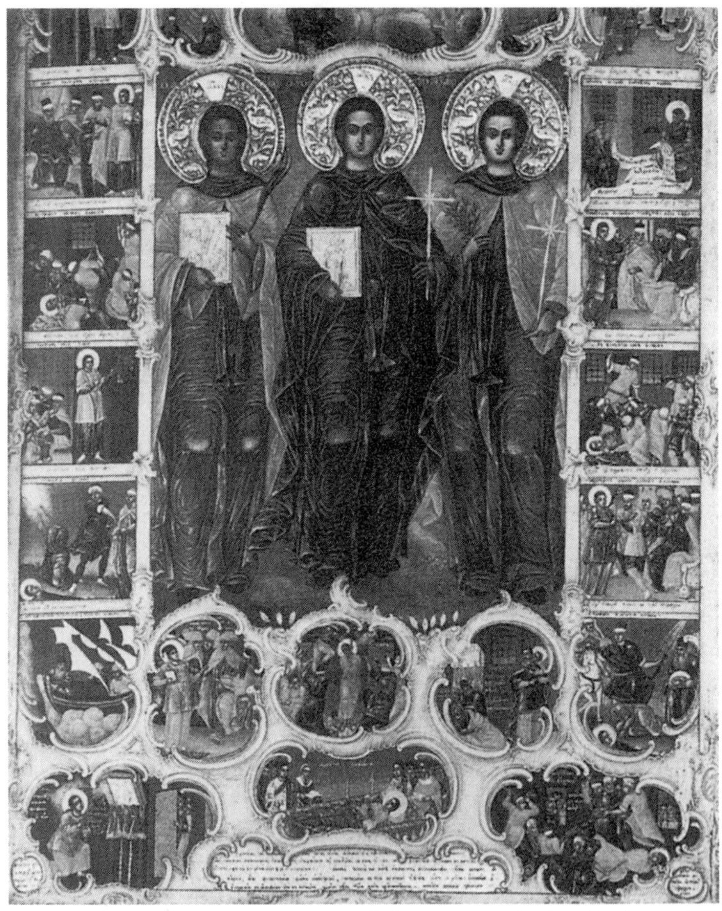

(L.) *Saint Akakios bears an icon of the resurrection and a branch of a palm tree.*
(C.) *Saint Ignatios has an icon of Christ and a cross of martyrdom.*
(R.) *Saint Efthymios holds palm fronds and a cross of martyrdom.*

In that place they interred the body reverently within the chapel, which was newly consecrated in honor of the two earlier contestants in martyrdom, the venerable Martyrs Efthymios and Ignatios.[217] They placed the recent relics before the sacred icon of the Mother of God, that is, the very spot where the holy Martyr Akakios earlier prophesied to the Elder Akakios, before he departed the skete on the way to martyrdom, that he would return thirty days after Pascha.[218]

---

[217] The holy skulls of all three new-martyrs are now treasured at Athos in the Russian Monastery of the Great-martyr Panteleimon.

[218] The icon of the three new-martyrs shown herein requires explanation. While the names and dedicatory inscriptions are in Greek, the silver haloes are in Serbian. The silver halo of Saint Akakios is assigned to Saint Efthymios and vice versa. The silver inscription must be in error, since Saint Akakios suffered martyrdom and won the palm of victory immediately after celebrating Palm Sunday and Pascha, while Saint Efthymios suffered and died on the very day of Palm Sunday. Moreover, those panels aligned vertically at the left are scenes from the martyrdom of Saint Akakios, whereas, the panels to the right depict scenes from the martyrdom of Saint Efthymios.

The scenes from the Life of Saint Akakios (commemorated the 1st of May), from the panels on the left, portray Saint Akakios speaking openly in the Muslim court to the governor, being tortured in prison, receiving holy Communion, and suffering beheading.

The scenes from the Life of Saint Efthymios (commemorated the 22nd of March), from the panels on the right, portray Saint Efthymios beholding the cross and the Mother of God, writing letters—to his brothers, Dositheos, Onouphrios, Akakios, Iakovos, and Kallinikos—showing the cross and palm branches before the Muslim ruler, being flogged in prison, sundering the green turban, and the severing of his head.

The scenes from the Life of Saint Ignatios (commemorated the 20th of October) may be seen in the nine panels at the bottom of the icon that are arranged in groups of three zones. The upper two portray Saint Ignatios in prayer, being crowned by the Theotokos, being presented to the ruler, being flogged in prison, being hanged, healing the paralyzed man, and returning the purse.

The three panels at the bottom contain three inscriptions, with the following in the central panel: "Having painted this venerable icon at the expense of hierodeacon lord Manasses from Gambrovo, having changed his name to Onouphrios, he was himself martyred at Chios on the 4th of January, in the year 1818. And he was placed in this venerable martyrium of the same three saints." [This New-martyr Onouphrios was a member of the synodia around Nikephoros, who suffered martyrdom at the age of thirty-two, being led by the Elder Gregory.]

At the bottom of the left panel is the following inscription: "By the hand of Dositheos, monk, from Peć in Serbia." Dositheos was a bilingual Serb. The bottom right panel contains the same inscription in Slavonic, with the addition of the date of 1818. The inscriptions in both languages relay the message to the two basic linguistic communities in the Balkans, in an earnest attempt to arrest the swelling tide of conversions to Islam. This icon is done on wood in egg tempera, measuring 74 x 55 centimeters. Dositheos, in all likelihood, learned iconography on Mount Athos, since

(continued...)

This, O beloved Christians, is the martyrdom of the righteous New-martyr Akakios who, for the love of the Lord Jesus Christ, endured much. Let us pray that through Saint Akakios' intercessions and entreaties we might be deemed worthy of the forgiveness of our sins and be vouchsafed the heavenly kingdom, by the grace and love for mankind of our Lord Jesus Christ, together with the unoriginate Father and the all-holy and good and life-creating Spirit, to Whom is due glory, dominion, honor, and veneration, now and ever and to the ages of the ages. Amen.

Rejoice, O trinity of new martyrs! Rejoice, O victor Efthymios, bearing palm-fronds, who confessed the divinity of Christ, denounced the antichrist, and refuted the falsehood of Islam! Rejoice, O glorious Ignatios, who emulated Christ's sufferings and strangled the devil with a noose! Rejoice, O honored Akakios, who dyed for thyself a robe of porphyry in thine own blood. O venerable crown-bearers from the Skete of the Forerunner, do ye entreat Christ that we may escape the harmful snares of the cruel adversary!

On the 1st of May, the holy Church commemorates our venerable and God-bearing Father NIKEPHOROS of Chios.[219]

Nikephoros, our righteous and God-bearing father, was born in 1750 at Kardamyla of Chios in the eastern Aegean.[220] He was the offspring of pious

---

[218](...continued)
he adheres to the style of Nikephoros of Agrapha and his group. The icon now resides at the Skete of Saint John the Baptist, a holding of Iveron.

This icon honors a group of brother monks who were disciples of the same elder, Akakios, and were escorted to their martyrdom by the same Elder Gregory the Peloponnesian. The icon was made only a year and one-half after the martyrdom of the third group. The icon was commissioned by a fellow monk who also underwent martyrdom while the same icon was being painted. Taken from *Treasures of Mount Athos*, 2nd ed. (Thessalonike, 1997), pp. 194, 195.

[219] The biography incorporated into *The Great Synaxaristes* (in Greek) was authored by Amilia George Zolotas (also know later as Emily Sarou). The divine office was composed by the Protosynkellos Kyril Trehakes of the metropolis of Chios. See *Akolouthia tou Osiou Nikephorou tou Chiou hypo tou Protosynkellou Kyrillou Trehake, kai Vios Aftou hypo A. G. Z.*, 2nd ed. (Chios, GR, 1907), in *Neon Chiakon Leimonarion* [*New Chian Spiritual Meadows*]. The aforementioned *Leimonarion* was expanded and revised by Ambrose Michalos (Athens, 1930) and, again, by Christopher K. Gerazounis (Athens, 1968). See also Constantine Cavarnos' work in Vol. 4 of Modern Orthodox Saints Series, entitled *Saint Nikephoros of Chios* (Belmont, MA: Institute for Byzantine and Modern Greek Studies, 1976).

[220] Chios Island (38°23′N 26°07′E) lies south of Lesvos (Mytilene). It covers an area of 842 square kilometers and has 213 kilometers of coastline. It is a separate prefecture

(continued...)

parents. In holy Baptism he was given the name of George. As a young boy, he succumbed to a pestilential disease. As he was in danger of dying, the parents hastened with tears to the most holy Theotokos. With heartfelt entreaties, they besought her with tear-beaded eyelashes to heal their ailing child. If he became well, they promised to dedicate him to her sacred monastery on the island, known to the Chiotes as Nea Moni.[221]

Since he was healed of the disease, his parents, in accordance with the vow pronounced over his sickbed, brought him to the monastery. At first, the lad performed obediences and services for the reverend and marvellous Elder Anthimos Agiopateritis. Since the youth showed a propensity for study and learning, he was sent to the island's capital, also named Chios, where he was

---

[220](...continued)
including the small islands of Oinousses, Psara, Antipsara, and Pasas. It is 146 nautical miles from Piraeus. Chios is semi-mountainous with several valleys intersecting the mountain ridges. The coast contains steep rocky cliffs in the west and north, but flat and sandy shores in the south and east. There is a mild climate that supports verdant vegetation. Chios, in 1566, was captured by the Turks. The conquerors granted the island special privileges which lasted until the 1821 War of Independence. The island's capital, Chios (but called Chora by the locals), is also its main port, located in the middle of the east coast. The north side of the island contains fewer and smaller villages than the south. In the north, the largest village, Kardamyla (twenty-seven kilometers from the capital, Chios), is built in a richly vegetated region. See E. Karpodini-Dimitriadi, *The Greek Islands* (Athens: Ekdotike Athenon S.A., 1987), pp. 130-136.

[221] The most important Byzantine monument on Chios is Nea Moni, some fifteen kilometers west of the main town. The monastery was founded in 1042 A.D. by Emperor Constantine the Duelist (Monomachos). It is a royal edifice, as many imperial *chrysobulls* have borne testimony. Its construction lasted twelve years (A.D. 1042-1056). It is dedicated to the Feast of the Dormition. Its octagonal *katholikon* is decorated with marble revetments and mosaics. Mosaics of Nea Moni compose a representative proof of austere Byzantine sacred art. They decorate the walls on the higher surfaces, the domes in the inner narthex, and the nave and the sanctuary. The multi-colored mosaics are made of natural stone and glass. The refectory, side chapel, underground cistern, and bastion on the west face have survived, as well as a few deserted cells and ruined buildings of the 18th and 19th C. The museum is installed in the upper floor of the building, which consists of two continuous rooms for the exhibition and one small room for the guards. At the ground floor there is a small oratory and a storeroom. On account of the pillage that the monastery suffered under the Turks during the massacres of Chios in 1822, the items exhibited are not numerous and date mostly after that time. Among them, post-Byzantine icons, ecclesiastical silverworks, ecclesiastical and popular embroideries, and woven textiles are included. See the web site, entitled "Nea Moni Photo Gallery," at http://www.chiosonline.gr/gallery_neamoni.asp. See also, herein, Life of the founders: Saints Niketas, John, and Joseph, who are commemorated on the 20th day of May.

enrolled in school. Chios, at that time, was one of the preeminent learning centers in the Hellenic community under the Ottomans. The school in the capital attracted students from all over the world. The young scholar had as his teacher the preacher and priest, Father Gabriel Astrakares.[222] This same cleric was also the parish priest of the Church of Saint Efstratios at Vounokion, which belonged to Nea Moni. The youth, during the entire time of his schooling in the capital, remained under the tutelage of that elder. That thirsty soul reaped benefit for both his soul and mind, so that they were shaped and beautified, while receiving instruction from that gifted educator. Together with the curriculum, he learned to love and revere God. He also received knowledge of the sacred writings and the wise sayings of the holy fathers. His respect and zeal for learning was an early indication that the child would succeed and bear fruit. It, furthermore, augured that a useful and good citizen was in the making. Throughout his life, he exhibited respect toward the Church and teachers. The deep love he harbored for the holy writings and the practise of virtue eventually brought him in the way of the acclaimed teacher Athanasios Parios (ca. 1722-1813). The youth's fervent desire of the Christian Faith also brought him into the milieu of Saint Makarios (1731-1805), Archbishop of Corinth,[223] who was sojourning on Chios. The fame of the exiled bishop extended throughout the island. These two saintly men, Makarios and Athanasios, were pillars of the Church and of education for that era.

After the goodly young man successfully completed his education, he returned to Nea Moni. It was there that he was ordained to the diaconate, and afterward to the dignity of the priesthood. Following this, he was appointed as a teacher in the schools of the island, as which post he proved to be more than a simple teacher. He daily infused his pupils with the fear of God. He was, concurrently, a preacher, proclaiming unceasingly the word of God. He admonished and exhorted the Christians to keep the commandments of Christ: love, almsgiving, righteousness, and doing good works. His own life was a prototype of virtuous conduct.

He had no notions of self-consequence but by the superiority of his virtue and the labors by which he attracted divine grace, he was accounted worthy of the abbacy of the monastery. The selection of a man of integrity for this dignity was critical at that time for Nea Moni. The monastery had accrued serious debts, due to inept administration of the monastery holdings and estates. The brotherhood's otherworldliness and world-denying mentality caused them

---

[222] George Zolotas (1845-1906), in his five-volume *History of Chios*, is of the opinion that it is likely that young Nikephoros also was under the tutelage of the educator and author Neophytos Kafsokalyvitis, an Hagiorite, who was a former Jew who converted to Orthodoxy and taught at the school for a time. See Cavarnos, pp. 12, 13.

[223] Saint Makarios (Notaras) is commemorated by the holy Church on the 17th of April.

Saint Nikephoros of Chios

not to bother with audits. Consequently, the monastery, in the year 1802, was expected to pay a penalty of six hundred thousand piasters (*grosia*). The monastery certainly did not have this tremendous sum of money. Nea Moni, therefore, needed to sell monastery lands and holdings. The debt owed was seen to be in the eyes of certain citizens as the result of glaring mismanagement. Though there was no evidence of anything nefarious, other than a dereliction of duty, yet some people imagined otherwise.

Now the name of Father Nikephoros circulated in the mouths of all. He was a man of irreproachable moral excellence. The bloom of grace induced all to honor and admire him; therefore, no one confuted his election. Together with his ascetical mode of living, he was adorned with modesty of spirit and love for neighbor. He could never be dunned for lack of trustworthiness. It was agreed that he could discharge all duties honorably and competently. He was already known as one who had expelled ambition from his soul and had trampled upon the tyranny of vainglory. Though he was always keen to hide his labors, his love of non-acquisition was no secret. None of the praise showered on him had been exaggerated. Thus, he was everywhere extolled. Their choice for hegumen, however, was his aversion. He had no wish for distinction but could not oppose the general will. The elevation afforded him no satisfaction. He acceded to their request and was installed as hegumen in 1802 or slightly thereafter.

Upon his coming into the office of superior, an annual audit was instituted for the monastery accounts. The elders of the city, every autumn, reviewed and examined the records. Father Nikephoros, thereupon, was entrusted with the shepherding of the rational sheep of Christ. The rank of hegumen was not an easy or light ministration. This was especially true in the case of Nikephoros, who was a humble and meek man. He was not familiar or accustomed to the concerns of such administration and management. Although he was a man who enjoyed meditation and delighted in the labors of solitude, still he was inexhaustible in the services he rendered to others. His conscientiousness toward his new servitude illustrated his character. He continued to put first the interests of the monastery and what was to its advantage. He also kindled and strengthened among the brethren a greater devotion for the ascetical life, so that the monks might make daily ascents. The new abbot, resplendent with gifts, fostered and manifested every form of virtue as he presided over the flock.

Father Nikephoros was also diligent in regularly teaching the monks, but he did not play the schoolmaster. Though he was articulate in teaching, yet added to his other perfections he was also splendidly adorned by action and vision. He actively pursued the virtues and deeds of righteousness and justice. His whole life bore eloquent witness to these occupations, for which he endeavored to train the men under his guidance. He especially pursued righteousness and justice, for which he had an inherent attachment and which education enhanced. Our paragon of virtue, however, had another vision for himself. At length, the toils that beset him and the perseverance required in occupations foreign to him wore him out. He was further wearied and torn by the ingratitude of those around him and subordinates. There was a great disparity in their minds and Nikephoros knew it. How were such men to be worked on?

It should be said that the conflict within him was a result of his character; for the nature and disposition of our venerable Father Nikephoros was altogether estranged from craftiness and contentiousness. His was a character unwounded by these emotions. Nikephoros was a true philosopher in Christ, caring little for the things of the world and having little acquaintance with its ways. He was unable to govern or control the ship of his pursuit of virtue in the midst of a tempest of passion. He, therefore, with full sails, sought refuge in the haven of virtue. As a familiar and emulator of Saint Makarios Notaras and an imitator and follower of the Christ-loving teacher Athanasios Parios, and one of like zeal with them, he disdained, as vain and transient, the things of this life. He had little care or concern for the mundane, spending life simply and frugally, possessing for himself neither field nor beast of burden. His main concern was purification from the passions and thoughts not pleasing to God. He believed that through the virtues one attains similitude to God. Through this similitude, *theosis*, or divinization, may be attained. Thus, this union by grace with God ushers in participation in God's energies. For Father Nikephoros this was the Orthodox Christian's goal. He believed the saints attained such *theosis* while in this life, and continued after this earthly sojourn to abide in the everlasting light.

His life as monastery superior was taxing him inordinately. In the anguish of his heart, it was, consequently, a stage or period of discernment for the venerable Nikephoros: should he remain in the thankless office of abbot or retire from it? Certainly with regard to such a withdrawal, he himself would say that he was a zealot of erudition. Even though he may have fallen short in governing the monks, still he did not fail in excelling in his own life and in leading by the hand many souls to virtue—even after his own repose. Let us for a moment turn back into history and we shall discover an abundance of such examples that certainly acquit Nikephoros of his withdrawal. It surely was a man of such a character as the righteous Nikephoros that the great Chrysostom had in his mind's eye when he thundered forth those deathless words: "For one to be able to disdain those things of this present sphere, and to consider virtue a great acquisition, and to strive not in worldly contests, but to withdraw and place one's hopes in what lies beyond it, and to possess one's soul and entrust it, intensely and eagerly, to such an attainment, so as not to let current sufferings and straits hinder hopes in those future things, how would such a one not be philosophical?"

The goodly Nikephoros, attending such divine words and having as a model those great and learned fathers of old and in his time who flourished in Chios, bore long without being immersed in the beauty he loved and participating in the vision of God. He, at first, threw himself into his work and tirelessly toiled. He spent his time at the monastery in a spiritually profitable manner and in God-pleasing works, acquitting himself very well, which helped him brave temptations and sorrows. He opened a path for himself, by allotting his time to the publication of much needed religious works. On account of his duties as abbot he found himself in the world, yet he kept treading steadfastly out of it toward immortality. An example of his godly diligence is the composition and publication[224] of "The Service of the Holy Fathers Niketas, John, and Joseph."[225] These three holy fathers have the distinction of being the founders of Nea Moni. Father Nikephoros' compilation also contains a synopsis and history of Nea Moni, wherein the church (*katholikon*) is described together with its iconographic adornment. In the prologue of this book he mentions that,

---

[224] "The Divine and Holy Akolouthia of Our Holy and God-inspired Fathers Niketas, John, and Joseph, Founders of the Venerable, Holy, Royal, and Cross-possessing Monastery Named the New, Which Is Dedicated to Our All-holy Lady Theotokos and Ever-virgin Mary, and the History of the Monastery and Certain Strange Miracles Performed by the Mother of the Lord" (Venice, 1804). A second edition, by Gregory Photeinos, appeared in *Writings Pertaining to Nea Moni* [*Ta Neamonesia*], Book I (Chios, 1865).

[225] Our holy Fathers Niketas, John, and Joseph are commemorated by the holy Church on the 20th of May. All three were natives of Chios who discovered the wonderworking icon of the Theotokos nestled on a myrtle branch. They constructed a chapel and struggled ascetically nearby. After the fathers foretold the rise of Constantine Monomachos to the imperium, they built Nea Moni or the "New Monastery."

during the time he was a student of Gabriel at Chora, his teacher remarked, "I, too, also desired to do one such work, but neither my circumstances nor my fellow dwellers, sickness and weakness, yielded or allowed me; and clearly, the work of the school and the ambo and other daily concerns would not defer. But the desire always abides in memory and, ofttimes, my conscience censures me, insofar as I did not constrain myself when I was younger to do at least one such good work. If God were to grant me life and progress in my lessons, I should not neglect to accomplish that which I had failed to do earlier."

Our venerable Nikephoros, listened to that sacred message as a word of command. As well as he could, he attempted to carry out this precept. Now the usefulness of that inestimable work concerning Nea Moni was clearly manifest. All will concede to its value. It was Nikephoros who collected information regarding Nea Moni, leaving a record of the monastery's heirlooms and treasures. In making this inventory, there flashed forth among the lot, as precious pearls, the *chrysobulls* (gold bullas)[226] of the emperors who endowed Nea Moni. All of us now would not have known even of the existence of such documents had not Nikephoros committed his discoveries to writing. Everything would have been lost to us, because, shortly after the saint's repose, all those treasures were destroyed by fires. The Turks set the monastery on fire in 1822 and again in 1828. We should also mention that the divine office written by Nikephoros is both full and beautiful. Among his other accomplishments are Church services[227] and special hymns[228] honoring the saints

---

[226] A *chrysobull* was a document, granting privileges, that bore the emperor's bulla (seal) and autograph in red or purple ink.

[227] His hymnographical compositions that are extant include:

(1) "Service of the Holy and Glorious New-martyr Nicholas of Chios," published in the *New Martyrologion* and *New Chian Leimonarion*. This new-martyr suffered in 1754 at Chios. He is commemorated by the holy Church on the 31st of October.

(2) "The Divine and Sacred Service to Our Venerable and God-bearing Fathers Niketas, John, and Joseph," *New Leimonarion*; *New Chian Leimonarion*; and *Ta Neamonesia*.

(3) "Service of the Holy Great-martyr Myrope," *New Leimonarion* and *New Chian Leimonarion*. She is commemorated by the holy Church on the 2nd of December.

(4) "Service to Saint Demetrios the Peloponnesian," *New Leimonarion*.

(5) "Service of the Holy and Great New-martyr George of Chios," *New Leimonarion* and *New Chian Leimonarion*. This new-martyr suffered in 1807 at Kydoniai. He is commemorated by the holy Church on the 26th of November.

(6) "Service of the Holy Martyr Theophilos," *New Leimonarion* and *New Chian Leimonarion*. This new-martyr suffered in 1635 at Chios. He is commemorated by the holy Church on the 24th of July.

(continued...)

and various occasions. There is, among these, one noteworthy spiritual masterpiece which is comprised of salutations addressed to Saint Matrona of Chios (d. 1462).[229]

---

[227](...continued)

(7) "Service of the Holy Great-martyr Mark the New," *New Leimonarion* and *New Chian Leimonarion*. This new-martyr suffered in 1801 at Chios. He is commemorated by the holy Church on the 5th of June.

(8) "Service of Holy New-martyr Angelis," *New Leimonarion* and *New Chian Leimonarion*.

(9) "Service of the Holy and Glorious New-martyr George Who Martyred at New Ephesus," *New Leimonarion*. This new-martyr suffered in 1801 at Ephesus. He is commemorated by the holy Church on the 5th of April.

(10) "Service of the Holy New-martyr Lazarus," *New Leimonarion*. This new-martyr, known as "the Bulgar," suffered in 1802 at Pergamon. He is commemorated by the holy Church on the 23rd of April.

(11) "Service of the Holy and Venerable Martyr Luke the New," *New Leimonarion*. This new-martyr suffered in 1802 at Mytilene. He is commemorated by the holy Church on the 23rd of March.

(12) "Service of Our Holy Father among the Saints, Archbishop Makarios Notaras of Corinth," *New Leimonarion*; *New Chian Leimonarion*; and *Great Synaxaristes* of Constantine Doukakes (1840-1908), published at Athens from 1889 to 1896.

(13) "Service for the Feast of the Discovery of the Honorable Head of Our Holy Mother Matrona of Chios," *New Leimonarion* and *New Chian Leimonarion*. She is commemorated by the holy Church on the 20th of October.

(14) "Service of the Holy Virgin-martyr Markella of the Island of Chios," *New Leimonarion*; *New Chian Leimonarion*; and a pamphlet (Hermoupolis, 1908). She is commemorated by the holy Church on the 22nd of July.

(15) "Service of Our Venerable and God-bearing Father Gerasimos the New." This work was actually corrected by our Saint Nikephoros. It has appeared in *New Leimonarion*. Saint Gerasimos dwelt at Kephalonia. He is commemorated by the holy Church on the 20th of October, though he reposed in peace on the 15th of August, in the year 1579.

[The lists with books and divine offices was gleaned from C. Cavarnos' chapter on "Works of the Saint," in Modern Orthodox Saints, IV:66-75.]

[228] Saint Nikephoros composed three *prosomoia*, honoring New-martyr Polydoros; as well as an *idiomelon* and *doxastikon* to Martyr Phanourios. These were printed in both the *New Leimonarion* and *New Chian Leimonarion*. He wrote six *idiomela* to the Theotokos in a work entitled "Service of the Life-giving Spring and that of the Nativity of the Theotokos," printed in *Ta Neamonesia*.

[229] Saint Matrona of Chios is commemorated by the holy Church on the 20th of October. See "Twenty-four Oikoi in Honor of Our Holy Mother and God-bearing Mother Matrona of Chios," *New Leimonarion* and *New Chian Leimonarion*.

All that he has authored is replete with religious ecstasy, revealing his mighty and lively spirit as one sufficiently versed in poetry. He was eminently endowed with a skill for writing, which is masterfully shown in his collection of the lives of the saints.[230] Although the initial compiler was Saint Makarios and his fellow worker, Athanasios Parios, Nikephoros was to add many hagiographies and with divine offices to these saints. It was a fortuitous alliance. Much of Nikephoros' development and motivation to become a religious writer is due to the encouragement of Archbishop Makarios. Second to the archbishop as a model of piety was Nikephoros' teacher, the theologian Athanasios Parios. Both Makarios and Athanasios were Kollyvades, that is, they were members of a movement toward strict Orthodox tradition, which included upholding the canons, frequency in taking holy Communion, and the practise of the Jesus Prayer. Just as the holy Makarios was to be translated from this life, he entrusted Nikephoros, adorned in mind with understanding, to take up the office of editor and publish their labors. Makarios was a warm admirer of Nikephoros' talents. But Nikephoros, too, desired to see the lives of the saints, with their feats, made readily available. He deemed it of great importance that the Orthodox had models of Christians practising right-believing and true Orthodoxy. He felt strongly about presenting these biographical accounts to those of his generation, since there were many subjects under the Ottomans who denied their Orthodox Faith in favor of Islam.[231] "The martyrs," he said, "are celestial wealth, a spiritual treasure,

---

[230] The lives of the new-martyrs, published under the title *Neon Leimonarion* (Venice, 1819; Syros 1855-1857; Athens, 1873 and 1913), was compiled with the collaboration of Archbishop Makarios, Father Nikephoros, and Athanasios Parios.

[231] Extant Writings of Saint Nikephoros include:

(1) "Life and Martyrdom of the Holy New-martyr Nicholas of Chios," *Neon Martyrologion* (Venice, 1799; Athens, 1856, 1961).

(2) "Life of the Holy and Glorious Virgin-martyr Myrope Who Contested in Chios," *New Leimonarion* and the *New Chian Leimonarion*.

(3) "Life of Saint Demetrios the Peloponnesian," *New Leimonarion*.

(4) "Life of the Holy and Venerable Martyr Luke the New," *New Leimonarion* and Doukakes' *Great Synaxaristes*, Vol. 7 (March).

(5) "Life of the Holy Martyr Theophilos," *New Leimonarion*; *New Chian Leimonarion*; and Doukakes' *Synaxaristes*, Vol. 11 (July).

(6) "Life of the Holy New-martyr John from Thessalonike," *New Leimonarion*. This new-martyr suffered in 1802 at Smyrna. He is commemorated by the holy Church on the 29th of May.

(7) "The Life of the Holy New-martyr Lazarus," *New Leimonarion* and Doukakes' *Synaxaristes*, Vol. 8 (April).

(8) "Martyrdom of the Holy and Glorious and Gloriously Triumphant New-

(continued...)

God-given saviors, helpers, and public benefactors."[232] Saint Nikephoros' writings also censured the Latin Church. He examined and refuted with clarity Rome's introduction of the *Filioque* into the Creed, as well as her doctrines on papal primacy and infallibility. In his own writings, Nikephoros reveals his intimacy with the writings and sayings of the holy fathers. His obvious favorites were the three great hierarchs—Basil the Great, John Chrysostom, and Gregory the Theologian—together with Mark of Ephesus. He also manifests his familiarity with some ancient Greek writers, though he offers a disclaimer. In the words of Saint Basil, in his "Address to Young Men," regarding the works of the ancient Greeks, Nikephoros agrees with what is written: "Select from them whatever is true, incites to virtue, and dissuades from vice; but pass over the rest."

As we said earlier, after a short term as abbot, he decided to have done with it all and take up the labors of reclusion. Hegumen Nikephoros, innocent of every imputation, decided to take himself away. They had no ground of complaint against him, but he was resolved that he should no longer trespass on their time. Therefore, after two years serving as superior, he left for quiet and rest, to a place called Resta, where he could take up the evangelical life unencumbered. He knew this was the right thing to do and that it could not be done too soon. In that place, he had a friend, a preacher of sacred subjects, named Father Joseph, a former native of Fourna of Agrapha in Thessaly.[233] This priest-monk abided in the vicinity of Saint Makarios' ascetical retreat. It was the latter with whom Father Nikephoros had kept up a regular communica-

---

[231](...continued)
martyr Angelis Who Contested at Chios," *New Leimonarion* and *New Chian Leimonarion*.

(9) "Martyrdom of the Holy New-martyr George of Chios," *New Leimonarion* and *New Chian Leimonarion*.

(10) "Life and Martyrdom of the Holy and Victorious Virgin-martyr of Christ, Markella, of the Island of Chios." This work was corrected by our Saint Nikephoros. It has appeared in *New Leimonarion*; *New Chian Leimonarion*; and Doukakes' *Synaxaristes*, Vol. 11 (July).

(11) "Life of our Venerable Mother Matrona the Wonder-worker." Though authored by another, our Saint Nikephoros corrected the text. It has appeared in *New Leimonarion* and *New Chian Leimonarion*.

[232] *Logos Enkomiastikos e Enkomion pros ten Philomouson Chion*, in G. I. Zolotas' *The History of Chios*, Vol. 3(1), p. 566. See Cavarnos, p. 78.

[233] Father Joseph had struggled ascetically on Athos. He was enjoined to leave after suffering as a Kollyvades, since he refused to participate in memorial services on Sundays. He at, one point, taught at the School of Chios. He also composed a divine office to New-martyr Nicholas the New (d. 1754), which was published at Venice in 1791. Saint Nicholas is commemorated by the holy Church on the 31st of October.

tion. This is borne out by ample evidence. There was also in that place an Hagiorite monk, Neilos Kalognomos, who hailed from Chios, who was a beloved fellow monastic of Makarios. Father Neilos had been living under the spiritual care and sacred influence of the holy Makarios. This same monk also was with Makarios during the final years of the archbishop's life. Hence, Nikephoros, Joseph, and Neilos shared Makarios as their spiritual father and touchstone of piety.

It would not be pious to omit that others also came to be instructed by Saint Makarios. In particular, there were those who came to be future new-martyrs. These new-martyrs took counsel from Makarios, as well as from Nikephoros, Joseph, and Neilos. One among the memorable martyric athletes of Christ was Demetrios the Peloponnesian.[234] Demetrios had actually made his confession to our venerable Nikephoros. This took place just before his martyrdom, in 1803, at Tripoli of Arkadia. There was also Saint Mark the New (d. 1801)[235] who sojourned with the fathers for a few days until he took ship to New Ephesus. Another pilgrim was Saint Angelis (d. 1813)[236] who, ofttimes, before his martyrdom, visited the venerable Nikephoros and other fathers, as well as the tomb of Saint Makarios. We should also mention that after the righteous Nikephoros went to live henceforth at Resta, his beloved teacher, the ever-memorable Athanasios Parios, also retired to that neighborhood in 1812. The former director of the schools of Chios, now aged, lived out the remainder of his life in that place. He was happy for his withdrawal, for some accused him of not being adequately progressive to suit the times.

It was in these quiet and small woods that Nikephoros found a philosophical retreat. He was fully aware of his God-given spiritual and moral strengths. He preferred, however, to take refuge and settle in this place of solitude, released of every pell-mell of life's happenings and circumstances. In his retirement he had the best of companions: the lofty faith of Saint Makarios and the august Christian instruction of Athanasios. With Father Joseph, Nikephoros, in the midst of fellow lovers of virtue and learning, found good anchorage at a place where the tanners of Chios honor majestically Saint George of Resta.

In that place called Resta, the venerable Nikephoros remained for almost twenty years. He struggled and labored in a superhuman manner. The number of toils and contests is alone known to God, Who is the Knower of all secrets. As a God-fearing monk, Nikephoros conducted daily services and vigils. He practised unceasing interior prayer or mental prayer, keeping strict

---

[234] Saint Demetrios is commemorated by the holy Church on the 14th of April.

[235] Saint Mark the New is commemorated by the holy Church on the 5th of June. This Life was actually recorded by Athanasios Parios.

[236] Saint Angelis is commemorated by the holy Church on the 3rd of December.

abstinence and making prostrations. He read books and wrote. In order to mortify his flesh and benefit other Christians at the same time, he became a living example of manual labor and industry to them. He began planting pine trees, to the right and to the left of the hillock. His agricultural concerns expanded into olive groves and fig trees. Together with the pines, he also grew cypresses and developed a nursery. He truly believed, as did Saint Kosmas Aitolos (1714-1779),[237] that the impoverishment of the Greeks ensued from their dearth of trees. The expenses of Father Nikephoros' undertaking were met by his father's inheritance; for he sold the property that he inherited from his father. Nikephoros thought to stem the material wretchedness of the island by urging the faithful to plant trees. He not only used to give away the young trees that he grew at his nursery but also paid men to plant them. In some instances, as part of a penance, the one whom he confessed was enjoined to plant a certain number of trees. In other instances, with his inheritance, he gave money to the poor that they might plant plenty of olive bushes and thereby have a livelihood. He also engaged in these works in his hometown of Kardamyla. He went about the villages, promoting this needful occupation to his fellow islanders. He did not merely speak the following words but also strived to keep them himself: "A distinguishing characteristic of every man who possesses the virtue of practical wisdom and prudence is to take care not only for his own good but also for that of others."[238] Thus, together with multiplying trees, he also spoke of the great importance of having schools in which both secular and spiritual studies were offered in the curriculum. He noted that schools help create worthy priests and confessors, together with wise lawgivers, judges, and teachers. Also, he advocated the printing of books, not only for school children but also for general consumption.

It was not unusual for one to observe Father Nikephoros frequently traveling from the city into the villages. He was wont to visit the sick and preach the word of God with clarity and simplicity. He encouraged them to remain faithful to their Orthodox Faith and close to the Church, saying, "The divine churches are works and signs of love for God."[239] His constant goal was to offer universal and pragmatic help to the villagers. To his Gospel-couched exhortations and admonitions, he also reminded the people of their environment and ecosystem. He urged them to keep planting trees. He did not hesitate reminding them of their stewardship bequeathed to them by God. He also could be heard saying, "If you do not love trees, you do not love God."

---

[237] Saint Kosmas is commemorated by the holy Church on the 24th of August.

[238] *Logos Enkomiastikos e Enkomion pros ten Philomouson Chion*, in G. I. Zolotas' *The History of Chios*, Vol. 3(1), p. 555, 556. See Cavarnos, pp. 77, 78.

[239] Ibid., Vol. 3(1), p. 558. See Cavarnos, p. 77.

The villagers so revered the saint, especially the Kardamylions, so that even to this day they commemorate his memory with special honor. During times of drought, they sought his mediation before the Lord. He proved to be a ready helper. As an excellent go-between, his prayers succeeded in nearly every instance to bring forth much-desired rain. Thus, he brought joy and gladness to the people. His biographer does not conceal that, on many occasions, the peasants sought his wonderworking entreaties before God. Nikephoros, always looking to be of service to others, was glad to work acts of benevolence among the people that ushered in refreshment and help. The people were further heartened when they perceived that while they importuned him to offer up his efficacious petitions for rain, their benefactor remained tireless.

Although he was an old man, he sped off to wherever there was need. In the Life of Saint Makarios one such situation is mentioned. At one time there was an infirm woman from Kallimasia.[240] She sought Father Nikephoros. But he was not then found at Chora in his lodging, where he usually spent the night. It so happened that he was absent that evening, having gone to Nenita.[241] Some persons, therefore, in her behalf, made haste thither in order to bring him back to the capital. When he was discovered at Nenita and learned the cause for their anxiety, the venerable man wasted no time in returning with them. Although it was already nine o'clock at night, still he would not put it off till the morning. Immediately, he went to the bedside of the ailing woman, bearing with him the relic of Saint Makarios. As soon as the precious relic was placed upon the sufferer, she was cured of her disease. Father Nikephoros was in the habit of always bearing about with him the relic of Saint Makarios, by means of whom many miracles were wrought.

Father Nikephoros, also, performed a multitude of miracles by divine grace. From the many cases, we shall narrate only a few that will be sufficient to demonstrate the grace that worked in him. The man of God was deemed a saint even in his own lifetime. The miracles, however, resulted in an earlier official recognition of his sainthood. He was conspicuous for his humility, gentle demeanor, almsgiving, and lack of anger and of remembrance of wrongs.

One case involved a severely mentally ill maiden who was completely healed. He also restored a madman to perfectly sound mental health. In both of these cases, the cures were permanent. There was also an occasion when

---

[240] Kallimasia is five miles south of the capital city of Chora (Chios). The village is on a knoll beside the Zevoi tower, where there stands the 13th-C. church to the Virgin of Sicily.

[241] Nenita (Neneeta) is three and one-half miles south of Kallimasia, and nineteen kilometers south of the capital. It is known for the Monastery of the Taxiarchs (Bodiless Host).

fiery stones fell. The venerable elder was invited to perform the Service for Holy Water that the evil which came upon the parish of Saint George at Vrontados[242] would cease. With the completion of that divine office—O Thy wonders, Christ King!—the stones began falling into the holy water where they were instantly extinguished. This took place until the last stone fell.

At another time, while Father Nikephoros was away and making the rounds through the villages, someone stole his only goat. Upon the reverend father's return, his disciple who was in obedience (*hypotaktikos*) to him was evidently distressed and even angry on account of the theft. The righteous Nikephoros, nevertheless, attempted to calm him and said, "Cease letting anger reign, because the thief must have been poor. We had the goat for an ample amount of time. Let someone else have her now." Even as he finished uttering these generous words, the thief himself arrived and stood before them. As he wept, he began confessing his wrongful deed. He then added, "I slaughtered the goat, but found it impossible to sell the meat." Father Nikephoros readily accorded forgiveness for the crime. He then said, "Go thou now, and thou shalt have sold the meat." When the man returned to his house, he was informed by his wife that during his absence all the meat was sold.

It is also said that Father Nikephoros foresaw and foretold the future sufferings that would befall the people.[243] He was also distinguished for his noble character and conduct, and, especially, his compassion. Whatsoever money he received from time to time, he would distribute it and help the poor; in the meantime, he was left in want. It should be noted that the kindhearted father did not dispense the alms personally. Instead, he entrusted the act through a trustworthy child. He bade the lad to leave the assistance for the suffering family and to take himself away quickly. In this manner, he was coinciding with the Gospel command wherein it is written: "But when thou art doing alms, let not thy left hand know what thy right hand is doing [Mt. 6:3]."

At the hermitage of Resta, Father Nikephoros, restored, repaired, and extended the cells. It eventually came to be a place of pilgrimage. Crowds of pilgrims were coming there that they might both esteem and assess the holiness and compassion of the righteous elder. They were coming to see Father Nikephoros either to make their confessions or to seek consolation. Each one came to hear the words of God. Nikephoros said, "Happy is the man who has come to have God as his helper and to have his hopes in Him alone. Let the devil bear malice toward him, let all men persecute him and plot against him, let all his adversaries fight against him. He never fears anyone, because he has

---

242 Vrontados is five kilometers north of the capital.

243 The catastrophe that struck Chios in 1822 involved the slaughter or captivity of most of the Orthodox population by the Turks. The Turkish admiral, Kara Ali, ordered the massacre.

God as his helper. He remains always a victor, always glorified, always happy, always rich, always cheerful, and ever joyful, even if he happens to fall into extreme poverty and into a great many adverse and grievous circumstances of the present life. For inasmuch as he hopes in almighty God, he does not despair, he is neither sorry nor anxious, but expects help from on High."[244] Thus, "To those who love God, everything is conducive to their good."[245]

We should also mention some of the holy man's disciples. The names of three men, living in obedience under him, have come down to us. There was Makarios Garis of Vrontados. He was trained and instructed by Father Nikephoros. In the year 1817, however, Makarios was ordained as an archdeacon. He, thereafter, went and served Metropolitan Platon, whom he followed to the end. Indeed, both metropolitan and archdeacon suffered martyrdom under the Ottomans in 1822. Another disciple of Father Nikephoros was Kyril Vavylos. He, after a time, became a preacher at Chora, the island's capital. A third disciple, named Michael Lagoutis, who originally hailed from Vrontados, is described as a teacher of music. The latter was probably skilled in the Byzantine chant.

It would not be reverent to pass over the memory of an incident which took place after the blessed man's repose. There was a man named Nicholas Lodis. He, too, came from Vrontados. Nicholas was suffering from a dreadful illness, for which he frequently called upon the elder's help. After showing constancy in his invocations, Nicholas was vouchsafed a night vision while asleep. He was commanded thus by Father Nikephoros: "Nicholas, go to my tomb. Take up some of the soil, and thou shalt find healing." This visitation at night by Saint Nikephoros to Nicholas took place during the days when the saint's relics were being translated. Nicholas, on the following day, despite his incapacitating infirmity, was conveyed to the tomb. He took up the soil as directed in his vision. A Holy Water Service was then conducted. Nicholas Lodis, thereafter, received sound health. Perceiving his restoration, Nicholas was gladdened in his heart. As a token of his gratitude, he was moved to commission an iconographer that he might make the venerable man's image. Nicholas had the saint portrayed exactly as he had seen him while he was among the living. He, consequently, furnished the artist with a careful description. This, accordingly, became the first icon painted of the saint.

The venerable Nikephoros, as it is recorded by tradition, was of medium stature, well-grown, and strong. He was pleasing of countenance. His complexion was somewhat pale and sallow. His aspect was gentle and kind. He was said to have had beautiful eyes and a rich black beard. He had the habit of

[244] *Neon Chiakon Leimonarion* (Athens, 1968), p. 300. See Cavarnos, p. 76.
[245] *Logos Enkomiastikos*, in G. I. Zolotas' *The History of Chios*, Vol. 3(1), p. 559.

covering up his beard inside his clothing. But as he turned his torso, it could be discerned.

The repose of Father Nikephoros came during harvest time, in the year 1821. The venerable man had predicted the time that his earthly sojourn would end. His departure from this life took place in a house near the Church of Saint Paraskeve. On account of his old age, when traveling about, he could not always return the same day to Resta. He, therefore, had the custom of passing the night in the capital. It was there that his seal was discovered. There was written out "Nikephoros." There were others that said "Nikephoros of Chios." His honorable relics were transferred from Chora to Resta. They were interred in the grave wherein was laid Athanasios Parios. Prior to that, the tomb had received the body of the Hagiorite Father Neilos Kalognomos. In fact, it had been Father Nikephoros who conducted the funeral of Father Neilos.

With the passing of a generation, in the year 1845, the saint's relics were discovered in the following manner. There was a monk at Resta. His name was Agathangelos. He originally came from Hydra of the Argo-saronic Gulf, some thirty-six nautical miles from Piraeus. Father Agathangelos was vouchsafed a dream in which he beheld the place of Father Nikephoros' burial. Upon arising, Father Agathangelos took a shovel in hand and began digging in the place that he beheld in his dream. He uncovered the relics, together with the saint's *epitrachelion*[246] and *epigonation*.[247] The then Metropolitan of Chios, Sophronios, who later became Patriarch of Alexandria, had the relics translated to the cathedral at Chora where they were preserved in a closed reliquary chest.

With the passage of years, the Guild of Tanners requested and received these sacred relics. The properties at Resta belonged to these craftsmen. Upon receiving the relics, they deposited them inside a costly reliquary within the holy Church of Saint George. To this day, the relics are venerated reverently

---

[246] The *epitrachelion* (stole), which is worn over the neck, is, according to Saint Germanos, a symbol of the rope about Jesus' neck. The right side symbolizes the reed set in Christ's hand; and the left side represents the Lord bearing the Cross. Since the *epitrachelion* symbolizes the grace of the priesthood, a priest should wear it in public, as confirmed by the Synod of Laodikeia. According to Saint Simeon of Thessalonike, if a priest is without a stole and the occasion demands one, he may take a piece of rope, or something similar. He then should bless it and wear it around his neck. Peter D. Day's *The Liturgical Dictionary of Eastern Christianity*, s.v. "Epitrachelion."

[247] The *epigonation*, which is worn over the knee, is a stiffened material, that may be embroidered with either a cross or the head of the Theotokos. At first, it was awarded as a privilege to bishops and some minor prelates. After the 12th C., however, the privilege was extended to other clergy. It is a mark of authority, symbolizing the two-edged sword of Christ [Rev. 1:16; 2:12] or the sword of the Spirit [Heb. 4:12]. Some suggest that it represents the napkin with which our Lord girded Himself at the Mystical Supper. Ibid., s.v. "Epigonation."

by those who come forth with faith. Now the sacred temple wherein the saint's earthly tabernacle was laid to rest was enclosed by latticed gates, around which is set a reliquary of carved marble. In recent times, that is, 1907, the Guild, which continued to revere and esteem Saint Nikephoros' holy memory, placed a beautiful icon of the saint in that very church. In the same year, when Protosynkellos Kyril Trehakes of the metropolis of Chios composed a divine office to the saint, it was decided that Saint Nikephoros should be commemorated by the holy Church on the 1st of May.

Such, O pious listeners, was the life of this righteous man who not only was educated in secular learning but also cultivated in himself the divine teachings of our Lord Jesus Christ. He faithfully and unalterably applied the Gospel practises to his own life. The saint said: "Earthly wisdom must be conjoined with heavenly wisdom; or, to speak more aptly, heavenly wisdom, which is reverence of God, must be the starting point and foundation of education, as the fear of the Lord is the beginning of wisdom [Prov. 1:7]."[248] He, moreover, stood as an example of love in action, sweetening and benefitting the lives of others. By his words of correct Orthodox teaching and his holy conduct and manners, he enlightened many and put them on the straight path of the Lord. He was much revered and blessed by those whom he helped both morally and materially. He became a pillar to the Greek nation and an adornment of the Orthodox Church of our Lord Jesus Christ, to Whom is due glory, honor, and veneration, together with the beginningless Father and the life-creating Holy Spirit, now and ever and to the ages of the ages. Amen.

On the 1st of May, the holy Church commemorates the right-believing and blessed TAMARA, Queen of Georgia.[249]

Tamara (Thamar or T'amara) the Great, the Queen of Georgia, the mighty mistress of the land of Iberia, was born between the years 1156 and 1165. She was descended from the ancient Georgian Bagratid Dynasty.[250] She was the only child of the beauteous Bourduhan and George III (r. 1156-1184). In the year 1178, Tamara became co-regent with her father, George III, who

[248] *Logos Enkomiastikos*, in G. I. Zolotas' *The History of Chios*, Vol. 3(1), p. 565. See Cavarnos, p. 77.

[249] The Life of Saint Tamara as taken from the *Great Horologion* and other sources as indicated herein.

[250] The Bagratids were an Armenian feudal family that gave royal dynasties to Armenia, Georgia, and Caucasian Albania. Some believe their origin to have been from Iran, while a later tradition traces them to the house of David. Bagrat III, in 1008, united Abchasia and Georgia to form a single kingdom. It reached its zenith under David II/IV the Restorer and Queen T'amara, who supported the empire of Trebizond and ruled Armenia through her Zak'arid viceroys. See *Oxford*, s.v. "Bagratids."

eventually gave up his throne in favor of his daughter at his repose. During the time of Tamara's mother, Christianity had already spread and thrived in various parts of Georgia. Tamara's learned aunt, named Rusudan, also participated significantly toward her niece's education.

When George III reposed in 1184, the young Tamara became ruler and queen. Her marriage, ca. 1185, to Jurij, son of Andrej of Bogoljubovo,[251] failed. Her husband was the dissolute scion of the Russian Bogolyubskoi family of Suzdal. She eventually divorced him on account of sexual misconduct of an unnatural kind with boys. The marriage was never consummated. The homosexual Jurij was expelled from the kingdom, though not without bloody civil strife.

Tamara, in 1189, as a virgin, married David Soslan.[252] He was an Ossetian prince with Bagration blood. On the occasion of her marriage, a musical performance was given. Numerous minstrels and even acrobats participated, as well as displays of knightly prowess. Tamara bore him the future King Giorgi Lasha (r. 1213-1223) and Queen Rusudan (r. 1223-1245).[253] Tamara, in 1191, aided by Byzantium, found it necessary to suppress a revolt of Georgian nobles who supported her former husband Jurij.

Tamara's reign came to be known as the Golden Age of Georgian history. She continued the initiatives of her great-grandfather, the holy King David, known as "the Builder" or "Restorer."[254] Queen Tamara ruled with much wisdom and godly piety. From the outset of her reign, however, there was a movement to limit the royal prerogative by setting up a kind of House of Lords, with authority matching that of the sovereign. But this Georgian constitutional movement came to nought, for it lacked popular support. Despite the fact that the Georgian feudal system reached its high point during her reign and the political organization was extremely complex, Tamara was a favorite

---

[251] Andrej of Bogoljubovo, prince of Suzdal and son of Jurij Dolgorukij, was born ca. 1111 and died in 1174.

[252] Some Georgian sources say that David was related to Tamara's father and her father's sister, Rusudan. When Tamara was under her aunt's supervision, she also was reared with David. Nevertheless, when Tamara came of marriageable age, she was forced into her first marriage with the Russian prince. Afterward, when she married David, it was a love match.

[253] See David Marshall Lang's *The Georgians* (UK: Thames and Hudson, 1966), pp. 114, 150.

[254] The Georgians commemorate their righteous King David of Iberia on the 26th of January. He had reigned from 1089 to 1125. He restored the power of the Georgian crown and reunited the principalities, taking Tblisi from the Muslims in 1122. His military victories and foundation of cultural and intellectual centers, such as the Monastery of Gelati, laid the foundation for Georgian power which later reached into Armenia and Azerbaijan. *Oxford*, s.v. "David II/IV the Restorer."

Saint Tamara

among her people.[255] She promoted Orthodoxy among her subjects, building for them both churches and monasteries. It is said that there was not a single case of capital punishment or corporal punishment during her reign, as she applied the Gospel commands. She was conspicuous for her continuous flow of alms among the needy, as well as her support and maintenance of widows and orphans. She called herself "the father of orphans and judge of widows." Her court and subjects addressed her as "king" (*mepe*) rather than "queen" (*dedopali*). She not only exhibited solicitous care to those in want but also did all she could to patronize the spiritual development of her subjects. She believed in education and learning. She, therefore, sponsored poets and writers.

Upon her coronation, she too, much like Emperor Constantine who advanced Christianity, convoked a holy synod. She honored the bishops as though she were a commoner in the midst of holy angels. Upon opening the synod conference, she urged the holy fathers in a twofold manner: to establish righteousness and to redress abuses which had crept in. She desired for them to end the confusion and replace unworthy hierarchs. In her humility, she exhorted them to remove all wickedness from the land, even if it meant beginning with herself and the throne if she were to make war against God. At the commencement of the synod, she addressed the prelates and said: "O holy fathers, you have been appointed by God to guide the people. Take this opportunity to investigate all things thoroughly. Establish truth and justice in our midst. Expose and depose all defilements and abominations in our land. Have before your hearts and minds only God. Think only to please the Lord and not men of lofty degree. Despise not the poor and needy on account of their low estate, for they are precious in the eyes of God. I beseech you to labor in the Gospel word and message, as I will in actual deeds—with God helping me. As you labor in teaching the message, I will uphold that teaching in my actions. I urge you to put forward the education of the people, for which I will do my part so that such programs should thrive. I beseech you, men of God, that we

[255] Lang, *The Georgians*, pp. 114, 116.

act in concert for the defense and furtherance of the Faith. Our holy Faith will be exalted by you as spiritual fathers and ones with authority given to you from on high, and by me as this fair country's ruler and vigilant guardian." This and many more wise words were uttered by the young sovereign. As a result of the council, not only unworthy hierarchs were retired but also corrupt governors were dismissed. Tamara also arranged for the churches in her realm to be tax exempt and free of other government restraints.

Due to her energetic programs within the government, she built her God-pleasing kingdom which spread and became stronger. Together with religious institutions and care for her subjects, she continued to foster the arts and letters. She also built the beautiful Vardziskiy Palace. By means of her many military and political triumphs, she expanded Georgian power into Armenia. When the Fourth Crusade left in 1203 and attacked Constantinople and its weak-willed Emperor Alexios III Angelos (1195-1203), the Frankish desperadoes and freebooters found the empire in disarray. Tamara took the opportunity to mount a Georgian expedition against Trebizond on the Black Sea. She succeeded and, thus, her army officers installed her kinsman, Alexios I Komnenos, as emperor (r. 1204-1222). Alexios had been educated in Georgia and placed at the head of the new and independent state. This empire continued to exist up to the year 1461, when the city was taken by Sultan Mohammed II. She, thus, founded the empire of Trebizond. Her men then advanced into Paphlagonia with Alexios' brother, David Komnenos.

Then, during her reign, the Georgian people were threatened by the inroads of Muslims in surrounding lands. In 1204, the governor of the Ruma sultanate, Rukn-en-Din, sent a demand to the pious Tamara that Georgia abandon Christianity and accept Islam. The queen replied with an emphatic negative. She invoked the name of God to help her defend her Christian subjects. The queen went herself, clad in armor at the head of her Georgian armies. Some of the men doubted that a woman could even lift a sword. But she wielded it very well and moved against the Muslims and fearlessly defeated them. With sword in hand, she gained unprecedented military triumphs over the neighboring Muslims. Thus, even in spirit, our queen held the sword of righteousness in her right hand and the shield of the Faith in her left, thereby vanquishing all the enemies of Orthodoxy. Finally, in a historic battle near Basiani, the Georgian army defeated a coalition of Muslim rulers. The enemies of Georgia, entire mountain tribes, on account of the reverence they had for Tamara the queen, renounced Islam and were baptized. She succeeded in uniting under her authority all the mountaineers of Abkhazia, Imeretia, and Kakhetia.

In one case, a Turkish military chief, observing how the Christian God fought for Tamara and her Orthodox Georgians, surrendered. She had become the fear and humiliation of the impious. He, thereupon, asked to receive holy Baptism. In other instances, Saracen prisoners of war were brought before her throne. Those infidels had been vouchsafed a vision of the supreme commander of the incorporeal hosts, the Archangel Michael. It was made known to them that his heavenly solicitude was directed toward the queen, so that he both protected her in battle and caused her campaigns to succeed. The Muslims so revered Tamara that they insisted that the keys of Karsa should only be entrusted to her and to none other. When she received their proposal, she obliged them and went forth personally to receive the keys to their city.

In 1208, the Georgians sent an expeditionary force into Persia. The cities of Khorosan, Erzerum, Tabriz, and Kazvin were vanquished by the queen. She succeeded in taking Aleppo, then held by Sultan Neredin, deemed as a terror by the Crusaders. She also occupied Ardebil, conquering its sultan. A Georgian dynasty, the Beshkenids, ruled the important district of Ahar in Persian Azerbaijan for several generations.[256] Thus, she expanded her kingdom for the sake of Orthodoxy and the curtailment of Islam. Her wise rule and valorous conduct won her the love of her nation and the respect of the infidel hordes. Even intractable mountaineers deferred to her rule and name, so that whole tribes were accepting the Mystery of Baptism. Although fearless in war and governing, her people extolled her gentleness, love of peace, wisdom, piety, and beauty. The holy and right-believing queen continued to shine forth with the light of good works and grace. In imitation of the saintly empress of old, Helen, this lover of Orthodoxy also built countless churches and monasteries throughout her kingdom, and was a benefactress also to the holy land, Mount Athos, and the sacred places in Greece and Cyprus.

She continued to retain the love of her people who wrote ballads and songs to her. Among the many descriptions accorded her by her people, she was called "radiant mother," "vessel of wisdom," "slender reed," "smiling sun," and many other epithets. The poem written in her honor by Shota of Rustaveli (ca. 1172-ca. 1216), entitled "The Knight of the Panther Skin," is a masterpiece of Georgian literature. He wrote a series of odes to his queen, when Georgia achieved her greatest power and influence. The queen appointed Rustaveli as treasurer of her court. It is alleged that he fell madly in love with her, but that she disdained his attachment for her. Sick with love, the rebuffed treasurer decided to withdraw from secular life and finish his days at the Monastery of the Cross at Jerusalem.[257] Although Tamara acquired much glory and admiration in her lifetime, still she did not exalt herself in her mind. For all things, whether accomplishments or vicissitudes, she gave thanks to Christ.

---

[256] Ibid., p. 115.
[257] Ibid., p. 173.

And though she surpassed all in physical beauty, the beauties of her soul were far more resplendent.

As for the renowned Tamara, she considered servitude to Christ to be honor. She deemed riches and her earthly dominion to be but a shadow and a dream, to which her heart was not attached. The venerable queen, therefore, as the wise and faithful servant of Christ, spent the final years of her life in the Bardzia Cave Monastery. She had her own cell which was connected to the church by a window, through which she could offer up prayer to God during the divine offices. She reposed in peace between 1207 and 1213, and soared into the heavens where she is numbered among the saints. Many Georgians venerate Saint Tamara as the healer of infirmities. The right-confessing Tamara, queen of the Georgians, is commemorated on the 1st of May, the day of her repose, as well as on the Sunday of the Myrrh-bearing Women. A Slavonic source gives the day of her repose as the 18th of January, in the year 1212. Even in her last moments, she thought only of her people and keeping them safe in Christ. She is recorded to have uttered these final words: "O Christ, my God, as Thou hadst entrusted me with the stewardship of this kingdom dedicated to Thee, so I commend to Thee the people who have been redeemed by Thy precious blood. To Thee, O my Christ, do I commit my spirit...." Tamara the all-great is the never-fading glory of the Iberians and the exquisite ornament of the Orthodox Church, for she tended well the portion of the Theotokos and cultivated well the vine of the enlightener Nina, by confirming her people in Orthodoxy and with right doctrine and practise.[258]

---

[258] After the descent of the Holy Spirit on Pentecost, when the apostles cast lots that they might determine where each should go and preach the Gospel, the Virgin-Mother also requested a lot for herself, so that she might share in the preaching. Thus, she said, "I, also, wish to take part in the preaching of the Gospel and cast my lot with you to receive the land that God will show." Then with fear and reverence, they cast for the Theotokos; and her lot fell on the Iberian land. The most pure Mother of God then joyfully accepted her lot.

After the day of Pentecost, the Theotokos was planning to set out for Iberia at once, but the Archangel Gabriel appeared to her, restraining her, saying, "Virgin Birth-giver of God, Jesus Christ Who was born of thee, thus commands: Thou shalt not depart from the land of Judaea, that is, Jerusalem. The place assigned as thy lot is not Iberia but Macedonia's peninsula, Mount Athos. After some time, thou shalt have the work of preaching in the land to which God shall guide thee. This place shall be greatly blessed and illuminated in the light of thy face." The archangel then revealed to her the following about the Iberian land: "The land which fell to thee shall be enlightened in the latter days, by another woman, and thy dominion shall be established there." These words were fulfilled three centuries later when the Virgin Mary sent Saint Nina, "Equal-to-the-apostles" (commemorated on the 14th of January), whom she blessed and

(continued...)

On the 1st of May, the holy Church commemorates our righteous and God-bearing Father PAPHNUTIOS, Wonder-worker of Borovsk, Priest and Hegumen of the Vyosky-Protection Monastery and Builder of the Church of the Nativity of the Virgin Mary (d. 1477).

On the 1st of May, the holy Church commemorates the holy New-martyr MARY of Crete (1826).[259]

Mary, the goodly virgin and new-martyr under the Turkish yoke, surnamed Methymopoula, was born of pious parents who were from the village of Kato Phourni in Merebellou County of Crete. She became the objective of an Albanian Turk, a land constable, who fell in love with her and attempted to entice her to marry him, thereby converting her to Islam. However, whenever she encountered him, the most sensible and faithful maiden (to the Faith of Christ) avoided him as if she saw a dreadful demon. Though the defiled one displayed kindness toward her, flattered her, and promised opulence and innumerable gifts, these were but paltry attempts to lure her into loving him. Indeed, the maiden loathed both his unwholesome craving and his riches, as he was an intemperate and savage man.

However, since that sinister and evil Turk attempted many times to break her resolve and failed, he decided to wreak his revenge upon her. Taking up the arms which he used as a constable, one day in May, he espied her high up among the branches of a mulberry tree nearby the village. As she was busy collecting leaves for feeding the silkworms, the Turk drew his weapon and fired at her. The bullet pierced her heart, which he could not subdue with his deception and flatteries. The blessed maiden fell from the tree, branch by branch, as a fowl downed by a hunter in the bush. Thus, she landed dead, slain because she would yield neither to the satanic lust of this inhuman Albanian Moslem nor to the acceptance of Islam. The authorities did not even inquire into this lawless act which took place in 1826.

Through the intercessions of Thy Saints,
O Christ God, have mercy on us. Amen.

---

[258](...continued)
helped in proclaiming the Gospel to the Iberians. See *The Life of the Virgin Mary, the Theotokos*, pp. 413, 414.

[259] The present martyrdom is recorded as having occurred during the first few days of May. The precise date is unknown according to the *Neon Martyrologion* of Gerasimos Doukakes (Athens, 1905). Therefore, our primary source, *The Great Synaxaristes* (in Greek), has placed it on the 1st of May. It is to be noted, however, that the Slavonic Calendar places our saint on the 3rd of May.

On the 2nd of May, the holy Church commemorates the Translation of the precious Relics of our holy Father among the saints, ATHANASIOS the Great, Archbishop of Alexandria.[1]

Athanasios the Great (b. 295-373) lived throughout the years of the illustrious Emperor Constantine the Great (306-337), and during the time of the latter's son, the Arian Emperor Constantius II (337-361), whom Athanasios said was "worse than Saul, Ahab, and Pilate,"[2] and through to the short reign of Emperor Julian the Apostate (361). Athanasios attended the First Œcumenical Synod in Nicaea (325), which put down the profane Arius. He was elected Archbishop of Alexandria on the 8th of June, in the year 328, following the illustrious Patriarch Alexander. Athanasios, the initiate of heavenly mysteries, also suffered five exiles (335, 339, 356, 362, and 365). He is commemorated today in remembrance of the translation of his relics, first to Constantinople and then to Venice; but we also honor the memory of his tireless labors and everlasting exhortations.

---

[1] The holy Church, on the 18th of January, commemorates Saint Athanasios with his fellow Alexandrian, Saint Kyril. The latter lived during the time of Emperor Theodosios II the Younger (408-450). Kyril attended the Third Œcumenical Synod in Ephesus (431), which denounced the blasphemies of Nestorios. The special feast day of Saint Kyril, champion of the Virgin Theotokos, is the 9th of June, the day of his falling asleep in the Lord. Today's feast was observed from ancient times by the Orthodox. Many are of the opinion that this latter date should be the main feast day, maintaining it was the day of the saint's repose. The shared date of the 18th of January is believed by them to be in response to the Feast of the Three Hierarchs (commemorated by the holy Church on the 30th of January). The history and sayings of Saints Athanasios and Kyril have been the subject of many Church writers. Those who have written about Saint Athanasios include Saint Gregory the Theologian, Saint Symeon the Metaphrastes, Theodoretos of Kyros, Socrates Scholasticus, Eusebius, Rufinus, Saint Epiphanios, Sozomen, and other ancient chroniclers. Two hagiographies of Saint Athanasios are extant, which are kept at the Athonite Monastery of the Great Lavra. An elegant encomium by Saint Gregory the Theologian has also been preserved, which is recounted in part below. Encomia praising the summit of the fathers, Athanasios the Great, are many. A poem was written by John Efchaita, published by Caesarios Dapontes [*Paterikon of our Holy Father Among the Saints, Gregory the Dialogist*...(Venice, 1780)]. A service concerning the translation of Saint Athanasios' sacred relics was composed by Nikodemos the Hagiorite. Editions of the work of this Hagiorite have been published by the Athonite Monastery of Iveron (Athens, 1903). The biography presented in our English January *Synaxaristes* presents the history, in its entirety, of our hero's famous flights and feats.

[2] Saint Athanasius, *History of the Arians*, Part VIII, § 68, Nicene and Post-Nicene Fathers, 2nd Series, Vol. IV, p. 295.

Saint Athanasios

Saint Athanasios addressed those questions pertaining to the Trinity, as well as to the incarnation of the Logos (Word) of God. His chief work, as champion of the Logos, was the disproving of Arian dogma in his four orations or discourses. The divinization of man was paramount to him, which was now made possible since the incarnate Logos put on human flesh. This was inconsistent with Arian ideas, but Athanasios refuted them and said that Jesus "was not a man Who later became God, but God Who later became man in order to divinize us."[3]

Saint Gregory the Theologian delivered an oration on this venerable father and pillar of right-believing Orthodoxy. It was a panegyric given at the Church of Constantinople at the annual feast in honor of Saint Athanasios. It is unknown whether Saint Gregory gave the oration on the 18th of January or the 2nd of May. He opens his address to the faithful saying, "In praising Athanasios, I shall be praising virtue. To speak of him and to praise virtue are identical, because he had embraced virtue in its entirety.[4]...To speak of and to admire him fully would perhaps be too long a task for the present purpose of my discourse, and would take the form of a history rather than of a panegyric.[5]...This I will say. In the discharge of his office, he was sublime in action, lowly in mind; inaccessible in virtue, most accessible in intercourse. He was gentle, free from anger, sympathetic, sweet in words, and sweeter in disposition. He was angelic in appearance, but more angelic in mind. He was calm in rebuke, persuasive in praise, without spoiling the good effect of either by excess; rather, he reproved with the tenderness of a father. He praised with the dignity of a ruler. His severity was not sour. In all his ways he was reasonable, prudent, and truly

---

[3] Idem, "Oration I," *Against the Arians* (*Kata Arianon* or *Contra Arianos*), *Patrologia Graeca* (*P.G.*) 26:92C-93A.

[4] Saint Gregory, "Oration XXI, On the Great Athanasius, Bishop of Alexandria (delivered ca. 379/380)," ¶ 1, Nicene, 2nd Ser., VII:269-280.

[5] Ibid., ¶ 5.

wise. His disposition sufficed for the training of his spiritual children, with very little need of words.[6]

"Let one praise him in his fasts and prayers; for Athanasios was as one disembodied and immaterial. Let another laud his unweariedness and zeal for vigils and psalmody. Let some extol his patronage of the needy, while others proclaim his dauntlessness toward the powerful or his condescension to the lowly. Let the virgins celebrate the friend of the Bridegroom. Let those under the yoke glorify their restrainer. Hermits recognize him who lent wings to their course. Coenobites acknowledge their lawgiver. Simple folk acclaim their guide. Contemplatives eulogize the heavenly-minded hierarch. The joyous commend their bridle. The unfortunate panegyrize their consolation. The hoary-headed reverence their staff. Youths applaud their instructor. The poor magnify their resource. The wealthy speak in high terms of their steward. Even the widows will, methinks, praise their protector, even the orphans their father, even the poor their benefactor, strangers their host, brethren the man of brotherly love, the sick their physician: in whatever sickness or treatment you will, the healthy the guard of health. Yea, he made himself all things to all men that he might gain almost, if not quite, all [cf. 1 Cor. 9:22]."[7]

Saint Gregory then touches upon the Ariomaniacs, describing life with them, saying, "O what Jeremias will bewail the confusion and blind madness that have befallen us? He alone could utter lamentations befitting our misfortunes.[8] The beginning of this madness was Arius (whose name is derived from frenzy). He paid the penalty of his unbridled tongue by his death in a profane spot, brought about by prayer not by disease. For he, like Judas, burst asunder for his similar treachery to the Logos."[9]

Simply put, the Arian position was that (1) God made the Son out of nothing, and called Him His Son; (2) the Word of God is one of the creatures; (3) there was a time when the Word was not; and (4) He is alterable, and He is capable, when it is His will, of altering.[10] We learn of Saint Athanasios' attitude toward heretics in his own words: "A heretic is a wicked thing in truth. And in every respect his heart is depraved and irreligious. For—behold!—though convicted on all points and shown to be utterly bereft of understanding, the heretics feel no shame. They, thereupon, losing their life in the objections which they advance, invent for themselves other questions, Judaic and foolish, and new expedients, as if Truth were their enemy. They, thereby, rather reveal

---

[6] Ibid., ¶ 9.

[7] Ibid., ¶ 10.

[8] Ibid., ¶ 12.

[9] Ibid., ¶ 13. Cf. Acts 1:18.

[10] See *De Synodis* or *Councils of Ariminum* (Italy) *and Seleucia* (Isauria), in Nicene, 2nd Ser., IV:448-480.

that they are Christ's opponents in all things....After so many proofs against them—at which even the devil who is their father had himself been abashed and gone back—they, as from their perverse heart, again mutter forth other expedients, sometimes in whispers and sometimes with the drone of gnats."[11]

In Athanasios' first letter to the Egyptian monks, the famed recorder of the laws of monasticism describes his hesitation and doubt upon writing. As a watchman [cf. Ez. 3:17] of the Church, however, he is enjoined to speak out against what the Church has undergone at the hands of the Arian madmen. "For the more I desired to write, and endeavored to force myself to understand the divinity of the Logos, so much the more did the knowledge thereof withdraw itself from me. Correspondingly, when I thought that I apprehended it, I concurrently perceived myself to have failed of doing so. Moreover, I was unable to express in writing even what I seemed to myself to understand; and that which I wrote was unequal to the imperfect shadow of the truth which existed in my conception....I, frequently, designed to have done and cease writing; believe me, I did. But I constrained myself to write briefly; for though it be impossible to comprehend what God is, yet it is possible to say what He is not. Accordingly, I have written as well as I was able; and you, dearly beloved, receive these communications not as containing a perfect exposition of the divinity of the Logos but as being merely a refutation of the impiety of the enemies of Christ. The words contained herein afford suggestions to those who desire to arrive at a pious and sound faith in Christ. And if in anything they are defective—and I think they are defective in all respects—pardon it with a pure conscience; and only receive favorably the boldness of my good intentions in support of godliness."[12]

The heretics, nonetheless, were bold and unabashed. The saint then puts the monks and solitaries on their guard in a second letter. "I have been compelled to write at once: that you may keep faithfully and without guile the pious Faith which God's grace works in you; and that you may not give occasion of scandal to the brethren. For when any sees you, the faithful in Christ, associate and communicate with such persons, or worshipping along with them, certainly they will think it a matter of indifference; and then, they, too, will fall into the mire of irreligion. Lest, then, this should happen, be pleased, beloved, to shun those who hold the impiety [of Arius]. Moreover, do avoid those who only feign not to hold with Arius yet worship with the impious. We are specially bound to fly from the communion of men whose opinions we hold in execration. But if any should pretend that he confesses the right Faith, but should appear to communicate with those others, exhort him to

---

[11] Saint Athanasius, "Discourse III," *Against the Arians*, Ch. XXX, §§ 58, 59, Nicene, 2nd Ser., IV:425.

[12] Idem, "Letter LII, First Letter to Monks (Written 358–360)," Nicene, IV: 563, 564.

abstain from such communion. If he should promise to do so, treat him as a brother; but if he should persist in a contentious spirit, him avoid. I urge you that, living as you do, you will preserve a pure and sincere Faith. Then those persons, seeing that you do not join with them in worship, will derive benefit, fearing lest they should be accounted as impious and as those who hold with the impious."[13] Elsewhere, he gives this counsel: "For we ought to walk by the standard of the saints and the fathers, and imitate them, and to be sure that if we depart from them we put ourselves also out of their fellowship."[14]

Saint Athanasios, as a result of the Arian controversy, authored four discourses or orations that form a single work, entitled *Against the Arians*, which were written between 356 and 360. There was a demand for such a treatise, for which our saint answered the call. While he eloquently penned a comprehensive refutation of the heresy, he also was made to endure countless tribulations while contending for piety. The saint favored using passages from Scriptures, since the heretics put the wrong explanations or meanings on the God-inspired words. He found that he needed to explain how Christ was begotten first and made or created afterward, with the proper interpretation of the terms "only-begotten" and "firstborn." He also found it necessary to discourse on why a creature could not redeem and why redemption was necessary at all. "As the namesake of immortality, Athanasios has clearly proven that the sound of his immortal dogmas have gone out into all the inhabited world."[15]

"If Jesus," he writes, "is also called 'the firstborn of the creation [Col. 1:15],' still this is not as if He were leveled to the creatures, and only first of them in point of time (for how should that be, since He is 'only-begotten?'), but it is because of the Logos' condescension to the creatures, according to which He has become the 'Brother' of 'many.'...Accordingly, it is nowhere written in the Scriptures either 'the firstborn of God' or 'the creature of God.' But 'Only-begotten' and 'Son' and 'Logos' and 'Wisdom,' refer to Him as proper to the Father. Thus, 'We beheld His glory, the glory as of the only-begotten from the Father [Jn. 1:14]'; and 'God sent forth His only-begotten Son [1 Jn.4:9]'; and 'O Lord, Thy Word endureth forever [Ps. 118:89]'; and 'In the beginning was the Logos, and the Logos was with God [Jn. 1:1]'; and 'Christ, God's power and God's wisdom [1 Cor. 1:24]'; and 'This is My beloved Son [Mt. 3:17]'; and 'Thou art the Christ, the Son of God, the living One [Mt. 16:16].'...He is only-begotten because of His generation from the Father, as has been said; and He is firstborn, because of His condescension to the creation

[13] Idem, "Letter LIII, Second Letter to Monks," Nicene, IV:564.
[14] Ibid., "Letter XLIX, To Dracontius (bishop in Egypt, written 354/355)," Nicene, IV:558.
[15] May 2nd, Orthros Canon, Ode Eight, Mode Three.

and His making the many His brethren....Moreover, the word 'firstborn' has again the creation as a reason in connection with it, which Paul proceeds to say, 'for in Him were all things created [Col. 1:16].' But if all the creatures were created in Him, He is other than the creatures, and is not a creature, but the Creator of the creatures."[16]

Saint Athanasios

Saint Athanasios believed the divinity of Father and Son is one. All things that can be said of the Father can also be said of the Son, excepting only that the Father is said to be Father. "And why are the things of the Son proper to the Father, except because the Son is the proper Offspring of His essence? And the Son, being the proper Offspring of the Father's essence, reasonably says that the things of the Father are His own also."[17]

Again, "So that when the Son is called firstborn, this is done not for the sake of ranking Him with the creation, but to prove the framing and adoption of all things through the Son....For as the Father is First, so also is He both First as image of the First, and because the First is in Him, and also Offspring from the Father, in Whom the whole creation is created and adopted into sonship."[18]

A true Orthodox teacher, he preached that the Only-begotten is equally worshipped and equally enthroned with the Father. "It is proper for the Son to be always, and to endure together with the Father....The Son is Offspring of the Father's essence (γέννημα τῆς τοῦ Πατρὸς οὐσίας), and He is Fashioner, while other things are fashioned by Him; and He is Radiance and Logos and Image and Wisdom of the Father, while originate things (having the capacity of perishing) stand and serve below the Triad (having eternal duration). Therefore, the Son is different in kind and essence from originate things, and on the contrary is proper to the Father's essence and one in nature with it."[19]

---

[16] Saint Athanasius, "Discourse II," *Against the Arians*, Ch. XXI, § 62, Nicene, IV:382.

[17] Idem, "Oration III," *Against the Arians*, *P.G.* 26:329BC.

[18] Idem, "Discourse III," *Against the Arians*, Ch. XXIV, § 9, Nicene, IV:398, 399.

[19] Idem, "Oration I," *Against the Arians*, § LVIII, *P.G.* 26:133B.

His words were like thunder that smote the ears of the heretics when he said, "The Son is begotten not from without but from the Father; and while the Father remains whole, the expression of His hypostasis (subsistence) abides forever, and preserves the Father's likeness and unvarying image, so that he who sees Him, sees in Him the hypostasis too, of which He is the impress (χαρακτῆρα). And from the energy of the impress we understand the true divinity of the hypostasis, as the Savior Himself teaches when He says, 'the Father Who abideth in Me, He doeth the works [Jn. 14:10] ' which I do; and 'I and the Father are one [Jn. 10:30],' and 'I am in the Father and the Father in Me [Jn. 14:11].' Therefore let this Christ-opposing heresy attempt first to divide the examples found in things originate, and say, 'Once the sun was without his radiance,' or, 'Radiance is not proper to the essence of light' or 'It is indeed proper, but it is a part of light by division.'"[20]

Elsewhere, he writes: "Our Lord did not come into, but became, man, and therefore had the acts and affections of the flesh....But—behold!—the Ariomaniacs, as if not wearied in their words of irreligion, but hardened with Pharaoh, with arrogant and audacious tongues say, 'How can Christ be the natural and true Power of the Father, Who near upon the season of the Passion says, "Now My soul hath been troubled; and what shall I say? 'Father, save Me from this hour'; but on this account I came to this hour [Jn. 12:27]. 'Father, glorify Thy name.' Then a voice came out of the heaven: 'I both glorified it and will glorify it again [Jn. 12:28].'" And He said the same another time, He said, "O My Father, if it is possible, let this cup pass from Me [Mt. 26:39]." And also, "Having said these things, Jesus was troubled in Spirit, and testified and said, 'Verily, verily, I say to you, that one of you shall deliver Me up [Jn. 13:21].'"' Then these perverse Arians argue, 'If He were Power, He had not feared, but rather He had supplied power to others.' Further they say: 'If He were by nature the true and own Wisdom of the Father, how is it written: "And Jesus kept on advancing in wisdom and stature, and in grace in the presence of God and men [Lk. 2:52]"?'...This too they urge: 'How can He be the own Word of the Father, without Whom the Father never was, through Whom He makes all things, as you think, Who said upon the Cross, "My God, My God, why didst Thou forsake Me [Mt. 27:46; Mk. 15:34; Ps. 21(22):1]?" And before that had prayed, "Father, glorify Thy name [Jn. 12:28]"; and "O Father, glorify Thou Me with Thyself, with the glory which I had with Thee before the world came to be [Jn. 17:5]."...And elsewhere He says, "Concerning that day or the hour, no one knoweth, not even the angels in heaven, nor the Son, except the Father [Mk. 13:32]."' Upon this again say the miserable men, 'If the Son were, according to your interpretation, eternally

---

[20] Ibid., "Oration II," *Against the Arians*, Ch. XVIII, § 33, *P.G.* 26:217AB.

existent with God, He would not have been ignorant of 'that day' but would have known as Word. Neither would He have been forsaken as being coexistent, nor would He have asked to receive glory as having it in the Father, nor would He have prayed at all; for, being the Word, He had needed nothing. But since He is a creature and originate, He thus spoke. He needed what He had not; for it is proper to creatures to require and need what they have not.'"[21]

"But they ought, when they hear 'I and the Father are one [Jn. 10:30],' to see in Him the oneness of the divinity and the propriety of the Father's essence. Again, when they hear, 'He wept [Lk. 19:41]' and the like, they ought to say that these are proper to the body; especially since on each side they have an intelligible ground, namely, that this is written as of God and that with reference to His manhood. For, in the incorporeal, the properties of body had not been—unless He had taken a body corruptible and mortal; for mortal was holy Mary, from whom was His body. Therefore, when He was in a body suffering, and weeping, and toiling, these things are proper to the flesh; they are ascribed to Him together with the body. If then He wept and was troubled, it was not the Word, considered as the Word, Who wept and was troubled, but it was proper to the flesh; and if too He besought that the cup might pass away, it was not the Divinity that was in terror, but this affection too was proper to the manhood. And that the words declared through the evangelists, 'Why didst Thou forsake Me [Mt. 27:46]?' are His, according to the foregoing explanations that these were proper to manhood; for the impassible Word suffered nothing. Now the Lord became man, and these things are done and said as from a man, that He might Himself lighten these very sufferings of the flesh, and free it from them. Whence neither can the Lord be forsaken by the Father, Who is ever in the Father, both before He spoke and when He uttered this cry. Nor is it lawful to say that the Lord was in terror, at Whom the keepers of Hades' gates shuddered [Job 38:7] and set open Hades, and the graves did gape, and many bodies of the saints arose and appeared to their own people [Mt. 27:52, 53]. Therefore, let every heretic be dumb. Let none of them dare to ascribe terror to the Lord Whom death, as a serpent, flees, at Whom demons tremble, and the sea is in alarm, and for Whom the heavens are rent and all the powers are shaken. For behold when He says, 'Why didst Thou forsake Me [Mt. 27:46]?' the Father showed that He was ever and even then in Him; for the earth knowing its Lord Who spoke, straightway trembled, and the veil was rent, and the sun was hidden, and the rocks were torn asunder, and the graves, as I have said, did gape, and the dead in them arose; and, what is wonderful,

[21] Idem, "Discourse III: Introductory to Texts from the Gospels on the Incarnation," *Against the Arians*, Ch. XXVI, § 26, IV:407, 408.

they who were then present and had before denied Him, seeing these signs, confessed that 'truly, this was God's Son [Mt. 27:54].'...[22]

"Therefore as man He utters this speech, and yet both were said by the Same: to show that He was God, willing in Himself; and that as man, He had a flesh that was in terror. For the sake of this flesh He combined His own will with human weakness, that destroying this affection He might in turn make man undaunted in face of death....Though the divinity was not in terror, yet the Savior took away our terror. For as He abolished death by death, and by human means all human evils, so by this so-called terror did He remove our terror, and brought about that never more should men fear death. His word and deed go together. For human were the sayings, 'Let this cup pass [Mt. 26:39],' and 'Why didst Thou forsake Me [Mt. 27:46]?' But divine were the acts whereby the Same did cause the sun to fail and the dead to rise. Again He said humanly, 'Now My soul hath been troubled [Jn. 12:27]'; and He said divinely, 'I lay down My soul, that I might take it again. No one taketh it from Me, but I lay it down of Myself. I have authority to lay it down, and I have authority to take it again [Jn. 10:17,18].' For to be troubled was proper to the flesh, and to have power to lay down His life and take it again, when He willed, was no property of men but of the Word's power. For man dies, not by his own power, but by necessity of nature and against his will. But the Lord—being Himself immortal, but having a mortal flesh—had power, as God, to become separate from the body and to take it again, when He would. Concerning this too speaks David in the psalm: 'For Thou wilt not abandon my soul in Hades, nor wilt Thou suffer Thy Holy One to see corruption [Ps. 15:10].' For it beseemed that the flesh, corruptible as it was, should no longer after its own nature remain mortal; but because of the Word Who had put it on, it should abide incorruptible. For as He, having come in our body, was conformed to our condition, so we, receiving Him, partake of the immortality that is from Him.[23]

Further on, he writes: "Idle then is the excuse for stumbling, and petty the notions concerning the Word, of these Ariomaniacs, because it is written, 'He was troubled,' and 'He wept.' For they seem not even to have human feeling, if they are thus ignorant of man's nature and properties. Indeed, it is the greater wonder that the Word should be in such a suffering flesh. He neither prevented those who were conspiring against Him nor took vengeance of those who were putting Him to death, though He was able. And this was He Who hindered some from dying, and raised others from the dead. And He let His own body suffer, for therefore did He come, as I said before, that in the flesh He might suffer, and thenceforth the flesh might be made impassible and immortal; and that, as we have many times said, contumely and other troubles

---

[22] Ibid., "Discourse III," *Against the Arians*, Ch. XXIX, § 56, IV:423, 424.

[23] Ibid., "Discourse III," *Against the Arians*, Ch. XXIX, § 57, IV:424, 425.

might determine upon Him and come short of others after Him, being by Him annulled utterly; and that henceforth men might forever abide incorruptible, as a temple of the Word. Had the fighters against Christ thus dwelt on these thoughts, and recognized the ecclesiastical scope as an anchor of the Faith, they would not have made shipwreck concerning the Faith."[24]

The saint, then, was wont to speak of our redemption, saying that "Mankind is perfected in the Son, and restored[25] as he was made in the beginning, and with a much higher grace. For, being raised from the dead, we no longer fear death, but reign eternally with Christ in the heavens."[26] The saint also speaks of the divinization of man, that is: "As the Lord put on the body and became man, so also we are divinized (θεοποιούμεθα) by the Logos."[27]

Athanasios was a great proponent of Baptism, for at that Mystery is "the Holy Spirit poured out. We are given the indwelling and intimacy of the Spirit."[28] He goes on to say that by virtue of bearing Jesus' body, "we receive the Spirit and thus are sanctified. By participation in the Spirit we become sons and one with Father and Son. It is the reception of the Holy Spirit into our hearts that empowers us to call God 'Father' and to become His children. Those who receive into their hearts, as the apostle says, 'the Spirit of His Son into your hearts, crying, "Abba, Father [Gal. 4:6],"' are they, who, receiving the Logos, gain power from Him to 'become children of God [Jn. 1:12].' For men cannot otherwise become sons, since they are by nature creatures, unless they receive the Spirit of the nature and true Son. That this might take place, the Logos became flesh, that He might make man capable of divinity."[29]

Saint Athanasios, therefore, urges the necessity for holy Baptism. For He believes that this Mystery ushers in both grace and consecration. It is the means of our adoption. He believes that its administration is not simply reciting the correct words but also with the correct understanding and the correct Faith that follows from such understanding. And the correct understanding and belief is that the divinity of the Son is the same as that of the Father.[30]

Why the need for redemption? Saint Athanasios answers: "The race of man was perishing; the rational man made in God's image was disappearing, and the handiwork of God was in a process of dissolution....For God had

[24] Ibid., "Discourse III," *Against the Arians*, Ch. XXIX, § 58, IV:425.

[25] He has set over all the same Head, Christ according to the flesh, both over angels and men. For the recapitulation [Eph. 1:10] of all things in Himself, Christ at the end of the times became a man. Christ summed up all things in Himself.

[26] Saint Athanasios, "Oration II," *P.G.* 26:289B.

[27] Ibid., "Oration III," *P.G.* 26:329BC.

[28] Ibid., "Oration I," *P.G.* 26:108B.

[29] Ibid., "Oration II," *P.G.* 26:273A.

[30] Ibid., *P.G.* 26:333A-240C.

ordained that man, if he transgressed the commandment, should die the death; but if after the transgression man should not die, God's word would be broken. For God would not be true, if, when He had said we should die, man died not. Again, it would be unseemly that creatures once made rational, and having partaken of the Logos, should go to ruin, and turn again toward non-existence by the way of corruption. For it would not be worthy of God's goodness that the things He had made should waste away, because of the deceit practised on men by the devil. Especially would it be unseemly to the last degree that God's handicraft among men should be done away—either because of their own carelessness or because of the deceitfulness of evil spirits.

"So, as the rational creatures were wasting and such works were in the course of ruin, what was God in His goodness to do? Was He to suffer corruption to prevail against them and death to hold them fast? And where would be the profit of their having been made, to begin with? For better were they not made, than once made only to be left to neglect and ruin. For neglect reveals weakness, and not goodness on God's part—if, that is, He allows His own work to be ruined when once He had made it—more so than if He had never made man at all. For if He had not made them, none could impute weakness; but once He had made them, and created them out of nothing, it would be most monstrous for the work to be ruined—and that before the eyes of the Maker. It was, then, out of the question to leave men to the current of corruption; because this would be unseemly and unworthy of His goodness."[31]

Athanasios, as the mouth of the Word of God, reveals: "For by His becoming Man, the Savior was to accomplish both works of love: first, in putting away death from us and renewing us again; secondly, being unseen and invisible, in manifesting and making Himself known by His works to be the Logos of the Father, and the Ruler and King of the universe."[32]

Athanasios' Spirit-filled words have the power to enlighten our hearts and flood us with the waters of the Spirit. He plainly speaks the mysteries of God, telling us, "Now even while present in a human body and Himself quickening it, He was, without inconsistency, quickening the universe as well, and was in every process of nature....For He was not bound to His body, but rather was Himself wielding it. So He not only was in it but also was actually in everything; and while external to the universe, He abode in His Father only. And this was the wonderful thing: that He was at once walking as man, and as the Word was quickening all things, and as the Son was dwelling with His Father. So that not even when the Virgin bore Him did He suffer any change, nor by being in the body was [His glory] dulled: but, on the contrary, He sanctified the body also. For not even by being in the universe does He share

---

[31] Idem, *Incarnation of the Word*, § 6, Nicene, IV:39.

[32] Ibid., § 16, Nicene, IV:45.

in its nature, but all things, on the contrary, are quickened and sustained by Him."[33]

Saint Athanasios

Some might ask, "Why could not God restore man by just a word?" "Restoration," Athanasios informs us, "by a mere fiat would have shown God's power; the incarnation shows His love. For it was not things without being that needed salvation, so that a bare command would suffice, but man, already in existence, was going to corruption and ruin. Therefore, He put on a body that He might find death in the body and blot it out. For how could the Lord have been proved at all to be the Life, had He not quickened what was mortal?...And if death had been kept from the body by a mere command on His part, if would nonetheless have been mortal and corruptible, according to the nature of bodies; but that this should not be, it put on the incorporeal Word of God, and thus no longer fears either death or corruption; for it has life as a garment, and corruption is done away in it."[34]

That we have the ability to call God "Father" is due to the presence of the Logos and the Spirit within us. It is the Son's good pleasure that we should call His Father our Father. The saint prefers the word "Father" to the word "unoriginate" as a name for God. He says, "We have not been instructed to baptize in the name of 'Unoriginate and Originate' or in the 'Uncreate and Creature,' but in the name of Father, Son, and Holy Spirit. For in this manner, when we are thus initiated, we also are truly made sons. When saying the name of Father, we, too, acknowledge also from that name the Word in the Father."[35]

While Athanasios was active in political leadership, he also had a contemplative side and love for the quiet life. Among the saint's ascetic and pastoral writings, he also compares virginity and marriage. "For there are two ways in life, as touching these matters. The one the more moderate and ordinary, I mean marriage; the other angelic and unsurpassed, namely

---

[33] Ibid., § 17, loc. cit.

[34] Ibid., § 44, Nicene, IV:60, 61.

[35] Idem, *Defense of the Nicene Definition* (*De Decretis*), Ch. VII, § 31, Nicene, IV:171.

virginity. Now if a man choose the way of the world, namely marriage, he is not indeed to blame; yet he will not receive such great gifts as the other. For he will receive, since he too brings forth fruit, namely thirtyfold [Mk. 4:20]. But if a man embrace the holy and unearthly way, even though, as compared with the former, it be rugged and hard to accomplish, yet it has the more wonderful gifts: for it grows the perfect fruit, namely an hundredfold."[36]

Saint Gregory the Theologian closes his oration saying that with loving and paternal concern, Athanasios knew when to employ praise and a gentle rebuke. He knew how to stir the lethargic from sluggishness and restrain the passion of others. Whether he was eager to prevent the fall of another or was busy devising means of recovery after a fall, he could be counted upon. Though he was simple in disposition, yet he was manifold in the arts of government. He was clever in argument, but more clever still in mind. While he condescended to the more lowly, he outsoared the more lofty. He was conspicuous for his hospitality. He was distinguished as a protector of suppliants. He was resourceful in averting evils. Furthermore, he was the patron of the wedded and virgin state alike. He was both peaceable and a peacemaker. O how many a title does his virtue afford me, if I would detail its many-sided excellence?

"After such a course, as one taught and a teacher, we discern," Gregory continues, "that Athanasios' life and habits form the ideal of an episcopate. What kind of reward shall these virtues, together with his teaching the law of Orthodoxy, win for his piety? It is not indeed right to pass this by. In a good old age he closed his life, and was gathered to his fathers, the patriarchs, and prophets, and apostles, and martyrs, who contended for the truth. To be brief in my epitaph, the honors at his departure surpassed even those of his return from exile to jubilant Alexandria. Yet, O thou dear and holy one, who didst thyself, with all thy fair renown, so especially illustrate the due proportions of speech and of silence, do thou stay here my words of praise, falling short as they do of thy true and fitting recompense, though they have claimed the full exercise of all my powers. And mayest thou cast upon us from above a compassionate glance, and conduct this people in its perfect worship of the perfect Trinity, Whom—as Father, Son, Holy Spirit—we contemplate and adore. And mayest thou, if my lot be peaceful, possess and aid me in my pastoral charge, or if it pass through struggles, uphold me, or take me to thee, and set me with thyself and those like thee (though I have asked a great thing) in Christ Himself, our Lord, to Whom be all glory, honor, and power forevermore. Amen."[37]

---

[36] Idem, "Letter XLVIII, To Amun (written before 354)," Nicene, IV:556, 557.

[37] Saint Gregory, "Oration XXI, On the Great Athanasius," ¶¶ 36, 37, Nicene, 2nd Ser., VII:280.

On the 2nd of May, the holy Church commemorates the holy Martyrs ESPEROS and ZOE and their children KYRIAKOS and THEODOULOS.

Saint Zoe

Esperos, Zoe, Kyriakos, and Theodoulos, the holy martyrs, lived during the years when Hadrian reigned (117-138). This Christian family hailed from Attaleia[38] of Pamphylia.[39] Esperos and Zoe, who had been Christians since childhood, were lawfully married. Their two sons were Kyriakos and Theodoulos, whom they also raised in Christian piety. In the year 125, at Attaleia, it happened that the whole family was sold into slavery to Catallus, a Roman of some standing, and Tetradia his wife. Catallus took Esperos and Zoe, together with their sons, back to Rome. Though the Christians were in bodily servitude, they considered themselves spiritually free as slaves of Christ. Bearing this in mind, the family endured a long period of servitude to impious and pagan masters who, instead of worshipping the Creator of all, worshipped senseless idols.

One day, Kyriakos and Theodoulos advocated to their parents that they should no longer dwell with the godless. They urged them that they all flee from their Roman masters lest they should be destroyed with them by remaining. Zoe responded, "What can we do, children, since Catallus is our master?" However, the sons answered, "We, O our parents, have been freed with the blood of Jesus Christ; and we are not in bondage to any man!" Zoe, enamored with the everlasting freedom of God, hearkened to their words and agreed with them. Mutually emboldening one another, they conceived the desire to approach Catallus. They confessed before him that the Lord Jesus Christ was the sovereign of their souls. They declared that providence only gave him power over their bodies. They, moreover, pointed out that it was

---

38 Present-day Antalya was founded by King Attalus II of Pergamon, as a port city before Christ. The impressive Roman structure of Hadrian's Gate was built by the Attaleian citizens to commemorate the visit of the Emperor Hadrian in A.D. 130. The marble structure, originally two-stories high, is now found in Ataturk Street. It has three arched entrances, separated by piers with Corinthian columns in front of each. The gate is flanked by two towers. The Duden River was used for Attaleia's irrigation.

39 Pamphylia was a Roman province on the southern coast of central Asia Minor. Perga, the largest city, was its capital. The Apostle Paul visited Perga twice, once when he sailed there from Paphos [Acts 13:13, 14], and some time later, when Barnabas and he made a second stopover [Acts 14:25].

more estimable to have authority over their souls, as the Master Christ, than his authority over their bodies. They brought to mind the words of the divine Apostle Peter who said, "It is needful to obey God rather than men [Acts 5:29]." Upon hearing these words, Catallus was astonished.

The sons with their mother were then sent back to their father, Esperos, who was at a place called Tritonion. Catallus was not ready to deal with them at that time. He was in the midst of celebrating the occasion of the birth of his son. Catallus then decided to send his Pamphylian slaves wine and meat, which had been prepared for the profane festivities of his son's birth. Catallus, engulfed in the darkness of polytheism, sent them foods offered to the idols as a test to determine if the Christian family would partake of them.

When the meats and wine arrived, those blessed boys, Kyriakos and Theodoulos, took counsel with their mother not to partake of the polluted food offered to the pagan goddess Fortunas, but to cast it all to the dogs. Zoe poured the wine out on the ground and threw the meat to the dogs. Now Catallus learned of this and ordered that the children be suspended from a tree and raked and flayed with iron claws. While this took place, Esperos and Zoe encouraged their children not to be fainthearted, but to gaze steadfastly upon their martyric crowns and to endure all, manfully, to the end.

Saints Zoe, Esperos, and Sons

Catallus then charged that the children be taken down and given a harsh beating with their mother. Devising new tests of endurance, Catallus commanded that a furnace be lit and that both children, with their parents, be cast inside. This being done, that holy family delivered their souls unto the Lord. Thus, they received the unfading laurels of martyrdom when they migrated to that life without misery and bondage.

The morning of the following day, chanting voices could be heard from within the furnace. The pagans opened the furnace door, and beheld the bodies of the saints which were completely intact and uncharred. Moreover, their precious bodies were all facing east as they appeared to be slumbering.

During the reign of Justinian (483-565), the emperor had their august relics transferred to Constantinople. They were then deposited in their holy temple, in the Defteron quarter, just southwest of the Phanarion quarter.

On the 2nd of May, the holy Church commemorates Saint JORDAN the Wonder-worker.

Through the intercessions of Thy Saints,
O Christ God, have mercy on us. Amen.

On the 3rd of May, the holy Church commemorates the holy and glorious Martyrs TIMOTHY and MAVRA.[1]

Saint Mavra

Timothy and Mavra (Maura), the holy couple and God-inspired martyrs, hailed from the Thebaïd of Egypt.[2] They lived during the reign of Emperor Diocletian (284-305) and when Arrianos was governor of the Thebaïd.[3] Today, for your love and edification, we shall set before you the lives of these glorious and sacred martyrs for our true God, the Lord Jesus Christ.

The holy Timothy was from the village of Panapeon (Penapeis), near Antinoë of the Thebaïd. He was the son of pious and upright parents. After Timothy was weaned from his mother's milk, he was given to a certain virtuous and God-fearing teacher that the lad might learn sacred Scriptures. Since Timothy was vouchsafed a well-ordered mind, in a short time, he learned whatever was needed to know his Creator, the only true God. He also quickly perceived the God-given nobility and immortality of the soul. The youth also came to understand the corruption and vanity of this present life. When Timothy came of age, according to the sacred laws of our holy Church, he took a wife from a Christian family. She was the ever-memorable and worthy of love Mavra. The couple lived a holy and blessed life, to the continual admiration of the faithful.

---

[1] Three Greek sources were used to present this beautiful account: (1) *The Great Synaxaristes* refers to the IV Codex of Κρυπτοφέρης 'Ακολουθία τῶν 'Αγίων, published at Venice (1769, 1802), Zakynthos (1858), and Athens (1895, 1915); (2) the pamphlet by the Metropolitan of Zakynthos, Panteleimon Bezenites, entitled "Saints Timothy and Mavra and Their Church at Machairado (Μαχαιράδο), Zakynthos" (Athens, GR: Apostolike Diakonia, 1986); and, (3) the text of the *Synaxarion* found in the *Menaion* for the month of May (Athens, GR: Apostolike Diakonia, 1977).

[2] The Thebaïd was in Upper Egypt near the Nile River.

[3] *The Great Synaxaristes* (in Greek) and the *Synaxarion* of the *Menaion* record Arrianos as governor. The Zakynthos biography of the saints, lists him as eparch (prefect) of the region.

Though a newly married couple, the Bishop of the Thebaïd observed Timothy's remarkable manner of life and zeal for piety which also was acknowledged by everyone. Thus, the bishop decided to honor Timothy by enrolling him in the clergy. Timothy, with the consent of Mavra, accepted this ministry. Thus, the bishop ordained Timothy to the priesthood.[4] Moreover, Timothy was appointed to teach and strengthen the Christians in the truth, so they might not be timid or fainthearted in the face of persecutions and torments. For it was a time when the enemies of truth oppressed and abused the devout Christians. Timothy was determined to emulate the Teacher, Christ. Together with instructing the God-fearing, he exhorted all through works and deeds. Thus, Timothy enthusiastically carried out his duties. Not one to tarry with the work of God, he counseled those among the faithful who were in turmoil or confusion that they should stand firm in the Orthodox Faith.

When the Christians heard Timothy's God-inspired words, they received delight in their souls, and were further confirmed in godliness. God also quickly blessed his endeavors when many idolaters were brought into the Church. When the pagans heard his sermons and observed his manner of life, they scorned the idols and became Christians. Timothy would admonish the idolaters to forsake their deceptive superstition. He urged them to believe in the one and only true God, known in three hypostases, Who, out of compassion, sent His only-begotten Son, our Lord Jesus Christ, into the world. Christ came that He might show us the path of salvation, and blot out the deception of the devil who had beguiled mankind. Thus, more and more idolaters abandoned their impiety and came to the Faith of Christ. They were baptized in the name of the holy, co-essential, and undivided Trinity.

Now a mere twenty days passed since he was united to the blessed Mavra in their God-consecrated marriage, when Governor Arrianos was set at variance with Timothy. Arrianos heard reports from pagan leaders of this cleric and teacher of the Christians. Arrianos himself was an irreconcilable and harsh persecutor of the Faith of Christ. The atrocities of Diocletian against the Christians were also cruelly enforced in Upper Egypt by Arrianos, a vessel of the devil and an enemy of godliness. He dispatched his minions of impious deceit to arrest Timothy and those Christians with him. Thus, the pious were made to stand before the tyrant who, without any previous questioning, singled out Timothy with a stern gaze. Arrianos commanded him to fetch the holy

---

[4] There appears to be a discrepancy whether he was ordained to the office of Priest or Reader. Both *The Great Synaxaristes* and Metropolitan Panteleimon Bezenites of Zakynthos (op. cit.) describe Timothy as a priest. Saint Dimitri of Rostov, whose account of Saint Mavra has significant differences, lists Timothy as a Reader. Nevertheless, one office to which he was appointed is agreed upon by all: Timothy was assigned to be a guide and teacher of the sacred writings.

books by which he instructed the Christians. The real motive of Arrianos, a son of the devil, was to destroy the precious and priceless handwritten books of the Christians. He supposed that the holy Timothy, without the books, would be unable to establish the Christians in the Orthodox Faith.

However, the great general of the heavenly kingdom, Timothy, cowered neither before the tyrant's angry countenance nor at his death threats. Instead, he courageously responded, "O governor, what prudent father delivers, voluntarily, his children to death? If that father, who loves his children, yields to the law of nature, he will in no wise surrender the children of his flesh to death. So then, how shall I give up my spiritual children, the sacred books, into thy profane hands? Nay, this will never be! I am ready to die rather than hearken to thy godless commands."

After the lawless tyrant heard Timothy's declaration, he was mightily incensed and directed that iron skewers be laid in the fire. When they were brought to a red-hot glow, they were used to puncture the ears of the martyr. Upon inserting the skewers into that glorious hero's ears, the pupils of his eyes dropped. Yet—O the boundless steadfast patience of the saint!—this excruciating punishment was valiantly borne by that blessed man for the name of Christ. Speaking of a martyr's courage, the divine Paul says, "Who shall separate us from the love of Christ? Shall affliction, or distress, or persecution, or famine, or nakedness, or danger, or sword [Rom. 8:35]?" Thus, what the martyr was saying is this: "O relentless and vindictive tyrant, dost thou think that such bitter torment can separate me from my Christ? Thou art deluded; for thou canst in no wise separate me from the love of my glorious Savior, even if thou shouldest mete out affliction, straits, hunger, exile, torture, prison, and even death. This is because 'the sufferings of the present time are not worthy in comparison to the future glory to be revealed in us [Rom. 8:18].'"

The saint, having uttered such words as these, kindled the tyrant's rage. Arrianos ordered that they bind the prisoner to a wheel designed to rend to pieces Timothy's bodily members. Timothy was told that if he persisted in not doing Arrianos' bidding, he could expect a death befitting his civil disobedience. Since the saint remained firm in his convictions, the ministers of deception bound him to that grisly wheel. They violently turned that contraption hither and thither, causing the notched-in nails to tear the athlete's flesh mercilessly. Nevertheless, Christ's soldier, once more, bravely withstood this barbarous punishment, while he chanted, "The Lord is my helper; and I will not fear what man shall do unto me [Ps. 117:6]"; and, he also uttered, "I will not be afraid of evils; for Thou art with Me [Ps. 22:4]."

In the interim, the Christians, including Mavra, were informed that Timothy had been captured. The pagans continued administering torture in their attempt to have him deny the Christian Faith. Straightway, a multitude of people converged upon the place where the martyr was being tested. Meanwhile, his companion in life, Mavra, prayed to God, seeking endurance and steadfastness for her husband. Moreover, she entreated God that He furnish relief for Timothy's pain. All the while, Arrianos could not help but admire the prisoner's capacity for pain. Finally, that dreadful wheel was brought to a halt by the executioners. The spectators beheld the martyr as a mass of bloodied flesh. His eyes were put out and his body sundered and shattered. He was gasping for breath. Then, suddenly, a miracle! Forthwith, Timothy recovered his strength. He opened his eyes. His wounds vanished without a trace. Before such a spectacle, all the bystanders were dumbfounded and astonished. There was, at first, a hush in the crowd; then all were filled with enthusiasm for the victory of the martyr and the power of God. This divine display of power brought many to confess the Faith of Christ. Mavra was stirred and joyous. She approached her husband and embraced him, glorifying God. Though many were enlightened by this miracle, Arrianos was engulfed in a dense darkness, and became more cruel. Though Christ revived His athlete, the governor was pondering how to deal with the prisoner. Indeed, he attributed the entire phenomenon to the powers of black magic. In fact, Arrianos was more determined than ever to do away with Christ's witness.

Saints Timothy and Mavra

Unmoved by the prisoner's prodigious recovery, Arrianos then charged that a huge wooden spool be placed inside the martyr's mouth. He then ordered that they bind a large stone about Timothy's neck. With these burdens, Christ's athlete was made to compass the village. Afterward, the martyr was suspended from a high tree. While all this took place, the saint persisted with much courage. Timothy then turned to the tyrant and, in spite of the spool in his mouth, bravely uttered, "O tyrant, imagine not that by such punishments thou canst cause me to waver from the right-worshipping Faith. I receive thy torments as refreshment, I accept thy punishments with joy. Indeed, all these trials will usher in everlasting good cheer and deathless joy. May God enable thee, O tyrant, to open the eyes of thy soul! Mayest thou behold the truth and renounce the devil! Would that thou mightest believe in the only true and almighty God!"[5]

Hearing these words issuing from the martyr's mouth, the tyrant was confounded by the prisoner's freedom of speech. Thus, giving reign to even greater anger, he bid that Timothy be kept in a dungeon until a second examination. The tyrant was then informed that the prisoner's wife was in the crowd. Arrianos then thought to use her as a means to break Timothy's resolve. He tested Mavra's disposition with flatteries and honeyed words, so he might deceive her into worshipping the idols. He then said to her, "O Mavra, consider well thy youth and the sweetness of life. Prepare and beautify thyself, for tomorrow thou shalt offer sacrifice unto the gods. Indeed, if thou wilt hearken to my words, thou shalt receive great honors and benefits. However, if thou shouldest disobey my advice, I will subject thee to torments and punishments as those of thy husband's!"

When Mavra heard these vile words from the mouth of the tyrant, she exhibited the same heroism as Timothy, and spoke words befitting the wife of a clergyman and martyr. She answered, "O impious man, filled with every lawlessness, I do not want thy favors. I refuse to pay homage to thine idols. I, moreover, am not afraid of thy punishments. I worship my Christ, the Creator of heaven, the earth, the sea, and everything visible and invisible. He it is Whom I revere, Whom I worship; and for His love I am prepared to die that I might live eternally with Him in the heavens. Now the idols which thou adorest as gods, I mock, since they are deaf and senseless wood, the works of men's hands. Moreover, I also scorn thee because thou art found in such mindless error. Thou must also know that my husband desired this martyrdom not only because it is his duty but also because he desires to be worthy of my love. What is between my husband and I is not a carnal love, but a spiritual one. Our love is not a temporal flame but an undying fire. We love each other so much that we desire that our love abide not only on earth but also throughout everlasting ages. Death for the sake of Christ is the surest perpetuation of a couple's togetherness and devotion. Therefore, I will not attempt to convince my husband to deny Christ; instead, I prefer to die with him for my God. Hence, the singular joy which I seek from thee is that when thou slayest my husband that thou slayest me also."

This unexpected response increased the transgressing governor's anger, so that he was rendered a wild beast. Needing time, he ordered that she remain quiet. He commanded his soldiers to cut off all of Mavra's luxurious locks of

---

[5] In 305, Governor Arrianos, after putting other Christians to death, finally repented and embraced the Faith of Christ. He also suffered martyrdom on behalf of Christ's name. The holy Church celebrates his memory on the 14th of December, together with the holy Martyrs Philemon and Apollonios.

raven-colored hair; for she had gorgeous tresses that splendidly crowned her head as a queen. Arrianos then ordered them to cut off the fingers of both her hands. Indeed, these were fingers that only knew to wipe the tears of orphans and to minister to sick maidens who were now bereft of her motherly solicitude; for she took many destitute maidens under her roof. The holy Mavra, by her superiority of virtue, had been well taught to bear violence; and, thus, she endured all these torments. All the while she kept entreating God, uttering, "O Lord, our God, Who for our salvation came down from the heavens and was crucified by Pontius Pilate for the redemption of the world, do now, O Master and King of all, look down upon Thy slave. Empower me in Thy love that I might abide to the end of the martyrdom and, thus, not only share Thy sufferings and Passion but also partake of Thy kingdom. Amen."

Praying thus during the severing of her fingers, God, as a ready helper, did not abandon those that put their hope in Him. He strengthened the holy woman so that she should put to shame the devil, the ruler of darkness. The tyrant, observing the courage of the sacred Mavra, then ordered another heinous affliction. He ordered that a large cauldron be filled with water and brought to a boil. He then charged that Mavra be cast naked within the bubbling waters, so she should suffer terrifying burns. Then God, Who once, in a paradoxical manner, caused dew to come upon the holy Three Children in the fiery Babylonian furnace [Dan. 3:25, 26], at this time, also changed the property of boiling water to that of a cool fountain. Hence, the holy woman, preserved unscathed in a miraculous manner, chanted, "We went through fire and water; but Thou broughtest us out into a place of refreshment [Ps. 65:12]." Now when the governor, that senseless man, observed this phenomenon, he could not believe his eyes. He thought that his servants, desiring to spare the woman, did not bring the water to a boil as he directed. He, consequently, in order to test the temperature, went up to the cauldron and said, "Mavra, sprinkle me with water that I might determine if it burns." The holy woman then filled her palms with water and poured it into the hands of the tyrant. He nearly fainted from the bitter pain of his scalded hands and dissolved flesh. As his body began to convulse, the overwhelmed ministers of the demonized Arrianos lost hope. Arrianos, although beside himself with pain, still managed to gasp out orders directing that two crosses be made and that the two Christian martyrs be crucified. When the holy ones heard their sentence of death, they joyfully thanked God Who counted them worthy, for His love, to receive death by crucifixion—just as the God-Man shed His undefiled blood upon the Cross for our love and salvation.

Straightway, Arrianos' minions set about constructing the crosses for Timothy and Mavra. The executioners then seized the holy couple and led them to the execution site. The martyrs were moved at the sight of the crosses upon which they would be transfixed; they, thereupon, bowed and piously kissed them, calling the Cross of Jesus "the Wood of salvation." Then they both, bravely and calmly, surrendered themselves to the executioners. Each contestant went and fell upon their cross as a bed of fragrant and dewy roses. Then, within moments, the soldiers hung the couple's young bodies upon their crosses. The spectacle of the young couple upon their crosses seemed a tragedy to many, but, in reality it was their loftiest moment. The two crosses were placed next to each other and were reminiscent to the Christians of the Passion of the God-Man. The pain and discomfort experienced by the martyrs was visibly hard to bear. However, undaunted, each kept their righteous conviction, their vigorous purpose, and the might of their faith. As their pangs increased, so much more did love heighten in their hearts. Instead of murmuring or complaining about their predicament to one another, each encouraged the other with heartfelt words of consolation which made manifest their mutual affection, their oneness of soul, their faith in God, and their hope of immortality.

The holy Timothy was heard saying to his blessed wife, "Do not fear, O Mavra, the temporal torments, because these shall usher in eternal glory in the heavens. Small is the pain, but great the reward. Bitter do the punishments appear, but sweet is Paradise. We, thus, for a moment endure and then gain everything forever. Our sinless Master Jesus condescended to be crucified upon the Wood of the Cross for our salvation. We, too, have become imitators of His Passion that we might be vouchsafed to be glorified with Him in His glory." After offering her these consoling words, the two stood firm, rejoicing with their minds turned heavenward.

Nevertheless, the malevolent devil, dissatisfied, now attempted a new machination upon the holy Mavra, since he is the hater of mankind.[6] As the saint was suspended upon her cross, the demons took on the guise of the impious tyrant Arrianos and others. They appeared to Mavra and offered her honey and milk, so she might quench her flaming thirst. The holy woman, however, perceived that this was a demonic contrivance. She asked the specter, "Who has inspired thee to do this?" The creature remarked, "I only had wished to lighten thy sufferings, for thou hast not eaten or drunk anything." She thought this response odd, that he should have a care that she was fasting. Mavra then took refuge in prayer, invoking the name of Christ. She next observed that the creature turned about and faced the west. By this, she understood it to be nought but a demonic delusion. She, therefore, continued steadfast in prayer until that foul demon disappeared.

However, the mischievous demon schemed again. This time, in a kind of trance, he transported Mavra to a river, flowing with milk and honey. By

[6] "And I will put enmity between thee and the woman [Gen. 3:15]."

bringing to her mind the remembrance of their taste, the devil anticipated ensnaring the holy woman with this delusion. However, the valiant martyr, enlightened by wisdom from above, said to him, "Accursed devil, though thou wouldest test me by so many ploys and assaults to deceive me, nonetheless, thou wilt succeed in none of these things. This is because of the power of my Christ Who has conquered thee in everything. On account of this, I have no desire for thy defiled drink; for I drink of that immortal cup which is offered to me by my Lord Jesus Christ." Put to shame, the devil departed, unable to bear his own defeat by one fragile and delicate woman.

Then our Lord Jesus Christ sent an angel from heaven who stood by the holy woman and emboldened her. He then took her by the hand and they ascended, as in a trance, into the heavens. Once there, the angel showed Mavra a lofty throne, beautifully adorned in white. He also revealed a brilliantly shining crown, and said, "All these the Lord has prepared for thee because of the torments thou didst endure for Christ's love." The angel and Mavra then ascended to a higher place. The angel exhibited another throne, also beautifully adorned in white, and a crown, saying, "These are allotted to thy husband Timothy whose place is higher than thine, because, as thou wilt testify, he was the agent of thy salvation." In this manner, the holy woman was informed of the glory prepared by the Lord for His holy martyrs. Returning to herself, she then related all these things to the blessed Timothy. Thus, with happiness and rejoicing, after nine days and nights in abstinence upon their crosses, they surrendered their thrice-blessed souls into the hands of our Lord on the 3rd of May, ca. 286. Hence, the Church chants: "Being joined together in an excellent marriage bond, you took up together the light yoke of Christ."[7]

Then certain devout Christians bribed the soldiers with money and took down the martyrs' precious relics from their crosses. They were honorably and reverently buried, to the glory of God Who enables His servants and handmaidens, without injury, to trample upon the serpent and scatter every device of the enemy. O the superhuman courageousness of the soldiers of the Gospel of peace! A church came to be dedicated to Saints Timothy and Mavra near the palace of Justinian (r. 527-565) in Constantinople.

The Saints' Church at Zakynthos

Today, a famous and ancient church, dedicated to Saint Mavra, is located in the lovely country town of Machairado on the picturesque Ionian island of Zakynthos.[8] The founding of this church began as follows. After a light emanated from a hidden icon, a shepherd from the village of Lagopodos discovered it to be the long-concealed icon of Saint Mavra. He returned to his village reverently bearing his new find, the mysterious icon. His fellow

---

[7] May 3rd, Orthros Canon, Ode Eight, Mode One.

[8] 37°47′N 20°54′E.

villagers desired to erect a church in honor of the martyr, but then the icon vanished in an inexplicable manner.

Shortly thereafter, the sacred icon was again recovered at the site of its first uncovering. After this miraculous event, the inhabitants of Machairado took this as a sign. They settled it in their minds to build a chapel at that site. Much later, on the same location, a large church and monastery were erected by the family of Davaria (or Tavaria). Though this church was destroyed by an earthquake, the structures were rebuilt in 1632. By permission of the all-wise Creator, Whose ways are past finding out, earthquakes and other calamities continued to befall the church. In 1938, it was converted into a parish church. After 1953, when it was destroyed by another earthquake, it was rebuilt by the donations of Christians and the relief of the Greek State.

Today, the famous icon (shown herein), after having survived all, is encased in a wood-sculptured icon stand, and surrounded by a large baroque-style iconostasion. Many miraculous cures have taken place at the intercessions of Saint Mavra. The finding of her miraculous icon is commemorated on the first Sunday of July.

Some Miracles of the Saint Mavra

Numberless miracles on the island of Zakynthos have taken place through the years at the holy church of these martyred saints. We shall recount two for the benefit of our beloved listeners.

In one case, there was a woman who was assaulted by the wicked devil. Her relatives decided to bring her to the church of these saints. Since the demon attempted to drown that thrice-unhappy woman, they bound her to the saint's icon. Then, one day, she managed to break loose of her fetters and the demon cast her into a well located near the church. Inside the well, the demonized woman remained for three or more hours. Finally, her relatives discovered her in the well and—O the wonder!—she was atop the water. The relatives asked her why she was not drenched. The woman then boldly confessed that Saint Mavra held her by the hairs of her head and would not let her sink. After she was removed from out of the well by the church, straight-

Saint Rodopianos

way, she was cured. The entire family then departed to their home glorifying God and the wonder-working martyr.

In another case, a miracle also occurred for a young demonized man. He, only upon gazing at the icon of Saint Mavra, was set free from the demon. Wondrously and effortlessly healed, he glorified God unceasingly and proclaimed everywhere the supernatural wonder of the holy woman, Saint Mavra.

Saint Diodoros

On the 3rd of May, the holy Church commemorates the holy Martyrs DIODOROS and RODOPIANOS the Deacon.

Diodoros and Rodopianos, the holy martyrs, lived during the years of Emperor Diocletian. In the year 302, the ever-memorable Diodoros and Rodopianos, demonstrated their mettle as they contended for the Faith. They underwent insults, outrages, and scourges, which were perpetrated against them by soldiers of Caria.[9] The site of their contest took place in the city of Aphrodisias.[10] The soldiers finally dispatched the martyrs from this life by

[9] Caria is located in southwest Asia Minor, which is situated directly opposite the Aegean islands of Samos and Rhodes.

[10] Aphrodisias was an ancient city of the Caria region of southwestern Asia Minor (Anatolia, or modern Turkey). It was situated on a plateau south of the Meander River (modern Büyük Menderes). During the Roman Empire, life in Aphrodisias was compared to that in Rome. The population reached fifty thousand, and the citizens were wealthy. The city dedicated to Aphrodite was known for its magnificent buildings and streets which intersected each other at right angles. Only the city guards were permitted to bear weapons. Apart from its cult to Aphrodite, the city was also a center of medicine and philosophy. With the advent of Christianity, the city became an episcopal see. The temple of Aphrodite was transformed into a triple-naved basilica with an atrium. The name of the city was changed to Stavropolis, thus indicating that it had come under the power and protection of the Cross and not the demon goddess of fertility and love. Today, the much-diminished city is known as the village of Geyre. Significant remains of a theater, a large paved square, baths, and pillars remain. The columned hall (portico) of the agora and even the ancient Ionic temple of Aphrodite

(continued...)

means of stoning. Diodoros and Deacon Rodopianos then surrendered their souls into the hands of God, from Whom they received crowns as victors of martyric contests.

On the 3rd of May, the holy Church commemorates our holy father among the saints, PETER the Wonder-worker, Archbishop of Argos and Nafplion.[11]

Saint Peter

Peter, the radiant and all-famed hierarch of the Church, flourished around the beginning of the ninth century after Christ. He was born in the queen of cities, Constantinople, of parents who were not only of notable lineage but also were distinguished for their virtues and piety. Their house was the scene of philanthropic endeavors. From childhood days, Peter dedicated himself to pondering the sacred writings. He gave himself over to esoteric studies. All were amazed at his keen spirit, his sharp apprehension, the breadth of his thoughts, and the correctness of his judgment. While still a youth he was, together with his younger brother Platon, garbed in the monastic Schema. Now both his parents and his two elder brothers, Dionysios and Paul, also forsook secular life. They, too, renounced the perishable things of this world and embraced the monastic conduct of life. They received the monastic tonsure in one of the sacred monasteries of Constantinople. It was

---

[10](...continued)
with early Byzantine apse are extant. The concert hall (odeum) may also be seen with the stadium that could hold thirty thousand spectators. There is a martyrium to the southwest of the acropolis, which may have been dedicated to a martyr or it may have been part of a cloister. It had been surrounded by a large Byzantine cemetery. For history and photographs, see Dr. U. Onen's *Caria: Southern Section of the Western Coast of Turkey*, printed by Akademia, and published in Turkey by Net Turistik Yayinlar A.S. (1989).

[11] Today's Saint Peter is not to be confused with another venerable Peter the Sign-bearer at Atroa, who is commemorated by the holy Church on the 3rd of January.

there that the divine Peter stripped as a wrestler to compete in ascetic contests. He came to be deeply esteemed by all. He was held as a model of the monastic life and conduct.

It was not possible that the excellences of such a man should be hidden away to the end. It was about that time that at the rudder of the Constantinopolitan Church was Italian-born Nicholas I, who was known as Mystikos.[12] He had been appointed by Emperor Leo VI. Nicholas I Mystikos served as patriarch from 901 to 907, and again from 912 to 925. Just before the death of Leo in May of 912, when Nicholas returned for a second term, the patriarch wished to provide an archbishop for the widowed see of Corinth. The patriarch was seeking for this office a man who shone forth in the virtues. He needed to place at Corinth a shepherd who could support and confirm the flock in piety. The patriarch had no need to look about. His choice was the Monk Peter. But Peter could only think of the burden of that office with its difficult decisions and manifold responsibilities and complications. He, therefore, declined the invitation, believing himself to be unfit. The patriarch was not put off. Instead, he persevered and pursued Peter's able brother, Paul, whom he persuaded to enter the rolls of the episcopacy.[13]

Following Paul's elevation, Patriarch Nicholas did not cease showing his warm interest in Peter. Indeed, with some measure of vehemence, Nicholas attempted to number Peter in the choir of the hierarchs. The blessed Peter, apprehensive that in the end the driving force of the patriarch would oblige him to accept such a lofty dignity, decided to take himself away and out of Constantinople. Peter, therefore, quit the city and followed his brother Paul to Corinth. Once there, Peter spent much time in ascetic struggles in the hermitages of that place. While Peter took flight that he might avoid the glory of men and continue his days in extreme humility, the all-good God, Who glorifies those who glorify Him, willed otherwise for this priceless treasure of the Church.

The good fame of Peter and the brilliancy of his virtues—though he was wont to conceal his achievements—spread throughout the Peloponnesos and even all of Greece. It was about that time that the hierarch of Argos and

---

[12] *Mystikos* was the title of a high-ranking functionary, that is to say, an office very close to the emperor. It is unclear in this instance whether such an office was secretarial with regard to the emperor's private correspondence or if it involved judicial duties. In any case, Nicholas (commemorated by the holy Church on the 16th of May) was well educated. His writings are a first-rate source of ecclesiastical affairs and of Byzantine relations with southern Italy, Bulgaria, and the Caucasus.

[13] See the Life of Saint Paul, Archbishop of Corinth, who is commemorated by the holy Church on the 27th of March.

Nafplion,[14] of northeastern Peloponnesos, migrated to the Lord. The Christians of that diocese sent an embassy to Archbishop Paul of Corinth. They besought him to persuade his brother Peter to accept the shepherding of their widowed see. Now Peter heard of their request and secretly departed. For a long while, despite the persistent search of Paul and others, Peter's hideaway was unknown. Ultimately, Peter was moved by the implorations and tears of the Christians. He received the episcopal ministry and was consecrated to the throne of Argos and Nafplion. With his mounting that throne, it was indeed as it is written in the Gospel regarding placing the lamp upon the lampstand that light might be given to all those in the house [cf. Mt. 5:15]. Straightway, as Peter received the administration of the Church, he made haste to render her magnificent as was meet.

After Bishop Peter put in order his diocese and clergy with remarkable understanding and wisdom, he undertook new spiritual contests. The loftiness of the episcopacy opened for the saint a broad course of operations. Until then he was able to remain hidden and alone, as best he could. He previously performed most of his deeds in obscurity, but now, and from henceforth, he needed to labor at bringing to perfection countless souls. At last the wealth of his wisdom was beginning to be amply shared with others. The treasury of his productive mind and fertile thoughts generated saving waters for those in need. His divine words flowed abundantly, springing forth correct and well-expressed Orthodox teachings. The saint's speech possessed the power of persuasion. He richly tilled and plentifully irrigated with much diligence and care the spiritual fields of his flock's souls, so that they brought forth the splendid fruits of virtue and piety. When he poured forth mellifluous words of exhortation, they were backed up by the practical example of his own life. His actions, which shone forth in every quarter, supported his teachings. This was effective in leading and guiding others to conform their conduct to the rhythm and order of a Christ-centered life. He was distinguished as a humanitarian, and thought nothing of giving everything away to those in want. This included, on occasion, even his own bed and blankets, which deed enjoined him thereafter to sleep on the floor. This act of charity, nonetheless, confounded his

---

[14] Argos (37°38′N 22°42′E) is the main city of the Argolid. In the 10th C., Argos was combined with Nafplia—(also Nauplia and Nafplion, 37°35′N 22°48), which is the port of Argos—as a bishopric. Most of Nafplion's history is shared with Argos. In 1188/1189, Isaac II promoted the see of Nafplia-Argos to the status of metropolis. That Nafplia shared a bishopric with Argos is stated both in the vita of Saint Peter of Argos [ed. Ch. Papoikonomos, ¶ 9, p. 64.1-9] and a letter of Theodore of Nicaea to Basil of Corinth [J. Darrouzès, *Epistoliers byzantins du X siècle*, 7:43.16-18 (Paris, 1960), p. 315]. Cited in *The Oxford Dictionary of Byzantium*, s.v. "Argos" and "Nauplia."

attendants at the diocesan house. But the saint would in no wise turn away anyone empty-handed, whether friend or enemy.

The saint was conspicuous as a vigilant guardian and unsleeping shepherd of Christ's flock. He was a zealot of the traditions of the holy fathers and of the sacred doctrines of the Faith. These he laid down as foundations during his tenure, keeping them whole, untouched, and inviolate. By reason of his steadfastness in this regard, the blessed one attained many brilliant trophies for Orthodoxy. Although many years had elapsed since the time of the distemper of the heresies, those dissident teachings that caused division in the Church on doctrinal grounds[15] still existed as pernicious roots hidden away. Dissent usually emerges when assisted by ignorance or presumption or demonic complicity or private interpretation apart from the Church fathers or linguistic peculiarities or translating difficulties. It is not rare even to uncover economic, political, national, and cultural factors that have found expression in adhering to heresies. Weeds periodically spring forth in the field of the Lord. It was, and is not, a strange phenomenon. But when such mutations spring forth and attempt to spoil or destroy the genuine seed of Gospel preaching, God raises up those approved by Him who cut in a straight line the word of the truth [2 Tim. 2:15]. Such a workman was our Saint Peter, who permitted nothing to thwart or sully the Gospel preaching.

There was one particular endeavor of the saint which endeared him deeply to his flock. The ardor of their love for their hierarch was excited and made sanguine by reason of his zeal for ransoming Christians taken captive by pirates. Their attachment to him was made stronger by reason of Peter's eagerness and readiness to assist those cities and garrisons that suffered from the inroads of the barbarians. In times of trouble and need, he was shown to be a sincere helper. He assisted and consoled those upon whom dire need had fallen. Peter of Argos could say with the Apostle Paul that, as a minister of Christ, he endured many sufferings and hardships. Beside things external, which rise up daily, he too had the care of all the churches in his diocese. Thus, he too declared, "Who is weak, and I am not weak? Who is made to stumble, and I am not set on fire [2 Cor. 11:28, 29]?" On account of his love for his flock, he endured all things and hoped all things. No matter how bad circumstances became, he would not allow himself to behave unseemly or be provoked or think evil. He never sought his own [cf. 1 Cor. 13:5, 7] advantage but that of his neighbor. Such was the saint's behavior and steadfast love for both God and his fellow man. He was accounted worthy of the gift of clairvoyance and to work miracles. He, consequently, foreknew and foretold many happenings, which events came to pass during the very times that he

[15] Arianism, Nestorianism, Monophysitism, Iconoclasm, etc.

predicted. It is fitting that we should cite some cases among his many miracles, which were wrought in the name of the Savior. By these few examples, we shall demonstrate how much access and boldness the saint acquired before the Lord. For the great works of power wrought by Bishop Peter are glorious and extraordinary.

There once occurred a severe and mighty famine that visited Argos and the surrounding area. A multitude had gathered together and hastened to the saint, seeking bread. The holy Peter had nothing left, since all of his inheritance and goods had been lavishly spent helping others. Actually, to be precise, all that was remaining was one single jar of wheat. Inwardly, however, he possessed a heart full of faith in God. His faith, in the midst of all those starving people and unrelenting famine, was not in the least shaky. The holy Peter called upon divine succor. Behold the miracle! That jar containing a little wheat was transformed into a never-emptying and inexhaustible mill flowing with grain. This occasion was not unlike that of Elias the Thesbite and the widow of Sarepta (Zarephath) [3 Kgs. (1 Kgs.) 17:9]. The prophet told her to be of good courage, though all she had left was barely enough for a little cake. Elias prophesied, "The pitcher of meal shall not fail, and the cruse of oil shall not diminish, until the day that the Lord gives rain upon the earth"; and this indeed came to pass [3 Kgs.(1 Kgs.) 17:13-16]. In like manner did Peter feed his flock until the famine passed. This incident surely bespoke the saint's boldness before the Lord.

In another case, there was a maiden who, for a long while, suffered under the influence of a wicked and unclean spirit. The demon-possessed girl was escorted by her kin to the saint that they might beseech him to help her. The venerable hierarch—by the power and authority granted to those who trust in the Lord Who said, "Behold, I give you the authority to tread upon serpents and scorpions, and upon all the power of the enemy; and nothing in anywise shall injure you [Lk. 10:19]" and to whom it is written according to the Evangelist Matthew that Jesus "gave to them authority over unclean spirits, so as to cast them out, and to cure every disease and every weakness [Mt. 10:1]"—stretched forth his hand and turned his heart heavenward. He rebuked the demon and commanded him to exit from the maiden. Lo, the wonder! The maiden who had been pitilessly tormented for so long was delivered and healed in an instant. She gave thanks and glory to God, Who bestows such authority upon men.

The divine Peter wrought numerous supernatural and prodigious wonders by means of prayer and his fervent faith in God. As a result, he healed the lame, cleansed the lepers, raised up the paralytics, and cured the largest number of diseases. These works of healing were accomplished by the laying on of hands, which he performed even as another apostle. We should also mention his paternal sympathy, affection, and provision for both widows and orphans, so that his exemplary handling of this downtrodden sector of society set a precedent and made him a model to be followed. The saint did not limit himself to any group. He made himself accessible to all. The oppressed and disenfranchised found in him a protector and defender. Those who were ill-treated or denied justice by the mighty found in him a fervid and invincible champion. This is due to the strength and power of his words, which were founded in piety and virtue. The saint came to be revered by all.

During the second tenure of Patriarch Nicholas, a synod was convoked in July of 920. Prior to this, during Nicholas' first tenure, he had, in his capacity as patriarch, opposed the fourth marriage of his sovereign, Emperor Leo VI (886-912), with Zoe Karbonopsina. The fourth marriage did much to undermine stability during Leo's reign, but the much-desired male heir resulted: Constantine VII Porphyrogennetos (b. 905-d. 959). Emperor Leo was displeased with Patriarch Nicholas' continual remonstrances against his union with Zoe. Leo, therefore, replaced Nicholas with Efthymios as patriarch, since the latter was willing to grant a dispensation. Nicholas was then sent into exile, but he was recalled just before Leo's death.

The restoration of Nicholas to the patriarchate created another controversy: a struggle ensued between the supporters of Nicholas and those of the deposed Efthymios. Reconciliation was only attained in 920 with the decision formulated in the Tomos (Tome) of Union. The synod of July 920, held in the presence of the papal legates, had decided the question of Leo VI's fourth marriage (tetragamy) in favor of the previous decision of Patriarch Nicholas. Thus, the fourth marriage was pronounced illicit. It was also resolved that a third marriage was admissible only in certain circumstances. The resolution of this synod took place while Zoe was still regent for her minor son, Constantine VII. It was then that Romanos I Lekapenos (920-944) succeeded in becoming emperor later that year. While Patriarch Nicholas was pleased with the moral victory, Romanos was also delighted at the synod's decision. Why? It detracted from Zoe and Constantine's claim to the throne. Even though young Constantine had been crowned co-emperor as early as 908 by his father Leo VI, he was excluded from power for nearly forty years. Then after many quarrels, the Byzantine Church was finally united. Patriarch Nicholas proclaimed his triumph in the Tomos of Union. As we said, the synod that produced that document convened to settle the conflict between the partisans of the two patriarchs: Efthymios and Nicholas. Fourth marriages were completely banned, while third marriages were restricted with the penalty of four to five years' deprivation of Communion. Only childless widowers, under the age of forty, were exempt, while those with issue from previous marriages were subject to the four-year penance. Since Leo had already been dead for eight years, the fourth marriage was not as much interest to the participants as the validity of episcopal appointments. Were the nominees of Nicholas or of Efthymios rightfully entitled to their sees? The latter question, however, was not mentioned in the Tomos, since Efthymios had already reposed in 917. Inasmuch as Nicholas, during the synod meeting, had the support of Romanos (then the *basileopater*[16]), he had the upper hand. According to Nicholas' correspondence,[17] provisions were made for restoring bishops expelled from their sees during the controversy. The Tomos, nevertheless, unified the Church and restored the alliance with Rome, since papal representatives approved this synod. Saint Peter also attended the 920 Synod of Constantinople.

Before we venture further, it is necessary to mention at this point the account of our venerable Father Theodosios the New,[18] who flourished at the time of the divine Peter. He, too, was a co-struggler with the saint in the advancement of piety. Our venerable Father Theodosios was born in 862 in the city of Athens. He later spent his time engaged in ascetic feats at Medeia (Midea), a prominent Mycenaean center of the Argolid, just northwest of Argos. He built a shrine to Saint John the Baptist and then began a monastery. Envy stirred some in the area to accuse the holy Theodosios of being an imposter and deceiving the people by means of sorcery. But works of power and grace wrought mightily in Father Theodosios by means of his patron, none other than the honorable Forerunner and Baptist John. Meanwhile, our beloved archbishop was ill-used and put upon by the words of Theodosios' calumniators, so that Peter guilelessly said he would look into the accusations against Theodosios. He was even considering a reprimand and expelling Theodosios from the diocese. While Peter was ruminating on what course to pursue in the matter, he was summoned by Patriarch Nicholas to the above mentioned synod in the capital. As Peter was journeying, one night he received a vision. He beheld Father Theodosios stating his case and reproving the archbishop for considering groundless allegations against him. Peter was roused from that

---

[16] The *basileopater*, lit. the "emperor's father," was the office of protector or tutor of a young emperor. It was actually Leo VI who created the office, according it the highest rung on the ladder of offices. Romanos' daughter, Helen, was the wife of Constantine VII. The marriage had taken place in 919. Romanos became *basileopater*, Caesar, and then was crowned in December of 920. He, thereafter, proceeded to crown his own sons as co-emperors, in order to diminish his son-in-law's role in government.

[17] *Tomos unionis—Nicholas I, Patriarch of Constantinople: Miscellaneous Writings*, ed. L. G. Westerink (Washington, D.C., 1981), Ep. 94, 361.20-22. See also *Oxford*, s.v. "Constantinople, Councils of," "Nicholas I Mystikos," and "Tomos of Union," and G. Ostrogorsky's *History of the Byzantine State*, pp. 240, 241.

[18] Saint Theodosios the New is commemorated by the holy Church on the 7th of August. A fuller account of the episode with Saint Peter is given in that vita.

vision and found himself trembling. That very same night, in Constantinople, Patriarch Nicholas was also vouchsafed a visitation. Father Theodosios appeared to him and protested the false charges made against him. When the hierarchs, Nicholas and Peter, met in the city, and it was uncovered that both received the same vision, both perceived divine testimony upholding the accused man's innocence and exposing the conspiracy.

After the 920 Synod was dismissed, Archbishop Peter returned to his see. He thought to go nowhere else save to the hermitage of Father Theodosios. He only wished to offer his sincere regrets and to ask for pardon. A reconciliation followed soon thereafter. Peter, also, learned of the wonderful virtues of Theodosios and wished to enroll him first in the diaconate and then in the priesthood; for the bishop was most desirous to enlist him as a fellow worker in the divine ministry of saving souls. The humble Theodosios, nevertheless, respectfully declined. Consequently, the actions of the archbishop caused all accusations against Theodosios to be judged as they truly were: perniciously frivolous. All charges were thrown out. The holy Theodosios continued his work for the Church until his peaceful repose soon thereafter in 921. Upon the falling asleep of the venerable Theodosios, the blessed Peter and his clergy went and buried the relics in a reverent manner. Saint Theodosios' monastic establishment may still be seen in Medeia. As for our archbishop, he thereafter treasured the memory of the holy Theodosios as his rule and model of virtue.

When Saint Peter reached seventy years old, he foreknew the end of his earthly sojourn. He delivered suitable paternal counsels and exhortations to his rational flock. He, thereafter, cheerfully surrendered his spirit into the hands of God Whom he loved. As for the faithful left behind, they lamented the loss of such a shepherd and benefactor. They buried the grace-flowing relics of the hierarch within the church, the one which they raised up and dedicated to his memory. His relics proved to be a limitless source of healing for those who came to him with faith. The saint's church, nevertheless, with the passage of time, fell into ruin. The pious of Argos, those lovers of Christ, erected another temple in the center of their city. It is still in the same location where it dominates a central square, not far from the original church. The magnificence and beauty of this church is said to be unrivaled among temples in Greece. The faithful Argolians who had honored the name of the saint, clearly testified to their esteem and reverence toward their honored and celebrated patron of Argos and the patron of the prefecture of Argolis.

Five hundred years later, the Venetians and the Franks raided Argos and Greece. They bore away the saint's relics, so that, to this day, no one knows where they may have been deposited. A few of his sermons have been preserved which disclose his profound spiritual insights. The few details that we do have concerning his life were recounted by his disciples, who experienced firsthand countless examples of his love and wisdom.

The biography of this glorious hierarch had been written down in ancient times. The original was richly endowed with accounts describing the saint's virtues and excellence and God-pleasing deeds. It was treasured with other heirlooms of Hellenic eloquence and piety. But all-consuming time and the inroads of aliens ushered in the disappearance or destruction of many such precious manuscripts. The scanty material that is extant, nevertheless, suffices to give us a trustworthy glimpse into the saint's manner of life and compassionate ways. In 1421, when his relics were transferred from Argos to Nafplion, they were exuding myrrh and performing miracles. This episode is further evidence of the glory and honor our holy Father Peter received from God. For years, and even to present times, there has been an ongoing search for his works and the recovery of his relics. By the intercessions of Saint Peter, may we be delivered from all necessity and affliction! Amen.

On the 3rd of May, the holy Church commemorates the holy TWENTY-SEVEN MARTYRS, who suffered martyrdom by fire.

On the 3rd of May, the holy Church commemorates the holy New-martyr AHMET.[19]

Ahmet, the holy new-martyr, hailed from Constantinople, having been reared in the ungodliness of the Moslems by his parents. By occupation, he was a scribe (*deftedar* or secretary) in the chief accounting department of the Ottoman Archives, which was being called Pat Souroumes. In accordance with the law of the Ottomans, since he did not have a wife, in her place he had a concubine slave—a certain woman from Russia. With her there lived another captive from Russia, an elderly woman who was also his slave. Both of these women were exceedingly pious.[20] Now on feast days this old woman would go

---

[19] The account of the martyrdom of New-martyr Ahmet was written by an anonymous author. It was collected and published by Nikodemos the Hagiorite in his *Neon Martyrologion*, 3rd ed. (p. 101). It was later incorporated into *The Great Synaxaristes* (in Greek). This holy new-martyr was also mentioned in Theodoretos' interpretation of Saint John the Theologian's Sacred Apocalypse (1800 edition, p. 7). The new-martyr is also named in a manuscript at the Kalamai Monastery of Deemiove, and in a footnote of that text by Bessarion Striftobola. See also Saint Ahmet's commemoration on the 24th of December in *The Great Synaxaristes* (in English), which records that he was finally slain by the sword.

[20] Regarding the spiritual condition of Christian slave women who were held as (continued...)

to the church of the Christians. She would take antidoron[21] and bring it to her fellow captive, the young woman. The latter partook of the blessed bread, together with holy water which was also given to her by the old woman.

Whenever this occurred and Ahmet was close by, he could perceive a most beautiful and ineffable fragrance coming forth from her mouth. He, therefore, on a number of occasions asked the young woman, "What hast thou eaten that thy mouth is so fragrant?" But she, not comprehending the matter, kept saying, "I have not eaten anything." He, however, was curious and persisted in asking that he might learn what caused the sweet scent. Then she finally said, "I have partaken of nought save the bread blessed by the priests, which the old woman brings me upon her return from the church of the Christians." Upon hearing this, Ahmet was filled with a great longing not only to see in what manner the Christians received the bread but also to view the order of their Church. What did he contrive? He invited a priest of the Great Church, that is, of Hagia Sophia, in order to consult with him. "Prepare a place," said he, "where I might stand in the church, in a place apart and private, when the patriarch is liturgizing." The priest fell in with his plan.

---

[20](...continued)
concubines by their masters, Saint Basil the Great in his 49th Canon states: "Deflorations performed by force entail no responsibility, thus a slave girl violated by her own master is free from responsibility." Saint Gregory the Wonder-worker comments in his 2nd Canon concerning a charge that female captives had been ravished, the barbarians violating their bodies, he writes: "But if the life of any particular one of them has been duly investigated and she has been found to have been following the lead of amorous glances, as is written [Ruth 3:10], it is plain that a propensity to fornication may be suspected also during the time of captivity; accordingly, such females ought not to be admitted offhand to communion of prayers. If, however, it is found that any particular one of them has lived a life of the utmost sobriety, and that her previous life has been pure and above suspicion, but that she has now fallen as a result of violence and necessity a victim to insult, we have the example to be found in Deuteronomy in the case of the damsel whom a man found in the plain (or field) and forced to sleep with him: 'Unto the damsel,' it says, 'you shall do nothing. There is in the damsel no sin deserving death; for this matter is like the case in which a man rises up against his neighbor and puts his soul to death....The damsel shouted, and there was no one responding to her appeal [Deut. 22:26, 27].' So much for these matters." *The Rudder*.

[21] Antidoron, literally "instead of the gift," is blessed bread (the unused prosphora) that is not consecrated during the Liturgy. The Byzantines cut it into small cubes and distribute it to the faithful at the dismissal of the Liturgy. The Russians prepare antidoron from the prosphora in excess of the five loaves used in the Oblation Service or Proskomide. Russian prosphora are small, approximately 2-inches in diameter and 1-½-inches in height. The Russians often keep it in their home, in a special container, partaking a small portion at the commencement of each weekday after their morning prayers. *The Liturgical Dictionary of Eastern Christianity*, s.v. "Antidoron."

Ahmet, therefore, garbed himself in Christian attire[22] and stood as a spectator at a patriarchal Liturgy.

Saint Ahmet

Now the Master of all, Who knows the secrets of the souls of men, added a second miracle to the first: He led Ahmet to the knowledge of the truth. Therefore, while in the church, Ahmet beheld—lo, the miracle!- Patriarch Iakovos[23] shining with a radiance and lifted above the floor as he passed through the Beautiful Gate to bless the people. As he gave the blessing, rays of light came forth from his fingers. Now the rays fell upon the heads of all the Christians, but none upon that of Ahmet. The patriarch, thereafter, again performed the same blessing two or three times. Each time, Ahmet was vouchsafed to behold the same manifestation. As a result of this vision, Ahmet believed without hesitation. He sent for the priest, who conducted the Mystery of Holy Baptism, thus granting him rebirth. After this event, he remained a Christian secretly for a considerable time.[24]

---

[22] During the time when the Orthodox were under the Ottoman yoke, the *raya*—the non-Muslim subjects of the Ottoman known as "the cattle people"—as the Christians were called, were subjected to many degradations and indignities in order to induce them to become Moslems. They were made to suffer confiscation of churches, heavy taxation, forcible abduction of male children to replenish the ranks of Janissaries, and kidnaping maidens for the royal and local harems. Christians were compelled to wear dull and drab clothing, while the Moslems arrayed themselves in costly garments, seeking to signify in this manner that, in contrast to the Christian Faith, that Islam was "bright" and "luminous." For all these great or petty indignities, many Christians gave thanks to God, welcoming this opportunity to witness to their Faith. Others, however, being weak in the Faith, allowed these humiliations to overcome them; and thus, many thousands submitted to Islam. *New Martyrs of the Turkish Yoke*, p. 176, note 4.

[23] Patriarch Iakovos of Constantinople served during the following years: 1679-1682, 1685-1686, 1687-1688.

[24] This was a common practise for those who wished to remain Christian, or who were converted from Islam. The Christians of inner Asia Minor all disappeared officially, most of them becoming crypto-Christians. Thus, on the surface, their names, language, customs, religion, etc., remained Turkish, yet secretly they continued to be Christians. If it was discovered that a former Muslim had converted to Orthodoxy, he was

(continued...)

Once, when Ahmet and certain grandees had come together, they dined and afterward sat about conversing while smoking the narghile,[25] as the Muslims are wont to do. In the course of the conversation, they began to discuss what the greatest thing in the world might be. Each man offered his opinion. The first to speak remarked, "The greatest thing in the world is for a man to possess wisdom." A second then commented, "Woman is the greatest thing in the world." A third man said, "Nay, the greatest thing in the world, and by far the most delightful, is pilaf with yoghurt. Is it not the food of the just in Paradise?" After this, it was Ahmet's turn to speak. They all set their gazes upon him, asking him, "What is thine opinion on the matter?" Then Ahmet, being filled with holy zeal, cried out as loudly as he could, "The greatest of all things is the Faith of the Christians!" This declaration was then followed up by his confession: "I myself profess to be a Christian." He, thereupon, boldly censured the falseness and deception of Mohammedanism. At first, upon hearing these things, his Muslim dinner mates stood aghast. Then being filled with unspeakable rage, they rushed upon the holy confessor and dragged him to the judge that he might be given the sentence of death. Throughout his martyric contest, Christ's struggler kept openly proclaiming the dispensation of the incarnation of the God-Man Jesus Christ. Thus, he received the crown of martyrdom, suffering decapitation by command of the *kadi* (Muslim judge) on the 3rd day of May, in the year 1682, at the place called Keaphane Baze. Such was the blessed end of the holy new-martyr, through whose holy prayers may we be deemed worthy of the kingdom of God. Amen.

Saint Oikoumenios

On the 3rd of May, the holy Church commemorates our holy father among the saints, OIKOUMENIOS the Wonder-worker, Bishop of Trikke.[26]

---

[24](...continued)
immediately sentenced to death. For this reason, also, we do not know the baptismal name received by Ahmet.

[25] A smoking apparatus used in the Middle East, the smoke being drawn through water.

[26] In a lengthy footnote within *The Great Synaxaristes* (in Greek), s.v. "May 3rd," the Greek compilers note that, in these latter times, the year in which the saint lived has been under discussion. Some maintain that he lived as early as the 4th C. Adding to the (continued...)

Oikoumenios (Ecumenius), our holy father among the saints, flourished at the end of the tenth century (A.D. 995). He always meditated upon the writings of the Church fathers, with whom he demonstrated himself to be an excellent interpreter of the holy Scriptures. He authored explanations for the Acts of the Apostles and the fourteen Epistles of Paul and the Seven Catholic Epistles. He followed faithfully the spirit of the homilies of the divine Chrysostom in his writings. Regrettably, with the passage of time, many of

---

[26](...continued)
confusion is the fact that there is another Oikoumenios, who was a lay philosopher and rhetorician. The latter was a Monophysite and follower of the ill-famed Patriarch Severos, Bishop of Antioch (512-538). Complications arose on account of the various writings bearing the name of Oikoumenios. The compilers of *The Great Synaxaristes* (in Greek) believe that today's saint is the 10th-C. father who wrote hermeneutics on Acts and the Epistles of the New Testament. As for the 6th-C. Oikoumenios, a heretic, they believe him to be the author of twelve books wherein he attempts to explain the Apocalypse.

The first edition of *The Great Synaxaristes* (in Greek) cites a 14th-C. manuscript (No. 226) of the Meteorite Monastery of Varlaam in Thessaly, written by Metropolitan Anthony of Larissa of Thessaly. The latter penned a divine office and encomium to Saint Oikoumenios. Within his text, he notes that the saint was a kinsman (ἀνεψιὸς) of Saint Achillios (commemorated the 15th of May) and participated in the First Œcumenical Synod. These points are preserved at the Athonite Monastery of Iveron (Codex 571) and at the Aedis Christi Library at Oxford (Codex 66). The existence of this Oikoumenios is also supported by others, including G. Papageorge, herald of two treatises, published under these titles: "Ὁ Ἅγιος Οἰκουμένιος" (Trikke, 1949); and "Συμβολὴ εἰς τὴν ἱστορίαν τῆς πόλεως Τρίκκης. Οἰκουμένιος Α΄ ὁ πολιοῦχος, Διονύσιος Β΄ ὁ ἐθνικὸς ἥρως" (Trikke, 1952). In his first treatise, Papageorge calls him Saint Oikoumenios. In his second treatise, he names him Oikoumenios I, patron. Simply put, the Greek compilers acknowledge that on account of such testimony there is no reason not to believe there were two holy fathers with this name—one who flourished in the 4th C. and another in the 10th C.

The saint whom we commemorate today—the 3rd of May—was not only a bishop but also a wonder-worker. His synaxis is celebrated at the sacred Monastery of the Holy Transfiguration at Meteora. Of the icons honoring the saint, there is one at the 16th-C. Meteorite Monastery of the Meeting in the Temple. There is also a portable one, from the 17th C., now residing at the Byzantine Museum in Athens. Iconographer Photios Kontoglu has listed Saint Oikoumenios among the most important bishops that may adorn the arch of the holy bema. He also notes that the saint is elderly with a pointed beard. For others who have written about this saint, see: (1) B. Stephanides in his *Ecclesiastical History* (Athens, 1948), p. 429; (2) N. Vees in "Zur Schrifstellerei des Antonios von Larissa," *Byzantinisch—Neugriechische Jahrbücher*, XLI (Athens, 1936), p. 308; (3) Photios Kontoglu, *Ekphrasis of Orthodox Iconography*, Vol. 1 (Athens, 1960), pp. 137, 313; (4) Θρησκευτικὴ καὶ Ἠθικὴ Ἐγκυκλοπαιδεία, Vol. 9 (Athens, 1966), pp. 876-878; and, (5) many other encyclopedias.

Oikoumenios' valuable commentaries have been destroyed.[27] During his lifetime, on account of his irreproachable morals and his profound erudition, he was deemed worthy of the episcopal throne of Trikke in Thessaly.[28] He adorned that see as a good shepherd and disciple of the Chief Shepherd Christ. He reposed in peace.

On the 3rd of May, the holy Church commemorates the Recovery of the Relics of our venerable and God-bearing Father LUKE of Mount Steirion of Greece.

On the 3rd of May, the holy Church commemorates XENIA the Great-martyr and Wonder-worker.

Xenia, the great martyr of Christ, was born in 291, at Kalamata (Kalamai) in the Peloponnesos.[29] Her parents, Nicholas and Despina, known for their upright and noble character, were also the offspring of Christian ancestors. They were especially hailed as being self-supporting and pious. The family originated from the eastern part of Italy. However, due to oppression and hardships during the years of the persecutions against the Christians, they found refuge in the city of Kalamai. They established themselves on rural property, outside the city, where Nicholas was a farmer. They, therefore, worked with their own hands; and, by the sweat of their brows, they ate their bread. It was amid these surroundings that their daughter, the grace-filled holy Xenia, was born. From a young age, Xenia revealed who she would be later. Instead of disorderly playing and occupying herself with chatter and unbecoming games, she stayed at home next to her mother. With attention and devotion, Xenia hearkened to her mother's exhortations and good counsels.

When Xenia reached marriageable age, the virtue of her prudence and wisdom that illumined her soul was much more evident. Indeed, as she increased in physical stature, so much more was her learning augmented and her remarkable comeliness enhanced. The blessed maiden's appearance was

---

[27] See *P.G.* 118:9-1256 ff.

[28] Trikke or Trikkala or Trikala (39°33′N 21°64′E) of Thessaly, where Larissa is the capital. The Byzantine fortress, the archaeological site near the Greek Orthodox Cathedral of Saint Nicholas, which is attributed to an Asklepeion, the old neighborhood of Varousi below the castle, and the old churches may be seen by visitors. Kalambaka, the site of Meteora, is 349 kilometers from Athens and twenty-two kilometers north of Trikkala.

[29] Kalamata (37°02′N 22°07′E) is the name derived from ancient Kalamai. It is a city in the *nomos* or department of Messenia near the head of the gulf of the same name. Peloponnesos is the name for southern Greece, the large peninsula sometimes known as the Morea.

Saint Xenia

indeed most exquisite. She had golden and curly hair. Her forehead was not broad, but handsome brows framed distinctively large and lively dark blue eyes. Her cheeks were always flushed with fresh virginal rosiness. Two dimples below her cheeks dispersed joy across her face. Though fair and statuesque, she was humble of demeanor. Her conversations were pleasant and simple, filled with virtue and grace. Whoever encountered her went away feeling cheerful. Never was gossip, condemnation, or a lie heard from her mouth. Due to her poverty and the distance of her farm from the city, Xenia was not a pupil at school. Nevertheless, she learned simple reading from her mother. Nothing pleased Xenia more than to learn the life and miracles of our Lord Jesus Christ and different prayers that her good and pious mother zealously taught. Xenia would also very regularly attend church on Sundays and feast days.

As an indispensable labor, blessed Xenia, from her earliest years, never neglected to adorn her soul with fasting, self-control, silence, regular prayer, modest conversations, tears, and vigils. As Xenia advanced in age, her virtues heightened as she added toil to toil. Xenia displayed unfeigned sympathy for poor people, widows, and orphans. If a needy person came to their home seeking alms, she never neglected them in whatever they required. Ofttimes, to furnish food for strangers, Xenia was left keeping abstinence; indeed, this practise of helping strangers befit her name which, in Greek, meant "stranger."

Her God-pleasing life, however, did not go unnoticed by the hater-of-good, the devil. He envied the holy maiden's progress in virtue. Unable to suffer his might being trampled upon, he raised warfare against her. Observing her to be a young and pure girl, he sought to cast her, if it were possible, into the gulf of sin. He waged his battle by making a direct hit to her heart by suggesting carnal and unclean thoughts toward a certain youth. The devil did not succeed, however, because that holy maiden had stalwart prudence as that of an old woman. The enemy then laid another snare in the following manner.

At that time, the prefect of Kalamai was Dometianos. He was a brutal and malignant man. Once, when he was returning from hunting, he passed by Xenia's farm where he happened to meet the virgin. So amazed was Dometianos at her comeliness and exceptional beauty, he was mastered by carnal love. Then that lawless and impious man considered how he would take her as his wife. Thereupon, Dometianos resorted to a celebrated sorcerer of those parts. He hoped that through the magic arts he might win the love of the all-modest Xenia. However, that righteous maiden, by the power of the honorable Cross, safeguarded herself. She was kept unharmed by assailing thoughts and brought to nought every violence of the enemy. Dometianos then ordered that the holy maiden be brought to the government house (Διοικητήριον).

As the prefect's men carried out the order and led the holy Xenia to the tyrant, she prayed as she was marched along the road. She invoked God as her helper that He might bestow understanding and power, so she might be true to the end. She called upon the Lord to uphold her conscience and dedication to Him. Anticipating reprisals, she supplicated God not only to help her overcome all punishments and torments but also to count her worthy of the crown of martyrs. When Xenia arrived at headquarters, the prefect bid that she be brought to him. When Xenia was made to stand before him, he asked her name, whence she came, and her religion. Xenia, making the sign of the honorable Cross, answered candidly and courageously, "My name is Xenia. I am the child of Christians living outside this city. I pray with my whole soul that I am vouchsafed to be a handmaiden of my Lord Jesus Christ Who made the world and all that is in the world."

All those who happened to be present could hardly believe her daring answer. Nevertheless, this answer only heightened Dometianos' lawless desire, because the tyrant's soul raged with lust. Therefore, he concealed his wrath and, in a flattering manner, said to the maiden, "O Xenia, by the might of the great gods, I marvel at thy youthfulness and comeliness; but I am also struck with consternation at thy wit. Due to thy charms, therefore, enter into a marriage-contract and be my wife. Then I shall bestow upon thee many rich gifts, countless wealth, and honor and glory which the immortal gods abundantly bestow upon those that revere them. If, however, thou wilt not obey my will, thou canst expect tortures and harsh punishments, and, in the end, a dreadful death!"

When the blessed maiden heard this pronouncement, she was in no wise agitated. Instead, with much hardihood, she answered, "Do not hope in vain that thou canst separate me from my Christ by whatever thou shouldest promise me or threaten against me! Nor is it possible for me to desire another bridegroom than Christ—especially a man who believes in handmade deities who are incapable of even protecting themselves. Therefore, thou canst torture me by whatever punishment thou desirest. But know this: although thou shouldest heap cruel torments upon me, still more shall I hope to be glorified by my Jesus Christ in that future blessedness, in life eternal. I, furthermore, do not sorrow for my fleeting and perishing life, since one day we must all die. Much rather, I, with all my soul, eagerly deliver my body up to death, for the sake of my immortal God and Master Who, for our sins, was crucified. Do not think, O governor, that I shall change my mind; for there is no human power sufficient to change my resolve and my firm belief in the only true God, my Savior Jesus Christ, in Whom I place my every hope for salvation."

Hearing these words, Dometianos was filled with fury. Nevertheless, he planned another demonic scheme when he charged that she be locked inside a dark chamber. Once immured, the holy maiden raised her mind and eyes heavenward and entreated the Lord for assistance that He might keep her to the end in her steadfast confession. The following day, the prefect's soul was still smitten with the desire to take her as his wife. Though she did not love him, and he knew it well, yet his desire for her had not abated. Thus, he attempted to prevail forcefully upon the undefiled bride of Christ. The profane one believed that, ultimately, he would obtain her consent. However, that deplorable man was again rebuffed. The holy maiden not only refused him but also, with indignation, rebuked his pitiless behavior. His mind benighted, the prefect, filled with rage, seized Xenia by the hairs of her head and dragged her out of the chamber. He remanded her to the guards, commanding them to strip her and suspend her upon a post. Dometianos bid that they sever her breasts and then cauterize the large wounds left by the amputations with lit torches. Moreover, they were to apply fire to her sides and all of her body.

Aflame with godly zeal, while the holy martyr awaited this fearful martyrdom, she prayed with an ardent heart, "My Lord Jesus Christ, Thou knowest that for Thy love I suffer these heinous mutilations. Neither abandon Thy handmaiden nor permit that most abominable man to conquer me that he might boast on my account. But deem me worthy to endure to the end that I might receive the crown." Indeed, that bitter punishment was carried out with exceeding harshness on the part of the soldiers of the foul prefect. All the while, the sacred maiden did not feel the least pain, because an angel of the Lord appeared and assisted Xenia—though only she was vouchsafed to behold that incorporeal being. The angel bedewed her in such a manner that Dometianos' soldiers then grew weary. The tyrant, supposing that his men had mellowed and moderated the holy maiden's torments, changed executioners many times.

Finally, the tyrant ordered that they loose the maiden and bring her to the first chamber. Indeed, he did not do this because he was sympathetically affected by the dread circumstances he had inflicted upon her. The rogue was determined to increase the torture, thinking that, perhaps, he could prevail over her convictions. Despite all the cruel injuries he wrought upon her, he still hoped that she would become his wife and renounce Christ. During that night, the holy Xenia called upon the Lord to come to her aid. Then—behold!—at midnight, she beheld a pleasant and heavenly light which illuminated the entire chamber. The Savior strengthened her, saying, "Cease fearing, Xenia, the torments, because My grace desires to be with thee and to deliver thee from every temptation." Then our Savior healed her every wound and pain, and ascended into the heavens. Saint Xenia, with tears of inexpressible rejoicing and good cheer, thanked and glorified our Lord and Savior Jesus Christ.

In the morning, the soldiers brought the maiden to the prefect. When he beheld her healthy and without a trace of the previous day's maiming and mutilations, he marvelled and said, "Dost thou see, O Xenia, how much the great gods love thee? Grieving for thy beauty, they healed thy wounds and granted thee health. Therefore, do not appear ungrateful before them. Much rather, do thou enter their temple with me that thou mightest pay them homage and receive yet greater favors, and, from me, many gifts." The holy maiden answered, "How, O governor, is it possible that thy gods, who are senseless and made by the hands of men, should have such power to restore me perfectly in one night, as thou dost see? Learn this, therefore, they did not grant me health. Instead, it was my Christ, the true God, Whom I worship with all my soul and heart: He healed me. However, since thou desirest to enter the temple of thy gods, let us see which gods thou dost wish me to adore."

Hearing this, Dometianos was overjoyed. He imagined that the holy maiden changed her mind regarding making obeisance before the gods. Therefore, he brought her to the temple. Straightway, as the holy Xenia entered the temple and stood in the midst thereof, she bent her knees and prayed unto the true God, saying, "Lord Jesus Christ, my God, Creator of heaven and earth, Who hearkens to the supplications of Thy believers, hearken unto Thy handmaiden this hour, and level and destroy these soulless and deceptive idols, so all the bystanders will know that Thou alone art true God." After praying thus, even before she completed her prayer, a great earthquake took place and—O the wonder!—all the idols were toppled and shattered. Dometianos, observing this miracle, instead of believing in the true God, was beside himself and commanded she again be subjected to punishments. As on the previous day, they burned the saint with lit torches but only with far more viciousness. Nonetheless, that unholy man toiled in vain, though he repeated these frightful and inhuman tortures for days. This is because the saint had Christ as her helper, Who never left off from sending His help to heal her as He did the first time.

Though continually subjected to torture, the holy martyr rejoiced and glorified God Who enabled her to undergo such torments for His holy name. Meanwhile, the prefect, void of understanding, saw that he was humiliated, because he could not succeed in defeating one simple girl. Therefore, he thought to punish the holy maiden with other torments. Again, he hoped that she would grow weary and agree to deny Christ and become his wife. Later, however, he charged his men to bring a wild horse. They were commanded to bind the maiden's legs behind the beast. Dometianos then gave orders that they have the horse drag her through a rocky terrain, thus tearing her flesh so she might cruelly die. Though this is what the tyrant planned, yet the all-good God, Who does the will of those who fear Him, dispensed otherwise. What did He permit to further shame that proud prefect and, at the same time, glorify the name of Christ Whom the saint proclaimed and confessed with boldness? Hearken. When they fettered Xenia's feet behind the horse, planning to let it run wild, instead of furiously racing about, as the tyrant intended, the beast would not move. Though the soldiers violently goaded the creature, it refused to run and obey the commands of Dometianos. Thus, Dometianos ascribed the horse's fixed position to the incompetency of his soldiers. He then furiously shook the horse's bridle in order to provoke the animal.

What followed is worthy of wonder. The horse spoke in a human tongue, which amazed that unfeeling prefect! The beast reprimanded Dometianos' savagery and inhumanity toward the handmaiden of the true God. O Thy wonders beyond words, O Christ! Let none wonder at this phenomenon, because "the things impossible with men are possible with God [Lk. 18:27]." Then, at that moment, the saint, freed from her bonds by a holy angel, was then raised from the ground and stood straight. The holy martyr of God, Xenia, glorified God and focused her eyes heavenward. Her lips moved with the chanting of hymns and thanksgiving to the all-good God Who, once again, rescued her from danger and shamed the pretentious Dometianos. All onlookers who beheld this wonder cried aloud, "Great is the God of the Christians!" Thus, many believed in Christ. Only the blinded eyes and benighted soul of Dometianos refused to believe. Instead, he commanded that the holy maiden be cast into prison. As this was carried out, she remained throughout that day and night in fasting and prayer.

With the passing of midnight, suddenly, inside the chamber where the saint was locked, a divine light blazed. Before an astonished Xenia came to herself, our Lord Jesus Christ appeared in the midst of many light-bearing holy angels. He spoke to the saint and said, "Rejoice, Xenia, faithful and pure handmaid of thy Lord Whom thou hast desired with all thy heart, for thou hast spurned every transient pleasure! Rejoice and be glad, for the day has arrived that thou shalt receive the crown of victory! With the wise virgins, thou shalt enter adorned into the heavenly bridal chamber of Thy Bridegroom and King. Shortly, thy contest shall come to an end that thou mayest receive an auspicious finish." After uttering these words, the Lord ascended into the heavens with the holy angels. The chamber was filled will an ineffable fragrance. Although the saint received joy of soul, still she was awestruck by the divine vision. She glorified the Lord because He counted her worthy to struggle and offer her life for His love.

The following day, Dometianos ordered that they bring the holy maiden before him. He wished to test her resolve one more time, peradventure he might succeed in separating the saint from love of our Lord Jesus Christ. He began complimenting her, and said, "It has not yet entered my mind, O Xenia, that thou wilt persist in thy previous foolish opinion. If only thou wouldest sacrifice to the immortal gods and consent to be my wife, thy future shall be bright and splendid; for I want thee to be very happy and to establish thee as my queen." To these words, the saint replied, "Do not believe that with such promises and false flatteries, O governor, thou canst overcome my steadfast faith and my decision to avow Christ. Thou knowest this well and art sufficiently persuaded even now that neither fire, nor sea, nor sword, nor any other torment frightens me. Therefore, do not labor for nought. That which thou desirest, do it quickly; for by doing so shall I be united with my Savior Christ more speedily."

By these utterances, Dometianos was convinced that nothing would succeed in changing her mind. He then determined to slay her, and handed down the following sentence: "Inasmuch as Xenia has denied our gods and believes in the crucified Jesus, I command that she die by the sword, and that her hard and insensible heart be removed and borne upon a wooden board. Afterward, her body is to be cut into small pieces and cast into pitch and fire to be burned." Sentencing her in this manner, the soldiers took the righteous maiden and brought her outside the city to the execution site. Once there, the holy Xenia besought them that while they prepared what was needful for a fire that she be left to pray; in this request, she was given leave.

Then Saint Xenia bent her knees and raised her hands and eyes heavenward. She uttered the following prayer: "Lord Jesus Christ, my God, Thou it was Who redeemed me from the rebellious Dometianos and brought to nought all his machinations and thoughts. It was Thou Who, by the might of Thy Cross, preserved me and saved me from being torn asunder when dragged. It was Thou Who strengthened me to conquer the many devices of the invisible adversary. While fortifying me in my martyrdom, do Thou, O Master, cleanse my soul from the filth of sins and redeem me from the pit of destruction. And when I depart this corruptible world, receive my pure and undimmed repentance favorably; and guide me to Thy divine and dread tribunal. Glorify

Thy holy name and strengthen me at my final hour against my visible and invisible enemies. Remember, O Lord, how I, Thy handmaiden, Xenia, invoked Thee with faith and was ever mindful of Thee during my martyrdom. Do Thou now grant help and salvation to my soul. Moreover, as Thou didst put an end to the magic and keep me untouched by the spells cast upon me by the impious prefect, do thou also lay waste all demonic contrivances for those seeking Thy help through me, Thy humble handmaiden. Destroy any witchcraft or artifice of the magical arts. Make away with every potion or device. Dispel every bewitchment, sorcery, or astrological work in whatever place and in every animate creature or soulless object, whether in the air, or on the earth, or in the ground. Indeed, do Thou dissolve them though they be charms cast into the waters of rivers, or lakes, or wells, or seas. As the wind sweeps and carries away dust from the face of the earth, similarly, scatter the works of magic wrought by envious ones: wherever the hex may be and in whatever symbol, organ, or material it is prepared, arranged, or built—dissipate it; or whatever number it is numbered and in whatever constellation it is marked or named, whether it be day or night, or in the light or the dark—eradicate it. Remember, O Lord, those who celebrate the memory of my martyric contest and requite them through the richness of Thy gifts. Hearken to them in the hour of entreaty, to the glory of Thy holy name that is glorified unto the ages. Amen."

Saint Xenia

Having uttered this prayer, the holy Xenia invisibly heard a voice, as thunder, mightily say, "I have hearkened to thine entreaty, Xenia, and I desire to fulfill what thou hast requested." Saint Xenia, filled with joy, then beckoned to the executioner. Now he was frightened before what sounded as thunder. Xenia then bid him carry out the command of his master. The righteous maiden then bent her neck, so she might more easily receive the blow of the sword. Then, with fear, the soldier struck off her sacred head on the 3rd of May, in the year of our Christ, 318. Her soul, replete with light, then ascended into the everlasting abodes to rejoice with the other holy women and martyrs. Her venerable body was then cut to pieces by the soldiers, according to the command of their abominable master. This was done, however, after they removed her heart and brought it on a board to that vile prefect. Afterward, a great fire was lit and slices of her relics were cast into the flames with pitch. As these august relics were consumed by the flames, an undescribable fragrance wafted forth as incense. This surely demonstrated that the relics were imbued with divine grace. Everything was immolated lest any member remain as a blessing for the Christians. Dometianos, however, was punished by divine judgment for his inhumanity and ungodliness. One day, while hunting, he was struck by a thunderbolt and blasted to a cinder.

It is noteworthy that Christians who happened to be in attendance at the venerable Xenia's execution and the immolation of her sacred relics, with faith, took up the ashes. This residue, through the intercessions of the Great-martyr Xenia, proved effective for the healing of incurable diseases for longtime sufferers. Thus, the good fame of the saint circulated in the mouths of all in Peloponnesos and throughout Greece. Now many other miracles and extraordinary wonders have taken place for those who invoke the help of Saint Xenia. This phenomenon takes place to this day for those who take refuge in her and with faith call upon her honorable name. We, therefore, shall narrate a few of these miracles to the glory of God, Who loves mankind and Who is glorified in His saint, and to the benefit of your love.

Some Miracles of Saint Xenia

At that time, there was a pious woman, name Maria, from Patras, in the northwestern Peloponnesos. She was afflicted with a severe illness. The physicians, to whom she resorted, could neither diagnose the illness nor remedy it. Thus, she lay abed for many months. She never ceased, however, to call upon the Lord's help and His saints. Once, her husband's cousin came to visit and comfort her. She was from Kalamai. When the cousin beheld Maria's pitiable condition and learned that physicians were incapable of healing or assisting her, she brought to mind the wonder-worker of her homeland, the Great-martyr Xenia. She recommended that Maria take refuge in her patronage and seek her help. As advised, the infirm Maria entreated the saint night and day with tears for a cure. Then, one night, as she ardently prayed after a critical stage of her disease, Maria beheld the saint in her sleep, who said to her, "Thy suffering cannot be cured by the physicians. Evil people have bound thee with a spell. However, if thou wilt meet with me, I shall loose thee from thine illness and heal thee. My name is Xenia." Maria awoke filled with joy and related the dream to her husband. Now he, without wasting any time, brought her to the newly built church honoring the saint. When Maria beheld the icon of Saint Xenia, she immediately recognized her. Thus, before her icon, Maria supplicated the saint with ardent faith and profound compunction. On the third day, the saint again appeared in a dream to the ill woman. The saint took oil from the oil lamp of her icon and anointed Maria's body, and uttered, "Glorify, O woman, God Who has granted thee thy health. Go now to thy house." Then, O the wonder! Maria arose and was exceedingly glad, for she sensed that she was completely restored. Then, with even greater reverence, Maria glorified our Lord Jesus Christ and the holy Great-martyr Xenia who saved her from a certain and grievous death.

During the Frankish domination, Saint Xenia healed the son of a farmer suffering from lunacy. As many times as he was troubled by the devil, he would cry out, "Saint Xenia torments me!" Due to this, his parents entreated the saint with faith to save their child. The merciful and benevolent martyr then appeared in a dream to the mother of the afflicted child. She counseled the mother to betake herself to the parish priest, promising to help heal her child. When the mother awoke, she immediately acted upon what she was advised by Saint Xenia. Then, in a short while, her son was healed and liberated from that frightful madness.

In like manner, the saint healed one named Nicholas, who was paralyzed in his feet. Nicholas had humbly, and with faith, invoked the wonderworking saint and great-martyr.

A young woman, suffering from facial paralysis, was immediately restored when, with fervent faith, she sought the help of the saint.

Therefore, O pious listeners and lovers of Christ, let us, with faith, take refuge in Saint Xenia. Let us repair to her in every difficulty and, especially, in those sicknesses which she, by the grace of God, specially helps and cures; for many have been healed by God at her behest. This includes sufferers from lunacy, heart disease, nervous disorders, and boils and ulcers. Moreover, she may be invoked for deliverance from charms and spells wrought through jealousy and envy. Indeed, she is able to dispel these demonic machinations and incantations for all those that call upon her with faith and piety; for she is able to save them through the honorable Cross of our Lord and Savior Jesus Christ, to Whom is due glory and dominion to the ages. Amen.

On the 3rd of May, the holy Church commemorates our venerable Father THEODOSIOS, Hegumen of the Caves Monastery in Kiev, who founded the coenobitic life in Russia.

Through the intercessions of Thy Saints,
O Christ God, have mercy on us. Amen.

On the 4th of May, the holy Church commemorates the holy Martyr PELAGIA of Tarsus.

Pelagia, the holy martyr, lived during the reign of Diocletian (284-305). Of pagan parentage, she hailed from Tarsus of Cilicia.[1] At that time, Bishop Linus[2] catechized and baptized many of the idolaters. Once, in a dream, the blessed Pelagia beheld the visage of this bishop who besought her to go and receive holy Baptism. When she awoke from sleep, she pondered upon the meaning of her dream. She then sought her mother's permission to visit her nanny. This, however, was a pretext so she could travel to the bishop and receive the Mystery of Baptism. From her youth, she consciously inclined toward the true Creator; for knowledge concerning God was placed in man from the beginning. Visible and perceptible objects provided guidance to the mind for the contemplation of the invisible. The majesty of the divine nature could be seen in the present harmony and ordering [Rom. 1:19-21]. The pagans

[1] Tarsus, the birthplace of the Apostle Paul [Acts 21:39, 22:3], was the chief city of Cilicia (a province of southeast Asia Minor). It is situated on the banks of the Cydnus River, about ten miles north of the Mediterranean Sea, and protected on the north by the Taurus Mountains. In the time of the Romans, Tarsus competed with Athens and Alexandria as the learning center of the world. North of Tarsus was also the famous Cilician Gates which was a narrow gorge in the Taurus Mountains. Through it ran the only good trade route between Asia Minor and Syria. The location of Tarsus in a fertile valley, close to the Cilician Gates, brought great wealth to the city.

[2] The Greek compilers of *The Great Synaxaristes* (in Greek) make the point that it is recorded in ancient *Synaxaristae* that Saint Pelagia lived during the time of Linus and Diocletian. They discuss a compatibility issue, saying that Linus was Bishop of Rome during the years of A.D. 67-76, whereas Diocletian reigned from 284 until 305. The compilers remark that if you accept that her martyrdom took place during the time of Linus, then it is necessary to believe that Nero was then reigning (54-68) or his successor. If one chooses to believe that her contest took place during the reign of Diocletian, then the bishop of that period was either Caius (283-296) or Marcellinus (296-304). Further difficulties arise when we learn that she was the fiancée of the emperor's son who later committed suicide. There is no record that either Nero or Diocletian had a son. Both men had one daughter each, yet one source says that Diocletian had adopted a boy. Other sources say that while Diocletian was traveling, he stopped in Tarsus. His son and heir was smitten with the virgin and wished to have her for his wife. Pelagia replied through her mother, a wicked woman, that she was already betrothed to Jesus Christ. Pelagia fled and found refuge with Linus. Thus, this would not be Linus of Rome, but another holy bishop in the environs of Tarsus. One source identifies him as Bishop Linus of Tarsus. Meanwhile, the heir to the throne, despairing, fell on his sword and dispatched himself to the next life. Then Pelagia's perverse mother denounced her daughter to the emperor, before whom she was made to stand trial. She was consigned to a brazen ox figure that was heated by fire. She was described as having melted like wax and reposed in the Lord in the year 287.

Saint Pelagia

knew that there was a God, but they corrupted the whole matter by their peculiar and mistaken ideas. As for Pelagia, she longed to know the true God and forsake her abominable religion. She was even prepared to spurn her mortal bridegroom, the emperor's son, for this discovery.

By God's grace helping her, this all came about. She then, at the behest of God, was instructed in the Faith and was vouchsafed the laver of divine Baptism and holy Communion. Filled with divine illumination, she exchanged her costly purple raiment for a plain white tunic. Her rich apparel and adornments were then distributed among the poor. Afterward, the newly-illumined Pelagia, indeed, paused for a short while to see her nurse. Pelagia still wore the same humble tunic with which she was dressed at holy Baptism.

After the visit, Pelagia departed and returned to her mother still garbed in that simple tunic. When her mother beheld her in such a poor dress, she felt an intolerable sorrow. But Pelagia received the word of God like rich and fertile soil. She disdained transitory things, and only sought to be strengthened with divine teachings. Now her worldly mother attempted to have her change her garb and renounce Christ, but was unable to convince her. The holy maiden's mother then made the matter known to Pelagia's betrothed, Diocletian's son. He deemed Pelagia's course of action as a rebuff to his avowals of love. Therefore, from his inordinate grief, he took his own life.

Saint Pelagia

When Diocletian was informed of the circumstances surrounding his son's demise, he was extremely wroth. He had Pelagia arrested. When the maiden was brought to him, he admired her exquisite beauty. He would fain have taken her for himself, but she rejected him. Though she spoke wisely to the tyrant about the Faith, he would in no wise hearken. Instead, he sentenced her to burn inside a bronze ox that had been fired to a red-hot glow. Set afire with the love of Christ in her soul,

Pelagia bravely entered the flames, saying, "Blessed art Thou in the temple of Thy glory, O Lord!" The virgin Pelagia, as a sacrifice of sweet savor for the Master Christ, received the vesture of incorruption with the sacred crown of martyrdom. When Diocletian directed that her remains be cast out of the city for wild beasts to devour, God preserved her relics intact. Bishop Linus recovered them and buried them honorably under a stone atop a hill. In the time of Emperor Constantine V Kopronymos (741-775), a beautiful church at that site was dedicated to her name.

On the 4th of May, the holy Church commemorates our venerable Father HILARION the Wonder-worker.

Hilarion, our righteous father, from an early age took upon his shoulders the cross of the Lord. He followed our crucified Lord Jesus Christ and subjected the passions of the flesh to the spirit and soul. For this cause was he enriched by God with the gift of working cures. He healed the diverse diseases and infirmities that assail mankind. Furthermore, he was able to expel demons from those afflicted by those wicked creatures. After a time of working miracles, Hilarion immured himself in a narrow and tiny hut. He chose a place far from this world's tumult and clamor. After he had been made even more radiant by the degree of impassiveness that he attained, he was vouchsafed the dignity of the priesthood. Some of the miracles he performed that could not be discounted by reason of the obvious evidence are as follows. He healed the withered hand of a Christian, so that there was no longer any trace of palsy. Another Christian, suffering from lameness and paralysis in the feet, received the straightening of both limbs so that he could walk with a steady gait.

The saint was not limited to working wonders among his fellow men. God also gave him the gift of commanding the elements. Whether a storm was raging or hail was falling, Saint Hilarion was able to abate the fury of the weather. If the land happened to be suffering from drought, by his mighty intercessions he could summon rain clouds. He was able to order away animals lest they cause injury to newly planted seeds or crops. If a river needed to be crossed, he could divide, as did Eliseos and Elias of old, the waters, hither and thither, and pass through to the other side. These and many other miracles were wrought by Hilarion the Wonder-worker, who ultimately migrated to the Lord in peace.

On the 4th of May, the holy Church commemorates the holy Fathers APHRODISIOS, LEONTIOS, ANTONINOS, MELES (MELDA), WALLERIANOS, and MAKROVIOS, together with a multitude of others, who suffered martyrdom at Skythopolis.

The synaxis of this venerable assembly of monastic fathers, who suffered martyrdom at Skythopolis,[3] is celebrated in the august temple of the holy and all-lauded Apostle Iakovos, the brother of the Lord. This temple is within the august house of our most holy Lady, the Theotokos, at Chalkoprateia,[4] which contains the martyrs' precious relics. Aphrodisios, Leontios, Antoninos, and Meles[5] were slain by the sword. Wallerianos and Macrovios were slain by both fire and the sword.

The Risen Christ
with the Theotokos and Saint Mary Magdalene

---

[3] Skythopolis (Heb. Beth Sh'an) was the largest city of northern Palestine. Its pluralistic society consisted of communities of pagans, Jews, Samaritans, and Christians. There were waves of intolerance. One significant persecution against the Christians took place in 361. *The Oxford Dictionary of Byzantium*, s.v. "Skythopolis."

[4] Chalkoprateia, situated west of Hagia Sophia, is the home to the basilical church of the Theotokos, which has been variously attributed to either Pulcheria or Verina the empresses. The church was later repaired by Justin II and Basil I. This church also treasured the relics of the Virgin's belt or girdle (*zonee*), which was in a special chapel (*soros*), as well as the wonderworking icon of Christ Antiphonetes. Some parts of the church are still preserved. *Oxford*, s.v. "Chalkoprateia."

[5] The *Synaxaristes* of the Athonite Monastery of Dionysiou records the name of Saint Meles as Melda.

On the 4th of May, the holy Church commemorates the Recovery of the sacred Relics of the holy and Righteous LAZARUS, friend of the Christ, and the Myrrh-bearer MARY MAGDALENE.

The recovery of these relics took place during the reign of Leo the Wise, in the year 890. The synaxis of these saints is celebrated in the holy Monastery of Saint Lazarus, which was founded by Leo. The consecration of the holy church of this same monastery is also celebrated on this day. The translation of the relics of the Righteous Lazarus is also celebrated specially by the holy Church on the 17th of October. Dositheos in his *Dodekavivlos*[6] adds that Leo the Wise brought to Constantinople the sacred relics of Mary, the sister of Lazarus.

The Raising of Lazarus

On the 4th of May, the holy Church commemorates our venerable Father NIKEPHOROS, Hegumen of the Monastery of Medikion, who reposed in peace.[7]

Nikephoros, our righteous father, flourished during the years of the iconoclasts. He was the scion of an affluent Constantinopolitan family. From a tender age, he nourished a love for the Christ. As he grew, he observed how

[6] Patriarch Dositheos II of Jerusalem (1669-1707), *Dodekavivlos* (Thessalonike, GR: Regopoulos, 1983), p. 1153.

[7] The unabridged Life of Saint Nikephoros begins, "Many people, ofttimes...." The author is anonymous. The text is preserved in the National Bavarian Library, as mentioned in "Ignatius Hardt Catalogus Codicum manuscriptorum Bibliothecae Regiae Bavaricae," Vol. 4, p. 85. There are other details in the biography of Saint Nikephoros that have been gleaned from the vita of our venerable Father Niketas, his disciple and his successor as hegumen of the Medikion Monastery. Saint Niketas, an iconodule confessor who suffered exile, is commemorated by the holy Church on the 3rd of April. In *Synaxaria*, sometimes, the holy Fathers Nikephoros and Niketas are confused. See also F. Halkin's "La Vie de Saint Nicéphore fondateur de Medikion en Bithynie (d. 813)," *Analecta Bollandiana* 78 (1960), pp. 396-430.

the heresy of Iconoclasm was thriving. He decided to forsake the things of this fleeting life and become a monk. He ascended a mountain where he took up the labors of asceticism. In his philosophical retreat, he embraced abstinence and vigilance. He kept fasts and all-night standing in prayer. He held converse with God, entreating for the peace of the inhabited world.

Saint Nikephoros of Medikion

When the madness of the iconoclasts abated somewhat, a number of monks besought the holy man to be their superior. In 780, Father Nikephoros founded the Bithynian Monastery of Medikion,[8] situated by the Moudania.[9] Medikion was located close to the southern coast of the Sea of Marmara, also known as the Propontis. At the site there was a ruined church that had been dedicated to the Archangel Michael, which building was restored by Nikephoros. The saint was described as a man of fervid piety and a devotee of things divine, both the perceived and the unperceived. He was notable for his moral excellence and virtue. He was distinguished as an elder and clairvoyant, moved and guided by the All-Holy Spirit. By reason of these gifts, he was vouchsafed to be a victor over the demons and to become a confessor of the Orthodox Faith.

Iconoclasm was started by those who denied veneration to the holy icons. The movement first gained momentum during the time of Emperor Leo III (r. 717-741), founder of the Isaurian Dynasty, who openly upheld their position in 726. Patriarch Germanos I (715-730) was forced to resign and Leo II commenced persecutions. Afterward, Emperor Constantine V Kopronymos (r. 741-775) wrote treatises against the icons and summoned a council in Hieria which condemned veneration as idolatry. He was hostile not only toward the icons but also toward relics and even the intercessory prayers of the Theotokos. More iconophiles underwent mistreatment and even death. Outside of the capital, however, Iconoclasm was irregularly supported. Persecutions, thereafter, declined with the death of Constantine V. Emperor Leo IV the

---

[8] Medikion Monastery, two kilometers from the sea, is one-half mile south of the Bithynian village of Trigleia (Turk. Tirilye).

[9] The Moudania, now Turkish Mudanya, is twenty-five kilometers northeast of Prousa (Bursa, 40°12′N 29°04′E). Mudanya is a city on the coast of the Marmara Sea, known for its fresh air. It has an open anchorage usable in calm weather. Summers are hot and dry, whereas winters are warm and rainy.

Khazar (r. 775-780) persecuted small groups. Finally, in 787, his widow, the Empress Irene, with her young son, Constantine VI, together with Patriarch Tarasios (784-806), condemned Iconoclasm at the Second Synod of Nicaea (also known as the Seventh Œcumenical Synod), where three hundred and fifty bishops were in attendance with two papal legates. Our Hegumen Nikephoros had also signed the acts of the Second Synod of Nicaea, which brought an end to the first period of Iconoclasm. It should be noted that when the venerable man signed the document, he referred to his monastery as "Saint Sergios of Medikion." The emperors of the much-later Amorian Dynasty (820-867)[10] revived Iconoclasm, though it was not as virulent as the first period.

During the end of Father Nikephoros' earthly sojourn, Leo V became emperor in 813 and restored the heresy. He deposed Patriarch Nikephoros I (806-815) and rehabilitated the wretched council at Hieria by renouncing the Synod in Trullo.[11] Now Medikion had reached its peak under Father Nikephoros' watch. His monastery was a center of resistance to Iconoclasm. Father Nikephoros never swayed from his position as one who venerated the sacred images. In the year 813, Father Nikephoros reposed in peace. Prior to his repose, Father Nikephoros had brought his disciple, Father Niketas, to Constantinople and to the patriarchate. Nikephoros introduced Niketas to Patriarch Tarasios, for the elder wished to have Niketas ordained to the priesthood. When Father Niketas with some hesitation received the prayer and blessing of Saint Tarasios, the latter persuaded him to take on the care and supervision of the monastery as a second to Father Nikephoros, that he might share with him the toils and concerns of such a ministration. One of the reasons that the patriarch wished to provide Elder Nikephoros with a young priest was on account of the advanced years of the infirm hegumen. Thus, Niketas could not refuse both, that is, his spiritual father and the patriarch. Afterward, both abbots and strugglers for the icons, Nikephoros and Niketas (d. 824), were interred in the narthex of the Church of the Archangel Michael. In the eleventh century, Medikion was also called the Monastery of the Holy Fathers.

On the 4th of May, the holy Church commemorates the venerable NICEPHORUS (NIKEPHOROS), who struggled in asceticism in the most remote places of Athos and reposed in peace.

---

[10] The Amorian Dynasty included Michael II, Theophilos, Theodora, and Michael III. It was Theophilos who had revived Iconoclasm, but which his widow overturned as regent for their young son Michael III. Thus, Iconoclasm ended with the Triumph of Orthodoxy.

[11] Emperor Justinian II had convoked the Synod in Trullo, which convened between 691 and 692. Among its resolutions was that, in iconography, Christ was to be depicted in His human form.

Saint Nicephorus of Athos

Nicephorus, the revealer of veiled teachings, had hailed from Italy and had first been brought up in papal error. At length, as one adorned in mind with understanding, he repudiated the cacodoxy of the Latin west. He left his homeland and traveled east to Byzantium. After he espoused the true Orthodox Faith, he bid farewell to all things transitory and foolish. He became a monk on Mount Athos. He seems to have taken up the eremitical life in a small hermitage rather than one of the coenobia on the peninsula.

Now he had lived during the time when Michael VIII Palaiologos (1259-1282) wielded the scepter. This emperor's foreign policy revolved around warding off Latin attempts to regain Constantinople. Byzantium's memories of the atrocities of the Fourth Crusade and the sacking of the capital in 1204 were still fresh. The ill-qualified emperor, therefore, in 1274, agreed to the Union of the Churches at Lyons (1274). On the 16th of January, in the year 1275, the Union of the Churches was solemnly proclaimed by profane lips in Constantinople. Michael thought by this union and political maneuvering to forestall the invasion of Charles I of Anjou. The union that Michael hoped to create was a false one. Together with the dread of Latin domination, there were the issues of papal centralization, scholastic theology, and the *Filioque*. The Palaiologan Dynasty also had an unwholesome craving for western military aid to ward off Turkish inroads. The papacy was thus motivated to declare Byzantium's complete ecclesiastical submission in return for their much-desired soldiers and munitions. While the Latin Church was unwilling to acknowledge Orthodoxy's practises, eastern monastic communities were mostly against the union and maintained their adamant opposition to the end. The specifics of the Union of the Churches spat forth strange and dangerous doctrines. Turkish conquest to the fathers was even preferable to submission to the Roman Catholics. This union of expediency had pierced the souls of many holy fathers who let out a strident cry of protest. Michael could not procure their good opinion. The emperor, thereupon, lost to all judgment, inflicted injuries and imprisonments. Our holy Father Nicephorus, who had lived among the westerners and understood them well, did not disguise his feelings. He had not a whit of sympathy for papal presumptions. He was vehemently opposed to the unionist policy and suffered the consequences, as had many other steadfast Orthodox monastics during that acrimonious dispute.

Now Father Nicephorus had become an instructor in divine mysteries and was one initiated into mysteries. Saint Gregory Palamas,[12] before he became Archbishop of Thessalonike, sojourned on the Holy Mountain at the Monastery of Saint Athanasios (the Great Lavra). During that period, he was under the spiritual direction of our Father Nicephorus. This elder for Saint Gregory was a guide in the art of silence that was undisturbed by worldly cares. Elder Nicephorus was very experienced in keeping attention within himself and in reaching the indescribable union with God. He made it his study to concentrate in himself untrammeled quietude. In this activity, he was united, in an ineffable manner, with the supramundane and the highest. He acquired the divine illumination and the light of grace which indeed dwelt in his heart.

The inimitable Nicephorus, a living example of a divinized man, was accounted worthy of divine gifts. As an expounder of mysteries, he has provided even us, in a paternal and abundant manner, with his treatise entitled "On Watchfulness and the Guarding of the Heart." He gives marked attention to this subject and unfolds the meaning of true prayer and perpetual intercourse with God that refuses to experience repletion. For those who desire to attain watchfulness and noetic stillness, he can lead the way as one experienced. He continues to help beginners who have difficulty stabilizing their intellect. "We cannot be reconciled to God and assimilated to Him," he tells us, "unless we first return or, rather, enter into ourselves, insofar as this lies within our power. That is why the monastic life has been called the art of arts and the science of sciences. For this holy discipline does not procure us what is corruptible so that we divert our intellect from higher to lower things and completely stifle it."[13]

---

[12] Saint Gregory Palamas is commemorated by the holy Church on the 14th of November.

[13] Nikiphoros the Monk, "On Watchfulness and the Guarding of the Heart," *The Philokalia*, Vol. IV, trans. and edited by Palmer, Sherrard, and Ware, pp. 204-206.

Further to this, he tells us that "some of the saints have called attentiveness the guarding of the intellect. Others have called it custody of the heart, or watchfulness, or noetic stillness, and others something else. Attentiveness is the sign of true repentance. It is the soul's restoration, hatred of the world, and return to God. It is rejection of sin and recovery of virtue. It is unreserved assurance that our sins are forgiven. It is the beginning of contemplation or, rather, its presupposition; for through it God, detecting its presence in us, reveals Himself to the intellect. It is serenity of intellect or, rather, the repose bestowed on the soul through God's mercy. It is subjection of our thoughts, the palace of the mindfulness of God, the stronghold that enables us patiently to accept all that befalls us. It is the ground of faith, hope, and love. For if thou hast not faith, thou canst not endure the outward afflictions that assail thee; and if thou bearest them not gladly, thou canst not say to the Lord, 'Thou art my helper and my refuge [Ps. 90:2].' And if the Most High is not thy refuge, thou wilt not lay up His love in thy heart."[14]

Saint Nicephorus of Athos

The venerable Nicephorus proposed a method, whereby novices can recollect their mind. He had a kind of psychosomatic method for restraining the intellect from wandering about and succumbing to surrounding distractions. This technique was to help beginners who were unable to restrain their intellect from fantasizing. This method may have already been handed down on the Mountain from spiritual father to disciple, for which Nicephorus gave the initial written description of the technique. Before praying the Jesus Prayer, he recommends an experienced teacher for bringing the intellect into the heart. "It is not that our mental faculties are located spatially inside the heart as a container.[15] But there is a correlation, a relationship of analogy participation,

[14] Ibid., IV:204, 205.

[15] Saint Gregory Palamas, *Triads* I, ii, 3. "Our soul is a single entity possessing many powers. It utilizes an organ of the body that by nature lives in conjunction with it. What organs, then, does the power of the soul that we call 'intellect' make use of when it is active?...Some locate it in the head, as though in a sort of acropolis. Others consider

(continued...)

between our physical modalities and our mental and spiritual state. 'After our fall our inner being naturally adapts itself to outward forms.'[16] Father Nicephorus wished to harness bodily energies for the work of prayer."[17] He commented that "the heart is the source of life and warmth for the body....Seat thyself, then, concentrate thine intellect, and lead it into the respiratory passage through which thy breath passes into thy heart. Put pressure on thine intellect and compel it to descend with thine inhaled breath into thy heart."[18]

Again, Saint Nicephorus was an advocate for finding a spiritual guide. Most, if not all of those who attain this greatest of gifts, do so chiefly through being taught. Very few, without being taught, receive it directly from God, by means of the ardor of their endeavor and their fervid faith. One should, therefore, search for an unerring guide, one who has been tested. The saint advises, "Brother, train thine intellect not to leave thy heart quickly; for at first it is strongly disinclined to remain constrained and circumscribed in this way. But once it becomes accustomed to remaining there, it can no longer bear to be outside the heart. For behold, the kingdom of God is within us [cf. Lk. 17:21]! When the intellect concentrates its attention in the heart and, through pure prayer searches there for the kingdom of the heavens, all external things become abominable and hateful to it. When thine intellect is firmly established in thy heart, it must not remain there silent and idle. It should constantly repeat and meditate on the prayer, 'Lord Jesus Christ, Son of God, have mercy on me.' This prayer protects the intellect from distraction. It renders it impregnable to diabolic attacks, and daily increases its love and desire for God. If, however, in spite of all thine efforts, thou art not able to enter the realms of the heart, compel thyself to repeat the Jesus Prayer. If thou wilt continue this for

---

[15](...continued)
that its vehicle is the center most part of the heart, that aspect of the heart that has been purified from natural life. We know very well that our intelligence is neither within us as in a container—for it is incorporeal—nor yet outside us, for it is united to us; but it is located in the heart as in its own organ. The Creator of man said, 'Not that which entereth into the mouth defileth the man; but that which goeth forth out of the mouth, this defileth the man [Mt. 15:11],' adding 'For out of the heart cometh forth evil thoughts, murders, adulteries, fornications, thefts, false testimonies, blasphemies [Mt. 15:19].'...Our heart is the shrine of intelligence and the chief intellectual organ of the body. When, therefore, we strive to scrutinize and to amend our intelligence through vigorous watchfulness, how could we do this if we did not collect our intellect, outwardly dispersed through the senses, and bring it back within ourselves—back to the heart itself, the shrine of the thoughts?" "In Defence of Those Who Practise a Life of Stillness," *Philokalia*, IV:334.

[16] Idem, *Triads* I, ii, 8.

[17] Nikiphoros the Monk, "Introductory Note," *The Philokalia*, IV:192, 193.

[18] Ibid., "On Watchfulness," IV:205.

some time, it will assuredly open for thee the entrance to thy heart. Then, together with the attentiveness thou hast so desired, the whole choir of the virtues will come to thee"[19]—that is, "love, joy, peace, long-suffering, kindness, goodness, faith, meekness, self-control [Gal. 5:22]." And, "through the virtues, all thy petitions shall be answered in Christ Jesus our Lord."[20]

The saint only desired to become a dwelling place of the Holy Spirit. He took to heart the apostolic utterance of Saint Paul: "But we all, with unveiled face reflecting as a mirror the glory of the Lord, are being transformed into the same image from glory to glory, even as from the Lord, the Spirit [2 Cor. 3:18]." Saint Nicephorus contended to the end in the labors of virtue and asceticism, always immeasurably cheered by the good promises of our Lord. He reposed in peace, splendidly adorned with both action and vision, probably before the year 1300, and adorned the godly choir of saints.

On the 4th of May, the holy Church commemorates our venerable Father ATHANASIOS, Bishop of Corinth, who fell asleep in the Lord during the days of Emperors Basil and Constantine (937).

Through the intercessions of Thy Saints,
O Christ God, have mercy on us. Amen.

[19] Ibid., IV:205, 206.
[20] Ibid., IV:206.

On the 5th of May, the holy Church commemorates the holy and Great-martyr IRENE.[1]

Irene, the holy great-martyr, was born in the city of Magedon or Magedo.[2] She lived during the reign of Constantine the Great (306-337). She was the sole offspring of her pagan parents, Licinius, who was a certain kinglet, and Licinia. Irene had been given the name of Penelope at birth. Since she was the most fair of maidens and surpassed in beauty all the others of her day, her father, who feared for his daughter, built a lofty tower to isolate Penelope. He also lodged thirteen other young maidens with her, amid whom she lived in luxury and wealth. She received such items as a throne, a table, and a lamp made of solid gold. She was six years of age when her father confined her to the tower. He also assigned a certain elderly Apellianos to supervise his sheltered little daughter's education.

Saint Irene

One day, the saint observed that a dove had entered the tower. The dove, bearing an olive branch in its beak, placed it on the golden table. Subsequent to this, she beheld an eagle fly into the tower. The creature was holding a wreath of plaited flowers in its beak, which it deposited on the table. Following close upon this delivery, she then noticed that a raven came in through the window, carrying a snake, which it

[1] The manuscript of the events surrounding the martyrdom of the saint, recorded by Apellianos, her teacher, begins: "In recent years, a certain kinglet ascended the throne...." The text is extant in the Athonite monasteries of the Great Lavra, Iveron, and in other places. At Lavra, there is also extant her martyric account which manuscript begins: "In those days...." The service to Saint Irene was composed by the Monk Kallinikos, the Lykaonian of Mount Athos, initially published at Hermopolis (1877). The most recent edition of this service was published in Athens (1954), under the guidance of the Athonite monk, Father Gerasimos Mikrayiannanites.

[2] This city was situated somewhere in the Sasanian state of Persia, as evidenced by the fact that Shāpūr II (309-379), king of the Persians, having heard reports of Saint Irene, ordered her death, which he would not have decreed unless it was within his jurisdiction.

also dropped on the golden table. Witnessing all this, the blessed virgin was perplexed and wondered at the meaning of these signs.

Apellianos interpreted all these signs for her, saying, "The dove makes known thy superior education; the olive branch signifies many wondrous events, and is a symbol of Baptism. The eagle, being the king of birds, foretells, by the royal crown of flowers, future success in notable endeavors. But the raven and serpent disclose thy future sufferings and anguish." By these hidden meanings, the elderly teacher revealed the great struggle of martyrdom, which the saint was to undergo one day for the sake of her love for God. All the events that followed concerning the holy Irene, which have been committed to writing, are indeed supernatural and paradoxical.

It is said that an angel of the Lord gave her the name of Irene, changing it from Penelope. That incorporeal being instructed her in the Faith of the Christ, and foretold that myriads of souls would be saved by means of her. Furthermore, Apostle Timothy, a disciple of Saint Paul, would visit her in a paradoxical manner and baptize her. When this latter prophecy was fulfilled, the blessed Irene cast her father's idols to the ground, shattering them. At first, Irene was questioned by her father who, upon seeing that she persisted in the beliefs of the Christian Faith, was intensely dissatisfied. He ordered that she be bound. Irene was then cast between many horses that they might trample upon her. However, one of the horses, instead of harming the saint, turned on Licinius. It struck him down, crushing his right hand and slaying him. The horse then magnified the saint with a human voice!

The martyr was thereafter released from her bonds. At the request of the bystanders, she prayed and resurrected her father. Licinius came to believe in God, as did his wife Licinia. In fact, another three thousand people received holy Baptism. Thenceforth, Irene's father abandoned his dominion and lived in the tower which he had built for his daughter, passing the rest of his life in repentance.

After her father renounced this world, another kinglet, named Sedekias, rose to power. He attempted to force the saint to sacrifice to idols. Since she opposed his demand, he ordered that the blessed maiden be cast headlong into a deep pit filled with a nest of venomous snakes and reptiles. The blessed maiden, nevertheless, persevered in that cavity of the earth. After fourteen days, she emerged unscathed. Following this trial, the pagans cruelly amputated her feet with a saw; yet, by the aid of a holy angel, she was restored to health and stood on her feet. Next, the idolaters bound her to a wheel that turned by the force of water. When the waters miraculously ceased flowing, the sacred damsel remained unharmed. As a result of this miracle, eight thousand people came to believe in Christ Jesus.

After Sedekias was ousted from his domain, Savor, his son, marched against those who had deposed his father. Saint Irene met Savor and his army in the city of Magedon. By her prayers, his entire army was stricken blind. Again, she prayed and their eyesight was restored by divine grace. Notwithstanding, those ungrateful ones, out of vengeance, pierced her heels with spikes and burdened her back with a cumbrous sack of sand. In this manner, she was led on a march for three miles. Then, suddenly, the earth was rent asunder, swallowing ten thousand infidels. Due to this, thirty thousand other souls accepted the Faith of Christ. Despite this, the kinglet stubbornly persisted as a pagan. Therefore, an angel of the Lord descended and smote him.[3] Consequently, the holy maiden was able to walk unhindered through the city, performing many miracles. She also went to the tower her father had built, accompanied by a priest, named Timothy. Through her God-inspired teachings, she succeeded in converting, to the Faith of Christ, five thousand idolaters who then received holy Baptism. Among them were thirty-three men who were designated to guard the tower.

Following this episode, the saint came to a city called Kallinikos (Callinicus).[4] It was the seat of Numerianos the kinglet, the son of Sebastianos. Once there, Irene appeared before him and proclaimed Christ. He, as a result, confined her to the interior of three bronze oxen, which figures were heated until they glowed red. He then had her transferred from the first to the second, and from the second to the third. The third ox, albeit it was inanimate, walked miraculously and then split asunder. The saint, thereupon, exited uninjured, without the least trace of a burn or singed hair and attire. Throngs of pagans who beheld this wonder accepted Christ, numbering as many as one hundred thousand souls.[5] As the kinglet was about to die, he left instructions to his prefect, named Vavdonos, to punish the holy Christian maiden in diverse ways. The prefect fettered her with chains and lit a great pyre under her. However, an angel of the Lord intervened and put out the fire, preserving the saint unharmed. The prefect, observing this, straightway believed in Christ. The venerable Irene then went further north, to Constantina.[6]

Hence, by 330, the fame of the saint's marvels reached the impious ears of Shāpūr II the Great, king of the Persians, who ordered the beheading

---

[3] In an older *Synaxaristes*, according to the Greek compilers of *The Great Synaxaristes* (in Greek), the angel slew also five thousand men.

[4] Callinicus could possibly be Callinicum, also known as Nicephorium or Raqqa on the Euphrates River in Syria.

[5] The *Synaxarion* of the *Menaion* records twenty thousand souls.

[6] Constantina is approximately eighty-five miles northeast of Callinicum, and forty miles northeast of Edessa (Urfa).

Saint Irene

of the saint.[7] The victorious champion of Christ, Irene, was apprehended and her head was struck off. Though the martyr was interred, yet was she was resurrected by an angel of God. He magnified her, because she had been martyred for Christ. Moreover, those who honor her name and commemorate the day of her martyrdom also bring blessings upon themselves. After her resurrection, it is said that she entered the city of Mesembria,[8] bearing an olive branch in her hand. Saint Irene appeared before the kinglet who, upon seeing her, straightway, accepted Christ and was baptized with myriads of other people by the Priest Timothy. When the holy one returned to her parental home in Magedon, she mourned the death of her father. After visiting and bidding farewell to her mother, Irene was caught up in a cloud and traveled to Ephesus,[9] tarrying there for a period of time and performing many miracles. She was honored there as an apostle. Thereafter, she also saw her teacher Apellianos.

Since Saint Irene had taught and exhorted the populace of Ephesus, she departed thence in the company of six followers, including Apellianos. Not too far from its outskirts, she came upon a newly constructed tomb wherein none had lain. She entered the tomb, and Apellianos sealed it with a stone. While Irene was still among the living, the saint ordered that, for four days, no one was to move the stone which Apellianos had placed over the grave. Two days later, he returned to the tomb, and—lo, the miracle!—he discovered the stone overturned and the body of the saint missing. All these accounts may seem improbable to the limited intelligence of man, but to God, they are possible.

---

[7] Shāpūr, in years of fighting, secured the frontiers of his empire against the Rhomaioi, wresting from them strongholds in the west. The dynasty of the Sasanians shaped a powerful empire that rivaled Rome and Constantinople until the 630s. Shāpūr's cruel persecution of Christians was also rooted in fear, since the Faith had been elevated to the rank of a state religion in the west. The Zoroastrians feared the missionary spirit of the Christian Faith.

[8] It is uncertain whether Mesembria (Bulgarian Nesebur, 40°39′N 27°43′E), a city on the Black Sea coast, is meant.

[9] Ephesus (37°57′N 27°21′E) is a seaport of Aegean Asia Minor.

To sum up her struggles, she stood before the following rulers and magnates: she was first summoned by her father Licinius, second by Sedekias, third by Savor, fourth by Numerianus, fifth by the Vavdonos, and sixth by Shāpūr of the Persians. Those cities where she contested and martyred for Christ were her hometown of Magedon, Kallinikos, Constantina, and Mesembria, until her second repose outside of Ephesus. Myriads were brought to repentance and embraced Christ by her preaching and example; and we, too, now beg to gain her powerful intercession.

Saint Efthymios

On the 5th of May, the holy Church commemorates our holy father among the saints, EFTHYMIOS the Wonder-worker, Bishop of Madytos.[10]

Efthymios, Bishop of Madytos and our holy father among the saints, was born at the beginning of the tenth century in Epivatas, a small town in Thrace on the shores of the

[10] The Life of Saint Efthymios, Bishop of Madytos, does not appear in the older *Synaxaria* and *Menaia*. It was inserted in *The Great Synaxaristes* (in Greek) for the first time in the second edition of the May volume. The divine office of the saint was composed by Father Gerasimos Mikrayiannanites, hymnographer of the Great Church of Christ, and published in 1961. This composition was edited by Protopresbyter John Ramphos. This work also contains a synopsis from the "Encomium to the Great Efthymios, Bishop of Madytos," by George the Cypriot, who later became Patriarch of Constantinople (Gregory II) from 1283 to 1289. This narrative was composed at the request of Meletios, Bishop of Athens, who presided over the Church at Madytos. It was translated and published into Russian (Moscow, 1889) by the Russian Archimandrite Arsenios. It was reprinted in 1892, but without the revised translation and introductory essays by Professor Antoniades of the Theological School at Chalke. On account of its great length, it was not possible to reprint the life in its entirety. A marvellous icon of Saint Efthymios is reproduced herein. It is a wall-painting from the Church of Saint George (Kypsely, Athens), painted by the renowned Photios Kontoglu. He based his depiction on a rare portable icon from Mount Sinai, dating to the 14th C., which was executed with the permission of the Patriarch of Alexandria, Christophoros Madytiou.

Propontis. His parents were pious and devout Christians, who engaged in farming and were prosperous at this occupation. While the saint was still a child, he was orphaned of his father. His mother then brought him to a monastery in Constantinople, where he remained for thirty years, distinguishing himself in his spiritual struggles. He acquired a reputation as an imitator of the ancient holy ascetics.

The blessed Efthymios, however, desired the eremitical life and total solitude and peace. He departed the monastery and retired to a place near Constantinople, where he struggled alone for four years, communicating with God. The sanctity of his life did not escape the notice of the Bishop of Perinthos[11] who ordained him to the diaconate, though it was against the latter's will. Later, Efthymios received the office of the Priesthood at the hands of another bishop. Eventually, he was elevated to the bishopric of Madytos.[12] He was chosen on account of his conspicuous attainment of the virtues. This reason as well as his exceptional pastoral experience acquired over forty years proved to be a successful combination.

While the saint was still among the living, he was honored by God with the performance of many miracles, rendered for both spiritual and bodily cures. Many women were delivered from difficult childbirth and severe fever at his supplications before the Lord. One of these mothers, in gratitude, named her son Efthymios. Others were rescued from demonic possession and influence. A man who was a deaf-mute and demoniac was cured by the saint, even as Efthymios was celebrating the Liturgy during the Feast of Saint Hermogenes the Martyr. A possessed nun was rendered free during the celebration of the martyred Saint Ephemianos. On another occasion, the saint healed a terribly afflicted leper. Toward the end of his life, the man of God saved the people of his diocese from the great famine that struck in the year 989. He fought the famine by personal self-denial and by collecting and distributing food supplies.

The saint's fame reached the ears of Emperor Basil II, who reigned from 976 to 1025. The emperor came to Madytos to visit the saint, who foretold the emperor's famous victory against Bardas Phokas in 989.[13] After Bishop Efthymios lived a saintly life, he reposed in peace at Madytos on the 4th of May between the years of 989 and 996. Many miracles occurred after his blessed repose, and the all-good God honored his sacred relics with myrrh that streamed forth from his tomb. Many sick people were cured by him, to the

[11] Perinthos was an ancient city of Thrace on the Propontis.

[12] Madytos (40°12′N 26°22′E) is a city in eastern Thrace on the Hellespont, now called Maintos, as well as Madyta. It is actually on the Dardanelles, across from Abydos.

[13] The 987 rebellion of Bardas Phokas, *doux* of Antioch, was overcome with aid from Vladimir I of Kiev, to whom Basil married his sister Anna. Bardas fell at Abydos in April of 989.

glory of Father, Son, and Holy Spirit, the one God, to Whom is meet all glory, honor, and veneration to the endless ages. Amen.

On the 5th of May, the holy Church commemorates the holy Martyrs NEOPHYTOS, GAIOS, and GAIANOS.

Neophytos, Gaios, and Gainos, the holy martyrs, suffered this day, manfully, for the sake of the Holy Trinity. Their synaxis (liturgical gathering) was celebrated in the church dedicated to the holy, glorious, and wonder-working Unmercenaries Kosmas and Damian, located in the Darius Quarter.

On the 5th of May, the holy Church commemorates the Consecration of the Church of the Most Holy THEOTOKOS in the Kyrou Quarter.[14]

On the 5th of May, the holy Church commemorates the holy New-martyr EPHRAIM, the Newly-appeared Wonder-worker (1426).

Ephraim, the holy great-martyr and wonder-worker, was born on the 14th of September, in the year 1384. At a young age, both he and his six siblings were orphaned of their father. The care of the family fell solely upon their pious mother. Ephraim loved God from an early age. The seal of his dedication, of course, was to be his awesome and glorious martyrdom at the end of his life.

When Ephraim was only fourteen years of age, God led his steps to the flourishing monastery at Amomon of Katharon near Nea Makri in Attike.[15] The monastery was dedicated to the Annunciation of the Theotokos and Saint Paraskeve. He strictly emulated, in that monastery, the Gospel bidding of our Lord Who says: "If anyone is willing to come after Me, let him deny himself, and take up his cross, and keep on following Me [Mt. 16:24]." This command was carried out by Ephraim with both gladness and eagerness. Now Ephraim's youthful heart was filled with divine love. Thus, he submitted himself willingly in obedience to Christ. By his monastic life, which was equal to that of the angels, he became an emulator of the great ascetics and fathers of the desert. He, thereupon, conducted his life in this saintly manner for twenty-seven years.

---

[14] See the Life of Saint Romanos the Melodist, commemorated the 1st of October, for a discussion on this church.

[15] Nea Makri, a coastal suburb of Athens, is on the northern coast of Attike. Historical Marathon is situated eight kilometers from Nea Makri. Nea Makri is approximately twelve kilometers north of Rafina port. Present-day Nea Makri, a seaside tourist town, overlooks the Aegean and the southern peninsula of Evia.

Saint Ephraim pursued Christ with much divine zeal as he renounced the joys and pleasures of the world. He shone forth with the brightness of his manner of life and in the burdens of his abstinence at Mount Amomon. With divine assistance and his own perseverance, he cleansed his soul and body from the soul-destroying passions. At length, he came to be deemed a worthy vessel of the Holy Spirit. He also was vouchsafed the Mystery of the office of the Priesthood. He, therefore, served in the holy sanctuary as an angel of God with much contrition and the fear of God.

Saint Ephraim

On the 14th day of September, in the year 1425, the day of the celebration of the holy Cross, when he had turned forty-one years old, he returned to his skete from one of its dependent *metochia*, that is, a monastery holding of his community. When he first laid eyes on his monastic retreat, he was stunned to find that the community had been completely devastated. All the fathers had been massacred by the barbaric Turks who had come by sea. They not only destroyed the monastery and the fathers but also they looted the surrounding area. Father Ephraim, too, was seen by the malevolent infidels and taken captive. It was then that his monstrous sufferings began over a period of months, which only ended on the 5th of May, in the year 1426, at nine o'clock in the morning. The holy martyr met his end at the age of forty-one. He was tortured in a most inhuman way, and surrendered his soul while praying. They hanged him from a tree (which can still be seen to this day), nailing his feet to it and driving nails into his head. At last, they drove a stake through his wounded body. At that point, he surrendered his soul to our Lord, from Whom he received the laurel of martyrdom.

More than five hundred years later, God granted many appearances to the Christians of Saint Ephraim. Numerous amazing events also took place. On the 3rd of January, in the year 1950, a discovery was made. The martyr's relics were confirmed to be those of Saint Ephraim. Hearken to how this remarkable finding came about. At the present-day site of Saint Ephraim's old monastery, there stood a convent headed by Hegumene Makaria. She had been taking a turn about the ruins of the monastery, meditating on the martyrdoms that took place about five hundred years earlier. She kept thinking how the ground upon which she was treading was soaked with the blood of Orthodox monastic martyrs. She entreated Christ that He would permit her to unearth one of the venerable fathers. After some time, she perceived that she was being told to dig in a certain spot. The abbess summoned a workman whom she had hired earlier to make repairs at the old monastery. He was somewhat cantankerous and did not wish to oblige the abbess as she wished. Being somewhat self-willed, he chose where he wanted to dig. She pleaded with him, but he remained obstinate. She then uttered a prayer secretly that in the place where he chose to dig, he would be impeded. Indeed, the workman began digging and quickly hit solid rock. Unabashed, he went to three and four other places of his own choosing. Headstrong as he was, he succeeded each time in striking a spot that had rock underneath it. She continued to bear with his wilfulness. He finally yielded to her pleas and dug in the place where she first indicated. She asked him to excavate in the ruins of an old *kellion* that was filled with debris and rubble. He was vexed as he began clearing it away. But when he had commenced, he was digging in a wild and angry manner. "Brother," she cried out, "do not excavate with such vehemence lest the relics should be harmed." He scorned the abbess' words and kept digging. He did not believe her that relics lay beneath him. When he dug as far down as six feet, he unearthed the head of the martyr. Straightway, an indescribably pleasant fragrance wafted forth that emanated from the relics. The cynical and contrary workman now turned pale at the discovery, so that he was unable to utter a word in his awe. Mother Makaria went to her knees. Her happiness was complete. She turned to the workman and said, "Thou mayest go now and leave me to myself." He obeyed and went forth. She, thereupon, began clearing away more soil. She then noticed sleeves from the martyr's *rason* (cassock). She observed that the fabric was thick. It clearly had been woven on a loom from an earlier period. She removed more and more dirt, until she discovered the rest of the bones and carefully extracted them from the earth. She was there until evening fell. At that juncture, she began to recite the office of Vespers.

Suddenly, she heard footsteps coming from the grave. It seemed to her that the sound of steps was then moving diagonally across the courtyard in the direction of the church. She discerned that the steps were that of a man with a strong and steady gait. Inexplicably, fear gripped her until she heard a voice addressing her and saying, "How long shalt thou leave me here?" She then beheld a tall monk. She gazed into his eyes, which were small and round. His beard reached to his chest. He bore in his left hand a bright light, while he gave a blessing with his right hand. When she observed him thus, her fright was transformed into joy. The abbess replied, "Forgive me, holy father, I will attend to thee tomorrow, even as soon as God should grant the dawn." The tall monk then vanished. Mother Makaria then resumed reading Vespers.

After the office of Orthros, when it was very early in the morning, the abbess remained true to her word. She reverently took up the sacred relics and washed them. After she stacked them nicely in a niche in the altar area of the convent church, she lit a candle before them. That same night, the same monk appeared to Mother Makaria and greeted her warmly. He thanked her for her solicitude toward his bones. He then introduced himself, saying, "My name is Father Ephraim." He next began to recount the story of his life. He also spoke to her of his martyrdom and that of his fellow monastics. The finding of Saint Ephraim's relics took place, as we said, on the 3rd of January.

Now the martyr's relics not only emit a divine and heavenly fragrance but also every kind of healing springs forth for those who venerate the relics with faith and seek the aid of the miracle-working Hieromartyr Ephraim. With his pure life and martyrdom, he honored the name of the triune God and was honored in return by the Lord Almighty. To those who call upon him, the saint bestows the grace of God, which gift the venerable Ephraim received abundantly. This is manifested clearly in the extraordinary and supernatural miracles he performs for both body and soul over sufferers. He is known to quickly answer the prayers of those who call upon him. Thus, our holy Father Ephraim is commemorated twice yearly: on the 3rd of January, the day of the recovery of his precious relics; and on the 5th of May, today, the date of his martyrdom.

A Few Miracles of Saint Ephraim the New

Abbess Makaria recalls that "a woman named Elisabeth (Vetta) Makris came to the convent and sewed clothing, free of charge, for the children of our institution. One day, as Vetta prostrated herself in prayer before Saint Ephraim's icon, she sensed a fragrance envelop her that she had never known before. Her eyes welled up with tears. She was filled with contrition, as she beheld the saint pass before her eyes. She was never seen again at the convent after that incident. Much later, a young woman, the one who used to accompany Vetta and helped her with the sewing, came to the convent. She cried out pitifully in her heartfelt appeal, saying, 'Mrs. Vetta, Mrs. Vetta! Perhaps it is too late!'

"At once," continued the abbess, "I took up the relics of Saint Ephraim and went to the hospital to see Mrs. Makris. The nurse in charge said to me, 'It is not possible to visit her. Her condition is critical!' But, in spite of the admonition, I entered the patient's room. It was self-evident that I was standing before a woman at the threshold of death. I then went aside, a small distance from the sickbed of the ailing Vetta, and pleaded with the saint to restore the dying woman to life. Vetta then opened her eyes and looked in my direction.

She cried out to me, 'O, mother, mother, thou hast come!' I, thereupon, lost no time in placing the relics on the woman's breast. She made the sign of the Cross and—behold!—real signs of life returned to her face, and she asked for food.

"Vetta's husband and children were present, too, as well as the nurses of the hospital and the physicians. All were astonished at the miraculous recovery and praised God, Who works such awesome and strange miracles. I should state here the condition of the patient: Vetta had not partaken of food for fifteen days. It was only after the placement of the relics that she regained her strength and appetite. She asked for something to eat. She recovered as if from a deep sleep. As one who always had the cares and concerns of others before her own needs, Vetta requested that I take the relics and make the sign of the Cross with them over a grandmother who was suffering in the next room. But instead, the elderly woman was called into Vetta's room. She required assistance, however. Someone led her by the hand, since the woman was manifestly blind. She was then escorted into Vetta's room. I made the sign of the Cross, with the relics of Saint Ephraim, over the grandmother. I then departed.

"Afterward, I learned that the grandmother, by the grace of God and the holy relics of Saint Ephraim, had completely regained her eyesight. I also heard that she returned to her family back home on Crete. I thought, what further proof is needed for one to believe in the wonders of God? Individuals near death have been restored to life; and the blind have regained their sight. There was another case, which I cannot recount at this point, for the sake of brevity, that dealt with deliverance from paralysis so that the patient stood upright. These supernatural cures that have occurred before witnesses—and indeed even in the presence of those with licensed medical backgrounds—have filled souls with amazement and awe. One cannot help but move their lips in praise of God, Who has wrought so many wonders by means of His saints!"

But let us return to Vetta who was on her deathbed. After she recuperated, she returned to her village in the Cyclades, on the Aegean island of Naxos. She lived in a small farmhouse by the sea. Years later, Vetta's daughter was vouchsafed a vision of Saint Ephraim. She observed him standing above the water, flanked by two angels. The holy priest-monk addressed her and said, "Anna, my child, hearken to me! I am come to take thy mother; but do not grieve over this. It is the will of God this time. Thou shouldest see the beautiful place that I am preparing for her." He then revealed to Anna a beautiful garden, dressed with sweet-scented flowers and fruit trees. It was truly a vision of Eden. "Cease sorrowing," he repeated, "for I shall always be with thee to protect thee." As he turned to depart, the young girl said, "Why dost thou not tarry with us, Saint Ephraim?" He looked upon her and said, "I cannot, my child, for the hospital sick are calling me." At that moment, the accompanying angels said to him, "Let us be off, Saint Ephraim! The sick are calling thee!" He then said to young Anna, "Dost thou hear, my child? The sick are calling. I cannot stay." Then he disappeared. Indeed, at that very moment, Mother Makaria was at the hospital with the saint's holy relics, because she was asked to visit certain people with them. Dearly beloved brethren, let us remain faithful and stand by the side of our Lord that we may maintain our strength for all of the difficulties of life.[16]

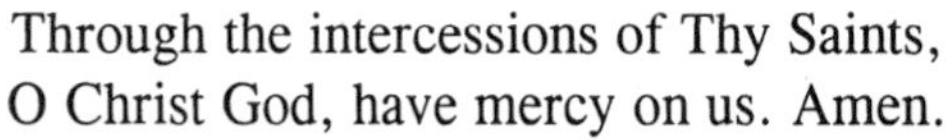

Through the intercessions of Thy Saints,
O Christ God, have mercy on us. Amen.

[16] More is known about the wonderful life and wondrous miracles of the Great-martyr Ephraim and can be found in the recent book, *Visions and Miracles of the Great-martyr Ephraim the Newly-appeared*, published by the Monastery of the Holy Mother of God, Nea Makri, in Attike, Greece. The proceeds from the book are said to go toward the completion of the first church ever dedicated to the glorious Saint Ephraim the New of our Orthodox Church. The book is available from Orthodox Kypsely Press, for those who wish to draw unto themselves the blessing of a wonderful and healing great-martyr of Christ. In the United States, a portion of his relics are kept at the monastery-church of Saints Raphael, Nicholas, and Irene, in Astoria, Long Island, New York.

On the 6th of May, the holy Church commemorates the holy and righteous Prophet JOB of many labors.[1]

Job, the righteous and wise man, was living in the land of Ausis, on the borders of Idumea and Arabia. He was the grandson of Esau and fifth from Abraham.[2] In the Old Testament book of his name, we learn how he loses his wealth, large family of ten children, and his health. Saint Andrew of Crete (ca. 660-740) writes: "Once Job sat upon a throne, but now he sits upon a dunghill, naked and covered with sores [Job 2:7, 8]. Once he was blessed with many children and admired by all, but suddenly he is childless and homeless. Yet he counted the dunghill as a palace and his sores as pearls."[3] The book records a number of debates, an extraterrestrial one between God and Satan, and an earthly one between Job and three of his acquaintances (Eliphaz the king of the Thaemanites, Baldad the sovereign of the Sauchaeans, and Sophar the king of the Minaeans). Job in the end acknowledges the sovereignty of God, and he is restored. God blesses Job, and the man of God receives more than what he had lost in cattle, sheep, camels, oxen, and she-asses. He also begot other children, three of whom were daughters. "And he [Job] called the first Day, and the second Casia, and the third Amalthaea's horn. And there were not found, in comparison with the daughters of Job, fairer women than they in all the world.

---

[1] Unpublished divine offices to the Righteous Job are found in the following codices: Paris [13, 1574, 1575, 1617, 1966]; Athonite Great Lavra [Δ 19, Δ 45, Θ 87, I 70]; and at Kafsokalyvia. Saint John Chrysostom had written four encomia, which are preserved in the *Patrologia Migne*, Vol. 56:563, 567, 570, and 576. The historian Meletios writes that in Capitolia, now named Souvete, of Coele-Syria, there lies the tomb of the Righteous Job.

[2] It is difficult to date the book of Job. In the Orthros Canon to the prophet, we chant, "Although thou knewest not the words of the law, thou dost testify to the fullness of the prophets and the law, O Job," which leads us to believe he lived before the time of Moses and the exodus. [See May 6th, Orthros Canon, Ode Seven, Mode Four, by either Saint Kosmas or John the Monk.] We also note Job's priestly role for his family [Job 1:5] and the measurement of his wealth in terms of livestock [Job 1:3], which place him in remote antiquity. Saint Epiphanios (ca. 315-403), Bishop of Salamis, comments: "When Esau departed for Idumea, a land which lies to the south and east of Canaan, he settled on Mount Seir and founded a city of Edom called Rekem or Petra. He had children who governed in Idumaea, each in succession, and who were called governors of Edom. Fifth in succession from him was Job, not counting Abraham but reckoning from Isaac. For Isaac begat Esau, Esau Reuel, Reuel Zerah, and Zerah Job, who was first called Jobab and later named Job shortly before his temptation. Now the rite of circumcision was being observed." Saint Epiphanius, "Judaism," *The Panarion*, §§ 4.1.6-10, trans. by P. A. Amidon (NY/Oxford: Oxford University Press, 1990), pp. 30, 31.

[3] *Triodion*, Tuesday in the First Week, Great Compline, Ode Four, Tone Plagal Two, by Saint Andrew of Crete.

And their father gave them an inheritance among their brethren [Job 42:14, 15]."

As far as the theme of this biblical book, the subject matter may be classified into three divisions: the dilemma of Job [Job Chaps. 1, 2], the debates of Job [Job Chaps. 3-37], and his deliverance [Job Chaps. 38-42]. The most compelling question the book prods the reader to ask is, "Why are the righteous permitted to suffer if God is loving and all-powerful?" Suffering is not the theme of the book: it is what Job learns through suffering; and, indirectly, his friends learn by his example. The debates from Chapters 3-37 deal with whether God should allow the innocent to suffer. Job's acquaintances believe that there is a direct correlation between righteous conduct and health and prosperity. It is revealed at the end, after a conversation between God and Job, that God is sovereign and worthy of worship in whatever He chooses to do. Satan and Job's acquaintances find a link between obedience and blessing. Satan contends that divine blessings extract human obedience. At the same time, Job's acquaintances maintain that, on the one hand, obedience earns God's blessings and that, on the other hand, disobedience merits punishment. God has a purpose in permitting suffering, though we may not understand it. Through suffering we should recognize God's infinite greatness and our mortality, and that His ways are oftentimes incomprehensible to us.

Saint Basil the Great (ca. 330-379) wrote in a letter that "the study of inspired Scripture is the chief way of finding our duty; for in it we find both instruction about conduct and the lives of blessed men, delivered in writing, as some breathing images of godly living, for the imitation of their good works. Hence, in whatever respect each one feels himself deficient, devoting himself to this imitation, he finds, as from some dispensary, the due medicine for his ailment....He is taught endurance by Job who not only remained the same and kept the disposition of his soul uncrushed throughout when the circumstances of life began to turn against him—for in one moment he was plunged from wealth into penury, and from being the father of fair children into childlessness—but also remained unstirred by anger against the friends who came to 'comfort' him. Much rather, they trampled on him and aggravated his troubles."[4] Elsewhere, Saint Basil remarks that "sometimes sickness afflicts us at the request of the evil one. Our benevolent Master condescends to enter into combat with our enemy, as if the devil were a mighty adversary; but it is so that God should confound the devil's boasts by the heroic patience of God's servants. This we learn in the case of Job [Job 2:6]. Then, too, God places

[4] Saint Basil, "Letter II to Gregory," The Nicene and Post-Nicene Fathers of the Christian Church, 2nd Ser., Vol. VIII:111.

those who are able to endure tribulation even unto death before the weak as their model."[5]

Righteous Job

Satan's idea of theology is that if Job were to be blessed by God, then Job would be faithful. If Job is not blessed by God, then he would be unfaithful. Job's friends believe that only when Job is faithful, shall he be blessed; but if he is unfaithful, he shall be punished. At God's challenge, Job could only humble himself. He was absent at creation and cannot explain the forces of nature. Conspicuously, Job admits his ignorance and keeps silence. Job also admits that neither can he overrule God's ways nor can he control the forces of nature. Thus, he confesses his presumption and repents. Saint Ambrose (ca. 339-397) observes that the devil knows that when the book of Job is explained, "the power of his temptations is shown and made clear."[6]

The Redeemer and Mediator, and the Resurrection

Job recognizes his Redeemer. In the Septuagint, we read these words of the venerable Job: "For I know that He is eternal (ἀένναός) Who is about to deliver me [Job 19:25]." Job acknowledges the resurrection, saying that he knows that the Eternal One shall "raise up (ἀναστῆσαι) upon the earth my skin that endures these sufferings [Job 19:26]." Blessed Jerome (ca. 342-420), in the Vulgate, wrote this of the Redeemer: "Listen to those words of thunder which fall from Job, the vanquisher of torments, who, as he scrapes away the filth of his decaying flesh with a potsherd, solaces his miseries with the hope and the reality of the resurrection, 'O, that,' he says, 'my words were written—O, that they were inscribed in a book with an iron pen, and on a sheet of lead, that they were graven in the rock forever! For I know that my Redeemer *(redemptor)* liveth, and that in the last day I shall rise from the earth, and again be clothed with my skin, and in my flesh shall see God, Whom I shall see for myself, and my eyes shall behold, and not another. This, my hope, is

[5] Idem, "The Long Rules: Q. 55. Whether recourse to the medical art is in keeping with the practise of piety," *Ascetical Works*, The Fathers of the Church Series, Vol. 9:335.

[6] Saint Ambrose, "Letter XX," *Letters and Select Works*, Nicene, 2nd Ser., X:424.

laid up in my bosom.' What can be clearer than this prophecy? No one since the days of Christ speaks so openly concerning the resurrection as he did before Christ. He wishes his words to last forever; and that they might never be obliterated by age, he would have them inscribed on a sheet of lead, and graven on the rock. He hopes for a resurrection; nay, rather, he knew and saw that Christ, His Redeemer, was alive. Job knew, at the last day, he would rise again from the earth. The Lord Jesus had not yet died, and the athlete of the Church saw his Redeemer rising from the grave. When he says, 'And I shall again be clothed with my skin, and in my flesh see God,' I suppose he does not speak as if he loved his flesh, for it was decaying and putrefying before his eyes; but in the confidence of rising again, and through the consolation of the future, he makes light of his present misery. Again he says, 'I shall be clothed with my skin.' What mention do we find here of an ethereal body?...'And in my flesh, I shall see God.' When all flesh shall see the salvation of God, and Jesus as God, then I, also, shall see the Redeemer and Savior, and my God. But I shall see Him in that flesh which now tortures me, which now melts away for pain."[7] Moreover, Job cries out for a mediator, saying, "Would that He our Mediator (μεσίτης) were present, and a Reprover (ἐλέγχων), and One Who should hear the cause between both [Job 9:33]!"

The Manifold Sufferings of the Righteous Job

Saint Cyprian (d. 258) counsels those with many children at home, saying, "You say there are many children at home; and the multitude of your children checks you from giving yourself freely to good works. And yet on this very account you ought to labor the more, for the reason that you are the father of many pledges. There are more for whom you must beseech the Lord. The sins of many have to be redeemed, the consciences of many to be cleansed, the souls of many to be liberated. As in this worldly life, in the nourishment and upbringing of children, the larger the number the greater also is the expense; so also in the spiritual and heavenly life, the larger number of children you have, the greater ought to be the outlay of your labors. Thus, Job offered numerous sacrifices in behalf of his children; and as large was the number of pledges in his home, so large also was the number of victims given to God. The holy Scripture proves this, saying, 'Job, a true and righteous man, had seven sons and three daughters, and cleansed them, offering for them victims to God according to the number of them, and for their sins one calf [Job 1:5].' If, then, you truly love your children, if you show to them the full and paternal

[7] Saint Jerome, "To Pammachius Against John of Jerusalem," *Letters and Select Works*, Nicene, 2nd Ser., VI:439.

sweetness of love, you ought to be the more charitable, that by your righteous works you may commend your children to God."[8]

Saint Ambrose describes the holy man thus: "Job, also, in prosperity and adversity, was blameless, patient, pleasing, and acceptable to God. He was harassed with pain, yet could find consolation."[9] And, speaking of how fortitude should be used in struggling for virtue, he writes: "What of all this was wanting in holy Job, or in his virtue, or what came upon him in the way of vice? How did he bear the distress of sickness or cold or hunger? How did he look upon dangers which menaced his safety? Were the riches from which so much went to the poor gathered together by plunder? Did he ever allow greed for wealth, or the desire for pleasures, or lusts to rise in his heart? Did ever the unkind disputes of the three kinglets, or the insults of the slaves, rouse him to anger? Did glory carry him away like some fickle person when he called down vengeance on himself if ever he had hidden even an involuntary fault, or had feared the multitude of the people so as not to confess it in the sight of all? His virtues had no point of contact with any vices, but stood firm on their own ground. Who, then, was so brave as holy Job? Can he be put second to any, on whose level hardly one like himself can be placed?"[10]

Saint Ambrose continues: "The three royal friends of Job declared him to be a sinner, because they saw that he, after being rich, became poor; that having many children, he had lost them all, and that he was now covered with sores and was full of welts, and was a mass of wounds from head to foot. But holy Job made this declaration to them, 'If I suffer thus because of my sins, why did the wicked live? They grow old also in riches, their seed is according to their pleasure, their houses are prosperous; but they have no fear; there is no scourge from the Lord on them [Job 21:7-9].' A fainthearted man, seeing this, is disturbed in mind, and turns his attention away from it."[11]

Elsewhere, Saint Ambrose remarks, "Job recognized that to be born is the beginning of all woes; and therefore, he wished that the day on which he was born might perish, so that the origin of all troubles might be removed, and wished that the day of his birth might perish that he might receive the day of resurrection."[12]

Saint John Chrysostom (ca. 347-407) adds here, "To Job, also, the reproaches of his friends appeared more grievous than the worms and the sores. For there is nothing, there is nothing more intolerable to those in affliction than

---

[8] Saint Cyprian, "The Treatises of Cyprian," The Ante-Nicene Fathers, Fathers of the Third Century, V:481.

[9] Saint Ambrose, "Duties of the Clergy," Nicene, 2nd Ser., X:19.

[10] Idem, Nicene, 2nd Ser., X:33.

[11] Ibid., Nicene, 2nd Ser., X:8.

[12] Ibid., "On the Belief in the Resurrection," Bk. II, Nicene, 2nd Ser., X:178.

a word capable of stinging the soul."[13] Saint Chrysostom also exhorts his congregation using the example left to us by the just Job: "Tell me," Saint John asks, "who conquered at the dunghill? Who was defeated? Job who was stripped of all, or the devil who stripped him of all? Evidently, it was the devil who stripped him of all. Whom do we admire for the victory, the devil that smote, or Job that was smitten? Clearly, Job. And yet he could neither retain his perishing wealth nor save his children. Why speak I of riches and children? He could not insure to himself bodily health. Yet nevertheless, this is the conqueror: he that lost all that he had. His riches indeed he could not keep; but his piety he kept with all strictness. 'But his children, when perishing, he could not help.'...Now had he not suffered ill and been wronged of the devil, he would not have gained that signal victory. Had it been an evil thing to suffer wrong, God would not have enjoined it upon us: for God enjoins not evil things. What, do you not know that He is the God of Glory? Do you not know that it could not be His will to encompass us with shame and ridicule and loss, but to introduce us to the contrary of these? Therefore, He commands us to suffer wrong. He does all to withdraw us from worldly things: to convince us what is glory and what is shame; what is loss and what is gain. 'But it is hard to suffer wrong and be spitefully entreated,' thou sayest. Nay, O man, it is not, it is not hard. How long will thy heart be fluttering about things present? For God, thou mayest be sure, would not have commanded this had it been hard. Just consider. The wrongdoer goes his way with the money, but with an evil conscience besides. The receiver of the wrong, defrauded indeed of some money, is enriched with confidence toward God; and this is an acquisition more valuable than countless treasures. Now it is no advantage that a man defeated in a trial endures it; for it becomes thenceforth a matter of necessity. What then is the splendid victory? When thou lookest down on it, when thou refusest to go to law."[14]

Saint Chrysostom then discusses Job's wife. "For when indeed the wife of Job speaks, a devil is at work. For of such sort the advice is."[15] Saint Chrysostom then addresses women who may have lost a child, and he asks, "Does not Job come into thy mind, O woman? Rememberest thou not his words at the misfortune of his children, which adorned that holy head more than ten thousand crowns, and made proclamation louder than many trumpets? Dost thou make no account of the greatness of his misfortunes, of that unprecedented shipwreck, and that strange and portentous tragedy? For thou hast possibly lost one, or a second, or third—but he so many sons and daughters: and he that had many children suddenly became childless. And not

---

[13] Saint Chrysostom, "Homily XII," *Second Corinthians*, Nicene, 1st Ser., XII:339.

[14] Ibid., "Hom. XVI," *First Corinthians*, Nicene, 1st Ser., XII:94, 95.

[15] Ibid., "Hom. IV," *Second Corinthians*, Nicene, 1st Ser., XII:292.

even by degrees were his bowels wasted away, but at one sweep all the fruit of his body was snatched from him. Nor was it by the common law of nature, when they had come to old age, but by a death both untimely and violent. Indeed, the children were dispatched all together, and when their father was not present nor sitting by them—that at least by hearing their last words he might have some consolation at so bitter an end as theirs. But contrary to all expectation and without his knowing anything of what took place, they were all at once overwhelmed and their house became their grave and their snare.

"And not only their untimely death, but many things besides these were to grieve Job: such as their being all in the flower of their age, all virtuous and loving. There was not one child of either sex remaining. They did not die natural deaths at a mature age. He was not aware if they had sinned in anything.... Now each of these circumstances is enough even by itself to disturb the mind. But when we find them even coinciding together, imagine the height of those waves, how great the excess of that storm! And what in particular is greater and worse than his bereavement, he did not even know why all these things happened. On this account then, having no cause to assign for the misfortune, he ascends to the good pleasure of God and says, 'The Lord gave, the Lord hath taken away: as it seemed good to the Lord, so hath it come to pass: blessed be the name of the Lord [Job 1:21].' And these things he said. Indeed, such a man as Job who had followed after all virtue in the last extremity. But, meantime, evil men and impostors were prospering, luxuriating, and reveling on all sides. And he uttered no such word as it is likely that the weaker sort would have uttered: 'Was it for this that I brought up my children and trained them with all exactness? For this did I open my house to all that passed by, that after those many courses run in behalf of the needy, the naked, the orphans, I might receive this recompense?' But instead of giving these complaints, he offered up those words better than all sacrifice, saying, 'I myself came forth naked from my mother's womb, and naked shall I return thither.' If, however, he rent his clothes and shaved his head, marvel not. For he was a father and a loving father. It was meet that both the compassion of his nature should be shown and the self-command of his spirit. Whereas, had he not done this, perhaps one would have thought this self-command to be of mere insensibility. He, therefore, indicates both his natural affection and the exactness of his piety; and in his grief he was not overthrown.

"Yea, and when his trial proceeded further, he is again adorned with other crowns on account of his reply to his wife, saying, 'If we have received good things of the hand of the Lord, shall we not endure evil things [Job 2:10]?' For in fact his wife was by this time the only one left. All else had been clean destroyed—both his children and his possessions and his very body. Only she was reserved to tempt and to ensnare him. And this indeed was the reason

Righteous Job

why the devil neither destroyed her with the children nor asked her death, because he expected that she would contribute much toward the ensnaring of that holy man. He, therefore, left her as a kind of implement, and a formidable one, for himself. 'For if even out of Paradise,' said he, 'I cast forth mankind by her means, much more shall I be able to trip him up on the dunghill.' And observe his craft. He did not apply this stratagem when the oxen or the asses or the camels were lost, nor even when the house fell and the children were buried under it. He suffers her to be silent and quiet. But when the fountain of worms on Job gushed forth, when his skin began to putrefy and drop off, and the flesh wasting away to emit most offensive discharge, then the enemy makes his move. Job had spent a long time in misery.[16] The enemy was preparing by wearing him out with pains sharper than gridirons and furnaces and any flame. He was consuming on every side and eating away Job's body more grievously than any wild beast. Then, after a long time, as I said, then he brings her to him, when he is seasoned and worn down. Whereas if she had approached him at the beginning of his misfortune, neither would she have found him so unnerved nor would she have had it in her power so to swell out and exaggerate the misfortune by her words. But now when she saw him through the length of time thirsting for release, and desiring the termination of what pressed on him vehemently, then does she come upon him. For to show that he was quite worn down, and by this time had become unable even to draw breath, yea, and desired even to die, hear what he says: 'For I know that death will destroy me; for the earth is the house appointed for every mortal. O then that I might lay hands upon myself, or at least ask another, and he should do this for me! Yet I wept over every helpless man; I groaned when I saw a man in distress [Job 30:23-25].'

"Notice, too, the wickedness of his wife. She asks, 'How long wilt thou hold out [Job 2:9]?' However, that we may see more clearly the engine which was brought against that adamantine wall, let us listen to the very words. 'How long wilt thou hold out?' says she. He replies, 'Behold, I wait yet a little while, expecting the hope of my deliverance [cf. Job 2:9]!' 'Nay,' says she, 'the time has exposed the folly of thy words, while it is protracted, yet shows

[16] The Greek compilers of *The Great Synaxaristes* (in Greek) tell us that Job was scourged for seven years.

no mode of escape.' And these things she said, not only thrusting him into desperation but also reproaching and jesting upon him. For he, ever consoling her as she pressed upon him, and putting her off, would speak as follows: 'Wait a little longer, and there will soon be an end of these things.' Reproaching him, therefore, she speaks: 'Wilt thou now again say the same thing? For a long time has now run by, and no end of these things has appeared.' And observe her malice, that she makes no mention of the oxen, the sheep or the camels, as knowing that he was not very much vexed about these; but she goes at once to nature, and reminds him of his children. For on their death she saw him both rending his clothes and shaving off his hair. And she said not 'thy children are dead' but very pathetically 'thy memorial is abolished from the earth [Job 2:9]'—the thing for which thy children were desirable. For if, even now after that the resurrection has been made known, children are longed for because they preserve the memory of the departed, much more in those days. 'But if thou,' says she, 'carest not for these, at least consider what is mine. The pains of my womb, and labors which I have endured in vain with sorrow [cf. Job 2:9].' Now what she means is this: 'I, who endured the more, am wronged for thy sake; and having undergone the toils, I am deprived of the fruits.'

"She also laments, 'I am a wanderer and a servant from place to place and house to house, waiting for the setting of the sun, that I may rest from my labors and my pangs which now beset me. But say some word against the Lord, and die [Job 2:9].' Perceivest thou here too her crafty wickedness? She first pitifully relates her misfortunes. Then having drawn out the tragedy at length, she couches in a few words what she would recommend. She does not even declare it plainly, but throws a shade over it. She then holds out to him the deliverance which he greatly longed for, and promises death, the thing which he then most of all desired. And mark from this also the malice of the devil: that because he knew the longing of Job toward God, he suffers not his wife to accuse God lest he should at once turn away from her as an enemy. For this cause she does not mention God, but the actual calamities she is continually harping on.

"What then did the blessed saint, firmer than adamant, do? Looking bitterly upon her by his aspect even before he spake, he repelled her devices. She, no doubt, expected to excite fountains of tears. But he, instead, became fiercer than a lion, full of wrath and indignation, not on account of his sufferings, but on account of her diabolical suggestions. He signified his anger by his looks. Then, in a subdued tone, he delivers his rebuke; for even in misfortune he kept his self-command. And what says he? 'Thou hast spoken like one of the foolish women [Job 2:10],' that is to say, 'I have not so taught thee. I did not so nurture thee. And this is why I do not now recognize even my own consort. For these words are the counsel of a foolish woman and of one beside herself.' Seest thou not here an instance of wounding in moderation, and inflicting a blow just sufficient to cure the disease? Then, after the infliction, he brings in advice sufficient on the other hand to console her, and very rational, thus speaking: 'If we have received good things of the hand of the Lord, shall we not endure evil things [Job 2:10]?'

"The words of this discourse let us engrave in our minds. Let us sketch upon our minds, as in a picture, the history of these sufferings: I mean the loss of wealth, the bereavement of children, the disease of body, the reproaches, the words of mocking, the devices of his wife, the snare of the devil—in a word, all the calamities of that righteous man. Let us provide ourselves with a most ample port of refuge: that, enduring all things nobly and thankfully, we may both in the present life cast off all despondency and receive the rewards that belong to this good way of taking things."[17]

Saint Chrysostom then discourses on Job's physical infirmities that could claim his life. He says, "And truly stouter than any armor is joy in God; and whosoever has it, nothing can ever make his head droop or his countenance sad, but he bears all things nobly. For what is worse to bear than fire? What is more painful than continual torture? Truly it is more overpowering in pain than the loss of untold wealth, of children, of anything; for, says he, 'Skin for skin, all that a man hath will he give as a ransom for his life [Job 2:4].' So nothing can be harder to bear than bodily pain; nevertheless, because of this joy in God, that which is intolerable even to hear of becomes both tolerable and longed for. And if thou shouldest take from the cross or from the gridiron the martyr yet just breathing, thou wilt find such a treasure of joy within him as admits not of being told."[18] In another discourse, Saint Chrysostom adds, "For this reason the blessed Job felt no severe suffering, when he heard of the death of his children all at once, because he loved God more than them. And whilst He Whom he loved was living, those things would not be able to afflict him."[19]

So, "Why then murmur? Because thou art poor? Yet think of Job. But thy child is dead? What then if thou hadst lost all thy children, and that by an evil fate, as he did? But there are some who revile thee? What then would be thy feelings if thy friends had come to administer consolation to thee, and they should speak like Job's friends? For, as it is, innumerable are our sins, and we deserve to be reproached; but in that case he who was true, just, godly, who kept himself from every evil deed, heard the contrary of those laid to his charge by his friends. Art thou afflicted with a disease? No disease you can name is worse than that of his, though you name ten thousand. It was so grievous that he could no longer be in the house and under a cover. Much rather, all men

[17] Saint Chrysostom, "Hom. XXVIII," *First Corinthians*, Nicene, 1st Ser., X:65-168.
[18] Idem, "Hom. I," *Second Corinthians*, Nicene, 1st Ser., XII:275.
[19] Idem, "Hom. VI," *First Thessalonians*, Nicene, 1st Ser., XIII:350.

gave him up. For if he had not been irrecoverably gone, he would never have taken his seat outside of the city. He was an object more pitiable than those afflicted with leprosy. For the diseased and lepers are both admitted into houses, and they do herd together. But Job was passing the night in the open air. He was naked upon a dunghill. Why? Because he could not even bear a garment upon his body. How so? Perhaps the chaffing and rubbing would only have been an addition to his pangs. For 'My body is covered with loathsome worms; and I waste away, scraping off clods of dust from my eruption [Job 7:5].' His flesh bred sores and worms in him, and that continually. Seest thou how each one of us sickens at the hearing of these things? But if they are intolerable to hear, is the sight of them more tolerable? And if the sight of them is intolerable, how much more intolerable to undergo them? And yet that righteous man did undergo them, not for two or three days, but for a long while; and he did not sin, not even with his lips. What disease can you describe to me like this, so exquisitely painful? For was not this worse than blindness? 'I perceive my food,' said Job, 'as the smell of a lion to be loathsome [Job 6:7].' And not only this, but that which affords cessation to others, night and sleep, brought no alleviation to him, nay, were worse than any torture. Hear Job's words: 'Thou scarest me with dreams, and dost terrify me with visions....Whenever I lie down, I say, "When will it be day?" And whenever I rise up, again I say, "When will it be evening?" And I am full of pains from evening to morning [Job 7:4].'

"And there was not only this; but reputation in the eyes of the world was added. For they, forthwith, concluded him to be guilty of endless crimes, judging from all that he suffered. And accordingly this is the consideration, which his friends urged saying to him that 'a just recompense of thy sins has come to thee from the Lord [Job 11:6].' Therefore, he himself said, 'But now the youngest have laughed me to scorn, now they reprove me in their turn, whose fathers I set at nought; whom I did not deem worthy to be with my shepherd dogs [Job 30:1].' And was not this worse than many deaths?

"Despite all, he remained unmoved in the storm, seated as it were in the midst of this surging flood, thus awful and overwhelming, as in a perfect calm. No murmur escaped him. He comported himself thus before the gift of grace, before anything was declared concerning a resurrection. Yet we—who hear both prophets and apostles and evangelists speaking to us, and who have innumerable examples set before us, and who have been taught the tidings of a resurrection—harbor discontent, though no man can say that such a lot as Job's has been his own. For if one has lost money, yet not all that great number of sons and daughters, or if he has, perchance it was that he had sinned; but for him, he lost them suddenly, in the midst of his sacrifices, in the midst of the service which he was rendering to God. And if any man has at one blow lost property to the same amount, which can never be, yet he has not had the further affliction of a sore all over his body, he has not scraped the humors that covered him; or if this likewise has been his lot, yet he has not had men to upbraid and reproach him, which is above all things calculated to wound the feelings, more than the calamities we suffer. For if when we have persons to cheer and console us in our misfortunes, and to hold out to us fair prospects, we yet despond, consider what it was to have men upbraiding him. If the words, 'And I waited for one that would grieve with me, but there was no one; and for them that would comfort me, but I found none [Ps. 68:20],' describe intolerable misery, how great an aggravation to find revilers instead of comforters! 'Poor comforters are ye all [Job 16:2],' he says to his visiting friends. If we did but revolve these subjects continually in our minds, if we weighed them well, no ills of this present time could ever have force to disturb our peace, when we turned our eyes to that athlete, that soul of adamant, that spirit impenetrable as brass. For as though he had borne about him a body of brass or stone, he met all events with a noble and constant spirit."[20]

Saint Kyril of Alexandria (378-444) praises Job, saying how he possessed the Holy Spirit, "This Spirit Job also had, that most enduring man."[21] Saint Andrew of Crete puts to melody the following words that the faithful may chant and be edified: "Thou hast heard, O my soul, of Job justified on a dunghill, but thou hast not emulated his fortitude [Job 1]. In all thine experiences and trials and temptations, thou hast not kept firmly to thy purpose but has proved inconstant."[22] And, "If he who was righteous and blameless above all men did not escape the snares and pits of the deceiver, what wilt thou do, wretched and sin-loving soul, when some sudden misfortune befalls thee [Job 2:3-6]?"[23]

Let us close with the counsel of Saint Basil, who speaks on detachment from worldly goods. This homily was prompted when a devastating fire had occurred in the neighborhood of the church. "Recall to your minds the patience of Job. No one should be led by his sufferings to think or to say that no providence rules our affairs. Nor should any man cast aspersion upon the government and decree of providence ruling our affairs. Nor should any man cast aspersion upon the government and decree of the Lord. Let him contemplate the athlete just mentioned and provide himself with an adviser of wiser

---

[20] Ibid., "Hom. VIII," *Philippians*, Nicene, 1st Ser., XIII:222.

[21] Saint Cyril of Jerusalem, "Lecture XVI," *Catechetical Lectures*, Nicene, 2nd Ser., VII:122.

[22] *Triodion*, Tuesday in the First Week, Great Compline, Ode Four, Tone Plagal Two, by Saint Andrew of Crete.

[23] *Triodion*, Thursday in the First Week, Great Compline, Ode Four, Tone Plagal Two, by Saint Andrew of Crete.

counsel. Let him review in his mind all the trials, one after another, in which Job distinguished himself and reflect that, for all the many shafts aimed at him by the devil, he did not receive a mortal blow. The devil took from him his domestic prosperity and planned to overwhelm him with reports of disasters, following closely upon one another. While the first messenger was announcing a heavy misfortune, another came, bringing news of more serious calamities. Evils were linked, one with another, and the catastrophes were like onrushing waves. Before the first lamentation had ceased, cause for another was at hand. That just man, however, stood firm as a rock, receiving the blasts of the tempest and reducing to foam the dash of the waves....He deemed worthy of tears none of the evils which were befalling him. But, when one came to report that, while his sons and daughters were feasting, a violent wind had blown down the chamber where the merrymaking was going on, he rent his garments, showing his natural sympathy and proving by the action that he was a father who loved his children. But even at that moment he set a limit and measure to his grief. And he graced with words of piety the misfortune that had occurred, saying that 'the Lord gave, the Lord hath taken away; as it hath pleased the Lord, so also is it done [cf. Job 1:21].' It was as if he were crying out: I was called a father for as long a time as He Who made me wished it. He willed, in turn, to take from me the crown of offspring. I do not resist Him in what belongs to Him. May that which seems good to the Lord prevail! He is the Maker of my children; I am His instrument. Why should I, a servant, give way to useless mourning and bitter complaints against a decree which I am powerless to avoid? With such words did this just man shoot down the devil. But, when the enemy saw that Job was winning the victory and that he could not be shaken by any of these disasters, he brought up another siege machine: temptations of the flesh. He flayed his body with unspeakable afflictions and made it exude streams of worms. From a kingly throne, he brought him down to a seat on a dunghill. Yet, although he was buffeted there by the woes I have just mentioned, he remained steadfast. His body was lacerated, but he kept inviolate in the depths of his soul the treasure of piety.

"The enemy, having now no further recourse and bethinking himself of an ancient device of treachery, seduced the mind of Job's wife with an impious and blasphemous notion whereby she hoped to shake the athlete's resolution. She stood beside that just man, haranguing him at great length. She prostrated herself and struck her hands together at what she saw, casting revilements at him for the rewards his piety had brought, recounting the ancient prosperity of their house, calling attention to his present misfortunes, the state to which he was reduced, and the fine reward he had received from the Lord for his many sacrifices. On and on she spoke, expressing sentiments worthy of this woman's cowardly heart; yet such sentiments are capable of disturbing any man and of subverting even a noble mind. She added that it would be a better and more beneficial thing for him to destroy himself utterly and to blaspheme, thus sharpening the sword of the Creator's wrath, rather than that he prolong the labor of the struggle for himself and for her by persevering in the patient endurance of his misfortunes. Grieved by her words as by none of the evils that had previously afflicted him, he turned to his wife a countenance full of wrath. And what are his words? 'Why hast thou spoken like one of the foolish women?' He says in effect, 'Repudiate, woman, this counsel. How long wilt thou desecrate our life together by thy words! Thou didst speak falsely—may God avert the evil!—of the way of life which was mine and thou didst plot against my life. Now I think that half of myself has committed an impious act, since marriage has made us twain one body and thou hast committed blasphemy. If we have received good things at the hand of the Lord, shall we not receive evil? Recall to thy mind our past blessings. Weigh our prosperity in the balance with these adversities. For no man's life is altogether happy. To prosper in all things belongs to God alone. But, if thou art made sorrowful by our present circumstances, console thyself by remembering the past....If we have received good things at the hand of the Lord, should we not receive evil? Do we compel our Judge to provide us always with the same abundance? Do we teach the Lord how He ought to arrange our life? He Himself holds the authority over His own decrees. He directs our affairs as He wills. But He is wise, and He metes out that which is profitable to His servants. Do not curiously examine the Lord's decrees; only love the dispensations of His wisdom. Whatever He may bestow upon thee, receive it with gladness. In adversity prove that thou art worthy of the joy that was previously thine.'

"Thus, Job repulsed the devil's attack and brought upon Satan the disgrace of total defeat. What happened then? His malady left him as if it had visited him to no avail and had gained no advantage. His flesh regained the health of a second youth. His life prospered again with all good things and doubled riches flowed in from all sides upon his house. One-half consisted of his former wealth, as if he had lost nothing, and the other half represented the reward of patience which is bestowed upon a just man. But why did he receive in double measure houses, mules, camels, sheep, fields, and all the accouterments of wealth, while the number of children born to him remained equal to those who had died? It was because brute beasts and riches of all kinds are completely destroyed when they perish. Children, on the other hand, even if they are dead, live on in the best part of their nature. Therefore, when he was favored by the Creator with other sons and daughters, he possessed this portion of his goods also in double measure—one family abiding with him to give joy to their parents, the other children gone before to await their father. All of them will stand about Job when the Judge of human life will gather together the universal Church, when the trumpet, which is to announce the coming of the King, calls loudly to the tombs and demands the bodies which have been entrusted to their charge. Then, they who now appear to be dead will take their place before the Maker of the whole world more quickly than will the living. For this reason, I think, the Lord allotted to Job a double portion of his other wealth, but judged that he would be satisfied with the same number of children as before. Do you see how many blessings the just Job reaped from his patience? Therefore, you, too, bear patiently any harm enkindled by a demon's treachery. Alleviate your feelings of distress over your misfortune with more courageous thoughts, in accordance with the words of the Scripture: 'Cast thy care upon the Lord, and He will nourish thee [Ps. 54:25].' To Him is due glory everlasting. Amen."[24]

We read in the Septuagint that "Job lived after his affliction a hundred and seventy years. And all the years he lived were two hundred and forty. And Job saw his sons and his sons' sons, the fourth generation [Job 42:16]."

And, "Sickness and health, riches and poverty, are become the glory of thy life, O blessed Job; for through all things thou art shown to be illustrious."[25]

On the 6th of May, the holy Church commemorates the venerable Fathers MAMAS, PACHOMIOS, and HILARION, who reposed in peace.

On the 6th of May, the holy Church commemorates the holy Martyr DEMETRION, who was shot with arrows.

On the 6th of May, the holy Church commemorates the holy Martyrs DANAX, MESIROS, and THERINOS, who were slain by the sword.

On the 6th of May, the holy Church commemorates the holy Martyr DONATOS, who was shot with arrows.

On the 6th of May, the holy Church commemorates the holy Martyr BARBAROS, who was slain by the sword.

---

[24] Saint Basil, "Hom. 21, On Detachment from Worldly Goods and Concerning the Conflagration Which Occurred in the Environs of the Church," *Ascetical Works*, FC, 9:501-505.

[25] May 6th, Orthros Canon, Ode Eight, Mode Four.

On the 6th of May, the holy Church commemorates the SYNAXIS of the aforesaid Saints in their Martyrium, situated in the Defteros Quarter.

On the 6th of May, the holy Church commemorates our venerable and God-bearing Father SERAPHIM, who struggled in asceticism on Mount Dombou of Levadeia.[26]

Seraphim, our righteous and God-bearing father, is calling us together, O Christ-loving people of the feast, to a radiant and joyous festival on this spring day. It is a time when life is brought back and renewed and when the sweet singing of the birds and the fragrance of the flowers gladden man. The Lord has appointed this bright time of spring and nature in its beauty, that the memorial of the saint whom we celebrate today may further adorn the season's splendor. This is the feast day of our venerable and God-bearing Father Seraphim, who arose as a brilliant star over the land of Greece. He has shone forth in both virtue and miracles, even during the gloomy days of enslavement.

Our holy and God-inspired father, Seraphim, conspicuous among the ascetics and glorified by wonderworkings, had as his homeland present-day Zeli, a small village in the district of Talantios of Voeotia in central Greece. It was during the sixteenth century that he became the offspring of pious and virtuous parents. While just a babe in his swaddling clothes, a certain phenomenon took place which very clearly indicated the saint's future advancement and contribution in things spiritual. It portended that he was to be an elect vessel and receptacle of the All-Holy Spirit. Indeed, while he was yet an infant—and for this reason could discern neither the day from the night nor the good from the evil—still the Holy Spirit, Who foreknew Seraphim's future spiritual ascents, enlightened and taught the babe. How was this revealed? When the day was either Wednesday or Friday, that is, the days of our Lord's Passion, which we should hold in esteem by abstaining from foods, the infant, during those two days of the week, remained in a state of fasting. He would not take milk from his mother, as she herself was telling the neighbors. Only during the time when the sun was setting, when the infant was no longer able to endure an empty stomach, he would nurse a little and then fall asleep.

---

[26] The Life and divine office of Saint Seraphim was composed by the then hierarch of Talantios, and later Metropolitan of Athens, Neophytos Metaxas, which were published at Aegina (1828) and at Athens (1855 and 1885). The Life presented in *The Great Synaxaristes* (in Greek) was incorporated from this source and revised and edited. The English translation herein is added to this Greek version. Additional notes were added to the translation, to aid and benefit English-speaking readers. The sections on the saint's miracles, those performed before and after his repose, were also chronologically placed in the English version.

When the holy child reached the age of seven, it is probable that his parents gave him over to the village parish priest that he might be taught the sacred letters. The lad, as a lover of learning and a proper child, being that he was good natured and very diligent, felt great thirst for the holy writings. With much zeal, he studied and learned those lessons assigned by the teacher. Who is able to aptly report the holy boy's attention and propriety in the classroom? Who can characterize his decorum toward his peers? Who can describe his extreme humility and unquestioning submission to his parents? How should one speak of the boy's modesty and exemplary behavior, for which not much time passed for the other villagers to take notice? In fact, all the inhabitants were saying that the holy boy was a model and pattern of upright conduct and decency. They, therefore, urged the other young people to have him as a model of emulation.

Saint Seraphim

As the saint advanced in years, so much more did his zeal increase for the holy writings. Hence, as an untiring honeybee, he took delight in the flower-laden meadow of the sacred Scriptures. He read the words with spiritual pleasure and joy inexpressible. Even as a magnet attracts iron, he also would not let himself be drawn away from such a sweet and life-bearing repast so as to turn aside to the cares and concerns of this life. Consequently, though he was young in years, he had no other enjoyment save one: to meditate upon how he might take himself away, that is, from the world, and serve unencumbered our Creator and Fashioner. For thereby he wished to imitate the seraphim and the choirs of the righteous, so he might be numbered with those who have attained everlasting blessedness.

The righteous youth, therefore, having conducted himself in a God-pleasing matter and mindful of our purpose here on earth, while still young, zealously read the lives of the saints. Finally, he decided it was time to have done with it all and go to the monastery, after forsaking parents, country, kinfolk, and friends. In that sacred place, where he would be clothed in the monastic Schema, he could dedicate himself, both soul and body, to God. In that manner, he thought to quench the spiritual thirst that he was sensing. He, therefore, on one of those days, went to his much-loved parents and kissed their right hands. He then began to ask them for their blessing, beseeching them with tears, that they might give their consent. He asked that their prayers and blessings might accompany him on his new course, the monastic one, which he had loved from his youth. He then said that he had promised God that he would pass his life in monasticism.

His parents, godly and moral people, when they heard the words of their beloved son, they, on the one hand, rejoiced on account of their son's fervent piety and his perfect dedication to Christ, but, on the other hand, they were exceedingly sorrowful. Why? The words of their child seemed to them as death-bearing darts that passed through their hearts. Previous to this, their hearts had been filled with joy over their son. They deemed his departure from them to be no small loss. The emptiness resulting from his absence was too great for them to bear. They were not only grieving at his leaving but also commiserating with all the villagers. They were wont to say that the man's manner of life, for all of them, was an excellent example of virtue and duty.

Such were the ruminations of the parents. They attempted to dissuade him from this decision, by the use of words full of emotion. They were speaking to him with tear-filled eyes and faltering voices, saying, "Child, if thou shouldest betake thyself to a monastery, what comfort shall we have in this world? Who shall be a staff to our old age? Who shall lighten the bitterness of this life, if not thee, and especially during these wicked days of our bitter enslavement to the alien Hagarene? By thy manner of life and thine excellent conduct toward us and all, O most longed-for and beloved child, thou hast become our comfort. Who then shall replace thy gentle disposition? If not thee, who shall refresh our wounded hearts with the sweet balm of consolation? If thou shouldest leave us now and depart for the monastery, according to thy desire, thou wilt be abandoning thine elderly and ailing parents. To whom then shall we look and to whom shall we expect to receive help? Do not decide, child, to leave us desolate in this world. But rather, remain here by us until thou shouldest surrender us to the earth. Then thou mayest go to the monasteries or to the deserts in order to find that quietude and rest in the Lord Whom thou dost desire."

Such were the utterances, amid copious tears, of the righteous youth's parents. They paused to measure the effect of their words, gazing at him longingly as they waited anxiously to receive his assent. As a solid diamond of virtue, the young man Soterios (Salvatore)—for that was what he was called at that time—remained firm in his resolve. He could not help but cast a sympathetic eye with filial love upon his weeping and grief-stricken parents. Indeed, his sensitive heart was shivered to pieces. He, nevertheless, maintained an unaltered decision. He hearkened more to the divine call, which was inviting him to the stadium of struggles. Indeed, for him the first contest already had begun: complete renunciation of kin rather than succumbing to his parents' voices that excited tender feelings. What then did he do? He threw himself into their arms and embraced them. He kissed their right hands and departed. He repaired to the small Monastery of Prophet Elias. It was situated on Mount Karkara, at a distance of one hour from the village.

Near this mountain, the venerable young man raised up a small chapel. He dedicated it to the name of our Savior. He also constructed a small cell within a certain cave found there. The remnants of these structures may be seen until this day. The natives of the surrounding villages call this place Saint Seraphim's Hermitage. Close to this precinct there is another church, named in honor of our most holy Lady Theotokos. There are also cells in the vicinity which, according to the elderly folks of that place, were later built by the inhabitants of Elateia during a plague. The Elateians, fleeing from this peril, took refuge in the church and sought the protection of the Theotokos and the help of Saint Seraphim. It was in that place, as in the cave mentioned earlier, that the saint had spent considerable time. He struggled with keeping vigil and saying prayers, as a good worker in the mystical vineyard of the Lord and a genuine friend of our Master Christ. However, since his spiritual quietude was disturbed by the frequent visits of his parents, relatives, and friends, he abandoned his agreeable cave. He took himself away to the sacred Monastery of the Holy Unmercenaries, nearby Talantios. But even here, he was again troubled by the regular visits of his kin. He was not able to remain there for more than six months.

He, thereupon, left that place and went seeking a desolate spot, as another turtledove that is a lover of wilderness habitats. He arrived at Mount Sagmata. At the summit there was a monastery, honoring the Transfiguration of the Savior. The monastery was lying between Thevai and Evia. It should be noted that this monastic establishment possessed a large portion of the precious and life-giving Cross, upon which the Savior of mankind commended His spirit into the hands of His Father.[27] This relic was donated to the monastery by the pious autocrat Alexios Komnenos,[28] by an imperial chrysobull, so that the monks struggling within that monastery might have the heavenly treasure as help and protection in their run on the course of their ascetical life.

It was to this monastery that Christ's most faithful servant resorted. He enlisted in that angelic choir of ascetics, who were famed for their virtue and discipline of austerity. He gave himself over entirely into the arms of that much-desired life of self-denial, even as a thirsty deer that had sought so many

[27] Lk. 23:46.

[28] The relic of the true Cross had been treasured in the Great Palace at the time of Emperor Alexios I Komnenos of Constantinople (1081-1118). He had given a portion to Henry IV, when he sought the western emperor's alliance against the Normans. In 1097, Alexios made the leaders of the First Crusade swear upon the relic that they would cede to Byzantium the cities and strongholds that they took in the east. Seven years later, Alexios presented a large fragment to the Transfiguration Monastery on Mount Sagmata in Voeotia, a gift that may have signaled recognition of the region's renewed significance for the imperial fisc (treasury).

places to quench a burning thirst. Who is able to narrate the toils he undertook and his striving after spiritual things? Who can describe how he, both night and day, was struggling in fasts, vigils, prayers, and tears? Who can speak of his unlimited obedience toward all or his patience in afflictions and tribulations or his complete dedication to spiritual cultivation? Therefore, in but a short time, because of his virtues, the humble-minded and meek saint surpassed all his fellow ascetics in virtue and spiritual exercises. For this reason, even as a radiant star is distinguished in the midst of lesser lights, in this case that spiritual choir of ascetics, all of them were illumined by the rays of his virtues; and so they set the rhythm to their spiritual conduct of life after his example.

The abbot—viewing the excellence and spiritual progress of the venerable young man, and perceiving distinctly those ascetical contributions and labors that were to follow—tonsured Soterios and renamed him Seraphim. Not much time passed before the abbot had Father Seraphim ordained to the diaconate. The humble Seraphim, with regard to accepting this dignity, yielded only after great persistence by the others, that is, the entreaties of the abbot and the other fathers. The brethren foresaw how Father Seraphim was to become a chosen vessel of the All-Holy Spirit and a guide to the erring. Thus, according to the word of the evangelist, "They do not light a lamp and put it under the bushel, but upon the lampstand, and it giveth light to all those in the house [cf. Mt. 5:15]." Therefore, after much pleading and persuasion, he accepted also the rank of the priesthood.

Upon being raised to the lofty rank of the priesthood, the righteous Seraphim reckoned it a grave responsibility that he had assumed before God and man. As one humble in spirit and simple in heart, he took into account his spiritual powers and found that he was wanting in meeting the needs of the Church. He, consequently, engaged in great labors. He performed very many vigils and prayers that he might attain to that measure of perfection by which his life would be commensurate with the considerable obligations which that office imposed on him. The God-inspired man remained at this Monastery of the Savior's Transfiguration for ten full years. During this period, he strived in the spiritual contest of virtue. He became a type and outline of emulation for his fellow strugglers. In like manner, he learned from them those counsels that are beneficial and soul-saving.

He, at length, was looking to avoid the acclaim that his virtues excited, since his reputation kept spreading. In his desire to shun the praise which men were showering upon him, he, thereupon, asked and received permission of the hegumen to depart the monastery. He bade farewell to his fellow ascetics, as well as the Spirit-bearing Germanos, a co-struggler of Saint Clement. The latter lived an eremitical life, striving after perfection, on Mount Sagmata. Father Seraphim had received from that venerable elder an abundance of teachings on salvation. Seraphim then went forth from the monastery, hastening to find solitude conducive to spiritual endeavors. After he had traversed for a long while on the road and crossed not a few mountains, he arrived at a place called Dombou (Dombos or Domvou), on the west side of Mount Elikon (Helikon),[29] about one hour above ancient Voulos situated on a hill. In this place, Seraphim built a small chapel to the name of the Savior and participated wholeheartedly in the labors of reclusion. Some cells were put up by those few monks who had gathered. Seraphim remained in that place for about ten years, practising the works of virtue and teaching his disciples the salutary instructions of the monastic conduct of life. The venerable man was tireless in his ascetic labors. He was like another Anthony of the Libyan desert, completely enveloping himself in the angelic life. Many lost souls were guided by him to the fair haven of salvation.

Close to the hermitage of the saint, about a quarter of an hour's distance in a northeasterly direction, at a place where the monastery is situated today, there were a few families of Albanian descent. These people were harsh and wild in their manners and customs. They lived by thievery and were a cause of alarm to all the inhabitants of the neighborhood. Seraphim took the initiative and went to speak with them. He instructed them with fruit-bearing words. He converted their harshness and wildness into gentleness. He persuaded them to repent of their former fierce and cruel life-style. Before the saint entered their lives, these savage Albanians had weapons and knives. By use of this arsenal, they were exacting their food. Hence, they were robbing and threatening murder and ill-treatment. But as soon as they heard the soul-saving counsels of the venerable Seraphim, they forsook their weapons. One by one they took up either the ax, or the plow, or some other bread-winning tool of honest work and toiled to sustain themselves. Many Christians from different quarters heard of the good reputation of the saint, so they called upon him to receive assistance. By Father Seraphim's prayers to God and his tear-filled invocations for divine succor, he healed both their spiritual and bodily infirmities.

The great multitude, however, of those coming to him daily, by reason of the saint's show of sympathy upon the infirm, troubled his quietude. These

---

[29] Elikon (38°18′N 22°53′E), a mountain of Voeotia that is also known as Zagaras or Mount of the Nymphs (ancient) or Paliovouna (mountaintop name), reaches an altitude of 1,748 meters. Elikon Mountain is southwest of the village of Hagia Anna, just southwest of Hagios Georgios, a small town of the municipality of Koronia, which belongs to the province of Levadeia (Livadeia), of the prefecture of Voeotia, of the region known as Sterea Hellas. Elikon has a number of peaks, apart from Paliovouna. There is Tsiveri (1,561 meters), Megali Loutsa (1,549 m.), Koliedes (1,487 m.), Xerovouni (1,182 m.), Prophetis Elias (1,091 m.), and Xero Vouno (1,077 m.).

visits, naturally, hindered his spiritual calm and stillness. These continual interruptions also prevented him from praying unceasingly and pursuing his spiritual contests. The righteous man sorrowed exceedingly at this disruption. For this very cause, he left his disciples in that small monastery where he had been dwelling for some ten years. Father Seraphim went to the northwest side of Elikon, which is about two hours distant from his former small monastery. It was his hope that he might find in that place much longed-for spiritual rest. This spot is now called the Kellion of Saint Seraphim.

On this isolated peak, Father Seraphim persevered as another Elias the Thesbite. When his soul had been purified, he heard a voice. It was that of our Lord Jesus Christ, Who was calling him to leave that peak and descend to the plain; and there he was to build a monastery. This sacred precinct was to be employed as another verdant oasis in the wilderness of Jordan. Hence, pious Christians, taking flight from the confusion and disorder of the world, could resort there for the salvation of their souls. Indeed, when Seraphim heard the voice of the Lord, he, straightway, came down from the peak. After he had gathered together some of his disciples, which he had left behind, he brought in builders and craftsmen. He, thereupon, began the construction of the monastery. The site, nonetheless, was unsuitable for the monks who later gathered. It was a wild place where there was little sunshine.

While the saint, by all means, was coordinating all the forces needed to complete the work, there appeared to him the most holy Theotokos. She commanded him to abandon any further building on that monastery structure. She told him it would prove unacceptable for those who were to come later. She ordered him to erect another structure in a place where the village of Dombou is situated. He fulfilled the command of the most holy Theotokos, by going to the inhabitants of the village of Dombou. He announced to them what he had been commanded by our Lady. He persuaded them to leave their huts and settle in another place. He, of course, paid them the equal worth of their private properties.

After the sale of the land from the people of Dombou, Seraphim went to Constantinople. He received a document from the œcumenical patriarchate, granting him permission to build the monastery. This document is preserved to this day in the monastery archives. Seraphim returned and began to build the church and monastery, now a patriarchal monastery or *stavropegion*.[30] The

---

[30] The term *stavropegion*, in a liturgical context, describes a site whereon a cross was fixed by a bishop for a new church. It was used chiefly to distinguish patriarchal monasteries. This meant that the monastery of Saint Seraphim was independent of the bishopric of Thevai (Thiva, Thebes) and Levadeia (Livadia). As a monastery founded by the patriarch, it was considered *stravropegial*. This means the monastery

(continued...)

monastery was named in honor of our Savior, even as the most holy Theotokos had bidden him. But the hater-of-good, the devil, employed machinations to bring to nought this God-pleasing work. He sowed darnel in the hearts of certain men; and they, in turn, yielded to the demon at work upon them. They became the instruments of the envious and malicious devil. Impelled by demonic complicity, they slandered the holy man as a fraud and deceiver. They went as far as to denounce the man of God to the Hagarene governor of Levadeia.[31] The saint's detractors said, "There is a certain unscrupulous monk who, by his scheming words, has persuaded the easily put-upon people of Dombou to alienate themselves from their homes and lands in return for the most paltry monetary recompense."

Upon hearing this accusation, the governor of Levadeia became extremely angry against Father Seraphim. He dispatched three Turkish soldiers to lead him bound to Levadeia, where he would be subjected to a fitting punishment. As the soldiers reached the place where the saint was working, they began to insult and abuse him with coarse words. One of the soldiers delivered such a fierce blow to Father Seraphim's head that the saint fell down half-dead. He suffered a skull fracture, the evidence of which may be seen today on the precious relic of his head. When the saint regained a little consciousness, they tied him and led him to Levadeia. As they were traveling on the road, the soldiers became thirsty. But they could find no water to drink, because the place was dry. They came to a place called Pamplouki, which is about one hour's distance from their point of departure, where they set upon the saint again. They threatened to slay him because, as they claimed, "It is on thine account that we are suffering thirst and toils. And we are in peril of dying in this dry wilderness."

Although the saint was sore stricken from both the blow to the head and the maltreatment, which resulted in his feeling sharp pains from the wound site, still he was moved to take compassion upon the soldiers. Indeed, he bore no

---

[30](...continued)
acknowledged the jurisdiction of the patriarch, commemorated him in the diptychs, and paid him the *kanonikon* (ecclesiastical tax).

[31] Thevai (38°19′N 23°19′E) of Voeotia (Central Greece) is eighty-four kilometers, or fifty-three miles by motorway, northwest of Athens. Levadeia (38°26′N 22°53′E), the capital of Voeotia, on the Delphi road, is forty-five kilometers northwest of Thevai. Vagia lies just southwest of Thevai. The Monastery of Hosios Seraphim at Dombou of Levadeia is thirty-two kilometers from Vagia. During the time of Saint Seraphim, Thevai was referred to as "a charming and healthy city producing an abundance of food." Levadeia was described as a bustling commercial center, "producing much that was useful to man." A. E. Vacalopoulos, *The Greek Nation: 1453-1669* (NJ: Rutgers University Press, 1976), p. 229.

remembrance of the wrong he suffered and was not resentful at their cruelty and inhumanity. Instead, he imitated our Savior Who, from His Cross, was praying for His crucifiers.[32] He requested leave from the arresting officers that he might pray to God Who was able to quench their thirst. Since his humility disarmed them, the parched Turks gave him their permission and loosed him from his bonds. Father Seraphim went to his knees and prayed to the Lord that He would demonstrate His divine might by bringing forth water from that arid spot, even as water once gushed forth from that barren and hard rock of Sinai, to the glory of His divine name.[33] Seraphim added, "Provide this consolation, O Lord, for Thy slave who suffers for Jesus' sake." After his prayer, he took his staff and struck the place where he had spilled a fountain of tears during his prayer. Then—O the wonder!—straightway, sweet and clear water sprang forth which, to this very day, continues to flow. It is available for all travelers to satisfy their thirst and glorify God, since it brings to mind this extraordinary wonder which was wrought by the prayer of Jesus' slave who was suffering ill from the aliens.

When the Turkish soldiers had drunk of the water and satiated their thirst, they continued on their way. At this juncture, they showed respect to the saint and even contrition for all the bad treatment they inflicted upon him. They now understood, by reason of the performance of this miracle, that the accused was not guilty of the charges alleged by his calumniators. A greater realization of this was made apparent to them by the following incident. As they were traversing, there flew by some wild doves. The Turkish soldiers attempted to fell some of the creatures. Despite the fact that they fired plenty of shots, they were unable to hit even one bird. At that point, Father Seraphim said, "Hold your fire!" He then said composedly that he would be able to offer them the doves live. Indeed, after Father Seraphim sent up prayer, he extended his hands and three doves flew down and alighted upon them. Thus, Father Seraphim gave one bird to each Turkish soldier. Beholding this miracle, the soldiers were astonished. They acknowledged among themselves how they had quite mistaken him. They, therefore, said to the man of God, "Thou art free to go about thy work. Do whatsoever thou dost wish and whatsoever God should command thee."

The Turks, then, followed the road that took them to Levadeia. As for Saint Seraphim, he returned to his monastery. He found his disciples in deep and inconsolable grief, on the taking away of their teacher and protector. The saint encouraged them, saying, "It is the will of God that the work on the monastery should be completed." At the same time, he urged them to give glory to God Who never abandons His faithful servants. He does not permit

[32] Lk. 23:34.

[33] Ex. 17:6; Num. 20:11; Ps. 113:8.

them to become the prey to the intrigues of evil men and the despotic madness of the mighty. God, much rather, preserves His servants even during the most critical times. As the venerable Seraphim was speaking to his disciples, he added the following: "Therefore, my children, it is necessary for us to labor resolutely and not shrink from the task before us, that we may come to the end of the work which we have commenced with divine condescension." In very truth, within a short time, the labor was finished.

The swift-winged renown of the saint's virtues spread abroad to every place under the sun. From many parts, numerous laborers of the mystical vineyard of the Lord collected. Thus, that rough and unfruitful wilderness of Dombou, formerly inhabited by rustic and harsh Albanians, now became a place of learning and melody, abounding in good and valorous men. Forthwith, as soon as the monastery had been established, men of virtue and learning congregated from all quarters. Nor was their assembling together by chance, as their talents were neither small nor ordinary. This has been demonstrated by their excellent monastic writings, of which portions of these works are preserved on parchment and paper, testifying to the worth of those men of excellence and virtue.

Such were the individuals who hastened to the monastery of Saint Seraphim, desiring the monastic life and training in spiritual contests. But the original structure proved inadequate to accommodate the number of desert-loving disciples who were arriving at all hours. As a result of the influx of disciples—many of whom were good and serious men devoted to letters and faithful servants of asceticism—they were unable to satisfy their spiritual needs. They, therefore, departed from the monastery and settled in the nearby wilderness, partaking of the isolation for which they yearned. They spent their lives in that place at their own *kathisma*, which is a small monastic habitation that houses only a few monks dependent on a larger monastery. They were occupied with their writings and keeping strictly all the rules of the monastic life. In these circumstances, the prophetic words of the great-voiced Esaias may be recited: "Rejoice, thou barren that bearest not! Break forth and cry, thou that dost not travail; for more are the children of the desolate than of her that has a husband [Is. 54:1]."

After the passage of three years from the completion of the work on the monastery, the time came when Saint Seraphim, this colonizer of the desert and teacher of the monastic discipline, was about to forsake this world and depart to the heavenly homeland. Once there, he would receive from God, the Bestower of recompenses, the reward of his labors which he undertook while on earth, to the glory of Christ's name. Foreseeing the hour of the end of his earthly sojourn, he called to himself his well-beloved disciples. With a tone most sweet and joyous, he said to them, "O lovesome children, the time of my earthly life has come to an end. As much as I was able, I fought the fight[34] which the Lord laid upon me. Therefore, all that remains is for me to die. Cease grieving, children dear to my heart, because I am leaving you. Much rather, rejoice and be glad! Why? Because we completed the work which shall abide on earth, to the glory of the name of God the Most High. Be not forgetful, children most loved, of the teachings which you have learned from me, the weak one; and never abandon the spiritual struggle of asceticism, inasmuch as by this means alone, as a kind of map giving him directions, a man may sail over the sea of life that swells with manifold waves, and arrive in the much-desired celestial harbor of everlasting life.[35] Children, most precious, prayer is that most sweet converse with the heavenly King, which issues in spiritual nourishment for the soul and whereby the gate of the heavenly kingdom is opened. Do not, therefore, my darling children, lose remembrance of prayer lest you should be deprived of that most sweet converse with God. For the abandonment of prayer is the spiritual death of the soul. Most beloved sons, let not earthly cares consume your souls or the fatal infirmity of pride overtake you, for this is proper to Lucifer; instead, be always humble-minded and inclined to be governed by few, imitating in this our Savior Who had nowhere that He might lay His head[36] and humbled Himself and became obedient even to death—indeed, the death of a cross.[37] Yet one more command I give to you, O amiable children, and I beseech you to fulfill it: when my soul exits my body, take my body and bury it at the old monastery, where the most holy Theotokos revealed herself. I also prefer that the place of my burial should remain unknown. With this arrangement, the confluence of visitors may be avoided."

After Saint Seraphim spoke these words, he sent up the final prayer. As he prayed, he departed to our God and Fashioner, Whom he longed for since infancy and Whom he had followed in self-renunciation. Taking upon his shoulders the cross of the Lord, he had walked the narrow and afflicted path, which the Lord had shown to those who love Him. After the repose of the saint, his disciples reverently and tearfully took up his worn out and wearied body in the pursuits of asceticism, and laid it to rest in the place where the saint had indicated while alive. Thus, he wished to fulfill that divine resolution of the Lord Who said, "For earth thou art, and unto earth shalt thou return [Gen. 3:19]." The brotherhood put a monk under a command to keep guard for two

---

[34] Cf. 2 Tim. 4:7.

[35] "Asceticism is the mother of saintliness; from it is born the taste of the first apperception of the divine and it is called the first period of spiritual knowledge." Saint Isaac the Syrian, "Treatise XXXIV," *Mystical Treatises by Isaac of Nineveh*, translated from Bedjan's Syriac text, by Arent Jan Wensinck, Volume One, p. 149.

[36] Mt. 8:20; Lk. 9:58.

[37] Phil. 2:8.

whole years this divine treasure lest it should be seized by sacrilegious hands. For this cause also, the recovery of the saint's sacred relics took place quickly. Indeed, though the saint's body was found beneath the earth, God did not leave off giving witness to His slave. Therefore, even as in this present life the Lord granted Saint Seraphim wonderworking grace, so also was he vouchsafed this grace for the two-year period when his body was resting in the earth. An extramundane light from heaven descended and illumined the tomb, thereby openly declaring the saint's boldness before God. This divine light also guided many pious Christians who came to the grave and fell to their knees before it in tears, invoking the saint to bestow help and assistance.

Again, after the passage of two years, the precious relics of Saint Seraphim were recovered upon their exhumation from the earth. The relics, as though they were the most fragrant roses and lilies, were transferred reverently to the old monastery. They were placed inside the sacred church, in a special place, where they are kept presently. They are preserved as a sacred heirloom and gratis treasure of the monastery, which the saint himself founded after multifarious toils and sufferings, to the glory of God and the spiritual benefit of the Christians. Saint Seraphim reposed on the 6th day of May, in the year of our Lord 1602, on the day of Mid-Pentecost at the hour of noon, after having lived seventy-five years.

In a few words, beloved brethren, have we presented the life of the venerable and righteous Seraphim whose memorial we celebrate today. These were the spiritual struggles of our Father Seraphim who shone forth among ascetics, for whom he became a standard rule of virtue. On account of these struggles, God accounted him worthy of great grace so that he might drive off the infirmities of men and work other wonders. We wish to recount a few miracles, to the glory of God Who glorifies His saints in such a manner. We also wish to honor the saint and make manifest the abundance of divine power supplied to him. We invoke his mediation in every situation of necessity, receiving speedy succor and assistance from on high. Come, then, you Christ-loving observers of the feast, you, who out of Christian piety, left your homes and your labors that you might honor Saint Seraphim. Come and do hearken with Christian attention to a few of the miracles wrought by him, while he was yet alive and after his blessed translation to the heavenly abodes. When you have carried away spiritual benefit for yourselves, return again to your hearths rejoicing and filled with gladness.

Miracles of Saint Seraphim During His Lifetime

As we said earlier, Father Seraphim, our saint among the saints, and the righteous one among the righteous, sought by all means to flee the praise of men. However, it was not possible for him to remain unknown. Why? The notability of his great virtues and his continuous spiritual struggles ran to and fro, as rays of the sun, throughout the inhabited earth. Reverent Christians, from all places, were converging that they might receive spiritual and bodily help from the saint. Thus did the Lord place the man of God as a lamp upon the lampstand, so that the light might shed forth without bounds. He was not only enlightening the souls that drew near to hear his salutary teachings but also healing their bodies of all manner of illness.

Near the monastery, a distance of about an hour and a half toward the southeast, close to the village of Hostia, there is another monastic house in honor of the supremely great archangels. In this place, there was a certain young man, named George, who was working therein. However, unfortunately, this young man was harrowed by the devil. By reason of this hostile influence, George was made to pass through perils more than one can tell. For the troublesome devil sought to slay George. There were times that he was cast into the water and, at times, into the fire; and on other occasions, when George was near precipices, the devil attempted to through him down headlong in order to slay him. The monks of the Archangels Monastery were unable to help him. They, therefore, were in a state of fear lest the devil should cast him over a cliff or into the fire which would end his life. But knowing the wonderworking power of Father Seraphim, they brought George before him. Putting forward positive expectations, they committed George to his effective protection. The saint, seeing the young man's pitiful condition, wept. Father Seraphim raised his hands in prayer, calling upon divine compassion for the sufferer's speedy cure. Straightway then—lo, the miracle!—after the saint's fervent prayer, the young man was healed. In showing his gratitude, George remained near the saint, as his subordinate, ministering to him in his daily needs. George, thereupon, struggled together with him in the spiritual exercises of asceticism.

Another hapless man, named Demos, from the village of Zeli (which was the saint's birthplace), was also possessed by a demon. Compelled by the demon, he went about, night and day, into precipitous places not frequented by men. He would tear his garments and walk about barefoot, even in the winter, when the relentless cold is bitter and icicles hang from the houses. His parents, driven to extremity, ran hither and thither, seeking their son. At times they would find him lying on the snow, naked and half-dead. At other times, they would find him running toward cliffs. And still other times, he was doing other senseless and disorderly actions. Seeing the wretched state of their son, they shed tears and could not be comforted. They had no sanguine expectations that their son's condition could be improved or remedied. Their dejection had no abatement. But while they were submerged in dismal thoughts about such a bleak lot, and had not one single hope in human assistance, they began to consider that surely it would be blessed to bring their son Demos to Saint Seraphim. By then the saint's popular repute had spread everywhere and his wonderworking powers were known to all. Hence, from the saint, the parents sought help and a cure for their son.

Therefore, they took their woeful son and went to the monastery. Their eyes welled with tears as they called upon the help of Father Seraphim. But Demos, forthwith as he observed the saint, began to insult and abuse him. Demos, with wild shouts, turned away from him and made foul gestures. Saint Seraphim, beholding Demos' turbulent and uncouth condition, recognized that the beclouded youth had long been plagued by the pitiless demon. He also knew well, based on that which had been written in the sacred Gospel, "that this kind goeth not out except by prayer and fasting [Mt. 17:21; Mk. 9:29]." Indeed, the man of God commanded that Demos be enclosed in a *kellion*.[38] As for himself, Father Seraphim kept constant for forty days in prayer and fasting. He entreated God to have mercy on His lamentable creature and to expel the demon that harassed Demos. After forty days had been completed, Demos was removed from the *kellion* and led into the church. Father Seraphim brought Demos before the icon of our Master and Savior. After Father Seraphim offered up prayer for many hours, Demos, who for quite a few years was disturbed by the demon, received healing. Demos then began to glorify God and to thank the saint; for Demos perceived that it was by the venerable man's prayer that he had been delivered. Later, Demos was recounting his immense terror and fear while he had been tormented by the demon.

Such miracles are wrought even to this day by means of Saint Seraphim's sacred relics. A considerable number who are afflicted by grave illnesses invoke the saint's mediation before God. After calling upon Saint Seraphim that they might obtain their longed-for health, they receive their requests. Saint Seraphim, nevertheless, through his prayers, does not only cure humans but also works miracles elsewhere. By his prayer, he halted a large boulder which had broken loose. As it rolled and gained momentum, the newly built church, which lay in its path, was threatened with a catastrophe. By his intercession, he also stayed a swarm of locusts and then drove them away. He even exercised authority over the most bold and fearsome of animals, slaying a particularly destructive one, as you will come to hear in the subsequent narrations that suffice to reveal the man's familiar access to God.

There occurred an incident when they were building the church of the sacred monastery that involved the builders who were cutting stones, at a distance of a few steps from the church. While engaged at that employment, suddenly, a boulder which had been cut and chiseled away began rolling down. There was no doubt that it would have damaged the church, which lay in its

---

[38] A *kellion* is either the cell of a hermit or a monastic at a lavra, or a cell in a coenobium capable of housing one or two dwellers. It was a place for praying, reading, and sleeping. It was forbidden to keep food in such cells.

path, if Father Seraphim were not found there at that crucial moment. The saint raised his staff and pronounced these words: "O most Holy Trinity, help us!" Then—behold the wonder!—the boulder, which was rolling downward, gaining momentum, was going directly toward the church. It would have carried away and ruined a great part of the building when, suddenly, it stopped in its track. Now this boulder, a height and width of at least ten meters, may still be viewed to this day. It is supported at the extreme edge toward the lower slope as a testimony to the wondrous event. Hence, so long as the monastery endures, the boulder bears silent witness to the virtue of the saint and his great boldness before God.

At another time, a swarm of locusts devoured the fruits surrounding the monastery. The insects also threatened the olive trees, together with the fig and almond trees. The saint was informed of the danger by the monastery steward (*oikonomos*). Father Seraphim emerged from the monastery and went to the very place where the insects were causing destruction and despoiling the fruits. The saint went to his knees and offered up prayer. Next, with his staff, he inscribed in the air the sign of the precious Cross. Following this action, he departed. The following day, it was reported to him that the entire swarm of locusts took flight and drowned in the sea.

East of the monastery, at a distance of about ten minutes away, the saint had established beehives and the monastery honeybees. He assigned someone to superintend the work, so as to guard and take care of it. But around the beehives, there was the den of a bear. The creature came out at night and attacked the colony of honeybees, since their nests contained large amounts of honey toward the top of the combs. The bear laid waste to the colony when it overturned the hives and seriously injured the bees. The overseer, observing the loss, went and made a report to the saint of the consumption and destruction wreaked by the bear. The saint told him to return to his ministration and that God would cast out that destructive creature. The following morning, Father Seraphim dispatched two monks to Makry Lithari, around the nests of the honeybees. He bade them take the hide of the bear, which they would find dead, and bring it back to the monastery. The monks went and fulfilled the command of the saint. They went to the appointed place and indeed found the bear dead, even as the saint described. After they flayed the animal, they brought the skin back to the monastery, a part of which is still preserved to this day, certifying the miracle of the saint.

Not only wild beasts that inflicted damage and loss to the environs and properties of the monastery were punished with the utmost penalty of death by God but also criminals and audacious persons who held nothing sacred or holy met an end proportionate to their just deserts. Such is the penalty imposed upon those who treat with insolence and violence the saints and the Schema.

A certain shepherd of sheep, tending his flock around the monastery, ushered in spoil and ruin not only to the sown seed and cultivation but also to the gardens and vineyards. The saint, taking notice of this carelessness and negligence, still remained meek and calm. The shepherd's destructive trespassing took place once, then twice, and then many times. On each occasion, when the sheep stamped out and trampled upon the crops, it imposed an unjust loss to the monastery. The shepherd, instead of acknowledging his error and asking pardon, insulted both the saint and the habit of the Angelic Schema in the most obscene of terms. The wretched shepherd gave no thought to the consequences of his uncivil conduct and vile speech. By this action he exchanged the saint for the saint's Master, that is, God Who glorifies His saints and Who punishes despisers and scorners. When the coarse language and irreverent insults of that boasting shepherd were heard by the saint, he was exceedingly grieved. Though the shepherd was vulgar and offensive in the extreme, yet the holy man left him to tend his flock as he wished. But divine judgment did not pardon the surly shepherd's insolence and did not permit his injustice to go any further. Why should the shepherd have spoken despitefully regarding Father Seraphim's holy and Angelic Schema? It is a sign which even the demons revere. Furthermore, when the demons see the saint, they tremble and flee when he performs exorcisms; for he had set up glorious trophies over them. The remorseless shepherd was punished speedily and severely, by means of a harsh and very painful death. Let this be a fearful example to those shepherds who dare to transgress the sacred boundaries of the monastery and allow their flocks to ravage its property.

At another time, the saint drove out of the monastery fields a swarm of locusts which threatened to bring about a complete catastrophe. The distinction that this wonderworking event brought to the saint made him known by all in every quarter. His fame extended—and has remained inextinguishable—as one who received from God the gift of casting out this destructive insect. Another outbreak and migration occurred at one time, while the saint was still living on earth. A numberless destructive swarm of locusts attacked the fields of Athens and caused extensive plant damage. The locust plague then threatened the trees. It was then that the Athenians brought to mind Saint Seraphim. They sought him out and brought him back to the afflicted fields that he, through his effectual prayers, might frustrate and drive away those short-horned creatures.

Saint Seraphim, thereupon, repaired to the Monastery of Saint Spyridon at Piraeus, the port of Athens. It was there that he conducted a litany and chanted the service for the blessing of the waters. When he chanted, "Save, O Lord, Thy people," and submerged the cross into the waters—lo, and behold!—the swarm of locusts, heaped up together, fell into the sea, and drowned. The waters of the deep wherein the honorable cross was dipped became a source of drinking not only for Christians but even the Hagarenes who were present. They partook of those waters and many were cured of long-standing diseases of whatever they were suffering. This supernatural event was witnessed by the Athenians who testified that the water from the sea of which they drank was converted into sweet water. They presented Saint Seraphim with a precious cross and gave him donations, so that he might finish constructing his church and adorning it.

The Athenians, thereafter and to this day, never forgot the marvel that transcended nature. Indeed, a church dedicated to Saint Seraphim was later built in upper Phaleron where they celebrate his memory on the 6th of May with the most festal celebration. In the countryside round about, agricultural orders and bodies among the Athenians, invoke his speedy succor in every necessity. His holy skull is conveyed from his reliquary on roads running from his monastery to sites near and far. Our audience should be aware that the saint's power to halt such destructive swarms, sporadic as they were, was not limited to the time in which he lived. Since the time of his repose, over the years, ofttimes, his sacred relics were brought to infected sites where, according to ancient ecclesiastical custom, a Service for the Blessing of Water is chanted for the sake of averting the dangerous threat from such injurious insects.

Truly, the ardor of each Christian's faith, coupled with the saint's intercession before God, energized the miracle in an ineffable manner so that the locusts vanished. Thus, according to the words of our Savior after He had withered the fig tree, "Verily I say to you, if ye have faith and doubt not, ye shall not only do that which was done to the fig tree, but even if ye should say to this mountain, 'Be thou taken away, and be thou cast into the sea,' it shall come to pass. And all things, whatsoever ye ask in prayer, believing, ye shall receive [Mt. 21:21, 22]." With such distinguishing faith as shown by the saint and the faithful, all things are possible. But it was not only the pious Christians who were accounted worthy of the wonderworking energies of the saint but even the Hagarenes, who were then lords in Greece, were vouchsafed the benefits of such grace. For many of them, observing the energy which wrought mightily through the sacred relics of Saint Seraphim while chanting the divine office for the Blessing of Water, asked and received from the Christians some of the holy water. They would take it and sprinkle it upon the locusts that were threatening their fields. They indeed, too, were granted the successful results of the miracle-working energy against those menacing insects.

Now after the saint had purchased the fields and other properties in the neighborhood of Dombou, he appointed farmers and overseers from among the monastic brethren. These monks were charged with cultivating the arable land and sowing wheat, barley, and fruits not requiring watering. This area, at that time, produced nought else but such products. There were two factors: there was little water and the earth in those parts was not very fertile. Now the saint was explicit with them regarding their return to the monastery on the eves of the feasts. They were instructed to leave off their labors and return to the monastery that they might be found with the other brethren and present at the readings during Vespers. On one such day, when the eve was a Saturday, those monks in the fields had not yet completed seeding the small farm. The hour of Vespers drew near. The fathers transgressed the elder's express order and remained to finish the sowing. After they finished, then they returned to the monastery. When those fathers were asked the reason for their tardiness, the steward answered, "A portion of one of the small farms was undone. Since we did not wish to lose the daylight, we stayed and worked that we might finish that small patch of land." The saint smiled benevolently and remarked resignedly, "May it be blessed! But never do it again."

The elder then said to the steward, "Go to the small farm and mark with flags that portion which you worked during Vespers, so you may differentiate it from the other parcels." When summer arrived and it was harvest time, the saint went with the steward to that small farm. They approached that section previously flagged by the steward. The elder, with not the least discomposure, turned to the harvesters and said, "Burn the fruits in this patch. It is not right that the fruits sown on work days and blessed by God should be united with those fruits sown on a feast. For the feast days have been consecrated by the Church for the glorification and worship of God and not for agricultural pursuits." The steward and the rest of the monks hesitated to lay fire to the field, saying, "If we should set this field afire, it will spread to another—and thus to other farms." But the saint was confident that only the fruit of the labor done on the feast day would burn. He did not believe that the crops made from labors performed on work days would be touched. He insisted that they obey his word. The steward, yielding to the elder's order, with a trembling hand, started a fire. He placed the burning torch on the patch that had been flagged. This section, as it burned, remained self-contained. It then self-extinguished without even singing the adjoining sown lands of the small farms.

This example, beloved brethren in Christ, is truly excellent. It certifies the sanctity of the feast days which we are obliged to honor, by visiting the churches and offering worship to our God and Fashioner. We ought to be giving Him thanks for all the good things He has granted us and continues to bestow. We must not forget, brethren, that "God finished on the sixth day His works which He made, and He ceased on the seventh day from all His works which He made [Gen. 2:2]." We are also told that "Six days thou shalt labor, and shalt perform all thy work. But on the seventh day is the sabbath of the Lord thy God; on it thou shalt do no work...[Ex. 20:9, 10]." Let us then esteem those festal days consecrated as holy by the Church, so that God should bless our labors and grant us the riches of His mercies. Let us now return to our narration.

The renown of the saint and his accomplishments came into the ears of the godly Christians. They were hastening from every place and visiting the monastery in order to behold and venerate the saint. Those who were in sore plight from diseases received healing from him. On one such day, two Christians from Thevai,[39] moved by piety, came on a pilgrimage to the monastery to receive the venerable man's blessing. While they were going their way on the road, they encountered a Hagarene soldier who took it upon himself to escort them to the monastery. The Turk did not make this gesture out of reverence but for the sake of his own amusement. The soldier remarked to the two pilgrims, "Come and make haste that we might reach and constrain the *kalogeros*—for with the Greek word signifying 'monk' that is how they were calling the saint—to prepare food for us and give us a good gratuity."

The Christians from Thevai, hearing these words, were astonished. Finding the soldier's words piteous, they attempted to exhort him not to speak ill of the saint. They also said, "Do not seek food and select drinks from the elder. Those people who go to the monastery, do so for the benefit of their souls and not for entertainment." The Turk gave not the least consequence to the Christians' sober admonitions. Instead, the soldier kept jeering at the two pilgrims as imbeciles and wanting in understanding. When they finally arrived at the monastery, the Christians from Thevai dismounted from their horses. They entered into the church in order to offer veneration. Meanwhile, the Turkish soldier, try as he might, could not alight from his beast so that he might swagger into the monastery and extort delicacies and fine drinks—as he had imagined—from the monastery pantry. Divine justice, the unsleeping eye, punished the Hagarene's arrogant presumptions, holding him tight in the saddle as an example to others.

The saint, beholding the soldier sitting and squirming on his horse in an attempt to dismount, approached him. He greeted the Turk and invited him to dismount from his horse. Then—behold the miracle!—he who only moments earlier could not budge from his mount, climbed down, forthwith, from the horse. He cordially thanked the saint and entered the monastery. The Turk, instead of asking for food and special drinks, knelt before the feet of the saint. His shamefaced apology consisted of requesting pardon for his former audacity and impiety, which he exhibited toward the saint by reason of his ignorance. With the bondage of evil broken by speaking the truth, the saint accorded

---

[39] In the 19th C., Thevai was destroyed by an earthquake and rebuilt. The present Voeotian city is the chief market town of a rich agricultural plain, trading in wheat, olive oil, wine, tobacco, and cotton, as well as silk manufacture.

pardon and acquitted him of his previous misconduct and undisciplined tongue. Thereafter, that Turkish soldier did not cease extolling the holy man for his meekness and the amnesty which he unstintingly bestowed upon him; for he also declared with shivering fear the predicament in which he had found himself trapped outside the monastery.

Miracles of Saint Seraphim After His Repose

At Amarousi,[40] a man of advanced years and an elder, recounted the following event which took place in those days. A certain Turk had a large and sprawling property, upon which he had planted six fruit-bearing trees. During the spring season there came a great swarm of locusts. The creatures threatened not only the tender leaves but also the branches and trunks of those trees. The Turk, however, had heard that the Christians, in such circumstances, were in the habit of invoking divine help through one of their priests. He, therefore, summoned one of the ministers of his religion who, in turn, called upon the assistance of Mohammed. The Ottoman cleric kept invoking the succor of Mohammed, believing him to be a great prophet. He cried out with mighty shouts from the morning until that evening. But that worshipper of Mohammed, that antichrist, was put to shame with his thunderous outpourings; for neither his prayer nor his uplifted voice was heard.

While the Turkish property owner was utterly in despair on account of the invasion of the insects and the continuing destruction of his property, a certain Christian furnished with wings his dashed hopes by reason of a promise. The Christian said that he was able to bring a Christian priest who could drive out the locusts by his prayer. It was during those days that there had been called to Amarousi, by reason of the locust swarm, a priest from the Monastery of Saint Seraphim. The priest brought with him to Amarousi the holy and grace-streaming skull of Saint Seraphim. The Christian who made the pledge to the Turk went to find the visiting priest. He located him and guided him back to the Turk's property. After the monastery priest conducted a Service for the Blessing of Holy Water, the insects rose up from the ground and disappeared. The Turkish owner, beholding this extraordinary phenomenon did two things. First he thanked the Christian priest. Then he went to the mystic of Mohammed and administered a merciless thrashing. Thereafter, that Turk did not cease proclaiming his gratitude toward Saint Seraphim. We are able to number with this episode a league of similar miracles that occurred after his blessed repose. For the sake of brevity, we shall pass over those accounts lest we should speak at great length.

But there are other wonders of this saint, histories within histories, in a class of their own. We wish to narrate some of them to the glory of God and

[40] Amarousi or Marousi (38°03′N 23°47′E) is a suburban city northeast of Athens, in the prefecture of Attike.

to the honor of the saint. After Saint Seraphim's ascent into the heavens, he did not leave off keeping a watchful eye and guarding his sacred monastery. For this reason, he did not permit, during the times of tyranny, the infidel to use violence and dash to the earth his monastery, which many among the Muslims bethought themselves and issued orders to this effect.

Odysseus Androutsos,[41] the hero of the Greek Revolution, when he served under Ali Pasha, came into the province of Levadeia. He made an abrupt entry at the monastery of Saint Seraphim, where he threatened the monks of pending violence and ill-treatment unless he and his men received money and gifts. Now the first thing Androutsos asked for was roasted lamb. The poor monks, unused to this type of fare, prepared such a table. Androutsos took a seat while the monks stood around the table in great terror. They were waiting, minute by minute, to hear the command that they were to be subjected to torture. Then, a sudden change came over Androutsos. Instead of partaking of the prepared lamb, he pushed the table away and went forth to go to sleep. How did this happen? Just as he was about to cut away the meat from the lamb, he heard—lo, the miracle!—the sound of a lamb coming from the head of the roasted main course. Now he was either angered or afraid, but he chose not to eat. The sound was heard by all others who were in attendance, both those at table with Androutsos and the monks standing by. It is from them that we have heard and have written down this episode in the monastery's annals.

---

[41] Odysseus (Odyssefs) Androutsos (1788-1825) was born in Ithaca. His family originally hailed from the village of Livadates in Phthiotis prefecture. His father was Andreas Androutsos, a *klepht* (lit., bandits who were pre-nationalist armed resistance). After losing his father, Androutsos joined the Albanian army of Ali Pasha and became an officer. However, in 1818, he joined the Friendly Society (Philike Etaireia) which was planning the liberation of Greece from the Ottoman Empire. In May of 1821, Omar (Omer) Vrioni, the Albanian commander of the Turkish army, advanced with eight thousand men. After crushing the resistance of the Greeks at the river of Alamana (Spercheios) and putting Athanasios Diakos to death, he headed south into the Peloponnesos to crush the Greek uprising. Androutsos, with a band of one hundred or so men, took up a defensive position at an inn near Gravia, supported by Panourgias and Diovouniotis and their men. Vrioni attacked the inn but was repulsed with heavy casualties (over four hundred dead). When he sought reinforcements and artillery, the Greeks managed to slip out before the reinforcements arrived. Androutsos lost two men in the battle and earned the title of commander-in-chief of the Greek forces in Roumeli (Central Greece). In the following year, 1822, Androutsos was accused of being in contact with the Turks; and he was stripped of his command. Finally, in 1825, the revolutionary government placed him under arrest in a cave at the Acropolis in Athens. The new commander, Yiannis Gouras, who once was Androutsos' second in command, had him executed on the 5th of June, in the year 1825. See http://wiki.phantis.com/index.php/Odysseus_Androutsos.

Athanasios Diakos,[42] revolutionary hero of Alamana and former hierodeacon, who was for a time serving with Androutsos, remarked at the incident to Androutsos' face: "It is a miracle of the saint, who is the patron and protector of the monastery, because, perhaps, thou hadst the intention of mistreating the monks, a deed that the saint would not countenance to take place in his monastery." The following day, Androutsos departed very early in the morning from the monastery. He still had not eaten anything and left fasting. He went directly to a church, the one dedicated to Saint Seraphim's memory. It was built in remembrance of the miraculous gushing forth of water, which we spoke of earlier, when the saint had offered up entreaty in that parched place. Androutsos fell prostrate to the ground, agitated by a shivering fit. To those around him, Androutsos remarked contritely and did not dissimulate, "The saint of this monastery is its fearsome and valiant champion, because I suffered many things this past night. And now I see that it is a chastisement of the saint. It is this punishment which agitates me. But may Saint Seraphim preserve me! And never will I ask for even a pin." Verily,

---

[42] Athanasios Diakos (born Athanasios Massavetas in 1788), with other revolutionaries and dignitaries of Eastern Roumeli, declared the Greek Revolution in the Byzantine Monastery of Hosios Loukas; and, on the 30th of March, entered Levadeia. Athanasios was an honest and good-hearted man. Prior to the 1821 War, he entered a monastery and was ordained a deacon ("diakos" in the Greek language). One day, a Turkish pasha came to his monastery and made some crude and suggestive remarks about Athanasios' good looks. When the perverse Turk attempted to seduce him, Athanasios slew him and fled to the mountains. He joined a band of *klephts* under Odysseus Androutsos, who made him second in command. Eventually, Athanasios headed his own band. In April 1821, Omar Vrioni, the commander of the Turkish army, advanced with nine thousand men from Thessaly to crush the revolt in the Peloponnesos. Athanasios and his band of followers, along with two other bands (a total of perhaps 1,500 men), took up defensive positions at the river of Alamana (Spercheios), near Thermopylae, while Panourgias and Diovouniotis were entrenched on the slopes of the surrounding mountains. They soon abandoned their positions, leaving alone Athanasios Diakos with Bishop Esaias of Salona and some dozen men. Athanasios' men fought for several hours before they were overwhelmed. The wounded Athanasios was taken to Vrioni, who offered to make Athanasios an officer in his army. Athanasios would not flee. All those Greeks were killed, and Athanasios, with broken sword, was taken alive. When Vrioni asked him to become a Muslim and fight with him, Athanasios rejected the offer telling him, "I was born a Rhomaios; and I will die a Rhomaios." Athanasios Diakos was impaled on a spit and roasted over a fire on the 23rd of April, in the year 1821. His service to the cause was short, but his memory as an revolutionary martyr is still strong. See also http://www.wiki.phantis.com/index.php/Athanasios_Diakos, as well as http://www.members.fortunecity.com/fstav1/1821/fort1821/struggle4.html. Omar Vrioni, largely antagonistic with Kutahye, the Turkish commander of Central Greece, was recalled in 1824 by the Porte and assigned a command in Macedonia.

thereafter, as many times as Androutsos came to the saint's monastery, he asked for nought. He could not think of his previous behavior without abhorrence. Certainly, he never again asked for meat at the saint's monastery, but instead ate the monastic fare of pulse and vegetables.

The Turks, on another occasion, threatened with despoliation and utter destruction the province of Levadeia and all of the region of Sterea Hellas over which they held sway. The monks, fearing the evils of those ferocious masters, took refuge in the Peloponnesos, the large mountainous peninsula to the south. The Turks, thereupon, then lorded it over the monastery. They wished to pull down the monastery and demolish the church. But no sooner had they marched inside the church, full of thoughts ripe for mischief, than they beheld standing in the midst of the temple a terrifying giant. It was the church's imposing patron, the venerable Seraphim. He raised his staff and extended it toward them, fixing on them a menacing gaze. As he threatened them with death, he gestured for them to exit the sacred temple without touching anything. He forewarned them not to be the cause of even the slightest damage or loss in the monastery. Indeed, who could exceed the saint's solicitude and care for the monastery?

The Turks, quite alarmed, beheld the saint thundering at them. They understood, to a man, that this must be the monastery's patron. With fear and trembling, they hastened out of the church and recounted to their compatriots the mysterious and extraordinary phenomenon that occurred within. All of them were smitten with terror. So frightened out of their wits were they that they abandoned the plan. One monk who happened to be found therein was given one order as the Turks retreated from the confines of the church: they bid him attend to lighting the lamp before the saint. Although the Turks were horror-stricken and stunned, still they tarried at the monastery. Then another miracle followed after the first one. The following day, throughout the morning, a thick cloud hovered over the monastery. Lightning and thunder could be perceived only from within the village of the monastery. Everything outside of these boundaries was quite the opposite. The weather was bright and clear, with a brilliant sun shedding its rays in a cloudless sky. Meanwhile, at the monastery and its village, it was hailing as if sand were falling out of the sky. So intense was the precipitation that the roof tiles on the monastic cells were breaking and falling down, so that the disjointed soldiers quartered within were in danger of losing their lives. Shaking from abject fear, they understood why this was befalling them. They implored the saint to cease his wrath, saying, "We are leaving, and we are not going to bring about any damage or loss to the monastery." The chief officer, with a wild and frantic shout summoned his men, asking for help from them. Petrified, he kept saying, "The *kalogeros* of the monastery!" For again, that is how they called Saint Seraphim.

Evidently, the saint would not permit the officer to take his ease; instead, the monastery's protector had used other means to induce him to go away. The holy elder chose to put the officer to the test, so that the latter felt he was on the rack. He thought he was about to die unless he agreed to decamp with his soldiers from the monastery, without causing the slightest loss to it.

The Turks, hearing and seeing all these happenings, were dispirited. They were not able to pillage or loot or pull down the monastery. They feared that unless they quit being billeted in the monks' cells, they might broker their own deaths. They, therefore, prepared to evacuate with their leader and take the road to Levadeia. Now as they arrived in Pamplouki, they found other Turkish soldiers who had been dispatched from Levadeia. These men were on their way to the saint's monastery. The soldiers from Levadeia, clearly recognizing that their comrades coming from the monastery were quivering and withdrawn, could not resist questioning the leader of the terror-crazed men. Thus, one among them asked, "Why do you appear haunted with fear? How came you hither in this state?" The Turkish leader said, "You may well ask!" He then began to recount his story, speaking with apprehension and a tremor in his voice. He explained that just as he was approaching the well that is there at the monastery (the one from the saint's time when he made a miracle and caused water to spring forth), he stretched forth his hand to take some water, in order to wash, according to their Islamic law of ablutions when, suddenly, there appeared the *kalogeros*, he said, meaning the saint. He described in an undisguised way how the saint, with a threatening look, said, "Defiled one, did it not suffice that you all have made desolate my house? And now thou comest to pollute the water which God made manifest, so as to provide drink for wayfarers?" He then paused a moment and continued his narrative, telling his listeners that the *kalogeros* gave no heed to his soldier's weapon which was before him. That audacious Turk then said that, at one point, as he felt for his weapon, the *kalogeros* showed not a trace of cowardice. Impenetrably calm, the *kalogeros* said to him, "Do not even think to touch thy weapon. Much rather, hasten to go down to the monastery and inform the others that they are to vacate the premises. Go, get you gone, otherwise not one among the troops shall survive!"

After the disquieted Turk spoke these words, he took a few short breaths and added the following, "Therefore, from what he spoke when he appeared before me, I understood that he was not a simple monk. Rather, he is the protector and champion of the monastery, which we seized and caused to suffer ruin. With fear and trembling, I rushed here to inform you to leave alone this monastery and go to some other place lest you should learn as I did from the same blunder and suffer any evil." The military leader and that Turk to whom he spoke went to Levadeia. They appeared before the *voivod* (prince),

Mufti bey,[43] declaring they had business of great moment. The military leader, still sensing his terror and fright, reported all that occurred. Mufti bey was then urged by that officer to cease the operation against the Monastery of Saint Seraphim, because the saint was an awesome guardian of his monastery and did not permit anyone to injure it. In truth, the monastery sustained not the least damage from the Turkish troops. It survived and stood throughout the period of the Turkish domination. Thus, it was found in the end to be as the saint had built it, though, ofttimes, the Turks were resolved to destroy it.

"It needs to be mentioned here that many of our chieftains (of the revolution)," remarks the biographer, "were coming to the monastery during the ethnic-saving revolution, invoking the help of Saint Seraphim. They found in him a helper and defender against Turkish expeditions and campaigns." One such example was the revolutionary hero, George Karaiskakis, who achieved stunning military successes against the Ottomans in Dombrena, Distomo, and Arahova.[44] After he passed through Amphissa (Salona), the main town of

---

[43] Bey signified the governor of a district or a minor province in the Ottoman Empire.

[44] George Karaiskakis, a leader of the Greek War of Independence, was born in Mavromati of the Karditsa prefecture, in 1782 to nun Zoe Dimiski and was known as the "son of the nun" for his entire life. During the early stages of the war, Karaiskakis served in the militia in the Morea (Peloponnesos), but was barred from fighting due to the intrigues that divided the Greek leadership. Nonetheless, he recognized the necessity of providing Greece with a stable government and was a supporter of John Kapodistrias who would later become Greece's first head of state. Karaiskakis' reputation grew during the middle and latter stages of the war. He suffered from tuberculosis most of his life. He attempted to lift the siege of Mesolonghi in 1823 and in 1826. That same year, he was appointed commander-in-chief of the Greek patriotic forces in Roumeli.

On one of his campaigns, Greek forces reached the village of Dombrena and attacked the following day. Turks defended themselves inside three towers. On the 30th of October, three hundred Greeks under Giannakis Androutsos, brother of Odysseus, were sent by the general to Zagaras, but they were defeated by the enemy forces. Giannakis was captured and later was decapitated. The Albanian Mustafa bey was the leader of the Ottoman forces. On 11th of November the heroic fighter, John Soultanis, who had survived the Mesolonghi siege, was killed at Dombrena. Mustafa bey joined his forces with Kehagia bey's and reached the monastery at Davlia. There he had discussions with his officers and decided to head to Salona, modern Amphissa to attack the forces of Diovouniotis and Panourgias. They decided to pass through a village near ancient Delphi, Arahova, where they achieved a memorable victory.

In 1827, Karaiskakis participated in the failed attempt to raise the siege of Athens. He also attempted to prevent the massacre of the Turkish garrison stationed in the Fort of Saint Spyridon. He was killed in action in a skirmish against the Turks at Neon Phaleron, near Athens, on the 23rd day of April, in the year 1827. See

(continued...)

Parnassos in central Greece, he came to Saint Seraphim's monastery. With Christian piety, Karaiskakis kissed the icon of Saint Seraphim. He then started weeping and calling upon the saint. He asked for his assistance, succor, and defense in the mission that he was planning. Truly, on account of that religious feeling that possessed him, the unforgettable Karaiskakis beheld his design gain upward momentum so that he succeeded. He entered into Arahova,[45] built on the rocky spur of Parnassos, where a fight opened against the enemies. All of his undertakings went well. A monk who spoke Albanian went in the night to Distomo and informed George Karaiskakis about the enemy's plans. On the 18th of November, Karaiskakis sent four hundred men under Gardikiotis Grivas and George Vagias to fortify the houses of Arahova. The enemy forces of 2,500 men approached the village on the 19th of November, in the year 1826, under the command of the Albanian Mustafa bey, his brother Kiamil bey and Kehagia bey. They immediately began to fight the few Greeks who were fortified inside Arahova. But after a while Karaiskakis came, as well as Christodoulos Hatzipetros, Iovouniotis from the Salona road, Panourgias, and Giannousis. The Turko-Albanians retreated to a hill over the village and continued to fight. Soon they realized that they were surrounded. Escape was not possible. They refused to accept the terms of surrender set by Karaiskakis. The next nights were very cold and a heavy snow was falling. While the Orthodox stayed inside the warm houses of Arahova, the enemy forces were frozen, hungry, and sick. Karaiskakis went after the Turks. Almost two thousand bodies were laying in the snow. The whole army was wiped out. Only eight Greek fighters were killed. The decapitated head of the leader of the Muslim army was sent to the Greek government as testimony to the Greek victory. This day, on the 24th of November, in the year 1826, was celebrated by the Greek government as the day of liberation of the whole Roumeli.

After the victory, Karaiskakis fortified Distomo and placed there Souliots under the command of Kostas Botsaris. On the 19th of January, in the year 1827, the Ottomans attacked Distomo, which was defended by four hundred Souliots. The Souliots fought bravely but they would have perished if

[44](...continued)
http://www.wiki.phantis.com/index.php/Georgios_Karaiskakis, as well as http://www.members.fortunecity.com/fstav1/1821/fort1821/struggle11.html. See also, David Brewer's *The Greek War of Independence* (Woodstock & NY: The Overlook Press, 2001), pp. 282-286 for the poignant account of the fall of Mesolonghi, and pp. 312, 313, for Karaiskakis' opposition to the march on Athens.

[45] Arahova, on the western slope of Mount Parnassos (8,061 feet or 2,457 meters), is some twelve kilometers from Delphi. Around Arahova, and eight kilometers from the village of Distomo, is the famous Monastery of Hosios Loukas (see the 7th of February in *The Great Synaxaristes*). One reaches Distomo via Levadeia.

reinforcements had not come from Salona. On the night of the 20th of January, there came Karaiskakis with his men to help the defenders. In order to reach the Greeks in time, he preferred to cross through the enemy camp. He chose to hazard the loss of his life. His risky and nimble deed gave courage to the defenders. The next morning, Omar Pasha decapitated all the guards who were responsible for the camp during the previous night. The war continued for some days. The tactical Turkish forces that arrived as reinforcements from Constantinople were defeated; and Omar Pasha decided to withdraw to Griponisi, modern Evia. The Turks abandoned the castle of Salona and many towns which they possessed. Hence, in February of 1827, Roumeli was almost liberated with the exception of Vonitsa, Epahtos (modern Nafpaktos) and Mesolonghi.[46]

By what had taken place, especially at Arahova, Karaiskakis rendered that splendid triumph to divine defense. He understood that it was upon God Whom he needed to hang all his hopes. Karaiskakis also showed no small gratitude toward Saint Seraphim, for he believed that it was through the holy man's intercession before God that he achieved what he did. In thanksgiving, he returned to the saint's monastery and poured out his heartfelt thanks. After January of 1827, George Karaiskakis was called away by the Greek government to return through Elefsina to Piraeus, in order to face Reshit Pasha, also known as Kioutahes. But so much for now regarding the saint's powerful mediation to help his monastery and assist the Greek cause in extricating the Orthodox from under the Ottoman yoke.

These events, beloved brethren, describing the wonders and miracles of our righteous and God-bearing Father Seraphim, have been presented herein today for your remembrance that we might glorify God Who glorifies His saints. Such were and are the grace and the spiritual gifts vouchsafed to Saint Seraphim by God. Although he had forsaken all things on earth when becoming a monk, and he now stands on high with the fiery seraphim, still he has not ceased working marvels and granting aid and succor to those who call upon him with reverence. We ask, O lovers of this feast, for Saint Seraphim's powerful entreaties and intercessions before God that we may be accounted worthy of His heavenly kingdom. May it be so for all of us, in Christ Jesus, to Whom is due glory and dominion unto the ages of the ages! Amen.

Through the intercessions of Thy Saints,
O Christ God, have mercy on us. Amen.

---

[46] The scanty synopsis given in *The Great Synaxaristes* (in Greek), adequate for Greek readers already acquainted with their history of the revolution, needed to be supplemented for our English readers. Facts were retrieved from www.members.fortunecity.com/fstav1/1821/fort1821/struggle11.html.

**On the 7th of May,
the holy Church commemorates
the Appearance of the
Sign of the Precious CROSS over Jerusalem.**[1]

The Veneration of the Cross

The sign of the precious and life-giving Cross appeared in the sky over Jerusalem during the days of Emperor Constantius (337-361), the son of Saint Constantine the Great. The apparition took place during the episcopacy of the holy Patriarch Kyril of Jerusalem.[2] Throughout the days of the Pentecost, the honorable sign of the Cross, filled with divine light, was made manifest over Jerusalem.

Saint Kyril, in his epistle to Emperor Constantius, speaks of the miraculous appearance of a luminous cross in the sky over Jerusalem. The epistle is dated the 7th day of May, in the year 351. "In these holy days of the paschal season, on the 7th of May at about the third hour, a huge cross made of light appeared in the sky above holy Golgotha (Calvary) extending as far as the holy Mount of Olives. It was not revealed to one or two people alone, but it appeared unmistakably to everyone in the city. It was not as if one might conclude that one had suffered a momentary optical illusion; it was visible to the human eye above the earth for several hours. The flashes it emitted outshone the rays of the sun....It prompted the whole populace at once to run together into the holy church, overcome both with fear and joy at the divine vision. Young and old, men and women of every age, even young girls confined to their chambers at home, natives and foreigners, Christians and pagans visiting from abroad, all together as if with a single voice raised a hymn of praise to God's only-begotten and wonderworking Son. They had the evidence of their own senses that the holy Faith of Christians is not based on the persuasive arguments of philosophy but on the revelation of the Spirit and power;[3] it is not proclaimed by mere human beings but testified from heaven by God Himself. Accordingly we citizens of Jerusalem, who saw this extraordinary wonder with our own eyes, have paid due worship and

[1] Concerning the miraculous apparition, the God-inspired Kosmas chants at the Feast of the Exaltation of the Cross: "The Cross, wondrously spread out, shot forth rays as the sun, and the heavens declared the glory of our God [Ps. 18:1]." Taken from the 14th of September, Orthros Canon, Ode Four, Mode Plagal Four, by Saint Kosmas.

[2] Saint Kyril, Patriarch of Jerusalem, is commemorated by the holy Church on the 18th of March.

[3] Cf. 1 Cor. 2:4.

thanksgiving to God the universal King and to God's only-begotten Son—and shall continue to do so."[4]

Again, in his letter, Saint Kyril speaks to Constantius of his father, Saint Constantine,[5] since the true Wood of the Cross was first found in Jerusalem during his reign. Moreover, certainly Constantius knew of an even earlier vision of the Cross. The first appearance took place slightly before October of 312, when his father, Constantine the Great, succeeded in his splendid victory over Maxentius at the Milvian Bridge near Rome. "The Cross, that mighty trophy, was revealed by heaven to the godly-minded emperor."[6] Constantine, afterward, became sole ruler and promoted Orthodoxy, thereby bringing to an end the vile persecution by the pagans against the Christians.

Now Kyril, in writing to Constantius, regarding the appearances of the Cross, did so, hoping to inhibit the emperor's inclination toward Arianism, which heresy taught that Christ was a mere creature and not God. In hymns written for today's divine office, the Church chants: "The Father...now delineates the luminous Cross to bear witness to the divinity of the crucified Son."[7] And, "Thy Cross has gladdened all who declare Thee to be God crucified; for it has shone forth with radiant and unapproachable beauty."[8]

Many people, despite the First Œcumenical Synod (Nicaea, 325) convoked by Constantine the Great, still foundered on the rocks of the Arian heresy. This left the Orthodox in the minority. Emperor Constantius, up until 350, was somewhat held in check by his brother: the powerful western emperor, Constans, who opposed Arianism and supported Athanasios the Great.[9] With Constans' assassination by Magnentius, Constantius, an inveterate adherent of the Arian heresy, began oppressing the Orthodox and aiding the Arian heretics in every way possible. Kyril, nevertheless, continued to urge Constantius to act as protector of the Church and the empire.

In appearances of the sign of the Cross in the heavens, we note that our Savior has overshadowed error and raised up the truth of right belief. One appearance, that which we commemorate today, confirmed Orthodoxy against the great heresy of Arianism. The sign of the Cross, shining more brilliantly than the sun and stretching a distance of about five and one-half miles, lasted

---

[4] See Edward Yarnold, S. J., "Letter to Constantius," *Cyril of Jerusalem*, The Early Church Fathers (London/NY: Routledge, 2000), pp. 69, 70; and *P.G.* 33:1165-1176.

[5] Saint Constantine and his mother, Saint Helen (who discovered the true Cross), are commemorated by the holy Church on the 21st of May.

[6] September 14th, Orthros Canon, Ode One, Mode Plagal Four, by Saint Kosmas.

[7] May 7th, Orthros Canon, Ode Five, Mode Four, by John the Monk.

[8] May 7th, Orthros Canon, Ode Three, Mode Four, by John the Monk.

[9] Saint Athanasios the Great is commemorated on the 2nd of May and the 18th of January by the holy Church.

for an entire week over the holy city. This appearance, together with confirming the articles at Nicaea, also led many pagans and Jews to Orthodoxy. "With the light that shone in the form of Thy Cross, O compassionate Savior, Thou didst triumph over the lawless daring of the God-slayers."[10]

The other appearance of the Cross confirmed the traditional Patristic Calendar of the Orthodox Church against the renovationists' papal Gregorian Calendar. On the 14th of September (according to the Julian Calendar), in the year 1925, on the eve of the Feast of the Exaltation of the Cross, an all-night vigil was being celebrated at the Athenian Church of Saint John the Theologian. By nine o'clock at night, more than two thousand faithful gathered. Civil authorities attended in order to keep the peace, in the event of any disorderly conduct. At 11:30 that same night, there gradually appeared in the sky above the church, in the direction of north-east, the sign of the Cross. The exact location was on the mountain of Hymettos above Holargos.[11] The celestial light illumined not only the church but also the churchyard. The rays emitted from the Byzantine-style Cross with three crossbars, made dim the stars in its path on that cloudless night. The duration of the heavenly phenomenon was one-half hour or until midnight. After midnight, the sign of the Cross gradually rose to a vertical position, even as the hands of the priest elevates a cross in the divine office. When the sign of the Cross was in an upright position, it started to fade. The vigil lasted until four in the morning. The earlier appearance, before 351, was manifested when the first great heresy of Arianism threatened the Church, while this appearance is connected with the greatest of all heresies, that is, ecumenism. This latter appearance in the heavens, on the day of the 14th according to the Traditional Calendar, confirmed what feast was being celebrated by the Church Triumphant in the heavens.

These apparitions of the Cross should also bring to our minds that final one, at the Second Coming of Christ: "And then shall the sign of the Son of Man appear in the heaven, and then the tribes of the earth shall mourn, and they shall see the Son of Man coming on the clouds of the heaven with power and great glory.[12] And He shall send forth His angels with a great sound of a

---

[10] May 7th, Orthros Canon, Ode Four, Mode Four, by John the Monk.

[11] The incident was reported in the Greek newspaper *Skrip* (15/28 September, 1925).

[12] Saint John Chrysostom comments: "'And then shall the sign of the Son of Man appear in the heaven (ἐν τῷ οὐρανῷ)': that is, the Cross, being brighter than the sun—since the latter shall be darkened and hide itself—will appear...far brighter than the rays of the sun." ["Homily 76," *Matthew*, *P.G.* 58:736 (col. 698).]

Blessed Theophylact: "What need is there for such a sensory light, since there is no night and the Sun of Righteousness has appeared? But even the powers of the heavens shall be shaken, that is, they shall be astounded and shudder seeing creation (continued...)

trumpet, and they shall gather together His elect from the four winds, from the uttermost parts of the heavens unto their extremities [Mt. 24:30, 31]."

Saint Akakios

On the 7th of May, the holy Church commemorates the holy Martyr AKAKIOS.[13]

Akakios, the holy martyr, hailed from Cappadocia of Christian parentage. He lived during the reign of Maximian (286-305). As Akakios' name in Greek bespoke guilelessness, he was, not only in name but also in reality, a stranger to evil. But Akakios, who led a life that was beyond reproach, was now led as a criminal to Firmos, the magistrate at Cappadocia, before whom he professed the name and divinity of Christ. Adorned with understanding, Akakios discoursed in a wise manner and shredded the arguments of the pagan sages and the iniquitous. He also stated that he had witnessed the miraculous cures performed at the shrines of the martyrs, which occurrences he could never deny. After Akakios was subjected to manifold tortures, they remanded him to another magistrate, named Vivianos, who brought Christ's confessor bound, with other prisoners, to Byzantion.[14] Akakios was harshly whipped and suffered dreadful scourges. The pagans also applied satanic instruments and tools to further tyrannize him, during which ordeal he entreated the unconquerable might of God. He was then condemned to starvation. The Lord, indeed, sustained His martyr, and empowered him so that he rejected the polluted drink of the idolaters. Christ's athlete remained

[12](...continued)
altered and all mankind, from Adam up till then, about to give account." [*P.G.* 123:132D (col. 413).]

[13] Unpublished divine offices to Saint Akakios, such as that of the poet Theophanes, are found complete in: Parisian Codices 13, 1566; and Lavreote Codices Γ 19, Γ 74, Δ 5, Δ 36, and Ω 147.

[14] Bishop Nikolai Velimirović, in *The Prologue From Orchid* [2:151], mentions that before he was taken to Byzantion, he first went to the Thracian city of Pyrrinthus, where he endured harsh torture. The synopsis given in Bishop Nikolai's work for the 7th of May also mentions that Saint Akakios was a soldier in the Roman army.

steadfast throughout the torments, wounds, blows, and severing of his members. When he was cast into prison, angels of the Lord visited and attended him. They restored him to health and gave him instructions. After his miraculous recovery, the pagans sent him forth to yet another magistrate, Phalkianos,[15] who gave the order to have the Christian's head severed by the sword. The holy Akakios, without any fear, went forth to the executioner and drowned that old serpent Satan in the torrents of his martyric blood.[16]

On the 7th of May, the holy Church commemorates the holy Martyr QUADRATUS (KODRATOS) and other MARTYRS with him.

Quadratus (Kodratos), the exemplary martyr and the holy martyrs who suffered with him, contested during the years of the irreverent Emperors Decius (249-251) and Valerian (253-259). A great persecution was launched against the Christians. Many were arrested from different places and transferred to Nikomedia.[17] They were incarcerated and kept in a high security environment. These measures were taken in order to constrain the prisoners to offer sacrifice to the idols. Those who consented were released and allowed to return to their homes. Those who refused to be persuaded were punished with many and diverse torments, which ended in death. Those Christians who were living in Nikomedia were filled with intense fear. Some of them took flight into the mountains, while others concealed themselves in hideaways. All those who were valiant and true slaves of the Christ continued conducting their lives fearlessly inside the city. Such brave Christians were joyous and glad, as they awaited the time when they might be vouchsafed the opportunity to glorify the Lord by means of martyric tortures.

Counted among those godly and courageous Nikomedians, at that time, was young Quadratus. He was noble, wealthy, handsome, educated, learned, and adorned with every virtue. Out of love for the brethren, he went to the

---

[15] Other sources record the name as Phalkinianos; and one source lists him as Phylakianos.

[16] The synaxis of Saint Akakios is celebrated at his martyric shrine in the temple dedicated to him, which is situated in Eptaskalo (or according to others, Paschalo), at which time they also commemorate the anniversary of the consecration of the same church.

[17] Nikomedia (now Izmit, 40°48′N 29°55′E), is a city of Bithynia, that is, northwestern Turkey, at the head of Izmit Gulf of the Sea of Marmara. Nikomedia, originally a Megarian city founded in the 8th C. B.C., spreads across several hills and over a narrow plain that contains both commercial and industrial sections. It served as the capital of the kingdom of Bithynia and later, under the Romans, was often the residence of emperors. It became the eastern capital of the Roman Empire under Diocletian (284-305).

warden and soldiers of the prison detaining the martyrs. Careless of his own safety, Quadratus brought with him many silver coins. By the use of such gifts to the pagans in charge, he received leave to enter within. He, thereupon, diligently cared and treated for the imprisoned brethren. Without feeling the least intimidated, Quadratus gave to each what was required. Those in the cells who were endued with more daring for martyrdom, Akakios besought them to remember him whensoever they should enter into the kingdom of the heavens. Those who were cowering, Akakios was emboldening and telling them not to be afraid of the tortures. He urged them to be eager and ready for martyrdom and, moreover, to be rejoicing on account of these things. He reminded them that most people pass through this life not in comfort and ease, but with abundant pain, suffering, affliction, and terrible torments; for "through many temptations it is necessary for us to enter into the kingdom of God [Acts 14:23]." He added strength to their souls by speaking these words, by exhorting them to be giving thanks always, even in affliction and tribulations, to God in the name of Christ.[18] He then recited those words which Saint Paul spoke: "For I reckon that the sufferings of the present time are not worthy in comparison to the future glory to be revealed in us [Rom. 8:18]."

One day, during that period that the blessed Quadratus was exercising such virtues, the proconsul[19] took his seat on the tribunal. He charged the soldiers to bring forward the Christian martyrs for judgment. When the martyrs were made to stand before him, the proconsul addressed them with these words: "Let each one of you state his name, station among his people, and his homeland." The blessed Quadratus, as one extremely devoted to piety and overcome by love of the Lord, possessed an incomparable longing for the kingdom of the heavens. He, therefore, in the secret recesses of his soul, was thinking to go to the Lord before the other brethren. This thought was impelled onward when he observed that some among the present brethren were hesitating to enter the contests of martyrdom. He considered they might become even weaker in their resolve to keep to the Christian Faith if fear or the tortures should drive them to deny the name of the Christ. For this reason, he wanted to go forth and inaugurate the contest, as the first contender and soldier

[18] Cf. Eph. 5:20.

[19] Proconsul (ἀνθύπατος or Lat. *pro consule*), in the ancient Roman Republic, was a consul whose powers had been extended for a definite period after his regular term of one year. During lengthy wars the need arose to extend the terms of certain magistrates; such extension was termed *prorogatio*. Initially prorogation was voted by the people, but soon the Senate assumed this power. Provincial governors were almost always prorogued magistrates or proconsuls. After 27 B.C., governors of senatorial provinces were called proconsuls. *Encyclopaedia Britannica Deluxe Edition 2004 CD-ROM*, s.v. "Proconsul."

of high calling, hoping in God that he should become a good example. So he thought, and thus he carried it out. Even though he was behind all the brethren and was held in bonds by no one, he, in but a moment, with an uplifted answer responded first to the proconsul, saying, "Know, O proconsul, that we are called Christians and that we are Christians in very deed. For this is our special and wondrous name. Our noble and highborn station is singular and it is this: we are all slaves of the Lord Jesus Christ, our heavenly and invisible God. As for our homeland, it is the heavenly Jerusalem, the mother of 'the festal assembly and Church of the firstborn ones who have been registered in the heavens [Heb. 12:23]';[20] and within does Christ establish those who hope in Him. Behold, thou hast heard all things concerning us! Henceforth, then, there is no longer any need to put forward questions concerning these things."

Saint Quadratus

The proconsul, hearing all these succinct declarations, was both astonished and shocked at what he deemed to be foolish bravado. Thinking the confessor's entrance precipitate, the proconsul turned to his soldiers and said, "Bring forward that self-chosen and impudent fellow, in order that I may decide how to deal with his shameless arrogance." The noble-minded Quadratus, hearing the directions given to the soldiers, cut through the crowd and presented himself, standing before all. After he made the sign of the precious and life-giving Cross, he addressed the proconsul and said, "I came, self-called, before thee, that I may enter the lists, in the name of all my fellow soldiers here present and against thy father, the devil. Therefore, cease delaying, and do with me as thou dost wish. In this way, thou mayest learn from my own examination and trial the following: we are all soldiers of the Christ; and, in the name of our Master Jesus Christ, we are unconquerable when we wage war against the machinations of Satan." The prefect replied, "Thy wilfulness has alienated the mirth of the gods. Who mayest thou be? Tell

[20] Saint John Chrysostom, "'Of *the* firstborn *ones* (πρωτοτόκων).' Of what firstborn does Saint Paul speak? All of the choirs of the faithful." ["Homily 32," *Hebrews*, *P.G.* 63:294 (col. 220).]

me first thy name and thy position in society." The venerable Quadratus replied, "I told thee already that we are Christians, both I and all of these," as he pointed significantly at the brethren. "We have no other title of nobility, except that we are slaves of our Lord Jesus Christ. This is our noble birth and title." The proconsul, imagining this might be a caprice on the part of the young man, remarked, "Thy conversation is ill-chosen. It is not in thine interest to call thyself a Christian. I say this since the command of our unvanquished emperors has pronounced that all Christians are to be put to death. By what I see, I perceive that thou art an educated man with much erudition and impeccable breeding. I judge this by thy pleasing address, clear delivery, and thy comely appearance. Indeed, from all the others, it is evident that thou art wellborn and not lowborn. Therefore, state when and where thou didst obtain such learning and wisdom. Do thou obey me, beloved friend, that thou mayest appear pleasing to the gods. And be assured that I shall recommend thee to the emperors in a dispatch; they will offer thee a governor's post."

The right-minded Quadratus, not in the least taken in by the praises and promises of the proconsul, came back to him with this admonishment: "O proconsul, cease referring to them as gods, for there are not many gods. Indeed, there is one God and Father, Maker of all, and one Lord Jesus Christ, 'through Whom all things came into being [Jn. 1:3],' and the Holy Spirit Who fills all things." The proconsul commented, "Though there are many gods, the emperors have decided that the people need only pay homage to the twelve gods. Thou art also under this obligation, that is, to offer them sacrifice and veneration." The holy Quadratus, with great boldness, then lifted up his voice and quoted Homer, saying, "The rule of many is not good; let there be one rule, one King." The proconsul rejoined, "Homer, however, says this regarding the gods, Poseidon (Neptune) the 'earth-shaker' and Zeus (Jupiter) the 'cloud-gatherer,' because the latter gathered clouds and agitated various winds, thus covering the sky. And so Homer wrote of more than one god, saying: 'Fearful thundering, O father of men and gods on high, but from beneath Poseidon shakes the earth.' Furthermore, the poet also speaks in regard to how Dia, that is Zeus, revealed himself as an ordinary mortal,[21] which transformation thou thyself dost understand, since thou dost claim it also for thy Christ. That being the case, thou shouldest perceive the greatness of the gods."

---

[21] According to Greek mythology, Zeus revealed himself as a man to Semele; she was the mother of the god of wine and of vegetation, Dionysus. Semele then asked Zeus to reveal his true form, but he hesitated since he knew the consequences of such a revelation. But on account of his prior promise to her to do whatsoever she asked, she was scorched by his heavenly radiance and died.

The blessed Quadratus then asked the proconsul, "Whatsoever Homer said concerning the gods, is it true or false?" The proconsul answered, "It is true." Quadratus then remarked, "I blush for you idolaters, since the gods to whom you pay obeisance are adulterers and homosexuals. Indeed, so says Homer. But those who do such things, that is, those who commit adultery and homosexuality, you have punished by law since the era you came into authority. But here, on the contrary, you consider as deities and worthy of worship those whom Homer clearly identifies with such crimes. If, therefore, thou dost wish it, be persuaded by your own poets that such gods are actually demons who are obscene, disorderly, fickle, dwellers of the nether world, spirits of sorceries and deceits." The proconsul, perceiving the irony, affected insensibility and retorted, "Mindless one, hast thou begun to insult and outrage the gods? I fear that, peradventure, the emperors shall become indignant with me, in view of the fact that I continue to be lenient with thee." The saint replied to this, saying, "My candor, O proconsul, neither thou nor another is able to take from me. Therefore, do whatsoever thou dost wish."

At this juncture, the proconsul, goaded by the censures, was exceedingly cross. He ordered his officers to remove the Christian's clothing and administer a flogging with raw bullwhips. As the punishment was being dispensed, the proconsul kept asking, "Tell me thy name." But since the blessed Quadratus gave no answer, the proconsul then asked the soldiers, "How is he called?" They answered him, "He is called Quadratus; and he is of an illustrious family." The proconsul said, "Leave him, cease scourging him; instead, raise him up from the ground." After this was done, the proconsul said to the martyr, "Why dost thou make us dishonor thy dignity and house?" The proconsul then summoned Quadratus to draw closer, at which point he continued talking and saying, "Why hast thou illogically forsaken thy dignity, reputation, and family? Why dost thou follow the empty and profane religion of the Christians?" Saint Quadratus then bravely answered, "I have chosen rather to be an outcast in the house of my God than to dwell in the tents of sinners [Ps. 83:11]." The proconsul remarked to this, saying, "Hearken to me, and sacrifice to the gods. Do it this day, especially the holy anniversary of the emperors, if thou wouldest be numbered among those in the Roman Senate and not undergo an evil demise as some malefactor. Hast thou not heard the command of the emperors and the sacred Senate, or even the counsels of myriads of men, who are virtuous and admirable? They have certified that it is not necessary for anyone to live as a Christian."

To this speech, the saintlike Quadratus gave answer, by first reciting David: "Blessed is the man that hath not walked in the counsel of the ungodly, nor stood in the way of sinners, nor sat in the seat of the pestilent. But his will is rather in the law of the Lord, and in His law will he meditate day and night

[Ps. 1:1, 2]." The proconsul remarked, "Do not deceive thyself, Quadratus, because the decree of the emperors is contrary to every Christian, whether poor or rich, whether an officer or a private citizen. Distinction of rank will not be observed. Simply put, every Christian, whosoever that person may be, will not in the least receive mercy at the tribunal; much rather death awaits each." Quadratus made this acknowledgment: "Thou hast spoken truly, so that even the Scriptures say, 'There is no Greek and Jew, circumcision and uncircumcision, barbarian, Scythian, slave and free, but Christ is all things and in all [Col. 3:11].' For this reason, all the Christians, with the grace of God, are one. I, therefore, beseech thee, quickly apply to me the penalty for those who disobey the decree of thine emperors and of the Senate; forasmuch as I am a Christian. Indeed, my own race and my rank are with the saints, those who possess glory in the heavens above."

The proconsul, astonished at what he was hearing, came back and said, "Listen to me and give the prescribed sacrifice to the gods that thou mayest enjoy the light of this world, otherwise thou art about to be put to death by means of a fearful martyrdom." As he was delivering this decision, the proconsul wept and sighed heavily. He drew out his handkerchief and began wiping his face. The saint, witnessing this show of emotion, invalidated the performance, saying, "O proconsul, thou rapacious despoiler, cease by these artificial means to employ the knavish tricks of the dragon, by shedding tears of the apostate! For thou shalt not succeed in bringing me, the slave of God, into error."

Present among the bystanders was Maximos, the governor, who, with a hostile glare, began to remonstrate with the saint and said, "O most evil man, hearken! My master, the most magnificent proconsul, has taken pity on thee. What is this effrontery and incivility? It ill becomes thee to insult him." Saint Quadratus contradicted him, saying, "Let him weep for himself and for the hour of his birth, seeing that I, as the humble slave of God, am worthy of neither mercy nor tears. If the proconsul is a judge, who art thou who speakest before him? This matter pertains to us. But if thou shouldest also wish to make a beginning, the Lord shall remove thee." That disputatious governor, inflamed by wrath, or rather by his father the devil, turned to the proconsul and said, "His conduct is unpardonable. I assure thee in the name of thy great fame and fortune, milord proconsul, that if thou shouldest let this fellow go unpunished, he will not hesitate to outrage even the emperors and, thereby, place us in enormous danger." The right-minded Quadratus, undisturbed by this outburst, said, "Verily, the divine writings speak the truth: 'Why have the heathen raged, and the peoples meditated empty things? The kings of the earth were aroused, and the rulers were assembled together, against the Lord, and against

His Christ [Ps. 2:1, 2].' Behold, therefore, that also now the slave of the Christ is judged by ungodly and vain men."

The proconsul, filled with rage against Quadratus, shouted at his soldiers, "Strip this ingrate and blasphemer. Thrash him without pity that he might awaken from the madness that has stricken and overthrown him. By corporal punishment, persuade him to adhere to the decree of the emperors which require him to sacrifice to the gods." The happy Quadratus, while they were beating him, was saying, "Glory to Thee, O God and Lord Jesus Christ, in that Thou hast vouchsafed even me, the sinner and unworthy one, to suffer these things for Thy holy name's sake, so that I also, Thy humble creature, may be numbered with Thy beloved slaves! Yea, my Lord Jesus Christ, account me worthy to enjoy richly the grace of Thy Holy Spirit. Moreover, grant me prudence to the end that I may preserve my Faith unshaken. For this is the moment that I need Thy protection. This is the season of Thy good will. Now is the time that I require Thy help. Strengthen me, O Lord. Support and set me right in accordance with Thy promise: 'Be taking heed to yourselves: For they shall deliver you up to councils...and ye shall be made to stand before governors and kings on account of Me, for a testimony to them. And it is needful for the Gospel first to be proclaimed to all the nations. But whenever they lead you away and deliver you up, cease taking thought before what ye should say, neither be meditating. But whatsoever shall be given to you in that hour, be speaking this; for ye are not the ones who speak, but the Holy Spirit [Mk. 13:9-11].' Do Thou receive me in Thy sanctuary above the heavens. Accept the sacrifice of Thy humble slave, to the glorification of Thy most holy name to the ages of the ages. Amen."

The officers administering this chastisement needed to be changed five times to refresh themselves. By reason of the prolonged torture, the tissues swelled about the ribs of the blessed martyr and a river of blood ran from his flesh. At that point, the proconsul interposed, "At least tell me now if thou art persuaded to sacrifice to the gods? Yea or nay?" The estimable athlete of Christ confuted him with this response: "The idols of the nations are of silver and gold, the works of the hands of men. They have a mouth, but shall not speak; eyes have they, and shall not see. Ears have they, and shall not hear; noses have they, and shall not smell. Hands they have, and shall not feel; feet have they, and shall not walk; they shall make no sound in their throat. Let those that make them become like unto them, and all that put their trust in them [Ps. 113:12-16]." The proconsul answered back, "Thou art speaking blasphemy with dark speech, fancying thou canst trick us. On this account, I command thee to offer sacrifice immediately to the gods; otherwise, I shall cast thy flesh in small pieces before thine eyes!"

Undaunted, Christ's sterling confessor explained, "Well said, for through dark sayings I spoke, because the speech of truth seems dark to thee, while error shines for thee. Those things which I have spoken 'have been from the beginning. Even those things that we have heard and have known and which our fathers have told us [Ps. 77:2, 3].' Now 'piety toward God is the beginning of discernment; but the ungodly will set at nought wisdom and instruction [Prov. 1:7].' Know this, then, that we are not worshipping thy gods; and we are not persuaded by the decisions or beliefs of Caesar and the Senate. Therefore, if it seems good to thee to torture me, carry on and do it quickly, so as to send me forth to my heavenly kingdom." The proconsul, with much shamelessness and indignation, said, "Thine evil fate punishes thee. Consequently, with the power of all the gods, I do not want to pity thee in the least. But rather, I wish to exterminate thee with manifold and diverse tortures, ending with a bitter death."

After this scene, the day had already been far spent. The proconsul charged his officers to lock up the martyrs inside the prison. With regard to the blessed Quadratus, the proconsul specified that sharp spear-like stones were to be spread on his wounded sides. A large rock, however, was to be set upon his chest. His feet were to be secured in wooden stocks. The other members of his body were to be placed in heavy irons. The minions of the proconsul executed those orders to the letter. Thus, they relinquished the man of God to painful bonds and acute afflictions, under which conditions he was extremely tormented for many days.

The heavenly-minded martyr, as a truly valiant athlete of piety, endured with magnanimity. Although the torments were terrible, still he neither altered nor withdrew his hope and love which he had toward God. Now after these proceedings, it happened that the proconsul was preparing to go to Nicaea.[22] He directed that the holy martyrs were to follow him. Among those who were being transferred to Nicaea was Quadratus. Even as a courageous and valiant commander in chief—who has confidence in his strength and ability, and who marches in front of his troops against the enemy host with the bright gleam of his armor and weapons—causes terror in his adversaries looking upon him, in like manner did the valiant and manly Quadratus go before all the holy martyrs, showing a countenance both gracious and full of strength. He was bearing his chains with dignity and gladness, as though he had precious ornaments. The solemn aspect of Quadratus and that of his fellow martyrs was such that the philosophers of the idolaters wondered and marvelled

---

[22] Nicaea of Bithynia, the ancient rival of Nikomedia, is present-day Iznik (40°27′N 29°43′E) on the eastern shore of Lake Iznik. In late antiquity Nicaea was a fortified city with civic and private buildings laid out on a regular plan. It was on major trade and military routes.

on account of the wisdom, self-possession, and patience exhibited by the Christians. They began to glorify God, saying, "Truly great is the Faith of the Christians!" In fact, many among them, came to believe in the Lord.

After they arrived in Nicaea and the hour drew nigh that the Christians were to appear before the proconsul's judgment seat, Quadratus besought the officers that they might present him first for examination. As Quadratus was led forth, the tyrant said to him, "Quadratus, sacrifice to the gods that thou mightest save thyself from the tortures that await to put thee to the test." The man of God said, "I am the slave of Jesus Christ Who spoke by His prophet, saying, 'Let the gods which have not made heaven and earth perish from off the earth, and from under this sky [Jer. 10:11].'" The proconsul persisted and said, "Thou must be obedient to the laws of the emperors and not the Christ." The upright Quadratus countered this, saying, "I am obedient to Christ, my King, Whom I confess openly. I am not obedient to men who know not God. It is, however, written for us that we ought to supplicate God in their behalf, that they might turn to the knowledge of God and acknowledge the truth.[23] But that we should sacrifice to idols is not at all written. Moreover, you also have no obligation to sacrifice to them. Offering sacrifice that you may be subject to Caesar, indeed, injures not only you but also him."

The proconsul sought to disprove this cleverly and conclusively when he said to that just man, "If it is written in your books that you ought to beseech God in behalf of the emperors, then thou art also obliged to obey their commands. Inasmuch as it has been written for you Christians, as thou knowest it: 'Render therefore the things of Caesar to Caesar, and the things of God to God [Mt. 22:21].'" Quadratus, always filled with good courage, declared, "I paid Caesar for my fields. I am, therefore, also bound to remit piety to my God. Now Caesar has commanded that we Christians either offer sacrifice or forfeit our lives. We are ready, then, by reason of our confession in Christ, to lay down our lives, not only once but even tens of thousands of times." The proconsul, thinking to expose Quadratus' weak point, commented, "Seest thou, O Quadratus, how a multitude of Christians offer sacrifice to the gods? Peradventure, thou dost think thyself more superior or noble than all of these?"

The holy minded one, with a brisk rejoinder, said to the tyrant, "Yea, I have been distinguished by the following: that I did not pay homage to thy gods. But where are these persons whom thou dost claim have offered sacrifice? Because I do not see any such persons." The proconsul gave the

[23] "I [Paul] exhort therefore, first of all, that entreaties, prayers, intercessions, and thanksgivings be made for all men, for kings and all those who are in authority, that we may pass a quiet and peaceable life in all piety and gravity. For this is good and acceptable before God our Savior, Who willeth all men to be saved and to come to a full knowledge of the truth [1 Tim. 2:1-4]."

command to present all those who made sacrifices to the idols. The righteous Quadratus, lest they should see him fettered, said to the proconsul, "I pray thee, give the order that they loose me from my bonds." The proconsul, hearing these words, imputed Quadratus' request to mean that he was going to make the mandatory sacrifice. He, thereupon, gave orders to have him unfettered. That seraphic-like man, as soon as he was released, made haste to their idol temple. He then proceeded to break in pieces all the idols, casting them down to the ground. The vile priests of the temple, beholding what was taking place, called the soldiers and, together, they seized Quadratus. Once again, Quadratus was brought before the proconsul whose fury waxed hot. He charged the executioners to suspend Quadratus upon a wooden pole and to lacerate and flay his flesh. As the martyr was suspended from the wood and the soldiers were stripping his flesh, Quadratus was glorifying God with a voice filled with fervor.

Now when those who had denied Christ entered, the peerless Quadratus rebuked them and said, "Alas! O most wretched ones and cowards, what great evil have you brought upon yourselves by denying the Master Christ and delivering yourselves up to death? Did you not believe that there is a resurrection of the dead and God's judgment? Did you not learn that there is an everlasting fire,[24] an unsleeping worm,[25] the deepest Tartarus,[26] and unending punishment?[27] Therefore, what kind of defense shall you give on that glorious and great day of the second coming of our Savior Jesus Christ? Open the eyes of your minds. See from what height of glory you have fallen down headlong. Look at the depths of ingloriousness into which you have plunged yourselves, since you have relinquished the kingdom of the heavens and everlasting life. By your actions, you have submitted yourselves to the devil, the unprofitable and paltry slave who, since he apostatized from the Master and God, strikes and slays his fellow slaves, men and women. Now whensoever the Master should come, He will divide the peoples in two; and those on the left shall be sent 'into the fire, the everlasting one, which hath been prepared for the devil and his angels [Mt. 25:41].' Do you not know, then, O miserable ones, the evil which you have committed? Do you not realize how you have handed yourselves over to everlasting punishments, owing to your fear of mere temporal chastisements? Have you not heard the commands of the Lord Who said, 'Do not become afraid because of those who kill the body, but are not able to kill the soul; but rather fear the One Who is able to send away both soul and body into Gehenna [Mt. 10:28]'?"

---

[24] Mt. 25:41.

[25] Mk. 9:44 ff.

[26] 2 Pe. 2:4.

[27] Mt. 25:46.

While Quadratus was making these utterances, the Christ-deniers were shouting aloud amid their tears: "O our master and teacher, we were frightened of the tortures. We were pulled to pieces as irrational animals, and, as lambs in the midst of wolves, lapsed into error. On account of our sins were we blinded, longing as we were to live this temporal life; and, as a result, we died to that future and true age. We, the distressed ones, therefore, do not know what to do from henceforth." The blessed Quadratus, filled with great joy upon seeing their tears and hearing their repentance, said to them, "Take courage, brethren! For our Lord Jesus Christ, as One compassionate Who loves mankind, accepts all of you who repent. Only weep and prostrate yourselves before Him, making a humble and heartfelt entreaty. Then stand courageously in the Faith and in the confession of Christ the Savior. Let each one purge his own sin by his own blood. If once you were vanquished by the flesh, overcome now by the resistance of the soul and your confession."

After Quadratus delivered those soul-saving words, which proved to be balm for their stricken souls, they did not disguise their misery and mortification. They began weeping, crying aloud, and wailing over their defection. They fell forward to the ground, striking their heads and beating their chests with rocks. None of the spectators were inured to this fearful exhibition. Not only those who were Christians but also those who were idolaters and heartless officers were moved to sympathy before such a sign of repentance. In fact, all of them thought that even the rocks were lamenting with the penitents. Such was the astonishment of the inhabitants of the city when they assembled together—that is, men, women, and children, whether they were Jews, idolaters, or Christians. There were so many in attendance that neither the marketplace nor the square could hold the crowds. The sight of this gathering maddened the proconsul. He issued another order to his executioner to flay Quadratus. After many hours of this savage stripping of his skin, they were instructed to burn his sides with lit torches.

Quadratus, the excellent contestant for Jesus, as one insensible to his torments, exhorted, with great boldness, the Christ-deniers who were repenting. Among his admonitions, he was saying the following to them: "Brethren, without ceasing, direct your appeals to our Lord Jesus Christ, and He shall bestow His mercy." They replied mournfully that they were not worthy. With plaintive expressions, they admitted that they could not bring themselves to bring forth the holy name of Christ out of their defiled mouths which previously had dishonored Him. The angel-like Quadratus resolutely encouraged them, saying, "Brethren, invoke God, call upon Him incessantly." Quadratus then added, "Draw nigh to me and cease fearing."

After they came close to him, they prostrated themselves and wailed aloud before God. Others standing by also wept for them. Then the matchless

Quadratus raised his voice and cried out with tears, saying, "O Lord God, Who art good, compassionate, and lovest mankind, Thou hast sent forth Thine only-begotten Son, Jesus Christ, through Whom Thou hast reconciled us to Thyself.[28] O Lord, Thou hast made all creation in wisdom,[29] fashioning it for man, who is according to Thine image, that he might enjoy Thy creations and govern the world in holiness and righteousness. O Lord, Thou didst not spare the apostate and man-hating tyrant, the devil, and his angels, but cast them into Tartarus;[30] for the devil is the father of the idols and the leader of darkness. But Thou, O God our Savior, in Thine incomparable goodness and love for mankind, invited all men to repentance and salvation; for Thou desirest not the death of any, but rather that all men be saved and come to a full knowledge of the truth.[31] I beseech Thee, O Master Christ, receive even now these, my fellow soldiers, who have repented with all their soul. Although they had been ensnared in the devil's trap and abjured Thee, yet now they take refuge in Thy goodness and love for mankind. Be not angered with them, O Lord, as those are with soldiers who desert. Although they were late in returning to their posts, still they now offer repentance and desire to abide immoveable in their belief in Thee, if Thou wouldest have mercy on them and receive them with gracious cheerfulness. Yea, my Lord Jesus Christ, accept the gift of Thine unworthy slave, and count them among those to be united and numbered with Thy heavenly and true army. Do Thou show them, this day, a sign for good that they might recognize that Thou dost have mercy upon those who repent and that Thou dost not abominate them. Yea, O Master Lord Jesus Christ, hearken to me, Thy slave, receive as their pledge my own soul, for to Thee is due glory to the ages. Amen."

Straightway, as they all cried out the "Amen," the torches, the ones used to burn the Martyr Quadratus, were extinguished. A radiant cloud then hovered over the holy martyrs. At that very moment a dark fog and acrid smoke enveloped the proconsul and idolaters. Such was the fear of the pagans and their councillors in that thick and pungent smoke that they were unable to articulate. They imagined that the city was about to collapse. In the midst of that silence, an angelic voice could be heard hymning and glorifying God. Two hours later, when the darkness started to disperse, the idolaters began looking intently at the holy martyrs, for they observed that a great light surrounded them. The penitents also began wailing and lamenting, shouting aloud, "We have sinned, we have transgressed Thy law, we have done wrong, we have

---

[28] Cf. 2 Cor. 5:18, 19; Rom. 5:10; Col. 1:20.

[29] Cf. Ps. 103:26.

[30] Cf. 2 Pe. 2:4.

[31] Cf. 1 Tim. 2:4.

separated ourselves from Thee. But do Thou expiate our sin, O Savior. Be merciful to us, O God! Become our expiation, O heavenly King!"

After these momentous experiences, since the proconsul composed himself, he charged his soldiers to lock up Quadratus and all the martyrs in the prison where they were to be kept under strict security. Only after this was the stalwart Quadratus taken down from the wooden pole. He, too, as earlier, was cast into prison. After these happenings, then a crowd from the city and the ranks of the proconsul's soldiers, together with the governor, kept watch outside of the prison. The following day, when the proconsul took his place at the tribunal, he asked that Quadratus be brought before him. He also bade them bring those who had recanted and converted by means of Quadratus. When they were all presented, the proconsul perceived their unshakeable boldness. He noted that they did not swerve in confessing Christ, and that they were ardent and inspired in the language they used. The proconsul then appointed a beating for all of them. This punishment did not reap any results. The proconsul then instructed his soldiers to lead the confessors to the places from which they hailed. Once there they were to be consigned, alive, to the flames. Those heavenly-minded ones, with much joy and without a backward glance, went with the soldiers, praising and glorifying God. When each was conveyed to his own place, every last one of them, filled with the grace and power of our Lord Jesus Christ, finished in the fire. Thus, God wisely contrived their salvation through the good offices of Quadratus.

After all these stirring events, the proconsul commanded that Quadratus was to be transferred with the others. First they would go to Apameia and, afterward, to Caesarea, the same cities which the proconsul was visiting. At Apameia, after the proconsul offered sacrifice to the idols, he ordered that the holy martyrs be brought before him. The proconsul, at that point, said to Quadratus, "Wilt thou at least perform the sacrifice now to the gods, O sorcerer and deceiver? Or wilt thou refuse again?" Quadratus answered, "Thy father, Satan, claims those words 'sorcerer' and 'deceiver.' But I am a Christian; and neither do I know magic, nor do I engage in deceit or fraud, nor do I offer sacrifice to demons—not ever." The proconsul then gave heed to the appearance of that unearthly Quadratus. His whole body looked like one wound. The proconsul then remarked to his friends, "I know not what other kind of punishment to apply so as to usher in an evil death for this one." But the others were stupefied, wondering at Quadratus' resilient alchemy and hair-breadth escapes, so they did not offer any suggestions. It was evident to all of them that there was nowhere that his flesh could receive a fresh injury. The proconsul then made up his mind to have Quadratus placed inside of a sack. He then enjoined his men to strike heavily upon the martyr in the sack. After they had administered blows for a long while, the proconsul demanded that they remove Quadratus from the sack; for he thought that surely the martyr had died.

When the men opened the sack, the holy martyr emerged on his own and stood upright. The proconsul, astounded, asked, "Wretched man, dost thou still not feel the torments?" The unworldly Quadratus gazed heavenward and uttered, "I give thanks to Thee, O Lord Jesus Christ, that to me their wounds are as the darts of infants; whereas Thou hast utterly weakened their strength, but Thou hast empowered me." Quadratus then looked at the proconsul and said, "Vain and sorry man, why look and not examine? Whatsoever, therefore, thou art able to do, carry it out quickly." The proconsul, chaffing at these words, felt his temper rising and responded in a vexed tone, "During the entire journey on the road I will be subjecting thee to torture, O miserable one, and thou mayest go on believing in thy sorceries." At this response, Quadratus privately gave thanks to the Lord and said, "Blessed art Thou, O Lord God, that thou hast delivered my life and not permitted the snares of death to overtake me!"[32] The proconsul issued a command to his soldiers that they escort the Christian to Caesarea. He then added that they were to leave immediately, which came to pass.

When the proconsul came into Caesarea, he had the Martyr Quadratus brought before him. Once again, the proconsul asked Quadratus if he were ready to offer sacrifice. Seeing the martyr refused to comply, the proconsul said, "Sufficient, O man, were the punishments to which thou wast subjected. Come, then, and sacrifice to the gods." Quadratus, again, answered with boldness and said, "Thou hast played with me by means of such chastisements, O proconsul, and hast not punished me." The proconsul flew into a rage at these words. His next word of command was to his soldiers, directing them to bring Quadratus to the stone pavement. He, thereupon, instructed them to bind Quadratus' hands and feet to the pillars. When he was thus secured, they were to chastise his entire body with raw bullwhips. The blessed man, while he was scourged for a very long time and suffered bitter torments, kept giving glory to God and said, "Many a time have they warred against me from my youth, and yet they have not prevailed against me. The sinners wrought upon my back, they lengthened out their iniquity [Ps. 128:2, 3]."

The Holy Martyrs Satorninos and Rufinos

When the saint finished reciting the psalm, he made this comment to the proconsul: "Thou hast lashed my humble skin. Thou art able to wrong my flesh. My soul, however, thou canst in no wise injure." The proconsul flashed back, "Wretched fellow, an evil demon lords it over thee." The saint parried, "My Lord Jesus Christ knows that I became lord and master over a very evil

---

[32] Cf. Ps. 17:5.

demon; and yet not only that one spirit but even a whole army of them, by the grace and power of my Lord Jesus Christ to Whom is glory due unto the ages." As he finished speaking, the crowd of Christian brethren gave the response of "Amen," which exceedingly enraged the proconsul. He, therefore, enjoined that two from among that company should be apprehended. He then charged the executioners to suspend those two men and flay their bodies. The two Christians selected were Satorninos and Rufinos. The executioners, consequently, abandoned, for the moment, Saint Quadratus, and they undertook the punishment of the other two. So brutal were the lacerations carried out by means of iron claws that the inward parts of the two martyrs were about to fall on the ground. Those two tormented martyrs besought Quadratus and all the other brethren present to pray in their behalf.

The saint, with a great voice, then sent up an entreaty to the Lord, uttering, "O Lord Jesus Christ, Son of the invisible Father, send forth Thy help to them and defend them. Do Thou, Who art the God of the humble, have mercy on Thy slaves and grant them patience to the end and victory." After considerable time passed, Satorninos and Rufinos still gave no answer. This was due to the many torments they sustained, leaving them unable to utter a word. The proconsul then told his men to take the two of them down from the wooden pole and hand them over to the executioners for beheading. The sentence was to be carried out on the road of the Hellespont.[33] On the way to execution, certain reverent lovers of Christ followed. The two holy Martyrs Satorninos and Rufinos received a sacred martyric end. The godly folk who witnessed the decapitations gave the executioners much money. They bribed them so that they might collect the precious and holy relics, thereby providing them with a fitting burial in their homeland.

The Repose of Saint Quadratus

In the meantime, the proconsul crossed over to Caesarea to attend to some business. When he was about to depart for Apollonia, he gave orders that Quadratus and the other martyrs were to follow him. As soon as he arrived, he entered into the temple of Apollo. He commanded the soldiers to bring the Christians to him. After they came, he again insisted that they offer sacrifice to the gods, that is, the unclean demons. Then he spoke in a sweet tone to Quadratus, saying, "Hearken to me, man, at least now offer the sacrifice to the gods. Why dost thou dishonor thy station and thy family? Come to know the gods and pay them homage that thou mightest save thy life. And be assured, I

[33] The Hellespont (Dardanelles or "the Stenon" or Canakkale Bogazi) was a strait between the Aegean Sea and the Sea of Marmara. It is thirty-eight miles (sixty-one kilometers) long. It is 3/4 to four miles wide and lies between the peninsula of Gallipoli (Kallipolis) in Europe (northwest) and the mainland of Asia Minor (southeast) with the cities of Abydos and Lampsakos.

will have the physicians provide expert care and treatment for thy wounds; only I tell thee, perform the prescribed sacrifice to the great gods."

The dear Martyr Quadratus affirmed what he had said from the beginning: "I pay homage to the true God and His only-begotten Son, Jesus Christ, and the holy and life-giving Spirit, hymning and glorifying the Trinity forever. As for the demons, I fear them not. With regard to the work of the hands of men, I do not make obeisance to such creations. Nor to thee, with thy temporal authority, do I render obedience; inasmuch as in a few days I shall pass over to my Lord Jesus Christ. As regards thee, thou shalt come to a bad death since thou dost not wish to know the true God Who granted thee authority. But thou art a son of Satan, a brother of the apostate devil, a partaker of the unclean demons, a most irrational swine, a mad dog, a blood-drinking dragon, a flesh-eating lion, and one more fierce even than the beasts! Art thou not ashamed before such a multitude of people to give sacrifice to stones that comprehend nothing? The cooks are more worthy of respect than you idolaters; they make themselves appear to be slaves of men and not of demons. You, however, shamelessly offer sacrifice, publicly, to insensate idols. On the one hand, you pay them homage; on the other hand, what is most awful, you eat the same sacrifices. Let the one who receives the offerings come forth. Let such a one be shown that we may see him. Let us ask such a one about the sacrifice he received and whether he consumed it. Let your stone god speak and tell us what he prefers as a sacrifice—goat or bull or bird—and which of these is of more value. The worship you render is absurd and errant nonsense. It is shameful, therefore, to compel us to offer sacrifice to the idols. For shame, O children of shame, inasmuch as you are out of your minds and think that we who are of sound mind are mindless!"

The proconsul, after hearing these words, was filled with wrath. He commanded his underlings to steep in vinegar and salt the wounds of the martyr. After bathing him with that solution, they were to take rough and bristly material, made of haircloth, and rub the same wounds. These orders were quickly dispatched and continued for many hours. Following the application of these torments, that savage and impious proconsul had the executioners burn the martyr's sides with red-hot irons. The hallowed martyr, Quadratus, endured with much long-suffering these pangs, praying calmly all the while with his lips moving. His voice was not heard. Since the soldiers had become exhausted after administering the tortures, the tyrant told them to cast Quadratus into the prison.

The following day, the proconsul enjoined the man of God to walk before his entourage. The proconsul also ordered that Quadratus be in a state of fasting as he went before all toward the Hellespont. After they passed over from there to the Reendaka River,[34] they were met in advance not only by the men in authority of that place but also a crowd of people from the villages thereabout. They came in order to confirm the reality of the triumphs of Christ's athlete. The fame of Quadratus' name had spread throughout Asia and nearly the inhabited world. The proconsul then commanded that they all go on ahead to the village of Seroukomeen, a place possessing many idols. It was there that the proconsul chose to rest for the remainder of the day. At dawn of the following day, he ascended the judgment seat. He ordered his men to bring forward Quadratus. A multitude of onlookers, in the meantime, had assembled. They were waiting to view the martyr as he contested.

Though the saint had sustained wounds all over his body, which caused his flesh to swell as a wineskin, yet his countenance was cheerful and pleasant. The soldiers, those who were assigned to accompany Quadratus, commented that his face was wont to bear a smile. At this critical point in the course of the martyr's contest, on account of the many tortures with which he had been inflicted, he was no longer able to walk. The soldiers, therefore, for the remainder of the journey, conveyed him by a four-wheeled wagon. When Quadratus was brought before the proconsul, the latter posed this question to the martyr: "Hast thou come to thy senses or not, Quadratus?" The saint, with a loud voice, answered, "I do possess a sound mind; and such has been my state from the time when I was very small and my fingernails were soft. And, indeed, I am a Christian from my mother's womb.[35] Another God I know not, save Jesus Christ. Do, then, whatsoever thou dost wish as soon as thou art able."

Upon this declaration, the proconsul, blazing with rage, commanded that a great fire be kindled. A brazier was placed over the fire. The coals underneath heated the pan of the brazier until it glowed red. The saint was about to be placed upon the brazier when the memorable Quadratus remarked, "O proconsul, I myself will go up to the brazier. There is no reason why thine underlings should catch fire." Quadratus then solemnly made the sign of the honorable and life-creating Cross, and then cast himself upon the fiery brazier. The servants of the devil began adding pitch, oil, and tow to the top of the brazier. The martyr began chanting this psalm: "O God, be attentive unto helping me; O Lord, make haste to help me. Let them be shamed and confounded that seek after my soul. Let them be turned back and brought to shame that desire evils against me [Ps. 69:1-3]."

---

[34] *The Great Synaxaristes* (in Greek) records the name of the river as Reendaka (Ρήνδακα). The *Synaxarion* of the *Menaion* records that they passed over the Roundakon (Ρουνδακόν) River and Hermoupolis.

[35] Cf. Jer. 1:5; Ps. 21:9, 10; Gal. 1:15.

After the saint completed the psalm and two hours had elapsed with him still upon the brazier, Quadratus began to deride the proconsul and declared, "Thy fire, O proconsul, is cool. The iron bars of the gridiron are softer than thy heart. Well didst thou to command that I should be thrown onto such a soft brazier that I might take my ease upon such comfortable bedding, since I became quite fatigued from our journey. But now I have collected myself and, once again, I have recovered my strength which I had at the commencement of thy tortures." Thus spoke the happy martyr as he turned from one side to the other. Since much time had passed and the fire in no wise touched the saint upon the brazier, the proconsul gave orders to lift Quadratus from the brazier. The proconsul, with brusque resolution, directed his men to remove the saint to a lofty spot slightly outside the village, where he was to have his head severed.

The blessed Quadratus, as he went, knew he was nearing the end of his martyrdom, which moved him to chant this verse: "Blessed be the Lord Who hath not given us to be a prey to their teeth [Ps. 123:5]." Now some of the brethren, those who had been following him, chanted along with him until they reached the execution site. When they arrived at the place, Quadratus stood and faced east, offering up the following glorification to God: "I give thanks to Thee, O Lord, that Thou hast vouchsafed me, Thine unworthy slave, to endure and undergo, for Thy name's sake, bonds and imprisonments and torments and manifold chastisements. O Lord God, the almighty One, the Father of Thy beloved Son and our Lord Jesus Christ Whom I glorify—for Thou hast accounted even me, the unworthy one, in this day and hour to be numbered with Thy holy martyrs—do Thou now, with the grace and power of the Savior Christ, bestow resurrection and life everlasting to both soul and body; for so it is written that 'he that soweth to the Spirit shall of the Spirit reap life everlasting [Gal. 6:8].' Would to God, then, that even I, the unworthy one, might be received with Thy holy martyrs before Thee, this day! Do Thou grant that I might appear before Thee with a sacrifice that is radiant and acceptable! For it was Thou, our unerring and true God, Who didst prepare and reveal it beforehand and perfect it. But so hast Thou promised by Thine apostle that 'after we suffer a little while, the God of all grace, the One Who called us to His eternal glory in Christ Jesus, shall perfect, set fast, strengthen, and found us. To Him be glory and might [Cf. 1 Pe. 5:10, 11],' now and ever and to the ages of the ages."

After Saint Quadratus gave thanks to God, his head was struck off by the sword on the 7th day of the month of May. Thus, the dashing imitator of the Master's love for men became the spokesman, elocutionist, mediator, and living prototype and monument for his fellow martyrs, for which he received the crown of martyrdom from our Lord Jesus Christ, to Whom is due glory and dominion forever. Amen.[36]

On the 7th of May, the holy Church commemorates the holy Martyrs RUFINOS and SATORNINOS, who were slain by the sword.[37]

On the 7th of May, the holy Church commemorates our venerable Father JOHN Psychaïtes, the Confessor.

John, our righteous father, flourished during the period of Iconoclasm.[38] From his youth, John chose to imitate the life of the Baptist John and Prophet Elias, so that he pursued a rough mode of asceticism. Courageously he vanquished the assaults of the demons. With abundant tears, he cleansed his soul. He expiated God with his offerings of all-night standing in prayer and keeping vigil. The ever-memorable man of God venerated and honored the august images of the Master Christ and of all the saints. He overturned and set at nought the proud designs and presumptions of the iconomachs, that is, those who fought against the icons. By his confession of the Faith and his tears, he made stale and parched the rivers of the heretics' teachings. This true confessor was made to undergo both exiles and imprisonments for the sake of his defense of the traditions of the holy fathers, since he disdained the laws of the

Saint John Psychaïtes

[36] The synaxis of the saint was celebrated near Xerokerkos.

[37] The account of the martyrdoms of Saints Rufinos and Satorninos is within the Life of Saint Quadratus, also commemorated this day. Saints Rufinos and Satorninos suffered lacerations and flaying by means of iron claws at Nicaea, after which they suffered decapitation on the road to the Hellespont.

[38] This iconodule monk, John the Psychaïtes, in all likelihood, reposed circa 825, according to the Dumbarton Oaks Hagiography Database. It was Patriarch Tarasios (784-806) who had ordained him to the diaconate. Afterward, Saint John took up the offices of *oikonomos* and then hegumen of the Psycha Monastery at Constantinople. He suffered persecution and was exiled to Cherson by Emperor Leo V (813-820). He did not die there, Instead, he was recalled and reposed in his monastery. See P. van den Ven, "La vie grecque de s. Jean le Psichaite," *Muséon* 21 (n.s. 3) (1902), pp. 103-125.

iconoclastic emperors. The venerable John was accounted worthy of the grace of working miracles, healing both souls and bodies of sufferers. After valiantly contesting in contests equal to those of the saints, he, too, rightfully received a crown.

On the 7th of May, the holy Church commemorates the holy Martyr MAXIMOS, who suffered stoning.

Maximos, the holy martyr, openly and boldly professed the Christ. While he guided many of the idolaters to piety, yet he also endured many chastisements at the hands of inexorable pagans. The latter finally put Maximos to death by stoning. When this took place, in an extraordinary way, some of the stones formed a crown about the martyr, even as he was being translated to the Lord from Whom he received the amaranthine crown of the contest.

On the 7th of May, the holy Church commemorates the Synaxis and the Recovery of the Relics of our venerable and God-bearing Father NEILOS the New, the Myrrh-streamer who struggled in asceticism on Mount Athos.[39]

Neilos, our holy father who struggled on Mount Athos, was born of pious parents during the last quarter of the sixteenth century in a town called Hagios (Aghios) Petros of Kynouria.[40] He was blessed with an uncle, a celibate

[39] The Life of Saint Neilos has been translated from *The Great Synaxaristes* (in Greek), with an extracted paragraph from a Russian translation, as noted, of a Greek manuscript from the saint's *kellion*. The aforesaid Greek compilers of *The Great Synaxaristes* constructed the saint's Life from information found in the 1847 Athonite edition of his divine office. The chief day of the saint's commemoration is the day of his repose, the 12th of November. The synaxis and the recovery of his sacred relics are commemorated today, the 7th of May.

[40] Kynouria is the name of the rugged coastal region of the Arkadia prefecture of the Peloponnesos. In ancient times, the region was contested by Argos and Sparta. The Argives controlled the north, and the Spartans the south. Hagios Petros and neighboring Kosmas lie in the Parnonas (Parnon) Mountains. The village-town of Hagios Petros developed, it is said, from the beginning of the 4th C. According to the tradition, Athonites were established there by the great Constantine. He wished to relocate them outside of Mount Athos. His object was to leave the Mountain dedicated solely to the worship of God, with places of refuge in a monastic setting. The Athonites who settled in Kynouria, with the passage of time and the corruption of the word Athonite, were called Tsakonitai or Tsakones; but now they are known as Kynourians. Hagios Petros has a wonderful landscape. It is a large village at an altitude of 950 meters. It is presently a tourist settlement, especially for lovers of hiking and mountain climbing. The festivals of Saint Neilos on the 7th of May and the Apostles Peter and Paul on the

(continued...)

priest, Father Makarios, who took the young boy Neilos under his guardianship. Father Makarios trained him well in the sacred letters and in the practise of good deeds. When Neilos came of age, both he and his uncle went to the Monastery of Kynouria, called Malevee (Malevi),[41] dedicated to the Feast of the Dormition of the Theotokos. In that monastery they stayed for a period of time. Later, Makarios, seeing the virtues of the young man, called the bishop of the diocese. The bishop, perceiving Neilos' worthiness, accepted the monastery's recommendation. The bishop ordained Neilos to the diaconate. Afterward, Neilos was raised to the dignity of the priesthood. He served as a priest-monk in the Malevee Monastery.

It was, though, their wish to find a more divine way of life, so they abandoned their homeland, friends, and kin, repairing to the Holy Mountain Athos. After they toured all the sacred places of refuge, at last they settled near the cave wherein dwelt the great Peter the Athonite.[42] Just as the hometown of the saint was Hagios Petros, thus by divine œconomy they dwelt in the vicinity of Saint Peter the Athonite. They desired to be imitators and heirs of his lofty ascetical life, equal to that of the angels. At that time, the spot was completely uninhabited. The Skete of Kafsokalyvia had been founded later, in the year 1740;[43] nor yet were there any monastic cells at Kerasia.[44] Only the hermitages of Saint Symeon existed, each one at a great distance from the other.

Observing this secluded and suitable spot, they were overjoyed. The fathers, thereupon, went to the Lavra of Saint Athanasios.[45] It was there that

---

[40](...continued)
29th of June, together with the Feast of our Lady of Malevee, the 23rd of August, are celebrated with special fervor in the town.

[41] Presently, the imposing Monastery of Malevee, thirty kilometers from Astros, is a nunnery surrounded by forests full of junipers, walnut trees, and cherry trees. Malevee houses the wonderworking icon of the Theotokos.

[42] Saint Peter is commemorated by the holy Church on the 12th of June.

[43] Kafsokalyvia, situated on an abrupt slope, is a dependency of Great Lavra. It resembles a village with widely scattered houses.

[44] Kerasia, a dependency of Great Lavra, is situated to its southwest at a high elevation of about 2,500 feet above the sea.

[45] Great Lavra is the earliest (963) and largest Athonite foundation, built on a rocky outcrop at the end of the peninsula. Its feast day is the 5th of July, commemorating the repose of Saint Athanasios. The number of monks dwindled by the early 16th C., on account of the change from the coenobitic to the idiorrhythmic way of life. The wall-paintings were executed by the famous Cretan iconographer Theophanes in 1535, which must have been of interest to Neilos and Makarios who were iconographers. Lavra returned to the coenobitic life after 1579, but the decline in numbers continued. By the beginning of the 17th C., there were only five or six monks. Subsequently, the
(continued...)

they paid the purchase price of one gold florin for the land. The task of clearing the site of foliage then lay ahead of them, which would be no mean accomplishment as can be seen in the testament of Saint Makarios (the saint's uncle). On account of the name of Saint Peter the Athonite and the homeland of the saints, Hagios Petros, is that place called Hagia (Aghia) Petra. They also built there a church to the most holy Theotokos, commemorating the Feast of the Meeting in the Temple. In view of the fact that the fathers were proficient in iconography, they admirably adorned the entire church. They also provided the sacred temple with the necessary vessels, vestments, and books. In fact, they used the last of the money they had taken from home.

Saint Neilos the Myrrh-streamer

Before his blessed repose, Father Makarios wrote his spiritual testament, by which he bequeathed the *kellia*[46] and all goods within—as his own personal property—to his disciple, the Priest-monk Neilos, his nephew. After the *kellia* were completed and Father Makarios finished the burden of his righteous labors, it was then that the holy man reposed peacefully in the Lord. His nephew, Father Neilos, as his successor, became his genuine heir in all lofty things and proved to be a worthy superior of the *kellia*.[47]

The divine Neilos was inflamed by the desire for solitude. He, therefore, sought a spot which was more desolate. He found a cave, flanked by sheer precipices on both sides, that held frightening views. With the utmost difficulty, he managed to reach this cave. The ever-memorable one remained there in quietude, praying to God and arriving at sublime contemplation. No one else knew of this, except the One Who guided him to that isolated retreat. It was there that the blessed man abided and struggled in anonymity to the end.

---

[45](...continued)
monastery again became idiorrhythmic.

[46] *Kelli* or *kellion* (pl. *kellia*) denotes the cell of a monk. It can also describe a monastic establishment that consists of a chapel and some surrounding land. Usually three monks dwell therein.

[47] The last five sentences were taken from a Russian translation of a Greek manuscript from the saint's *kellion*.

It is not possible to know how many were the tears he shed and the contests in which he engaged. Who can speak exactly of his all-night standing in prayer and keeping vigils, making prostrations, and observing fasts? Can anyone describe the apparitions, appearances, and threats of the demons, who kept attempting to drive him away from that cave? Again, can anyone adequately narrate the angelic visions and consolations that he was vouchsafed? Why attempt impossibilities? These facts are unobtainable here. We do know that within the cave itself, Father Neilos constructed an altar in honor of the Feast of the Meeting of the Lord in the Temple (2nd of February).

The all-benevolent God, knowing Neilos' heart and his patience, glorified him with a righteous end. This occurred on the 12th of November, in the year 1651 of our Lord Christ. His sacred body was buried near the cave. As we know, Saint Neilos fled human glory. He desired it neither during his lifetime nor after his death. On his deathbed, in order that none should venture to remove his remains, he made a testament. Out of respect to the wishes of the testator, the reverent mourners interred the saint's body in a small cave that was located underneath the saint's dwelling place. There is an inscription therein forbidding the removal of the saint's body. This, indeed, was in accordance with the saint's instructions.

Nevertheless, the Lord, Who places lamps upon the lampstands that it might give light to all those in the house,[48] glorified His saint in this manner. Neilos' virginal body, consecrated to the Lord from his youth, purified by fasts and tears, and made fragrant by prayer, was transformed by God into a vessel streaming with myrrh. The myrrh exuded through a small aperture from the grave and flowed down that perpendicular cliff to the sea. When the course of the myrrh was noticed by men, the unheard-of miracle and the venerable man's fame soon spread far and wide. Saint Neilos' fame spread abroad. Ships, consequently, were coming and collecting the myrrh as if drawing it from an ever-flowing spring. The miraculous myrrh healed every malady. That place came to be known as Karavostasion ("the boat-stop"), an apt name. It was at that same location where the ship stood in which Saint Peter the Athonite came to the Holy Mountain. The vessel could not sail away from that very spot until the sailors permitted the saint to disembark. Now it was precisely there that Saint Peter strived ascetically in that cave, even as it is recorded in his history.

Saint Neilos, consequently, was called Myrovleetes or Myrrh-streamer, due to the myrrh that gushed forth from his holy relics. But the precise location of his tomb remained unknown for many years. The reason for this is as follows. Once it happened that two monks from nearby cells wished to find the relics of the righteous one. They came with a mattock and a pickaxe.

---

[48] Mt. 5:15.

They began to dig the surface of the ground when, suddenly, a great rock from above tumbled down. It crushed the leg of one of the monks, who, as a result of the pain from his broken leg, lay there as one dead. The other monk could neither assist him nor carry him. He, thereupon, went for help, bringing another monk with his mule to convey the injured monk away from that place.

Now while that brother stayed there alone, groaning aloud and heaving heavy sighs, for a moment he saw the form of a monk. Suddenly the righteous Neilos appeared to him in the habit of a monk, asking him, "What ails thee, brother? What art thou seeking here? What has befallen thee?" The brother disclosed his purpose for coming to that place and what transpired. The saint remarked, "And how dost thou dare, impoverished one, without the express counsel of the saint, to undertake such a perilous work? But behold, the saint cures thee! Take heed, henceforth, that without the divine will thou oughtest not to venture into that which is beyond thy power." At the same time, the venerable Neilos touched the crushed bone of that brother and, forthwith, he was sound and whole. The saint then disappeared. The brother, filled with joy, jumped to his feet and went in the direction of his cell. On the way, he met the other monk, who was leading the mule. When that monk beheld him completely restored, he was beside himself in a state of ecstasy. Together, therefore, they glorified God and gave heartfelt thanks to the saint. Thereafter, no one ever attempted a similar undertaking.

In the year 1815, a monk called Aichmalotos ("Prisoner" or "Captive")[49] suffered from a demon that oppressed him and ruptured his testicles. After Saint Neilos healed him, he showed him many visions, foretelling future happenings, that is, what would befall Mount Athos, the coming of the Greek Revolution, the attacks of the Hagarenes, and many other predictions which were all recorded in a book. Saint Neilos charged him to repair the path to the cave, so that the brethren could traverse easily and offer veneration, which would be for their spiritual benefit. He also commanded that Liturgies be served in the church, the one Neilos had built alone when he dwelt there at the cave.

---

[49] In the article "Saint Neilos' Posthumous Discourses," translated from the Russian, the monk's name appears to have been Theophanes. When Theophanes received the Great Schema, it was Saint Neilos who charged that he be named "Prisoner" as a sign that he was taken captive by the saint, who had delivered him from his captor, the devil. This monk, in desperate straits and suffering from a serious rupture, was visited by Saint Neilos who healed him and protected him from demonic attacks. Saint Neilos delivered to Theophanes an accusatory discourse for monks. Theophanes recorded the words of the saint, which have been left for us. Some edifying excerpts will be placed at the end of this account. See Archimandrite Alexander, "Saint Nilos' Posthumous Discourses," *The Orthodox Word*, Vol. 4, No. 4(21) (July-August 1968):143, 144.

The fathers, therefore, were notified. No sooner had they heard than they made haste and cleared the area of the briars and undergrowth. They were desirous of building a new church in the name of the saint. As they dug away in order to lay the foundations, they came upon the tomb of the saint. His august relics were emitting an indescribable fragrance. This took place on the 7th of May, in the year 1815, the day upon which we now commemorate the recovery of his relics. The fathers were filled with immense joy at the discovery. They, straightway, sent tidings of the recovery to the Lavra. Those fathers came with candles, lamps, and incense. They effected the transfer of the saint's relics to the Great Lavra, leaving only the jaw at the cell for the sanctification of those who came on pilgrimage. Numerous miracles took place during the translation of the holy relics. Many who participated and were ailing were healed of various infirmities. The saint's tomb was beautified and positioned behind the sacred bema, as can be seen to this day. The precious head of the saint is at Great Lavra, while a part of his arm is at Kafsokalyvia Skete.

Posthumous Discourses

When Theophanes (later Aichmalotos) was dwelling on the Holy Mountain, he bethought himself to repair to the city, Constantinople. Saint Neilos, on the eve of Theophanes' departure, appeared to him in the form of an elder—one unknown to Theophanes. The saint promised to help him and showed him an abandoned hut in which to dwell. Now when Theophanes was commanded to write the sayings of the saint, he was barely literate. Therefore, a certain priest-monk, Gerasimos from Constantinople, assisted Theophanes. The writings took place between 1813 and 1819. The saint foretells the tribulations in store for future generations of monks. The saint urges the monks of Theophanes' time to labor, saying, "Now is the time of salvation! Now is the time for him to be saved who desires to receive salvation; for ahead there is coming upon us a most severe winter. Then we shall not find such freedom for salvation as we have now."[50]

Although Theophanes had personal sins, he had preserved his Orthodox Faith unfailingly. He maintained simplicity of heart and repented for his sins. In fact, Theophanes is a type of the monk of the latter times. Though he had departed from God's commandments, the merciful God, seeing the sincerity of Theophanes to repent, sent Sant Neilos to aid him.[51] The book entitled *The Posthumous Discourses of Saint Neilos* comprises some five hundred pages. The following excerpts, the words of Saint Neilos from the other world, are a warning and encouragement to present-day monastics.

---

[50] Ibid., "Posthumous Discourses: The Autumn of Monasticism" (pp. 170, 173-175), *The Orthodox Word*, 146.

[51] Ibid., "Introduction," *The Orthodox Word*, 145.

"Now is the time for gathering into the granary the fruits of the monastic life. Now let whoever wishes to cultivate the monastic life, cultivate it; for autumn is coming and severe winter has drawn nigh....Therefore, while we still have spring in our nature, let us strive to work in the vineyard of monastic life, before the fruit of this life perishes. Let us strive to gather the harvest of mutual love! Let us strive to treasure the fruit of the monastic life!...Now is the time of sorrow, that we may sorrow over the evils we have committed. Now is the time of repentance with the sorrow of contrition for our lawless deeds! Now is the time of sighing, that we may sigh from the depths of our heart and soul over the deeds of impurity we have committed!...Winter draws nigh! The queen of perdition has heard that the monastic life has become desolate. She has called the seven-headed beast of lawlessness.[52] She has mounted this beast and commanded him, 'Take possession!' And he has taken possession of the first bridle of insubordination [that is, the obedience of monks to the monastic rule and elders]."[53]

Saint Neilos the New

Next, it is written: "The power of the monk is prayer. If prayer in a monk grows feeble, then too the gifts of prayer grow feeble....If a monk, when he is tonsured, will not constantly pray [the Jesus Prayer], he will perish by perdition....If a monk receives the Angelic Habit but will not avail himself of prayer, then of what profit is the Schema to him? Prayer is breath. If breath is lost, how can a man live? Let him read all of the Church *Menaia*, the *Psalter*, and the *Triodion*; but if he will not pray, this reading profits him nothing."[54]

The author then presents a riveting section on the Theotokos and her icon at the Athonite Monastery of Iveron,[55] beginning: "As the Father glorified

---

[52] Cf. Rev. 12:3; 13:1; 17:3 ff.

[53] Alexander, "Posthumous Discourses: The Autumn of Monasticism," *The Orthodox Word*, 146, 147.

[54] Ibid., "Posthumous Discourses: The Power of the Monk is Prayer" (p. 231), *The Orthodox Word*, 147, 148.

[55] Iveron is on the northeastern side of the Athos peninsula, a short distance from the (continued...)

His Son, so has the Son glorified His Mother. The Theotokos then begged of Him that, for her sake, men, too, might be glorified. She requested a province for herself on earth. This beautiful land and high garden of Athos would be her province. The Queen then said to her servants, 'Build twenty-four towers, for the twenty-four written letters, so that the alphabet might be filled and perfectly adorned with human souls.' Then her servants accomplished the building of the twenty-four towers. [This was the establishment of the twenty-four chief monasteries on Athos.] The Queen next commanded her servants, saying, 'Divide this province and make in it seven sowings that they may crush the seven heads of the queen of perdition.' The servants of the Queen of Salvation did as she charged them. She then commanded that each sowing be named by its name: faith, love, oneness of soul, non-acquisitiveness, fear of God, chastity, and continence.

"She, thereupon, sent forth her servants anew and said, 'Go to the ends of the universe, go to the crossroads to find slaves who would serve in my province and bring to fruition the seven blossoms of salvation. When you seek these slaves, take not the healthy and strong, but the sick, the shriveled, the lame, the bent, the cross-eyed, the leprous, and the naked. Such persons are you to gather into my province so that, laboring in it upon these seven sowings of salvation, they might be healed.'

"The Queen of Salvation saw that her servants [that is, the first generations of monks] were faithful, and said to them, 'O, my beloved and faithful servants, cultivate my province without murmuring until evening! And when the day shall grow dark, then you shall freely enter into my glory, that you may rejoice and be glorified together with me.'"[56]

Thus, the monks are exhorted not to lose faith in the protection of the Theotokos. They are told not to leave Athos until the Iveron icon of the Mother of God should leave. He writes: "On account of men's ruinous deeds, the Mountain is threatened by the danger of losing the Queen of Salvation. And so I say unto you, 'When the Queen of Salvation departs from this Mountain, then—woe to this Mountain!—there will follow a great disturbance (overturning) in this honorable and Holy Mountain.'" The writer then goes on to explain how demonic temptations and human animosities, as pirates, will gain access and spread as they please.

Continuing, he writes: "The departure of Salvation will be thus: First, a short time beforehand, the monastery in which dwells the image of the Queen

---

[55](...continued)
sea. It was founded in 980. It is dedicated to the memory of the Feast of the Dormition of the Theotokos.

[56] Alexander, "Posthumous Discourses: The Mother of God, Protectress of Athonite Monasticism" (pp. 178-189), *The Orthodox Word*, 148.

of Salvation [the Monastery of Iveron] shall be shaken. This means that senseless earth shall sense that it is about to be impoverished of its guardian, who has guarded it to this day. After this shaking, all trees that have been planted shall quake greatly; and everything planted, that is, everything rooted, shall be bent into captivity for the sake of the Queen. Athos shall be shaken by a fearful roar, and a gentle sound shall go out. At the time of the departure of the image of our Lady, the Mother of God, there will be a fearful and trembling sign. The sign will be this: By reason of the departure of Salvation [the Theotokos], all churches will be bent as escorts of Salvation and as a bow of salutation. Therefore I say to you, insensible [nature] shall sense, but [those with] feeling shall be darkened and shall not be aware that Salvation is departing. And so I say to you, most worthy fathers, as long as the image of our Lady the Mother of God remains within this Mountain, let none move to leave; as soon as any moves to leave, he shall immediately find in himself chastisement of soul and body. But when it is seen that the icon of the Panagia (All-holy one) has departed this honorable Mountain, then depart you also, whither you will; only preserve your vow of monastic life whole and pure."[57]

A Prophecy Attributed to Saint Neilos,
the Ascetic of Mount Athos, Concerning the End Times

"From the year 1900, toward the middle of the twentieth century, the people and the world will begin to become unrecognizable. As the time of the advent of the Antichrist draws nigh, the minds of people shall be darkened due to the passions of the flesh. Ungodliness and iniquity are going to increase.

"Then will the world become unrecognizable. The faces of people are going to be changed. Men will not be distinguishable from women, on account of their shamelessness in dress and style of hair. These people will become wild, becoming like beasts because of the temptations and the deception of the Antichrist.

"There will be no respect toward parents and elders. Love is going to disappear. Christian shepherds, that is, bishops and priests, are going to be filled with vainglory (with some exceptions), utterly failing to distinguish the right way from the left. The customs and traditions of the Christians and of the Church are going to change. Purity will depart from society, and immorality is going to reign.

"Falsehood and greed are going to attain great proportions. And woe to those who lay up treasures of silver! Fornications, adulteries, homosexuality, theft, and murders are going to prevail at that time. Due to the power of such great crimes and licentiousness, people are going to be deprived of the grace

---

[57] Ibid., "Posthumous Discourses: The Departure of the Queen of Salvation, the Iveron Icon, from Mount Athos" (pp. 310-318), *The Orthodox Word*, 173.

of the Holy Spirit, which they received at holy Baptism, as well as remorse of conscience.

"The Churches of God are going to be deprived of godly and pious shepherds. And woe to the Christians remaining in the world at that time! And woe to those who would be utterly deprived of their faith, because they should not see the Light of knowledge in anyone! The Christians are going to then separate themselves from the world in holy places of refuge that they might lighten their spiritual sufferings and find relief. Everywhere they are going to encounter obstacles and distress.

"All these things are going to occur because the Antichrist would lord it over everything. He will take control of the whole earth. He will work signs and wonders. He will also give depraved wisdom to wretched men so that they would invent ways of speaking one to another from one part of the earth to the other. As birds, they are going to fly through the air and, as fish, they are going to penetrate the depths of the sea.

"Humanity that will be living in comfort shall be unfortunate, not knowing that all these things are the deception of the Antichrist. The Antichrist is going to advance to such an extent in the field of science that he will deceive men, so that they might not believe in the existence of the tri-hypostatic God.

"Then God, the all-good One, seeing the destruction of the human race, shall shorten those days for the sake of those few who are being saved,[58] because, if possible, the Antichrist would deceive even the elect.[59] Then suddenly the two-edged sword[60] shall appear and shall slay the deceiver and his followers."[61]

Epilogue

The saint's biographer closes, saying: "Behold, therefore, even in these latter days, when the Eastern Orthodox Church was in captivity and many anomalies existed, nevertheless she triumphed, and is triumphant against the apostate Lucifer and all his hostile demons of ill-will! She now may boast of additional saints, new trophies, and splendid standards of victory. The three-sunned Divinity on high has spread out gleaming gold rays of heavenly gifts of grace, by means of newly-revealed saints to the very ends of the inhabited earth. Behold also how the heaven redounds and proclaims to all the nations the many-lighted grace of the Orthodox Faith and the invincible truths of the holy Gospel!

---

[58] Cf. Mt. 24:22; Mk. 13:20; Rom. 9:28.

[59] Cf. Mt. 24:24; Mk. 13:22.

[60] Cf. Rev. 1:16; 2:12; 19:15.

[61] See the Greek text of D. Panagopoulos, *Saints and Sages Concerning Future Events* (Athens, GR), p. 80.

"Behold even now the unrestrained mouths of the heretics are fenced off! We speak of those who rave that, after we lost the empire, we also lost wonderworking men, and the goodness of God as well. Behold the goodness of God! It pours out richly upon those accounted worthy of illuminating the Orthodox Church! We have testimony of this in the sanctity of her glorious new-martyrs and myrrh-streamers and righteous fathers who have been conspicuous for their glorious and supernatural accomplishments. Indeed, until the consummation of the age, there shall not fail to be valiant soldiers of Jesus Christ. In every generation of faithful Orthodox, there shall be luminaries shining forth in the world.

"With what hymns of praise can we extol the most holy Neilos? By his manner of life and his God-sent words, he showed himself to be the pillar of humility, the foundation of the monastic discipline, the unbroken rock of patience and perseverance, the glory of the Church, the consolation of the afflicted, the comfort of the misfortunate, the guide of sinners to repentance, the salvation of the Peloponnesos and his hometown of Kynouria, and the unsleeping protector and patron of all the world. Thou hast shown thyself to be a veritable treasury of spiritual gifts, a never-emptying fountain of miracles, an ever-flowing spring of healings, a resolute fulfiller of all the supernatural gifts of the Spirit, a joint heir of those adorned with ornamental fillets full of light. Thou art one who illuminates with those sweet rays of divine effulgences. Thou art a blockading wall for all Orthodox Christians. Thou art the boast of Athos, the expeller of wicked demons, and the storehouse of divine mysteries.

"We entreat thee and beseech thee, most holy Father Neilos, to have compassion upon us sinners, we who are thine unworthy slaves. Send down upon us, who honorably reverence thee, the rich mercy and compassion of the Lord. Intercede for us that we may receive the grace and power from on high of the Holy Spirit, by means of thine acceptable and thy holy intercessions before God. We ask this that we might be able to vanquish the flesh, the world, and the evil ruler of this world. By thy prayers we hope to overcome the devouring passions and receive enlightenment to the senses of our bodies and souls that they might be set aright. May our minds be fixed upon Paradise and the struggles and contests of the saints! May our imaginations dwell on nought else but that exceedingly bright glory of that future blessedness! Strengthen us, O saint of God, that we may conduct our lives in a God-pleasing manner, so that we might be accounted worthy to be numbered with the choirs of the righteous, together hymning and glorifying Father, Son, and Holy Spirit, to Whom is meet all glory, honor, and veneration to the endless ages. Amen."

On the 7th of May, the holy Church commemorates the holy and venerable New-martyr PACHOMIOS, who suffered martyrdom by the sword at Ousaki of Philadelphia on Ascension Thursday (1730).[62]

Pachomios, the memorable new-martyr, born in Byelorussia, was the son of pious parents. While still young, he was taken prisoner by the Tartars.[63] They, in turn, sold him to a Turkish tanner who brought him to his homeland at Ousaki near Philadelphia. In that place, the Muslim taught the youth not only his trade but also his religion. He observed, however, that though Pachomios was eager to learn the trade, yet the Islamic religion he detested and abhorred. So the Turk terrorized him with beatings and taunts, threatening to deprive him even of his food. But the valiant soldier of Christ endured all these things happily for the Orthodox Faith for twenty-seven long years, serving his master with eagerness and trustworthiness, so that the latter was moved to offer him his daughter in marriage and make him his heir—if only he would deny Christ.

The goodly youth though, as an adherent of prudence, considered marriage and wealth as insignificant attainments. He pondered on the apostolic words that said: "Who shall separate us from the love of Christ? Shall affliction, or distress, or persecution, or famine, or nakedness, or danger, or sword [Rom. 8:35]?" When his master perceived Pachomios' irreversible stand, he set him free. As Pachomios was preparing to depart his master's house, he became ill. The Turks, those who were visiting him, then took the opportunity to fabricate a lie. They said that Pachomios expressed the wish to deny Christ and become a Muslim. Thus, following the illness, they dressed

---

[62] The martyrdom herein of the venerable New-martyr Pachomios was taken from Nikodemos the Hagiorite's *Neon Martyrologion*, 3rd ed. (pp. 115-118), and incorporated into *The Great Synaxaristes* (in Greek). The text had originally been collected by Nikodemos from a composition of Makarios of Patmos contained in *Evangelikeen Salpinga*, which includes an encomium to the saint. The compilers of *The Great Synaxaristes* (in Greek) note that in older editions, the saint is listed under the 21st of May, but that is an error. They affirm that Ascension Thursday, in the year 1730, fell on the 7th day of May. This latter date is also when this Athonite father is celebrated on the Holy Mountain. A service to the saint is found at the Athonite Monastery of Saint Panteleimon [Codices 6008 (501), 6375 (868)], which have been in print. Another divine office was composed by the hymnographer of the Great Church, Father Gerasimos Mikrayiannanites. The sacred relics of the New-martyr Pachomios are treasured at the Monastery of Saint John the Theologian on Patmos. A portion of the saint's precious relics from the aforesaid monastery is also at the Athonite Monastery of Saint Paul, since the year 1953.

[63] During this same period, another who was taken captive by the Tartars was Saint John the Russian. He, too, is commemorated by the holy Church in the month of May, on the 27th day.

Pachomios in Turkish garments but did not circumcise him. Christ's athlete was repulsed by this and, taking nothing with him, departed for Smyrna. He took up, for a time, working as a merchant. After he discarded those Turkish garments, he sailed to Mount Athos. When he arrived in the vicinity of the Monastery of Saint Paul, he encountered a priest-monk. This was the virtuous Joseph, to whom he confessed all. Pachomios then persuaded the priest to take him under his direction and make him a monk. This all came to pass. Thus, Pachomios stayed with him for twelve years, imitating his every virtue.

After this passage of time, Pachomios heard of the wonderful life of Saint Akakios at Kafsokalyvia. He relocated to that skete, supporting himself by his own labors for six years. Even as an industrious bee collects pollen from flowers, so did Pachomios obtain every virtue. He became a prime example of the monastic life for all the fathers. He was so sweet-tempered and filled with grace, that he was loved by all. However, in spite of the acquisition of all these virtues, he was not content in heart. Why? He kept yearning to suffer martyrdom for Christ. He felt this way, on the one hand, out of divine love; but, on the other hand, he feared that in time of infirmity, he might carelessly let slip a heedless word of denial, for which the Turks would drape him with the green garments that they were accustomed to wearing.

Pachomios disclosed his desire for martyrdom to his elder, who immediately reprimanded him because he assumed that this thought came to him out of pride. But Pachomios insisted, so the elder tried him for an entire year with various rules and obediences. In all this he found him willing to endure all these tests. So they both besought God through vigils and fasting to reveal to them if this endeavor was His divine will. Then they consulted the most virtuous fathers of Mount Athos and announced Pachomios' intention. They were all found to be in agreement with that which he desired. Therefore, with their prayers and advice (especially those of Saint Akakios), Pachomios and his Elder Joseph left Mount Athos and traveled to Ousaki, the homeland of Pachomios' former Turkish master. While the Elder Joseph stayed at an inn, Pachomios went straight to the house of his former master. Afterward, he betook himself to the marketplace, so that everyone should take notice of him.

Indeed, the Hagarenes recognized him. They seized and led him to the judge, charging that he was the servant of the aforementioned Turkish master. They claimed that, during a time of illness, Pachomios had denied Christ. After his recovery they had clothed him in green garb. "And now, O judge," they cried out in indignation, "behold what garments he is wearing!"[64] The judge questioned Pachomios if this were true. The martyr of Christ, with a jovial countenance and outright boldness, proclaimed that he had never denied the

---

[64] It was customary for monastics going to martyrdom to put on secular Christian garments in order to avoid reprisals against the Holy Mountain.

Lord Jesus Christ at any time, neither in word nor in thought. Much rather, he confessed Jesus as true God and true Man. For this confession he affirmed that he was ready to endure myriads of sufferings as well as any type of death.

When the judge heard this, witnessing the magnanimous spirit of the saint, he threatened and cursed him. "Since thou didst deny thy religion once already," the judge began, "it is impossible to wear Christian garments henceforth. Two choices, therefore, are before thee: thou must either deny Christ or partake of a harsh death." Christ's contestant answered, "God forbid! May it not be! Never will I renounce Thy name, my Christ King, even in my slightest thoughts; for I am prepared to be cast into fire and accept death gladly for Thy love." Upon hearing this utterance, the judge ordered that Pachomios be thrown into the darkest jail. The martyr dwelt therein as if in Paradise, even though he was famished, sleepless, and bereft of all comfort, being sustained only by divine hope.

On the third day, a sentence of death was issued against Pachomios. Thus, the guard brought him the sweet tidings of death. As the martyr received the news, he rejoiced and glorified the name of the Lord. Throughout the course of the night, he kept constant in prayer. At dawn, he was escorted from jail and brought before the judge who said to him, "Behold, for thy stubbornness, thou shalt suffer death. I am warning thee, therefore, do not wait to change thy mind later; for it shall be in vain." The holy Pachomios answered fearlessly as before, "O judge, I will never deny Christ, even if thou shouldest subject me to ten thousand harsh deaths. Only that which thou hast decided, do quickly." At these words the judge gave his final decision.

The Hagarenes, those who were in attendance, bound the martyr. They proceeded to push him to the site of execution that was located outside the city, at the place where sheep were slaughtered. A throng of Christians and Turks followed. Some of the Turks jeered at the martyr; others spat upon him, while still others urged him to deny Christ. The martyr fastened his mind on prayer as he hastened to his desired martyrdom. Finally, when they arrived at the spot, he knelt down. The executioner, in the meantime, was not only afraid to behead the holy martyr but he even whispered in his ear prompting him to forsake Christ. The valiant athlete of Christ urged the executioner and boldly said to him, "Do that which thou wast ordered. Do not lose time for nought." The executioner gathered strength and struck off Pachomios' sacred head. Thus, the ever-memorable one received the crown of martyrdom on the day of the Ascension of our Lord Jesus Christ, that is, the 7th day of May, in the year 1730.

Three days later, the Christians took his honorable relics and buried them with reverence. Following this, the executioner became demonized. He ran amok in the city, sending forth loud cries and shrieks. He foamed at the mouth until a few days later he died. In the interim, the saint's elder heard of his disciple's gallant death, for which he offered thanksgiving to God with tears of joy. He came out of his hideout and went to the place where the body of the martyr lay. Seeing Pachomios, the elder wept. He greeted him, "Thou hast achieved that which thou hadst desired, my dear Pachomios. Intercede for me before the Lord and for all those who call upon thee!"

Truly this occurred. A few days later, the Elder Joseph was seized by a terrible fear and indecision, wondering how to flee that area without being detected. The Martyr Pachomios appeared to the elder in his sleep. His countenance was radiant and joyous, and he said to him, "Fear not, O elder, and no harm will come upon thee." Immediately then, by this word, fear vanished from the elder's heart.

Also, a certain local Christian woman was tormented from her youth with incurable headaches. She invoked the assistance of the righteous martyr with faith, anointing her head with his blood. Thereupon, she fully recovered from this unending illness. In memory of this benefaction, the pious woman sent a message to the fathers at Mount Athos, who knew the martyr's bodily characteristics. She commissioned for the painting of a holy icon of Saint Pachomios. When she received the desired icon, she observed annually the memory of the righteous Martyr Pachomios devoutly, by whose intercessions may we be granted the kingdom of the heavens. Amen.

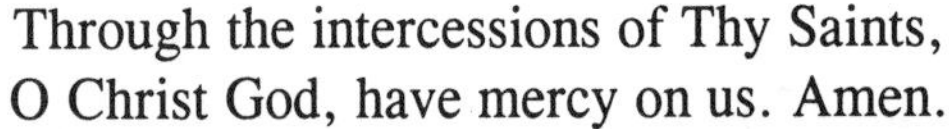
Through the intercessions of Thy Saints,
O Christ God, have mercy on us. Amen.

On the 8th of May, the holy Church commemorates the Synaxis of the dispatch of holy dust, that is, the manna, from the tomb of the holy and glorious Apostle and Evangelist JOHN THE THEOLOGIAN.[1]

John the Theologian, the divine apostle and evangelist, the beloved disciple of the Lord, was born in Bethsaida of the Galilee. He was translated to the Lord, while preaching the word of God at Ephesus, in deep old age during the days of Emperor Trajan (98-117). When the blessed John was about to depart from this present life, to that which is perpetual and eternal, he foreknew it by the indwelling of divine grace. He took his disciples and went outside of the city of Ephesus. John, according to Prochoros his disciple, had assembled seven of his disciples: Prochoros and six others. John said to them, "Take spades in your hands and follow me." They followed him outside the city to a certain place, where he said, "Sit down." He then went a little apart from them to where it was quiet and began to pray. It was very early in the morning; the sun had not quite risen. After his prayer, he said to them, "Dig with your spades a cross-shaped trench as long as I am tall." This was done while the evangelist prayed. After he had finished his prayer, he set himself down in the trench that had been dug. John then said to Prochoros, "My son, thou shalt go to Jerusalem. That is where thou must end thy days." The evangelist then gave them instructions and embraced them, saying, "Take some earth, my mother earth, and cover me." The disciple embraced them again and, taking some earth, covered him only up to his knees. Once more, he embraced them, saying, "Take some more earth and cover me up to the neck." So they embraced him again and then took some more earth and covered him up to his neck. Then he said to them, "Bring a thin veil and place it on my face, and embrace me again for the last time, for you shall not see me any longer in this life." So they, stricken with grief, embraced the apostle again. As he was sending us off in peace, the disciples,

Burial of the Evangelist John

[1] See also the full Life of Saint John presented on the day of his repose, the 26th of September.

lamenting bitterly, covered his whole body. The sun rose just then, and he surrendered his spirit.[2]

Saint John the Theologian

The disciples returned to the city and were asked, "Where is your teacher?" So they explained what had just occurred in great detail. The Ephesians begged them that they show them the site. They, therefore, went back to the grave with the brethren, but John was not there. Only his shoes were left behind. Then they remembered the words of the Lord to the Apostle Peter, 'If I wish him to tarry while I am coming, what is that to thee [Jn. 21:22]?' And they all glorified God, the Father, and the Son, and the Holy Spirit, to Whom is due glory, honor, and worship, unto the ages of ages. Amen. Each year, on the 8th day of May, the grave of the saint was decorated with roses.

Saint Hippolytos, Pope of Rome, in his narration on how the apostles departed this life, notes that John "went to Ephesus and there reposed. When his relic was sought by the inhabitants of Ephesus, it could not be found." Saint Gregory the Theologian, in answering a question put to him by his brother Caesarios, comments: "The great John, at the end of his Gospel, writes that the Lord said to Peter, 'Follow thou Me.' And Peter, having turned about, seeth the disciple, whom Jesus loved, following—who also leaned back on His breast at the supper—and said, 'Lord, who is the one who is delivering Thee up?' After Peter saw him, he saith to Jesus, 'But Lord, this man—what?' Jesus saith to him, 'If I wish him to tarry while I am coming, what is that to thee? Do thou

[2] The publisher of this present volume of the *Synaxaristes* notes that the phrase "the sun rose just then, and he surrendered his spirit" is not recorded thus, but was incorporated into the text from the work of Maximos the Margounion. Furthermore, we wish to make mention herein that, according to the blessed Jerome, the apostle and evangelist reposed in the third year of the reign of Trajan, that is, A.D. 101. This is sixty-eight years after the Passion and resurrection of the Lord. This is confirmed by Clement of Alexandria, Irenaeos, and many holy fathers of the Church. It is believed he was about six to eight years younger than the Lord, which made him ninety-three or ninety-five years of age upon his repose.

be following Me.' Then this saying went out among the brethren that 'that disciple dieth not'; and yet Jesus did not say that 'he dieth not,' but, 'If I wish him to tarry while I am coming, what is that to thee [Jn. 21:19-23]?' Now some use this passage as a pretext that John still has not tasted death, but rather was transposed live as were Enoch and Elias. However, this is not the truth. Christ spoke enigmatically when He said, 'If I wish him to tarry,'...meaning that the Lord did not intend for Peter and John to be in one another's company to the end. Their future work would take each one to different places. The Lord also reveals here that John would not die in the same manner as the other apostles." Saint Gregory then describes to Caesarios the fine dust which has wrought cures for a multitude of sufferers.[3]

Saint John

Saint Bede remarks that "Jesus did not love John alone in a singular way to the exclusion of others, but He loved John beyond those whom He loved, in a more intimate way as one whom the special prerogative of chastity had made worthy of fuller love. Indeed, Jesus proved that He loved them all when before His Passion He said to them, 'Even as the Father loved Me, I also loved you; abide in the love, that which is Mine [Jn. 15:9].' But beyond the others He loved the one who, being a virgin when chosen by Him, remained forever a virgin. Accordingly, when Christ was about to die on the Cross, He commended His Mother to John [Jn. 19:26, 27], so that virgin might watch over virgin; and when He Himself ascended to heaven after His death and resurrection, a son would not be lacking to His Mother whose chaste life would be protected by his chaste services."[4] Further on, Saint Bede writes: "Mystically speaking, we can take these things which are predicted by the Lord to Peter and John, as designating the two ways of life in the Church which are carried out in the present, namely the active and the contemplative....Christ

[3] *The Great Synaxaristes* (in Greek), September Volume, 5th ed. (Athens, 1978), pp. 554, 555.

[4] The Venerable Bede, "Homily I.9, Feast of St. John the Evangelist," *Homilies on the Gospels*, Bk. One, 87.

saying this about John suggests the state of contemplative virtue, which is not to be ended through death, as the active life is, but after death is to be more perfectly completed with the coming of the Lord."[5]

Saint John

As we said, after the evangelist's falling asleep in the Lord, his tomb was shown to be another pool of Siloam. Since our all-good and man-befriending Lord not only glorifies the saints—that is, those who for love of Him engaged in struggles such as the disciples and apostles, the prophets, and martyrs, and all those who led God-pleasing lives—accounting them worthy of the kingdom of the heavens and those everlasting good things, but also grants, by the free gift of divine gifts of grace, manifold and splendid miracles then and now and forever.

We, therefore, at the empty tomb of John the Theologian celebrate the great evangelist. He was granted Christ's grace by which he is adorned with many wonderworkings. His tomb, yearly and to the day of this writing, in a sudden and mysterious manner, spouts up dust. The natives have named the dust "manna." The dust has been called so because it is used for the deliverance and recovery from every disease. It is employed for the health of both souls and bodies, to the glorification of God and His servant John.

We have learned, by means of the encomium of Sophronios, Patriarch of Jerusalem, as noted in Nikodemos the Hagiorite's *Synaxaristes*, that Zebedee was John's father and Salome was his mother. Salome was the daughter of Joseph, the betrothed of the most holy Virgin Mary. Joseph, by his first wife, had four sons: Iakovos (James), Symeon, Jude, and Joses. He also had three daughters: Esther, Martha, and Salome. Salome, as the daughter of Joseph, was, therefore, the Lord's stepsister, since Joseph was the putative father of Jesus. This also means that our Lord was John's uncle.

The encomium then mentions that, at the time of our Lord's Passion and crucifixion, all the disciples fled. John alone was present, as one beloved and who loved the Lord with perfect love; for even John himself says, "Perfect

[5] Ibid., 90, 92.

love casteth out fear [1 Jn. 4:18]." He alone remained to witness all the torments of Christ on the Cross, suffering with Him in his heart, weeping and lamenting with the all-pure Theotokos. Jesus, then, from the Cross, "having seen His Mother and the disciple whom He loved standing by, saith to His Mother, 'Woman, behold thy son!' Then He saith to the disciple, 'Behold, thy Mother!' And from that hour the disciple took her into his own home [Jn. 19:26, 27]." And he, indeed, regarded her as his own mother, and served her with much respect. When Saint Magdalene ran and came to "Simon Peter, and to the other disciple, whom Jesus was regarding with affection," that is, John, she said to them, "They took away the Lord out of the sepulcher, and we know not where they laid Him." Peter and John went forth to the sepulcher. "And the two were running together, and the other disciple ran ahead of Peter more quickly, and came first to the sepulcher. And he, having stooped to look, seeth the linen cloths lying; yet he entered not. Then Simon Peter cometh, following him, and entered into the sepulcher [Jn. 20:1-6]." We also read in the encomium that only John among the earthborn had three mothers: first, Salome from whom he was physically born; second, the thunder, since the Lord gave to Iakovos and John the name of Boanerges, that is, "Sons of Thunder [Mk. 3:17]"; third, by grace, he received as his Mother the Lady Theotokos, in accordance with the Lord's word, "Behold, thy Mother [Jn. 19:27]!"

Saint John the Theologian

The Apostle John remained with the Theotokos until her holy dormition. Afterward, he left Jerusalem and went to Asia Minor; for when the lands of the earth were divided among the apostles, John chose the last lot—that of Asia Minor. He, therefore, repaired to Ephesus and other places. Ephesus was the most important Greek city in Ionian Asia Minor. The colossal temple of Artemis, or Diana, to which Ephesus owed much of its fame, was demolished by the lever of John's prayers. The idol worshippers, thereupon, were delivered from their error as they were guided to the light of the knowledge of God by John. The number of them was forty myriads, that is to say, four hundred thousand people who worshipped the false goddess Artemis. At length, they built and named a church after Saint John the Theologian. The church is situated atop a mountain that the Ephesians called Elivaton, which was situated in ancient Ephesus.[6]

Now toward the western slope of that mountain was also the grave of the holy Apostle Timothy.[7] In the mountain near to Elivaton, there is also the tomb of Saint Mary Magdalene,[8] as well as the Cave of the Holy Seven Sleepers,[9] which is called Heileton or Heileon. The adjoining mountain hosts the tomb of Saint Hermione,[10] one of the four prophetesses [Acts 21:9] and daughter of Philip (one of the seven deacons [Acts 6:5]). In addition, there are also the relics of the Martyr Avdaktos and his daughter Kallisthene,[11] as well as these holy martyrs and bishops: Aristonos, Aristoboulos, and Paul the Hermopolite.

The synaxis of the holy apostle and Evangelist John is celebrated in his august apostolic church, which is located at Evdomon (Hebdomon).[12]

On the 8th of May, the holy Church commemorates our venerable Father ARSENIUS the Great.[13]

---

[6] Ancient Ephesus was situated on the northern slopes of the hills Coressus and Pion and south of the Cayster River. Since then, while the silt from the river has formed a fertile plain, it has also caused the coastline to move ever farther west by three miles.

[7] Saint Timothy is commemorated by the holy Church on the 22nd of January.

[8] Saint Mary Magdalene is commemorated by the holy Church on the 22nd of July.

[9] The Seven Sleepers of Ephesus are commemorated by the holy Church on the 4th of August. The grotto is located on the northern slopes of Mount Pion, near Ephesus. It is located eighteen kilometers from Kusadasi.

[10] Saint Hermione is commemorated by the holy Church on the 4th of September.

[11] Saints Avdaktos and Kallisthene are commemorated by the holy Church on the 4th of October.

[12] Evdomon (lit. "seventh"; Turk. Bakirkoy), a suburb of Constantinople, is situated on the Sea of Marmara. The church to the evangelist was built before the year 400. In the year 673 and 717, Arab fleets put in there at Hebdomon. Emperor Basil I (867-886) rebuilt the churches of Saint John the Evangelist and Saint John the Baptist, which had fallen into ruins. The evangelist's church, thereafter, was transformed into a monastery. By 1260, it was again in ruins. [*The Oxford Dictionary of Byzantium*, s.v. "Hebdomon."] At least eight churches in Constantinople were dedicated to Saint John.

[13] The Life of Saint Arsenius was immediately recorded by his disciples. The manuscript was not preserved, which may be due to the righteous Arsenius' prohibition against such an endeavor, since he stood aghast at the praise of men. There are, however, plenty of circumstances of his life which may be found in the sayings and writings of different books. An account with full biographical details is not extant. We may only gather up the synopses of the variously described episodes and construct a satisfactory biography well worth the telling. Such a collection was made in a Greek text found in a few Athonite monasteries: at Great Lavra; in the seventh panegyric at

(continued...)

Arsenius, the marvellous and notable father among ascetics, hailed from far-famed and glorious Rome. He was born during the first half of the fourth century. His father was a senator and judge. Both his parents were righteous and honorable Christians. Arsenius also had a sister, named Aphrositty, who was pious from girlhood. Arsenius' parents wished their son to have an excellent education. He studied Greek letters and writings and all the sciences, applying himself with the utmost diligence. Since he was endowed with a well-ordered and agile mind, which was coupled with his exertion and much toil, he learned philosophy in but a short time, together with rhetoric and logic. He also had a wonderful foundation in the other sciences.

The Deacon at Rome

Despite all his study and scholarship, and his mastery of both the Greek and Latin tongues, he was not neglectful of his private devotions and asceticism. Indeed, he preferred such discipline as far more salutary for the soul. From his youth, he led a life that was virtuous. At length, as a man of prudence and sense, he came to disdain profane Greek learning. He reckoned it of small account when compared to the God-inspired Scriptures and the sacred teachings, which were his great love and happiness. He also relished reading the writings of Rophenius, a monastic historian, who wrote about the Egyptian monastic fathers at Sketis or Wadi Natrun, west of the Nile Delta, so that Arsenius cherished a hope to meet the athletes of virtue of that famed monastic center. When comparing the wisdom that was profane to that which descends

---

[13](...continued)
Vatopedi; and at Iveron. The text begins, "But men who are earnest and lovers of virtue...." There is also an account in the Monastery of Chalke, numbered Codex 100. There are other biographies preserved in both the Parisian and Vatican codices. The Life of the righteous Arsenius also was published in the periodical of the Alexandrian Patriarchate, entitled *Ecclesiastikos Pharos* [No. 34 (1935), pp. 37-55 and 189-201]. An encomium to this venerable elder was composed by Saint Theodore the Stoudite, which is kept at the Great Lavra and begins, "A star ever-shining for us...." This was published in the *Greek Patrology* of Abbe Migne [*P.G.* 99:849-881]. One may also find many words and deeds of this holy father in the sayings of the fathers, such as the *Gerontikon*, *Apofthegmata Pateron*, and *Evergetinos*, as well as in other places. See also the Greek Library of Anthimos of Gaza [Vol. 2, p. 124], who mentions the writings of the righteous Arsenius. The saint's principal works include the *Didaskalia kai Parainesis* (*Instruction and Exhortation*), which was written as a guideline for monks. His commentary on the Gospel according to Saint Luke, *Eis ton Peirasteen Nomikon* (*On the Temptation of the Law*), in effect is also a treatise describing the contemplative life. Both Greek texts are contained in the Migne series: *P.G.* 66:1617 and 1621, respectively. See also, in English, *The Paradise of the Fathers*, Vol. II, translated from the Syriac by E. A. Wallis Budge (Seattle, WA: Saint Nectarios Press); and *The Evergetinos* (Etna, CA: Center for Traditionalist Orthodox Studies, 2000).

from above, he understood the former was earthly and material-minded. "But the wisdom from above indeed is first pure, then peaceable, equitable, easily entreated, full of mercy and of good fruits, impartial and without hypocrisy [Jas. 3:17]." Even as a young man, Arsenius sought to be of service to the Church. While he shone forth brilliantly in the virtues, moral excellence, and a God-pleasing life, Pope Damasus of Rome (366-384) ordained Arsenius to the diaconate. In that office, Arsenius strived to preserve without blemish the image of Jesus with which God had foreordained that we be conformable.[14] So much so did Arsenius keep this heavenly image that he rendered honor to the priestly services or he was rendered worthy of honor by it. Arsenius, as one conspicuous for his wisdom and probity, was respected by all and everywhere known.

After the repose of his parents, both Arsenius and Aphrositty gave all their family wealth to the poor. Thereupon, both siblings engaged in greater ascetic struggles. During that time, Gratian was emperor in the west (r. 367-383). He was a man who respected the Senate and maintained traditional cultural values. Since Gratian believed that God's wrath was upon his people due to their belief in Arianism, he, on account of the influence of Bishop Ambrose of Milan,[15] became a supporter of Orthodoxy. Gratian sought an alliance with Theodosios I (r. 379-395), whom he believed to be staunchly Orthodox. He appointed him ruler of the east in the year 379. In 380, Theodosios issued an edict declaring Orthodoxy the true Faith. He had Arianism condemned at the First Synod in Constantinople (381).

Theodosios' first wife, Aelia Flacilla,[16] was the mother of Pulcheria (d. ca. 385), Arkadios (b. ca. 377/378), and Honorius (b. 384). Now Theodosios was in search of a tutor for his children. His son would one day reign in his place; and, moreover, he expected to have more children. "I very much want my children to be taught philosophy and every branch of learning, so that they should become moral and useful leaders. I may, thus, rest in peace with the knowledge that, after my death, they will govern the empire both piously and wisely. I need to find a teacher who is practised and erudite in such pursuits. I must entrust this delicate commission to one who is wise not only in secular letters but also experienced in disciplining them that they might comport themselves with decency and orderliness. He needs to be competent in bringing into proportion inclinations, judgments, and pursuits. I desire to find a man who can couple both majesty and modesty." Such were the thoughts of

---

[14] Rom. 8:29; 1 Cor. 15:49; 2 Cor. 3:18; Col. 3:10.

[15] Saint Ambrose is commemorated by the holy Church on the 7th of December.

[16] Saint Flacilla or Plakilla, is commemorated by the holy Church on the 4th of September. Her husband, Theodosios the Great, is commemorated on the 17th of January.

Theodosios while he sought a tutor. But the results of his emissaries' investigations and interviews were unsatisfactory. The candidates for the post were either learned men not living godly lives or godly men unqualified in all profane knowledge. Despite the seeming failure of the emperor to discover such a paragon, God was about to send just the man that was in accordance with the emperor's desire and even more. Hearken to how the royal children were found the best possible educator and trainer.

Saint Arsenius the Great

Theodosios, thereupon, thought to consult with Gratian over the matter. The emperor of the west, in turn, took counsel with the saintly Pope Damasus, who had a reputation for upholding the Faith against Apollinarianism, Makedonianism, Arianism, and Priscillianism. "Whom shall we send?" asked Gratian, "For we should be held in contempt if our realm in the west cannot produce even one man of virtue and erudition, such as Theodosios seeks. Indeed, no effort must be spared to locate a tutor for the royal children that they may learn philosophy and the fear of God, not only from books but also by having a living example of such." The pope had in mind for the position one man, who far surpassed anyone else. His choice was fixed exactly on Arsenius, a man set apart by education, intellect, superior abilities, and piety. Gratian asked to be introduced to the one to whom the education of kings and princes would be entrusted. The pope commented, "The Deacon Arsenius is from a senatorial family. He is a mature man, not young in years, who is proficient in both sacred and secular learning. His manner of life is ascetical. With his sister he lives a life most holy and pure." Gratian, upon beholding the countenance of Arsenius, his orderliness and discipline, as well as his modest and reverent disposition and character and dress, was impressed. When Arsenius opened his mouth and his all-wise and eloquent tongue gave utterance, Gratian praised him much and remarked, "Even as we heard, so we also see that nothing is wanting in thee of all the good things we have heard concerning thee. Do, therefore, take the trouble to go as far as Constantinople so as to undertake the education of the emperor's children. In so doing, thou shalt have thy reward: first from God; and second from the eastern emperor who shall befriend thee and grant thee many gifts and privileges."

The humble-minded Arsenius, after hearing such words, kept giving pretexts, speaking in a constrained voice, "I am not worthy of such a dignity." He also was saying, "Since I became a deacon, I left off Greek studies. I turned all my attention and mind to the Church offices and services. Besides that, I have completely forgotten Hellenic philosophy. I, therefore, am unqualified. Others are fitter for the post." Now Arsenius spoke thus by reason of his modesty and his profound desire to attain both silence and quietude, which he preferred to temporal wealth, ease, and opportunity. He cherished no worldly ambition. He was not seeking a future of power and plenty. Although both the emperor and the pope discerned well his thoughts, still they believed he underestimated himself. They persisted, imploring him not to disobey them on this issue. "Consider," they said to him, "the benefits that could be derived by instructing the royal children in godly piety and right Faith. One day, they will come into their own and confirm what they had been taught as children. Therefore, hearken to our counsel. Shouldest thou like to be estranged by us? Certainly, thou shouldest not like it if we were to send thee by force." Consequently, since they insisted and lest the matter should end in violence, Arsenius gave place. He accepted the teaching post, only because the pope kept pressing him to the end to undertake the commission of educating the princes. First, however, Arsenius placed his sister in a convent and arranged for her maintenance with whatsoever she should need or require. He then departed, being sent away by both emperor and pope with no small honor.

The Schoolmaster at Constantinople

The man of God, Arsenius, arrived in Constantinople ca. 384.[17] He handed over his letters of introduction, which were in Gratian's handwriting. When Theodosios read the commendations and praises within, regarding the wise Arsenius, he was filled with great joy. With an earnest and steadfast gaze,

---

[17] Emperor Theodosios' son, Prince Honorius, was born on the 9th of September in the year 384. Since Pope Damasus speaks of Theodosios' sons both requiring instruction, we must assume that Arsenius entered Constantinople just after the birth of the second son, that is, Honorius. Pope Damasus reposed on the 11th of December in the same year. Thus, Arsenius must have entered the queen of cities before the repose of Damasus. The pope's successor, Siricius (384-399), was consecrated later during that same December. As for Emperor Gratian, he had already died by assassination in Lyons on the 25th of August, a year earlier, in 383. Gratian's half-brother, the child-emperor Valentinian II (b. 371, r. 375-392), had been kept in a subordinate position. Hence, after Gratian's murder, Justina, Valentinian's mother, ruled in his name. Both Valentinian and Justina must have agreed to the choice of Arsenius. Arsenius was the royal tutor for eleven years, during the last three of which he also had charge of his pupil's brother Honorius.

Theodosios looked at Arsenius with admiration. The emperor perceived Arsenius' noble character, modesty, and orderliness. When he heard his mellifluous words, he marvelled even more at the man. He chose to regard Arsenius as his own father.[18] The emperor then introduced Arsenius to his charges, saying to him, "I, with God, deliver them into thy hands. From this day, they have thee as their father. May thy holiness regard them as thy genuine offspring! Furthermore, I adjure thee not to be negligent or careless. But by all means teach them well, instructing them in that which is good, moral, virtuous, and upright. This is a more fatherly work than simply to father them. I beseech thee, therefore, my beloved Arsenius, instruct them how to come to thy similitude in virtue. Exhort and admonish them as thine own children lest they should become corrupted by some youthful desire or fancy. Give no heed that they are of the royal family, for they are to be subject to thee." The emperor then uttered a prayer aloud to God, saying, "Yea, my God and almighty Master, strengthen them and vouchsafe them to become as their teacher, genuine slaves of Thee."

Such were the tear-filled words of Emperor Theodosios' prayer to Christ. He then turned and resumed his conversation with Arsenius, saying, "Take heed, brother most-loved and reverend father, not to reckon in the least that they bear the royal crown on their brows. Whenever they transgress, thou art to be strict and punish them even as thou wouldest thine own children lest they should develop a flawed perception of the world and life. Thou hast my full and explicit approval. And do not bestow upon them the least honor or deference, which command I pronounce before their faces. The distinction of rank will not be preserved. We will dispense with convention. Thou shalt not stand on ceremony with any of thy students. If I should see that thou hast not observed this express order of mine, I shall be offended and scandalized. I shall even hate thee, as one plotting and laying snares against my reign." These and many other directions were given by the emperor. A suitable building, close by the palace, was established as the children's school. It was Theodosios' desire to frequently see the children and follow their progress. He held the divine Arsenius in very high esteem, so that he counted him first in the Senate. Theodosios also charged that everyone was to call Arsenius not only the genuine father of his sons but also his own father. As a result, Arsenius came to be known as "father of the sovereign and his sons." All complied and used this appellation, which brought honor rather to Theodosios than to Arsenius.

Arsenius took up his duties with his usual diligence, so as to mold the children as Theodosios desired. The curriculum and lectures on diverse

[18] Theodosios I was born in northwest Spain ca. 346-347. He was a military man until he was summoned by Gratian and proclaimed emperor in the east. He is described as a gracious man with blond hair and eagle-like nose.

branches of learning varied. There were times he gave them Greek studies. There were other times that he was teaching them the sacred Scriptures, which were more beneficial and edifying than the other writings. There were times that he exhorted them on how they should proceed in temporal matters or how they ought to submit to all their father's commands. He discoursed on how they should love their subordinates and subjects. These and a multitude of other fields of study were covered in his schoolroom. But most of all, he wished to impress upon the children what was beneficial for the soul. He especially urged them not to succumb to pride and arrogance on account of their imperial rank. He encouraged them to exercise humility, being mindful of the extreme humility of the King of kings. Arsenius also inculcated his pupils with the importance of showing sympathy toward the poor and needy. He enlightened them further by saying that by giving alms they too, in like manner, would find mercy with God on the day of judgment. Upon these things and many other themes did that most wise man expound in order to imbue and foster Christian virtues and behavior in the royal children. They, indeed, profited by his nurturing and cultivation while they were in his charge, so that they advanced not only in their lessons but also in morals and good conduct.

Now it happened one day that the emperor entered the class before the appointed time. Seeing that his visit was unforeseen, he found the children sitting upon thrones while their venerable teacher was standing before them. Arsenius allowed this system not only because he was a lover of humble-mindedness but also because he respected the imperial rank. He had, it seems, reverted to his old inherited ideas about royalty and rank. Now when Theodosios observed what was happening, he did not disguise his displeasure. He went to his children and removed their royal garb, that is, he stripped them of the tokens of the imperium which included the gold chain and crown. Thus, the children were reduced to simple dress. He then charged Arsenius to take a seat. He turned to the children and ordered them to stand before their teacher, which was the custom for all pupils with their tutors. Theodosios then said to Arsenius, "If they should learn to preserve the law of God and His soul-saving commandments, God will vouchsafe them to receive the empire from His holy right hand. If they show themselves to be unworthy of this administration, better that they should die rather than govern badly and stupidly. I pray God that they should be taken from this life, even while they are young, rather than grow up evil into adulthood. Such a calamity would usher in destruction not only to their souls but to others as well."[19] The sagacious Arsenius, hearing

[19] Arkadios became augustus in 383. He was dominated by his wife Evdoxia. His reign participated in the vile deposition of Saint John Chrysostom. Arkadios died in 408. He was about thirty-one years of age. Two of his five children were left to reign, Pulcheria

(continued...)

such a pious opinion from the emperor, marvelled inwardly. With all due deference and humility, he extolled the emperor's declaration as rational, prudent, and God-revering. Arsenius also obeyed the emperor's bidding that he should sit as he taught, while the children stood in his presence.

Despite all the prestige and honor that were accorded to the eminent elder, it afforded him neither gratification nor rest. All he desired was to find solitude and quiet in an untroubled and trackless wilderness retreat. He, thereupon, ofttimes, entreated God with fervent and hot tears to show him a dignified way, consistent with honor, and a blessed reason to flee quickly from his bondage. For Arsenius had no wish to offend or scandalize Theodosios. He also did not want to put his own life in peril, since he wished to live in repentance as a monk before God. Now God did not look askance at Arsenius' ardent and pious request. He hearkened to His servant's supplication and delivered him in the following manner. It so happened that Arkadios fell into a severe transgression. The venerable Arsenius could not allow the prince to go unpunished. He judged the youth's trespass to be wanton violence which he deprecated. He, therefore, had the disagreeable duty of administering a thrashing in order to bring the prince to prudence, as was meet and right. As for Arkadios, upon receipt of the warranted punishment, he bore malice and secretly meditated revenge against Arsenius. His hatred festered to such a degree that he was thinking of putting him to death in order to avenge what he deemed to be a pointed insult to his person.

Arkadios had a sword-bearer (*spatharios*) who served the young prince faithfully. Arkadios entrusted him with all his secrets. The prince charged him to slay Arsenius in whatsoever way he could. But the sword-bearer was a very religious man and feared the heavenly King, not to mention the earthly one also, that they might put him to death as a wrongdoer. Discreetly, then, the sword-bearer disclosed the deep secret to Arsenius that he had been ordered by Arkadios to dispatch him to the next life. "I advise thee, therefore," confided the sword-bearer, "to take flight this very night in a clandestine manner; for thy life is in danger." This impasse, manifestly, was a dispensation of God. This was His providence at work in Arsenius' life, so that the venerable teacher could exchange the schoolroom and the clamor and tumult of the world for that

---

[19](...continued)
(see her dates of commemoration, the 10th of September and the 17th of February) and Theodosios II. Honorius was summoned to the west by Theodosios in 394 and assumed power after his father's repose in 395. He was married twice: to two sisters, the daughters of the *magister militum* Stilicho. Honorius was childless. His reign saw the sacking of Rome by Alaric. He died in 423 at thirty-nine years of age. Neither Arkadios nor Honorius were of any real credit to their father or tutor. Abba Arsenius continued to pray for their souls.

which he really desired: a quiet cell away from everything. That very night, the same sword-bearer secretly assisted the holy man in his escape from the city.

When Arsenius was left on his own, he sent up urgent entreaties to the Lord that He might preserve him from danger and enlighten him where he should go, far from the crowds, that he might live in a wilderness retreat. While he was engaged in fervent prayer, he heard a voice from on high that said, "Arsenius, flee from men and do thou save thyself!"[20] When he heard these words, he was elated because they coincided with his desire to quit the present realm and take up the retired life. He, without a moment's delay, removed his costly raiment, which he still was wearing, and donned a tattered *rason* (cassock). He made haste to the harbor where divine providence arranged that a ship, sailing that very hour, was bound for Alexandria. Arsenius boarded the vessel and arrived, within a few days, in that major intellectual and cultural center where Greek and Coptic were spoken. With God helping him, Arsenius directed his steps, forthwith, to Sketis that he might be numbered with the solitaries.

The Novice Arrives at Sketis

When Arsenius first introduced himself to the superiors of the monks at Sketis, including the great Abba Makarios (301-391),[21] he called himself a wretched wanderer. The fathers asked, "Who mayest thou be? Whence comest thou?" Arsenius answered, "I am a stranger and a poor fellow." The desert fathers, nonetheless, spotted him immediately as a man of culture and education. After deliberating together, they recommended him to the supervision of Abba John the Kolovos (that is, "the Short," ca. 339-ca. 407).[22] When Abba John was first informed about the new man and that he needed testing, he remarked, "May the Lord's will be done!" Arsenius was then led to Abba John who wished to test the novice's mettle. The ninth hour (3:00 p.m.) had come and the monks were sitting down to take their meal. Abba John also took his seat, but Arsenius was left standing in their midst. No one invited him to take a seat. There was no effort to show the least civility. In fact, no one took notice of the newcomer. The ex-courtier and father of kings, nevertheless, showed no resentment at the obvious slight. His head slightly bowed, he believed himself to be in the presence of God and His holy angels. Halfway through the repast, Abba John then took a loaf of bread from the table and tossed it at Arsenius. When the loaf fell to the floor, Abba John said to him in a tone of indifference, "Eat it if thou wilt." Though it might appear to some to

---

[20] The famous line is: 'Αρσένιε, φεῦγε τοὺς ἀνθρώπους καὶ σῴζου (the verb *sozou* parsed is present middle/passive imperative 2nd person singular).

[21] Saint Makarios the Great is commemorated by the holy Church on the 19th of January.

[22] Saint John the Kolovos is commemorated by the holy Church on the 9th of November.

have been a stern and offensive test, yet Arsenius did not display the slightest vexation. Much rather, he thought to himself that his abba must be a clairvoyant, saying to himself, "He perceives that I am but a dog and not fit to eat with the brotherhood." He, therefore, cheerfully sat on the ground and took his meal. Abba John was pleased with Arsenius' humility and grit. Reflecting with satisfaction upon the neophyte's conduct, he acknowledged his merits. Persuaded that Arsenius was predisposed to their manner of life and conduct, he said to the other fathers, "He will require no further trial to be admitted. This man will make a monk." Arsenius was then tonsured a monk. With the snipping of the hairs of his head, he also cut off every earthly concern, care, and vanity. He was next clothed in angelic comeliness, that is, the monastic Schema of holy name and salvation. Following this, Abba Arsenius was sent to a lofty mountain where other hermits were also dwelling in quiet and solitude. He participated in ascetical and spiritual struggles, thereby receiving the benefits of silence.

Imperial Attempts

Meanwhile, back in the capital, Emperor Theodosios understood that Arsenius had taken flight secretly. He was not angry with Arsenius, but he deeply missed his company and counsel since the schoolteacher and surrogate father had a claim on his affections. He, therefore, sent forth men everywhere to find him. This they did with much thoroughness, examining all the caves, as well as clefts of the rocks and the ravines; but the Lord covered Arsenius lest they should discover him. The investigation lasted as long as Theodosios lived. The emperor reposed in Milan on the 17th of January, in the year 395. With his death, Arkadios wielded the scepter. Arkadios had learned, in the interim, where Arsenius could be found. He was also apprised of the state of virtue which the venerable man had attained. Arkadios, thereupon, dispatched an epistle. It was written in a humble style. Gifts were also sent, beseeching the righteous man to forgive him for both the unjust plot and hatred which Arkadios admittedly felt previous to Arsenius' departure. He besought Abba Arsenius for his prayers before God in his behalf. Arkadios asked that God might grant him length of days, victory against the adversaries, and strength to keep strictly the Lord's commandments. Before all else, however, Arkadios entreated the abba with warm tears to accord him pardon with all his heart for his transgression. He also besought him to accept the gift which he was offering, that is, the tribute money of Egypt. Arkadios desired to entrust these monies with Arsenius to be distributed, at the abba's discretion, among the poor and the monasteries.

The man of God read the epistles and bestowed honor upon the imperial messenger, as was proper. Abba Arsenius, nevertheless, did not wish to make a written reply; nor would he accept the tribute money into his hands.

He bid the messenger deliver his oral reply to Emperor Arkadios, saying, "From my soul, I excuse the sinful action; and I pray to God to have mercy on the sovereign with all his subjects. But in regard to the money, I will not take charge of it; for I have already renounced all things of the world and am dead in body. Therefore, as a dead man, it is not seemly that I should provide for earthly good things." Such were the words that the great Arsenius sent by messenger to the emperor. By reason of Arsenius' conduct in this affair, he set the goal of emulation. He became the fitting model for all the ascetics. He, at length, became their chief, as one most learned and expert. Though he was endowed with superior abilities and excellences, yet he never fell into pride. Much rather, he was humbling himself before them all. Moreover, despite all his wisdom, he kept saying, in accordance with the words of the apostle: "I decided not to know anything among you, except Jesus Christ, even this One Who was crucified [1 Cor. 2:2]."

Learning to Sit Properly

Now when Arsenius had first come to the ascetical life, he still had a few habits that he used to practise when he was in the world. For instance, Arsenius used to sit in a cross-legged manner. This seemed to the monks to savor of levity or lack of physical recollection. The senior fathers, since they respected him, did not wish to correct him before the whole company, even though it unwittingly escaped him that no one else sat in that fashion. They agreed among themselves that one of them would sit cross-legged, while another would reprove him for his immodest and unbecoming posture. The one who should accept the rebuke, of course, agreed not to offer any pretext. This skit was carried out before Arsenius, who perceived the blind to conceal the real situation. Knowing, then, that the performance was done for his benefit, he took the hint and quickly quit the habit of sitting with one leg folded over the other.

Seeking Quiet by the Reeds

On one occasion, Abba Arsenius went to see the brethren. They were at a location where an abundance of reeds grew. When Abba Arsenius found them sitting in the midst of the rushes, the wind was blowing. The multitude of reeds was shaking and rustling loudly in the breeze. Arsenius remarked, "Whence cometh this rustling sound?" The others replied, "The rushes are being shaken by the wind." Arsenius asked, "Why are you sitting and listening to the din of these great grasses? If a man dwells in silence and hears but the chirping of a sparrow, he cannot attain to repose in his heart. How much less can you do so sitting in the midst of this commotion?"

Some Spiritual Counsels

The saint repaired to his cell and dwelt there in silence. He left only on special occasions when invited to speak to others on monastic conduct. The desert fathers at Sketis had the custom of gathering for Liturgies on the Lord's day, as well as for the feasts of the Lord, and conducting an all-night vigil. During one of the feast days, the fathers besought Abba Arsenius to teach them and deliver a divine sermon on what was beneficial for the soul. In order to show obedience, he obliged them and spoke the following words which were instructive and fruitful.

"Brethren and fathers: Whosoever endeavors to take up this conduct of life must give much thought to its evident goal. The aim for such as we who have fled the world was that we might save, by means of the departure, our precious and deathless soul. It is, therefore, needful that we bestir ourselves and diligently cleanse the soul. Why? The passions that afflict the soul are more difficult to correct than those of the body. Now there are some who demonstrate virtue and continence with regard to the body, that is, by means of fasts, vigils, and austerities. In order to purify the soul and thoughts, however, of sordid and unclean thoughts, not one passion is put down in a desultory manner. It is immeasurable folly and thoughtlessness on the part of those who avoid fornication and living luxuriously, but do not exercise self-control over the most hidden passions of the soul, such as envy, vainglory, avarice, self-conceit, and pride, which is the worst of all the sins. Such persons are half dirty; or rather it is better to say that they, in large part, resemble idols. The outside is gold or silver, and they shine brilliantly. The inside is full of uncleanness and badness. They may also be likened to tombs. Their bodies are outwardly unpolluted but within their souls are sullied.

"From these hidden passions, let us hasten to be cleansed. Let us bethink ourselves always that the demon is attempting to cast man into error. Let us be mindful of this that we may not be deceived and err. Thus, it frequently happens, under a good pretext, that the treacherous one makes us sin. Let us cite an example. Whensoever a stranger should come to us, we, using the excuse of offering hospitality, dispense with the fast and become extravagant. Then, as mindless ones, we indulge in immoderate drinking and eating—even to excess. In another instance, the malevolent one instigates avarice lest we should have mercy on the needy. In other cases, that rogue counsels those who listen to his suggestions that they leave their place of quiet so that they might profit the people with teaching. Such persons even imagine that they have attained to dispassion. They hold converse, even with women, in a carefree manner. As such, these unfortunate ones fall in with passions bent on pleasure. But, again, there are those whom the inventive enemy leaves alone, even for many years without temptation and harassment. These individuals fancy that they have reached the summit of virtue; but these senseless and vainglorious ones are soon chastised. There are others, again, who are persuaded to accept their thoughts and, at the same time, hear the confessions of sinners, since they supposedly have attained to dispassion and are counted worthy as passionless ones able to govern the impassioned. But such persons, in the end, are plunged into destruction by reason of their wilfulness and arrogance. They eventually fall into sins of the flesh, being reduced to a laughingstock of men and a plaything of the demons. Since the attacks of the troublemaker are diverse and ingenious, it is necessary that we be watchful and diligent and attend to ourselves with exactness. It is needful that we keep constant in prayer to God, with humility, that we might be granted enlightenment and understanding, so that we might discern well and prefer that which is soul-benefitting and in our interest."

These exhortations and many others made up the discourses of Arsenius. He knew very well the assaults and artifices of the demons. He took care each day to stand before God without sin. He would draw nigh to God with tears as did the sinful woman. He would say that one ought to pray to God as if the Lord were standing before one; for He is near and looks at us carefully.[23] And, "If we seek God, He will be revealed to us. And if we lay hold upon Him, He will remain with us."[24] Abba Arsenius told a brother, "Labor with all thy might in the work of righteousness. Toil with the labors of the mind more than with all the various kinds of work of the body. For the labors of the body only incite and gratify the passions of the body. But the labors of the mind—that is to say, the thought which is in God and prayer without ceasing and the suppression of the thoughts with humility—liberate one from all the passions. Labors of the mind vanquish devils, and purify the heart, and make perfect love, and make one worthy of the revelations of the Spirit."[25] He also said, "Thou shalt do nothing without the testimony of the Scriptures."[26]

A favorite of Abba Arsenius, as a model of patient endurance, was the righteous Patriarch Joseph the All-comely. The abba was wont to say that "when an unburned or undried brick is laid in the foundations of a building by the riverside, it will not lend support since it is still moist. But if the same brick should be heated in the kiln, it can support the building as a stone. In like manner, the man who possesses a carnal mind can be compared to a moist brick. If that man does not become hot and burn with heat—even as did Joseph with the word of God—when such a man comes to have dominion, he will be found to be wanting. For very many, upon whom trials have come, straightway, were either swept away or made to fall. It is, therefore, a good thing for a man to know the gravity of dominion. It is good for a man to be required to

---

[23] See E. A. Wallis Budge, *The Paradise of the Fathers*, Vol. II, "Questions and Answers on the Ascetic Rule," p. 246, ¶ 450.

[24] Ibid., p. 197, ¶ 203.

[25] Ibid., p. 316, ¶ 654.

[26] Ibid., p. 197, ¶ 202.

bear trials, which are like the onset of many mighty waters. He then learns to remain firm and unmoved. As for Joseph, he was not at all a being of this earth, so much was he tempted. And consider this also: in the country of Egypt, wherein he was held in bondage, there was not, during former times, even a trace of the fear of God! Nevertheless, the God of his fathers was with Joseph; and He delivered him out of all his tribulations. Joseph is now with his fathers in the kingdom of the heavens. Let us entreat with all our might, then, that we, in the same manner, may be able to flee from, and escape, the righteous judgment of God."[27]

Warfare with Demons

Now Abba Arsenius had two disciples who lived in the neighborhood. Their names were Alexander and Zoilos. He, afterward, admitted a third to their company, one named Daniel (also his sometime biographer). All three of his disciples became famous for their sanctity. They, too, are mentioned in the accounts of the Egyptian desert fathers.

Arsenius, ofttimes, beheld the demons come to his cell—as recorded by the Monk Daniel, one of the venerable man's disciples—and they gave him great trouble. Arsenius endured the temptations of the demons, showing them that he did not fear them. Arsenius would solely pray to the Master, in a humble manner, and say, "O my God, forsake me not; for I have never done before Thee any good thing; but grant to me, by Thy goodness, to put forth a beginning." Now he was heard to say this when the devils rose up against him and vexed him. Those who used to minister to him, as they stood outside of his cell, heard him cry out to God in this manner.

The righteous man was so above human passions and the mightiest of necessities that he endured not only thirst and hunger but also wakefulness so that with regard to sleep he was very temperate. For there is nothing more drastic, and yet efficient, in pressing down the body. The thrice-blessed man, hence, was spending the whole night without sleep while engaged in unceasing prayer. Only in the morning, on account of the weakness of the flesh, when it is no longer able to struggle, he would take his ease for one hour. He would address the coming sleep, saying, "Come, O evil slave!" Then, after he slumbered for that short space, he rose up and kept constant in prayer. He used to say to those who were there that "one hour's sleep is sufficient for a monk, if he is a struggler and of approved ability to do so."

Abba Arsenius, one day, called Abbas Alexander and Zoilos, his disciples. They showed a right and proper feeling to their elder. They would one day become the heirs of his virtue, since they endeavored to deserve such a distinction. He said to them one night, "Behold, the demons are striving with

[27] Ibid., "Of Patient Endurance," p. 49, ¶ 220.

me! I do not know if they may carry me off to sleep, so toil with me this night and keep vigil. Let me know if I should fall asleep during the vigil." So they sat down, one to his right hand and the other to his left. They remained from the evening until the morning. While the disciples were awake, Arsenius did not sleep. Sleep, however, overcame Alexander and Zoilos, so they knew not whether their elder had succumbed. In the morning the disciples admitted afterward to others, "We did fall asleep. We, therefore, did not observe whether the elder slept at all; but he did not appear so when we awoke. When it began to be light, we heard the sound of heavy breathing through his nostrils thrice. Whether he did this purposely or slumber overtook him, we know not. The elder then stood up and said, 'Have I been asleep?' But we were not certain and said to him, 'We know not, abba, for we ourselves had fallen asleep.'"[28]

Saint Arsenius

Abba Daniel used to say that "on one occasion, Abba Arsenius called me and said, 'Make thy father to be gratified, so that when he goes to our Lord, he may make entreaties to Him in behalf of thee; and good shall be to thee.'"[29]

Abba Arsenius' Attire and Abstinence

Arsenius was also very humble in his attire; for as he appeared outwardly, so was his inner man. His *rason* was old and needed to be cast off. If one caught sight of him and did not know him from a previous acquaintance, one might assume he was but a simple and unlettered monk. This was due to his utter lack of attention to his flesh, though this was the same man who once knew of the luxuries and amenities of palace life. Though his apparel was very fine in the palace, he now wore garments which were inferior to all the other inhabitants of Sketis. His garb did not differ from that of a poor peasant in tattered and worn garments. But on account of his despising those things of this world and preferring mortification of the passions, Arsenius preferred to adorn his soul with the splendid raiment of dispassion. He, therefore, passed his life in hardships, for which he rejoiced and gave thanks to God. Despite his

---

[28] Ibid., "On Reading, Vigil, and Prayer," pp. 25, 26, ¶ 113.

[29] Ibid., "Of Obedience," p. 54, ¶ 243.

threadbare clothing and his poor and needy fare, which was his usual food, his aspect was grace-filled. His pleasant countenance appeared as though he were partaking of a variety of savory dishes.

Abba Daniel was saying, as well as the neighbors of Abba Arsenius, that the elder fasted to a very great degree. Though no one knew exactly how strict was his abstinence, it must have been prodigious; for the measure of wheat sent him for the year was very small. This amount would suffice not only him but also others to whom he gave from it. As for fruits, Abba Daniel used to say this about the abba. When Arsenius learned that the fruits were ripe on the tree, he was desirous to partake of some. He did so once yearly of every kind of fruit, so as to give thanks to God and for the sake of condescension.

Abba Arsenius' Handiwork

Abba Arsenius was never idle. He was about thirty-two miles from the church.[30] While he never went anywhere, others brought him what he needed. If he was not engaged at his handiwork, he was praying. He used to plait baskets and mats of the fronds of the date palms. The fronds needed to be steeped in water that they might be made malleable, so he could twist and weave them. He also used the leaves, entwining them into ropes. He worked daily with the palm leaves, sewing them together, until the sixth hour. Since he never changed the water, but only added to it as he needed it for the work, a rank odor exhaled from the bowl. The brethren and fathers, supposing that he left the stagnant water on account of negligence, reproached him and asked, "Why not change that water used for soaking the palm fronds, for it is very foul?" The elder answered, "When I was living in the world, I indulged myself and used to enjoy many delightful aromatic fragrances and oils. In order, therefore, that I might blot out that sin, I now endure these harmful whiffs." In fact, the elder lived in such utter poverty, not wishing to possess anything, that once, when he fell ill, he had not even a lamp for his needs which caused others to pity him.

The Occupation and Conduct of a Monk

A certain monk besought the righteous man to speak to him a profitable word, to which request the abba exhorted him and said, "Be in earnest and be struggling as much as possible to please God in the work of the inner man of the soul; and then it is possible to vanquish the outward man and passions of the flesh. For vain and to no benefit are the toils and pains of the flesh, if we have not conquered in the interior warfare."[31] These and many other sayings were

[30] Ibid., "Of Patient Endurance," p. 46, ¶ 207.

[31] *The Great Synaxaristes* (in Greek) provides a note saying that divine Gregory of Thessalonike mentions these words ofttimes that every effort should be made to achieve the interior works according to God in order to vanquish the exterior passions. This is (continued...)

uttered by the great Arsenius to that monk, which caused the listener and others to marvel at all of the elder's counsels.

At another time, the venerable man was asked by a monk, "How should they conduct themselves who journey to a strange city or land?" The elder remarked, "When a monk travels to a city, let him not make any acquaintance. He should be neither outspoken nor familiar with any, that he may keep his soul from harm." He also said elsewhere, "The monk is a stranger in a foreign land. Let him not occupy himself with anything therein; and he will find rest."[32]

On one occasion, seven brethren came to visit Abba Arsenius. They entreated him to speak a few words in answer to their question: "What is the work of a monk?" The elder said, "Indeed, when first I came to this place I also went and posed the same question to two old men. They answered me and said, 'Dost thou believe in what we are doing?' I said, 'Yea.' Then they said to me, 'Go, then, and whatsoever thou hast seen us do that also do thyself.'" Then the seven brothers asked in unison, "Abba, what was their work?" Arsenius then remarked, "The one old man had acquired great humility and the other obedience." The seven then asked, "What is thy work, abba?" The elder commented, "According to my mind, it is a great thing for a man not to bind himself with any matter." The seven then departed, greatly profited by what they heard, and gave thanks to God.[33]

At another time, a certain virtuous monk, named Abba Makarios,[34] posed this question to Abba Arsenius: "Well then, is it good for one not to have even one pleasurable thing in his cell? I ask this because I know of a monk who used to have a few garden herbs in his cell. But in order to avoid any source of delight or enjoyment, he pulled them out by the roots." The righteous Arsenius gave his opinion, saying, "This is good, but such a one henceforth needs to maintain the same virtue. If, however, he cannot thereafter maintain perfection and if he should be inclined to draw back to the first things, let him plant others."

It was customary for the marvellous Arsenius to profit the fathers with the telling of sacred feats and stories, speaking in the third person. For instance, if he wished to recount a certain vision which he beheld, he would frame his story as though another father had seen it. He spoke thus that he

---

[31](...continued)
needful for all those wishing to be saved. The interior works include sacred prayer and sobriety that is pure and solely for the sake of God. If the interior work is energized purely, we shall easily vanquish the outward passions of the flesh.

[32] See Budge, *Paradise*, "Questions and Answers on the Ascetic Rule," p. 166, ¶ 47.

[33] Ibid., "Of Humility," p. 120, ¶ 527.

[34] The name Mark is given elsewhere.

might avoid vainglory. Abba Daniel confirms this, saying that Abba Arsenius would tell a story as if he were speaking of some other man. Hearken to one such narration. "A certain elderly monk, while he was sitting in his cell, heard once a voice saying to him, 'Come hither and I shall show thee how it is with the works of men.' The old man, thereupon, went outside, following the angel. When they arrived at a certain place, the angel showed him a man who was cutting wood. After he bound up the loose wood to be carried off, he found he was unable to lift the bundle. Instead of making the bundle smaller and lighter, he busied himself with cutting more wood. Thus he added even more wood to the bundle and, indeed, kept at it. Then the angel took the monk off a little further. This time he showed him another man who was standing nearby a pit and drawing forth water and putting it in a sieve. The result was that the water ran down again into the pit. The angel then proceeded a little further and showed the monk a huge church. The monk observed that there were two men on horseback outside of the church. Between them they were bearing a very large piece of wood, which they held parallel, and not endways, to the building. They attempted to enter therein without changing their position, but the wood was as long as the width of the building. Try as they might, they were unable to enter into the temple. The length of the wood did not permit passage through the door. Neither man would stoop before the other. Neither would give place to the other to enter one after the other. Neither would consider bringing the wood in endwise through the door. They kept holding it parallel to the building, which prevented access to either man. Thus, both men remained outside.

"After the angel showed the elder these three sketches, he revealed the meaning of each vision and said, 'Those who were bearing the wood are as many who believe and are righteous, but, on account of pride, the path of humility has become untraversable for them. Thus, those mindless ones remain outside of the heavenly kingdom. The one who was drawing water into the vessel with holes, is one who cultivates the virtues—that is, fasting, prayer, almsgiving, and other such practises—but he is a man-pleaser. He wishes, therefore, to exhibit his deeds before men. He is not thankful that only God should know of these deeds; for he seeks rather the praise of men. It is by reason of this, and justly, that God loathes such a man's practises and does not give him any reward. As for the other man, the one who could not lift the wood, he is like one who has many sins. Instead of repenting and casting them off, the foolish one adds other sins to the pile. Verily, it is needful that a man should be watchful in his labor and examine himself lest he should toil in vain.'" Such were the words of the divine Arsenius, which brought healing treatments to each listener with the respective passion. All were benefitted to a great degree by his admonitions, exhortations, and teachings.

The Vision at the Divine Liturgy

At another time, the divine Arsenius recounted to the fathers the following history. But it was Abba Daniel Parnaya, the abba's disciple, who used to speak of it. The narrative concerning a certain monk is as follows. There lived at Sketis an uneducated elderly monk of simple faith, who had performed great and wonderful labors. The devil, taking advantage of that elder's rusticity and lack of learning, sowed in him thoughts like unto darnel, so that the old man was saying that the holy bread or Lamb of which we were partaking is not the actual body of the Lord, nor the holy wine the Lord's blood; but these were antitypes. Now some of the senior fathers heard these words and were grieved. They desired to correct the error of that elder's opinion, because they knew of his lofty works. They, therefore, thought that the elder spoke thus on account of his simplemindedness. Two of these fathers went to that elder's cell. As they spoke, the two visitors mentioned a conversation that they heard being bruited about. They said, "We, O abba, have heard a story about an elder who has mistakenly uttered blasphemous words concerning the immaculate Mysteries. He was saying that the holy Communion, of which we partake, is not the very blood and body of Christ, but rather an antitype of these." That abba then made a prostration before the two visitors, saying, "Give the blessing, holy fathers! I am he who uttered this; and I said this because I do not believe that it is actually the body of Christ."

The two visiting fathers said, "Cease blaspheming, elder, and bringing punishment upon thy head. According to what is taught by the holy Church, the divine transformation of the essence of the bread is truly the body of Christ; and the wine is truly the divine blood. These are not mere similitudes. Even as God took dust from the earth and fashioned man in His image—and no man is able to say that he is not the image of God—so also is the case of the bread of which Jesus said that 'this is My body.'[35] This is not merely a commemorative practise. We believe that this is indeed the body of Christ." Then the visitors said, "Thus has the Lord dispensed in His œconomy that we participate in this manner, because He knew that human nature would be repulsed at partaking of raw flesh and blood. For this reason, we receive the body and blood in these forms. But it is at the prayer and *epiklesis* (invocation) of the priest, through the presence of the Holy Spirit, that the bread and wine are transformed in a marvellous manner. It is exactly the same case in regard to holy Baptism. According to appearance, we see water. But by the prayers and the performance of the sacred Mystery, the Holy Spirit sanctifies those waters. So what appears as plain water actually regenerates and refashions the baptismal candidate who is delivered of all his sins."

---

[35] Mt. 26:26; Mk. 14:22; Lk. 22:19; 1 Cor. 11:24.

The old man, however, was not much the wiser for what he had heard and said, "Unless I should be convinced of this transformation with my own eyes, I will not hearken." The visitors then said, "Let us offer up prayer to God for one whole week, so that He might reveal this Mystery; and we trust that He will reveal it to us." The old man, pleased with this recommendation, agreed happily. Then each father went to his own cell. The old man, when left alone, besought God in a frankhearted manner as follows: "Thou knowest, O Lord, that it is not out of a vitiated mind or a perverseness on my part to be contradictory that I do not believe what they are uttering. But lest I should go astray through ignorance, do Thou, O Lord Jesus Christ, reveal this Mystery to me." The two sincere fathers also remained in prayer, entreating the Lord for the elder's enlightenment, "O Lord Jesus Christ, bring this old man to the knowledge of the truth regarding this Mystery lest he should lose his previous ascetic toils attained by much sweat."

When the week ended, all three fathers went to church in order to attend the divine Liturgy. The three sat down by themselves on one bench, with the erring elder between the other two. When the priest lifted up his voice during the anaphora, saying, "Especially our all-holy, immaculate, most blessed, glorious Lady Theotokos and ever-virgin Mary," the three fathers noticed the holy paten. O Thy most kind and wonderful power, O Christ! A little infant, living and gracious, was seen.

When the priest stretched forth his hand in order to break the holy bread or Lamb, the three elders observed a holy angel having a knife in his hands. He slaughtered the holy Infant and poured His precious blood into the holy chalice. When the priest broke the holy Lamb into small pieces, the angel cut the flesh of the divine Infant into the same portions. Now when the elder, the one who held that erroneous belief, approached to commune the immaculate Mysteries, he was sensible of partaking of raw flesh which was dripping with blood. The elder beheld this and cried out from his joy, saying, "I believe, O Lord, that the bread is Thy body, and that the cup is Thy blood!" Thus, he utterly cast off his former delusion, the incontrovertible truth having been shown positively. Likewise, the two other fathers were gladdened when they, too, beheld such a wonder. The two then said to the converted elder, "God knows the nature of men and that it is unable to eat living flesh. So although we may perceive bread and wine, yet in truth it is His body and blood." After the dismissal, all three returned to their cells filled with gladness. Now the two fathers gave thanks to the Lord not only for the vision but also for the old man and his labors that were not destroyed by Satan.

Ineffable Contemplation and Amiable Hospitality for the Lord's Sake

Another monk, named Mark, questioned the venerable Arsenius, saying, "How come thou hatest men and avoidest us?" The elder answered, "O venerable Mark, God knows how much I love you all. But I am not able to divide myself in two. I cannot remain alone with God at the same time I am with you. I, therefore, prefer to please God rather than men. Consider this. On the one hand, all the myriads of the angels have one goal and one will. It is to hymn God unceasingly and to accomplish His commands strictly. On the other hand, men possess other desires. Each man has his own will and thoughts. Each man has his own inclinations and opinions. If we would seek God with a pure and blameless manner of life, as is meet, He shall abide in us. I, therefore, cannot leave God to be with men." Though the saint maintained this disposition, yet when enjoined by the brethren he offered spiritual instruction. But his speech was framed as though he were speaking the words of another father lest he appear to be acting as the schoolmaster again.

On another occasion, a certain brother desired to behold the great Arsenius. He repaired to the church building (*kyriakon*) at Sketis. He besought the fathers to show him Abba Arsenius. The priests suggested that he refresh himself a little and then he could see Arsenius. That brother, nevertheless, was impatient. He protested, saying, "I will neither eat nor sleep unless I first see the man of God." The clergy then dispatched another monk to show him the way to Arsenius' cell, which was a long way off, some seven miles from Sketis. Finally, when they arrived and knocked at the door, the venerable man emerged. He welcomed them and saluted them. They, next, all sat down but not a word was spoken. After a long time passed, the monk who escorted the visiting brother said to him, "I shall return to my cell, but do thou remain here if thou hast further need." As that monk rose up, the visiting brother followed him, saying, "I, too, shall accompany thee." Thus, the two bowed to the elder and went out. The visitor, after they walked a little, said to the monk, "I should like to see Abba Moses the Ethiopian.[36] Do thou take me to him who was once a thief." The monk fell in with the visitor's plan and they went. Abba Moses received them with joy. He washed their feet and set a table before them with food and drink. He also edified them with soul-befitting conversation. After he entertained them, he dismissed them in peace.

As they were on their way, the monk asked the visiting brother, "Behold, I have brought thee to two men this day! One was from a foreign land and the other is from here. Tell me, which of the two seems to be more virtuous?" The visitor, impressed with the kindly bestowed solicitude given by Abba Moses, answered, "The latter, the one who just refreshed us." Now one of the renowned elders heard about this discordant episode, which caused him some degree of consternation. He wished to know which one of the two, that is, Arsenius or Moses, committed that which was superior. He, therefore,

---

[36] Saint Moses is commemorated by the holy Church on the 28th of August.

supplicated the Lord and uttered, "O Lord, reveal to me this matter. For one man flees from men for Thy name's sake, while another receives strangers and is gracious to them for Thy name's sake." Then that elder entered into a state of ecstasy, being drawn out of himself by the power of God. He beheld in a vision two feluccas running on the river. In the one vessel was Arsenius, sailing alone and unperturbed, being protected, guarded, and led by the Spirit of God. In the other vessel was Moses, whom the angels of God were feeding honey from the comb. That elder, upon seeing these things, understood that both abbas were most worthy laborers of God, but the silence of Arsenius was preferred to the hospitality of the Ethiopian. He came to this conclusion since Arsenius was with the Holy Spirit, while Moses was with the holy angels who were feeding him honey on account of his love and hospitality. The fathers understood, thereupon, that the life of silent contemplation is exalted above alms and ministrations. But all in all, both virtues are good and God-pleasing.

There was another occasion when an uninvited visitor intruded upon Arsenius. A certain father had come to Arsenius and knocked at the door of the abba's cell. The elder opened the door, straightway, thinking it was his disciple. When he saw that the man who stood before him was a stranger, he prostrated himself prone on the ground that he might not see the man. The visitor then said, "Abba, rise up that I may give thee the salutation of peace." But Arsenius remained prone to the ground, saying, "I will not stand up until thou hast departed." The visitor kept pleading with Arsenius to rise up, but he would not hearken. Thus, the importunate visitor departed so that Arsenius might continue the labors of reclusion.[37]

Abba Arsenius Suffers Illness

Abba Arsenius, at another time, fell sick while he was at Sketis. He was in need of a bowl of pottage which was nowhere to be found. He, therefore, took the remains of the Eucharist and said, "I give thanks to Thee, O Christ, that, because of Thy name, I am able to receive the food of grace."[38]

There was another time that the wondrous man succumbed to illness. One of the priests went to his cell and brought Arsenius back to the infirmary that was adjacent to the church. He spread out a mat made of palm fronds and skins that he might convalesce. He also placed a pillow under the abba's head. Now while this was taking place, there came in one of the elders. When that elder observed Arsenius reclining on the mat with a pillow under his head, he was scandalized at the sight. The priest saw the elder's reaction and, in turn, by that admonitory glance, the elder perceived his accusing thought was discovered. He, therefore, said to the priest, "This is Abba Arsenius? Is he taking his ease upon such things? I can scarcely believe it." The priest then

[37] See Budge, *Paradise*, "On Retreat from the World and Contemplation," p. 6, ¶ 13.
[38] Ibid., "Of Voluntary Poverty," p. 35, ¶ 158.

took that elder aside, away from Arsenius' hearing, and asked him, "Before thou camest to the monastic state, what was thine occupation in thy village?" The old man said, "I was a shepherd." The priest continued and asked, "Tell me the manner of thy life that thou didst lead in the world." The elder replied, "It was a life of sore distress and hardship, on account of my poverty." The elder then described some of his toils. The priest then asked, "Tell me the manner of thy life here." The elder admitted the following, saying, "I am quite comfortable in my cell. In fact, I have more than I want." The priest then said, "But this one, Abba Arsenius, whom thou seest lying here, consider his position when he was in the world. He was the father of the emperors. He possessed wealth in abundance. He had a life of ease, comfort, and every convenience at his disposal. As for his apparel, he was girt with soft garments made of silk. Even the servants who stood before him to do his bidding wore necklaces and ornaments of gold; and they, too, were arrayed in silken garments and gold-embroidered vests. His commodious bedchamber had luxurious appointments. He possessed costly couches and cushions to take his ease. So, just reflect a moment: the comforts which thou never hadst in the world, thou hast found here. But Arsenius has none of the comforts he had in the world. He now loathes the world and disdains all such things that he once had ready at hand. Moreover, for the love of Christ, he has renounced all and is in the midst of straits. And even now he is suffering while thou art at thine ease. In fact, thy life now, my father, according to thine own words, is free from care and affords thee rest and comfort previously unknown to thee." When the elder heard these words, he understood his earlier ill judgment and ignorant presumptions. Pricked in his heart, he became contrite and said plaintively to the priest, "Father, forgive me, I have sinned. What thou sayest is certainly the truth. Abba Arsenius has come to a state of humility, while I have only attained to leisure." Thus, that elder went away greatly profited.

Abba Alexander

At another time Abba Arsenius said to Abba Alexander, "Whensoever thou hast finished thy handiwork, come and we shall eat together. But should strangers come, take thy meal with them and do not come to me." Alexander then went about his employment, working late. When the time for the meal arrived, he still had palm leaves set before him. He felt more or less betwixt and between whether to carry on. He, on the one hand, was anxious to keep the appointment with the elder and not make him wait; but, on the other hand, he wanted to complete the leaves and then go and eat with him. Meanwhile, Abba Arsenius noticed that Abba Alexander was late in coming. He assumed that strangers must have come visiting and that his disciple was enjoined to remain and refresh them. When Abba Alexander finished the palm leaves, he rose up and went forthwith to his elder. Arsenius, straightway, inquired, "Did strangers visit with thee?" Alexander said, "No, father." Arsenius then asked, "Then why wast thou delayed in coming here?" Alexander replied, "Because thou didst say that I might come whensoever I should finish the palm leaves. I gave heed to thy word and finished the work. Behold, I am come!" The elder marvelled at Alexander's over-scrupulous obedience. Arsenius then said to Alexander, "Make haste, then, and recite the prayer before a meal. Then drink some water, for if thou dost not do it quickly, thy body shall sicken from weariness."[39]

Abba Arsenius Aflame at Prayer

It was said about Abba Arsenius that no one could attain to his mode of life that he kept in his cell. The fathers also said that on Saturday evening until the end of dawn on Sunday, he would stretch forth his hands heavenward, facing east in prayer. He would leave the sun behind him until it rose again and beamed on his face. Only then, did he give a little rest to his eyes.

At another time, a certain elder came to see the righteous Arsenius while he was in Sketis. He desired to hear some spiritually profitable words from the abba. Since he found the door closed when he arrived, he chose not to knock at the door lest he should disturb the holy occupant within. He, therefore, peered in through a small opening. He saw the venerable Arsenius standing upright. His appearance was changed into fire. The visiting elder remained a long while, wholly in a state of fear. After he composed himself, he plucked up courage and knocked at the door. The venerable Arsenius opened the door. He immediately perceived that his visitor was in a state of wonder. Arsenius, always keen to hide his labors, asked him with a tinge of anxiety of mind, "How long hast thou been waiting outside? Hast thou seen something?" For Arsenius wished to ascertain if he had seen any vision. The visiting elder denied seeing anything. He admitted nothing lest he should discomfit Arsenius. The righteous man then spoke with his guest and dismissed him in peace. But that you may know to what extent Abba Arsenius renounced the world and forsook its delights—for he despised everything earthly since, in accordance with the apostle's words, "through Jesus the world had been crucified to him, and he to the world [Gal. 6:14]"—hearken to the following account.

Abba Arsenius is Named as Heir

One of the emperor's officers of high rank was dispatched from Rome, bearing a last will and testament of a certain kinsman of Arsenius. A deceased senator left a large inheritance to his heir, namely, Arsenius. When the abba received the document into his hands, he was about to tear it to pieces. The officer fell before Arsenius' feet and shouted aloud, "If thou shouldest destroy the document, I am in danger of losing my life." The abba then handed over the

---

[39] Ibid., "Of Watchfulness," pp. 68, 69, ¶ 305.

document to the officer, stating the following: "I am no longer interested in temporal affairs. In fact, I am no longer among the living, because I died long ago and cannot be his heir. I, indeed, died before the decedent though his death is but recent." Thus, Arsenius refused the estate and took nothing from him. The officer, upon hearing this declaration, went his way. Who would not marvel at hearing this account of the wondrous virtues of the great Arsenius?

Abba Arsenius is Visited by Hierarchs and Dignitaries

The fame of the righteous Arsenius spread to nearly every city and land, which resulted in visitors coming to his cell that they might receive benefit from his words. There visited not only lay people but also superiors and hierarchs. They had Arsenius as their boast and would say as much for having had a conversation with him.

On one occasion, it happened that Elder Arsenius fell ill when he was living in Patara of Estoris.[40] Certain fathers from Alexandria, according to Abba Daniel's recollection, came to see the abba. One of the pilgrims was the brother of Patriarch Timothy of Alexandria (380-385). Another in the group was his nephew. Since Arsenius was feeling unwell, he did not wish to spend much time with them lest they should come again and trouble him. As a result of the visit, those pilgrims left feeling sorrowful.

Now it happened that barbarians came into the country and committed blood-chilling atrocities. It was then that Abba Arsenius left and dwelt in the lower countries. Those same fathers out of Alexandria heard of his arrival and went to see him. Abba Arsenius, this time, greeted them gladly. Then the patriarch's brother said to Arsenius, "Abba, when last we came and saw thee that first time at Estoris, I noticed that thou didst not speak to us at any length. Why is that?" The elder remarked, "My son, while you all ate bread and drank water, I refused to partake of anything. I would not take my ease and sit, even upon my legs. I tortured myself all the while until I knew, that is, after calculating the distance by experience, that you should have arrived at your homes safely. For I knew in my heart that it was for my sake that you undertook the trouble, traversing no easy distance, to see me." Upon hearing these words, all in the party were pleased and gratified in their hearts. They departed rejoicing on account of the saint's gracious concern for their well-being.[41]

On another such occasion, there came to him both the governor of Alexandria and Patriarch Theophilos (385-412). After they exchanged greetings, the visitors besought the venerable elder to speak to them salutary words to their benefit, because this is what they desired and this is why they

---

[40] Patara of Sketis was some forty miles distant from the church, and twelve miles from the closest spring.

[41] See Budge, *Paradise*, "Of Watchfulness," p. 71, ¶ 317.

exerted themselves to come this far. Arsenius then asked them, "If I should say something to you, will you be disposed to hearken?" They replied, "Yea." Then the most wise abba said, "Wheresoever you should hear that Arsenius is found, you will not draw nigh." When the visitors heard this statement, they were scandalized initially. But then they were glad, as they understood what he was saying by these words lest his solitude should be disturbed. The saint also thought to spare them the trouble of coming after him.

The same hierarch, at another time, sent a written message to Arsenius and asked this of the elder: "Wilt thou open thy cell in the event that I should come? If the answer is 'nay,' say as much lest I should toil for nought in the coming." Arsenius sent back these words, saying, "If I should receive thy prelacy, then I shall be enjoined to receive everyone. And then it will be needful for me to depart this place lest they should trouble me." The patriarch, hearing this response, in no wise ventured to see the venerable man and said, "If my going would drive away the old man, I should not go."

Abba Arsenius' Hardly Discernible Appearance

Abba Arsenius' humility and self-effacing ways were no vain show. While some hanker after approbation and notice, he yearned for obscurity and invisibility. For this reason, also, he never entered the sanctuary, though he was a deacon. Instead, he received holy Communion with the monks who were not ordained. He, therefore, attempted to flee every possibility of seeing others or being seen or seeming to show off. For this same reason, at the gatherings or assemblies and the feasts of the Church, he usually stood behind either a column or a veil. There were other times that he stood in the corner. He did all these things to be as inconspicuous as possible. While he stood reverently, he prayed continually. He calmly and easily raised his mind to God. He had the habit of asking himself, "Arsenius, why didst thou leave the world?" He was also asking himself, "Arsenius, why didst thou come to the wilderness and forsake the world? Certainly for no other reason save to please God. Therefore, as much as thou art able, diligently apply thyself to whatsoever Christ desires." Regarding his flight from men and his love of silence, when he was living the ascetic life at first in the monastery, he had prayed to the Lord the same prayer that he was wont to utter in the palace, that is, "O Lord, direct me how to live." Again, he heard a voice saying to him, "Arsenius, flee, keep silence, and lead a life of silent contemplation." The ever-memorable man was also wont to say that "ofttimes, I repented of that which I had spoken, but by holding my peace I have never had need to repent."

The Gift of Tears

The unforgettable Arsenius also possessed the gift of blessed mourning. The gift of tears was with him during his uninterrupted hours of work. Tears were ever welling up in his eyes, so that he kept at his breast a patch of material from his cassock that he might wipe them away. He observed this habit in his dress, especially since he did not wish for tears to fall upon any book he was reading. Now Abba Poemen noticed this when he visited Arsenius in his cell. Poemen said, among many other things to Arsenius, this: "I call thee fortunate, O Arsenius; and verily thou art happy because thou hast wept sufficiently in this life and, thus, in no wise, art thou going to mourn in the one to come but rather thou art going to ever rejoice." Furthermore, at another time, when Patriarch Theophilos of Alexandria was about to depart from this world, he commented, "Blessed art thou, O Arsenius, because always thou hast in remembrance this hour of death."

Barbarian Raids Bring the Desert Fathers to Troe

Barbarians, about that time, made inroads upon Sketis.[42] While the other fathers took flight lest they be slain, Arsenius in no wise was terrified since he had authority over demons and the ungodly were afraid of him. He, therefore, remained in his cell but said, "If God does not have a care for me, why should I want to live?" Thus, he continued to abide unconcerned. Meanwhile, the barbarians came but did not notice his *kellion*.

On another occasion, in order to flee the praise of the fathers, he left with the others for the rock or Mountain of Troe (Troë) as the barbarians had raided Sketis. Though Arsenius passed through the midst of them, yet he was invisible to them. For he was under the protection and providence of God. Arsenius wept copious tears over the desolation of Sketis. Since Rome had been sacked shortly before by the Visigoths,[43] he commented, "The world has lost Rome, and the monks have lost Sketis!" Finally, when the barbarians departed, the fathers returned to their cells.

At the Lower Lands and Near Alexandria

During the time that Abba Arsenius was dwelling in the lower lands, he was troubled in his soul. Many were coming to see him in his cell, thereby interrupting his inner quietude and interior mental prayer. Such was his disturbance that he was determined to exit his cell, abandoning everything in it. He then departed and went to his disciples, that is, Alexander and Zoilos. Arsenius said to Alexander, "Get thee up into the place where I had sojourned." Alexander obeyed and went ahead. As for Zoilos, Arsenius said to him, "Accompany me to the river. Find me a ship bound for Alexandria. Then thou mayest return and go to thy brother." Zoilos was surprised at these words, but he did not question his elder. Neither disciple, in fact, dared to ask the abba

---

[42] Saint Arsenius was forced to flee to Troe (Troë, Troes, Troja), near ancient Memphis, Egypt, in order to escape the devastating incursions of the Libyan Mazici tribesmen, whom he likened to the Goths and Huns who ravaged Rome.

[43] King Alaric I, ruler of the Visigoths, sacked Rome on the 24th of August, in the year 410.

why he was leaving them. Thus, when Arsenius parted from Zoilos at the river, Arsenius left for Alexandria where he later succumbed to a serious illness. Meanwhile, Alexander and Zoilos returned and met in the same place where they formerly dwelt. When they were together, they each, somewhat disheartened, said to the other, "Perhaps one of us has offended the elder? What other reason could there be for his departure from among us?" They carefully examined themselves, but could not imagine what might have offended the abba to such a degree that he should leave everything. At length, Abba Arsenius recovered from his infirmity. He was then prompted to return to the fathers. He, therefore, traveled to Patara where his disciples were sojourning.

Saint Arsenius

Now it happened during the journey back that he was passing near the riverside. As he was going along, a dark-skinned woman took hold of his mantle and pulled at it. Arsenius, in disproportionate anger, said sharply, "Leave go of me!" and he insulted her. Her seemingly arbitrary act had provoked an unbidden reaction in him. She responded without the least tremor in her voice, saying, "It is not meet that thou shouldest become angry, O Arsenius, so easily; but rather, if thou art a monk, abide in thy cell." Upon hearing her lucid words, the venerable man was startled but benefitted. He, shamefaced, reproached himself. He thought his conduct toward her and loss of self-possession would ill bear examination. By means of her brisk rejoinder, he avowed, "Arsenius, if thou art a monk, get thee to the mountain."

This encounter spurred him on. He went directly to Alexander and Zoilos who met him. The disciples, spontaneously, made a prostration at the elder's feet. He, in turn, made a full prostration to the ground. A hot wave of tears befell all three fathers. Then the elder said, "I suppose you did not hear that I was unwell, did you?" They replied, "Indeed, abba, we had heard." Arsenius then asked, "Why did you not come and see me?" Alexander answered cautiously, "The manner in which thou didst depart from us, it was, well, so sudden. By reason of it, many were scandalized. Some even accused us of having oppressed thee or disobeyed thee; for otherwise they believed that thou wouldest never have gone away so abruptly." Arsenius remarked in mildly disparaging good humor, "I, too, thought that there would be some fathers who would thus interpret my departure. This is why I have returned to you. But let the fathers now say this of me: 'The dove could not find rest for her feet, so she returned to Noah in the ark.'"[44] The disciples took delight in the comparison and were consoled. Thus, they resumed dwelling together in harmony.

The Abba Teaches and Learns

Among the other virtues of the thrice-blessed man, he, with regard to the divine Scriptures, never made queries nor accepted them. It was not, however, that he did not know how to give an answer. As we know, he was most wise and eloquent. He knew well how to solve every difficult passage of sacred Scriptures. But out of humble-mindedness, he did not want to display his knowledge that he might keep watch over silence. Since he did not wish to reveal that he was wise in book-learning, he did not write letters. He chose to comport himself as a simple monk. Despite his fixed opinion on this subject, he was not inflexible or undeviating when a brother came to him and sought help. Such encounters had occasioned an opportunity for him to speak a word or two in season, neither with embellishment nor with stock phrases. Once, a certain brother said to Abba Arsenius, "Honorable father, I wish to disclose to thee that I have studied many sacred books and psalms. Though I desire to read them with compunction of heart, yet I have no compunction. Furthermore, ofttimes, I have no comprehension of what I am reading in the sacred texts. Believe me, this is no small grief to me." The venerable elder, perceiving his sincere regret and consternation, advised him in this wise: "Son, we are told to 'keep on searching the Scriptures [Jn. 5:39].' Spiritual reading requires great attention. Study the word of God continually, even if for now thou hast not attained to understanding or compunction. I have heard Abba Poemen (d. ca. 450)[45] and, indeed, other fathers, address this very problem, giving this example. Even though snake charmers do not understand the words they speak,

---

[44] Gen. 8:8, 9.

[45] Saint Poemen is commemorated by the holy Church on the 27th of August.

yet the serpents, hearing their words, succumb to their sounds as if they understood the words. We may do the same by consecrating our tongues. What I mean to say is that although we do not always comprehend what we are reading in the Scriptures, still we have the God-inspired words on our lips. When we articulate these words, the demons, in their dread of hearing them, are dispelled. Thus, our enemies, not enduring the words of the Holy Spirit speaking through the prophets and apostles, are put to flight."

Abba Arsenius was also not ashamed to take instruction from simple monks, uneducated by the standards of the world. When he was conversing with such an Egyptian father, he asked him, "How can I expel sinful thoughts?" He, thereupon, received a helpful response. Afterward, when another brother had heard that the great abba humbly sought advice from a simple monk, he asked Arsenius, "Father, thou art a man of learning, well-versed in the sciences, and knowledgeable in both the Greek and Latin tongues. How is it that thou hast asked the counsel of a simple monk?" Arsenius, without evincing the slightest elevation, replied, "I am not unacquainted with Greek and Latin learning, but I have not yet learned the alphabet of virtue of which this father has command." At another time, Arsenius remarked, "We make no progress because we dwell in that exterior learning which puffs up the mind. These seemingly illiterate Egyptians have a true sense of their own infirmities, blindness, and inadequacies. By that very acknowledgment of their weakness, they are empowered from on high to labor with success in attaining the virtues."

Abba Arsenius is Visited by a Roman Lady at Canopus

While Abba Arsenius was living near Canopus (one of the seven mouths of the Nile), a great lady of the Roman nobility and senatorial class came to Alexandria. She was wealthy not only materially but also spiritually as one virtuous and beloved by God.[46] She nurtured a great desire to behold Arsenius that she might hear from his mouth salutary words for her soul. Patriarch Theophilos was informed of the lady's noble heritage. He received her gladly and treated her hospitably. The lady besought the archbishop that they might go together and visit Abba Arsenius. He went to Arsenius and entreated him, saying, "A noble lady from Rome has come hither and requests a conference with thee. She wishes to receive thy blessing. She is very pious and quite the gentle woman. Moreover, she has undergone many toils and hardships, traversing land and sea by reason of her reverence and regard for

---

[46] In *The Paradise of the Fathers* ["Of Watchfulness," p. 57, ¶ 253] she is described as a virgin, while elsewhere she is identified as a senator's wife [*Evergetinos*, Vol. III of The Second Book, pp. 48, 49]. *The Great Synaxaristes* (in Greek) is silent on her marital state.

thee." These tidings, nevertheless, gave Arsenius dissatisfaction. He would in no wise agree to meet with her.

The patriarch, therefore, returned to the Roman lady, telling her of his lack of success. She, however, did not wish to depart. Her purpose was too decided. She obeyed the first impulse of her heart and remarked, "By God, I believe that I shall see him! I came not to see a simple man, for there are men in Rome; but I came all this way to see a prophet." She then gave the order to make ready her animals for traveling. She would wait outside the abba's cell and bide her time. She figured that eventually he had to exit his cell. By the working of God, when she came, he happened to have been outside of his cell. She hastened to him and knelt before his feet, entreating him with tears to speak to her a word of salvation. The saint raised her from the ground to her feet, being somewhat vexed, and said with no very benignant expression, "If thou hast come to behold my face, gaze upon it!" But modesty prevented her from looking directly at him. Then Arsenius asked her, "Hast thou not heard of my works, that I am a sinful man? Why, then, was it necessary for thee to put thyself in peril, making this long journey to a barren and blazing wasteland, merely for me? This unconventional behavior does not become a well-bred lady. Hast thou come so thou mayest gain distinction by recounting to other women, upon thy return to thy homeland, that thou hast seen and conferred with Arsenius? For by doing so, dost thou not know that other women will gather here?" The noblewoman, with a blush of surprise, quickly interposed, "Why dost thou think so? Truly, holy father, I had no intention of bringing other women hither. I came solely on account of my profound reverence for thy sanctity. I came to take thy blessing and to ask that thou mightest remember me in thy holy prayers." The saint remarked, "And I beseech God to blot out thy remembrance from my heart." When she heard him speak thus to her, she was stupefied. She had no heart or will to incommode him any further. She quit that heavy scene. Afterward, she became so dejected by that mortifying interview that she was stricken with a fever. Her low spirits caused her health to decline. Mutual acquaintances reported her grief to the patriarch, saying, "The noble lady has taken ill." The archbishop went off to visit her and inquire after the cause of the break in her health. Discomposed, she replied fretfully, "Would to God that I had never journeyed to the abba's cell! When I asked the old man to remember me in his prayers, he said with astonishing celerity that he would beseech God to blot out the remembrance of me from his heart. When I heard those words, I thought I should die of grief." The patriarch, for his part, attempted to console her and said, "Cease grieving, milady. Thou hast quite mistook the holy man. Do not give the words he spoke a turn which he by no means intended. He did not speak out of contempt or hatred. But he spoke this way because the evil one troubles and scandalizes the ascetics with the remembrance of women. This is the reason why he spoke as he did to thee. However, be assured of this: he will always remember thy soul in his prayers." She carefully listened with admirable equanimity to the archbishop's words and kept them in her mind. Comforted by this explanation, she rapidly recovered her spirits and rose up. She then returned to Rome with a gladsome heart.

The war of fornication has caused great and famous fathers to be on their guard. Many of them endured this war, in all its severity, for a long time. They were, as a result, in a state of fear and trepidation as was also Abba Arsenius who was a man well over eighty years of age when the Roman noble lady came visiting. When he spoke to her as he did, calling upon God to blot the remembrance of her face, he put to shame the demon of fornication. He showed how much he detested this unclean passion that wars against the holy men.[47]

Abba Arsenius Counsels a Brother Wishing to Leave

Arsenius' call for retreat from the world and love of contemplation was not advice that he reserved only for himself, but he counseled others in the same manner who came to him. A much-tried brother came to Abba Arsenius, complaining to him that his thoughts were vexing him. "My thoughts," he disclosed to Arsenius, "tell me that it is too hard for me to fast or labor. Therefore, I have given thought to visiting the sick, which is also a great commandment of the Lord."[48] Abba Arsenius listened quietly as he recognized whence this warfare was emanating. He knew that his brother was being tempted by the inexorable demons, so he said to him, "Where is the difficulty? I tell thee this: do eat, drink, sleep, and engage not in labor. But in no wise exit thy cell." Now Arsenius' advice to take up this seemingly incompatible regime for an ascetic was not without purpose. Arsenius knew that at least by dwelling constantly in a cell, little by little, the ways of the solitary life would become impressed upon that man. The brother agreed to try and follow Arsenius' proposed course of action. After three days of eating, drinking, sleeping, and not toiling, he became weary of doing nothing. Idleness was tiresome. It was becoming disagreeably tedious to spin out the time between meals. He, therefore, took up a few palm leaves that were lying on the ground and broke them apart, thinking to weave a basket. The next day, he placed the palm fronds into water and allowed them to soak as needed. Afterward, he began weaving a basket; but then the time to eat arrived. Yet he was so caught up in his work that he said, "I will do one more row of weaving, and then I shall eat." He then also thought to help pass the time with some reading. As he was chanting the psalms and saying a few prayers, he found comfort in his soul; but then the time to eat arrived once again. Yet he said to himself, "I will sing a

[47] See Budge, *Paradise*, "Questions and Answers on the Ascetic Rule," p. 301, ¶ 629.
[48] Cf. Mt. 25:36.

few more psalms and utter a few more prayers, and then break to eat." Thus, gradually, by the working of God, he became engulfed in the full tide of prayer and work. This brother, therefore, advanced in the ascetical life. Indeed, in time, he attained to the first rank, so that he received power from on high to resist thoughts and vanquish them as well.[49]

The Repose of Abba Arsenius

Such are some of the struggles, feats, and sayings of the great Arsenius, even as they are found in various books which are extant to this day. An exact chronology of these events has not been left to us. It appears that we owe the evasion of putting the anecdotes sequentially to the strict command of the venerable man himself. For he had bidden his disciples that nothing of his biography was to be recorded. This again was his customary modesty at work within him, which trait he maintained during his lifetime. He exerted all his powers to keep his virtues concealed, all for the sake of fleeing the vain and empty glory of the world and the praises of men. Nevertheless, the stories available are sufficient to demonstrate how he soared above this earthly sphere. The old men used to say about Abba Arsenius that he possessed, in a far greater degree than most monks, a dread of the admiration of men. Abba Arsenius, therefore, was never pleased at meeting and conversing with others. Nevertheless, it was not enough for him that he should shun such things while alive, but he also wished that he should observe this rule even in death. In fact, such was his humility that he thought he was unworthy of burial. Let us say a few words about this in what follows.

When the blessed Arsenius knew that the time had arrived for his happy departure and translation from this world, he revealed it to his disciples. When the abba divulged these tidings, they mourned inconsolably. Arsenius attempted to comfort them, saying, "Cease grieving, brothers, lest you appear pusillanimous. I wish for you to lament neither before the time nor when it arrives. However, I do charge and command the following, for which any omission carries a grave penance with no concessions. Let none dare among you, after my death, to give away even the least part of my relic. If you should transgress this command, then know this: I will bring a charge against you at the dreadful throne of the Master Christ. Moreover, I will ask for a terrible punishment for your souls." He, also, added this admonition. He said to his disciples that they were forbidden to host a memorial dinner for his sake. "Do not invite the brethren for a funeral meal." This directive visibly saddened his disciples. He then added, "I only ask that my name be mentioned in the offering at divine Liturgy for the sake of my sinful soul." The disciples then asked, "Well, then, how wouldest thou have us arrange thy funeral? What

---

[49] See Budge, *Paradise*, "On Retreat from the World and Contemplation," pp. 4, 5, ¶ 7.

wouldest thou have us do with thy remains?" The saint, in deep earnest, replied, "Do you not know how to bind my feet with a rope and drag me carefully until you come to the mountain? From that high spot, you can cast me off the edge of the cliff. In this way, no man will be able to approach that harsh place." Since he was distinguished and notable in virtue and moral excellence, he was dismayed with even the thought that after death men might extol him. He was apprehensive that temporal honor might become a hindrance for him or lessen his boldness before the Lord or cost him a diminution of those everlasting rewards.

When the hour of his migration from this world arrived—O what a disquieting account!—Arsenius was wanting in confidence before death. The man who was a familiar of the angels shed hot tears. The disciples wondered at him and asked him, "Woe to us, O father, that even thou art filled with fear and dread of death!" The saint answered solemnly, "This fear has not left me even for a moment from the time that I became a monk." Having spoken thus, he bid the brethren farewell, as well as he was able. He then surrendered his blessed soul into the hands of the angels, who escorted him on high with joy. His disciples chanted the Funeral Service. They interred his angelic relics, precious and venerable, with the mantle and the hair shirt which he wore. He was laid to rest in a place that was hidden. When Abba Poemen learned of Abba Arsenius' repose, he said, "Blessed art thou, O Abba Arsenius, for thou didst weep over thyself in this world! For this cause shalt thou rejoice eternally. Indeed, the one who weeps not here of his own volition is going to lament after death while in the midst of torments. But then such lamentation can be of no benefit."

Abba Arsenius had lived fifty-five years as a faithful ascetic in Christ. We bring to mind that he was sixty-five years of age when he quit the palace. Therefore, he departed to the Lord Jesus when he was one hundred and twenty years old.[50] His habitations changed from time to time. He began in the desert of Sketis and then transferred to more desolate places, distancing himself from mankind. He spent about forty years at Sketis. After the barbarian devastation of Sketis, he repaired to the Mountain of Troe, situated near Babylon, that is, Cairo, and opposite Memphis. He sojourned about ten years in that place. Afterward, he dwelt on the island of Canopus,

---

[50] The anecdotes scattered throughout the books diverge regarding Saint Arsenius' age at the time of his repose. Some give his age at death as ninety years old, while others list him as one hundred and twenty years old. The newer *Hagiologion* [p. 58] of Sophronios Efstratiades records his age as one hundred and five years old. The Greek text of *Religious and Ethics Encyclopaedia* [Vol. 3, pp. 229, 230] writes that he was born in the year 354 and reposed in 445, thus making him about ninety-one years of age.

near Alexandria, where he resided for three years. Following this, he returned to Troe. He took up his abode there for two years until his repose.

The brethren asked, "How come in the first book and in the first chapter of the sayings of our desert fathers, they cite Abba Arsenius first as an example of the monk's flight from men?" This book and leading chapter, of course, to which they were referring, was the history composed by Bishop Palladius for the Prefect Lausus. This is how the brethren were answered: "Abba Arsenius was called by God from the palace to the monastery, and from the monastery to the cell. It is certain that these two calls were according to the will of God. It was a well-selected history for the beginning of the doctrine of the old men."[51]

The brethren then said, "Explain to us these two calls of Abba Arsenius. What is the meaning of those words that he received in the first call: 'Flee from the children of men and thou shalt live'? And what is the signification of that which was said at the second call, 'Flee, keep silence and live a life of contemplation in silence, for these are the principal things which keep a man from sinning'?" The elder conducting the question and answer session, said, "The meaning of the first call is this: If thou dost wish to be delivered from the death which is in sin, and thou dost wish to live the perfect life which is in righteousness, leave thy possessions, family, and country. Depart into exile, that is, to the desert and mountains and holy men. Cultivate with them the Lord's commandments; and thou shalt live a life of grace.

"And the meaning of the second call is this: When thou wast in the world, thou wast drawn toward anxieties about the affairs thereof. Christ has made thee to come out from the world. He has sent thee to the habitation of monks, so that after a short time of dwelling in the coenobium thou mayest be drawn to the following. First, thou mayest be drawn to the cultivation of Jesus' commandments openly; and secondly, thou mayest be drawn to contemplation in silence. When thou art trained in the former sufficiently, thou mayest flee, that is to say, get thee forth from the monastery of the brethren. Then thou mightest enter into thy cell—just as thou didst go forth from the world and didst enter into the monastery.

"Furthermore, the meaning of 'keep silence, and lead a life of contemplation in silence,' is this: having entered into thy cell to contemplate in silence, thou shalt not give the multitude an opportunity of coming in to thee, and talking to thee unnecessarily, except on matters which relate to spiritual excellence. For, through the sight and the hearing and the converse of the multitude who shall come in to thee, the captivity of wandering thoughts will carry thee off. Then shall thy silence and thy contemplation be disturbed. But

---

[51] See Budge, *Paradise*, "Questions and Answers on the Ascetic Rule," p. 318, ¶ 658; and see also p. 3, ¶¶ 1, 2.

do not imagine that the mere fact of having left the brethren in the monastery, or not bringing other men into thy cell to be disturbed by them, will be sufficient to make thy mind to be composed. Do not think it will be sufficient to enable thee to meditate upon God, and to correct thyself, unless thou dost take good heed not to occupy thy mind with them in any way whatsoever when they are remote from thee.

"A man must strive to arrive at a state of impassibility. He must strive to overcome the passions and the devils....It is also thus in the case of a neophyte. For whensoever during his contemplation in silence he should remember women, he falls into the lust of fornication. And whensoever he should remember men, either he is wroth with them in his thoughts—accusing, blaming, and condemning them—or he demands from them vainglory. Hence, he inclines toward passibility. Therefore, let no monk, when he is in his cell, have any remembrance whatsoever of any man; for he cannot profit in any way in restraining his feelings from the conversation of men, except he take care to withhold his thoughts from secret intercourse with them. This, then, is the meaning of the words, 'Flee, keep silence, and contemplate in silence.'"[52]

Now Saint Arsenius was never subjected to a grave illness. Neither his eyes waxed dim nor his bodily members weakened. He, generally, enjoyed good health on account of his temperance and self-discipline which he always observed. Those illnesses that attacked his sacred body, from time to time, were allowed by the God of the universe in order to reveal undisguised the endurance of that godly soul. His long and comely white beard went down to his abdomen. He was a tall man, with a graceful carriage, though in his old age he stooped a little. He had worn away his eyelashes from the copious tears he shed. His countenance had an air of both beauty, majesty, and meekness.

"With what kind of praises," asks the biographer, "can we extol this excellent and thrice-happy struggler who vanquished the passions? What recompense is in accordance with his pangs and toils? If the blessed Paul says that he 'reckons that the sufferings of the present time are not worthy in comparison to the future glory to be revealed in us [Rom. 8:18],' what kind of blessedness will the venerable Arsenius enjoy? For he exerted himself to such a degree that he manfully overcame the three great enemies: the world, the flesh, and the devil, which he spurned.

"For the one who has renounced the world and become a monastic, let such a one have the righteous Arsenius as one's pattern, outline, and archetype. Let such a one copy such practises. Let such a one, as much as one is able, emulate the saint in poverty, frugalness, calmness, silence, humble-mindedness, self-control, industriousness, perfect denial of the world and his body,

[52] Ibid., pp. 318, 319, ¶ 659.

remembrance of death and what was profitable for the souls of all. Let us imitate, for the love of Christ, how Arsenius united himself to Christ, so that he no longer lived but Christ lived in him.[53]

"But let all those, then, who have provoked God's wrath by their continual sins but who wish to repent—even as I, the unworthy one—make provision to obtain a mediator, such as this great Arsenius, before the man-befriending God. For the thrice-blessed one endured martyrdom—and not for one month or one year. But rather, he persevered for fifty-five whole years, harshly chastening his flesh. He, therefore, is counted worthy of many crowns." Though in life he loved to be forgotten, in death he is not forgotten. Through Saint Arsenius' intercessions may we be vouchsafed the forgiveness of sins and the kindness and love of God, to Whom is due all glory, honor, and veneration to the ages of the ages. Amen."

On the 8th of May, the holy Church commemorates our venerable Father MELES the Hymnographer, who reposed in peace.

On the 8th of May, the holy Church commemorates a whole COMPANY OF SOLDIERS who were slain by sword.[54]

On the 8th of May, the holy Church commemorates the accomplishment of a supernatural wonder by the most holy THEOTOKOS and EVER-VIRGIN MARY, wrought through her august Icon at Kassiope, in behalf of Stephen who was unjustly blinded but then received orbs (oculi) in an extraordinary and mysterious manner.[55]

The most holy Theotokos performed this miracle which we will speak of today. It occurred during the governorship of Simon Leone Balbi (Bayilos) on the Ionian island of Corfu or Kerkyra, in the year 1530 after Christ. During that time there was a youth named Stephen. He was returning to his village

---

[53] Gal. 2:20.

[54] The Greek word *speira* (σπεῖρα) is a word that describes a tactical unit in the Ptolemaic army. The word was often used to translate the Roman *manipulus* (a company of soldiers, one-third of a cohort). The standard of the latter originally bore a wisp of hay. It is revealed to us in the introductory two-line or couplet verses (*distichon*) given in the *Synaxarion* and *Synaxaristes* that the warriors of this Christ-minded company of soldiers were beheaded on account of their refusal to imitate other companies of soldiers who were Christ-slayers, that is, under orders to slay Christians.

[55] This miracle was taken from the published divine office, entitled *Hymologidion* (Venice, 1724), and incorporated in *The Great Synaxaristes* (in Greek).

from the city, they encountered certain youths who were returning from the mill carrying flour. Those travelers in Stephen's company, being wicked men and ill-disposed, said to one another, "What prevents us from snatching their flour and dividing it among ourselves? No one is going to see us."

But Stephen, as one righteous, as soon as he heard their words, he attempted, as much as he was able, with exhortations and admonitions, to check their proposed deed. He addressed them, saying, "What you are contriving to do is a beastly act. If you should carry it out, you, as thieves and malefactors, shall not escape just punishment." But they, as asps that are deaf and stop their ears,[56] would not listen to counsel. Much rather, they preferred to incite Stephen to cooperate as an accomplice in the robbery. He, in no wise, would consent. The perpetrators, therefore, attacked and beat the youths from the mill. They seized the flour from them and went to their homes quite pleased with themselves. The youths who were assailed and robbed returned to their own homes, weeping and with empty hands. They recounted to their kinfolk how they were accosted and robbed. This resulted in a diligent investigation by them to learn the identity of the thieves and refer the matter to the governor.

Stephen, therefore, was accused together with the other thieves. This came about only because the victims of the crime had seen Stephen walking with the perpetrators. They did not realize, however, that Stephen, on the contrary, had attempted to hinder their assailants and that he refused to assist them in the crime. Those guilty of the theft, knowing they were liable, concealed themselves lest they should be apprehended and subjected to punishment by the criminal justice system. Stephen, nevertheless, since he was innocent, went about without any fear. When the governor's soldiers approached him, inasmuch as he was recognized, they apprehended him and cast him into prison. Following this, he was bound and led before the governor for an examination. When he was questioned, Stephen explained what took place and affirmed that all he said was the truth. "I had been walking," he stated, "with those who committed the theft," he admitted, "but I did not join with them in the deed. I have been wrongly accused." Whatsoever he said was in vain. The words of his testimony were deemed to be false in the opinion of the judge, who thought that Stephen must have participated with the others.

Consequently, he was wrongly convicted by the governor. Balbi imputed a crime to him of which he was guiltless. (Harsh were the penalties of the Middle Ages, involving various forms of corporal punishment that included mutilation, branding, flogging, amputation for theft, as well as execution.)

---

[56] Cf. Ps. 57:4.

Stephen was then permitted to choose which penalty he preferred: either the loss of his eyes or the severance of his hands. Since the privation of his eyes seemed to him to be the lighter sentence, he chose that punishment. He was taken to the customary execution site. The innocent youth bewailed his plight as they escorted him. His both eyes were gouged out in the presence of a considerable crowd. His mother kept weeping and lamenting aloud, even after he was blinded. She then led him forth to the Church of Saint Lazarus for the sake of seeking alms.

Now most of the inhabitants of that place scorned and reproached Stephen, saying, "Justly hast thou suffered punishment; for, as a thief, thou hast seized that which was not thine." As it happened, very few folks were pitying him. He, therefore, thought, at the prompting of divine providence, to go with his mother to the Church of the Theotokos in the city of Kassiope (Cassiope),[57] which had a harbor some eighteen miles distant from the capital city, Corfu. Within that church there was housed the wonderworking icon of the most holy Theotokos, known as the Unfading Rose.[58] The icon depicted the Theotokos holding a rose in her right hand and the infant Christ in her left. Since the church was by the sea and possessed a suitable harbor, the ships, out of reverence for the most holy Theotokos, secured their boats by mooring there. In that place Stephen thought to abide and seek alms from those entering the church to venerate the holy icon of the Theotokos. His mother agreed.

Mother and son, therefore, went to the Church of the Mother of God. After they offered the customary veneration, they recounted to the monk residing there what had occurred. Bewailing themselves and sighing heavily, they described the unjust misfortune that they had undergone. They also told

---

[57] The town of Kassiope, situated thirty-seven kilometers north of the capital city (also called Corfu), has a population of 1,200 inhabitants. It is built upon the cape of Kassiope, opposite the Albanian coast. Kassiope's inhabitants are occupied mainly with sailing and fishing. According to history, the town was founded by Pyros who transferred Epirotians there from Kassiopia in order to solve the problem of the scarce population on the island. According to another tradition, the town was founded by the Epirotians after the destruction of Epiros by the Romans. It is said that in the current location of the Church of Panagia Kassiopitissa, during the Roman years, stood the Temple of Cassius Zeus after whom the town was named. During antiquity, Kassiope was the second largest town on the island, and it thrived during the Roman years. From the walls (preserved until the 17th C.) and the medieval castle, built by the Andegaves, only ruins are currently called Pirgos. Apart from the beach of Kassiope, the surrounding area is characterized by developed beaches of unique natural beauty, attracting a multitude of tourists in the summer. Taken from http://www.hri.org/infoxenios/english/ionian/corfu/towns.html.

[58] This appellation addressed to the Virgin Theotokos is derived from the Service of the Saturday of the Akathist during the Great Fast, Canon, Ode One.

him the reason why they were looking for refuge at Kassiope. They sought from him a small *kellion* or cell in which to dwell. "There is a cell," he replied, "to which a certain brother monk has the key. Since he is presently absent, you may stay in the church." The mother of Stephen, very wearied from the journey by foot, thereafter, fell asleep quickly.

Stephen, however, by reason of the pains he was experiencing from the digging out of his eyes, was unable to take his ease. But at length, a very light slumber overtook him for only a short time. During the night—O thy marvels, most holy Lady Theotokos!—Stephen sensed hands touching and pressing against his empty sockets. He was awakened by the pressure that he felt, shouting and pondering aloud, "Who has touched my eyes so strongly?" He beheld a Woman, resplendent and dazzling with light, who vanished after a few moments. He considered it to be but a dream and not an actual event. But then he turned and noticed the lit oil lamps. He marvelled and wondered, "How and what has taken place?" After he awakened his mother, he asked, "Who has lit the lamps?" She, thinking that her son was digressing in his sleep, did not turn to look at him and said plaintively, "Hush, son, go to sleep!"

Stephen, however, would not keep silence. He kept insisting and saying, "Mother, I truly see the oil lamps. Indeed, I also see the holy icon of the Mother of God. What I am telling thee is not an apparition." He then told his mother what had taken place earlier. He explained that he had cried out, but she did not hear because she was sound asleep. His mother was thinking, "Surely, this is divine assistance at work." She then rose up, forthwith, and looked inquisitively upon Stephen's face. She observed that he truly had orbs in the recently excised sockets. She also noticed that while previously he had brown eyes, now they were blue. From her abundant joy and reverential fear, she began to shout aloud and weep. She kept glorifying and calling continually upon the name of the Mother of God. Together with her son, they clapped their hands and magnified the most holy Theotokos.

The shouts and clamor were certainly heard by the monk, who was the sacristan of the church, since he had arisen not long before in preparation of the coming Orthros Service. He became angry and reproved their conduct, saying from a distance, "You are disorderly and wicked people, for which you have justly suffered so wretched a plight." But Stephen and his mother began narrating the magnificent work of God. The sacristan, wondering at what was being recounted, disbelieved on account of the awesomeness of the miracle. He drew closer and entered into the main part of the church. He approached and beheld Stephen, who shortly before was eyeless. The monk, in his astonishment, now discerned that Stephen had both orbs and vision.

Filled with divine zeal, the monk departed immediately and hastened to the city. Arriving early in the morning, he was looking for Governor Balbi in the courthouse. The monk found him and raised his voice at him, calling him a lawless man. Those standing by drove out the monk, saying to him, "This audacious act before the face of those in authority, which thou hast dared, is both unlawful and shows thee to be haughty." But the monk cried out louder, saying, "If the punishment of blinding imposed upon Stephen was not unjust, then God would not have granted him other eyeballs through the mediation of the Mother of God." The governor, hearing this statement, dispatched certain notable and trustworthy men to confirm the report. Upon their return, they confirmed the veracity of the monk's words. The governor had his small private ship, a caravel, with at least three masts, prepared. He entered the vessel with his dignitaries from Corfu. They set sail bound for the harbor of Kassiope. When they arrived and beheld with their own eyes this great miracle, they marvelled greatly as was fitting.

Governor Balbi, nevertheless, still had doubts. He was thinking, "This fellow is not Stephen or, perhaps, he was not truly blinded." Thus, he was in concert with the Jews who had not believe that the Lord fashioned eyes for the man born blind.[59] On account of the magnitude of the miracle, the governor and some others did not permit themselves to believe straightway. Balbi then returned to the capital. He summoned the executioner and questioned him, saying, "Didst thou gouge out the eyes of Stephen, even as I had ordered?" He assured the governor, saying, "Verily, I blinded him and, indeed, the eyes that I dug out are still found inside the basin." The executioner went and fetched the basin. He showed the contents to Balbi, who then believed that the miracle was true. At length, he remembered also that the eye color was different. He also brought to mind that he had seen the marks from the iron implement used for the excision; for they were still discernible on Stephen's eyelids.

This verification came to pass by divine providence, so that the miracle should be heralded and believed as indubitable. Hence, this was proved both by the sign of the iron marks and the eyes of a different hue. For if the eyes had been the same color, many would be saying, "They are the original eyes. They were not truly gouged out." On account of such incontrovertible evidence, therefore, the miracle was much talked of throughout Kerkyra; and it was generally believed. It was then that Balbi summoned Stephen and sought his forgiveness for the wrongful act, adding that "I brought it upon thee out of ignorance." The governor then thought to recompense the youth with rich gifts. He also attended him with much care and kindness. After this episode, the governor was diligent in having the courtyard of the Church of the Theotokos renovated.[60]

---

[59] See Jn. 9:1 ff.

[60] In 1537, during the failed Turkish siege of Corfu, the church, because it was situated (continued...)

Many of the people, those who were weak in the Orthodox Faith of our Lord Jesus Christ, were confirmed by means of this supernatural wonder. With their faith thus strengthened, they also came to believe in those things mentioned in the divine writings that are usually believed in the hearing alone. As for those who still remained unbelieving, not wishing to honor this exceptional wonder, they were put to shame. Such iniquitous persons were spoken of by the Lord through the Prophet Ezekiel who said that they "have eyes to see, and see not; and have ears to hear, and hear not [Ez. 12:2]."

Let us all hasten, with faith and reverence, to the light-providing Virgin Mary and Theotokos. Let us supplicate her to illumine the eyes of our understanding lest we should walk in the darkness of sins. As she is one possessed of boldness with the One born of her, let us beseech her mediation that we might be delivered from every temptation of the evil one and that we might be deemed worthy of the heavenly kingdom of our Lord Jesus Christ, to Whom is due glory, thanksgiving, honor, and veneration, with the unoriginate Father and the all-holy and good and life-creating Spirit, now and ever and to the ages of the ages. Amen.

Through the intercessions
of Thy Saints,
O Christ God,
have mercy on us. Amen.

---

[60](...continued)
on the coastline, suffered destruction. In 1590, it was rebuilt and expanded by the Venetian Admiral Nicholas Suriano. It was about that time that the church and icon came into the possession of the Venetians who were Roman Catholics. The icon, nevertheless, sometime between 1530 and 1590, was relocated to the capital, Corfu, in the Latin church of Tenedos. The Ionian islands—Kerkyra, Paxos, Lefkas, Ithaca, Kephalonia, and Zakynthos—were under Venetian rule until seized by Napoleon in 1797, when the icon was returned to the Orthodox. The icon still remained in the capital, but at the Orthodox Cathedral of the Archangel Michael. In 1940, during World War II, the icon was transferred to the metropolitan's residence. The 14th-C. cathedral was destroyed during the Italian bombardment. In 1967, the icon was returned to its home at Kassiope.

On the 9th of May, the holy Church commemorates the holy Prophet ESAIAS (ISAIAH).[1]

Prophet Esaias "knew more perfectly than all others the mystery of the religion of the Gospel," says Saint Gregory (ca. A.D. 335-395),[2] Bishop of Nyssa.[3] Blessed Jerome (ca. 342-420) also lauds the Prophet Esaias, saying, "He was more of an evangelist than a prophet, because he described all of the mysteries of the Church of Christ so vividly that you would assume he was not prophesying about the future, but rather was composing a history of past events."[4]

A Brief Introduction of the Prophet's Life With Historical Background

The holy Esaias (pronounced Ēsaēa in Greek), whose Hebrew name is an approximate transliteration of the abbreviated form *Yĕsha'yāh*, is derived from the fuller and older form *Yĕsha'yāhû*, meaning *"'J' is salvation."* It is therefore synonymous with Joshua or Jeshua (Jesus) or "God is salvation" or "God of salvation." This grandiloquent prophet, born ca. 765 B.C., hailed from Jerusalem. His family was related to the imperial house of Juda. He was the son of Amos [Is. 1:1], who was the brother of King Amessias or Amaziah (796-767 B.C.) of Juda. From his writings, it is safe to presume he was well educated and that he probably came from an upper-class family. Israel and Juda, under Jeroboam II (793-753 B.C.) and Ozias or Uzziah (791-739 B.C.), enjoyed a time of prosperity during the prophet's boyhood, with little interference from foreigners. He was called to the prophetic ministry at a young age, in his twenties, through a divine vision during the last year of the

---

[1] An encomium to Prophet Esaias was eloquently plaited by Niketas the Rhetor, which text is extant in the Athonite Monastery of Dionysiou. The *Synaxarion of Constantinople* (9th of May) identifies the prophet as a martyr. His relics were transferred to Constantinople and treasured in the Church of Saint Laurence near Vlachernai. The prophet wrought many miracles, including those for a vinedresser, a fisherman, a silversmith, and others [see H. Delehaye, *Analecta Bollandiana* 42 (1924), pp. 257-265.]

[2] Years before Christ are indicated herein as such—B.C. Years after the Lord (Latin, *Anno Domini*) are shown once as A.D., but will apply to all dates given for holy fathers and the patristic commentary.

[3] Saint Gregory of Nyssa, *Dogmatic Treatises: Against Eunomius*, Bk. V, The Nicene and Post-Nicene Fathers of the Christian Church Series, 2nd Ser., Volume V, edited by Philip Schaff, D.D., LL.D and Henry Wace, D.D., p. 173. [Henceforth the Series' name will be abbreviated as Nicene, 2nd Ser., with the volume number preceding the page number by a colon.]

[4] Saint Jerome, *Dogmatic and Polemical Works: Against Rufinus*, The Fathers of the Church Series, Vol. 53, pp. 156, 157. [Henceforth the Series' name will be abbreviated as FC, with the volume number preceding the page number by a colon.]

reign of King Ozias [Is. 6:1], in about 740. Esaias was married to a woman described as **"the prophetess** [Is. 8:3]**."** They had two sons, naming one Jasub (meaning **"A remnant shall return** [Is. 7:3]") and the other Maher-Shalal-Hash-Baz (meaning **"Spoil quickly, plunder speedily** [Is. 8:3]").

Prophet Esaias admits, **"The instruction of the Lord, even the Lord, opens mine ears, and I do not disobey, nor dispute** [Is. 50:5]**."** "Comprehend what the prophet means," says Blessed Jerome, "'The Lord has given me an ear. Because I did not possess that ear which is of the heart, He gave me one that I might hear God's message.' Whatever the prophet hears, therefore, he hears in his heart."[5]

Prophet Esaias

Possessed of considerable literary skill by the grace of the Holy Spirit, the prophet's devotion to God is manifest. He is one of the four Major Prophets, that is, those with longer writings extant. His prophecy is the third longest book in the Bible, sixty-six chapters, being exceeded only by the books of the Prophet Jeremias and the Psalms. His long ministry, approximately forty years, extended from about 740 until at least 701 B.C. [Is. 37-39]. The life and times of the prophet are also mentioned in two other books of sacred Scriptures, namely, 2 Chronicles [32:20, 32] and 4 Kings (2 Kgs.) [20:1-19]. He is depicted in sacred icons as approaching old age and having gray hair and a long pointed beard. This prophet was a contemporary of the great Prophets Hosea and Michaeas.

In 745 B.C., Tiglath-pileser III (Thalgath-phellasar, also known in Babylon as Pul) came to the Assyrian throne. Assyria then sought to extend the western border of her empire into Syria, Israel, and Juda. Damascus fell in 732 B.C., and then much of Galilee, to Tiglath-pileser. Shalmaneser V (727-722 B.C.) and Sargon II (722-705 B.C.) then attacked Samaria, and the latter captured her in 722 or 721 B.C. In the last decade of the century, Egypt restored herself somewhat after decades of weakness, while Assyria had difficulties with Babylon. This international scene moved Juda and other neighboring states to rebel against the Assyrians. Sennacherim (Sennacherib, 705-

[5] Saint Jerome, "Homily 17," *1-59 On The Psalms, Vol. 1*, FC, 48:130.

681 B.C.) invaded Juda and took her [Is. 36:1], but God spared Jerusalem during King Ezekias' reign (729/728-699 B.C.).

Esaias delivered the words of God during an era of great moral and political upheaval among his people. In about 722 B.C., when the northern kingdom of Israel fell to the Assyrians, it appeared that Juda to the south would likely follow. In spite of this, Esaias forewarned the rulers of Juda not to have pagan foreigners as allies in the event of an Assyrian assault. He counseled his people to put their trust in God Who could deliver them. He said, **"Woe to them that go down to Egypt for help, who trust in horses and chariots, for they are many;...and have not trusted in the Holy One of Israel, and have not sought the Lord** [Is. 31:1]**."**

The holy man's prophecies are not reserved only for Juda, but include God's judgment upon her neighbors: Prophecies against Babylon [Is. 13:1-14:23; 21:9], Assyria [Is. 14:24-27], Philistia [Is. 14:28-32], Moab [Is. 15:1-16:14], Damascus and Syria [Is. 17:1-14], Ethiopia [Is. 18:1-7], Egypt [Is. 19:1-20:6], Idumea [Is. 21:11-17], and Tyre [Is. 23:1-18]. He again warns Juda not to seek help through vain alliances with Egypt [Is. Chaps. 30, 31]. Heedless, the king of Juda sought to protect the nation's interests by forming an alliance with Egypt. The prophet also predicted that the invading Assyrians would be turned back by God before they succeeded in overthrowing Juda [Is. 30:27-33].

Kings Ozias and Joatham

The man of God prophesied unto the days of Ozias' successors, Joatham (Jotham, 752-736 B.C.), Achaz (Ahaz, 736-720 B.C.), Ezekias (Hezekiah, 729/8-699 B.C.), and Manasses (Manasseh, 698-643 B.C.), that is, five kings in all. Ozias, a leper [2 Chr. 26:21], died in about 739/740, though Joatham was regent for some years before this occurrence. Ozias had been a godly man until "his heart was lifted up to his destruction" in his latter days [2 Chr. 26:16-21]. Joatham died in 736, leaving an effective government to his son Achaz. Neither Ozias nor Joatham removed the idolatrous high places that littered the countryside of their realm.

King Achaz

In about 734, when Achaz was on the throne, an impending attack brought Syria and Israel into a coalition. Juda refused to enter the alliance. **"And it came to pass in the days of Achaz...there came up Rasin (Raasson) king of Aram, and Phakee (Pekah) son of Romelias, king of Israel, against Jerusalem to war against it, but they could not take it** [Is. 7:1]**."** The prophet, with words from God, encouraged Achaz to trust in the Lord, and said, **"Take care to be quiet, and fear not, neither let thy soul be disheartened because of these two smoking firebrands: for when My fierce anger is over, I will heal again** [Is. 7:4]**."** Nevertheless, Achaz called on Syria for help, but the capital city of Syria, Damascus, was taken by the Assyrians in 732, and most of Galilee was conquered. "In the days of Phakee (Pekah) king of Israel came Thalgath-phellasar king of the Assyrians; and he took Ain, and Ael, and Thamaacha, and Anioch, and Kenez, and Asor, and Galaa, and Galilee, even all the land of Nephthali, and carried them away to the Assyrians [4 Kgs. (2 Kgs.) 15:29, 30]."

"Then Raasson king of Syria and Phakee son of Romelias, king of Israel, went up against Jerusalem to war, and besieged Achaz, but could not prevail against him [4 Kgs. (2 Kgs.) 16:5]." At that time, however, Syria managed to recover Aelath, so "Achaz sent messengers to Thalgath-phellasar, king of the Assyrians, saying, 'I am thy servant and thy son: come up, deliver me out of the hand of the king of Syria, and out of the hand of the king of Israel, who are rising up against me [4 Kgs. (2 Kgs.) 16:7].'" He then sent gifts to the king; and the king of the Assyrians hearkened and took Damascus, killing Raasson [4 Kgs. (2 Kgs.) 16:9]. Phakee (Pekah, 740-732 B.C.) the king of Israel was murdered by Osee (Hoshea, 732/731-722 B.C.), who replaced him on the throne.

Grave aftereffects arose with the alliance between Juda and Assyria. When "Achaz went to Damascus to meet with the king of the Assyrians, he saw an altar there. And King Achaz sent to Urias the priest the pattern of the altar, and its proportions, and all its workmanship. And Urias the priest built the altar, according to all the directions which King Achaz sent from Damascus [4 Kgs. (2 Kgs.) 16:10, 11]." Achaz's religious innovations bespoke his deepening apostasy, which would go further, as we read: "Achaz removed the vessels of the house of the Lord, and cut them in pieces, and shut the doors of the house of the Lord, and made to himself altars in every corner in Jerusalem. And in each several city in Juda he made high places to burn incense to strange gods. And they provoked the Lord God of their fathers....And Achaz slept with his father, and was buried in the city of David; for they did not bring him into the sepulchers of the kings of Israel [2 Chr. 28:24, 25, 27]."

Thalgath-phellasar died in 727 B.C.; and Achaz died shortly thereafter. The prophet uttered a prophecy warning Philistia of the consequences of revolt [cf. Is. 14:28-31]. He also counseled Juda not to follow after her, for **"the Lord has founded Sion, and by Him the poor of the people shall be saved** [Is. 14:32]**."**

Meanwhile, in the northern kingdom, King Osee (Hoshea) held back the tribute due Shalmaneser V who, for three years, besieged Samaria; but Samaria was later taken by his successor, Sargon. According to the Assyrians, twenty-seven thousand Israelites were then deported and resettled in the northern regions of the Assyrian Empire.

King Ezekias

A decade later, Egypt encouraged the Philistines and others to form a new coalition against the Assyrians. In 711, Sargon, at the Egyptian border, crushed the uprising. Juda, meanwhile, under King Ezekias, avoided this fray, hearkening to the words of the prophet "who for three years walked naked and barefoot [cf. Is. 20:3]," and said, **"There shall be three years for signs and wonders to the Egyptians and Ethiopians; for thus shall the king of the Assyrians lead the captivity of Egypt and the Ethiopians, young men and old, naked and barefoot, having the shame of Egypt exposed** [Is. 20:4]**."**

With the death of Sargon (ca. 705 B.C.) and his replacement by Sennacherim, there was unrest in the Assyrian Empire that was incited by both the Ethiopian monarchs instigating the Egyptians and also by the Chaldean Marodach Baladan (Merodach-Baladan) of Babylon. Ezekias heeded not the prophet's warnings, but desired to take up arms and to prepare Jerusalem for a siege. The prophet uttered this word to the "Valley of Sion," saying, **"The Elamites took their quivers, and they were men mounted on horses, and there was a gathering for battle. And it shall be that thy choice valleys shall be filled with chariots, and horsemen shall block up thy gates. And they shall uncover the gates of Juda, and they shall look in that day on the choice houses of the city. And they shall uncover the secret places of the houses of the citadel of David. And they saw that they were many, and that one had turned the water of the old pool into the city; and that they had pulled down the houses of Jerusalem, to fortify the wall of the city. And ye procured to yourselves water between the two walls within the ancient pool, but ye looked not and regarded not Him that created it. And the Lord, the Lord of hosts, called in that day for weeping, and lamentation, and baldness, and for girding with sackcloth...**[Is. 22:6-12]**."**

Ezekias Builds the Siloam Water Tunnel

As a defense against the attacks perpetrated by Assyria, which climaxed in Sennacherim's campaign of 701 [cf. 2 Chr. 32:4], King Ezekias of Juda constructed the Siloam water tunnel from the Gihon (Gion) spring, southwestward through the rocky core of Mount Sion, and out into the Tyropoeon Valley of Jerusalem. The tunnel is square cut, averaging two feet wide and six feet high. It follows an S-shaped course, so that the direct distance of 1,090 feet involves 1,750 feet of actual tunneling. While the pool may have remained outside the city walls as a covered cistern, with additional concealed access tunnels and overflow channels, the water seems actually to have come into the city [cf. 4 Kgs. (2 Kgs.) 20:20].[6]

---

[6] *The Zondervan Pictorial Encyclopedia of the Bible*, Vol. 5, Merrill C. Tenney, Gen. Ed. (Grand Rapids, MI: Regency Reference Library, 1976), s.v. "Siloam."

The Fountain of the Virgin (Ain Sitti Mariam), an intermittent spring in the Valley of Kidron and the only true one at Jerusalem, is identified with Gihon; and the changes made in the distribution of the waters are intimately connected with the history of Siloam. After the capture of Jerusalem by the Hebrews, the water of the spring was impounded in a reservoir of the Kidron Valley. It was used to irrigate the king's garden, which filled the valley to the south. This reservoir, the site of which is lost, is called by Josephus "Solomon's Pool." After a while, the water was carried by a rock-hewn conduit down the west side of the Kidron Valley, and through the extremity of Mount Moriah, to a pool in the Tyropoeon, so that it might be more accessible to dwellers in the lower parts of the city. To this conduit, with its slight fall and gently flowing stream, Prophet Esaias possibly referred: **"Because this people chooses not the water of Siloam that goes softly...**[Is. 8:6]**."** At a later period, the winding rock-hewn tunnel which connects the Fountain of the Virgin with the Birket Silwan was made, and the water of the spring was collected in the two reservoirs in the Tyropoeon Valley. The execution of this remarkable work may be ascribed with much probability to Ezekias who, prior to the Assyrian invasion, we read how "he collected many people, and stopped the wells of water, and the river that flowed through the city, saying, 'Lest the king of Assyria come, and find much water, and strengthen himself [2 Chr. 32:4].'" And, "The same Ezekias stopped up the course of the water of Gion above, and brought the water straight south of the city of David. And Ezekias prospered in all his works [2 Chr. 32:30]." And, "Ezekias fortified his city, and brought in water into the midst thereof: he dug the hard rock with iron, and made wells for waters [Wis. of Sir. 48:17]."

The Prophet Esaias speaks of the city's **"water between the two walls within the ancient pool** [Is. 22:11]**."** This latter pool may refer to the original **"pool of the upper way of the fuller's field** [Is. 7:3]**."** There also appears to be a lower or **"old pool** [Is. 22:9]**"** at the southern tip of the pre-Hezekian city. This was known to have received water via a surface conduit. The course of its upper two hundred feet had a minimal drop along the east side of Mount Sion. By post-exilic times, the lower pool came to be called Siloah (Shelah) with the same meaning of Siloam, meaning the sending one, since it seems to have continued in use for overflow from Ezekias' newer pool. By the Christian era, the name Siloam was transferred to the newer pool.

The Foulmouthed Rabsaces, the Assyrian

The Assyrian army invaded Juda, taking forty-six walled cities and spoiling the countryside. The Assyrian menace had already destroyed all Judaean resistance outside of Jerusalem, which was blockaded. Sennacherim's field commander, Rabsaces, went to speak with King Ezekias, but was met by three of the king's officers at the upper pool. The field commander challenged

Ezekias' military strategy, and demonstrated the king's weak position. He indicated that Egypt is unreliable as a bruised staff of reed. When one leans on it, he maintained, it pierces the hand. He attempted to have the refugees and Jews hear his speech by speaking in the Hebrew tongue. He warned them not to trust Ezekias. He said the king of Assyria shall deliver them and not God; for no one has been delivered out of the hands of the Assyrians. He recklessly blasphemed God Whom he said he obeyed when commanded to go up against this land and destroy it [Is. 36:10]. Rabsaces' propaganda speech quickly hastened the return of the three royal emissaries to Ezekias. When the king was apprised of the meeting, he rent his clothes and put on sackcloth. He then went up to the temple, and sent the steward, the scribe, and the elders of the priests clothed with sackcloth, to Esaias the prophet.

The Downfall of Sennacherim

The prophet then made a reply, **"Thus shall ye say to your master, 'Thus saith the Lord, "Be not thou afraid at the words which thou hast heard, wherewith the ambassadors of the king of the Assyrians have reproached Me. Behold, I will send a blast upon him, and he shall hear a report, and return to his own country, and he shall fall by the sword in his own land** [Is. 37:6, 7]**!"'"** And indeed Rabsaces returned to find his king besieging another place. The Assyrians received a report about the Ethiopian king who was coming to attack them, so they turned aside. The Assyrians, however, sent Ezekias a note and told him not to find relief and trust that God delivered them. The pagan then reproached God, and Ezekias took himself away to the temple that he might pray for deliverance. Prophet Esaias was then sent to him, and said, "Thus saith the Lord, the God of Israel, 'I have heard thy prayer to Me concerning Sennacherim, king of the Assyrians. This is the word which God has spoken concerning him: The virgin daughter of Sion has despised thee, and mocked thee; the daughter of Jerusalem has shaken her head at thee....Thou hast reproached the Lord by messengers....Thus saith the Lord concerning the king of the Assyrians: He shall not enter into this city, nor cast a weapon against it, nor bring a shield against it, nor make a rampart round it. But by the way that he came, by it shall he return; and he shall not enter into this city....I will protect this city to save it for My own sake, and for My servant David's sake [cf. Is. 37:21-35].'" An angel of the Lord then went forth, and slew 185,000 out of the Assyrian camp. They were found the following morning. Sennacherim then returned to Nineve. While there, he was worshipping his country's god; and his sons rose up and slew him with swords in the house [Is. 37:36-38]. God indeed rescued Jerusalem this time, however, she fell over a century later to a renewed Babylon.

This Sennacherim was used as an axe and a saw in God's hands. But the "tool" prided himself on his own strength and ability. Saint Aphrahat (early

4th C.) speaks of Sennacherim as God's tool for judgment, and writes: "For thou, Sennacherim, art the axe in the hands of Him that cuts, and thou art the saw in the hands of Him that saws, and the rod in the hands of Him that wields thee for chastisement. Thou art the staff for smiting. Thou art sent against the fickle people, and again thou art ordained against the stubborn people, that thou mayest carry away the captivity and take the spoil. And thou hast made them as the mire of the streets for all men and for all the Gentiles. And when thou hast done all these things, why art thou exalted against Him Who holds thee, and why dost thou boast against Him Who saws with thee, and why hast thou reviled the holy city? And thou hast said to the children of Jerusalem, 'Can your God deliver you from my hand [cf. 4 Kgs. (2 Kgs.) 18:35]?' And thou hast dared to say, 'Who is the Lord that He shall deliver you from my hands?' Because of this, hear the word of the Lord, saying, 'I will crush the Assyrian in My land; and on My mountains will I tread him down [cf. Is. 14:25].' And when he shall have been crushed and trodden down, the virgin, the daughter of Sion, will despise him, and the daughter of Jerusalem will shake her head and say: 'Whom hast thou reviled and blasphemed? And against Whom hast thou lifted up thy voice? Thou hast lifted up thine eyes toward heaven against the Holy One of Israel; and by the hands of thy messengers thou hast reviled the Lord. Now see that the hook has been forced into thy nostrils, and the bridle into thy lips; and thou hast turned back with thine heart crushed, who camest with thine heart uplifted [4 Kgs. (2 Kgs.) 19:21-23, 28; Is. 37:22-24, 29].' And his slaying was by the hands of his loved ones. And in the house of his confidence [4 Kgs. (2 Kgs.) 19:37; Is. 37:38], there was he overthrown and fell before his god. And truly it was right, my beloved, that his body should thus become a sacrifice and offering before that god on whom he relied, and in his temple, as a memorial for his idol."[7]

Marodach Baladan, in the meantime, had assumed power in Babylon from 721. He declared it independent of the Assyrians. Sargon entered Babylon in 711 or 710 without a fight. But after Sargon's demise, Marodach Baladan became a leader of the rebelling party against Sennacherim, and even sought to enlist Ezekias. Sennacherim overcame and dethroned Marodach Baladan. However, before this happened, in about 703, Marodach Baladan sent ambassadors and gifts to Ezekias when he learned of the latter's miraculous recovery from near death [Is. 39:1]. The following is the account of the king's miraculous healing through Prophet Esaias.

Ezekias' Miraculous Recovery

"And it came to pass at that time, that Ezekias was sick even to death. And Esaias the prophet, the son of Amos, came to him, and said to

---

[7] Saint Aphrahat, "Demonstration V.—Of Wars," § 4, *Select Demonstrations*, Nicene, 2nd Ser., XIII:353, 354.

him, 'Thus saith the Lord, "Give orders concerning thy house: for thou shalt die, and not live."'

"And Ezekias turned his face to the wall, and prayed to the Lord, saying, 'Remember, O Lord, how I have walked before Thee in truth, with a true heart, and have done that which was pleasing in Thy sight.' And Ezekias wept bitterly [Is. 38:1-3]."

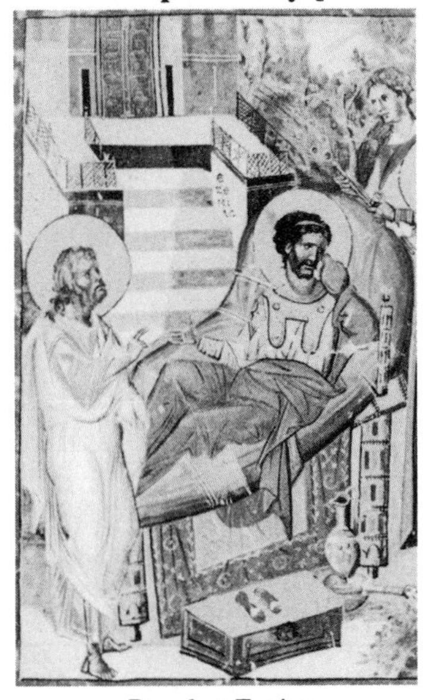

Prophet Esaias and King Ezekias

Saint Kyril of Jerusalem (ca. 316-386), reminds us of the following: "Wouldest thou know what power repentance has? Wouldest thou know the strong weapon of salvation, and learn what is the force of confession? Ezekias, by means of confession, routed a hundred and fourscore and five thousand of his enemies. A great thing verily was this, but still small in comparison with what remains to be told: the same king by repentance obtained the recall of a divine sentence which had already gone forth."[8]

And the word of the Lord came to Esaias, saying, **"Go, and say to Ezekias, 'Thus saith the Lord, the God of David thy father, "I have heard thy prayer, and seen thy tears: behold, I will add to thy time fifteen years. And I will deliver thee and this city out of the hand of the king of the Assyrians: and I will defend this city** [Is. 38:4-6]."

"""And this shall be a sign to thee from the Lord, that God will do this thing; behold, I will turn back the shadow of the degrees of the dial by which ten degrees on the house of thy father the sun has gone down—I will turn back the sun the ten degrees; so the sun went back the ten degrees [Is. 38:8].""""

Saint Hippolytos (ca. 170-ca. 236) narrates that when the clock had run its course and then returned again, "Marodach the Chaldean, king of Babylon, being struck with amazement at that time [Is. 39:1]—for he studied the science of astrology, and measured the courses of these bodies carefully—on learning the cause, sent a letter and gifts to Ezekias, just as also the wise men from the east did to Christ [Mt. 2:10, 11]."[9]

---

[8] Saint Cyril of Jerusalem, "Lecture II," *Catechetical Lectures*, Nicene, 2nd Ser., VII:11, 12.

[9] Saint Hippolytus, *Fragments from Commentaries: On the Prophet Esaias*, The Fathers

(continued...)

Saint Kyril of Jerusalem continues, saying, "And he, who could not hope to live because of the prophetic sentence, had fifteen years added to his life; and for the sign, the sun ran backward in his course. Well then, for Ezekias' sake the sun turned back [Is. 38:8], but for Christ the sun was eclipsed, not retracing his steps, but suffering eclipse, and therefore showing the difference between them, I mean between Ezekias and Jesus. The former prevailed to the canceling of God's decree; and cannot Jesus grant remission of sins?"[10]

Now Marodach Baladan sent letters, ambassadors, and gifts to Ezekias, since he recovered from his life-threatening sickness. Ezekias welcomed them, according to the Scriptures [Is. 39:1, 2]. Saint Aphrahat comments that "Ezekias had great wealth, and he went and boasted of it before the Babylonians; yet it was—all of it—carried away and gone to Babylon. And if thou gloriest in thy children, they shall be led away from thee to the Beast, as the children of Ezekias were led away, and became eunuchs in the palace of the king of Babylon [4 Kgs. (2 Kgs.) 20:18; Is. 39:7]."[11]

Blessed Jerome tells us that "Ezekias showed the Babylonians all the storehouses of his aromatical spices, and of his gold and silver, and the storehouses of his vessels. There was nothing that Ezekias did not show them in the house of the Lord and in all his dominions [Is. 39:2; 4 Kgs. (2 Kgs.) 20:13]. From this we see that even the vessels of the temple were shown to the ambassadors of Babylon. Consequently, the wrath of God was also kindled. It was subsequently revealed to him by the prophecy of Esaias that his sons shall be eunuchs, and all the vessels of the temple shall be carried into Babylon [Is. 39:6, 7; 4 Kgs. (2 Kgs.) 20:17, 18]. Moreover, it is written in the book of Chronicles: 'Ezekias did not recompense the Lord according to the return which He made him, but his heart was lifted up: and wrath came upon him, and upon Juda and Jerusalem [2 Chr. 32:25].' Certainly, no one but the ungodly will deny that Ezekias was a just man. You may say, 'He sinned in certain things and, therefore, he ceased to be just.' But Scripture does not say this. For he did not lose the title of just because he committed small sins, but he possessed the title of just because he performed many good deeds. I say all this to prove with the testimonies of sacred Scripture, that the just are not sinners

---

[9](...continued)
of the Third Century, The Ante-Nicene Fathers Series, Volume 5, p. 176. [Henceforth, the Series name will be abbreviated as Ante-Nicene, with the volume number preceding the page number by a colon.]

[10] Saint Cyril of Jerusalem, "Lecture II," *Catechetical Lectures*, Nicene, 2nd Ser., VII:12.

[11] Saint Aphrahat, "Demonstration V.—Of Wars," § 7, Nicene, 2nd Ser., XIII:354.

simply because they have sinned on occasions, but they remain just because they flourish in many virtues."[12]

The Great Synaxaristes of the Orthodox Church (in Greek) has the following account: "Toward the eastern part of Sion, near the gate entering Gabaon, Solomon built the tomb of David his father. After the return from exile, King David's sepulcher nearby Siloam was pointed out: 'The garden of David's sepulcher, and as far as the artificial pool, and as far as the house of the mighty men [cf. Neh. 3:16]'; and the Apostle Peter makes mention of the presence of the prophet-king's tomb on the day of Pentecost [Acts 2:29]). Solomon constructed this gate with winding or spiral forms as the design of a shellfish with a spiral shell, so that none could locate it easily. This fact is not known by most of the priests or people, even to this day. King Solomon had overlaid the gate with gold which he brought from Ethiopia, together with precious scents, spices and perfumes."

Now an over-enthusiastic King Ezekias revealed this hidden treasure of the tombs of the kings, David and Solomon, to the Babylonians who defiled the place and the bones in the tombs by their presence. For this cause, God's wrath was moved against Ezekias; and his seed would be in the company of the deportees into Babylon.[13]

Gradually, the Babylonians revived during the seventh century to become the dominant force of Mesopotamia. Ultimately, Juda became subject to Babylon with the fall of Jerusalem in 587 B.C. This takeover was another prophecy of Esaias who predicted that the kingdom of Juda would experience utter devastation; and this took place about one hundred years later. Following the sack of the city, the deportation of the Jews into Babylon took place. This left the land desolate [Is. 6:12]. However, there would be a remnant: **"There shall be a tenth upon it, and again it shall be for spoil, as a turpentine tree, and as an acorn when it falls out of its husk** [Is. 6:13]**."**

King Manasses

The Prophet Esaias had outlived King Ezekias by a few years. Manasses (Manasseh), the son of Ezekias, reigned fifty-five years, longer than any other Israelite king. Ezekias was succeeded by his son in 686 B.C. This apostate king, who was unaffected by his father's godly influence, chose to backslide into the ways of his notorious grandfather—Achaz (Ahaz). Devoted to idol madness, he reintroduced all that his father had quashed. Manasses built altars to Baal and erected an image of Asherah in the temple. He worshipped the sun, moon, and stars. He acknowledged Molech, an Ammonite god, and

---

[12] Saint Jerome, *Dogmatic and Polemical Works: Against the Pelagians*, FC, 53:331, 332.

[13] "Prophet Esaias," *The Great Synaxaristes of the Orthodox Church* (in Greek), s.v. "May 9th."

offered his children: "And he caused his sons to pass through the fire, and used divination and auspices, and made groves, and multiplied wizards, so as to do that which was evil in the sight of the Lord, to provoke Him to anger. And he set up the graven image of the grove in the house of the Lord [4 Kgs. (2 Kgs.) 21:6, 7]." His reign is summarized thus: He led the people "astray to do evil in the sight of the Lord, beyond the nations whom the Lord utterly destroyed from before the children of Israel [4 Kgs. (2 Kgs.) 21:9]."

The Martyric Repose of the Prophet

During the years of King Manasses, son of Ezekias, the prophet was sawn in pieces and finished his life by martyric contest. This is further confirmed by the Church fathers and sacred hymnography. He rebuked Manasses and the leaders of the people for their pagan practises. Saint Paul in his Epistle to the Hebrews supports this tradition of the prophet's martyrdom [Heb. 11:37]. He was one of those spiritual heroes **"of whom the world was not worthy** [Heb. 11: 38]**."** Saint Kyril of Jerusalem confirms the manner of Esaias' death: "Esaias was sawn asunder; yet after this the people were restored."[14] Palladius (ca. 365-425) also attests that "Esaias was sawn into pieces."[15] In the sacred music of Wednesday of Mid-Pentecost, the holy Church chants: *They sawed Esaias asunder with a saw fashioned out of wood.*[16]

The Martyrdom of Prophet Esaias

Saint Hilary of Poitiers (ca. 315-358) mentions the cause of the prophet's execution: "Esaias did see God [Is. 6:1], even though it is written: **'No one hath seen God at any time. The only-begotten Son, Who is in the bosom of the Father, that One declareth Him** [Jn. 1:18]**.'** It was God Whom the prophet saw. He gazed upon the divine glory, and men were filled with envy at such honor vouchsafed to his prophetic greatness; for this is why the Jews passed the death sentence upon him."[17]

---

[14] Saint Cyril of Jerusalem, "Lecture XIII," *Catechetical Lectures*, Nicene, 2nd Ser., VII:85.

[15] Palladius, *Palladius: Dialogue on the Life of Saint John Chrysostom*, Ancient Christian Writers, No. 45, trans. & ed. by Robt. T. Meyer (NY, NY: Newman Press, n.d.), p. 122. Note: cf. Justin Martyr, *Dialogus cum Tryphone* 120. [Henceforth the Series' name will be abbreviated as ACW.]

[16] Wednesday of Mid-Pentecost, extract of Orthros Praises, Mode Four.

[17] Saint Hilary of Poitiers, *On the Trinity*, Bk. V, § 33, Nicene, 2nd Ser., IX:95.

Saint Ambrose of Milan (ca. 339-397) also affirms that "the prophet saw the glory of Christ and spoke of Him, as the Gospel says plainly [Jn. 12:41]."[18]

Saint Ephraim the Syrian (ca. 306-383) cites another cause for the Jews' anger, noting that "it was a great source of scandal to them (certain Jews) that a virgin should give birth, because they were convinced that, through her birth-giving, their city would be destroyed, and that their kingdom, priesthood, and prophecy would be abolished. It was for this reason, too, that they also killed the Prophet Esaias who announced these things, that a virgin would give birth [Is. 7:14]."[19]

The Martyrdom of Prophet Esaias

The apocryphal book, entitled *Martyrdom and Ascension of Esaias*, describes the prophet's gruesome execution, as such: "Because of the visions of the prophet, Beliar was angry with Esaias; and he dwelt in the heart of Manasses; and he sawed Esaias in half with a wood saw....The false prophets stood by, laughing and maliciously joyful because of Esaias. His accusers stood by, laughing and deriding....And Esaias was in a vision of the Lord; but his eyes were open, and he saw them....Manasses, the false prophets, the princes, and the people were present....And while Esaias was being sawn in half, he did not cry out, or weep, but his mouth spoke with the Holy Spirit until he was sawn in two."[20]

Saint Epiphanios (ca. 315-403) confirms this account and says that, while they were sawing the prophet, he grew weary and thirsty. He besought God to send him water that he might drink. And—O the wonder!—straightway, God sent him living water out of the spring of Siloam. The spring, for this cause, was called Siloam, which is interpreted as "He who had been sent

---

[18] Saint Ambrose, *Select Works and Letters: Of the Christian Faith,* Bk. I, Ch. XVII, Nicene, 2nd Ser., X:220.

[19] *Saint Ephrem's Commentary on Tatian's Diatessaron*, Journal of Semitic Studies Supplement 2, an English trans. of Chester Beatty, Syriac MS 709, p. 64.

[20] *The Old Testament Pseudepigrapha*, Vol. 2, ed. by James H. Charlesworth (NY: Doubleday, 1985), pp. 159, 160.

(ἀπεσταλμένος)."[21] Saint Epiphanios states that an angel had appeared to the prophet from out of heaven. He quenched his thirst, as a pledge of eternal life, from the water of the spring of Siloam which suddenly began flowing abundantly.

Saint Irenaeos (ca. 130-ca. 200) records that "this spring gushes forth more abundantly on Saturdays. Therefore, when Christ sent the man born blind [Jn. 9:7] to the pool of Siloam on a Saturday to wash or rather to drink, He did so that the man might receive his vision—even as the water of Baptism is illumination."[22]

Esaias was interred in a place called Aroēl or Rogēl, beside the crossover of the waters of Siloam. According to some, this same pool was used by Solomon and was named Gihon, of which Siloam lies in the adjoining area.

As we mentioned earlier, it is written in Scripture that Ezekias "fortified his city, and brought in water into the midst thereof: he digged the hard rock with iron, and made wells for waters [Wis. of Sirach 48:17]." However, before these construction projects were undertaken, according to a tradition, the prophet had besought God to gush forth a little water from the Siloam spring lest the city perish from thirst. God granted the request and the city became impregnable against foreigners. Thus, the prophet showed himself to be a wonder-worker. When aliens asked whence the Jews drank water and learned it came from the spring of Siloam, they sat nearby and partook of the little flow of water therefrom. But when the Jews with Esaias approached to draw water, it gushed forth plentifully. Since this spring appeared through the prayer of this prophet, the people, upon his repose, diligently buried his glorious and honorable relics nearby the spring in order that through his intercession, even after death, they might have water. "The prophet," says Saint Ephraim, "sent them to the spring; but the One Who fulfills the prophets' words invited them to drink, saying, 'If anyone thirst, let him come to Me and drink [Jn. 7:37].'"[23]

The tomb of the prophet is found close by the tombs of the kings, as he himself was of the royal house, and behind the memorials of the priests, south of Jerusalem. Later, the synaxis of the holy prophet was celebrated at the Church of the Holy Martyr Laurence (Lavrentios), near Vlachernai, where the prophet's sacred relics were interred, after being brought to Constantinople.[24] Through his august relics, miracles were worked for many.[25]

---

[21] *Great Synaxaristes* (in Greek), pp. 218-220.

[22] Ibid., p. 220, notes 1 and 2.

[23] *Saint Ephrem's Commentary on Tatian's Diatessaron*, p. 256.

[24] *Great Synaxaristes* (in Greek), p. 221.

[25] *The Oxford Dictionary of Byzantium*, s.v. "Isaiah."

A commemorative Byzantine church was constructed just northwest of the reservoir in A.D. 440, by the Byzantine Empress Evdokia, together with elaborate porticoes about the pool. Only fragments now remain visible, and the pool itself rests eighteen feet below the surrounding ground level.

The surviving pool, an artificial one, carries the title Birket Silwan, situated in the narrowest part of the Tyropoeon ravine, and receives its supply of water, by transmission through a rock-hewn tunnel, from the Fountain of the Virgin. It may be reached by a steep flight of stone steps, and measures 16-feet by 50-feet. A small mosque stands over the ruins of the church; and the name Silwan has become attached to the Arab village across the Kidron Valley to the east.[26]

King Manasses' End

After the prophet's martyrdom, Manasses was temporarily deported to Babylon where he humbled himself before God in repentance: "And the Lord brought upon them the captains of the host of the king of Assyria, and they took Manasses in bonds, and bound him in fetters, and brought him to Babylon. And when he was afflicted, he sought the face of the Lord his God, and was greatly humbled before the face of the God of his fathers. And he prayed to Him, and He hearkened to him, and listened to his cry, and brought him back to Jerusalem to his kingdom. And Manasses knew that the Lord He is God [2 Chr. 33:11-13]." Upon Manasses' return to Jerusalem, he tried to reverse the trends he had set; "and he removed the strange gods and the graven image out of the house of the Lord, and all the altars which he had built in the mount of the house of the Lord, and in Jerusalem, and without the city. And he repaired the altar of the Lord, offering upon it a sacrifice of peace-offering and thank-offering, and he told Juda to serve the Lord God of Israel. Nevertheless, the people still sacrificed on the high places, only to the Lord their God....However, his reforms were quickly reversed after his death by his wicked son Amon, who sacrificed to all the idols which his father Manasses had made; and he served them [2 Chr. 33:15-17, 22]."

God Permits Evils to Befall His People

"I am He that prepared light, and formed darkness, Who make peace, and create evils; I am the Lord God, that does all these things [Is. 45:7]**."**

We have just recounted briefly the immediate history of God's people which lead to the deportation to Babylon. The many vicissitudes permitted to come upon Israel and Juda, and on all of us, are explained by the holy fathers. Saint Irenaeos remarks, "He makes peace and friendship with those who repent

---

[26] *The Zondervan Pictorial Encyclopedia of the Bible*, s.v. "Siloam"; *A Dictionary of the Bible*, edited by James Hastings, M.A., D.D. (Peabody, MA: Hendrickson Publishers, Nov. 1988), Vol. 4, s.v. "Siloam."

and turn to Him;...but for the impenitent, those who shun the light, He prepares everlasting fire and outer darkness, which are evils indeed to those persons who fall into them....One and the same Lord has pointed out that the whole human race shall be divided at the judgment, 'as the shepherd separateth the sheep from the kids [Mt. 25:32].'"[27] Saint Hippolytos briefly says that the prophet means by this, "I maintain peace, and permit war."[28]

Saint John Chrysostom (ca. 347-407) confirms, "By 'evil' here He means, not wickedness, far from it, but affliction, and trouble, and calamities; much as in another place also He says, 'Shall there be evil in a city which the Lord hath not wrought [Amos 3:6]?' He does not mean rapines, nor injuries, nor any thing like these, but the scourges which are borne from above. And again, **'I,'** saith He, **'make peace, and create evils** [Is. 45:7]**.'** For neither in this place does He speak of wickedness, but of famines, and pestilences, things accounted evil by most men—the generality being wont to call these things evil."[29]

In the midst of these troubles, God's unsurpassing love is ever present, though Sion said, **"The Lord has forsaken me,"** and **"The Lord has forgotten me** [Is. 49:14]**."** The Lord answers, **"Will a woman forget her child, so as not to have compassion upon the offspring of her womb? But if a woman should even forget these, yet I will not forget thee** [Is. 49:15]**."**

Abbot Chaeremon, in his conference with Saint John Cassian (ca. 360-435), speaks: "This providence and love of God, therefore, which the Lord in His unwearied goodness vouchsafes to show us, He compares to the tenderest heart of a kind mother, as He wishes to express it by a figure of human affection, and finds in His creatures no such feeling of love, to which He could better compare it. And He uses this example, because nothing dearer can be found in human nature, saying, 'Can a mother forget her child, that she should not have compassion on the son of her womb?' But not content with this comparison, He at once goes beyond it and subjoins these words: 'And though she may forget, yet will not I forget thee [cf. Is. 49:15].'"[30]

The Prophet's Vision and Calling [Is. 6:1-8]

1. God is Seen by Condescension and Accommodation.

"I saw the Lord sitting on a high and exalted throne, and the house was full of His glory [Is. 6:1]**."**

---

[27] Saint Irenaeus, *Against Heresies*, Bk. IV, Ch. XL, Ante-Nicene, I:523, 524.

[28] Saint Hippolytus, *Fragments from Commentaries*, Ante-Nicene, V:172.

[29] Saint Chrysostom, "Hom. XXII," *Matthew*, Nicene, 1st Ser., X:153, 154.

[30] Saint John Cassian, "The Third Conference of Abbot Chaeremon," *Cassian's Conferences*, Ch. XVII, Nicene, 2nd Ser., XI:434.

Saint Irenaeos says, "The prophets did not openly behold the actual face of God, but they saw the dispensations and the mysteries through which man should afterward see God."[31]

Prophet Esaias

Saint Gregory the Theologian (ca. 329/330-ca. 390) asks, "What would you say of Esaias or Ezekiel, who were eyewitnesses of very great mysteries, and of the other prophets? For one of these saw the Lord of Sabaoth sitting on the throne of glory [Is. 6:1], and encircled and praised and hidden by the six-winged seraphim, and was himself purged by the live coal, and equipped for his prophetic office....And whether this was an appearance by day, only visible to saints, or an unerring vision of the night, or an impression on the mind holding converse with the future as if it were the present, or some other ineffable form of prophecy, I cannot say; the God of the prophets knows, and they know who are thus inspirited. But neither these of whom I am speaking nor any of their fellows ever stood before the subsistence (*hyposteemati*) and essence of God, as it is written, or saw, or proclaimed the nature of God."[32]

"No one hath seen God at any time [Jn. 1:18]." "By what connection," inquires Saint Chrysostom, "does the apostle come to say this?...What then shall we answer to the most mighty of voice, Esaias, when he says, **'I saw the Lord sitting upon a high and exalted throne** [Is. 6:1]'?...And others have seen Him [cf. Ex. 33:13; Ez. 1, 10; Dan. 7:9]. Why does John say this then? It is to declare that all these were instances of His condescension, not the vision of the essence itself unveiled. For had they seen the very nature, they would not have beheld it under different forms, since it is simple, without form, or parts, or bounding lines. It sits not, nor stands, nor walks: these things belong to all bodies. But how He is, He only knows. And this He has declared by a certain prophet, saying, 'I have multiplied visions, and used similitudes by the hands of the prophets [Hos. 12:10],' that is, 'I have condescended, I have not

[31] Saint Irenaeus, *Against Heresies*, Bk. IV, Ch. XX, Ante-Nicene, I:490.

[32] Saint Gregory Nazianzen (the Theologian), "Oration XXVIII, The Second Theological Oration," *Orations*, Nicene, 2nd Ser., VII:295.

appeared as I really am.' For since His Son was about to appear in very flesh, He prepared them from old time....But what God really is, neither have the prophets seen, nor angels, nor archangels....Does this special attribute belong to the Father only, not to the Son? Away with the thought! It belongs also to the Son. And to show that it does so, hear Paul declaring this point, and saying, that He 'is the image of the invisible God [Col. 1:15].' Now if He is the image of the invisible, He must be invisible Himself; for otherwise He would not be an 'image.' And wonder not that Paul says in another place, 'God was manifested in the flesh [1 Tim. 3:16]'; because the manifestation took place by means of the flesh, not according to (His) essence. Besides, Paul shows that He is invisible, not only to men but also to the powers above; for after he says, 'was manifested in the flesh,' he adds, 'was seen of angels [1 Tim. 3:16].'"[33]

Saint Kosmas the Melodist and Bishop of Maiuma (7th C.), hymning the incarnation of our Lord, sings: *In a figure, Esaias saw God upon a throne...and he cried, "Woe is me! For I have beheld beforehand the incarnate God, the Light that wanes not, and Master of peace* [Is. 6:1-5]. *"*[34]

Saint Chrysostom, explaining the word "glory" in the context used by the prophet, says, "The prophet calls 'glory,' that vision, the smoke, the hearing unutterable mysteries, the beholding of the seraphim, the lightning which leaped from the throne, against which those powers could not look."[35]

Blessed Jerome observes: "Whenever God is represented as seated, the portraiture takes one of two forms: He appears either as the Ruler or as the Judge. If He is like a king, one sees Him as Esaias does, 'I saw the Lord seated on a high and lofty throne [cf. Is. 6:1].'"[36]

Saint John of Damascus (ca. 675-ca. 749), in his *Exposition of the Orthodox Faith*, writes concerning the place of God and that the Deity alone is uncircumscribed: "There is a mental place where the mind dwells and energizes, and yet it is not contained in a bodily but in a mental fashion. For it is without form, and so cannot be contained as a body is. God, then, being immaterial and uncircumscribed, has not a place. For He is His own place, filling all things and being above all things, and Himself maintaining all things. Yet we speak of God having a place and the place of God where His energy becomes manifest. For He penetrates everything without mixing with it, and imparts to all His energy in proportion to the fitness and receptive power of each: and by this I mean, a purity both natural and voluntary. For the immaterial is purer than the material, and that which is virtuous than that which

---

[33] Saint Chrysostom, "Hom. XV," John, Nicene, 1st Ser., XIV:51, 52.

[34] February 2nd, Meeting of Our Lord in the Temple, extract of Orthros Canon, Ode Five, Mode Three.

[35] Saint Chrysostom, "Hom. LXVIII," *John*, Nicene, 1st Ser., XIV:252, 253.

[36] Saint Jerome, "Hom. XIV," *1-59 On The Psalms, Vol. 1*, FC, 48:103.

is linked with vice. Therefore, by the place of God is meant that which has a greater share in His energy and grace. For this reason heaven is His throne. In it are the angels who do His will and are always glorifying Him [Is. 6:1 seq.]. This is His rest and the earth is His footstool [Is. 66:1]. In it He dwelt in the flesh among men [Bar. 3:38]. And His sacred flesh has been named the foot of God. The Church, too, is spoken of as the place of God. For we have set this apart for the glorifying of God as a sort of consecrated place wherein we also hold converse with Him. Likewise also the places in which His energy becomes manifest to us, whether through the flesh or apart from flesh, are spoken of as the places of God. But it must be understood that the Deity is invisible, being everywhere wholly in His entirety and not divided up part by part like that which has body, but wholly in everything and wholly above everything."[37]

Saint Gregory Palamas (ca. 1296-1359), Archbishop of Thessalonike (1347), agrees with Saint Chrysostom that "whenever you hear the prophet saying, 'I saw the Lord seated upon a throne,' do not suppose that he saw the essence (*ousian*), but rather the condescension, and this even more obscurely than the supreme powers."[38]

At the Midnight Office, we sing: *As Esaias saw in figure God, the One divine Lordship, glorified in Three Persons by the undefiled voices of the seraphim* [Is. 6:1], *this sent him straightway to proclaim the thrice radiant essence and the One threefold Sun.*[39]

2. The Seraphim.

"And the seraphs stood round about Him. Each one had six wings: and with two they covered their face, and with two they covered their feet, and with two they flew [Is. 6:2].

"And one cried to the other, and they said, 'Holy, Holy, Holy, is the Lord of Hosts: the earth is full of His glory [Is. 6:3].'"

Saint Dionysios the Areopagite (1st C.) writes in *The Celestial Hierarchies*: "Theology has given to the celestial beings nine interpretative names, and among these our divine initiator distinguishes three threefold orders. In the first rank of all he places those who, as we are told, dwell eternally in the constant presence of God, and cleave to Him, and above all others are immediately united to Him. And he testifies that the teachings of the holy Word testify that the most holy thrones and many-eyed and many-winged ones, named in the Hebrew tongue cherubim and seraphim, are established immediately about God and nearest to Him above all others.

---

[37] Saint John of Damascus, *Exposition of the Orthodox Faith,* Bk. I, Ch. XIII, Nicene, 2nd Ser., IX:15.

[38] Saint Gregory Palamas, *The One Hundred and Fifty Chapters*, Ch. 77, p. 173. See also Saint Gregory's cite, Saint John Chrysostom, *In Isaiah* 6, *P.G.* 56:68 (6:1).

[39] Sunday, The Midnight Office, Canon to the Holy Trinity, Ode Five, Mode Three.

"Our venerable hierarch (Saint Hierotheos) describes this threefold order as a co-equal unity, and truly the most exalted of the hierarchies, the most fully godlike, and the most closely and immediately united to the first light of the Divinity."[40] Hence, "The first order of celestial beings...is established about God, immediately encircling Him. And in perpetual purity, they encompass His eternal knowledge in that most high and eternal angelic dance, rapt in the bliss of manifold blessed contemplations, and irradiated with pure and primal splendors,...they are deemed worthy of communion and co-operation with God by reason of their assimilation to Him, as far as is possible for them, in the excellence of their natures and energies. For they know preeminently many divine matters, and they participate as far as they may in divine understanding and knowledge. Theology, therefore, has given those on earth its hymns of praise in which is divinely shown the great excellence of its sublime illumination. For some of that choir (to use material terms) cry out as with a voice, as the sound of many waters [Ez. 1:24], **'Blessed be the glory of the Lord from His place** [Ez. 3:12]'; others cry aloud that most renowned and sacred hymn of highest praise to God, **'Holy, Holy, Holy, Lord of Sabaoth, the whole earth is full of His glory** [Is. 6:3].'"[41] He explains that "when the prophet says 'the seraphim's feet [cf. Is. 6:2],' they signify the power of motion, swiftness, and skillfulness in the ever-moving advance toward divine things. The prophet, therefore, described the feet of the celestial intelligences as being covered by their wings which symbolize a swift soaring to the heights, and the heavenly progression up,...and the exemption from everything earthly through the upward ascent. The lightness of the wings shows that they are altogether heavenly and unsullied and untrammeled in their upliftment on high. The naked and unshod feet symbolize their free, easy, and unrestrained power, pure from all externality, and assimilated, as far as is attainable, to the divine simplicity."[42]

In *The Ecclesiastical Hierarchy*, Saint Dionysios remarks, "I think their numberless faces and many feet symbolize their outstanding visual capacity when face to face with the most divine enlightenment. They symbolize an ever moving, ever active conception of the divine goodness....The seraphim have wings everywhere and therefore they have in the highest degree the power to be lifted up toward true Being. If they hide their faces and feet with their wings, if they fly only with their middle wings, know reverently that this most outstanding order among the transcendent beings looks with caution on

[40] Saint Dionysius the Areopagite, *The Mystical Theology and the Celestial Hierarchies of Dionysius the Areopagite*, Ch. VI, trans. by the Editors of The Shrine of Wisdom, p. 37.

[41] Idem, Ch. VII, pp. 41, 42.

[42] Ibid., Ch. XV, p. 64.

whatever is higher and deeper than what its own intelligence can grasp, that is it uplifted by its middle wings to the proportionate sight of God, that it submits its own life to the divine constraints, and that it thereby allows itself in all reverence to be led to a recognition of its own limitations."[43]

God is unapproachable not only for men but also for the powers above. Saint Chrysostom says, "Listen to what Esaias says, I mean what the Spirit states, for every prophet speaks through the action of the Spirit." The prophet's vision takes place in the temple at Jerusalem. What now will be important to Saint Chrysostom is that the seraphim cover their faces, since the theophany is too much for them to gaze upon. "What does Esaias say? **'And it came to pass in the year in which King Ozias died, that I saw the Lord sitting...**[Is. 6:1, 2]**.'** Why, tell me, do they stretch forth their wings and cover their faces? For what other reason than that they cannot endure the sparkling flashes nor the lightning which shines from the throne? Yet they did not see the pure light itself nor the pure essence itself. What they saw was a condescension accommodated to their nature. What is this condescension? God condescends whenever He is not seen as He is, but in the way one incapable of beholding Him is able to look upon Him. In this way God reveals Himself by accommodating what He reveals to the weakness of vision of those who behold Him.

"And it is clear from Esaias' very words that, in his case, he saw God by such condescension....But God is not sitting. This is a posture for bodily beings. And Esaias said, 'on a throne.' But God is not encompassed or enclosed by a throne; divinity cannot be circumscribed by limits. Nonetheless, the seraphim could not endure God's condescension even though they were only standing near. For **'the seraphim stood round about Him** [Is. 6:2]**.'** It was especially for this very reason that they could not look upon Him, namely, because they were near. But Esaias is not speaking of being near in place. He said, **'And the seraphs stood round about Him** [Is. 6:2]**,'** because he wished the Holy Spirit to make it clear that even though the seraphim are closer to God's essence than we men are, they still cannot look upon it just because they are closer. He is not hinting at place in a local sense. When he speaks of closeness in place, he is showing that the seraphim are nearer to God than we men are.

"And the fact is that we do not know God in the same way in which those powers above know Him. Their nature is far more pure and wise and clear-sighted than man's nature....So, even if you hear the prophet say, **'I saw the Lord** [Is. 6:1]**,'** do not suspect that he saw God's essence. What he saw was this very condescension of God. And he saw that far less distinctly than did the powers above. He could not see it with the same clarity as the

---

[43] Saint Dionysius found in Pseudo-Dionysius, *The Complete Works: The Ecclesiastical Hierarchy*, Ch. Four, trans. by C. Luibheid and P. Rorem, p. 230.

cherubim. And why do I speak of that blessed essence of God? A man cannot even look upon the essence of an angel without fear and trembling [cf. Dan. 10:8]."[44]

Saint Chrysostom informs us that "the angels are not party to the counsels of God. They are to stand in waiting and fulfill sacred ministry. Listening to Esaias, it is obvious that they could not bear the radiance beaming from that source, but stood in great fear and trembling. To stand in waiting before the Lord is, after all, proper to creatures."[45]

3. The Mystery of the Holy Trinity.

A. "And one cried to the other, and they said, 'Holy, Holy, Holy, is the Lord of Hosts: the earth is full of His glory [Is. 6:3]**.'"**

"The scriptural declaration, **'they cried out to one another** [Is. 6:3]' means, I think," says Saint Dionysios the Areopagite, "that they ungrudgingly impart to each other the conceptions resulting from their looking on God. And we should piously remember that, in Hebrew, the Scripture gives the designation of seraphim to the holiest beings in order to convey that these are fiery-hot and bubbling over forever because of the divine life which does not cease to bestir them."[46] Thus, "I think, it is clear that the first impart to the second their knowledge of divine things."[47]

Saint Gregory the Theologian says, "Glorify Him with the cherubim who unite the Three Holies into One Lord [Is. 6:3]."[48]

Saint Basil the Great (ca. 330-379) asks, "How could the seraphim cry, **'Holy, Holy, Holy** [Is. 6:3]**,'** were they not taught by the Spirit how often true religion requires them to lift their voice in this ascription of glory?"[49]

Saint Gregory of Nyssa says that it was by Esaias' seraphim [Is. 6:3] that "the mystery of the Trinity was luminously proclaimed when they uttered that marvellous cry, 'Holy,' being awestruck with the beauty in each Person of the Trinity."[50]

Saint Ambrose asks, "What means this threefold utterance of the same name 'Holy'? If thrice repeated, why is it but one act of praise? If one act of

---

[44] Saint John Chrysostom, "Hom. III," *On the Incomprehensible Nature of God*, FC, 72:101-105.

[45] Saint John Chrysostom, "Hom. 8," *Homilies on Genesis*, FC, 74:108.

[46] Saint Dionysius, *The Complete Works: The Ecclesiastical Hierarchy*, Ch. Four, Luibheid & Rorem, loc. cit.

[47] Idem, *The Mystical Theology and the Celestial Hierarchies of Dionysius the Areopagite*, Ch. X, The Shrine of Wisdom, p. 50.

[48] Saint Gregory Nazianzen (the Theologian), "Oration XXXIV, On the Arrival of the Egyptians," Nicene, 2nd Ser., VII:337.

[49] Saint Basil, *On the Spirit*, Ch. XVI, Nicene, 2nd Ser., VIII:24.

[50] Saint Gregory of Nyssa, *Against Eunomius*, Bk. I, Nicene, 2nd Ser., V:64.

praise, why a threefold repetition?"[51] He expounds, "The Father is holy, the Son is holy, and the Spirit is holy, but they are not three holies; for there is one holy God, one Lord. For the true holiness is one, as the true Divinity is one, as that true holiness belonging to the divine nature is one....The cherubim and seraphim with unwearied voices praise Him....They say it not once, lest you should believe that there is but one—and exclude the Son; not twice, lest you should exclude the Spirit. They say not holies (in the plural), lest you should imagine that there is plurality; but they repeat thrice and say the same word, that even in a hymn you may understand the distinction of Persons in the Trinity and the oneness of the Divinity; and while they say this they proclaim God."[52] And, "Furthermore, to show that the divinity of the Trinity is One, he, after the threefold 'Holy,' added in the singular number 'the Lord God of Sabaoth.' Holy, therefore, is the Father, holy the Son, holy likewise the Spirit of God; and therefore is the Trinity adored, but adores not, and is praised, but praises not."[53]

Saint Chrysostom says, "They pronounce that name with dread and awe, while glorifying and praising Him"[54] Elsewhere, he asks, "What, then, do you think? Do you think that the angels in heaven talk over and ask each other questions about the divine essence? By no means! What are the angels doing? They give glory to God, they adore Him, they chant without ceasing their triumphal and mystical hymns with a deep feeling of religious awe. Some sing, 'Glory to God in the highest [Lk. 2:14]'; the seraphim chant, **'Holy, holy, holy** [Is. 6:3]**,'** and they turn away their eyes because they cannot endure God's presence as He comes down to adapt Himself to them in condescension. And the cherubim sing, 'Blessed be the glory of the Lord from His place [Ez. 3:12],' not that God is surrounded by a place—heaven forbid!—but they are speaking after the fashion of men, just as if they were to say, 'wherever He is,' or 'in whatever way He is'—if, indeed, it is safe to speak in this way of God. For our tongues speak with the words of men. Did you see how great is the holy dread in heaven and how great the arrogant presumption here below?"[55]

Saint Gregory the Great comments, "Truly, Esaias heard angelic hosts in heaven, crying, **'Holy, Holy, Holy, is the Lord of Hosts** [Is. 6:3]**.'**...Then in order that the essence of the Trinity appear as One, it is said 'the whole earth is full of His glory.'"[56]

---

[51] Saint Ambrose, *Of the Christian Faith,* Bk. II, Ch. XII, Nicene, 2nd Ser., X:238.
[52] Idem, *Of the Holy Spirit,* Bk. III, Nicene, 2nd Ser., X:151.
[53] Idem, *Of the Christian Faith*, loc. cit.
[54] Saint Chrysostom, "Hom. VII," *Homilies on the Statues,* Nicene, 1st Ser., IX:394.
[55] Idem, "Hom. I," *On the Incomprehensible Nature of God*, FC, 72:66.
[56] Saint Gregory the Great (the Dialogist), "Hom. IV," *The Homilies of Saint Gregory*
(continued...)

Thus Saint Theophanes sings of the triune unity with the unoriginate Father as the Source: *The pious Esaias hath proclaimed, to the ignorant, the one Trinity in a single Essence: the Logos and the Holy Spirit Who have Their origin in God the Father* [Is. 6:2, 3].[57]

B. Elsewhere, the prophet speaks of the Holy Spirit, saying, **"And the light of Israel shall be for a fire, and He shall sanctify him with burning fire, and He shall devour the wood as grass** [Is. 10:17]**."** Saint Ambrose of Milan says that "Esaias shows that the Holy Spirit is not only light but also fire, saying, 'And the light of Israel shall be for a burning fire [cf. Is. 10:17].' So the prophets called Him a burning fire, because in those three points we see more intensely the majesty of the Divinity: since to sanctify is of the Divinity, to illuminate is the property of fire and light, and the Divinity is wont to be pointed out or seen in the appearance of fire, 'For our God is a consuming Fire,' as Moses said [cf. Deut. 4:24]."[58]

4. The Prophet Acknowledges Unclean Lips.

"And the lintel shook at the voice they uttered, and the house was filled with smoke. And I said, 'Woe is me, for I am pricked to the heart; for being a man, and having unclean lips, I dwell in the midst of a people having unclean lips; and I have seen with mine eyes the King, the Lord of hosts [Is. 6:4, 5]**.'"**

Saint Irenaeos declares God's Logos has shown that in many modes He may be seen and known. "The prophets used not to prophesy in word alone, but in visions also, and in their mode of life, and in the actions which they performed, according to the suggestions of the Spirit. After this invisible manner, therefore did they see God, as also Esaias says, **'I have seen with mine eyes the King, the Lord of hosts** [Is. 6:5]**,'** pointing out that man should behold God with his eyes, and hear His voice."[59]

"The word 'holy,'" explains Saint Chrysostom, "has not force to give the same meaning in every case to which it is applied; since God is called 'holy,' though not as we are (as His people). What, for instance, does the prophet say, when he heard that cry raised by the flying seraphim? **'Woe is me, for I am pricked to the heart; for being a man, and having unclean lips** [Is. 6:5]**'**; though he was holy and clean. But if we should be compared with the holiness which is above, we are unclean. Angels are holy, archangels are holy,

---

[56](...continued)
the Great On the Book of the Prophet Ezekiel, Bk. II, p. 198.

[57] May 9th, Prophet Esaias, Orthros Canon, Ode Five, Mode Four.

[58] Saint Ambrose, *Of the Holy Spirit*, Bk. I, Ch. XIV, Nicene, 2nd Ser., X:112.

[59] Saint Irenaeus, *Against Heresies*, Bk. IV, Ch. XX, Ante-Nicene, I:490.

the cherubim and seraphim themselves are holy, but of this holiness again there is a double difference; that is, in relation to us, and to the higher powers."[60]

Abbot Theonas, in his conference with Saint John Cassian, declares: "All the saints have confessed with truth that they were unclean and sinful....And so they have recognized that man's righteousness is weak and imperfect and always needs God's mercy....When Esaias says, 'Woe is me! for I am a man of unclean lips,' he shows that his confession that follows refers to his own lips, and not to the uncleanness of the people. But even when in his prayer he confesses the uncleanness of all sinners, he embraces in his general supplication not only the mass of the wicked but also of the good, saying, **'We are all become as unclean, and all our righteousness as a filthy rag** [Is. 64:6].'"[61]

Saint Maximos the Confessor (580-662) says, "When through love the mind is ravished by divine knowledge and in going outside of creatures has a perception of divine transcendence, then, according to the divine Esaias, it comes in consternation to a realization of its own lowliness and says with conviction the words of the prophet [Is. 6:5]."[62]

5. The Coal: A Type of Christ.

"And there was sent to me one of the seraphs, and he had in his hand a coal, which he had taken off the altar with the tongs [Is. 6:6]."

Saint Ephraim the Syrian uses the phrase "Coal of Fire" with reference to both Christ and the Eucharist: "The Coal of Fire that came to burn away thorns and thistles [Gen. 3:18] dwelt in a womb, refining and sanctifying that place of pangs and curses [Gen. 3:16]."[63] In the prophet's vision the coal is held by the seraph in tongs, and it merely touches Esaias' lips, but Christians hold and consume Christ the new Coal of Fire: "The seraph could not touch the coal of fire with his fingers; and the coal merely touched Esaias' mouth. The seraph did not hold it; Esaias did not consume it; but our Lord has allowed us to do both."[64] For Saint Ephraim the coal of fire is but a specific example in which the Divinity may be spoken of as fire: "In Thy bread, Lord, there is hidden the Spirit Who is not consumed, in Thy wine there dwells the fire that

---

[60] Saint Chrysostom, "Hom. XIV," *John,* Nicene, 1st Ser., XIV:49.

[61] Saint John Cassian, "Third Conference of Abbot Theonas," Ch. XVII, Nicene, 2nd Ser., XI:529.

[62] Saint Maximus Confessor, *Selected Writings: The Four Hundred Chapters on Love—First Century*, no. 12, trans. by G. C. Berthold, p. 37.

[63] Saint Ephraim the Syrian, *The Luminous Eye: The Medicine of Life*, Cistercian Studies Series: Number One-Hundred Twenty-Four, p. 103 (*Commentary on the Diatessaron* 1:5).

[64] Idem, p. 104 (Faith 10:10).

is not drunk: the Spirit is in Thy bread, the fire in Thy wine—a manifest wonder that our lips have received."[65]

"What interpretation," asks Saint Kyril of Alexandria (378-444), "then are we to put upon the coal which touched the prophet's lips, and cleansed him from all sin? Plainly it is the message of salvation, and the confession of faith in Christ, which whosoever receives with his mouth is forthwith and altogether purified....We say then that the power of the divine message resembles a live coal and fire."[66]

Saint John of Damascus, discoursing on the holy and immaculate Mysteries of the Lord, urges us to "draw near to It with an ardent desire, and with our hands held in the form of the Cross. Let us receive the body of the crucified One...that we may be inflamed and divinized by the participation in the divine fire. Esaias saw the coal [Is. 6:6]. But coal is not plain wood, but wood united with fire: in like manner also the bread of the Communion is not plain bread but bread united with divinity. But a body which is united with divinity is not one nature, but has one nature belonging to the body and another belonging to the divinity that is united to it; so that the compound is not one nature but two."[67]

6. The Tongs: A Type of Mary Theotokos [Is. 6:6].

The hymnographers of the Church, during the Feast of the Meeting of the Lord in the Temple, compare the arms of Mary Theotokos with the tongs and Christ as the Coal, chanting: *Christ the coal of fire, Whom holy Esaias foresaw, now rests in the arms of the Theotokos, as in a pair of tongs* [Is. 6:6], *and He is given to the elder.*[68] Saint Kosmas the Melodist also voices: *Mary, thou art the mystic tongs, who hast conceived in thy womb Christ the live Coal* [Is. 6:6].[69]

The Virgin is also perceived as the censer, as in this hymn of Saint Joseph of Thessalonike (810-866): *We call thee...the censer of the immaterial Ember* [Is. 6:6, 7], *O pure one.*[70]

---

[65] Ibid., p. 104 (Faith 10:8).

[66] Saint Cyril of Alexandria, "Hom. 94," *Commentary on the Gospel of Saint Luke*, p. 378.

[67] Saint John of Damascus, *Exposition of the Orthodox Faith,* Bk. IV, Ch. XIII, Nicene, 2nd Ser., IX:83.

[68] February 2nd, Meeting of Our Lord in the Temple, Small Vespers Aposticha, Mode Two.

[69] February 2nd, Meeting of Our Lord in the Temple, Orthros Canon, Ode Nine, Mode Three.

[70] *Pentecostarion*, Sunday of the Samaritan Woman, extract of Theotokion of Orthros Canon, Ode Five, Mode Four.

7. The Prophet is Purified.

"And there was sent to me one of the seraphs, and he had in his hand a coal, which he had taken off the altar with the tongs. And he touched my mouth, and said, 'Behold, this has touched thy lips, and will take away thine iniquities, and will purge away thy sins [Is. 6:6, 7]**.'"**

Saint Gregory of Nyssa tells us that the prophet's goal was purification and that he was not harmed by a burning coal, but he was glorified for being illumined: "Esaias saw One sitting in magnificence upon a lofty, exalted throne, though he could not see His form and greatness. (Esaias would have spoken of this if he could when he saw the other things, such as the number of the wings of the seraphim, their location, and movement.) He only speaks of the voice he heard, the lintels raised because of the seraphim's singing, and the house filled with smoke. One of the seraphim touched his mouth with a fiery coal; not only were his lips purified but also were his ears to receive God's word....The lintel was removed so that Esaias' contemplation may not be hindered."[71]

Saint Ambrose insists "that the Spirit forgives sin is common to Him with the Father and the Son, but not with the angels....Who rather forgives sin? Does an angel forgive? Does an archangel? Certainly not, but the Father alone, the Son alone, and the Holy Spirit alone. But perhaps someone will say that the seraph said this to Esaias [Is. 6:7]. The seraph said 'This shall take away,' and, 'This shall purge,' not, 'I will take away,' but that fire from the altar of God, that is, the grace of the Spirit. For what else can we piously understand to be on the altar of God, but the grace of the Spirit? Certainly not wood of the forests, nor the soot and coals. Or what is so in accordance with piety as to understand according to the mystery that it was revealed by the mouth of Esaias that all men should be cleansed by the Passion of Christ....But even if the seraph had taken away sin, it would have been as one of the ministers of God appointed to this mystery."[72]

Saint Gregory the Great (ca. 540-604), Pope of Rome, describing the action of the seraphim, writes: "The prophet wishes us to understand that those spirits which are sent receive a name indicative of their service. Since the angel carried a burning coal from the altar to burn away sins of speech, it is called a seraphim, because the name indicates burning."[73]

The image of the ember as a source of purification is confirmed in Church hymns. Saint Joseph of Thessalonike takes up this point: *By a live coal was Esaias cleansed* [Is. 6:6, 7], *thereby proclaiming aforetime the noetic*

---

[71] Saint Gregory of Nyssa, *Commentary on the Song of Songs*, pp. 224, 225.
[72] Saint Ambrose, *Of the Holy Spirit*, Bk. I, Ch. X, Nicene, 2nd Ser., X:108.
[73] Saint Gregory the Great, "Hom. 34," *Forty Gospel Homilies*, Cistercian Studies Series: One Hundred Twenty-Three, p. 292.

Ember that was incarnate of thee, O Virgin, in a manner surpassing comprehension, and that burneth away all the substance of the sins of mortal men, and divinizes our nature in His compassion, O all-blameless one.[74] During the Theophany this idea of cleansing is reiterated in the following hymn: *The living Coal that Esaias foresaw is inflamed in the waters of the Jordan; He will burn up all the tinder of sins and grant restoration to the broken.* [Is. 6:6, 7].[75]

8. The Voluntary Consent.

"And I heard the voice of the Lord, saying, 'Whom shall I send, and who will go to this people?' And I said, 'Behold, I am here, send me.' And He said, 'Go, and say to this people...[Is. 6:8].**'"**

Saint Athanasios the Great (ca. 296-373) gives the following dramatic representation of the Son's voluntary condescension, taking on of flesh, and His mission, all prefigured here in the word and action of the prophet: "Man sinned and is fallen, and by his fall all things are in confusion: death prevailed from Adam to Moses, the earth was cursed, Hades was opened, Paradise was shut, heaven was offended, man was corrupted and brutalized, while the devil was exulting against us. Then God, in His loving-kindness, not willing that man—made in His own image—should perish, said, **'Whom shall I send, and who will go** [Is. 6:8]**?'** But while all held their peace, the Son said, 'Here am I, send Me.' And then it was that saying 'Go Thou' that He 'delivered' to Him man, that the Logos Himself might be made flesh; and by taking the flesh, restore it wholly. For to Him, as to a physician, man 'was delivered' to heal the bite of the serpent: as to life, to raise what was dead; as to light, to illumine the darkness; and, because He was the Logos, to renew the rational nature. Since then all things 'were delivered' to Him, and He is made man, straightway all things were set right and perfected. Earth receives blessing instead of a curse, Paradise was opened to the robber, Hades cowered, the tombs were opened and the dead raised, the gates of heaven were lifted up to await Him...."[76]

Saint Ambrose of Milan believes that "Esaias offered himself of his own accord."[77] Blessed Jerome explains the meaning of the following words: "Where we say 'sent,' the Hebrews say, 'one sent forth.' In Greek, the word is *apostolos*, in Hebrew *siloas*....Esaias is sent; he was an apostle. 'Here I am, send me [cf. Is. 6:8]!'"[78]

---

[74] *Pentecostarion*, Sunday of the Samaritan Woman, Theotokion of Orthros Canon, Ode Eight, Mode Four.

[75] January 5th, Orthros Canon, Ode Eight, Mode One.

[76] Saint Athanasius, "On Luke 10:22 (Mt. 11:27)," *Select Works and Letters*, Nicene, 2nd Ser., IV:87, 88.

[77] Saint Ambrose, *Seven Exegetical Works: Joseph*, FC, 65:193.

[78] Saint Jerome, "Hom. 87," *60-96 On The Psalms, Vol. 2*, FC, 57:216.

9. The Prophet's Conclusions.

"The prophet," sums up Saint Dionysios, "learns from his visions that God bears no likeness even to these first-subsisting beings. Moreover, he learns that He is the principle and cause of all being, and the immutable foundation of the abiding stability of things that are, from which the most exalted powers have both their being and their well-being."[79]

Saint Dionysios, continuing, speaks of the seraphim, "The sacred image of their six wings signifies an endless, marvellous upward thrust toward God by the first, middle, and lower conceptions. Seeing the limitless number of feet, the multitude of faces, those wings blocking out the contemplation of their faces above and their feet below, and the unending beat of the middle set of wings, the sacred theologian was uplifted to a conceptual knowledge of the things seen. There was shown to him the many facets of the most exalted of the intelligent minds....He witnessed that sacred caution of theirs which, in an unearthly fashion, they maintain regarding any brash, bold, and unpermitted search of the highest and the deepest things. He saw the harmony among them, as they acted to be like God amid a stirring that was ceaseless, exalted, and forever."[80]

"Moreover," says Saint Dionysios, "he also learned that divine and most glorious song of praise. For the angel who fashioned the vision gave, as far as possible, his own holy knowledge to the prophet. He also taught him that every participation in the divine light and purity, as far as this may be attained, is a purification, even to the most pure. Having its source in the Most High God, it proceeds from the most exalted causes in a superessential and hidden manner, traversing the whole of divine intelligences, and yet it shows itself more clearly, and imparts itself more fully to the most exalted powers around God."[81]

Esaias was thus commissioned as a prophet after this vision, according to the hymnographer and bishop, Saint Theophanes (d. 845): *To thy fearful lips, O Esaias, did the seraph bear the burning ember, carrying it with tongs; and he made thee a prophet of God, mystically consecrated.*[82] And, *Having seen and been taught of the divine seraphim, who unceasingly glorify the single dominion of the Divinity in three hypostases* [Is. 6:2, 3], *thou wast assured of*

---

[79] Saint Dionysius the Areopagite, *The Mystical Theology and the Celestial Hierarchies of Dionysius the Areopagite*, Ch. XV, The Shrine of Wisdom, p. 58.

[80] Idem [Pseudo-Dionysius], *The Complete Works: The Celestial Hierarchy*, Ch. Thirteen, Luibheid & Rorem, pp. 179, 180.

[81] Idem, *The Mystical Theology and the Celestial Hierarchies of Dionysius the Areopagite*, Ch. XV, The Shrine of Wisdom, pp. 57-59.

[82] May 9th, Prophet Esaias, Orthros Canon, Ode Six, Mode Four.

the grace of prophecy, O wondrous one; therefore, celebrating thy most sacred memory, we bring thee before Christ as a most powerful advocate.[83]

The Prophet's Prophetic Actions in Life

[Is. 8:1-4; 20:2, 3; 30:1, 8]

1. The Prophet Writes Down His Oracles [Is. 8:1, 2].

It was in the midst of the war between Syria and Ephraim (northern Israel), which was not quite at an end, when Esaias received from God the command to perform a prophetic action. **"And the Lord said to me, 'Take to thyself a volume of a great new book, and write in it with a man's pen concerning the making a rapid plunder of spoils; for it is near at hand. And make Me witnesses of faithful men, Urias, and Zacharias the son of Barachias** [Is. 8:1, 2]**.'"** The writing served as a public record. Urias was undoubtedly the priest during the time of King Achaz, who built an altar for that king [4 Kgs. (2 Kgs.) 16:10]. This Zacharias was not the prophet of the times after the captivity, but another one. These two men were reliable witnesses insofar that their testimony carried weight with the people.

Blessed Jerome interprets this passage as one speaking of Christ, writing: "This young Child, this mere Boy, Who is fed on butter and honey [Is. 7:14, 15], and Who is reared among curdled mountains [Ps. 67:16 LXX], quickly grows up to manhood, speedily spoils all [Is. 8:1] that is opposed to Him in you; and when the time is ripe, He plunders the spiritual Damascus and puts in chains the king of the spiritual Assyria."[84]

According to Saint Chrysostom, "The prophets not only had foretold what would come to pass but even had witnesses of what they were doing. Again it was Esaias who said, **'Make Me witnesses of faithful men, Urias, and Zacharias the son of Barachias** [Is. 8:2]**.'** He set his prophecy down in writing in a new book, so that after his prophecy was fulfilled, what he had written might bear witness against the Jews of what the inspired prophet predicted to them a long time before. This is why he did not simply write it in a book, but in a new book, a book capable of staying sturdy for a long time without easily falling apart—a book which could last until the events described in it would come to pass [cf. Is. 30:8]."[85]

2. The Prophetess and Son.

"And I went in to the prophetess; and she conceived, and bore a son. And the Lord said to me, 'Call his name, "Spoil quickly, plunder speedily." For before the child shall know how to call his father or his

---

[83] May 9th, Prophet Esaias, Vespers Sticheron, Mode Four.

[84] Saint Jerome, "Letter LXVI to Pammachius," Nicene, 2nd Ser., VI:138.

[85] Saint John Chrysostom, "Discourse V," *Discourses Against Judaizing Christians*, FC, 68:112, 113.

mother, one shall take the power of Damascus and the spoils of Samaria before the king of the Assyrians [Is. 8:3, 4].'"

A representative name is given to Esaias' son who is a type of Christ. Esaias' son was a symbol of the approaching plunder of Syria and the northern kingdom of ten tribes. Before his son was able to stammer out the name of father and mother, Tiglath-pileser III (732 B.C.) conquered Damascus, and took from the Samarian King Phakee (Pekah) [4 Kgs. (2 Kgs.) 15:29] the land beyond the Jordan, and on this side also. He then took the spoils to Assyria.

Saint Gregory of Nyssa says that in the reading of Scriptures, "We must pass to a spiritual and intelligent investigation of Scripture, so that considerations of the merely human element might be changed into something perceived by the mind once the more fleshly sense of the words has been shaken off like dust....If we stay only with the mere facts of the text, the historical narratives (of Scripture) do not offer us examples of a good life. For what benefit to virtuous living can we obtain from...Esaias having intercourse with the prophetess [Is. 8:3], unless something else lies beyond the mere letter?"[86]

The spiritual meaning is often interpreted as the prophetess being a type of the Virgin Theotokos and the son, "Spoil quickly, plunder speedily," as Christ plundering the noetic Amalek, or even the taking of the Gentiles according to Saint Ambrose, who says this was a prefigurement of the "calling forth of the Gentiles that He might gain a kingdom for the Father out of a holy and devout worship."[87]

Saint Irenaeos says that "the Infant Whom Symeon was holding in his hands, Jesus, born of Mary, was Christ Himself, the Son of God, the light of all, the glory of Israel itself, and the peace and refreshing of those who had fallen asleep. For He was already despoiling men, by removing their ignorance, conferring upon them His own knowledge, and scattering abroad those who recognized Him, as Esaias says, 'Call His name, "Quickly spoil, rapidly divide [cf. Is. 8:3]."' Now these are the works of Christ....It was He to Whom the Magi, when they had seen Him, adored and offered their gifts to Him....And prostrating themselves to the eternal King, they departed by another way, not returning by the way of the Assyrians. **'For before the child shall know how to call his father or his mother, one shall take the power of Damascus and the spoils of Samaria before the king of the Assyrians** [Is. 8:4].'

"This declares in a mysterious manner indeed, but emphatically, that the Lord did fight with a hidden hand against Amalek [Ex. 17:16]. For this cause, too, He suddenly removed those children belonging to the house of

[86] Saint Gregory of Nyssa, *Commentary on the Song of Songs*, pp. 36, 37.

[87] Saint Ambrose, *Seven Exegetical Works: The Prayer of Job and David*, FC, 65:408.

David whose happy lot it was to have been born at that time, that He might send them on before into His kingdom. Since He was Himself an infant, it was so arranged that human infants should be martyrs for the sake of Christ, Who was born in Bethlehem of Juda, in the city of David [Mt. 2:16-18]."[88]

Saint Athanasios, describing Christ's sovereignty, writes: "But what king that ever was, before he had strength to call father or mother, reigned and gained triumphs over his enemies [cf. Is. 8:4]?...Who, then, is there that was reigning and spoiling His enemies almost before His birth? Or what king of this sort has ever been in Israel and in Juda—let the Jews, who have searched out the matter, tell us—in Whom all the nations have placed their hopes and had peace, instead of being at enmity...on every side?"[89]

Saint Chrysostom, speaking of the significance of the appellation with relation to the issue of events, says: "This is customary in Scripture, to substitute the events that take place for names. Therefore, to say, 'They shall call Him "Emmanuel [Mt. 1:23]"' means nothing else than that they shall see God among men. For He has indeed always been among men, but never so manifestly. But if Jews are obstinate, we will ask them, when was the child called, 'Make speed to the spoil, hasten the prey [Is. 8:3]'? Why, they could not say. How is it then that the prophet said, 'Call his name Maher-shalal-hashhaz?' Because, when he was born, there was a taking and dividing of spoils, therefore the event that took place in his time is put as his name."[90]

3. The Prophet Goes About Naked, Signifying the Coming Captivity.

"Then the Lord spoke to Esaias the son of Amos, saying, 'Go and take the sackcloth off thy loins, and loose thy sandals from off thy feet, and do thus, going naked and barefoot [Is. 20:2].**'**

"And the Lord said, 'As My servant Esaias has walked naked and barefoot three years, there shall be three years for signs and wonders to the Egyptians and Ethiopians; for thus shall the king of the Assyrians lead the captivity of Egypt and the Ethiopians, young men and old, naked and barefoot, having the shame of Egypt exposed [Is. 20:2, 3].**'"**

Saint Ambrose of Milan comments, "Review with me the well-known case of Esaias, how he was naked before the people, not in mockery but gloriously, as one who uttered with his mouth the words of the Lord. Someone perhaps will say, 'Was it not disgraceful for a man to walk naked among the people, since he must meet both men and women? Must not his appearance have shocked the gaze of all, but especially that of women? Do we not ourselves generally abhor the sight of naked men? And are not men's genital

[88] Saint Irenaeus, *Against Heresies*, Bk. III, Ch. XV, Ante-Nicene, I:441, 442.
[89] Saint Athanasius, *On the Incarnation of the Word*, § 36, Nicene, 2nd Ser., IV:55.
[90] Saint Chrysostom, "Hom. V," *Matthew*, Nicene, 1st Ser., X:32.

parts covered with clothing that they may not offend the gaze of onlookers by their unsightliness?'

"I agree, but you must consider what this act represented and what was the reason for this outward show: It was that the young Jewish youths and maidens would be led away into exile and walk naked, **'As My servant Esaias hath walked,'** He says, **'naked and barefoot** [Is. 20:3]**.'** This might have been expressed in words, but God chose to enforce it by an example that the very sight might strike more terror, and what they shrank from in the body of the prophet they might utterly dread for themselves. Wherein lay the greater abhorrence: in the prophet's body or in the sins of the disbelievers who deserved by their deeds that calamity of captivity?

"Why was there no ground for reproach in the body of the prophet? He was intent not upon bodily but spiritual affairs, for in his ecstasy he did not say, 'I shall listen to what I say,' but 'I will hear what the Lord God will speak in me [Ps. 84:8].' He paid no attention to whether he was naked or clothed. The prophets looked not to themselves, nor what lay at their feet, but to heavenly things. And, so, too, Esaias did not notice his nakedness, but made himself the instrument of God's voice, that he might proclaim what God spoke within him.

"Why should the prophet feel shame when one thing is being enacted, but another prefigured? The Jews, who were abandoned by the Lord God because of their wickedness and were soon overwhelmed by their enemies, would have liked to align themselves with the Egyptians as a protection against the Assyrians, whereas they might have returned to the faith had they consulted their own good. The Lord in anger showed them that they indulged a vain hope,...for the very persons whose help the Jews trusted were themselves to be conquered. This is a matter of history. Figuratively, he who trusted the Egyptians was he who was given to wantonness and enslaved to pleasure."[91]

4. A Perennial Tablet for the Apostate and Disobedient Children.

"'Woe to the apostate children,' saith the Lord, 'Ye have framed counsel, not by Me, and covenants not by My Spirit, to add sins to sins...[Is. 30:1]**.**

"'Now then sit down and write these words on a tablet of boxwood and in a book; for these things shall be for many long days, and even for ever [Is. 30:8]**.'"**

Saint Ambrose of Milan informs us, "The boxwood tree, because of its light material, trains the child's hand when it is used for forming the outlines of the letters of the alphabet. Hence, Scripture says, 'Write upon a box [cf. Is. 30:8],' in order that you may be admonished by the wood itself (which is an

---

[91] Saint Ambrose, "Letter 28 to Sabinus, Bishop (ca. 395)," *Letters*, FC, 26:146-149.

evergreen and is never devoid of foliage) never to be deprived of the support of your hope, but rather that the hope of salvation may be generated by faith."[92]

The Apostasy of Israel

[Is. 1, 3, 10, 22, 25, 26; 22:4; 30:9, 10; 48:4; 59:20; 65:2]

1. The People of the Synagogue [Is. 1; 30:9, 10].

A. "Hear, O heaven, and hearken, O earth: for the Lord has spoken, saying, 'I have begotten and reared up sons, but they have set Me at nought [Is. 1:2]**.'"**

Saint Athanasios the Great comments, "Of course, since they were not sons by nature, therefore, when they altered, the Spirit was taken away and they were disinherited; and, again, on their repentance, that same God Who thus at the beginning gave them grace, will receive them, and give light, and call them sons again."[93]

B. They Know Not God:

"The ox knows his owner, and the ass his master's crib: but Israel does not know Me, and the people do not perceive Me (οὐ συνῆκεν) [Is. 1:3]**."** Saint Justin, philosopher and martyr (ca. 100- ca. 165) tells us that even now in his own time "all the Jews teach that the nameless God spoke to Moses. The Spirit of prophecy accuses them by Esaias the prophet [Is. 1:3]. Jesus Christ also, because the Jews knew not what the Father was and what the Son, in like manner accused them; He Himself said, 'No one doth fully know (ἐπιγινώσκει) the Son, except the Father; nor doth anyone fully know the Father, except the Son, and he to whomsoever the Son is willing to reveal Him [Mt. 11:27].' And He is called angel and apostle; for He declares whatever we ought to know, and is sent forth to declare whatever is revealed."

Continuing he says that "the Angel of the Lord that spoke to Moses, in a flame of fire out of the bush, was the Son of God...[Ex. 3:2]. But so much is written for the sake of proving that Jesus Christ is the Son of God...being of old the Logos, and appearing sometimes in the form of fire, and sometimes in the likeness of angels....Yet they maintain that He Who appeared and spoke was the Father and Creator of the universe. Whence also the Spirit of prophecy rebukes them, and says, **'Israel does not know Me, and the people do not perceive Me** [Is. 1:3]**.'**"[94] Saint Justin also classifies the prophet's words [Is. 1:3] among those spoken from the person of the Father.[95]

---

[92] Idem, *Hexaëmeron*, Bk. Three, Ch. 13, FC, 42:109.

[93] Saint Athanasius, "Discourse I," *Four Discourses Against the Arians*, Nicene, 2nd Ser., IV:328.

[94] Saint Justin Martyr, *The First Apology of Justin*, Ch. LXIII, Ante-Nicene, I:184.

[95] Idem, Ch. XXXVII, Ante-Nicene, I:175.

C. They Desire to Hear Errors:

"For this people is disobedient, false children, who would not hear the law of God, who say to the prophets, 'Report not to us,' and to them that see visions, 'Speak them not to us, but speak and report to us error otherwise than should be (ἑτέραν πλάνησιν)[Is. 30:9, 10]**.'"**

Saint Kyril of Jerusalem remarks that "after Christ's crucifixion and burial, when the soldiers came into the city to the chief priests and Pharisees, and told them all that had come to pass, they said to them, 'Say, "His disciples came by night and stole Him while we were sleeping [Mt. 28:13]."' Well, therefore, did Esaias foretell this also, as in their persons, 'But tell us, and relate to us another deceit [cf. Is. 30:10].'...And for a gift of money they persuade the soldiers, who surrendered truth for silver."[96]

D. Their Ways Are as Those of Sodom and Gomorrah [Is. 1:10]**.**

Addressing the rulers of Israel, it is written: **"Hear the word of the Lord, ye rulers of Sodom; attend to the law of God, thou people of Gomorrah** [Is. 1:10]**."** He is not addressing those in Sodom and Gomorrah. Saint Irenaeos remarks that "Esaias, when preaching in Judea, and reasoning with Israel, terms them **'rulers of Sodom'** and **'people of Gomorrah** [Is. 1:10]**.'** He intimates that they were like the Sodomites in wickedness, and that the same description of sins was rife among them, calling them by the same name, because of the similarity of their conduct."[97]

Nonetheless, though they behave as those people of ill repute, some were delivered. **"And if the Lord of Sabaoth had not left us a seed, we should have been as Sodom, and we should have been made like to Gomorrah** [Is. 1:9]**."** Saint Chrysostom remarks, "God had used much kindness to them, and had saved them by faith. And this happened also in the case of the visible captivity, the majority having been taken away captive and perished, and some few only being saved."[98]

E. A Watered Tradition:

"Your silver is worthless, thy wine merchants mix the wine with water [Is. 1:22]**."**

Saint Irenaeos explains that "this shows that the elders were in the habit of mingling a watered tradition with the simple command of God; that is, they set up a spurious law, and one contrary to the true law."[99]

Saint Chrysostom agrees that this bespeaks those who corrupt the word of God. "For this is 'to corrupt,' when one adulterates the wine; when one sells

---

[96] Saint Cyril of Jerusalem, "Lecture XIV," *Catechetical Lectures*, Nicene, 2nd Ser., VII:97.

[97] Saint Irenaeus, *Against Heresies*, Bk. IV, Ch. XLI, Ante-Nicene, I:525.

[98] Saint Chrysostom, "Hom. XVI," *Romans,* Nicene, 1st Ser., XI:470.

[99] Ibid., Bk. IV, Ch. XII, Nicene, 1st Ser., XI:475.

for money what he ought to give freely. For he seems to me to be here taunting them in respect to money."[100]

F. The Synagogue Shall be Purged:

"And I will bring My hand upon thee, and purge thee completely, and I will destroy the rebellious, and will take away from thee all transgressors [Is. 1:25].

"And I will establish thy judges as before, and thy counselors as at the beginning: and afterward thou shalt be called the city of righteousness, the faithful mother-city Sion [Is. 1:26]."

Saint Kyril of Alexandria explains this promise, saying, "God, by the voice of Esaias, says these words [Is. 1:25, 26] to the mother of the Jews, that is, the Synagogue....And by 'judges and the counselors,' are signified the preachers of the new covenant [Is. 1:26]."[101] Continuing, he says, "The chiefs...of the Synagogue of the Jews were cast out for resisting the Lord's will by rendering the vineyard which had been entrusted to them unfruitful. For God said, 'Many shepherds have destroyed My vineyard, they have defiled My portion, they have made My desirable portion a trackless wilderness; it is made a complete ruin [Jer. 12:10, 11].'...And why have they burned My vineyard [cf. Is. 3:14]? Therefore, as those who had rendered the land sterile, being evil, they perished evilly. For it was just, most just, that as being slothful, and murderers of the Lord, they should be the prey of extreme miseries....'And He will come and destroy these vinedressers, and will give the vineyard to others [Lk. 20:16].' And who are they? I answer, the company of the holy apostles, the preachers of the evangelic commandments, the ministers of the new covenant, who were the teachers of a spiritual service, and knew how to instruct men correctly and blamelessly, and to lead them most excellently unto every thing whatsoever that is well pleasing to God."[102]

2. The Word of the Valley of Sion [Is. 22].

Blessed Jerome says, "Let us call upon the testimony of Esaias when Sion had fallen into sin, in which after many visions, the prophet mentions one against Idumea [Is. 21:11], one against Moab [Is. 15], one against Edom and the sons of Ammon, and lastly, 'A vision of the valley of Sion [cf. Is. 22:1],' because she had descended from sublime faith and fell recklessly from the mountain into the valley."[103]

3. The Prophet's Genuine Grief for His People [Is. 22:4].

Saint Chrysostom says the prophet was continually saying, **"Let me alone, I will weep bitterly; labor not to comfort me for the breach of the**

[100] Saint Chrysostom, "Hom. V," *Second Corinthians*, Nicene, 1st Ser., XII:302.

[101] Saint Cyril of Alexandria, "Hom. 134," *Commentary*, pp. 533, 534.

[102] Ibid., p. 533

[103] Saint Jerome, "Hom. 45," *1-59 On The Psalms, Vol. 1*, FC, 48:339.

daughter of my people [Is. 22:4]." "Oftentimes," observes the saint, "sadness is the bearer of consolation."[104]

4. "I know that thou art stubborn, and thy neck is an iron sinew, and thy forehead brazen [Is. 48:4]."

Saint Chrysostom explains that "iron sinew means the Jewish people are unbending. Their forehead is bronze, that is, incapable of blushing."[105]

5. Saint Chrysostom comments upon this: "**'To Israel He says, "The whole day I stretched forth My hands to a disobedient and contradicting people** [Is. 65:2; Rom. 10:21]."' By 'day' he means the whole period of the former dispensation. But the stretching out of the hands means calling and drawing them to Him, and inviting them. Then to show that the fault was all their own, He says, **'to a disobedient and contradicting people** [Is. 65:2].' You see what a great charge this is against them! For they did not obey Him even when He invited them, but they contradicted Him—and that when they saw Him doing so, not once or twice or thrice, but the whole period."[106]

"This is the people that provokes Me continually in My presence; they offer sacrifices in gardens, and burn incense on bricks to devils that exist not. They lie down to sleep in the tombs and in the caves for the sake of dreams, even they that eat swine's flesh and the broth of their sacrifices. All their vessels are defiled [Is. 65:3, 4].

"Behold, I will not be silent until I have recompensed into their bosom, their sins and the sins of their fathers, who have burnt incense on the mountains, and reproached Me on the hills [Is. 65:6, 7]."

6. Deliverance for Sinners: "And the Deliverer shall come for Sion's sake, and shall turn away ungodliness from Jacob [Is. 59:20]."

Saint Kyril of Alexandria says, "Christ arose to deliver the inhabitants of the earth from their sins, and to seek them that were lost, and to save them that had perished. For this is His office...."[107]

The Waywardness of the People

[Is. 3:16-26; 5:1-7; 42:18, 19; 58:1-9]

1. God Planted a Vineyard.

"Now I will sing to My beloved a song of My beloved concerning My vineyard [Is. 5:1]." "Who is this well-beloved but the only-begotten Son?" says Saint Athanasios.[108] Saint Ambrose of Milan adds, "For only in the

---

[104] Saint Chrysostom, "Hom. XVIII," *Homilies on the Statues,* Nicene, 1st Ser., IX:461, 462.

[105] Idem, "Discourse V," *Against Judaizing Christians*, FC, 68:111, 112.

[106] Idem, "Hom. XVIII," *Romans*, Nicene, 1st Ser., XI:479, 480.

[107] Saint Cyril of Alexandria, "Hom. 127," *Commentary*, p. 507.

[108] Saint Athanasius, "Discourse IV," *Four Discourses Against the Arians*, Nicene, 2nd

(continued...)

only-begotten Son of God the Church flourishes, keeping the unique Word of God, in Whom there is the fullness of power and wisdom, and from Whose abundance there sprouted a crop of faith. This is the Word the saints follow."[109]

The Jews, being on the point of complete ruin and ready to be given over to extreme punishment lest any slander God's providence, God speaks through the prophet: **"And now, ye dwellers in Jerusalem, and every man of Juda, judge between Me and My vineyard** [Is. 5:2]**....What shall I do any more to My vineyard, that I have not done to it? Whereas I expected it to bring forth grapes, but it has brought forth thorns** [Is. 5:4]**."**

"Let no one," warns Saint Chrysostom, "accuse God; for unbelief comes not of Him that calls, but of those who start away from Him. But some man will say, 'He ought to bring men in, even against their will.' Away with this. He does not use violence, nor compel. For who that bids to honors, and crowns, and banquets, and festivals, drags people, unwilling and bound? No one. For this is the part of one inflicting an insult. Unto Gehenna He sends men against their will, but unto the kingdom He calls willing minds. To the fire He brings men bound and bewailing themselves; to the endless state of blessings not so. Else it is a reproach to the very blessings themselves, if their nature be not such as that men should run to them of their own accord and with many thanks. 'Whence it is then,' say you, 'that all men do not choose them?' From their own infirmity. 'And for what purpose does He not cut off their infirmity?' And how tell me—in what way ought He to cut it off? Has He not made a world that teaches His loving-kindness and His power?...Has He not also sent prophets? Has He not both called and honored us? Has He not wrought signs and wonders? Has He not given a law both written and natural? Has He not sent His Son? Has He not commissioned apostles? Has He not threatened Gehenna? Has He not promised the kingdom? Does He not every day make His sun to rise [cf. Is. 5:4]?"[110]

Saint Aphrahat writes: "The Son of Man came to free them (the children of Israel) and gather them together, but they did not receive Him. For He came to obtain fruit from them, and they did not give it to Him. For their vines were 'of the vine of Sodom and of the stock of Gomorrah,' a vineyard [cf. Deut. 32:32] in which thorns grew, and which 'bore wild grapes [Is. 5:2].' Their vine was bitter, and their fruit sour. The thorns could not be softened, nor could the bitterness change to the nature of wine, nor could the sour fruit change to a sweet nature. For Esaias speaks of how God planted His vineyard

---

[108](...continued)
Ser., IV:442.

[109] Saint Ambrose, *Seven Exegetical Works: The Patriarchs*, FC, 65:272.

[110] Saint Chrysostom, "Hom. II," *First Corinthians*, Nicene, 1st Ser., XII:8.

with vine scions, but they became strange vines. 'I surrounded it with a fence' of heavenly watchers 'and I built its tower'—the holy temple. 'And I dug out its winepress'—the baptism of the priests. 'And I brought down rain upon it'—the words of My prophets. 'And I pruned it and trimmed it from the works of the Amorites. I looked that it should produce grapes of righteousness, and it produced wild grapes of iniquity and sins. I looked for judgment and, behold, oppression; and I looked for righteousness, and there was a cry. **"And I will forsake My vineyard; and it shall not be pruned, nor dug, and thorns shall come up upon it as on barren land; and I will command the clouds to rain no rain upon it** [Is. 5:6]**."'** For the heavenly watchers departed from the fence of the vineyard; and the mighty tower on which they relied was torn down. The winepress, the cleansing away of their offenses, was overthrown."[111]

Saint Irenaeos explains that "they shall no longer have the dew of the Holy Spirit from God....This Spirit He did confer upon the Church, sending throughout all the world the Comforter from heaven, from whence also the Lord tells us that the devil, as lightning, was cast down [Is. 14:12]. We, therefore, have need of the dew of God, that we be not consumed by fire, nor be rendered unfruitful, and that where we have an accuser there we may have also a Paraclete [1 Jn. 2:1]."[112]

Saint Ambrose of Milan asserts that "the dew of moistening faith dried up in the breasts of the Jews, and that divine Fountain [Jer. 2:13] turned away its course to the hearts of the Gentiles. Thus it has come to pass that now the whole world is moistened with the dew of faith, but the Jews have lost their prophets and counselors. Nor is it strange that they should suffer the drought of unbelief, whom the Lord deprived of the fertilizing of the shower of prophecy, saying, 'I will command My clouds that they rain not upon that vineyard [cf. Is. 5:6].'"[113]

2. The Daughters of Sion [Is. 3:16-26].

The prophet rebukes women in particular, though, as Saint Chrysostom notes, "The laws which God appoints are in every case in common to men and women....For woman and man He knows as one living creature, and nowhere distinguishes their kind. Listen to Esaias, in many words inveighing against them, and deriding their habit, their aspect, their gait, their trailing garments, the sporting with their feet...[Is. 3:16-26]."[114]

Saint Paulinus of Nola (353/354-431) also warns a Christian maiden, saying, "A woman adorning herself with such a range of disguises will gain no credence when she claims she is chaste. Esaias threatens [Is. 3:24] that women

---

[111] Saint Aphrahat, "Demonstration V.—Of Wars," § 22, Nicene, 2nd Ser., XIII:360.
[112] Saint Irenaeus, *Against Heresies*, Bk. III, Ch. VXII, Ante-Nicene, I:445.
[113] Saint Ambrose, *Of the Holy Spirit*, Bk. I, Nicene, 2nd Ser., X:94.
[114] Saint Chrysostom, "Hom. LXXXIX," *Matthew*, Nicene, 1st Ser., X:528.

now clad in ensembles of white silk and purple garments, who wear long dresses bright with purple and rustling with gold, with folds flowing down to the ankles, are to be fastened with a rope tight-drawn; thus girt with ropes, they will wear sackcloth forever, and will turn huge grindstones in their prison of a mill. And those who pile their heads high with hair long-grown will have them uncovered in shameful baldness. Avoid the adornment of such endowments,...for these are the delights of an empty mind. Do not wander abroad with perfumed clothes and hair, seeking recognition from men's nostrils wherever you pass. Do not sit with your hair structured and castellated, with layers and ropes of interwoven locks. Do not through your luster be a cause of unhappy vexation to many, nor an evil cause of baneful attraction. You must not seek with foul purpose to delight even your own husband by thus adding inches to your person."[115]

3. A Blind and Deaf People.

Abbot Chaeremon, in a conference with Saint John Cassian, says, "The Lord, by the prophet, rebukes the unnatural but freely chosen blindness of the Jews, which they by their obstinacy brought upon themselves, saying, **'Hear, ye deaf, and look up, ye blind, to see. And who is blind, but My servants? And deaf, but they that rule over them? Yea, the servants of God have been made blind** [Is. 42:18, 19]**.'** And that no one might ascribe this blindness of theirs to nature instead of to their own will, elsewhere He says, **'I have brought forth the blind people; for their eyes are alike blind, and they that have ears are deaf** [Is. 43:8]'; and again, 'having eyes, but ye see not; and ears, but ye hear not [cf. Jer. 5:21].'"[116]

4. Dumb and Insatiable Dogs.

"See how they are all blinded. They have not known. They are dumb dogs that shall not be able to bark, dreaming of rest, loving to slumber. Yea, they are insatiable dogs, that know not what it is to be filled; and they are wicked, having no understanding. All have followed their own ways, each according to his own will [Is. 56:10, 11]**."**

Saint Chrysostom says the fact that "Esaias called the Jews dogs [Is. 56:10, 11] and Jeremias called them mare-mad horses [Jer. 5:8], this was not because they suddenly changed their natures with those beasts, but because they were pursuing the lustful habits of those animals."[117] And, "Scriptures in many places applies the names of brutes and of wild beasts to those gifted with

---

[115] Saint Paulinus, "Poem 25," *The Poems of Saint Paulinus of Nola*, ACW, 40:247, 248.

[116] Saint John Cassian, "The Third Conference of Abbot Chaeremon," Ch. XII, *Cassian's Conferences*, Nicene, 2nd Ser., XI:428, 429.

[117] Saint John Chrysostom, "Discourse IV," *Against Judaizing Christians*, FC, 68:88.

reason: sometimes it calls them dogs on account of their shameful and headstrong behavior—**'they are dumb dogs that will not bark** [Is. 56:10].'"[118]

5. The Sins of God's People and the Remedy [Is. 58:1-3].

A. "Cry aloud, and spare not; lift up thy voice as with a trumpet, and declare to My people their sins, and to the house of Jacob their iniquities [Is. 58:1].

"They seek Me day by day, and desire to know My ways, as a people that had done righteousness and had not forsaken the judgment of their God. They now ask of Me righteous judgment, and desire to draw nigh to God, saying, 'Why have we fasted, and Thou regardest not? Why have we afflicted our souls, and Thou didst not know it [Is. 58:2, 3]?'"

Saint Chrysostom says, "The Jews fasted and profited nothing, nay, they departed with blame."[119] Saint John Cassian, in a conference with Abbot Theonas, counsels: "You see then that fasting is certainly not considered by the Lord as a thing that is good in its own nature, because it becomes good and well pleasing to God not by itself, but by other works; and again from the surrounding circumstances it may be regarded as not merely vain but actually hateful, as the Lord says, 'When they fast I will not hear their prayers [cf. Is. 58:3-9].'"[120]

B. "'If ye fast for quarrels and strifes, and smite the lowly with your fists, for what purpose do ye fast to Me as ye do this day, so that your voice may be heard in crying [Is. 58:4]?...

"'I have not chosen such a fast,' saith the Lord, 'but do thou loose every burden of iniquity, do thou untie the knots of hard bargains, set the bruised free, and cancel every unjust account [Is. 58:6].

"'Break thy bread to the hungry, and lead the unsheltered poor to thy house: if thou seest one naked, clothe him, and thou shalt not disregard the relations of thine own seed [Is. 58:7].'"

Saint Cyprian powerfully exhorts the manifestation of faith by works: "Finally, beloved brethren, the divine admonition in the Scriptures, old as well as new, has never failed, has never been silent in urging God's people always and everywhere to works of mercy. And in the strain and exhortation of the Holy Spirit, everyone who is instructed into the hope of the heavenly kingdom is commanded to give alms. And when He had commanded the Jews' sins to be charged upon them—and with the full force of His indignation He had set forth their iniquities—and had said that not even though they should use supplications, and prayers, and fasts, would they be able to make expiation for

[118] Idem, "Hom. 12," *Homilies on Genesis*, FC, 74:162.

[119] Saint Chrysostom, "Hom. III," *Homilies on the Statues,* Nicene, 1st Ser., IX:358.

[120] Saint John Cassian, "First Conference of Abbot Theonas," Ch. XIV, *Cassian's Conferences*, Nicene, 2nd Ser., XI:509.

their sins, nor if they were clothed in sackcloth and ashes would they be able to soften God's anger, yet in the last part it is shown that God can be appeased by almsgiving alone [Is. 58:1-9]."[121]

C. "Then shalt thou cry, and God shall hearken to thee; while thou art yet speaking He will say, 'Behold, I am here.' If thou remove from thee the band, and the stretching forth of the hands, and the murmuring speech [Is. 58:9]**."**

"Then as our sins separate us from Him," admonishes Saint Chrysostom, "so does our righteousness draw us nigh unto Him. For **'while thou art yet speaking,'** it is said, 'I will say, **"Behold, I am here** [Is. 58:9]**."'**...God stands continually waiting, if any of His servants should perchance call Him; and never, when we have called as we ought, has He refused to hear. Therefore He says, **'While thou art yet speaking** [Is. 58:9], I do not wait for thee to finish, and I straightway hearken.'"[122]

Saint Paulinus of Nola says, "Our Lord is everywhere close to us, and says, 'In every place, even as you address Me, I am there [cf. Is. 58:9].'"[123]

Sacrifices and Temple Rituals

On account of the Jewish fixation and dependency on the physical temple in Jerusalem, we read in the *Epistle of Barnabas*: "I will tell you concerning the temple, how the wretched Jews, wandering in error, trusted not in God Himself but in the temple as being the house of God. For almost after the manner of the Gentiles they worshipped Him in the temple. But learn how the Lord speaks, when abolishing it: 'Who hath meted out the heaven with a span, and all the earth in a handful? Have not I [cf. Is. 40:12]?' **'Thus saith the Lord, "Heaven is My throne, and the earth is My footstool." What kind of house will ye build Me? And of what kind is to be the place of My rest** [Is. 66:1]**?'** You perceive that their hope is vain."[124]

1. The Ancient Sacrifices [Is. 1:11-18; 66:3]**.**

A. "But the transgressor that sacrifices a calf to Me, is as he that kills a dog; and he that offers fine flour, as one that offers swine's blood; he that gives frankincense for a memorial, is as a blasphemer [Is. 66:3]**."**

Saint Irenaeos tells us, "Sacrifices, therefore, do not sanctify the man, for God stands in no need of sacrifice; but it is the conscience of the offerer that

[121] Saint Cyprian, "Treatise VIII," *The Treatises of Cyprian*, Ante-Nicene, V:476, 477.
[122] Saint Chrysostom, "Hom. LIV," *Matthew*, Nicene, 1st Ser., X:227.
[123] Saint Paulinus, "Letter 17," *Letters of Saint Paulinus of Nola, Vol. 1*, ACW, 35:166.
[124] *The Epistle of Barnabas*, Ch. XVI, Ante-Nicene, I:147.

sanctifies the sacrifice when it is pure, and thus moves God to accept the offering as from a friend."[125]

B. Who Has Required These Sacrifices?

The ancient sacrifice should be made void and a new one ought to be celebrated. Saint Irenaeos asserts that "God stands in need of nothing; but He exhorts and advises them to those things by which man is justified and draws nigh to God. This same declaration does Esaias make: **'"Of what value to Me is the abundance of your sacrifices?" saith the Lord: "I am full of whole-burnt-offerings of rams; and I delight not in the fat of lambs, and the blood of bulls and goats. Neither shall ye come with these to appear before Me; for who has required these things at your hands? Ye shall no more tread My court** [Is. 1:11, 12]."' And when He had repudiated holocausts, and sacrifices, and oblations, and likewise the new moons, and the sabbaths, and the festivals, and all the rest of the services accompanying these, He continues, exhorting them to what pertains to salvation: **'"Wash you, be clean; remove your iniquities from your souls before Mine eyes; learn to do well; diligently seek judgment, deliver him that is suffering wrong, plead for the orphan, and obtain justice for the widow. And come, let us reason together," saith the Lord** [Is. 1:16-18].'"[126]

Saint Athanasios declares: "God does not need anything; and since nothing is unclean to Him, He is full in regard to them, as He testifies, by Esaias, saying, **'I am full** [Is. 1:11].'"[127] He gives this opinion: "Now it appears to me,...that the remarks I presume to make may not be far from the truth—that not at first were the commandment and the law concerning sacrifices, neither did the mind of God, Who gave the law, regard whole burnt-offerings, but those things which were pointed out and prefigured by them. For the law contained a shadow of good things to come. And those things were appointed until the time of reformation [cf. Heb. 10:1]."[128]

Saint Chrysostom believes that "if He made sacrifice a necessity, He would also have subjected the Jews to this way of life and all the patriarchs who flourished before the Jews of Esaias' day....This is what God did. He saw the Jews choking with their mad yearning for sacrifices. He saw that they were ready to go over to idols if they were deprived of sacrifices. Indeed, I should say that He saw that they already had done so. So He let them have their sacrifices....But even if He permitted sacrifices, this permission was not to last

[125] Saint Irenaeus, *Against Heresies*, Bk. IV, Ch. XVIII, Ante-Nicene, I:485.
[126] Ibid., Bk. IV, Ch. XVI, Ante-Nicene, I:482, 483.
[127] Saint Athanasius, "Letter XIX," Nicene, 2nd Ser., IV:545.
[128] Ibid., Nicene, 2nd Ser., IV:546.

forever; in the wisdom of His ways, He took the sacrifices away from them again."[129]

Now Moses was speaking of Jerusalem when he enjoined the people not to sacrifice the passover in any other city [Deut. 16:5, 6]. "Do you see how God confined the festival to one city, and later destroyed the city so that, even if it were against their wills, He might lead them away from that way of life?" inquires Saint Chrysostom. "Surely, it is clear to everybody that God foresaw what would come to pass. Why then, did He bring them together to that land from all over the world if He foresaw that their city would be destroyed? Is it not very obvious that He did this because He wished to bring their ritual to an end? God did bring the ritual to an end."[130]

The Prophet-King David uttered, "If Thou hadst desired sacrifice, I had given it [Ps. 50:16]." Saint Chrysostom says, "By this, also, David makes it plain that God does not desire it. Therefore, sacrifices are not God's will; much rather, He desires the abolition of sacrifices. So they sacrifice contrary to His will. To do God's will and to give up ourselves, this is the will of God, by which we will be sanctified. Sacrifices do not make men clean, but the will of God. Therefore to offer sacrifice is not the will of God. And why dost thou wonder that it is not the will of God, now, when it was not His will even from the beginning? For **'who'**, saith He, **'has required these things at your hands** [Is. 1:12]**?'**"[131]

Saint Kyril of Alexandria says, "Understand, therefore, that he says He hated their festivals, and that as well their praises, as their sacrifices were rejected by Him."[132] **"Though you bring fine flour, it is vain. Incense is an abomination to Me. I cannot bear your new moons, and your sabbaths, and the great day. Your fasting, and rest from work, your new moons also, and your feasts My soul hates. Ye have become loathsome to Me. I will no more pardon your sins** [Is. 1:14]**."**

When they stretched forth their hands, we read, **"I will turn Mine eyes away from you** [Is. 1:15]**,"** because their hands were bloodstained. "These words," Saint Chrysostom tells us, "are not an accusation made against the sacrifices. They are an indictment of the sinfulness of those who offered them. God rejected their sacrifices because they offered them with **'hands full of blood** [Is. 1:15]**.'**"[133]

---

[129] Saint John Chrysostom, "Discourse IV," *Against Judaizing Christians*, FC, 68:89, 90.

[130] Ibid., FC, 68:57, 58.

[131] Idem, "Hom. XVIII," *Hebrews*, Nicene, 1st Ser., XIV:451

[132] Saint Cyril of Alexandria, "Hom. 96," *Commentary*, p. 388.

[133] Saint John Chrysostom, "Discourse VII," *Against Judaizing Christians*, FC, (continued...)

2. A Law Proceeds From the Christ [Is. 51:4].

Saint Justin asserts that the law is abrogated, but the New Testament was promised and given by God. He tells his opponent, Trypho the Jew, "We Christians do not think that there is one God for us, another for you, but that He alone is God Who led your fathers out from Egypt with a strong hand and a high arm....But now...I have read that there shall be a final law, and a covenant, the chiefest of all, which is now incumbent on all men to observe, as many as are seeking after the inheritance of God. For the law promulgated on Horeb is now old, and belongs to yourselves alone; but this is for all universally.

"Now law placed against law has abrogated that which is before it, and a covenant which comes after in like manner has put an end to the previous one; and an eternal and final law—namely, Christ—has been given to us, and the covenant is trustworthy, after which there shall be neither law, nor commandment, nor ordinance. Have you not read that which Esaias says, **'Hearken to Me: for a law shall proceed from Me...**[Is. 51:4]'?"[134]

The Jews After the Coming of Christ
[Is. 5:20; 6:9, 10; 8:13, 14; 9:5, 10; 28:16;
29:13, 18; 45:15, 16; 52:5; 65:13, 14]

1. The Jews Call What is Good Evil [Is. 5:20].

The Jews did not recognize Him, and treated Him shamefully, according to Saint Justin. "And that it was foreknown that infamous things would be uttered against those who confessed Christ, and that those who slandered Christ and said that it was well to preserve the ancient customs would be miserable, hear what was briefly said by Esaias: **'Woe to them that call evil good, and good evil, who make darkness light, and light darkness, who make bitter sweet, and sweet bitter** [Is. 5:20]!'"[135]

Saint Paulinus of Nola believes there is a peculiarity known as "wicked humility." He characterizes it, as such: "That humility, that is, wicked humility, is condemned which is complaisant to men not from faith but from mental cowardice, which cares more for popularity with men than for salvation. It is the servant of lies, the enemy of truth, a stranger to freedom, a subject of injustice; it mixes water with wine, weakening the wine of truth with the water of flattery [Is. 1:22]. I think it is humility of this kind which is specifically attacked and condemned by these words of Scripture: 'Woe to you

---

[133](...continued)
68:189.

[134] Saint Justin Martyr, *Dialogue with Trypho*, Ch. XI, Ante-Nicene, I:200.

[135] Ibid., *The First Apology*, Ch. XLIX, Ante-Nicene, I:179.

that call evil good, that proclaim the sweet for those who are bitter, and righteousness for the wicked [cf. Is. 5:20, 23].'"[136]

Saint Kyril of Alexandria charges the scribes and Pharisees with the prophet's words [Is. 5:20]. "Such was the character of the Israelites, and especially of those whose lot it was to be their chiefs, the scribes, namely, and Pharisees."[137]

2. The Jews Shall Neither Understand Nor Perceive.

"Ye shall hear indeed, but ye shall not understand; and ye shall see indeed, but ye shall not perceive [Is. 6:9]**."**

"See," says Saint Chrysostom, "how the prophet accuses them with the same accuracy as Christ [Mt. 13:14, 15]. For neither did he say, 'Ye see not,' but 'Ye shall see and not perceive'; nor again, 'Ye shall not hear,' but 'Ye shall hear and not understand.' So that they first inflicted the loss on themselves, by stopping their ears, by closing their eyes, by making their heart fat. For they not only failed to hear but also 'heard heavily,' and they did this, He says, 'Lest ever...they should be converted; and I shall heal them [cf. Mt. 13:15].'"[138]

3. The Jews' Ears are Dull of Hearing and They Have Closed Their Eyes.

"For the heart of this people has become gross, and their ears are dull of hearing, and their eyes have they closed; lest they should see with their eyes, and hear with their ears, and understand with their heart, and be converted, and I should heal them [Is. 6:10]**."**

"For how were they not," asks Saint Kyril of Alexandria, "heavy and without understanding, and of a mind past helping, who when they might have perceived that He was the Christ by His teaching being superior to the law, and by the wonderful works that He wrought, were obdurate, and regarded only their own preconceived idea of what was right—or rather they were concerned only with that which brought them down to the pit of destruction?"[139]

4. The Jews Have Stumbled at the Stumbling Stone.

A. "Sanctify ye the Lord Himself; and He shall be thy fear. And if thou shalt trust in Him, He shall be to thee for a sanctuary; and ye shall not come against Him as against a stumbling stone, neither as against the falling of a rock [Is. 8:13, 14]**."**

---

[136] Saint Paulinus, "Letter 12," *Letters of Saint Paulinus of Nola, Vol. 1*, ACW, 35:112.

[137] Saint Cyril of Alexandria, "Hom. 39," *Commentary*, p. 165.

[138] Saint Chrysostom, "Hom. XLV," *Matthew*, Nicene, 1st Ser., X:285.

[139] Saint Cyril of Alexandria, "Hom. 101," *Commentary*, p. 408.

"The phrase," advises Saint Kyril of Alexandria, "that God is hallowed by us, is a confession of our regarding Him as Holy of Holies, and does not bestow on Him any additional holiness, thou mayest understand hence."[140]

Saint Kosmas the Melodist chants: *Thou hast been set up in Sion as a stumbling stone and rock of offense for the disobedient* [Is. 8:14; Lk. 2:34; Rom. 9:33], *and the unbroken salvation of the faithful.*[141]

B. Christ, the Cornerstone:

"Behold, I lay for the foundations of Sion a costly stone, a choice, a cornerstone, a precious stone, for its foundations; and he that believes on Him shall by no means be ashamed [Is. 28:16]**."**

Blessed Jerome chides the Jews: "O truly unhappy Jews, O truly wretched and pitiable Jews, who failed to realize that the Stone, which Esaias promised would be laid in the foundations of Sion [Is. 28:16] and would unite both peoples, was the Lord Savior, the Son of God! That is the Stone you rejected when you were building the congregation of the Lord and were the custodians of the sacred rites of His temple. Rejected by you, He has become the Cornerstone; and the first Church, gathered from among the Jews and the believers from the nations, He has united into one flock and into one divine mystery."[142]

Saint Kyril of Alexandria indicates that "those then who trusted in Him were not ashamed, but those who were unbelieving and ignorant, and unable to perceive the mystery regarding Him, fell, and were broken in pieces." Moreover, "The Savior, although He was a chosen stone, He was rejected by those whose duty it was to build up the Synagogue of the Jews in everything that was edifying; and yet He became the head of the corner. Now the sacred Scripture compares to a corner the gathering together, or joining of the two people, Israel I mean, and the nations, in sameness of sentiment and faith. 'For the Savior has built the two people into one new man, by making peace and reconciling the two in one body unto the Father [cf. Eph. 2:15].' And the so doing resembles a corner, which unites two walls, and, so to speak, binds them together. And this very corner, or gathering together of the two people into one and the same, the blessed David wondered at and said, 'The stone which the builders rejected has become the head of the corner. This—that is, the corner—has been done of the Lord, and is marvellous in our eyes [cf. Ps. 117:22].' For Christ, as I said, has girded together the two people in the bonds of love, and in sameness as well of sentiment as of faith.

---

[140] Ibid., "Hom. 72," *Commentary*, pp. 304, 305.

[141] February 2nd, Meeting of Our Lord in the Temple, extract of Orthros Canon, Ode Six, Mode Three.

[142] Saint Jerome, "Hom. 94," *60-96 On The Psalms, Vol. 2*, FC, 57:252.

"The stone, therefore, is the safety of the corner which is formed by it: but breaking and destruction to those who have remained apart from this rational and spiritual union. For, 'Everyone who falleth upon that stone shall be broken; but on whomsoever it shall fall, it will crush him [Lk. 20:18].' For when the multitudes of the Jews stumbled at Christ, and fell against Him, they were broken; for they would not hearken to the voice of Esaias, where he says, **'Sanctify ye the Lord Himself; and He shall be thy fear....And ye shall not come against Him as against a stumbling stone, neither as against the falling of a rock** [Is. 8:13, 14].**'** Those, therefore, who did not believe were broken; but Christ has blessed us who have believed in Him."[143]

Saint Theophanes the Confessor (d. 845) explicitly names Christ as the Cornerstone in his majestic hymns: *Esaias prophesied Christ the Master, Who sustaineth the universe, as the all-precious Cornerstone set in Sion* [Is. 28:16].[144] And, *When Christ, the chief Cornerstone* [Ps. 117:22; Is. 28:16; Mt. 21:42; 1 Pe. 2:6], *not cut by the hand of man, was cut from thee, the unhewn mountain* [Dan. 2:34, 35], *O Virgin, He joined together the separate natures.*[145] Saint Joseph the Hymnographer also makes mention of Christ in his penitential hymn: *O divinely inspired apostles of the Lord, stones built upon the chief Cornerstone* [Is. 28:16], *intercede with Him Who is all-merciful that He may take away the heavy stone from my heart.*[146]

5. The Jews Are Willing to be Burnt with Fire.

"And they shall be willing, even if they were burnt with fire [Is. 9:5]**."** Saint Irenaeos informs us that the words "'they shall wish that they had been burnt with fire [cf. Is. 9:5],' refer to those who do not believe Him, and who have done to Him all they have done; for they will say in the judgment, 'O, that we had rather been burnt with fire before the Son of God was born, than not to have believed Him when born!' For those who died before the appearance of Christ have hope of attaining salvation in the judgment of the risen Christ—whoever feared God and died in justice and had the Spirit of God within them, such as the patriarchs and the prophets and the just. But for those who after the manifestation of Christ have not believed Him, there is in the judgment inexorable vengeance."[147]

---

[143] Saint Cyril of Alexandria, "Hom. 4," *Commentary*, p. 61; and "Hom. 134," pp. 534, 535.

[144] May 9th, Prophet Esaias, Orthros Canon, Ode Three, Mode Four.

[145] Wednesday of Mid-Pentecost, Eirmos of Orthros Canon, Ode Nine, Mode Four.

[146] *Triodion*, Thursday in the Sixth Week, Orthros Canon, Ode Eight, Mode Plagal One.

[147] Saint Irenaeos, *Proof of the Apostolic Preaching*, ¶ 56, ACW, 16:84.

6. The Jews Shall Fall.

"The bricks are fallen down, but come, let us hew stones...[Is. 9:10]**."**

Saint Gregory the Great comments that "surely when the Prophet Esaias realized that the people of the Jews would be lost to the faith, and foresaw that there would arise in the Church holy apostles through whom many from among the Gentiles would be confirmed in the courage of faith and life, spoke in great consolation: **'The bricks are fallen down, but come, let us hew stones...**[Is. 9:10]**.'** Then seeing apostles, martyrs, and teachers rise in Holy Church, he grieved less about the fall of the bricks, that is, the destruction of the Jewish people, because he perceived that the building of almighty God, namely, Holy Church, is made from square stones."[148]

7. The Commandments of Men.

"And the Lord has said, 'This people draw nigh to Me with their mouth, and they honor Me with their lips, but their heart is far from Me. But in vain do they worship Me, teaching the commandments and doctrines of men [Is. 29:13; cf. Mt. 15:8, 9]**.'"**

Saint Justin tells Trypho the Jew that the latter's teachers "beguile themselves and you teaching the commandments of men, and supposing that the everlasting kingdom will be assuredly given to those of the dispersion who are of Abraham after the flesh, although they be sinners, and faithless, and disobedient toward God."[149]

Saint Irenaeos says that the prophet "does not call the law given by Moses 'commandments of men,' but the traditions of the elders themselves which they had invented, and in upholding which they made the law of God of none effect, and were on this account also not subject to His Logos. For this is what Paul says concerning these men: 'For they being ignorant of the righteousness of God, and seeking to establish their own righteousness, submitted not to the righteousness of God. For Christ is the end of the law in regard to righteousness for everyone who believeth [Rom. 10:3, 4].'"[150]

Saint Gregory of Nyssa asks, "What is the meaning of 'This people honoreth Me with their lips, but their heart is far from Me [cf. Is. 29:13]'? That the right attitude of the soul toward the truth is more precious than the propriety of phrases in the sight of God, Who hears the groanings that cannot be uttered [cf. Rom. 8:26]. Phrases can be used in opposite senses: the tongue

[148] Saint Gregory the Great, "Hom. IX," *The Homilies of Saint Gregory the Great On the Book of the Prophet Ezekiel*, Bk. II, p. 261.
[149] Saint Justin Martyr, *Dialogue with Trypho*, Ch. CXL, Ante-Nicene, I:269.
[150] Saint Irenaeus, *Against Heresies*, Bk. IV, Ch. XII, Ante-Nicene, I:476.

readily serving, at his will, the intention of the speaker; but the disposition of the soul, as it is, so is it seen by Him Who sees all secrets."[151]

8. Christ is God.

"**For Thou art God, yet we knew it not, the God of Israel, the Savior** [Is. 45:15].

"**All that are opposed to Him shall be ashamed and confounded, and shall walk in shame: ye isles, keep a feast to Me** [Is. 45:16]."

Saint Cyprian cites these verses as showing "that Christ is God."[152] Saint Gregory of Nyssa declares, "Who of all that are conversant with prophecy is unaware that Esaias, among other passages, thus openly proclaims the divinity of the Son, where he says, '**Sabeans, men of stature, shall pass over to Thee, and shall be Thy servants; and they shall follow after Thee bound in fetters, and shall pass over to Thee, and shall do obeisance to Thee, and make supplication to Thee, because God is in Thee, and there is no God beside Thee** [Is. 45:14]'? For what other God is there Who has God in Himself, and is Himself God, except the Only-begotten? Let them say who hearken not to the prophecy."[153]

9. The Lord's Name is Blasphemed [Is. 52:5].

Saint Justin accuses the Jews as "authors of the wicked prejudice against the just One, and us who hold by Him....After then you knew He had risen from the dead and ascended to heaven, as the prophets foretold He would, you not only did not repent of the wickedness which you had committed but also, at that time, did select and send out from Jerusalem chosen men through all the land to tell that the godless heresy of the Christians had sprung up....So that you are the cause not only of your own unrighteousness but also, in fact, that of all other men. And Esaias cries justly, '**On account of you My name is continually blasphemed among the nations** [Is. 52:5].'"[154] "This passage," says Saint Chrysostom, "is a fearful statement, fraught with terror."[155]

10. Israel to be Provoked to Jealousy by the Foolish "No Nation."

Saint Chrysostom, discussing the disposition of both the Jews and the Greeks, makes the following observations: "First Moses says, 'I will provoke you to jealousy by them that are no people, and by a foolish nation I will anger you [cf. Deut. 32:21].' And so they ought even from Moses to have been able to distinguish the preachers,...not from the fact of their preaching peace, not from the fact of their bringing the glad tidings of those good things, not from

---

[151] Saint Gregory of Nyssa, *Dogmatic Treatises: Against Eunomius,* Bk. I, Nicene, 2nd Ser., V:85.

[152] Saint Cyprian, "Testimonies," § 6, *The Treatises of Cyprian*, Ante-Nicene, V:517.

[153] Saint Gregory of Nyssa, *Against Eunomius*, Bk. XI, Nicene, 2nd Ser., V:232.

[154] Saint Justin Martyr, *Dialogue with Trypho*, Ch. XVII, Ante-Nicene, I:203.

[155] Saint John Chrysostom, "Hom. 7," *Homilies on Genesis*, FC, 74:92, 93.

the word being sown in every part of the world, but from the very fact of their seeing their inferiors, those of the Gentiles, in greater honor. For what they had never heard, nor their forefathers, that wisdom did these on a sudden embrace. And this was a mark of such intense honor, as should gall them and lead them to jealousy and to recollection of the prophecy of Moses, which said, 'I will provoke you to jealousy by them that are no nation [Deut. 32:21].' For it was not the greatness of the honor alone that was enough to throw them upon jealousy, but the fact too that a nation had come to enjoy these things which was of so little account that it could hardly be considered a nation at all. 'For I will provoke you to jealousy, by them which are no nation, and by a foolish nation will I anger you [Deut. 32:21].' For what more foolish than the Greeks? Or what of less account?...And now the Jews see those in the enjoyment of countless blessings, who had formerly been objects of their contempt....Saint Paul also, 'But Esaias is very bold, and saith, "I was found by those not seeking Me; I became manifest to those not asking after Me [Rom. 10:20; cf. Is. 65:1]."'...Who then are they that sought not? Who are they that asked not after Him? Clearly, not the Jews, but they of the Gentiles, who hitherto had not known Him. As then Moses gave their characteristic mark in the words 'no people' and 'a foolish nation,' so here also he takes the same ground to point them out from, namely, their extreme ignorance. And this was a very great blame to attach to the Jews, that they who sought Him not found Him, and they who sought Him lost Him....

"How then and whence came it to pass? Hear Paul telling you....'For they being ignorant of the righteousness of God, and seeking to establish their own righteousness, submitted not to the righteousness of God [Rom. 10:3].'...For when the Jews were having greater privileges than the Greeks, through having received the law, through knowing God, and the rest which Paul enumerates, they, after the coming of Christ, saw the Greeks and themselves called on equal terms through faith. And, after faith, they received one circumcision, thereby in nothing preferred to the Gentile, they came to envy and were stung by their haughtiness. They could not endure the unspeakable and exceeding loving-kindness of the Lord. So this has happened to them from nothing else but pride, wickedness, and unkindness. And not only this but even the Jews have been the cause that God 'is continually blasphemed among the nations [cf. Is. 52:5; Rom. 2:24].'"[156]

11. Therefore, thus saith the Lord, "Behold, My servants shall eat, but ye shall hunger. Behold, My servants shall drink, but ye shall thirst. Behold, My servants shall rejoice, but ye shall be ashamed [Is. 65:13].

---

[156] Idem, "Hom. IX," *John,* Nicene, 1st Ser., XIV:32, 33.

"Behold, My servants shall exult with joy, but ye shall cry for the sorrow of your heart, and shall howl for the vexation of your spirit [Is. 65:14]**."**

Saint Cyprian expounds on these verses [Is. 65:13-16], saying that "the Jews would lose while we should receive the bread and the cup of Christ and all His grace; and that the new name of Christians should be blessed in the earth."[157]

12. The Jews in the Latter Days [Is. 29:18]**.**

Though the Jews would not understand the holy Scriptures, Saint Cyprian predicts, "that they would be intelligible in the last times, after that Christ had come. For Esaias says, **'In that day the deaf shall hear the words of the book, and they that are in darkness, and they that are in mist: the eyes of the blind shall see...**[Is. 29:18]**.'**"[158]

The Son of God

[Is. 41:4; 43:10; 45:5; 48:13, 15; 49:5, 6]

1. "I AM [Is. 41:4]**."**

Prophet Esaias prepared the people for the Coming One. He speaks of the One Who spoke to Moses and reveals His divine name, saying, **"'I AM THE BEING'; and He said, 'Thus shall ye say to the children of Israel, THE BEING has sent Me to you** [Ex. 3:14]**.'"** God's *parousia* shall be for all the human race. **"Who has wrought and done these things? He has called it Who called it from the generations of old; I God, the first and to all futurity, I AM** [Is. 41:4]**."** Saint Justin explains the name: "God cannot be called by any proper name, for names are given to mark out and distinguish their subject-matters, because these are many and diverse; but neither did anyone exist before God Who could give Him a name, nor did He Himself think it right to name Himself, seeing that He is One and unique, as He Himself also by His own prophet testifies [Is. 44:6]. On this account, God did not, when He sent Moses to the Hebrews, mention any name, but by a participle He mystically teaches them that He is the one and only God. 'For,' says He, 'I AM THE BEING [Ex. 3:14]'; manifestly contrasting Himself, 'the Being,' with those who are not (the not-beings)....By the participle 'Being' He might teach the difference between God Who is and those who are not (that is, the God-being and not-beings)."[159]

Saint Ambrose says that "the Son of God had no beginning, seeing that He already was at the beginning, nor shall He come to an end, Who is the Beginning and the End of the universe; for being the Beginning, how could He

---

[157] Saint Cyprian, "Testimonies," § 22, *Treatises*, Ante-Nicene, I:514.

[158] Ibid., "Testimonies," § 4, *Treatises*, Ante-Nicene, I:509.

[159] Saint Justin Martyr, *Justin's Hortatory Address to the Greeks*, Ch. XXI, Ante-Nicene, I:281.

take and receive that which He already had, or how shall He come to an end, being Himself the End of all things, so that in that End we have an abiding-place without end? The divine generation is not an event occurring in the course of time, and within time's limits; and therefore, before it (the divine generation) time is not, and in it time has no place."[160]

2. "There is No Other God Beside Me [Is. 45:5]**."**

Not wishing the Jews to fall into polytheism "this is why the prophets revealed the Son of God to the Jews in a somewhat dim and scanty fashion," says Saint Chrysostom, "rather than with clear and obvious statements. After the Jews had just been set free from the error of polytheism, they would have fallen back into the same disease if they were again to have heard of one Person Who is God and another Person Who is God. This is why, throughout the Old Testament, the prophets are constantly saying, 'There is one God, and there is no God except for Him [cf. Deut. 4:35; Is. 45:5, 21].' The prophets were not denying the Son—God forbid!—but they wished to cure the Jews of their weakness and, meanwhile, to persuade them to give up their belief in the many gods which did not exist.

"Therefore, when you hear the words 'one' and 'no one' as in, **'I am the Lord God, and there is no other God beside Me** [Is. 45:5]**,'** and similar expressions, do not diminish the glory of the Trinity but, by these terms, learn the distance which separates the Trinity from created beings. As Scripture also says in another place, **'For who has known the mind of the Lord** [Is. 40:13]**?'**...And, 'No one knoweth the things of God, except the Spirit of God [1 Cor. 2:11].' And again, it is the Son Who says, 'No one doth fully know Who the Son is, except the Father, and Who the Father is, except the Son...[Lk. 10:22].' And indeed in another text He also says this same thing: 'Not that anyone hath seen the Father, except the One Who is from God, that One hath seen the Father [Jn. 6:46].'"[161]

3. The Chosen Servant (Παῖς).

"'Be ye My witnesses, and I too am a witness,' saith the Lord God, 'and My Servant Whom I have chosen, that ye may know, and believe, and understand that I am He. Before Me there was no other God, and after Me there shall be none [Is. 43:10]**.'"**

"But lest these words," says Saint Hilary of Poitiers, "'For I am, and before Me there is no other God, nor shall be after Me,' be made a handle for blasphemous presumption, as proving that the Son is not God, since after the God, Whom no God precedes, there follows no other God, the purpose of the passage must be considered. God is His own best interpreter, but His chosen

[160] Saint Ambrose, *Of the Christian Faith,* Bk. IV, Ch. IX, Nicene, 2nd Ser., X:276.

[161] Saint John Chrysostom, "Hom. V," *On the Incomprehensible Nature of God*, FC, 72:147, 148.

Servant joins with Him to assure us that there is no God before Him, nor shall be after Him. His own witness concerning Himself, is, indeed, sufficient, but He has added the witness of the Servant Whom He has chosen. Thus we have the united testimony of the Two, that there is no God before Him; we accept the truth, because all things are from Him. We have Their witness also that there shall be no God after Him."[162]

Saint Chrysostom asks, "What do these expressions mean? For if the Son be not of the same essence, there is another God; and if He be not co-eternal, He is after Him; and if He did not proceed from His essence, clear it is that He was made....In saying 'after Me is no other God,' He does not exclude the Son; but He says that 'after Me there is no idol God,' not that 'there is no Son....' And how again, since He is 'Life [Jn. 1:4],' was there ever when He was not? For all must allow that Life both is always and is without beginning and without end, if It be indeed Life, as indeed It is. For, if there be when It is not, how can It be the life of others, when It even Itself is not?"[163] Saint Hilary agrees that the passage was spoken with regard to "the destruction of idols and those who are no gods."[164]

4. The Son of God was Sent by the Father.

" My hand also has founded the earth, and My right hand has fixed the sky [Is. 48:13]**.**

"I have spoken, I have called, I brought (ἤγαγον) **Him, and made His ways prosperous** [Is. 48:15]**."**

Saint Ambrose of Milan comments, "Here, indeed, He Who made the heaven and the earth Himself says that He is sent by the Lord and His Spirit. Ye see, then, that the poverty of language takes not from the honor of His mission. He, then, is sent by the Father...."[165]

5. The Father Speaks to the Son [Is. 49:5, 6]**.**

"And He said to Me, 'It is a great thing for Thee to be called My Servant (Παῖδά Μου), **to establish the tribes of Jacob, and to recover the dispersion of Israel. Behold, I have given Thee for the covenant of a race, for a light of the Gentiles, that Thou shouldest be for salvation to the end of the earth** [Is. 49:6]**.'"**

Saint Irenaeos says that Christ reports in the first person the Father's speech with Him. "For here, in the first place, we have that the Son of God was pre-existent, from the fact that the Father spoke with Him, and caused Him to be revealed to men before His birth. Next, we have that the Son had to

---

[162] Saint Hilary of Poitiers, *On the Trinity*, Book IV, §§ 35, 36, Nicene, 2nd Ser., IX:82.

[163] Saint Chrysostom, "Hom. IV," *John,* Nicene, 1st Ser., XIV:17, 18.

[164] Saint Hilary of Poitiers, *On the Councils,* § 56, no. XXIII, Nicene, 2nd Ser., IX:19.

[165] Saint Ambrose, *Of the Christian Faith*, Bk. II, Ch. IX, Nicene, 2nd Ser., X:233.

become man, born of mankind, and that the very God Himself forms Him from the womb, that is, that He would be born of the Spirit of God. And we have that He is Lord of all men, and Savior of those who believe in Him, Jews and others. For 'Israel' is the name of the Jewish people in the Hebrew language, from the Patriarch Jacob, who was also the first to be called 'Israel'; and 'Gentile' He calls all men. And that the Son calls Himself the Father's Servant is because of His obedience to the Father, every son being a servant of his father among men too."[166]

Saint Athanasios explains, "The Logos is not created into existence, but 'In the beginning was the Logos [Jn. 1:1]'; and He is afterward sent 'for the works' and the œconomy toward them. For before the works were made, the Son was ever; nor was there yet need that He should be created. But when the works were created and need arose afterward of the œconomy for their restoration, then it was that the Logos took upon Himself this condescension and assimilation to the works, which He has shown us by the word 'He created.' And through the Prophet Esaias, willing to signify the life, He says again: **'And now, thus saith the Lord that formed Me from the womb to be His own Servant** (Δοῦλον Ἑαυτῷ), **to gather Jacob to Him and Israel. I shall be gathered and glorified before the Lord...**[Is. 49:5]**.'** So here too, He is formed, not into existence, but in order to gather together the tribes, which were in existence before He was formed....[Thus when] the works were made and the need required, then 'He created' was said...."[167]

6. The Jews Do Not Understand the Divinity.

Saint Hilary of Poitiers tells us that "the Jews, unaware of the typical meaning of their mysteries, and therefore ignorant of God the Son, worshipped God simply as God, and not as Father; for, if they had worshipped Him as Father, they would have worshipped the Son also....The mysteriousness of His incarnation was to blind the eyes of some to His true divinity."[168]

Messianic Prophecies

Prophet Esaias lived about seven hundred years before our Lord's incarnation. The holy prophet's most conspicuous prophecies dealt with: 1. The Incarnation—2. The Magi—3. Jesus' Flight into Egypt—4. Jesus' Childhood and Youth—5. The Coming of the Forerunner—6. Jesus' Manner and Conduct—7. Christ's Message—8. Christ's Miracles—9. Christ, the Shepherd—10. Palm Sunday—11. The Passion—12. Christ's Descent into Hades—13. Death is Swallowed Up—14. Broken Brazen Gates—15. The Dead Shall Rise—16. The Myrrh-bearers—17. Christ's Ascension—18. Christ's

---

[166] Saint Irenaeus, *Proof of the Apostolic Preaching*, ¶ 51, ACW, 16:80.
[167] Saint Athanasius, "Discourse II," Chaps. XIX and XX, *Four Discourses Against the Arians*, Nicene, 2nd Ser., IV:376.
[168] Saint Hilary of Poitiers, *On the Trinity*, Book V, § 27, Nicene, 2nd Ser., IX:93.

Eternal Kingdom. Thus, Prophet Esaias set forth every aspect of the glory and ministry of Jesus Christ.

1. The Incarnation.

A. God Becomes Man [Is. 40:5; 63:8, 9].

1) "And the glory of the Lord shall appear, and all flesh shall see the salvation of God: for the Lord has spoken it [Is. 40:5]**."**

Saint Kyril of Alexandria briefly states that "the meaning of **'all flesh shall see the salvation of God** [Is. 40:5]**'** is that every man shall see it. While, therefore, the immutable retains that which He was, yet as having under this condition assumed our likeness, He is said to have been made flesh. Behold Him, therefore, as a man, enduring with us the things that belong to man's estate, and fulfilling all righteousness, for the plan of salvation's sake."[169]

2) "He became to them deliverance out of all their affliction: not an ambassador, nor a messenger (angel), but He Himself saved them, because He loved them and spared them. He Himself redeemed them, and took them up, and lifted them up for all the days of eternity [Is. 63:8, 9]**."**

Saint Irenaeos says, "He was Himself to bring about these blessings in person."[170] And, "Again, that it should not be a mere man who should save us, nor one without flesh—for the angels are without flesh—Prophet Esaias announced, saying that God Himself would become very Man, visible...."[171]

Saint Cyprian also believes this passage signifies that "Christ our God should come, the Enlightener and Savior of the human race."[172]

B. "And the Lord again spoke to Achaz, saying, 'Ask for thyself a sign of the Lord thy God in the depth or in the height.' And Achaz said, 'I will not ask, neither will I tempt the Lord.' And He said, 'Hear ye now, O house of David: Is it a little thing for you to contend with men? And how do ye contend against the Lord [Is. 7:10-13]**?'"**

Saint Irenaeos explains the prophet's words: "'From the height above, or from the depths beneath [cf. Is. 7:11],' was meant to indicate, that 'the One Who descended is the same also Who ascended [Eph. 4:10].'"[173]..."When He says, 'Hear, O house of David [cf. Is. 7:13],' He performed the part of one indicating that He Whom God promised David that He would raise up from 'the fruit of his belly [Ps. 131:11]' an eternal King, is the same Who was born

[169] Saint Cyril of Alexandria, "Hom. 11," *Commentary*, p. 78.

[170] Saint Irenaeus, *Proof of the Apostolic Preaching*, ¶ 88, ACW, 16:102.

[171] Idem, *Against Heresies*, Bk. III, Ch. XX, Ante-Nicene, I:450, 451.

[172] Saint Cyprian, "Testimonies," § 10, *Treatises*, Ante-Nicene, V:518.

[173] Saint Irenaeus, *Against Heresies*, Bk. III, Ch. XXI, Ante-Nicene, I:453.

of the Virgin, herself of the lineage of David."[174] On this point, he adds, "He therefore, the Son of God, our Lord, being the Logos of the Father, and the Son of Man, since He has a generation as to His human nature from Mary—who was descended from mankind, and who was herself a human being—was made the Son of Man. Therefore, also, the Lord Himself gave us a sign, in the depth below, and in the height above, which man did not ask for, because he never expected that a virgin could conceive, or that it was possible that one remaining a virgin could bring forth a son, and that the child should be 'God with us,' and descend to those things which are of the earth beneath, seeking the sheep which had perished, which was indeed His own peculiar handiwork, and ascend to the height above, offering and commending to His Father that human nature which had been found, making in His own person the firstfruits of the resurrection of man. So that, as the Head rose from the dead, also the remaining part of the body."[175]

"Therefore the Lord Himself shall give you a sign: Behold, the Virgin (ἡ Παρθένος) **shall conceive in the womb, and shall bring forth a Son; and thou shalt call His name Emmanuel** [Is. 7:14]**."**

Saint Ignatios the God-bearer (ca. 35-ca. 107) writes about three celebrated mysteries: "Now the virginity of Mary was hidden from the prince of this world, as was also her Offspring, and the death of the Lord; three mysteries of renown, which were wrought in silence by God."[176]

Saint Justin remarks that "it is evident to all that, in all the race of Abraham according to the flesh, no one has been born of a virgin, or is said to have been born of a virgin, save this our Christ."[177] Now the prediction of the manner of Christ's birth, says Saint Justin, "was incredible and seemed impossible with men....These things God predicted by the Spirit of prophecy as about to come to pass, in order that, when they came to pass, there might be no unbelief, but faith, because of their prediction....The prophecy signifies that the Virgin should conceive without intercourse. For if she had had intercourse with anyone whatever, she was no longer a virgin; but the power of God having come upon her, and caused her while yet a virgin to conceive....It is wrong, therefore, to understand the Spirit and the power of God as anything else than the Logos, Who is also the Firstborn of God, as Prophet Moses declared [Gen.

---

[174] Ibid., Ante-Nicene, I:452, 453.

[175] Ibid., Bk. III, Ch. XIX, Ante-Nicene, I:449.

[176] Saint Ignatius, *The Epistle of Ignatius to the Ephesians*, Ch. XIX, Ante-Nicene, I:57.

[177] Saint Justin Martyr, *Dialogue with Trypho*, Ch. XLIII, Ante-Nicene, I:216.

49:10]; and it was this which, when it came upon the Virgin and overshadowed her, caused her to conceive, not by intercourse, but by power."[178]

Saint Irenaeos, speaking of the sign, asks the skeptics, "For what great thing or what sign should have been in this, that a young woman conceiving by a man should bring forth—a thing which happens to all women that produce offspring? But since an unlooked-for salvation was to be provided for men through the help of God, so also was the unlooked-for birth from a virgin accomplished—God giving this sign, but man not working it out."[179]

Prophet Esaias

Saint Irenaeos also charges "those men who would make different translations to be impudent and presumptuous."...He then adds, "Carefully, then has the Holy Spirit pointed out His (Jesus') birth from a virgin, and His essence, that He is God (for the name Emmanuel indicates this)....God promised David that He would raise up from the fruit of his belly an eternal King, is the same Who was born of the Virgin, herself of the lineage of David. For on this account also, He promised the King should be 'of the fruit of his belly [Ps. 131:11],' which is appropriate to a virgin conceiving, and not 'of the fruit of his loins,' nor 'of the fruit of his reins,' which expression is appropriate to a generating man, and a woman conceiving by a man. In this promise, therefore, the Scripture excluded all virile influence....But Scripture has fixed and established 'the fruit of the belly,' that it might declare the generation of Him Who should be born from the Virgin, as Elisabeth testified when filled with the Holy Spirit, saying to Mary, 'Blessed art thou among women, and blessed is the fruit of thy womb [Lk. 1:42]'; the Holy Spirit pointing out to those willing to hear, that the promise which God made, of raising up a King from the fruit of the belly, was fulfilled in the birth from the Virgin, that is, from Mary. Let those, therefore, who alter the passage of Esaias thus, 'Behold, a young woman shall conceive,' and who will have Him to be Joseph's son, also alter the form of the promise which was given to David, when God promised to raise up from the fruit of his belly the

[178] Ibid., *The First Apology*, Ch. XXXIII, Ante-Nicene, I:174.

[179] Saint Irenaeus, *Against Heresies*, Bk. III, Ch. XXI, Ante-Nicene, I:453.

horn of Christ the King. But they did not understand, otherwise they would have presumed to alter even this passage also."[180]

Saint Athanasios, expounding upon this verse [Is. 7:14], proclaims, "But what does that mean, if not that God has come in the flesh?"[181] He also supports the Virgin's humanity: "Gabriel is not simply sent to a virgin, but 'to a virgin who was espoused to a man [Lk. 1:27],' in order that by means of the betrothed man he might show that Mary was really a human being."[182] He observes, "All of Scripture teems with refutations of the disbelief of the Jews. For which of the righteous men and holy prophets and patriarchs, recorded in the divine Scriptures, ever had his corporal birth of a virgin only? Or what woman has sufficed without man for the conception of humankind?"[183]

Saint Kyril of Jerusalem also remonstrates with the Jews, arguing, "The Jews contradict this prophecy [Is. 7:14]. For of old, it is their wont wickedly to oppose the truth, and they say that it is not written 'the Virgin,' but 'the damsel.' But though I assent to what they say, even so I find the truth. For we must ask them, 'If a virgin be forced, when does she cry out and call for helpers, after or before the outrage?' If, therefore, the Scripture says, 'The betrothed damsel cried, and there was none to save her [cf. Deut. 22:27],' does it not speak of a virgin? But that you may learn more plainly that even a virgin is called in holy Scripture a 'damsel,' hear the book of Kings, 'And the damsel was very fair [3 Kgs. (1 Kgs.) 1:4]': for that as a virgin she was chosen and brought to David is admitted."[184]

Blessed Jerome writes: "Now that the Virgin [Is. 7:14] has conceived in the womb and has borne to us a Child, of Whom the prophet also says that 'Government is upon His shoulder, and His name shall be called the mighty God, the everlasting Father [Is. 9:6 Vulg.],' now the chain of the curse is broken. Death came through Eve, but life has come through Mary. And thus the gift of virginity has been bestowed most richly upon women, seeing that it has had its beginning from a woman."[185]

Taking the issue up with the Jews, Blessed Jerome declares: "I know that the Jews are accustomed to meet us with the objection that in Hebrew the word *almah* does not mean a virgin, but 'a young woman.' And, to speak truth, a virgin is properly called *bethulah*, but a young woman, or a girl, is not *almah*, but *naarah*! What then is the meaning of *almah*? A hidden virgin, that

---

[180] Ibid.

[181] Saint Athanasius, "Letter LX," Nicene, 2nd Ser., IV:577.

[182] Ibid., "Letter LIX," Nicene, 2nd Ser., IV:572.

[183] Ibid., *On the Incarnation of the Word*, § 35, Nicene, 2nd Ser., IV:55.

[184] Saint Cyril of Jerusalem, "Lecture XII," *Catechetical Lectures,* Nicene, 2nd Ser., VII:78.

[185] Saint Jerome, "Letter XXII to Eustochium," Nicene, 2nd Ser., VI:30.

is, not merely virgin, but a virgin and something more, because not every virgin is hidden, shut off from the occasional sight of men. Then again, Rebecca, on account of her extreme purity—for which she is a type of the Church, which she represented in her own virginity—is described in Genesis as *almah*, not *bethulah* [Gen. 24:42 sq.]....Where he speaks of the maiden coming forth to draw water, the Hebrew word is *almah*, that is, 'a virgin secluded,' and guarded by her parents with extreme care. Or, if this be not so, let them at least show me where the word is applied to married women as well, and I will confess my ignorance. It is written that the Virgin shall conceive and bear a Son; now if virginity be not preferred to marriage, why did not the Holy Spirit choose a married woman or a widow?"[186]

Saint Chrysostom, discussing the word "virgin" as translated by the Seventy, remonstrates with those "other translators who used not the term 'virgin,' but 'young woman.' In the first place we will say this, that the Seventy were justly entitled to confidence above all the others. For the others made their translation after Christ's coming, continuing to be Jews, and may justly be suspected as having spoken rather in enmity, and as darkening the prophecies on purpose; but the Seventy, as having entered upon this work a hundred years or more before the coming of Christ, stand clear from all such suspicion, and on account of the date, and of their number, and of their agreement, would have a better right to be trusted."[187]

The name "God" is not greater than the name "Lord," nor is the name "Lord" inferior to the name "God." Saint Chrysostom says, "You have heard, therefore, that the Father is called Lord. Come now, and let me show you that the Son is called God. 'Behold, the Virgin shall be with child, and shall bring forth a son; and they shall call His name Emmanuel, which is, being interpreted, "God with us [Mt. 1:23]."' See now how both the name 'Lord' is given to the Father, and the name 'God' is given to the Son: In the Psalm, the sacred writer said, 'Let them know that Thy name is Lord [Ps. 82:17].' Here Esaias says, **'They shall call His name Emmanuel** [Is. 7:14]**.'** And again, he says, 'A Child is born to us, and a Son is given to us;...and His name is called the Angel of Great Counsel, God the Strong, the Mighty One [cf. Is. 9:6].'"[188]

Jesus was not called Emmanuel by His disciples, friends, or enemies. "What then? Did the prophet speak falsely? By no means," says Saint Chrysostom. "But how is it that Esaias says, **'Thou shalt call His name Emmanuel** [Is. 7:14]'?" He explains that "the name was a kind of expression according to the issue of the event of His incarnation that now 'God is with us,' as the meaning of Emmanuel portends. The prophets are wont to do this. Yes, Christ

---

[186] Ibid., *Against Jovinianus.—Book I*, Nicene, 2nd Ser., VI:370.
[187] Saint Chrysostom, "Hom. V," *Matthew*, Nicene, 1st Ser., X:33.
[188] Idem, "Hom. V," *On the Incomprehensible Nature of God*, FC, 72:142-144.

too should be called Emmanuel, yet was He not so called. But the facts utter this voice."[189]

Saint Joseph the Hymnographer also praises the Theotokos: *Having inexplicably conceived in thy womb the God of all, O Virgin Mother, thou didst give birth in a manner surpassing mind and speech, and didst remain a virgin, even as thou wast before giving birth, O Bride of God* [Is. 7:14].[190] Speaking of her virginity before, during, and after childbirth, Saint Joseph continues: *We praise thee, for thou alone didst give birth as a virgin and didst keep thy womb incorrupt, O pure one* [Is. 7:14].[191] Also, extolling her virginal delivery, we chant from the resurrection hymns: *Behold, fulfilled is the prophecy of Esaias* [Is. 7:14]*! For as a virgin hast thou given birth, and after giving birth, thou hast remained as thou wast before childbirth; for He that was born was God.*[192]

C. The Painless Birth-giving of the Virgin Theotokos:

"Before she that travailed brought forth, before the travail-pain came on, she escaped it and brought forth a male [Is. 66:7]**."**

Saint John of Damascus informs us that "He Who was of the Father, yet without mother, was born of woman without a father's cooperation. And so far as He was born of woman, His birth was in accordance with the laws of parturition; while so far as He had no father, His birth was above the nature of generation. And in that it was at the usual time (for He was born on the completion of the ninth month when the tenth was just beginning), His birth was in accordance with the laws of parturition; while in that it was painless, it was above the laws of generation. For, as pleasure did not precede it, pain did not follow it, according to the Prophet Esaias [Is. 66:7]. The Son of God incarnate, therefore, was born of her—not a God-bearing man, but God incarnate...."[193]

D. The Sealed Book, the Theotokos:

"And all these things shall be to you as the words of this sealed book, which if they shall give to a learned man, saying, 'Read this,' he shall then say, 'I cannot read it, for it is sealed [Is. 29:11]**.'"**

Saint Hippolytos remarks that "the things spoken of old by the law and the prophets were all sealed; and that they were unknown to men, which Esaias declares [Is. 29:11]. It was meet and necessary that the things spoken of old by

---

[189] Idem, "Hom. XLI," *First Corinthians,* Nicene, 1st Ser., XII:252.

[190] *Pentecostarion*, Sunday of the Samaritan Woman, Theotokion of Orthros Canon, Ode Three, Mode Four.

[191] *Pentecostarion*, Sunday of the Samaritan Woman, extract of Theotokion of Orthros Canon, Ode Six, Mode Four.

[192] *Anastasimatarion*, Resurrection Theotokion of Vespers Aposticha, Mode One.

[193] Saint John of Damascus, *Exposition of the Orthodox Faith,* Bk. IV, Ch. XIV, Nicene, 2nd Ser., IX:86.

the prophets should be sealed to the unbelieving Pharisees who thought that they understood the letter of the law, and be opened to the believing. The things, therefore, which of old were sealed, are now, by the grace of God the Lord, all open to the saints."[194]

What is the significance of this sealed book? The Virgin Mary. Hearken to the hymnographers of the Church: During the Feast of the Conception of the Virgin by Righteous Anna, we sing: *Anna, holding in her womb the Book* [Is. 29:11] *that the prophet foretold and that was sealed by the divine Spirit, cried out to all, "All Scriptures proclaim her! I am magnified putting her forth this day!"*[195]

At the Virgin Mary's nativity, Saint Joseph the Hymnographer honors her: *Most manifestly did the prophet describe thee as a new and divine scroll, whereon the Word is written by the finger of the Father, O Virgin.*[196] And, *Now is the sealed Book born* [Is. 29:11], *which it is impossible for mortals to read by the nature of the law, and which is kept in the dwelling place of the Word. For by the Spirit hath she revealed the books of the divinely eloquent.*[197]

Saint Athanasios, Patriarch of Constantinople, in his canon, writes: *Rejoice! Living Book of Christ.*[198] From the Canon of the Akathist Hymn, we magnify her: *O Christ's Book* [Is. 29:11] *endowed with life and clearly sealed with the Spirit's grace.*[199]

We end this section with this hymn of Saint John, Metropolitan of Evchaïta, and together with him implore her unassailable protection: *O sealed Book of God* [Is. 29:11], *I set thee as a divine seal on my hymn: I offer thee my praises, Virgin.*[200]

E. "For a Child is born to us, and a Son is given to us, Whose government is upon His shoulder: and His name is called the Angel of Great Counsel [Is. 9:6],

"Wonderful, Counselor, Mighty One, Potentate, Prince of Peace [Alexandrian Text Is. 9:6]**."**

---

[194] Saint Hippolytus, *Fragments from Commentaries*, Ante-Nicene, V:181, 182.

[195] December 9th, Conception of the Virgin Mary by Righteous Anna, Orthros Canon II, Ode One, Mode One.

[196] September 7th, Feast of the Forefeast of the Nativity of the Virgin Mary, Orthros Canon, Ode Five, Mode Four.

[197] September 7th, Feast of the Forefeast of the Nativity of the Virgin Mary, Orthros Canon, Ode Five, Mode Four.

[198] Extract of Canon at Small Compline, Ode Nine, Mode Two, by Saint Athanasios, Patriarch of Constantinople.

[199] Extract of Canon of the Akathist Hymn, Ode One, Mode Four.

[200] *Triodion*, Saturday in the First Week, extract of Orthros Canon Theotokion, Ode Nine, Mode Four, by Metropolitan John of Evchaïta.

Saint Justin believes this verse "is significant of the power of the Cross; for to it, when He was crucified, He applied His shoulders."[201] And he says that when "Esaias called Him the Angel of Mighty Counsel, did he not foretell Him to be the Teacher of those truths which He did teach when He came to earth? For He alone taught openly those mighty counsels which the Father designed both for all those who have been and shall be well pleasing to Him, and also for those who have rebelled against His will, whether men or angels."[202]

The "Angel of Great Counsel of the Father," says Saint Irenaeos, "is the Son of God, Jesus Christ, Who was announced by the prophets, Who from the fruit of David's body was Emmanuel, through Whom God caused the Dayspring [Zach. 6:12] and the just One to arise to the house of David, and raised up for him a horn of salvation and established a testimony in Jacob [Lk. 1:69]."[203] Moreover, Saint Irenaeos says that "the words 'Whose government is set upon His shoulder' means allegorically the Cross, which He held on His back when He was crucified; for what was and is an ignominy for Him, and because of Him, for us, the Cross, that, he says, is His government, that is, a sign of His empire. And he says 'Angel of Great Counsel': Messenger of the Father, Whom He announced to us."[204] And here, Saint Cyprian agrees: "In the Passion and the sign of the Cross is all virtue and power."[205]

Saint Irenaeos also points out: "Esaias calls Him 'Wonderful, Counselor,' even of the Father, whereby it is pointed out that it is with Him that the Father works all things whatsoever, as we have in the first of the Mosaic books: 'And God said, "Let us make man according to our image and similitude...[Gen. 1:26]."' For He is here seen clearly, the Father addressing the Son, as Wonderful, Counselor of the Father. Now He is also our Counselor, giving counsel—not constraining, as God, and nonetheless being 'God the Mighty,' he says—and giving counsel to leave off our ignorance and receive knowledge, and to go forth from error and come to truth, and to cast forth corruptibility and receive incorruptibility."[206]

In his commentary, Saint Ambrose remarks, "He bowed His shoulder to labor, bowed Himself to the Cross, to carry our sins. For that reason the prophet says, **'Whose government is on His shoulder** [Is. 9:6]**.'** This means, above the Passion of His body is the power of His divinity, or it refers to the Cross that towers above His body. Therefore, He bowed His shoulder,

---

[201] Saint Justin Martyr, *The First Apology*, Ch. XXXV, Ante-Nicene, I:174.
[202] Ibid., *Dialogue with Trypho*, Ch. LXXV, Ante-Nicene, I:236.
[203] Saint Irenaeus, *Against Heresies,* Bk. III, Ch. XVI, Ante-Nicene, I:441.
[204] Idem, *Proof of the Apostolic Preaching*, ¶ 56, ACW, 16:84.
[205] Saint Cyprian, "Testimonies," § 21, *Treatises*, V:524.
[206] Saint Irenaeus, *Proof of the Apostolic Preaching*, ¶ 55, ACW, 16:83.

applying Himself to the plow—patient in the endurance of all insults, and so subject to affliction that He was wounded on account of our iniquities and weakened on account of our sins [cf. Is. 53:3-5]."[207]

Saint Chrysostom contends: "No one would say this of a mere man, as is obvious even to those who are very eager to show how stubborn they can be. No man from the beginning of time has been called God the Mighty, nor Father of the world to come, nor the Prince of Peace."[208] He defines the **"Angel of Great Counsel** [Is. 9:6]**"** as a name which "the Son of God is called, because of the other things which He taught, and principally because He announced the Father to men, as also now He says, 'I manifested Thy name to the men whom Thou hast given Me out of the world [Jn. 17:6].'"[209]

In his homilies on the incomprehensible nature of God, Saint Chrysostom explains, "Though Saint Paul wishes to show that the Father needs no counselor [Rom. 11:34; Is. 40:13], yet the prophet wishes to show the equal honor of the Only-begotten. And this is why, in the text from Genesis, the Father did not say, 'Make this,' or 'Do this,' but rather, 'Let Us make [cf. Gen. 1:26].' For to say 'Make this' is to us words proper to a command given to a servant."[210]

F. "And there shall come forth a rod out of the root of Jesse, and a blossom (ἄνθος, 'flower') **shall come up from his root** [Is. 11:1]**."**

Saint Irenaeos pronounces, "Thereby he says that it is of her, who is descended from David and from Abraham, that He is born. For Jesse was a descendant of Abraham, and father of David; the descendent who conceived Christ, the Virgin, is thus become the 'rod.' Moses, therefore, worked his miracles before Pharaoh with a rod; and among others, too, of mankind, the rod is a sign of empire. And the 'flower' refers to His body, for it was made to bud forth by the Spirit."[211]

Saint Chrysostom remarks, "So Esaias predicted that He Who was to come will come not only from the tribe but even from the house of Jesse [Is. 11:1]. For the prophet was not simply speaking of the rod, but of Christ and His kingdom. The words which follow make it clear that Esaias did not say this about the rod; for when Esaias had said 'a rod shall come forth,' he went on to add that **'there shall rest upon Him the Spirit of wisdom and understanding** [Is. 11:2]**.'** No man, even if he is extremely senseless, will say that the grace of the Spirit came down on a rod of wood. It is quite obvious that the grace of

---

[207] Saint Ambrose, *The Patriarchs*, FC, 65:259.

[208] Saint John Chrysostom, *Apologist: Demonstration Against the Pagans*, Ch. III, FC, 73:195.

[209] Idem, "Hom. LXXXI," *John*, Nicene, 1st Ser., XIV:299.

[210] Idem, "Hom. XI," *On the Incomprehensible Nature of God*, FC, 72:276.

[211] Saint Irenaeus, *Proof of the Apostolic Preaching*, ¶ 59, ACW, 16:87.

the Spirit came down on that spotless temple of the Spirit. This is why Esaias did not say, 'He will come,' but 'He shall rest for Himself,'[212] because after the Spirit came He did not depart but remained. This is what John the evangelist made clear when he quoted the words of the Baptist: 'I have beheld the Spirit descending out of heaven as a dove, and He abode upon Him [Jn. 1:32].'"[213]

Saint Ambrose of Milan declares, "The flower from the root is the work of the Spirit, that flower, I say, of which it was well prophesied: **'A rod shall come forth out of the root of Jesse, and a flower shall rise from his root** [Is. 11:1]**.'** The root of Jesse the patriarch is the family of the Jews, Mary is the rod, Christ the flower of Mary, Who, about to spread the good odour of faith throughout the whole world, budded forth from a virgin womb, as He Himself said, 'I am the flower of the plain, a lily of the valleys [Song 2:1].'"[214]

Blessed Jerome, a biblical scholar who knew Hebrew, makes this observation, "The evangelist writes: 'And he (Joseph) came and dwelt in a city which is called Nazareth, in order that it might be fulfilled that which was spoken by the prophets, that He (Christ) shall be called a Nazarene [Mt. 2:23].'...Where are these words? Let me tell them that they are in Esaias [Is. 11:1]. For in the place where we read and translate, 'There shall come forth a rod out of the stem of Jesse, and a branch shall grow out of his roots,' in the Hebrew idiom it is written thus: 'There shall come forth a rod out of the root of Jesse and a Nazarene shall grow from his root.'"[215] In a letter he calls "Nazareth, as its name denotes, 'the flower of Galilee.'"[216] Yet elsewhere, Blessed Jerome declares: "The rod is the Mother of the Lord—simple, pure, unsullied; drawing no germ of life from without, but fruitful in singleness like God Himself. The flower of the rod is Christ, Who says of Himself, 'I am the rose of Sharon and the lily of the valleys [Song 2:1].'"[217]

Saint Ephraim, commenting upon the Gospel verse, "He shall be called a Nazarene [Mt. 2:23]," says that "the word *nezer* or *neser* in Hebrew means a 'scepter.' The prophet calls Him a 'Nazarene,' because he is the Son of the Scepter; and because He was brought up in Nazareth, the evangelist notes this prophecy."[218]

Most of the hymnographers of the Church are in agreement that Mary Theotokos is signified by 'the rod' of which Christ is her fruit. Saint Andrew of Crete sings, Thou, *O Lord, hast made to flower an undefiled fruit from the*

---

[212] The verb "rest" *(anapavsetai)*: Future Tense, Middle Voice, Indicative Mood.
[213] Saint John Chrysostom, *Demonstration Against the Pagans*, Ch. II, FC, 73:194.
[214] Saint Ambrose, *Of the Holy Spirit,* Bk. II, Ch. V, Nicene, 2nd Ser., X:119.
[215] Saint Jerome, "Letter LVII to Pammachius," Nicene, 2nd Ser., VI:115, 116.
[216] Ibid., "Letter XLVI, Paul and Eustochium to Marcella," Nicene, 2nd Ser., VI:65.
[217] Ibid., "Letter XXII," Nicene, 2nd Ser., VI:29.
[218] *Saint Ephrem's Commentary on Tatian's Diatessaron*, p. 78.

barren root of holy Anna, even the rod that is the Theotokos.[219] At her conception he chants, *Anna now beginneth to put forth the divine shoot which shall give rise to Christ, the mystic Flower, the Creator of all.*[220] And at her nativity, he says, *The rod is born, from whom the flower sprang forth: Christ, the only deliverer of Adam.*[221] Saint Kosmas concurs at our Lord's nativity: *Rod of the root of Jesse, and flower that blossomed from his stem, O Christ, Thou hast sprung from the Virgin.*[222]

Saint Theodore the Stoudite interchangeably identifies Christ and the Virgin Birth-giver as the rod: *Thou hast borne the Rod* [Is. 11:1].[223] Yet, in the next hymn, he magnifies her as the rod: *Esaias proclaimed thee as the rod that blossomed from the root of David.*[224] Here, he calls her the root: *O Virgin Mother undefiled, Thou art the root of Jesse from which has sprung Christ the flower.*[225] And also in the following hymn: *Thou art the root from whence Christ, the Rod of Jesse, sprung* [Is. 11:1].[226]

However, in most cases,[227] Christ is represented as the flower: *As it is written, the mystic rod doth gradually blossom forth a divine flower* [Is. 11:1], *manifesting it to us from the root of Jesse.*[228] On the other hand, a resurrectional hymn celebrates Christ as both rod and flower, Who sprung from the Virgin: *The Virgin, O Christ, hath blossomed forth with Thee, the rod of the root of Jesse, as was prophesied, and hath sprouted Thee forth as a flower for us; holy art Thou, O Lord.*[229]

---

[219] September 8th, Feast of the Nativity of the Virgin Mary, Orthros Canon, Ode Eight, Mode Plagal Four.

[220] December 9th, Conception of the Virgin Mary by Righteous Anna, Orthros Canon I, Ode Five, Mode One.

[221] September 8th, Feast of the Nativity of the Virgin Mary, Orthros Canon, Ode Five, Mode Plagal Four.

[222] December 25th, Feast of the Nativity According to the Flesh, extract of Katavasia, Ode Four, Mode One.

[223] *Triodion*, Saturday in the Second Week, Extract of Theotokion of Orthros Canon, Ode Nine, Mode Three.

[224] *Triodion*, Wednesday in the Second Week, extract of Orthros Canon, Ode Nine, Mode Three.

[225] *Triodion*, Wednesday in the Sixth Week, Theotokion of Orthros Canon, Ode Three, Mode Three.

[226] December 9th, Unexpected Joy Icon of the Theotokos, Orthros Canon I, Ode Six, Mode Four.

[227] September 8th, Feast of the Nativity of the Virgin Mary, extract of Orthros Sessional Hymn, Mode Plagal Four; Small Vespers Sticheron, Mode One.

[228] March 24th, Annunciation Forefeast, Canon of Forefeast, Ode Five, Mode Four.

[229] *Anastasimatarion*, Resurrection Canon to the Mother of God, Ode Three, Mode

(continued...)

G. "We brought a report as a child before Him, as a root in a thirsty land [Is. 53:2]**."**

Saint Ephraim the Syrian writes in a nativity hymn: "A wonder it is that God as a babe should show Himself. By the word 'Worm' did the Spirit foreshow Him in a parable [Ps. 21:6], because His generation was without marriage....He came up as a root before Him, as a root of parched ground [Is. 53:2]."[230] And, "She conceived Thee within her without marriage. There was milk in her breasts, not after the way of nature. Thou madest the thirsty land suddenly a fountain of milk....How meek art Thou! How mighty art Thou, O Child! Thy judgment is mighty, Thy love is sweet! Who can stand against Thee? Thy Father is in heaven, Thy Mother is on earth; who shall declare Thee [Is. 53:8]?"[231]

H. "Who shall declare His generation [Is. 53:8]**?"**

Saint Athanasios, in the *Statement of Faith*, declares this of the Son: "He was begotten ineffably and incomprehensibly, for **'who shall declare His generation** [Is. 53:8]**?'**; in other words, no one can. He it was Who, at the consummation of the ages [Heb. 9:26], descended from the bosom of the Father and took our humanity from the undefiled Virgin Mary...."[232]

Saint Chrysostom, speaking of Christ's nativity, declares, "Even the prophets from the first were amazed at this, that 'He did show Himself upon earth, and conversed with men [Bar. 3:37].' Yea, for it is far beyond all thought to hear that God, the Unspeakable, the Unutterable, the Incomprehensible, and He that is equal to the Father, has passed through a virgin's womb, and has vouchsafed to be born of a woman, and to have Abraham and David for forefathers....Hearing these things, arise, and surmise nothing low; but even because of this very thing most of all shouldest thou marvel, that being Son of the unoriginate God, and His true Son, He suffered Himself to be called also Son of David, that He might make thee son of God. He suffered a slave to be father to Him, that He might make the Lord Father to thee a slave....Thus, He was born after the flesh, that thou mightest be born after the Spirit; He was born of a woman, that thou mightest cease to be the son of a woman. The birth, therefore, was twofold, both made like unto us, and also surpassing ours. For to be born of a woman indeed was our lot, but to be 'begotten not of blood, nor of the will of flesh, nor of the will of man [Jn. 1:13],' but of the Holy Spirit,

---

[229](...continued)
Three.

[230] Saint Ephraim, *Hymns on the Nativity,* Nicene, 2nd Ser., XIII:223.

[231] Ibid., Nicene, 2nd Ser., XIII:242.

[232] Saint Athanasius, *Statement of Faith*, Nicene, 2nd Ser., IV:84.

was to proclaim beforehand the birth surpassing us, the birth to come, which, freely, He was about to give us of the Spirit."[233]

Blessed Jerome writes: "If His generation has been hidden in God from heavenly creatures, what wonder if it seems unknown to us who have been made from the slime of the earth?"[234]

Regarding the divine maternity, Blessed Jerome asks, "Should you like to know how He is born of a virgin and, after His nativity, the mother is still a virgin? 'The doors were closed and Jesus entered [cf. Jn. 20:19, 26].' There is no question about that. He Who entered through the closed doors was neither a ghost nor a spirit; He was a real man with a real body. Furthermore, what does He say? 'Touch Me and see, for a spirit hath not flesh and bones, even as you see Me having [Lk. 24:39].' He had flesh and bones, and the doors were closed. How do flesh and bones enter through closed doors? The doors are closed and He enters, Whom we do not see entering. Whence has He entered? Everything is closed up; there is no place through which He may enter. Nevertheless, He Who has entered is within and how He entered is not evident. You do not know how His entrance was accomplished, and you attribute it to the power of God. Attribute to the power of God, then, that He was born of a virgin, and the Virgin herself after bringing forth was a virgin still."[235]

Saint Leo the Great (d. 461), Pope of Rome, writes: "We believe that when Esaias says, **'Who shall declare His generation** [Is. 53:8]**?'** applies not only to that mystery, whereby the Son of God is co-eternal with the Father, but also to this birth whereby the Word became flesh."[236]

I. Jesus' Name From His Mother's Womb: "'Hearken to Me, ye islands, and attend, ye nations, after a long time it shall come to pass,' saith the Lord, 'from My Mother's womb He has called My name [Is. 49:1].

"'And He has made My mouth as a sharp sword, and He has hid Me under the shadow of His hand...[Is. 49:2]**.'**

"And He said to Me, 'Thou art My servant, O Israel, and in Thee I will be glorified [Is. 49:3]**.'"**

Saint Ambrose says that "the Son of God Himself is speaking."[237]

Saint Kyril of Jerusalem says, "There is One Lord Jesus Christ, a wondrous name, indirectly announced beforehand by the prophets....Now Jesus in Hebrew is by interpretation 'Savior.' For the prophetic gift, foreseeing the murderous spirit of the Jews against their Lord, veiled His name, lest from

---

[233] Saint Chrysostom, "Hom. II," *Matthew*, Nicene, 1st Ser., X:9, 10.
[234] Saint Jerome, "Hom. 69," *60-96 On The Psalms, Vol. 2*, FC, 57:90.
[235] Ibid., "Hom. 87," FC, 57:217, 218.
[236] Saint Leo the Great, "Sermon XXIII on the Nativity," Nicene, 2nd Ser., XII:132.
[237] Saint Ambrose, "Letter 27 to Sabinus (ca. 389)," *Letters*, FC, 26:141.

knowing it plainly beforehand they might plot against Him readily. Now He was openly called Jesus, not by men but by an angel who came by the power of God and not by his own authority....The angel said to Joseph, 'And she shall bring forth a Son and thou shalt call His name Jesus, for He shall save His people from their sins [Mt. 1:21].'...Consider how He Who was not yet born could have a people, unless He was in being before He was born. This also the Prophet Esaias says in His person, **'From My Mother's womb He has called My name** [Is. 49:1]**'**; because the angel foretold that He should be called Jesus. And again concerning Herod's plot, the Lord says, **'And under the shadow of His hand hath He hid Me** [Is. 49:2]**.'**"[238]

2. The Magi [Is. 45:14; 60:3, 6]**.**

A. "Thus saith the Lord of hosts, 'Egypt has labored; and the merchandise of the Ethiopians, and the Sabeans, men of stature, shall pass over to thee, and shall be Thy servants. And they shall follow after Thee bound in fetters, and shall pass over to Thee, and shall do obeisance to Thee, and make supplication in Thee, because God is in Thee; and there is no God beside Thee [Is. 45:14]**.'"**

Saint Hilary of Poitiers, says, "Let us call to mind how the Magi of the east worshipped and paid tribute to the Lord. Let us estimate the weariness of that long pilgrimage to Bethlehem. In the toilsome journey of the Magian princes, we see the labors of Egypt to which the prophet alludes. For when the Magi executed, in their spurious and material way, the duty ordained for them by the power of God, the whole heathen world was offering in their person the deepest reverence of which its worship was capable. And these same Magi presented gifts of gold and frankincense and myrrh from the merchandise of the Ethiopians and Sabeans; a thing foretold by another prophet [Ps. 71:9, 10]. The Magi and their offerings stand for the labor of Egypt and for the merchandise of Ethiopians and Sabeans; the adoring Magi represent the heathen world, and offer the choicest gifts of the Gentiles to the Lord Whom they adore. As for the men of stature who shall come over to Him and follow Him in chains, there is no doubt who they are. Turn to the Gospels: Peter, when he is to follow his Lord, is girded up. Read the apostles: Paul, the servant of Christ, boasts of his bonds...."[239]

B. "And kings shall walk in Thy light, and nations in Thy brightness....And the camels of Madiam and Gaepha shall cover thee: all from Saba shall come bearing gold, and shall bring frankincense, and they shall publish the salvation of the Lord [Is. 60:3, 6]**."**

---

[238] Saint Cyril of Jerusalem, "Lecture X," *Catechetical Lectures,* Nicene, 2nd Ser., VII:60, 61.

[239] Saint Hilary of Poitiers, *On the Trinity*, Bk. IV, §§ 38, 39, Nicene, 2nd Ser., IX:83.

Saint Kosmas the Melodist adds: *Babylon despoiled Sion the Queen and took her wealth captive. But Christ, by a guiding star, drew to Sion the treasures of Babylon, with her kings who gazed upon the stars* [Is. 60:3, 6].[240]

3. Jesus' Flight into Egypt.

"Behold, the Lord sits on a swift cloud, and shall come to Egypt: and the idols of Egypt shall be moved at His presence, and their heart shall faint within them [Is. 19:1]**."**

Saint Kyril of Jerusalem also confirms that this [Is. 19:1] is a prophecy fulfilled by Christ's flight into Egypt, "that He might overthrow the gods of Egypt made with hands."[241]

Blessed Jerome comments upon this passage, writing: "'See, the Lord is riding on a swift cloud on His way to Egypt [cf. Is. 19:1].' We must think of that swift cloud as befitting either the body of the Savior—because His body was light, not weighed down by any sin—or holy Mary, certainly, who was heavy with child by no human seed. Behold, the Lord has entered the Egypt of this world on a swift cloud, the Virgin!"[242] In another homily, he expounds further: "'The Lord is riding on a swift cloud on His way to Egypt [cf. Is. 19:1].' Appreciate what that means: The Lord comes, the Lord and Savior, into the Egypt in which we live; the Lord comes into the land of darkness where Pharaoh is. But He does not come, save riding on a swift cloud. Now what is this swift cloud? I think it is holy Mary with child of no human seed. This swift cloud has come into the world and brought with it the Creator of the world. What does Esaias say? 'The Lord will enter into Egypt upon a swift cloud, and the idols of Egypt shall be shattered [cf. Is. 19:1].' The Lord has come, and the false gods of Egypt tremble violently, crash together, and are destroyed."[243]

Saint Kosmas the Melodist distinguishes Mary Theotokos as that cloud, chanting, *Thou art the swift cloud* [Is. 19:1], *from whom the Most High God, the Sun of righteousness, shone forth upon those that were in darkness and shadow.*[244]

Saint Theodore the Stoudite (759-826), in his *Triodion* canons, glorifies the Virgin thus: *Rejoice, radiant cloud* [Is. 19:1] *of everlasting Light; from thee, Christ our God has shone out as the dawn* [Mal. 4:2].[245] Elsewhere he

---

[240] December 25th, Feast of the Nativity of our Lord, extract of Orthros Canon, Ode Eight, Mode One.

[241] Saint Cyril of Jerusalem, "Lecture X," *Catechetical Lectures,* Nicene, 2nd Ser., VII:60.

[242] Saint Jerome, "Hom. 11," *1-59 On The Psalms, Vol. 11*, FC, 48:88.

[243] Ibid., "Hom. 24," FC, 48:193.

[244] August 15th, Dormition of the Theotokos, Orthros Canon, Ode Five, Mode One.

[245] *Triodion*, Monday in the Third Week, Theotokion of Orthros Canon, Ode One, (continued...)

also lauds her, saying, *Let us all magnify the radiant cloud* [Is. 19:1], *in which the Master of all descended, as dew from heaven upon the fleece* [Jdg. 6:37, 38], *and for our sake took flesh and was made man. He Who is without beginning: for she is the pure Mother of our God.*[246]

Saint Theophanes declares at the prophet's feast day: *O Lord, Esaias clearly saw Thee sitting on the cloud of Thy most hymned Mother, casting down the idols of Egypt.*[247] And in the Akathist we hear: *Shining upon Egypt with the light of truth* [Is. 19:1; Mt. 2:14], *Thou hast dispelled the darkness of falsehood; for the idols of that land fell down, unable to endure Thy power, O Savior.*[248]

4. Youth [Is. 7:15, 16]; **Energies** [Is. 11:2, 3]; **No Comeliness** [Is. 53:2].

A. "Butter and honey shall He eat before He knows either to prefer evil or choose the good. For before the Child shall know good or evil, He refuses evil to choose the good; and the land shall be forsaken which thou art afraid of because of the two kings [Is. 7:15, 16]."

Saint Irenaeos comments, "He shows that He is a man, when he says, '**Butter and honey shall He eat** [Is. 7:15]'; and in that He terms Him a child also, in saying, 'before He knows good and evil'; for these are all the tokens of a human infant. But that 'He will not consent to evil, that He may choose that which is good,' this is proper to God; that by the fact that He shall eat butter and honey, we should not understand that He is a mere man only, nor, on the other hand, from the name Emmanuel, should we suspect Him to be God without flesh."[249]

Saint Cyprian affirms that "this shall be the sign of His nativity, that He shall be born of a virgin—Man and God—Son of Man and Son of God. Now this 'Seed' God foretold would proceed from the woman that should trample on the head of the devil [cf. Gen. 3:14, 15]."[250]

Saint John of Damascus tells us that "we cannot, if we wish to be accurate, speak of Christ as having a means of knowing (the saint later gives variants of the Greek word *gnomee*, as meaning sometimes judgment, decree, belief, opinion, or purpose) and preference. For judgment is a disposition with reference to the decision arrived at after investigation and deliberation concerning something unknown, that is to say, after counsel and decision. And

---

[245](...continued)
Mode Plagal Four.

[246] *Theotokarion*, Eirmos of Saturday Canon sung at Small Compline, Ode Nine, Mode One.

[247] May 9th, Prophet Esaias, Theotokion of Orthros Canon, Ode Four, Mode Four.

[248] *Triodion*, Saturday of the Akathist, Orthros Canon, Oikos Six.

[249] Saint Irenaeus, *Against Heresies*, Bk. III, Ch. XXI, Ante-Nicene, I:452.

[250] Saint Cyprian, "Testimonies," § 9, *Treatises*, Ante-Nicene, V:519.

after judgment comes preference, which chooses out and selects the one rather than the other. But the Lord being not mere man but also God, and knowing all things, had no need of inquiry and investigation, and counsel, and decision. And, by nature, He made whatever is good His own and whatever is bad foreign to Him. For thus says Esaias [Is. 7:16]. For the word 'before' proves that it is not with investigation and deliberation, as is the way with us, but as God and as subsisting in a divine manner in the flesh, that is to say, being united in subsistence to the flesh, and because of His very existence and all-embracing knowledge, that He is possessed of good in His own nature."[251]

B. The Divine Energies:

"And the Spirit of God shall rest upon Him, the Spirit of wisdom and understanding, the Spirit of counsel and strength, the Spirit of knowledge and godliness shall fill Him; the Spirit of the fear of God [Is. 11:2, 3]**."**

The Jew Trypho asks Saint Justin about this phrase [Is. 11:2], who replies: "The Scripture says that these enumerated powers of the Spirit have come on Him (Christ), not because He stood in need of them, but because they would rest in Him, that is, would find their accomplishment in Him, so that there would be no more prophets in your nation after the ancient custom: and this fact you plainly perceive. For after Him no prophet has arisen among you....Accordingly, He (the Spirit) rested, that is, ceased, when He (Christ) came, after Whom, in the times of this dispensation wrought out by Him amongst His people, it was requisite that such gifts should cease from you; and having received their rest in Him, should again, as had been predicted, become gifts which, from the grace of His Spirit's power, He imparts to those who believe in Him, according as He deems each man worthy thereof. I have already said, and do again say, that it had been prophesied that this would be done by Him after His ascension into the heavens. 'Therefore He says, "Having ascended on high, He led captivity captive, and gave gifts to man [cf. Ps. 67:19; Eph. 4:8].'""[252]

Saint Irenaeos says that Jesus, God's Anointed, showed Himself to be the One Who had been preached in advance by the prophets. "And as precursor there went before Him John the Baptist, preparing in advance and disposing the people to receive the Word of life, declaring that He was the Christ, on Whom rested the Spirit of God [Is. 11:2; Mt. 3:16; Jn. 1:32], united with His body."[253]

---

[251] Saint John of Damascus, *Exposition of the Orthodox Faith,* Bk. III, Ch. XIV, Nicene, 2nd Ser., IX:60.

[252] Saint Justin Martyr, *Dialogue with Trypho*, Ch. LXXXVII, Ante-Nicene, I:243.

[253] Saint Irenaeus, *Proof of the Apostolic Preaching*, ¶ 41, ACW, 16:73.

Saint Irenaeos also discusses seven heavens, as he interprets this verse, as follows: "The earth is encompassed by seven heavens, in which powers and angels and archangels give homage to almighty God, Who created all things—not as One having need of anything, but lest they too be idle and useless and accursed. Therefore, the Spirit of God in His indwelling is manifold, and is enumerated by Esaias the prophet in seven *charismata* resting on the Son of God, that is, the Logos, in His coming as man. For he says, **'The Spirit of God shall rest upon Him, the Spirit of wisdom and understanding, the Spirit of counsel and strength, the Spirit of knowledge and godliness shall fill Him; the Spirit of the fear of God** [Is. 11:2]**.'** Hence, the first heaven from the top, which encloses the others, is wisdom; and the one after it, that of understanding; but the third is that of counsel; and the fourth, counting from the top downward, that of fortitude; and the fifth that of knowledge; and the sixth that of godliness; and the seventh, this firmament of ours, full of the fear of this Spirit, Who lights up the heavens. For after this pattern Moses received the seven-branched candlestick always burning in the sanctuary; since it was on the pattern of the heavens that he received the liturgy, as the Logos says to him, 'Thou shalt do according to all the pattern of what thou hast seen on the mount [cf. Ex. 25:9, 40; Num. 8:4].'"[254]

Saint Hippolytos, discussing this passage [Is. 11:2, 3], says, "Christ, the wisdom and power of God the Father [1 Cor. 1:24], has builded His house, that is, His nature in the flesh derived from the Virgin....He assumed the temple of the body. He has raised (hewn out) her seven pillars [cf. Prov. 9:1], that is, the fragrant grace of the All-Holy Spirit, as Esaias says [Is. 11:2]."[255]

Saint Kyril of Jerusalem says that "this verse [Is. 11:2] signifies that the Spirit is one and undivided, but His operations various."[256] And, "It is established, that though the titles of the Holy Spirit be different, He is one and the same: living and subsisting, and always present together with the Father and the Son; not uttered or breathed from the mouth and lips of the Father or the Son, nor dispersed into the air, but enhypostatic, Himself speaking, and working, and dispensing, and sanctifying, even as the œconomy of salvation which is to us from the Father and the Son and the Holy Spirit is inseparable and harmonious and one....I wish you to keep in mind...and to know clearly that there is not one Spirit in the law and the prophets, and another in the

[254] Ibid., ACW, 16:53.
[255] Saint Hippolytus, *Fragments from Commentaries*, Part II, Ante-Nicene, V:175.
[256] Saint Cyril of Jerusalem, "Lecture XVI," *Catechetical Lectures*, Nicene, 2nd Ser., VII:123.

Gospels and apostles, but that it is one and the self-same Holy Spirit Who, both in the Old and in the New Testaments, spoke the divine Scriptures."[257]

Saint Ambrose of Milan points out, "The Father, the Son, and the Holy Spirit are One in counsel. For the Spirit Himself is Power, as you read, 'The Spirit of Counsel and of Power (or might) [cf. Is. 11:2].' And as the Son is the Angel of Great Counsel, so, too, is the Holy Spirit the Spirit of Counsel, that you may know that the Counsel of the Father, the Son, and the Holy Spirit is One. Counsel, not concerning any doubtful matter, but concerning those foreknown and determined."[258]

Abbot Chaeremon, in his conference with Saint John Cassian, writes about fear which is the outcome of the greatest love. "Whoever then has been established in this perfect love is sure to mount by a higher stage to that still more sublime fear belonging to love, which is the outcome of no dread of punishment or greed of reward, but of the greatest love. For by this a son fears with earnest affection a most indulgent father,...or a wife her husband. For though there is no dread of his blows or reproaches, there is fear of only a slight injury to his love; so that in every word, as well as act, there is ever care taken by anxious affection, lest the warmth of his love should cool in the very slightest degree....To this fear, then, not sinners, but saints are invited by the prophetic word where the psalmist says, 'O fear the Lord, all ye His saints; for there is no want to them that fear Him [Ps. 33:9].' For where a man fears the Lord with this fear, it is certain that nothing is lacking to his perfection. For it was clearly of that other penal fear that the Apostle John said that 'There is no fear in love; but perfect love casteth out fear, because fear hath chastisement; and the one who feareth hath not been made perfect in love [1 Jn. 4:18].' There is then a great difference between this fear, to which nothing is lacking, which is the treasure of wisdom and knowledge, and that imperfect fear which is called 'the beginning of wisdom [Ps. 110:9].'...And in truth, if the beginning of wisdom consists in fear, what will its perfection be, except in the love of Christ?...And therefore there is a twofold stage of fear....

"'And the Spirit of the fear of the Lord shall fill Him [cf. Is. 11:3].' We must in the first place notice carefully that he does not say 'and there shall rest upon Him the Spirit of fear,' as he said in the earlier cases. For such is the greatness of its richness that when once it has seized on a man, by its power, it takes possession not of a portion but of his whole mind. And not without good reason. For as it is closely joined to that love which never fails, it not only fills the man but also takes a lasting and inseparable and continual possession of him in whom it has begun, and is not lessened by any allurements of temporal joy or delights, as is sometimes the case with that fear which is cast

[257] Ibid., "Lecture XVII(5)," *Catechetical Lectures*, Nicene, 2nd Ser., VII:125.

[258] Saint Ambrose, *Of the Holy Spirit*, Bk. II, Ch. II, Nicene, 2nd Ser., X:117.

out. This then is the fear belonging to perfection with which we are told that the God-Man, Who came not only to redeem mankind but also to give us a pattern of perfection and example of goodness, was filled. For the true Son of God—Who did no sin, neither was guile found in His mouth—could not feel that servile fear of punishment."[259]

Saint Gregory the Great looks at this list, and says, "The heavenly life is opened to us through the sevenfold grace of the Holy Spirit. Esaias, recounting this sevenfold grace on our Head Himself (Jesus) or in His body, enumerated these steps by descending rather than ascending, namely, wisdom, understanding, counsel, fortitude, knowledge, godliness, fear, since it is written: 'The fear of the Lord is the beginning of wisdom [Ps. 110:9].' It is undoubtedly established that the way ascends from fear to wisdom, but does not return from wisdom to fear, because wisdom truly has perfect love."[260]

Saint Photios the Great (ca. 897) states: "The All-holy Spirit is sacredly named the Spirit of wisdom, the Spirit of understanding, the Spirit of knowledge, the Spirit of love, the Spirit of a sound mind, the Spirit of adoption [cf. Rom. 8:15]....Indeed, the Spirit is also called the Spirit of faith, and of promise and of power and of revelation, of both counsel and strength, and piety and meekness [cf. 2 Cor. 4:13; Eph. 1:13, 17; Gal. 6:1]....He is also the Spirit of judgment and of burning [cf. Is. 4:4]....Will you blasphemously declare that the All-Holy Spirit proceeds from the gifts which He distributes and grants? That He derives His existence and procession thence?"[261]

Saint Gregory Palamas states, "Esaias names these divine energies as seven; but among the Hebrews the word seven indicates many. There are those who foolishly contend that these seven spirits are created....But Gregory the Theologian, when he called to mind these divine energies of the Spirit, said, 'Esaias was fond of calling the energies of the Spirit spirits.' And this most distinguished voice among the prophets clearly demonstrated through this number not only the distinction with respect to the divine substance but also the uncreated character of these divine energies by means of the word 'rested upon,' for resting upon belongs to a preeminent dignity. As for those spirits that rested upon the Lord's human nature which He assumed from us, how could they be creatures?

"According to Luke," he continues, "our Lord Jesus Christ says He cast out demons by the finger of God [Lk. 11:20], but according to Matthew it is by the Spirit of God [Mt. 12:28]. Basil the Great says that the finger of

---

[259] Saint John Cassian, "The First Conference of Abbot Chaeremon," *Cassian's Conferences*, Ch. XIII, Nicene, 2nd Ser., XI:421, 422.

[260] Saint Gregory the Great, "Hom. VII," *The Homilies of Saint Gregory the Great On the Book of the Prophet Ezekiel*, Bk. II, p. 234.

[261] Saint Photios, *On the Mystagogy of the Holy Spirit*, pp. 93, 94.

God is one of the energies of the Spirit. If then one of these is the Holy Spirit, the others too certainly are, since Basil has also taught us this. But on this account there are not many Gods or many Spirits, for these realities are processions, manifestations and natural energies of the one Spirit, and in each case the Agent is one. When the heterodox call these creatures, they degrade the Spirit of God to a creature sevenfold. But let their shame be sevenfold, for a prophet again says of the energies, 'Those are the seven eyes that look upon all the earth [Zach. 4:10].' And it is written in the book of Revelation, 'Grace to you and peace from God, the One Who is and the One Who was and the One coming, and from the seven Spirits which are before His throne, and from Jesus Christ [Rev. 1:4, 5].' It is clearly demonstrated to the faithful that these are the Holy Spirit."[262]

C. "We brought a report as a child before Him, as a root in a thirsty land. He has no form nor comeliness. And we saw Him, but He had no form nor beauty [Is. 53:2 LXX]**."**

Saint Justin says that the Prophet Esaias "speaks as if he were personating the apostles when they say to Christ that they believe not in their own report, but in the power of Him Who sent them. But when the passage speaks as from the lips of many, 'We have preached before Him,' and adds, 'as a child,' it signifies that the wicked shall become subject to Him, and shall obey His command, and that all shall become as one child. Such a thing as you may witness in the body: although the members are enumerated as many, all are called *one*, and are a *body*. For, indeed, a commonwealth and a church, though many individuals in number, are in fact as one, called and addressed by one appellation."[263]

Saint Gregory the Theologian notes that "Christ has not form nor comeliness in the eyes of the Jews [Is. 53:2]—but to David He is fairer than the children of men [Ps. 44:2]. And on the Mountain (Tabor), He was bright as the lightning; and He became more luminous than the sun [Mt. 17:2], initiating us into the mystery of the future."[264]

Saint Chrysostom observes the following about Christ: "For not by any means in working wonders only was He wonderful, but even when merely showing Himself, He was full of great grace; and to declare this the prophet said, 'Comely art Thou in beauty more than the sons of men [Ps. 44:2].' And

---

[262] Saint Gregory Palamas, *The One Hundred and Fifty Chapters*, Chaps. 70, 71, pp. 165, 167. Also for cites mentioned by Saint Gregory, see Saint Gregory Nazianzen, "Or. 41.3," *P.G.* 36:432C and Saint Basil, *Adversus Eunomium* 5, *P.G.* 29: 716C-717A.

[263] Saint Justin Martyr, *Dialogue with Trypho*, Ch. XLII, Ante-Nicene, I:215, 216.

[264] Saint Gregory Nazianzen (the Theologian), "Oration XXIX, On the Son," Nicene, 2nd Ser., VII:308.

if Esaias says, **'He hath no form nor comeliness** [Is. 53:2],**'** he affirms it either in comparison of the glory of His divinity—which surpasses all utterance and description—or as declaring what took place at His Passion, and the dishonor which He underwent at the season of the Cross, and the mean estate which throughout His life He exemplified in all respects."[265]

Saint Jerome gives his opinion, regarding, "'We have seen Him, and there was no stately bearing in Him [cf. Is. 53:2].' Why? Because His flesh has become wasted for 'want of oil [Ps. 108:23].' There was nothing appealing about His body, only about His spirit."[266] In another homily, he compares this verse [Is. 53:2] with that in Psalms, "The Lord reigneth as King, He clothed Himself with majesty [Ps. 92:1]," and advises us: "The meaning, then, is that He Whose appearance before had been frightful in the meanness of the flesh, now is resplendent in the majesty of the Divinity, for whatever unsightliness there is in Him is to be ascribed to our estate, but whatever there is of beauty shall be applied congruently to His majesty."[267]

Saint Isaac (d. ca. 700) says, "Though the legions of the angels are not able to look upon the glory surrounding His majestic throne, yet for thy sake He has appeared before the world...with no form nor comeliness [Is. 53:2]."[268]

5. The Coming of the Forerunner, Saint John the Baptist.

"The voice of one crying in the wilderness, 'Prepare ye the way of the Lord, make straight the paths of our God [Is. 40:3].**'"**

Saint Ephraim says that "the daughter (Elisabeth) of Aaron gave birth to the voice in the desert [Is. 40:3; Mt. 3:3], and the daughter (Mary) of King David to the Word of the heavenly King."[269]

Saint Chrysostom identifies also the voice in the wilderness as Saint John the Forerunner and Baptist. "Conceive, for example, how great a thing it was to see a man after thirty years coming down from the wilderness, being the son of a chief priest [Lk. 1:13], who had never known the common wants of men, and was on every account venerable, and had Esaias with him. For he too was present, proclaiming him, and saying, 'This is he who I said should come crying, and preaching throughout the whole wilderness with a clear voice [cf. Is. 40:3].' For so great was the earnestness of the prophets touching these things, that not their own Lord only, but him also who was to minister unto Him, they proclaimed a long time beforehand. And they mentioned not only him but also the place in which he was to abide, and the manner of the doctrine

---

[265] Saint Chrysostom, "Hom. XXVII," *Matthew*, Nicene, 1st Ser., X:186.

[266] Saint Jerome, "Hom. 35," *1-59 On The Psalms, Vol. 1*, FC, 48:264, 265.

[267] Idem, "Hom. 70," *60-96 On The Psalms, Vol. 2*, FC, 57:95.

[268] Saint Isaac the Syrian, "Treatise III," *Mystical Treatises by Isaac of Nineveh*, translated from Bedjan's Syriac text, by Arent Jan Wensinck, Volume One, p. 28.

[269] *Saint Ephrem's Commentary on Tatian's Diatessaron*, p. 58.

which he had to teach when he came [Mt. 3:8], and the good effect that was produced by him."[270]

Saint Kyril of Alexandria says, "The blessed Esaias was not ignorant of the scope of John's preaching, but of old, even long before the time, bearing witness of it, he called Christ Lord and God; but John he styled His minister and servant, and said that he was a lamp advancing before the true light, the morning star heralding the sun, foreshadowing the coming of the day that was about to shed its rays upon us; and that he was a voice, not a word, forerunning Jesus, as the voice does the word."[271]

6. His Manner and Conduct [Is. 11:2, 3; 42:2, 3].

A. "He shall not judge according to appearance, nor reprove according to report [Is. 11:3]:

"But He shall judge the cause of the lowly, and shall reprove the lowly of the earth: and He shall smite the earth with the word of His mouth, and with the breath of His lips shall He destroy the ungodly one [Is. 11:4].

"And He shall have His loins girt with righteousness, and His sides clothed with truth [Is. 11:5]."

Saint Irenaeos indicates that "this shows His divinity more strongly. For to judge without acceptance of persons or partiality, not favoring the noble, but rendering to the lowly what is right and equitable and fair, corresponds to the exaltation and sublimity of God's justice, for God is not subject to influence, and favors none but the just man; and to have pity is especially proper to God, to Him Who can also save out of pity. And also, 'He shall strike the earth with a word and slay the ungodly [cf. Is. 11:4],' by a word alone; this is proper to God, Who works all things whatsoever by His Logos. But in saying, 'His loins shall be girded with justice, and His flanks clad in truth [cf. Is. 11:5],' he announces His outward human form, and His inward supreme justice."[272]

B. "He shall not cry, nor lift up His voice, nor shall His voice be heard without [Is. 42:2].

"A bruised reed shall He not break, and smoking flax shall He not quench; but He shall bring forth judgment to truth [Is. 42:3]."

Saint Chrysostom characterizes Christ in the same manner as the prophet, and so refers us to the Lord's very words: "I came not that I might judge the world, but that I might save the world [Jn. 12:47]."[273]

---

[270] Saint Chrysostom, "Hom. X," *Matthew,* Nicene, 1st Ser., X:63.

[271] Saint Cyril of Alexandria, "Hom. 6," *Commentary*, p. 69.

[272] Saint Irenaeus, *Proof of the Apostolic Preaching*, ¶ 60, ACW, 16:87.

[273] Saint Chrysostom, "Hom. XXIV," *John*, Nicene, 1st Ser., XIV:84.

7. Christ's Message.

"The Spirit of the Lord is upon Me, because He has anointed Me; He has sent Me to preach glad tidings to the poor, to heal the broken in heart, to proclaim liberty to the captives, and recovery of sight to the blind [Is. 61:1]**."**

"The meaning implied in the name 'Christ,'" observes Saint Irenaeos, "is 'He that anoints,' 'He that is anointed,' and the 'unction' itself with which He is anointed. And it is the Father Who anoints, but the Son Who is anointed by the Spirit, Who is the unction, as the Logos declares by Esaias: **'The Spirit of the Lord is upon Me** [Is. 65:1]**'**—pointing out both the anointing Father, the anointed Son, and the unction, which is the Spirit."[274] Also, according to Saint Irenaeos, this verse spoken by the prophet shows Jesus is Savior and "that He became the cause of salvation to those who were at that time freed by Him from all manner of ills and from death, and to those to be, who believed after them, and the Conferrer of eternal salvation."[275]

Saint Athanasios explains this verse saying that "He is anointed with the Spirit in His manhood to sanctify human nature. Therefore the Spirit descended on Him in Jordan, when in the flesh. And He is said to sanctify Himself for us, and give us the glory He received....We hear, 'The Spirit of the Lord is upon Me, because the Lord has anointed Me [cf. Is. 61:1],' and the apostle, 'Ye know...how God anointed Him, Jesus, the One from Nazareth, with the Holy Spirit...[Acts 10:37, 38].' When then were these things spoken of Him, but when He came in the flesh and was baptized in Jordan and the Spirit descended on Him? And indeed the Lord Himself said, 'The Spirit shall receive of Mine [cf. Jn. 16:14]'; and 'I will send Him (the Paraclete) [Jn. 16:7]'; and to His disciples, 'Receive ye the Holy Spirit [Jn. 20:22].' And, notwithstanding, He Who, as the Logos and Radiance of the Father, gives to others, now is said to be sanctified, because now He has become Man, and the body that is sanctified is His. From Him then we have begun to receive the unction and the seal, John saying, 'And ye have an anointing from the Holy One [1 Jn. 2:20]'; and the apostle, 'And ye were sealed with the Holy Spirit of promise [Eph. 1:13].' Therefore because of us and for us are these words."[276]

In the same discourse, Saint Athanasios later says that "in no wise should we have partaken of the Spirit and been sanctified had not the Giver of the Spirit, the Logos Himself, spoken of Himself as anointed with the Spirit for

---

[274] Saint Irenaeus, *Against Heresies*, Bk. III, Ch. XVIII, Ante-Nicene, I:446.

[275] Idem, *Proof of the Apostolic Preaching*, ¶ 53, ACW, 16:82.

[276] Saint Athanasius, "Discourse I," *Four Discourses Against the Arians,* Nicene, 2nd Ser., IV:334.

us....And since as Man the flesh was sanctified in Him,...we have the sequel of the Spirit's grace, receiving 'of His fullness [Jn. 1:16].'"[277]

Saint Kyril of Jerusalem, in his lecture regarding Chrism, writes: "Having been baptized into Christ, and put on Christ [cf. Gal. 3:27], ye have been made conformable to the Son of God....We have become partakers of Christ [Heb. 3:14]....He washed in the river Jordan, and having imparted of the tincture and flavor of His divinity to the waters, He came up from them; and the Holy Spirit in the fullness of His Being lighted on Him, like resting upon like. And to you in like manner, after you had come up from the pool of the sacred streams, there was given an Chrism, the antitype of that wherewith Christ was anointed; and this is the Holy Spirit of Whom the blessed Esaias, in his prophecy respecting Him, spoke of in the person of the Lord [Is. 61:1]. For Christ was not anointed by men with oil or material ointment, but the Father having before appointed Him to be the Savior of the whole world, anointed Him with the Holy Spirit....And as Christ was in reality crucified, and buried, and raised, and you are in Baptism accounted worthy of being crucified, buried, and raised together with Him in a likeness, so is it with the Chrism also. As He was anointed with a noetic oil of gladness, that is, with the Holy Spirit, called 'oil of gladness [Ps. 44:6],' so you were anointed with ointment, having been made partakers and fellows of Christ."[278]

Saint Ambrose of Milan speaks of the unity of the Trinity, as follows, "Bethink you that our Lord Jesus Christ said in Esaias that He had been sent by the Spirit [Is. 61:1]? Is the Son, therefore, less than the Spirit because He was sent by the Spirit? Thus you have the record, that the Son declares Himself sent by the Father and His Spirit. **'I am the first, and I endure for ever. My hand also has founded the earth, and My right hand has fixed the sky; I will call them, and they shall stand together** [Is. 48:12, 13]'; and further on, **'I have spoken, I have called, I have brought Him, and made His way prosperous. Draw nigh to Me, and hear ye these words. I have not spoken in secret from the beginning; When it took place, there was I, and now the Lord, even the Lord, and His Spirit, hath sent Me** [Is. 48:15, 16].' Here, indeed, He Who made the heaven and the earth Himself says that He is sent by the Lord and His Spirit. You see, then, that the poverty of language takes not from the honor of His mission. He then is sent by the Father; by the Spirit also is He sent. And that you may gather that there is no separating difference of majesty, the Son in turn sends the Spirit, even as He Himself has said [Jn. 15:26]. That this same Comforter is also to be sent by the Father He has already taught

[277] Ibid., Nicene, 2nd Ser., IV:336.
[278] Saint Cyril of Jerusalem, "Lecture XXI," *Catechetical Lectures*, Nicene, 2nd Ser., VII:149.

saying, **'But the Paraclete (Comforter), the Holy Spirit, Whom the Father will send in My name...**[Jn. 14:26]**.'** Behold their unity."[279]

Furthermore, he adds: "Jesus says in the Gospel, 'Today this Scripture [Is. 61:1] hath been fulfilled in your ears [Lk. 4:21],' that He might point out that it was said of Himself. Can we then wonder if the Spirit sent both the prophets and the apostles, since Christ said, **'The Spirit of the Lord is upon Me** [Is. 61:1]'? And rightly did He say 'upon Me,' because He was speaking as the Son of Man. For as the Son of Man He was anointed and sent to preach the Gospel."[280]

8. Christ's Miracles.

"Then shall the eyes of the blind be opened, and the ears of the deaf shall hear. Then shall the lame man leap as an hart, and the tongue of the stammerers shall speak plainly; for water has burst forth in the desert, and a channel of water in a thirsty land [Is. 35:5, 6]**."**

Saint Justin counters those who say that the deformed rise deformed. "For if on earth Jesus healed the sicknesses of the flesh, and made the body whole, much more will He do this in the resurrection, so that the flesh shall rise perfect and entire. In this manner, then, shall those dreaded difficulties of theirs be healed."[281]

Saint Athanasios, speaking of clear prophecies of the coming of God in the flesh, writes: "Now what can they say to this [Is. 35:3-6], or how can they dare to face this at all? For the prophecy not only indicates that God is to sojourn here but also announces the signs and the time of His coming. For they connect the blind recovering their sight, and the lame walking, and the deaf hearing, and the tongue of the stammerers being made plain, with the divine coming which is to take place. Let them say, then, when such signs have come to pass in Israel, or where in Jewry anything of the sort has occurred."[282]

"Esaias shows," declares Saint Chrysostom, "how Christ cured the lame, how He made the blind to see, and the mute to speak [Is. 35:5; cf. Mt. 15:30]. And thereafter he spoke of other marvels [Is. 35:6; Mt. 11:5; Mk. 7:37; Lk. 7:22]. And this did not happen until His coming."[283]

9. Christ, the Shepherd.

"He shall tend His flock as a shepherd, and He shall gather the lambs with His arm, and shall soothe them that are with young [Is. 40:11]**."**

---

[279] Saint Ambrose, *Of the Christian Faith,* Bk. II, Ch. IX, Nicene, 2nd Ser., X:233.

[280] Ibid., Bk. III, Ch. I, Nicene, 2nd Ser., X:135, 136.

[281] Saint Justin Martyr, *On the Resurrection*, Ch. IV, Ante-Nicene, I:295.

[282] Saint Athanasius, *On the Incarnation of the Word*, § 38, Nicene, 2nd Ser., IV:56, 57.

[283] Saint John Chrysostom, *Demonstration Against the Pagans*, Ch. III, FC, 73:200.

Saint Kyril of Alexandria says, "Our Lord Jesus Christ showed Himself to us having divine strength, and His arm with authority, that is, with power and dominion. For that very reason, He said to the leper, 'I will; be made clean [cf. Mt. 8:3].' For that reason, He touched the bier and raised up the dead son of the widow [Lk. 7:12-15]. And He gathered together the lambs, for He is the good Shepherd Who laid down His life for His sheep."[284]

10. Palm Sunday [Is. 8:18; 40:9].

A. "Behold I and the children which God has given Me. And they shall be for signs and wonders in the house of Israel from the Lord of host, Who dwells in Mount Sion [Is. 8:18]."

Blessed Jerome apprises us that "since the seniors and the elders of the Jews are silent, and the Pharisees, too, in the gnawing of envious malice, children cry out and acclaim Christ [on Palm Sunday, Mk. 11:9, 10]. Even if they had been silent, the very stones would have shouted."[285]

B. "O thou that bringest glad tidings to Sion, go up on the high mountain. Lift up thy voice with strength, thou that bringest tidings to Jerusalem. Lift up, fear not. Say unto the cities of Juda, 'Behold your God [Is. 40:9]!

"'Behold the Lord! The Lord is coming with strength, and His arm is with power. Behold, His reward is with Him, and His work before Him [Is. 40:10].'"

For Palm Sunday, we sing exultantly: *Go up the mountain, Thou that bringest good tidings to Sion; and Thou that preachest to Jerusalem, lift up Thy voice with strength* [Is. 40:9]. *Glorious things are spoken of thee, O city of God* [Ps. 86:3]: *Peace be upon Israel* [Ps. 127:6] *and salvation to the nations.*[286]

11. The Passion [Is. 1:21; 3:10, 13, 14; 5:26; 50:6; 53:3-12].

A. "I gave My back to scourges, and My cheeks to blows; and I turned not away My face from the shame of spitting [Is. 50:6]."

Saint Irenaeos tells us that "by the obedience, whereby He obeyed unto death [cf. Phil. 2:8], hanging on the tree, Christ undid the old disobedience wrought in the tree. And because He is Himself the Logos of the almighty God, Who in His invisible form pervades us universally in the whole world, and encompasses both its length and breadth and height and depth—for by God's Logos everything is disposed and administered—the Son of God was also crucified in these, imprinted in the form of a Cross on the universe. For He had necessarily, in becoming visible, to bring to light His cross-sharing with the

---

[284] Saint Cyril of Alexandria, "Letter 1 to Priests, Deacons, Fathers of Monks and Solitaries," *Letters 1-50*, FC, 76:27, 28.

[285] Saint Jerome, "Hom. 94," *60-96 On The Psalms, Vol. 2*, FC, 57:254.

[286] Palm Sunday, Eirmos of Orthros Canon, Ode Five, Mode Four, by Saint Kosmas or Saint Andrew of Crete.

universe, in order to show openly through His visible form that activity of His: that it is He Who makes bright the height, that is, what is in heaven, and holds the deep, which is in the bowels of the earth, and stretches forth and extends the length from east to west, navigating also the northern parts and the breadth of the south, and calling in all the dispersed from all sides to the knowledge of the Father."[287]

Saint Athanasios says, "Thus our Lord and Savior Jesus Christ comes before us. He would show men how to suffer. When He was smitten, He bore it patiently. When He was reviled, He reviled not again. When He suffered, He threatened not. But He gave His back to the smiters, and His cheeks to buffeting, and turned not His face from spitting [Is. 50:6]. And He was willingly led to death, that we might behold in Him the image of all that is virtuous and immortal, and that we, conducting ourselves after these examples, might truly tread on serpents and scorpions, and on all the power of the enemy."[288]

In another letter, Saint Athanasios writes: "The incorporeal Logos made His own the properties of the body, as being His own body. What the human body of the Logos suffered, this the Logos, dwelling in the body, ascribed to Himself, in order that we might be enabled to be partakers of the divinity of the Logos [cf. 2 Pe. 1:4]. And verily it is strange that He it was Who suffered and yet suffered not. Suffered, because His own body suffered, and He was in it, which thus suffered; suffered not, because the Logos, being by nature God, is impassible. And while He, the incorporeal, was in the passible body, the body had in it the impassible Logos, which was destroying the infirmities inherent in the body. But this He did, and so it was, in order that Himself taking what was ours and offering it as a sacrifice, He might do away with it, and conversely might invest us with what was His, and cause the apostles to say: 'For it is needful for this corruptible to put on itself incorruption and this mortal to put on itself immortality [1 Cor. 15:53].'

"Now this did not come to pass putatively, as some have supposed—far be the thought!—but the Savior, having in very truth become Man, the salvation of the whole man was brought about. For if the Logos were in the body putatively, as they say, and by putative is meant imaginary, it follows that both the salvation and the resurrection of man is apparent only, as the most impious Manichaeos held. But truly our salvation is not merely apparent, nor does it extend to the body only, but the whole man, body and soul alike, has truly obtained salvation in the Logos Himself. That then which was born of Mary was according to the divine Scriptures human by nature, and the body of

---

[287] Saint Irenaeus, *Proof of the Apostolic Preaching*, ¶ 34, ACW, 16:69, 70.
[288] Saint Athanasius, "Letter X," Nicene, 2nd Ser., IV:530.

the Lord was a true one; but it was this, because it was the same as our body, for Mary was our sister inasmuch as we all are from Adam."[289]

"If God," Saint Makarios of Alexandria (330-390) reminds us, "condescends to such insults and sufferings and humiliations, thou, who art by nature clay and mortal, howsoever thou mayest be humbled, thou wilt never do anything like Thy Master. God for thy sake humbled Himself, and thou wilt not be humbled for thine own sake, but art proud and puffed up. He came to take upon Him thine afflictions and thy burdens, and to give Thee His own rest; and thou art unwilling to bear troubles and to suffer in order to gain healing for thy wounds. Glory be to His patience and long-suffering forever!"[290]

Saint Kyril of Alexandria, in a letter, writes concerning the divine nature of the Logos: "For He remains what He is always, and He is not changed....Each of us confesses that the Logos of God is, moreover, impassible, even though He Himself is seen arranging the dispensation of the mystery all-wisely by assigning to Himself the sufferings that happened to His own body. And in this way, also, the all-wise Peter speaks, 'since Christ suffered for us in the flesh [cf. 1 Pe. 4:1]' and not in the nature of His ineffable divinity. For in order that He might be believed to be the Savior of all, according to incarnational appropriation, He assumes, as I said, the sufferings of His own flesh."[291]

What purpose was achieved by our Savior's self-emptying and suffering? Saint Andrew of Crete (ca. 660-740) tells us: *The Lamb Whom Esaias proclaimed goes of His own will to the slaughter* [Is. 53:7]. *He is condemned to a disgraceful death. Though sinless, He accepts all these things willingly, that He may grant to all men resurrection from the dead.*[292]

B. Christ is Despised:

"But His form was ignoble, and inferior to that of the children of men; He was a man in suffering, and acquainted with the bearing of sickness, for His face has been turned away (ἀπέστϱαπται) **He was dishonored and not esteemed** [Is. 53:3]**."**

Saint Kyril of Alexandria notes, "'He was despised and not esteemed [cf. Is. 53:3],' as it is written, that He might make us honorable. He did no sin, that He might crown our nature with similar glory."[293]

The following hymn by the holy hymnographer Joseph, during the *Triodion* period, expresses the Theotokos' maternal grief: *"I see Thee lifted on*

---

[289] Ibid., "Letter LIX," Nicene, 2nd Ser., IV:572, 573.
[290] Saint Macarius the Great, "Hom. XXVI," *Fifty Spiritual Homilies*, pp. 198, 199.
[291] Saint Cyril of Alexandria, "Letter 39 Theognostus and Charmosynus, Priests, and to Leontius, the Deacon," *Letters 1-50*, FC, 76:151.
[292] Holy Thursday, Orthros Doxastikon, Mode Two.
[293] Saint Cyril of Alexandria, "Hom. 153," *Commentary*, pp. 608, 609.

high," cried the holy Virgin, "and because of Thy suffering there is neither form nor beauty in Thee [Is. 53:2]; *yet when first I saw Thee incarnate in the flesh, only-begotten Son, Thou wast fairer than all the sons of men* [Ps. 44:2]. *O salvation of all, manifest Thy glory.* "[294] And, *At Thy Passion, O Logos, there was neither form nor beauty in Thee* [Is. 53:2]: *but Thou hast risen in glory, and with Thy divine light Thou hast given beauty to mortal men.*[295]

Saint Chrysostom comments, "For neither did He fail in any things of gentleness nor did they fail in acts of insolence and cruelty in what they did and in what they said. All these things did the Prophet Esaias foretell, thus proclaiming beforehand, and by one word intimating all this insolence; for he said, **'As many shall be astonished at Thee, so shall Thy form be held inglorious of men, and Thy glory of the sons of men** [Is. 52:14 LXX].'"[296]

C. Christ Bears Our Sins and Sorrows:

"He bears our sins, and is pained for us: yet we accounted Him to be in trouble, and in suffering, and in affliction. But He was wounded on account of our sins, and was bruised because of our iniquities. The chastisement of our peace was upon Him; and by His bruises we were healed [Is. 53:4, 5]."

In a letter, Saint Athanasios writes: "He bore our sins, as the prophet says [Is. 53:4], and was afflicted for us, that He might put away from all of us grief, and sorrow, and sighing."[297] He explains that when we hear "'Christ became a curse for us [cf. Gal. 3:13]' and 'He made Him to be sin on our behalf, Who knew not sin [cf. 2 Cor. 5:21],' we do not simply conceive this, that whole Christ has become curse and sin, but that He has taken on Him the curse which lay against us, as the apostle has said, 'Christ redeemed us from the curse of the law [Gal. 3:13]' and 'bears (φέρει),' as Esaias has said, **'our sins** [Is. 53:4]**,'** and as Peter has written: 'He Himself carried up (ἀνήνεγκεν) our sins in His body on the tree [cf. 1 Pe. 2:24].'"[298]

Saint Hilary of Poitiers informs us that Christ "was esteemed 'stricken, smitten, and afflicted.'...Though He was wounded, it was 'for our transgressions.' The wound was not the wound of His own transgressions; the suffering not a suffering for Himself. He was not born man for His own sake, nor did He transgress in His own action. The apostle explains the principle of the divine plan when he says, 'We beseech on behalf of Christ, be ye reconciled to God. For He Who knew no sin He made to be sin on our behalf [cf. 2 Cor. 5:20,

---

[294] *Triodion*, Wednesday in the Fourth Week, Stavrotheotokion of Orthros Canon, Ode Eight, Mode Plagal Two.

[295] Holy Saturday, Orthros, Encomia, Second Stasis, Mode Plagal One.

[296] Saint Chrysostom, "Hom. LXXXV," *Matthew*, Nicene, 1st Ser., X:506.

[297] Saint Athanasius, "Letter XX," Nicene, 2nd Ser., IV:548.

[298] Ibid., "Discourse II," *Four Discourses Against the Arians,* Nicene, 2nd Ser., IV:374.

21].' In order to condemn sin through sin in the flesh, He Who knew no sin was Himself made sin;...and therefore was wounded because of our transgressions."[299]

Saint Makarios the Great expresses the following: "See to what humiliation He came, having taken the form of a servant [Phil. 2:7], Who is God, the Son of God, King, the Son of the King, giving healing remedies and curing those that are wounded, when He Himself appeared outwardly as one of the wounded [Is. 53:5]."[300]

Saint Gregory the Theologian points out, "He is bruised and wounded, but He heals every disease and every infirmity [Is. 53:5]."[301]

Saint Ambrose of Milan writes: "By hunger Christ proved to us that He had verily taken upon Himself a body, so that He might teach us that He had taken not only our body but also our bodily weaknesses, as it is written: 'Surely He hath taken our infirmities and borne our sicknesses [cf. Is. 53:4].' It was then a weakness of ours that He hungered. When He wept and was sorrowful even unto death, it was of our nature. Why ascribe the properties and incidents of our nature to the divinity?"[302] More importantly, he affirms, "He is not weak, for though in the flesh He suffered weakness for our sins, yet that was the chastisement of our peace upon Him [Is. 53:5], not lack of sovereign power in Himself."[303]

D. Christ is Given Up for Our Sins:

"All we as sheep have gone astray; every one has gone astray in his way; and the Lord gave Him up for our sins [Is. 53:6]**."**

"The Lord gave Him up for our sins [Is. 53:6]**,"** means, according to Saint Irenaeos that "it is clear that it came about by the will of the Father that these things happened to Him, for the sake of our salvation."[304]

"What profit came from that death on the Cross?" asks Saint Chrysostom. He answers, "These are the blessings it achieved: evil was destroyed, the wounds of the soul were set right by a wondrous cure and a healing beyond belief."[305] Continuing, he says: "'He Himself took our weaknesses and bore our diseases [Mt. 8:17].' He said not, 'He did away with them,' but 'He took

---

[299] Saint Hilary of Poitiers, *On the Trinity*, Bk. X, §§ 47, 48, Nicene, 2nd Ser., IX: 194, 195.

[300] Saint Macarios the Great, "Hom. XXVI," *Fifty Spiritual Homilies*, 198.

[301] Saint Gregory Nazianzen (the Theologian), "Oration XXIX, On the Son," Nicene, 2nd Ser., VII:309.

[302] Saint Ambrose, *Of the Christian Faith,* Bk. III, Chaps. I, II, Nicene, 2nd Ser., X:243.

[303] Ibid., Bk. IV, Ch. V, Nicene, 2nd Ser., X:269.

[304] Saint Irenaeus, *Proof of the Apostolic Preaching*, ¶ 69, ACW, 16:92.

[305] Saint John Chrysostom, *Demonstration Against the Pagans*, Ch. IV, FC, 73:206.

and bore them,' which seems to me to be spoken rather of sins, by the prophet, in harmony with John, where he says, 'Behold the Lamb of God Who taketh away the sin of the world [Jn. 1:29]!' How then does the evangelist here apply it to diseases? Either as rehearsing the passage in the historical sense or as showing that most of our diseases arise from sins of the soul. For if the sum of all, death itself, has its root and foundation from sin, much more the majority of our diseases also, since our very capability of suffering did itself originate there."[306]

Saint Kyril of Alexandria indicates, "Thus Christ became a victim 'for our sins according to the Scriptures [Is. 53:4-6; 1 Cor. 15:3].' For this reason, we say that He was named sin. Therefore, the all-wise Paul writes: 'For our sake He made Him to be sin Who knew nothing of sin [cf. 2 Cor. 5:21].' For we do not say that Christ became a sinner, far from it, but being just, or rather in actuality justice, for He did not know sin, the Father made Him a victim for the sins of the world."[307]

Saint Paulinus of Nola, in a poem, writes of the Son of Man: "So Christ has healed the vices of my soul, and taken on Himself the sicknesses of my body [Is. 53:4]—Man by His Mother, God by His Father. He bore the weaknesses of the flesh that are appointed by nature [cf. Heb. 5:2], and evinced the feelings of the human body. He ate and drank, and closed His eyes in sleep, and grew weary with journeying in accordance with His human sensibilities. He shed tears over the death of a friend like a man, but then as God raised him from the tomb [cf. Jn. 11:35, 44]. As a man He sailed on a ship, and as God He governed the winds; by His strength as God, the Man walked over the sea [cf. Mt. 14:24 ff.]. With His human mind He feared the hour of imminent death, but with His divine mind He knew that the moment of execution was at hand. As Man He was nailed to the Cross, and as God He terrified the world from the Cross [Mt. 27:51]. The Man endured death, but death itself endured the true God. The Man hung on the Cross, but as God He forgave sins from the Cross, and by dying destroyed the life of sin. He Who was counted among the guilty [cf. Mk. 15:28], and was assessed as worse than the thief, whom the Jews ranked before their devoted Lord [cf. Mt. 27:21], gave the kingdom of the heavens to the thief who believed [cf. Lk. 23:43], and while still confined to earth opened the gates of Paradise."[308]

Saint Leo the Great, Pope of Rome, writes: "The saving of all through the Cross of Christ was the common will and the common plan of the Father and the Son; nor could that by any means be disturbed which before eternal ages had been mercifully determined and unchangeably foreordained.

---

[306] Idem, "Hom. XXVII," *Matthew*, Nicene, 1st Ser., X:185.

[307] Saint Cyril of Alexandria, "Letter 41 to Bishop Acacius," *Letters 1-50*, FC, 76:174.

[308] Saint Paulinus, "Poem 31," *The Poems of Saint Paulinus of Nola*, ACW, 40:313.

Therefore, in assuming true and entire manhood, He took the true sensation of the body and the true feelings of the mind. And it does not follow because everything in Him was full of sacraments, full of miracles, that therefore He either shed false tears or took food from pretended hunger or feigned slumber. It was in our humility that He was despised, with our grief that He was saddened, with our pain that He was racked on the Cross. For His compassion underwent the sufferings of our mortality with the purpose of healing them, and His power encountered them with the purpose of conquering them. And this Esaias has most plainly prophesied, saying, 'He carries our sins and is pained and in vexation. But He was wounded for our sins, and was stricken for our offenses, and with his bruises we are healed.'"[309]

E. The Lamb of God's Voluntary Acceptance:

"And He, because of His affliction, opens not His mouth; He was led as a sheep to the slaughter, and as a lamb before the shearer is dumb, so He opens not His mouth [Is. 53:7]**."**

Saint Justin to Trypho the Jew says, "Our suffering and crucified Christ was not cursed by the law, but made it manifest that He alone would save those who do not depart from His faith. And the blood of the passover, sprinkled on each man's doorposts and lintel [Ex. 12:22, 23], delivered those who were saved in Egypt, when the firstborn of the Egyptians were destroyed. For the Passover was Christ, Who was afterward sacrificed, as also Esaias said, **'He was led as a sheep to the slaughter** [Is. 53:7]**.'** And it is written, that on the day of the passover you seized Him, and that also during the passover you crucified Him. And as the blood of the passover saved those who were in Egypt, so also the blood of Christ will deliver from death those who have believed. Would God, then, have been deceived if this sign had not been above the doors? I do not say that; but I affirm that He announced beforehand the future salvation for the human race through the blood of Christ. For the sign of the scarlet thread, which the spies, sent to Jericho by Jesus of Navee, gave to Rahab the harlot, telling her to bind it to the window through which she let them down to escape from their enemies [Josh. 2:18], also manifested the symbol of the blood of Christ, by which those who were at one time harlots and unrighteous persons out of all nations are being saved, receiving remission of sins, and continuing no longer in sin."[310]

Saint Athanasios contends that "when Patriarch Abraham was tried, by faith he offered up Isaac, and sacrificed his only-begotten son—he who had received the promises. And, in offering his son, he worshipped the Son of God. And, being restrained from sacrificing Isaac, he saw the Messiah in the ram [Gen. 22:13], which was offered up instead as a sacrifice to God. The patriarch

---

[309] Saint Leo the Great, "Sermon LVIII on the Passion," Nicene, 2nd Ser., XII:170.

[310] Saint Justin Martyr, *Dialogue with Trypho*, Ch. CXI, Ante-Nicene, I:254.

was tried through Isaac, not however that he was sacrificed, but He Who was pointed out in Esaias: **'He was led as a sheep to the slaughter, and as a lamb before the shearer is dumb, so He opens not His mouth** [Is. 53:7]'; but He took away the sin of the world. And on this account Abraham was restrained from laying his hand on the lad, lest the Jews, taking occasion from the sacrifice of Isaac, should reject the prophetic declarations concerning our Savior, even all of them, but more especially those uttered by the psalmist: 'Sacrifice and offering hast Thou not desired, but a body hast Thou perfected for Me [Ps. 39:9]'; and should refer all such things as these to the son of Abraham."[311] Also; Saint Athanasios believes that "the wound in the side by the spears answers to **'He was led as a sheep to the slaughter** [Is. 53:7]**.'**"[312]

Saint Ephraim the Syrian observes the ordering in this verse, as follows, "Like a lamb He went to the slaughter and like a sheep before the shearers [cf. Is. 53:7]," and says, "It is difficult to perceive logically that He should be killed first, and then shorn. But that was said of the Lord, because He was killed by that sentence which came forth from the judge's mouth, and after that they then came and stretched Him out on the Cross. Spread out thus over the earth, He was like a sheep before the shearers."[313] Elsewhere, Saint Ephraim exults: "Let Isaac praise the Son, for by His goodness he was rescued upon the mount from the knife; and in his stead there was the victim, the type of the Lamb for the slaughter. The mortal escaped [Heb. 11:19], and He Who quickens all died [Is. 53]. Blessed be His offering!"[314]

Saint Kyril of Jerusalem explains that "though He is called a Sheep, not an irrational one, but the One which through His precious blood cleanses the world from its sins, Who is led before the shearers, and knows when to be silent. This Sheep again is called a Shepherd, Who says, 'I am the good Shepherd [Jn. 10:11].' He is a Sheep because of His manhood, a Shepherd because of the loving-kindness of His divinity."[315]

Saint Ambrose of Milan writes: "Well does he say **'before the shearer** [Is. 53:7]**,'** for He laid aside what was additional, not His own essence, on the Cross, when He laid aside His body, but lost not His divinity."[316]

---

[311] Saint Athanasius, "Letter VI," Nicene, 2nd Ser., IV:522.

[312] Ibid., "Discourse II," Ch. XV, *Four Discourses Against the Arians,* Nicene, 2nd Ser., IV:356.

[313] *Saint Ephrem's Commentary on Tatian's Diatessaron*, p. 324.

[314] Saint Ephraim, *Hymns on the Nativity,* Nicene, 2nd Ser., XIII:249.

[315] Saint Cyril of Jerusalem, "Lecture X," *Catechetical Lectures,* Nicene, 2nd Ser., VII:57.

[316] Saint Ambrose, "Letter LXIII, to the Christians at Vercellae," Nicene, 2nd Ser., X: 470.

Saint Chrysostom says that "Esaias foretold Christ's death....Notice that the Lamb was not mentioned merely as a lamb, for John (the Baptist) added the words 'of God [Jn. 1:29].' Since there was another lamb, namely, the Jewish lamb, John spoke in this way to show that the Lamb of which he was speaking is the Lamb of God. The Jewish lamb was offered only for the Jewish nation; the Lamb of God was offered for the whole world."[317]

Elsewhere, Saint Chrysostom remonstrates with Christ's accusers, certain Jews who declared, "We have a law and, according to our law, He ought to die because He made Himself Son of God [Jn. 19:7]." "Tell me," asks Chrysostom, "is this a ground of accusation, that He Who performed the deeds of the Son of God should call Himself the Son of God? What then does Christ? While they held this dialogue one with the other, He held His peace, fulfilling that saying of the prophet, that, **'He openeth not His mouth** [Is. 53:7]' and **'In His humiliation His judgment was taken away** [Is. 53:8].'"[318] Now, "The prophet foretold that He should not even plead For Himself, 'For this Man,' he saith, **'openeth not His mouth** [Is. 53:7]'; and that He should be unjustly condemned, **'For in His humiliation,'** says he, **'His judgment was taken away** [Is. 53:8].'"[319]

Saint Chrysostom wishes to show the similitude between Christ and Isaac. Isaac "was even bound and lifted up and laid upon it, and endured all in silence, like a lamb, yea, rather like the common Lord of all. For of Him he both imitated the gentleness and kept to the type. And yet Isaac spake; for his Lord spake also. How dumb then? This meaneth, he spake nothing wilful or harsh, but all was sweet and mild, and the words more than the silence manifested His gentleness. For Christ also said, 'If I spoke evilly, bear witness concerning the evil; but if well, why smitest thou Me [Jn. 18:23]?' And He manifested His gentleness more than if He had held His peace. And as this one speaks with his father from the altar, so too does He from the Cross, saying, 'Father, forgive them; for they know not what they do [Lk. 23:34].'"[320]

---

[317] Saint John Chrysostom, "Hom. VII," *On the Incomprehensible Nature of God*, FC, 72:202.

Saint Chrysostom also notices the tense used by the prophet, remarking, "This was the custom of the prophets of old, to speak of the future as of the past; for he does not say 'shall be,' but 'was.' Thus, Esaias speaking of His slaughter, does not say, 'He shall be led (which would have denoted futurity) as a sheep to the slaughter'; but 'He was led as a sheep to the slaughter [Is. 53:7]'; yet He was not yet incarnate, but the prophet speaks of what should be as if it had come to pass." Idem, "Hom. XIII," *John*, Nicene, 1st Ser., XIV:46.

[318] Idem, "Hom. LXXXIV," *John*, Nicene, 1st Ser., XIV:314.

[319] Idem, "Hom. XXXVI," *Matthew*, Nicene, 1st Ser., X:240.

[320] Idem, "Hom. III," *Second Corinthians*, Nicene, 1st Ser., XII:293.

Saint Paulinus of Nola writes: "The Lamb was led to the slaughter for us, and was dumb before His shearer [Is. 53:7], allowing His fleece, which are the spoils of His flesh, to be torn from Him. For He laid down His soul and body for us, and for us He regained them [cf. Jn. 10:17 f.]. He is Priest, Victim, Lamb, and Shepherd. As Shepherd, He died for His sheep; as Lamb, He was killed for His shepherds, for the Lord Himself is the sacrificial Victim of all priests [cf. Heb. 10:10 f.]. Offering Himself to the Father to win back all mankind, He was the Victim which His priesthood offered, and the Priest Who offered Himself as Victim. To Him now, as the one Lord of all, each new creature is a sacrifice, and the priests themselves are victims. If we now offer ourselves to be shorn with that silent humility and patience in which He offered Himself for us, He will take on Himself the burdens of our fleeces, and will not disdain to carry the wool of His sheep. For He condescends to bring back to the fold on His shoulders the sheep which He has called back from sin."[321]

Saint John of Damascus, in his famous Paschal canon, affirms: *Christ is the new Pascha, the living sacrificial Victim, the Lamb of God that taketh away the sin of the world* [Is. 53:7].[322]

F. His Judgment Was Taken Away:

"In His humiliation His judgment was taken away. Who shall declare His generation? For His life is taken away from the earth: because of the iniquities of My people He was led to death [Is. 53:8]**."**

Saint Justin asks Trypho the Jew, "The passage which Esaias records, **'Who shall declare His generation? For His life is taken away from the earth** [Is. 53:8],' does it not appear to you to refer to One Who, not having descent from men, was said to be delivered over to death by God for the transgressions of the people? Of Whose blood Moses, when speaking in parable, said that He would wash His garments in the blood of the grape [Gen. 49:11], since His blood did not spring from the seed of man but from the will of God."[323]

By these words [Is. 53:8], Saint Chrysostom says the prophet wished "to show that the court was corrupt and the sentence unjust."[324] And "where can we see that all these things came true? In Pilate's unlawful court of law. Although they testified to so many things against Him, as Matthew said, Jesus made no answer to them. Pilate, the presiding official, said to Him, 'Hearest Thou not how many things they bear witness against Thee [Mt. 27:13]?' And He made no answer but stood there silent. This is what the heaven-inspired

[321] Saint Paulinus, "Letter 11," *Letters of Saint Paulinus of Nola: Letters 1-22, Vol. 1*, ACW, 35:98.

[322] Sunday of Pascha, Canon of Pascha, Ode Nine, Megalynarion, Mode One.

[323] Saint Justin Martyr, *Dialogue with Trypho*, Ch. LXIII, Ante-Nicene, I:229.

[324] Saint John Chrysostom, *Demonstration Against the Pagans*, Ch. IV, FC, 73:205.

prophet meant. Then he showed the lawlessness of the law court when he said, **'In His humiliation His judgment was taken away** [Is. 53:8].**'** No one at that time cast a truly just vote against Him, but they accepted the false testimony against Him. What was the reason for this? Because He did not wish to proceed against them. If He wished to do so, He would have stirred up everything and shaken the world to its depths. When He was on the Cross, He split the rocks, darkened the earth, turned aside the rays of the sun, and made night out of day over the whole world [cf. Mt. 27:51]. If He did this on the Cross, He could have done it in the courtroom. Yet He did not wish to do it, but, instead, showed us His mildness and moderation. This is why Esaias said, 'In His humiliation His legal trial was taken away.' Then, to show that Jesus was not just anybody, he went on to say, **'Who shall declare His generation** [Is. 53:8]**?'**"[325] Saint Chrysostom, speaking further on Jesus's trial, says, "He replies to nothing, but holds His peace. Yet He did answer briefly, so as not to get the reputation of arrogance from continual silence, when the high priest adjured Him or when the governor made inquiry. But in reply to their accusations, He no longer spoke anything; for He was not now likely to persuade them. Thus Esaias says, **'In His humiliation His judgment was taken away** [Is. 53:8].**'**"[326]

G. Christ is Judged by His People:

"But now the Lord will stand up for judgment, and will enter into judgment with His people. The Lord Himself shall enter into judgment with the elders of the people, and with their rulers: 'But why have ye set My vineyard on fire, and why is the spoil of the poor in your houses [Is. 3:13, 14]**?'"**

Saint Kyril of Jerusalem explains this verse as a sign of "what the Lord will do when He comes," as follows: "A notable sign! The Master judged by His servants—the elders—and submitting to it!"[327] Later, he adds, "But the high priest having questioned Him, and heard the truth, is wroth; and the wicked officer of wicked men smites Him; and the countenance, which had shone as the sun, endured to be smitten by lawless hands. Others also come and spit on the face of Him, Who by spittle had healed the man who was eyeless from his birth."[328]

H. Christ is Rejected and Bound [Is. 3:10]**.**

Saint Justin writes: "The Jews, in rejecting Christ, rejected God Who sent Him...." He chides them, saying, "You neither suffer Him when He calls

---

[325] Idem, "Discourse VI," *Against Judaizing Christians*, FC, 68:162-165.
[326] Idem, "Hom. LXXXVI," *Matthew*, Nicene, 1st Ser., X:511.
[327] Saint Cyril of Jerusalem, "Lecture XII," *Catechetical Lectures,* Nicene, 2nd Ser., VII:75.
[328] Ibid., "Lecture XIII," Nicene, 2nd Ser., VII:86.

you, but have done evil in the presence of the Lord. But the highest pitch of your wickedness lies in this, that you hate the righteous One, and slew Him; and so you treat those who have received from Him all that they are and have, and who are pious, righteous, and humane. Therefore, **'Woe to their soul, for they have devised an evil counsel against themselves, saying against themselves, "Let us bind the just, for He is inconvenient** (δύσχρηστος) **to us." Therefore shall they eat the fruits of their works** [Is. 3:10]**.'** For indeed you are not in the habit of sacrificing to Baal, as were your fathers, or of placing cakes in groves and on high places for the host of heaven, but you have not accepted God's Christ. For he who knows not Him, knows not the will of God; and he who insults and hates Him, insults and hates Him that sent Him. And whoever believes not in Him, believes not the declarations of the prophets who preached and proclaimed Him to all."[329] Further, he explains, "God, knowing beforehand that you Jews would do such things, pronounced this curse upon you by the Prophet Esaias [3:9-15]....For verily your hand is high to commit evil, because you slew the Christ, and do not repent of it. But so far from that, you hate and murder us who have believed through Him in the God and Father of all, as often as you can. And you curse Him without ceasing, as well as those who side with Him, while all of us pray for you and for all men. For our Christ and Lord taught us to do this, when He enjoined us to pray even for our enemies and to love them that hate us and to bless them that curse us."[330]

I. Christ's Couching:

"How has the faithful city Sion, once full of judgment, become a harlot! Righteousness couched (ἐκοιμήθη) **in her, but now murderers** [Is. 1:21]**."**

Saint Hippolytos informs us that "even as the expression 'He stooped down, He couched as a lion, and as a lion's whelp [cf. Gen. 49:9],' refers to the three days' sleep (death, couching) of Christ, so also as Esaias says [Is. 1:21]."[331]

J. Christ's Burial:

"And I will give the wicked for His burial, and the rich for His death; for He practised no iniquity, nor guile with His mouth [Is. 53:9]**."**

Saint Kyril of Jerusalem, commenting on Christ's sinlessness, says, "It is not Peter [1 Pe. 2:22] who says this, for then we might suspect that he was partial to his Teacher, but it is Esaias, who though he was not present with Him in the flesh yet in the Spirit foresaw His coming in the flesh. Yet why bring only the prophet as witness? Take for a witness Pilate himself, who gave

---

[329] Saint Justin Martyr, *Dialogue with Trypho*, Ch. CXXXVI, Ante-Nicene, I:267, 268.
[330] Ibid., Ch. CXXXIII, Ante-Nicene, I:266.
[331] Saint Hippolytus, *Treatise on Christ and Antichrist*, Part II, Ante-Nicene, V:206.

sentence, saying, 'I did not find even one charge in this Man of which ye bring as an accusation against Him [Lk. 23:14].'"[332]

Saint Chrysostom warns, "Now the Jews are enduring their present troubles because of Christ. It is time now to bring in my witness, Esaias, who spoke these words. Where then did he say this? After he spoke,...**'His life is taken from the earth** [Is. 53:8],**'** he went on to say, **'And I will give the wicked for His burial, and the rich for His death** [Is. 53:9].**'** He did not simply say 'the Jews,' but the ungodly. What could be more ungodly than those who first received so many good things and then slew the Author of those blessings?"[333]

Saint John of Damascus writes concerning the fact that "the divinity of the Logos remained inseparable from the soul and the body, even at our Lord's death, and that His subsistence continued one. Since our Lord Jesus Christ was without sins (for He committed no sin, He Who took away the sin of the world, nor was there any deceit found in His mouth [Is. 53:9; Jn. 1:29]), He was not subject to death, since death came into the world through sin [Rom. 5:12]. He dies, therefore, because He took on Himself death on our behalf, and He makes Himself an offering to the Father for our sakes. For we had sinned against Him, and it was meet that He should receive the ransom for us, and that we should thus be delivered from the condemnation. God forbid that the blood of the Lord should have been offered to the tyrant. Death, therefore, approaches and swallows up the body as a bait. Death is transfixed on the hook of divinity, and after tasting of a sinless and life-giving body, perishes, and brings up again all whom of old he swallowed up. For just as darkness disappears on the introduction of light, so is death repulsed before the assault of life, and brings life to all, but death to the destroyer.

"Therefore, although He died as man...yet His divinity remained inseparable from both, I mean, from His soul and His body, and so even thus His one hypostasis was not divided into two hypostases. For body and soul received simultaneously in the beginning their being in the subsistence of the Logos. And although they were severed from one another by death, yet they continued, each of them, having the one subsistence of the Logos....For at no time had either soul or body a separate subsistence of their own, different from that of the Logos, and the subsistence of the Logos is forever one, and at no time two. So that the subsistence of Christ is always one. For, although the soul

---

[332] Saint Cyril of Jerusalem, "Lecture XIII," *Cathechetical Lectures*, Nicene, 2nd Ser., VII:82, 83.

[333] Saint John Chrysostom, "Discourse VI," *Against Judaizing Christians*, FC, 68:loc. cit.

was separated from the body topically, yet hypostatically they were united through the Logos."[334]

K. Christ Serves Many Well:

"The Lord also took counsel to purge Him of His stroke. If ye can give an offering for sin, your soul shall see a long-lived seed: the Lord also is pleased to take away from the travail of His soul, to show Him light, and to form the understanding; to justify the just One Who serves many well; and He shall bear their sins [Is. 53:10, 11]**."**

"David," Saint Chrysostom informs us, "made it clear that Christ would be buried when he said, 'They laid Me in the lowest pit, in darkness and in the shadow of death [Ps. 87:6].' Nor was David silent about the spices used on His shroud. Since the women brought myrrh, spice, and cassia, hear what the prophet said, 'Myrrh and stacte and cassia exhale from Thy garments, from the ivory palaces, whereby they have made Thee glad, they the daughters of kings in Thine honor [Ps. 44:7].' See how he also predicted that Christ would rise again: 'For Thou wilt not abandon My soul in Hades, nor wilt Thou suffer Thy Holy One to see corruption [Ps. 15:10].' Esaias expressed the same thing in a different way. For he said, 'The Lord also took counsel to purge Him of His stroke....to show Him light,...to justify the just One Who serves many well...[Is. 53:10, 11].'"[335] He served many well? Saint Gregory the Great says, "When He took on our human nature He Himself bore our sins [Is. 53:11]."[336]

L. Christ Would Bear the Sins of Many:

"Therefore He shall inherit many, and He shall divide the spoils of the mighty, because His soul was delivered to death. And He was numbered among the transgressors, and He bore the sins of many, and was delivered because of their iniquities [Is. 53:12]**."**

Saint Ephraim the Syrian asks, "Does Christ possess a will other than the will of His Father?...Esaias says, **'The Lord took counsel to purge Him of His stroke** [Is. 53:10],**'** and he also said, 'Because He handed over His soul to death [cf. Is. 53:12],' showing that this was His will....He wished to show that He was from the Father, and He attributed everything to the Father. And although He had made everything by His will, He appeared Himself as in need, for the sake of His Father's honor. It was not necessary that He should have humbled Him (but it is said), so that those who say that the powers of darkness have conquered Him might be confounded."[337]

---

[334] Saint John of Damascus, *Exposition of the Orthodox Faith,* Bk. III, Ch. XXVII, Nicene, 2nd Ser., IX:71, 72.

[335] Saint John Chrysostom, *Demonstration Against the Pagans*, Ch. IV, FC, 73:207.

[336] Saint Gregory the Great, "Hom. 34," *Forty Gospel Homilies*, p. 282.

[337] *Saint Ephrem's Commentary on Tatian's Diatessaron*, p. 297.

Saint Kyril of Jerusalem says, "Concerning the robbers who were crucified with Him, it is written, 'And He was numbered with the transgressors [cf. Is. 53:12].' Both of them were before this transgressors, but one was so no longer. For the one was a transgressor to the end, stubborn against salvation, who, though his hands were fastened, smote with blasphemy by his tongue."[338]

In a homily, Saint Chrysostom writes: "They crucified Him with robbers, in this also unintentionally fulfilling prophecy; for what they did for insult contributed to the truth, that thou mayest learn how great is its power, since the prophet had foretold of old, that **'He was numbered among the transgressors** [Is. 53:12]**.'** The devil therefore wished to cast a veil over what was done but was unable; for the three were crucified, but Jesus alone was glorious, that thou mayest learn that His power effected all. Yet the miracles took place when the three had been nailed to the cross. But no one attributed anything of what was done to either of those others, but to Jesus only; so entirely was the plot of the devil rendered stale, and all returned upon his own head. For even of these two, one was saved. He therefore did not insult the glory of the Cross, but contributed to it not a little. For it was not a less matter than shaking the rocks to change a robber upon the cross and to bring him unto Paradise."[339]

Saint Chrysostom commenting further, says, "Esaias also established that the slaying of Christ was the ransom for man's sins by saying, **'He bore the sins of many** [Is. 53:12]**.'** And He freed mankind from demons; for, as Esaias said, **'He shall divide the spoils of the mighty** [Is. 53:12]**.'** And the same prophet spoke out clearly that Christ did this through His death when he said, **'Because His soul was delivered to death** [Is. 53:12]**.'** That Christ would be put in charge over the whole world, he revealed by these words of his: **'He shall inherit many** [Is. 53:12]**.'**"[340]

N. Christ's Cross:

"There shall He lift up a signal to the nations that are afar, and shall hiss [cf. Num. 21:8, 9] **for them from the end of the earth and, behold, they are coming very quickly** [Is. 5:26]**."**

Saint Ignatios, Bishop of Antioch and God-Bearer names this "signal or standard" as spoken by Esaias as the Cross of Christ.[341] The brazen serpent lifted up on a pole by Moses in the desert is acknowledged by Saint Basil and

---

[338] Saint Cyril of Jerusalem, "Lecture XIII," *Catechetical Lectures*, Nicene, 2nd Ser., VII:90.

[339] Saint Chrysostom, "Hom. LXXXV," *John*, Nicene, 2st Ser., XIV:317.

[340] Idem, *Demonstration Against the Pagans*, Ch. IV, FC, 73:207, 208.

[341] Saint Ignatius, *The Epistle of Ignatius to the Smyrnaeans*, Ch. I, Ante-Nicene, I:86.

the holy fathers "as a type of the Passion of salvation accomplished by means of the Cross."[342]

12. Descent Into Hades.

"Drink this first. Act quickly, O land of Zabulon, land of Nephthaleim, and the rest inhabiting the seacoast, and the land beyond Jordan, Galilee of the nations [Is. 9:1]**."**

Saint John of Damascus, concerning Christ's descent into Hades, says, "Just as the Sun of righteousness [Mal. 4:2] rose for those upon the earth, so likewise He might bring light to those who sit under the earth in darkness and in the shadow of death [Is. 9:2; 1 Pe. 3:19]. For just as He brought the message of peace to those upon the earth, and the news of release to the prisoners, and sight to the blind—and He also became the Author of everlasting salvation to those who believed, but a reproach to those who did not believe—so might He become the same to those in Hades, 'That in the name of Jesus every knee should bow, of those in heaven and on earth and under the earth [cf. Phil. 2:10].' And thus after He had freed those who had been bound for ages, straightway, He rose again from the dead and showed us the way of resurrection."[343]

The holy Theodore the Stoudite chants: *O all-destroying death, expect now thine own dissolution. Let thy doorkeepers look to the bolts and bars; for Christ shall raise up Lazarus and shatter thy gates by His word. With us the prophet cries to thee, "O Hades, drink this first* [Is. 9:1]. *"*[344]

13. Death is Swallowed Up.

"Death has prevailed and swallowed men up, but again the Lord God has taken away every tear from every face. He has taken away the reproach of His people from all the earth, for the mouth of the Lord has spoken it [Is. 25:8]**.**

"And in that day they shall say, 'Behold our God in Whom we have trusted, and He shall save us. This is the Lord; we have waited for Him, and we have exulted, and will rejoice in our salvation [Is. 25:9]**.'"**

Saint Ambrose of Milan notes, "In the Old Testament the jaw of death is bitter, since it is said, 'Strong death is all devouring [cf. Is. 25:8].' In the New Testament the jaw of death is sweet, for it has swallowed death, as the apostle says, 'But whenever this corruption should put on itself incorruption, and this mortal should put on itself immortality, then the word which hath been written shall come to pass: "Death is swallowed up in victory. O death, where

---

[342] Saint Basil, *On the Holy Spirit*, Ch. XIV(31), Nicene, 2nd Ser., VIII:20.

[343] Saint John of Damascus, *Exposition of the Orthodox Faith,* Bk. III, Ch. XXIX, Nicene, 2nd Ser., IX:73.

[344] *Triodion*, Thursday in the Sixth Week, Orthros Canon, Ode Nine, Mode Plagal Two.

is thy sting? O Hades, where is thy victory [1 Cor. 15:54, 55; cf. Is. 25:8; cf. Hos. 13:14]?"'"[345]

Saint Chrysostom, in his catechetical homily for the Sunday of Pascha, believes the following: "He Who came down into Hades, despoiled Hades; and Hades was embittered when he tasted of Christ's flesh. Esaias, anticipating this, cried out and said, 'Hades was embittered when below he met Thee face to face [cf. Is. 25:8].'"

Saint Kyril of Alexandria explains the passage, "He has taken away the reproach of His people," saying, "By reproach of the people he means sin, which disgraces and depraves men, and which, together with destruction, shall be slain, and sorrow and death shall perish, and the tears cease which are shed on its account."[346]

14. The Brazen Doors Will be Broken to Pieces.

"Thus saith the Lord God to My anointed Cyrus (Ὁ Θεὸς τῷ χριστῷ Μου Κύρῳ), **whose right hand I have held, that nations might be obedient before him; and I will break through the strength of kings; I will open doors before him, and cities shall not be closed** [Is. 45:1].

"I will go before thee, and will level mountains: I will break to pieces brazen doors, and will burst iron bars [Is. 45:2].

"And I will give thee the treasures of darkness, I will open to thee hidden, unseen treasures, that thou mayest know that I, the Lord thy God, that call thee by name, am the God of Israel [Is. 45:3]."

The *Epistle of Barnabas* (A.D. 100) reads this as follows: "The Lord said to Christ, My Lord,..."[347] The Sinai Codex reads this as "Cyrus," as in the Septuagint. The *Epistle* also ascribes these verses to Christ shattering the gates of Hades.[348] Cyrus who bears the Lord's name *Kyr* could be thought of as a type of Christ.

Saint Irenaeos reads this verse, as follows: "'Thus saith the Lord to My anointed Lord, Whose right hand I have held, that the nations hearken before Him.'" The variant of *Kyrio* instead of *Kyro*, that is "to my anointed *Lord*" instead of "to my anointed *Cyrus*," is a reading found before Saint Irenaeos in the *Epistle of Barnabas*, and after him in other early writers as Saint Cyprian, Tertullian, and Lactantius. Continuing with Saint Irenaeos' explanation, he says, "And for how the Son of God is called both the 'anointed' and King of nations, that is, of all men, David also says that He both is called and is Son of God and King of all, as follows: 'The Lord said unto Me: "Thou art My Son,

[345] Saint Ambrose, "Letter 50 to Priest Horontianus (Spring, 387)," *Letters*, FC, 26:268.

[346] Saint Cyril of Alexandria, "Hom. 36," *Commentary*, p. 154.

[347] *The Epistle of Barnabas*, Ch. XII, Ante-Nicene, I:145.

[348] Ibid., Ch. XI, Ante-Nicene, I:144.

this day have I begotten Thee [Ps. 2:7]. Ask of Me, and I will give Thee the nations for Thine inheritance, and the uttermost parts of the earth for Thy possession [Ps. 2:8].''' These things were not said to David, for he did not have dominion over 'the nations,' nor over 'the whole earth,' but only over the Jews. So it is clear, the promise to the 'Anointed,' that He should be King over the whole earth, is made to the Son of God, Whom David himself acknowledges as his Lord, saying, 'The Lord said unto My Lord: "Sit Thou at My right hand, until I make Thine enemies the footstool of Thy feet [Ps. 109:1].''' For he means that the Father is speaking with the Son,...because the promise is the same through both Prophets David and Esaias, that He would be King, so consequently God is addressing one and the same Person, that is, I say, Christ the Son of God."[349]

Saint Chrysostom writes: "After He descended into Hades, He threw all things into an upheaval. He filled everything with tumult and confusion. He destroyed the citadel. The prophets did not remain silent on this, but David exclaimed and said, 'Lift up your gates, O ye princes; and be ye lifted up, ye everlasting gates, and the King of Glory shall enter in [Ps. 23:7]. 'Who is this King of Glory? The Lord strong and mighty, the Lord, mighty in war [Ps. 23:8]. Lift up your gates, O ye princes; and be ye lifted up, ye everlasting gates, and the King of Glory shall enter in [Ps. 23:9]. Who is this King of Glory? The Lord of hosts, He is the King of Glory [Ps. 23:10].' Esaias put it another way: **'I will break to pieces brazen doors, and will burst iron bars** [Is. 45:2]**. And I will give thee the treasures of darkness, I will open to thee hidden, unseen treasures, that thou mayest know that I, the Lord thy God, that call thee by name, am the God of Israel** [Is. 45:3]**.'**

"Even if it were Hades," continues Saint Chrysostom, "it still preserved the sacred souls and precious vessels, Abraham, Isaac, and Jacob. This is why Esaias called it a place of treasures, even if in darkness, because the Sun of righteousness had not yet penetrated there with its rays nor with any message on the resurrection. But hear how David made it clear that, after Christ's resurrection, He would not remain on earth but would ascend into the heaven: 'God is gone up in jubilation, the Lord with the voice of the trumpet [Ps. 46:5].' By speaking of the shout and the trumpet, David showed how manifest Christ's ascension would be. Christ would not stand with the angels, nor with the archangels, nor with any other ministering power, but would be seated on the royal throne. Hear again what David said: 'The Lord said unto My Lord: "Sit Thou at My right hand, until I make Thine enemies the footstool of Thy feet [Ps. 109:1].''''[350]

---

[349] Saint Irenaeus, *Proof of the Apostolic Preaching*, ¶ 49, ACW, 16:79, 80.

[350] Saint John Chrysostom, *Demonstration Against the Pagans*, Ch. IV, FC, 73:208,

(continued...)

15. The Dead Shall Rise [Is. 26:19-21].

A. "Esaias," says Saint Chrysostom, "made it clear that Christ will raise up all men when he said, **'The dead shall rise, and they that are in the tombs shall be raised, and they that are in the earth shall rejoice; for the dew from Thee is healing to them, but the land of the ungodly shall perish** [Is. 26:19].**'** That was not all. After His Cross, after His slaughter, His glory will shine forth more brightly; after His resurrection, He will advance the message of His Gospel still more."[351]

Saint Kyril of Alexandria says, "And by dew I imagine he means the life-giving power of the Holy Spirit...."[352]

Saint Aphrahat says this passage clearly speaks of the resurrection of the dead, and graphically depicts for us what took place: "When Death heard all these things, amazement seized him, and he sat him down in mourning." Continuing, he says, "And when Jesus, the slayer of Death, came, and clothed Himself in a body from the seed of Adam, and was crucified in His body, and tasted death, and when Death perceived thereby that He had come down unto him, he was shaken from his place and was agitated when he saw Jesus. And he closed his gates and was not willing to receive Him. Then Jesus burst his gates, and entered into him, and began to despoil all his possessions. But when the dead saw light in the darkness, they lifted up their heads from the bondage of death, and looked forth, and saw the splendor of the King Messiah. Then the powers of the darkness of Death sat in mourning, for he was degraded from his authority. Death tasted the medicine that was deadly to him, and his hands dropped down, and he learned that the dead shall live and escape from his sway. And when Jesus had afflicted Death by the despoiling of his possessions, Death wailed and cried aloud in bitterness, and said, 'Go forth from my realm and enter it not. Who then is this that comes in alive into my realm?' And while Death was crying out in terror (for he saw that his darkness was beginning to be done away, and some of the righteous who were sleeping arose to ascend with Him), then He made known to him that when He shall come in the fullness of time, He will bring forth all the prisoners from his power, and they shall go forth to see the light. Then when Jesus had fulfilled His ministry amongst the dead, Death sent Him forth from his realm, and suffered Him not to remain there. And to devour Him like all the dead, he counted it not pleasure. He had no power over the Holy One, nor was He given over to corruption.

"And when he had eagerly sent Him forth and He had come forth from his realm, He left with him, as a poison, the promise of life, that by little and

---

[350](...continued)
209.

[351] Ibid., Ch. IX, FC, 73:222.

[352] Saint Cyril of Alexandria, "Hom. 136," *Commentary*, p. 541.

little his power should be done away. Even as when a man has taken a poison in the food which is given for (the support of life), when he perceives in himself that he has received poison in the food, then he casts up again from his belly the food in which poison was mingled; but the drug leaves its power in his limbs, so that by little and little the structure of his body is dissolved and corrupted. So Jesus dead was the One Who brought to nought Death; for through Him life is made to reign, and through Him Death is abolished, to whom it is said, 'O Death, where is thy victory [cf. 1 Cor. 15:54]?' Therefore," counsels Saint Aphrahat, "ye children of Adam, all ye over whom Death has ruled, be mindful of Death and remember Life; and transgress not the commandment as your first father did."[353]

Saint John of Damascus says these words of the Prophet Esaias make "it clear that not the souls, but the bodies, lie in the graves."[354]

Saint Kassiane the Poetess (9th C.) sings during Great and Holy Saturday: *Esaias, as he watched by night, beheld the light that knows no evening, the light of Thy Theophany, O Christ, that came to pass from tender love for us; and he cried aloud, "The dead shall arise and they that dwell in the tombs shall be raised up, and all those born on the earth shall rejoice exceedingly* [Is. 26:19]. *"*[355]

B. "Go, My people, enter into thy closets, shut thy door, hide thyself for a little season, until the anger of the Lord have passed away [Is. 26:20]**."**

Saint Hippolytos believes this speaks prophetically of the judgment and the coming of the Lord.[356]

Blessed Jerome in a letter comments: "'An hour cometh, and now is, when the dead shall hear the voice of the Son of God, and they who hear shall live [Jn. 5:25].' They shall hear with ears, and come forth with feet. This Lazarus had already done. They shall, moreover, come forth from the tombs; that is, they who have been laid in the tombs, the dead, shall come, and shall rise again from their graves. For the dew which God gives is healing to their bones. Then shall be fulfilled what God says by the prophet, 'Go, My people, into thy closets for a little while, until Mine anger should pass [cf. Is. 26:20].' The closets signify the graves, out of which, of course, is brought forth that which had been laid therein. And they shall come out of the graves like young mules free from the halter. Their heart shall rejoice, and their bones shall rise

---

353 Saint Aphrahat, "Demonstration XXII.—Of Death and the Latter Times," § 6, Nicene, 2nd Ser., XIII:403.

354 Saint John of Damascus, *Exposition of the Orthodox Faith,* Bk. IV, Ch. XXVII, Nicene, 2nd Ser., IX:100.

355 Holy Saturday, Orthros Canon, Eirmos of Ode Five, Mode Plagal Two.

356 Saint Hippolytus, *Treatise on Christ and Antichrist*, Ante-Nicene, V:218.

like the sun. All flesh shall come into the presence of the Lord. And He shall command the fishes of the sea, and they shall give up the bones they had eaten. And He shall bring joint to joint, and bone to bone. And they who slept in the dust of the earth shall arise [Dan. 12:2], some to life eternal, others to shame and everlasting confusion."[357]

C. "Esaias," says Saint Ambrose of Milan, "proclaims the resurrection to the people, saying that he is the announcer of the Lord's coming....How well did he by the chambers point out the tombs of the dead, in which for a brief space we are hidden, that we may be better able to pass to the judgment of God, which shall try us with the indignation due for our wickedness. He then is alive who is hidden and at rest, as though withdrawing himself from our midst and retiring lest the misery of this world should entangle him with closer snares, for whom the heavenly oracles affirm by the voices of the prophets that the joy of the resurrection is reserved, and the soundness of their freed bodies procured by the divine deed. And dew is well used as a sign, since by it all vital seeds of the earth are raised to growth. What wonder is it, then, if the dust and ashes also of our failing body grow vigorous by the richness of the heavenly dew, and by the reception of this vital moistening the shapes of our limbs are refashioned and connected again with each other?"[358]

D. "Thus saith the Lord, 'In an acceptable time have I heard thee, and in a day of salvation have I succored thee: and...saying to them that are in bonds, "Go forth"; and bidding them that are in darkness to be made manifest (ἀνακαλυφθῆναι) [Is. 49:8, 9].'"[359]

"Whomsoever," declares Saint Hippolytos, "Satan bound in chains, these did the Lord on His coming loose from the bonds of death, having bound our strong adversary and delivered humanity."[360]

Saint Kyril of Alexandria, in a letter, writes: "For He rose again, despoiling death and saying to the prisoners, 'Come out' to those in darkness, and 'Show yourselves [cf. Is. 49:9]'; and He ascended to His Father above in the heavens to a position inaccessible to men, having taken upon Himself our sins and being the expiation for them."[361]

E. Death is Despoiled:

"For thus saith the Lord, 'If one should take a giant captive, he shall take spoils, and he who takes them from a mighty man shall be

---

[357] Saint Jerome, "To Pammachius Against John of Jerusalem," Nicene, 2nd Ser., VI:441.

[358] Saint Ambrose, *On Belief in the Resurrection,* Bk. II, Nicene, 2nd Ser., X:185.

[359] Aorist passive infinitive of αναχαλύπτω.

[360] Saint Hippolytus, *Fragments from Commentaries*, Ante-Nicene, V:181.

[361] Saint Cyril of Alexandria, "Letter 41 to Bishop Acacius," *Letters 1-50*, FC, 76:175, 176.

delivered: for I will plead thy cause, and I will deliver thy children [Is. 49:25].'"

Death and Hades is the giant. Saint Ephraim the Syrian writes: "Let Moses praise Him with us, since he was afraid and fled from his murderers. Let him praise the Lord that bore the spear and that received the nails in His hands and in His feet. He entered into Hades and spoiled it, and came forth. Blessed be Thy resurrection!"[362]

16. The Myrrh-bearing Women at the Tomb.

"Come hither, ye women that come from a sight; for it is a people of no understanding; therefore He that made them shall have no pity upon them, and He that formed them shall have no mercy upon them [Is. 27:11]."

"Though chief priests and Pharisees," remarks Saint Kyril of Jerusalem, "through Pilate's means sealed the tomb, yet the women beheld Him Who was risen. And Esaias knowing the feebleness of the chief priests, and the women's strength of faith, says, 'Ye women, who come from beholding, come hither; for the people have no understanding;—the chief priests want understanding, while women are eyewitnesses.'"[363]

17. Christ's Ascension [Is. 33:10, 11; 63:1-3].

A. "Who is this that is come from Edom, with red garments from Bosor (Bozrah)**? Thus fair in His apparel, with mighty strength? 'I speak of righteousness and saving judgment.' Why art Thy garments red, and Thy raiment as if fresh from a trodden winepress? 'I am full of trodden grape, I have trodden the winepress utterly alone, and of the nations there is not a man with Me** [Is. 63:1-3]**.'"** The foregoing is also a Reading from the Vespers Service of the Feast of the Ascension.

Saint Cyprian points out that Scripture says, "'He shall wash His robe in wine, and His garment in the blood of the grape [Gen. 49:11].' But when the blood of the grape is mentioned, what else is set forth than the wine of the cup of the blood of the Lord?" Continuing, he says: "In Esaias...the Holy Spirit testifies...concerning the Lord's Passion, saying, **'Why art Thy garments red, and Thy raiment as if fresh from a trodden wine press** [Is. 62:2]**?'** Can water make garments red? Or is it water in the winepress which is trodden by the feet, or pressed out by the press? Assuredly, therefore, mention is made of wine, that the Lord's blood may be understood, and that which was afterward manifested in the cup of the Lord might be foretold by the prophets who announced it. The treading also and pressure of the winepress is repeatedly dwelt on, because just as the drinking of wine cannot be attained to unless the

---

[362] Saint Ephraim, *Hymns on the Nativity*, Nicene, 2nd Ser., XIII:249.

[363] Saint Cyril of Jerusalem, "Lecture XIV," *Catechetical Lectures*, Nicene, 2nd Ser., VII:97.

bunch of grapes be first trodden and pressed, so neither could we drink the blood of Christ unless Christ had first been trampled upon and pressed, and had first drunk the cup of which He should also give believers to drink."[364]

Saint Kyril of Jerusalem notes that when Christ "had been judged before Pilate, He was clothed in red; for there they put on Him a purple robe. Is this also written? Esaias says, 'Who is this that cometh from Edom? The redness of His garments is from Bosor [cf. Is. 63:1, 2].'"[365]

Saint Ambrose of Milan makes the following point of interest: "The angels, too, were in doubt when Christ arose; the powers of heaven were in doubt when they saw that flesh was ascending into heaven. Then they said, 'Who is this King of Glory?' And some said, 'Lift up your gates, O ye princes; and be ye lifted up, ye everlasting gates, and the King of Glory shall come in [Ps. 23:7].' In Esaias, too, we find that the powers of heaven doubted and said, 'Who is this that cometh up from Edom, the redness of His garments is from Bozrah, He Who is glorious in white apparel [cf. Is. 63:1]?'"[366]

Blessed Jerome says, "Even the graves were opened [Mt. 27:52] at our Lord's Passion when the sun fled, the earth trembled, and many of the bodies of the saints arose, and were seen in the holy city. 'Who is this,' says Esaias, 'that cometh up from Edom, with shining raiment from Bozrah, so beautiful in His glistening robe [cf. Is. 63:1]?' Edom is by interpretation either 'earthy' or 'bloody'; Bozrah (Bosor) means either 'flesh,' or 'in tribulation.' In few words he shows the whole mystery of the resurrection, that is, both the reality of the flesh and the growth in glory. And the meaning is: Who is He that cometh up from the earth, cometh up from blood? According to the prophecy of Jacob [Gen. 49:11], He has bound His foal to the vine, and has trodden the winepress alone, and His garments are red with new wine from Bozrah, that is from flesh, or from the tribulation of the world: for He Himself has conquered the world [Jn. 16:33]. And, therefore, His garments are red and shining, because He is beauteous in form more than the sons of men [Ps. 44:2]; and on account of the glory of His triumph they have been changed into a white robe."[367]

Saint Kyril of Alexandria, notes that when the only-begotten Logos of God returned to the heavens with the flesh united unto Him: "Strange was the sight in heaven, yea, the throng of angels marvelled when they saw the King of earth and the Lord of Might in a form like unto us. Moreover they said, 'Who is this that cometh from Edom (meaning thereby the earth)? The redness

---

[364] Saint Cyprian, "Epistle LXII," *The Epistles of Cyprian*, Ante-Nicene, V:360.

[365] Saint Cyril of Jerusalem, "Lecture XIII," *Catechetical Lectures*, Nicene, 2nd Ser., VII:89.

[366] Saint Ambrose, *Of the Mysteries,* Ch. VII, Nicene, 2nd Ser., X:322.

[367] Saint Jerome, "To Pammachius Against John of Jerusalem," Nicene, 2nd Ser., VI: 441.

of His garments is from Bosor (the interpretation of which is flesh, as being a narrowing and pressing) [cf. Is. 63:1].'"[368] Continuing, Saint Kyril says, "For just as after His return to life from the dead, when showing, with most wise purpose, His hands unto Thomas, He bade him handle both the prints of the nails and the hole bored in His side, so also when He arrived in the heavens, He gave full proof to the holy angels, that Israel was justly cast out and fallen from being of His family. For this reason, He showed His garment stained with blood, and the wounds in His hands—and not as though He could not put them away. For when He rose from the dead, He put off corruption, and with it all its marks and attributes. He retained those things, therefore, that the manifest wisdom of God, which He wrought in Christ, might now be made known by the Church, according to the plan of salvation, to principalities and powers."[369]

Prophet Esaias

Saint Gregory the Great writes: "Thus it is also said through John: 'And He hath on His outer garment and on His thigh a name having been written: "King of Kings, and Lord of Lords [Rev. 19:16]."' What then is His garment if not the body He assumed from the Virgin?...But Esaias, looking long ago upon His garment stained by the blood of His Passion on the Cross, said, **'Why art Thy garments red, and thy raiment as if fresh from a trodden winepress** [Is. 63:2]**?'** Thereupon, He replied, **'I am full of trodden grape, and of the nations there is not a man with Me; and I trampled them in My fury, and dashed them to pieces as earth, and brought down their blood to the earth** [Is. 63:3]**.'** So He trod alone the winepress on which He was downtrodden, He Who by His power overcame the Passion which He endured. For He Who suffered even unto the death of the Cross rose from the dead with glory. Then," continues Saint Gregory, "it is well said, **'and of the nations there is not a man with Me,'** because those for whom He had come to suffer should have been partakers in His Passion; insofar as at that time they

[368] Saint Cyril of Alexandria, *Commentary*, Ch. 5, p. 108.
[369] Ibid.

had not come to belief, He laments in His Passion for them whose life He sought in that Passion."[370]

B. "'Now will I arise,' saith the Lord, 'now will I be glorified; now will I be exalted [Is. 33:10].

"'Now shall ye see, now shall ye perceive; the strength of your breath shall be vain; fire shall devour you [Is. 33:11].'"

"This indicates," according to Saint Cyprian, "that after Christ had risen again He would receive from His Father all power, and His power would be everlasting."[371]

18. Christ's Eternal Kingdom.

"His government shall be great, and of His peace there is no bound. It shall be upon the throne of David, and upon his kingdom, to establish it, and to support it with judgment and with righteousness, from henceforth and for ever. The zeal of the Lord of hosts shall perform this [Is. 9:7]."

Saint Kyril of Jerusalem remarks, "The prophet says **'and of His peace there is no bound** [Is. 9:7].' The Romans have bounds, but concerning the kingdom of the Son of God there are no bounds. The Persians and the Medes have bounds, but the Son has no bounds. Then next, **'upon the throne of David, and upon his kingdom, to establish it** [Is. 9:7].' The holy Virgin, therefore, is from David."[372]

Saint Chrysostom, proclaiming Esaias' words, writes: **"'Of His peace there is no bound** [Is. 9:7].' And what did happen makes it clear that this peace has spread over the whole earth and sea, over the world where men dwell and where no man lives, over mountains, woodlands, and hills, starting from the day on which He was going to leave His disciples and said to them, 'Peace I leave to you, My peace I give to you [Jn. 14:27].' Why did Christ speak in this way? Because the peace which comes from man is easily destroyed and subject to many changes. But Christ's peace is strong, unshaken, firm, fixed, steadfast, immune to death, and unending. No matter how many wars assail it, no matter how many plots rise against it every passing day, His peace is always the same. And it was His word, which accomplishes all things, that accomplished this along with His other blessings."[373]

---

[370] Saint Gregory the Great, "Hom. I," *The Homilies On the Book of the Prophet Ezekiel*, Bk. II, p. 164.

[371] Saint Cyprian, "Testimonies," § 26, *Treatises*, Ante-Nicene, V:525.

[372] Saint Cyril of Jerusalem, "Lecture XII," *Catechetical Lectures*, Nicene, 2nd Ser., VII:79.

[373] Saint John Chrysostom, *Demonstration Against the Pagans*, Ch. II, FC, 73:195, 196.

Symbols of Christ's Passion

[Is. 11:10; 33:14-17; 60:13; 65:2]

1. Christ's Cross.

A. The Cross of Three Types of Wood:

"And the glory of Libanus shall come to thee, with cypress, and pine, and cedar together, to glorify My holy place [Is. 60:13]**."**

This verse from the prophet lauds the precious and life-saving Cross. Saint Theodore the Stoudite chants: *Let us sing the praises of the Cross, made from three kinds of wood* [Is. 60:13] *as a figure of the Trinity; and venerating it with fear, let us raise our cry, as we bless, praise, and exalt Christ above all forever.*[374] And, *Thou wast crucified, O Son of God, on the pine, the cedar, and the cypress. Sanctify us all, and count us worthy to look upon Thy life-giving Passion.*[375]

Saint Joseph the Hymnographer also solemnly sings: *Let us venerate the Cross of the Lord, offering our tender affection as the cypress, the sweet fragrance of our faith as the cedar, and our sincere love as the pine; and let us glorify our Deliverer Who was nailed upon It* [Is. 60:13].[376] We also have this hymn from the *Triodion*: *Rejoice, divine Cross, formed from three different kinds of wood* [Is. 60:13]: *on Thee One of the Trinity was nailed.*[377]

2. "I stretched forth My hands unto a disobedient and contradicting people [Is. 65:2]**."**

Saint Justin explains the verse as one predicting the crucifixion of Christ where He applied His shoulders [Is. 9:6] and hands.[378] In his *Dialogue With Trypho*, he again reiterates this in a prediction of the Cross "and the manner in which He would die."[379] The *Epistle of Barnabas* also agrees with this interpretation of Christ stretching forth His hands upon the Cross.[380] "Concerning the stretching forth of His hands [Is. 65:2], spoken of by Esaias, this is a figure of the Cross."[381] Saint Cyprian remarks that this verse signifies "that the Jews would fasten Christ to the Cross."[382]

---

[374] *Triodion*, Tuesday in the Fourth Week, Orthros Canon, Ode Eight, Mode Plagal Fourth.

[375] *Triodion*, Friday in the Fourth Week, Orthros Canon, Ode Five, Mode Four.

[376] *Triodion*, Wednesday in the Fourth Week, Orthros Canon, Ode Seven, Mode Plagal Two.

[377] *Triodion*, Thursday in the Fourth Week, Orthros Canon, Ode Eight, Mode One.

[378] Saint Justin Martyr, *The First Apology*, Ch. XXXV, Ante-Nicene, I:174.

[379] Ibid., *Dialogue with Trypho*, Ch. XCVII, Ante-Nicene, I:247.

[380] *The Epistle of Barnabas*, Ch. III, Ante-Nicene, I:145.

[381] Saint Irenaeus, *Proof of the Apostolic Preaching*, ¶ 79, ACW, 16:97.

[382] Saint Cyprian, "Testimonies," § 20, *Treatises*, Ante-Nicene, V:524.

Saint Kyril of Jerusalem repeats, "He stretched out His hands on the Cross, that He might embrace the ends of the world; for this Golgotha is the very center of the earth. It is not my word, but it is a prophet who has said, 'He hath wrought salvation in the midst of the earth [Ps. 73:13].' He stretched forth human hands, Who by His spiritual hands had established the heaven. And they were fastened with nails, that His manhood, which bore the sins of men, having been nailed to the tree, and having died, sin might die with it; and we might rise again in righteousness."[383]

3. Golgotha.

"Who will tell you of the eternal place [Is. 33:14]?

"He that walks in righteousness, speaking rightly, hating transgression and iniquity, and shaking His hands from gifts, stopping His ears that He should not hear the judgment of blood, shutting His eyes that He should not see injustice [Is. 33:15];

"That One shall dwell in a high cave of a strong rock; bread shall be given Him, and His water shall be sure [Is. 33:16].

"Ye shall see a King with glory [Is. 33:17]."

The *Epistle of Barnabas* mentions that Golgotha and the tomb are prefigured in the words, **"He shall dwell in the lofty cave of the strong rock"**; and the words **"His water shall be sure** [Is. 13:16]" refers to holy Baptism.[384]

Saint Justin believes: "Now it is evident, that in this prophecy (allusion is made) to the bread which our Christ gave us to eat, in remembrance of His being made in the flesh for the sake of His believers, for Whom also He suffered; and to the cup which He gave us to drink, in remembrance of His own blood, with giving of thanks. And this prophecy proves that we shall behold this very King with glory. And the very terms of the prophecy declare loudly, that the people foreknown to believe in Him were foreknown to pursue diligently the fear of the Lord."[385]

Saint Hippolytos describes the two advents of our Lord and Savior: "As indicated in the Scriptures, the one being His first advent in the flesh, which took place without honor by reason of His being set at nought, as Esaias spoke of Him aforetime [Is. 53:2-5]. But His second advent is announced as glorious, when He shall come from heaven with the host of angels, and the

---

[383] Saint Cyril of Jerusalem, "Lecture XIII," *Catechetical Lectures*, Nicene, 2nd Ser., VII:89.

[384] *The Epistle of Barnabas*, Ch. XI, Ante-Nicene, I:144.

[385] Saint Justin Martyr, *Dialogue with Trypho*, Ch. LXX, Ante-Nicene, I:234.

glory of His Father, as the prophet says, 'Ye shall see the King of Glory [cf. Is. 33:17].'"[386]

4. The Holy Sepulcher, Christ's Rest Shall be Glorious.

"And in that day there shall be a root of Jesse, and He that shall arise to rule over the Gentiles; in Him shall the Gentiles trust, and His rest shall be glorious [Is. 11:10]**."**

Saint Chrysostom defines "the root" as Christ.[387] Even though He would undergo torments, "Christ roused up those who would listen," observes the saint. "He stirred them to courage by saying, 'Do not be afraid of these things which they did to Me. I was crucified, I was scourged, I was outraged and insulted by robbers, I was arrested on suspicion of blasphemy and of being a king. But after My death and resurrection, people will look on My sufferings in such a way that no one will say that they were not filled with abundant value and honor.' Certainly this did come to pass. And a prophet predicted it long beforehand [Is. 11:10]. This kind of death is more glorious than a crown. Certainly, kings have laid aside their crowns and taken up the Cross, the symbol of His death. On their purple robes is the Cross, on their crowns is the Cross, at their public prayers is the Cross, on their weapons is the Cross, on the sacred Table of their Altar is the Cross. Everywhere in the world, the Cross shines forth more brightly than the sun. **'And His rest shall be glorious** [Is. 11:10]**.'**"[388] In the following, Saint Chrysostom has applied the "resting place" of Christ to the Cross and to His sepulcher: "Although the place which received His slain body was very small and narrow, it is more venerable than royal palaces, and the emperors themselves hold His tomb in higher honor. **'His resting place shall be glorious** [Is. 11:10]**.'** And this is true not only of His tomb but also of the tombs of His apostles."[389]

Blessed Jerome explains that the glory of the holy sepulcher of our Lord "was foretold by Esaias' prediction, **'His rest shall be glorious** [Is. 11:10]**,'** meaning that the place of the Lord's burial should be held in universal honor."[390]

The Holy Apostles

[Is. 28:11; 52:6, 7; 61:5, 6]

1. Preachers of the Good News.

"Therefore shall My people know My name in that day, for I am He that speaks [Is. 52:6]**:**

---

[386] Saint Hippolytus, *Treatise on Christ and Antichrist*, Ante-Nicene, V:213.

[387] Saint Chrysostom, "Hom. V," *John*, Nicene, 1st Ser., XIV:23.

[388] Idem, *Demonstration Against the Pagans*, Ch. VIII, FC, 73:222, 223.

[389] Ibid., Ch. IX, FC, 73:225.

[390] Saint Jerome, "Letter XLVI," Nicene, 2nd Ser., VI:62.

"I am present, as a season of beauty upon the mountains, as the feet of one preaching glad tidings of peace, as one preaching good news: for I will publish thy salvation, saying, 'O Sion, thy God shall reign [Is. 52:7].'"

"The man," notes Saint Ambrose, "who seeks the good is praised, not for his sandals, but for the swiftness and grace of his feet, as Scripture says, 'How beautiful are the feet of those preaching the glad tidings of peace, of those preaching the glad tidings of good things [Rom. 10:15; cf. Is. 52:7]!' Therefore, remove the sandals from your feet, that they may be beautiful for preaching the Gospel."[391]

Saint Ambrose continues, "Therefore, know yourself and the beauty of your nature, and go forth as if your foot had been freed of bonds and were visible in its bare step, so that you may not feel the fleshly coverings, that the bonds of your body may not entangle the footstep of your mind, that your foot may appear beautiful. For such are they who are chosen by the Lord to announce the kingdom of the heavens....Such was Moses [Ex. 3:5],...so that when he was about to call the people to the kingdom of God he might first put aside the garments of the flesh and might walk with his spirit and the footstep of his mind naked."[392] In a letter, Saint Ambrose writes concerning this passage: "Who are those who preach except Peter, Paul, and all the apostles? What do they preach to us, except the Lord Jesus?"[393]

Saint Chrysostom, lauding the Apostle Paul, declares, "For what could be more 'beautiful' than these 'feet' which visited the whole earth under the sun? This same 'beauty' the prophet also from of old proclaims [Is. 52:7]. Hast thou seen how fair are the feet?"[394] Elsewhere, he comments, "They did preach, and there were many sent forth for this very purpose. And whence does it appear that these are those persons sent? Then he brings the prophet in next [Is. 52:7]. You see how by the kind of preaching he points out the preachers."[395] The mission of the apostles is foretold in the foregoing words. "After the resurrection and the ascension," Saint Chrysostom continues, "He would send forth His apostles, as Esaias foretold [Is. 52:7]. Look what part of the body he praised. He lauded their feet, which took them everywhere they went. Furthermore, David showed the manner and source of their strength and

[391] Saint Ambrose, *Seven Exegetical Works: Flight from the World*, FC, 65:301.
[392] Ibid., *Seven Exegetical Works: Isaac, or the Soul*, FC, 65:21.
[393] Saint Ambrose, "Letter to Layman Irenaeus (Summer, 393)," FC, 26:439.
[394] Saint Chrysostom, "Hom. XIII," *First Corinthians*, Nicene, 1st Ser., XII:75.
[395] Idem, "Hom. XVIII," *Romans*, Nicene, 1st Ser., XI:478.

success when he said, 'The Lord shall give speech with great power to them that bring good tidings [Ps. 67:12].'"[396]

2. The Lord Shall Speak to Them "By Means of Another Language [Is. 28:11]**."**

"Someone might well say," remarks Saint Chrysostom, "'How did the apostles draw to themselves all these people?' And, 'How did men who spoke only the language of the Jews win over the Scythian, the Indian, the Sarmatian, and the Thracian?' Because they received the gift of tongues through the Holy Spirit [Acts 2:4]....The prophets made clear both facts, namely, that the apostles received the gift of tongues and that they failed to win over the Jews, for **'this is the calamity: and they would not hear** [Is. 28:12]**.'**...The Jews would reject the faith and the nations would rush to embrace it."[397]

3. New Teachers and Instructors [Is. 61:5, 6]**.**

Saint Kyril of Alexandria tells us that "Esaias signifies the preachers of the new covenant when he says, **'And strangers shall come and feed thy flocks, and aliens shall be thy plowmen and vinedressers** [Is. 61:5]**.'** Now that the farm was given to other husbandmen, and not solely to the holy apostles, but to those also who come after them, even though not of Israelitish blood, the God of all plainly reveals when He speaks this [Is. 61:5] by the voice of Esaias unto the Church of the Gentiles and to the remnant of Israel. For many indeed of the Gentiles were called, and holy men of their number became teachers and instructors; and even unto this day men of Gentile race hold high place in the churches, sowing the seeds of piety unto Christ in the hearts of believers, and rendering the nations entrusted to their charge as beautiful vineyards in the sight of God."[398] And, **"Ye shall be called priests of the Lord, the ministers of God. Ye shall eat the strength of nations, and shall be admired because of their wealth** [Is. 61:6]**."**

Hearken to Saint Kosmas the Melodist's hymn: *O My disciples and friends, ye shall eat the strength of the nations and their riches shall be your boast* [Is. 61:6]! *For when I shall appear shining brighter than the sun, ye shall be filled with glory and cry out for joy, "Let us sing unto our God, for He has been glorified."*[399]

The Gospel Message

[Is. 10:22; 11:9; 45:12, 13; 55:1]

1. A Remnant Shall be Saved by Faith.

"And though the people of Israel be as the sand of the sea, a remnant of them shall be saved [Is. 10:22]**."**

---

[396] Idem, *Demonstration Against the Pagans*, Ch. V, FC, 73:210.

[397] Ibid., Ch. VII, FC, 73:215, 216.

[398] Saint Cyril of Alexandria, "Hom. 134," *Commentary*, p. 534.

[399] August 6th, The Transfiguration of our Lord, Orthros Canon, Ode One, Mode Four.

Saint Chrysostom remarks, "When the prophet says thus, it means that 'the multitude will never prevail with Me.'...For what advantage, I ask, does a multitude bring, if their system of living be vicious? Nay, on the contrary, even injury results from it."[400] Now, "Why only a remnant?" he asks. He then compares the prophet's words with those of Saint Paul, "For God said to Moses, 'I will have mercy on whomsoever I will have mercy, and I will have compassion on whomsoever I will have compassion [Ex. 33:19; Rom. 9:15].' He then says, 'Now tell me, O thou Jew that hast so many perplexing questions and art unable to answer any of them, how thou comest to annoy us on account of the call of the nations? I, however, have a good reason to give you why the Gentiles were justified and you were cast out. And what is the reason? It is that they are of faith, you are of the works of the law. And it is owing to this obstinacy of yours that you have in every way been given up. "For they being ignorant of the righteousness of God, and seeking to establish their own righteousness, submitted not to the righteousness of God [Rom. 10:3]."'"[401]

Continuing, Saint Chrysostom asks, "Do you see that he too does not say that all are to be saved, but only those that are worthy? 'For I regard not the multitude,' means, 'that a race diffused so far distresses Me not, but those only do I save that yield themselves worthy of it.' And He does not mention the 'sand of the sea' without a reason, but to remind them of the ancient promise whereof they had made themselves unworthy. Why then are you troubled, as though the promise had failed, when all the prophets show that it is not all that are to be saved? Then he mentions the mode of the salvation also. Observe the accuracy of the prophet—and the judgment of the apostle—what a testimony he has cited, how exceedingly apt! For it not only shows us that those to be saved are some and not all but also adds the way they are to be saved. How then are they to be saved, and how will God count them worthy of the benefit? **'He will finish the work, and cut it short in righteousness,'** he says, **'because a short work will the Lord make upon the earth** [Is. 10:23].**'** What he means then is somewhat of this sort. There is no need of...trouble, and the vexation of the works of the law, for the salvation is by a very short way. For such is faith, it holds salvation in a few short words."[402]

Saint Cyprian, in his treatise *On The Lord's Prayer*, asks, "What wonder is it, beloved, brethren, if such is the prayer which God taught, seeing that He condensed in His teaching all our prayer in one saving sentence? This had already been before foretold by Esaias the prophet, when, being filled with the Holy Spirit, he spoke of the majesty and loving-kindness of God, 'consummating and shortening His word,' He says, 'in righteousness, because

[400] Saint Chrysostom, "Hom. XVII," *On the Statues*, Nicene, 1st Ser., IX:457.
[401] Idem, "Hom. XVI," *Romans*, Nicene, 1st Ser., XI:465.
[402] Ibid., Nicene, 1st Ser., XI:469, 470.

a shortened word will the Lord make in all the earth [cf. Is. 10:23].' For, when the Word of God...came unto all,...He taught what is life eternal. He embraced the sacrament of life in a large and divine brevity, saying, 'And this is the eternal life, that they may know Thee, the only true God, and Jesus Christ Whom Thou didst send [Jn. 17:3].' Also, when He would gather from the law and the prophets the first and greatest commandments, He said, 'Thou shalt love the Lord thy God with all thy heart, and with all thy soul, and with all thy mind [cf. Deut. 6:5; 10:12; 30:6]. This is the first and great commandment. And the second is like it, "Thou shalt love thy neighbor as thyself [Lev. 19:18]." On these two commandments hang all the law and the prophets [Mt. 22:37-40].' And again: 'All things whatsoever ye wish that men be doing to you, so also be ye doing to them; for this is the law and the prophets [Mt. 7:12].'"[403]

2. The Gospel Message Fills the World [Is. 11:9].

"'**The whole world is filled with the knowledge of the Lord, as much water covers the seas** [Is. 11:9],' we read in Esaias," says Saint Chrysostom. "And in the Psalms and Romans, we read: 'Their sound hath gone forth into all the earth, and their words unto the ends of the world [Ps. 18:4; Rom. 10:18].' This is the meaning of 'they shall not teach every man his neighbor, and every man his brother, saying, "Know the Lord": for all shall know Me, from the least to the greatest [cf. Heb. 8:11; Jer. 38:34 LXX; 31:34 KJV].'"[404] For the prophet wrote: **"And I will cause all thy sons to be taught of God, and thy children to be in great peace** [Is. 54:13]."

Saint Kyril of Alexandria observes, "It is not difficult to see that the message of the Gospel preaching, being small at first, was soon to leap forth as it were unto great increase, inasmuch as God had foretold it by the voice of Esaias that 'the whole earth has been filled with the knowledge of the Lord, as the deep waters that cover the seas [cf. Is. 11:9].' For the preaching of salvation is everywhere poured forth like a sea, and its onward course is irresistible. This, too, the God of all clearly told us by the voice of the Prophet Amos, 'And judgment shall roll as the waters, and righteousness as an impassable flood [cf. Amos 5:24].'"[405]

3. Freely Are We Saved.

"'**I have made the earth, and man upon it; I, with My hand, have established the heaven; I have given commandment to all the stars** [Is. 45:12].

---

[403] Saint Cyprian, "Treatise IV, On the Lord's Prayer," § 28, *Treatises*, Ante-Nicene, V:455.

[404] Saint Chrysostom, "Hom. XIV," *Romans*, Nicene, 1st Ser., XI:436.

[405] Saint Cyril of Alexandria, "Hom. 98," *Commentary*, p. 395.

"'I have raised Him up to be King with righteousness, and all His ways are right; He shall build My city, and shall turn the captivity of My people, not for ransoms, nor for rewards,' saith the Lord of hosts [Is. 45:13]."

Saint Hilary of Poitiers asks, "Is there any opening left for gainsaying, or excuse for ignorance? If blasphemy continue, is it not in brazen defiance that it survives? God from Whom are all things, Who made all by His command, asserts that He is the Author of the universe; for unless He had spoken, nothing had been created. He asserts that He has raised up a righteous King, Who builds for Himself, that is, for God, a city, and turns back the captivity of His people for neither gift nor reward; for freely are we all saved."[406]

4. Grace is Free; Go to the Writings of the Evangelists.

"'Ye that thirst, go to the water, and all that have no money, go and buy; and eat and drink wine and fat without money or price [Is. 55:1].'"

Saint Cyprian says "that the grace of God ought to be without price."[407] Saint Ephraim the Syrian calls Christ, "O Gift that camest up without price [Is. 55:1]!"[408]

"The Prophet Esaias," comments Saint Kyril of Alexandria, "says, **'Ye that thirst, go to the water** [Is. 55:1].' For he sends us to the writings of the holy evangelists, as to fountains of water....Let us, therefore, draw from the sacred springs, the living and life-giving waters, even those that are rational and spiritual. Let us take our fill, and weary not in the drinking; for in these things more than enough is still for edification, and greediness is great praise."[409]

Holy Baptism Prefigured

[Is. 1:16-18; 12:3-6; 13:16; 35:1, 2; 43:18-21; 48:21; 55:1; 61:10]

1. "Wash you, be clean; remove your iniquities from your souls before Mine eyes. Learn to do well. Diligently seek judgment. Deliver him that is suffering wrong. Plead for the orphan, and obtain justice for the widow [Is. 1:16, 17]."

Saint Hippolytos asks, "Do you see, beloved, how the prophet spoke beforetime of the purifying power of Baptism? For he who comes down in faith to the laver of regeneration, and renounces the devil, and joins himself to Christ, and who denies the enemy and makes the confession that Christ is God, and who puts off the bondage and puts on the adoption, comes up from the

---

[406] Saint Hilary of Poitiers, *On the Trinity*, Bk. IV, § 38, Nicene, 2nd Ser., IX:83.

[407] Saint Cyprian, "Testimonies," § 100, *Treatises*, Ante-Nicene, V:554, 555.

[408] Saint Ephraim, "Hymn V," *The Pearl, Seven Hymns on the Faith*, Nicene, 2nd Ser., XIII:297.

[409] Saint Cyril of Alexandria, "Hom. 65," *Commentary*, p. 277.

Baptism brilliant as the sun, flashing forth the beams of righteousness. And the chief thing indeed is this: he returns a son of God and joint-heir with Christ."[410]

"The Jews, by this alone," says Saint Cyprian, "can receive pardon of their sins, if they wash away the blood of Christ slain, in His Baptism, and, passing over into His Church, obey His precepts."[411]

Saint Ambrose of Milan warns that "in the judgments of God, the Jews are set forth as having offended the Lord in nothing more than violating what was due to the widow and the rights of minors. This is proclaimed by the voices of the prophets as the cause which brought upon the Jews the penalty of rejection. This is mentioned as the only cause which will mitigate the wrath of God against their sin, if they honor the widow, and execute true judgment for minors, for thus we read: **'"Judge the fatherless, deal justly with the widow; and come, let us reason together," saith the Lord** [Is. 1:17]**.'**"[412]

Saint Chrysostom also notes this point: "There is frequent mention in the Scriptures of widows and orphans, but we make no account of this. Yet consider how great is the reward. **'And though your sins be as purple, I will make them white as snow; and though they be as scarlet, I will make them as white as wool** [Is. 1:18]**.'**"[413]

During the Feast of the Theophany, we chant: *Esaias, rising at dawn out of the night, beholding the never-waning light of Thy Theophany, O Christ, that compassionately came to pass for us, cried aloud, "O ye who are illumined, come ye and wash yourselves; make yourselves clean in soul and body through the divine water and the Spirit* [Is. 1:16]*.*"[414]

2. "Draw ye therefore water with joy out of the wells of salvation. And in that day thou shalt say, 'Sing to the Lord, call aloud upon His name, proclaim His glorious deeds among the nations, make mention that His name is exalted. Sing praise to the name of the Lord, for He has done great things; declare this in all the earth. Exalt and rejoice, ye that dwell in Sion, for the Holy One of Israel is exalted in the midst of her [Is. 12:3-6]**.'"**

At the Great Blessing of Waters, we chant: *Let us then draw water in gladness* [Is. 12:3], *O brethren: for upon those who draw with faith, the grace of the Spirit is invisibly bestowed by Christ the God and Savior of souls.*[415] At Mid-Pentecost, we chant: *He that thirsteth, let him come unto Me and drink*

---

[410] Saint Hippolytus, *Discourse on the Holy Theophany*, Ante-Nicene, V:237.
[411] Saint Cyprian, "Treatise XII," § 24, *Treatises*, Ante-Nicene, V:514.
[412] Saint Ambrose, Concerning Widows, Ch. II, Nicene, 2nd Ser., X:393.
[413] Saint Chrysostom, "Hom. LXX," *John*, Nicene, 1st Ser., XIV:259.
[414] January 5th, Canon at Compline, Ode Five, Mode Plagal Two.
[415] Theophany, Great Blessing Of Waters, Mode Plagal Two.

living water, and he shall never thirst unto eternity. He that believeth in My goodness, rivers of eternal life shall pour forth from his belly.[416]

3. The *Epistle of Barnabas* mentions that the words **"His water shall be sure** [Is. 13:16]" refer to holy Baptism.[417]

4. Saint Gregory of Nyssa exclaims that "in the Baptism of Jesus, all of us who are putting off our sins like some poor and patched garment are clothed in the holy and most fair garment of regeneration. And where shall we place that oracle of Esaias? It cries to the wilderness, **'Be glad, thou thirsty desert, let the wilderness exult and flower as the lily. And the desert places of Jordan shall blossom and rejoice. The glory of Libanus has been given to it, and the honor of Carmel; and My people shall see the glory of the Lord and the majesty of God** [Is. 35:1, 2].**'** For it is clear that it is not to places without soul or sense that he proclaims the good tidings of joy, but he speaks by the figure of the desert, of the soul that is parched and unadorned."[418]

A resurrectional hymn proclaims: *The desert, the barren Church of the nations, hath blossomed as a lily by Thy presence* [Is. 35:1].[419]

5. "Remember ye not the former things, and consider not the ancient things. Behold, I will do new things, which shall presently spring forth, and ye shall know them. And I will make a way in the wilderness, and rivers in the dry land. The beasts of the field shall bless Me, the owls and young ostriches; for I have given water in the wilderness, and rivers in the dry land, to give drink to My chosen race, even My people whom I have preserved to tell forth My praises [Is. 43:18-21]."

Saint Cyprian states: "As often as water is named alone in the holy Scriptures, Baptism is referred to, as we see intimated in Esaias [Is. 43:18-21]. It is there that God foretold, by the prophet, that among the nations, in places which previously had been dry, rivers should afterward flow plenteously and provide water for the elected people of God—that is, for those who were made sons of God by the generation of Baptism."[420] He also says, "The old baptism was to cease, and a new one was to begin."[421]

6. Water Out of the Rock, Christ.

Saint Cyprian says, "It is predicted and foretold that the Jews, if they should thirst and seek after Christ, should drink with us, that is, should attain

---

[416] Wednesday of Mid-Pentecost, Vespers Aposticha, Mode One, by John the Monk.

[417] *The Epistle of Barnabas*, Ch. XI, Ante-Nicene, I:144.

[418] Saint Gregory of Nyssa, *Dogmatic Treatises: On the Baptism of Christ,* Nicene, 2nd Ser., V:523.

[419] *Anastasimatarion*, Orthros Eirmos of Resurrection Canon, Ode Three, Mode Two.

[420] Saint Cyprian, "Epistle LXII, To Caecilius, On the Sacrament of the Cup of the Lord," ¶ 8, *Epistles*, Ante-Nicene, V:360.

[421] Ibid., "Testimonies," § 12, *Treatises*, Ante-Nicene, V:511.

the grace of Baptism. The Prophet Esaias says, **'And if they shall thirst, He shall bring forth water to them out of the rock: the rock shall be cloven, and the water shall flow forth, and My people shall drink** [Is. 48:21]**.'** And this is fulfilled in the Gospel, when Christ, Who is the Rock, is cloven by a stroke of the spear in His Passion. Christ also, admonishing what was before announced by the prophet, cries and says, **'Ye that thirst, go to the water** [Is. 55:1]**.'**...For by Baptism the Holy Spirit is received."[422]

7. "Let my soul rejoice in the Lord; for He has clothed me with the robe of salvation, and the garment of joy [Is. 61:10]**."**

Saint Kyril of Jerusalem declares in a lecture to the newly-illumined that "thou shalt no more mourn, now that thou hast put off the old man; but thou shalt keep a panegyric, clothed in 'the garment of salvation [cf. Is. 61:10],' even Jesus Christ."[423]

The Church of the Nations

[Is. 1:2, 3, 4; 2:4; 9:1; 10:33, 34; 11:6, 7, 10; 14:1; 19:24, 25; 24:15; 35:7, 8; 41:18, 19, 20; 42:10-12; 43:15, 19; 45:20; 49:20; 52:15; 54:1; 60:4, 8; 62:2, 12; 65:15, 16; 66:8, 12, 18-21]

This section includes: 1. The Mountain of the Lord—2. Many Nations Will Come—3. Christ is the Light—4. The Diversity of People—5. The Lofty Will Fall—6. Christ Will Rule Over the Nations—7. The Christians are the True Israel—8. Another Israel—9. The Islands, the Churches—10. The Knowledge of God—11. Waters of the Gospel—12. Dry Land Watered—13. The Orchard of the Church—14. Those of the Nations Being Saved—15. Kings and Nations Will See and Consider—16. The Barren Has More Children—17. The Populous Church—18. The Name of Christian—19. A Nation Born At Once—20. New Priests and Levites.

1. The Mountain of the Lord.

"For in the last days, the mountain of the Lord shall be glorious, and the house of God shall be on the top of the mountains, and it shall be exalted above the hills; and all nations shall come to it [Is. 2:2]**."**

Saint Kyril of Jerusalem says, "The Church is called a mountain."[424] Saint Chrysostom says that "Esaias shows how indestructible the Church would be [Is. 2:2]."[425]

2. "And He shall judge among the nations, and shall rebuke many people; and they shall beat their swords into plowshares, and their spears into

---

[422] Ibid., "Epistle LXII, Caecilius, on the Sacrament of the Cup of the Lord (dated A.D. 253)," ¶ 8, Ante-Nicene, V:360.

[423] Saint Cyril of Jerusalem, "Lecture XIX," *Catechetical Lectures*, Nicene, 2nd Ser., VII:146.

[424] Ibid., *Lecture XXI*, Nicene, 2nd Ser., VII:150.

[425] Saint John Chrysostom, *Demonstration Against the Pagans*, Ch. VI, FC, 73:213.

sickles: and nation shall not take up sword against nation, neither shall they learn to war any more [Is. 2:4]."

Saint Justin calls this a direct prediction by the Spirit. "And that it did so come to pass, we can convince you. For from Jerusalem there went out into the world, men, twelve in number, and these, illiterate and of no ability in speaking; but by the power of God, they proclaimed to every race of men that they were sent by Christ to teach to all the word of God. And we who formerly used to murder one another do not only refrain now from making war upon our enemies but also willingly die confessing Christ that we may neither lie nor deceive our examiners."[426]

Saint Irenaeos says that "those that bring good tidings of peace [cf. Is. 52:7] were to come from Judaea and from Jerusalem to announce to us the word of God, which is also for us the law [Is. 2:3]."[427] Moreover, "If, therefore, another law and word, going forth from Jerusalem, brought in such a reign of peace among the Gentiles which received the word, and convinced, through them, many a nation of its folly, then it appears that the prophets spoke of some other person. But if the law of liberty, that is, the word of God, preached by the apostles who went forth from Jerusalem throughout all the earth, caused such a change in the state of things, that these nations did form swords and war-lances into plowshares, and changed them into pruning-hooks for reaping corn, that is, into instruments used for peaceful purposes, and that they are now unaccustomed to fighting, but when smitten, offer also the other cheek [Mt. 5:39], then the prophets have not spoken these things of any other person, but of Him Who effected them....Now He has finally displayed the plow, in that the wood (of the Cross) has been joined on to the iron (nails), and has thus cleansed His land; because the Logos, having been firmly united to flesh, and its mechanism fixed with pins (the nails), has reclaimed the savage earth."[428]

Saint Athanasios brings out this point: "Who then is He that has done this, or Who is He that has united in peace men that hated one another, save the beloved Son of the Father, the common Savior of all, even Jesus Christ, Who by His own love underwent all things for our salvation? For even from of old it was prophesied of the peace He was to usher in [Is. 2:4]. And this is at least not incredible, inasmuch as even now barbarians with savage manners, who still sacrifice to the idols of their country, who are mad against one another, and who cannot endure to be a single hour without weapons, yet when they

[426] Saint Justin Martyr, *The First Apology*, Ch. XXXIX, Ante-Nicene, I:175, 176.

[427] Saint Irenaeus, *Proof of the Apostolic Preaching*, ¶ 86, ACW, 16:101.

[428] Idem, *Against Heresies,* Bk. IV, Ch. XXXIV, Ante-Nicene, I:512. The Oxford editors and translators complain in a footnote [4] that "the whole passage is almost hopelessly obscure, though the general meaning may be guessed."

hear the teaching of Christ, straightway, instead of fighting they turn to husbandry, and instead of arming their hands with weapons, they raise them in prayer. And, in a word, in place of fighting among themselves, henceforth they arm against the devil and against evil spirits, subduing these by self-restraint and virtue of soul. Now this is at once a proof of the divinity of the Savior, since what men could not learn among idols they have learned from Him. And this is no small exposure of the weakness and nothingness of demons and idols. For demons, knowing their own weakness, for this reason formerly set men to make war against one another, lest, if they ceased from mutual strife, they should turn to battle against demons."[429]

3. Christ is the Light and Delivers the Gentiles from Error [Is. 9:1].

"Act quickly, O land of Zabulon, land of Nephthaleim, and the rest inhabiting the seacoast, and the land beyond Jordan, Galilee of the nations [Is. 9:1]."

Zabulon (Zebulon) and Nepthaleim (Naphtali) were in northern Palestine, which was first to be attacked by the Assyrians. God, however, would redeem it as He redeemed all His people. The "seaward road" ran from Damascus, across southern Galilee, to the Mediterranean. The "district of the Gentiles" was in northern Galilee, and was inhabited by pagans. In these words [Is. 9:1, 2], "Esaias," affirms Saint Chrysostom, "revealed that Christ came to those places, that He taught in those lands of Zabulon and Nephthaleim, and that He was recognized by the wonders He wrought."[430]

Saint Irenaeos acknowledges by the following how Christ was typified: "He was prefigured in Joseph. Then from Levi and Juda He descended according to the flesh, as King and Priest. And He was acknowledged by Symeon in the temple. Through Zabulon He was believed in among the Gentiles, as says the prophet, 'the land of Zabulon [cf. Is. 9:1]'; and through Benjamin, that is Paul, He was glorified, by being preached throughout all the world."[431]

The Jews thrust out Christ into Galilee of the Gentiles. "But mark, I pray thee," says Saint Chrysostom, "how in every case when He is about to depart unto the Gentiles, He has the occasion given Him by Jews [cf. Mt. 4:12]. For so in this instance, by plotting against His forerunner, and casting him into prison, they thrust out Christ into the Galilee of the Gentiles. For to show that He neither speaks of the Jewish nation by a part of it nor signifies obscurely all the tribes, mark how the prophet distinguishes that place, saying, 'O land...of Nephthaleim, and the rest inhabiting the seacoast, and the land

---

[429] Saint Athanasius, *On the Incarnation of the Word,* § 52, Nicene, 2nd Ser., IV:64.

[430] Saint John Chrysostom, *Demonstration Against the Pagans*, Ch. III, FC, 73:200.

[431] Saint Irenaeus, *Fragments from the Lost Writings of Irenaeus*, Ch. XVII, Ante-Nicene, I:571.

beyond Jordan, Galilee of the nations,...the people who sit in darkness saw a great light [cf. Is. 9:1; Mt. 4:16].' By darkness here he does not mean that which is sensible, but men's errors and ungodliness. He, therefore, also added, **'O people walking in darkness, behold a great light: ye that dwell in the region and shadow of death, a light shall shine upon you** [Is. 9:2; cf. Mt. 4:16]**.'** For that thou mightest learn that neither the light nor the darkness which he speaks of are sensible, in discoursing of the light, he called it not merely light, but 'a great light,' which elsewhere he expresses by the word 'true [Jn. 1:9]'; and in describing the darkness, he termed it 'a shadow of death [Is. 9:2; Mt. 4:16].'"[432]

Saint Romanos the Melodist (ca. 490-ca. 556) calls this light Christ at the canon during our Savior's theophany: *Upon Galilee of the Gentiles, upon the land of Zabulon and the land of Nephthaleim, as the prophet* [Is. 9:1] *said, "A great light has shone, even Christ." To those that sat in darkness a bright dawn has appeared as lightning from Bethlehem.*[433] This light and grace Saint Paul speaks of, writing: "The grace of God which bringeth salvation appeared to all men [Tit. 2:11]." Also at our Lord's theophany: *Light has now shone on those in darkness, and grace has shed its bright rays upon all* [Is. 9:2; Tit. 2:11].[434] Saint Kosmas also identifies Christ as the Light to those in darkness: *I shall declare the divine and ineffable beauty of Thine excellencies, O Christ. For Thou hast shone forth in Thine own Person as the coeternal brightness from the eternal glory; and taking flesh from a virgin's womb, Thou hast arisen as the sun* [Mal. 4:2], *giving light to those that were in darkness and shadow* [Is. 9:2].[435] Saint Ambrose of Milan identifies that Light as the Son of God.[436]

The hymnographers also praise the Theotokos as the Mother of Light. Saint Romanos: *Rejoice, thou who ineffably gavest birth to the Light.*[437] Saint Theodore the Stoudite, during the *Triodion* period, invites us also to extol her: *Let us sing the praises of the holy mountain of God* [Ps. 67:17], *Mary undefiled. From her shone forth upon those in darkness* [Is. 9:2] *the Sun of righteousness* [Mal. 4:2], *Christ the Life of all.*[438] And, *From thy womb, filled with radiance, Christ has come forth as a bridegroom from His chamber* [Ps. 18:6], *and as a great light He has illumined those in darkness* [Is. 9:2]. *As*

---

[432] Saint Chrysostom, "Homily X," *Matthew*, Nicene, 1st Ser., X:86, 87.

[433] Theophany, Orthros Canon, Oikos.

[434] January 5th, Orthros Aposticha, Mode Two.

[435] August 15th, Dormition of the Theotokos, Katavasia, Ode Five, Mode One.

[436] Saint Ambrose, *Of the Holy Spirit,* Bk. I, Ch. XIV, Nicene, 2nd Ser., X:112.

[437] Extract of Akathist Hymn, Stanza Two.

[438] *Triodion*, Monday in the First Week of the Great Fast, Orthros Canon, Theotokion of Ode One, Mode Two.

lightning has the Sun of righteousness [Mal. 4:2] *shone out, O pure Virgin, and given light to the world.*[439]

4. The Diversity of People in the Church.

"And the wolf shall feed with the lamb, and the leopard shall lie down with the kid; and the young calf and bull and lion shall feed together; and a little Child shall lead them [Is. 11:6].

"And the ox and the bear shall feed together; and their young shall be together; and the lion shall eat straw like the ox [Is. 11:7]."

Saint Chrysostom comments that "the prophet foretold the kinds of people for whom the Church would be established. Not only the meek and the mild and the good would form the Church but also the wild, the inhuman, and men whose ways were like those of wolves and lions and bulls would flock together with them and form one Church."[440] Continuing, he says, "Since this text did not literally refer to wild beasts, let the Jews say when this actually happened. For a wolf has never pastured with a lamb. If it were to happen that they would pasture together, how would this benefit the human race? The text referred not to wild beasts but to wild men. It referred to Scythians, to Thracians, to Mauritanians, to Indians, to Sarmatians, to Persians."[441] Giving a further explanation, he says, "He meant that incongruities of character are blended into one and the same evenness of self-restraint, so also there, by the characters of the brute animals indicating the different dispositions of men, he again spoke of their being linked in one and the same harmony of godliness."[442]

Blessed Jerome confers, "The leopard lies down with the kid and the lion eats straw like the ox [cf. Is. 11:6-8]; not of course that the ox may learn ferocity from the lion, but that the lion may learn docility from the ox."[443]

Saint Kyril of Alexandria writes: "Consider, my beloved, and understand that those who were sanctified by faith did not conform to the habits of the heathen, but, on the contrary, those who were called of the heathen conformed to them. For such beasts as the wolf and lion, the bear and leopard, are eaters of flesh; but those animals which are of a gentle nature, kines and lambs, and steers, feed upon grass. But those of prey, he says, shall graze with these gentle ones, and eat their food. It is not, therefore, the gentle ones who have conformed to the habits of the savage; but, on the contrary, as I said, the savage who have imitated them. For they have abandoned their cruel disposition for the gentleness that becomes saints; and they have been changed by

---

439 *Triodion*, Sunday of the Last Judgment, Orthros Theotokion, Ode Eight, Mode Plagal Two.

440 Saint John Chrysostom, *Demonstration Against the Pagans*, Ch. VI, FC, 73:214.

441 Ibid.

442 Idem, "Hom. X," *Matthew*, Nicene, 1st Ser., X:64.

443 Saint Jerome, "Letter CXXX to Lady Demetrias," Nicene, 2nd Ser., VI:265, 266.

Christ, so that the wolves have become lambs; for He is the One Who has made them gentle."[444]

"The promise of the Church," says Saint Gregory the Great, "may be plainly seen to be fulfilled in this verse [Is. 11:6]. For through the bowels of charity, the wolf dwells with the lamb because those who were predators in this world rest in peace with the tame and the gentle. And the leopard lies down with the kid, because he who was mottled by the stains of his sins consents to be abased with him who despises himself and admits he is a sinner...."[445] Then, regarding the calf, bull, and lion [though Saint Gregory lists them as calf, lion, and sheep], he continues, "Because one, through a contrite heart, prepares himself for daily sacrifice to God, another is like a lion,...and the third is like a sheep, continuing in the simplicity of innocence. These have come together in the folds of Holy Church. Behold! What is the nature of charity which kindles, consumes, fuses and, as it were, reshapes diversities of minds into a single appearance of gold?...For the Lord and our Savior is One. It is He Who here binds the hearts of His elect in unanimity and always stimulates them to heavenly love through inner yearning. Hence, it is added **'and a little Child shall lead them** [Is. 11:6].' Who is that little Child if not He of Whom it is written: **'A Child is born to us, and a Son is given to us** [Is. 9:6].'"[446]

5. The Lofty Will Fall.

"Behold, the Lord, the Lord of hosts, will mightily confound the glorious ones; and the haughty in pride shall be crushed, and the lofty shall be brought low; and the lofty ones shall fall by the sword, and Libanus shall fall with his lofty ones [Is. 10:33, 34]."

"According to Esaias," says Saint Gregory of Nyssa, "this...Lebanon falls with the lofty ones when the blossom of Jesse's root springs up [Is. 11:1]. When His rod of authority goes up, it will change a lion, a leopard, and serpent into a tame and gentle animal. Thus, the lion will dwell together with the calf, and the leopard will lie down with the kid; and that little Child born for us will have charge over them. **'And an infant shall put his hand on the hole of asps, and on the nest of young asps** [Is. 11:8].' He will place His hand in the asp's hole and touch its offspring, thereby blunting its poison [cf. Is. 11:6, 8]. As the prophet says [Is. 10:34], Lebanon will fall with the lofty ones. Prophesy reveals these things by symbols. It would be superfluous to carefully explain them all since they are clear to everyone. For who does not know that the Child born for us touched the asp? His authority destroys beasts; dwelling under the same roof with tame beasts, He has blotted out their harsh nature. Because

---

[444] Saint Cyril of Alexandria, "Hom. 61," *Commentary*, p. 265.

[445] Saint Gregory the Great, "Hom. IV," *Homilies On the Book of the Prophet Ezekiel*, Bk. II, p. 195.

[446] Ibid.

Lebanon, that is, wickedness, falls by this Child's actions; that which exalted itself against the truth will fall along with the very beginning of evil."[447]

The virginal womb hath shamed the tyrant's mind; for an Infant hath thoroughly probed the serpent's soul-destroying lair with His hand [Is. 11:8]. *And having destroyed the haughty apostate, He hath brought him under the feet of the faithful.*[448]

6. Christ Will Rule Over the Nations: "And in that day there shall be a root of Jesse, and He that shall arise to rule over the Gentiles; in Him shall the Gentiles trust, and His rest shall be glorious [Is. 11:10]**."**

Saint Chrysostom comments upon **"In Him shall the Gentiles trust** [Is. 11:10]**,"** writing: "He everywhere declares that the power and knowledge of our Gospels would be poured out to the ends of the world, converting the human race from a brutish disposition and a fierce temper to something very gentle and mild."[449]

7. The Christians are the True Israel [Is. 14:1; 42:4-7, 16; 43:15; 62:12]**.**

A. "And the Lord will have mercy on Jacob, and will yet choose Israel, and they shall rest on their land. And the stranger shall be added to them, yea, shall be added to the house of Jacob [Is. 14:1]**."**

Saint Justin says the Jews understand this to mean the proselytes, but they are mistaken. "You think that these words refer to the stranger and the proselytes, but in fact they refer to us who have been illumined by Jesus. For Christ would have borne witness even to them; but now you are become twofold more the children of Gehenna, as He said Himself [Mt. 23:15]." Continuing, he then remonstrates with the "ridiculous interpretations of the Jews, because Christians are the true Israel." He writes: "It is ridiculous for you to imagine that the eyes of the proselytes are to be opened while your own are not, and that you be understood as blind and deaf while they are enlightened. And it will be still more ridiculous for you, if you say that the law has been given to the nations but you have not known it."[450]

B. The Christians, "In His Name Shall the Gentiles Trust [Is. 42:4]**."**

"As therefore from the one man Jacob," remarks Saint Justin to Trypho the Jew, "who was surnamed Israel, all your nation has been called Jacob and Israel, so we from Christ, Who begat us unto God, as Jacob, and

[447] Saint Gregory of Nyssa, *Commentary on the Song of Songs*, p. 255.
[448] *Anastasimatarion*, Resurrection Canon to the Theotokos, Ode Five, Mode Four.
[449] Saint Chrysostom, "Hom. X," *Matthew,* Nicene, 1st Ser., X:64.
[450] Saint Justin Martyr, *Dialogue with Trypho*, Ch. CXXIII, Ante-Nicene, I:261.

Israel, and Juda, and Joseph, and David, are called and are true sons of God, and keep the commandments of Christ."[451]

C. Christ is King of Israel:

"I am the Lord God, your Holy One, Who have appointed for Israel your King [Is. 43:15]**."**

Saint Justin asks Trypho the Jew, "Will you not understand that truly Christ is the everlasting King? For you are aware that Jacob the son of Isaac was never a king. And therefore Scripture again, explaining to us, says what 'King' is meant by 'Jacob and Israel': **'Jacob is My servant, I will help Him. Israel is My chosen, My soul has accepted Him. I have put My Spirit upon Him. He shall bring forth judgment to the Gentiles** [Is. 42:1]**. He shall not cry, nor lift up His voice, nor shall His voice be heard without** [Is. 42:2]**. A bruised reed shall He not break, and smoking flax shall He not quench; but He shall bring forth judgment to truth** [Is. 42:3]**. He shall shine out, and shall not be discouraged, until He should set judgment on the earth; and in His name shall the Gentiles trust** [Is. 42:4]**.'** Then is it Jacob the patriarch in whom the Gentiles and yourselves shall trust? Or is it not Christ? As, therefore, Christ is the Israel and the Jacob, even so we, who have been quarried out from the bowels of Christ, are the true Israelitic race."[452]

D. A Holy People:

Saint Justin Martyr explains that "after the just One was put to death, we (the Christians) blossomed forth as another people, and sprang up like new and thriving corn [cf. Hos. 2:23]....But we Christians are not only a people but even a holy people, as we have already shown: **'And one shall call them the holy people, the redeemed of the Lord. And thou shalt be called a city sought out, and not forsaken** [Is. 62:12]**.'** We, therefore, are not a contemptible people, nor a tribe of barbarians, nor just any nation,...but the chosen people of God Who appeared to those who did not seek Him. **'I became manifest to them that asked not for Me. I was found of them that sought Me not** [Is. 65:1]**.'** For this is really the nation promised to Abraham by God, when He told him that He would make him a father of many nations, not saying in particular that he would be father of the Arabs or the Egyptians or the Idumaeans....We shall inherit the holy land together with Abraham, receiving our inheritance for all eternity, because by our similar faith we have become children of Abraham. For just as he believed the voice of God, and was justified thereby, so have we believed the voice of God (which was spoken again of us by the prophets and the apostles of Christ), and have renounced even to death all worldly things. Thus, God promised Abraham a religious and

---

[451] Ibid.

[452] Ibid., Ch. CXXXV, Ante-Nicene, I:267.

righteous nation of like faith, and a delight to the Father; but it is not you [Trypho and the Jewish nation] 'in whom is no faith [Deut. 32:20].'"[453]

8. Another Israel.

"In that day shall Israel be third with the Egyptians and the Assyrians, blessed in the land which the Lord of hosts has blessed, saying, 'Blessed be My people that is in Egypt, and that is among the Assyrians, and Israel Mine inheritance [Is. 19:24, 25]**.'"**

Saint Justin notes that "Esaias speaks thus concerning another Israel.... Since then God blesses this people, and calls them Israel, and declares them to be His inheritance, how is it that you repent not of the deception you practise on yourselves, as if you alone were the Israel, and of execrating the people whom God has blessed?"[454]

9. The Islands, the Churches [Is. 24:15; 42:10-12, 15]**.**

A. "The glory of the Lord shall be in the isles of the sea; the name of the Lord shall be glorious [Is. 24:15]**."**

Blessed Jerome comments, "We might say that the many isles are separate provinces or cities of the faithful, or interpret them as the individual churches."[455]

B. "Sing a new hymn to the Lord, ye who are His dominion, glorify His name from the sea, and sail upon it, the islands, and they that dwell in them [Is. 42:10]**."**

Again, Blessed Jerome interprets for us: "Let us speak also of the churches as islands....Even as islands have been set in the midst of the sea, churches have been established in the midst of this world, and they are beaten and buffeted by different waves of persecution. Verily, these islands are lashed by waves every day, but they are not submerged. They are in the midst of the sea to be sure, but they have Christ as their foundation, Christ Who cannot be moved."[456]

C. "They shall give glory to God, and shall proclaim His praises in the islands [Is. 42:12]**."**

At the dedication of the Church of the Holy Sepulcher, we chant, *"The islands are renewed for God* [Ps. 42:12]," *as saith Esaias* [Is. 42:10, 12; 24:15], *"by which we should understand the churches now built by the nations,*

---

[453] Idem, *Writings of Saint Justin Martyr: Dialogue with Trypho*, Ch. 119, FC, 6:331, 332.

[454] Idem, *Dialogue with Trypho*, Ch. CXXIII, Ante-Nicene, I:261.

[455] Saint Jerome, "Hom. 73," *60-96 On The Psalms, Vol. 2*, FC, 57:110.

[456] Idem, "Hom. 24," *1-59 On The Psalms, Vol. 1*, FC, 48:192.

which receive a firm foundation from God. Therefore, let us spiritually celebrate these present festivities."[457]

10. The Knowledge of God Through the Gospel [Is. 35:7, 8].

"And the dry land shall become pools, and a fountain of water shall be poured into the thirsty land; there shall there be a joy of birds, ready habitations and marshes [Is. 35:7]."

Saint Justin says to Trypho the Jew that "the spring of living water which gushed forth from God in the land destitute of the knowledge of God, namely the land of the Gentiles, was this Christ, Who also appeared in your nation, and healed those who were maimed, and deaf, and lame in body from their birth, causing them to leap, to hear, and to see, by His word."[458]

Saint Kyril of Alexandria remarks, "The blessed Prophet Esaias, when revealing the way of salvation by the preaching of the Gospel, thus speaks, **'There shall be there a pure way, and it shall be called the holy way** [Is. 35:8].' For it leads those who walk thereon unto holiness by spiritual service, and a righteousness superior to the law."[459]

11. Waters of the Gospel for the Barren Gentiles.

"I will open rivers on the mountains, and fountains in the midst of plains: I will make the desert pools of water, and a thirsty land water-courses [Is. 41:18]."

Saint Gregory the Great comments that "through Esaias the Lord promises to the forsaken people of the Gentiles, that is to Holy Church, the merits of spiritual virtues like longed-for orchards.... The Lord made the desert into a pool of water, and the dry land into streams of water. He gave the Gentiles, who because of their aridity had earlier borne no fruit in good works, the flowing waters of holy preaching. This way which was formerly closed to preachers, because of its roughness and dryness, later flowered with brooks of teaching."[460]

12. The Dry Land of the Gentiles Watered with the Spirit.

"I will make a way in the wilderness, and rivers in the dry land [Is. 43:19]."

Saint Irenaeos says, "'Dry land' is what the calling of the Gentiles was previously; for the Logos neither passed among them, nor gave them to drink the Holy Spirit Who prepared the way of godliness and justice. And He has poured forth rivers in abundance, to disseminate the Holy Spirit upon earth, as

---

457 September 13th, Feast of the Dedication of the Church of the Holy Resurrection of Christ our God, Vespers Sticheron, Mode Plagal Two.

458 Saint Justin Martyr, *Dialogue with Trypho*, Ch. LXIX, Ante-Nicene, I:233.

459 Saint Cyril of Alexandria, "Hom. 76," *Commentary*, p. 315.

460 Saint Gregory the Great, "Hom. 6," *Forty Gospel Homilies*, pp. 44-47.

He had promised through the prophets to pour forth the Spirit on the face of the earth in the end of days [cf. Joel 2:28, 29]."[461]

13. The Orchard of the Church.

"I will plant in the dry land the cedar and box, the myrtle and cypress, and white poplar: that they may see, and know, and perceive, and understand together, that the hand of the Lord has wrought these works, and the Holy One of Israel has displayed them [Is. 41:19, 20]**."**

Saint Gregory the Great explains the significance of each tree, saying, "The cedar owing to its strong aroma and indestructible nature, we may take to refer to the promise....The cedar designates those who show forth virtues and signs in their deeds, those who can say with Paul, 'We are to God a sweet smelling fragrance of Christ [2 Cor. 2:15],' whose hearts are so firmly grounded in everlasting love that they are uncorrupted by earthly love....Myrtle is soothing; by soothing them it contracts muscles which have been stretched. What then does myrtle represent? Those who are able to sympathize with the sufferings of their neighbors, and who soothe them in their afflictions by their sympathy....When they bring a word, assistance or comfort to their troubled neighbors, they bring them back to grace and keep them from falling into despair because of their excessive suffering....And what does the boxwood signify? It does not grow very tall; and, even though it lacks fruit, it remains always green. It signifies those who, owing to the weakness of age, can no longer produce good works in the Church, but who still follow the belief of their faithful parents and so remain eternally green....And so, after all the trees have been listed, he wisely concludes: 'That men may see and know, and consider and understand,' and then most appropriately adds, 'together.' Since there are in our Holy Church different functions and different ministries, it is necessary that all learn together; in the Church spiritual men, with a variety of characters, ages and ministries, all appear to have something to teach."[462]

14. Those of the Nations Being Saved.

"Assemble yourselves and come; take counsel together, ye that are being saved (σωζόμενοι)[463] **of the nations** [Is. 45:20]**."**

Saint Kyril of Alexandria comments, "It is easy to see from sacred Scripture that the multitude of the Gentiles was also summoned unto repentance and obedience by the holy prophets."[464]

15. Kings and Nations Will See and Consider [Is. 52:15]**.**

Saint Justin exhorts the Jews to repentance before Christ comes. Believing in Christ, Christians are far more religious than Jews. Jesus "is the

---

[461] Saint Irenaeus, *Proof of the Apostolic Preaching*, ¶ 89, ACW, 16:102.

[462] Saint Gregory the Great, "Hom. 6," *Forty Gospel Homilies*, loc. cit.

[463] Present passive participle of "save."

[464] Saint Cyril of Alexandria, "Hom. 130," *Commentary*, p. 516.

chosen Priest and eternal King, the Christ, inasmuch as He is the Son of God. And do not suppose that Esaias or other prophets speak of sacrifices of blood or libations being presented at the altar on His second advent, but of true and spiritual praises and giving of thanks. And we have not in vain believed in Him, and have not been led astray by those who taught us such doctrines. But this has come to pass through the wonderful foreknowledge of God; in order that we, through the calling of the new and eternal covenant, that is, of Christ, might be found more intelligent and God-fearing than yourselves, who are considered to be lovers of God and men of understanding, but are not. Esaias, filled with admiration of this, said, **'Thus shall many nations wonder at Him; and kings shall keep their mouths shut. For they to whom no report was brought concerning Him, shall see; and they who have not heard, shall consider** [Is. 52:15]**.'**"[465]

16. The Barren Has More Children [Is. 54:1]**.**

Saint Justin explains: **"Rejoice, thou barren that bearest not! Break forth and cry, thou that dost not travail. For more are the children of the desolate than of her that has the husband** [Is. 54:1]**."** "This predicted that there shall be more believers from the Gentiles than from the Jews and Samaritans. For all the Gentiles were 'desolate' of the true God, serving the works of their hands, but Jews and Samaritans, having the word of God delivered to them by the prophets, and always expecting the Christ, did not recognize Him when He came, except some few, of whom the Spirit of prophecy by Esaias had predicted that they should be saved. He spoke as from their person, **'And if the Lord of Sabaoth had not left us a seed, we should have been as Sodom, and we should have been made like to Gomorrah** [Is. 1:9]**.'**...And to show how those from among the Gentiles were foretold as more true and more believing, we cite, 'All the Gentiles are uncircumcised in flesh, and all the house of Israel are uncircumcised in their hearts [Jer. 9:26].'"[466]

Saint Irenaeos explains that "'the barren one' is the Church, which in previous times did not at all bring forth children to God,...and the former Synagogue had the husband, the law."[467]

Saint Isaac the Syrian tells us: "First He will free this whole [world] from its state....How suddenly this wonderful order will be destroyed and how a new world will begin in which no recollection whatever of the first creation will occur to any man's mind, in which there will be a different mode of life, different deliberations and different thoughts. Then human nature will no longer recollect this world nor the former way of life in it. For the gaze of their mind

[465] Saint Justin Martyr, *Dialogue with Trypho*, Ch. CXVIII, Ante-Nicene, I:258.
[466] Ibid., *The First Apology*, Ch. LIII, Ante-Nicene, I:180, 181.
[467] Saint Irenaeus, *Proof of the Apostolic Preaching*, ¶ 94, ACW, 16:105.

will be captivated by the sight of that [new] order, and it will not be able to turn in its memory towards the races of flesh and blood; for as soon as this world is destroyed, the new one will begin. O mother that suddenly has been forgotten by the sons which she has borne and educated and instructed—and in the twinkling of an eye they are gathered unto another bosom, and have become real sons of the barren one that which has never borne. 'Rejoice, O barren, thou that didst not bear [Is. 54:1],' at the sons which the earth has borne to thee."[468]

Saint Kosmas the Melodist explains this verse in his Theophany hymn: *Rejoice today, O Church of Christ, that before wast barren and sadly childless* [Is. 54:1]! *For through water and the Spirit* [Jn. 3:5], *sons have been born to Thee.*[469]

17. The Populous Church [Is. 49:20; 60:4, 8; 66:12].

"Lift up thine eyes round about, and behold thy children gathered: all thy sons have come from afar, and thy daughters shall be taken on shoulders [Is. 60:4]**."**

"The Prophet Esaias," declares Saint Gregory of Nyssa, "is predicting the establishment of the Church, and describes it as a certain procession—**'For thus saith the Lord, "Behold, I turn toward them as a river of peace, and as a torrent bringing upon them in a flood the glory of the Gentiles: their children shall be borne upon the shoulders, and comforted on their knees** [Is. 66:12]**."'"**[470]

And, **"Who are these that fly as clouds, and as doves with young ones to Me** [Is. 60:8]**?"** Saint Gregory of Nyssa remarks, "For virtue is a light and buoyant thing, and all who live in her way **'fly like clouds** [Is. 60:8]**,'** as Esaias says, **'and as doves with their young ones'**; but sin is a heavy affair...."[471] Elsewhere, Saint Gregory says that by these words the prophet "proclaimed from afar off, addressing by anticipation the Church with her fair and numerous children. Yes, and he adds moreover this also: **'Thy sons shall say, "The place is too narrow for me; make room for me that I may dwell** [Is. 49:20]**."'** For these predictions the power of the Spirit made with reference to the populous Church of God, which was afterward to fill the whole world from end to end of the earth."[472]

---

[468] Saint Isaac the Syrian, "Treatise XXXV," *Mystical Treatises by Isaac of Nineveh*, trans. from Bedjan's Syriac text, by Arent Jan Wensinck, Volume One, pp. 172, 173.
[469] Theophany, extract from Orthros Canon, Ode Three, Mode Two.
[470] Saint Gregory of Nyssa, *Commentary on the Song of Songs*, p. 63.
[471] Idem, *Dogmatic Treatises: Ascetic and Moral, On Virginity*, Nicene, 2nd Ser., V:364.
[472] Ibid., *Dogmatic Treatises: Oratorical, On the Baptism of Christ,* Nicene, 2nd Ser., V:519.

18. The Name of Christian [Is. 62:2; 65:15, 16].

A. "And the Gentiles shall see Thy righteousness, and kings Thy glory: and one shall call thee by a new name, which the Lord shall name [Is. 62:2]**."**

Saint Ignatios the God-bearer declares, "Let us prove ourselves worthy of that name which we have received. For whosoever is called by any other name besides this, he is not of God. For he has not received the prophecy which speaks thus concerning us: 'The people shall be called by a new name, which the Lord shall name them, and they shall be a holy people [cf. Is. 62:2].' This was first fulfilled in Syria; for 'the disciples were called Christians first in Antioch [Acts 11:26],' when Paul and Peter were laying the foundations of the Church. Lay aside, therefore, the evil, the old, the corrupt leaven [cf. 1 Cor. 5:7], and be ye changed into the new leaven of grace. Abide in Christ, that the enemy may not have dominion over you. It is absurd to speak of Jesus Christ with the tongue, and to cherish in the mind a Judaism which has now come to an end. For where there is Christianity there cannot be Judaism. For Christ is one in Whom every nation that believes and every tongue that confesses is gathered unto God. And those that were of a stony heart have become the children of Abraham, the friend of God [cf. Is. 41:8]; and in his seed all those have been blessed [Gen. 28:14] who were drawn up unto eternal life in Christ [Acts 13:48]."[473]

Blessed Jerome in a homily writes: "'You shall be called by a new name [cf. Is. 62:2].' A new name is deserving of a new son. So in the Apocalypse, 'To him who overcomes I will give a white pebble, and upon the white pebble a new name written [cf. Rev. 2:17].' The new name is that of Christians."[474]

B. "For ye shall leave your name for a loathing to My chosen, and the Lord shall destroy you: but My servants shall be called by a new name, which shall be blessed on earth; for they shall bless the true God [Is. 65:15, 16]**."**

Saint Kyril of Jerusalem proclaims that "Jesus Christ, being the Son of God, gave us the dignity of being called Christians....Let us question the Jews: Are ye servants of the Lord, or not? Show then your new name. For ye were called Jews and Israelites in the time of Moses, and the other prophets, and after the return from Babylon, and up to the present time: where then is your new name? But we, since we are servants of the Lord, have that new name,... for it is the name of the only-begotten Son of God that is proclaimed."[475]

---

[473] Saint Ignatius, *The Epistle of Ignatius to the Magnesians*, Ch. X, Ante-Nicene, I:63.

[474] Saint Jerome, "Hom. 25," *1-59 On The Psalms, Vol. 1*, FC, 48:197.

[475] Saint Cyril of Jerusalem, "Lecture X," *Catechetical Lectures*, Nicene, 2nd Ser.,

(continued...)

19. A Nation Born At Once.

"Who has heard such a thing? And who has seen after this manner? Has the earth travailed in one day? Or has even a nation been born at once, that Sion has travailed, and brought forth her children [Is. 66:8]?"

Blessed Jerome explains that the desert in the verse, "'The voice of the Lord Who shaketh the wilderness [Ps. 28:8],' was the Church that, at first, had no children. By the preaching of Christ, this wilderness 'was shaken,' and 'came to labor and gave birth, and there was born in a single day an entire nation [cf. Is. 66:7].' She, who before was called the 'wilderness of Kaddis [Ps. 28:8],' the desert of holiness—inasmuch as she had been barren of virtues—begins 'gathering the harts [cf. Ps. 28:9]' and sends out in throngs her holy men who kill the serpents on earth, contemptuous of their poisons. While they are running throughout the world proclaiming the Gospel of Christ, **'and in His temple every man uttereth glory** [Ps. 28:9].'"[476]

20. New Priests and Levites.

"'I am going to gather all nations and tongues; and they shall come, and see My glory. And I will leave a sign upon them, and I will send forth them that have escaped of them to the nations, to Tharsis, and Phud, and Lud, and Mosoch, and to Thobel, and to Hellas, and to the isles afar off, to those who have not heard My name, nor seen My glory. And they shall declare My glory among the Gentiles. And they shall bring your brethren out of all nations for a gift to the Lord with horses, and chariots, in litters drawn by mules and awnings, to the holy city Jerusalem,' said the Lord, 'as though the children of Israel should bring their sacrifices to Me with psalms into the house of the Lord. And I will take of them priests and Levites,' saith the Lord [Is. 66:18-21]."

"Even so we (the Christians)," says Saint Justin, "who through the name of Jesus have believed as one man in God the Maker of all, have been stripped, through the name of His first-begotten Son, of the filthy garments, that is, of our sins. And being vehemently inflamed by the word of His calling, we are the true high priestly race of God, as even God bears witness, saying that in every place among the nations sacrifices are presented to Him well pleasing and pure. Now God receives sacrifices from no one, except through His priests [Is. 66:21]....Accordingly, God—anticipating all the sacrifices which we offer through this name and which Jesus the Christ enjoined us to offer (that is, in the Eucharist of the bread and the cup), and which are presented by Christians in all places throughout the world—bears witness that

---

[475](...continued)
VII:61, 62.

[476] Saint Jerome, "Hom. 89," *60-96 On The Psalms, Vol. 2*, FC, 57:231.

they are well pleasing to Him. But He utterly rejects those presented by you and by those priests of yours."[477]

The Sufferings of Christ and of the Christians

1. "See how the just man has perished, and no one lays it to heart. And righteous men are taken away, and no one considers; for the righteous has been removed out of the way of injustice [Is. 57:1].

"His burial shall be in peace: He has been taken away out of the midst [Is. 57:2]."

Christ's death is "predicted by the Spirit of prophecy," according to Saint Justin, "that He and those who hoped in Him should be slain, according to the words of Esaias [Is. 57:1, 2]."[478] He says to Trypho the Jew, "It is plain that, though beheaded, and crucified, and thrown to wild beasts, and chains, and fire, and all other kinds of torture, we do not give up our confession; but the more such things happen, the more do others and in larger numbers become faithful, and worshippers of God through the name of Jesus."

Saint Irenaeos asserts that "these things [Is. 57:1], which were acted beforehand in Abel, were also previously declared by the prophets but were accomplished in the Lord's person; and the same is still true with regard to us, the body following the example of the Head."[479] Also, regarding the sufferings of Christ, he asks, "Who else is the just man to perfection, but the Son of God, Who perfects by justifying those who believe in Him, who, as Him, are persecuted and slain? But in the saying, **'His burial shall be in peace** [Is. 57:2],' he tells how He died for the sake of our salvation—for 'in peace' means, in that of salvation—and that by His death, those who were before mutually hostile and opposed, believing with one accord in Him, will have peace with one another, made well-disposed and friendly because of common faith in Him as also happens. But these words, **'He hath been taken away out of the midst** [Is. 57:2],' refer to His resurrection from the dead—for He was no more seen as one dead, after His burial."[480]

Saint Kyril of Jerusalem brings out that "the Savior then was buried, ye have heard distinctly, as says Esaias, **'His burial shall be in peace** [Is. 57:2]': for in His burial He made peace between heaven and earth, bringing sinners unto God."[481]

---

[477] Saint Justin Martyr, *Dialogue with Trypho*, Chaps. CXVI, CXVII, Ante-Nicene, I:257.

[478] Ibid., *The First Apology*, Ch. XLVIII, Ante-Nicene, I:179.

[479] Saint Irenaeus, *Against Heresies*, Bk. IV, Ch. XXXIV, Ante-Nicene, I:512.

[480] Idem, *Proof of the Apostolic Preaching*, ¶ 72, ACW, 16:94, 95.

[481] Saint Cyril of Jerusalem, "Lecture XIV," *Catechetical Lectures*, Nicene, 2nd Ser., VII:95.

Saint Gregory the Great, Pope of Rome, was asked a question: "Why is it, do you think, that good people are usually taken from us, and those who might be an inspiration to many by their good lives are extremely rare or cannot be found at all?" The saint answered, "The malice remaining in the world deserves no better than to have those who could be of profit quickly taken away. It is to spare the elect the sight of worse evils that they are removed when the end of time approaches. With this in mind, the Prophet Esaias spoke [Is. 57:1]."[482]

2. Resting place Among the Saints.

"Thus saith the Most High, Who dwells on high for ever, Holy in holies (Ἅγιος ἐν ἁγίοις) **is His name, the Most High resting in the saints** (ἐν ἁγίοις ἀναπαυόμενος), **and giving patience to the fainthearted, and giving life to the brokenhearted** [Is. 57:15]."

God is wondrous in His saints [Ps. 67:35] and has a resting place among them, according to the prophet, and Saint Kosmas the Melodist in his Dormition hymn: *O Christ, the Wisdom and the Power of God* [1 Cor. 1:24], *Who dost create and uphold all, establish the Church unshaken and unwavering: for only Thou art holy, Who hast Thy resting place among the saints* [Is. 57:15].[483]

The Devil and Antichrist

[Is. 10:12-16; 11:14; 14:12-17; 18:1, 2; 23:4, 5]

1. The Haughty Ruler of the Assyrians [Is. 10:12-16].

A. "And it shall come to pass, when the Lord shall have finished doing all things on Mount Sion and Jerusalem, that I will visit upon the proud heart, even upon the ruler of the Assyrians, and upon the boastful haughtiness of his eyes [Is. 10:12]."

The Jews have not chosen the water of Siloam that goes softly [Is. 8:6], that is, they have not chosen Him Who is sent; thus the Lord shall bring upon them the king of the Assyrians, and his glory. According to Saint Hippolytos, "By king, Esaias means metaphorically Antichrist."[484] Saint Gregory Palamas says that "by 'Assyrian' is meant a bad use of knowledge. Each evil angel is an intelligence, but, as the prophets say, an 'Assyrian' intelligence [Is. 10:12], which makes a bad use of knowledge."[485]

B. "For he said, 'I will act in strength, and in the wisdom of my understanding I will remove the boundaries of nations, and will spoil their strength [Is. 10:13].

---

[482] Saint Gregory the Great, "Dialogue Three," *Dialogues*, FC, 39:185.

[483] August 15th, The Dormition of the Theotokos, Katavasia, Ode Three, Mode One.

[484] Saint Hippolytus, *Treatise on Christ and Antichrist*, Ante-Nicene, V:216.

[485] Saint Gregory Palamas, *The Triads*, p. 101.

"'And I will shake the inhabited cities. And I will take with my hand all the world as a nest; and I will even take them as eggs that have been left. And there is none that shall escape me, or contradict me [Is. 10:14]**.'"**

Saint Athanasios explains that "when of old Satan deceived the first man Adam, thinking that through him he should have all men subject unto him, he exulted with great boldness and said, 'My hand hath found as a nest the riches of the people; and as one gathereth eggs that are left, have I gathered all the earth. And there is none that shall escape me or speak against me [cf. Is. 10:14].' But when the Lord came upon earth, and the enemy made trial of His human œconomy, being unable to deceive the flesh which He had taken upon Him, from that time forth, he, who promised himself the occupation of the whole world, is for His sake mocked even by children....For now the infant Child lays his hand upon the hole of the asp [Is. 11:8], and laughs at him that deceived Eve."[486]

Blessed Jerome warns that "for everyone who glorifies himself in his heart is partner to the devil, who used to say, 'By my own power I have done it, and by my wisdom, I am shrewd. I have moved the boundaries of peoples [cf. Is. 10:13].' The rest of the passage, in which the prophet describes the pride of the devil, is too long to quote. All other failings deserve the mercy of the Lord because, in humility, they are submitted to the tribunal of God; pride alone, because it honors itself beyond its power, resists God. The adulterer or the fornicator does not dare to raise his eyes to heaven. In dejection of soul, he looks for God's mercy; yet this man whom conscience bows down and humbles to the ground, it also elevates to heaven. When pride and inordinate desire for glory raise up a man, they, at the same time, abase him, for by his sin they make him an enemy of God."[487]

Saint Kyril of Alexandria notes, "For of old, that is before the time of the advent of Christ the Savior of all, the universal enemy had somewhat grand and terrible notions about himself; for he boastfully exulted over the infirmity of the inhabitants of the earth, saying, 'I will hold the world in my hand as a nest, and as eggs that are left I will take it up. And no one shall escape from me or speak against me [cf. Is. 10:14].' And in very truth there was no one who could rise up against his power; but the Son rose up against him and contended with him, having been made like unto us. Therefore, human nature,...as victorious in Him, wins the crown. And this in old time the Son Himself proclaimed. Through one of the holy prophets, He thus addresses Satan:

---

[486] Saint Athanasius, "To The Bishops of Egypt," Nicene, 2nd Ser., IV:223, 224.

[487] Saint Jerome, "Hom. 71," *60-96 On The Psalms, Vol. 2*, FC, 57:100, 101.

'Behold, I am against thee, O corrupting mountain, that corruptest the whole earth [cf. Jer. 28:25 LXX; 51:25 KJV].'"[488]

C. "Shall the axe glorify itself without him that hews with it? Or shall the saw lift up itself without him that uses it, as if one should lift a rod or staff? And it shall not be so [Is. 10:15]**; but the Lord of hosts shall send dishonor upon thine honor, and burning fire shall be kindled upon thy glory** [Is. 10:16]**."**

Saint Hippolytos, in his *Treatise on Christ and Antichrist*, warns us "that these things...are said of no one else but of that tyrant and shameless one and adversary of God...."[489]

Saint Cyprian also agrees that these verses [Is. 10:13-16] refer to Antichrist "whom the Lord rebukes by His prophet."[490]

2. Antichrist Proclaimed by Ammon.

"And they shall fly in the ships of the Philistines. They shall at the same time spoil the sea, and them that come from the east, and Idumea. And they shall lay their hands on Moab first; but the children of Ammon shall first obey them [Is. 11:14]**."**

Saint Hippolytos also interprets here, saying that Antichrist "shall be proclaimed king by them (the children of Ammon), and shall be magnified by all, and shall prove himself an abomination of desolation to the world, and shall reign for a thousand two hundred and ninety days."[491] He also reminds us that "Ammon and Moab are the children born to Lot by his daughters, and their race survives even now. Daniel the prophet also says, 'These shall escape out of his hand: Edom, and Moab, and the chief of the children of Ammon [Dan. 11:41].'"

3. Antichrist Troubles the Church.

"Woe to you, ye wings of the land of ships, beyond the rivers of Ethiopia [Is. 18:1]**.**

"He sends messengers by the sea, and paper letters on the water: for swift messengers shall go to a lofty nation, and to a strange and harsh people. Who is beyond it? A nation not looked for, and trodden down [Is. 18:2]**."**

According to Saint Hippolytos, Antichrist "will be so puffed up by the subserviency of others, he will begin to dispatch missives against the saints, commanding to cut them all off everywhere, on the ground of their refusal to reverence and worship him as God, according to the words of Esaias [Is. 18:1, 2]. But we who hope for the Son of God are persecuted and trodden down by

---

488 Saint Cyril of Alexandria, "Hom. 12," *Commentary*, p. 85.

489 Saint Hippolytus, *Treatise on Christ and Antichrist*, Ante-Nicene, V:207.

490 Saint Cyprian, "Epistle LIV," *Epistles*, Ante-Nicene, V:339.

491 Saint Hippolytus, *Fragments from Commentaries*, Part II, Ante-Nicene, V:184.

those unbelievers. For the 'wings of the vessels [cf. Is. 18:1]' are the churches; and the sea is the world in which the Church is set, as a ship tossed in the deep, but not destroyed; for she has with her the skilled Pilot, Christ. And she bears in her midst also the trophy (which is erected) over death; for she carries with her the Cross of the Lord (like a mast)."[492]

4. Having Mastered Egypt, Libya and Ethiopia, Antichrist Will Be Against Tyre and Sidon.

"Be ashamed, O Sidon: the sea has said, yea, the strength of the sea has said, 'I have not travailed, nor brought forth, nor have I brought up young men, nor reared virgins [Is. 23:4].'

"Moreover when it shall be heard in Egypt, sorrow shall seize them for Tyre [Is. 23:5]."

Saint Hippolytos, speaking of Antichrist, says, "In those times, he shall arise and meet them. And when he has overmastered three horns out of the ten in the array of war, and has rooted these out, namely, Egypt, and Libya, and Ethiopia, and has gotten their spoils and trappings, and has brought the remaining horns which suffer into subjection, he will begin to be lifted up in heart, and to exalt himself against God as master of the whole world. And his first expedition will be against Tyre and Berytus, and the circumjacent territory. For by storming these cities first he will strike terror into the others, as Esaias says [Is. 23:4, 5]."[493]

5. The Evil One Falls [Is. 14:12-17].

A. "How has Lucifer, who rose in the morning, fallen from heaven! He that sent orders to all the nations is crushed to the earth [Is. 14:12].

"But thou saidst in thine heart: 'I will go up to heaven, I will set my throne above the stars of heaven; I will sit on a lofty mount, on the lofty mountains toward the north [Is. 14:13];

"'I will go above the clouds; I will be like the Most High [Is. 14:14].'

"But now thou shalt go down to Hades, even to the foundations of the earth [Is. 14:15]."

Saint Ephraim comments upon this verse in the Gospel: "I was looking at Satan, who fell like lightning from the heavens [cf. Lk. 10:18]," and writes: "It was not that he was actually in them; nor was he in them when he said, 'I will place my throne above the stars [cf. Is. 14:13],' but he fell from his greatness and his dominion. 'I was looking at Satan, who fell like lightning from the heavens.' He did not therefore fall from heaven; for lightning does not fall from heaven, since it is the clouds which engender it. Why then did he say, 'from the heaven'? This was because it was as though it were 'from the

[492] Ibid., *Treatise on Christ and Antichrist*, Ante-Nicene, V:216, 217.

[493] Ibid., Ante-Nicene, V:215.

heaven,' like lightning which comes suddenly. For in one instant Satan fell beneath the victory of the Cross. After ordinary people had been anointed, and sent forth by reason of their mission, and were highly successful in an instant, through miracles of healing those in pain, and sickness and evil spirits, it was affirmed that Satan suddenly fell from his dominion, like lightning from the clouds. For just as lightning goes forth and does not return to its place, so too did Satan fall and did not again hold sway over his dominion."[494]

Blessed Jerome notes: "Adam died; we, too, are subject to death; but the devil, who was a prince and fell, did not die. It is not possible for the angelic order to submit to death, but only to damnation. Hence, He said you shall fall like one of the princes. 'How has the morning star fallen, the son of the dawn [cf. Is. 14:12]?' Behold, here he fell, and there he fell! He fell, for his dwelling place was always in heaven."[495]

Saint Paulinus of Nola writes: "Lucifer was one of the angelic princes before he fell and became the devil by defection. To him the words of Scripture are addressed, 'How is Lucifer fallen from heaven, when he did rise in the morning [cf. Is. 14:12]?' But we are not condemned to everlasting death as he is, for he was the author of sin. He will be punished both on his own account and for the man who died by the sin with which the devil killed him. This is because man did not deserve to be finally excluded from Paradise and from the earth, for the justice of God more indulgently decreed that he sinned not through his own design but through another's. It is more sinful to deceive than to be deceived, to devise a sin than to execute it. So he who consented to the deceit was punished for a time for his improvement, but the deviser of death was doomed to everlasting punishment. This punishment for his sin will never end, because the sin never ceases."[496]

Saint Gregory the Great also writes: "The angels were created such that if they wished they could continue steadfast in the light of blessedness, but if they did not wish they could also fall. Consequently, even Satan fell with his legions of followers [Is. 14:12-15]. But after his fall, the angels who remained steadfast were strengthened so that they certainly could not fall. This is well documented in the historical account at the very beginning of the book of Genesis, because God created heaven which He then called the firmament. Therefore, the heavens were those which were first well made, but then called

---

[494] *Saint Ephrem's Commentary on Tatian's Diatessaron*, p. 172.

[495] Saint Jerome, "Hom. 14," *1-59 On The Psalms, Vol. 1*, FC, 48:107.

[496] Saint Paulinus, "Letter 23," *Letters of Saint Paulinus of Nola: Letters 23-51, Vol. 2*, ACW, 36:47.

the firmament because they received the virtue of immutability so that they certainly should not fall."[497]

Elsewhere, he notes: "Archangels are distinguished by personal names to indicate by the word the service they are able to perform....Michael means 'Who is like God?'...As often as something requiring wonderful courage is to be done, Michael is said to be sent. We are to understand from the very action and name that no one can do what is possible to God. The ancient enemy, who in his pride desired to be like God, said, 'I will ascend to heaven; above the stars of heaven I will set my throne on high; I will sit on the mount of the testament in the recesses of the north; I will ascend above the heights of the clouds, I will be like the Most High [cf. Is. 14:13, 14].' At the end of the world, when he is left to his own strength, he is to be destroyed by a most dreadful punishment when he does battle with the Archangel Michael [Rev. 12:7], so that the one who proudly elevated himself to likeness to God may learn, after he has been destroyed by Michael, that no one can rise to likeness to God by pride."[498]

B. "They that see thee shall wonder at thee, and say, 'This is the man that troubled the earth, that made kings to shake, that made the whole world desolate, and destroyed its cities, he loosed not those who were in captivity [Is. 14:16, 17]**?'"**

Although this also applies to Lucifer, Saint Cyprian also sees Lucifer's servant, Antichrist, depicted here, affirming that "he shall come as a man who stirs up the earth, who disturbs kings, who makes the whole earth a desert [cf. Is. 14:16]."[499]

The Day of Judgment

[Is. 13:9-13; Is. 24:19-22; 61:7; 66:14-16, 22, 24]

1. "For behold! The day of the Lord is coming which cannot be escaped, a day of wrath and anger, to make the world desolate, and to destroy sinners out of it [Is. 13:9]**."**

"Concerning that day," says Saint Chrysostom, "hear the prophets, saying, 'The day of the Lord is incurable, full of anger and wrath [cf. Is. 13:9].' For there will be none to stand by, none to rescue, nowhere the face of Christ, so mild and calm. But as those who work in the mines are delivered over to certain cruel men, and see none of their friends, but those only that are set over them, so will it be then also; or rather not so, but even far more grievous. For here it is possible to go to the king, and entreat, and free the condemned person. But there, no longer; for He permits it not, but they

[497] Saint Gregory the Dialogist), "Fragment I: On Angels," *The Homilies of Saint Gregory the Great On the Book of the Prophet Ezekiel*, p. 287.
[498] Idem, "Hom. 34," *Forty Gospel Homilies*, p. 287.
[499] Saint Cyprian, "Testimonies," § 118, *Treatises*, Ante-Nicene, V:556.

continue in the scorching torment, and in so great anguish, as it is not possible for words to tell. For if, when any are in flames here, no speech can describe their sharp pangs, much less theirs, who suffer it in that place. Since here indeed all is over in a brief point of time, but in that place there is burning indeed—but what is burnt is not consumed. What then shall we do there? For to myself also do I say these things."[500]

Elsewhere, speaking of the second coming and judgment, Saint Chrysostom ponders the following: "I say that a far more severe punishment than Gehenna is exclusion from the glory of the other world, and I think that one who has failed to reach it ought not to sorrow so much over the miseries of Gehenna, as over his rejection from heaven; for this alone is more dreadful than all other things in respect of punishment....For this King does not come to judge the earth drawn by a pair of white mules, nor riding in a golden chariot, nor arrayed in a purple robe and diadem. How then does He come? Hear the prophets crying aloud and saying as much as it is possible to tell to men: for one says, 'He shall judge the world with righteousness, and the peoples with His truth [Ps. 95:13]....Fire shall go before Him, and shall burn up His enemies round about [Ps. 96:3].' But Esaias depicts the actual punishment impending over us speaking thus: **'For behold! the day of the Lord is coming which cannot be escaped, of wrath and anger, to make the world desolate, and to destroy sinners out of it** [Is. 13:9]. **For the stars of heaven, and Orion, and all the host of heaven, shall not give their light; and it shall be dark at sunrise, and the moon shall not give her light** [Is. 13:10]. **And I will command evils for the whole world, and will visit their sins on the ungodly; and I will destroy the pride of transgressors, and will bring low the pride of the haughty** [Is. 13:11]. **And they that are left shall be more precious than gold tried by fire; and a man shall be more precious than the stone that is in Suphir** [Is. 13:12]. **For the heaven shall be enraged, and the earth shall be shaken from her foundation, because of the fierce anger of the Lord of hosts, in the day in which His wrath shall come on** [Is. 13:13].' And again, **'The earth shall be utterly confounded, and the earth shall be completely perplexed** [Is. 24:19]. **It reels as a drunkard and one oppressed with wine. And the earth shall be shaken as a storehouse of fruits; for iniquity has prevailed upon it, and it shall fall, and shall not be able to rise** [Is. 24:20]. **And God shall bring His hand upon the host of heaven, and upon the kings of the earth** [Is. 24:21]. **And they shall gather the multitude thereof into prisons, and they shall shut them into a stronghold** [Is. 24:22].'

[500] Saint Chrysostom, "Hom. XLIII," *Matthew*, Nicene, 1st Ser., X:276.

"Then all the gates of the heavenly vaults are opened, or rather the heaven itself is taken away out of the midst 'for the heaven,' we read **'shall be rolled up like a scroll** [Is. 34:4]**,'** wrapped up in the middle like the skin and covering of some tent, so as to be transformed into some better shape. Then all things are full of amazement and horror and trembling; then even the angels themselves are held by much fear—and not angels only but also archangels and thrones, and dominions, and principalities and authorities. 'For the powers' we read 'of the heavens shall be shaken,' because their fellow servants are required to give an account of their life in this world [cf. Mt. 24:29]."[501]

2. "And all the powers of the heavens shall melt and the sky shall be rolled up as a scroll; and all the stars shall fall as leaves from a vine, and as leaves fall from a fig tree [Is. 34:4]**."**

"Our Lord Jesus Christ shall come with glory at the end of this world, in that last day," says Saint Kyril of Jerusalem. "For of this world there is to be an end, and this created world is to be re-made anew. For, since corruption and theft and adultery, and every sort of sin has been poured forth over the earth, and blood has been mingled with blood [cf. Hos. 4:2] in the world, therefore, that this wondrous dwelling place may not remain filled with iniquity, this world passes away, that the fairer world may be made manifest. And wouldest thou receive the proof of this out of the words of Scripture? Listen to Esaias, saying, 'And the heaven shall be rolled together as a scroll; and all the stars shall fall, as leaves from a vine, and as leaves fall from a fig tree [cf. Is. 34:4].' The Gospel also says, 'The sun shall be darkened, and the moon shall not give her light, and the stars shall fall from the heaven [cf. Mt. 24:29].' Let us not sorrow, as if we alone died, the stars also shall die, but perhaps shall rise again. And the Lord rolls up the heavens, not that He may destroy them, but that He may raise them up again more beautiful. Hear David the prophet saying, 'In the beginning, O Lord, Thou didst lay the foundation of the earth, and the heavens are the works of Thy hands. They shall perish, but Thou abidest [Ps. 101:25, 26].' But some will say, 'Behold, he says plainly that "they shall perish"!'It is plain from what follows: 'And all like a garment shall grow old [Ps. 101:26]. And as a vesture shalt Thou fold them, and they shall be changed; but Thou art the same, and Thy years shall not fail [Ps. 101:27].' For as a man is said to 'perish,' according to that which is written: **'See how the just man hath perished, and no one lays it to heart** [Is. 57:1]**,'** and this, though the resurrection is looked for. So we look for a resurrection, as it were, of the heavens also. 'The sun shall be turned into darkness, and the moon into blood [Joel 2:31].'...And again hear the Lord saying, 'The heaven and the earth shall pass away, but My words in no wise shall pass away [Mt. 24:35]';

---

[501] Idem, "Letter I," *An Exhortation to Theodore After His Fall*, Nicene, 1st Ser., IX:100, 101.

for the creatures are not as precious as the Master's words. The things then which are seen shall pass away, and there shall come the things which are looked for, things fairer than the present; but as to the time, let no one be curious....And venture thou not to declare when these things shall be, nor on the other hand supinely slumber."[502]

3. The Individual and General Judgment.

"Thus shall they inherit the land a second time, and everlasting joy shall be upon their head [Is. 61:7]**."**

Saint Gregory the Great, Pope of Rome, was asked, "If the souls of the just are already in heaven, how is it that they will receive the reward for their righteousness on the day of judgment?" The saint replied, "The just will indeed see an increase in their reward on the day of judgment, inasmuch as up till then they enjoyed only the bliss of the soul. After the judgment, however, they will also enjoy bodily bliss, for the body in which they suffered grief and torments will also share in their happiness. In regard to this double glory the Scriptures say, 'They shall receive double in their land [cf. Is. 61:7].' It is in reference to a time before the day of resurrection that they say of the elect, 'Thereupon a white robe was given to each of them; and they were bidden to take their rest a little while longer, until their number had been made up by those others, their brethren and fellow servants [cf. Rev. 6:11].' Those, therefore, who receive each a single robe are going to receive a double robe on the day of judgment. Just as they rejoice now only in the glory of their soul, they will then rejoice in the double glory of body and soul."[503]

4. Punishment and Reward.

Saint Justin tells us how it shall be in that day, saying, "What the people of the Jews shall say and do, when they see Him coming in glory, has been thus predicted: **'Why hast Thou caused us to err, O Lord, from Thy way** [Is. 63:17]**? The house, our sanctuary, and the glory which our fathers blessed, has been burnt with fire; and all our glorious things have gone to ruin** [Is. 64:11]**.'**"[504]

That the dead shall arise to judgment, we read herein: **"And ye shall see, and your heart shall rejoice, and your bones shall spring up as grass; and the hand of the Lord shall be known to them that fear Him, and He shall threaten the disobedient** [Is. 66:14]**."** Saint Irenaeos cites this as proof of the resurrection that God Who created us shall raise us up.[505] **"For, behold, the Lord will come as fire, and His chariots as a storm, to render His**

[502] Saint Cyril of Jerusalem, "Lecture XV," *Catechetical Lectures*, Nicene, 2nd Ser., VII:105.

[503] Saint Gregory the Great, "Dialogue Four," *Dialogues*, FC, 39:219.

[504] Saint Justin Martyr, *The First Apology*, Vol. I, Ch. LII, Ante-Nicene, I:180.

[505] Saint Irenaeus, *Against Heresies*, Bk. IV, Ch. XV, Ante-Nicene, I:542.

vengeance with wrath, and His rebuke with a flame of fire [Is. 66:15]**. For with the fire of the Lord all the earth shall be judged, and all flesh with His sword: many shall be slain by the Lord** [Is. 66:16]**.**"

Saint Aphrahat writes: "Accordingly, beloved, the righteous shall be tried by the fire, like gold and silver and goodly stones, and the wicked shall be burned in the fire like straw and reed and stubble, and the fire shall have power upon them and they shall be burned [cf. 1 Cor. 3:12-15]; even as the Prophet Esaias said, 'By fire shall the Lord judge and by it shall He try all flesh [cf. Is. 66:16].' And again he said: **'And they shall go forth and see the carcasses of the men that have transgressed against Me. For their worm shall not die, and their fire shall not be quenched; and they shall be a spectacle to all flesh** [Is. 66:24]**.'**"[506] Saint Basil the Great describes the worms, as follows: "They are a venomous and flesh-devouring class of worms, which eat greedily and are never satiated and cause unbearable pains by their voracity."[507]

Saint Cyprian thus admonishes us: "When the day of judgment shall come, what joy of believers! O what sorrow of unbelievers, that they should have been unwilling to believe here, and now that they should be unable to return that they might believe! An ever-burning Gehenna will burn up the condemned, and a punishment devouring with living flames; nor will there be any source whence at any time they may have either respite or end to their torments. Souls with their bodies will be reserved in infinite tortures for suffering."[508]

Saint Aphrahat also cautions us that "in respect of penalty, I say, that all men are not equal. He that has done great wickedness is greatly tormented. And he that has offended not so much is less tormented. Some 'shall be cast into the darkness, the outer one; there shall be there the weeping and the gnashing of the teeth [Mt. 8:12].' Others shall be cast into the fire, according as they deserve; for it is not written that they shall gnash their teeth, nor that there is darkness there. Some shall be cast into another place, a place where 'their worm shall not die... [cf. Is. 66:24].' In the faces of others the door shall be closed and the Judge will say to them:—'I know ye not [Mt. 25:12].'"[509]

"'For as the new heaven and the new earth, which I will make, remain before Me,' saith the Lord, 'so shall your seed and your name continue [Is. 66:22]**.'"** Saint Ambrose of Milan asks, "If the earth and heaven

---

506 Saint Aphrahat, "Demonstration I.—Of Faith," § 12, Nicene, 2nd Ser., XIII:349, 350.

507 Saint Basil, "Hom. 16 on Psalm 33," *Exegetic Homilies*, FC, 46:263.

508 Saint Cyprian, "Treatise V," § 24, *Treatises*, Ante-Nicene, V:464.

509 Saint Aphrahat, "Demonstration XXII.—Of Death and the Latter Times," § 22, Nicene, 2nd Ser., XIII:409.

are renewed, why should we doubt that man, on account of whom heaven and earth were made, can be renewed? If the transgressor be reserved for punishment, why should not the just be kept for glory? If the worm of sinners does not die, how shall the flesh of the just perish? For the resurrection, as the very form of the word shows, is this, that what has fallen should rise again, that which has died should come to life again."[510]

The Heavenly Jerusalem

1. "Behold the city Sion, our refuge: thine eyes shall behold Jerusalem, a rich city, tabernacles which shall not be shaken, neither shall the pins of her tabernacle be moved forever, nor shall her cords be at all broken [Is. 33:20]**."**

Saint Kyril of Alexandria notes that the city above of which Esaias bore witness is that "tabernacle in heaven which is immoveable; and, unending joy is the lot of those that dwell therein."[511]

2. "They shall...come to Sion with joy, and everlasting joy shall be over their head, for on their head shall be praise and exultation, and joy shall take possession of them; pain and sorrow and sighing have fled away [Is. 35:10]**."**

Saint Chrysostom correctly views this as some other rest: "For of Palestine we have not to speak; for they were already in possession of it. Nor can he be speaking of the seventh day; for surely he was not discoursing about that which had taken place long before. It follows therefore that he hints at some other, that which is rest indeed. For that is indeed rest, where **'pain, sorrow and sighing have fled away** [Is. 35:10]**,'** where there are neither cares, nor labors, nor struggle, nor fear stunning and shaking the soul; but only that fear of God which is full of delight." No more of Gen. 3:17-19. "All is peace, joy, gladness, pleasure, goodness, gentleness. There is no jealousy, no envy, no sickness, no death whether of the body or that of the soul. There is neither darkness nor night; all is day, all light, all things are bright. It is not possible to be weary, it is not possible to be satiated: we shall always persevere in the desire of good things."[512]

Elsewhere, he asks, "What then could be more blessed than this life? It is not possible there to fear poverty and disease, nor to see anyone injuring, or being injured, provoking, or being provoked, or angry, or envious, or burning with any outrageous lust, or anxious concerning the supply of the necessaries of life, or bemoaning oneself over the loss of some dignity and power. For all the tempest of passion in us is quelled and brought to nought. All will be in a condition of peace and gladness and joy; all things will be

---

[510] Saint Ambrose, *On Belief in the Resurrection,* Bk. II, § 87, Nicene, 2nd Ser., X:88.
[511] Saint Cyril of Alexandria, "Hom. 91," *Commentary*, p. 366.
[512] Saint Chrysostom, "Hom. VI," *Hebrews*, Nicene, 1st Ser., XIV:396, 397.

serene and tranquil. All will be daylight and brightness, and light, not this present light, but one excelling this in splendor as much as this excels the brightness of a lamp. For things are not concealed in that world by night, or by a gathering of clouds. Bodies there are not set on fire and burned; for there is neither night nor evening there, nor cold, nor heat, nor any other variation of seasons but the condition is of a different kind, such as they only will know who have been deemed worthy of it. There is neither old age there nor any of the evils of old age, but all things relating to decay are utterly removed; and incorruptible glory reigns in every part.

"But greater than all these things is the perpetual enjoyment of intercourse with Christ in the company of angels, and archangels, and the higher powers. Behold now the sky, and pass through it in thought to the region beyond the sky, and consider the transfiguration to take place in the whole creation! For it will not continue to be such as it is now, but will be far more brilliant and beautiful; and just as gold glistens more brightly than lead, so will the future constitution of the universe be better than the present."[513]

On the 9th of May, the holy Church commemorates Saint CHRISTOPHER the Great-martyr and those with him.[514]

Christopher, the holy and great-martyr of Christ, was vouchsafed the crown of martyrdom during the reign of the unjust Emperor Decius (249-251).[515] From his youth the saint had been called Reprobus. During that epoch, the rulers were possessed by a frenzied madness against the pious Christians. The lawless emperor had issued an outrageous decree. His foul command urged the ill use of the righteous and godly slaves of the Christians, with the application of violence, if they could not be coerced into eating meats offered and sacrificed to idols. These foods had been defiled by the sprinkling of the

---

[513] Idem, "Letter 1," *An Exhortation to Theodore After His Fall,* Nicene, 1st Ser., IX:99, 100.

[514] The Greek text of the martyrdom is extant in the Athonite monasteries of the Great Lavra, Iveron, and in other places. The manuscript begins, "In the fourth year of the reign of Decius." The melodic divine office to the saint was composed by Christopher the Prodromite, which was published in the *Panegyrikon* of Abimelek (pp. 10-19), which also contains two canons dedicated to the saint, one festal and one supplicatory (pp. 19-28). The ancient Greek Life is translated into English and presented first. It is followed by another similar version, taken from other pious sources, which is borne out in Orthodox iconography. The story of the river and the weight of the Christ Child upon Saint Christopher came to denote the trials and tribulations of the soul that takes up the yoke of Christ in this world. "In the world," Christ said, "ye shall have affliction; but be of good courage, I have overcome the world [Jn. 16:33]."

[515] The *Roman Martyrology* also places his martyrdom during the Decian persecution.

blood of sacrificial victims. Those who consented not to deny Christ were to be subjected to ten thousand torments, which led to death in a most horrifying manner. All the rulers and governors of the cities of the realm made it a point to appear compliant and obedient to the crown. The impious, as a result, were afforded no small protection by law while the pious were being persecuted.

The Christ Child and Saint Christopher

One of the emperor's military commanders, at that time, who was engaged in a campaign against other nations, encountered the blessed Reprobus. The latter hailed from the tribe of the dog-faced,[516] whom the general apprehended. The blessed Reprobus did not bear the least character resemblance to his countrymen. Indeed, he may be described as prudent and noble-minded, and as one who kept the divine words in his heart. The man of God observed how the idol-worshippers were torturing each of the Christians, which was ushering in no small grief for such a one as Reprobus

---

[516] The dog-faced one, according to the Greek compilers, must signify that the saint was not comely but rather had an ill-favored facial appearance. He features were not deformed so that he had the aspect of a canine, even as some unlearned painters have depicted him. He possessed a human countenance, as other men. Although he had a look that was displeasing to the senses, and even frightening and wild looking, yet his inner man was Christ-like. God created men with one image and one nature, while there are certain small differences one from the other according to similitude or likeness. For there are many nations which were and are, even to this day, cannibalistic. This fact is borne out by both ancient and modern historians. [Taken from note 1, on p. 224, of *The Great Synaxaristes*, s.v. "May 9th."] He should not be depicted with the head of a dog, as some iconographers have portrayed him. The Slavonic Prologue rejects such a visual representation. Nikodemos the Hagiorite attributed to him only a disfigured appearance. The Spanish version of his Life, however, describes Christopher as extremely handsome; but after Baptism, so as not to be troubled by women who would not leave him in peace, he prayed to be transformed into an ugly man with a garbled manner of address. See also English translation from the Spanish by Timothy Nikolau, "Great-martyr Christopher," *Orthodox Life*, Vol. 42, No. 3 (May-June 1992):11.

who was predisposed toward sympathy. With such a compassionate turn of mind, his fellow-feeling toward the sufferers stirred him. Since, however, he was ignorant of the language of the idol madmen who had captured him, he was unable either to reason with or to rebuke the benighted ones. There was not one with whom he could speak and come to an understanding. He, consequently, managed to betake himself to a place contiguous but outside of the city. He prostrated himself to the ground, supplicating the Lord with tears that he might be endowed with the power to converse with his pagan captors. He noetically offered up this prayer: "O Lord God, the Almighty, hearken to my low estate and humiliation. Show Thy compassion to me, the unworthy one. Open my lips and grant me to speak as the men of this place that I might be able to reprove the tyrant." While Reprobus was praying in this manner, he found before him a certain light-bearing youth who addressed him and said, "Thine entreaty has been heard, O Reprobus. So then, rise up and receive grace from the Lord."

Saint Christopher

The holy man rose up, at which point the light-bearing being touched Reprobus' lips. Straightway, as the angel breathed upon his mouth, Reprobus was enabled to speak freely. He then, at once, marched into the city. He viewed the Christians undergoing punishment, which sight pained his heart. It was as if he were receiving those scourges. He, thereupon, directed his words to the idolaters, speaking on behalf of his fellow Christians, saying, "O guides of the darkness and those full of every transgression, does it not suffice to surrender your own souls to Satan, but must you compel even us, who fear the one God, to perish along with you? I am a Christian and I do not condescend to venerate your vain gods and useless abominations." As the holy Reprobus was speaking, Vachthios, one of the pagan officers, happened to be near him. He struck Reprobus on the mouth. The blessed man, not giving reign to anger, turned to him and said modestly, "My Savior Christ is preventing me from retaliating; thus, I shall not render a fitting recompense. But should I become angry, all of thy perverse kingdom would not be able to vanquish me."

Vachthios, goaded by this statement, turned on his heel and departed for the city where the emperor was abiding. He submitted his report to the emperor, adding the following verbal declarations: "Sire, a few days ago, while the authorities were punishing the Christians, in accordance with thy divine command, there appeared a young man in the midst of the people. He can only be described as a huge and dreadful giant. He has the form and look of a wild man. His teeth jut out from his mouth, even as a swine. He has a head like a dog. Simply put, he is so unsightly that he defies description. Now this very tall fellow was blaspheming both the gods and thy realm. For that reason, I slapped him on the face. Instead of guarding his conduct, I then heard the most confounded piece of insolence. He had the cheek to boast that he did not fear thine entire kingdom. I, therefore, thought it prudent to announce these things to your majesty; for the idea came to me that the God of the Christians perhaps has heard their entreaty and has ventured to send a champion to their aid." The wrath of the emperor, while hearing this report, waxed hot. Losing his temper, he lashed out at Vachthios and said, "Peradventure, O thou fool, thou hast a demon and for this reason the scene appeared to thee in this way?" Although he spoke in this fashion, still Decius deemed it prudent to investigate the matter. He, immediately, summoned two hundred soldiers and dispatched them with these orders: "Bind this giant, named Reprobus, and conduct him here before me. In the event he should resist, cut him into a thousand pieces. Only bring forward his head that I may see for myself if he is the frightening ogre that this coward claims."

The sacred Reprobus, meanwhile, went forth to the church of the Christians. He took a seat outside the doors, where he planted in the earth his staff. Reprobus then bowed his head and touched it to the ground, as he offered up his petition that rose powerfully to Christ: "O Lord God, the Ruler of all and the Almighty, Who is carried upon the cherubim and glorified by the seraphim and is hymned by all the saints, hearken unto me, the unworthy one, and let this staff of mine blossom as that of Thy holy Prophet Aaron. And thus do Thou make manifest to me Thy great goodness. In so doing, I will be more eager in Thy confession in order that I might glorify Thee: the Father, the Son, and the Holy Spirit, to the ages. Amen." After praying in this manner, straightway—O the wonder!—the staff blossomed. When Reprobus beheld this wonder, he was empowered the more and kept praying, giving thanks to the Lord.

Now the soldiers, whom Decius dispatched to arrest the righteous man, arrived there the very moment Reprobus was engaged in prayer outside the church. From a distance, they descried his features and became frightened. As a result, they did not dare to draw nigh. But one of the soldiers plucked up courage and rallied his comrades, saying, "Why should we fear one lone man who is unarmed?" Thus, they approached and questioned him in this wise: "Whence comest thou and why weepest thou?" Reprobus gave answer, speaking with a humble tone, "I weep for the sake of men who are wanting in understanding. Such ones have left off venerating the true God for senseless graven images." When the soldiers, therefore, heard him speak to them with meekness, they waxed bold and declared unto him: "Our emperor has commissioned us to bind thee and lead thee before his presence, because thou wilt not pay homage to the ancient gods but rather a new one."

Reprobus replied, "If you will let me, I will come of my own volition; for thou shalt not be able to drag me bound before him. The reason for this is that my Master Christ loosed the bonds of my iniquities and delivered me from Satan, your father." The soldiers responded, saying, "If thou dost not wish to come, get thee hence wheresoever thou wilt. As for us, we shall tell the emperor that we were unable to find thee." The saint remarked, "Tut, tut! I only implore you to tarry a little while, that is, until I should receive holy Baptism. And thereafter we shall go together." The soldiers, still attempting to oblige him, answered, "Our expedition is finished, because for many days we have been searching for thee and, furthermore, we hardly have any rations." The saint remarked, "Bring what little remains that you may see the power of my God." The soldiers saw no reason not to accommodate him and brought forward their contemptibly small supply. Reprobus went to his knees and besought the Lord, saying, "O Lord God, Who blessed the five loaves and filled countless crowds, hear Thy slave! Multiply these few slices of bread that they may behold Thy wonders and may believe that Thou only art true God Who art able to do all things."

Forasmuch as the saint supplicated God with such words as these, an angel of the Lord came to him and said, "Take courage, O athlete of Christ, Christopher! For He has sent me forth to come unto thine aid, commanding me to fulfill all thou hast set thy heart upon." After the angel blessed the soldiers' bread, they were marvellously multiplied. The saint then bade the soldiers, "Eat now, brothers, as much as you wish. Moreover, by this act, come to know the power of my God, Who grants not only earthly good things to those who believe in Him but also heavenly things, as He is mighty and the all-good One." The soldiers, witnessing this wonderworking, were astonished and cried aloud with one mouth: "Great is the Christians' God, the One Who saves His slaves!" They began revering the saint and saying, "We, too, believe in the only true God. We worship Him as the Almighty. We, also, give thanks to thee because thou didst make Him manifest unto us, the benighted ones. Thou hast become unto us a brilliantly shining lamp. Thou hast led us out of the shadows of error and deceit. Thou hast guided us toward the light of truth. We are, therefore, with thee; so do thou command us to perform whatsoever thou dost wish." Then the saint, becoming filled with joy, began teaching them sufficiently the saving preaching of the Lord. He instructed them according to that which is contained in the divine and sacred Gospel. After this took place, Reprobus led them all forth to Antioch and to the sainted Babylas,[517] bishop of that city. Once there, Reprobus recounted the entire matter. When the hierarch was apprised of the history, he offered up heartfelt thanksgiving to God. He catechized and baptized all the soldiers, including the former Reprobus whom he named Christopher.

When this was completed, Christopher counseled the soldiers to return to headquarters at the palace. As they marched on their way, Christopher was strengthening them with these words of advice: "My beloved children and brethren, you acknowledged the God in Whom we believed. Let us endure, therefore, for His sake, both wounds and scourges in this vain world. And let us not deny Him, no matter what they should perpetrate against us. But rather, let us stand manfully, without displaying the least cowardice before the threats or the torments of the tyrants. For the Master Christ, in Whom we believe, shall render us help. Bind me, then, in order that you may lead me before Decius, even as he had given thee express orders. If, however, you fear the tortures, flee to wheresoever it pleases you. But be diligent in giving heed to the salvation of your souls." Upon hearing these admonitions, the soldiers began to weep. They were in no wise inclined to accept the idea of fettering their instructor and guide in the true Faith. Nevertheless, since Christopher stood there waiting, they bestirred themselves and bound him as he charged them. When they arrived at the palace and Decius clapped his eyes on the righteous man, the emperor cringed. He was seized with such fright that he nearly fell off his throne. It was then that the saint addressed the sovereign and said, "O most unfortunate one and perverse emperor, if thou fearest me, the weak one and slave of God, how shalt thou bear His wrath at the fearful hour of the judgment? How shalt thou endure it when the demons drag thee, that thou mayest give a defense at that fearful tribunal for all the souls thou hast destroyed?"

After the tyrant composed himself from his fear, he forced himself to address Christ's witness. "State thy religion, race, and name," said Decius. The holy martyr answered, "I am a Christian and my former name was Reprobus; but now, through holy Baptism, I was named Christopher. My race appears on my face. I am engaged in a struggle for the sake of the Christ and will not be persuaded to comply with thy godless commands." The sinister Decius recoiled and said, "They have given thee a cold and an evil appellation, which brings thee no benefit, O wretched one." The saint rejoined, "Cold is

---

517 Hieromartyr Babylas of Antioch is commemorated by the holy Church on the 4th of September.

thine own name, because thou art ignorant of God and thou, as one of the mindless ones, makest obeisance to stones." Moved to wrath, Decius retorted, "Take pity on thy body, O miserable one, and offer sacrifice to the gods, so that I may honor thee with a host of honors and even elevate thee as a priest of the gods; do so lest thou shouldest perish wrongfully." The righteous one replied, "God forbid! May it not be that I should ever deny the true God and venerate, O most lawless tyrant, vain graven images! Keep thy pleasant things for thyself. Let those vacuous and senseless ones of like mind with thee also keep their good things. I speak in this fashion because I do not grieve for my body, as thou dost presume; but rather, as one prudent, I am concerned for the soul. For this reason, then, do I worship and revere the immortal God. But your falsely-named gods are demons. They are leading your souls into perdition. Do not, then, entertain any hope that I ever will believe in those pseudo deities. Do whatever thou dost intend without delay."

Decius, having then become exceedingly displeased, ordered the hanging of the saint and said to the executioners, "Suspend him by the hairs of his head. Bind a heavy stone to his feet. Submit his whole body to a thrashing with the flat side of the sword." The saint, suffering such piercing pain, endured courageously and remarked to the tyrant, "I neither obey thee nor give thee ear, O most irreverent one. I am not going to pay homage to thy gods. Nor do I take into account the tortures, however dreadful they may be, because they are temporal. As for thee, however, there awaits an everlasting fire. Thou shalt inherit it together with the demons, the ones to whom thou dost offer worship, O most wretched man." The emperor's churlishness was raised with this rebuke. He commanded that lit torches be applied to the martyr's armpits. After the saint was savagely burned, some of the noblemen began urging Decius to alter his strategy. "Flatter the Christian," they were saying, "peradventure thou canst bring him around to thee with a kindly manner. If he should hearken, then thou canst employ his help in the wars."

The emperor fell in with their plan and had Christopher unfettered. Decius then started to ply Christopher in an affected and beseeching manner, saying, "Confess the deities, my good man, for I should desire to have thee as a driver for my chariot." The saint answered this appeal, saying, "Do thou become a Christian that thou mayest not only acquire me as a driver for thy chariot but also reign unto the ages with the Christ." The emperor, perceiving that he was toiling only to his own vexation, contrived another scheme. He gave orders that two harlots be brought forward. They were exceedingly beautiful, bedecked with costly raiment and wearing the most fragrant of sweet perfumes. When the two women were presented to Decius, he charged that they be placed in one of the imperial chambers with the saint. The guileful Decius gave them his pledge, saying, "I promise you much money, should you persuade the Christian to venerate the idols." The women were led into the chamber and locked therein with Christopher. Straightway, Christopher, although he perceived their object and interest, still had his own settled purpose. He went to his knees in prayer, uttering, "Behold, O Lord, as I stand, in what fashion they have enmeshed my feet and devised stumbling blocks! Rescue me from this secure detention, where they are playing me foul and putting me to a test that shows no outward wounds. Yea, O Lord, abandon me not, for Thine is the glory forever. Amen." Christopher then rose up from that entreaty. He then turned and faced the women, addressing them and saying, "What do you seek?"

The harlots, upon seeing the holy Christopher facing forward, became frightened. They turned their faces toward the wall. The saint, speaking in a gentle tone, inquired again, "What do you seek?" The women replied, "The emperor sent us that we might counsel thee to obey him, so that he need not deliver thee up to a painful demise." The saint commented, "Keep your counsel. I fear not a temporal death, because I desire to reign with my Christ eternally. Furthermore, if you should come to the Christian belief, joy shall be yours. For you shall inherit every enjoyment and pleasure; and thereupon, you shall rejoice with the saints in Paradise." The women became more alarmed and consulted with each other, saying between themselves, "If we come to believe in Christ and Decius should learn of it, the emperor will take it ill and slay us. Then again, if we choose not to believe, this fellow here will slay us on the spot. It is preferable, therefore, that we believe in the Christ. If we should die for Him, He will grant us everlasting life and deathlessness after our death." The women then turned to Christopher and declared with no doubts and no demurs, "We believe in the Christ; and we entreat Him to pardon our many lawless deeds."

The saint followed their acknowledgment with this question: "Have you murdered anyone or practised witchcraft?" Both answered, "No, sir, much rather we have purchased the freedom of many slaves with the sums we have received for prostitution. Apart from our harlotry, we have committed no other evil act." The saint then stretched forth his hands in prayer. He placed his arms crosswise on the two women's heads[518] and supplicated God with these words, "O Lord Jesus Christ, help Thy slaves Aquilina and Kallinike. Do Thou also situate them among the sheep of Thy flock. Number them with Thy saints. And do Thou pardon whatever sins they may have committed in ignorance; for Thine is the glory to the ages. Amen." After this invocation, he began teaching the women the truths of the Faith of the Christ. As for Aquilina and Kallinike—

[518] Cf. Gen. 48:14. Israel (Jacob) also stretched forth his hands, guiding them crosswise, over the heads of Ephraim and Manasse.

the namesakes, respectively, of "eagle" and "noble victory"—they kept glorifying the true God Whom they had come to know.

The two women, the following day, were brought before Decius. He asked them, "Have you succeeded in persuading Christopher to venerate the idols?" Aquilina and Kallinike, grateful to Christopher for having rescued them from wretchedness, answered, "We, rather, have come to believe in the Christ Who is true God and Savior." Decius, sorely astonished at this admission, with a surly demeanor, commented, "As I see, he also has bewitched you." Aquilina, feeling herself heroically disposed by grace, then stated openly: "There is one God Who made the heaven and the earth; and it is He Who saves those who believe in Him. Thy gods, nevertheless, are the commonest dust. They not only are unable to help you but also are leading you all to destruction and perdition." Decius, falling into a rage, charged his officers to seize Aquilina and said, "Take her and hang her from the hairs of her head. Then attach two large millstones to her feet, in order to weigh her down." These instructions were carried out. This heinous punishment caused the inward parts of the martyr to disband and part asunder from the burden of the hanging stones. Her scalp was also tearing away. Consequently, she was feeling the most sharp and bitter of pangs. She managed to turn toward Christopher, who witnessed this barbarous torture, and said, "I beseech thee, O slave of God, make entreaty on my behalf, because I am in much pain and suffering." The saint raised his hands heavenward and began praying and saying, "O Lord Jesus Christ, have mercy on Thy slave and permit her not to be chastised further; instead, do Thou receive her spirit in peace." As he prayed this prayer, the Martyr Aquilina, after running the course, surrendered her soul into the hands of God and reached the expanse of heaven. It was then the 1st of April.

The tyrant then cast a malevolent gaze toward Kallinike and spoke sternly, saying, "Dost thou see what thy companion has suffered, since she showed herself to be disobedient and contentious? Though thou dost not deserve consideration, yet, at least, do thou be induced to come to thy senses and sacrifice to the gods, if thou dost not wish to experience the same torments and more." But the sagacious and goodly Kallinike, wishing to mock and bait the tyrant said to him, "Inasmuch as thou hast issued to me a command, convention enjoins me to hear thee in thy kingly office. Therefore, lead me to the temple that I might assess thy gods, as is meet, according to thy word." The vain-minded emperor, cheered by her response, took the meaning of the saint's words literally. So wanting in understanding and perception, Decius even had bidden that white carpets be strewn from the path leading from the palace to the temple of the idols. Kallinike was escorted by bodyguards who accompanied her happily. As they proceeded, the way they traversed was sprinkled with a fragrant and expensive myrrh.

When the saint arrived at the altar of abomination, she asked the profane priests, "Which god is the greatest?" They indicated the idol of Dios, that is, Zeus or Jupiter. Kallinike took up the graven image into her hands and addressed it, saying, "If thou art a god, speak to me and tell me what thou dost wish of me; because I am come in order to render thee a service." Seeing as it was natural that there would be no response, Kallinike, at the top of her voice, persisted and said vehemently, "O god of the idol worshippers, talk to me!" But there was no voice or hearing. Kallinike then laughed and remarked sarcastically, "Woe to me, the sinner! The gods are incensed against me, because I have disdained them; for which they do not wish to quit blaming me." She disported further and pertly commented, "O well, perhaps, they are sleeping and do not hear!" The vile priests, thinking her to be in earnest, then said to her, "Offer repentance with all thy soul that they may pardon thee." The martyr, discerning that they were obtuse to her derision, ceased this diversion and removed her belt and handkerchief. She bound them around the idol and then gazed heavenward, uttering this prayer, "O Lord God, the Savior of our souls, help me in this same hour!" Kallinike, then, with a sweeping motion, pulled and dragged the idol with all the strength she could muster until she broke into pieces the image of Dios. With this same movement, she also toppled and shivered the images of Hercules and Apollo and whatsoever other idols came into her path. After she shattered the others, as many as she encountered, she declared, "Begone and vanish, O gods of the idolaters!" Finally, the stunned priests of the idols understood how mistaken they were from her manner of speech. They apprehended her lest all of the idols found in that temple should be dashed to the floor. As they attempted to restrain her, she mocked them and said with self-command, "Collect the bones of your gods. And bring forth salt and oil that you may administer treatment and heal them!" Thus did Kallinike set up glorious trophies over the malefic enemies.

Then did all the priests and lay people proceed to Decius. They informed against Christ's witness, pointing out and saying, "This demonized woman had the effrontery to demolish our gods and lay waste our most important deities. If we had not overtaken her and fettered her, this shameless hussy would have ruined all." The emperor, hearing their accusation, became mad with fury. With a booming voice, he shouted, "This is beyond all bounds. Didst thou not promise me, O evil woman, that thou wouldest offer sacrifice to the idols? How hast thou, therefore, dared to wreck them in this indecent manner?" The holy martyr replied with this quick rejoinder: "I did not pull to pieces gods but only pulled down stones that you might have building materials, should the need arise. Since, however, you name them gods, woe to you, O mindless ones, for your gods were overturned by a woman! And if they were unable to guard themselves, how then do you hope to receive their help?"

The vindictive tyrant, now exceedingly splenetic, commissioned a certain carpenter to construct a wooden frame, in the shape of a square, upon which to hang the saint. It was then ordered that a long skewer be inserted from her heel to her shoulder. The executioners also suspended two heavy stones from her feet and another two weights from her hands. The impalement came to pass as the twisted and ill-balanced mind of Decius imagined. The holy Kallinike, the martyr of many acute labors, underwent manifold pains that were excruciating and unspeakable. She glanced at Saint Christopher and said, "Pray for me, O slave of God, for I am much burdened." The hallowed Christopher, raising his eyes on high, uttered this prayer, "O Lord God of Thy saints, receive also this Thy slave; for Thou only art merciful and the Lover of mankind to the ages. Amen." Then the slave of God and gloriously triumphant Kallinike, after quaffing a cup of bitter temptations, uttered these words with impenetrable calmness, "O Lord, into Thy hands do I commit my spirit." As she spoke thus, she surrendered her holy soul into the hands of God. It was then the 2nd of April.

The blackhearted Decius, convulsing with rage at Christopher, roared at him and said, "Thou, much rather, and not these beautiful women, shouldest have been destroyed, O ill-named, dog-faced, and foreign-formed one! But they were deceived and led astray by thy sorceries. Well, what sayest thou now? Wilt thou sacrifice to the idols or dost thou insist upon abiding in thy former foolishness?" The martyr, laughing and shaking his head, then answered with gravity and reserve, "Meet and right it is that thou art named Decius, as the Greek word *dektikon*, for this bespeaks thee as one who accepts and joins in working together with thy father, Satan, who possesses thee as a vessel and organ for whatsoever he desires. Why wilt thou, in vain, put me to the test and lose thy time to no purpose? I have spoken to thee, ofttimes, that I do not pay homage to stupid demons. I wish I were able to bring thee also to the truth. But thou, as one blind and bedeviled, art not worthy to behold the splendid Sun of righteousness.[519] Play the man, therefore, O underling of the devil, and torment the righteous unrighteously."[520]

As he was speaking in this manner, the saint caught sight of the arresting officers and soldiers who had come to believe in Christ. They had gathered together in one spot and were praying. Christopher called out to them, saying, "Come ye children, hearken unto me; I will teach you the fear of the Lord [Ps. 33:11]." The soldiers, as a result, cast down their weapons and their military mantles. Then, falling prostrate, they saluted the saint with these

---

[519] Mal. 4:2.

[520] "The one doing wrong, let him do wrong still; and the filthy one, let him be filthy still; and the righteous one, let him do righteousness still; and the holy one, let him be made holy still [Rev. 22:11]."

words, "Rejoice, O luminary that has guided us to the light of the full knowledge of the Christ!" The emperor, observing that all were reverencing the saint, became panic-stricken. Yielding to the demon at work in him, who whispered to his mind, he asked himself, "Peradventure, Christopher is intending to seize my scepter?" Decius then asked aloud, "Hast thou become an insurgent to me?" But Christopher, making a wry face, answered, "Cease fearing, because only thou shalt inherit the fire, the everlasting one, and those with thee who are deceived."

Then the soldiers said to the emperor, "Sire, we came to believe in the Christ when thou hadst dispatched us to bring in His slave. We have also partaken of the heavenly bread. We, thereupon, do not deny this Faith, despite however many torments we should be subjected to by thee." Decius grumbled by way of complaint, saying, "How have I failed you that you should forsake me, my children? Perhaps you lacked horses, raiment, or money? Come, I beseech you, and you shall have double of whatsoever you require; only, do not abandon me and desert." The soldiers declared, "Keep thy wealth that thou mayest rejoice over thy good things in this life; for in the midst of these things, the demons, to whom thou dost offer obeisance, will drive thee into Tartarus. As for us, we have neither need of thy good things nor fear of thy chastisements." Decius, vexed, or rather besieged with alarm lest others among the bystanders should become emulous and come to believe in the Christ, was resolved to pass the death sentence against them. Thus, the soldiers were beheaded outside of the city. Their sanctified bodies were cast into a furnace where, in compliance with the tyrant's command, they were to be incinerated. But the fire in no wise touched the sacred relics. The pious Christians then collected the relics secretly, by night, and interred them. It was the 7th of April.

The unjust Decius returned Christopher to prison. After some days, the martyr was led before the emperor's judgment seat. Decius opened the examination, making the following demand: "If thou, O mindless one, wilt not obey me and render veneration to the gods, I shall not tarry even an hour longer. But I shall destroy thee by means of ten thousand torments." The saint then said, "Cease threatening me, O son of the devil and heir of everlasting punishment, because I have God as my helper and I have no terror of thy chastisements." Decius then ordered that a shirt, fabricated of copper, be fashioned. The shirt was designed to have four holes that the executioners might pin down the martyr. Meanwhile, a great deal of wood was collected, upon which was cast oil from twenty jars.

After this was carried out, a fire was lit. The saint was cast into the blaze. Though the flames soared to a lofty height, which filled the spectators with trepidation, yet Christopher was standing in that conflagration utterly unharmed. He was reverently engaged in prayer, conversing alone with the

Master Christ as if he were in a dewy and agreeable environment. When much time had elapsed and that devouring element was quenched, the saint emerged both healthy and uninjured. Nothing was even singed, not so much as a hair of his head or a thread of his garments. Those standing by, consequently, who witnessed this wonderworking, came to believe in the Christ. There were approximately one thousand people who were crying out, "Great is the God of the Christians! Help us, O heavenly King, for we also believe in Thee!" They, afterward, kneeled before the feet of the martyr and said, "Rightly art thou named Christopher, for thou bearest the Christ completely in thy heart. Moreover, we see that in no wise dost thou give any consequence to the punishments of the godless tyrant." Then the crowd began shouting at the emperor, "Shame on thee, O Decius, for Christ has conquered thee!"

When the tyrant heard the voices in unison, he was filled with such apprehension that he took to his heels and fled to the palace. As for the saint, he remained in the marketplace. He fearlessly kept teaching those who believed, that he might better establish them in the Faith. But the idol madmen continued urging the emperor to put to death the Christian holy man lest Decius should lose his kingdom. The next day, when the pagans were celebrating a great festival, Decius resumed his seat at the tribunal. He charged a numberless multitude of soldiers to bind all those who were Christian believers and sever their heads. Christopher, in the meantime, emboldened the faithful in their Christian confession. He kept teaching them not to cower before temporal death, so that they could live forever in Paradise. The faithful, as blameless lambs, listened to his words and eagerly completed their earthly sojourn. This took place on the 9th of April.

The most wicked and unrighteous Decius was thinking of diverse methods to inflict a violent death upon Christ's witness. He, thereupon, ordered that a huge stone—necessitating thirty men to drag it—be brought to him. A hole was bored into the stone, through which a chain was passed. One end of the chain was tied around the neck of the saint. After they fettered the hands and feet of Christopher, he was cast inside a deep well. The idolaters thought it impossible that he should ever exit from that darkest of places. But in vain did they meditate these things. This is because an angel of the Lord descended and led forth the saint, alive and unwounded. Decius, beholding such an extrication, became demonized from his own perniciousness. Why? Because he saw he was unable to put to death one naked and unarmed man. Decius then asked the saint, "Until when shall thy magic arts keep thee intact? Is it not possible, then, to blot thee out of existence by the many tortures to which I have thrown upon thee?" The saint replied, "Christ sustains me to the end of this life, my temporal one; for I have Him for my helper. While I am in this life, I despise thine inventions."

The tyrant, whose thoughts were bent to contrive means to be rid of Christopher, responded by giving instructions for the making of the garment of copper. After it was constructed, it was mightily heated. Christopher was fitted with the shirt. The heat of red-hot copper, nonetheless, never touched Christopher; thus, he remained unscathed. The deranged and violent tyrant, once more began uttering soul-damaging and vain words to the man of God, attempting to incite him to pay homage to his polluted abominations. The martyr answered him with prudence, "Thou hast heard me say many times that, even if thou wert to condemn me to ten thousand torments, I will not change my mind with regard to reverencing dumb statues. To what end, then, art thou toiling and punishing thyself to no purpose? Thou hast urgent demands on thy time. Why art thou trespassing on thy valuable time wrongly? I told thee that I revere and worship my Christ always, as He is pre-eternal God and the all-good One. Why the wrangling and disputation? I pray thee earnestly to do that which thou dost wish." Decius, perceiving the immoveable resolution of the saint, pronounced wrongfully and unjustly against the martyr, handing down his final decision when he said, "Since this most incorrigible and useless fellow foolishly slights my own commands, I command the severing of his revolting and ugly head."

The beheaders, thereupon, drew him to the place of execution. A multitude of people, both idolaters and Christians, followed after the saint. When they arrived at the site, Christopher requested leave from the headsman that he might first pray. Having received permission, Christopher prayed to God in the hearing of the whole company. He uttered these words: "O Lord God, the Almighty, I give thanks to Thee. For Thou hast helped me in all things, putting to shame my enemy together with his minions. Therefore, do Thou also come now as my supporter and flank me, O all-good Lord. Receive my spirit in peace and number me with the least of Thy slaves. As for the unjust Decius, render to him the deserving reward of his irreverence. May he be delivered up to Satan for the devouring and destruction of the flesh![521] Again, I beseech Thy goodness, O all-powerful King, help these Christians here and all others who are found in every place of Thy dominion; and do Thou deliver them from the stumbling blocks of the devil. Grant, too, O most compassionate Lord, grace to my body, so that, wheresoever the least portion of my relics should be found, demons would be dispelled, and, moreover, that neither famine nor hail would harm that place. Indeed, do not permit any other affliction ever to occur in that place. All those who celebrate the feast of my martyric contest and read of it, preserve them safe and sound, that they may

[521] Cf. 1 Cor. 5:5.

glorify Thee, the most good Lord; for blessed art Thou to the ages of the ages. Amen."

After the saint prayed in this manner, there came forth a voice out of the heavens, saying, "All, of whatsoever thou didst ask of Me, was My will to fulfill that I not sorrow thee. But this also do I say: if anyone should be found in need and invokes Me, in remembrance of thy name, I shall offer such a one speedy help. Do thou, therefore, come that thou mightest enjoy the good things and the gladness which have been prepared for thee." Christopher, hearing these promises, rejoiced and said to the executioner, "Child, do that which thou hast been charged to perform." The decapitator, drawing nigh to Christopher with much fear and reverence, then swung his sword and severed that honorable head. It should be noted that, after the execution, the same executioner took his own life and died upon the sacred body of the martyr. The day of the martyrdom was the 9th day of May.

After the martyric repose of the saint, Bishop Peter of Attaleia on the Mediterranean ventured forth.[522] He bribed the soldiers with sufficient silver coins for the purchase of the martyr's body. Bishop Peter wrapped the relics in spice and transferred them to his own city. Now Attaleia, which was near a river, from time to time, experienced flooding especially when the port was subjected to heavy rains. During those periods of inundation, the city sustained heavy damage. Consequently, the bishop trusted in the saint to remedy this perilous situation. The relics of Saint Christopher were placed on the bank of the river. Lo, the miracle! From that hour the river Catarrhactes no longer rose up and submerged the city—and so it is, even to this day. Thus, the Lord glorifies those who glorify Him.

But heavenly wrath and righteous judgment overtook and fell upon the unrighteous Decius, in order that the request of the righteous one might be fulfilled. The ruthless emperor, thereupon, contracted a dreadful and terrible disease. As he witnessed the wasting away of his flesh, he declared aloud, "Woe to me, the wretched one! For I unjustly put to death the slave of Christ, Christopher, for which I am now receiving this fearful illness in retribution." The empress, Herennia, said to him, "Was I not telling thee to take heed at that time, but thou wouldest not hearken to me? What will now become of me, the miserable one?" Decius, consequently, not knowing what else to do, summoned some soldiers and gave them these orders, "Make haste, I beseech you,

[522] Attaleia (mod. Antalya) is a Mediterranean port, on the Gulf of Antalya, at the mouth of the river Catarrhactes, which handled the commerce of Egypt and Syria. It is a suffragan bishopric of Perge of Pamphylia (southwestern Turkey). This walled Roman city, standing on a limestone terrace overlooking the sea, is surrounded by gardens and orchards. The city was visited by the Apostles Paul and Barnabas, who embarked from the seaport on their evangelical mission to Antioch [Acts 14:25].

and search for a portion of Christopher's relic or a piece of his garment, and bring it to me." The soldiers went forth and conducted a diligent investigation. When they could find nothing of the requested remains, they took up some of the soil from the execution site where his blood had been shed. Decius took the soil and mixed it with a cup of water, from which he partook. Soon thereafter, the unholy villain delivered over his vile soul to judgment and unending punishment.[523] May we the faithful be delivered from such an end by the intercessions of our ever-virgin Lady Theotokos, the holy and Great-martyr Christopher, and all the saints! Amen.

The Life and Sufferings of Saint Christopher According to Other Sources

Saint Ambrose (ca. 339-397), in his *Preface*, lauds the martyr with these words: "O Lord, Thou hast granted such a wealth of virtue and such grace of teaching to Christopher that by his gleaming miracles he recalled forty-eight thousand men from the error of paganism to the belief of Christian

---

[523] Decius (Gaius Messius Quintus Trajanus) was born ca. 201, Budalia, Pannonia Inferior [near modern Sremska Mitrovica, Serbia, Yugoslavia]. He was married to Herennia Etruscilla and had two sons Herrenius Decius and Gaius Valens Hostilianus. During his reign he fought the Gothic invasion of Moesia. He also had the ill-fame of having instituted the first organized persecution of Christians throughout the empire. Before this former senator and consul acceded to the throne, persecution of the Christians had been sporadic and local. In the beginning of January of 250, Decius issued an edict ordering all citizens to perform a religious sacrifice in the presence of commissioners. The edict obliged all subjects of the empire to offer a pagan sacrifice, by a specified date, on behalf of the emperor's well-being. A number of Christians were slain, among them Pope Fabianus at Rome, as well as the bishops of Jerusalem and Antioch. Countless others lost their lives and many others were arrested. The Christian movement progressed, despite the gruesome deaths. Public opinion even condemned the government's violence and more times than not applauded the passive resistance of the martyrs. When punishments became totally vile and loathsome, they much rather brought shame to those who dispensed them. Decius was killed by the Goths just south of the Lower Danube at Abrittus. It was June of 255. He was the first emperor to die in battle against a foreign enemy. His eldest son also perished. Decius was succeeded by Gallus (251–253). Decius, around whom whirled the maelstrom of sin, provided a vicious model for more atrocities against the Christians. Christian polemicists described Decius' body being stripped and left on the battlefield to be devoured by animals. [Lact. *Mor. Pers.* 4, quoting Jer. 22:19 and 36:30.] See Chris Scarre, *Chronicle of the Roman Emperors* (NY/London: Thames & Hudson, 2001, repr.), pp. 168-170; and *Chronicle of the Roman Emperors*; *Encyclopaedia Britannica 2004 Deluxe Edition CD-ROM*, s.v. "Decius." See also http://www.roman-emperors.org/decius.htm.

dogma. Kallinike[524] and Aquilina had been engaged in prostitution in a public brothel, but Christopher won them over to the practise of chastity and schooled them to receive the crown of martyrdom. For this he was strapped into an iron chair. A fire was set all about, but the blazing heat and flames were to him no cause for fear. Afterward, for a whole day, the storm of arrows shot by the soldiers could not pierce him. Yet one arrow struck an executioner in the eye.[525] The blessed martyr's blood mixed with earth restored his sight. In removing the body's blindness also was that man's mind illumined. The saint entreated for the forgiveness of his persecutor. Moreover, for us who resort to Saint Christopher in faith, by his supplications, we, too, may obtain cure of diseases and infirmities."[526]

Hymns from the Greek *Menaion* assure us also of his powerful intercession, chanting, "The holy dust of thy relics streameth with miracles. It driveth off the threatening of calamitous lightning and granteth us deliverance from perils and plague....And the infirm and suffering do richly abound in good health through thy holy prayers."[527]

Before Christopher received holy Baptism, he was called Reprobus, from the Latin for "castaway." It was not without significance that he was called Christopher by Christ Himself and given that name in holy Baptism by Saint Babylas of Antioch. He bore Christ in at least four ways: (1) on his shoulders when he carried Jesus across the river; (2) in his body by mortification; (3) in his mind by devotion; and, (4) in his mouth by confessing Christ and preaching Him.[528]

There is considerable material, some confused and contradictory, associated with the life and times of Saint Christopher.[529] His existence cannot

---

[524] In accounts, not in the Greek language, Saint Kallinike is also named Nikaea or Nicaea.

[525] The Slavonic *Menaion* confirms this history and records that, after Saint Christopher was "assailed by fire and wounds," he was "shown victorious," when he "cast down at the tribunal the archer who was his foe." May 9th, Vespers Sticheron, Mode Four.

[526] Page 14 of Jacobus de Voragine's *Golden Chain*, Vol. 2, trans. by W. G. Ryan, s.v. "100. Saint Christopher."

[527] May 9th, Vespers Sticheron from the Greek *Menaion*, Mode One.

[528] *Golden Chain*, II:10.

[529] The earlier Greek account may belong to the 6th C. About the middle of the 9th C., the history spread through France. The Greek and Latin *passio* soon gave way to more elaborate accounts. There is extant the 983 Latin edition, in prose and verse, by the Subdeacon Walter of Speyer, *Thesaurus anecdotorum novissimus* (Augsburg, 1721-1723), II, 27-142, and Harster, *Walter von Speyer* (1878). An 11th-C. edition is found in the *Acta Sanctorum* [July, vol. vi], and another in the *Golden Legend* of Jacobus de Voragine. The account from the *Golden Legend* was put into English by

(continued...)

be discounted or denied. A church, in 452, was dedicated to him in Bithynia of northwest Asia Minor. Saint Gregory the Great (d. 604) speaks of a monastery dedicated to Saint Christopher. The Mozarabic Breviary and Missal, ascribed to Saint Isidore of Seville (d. 636), contains a special office in Saint Christopher's honor.[530] He became one of the most popular saints in the east and west, for whom many strange legends arose. But we may, nonetheless, comprehend the nature of the whole from the parts. All accounts agree that he was extraordinary in size and strength. Variations arise in descriptions of how he supposedly wished the distinction of being in the service of the mightiest of kings. He, thereupon, bound himself successively to a mighty king and then to Satan himself. He found both masters lacking in courage, which debased them in his eyes. The mighty earthly king dreaded the name of the devil. He said to Reprobus, "Whensoever I hear the devil named, I fear that he should attain power over me. I, therefore, garnish myself by making the sign of the Cross lest he sorrow or harass me." Reprobus then imagined that Satan was mightier and greater than his present master. He went seeking after the devil who disguised himself as a mighty knight. Reprobus, thinking Satan was some eminent lord, entered into his service. Reprobus soon discovered that his new master was terrified by the sight of the Cross, for which Satan exercised extreme caution to avoid an encounter with the sign. After making a long detour into the stark desert in order to avoid a cross on the roadside, Satan finally admitted that he was sore afraid of the Cross and fled from it wheresoever he saw it. Reprobus again understood that he had not yet found the most powerful and bravest of kings in the world. He quit that sphere of Satan's

Saint Christopher

[529](...continued)
William Caxton. This version came to be known all over Christendom, both in the east and the west. See also *Analecta Bollandiana*, vol. i, pp. 121-148, and x, 393-405; as well as H. Usener's Acta *S. Marinae et St. Christophori*. There is also a Syriac text among the manuscripts of the British Museum [Addit. 12, 174].

[530] *Catholic Encyclopedia*, s.v. "Christopher, Saint."

service, saying, "If only the sign of the Cross fills thee with dread and pain, surely He Who was suspended on the Cross has superior strength. I, therefore, will seek Him and serve Him." Uttering these words, Reprobus, without a backward glance, departed. After yearning and searching for some time to find Christ, God led him to the discovery of a hermit in the desert.

Reprobus implored the hermit to tell him about the King Christ. The hermit imparted faithfully what instructions he knew. The hermit then said to him, "The King Whom thou desirest to serve requires thee to fast often." Reprobus considered this direction but then declined, saying, "Ask of me some other work which I can do, for that which thou requirest would compromise my considerable strength." The hermit then bade him pray, saying, "Thou must keep vigil and recite many prayers." Reprobus then confessed, "I do not perfectly understand this word—prayer. I do not know what it may be. But again, I cannot engage in it continually." The hermit persisted and prayed noetically for discernment in regard to Christopher, a soul of unaffected manliness. The venerable desert dweller then made this recommendation: "I see that thou art noble and good-hearted, of great stature, and possessed of bodily members both prodigious and strong. Do thou, then, go and dwell by the river near to this place. Dost thou know it? Hast thou heard tidings that many, attempting to traverse its rushing waters, are overtaken by the current and drowned? Do thou keep watch there, for it is deep and wide, and act as a human ferry for those who wish to pass over to the other side. In doing this labor, thou shalt appear right pleasing to our Lord Jesus Christ Whom I know thou dost wish to serve. In remaining at thy post and keeping this obedience, I believe thou shalt not be ill rewarded; for I have hope that Christ the King will show Himself to thee." Yearning to please Christ, with a purpose which would give shape and meaning to his life, Christopher did not ponder long before he agreed wholeheartedly saying, "H'm, this is indeed very good. This is the kind of service that I may well do. I am up to the task. I pledge myself to serve Christ in this manner."

Reprobus, thereupon, without further waste of time, hastened to the famous river. He constructed a small and scanty shelter near the river's edge, where he found good anchorage and lodged there. He next took up the business of selflessly assisting travelers. Reprobus employed a great pole by which he steadied himself in the troublous waters. Wayfarers came daily and at all hours to make the crossover. He cheerfully received all with the utmost civility, as he bore over each one and his burdens, without ceasing or murmuring. Abundantly serving every need, there was no form of service which he himself was not eager to undertake. He was thus occupied in doing such labors for many days, by which he attracted divine grace.

Saint Christopher

At one time, when it was cold and windy, as he was taking his ease in his little dwelling place, the voice of a child called out and said, "Christopher, come forth and bear Me over!" Stirred from his slumber, Reprobus went forth but saw nobody. As soon as he returned to his place indoors, he heard the same voice. He sped out the door but still found no one. Perplexed, he returned to his little house. When he heard the voice for a third time, he went outside with amazing celerity and espied a child by the brink of the river. When he drew closer, the Child spoke to him affably, saying, "I pray thee, bear Me across the water." Reprobus was happy to oblige. He lifted up the Child onto his shoulders. He felt the Child to be the normal weight for a lad His size and age. Reprobus took up his pole and stepped into the rushing waters.

As he tread, the rapids became boisterous. The waters rose significantly and swirled wildly roundabout. The undercurrent proved turbulent. Reprobus had difficulty maneuvering as the water frothed and raged. Added to his anxieties, as he went farther, was his sense that the Child was waxing heavier and heavier. Reprobus, despite his formidable size, felt as if he were carrying lead on his shoulders. The Child burdened Reprobus who had the real fear that both of them would be taken away down river and drowned. Reprobus was now in dire straits. The waves were rising higher, while the weight on his shoulders was near to crushing him. He staggered but endured to the end, despite his anguish for the Child, until he made it across. He struggled out of the water and was breathing rapidly. His muscles ached as he felt the ground firm beneath his feet. He gently drew the Child off his shoulders and placed Him safely on dry land. Reprobus then said to the Child, "My Boy, Thou hast put me and Thyself in no small peril. I must confess that, while transporting Thee across, it was as if I had all the world on my back. We nearly foundered. A burden greater than Thee have I never borne across the river. I could not have borne a burden greater than Thee." The Child spoke calmly and answered him, saying, "O Christopher [Christ-bearer], why dost thou marvel? Thou hast not only borne all the world upon thy shoulders but even the One Who created the world and all that is in it! I am Jesus Christ, the

King Whom thou seekest and for Whom thou servest in this labor of love. That thou mightest know that what I declare is the truth, do this: return to thy house and set thy staff in the earth. Tomorrow, upon arising, thou shalt see that the barren pole has blossomed forth fruit and flowers." Upon uttering this promise, the Lord Jesus disappeared before the eyes of Reprobus. The rapids, thereupon, subsided and Reprobus traversed the waters with ease. He obeyed and planted his staff in the soil by his house. In the morning, he found snow on the ground but the wooden pole was like unto a palm tree, bearing bright flowers, leaves, and dates.

Saint Christopher

The account then describes his entry into a city of Lycia[531] where Reprobus did not understand the language spoken.[532] Reprobus prayed for understanding and the ability to converse in the local tongue, which fluency the Lord granted to him. His second request was that he might be vouchsafed the regenerating waters of holy Baptism. With his God-endowed ability to speak their tongue, Reprobus went out among the heathen and remonstrated with them for persecuting Christians who taught love, peace, and mercy. Bacchus (Vachthios), a pagan general, admonished him and even smote Reprobus in the face. "If I were not a

---

[531] Lycia, an ancient maritime district of southwestern Anatolia, lay along the Mediterranean coast between Caria and Pamphylia, and extended inland to the ridge of the Taurus Mountains. In A.D. 43, it was annexed to Roman Pamphylia. After the 4th C., it became a separate Roman province. Its metropolis was at Myra.

[532] "The Lycian language is an extinct language of southwestern Asia Minor, written in an indigenous Lycian alphabet based on a West Greek prototype. Inscriptions in the language date from about 500 B.C. to about 200 B.C. In 1945, Holger Pedersen, a Danish linguist, published a convincing monograph indicating that Lycian belonged to the Anatolian group. Later, other scholars, among them the Frenchman Emmanuel Laroche, showed Lycian to be related to Luwian. It is now believed that Lycian descended from a West Luwian (Luvian or Luish) dialect. This, too, is an extinct Indo-European language primarily of the southern part of ancient Anatolia. It was closely related to Hittite, Palaic, and Lydian; and it was a forerunner of the Lycian language." *Encyclopaedia Britannica*, CD-ROM, s.v. "Lycian language" and "Luwian language."

Christian," remarked Reprobus, "I should avenge my injury." Reprobus then pitched his wooden staff in the earth. He prayed for the conversion of the people in those parts. He also implored God that a staff—another one—might bud and produce flowers and fruits. This came to pass, at which time eight thousand men came to believe in the Christ. Decius soon learned of these activities and dispatched two hundred soldiers, former comrades of Reprobus.[533]

They came and found him as he was in prayer. Reprobus turned toward them and asked, "Whom do you seek?" The soldiers replied, "The emperor has commissioned us to bring thee bound before him." Christopher remarked, "You could not, whether I was bound or unbound, lead me before him if I did not wish it." They said to him, "Well, then, if thou wilt not come with us, go thine own way wheresoever thou wilt. We shall tell Decius that thou hast eluded discovery." But Reprobus said to the soldiers, "Nay, it shall not be so. I will go with you." As he walked in their midst, he began discoursing on the Faith of Christ. When the soldiers complained that they did not have enough bread, Reprobus said, "Bring to me the pieces of remaining bread." As he prayed over them, they miraculously multiplied. Hence, there was food for all the men, including Bacchus who was in their ranks. As a result of witnessing the budding staff of flowers, the multiplication of the loaves, and his preaching, they all converted to the Faith. The soldiers were not ready to deliver up Reprobus to their sovereign. Thus, they all decided to accompany Reprobus into Antioch of Syria. It was Reprobus' earnest desire to visit Bishop Babylas of that city and receive Baptism with his fellow soldiers. They met with Saint Babylas. Reprobus described his past endeavors to serve the greatest of kings. After Babylas heard Reprobus' confession, he baptized and named him Christopher—the name given to him by Christ Himself—which name means Christ-bearer.

Christopher then addressed the soldiers and commanded them to bind his hands behind his back and lead him thus bound to the emperor. They were not keen on performing his word, but he implored them and said, "I should not like to have on my conscience your suffering under Decius' anger and vindictiveness were he to learn that you did not follow his orders." Although they were reluctant to deliver him up to the unjust emperor, yet they obeyed Christopher. He was brought before Decius who, fearing Christopher's visage, fell off his throne. His servants lifted him up. When the emperor recovered, he attempted to coerce Christopher to renounce Christ in favor of the idols. When he asked Christopher to state his name, the saint said, "Before I was baptized, I was named Reprobus. Afterward, I received the name Christopher. Before

[533] According to the Spanish version, Reprobus had served in the Roman legion for a time under Decius.

Baptism I was a Canaanee,[534] but now I am a Christian." The emperor interrupted and said, "Thou hast a foolish name, man. Why art thou called after the crucified One Who could not help Himself? So how may He profit thee? Therefore, O cursed Canaanite, offer sacrifice to our gods." The emperor then attempted to entice Christopher with wealth, luxury, power, position, and honor. The wily emperor labored for nought. Christopher was then sent to prison. As for the soldiers who were sent to apprehend Christopher, they were beheaded for avowing allegiance to Christ. They all declared with one voice that their God was the God of Christopher. Those Christian soldiers then bowed before Christopher and remained in that position, until executioners came forth and beheaded them. Afterward, their precious bodies and heads were cast into a furnace for incineration.

Decius then sent forth two fair and shapely young women, Kallinike and Aquilina. He thought that rather than use violence, he would break the resolve of Christopher by means of the beautiful faces of the harlots. The women were promised great gifts if they could lure Christopher into illicit relations. "Seduce him and persuade him to sacrifice to our gods," instructed Decius. When they entered Christopher's chamber, he immersed himself in prayer. When they attempted to embrace him, he did not allow their attentions. He rose up and asked, "What do you seek? Why have you come hither?" The women became frightened at his visage, which appeared radiant to them. The sight cast a pall over their brazen intentions. Collecting their minds, they, with startling lucidity, cried out, "O holy man of God, take pity on us that we may learn and believe in the God Whom thou dost revere and proclaim!" Christopher then went to the heart of the matter: their salvation. They listened composedly and brightly to his every word. Not long after, the emperor, having a carping sense that his scheme failed, learned of their conversion. The women, prepared for imputations, professed Christ before him. "So then, my pretties," he snarled, "you were rather seduced by him!" Decius, therefore, was utterly dejected in mind. He sickly glared at them and spoke with a strident voice to Kallinike and Aquilina. "You will do well to regulate your behavior accordingly. I am out of patience. Sacrifice to the gods lest you perish by an evil death."

An idea then struck the women forcibly. They agreed to enter the temple only if all the people would be summoned also. "Clear the streets," they

---

[534] The epithet "Canaanee" or "man-eater" does not imply that Saint Christopher's family members were cannibals. Some authors have even made the absurd claim that they were part canine. What is meant is that they were pagans, who offered up human sacrifices to their deities. [Note found in T. Nikolau's "Great-martyr Christopher," *Orthodox Life*, p. 9.] The memory of Saint Christopher was venerated in the east but more so in the west, particularly in Spain.

said decidedly to Decius, "and make the people assemble in the temple." They succeeded in imposing on his credulity. Decius agreed and the royal progress to the temple commenced. Kallinike and Aquilina entered the temple. They placed their belts about the necks of the graven images and dashed them to the ground. Thus, without an afterthought, they boldly engaged to forfeit their lives as a kind of expiation for their former imprudence. Seeing the idols broken to pieces, the women, with much ease and self-possession, lifted up their voices in the hearing of all and said with a tinge of disdain, "Make haste and summon your physicians and leeches, that you might heal your gods!" Packs of onlookers stood stupefied with incredulous disgust. A startled look ran from pagan eye to pagan eye. The emperor, fixing a rapt eye on his gods turned into dust on the floor, was moved to insane rage as he quivered and shrieked, "This is hateful! Your folly will cost you your lives! You will meet ends proportionable to your deserts!" His voice shook as he ordered their execution, to which pronouncement the women were impervious and detached. Aquilina, according to this account, was suspended by her wrists with a heavy boulder tied to her feet. The consequence of this torture was the breaking of all her limbs. She breathed her last with Christ's name on her lips. As for Kallinike, she was cast into the fire but made her exit untouched by the roaring flames. Decius, witnessing her issue out without the least injury, then ordered that her head be struck from her shoulders.

This history then continues with how Decius continued to put Christopher to the test. Christopher was cast into a well, but an angel drew him up unharmed. The emperor gave orders that Christopher should be beaten with rods of iron. He then commanded that a red-hot iron cross be placed on the martyr's head, so that it was fitted as a helmet. Christopher underwent that contest as one standing under a cool and refreshing waterfall. The saint was vouchsafed a vision, wherein he beheld a tall and comely Man, clad in a white robe, shining more brilliantly than the sun. A crown adorned His brow. A radiant angelic host stood about Him. Christopher discerned that the angels were rebuking fetid and blackened demons who fled in haste. Christopher recounted this vision to those standing by, saying that he was now endowed with greater strength to endure the heated contraption on his head. Some thought the saint deluded, but others justified him. Afterward, they fabricated a seat of iron upon which they tied Christopher. A fire, stoked with pitch, was laid beneath the seat; but, again, Christopher survived this ordeal intact. Meanwhile, the seat was seen by all to have melted from the intensity of the heat. Although the emperor witnessed these wonderworkings, he still sought to contrive new modes of suffering. A garment of heated bronze was made for Christopher, in which he was attired but suffered nought. The divine office to Saint Christopher adds this information regarding the martyr's suffering:

"While thy flesh was cut in pieces by torture, thy God-loving soul was nourished with love....Befittingly loving the uttermost Desire, thou, O prize-bearer, didst not feel the pain when thou wast lacerated and mangled, ever inclining thy mind to the Master."[535]

The relentless Decius then had Christopher bound to a stake. He instructed archers to aim and shoot their arrows at Christopher. The bowmen, all four hundred,[536] obeyed. Their arrows, nevertheless, remained suspended in mid air, near to Christopher, but in no wise touched him. Decius did not see this clearly at first. He presumed that the martyr was riddled with arrows. He, therefore, openly gloating with much relish, rose up from his throne and went toward the stake in order to mock Christopher. But his was a hollow victory. One of the arrows, suddenly, ricocheting, smote an executioner in the eye and blinded him. According to Saint Ambrose, "for a whole day the storm of arrows shot by the soldiers could not pierce Christopher. Nevertheless, one arrow struck an executioner in the eye. Christopher advised that executioner, who was humbled before the whole company, saying, 'I shall die on the morrow. Take up, then, a little clay mixed with my blood. Make it into a paste and anoint thine injured eye that thou mayest find thy health.' This is what took place, and the sight was returned to the eye. The spiritual eyes of the man were also opened and he was illumined."[537]

Thus, by order of the inexorable Decius, Christopher was sentenced to decapitation. The memory of Saint Christopher, and those martyrs with him, is commemorated at Kyparission of Constantinople on the day of his repose, not long after the Feast of Saint George. The oldest icon of the saint, in the monastery on Mount Sinai, dates from the time of Justinian (527-565). Christians from Lycia, according to the Spanish version, were said to have brought the relics of Saint Christopher to Toledo, Spain. The relics remained there for five hundred years. During the Moorish period (712–1085), the relics were translated to safety at Saint Denis in Paris.

Great veneration was shown to the saint in Venice, as well as along the shores of the Danube, the Rhine, and other rivers where floods or ice-jams caused frequent damage. As may be expected, he is called upon in perils from water and tempests. In addition to being the patron and protector of all travelers, he is also the guardian of bookbinders, gardeners, and mariners. He is invoked against lightning, storms, famine, epilepsy, pestilence, plagues

---

[535] May 9th, Orthros Canon, Odes Three and Six, Mode Four, by Saint Theophanes, Bishop of Nicaea (d. 845).

[536] Some accounts number forty archers.

[537] *Golden Chain*, loc. cit. Some versions identify the foul-tempered tyrant himself to have received the wound and repented [Ibid., and Alban Butler (*The Lives of the Saints*, s.v. "July 25th")], but such a claim of Decius' conversion is not borne out historically.

(black death), and sudden death. In times of old, people believed that whosoever should gaze upon the image of Saint Christopher would neither faint nor fall on that day. In recent times, he has also become the patron of motorists. Thus, Christians carry icons of him to help them on their journeys.

Saint Christopher, after treading the path of martyrdom without faltering, now rejoices in "the bridal chamber of virgins." We ask thee, "O glorious martyr, not to cease asking for the peace of the world."[538]

On the 9th of May, the holy Church commemorates the holy Martyrs KALLINIKE and AQUILINA, who, having come to believe in Christ through the testimony of Saint Christopher, suffered martyrdom when Kallinike was impaled with a skewer from heel to shoulder and Aquilina was suspended from the hairs of her head with two large millstones dangling from her feet.[539]

On the 9th of May, the holy Church commemorates the holy venerable Martyr NICHOLAS the New of Vounenee, who was slain by the sword.[540]

Nicholas the New, the famous and invincible soldier of Christ, hailed from the parts of Anatolia (Asia Minor). He was the offspring of wellborn and godly parents. Early in life, his soul manifested a high degree of noble-mindedness and prudence. He chose not to keep company with unruly children or to participate in their games. He shunned the company of those who were foulmouthed and babblers, as is often found among youths. It was his happiness and love to converse rather with people who were wise and discerning, as well as his senior in age. This presence of mind that he displayed was in concert with his desire to hear words that were salutary, useful, and beneficial to the soul. Such was his pursuit as he progressed through childhood. When he came of age, he was drafted into the army. The recruiters selected him, discerning his manliness and dexterity. Nicholas advanced through the ranks, by reason

---

[538] May 9th, Orthros Canon, Ode Nine, Mode Four, by Saint Theophanes.

[539] The biographies and martyrdoms of Saints Kallinike and Aquilina are given in the Life of Saint Christopher, also commemorated today.

[540] The author of this Life is unknown. The text was published with the divine office many times. Those editions that are known are given herein chronologically: Venice, 1657; Moscow, 1736; Venice, 1791; Athens, 1845; Patras, 1866; Athens, 1873; Patras, 1875 and 1905; Tripoli, 1906; Corinth, 1908; and Athens, 1930, by the Thessalian Ezekiel Velanidiotes. It is from this source that the Life was taken and revised and edited for incorporation into *The Great Synaxaristes* (in Greek).

of his bravery, manly virtue, and uprightness. Thus, it was not long before he achieved a reputation that was admired and celebrated all around.

The emperor at that time heard of Nicholas' good fame. From many people he was further informed that Nicholas was capable, amiable, and a competent advisor. Another such as Nicholas, they claimed, was not to be found. The emperor was resolved to summon the highly commended soldier to the royal palace. After they had a private interview, the emperor was exceedingly pleased. He saw that Nicholas was a man possessed of both learning and practical wisdom. The emperor bestowed upon Nicholas the office of commander (*doux* or *dux*).[541] He received his orders, assigning him to a province with men under his command as was fitting.

Saint Nicholas

With the attainment of his post, he also undertook the duties as military governor. With each passing day, Nicholas exercised and drilled his soldiers. He never failed daily to train them in the tactics and strategy of warfare, especially since this was incumbent upon his rank and position. His admonitions and exhortations were not only of a military nature. He also advised and taught the men under his command the works of a Christian state and body of soldiers. His instructions included how to pray and make entreaty to the Master Christ, to give them strength and power against their adversaries in the midst of combat. He also, ofttimes, imparted at his briefings the histories of renowned men of old and courageous deeds. He described how such warriors fought and delivered cities or how they overcame fortifications or how they won trophies. At the recapitulation of all these edifying historical gleanings, he urged his men to always have the fear of God and to commit no wrong against either a poor person or a rich one. As a result of his meticulousness and solicitousness for their welfare, not one of his men infringed the law or was disorderly. Wheresoever Nicholas and his troops

[541] The Latin term *dux* designated the military commander of *limitanei* (the empire's frontier soldiers) stationed within the border of a province. Mobile troops were put under the command of the *doux* by Anastasios I (492). The *doux* normally functioned apart from the civil administration. Only in Isauria, Mauritania, and the Thebaid did the governor combine both military and civil duties. With the decline of the Roman administrative system, the term *doux* came to indicate a subaltern officer, *merarches* or commander of a *moira*, while the governors of *themes* came to be called *strategoi*. The *doux*, from the second half of the 10th C., was the military commander of a larger district sometimes called *doukaton*. *Oxford*, s.v. "Doux."

passed through, no one could say that he was either wronged or suffered loss or injury, in the least, at the hands of one of his men.[542]

---

[542] The Byzantine state had enemies or potential enemies on virtually every front. There was also a need to fight wars on more than one front at a time. "The 6th-C. Byzantine *Treatise on Strategy* states: 'I know well that war is a great evil and the worst of all evils. But since our enemies clearly look upon the shedding of our blood as one of their basic duties and the height of virtue,...we have decided to write about strategy. By putting it into practise we shall be able not only to resist our enemies but even to conquer them.' Throughout military handbooks, the authors refer constantly to the help given to the Rhomaioi, by God and the Virgin's protection, to fight. Successful warfare without God's help is impossible, as the writer of the *Strategikon* emphasizes: 'We urge upon the general that his most important concern be the love of God and justice. Building upon these, he should strive to win the favor of God, without which it is impossible to carry out any plan, however well devised it may seem, or to overcome any enemy, however weak he may be thought. [*Proem.* 9, trans. by Dennis.]

"During the 6th C., and on numerous occasions thereafter, religious images were taken with the armies on their campaigns, designed to ensure divine support for the expedition and to encourage the soldiers against the non-Orthodox foe. The wars with the Persians were frequently presented both to the soldiers of the armies of the Rhomaioi and to the wider populace in the light of a struggle between Christianity and the forces of evil. All wars were holy wars, for the very survival of the God-protected realm of the Chosen People under threat. The soldiers were told, 'By the grace of Christ, you will annihilate them.' The Byzantine self-image was one of a beleaguered Christian state, fighting the forces of darkness.

"Texts of the 7th C. dealing in particular with the events of the Arab conquests explain the defeats of the Rhomaioi as a result of God's anger with the Rhomaioi, the Chosen People, who are thus being punished for their sins. Public petitions for peace or success in war were enunciated in the Orthodox Liturgy. Icons and relics often accompanied Orthodox soldiers into battle. Liturgies for the troops were often held before battles. Supplicatory prayers before, and prayers of thanksgiving after, battle were recommended. Priests accompanied the army, at least on major expeditions, and played an important role in maintaining the soldiers' morale. Whether the enemy was pagan or Christian (for example, the Bulgars) these tokens of Byzantine Orthodoxy and God's support against those who threatened the empire were regularly employed. War with other Orthodox Christians was, of course, to be avoided, yet it could be justified if the one true empire, that of the Rhomaioi, were to be attacked by the misguided rulers of such lands, a position perfectly exemplified in the letters of the Patriarch Nicholas I in the early 10th C. to the Bulgar Tsar Symeon.

"When the soldiers went into battle, they were instructed to remain as silent as possible until the command was given to shout the battle-cry. But they should also cry out, in unison, on leaving camp, either 'God is with us' or 'Lord have mercy' and invoke Christ as the Lord of battles before advancing in formation upon the enemy. These values are constants throughout the existence of the empire.

(continued...)

542(...continued)

All fighting was for Orthodoxy and the empire. All warfare was, thus, holy war. And while it was to be regretted, and avoided wherever possible, it was also part of daily life for the empire and many of its inhabitants. The Orthodox Christian Empire was—as the earthly version of the kingdom of the heavens—quite justified in fighting to defend itself against external aggressions. Defensive warfare was, in this view, God's struggle, and was perfectly acceptable. Aggressive warfare and the needless shedding of blood of even barbarians should be condemned, according to Emperor Leo VI (886-912) in the preface to his treatise on military tactics and strategy. Emperor Justin II, on the elevation of Tiberius Constantine, to the rank of Caesar, exhorts him to eschew acts of bloodshed and yet to look after the soldiers.

"Saint Athanasios the Great was often quoted, who wrote: 'It is not permissible, to murder anyone [Ex. 20:13], yet in war it is praiseworthy and lawful to slay the adversaries. Thus, at any rate, those who have distinguished themselves in war are entitled to, and are accorded, great honors; and columns are erected in memory of them reciting their exploits. So that the same matter in some respect and at some time or other is not permitted, but, in another respect and at some other time, when there is a good occasion for it, may be allowed and permitted.' ['First Epistle of Athanasios the Great, Addressed to the Monk Amun, quoted at the holy and œcumenical Quinisext, that is, Fifth-and-sixth or Sixth Synod.']

"In the 10th-C. treatise on tactical organization and battle dispositions, Emperor Nikephoros II recommends that the whole army, officers and men, should fast for three days before battle, banishing all evil thoughts, repenting of their sins, and promising God not to take up their bad habits should they survive the fighting. The need to go into battle with a pure spirit was essential to victory, of course. Yet the desire to purify the souls of the soldiers was also intimately connected with the anxieties associated with the taking of life, which all Christians were supposed to feel. [*Praecepta*, vi, 31-48.] Imperial ideology had constantly to balance two extremes: to maintain a sufficient element of threat, together with confidence in the military strength of the empire, and to represent the Rhomaioi and their rulers as peace-loving and war-avoiding, because that is what their beliefs and their view of themselves actively demanded.

"Leo in the *Tactica*, writes: 'For we have always welcomed peace, both for our subjects and for the barbarians, through Christ, God and Ruler of all, if the foreigners enclosed within their own bounds are content, professing no injustice, while you yourself (the general) withhold your hand from them, sprinkling the earth neither with foreign nor with our own blood....But if the foe is not sensible, and himself commences the injustice, then indeed there is a just cause present—an unjust war having been begun by the enemy—to undertake war against them with good courage and with eagerness, since they furnish the causes, raising unjust hands against our subjects. So take courage, for you have the God of righteousness as a help; and taking up the fight on behalf of your brethren, you will achieve complete victory.'

"One prayer recited to the troops as they marched to attack the enemy is as (continued...)

At that time, the inhabitants of Thessaly[543] formed a sedition. They refused to submit to the emperor at Constantinople whom they deemed to be in the east. They renounced Constantinopolitan rule and refused to pay their regular taxes. They rose up and plundered Macedonia, taking many captives. Due to the state of discord, the emperor dispatched decrees throughout Anatolia. The governors of those districts traveled west with their armies. Among them was our marvellous Nicholas. Both he and his subordinates were transferred to Thessalonike. A battle ensued, but Nicholas and his men brought the Thessalonians into submission. They again resumed paying their taxes, even as earlier. After this engagement, Nicholas moved further south into Thessaly. When they came to the right bank of the Peneios River, at the junction of the major Thessalian routes, they approached Larisa. The city was both the administrative and ecclesiastical center of Thessaly. A castle on its acropolis was both mighty and handsomely embellished. The castle at that time was guarded with many strong towers. Nicholas and his men were unable to

---

[542](...continued)
follows: 'Lord Jesus Christ, our God, have mercy on us. Come to the aid of us Christians and make us worthy to fight to the death for our Faith and our brothers. Strengthen our souls and our hearts and our whole body, O mighty Lord of battles, through the intercession of the immaculate Theotokos, Thy Mother, and of all the saints. Amen.' [*Tactica*, § 61.11]. The Byzantines fought under the symbol of the Cross. Soldiers actively invoked the military saints, such as George, Theodore the Recruit, Demetrios, Anastasios the Persian, and Mercurios, for whom there was popular devotion. Public and private prayers always played a significant role.

"The military treatise compiled by Leo VI, the *Tactica*, said that the reward of the soldier who fights for the Faith is expressed in terms not simply of doing his duty as the companion in arms of the emperor but also in spiritual terms: fighting the enemies of Christendom brings immediate spiritual benefit, and for those who die in battle perpetual contentment." See John Haldon's *Warfare, State and Society in the Byzantine World 565-1204* (NY: Routledge, 1999), pp. 17-33; George T. Dennis' translation of *Maurice's Strategikon: Handbook of Byzantine Military Strategy* (Philadelphia, PA: University of Pennsylvania Press, 1984), p. 19; cf. Haldon, *Byzantium at War 600-1453* (UK: Osprey Publishing, 2002).

[543] Thessaly is a region of central Greece. It is situated south of Macedonia and north of Hellas. On the west it is separated from Epiros by the Pindos Mountains. It possesses a central plain formed by the Peneios River. On all sides, Thessaly is surrounded by high mountains. The main city is Larisa (Larissa), followed by centers at Trikkala and Stagoi in the west, Lamia and Neopatras in the south, Demetrias and Neopatras on the sea to the east. The major north-south road ran from Thermopylae north to Larisa, continuing to Macedonia, either through Servia or along the coast to Thessalonike. The main east-west road ran to Trikkala and then either north to Grevena and Kastoria or west to the pass of Porta or the pass of Metsovo. *Oxford*, s.v. "Thessaly."

take the city's defenders. Instead, the Larisai beat Nicholas roundly when they exited and gave rise to a great fight. Many soldiers lost their lives.

Nicholas saw that his men, the Rhomaioi, were subdued and worn out. The enemy was victorious. He, thereupon, reasoned within himself, "Behold, our men have been vanquished! If I should fall into the hands of our enemies, they will put me to death unjustly even as the other hapless ones. This being so, what benefit is the temporal honor and transitory rank of a military commander? It is better that I should live as one unimportant, rather than one who must make determinations for so many soldiers—and receive a dishonorable death into the bargain. What worth any longer has my body to me? Or what kind of profit shall my soul find whensoever I should disappear, and before my time, from this life of mine? It is to be preferred, therefore, that I should pass over to rest and quiet in some desert place, where I might weep by reason of my sins. In that way, perhaps, I shall succeed in gaining pardon from God in that fearful hour of judgment."

Such were the deliberations of Nicholas. He, therefore, repaired to the mountain of Vounenee.[544] It was the location of a large forest which hosted cells of wilderness dwellers, that is, anchorites and ascetics pursuing virtue. When Nicholas' eyes lit upon them, he was overjoyed. He gave thanks to the Lord who enlightened him and led him to such a soul-saving land. Nicholas lived with them and struggled alongside them, laboring for virtue according to God. Those wonderful ascetics of Vounenee soon perceived Nicholas' eagerness and love for God. They observed how he toiled without measure in asceticism, with its accompanying fasts, prayers, and vigils. Those athletes of virtue often conversed with such an eager pupil, inciting him with soul-benefitting narratives for making greater progress in attaining excellence and the virtues. Nicholas was careful to meditate upon all their advisements and warnings. He, thereupon, engaged in the struggles of the monastic conduct of life, as much as he was able. All of his fellow strugglers were marvelling at how he made great strides, so that many strived lest such a young man should surpass them.

But the malevolent devil, seeing the life in God led by that assembly of the pious, that is was wonderful and worthy of praise, was unable to bear with it to the end. The thrice-accursed one, as a hater-of-good and full of treachery, in his usual fashion of thwarting uprightness, harassed those virtuous fathers.

---

[544] Vounenee was an ancient city of Thessaly. Its exact location is unknown. From various ecclesiastical writings, it was an acknowledged seat of a bishop under the Metropolitan of Larisa. Evidently, Vounenee was left desolate before the Turkish domination of Thessaly in 1393. One can only conjecture what became of it, because after 1371 the name appears to have vanished.

He raised up the godless Avars[545] who laid waste to many parts of the west. They overwhelmed the castle at Larisa and the surrounding areas, taking many captives. When they came into Larisa, they became masters of it and all the surrounding parts in but a few days.[546] They humbled the people of those neighborhoods, compelling many to deny the Master Christ, the only true God, and to pay homage to their do-nothing idols. Those Orthodox who would not betray piety were put to death. Those blessed souls and lovers of Jesus

---

[545] The Avars of Central Asia came west first, north of the Caucasus. They gradually moved across the steppes of southern Russia, till they reached the Dnieper and then the Danube. Toward the close of the reign of Emperor Justinian, a hundred years after the fall of the Huns, this Asiatic people, ethnologically akin to the Huns, resembling them in character and manners, arrived. They made an agreement with the Byzantines and fought against, and defeated, Turkish tribes (such as the Sabiri, Onogurs) on behalf of the Byzantines. They expanded to the banks of the Danube River, over the lands of the Antae, a Slavic tribe. From time to time, they made raids throughout the Balkans and even as far as the Peloponnesos in Greece. The borders of the Avar Empire extended from the Dnieper to the Elbe River and from the North Sea to the Adriatic Sea during the reign of their famous ruler Baian (Bayan) Khan. In one of their incursions, the Avars placed under their control all of Thessaly and Greece, Old Epiros, Attike, and Evia. They attacked and forcibly subjugated the Peloponnesos, expelling and destroying the Hellenes; and they themselves settled there. Those who were able to flee went to Rhegium Calabria, Orobe, Aegina, Monemvasia, and Sicily. Thus the Avars, after they had conquered the Peloponnesos and settled there, held it for 218 years, that is from the year 587 until 805. During the reign of Justin II, ca. 573/574, the Avars came to the regions of the Danube. The emperor dispatched Tiberius. The Byzantines sustained a sudden attack and were defeated, retreating with heavy losses. Emperor Maurice (582-602) attempted to stop them, but he was unsuccessful. The Avars also besieged, with the Persians, Constantinople in 626, which assault failed. The Avar Empire collapsed between 776-805 due to the concurrent attacks of Krum Khan, the leader of the Bulgarians. It survived until 805, when it submitted to Charlemagne. Survivors of the Avars are mentioned for the last time ca. 950. See also J. B. Bury's *The Invasion of Europe by the Barbarians* (NY and London: W. W. Norton & Company), pp. 262, 263.

[546] The Avars depended on the armament of their cavalry. Troopers in the heavy cavalry were protected by long coats of mail, down to the ankle. They wore throat-guards and decorated clothing, covered with a felt coat. They had Hunnic bows, Persian-styled quivers and bowcases, cavalry swords, and horses armored in front with a skirt and neck-covering, of either iron or felt. The best of the heavy infantry wore greaves of iron or wood and helmets. They carried a spear, shield, and sword. Light infantry had a small shield, sling, javelins, bow, and arrow-guide. See Haldon, pp. 129, 130; and Warren Treadgold's *Byzantium and Its Army 284-1081* (Stanford, CA: Stanford University Press, 1995), pp. 19, 20. See also illustrations and explanations in *Romano-Byzantine Armies 4th-9th Centuries* and *Byzantine Armies 886-1118*, in the Men-at-Arms Series, Numbers 89 and 247 (UK: Osprey Publishing).

underwent myriads of cruel and harsh chastisements and tortures for the love of their most sweet Christ. Nevertheless, by means of temporal ill treatment, they became heirs of everlasting delight and joy in His heavenly kingdom.

When these events were taking place, the blessed Nicholas was still sojourning with the other fathers in the small monastery or Skete of Vounenee. The names of his companions in piety were Gregory, Armodios, John, Demetrios, Michael, Akindynos, Theodore, Pancratios, Pantaleon, Aimilianos, and Naoudios. One night, while they were praying, an angel of the Lord came and said to them, "Prepare yourselves to stand valiantly, because in a few days you are about to undergo martyrdom that you may receive the rewards and the crowns of the contest and, thus, inherit the heavenly kingdom."

The bloodsucking dogs, the barbarian Avars, within a few days learned that there were Christian ascetics abiding on the mountain of Vounenee. They were told that the monks engaged in fasts and spent days and nights in unceasing prayer to the Lord. The Avars armed themselves and went forth in order to slay them. The blessed Nicholas exhorted his brethren and fellow ascetics, counseling them and saying, "Fear not, brothers, mundane death, nor cower before it. Because the hour has now come for us to demonstrate our courage that we might become inheritors on high. Thus, with a small and short-lived punishment, endless delight and everlasting rest await us."

These and many other words of encouragement for the strengthening of the brethren flowed forth from the lips of the man of God. Finally, those greedy for blood arrived. They were as untamed beasts. They apprehended the saints and proceeded to inflict pitiless and merciless punishments. They utilized wheels and racks for twisting and wrenching limbs. They applied rods and diverse methods of torture on their members. Those venerable men endured manfully and bravely all that the barbarians devised against them. Not one of them betrayed their piety. The barbarians, therefore, severed the heads of those holy fathers. With that temporal death, these holy martyrs received everlasting life and the kingdom of the heavens. As for Nicholas, the barbarians took note of his youth, comeliness, understanding, and manly courage. They chose not to inflict any physical injury upon him. With words that were both fraudulent and fitting for the rogues that they were, those mindless madmen were hoping, by means of blandishments, to convert him to their vile religion.

In vain, however, and falsely, did they contrive this against the stalwart soldier of Christ. Not even for a moment were they able to draw away the saint from right belief. He prudently addressed the flatteries they used and said, "I am not a small child that I should be deceived into denying the true God Who fashioned me, so as to venerate idols that are deaf and senseless. But even as from the beginning I was a devout Orthodox Christian, thus shall I remain until I deliver up my soul into the immaculate hands of our Lord Jesus Christ, Who, as true God and my Savior, I venerate, worship, and revere. For the sake of His love I feel profound readiness and desire to shed my blood. As for your deities, I disdain them and deem them beneath contempt; moreover, they are made of inanimate stone and wood or of materials that are cheap and useless."

The barbarians, however, kept complimenting the saint, saying, "Nicholas, do not despise for nought, and to no aim, the courage and comeliness with which thou hast been endowed, because thy Christ is not going to afford thee the least assistance. Only do that which we have bidden thee and become of one mind with us and have fellowship with us. Just offer homage to the gods that we might not deprive thee of this sweet life with the application of harsh tortures, which thou art about to receive, this very day, from us if thou shouldest regard slightly our words." The venerable Nicholas replied, "Those things by which you are attempting to threaten me, I very much desire to prove for myself. For if you should separate me from this vain and evanescent life, you will offer to me the heavenly kingdom and life without ending, so as to be glorified together perpetually with my Christ and receive indescribable happiness, delight, and joy in Paradise."

When they perceived that it was not possible to draw off the holy man from his Faith, they decided to exact revenge with a terrifying and painful death. They administered a thrashing, exercising no leniency, until the ground beneath the saint was reddened with his blood. They prolonged the scourging by changing the executioner two and three times. The saint, for his part, stood his ground nobly and prayerfully, as he began to say, "With patience I waited patiently for the Lord [Ps. 39:1]." Such was his endurance in that torment that it appeared as though another were suffering in his place. Afterward, the barbarians bound the saint to a tree. They tortured him with a spearhead and other horrid inflictions. They kept insisting that he renounce the Christ and make obeisance to the idols. Nicholas continued to answer them fearlessly. He outraged his tormentors when he said, "O beastly-minded ones and savages, you only retain the form of men, but you have no share in human understanding or intelligence. You do not have a single hope in separating me from the love of my Christ. For as many evils as you perpetrate against me, so much the more crowns do you weave for me. My Lord Jesus Christ stands here as my helper and lightens my trials, so that I do not feel any pain."

The barbarians, hearing these declarations, became disheartened. They were finally persuaded that they would be unable to alter his resolve, even if they were still to usher in myriads of wounds. It was the 9th of May when they struck off his head. Hence, Nicholas' blessed soul, replete with light, ascended to the heavenly tabernacles escorted by radiant angels with whom he rejoiced and chanted. His holy and most august relic remained, unburied and uncared for, on that mountain. However, by the grace of the munificent and almighty

God, his relic was revealed in a wondrous manner. For as many as glorify God and who struggle on behalf of His all-holy and highly extolled name, the all-good God rewards richly, establishing them as sons and heirs of His heavenly kingdom.

Miracles of Saint Nicholas the New

The Lord recompensed those who toiled and were wearied for His sake, not only in the heavens but also in the earth. This was made manifest by the performance of miracles and wonders through relics. This grace and power both glorifies those who struggled for the Lord and prompts others to imitate, according to their means and strength, such deeds. The venerable Martyr Nicholas was established as an apt wonder-worker, which exhibited to each how much boldness and glory he was vouchsafed before the all-good and all-powerful God of the universe. Hearken, therefore, to one of the many miracles wrought by Saint Nicholas the New, so that you might understand the caliber of the rest of his achievements.

Saint Nicholas of Vounenee

In those parts of Anatolia, where the righteous Martyr Nicholas was born and raised, there was a notable and affluent grandee of power and property. He contracted a chronic and infectious disease, leprosy, which for a long while had been consuming his flesh, leaving him disfigured and with physical disabilities. Despite the considerable sums he expended on physicians and treatments, he did not enjoy the least benefit. On the contrary, though he spent very much, the lesions worsened with accompanying sensory loss and thickened nerves. The affliction and crushing feeling that he felt were inexpressible. One night, as he lay asleep, the saint appeared to him and said, "Why dost thou toil and spend thy means to no effect? Betake thyself to Larisa, and thither thou shalt ask to be shown the mountain of Vounenee. Search the place well and thou shalt find, at a certain spring, my relic that shall grant thee the cure for the dangerous disease from which thou dost suffer."

In the morning, when the ailing man arose from his bed, he related nothing of what he experienced during the night. He went to the harbor where he found a ship laying a course near Larisa. When he arrived, he was shown the area of the spring spoken of by the saint. This discovery made the Anatolian pilgrim very happy. But afterward, there followed a laborious search on account of the thick bushes and shrubs, towering trees, and a dense forest. By divine help he uncovered the most precious relic of the martyr that—lo, the miracle!—appeared untouched, unravaged, whole, and fragrant, though many years had elapsed. The grandee, after first washing in the spring, embraced that sacred relic with reverence and faith. Straightway—O the wonder!—his disease fled from him even as darkness vanishes before the light. In but one moment he was completed healed, without a trace of any ugly scarring on his flesh. Then, lest he should appear ungrateful at such a grand benefit, he cleaned the entire area where he made the discovery of that invaluable treasure. It was there that he constructed a church dedicated to the saint. He, afterward, returned to his own house full of joy, giving glory to God and thanks to Saint Nicholas. He, furthermore, had taken with him a small portion of the sacred relics, as well as soil from the site. All those who embraced these things were healed of every infirmity.

Not only this wondrous miracle was performed by the saint of Christ, venerable Martyr Nicholas, but also many more worthy of recounting. Now when the grandee was cured, he proclaimed the event in every quarter. Hence, not only were all the Anatolians made aware of the martyr's sanctity but also the westerners learned of his fame. The sick hastened from every direction. All those who came received instant healing, according to each one's faith toward God and reverence toward the saint. It is important to say here that the wonder-working saint did not confine his cures to days of old. Even in these times, he still energizes great miracles for those who possess faith, pure and genuine, toward the Master Christ and ardent reverence toward the saint.

It would not be proper to pass by in silence what took place on the Cycladic Island of Andros.[547] There is a sacred and august monastery, dedicated to Saint Nicholas, Bishop of Myra. Within that sacred precinct there is also treasured the wonderworking and grace-flowing skull of our righteous Martyr Nicholas the New. It was transferred there when monastic fathers from Constantinople were passing through Andros frequently, visiting the *metochion* of that monastery at Vlachsaragi. Boundless miracles have taken place through this precious skull.

Let us, today, rejoice and be glad. Let us honor the saint and praise him with a pure heart and prudent thoughts. Let us celebrate his feast day in a Christian manner, not with overeating and drinking, dancing, and disorderly

---

[547] Mountainous Andros is the greenest island of the Cyclades, only one and one-half hours from the harbor of Piraeus. At Apoikia (northwest of Chora or Andros, the capital of the island of the same name) are the Sariza springs and, to the north, the Monastery of Saint Nicholas (18th C.).

shouting. Let us give alms. Let us pray with tears. Let us perform other God-pleasing works. By commemorating the saint in this manner shall we have a reward. Let us conduct ourselves worthily of the Gospel of the Christ. Let us not be frightened by those who oppose it. For to us it was granted on behalf of Christ, not only to believe in Him but also to suffer on His behalf.[548]

Let us hearken to the words of Saint Paul which were continually recalled by Saint Nicholas in his martyrdom: "Who shall separate us from the love of Christ?" The martyr feared neither affliction, nor distress, nor persecution, nor famine, nor nakedness, nor danger, nor sword. For it had been written aforetime that on account of Thee, O Lord, we are being put to death the whole day; we were counted as sheep of slaughter [Ps. 43:23]. But the martyr said with the apostle: "But in all these things we more than conquer through the One Who loved us. For I have been persuaded that neither death, nor life, nor angels, nor principalities, nor powers, nor things present, nor things coming, nor height, nor depth, nor any other created thing, shall be able to separate us from the love of God, which is in Christ Jesus our Lord [Rom. 8:35-39]."

Therefore, when we encounter persecutions and suffering, let us believe that the Lord shall deliver us. Let us remember that "all those who wish to live piously in Christ Jesus shall be persecuted [2 Tim. 3:12]." Evil men and cheats shall advance to the worse, leading astray and being led astray. But we are told to keep on abiding in what we learned and were assured of [2 Tim. 3:13, 14]. We are joint-heirs of Christ, if we, indeed, suffer with Him in order that we might also be glorified together. Saint Nicholas the New reckoned that the sufferings of the present time were not worthy in comparison to the future glory to be revealed in us [Rom. 8:16-18].

O brethren and Christians, let us exercise ourselves in the virtues that we may rejoice in the kingdom of the heavens with the saints and not come to Gehenna of the unquenchable fire to burn for all eternity. Let us keep the commandments of Christ, loving our enemies and giving alms to those in need. Let us have done with fornication, drunkenness, blasphemies, false oaths, and avarice. If you wish to honor Saint Nicholas on his feast day, do not call to your table the rich and those from whom you expect a reciprocal invitation; invite, rather, the poor, needy, and disabled. Treat them with mercy and kindness, so that the all-good Lord may recompense you for the benefit both here in this present life and also there in the life to come, granting you His heavenly kingdom. Amen.

---

[548] Cf. Phil. 1:27-30.

On the 9th of May, the holy Church commemorates the holy Martyrs EPIMACHUS the New and GORDIAN of Rome, who were slain by the sword.

Epimachus and Gordian, the holy martyrs, hailed from Rome. After they were arrested and brought before the idol-mad ruler, they boldly and openly professed the Christ. The ruler attempted to compel them to deny Jesus and offer sacrifice to the graven images. Although the two martyrs were tried and proven with many tortures, still they could not be persuaded to renounce the Faith. With their continual denouncement of the worship of idols, the idolaters finally decided to behead the two confessors. Epimachus contended to the end as a mighty warrior against error. Gordian remained impervious to the threat of the sword, being instilled with courage at the thought of the crown that awaited him. Thus, both were beheaded and, indeed, received the crowns of the contest from Christ. The synaxis of Saints Epimachus and Gordian was celebrated in the Church of the Holy Martyr Stratonikos.

Through the intercessions of Thy Saints,
O Christ God, have mercy on us. Amen.

On the 10th of May, the holy Church commemorates the holy Apostle SIMON the Zealot.[1]

Simon, the holy apostle, hailed from Cana of the Galilee.[2] Tradition holds that he was the bridegroom in the wedding at Cana, which marriage is spoken of by the Evangelist John in his Gospel [Jn. 2:1-11]. Saint Romanos the Melodist, in divine chant, has the Savior pronounce these words: "At the wedding in Cana, I made water into wine at the behest of Mine all-pure Mother. There also, O Simon, I made thy heart zealous to follow Me in faith; I Who alone know what is in the heart." Thus, it is also believed that Simon was acquainted personally with his wedding guests, Jesus and His Mother, who were then residing in Nazareth. Cana (Kefr Kenna) is only five miles northeast of Nazareth.

---

[1] An encomium to Apostle Simon was composed by Niketas the Rhetor, which manuscript begins, "This brilliantly joyous day." The text is extant in the Athonite monasteries of the Great Lavra and Dionysiou. The Zealot Simon should be distinguished from two other disciples named Simon or Symeon mentioned in the New Testament: Today's Simon is neither Simon Peter, one of the Twelve, nor Simon, the kinsman of the Lord according to the flesh [Mt. 13:55; Mk. 6:3], who belonged to the Seventy Apostles. This latter Simon was also successor of the Apostle Iakovos, the brother of the Lord according to the flesh. Saint Simon the Zealot is also commemorated by the holy Church on 30th of June.

[2] *The Great Synaxaristes* (in Greek) for this day notes, furthermore, that some have confused this apostle with Nathanael who was also of Cana [Jn. 21:2]. See explanatory lead note for the Life of Saint Nathanael (also known as Bartholomew) on the day of his commemoration, the 22nd of April. The name Bartholomew appears in Mt. 10:3; Mk. 3:18; Lk. 6:14; and Acts 1:13. The name Simon, with the surname "Zealot," appears in Lk. 6:15 and Acts 1:13. The name Simon, with the surname "Cananite" appears in Mt. 10:4 and Mk. 3:18. According to sacred interpreters, the word "cana" signifies "zealot."

Thus, when the evangelists provide a register of the Lord's disciples, we note that Simon Cananite and Simon Zealot are not listed together, since he is one and the same person. When Simon Cananite is mentioned by the Evangelists Matthew [10:4] and Mark [3:18], they also list Bartholomew, leading us to believe that Simon Cananite and Bartholomew are two different disciples. When the Evangelist Luke in his Gospel [6:14] and in Acts [1:13] mentions Bartholomew in his list of disciples, he also mentions Simon the Zealot; again, we are led to believe that these are two different disciples.

From the foregoing facts, we note: that the name "Bartholomew" never occurs in the Fourth Gospel, while Nathanael is not mentioned in the synoptics; that Bartholomew's name is coupled with Philip's in the lists of Matthew and Luke, and found next to it in Mark, which agrees well with the fact shown by Saint John that Philip was an old friend of Nathanael's and brought him to Jesus [Jn. 1:45 ff.]. Thus, we cannot justify that the Apostle Nathanael was also named Simon the Zealot.

"On the third day[3] a marriage took place in Cana of Galilee,[4] and the Mother of Jesus was there. Jesus also was invited, and His disciples, to this marriage.[5] In the course of the festivities they fell short of wine.[6] The Mother of Jesus saith to Him, 'They have no wine.'[7] Jesus saith to her, 'What is it to

---

[3] Saint Bede: "It is not devoid of mystical meaning that the marriage is reported to have taken place on the third day [Jn. 2:1]....This indicates that the Lord came to link the Church to Himself during the third age. Indeed, the first age shone brightly in the world with the examples of the patriarchs before the Law, the second with the writings of the prophets under the Law, the third with the proclamation of the evangelists in the time of grace, as if by the light of the third day." ["Homily 1.14, After Epiphany," *Homilies on the Gospels*, Bk. One, 135, 136.] Saint Kyril of Alexandria: "The nuptials are celebrated on the third day, that is, in the last age of the world. For the ternary number signifies for us a beginning, a middle, and an end." [*Explanation on the Gospel of St. John*, *P.G.* 73 (cols. 223-226), in Toal, I:277.]

[4] Saint Bede: "The marriage was performed in Cana of Galilee [Jn. 2:1], by interpretation meaning, in the 'zeal' of 'emigration.'" ["Hom. 1.14," op. cit., 136; cf. Bl. Jerome, *Interpretation of Hebrew Names*, in *CCL* 72: 131, 2.] Saint Kyril of Alexandria: "The careful listener will notice that the celebration was not held in Jerusalem, but outside Judaea, so that the gathering was celebrated in the country of the Gentiles [Mt. 4:15]. For it is very plain that the Synagogue of the Jews had rejected the heavenly Bridegroom, but by the Church of the Gentiles He was received with a joyful heart." [*Explanation*, loc. cit.]

[5] Saint Bede: "Jesus, the Bridegroom, came to a marriage celebrated on earth in the customary fleshly way, since He descended from heaven to earth in order to connect the Church, His Bride, to Himself in spiritual love. His nuptial chamber was the womb of His incorrupt Mother, where God was joined with human nature; and from there He came forth like a bridegroom to join the Church to Himself." ["Hom. 1.14," 135.] Saint Kyril of Alexandria: "He came, not so much to partake of the wedding feast as to perform His miracle; and furthermore, that He might sanctify the beginning of human generation in that which pertains to the flesh. It was but fitting that He Who was about to restore the nature itself of man, and bring it wholly to a better state, should give His blessing, not alone to those already born but also to those who were afterward to be born, sanctifying their coming into this world....By sanctifying marriage, He has taken away the ancient sadness of childbearing." [*Explanation*, in Toal, I:276.]

[6] Saint Bede: "If we seek the mystical meaning in this, when the Lord appeared in the flesh, the undiluted sweetness of legal meaning had gradually begun to 'run short' [Jn. 2:3] of its former virtue because of its fleshly interpretation by the Pharisees. Christ soon turned those mandates which seemed fleshly to spiritual teaching; and He changed the whole exterior appearance of the letter of the Law to the Gospel virtue of heavenly grace—which is the meaning of His having made wine from water." ["Hom. 1.14," 136.]

[7] Saint Kyril of Alexandria: "His Mother asks [Jn. 2:3], desiring Him, that He use His wonted goodness and kindness. Since it was in His power to do all things whatsoever

(continued...)

Me and to thee, woman?[8] Mine hour is not yet come.'[9] His Mother saith to the

---

[7](...continued)
He wished, she urges Him to perform a miracle....But the most bountiful God does not despise us who are striving with the hunger for good things. He offers us a wine far better than we had." [*Explanation*, 276, 278.]

[8] "What is it to Me and to thee, woman [Jn. 2:4]?" (Τί Ἐμοὶ καὶ σοῖ, γύναι;)

Saint Gregory the Great: "At the marriage,...because the Virgin Mother, when wine was wanting, wished a miracle to be done by Him, it was at once answered her,...as if to say plainly, 'That I can do a miracle comes to Me of My Father, not of My Mother.' For He Who, of the nature of His Father, did miracles had it of His Mother that He could die. Whence also, when He was on the Cross, in dying, He acknowledged His Mother, whom He commended to the disciple, saying, 'Behold thy Mother [Jn. 19:27]!' He speaks then, 'What is it to Me and to thee, woman? Mine hour is not yet come'—that is, 'In the miracle, which I have not of thy nature, I do not acknowledge thee. When the hour of death shall come, I shall acknowledge thee as My Mother, since I have it of thee that I can die.'" ["Epistle XXXIX, to Eulogios, Patriarch of Alexandria," Bk. X, in *Nicene*, 2nd Ser., XIII:48.]

Saint Bede: "What He is saying is that 'there is nothing in common between the divinity which I have always possessed from the Father, and thy flesh, from which I adopted flesh. Mine hour has not yet come when, by dying, I may demonstrate the weakness of the humanity taken from thee. First I must disclose the power of Mine eternal Deity by exercising My powers.' The hour came, however, to show what was in common between Him and His Mother when, as He was about to die on the Cross, He took care to commend her, a virgin, to the virgin disciple. When He was enduring the weakness of the flesh, He dutifully acknowledged His Mother, from whom He had received it; but when He was about to do divine things, He pretended not to acknowledge her because He recognized that she was not the source of His divine nativity." ["Hom. 1.14," 137.]

[9] Saint Chrysostom: "He desires to show this: that He works all things at their due season, not doing everything at once, because a kind of confusion and disorder would have ensued, if, instead of working all at their proper seasons, He had mixed all together, His nativity, resurrection, and judgment....He was not subject to the necessity of seasons, but rather settled their order, since He is their Creator; and therefore, He says, 'Mine hour is not yet come [Jn. 2:4].' And His meaning is that as yet He was not manifest to the many, nor had He even His whole choir of disciples....'Moreover, I ought not to have been told it from thee; thou art My Mother, and renderest the miracle suspicious. They who wanted the wine ought to have come and entreated Me—not that I need this—so that they might, with an entire assent, accept the miracle. For one that knows that he is in need is very thankful when he obtains assistance; but one who has not a sense of his need, will never have a plain and clear sense of the benefit.'" ["Hom. 22," *P.G.* 59:126, 127 (cols. 133, 134).]

Saint Kyril of Alexandria: "It was not becoming that Christ should hasten, or freely offer, to perform miracles....Things asked for are more gratefully re-
(continued...)

Saint Simon the Zealot

servants, 'Whatsoever He saith to you, do it.'[10] And there were standing there six stone waterpots, according to the purification of the Jews,[11] containing two or three measures each. Jesus saith to them, 'Fill the waterpots with water.' And they filled them up to the top. And Jesus saith to them, 'Draw out now, and bear it to the master of the feast.' And they brought it. Now when the master of the feast tasted the water that had become wine, and knew not from what place it was—but the servants who had drawn the water knew—the master of the feast called the bridegroom, and saith to him, 'Every man first setteth forth the good wine, and whenever they have drunk freely, then the inferior. As for thee, thou hast kept the good wine until now.'[12]

---

[9](...continued)
ceived....Here, too, Christ gives us an example that the greatest honor is due to parents, since it is out of reverence for His Mother that He now undertakes to do that which He had not yet desired to do." [*Explanation*, loc. cit.]

[10] Saint Kyril of Alexandria: "The Woman, having, as was fitting, great weighty influence over the Lord, her Son, persuades Him to work a miracle. She also prepares the way for it [Jn. 2:5], bidding the waiters of the feast to be at hand, and to have prepared that which the Lord will presently command." [Ibid.]

[11] Saint Chrysostom: "In order that none of the unbelievers might suspect that lees were left in the vessels, and water was poured upon and mixed with them, and a very weak wine had been made, the evangelist shows that those vessels were never receptacles for wine, when saying 'according to the purification of the Jews.'" ["Hom. 22," *P.G.* 59:127 (col. 135).]

[12] Saint Bede: "It is proper to teachers to recognize the difference between the Law and the Gospel, between the shadow and the truth, and to bring forward for all of the earthly kingdom—as promised by all the ancient teachings—the new grace of the Gospel faith and the everlasting gifts of the heavenly fatherland." ["Hom. 1.14," loc. cit.]

Saint Kyril of Alexandria: "The Law had no completeness in good things, but the teaching of the Gospel has in it the fullness of every blessing." [*Explanation*, loc. cit.]

This did Jesus in Cana of Galilee as the beginning of the signs, and it made manifest His glory; and His disciples believed in Him [Jn. 2:1-11]."[13]

Saint Romanos the Melodist says that "at the marriage feast, the crowd of guests was faring sumptuously. The supply of wine failed them, and their joy was turned to distress. The bridegroom was upset. The cupbearers muttered unceasingly. There was this one sad display of penury. And there was no small clamor in the room."[14] When the change of water to wine took place suddenly and quickly, Saint Romanos has Christ address the servants, saying, "Draw the wine which was not harvested. And after that, offer drink to the guests. Replenish the dry cups. Let all the crowd and the bridegroom himself enjoy it. For I have in marvellous fashion given pleasure to all. I Who have in wisdom created all things."[15]

The Marriage at Cana

Indeed, the bridegroom witnessed what had taken place. Awed by this miracle, he came to believe in the Lord Jesus Christ as the true God. He, therefore, quit his wedding festivities and his very house. Indeed, he forsook his bride for love of Christ, preferring to wed his soul to the heavenly Bridegroom. He followed the Lord with such zeal that he, henceforth, received the name "Zelotes," or "the Zealot," which was in concord with his ways. For these reasons, Simon was numbered among the choir of Jesus' disciples and became one of His holy Twelve Apostles.

After the crucifixion and resurrection of our Lord, when the disciples were assembled together, Jesus ordered them not to depart from Jerusalem. He bid them wait for the promise of the Father, that they should be baptized in the Holy Spirit not many days after these. Although the disciples kept questioning

[13] Saint Romanos the Melodist: "When Christ, as a sign of His power, clearly changed the water into wine, all the crowd rejoiced, for they considered the taste marvellous. Now we all at the banquet in the Church partake of Christ with holy joy from the wine changed into His blood, praising the great Bridegroom." ["On the Marriage at Cana," *Kontakia of Romanos*, Strophe 20, I:74.]

[14] Ibid., Strophe 5, I:69.

[15] Ibid., Strophe 19, I:74.

the risen Lord, regarding the restoration of the kingdom to Israel, He said to them, "It is not yours to know times or seasons which the Father Himself put in His own authority. But ye shall receive power, after the Holy Spirit is come upon you; and ye shall be witnesses to Me both in Jerusalem, and in all Judaea and Samaria, and unto the ends of the earth." After the Lord spoke these words, while the disciples were yet looking upon Him, Jesus was taken up; and from before their eyes, a cloud took Him up from under.

While the disciples were gazing intently into the heaven as He went, then two men stood by them in white raiment, who also said, "Men, Galilaeans, why do ye stand looking into the heaven? This Jesus, the One Who was taken up from you into the heaven, so shall He come in the manner ye beheld Him going into the heaven." Then they returned to Jerusalem from the mount which is called the Mount of Olives, which is near Jerusalem. The disciples then entered the upper chamber where they were staying, both Peter and Iakovos, and John and Andrew, Philip and Thomas, Bartholomew and Matthew, Iakovos the son of Alphaeos and Simon the Zealot, and Judas [Jude] the brother of Iakovos. These all were persevering with one accord in prayer and in entreaty, with the women and Mary the Mother of Jesus, and with His brethren [cf. Acts 1:4-14].

While the day of Pentecost was being fulfilled, Simon was with the other faithful. They were all with one accord in the same place. Suddenly there came to be a sound out of the heaven, like as of a violent wind borne along; and it filled the whole house where they were sitting. There appeared to them tongues, as if of fire, being distributed; and it sat upon each one of them. Thereupon, were they all filled with the Holy Spirit. They began to speak in other tongues, even as the Spirit was giving them to utter [cf. Acts 2:1-4]. Thus, they were endowed from on High to preach the Gospel to all nations. Simon, together with the rest, received the Holy Spirit. It is not possible to reconcile the various traditions with the meager information that is available. All sources agree that he preached lofty theology in many lands, "kindly feasting men on the full knowledge of Christ, setting forth His feats as a delightful and complete banquet at which nothing fails."[16]

Various Traditions of the Apostle's Missionary Fields and Martyrdom

Some of the places which he passed through were Egypt, Mauritania, Libya, Numidia, Cyrene, and Abkhazia. The latter place is a region around the northeastern shore of the Black Sea.

1. Britain.

The apostle, also, was believed by some to have come into western parts, as far as Great Britain, which journey was by no means unreasonable.

---

[16] May 10th, Vespers Sticheron, Mode Four.

He converted great multitudes, while enduring manifold hardships and persecutions. He was crucified by idolaters and buried there. This is one of the earliest traditions, the principal authority for which is Bishop Dorotheos (ca. 255-362) of Gaza, who wrote ca. 300. His testimony is considered decisive by many: "Simon Zelotes traversed all Mauritania, and the regions of the Africans, preaching Christ. He was at last crucified, slain, and buried in Britain. Crucifixion was a Roman penalty for runaway slaves, deserters, and rebels. It was not known to British laws. We conclude that Simon Zelotes suffered in the east of Britain, perhaps, as tradition affirms, in the vicinity of Caistor, under the Roman officer whose atrocities were the immediate cause of the Boadicean war. Two things strike the investigator of early Christian history: the marvellous manner in which Christian seed is found growing and fructifying in unheard-of places; and, the indifference of the sowers of perpetuating their own name and labors."[17]

Saint Simon

Another source for this tradition of evangelizing Britain is Patriarch Nikephoros I (806-815) of Constantinople. As a Byzantine historian, he also confirms this apostle's visit to Britain. He writes: "Simon was born in Cana of Galilee. He was, for his fervent affection for his Master and great zeal that he showed by all means to the Gospel, named Zelotes. After having received the Holy Spirit from above, he traveled through Egypt and Africa, then through Mauritania and all Libya, preaching the Gospel. He taught the same doctrine to the Occidental Sea, which was also proclaimed in the Isles called Britanniae."[18]

The one tradition holds that Simon arrived in Britain during the first year of the Boadicean war (A.D. 60), when the whole island was convulsed in a deep and burning anger toward the Romans. It was an anger which was never equaled before or after in the long years of conflict between the two nations. Tacitus states that from A.D. 59 to 62 the brutalities

[17] Dorotheus, *Synod. de Apostol.; Synopsis ad Sim Zelot.*, as quoted in R. W. Morgan's *Saint Paul in Britain* (London: The Covenant Publishing Co., 1860), p. 79, cited in W. S. McBirnie's *The Search for the Twelves Apostles*, 6th ed. (Wheaton, IL: Tyndale Publishers, 1975), p. 212.
[18] Saint Nikephoros, Bk. II, c. 40.

of war were at their worst. Atrocities occurred on both sides, but the Romans carried their vicious perpetration to such an extent that even Rome was shocked. Bearing this in mind, we can readily understand that any Christian endeavor at evangelizing outside the British shield would be fraught with imminent danger. At all times the disciples of Christ were oblivious to danger. But when the pressure became too severe, they were known to depart until matters quieted. In A.D. 44, a Claudian edict expelled the Christian leaders from Rome. Many of them sought sanctuary in Britain. Among those who fled to Britain from Rome was Peter.

One source reports that "the south of England was sparsely inhabited by the native Britons and, consequently, more heavily populated by the Romans. It was far beyond the strong protective shield of the Silurian arms in the south and the powerful northern Yorkshire Celts. In this dangerous territory, Simon was assuredly at risk. Undeterred, with infinite courage, he began preaching the Christian Gospel right in the heart of the Roman domain. His fiery sermons brought him speedily to the attention of Catus Decianus, but not before Simon had sown the seed of Christ in the hearts of Britons and many Romans who, despite the unremitting hatred of Decianus for all that was Christian, held the secret of the truth locked in their hearts.

"But the evangelizing mission of Simon was short-lived. He was finally arrested under the orders of Catus Decianus. As usual, such trials were a mockery of justice. Simon Zelotes was condemned to death and was crucified by the Romans at Caistor, Lincolnshire. He was there buried, circa the 10th of May, in the year 61.

"The day of the martyrdom of Simon Zelotes, the devoted disciple of Christ, is officially celebrated by the Eastern Church and Western Church on the 10th of May, and so recorded in the Greek *Menology*. Cardinal Baronius, in his *Annales Ecclesiastici*, gives the same date in describing the martyrdom and burial of Simon Zelotes in Britain."[19]

The *Menology* of the Greek Orthodox Church supports the statements of the apostle's preaching and martyrdom in Britain.[20] We, therefore, hear of this tradition in the *Synaxarion* read at the Sixth Ode of the Orthros Canon. Though Saint Aristoboulos is generally believed to have been England's first apostle, another source notes that, in A.D. 60, Saint Joseph of Arimathea went to Gaul and returned to Britain with another band of recruits, among whom is particularly mentioned Simon Zelotes, one of the original Twelve. This was the second journey of Simon Zelotes to Britain—and his last. According to

---

[19] G. F. Jowett, pp. 157-159, cited in McBirnie, pp. 213, 214.

[20] *Annales Ecclesiastici*, Baronius under A.D. 44, § XXXVIII, cited in L. S. Lewis; *Saint Joseph of Arimathea at Glastonbury*, 4th ed. (London: James Clarke & Co., Ltd., 1964), p. 117.

Cardinal Baronius and Hippolytos, Simon's first arrival in Britain was in A.D. 44, during the Claudian war. He remained a short time and returned to the continent.[21]

2. Persia.

Another very strong tradition places the apostle's martyrdom and death in Persia. This tradition, however, does not preclude a missionary trip of the apostle to Britain. Afterward, he may have fled to the Middle East because of the destruction of London[22] at the hands of anti-revolutionaries led by British Queen Boadicea. Travel in the first century was relatively easy, since it was made possible by the vast network of Roman roads all over the empire from the Persian frontier to Britain. Not only did the Romans charge the local people in each area to build the roads but even the Romans themselves built and protected the roads.

The *Menology of Saint Basil* writes that this apostle reposed in peace at Edessa. Western tradition, recognized in the Roman liturgy, is that Simon preached in Egypt. Thereafter, he accompanied Saint Jude who had come from Mesopotamia. Together, these two apostles heralded Christ for some years to the Persians. It is there that Simon suffered martyrdom. In the west, both Saints Simon and Jude are commemorated on the 29th of October. This account is upheld by Fortunatus of Poiters (6th C.), who writes that both apostles underwent martyrdom at Suanir in Persia. The Venerable Bede also places Simon's martyrdom in Persia, at a city called Suanir, where they say the idolatrous priests slew him. Bede, Vsuardus, and Ado alleged the authority of Eusebius, whose *Martyrology* was translated by Blessed Jerome. Suanir is not known to geographers. It might be the country of the Suani or Surani, or a little higher in Sarmatia. The names of Simon and Jude are seen together in the *Hieronymianum* for the 28th of October. The place of martyrdom, again, for the two apostles is said to be "Suanis, civitate Persarum."[23]

Thus, from the foregoing, it is possible that Saint Simon visited Britain and Glastonbury, in company with Joseph of Arimathea. From Glastonbury he could have gone to London, the little colony that had become the capital of the new Roman conquest. When Queen Boadicea's revolutionaries moved against the Roman occupation force, rumors of her destruction of all Romans and London may have caused Simon to leave for the south of Britain and board a ship to Palestine. Again, the strong tradition that he suffered martyrdom in Persia is also possible. Simon, together with Jude, went as far as Persia, where

---

[21] See George F. Jowett, *The Drama of the Lost Disciples* (London: Covenant Publishing Co., Ltd., 1970).

[22] London was founded in A.D. 43.

[23] See H. Delehaye's "Commentary on the Hieronymian Martyrology," in the *Acta Sanctorum*; and Gutschmid, *Kleine Schriften*, vol. ii, pp. 368, 369.

Simon was sawn asunder and Jude was killed with a halberd. The Roman and Celtic tradition is that the apostles were buried in Babylon. The tradition of the Church of Rome maintains that the bodies of Jude and Simon were buried together. Their bones were intermixed. The major tomb of these two apostles is at Saint Peter's in Rome, with fragments in the Churches of Saint Saturninus (Tolosa, Spain) and Saint Sernin (Toulouse, France), and, until World War II, in the monastery chapel of Saint Norbet (Cologne, Germany).[24]

3. Black Sea.

Still others claim that Saint Simon was buried in the city of Nikopsia, near Dzhigentia. The ruins of this city are pointed out by the local inhabitants some thirteen miles from Sukhumi, not far from the shore of the Black Sea. A church was later raised up on the site of the apostle's martyric death. This building was renovated in 1875, by the generous means of a Russian grand duke.

4. Slain by Crucifixion.

It is possible that the apostle made missionary journeys to all these lands mentioned earlier. It is also probable that he suffered abuses and outrages in many, if not all, of these places. In the Praises sung to the saint, he emulated the Lord's Passion, thus becoming an heir of the Lord's glory.[25] This is also evidenced in the couplet verses dedicated to Simon in the reading of the *Synaxarion*,[26] which says, "Simon's zeal is analogous to such speech as this to Christ: 'In my zeal for the suffering of Thy Passion, I suffer the cross resolutely.' On wood, was the great-hearted Simon enwrapped." According to the Orthros Canon written by Saint Theophanes (d. 845), the apostle was revealed to be a worker of divine wonders,[27] for which we beg his holy prayers that we may partake of his zeal and turn away from the pleasures of this age.

On the 10th of May, the holy Church commemorates the holy Martyrs ALPHAEUS, PHILADELPHUS, and CYPRIAN of the Basques.[28]

---

[24] See Mary Sharpe's *A Traveller's Guide to Saints in Europe* (London: The Trinity Press, 1964), p. 198.

[25] May 10th, Praises, Mode Four.

[26] May 10th, *Synaxarion* Reading after the Sixth Ode of Orthros.

[27] May 10th, Orthros Canon, Ode Six, Mode Plagal Four.

[28] The Basque martyrs appeared to Euthalia of Sicily, the mother of the virgin-martyr of the same name (commemorated by the holy Church on the 2nd of March), and healed her of a bloody flux. In the year 1517, the incorrupt relics of today's martyrs were found at Leontini (mod. Lentini) of eastern Sicily, about 20 miles (32 kilometers) south of Catania.

Alphaeus (Alphius), Philadelphus, and Cyprian (Cyprianus), the holy martyrs and brothers according to the flesh, were from the Basque Country.[29] They were of noble lineage and scions of an affluent family. They were the sons of Vitalius, governor of the prefecture. The brothers were reared in piety and in meditation of the divine Scriptures. Their tutor was a certain teacher, named Onesimos, who was a most holy man that heralded the Christ.[30]

They were submitted to questioning by Aneengelion,[31] the prefect, who remanded them to Rome with royal dispatches by him to Licinius (308-324). Licinius sent the prisoners to Valerian, who examined them. He, in turn, referred the matter to Governor Diomedes. He moved the case to Tertullus, who was governor of Sicily.

As the venue and courts and judges kept changing in this action against the defendants, the stalwart martyrs were subjected to different kinds of tortures by the governors and judges. The chastisements were so harsh and unbearable, that one punishment alone was certainly sufficient to sap the strength of any other person; indeed, it is more precise to say that such treatment would have slain anyone else. In one such torture, they severed the tongue of Alphaeus which caused him to hemorrhage. But the ever-memorable and hardy confessor endured to the end. They, finally, ended their martyrdom in Sicily under Tertullus. Alphaeus was beheaded. Philadelphus was stretched out on a fiery brazier. Cyprian was placed in a red-hot frying pan. Thus, these three martyrs ascended victorious into the heavens.

On the 10th of May, the holy Church commemorates our venerable Father HESYCHIOS the Confessor.

Hesychios, our righteous father and confessor, originated from Andrapa of Galatia of central Anatolia. He was a man noted for his goodness and meekness. Even as he bore the name Hesychios—having the Greek meaning of one who is quiet, gentle, and peaceful—so he was in his manner

[29] The Basque Country borders the Bay of Biscay to the north, while the Pyrenees Mountains separate the region from the Basque Country of France to the northeast; however, the ethnically similar autonomous community of Navarre, which adjoins the (Spanish) Basque Country on the east, makes up most of the border with the French Basque region. To the south and southwest lie the Ebro River basin. *Encyclopaedia Britannica Deluxe Edition 2004 CD-ROM*, s.v. "Basque Country."

[30] Onesimos, together with fifteen other Christians, including one named Erasmus, were also brought and tried at Rome with the three brothers. Afterward, Onesimos, Erasmus, and the other confessors suffered martyrdom at the maritime city of Pozzuoli, near Naples. The chest of Onesimos was crushed by a boulder placed by the idolaters. His companions underwent decapitation. They, also, are commemorated today.

[31] The Dionysiou manuscript reads Angelion, whereas some *Menaia* record Lingelion.

and conduct. He supplicated the Lord to show him a place of repose and stillness that he might lead a life pleasing to God. He, thereupon, was commanded, by a divine revelation, to go down to the parts by the sea and dwell on Mount Maiyonos (Μαΐωνος). He hearkened and retired to that quiet abode where he spent many years. Afterward, he departed and went to a spot closer to the water. He built a small church, dedicated to Saint Andrew. He passed the rest of his days persevering in virtue and asceticism. After he wrought many wonders and miracles, he was translated to the Lord.

On the 10th of May, the holy Church commemorates our venerable Father LAURENCE, who reposed in peace.[32]

Laurence, our righteous father, became a monk on the Holy Mountain at the Great Lavra, the earliest (963) and largest foundation on that peninsula. On account of the prevailing controversy over the Palamism of Saint Gregory Palamas (ca. 1296-1359),[33] Laurence left Athos.

The main feature of this teaching is the distinction between the inaccessible and unknowable essence of God and His uncreated energies. The goal of contemplative prayer is the vision of the uncreated light of God, exemplified by the Taboric light. By means of this light or energy, salvation or divinization (*theosis*) is realized. Since the contemplative can experience God's own uncreated grace (*energeia*), as distinct from His unknowable essence, the hesychast encounters the living God. Such a one has communion with God through His divine energies which are accessible to human experience. Those Athonite monks who asserted the possibility of seeing the divine uncreated light

---

[32] The Life of Saint Laurence, regrettably, has not been preserved. From the physical evidence that exists, he was, undoubtedly, an energetic and active man. The remains of his foundations can still be viewed on the west side of the cliffs of Mount Pelion of Thessaly, Greece. The village-town of Hagios Lavrentios, named for the martyred Archdeacon Laurence of Rome, is at a higher elevation and further east. Marble tiles on the walls reveal the following inscription regarding the sacred monastery of our venerable saint for today: "The Skete of the Imperial Monastery, raised up by Laurence the Great, in the name of the Metamorphosis of the Lord and of the Prophet Elias." The reference to "Laurence the Great" discloses the venerable man's strength and efficacy. However, as a result of the inroads of the Turks and the long enslavement of the nation under the Ottomans, details regarding the saint's activities have vanished. The information placed within the *Synaxarion* of the venerable Laurence was taken from marble tiles, dated 1865, found at the perimeter, in the chapel by the place of Prophet Elias, as well as an inscription on the north wall above the door of the Monastery of Saint Laurence. A divine office was composed to the saint, published at Athens in 1901, by the Esphigmenite Monk Zosimas who originally hailed from Volos, Thessaly.

[33] Saint Gregory Palamas is commemorated by the holy Church on the 14th of November.

were subjected to heavy criticism. Two of Saint Gregory's greatest critics were Barlaam of Calabria (ca. 1290–1348) and Akindynos of Prilep (ca. 1300-1348). Barlaam believed such hesychasm as taught by Palamas was Messalianism, insofar as it eliminated the distinction between the Creator and His creation. Akindynos stressed the simplicity of God Who admits of no distinctions, except the properties of the three hypostases. Saint Gregory made a defense of his teachings in his *Triads*.[34]

Saint Laurence, in order to avoid the heresy of Barlaam and Akindynos, departed and went to the Volos eparchy on the east coast of Thessaly,[35] to the village of Hagios Lavrentios.[36] He founded a holy monastery in honor of the Hierodeacon Laurence, commemorated by the holy Church on the 10th of August. At that time, Alexios III Komnenos, the emperor of Trebizond (1349-1390), sent a chrysobull to the venerable elder. Other gifts required to build up the new foundation were also sent, together with gold and sacred vessels for the construction of the temple. The work was completed in the year 6886 from Adam, that is, in the year of our Lord 1378.[37] The same righteous Elder Laurence also founded the Skete of the Transfiguration of Christ and of the Prophet Elias.[38] Saint Laurence reposed in peace, after undergoing many labors and pains for which he received the Eden that is beyond labors.

---

[34] See *The Oxford Dictionary of Byzantium*, s.v. "Palamism."

[35] Volos (39°22′N 22°57′E) was ancient Iolkos (Iolcus). The old town, a suburb with houses built up to 2,500 feet (750 meters) above sea level, rises on the spurs of Mount Pelion on the Magnesia peninsula of southeastern Thessaly. Pelion rises to 5,417 feet (1,651 meters) at its highest point. Pelion peak (5,075 feet), just northeast of Volos, has a wooded western flank overlooking a gulf whose ancient ports were Iolkos and Pagasae. *Encyclopaedia Britannica, CD-ROM*, s.v. "Volos" and "Pelion, Mount."

[36] Hagios Lavrentios (39°33′N 23°18′E) is a traditional village on Mount Pelion, approximately 20 kilometers from Volos, at an elevation of 600 meters. There are about seven hundred permanent residents in this typical, yet most beautiful village with its luxuriant vegetation. Not far from this village of traditional cobbled stone paths is the Byzantine Monastery of Saint Laurence, which is dated from 1378.

[37] This same building was expanded and heightened first in 1764, which modification can be seen to this day. The cells of the monks, however, have not been immune from neglect and the ravages of time. The eastern side was preserved until 1853; thereafter, it collapsed and left a monastery void of cells. Presently, the north side, where the *archontarikion* or reception room is located, still remains. Beneath this floor is the basement, containing the wine cellar and storage for oil. However, these chambers are now empty and in a ruinous state.

[38] The skete of this monastery was founded at the present-day spot of Prophet Elias.

On the 10th of May, the holy Church commemorates our venerable Father SIMON, Bishop of Suzdal and Vladimir, Wonder-worker of the Kiev Caves (1221).

On the 10th of May,[39] the holy Church commemorates the holy Virgin-martyr BASIL of Mangazeya and the translation of his relics.[40]

Basil or Vasili was born in the ancient Volga town of Yaroslavl in about 1587. His father, Theodore, was a very poor merchant. The family lived in poverty and deprivation. From his earliest days, Basil found consolation from his harsh childhood in God's holy temple. He would joyfully run to the church for every divine service; and he was often found deep in prayer.

On account of his family's great impoverishment, when he reached the age of twelve, Basil set out to earn his own living. The young boy chose to go east to Siberia. It was a perilous land, full of wild beasts, belligerent tribes, and unprincipled men. After a long and arduous journey through the wild forests on little-traveled roads, he reached the Russian settlement of Mangazeya (Magazea or Magazeya). The village was situated on the river Taz, which was surrounded by Mongols and Siberian tribesmen.

Having gone to the village church to pray and to give thanks for his safe passage, Basil, afterward, began to look for employment as an apprentice. Being a bright and quiet lad, he found employment as a clerk for a local merchant. Basil was a conscientious and thoughtful worker. The owner of the store was happy to make use of the boy's good work habits. Now, since Siberia was a frontier area, there were few women. Some licentious men, ruled by unnatural desires, engaged in homosexual acts with young men and boys.

---

[39] We are told that the child-martyr Basil of Mangazeya suffered for the sake of righteousness on the first day of Pascha. Some sources give 1600 as the year of his repose. Pascha was then celebrated on the 23rd of March (Julian Calendar) or the 2nd of April (Gregorian) Calendar. There was, at that time, a 10-day difference between the calendars. Other sources give 1602 as the year of his repose, when Pascha was on the 4th of April (Julian Calendar) or the 14th of April (Gregorian Calendar). If he met death in 1600, the date of his martyrdom would be the 24th of March; if he reposed in 1602, the date would be the 5th of April. All sources, nevertheless, agree on the day of the translation of his relics from Mangazeya to Turakhanov, that is, the 10th of May. The patron of today's Saint Basil was Hieromartyr Basil, a presbyter of Ankyra, commemorated by the holy Church on the 22nd of March.

[40] This Life has been presented in *The Great Synaxaristes* (in English), courtesy of the editor of the bi-monthly periodical, *Orthodox Life*, published by Holy Trinity Monastery, Jordanville, NY. See "The Holy Innocent, Vasili of Magazeya," *Orthodox Life*, Volume 22, Number 2, March-April 1972:8-11. The article was revised, edited, and expanded slightly for incorporation into *The Great Synaxaristes*.

Basil's employer was one of these perverse men. Not much time passed before Basil's employer attempted to entice the boy into homosexual relations. At first he tried flattery and a gift of money. When the lad refused, his employer threatened him with punishment. Basil responded by fasting and praying, imploring God's help that he remain pure from the older man's sexual harassment. The merchant, being an atheist and a person of very low morals, could not countenance the prayerful and religious attitude of the boy. He especially despised Basil for his meek and humble personality, which betokened his pureness. Satan, the enemy of mankind, also was enraged by the God-fearing life of this blessed youth. He chose to attack Basil through this evil and godless merchant, who came to detest his quiet and pious clerk more and more. He, consequently, began to mistreat and persecute the boy. Finally, the merchant's mounting antipathy and verbal abuse reached a terrible point.

Saint Basil

Then, when the holy Church was celebrating Orthros of Pascha, thieves robbed the shop where Basil worked. The merchant, discovering the robbery, went immediately to the governor, Pushkin, and reported the crime. But then a terrible deed occurred: the merchant hated Basil so much—and so strong was the evil working in his members—that he formally accused the innocent boy of being one of the thieves.

Thus, on the first day of Christ's bright Pascha, when the holy Church calls all people to peace and love, this innocent and God-fearing youth was betrayed by a false witness, just as Christ had been betrayed by false witnesses. The governor did not even investigate the charges. He, instead, called for Basil's arrest. He dispatched officers who went and dragged the youth from the Church service he was attending. The governor and Basil's employer began to torture him, in order to force a confession from him. In spite of all the fierce punishments inflicted upon the adolescent, the blessed youth would only reply meekly, "I am innocent." The pain from the tortures became so unbearable that the boy fainted; but when he regained consciousness, he again quietly repeated, "I am innocent."

The meek, humble, Christ-like endurance and the quiet reply of the blessed one enraged the malignant merchant even more. Finally, he flew into a demonic rage and struck the innocent one in the temple with a heavy chain of keys. Basil fell to the floor, sighed heavily, and gave up his pure and innocent soul into the hands of the Lord. He was then about thirteen years of age.

In order to hide this foul crime, the governor ordered the body of the holy innocent to be put into a rough coffin. It was lowered into a nearby swamp, after being weighed down with rocks. Rumors of the brutal murder went about Mangazeya almost immediately after the slaying, but God chose to conceal the sacred relics for fifty-two years.[41] Circa 1652, during the tenure of the military governor Ignaty Stepanovich Korsakov, God chose to reveal the relics of His sacred martyr. In that year, numerous wondrous events began to occur in the neighborhood about Mangazeya. Many pious Orthodox Christians were vouchsafed dreams of a beardless youth. He appeared to them, and not a few were healed by his salutary intercessions. There was also a strange light seen over the marsh, with the sound of invisible beings chanting.

Slowly, the coffin arose to the top of the mud. A devout believer, named Stefan Shiryaev, noticed the coffin but did not investigate. The virgin-martyr appeared to him in a vision, charging him to open the coffin. Only then was the full account of Saint Basil's martyrdom made manifest. Governor Pushkin's servants, who had disposed of the body, could not keep silent about the terrible crime. Soon, all the residents of Mangazeya knew that the relics of the blessed one were resting in the marsh. The terrible murder had been committed in secret, but soon all the people of Siberia and Russia were to know of it; for wonderful things began to happen over the place where the relics of Basil, the holy innocent, were reposing. While his precious relics were cast into the darkness of a swamp by his cruel tormentors, his soul ascended to the heights. God had received the soul of the blessed one into the heavens among the ranks of the saints, glorifying him in the heavenly Church. Now He was revealing this to the Church on earth. For this reason, many signs were given to the faithful of Siberia. Soon people all over the country were addressing prayers to Basil, the holy innocent, and were receiving his help and intercessions.

The coffin was drawn out of the marsh and opened. Within were found the sacred relics, whole and incorrupt, of the child martyr. A chapel was built over the relics by an archer, Timothy Sechenkov. Many suffering from infirmities received cures through the intercessions of the young martyr.

---

[41] Some sources record forty-two years.

In 1670, on the 10th of May, Hieromonk Tikhon, the founder of the Holy Trinity Monastery near Turakhanov, solemnly carried over the holy relics of the saint into the wooden monastery church.

In 1719, Metropolitan Philotheos, the enlightener of Siberia, sent a beautifully carved reliquary to the monastery for the relics. Countless miracles took place near the shrine; and Saint Basil helped Metropolitan Philotheos on many occasions.

In 1787, a new stone church was built in the Holy Trinity Monastery; and the relics of the holy innocent were transferred there.[42]

Saint Basil is portrayed in icons as a youth with light brown hair. He is seen barefooted and wearing only a long shirt. The martyr is also depicted on the Abaletsk Icon of the Sign.

Thus, to the glory of virginity, Saint Basil witnessed unto death. He is invoked as the patron of missionaries and protector of those struggling for the sake of chastity. We see thee, O Basil, as a radiant lamp in the darkness of a wicked and perverse generation. Free from the passions those who cry to thee, "Rejoice, holy Martyr Basil, radiant light of virginity!"

Through the intercessions of Thy Saints,
O Christ God, have mercy on us. Amen.

---

[42] In September of 1970, a three-year excavation was completed on the site of Mangazeya, a 17th-C. city in the northern part of the Tiumen Region between the Ob and Yensei Rivers. The city was built by Russian traders and the troops of Tsar Boris Gudunov, and it played an outstanding role in the conquest of Siberia. After seventy years it was abandoned when the tsar ordered the troops to settle elsewhere. Traces of the city's defense structure, the governor's court, the town hall, three churches, and one chapel were unearthed, as well as the main commercial buildings and several workshops. The large trading center, a two-story building near the eastern wall of the fortress, was of great importance. Here Russian merchants, native Nenets and representatives of western European trading houses, came to trade—the primary item being fur. A lead stamp with the inscription "Amsterdam And Other Trading Houses" was found at the center, indicating that the famous Dutch trading company bought Russian sables in Mangazeya.

In 1971, the palace of Governor Andrei Palitsyn was discovered and studied. A large structure, it spread over an area of more than 4,300 square feet and was built in western style. Palitsyn had lived in Poland as the tsar's ambassador for many years. Among the finds from the palace was a man's beautiful silver ring, and table knives with ivory handles.

The site of new Mangazeya on the Yenisei River was also investigated and future explorations are planned for other sites in the area. [Reprinted from the *Archeology Journal*, Vol. 24, No. 1 (January 1972):61, as cited in *Orthodox Life*, loc. cit.]

On the 11th of May, the holy Church commemorates the holy Hieromartyr MOKIOS.[1]

Mokios, the sacred hieromartyr, flourished during the reign of Emperor Diocletian (284-305). His parents were Efratios and Efstathia, wellborn and wealthy, who hailed from old Rome. After the virtuous Mokios completed his education, he was ordained to the priesthood for the Church at Amphipolis.[2] Father Mokios always gave his attention to teaching and proclaiming Christ, calling the people to shed the error of the idols. His holy life, acts of kindness, and zeal were a source of illumination to many. While he exhorted and inspired the Christians to stand firm for the Faith, in the face of persecution, many of the pagans, also, were enlightened and pleased with his preaching so that they believed in Christ and received holy Baptism.

The proconsul, named Laodikios, after receiving his office from Diocletian, came into Thrace. Soon after his arrival, Laodikios and other idolaters were offering sacrifice to the falsely-named god Dionysos, who was the favored deity of that place.[3] While the proconsul and his company were engaged in their devotions, Father Mokios appeared. He destroyed their profane altar, casting the votive offerings to the ground. By reason of this deed, the crowd lunged at him and would have rent him to pieces had not the proconsul intervened. Laodikios had the man of God arrested by the guards.

---

[1] The divine office of Hieromartyr Mokios was composed by George of Nikomedia. The text is extant in the Lavreote Codices Γ 19, fol. 34, and Δ 45, fol. 72.

[2] Amphipolis (40°48′N 23°52′E), of the Serres prefecture, is near the mouth of the Strymon River and Mount Pangaion. It was originally a Thracian town called Ennea Odoi or "Nine Roads." It was founded as an Athenian colony in 437-436 B.C. In Roman times, it was capital of Macedonia I or Macedonia Prima. By late antiquity it was subject to Thessalonike. When Rome had captured it from the Macedonians, it was made a free city and the headquarters of the Roman governor of Macedonia. The city thrived as a staging post on the Via Egnatia. Traces of ancient fortifications and a Roman aqueduct are on the city's site. Mineral-rich Pangaion was known as the "holy mountain" to the ancient pagans by reason of the cult of Dionysos (Dionysus) and his followers, the Maenads, as well as for its gold mines and thick forests. Saint Paul went through Amphipolis, ca. A.D. 50, which marked the beginning of the Christian era, though the Bishop of Amphipolis, first mentioned in 553, was suffragan of Thessalonike. From the 12th to the 14th C., authors still used the name of Amphipolis as a geographic designation. When the late antique city ceased to exist, its place was taken by Chrysopolis.

[3] Dionysos or the Roman Bacchus is famous as the god of wine. But he was also the god of vegetation and ecstasy. He was originally worshipped in Thrace and Phrygia, but the cult soon permeated Greek culture. Dionysos had female disciples, the Maenads, that is, "the mad ones" or bacchantes. They indulged in states of ecstatic intoxication. Many of this god's followers reached such states through the use of alcohol and drugs.

Mokios, as one self-called to the contest, confessed Christ as true God before the idol madmen. Setting aside any court proceedings, they straightway subjected the priest to torture. First they suspended him from a wooden pole. With iron claws, they flayed his scalp, cheeks, jaw, and sides. After this brutal skinning, they ignited a furnace, using the coarse fiber of flax and vine-twigs and branches for kindling. After stoking the fire, the flames reached a height of seven cubits or ten feet and more. It was then that the guards hurled in the venerable Mokios. His constancy was proved as he prayed silently to God, enduring all with valor. He rejoiced since he was suffering for the sake of Christ. The saint was preserved safe and whole from the flame when Christ bedewed Him, even He Who in the form of an angel once kept the holy Three Children. Meanwhile, outside the furnace, the pagans witnessed three other men, glorious to behold, walking about in the midst of the fire. The countenance of one Man was more brilliant than a lightning flash. Though it was plainly seen that the holy priest was in the midst of that roaring fire, still the scorching heat in no way harmed him; not even a hair was singed. But then the fire leaped out of the furnace, burning both Laodikios and nine of his guards. In but a short time, all ten were consumed by the devouring flames so that not even the least trace of their bodies or clothing survived. Mokios continued treading through the flames in the furnace, with a radiant countenance and praises upon his lips. Many of the spectators came to believe in Christ. Mokios then emerged from that martyric crucible, unscathed and unharmed.

Saint Mokios

With the immolation of Laodikios, a quick replacement was found in Thalassios, a prince. The latter ordered that Mokios be kept in prison. At length, some twenty-six days later, there came to Thrace another proconsul. His name was Maximos. Since he was an avid follower of the case, he had the martyr summoned and presented to him for further examination. The new proconsul imagined that he could dissuade the holy priest from his devotion toward Christ. What actually took place was not what Maximos had expected. Father Mokios proclaimed Christ clearly and splendidly. After Maximos commanded him to deny Jesus and offer sacrifice to the gods, Mokios contradicted him and taught the crowds that had gathered. Those present were there for a number of reasons. Some came to see the Christian martyr perform another wonderful feat. Others came to view the new proconsul or attend the sacrifices at the temple of Dionysos. Maximos was brought quickly to the end of his wit as he bellowed out this order to his men: "Take this fellow and bind him between two wheels of torture." Now this was an apparatus that could tear to pieces its victim as the wheels made revolutions. As soon as Mokios was strapped onto that heinous machine, the wheels were set in motion. Mokios was chanting all the while, as his blood flowed and fell to the ground below. Suddenly, the wheels of that contraption were cleaved. The martyr, as a result, walked away unharmed. Thus, by divine grace, the athlete of Christ was rendered uninjured in a mysterious and extraordinary manner.

Saint Mokios

Maximos, in a rage, gave other directions: "Make arrangements that the old man be cast to the wild beasts in the amphitheater." Three days later, the holy priest was thrown to the animals as prey. While all expected the semi-starved beasts to devour the elder, the grace of God shielded him. The animals in no wise attacked him; rather, they fawned on him. The crowds, heeding this spectacle, cried out, "Leave off torturing the soldier of Christ! Cease the punishment! Spare him!" Maximos could do nought but oblige popular opinion. He, thereupon, dispatched Mokios to Perinthos.[4] After Mokios was incarcerated for a fortnight, he was made to stand before Prefect Philippisius. The latter, for fear of the people, directed the case to Byzantion,[5] the name of the Megarian colony at the southern mouth of the Bosporos. At the decision of the curia (*voulefterion*) of Byzantion, the saintly Mokios quickly received the death penalty, that is, before the Christians learned of his appearance in that city. At his sentencing, he offered a hymn of thanksgiving to Christ. Just before

---

[4] Herakleia, or ancient Perinthos (Marmara Eregli, 40°59′N 27°57′E) in Thrace, is situated on the north shore of the Sea of Marmara. It is at the junction of the Via Egnatia and the main Balkan road to Naissus (Serb. Nis). Actually Diocletian had renamed this important city, giving it the name Herakleia, since the emperor was a devotee of Hercules.

[5] Not much time would pass before Emperor Constantine I would choose Byzantion as the site of his new capital, which later was absorbed into Constantinople.

the valiant contestant had his head severed by the executioner's sword, he prayed that God forgive the ignorance of his persecutors and asked that they come to a knowledge of the truth. As the saint's head fell under the sword, in 304, a divine voice from on high could be heard by the bystanders, welcoming Mokios' entrance into the heavens among the choir of saints. Saint Mokios received a double crown from Christ: as a priest and as a martyr of the Lord. The hieromartyr's relics were taken by some bishops who interred them one Roman mile[6] outside of Byzantion. His veneration, at an early date, became popular in Byzantium as a holy unmercenary healer. A part of his relics is now found at the Russian Monastery of Saint Panteleimon on the Holy Mountain Athos.

Sozomen mentions a shrine by the fifth century.[7] Later tradition ascribes the building of the martyr's church by Constantine I, who constructed it on the site of the temple of Zeus (or Herakles). The exact location of the large church and later monastery (9th-12th C.) of Saint Mokios is not known. It is generally believed to have been situated near the cistern of Mokios that was built on the seventh hill, beyond the walls of Constantine and not far from the Golden Gate.[8]

On the 11th of May, the holy Church commemorates the INAUGURATION or CONSECRATION of the divinely preserved and extolled City of CONSTANTINOPLE, specially dedicated to the protection of our all-immaculate Lady, the Theotokos and Ever-virgin MARY.[9]

---

[6] A Roman mile consisted of 1,000 paces of 5 feet each, and was therefore 5,000 feet.

[7] Sozomen, *H.E.* 8:17:5.

[8] The church, over the years, suffered many times from earthquake damage that required rebuilding. After a section of the church was destroyed in the 9th C., it was restored to a glorious state by Basil I. The church was also the scene of important court ceremonies. It housed the relics of Saint Efthymios the Younger (commemorated the 4th of January) and Saint Samson the Hospitable (27th of June). At the beginning of the 13th C., the church was mentioned as still splendid; but it came to be in a state of ruin by the end of the 14th C. John V used its stones to repair the walls near the Golden Gate. *The Oxford Dictionary of Byzantium*, s.v. "Mokios"; *The Great Synaxaristes* (in Greek), s.v. "May 10th."

[9] The mosaic—shown herein—over the southwestern entrance of Hagia Sophia, above the vestibule bronze door, portrays Emperor Constantine proffering a model of the city to the Mother of God. The inscription reads: "Great Emperor Constantine among the Saints." He is not clad in garments of his period, but those of the making of the mosaics, between the years 968 and 984, during the reign of Basil II. On the right of

(continued...)

Saint Constantine the Great Presenting Constantinople to Christ and the Theotokos

Constantine the Great, the first Christian emperor, when he arrived and overtook Byzantion, planned to build a larger city. Constantine was going to build "New Rome." After his victory over Licinius, he started some construction work in the small but strategic town of Byzantion. He already knew the neighborhood well, since he lived there for ten years while in the service of Diocletian and thereafter, for a short while, of Galerius. Constantine could not help but observe the town's unique and well-situated location. The two continents of Europe and Asia were separated at that point by less than two miles, and, at some points by less than one mile. The inlet known as the Golden Horn was a natural harbor. The small peninsula from the Golden Horn to the Propontis was surrounded by water on three sides, leaving only one side to be buttressed with strong walls. The city was also within comfortable reach of the Danube and Euphrates frontiers. Communication between the capital and all parts of the empire was far easier at Byzantion than it ever had been with Rome. In years to come, as a military base for the Striking Force, the whole history of Europe was altered by this factor.[10] Constantine, therefore, laid the first stone in the foundation of the wall, which was to mark the bounds of the new city or "New Rome" on the 4th day of November, in the year 326. The intention was to call it "New Rome," but this appellation failed. Before Constantine's death, the name Constantinople had been evolved by public opinion; and it abided.

After four years of work, the city was officially opened on the 11th of May, in the year 330. The regnant party formed a procession through the city, followed by multitudes. Hymns to the Theotokos, as patroness, were chanted. It would remain the "Queen of Cities" until, after a prolonged blockade and a foolish union with the Papists, it was overrun by the Ottomans on Tuesday, the

---

[9](...continued)
the Virgin there is depicted Emperor Justinian the Great (527-565)—who is not shown herein—proffering Hagia Sophia to the Theotokos.

[10] D. G. Kousoulas, *The Life and Times of Constantine the Great* (Danbury, CT: Rutledge Books, Inc., 1997), p. 389; and G. P. Baker, *Constantine the Great and the Christian Revolution* (NY, NY: Cooper Square Press, 1992), p. 260.

29th of May, in the year 1453, about two and a half hours after dawn. The Byzantines could hardly believe that their God-guarded city had fallen into the hands of the infidel after one thousand, one hundred and twenty-three years.

The festivities and ceremonies for the city's inauguration lasted forty days. During one of those festive days, a colossal statue of Apollo, transferred from Athens, was brought to the Hippodrome.[11] The head of Apollo was skillfully removed and replaced with that of Constantine. After the parade, the statue was set upon a lofty porphyry-colored marble column in Constantine's Forum. Its height loomed eighty feet over the crowd, while it rested on a pedestal of white marble that was about nineteen feet high, which stood on a base of four wide steps.[12] At the foot of this column, we are told, there was the following inscription: "O Christ, Ruler and Master of the cosmos, to Thee have I dedicated this obedient city. Guard and deliver her from every harm."[13] The precious nails with which Christ was crucified were placed in the statue's head. At its feet were enclosed the twelve baskets from which the fragments remained after the miracle of the loaves and fish. Every year, on the first day of September, Constantine's successors, with the Patriarch of Constantinople at their side and with priests chanting hymns, assembled in front of the column to pay homage to the founder of the city.

On the last day of the inaugural festivities, columns of pagan soldiers in dress uniform, carrying white candles, escorted a statue of the goddess Fortuna now under its Greek name "Tyche." Large crowds of spectators along the avenue of the Hippodrome acclaimed the procession. The pageant circled the Hippodrome and stopped before the imperial box, the *kathisma* (Greek for seat). Constantine rose from his seat in order to address the burgeoning multitude,...proclaiming that a parade was to be held every year on the city's inauguration anniversary. The festivities ended with the traditional chariot races in the magnificent circus (Hippodrome). At the same time coins were minted showing Constantinople with a ship as the "Queen of the Seas." The new city was a magnificent sight. Constantine had removed statues and works of art from Greece and other parts of the empire to embellish his city.[14]

There was, at that time, no recognized Christian way to found a city, much less the capital of an empire. Constantine also was aware of the sensibilities of the pagan population of Byzantion and much of the military. He

---

[11] The Hippodrome of Constantinople was not only the sports arena but also the scene of royal proclamations, triumphal celebrations, and the city's public life.

[12] The column still stands today, though badly damaged by fire. The statue is long gone. It came crashing down to earth in 1105, killing a number of persons in its fall. Kousoulas, p. 393.

[13] Ibid.

[14] Ibid., p. 394.

felt that to some degree he needed to accommodate them. But he also wished to impress on them the fact that he had important plans for their city, for which he perceived that in order to succeed with them he would do it in terms that they could understand. Nonetheless, he would not allow them to interfere with the Christianization of the city. In some cases, a more drastic treatment was employed: the temples of Artemis-Selene, of Aphrodite, and of Apollos-Helios were all stripped of their treasures and revenues, and left with a neutralized cult. Inside of fifty years, paganism in Constantinople had no popular roots. It is generally agreed that Constantine never permitted the idolaters to offer sacrifice in his new capital.[15]

Constantinople was the first purely Christian city ever built. No pagan temple was open for public worship within its bounds. The old temples of Byzantion were preserved as public monuments. It is true that Constantine collected a number of important memorials of the old religion, especially those of artistic or historical interest, and preserved them in his city, where they formed a striking link with the famous past of Hellas.

At the new city's center, the emperor constructed a vast plaza—the Augusteum. It was paved in marble, adorned with classical statuary, and surrounded by imposing buildings. To the north was the ongoing construction of the Church of Hagia Sophia (Holy Wisdom). To the east was the Senate building. To the south, overlooking the Propontis, was the imperial palace[16] next to the Hippodrome. To enter the palace, one had to pass through an enormous bronze gate known as Chalke ("of bronze"). Right next to the palace were the so-called baths of Zeuxippus.[17]

In the Augusteum, Constantine had installed a marble column known as the Million. It was designed to display the distances of all parts of the empire from Constantine's city. There was a wide avenue, known as the *mesi*, that is "the middle street," that connected the Augusteum with the Forum of Constantine, an elliptical plaza surrounded by colonnades. They ended at either end in two spacious porticos in the shape of a triumphal arch. In the middle—which tradition held was the exact spot where the emperor had pitched his tent when he was besieging Licinius inside Byzantion—was Constantine's porphyry column.[18]

The imperial palace, known as the Great Palace (*Mega Palation*), was a complex of buildings spread over a large area, with mighty walls and towers, so that it resembled a city within the city. One of the buildings, covered in

---

[15] T. G. Elliott, *The Christianity of Constantine the Great* (Scranton, PA: University of Scranton Press, 1996), pp. 256, 257.

[16] The palace was located where the Blue Mosque is today. Kousoulas, p. 394.

[17] Ibid., pp. 394, 395.

[18] Ibid., p. 395.

porphyry marble brought from Rome, was set aside for women with child, that is, those ladies who were part of the imperial household. This maternity ward and retreat provided them with serenity and every comfort, far from the strain of everyday life.[19]

Since Constantinople had few natural springs, water was needed for the citizens. Below the city, Constantine constructed underground cisterns. The water was brought in over a long aqueduct, but it was also collected from rainfall. The colonnaded cisterns, many of them enormous in size, were costly. Two of the largest cisterns remain in good condition, even after so many centuries. One of them, the "Cistern of Philoxenos," had eighteen-foot columns arranged in sixteen rows of fourteen columns each. The cistern was named after Philoxenos, the rich Greek patron who underwrote the cost. Indeed, Constantine had many wealthy Romans and Greeks contribute lavish sums for the construction of the cisterns. In return, he had the names of the donors chiseled on stone. Practically all the names are Greek, an interesting piece of evidence that the Latin-speaking emperor's new Rome was rapidly becoming a Greek city. The second cistern, known as the "Underground Palace," is 390-feet long and 174-feet wide. This ancient cistern still supplies water as clear as when it was first opened. Both cisterns can be visited today by tourists.[20]

Of the renowned Hippodrome—made known throughout the inhabited world both by secular history and the sermons of Saint John Chrysostom—little remains today. There is an Egyptian obelisk, a marble column in the shape of a twisted serpent,[21] and a crumbling stone pillar. These three stone monuments that have survived define the outline of the *spina*, around which the charioteers raced their chariots. The obelisk stood in the exact center of the racetrack, which followed the traditional lines of an elongated ellipse. Tiers of marble seats were on both sides of the track, embellished with statues and works of art. At the northern end of the *spina* was a large building, housing the stables and the storehouses for supplies and chariots. At the middle point of the long side of the arena, adjacent to the Great Palace, was the imperial box containing the *kathisma* (the emperor's throne). There was a pillared platform right in front of the throne, for the emperor's standard-bearers. Immediately behind the imperial box was the Church of Saint Stephen; it, too, was part of the Great Palace. To reach the imperial box, the emperor strolled through the church down a spiral staircase. It was designed for the impressive entry of the

---

[19] Ibid.

[20] Ibid., pp. 395, 396.

[21] This column was brought in from Delphi where it was erected centuries ago to commemorate the victory of the Greeks over the Persians at Plataea in 479 B.C. Kousoulas, p. 396.

emperor. Around the *kathisma* were seats for his high-ranking dignitaries. The first tier of seats, reserved for the more distinguished spectators, was some thirteen feet above the arena with several more tiers rising behind. Above and behind the seats at the top was a wide promenade which ran all around the arena, a spacious avenue of some 2,740 feet above ground, with a magnificent view of the Bosporus. People walking on it were protected from falling off by a solid marble railing reaching almost to a man's breast.[22]

Eusebius writes in his Life of Saint Constantine that the emperor "consecrated Constantinople to the Christian martyrs' God. He gave favorable and special treatment and attention by embellishing it with numerous sacred edifices, buildings, and memorials on the largest scale. He determined to purge the city from idolatry of every kind."[23]

It is true that Constantine spent large sums for the construction of churches. One of them, as mentioned earlier, was Hagia Sophia. Another important church was dedicated to the Holy Peace (Hagia Ireenee), the Peace of God. It, too, was half-finished at the time of the city's inauguration. One church that was finished was that of the Holy Apostles, initially dedicated to the Holy Trinity.[24]

Eusebius tells us that "Constantine, ever the builder for Christ, erected a magnificent church to the holy apostles in Constantinople. It was of a vast height, its walls encased from the foundation to the roof with marble slabs of various colors. He also formed the inner roof of finely fretted work, and overlaid it throughout with gold. The external covering was of brass, and splendidly and profusely adorned with gold, and reflected the sun's rays with a brilliancy which dazzled the distant beholder. The dome was entirely encompassed by a finely carved tracery, wrought in brass and gold."[25]

Now buried under the great altar of the Church of the Holy Apostles were the relics of Saints Timothy, Andrew, Luke, Matthias, Iakovos the brother of the Lord, and the head of Saint Ephemia. Around a rotunda inside the church stood the memorials of the Twelve Apostles; and in their midst Constantine had placed the sarcophagus where his body was to be placed after his death. In later years, the Church would accord him the title *Isapostolos* (Equal-to-the-apostles), since, by his actions, he had lifted the Christian Faith

---

[22] Ibid., pp. 395, 396.

[23] Eusebius, *The Life of the Blessed Emperor Constantine*, Book III, Ch. XLVIII, *Logos Research Systems* on CD-ROM.

[24] Kousoulas, p. 397.

[25] Eusebius, Bk. IV, Ch. LVIII.

from obscurity and persecution. He now made it the dominant religion in the Roman Empire.[26]

What was the emperor's intent in being buried in this way among such august company as the Lord's apostles? In the 330s, when the church was being built, the main attraction in it for most of the population of Constantinople was going to be the coffin of Constantine. The emperor, perceiving the spiritual level of the populace, took this into account. He knew that anyone visiting the church to see the emperor's tomb would necessarily find himself surrounded by the tombs of the apostles. This was Constantine's intention. But with the passage of time, and the further Christianization of the city, Constantius II (Constantine's son) built the imperial mausoleum adjacent to the church and had his father's coffin moved into it.

There was another problem that Constantine needed to deal with squarely. This city was going to be the empire's capital, but not many people lived in it. "To bring people to his city, Constantine used every practical inducement. To the poor, he promised handouts of food and clothing; to the rich, tax relief. He required all the officials in the imperial administration to reside within the walls of the city. He invited old patrician families from Rome to move to his new city and receive large tracts of land in Asia Minor, but not many responded at first. At length, a multitude of the emperor's friends from Rome and Milan came. They were soon to find that the new capital was flourishing rapidly. It offered openings for the investment of capital and for commercial enterprises. While Rome continued in the imposing grandeur of a dying city, Constantinople was growing into an active and progressive commercial capital. Thus, Constantine succeeded in transferring the center of the empire to the east."[27]

He created a new aristocracy, the class of *clari*, and elevated new senators for his Senate. Within a short time, many Christians, especially from Asia Minor and the Balkans, moved to the city on their own to live in a place where the emperor and the majority of the residents shared their religious beliefs. Using the Greek language, Constantine named the city after himself, Constantinoupolis, the "City of Constantine." It, eventually, simply came to be called "The Polis," that is, "The City." Even when the Turks changed the name to Istanbul, they still used, somewhat distorted, the Greek words *is tin poli*, meaning "to the city."[28]

The City's Patroness

On the birthday of the city, it was dedicated to our Lady Theotokos. New Rome's patroness has, ofttimes and in diverse ways, preserved and

---

[26] Kousoulas, loc. cit; Eusebius, Bk. IV, Ch. LVIII.
[27] Baker, pp. 266, 267.
[28] Kousoulas, p. 398.

protected her city from perils. Among these many inspiring events demonstrating her care and solicitude, we shall cite three stunning incidents.

I. In 626, the icon of the Theotokos dispersed the hordes of Avars (western Huns) and Persians who had come against Constantinople. This took place during the reign of Herakleios, when Chosroes ruled over the Persians, and Sergios was Patriarch of Constantinople. Saint Theophanes, in his *Chronographia*, writes: "With God's help, by the mediation of the all-praised Theotokos, when engaged in battle, a storm of hail fell unexpectedly on the barbarians and struck down many of them, whereas the soldiers of the Rhomaioi enjoyed fair weather. So the Rhomaioi routed the Persians and slew a great multitude of them....When the Avars approached the city by way of Thrace, with a view to capturing it, they set in motion many engines against it. They filled the gulf of the Horn with an immense multitude, beyond all number....But they were vanquished by God's might and help, and by the intercession of the immaculate Virgin, the Mother of God. Having lost great numbers, both on land and on sea, they shamefully returned to their country."[29]

When the icon of the Theotokos was reverently borne aloft on the city's walls, the Theotokos herself defended Constantinople. If Judith proved to be a citadel for the city of Bethulia, how much more is the city of Constantinople kept by the most holy Theotokos? In the Song of Songs, we find: "I am a wall, and my breasts are as towers [Song 8:10]." From this event, that is, the lifting of the Avar siege of Constantinople, did the Church commence chanting the Akathist Hymn to the Theotokos and unwedded bride, the champion leader of the Orthodox. The Akathist Hymn consists of twenty-four stanzas, during which the congregation stands (since *akathistos* means "not seated").

II. In 716/717, during the reign of Leo the Isaurian, when Germanos was Patriarch of Constantinople, the Saracens had laid siege to the city for many months, but "God brought to nought the counsel of Caliph Souleiman through the intercession of the all-pure Theotokos."[30]

Saint Theophanes comments that "the winter proved very severe in Thrace, so that for a hundred days the earth could not be seen beneath the congealed snow. In the meantime, the enemy Suphiam arrived with a fleet, that is, four hundred transports laden with corn, as did Izid with another fleet with three hundred and six transports, a store of arms, and provisions. When some of the Egyptian crew of the enemy sought refuge in the city, the emperor was informed that the two fleets were hidden in the bay. With God's help, thanks to the intercessions of the all-pure Theotokos, the adversaries were sunk on the spot. The Arabs suffered a severe famine, so that they ate all of their dead

[29] *The Chronicle of Theophanes Confessor*, ed. by Mango & Scott (Clarendon's Press, Oxford), AM 6117 (A.D. 624/625), p. 446, 447.
[30] Ibid., AM 6209 (A.D. 716.717), pp. 541-545.

animals, namely horses, asses, and camels. A pestilence fell upon them also and killed an infinite number of them.[31] Furthermore, the Bulgarian nation made war on them and massacred 22,000 Arabs. Many other calamities befell them at that time and made them learn by experience that God and the all-holy Virgin, the Mother of God, protect this city and the Christian Empire; and that those who call upon God in truth are not entirely forsaken, even if we are chastised for a short time on account of our sins."[32]

III. On the 18th day of June, in the year 860, Russians, hoping to capture the capital, came down from the north in two hundred ships. Both the emperor and the army were absent from Constantinople. They were engaged in warding off the Arabs. Hence, the inhabitants offered no resistance. Patriarch Photios spoke later of the appalling slaughter and destruction: "The wrath of God comes upon us for our transgressions;...the assault of the invading nation has given clear proof of the abundance of our sins. That nation was obscure, insignificant, and not even known until the incursion against us....They have ravaged the environs, they have laid waste the approaches to the town, they have harshly destroyed those who fell into their hands....We have become the plaything of a barbarous tribe....Suddenly, in the twinkling of an eye, like a wave of the sea poured over our frontiers, and as a wild boar devours the inhabitants of the land like grass, or straw, or a crop,...they spared nothing from man to beast....Everything was full of dead bodies; the flow of rivers was turned into blood.[33]...

"At that time, denuded of all help and deprived of human alliance, we were spiritually upheld by holding fast to our hopes in the Mother of the Logos our God. We urged her to implore her Son, invoking her for the expiation of our sins. We sought her intercession for our salvation and her protection as an impregnable wall. We begged her to break the boldness of the barbarians, to crush their insolence, to defend the despairing people, and to fight for her flock."[34]

Addressing his flock, the patriarch continued: "Beloved ones, the time has come to have recourse to the Mother of the Logos, our only hope and refuge. Imploring, let us cry out to her, 'Save thy city, as thou knowest how, O Lady!' Let us set her up as our intermediary before her Son our God. Let us

---

[31] *The Great Synaxaristes* (in Greek) reports that a deadly plague slew two hundred thousand. By reason of disease and hunger, the barbarians were compelled to take flight.

[32] *The Chronicle of Theophanes Confessor*, AM 6209 (A.D. 716/717), p. 546.

[33] "Homily IV, Departure of the Russians," *Homilies of Photius*, trans. by C. Mango (Cambridge, MA: Harvard University Press, Dumbarton Oaks Studies Three, 1958), pp. 96-99.

[34] Ibid., p. 102.

make her the witness and surety of our compact. It is she who conveys our requests and rains down the mercy of her Offspring, scattering the cloud of enemies and lighting up for us the dawn of salvation."[35]

Patriarch Photios and the inhabitants of the city then carried the Virgin's garment (*maphorion*) about the walls. Upon this occasion, the holy Photios said: "As the whole city was carrying with me her raiment for the repulse of the besiegers and the protection of the besieged, we offered freely our prayers and performed the litany." Continuing, he says, "Thereupon, with ineffable compassion, she spoke out in motherly intercession: God was moved, His anger was averted, and the Lord took pity on His inheritance. Truly is this most holy garment the raiment of God's Mother! It embraced the walls, and the foes inexplicably showed their backs;...for, immediately, as the Virgin's garment went round the walls, the barbarians gave up the siege and broke camp, while we were delivered from impending capture and were granted unexpected salvation. Thereupon, the Lord looked not upon our sins but upon our repentance. He did not remember our iniquities [Ps. 78:8], but looked on the affliction of our hearts, inclining His ear [Ps. 114:2] to the confession of our lips.[36]...

"Since we have been delivered from the threat, and have escaped the sword, and the destroyer has passed by us, who have been covered and marked out with the garment of the Mother of the Logos, let us all, in unison with her, send up songs of thanksgiving to Christ our God Who was born of her.... Indeed, those to whom a common destruction was impending ought to consecrate and offer to God and His Mother a common hymn. We have enjoyed a common deliverance: let us offer common thanks. With rectitude of mind and purity of soul, let us say to the Mother of the Logos, 'Unhesitatingly, we keep our Faith and our love for thee. Do thou save thy city, as thou knowest how and willest. We put thee forward as our arms, our rampart, our shield, and our general: do thou fight for thy people. We shall take heed to the best of our strength to make our hearts pure before thee, having torn ourselves away from filth and passions. Do thou dispel the plots of them who rise up arrogantly against us. For even if we are amiss in the commandments made unto us, it is thine to set us straight; it is thine to proffer a hand to us who are kneeling and to raise us up from our fall.' Thus, let us address the Virgin, and let us not speak falsely."[37] After the Russian ships departed they were destroyed by a storm, and only a few escaped total wreckage. Saint Photios, enlightened by God, thought it prudent to Christianize these pagans. Indeed, this is what he did.

---

[35] "Homily III, The Russian Attack," *The Homilies of Photius*, p. 95.

[36] "Homily IV, Departure of the Russians," loc. cit.

[37] Ibid., pp. 109, 110.

On the 11th of May, the holy Church commemorates the holy Martyr DIOSCOROS the New, who was slain by the sword.[38]

Dioscoros, the holy martyr, came from the great city of Smyrna. By reason of his belief in the Faith of Christ, he was led before the pagan governor. Since Dioscoros was constant in his profession as a Christian, he was cast into prison. He was made to undergo a second examination. He, once more, persisted in the same testimony and heralded Christ, which brought down a sentence from the governor. The blessed Dioscoros, having suffered the cutting off of his head, received the crown of martyrdom. Unlike the Dioscuri of myth, Castor and Polydeuces, who divided the gift of immortality, alternating their days between Olympos and the underworld, our Dioscoros, beheaded, verily possesses eternal life.

On the 11th of May, the holy Church commemorates our holy fathers among the saints, KYRIL and METHODIOS of Thessalonike, the Equals-to-the-apostles and Enlighteners of the Slavs.

Kyril (Cyril) and Methodios hailed from ninth-century Thessalonike. They were two of the seven children of Leo and Mary. Their youngest child, Kyril, was born ca. 815. His baptismal name before his monastic tonsure was Constantine (Konstantin). It is unknown whether Methodios was the elder brother's baptismal name or his monastic one. Methodios was born ca. 815. This well-known Thessalonian family was affluent and of noble lineage. Leo served as *droungarios*, a high military rank, having as many as one thousand men under his command. Mary was the scion of good and distinguished stock. The family was also known in the emperor's circle.

Constantine, the youngest in the family, showed marked inclinations toward study and the virtuous life. At seven years of age, he was vouchsafed a heaven-sent dream. He beheld the governor of Thessalonike arranging a bride show, from whom Constantine was to select a wife from among the most beauteous and notable maidens. As the youth looked upon them, his eye was drawn to the most beautiful damsel. Her countenance was radiant with light. She was arrayed in splendid attire, embellished with gold necklaces and pearls. He, therefore, chose for his wife the one that was named Sophia, which in the Greek language means "wisdom." Thus, the vision portended that Constantine would choose Wisdom as his life's companion and not a mortal woman.

---

[38] In other books, such as the *Menaion* and *Synaxaristes*, the name is recorded as Dioscorides, perhaps by way of endearment to call him by a soft name, or to distinguish him from the older holy Martyr Dioscoros who is commemorated by the holy Church on the 13th of October.

Saints Kyril and Methodios

The young scholar Constantine was taught by tutors. He, immediately, shone forth in his studies. His accurate memory and sharp mind excelled in grammar, poetry, and rhetoric. At the age of fourteen, he learned by heart the poems of Saint Gregory the Theologian. When he implored his instructors to teach him Homeric Greek and advanced grammar, he was turned away at first. It simply was difficult to find such a teacher in his home city at that time. Even so, he received a reasonably good education locally. Cosmopolitan and polyglot Thessalonike, gateway to the west, was the empire's second city after Constantinople, linking Rome with New Rome. Thessalonike was a center of both spiritual and cultural activities. Both brothers were familiar with the Slavs' attacks and uprisings, and the problems that they created for the empire. The brothers' father, Droungarios Leo, a military man, would have certainly been involved in state operations and security surrounding the 836 uprising of the Slavs who lived to the east of Thessalonike. By the ninth century the Slavs of diverse tribes had settled in various parts of Macedonia. Though the Slavic tribes had a common tongue, yet they remained separated from one another. The merchants of Thessalonike, by reason of their flourishing commercial enterprises, learned the language of their customers. The uncultured Slavs had difficulty communicating in Greek, so businessmen took it upon themselves to learn Slavic. Every morning, when the great gates in the city walls were opened, groups of Slavs entered Thessalonike to buy and sell and pursue other business. Slavic was, therefore, used in the city, so that the Greeks could speak with the former invaders in the course of their transactions.[39]

Formative Years

Due to the eminent position of the family in Thessalonian society, the elder brother, Methodios, left home and pursued a government-appointed position. By reason of his intellect, amiability, and an appearance that showed

[39] See interesting discussion on the celebrated city of Thessalonike and the Slav presence in Anthony-Emil N. Tachiaos' *Cyril and Methodius of Thessalonica* (Crestwood, NY: Saint Vladimir's Seminary Press, 2001), p. 16.

him to be a man of refinement, the emperor appointed him with the governance of a Slavic province that was situated within the Byzantines' jurisdiction. As a result of this office, Methodios, on a daily basis, not only came to see Slavic customs and traditions firsthand but also came to hear the Slavic language in all its nuances within that Slavic enclave. He gradually habituated himself to their ways and tongue.

In the meantime, in Thessalonike, Constantine had completed his general education at the age of fifteen. This brilliant student of astute intellect received an offer to further his studies in the capital. A personal invitation was sent by the *Logothetes tou Dromou*, a subaltern official under the *Magister Officiorum* in charge of the public post. This official, who was involved in the state mail network, heard of the promising young scholar's diligence, grace, and wisdom. The adolescent, thus, had an opportunity to study with the emperor. When Constantine entered into studies with the young emperor, he uttered, "Grant that I may understand what is pleasing unto Thee, O Master Christ!" The Lord, thereupon, in addition to bestowing upon Constantine the knowledge of profane philosophy, also received the wisdom of the Holy Spirit and the reverent fear of God. Constantine's arrival in Constantinople came at a time when Empress Theodora was acting as regent to her young son, Michael III (b. 840-867). She, together with the Orthodox Patriarch Methodios I (843–847), brought an end to the iconoclastic era of her husband, Emperor Theophilos (d. 20th of January, 842). After three months in the capital, Constantine mastered grammar. He then gave heed to other studies. He took up Homer and geometry with Leo the Mathematician.[40] He studied dialectic and all the branches of philosophy with Saint Photios the Great.[41] His curriculum, among other Greek sciences, also included rhetoric, arithmetic, astronomy, and music. He learned his lessons easily and quickly. Constantine, a youth gifted with a lofty intellect, also grew into a man of good morals.

He came to the attention and admiration of the eunuch and *logothete* (a high official), Theoktistos (d. 855),[42] regent for Michael III and adviser to Theodora. He, too, helped bring about the Triumph of Orthodoxy over

---

[40] This Leo had been the former Metropolitan of Thessalonike (840-843). He lost his office when his patron, Patriarch John Grammatikos, was deposed for his cooperation with Iconoclasm. Leo, therefore, returned to the capital and resumed his former career as a teacher.

[41] The Professor Photios, future Director of the Imperial Secretariat and Patriarch of Constantinople, had a flock of distinguished students who were taught not only secular studies but also the highest philosophy and spiritual learning. Saint Photios, Patriarch of Constantinople (858-867, 877-886), is commemorated by the holy Church on the 6th of February.

[42] Saint Theoktistos is commemorated by the holy Church on the 20th of November.

Iconoclasm in 843. Theoktistos also was involved in the elections of two patriarchs: Methodios and, later, Ignatios. "Philosopher," he once addressed Constantine, "I should like to know what is philosophy." Constantine replied, "Knowledge of things human and divine, insofar as man is able to approach God; for it teaches man, by his actions, to become the image and similitude of his Creator." After that response, Theoktistos always addressed him as "Philosopher," so that the name remained. Constantine was not smitten with pride over this distinction. He, also, never made a display of either the title or his learning. Thereafter, Constantine passed his examinations. At that point, Theoktistos wished to make a match between Constantine and his niece who was also his goddaughter. Theoktistos assured Constantine that such a marriage would put him in the way of a high administrative office and the best circles. Theoktistos even offered Constantine the exalted rank of *strategos*, or governor of a *theme*. It was a post that would give him military and civil authority over a large territory. Constantine declined all the offers, attractive though they were. "I have no such ambitions," he told Theoktistos, "I desire knowledge, and knowledge alone." Theoktistos, nevertheless, with the empress' approval, had Constantine appointed as the director of the patriarchal secretarial. One of the necessary qualifications for such a post was that the candidate hold the Church office of either Deacon or Reader. As important as the post was in the patriarchate, this administrative work was not to his liking. Constantine resigned and entered a monastery on the Bosporos. It is likely he withdrew to the Kleidion Monastery, but he was not tonsured there. He was known to enter into debates with the former Patriarch John Grammatikos, who lived in a private house in the neighborhood. Constantine was hopeful in converting the backslider to again accept the veneration of the sacred images.

Constantine resided at the monastery for six months. Theoktistos continued to pursue the gifted young man. He brought him back to the capital and gave him a professorship, for which Constantine received payment from the state that he might teach philosophy. Although only twenty-four years of age, Constantine was drawn into missionary circles that worked close with the government.

Middle East Talks

It was at that time that the young Arab Caliph al-Mutawakkil (847-861) intruded on Byzantine territory. Straightway, the Byzantines launched a diplomatic mission, in which Constantine was also dispatched. Byzantine-Arab relations were at a sensitive juncture. The two delegations met at Samarra on the upper Tigris, some sixty miles north of Baghdad. While matters between the two realms were certainly discussed, the conversation also took a religious turn.

The religious sages of the Saracens, then, confronted Constantine with this question: "Why is it that among you Christians, who worship one God, that there are so many variances between your Faith and your manner of life, whilst we Mohammedans strictly adhere to one law and do not transgress it?" Constantine replied, "Our God is as a vast ocean, Whose depth is immeasurable and inconceivable to the human mind. Many probe into the immense greatness, seeking the Lord, sailing in the leaky boats of their own intellect. They fall into errors and heresies. Some strong in mind and in faith, and supported by the grace of God, find riches of wisdom and salvation. Still others, weak and deprived of the help of God, on account of their pride and self-conceit, endeavor to sail across this vast ocean, but they fail for the want of strength. They are buffeted by incomprehension and doubts, so that they either become lost or exhausted by hardships. God, having created man, adorned him with free will. Each one may select one's own way. One may rise with one's mind and resemble the angels, serving God and fulfilling His law. One, also, may lower oneself to the level of an animal, feeding one's desires and binding oneself in passions. In order to serve God, one must struggle with oneself; one must endeavor to grow in perfection, to conquer one's passions, and to bridle one's evil habits. But this is a difficult task. Your religion, on the other hand, as a small stream, is rationally comprehensible to anyone: everything in it is human and there is nothing divine. It does not demand of you any struggles or hardships. It does not make it your duty to constantly advance to a higher perfection, and, therefore, it is easily fulfilled by anyone. Without any labor, one may fulfill the whole of your law."[43]

The Arabs, furthermore, refused to accept the trihypostatic nature of God. Constantine rose to the occasion and refuted the Arabs' heretical notions by explaining the mystery in this wise. He gave the example of the visible and created sun in the sky as an image of the Holy Trinity, saying, "The solar disc is as an image of God the Father Who has neither beginning nor end. A ray of light issuing forth from the solar disc, illuminating the earth, is as the Son, Jesus, Who is the effulgence of the Father and begotten of the Father. The warmth pouring forth from that same disc is as the Spirit, Who is proceeding from the same Father." This served to close the Muslims' blasphemous lips. The Arabs, thereafter, were very interested in what he had to say. In fact, they had long been interested in anything Greek. They had already embarked on having the great Greek writers translated into Arabic. The Muslim palace at Samarra was even being adorned with wall-paintings done by Byzantine painters. Constantine found these Muslims to be educated and well versed in geometry, astronomy, and other sciences.

---

[43] "Saints Kyril and Methody, Evangelizers of the Slavs" (Juneau, AK: Saints Kyril and Methody Society), p. 2.

The Arab Muslims, for the most part, were amazed with the breadth of the young man's learning. "How dost thou know all this?" they asked. Constantine told them a parable and then concluded, "All the sciences started with us." After the talks finished, and the Arabs made every effort to impress the Byzantine diplomats, the delegation was given the grand tour of Samarra's palaces and gardens.[44]

Following this mission, Constantine returned to the capital. Not much time passed before he longed to find a place of quietude and stillness. He thought to forsake his position and renounce the world. He began by distributing all that he had to the poor. He kept only one manservant. Together they suffered deprivation and poverty. His patron, Theoktistos, the *Great Logothete*, was murdered as part of a conspiracy devised by Caesar Bardas, Theodora's brother, to remove her and Theoktistos from power, so that he could direct his nephew, Emperor Michael III.

The Brothers at Mount Olympos, Asia Minor

After Theoktistos, Constantine's patron, was brutally removed from office in November of 855, the two brothers were to meet again. Methodios had already resigned his government post over the Slavs. He, thereafter, repaired to the famed monasteries on Mount Olympos of Bithynia, which province was opposite the capital in northwest Asia Minor. Olympos was the Holy Mountain southeast of Prousa. During the time of Iconoclasm this "Mountain of the Monks," as it was called, struggled against the iconoclasts. Methodios made the decision to enter the monastic life, abandoning all the beauties and delights of this world, after living a number of years among the Slavs. Those years of governing were a time of turmoil and agitation. He now yearned for the life of a monk, after hearing with the ear of his heart those words of Jesus: "If anyone is willing to come after Me, let him deny himself, and take up his cross, and keep on following Me [Mt. 16:24; Mk. 8:34; Lk. 9:23]." Methodios, therefore, was clad with the habit of the monastic and remained in obedience, fulfilling all of the monastic rule. He adorned his soul with prayers, vigils, and fasts, living as an earthly angel. He also spent much time studying the sacred books. Constantine, of course, learned that his brother was on Olympos. The eloquent brother who loved philosophy, Constantine, went to visit Methodios, the lover of the wilderness, and stayed with him. They spent their time in prayer and reading books and writing. Although Constantine lived the life of a monk, praying in the wilderness with his brother, still he was

---

[44] One Slavonic hymn chanted on this day mentions that some disgruntled Muslims offered Constantine a deadly poison to drink. But the saint was preserved whole and unharmed by the One Who said that if should His disciples drink anything deadly, in no wise shall it harm them [cf. Mk. 16:18]. May 11th, Orthros Canon, Ode Six, Mode Three.

not tonsured. In Bithynia, at that time, there was a large population of Slavs, in fact, hundreds of thousands, who had been transferred there.

The Crimea and the Khazars

After Father Methodios and Constantine lived on Olympos for a number of years, in 860, Michael III dispatched Constantine to the Khazars. Their leader, or *khagan*, was being pressed by both Jewish and Arab advocates to convert to one or the other religion. The *khagan* took counsel with the Byzantines, asking that a learned man come and debate the Khazars. If the Orthodox representative could successfully disprove the arguments of the Jews and Arabs, he would lead his people to accept the Faith of the Rhomaioi. Michael III wasted no time sending forth Constantine the Philosopher, since he was confident in his abilities to rout the heterodox and bring these allies in the northern Caucasus to right belief. Constantine took along his elder brother, Father Methodios. The mutual enemy of the Byzantines and Khazars, the Russians or Rus, was ever a threat. It was Byzantium's wish to renew the Byzantino-Khazar treaty. Thus, both the state and the Church had interests in this important mission. The mission to Khazaria took them by way of Cherson. But in 860, the Rus had attacked Constantinople.

The first impact of the Rus, Russian barbarians whose very name previously had been unknown, appeared suddenly to the Byzantine world on the 18th day of June, in the year 860. Hoping to capture the capital, the Russians came down from the north in two hundred ships. With so unexpected a raid, there was general consternation because the emperor and the army were absent, having departed to ward off the Arabs. Hence, no resistance was offered. Saint Photios reproached the citizenry for cowardice and dejection. The barbarians were successful,[45] making themselves rich with booty. Leaving the outskirts of Constantinople, they ravaged and devastated the Black Sea coast and the Bosporos strait, and extended their depredations to the Princes' Islands, on which ex-Patriarch Ignatios was then living in exile.[46]

Though the Russians were not well organized, yet their attack, both swift and inhumane, was unprecedented. The patriarch and people of Constantinople invoked the aid of their champion leader, the Theotokos. The Virgin's garment was borne aloft about the city's walls. As this took place, the barbarians gave up the siege and broke camp. The capital was delivered from impending capture. After the Russian ships departed they were destroyed by a storm, and only a few escaped total wreckage.

Saint Photios, devoted to the spreading of Christ's Gospel among people who had not as yet heard it, thought it prudent to act quickly and work

---

[45] *The Homilies of Photius, Patriarch of Constantinople*, trans. by Cyril Mango, p. 77.

[46] Ibid., p. 76, according to Niketas Paphlagon, the *Brussels Chronicle* and the *Theophanes Continuatus*, *Chronographia* (Bonn).

toward the Christianization of these pagans. Byzantium was surrounded by numerous non-Christian peoples. It was far better to have them become friends of Byzantium, and thus avert future danger. To allow them to remain in darkness would only invite other political and ecclesiastical powers to establish their authority and leadership at Byzantium's borders. Hence, it was the Russian attack that prompted the Byzantines to renew relations with the Khazars, a Turkish people, in the south of Russia. An embassy, therefore, was sent, led by Constantine, who championed the cause of Orthodoxy in the face of Jewish and Islamic influences. The emperor said to Constantine, "Thou art aware of the empire's power and prestige. Go, then, with the esteem and aid of the emperor."

At the commencement of the mission, George was elected Bishop of Cherson. Constantine and Methodios, ca. 861, appeared on the peninsula.[47] They spent some time in the Crimea that they might learn the language of the people. Since the holy brothers were acquainted with the account of a local martyr, Saint Clement, Bishop of Rome,[48] who had suffered under Trajan (98-117), they made a diligent inquiry as to the whereabouts of his relics. It was exceedingly difficult to reconstruct the incidents and discover the locality, since successive barbarian invasions had swept over the land and all but wiped out the memory of it. Bishop George, at the brothers' prompting, traveled to the capital and made a report with the emperor and Patriarch Photios (858-867). He returned with clergy to Cherson, where they conducted entreaties and prayers. The relics of the saint were then made manifest in a wondrous manner. One account relates that the relics floated miraculously from the depths after much prayer. Many miracles of healing and release from demonic possession

---

[47] Chersonese Taurica or Chersonesus (known as Kherson in the Middle Ages and as Korsun in Slavic sources) had once been a Greek city and city-state in the southwestern part of the Crimea, near present-day Sevastopol (Sebastopolis) on the east coast of the Black Sea. Christianity had been established in Cherson by the beginning of the 4th C. At the end of the 4th C., the city became part of the Byzantine Empire. It went on to become the largest city on the northern coast of the Black Sea and an important center of Byzantine culture. It had been a place of exile for Pope Martin I and Emperor Justinian II. In the 8th C. , it was under Khazar rule. Theophilos, Theodora's husband, had established Byzantine rule, ca. 832, and created the *theme* of Klimata. From the 10th to the 12th C., it enjoyed great prosperity. At the end of the 10th C., Chersonese was captured and held briefly by the Kyivan Prince Volodymyr the Great. From that point and onward, Byzantine cultural influences entered Kyivan Rus through Chersonese. Ruins of the former city revealed over fifty Christian churches, palaces, and a theater seating over three thousand people. See *Oxford*, s.v. "Cherson"; and M. Labunka's article at http://www.encyclopediaofukraine.com/pages/C/H/Chersonese Taurica.htm.

[48] Saint Clement is commemorated by the holy Church on the 24th of November.

took place through the saint's relics. Another account relates that, after much prayer, Constantine was directed in a vision to a certain island lying off the coast. He obeyed and went. Both he and his companions dug in a mound and found the saint's relics, and even an anchor. The relics emitted a fragrance of unsurpassed sweetness.

The relics were later translated to Constantinople and were housed, successively, at the Church of Saint Sozon, then the Church of Saint Leontios, and, subsequently, in the Cathedral of the Holy Apostles. When Constantine and Methodios were in the capital, they received a portion of the relics of Saint Clement.[49] They were then summoned to Rome by Pope Nicholas I (858-867), but he died and left as his successor Hadrian II (also Adrian, 867-872). When the latter learned that the brothers bore with them the relics of Saint Clement of Rome, then, the pope, clergy, and people went forth in a solemn procession to meet the missionary brothers outside the city walls and escort them into the city. The relics of Saint Clement were deposited in his own basilica, after an absence of nearly eight centuries.

After the embassy's arrival in the Crimea, but before they reached Khazaria, two incidents disrupted the mission. The Khazars launched an attack on a Christian town. By the prayers of the holy Constantine, the expedition was deflected. Then a Hungarian horde, howling as wolves, assailed the envoys. They tried to slay Constantine even as he was engaged at prayer. As he continued constantly in his prayers, the Ugrian hordes were miraculously pacified and dispersed. After these two wondrous escapes, the Byzantine ambassadors continued their journey. Coming over the Sea of Azov and sailing up the river Don, they passed the Caspian Sea. They continued southward, through the Caspian Gate in the Caucasus.

Constantine engaged in theological talks that were lengthy. Methodios later translated the full text of the talks into Slavonic. The discussions addressed mostly the views of the Jews rather than the Muslims. Evidently, the *khagan* by then had embraced Judaism. After the discussions, two hundred people accepted the Orthodox Faith and received holy Baptism. The *khagan* and Khazar leaders were pleased with the discussions, believing Constantine to be a holy man. When the *khagan* wished to give Constantine and Methodios gifts, they refused to receive anything for the grace of God in preaching the Gospel among them. Constantine only asked for the release of two hundred Greek prisoners, which captives were immediately set free. The Orthodox delegation then headed home to Constantinople.

---

[49] Later, the precious skull of Saint Clement was translated to Kiev by the holy Prince Vladimir, the equal-to-the-apostles (d. 1015). The relic was placed in the Tithe Church, together with the relics of Saint Phoebus, where a side-chapel was built in the name of Saint Clement.

As they crossed the barren steppes of the Northern Caucuses, Constantine entreated God to send relief for a drought. The Lord hearkened to his entreaties. When the brothers returned again to Cherson, they were greeted most warmly by the Archbishop of Cherson. While at a banquet, Constantine predicted the coming death of the prelate. This event, indeed, happened soon thereafter.

The brothers did not spend all their time in Cherson, but they brought the word of God to the whole Tauric Peninsula. Their travels brought them into the city of the Phullae, where some unusual traditions were being observed along with Christian rituals. Although the people had previously converted to Christianity, still they had interspersed some of their pagan customs. One such tradition involved offering homage to a tree which they named Alexandron. They allowed none of their women to approach it. Constantine, seeing the errant nonsense that had crept in among them, preached a sermon. By God-inspired arguments, he persuaded them to cut down the tree and burn it. After they obeyed, he then gave them the Gospel. The leader of the Phullae kissed the sacred book. He was followed in this by his subordinates. Henceforth, they abandoned their ancestral deception completely and observed only the Christian Faith unadulterated.

While engaged in this missionary outreach, Constantine also undertook private study. One source says that while he was in the Crimea he learned three languages: Hebrew, Samaritan, and Russian. Another source says that he tarried awhile to learn the speech of the Crimeans. If Constantine already had a handle on the Slavonic tongue, then he certainly was looking to learn dialectal differences that existed between the spoken language of the Balkan Slavs and that of the Russian Slavs.

The brothers returned to Constantinople. Constantine went to the emperor and reported what the mission achieved in the Crimea and Khazaria. It was his intention, afterward, to settle in a dependency of the Church of the Holy Apostles. As for Methodios, he had no wish to remain in the capital. He longed to return to Mount Olympos. The emperor and the patriarch took counsel together, remarking over Methodios' noble and godly enterprises. They besought Methodios to accept consecration, saying, "A man such as thyself is needed for the Church. Consent to be consecrated as archbishop for a key place." Methodios, nonetheless, would not consent. They disregarded his pleas for retirement, appointing him as hegumen of the *stavropegial*[50] Monastery of Polychroniou.[51]

---

[50] Stavropegial monasteries acknowledged the jurisdiction of the patriarch and commemorated him in the diptychs.

[51] At this juncture, Theophylact of Ohrid in his Long Life of Clement of Ohrid opens

(continued...)

Great Moravia

However, greater labors lay in store for Constantine and Methodios. The light of the Gospel needed to be brought to those who sat in the darkness of ignorance and the shadow of death.[52] The Moravian Prince Rastislav sent an embassy to the capital to request missionaries from Emperor Michael. The Slavonic *vita* or *Life of Constantine* records these words of the prince: "Since our people rejected idolatry and came under Christian law, we have not had a teacher capable of explaining this Faith to us in our own tongue, so that other countries, seeing our example, might emulate us. Therefore, sire, send such a bishop and teacher; for it is from your majesty that the good law ever flows out to all the lands."[53]

In the Slavonic *Life of Methodios*, we read: "Rastislav and Sventopulk (Svatopluk) sent a letter from Moravia to Emperor Michael, saying: 'By the mercy of God we are well, and many Christian teachers have come to us from the Latins, the Greeks, and the Germans, who teach us various things. We Slavs are simple people. We have no one to instruct us in the truth and teach us knowledge. Therefore, sire, send us such a man that can teach us the full truth.'"[54] Great Moravia was the first known organized Slavic state in Central Europe, though its origins remain obscure and the location of its borders is still under discussion.[55] They requested that the missionaries and the clergy know the Slavonic language, so that the evangelical Faith could be established among

---

[51](...continued)
with a panegyric of Clement's teachers, Constantine-Kyril and Methodios. Theophylact also relates some details that are not found in either the *Vita Constantini* or the *Vita Methodii*. Theophylact mentions that Methodios "had previously made King Boris of the Bulgarians his spiritual child. The latter lived during the reign of Emperor Michael III of the Rhomaioi....Methodios continually lavished upon him the bounty of his words." No other early medieval source mentions this news. Saint Clement, in his encomium of Saint Kyril, written in Bulgaria, mentions nothing about it. Theophylact implies that Boris' Baptism and instruction took place before 863. See discussion in Dimitri Obolensky's "Theophylact of Ohrid," *Six Byzantine Portraits* (NY: Oxford University Press, 1988), pp. 63-65.

[52] Cf. Is. 9:2; Mt. 4:16; Lk. 1:79.

[53] *Life of Constantine*, Ch. 14, in F. Grivec and F. Tomsic, 95-143.

[54] *Life of Methodios*, Ch. 5, in Grivec-Tomsic, 147-167.

[55] Where was Great Moravia? Some suggest the upper reaches of Moravia, where the river flows through Moravia; from there, Great Moravia spreads toward Slovakia, Pannonia, southern Poland, Bohemia, and parts of eastern Germany. Another theory places it in the area of ancient Sirmium, where Slavonia is today. Yet another places it toward the vast plain of the river Tisza, which stretches from Eastern Hungary to western Romania. See Tachiaos, p. 57.

the Slavs in Moravia. By the gracious providence of God, Rastislav chose to turn to Byzantium to bring the true Orthodox Faith to his people.

Now Rastislav also possibly had apprehensions of the influence of the Frankish clergy. Politically, also, Rastislav may have desired to find in Byzantium an equal and opposite force or power against the possibility of being surrounded by Franks, Germans, and Bulgarians. Byzantium was pleased with the possibility of expanding her Orthodoxy and influence into this new and remote territory. This would certainly apply pressure to the Bulgars, who were wedged in the middle.

Though the letter was addressed to Emperor Michael, who can doubt that Patriarch Photios, whom Michael had as his advisor in all spiritual and ecclesiastical questions, had not himself selected the brothers as he had done for earlier missions? As we know, Constantine had been a pupil of Photios; he later became his colleague at the University of Constantinople, having been appointed Professor of Philosophy in the reign of Empress Theodora. He was, moreover, a close friend of Photios, according to the Roman Anastasius the Librarian.[56] Constantine had traveled with Photios, in 856, to the Crimea and Khazaria. In his return from this mission in 861, Constantine had his seat in the Church of the Holy Apostles, that is, he took up a professorial chair in the Patriarchal School, which operated on that church's premises.

In the case of Father Methodios, the fact that he was appointed hegumen of Polychroniou Monastery does not mean that he was friendly toward the deposed Patriarch Ignatius. Indeed, given the fact that his appointment was made during Photios' tenure as patriarch—an office obviously sanctioned by the patriarch—it seems likely that it was made precisely to mollify the monks who supported Ignatius and to change their sentiments. The appointment followed directly upon the two brothers' return from Khazaria and the Crimea, after Photios had offered Methodios an episcopal see which the latter had declined. It is clear from what has been said above that Photios must have been part of the deliberations concerning the mission to Central Europe.[57]

---

[56] "Epist. VII, to Pope Hadrian," *Monumenta Germaniae Historica*, p. 407.

[57] The fact that the name of Saint Photios is missing from the *Life of Constantine the Philosopher* is due to the hagiography being written in Rome shortly after Constantine-Cyril's death in 869 by a companion of his and of Methodios. Its purpose was to present clear evidence that Pope Hadrian approved the use of the Slavonic language in the Liturgy and thus forestall the charges being brought against Methodios. The *Life of Methodios* was written at Moravia, in 885, with the aim of persuading the ruler, Prince Svatopulk, who was both a Latinophile and a Germanophile, that the mission was the work of the emperor of Byzantium, and that those who reacted against it were therefore opposing the plans of the emperor. It would have been impossible, in the *Life*

(continued...)

Rastislav desired his country's Church to become independent of the ecclesiastical jurisdiction of Bavaria. German clergy came from a land that had vulturous territorial designs. Rastislav wished that the Church of Moravia should be raised to the rank of an episcopate. He needed at his side an independent Church leader that, of course, supported his own sovereignty. He asked the Byzantines, knowing they had no predatory plans over Moravia. As far as his southern border, he knew that the Byzantine emperor could apply pressure upon any rapacious Bulgars. Above all, he wanted a bishop familiar with Slavonic and a Bible in the Slavonic tongue spoken by Moravians.[58]

Emperor Michael sent for Constantine the Philosopher, who appeared before the imperial Senate. It should be noted that Constantine's health was flagging. After some talk about the Moravians' earnest appeal, the emperor said to Constantine, "I know that thou art yet weary from thy previous mission. But it is imperative that thou goest to Moravia; for no one else is capable of carrying out this task." Constantine agreed but expressed one condition, "Sire, I will go if they have letters for their language." The emperor remarked, "Indeed, my grandfather and my father[59] and many others have sought the Slavonic alphabet, but not one of them found it. How, then, shall I find it?" The philosopher answered, "How can I teach them? It would be like writing upon water. If I should invent letters myself, I fear that I may be called a false teacher." Michael and Caesar Bardas (the emperor's maternal uncle) replied,

---

[57](...continued)
of Constantine, to make much of Photios' role. Reference to his part in events would have undermined the whole purpose of the work; for Photios was hated in Rome and in the west generally, and had now been deposed in the east. Although Photios was returned to the patriarchal throne and had mended his differences with Rome, he still had not done so with the Germans who were continuing to promote the *Filioque*. It would, therefore, have been most unwise to present Photios as the person behind the brothers' mission. It is for the same reason that no mention is made of Photios' role in Constantine-Cyril's mission to the Caliphate, although they probably went together, the one being responsible for religious and the other for civil affairs. In this context, too, such a reference would have been seen in the west as provocative. See the following article of Panayiotis Christou: "Who Sent Cyril and Methodius into Central Europe, the Emperor or the Patriarch?" http://www.myriobiblos.gr/texts/english/christou_kyrmeth. html.

[58] Tachiaos, p. 67.

[59] Michael III is referring to his grandfather, Michael II (820-829), and his father, Theophilos (929-842). There is no historical record extant that these former emperors sought a Slavonic alphabet. Either the Byzantines had the matter investigated and found no alphabet or they had composed one for the Slavs that did not succeed. Tachiaos, p. 69.

"If thou dost desire it, God shall grant it to thee; for He gives to all those who ask with faith and He opens up to those who knock."[60]

Saints Methodios and Kyril

The Alphabet

Constantine agreed to undertake the emperor's commission. He first fetched his elder brother, Methodios, and then those associates who were of the same spirit as themselves.[61] They all applied themselves to prayer. The brothers were firm in the hope of obtaining God's blessing. Constantine fasted strictly for forty days, praying very earnestly. Then, immuring himself in his cell with a few disciples, those with whom he was to share his future apostolic journey, he set himself to the task of inventing an alphabet, that the Slavic people might retain the word of God written down for them, as teaching by word of mouth alone could be quickly forgotten or corrupted. God, verily, right soon, revealed the Slavic script to the Philosopher. Once the letters were constructed, written words were formed.[62] Constantine began to write the first words, taken from the Gospel: "In the beginning was the Logos, and the Logos was with God, and the Logos was God [Jn.

[60] Cf. Mt. 7:7; Lk. 11:9.

[61] The associates may have been Greek speakers of Slavic and Slavic speakers of Greek, but they were all under the guidance of the patriarchal official, professor, diplomat, and linguist, Constantine the Philosopher. Was a rough-and-ready alphabet by the brothers available from the time they were on Mount Olympos in Bithynia, a province with a heavy Slav presence? Was the translating continued at Polychroniou Monastery, which the author of the *Life of Methodios* speaks of in the present tense that the work was proceeding? A number of Greek words passed untranslated into the Old Slavonic texts. These Greek words do not attest the influence of northern Greek idioms, as one might expect from the Thessalonian brothers, but rather reflect the phonetic characteristics of Greek idioms of Asia Minor. Were some of the associate translators from Asia Minor? When Methodios served as *archon* or *comes*, was it in Bithynia of the Opsikion *theme*? Was the rough-and-ready alphabet used on the mission to the Khazars where Constantine knew he would encounter Russians? Tachiaos, pp. 69, 70.

[62] *Life of Methodios*, Ch. 6; "Saints Kyril and Methody, Evangelizers of the Slavs," p. 3.

1:1]," and the rest.[63] This account of the creation of the alphabet is similar to that given in the *Life of Methodios*. When this great work was finished, in 862, the whole ecclesiastical council held a general service of thanksgiving (*moleiben*) to glorify God.

The script invented was the so-called Glagolithic[64] or Cyrillic alphabet. Constantine then translated the Bible into Slavonic, using the Macedonian-Slavonic dialect. The two brothers also brought the divine Liturgy, in the Slavonic tongue, into Moravian. Through these methods, their mission was assured of success.[65] Thus, the Greek missionaries did not have as their purpose the changing of the ethnic consciousness of the people, but ushering in their Christianization. As a result of the works of the two brothers, the internal structure of the state of Great Moravia and the country's position among nations that were culturally advanced were transformed in every sphere.

All the evidence given leaves us no doubt that Constantine-Kyril created the Slavic alphabet with divine enlightenment. It was a proper alphabet that coped with the whole phonetic range of the Slavonic tongue. Apart from the alphabet, however, the hardest task facing Constantine's team was to create a scholarly language for the simple and unsophisticated tongue of the Slavs, for they lacked one. Terminology, both theological and ecclesiastical, was required for the translations of basic books for the divine offices and instruction. Their unwritten and underdeveloped language simply did not have all the words and expressions needed to convey the full spectrum of thought in such books. "A people without spiritual cultivation or education naturally lacked abstract concepts too. Such were the concepts that needed to be created in the Slavonic tongue, so that they would then pass from Greek into Slavic. There lay before them a monumental task. The knowledge and experience of the two brothers were vital to it. In order to render the Gospel in Slavic, it was necessary to build up an enormous stock of abstract nouns and adjectives, and even compound words, none of which existed in Slavic. These words and concepts came straight out of molds furnished by the rich Greek language, which had been worked on for centuries by scholars and intellectuals. In this way, limitless wealth flowed forth from the treasure house of the Greek language and was offered to the Slavic world as a permanent, sacred gift. Transcending time, it stamped its presence forever on the Slavic language, which, alive and flexible as it was, now acquired greater plasticity and movement from this benevolent influence, as well as sufficient depth to become a highly expressive organ.

[63] *Life of Constantine*, loc. cit.

[64] Glagolitic (Glagolithic) script, which comes from the Slavonic word *glagol*, meaning "verb."

[65] George Ostrogorsky, *History of the Byzantine State*, trans. from the German by Joan Hussey (NJ: Rutgers University Press, 1957), pp. 203, 204.

Constantine-Kyril, then, did not simply create an alphabet, but shaped the Slavic language in such a way as to enable it to assimilate the conceptual wealth of the Greek language; and this was much more important than devising the alphabet. Thus formed, the Slavic language became the basis for the creation of a self-sufficient Slavic learned culture; and it is precisely here that the significance of Kyril and Methodios' historic work may be found."[66]

The first book Constantine translated was the *Evangelion*, the daily and festal Gospel pericopes read in Church services. He also wrote an introduction with an address—not so much to the Slavs as to the imperial and patriarchal authorities. "The words," Constantine wrote, "were not rendered blindly with their Slavic equivalents; for it was not the words that we required, but their meaning. For this reason, wherever the meaning in both Greek and Slavic chanced to coincide, we used the same word to translate it; but where the expression was longer or caused the meaning to be lost, we did not forsake the meaning, but rendered it with another word. When translated into another tongue, Greek cannot always be rendered in the same words, and this is true of all the languages into which it is translated. It frequently happens that a word which is elegant in one language is not so in another, and a word which is impressive in the one is not in the other, and a word which is of capital significance in the one is not in the other....Thus, it is not always possible to follow the Greek expression, but what must be preserved is the meaning."[67]

The missionaries, thereupon, left for Great Moravia in the spring of 863, bearing gifts and an epistle from Emperor Michael III to Prince Rastislav. Here is a summary of this letter given in the *Life of Constantine*: Michael assured Rastislav and the Moravians that God, seeing his faith, "has now, in our time, revealed letters in your tongue, a thing which has not happened for a long time, but only in ancient days, so that you may be included among the great nations which praise God in their own tongue. Moreover, we are sending you the one to whom He has revealed them, a virtuous and devout man and a most learned philosopher. Therefore, accept a gift greater and more valuable than gold and silver and precious stones and all transient riches."[68]

The holy brothers, together with Saint Photios and Caesar Bardas, share the credit for the conversion of the Slavs to Orthodoxy. While the Byzantine missionaries were received with great honor, Constantine and Methodios' labors were not without temptations among their new spiritual children. Constantine immediately set about translating the daily Church services and Liturgy into the Slavic tongue. This was done in order to replace the Latin offices. Rastislav had selected a number of men to study, under the

---

[66] Tachiaos, p. 73.

[67] *Life of Constantine*, Ch. 14; Tachiaos, 75.

[68] Tachiaos, loc. cit.

brothers, the Slavic script. Those who completed the program were to eventually succeed the Latin clergy. One student who excelled from the start was Gorazd. We shall speak of him later.

German Interference

Meanwhile, the German clergy within Moravia, jealous of the Byzantine missionaries, proved to be adversaries. Among the many disputes, two points stand out. First, the Germans were teaching the Moravians obsolete cosmographic and anthropological doctrines.[69] Second, the Germans promulgated a heretical theory. They said that there were only three sanctified languages in which the name of God ought to be praised and the Eucharist celebrated. They were the three languages used for Pilate's placard, atop the Cross of Christ: Hebrew, Greek, and Latin.[70] This became the most serious cause of controversy, known as the doctrine of Trilingualism (Triglossites), between the Germans and the two Greek brothers. Although it had been condemned in the west by Church councils, still the German clergy held fast to it. Naturally, Slavonic would then be disqualified as a sacred language. Constantine and Methodios comprehended the seriousness of German claims against their work; nevertheless, the brothers persisted. The fact that they had with them the relics of Saint Clement, whom they recovered in the Crimea, was of no small moment to the Moravians. They built a church, "Klimentka," to the hieromartyr, east of Velehrad, where they treasured the relics.

Pannonia and Venice

The disciples of Constantine and Methodios needed to be ordained to the clergy. In this way the foundations of an independent Moravian Church could be realized. After more than three years, the two brothers, with the ordinands, set off for Venice, a port with constant links to Constantinople.[71] The indefatigable brothers now created the basis of Slavonic education that would replace Latin in the Church of Moravia. On their way to the Italian port, they needed to pass through Slav-populated Pannonia,[72] under the archdiocese of Salzburg, with German clergy, headed by a protopresbyter. Prince Kocel (Kotsel) welcomed the brothers and their Slavic letters. The prince learned them and had some fifty pupils tutored also.[73]

---

[69] Ibid., 77.

[70] Cf. Lk. 23:38; Jn. 19:20.

[71] The land route to Constantinople would have been dangerous, due to the poor relations between the Rhomaioi (Byzantines) and the Bulgars. They went via Venice in order to journey by sea.

[72] Pannonia then covered the western part of present-day Hungary, eastern Austria, and northern Yugoslavia.

[73] *Life of Constantine*, Ch. 15.

The tireless new apostle, Constantine, out of love for his neighbor, translated the book of Psalms, and other portions of the Bible, and all the Church services. Again, as with the Khazars, Constantine and Methodios would take no gifts and accept no acknowledgment of their labors. They only besought Prince Kocel to release nine hundred captives. When Constantine imparted this precious gift, that is, the word of God, to the Slavic people in their own tongue, he told them, in his preface in the book of the Gospels: "O Slavic peoples, hear ye the word which feeds the soul of man, the word which strengthens the heart and mind."[74]

It is also important to note that the prince was interested not only in neighboring Moravia's educational program but also in her plans to create an independent Church. He, too, desired Slavonic letters and a Church free of the German stranglehold. Meanwhile, Protopresbyter Richbald returned to Salzburg, complaining that Methodios arrogantly displaced Latin with Slavic letters, and that he degraded Latin in the eyes of the Pannonians. Upon the brothers' arrival in Venice, they became the topic of a lively controversy initiated by complaints from Latin clergy. The Latin bishops, priests, and monks descended upon Constantine as crows upon a hawk. They advocated Trilingualism, saying, "Tell us, O man, how is it that thou hast created a script for the Slavs and dost teach it to them? What thou hast invented is a script such as none other—whether apostle, or pope, or even Gregory the Theologian or Jerome or Augustine—has founded. We know of only three tongues in which is meet to offer praise to God in writing: Hebrew, Greek, and Latin."[75] Now the doctrine of Trilingualism was unknown in Byzantium, but this body of Latin ecclesiastical authority sought to undo the Byzantine mission.

Part of Constantine's defense has been left to us. It was originally written in Greek and then translated into Slavic. "Does the rain," he began, "not fall equally upon all people? Does the sun not shine for all? Do we not all breathe the air in equal measure? Wherefore, then, are you not ashamed to recognize but three tongues and command the other nations and races to be blind and deaf? Will you say that God is weak, as though He were unable to bestow this script? Will you say that God is jealous, that He does not wish to bestow it? For we know many peoples who have a script and give glory to God, each in its own tongue. It is known that such are the Armenians, Persians, Abasgians, Iberians, Sogdi, Goths, Avars, Turks, Khazars, Arabs, Egyptians, Syrians, and many others besides."[76] Constantine then cited a lengthy list of verses from the sacred Scriptures, defending the right of peoples to use their own language to worship God. He especially noted the passage describing how

[74] "Saints Kyril and Methody, Evangelizers of the Slavs," p. 4.

[75] *Life of Constantine*, Ch. 16; Tachiaos, p. 82.

[76] *Life of Constantine*, loc. cit.

the gift of tongues was bestowed upon the apostles at Pentecost,[77] a sign of God's blessing upon all human languages, and a sign that the Gospel was to be preached in every tongue.[78]

Rome

Now Pope Nicholas learned of the heated debate in Venice. Such an important issue and its outcome, he felt, needed to be under Rome's supervision. Nicholas invited them to Rome, and Constantine and Methodios were pleased to defend their views before the west's ultimate Church authority.[79] By the time the brothers arrived in Rome, Nicholas had reposed in November of 867. His successor, Pope Hadrian II, was installed on the 14th of December, in the same year. Hadrian, too, was more than happy to intervene. He welcomed the brothers cordially. The brothers were carrying with them the relics of Saint Clement of Rome, which they had transferred from the Crimea. When the pope learned of this, the brothers were assured of a triumphal welcome. The reception was magnificent. The pope and his retinue came forth with tapers and candles to meet the relics and their bearers at the gates of the city. The populace was ecstatic and many miracles were wrought. Afterward, the pope happily took the Slavic books from the brothers and placed them upon the altar. He consecrated them, thus signifying his approval. Hadrian also participated in a Liturgy in which the Slavic books were utilized. Rome, consequently, helped contain those who opposed the Slavic books as contemptible, profane, and blasphemous. The pope's actions and authority were to resolve the issue decisively. Hadrian also ordained Father Methodios as a priest.[80] Bishop Formosus of Porto and Bishop Gauderich of Velletri were charged with the ordination of the brothers' disciples; three pupils became priests and two became lectors.[81] One of the disciples was Clement who was ordained to the

---

[77] Cf. Acts 2:4-6.

[78] "Saints Kyril and Methody, Evangelizers of the Slavs," p. 5.

[79] The pope was informed about Constantine. It was the pope who sent and asked for him. This means that Constantine had not originally intended to go to Rome, but did so at the pope's invitation. When he reached Rome, however, he was received not by Nicholas, but by his successor, Hadrian II, who was well disposed toward him. Had it not been for the invitation, he would have gone to Constantinople. Indeed, what the two brothers failed to do then, Methodius did alone fifteen years later when Photius was again patriarch. See P. Christou, loc. cit. at the http://www.myriobiblos.

[80] The Slavonic hymns of the day, in the same Orthros Canon, indicate that Constantine-Kyril received the rank of priest just before devising the alphabet [Odes Five and Eight].

[81] "These two bishops were deliberately selected: Formosus had been involved in Bulgarian ecclesiastical affairs and had been sent to Bulgaria by the pope as apostolic legate in 864,while Gauderich was an exceptionally learned prelate with a particular

(continued...)

priesthood. He had been with the brothers in Moravia and supported their efforts to provide the Moravians with a complete cycle of liturgical offices in Slavonic translation. He also assisted in the training of a local Slav-speaking clergy. He was also on hand to repel the Frankish assaults on the Byzantine mission. Such were his years of apprenticeship.[82]

The new priests and lectors were called upon to take part in a Liturgy in the Slavic language in the Basilica of Saint Peter. In the days which followed, they also celebrated in the Churches of Saint Petronila and Saint Andrew and, subsequently, in the Church of Saint Paul the Apostle *extra muros*, where they concelebrated with Bishop Arsenius and Anastasius Bibliothecarius in a Slavic vigil over the saint's tomb.[83] The common intellectual interests of Anastasius and Constantine ushered in a close friendship. Anastasius called him "Constantine the Philosopher, a most holy man" and "Constantine the Philosopher from Thessalonike, a man with an apostolic life."

Thus, the brothers' visit resulted in the triumph of the Slavic script. Papal sanction not only made Slavic a liturgical language but also made Rome, and no longer Byzantium alone, a supporter and benefactor of national languages in Church liturgical life. Rome also gained the favor of the Slavic world by granting their language international recognition, something that the sees of Salzburg and Bavaria had begrudged them. Constantine and Methodios also gained a higher profile among the Slavs, since the brothers had championed the Slavic cause for recognition and ecclesiastical integrity. However, the pope did not want to give unnecessary offense to the powerful Germans who could apply an uncomfortable level of pressure. Hadrian, therefore, refrained from ordaining a bishop and granting the Moravians independence.

---

[81](...continued)
devotion to Saint Clement. It was this latter sentiment that made him give Anastasius Bibliothecarius the task of collecting information about the discovery of the saint's relics. This, ultimately, led to the composition of the *Legenda Italica*, that valuable Latin source about Cyril and Methodius." Tachiaos, p. 85; F. Dvornik, *Les légendes de Constantin et de Méthode vues de Byzance* (Prague, 1933), pp. 195, 196.

[82] D. Obolensky, "Clement of Ohrid," *Six Byzantine Portraits*, p. 16.

[83] "Once again, these two clerics were carefully selected. Arsenius, Bishop of Orte, was a member of a seven-man permanent papal advisory committee, which later became the College of Cardinals. Anastasius Bibliothecarius was Bishop Arsenius' nephew and supervisor of the Papal Secretariat and Archive. He was an exceptionally learned man with an excellent command of the Greek language, which tongue he admired greatly. He was also responsible for the pope's official correspondence with the Byzantine Imperial and Patriarchal Secretariats. As a scholar, Anastasius was active in the literary sphere, producing notable Latin translations of Greek historical and hagiological works." Tachiaos, loc. cit.

The Tonsure of Saint Kyril and His Repose

While in Rome, the two brothers and their associates sojourned in one of the city's Greek monasteries. There were many such Greek monastic houses and churches, such as the Church of Santa Maria in *Cosmedin*. They were located around the foot of the Palatine and Aventine Hills. The Greek monastics abiding in Rome were active in Church affairs. Constantine, at that time, fell ill. He had become exhausted from continual traveling and hard work. He perceived that his end had drawn nigh and wrote a poem: "Never more shall I be the servant of either emperor or any other on this earth, only of almighty God have I been and shall be forevermore." Constantine then asked that he receive the monastic tonsure before his death. Upon being clothed with the Great Schema by Pope Hadrian, he was renamed Kyril. He tarried another fifty days, humbly uttering this final prayer with tears: "Lord, ...hearken to my prayer and guard Thy faithful flock that Thou hast entrusted to me, Thy vile and unworthy servant; and do Thou deliver it from all profane and heathen wickedness, as well as from all loose and blasphemous language that speaks injuriously of Thee."[84] He also implored God to destroy the heresy of Trilingualism, which he believed to be the weapon of those against the spiritual freedom of the Slavs.

Just before his departure from this earthly sphere, he spoke to his brother and said, "Thou knowest, O brother, that we have been as a contented yoke of oxen plowing the same furrow; but now I am fallen in the harness, having early finished my day in the field. I know that thou lovest the holy Mountain [that is, Olympos], yet thou mayest not forsake thy teaching for the Mountain's sake; for it is through this teaching, more than anything else, that thou shalt be saved."[85] Father Kyril then exchanged the final kiss of love and forgiveness with Father Methodios and his associates. He, thereupon, reposed in a Greek monastery at Rome on the 14th of February, in the year 869. He was about forty-two years of age.

Hadrian commanded that all in Rome, both Greeks and Romans, were to assemble. The faithful bore tapers and candles, as they chanted hymns and escorted the body. The bishop of Rome, with all the prelates and dignitaries of the western capital, was present. The attendance and reverence at the funeral were such that one would have thought it was for the pope himself. Father Methodios told Hadrian that their mother had made them promise that whosoever should repose first, the surviving brother would return the relics to the monastery where they had lived together on Mount Olympos. The pope

---

[84] *Life of Constantine*, Ch. 18; "Saints Kyril and Methody, Evangelizers of the Slavs," p. 6.

[85] *Life of Methodios*, Ch. 7; "Saints Kyril and Methody, Evangelizers of the Slavs," loc. cit.

respected Methodios' promise to his mother.[86] Hadrian, therefore, charged that the body be placed in a coffin, which was sealed with iron nails. The newly reposed remained interred for seven whole days. Nonetheless, the bishops at Rome protested. "He reposed in Rome," said they, "and in Rome should he be buried." Hadrian fell in with their plan. Hadrian had the holy Kyril buried in his own tomb in the Basilica of Saint Peter. Father Methodios, for his part, thought that the Church of Saint Clement would be the next best place after Bithynian Olympos. Again there was opposition, but Father Methodios pleaded for the church which housed the relics he and his brother had recovered. The venerable Kyril was finally laid to rest in the Church of Saint Clement. Thus, his reliquary was laid in the tomb, on the right-hand side of the sanctuary, in the Church of Saint Clement.[87] Many miracles were wrought at his tomb. The man of God, forthwith, was venerated as a saint. An icon, also, was immediately painted and placed upon his tomb.[88] A fragment of the relic is now at the Church of Saints Kyril and Methodios in Thessalonike.

An Archbishop and Teacher for the Slavic Peoples

Now Prince Kocel, the ruler of Pannonia, appealed to the pope to return Father Methodios back to his land. After this took place, Kocel, at length, returned Father Methodios to Rome for the purpose of having him consecrated as a bishop. A papal bull was dispatched, addressed to Rastislav of Moravia, his nephew Sventopulk of Nitra, and Kocel of Pannonia.[89] They were informed that Methodios was to become not only the instructor of the Pannonians but even of all the Slavic lands. The pope wrote: "Methodios is sent to the Slavs by God and by the first apostle, Peter, keeper of the keys of the kingdom of the heavens." The official letter still survives, wherein it is written: "You did not seek a teacher from this pontifical seat alone, but, since we ourselves were not yet ready, you asked the most revered Emperor Michael to send you the blessed Constantine the Philosopher and his brother. Learning that your countries are under the jurisdiction of the apostolic throne, these men

[86] One source says that Saint Methodios was desirous "to carry the relics back to Salonika," and not Olympos. "Saints Kyril and Methody, Evangelizers of the Slavs," loc. cit.

[87] *Life of Constantine*, loc. cit.

[88] In 1677, the Church of Saint Clement came under the control of Irish Dominican monks. In 1798, during the French occupation, Saint Kyril's relics disappeared. A small portion of the relics, however, was in the possession of the noble Italian Andici-Mattei family that had rescued other relics. In 1963, Princess Andici-Mattei and other family members gifted the fragment to Pope Paul VI. In 1976, the same pope offered the precious relic to the birthplace of the saint, Thessalonike, where a newly built church to the brothers was constructed. Tachiaos, p. 91.

[89] *Life of Methodios*, Ch. 8.

in no wise transgressed the laws, but came to us, bringing with them the sacred relics of Saint Clement." The pope also informed the Slavic princes that he was most pleased to be sending them Methodios, now an ordained priest, and his followers that "they might teach you, as you have asked, rendering the books in your language, in complete accordance with your Church rite, with the divine Liturgy and the Church services and Baptism, as the Philosopher Constantine instituted them."[90]

The venerable Methodios was authorized by the pope to educate other teachers. As a concession to the German clergy, the pope instructed Methodios to have the Epistle and Gospel Readings, in the divine offices, first read in Latin and then in Slavonic. The pope also issued a stern condemnation against those who would corrupt the Slavs by defiling the books of their language. As we can see, the pope wished to establish jurisdiction over the western Slavic world and to diminish the roles of the archbishops of Salzburg and Regensburg.[91]

Kocel, after deliberations, sent Methodios back to Rome with a twenty-member embassy. Father Methodios was consecrated bishop on the throne of the holy Apostle Andronikos.[92] The see of Archbishop Methodios was Sirmium (present-day Sremska Mitrovica), northwest of Belgrade. Thus, Methodios became a papal legate over the whole of Moravia and Pannonia, that is, both countries. The pope desired to restrict the German clergy and avoid a national Slavic Church.

In early 870, Sventopulk had become a vassal of the Germans and delivered up his uncle, Rastislav, to them. Rastislav was blinded and, thus, incapacitated for rule. The Germans, predictably, moved into Moravia.

---

[90] Tachiaos, p. 94.

[91] Methodios was compelled to accept consecration. Many power-loving Latin teachers were entering the missionary field where he and his brother had labored. By receiving consecration at the hands of the pope, who was still united with the holy Church, it was thought that by obtaining letters from Rome and securing authority from the west, these foreign and non-Orthodox teachers—especially from Germany—might be curtailed from entering Slavic countries. Moreover, Methodios felt it important to preserve Slavic history, culture, and future identity. "Saints Kyril and Methody, Evangelizers of the Slavs," loc. cit.

[92] Apostle Andronikos, one of the Seventy (commemorated on the 4th of January and the 17th of May), was a kinsman of the Apostle Paul [Rom. 16:17]. He is remembered with Saint Junia. Andronikos was made Bishop of Pannonia, where he preached throughout the land. With Junia, he brought many to the knowledge of the truth in Christ. Both of these apostles wrought many miracles, expelling both demons and diseases. Both suffered for Christ and received the crowns of apostleship and of martyrdom. Their precious relics were also found in the excavations in Evgenios (commemorated on the 2nd of February).

Archbishop Methodios was summoned to their court, at which King Louis the German was present. The holy man was accused of usurping episcopal rights in another's see—in this case, the Archbishop of Bavaria. Methodios was subjected to false charges and threats. One German bishop, named Hermanrich, tried to lash him with a whip but he was restrained by his cohorts. Methodios affirmed his innocence. "Under no circumstances," he said, "have I entered another's province. The diocese which I administer, appointed by the successor of Saint Peter, is under the jurisdiction of Rome." As a result of this affair, the Germans were now in conflict with the pope.

Saints Methodios and Kyril

Methodios was innocent and not in violation of any canons. The German court, nevertheless, exiled him in Swabia (Souabe) of southwestern Germany. It is believed that he was detained at a monastery in Ellwangen. He spent two years confined. It is suggested that he suffered punishment under Bishop Hermanrich who was put in charge of Methodios. The holy archbishop attempted to communicate with Rome. The messenger to the pope was waylaid and slain by the Germans. At length, Hadrian reposed toward the close of the year 872. He never learned of Methodios' imprisonment. His successor, John VIII, only learned of it after a significant delay. But as soon as he heard the report that Methodios had been immured, he wrote the German King Louis and demanded Methodios' immediate release. He, furthermore, suspended the bishops who sat in judgment of Methodios and sentenced him. None were allowed to officiate until Archbishop Methodios was released. The pope deemed the Germans' conduct reprehensible and an utter disregard of Rome's sovereignty. The Bavarian bishops were not about to challenge Rome. They released Methodios in the spring of 873. In their resentment, they threatened Kocel if he accepted Methodios. The holy archbishop left for Moravia, by avoiding going through Bavaria. He tarried for some time at the Reichenau Monastery. There is extant a Greek manuscript, bearing his illustrious name, together with his associates, Leo, Ignatios, Joachim, Symeon, and Dragain. Evidently, the blessed archbishop was not alone in exile.[93]

Methodios arrived in Moravia that spring. He found that the Moravians had driven out the Germans and the German clergy from Moravia. King Louis was compelled to sign a peace treaty with the Moravians, but he sent back his German clergy who reinstated Latin in the Church services. While the inconstant Prince Sventopulk only attended services when the Germans were serving, still he did not thwart Methodios and his activities. Sventopulk extended his territory into the upper basin of the river Visla in Poland by the capital Cracow. Methodios already urged the ruler of that land to quit persecuting the Christians and receive Baptism lest he lose all. This indeed came to pass.

Methodios' time in Moravia proved fruitful. Based on his literary activity in Slavic, it is plain that he possessed a better command of Slavic than his younger brother. This, of course, may be due to the time that he had lived among them and heard it spoken daily, before taking the monastic tonsure. He certainly had a feeling for their language and understood all its features. Kyril, however, the golden clarion of theology, excelled in those cases requiring specific theological knowledge and the ability to translate doctrinal concepts into Slavic. Methodios, with unity of spirit, aided his brother with prayers and signs. Methodios appears to have addressed problems with organization and administration in the Church, which he handled well. But he already had previous legal and administrative training, which served him well then and at this point in his life. Skilled Slavicists studying Methodios' work commend him unequivocally for having an excellent command of the Slavic language. Although there are times that he transferred the Greek mode of expression into Slavic, since the Slavic language did not have the needed sophistication, he is clearly comfortable with Slavic vocabulary and concepts. This is especially evident in his hortatory document addressed to the ruler of Great Moravia. He also composed the *Law for the Adjudication of the People*, based on the *Ecloga* ("Selection of the Laws") of the Isaurians. Methodios proves by his writing that he is a consummate legislator. He significantly contributed to the improved organization of the state of Great Moravia by transposing Byzantine principles of law.[94]

The German clergy campaigned against Methodios. They never relaxed for a moment. Pressure was put on Sventopulk, while attempts to slander the man of God's name in Rome were relentless. As Methodios endured the false witnesses and calumniators, he rejoiced that God, in His mercy, had granted

---

[93] Tachiaos, p. 96.

[94] Ibid., p. 98.

His servant the privilege of suffering in likeness of Christ.[95] Sventopulk, influenced by the German priest named Wiching, sent a Venetian clergymen, named John, to request a solution from John VIII. The pope, consequently, summoned Methodios.[96] This took place in 879. Inexplicably the pope remonstrated with Methodios for celebrating the Liturgy in the "barbaric Slavic tongue." Methodios was told to use either Greek or Latin, but that he was free to preach in Slavonic. Methodios was perplexed but understood that the reversal in papal policy was due to difficult relations between the pope and the Germans. When Methodios came to Rome, Wiching arrived simultaneously and plotted against the venerable archbishop. Since the German priest presumed that he had undone Methodios at Rome, he raced back to Moravia to boast that Methodios was to be condemned. While Wiching was absent from Rome, Methodios took the opportunity to speak with the pope. After Methodios explained everything and removed any doubts in the pope's mind, papal policy returned to its former and proper position. But Wiching had created an uncongenial atmosphere against Methodios. Even though Wiching had German supporters for Trilingualism, Methodios had the numberless Slav populace behind him. The people were in favor of their archbishop who brought them religious and spiritual freedom, self-determination, and autonomy. When the archbishop returned in June of 880, he carried with him an epistle from John VIII to Sventopulk. Wiching and those with him smugly thought the letter condemned Methodios. Much to their surprise, when the letter was read before the assembled populace, they heard that Rome had resumed her initial stance. The Slavic Liturgy and the reading of the Scriptures in Slavic were reinstated. "The Slavic language," wrote the pope, "is not less acceptable than Hebrew, Greek, and Latin." Thus, the Germans were defeated.

Wiching would not accept the papal decision. He persuaded his supporters of the necessity to keep fighting Methodios and to make a new appeal to the pope. Accusations were hurled again at the holy man, so that Methodios needed to defend himself in writing. John VIII summoned the archbishop to Rome again. But soon thereafter Methodios repaired to Constantinople.[97] What took place on that journey has not been left to us. We

---

[95] "Saints Kyril and Methody, Evangelizers of the Slavs," p. 7.

[96] It was the pope's intention to use Saint Methody's obedience to his summons as a demonstration of papal overlordship. After questioning the saint concerning the orthodoxy of his teaching, the pope let him go, with a commendation. Ibid.

[97] Elsewhere, it is written: "When the enemies of the great evangelizer saw that they had failed against him at Rome, they next accused him at Constantinople. Indeed, now the venerable old bishop had to make his way to Constantinople, to defend not only the work of his glorious brother and himself but also the Slavonic Church. But the saint's

(continued...)

can confidently surmise, nevertheless, that Methodios wished to inform Emperor Basil I and Patriarch Photios about what was transpiring inside Moravia. Doubtless, he spoke to them of German aggression and animosity and of papal hesitation and equivocation. Both Basil I and Photios, with love and honor, welcomed Archbishop Methodios heartily. The emperor refused Methodios nothing and gave him gifts and assurances. After all, the Moravian mission and the creation of Slavic script were Byzantine projects. It should be noted that relations between Photios and Rome were then cordial. The pope's relations with the Germans were in turmoil.

From the evidence, it appears that Methodios went to Constantinople with a large retinue and many manuscripts translated into Slavic. The emperor was so impressed that he retained some of the archbishop's party, namely one priest and one deacon. He also kept some of the Slavic books. It is likely that Basil was planning a new missionary project. The manna of the divinely wise teaching in the Slavic language could now feed the Slavic peoples who were perishing out of hunger for the word of God. When it was all said and done, it was clear that Methodios felt he was at home and in unity with the Mother Church of Constantinople.[98]

While Saint Methodios was received very cordially by Saint Photios in 882, Photios himself was busy helping the Slavs. He established a school for Slavonic studies, which became a refuge for Slavonic priests who had been sold into slavery by a hostile prince and then freed by the Venetians. In fact, Saint Photios even maintained the Institute for Slavonic Studies in Thessalonike, to educate the Byzantines in the ways and culture of the Slavic people.

The much-suffering Methodios set out for his flock once more. Methodios returned to Moravia with an iron will. Again the people of Pannonia and Moravia were elated to see their beloved shepherd. The triumphs of Saint Methodios helped to raise the morale and energy of his disciples, who were continually preaching and translating. His attitude toward German harassment was impassible. He concentrated on his translations and writings that he might leave the Moravians a heritage in their own language, a gift from Byzantium. In the few remaining years of his life, until his repose in 885, two of his priests, who knew tachygraphy or stenography, assisted him. His biographer notes that, in six months, Methodios translated all the Scriptures save the Book of Maccabees. He also prepared the *Nomokanon*, and translated *Books of the*

[97](...continued)
enemies, inspired by the demon of envy, failed again. The saint received a warm welcome in the imperial city, from patriarch and emperor alike. The patriarch happily received the books in the Slavonic language and hastened to put them to use in teaching the Bulgarians." "Saints Kyril and Methody, Evangelizers of the Slavs," loc. cit.

[98] Tachiaos, 101.

Fathers. The latter title was a collection of writings by the holy Church fathers. Just before the day of the Feast of Saint Demetrios of Thessalonike, Methodios completed his translation of the Old Testament. Then, on the day of the patron saint of his native city, he conducted a great service of thanksgiving to God and a celebration with all the services being sung in Slavonic. As a true son of Thessalonike, he also introduced a deep veneration for his city's patron, that is, Saint Demetrios of Thessalonike, so that he left the Moravians a splendid canon to the martyr.

Now Saint Methodios perceived his earthly sojourn was coming to an end. He was constrained to anathematize Wiching who had been preaching heretical doctrines. Wiching was advocating the *Filioque*, that is to say, that the Holy Spirit proceeded not only from God the Father but also from the Son. Both Sventopulk and the rational flock of Christ approved of the archbishop's action.

During sixteen years of episcopal service, Methodios traveled throughout the Slavic provinces, disseminating the Faith. Meanwhile, as German warriors and Latin monks raged through Europe together, with fire and sword, the holy archbishop labored hither and thither, in small communities, establishing his disciples as teachers and pastors.[99]

The Repose of Saint Methodios

But overwork, afflictions, imprisonment, persecutions, and tribulations took their toll. The archbishop chose his Moravian disciple Gorazd as his successor, a man most competent in both Greek and Latin. Thereafter, Methodios' repose came quickly on Palm Sunday in the year 885. As the blessed man was entering church to celebrate the Liturgy, he suddenly felt unwell. He uttered a blessing over the emperor, then one over Sventopulk, followed by the clergy and the faithful. Three days after this incident, on the 6th of April, he reposed in the Lord. There was universal mourning of the people for their selfless archbishop, as the funeral service was conducted in Latin, Greek, and Slavic. "Countless people congregated. They were holding tapers and weeping, men and women, young and old, rich and poor, freemen and slaves, widows and orphans, foreigners and natives, infirm and healthy. All came that they might escort their good teacher and shepherd; for he had won their hearts, having become all things to all."[100] The biographer simply states that Saint Methodios was buried in the cathedral, but the church's location is presently unknown.

The *Filioque* and Aftermath

Afterward, Methodios' disciples still encountered many troubles with the Germans and the pagan Magyars. Wiching gained the patronage of Pope

---

[99] "Saints Kyril and Methody, Evangelizers of the Slavs," pp. 7, 8.

[100] Cf. 1 Cor. 9:22.

Stephen V, who had succeeded Hadrian III, in 885. Stephen sent an epistle to Moravia upholding Wiching's arguments and doctrine, which Saint Methodios had condemned. The Frankish Church was firmly committed to the doctrine of the *Filioque*. In Rome, the *Filioque* was not formally accepted until the early eleventh century. Though some of the popes believed that the addition of the words "and from the Son" was justified, they were not yet prepared to corrupt the Creed that had been accepted by the whole of Christendom. The Byzantines stood firm against any tampering with the synod-sanctioned Creed, especially against adding words which were erroneous. Although Methodios could be considered a papal legate, yet he agreed with Patriarch Photios who condemned the Frankish doctrine as heretical.

Gorazd and another disciple, a Bulgarian Slav, named Clement, attempted to check events, but they were overwhelmed. In fact, it had been mostly Gorazd and Clement who publicly argued the case against the *Filioque*. The two disciples expounded Orthodox doctrine on the Trinity in homilies addressed to the Frankish clergy and to Prince Sventopulk.[101]

In this same letter, the pope also had forbidden the use of Slavic in the divine offices. Sventopulk, under political pressure, sided with Wiching. Rome even appointed Wiching as the Frankish Bishop of Nitra, who continued seeking the suppression of the Slavonic Liturgy. While returning the German clergy to his land, the fickle Sventopulk delivered up the two hundred followers of the sacred twain, Kyril and Methodios, into German hands. They suffered thrashings and being dragged through briars. The younger ones, whom the Germans did not sell into slavery at the Venice market, were imprisoned. The five imprisoned champions of the Slavonic Liturgy were Gorazd, Clement, Nahum, Laurence, and Angelarios.[102] Emperor Basil ransomed the slaves and brought them back to Constantinople. Those who suffered incarceration were later exiled to the Danube region, where many died from the hardships encountered. Gorazd and a few others returned to Moravia, which was overrun by the Magyars in 907. The land was not only laid to waste but also came to be

---

[101] Obolensky, "Clement of Ohrid," p. 18.

[102] Their detention was brief, but they were sentenced to perpetual exile. They were escorted to the borders of the Moravian state by a detachment of Sventopulk's German soldiers. Clement, Nahum, and Angelarios crossed the Danube on a makeshift raft during the winter of 885-886. They reached Belgrade, which was then on Bulgarian territory. The ejection from Moravia signaled the final collapse of the Cyrillo-Methodian mission in that country. Within two centuries, the Slavonic Liturgy was wiped out of central Europe. Their linguistic and cultural tradition, however, was saved for Europe and the Slavs by the Bulgarians. It was in these initial stages that Saint Clement (commemorated by the holy Church on the 22nd of November) played the leading role. Ibid., p. 19.

under Latin domination. Gorazd sought refuge in Poland, while others went into Bohemia. While the work of Saints Kyril and Methodios flourished in their generation, it withered with coming generations in Moravia. The seed of their teaching took root elsewhere, in Bulgaria, just as Sventopulk betrayed the followers of Saints Kyril and Methodios.[103] Hence, as a wild olive-tree, they were grafted onto the fruitful root of Orthodoxy.[104]

Epilogue

Despite all these setbacks, the labors of "the Apostles of the Slavs," Kyril and Methodios, who found the Slavic peoples like a lost coin,[105] firmly established Byzantine culture on Slavic soil. The translating of Christian works into Slavonic went on and contributed greatly to the spread and nourishment of the Faith in Bulgaria and, after 950, into Russia. The Gospel of Christ then spread, not only among the Slavs of Moravia but also throughout the Balkans and surrounding areas.

Saint Clement of Ohrid praised the brothers, especially Constantine-Kyril, in an encomium that is both warm and most personal. It is written that the intensity of Clement's devotion to his master's memory "repeatedly breaks through the sober etiquette of conventional hagiography. Based in part on the *Vita Constantini*, it illustrates, with the help of techniques borrowed from medieval Greek rhetoric, the underlying features of the Cyrillo-Methodian tradition: an awareness of its Byzantine origins; veneration for the apostolic city of Rome; recognition of the immense debt owed by the Slavs to Constantine-Kyril, who, by giving them a Liturgy and Scriptures in their own language, placed them among the chosen peoples of the earth; and a Christian universalism seeking to unite Byzantium and the Slavs within a single religious and cultural community. Fittingly enough, Constantine-Kyril's achievement of teaching 'all nations' is likened by Clement to that of Saint Paul, the 'apostle of the nations,' whose work was brought to fulfillment by 'Kyril the philosopher, the teacher of the Slavs,' who 'overflew all countries, from east to west, and from north to south.'...Clement's panegyric says that by acquiring the Scriptures and Liturgy, the Slavs have gained direct access to the knowledge of God. This heritage is seen as an outpouring of divine bounty, which Clement, together with other writers of the Cyrillo-Methodian school, makes concrete through the image of rain: 'Thanks to Saint Kyril,' he writes, 'the rain of divine understanding came down upon my people.' The idea of ethnic self-determination implicit in these words provides the second ideological link between Clement's encomium and other works of the Cyrillo-Methodian school. Thus, the Slavs have 'been numbered among the great nations which

[103] Tachiaos, pp. 107, 108; Obolensky, pp. 17, 18.
[104] Cf. Rom. 11:17, 24.
[105] Lk. 15:8, 9.

praise God in their own languages,' and 'by entering this community, the Slavs underwent a spiritual rebirth, becoming "a new people."'"[106]

On the 11th of May, the holy Church commemorates the holy New-martyr ARGYROS of Thessalonike (1806).[107]

Argyros (or Argyres), the new athlete of Christ, hailed from Aponome of Thessalonike.[108] The names of his parents or family are unknown. Before Argyros underwent martyrdom, he was in service to a tailor at Thessalonike. He was a young man who had been shown grace by God. This is how, without any dispute, he is described by trustworthy Thessalonians who knew him personally. His virtue and Orthodoxy were beyond reproach, for which God accounted him worthy of grace to sustain martyrdom. We shall now briefly recount those events that ushered in his blessed end, based on the written information of reliable witnesses at Thessalonike.

Saint Argyros

Now there was a Christian, hailing from Soho of Thessalonike, who found himself in a Thessalonian jail. He was in arrears with his payments to his creditors. The pasha, when he demanded that the debtor remit the monies he owed, learned that the accused had not the means. The pasha decided that the prisoner committed a hanging offense. When the sentence was handed down, the Christian was told that there was only one way he could find amnesty: he needed to espouse Islam and become as one of the Turks. The miserable debtor, as one losing his senses when seized with fear of death, committed a great folly. He said that he would become a Turk. After making such a promise, he was released from jail. Thus, as he exited, he bore the burden of denial of our most divine and holy Faith. Woe to the wretch! For he changed our Orthodox confession for the antichrist error of the Hagarenes.

---

106 Obolensky, "Clement of Ohrid," p. 32.

107 The martyrdom of Saint Argyros was taken from the *Neon Leimonarion*, and incorporated into *The Great Synaxaristes* (in Greek), revised and edited.

108 Aponome probably is situated in the vicinity of Epanome, a suburb of present-day Thessalonike. In the more recent hagiologies, in the Greek language, such as Sophronios Efstratiades' *Hagiologion of the Orthodox Church* [p. 53] and the *Religion and Ethics Encyclopaedia* [Vol. 3, p. 68], the name of Apanome is recorded. In all likelihood there was a village bearing that name.

He was accompanied by some Hagarenes who brought their new convert to the coffeehouse in order to exhort him regarding their religion.

As it happened, Argyros was close at hand and observed them enter that establishment. Argyros, the namesake of "silver" but who was more precious than all the silver and gold and precious stones—or rather should we say incomparably of more value—was aglow with fervor, inspired by God, for the Faith. Argyros' soul and heart were filled with divine zeal and enthusiasm, so that in such a state of ecstasy he cast off every sense of fear and looked down upon every attachment and delight of this life. Argyros, with great courage and wondrous valor, entered inside the coffeehouse. There was a press of people, as the place was filled with Janissaries and other customers. Argyros' eyes caught sight of that pitiful Christ-denier, who was surrounded by a crowd of wild and tough Janissaries. Argyros went directly to the apostate, giving no consequence to others present, and addressed him boldly and openly before the all: "Wherefore hast thou committed this bad thing, brother? Why shouldest thou forsake the Christ, our Creator and Savior? What great evil, O wretched one, hast thou brought upon thy soul so as to deliver it up to punishment, that is, everlasting and unending death? What was it for? That thou mightest escape temporal death? Come, come, brother, to thy senses! Come to thyself! Do thou repent and confess Christ again. What? Thou fearest they will slay thee? So lay down thy life. Offer thy blood for the sake of Christ; for we are all obliged to die for His love, whensoever there is need, because that One also sacrificed Himself for our love."

Bravo, to thy divine zeal! Well done, O Argyros, ardent lover of Christ. Thou, O silvery martyr, hast a soul made of adamant. Hear, hear, to thy marvellous manliness and thine indescribable outspokenness! Beloved Christians and brethren, these were the only sacred and saving words that the blessed Argyros managed to speak. What followed inside of that coffeehouse each listener is able to surmise. Straightway, that dreadful group of Janissaries, raising a war-cry, lunged at the holy Argyros. As they kept shouting and shrieking barbarously, they struck him and beat him with much ferocity. It is fitting here to describe the blessed Argyros' demeanor and disposition, which was spoken of prophetically by David on behalf of our Savior Jesus Christ: "Scourges were gathered together upon me, and I knew it not [Ps. 34:18]." They certainly were prepared to slay the man of God at that moment, if it had not been for the notion that they should attempt to convert him from our reverential piety to their vile impiety. It was only this expectation that stayed their hands from pummeling him to death. The Janissaries then circled about Argyros, brandishing their knives and pistols, and shouted loudly, "Either say thou wilt become a Turk or, this second, we are going to kill thee."

That is what they said, and that is what they meant. As for Christ's athlete, he deemed their threatening ultimatum to be as a dart cast by an infant. In no wise did he cower as he cried aloud, "I am a Christian; and I will not renounce my Faith whatsoever you should do. Indeed, whatsoever you should contrive will work toward my glory and honor, for I greatly desire to die for the sake of the Orthodox Faith and the love of Christ." After hearing these words, the Janissaries, filled with fury and rage, dragged and pushed Argyros violently. They led him to the judge and denounced his bold act as an effrontery to Islam. Argyros was subjected to a relentless and merciless beating. Using force, they attempted by all means to make him forsake his sacred Faith and confess their own superstition. This strategy, however, came to be seen by them as much toil that came to nothing. It was evident that Argyros' resolve was firm and even immoveable. They, therefore, left off flogging him and changed their tactics. They began using flattering speech in order to coax and cajole him into a conversion. They also did not stop at making all kinds of promises of gifts and posts. They entertained evil hopes to lure him in this wily manner that they might make him change his mind. But they did not succeed by using such ploys. They, therefore, cast him in prison, leaving him covered with wounds, until a second examination.

After two days, the saint was removed from prison and put to the test afresh. The Janissaries, observing that he remained steadfast and unaltered in his beliefs, sought his hanging from the judge. But the judge did not think their request was reasonable or fair, and said as much: "In advocating his religion, it is not a crime worthy of such a decision as death; inasmuch as this type of profession of one's beliefs is demanded by every sect. Every faith requires that its members be zealous and sanguine defenders. The defendant, therefore, following what every denomination urges upon its devotees, merely demonstrated his zeal and love for his own religion. You, too, are known to be hot-headed zealots—but for our Islamic faith. Should your lives be sought? Should you, though not liable for any crime, be guilty of death for professing what you believe? Instead of burdening the court with this man's punishment, why do you not rather, as much as you are able, win him over to our faith?"

So spoke the judge. The Janissaries, confounded by the judge's words, were in an upheaval. As wild beasts, consumed with wrath, they raised their voices against him and gave an impassioned argument: "What art thou saying? Art thou justifying the enemy of our faith? Dost thou judge it fair and reasonable that the defendant, on the one hand, praises his religion, but, on the other hand, insults and blasphemes our faith—and, moreover, in our presence? Thou dost not judge this deed to be worthy of death?" The judge heard their argument and ruminated a short while upon it. He then said, "Since, then, the accused blasphemed our religion, he is guilty. Now behold! I also hand down a judgment: he is to be taken to the place of execution, where he shall be hanged by the neck."

Those beastly Janissaries took hold of the righteous Argyros and hanged him at a place called Kaban. The gloriously triumphant athlete of Christ, Argyros, received the inviolate crown of martyrdom, in the year of our Lord 1806, on the 11th day of May. It was a Friday. He was eighteen years of age. He now rejoices together with all the glorious martyrs of Christ, inasmuch as he exhibited that double love required by God: that one love God and one's neighbor. With regard to showing love to his neighbor, Argyros did so, to the peril of his own life, for the sake of that unhappy Christ-denier. With regard to his Lord, he manifested a love both perfect and incomparable since he died for the holy name of Jesus. Thus, we bring to mind the words of the evangelist: "This is My commandment, that ye be loving one another, even as I loved you. Greater love hath no one than this, that one should lay down his life for his friends [Jn. 15:12, 13]."

A similar martyric account to that of Saint Argyros took place in the same city but a little earlier. In the year 1777, New-martyr Christodoulos, on the 28th of July, in his attempt to return to piety a Christ-denier from the error of his way, also struggled and received the crown of the contest.

It would not be pious to pass over the observations of those who beheld the dead body of the blessed Argyros. All were in symphony that not one mark or sign of a wound appeared on his body, which underwent torture and wounding. Much rather, they described his appearance as one alive and sleeping. Each witness was amazed at this mysterious and extraordinary manifestation; for they had seen his much-tried flesh prior to his hanging. The body was left hanging for three days, in accordance with the custom of the Hagarenes. No one could explain the miraculous occurrence of the martyr's restored flesh.

As much as we have been informed, so have we committed in this writing toward the remembrance of the struggle of the ever-memorable athlete Argyros for the love of Christ (Who also suffered for us, leaving behind an example that we should follow His footsteps. But He committed no sin, neither was guile found in His mouth. When He was reviled, He reviled not in return. When He suffered, He threatened not, but kept on giving Himself over to Him Who judges righteously [1 Pe. 2:21-23]), to Whom is due all glory, honor, and veneration, together with the unoriginate Father and the All-Holy Spirit, to the ages of the ages. Amen.

Through the intercessions of Thy Saints,
O Christ God, have mercy on us. Amen.

On the 12th of May, the holy Church commemorates our holy father among the saints, EPIPHANIOS, Bishop of Cyprus.[1]

Epiphanios, our holy father among the saints, was born circa 310. He hailed from the Palestinian village of Veesandouk, a distance of three miles from Eleftheropolis.[2] His parents were Hebrews. The occupation of Epiphanios' father was farming, while his mother was engaged in the spinning of linen thread. There were two children: Epiphanios and his sister, Kallitrope. Now it came to pass that the father of Epiphanios died. This took place when Epiphanios was young, being about ten years of age. This tragic loss left not only the mother widowed and the two children fatherless but also the household in appalling straits, lacking even the most meager necessities of life.

Early Life in Palestine

For the sake of their needs, Epiphanios' mother was considering selling one unruly donkey which they owned. The mother, therefore, said to

[1] The Greek Life of our holy father among the saints, Epiphanios, was written down by his disciples: first, Priest John, and then Bishop Polyvios who resumed the account. The text was rendered into simpler Greek and published by Nikodemos the Hagiorite, who included it in his work, entitled *Neon Eklogion*, which was revised and incorporated into the Greek text of *The Great Synaxaristes*. The Life was also published by Caesar Dapontes in *Paterikon of Saint Gregory*. The canon in the divine office to the saint was composed by Saint John of Damascus. Various hymnological works and additional anecdotes of Saint Epiphanios are found in the following codices: Parisian 1566, 1574, and 1575; and Lavreote Γ 19, Γ 74, Δ 5, Δ 19, Δ 45, Θ 87, I 70, and Λ 164.

Recent critics (Loupinos, Abba Rakinas) doubt that the authors of the saint's Life were his disciples. They attribute the text to Saint Symeon Metaphrastes. This contention, however, is incorrect. Fathers of old have upheld that Saint Epiphanios' disciples composed the biography. One example is Saint John the Merciful, who lived from 555 to 619. Thus, it is not possible for Saint Symeon to have written an eyewitness account since he lived during the days of Leo VI the Wise (886 to 912). Modern critic Constantine Kontogones also agrees with this conclusion [see *Philologike and Kritike Historia ton Agion tis Ekklesias Pateron, 4th C.*, p. 329].

For other sources relative to various controversies involving Saint Epiphanios: See Saint Jerome, "Contra Joannem Hierosolymitanum," in *P.L.*, 23:355; Idem, "Ad Theophilum," *P.L.*, 22: 736; Epiphanios, "Ad Joannem Hierosolymitanum," *P.G.* 43:379; Socrates, *Hist. eccl.*, VI, x-xiv; Sozomen, *Hist. eccl.*, VIII, xiv-xv. The chief editions of Epiphanios' works are those of Petavius (Paris, 1622); Greek text, Latin tr., and notes reproduced with additions in *P.G.* 41-43; and of Dindorf (Leipzig, 1859-1862), 5 vols., giving only the Greek text, improved in some parts.

[2] Eleftheropolis, the seat of a bishopric, was an ancient city of western Palestine, situated between Jerusalem and Gaza. It lies a distance of some forty kilometers from Jerusalem.

Epiphanios, "Take, my child, the beast of burden and go to the festival in order to sell it that we might purchase necessary food for ourselves." Epiphanios, familiar with that creature's intractability, knew he would have difficulty handling it. He, thereupon, remarked to his mother, "Thou knowest, mother, that our donkey is untamed. And if I attempt to sell it to those who have gathered at the festival and they observe how rebellious it acts, they will reprove me." The mother insisted, saying, "Go, child, and the God of our fathers—Abraham, Isaac, and Jacob—will control the animal in order for thee to sell it and receive money. With the sale, we shall be able to steer ourselves out of our neediness." Epiphanios, then, invoked God's help. He took the animal and went forth to sell it, in obedience to his mother's bidding.

When Epiphanios arrived at the place where the festival was taking place, the donkey became calm and obedient. A certain Jewish business representative, named Jacob, said to Epiphanios, "Art thou selling the beast of burden, child?" Epiphanios answered, "Yea, it is for sale. It is for this reason that I have brought it here." Jacob next asked, "What is thy religion, boy?" Epiphanios replied, "I am a Hebrew." Then Jacob said, "Since we are of one faith, child, and righteous slaves of God, let us appear just in the price of the donkey, so that neither thou shouldest suffer wrong nor I shouldest bear a loss. For then we may provoke God's curse and indignation against us. We, rather, ought to try to gain a blessing, since God said, 'The one blessed of Him is blessed, and the one cursed of Him is accursed.'"[3]

Hearing these words, Epiphanios very much dreaded receiving a curse from Jacob, bringing to mind the words of Jacob of old.[4] For he feared to be deceptive about the donkey lest he bring a curse upon himself and not a blessing—especially if the donkey injured the older man. So the business agent asked the youth, "Why, my boy, wilt thou not sell to me?" Epiphanios would not prevaricate and said, "Because the animal is rebellious. But my mother ordered me to sell it that we might provide for much-needed food. Indeed, since the death of my father, we have come into great distress. Furthermore, after hearing thy words that it is evil to render an injury to one's neighbor, I am fearful of God. Peradventure, He should punish me for knowingly bringing harm to another by this wild and heedless donkey." When Jacob heard the youth's honest disclosure, he marvelled. He dipped into his purse and removed three silver coins, saying, "Receive this blessing, child. And whensoever thou shouldest see thy mother, give her these coins that she might buy food. In the meantime, take thy beast of burden. If the animal does not misbehave, hold on

---

[3] Cf. Ps. 37:22 KJV—"For such as be blessed of Him shall inherit the earth; and they that be cursed of Him shall be cut off."

[4] Cf. Gen. 27:12 KJV—"My father [Isaac] peradventure will feel me, and I shall seem to him as a deceiver; and I shall bring a curse upon me, and not a blessing."

to it for thy work. If the creature becomes uncontrollable, drive it far from your house lest it should do violence and kill someone."

Epiphanios, taking the donkey and the three coins, went in the direction of his village. On the road, he encountered a certain Christian, named Kleovios, who asked, "Art thou selling the donkey, child?" Epiphanios replied, "Nay, it is not for sale." Kleovios continued, "If thou sellest him, receive what it is worth and give him to me." While Kleovios was speaking, the donkey became uncontrollable. The beast was attempting to throw the youth. It bucked until it cast him to the ground. Before it scampered away, the donkey gave a mighty kick to the thigh of Epiphanios. Crying, Epiphanios was sprawled out on the ground. He was unable to rise up due to the sharp pangs he felt. Kleovios thrice made the sign of the life-creating Cross over Epiphanios' thigh, on the spot where the animal struck. O the wonder! Epiphanios quickly arose without feeling the least discomfort.

Saint Epiphanios

Kleovios then turned toward the escaping donkey and said, "In the name of Jesus Christ the crucified, O contrary animal, since thou wouldest slay thy master, thou shalt not move any further than that spot." Straightway, with the pronouncement of those words by Kleovios, the animal fell to the ground and expired. Epiphanios was astonished at what took place and asked, "Who is Jesus the crucified, in Whose name thou hast wrought such signs and wonders?" Kleovios answered, "This Jesus is the Son of God, Who was crucified by the Jews." Epiphanios was afraid to reveal to Kleovios that he was a Jew. At length, Kleovios continued on his way. Epiphanios, meanwhile, went off to his mother, pondering upon the crucified Jesus and wishing to know more of Him. When he returned home, he recounted to his mother all of the day's events.

After the passage of a little time, the mother of Epiphanios said, "Behold, my child, how we are unable to cultivate our field and collect any crop from it! While thy father was alive he was able to till it and have it yield a crop for our sustenance. But let us now sell the land so that thy sister and I may find some relief from poverty. As for thee, my son, betake thyself to some

God-fearing artisan or craftsman in the city. Apprentice thyself and learn some trade, by which thou mightest be able to feed thyself and to help us in our want and misery."

At Eleftheropolis, there was a certain Hebrew, an extraordinary teacher of the Mosaic law, who was devout in his religion. His name was Tryphon. He had substance and property in Epiphanios' village. Tryphon was also acquainted with the parents of Epiphanios. When he came to Veesandouk to inspect his holdings, he paid a courtesy call to the home of Epiphanios. He perceived their impoverishment and proffered the following solution to the widow: "Wilt thou consider giving Epiphanios into my care that I might make him my ward and have him as my son? I can try to compensate thy loss by providing maintenance for thee and thy daughter." This opportunity for her son gave her great joy. She, straightway, handed over Epiphanios to Tryphon that he might be received into his home.

Now Tryphon had an only child, a daughter, whom he wished to join in marriage to Epiphanios. Tryphon, consequently, having brought Epiphanios into his home, laboriously and with all exactness, taught him all the Mosaic law and Jewish writings. Now after a time the daughter of Tryphon died. Epiphanios, by that time, had advanced in age and in the wisdom of the Jews. Not long after, Tryphon also died, leaving his entire estate to Epiphanios. The death of Epiphanios' mother soon followed, leaving Epiphanios alone with his sister in the house of Tryphon. Thus, the two siblings were sole heirs to all his substance and properties. Epiphanios took care to raise his sister properly.

One day, while Epiphanios was returning to his village to visit the properties which he had inherited from Tryphon, he met a certain monk whose name was Lucian. He was a learned and splendid man, who practised the art of calligraphy. From his earnings he supported himself. If any part of his wages remained, he donated it to the poor and needy. Now while Epiphanios was on horseback and the monk was proceeding on foot, there came toward Father Lucian some indigent man. The latter kneeled before the feet of the monk, saying, "O man of God, have mercy on me! For I have been without food for three days." The blessed Lucian, not having any money to give him, removed his outer garment. He gave it to the poor man and said, "Go to the village and sell it so thou canst buy loaves of bread." Even as the monk was offering his garment to the fellow in need, Epiphanios witnessed a white robe descending out of heaven and covering Father Lucian.

Great fear then seized Epiphanios. He dismounted and fell to his knees before the feet of Lucian, saying, "I beseech thee, O man, tell me, who art thou?" The venerable Lucian answered, "Do thou tell me, first, what religion dost thou follow? Then shall I tell thee in what religion I believe." Father Lucian, as one divinely endowed with the gift of clairvoyance, perceived in the meantime that the grace of God came upon Epiphanios, so that he spoke again and said, "How is it that thou, being a Hebrew, dost question a Christian so as to learn who I am? As thou knowest, the Jewish religion is an abomination to the Christians, and Christianity is a cause of reproach to the Jews. Behold, and hearken, that I am a Christian! At this point thou needest not hear anything else from me." As for Epiphanios, who maintained a good disposition throughout their conversation, he asked, "And what hinders me from becoming a Christian? Tell me, I beseech thee." Lucian remarked, "The only hindrance would be if thou shouldest lack volition, because, if thou willest, thou art able to become one."

Epiphanios was moved to compunction at the words of Lucian. Instead of inspecting his properties in his village, Epiphanios escorted Lucian to the house he had received by inheritance. Epiphanios did not disguise his wealth. Inside the house, Epiphanios said to Lucian, "All these things which thou dost see are my substance, father. This here is my sister. I, nonetheless, wish to become a Christian and take up the monastic life. What sayest thou regarding this?" The blessed Lucian, at that declaration, remarked, "Thou art not able, child, to live the monastic conduct of life if thou dost possess all these fine things. But if thou wilt bring thy sister to the Faith and arrange for her marriage with a Christian, giving her what is her due as a dowry, and leave the rest for the poor, then thou canst live the monastic life as is meet." Epiphanios then said to him, "First, father, make me a Christian and, afterward, I shall put into action what thou hast commanded of me." Lucian then remarked, "I am not able to make thee a Christian, for the bishop of the Christians should be apprised of thy case that he may perform the Mystery of holy Baptism. I will bring thy matter before him, only do thou remain constant in thy zeal toward the Christ."

Thus spoke Lucian and they came to an agreement. Lucian then exited that house and went directly to the bishop. Epiphanios, without a moment's delay, turned to his sister and said, "I want to become a Christian and lead the monastic life." Kallitrope responded that very moment and said to him, "Even as thou dost wish, so also do I wish to do the same; and so I will." In the meantime, Lucian went to the bishop and announced the intention of Epiphanios. The bishop said to the monk, "Go and catechize him. Whensoever next I am in church, lead him therein that he might prostrate himself before the man-loving God." Lucian, therefore, went to the house of Epiphanios. The moment Epiphanios and Kallitrope caught sight of the monk, they fell to their knees before his feet. Both were weeping and began to say, "We implore thee, O father, to make us Christians." Lucian, subsequently, catechized them and guided them both to the Church. He taught them continually as their insatiable desire to learn never waned.

Brother and Sister are Baptized

Lucian then made ready to escort the siblings to the church. On the way they met with the bishop who was also going to the church. Forthwith, Epiphanios and Kallitrope made a prostration before the prelate's feet, beseeching him to baptize them. Hence, they went all together to the church. When Epiphanios arrived at the outer door of the church and, immediately, went up to the first step of the flight of steps, the sandal from his left foot fell off. As he lifted his right foot to continue his ascent, that sandal also dropped. As a result, both of Epiphanios' sandals were found outside on the steps leading into the church. Now Lucian observed this phenomenon and wondered at it. The blessed Epiphanios neither looked to his sandals nor desired to retrieve them. The place in which they fell is where they remained. In fact, for the rest of his life he did not wish to be clad in sandals.[5]

As brother and sister stood in the church and listened to the reading from the sacred Scriptures, the bishop noticed the countenance of Epiphanios. It appeared glorified and radiant. He also beheld a crown on Epiphanios' head. After the Gospel Reading, the bishop entered the baptistry. He invited Epiphanios, Kallitrope, and Lucian to enter. Moreover, Father Lucian was made Epiphanios' spiritual father. After the bishop exhorted and taught them all that was necessary, he baptized them. They also communed the immaculate Mysteries. Following the Mystery of holy Baptism, the bishop invited them to the episcopal house to take lunch together. They also, according to custom, remained there for seven days.

After the passage of seven days, Epiphanios brought to his home both Lucian and a certain virgin named Mother Veronike, the abbess of a convent. The latter became the spiritual mother of Kallitrope. Epiphanios gave Veronike one thousand gold coins for his sister's support and maintenance at her convent. It was there that his sister could live the monastic life with other virgins. Epiphanios, following this, sold all his belongings—both moveable and stationary—and distributed the proceeds among the poor. He retained only four hundred coins for the purchase of divine and life-giving books. Next, he departed the city with Lucian. They went directly to a monastery, one where there were ten monks living in quietude. They supported themselves through their calligraphic efforts. It was there that Epiphanios became a monk at the age of sixteen.

Saint Epiphanios Enters the Monastery

At that monastery there was living a certain monk, named Hilarion,[6] who was Lucian's second. This monk was adorned with virtues and spiritual gifts. Emulating his mode of life was another monk, named Claudios. The

---

[5] Cf. Ex. 3:2-6.

[6] Saint Hilarion is commemorated on the 21st of October.

young Epiphanios, seeing his superiors engaged in such practises, also sought to imitate them. For Epiphanios had been assigned to the divine Hilarion by Father Lucian. It was Father Hilarion who taught Epiphanios the sacred Scriptures. Epiphanios greatly exerted himself to imitate Father Hilarion's useful disposition and moral character. With the grace of God working with him, Epiphanios progressed in the monastic state. Not much time passed before the great Lucian migrated to the heavenly mansions. Father Hilarion, thereupon, became superior of the brotherhood. A comment should be made regarding the fare of Hilarion, which also influenced Epiphanios' eating habits. Father Hilarion partook of very little bread with salt and a moderate amount of water. He ate once every two days. Ofttimes, he only ate once every three or four days. It also was not unusual for him to take food once a week. Epiphanios also chose to take up this diet, which he kept for the rest of his life.

The place in which the monastery was located was arid and bereft of water. The fathers fetched water from a distance of five miles (or eight kilometers). On account of oven-like heat during daylight hours, the fathers were constrained to convey the water to the monastery by night. On one such occasion, before the fathers had gone out at night to bring water, some wayfarers passed by the monastery. They came with beasts of burden laden with wine. They halted to rest and refresh themselves since that wasteland heated up like a furnace, which ushered in universal thirst to both man and beast. When the travelers entered the monastery grounds, they requested water for drinking. But at that hour, it so happened that the fathers had not even a drop of water to offer them. So sorrowed was the brotherhood that they could not assist their guests that they even wept at their predicament. The divine Epiphanios, taking into his right hand the skins that contained wine, said, "Just believe, brothers, that our Lord Jesus Christ Who transformed the water into wine in Cana of the Galilee can also change wine into water." Lo, the miracle! The skins, which were plump with wine, became filled with water. Hence, both the wayfarers and their animals were refreshed by that clear and fresh water. At the sight of that wonderworking, both the monastery brethren and those who had journeyed were beside themselves.

From that day and henceforward, the saint no longer wished to dwell in that place. Why is that? Because those wayfarers celebrated the wonderworking and proclaimed it wheresoever they went. As a result thereof, the fame of the saint came to be known in all places. The modest Epiphanios was unable to endure the distinction and reverence paid to him by both the brotherhood and the visitors. He, therefore, secretly departed from that place, finding solace in a region more wild than his present wilderness site. The brethren back at the monastery grieved for Epiphanios, for they knew not where he had taken himself. After spending three days of eating nothing in that parched and sunbaked location, it was about that same time that forty Saracens came to that region. They spotted Epiphanios trying to survive in that place. They mocked him for the conditions in which he was living. Now one of them, who was blind in one eye, had a beastly and savage temper. He drew his dagger from its scabbard. Drawing near to the holy man, the Saracen raised his murderous hand in order to strike a blow. But behold the wonder! The vision in the blind eye was miraculously restored. Such fear seized that Saracen that he cast the dagger down to the ground and stood rooted to the spot. His cohorts, seeing him motionless, drew closer to him and to the monk. When they observed that their comrade's former blind eye had the power of sight, they were ecstatic.

The saint detected that a commotion was in the making. He began to speak to them with unfeigned cheerfulness and humility. His words succeeded in calming their excitement and agitation, telling them that this wonderworking came about by the holy God. But they seized him, taking him along with them, and said, "Thou art our god. Keep following us that thou mayest preserve us from every evil likely to beset us by reason of those who are pursuing us." The saint, therefore, having no other choice, went away with them. During the three months that he was in their company, he kept them from committing any violent or profligate deed. The Saracens perceived that, on account of the holy monk's admonitions and counsels, they were becoming frustrated. Father Epiphanios, repeatedly, warned them against committing thefts and seizures. As long as he was with them, they committed no criminal acts. The Saracens, finally, in straits since they could not act upon every whim and fancy that entered their minds, went to their knees before Epiphanios and besought him to depart. The holy man, after advising them, cautioned them with these final words: "If you do not cease performing these evil deeds, you shall come to have neither good days nor success in this present life." After exhorting and admonishing them in this manner, all forty Saracens escorted Father Epiphanios back to the place where they first encountered him. Following this, they built for him a small habitation. Then, taking their leave, they departed in peace.

"And I," remarks the biographer of this Life, "was one of those Saracens. I decided to remain with the man of God. I was catechized by him with the word of the truth and the Faith of the Christ. After six months went by, the saint led me to the monastery—the one of the great Hilarion. When the brotherhood beheld him again, there was universal joy. After three days, the saint besought the Elder Hilarion to baptize me, for Hilarion had attained to the dignity of the priesthood. After I was instructed in all that was necessary, I received holy Baptism and the name of John. We tarried at the monastery for ten days, after which the brethren begged the holy Epiphanios to remain with them in the monastery. He, however, did not wish this. Since I had no intention of being parted from Epiphanios, we returned together to our habitation. On the way back, we encountered a certain young man who was sorely afflicted by a terrible demon. The saint espied the troubled youth as the latter was running about hither and thither, naked and in a disturbing manner. Epiphanios was saddened by the youth's sore plight and called out, 'In the name of the crucified Jesus Christ, I command thee, O unclean demon, to come forth from the creation of God!' Immediately, then, the youth came to his senses completely. He next went and kneeled before the saint. The venerable man raised him to his feet, telling him to give thanks to God. Following this, he sent him to his house in peace and in health."

Saint Epiphanios and the Persians

The biographer continued: "That same wicked demon went into Persia and entered into the daughter of the king. He tormented her, even as he had the young man, so that he caused her to cry out and say, 'If there does not come here, O king, Epiphanios who sent me to thy daughter, I am not withdrawing from her.' And then that vile spirit began to say, 'O Epiphanios, thou who art in Phoenicia, come here that I might depart from the king's daughter!' The king, hearing this last utterance of the demon, dispatched a multitude of elite men to Phoenicia. They searched for the holy man in every quarter, but they could not find him. They, therefore, returned to their kingdom unsuccessful. In fact, some of those Persians suffered ill at the hands of the Rhomaioi, since the latter deemed them to be spies. The demon inhabiting the princess then divulged a further detail saying, 'Epiphanios dwells in a place called Spanydrion.' The king, hearing this new information, outfitted another company of men that numbered thirty. He charged them to exchange their Persian garb for the dress of the Rhomaioi. They were told to go to Phoenicia and conduct their investigation in a place known as Spanydrion, in which location dwelt one called Epiphanios. The envoys, therefore, were clad in the attire of Rhomaioi and made their way to Phoenicia. They carefully and diligently discovered the exact location of Spanydrion.

"The Persians came and reached the door of the saint's cell during the night. They knocked at the door at the hour when the saint was at his prayers. He neither opened the door to them nor made the least stirring. Despite the pounding at the door, Epiphanios was unwilling to cut off his prayer to the Lord. The Persian envoys, nevertheless, were angered and wished to break down the door. One of the Persians drew his dagger and spread forth his hand in order to rend asunder the door. But his hand, rendered motionless, became withered. His fellows, seeing what befell him, trembled with fear and backed away from the door of the cell. Since the saint had finished his prayer, he opened the door. When Father Epiphanios saw the man with the shriveled hand, that Persian prostrated himself before the saint's feet and said, 'Have mercy on me, O slave of the immortal gods!' The saint remarked, 'What art thou asking from a sinful man?' The Persian replied, 'I came to this place in full health. Behold how my hand has withered!' The righteous one said, 'Thou camest healthy, do thou become healthy again.' Instantly, as soon as Epiphanios touched the hand of the sufferer, the Persian was delivered of his affliction. His companions, after they witnessed the miracle, made obeisance before the feet of the saint. But Epiphanios admonished them, saying, 'Rise up and give glory to the one and true God, Christ, for I am but His slave.' After they reverenced Epiphanios, they revealed the cause of their visit to find him.

"When the venerable man heard the explanation of the envoys, he understood that the same demon that he had dispelled from the young man had entered into the Persian princess and was now tormenting her. The righteous one then turned and said to me, 'Let us be off, child, and go thither with these men into Persia.' The envoys said, 'The king, O father, did not send us for another save thee. We have brought an animal for thee to sit upon.' The saint responded and said, 'I shall travel on foot. As for my disciple, however, I will not leave him here alone.' The Persians said, 'Very well. We have two animals here; only we beseech thee to follow us, your slaves.' Straightway, one of the envoys, a young man, with a gracious countenance, venerated the saint and said, 'Pardon me, father.' The saint then said sweetly, 'May God bless thee, child!' Then the young man, with much reverence, embraced the righteous man and lifted him up that he might sit upon one of the camels which he had. Then he came toward me and did the same by helping me up. We then departed, while that young man walked before the camels.

"After we traveled for thirty days, we arrived in the king's realm. We waited in a place called Ourion. Now three of the party with whom we were journeying went ahead in order to announce our arrival to the king. He sent back the order that we should come forward to him. The righteous Epiphanios proceeded with great courage and boldness, as if he were not meeting a king at all. I, however, beholding such a great crowd of people standing about the king, was in no small way afraid. As the saint approached the king, the latter arose from his throne. The saint then addressed the king and said, 'Take thy seat, child, on thy throne and cease grieving for thy daughter; for I have the help of the man-loving God Who will drive out the wicked demon. Only believe in Him, and thou shalt behold thy girl sound and whole. That most malevolent demon, since he was dispelled from that place whence he was found, came hither into thy daughter. Nonetheless, if thou wilt believe in the crucified Jesus Christ, that One will cast him out even from here. Bring forth, then, to this place, thy daughter; and thou shalt behold the grace of the man-loving Jesus.'

"The king then gave the command to have the princess escorted. Straightway, as soon as she came, the saint addressed her and said, 'Come to thy senses, O damsel, and revere thy father, because the wolf no longer lords it over thee.' He then made the sign of the honorable and life-giving Cross over the lass, and said to the demon, 'Badly hast thou done to enter into the daughter of the king. Depart from her, and take thyself away to uninhabitable regions.' Forthwith, the demon quit the damsel and fled. The saint, beholding how the king was beside himself in the face of this miracle, said to him, 'Rejoice, O king, because the wolf has departed from thy girl. And do thou, O daughter, go to thy mother and rejoice with her. Only take heed well to preserve thy body pure and inviolate from sins; and then no longer will the villainous devil approach thee.' Then the king and all those standing fell down before the feet of the saint and made obeisance to him. They pleaded with the man of God to take up his abode among them, that they might adopt him as father of the king.

"One of the chief magicians of Persia then commented, 'O blessed Epiphanios, beloved sorcerer, thou hast come here in order to perform many achievements. Do thou teach thine art to us, the Magi, and we will hearken to thee.' But the saint, hearing such words as these, addressed him and said, 'O magus, enemy of the truth, learn not to speak with muddled words! Do not even begin to think that the slave of the one God is a magician of injustice and wrong. Therefore, toward thy correction to render thee wise, I say that thou shalt remain dumb and no longer shalt thou be able to speak.' Then—lo, the wonder!—instantly, with the utterance of the saint, the magus remained voiceless and motionless. The king, as well as the multitude of spectators, witnessed these events. Such was their terror that they fell prone to the ground. The saint, stretching forth his hand, took hold of the king and said to him joyfully, 'Rise up, O king, compose thyself, and cease fearing.' Thus, all of them went to their feet. The saint then turned to the stricken magus and said, 'Reckon well what thou hast seen and heard, and take heed to the truth, so as not to entertain any notion that I am a sorcerer. For I am a slave of the crucified Jesus Christ and, in His name, I bid thee speak again and hear as before and become a friend of the truth.' Straightway, then, the magus began to speak. Acknowledging his fault, he also asked forgiveness from the saint.

"After this incident, the king issued orders and they brought forth gold, silver, pearls, and precious stones which were laid down before the saint. The king then said to the venerable elder, 'Receive these, father, and keep me in thy memory.' The unacquisitive saint, nevertheless, replied, 'We think slightly of all these things, as false and trivial goods of fortune in this world, so that we may enjoy the true and everlasting good things of heaven. Do not, therefore, show concern for me by means of such dainties, for the Christ taught me not to have any need of such earthly treasures. Therefore, take them and bury them again in thy treasury. Do thou know, however, that, as long as they are found therein, they are dead and inefficacious. Why? Because thou dost give heed to these things and thou dost lavish much care upon them, but thy soul does not receive the least benefit from all this care. Indeed, by reason of gold, have many souls been lost! This wealth, given to thee by the Lord, was meant to be distributed among those in need. Become, therefore, just and righteous. Approach thou the God of all, even the God Who bestowed all this gold upon thee. Give to the poor that thou mayest not be condemned to the everlasting darkness in the coming judgment. For then shalt thou bring to mind my very words, but such remembrance will be to no benefit. But listen to my words now that thou mightest then rejoice perpetually. Cease having thy sights on this world and its delights, and then all the world shall be subject to thee. Guard thyself carefully from the Magi, for they deceive and mislead thee by means of their dark practises.'

"After these occurrences, the saint, seeing that the hour of lunch had arrived, said to the king, 'I should like to speak with thee further on this and regarding other matters, but I perceive thou art not attentive. I know that thy thoughts at this hour are bent on the meal at table. Therefore, go, eat of all the foods with moderation; for to such things is thy mind turned.' The king then said to the saint, 'Come, father, that we might eat together.' But the saint answered, 'Go thou to the table and eat, even as I said, of all the food thou desirest to taste. The only thing is to avoid undisciplined eating. As for me, a little bread made from bran and a little salt are sufficient for the needs of my body.' The king then dismissed all the others and bade us come with him into the canopied area, where various fine foods were set out for us. The saint, taking only one loaf of bread, declined the other dishes. He partook of the bread and was satisfied, giving thanks to the God of the universe.

"The following day, the king invited the saint to an audience with him. As the venerable elder approached the throne room, the king rose up and placed the royal scepter on the floor. The saint said, 'Take up, O king, the exercise of thy royal office and give thanks to God Who granted it.' The king remarked, 'I beseech thee, father, remain here among us; and whatsoever thou wilt bid me do, that shall I do.' The saint remarked, 'If thou keepest my words, I also will remember thee wheresoever I shall be found.' We stayed in the royal palace for ten days. The man of God preached to the king, but the seed of the Gospel teaching fell among thorns in his heart that was replete with the cares of this world and the deceitfulness of riches.[7] He was so full of the ancestral belief of the Persians that it choked the word of truth. Nevertheless, Epiphanios thought it prudent to counsel the king and his judges regarding mercy and judgment in

[7] Mt. 13:22.

governing. After this period of time, the saint said to the king, 'I should like to depart for my land, for I am being sought by those found there. As for thee, O king, sit on thy throne, tranquilly and serenely, and do not declare war on the Rhomaioi. For if thou shouldest become their enemy, thou shalt become an enemy of the crucified Jesus Christ. Moreover, if thou shouldest become an enemy of the crucified Jesus, thou shalt perish in a bad way at the hands of thine adversaries.' The king, still very amiable toward us, went ahead of us, followed by his household, escorting us till we departed the palace.

"When we emerged from the royal palace, with the king and his retinue still accompanying us, we met with the remains of a certain dead child of a Persian grandee. Those star-gazing people were bearing the corpse on a bier, so as to cast it at the astrological time of the astral deity Dog Star (Sirius, Tishtrya) in order for the dogs to devour it. At that time, this was the custom among the Persians. They cast their dead to the dogs, an animal held in esteem by them, for their consumption. The saint then addressed those people who were conveying the body and said, 'O children, place the remains on the ground that we too may view the dead.' They obliged the elder in his request. The saint then turned to the king and said to him, 'Sire, thou oughtest to commit the bodies of your dead to the earth and not cast them to the dogs for them to eat. Thou needest to know that thou hast many bad men in thy realm who slay people before their time. Take this dead person before us: his wrongful death was committed by a man of ill-intent who used magic. Nonetheless, my God, Who was crucified on the wood of the Cross, desires to resurrect this child before the eyes of all.'

"As the saint spoke these words, he touched the dead child with his hand. He prayed to the man-befriending God and said, 'O Lord Jesus Christ, Son of God, Who raised the four-day dead Lazarus, raise up this youth.' The holy man then removed his outer garment and clad the youth with it. He did this because it was the custom of the Persians to bury their dead naked. Straightway, then—O the wonder!—the dead youth arose and thanked the saint. The astonishment of the Persians led them to think that the man of God was one of the gods in the flesh. Our venerable elder quickly corrected them, stating he was a slave of the triune God. The saint then said to the youth, 'Go, child, to thy house and don thine usual clothing; and return to me my outer garment.' This is what he said because the saint was left in his hair shirt. Now those Persians listened to the saint's preaching, but were not of a mind to become Christians. Some understood the teachings, but it fell on stony places in their hearts. Others did not understand, and so the word fell by the wayside.[8]

[8] Cf. Mt. 13:4, 5; Mk. 4:4, 5.

"The king, beholding this miracle wrought by the saint, was taken with the idea that Epiphanios was God. The saint said to him, 'Do not reason thus about me, O king! For I am a man as thee of like passions and feelings,[9] and, I, too, am mortal. But my God, in Whom I believe, concedes such signs to those who love Him.' After speaking these words, the saint added many pertinent others. He then concluded and said, 'Return, child, to thy palace; and we shall depart for our homeland.' The king asked the saint, 'How many armed men needest thou, father, to accompany and guard thee on the road?' The saint replied, 'I have God and His soldiers, the holy angels, that guard me.' Next the king made obeisance to the saint and said, 'Go in health, Epiphanios, thou glory of the Rhomaioi, and remember us also who are found in Persia.'"

Saint Epiphanios Returns to Spanydrion

The biographer, continuing, writes: "Departing from that land, we finally came to our habitation. It was three days since we drank any water. The righteous man turned toward the east, sending up prayer to God with words such as these: 'O Lord God, even as Thou didst direct Moses to smite the barren rock in the wilderness, inscribing the Cross thereon, and water gushed forth out of the rock for the people to drink,[10] so do Thou smite this ground and cause water to spring forth for the sake of the poor men who dwell here.' After uttering this prayer, an ineffable fragrance permeated the area. Three times he bowed down to the ground and prayed. He then took up a mattock and dug a little into the earth. Immediately, then, a small amount of water bubbled up. After he applied the digging tool a little more, an abundance of water sprang forth. There was enough water, thenceforth, to plant plenty of vegetables for our enjoyment and nourishment.

"Since, however, wild animals were coming and eating the vegetables, the saint stood in the midst of the garden patch and conversed with the beasts, as though they were humans, saying, 'Why, O beasts, are you giving toil and trouble to us? I, being a sinner and impoverished, came to this place that I might weep for the multitude of my sins. And it is God Who has given me this consolation of vegetables for food. But you have come and have continued to devour them. Therefore, the same God commands you intruders not to come here any longer and injure the plants.' Straightway, as if the beasts heard and understood those admonitory words, even as rational beings, they took themselves away from that day and no longer tread on our land. Now those Saracens who had built the *kellion*, that is, the hermit's cell, heard the news that the saint had returned from Persia. They, therefore, came in order to take his blessing. The Saracens then built for us another three *kellia*, after which they departed into their own lands. It then was bruited about all of Phoenicia

[9] Cf. Acts 14:15.

[10] Ex. 17:6.

that the saint was dwelling at Spanydrion. Men gathered to that place; and so the brotherhood came to number eight in all.

"One day, when the saint had called me, we went to visit the brethren at the Monastery of Saint Hilarion. They received us with great joy and offered us hospitality for many days. But the devil, who from the beginning has persecuted the slaves of God, transformed himself into the appearance of Saint Epiphanios. While we were away, the devil, in the guise of the elder, went to our monastery. One of the brethren, one of the most unpractised and negligent of monks, hastened to reverence him. That brother, after prostrating himself to the ground before that most roguish demon, became demonized. He ran here and there in a rambunctious manner. The other fathers could not understand how that brother, hitherto of sound mind, was suddenly out of his mind. The saint, discerning the event by the power of the Spirit, spoke of it to the great Hilarion and said, 'A wolf has entered the monastery and has agitated all the brothers.' Consequently, Epiphanios, taking his leave after embracing all the brothers, returned to our monastery. He sent up fervent prayer to the man-loving God on behalf of the brother in tribulation. The sufferer, by the presence of the saint, was delivered from that demon which troubled him. As a result of this incident, the elder exhorted the brethren how to be on their guard against such demonic assaults.

"At another time, three rustics came to the monastery. In one of them there dwelt a demon. The two other companions supplicated the saint to drive out the demon. The saint said, 'Take your friend, children, and depart in peace. For, in the name of Jesus Christ, there will no longer abide an evil spirit in him.' Those countryfolk believed the word of the saint and departed. As soon as they arrived at their houses, the demon took flight from their afflicted friend. Hence, he was completely healed from that same hour.

"Now there was a certain spot in the desert, at a distance of sixty stadia (almost seven miles), where a lion would emerge from its lair and devour many passersby. Consequently, those who needed to traverse that area did so in large caravans for safety. The majority of them conceived the idea to visit the saint's monastery and seek his help. With tear-filled eyes, they besought the righteous man to send up prayer to God and drive out the lion from those parts. The saint remarked, 'In the name of the Lord, let us go thither and have a look at this man-eating lion.' When they all arrived at the thicket where his lair was situated, those with the saint went a comfortable distance away and looked on from that vantage point. It was then that the lion exited from that bushy area. The moment the beast cast its glance upon Father Epiphanios, it fell down to the ground and expired. Those who had accompanied the saint and witnessed this miracle marvelled at the spectacle. The saint then addressed them and said,

'If you have faith in Jesus Christ, in like manner can you all bring down those who form designs against you.'"

Among the many virtues that God bestowed upon the saint, He granted also this one. The saint could explain and interpret the divine writings with all truth. Whether he read to the brethren from the Old or the New Testaments, he expounded upon all the passages. Now there was a philosopher, also named Epiphanios, at Edessa. He was a skilled orator who had heard of the saint's reputation for learning and articulating on scriptural verses. He, consequently, desired to converse with Father Epiphanios. He, therefore, moved out of Edessa and came to the saint's monastery. When the philosopher first caught sight of the man of God, he understood that the saint was the one for whom he had undertaken this pilgrimage. He went to the elder in order to reverence him. The saint then said to him, "I marvel, O philosopher, and I wonder for what cause that such a one as thyself, a great rhetorician, should undertake such a journey. Why wouldest thou traverse long roads in order to come to me, a man ignorant and a sinner?" The philosopher replied, "Cease marvelling regarding this, O much longed-for teacher, for the conversation of sages usually demands verbosity; but that which thou hast just uttered speaks volumes. From that one utterance, one may obtain a lesson on diverse subjects."

So spoke the philosopher and then he held his peace. The saint then began reading aloud the first book of the Old Testament, Genesis. The philosopher, on the one hand, was accepting some things that were written, but, on the other hand, was gainsaying others. After three days of discussions, still no concord was reached. Nevertheless, the philosopher, taking note of the saint's pure and holy conduct of life, as well as his morals and ethics, came to love and respect very much the man of God. On the fourth day, the philosopher said, "O teacher, my stay in this place is pleasant and I should love to dwell here also." The saint remarked, "This is of thine own choosing. So if this is what thou hast resolved to do, dwell here." The philosopher then asked, "Shall I bring my books?" The saint answered, "Bring them." The philosopher then declared, "I will not depart from this place, but I beseech thee to send Callistus that he might bring back my books and belongings." The biographer then says, "Let us now say something about Monk Callistus." Hearken!

The number in the monastery swelled to fifty. Among the fathers there was one named Callistus, who was the son of Aetius, the prefect of Rome. Before Callistus joined the monastery, he, when he was a young man, had become demonized. One night, in his sleep, though he did not know the elder, he dreamed that he saw Father Epiphanios. The holy man said to him, "Callistus, wilt thou be made whole? Desirest thou to be delivered from the unclean spirit that troubles thee?" The youth asked, "Who art thou, milord? Canst thou expel the demon?" Then the elder said, "I am Epiphanios. I dwell in Phoenicia of Palestine, at the monastery retreat called Spanydrion. If I drive out the demon that torments thee, shalt thou come to my monastery and dwell with me as a monk?" Callistus answered, "Cast out the demon, milord, and I will gladly dwell with thee." Epiphanios then cautioned him, "Take care not to do otherwise, for the demon will come again into thee!"

With these words ringing in his ears, Callistus was stirred from his sleep. He perceived that the demon had been driven away and that he was restored. He went and told his father the gladsome tidings of his liberation. He, after three months, disclosed to his father the whole of what had transpired in his dream and of the agreement he entered into with the saint. "I wish, father," said he, "to go to Phoenicia and find Epiphanios that I might dwell with him at Spanydrion." The young man explained that he feared the return of that relentless demon if he did not keep his pledge. He believed that a second attack by the demon would be worse than the first.[11] His father yielded before his son's promise to the saint, furnishing him with many silver coins. He, thereupon, sent him forth with menservants to protect Callistus on his journey. Callistus discovered Father Epiphanios in Phoenicia. He described all that he had seen and experienced. He, as a result, lived at the monastery and received the monastic tonsure. As for the money which he brought, it was used to build a proper monastery complex. His father's menservants were directed to return to Aetius. Hence, it was to Father Callistus that the obedience was given to retrieve the books and goods of the Edessene philosopher. Callistus took with him two novices and three camels. He went, by command of the saint, to Edessa and brought back to the monastery the philosopher's books. Thereafter, the saint and the philosopher, on a daily basis, found themselves in no small contention. The saint, one day, spoke these words of Scripture to the philosopher: "Thus says the Prophet Daniel: 'The court of judgment sat and the books were opened [Dan. 7:10].'" The elder then added, "Bring to me, then, thine own books and I will bring mine, that is, those given by God to me. And let us sit down that we might form a judgment between us."

The saint placed the divine Scriptures to the right and the books of the philosopher were set to the left. The two then began with the creation of the cosmos. The saint, on the one hand, used the text of Genesis that was written by Moses. The philosopher used the writings of Hesiod.[12] Readings took place from both books, which resulted in a dispute. However, light is light and darkness is darkness. Moses' book of Genesis is truth, and Hesiod's book of

[11] Cf. Mt. 12:45.

[12] The story of the creation in early Greek cosmology, as told by the Greek poet Hesiod (ca. 700 B.C.) in his *Theogony* (and the later Roman version of the same event given in Ovid's *Metamorphoses*), speaks of Chaos, then Gaea (Earth) and Eros (Desire). He speaks of thirty gods in his fable-filled poetry.

the generation of the gods is false. This is because Moses wrote Genesis with the grace of God, while Hesiod, though he had life of God, yet he had error and deception from the demons.

For one whole year, the argument surrounding this theme ensued between the saint and the philosopher. The philosopher had no success in prevailing over the saint. While the saint was attempting to bring around the philosopher to the truth, seven rustics came to the monastery. They brought with them a certain demonized young man. Since they were unable to constrain him, they bound him with chains. The saint then challenged the philosopher, saying, "Invoke the multitude of thy gods and expel the demon from the youth." The philosopher, hearing this charge, thought that he had finally vanquished the saint. But since the philosopher knew he could do nought of what was asked of him, and knew not how to counter the elder, he made the same request of him. The saint understood this evasion and said to the philosopher, "What sayest thou, O philosopher, concerning this youth? Shouldest thou heal him by thy gods, then I would believe in them. But should he be made well by my God, the Crucified, then thou wilt believe in Him." The philosopher, however, did not believe that Epiphanios truly meant what he was proposing. In fact, he thought it was some kind of jest. The saint, nevertheless, approached the demonized man and asked, "Dost thou wish that I should loose the irons from thy hands?"

The philosopher, hearing these things, made haste inside of one of the cells. He closed the door tight and reasoned within himself and said, "That monk, as one inexperienced, wishes to loose the bonds of the afflicted youth. Let me leave from that spot lest I should suffer some evil when he is loosed." The saint, in fact, removed the irons from the sufferer. Epiphanios then made the sign of the life-giving Cross thrice over the youth, addressing the demon and saying, "I, the sinner, Epiphanios, the slave of the Lord, command thee in the name of Jesus Christ, the crucified Son of God, to come forth from that man and no longer trouble him." Straightway then—behold the miracle!—the demon went out of the youth, leaving him sound of mind and restored to a good condition. The philosopher opened the door and beheld that the youth was healed. He hastened to venerate the saint, saying to him, "O Epiphanios, victor and crown-bearer, I believe in thy words! Yea, I believe by means of the deeds which thou hast wrought, that is to say, this miracle performed before my eyes. For, while words just fly and fade in the air, works are fruit-bearing and are manifest. For this cause do I also wish to become a slave of the Crucified." The saint then said to him, "Why dost thou think to marvel at this, O philosopher, as though I executed the wonder? Nay, I did not energize this miracle, but the Son of God performs all these good things by means of those who believe in

Him." The philosopher, hearing this response, implored the saint to baptize him.

"The saint," continues the biographer, "then led him and me to the great Hilarion, who administered holy Baptism. After this took place, the saint requested the great Hilarion to send one of the brethren with Epiphanios, the newly-illumined, to the Bishop of Eleftheropolis that he might be ordained to the priesthood. When this was arranged, we then departed for our monastery. The elder then summoned all the brotherhood and announced, 'Behold, the one whom it was formerly thought that he was a great philosopher—even though he was not—has now, with the grace of the Christ, become truly a philosopher and worthy priest! He, from henceforth, shall become your spiritual father.' Epiphanios, therefore, the former philosopher, was accounted worthy by God to receive such extraordinary grace that he also became abbot of the brethren."

Saint Epiphanios in Egypt

Since many were coming to the monastery and not giving the saint any peace and quiet, he decided to leave those parts for Egypt. He, thereupon, called the brethren to himself and said, "I wish, children, to go to the monastery of the great Hilarion and visit with him and the brothers there." The saint's disciples, nevertheless, grasped what was about to happen. They understood that his flight was imminent. They fell before his feet and begged him, with much weeping and lamenting, not to depart. The saint took pity on them and said he would not leave. "But then with the passage of ten days and nights, he called me to follow him. We set out in the direction toward Jerusalem where we venerated our life, that is, the precious Cross of the Lord. After we made a pilgrimage throughout the holy land and offered up prayer and reverence at the shrines and holy sites, we went forth from Jerusalem and toward Egypt. On the way, we encountered a demonized woman, who lunged at the saint and began tearing at his outer garment. The demon then immediately left the woman. She kneeled before the feet of the saint, beseeching him to forgive her and not to be angered with her. The saint then said to the woman, 'Go in health to thy house, for the one who rent my garment is gone.' Thus, the woman, restored whole, returned to her house. We, consequently, went on to Joppa, which was commonly called Jaffa or Yafo. From there we entered into a ship, setting sail for Alexandria.

"It was there that we met Aquila, a certain teacher of the law of the Jews. It was he with whom the elder entered into a discussion over certain sections of the Old Testament. A rivalry ensued that day and into the following day. The debate was lengthened until Aquila was persuaded by the saint's words. He finally asked to be made a Christian. Epiphanios, therefore, took him and led him before Patriarch Athanasios the Great (b. 295-373),[13] the pope of the Alexandrian see, in order to catechize him. Saint Athanasios joyfully received the Jew who wished to convert to the Faith of the Christ. We, then, exited the city and went to those parts of the upper Thebaid.[14]

"On the way we met a certain disciple of the great Anthony (d. 356).[15] His name was Paphnutios, to whom the saint said, 'Bless us, father!' He replied, 'May you be blessed in the name of the Lord!' Since Paphnutios uttered this blessing, we embraced one another and then sat down in that same place that we might take refreshment. The saint then questioned Paphnutios about all the accomplishments of the great Anthony. Abba Paphnutios recounted that venerable elder's history. Afterward, the holy Epiphanios said, 'I wish, father, to dwell in Nitria.'[16] Paphnutios remarked, 'Go in health and

---

[13] Saint Athanasios the Great is commemorated by the holy Church on the 18th of January and the 2nd of May.

[14] The Thebaid, administratively, was the southern province of Upper and Lower Thebaid, with its capital at Antinoöpolis (modern Sheikh 'Ibade, 177 miles or 285 kilometers south of Cairo). It was the heartland of Egyptian monasticism and center of the classic literary dialect of classic Coptic known as Sahidic. Under Emperor Valens (r. 364–378), Antinoöpolis became the seat of two bishops: one Orthodox and the other Monophysite.

[15] Saint Anthony the Great is commemorated by the holy Church on the 17th of January.

[16] Nitria itself probably lies under the modern village of el-Barnudj in the upper eastern delta. The unknown author of the *History of the Egyptian Monks* (perhaps Flavius Rufinus) visited the area at the end of the 4th C. He tells us: "Then we came to Nitria, the best-known of all monasteries of Egypt, about forty miles from Alexandria; it takes its name from a nearby town where nitre (nitrate) is collected....In this place there are about fifty dwellings, or not many less, set near together and under one father. In some of them, there are many living together, in others a few and in some there are brothers who live alone. Though they are divided by their dwellings, they remain bound together and inseparable in faith and love."

Another early visitor to the monastery was Palladius, writer of *Lausiac History*, who tells us that: "I...crossed over to Mount Nitria. Between this mountain and Alexandria there lies a lake called Marea, seventy miles long. I was a day and a half crossing this to the mountain on its southern shore. Beyond the mountain stretches the great desert reaching as far as Ethiopia, Mazicae, and Mauritania. On the mountain live close to five thousand men following different ways of life, each as he can or will. Thus some live alone, others in pairs, and some in groups. There are seven bakeries on this mountain serving these men as well as the anchorites of the Great Desert, six hundred in all....On this mountain of Nitria there is a great church....The guesthouse is close to the church. Here the arriving guest is received until such time as he leaves voluntarily. He stays here all the time, even for a period of two or three years. They allow a guest to remain at leisure for one week; from then on he must help in the (continued...)

enjoy the sayings of the fathers in that desert. Collect their spiritual conversations and satiate thyself with them. But afterward, get thee to Cyprus and nourish the sheep for wool and esteem children that thou mayest have lambs.[17] After they had offered up prayer for a considerable time, we left to go on our way."

The words of divine Abba Paphnutios, reminiscent of the proverb, were prophetic and were for the benefit of Saint Epiphanios regarding what would happen in the future. The saying is explained in this fashion. He was told to go to Nitria and meet the fathers that he might put into practise their holy actions and spiritual concepts, for future use, when he would later shepherd the rational flock of Christ, that is to say, the Christians, in Cyprus. Thus, what he would gather among the fathers in Nitria, he would cover, as a garment, and adorn before Christ, the Cypriots as a true flock. As for esteeming or honoring children, Epiphanios is exhorted to treat and care for the unruly idolaters of the island that he might bring them to orderliness and gentleness, which is what took place. He took an interest in them and converted them to the knowledge of God, thus making them lambs in the flock of Christ.

It was in the neighborhood of Leontopolis[18] that a certain monk, named Hierax, was conspicuous for his severe abstinence. He partook of neither oil nor wine. Many people thought that he was a man good and pure and a clairvoyant too. The saint heard of his reputation, and desired to see him. He,

---

[16](...continued)
garden, bakery, or kitchen. Should he be a noteworthy person, they give him a book, not allowing him to converse with anyone before the sixth hour. On this mountain there are living also doctors and pastry cooks. They use wine, too, and wine is sold. All these work with their hands at making linen, so that none of them is in want. And indeed, along about the ninth hour one can stand and hear the divine psalmody issuing forth from each cell and imagine one is high above in Paradise. They occupy the church on Saturdays and Sundays only. Eight priests have charge of the church; while the senior priest lives, none of the others celebrates or gives the sermon. They, rather, simply sit quietly by him." See description and photographs at http://www.touregypt.net/featurestories/kellia.htm.

[17] See Prov. 27:25, 26 LXX: "Take care that thou mayest have wool of sheep for clothing: pay attention to the land (*pedion*), that thou mayest have lambs." Paphnutios, using the similar sounding word παῖδας (children) instead of πεδίον (a plain or flat open country) said, "Nourish the sheep for wool; and esteem children (*pedas*) that thou mayest have lambs," foretold how Epiphanios would make the sons of the Cypriots prolific and fertile in the Faith.

[18] At Leontopolis, about ten kilometers (6.25 miles) southeast of the modern town of Mit Ghamir on the Damietta branch of the Nile, are the several mounds that represent all that is left of ancient Taremu (Leontopolis, or "City of the Lions"). The ancient Egyptian name for the site means "Land of the Fish."

therefore went to Hierax's monastery. Upon arriving, Epiphanios found a multitude of people hearkening to Hierax's teaching. Hierax, when he caught sight of the saint, asked, "Whence comest thou and what is thy name?" When Hierax learned that the elder was from Palestine and that his name was Epiphanios, he became very timid; for he had heard of the fame of the same, that Epiphanios was learned and had the gift of foresight. Despite his faintheartedness, he kept teaching the people. He was discoursing on the resurrection of the dead, saying that, in the future age, the same flesh of man is not going to rise but rather another. He explained the reason for this is that the one we now possess dissolves into the earth, in accordance with the scriptural passage, "For earth thou art and to earth thou shalt return [Gen. 3:19]." He also claimed that, in the resurrection, children that have died would not attain perfection.

The saint, hearing these errors, was displeased. He reproved him before the whole company, saying, "May thy mouth be rendered without speech so that thou mayest learn not to blaspheme!" Straightway, with the pronouncement of the saint, Hierax remained fixed in his tracks and could not speak. His audience, beholding the miracle at that point, was ecstatic with what Epiphanios wrought upon Hierax. The saint then addressed the people, teaching them the Church's position concerning the resurrection, bringing forth testimony from the divine writings. After the passage of about three hours, while Hierax was still speechless, the saint said to him, "Hearken to the Faith, the sure and steadfast one, and speak henceforth the word of truth." Forthwith, the bond of Hierax's tongue was loosed and he began to speak. He professed his fault and repented of his erroneous thought on the subject of the resurrection of the dead.

Epiphanios left that place and moved toward the Upper Thebaid, toward a wonderful man named John who was distinguished for his virtue. "He received us with much love and cheerfulness. Some men from that place had brought near to John a demonized youth, whom they had bound first. Now when the afflicted youth beheld that Epiphanios was in the midst of the company, he said with a great voice, 'Why hast thou come here, O Epiphanios, slave of God?' Thus, the demonized youth shouted from the sixth hour to the ninth hour. After that time period, he suddenly managed to cut free of his bonds. He ran straight toward the venerable elder, touching the feet of Epiphanios and crying aloud, 'O slave of God, deliver me by the God in Whom thou believest!' Prior to his pleas, the saint had uttered to the demon not to come forth from the youth lest John should think that he casts out demons. The saint then said to the youth, 'Rise up, man, why dost thou trouble me?' Forthwith—behold the wonder!—the demon emerged. The youth rose up healthy and sound, giving thanks to the saint. We stayed close to John for three days.

Afterward, we went down to Voukolia (Bucolia) where we sojourned for seven years. But even there the righteous man was troubled by visitors.

"There once came to the saint a certain philosopher, named Evdaimon, with whom he conversed over a ten-day period. The saint demonstrated the truth from the divine Scriptures. The philosopher contended and contradicted him unsuccessfully. Now Evdaimon had his son with him, a child who was blind in one eye. One day the saint asked him, 'I see, O philosopher, that thou art adorned with elegance and opulence. I see also that still thou hast many gods. But how come thou hast not provided for thy child? Why hast thou not taken care to have his eye treated?' The philosopher chuckled at what he heard and said to the venerable man, 'If in all the inhabited world my son were the only one not having sight in one eye, I would attend to it. But since there are numberless persons in the world who have no vision at all, why should I bother since he has the one good eye?' The saint then remarked, 'If, however, thine own child solely had this impairment, wouldest thou pursue his healing?' Evdaimon commented, 'Nothing more than to keep telling myself that no one in all the world is like unto my child.' The saint continued and said, 'Do not take my words, O philosopher, as a jest, because in our midst is God Himself. But bring thy boy here; and thou shalt behold the glory of God.' Straightway, the saint took hold of the lad's hand. The saint then made the sign of the life-creating Cross over the blind eye. After he did this three times—lo, the miracle!—immediately, he regained his sight. As Evdaimon himself witnessed this wonderworking, he besought the saint to make him a Christian. But the saint told him to go to the bishop who could baptize him."

Saint Epiphanios Returns to the Monastery of Hilarion the Great

The biographer then says, "The saint became renowned in all of Egypt, so that the bishops were looking for an opportunity to consecrate him to the episcopacy. But God, Who was the guide of the saint, revealed their intent to him. The holy man, therefore, decided to depart from that place. We returned to our own homeland and went to the monastery of Hilarion the Great. When the brethren at that monastery detected the saint coming, they rejoiced greatly. The man of God's coming was no small consolation to them since their own elder, that is, the venerable Hilarion, had left the monastery. Hilarion, desiring rest and quiet, longed to flee both the approbation and the harassment of men. Hilarion, therefore, had sailed to the parts around Paphos on the island of Cyprus.[19] We, nevertheless, stayed forty days at that monastery and then left

[19] Paphos (Gk. Pafos) is presently located in the southwestern Republic of Cyprus. Paphos was also the name of two ancient cities that finally formed the modern town. The older town, Palaipaphos, was located at modern Pirgos (Kouklia); New Paphos, which had superseded Old Paphos by Roman times, was ten miles (sixteen kilometers) (continued...)

for our own monastery. I am speaking of the monastery in which the saint had made the Edessene Epiphanios abbot. In the meantime, a multitude of monks had settled there, for Abbot Epiphanios proved to be a diligent and marvellous man. The saint, upon viewing the brethren, was exceedingly glad and kept glorifying God for the growth at Spanydrion."

At about that time, by reason of a severe drought, famine struck all of Phoenicia. People in droves were coming to the saint, begging him to send up prayer to the man-loving God that He might grant rain so that the earth might yield her fruit. The saint said to them, "Why do you people trouble me? I, too, am a sinful man." They would not desist importuning him, but rather they increased their petitions until the ninth hour of the day. The saint then said to the abbot, "Command the brethren to prepare the refectory, so these people may eat and be filled with good cheer; and then they will return to their homes." As the fathers prepared the table, the saint retired to his cell and went to his knees, entreating God to send down rain upon the thirsty earth.

Immediately with the prayer of the saint, the sky was filled with clouds. Flashes of lightning and rolls of thunder preceded a downpour of rain. The people rose up from the table and gave thanks to God. It rained heavily for three days throughout Phoenicia. The people, therefore, went to the cell of the saint and requested that he supplicate God to halt the precipitation. The saint said to them, "Why, my children, do you possess such thoughts regarding me? I am but human even as you. Nevertheless, our benefactor and God knows that we have need and He will provide for it." But they besought him with greater persistence. The man of God then said to the abbot, "Command that the brethren prepare a table for the people, that they may eat and drink and afterward return to their places." After the table was readied, they went in. The people asked that the saint might give the blessing. The saint bowed to the general request and said, "Blessed be the Lord!" Straightway, the thrashing rain was arrested. Owing to the significant interruptions and intrusions visited upon the saint by visitors, he again sought to leave from that place.

It was also about that time that the bishops of the land assembled in order to consecrate a prelate for a widowed bishopric. They examined the problem of finding someone worthy of the dignity. They judged it blessed to

---

[19](...continued)

farther west. New Paphos and Ktima together form present-day Paphos. Old Paphos, which was settled by Greek colonists in the Mycenaean period, contained a famous temple of Aphrodite. In Hellenic times, Paphos was second only to Salamis in extent and influence. Old Paphos, eventually, dwindled in influence until it was finally deserted after the 4th C. New Paphos, which had been the port town of Old Paphos, became the administrative capital of all of Cyprus in both Ptolemaic and Roman times. *The Encyclopaedia Britannica 2004 Deluxe Edition CD-ROM*, s.v. "Paphos."

consecrate Epiphanios. The bishops summoned a certain monk, an extremely pious man, named Polyvios, who was acquainted with the saint. They charged him with the following commission: "Quickly mount a beast of burden and go to the monastery to see if Epiphanios is there. Then hurry back and inform us. Take heed lest thy mission should be made manifest to anyone, even Epiphanios. Let no one know that thou wast dispatched by us."

Polyvios arrived at the monastery and went to the saint in order to greet him. The saint inquired of him, "For what reason, child, hast thou come here?" Polyvios answered, "I, my father, wish always to tell the truth." The saint then commented, "Thou camest, child, because the bishops sent thee to see whether or not I was here. The sinner Epiphanios, however, walks from place to place. He sighs and trembles on account of his sins. I am not worthy to become a bishop. But do thou, my child, remain here and leave the bishops to seek those worthy of the office of Bishop." Polyvios accepted the word of the saint. He, thereupon, sent back the beast of burden and remained there. The Lord, Who guided the saint, enlightened him to go to Cyprus. "That very night, he took along Polyvios and exited the monastery. We," continued John, the saint's biographer, "went to Jerusalem in order to venerate the vivifying and precious Cross."

Saint Epiphanios in Cyprus

The biographer writes: "After three days, we came down to the shore. Upon entering a ship, we voyaged to Paphos. We made inquiries and learned the whereabouts of the great Hilarion. When we met, there was general happiness all around. We took up our abode there for two months. Hilarion, for his part, was abundantly overburdened by visitors coming to see him. When the holy Epiphanios decided to depart from that place, Hilarion asked him, 'Whither dost thou wish to go, child?' The saint replied, 'I wish to go to Gaza.' Hilarion then said, 'Thou shouldest go to Salamis.[20] It is there that thou shalt find a place to dwell.' But the saint had no wish to go to there. The great Hilarion remarked, 'I tell thee, child, it is there that thou needest to go and to dwell. And do not disobey my words lest thou shouldest suffer peril in the sea.'" But Epiphanios, knowing that an episcopacy was awaiting him in that place, did not wish to comply.

---

[20] Salamis was a principal city of ancient Cyprus. It is situated on the island's east coast, north of modern Famagusta. Salamis, on account of its excellent harbor, grew and became the chief Cypriot outlet for trade with Phoenicia, Egypt, and Cilicia. The city suffered repeatedly from a series of devastating earthquakes, so that it was completely rebuilt and renamed Constantia by Emperor Constantius II (337–361). Under Christian rule, Salamis was the metropolitan see of Cyprus. It had been honored, until the Latin occupation of the island (1191-1571), with an autocephalous archbishop under whom there were fourteen bishops. Today the see of the Archbishop of Cyprus is at Lefkosia.

"We therefore went down to the shore and found two ships. One was bound for Gaza and the other for Salamis. We entered the ship sailing for Gaza. As we were traveling, mighty swells broke against the ship; so that it was in danger of shattering. For three days we were in despair. On the fourth day the ship was forced to put in at Salamis. We all disembarked from the ship and fell to the ground, as dead men, on account of much weariness and abstinence from food. After we tarried there for three days, we, by the grace of God, recovered and were restored to a good condition. But again, the saint, wished to depart from that place.

"Now it happened at that time that all the bishops of Cyprus had gathered together. This was due to the death of the Bishop of Salamis, for which the hierarchs desired to elect another in his place. They besought God to reveal to them who had the strength to shepherd the flock of Christ in a God-pleasing manner. Now there was present the Bishop of Kythrea,[21] a man of much sanctity. He was accounted worthy of martyrdom, but he survived it. He suffered many tortures, for the sake of Christ, at the hands of the idolaters. It was he who was vouchsafed a divine revelation regarding the much-needed consecration. We should also add that he was an ancient man, having served fifty-eight years as a bishop. All the other bishops reckoned him as their father, because, together with his other virtues, this confessor and elder was also a clairvoyant. It was to this most holy hierarch, therefore, named Pappos,[22] that God revealed that Epiphanios should be ordained Bishop of Salamis.

"Now it was the time of the harvesting of the grapes. The saint, as he was resolved to enter the ship with the course set for Gaza, said to Polyvios, 'Let us go to the marketplace and buy grapes that we might have them for our voyage.' So they went into the city. The saint selected two beautiful clusters and said to the seller of grapes, 'How much dost thou want for these?' The saint had the custom of not disputing with a seller, but giving the price asked. While the seller was declaring the cost of the grapes, there arrived the venerable Pappos being supported by two deacons. In his company there were also three other bishops. Pappos said to Epiphanios, 'Abba, leave the grapes[23] and follow us to the church.' Epiphanios then brought to mind the divine verse which says, 'I was glad because of them that said unto me: Let us go into the

---

[21] In other texts, it is written that he was Bishop of Chytron (Chitron). See Delehaye, *Les saints de Chypre*, p. 243.

[22] This venerable Pappos, in all likelihood, is the saint commemorated by the holy Church on the 3rd of June. In the Sinaite Codex 140, there is a commemoration on the 24th of October for a venerable Bishop Pappos of Skythros in Cyprus.

[23] When the blood of the grape is mentioned, the wine of the chalice of the blood of the Lord is signified—the saving drink prefigured in the Old Testament [cf. Num. 13:24; Deut. 32:14].

house of the Lord [Ps. 121:1].' He, consequently, followed Pappos to the church. Then Pappos said, 'Say a prayer, father.' Epiphanios then replied, 'Forgive me, father, for I am not consecrated to the priesthood.'

"Hearing this response, Pappos intoned, 'Peace to all.' Straightway, one deacon took Epiphanios by the head, assisted by many other deacons. Forcing Epiphanios, they led him into the altar and to Pappos. First, Epiphanios was ordained to the office of Deacon. The following day, he was elevated to the priesthood. The day after that he was consecrated to the episcopacy. Then, after the dismissal, while they were entering the episcopal house, Pappos said to Epiphanios, 'Give the command that they prepare a table for the fathers that they might eat and rejoice because of thy consecration as archpastor.' Epiphanios, nonetheless, by reason of the burden of the high priesthood, was so sorrowful that he wept and lamented inconsolably.

"Pappos, seeing him weeping, remarked, 'I ought to keep silence, but thou, child, givest me cause to be foolish and to reveal the following events. Thou shouldest know, then, that all the bishops gathered here with the aim of finding a worthy ordinand to consecrate as archbishop. They laid this onerous task upon me, the sinner, charging me to supplicate God to uncover the one worthy for the office. After immuring myself within my cell, I entreated God about this. A lightning-like radiance shone forth in my cell and I heard a voice saying to me, the sinful one, "Pappos, Pappos, hearken!" I was very much filled with fear and said, "What commandest thou me, O Lord?" The voice then responded in a joyful tone, "Take along with thee the deacons and go down into the marketplace. There thou shalt find a certain monk buying grapes. His countenance is like unto the one depicted in the icon of Prophet Elias. This monk's name is Epiphanios. In his company thou shalt find two monks. But do not immediately make manifest to him what thou art about to do lest he should take flight." Behold, I have become foolish in speaking thus, but thou hast compelled me! Therefore, give thought what thou art doing and take heed well to thyself lest thou shouldest appear to oppose the will of God. Because I was sent forth from God and performed that which I was obliged to do. I am even innocent regarding this. Keep in mind all these things.'

"The saint, hearing these circumstances, made a prostration to the ground before the venerable Pappos then said, 'Cease being angry, father, against me; because I am a sinful man and am not worthy of the loftiness of the episcopacy, for which dignity I am saddened.' So he spoke and then venerated all the bishops. He then directed that a table be set for them. They ate and were refreshed and, subsequently, each bishop returned to his diocese."

After three days passed, a certain good and reverent Christian was taken into custody. His name was Evgnomus. He was jailed by the affluent Drakos. This was owing to a past due debt of one hundred gold coins. Since

Evgnomus was from Rome, as a stranger in the city, he knew no one who could deliver him from prison. When the saint learned of the dilemma, he paid a visit to Drakos. He besought him to have Evgnomus released from prison. But Drakos, possessed of a beastly and untamed disposition, replied to the saint, "Begone, thou dost transgress the laws of our state! Bring me one hundred gold coins, which thy friend owes me, and afterward take him in hand." The saint returned to the episcopal house. He took up one hundred gold coins, which were in the house for the needs of the church. He gave the money to Drakos, which brought about Evgnomus' release from prison. Now a certain deacon of the church, Harinos (Charinos) by name, was most undisciplined. He stirred up all the clergy against the saint, saying such words as these against Epiphanios: "This stranger wishes to consume all the substance of the Church. Come, then, that we might expel him; otherwise we, too, shall be guilty of this sin of plunder." As for Harinos, he was a very rich man who was desirous of having the saint driven out that he might become archbishop in his stead.

The clergy then went forth to confront the saint. Harinos spoke up and said to the archbishop, "Wast thou not sufficiently pleased, Epiphanios, O thou who camest among us without even an overcoat, to take charge of the Church? But rather, as a stranger, thou hast scattered her belongings? Who can endure this? Either return every coin of the Church or go back to thy homeland." Evgnomus learned of the archbishop's predicament and took action. He returned to Rome where he sold all his goods and property. Whatever money Evgnomus received, he took every coin with him to Cyprus and to the saint. He entrusted all of it in the hands of Epiphanios, which was well over the amount of one hundred coins which was paid for his freedom. Evgnomus, as he relinquished all his wealth, was also resolved to remain with the saint and serve the Church for the rest of his days. (This he did until his repose.) Now when Evgnomus delivered up the money to the archbishop, Epiphanios wasted no time giving one hundred of the coins to Harinos. As for the rest of the money donated by Evgnomus, it was distributed among the poor. Harinos, rogue that he was, called the clergy to him and boasted, "Receive the gold which I have kept safe from Epiphanios who had squandered it." The clergy, having come to know the truth, in no wise wished to take hold of the one hundred coins. They said to the deacon, "Return the money to the holy man, which thou hast wrongfully retained." They had become annoyed with the deacon for inciting them to grumble against the archbishop. They reminded the deacon that the archbishop has authority over the property of the Church. If the precious souls of human beings ought to be entrusted to him, there is little need of any special injunction concerning money. Everything may be entrusted to be governed in accordance with his authority. It is he who has the care of ecclesiastical matters; so let him manage them, on the understanding that God is overseeing and supervising.[24] Despite what the other clergymen said to Harinos, he paid no heed to their words. The deacon did not return the money to the saint; instead, he kept it all. This deacon, in fact, committed many misdeeds. The knave was unscrupulous and self-indulgent, treating slightingly his archbishop. As for Epiphanios, he in no wise remembered these wrongs against himself which the deacon recklessly perpetrated. The saint bore everything with magnanimity and meekness.

One time, while all the clergy were at the episcopal residence and receiving hospitality at table, the saint, in his customary manner, was teaching them. In so doing, it was his habit always to be holding in his hands the holy Gospel. He was wont to discourse night and day on the word of God. On that particular occasion, a crow was cawing loudly. Harinos, consequently, commented to the whole company, "Who among us knows what the crow is saying?" The clergymen, however, were giving heed to the word of God and the exhortation of the saint. They, in no wise, paid any attention to the loud bird. Harinos then raised his voice and repeated the question again for a second time. When the obnoxious one received no response, he shouted aloud a third time, "I ask you all, who among you knows what the crow is communicating?"

The saint, without the least agitation, but rather with much cheerfulness, replied to Harinos, "I know what the crow is saying." Harinos remarked, "Reveal to me what the crow is saying; and I shall empower thee with all my goods." The saint declared, "The crow said that thou art not worthy to be a deacon." Straightway, with that utterance of the saint, fear and trembling overtook Harinos. He could no longer speak, nor eat, nor drink. His menservants propped him up and conveyed him to his own house where he was deposited in his bed. The following day, he expired. The former deacon had been a married man. His very pious wife was a good and innocent woman. Since she had no children, she offered all her goods to the man of God. Having renounced the world, she became a deaconess of the Church. Now she had suffered paralysis in her right hand for the past ten years. The archbishop made the sign of the life-creating Cross over the afflicted hand, which action brought about immediate healing. Thereafter, all the clergy at the diocesan house submitted themselves to the venerable man with fear and reverence.

The following practise was also preserved by the blessed Epiphanios. Whensoever he performed the divine Liturgy—at the moment that he offered the holy gifts to God and entreated Him with these words, "Make this bread..."—if he did not behold a vision,[25] he did not finish the sacred Liturgy.

---

[24] See *The Rudder*, Canons XLI and XXXVIII of the Apostles.

[25] This vision was the movement of a wooden dove which was suspended over the holy Table. Mention of this phenomenon is made in the *praktika* (minutes) of the Seventh

(continued...)

On one occasion, then, at that very moment when the saint was pronouncing those words, he beheld no vision. With tears, he besought God to reveal to him the cause. He glanced at his deacon, who was to his left, holding the *ripidion.*[26] Epiphanios noticed that the deacon had a leprous lesion on his forehead. The archbishop understood that this was the cause for the absence of the vision. Epiphanios went over to the deacon and took the fan from him, saying cheerfully, "Go, child, to thy house without receiving the Mysteries today." Another deacon then took up the fan. Epiphanios then resumed his stance and repeated the customary divine words with fear and tears. He beheld the vision and, only then, continued the divine Liturgy.

After the dismissal of the divine Liturgy, the saint summoned the deacon and asked him about the leprosy that he might learn the cause. The deacon then confessed that the previous night he had marital relations with his wife. The saint then summoned the body of priests. He spoke with a bright countenance and gladness, saying, "My children, all those who have been vouchsafed to receive the grace of the priesthood ought to keep themselves pure from every bodily and spiritual defilement lest they celebrate unworthily the divine Mysteries." Henceforth, the saint did not ordain men who had wives. He preferred monastics, venerable men, or widowers, those who had been tried and approved. And, in reality, whosoever beheld this Cypriot Church beheld her as a beautiful bride adorned by a priesthood holy and virtuous.

---

[25](...continued)
Synod and in the *Gerontikon*. The energy and manifestation is that of the Holy Spirit. The Spirit manifested Himself in this manner to the saint during the time of the sanctification of the precious gifts. The divine Amphilochios, regarding the great Basil, speaks of it in the *Leimonarion* [Ch. 150]. Saint Basil (commemorated by the holy Church on the 1st of January) had a goldsmith fashion a dove of pure gold, as an image of what took place at the Baptism of Christ, when John the Baptist bore witness and said, "I have beheld the Spirit descending out of heaven as a dove, and He abode upon Him [Jn. 1:32]." Basil, therefore, suspended it above the holy Table as a receptacle in which to store the Mysteries. Whenever the saint served the divine Liturgy and elevated the holy gifts, that golden dove, which was suspended above the holy altar, shook thrice by the power of God.

[26] Evidently, Saint Epiphanios heard about the same situation that occurred to Saint Basil who wondered why no vision was forthcoming. Basil then gazed at one of his deacons, the one holding the fans (*rhipidia or ripidia*). The deacon's attention was not on the Liturgy but was rather fixed on a pretty woman standing in the church. Basil dismissed that deacon and gave him a penance. He was to pray and fast for seven days, and distribute alms to the poor. As a result of this incident, Saint Basil commanded that a veil be hung and a partition (icon screen or iconostasion) be constructed before the sanctuary.

Saint Epiphanios' Disciples and Biographers

Up to this point in the account, the history of Saint Epiphanios' life, written by his disciple, the Priest John, has been interrupted by reason of the biographer's illness and repose. The biography was continued by another disciple, Bishop Polyvios, Bishop of Rinokoura.[27]

"May the almighty God be glorified, Who grants life to us and glorifies those who glorify Him. It was about this time that the venerable Father John, the disciple of Saint Epiphanios, contracted a grave disease that left him bedridden. He invited me to his bedside and said, 'Since the saint did not wish to have his wonderworkings recorded, those miracles that God wrought through Him, for this reason, child Polyvios, do thou take up the notes that I have kept of these accounts. I am speaking of those deeds which I saw him perform to this day. Although I did not inform him about my journal, I ask that thou makest an end of it. Take up this work today and continue to the end, because God shall add years to thy life that thou mightest remain by the side of the archbishop for as long as he shall live. Take heed, then, that thou be not negligent or careless in the task, because I have been moved by God to put in writing these events. I am already near death, so thou must take up thy pen and continue where I left off.' Then he paused and said to me, 'Do thou call to my side our venerable Father Epiphanios.'

Saint Epiphanios

"The desire of John was reported to the saint. The archbishop, therefore, went to him and said, 'Trouble not thyself, Father John, to beseech God by means of the sinner Epiphanios.' But John answered, 'Utter, father, a prayer, for I wish thee to speak for me.' The saint made a prayer and we said the 'Amen.' John then said to him, 'Lay thy hand upon me, father.' The saint then touched him. Again he said, 'Place thy hands upon my eyes, father, and give me the kiss of peace, for in but a short while I shall die.' The saint then set his hands upon John's eyes and also gave him the final kiss. Straightway, John surrendered his spirit. The saint, thereupon, fell upon the deceased's neck and

[27] Rinokoura is on the road to Egypt on the border of Palestine, some thirty-four miles from Rafia (Raphia). See also Is. 27:12 LXX for Rhinocorura. It was a titular see in Augustamnica Prima, suffragan of Pelusium. Rhinocolura or Rhinocorura was a maritime town identified usually with the present fortified village El Anish.

wept much. He was extremely sorrowful at John's repose. The archbishop then conducted the Funeral Service."

Saint Epiphanios Builds

Not much time passed before the saint went to his knees on the ground and supplicated the Lord to send forth help for the building of a church to God's holy name. The original church was small with inadequate room to receive all the faithful when they gathered together. The saint, while he was supplicating God, heard from on high: "Epiphanios!" Even though the saint heard this voice many times, he was not disturbed but said, "What hast thou marked out, my Lord?" And the Lord said, "Commence building the church." The saint, immediately, went to the place where he desired to build the temple. He, consequently, offered up the appropriate service in its entirety. Thereafter, he went straightaway to bring sixty builders and many other workers who began the construction.

There was in that city a certain idolater, very wealthy and mighty, named Drakon. He had a son bearing the same name. The younger Drakon suffered from a terrible infirmity to his right side, for which treatment his father spent much money on physicians. But the son did not receive the least relief. One day, as the saint was passing by their house, the elder Drakon was sitting outside with his sick son and other people. The archbishop greeted them all. He next took the hand of the ailing younger Drakon and remarked, "Drakon, do thou become well, even as these others." Then—lo, the wonder!—Drakon was instantly healed as Epiphanios went his way. Those standing by, beholding the miracle, were beside themselves with awe. Then the father was filled with fear and trembling, on account of which he was unable to enter the house with his own two feet. His menservants were called upon to bear him up. They conveyed him within his bedchamber and placed him on his couch.

The following day, the wife of Drakon went to the saint. She begged him to come to her home that he might send up prayer to God and raise up her ailing spouse from his bed. Therefore, the saint went to the house of Drakon. He uttered a prayer in his behalf before God. Forthwith, Drakon rose up from his bed. The following morning, Drakon took five thousand coins and brought them to the saint. The archbishop said to him, "For me, my child, sufficient is one garment to cover my body and the least amount of bread and water to sustain me. Why then dost thou offer this burden to me? If, however, thou dost wish to be glorified, go to the building of the temple of God and dispose of this money to those working at the site." Drakon, therefore, did as he was directed. Afterward, he besought the saint to baptize him and his wife.

Another idolater, the wealthy Synesios, had one child, a thirteen-year-old boy, named Efstorgios, who contracted a terrible disease around his throat.

The result was that his breath was pent up and he expired. Great lamentation and mourning came upon his house. A certain Christian, named Hermias, acquainted with the saint, said to the mother of the dead boy, "If thou shouldest call the holy Epiphanios to come here and utter a prayer for the sake of thy child, he could raise him." The bereaved mother, believing the words of Hermias, asked him to go in her behalf to the man of God. Hermias went and informed the saint with these words: "My master Synesios beseeches thee to come to his house, that thou mightest entreat God to resurrect his child who has died." The archbishop said to him, "Let us be off to the house of Synesios." And so they departed together.

When the wife of Synesios descried the saint's approach, she fell to her knees before the archbishop's feet and said, "O great physician of the Christians, thou hast come here! Demonstrate thine art and raise up our boy that we, too, may see and believe in thy Christ." The saint remarked to her, "If thou wilt believe in the crucified Jesus Christ, thou shalt see thy son rise from the dead." The mother replied, "Nothing else is found in my thoughts except to pray to the crucified Jesus." The saint, then, approached the bed of Efstorgios. Epiphanios stretched forth his hands and touched the throat of the deceased, turning it gently. He then addressed the boy with a gladsome voice, saying, "Efstorgios." Straightway—lo, the wonderworking!—the lad opened his eyes and sat up in the bed. All the bystanders, witnessing this wonder, remained ecstatic. The mother then had three thousand gold coins brought and given to the saint. The blessed man said to the woman, "I have no need of these coins; but do thou give them to thy spouse, Synesios. Let him bring the money to the temple of the Lord, the One Who raised thy son, and distribute it among those toiling there in the construction." Synesios, indeed, took up the task. Afterward, Synesios and his wife, as well as the child, received holy Baptism. Consequently, the new church was handsomely adorned with the contribution of Synesios. As to the priest for this new church, it was Polyvios, the saint's disciple, who was appointed.

"Since," comments Polyvios, "with the recent repose of our holy Father John, the need arose to ordain another priest for the new church, Archbishop Epiphanios desired to ordain me. But I, thinking upon the great burden of the dignity of the priesthood, did not accept his offer. Now the hour arrived for the divine service when I went together with the sacred archbishop into the church. I had in my mind to take flight prior to the moment of my ordination. But, when we arrived inside the church, the saint took me by the hand and said, 'Remain in this place until the time comes.' Now everyone there heard him speak these words. As I stood in that place, it became evident to me and those there that I was unable to move my feet from that spot. They remained riveted as though fastened with iron nails to the floor. When the moment came for my ordination, a deacon was dispatched who was to escort me to the holy bema: for, on that day, I was to be made a deacon; and the following day, I was scheduled to be ordained to the priesthood. When the deacon took hold of me, only then was I released from my stationary position. Following my ordination, I fell sick. The cause was from my intense fear of the office. I remained in my bed until the saint came. After he prayed to God over me, I immediately rose up from my bed completely well and whole."

Saint Epiphanios at Jerusalem

The biographer writes: "After a time, a deacon from Jerusalem came to the saint and said, 'John the Patriarch of Jerusalem is avaricious and hordes money, providing nought for the poor from the treasury.' Now Patriarch John was formerly at the monastery of the great Hilarion, at whose place he had dwelt together with Saint Epiphanios. Epiphanios wrote a letter to John, beseeching him to have mercy upon those in need, but John did not hearken. The saint, on this account, took me and we went together to Jerusalem where we venerated the holy places and shrines. When the patriarch beheld the saint, he rejoiced with profound joy. We were given a well-appointed domicile. John also extended a daily invitation to us to share his table. We, therefore, were offered many diverse foods and drinks, while the poor were deprived of all of these things and complained of their want.

"During one of those repasts, when the best silver was used, the saint said to John, 'Give to me, father, as many silver vessels and adornments as thou hast. But, I beseech thee, only give me the best, to thine own glory.' The patriarch asked, 'Why is that father?' The saint said, 'I have high-ranking dignitaries visiting me from my island. Since I need to refresh them in my own quarters, let them see thy silver service. Then I might have the opportunity to show them the house given for my use and thine exceeding generosity and kindness by letting me use thy silver vessels and dinnerware. When they return to Cyprus, they surely shall speak of thine unfeigned love toward me as well as praise thine own resplendence and riches. I shall use the silver only for a short space.' The patriarch was pleased with the idea and brought forth many good pieces and presented them to the saint. The miserly John asked, 'Surely what I have brought is sufficient for thy purpose!' Epiphanios then asked John, 'Nay. If thou hast any other vessels or utensils, father, bring them to me. Thus, we will show them to these friends who are sure to be filled with awe and astonishment at thy glory. Only do thou remember all thou hast given me that I might return them afterward.' John, with this assurance, brought out other vessels of the finest workmanship and quality. The patriarch then remarked, 'Take all of these elegant pieces that thou mightest offer hospitality to thy friends, even those whom thou lovest.' The saint took these exquisite silver vessels and plates of John. Their value came to about one thousand five hundred litrae or ninety-four pounds of silver.[28] Epiphanios sold to one dealer, the Roman Asterius, all the silver he collected from the patriarch. The silver merchant then returned to Rome. The money that Epiphanios received in that exchange was distributed, night and day, to the poor. After the passage of considerable time, John asked Epiphanios, 'What has become of my silver objects?' The saint answered, 'Have a little patience, father, because I still have need to entertain some strangers. Afterward, I shall return them.'

"Then one day, after much time, when the patriarch and the archbishop were found inside of the church of the Lord, where the saving Tree of the life-giving Cross was treasured, John again inquired of the saint, 'When shall I receive the silver service and plate that I loaned thee?' Epiphanios answered calmly, 'I shall give them to thee, father.' John, thereupon, became very angry. He seized the saint by his outer cassock in a tight stranglehold and said, 'Epiphanios, unjust one, thou shalt not exit from here, nor rest, nor find peace, if thou dost not return to me the silver vessels which I gave thee.' For two hours he applied force and suppressed the archbishop's movements. He denounced the holy man and insulted him in such a way that witnesses were horrified at the harsh language employed by John. As for the saint, he in no wise was either distressed or dismayed. Much rather, at one point, he breathed upon the face of John who, instantly, was blinded in both eyes. Fear gripped all the onlookers. John then fell down before the saint, imploring him to pray to God that he might recover his eyesight. The saint remarked, 'Go and venerate the precious Cross; and thou shalt receive that which thou hast requested.' But John would not leave off begging him. The saint, consequently, exhorted him in that which was needed. Epiphanios then rested his hand on John. Forthwith, the vision in the patriarch's right eye returned. John continued to supplicate the saint to heal his left eye as well. The saint commented, 'This is not my work, father. God closed it, so He will open it and make it well as it pleases Him, that thou mightest come to prudence.' After this episode, since John was chastised and censured by the saint, he amended his former acquisitiveness and cupidity. He became merciful, openhanded, and virtuous in all his affairs."

Saint Epiphanios Returns to Cyprus

The biographer then tells us: "As we exited Jerusalem to return to Cyprus, two men, wanting in understanding, agreed between themselves to mock the saint. One of them pretended that he was dead, by lying on the ground. The other fellow, standing over him, said to the saint, 'Venerable father, take pity on this dead man and place upon him some covering.' The saint, hearing these words, stood still and faced east. He entreated God for the

[28] As a weight, one litra is twelve ounces.

man on the ground, as though he were dead, so that the Lord would give him rest in the tabernacles of the righteous. The archbishop then removed his outer cassock and cast it upon the dead man.

"The saint then went on his way. After he traversed some distance, the one who asked the archbishop for a covering laughed and said to his companion on the ground, 'Get up because that fool has departed.' But the man on the ground gave no answer. Then the other fellow, attempting to stir with his hand the one lying prone to the ground, discovered that his companion really was dead. He, thereupon, hastened after the saint. At length, he overtook Epiphanios on the road and knelt before him. He revealed the whole truth regarding their scheme. The man besought Epiphanios to look askance at their prank and resurrect his dead companion. He also urged the archbishop to take back his cassock. The man of God then remarked, 'Go, child, and bury him, for he died first and then thou didst seek the garment.' After this startling event, we went down to the shore. We put out to sea, traveling to Cyprus. When we arrived, the brethren received us with great joy.

"Now there was a certain lawyer, a Hebrew, named Isaac. He was devout and kept with exactness the law of Moses. He was converted by the saint and catechized by him. He received holy Baptism and remained with us."

At that time, the sister[29] of Emperors Arkadios and Honorius was suffering from an incurable disease. The flesh on her right hand was gradually being consumed. She heard of Saint Epiphanios and that, by his mediation, God cured the sick. She sent a letter and men of the palace to the archbishop. She wished to have him come and stay in Rome in order to heal her. The envoys reached Cyprus and gave the letter to the saint. Now tidings of their arrival came into the ears of a certain wealthy idolater, named Faustinianos, who harbored an intense enmity toward the holy archbishop. Faustinianos went and

[29] The brothers Arkadios (r. 395-408) and Honorius (r. 395-423) were born of Theodosios I and his first wife, Aelia Flacilla. Arkadios and Honorius had two sisters: Pulcheria and Aelia Galla Placidia. Pulcheria (d. ca. 385) was the daughter of Theodosios I and his first wife, Aelia Flaccilla (or Plakilla). Pulcheria, therefore, was the eldest and the full sister of Arkadios and Honorius. Aelia Galla Placidia (b. 388), augusta of the Western Roman Empire (421-450), was the daughter of Theodosios I (r. 379-395) and his second wife, Galla. She was, therefore, the half-sister of Arkadios and Honorius. Galla Placidia married the Visigothic chieftain Ataulf (Ataulphus). She was captured in Rome when the city fell to the Goths in 410. She was carried off to Gaul and married to Ataulf (414), who was assassinated in 415. Galla Placidia, in 416, was restored to the Romans. The following year, she was married to Constantius III and gave birth to Valentinian III (b. 419-455). She was Orthodox in her faith and a generous donor to churches, especially in Ravenna. When Valentinian was made Caesar (424) and Augustus (425), she dominated the western court during her son's minority. It is likely that the half-sister is spoken of in this account.

welcomed the envoys, offering them hospitality. They accepted his invitation. During their stay at his house, Faustinianos ceased not decrying the man of God. He spoke such things as these: "Why do you pay heed to that hypocrite as though he were a god? He speaks only chilling words and nought else."

Meanwhile, during that time, the saint went to supervise the builders who were working on the new church. Close by were the royal envoys from the palace. Faustinianos was also present. Suddenly, one of the builders, falling from a great height, struck Faustinianos on the head. Now the builder sustained no injuries, but rather rose up immediately. As for Faustinianos, he collapsed to the ground. He remained there—dead. The saint approached him and placed his hand upon him, saying, "Child, in the name of the Lord, rise and go to thy house in health." Immediately, Faustinianos rose up and went to his house. His spouse, hearing the miracle which was wrought by the saint, took one thousand coins and offered them to the saint. The saint directed her not to hand them over to him but to the laborers working on the church. In this manner, therefore, did the wife show her gratitude.

Saint Epiphanios at Rome

Now there was a deacon, named Philon, who was pious and virtuous. Since the Bishop of Karpasion departed to the Lord, God revealed that this deacon should be consecrated as his successor. It happened, thereafter, that Archbishop Epiphanios needed to go to Rome. He, therefore, entrusted the governance of his diocese to Philon. He also entrusted him with the responsibility of ordaining should the need arise.

"The saint took along me (Polyvios) and Isaac. We departed and sailed for Rome. At the imperial palace there was much sorrow, by reason of a disease afflicting the emperors' sister. Physicians were called in and performed many treatments, without reaping any benefit. She suffered to such an extent from her many pangs, that the emperors were provoked. In their ill-judgment from grief, they suggested to the treating physicians that poison be administered that she might drink thereof and die sooner so as to quit her torments.

"When the saint arrived in the palace, he went straight to the imperial bedchamber where the sister of the emperors was reclining. When the emperors beheld the archbishop, they rose up quickly from their thrones and venerated the saint. The archbishop said to them, 'This honor you should offer to God, the Benefactor, Who desires to see thy sister well. Hope in Him and He shall deliver you from every evil.' The emperors, however, hesitated to believe in the words of the saint. He perceived this and commented, 'Why do you doubt, children, in those things which I have uttered? Now shall you behold the grace of God.' The archbishop then drew nigh to the sufferer and spoke to her with a cheerful countenance, saying, 'Cease sorrowing, child, on account of thy malady. But do thou have faith in God, so thou mightest behold thyself made healthy by Jesus Christ Who shall heal thee this very moment. Behold how the pains of thy body have ceased! Give glory, therefore, to God, Who grants thee this gift. Always have Him in thy mind and in thy remembrance, in whatsoever thou doest, that He may preserve thee throughout thy life.' Having spoken thus, he took up her ailing hand and traced over it, thrice, the sign of the life-giving Cross. Forthwith—behold the wonderworking!—she was delivered from her pains and completely made whole."

Then, on yet another occasion, the son of the emperors' sister[30] was found on his deathbed, though he had no prior illness. When he died there was abundant wailing in the imperial palace. The emperors besought the saint to raise up the child. Epiphanios made the sign of the precious and life-creating Cross over the entire body of the child and supplicated God. He then addressed the deceased, saying, "Rise up, child, in the name of Jesus Christ the Crucified." Straightway—lo, the marvel!—the child was resurrected. He sat up on his bed to the wonder of eyewitnesses. All those who were as yet unbaptized sought Baptism from the saint.

After the rite was performed, the saint tarried there for seven days with the newly-illumined. After he taught them appropriately and they changed their baptismal garments, he counseled them and said, "Abide, children, in tranquility. The wolf will no longer lord it over you. All pain, sorrow, and sighing have fled. However, while considering upon the resurrection of the dead, do not grieve for those who have died. For those who believe in Christ and are baptized, they have put on Christ and have Him as their helper. The child which had previously expired was resurrected that he might receive the grace of the Holy Spirit and that he might go before the Savior Christ and behold His great glory that is hymned by the angels." The following day, while the saint was preaching to the royals, an ineffable fragrance wafted forth. "The saint commented to the royals, 'Rise up, O sons of light, that we might pray.' When they finished the prayer, we all heard, that is, those present, the 'Amen,' as though a multitude of voices had uttered that word. It was then that the child of the emperors' sister surrendered his soul, even as the saint had foretold."

The saint passed one entire year at Rome, where he wrought many other miracles. When he decided to return to Cyprus, the emperors told him to

---

[30] The account in *The Great Synaxaristes* (in Greek) names neither the sister nor the son. On the one hand, the emperors' elder sister, Pulcheria, had died early. She could not have been more than ten, and no issue from her is known. On the other hand, the sister mentioned could not have been the brothers' younger sister, Galla Placidia, who gave birth to Valentinian III (419) well after the repose of Saint Epiphanios (403). Thus, the identity of the "emperors' sister" is not clearly known. But it is not incredible to suppose that the kinswoman referred to herein could have been a godsister or another very close relation of the royal family.

take plenty of gold for the need of the Church and to use it for its necessities. The saint, however, did not wish to receive anything and said, "You, my children, donate the gold to the poor, even as the Lord commanded. In this act will I rejoice for the sake of your almsgiving. As for me, however, do not place this burden upon me, because God is disposed to provide all and to sustain all in this present life." After saying these things, the saint departed from Rome. "When he came to Cyprus, we, the brethren, received him with great joy."

Saint Epiphanios and the Famine on Cyprus

Now the saint had the custom of visiting, by night, the cemeteries, that is, those tombs with the relics of the holy martyrs. It was there that he was wont to supplicate God for each and every one of those among the living that were afflicted and in straits. Even as a friend gives to a friend when asked, so did God yield to the holy man that which he sought.

It was also about that time that the island suffered from a severe famine. Such was the lack of food that one could not find bread at the marketplace. The aforementioned rich idolater Faustinianos, the one who suffered the blow to the head at the building site, had plenty of wheat and barley. As one with no pity, he raised the price enormously. If a buyer did not place the money in his hands, that one did not receive any grain. Especially great was the hunger and distress among the indigent. The saint went to Faustinianos and besought him to give him grain. Epiphanios disclosed that he needed the grain that he might be able to handle the needs of the starving poor. Epiphanios, furthermore, promised Faustinianos that he would reimburse him. But Faustinianos quipped, "Go and beseech the God Whom thou dost venerate, and let Him give thee wheat in order to maintain thy friends." The man of God went that night to the cemeteries. It was there that he entreated God to grant him food for all those in need, in the manner in which His all-wise providence knew to be best. The saint then heard an invisible voice responding to his request and saying, "Epiphanios, go to the temple, the one called Dios (Zeus). The doors that have been secure and closed for years shall be opened to thee. When thou enterest therein, thou shalt find an abundance of gold. Take it and buy all the wheat and barley of Faustinianos that thou mightest feed the poor." Upon hearing these words, he put them into action. The temple, or fortress of Dios, had been locked and sealed by the imperial authority lest the pagans should resume their profane sacrifices. It was generally believed among the populace that the temple was the haunt of evil and violent spirits that slew trespassers. Already some pagans, and even Christians, by God's permission, lost their lives at the site. When the holy archbishop approached, the doors opened of themselves. Indeed, within, the saint discovered an immense amount of gold and silver—more than enough to pay Faustinianos and empty out the granaries. The saint, thereupon, came to an agreement over the price in the purchase of all of Faustinianos' wheat, barley, and oats, which the latter was more than happy to sell. The saint took the grain and had it distributed among the indigent and destitute. The hungry, consequently, found relief.

Meanwhile, Faustinianos' household, within a short time, was found in dire straits. By reason of his greed, he, as we said, sold everything. Upon selling all his inventory, he gave no thought to retaining some for the needs of his own house as the gold and silver shined in his eyes. Faustinianos was distraught because he did not dare ask the saint for wheat, either for himself or for those living with him. He had the notion that should he ask, he would suffer an indignity. What did he do then? He had five of his own ships and hired five others, for which he paid a considerable sum. He, next, secured the services of a trustworthy man named Longinos. He dispatched him to Calabria of southern Italy, in order to purchase wheat in that city and return with it to Cyprus. Longinos sailed to Calabria with all the ships and made the wheat acquisition. The ships were heavily laden when he began thc return voyage. When the ten ships arrived opposite that province, a storm of frightening magnitude and gale-force winds struck them, submerging all the ships. As for the stores of wheat, they were cast up on the shore of Salamis in Cyprus. The poor of that area collected the grain.

Faustinianos was apprised of the loss. He, immediately, went down to the shore. Upon beholding what took place, Faustinianos, enraged with God, began shouting blasphemies against the Most High God and insulting the saint. He spoke such things as these against the archbishop: "O, how I should like to be rid of that sorcerer! Was he not pleased with all the evil he wrought against me on dry land, when he bought up all my grain? Must he also, even at sea, send demons to capsize my grain ships which were bringing provisions for my people? Woe! What kind of wind brought that magician here and confounded us so?" After Faustinianos said these things and more besides, he went to his house uttering threats against the saint. As for all the poor folk, those found in the city, including men, women, and children, they kept going down to the shore and fetching the grain and bringing it back to their houses. Indeed, some managed to collect a supply for one year and others enough for two years. The wife of Faustinianos, possessed of a good disposition, performed many good works. She, secretly and unbeknownst to her husband, sent the saint two thousand coins. She requested wheat from him for those of her household. The saint said to her, "Keep thy money and take wheat, as much as thou needest. And when your fields yield their crop, then reimburse me for the wheat which thou hast taken." Thus it came to pass. The good-intentioned wife of some understanding, as another Abigail of a churlish husband,[31] found to be true

[31] Cf. 1 Kgs. (1 Sam.) 25:3 ff.

those words of the Psalmist David: "Rich men have turned poor and gone hungry; but they that seek the Lord shall not be deprived of any good thing [Ps. 33:10]."

Saint Epiphanios Hands Down Judgments

At the episcopal house, a certain deacon, Savinos, was a calligrapher. He was meek and virtuous. Out of the seventy brethren who were at the episcopal house, Savinos shone forth in every virtue. He also kept a journal of the archbishop's life, noting the man of God's vigils, prostrations, and wonderworkings. The hierarch gave him full powers to deal with Church affairs. On one such occasion, Savinos was judging between two men. One was wealthy and the other poor. The man who had right on his side happened to be the wealthy one. Now the saint, standing concealed from Savinos, heard the merits of each case and listened to his deacon pronounce judgment. He saw that Savinos took the part of the poor man, because he felt sorry for his poverty. Thus, he gave his decision in favor of the poor man. It was then that Epiphanios stepped forward from the back of the chamber and addressed Savinos, saying, "Go, child, to thy calligraphy and bring to thy remembrance the divine Scriptures that thou mayest become perfect in rendering judgment and justice. Hear the words of our benefactor and God Who said, 'Thou shalt not spare a poor man in judgment.'[32] And, 'Thou shalt not act unjustly in judgment. Thou shalt not accept the person of the poor, nor admire the person of the mighty; with justice shalt thou judge thy neighbor.'[33] Thenceforth, the saint judged the cases that came before the Church. From dawn to the ninth hour of the day, he heard matter after matter. But from the ninth hour until the following dawn, no one was appearing before him with such affairs and concerns."

Saint Epiphanios' Enemies Seek to Slay Him

Now there was another deacon, also a calligrapher, at the episcopal house. His name was Rufinos. The man had a wild face and beastly disposition. He was, in fact, in agreement with the above mentioned Faustinianos insofar as his many daily insults that he hurled at the holy archbishop. The archbishop, perceiving the deacon's surliness, allayed Rufinos' audacity with his extreme meekness. The deacon, nevertheless, was instigated by Faustinianos. The latter urged him to commit violence against the archbishop, saying, "If thou wilt slay that irksome old man who vexes us, I will have thee seated on the throne of his episcopacy. I have the means and the connections." For thus was Faustinianos driven by the devil in seeking the slaying of the saint. Since, then, Rufinos was the youngest deacon of the Church, he had the ministration of preparing the hierarch's throne. Rufinos, therefore, took a sharp knife and set it straight up in the seat of the throne. He covered it with the seat cushion. Thus, when

[32] Ex. 23:3.

[33] Lev. 19:15; Sir. 4:27.

Epiphanios took his place on the throne during the appropriate moment of the divine office, he would sustain a deadly stabbing. And so, with everything in place, the moment came during the service when the archbishop customarily takes his seat. At that moment, Epiphanios called to himself Rufinos and said to him, "Lift up, child, the cushion on the throne." But Rufinos did not take it up in accordance with the saint's bidding. He pretended not to hear, though the archbishop asked him thrice. Then, straightway, the knife, of its own accord, fell down on the foot of Rufinos. It struck and punctured his right foot. The saint, beholding this occurrence, remarked, "Cease, child, thy waywardness lest thou shouldest very quickly come to be in danger. Moreover, go forth from the church; because thou art not worthy to partake of the divine Mysteries." Rufinos limped out of church and went to the episcopal house. He fell on his bed, after which he died in three days' time.

Not much time passed before God's judgment overtook the other perpetrator of the crime against the bishop. Faustinianos was charged with some offense, for which he was detained in one of the jails in the capital. Epiphanios, who bore no grudge against such a hostile enemy, much rather attempted to mediate for his release. The emperor, nonetheless would not countenance the hierarch's petition for an appeal. The saint, realizing he could do nought to move earthly powers, prayed to God for Faustinianos and even wept for him. Faustinianos soon died, leaving all his property and goods to his wife. She desired to relinquish all her wealth and serve the Church. Epiphanios made her a deaconess.

Saint Epiphanios at Constantinople with Emperor Theodosios the Great

Also at that time, the great Theodosios, who reigned as emperor (379-395), was suffering sharp pains in his feet. From his knees to his feet, he even suffered paralysis. As a result of this debilitation, he took to his bed for seven months. He, thereupon, sent men with letters from the palace to Cyprus. The content of the messages were supplications to the saintly archbishop that he visit them in Constantinople for the healing of the emperor. The envoys arrived on the island and delivered the royal missives. Epiphanios agreed to accompany them. When the envoys were ready to escort the archbishop back to Constantinople, they hesitated to follow through with the mission. The tribulation and the tears of the faithful thwarted the departure of the saint from the island. When the saint prepared to depart, all the Christians concentrated around him and wept. Such was the press of the crowd that they nearly brought about his death. The archbishop then charged the emperor's men to depart without him, saying, "Depart, children, to the palace and I will come later." The envoys responded: "Hold no anger against us, father, because we are not leaving without thee. It is an imperial command that we travel together, for which we cannot do otherwise lest we put ourselves in peril—especially now that the emperor is unwell and awaits the arrival of thy holiness." Epiphanios then summoned the aforementioned Bishop Philon, to whom he entrusted the archdiocese in his absence. He asked him to render his services in whatsoever ecclesiastical need should arise. Afterward, Epiphanios exhorted all the Christians in those things proper. He bade all farewell and departed with the envoys for Constantinople.

"When we arrived in Constantinople and came into the royal palace, the saint went forth with boldness to the emperor. Theodosios was lying in his bed, enduring such bitter pains that he was rendered speechless. When the saint approached his bedside, the emperor forced himself to say, 'Supplicate God, father, that I might see my health again, because I am gravely ill.' The saint replied, 'Believe, child, in the power of the crucified Jesus Christ and thou shalt always have thy health. Have God in thy mind that thou mayest not be troubled by any evil. Become merciful to the afflicted and thou shalt have mercy from God. Honor God Who granted thee the realm; for it is His will to grant thee much more favor.' As the archbishop was speaking these words to the emperor, he touched Theodosios' feet and made the sign of the precious and life-creating Cross and said, 'Rise up, child, from thy bed, for the pains in thy feet shall trouble thee no more.' And—lo, the miracle!—immediately, the emperor arose from his sickbed. He did not feel the least twinge in his feet. He then commented to the saint, 'Give the command, father, and whatsoever thou shouldest determine, I will obey in all.' The saint then answered, 'Have in thy soul the words of God and keep them that thou mightest have no need for Epiphanios; but give glory to God, thy benefactor.'

"Now while we were still in Constantinople, there came from Rome both Arkadios and Honorius. They said to their father, Theodosios, 'The man of God had been in Rome where he healed thy daughter and raised her son who was found dead.' When the emperor heard these tidings, he was even more joyous and from thenceforth considered the saint as his father. Now it was during that time, that an imperial order remanded Faustinianos from Cyprus to Constantinople, where he was incarcerated in the city prison and charged with insulting the emperor. The holy Epiphanios learned of the extradition and went to visit him in prison. The archbishop asked him, 'Dost thou wish that I should mediate for thee before the emperor and have thee released from condemnation?' But Faustinianos did not wish it and said to the holy man, 'Go, thou deceiver, and delude the gullible and inexperienced; but do not make such offers to me. I know thou hast come here not to help me but to gloat and rejoice over my misfortune. However, the hour has come for thee to leave Cyprus and go to Phoenicia, thy homeland. There thou canst perform as much magic and wicked deeds as thou dost like.'

"The saint, then, left the jail, and went to the emperor in order to bid him farewell, since we were about to leave for Cyprus. The emperor, however, besought the saint to tarry a few days longer in the capital. The saint accepted. The following day, the *apokrisiarios*[34] came to the emperor and announced that Faustinianos had died. When the saint heard this news, he was much sorrowed for the man's double death: both physical and spiritual. Now the emperor was desirous to confiscate all of Faustinianos' possessions for the imperial treasury, especially since he had no children. The saint intervened and said, 'Take heed, child, not to commit a sin, because Faustinianos' widow reveres God with all her heart and she wishes to distribute all of her husband's wealth to the poor. Be persuaded, therefore, by my words and leave the estate to the wife, for which thou shalt receive grace from the Most High God.' The emperor then gave the saint full authority over the property and belongings of Faustinianos. The saint, nevertheless, predicated his acceptance, saying, 'I, child, have God Who gives me all that I need; but as for all these properties, in accord with the widow's judgment, we shall distribute everything among the poor.'

"When the time came for us to depart, the emperor said to the saint, 'Ask, father, for those things thou needest and I will gladly give them.' The archbishop answered, 'I seek this from thee, child: that thou keepest the promises that thou hast made and that thou rememberest me always.' The emperor then came forth from the imperial palace, so as to escort us. He then besought the archbishop to bless him. The saint, forthwith, uttered a prayer and blessed the emperor; and then he embraced him. Then, as the emperor returned to his palace, we entered a ship bound for Cyprus. We were received by all the Christians with great joy. We did find the wife of Faustinianos weeping, on account of her husband's death. While in this afflicted state, the saint comforted her sufficiently. Afterward, we baptized her and consecrated her to the diaconate. As she previously pledged, she gave all her substance and that of Faustinianos, in consultation with the saint, to those having need."

Saint Epiphanios Fights the Heretics

In the saint's diocese, there was a multitude of people who followed the heresy of Valentinian who were pleased to call themselves Gnostics.[35] The

---

[34] The *apokrisiarios* or *responsalis* was the messenger or representative of a bishop.

[35] Valentinian (d. ca. 165), an Alexandrian, wished to produce thirty aeons, which he also calls 'gods,' saying that there are fifteen male and as many female [i.e., Depth and Silence, Mind and Truth, Logos and Life, Man and Church, Paraclete and Faith, Paternal and Hope, Maternal and Charity, Ever-Mind and Intelligence, Willed (also known as Light) and Beatitude, Ecclesiasticus and Wisdom, Deep and Combination, Ageless and Union, Self-originate and Blending, Only-begotten and Unity, and Unmoved and Pleasure]. Epiphanios notified us that Valentinian preached in Egypt and

(continued...)

bishop of these heretics was one called Aetios. One day it happened that the archbishop was speaking to Aetios about his heresy. The latter was contentious and speaking nonsense. Hearing him utter many blasphemies regarding the Most High God, the archbishop cut him off and said, "O most impious Aetios, put a bit and bridle to thy mouth and cease speaking blasphemies!" Immediately, with that spoken word of the saint, Aetios was rendered without speech. He was unable to articulate one word. Then those of his sect, beholding how the saint by solely a word curbed and rendered speechless the mouth of Aetios, knelt before the saint and anathematized their heresy. They became Orthodox Christians. As for Aetios, he remained dumb for six days. On the seventh day, he expired.

Now there were many other heretics living on the island of Cyprus, such as the Sophists, Sabellians,[36] Nikolaitans,[37] Simonians,[38] Vasileidians,[39]

---

[35](...continued)
Rome. He then came to Cyprus and corrupted the island with his impiety. He tells us that the Valentinians believe that Christ is Savior but that He is not the first Logos. They considered His passage through the Virgin Mary to have been as like water through a channel and that He partook of nothing from the virginal womb. Nor do they believe in a resurrection. They think that gnosis is given only to the spiritual and not the material. And, of course, the spiritual to them are the Valentinians who are destined to return to the Pleroma. Other Christians, by faith and good works, can attain to a form of salvation, but in a lower realm below the Pleroma. As for the rest of mankind, they are doomed to everlasting perdition. Saint Epiphanios, *The Panarion of Saint Epiphanius, Bishop of Salamis, Selected Passages*, § 31, trans. by Philip R. Amidon, S. J. (NY/Oxford, Oxford University Press, 1990), pp. 108-114. Amidon uses the text of K. Holl, *Epiphanius*, in the Griechische Christliche Schriftsteller (GCS) series, 3 vols. (1915, 1922, and 1931-1933).

[36] The Sabellians, from Sabellius (3rd C.), teach that He Who is the Father is the same One Who is the Son and the same One Who is the Holy Spirit, so that there are three names in one hypostasis. They accept the Bible, but they choose certain verses according to their own bogus nonsense and insanity. *Panarion*, § 62, pp. 209, 210.

[37] The Nikolaitans came from Nicholas, one of the seven deacons chosen by the apostles. The devil entered into Nicholas and deceived him. He had a beautiful wife, from whom he was abstaining in imitation of those whom he had seen who were devoted to God. He persevered for a time, but did not manage to control his intemperance to the end. He, therefore, thought up poor excuses in defense of his own passion of licentiousness. He failed in his resolve and had relations with his wife. But ashamed of his failure and suspecting that he might be detected, he dared to say that unless one engaged in sex daily one could not participate in eternal life. He went from excuse to excuse. Now seeing that his spouse was of outstanding beauty but humble demeanor, he became jealous of her. Supposing that others were like him in his lewdness, at first he never stopped acting offensively to his own wife and slandering

(continued...)

Karpokratians,[40] and all sorts of others whom the saint wrote about in an epistle to the emperor, requesting that they be expelled from Cyprus. Since many among these heretics were wealthy, they bought public offices of authority and

---

[37](...continued)
her in various ways by what he said. He finally pulled himself down to carnal practise and blasphemy. The Gnostics came to be united with these sectarians. "What can I say to you, Nicholas? How can I talk with you? From where do you come to us, sir, with this business about a foul aeon, a root of wickedness, a generative Womb, and many gods and demons?" Ibid., § 25, pp. 72-74.

[38] Simonians, named after Simon Magus, do dreadful things in their depravity. Simon would tell the Samaritans that he was the Father, and to the Jews that he was the Son. He was devoted to shameful gain and greed. Christ's name was a screen for the demonic seduction in his magic. A carnal man, he married a woman named Helen and kept the relationship secret. In fact, he told people she was the original Helen of Troy. He spun other fables that he was the great power of God. He taught the corruption and perdition of the flesh and that only souls could be purified. Thus begins the error of those called Gnostics. He said the law was not of God but of a power of the left. He said that prophets were not from the good God but from one or another power. The prophets of the Old Testament were assigned to different powers, but all are from the power on the left and outside the Pleroma. Anyone who believes in the Old Testament is subject to death. "He calls himself the great power of God. And how is it that when his time came, his life reached its end in Rome when the wretch fell down and died right in the middle of the city?" Ibid., § 21, pp. 61-63.

[39] Vasileidians (Basilidians), from Vasilides, say that the Unbegotten was one Who alone is Father of all. From it proceeds, he says, Mind, from Mind Logos, from Logos Prudence, from Prudence Power and Wisdom, and from Power and Wisdom principalities, authorities, and angels. He also says there are 365 heavens. He thinks the God of the Jews was an angel, and that the angels divided up the world by lot according to their number; and so, the God of the Jews got the Jewish people. He believes that Christ's appearance is a phantasm, not a man, and that He did not take flesh; in fact, according to him, Jesus did not suffer on the Cross but Simon of Cyrene. Such are the poetic fables of this imposter. He allows his disciples lustful deeds; because of this self-indulgence, many fall into this sect. Ibid., § 24, pp. 68-71.

[40] Karpokratians (Carpocratians), of Karpokrates, started an abominable school of their founder's falsely named "knowledge," being worse in his ways than all the rest. He said that the world, and what is in it, was produced by angels far inferior to the unknown Father. He also believed that Jesus was engendered from Joseph. Those of this sect attempt all sorts of dreadful and pernicious deeds. They are involved in the magical arts and incantations used for deception and seduction. They live in continual profligacy and bodily enjoyment. Their writings amaze and shock the sensible reader, making one doubt if such things are done by human beings. They behave like dogs and swine. They hold to the transmigration of souls. To them, salvation is for only the soul and not the body. They also keep figures of Jesus with Pythagoras, Plato, Aristotle, and the rest, before whom they worship and perform pagan rites. Ibid., § 27, pp. 83-86.

brought injury and loss to the Orthodox. When the emperor received the archbishop's epistles, he replied with a document ordering the following: "Whosoever among the heretics does not obey Archbishop Epiphanios and his divine words, let such a one depart from the island of Cyprus and dwell wheresoever he wants. But if anyone among them wishes to repent and confess before the common father of the island that he was deceived and now wishes to come to the path of the truth and become Orthodox, let such a one remain in Cyprus and be taught by our common father—the divine Epiphanios." Such was the wording of the imperial command that was delivered by the emperor's envoy to Cyprus. It was read in the general hearing of all. Now many of the island's heretics hastened to the saint and became Orthodox Christians. Those who had no desire to leave their heresy were banished from Cyprus.

Theophilos and Saint John Chrysostom

The then Patriarch of Alexandria was Theophilos (385-412), who was acquainted with Saint Epiphanios. Now in Alexandria there were three brothers, the sons of Herakleonos, the superintendent at Alexandria. When the father died, the brothers conceived the good thought to become monks. All three of them repaired to the wilderness, received the Angelic Schema of the monks, and lived in quietude. They conducted their lives in a manner befitting the monastic habit. Theophilos knew the brothers and drew them by a deceptive device back into Alexandria. The eldest brother was consecrated to the episcopacy of some region in Egypt, whereas the two other brothers were made deacons and *oikonomoi*[41] of the Church. They served the church in these capacities for three years. They perceived that by taking on these offices they relinquished their solitude and felt they were even being deprived of divine grace. They shared their concerns with Theophilos and begged him to give them a release that they might go to where they formerly dwelt.

Theophilos, however, would not give them leave to go. They, consequently, departed secretly and returned to their former retreat of rest and quiet. Theophilos excommunicated them for three years without holy Communion. They greatly implored the hierarch to forgive them, so that they could commune the divine Mysteries. Theophilos, however, would not pardon them.

In the meantime, Saint John Chrysostom,[42] Patriarch of Constantinople (398-404), wrote to Theophilos, requesting him to loose the bond of excommunication. Theophilos would not hearken to the supplications of the divine Chrysostom. Chrysostom then wrote a second time, again beseeching him to

---

[41] The *oikonomos*, a cleric, was responsible for managing the property, income, and expenditure of a see. *The Oxford Dictionary of Byzantium*, s.v. "Oikonomos."

[42] Saint John Chrysostom is commemorated by the holy Church on the 13th of November. Much of what follows herein pertaining to him is spoken of in greater detail in that saint's Life.

relent. Once again, Theophilos refused to yield and lift the excommunication. The holy Chrysostom, thereupon, loosed the bond of excommunication. This action by the Patriarch of Constantinople brought about a considerable cooling of relations between Theophilos and the hallowed Chrysostom.[43]

In the capital during that period, there was a senator, Theognostos, who was a good Christian and possessed continual fear of God. By reason of his piety he was much loved by the emperor, Arkadios. But there was another senator, named Dorotheos, an Arian by persuasion, who was envious of Theognostos. He calumniated the latter, claiming that Theognostos had denounced the emperor. Dorotheos also arranged to bring forward two false witnesses who censured Theognostos to his face. The emperor, thereupon, decided to exile Theognostos and to confiscate his fortune. There was left to the wife of Theognostos one property that she might have some means for her necessities. As for Theognostos, while he was in exile, he died. Now it happened that the empress, Evdoxia, had taken a walk. As she went about during the season of the grape gathering, she found herself on the property of Theognostos' widow. It was not known for what reason she entered the widow's vineyard and cut a cluster of grapes. According to the custom at that time, if the emperor or the empress stepped into a strange place and cut fruit from any tree, no one but the emperor and empress could exercise authority over the property. It became an imperial holding.

The widow of Theognostos, hearing that the empress had entered her property, wrote a petition to the divine John Chrysostom. At that point in time, he was still beloved by both emperor and empress. The widow asked for the patriarch's mediation in the case that she might have her vineyard returned. The blessed patriarch sent the Archdeacon Eftychios, a learned man who was adorned with every virtue. He made the application to Evdoxia for the return of the property to the widow. The archdeacon conveyed all that the divine Chrysostom had bidden him speak. Evdoxia commented that she was unable to return the property, for it was an imperial law to which she was held. She did offer to give the widow whatever other property she desired. The archdeacon returned to the patriarch and imparted the empress' answer.

---

[43] Saint Theophanes the Confessor remarks, "While John Chrysostom was loved by the whole congregation,...some collaborated to make war on him. At this juncture occurred the affair of the eunuch Eftropios, and furthermore the rivalry between Severianos of Gabala and John's Archdeacon Serapion, the matter of the Tall Brothers who fled Egypt because of Theophilos, and Theophilos' correspondence with Epiphanios. In all of these John, the servant of God, was being plotted against." *The Chronicle of Theophanes Confessor*, AM 5896, A.D. 403/404, trans. by C. Mango and R. Scott (Oxford: Clarendon Press, 1997), pp. 119, 120.

Chrysostom himself decided to go the empress and speak with her regarding the matter. He urged her to return the widow's vineyard. The empress retorted, "Learn, father, first the cause; and then say whether or not I plotted against the widow to seize her property, lest thou shouldest censure the royals to their faces." The divine Chrysostom responded: "Return the property to the widow, for thou knowest how the sacred Scripture condemns, even to this day, Jezebel who unjustly took the vineyard of Nabouthai."[44] When the empress heard this comparison spoken of by the archbishop, she ordered that he be escorted out of the imperial palace. The holy Chrysostom exited from that place and went to the church, remarking to Eftychios, "When the empress comes to the church, command the deacons and the servants of the church to stand at this door, the one through which the empress is wont to enter; and do not allow her entry into the church, saying that 'John commands that thou not enter into the church.'" Eftychios, therefore, at the appearance of the empress for the divine service, did exactly as the patriarch had directed him. By reason of this episode, she was incited to have the patriarch banished.

Saint Epiphanios and Saint Chrysostom at Constantinople

Theophilos, learning that the empress was intent on banishing the divine Chrysostom, also raised up many treacherous designs against the Constantinopolitan patriarch. Included among his many insidious designs were his written letters to Saint Epiphanios. Theophilos accused Chrysostom of having an Origen mentality and that for this the empress was bent on exiling him. The holy Epiphanios, having a serious reason to go to Constantinople, read these assertions of Theophilos regarding the divine Chrysostom. Epiphanios was stirred the more to make the trip to the capital. But he thought to go not so as to harm the divine Chrysostom but rather to help him.[45] "He,

---

[44] Cf. 3 Kgs. (1 Kgs.) 20.

[45] Saint Epiphanios, in his heresy-hunting pursuits, was a strong opponent of Origenism. Socrates comments that "when Theophilos professed to be friendly with Epiphanios, he then, by letter, managed it so that Epiphanios should convene a synod of the bishops in Cyprus in order to condemn the writings of Origen. Epiphanios, a man of extraordinary piety, possessed of simplicity in mind and manners, was easily influenced by the letters of Theophilos. Having, therefore, assembled a council of bishops in that island, he caused a prohibition to be therein made of the reading of Origen's works. He also wrote to John, exhorting him not only to abstain from the study of Origen's books but also to convoke a synod for decreeing the same thing as he had done." Socrates Scholasticus, *The Ecclesiastical History*, Bk. VI, Ch. X, Logos Research Systems on CD-ROM (1997).

Sozomen speaks of the perversity of Theophilos. He also talks of Epiphanios' residence in the city, some seven milestones from the capital. He writes: "Theophilos kept his designs against John as secret as possible. He wrote to the bishops of every

(continued...)

therefore, took Isaac and I, and we left for Constantinople. Great confusion ensued with the persecution against the divine Chrysostom. Since the citizens loved him dearly, we took up our abode in a monastery outside of Constantinople.

"The monastery where we resided happened to be one of those monasteries which received its wheat maintenance from the empress.[46] Thus,

---

[45](...continued)
city, condemning the books of Origen. It also occurred to him that it would be advantageous to enlist Epiphanios, Bishop of Salamis in Cyprus, on his side, a man revered for his life and who was the most distinguished of his contemporaries. Theophilos, therefore, formed a friendship with Epiphanios, though previously the two hierarchs held different theological opinions regarding whether God possessed a human form. Theophilos wrote to Epiphanios to acquaint him that he now held the same opinions as himself. Theophilos also urged Epiphanios to move attacks against the books of Origen, as the source of such nefarious dogmas. Epiphanios had long regarded the writings of Origen with peculiar aversion. He was, therefore, easily led to attach credit to the epistle of Theophilos. Epiphanios, soon after, assembled the bishops of Cyprus together, and prohibited the examination of the books of Origen. He also wrote to the other bishops, and, among others, to the Bishop of Constantinople, exhorting them to convene synods and to make the same decision. Theophilos, perceiving that there could be no danger in following the example of Epiphanios who was the object of popular praise and who was admired for the virtue of his life, passed a vote similar to that of Epiphanios with the concurrence of the bishops under his jurisdiction. John, on the other hand, paid little attention to the letters of Epiphanios and Theophilos. Those among the powerful and the clergy, who were opposed to John, perceived that the designs of Theophilos tended to John's ejection from the bishopric; and therefore, they endeavored to procure the convocation of a council in Constantinople in order to carry this measure into execution. Theophilos, knowing this, exerted himself to the utmost in convening this council. He commanded the bishops of Egypt to repair by sea to Constantinople; he wrote to request Epiphanios and the other eastern bishops to proceed to that city with as little delay as possible; and he himself set off on the journey thither by land. Epiphanios was the first to sail from Cyprus. He landed at Hebdomon, a suburb of Constantinople." Sozomen, *The Ecclesiastical History*, Book VIII, Ch. XIV, Logos Research Systems.

Now Epiphanios had come to Constantinople in 400, after corresponding with Theophilos of Alexandria. Bishop Epiphanios brought with him a copy of the synodical decree in which the Cypriot Church did not excommunicate Origen himself but condemned his books. Socrates, Bk. VI, Ch. XII.

[46] Sozomen mentions that there took place an encounter between the empress and Saint Epiphanios, as well as a conference with the "Tall Brothers" prior to the saint's re-embarkation for Cyprus. "About this time, the son of the empress was attacked by a dangerous illness. The mother, apprehensive of consequences, sent to implore Epiphanios to pray for him. Epiphanios returned for an answer that the sick one would

(continued...)

this was a monastery that did not receive the divine Chrysostom. Now since the church of the same monastery lacked a deacon, the fathers of that monastery very much importuned the holy Epiphanios to ordain one for them. It was not long before the divine Chrysostom learned of the ordination officiated by Saint Epiphanios, especially a service conducted in another diocese without the resident bishop's permission. The patriarch expressed his sorrow in a letter to Epiphanios who, in turn, wrote back to the divine Chrysostom.

"The empress, apprised of what had taken place and the displeasure between Chrysostom and Epiphanios, summoned Epiphanios and said to him, 'All the realm of the Rhomaioi, father, is mine and under my authority, as well as all the priests and the hierarchs of the Church that are in my kingdom; they are mine and under my authority. Therefore, since John does not preserve the proper order toward his bishops, but rather brings forth disorderly ways against the realm, for this reason after many days of deliberation I have given thought to assembling the hierarchs in order to depose him as one unworthy of the high

---

[46](...continued)
live, provided that she would avoid all intercourse with the heretic Dioscoros and his companions. To this message the empress replied as follows: 'If it be the will of God to take my son, His will be done. The Lord Who gave me my child, can take him back again. Thou hast not power to raise the dead, otherwise thine archdeacon would not have died.' She alluded to Chrispion, the archdeacon, who had died a short time previously....

"Then Ammonios and his companions went to Epiphanios, at the permission of the empress. Epiphanios inquired who they were, and Ammonios replied, 'We are, O father, the Tall Brothers. We come respectfully to know whether thou hast read any of our works or those of our disciples?' On Epiphanios replying that he had not seen them, Ammonios continued, 'How is it, then, that thou dost consider us to be heretics, when thou hast no proof as to what sentiments we may hold?' Epiphanios said that he had formed his judgment by the reports he had heard on the subject. To this Ammonios replied, 'We have pursued a very different line of conduct from thine. We have conversed with thy disciples. We have read thy works frequently and, among others, that entitled *The Well-anchored*. When we have met with persons who have ridiculed thine opinions, and asserted that thy writings are replete with heresy, we have contended for thee and defended thee as our father. Oughtest thou then to condemn the absent upon mere report, and of whom thou knowest nothing with assured certitude, or return such an exchange to those who have spoken well of thee?' Epiphanios was measurably convinced, and dismissed them.

"Soon after, Epiphanios embarked for Cyprus, either because he recognized the futility of his journey to Constantinople or because, as there is reason to believe, God had revealed to him his approaching death; for he died while on his voyage back to Cyprus. It is reported that he said to the bishops who had accompanied him to the place of embarkation, 'I leave you the city, the palace, and the stage, for I shall shortly depart.'" Ibid., Bk. VIII, Ch. XV.

priesthood. Let another be appointed as archbishop, one who is able to govern the Church as is meet, that peace be restored in all quarters of my realm. Now, however, that thou art found here by God's providence, there is no need to subject the hierarchs to such toils; but rather, do thou determine who shall be patriarch as God may reveal to thee that we may send forth that one from Constantinople.'

"After speaking in this manner, the empress was extremely agitated from anger. The divine Epiphanios, hearing what she spoke, exercised forbearance without the least vexation and said, 'Hearken, child. If, on the one hand, the archbishop is a heretic, as thou hast imputed, and is censured publicly, and he does not confess his error, then he is unworthy of the high priesthood. Consequently, that which thine authority has determined shall I carry out. If, on the other hand, thou art seeking to drive out John from the Great Church for hurt feelings or an insult against your majesties, your own Epiphanios will not ever consent. Much rather, child, it is the obligation of princes, whensoever they are insulted and dishonored, to pardon those who reproach. For you emperors have the King in the heavens, before Whom you commit sins in many ways. He, however, desires to forgive you when you forgive those who fail and despitefully use you, even as it is written in the divine and sacred Gospel: "Keep on becoming compassionate, even as your Father also is compassionate [Lk. 6:36]."' The frustrated empress then uttered this rejoinder to the saint, 'If perhaps, father, thou shouldest become a hindrance to John's exile, I will open the temples of the idols and will make the people pay homage to the idols. This and much worse will I do.' She spoke these words, shaking and sobbing from the intense wrath that filled her. The saint remarked, 'I, child, am innocent of this sin.' Speaking thus, he departed from the palace. Now Isaac had fallen ill, so he was not with us.

"The following rumor was then bruited throughout the city: that the great Hierarch Epiphanios went to the empress and cooperated in ushering in the banishment of the divine Chrysostom. When Isaac heard this, he fled from the saint and went to a monastery. The holy Epiphanios was much grieved on account of Isaac. He, therefore, entreated God to reveal to him where he had taken flight. God, indeed, uncovered the place where the saint could find Isaac; and so the archbishop went to him. Isaac, nevertheless, turned away from the saint and said, 'I do not wish to be with thee any longer, by reason of the sin which thou hast committed against the divine Chrysostom.' We remained at that monastery for three days. Only by forceful words was the saint able to persuade Isaac that he had no share in the reckless venture to banish the divine Chrysostom. Thus induced, Isaac followed us and we returned to our habitation. Nevertheless, the divine Chrysostom believed that Epiphanios was in agreement with his exile and wrote about it to him, saying: 'O wise Epiphanios, thou hast agreed to my banishment; however, even thou shalt no longer sit on thy throne.' Then did the venerable Epiphanios respond to the epistle of the divine Chrysostom, saying: 'O athlete, do thou thrash and be triumphant! Since thou hast believed that I agreed with thy banishment, thou shalt not arrive at the place of thine exile.' He wrote these words, brethren, that none might reproach the saint. Because for one who practised so many good deeds, it is not ever possible to fall into such spite."[47]

---

[47] Sozomen continues and says that "after Epiphanios prayed in the church erected at that place, he proceeded to enter the city. In order to do him honor, John went out with all his clergy to meet him. Epiphanios, however, evinced clearly by his conduct that he believed the accusations against John; for, although invited to reside in the ecclesiastical residences, he would not continue there; and he refused to meet with John in them. He also privately assembled all the bishops who were residing in the capital, and showed them the decrees which he had issued against the discourses of Origen. He persuaded some of the bishops to approve these decrees, while others objected to them.

"Theotimos, Bishop of Scythia, strongly opposed the proceedings of Epiphanios....John still had respect for Epiphanios. He invited him to join in the meetings of his church, and to dwell with him. But Epiphanios declared that he would neither reside with John nor pray with him publicly, unless the latter would denounce the works of Origen and expel Dioscoros and his companions. Not considering it just to act in the manner proposed until judgment had been passed on the case, John tried to postpone matters. When the assembly was about to be held in the Church of the Apostles, those ill-disposed to John planned that Epiphanios should go beforehand and publicly decry not only the books of Origen but also the partisans of this writer—Dioscoros and his companions. They would also have him attack Chrysostom as the abetter of those heretics. By this did some suppose that the affections of the people would be alienated from their bishop, John. The following day, when Epiphanios was about to enter the church in order to carry his design into execution, he was stopped by Serapion, at the command of John, who had received intimation of the plot. Serapion proved to Epiphanios that while the project he had devised was unjust in itself, it could be of no personal advantage to him; for that if it should excite a popular insurrection, he would be regarded as responsible for the outrages that might follow. By these arguments Epiphanios was induced to relinquish his attack." Sozomen, *The Ecclesiastical History*, Book VIII, Ch. XIV, Logos Research Systems.

Socrates notes that "John was not offended because of Epiphanios....But John's adversaries led Epiphanios to adopt another course. For they contrived it so that as a meeting was in the church named the Apostles, Epiphanios came forth and, before all the people, condemned the books of Origen, excommunicated Dioscoros with his followers, and charged John with countenancing them. These things were reported to John. Therefore, on the following day, he sent the appended message to Epiphanios just as he entered the church: 'Thou dost many things contrary to the canons, Epiphanios. In the first place thou hast made an ordination in the churches under my jurisdiction: then, without my appointment, thou hast on thine own authority officiated in them.

(continued...)

Saint Epiphanios Departs Constantinople and Reposes

The biographer tells us that "following this exchange, we went back again to the palace. The saint bid farewell to the emperors, since we were about to depart. Emperor Arkadios then asked the saint, 'How old art thou, father?' The saint answered, 'I am one hundred fifteen years old and three months. I became a bishop when I was sixty years of age. I have served in the episcopacy fifty-five years and three months.'[48] Following this, we entered into a ship. The saint took a seat. We then took the seats next to him. He had the custom of always holding in his hands the sacred Gospel. He then sighed thrice and wept. He again opened and closed the Gospel, after which he wept as he prayed. After he finished the prayer, he wept once more and then addressed us.

"'O children, if you love me, keep my commandments and may the love of God abide among you. You know by how many afflictions was I proved in this life and that I, in no wise, counted them as such; but I always rejoiced and looked to God. He did not abandon me. But He preserved me from every assault of the evil one; for "we know that to those who love God all things work together for good [Rom. 8:28]," even as the divine Paul says.

"'There was one time, my beloved children, when I was in a wilderness place and praying to God to deliver me from the assaults of the enemy, that there came against me a multitude of demons. They attempted to rend me asunder on the ground. They took hold of my feet and were dragging me along. Some among them took up staves and began thrashing me. This continued for ten days. Thereafter, I no longer saw a demon personally; but by means of wicked people they instigated countless evils.

"'How many and what evils did they not introduce to me in Phoenicia, those unruly Simonians! In Egypt those unclean Gnostics! And in Cyprus those lawless Valentinians and the rest of the heretics! Take heed, children, and hearken to the speech of the sinner Epiphanios. Be not desirous ever for wealth,

---

[47](...continued)
Moreover, when heretofore I invited thee hither, thou didst refuse to come; and now thou takest that liberty thyself. Beware, therefore, lest a tumult being excited among the people thou thyself shouldest also incur danger therefrom.' Epiphanios, becoming alarmed on hearing these admonitions, left the church. After accusing John of many things, he set out on his return to Cyprus." Socrates, Bk. VI, Ch. XIV, Logos Research Systems.

Saint Theophanes writes: "Epiphanios came to the Hebdomon, and held ordinations and services contrary to John's wish. But although John overlooked this because of his holy love and indeed invited Epiphanios to stay in the episcopal residence with him, Epiphanios did not choose to do so, having been won over by Theophilos' slander against the blessed John." See Mango & Scott, *The Chronicle of Theophanes Confessor*, AM 5896, A.D. 403/404, pp. 119, 120.

[48] Others calculate the time of his repose in his nineties.

and much shall be given you. Do not hate any man, and you shall be loved by God. Do not speak against your brother, and in no wise shall a diabolic passion lord it over you. Alienate yourselves from all the heresies, as venomous and deadly beasts, of which I have written in the book I gave you, the one entitled *Panarion*. Turn away and keep yourselves from the pleasures which arouse the body and darken the thought. These are the temptations of Satan. For ofttimes, though the flesh is at rest, the thoughts of the unwatchful incline toward the unseemly. When, however, our mind is watchful, and within it there is the remembrance of God, it is easy for us to vanquish the enemy.'

"After the saint spoke these words and many others, he called to himself all the people found in the ship and addressed them and said: 'It is incumbent upon all of us, brethren, to beseech God with all of our soul to preserve us lest any among us in this vessel should perish. I say this because there is about to occur a great storm. But remain calm and rejoice, because not one tribulation shall approach any of us.' Next he said this to me: 'Child Polyvios, if we come out in Constantinople, remain there seven days; and afterward, go to Egypt and ascend to the Upper Thebaid in order for thee to shepherd the flock of Christ. But take heed, child, not to do anything else. For if thou wilt disobey my words and not go, thou wilt be lost; as much as thou shouldest build, all would be in vain; and thou wilt be unprofitable before all the people. If, however, thou shouldest hearken to my words and keep the command of our Lord Jesus Christ, the One Who commanded me to speak these words to thee, thou shalt be blessed by Him all the days of thy life and thou shalt gain Paradise.' Such things did he speak to me and then he embraced me.

"Next, he said to Isaac: 'And thou, child, remain in Constantia[49] until thou art commanded to go to the place of the Kitions.'[50] After he embraced him, the man of God summoned all the seamen and said, 'Have no fear, children, regarding the looming tempest which is about to follow. Rather, supplicate God and He shall help you.' The saint paused and then turned to one mariner and said, 'And do thou not trouble anyone lest thou shouldest suffer loss or damage.' It was then afternoon, one hour before the setting of the sun, when this assembly took place.

"During the setting of the sun, a storm raged against us and made the sea turbulent. As for the saint, he was inside the ship and reclining. His hands were spread out, the sacred Gospel was on his chest, and his eyes were wide open. But his voice was barely audible. As for us, though we were deeply frightened, we concluded that the holy man was praying to God for the cessation of the furious weather and waves. The commotion and clamor held

---

[49] Constantia was another name for ancient Salamis.

[50] Kiti is seven miles southwest of Larnaka in Cyprus.

out for two days and nights. On the third day, the saint said to me, 'Child, Polyvios, tell the seamen to light some wood, prepare charcoal, and to bring it here.' When his charge was carried out, he burned incense and said, 'Pray, children.' Immediately, then, he took to prayer. Even as he was lying there and looking upward, he spoke again after the prayer and said, 'Work out your salvation, children, because you will no longer see Epiphanios in this life.' He then surrendered his soul and, straightway, the fury of the sea abated. It was then the 12th day of May, in the year 403.[51]

"Both Isaac and I fell on the saint's neck and wept bitterly. Darkness covered our eyes during that hour. As for that mariner, the one whom the saint had told not to trouble anyone lest he suffer loss or damage, he kneeled before the saint's feet in an attempt to lift the venerable man's garment to see whether or not he had been circumcised. The deceased, as he lay there dead, raised his right foot and smote that perverse seaman in the face. Indeed from the interior of the ship that mariner was cast forth toward the stern, where he laid for two days. After that time, his fellow seamen brought him close to the saint that they might have him touch the feet of the saint. Straightway, that mariner rose up sound and whole. Fear gripped all those found on board.

"When we arrived in Constantia, the crew exited the ship. They kept shouting loudly throughout the city, 'Men, brethren, inhabitants of this populous metropolis of Constantia, come down to the sea in order to take up the precious relics of our righteous Father Epiphanios, because he has finished the course of this life.' Then darkness covered the entire city. People, holding hands with one another that they might be guided down to the shore, came weeping and wailing. With the gathering of all the clergy and the people, they took up the holy relic in the midst of candles, incense, and chanting. The body was transferred to the church that the final kiss might be given by the faithful. Those in the countryside also heard the tidings of the archbishop's repose. They sped into the city from practically all over the island of Cyprus. People were making haste that they might venerate the sacred relic before interment.

"Despite the crowds of faithful that converged, three blind men from the village of Skortike also set out to pay their respects. They, too, were inspired to come and venerate the sacred relic. Since they had no one to lead them on the road that they might find their way into the city sooner, one of them, named Prosechios, called upon the saint and said, 'O saint of God, Epiphanios, grant light to our eyes that we might come and venerate thine honorable relic.' Forthwith, then—lo, the marvellous wonder!—the three blind men recovered their eyesight. They came running into the city and venerated

[51] The prophesies of both hierarchs, Epiphanios and John, came to pass. For Epiphanios did not reach his see, having died en route to Salamis, and John, a short time afterward, was driven from his see.

the honorable relic of the saint, rendering thanks to him and recounting the wonderworking wrought in their behalf. The people, hearing this incontestable report, brought forth continual glorifications to God Who gifted such wonders to His worthy slaves.

"As for me, I abided inside the church for seven days, by reason of the great press of people who were praying and venerating the saint. On the eighth day, I took leave of the sacred relic with profound grief in my heart. I did not wish to disobey the command of the saint, so I entered a ship and came into Egypt. I ascended the Upper Thebaid where I sojourned for one year. There came down to those parts the great Herakleion, the superintendent of Egypt. He entered Rinokoura, because that is where he dwelt. When he learned that I was a disciple of Saint Epiphanios, he sent soldiers after me. They came suddenly and seized me. They escorted me, though it was against my will, to Rinokoura.

"The bishops had assembled there that they might choose a bishop for the church, since the throne of the bishopric of that city was widowed. They consecrated me as Bishop of the Church of Rinokoura. After the passage of a little time, I dispatched the honorable Deacon Kallistos through whom I learned the day and place of the burial of the precious relic of our holy father among the saints, Epiphanios, through whose intercessions may we be vouchsafed the kingdom of the heavens."

Epilogue

Saint Epiphanios, according to Blessed Jerome (ca. 341-420), was "a last relic of ancient piety." In Jerome's "Epistle to Pammachios," he names Epiphanios "Father of the Bishops." At the Seventh Œcumenical Synod (or Nicaea II in 787), Epiphanios was called "Father and Teacher of the whole Church."[52] He had been instructed from adolescence by the most celebrated ascetics. He spent much time in Egypt and became renowned both there and in Palestine by his attainments in monastic philosophy. Sozomen remarks, "I think he is the most revered man under the whole heaven, so to speak. For he fulfilled his priesthood in the concourse of a large city and in a seaport. And when he threw himself into civil affairs, he conducted them with so much virtue that he became known in a little while to all citizens and every variety of foreigner: to some, because they had seen the man himself, and had experience of his manner of living; and to others, who had learned it from these spectators."[53]

His zeal for monasticism, ecclesiastical learning, and Orthodoxy gave him extraordinary authority even beyond the boundaries of his island. His advice was sought on numerous occasions. He went to Antioch, ca. 376, to

---

[52] Seventh Synod, Prax. 6.

[53] Sozomen, Bk. VI, Ch. XXXII, Logos Research Systems.

investigate Apollinarianism[54] and to intervene in the schism that divided that Church. He decided in favor of Bishop Paulinus, who was supported by Rome, against Meletios, who was supported by the episcopate of the east. In 382, he assisted at the Council of Rome to uphold the cause of Paulinus of Antioch.

Saint Epiphanios also denounced John II, Bishop of Jerusalem (386/387-417), for his Origenist sympathies. Epiphanios delivered a sermon in John's presence at Jerusalem in 392 and in two letters, one of which survives in a Latin translation made by Jerome.

It was at the instance of Epiphanios' correspondents that he compiled his works. The earliest (374) is the *Ankyrotos* ("holding fast like an anchor"), that is, the Christian firmly fixed against the onslaughts of error. The Trinity and the dogma of the resurrection are particularly treated by the author, who pointedly remonstrates with the Arians and the Origenists. There are two Symbols of the Faith at the end of the work: the first, which is the shorter, is very important in the history of Symbols, or professions of the Faith, being the Baptismal Creed of the Church of Constantia. The second is the personal work of Epiphanios, and is intended to fortify the faithful against current heresies. In the *Ankyrotos*, Epiphanios confines himself to a list of heresies. Some readers desired to have a detailed work on this question, and, Epiphanios, as a rigorous pro-Nicene, composed (374-377) the *Panarion*, that is, a medicine-chest stocked with antidotes against the poisons of many a heresy. This work, formally addressed to the Syrian Abbots Paul and Akakios, is divided into three books comprising in all seven volumes and treating eighty heresies. The first twenty heresies are prior to Jesus Christ; the other sixty deal with those heresies during the Christian era. Some of the saint's information within is on hearsay, but there is furnished very valuable and unique information concerning the religious history of the fourth century, either because the author confines himself to transcribing documents preserved by him alone or because he writes down his personal observations.

Another title of the saint is *On Measures and Weights*, which supplies the reader with an introduction to the holy Scriptures, as it provides the history of biblical texts and sacred archaeology. The treatise entitled *On the Twelve Precious Stones* is an explanation of the ornaments of the high priest's breastplate.[55]

---

[54] The Apollinarians, from Apollinaris of Laodikeia, say that while Christ took flesh and a soul when He came, He did not take a mind. Thus, these "Two-thirdsers" believed Jesus had only two of three parts of human nature, missing human intellect. Apollinaris, therefore, denies the full incarnation of Christ. *Panarion*, § 77, pp. 339 ff.

[55] Ex. 28:17.

In theological matters, the holy archbishop teaches Orthodox doctrine in the vocabulary of the Greeks regarding Trinitarian theology. Thus, he speaks of three hypostases in the Trinity. He is also one of the chief authorities of the fourth century for the devotion to the Virgin Theotokos.

He was conspicuous for his tenderness, love, and generosity toward the poor. He also took seriously one of his primary responsibilities: to protect the flock from heresies. He zealously overturned the babbling of the heretics and anchored the faithful in Orthodox doctrine. He is the ornament of the Orthodox and a model for the hierarchy, opposing impiety and standing vigilant as a watchman[56] of the Church. To Epiphanios, who also received the gift of working miracles in the midst of diseases hard to cure, we ask for his salutary intercessions before Christ our God.

On the 12th of May, the holy Church commemorates our holy father among the saints, GERMANOS, Archbishop of Constantinople.[57]

Germanos, our father among the saints, hailed from Constantinople. He was born circa 650, sometime during the reign of Constans II Pogonatos (r. 641-668)[58] the emperor who was also known as Constantine III. Constans II was the son of Herakleios Constantine and the grandson of Herakleios (r. 610-641). Now Germanos' father, Justinian, noted for his virtue, held the high-ranking dignity of patrician (*patrikios*). During the reign of Herakleios, Justinian received much public distinction and authority. All the grandees of the palace esteemed his piety and virtue. Now it happened that Herakleios' great grandson, Constantine IV (668-685),[59] was jealous of the patrician. He ushered in the death of Justinian, giving the pretext that the illustrious man was supporting sedition against his throne.

---

[56] Cf. Ez. 3:17; 33:7.

[57] Saint Germanos was one of the prominent and distinguished hierarchs of Constantinople. He adorned the throne by reason of his holy life and pure Orthodox Faith. His excellence and virtue were commended at the Holy Seventh Œcumenical Synod in 787, some forty-seven years after his translation to the Lord. He was recorded to have been as another Samuel, a nursling of God, dedicated to Him as a votive offering. He was equal to the wonderful Church fathers, so that his writings were disseminated throughout the inhabited world. A divine office was composed in his honor by a fellow iconophile, Saint Theophanes the Branded. Other hymns were also dedicated to the saint, which are preserved in the following places: Parisian Codex 1566; Lavreote Γ 74, Δ 5, Δ 45, Θ 87, Ι 70; and in the codices of Kafsokalyvia.

[58] Pogonatos was a nickname meaning "thick beard."

[59] In the 19th C., many scholars identified Constantine IV with his father, Constantine Pogonatos, also known as Constans II.

After the murder of that exceptional patrician and senator, it was the emperor who, forthwith, had the son of Justinian castrated. We are speaking here of the blessed Germanos, who was emasculated well beyond the age that such operations were performed.[60] Germanos, afterward, was given over to service in the Church. He was enrolled in the ranks of the clergy of the Great Church (Hagia Sophia). By way of command, Pogonatos brought this about with a vote. The emperor reckoned that should Germanos take up a secular career and enter into the ranks of the patricians and senators, he might take revenge on Pogonatos' progeny for the slaying of his father. As for Germanos, a devout man, he dedicated himself to the service of the Church and not to retribution or vengeance.

The blessed Germanos passed through the clerical ranks. His manner of life was as an angel of God. He hated every passionate attachment and vanity of this world. He, thereupon, dedicated himself to the study and contemplation of the divine Scriptures. He also had the praise of the Lord continually in his mouth, so that he came to be a vessel of the Holy Spirit. He drew forth living waters and God-inspired teachings, by which he gave to drink Christ's Church. His character was made manifest when he served as her shepherd and teacher. Now this came to pass by reason of his manner of life, which was a model of virtue, so that he shone forth as a most radiant lamp.

Germanos was consecrated Bishop of Kyzikos, a city on the southern coast of the Sea of Marmara, which was the metropolitan bishopric of Hellespont.[61] It was in Kyzikos that Bishop Germanos struggled against the

---

[60] Eunuchs still served in critical positions within the Church, military, and civil service. Other patriarchs who were eunuchs include Methodios and Ignatios. General Narses, also, proved himself to be a competent military commander. Civil officials included such famous names as Eftropios, Samonas, Joseph Bringas, Basil Lekapenos, and John the Orphanotrophos. Eunuchs often held palace dignities. Although legislation prohibited castration [Leo VI, No. 60], social convention still countenanced surgery performed on both boys and men. Some eunuchs were imported from the Caucasus, the caliphate, and Slavic countries. At times, eunuchs attained lofty dignities; at other times, they were pushed out of the highest posts. Monastic leaders, fearing that the presence of "beardless" monks might instigate homosexual acts, sometimes excluded eunuchs' entry into their monasteries. The Monastery of Saint Lazarus in the capital was reserved for eunuchs. *Oxford*, s.v. "Eunuchs."

[61] Kyzikos (Cyzicus), an ancient Greek town, is now Blakiz near Erdek. Among Kyzikos' ruins are the substructures of the Temple of Hadrian, sometimes ranked among the Seven Wonders of the World. Later, the region contained many monasteries; among the most noteworthy was Megas Agros on the mountain of Sigriane, the home of the historian Saint Theophanes Confessor (d. 817) who is often quoted herein. Kyzikos was occupied by the Arabs, from 671 to 678, during one of their attacks on the

(continued...)

heresy of the Monothelites.[62] He labored conscientiously with Patriarch Kyros of Constantinople (706-711). When Philippikos (baptismal name Bardanes) was acclaimed emperor, he was supported by the Khazar *khagan* and rebellious Byzantine troops. He entered Constantinople in November of 711. He wasted no time actively supporting Monotheletism. Philippikos first deposed Patriarch Kyros that same year and, soon thereafter, appointed John VI (712-715) in his place. John was his fellow mystic and fellow heretic. The new emperor convened a council and had Constantinople III (that is, the Sixth Œcumenical Synod) anathematized. The emperor removed from the palace that synod's inscriptions and representations. He had rehabilitated those who were excommunicated, such as Patriarch Sergios I who developed the formula of Monoenergism (633) that was later altered into the concept of one will in Christ or Monotheletism. Germanos, during the reign of that tyrant and persecutor of proven cacodoxy, Philippikos, suffered exile together with Patriarch Kyros.

There is conflicting evidence about Germanos' position during the reign of the infamous Philippikos. According to historians Theophanes and Nikephoros, Germanos was present at the 712 Council, at the insistence of Philippikos who favored Monotheletism. Some claim that Germanos, with the majority of the Greek bishops, submitted to the imperial will.[63]

Saint Theophanes Confessor writes in his *Chronicle*: "In this year (704),...Philippikos was not ashamed to move insanely against the Sixth Holy Œcumenical Council, and was eager to overturn the holy doctrines it had secured. Philippikos even imprisoned Patriarch Kyros in the Monastery of the Chora. He found that John, whom he had made Bishop of Constantinople when he condemned his predecessor Kyros, was of his imperial opinion. Also of his party were Germanos (who later held the throne of Constantinople, but was at that time Bishop of Kyzikos), Andrew (who was Bishop of Crete), Nicholas (who knew a great deal about medicine and was at that time quaestor), Elpidios

---

[61](...continued)
capital at Constantinople. By 675, the Arabs had partly destroyed Kyzikos. After the destruction, Justinian II, in 688, brought in Cypriote refugees. The settlement was renamed Nea Ioustinianoupolis. *Oxford*, s.v. "Kyzikos."

[62] The Monothelites confessed only one will in the God-Man. In the Constantinopolitan Synod of 680, the decisions of the synod at Rome (679) were upheld and the Monothelite formula and its adherents were condemned. The 680 Synod proclaimed the existence of two wills in Christ, divine and human. However, Emperor Philippikos repudiated the condemnation against Monotheletism. It was only when this emperor was overthrown that the 7th-C. movement finally vanished.

[63] Mansi, *Conc. Coll.*, XII, 192-196; *Oxford*, s.v. "Germanos."

the deacon of the Great Church, Antiochos the *chartophylax*, and many others of similar stripe. They anathematized in writing the holy Sixth Synod."[64]

Saint Germanos

Philippikos Bardanes was soon deposed and blinded in June of 713. Patriarch Kyros did not return to his rightful throne, having died in exile. The next emperor, Anastasios II (713-715), whose baptismal name was Artemios, reversed his predecessor's support of Monotheletism. Eventually, toward the end of Anastasios' reign, he rid the patriarchate of the false Patriarch John, by having him deposed in 715. In his place, our holy father Germanos was installed on the patriarchal throne of Constantinople on the 11th of August, in the year 715. *The Great Synaxaristes* (in Greek) maintains that Germanos was raised to the patriarchal dignity by a Constantinopolitan synod. They refute the papists who say that Germanos was selected by Pope Gregory II.[65] In any event, the installation of Germanos brought much joy to the Orthodox. In either 715 or 716, Germanos convened a synod of Greek bishops in the capital. They acknowledged and proclaimed anew the doctrine of the two wills and the two operations in Christ. Then, for a short time, Germanos entered into communi-

---

[64] *The Chronicle of Theophanes Confessor*, Annus Mundi 6204 (September 1, 712-August 31, 713), trans. by Harry Turtledove (Philadelphia, PA: University of Pennsylvania Press, 1982), p. 78. Turtledove comments in note 154, loc. cit.: "It is interesting to note that, according to Theophanes, Germanos subscribed to Bardanes Philippikos' council which briefly overturned the antimonothelite Third Council of Constantinople, but proved a champion of Orthodoxy against Iconoclasm after he became Patriarch of Constantinople."

[65] After the blinding and dethronement of Philippikos, it was then that Anastasios II restored Orthodoxy. If Germanos really yielded temporarily to Philippikos' will, he now acknowledged the Orthodox definition of the two wills in Christ. The previous false patriarch, John, who sent to Pope Constantine a letter of submission and accepted the true doctrine of the Church promulgated at the 680 Synod, was recognized by the pope as Patriarch of Constantinople. Again there is conflicting evidence whether it was John's deposition or death that brought about the elevation of Germanos to the patriarchal see. *The Great Synaxaristes* (in Greek) contends that Germanos suffered exile with the Orthodox Patriarch Kyros and that John was deposed.

cation with the Armenian Monophysites. It was his aim to restore them to unity with the Church, but this rapprochement proved unsuccessful.

The chronicler Theophanes has preserved for us Germanos' splendid elevation during the reign of Emperor Anastasios Artemis: "In the second year of Artemios (who was also called Anastasios)—the thirteenth indiction—on the 11th of August, Germanos was translated from the metropolis of Kyzikos to Constantinople. On that occasion a decree of transfer was announced: 'By the decision and determination of the pious priests and deacons, of all the pious clergy, of the holy Senate, and of the Christ-loving people of this God-guarded imperial city, divine grace (which ministers to infirmity and fulfills the incomplete) translates the most holy president of the metropolitanate of the Kyzikenes so he can become bishop of this God-guarded and imperial city.' This translation took place in the presence of Michael (a holy priest who was legate of the apostolic throne) and of other priests and bishops, and occurred during the reign of Artemios."[66]

The Great Synaxaristes (in Greek) also includes the report of Saint Theophanes, and adds that Germanos was escorted to the Cathedral of the Holy Wisdom that he might ascend the throne. Crowds of faithful converged and met at the church, very desirous to behold the newly elected patriarch. Their new chief shepherd was both distinguished and noble. He was one preeminent in every virtue and sanctity. God, also, vouchsafed Germanos the prophetic gift, so that he could foretell future events. We shall recount one example of this spiritual gift which was made manifest even as Germanos was entering Hagia Sophia to serve.

A certain woman, named Anna, approached the saint and cried out with faith, "Give the blessing, *despota*, for that which I have conceived in my womb!" The patriarch, gazing intently upon her, foresaw with clairvoyant eyes that which would come to pass and uttered, "May the Lord bless, by the intercessions of the holy Protomartyr Stephen, that which thou hast conceived!" By means of such words did the man of God prophesy that the child that she should bear would be a male who was to take Saint Stephen as his patron. The saint's manner of foretelling, in this instance, came about in a marvellous manner. The woman with child, who attested on oath, affirmed that as the reverend patriarch was prophesying to her, she beheld a flame of fire issue from his mouth. By reason of this manifestation, she believed in his words without doubting. When the fullness of days was accomplished, Anna brought forth a male child. They called him Stephen, according to the saint's prophecy. This same Stephen, when he came of age, took up the angelic life of monasticism on Mount Afxentios. In his lifetime, he showed his mettle as an

---

[66] H. Turtledove, *The Chronicle of Theophanes Confessor*, AM 6207 (September 1, 714-August 31, 715), p. 80.

iconophile. He confessed the properness of venerating the holy icons, for which conviction he suffering martyrdom.[67] This took place during the reign of Constantine V Kopronymos or the "dung-named" (r. 741-775).

Saint Germanos also predicted what would befall the Church while Constantine V Kopronymos held the scepter of the empire. The patriarch annunciated how the little prince Constantine would one day become a terrible persecutor and tyrant of the Orthodox. The circumstances surrounding this prophesy took place at the Baptism of Constantine V, which event foreshadowed the profane future deeds of the prince. Saint Theophanes, in his *Chronographia*, describes the scene for us that took place during Germanos' fifth year: "In the year 718 [at Constantinople], a son was born to the impious Emperor Leo, namely, the yet more impious Constantine, the precursor of the Antichrist. On the 25th of the month of December, Leo's wife, Maria, was crowned in the Augusteus hall and solemnly processed alone to the Great Church, without her husband. After praying in front of the sanctuary doors, she went over to the Great Baptistery [north of Hagia Sophia],[68] which her husband had entered earlier along with a few members of his household. While Archbishop Germanos was baptizing therein the successor to their wicked rule, namely Constantine, a terrible and evil-smelling sign was manifested in his very infancy. The babe defecated in the holy font, as affirmed by actual eyewitnesses. Consequently, the most holy Patriarch Germanos declared prophetically that the sign of his defecation denoted the great evil that would befall the Christians and the Church on account of Constantine. When Constantine had been baptized, the chief men of the *themes* (*themata*)[69] and of the Senate received him as sponsors. After the holy Liturgy, the Augusta Maria returned in procession with her baptized son and distributed largess on her way from the church to the Bronze Gate of the palace." Thus, Germanos perceived in the Spirit that when the lad came of age, he would try to defile the sanctity of the Church by means of vile heresy. He also foresaw that Kopronymos would shed the blood of many of Christ's pious slaves who revered the sacred images, among whom was Saint Stephen—and so it came to pass as Germanos prophesied.

The hideous heresy of Iconoclasm was restored during the reign of Emperor Leo III the Isaurian (717-741), the father of Constantine Kopronymos.

---

[67] The venerable Martyr Stephen the Confessor is commemorated by the holy Church on the 28th of November.

[68] *The Chronicle of Theophanes Confessor*, AM 6211, A.D. 718/719, trans. by C. Mango and R. Scott, pp. 551, 552.

[69] A *theme*—and the system of the *themes*—was a term for a military division and a territorial unit administered by a *strategos*, who combined both military and civil power. *Oxford*, s.v. "Theme."

Before donning the purple, Leo had received the rank of *spatharios*[70] from Justinian. He followed that emperor to Constantinople and rose to prominence. After he served in the Caucasus, Leo was elevated to *strategos*.[71] Following the deposition of Emperor Anastasios II, Leo joined forces with Artabasdos. Both had been thematic generals under Anastasios II. They revolted against Emperor Theodosios III the Atramyttion, who was compelled to abdicate. Leo entered the capital in March of 717, which throne he was able to secure while successfully resisting the Arab siege of Maslamah. The latter was a general and brother of caliphs who moved an army against Constantinople, which he besieged with Suleiman's navy in August of 717. Maslamah's army fell victim to Greek fire, famine, and a Bulgarian attack.[72] As for Artabasdos, he received Leo's daughter in marriage. Initially, Leo appeared to be devout. In his tenth year, he vomited the poison of his evil heresy and fought against the icons. He issued an impious decree to every quarter of his realm, commanding that the holy icons be prohibited from the churches of God. This casting out of the images was executed when the icons were either trampled upon or consigned to the flames. That wretched and paltry emperor called the icons idols and those who venerated them idolaters.

---

[70] *Spatharios* (lit. "sword-bearer") was a bodyguard, either private or imperial.

[71] *Strategos* was an ancient term for general. The term, in the 8th C., designated the military governor of a *theme*, who possessed local financial and judicial administration.

[72] During Germanos' third year as patriarch (716/717), Maslamah wrote to the Caliph Suleiman that the latter should come with the fleet against Constantinople. After Maslamah devastated the Thracian forts, he laid siege to Constantinople on the 15th of August. The Arabs fenced the land walls all round by digging a wide trench and building above it a breast-high parapet of dry stone. On the 1st of September, Christ's enemy, Suleiman, sailed up with his fleet and emirs. He had enormous ships, military transports, and *dromones* (warships) to the number of 1,800. These vessels found themselves becalmed in the midst of the current and, when a slight breeze blew down the strait, they were pushed back. The emperor sent against them the fire-bearing ships from the Akropolis and, with divine help, set them on fire. Some of them were cast up burning by the sea walls; some sank to the bottom with their crews; and others were swept down, in flames, as far as the islands of Oxeia and Plateia. As a result, the inhabitants of the city took courage, whereas the enemy cowered with fear after experiencing the efficacious action of the liquid fire. Thus, God brought the infidels' counsel to nought through the intercession of the all-pure Theotokos. Afterward, with God's help, thanks to the intercession of the Theotokos, the enemy was sunk on the spot. The Arabs, thereupon, suffered a multitude of losses that winter. Many other calamities befell them at that time and made them learn by experience that God and the all-holy Virgin protect that city and the Christian Empire—"even if we are chastised for a time on account of our sins." See Mango & Scott, *The Chronicle of Theophanes Confessor*, AM 6209, A.D. 716/717, pp. 545, 546.

Saint Germanos

The holy Germanos, together with other Orthodox hierarchs, mightily resisted the emperor. They demonstrated the error of that corrosive heresy. The man of God kept sending wise men and teachers to the emperor that they might enlighten his dark and erroneous reasoning. At other times, Germanos himself went alone to the emperor that they might converse privately. Saint Germanos was a chief expositor of iconographic tradition. The patriarch firmly stated: "We make no icon or likeness or figure of the invisible divinity upon which even the sublime orders of angels themselves cannot look or comprehend; but because the only-begotten Son, Who is in the bosom of the Father, accepted to become man by the merciful will of the Father and the Holy Spirit, we draw His human face and the icon of His human form, according to the flesh and not of His incomprehensible and invisible divinity."[73] Germanos exhorted Leo to put an end to his evil arbitrariness and imperiousness. Nevertheless, Leo would not hearken.

Bishop Constantine of Nakoleia in Phrygia, who condemned the veneration of the images of Christ and the saints, went to Constantinople. Naturally, he visited with the patriarch. They conversed on the subject of the veneration of the icons. The patriarch represented their traditional purpose and use in, and by, the Church. Germanos attempted to persuade Constantine of the propriety of offering the images reverence. His godly words converted Constantine to the right teaching of the Church. But when Constantine failed to deliver Germanos' letter with which he was entrusted to the Metropolitan of Synnada, he was excommunicated.

Also, about that time, the learned patriarch wrote to the iconoclast Bishop Thomas of Claudioupolis. Germanos countered the recent innovation that attacked the sacred images, by developing in detail the sound principles underlying the reverencing of icons. Emperor Leo III, however, did not recede from his misguided position; instead, he encouraged the iconoclasts, in every

---

[73] Saint Germanos of Constantinople is quoted in: Grumel, V., "Images (Cult des)," *Dictionnaire de Theologie Catholique*, 7,1 (Letouzy et Ane, Paris, 1927), p. 838, as reproduced in Father Stephen Bigham's *The Image of God the Father in Orthodox Theology and Iconography and Other Studies* (Torrence, CA: Oakwood Publications, 1995), pp. 27, 28.

quarter, to advance. Then, when a volcanic eruption between the islands of Thera and Therasia took place, Leo believed he beheld divine judgment against image-veneration. In his 726 Edict, he sought to explain how the icons of the Christians had taken the place of the idols of old. He named as idolaters the Orthodox venerators of images, since, according to his private interpretation of the law of God [Ex. 20:4], no product of the hand of man may receive homage. This edict sparked iconoclastic disturbances in the capital.[74]

Now it happened on one such occasion that Germanos, during his fifteenth year and Leo's thirteenth year (728/729), was summoned by the lawless emperor. "In Leo's raging against the correct Faith," records Saint Theophanes, "the emperor attempted to entice the patriarch with flattering words. The blessed bishop said to him, 'We have heard it said that there will be a destruction of the holy and venerable icons, but not in thy reign.' When the emperor compelled the patriarch to declare in whose reign such destruction would be, Germanos said, 'That of Conon.' Then Leo said, 'Truly, my baptismal name is Conon.' The patriarch replied, 'May this evil not be accomplished in thy reign, O sire! For he who commits this deed is the precursor of the Antichrist and the subverter of the divine incarnation [cf. 1 Jn. 4:3; 2 Jn. 1:7].' The tyrant, Leo, irritated at this remark, assailed the blessed patriarch as Herod had once done to the Forerunner."[75] The patriarch, nevertheless, reminded Leo of the covenants he had made before becoming emperor, namely, that he had sworn by God not to undermine the Church with respect to any of her apostolic and God-given rights. "O emperor, I remind thee," said he, "that thou didst pledge to preserve the holy Faith inviolate, according to the tradition of the holy apostles and the God-bearing fathers, neither taking away nor adding anything." Not even then, upon being reminded, was that wretched man put to shame. The emperor spied on the patriarch and tried to put in Germanos' mouth certain statements against Leo's imperial majesty. For Leo thought that if, by chance, he should find Germanos making such statements, he could have him deposed on charges as a mover of sedition and not as a confessor of the Faith. In this sorry affair to discover evidence that Germanos was a conspirator, Leo had an ally and a partner in the person of the pliant Anastasios. The latter was a disciple and *synkellos*[76] of Germanos. Leo had promised Anastasios—inasmuch as Anastasios shared in the

[74] *The Catholic Encyclopedia*, s.v. "Germanus I."

[75] Mango & Scott, *The Chronicle of Theophanes Confessor*, AM 6221, A.D. 728/729, p. 564.

[76] A *synkellos* (literally, one who shares a cell) was, at first, a monk who lived with his bishop. His function was to be a witness to the purity of his bishop's life. The *synkelloi* became patriarchal advisers with considerable powers. They had both seats and votes of their own at Church synod meetings.

emperor's impiety—to make him succeed adulterously to the episcopal throne. Meanwhile, the blessed Germanos was not unaware that Anastasios was crooked and maintained such a perverse position. Germanos chose to imitate our Lord. Germanos, wisely and gently, kept bringing to the attention of his disciple—as to a second Judas—the circumstances of the betrayal.

"Germanos," continues Saint Theophanes, "seeing Anastasios, however, to be irrevocably in error, once passed a remark regarding Anastasios' design. While Germanos was on his way to visit the emperor, Anastasios had proudly stepped on the hind part of the patriarch's vestments. Germanos turned to Anastasios and commented, 'Do not make haste, thou shalt enter the Diippion in good time!'[77] Then was Anastasios disturbed, only momentarily, by these words. Although both he and the others who heard the patriarch's comment were troubled, still they were unaware of the nature of Germanos' prediction. They understood the words properly and fully after the passage of fifteen years. It was in the third year of the persecutor and iconoclast emperor, Constantine Kopronymos, who had obtained the empire after the sedition of his brother-in-law Artabasdos. He had ordered Anastasios flogged, along with other enemies who supported Artabasdos, and paraded him naked in the Hippodrome, by way of Diippion. Anastasios was made to sit backwards on a donkey. Constantine did this because Anastasios had cursed him, as did his other enemies, and had crowned Artabasdos in his place. And so," concludes Saint Theophanes, in his *Chronographia*, "the holy and admirable Germanos was prominent in defending pious doctrine in Byzantium. He fought the wild beast, Leo (fitly named) and the latter's supporters....At length, Leo ejected Germanos, who was subject to him, from the episcopal throne."[78]

Germanos, before his resignation, sought assistance from his fellow bishop in Rome: Pope Gregory II (715-731). Despite much provocation, Gregory opposed all of Leo's efforts to destroy even one article of catholic Faith. By Gregory's letters, which were sent in every direction, he warned the people against the teachings of the emperor. Gregory convoked a council at Rome, in 727, that proclaimed the true doctrine on the question of the veneration of the images. Later, to the best of his power, Gregory also supported Germanos in the resistance the patriarch was making to the "gospel of Leo." Gregory, furthermore, threatened to depose Anastasios, who had replaced the saint in the see of Constantinople, if he did not renounce his heresy.

---

[77] The Diippion are the gates of the Hippodrome, and the space immediately before them, through which ride the chariots.

[78] Mango & Scott, *The Chronicle of Theophanes Confessor*, AM 6221, A.D. 728/729, pp. 562-564.

But before resignation from the patriarchal throne and exile came to pass, Germanos manfully fought with the sword of the Holy Spirit,[79] that is, the word of God, as a good soldier of Jesus Christ, for the sake of the reverence and honor due to the sacred images. He muzzled the foul mouths of the heretics, boldly speaking such words as these to the emperor's face. "It is not fitting for thee, O emperor, to rise up disobediently against thy God and Fashioner, the One Who gave thee life and the kingdom. Simply put, it behooves thee not to move that which is immovable. It is unseemly for thee to transgress those boundaries established by the holy fathers, inasmuch as such landmarks were foretold, decreed, and set from times of old.[80] For by reason of the Logos of God taking on flesh, and that from the all-immaculate blood of the most holy Theotokos, sacrifice to the demons was abolished and idolatry was set at nought. The tradition of portraying with color paints in the icons the likeness of the Christ and of her who ineffably bore Him, as well as the depiction of the saints of God, was handed down to us from the holy apostles, fathers, and teachers of the Church. The reason was so that the sacred images should continue to be venerated not only then but also now, seven hundred years after our Lord appeared in the form of man, showing Himself upon earth and conversing with men.[81] Furthermore, together with the above, the holy Church resumed this custom of depicting holy icons and venerating them reverently, since this sacred art had as its originator the Lord Himself. It was the Lord Who first made an icon, but one produced without hands, when He impressed His countenance on a napkin and sent it forth to Avgaros the Edessene.[82] Following this event, after the ascension of Jesus, the woman who had touched the hem of our Lord's garment and was healed[83] showed her gratitude by having the likeness of Jesus Christ fashioned out of bronze.[84] Next, mention should be made of how the holy Evangelist Luke painted many icons of the most holy Theotokos, that is, when she was still living on the earth. When the Panagia (all-holy one) beheld the icons depicting her, holding in her arms the pre-eternal Infant Jesus, she remarked with joy, 'May the grace of Him Who was born of me, through me, be imparted to them!'[85]

"It is in this way, O emperor, that the pious work of depicting Christ, His Mother, and the saints came to pass. By means of the holy icons do the

[79] Eph. 6:17.
[80] "Remove not the everlasting landmarks, which thy fathers placed [Prov. 22:28]."
[81] "He showed Himself upon earth, and conversed with men [Bar. 3:37]."
[82] See the 16th of August for this account.
[83] Cf. Mt. 9:20. This is the diseased woman who, after suffering twelve years with an issue of blood, came behind Jesus.
[84] See the 12th of July.
[85] See the 18th of October.

Orthodox Christians adorn the temples of God and their own homes.[86] This practise was accepted and sanctioned by the holy œcumenical synods, so that they have commanded that we revere and offer veneration to the icons. But we do not worship them, as the mindless, in their foolish talk, contend. Nay, rather honor is paid relatively to the icons, so that the honor paid to the image passes over to its prototype; and whoever venerates the icon, also venerates the hypostasis of the one depicted. Saint Basil the Great speaks in this manner. But we do not make gods of the icons.[87] Therefore, sire, if thou shouldest usher in

---

[86] To the Eastern Orthodox Christian of Byzantine times such acts as prostrations, kisses, and burning incense were perfectly natural ways of showing honor to anyone. The Byzantine was used to such things, and even applied such practises to his civil and social superiors. He, therefore, was accustomed to treat symbols in the same way, giving them relative honor that was obviously meant really for their prototypes. And so he carried his normal habits with him into church. Tradition gradually sanctioned such practises, till they were written down as rubrics and became part of the ritual. Nor is there any suspicion that the people who practised such outward signs of reverence were confusing the image with its prototype or were forgetting that to God only supreme homage is due. The forms they used were as natural to them as saluting a flag is to us. The Byzantine Christian believed that the honor shown to the image is referred to the prototype. The holy fathers of Nicaea II further distinguished between absolute and relative worship. Absolute worship is paid to any person for his own sake. Relative worship is paid to a sign, not at all for its own sake, but for the sake of the thing signified. An insult to the sign (a flag or statue) is an insult to the thing of which it is a sign; so also we honor the prototype by honoring the sign. The sign provides us with a visible direction for our reverence. Everyone knows the use of such signs in ordinary life. People salute flags, bow to empty thrones, uncover to statues, and so on; nor does anyone think that this reverence is directed to colored bunting or wood and stone. *The Catholic Encyclopedia*, s.v. "Veneration of Images."

[87] Images are to receive veneration (*proskynesis*), not adoration (*latreia*); the honor paid to them is only relative (*schetike*), for the sake of their prototype. The word relative veneration or *schetike proskynesis* became a technical term in the iconoclastic controversy. Relative or qualified veneration was contrasted with outright worship. Irrelative veneration is what is done when one reverences only the one represented by the picture, and not both the picture and the one portrayed therein. There are many kinds of images which are unvenerated, which serve to preserve in the mind memories of certain persons or things. Relative veneration, on the other hand, standing midway between worshipping adoration and irrelative veneration, is that which is paid to the holy icons. It is called relative because of the fact that in this case the image itself is not called such in itself (or by itself) and absolutely, but with respect (or in relation) to something else and relatively. For a picture is the picture of that which is pictured, or represented by it. Hence, on account of this relation and reference which it bears to that which is pictured, with respect to the likeness, that is to say, of the hypostasis, and with respect to the name in the inscription inscribed upon it, it is honored and venerated

(continued...)

Iconoclasm, know that I will be the first to oppose it. I am ready not only to suffer ill for the images but even to die for the icon of my Christ. For He shed His blood in order to restore my soul's fallen image. It is, therefore, manifest, that the image of Christ bears the name of the same Christ, Who was incarnate of the ever-virgin Mary, and Who lived among men on earth. Each Orthodox Christian ought to be prepared to die for Christ's holy icon. Moreover, whosoever dishonors the icons, dishonors the same depicted thereon.[88]

---

[87](...continued)

conjointly with the one who is pictured, with a single act of veneration, true enough, yet equivocally and relatively, and not this in all respects and in identically the same respect, as Theodore the Stoudite says in his letter to Athanasios. For, as we have said, we adore the person represented in the picture by paying Jesus worshipping adoration as Christ but we venerate Jesus' picture, or icon, relatively on account of its reference to Him. Likewise as for the saints and their relics, we venerate them as servants and slaves of Christ with servile veneration, that is to say, with slavish veneration, or veneration befitting a slave (as venerator), and not a freeman, on account of familiarity or association with Christ. But as for their pictures, or icons, we venerate these only relatively, on account of the reference which they bear to the persons themselves whom they are intended to represent to the eye, by reason of the likeness of their hypostasis, and by reason of the name inscribed upon them, or the title bestowed upon them, just as the above synod held during the patriarchate of Nicholas decreed. Likewise, as for the Theotokos herself, we revere with most servile honor, as most holy Mother of God; while, on the other hand, as regards her icon, we accord it relative veneration [see also Dositheos, *Dodekavivlos*, p. 655].

Do you see that the prayer which is read over holy pictures is a papal affair, and not Orthodox? Do you see that it is a modern affair, and not an ancient one? For this reason no such prayer can be found anywhere in the ancient manuscripts of the *Efchologia*. In fact, we have noticed that this prayer is not even found in *Efchologia* printed only a hundred years ago. It becomes evident that holy icons do not need any special prayer or application of myrrh, because the pictures painted on the walls of churches, and in their naves and in their aisles, and in general in streets and on doors, and on the holy vessels, are never anointed with myrrh and never have any special prayer recited over them. And yet, in spite of this, veneration is paid to them by all relatively and in an honorary manner on account of the likeness they bear to the originals. [Footnotes to Seventh Synod, see *The Rudder*.]

[88] The text of the decision of the seventh session of Nicaea II is: "We define (*orizomen*) with all certainty and care that both the figure of the sacred and life-giving Cross, as also the venerable and holy images, whether made in colors or mosaic or other materials, are to be placed suitably in the holy churches of God, on sacred vessels and vestments, on walls and pictures, in houses and by roads; that is to say, the images of our Lord God and Savior Jesus Christ, of our immaculate Lady the holy Mother of God, of the honorable angels, and of all saints. For as often as they are seen in their pictorial representations, people who look at them are ardently lifted up to the memory

(continued...)

"Let it not be, sire, that thy reign should usher in such dishonor toward the Master Christ, even as thou wouldest not tolerate a coin bearing thine image to be trampled underfoot. Hear me cheerfully and do not agitate the Church of God. If thou shouldest think that I alone reason thus, cast me, as Jonas, into the sea.[89] But do thou know that all the realm testifies with me and respects the veneration of the sacred icons. Without an œcumenical synod, I, alone, can neither innovate that which concerns the Faith nor dispense laws. Therefore, let not thy reign become unfaithful to the truth lest thou shouldest be numbered with the unbelieving Hebrews who hate the icon of the Christ. Bring to remembrance the other things that I told thee at a previous time, with so many creditable testimonies. I am referring to that miracle which took place in the city of Beirut, where there was the discovery of a miraculous icon of the Christ. When it was struck with a dagger on its right side—lo, the wonder!—so much blood came forth that it flowed outside of the house.[90] All, however, did not believe but only some. Do not, then, let it happen that thou shouldest be numbered with the unbelievers who shall inherit everlasting punishment."

The emperor, hearing such a censure from Patriarch Germanos, became angry. Since he could not gainsay the truth, he raised his hand and mightily struck the countenance of the saint and said wrathfully, "Begone, O evil head, from my sight lest thou shouldest also lose thy life!" The saint endured the slap, even as once did Christ,[91] and departed being driven out.

The emperor, beholding the impossibility of bringing the patriarch to his way of thinking, summoned the most wise gymnasiarch and œcumenical teacher.[92] He conferred with him regarding his decision, that is, the abolition

---

[88](...continued)
and love of the originals. They are induced to kiss them and honor with veneration (*aspasmon kai timetiken proskynesin*) but not real worship or adoration (*alethinen latreian*) which, according to our Faith, is due only to the divine nature. So that offerings of incense and lights are to be given to these as to the figure of the sacred and life-giving Cross, to the holy Gospel books, and to other sacred objects in order to do them honor, as was the pious custom of ancient times. For honor paid to an image passes on to its prototype; the one who venerates (*ho proskynon*) an image venerates the reality of the one who is painted in it [Mansi, XIII, pp. 378-9; Harduin, IV, pp. 453-456]."

[89] Jon. 1:12 ff.

[90] In regard to this miracle, which was recounted by the great Athanasios, see the note in *The Great Synaxaristes* under the Life of the holy Martyr Varypsavas who is commemorated by the holy Church on the 10th of September.

[91] Cf. Lk. 22:64; Jn. 18:22.

[92] At the most august Church of Hagia Sophia, which possessed a far famed library, it is said that there were approximately seven hundred thousand books. Inside this library
(continued...)

of the sacred icons. The teacher gave his response to the emperor, which answer was in concord with the words of Patriarch Germanos. The teacher, however, added even more histories and miracles which were wrought by the holy icons by reason of divine grace which dwelt within them. With regard to their veneration, the œcumenical teacher confirmed that it was an ancient tradition delivered by the holy apostles. The teacher indicated that Avgaros of Edessa, with faith and piety, venerated the Lord's image, the one not made by hands, and was healed of leprosy. Leo, nonetheless, deemed the teacher's exhortations to be nonsensical babbling.

The lawless tyrant, determined to show his relentless stubbornness, since the devil dwelt within him, commanded his army to encircle the school by night. The same teacher was inside when the imperial order was given to set fire to everything. The teacher was burned to death and the famous library was consumed. Other teachers and students within the school also lost their lives. Anyone else within the school perished. Neither person nor book survived. The following morning, Leo charged that all the sacred icons were to be removed from the churches. Some of the images were burned, while others were cast into the sea. Then, when Saint Germanos beheld the beginning of the destruction of the holy icons, he entered the church. As he prayed, he shed many tears. The patriarch then placed his *omophorion* upon the holy Table within the sanctuary. Germanos then took up in his hands a large icon of Christ, one that was in the patriarchate, and went down to the shore and to a place called Mandeion.

Germanos wished to convey that holy icon from the patriarchate to the then pope of Rome, whose name was Gregory, a pious and holy man. Germanos considered carrying out this action since Rome was not under the rule of Leo the Isaurian. Germanos wrote to Gregory the following letter: "Germanos, Patriarch of Constantinople, to Gregory, Pope of Rome: Know that here there is great confusion in the Church of God, since a fearful persecution has unfolded against those who venerate the holy icons. Inasmuch as the danger is great for the sacred images here but quiet exists in thy parts, I am sending thee the holy icon of the Christ. I ask thee to accept it." When Germanos completed the epistle, he dug out the back of the icon and placed

---

[92](...continued)
there were also twelve schools that were under the supervision of twelve wise teachers. These schools and teachers, in imitation of our Lord Jesus Christ and the holy twelve apostles, were pupils of the head teacher who resided within the imperial household. He was known as the œcumenical teacher since he lived in Constantinople, the capital of the empire. This office and honor, with the blessing of the patriarch, were in the emperor's gift to bestow. It was this teacher that Leo had summoned to have a consultation.

within the letter securely. He then wept profusely, praying and entreating God to put an end to the confounding of the Church. He supplicated for the Church's deliverance from such an evil emperor, as well as the peace of the world and many other things. He extended his arms with the icon in his hands and addressed the Savior portrayed thereon, saying, "O Master Christ, Who art depicted in this holy icon, preserve Thine image! Do Thou also save us, for we are perishing!" These were the words he uttered, and then he respectfully cast the icon into the sea.

Behold the miracle! The icon inclined neither to the right nor to the left. Much rather, it stood upright and hastened on top of the crests of the waves as though traversing a well-paved walkway. In fact, in one day's time, the icon arrived outside of Rome, in the Tiber River. During that night, while Pope Gregory slumbered, he beheld an angel of the Lord who said, "Rise up that thou mightest go and meet the King, because He is coming!" Gregory, at that message, was stirred from his sleep. He began wondering to himself, "Who is the King?" and "What hour is He coming?" As he pondered, he was overtaken by sleep. Once again, the angel appeared to him and said, "He Who is coming is Christ God, the King of those who rule as kings. Go down to the river Tiber and there thou shalt behold Him." In the morning, the pope called to himself both clerics and princes. Together, they descended to the river, bearing incense and candles. The entourage entered a ship, from which they caught sight of the Master Christ's icon; for it was standing straight in the waters. The pope then spoke aloud and said to the icon, "O Master Christ, if Thou hast come to us, do Thou enter the ship by Thyself, since I am unworthy to take Thee up into my arms." Forthwith, the holy icon entered the ship. The pope received the icon and found the letter. He, thereupon, deposited the icon within the church. From the time the icon arrived, it was streaming forth holy water, albeit, salt water, that was working many wonders.

Saint Germanos

Let us now return to the matter at hand. Let us speak of the saint's banishment. After the conflagration, which incinerated both men and library, the icons were cast out. The raving and lawless Leo then dispatched soldiers, armed as though for battle, to apprehend the patriarch. They seized Germanos, buffeting him, as they pushed him outside of the patriarchate. They insulted and wounded the man of God. This expulsion took place in 729. Such an outrage did not pass by unnoticed. All of Constantinople learned of the disrespect shown to the patriarch and his office. All those who were in favor of venerating the icons were in straits, feeling much sorrow and affliction. There was none among the faithful who did not lament and sigh for the great dishonor heaped upon their beloved patriarch. The iconoclasts, meanwhile, continued breaking in pieces the icons. Many of the images were exposed to foul abuse, cast into filth, trampled upon, or consumed in the fire. The effects of these events, together with the catastrophic loss of thousands of books and the untimely destruction of wise and learned teachers, were further worsened with the unjust expulsion of the most holy Patriarch Germanos. After the saint went into exile, the aforementioned Anastasios ascended the patriarchal throne. As we said earlier, this new traitor and Judas was in complete concord with both Leo and his son Kopronymos in regard to Iconoclasm and plotting against the lawful patriarch and Anastasios' elder. Anastasios, anxious to please his sovereign, threw outside of the Great Church all of her holy icons. The thrice-accursed one then ordered the flock to do so in like manner.

At the Chalke Gate, that is, the main entrance vestibule of the Great Palace of Constantinople, there was an icon of Christ that adorned its facade. This gold-leafed icon of Christ Chalkites, situated above the main door, depicted our Savior standing full-length on a footstool. Leo III gave orders for the removal of the icon, as his first public act of imperial Iconoclasm, together with its destruction and burning. Now as the emperor's *spatharios* set the ladder against the wall and clambered up, in order to cast down to the earth the sacred icon, his actions could scarcely be missed by passersby. The Christians—men and women, monks and nuns, hastened to the spot and implored the *spatharios* to desist and not destroy the icon.[93] He gave no consequence to their earnest entreaties. He carried out his orders with a deaf ear to their touching pleas. Some of the Christians, thereupon, took hold of the ladder. They cast it to the ground, with the *spatharios* still aloft on one of the upper rungs. When the ladder struck the ground with its rider, the *spatharios* was killed in the fall. Next, those Christians moved toward the patriarchate. They took up stones and pelted the irreverent iconomach, Anastasios. They shouted aloud their accusations against the emperor, calling him an antichrist and anathematizing him. Leo certainly heard what had transpired and his anger waxed hot. He

[93] See the Life of our venerable Mother Theodosia, commemorated by the holy Church on the 29th of May.

directed that all those present have their heads struck off. Only the Lord knows how many were in that great multitude.

Meanwhile, the holy Germanos was driven out of the patriarchate, as we said. He took up residence in his paternal house in a place called Platanion (an area planted with plane trees). In that retreat he found rest and quiet, enjoying fellowship with other spiritual men in his company or synodia. He was an example of celestial stillness and godly freedom from care.

Saint Theophanes reports the events as follows. In the year 730, on a Tuesday in January, the irreverent Leo convened a *silentium* against the holy and venerable icons.[94] That assembly of impiety was held in the Tribunal of Nineteen Couches. Leo had also invited the most holy Patriarch Germanos. Leo thought he could persuade Germanos to sign a condemnation of the icons. Nevertheless, Christ's courageous slave, Germanos, in no way was persuaded by Leo's abominable error. After the patriarch expounded correctly the true Orthodox doctrine, Germanos resigned from the episcopacy and surrendered his pallium. After many words of instruction, Germanos then repeated, "If I am Jonas, cast me into the sea. For without an œcumenical synod, it is impossible for me, O emperor, to innovate in matters of the Faith." Germanos then retired to his family house at the so-called Platanion. Germanos served as bishop fourteen years, five months, and seven days.

"In that same month, on the 22nd of January, Anastasios, the spurious pupil and *synkellos* of the blessed Germanos, who, on account of his worldly ambition, had adopted Leo's impiety, was ordained and appointed false Bishop of Constantinople....Leo, thereafter, intensified his assault on the holy icons. Many clerics, monks, and pious laymen faced danger on behalf of the true Faith and won the crown of martyrdom."[95]

---

[94] In the east, icons were taken on journeys as a protection, they marched at the head of armies, and presided at the races in the Hippodrome; they hung in a place of honor in every room, over every shop; they covered cups, garments, furniture, rings; wherever a possible space was found, it was filled with a picture of Christ, our Lady, or a saint. God worked miracles through and by the icons. The icons were crowned with garlands, incensed, and kissed. Lamps burned before them, hymns were sung in their honor. They were applied to sick persons by contact, and were set out in the path of a fire or a flood to halt it. The iconoclast complained about these practises and that psalms were sung before images and prostrations were made before them, while the supplicant implored their help. They disapproved that many iconophiles dressed up images in linen garments and chose them as godparents for their children. Others who became monks let their tonsured hair fall upon the icon as into the hands of a distinguished person. Some priests scraped the paint off images, mixed it with the consecrated bread and wine, and gave it to the faithful [Mansi, XIV, 417-422].

[95] Mango & Scott, *The Chronicle of Theophanes Confessor*, AM 6221, A.D. 728/729,

(continued...)

During the time of Leo and Anastasios, as well as Leo's son, Constantine, the Byzantines suffered many terrible events. The Arabs attacked their realm and took many captives. The false Patriarch Anastasios swore to the people, while holding the venerable and life-giving Cross, that "by Him Who was nailed to this," said he, "thus did the Emperor Constantine say to me, namely, 'Do not regard Mary's Offspring, Who is called Christ, as the Son of God, but as a mere man. For Mary gave birth to Him just as my mother Mary gave birth to me.'" When the people heard this, they cursed Emperor Constantine. It was spoken in the first year of Constantine's reign of terror.[96] From the 10th to the 15th of August, in 742/743, there appeared in the north and in some places dust that fell from the sky. In 745 there was a misty darkness. On the 15th of January, in 746, numberless died in an earthquake that rent asunder Palestine, by the Jordan and all Syria. In 746, a pestilence started in Sicily and Calabria. It spread to Monemvasia, Hellas, and the adjoining islands, thus scourging in advance the impious Constantine and restraining his fury against the Church and the holy icons, even though he remained unrepentant like Pharaoh of old. This disease of the bubonic plague spread to the imperial city. All of a sudden, without cause, there appeared many oily crosslets upon men's garments, on the altar cloths of churches, and on hangings. The mysteriousness of this presage inspired great sorrow and despondency among the people. Then God's wrath, according to Saint Theophanes, destroyed not only the inhabitants of the city but also those of all its outskirts. Men suffered from hallucinations. In the spring the plague intensified. Entire households were closed up. There was no one to bury the dead. The urban and suburban cemeteries were filled. Many vineyards were dug up and even orchards to make room for the burial of human bodies. When every household had been destroyed by this calamity, on account of the impious removal of the holy icons by the rulers, straightway, the fleet of the Hagarenes sailed from Alexandria to Cyprus where the fleet of the Rhomaioi happened to be. Many Byzantines died.[97]

But let us now say a few words regarding the saint's prophecy for Anastasios, the pseudopatriarch, which came to pass in the following manner. With the death of the impious Leo the Isaurian at Constantinople on the 18th of June, in the year 741, his unholy son, Constantine V Kopronymos, succeeded to his throne. Kopronymos, however, was briefly driven out of Constantinople by Artabasdos, who had married Leo III's daughter, that is Constantine V's sister, Anna. Artabasdos had revolted against Constantine V and defeated him. He, for a time, brought back the restoration of the icons. Artabasdos ruled with

---

[95](...continued)
p. 565.

[96] Ibid., AM 6233, A.D. 740/741, p. 576.

[97] Ibid., pp. 576-586.

his eldest son, Nikephoros, as a co-emperor. Now in Artabasdos' takeover, Patriarch Anastasios assisted him and crowned him emperor. A civil war ensued, since Kopronymos was able to recruit a large army and take back the capital. When Kopronymos regained his throne in November of 743, he took his brother-in-law Artabasdos and the latter's two sons, that is, Kopronymos' nephews, and had them blinded. As for Anastasios, who had condoned Artabasdos' deeds, he contrived another form of punishment. The patriarch was stripped and thrashed in public. After this punishment was meted out, Anastasios was made to sit backwards on an ass that was driven into the stadium to be made a spectacle of before the entire city. Thus was fulfilled the prophecy of Saint Germanos, who told Anastasios when he had stepped on the back part of the patriarch's vestments, "Do not make haste, thou shalt enter the Diippion in good time!" In truth, that was the name of those gates leading into the Hippodrome. Kopronymos reckoned that was where the greatest concourse of people might assemble so that the patriarch might fully experience both shame and humiliation. Since the emperor could not find another more groveling toward him and avid for the destruction of the icons, he allowed him to keep his throne. Anastasios, at length, came to a bad end, because of his blasphemous language against the sacred icons and treachery to his elder. Anastasios fell victim to a disease which was called then *chordapsos* or ileus, a disease of the ileum which is the last division of the small intestine. Thus, with his bowel obstructed, Anastasios had a painful and distended abdomen. With his intestinal contents backed up, he vomited dark or fecal matter that resulted in toxemia and dehydration. Hence, in 754, after twenty-four years on the throne, he surrendered his wretched soul.[98]

In that same year, in the palace of Hiereia, the irreverent Constantine convened an illegal assembly of 338 bishops. They sat and ruled against the holy and venerable icons, under the leadership of Theodosios of Ephesus and Pastillas of Perge. Then Emperor Constantine, holding a monk named Constantine (former Bishop of Syllaion), said in a loud voice, "Long live Constantine, the œcumenical patriarch!" Shortly thereafter, Emperor Constantine went up to the Forum together with the unholy Bishop Constantine and the other bishops. They proclaimed their misguided heresy in the presence

---

[98] Saint Theophanes records: "In 752/753, that is, the 13th year of Constantine and the 24th year of Anastasios, the unholy patriarch who held in unholy fashion the episcopal throne of Constantinople, died a spiritual as well as a bodily death. He perished from a dreadful disease of the guts, after vomiting dung through his mouth. Thus, it was a just punishment for his daring deeds against God and his teacher." Ibid., AM 6245, A.D. 752/753, p. 591.

of all the people, after anathematizing the most holy Germanos, George of Cyprus, John Damascene, and other holy men and teachers.[99]

Saint Germanos, meanwhile, lived in quietude for a considerable time, leaving behind a great many writings. He wrote a narrative sermon to Deacon Anthimos concerning the years when he presided over the holy synod.[100] There are other works that include various hymns for the great feasts of the Master Christ and the Mother of God. He also authored compositions honoring the memory of certain saints, that is, hymns for the offices of Vespers (*stichera*), Lity, and Orthros (Praises). There are also festal sermons for some feasts. He penned discourses on the Feasts of the Virgin's Entrance into the Temple, of the Annunciation, of the Nativity,[101] of the Meeting,[102] of the Dormition,[103] and

[99] Ibid., pp. 591, 592. The Seventh Synod pronounced anathemas against the iconoclast leaders, while Germanos, John Damascene, and George of Cyprus were praised. In opposition to the formula of the iconoclast council, the fathers of the Seventh declared: "The Trinity has made these three (fathers) glorious (*he Trias tous treis edoxasen*)." See the 11th of October for the account of this holy Seventh Synod.

[100] At the Seventh Œcumenical Synod (787), the name of Patriarch Germanos was included in the diptyches of the saints. He is known to have written an explanation of difficult passages of Scriptures. Several writings of Germanos have been preserved [Migne, *P.G.* 98:39-454], viz., *Narratio de sanctis synodis*, a dialogue *De vitae termino*, that is, on the rewards of the righteous after death, as well as a letter to the Armenians, and three letters on the reverencing of images that were read at the Seventh Synod, as well as nine discourses in the extravagant rhetorical style of the later Byzantines. He wrote a "Meditation on Church Matters or Commentary on the Liturgy." This commentary on the Liturgy is preserved under the peculiar title of *Church History*, but the *Historia ecclesiastica et mystica* attributed to him [*P.G.* 98:383-454] is of doubtful authenticity. It was his work concerning the various heresies that rose up from apostolic times, together with the Church synods during the reign of the iconoclast Leo, that provided much historical data. The dialogue *On Foreordained Terms of Life* is sometimes ascribed to Saint Photios. See *On Predestined Terms of Life*, ed. C. Garton, L. Westerink (Buffalo, NY, 1979); and P. Meyendorff, *On the Divine Liturgy* (Crestwood, NY, 1984).

[101] December 25th, Nativity Vespers Sticheron, Mode Two, by Saint Germanos: "The express image of the Father [Heb. 1:3], the imprint of His eternity, takes the form of a servant and, without undergoing change, He comes forth from a mother who knew not wedlock. For what He was, He has remained, true God: and what He was not, He has taken upon Himself, becoming man through love for mankind."

[102] February 2nd, Meeting in the Temple, Vespers Sticheron, Mode One, by Saint Germanos: "Symeon, tell us: 'Whom dost thou bear in thine arms, that thou dost rejoice so greatly in the temple? To Whom dost thou cry and shout: "Now I am set free, for I have seen my Savior?"' And the elder answered, 'This is He Who was born of a virgin: This is He, the Logos, God of God, Who for our sakes has taken flesh and

(continued...)

of the Deposition of the Virgin's Girdle or *Zonee*. There exist verses in the Slavonic tongue, full of beauty and compunction, that can evoke abundant tears and inspire continual mourning for sins.[104]

Germanos was an early champion of the Theotokos. He upheld the tradition of how the Virgin was brought up in the temple, fed by angels, and given into the care of Joseph after the priests drew lots. He addressed her with the title of Theonymphe, that is, God's bride. Among his works what particularly engages interest is his sermon on the Annunciation and the dialogue between the Archangel Gabriel and the Virgin Mary. This type of dramatic sermon would be widely used in the pulpit.[105] The saint, a proficient hymnographer, also wrote canons. The Akathist Hymn has been attributed to him by some scholars.[106]

---

[102](...continued)
has saved man.'"

[103] Saint Germanos commented upon the palm branch that was given to the Theotokos prior to her falling asleep. It was a symbol of victory, which was given to persuade her that in leaving this life she would overcome corruption, just as Christ conquered Hades. Such palms had the God-loving children of the Hebrews held when Christ was approaching His Passion, and was soon to become victorious over death. "Sermon 3, On the Dormition," *P.G.* 98:364.

[104] It is also noted in *The Great Synaxaristes* (in Greek) that a certain terrifying narration on repentance, mentioned by Nikodemos the Hagiorite in the *Neon Eklogion*, which is in the *Evergetinos* [Vol. 1 of the First Book] was cited under the name of Saint Amphilochios but should be Saint Germanos.

[105] Saint Germanos starts out with Joseph's sense of repulsion and wounded honor. He puts these words into the betrothed's mouth: "Leave my home straightway and betake thyself to thy new lover! I do not intend to feed thee any longer! Thou shalt not eat the bread from my table, since, instead of joy, thou hast given me sorrow, disgrace, and dishonor in my old age!" He then reminds her of the judgment and condemnation of the Jewish Synagogue, and that they will be tested by the "water of conviction [Num. 5:11-30]." Saint Germanos gives expression, in a poignant narration from his pulpit, of Mary's pleas with her betrothed, saying, "Be penitent, O Joseph! Do not drive me in secret from thy home! I am now in a strange place, and am not accustomed to it. I know neither right from left, and I do not know with whom I might find refuge." And, "As the Lord lives, I have not known a man! The stain which comes from a forced bed, and the blemish which comes from carnal desire, I know not!" Saint Germanos, "Sermon on the Annunciation of the Most Holy Theotokos," *P.G.* 98:332D.

[106] The author and date of the composition of the Akathistos Hymn remain uncertain. The famous *prooimion*, "To thee the champion leader," and hence the entire Akathistos Hymn, is attributed in the *Synaxaria* to Patriarch Sergios I in 626, after the lifting of the Avar siege of Constantinople; but in the Latin translation (8th or 9th C.), it is attributed to Patriarch Germanos I in 717/718, after the destruction of the Arab fleet (continued...)

Saint Germanos lived to be ninety years old, when he reposed in the Lord ca. 740. His sacred relics, as they were being borne away to burial, delivered many from diverse maladies. His relics continued to spring forth healings of every kind for those who hastened to the saint with faith. He was interred in the holy and lofty Chora Monastery in the northwestern region of Constantinople. Afterward, his precious relics were conveyed to France. As a reward for his pangs—having endured buffeting, maltreatment, imprisonment, and exile—he attained to life everlasting where he delights without end in divine vision. Through the intercessions of Saint Germanos, may we attain to the kingdom of the heavens. Amen.

On the 12th of May, the holy Church commemorates the holy New-martyr JOHN the Wallachian, who suffered martyrdom by hanging in Constantinople (1662).[107]

John, the holy new-martyr, was from Wallachia. He was born during the reign of Sultan Ibrahim (1640-1648). During that dark period, Wallachia was ruled by princes called voevods, who were subject to the Ottoman sultan. In the days of Sultan Mehmet IV (1648-1687), it happened that the voevod of Wallachia, one named Michna Tzivan, revolted against the Turks since they had imposed an unreasonable tribute which he could not pay. Therefore, wheresoever Tzivan found a Turk, he put him to death. He penetrated Turkish territory, where he burned, slew, and imprisoned many Turks. On hearing these reports, the Sultan Mehmet deployed an army, consisting of Turks and Tartars. Tzivan could not match this army, so he retreated while the Tartars and Turks stormed Wallachia. The Muslim soldiers massacred many Christians and imprisoned vast numbers of men and women. Among the captives was the blessed John, of a noble and wealthy family, who was abducted and imprisoned in the year 1662.

Saint John

[106](...continued)
that had threatened the city. Metrical patterns and theological considerations, however, point rather to a date in the early 6th C. *Oxford*, s.v. "Akathistos Hymn"; Oliver Strunk, *Essays on Music in the Byzantine World* (NY: W. W. Norton & Co.), p. 316.

[107] The account of the martyrdom of New-martyr John was written by John Karyophylles. It was published in Nikodemos the Hagiorite's *Neon Martyrologion*, 3rd ed. (pp. 82, 83), and incorporated into *The Great Synaxaristes* (in Greek).

However, a certain soldier of the Hagarenes noticed that John was particularly handsome. The Muslim then bought John for an evil purpose. Although the Muslim tried to seduce John, yet the young man, being a prudent and pure Orthodox Christian, resisted manfully. The Hagarene then tied John to a tree until the opportunity arose to fulfill his perverted purpose. John felt great sorrow in his heart at his predicament. He, also, feared that he might be seduced by force. When he found the opportunity, he killed that vile and indecent Turk. It was not long before that Turk's fellow soldiers investigated and found out what had happened. They bound John and brought him to Constantinople, where they delivered him up to the wife of the slain homosexual soldier. She brought John to the vizier who questioned him. Then John admitted the whole truth. The vizier promptly turned him over to the wife of the slain one, to do with him as she pleased. Meanwhile, seeing that he was very comely, she used deceptive methods to win him over. She promised that, should he became a Moslem, she would make him her husband and settle all her belongings on him.

When the blessed John heard her proposal, he made the sign of the Cross. He begged Christ to strengthen and safeguard him, to the end, in the true Faith of the Orthodox Christians. When the new "Delilah" saw what he had done, she surrendered him to the prefect who confined him to jail. There they tortured John excessively. Only thinking about what he suffered in that odious dungeon would terrify and appall one. They exposed the martyr to ill treatment for many days, during which time that most profane woman never ceased to flatter and entice John to sin, all the while hoping to separate him from the Faith of Christ. But the young man, as a solid diamond, stood unbending and firm in the Faith and in virtue; for he desired only our Lord Jesus Christ from Whom he drew strength. John, thereupon, succeeded in vanquishing all his visible and invisible enemies. Finally, seeing that they accomplished nothing, they asked the vizier to pass the death sentence. After the vizier issued the judgment, by which he condemned to death John of Wallachia, the prefect was ordered to carry out the execution. The executioners then led John to Parmak Kapi, near the covered bazaar, where they hanged him by the neck on the 12th day of May, in the year 1662. Thus, the blessed John received the crown of martyrdom from the hands of God. By the intercessions of Saint John, may we be vouchsafed strength against atypical sexuality and abandonment of the Faith for the sake of a temporally advantageous marriage, so that we might be deemed worthy of everlasting blessings.

On the 12th of May, the holy Church commemorates our venerable and God-bearing Father THEODORE, the Deacon of Korone, who struggled in asceticism on the island of Kythera.[108]

Theodore, our righteous father, flourished at the time of Emperor Romanos.[109] His homeland was in Korone (Koroni)[110] of the southern Peloponnesos. His parents were notable, distinguished, and God-fearing. His mother had been barren prior to his birth. The conception of Theodore was granted by God through fervent supplication. For this cause was he also named Theodore, signifying "God's gift." Young Theodore was nurtured "in the instruction and admonition of the Lord [Eph. 6:4]." He was taught the sacred writings when his parents had him study under the then Bishop of Korone. The bishop gladly

---

[108] The Life and divine office of Saint Theodore were published in a special issue, as follows: the 1st ed. was at Venice in 1747; the 2nd ed. was at Smyrna in 1841; and the 3rd ed. was at Athens in 1899. The version herein was taken from this source, which the compilers edited and revised for incorporation into *The Great Synaxaristes* (in Greek). The service to the saint was composed by Father Gerasimos Mikrayiannanites of the Great Church, at the behest of Metropolitan Meletios of Kythera, since the old text was unfinished. The new divine office, with the saint's biography and narratives of his wonderworkings, was published at Athens in 1961.

The icon shown herein of Saint Theodore is found in a wall-painting in the village of Mylopotamos on the west side of Kythera, seventeen kilometers from the capital at Chora, in the Church of Saint Sophia, outside a cave with spectacular stalagmitic and stalactitic formations.

[109] The present *Synaxarion* does not mention exactly when Saint Theodore flourished, other than this statement that Emperor Romanos was reigning. But since there were three emperors who bore that name, we must deduce that it was during the reign of the one that was concurrent with the captivity of Crete, which event is certainly referred to in the biography. The compilers of *The Great Synaxaristes* (in Greek) believe the likely sovereign to be Romanos II, son of Constantine Porphyrogennetos, who reigned from 959 to 963. Saint Theodore may have been born during the reign of Emperor Romanos I Lekapenos (920-944). But since the mastery of Crete by the Muslims took place during 960, it is probable that Romanos II is meant as the time in which Theodore flourished and then reposed.

During the reign of Romanos II, in the summer of 960, Nikephoros Phokas, at the head of a large squadron, campaigned for the recapture of Crete. After a hard and protracted siege that lasted all winter long, in March of 961, Phokas' troops stormed the capital of Chandax (Candia). The offensive was successful. The corsairs were destroyed, enabling Crete to come under Byzantine rule after belonging to the Arabs for nearly a century and a half.

[110] The little port of Korone (36°48′N 21°57′E) is forty-two kilometers or twenty-six miles southwest of Kalamata on the west side of the Gulf of Messenia. It occupies the site of ancient Asine.

took the youth under his tutelage, training him for the sacred clergy so that he appointed him to the office of Reader.

Within a short time, however, the parents of Theodore reposed. Since Theodore was not yet of an age to keep himself, his parents, before they died, entrusted him to the archpriest of Nafplion.[111] This priest was a family friend who took in Theodore and raised him as his own child. When Theodore reached his majority, the priest encouraged the young man to enter into marriage. Theodore wedded and became the father of two children. He continued to love God with all his heart and maintain a God-pleasing life and household. The cares and concerns of marriage and raising children were no hindrance to his pursuit of virtue and progress therein. The fear of God was never absent from his heart. He was very mindful of those words of Saint Paul who said that "the time hath been shortened henceforth, that even they who have wives be as though they did not have [1 Cor. 7:29]." And so, our Theodore deemed all things to be a loss for the excellency of the knowledge of Christ Jesus. He wished to come to know Christ, and the power of His resurrection, and the partaking of His sufferings, being conformed to His death.[112] This is what he wished to pursue and apprehend. He wished to forget the things which were behind, and stretch forth to those things which were before, that he might say with Saint Paul: "I pursue toward the mark for the prize of the high calling of God in Christ Jesus [Phil. 3:13, 14]."

The Bishop of Argos,[113] learning of the virtues of Theodore and his reverence to things holy, constrained him to be ordained to the diaconate. Theodore's desire for God was increased. He found that his mind was always riveted upon death and the hour of judgment. He, therefore, departed the Peloponnesos and went on a pilgrimage to Rome to see the churches of the holy apostles and the sacred relics of the saints and righteous. Theodore spent four years there and conversed with the holy fathers in that place. He then returned to the Peloponnesos and remained at Monemvasia.[114] He kept himself hidden from the eyes of men, biding his time until he should cross over to the island

[111] Nafplion (Nafplio, Nauplia) is situated on a rocky peninsula projecting into the Argolic Gulf. It lies some sixty-four kilometers or forty miles south of Corinth.
[112] Phil. 3:8, 10.
[113] Argos (37°37′N 22°43′E), located in the Peloponnesos, is near its harbor of Nafplion.
[114] Monemvasia (36°41′N 23°3′E), founded in the 6th C., is located on a steep and rocky peninsula off the east coast of the Peloponnesos in the Greek prefecture of Laconia. It is surrounded by walls and built on the southern slopes of the headland, which the Byzantines separated, leaving only a narrow causeway (hence its name in Greek, "single passage").

of Kythera.[115] At that time, this island of coves and sandy beaches, known as the crossroads of the sea routes to the Ionian, Aegean, and Cretan seas, was desolate. The reason that this island, inhabited since earliest times, had been evacuated was due to the inroads of the Muslims who held sway then also in neighboring Crete.

Saint Theodore

After Theodore sojourned a considerable time in Monemvasia, his hideaway was uncovered. His presence was discovered in a small church dedicated to the Theotokos. Nevertheless, he remained invulnerable before the entreaties of his wife and friends. His wife secured the intervention of the bishop, who sympathized with Theodore's children. Theodore's wife hoped that the bishop might compel him to return home, if only to give his consent that she might become a nun. Theodore believed this to be an artifice, nay an assault, of the most crafty devil. He remembered the words of the Apostle Peter who said, "Be sober, watch; because your adversary, the devil, as a roaring lion, walketh about, seeking whom he might devour [1 Pe. 5:8]." With regard to his children, he answered that God, Who is Father and takes thought and care for all His creatures, also watches over his children. Theodore, thereupon, gave no consequence to their pleas. He remained in solitude and silence, resting, having only one goal: to please God. He recited the Psalter at every hour of the day and night, while living a very simple existence in a hair tunic.

The opportunity arose for him to migrate to Kythera, even though it was deserted during that period because of the islanders' fear of the Hagarenes. A warship came by Monemvasia, planning to pass by Kythera on an expedition against the Muslims. The venerable man boarded the ship with a man named Anthony, a fellow ascetic, who wished to follow him. They remained on the windswept

[115] Kythera or Kythira or Cythera (36°10′N 22°59′E), geographically, culturally, and historically belongs to the Ionian islands. It lies opposite the eastern tip of the Peloponnesos peninsula. The rugged landscape is a result of prevailing winds from the surrounding seas which have shaped its shores into steep rocky cliffs with deep bays. It is administered and belongs to the prefecture of Piraeus in Attike. The island's main port is Diakofti and its capital is Chora.

island for three months, after which Anthony could no longer endure the toils, hardships, and struggles that he shared with Theodore. He, therefore, returned alone to Monemvasia and spoke of the saint's feats. Theodore abided alone in the abandoned Church of Saint Sergius and Bacchus. He persevered in his ascetic contests, conducting himself in a God-pleasing manner until he surrendered his soul. He fell asleep in the Lord in front of that same church. He foretold the day of his death, by leaving an inscription that gave the day of his death as the 12th of May.[116]

What tongue is able to describe all the ascetic struggles of the saint in such isolation? He endured hunger and thirst, as well as cold winters and scorching summers. Who can tell us of the attacks of the guileful devil and the apparitions and phantoms of the night which Satan instigated in order to frighten the man of God? Theodore courageously withstood all opposition, having as his mighty weapons both prayer and continence. For this reason, he was vouchsafed to know the end of his earthly life. In advance of his illness, he left a record of his last day. His relics were discovered by seamen who were too frightened to touch the holy man. Three years later, hunters from Monemvasia discovered the relics and the inscription written by the saint. His relics were intact and incorrupt.

Even in death, Saint Theodore glorified God. He performed many wonderworkings for those who invoked his name with faith and venerated with piety his honorable relic. He has wrought all kinds of healing. His relics were laid to rest in the church, formerly known as Saints Sergius and Bacchus but now named in his honor. This small church, wherein the recluse Theodore had been living, later became a monastery. Together with Saint Elesa (commemorated by the holy Church on the 1st of August), he is considered a patron of the Kytherans.

Through the intercessions of Thy Saints,
O Christ God, have mercy on us. Amen.

[116] The suggested year is 961.

On the 13th of May, the holy Church commemorates the holy Martyr GLYKERIA.[1]

Glykeria, the holy martyr of Christ, was in her prime during the years of Emperor Antoninus (138-161). This was the same time that Savinos was governor of Trajanoupolis in Thrace.[2] Glykeria, hailing from Trani,[3] a seaport on the Adriatic Sea, was the daughter of a high-ranking Roman official. Upon her father's death and loss of his support, she came to be in reduced circumstances and departed for Trajanoupolis. Once, as Governor Savinos sacrificed before the idols, the holy Glykeria made the sign of the honorable Cross on her forehead. She then went before the governor, proclaiming herself a Christian and handmaiden of Christ, saying, as she traced the Cross on her forehead, "This is my lamp." The governor summoned Glykeria to sacrifice to the idols. When she entered the temple of the idols, she prayed to Christ. Straightway, the idol of Dios (Zeus) was destroyed when it broke to pieces. The pagan bystanders, enraged, cast stones at Christ's witness. However, none of the stones struck the holy maiden. Standing unharmed, the pagans seized Glykeria and hanged her by the hairs of her head as they lacerated her body.

Saint Glykeria

[1] The holy Saint Theophanes the Branded (d. 845), hymnographer of the Church, composed a service dedicated to Saint Glykeria. Manuscripts may be found in the Parisian Codices 1569 and 1574, and those at Lavra Δ5, Δ36, Δ45, Θ87, and Θ147 and 170.

[2] Trajanoupolis was built by Emperor Trajan (98-117). In ancient times, Thrace was a part of the Balkan Peninsula. It was a territory somewhat indefinite, but which comprised the region north of Macedonia, including Scythia. Though understood differently at various times, it was later delineated as the country between the northern boundary of Macedonia and the Danube and that which lies between the Black Sea, the Bosporos, the Propontis and the Hellespont, the Aegean Sea and the Strymon River. The Balkans divided it into two parts—the Romans recognized only the southern division as Thrace. Its largest river is the Hebros or Maritza.

[3] Trani is a seaport in the province of Bari.

Afterward, they imprisoned the saint in a dungeon. Intending to starve her, they did not give her any food or drink for many days. An angel of the Lord brought Glykeria nourishment; and so, no evil befell her. Indeed, when the governor and his company entered her dungeon, they were astonished to find a platter and vessels containing bread, milk, and water, though the cell was locked securely and no one entered therein.

The governor then sentenced the holy woman to be burned in a fiery furnace. A cool dew, however, descended from on high and extinguished the fire. Glykeria exited the furnace unscathed. The executioners then flayed the skin of her scalp to her forehead. Following this, they bound her hands and feet. Next, they cast her upon a layer of rocks in prison. In her dungeon, an angel of the Lord descended and loosed the saint's bonds. The angel then healed the injuries to her skull. Now this restoration was witnessed by the warder, Laodikios. Amazed at this miracle, he, too, confessed Christ. He, forthwith, was beheaded and received the crown of martyrdom.

Glykeria was then led before Savinos. The governor ordered her thrown to the wild beasts that they might devour her. Without incurring any life-threatening wounds or bruises, except only a tiny bite, that blessed young woman surrendered her soul into the hands of God. Thus, after her manifold struggles, Glykeria, the namesake of sweetness,[4] now delights in the incorruptible sweetness of Paradise.

Now we shall recount a miracle that suffices to manifest the maiden's access to God. Patriarch Dositheos II of Jerusalem (1669-1707), in his *Dodekavivlos*,[5] records that her holy relics were interred at Herakleia in Thrace.[6] At Herakleia, a copper pot was used to collect divinely-flowing myrrh which gushed from the saint's tomb. By means of this streaming myrrh, many received miracles, as also attested by Theophylact.[7] The Metropolitan of Herakleia,[8] while in Constantinople, found an impressive gold pot. He bought

---

[4] The feminine form for the Greek word meaning sweetish is *glykera* (γλυκερά); compare it with the English word "glycerine."

[5] *Dodekavivlos* or *Twelve Books* (Thessalonike: Regopoulos, 1983), p. 519.

[6] Herakleia of Thrace is ancient Perinthos or modern-day Marmara Eregli, on the north shore of the Sea of Marmara, at the junction of the Via Egnatia and the main Balkan road to Naissus. It was actually Emperor Diocletian Herculius (284-305) who renamed the city from Perinthos to Herakleia.

[7] The holy Theophylact (Theophylaktos) was an 11th-C. Byzantine exegete from Evia. In 1078, he was made Archbishop of Achrida (Ohrid) in the country of the Bulgarians, who commemorate him on the 31st of December.

[8] Herakleia, once the most important city in Europa, was replaced by Constantinople, which was originally its suffragan. Herakleia became a bishopric in 325 and appeared as a metropolis in notitiae. The number of suffragans increased. Constantinople became

(continued...)

it with the intention of substituting it for the copper vessel that received that sanctified outflow from the saint's tomb. However, when the exchange was made, the wonderworkings also ceased. After shedding tears and uttering many prayers, the Lord revealed to the Herakleian bishop that the gold pot was unclean. The vessel was then brought to the œcumenical patriarch at Constantinople, Saint John the Faster (d. 595).[9] The patriarch discovered that the learned chief magician, Paulinos, an idolater, when casting a spell, shed blood into that vessel as a sacrifice to devils. When this event was recounted to Emperor Mavrikios (Maurice Tiberius, 582-602), the patriarch sought legal remedy against such demonic practises. The emperor sentenced the magician to be bound to a pillar until he died. Furthermore, the man's sons were beheaded as accomplices in their father's wizardry. O reader, mind the severe punishment received by magicians and sorcerers!

On the 13th of May, the holy Church commemorates Saint LAODIKIOS, the prison-guard of Saint Glykeria, who was slain by the sword.

On the 13th of May, the holy Church commemorates our righteous Father SERGIOS the Confessor.

Sergios, our righteous father, the Confessor, was the scion of a glorious and distinguished Constantinopolitan family. Great in spirit, this married man with children lived during the cruel era of Theophilos the iconoclast, who reigned from 829 to 842. Sergios, who venerated the sacred images in true Orthodox manner, was haled before the persecutor and iconomach emperor. As part of this confessor's punishment, he was paraded in the marketplace with a rope about his neck that he might be subject to countless insults, scorn, and derision. All of the goods and property of the ever-memorable Sergios were confiscated by the state, as he was cast into prison. He, afterward, was banished with his wife, Irene, and their children. They courageously endured the diverse afflictions and tribulations of exile. When Sergios was finally called by God to leave this earthly sphere, his soul ascended into the heavens and received the imperishable crown of confessor of the Faith.

On the 13th of May, the holy Church commemorates our venerable Father PAFSIKAKOS, Bishop of Synnada.

---

[8](...continued)
independent of Herakleia in 330 or 381. *The Oxford Dictionary of Byzantium*, s.v. "Herakleia."

[9] Patriarch John IV the Faster (585-595) is commemorated by the holy Church on the 2nd of September.

Pafsikakos, our righteous father, flourished during the reign of Emperor Maurice (582-602). Pafsikakos originated from Apameia[10] of parents that were wellborn, renowned, and dedicated to the true Faith of the Christians. From an early age, he tamed the impulses of the body with fasting and prayer. He mortified his flesh with other hardships and ascetic struggles. Following this early period of preparation, he became a monk. From that point, he nourished himself solely on bread and water. By the grace of God, he was vouchsafed the gift of healing. He wrought cures for maladies afflicting both bodies and souls. He dispelled demons from the possessed. He was, however, especially known for working wonders with children having severe birth defects that left them handicapped or malformed. He was known to correct, in a marvellous manner, kyphosis (hunchback) and other deformities.

On account of his great fame, he came to be introduced and known to Patriarch Kyriakos of Constantinople (596-606).[11] Kyriakos entrusted Pafsikakos with the Bishopric of Synnada of Phrygia.[12] True to his name, which in Greek means "cessation of evil," Pafsikakos rooted out what was bad. Upon entering his diocese of Synnada, he first cast out the noetic wolves, that is to say, the heretics. He accomplished this by his words which struck like a moving sling and his teachings which cut like a sharp knife into arguments of the heterodox. He, thereby, rendered healthy the Christian body of the faithful by excising the heretics from the Church as the gangrenous members that they were. In this fashion, he secured the safety and soundness of his flock, as well as its salvation, from injury or loss.

After these bouts with the enemies of the Church, Pafsikakos visited the capital where he healed the ailing emperor, Maurice, of disease. On account of this benefaction, the emperor did not show himself to be ungrateful. He issued a *chrysobull* assigning Synnada with a yearly sum of one litra or twelve ounces of gold. Upon the holy bishop's return to his see, he passed by a place called Solona. Since those in his traveling party were in danger of dying from thirst, he uttered a prayer. Miraculously, a spring of clear and fresh water gushed forth from the barren earth. Thus, the thirst of his companions was delightfully slaked.

The venerable bishop passed the days of his life practising the virtues and becoming the cause of salvation for many. He departed from this present

---

[10] *The Great Synaxaristes* (in Greek) places this Apameia in the Black Sea area. There were other cities with this same name in Phrygia (where Apameia is also known as Dinar), Bithynia, Cappadocia, and Syria (on the river Orontes).

[11] Saint Kyriakos is commemorated by thy holy Church on the 27th of October.

[12] Synnada or Synada (38°31′N 30°29′E), present-day Suhut, was a barren region that needed to import olives, wine, and wheat. But the region had wealth in its cattle raising, as well as its marble trade from the nearby quarries.

life and migrated to the future one that is everlasting, rejoicing together with the saints, through whose intercessions may we be delivered from every evil, to the glory of God.

On the 13th of May, the holy Church commemorates Hieromartyr ALEXANDER, Bishop of Tiberiani, who was slain by the sword.

On the 13th of May, the holy Church commemorates the venerable NIKEPHOROS, Presbyter of the Monastery of the Efapsis, who reposed in peace.

On the 13th of May, the holy Church commemorates the consecration of the august and divine Church of Our Most Holy Lady the THEOTOKOS PANTANASSA (QUEEN OF ALL) on the island of Saint Glykeria.[13]

On the 13th of May, the holy Church commemorates the venerable EFTHYMIOS the New of Georgia, Builder of the Athonite Monastery of Iveron.

Efthymios Mt̔ac̀mindeli (of the Holy Mountain),[14] our holy father, was born ca. 960 in the Iberian (Georgian) city of Tao.[15] He was the son of devout, notable, and affluent parents. At one point, Efthymios' father, a valiant soldier, moved to Constantinople. Within a short while, his father renounced the temporal and perishing splendor and glory of the world. The father resolved to follow Christ in that poverty that yields heavenly wealth. Upon taking the Angelic Schema of the monastics, he was renamed John. The former soldier, robust and handsome, now amazed all by his spiritual struggles and charitable

---

[13] The island of Saint Glykeria is in the Gulf of Bithynia.

[14] This version of the Life of Saint Efthymios was written in Greek by Manuel the Great Rhetor, who also composed a divine service to the saint; both of these works survive today in the Holy Monastery of Iveron. His hagiographic version was rendered into simpler Greek by Nikodemos the Hagiorite, who incorporated it into his work entitled *Neon Eklogion*. It is this rendering that was borrowed and edited by the compilers of *The Great Synaxaristes* (in Greek). The original Life of Saint Efthymios, with his father, the holy John, was written in Georgian by the Georgian translator and hagiographer George Mt̔ac̀mindeli (1009-1065; superior of Iveron ca. 1045), which includes valuable information about the revolt of Bardas Skleros.

[15] Tayk'/Tao is the Armenian and Georgian name for a region on the upper Coruch, west of the source of the Kura River. The Armenian Tayk' was more comprehensive than Georgian Tao, including the area to the southeast toward Kar.

soul. His son, Efthymios, who was still quite young, abided with his grandfather,[16] a man who was conspicuous for his good repute and virtue. He raised and nourished the lad in the instruction and admonition of the Lord.

Saint Efthymios

With the passage of a little time, the grandfather, taking Efthymios, repaired to Constantinople and sought his son John.[17] Finding him, he urged him, with many laments and tears, to return to their homeland. Though John remained unpersuaded, he, by all means, sought to hold on to his son. The grandfather was unwilling to release the child. Hence, this matter ushered in exceeding sorrow betwixt the father and grandfather of Efthymios.

Emperor Nikephoros II Phokas (r. 963-969) was informed of the contention separating John and his father over the lad. The emperor ordered that the two men appear before him. They, also, were to bring the young Efthymios with them. When the three approached the throne, and Nikephoros learned in greater detail of the rivalry for the child, he directed each not to snatch the boy by force. He counseled the adults to entrust the matter to God's penetrating discernment, saying, "Allow the lad to choose where he might go—and then let him go." After John and his father conceded, the child speedily ran into the arms of his father whom he never knew till that very hour. The child's choice, a source of amazement to the court, left tears in the eyes of all present. Thereupon, the blessed John received his son, as from the hands of God. After he clothed him in the

[16] Evidently, John was a widower left with a young son. After examining other sources, Efthymios was possibly left with John's brother-in-law.

[17] Other sources note that Father John was struggling on Mount Olympos when his relatives came to Constantinople. The Greeks, in order to secure the allegiance of David, dynast of upper Tayk'/Tao, relinquished the borderland territories of Tao and Clardzhetia. As an earnest of good faith, David was required to supply highborn "hostages" to the emperor. Among those of the hostage party were members of John's immediate family. This is what might have drawn him to the imperial capital in order to claim his son.

monastic Schema, they went to Mount Olympos of Bithynia.[18] At length, Father John sent the lad to Constantinople where instructors might teach him suitable lessons.

The goodly Efthymios, having a sharp mind, genuine zeal, and diligence, learned, in but a short time, both secular philosophy and knowledge of things divine. He appeared as a river of teachings of the Holy Spirit. Efthymios received a full education in the Georgian language and its literature, and later he studied Greek.

With the passage of time, after his schooling, Efthymios returned to Mount Olympos where he succumbed to a grave illness. His father, trusting not "in the sons of men, in whom there is no salvation [Ps. 145:2]," resorted to church where he implored the Theotokos for his son's deliverance. Father John then besought the priest to bring the Mysteries to his son's cell. As they entered the chamber, they perceived an ineffable fragrance. Efthymios, meanwhile, restored to health, was sitting upon his bed. When asked how he recovered, the young man answered that the Queen (the Theotokos) stood before him. She had asked him, in the Georgian tongue, "What ails thee?" He said that he told her that "I am dying." He then described how she approached him and, taking him by the hand, uttered, "Fear not, no longer shalt thou suffer illness." Afterward, she vanished and, "as you can see," said he, "I am completely well!" Learning of his restoration, Father John prostrated himself and offered up thanks before the icon of the Queen of all, the Virgin and Mother of God, whose lot on the day of Pentecost was their Iberian homeland.[19]

---

[18] Mount Olympos was a holy mountain (modern Ulu Dag, 2,237 meters). It is situated southeast of Prusa (present-day Bursa of Turkey). It was an important monastic center, especially from the 8th to 10th C. Despite Arab attacks in the 9th C., an important group of monasteries continued to function on Olympos in the 10th C. This sacred region occupied first place in the lists of holy mountains established by historians of this period. Among the monasteries of this region were Atroa, Medikion, Pelekete, Chenolakkos, Heliou Bomon, Sakkoudion, and the Lavra of Symboloi (Symbola). Renowned fathers of this center, including the holy Plato of Sakkoudion, Theodore of Stoudios, Ioannikios, Methodios (later Patriarch of Constantinople), and Efthymios the Younger, spent either part or all of their monastic careers on Olympos. *Oxford*, s.v. "Olympos, Mount."

[19] After the descent of the Holy Spirit on the day of Pentecost, the apostles cast lots that they might determine where each should go and preach the Gospel. The Theotokos also requested a lot for herself, so she might participate in the preaching. Then, with fear and reverence, they cast for the Theotokos; and her lot fell on the Iberian land, now Georgia in southern Russia. The pure Mother of God accepted her lot joyfully. At length, the Archangel Gabriel informed her that "the land which fell to thee will be enlightened in the latter days by another woman; and thy dominion will be established

(continued...)

From that sublime visitation, with the help of the most holy Theotokos, Efthymios was not only delivered from his illness but also endowed with proficiency in the Georgian tongue and surfeit of every virtue. The extraordinary grace and wisdom that Efthymios received from on high caused his father to suggest translating the Greek sacred texts into Georgian. Efthymios, obedient to his father's will in everything, undertook the task. A copy of the translated Gospel was sent to the Georgian King David of Tayk'/Tao, who remarked, "I thank God Who, in these times and for our sakes, has raised up a second Chrysostom!" Not only had he completed the Scriptures, but also, with the passage of time, Efthymios purged the errors that crept into the service books. From his advancement in wisdom, grace, and other prodigious talents, many understood that he would one day be a marvellous man. We must now recount one of his accomplishments, so that the reader might conclude the rest.

Once, a Hebrew came seeking to converse with Efthymios on matters of the Faith. In no wise did the blessed Efthymios wish to enter into a dialogue with the Hebrew, saying that such conversations were for nought. Nevertheless, his father urged him vehemently; so that only after much constraint was he persuaded. Efthymios then commenced refuting the Hebrew by showing forth proofs from the Old Testament. The Hebrew was unwilling to give way and accept defeat. Consequently, that profane man dared to utter blasphemies against our Lord Jesus Christ. Efthymios, stirred by divine zeal, said, "Thou shouldest close the mouth that utters blasphemies against our Lord and God!" Then—O the wonder!—forthwith, the Hebrew was rendered dumb and fell prone to the earth, as he slavered from his blasphemous mouth. Thus, he was a piteous sight as he lay there till the following day. Then, violently, he gave up his defiled soul. This miracle ushered in great fear and astonishment, so that all of Constantinople talked about the wondrous Efthymios.

However, the blessed man despised the glory of men, as being contrary to the glory of God. Straightway, in the 960s, he departed with his father for the Holy Mountain. Lighting upon the righteous Athanasios,[20] they wished to live with him in the Great Lavra. Of a truth, the divine Athanasios, with the discerning eyes of the soul, perceived the grace of the indwelling Holy Spirit in Efthymios. Thus, he urged Efthymios to receive the dignity of the priesthood. Efthymios, initially, would not accept, deeming himself unworthy of the office; yet, ultimately, he obeyed the words of the righteous Athanasios. Then,

---

[19](...continued)
there." Three centuries later, the blessed Virgin Mary sent Saint Nina, Equal-to-the-apostles (commemorated on the 14th of January), whom she blessed and helped in proclaiming the Gospel to the Iberians.

[20] Saint Athanasios, who builder of the Great Lavra, is commemorated by the holy Church on the 5th of July.

from the time he was ordained a priest, he added struggle upon struggle and discipline upon discipline, thus increasing exceedingly all the virtues he already possessed. For this reason, he became a divine vessel of the Holy Spirit and translated the entire sacred Scripture into the Georgian tongue. Moreover, he also penned many books filled with teachings on morals and the virtuous life. He constructed numerous temples, as well as infirmaries, and adorned Athos with hermitages.

The Iveron Monastery

With what words can we narrate worthily the nobleness and goodness that he radiated upon all who associated with him? Moreover, how can we adequately characterize his incomparable humility when, for fourteen years, he served not only the great Athanasios but also his ailing father?

Present-day Iveron from the Sea

Now in the latter half of the tenth century, the *magistros* Bardas Skleros was one of the most competent generals of Emperor John I Tzimiskes (969-976). In 971, he defeated the Kievan prince Svjatoslav, but later he fell from imperial favor and was accused of conspiracy. In 976, when the army in Mesopotamia proclaimed Bardas *vasilefs* (emperor), he marched against Constantinople. Though he was victorious in 977, the rebel was vanquished[21] in the Battle of Pankgalia in 979 by the ascetic-general John Tornikios. Yet before we describe the exploits of Tornikios, our readers must know that the latter was not only a vassal of David of Tayk'/Tao[22] but also Father John's brother-in-law (his wife's brother). While Tornikios was in Georgia, he had become a monk. At length, he sought his kinsman, Father John, on Mount Olympos. Now John and Efthymios had long since left and were living at the Great Lavra with Saint Athanasios. Tornikios, thereupon, repaired for Athos and the Lavra where he met his illustrious kinsmen.

When Bardas Skleros rebelled, Emperor Basil II (976-1025) desired to solicit aid from the Georgian king; but he was unable to inform him. When the emperor learned that two eminent Georgian warriors, John and Tornikios, were at the Great Lavra, straightway, he submitted letters requesting their assistance.

---

[21] Bardas Skleros fled to the Arabs and rebelled again in 987. Bardas Phokas, another usurper, took him captive. With the death of Phokas, Skleros kept fighting Basil II until 989 when he was reconciled and granted lands. He died in 991.

[22] David (d. 1000), from 961, was the junior member of the Iberian Bagratid house and ruler of the Armeno-Iberian marchlands. Georgian inscriptions identify him as "David Magistros" and "King Bagrat, duke of dukes."

After much prayer, Saint Athanasios and Father John decided that Tornikios should receive the commission from the imperial court. Trusting in their prayers, the monk and soldier Tornikios entered the capital. The empress presented Tornikios with a petition to David of Tayk'/Tao. In exchange for military aid, the empress agreed to relinquish to David, during his lifetime, those territories that formerly had been under his Church's jurisdiction. Reaching David, Tornikios was given a command of twelve thousand Georgians and Armenians. Tornikios fought a gallant battle against Skleros on the plain that is watered by the Falis River. With the help of God, Tornikios routed the enemy and took prisoners. Tornikios returned in triumph and received rich gifts and accumulated vast sums of booty.

Since David's support, through his man Tornikios, of Emperor Basil II decisively defeated Skleros, he not only won the title of *kouropalates*[23] but also extensive territories along the Armeno-Byzantine border from Tayk'/Tao by way of Theodosioupolis to Mantzikert.[24] When Tornikios returned to Athos, he resolved to establish a new lavra for the Iberians at the site of the Monastery of Klemes (*tou Klementos*).[25] At this time, Tornikios also received the Kolovou Monastery[26] from Emperor Basil II (976-1025).

---

[23] The *kouropalates* was a high-ranking dignity. In Justinian's time (6th C.) it was a title conferred upon members of the imperial family and foreign princes, such as Armenians and Georgians. In the official lists and titles (*Taktika*) of the 9th and 10th C., *kouropalates* follows the offices of Caesar and *Nobilissimos*. By the 11th C., the title was bestowed on several generals outside the imperial family.

[24] David had to retake the land from the Arabs between the years 992 and 994. His prominent position rendered him the role of arbiter in both Armenia and Georgia. His bilingual court was a great intellectual and artistic center.

When David supported Bardas Phokas, in 989, Basil II enjoined him to will his lands to Byzantium upon his death, since David was childless. Upon David's death, Basil annexed Tayk'/Tao and transformed it into the core of the new theme of Iberia, the most northeastern theme of the Byzantine Empire. This occasioned the beginning of the Byzantine conquest of the Armenian plateau. Nonetheless, the area fell under Turkish control after the battle of Mantzikert (1071). At the beginning of the 12th C., David II/IV the Restorer brought back Tao into Georgian control.

[25] The present-day monastery was built on the ruins of the pre-Christian town of Kleonai. As the site was called Klemen's Harbor, this monastery was also called Klementos. The Athonite Monk Nicholas, who compiled the Life of the first Athonite monk Saint Peter, in about 975, refers to a monastery called Ta Klementos. There is a tradition that the old *katholikon* honored Saint John the Baptist, but the monastery was destroyed by various robber-pirates. It was refounded by the Iberian General John Tornikios and his nephews, Efthymios and George, in 980.

[26] Kolovou Monastery, dedicated to Saint John the Baptist, was founded by the Monk John Kolovos between 866 and 883. It is located just outside the precinct of the Holy

(continued...)

The presence of such renowned Iberian men on Athos inspired other Georgians to enter the Great Lavra. In a short time, the number of Georgians grew amid the brotherhood. The Georgian fathers brought great wealth and fabulous donations to the Great Lavra. Nonetheless, to avoid factions and controversies, the holy fathers deemed it prudent that the Georgians have their own monastery. Saint Athanasios gave them a place that was one thousand paces away from Lavra, where they might build their *kellia* (cells) and live as a separate community. Hence, a plot of land was purchased, and the Monastery of the Iberians, dedicated to Saint John the Baptist, was established on the northeast coast of the peninsula, approximately four kilometers from Karyes. By common consent, the first superior was John the Iberian (980-1005). All the gifts and booty that Tornikios acquired, he presented to Father John who managed all the monastery's properties. Meanwhile, Tornikios resumed his life as an Athonite monk. By 982, cells and a fortified wall were built around the church. The empress endowed the monastery with an imperial charter, bearing a gold seal, establishing the independence of the Iberian monastery from the Great Lavra. David (*kouropalates*) also lavished monies and Georgian estates upon the new Iberian brotherhood.

A Drought

A drought, at one time, befell the Holy Mountain. All the fathers sustained immeasurable sorrow because of the lack of water. They, therefore, besought the righteous Efthymios to send up entreaties to God that He might bestow rain. The holy man, upon being compelled by the brethren, ascended to the Church of Prophet Elias which is near the holy Monastery of Iveron. With tears, the Elder Efthymios made supplications to the all-compassionate God when offering Him the rational and bloodless Sacrifice. Then—lo, the miracle!—straightway, so much rain fell that the dehydrated earth was saturated. All glorified God Who glorifies them that glorify Him.

The Feast of the Transfiguration

The monks of the Holy Mountain had an ancient custom, which they kept for the luminous Feast of the Transfiguration of our Savior. The fathers would ascend to the summit of the Holy Mountain where they conducted an all-night vigil. After they celebrated the divine Liturgy, they would descend. One time, when the 6th of August approached, the holy John and Efthymios with other brethren made the ascent. When the time came to celebrate the divine Liturgy, all, with one voice, besought the saint to celebrate the sacred

---

[26](...continued)
Mountain of Athos, on the isthmus that links the peninsula with the mainland. The monastery owned substantial estates, but was involved with frequent property disputes with the inhabitants of Ierissos and Athos. Its prominence continued until 979/980, when it was absorbed by the newly founded Monastery of Iveron.

Mysteries. The holy Efthymios, with unfeigned humility, hearkened to their request. As he was celebrating the Liturgy, the moment came when the celebrant says aloud, "Singing the triumphal hymn, shouting, crying, and saying...." When the chanters responded, singing, "Holy, Holy, Holy, Lord of Sabaoth,..." suddenly, immeasurable light enveloped all and the earth quaked. Everyone fell prone to the floor, save the blessed Efthymios. He appeared as a pillar of fire standing motionless before the holy altar.

Summit of Mount Athos

This miraculous phenomenon spread the good fame of the saint everywhere. For this reason, when the Archbishop of Cyprus was translated to the Lord, the soldier and Emperor Basil II, the Bulgar-Slayer (976-1025), sent ambassadors with epistles to the blessed Efthymios. The emperor fervently invited him to accept the leadership and charge of this archbishopric. The saint not only refused but he did not even want to hear about it. Instead, he remarked that he was altogether unworthy for such headship and authority. He also added that he rather had need to be shepherded than to shepherd others. It was evident from this incident that in Efthymios' heart was rooted true humble-mindedness, the mother of all virtues.

The Repose of Saint John

In 998, John the Iberian put his signature to a document for the last time. Advanced in years, he fell sick when his legs began to swell. Bedridden, he suffered greatly, though he thanked God for everything. Since he was disabled, he turned over the supervision of the monastery to Efthymios. Though at first he refused, Efthymios, ever obedient to his father, undertook the administration of the brethren. With his repose imminent, Father John summoned the brotherhood that he might exhort them. He directed that, upon the repose of each abbot, a new one should be appointed quickly. He also stated that if one resisted the authority of the abbot, then that man was to be dismissed from the monastery. He also bequeathed that the monastery be entrusted to the sovereign, since John personally enjoyed many boons from him. Urging them to maintain obedience, peace, and harmony in the brotherhood, he admonished them not to neglect hospitality and alms to the poor. He also besought his spiritual children to forgive him and to remember him, together with John Tornikios and the holy Athanasios, at every divine Liturgy. Then, after having penned his will, he communicated the Mysteries, and delivered his soul into the hands of his Lord on the 14th of June. His august relics were interred in the monastery where many received healing, including those troubled by unclean spirits, when they were anointed with oil from the oil lamp over his tomb.

The Abbacy of Saint Efthymios

Succeeding to the office of John's abbacy was Efthymios (1005-1019), followed by Efthymios' cousin George (1019-1029). During their abbacies, a scriptorium was established for both the translation of the Greek holy texts into Georgian and the copying of Greek and Georgian manuscripts. Thus, Iveron became an important center of Byzantine-Georgian interaction and the dissemination of the sacred texts in Georgian. Saint Efthymios contributed much to the translation of Greek theological and hagiographical works into the Georgian tongue. The holy man also wrote the monastery *Typikon*. Thus, from the eleventh century, a large number of Greek texts were translated into Georgian as were some Georgian texts into Greek.[27]

Saint Efthymios

When both Saint Athanasios (d. ca. 1004) and the holy John reposed, the leadership and the concerns of the sacred Great Lavra were left to the blessed Efthymios, as a kind of commissioner. He, moreover, not only exercised authority over the Great Lavra but even over the entire Holy Mountain. This was due to his devotion, willingness, and dexterity in the dual treatment and management of both the souls and bodies of the brethren. His divine mouth continually flowed with rivers of wisdom and teaching to the glory of God.

The Elder Efthymios served as abbot for about twenty years. During this time, with the cares and concerns of the monastery upon his shoulders, he no longer could devote long hours to translating. Due to his excessive asceticism, he grew physically weaker. He would remain in his cell on Mondays, Wednesdays, and Fridays. He would not partake of bread and water until sunset. Unless he had some need, he never partook of wine. The saint was solicitous for those entrusted to his care. He was strict about the correct and

[27] There is strong evidence in Latin and Georgian, as well as in Greek, that it was the Georgian Saint Efthymios who caused the biographies of Saints Barlaam and Ioasaph (attributed to Saint John of Damascus) to be translated from Georgian into Greek, the whole being reshaped and supplemented.

pious carrying out of obediences. If the cook prepared a poor meal, he admonished him not to lose his reward due to negligence or indifference. Talking during the refectory meal was not allowed unless a guest required something. Even so, his request would be filled quietly by a novice attending the tables. If any broke the rule of silence, the infractor was appointed an obedience on a Sunday or a feast. Letters were read before the general assembly. Twice monthly, the saint gave sermons at the coenobium when he would encourage his spiritual children to struggle lest they pass their lives unprofitably. Though he was now advanced in years, he punctually attended, before all others, the Midnight and Orthros Offices. He neither sat nor leaned against the wall during the divine services, though he would support himself with his staff. His attention and concentration during Church services was an inspiration to the brethren.

Saint Efthymios at Thessalonike

At one time, the venerable Efthymios went to Thessalonike where he was received with much kindness and cordiality by the hierarch. This wondrous archbishop, replete with the virtues, marvelled at all the talents of the Athonite elder. Now there was a certain Hebrew who was bound by friendship to the hierarch. The Hebrew attended to all the wants and comforts of the archbishop. Therefore, the archbishop, because of their friendship, wished to repay the man. The archbishop continually counseled and urged the Hebrew, by many exhortations, to believe in Christ. He, however, in no wise would allow himself to be swayed. All the time that the holy Elder Efthymios visited with the hierarch, the Hebrew came around, as was his custom; and the hierarch persisted in counseling the Hebrew to his salvation. The Hebrew not only remained unpersuaded but even defended Judaism in his conversation with the archbishop on the Orthodox Faith. Furthermore, he displayed great wilfulness and surliness, as he scorned the words of the hierarch. As a result, the hierarch besought the saint to confound the swelling words of the Hebrew with the wisdom of his words. The saint, as a true disciple of the meekness and humility of Christ, spoke of himself as earth and dust. Furthermore, he said that such a role was fitting for the hierarch and not himself.

The hierarch then said to the saint, "Even if thou wilt persist in not hearkening to my words, I shall still not desist from importuning thee." Thus, only after much constraint, Efthymios was compelled to make a defense. Thereupon, all that the Hebrew set forth, straightway, was abrogated by the elder who, with the indubitable proofs of the prophets and persuasive words, indeed, stopped his mouth; for he brilliantly and firmly preached the dispensation of the incarnation. The Hebrew, unable to endure the shame which he received, began to utter blasphemous words against Christ. The saint, gazing upon him sternly, said, "May thy tongue be cut off, O accursed one, because thou speakest falsely and blasphemously against Christ, the Creator and Master of all!" Forthwith—behold, the wonder!—the Hebrew remained speechless and fell to the ground with his eyes turning round and his mouth becoming twisted.

This spectacle was seen by all the bystanders, both Hebrews and Christians, who were filled with great astonishment and fear. They fell to their knees before the holy elder and besought him to take pity on the Hebrew and heal him. The saint, moved to compassion, hearkened to their entreaties and made the sign of the life-creating Cross over the fallen man. As a result, he was cured and his health was restored. Then, the Hebrew proclaimed in a loud voice that Jesus Christ is true God, the Creator of all, the Guardian, the Protector, and the Governor of all living. Straightway, both he and all his house were baptized. Indeed, not only he accepted Christ but also the Hebrews who witnessed this miracle. Moreover, many other Hebrews learned of this wonder and believed in Jesus Christ. The Hebrew who was healed, both in soul and body, out of thanks, offered a great sum of money to the holy Efthymios. The saint, however, in no wise accepted it; but rather he charged him to distribute it among the poor.

The apostate devil, meanwhile, who ever bears malice and contends with all good and God-pleasing works, could not bear to behold the virtues of the saint. Indeed, the saint advanced in all the virtues in a most God-pleasing manner and accomplished all to the glory of our Lord and God Jesus Christ. Therefore, out of envy and malevolence toward Efthymios, the enemy even more so wore himself away.

Murder in the Monastery

The hater-of-good, at length, found one of his own: he was a monk, but only in appearance, whereas his heart, all defiled and unclean, proved to be a fitting dwelling place for the evil one. Having entered the heart of that monk, he whispered in his ear and persuaded him to murder the saint. The devil convinced the monk that if he slew Efthymios, he would be the recipient of great benefits. Thus, that guileful monk, willing to commit homicide, readied the dagger and went to the elder's cell. However, Saint Efthymios, in no wise, gave him leave to enter. The murderer, not obtaining his victim, appeased his bloodthirstiness toward the saint by quickly knifing Efthymios' disciple. As the manslayer fled the scene, making disorderly cries and shouts, he encountered another disciple of that righteous man and downed him also! Afterward, as that demonized monk walked a short distance, he fell prone to the earth confessing those words spoken by the devil to him. Then, with violence, he cast forth his bloodstained soul. Meanwhile, the saint, through the grace of the Holy Spirit, knew that what befell his disciples was by the collaboration of the devil. He descended the tower and hastened that he might pronounce the prayers of the taking of the Great Schema over his fallen disciples. After having tonsured them, the two wounded brethren were translated unto the Lord.

The shameless, reckless, and ruthless devil, as a filthy dog, could not bear the saint's accomplishments wrought for the glory of God. Therefore, he incited the gardener to slay the saint. The assassin prepared the knife. He then drew near to the saint and jabbed him in the stomach! Yet—O the extraordinary wonder!—the saint remained uninjured, for the tip of the blade turned back as though it were wax. Indeed, the hand that perpetrated this heinous stabbing withered and remained motionless. The gardener, then, collapsed and shed tears before the saint. He confessed the demonic assault and ardently implored the saint's forgiveness and made a request for healing. The saint, taking pity upon his assailant, sent up prayers to the Lord on behalf of the gardener; in consequence of which, the gardener received healing of both soul and body.

What words can amply recount the virtues of Saint Efthymios, such as his sympathy and fellow feeling toward all? How can one characterize his compassion, cheerfulness, lack of a bad temper, and tranquility? Is it possible to describe his all-night standing, unceasing prayer, and humility? What of his moderation in everything, including food and clothing and bodily privations? In fact, he wore a garment of heavy iron chain mail under his monk's mantle. Indeed, from what little we have said, he was truly an angel in the flesh and an unwavering beacon to the world reflecting in his own person the word of life.

At length, however, the holy man, overcome with love for extreme quietude, established his cousin George as the hegumen of the Iberian lavra.[28] Efthymios then, in a God-pleasing manner, day and night, remained alone in stillness and quiet. No one knows his spiritual labors and the fruits reaped therefrom. This is because the saint tried to keep his asceticism concealed so that none might learn of his labors, save God Who desired to reveal the many accomplishments whereby His servant shone forth.

Saint Efthymios at Constantinople

In the latter years of the saint's life, scandals and offenses abounded in the earth. Troubles also overtook the Holy Mountain, especially at the Great Lavra of Saint Athanasios where Efthymios exercised supervision. As a result, all the fathers besought the saint to travel to Constantinople. They hoped, by imperial decree, that the scandals could be dispersed and that complete peace would be brought back to Athos. The holy man, hearkening to the words of the fathers, journeyed to the capital. Upon arriving, Emperor Constantine VIII (1025-1028) convened the Senate and assembled the nobles. They rendered

---

[28] Saint George of Iveron, a builder of the Iveron Monastery, reposed in peace. He is also commemorated by the holy Church on the 13th of May. He had stayed with sixty Georgians at Wonderful Mountain (Gk. Thavmaston Oros, or Turk. Saman Dagi), established earlier by Saint Symeon (commemorated the 24th of May).

extreme reverence to the Athonite elder, whom they not only received with great kindness but also fulfilled his requests quickly.

Then, one day, while on an errand with another monk, the holy man rode a mule through Constantinople. As they proceeded, they came to a certain section of the city called Plateia. In the road, they encountered a beggar who was sitting and begging alms. The saint espied him and was moved to compassion. As the elder prepared to offer him alms, the mule, as it caught sight of the beggar, became frightened and went wild. It ran kicking its legs, as it carried off the saint violently. It only came to a stop when it threw the saint to the ground, thereby shattering his bones. Christians that witnessed his multiple injuries hastened to assist him. They took up the broken body of that venerable man and bore him aloft to the house where he was staying. Within a few days, Saint Efthymios, after receiving the holy Mysteries, delivered his holy soul peacefully into the hands of God. It was the 13th of May, in the year 1028. Saint Efthymios was in his sixties when he reposed.

Upon his repose, his precious relics, to the glory of God, proved to be a source of cures and miracles that demonstrated both his sanctity and his boldness with God. His relics were translated and interred in the holy monastery that he dedicated to the honorable Forerunner and Baptist John. Later, the blessed George translated Saint Efthymios' relics to a marble sepulcher in the main church of the Dormition of the Mother of God. After the translation of his relics, the monastery was renamed the "Lavra of the Iberians" or "Iveron." Prior to this, from 1010 to 1020, it was called the "Monastery of the Iberian" or "of Efthymios." Therefore, we, too, entreat his intercession, to the glory of Father, Son, and Holy Spirit—one Divinity and kingdom—to Whom is due glory, honor, and worship, now and ever and unto the ages of ages. Amen.

Brief History of the Iveron Monastery

Tradition tells us how the Virgin Theotokos departed Palestine, but a violent sea storm forced her vessel off course. The Theotokos, together with Christ's beloved disciple, John, and others, who reverently accompanied them, set sail for Cyprus and Saint Lazarus.[29] The year was A.D. 52. It happened that, after a time at sea, a violent sea storm raged and the sailing vessel was forced off course. By divine intervention, as the storm abated, they found themselves outside the port of Klemes (Klementos) on Athos. At that time,

[29] As stated by Stephen of the Holy Mountain, cited in "The Dormition of Our Most Holy Lady," *The Orthodox Teachings of the Mother of God*, translated from the Menology of Saint Dimitri of Rostov (Moundsville, WV: Fr. Demetrios Serfes Publications), p. 36.

Athos was inhabited by pagan tribes.[30] Agapios the Cretan writes that when the ship carrying the Virgin Mary approached Athos, a statue of Jupiter (Zeus), at the top of the Mountain, fell and shattered to pieces in a thunderous noise.[31]

The Theotokos Approaches Athos

It is said that they came ashore close to the present Monastery of Iveron. There, the holy Virgin rested for awhile and, overwhelmed by the beauty of the place, she asked her Son to give her the Mountain, despite the fact that the inhabitants were pagans. A voice was then heard saying, "Let this place be thine inheritance and garden, a paradise and a haven of salvation for those seeking to be saved."[32] Thus, Athos was consecrated as the inheritance and garden of the Mother of God;[33] it immediately acquired the name Hagion Oros or Holy Mountain, because our Lady the Theotokos chose this Mountain and placed it under her personal protection. Upon asking and receiving Athos as a heavenly gift, in that moment, the

[30] In ancient times, the citizens of that region were mostly young virgins dedicated to the goddess Diana and destined to become priestesses to serve in the idolatrous temples of Greece. To this purpose, young girls were sent there from all parts of Greece. It was forbidden, under penalty of death, for men to enter; especially "Kerasia," which is today the area of the Holy Monastery of Great Lavra. The name "Kerasia" is a corrupted form of the Greek word *korasia*, meaning "virgin maiden." Trygonis Lavriotis, Macarios, *Pilgrimage Book of Lavra* (Venice, 1772).

[31] Agapios the Cretan, Monk, *Amartolon Sotiria* (Athens: Saint Nikodemos Pub., 1899). The presence of this statue is mentioned in ancient history. Plutarch and Anaximander and others also mention that at the top of Athos there was a great gold-ivory statue of Jupiter which, instead of eyes, bore two large gems, reflecting the starlight. Emitting flashes by night, they served as lighthouses to the seamen sailing around Athos. Andrew Simonopetritis Hagioritis, Monk [Haralampos Theophilopoulos], *Bulwark of Orthodoxy and of the Greek Nation* (Thessalonike: Basil Regopoulos Bookstore), pp. 30, 38.

[32] The Virgin then brought to mind the words of the Archangel Gabriel, who told her some twenty years earlier, after the Pentecost, that her lot would be a Macedonian peninsula of Mount Athos.

[33] Kadas, Archaeologist, *Mount Athos* (Athens: Ekdotike Athenon S.A., 1980), p. 10.

ground shook and the pagan statues in all the temples fell prostrate and broke into pieces. Then, even the trees of the peninsula bent forward, as though offering veneration to the Theotokos who had reached the port of Klemes.

On the peninsula there was also a great temple and shrine to Apollo. Diabolic works such as fortune telling, divining, and witchcraft took place here. All the pagans greatly honored this place as one chosen by the gods. In fact, people from all over the world gathered there to worship. Therein, they would receive answers to their questions from the diviners. Therefore, when the Mother of God entered port and all their idols had collapsed, shouting, confusion, and uproar were heard from the idols inhabiting Athos. Cries could be heard, saying, "Men of Apollo, get ye all to the harbor of Klemes and welcome Mary, the Mother of the great God Jesus!" Thus, all the demons inhabiting the idols, forced against their will, could not resist the power of God; and they proclaimed the truth.

Consequently, all the inhabitants of Athos hastened from all parts to that port. Once there, they welcomed the Theotokos. Meeting her with honor, they escorted the Theotokos, Saint John, and all their fellow passengers to the common hall (called the Synagogeion, a kind of meeting house or assembly room). They then asked her, "What God didst thou bear and what is His name?" Opening her divine lips, she explained, in detail, to the people everything about Christ. The natives diligently posed questions concerning the mystery of providence in the divine incarnation. They even wondered at how she, a Hebrew woman, explained everything to them in the Greek language. As a result of all the excellent and supernatural occurrences attendant with her arrival, they believed. Upon being catechized by her teaching, they accepted the Christian Faith. They then fell down to the ground and worshipped the God Who was born of her and showed great respect to the Virgin who bore Him in the flesh. The Mother of God also worked many miracles on the Holy Mountain. After they were baptized, she appointed a leader and teacher for the newly-illumined from among them that were in her traveling party.

Most pleased with the place, she prayed for it and said, "My Son and my God, bless this place, this lot of mine. Pour Thy mercy upon it and keep it free from harm till the end of this world, together with them that dwell therein for Thy holy name and mine. And, through their little fatigue and through the struggle of repentance, may their sins be forgiven! Fill their lives with every good and necessity in this age, and with eternal life in the future age. Glorify this place above every other place and show Thy miraculous power in every way. Fill it with men from every nation under the sky, who are called by Thy name and extend their habitations in it from end to end. Exempt them from everlasting punishment. Deliver them from every temptation. Rescue them from visible and invisible enemies and from every heresy. Fortify them in right worship (Orthodoxy)."[34]

After praying for the new flock on the Holy Mountain, the Theotokos, and those with her, entered the ship with joy and set sail for Cyprus. Upon arriving in Cyprus, she found the holy Lazarus in great sorrow, for he feared that her delay had been caused by a storm. He was unaware that divine providence had brought her to Mount Athos. However, her arrival speedily changed his sadness into joy.[35]

Tradition goes on to inform us that, later, this same haven was visited by Clement, Bishop of Jerusalem (318-ca. 386). He preached Christianity and founded a small cloister, calling it after his name. In the seventh century, the place was completely ruined by pirates, but rebuilt by Emperor Constantine Pogonatos. It was this site (*tou Klementos*) where the Georgian courtier and Byzantine dignitary John Tornikios founded the Iberian Monastery.[36] After the tenth century, the Iberians increased in numbers gradually. For many years, the monastery was the spiritual center of Iberia.

Circa 1356, it was established by the Athonite Protos Arsenios and by the Patriarch Kallistos I of Constantinople (1350-1354, 1355-1363) that the Greek language was to be spoken, since the Greek monks outnumbered the Iberians. In the fourteenth century, the following monasteries were annexed to Iveron Monastery lying within its bounds: Kaspakos, Saravaris, and Magoulas Skete (in olden times called Saint Savvas of Haldou). After armies of the unionists (with the papacy) and, in the early fourteenth century, the Catalan mercenaries devastated Iveron, the Palaiologoi emperors, Serbian ruler Stephen IV Dushan, and especially Gorganis, ruler of Georgia, and his heirs, from the fifteenth century onward, contributed to the restoration of Iveron.

At the end of the sixteenth century, Iveron was burdened with enormous debts. By the grace of God, the fathers were able to meet their obligations only through the munificent donation of the Georgian ruler, Alexander VI. Moreover, the monastery received moral and material assistance

---

[34] Andrew Simonopetritis Hagioritis, *Bulwark of Orthodoxy and of the Greek Nation*, p. 39; "The Dormition of Our Most Holy Lady," *The Orthodox Teachings of the Mother of God*, p. 37.

[35] This account of the arrival of the Virgin on Athos is given in its entirety in *The Life of the Virgin Mary, the Theotokos* (Buena Vista, CO: Holy Apostles Convent, 1990, repr.), pp. 432-434.

[36] Christou, Pan. C. and Tom. M. Provatakis, *Athos* (Thessalonike: Patriarchal Institute for Patristic Studies, 1970), p. 51; T. Provatakis, *Mount Athos*, trans. by Paul Markouisos (Thessalonike: John Rekos and Co. Pub. House, n.d.), p. 32.

from a number of patriarchs: from Kyrillos I (1622) to the Greek New-martyr Patriarch Gregory V,[37] who even lived at Iveron for a time.

In the eighteenth century, Iveron flourished. In 1821, during the Greek Revolution, it made many loans to poor monasteries. The monastery even contributed its own *skevophylax* (the keeper of the vessels), who served as deputy to the commander of the Greek forces in Macedonia, Emmanuel Pappas. There was a serious fire in 1845 that was followed by one in 1865 that reduced the holy monastery to ashes, leaving only the treasury intact. The main church or *katholikon*, dedicated to the Dormition of the Theotokos, was restored by Abbot George Varasvatzes in 1513. On the floor inlaid with marble can be viewed the circular Greek inscription which, translated, reads: "I established the columns of this Church and they shall not be moved to the end of time. Georgios the Iberian, Monk and Founder."

Presently, the *katholikon* is adorned with frescoes painted by various iconographers of the sixteenth and nineteenth centuries. Together with the old *katholikon*, named after Saint John the Baptist, this monastery also has thirteen holy churches. The most acclaimed is that of Portaïtissa, because of the wonderworking icon of the Theotokos. In addition to the *katholikon*, there are sixteen small chapels within the monastery enclosure. Outside the monastery are eleven *kathismata*,[38] thirteen *kellia* in the direction of Karyes, another three toward Philotheou, and ten more in or near Karyes. The monastery also holds properties outside of Mount Athos. Lying near the ancient Skete of Magoulas is now a skete dedicated to Saint John the Baptist. At one time, Magoulas Skete was the spiritual center and training ground of the great mystic Saint Gregory Palamas, Saint Kallistos, and others. The well-organized Iveron library is considered one of the richest in all the Balkans.

The great Monastery of Iveron lies at the mouth of a large mountain torrent, amid verdant landscape. Today, when the pilgrim enters the courtyard, the *katholikon* is in the center and the Chapel of Portaïtissa is to the left. The second noteworthy chapel, that of the Timiou Prodromou (Honorable Forerunner), built in 1711, is to the east of the other one, on the site of the old church of the Monastery of Klementos.

In the *Typikon* of Monomachos (1045), the Iveron monastery occupied the third place in the Athonite hierarchy. It has held this place ever since the eleventh century. The last Iberian monk reposed in 1955. As of 1990, eighty monks were dwelling at the monastery, its skete, and the different *kellia*.

---

[37] Patriarch Gregory V of Constantinople, commemorated by the holy Church on the 10th of April, had three tenures: 1797-1798, 1806-1808, and 1818-1821.

[38] A *kathisma* is a small monastic habitation for a few monks dependent on a larger monastery.

On the 13th of May, the holy Church commemorates the venerable JOHN of Iveron, the kinsman of Saint Efthymios the New, who reposed in peace.

On the 13th of May, the holy Church commemorates the venerable GEORGE of Iveron, the kinsman of Saint Efthymios the New, who reposed in peace.

On the 13th of May, the holy Church commemorates the venerable GABRIEL of Iveron, who reposed in peace. He had heard a divine voice and went into the sea to retrieve the wonderworking Portaïtissa Icon (Keeper of the portal).

Portaïtissa Icon

Gabriel, the venerable priest-monk from Iveron, was conducting the ascetic life on the Holy Mountain of Athos. He lived during the same time of our holy Father Efthymios, whom we also commemorate today. Our Father Gabriel hewed a cell out of rock not far from Iveron Monastery. The Elder Efthymios, ofttimes, visited and discussed spiritual matters with the Elder Gabriel whom he respected. Now the Virgin Theotokos had a special commission in store for Gabriel. However, we must first preface the account of the miraculous icon of Iveron with the following background information.

During the iconoclast period, when Emperor Theophilos reigned (829-842), a dire persecution raged against the Orthodox. Many of the faithful were subjected to punishments and tribulations. The icons were discarded from the sacred temples and eradicated by fire. Throughout the empire, the emperor dispatched spies to uncover the icons and destroy them.

In the Bithynian city of Nicaea (mod. Iznik of Turkey), there was a wealthy, pious, and virtuous widow. She had one child, a son. This widow also possessed a wonderworking icon of the Mother of God. She cherished an extraordinary faith and devotion toward the Theotokos. Nearby her home, she erected a small chapel and placed the holy icon therein. She continually went to this chapel and offered up fervent entreaties before the icon. In the meantime, the imperial spies entered her house and observed the small temple through the window. In a threatening manner, they said, "We want money. If thou dost refuse, we will quickly execute the imperial decrees and punish thee till death overtakes thee!" The widow promised to give them what they required—but the following day. The avaricious ones agreed to wait.

After the soldiers departed, the widow, by night, went with her son to the chapel. After many hours of prayer on her knees, with eyes and hands raised heavenward, the ground about her became soaked with tears. Upon completing her prayer, she arose trembling. With reverence, she took up the icon and brought it to the seashore. Again, she prayed with compunction to the heavenly Queen and said, "O Mistress of the universe, thou, as Mother of God, hast authority over all creation. Thou art able to deliver us from the imperial wrath and thy holy icon from sinking into the sea!" Straightway, after uttering these words, she cast the holy icon into the deep. Behold the marvellous result! The icon did not sink beneath the waves or float on the waters. Nay, it stood upright upon the crests of the waves, making a straight line toward the west.

The widow was heartened by this sight, and gave exceeding thanks unto the Lord and His all-immaculate Mother. Nevertheless, she lamented the loss of her treasure. The Mother of God then appeared to her, and consoled her, saying, "I will send my icon to a monastery, so that people, races, and languages may honor it through the centuries; and I will send thy son there also. As for thee, I shall take thee with me that thou mayest see me and not my icon." The widow then turned to her son and said, "Lo, my child! Fulfill our desire and hope. For our piety and reverence for the most-holy Theotokos shall not prove to be in vain. Behold, I am prepared—for her love—to die at the hands of the tyrant! But I desire not to witness thine own death. I cannot leave this place. I, however, beseech and entreat thee to depart for the regions of Greece." The son hearkened to his mother's counsel and, after receiving her blessing, he left immediately for Thessalonike. Once there, guided by God, he repaired to the Holy Mountain of Athos, nearby present-day Iveron. He became a monk, lived a God-pleasing life, and reposed in peace. Without a doubt his living on Athos was by divine providence, because, during his stay, he disclosed to the hermits, with the utmost detail, his mother's actions regarding the most holy icon. The monks noted the date and recorded the entire history. Where this wonderworking icon was hidden for decades is known only by the all-seeing One.

Then, in April of 1004, a column of fire, with a flame that reached from the sea to heaven, was espied by the monks of Iveron Monastery. Taken aback at this dread sight, they remained motionless and only cried out, "Lord, have mercy!" This phenomenon occurred during a number of successive days and nights. Consequently, the monks of the surrounding monasteries gathered at the beach; for they were astounded at beholding a fiery column rising above the icon of the Theotokos that stood upright upon the waters. Some put to sea in small skiffs that they might take hold of the icon. Though each besought the

Theotokos to allow him to receive her icon, yet, as each approached, the icon drew away.

Father John, abbot at Iveron, then summoned the brotherhood into the church. With tears, they conducted prayers and vigils, beseeching the Lord to vouchsafe their monastery the priceless treasure of the icon of His all-immaculate Mother. This continued for three days, until the Lord hearkened to their heartfelt entreaties and supplications. At that time, the Monk Gabriel dwelt at Iveron. He was of Georgian descent and distinguished for his discernment and austere conduct of life, together with his guilelessness and unaffected manner. During autumn, he would depart for the summit of the mountain where he found quietude in a rough and untrodden place. During wintertime, he came down and stayed either by the shore or inside the monastery. He always wore a hair shirt, and partook only of vegetables and drank simple water. In a word, he was as an earthly angel and a heavenly man.

The most holy Theotokos chose to honor the elder when she manifested herself unto him. Appearing in rays of heavenly light, she uttered, "Say unto the abbot and the brethren that I wish to give them my icon, as a protection and help for them. Enter the sea and walk upon the waves, so then all shall know my will and good pleasure for thy monastery. I have chosen thee because thou dost bear the name of my annunciation archangel, Gabriel. Thus, thou shalt retrieve my icon." The Elder Gabriel then related this vision to the abbot.

Saint Gabriel, on Bended Knees, Retrieves the Icon from the Sea

The following day, according to the command of the abbot, all the monastery brethren proceeded to the seashore praying, chanting, censing, and bearing candles. Gabriel, out of profound reverence, entered the sea upon his knees and, miraculously, he hastened upon the waters as on dry land. Indeed, he was counted worthy to embrace the august icon in his arms. With extreme reverence and joy, the monks met the icon at the shoreline. When Father Gabriel placed the icon upon the shore—O Thy glorious wonders, O Lord!—a spring flowing with pure water gushed forth from that place. Even today, one may behold this wondrous phenomenon where fresh water springs forth within twenty feet of the briny sea. This miraculous spring also proved to be a source of healing for those suffering from diverse diseases. Straightway, the Iveron monks, chanting a doxology and bearing many candles, escorted the Virgin Theotokos' icon to the main church of the monastery. Then, for three days and nights, they offered prayers of thanksgiving and supplication before the holy icon. At length, it was installed inside the bema of the main church.

On the following day, when the sacristan prepared to light the lamps for Orthros as was his custom, he failed to find the newly-appeared icon in the church. Now he and the brethren, for a long time, looked about in search of the icon. Finally, the brothers found it by the column at the monastery gate. Hence, with tear-filled eyes and prayers, they took it and bore it back to the same place inside the main church. However, again, the following morning, they found the icon by the monastery gate. Once more, the brethren took hold of the icon and returned it to the church. Nonetheless, this incident was repeated three times. Finally, the Theotokos appeared again to the Elder Gabriel and said, "Say to the abbot and the brethren not to hinder me hereafter. Because I do not wish to be protected by you, for I wish to protect you—not only in this life but even in the future one. All the monks in this Mountain who live virtuously, piously, and in the fear of God might take hope in the compassion of my Son and Master of all; for this grace I sought and received from Him for the sake of the monks. And, lo, I give you a sign! As long as you behold my icon in the monastery, the grace and mercy of my Son shall not depart from you." When the brethren learned this message from Gabriel, they were filled with inexpressible joy. Therefore, they blocked off this entrance to the monastery, and built a chapel by the monastery gate where they placed the wonderworking icon in an icon stand.

To this day, the icon of the Theotokos has chosen to rest within this chapel. It has been named Portaïtissa, meaning "Keeper of the portal," because she chose to be placed by the gate or portal of the monastery. A specially assigned priest-monk, called *prosmonarios*, conducts Liturgy and a special office and prayer in this church daily. The monks have also made a new door, close to the old one, through which they may enter and exit. The icon has wrought boundless miracles, so that cures are received by demoniacs, the lame, the blind, and those suffering with every manner of sickness. This Odegetria (Directress)-type icon has been adorned with gold rizas (chasings/enchasings) from Russia, and embellished with precious stones donated by the tsars.

The Iveron monks have also built a church at the site where the icon first touched land. Annually, on Bright Tuesday (the Tuesday after Pascha), the holy icon of Portaïtissa is taken from the chapel and a procession with litany is made around the monastery. The divine Liturgy is also conducted at this seaside church where *agiasma* or holy water is found.[39]

---

[39] The account of the Portaïtissa icon was taken from the "Pentecostarion," pp. 86-91,
(continued...)

The Keeper of the Portal and Saint Barbaros

After the time of the Elder Gabriel there took place an event, worth mentioning herein, the results of which may be seen to this day. Now a close look at the Portaïtissa icon will reveal distinct and vivid facial features. But below the Virgin's chin can be observed a wound with dried blood which was sustained as follows. An Arab infidel and chief of the pirates, named Rachai or Rahahaee, sent his men to plunder Iveron. When they returned empty-handed, he asked the reason for their failure. They explained that a woman halted their assault upon the monastery. He scoffed at their explanation. Then wielding his sword, he hastened to Iveron. When he beheld the Portaïtissa icon, he angrily struck the sublime image of the Theotokos with his sword. When blood poured forth from the cut, he was aghast and quaked with fear. He then implored her forgiveness. Moved to profound repentance, he resolved to become a monk at Iveron. He entreated the fathers not to call him by his monastic name, that is, Damaskenos, but "Barbaros" or "barbarian." Thus, he finished his life in a God-pleasing manner, and came to be known as Saint Barbaros.[40]

The Keeper of the Portal and Holy Russia

In 1651, there were 365 monks dwelling at Iveron. Since they were suffering economic hardships, they entreated the Theotokos for her succor. The Mother of God also desired to deliver them from financial concerns lest they be overburdened. Hence, she wrought the following miracle. Tsar Alexei's daughter suffered from paralysis in her legs. Her condition, diagnosed as permanent, was a great grief to her parents. Amid all this sorrow, the Queen of all appeared to the maiden and uttered, "Tell thy father to bring my icon, known as Portaïtissa, from Iveron Monastery on Mount Athos; then thou shalt receive healing." As soon as the maiden disclosed her vision to the tsar, he immediately sent an embassy to Patriarch Ioannikios II of Constantinople, requesting his assistance. The patriarch, straightway, ordered the fathers of Iveron to escort the Portaïtissa icon to the royal palace in Russia.

Now the truth is that the Iveron fathers feared to send the original icon lest they should lose their spiritual treasure to the Russians. What did they decide to do? They resolved to have a copy made by the pious iconographer and Priest-monk Iamvlihos. The fathers conducted a vigil and performed the Blessing of Waters. With this same holy water, they washed the original icon. Then, with the same water, they washed the cypress wood board for the new

---

[39](...continued)
in the Greek series of *The Great Synaxaristes*, 5th ed., Vol. XIV (Athens: Arch. Matthew Langes, Pub., 1979), s.v. "Tuesday of the Renewal Week"; and Andrew Simonopetritis, *Holy Mountain: Bulwark of Orthodoxy and of the Greek Nation*, trans. by John-Electros Boumis (Athens: Eptalofos Co., Ltd., 1967), pp. 173-176.

[40] Andrew Simonopetritis, *Holy Mountain: Bulwark of Orthodoxy*, p. 176.

icon. The iconographer was then given pulverized holy relics to mix with the colors. Then they directed the iconographer to work while fasting, whereas the brotherhood would conduct an all-night vigil every week.

Upon completion, the new Portaïtissa icon was brought to Russia, escorted by Archimandrites Pachomios, Cornelios, Ignatios, and Damaskenos. When the company of Iveron fathers arrived in the capital, they were met by the royal couple, dignitaries, and the people. However, the princess who was suffering with paralysis was unaware what was taking place. When the chambermaid revealed that the Portaïtissa icon arrived, the former paralytic leaped from her bed and exclaimed, "What? Has the Mother of God come? Have they left me behind?" She then quickly dressed and ran through the streets seeking the icon and her parents. When she caught sight of her parents, she complained how they left her behind. No one answered, for they were astounded at the sight of her running. Hence, the Virgin Theotokos healed the little princess.

As the fathers had expected, the tsar requested if it were possible to leave the miraculous icon for him and his people. Moreover, the tsar inquired what the Iveron fathers might ask in return for such a benefit. The envoys, replying that they required economic relief, requested a Russian estate. They also promised to pray for him and his successors. The tsar more than granted their request by donating the Church of Saint Nicholas in Moscow, near the Royal Palace. From his treasury, he also made other contributions. Wishing to honor the Portaïtissa icon, the tsar built a beautiful temple near the city gates, as the divine gatekeeper and protectress of all Russia. Hence, the princess received a cure, the Russian people were endowed with a priceless treasure, and the Iveron monks were assured of a considerable yearly income. In 1932, the God-hating Soviets confiscated the Church of Saint Nicholas.[41]

On the 13th of May, the holy Church commemorates the venerable and righteous MONK-MARTYRS of Iveron Monastery who were drowned in the sea (1280).

During the reign of Emperor Michael VIII Paleologos (1259-1282) and the first pro-unionist with the Latins and azymite Patriarch of Constantinople, John Veccos (1275-1282),[42] both Iveron's abbot and thirteen monks were cast

---

[41] Ibid., pp. 177-179.

[42] It was Michael VIII Palaiologos who opened negotiations on union with the Church of Rome. In 1273, despite the protests of Patriarch Joseph (1268-1275; 1282-1283), Michael browbeat a council into admitting the full primacy of the see of Rome. It was also decided that every churchman had the right to appeal to Rome and that the pope's name was to be mentioned in the Liturgy. The following year, Michael sent a (continued...)

The Holy Martyrs of Iveron

from one of the monastery's small boats into the sea. Thus, they received martyrs' crowns when they were drowned at the hands of the papal heretics, because they refused to accept the false union of the pope and Veccos. The other monks were taken as slaves to Italy. In addition, the Monastery of Iveron was sacked and ruined. It was during this period that Latin and pro-unionist forces invaded the Holy Mountain and put to death many monks of Athos who refused to commemorate the pope. The most notable places where the martyrdoms took place were at Protaton, Iveron, Vatopedi, and Zographou.[43]

Through the intercessions
of Thy Saints,
O Christ God,
have mercy on us. Amen.

---

[42](...continued)
delegation to announce his submission to the council that Pope Gregory X (1271-1276) was holding at Lyons. Ships were sent to Italy. The one carrying two high court officials, with a number of clerks and secretaries, and all the imperial gifts to the pope, was wrecked with a heavy loss of life off Cape Malea. No bishop of quality would go on this mission of the emperor. The delegation handed the letters from Michael to the pope, with no theological debates. At a bilingual service, the Creed was recited with the *Filioque*. Emperor Michael remained loyal to the Union of Lyons, though he could not force the union upon his Orthodox subjects. Patriarch Joseph's refusal to accept union necessitated a change in ecclesiastical leadership.

The *chartophylax*, John Veccos, was then appointed patriarch. As the first pro-unionist Patriarch of Constantinople, he wrote several tracts attempting to prove that when certain Greek fathers wrote concerning the procession of the Holy Spirit as "through the Son," they really meant "from the Son." Meanwhile, the emperor cruelly persecuted those that opposed him. The prisons were crowded with both high and humble alike. The schism affected everyone, including members of the imperial family. See "Causes for Anti-Union Feeling Among the Byzantines," *The Lives of the Pillars of Orthodoxy* (Buena Vista, CO: Holy Apostles Convent, 1990), p. 170-172.

[43] A fuller account of the venerable martyrs and confessors of Mount Athos who suffered at the hands of the Latinizers may be found in *The Great Synaxaristes*: on the 4th of January, when the holy Church remembers the hegumen and twelve monks of Vatopedi who suffered martyrdom; on the 5th of December, for the commemoration of the venerable monks and confessors of Athos; and on the 22nd of September, for the commemoration of the martyrs of Zographou.

On the 14th of May, the holy Church commemorates the holy Martyr ISIDORE of Alexandria, who was beheaded at Chios.[1]

Saint Isidore

Isidore, the glorious martyr of Christ, lived during the reign of Emperor Decius (249-251). The renowned athlete of Christ had as his home Alexandria of Egypt. He served as an officer in the Roman army. On one occasion, he sailed to the eastern Aegean island of Chios on a military exercise, under the military governor and command of Numerius. While on maneuvers, Isidore was accused of being a Christian by a centurion named Julius. The centurion maintained that Isidore, who rendered honor to Christ, did not revere their own gods.

Numerius summoned and questioned Isidore as to whether he was, as Julian alleged, a Christian. Isidore then, freely and without fear, answered, "Know this, O governor, that in truth I revere Christ and venerate His icon. I worship only Him as God, my ultimate desire, Whom I yearn to attain. The one who wishes to delight in knowledge of Him desires nought else; for He is the true God. Moreover, for our salvation, He became perfect Man. At the same time, He retained His divinity, as perfect God, without changing the essence and nature of it in the least."

Upon hearing the martyr's words, Numerius was deeply wounded in his heart and became insane from his wrath. He, therefore, charged that the saint be stretched out and tied to four posts by his hands and feet. In this fettered position, Isidore received a merciless lashing with a bullwhip. It was

[1] The Greek manuscript of this martyrdom begins: "According to the honored and godly teaching...." It is extant in the Athonite monasteries of the Great Lavra and Iveron. It was printed in vernacular Greek in the *Neon Leimonarion*, whence it was borrowed, revised, and included in *The Great Synaxaristes* (in Greek). In addition to this account of the martyrdom, there exist others, though abridged and unpublished in Vatican and Parisian Codices. Two encomia have been composed to this saint by the orator Niketas the Paphlagonian. A service to this saint was published in the *Neon Leimonarion of Chios*, and in a separate text published at Athens (1919).

an awesome spectacle to see the martyr, mutilated by the cruel beatings, maintaining his composure and joy bravely. He was able to undergo the torment with good cheer because of his love of Christ. Following this brutal scourging, the tyrant ordered that a furnace be kindled. After they had fired it sufficiently, the martyr was consigned to its flames. Yet, with the help of God, he suffered no harm in that blazing oven. They, thereupon, removed him and cast him into prison until the next examination.

In the meantime, Isidore's father, then at Alexandria, learned that his son had renounced the idols and worshipped Christ. He, consequently, made a swift voyage to Chios. He found his son not only contending valiantly but also persevering in the diverse contests of martyrdom. He attempted to change Isidore's mind and convince him to deny Christ and worship the idols, but he failed to do so. Therefore, he appeared before the tyrant and suggested to him, "Turn this deceiver and sorcerer over to me, O governor! With the punishment that I will mete out, I shall honor the gods whom my obstreperous son dishonors!" Such was the degree of delusion to which his father's mind had sunk, due to the darkness of idolatry. After the martyr was placed in his father's custody, he tried to convert him with flattery to the worship of idols. With a mild manner, he said, "My son, do not abandon thine ancestral faith so inconsiderately by espousing the crucified Jesus as God. He was but a man that suffered many things at the hands of the Jews; and, in the end, being unable to save Himself, He was put to an ignominious death by them!"

But on hearing this, the holy one sighed from within and, tearfully, answered, "O father, I should seem more thoughtless and foolish, indeed, than the senseless animals if I were to deny the true God, the Creator of the world, and sacrifice to lifeless deities and deaf idols which are the works of men's hands. If thy mind were not befuddled by the worship of graven images, I could demonstrate, in but a few words, the power of Him Who died upon the Cross. I could show thee how many good things were bequeathed to us as a result of His death." The saint uttered these words, but his misguided father would not heed them in the least. Observing the unyielding resolve of the blessed one, he changed his mildness to rage and his paternal love to hatred. Therefore, no longer as a father, but as a pitiless and inhuman tyrant, he ordered that his son be bound to wild horses. In such a manner, Christ's athlete was dragged and, thus, his flesh and tissues were wounded and cut to shreds on the rough terrain.

The blessed martyr endured his pangs in silence and with inner gladness; he solely appealed to the Lord Jesus Christ for help. Though they had protracted the punishment, the indomitable one still had not surrendered his soul. He continued to draw breath and bear all. At this juncture, the pagans cut off his honored head. Instead of blood—lo, the miracle!—milk flowed forth from the wound, to the astonishment and awe of the bystanders. When the martyr ended his life, they cast forth his sacred body in an area covered with dense underbrush. They abandoned him to be devoured by birds of prey. Nonetheless, they also took the precaution to post sentries, according to the command of the tyrant, so that the Christians would be prevented from taking up his relics.

Saint Isidore

However, at that time a certain pious and devout Ephesian virgin, named Myrope,[2] came to dwell in Chios. She had lost her father at an early age and was raised only by her mother. After Myrope received holy Baptism, she remained near the sepulcher of Saint Hermione, one of the four daughters of the Apostle Philip, who was a virgin and prophetess.[3] The blessed Myrope collected the myrrh, which miraculously flowed forth from that virgin's tomb, and distributed it generously to all who hastened to the site. Hence, she received the name Myrope which bespoke her sweet-scented activity.

Her mother, fearing Emperor Decius who vehemently persecuted the Christians, was constrained to take the maiden to Chios. It was there that the mother had her ancestral home and property. Thus, both mother and daughter remained at their home in constant prayer to God. Upon the martyrdom of Saint Isidore, Myrope was consumed by divine zeal and devotion for the martyr; and she wished to recover his body and bury it. Therefore, she drew nigh after dark with her maidservants. Finding the soldiers sleeping, she, secretly, together with her maidservants, took up his relics and departed. Later, she anointed the relics with sweet ointments and interred them in a fitting place, as was meet.

When the prefect learned that the relics of the saint had been stolen, he bound and shackled the guards in irons. Meanwhile, he ordered other guards to search for the body of the martyr. If they did not recover the remains within a certain time, he would have the shackled guards beheaded. While this took place, the virtuous Myrope witnessed the suffering of the soldiers caused by the cumbersome and weighty fetters which they bore. She also observed how tormented they were by the constant fear of death. She, therefore, took pity upon them and their plight. She said to herself, "If they are punished for my actions, my soul shall surely be burdened. For I would have been the cause not

[2] Saint Myrope is commemorated by the holy Church on the 2nd of December.

[3] See Acts 21:8, 9. Saint Hermione is commemorated by the holy Church on the 4th of September.

only for their execution but even for their death without the benefit of conversion and salvation. Woe unto me when the day of judgment should come!" Therefore, she straightway informed the soldiers and said, "My dear friends, it is I who took the relics which you missed as you slept." Thereupon, although they wondered greatly, they still laid hold of her and brought her before the prefect and declared, "Master, this woman stole the body of that man who died an evil death!" The prefect said to the holy Myrope, "Is it true what they say of thee? Didst thou steal the remains?" And she replied, "Of a truth, it was I!" The prefect then berated her: "And how didst thou dare, O cursed woman, to do such a thing as this?" Filled with courage and faith, the holy maiden replied, "I dared because I scorn and spit upon thy depravity and godlessness!"

These bold and defiant words of the saint sent the arrogant prefect into a maniacal and unrestrained rage. Thereupon, immediately, with a savage and shrill voice, he ordered, "Beat her mercilessly with heavy rods!" After she was scourged to the executioners' exhaustion, they dragged her by the hairs of her head through the city while others thrashed her body. As the soldiers carried out their orders, they struck her cruelly and brutally until she was nearly dead. When they finished with her, they thrust her into prison.

However, nigh toward midnight, while the saint was praying, a great light appeared and illumined the gloomy cell. Forthwith, a choir of angels appeared chanting the Trisagion Hymn. The holy Martyr Isidore stood in their midst. As he looked intently upon the Martyr Myrope, he uttered, "Peace be unto thee, for thy supplication to God has been granted. Thou shalt join us and receive the crown of martyrdom, which has been prepared for thee!" As the saint spoke these words, the Martyr Myrope surrendered her soul into the hands of God and ended her earthly sojourn. The jail then was filled with an indescribable fragrance, so that the guards were astonished and awestruck by such a wonder.

These wondrous marvels were disclosed by a prisoner who was also confined to that prison. He had been roused from sleep and recorded all that he saw and heard. On account of this, he also came to believe and was baptized. Later, he suffered martyrdom for Christ. The holy relics of the Virgin-martyr Myrope were interred where she had earlier buried the relics of Saint Isidore. Both tombs, separated by a single wall, may be seen to this day. According to tradition, Constantine Pogonatos,[4] emperor of the Rhomaioi, built a splendid royal church at the site. In all likelihood, it was constructed from the abundant and excellent marble that existed in the earth surrounding this church, which survives to this day over the tombs of the Martyrs Isidore and Myrope.

---

[4] Constantine IV (668-685) was identified by many 19th-C. scholars with Constantine Pogonatos, who in reality was his father, Constans II (641-668).

It is known that the holy relics were abducted by the Franks, who held sway over Chios,[5] and that the Christians have since venerated only the vacant tombs with awe, respect, and honor for the martyrs, through whose intercessions, O Christ God, have mercy on us and save us. Amen.

Saint Therapon

On the 14th of May,
the holy Church commemorates
the holy Hieromartyr
THERAPON.[6]

Therapon, the sacred hieromartyr, whom we commemorate today, possesses an origin and parentage that is unknown. We know neither the years in which he lived nor the governors and kings before whom he confessed Christ and attained the laurel wreath of martyrdom. This dearth of information describing any anecdote from his life is due to the ravages of all-consuming time. Only by reason of his sacred icon, wherein he is depicted as a monk, do we deduce that he received the Schema of the monastics.

---

[5] The sacred relics of the holy Martyrs Isidore and Myrope were stolen from their church in Chios, where they had laid in state, and were sold to the ambassador of Venice in Constantinople. Consequently, the Doge, Michael Dominic, transferred them to Venice in the year 1130. He, thereafter, deposited them in the Church of the Holy Apostle and Evangelist Mark, in a separate chapel built to the honor of Saint Isidore.

Recently, however, a portion of these holy relics, that is, the right thigh bone, was returned by the Latins to the diocese of Chios. When the relic arrived at Piraeus, it was taken to the Church of Saint Spyridon where it remained four days for public veneration. Thereafter, it was transferred to Chios on the 17th of June, in 1967, in a Greek naval vessel, the destroyer *Panther*, with all due ceremony and formality. The relics were placed temporarily in the Chapel of Saint Isidore by the Church of Saint Menas, until the new and splendid church, dedicated to Saint Isidore, could be built. Contributions made by the wealthy shipowners of Chios were collected to treasure the relics permanently upon its completion.

[6] The *Synaxarion* for this saint, as we mentioned, in the Life, discloses virtually nothing concerning his martyrdom. Together with this Saint Therapon, we also commemorate another of the same name on the 27th of May. A complete service to these two homonymous saints has been composed by Nikodemos the Hagiorite. Another service, consisting of three canons—two by Joseph the Hymnographer (ca. 812-886), and one by an anonymous author—is extant in the following Parisian Codices: 1566, 1574, and 1575; and those of the Great Lavra, Δ 5, Δ 45, Ι 170, and Ω 147. His service appeared in print for the first time at Venice in 1891, and at Athens in 1904.

Saint Therapon of Cyprus

The pious claim that he served as a bishop in Cyprus, offering himself to Christ as a martyr by which he met his end, is part of a tradition that has been handed down to us and survives to this day. We, too, believe it to be true, inasmuch as what is well known has been kept alive by oral transmission. The venerable man's relics were transferred to Constantinople when the Hagarenes were about to lay waste to Cyprus. It is said that the saint appeared to those who guarded his relics, ordering them to transfer them to Constantinople. So it is now that the site where they are treasured is a source of miracles for those who flock to the saint with faith.

On the 14th of May, the holy Church commemorates the holy Martyr ALEXANDER at Kentoukellai.[7]

---

[7] This holy Martyr Alexander is considered by many to be the saint of the same name commemorated on the 13th of May, who is identified as the bishop of the Tiberiani, as well as with the holy Martyr Alexander of Drizipara in Thrace, who is commemorated on the 25th of February. This view is supported by modern hagiologists who attribute his triple appearance in the *Synaxaristes*—the 25th of February, the 13th of May, and the 14th of May—to the discrepancies among the various codices. Moreover, Sophronios Efstratiades, in his *Hagiologion* [(Athens, 1960), pp. 25, 26] introduces evidence from a number of codices in which this view is amply supported. The evidence produced by him includes the present *Synaxarion* of the saint, which was selected from Codex K 195 at Lavra and assigned to the *Synaxaristes*. In this *Synaxarion*, the same information is given as found herein. The saint's synaxis (liturgical gathering) is observed at Kentukellai (according to Delehaye). In the Parisian Codex, Supplement 152, is written the following: "Alexander the Roman at Kellai, Bishop of Tiberiani." In Codex I 70 at Lavra, folio 238β, Sophronios found the following: "Alexander the saint lived at the time of Maximian, emperor of Rome, in Kentoulai; a soldier by profession under Tiberian the *comes* (military commander)." In Codex 266 at Patmos, he uncovered the following: "The contest of the holy Martyr Alexander: he was a soldier under *comes* Tiberian at the time of Maximian, emperor of Rome."

According to the above, it is certain that Kentukellai is none other than the location where the synaxis of the saint was conducted. This fact is mentioned at the end of the present Life herein. It is argued that due to the phrase "in" or "at Kentukellai" that this may be another Alexander and, that the title, "Bishop of the Tiberiani," is an erroneous rendering of an unclear passage. For instance, the phrase, "during Tiberian

(continued...)

Alexander, the holy martyr, lived during the reign of Maximian, who ruled between the years 286 and 305.[8] He was a Roman by birth, serving in the army of the commander Tiberian. When Tiberian decided to sacrifice to the idols with his entire host, the holy Alexander not only refused to sacrifice with them but also mocked them all as madmen wanting in understanding; for the pagan soldiers were as men who had lost their minds, inasmuch as they forsook the Creator of the world in order to worship unclean demons. Therefore, on account of his treating the order scornfully, he was led before Emperor Maximian.

As they escorted him, an angel of the Lord appeared to Alexander. He spurred on Christ's soldier to martyrdom, giving him courage and strength of heart. At first, the emperor attempted to separate the saint from the Faith of Jesus Christ. But he toiled in vain; for Alexander, the athlete of Christ, remained adamant in his convictions. Furthermore, it is also said that he witnessed the heavens having been opened. And, having beheld the Son of God sitting at the right of the Father, as did the First-martyr Stephen,[9] Alexander's face shone more than ever. Though he was handsome by nature, yet now he possessed the visage of an angel. The emperor lost all hope of converting him. He had no wish to question him further. He, therefore, remanded him to Tiberian, whom he had appointed as prefect and entrusted with the persecution of the Christians.

When Alexander was delivered to Tiberian, the latter was commanded to punish him by many scourges, even on the way as they marched. If Alexander still could not be persuaded to sacrifice to the idols, Tiberian was to put him to death forthwith. When Tiberian began advancing on the road, he subjected the holy one to an interrogation. Since he, too, could not dissuade Alexander from his course, he had him chastised. His sides were burned with lit torches. Tiberian then ordered that the road be overlaid with prickly plants. The holy martyr was cast upon them and beaten with rods. While this was

---

[7](...continued)
the *comes*," was read as "Bishop of the Tiberiani." This above mentioned view of Sophronios Efstratiades is shared by the newly published, *Religious and Ethical Encyclopedia* [Vol. II, p. 95]. A complete service to this holy Martyr Alexander may be found in the Parisian Codex 1566, folio 43.

[8] The emperor's full name in Latin is Marcus Aurelius Valerius Maximianus (d. 310), who ruled with Diocletian but as a junior emperor. He was of humble parentage and rose in the army due to his military skill. He was assigned the government of the west. Constantius Chlorus, appointed caesar under Maximian in 293, took charge of these areas while Maximian continued to govern Italy, Spain, and Africa. This Maximian was the father-in-law of Saint Constantine the Great who had married Fausta.

[9] Saint Stephen saw the glory of God, and Jesus standing on the right of God [Acts 7:55].

carried out, an angel of the Lord appeared and strengthened Alexander. Thus, the martyr endured all his tortures with ease, though his body was covered with wounds and lacerations.

Accompanying the holy martyr was his mother Pimainia. She was grieved and besought God on behalf of her son's plight. She was apprehensive lest he should cower for a moment. When they reached Philippopolis,[10] the entire Christian population came out to greet the saint. They even kissed his chains. The holy martyr gave thanks to God for such a kind reception. As soon as they arrived at a place called Paremvolae, the prefect subjected the martyr to further questioning and had him thrashed cruelly. As they approached Veroe,[11] the righteous one observed that there was no water in that vicinity. By his efficacious prayer, he caused water to spring forth from the ground. It is said that as the executioners were about to pour boiling oil upon his back and shoulders, the cauldron overturned. The oil, then, spilled out and seriously burned many of the prefect's servants.

Following this, the holy one was beaten with heavy and thick staves. Since he persisted in the Faith of Christ, he was cudgeled again. When they arrived at a Thracian site called Drizipara,[12] the decision was made to dispatch him with a sword by the waters of the river. However, the executioner who was assigned to behead him at the prefect's order, dared not raise his sword. This was due to his vision of angels standing about and guarding the saint. Therefore, the holy Alexander uttered a prayer and besought the angels to stand off a little. After they withdrew from him, the headsman was able to behead him. Thus, the blessed Alexander ascended victorious into the heavens. The translation of his relics and his commemoration are celebrated at a location called Kentoukellai.

On the 14th of May, the holy Church commemorates the holy Martyrs ALEXANDER, BARBAROS, and AKOLOUTHOS. Their Synaxis and feast is celebrated in the august Church of Saint Irene by the sea.[13]

[10] Philippopolis (42°08′N 24°45′E), a major city, is Thracia Pulpudeva or modern-day Plovdiv (Bulgaria) on the right bank of the Hebros or Marica River.

[11] The saint is still in Thrace at Veroe-Stara Zagora, which is not to be confused with Verea in Macedonia or Syria.

[12] Drizipara or Mistui in Mediterranean Thracia toward Constantinople.

[13] The Church of Hagia Eirene or Saint Irene, dedicated to "Holy Peace," was a contemporary and neighbor of Hagia Sophia ("Holy Wisdom").

On the 14th of May, the holy Church commemorates our holy father among the saints, LEONTIOS, Patriarch of Jerusalem, who reposed in peace.[14]

Leontios, our holy and God-bearing father, was born in Stromnitsa[15] (formerly known as Tiberiopolis). On receiving regeneration in the waters of holy Baptism, he was named Leo. During his childhood, he attended school and was educated in the holy Scriptures. The reading of the lives of the saints cultivated his soul. Their accounts and feats stimulated within him the desire to renounce the world and to become a monastic in service to the Lord.

On his father's repose, Leo departed his homeland for a tiny village. In that small corner of the world, he found a venerable priest. The latter was a friend of his father, who perceived well the lad's virtue and took a liking to him. He received the youth into his home and cared for him. When Leo saw the arrangement of holy icons in the priest's house, he approached and began to converse with the sacred images as if they were living beings in this world. He implored the saints that were depicted before him to direct him to the path of salvation. After this, he reclined in order to rest from his arduous journey. Nevertheless, he was awakened from his sleep in the night. He took up into his

---

[14] The Monk Theodosios of Constantinople (Theodosios Goudelis) was the author of the Life of our venerable Father Leontios, which was paraphrased into the vernacular by Nikodemos the Hagiorite. Father Theodosios was a younger contemporary of Saint Leontios and was personally acquainted with him. The author, providentially, met others who knew the saint very well, namely Anthony (later Father Arsenios). The latter was the saint's disciple and future hegumen of the Patmian monastery. Others whom the author came to receive information probably include the Monk Hilarion, who had met Leontios in Cyprus, as well as the Priests Evlogios and Andronikos.

The vernacular version of Nikodemos the Hagiorite was published in his *Neon Eklogion*; it was taken therefrom [(Venice, 1803; repr. Constantinople, 1863), pp. 253-270] and presented, in revised form, in *The Great Synaxaristes* (in Greek). A liturgical office to Saint Leontios was published at Jerusalem in 1912.

For further reading, see the study of Dimitris Tsougarakis' *The Life of Leontios Patriarch of Jerusalem: Text, Translation, Commentary*, The Medieval Mediterranean: Peoples, Economies and Cultures, 400-1453 (Leiden/NY/Koln: E. J. Brill Academic Publishers, August 1993), which provides a critical edition of the Life's text and an extensive commentary on various subjects such as history, language, theology, monasticism, and prosopography. This latter work was translated from Patmos Codices 187 (dated in the 13th C. with 177 folia) and 896 (ca. 12th/13th C. with some missing text), which are similar in content. Codex 187 follows with two manuscripts ascribed to Saint Leontios: *Chapters on the Holy Trinity* and *On Various Loves*. The Life of this saint supplies us with historical information of a period in which few Byzantine historiographies exist.

[15] Stromnitsa (Stromnitse), in former south Yugoslavia, is southeast of Skopje and 104 kilometers north of Thessalonike.

hands one small icon, portraying our Lord Jesus Christ as an infant. He then quietly exited the house, without being seen by anyone, and went to the nearby mountain. He set the icon upon a crag and kneeled down before our Lord in prayer, uttering these words, "O Lord instruct me in the path that I should take; for unto Thee have I lifted up my soul. Lead me and implant me in Thy holy mountain and make me Thy ready habitation. Lo, I have fled afar off and know not where to lodge! On Thee was I cast from my mother's womb. Forsake me not in the end." With such words and others from the psalms did he address the icon, again, as though he were conversing with a live person.

Leo fasted till evening. When darkness fell, he did not wish to sleep. He constrained himself to lie completely naked on a bed of thorns, which pricked his tender flesh and even penetrated the skin. This caused intense pain and moderate bleeding. For three days he subjected himself to abstinence and physical exposure by reclining on a bed of thorns, shedding fervent tears. Afterward, Leontios returned to the priest's house. But he was refused further hospitality, which led him to bid farewell to the priest. He then pushed on toward Constantinople without even a slice of bread.

Saint Leontios in Constantinople

When he drew nigh to Constantinople, he went to a certain monastery of the Theotokos called Ptelidion. It was there that he was tonsured with the name of Leontios. He had become a monk not only in the outward sense of the word but also in the inward sense as well. He had entered Constantinople a total stranger and was of no mind to greet anyone or to make acquaintances with either young or old folk. He began immediately to struggle against the princes and powers of darkness. He feigned madness, a kind of fool for Christ, and appeared to the citizenry a freak of sorts; some would strike him, others would rain blows down upon him, and still others mocked him to scorn.

Desiring to see if he derived any benefit from this pretense and from the insults with which he was pelted, he put hot burning coals in his hands with incense. He, then, ran out into the marketplace and began censing all the people in the streets and, especially, the sacred icons of Christ and the Theotokos that were set up at various sites. But—lo, the wonder!—the burning embers did not singe his hands in the least. They felt like cold rocks on the palms of his hands. Suspecting that this was a demonic wile to beguile those that watched him, he put his hands to the test while he was alone. Seeing that his hands were not burnt by the coals, he assayed the following: in a corner of his *rason* (cassock), with his own hands, he placed many lighted coals. Even though the embers consumed the incense, emitting a pleasant fragrance, they neither blistered his hands nor scorched his garment in the least.

Beholding this miracle, he marvelled, reasoning that he had attained a level of great sanctity. Straightway, he cast out these thoughts. He called himself dust and ashes. He tugged at his hair and shed copious tears. He poured dirt on his head. He kept invoking divine assistance to help him in his frailty. In this manner, he put all vainglorious thoughts to flight. He did not stop, however, at these demonstrations of proof. One day, as he was coming out of the public bath, he removed his mantle and cast it into the fire that heated the waters for the facility. Again, the miracle was repeated over and over; for as often as his mantle was cast into the fire, it would remain unscathed by the flames. Thus, he concluded that he was being mocked by the demon of pride. He began weeping with more intensity and striking his head on the walls. Fear seized him when he considered that through pride he might be forced to cede all that he had gained by his feigned madness.

Saint Leontios

Such were the acts and deeds of the righteous man during his short stay in Constantinople. As a result, he evoked mixed feelings in viewers. Some admired and declared him to be a servant of God; others ridiculed him and called him a fool. At that time, the Bishop of Tiberias,[16] a man of extreme virtue and excellence, arrived in Constantinople. Leontios, at once, attached himself to him and obeyed him in everything. The bishop, who became his spiritual father, was pleased by this and rejoiced. He blessed Leontios for his wisdom and obedience, perceiving that he was truly bearing the yoke of Jesus, although only a youth. The blessed one cultivated the virtue of obedience to such an extent that he was able to perform great and extraordinary signs because of it.

His elder, however, did not live in Constantinople, but on the slopes of Mount Afhenolakkos, in a rough and densely wooded place.[17] Leontios' new

[16] Tiberias of the Galilee, in the province of Palestina Secunda, is meant.

[17] According to what is said in the Life, Afhenolakkos (Auchenolakkos) should be on the Asiatic coast of the Bosporos; it is approximately opposite to Anaplous. A monastery with this name is not mentioned in other sources. As for the place-name, it (continued...)

home was in a remote place that was ideal for quietude. It was here that the bishop imparted to his disciples soul-saving instructions. But once, the need arose to send Father Leontios to Constantinople. Therefore, the blessed Leontios was dispatched to the capital and directed to conduct all business in one day. Without further ado, he was to return to his cell. This condition was enjoined upon him in order to protect him from temptations that infest the cities. Notwithstanding, as the expression goes, it is detrimental for the fish to remain out of water for any extended period of time.

Leontios obeyed and went into the city, Constantinople. He attempted to accomplish his appointed task as quickly as possible; therefore, when he had completed his business, he went down to the shore to board a ship to return to his elder. However, no vessel was available for sailing that late in the day. Nevertheless, so as to comply with his elder's instructions, he sought diligently to book a passage. He managed to find one boat that sailed the channel as far as Mega Revma. Once there, he needed to change and catch another boat. Since the sun had already set, there was not a soul to be found on the beach to help him reach the opposite shore. It was then that he descried a married priest. He was a friend of his elder, who also was engaged in the occupation of sea merchant. Leontios besought him to take him across as soon as possible, because he had a command not to sleep outside his cell. The priest replied that the hour had long passed to travel. The priest reminded him that everyone was in their home, including those who could take him across. The priest then suggested that Leontios come to his own home for food and rest.

Now the blessed Leontios knew that the priest had beautiful daughters. Therefore, he calculated the looming spiritual danger that threatened him. Moreover, he chose to perform his elder's command—even if it meant drowning—rather than risk coming to spiritual harm. Therefore, placing his hope in God and in his elder's prayers, he leapt into the sea! And—lo, the wonder!—God, Who helped Peter as he walked on the water,[18] also aided His servant, Leontios. He preserved him from the deep and chilly waters of the sea, for the undercurrent could easily have dragged him down. Indeed, Leontios tread the waves as if he were on dry land. Now, in what way he walked through the waters which enveloped him, he was unaware. He was aware that the waters covered him, at least the length of a span over his head. Such was his passage through the sea until he emerged on the opposite bank.

Is it possible to describe the great faith that the youth placed in God, or the wonderworkings wrought through him? If one wishes to question why God did not have the righteous lad to walk on top of the water, or dry shod, as

---

[17](...continued)
could be translated as "neck" for *afhen* and "pond," "pit," or "reservoir" for *lakkos*.

[18] Mt. 14:29.

the Israelites of old, but rather through the water, we answer in this manner: first, that he might not fall into pride and think that he attained sanctity; and second, that it might be impressed upon him that, if one is permitted to walk on the waves of the sea, this follows many a struggle and toil for virtue. Therefore, though he was drenched, he ultimately reached his elder at a late hour. The latter rejoiced upon seeing Leontios. He commended his disciple when learning of the miracle which God had performed. He further praised him for his love and faith in God, giving him his sanguine approbation for his obedience to him. Leontios was also glad; for he had found a spiritual director capable of rescuing his disciples from spiritual death.

Saint Leontios at Patmos

Now his teacher and elder decided to return to his diocese. He took Leontios with him. After they put out into the Aegean Sea, a tempest compelled them to land at one of the Dodekanese Islands: the harbor at Patmos. They traveled by foot on the path upward to the imposing and massive walls of the fortress-monastery of Saint John the Theologian and the Cave of the Apocalypse. Leontios and his elder sojourned for several days behind the defensive walls and battlements of that sacred monastery. Then they boarded the ship again and set sail for Cyprus, where it was their intention to stay until winter's end. They were, with the advent of spring, to go to Jerusalem and thence to Tiberias, the cathedra of his elder. But, God, foreknowing the deeds Leontios was to perform in Patmos, did not permit him to sail past Cyprus. Perceiving the divine will, he knew it was not in his best interest to remain on Cyprus. He, too, wished to return to Patmos and abide at the Monastery of the Theologian. Not only the location pleased him but also the manner of life led by the fathers who dwelt therein. It, therefore, seemed that the best thing to do was to ask permission from the hierarch to depart. God, Who had incited the venerable disciple to do this, also prompted the teacher to give his permission. Consequently, Leontios returned eagerly to Patmos wearing only his old *rason*.

When he arrived at the monastery, he was welcomed by Abbot Theoktistos.[19] The latter was a truly spiritual man and servant of God, capable of knowing the inner man from the outer. Although he accepted the young Leontios, still he directed him neither to associate with the brethren nor to attend the regular church meetings. Leontios was to remain in his own cell and observe the rule given to him. The abbot's reason for this isolation was simple: the lad was as yet beardless and might,[20] perhaps, have provided the means

[19] Abbot Theoktistos wrote a *Testament* in 1157, when he had been superior at the monastery for thirty years. He appointed Leontios as his successor.

[20] D. Tsougarakis notes that "dates concerning the age of Leontios can be computed only by approximation, due to lack of concrete information. The phrase regarding his

(continued...)

whereby the devil could create a scandal. Meanwhile, in his cell, Leontios never neglected his rule of prayer. Indeed, he prayed unceasingly. He read the sacred Scriptures, chanted, zealously pursued virtue, and wept constantly. However, tears did not come to him easily; therefore, while the other brethren slept, he would take a strap and flog his naked body. He, thus, lacerated himself with a whip. It was made from the tail of a crocodile, which was full of bony scales like spikes. On account of the pain from the flagellation, he would weep perforce. In the strap were set a number of studs, so that when he lashed his back his flesh was laid open and blood flowed. The blows that smote his wounds and bruises caused him acute agony. His pangs caused him to shed bitter and fervent tears, making it impossible for him to recline on the hard beaten earth. He, consequently, appeared sickly and weak to those that saw him—but none knew the reason.

The thought of death was always with him. Ofttimes, at dawn, he would leave his cell and go to the monastery cemetery. Among the dead, he would put off his clothes and secretly enter one of the tombs filled with bones. Once there, he would lie down like one dead. Naked, he would weep and lament. He would bedew with his tears the remains of the dead therein. Now this he did not once, twice, or even ten times, but constantly and for many years.[21] Indeed, these activities did not pass unremarked by certain brethren.

Following this, the abbot assigned Leontios as assistant ecclesiarch.[22] Even though he was given this task of serving in the church, he never ceased to pray secretly, to study, and to weep. Due to the constant exposure to hardship and strain, he fell prey to the unavoidable weaknesses of the body—especially sleep. If the abbot caught him leaning against the wall and dozing off in church, he would take Leontios by the chest and knock his head on the wall thereby creating a loud thud. Thus, the abbot not only kept Leontios awake but also roused the other brethren to remain wakeful and attentive.

---

[20](...continued)
lack of a beard means that at the time when he was accepted as a monk in Patmos he could not have been over 17-18 years old, if not younger still. If he was about 70-75 years old when he died in 1185, then he should have been born around 1110-1115. Consequently, he became a monk in Patmos certainly after 1127/1128 (when Theoktistos became abbot) and probably tonsured around 1132—at any rate not very long after Theoktistos had taken charge of the monastery. His young age when he entered the monastery of Patmos means that Leontios' stay in Constantinople must have been very short, probably a year or even less, between 1127 and 1130/1131." "Commentary," *The Life of Leontios, Patriarch of Jerusalem*, pp. 172, 173.

[21] The coffins were probably in a crypt or a subterranean room under a cemetery chapel, which was used as an ossuary. Tsougarakis, p. 174.

[22] Tsougarakis [loc. cit.] notes that Leontios took care of the church and served the chanting master.

But when the abbot was informed of the secret toils and hardships, as well as the self-inflicted punishments, that Leontios underwent, he left off hitting Leontios. Nevertheless, the abbot continued to test him in various ways. There were times when the abbot would promote him to ecclesiarch; and there were other times that he would demote him to the lowest place among the brethren. Regardless of the test, the lad was solid as a diamond and never complained. Notwithstanding, the blessed one neither gave much thought to these vicissitudes nor grumbled; much rather, he remained unmoved in his soul. Also, he continued to flog himself at night in a place outside, where he could not be observed by the brethren. With this bodily chastisement, he would say to himself: "Open the eyes of my heart, O Lord, and enlighten them by the light of Thy knowledge; for with Thee is the source of life, and in Thy light we shall see light." In this manner would he entreat God with fervent tears.

He, one night, beheld a hand and heard a voice say, "Receive this bread and eat it." It tasted like a mix of flour and honey that was mellow and delicious. When he came to himself, just as water races downhill, his mind was inclined to the holy writings. There was no Orthodox spiritual book that was not sweet or interesting to him. He eloquently expressed all that sprang from his heart by the grace of the all-enlightening Holy Spirit. He could easily recite by heart entire books, from not only the lives of saints and martyrs but also the sayings of the holy fathers. Moreover, his knowledge encompassed the most sublime doctrines of the Faith. He wrote with adeptness. He expounded in such a manner that those around him had the impression that he was reciting from a book in his hands. His favorite readings included especially the *Panoplia Domatike* ("Panoply of Dogmas").[23] His mind, thereupon, was enveloped with the light of divine knowledge and sublime doctrine.

Although endowed with the superabundant grace of the Holy Spirit, the thrice-blessed one never entertained high thoughts of himself. On the contrary, despite his voluntary inflictions, he wished to humble himself further and to mortify the flesh by fasting, indeed, to the point of total abstinence. Since Leontios lived in a coenobitic monastery and did not wish to scandalize the brethren, while he sat at table in the refectory he would only pretend to partake of the meal. Though he put food in his mouth, yet he did not swallow it. He, afterward, removed the morsels with his hand and stored them away in his pocket until he rose from the table. Thus, he left the refectory without eating and went to cast his food to the birds.

Learning of this exercise, Leontios' abbot thought he was no ordinary man. As the abbot considered him worthy of the priesthood, he made this fact known to him. At first, the holy one would not hear of it; but later, because of

---

[23] This is a well-known work of the 11th to 12th C., which refuted a collection of heresies. The author was the Monk Efthymios Zigabenos (Zigadenos).

pressure from the abbot and not wanting to appear disobedient, he accepted the Great Schema of the monastics and the rank of the priesthood. Even though he had the grace of the priesthood and was elevated to be an instructor of others, he still did not succumb to pride. He neither assumed the duties of a teacher nor looked down upon the younger monks. On the contrary, he was an example of humility to all. He toiled with the strugglers and comforted the suffering; he uplifted the fallen and took care of those who had stumbled.

Following this episode of his elevation, Leontios was again pressed by the abbot. With the approval of the entire brotherhood, he became the monastery steward. Indeed, he now had taken on many responsibilities and burdens, which tested his ability. But he never neglected his secret struggle, that is, his customary bodily mortification. At night, he would keep vigil by reading the Scriptures, chanting, and praying with tears. He slept for one hour nightly—and that, just before dawn.

By God's grace, the Lord visited him in the following manner: During the Feast of Saint John the Theologian, shortly after the vigil, Leontios went to his cell to rest a little. As he lay in bed and took up a book to read—lo, the miracle!—the disciple of Christ, the beloved John, appeared to him in the guise of the abbot and said, "My son, Leontios, go and serve the divine Liturgy tomorrow earlier than usual because I shall be going to Ephesus!"[24] The righteous one would not think of disobeying the wishes of the abbot, but wondered within himself why the abbot had not mentioned before that he intended to travel. Nevertheless, he went to make the usual bow before the abbot of the monastery and ask his blessing to commence the service. The latter was perplexed and said, "What has come over thee, brother, that thou dost wish to start now?" Leontios replied, "Didst thou not order me, holy father, to serve the Liturgy earlier, because thou art departing, thereafter, for Ephesus?" Now, when the abbot heard this explanation, it occurred to him that it was Saint John the Theologian who had thus instructed the righteous one. The abbot said to Leontios, "Go, my son, and do what thou wast bidden; for Saint John wishes to go to Ephesus and to concelebrate with us as well." Thus was the venerable Leontios accounted worthy to see and hear the Theologian.

Saint Leontios at Crete

It was decreed by the emperor that the Monastery of the Theologian should receive a subsidy from the revenues that the island of Crete paid to the

---

[24] Ephesus was one of the seven Churches addressed in the Apocalypse [Rev. 1:11; 2:1]. It was the chief city of the Ionian confederacy [Mysia, Lydia, and Caria], situated opposite the eastern Aegean island of Samos. It was the center from whence Saint John the Theologian oversaw the adjoining churches [Eusebius, *The Church History*, Bk. III, Ch. XXIII]. The distance from Patmos to Ephesus is about forty kilometers. Ephesus had one of the most famous shrines of Saint John, which was visited by pilgrims.

imperial treasury.[25] During the tenure of John Stravoromanos, the imperial tax collector at Crete,[26] Leontios went to that island with several monks in order to receive the monastery's portion of goods and to purchase certain items necessary for the brotherhood. When he was at Crete, the saint usually sojourned with a man named George. (This Christian had not yet become head of a monastery, but later founded one to the Great-martyr George.[27]) Now one evening, while Leontios tarried there, Constantine Skanthes—a man who pretended loss of his reason—was reputed to be a clairvoyant and cured many spiritual and physical ailments, suddenly began to cry aloud, "Lord, have mercy!" Many people were alarmed by this and supposed that some great evil was about to visit the island, so they gathered around him and asked him what was wrong that he cried out so loudly. But he, keeping silence, explained nothing; he, instead, continued to exclaim, "Lord, have mercy!"

Saint Leontios wished to go to him and ascertain why he was thus shouting. As soon as Leontios set out to see him, Skanthes stopped shouting "Lord, have mercy." Rather, he began, curiously, to raise his voice even louder and say, "Make way, stand aside! He comes! Woe unto you, ye lowly! Woe unto you if he had not come! What would ye have done?" When Leontios arrived, Skanthes changed his exclamations and remarked, "Welcome, my Chrysostom!" Then he fell at the saint's feet and kissed them. He then lifted his voice, saying enthusiastically, "Welcome!" Now why Skanthes behaved in such a manner, no one knew. Even he did not explain himself to anyone; but, by his actions, he indicated that Leontios was great in God's sight and a saint.

Saint Leontios Returns to Patmos

At another time, the abbot of the monastery fell ill. His malady grew so serious that he was bedridden and nigh unto death. The blessed Leontios

---

[25] Metropolitan Titus M. Sylligardakis of Rethymon, in his *Cretan Saints*, writes: "Whenever the saint visited Crete, he abided in the ancient city of Aptera (present-day Palaiokastro or Old Kastro). He stayed at the Monastery of Saint John the Theologian, atop a steep hill above the Turkish fortress Izsedin (Kalami) [p. 187]." Tsougarakis [p. 180] notes that "the monastery must have been in the vicinity of Chandax (Herakleion), the capital of Crete during the period....In later times there is mention of at least three old monasteries and one church in or near Chandax dedicated to Saint George."

[26] Tsougarakis [p. 179] notes that the author means that "Straboromanos (Stravoromanos) was the *doux* or provincial governor of the island....Leontios was *oikonomos* of Patmos,...so this visit must date before 1157, when the Abbot Theoktistos died and Leontios was elected as the new abbot; but it must have been after 1143, when Manuel I ascended the throne." The *oikonomos*, after the $9^{th}/10^{th}$ C., was the second in command after the hegumen whom he ofttimes succeeded. He was responsible for the administrative affairs of the monastery, particularly fiduciary and real estate matters.

[27] Tsougarakis notes where the saint sojourned while in Crete. "Text and Translation," *The Life of Leontios*, p. 67, § 30.

grieved over the condition of his spiritual father. One day, after the celebration of Liturgy at which a number of lay people also attended, Leontios accompanied the brethren to the communal table to eat. He asked what was being served, and if the abbot had any appetite. The monk who was serving reported that the abbot not only lacked an appetite but also suffered intensely. Leontios was deeply grieved and sighed, as his lips moved in prayer. He arose and went to the abbot's cell. He made the customary bow and asked for his blessing. The abbot was in such a degree of pain that he was unable to give the response. What did the righteous one do? He found a small gourd containing wine. Leontios filled a glass and offered the wine to him. The sick abbot, observing Leontios' insistence, said in a quiet voice that if he drank the wine he should most certainly die. The righteous one bade him drink because it was blessed by Christ, saying also, "As soon as thou partakest, thou shalt recover."Leontios proceeded to make the sign of the Cross over the glass and mystically supplicate the Lord. He then entreated aloud with these words: "My beloved Christ and much-desired Master, if Thou lovest Thy Mother, my Lady, hearken to the words of Thy poor servant and restore unto my spiritual father his health." The abbot heard these words. He respected the simple prayer of Leontios. He, therefore, was prevailed upon to drink the wine when—behold, the wonderworking!—his cure followed. As soon as he partook of the wine, he vomited up a great deal of gall—enough to fill a basin. In this manner was the miracle confirmed; for the abbot would not have lived much longer if so much poisonous matter had remained within. Since the abbot beheld the boldness that the saint enjoyed before the Lord, he constrained him thereafter to assume the rank of superior. The abbot commented that he would be pleased to submit in obedience to Leontios, claiming that, after all, he not only granted him life but also possessed much boldness before God. But the righteous one would not even hear of changing places with his elder. He, instead, remained in obedience to the elder. At the same time, he cared for, and ministered to, the sickly man.

Saint Leontios Visits the Monastery of Saint Daniel the Stylite

At one time, Father Leontios went to Constantinople to purchase certain materials for the monastery since he was now second to the abbot.[28] Having concluded his business, he visited the Monastery of Saint Daniel the Stylite.[29] Beholding its remote and serene location, he desired to live there

[28] Tsoungarakis ["Commentary," *Life*, p. 182] notes that "Leontios must have been in Constantinople in September 1157, as he was absent from the monastery at the time when Theoktistos dictated his *Testament*. We have no clues as to what were the affairs of the monastery which needed looking after in the capital."

[29] The 5th-C. stylite, Saint Daniel, is commemorated by the holy Church on the 11th of December. The monastery was near Sosthenion, on the left coast of the Bosporos as (continued...)

unencumbered for the rest of his days. He made this known to the monks who dwelt there. Upon their agreeing to accept him, he gave them his word that he would return. But first, he informed them, he needed to return to Patmos and settle his affairs with the brotherhood. He then, straightway, would return and make his abode with them. Thus, he set sail for Patmos. God, however, Who does all things for our own good, summoned Leontios' Patmian abbot to the everlasting abodes. God also enlightened the abbot to leave behind a written order, appointing Leontios as his successor at the Theologian's Monastery.[30]

Hegumen of the Monastery on Patmos

When the righteous one arrived at Patmos, he found the monastery in disarray. Its state of affairs was such that he did not know what to do first. Since the brethren were like abandoned orphans, he was moved in his heart to remain. But, again, he remembered his promise to God and his vow to Saint Daniel whose heir in virtue he desired to become. Thus, Leontios was sorely tempted to return to the Monastery of the Stylite. Nevertheless, both the tears of the Patmian brethren and the written testament of the late abbot, or rather God, prevailed over him. He agreed to shepherd the brethren, though acceptance of the office was against his will. He, henceforth, added pains upon pains, and vigils upon vigils, declaring inwardly, "If the vigilance and care that elders have for their spiritual children incite the latter to be obedient and mindful of their superiors, according to the apostle,[31] therefore if I am vigilant with myself and those that are in obedience to me, I pray that I shall be able to persuade them to do all the things that I order." For this cause, all they that were disobedient to him received the appropriate punishment—and not from man but from the evil demons,[32] as the following story will reveal.

There is a small desert island nigh unto Patmos, called Leipso, where the monks kept domestic animals. During the summer, they went there and slaughtered those that were too numerous. Afterward, they would dry the hides of the slain beasts and sell them to earn extra income for the monastery. This obedience was entrusted to a monk named Prochoros, who was ill-tempered

---

[29](...continued)
one sails northward.

[30] Theoktistos' *Testament* (dated the 23rd of September, in the year 1157) reads: "And I go to the other world and the common Judge, leaving to you the monk and *Oikonomos* Leontios to be abbot and master in my place, and to have authority over the whole monastery. And if perhaps he does not accept this, even if he is pressed by you, because of his piety, let another one be put forward...." See Miklosich F.-Muller J., *Acta and diplomata graeca medii aevi sacra et profana*, Vol. VI (Vienna, 1890), p. 108, cited in Tsougarakis, "Commentary," p. 183.

[31] Heb. 13:17.

[32] Cf. 1 Cor. 5:5.

and of a harsh disposition. He was very disobedient and, in front of everyone, would pester the saint in a disrespectful manner to buy him brand new sandals. Now, the righteous man had inquired into this matter with the monastery tanner. After asking if there were any new sandals available, the tanner answered Leontios that he did not have any ready. In a meek voice, Leontios told Prochoros exactly how he had been informed by the tanner. Leontios added that when he returned from Leipso, he would bring him new sandals. Nonetheless, the audacious Prochoros began to complain and shout in a manner utterly disrespectful. The saint told him to go about his chores in peace lest any mishap should befall him. But Prochoros would not depart in peace. The holy one then thought that Prochoros should be chastised, like a disobedient lamb, and said to him: "Go, and may thy way become darkness and a sliding! May the angel of the Lord also pursue thee [Ps. 34:7]!" These were his only words, and God sealed them by their fulfillment. Toward the middle of the day, when the stubborn Prochoros entered the boat bound for Leipso, stones fell like hail from heaven on the boat. The most remarkable thing was that the stones struck and wounded only his person and none of the others on board. All the while, voices could be heard declaring, "The obstinacy! The stubbornness!"

As a result of this experience, Prochoros surmised that demonic powers were at work. He had the thought that he was being punished for his earlier folly and the disobedience he had shown to his spiritual father. Sorrowing over these probable causes, he disembarked from the boat. For a time, he was rescued from the stones. He, nonetheless, kept wondering why this had befallen him alone. Now if the stones had continued to pelt him, he would have perished or lost his mind. A while later, when he attempted to take a little food, the stones again began to fall and to strike his plate. The soup spilt and his wine cup was smashed. The demons called him by name and kept saying: "The spite! The stubbornness!" The wretched Prochoros' spirit was shattered by all these occurrences. He did not know what to do. He forgot the food and wine. He returned to the monastery, after sustaining bruises all over his body caused by the falling stones. He showed the injuries to the saint, admitting that they were a recompense for his insubordination.

Now another monk overheard Prochoros speak thus. This monk had the presumptuous thought that he was capable of confronting those demons. He, therefore, he stood up and pridefully announced to the brethren: "These things happened to this monk because he was illiterate and lacked the knowledge to drive the demons away!" He took the Psalter and made the customary bow before the saint and departed for Leipso. Nonetheless, the same downpour of stones befell him also. Suddenly, he cowered and returned to the monastery. The great Leontios, deeming that they had suffered sufficiently, took several pious monks with him and went to Leipso. He read exorcisms to drive the demons away and allay the fears of those who had been justly punished—that is, the one for his disobedience the other for his pride.

At another time, corsairs invaded the monastery. The saint received them with kindness. But, as barbarians, they demanded the usual things—roasted lambs, choice foods, bread, and wine. The righteous one told the brethren to offer whatever the monastery could afford. However, this did not satisfy the marauders; they wanted more. Leontios, thereupon, stood in the midst of them. With a calm voice, he urged them to accept those things that were offered because that was all that the monastery possessed. This was still unacceptable to them, so they started to taunt the abbot and threaten the monks. Following this, the corsairs went down to the shore and set fire to the monastery's ship. The monks espied this from on high and notified the saint. He was terribly grieved and, taking up the icon of the Theologian, said, before the entire brotherhood: "My beloved John, if thou dost not hearken to me and punish those criminals for the damage they have wrought upon thy servants, know this: I shall not remain in thy monastery as abbot!" Thus, his words became deed! For, as the sea-raiders sailed out of the port bound for Ikaria, the sea grew calm and their ship came to a halt; then a storm arose, troubling the waters and creating mighty waves which sank the ship with its crew. Those who made it to shore on Ikaria were slain by the inhabitants. Indeed, only one woman survived to tell of the miracle to other pirates and, henceforth, they had great respect for the great Leontios.

There arrived from Crete a certain disciple of Leontios, named Anthony,[33] whom he instructed to confess his thoughts every evening. So, at eventide, Anthony would go to the saint's quarters and confess his thoughts, as well as their origin. A certain idea, one day, came to Anthony. He considered it trivial; therefore, he did not reveal it to the saint. Instead, he made a bow and attempted to depart from Leontios' cell. Yet the advice of his spiritual father was to confess that idea also, but he stood there undecided whether to return or retire to his cell. The righteous one then said to Anthony, "Come out with it, child, and consider it not unimportant or inconsequential; for they that disregard small things will later disregard weightier matters." Anthony never expected to hear this from the saint; for the saint told him the nature of his temptation and its potential. So the novice fell to his knees before the feet of Leontios, berating himself, asking and receiving forgiveness.

Furthermore, the blessed one knew things afar off, as will be seen in the following account. There was a certain monk named Athanasios, who hailed from Constantinople but dwelt in Crete. He decided to live the

[33] This Anthony, whose monastic name was Arsenios, came to be a well-known figure. He became *oikonomos* and then abbot of Patmos. He also was a main source for the biographer, Monk Theodosios, regarding Leontios' life and deeds.

remainder of his life repenting for his sins. Therefore, he went to the monastery at Patmos. By and by, he was tonsured to the Great Schema. However, through the enmity of the devil, he found no rest at the monastery and felt compelled to return to Crete—which he did. Once, when the saint visited Crete, Athanasios promised him that the following year, if he should send Anthony, he would return with him to Patmos. Now, when Leontios returned from his trip to Crete, he disclosed to Anthony that Athanasios had reposed. Anthony asked where he learned this. The saint said he learned the news from a ship coming from Crete. Indeed, Athanasios had reposed, but no ship had yet arrived from Crete; for it arrived after Saint Leontios imparted the news of Athanasios' death. Then Anthony went and told the others.

On another occasion, Anthony was set upon by evil thoughts of blasphemy, instigated by the devil, which were directed against the Lady Theotokos. The fear of such a grave sin cast him into confusion; and so he confessed the blasphemous thoughts to the saint. The latter told him that they were demonic suggestions and said, "Be of good courage, my son, and fear not. Leave the dog to bark, but say: 'Cease thy growling, O accursed one! For it is not meet that I insult or utter inferences against her who is my only hope of salvation, nor can I refrain from glorifying or honoring, as is meet, my Mistress and Lady the Theotokos!'"

These words encouraged Anthony. Nevertheless, the vile demon did not withdraw but haunted Anthony even more. Anthony found it impossible to rid himself of the abominable creature, except during Church services and in the refectory. When he would return to his cell, these thoughts were waiting to possess him. At one point, he feared to enter his cell. So he hastened to the saint's cell and again related the matter to him. He told him, "Thy previous advice was to no avail. I do not want to go back to my cell. I am afraid to enter it." He then confessed emphatically, "Father, I cannot go to my cell until I am rid of this temptation from the enemy. Where can I go? To my cell? But that place is the den of temptation!"

Seeing that there was nothing else to do, Leontios rose up from his stool and went to the icon stand. He besought the Lord and the Theotokos on behalf of the brother. Then he took Anthony's right hand and put it on his neck and said: "This sin, my child, let it be on my neck. If the enemy assails thee again, say to him, 'By the prayers of the lowly sinner, Leontios, I hold thee to be a filthy dog!'" Anthony was further instructed on this type of warfare and came to profound contrition. As he left the saint's cell, straightway, the blasphemous thoughts vanished as though they never had been. However, that evening he heard certain voices insult the righteous Leontios and threaten him. They also said to him: "Thou art fortunate to have taken recourse in Leontios; for if thou hadst not done so, it would have been much worse for thee!"

The great Leontios also overcame the passion of anger, as we shall see. The monastery at Patmos harbored many monks of various nationalities and races. They, ofttimes, disagreed among themselves and neglected their duties in the community. As a result, the saint imposed a severe penance and rebuked them for their indolence and carelessness. Only outwardly did he speak in this stern manner; but in his heart, he was never troubled. At all times he remained serene. Even when circumstances seemed to demand it, he would not abstain from the divine Mysteries. He would proceed as if nought had happened. In such a calm state, he would enter the sanctuary and celebrate the divine Liturgy. The monastery's steward, Anthony, asked him one day, "Art thou not vexed by the dissension that has broken out among certain monks? How canst thou liturgize, while seeming to foster such indignation." He replied: "Believe me, my son, that my own seeming displeasure is limited solely to words: the purpose of which is correction. If one does not display anger, how will he be able to correct them that are at fault?"

Saint Leontios Visits Constantinople

It happened that the holy Leontios decided to go to Constantinople. On his way, a tempest arose. He put in at an islet over against Phokis,[34] on which dwelt a wealthy man named Maurice. When Maurice was informed that the saint was aboard the ship, he was overjoyed; for he had heard a great deal about him. Thus, Maurice believed that he had found a great treasure. He asked Leontios to go to Phokis and bless his home. The venerable one went to the house of Maurice, accompanied by his disciples Anthony and Andronikos. He invoked the blessings of God upon Maurice and his household. He also exhorted them with soul-saving counsels. As he was about to depart, Maurice and his wife knelt at Leontios' feet. They besought him to pray in their behalf that God would grant them a child, as they were childless and sorely distressed. The saint said, "I am a sinner and in need of divine assistance just as yourselves. According to your faith, may God grant you a child next year." This occurred just as the holy man foretold. The following year, the wife of Maurice gave birth to a girl. She was named Leontina, in honor of the venerable man.

Saint Leontios Near Death

On another occasion, the righteous one set out for Constantinople with regard to reasons that concerned the monastery; but since the wind was contrary, he had to turn back to Patmos. While he waited aboard the ship until the wind abated, he fell ill. They carried him on a litter to the monastery. He suffered intensely, as he could neither eat, drink, or sleep. During the

[34] Phokis actually means the town of Phokea (Foca) on the coast north of Smyrna. There are seven small islands in the Gulf of Phokea, of which the one nearest to the coast is today called Incik, while the one called Orak is the largest of all and second closest to the coast. Either of these islands could have been where the ship laid anchor.

following fourteen days, it could be determined only from his breathing that he was still alive; for his powers flagged and he was near death.

They, therefore, made preparations for his funeral. But the Lord, Who heals those who are contrite and infirm, added another thirteen and a half years to the saint's earthly sojourn—as many as the days of his illness.[35] At the close of the fourteenth day, it was revealed to him alone that thirteen years would be added to his life. Straightway, he recovered and began to take food. The adverse wind, meanwhile, had subsided. The sailors were eager to set sail, so they came to the monastery and asked the saint whom he wished to send in his stead. The latter, in a barely audible voice, appointed Anthony as superior of the monastery. But the sentence fell like a stake into Anthony's heart, and he answered, "What have I done, father, that I must be deprived of thy final prayers? In but a little while, thou art going to repose and leave us orphans. Is it not enough that our separation is unbearable? The idea, to me, of losing thy last blessings is insufferable not only to hear it but even to think it!"

Thus spoke Anthony in his sorrow. The blessed one motioned to him to draw near and said, "O Anthony, dost thou truly believe that my years are at a close? Christ has renewed them! He appeared to me in His ineffable loving-kindness and has granted me an additional thirteen and a half years of life. Go, therefore, and rejoice, and be certain that thou shalt have me near thee for thirteen and a half years to come!" Thus spoke the righteous one—and thus it also came to pass. During the years that God granted to Leontios, he performed other miracles and also became Patriarch of Jerusalem as we shall see below.

In Search of Wheat at Constantinople

The following year, by the will of God, the saint went to Crete in the company of Anthony. Their purpose was to bring back the grain that was raised on the monastery estates. The custom officials of Crete, however, withheld the entire wheat crop.[36] Hence, the fathers returned to Patmos empty-handed. The brethren needed this wheat, so they asked the blessed one to go to Constantinople and report the matter to the emperor lest they should lose this crop which belonged to them. But the saint kept silent, withholding any reply, for he wished to receive enlightenment from the Holy Spirit Who would determine what would be the outcome of a trip to Constantinople. The brethren pressed him urgently though, and he appeared vexed. Before all, he uttered the following, "Let me be! Do not force me! For, believe me, if I go to Constantinople, I will only see Patmos as a visitor!" No one knew what these words could mean, until the prediction of the saint was fulfilled. Notwithstanding,

[35] Tsougarakis ["Commentary," p. 190] notes here that he believes the saint reposed in 1185, so that this event took place in November 1171.

[36] Tsougarakis [loc. cit.] notes that Patmos received from Crete seven hundred *modioi* or *modii* of wheat and forty-eight (*nomismata*) gold pieces.

they prevailed upon him; and he finally yielded. Therefore, he appointed one of the brethren to govern the monastery during his absence. He then prepared himself and departed for Constantinople.

On arriving in the city, he met a notable man who was well-versed in divine matters but even more so in worldly affairs. He was a close friend of the emperor and held the office of *Droungarius* (a high-ranking military officer). Our saint conversed with him for a considerable length of time. As their acquaintance grew, the officer came to respect Leontios as a father and a man of God. He sought to introduce him to Emperor Manuel I Komnenos (1143-1180). The officer prefaced the introduction with these words: "Behold, your majesty! I present to thee a man of God who will pray for thy kingdom. I believe that he can open the bosom of God for thee, if he so wishes." The emperor believed that the godly Leontios was as the *droungarius* represented. He gained ocular proof by Leontios' withered face and ascetical aspect. The interview was further enhanced with an audible demonstration. The emperor listened with pleasure at Leontios' discourse. He was impressed with the readiness with which he answered all questions. But that which made a deeper impression upon the emperor was the ease with which Leontios interpreted certain scriptural passages. Indeed, Manuel was overjoyed and certain that he had discovered a great spiritual treasure worthy of a king. He, therefore, was resolved to nominate the holy Leontios as hierarch and shepherd of the faithful.

In those days, the archbishop of the Russians reposed, and the emperor nominated Saint Leontios as primate of the Russian nation. He made this known to him by way of an emissary. The saint, however, did not respond to the suggestion. Suddenly, the see of Cyprus also fell vacant.[37] The emperor, again through the *droungarius*, tried to ascertain if the saint might be willing to accept the primacy of Cyprus. But Leontios declined again; for, by the grace of the Holy Spirit, he knew the future and when he would become a bishop. His disciples, meanwhile, pressed him to accept the position—especially Anthony, who said, "We believe, O father, that thou wilt benefit neither thyself, nor the monastery, nor us who set our hope in thee next to God if thou shouldest refuse this elevation. How will the emperor meet thy request in behalf of the monastery if thou hast disobeyed him twice? If thou shouldest become Archbishop of Cyprus, we would have thee as our sure aid; and the monastery would grow and flourish!"

When the blessed one heard this, he said to Anthony, "Why dost thou insist, my son, that I disclose what God alone knows concerning me, the lowly

[37] The prelate of Cyprus was John "the Cretan," who is last mentioned in the 1170 Synod. Barnabas II was elected archbishop upon Leontios' refusal.

one, and what neither the emperor nor thyself can learn?" Anthony then asked him, "What may this intelligence be, O honorable father?" The saint replied, "The heavenly King has foreordained me to become a patriarch. How then does the earthly king contemplate making me a bishop?" Nevertheless, Anthony continued, "And on which throne, O holy father, does God plan to set thee as patriarch?" The holy one replied, "As pertains to becoming patriarch, I have been fully assured by the Lord; yet on which throne, this has not been revealed to me."

Saint Leontios

Saint Leontios Becomes Patriarch of Jerusalem

In accordance with his prediction and in the fullness of time, God granted that Leontios be consecrated Patriarch of Jerusalem.[38] Moved by the Holy Spirit Who guided Leontios, Anthony was assigned steward of the Monastery at Patmos. Leontios also foretold him of his elevation to the abbacy, that is, after the one whom Leontios had earlier appointed to this office. Thus, at length, did it come to pass. When the righteous one was elected patriarch, he took ship for the holy land. As he sailed by Patmos, he stopped and visited the Monastery of Saint John the Theologian. He blessed the abbot of recent appointment with his own precious hands, and departed after two days. Then the brethren remembered the prophecy that he had made on his way to Constantinople, that he would see Patmos again only as a visitor.

Saint Leontios at Rhodes

On his arrival at the Dodekanese island of Rhodes, winter fell; so he decided to remain there until spring.[39] He sent a letter to Anthony, apprising

[38] The official registry of Jerusalem patriarchs gives his tenure from 1170 to 1190. See note at end herein discussing the problem with dating the saint's repose and the years of his tenure. Tsougarakis ["Commentary," p. 196] notes that "Leontios' appointment must have taken place between April 1176 and the autumn of the same year, and nearer to the former date than to the latter. His acceptance of the throne of Jerusalem, and the issuing of Manuel's *prostaxis* [ordinance, command] concerning Patmos practically coincided in April 1176, as Leontios may have accepted the offer and at the same time asked for the restoration of the damage that the monastery suffered in 1172." He then goes on to say that he does not believe that Leontios remained abbot of Patmos after he was appointed Patriarch of Jerusalem [p. 196].

[39] Tsougarakis ["Commentary," p. 198] notes that "Leontios must have traveled from Rhodes to Cyprus in the spring (March or April) of 1177."

him that all their provisions were exhausted and that they could not make any purchases. Leontios called upon Anthony to assume the responsibility of bringing them whatever they needed. The blessed Anthony was still obedient to the saint. He, thereupon, crossed over into Anatolia where he purchased all the necessities and set sail for Rhodes. But they met with adverse winds, and the ship was blown off course. Then Anthony and the others besought God, through the intercessions of the holy Leontios, to come to their aid. Lo, the miracle! The contrary winds ceased and, shortly thereafter, the ship sailed into the harbor of Rhodes. Now, by the grace of the Holy Spirit, the saint could see things afar off as though they were nigh. Therefore, Leontios declared to those around him, "Let us go down to the shore, for the steward of the monastery has arrived and brought us what we require." Forthwith, they went down to the harbor and found Anthony and the monks that had accompanied him just to have dropped anchor; and they marvelled at the clairvoyance of the holy man.

Saint Leontios and His Visits to Cyprus

With the arrival of spring, the blessed Leontios sailed to Cyprus and to the Jerusalemite *metochion*, a dependent monastery, at which the patriarchs would stay and rest during their visits. This monastery was neglected by that time and was occupied by two monks who were not true monastics; for they lived with two women and cared for nothing save to indulge in fornication. Leontios was deeply grieved by this situation. He advised them to avoid sin and repent lest death should visit them unexpectedly and they be damned to perdition. But they persisted in their evil ways, using as a pretext that they were inured to the habit. After the monks continued to make light of the canons, the holy Leontios sighed deeply and said, "My children, I have done my duty and advised you for your own good. But because you disdain both me and my words, God shall judge you in the end." And—lo, to their misfortune!—one day divine justice visited them. Both monks died without any prior symptoms of illness; for the justice of God punishes those that sin and do not repent.

At that time, a Cypriot monk, named John, became a disciple of our saint. But—alas!—he fell into fornication, thinking that Leontios would not find him out. Thus, John remained unrepentant. Nevertheless, his spiritual father uncovered his deed and reprimanded him. He urged John to repent and correct himself, but that fornicator did not wish to amend his ways. For this obstinacy and indifference, he sustained a twofold rebuke from God for his vice. As the saint raised his hand and made the sign of the Cross over the face of the sinful monk, straightway, the wretched one was blinded. Not only this but also—woe unto him!—the unfortunate one, after two days, died in both body and soul.

After the death of his predecessor, the imperial tax collector in Cyprus, Kyriakos, had all the revenues of the patriarchate of Jerusalem confiscated: this included the harvest of the patriarchal *metochion*. Therefore, our saint was unable to find the things necessary to sustain himself and those with him. It was a terrible wrong that a great hierarch should find himself, in the midst of an Orthodox empire, lacking not only the luxuries—which he did not seek—but even the bare essentials of life. The holy Leontios endured this deprivation with great longsuffering. Nevertheless, the devil—in an attempt to try our Leontios and to see if the saint weakened amid these temptations—stirred up the servant of the tax collector, Triantaphyllos, who presented himself before the saint with great impertinence. He demanded all the crops of the estate of the patriarchate on Cyprus. Furthermore, he threatened Leontios' life and promised he would mistreat both the patriarch and his men if denied this request.

The saint charged him to exercise a little patience. Despite this, Triantaphyllos got up to leave and, as he approached the stairwell to descend, divine justice overtook him. His mind became clouded. He, unexpectedly, began to strike his head against the walls. Triantaphyllos considered his symptoms to be a mere temporary lapse in self-control. He, therefore, went on to order his servants to confiscate the patriarch's mule. After Triantaphyllos mounted his steed and rode a little, the horse reared up on its hind legs and cast its rider to the ground. The fall caused Triantaphyllos to go blind. It was only then that he acknowledged his error. Triantaphyllos ordered his servants to bring him before the saint. When Triantaphyllos was brought in the venerable man's presence, he fell before the holy one's feet. He admitted his mistake and begged forgiveness. The saint, ever ready to forgive, made the sign of the Cross over him and kissed him. He, thereby, restored him to health and released him from blindness.

Saint Leontios went to a *metochion* of the Church of the Holy Sepulcher in order to visit the brethren dwelling there. He was well known in those parts, and numerous Christians flocked to receive his blessing and show him reverence. Among the people was a monk—however, only in name—that was in thrall to the demon of fornication. Although he was aware of his fault and ever grieved, yet was he still overcome by the evil habit. The holy Leontios looked at him directly and, in the presence of all, said, "Brother, thou art a victim of a spiritual illness that leads to damnation." The monk was wounded by these words and, prostrating himself before the saint, implored that he be cured. All the saint needed to do was to lay his hands upon him. After he blessed the monk, the latter was healed and abstained henceforth from that evil deed. Later, compatriots of the former wayward monk inquired why he was reprimanded. He confessed openly before them that he had succumbed to fornication only the previous night. Upon hearing his disclosure, they yearned to repent and save themselves. In their desire to be delivered of their sins, they, too, confessed their sins and reformed.

The steward in charge of the Cypriot estate of the Holy Sepulcher reported to the patriarch that the Cypriot Bishop of Amathounda[40] had branded all of the patriarch's livestock with his own seal. The saint summoned this bishop to appear before him. However, this bishop was arrogant and insolent. Indeed, he reveled in injustice and refused even to present himself. He was summoned three times before he finally appeared. The saint was calm and not in the least indignant. Leontios simply requested that he cease branding the livestock of the Jerusalem estate lest the bishop should fall victim to divine wrath and suffer a rebuke—not by man but by God Himself. The bishop showed no regard whatsoever for the patriarch's words; instead, he rose up angrily and departed. Moreover, he continued to retain the branded animals. God, nevertheless, did not neglect to visit him. A few days later, the bishop, while crossing a small river on horseback, was cast into the water and died. Indeed, he became a lamentable sight and example!

Archbishop Barnabas of Cyprus had profound respect for the holy Leontios and visited him of his own accord. He bade him come to Cyprus in order to concelebrate with him and his bishops, saying, "Holy father, we wish to be sanctified by thy presence!" Saint Leontios accepted the invitation and journeyed to Cyprus. When the divine Liturgy was being celebrated and all the clergy stood before the sacred bema according to rank—lo, the purity of Thy servant, O Lord!—the holy man, observing the participating celebrants, beheld the Archbishop Barnabas of Cyprus and Bishop Theophylact of Trimythous shining as brightly as the sun. Their faces were radiant with the overabundance of the grace of God which dwelt within them. The other hierarchs, however, he noticed, had darkened faces; and the faces of some were even as dark as coal! Other countenances, he observed, were not only swarthy but even leprous! Indeed, one of them was the Bishop of Lapitha, a cousin, according to the flesh, of Anthony, the disciple of Saint Leontios, as he himself had disclosed to him when they met in Constantinople.

Saint Leontios in the Holy Land

Following this concelebration, Patriarch Leontios left Cyprus[41] for the seaport of Acre,[42] which is eight miles north of Mount Carmel and thirty miles

---

[40] Tsougarakis ["Commentary," p. 200] identifies this bishop as Theodoulos, who is known from this incident alone; for he is not included in the older lists of Cypriot bishops. He died in 1177.

[41] Tsougarakis [p. 201] notes that "Leontios must have remained in Cyprus during the spring and summer of 1177....He reached Acre in August of that year."

[42] Acre (Akko) is on the Mediterranean Sea at the north end of the Bay of Haifa. It was conquered by the Crusaders (1104), who named the city Saint Jean d'Acre and made it their last capital. Its capture in 1291, by the Mamluk Sultan al-Ashraf Khalil (r.

(continued...)

south of Tyre. When news of his arrival was discovered, great throngs of people visited him. Some received his blessing, while others were healed of their infirmities after sprinkling themselves with holy water blessed by the venerable hierarch. His fame spread throughout Syria and Phoenicia. One pilgrim after the other hastened to venerate the saint and receive his blessing. During that period, the Latins ruled Palestine. They would not allow the patriarch to enter Jerusalem. Therefore, he remained in Acre.

Now there was a certain deacon, in the prime of life, who had been married for three years, yet he was unable to engage in marital relations with his wife. The reason for this was that he was hampered by the wiles of the demons. He went to the saint and confided the matter to him. Then the holy hierarch blessed water in the name of the Holy Trinity and gave it to the deacon and his wife to drink. When they partook—lo, the miracle!—they were unbound from the spell and loosed from this restraint.

As the saint passed through Nazareth on his way to Jerusalem, it was noon and the sun was very hot. All were weary from the journey, so he directed the men to stop and rest that they might eat a little bread in a roadside garden. While they looked about for the gardener, instead, a woman emerged. He asked her if she had a husband. She replied, with terrible grief in her voice, that her husband had been bedridden for many years. Indeed, his bed had become a tomb for both of them; for she also suffered. At these words, the saint sighed deeply within and was moved to pity. As they were about to depart, he went up to the invalid. Facing toward the east, Leontios invoked the Physician of our souls and bodies to come to the aid of the bedridden man. He touched the gardener's head to confer a blessing and departed. Not long after—lo, the miracle!—the sick man rose from bed completely cured, as though he had never been ill. In gratitude, when the blessed hierarch returned again from Jerusalem to Acre, the gardener offered him vegetables and fruits from his garden as a token of his appreciation for the great boon that he had received.

The holy Leontios arrived in Jerusalem at night. He entered the Church of the Holy Resurrection, where he worshipped alone at the sepulcher of our Savior. He took it for granted that his presence would go completely unnoticed, but such was not the case; for, by the miracles that he performed, he was well known to all. At that time, Jerusalem was stricken by drought, and the Christians of the city had need of another Prophet Elias to rescue them from their plight. For this, God sent the great Leontios. By the prayers of the man of God, it rained so heavily that the cisterns overflowed and the parched farms received ample water. Not less interesting, and vastly more important, was that

---

[42](...continued)
1290–1293), marked the end of the rule of the Crusaders in the holy land.

the hopes of all were revived that they would have an abundant crop of wheat, wine, and the other blessings of the Lord. The wondrous Leontios was extolled and praised by all. The lips of all exclaimed that this saint of God had come to their land to liberate them from the threat of destruction. (Let us, too, fall at his feet, that we may have him as our helper!)[43]

When the more fanatical Latins of Jerusalem learned of this wonder, they became envious—especially, their bishop,[44] who was overcome by hatred. It was he who plotted to murder the saint who, of course, had never harmed him. At night, therefore, the Latin hierarch dispatched men to the saint's chambers in order to murder him. Upon approaching, they detected a light in the saint's lodgings. They tried to enter, but when they searched for the door they were unable to find it. God, moreover, preserved Leontios; for it was He Who blinded the assassins. All night long they tried to find the entrance. After accepting their failure, they returned to the Latin bishop. They insisted that Leontios was guarded by God and that no one could harm him! This remarkable event was recounted everywhere, to the amazement of all. Indeed, the fame of the holy man reached even the queen of cities, Constantinople.

The emperor, Manuel I Komnenos, learned of this phenomenon and sent a messenger to Leontios. The emperor invited him to Constantinople that the world might not be deprived, prematurely, of so great a benefactor. The caliph of Damascus, though a Moslem, had great respect for the saint. He, too, sent a letter to the holy man and invited him to Damascus. He also promised to provide both Leontios and his retinue with gold and ample wheat. He added that he would make a place for the Christians in the Church of the Theotokos, which is located in Damascus. The holy man sent a letter, thanking him for his good intentions. Leontios indicated he could not accept the generous offers in his missive, because the emperor had invited him to Constantinople. However, Leontios asked him to send a letter ordering the corsairs (privateers) not to mistreat him and those who traveled with him. As soon as the caliph received the saint's letter, he dispatched the requested epistle for safe conduct. He considered himself the recipient of a favor rather than the dispenser of one.

Saint Leontios Visits Constantinople

The holy Leontios brought this letter with him when he went to Constantinople. He showed it to the emperor, to the censure of the Latins who, even though they called themselves Christians, did not show him as much good will as the infidel in the person of the caliph of Damascus. He also reported that he strenuously labored to secure permission from the Latins that he might serve

---

[43] Tsougarakis ["Commentary," p. 203] notes that "1177/1178 and 1178/1179 were bad years for the crops due to drought and, at least as far as Syria was concerned, there was a severe scarcity of foodstuffs."

[44] Patriarch Almaric.

the divine Liturgy at the holy sepulcher of our Lord. The Latins, nevertheless, had only granted him permission to enter and worship like any other pilgrim.[45] His retinue decided to depart Jerusalem, for the time being, that the Latins might not do him any harm since they controlled the holy city. Now before the saint entered the capital, we must say that his voyage was not uneventful. En route, he boarded a ship bound for Rhodes.[46] As they set sail, they were caught by a storm. The ship sustained damage and was in danger of capsizing. Those on board wept and lamented as they awaited death. When they saw that the one and only lifeboat had broken away with a few survivors, their cries intensified and they lost all hope. The holy man, observing the despair of both the crew and passengers alike, was moved to compassion. Therefore, he withdrew to a tiny cabin and besought God's help. The merciful and loving God hearkened to the saint's prayer to save the beleaguered souls on that ship and its lifeboat.

The deliverance and grace of God was revealed to the venerable Leontios even as he grew weary and fell into a light sleep on the ship. Suddenly, he roused himself and addressed his weeping fellow passengers: "Be of good cheer, and fear not! None will perish. By the grace of God, we shall all be saved; even this vessel and the lifeboat, which was considered lost, will be preserved. Tomorrow, the lifeboat will drift back to us, including its passengers." Now all those that were acquainted with the holy man and his virtues believed his words. Others, however, placed no credence in them—especially the captain, to whom the righteous one remarked, "Fear not, my good man! By God's providence, all aboard the ship and lifeboat will be saved!" Nevertheless, the captain construed the comforting words of our saint merely as a device to console him. Therefore, he wept over his misfortune as he beheld the fury of the storm, the seemingly vast expanse of sea that separated him from land (two miles), and the imminent wreckage of their ship.

The ship, piloted by divine providence through gale force winds, drew nigh to the shore. All that the saint had predicted came to pass. The tempest and the turbulence of the sea subsided. The lifeboat also survived and returned to the mother ship. All glorified God and deemed the patriarch a holy man and

---

[45] Leontios never received permission to officiate in the Church of the Holy Sepulcher, or anywhere in Jerusalem, in his capacity as the Orthodox patriarch. Almaric, the Latin patriarch, nevertheless, did allow prelates of other denominations, such as the Armenians, into the holy city.

[46] Tsougarakis ["Commentary," p. 205] notes "there is a hint here that the continuing ill-treatment of Leontios by the Latins could lead to violence between the Orthodox and Latin elements in Jerusalem, so he preferred to leave in order not to become the cause for such a confrontation. He sailed away since Saladin was in Syria from late spring of 1178. Leontios must have left a little later, during the summertime. His stay in Palestine lasted for about one year, that is, between ten and twelve months."

a prophet. They also held themselves fortunate to have been in the company of such a saint (verily, an angel of God). When they arrived in Constantinople, the emperor was apprised of what had transpired. He was so elated that he kissed the saint's hands and eyes, rejoicing that the Almighty had sent such a gift to his empire. Not long afterward though, Emperor Manuel reposed (1180) and passed on to the Lord. But the great Leontios lived to see the days of Andronikos I, the cousin of Manuel (r. 1183-1185), and even after this.[47]

A short while later, the steward of the Monastery of Patmos, Anthony, came to Constantinople and asked the holy Leontios if he would intercede in his behalf before the emperor, that is: the issuance of a *chrysobull* exempting his monastery from the boat tax. However, because the saint was not on good terms with the emperor, due to the latter's unlawful cohabitation,[48] he said in a stern voice to Anthony: "What sayest thou, Anthony? The things that I built

---

[47] Tsougarakis ["Commentary," pp. 205, 206] notes that "Andronikos I Komnenos, regent from May 1182, was crowned as co-emperor of the young Alexios II in September 1183; and he remained sole ruler two months later, after having the young emperor murdered. So the phrase does not of course mean that Leontios survived Andronikos I (who was executed in September 1185), but that he lived for some time after the accession of this emperor on the throne." Leontios, moreover, predicted that this emperor's death would follow his own quickly—whereas, in the final paragraph of the Life, it is said that the Emperor Andronikos "honored the man of God with a becoming coffin and great honors."

[48] Cohabitation (συνοικέσιον). Andronikos I Komnenos first married a Byzantine aristocrat. His second wife was Agnes (Anna) of France who had been married to the son and heir of Manuel I, that is, Alexios II. Manuel was Andronikos' cousin. In addition, Andronikos had Alexios II murdered. Andronikos' favorite mistress, Theodora Komnene, was the widow of Baldwin III of Jerusalem. Tsougarakis [loc. cit.] notes here that Andronikos' marriage "was discordant and deficient in the exact laws of wedlock. The marriage in question was the one between Alexios (illegitimate son of the late Manuel I and his niece Theodora) and Eirene (illegitimate daughter of Andronikos I and his niece Theodora—daughter of Manuel I and widow of Baldwin III of Jerusalem). The bridegroom, by this marriage, would become the son-in-law of his half-sister. Andronikos I asked the synod to consent to this marriage but Patriarch Theodosios I Boradiotes (1179-1183), considering such a union illegal, refused to do so and resigned (August 1183). Andronikos I then proceeded to the marriage, which was performed by the Archbishop of Bulgaria. Andronikos appointed a new patriarch, Basil II Kamateros, who legitimized it in September 1183. According to Choniates [*Nicetae Choniatae Historia* (Berlin/NY, 1965), pp. 260-262], few of the archpriests and a small number of the senators were honest and courageous enough to oppose the marriage. As for the rest, they were corrupted by money and honors in order to proclaim that there existed no legal impediment for the marriage....Later, in April 1186, Patriarch Niketas II Mountanes and the synod condemned Basil Kamateros for the consecration of this marriage and dissolved it."

in my youth must I now tear down in a moment, thereby offending God and His commandments, because of thy monastery? Depart from me! I shall never serve the mortal king instead of the immortal One!"

Anthony was sorely grieved at this response. Nevertheless, the saint smiled and encouraged him by saying: "Anthony, why art thou now grieved? Why such a sullen countenance? Know that after my death and that of this emperor,[49] which will come soon, what thou seekest will come to pass." Anthony remarked, "When thou reposest, this will never happen." The saint continued: "Hast thou no faith, Anthony? By the grace of the Holy Spirit, I tell thee that thou shalt accomplish thy desire by thine own means in the giving of gold coins." (All this did happen, just as the righteous one foretold, during the reign of the Emperor Isaac II Angelos.)[50]

The saint cured Anthony of a certain growth on his tongue, about the size of a pea, which had prevented him from speaking clearly and eating with ease. Anthony, previously, had consulted several physicians; and they were all of the opinion that the tumor needed to be excised. When the patriarch heard of his illness, he said, "Come, let us chant together to our God, and then I shall examine it." Anthony opened a book and began to read, though he stammered, while the saint chanted. Leontios, at the end of the service, smiled and said, "Now show me thine affliction." Anthony opened his mouth with difficulty and was hesitant to show the saint. But—lo, the miracle!—not a trace of the growth remained. It had disappeared from Anthony's tongue while the patriarch had been chanting.

It was to this Anthony that Leontios foretold many events, among which he confided that two monks of the monastery in Patmos led the life of monastics in appearance only, but, in reality, conducted themselves in a manner contrary to their holy Schema that led to perdition. Anthony, hearing these tidings, sighed deeply. Tears came to his eyes as he asked their identity. Anthony also inquired if they would come to knowledge of the truth and repent. The saint divulged their names and said, "If they do not repent, well then, woe to their misfortune!" He hesitated to continue and Anthony began to weep again. (I, the author of this life, also wept; for it is worthy of tears when one sins all one's life and does not come to repentance.)

Saint Leontios Commands an Angel

Indeed now, the great Leontios had received authority even to reprimand angels. This will be shown by the following event, which was spoken of by the Apostle Paul in his Epistle to the Corinthians: "Ye know that

---

[49] Andronikos was cruelly put to death in September 1185.

[50] Isaac II Angelos reigned from 1185 to 1195, and from 1203 to 1204.

we shall judge angels, do ye not [1 Cor. 6:3]?"[51] Patriarch Kyril of Antioch Theoupolis[52] fell gravely ill and was bedridden with barely a trace of life in his limbs. Many hierarchs and dignitaries gathered about him, to visit and bid him farewell. Among them was Patriarch Theodosios of Constantinople,[53] a man so virtuous that he performed more good works than he drew breath! The great Leontios was also present when all stood about, unable to assist the holy patriarch or to converse with him (for in his last moments he was only semi-conscious). What did the two patriarchs conceive to do in order to help him? What other than to hasten his death, that he might not suffer any further delay of the separation of body and soul? Therefore, the one urged the other to summon an angel to take his soul as soon as possible.

Saint Leontios called upon Patriarch Theodosios to entreat God that the angel of the Lord might come, since he was "first among equals." But the Patriarch of Constantinople replied that rank did not precede virtue, since virtue is an honor in itself. Time did not permit them to continue their dispute, for the dying one was suffering. The great Leontios obeyed. He raised his hands heavenward and, making the sign of the Cross, said to the angel of the Lord, "In the name of the holy and life-creating Trinity, I call upon thee, O angel of the Lord and our fellow servant, not to delay any longer the separation of the soul of our brother from his body. Neither ascend into the heavens, nor appear before the Lord, nor carry out any of the commands of God if thou dost not first accomplish this!" The holy angel obeyed and complied with the entreaty because it was made by a great and virtuous man. Straightway, the body and soul of the patriarch were separated; and his soul was transported to a place of rest.

---

[51] Saint Chrysostom makes this comment about the Pauline passage: "His speech is about demons." ["Hom. 16 on 1 Corinthians," *P.G.* 61:138 (col. 133).]

[52] There is no record, in the official registrar, of a Patriarch Kyril of Antioch during the years of 1179 to 1183. Those who served during this period are, as follows: Athanasios (1166-1180); Theodosios III (1180-1182); Elias III (1182-1184); Christopher II (1184); and Theodore IV (1185-1199). Regarding Patriarch Kyril, Tsougarakis ["Commentary," p. 210] notes: "There is only one other mention of this prelate, Patriarch Cyril II of Antioch: a synodical act of Patriarch Michael III (1170-1178) [published by Athenagoras, Metropolitan of Paramythia and Filiates in *Orthodoxia* 5 (1930), pp. 543, 544] notes the presence of Cyril of Antioch on 2 July of the year 1173. Cyril's death cannot be precisely dated, though, since the Patriarch Theodosios Boradiotes was also present, it must have taken place before or in August 1183 at the latest. On the throne of Antioch, Cyril II was the successor of Athanasios (d. 1170 and not 1171) and was succeeded by the celebrated canonist Theodoros Balsamon ca. 1185."

[53] Patriarch Theodosios I Boradiotes of Constantinople served from 1179 to 1183.

Saint Leontios' Clairvoyance

The holy Leontios himself once fell ill, bathed in hot springs, and recovered. As he sat on a bench, he said to his servant in jest, "What sayest thou, O Evlogios, shall we go to Cyprus and visit the properties of the patriarchate?" Evlogios, however, said nothing, but thought within himself: "Just imagine, this old man is nigh to death, yet he is of a mind to go to Cyprus!" But before he could finish his thought, the saint interrupted: "Dost thou think, O Evlogios, that I do not know thy thoughts concerning me? So thou supposest that I am old, sick, and near death, and am in no wise able to travel to Cyprus? Nay, Evlogios, think not that I do not know the thoughts of thy heart!" When Evlogios heard this, he was abashed and rendered speechless. He marvelled at how the saint perceived his hidden thoughts, which he himself had not even completed. For this reason, he never wished to say or to think anything about him lest he should suffer something unexpected; for he felt deeply the rebuke of the holy Leontios. Many more miracles did the great one perform, which we shall not mention lest we become tiresome to our pious readers. Thus, we come to the end of the saint's life. With the help of God, we might bring a conclusion to our narrative.

Saint Leontios Succumbs to Illness

When the thirteen and one-half years that God added to the saint's life came to a close, Leontios fell ill and lay abed. Knowing that the time of his repose was imminent, he hastily bade all farewell; for he was eager to go to the Lord Whom he had ever desired. They that were present bewailed his departure, for they would see him no longer in this life. On the 14th day of May, he surrendered his blessed soul into the hands of God without requesting anything for himself. Until the very end of his life, he was still meticulous in keeping to his rule of prayer and abstinence. His close companions placed his sacred relics in a wooden chest. They set them in the Church of the Archangel Michael until the matter was made known to the emperor.

While the Funeral Service was chanted by nearly the entire clergy of Constantinople, Evlogios and the saint's other disciples commissioned an artist to make a portrait of the holy one on a wooden panel. The artist stood opposite the bier and began closely to observe Leontios' godly countenance. He continually repositioned himself, attempting to determine the best possible angle from which to observe the saint's features; but the painter's efforts were in vain, for it proved impossible for him to depict Leontios. Even after death, the holy one would not allow his image to be painted. For this reason, his holy face was not drawn by the artist. For—O the wonder!—at one time, he would appear one way and then, at another time, another way. But he never appeared in the same manner. The saint retained his humility even after death in order to teach us to strive to escape the snares of the devil. The miracles worked after the burial of our righteous Father Leontios are indeed countless.

Beneath the coffer, where the relics of the righteous one were laid to rest, those who buried him placed ceramic pots and tiles.[54] They presumed this would absorb any foul odor that perchance might be emitted from the chest. After four days elapsed, they approached the chest and distinguished a particularly pleasant scent wafting from the sacred relics. Indeed, what was all the more wondrous was that they beheld that blood streamed forth from the holy relics, as if from a freshly cut wound. The blood ran out onto the marble slabs and appeared bright red against the marble. But the most wondrous fact was that the wooden chest was within a chest. The blood ran so profusely that it overflowed from and through both chests and onto the ground in four parts, that is, the blood formed the sign of the Cross. From this miracle, it may be surmised that Saint Leontios was as one living among the dead—and numbered among the martyrs also, as demonstrated by the voluntary martyrdom that he imposed on himself as he was lashed by the leather belt covered with studs.

Emperor Andronikos Komnenos[55] was moved by the miracles of Saint Leontios and had an imposing sepulcher constructed, wherein his honored relics were interred with due reverence and respect. Thus, this just man, Leontios, was numbered among the just. As one righteous, he is among the righteous. As a voluntary martyr, he is counted in the choir of the martyrs. As a great archpastor, he ranks with the hierarchs. He is now in the heavens, enjoying the reward of his labors, to the glory of the Father and the Son and the

---

[54] Tsougarakis ["Commentary," p. 212] suggests that by *ostrakos* is meant vessels containing unguents or perfumes. The modern Greek version of the Life [*Neon Eklogion* (Constantinople, 1863), p. 269] states at this point that "what was placed under the coffin was a lot of ground pottery...so that, if some bad-smelling matter happened to come forth from the coffin, it would be quenched by the pottery."

[55] The compilers of *The Great Synaxaristes* (in Greek) note that the year of Saint Leontios' repose is somewhat puzzling. The register of the Jerusalem patriarchate shows that his tenure was from 1170 to 1190. The problem with the 1190 date is that Emperor Andronikos, who is identified as having constructed a marvellous reliquary, died ca. September 1185. The emperor after him was Isaac II Angelos. The biographer mentions that the saint lived "even after" the reign of Andronikos. Sophronios Efstratiades [*Hagiologion*, p. 272] also notes that the death of the saint is not exact. Additionally, given the troublesome times then for the Church of Jerusalem—war raged between the Crusaders and the Arabs, and the patriarch sojourned in Constantinople and not in his see—this also could have contributed to the confusion in dating the year of his repose. Tsougarakis' explanation seems the most logical (see earlier notes): in 1185, the saint reposed in May and Andronikos in September. His coming to the throne actually began in 1182, when he was regent of young Alexios II and then crowned co-emperor with him the following year.

Holy Spirit, the One God and Dominion, to Whom is due all honor, glory, and worship, now and ever, and to the ages of ages. Amen.

On the 14th of May, the holy Church commemorates the holy New-martyr MARK of Crete, who was slain by the sword at Smyrna (1643).[56]

Mark, the holy new-martyr, hailed from Crete.[57] Since the youth was handsome in appearance, the Turks abducted him and made him a Moslem by force. He ever sought the opportune moment to flee or to become a martyr for the love of Christ. He left Smyrna and went to Constantinople, where he met a certain teacher of piety. It was to him that he confessed his ardent desire to become a martyr. The teacher advised and encouraged the young man, wholeheartedly, to seek martyrdom. He strengthened him further by his blessing.[58] Mark then returned to Smyrna. There, with great daring and

---

[56] The account of the martyrdom of New-martyr Mark was written by the venerable and learned Cretan Priest-monk Meletios Syrigos, a contemporary of the saint. Syrigos was a friend and neighbor of the saint at Constantinople. The scholar-vicar of the Western Church at Smyrna, John Foskaro, also recorded details of the martyrdom since he was an eyewitness. Syrigos' work was published in Nikodemos the Hagiorite's *Neon Martyrologion*, 3rd ed. (pp. 70, 71), and incorporated into *The Great Synaxaristes* (in Greek). The details of the mood at Smyrna were noted by Foskaro, a spectator of the martyrdom, which are found in the work of Metropolitan Titus M. Sylligardakis, in his work, entitled *Cretan Saints*, trans. by T. Andrews (West Brookfield, MA: The Orthodox Christian Center).

[57] According to the *Acta Sanctorum*, V (Palermo, 1644), Mark was born in Crete but grew up in Smyrna. While still a child he was Islamized by force. Cited in *Cretan Martyrs*, p. 189.

[58] Metropolitan Titus, as we said, draws upon the accounts of both Syrigos and Foskaro. The latter tells us that the family name of Saint Mark was Kyriakopoulos. Mark's father originated from Zakynthos, but his mother was Cretan. She reposed when Mark was eight years old, leaving him, together with a brother and sister, to his father's care. We learn from the metropolitan's book that the sternness and severity of Mark's father caused him, at the age of thirteen, to rebel. Perhaps the words of Saint Paul would have been helpful to the father: "Fathers, cease provoking your children, that they may not be disheartened [Col. 3:21]." Mark was made a Muslim and received the name of Moustafas. He was maintained and educated by a childless but wealthy corsair. Although the father begged Mark to return home, the youth refused. Moustafas continued to live as a Mohammedan for four years. At the age of seventeen, he wished to be rid of Islam. He, with his sister, left Smyrna bound for Zakynthos. Nevertheless, we find him next in Crete. He visited the Monastery of the Theotokos Akrotiriani of Toplou at the eastern end of the island. He was encouraged to repent of his folly committed as a young adolescent. Mark left Crete in the direction of Constantinople.

(continued...)

boldness, he declared before all that Christ was the true God. Without the least fear of Hagarene wrath, he derided the Muslims' deluded prophet and refuted their defiled religion.

Saint Mark

When the Hagarenes heard his derision of Islam and Mohammed, and also observed how he again embraced Christianity with a resolute denial of their religion, they crowded around him in rage. Seizing Mark, they struck him with staves and pushed him along to the judge of that place. They testified that he was a former Turk, who denied their faith. They accused him of becoming a Christian, who hurled insults at their Islamic faith and prophet. The judge, hearing these charges, was extremely embittered. He asked Mark impatiently, "Art thou a Christian or a Turk?" Christ's confessor answered, "I had been a Christian and a Christian have I become again. I revere my Christ and worship Him as true God. As for your religion, I renounce it and turn from it." Infuriated by this public confession, the judge ordered his men to thrash Mark mercilessly. They, afterward, pitched him into a dungeon and tortured him in diverse ways.[59] The martyr, nevertheless, received strength by the grace of God. While they labored at tormenting the martyr, he received the punishments as pleasures. He preferred death to life that he might enjoy those everlasting good things in the heavens. Finally, seeing that they could not convince him to deny his Orthodoxy, they led him

---

[58](...continued)
He took himself into the Galata neighborhood of the capital, to the learned parish priest of Chrysophighe, Father Meletios Syrigos, who counseled him to witness for Christ. Foskaro, the western biographer and eyewitness, later added some other details unknown in Syrigos' manuscript, which we will soon mention. *Cretan Saints*, p. 42.

[59] Foskaro describes the scene at Smyrna. He adds here that when Mark presented himself as a Christian in Smyrna, a terrified Venetian acquaintance attempted to distance himself from the martyr lest he should be destroyed with him by the Muslims. Former Turkish friends of Mark urged him to recant. There were also Jewish and English acquaintances of his who encouraged him to escape from prison. A Cretan tailor at Smyrna, seeing Mark's tribulation and coming martyrdom, spoke to him tearfully and said, "Mark, my little compatriot, pray for me too!" While he was in prison, he was not denied visitors. Orthodox and heterodox made free to see and speak with him. Some encouraged him, while others tried to console him with food and water. Roman Catholic women, upon seeing him, cried out for mercy from their windows. Foskaro makes the point that reactions toward Mark's confession of Orthodoxy varied inside Smyrna. Ibid., pp. 44, 45.

back to the judge. He spoke many harsh things to Mark, threatening him with worse martyric chastisements. But Mark gave the judge's words no consequence. With much self-possession, he calmly addressed the court and Muslims: "Do whatever you wish. Even if you were to give me over to ten thousand tortures and death, I will not deny my sweet Jesus Christ. Therefore, tarry not. But carry out what you have decided. Then shall you see the strength and power Christ bestows upon those who suffer for His name."

The judge, seeing that the young martyr's conviction and resolve were immovable, ordered that he be escorted to the execution site. Once there, the martyr readily complied and bent his head before the executioner's whirling sword. He received his blessed end by one fell swoosh, so that his crown-bearing soul soared into the heavens. As for his precious relics, after tremendous exertion and an exchange of money too much to make an accounting, the Christians retrieved the relics. New-martyr Mark was interred in the cathedral Church of Saint Photine at Smyrna. The sacred relics were proven to be by our most compassionate God a source of inexhaustible healing to those who hastened to Saint Mark with faith. The memory of Saint Mark is celebrated yearly by the Christians to the glory of Christ, to Whom is due all glory, honor, and veneration, to the ages of the ages. Amen.[60]

On the 14th of May, the holy Church commemorates the holy New-martyr JOHN the Bulgarian (1802).[61]

John the Bulgarian, the young athlete of Christ and gloriously triumphant martyr, hailed from the large Bulgarian city of Sumla.[62] It has not

---

[60] The *Acta Sanctorum* notes that Meletios Syrigos wrote a canon to the saint. Isaac D'Aultry, a Jesuit contemporary living in Constantinople, also gave an account of the martyrdom which was later placed in the *Acta Sanctorum*, a Roman book of the acts of the martyrs. A special treatise on the new-martyr was also written by Professor Mario Vitti, entitled "Mark Kyriakopoulos, the New-martyr, who was beheaded at Smyrna in 1643—one western source." It can be found in the periodical "Micrasiatica Chronica," X (1962), pp. 89-103. Cited in *Cretan Martyrs*, p. 189. See also Efstratiades, p. 304; and *Religious and Ethics Encyclopedia*, 8, col. 763.

[61] The account of the martyrdom of New-martyr John was written by the venerable Nikephoros of Chios (1750-1821, who is commemorated by the holy Church on the 1st of May), which was printed in his publication *Neon Leimonarion* (Venice, 1819). This work was revised and edited for incorporation into *The Great Synaxaristes* (in Greek).

[62] Sumla of Oblast Shumen region has many names and spellings: Sumen, Choumen, Kolarovgrad, Shumla, Sumla, Schumen, or Shoumen. It is located in the central part of northeast Bulgaria on the main roadways of Sofia-Varna and Ruse-Burgas-Istanbul. The Shumen municipality is the tenth largest in Bulgaria. Its town is an administrative center of the region. The terrain of this municipality varies with its hills, plateaus, and

(continued...)

been possible to learn either his family name or his parents' names. In the Bulgarian dialect he was called Raïkos which, being interpreted, means John.

John was a goldsmith by trade. Both his home and place of business were in Sumla. Our story opens when John was about eighteen years of age. The beauty of his soul was complemented with a handsome face. In matters of the Faith of Christ, his love, fervor, and firmness were unswerving. His belief was shown in a clear and palpable manner. His confession of the Faith was demonstrated in actual deed. The unyielding resolution that dwelt in his mind and in his heart was the same as that declaration made by Peter to Jesus: "Even if it should be necessary for me to die with Thee, in no wise will I deny Thee [Mt. 26:35]." Our John also showed himself to be an imitator of the Patriarch Joseph the All-comely, by reason of his wondrous prudence and self-control which he did not allow to rove.[63] On account of John's Orthodox convictions and values he entered into martyric contests. In feats both splendid and manly, before visible and invisible powers, he crossed the finish line as a victor and trophy-bearer on behalf of Christ. It is worthwhile here to relate how he endured a martyric death for the sake of continence, chastity, and temperance. "The history of this new-martyr has come to us," comments the biographer, "by means of a priest-monk who happened to be visiting among us."

As we said, John, the namesake of grace, was practising the craft of goldsmith and making jewelry at Sumla. Opposite his workshop was a Turkish residence. The daughter of that house was unmarried. That daughter of Islam, as one accursed, observed that John was handsome in form and exceedingly beautiful in countenance. Her unguarded gazing at his physical good looks caused her heart to be smitten with satanic lust. She thought she was consumed with love for him. There was no other way for her to succeed in her aim and to fulfill her wicked desire than by some contrivance and plan. Thus, she devised the following artifice in order to converse with him. One day, as she stood slightly outside the door of her house, she called out to John to come over to her. John, unaware that he was the object of her desire in a treacherous design, did not know what else to do other than acknowledge her request. Even though it was said among the Orthodox that the manner of life of the Turks tends to wickedness, blood, and slaying, and the Muslims showed themselves to be harsh tyrants toward those living as Christians, still he did not know how to avoid her. He went over and stood outside the door.

She asked him to draw a little closer that he might take the measurement of her finger for a gold ring that she wished for him to fashion for her.

---

[62](...continued)
plains. It is characterized by a typical continental climate. The warmest month is July and the coldest one is January.

[63] See Gen. 39:6 ff.

The goodly youth approached her. He was uncomfortable in her presence and stood before her somewhat apprehensively. She then, as one bereft of wits, pulled him with all her might and pushed him into the entranceway of her house. Such was her forwardness, licentiousness, and intemperance toward this new Joseph, that is, John, who resisted her with his greater strength. He broke the grip that she had on his hand. After releasing her hold on him, she fell backwards. Even as the Egyptian temptress of old, Potiphar's wife, her love turned to hate. She began to shout as loud as she could. This drew the attention of others immediately. She slandered John, he who was worthy of ten thousand praises. The spurned girl told those who came to answer her calls for help that John, with shameless boldness, attempted to rape her.

This hideous false accusation, when it came into the ears of her coreligionists, stirred up the bloodthirsty Hagarenes. They conducted themselves exactly as we mentioned earlier. They apprehended the blessed John and brought him before the judge. The latter gave his opinion, that is, after consulting with the father of the girl, that John had before him two choices: Either he could become a Turk[64] and take her as his wife or, if he did not wish that, he would be subjected to a thrashing until he gave up the spirit. The judge followed upon these two options with a question to the holy youth. "Which of these two choices dost thou prefer?" The ever-memorable one gave his answer: "It is much better to prefer death than to deny Christ." John was then encouraged by the judge and the bystanders—more so by the father of the girl—that his daring deed was pardonable. They kept saying that it would be sufficient only that he should embrace Islam and become the son-in-law to the girl's father. "He will treat thee as his son," they assured John, "and thou shalt inherit all of his estate and belongings." John, steadfast in virtue and piety, could not be converted to their way of thinking. Although they offered him money, means, property, and a spirited vixen into the bargain, he still repeated, "A Christian I am, and a Christian will I die."

Well done was thy firm objection, O most blessed John! Hooray for thy courageous resolution! Bravo to thy fervent and ardent love toward Christ! In but a short space of time, John demonstrated wonderfully the wealth he possessed in four general virtues: prudence, temperance, bravery, and righteousness. By prudence, he showed himself to be possessed of his senses by preserving as his chief commandment love of God and piety. By temperance, he proved his chastity by not allowing himself to become enslaved to the pleasures of the new Egyptian woman. He exhibited bravery by not fearing death to his body lest his soul should die. He manifested righteousness by his willingness to die for Christ. They offered him tempting expedients to save his

[64] He could become a Turk by being Islamized, that is, by converting to Islam.

skin, but he set them at nought. He was mindful of three godly virtues: faith, hope, and love.[65] He, therefore, put on the breastplate of faith and love, and, for a helmet, the hope of salvation.[66] He understood the meaning of the work of faith, and the labor of love, and the patience of hope in our Lord Jesus Christ.[67] He deemed all things to be dung that he might win Christ.[68] Thus, he disdained all the temporal promises and offers of the ungodly. He, rather, having placed his hope in the Lord's promises of those future good things, was determined to guard his faith until his last breath; and so, he was fully willing to undergo a harsh and terrifying death on account of his love for God.

The sentencing by the tyrant was fixed: death by beating, flogging, and bastinadoing. The martyr first had the soles of his feet cudgeled in a pitiless manner, until his toenails fell off. It was the hope of the Muslims to bring John to Islam by corporal punishment. Seeing that the bastinadoing was unsuccessful, they shackled John from under his arms and suspended him on high. He was kept in this excruciatingly painful position for the rest of that day until evening. After they removed him from hanging from his armpits, more psychological warfare ensued. They fluctuated from flattering him inordinately to threatening him with worse torments and a bitter death. In vain did the vain and foolish ones toil, thinking that they would soon bring him to heel. He, however, would not subscribe to their offers. No cringing submission was forthcoming, for John had already resisted as far as blood.[69] He remained unfaltering throughout. They had seen that beforehand, had they not? Any kind of torture, now, seemed laughable to the holy martyr. He was minded to die. But evening had drawn nigh, and there was no longer time to continue the chastisements. He was flung into prison and directed to ponder well upon how he was going to conduct himself thereafter. He spent two days in that prison. We are not told what he underwent in that time frame. No further news could be learned outside of the prison. But after two days, they removed John from his cell and put him to the test in manifold ways.

Since his resolve abided firm and unshaken, once again, they suspended him from the armpits. He remained aloft until evening of that day. When they lowered him from that height that was nearly as bad as a hanging, they hurled him back into his cell. He was taken out the following day. Again they commenced with their blandishments and promises of rich presents and pleasures. This was immediately followed by a string of threats of the most dreadful torments. As for our holy martyr, neither were their praises received,

---

[65] 1 Cor. 13:13.

[66] 1 Thess. 5:8.

[67] 1 Thess. 1:3.

[68] Phil. 3:8.

[69] Heb. 12:4.

nor were their pledges accounted as anything, nor were their intimidations to be feared by him. Throughout these proceedings, the blessed man had not cowered. He retained but one expression for his defense: "I am a Christian, and I am not becoming a Turk." What was the outcome of all these happenings? The Muslims raised him up, for a third time, passing a rope underneath his arms. After this brutal and cruel exercise that nearly strangled him, they devised a more heinous torture. They had a contraption which consisted of a wheel with sharp cutting blades, as those of a saw. When the wheel was spun, it devoured the flesh of its victim in a monstrous fashion. All the time that he was subjected to this brutal and bitter torture, the Turks did not hold their tongues. They kept urging him to become a Turk. Some were flattering him, while others were threatening more piercing and smarting trials. The valiant martyr endured that apparatus. He spoke nought save this, repeatedly, "I am a Christian." The Turks then summoned a medical doctor who, despite the easily discernible life-threatening wounds the martyr sustained, remarked, "Have no fear, death is still not imminent! Thy wounds can be healed." Similarly, the bystanders, desiring to persuade John that it was not too late to change his mind, began to say to him, "Behold, it is still possible to be healed! So say that thou wilt become a Turk that thou mightest be delivered; and then shall they make thee a great agha, a lord and master among the Turks." The martyr gainsaid them and remarked, "I believe in Christ, and I am a Christian. So how should I become a Turk?"

As the saint kept standing firm in the Faith, still more did the shamefaced Muslims harden. They, therefore, contrived worse punishments. What kind? A strip of skin was flayed from the top of his navel to his neck! O such harshness and savagery! They did it again from his back parts to his neck. Their bloodthirstiness was not sated with this torturous procedure. They thought to intensify the punishment by sprinkling plenty of salt over the area that had been sliced away! After this, they took lit candles and burned John ruthlessly! Who would not be horrified at their inexorable hardness of heart and beastly relentlessness? Who would not marvel, verily, at the wondrous and supernatural patient endurance of the martyr? Who would not be astonished by the power of God that filled the weakness of that youth's flesh that was tender, soft, and delicate?

The gloriously triumphant martyr of Christ bore those terrifying mutilations. So what still remained? Though his feet had been subjected to an excessive and inhuman beating, yet they were well empowered so that he could run unhindered on the heavenly path. Though his hands were hanged, yet they were sanctified so that he could raise them boldly before the divine majesty as holy and clean. Though his flesh was cut to pieces, yet he passed through the narrow gate and straitened way leading to heaven.[70] His abdomen was sliced that he might exhibit the divine fear he possessed in his inward parts. His chest was opened that he might reveal the fire of divine love kindled inside his heart. He was salted and subjected to fire that he might become worthy food for the heavenly table. What else, then, was left? The crowning of John as a most radiant, excellent, and victorious athlete. The enemies of the Cross, consequently, not having anything else they could devise against him, placed upon his head a surgical appliance, which resembled a crown of riveted iron spheres. Next they proceeded to wrap a rope about his head, which they tightened by the turn of two attached pieces of wood. This would be their final torture.

The Judge of the contest, that is, Christ, however, did not permit the contestant to suffer further. Straightway, that very same hour, the *mufti*[71] gave the order that the tortures were to cease and the prisoner was to be decapitated. Hence, the holy John had his head struck off, yet he was joined to the noetic and deathless Head, Jesus Christ, together with Whom John now lives and reigns. It was John's desire to complete this temporal life and commence the everlasting and unending one. The beheading took place in 1802, on the 14th day of May. It is not known what had become of the martyr John's much-tried body. Likewise, it has not been left to us as to how God, Who is glorified in His saints, glorified the martyr through miracles which is usually the case in such instances. The present account by the hieromonk, who was present to see and hear these events, related all this to us, to the glory of Father, Son, and Holy Spirit, and to the honor of the much-laboring and glorious victor John, through whose holy intercessions may we be delivered from everlasting condemnation and be vouchsafed the kingdom of the heavens. Amen.

**On the 14th of May, the holy Church commemorates
Saint ISIDORE the Prussian,
the Fool for Christ and Wonder-worker of Rostov (1474).**

**On the 14th of May, the holy Church commemorates
Saint NIKETA, Bishop of Novgorod,
the Recluse of the Kiev Far Caves (1109).**[72]

Through the intercessions of Thy Saints,
O Christ God, have mercy on us. Amen.

[70] Cf. Mt. 7:13.

[71] A *mufti* is a professional jurist who interprets Islamic religious laws.

[72] Saint Niketa is commemorated today at Novgorod, where his relics are located. He is also commemorated on the 31st of January, the day of his repose, and on the 30th of April for the uncovering of his relics in 1558.

On the 15th of May, the holy Church commemorates our venerable Father PACHOMIOS the Great.[1]

Saint Pachomios

Pachomios (Pachomius), our venerable father and colonizer of the wilderness, was born circa 290 in the Thebaid of Egypt. He was the offspring of parents who were idolaters—even as from the useless is born the useful, and from thorns the rose, and from the ill-smelling the fragrant. As a child, therefore, he was in obedience to his parents and venerated the idols in ignorance though he had an aversion to the profane ceremonies of the idolaters. On one occasion, when they passed over to the idol's temple in order to offer the profane sacrifice to the demons, Pachomios was in his parents' company. As they approached the unhallowed temple, the minister of the demons, pointing at young Pachomios, cried out as one demonized, "Drive out from the temple the enemy of the gods!" This charge grieved Pachomios' parents since

---

[1] The Greek Life of the venerable Pachomios survives in the Athonite monasteries of the Great Lavra, Iveron, and in other places. The manuscript begins, "True indeed is the common proverb." This text was rendered in simpler Greek by Agapios the Cretan, who included it in the work entitled *Kalokairine*. It is from that source that it was borrowed and presented in *The Great Synaxaristes* (in Greek), revised and edited. The hymns of the divine office to Saint Pachomios were excellently composed by the very erudite teacher Christopher the Prodromite. Another full service to the saint was that composed by the Monk Ioasaph, which is yet unpublished in codices of the Athonite Monastery of Kafsokalyvia. There are other versions of the Life in English. See "The First Greek Life of Pachomius," which is presented in *Pachomian Koinonia*, Volume One, of the Cistercian Studies Series: Number Forty-Five, trans. by Armand Veilleux (Kalamazoo, MI: Cistercian Publications, Inc., 1980). This text also contains the "Bohairic Life" and the "First Sahidic Life" in English. It is a three-volume set, in which Volume Two contains the "Pachomian Chronicles and Rules"; and Volume Three contains "Instructions, Letters, and Other Writings of the Saint and His Disciples." See also English anecdotes of the saint's life and times in: *The Paradise of the Fathers*, trans. by Ernest A. Wallis Budge, in two volumes (Seattle, WA: Saint Nectarios Press, 1978, repr.), *passim*; as well as *The Evergetinos*, trans. by Hieromonk Patapios, et soc. (Etna, CA: Center for Traditionalist Orthodox Studies), *passim*.

their son was deemed an adversary of what they held sacred. Their sorrow increased when, on another occasion, Pachomios was given to drink from the blood of the sacrifices. The child Pachomios partook and immediately vomited what he had drunk. This episode was related by Pachomios himself, which he recounted when he became a monk. He explained to the monks, who had gathered about him, that the demons, as ones wicked and horrible, perceive the manner and disposition of each one—even from the smallest acts. When they see the natural and unaffected soul and man's hatred of evil, they, as ones evil, try to foretell what the future might bring. Pachomios then said, "Do not even begin to think that the demons desired to cast me out because they knew I was going to receive mercy from God through the true Faith. Nay, they perceived that I hated evil even then; for 'God made man upright; but they have sought out many devices [Eccl. 7:29].' Thus, for this reason did the demons' minions chase me out, for they reasoned among themselves that I might become one who feared God afterward."

Life in the Military

When the young Pachomios reached the age of twenty, he was inducted into the military. Emperor Constantine, who had ascended the throne, had ordered many conscripts to be impressed. This was on account of his struggles against the impious tyrants and his dire need for substantial levies to build a great army.[2] Those drafted into the army were among the most courageous and manly of the young men. The recruiting officers enlisted Pachomios with other Egyptians, distinguishing them as ones suited for military service. The officers brought the new recruits to a location near to Thebes of Egypt. The men were placed under guard, as was commonly the practise, lest any should abscond. Now during the night, some Christians, as ones who loved both Christ and the stranger, went among the newly selected soldiers who were kept close confined. They gave the recruits food and drink lest they suffer distress inside the stockade. Pachomios marvelled at the compassionate sensitivities of those visiting men. The young Pachomios questioned those about him, "Who, pray, are these men who are ready to offer alms?" They, then, answered him and said, "They are those who believe in the Christ Who has promised to recompense in the future age, one hundredfold, all those who perform acts of charity in this world upon strangers and poor folk out of love to that One, that is, Jesus. These men are known as Christians, bearing the name of the only begotten Logos of God. They have put their hope in Christ Who made heaven and earth and us men; and so, in imitation of Him, they do good to everyone."

[2] It is suggested that Pachomios was pressed into military service for the war between Maximinus Daia and Licinius (313). From the details given in his life, we learn that he prayed for Saint Constantine's victory and that he never engaged in combat.

These words inflamed divine desire in Pachomios. He was favorably impressed with the magnanimity of the Christian Faith. He, thereupon, was enlightened in his mind and rejoiced in his spirit. He withdrew to the most quiet place in that detention camp. He raised up his hands and eyes, praying to that God Whom he did not yet know, and said, "O Lord, O Thou Who hast made the heaven and the earth, if Thou wilt look upon my lowliness and grant to me full knowledge of Thy wisdom and Thy divinity, I will become Thy soldier and Thy slave and keep Thy commandments until the end of my life." By means of these words he offered up prayer to the true and real God Whom, as we said, he did not yet know. Now when the time came for the troops to be moved from that site, Pachomios was transported with the others to the position assigned them. When they entered a certain city, they were given leave. It was then that some of the soldiers went about in a disorderly manner, seeking physical enjoyments. But the blessed Pachomios, took heed to how he comported himself. This is because from his youth, by nature, he loved prudence and continence. God also hearkened to the prayer of Pachomios who entreated the Lord to grant victory to the great Constantine. The emperor's triumph led to the discharge of the conscripts by imperial edict, as their service was no longer required. The regiment in which the blessed Pachomios served was called the *tagma*[3] of the Tyrones.

Pachomios Becomes a Christian

After his discharge, Pachomios returned quickly to his homeland. He, however, did not set foot into his parents' house. He forsook mother, father, siblings, friends, and fortune. He made haste to the Upper Thebaid, to a certain village called Chenovoskion (Chenovoskia or Seneset), the site of a church of the Christians. Pachomios entered that church and prostrated himself before the priest, confessing faith in our Lord Jesus Christ. Pachomios fervently sought to be initiated by holy Baptism. After he was vouchsafed that which he desired, that same night he beheld vision. He was standing in the road where an abundance of dew descended out of heaven that filled his right hand. He next observed how the moisture that collected in his palm crystalized and became as honey in the comb. He soon heard a voice that said, "Pachomios: understand that which thou seest, because it is in regard to a work that will produce change to the end." This experience, as one is able to surmise, portended the condition of the monastic life, which conduct Pachomios was about to follow. The righteous man, therefore, was enlightened by divine grace to adapt himself to austere but sweet asceticism, in the hope of a bountiful reward and for the sake of illumination by divine knowledge. As a result of this occurrence, the heart of Pachomios was further consumed by divine love and

---

[3] A *tagma* had from 2,000 to 4,000 soldiers.

the longing to become a monastic that he might pass his life quietly and unperturbed.

Life with Abba Palamon

Pachomios, therefore, upon hearing of the good fame of the hesychast Palamon, sped off to his cell that he might share with him the anchoritic life. As Pachomios knocked at the door, it opened and the elder exited. Palamon, with a severe and gruff tone of voice, asked, "What dost thou wish?" Now the elder spoke in this abrupt manner on account of the long years of isolation; for reclusiveness sometimes engenders harsh and abrupt manners. Pachomios, nevertheless, answered calmly and gently, "The Lord sent me forth that thou mightest make me a monk, because I am very desirous of this Schema of the monastics as something sacrosanct." But Palamon, as one wise and a man of experience, intended to put Pachomios to the test. The elder, therefore, said, "Go wheresoever thou willest, because here with me thou wilt not be able to submit to such labors and ascetic exercises with which I am engaged. Thou shouldest know that many others have come here, promising to remain, but they were unable to withstand the rigors and the regimen. They had not the strength for the strife. Also, be informed that during the summer months I partake of food once daily with a fare consisting of bread and salt only. During the winter season, I eat only every other day. As for oil and wine, they never touch my lips. I keep vigil for half the night, praying continually. Therefore, go and first see if thou canst endure such austerities and then return to me."

So spoke the elder to the young man in order to intimidate him by means of such hardships. Pachomios was surprised but not dismayed. Dauntless Pachomios, though he heard these toils enumerated, became even more eager. He, in no wise, gave any indication of withdrawal. He then said to the elder, "I hope in God and in thy prayers that I will readily observe all that thou didst tell me, O honorable father." Thus, Pachomios was retained at the monastery. It followed a coenobitic style of monasticism in all things, both in meals and ascetic practises. They were engaged in the making of hair sacks, that they might remember the poor[4] and give to those who came to them in that isolated wilderness. Pachomios was fervent in his prayers. Above all things, he entreated for purity of heart; so that being dispassionate from all secret attachment to creatures, he might love God with all his heart, soul, mind, and strength.[5] He strived to destroy the roots of all inordinate passions, seeking first to attain to profound humility, meekness, and patience. It was his habit to pray with his arms outstretched in the form of the Cross. Whensoever they felt that sleep was overtaking them, that they might keep awake for prayer, each one would take up a basket and convey sand from place to place. They did this until

[4] Gal. 2:10.

[5] Mk. 12:30.

they were overcome by harassing sleep deprivation. But ofttimes the elder would remark to Pachomios, "Keep vigilant, my child, that the adversary may not find thee asleep; for should he inflict a wound, thou wouldest be in danger of losing all thy toils." Palamon took notice of Pachomios' great obedience, for which he rejoiced and gave thanks to the Lord.

The young Pachomios was obedient to his elder and, without contradicting him, followed him with humility of heart in all of his preeminent and praiseworthy acts of austerity. Apart from other hardships to which Pachomios willingly submitted, he was often sent to a hill to gather wood. Since Pachomios used to walk barefoot, the thorns would pierce his feet like nails. Nevertheless, he endured this trial of suffering with joy, mindful of the nails with which they affixed our Savior's hands and feet to the Cross.[6]

Now on the day of the Feast of the Holy Pascha, Palamon said to Pachomios, "Today is the feast. Go thou and prepare a meal for us." After Pachomios boiled some vegetables, he poured a little oil on the dish. When they were about to taste the food, the elder detected the oil. Tears welled up in Palamon's eyes as he commented, "It was yesterday that my Master was crucified; and should I partake of oil today?" Pachomios begged the elder to eat, since it was the feast. The ever-memorable Palamon, nevertheless, would not accept. Consequently, they brought him another plate of vegetables without oil. Such was the abstinence preserved by the blessed Palamon.

On account of the holy Elder Palamon's extreme humility and discernment, he recognized the wiles of the demons. One night, as they were keeping vigil, a certain monk came visiting among them. When the visitor cast his eye on the charcoals lit for the vigil, he said to them, "Whosoever among you has faith, let him stand on these charcoals and utter the prayer given to us by Christ in the Gospel."[7] The old man, the Elder Palamon, knew that this monk was being lorded over by the demon of pride. Palamon, thereupon, in a brotherly manner, exhorted that monk not to mind such soul-injuring and vain antics. That monk, nonetheless, as one without sense, would not be benefitted by the counsels of the elder so as to repent of such demonic boasting and arrogance. Instead, he leaped onto the glowing charcoals with his bare feet. As he stood atop the burning charcoal, he recited the Lord's Prayer to the end. By demonic collaboration, he suffered no injury. He then removed himself from the fire, thinking that he had achieved some great feat. But the wretched one knew not that he was being consumed by another fire, that of pride, which was overturning his soul. That vain man departed in the morning, mocking the saints as those who were imperfect, and said, "Where is your faith?"

---

[6] This paragraph was taken from *The Evergetinos*, Volume III of The First Book, "Hypothesis XXXIII," p. 128.

[7] See Mt. 6:9 for the Lord's Prayer.

When the wicked demon, who delights in evil, was persuaded that the monk was engulfed in the darkness of pride and was entirely in captivity to this passion, he wished to cast him also into lawless fornication that he might better master him. The demon, therefore, transformed himself into a comely woman, fair of form. In this guise, the demon knocked at the cell door of that monk. In order to constrain that solitary to come forth, she said to him, "I owe money to certain men. These creditors are pursuing me to consign me to prison, for I have not wherewithal to repay them. Do thou let me hide here for a little while, until they have gone far from here." The monk believed the deceptive words of her story and let her, that is, the sinister demon, enter into his cell. The mindless monk did not consider the ambushes and the assaults of the hater-of-good. Why? Because a proud man is hurled down headlong into darkness.

The leader of licentiousness, thereupon, entered into the cell. He ignited such carnal warfare in him, that he ensnared the miserable man's heart. Thus, he entirely agreed to fornicate with the woman. As he drew near to her, the devil seized him and threw him down to the ground. That sorry man lay prone, as one dead, for a long while. For the demon entered into him completely, striking him and tormenting him until he left him out of his wits. Afterward, that is, with the passing of many hours, he finally rose up, as best as he was able, and understood his sin. He repaired to the venerable Palamon. Still trembling from his ordeal, he wept before the elder. He confessed his sin, saying, "I myself, the senseless one, O father, have become the cause of my own ruin. For even though thy holiness did wisely and prudently admonish me, I, the vain one, did not hearken. For this reason have I carried away together with me the fruits of my disobedience. But I beseech thee to help me, because I am in danger of being wasted by the demon." Having spoken in this fashion, the righteous Palamon and Pachomios, being sympathetic, wept. Meanwhile, the demon-possessed man leaped outside the door with a rapid and vehement motion forward, as though he were being goaded by a skewer. Under the demon's influence, he was drawn away and ran toward the mountain. When he arrived in a city called Panos (Smin in Coptic), he went inside a bathhouse. He then fell upon the hearth, where the unfortunate one was severely injured by the fire. This terrifying event served as an example for Pachomios and the others of the need for humble-mindedness in order to avoid the punishment that follows the lack thereof.

Thenceforth, there was rooted in the soul of Pachomios the fear of God. He did not retreat before, or surrender to, any passion. Instead, he produced the fruits of virtue. Such was his increase that the elder greatly marvelled, seeing that Pachomios surpassed him in the virtues inspired by God. He, therefore, permitted Pachomios to contest alone in whatsoever struggles the Lord wished to direct him. Pachomios, in those days, took himself away to a desolate place, named Tabennesi, in the diocese of Tentyra, between the Great and Little Diospolis. He spent many days in that isolated wasteland, sojourning in silence. While he was praying, he heard a voice from God commanding him to abide in that remote spot and build a monastery, for many were about to gather in that location and work out their salvation by means of him. The righteous Pachomios, distinguishing this command to be from God, went to the elder. He revealed to him the vision and sought acquiescence. The elder, indeed, went to assist him at the start when everything is difficult. When they built a *kellion*, or cell, the elder returned to his own little hermitage. They did, however, agree to visit one another from time to time, whensoever the Lord enlightened them, that they might converse and partake of the spiritual gifts of one another.

After a little while, Palamon succumbed to illness. He suffered from edema by reason of his eating habits, which had damaged his spleen. He, at times, ate bread without drinking water; and he, at other times, drank without eating any bread. He was advised to have done with such a hardy regimen lest he should die before his time. The thrice-blessed ascetic remarked, "If the holy martyrs persevered bravely, while being cut to pieces under iron instruments and being tormented with the twisting and wrenching of limbs, how should I now turn coward before a superficial bodily affliction and not endure a few bodily pangs? So should I prefer sumptuous fare and refreshment? But I was already persuaded to alter my diet, being assured that such a change would remedy the condition, and yet I have felt no improvement." The Elder Palamon, as a result, returned to the rigors of his previous abstinence. The blessed man courageously struggled with his gastric disorders. He fell seriously ill after one month. Pachomios was with him to the end, sitting at his side. After the holy ascetic was translated to the Lord, Pachomios committed his body to the earth; and, thereafter, he returned to Tabennesi.[8]

At Tabennesi with Brother John

At that site where Pachomios was toiling, his brother, according to the flesh, named John, came to him. He was older and bigger than Pachomios. After John became a monk, the brothers took up together the good struggle of asceticism with one purpose and will. They constructed cassocks (*rasa*), having only one garment each, in accordance with the Gospel command,[9] so that they had no second tunic while they washed the original. Pachomios, however, would also put on a hair garment to further mortify his flesh. Whatsoever they obtained from laboring at their handiwork, they gave the money to the poor. They only retained what was necessary for their meager sustenance. Pachomios did not take his ease on a bed. Instead, he would sit upon a small stool in the

---

[8] Saint Palamon is commemorated by the holy Church on the 12th of August.

[9] Cf. Lk. 3:11.

middle of the cell. He leaned against nothing. He was sleeping only for a little refreshment and when wearied after keeping a long vigil of watchfulness or undergoing hardships. In this manner did he conduct his life for some fifteen years, so that he became an example to many of how to humble the body for the redemption of the soul.

But the righteous Pachomios remembered the voice from on high. He brought to mind the words spoken to him, charging him to build a monastery. Therefore, in concert with his brother, he began construction. Now John, on the one hand, planned to erect something small, because he did not wish to usher in much disturbance; Pachomios, on the other hand, intended to design a large-scale facility. Pachomios was mindful of the words he heard that many monks would collect there. For this cause, the brothers had a slight contention between them. On account of their opposing endeavors, John wrongly insulted Pachomios. He accused Pachomios of being conceited and putting on airs. He told Pachomios that his idea was nonsense and silly talk. Pachomios, as a man, was offended. Nevertheless, as one sober-minded and virtuous, he endured the affront and kept silence. That same night, however, Pachomios reproached himself and said, "Woe is me, the wretched one! How a single utterance scandalized me and made me angry, after so many ascetic labors. Have mercy on me, O Lord, for I have not yet mortified my flesh! But rather have I become the slave of the enemy, the paltry one. How shall I teach others meekness when I myself have not attained to it?" He chided himself with these and many other self-recriminations throughout that night, weeping and extending his arms in prayer. He did not rest that hot summer night, but wept and perspired so that the ground under his feet turned to mud. With such humble-mindedness and meekness was the blessed man adorned.

Warfare Against the Demons

Not much time passed before John fell asleep in the Lord, leaving Pachomios to struggle alone as earlier. The demons harassed him ofttimes, teeming with schemes in an attempt to frighten him that he might depart from that ascetical retreat. Thus, whenever Pachomios was about to do his rule of prayer (*kanona*), there appeared before him an apparition. He seemed to find himself before a deep pit. The enemy presented such a sight to him in order to prevent Pachomios from taking a kneeling position in prayer. The righteous man, nonetheless, recognized the knavish trick. Pachomios, therefore, proved to be a pertinacious opponent of the adversaries so that he increased the number of full prostrations. His *kellion*, on one occasion, was made to shake and tremble for a long time so that the building was ready to collapse on top of him. At another time, the demon transformed himself into a cock and kept crowing in his face. At yet another time, the demons marched in front of him, hither and thither, as though they were escorting some great commander. They shouted to one another, "Make way for the man of God!" On another occasion, the demons, using a long post as a lever, comically attempted to lift one leaf on a tree. They feigned failure that they might provoke a laugh from the venerable man. But the man of God paid no attention to any of their pranks. In another instance, they took on the guise of naked women who began sitting next to him as he ate. He, however, would not lift his eyes to them or show any interest in them. He kept constant in prayer, reciting the psalm of David that begins with these words: "Let God arise and let His enemies be scattered...[Ps. 67:1]."

When the demons saw that he was invincible against their apparitions and phantoms, they were filled with wrath. One night, therefore, they came and administered a fierce thrashing. They smote Pachomios from the first hour of the night until dawn. Consequently, he fell gravely ill and lay abed. Let no one marvel why God permits the demons to strike the saints; for by these trials, the saints become more perfect. They gain experience of temptations and trials. The all-wise One dispenses these chastisements, even as it occurred to Job[10] and to Anthony[11] and to a multitude of holy men. Again, by these tests and tribulations, they become more perfect as wrought gold. So speaks Job of God: "For He knows already my way; and He has tried me as gold [Job 23:10]."

During the time that the righteous one found himself bedridden, he received a visit. There came to him a certain ascetic, named Ierakopollon. He was an active and practical hesychast, who exhorted him in this fashion: "Play the man, my child, and do not cower before temptations. For if the demons think that thou art frightened, they will do even worse things against thee. If, however, they should see that thou givest them no consequence, they will retreat and leave thee at peace." The Elder Ierakopollon remained as Pachomios' companion, that is, until he reposed and was buried by the righteous Pachomios. Henceforth, Pachomios remained untroubled by the enemy. He tread upon serpents and scorpions,[12] without suffering the least harm. When it was needful, he crossed the river sitting on the back of a crocodile. He dwelt in harmony with wild beasts, living and associating with them fearlessly and without incurring any injury. He also received from God the gift of discernment, so that he knew the divine will. He besought God regarding the matter of sleep: he desired that he should no longer require sleep that he might pray unceasingly and bring low the might of the enemy. This free spiritual gift was vouchsafed him for a considerable time—even as it was to the great Anthony.[13]

---

[10] Righteous Job is commemorated by the holy Church on the 6th of May.
[11] Saint Anthony the Great is commemorated by the holy Church on the 17th of January.
[12] Cf. Lk. 10:19.
[13] See E. A. Wallis Budge, *Paradise*, Volume I, "On Reading, Vigil, and Prayer," p.
(continued...)

He, therefore, prayed amply and with all his soul, so that as it is written "blessed are the pure in heart, for they shall see God [Mt. 5:8]," so it was with Pachomios that God was visible to his mind's eye, as it were, seeing the invisible God in a mirror.[14] As many more brethren arrived and became his fellow ascetics, imitating his conduct of life, he received each one with joy. Afterward, however, seeing that many cares and concerns confounded him and that he no longer had solitude and quiet, as before, he was ruminating upon which of two modes of conduct was the more God-pleasing: keeping silence as a solitary or protecting the brethren and standing at their head. He continued entreating God to give him assurance concerning this.

The Koinonia

Then an angel of the Lord came and said to the venerable Pachomios: "The will of God is that thou shouldest serve thy brothers, O Pachomios, and, as much as thou art able, keep peace among them that they may have love toward that One and toward one another." Having spoken thus, the brethren that came multiplied; "for it is by a favor from God that there appeared upon earth the holy Koinonia,[15] by which God made known the life of the apostles

---

[13](...continued)
24, ¶ 108.

[14] "The First Greek Life of Pachomius," ¶ 23, *Pachomian Koinonia*, Volume One, p. 311; Budge, *Paradise*, Vol. I, "On Reading, Vigil, and Prayer," p. 25, ¶ 108.

From the hymns to the saint, we also read that he was raised above all things of sense and perception, purely conversing with the Master, having passed far beyond the flesh, for his valiant mind conquered passions and trampled upon the demons' audaciousness. [May 15th, Vespers Sticheron, Mode Plagal Two]. Saint Theophanes, who composed the Orthros Canon, chants that Pachomios acquired a heart exceedingly pure and was vouchsafed to behold Jesus. [Ode Seven, Mode Two.]

[15] Koinonia (pronounced Keenonia) is the name given to all the Pachomian coenobiums (coenobia), though the word in Greek literally means communion or association—thus giving us an image of the Church's eucharistic congregation. The term, however, herein, is also used to characterize the manner of life in the Pachomian monasteries. Derwas J. Chitty notes that "the whole community is called in the *Vita Prima* [G1] coenobium (in the singular) or koinonia. The use of the term coenobium died out very early: the Coptic Lives always replace it with koinonia. In Jerome's introduction to the 'Rule' (A.D. 404) and in his translations of the 'Letter of Theodore' and the 'Book of Horsiesius,' and even once in the 'Paralipomena,' coenobia is used in the plural of a number of monasteries. But it seems to be found in Cassian's account [*Inst.* IV.1], where it makes credible his numbers for the Tabennesiotes—more than five thousand brethren under one abbot. Palladius, in his *Lausiac History* (A.D. 420) [*H.L.* c. 32(93.8)] gives the total numbers of the community as seven thousand in his own day, and three thousand already under Pachomius." *The Desert a City*, pp. 24, 25.

Rodolph Yanney, M.D., in his article "Monastic Settlements in Fourth-

(continued...)

to those who desire to follow their model forever before the Lord of all. Indeed the apostles left all[16] and, with all their heart, followed Christ. They stood steadfast with Him in His trials. They shared with Him in the death by the Cross, after which they deserved to be seated on the twelve thrones and to judge the twelve tribes of Israel."[17] Now, it was necessary that the Koinonia have the wisest leadership and governance. The angel, again, appeared and instructed Pachomios sufficiently in the order to be followed, that is, how they should proceed, as will appear in subsequent points in this writing.

The venerable man, thereupon, was enlightened by all that he heard from the angel. Pachomios accepted each man that came to him. There were those who came of their own will, as well as those who were brought by their parents. Pachomios, for his part, did not immediately tonsure them to the monastic state. But rather, he first put the novices to the test. He was teaching them to disdain attachment to properties, possessions, money, glory, honor, love of parents, the will of the flesh, and all that follows upon these desires. He especially taught them that they should preserve obedience to the superior and that they should take thought with regard to guiding their own wills as by bit and bridle—a virtue in which all other virtues are enclosed. By these means and similar other methods was he exercising and training them beforehand, that is, prior to making them monks and giving them the Schema. That most wise man served and ministered alone, with much diligence and wonderful eagerness. He provided for all the needs of the brethren that they might not be deprived of a single necessity lest, from a lack of essentials, they should dishearten.

---

[15](...continued)
Century Egypt," writes: "Saint Pachomius was the first monastic founder to transform the invisible wall between the ascetic tradition and the world into a visible entity. We owe to him the change of the meaning of the word 'monk,' literally a solitary, to one associated with a community and not a hermit living in seclusion. The Pachomian monastery wall facilitated the control of the monks within, while it limited access to outsiders including family members, neighboring farmers, and invading barbarians. Pachomius has succeeded in creating a koinonia of the Spirit sharing the common prayers, meals, and labor, while its members were bound together by an obedience to one father, which was understood as a way of obeying the heavenly Father. A significant number of his rules and customs remain in use in religious communities now both in the East and in the West." *Coptic Church Review*, Vol. 6, No. 2, Summer 1985, p. 43.

[16] Mk. 10:28.

[17] Mt. 19:28; Lk. 22:30. This succinct quote regarding the appearance of the Koinonia on earth was made by the saint's disciple, Abba Theodore, in "Instruction Two," *Pachomian Koinonia*, Volume Three, Cistercian Studies Series: Number Forty-Seven (Kalamazoo, MI: Cistercian Publications Inc., 1982), pp. 91, 92.

"In this Schema shall all flesh be saved, O Pachomios."

Even though he had mortified his flesh, no detail was beneath his notice. He prepared the meals. He watered, collected, and soaked the vegetables. If someone knocked at the door, it was he who answered. If anyone was ill, Pachomios nursed them at night. Since he perceived that the newcomers were not yet disposed to serve each other, he took on the work himself and freed them from all care.[18]

So much toil did he expend upon his disciples and such love did he show them that they all marvelled. Seeing such care and devotion, they honored and revered him as a tender and affectionate father who loves his children. As much as his disciples were able, they strived to emulate Pachomios in serving one another. On one occasion they dared to pose the following question to him: "Why, father, dost thou toil alone, serving us, the unworthy ones, with such

[18] "The First Greek Life," ¶ 24, p. 312.

labors and hardships?" The venerable man answered, "Whatever I do, it is so that you do not neglect spiritual matters. It is my hope that you pray resolutely with all your soul and assiduously perform your rule of prayer. Believe me, I am not better than the Master Christ Who ministered to His apostles.[19] Therefore, even as thou seest my example, you ought to do the same. Maintain love in the brotherhood by helping one another as much as you are able."

As for me, let me ask you something first: "What man yokes his beast of burden to the water wheel and then walks away, neglecting the creature until it should fall from exhaustion? I believe you know the answer. And so it is with our merciful Lord. I know He looks upon my poverty. Either He will strengthen you or He will bring others who can help in the care of this monastery."[20]

Now, among the brethren, there was a youth named Theodore. He had come to the monastery as a small child (ca. 328). He was one who exceedingly imitated the excellences of Pachomios. It was he whom Pachomios loved more than the others for his virtues, treating him as a genuine son.

Therefore, as time passed, more and more brethren gathered at Tabenna. The good fame and perfections of Pachomios drew them, even as a magnet attracts steel. Once again, the angel of the Lord descended. This time, while he was in his cell, he gave the venerable man a writing-tablet of copper.[21] It was in the shape of a small slab upon which was written the following words: "Thou shalt permit each one to eat, drink, and work, according to one's strength. This means that as many of those who are able-bodied, let them eat and work more. As many of those who practise quiet and are at rest and abstain from food, do not hinder them from such asceticism; but also build the *kellia* (small monasteries) accordingly, having them dwell together three by three. Let the meals be taken in common. Let them sleep in seats that support their heads, but they shall not lie down. Also have their loins girded with belts. Upon their

---

[19] Cf. Jn. 13:5-15.

[20] "The First Greek Life," ¶ 25, p. 313.

[21] D. J. Chitty notes that "before a hundred years had passed, Palladius (ca. 365-425) [*H.L.* c. 32 (88-89)] was giving the story of a brazen tablet delivered by the angel to Pachomius at the beginning, with the rule inscribed upon it. Early 5th-C. Sozomen [*H.E.* III.14.9] goes further and says that the tablet was still preserved. But the rule which Palladius then gives seems certainly to belong to a later stage in the development of the community. It has little direct connection with the surely genuine rule (though we cannot be sure that even this represents Pachomius' own rule unaltered), which survives in Jerome's (ca. 342-420) Latin translation of a Greek version [*Pachomiana* Latina (ed. Boon), pp. 3-74, 155-168] and in fragments of the Coptic original. This last one bears every sign of being a gradual accretion of *ad hoc* rule to be fitted into a framework of daily life...." "The Institution," *The Desert a City* (Crestwood, NY: St. Vladimir's Seminary Press, 1966), p. 21.

heads, let them wear cowls (*koukoulia*) signed with a Cross of red. Divide the community into twenty-four classes,[22] each of which is to be distinguished by one of the letters of the Greek alphabet, starting with Alpha (A) up to and including Omega (Ω). Arrange the men under the letter that is in accordance with their condition and situation. For example, the simpler ones place in Iota (I), and the more difficult ones in Ksi (Ξ); and do for the others in like manner. According to their disposition, so let each have a fitting cognomen. No order is to accept the monk of another monastery. As for those secular men who wish to become monks, they are to be tested for three years. When the brethren dine together in the refectory (*trapeza*), let them cover their heads with the *koukoulia* lest they should gaze upon one another and converse." These counsels and much more were written upon the tablet, the one that Pachomios received from the angel. Thus, he governed the brethren according to the divine command.[23]

---

[22] *Tagmata*.

[23] Church historian Salmaninius Hermias Sozomenus of Palestine, who was a lawyer at Constantinople, in his *Ecclesiastical History*, writes: "Pachomios was the founder of the monks called the Tabennesians. The attire and government of this sect differed in some respects from those of other monks. Its members were, however, devoted to virtue. They contemned the things of earth, excited the soul to heavenly contemplation, and prepared it to quit the body with joy. They were clothed in skins in remembrance of Elias. It appears to me that they were so clad because they thought that the virtue of the prophet would be thus always retained in their memory. Thus, they would be enabled like him to resist manfully the seductions of amorous pleasures and to be influenced by similar zeal and to be incited to the practise of sobriety by the hope of an equal reward. It is said that the peculiar vestments of these Egyptian monks had reference to some secret connected with their philosophy, and did not differ from those of others without some adequate cause. They wore their tunics without sleeves, in order to teach that the hands ought not to be ready to do presumptuous evil. They wore a covering on their heads called a cowl, to show that they ought to live with the same innocence and purity as infants who are nourished with milk, and wear a covering of the same form. Their girdle, and a species of scarf, which they wear across the loins, shoulders, and arms, admonish them that they ought to be always ready in the service and work of God. I am aware that other reasons have been assigned for their peculiarity of attire, but what I have said appears to me to be sufficient.

"It is said that Pachomios at first practised philosophy alone in a cave, but that a holy angel appeared to him and commanded him to call together some young monks and to live with them. For he had succeeded well in pursuing philosophy by himself. He was told that he was to train them by the laws which were about to be delivered to him. He was to guide and benefit many as a leader of communities. A tablet was then given to him, which is still carefully preserved. Upon this tablet were

(continued...)

---

[23](...continued)
inscribed injunctions by which he was bound to permit each one to eat, to drink, to work, and to fast, according to one's capabilities of so doing. Those who ate heartily were to be subjected to arduous labor; and the ascetics were to have more easy tasks assigned them. He was commanded to have many cells erected, in each of which three monks were to dwell. They were to take their meals at a common refectory in silence, and to sit around the table with a cowl over their head, so that they might not be able to see each other or anything but the table and what was set before them. They were not to admit strangers to eat with them, with the exception of travelers, to whom they were to show hospitality. Those who desired to live with them were first to undergo a probation of three years, during which time the most laborious tasks were to be done; and by this method they could share in their community. They were to clothe themselves in skins, and to wear linen tunics and girdles. They were to sleep in their tunics and garments of skin, reclining on long chairs specially constructed by being closed on each side, so that it could hold the material of each couch. They were to be provided with skull-caps without any nap upon them. Each skull-cap was to have in the front thereof a cross worked in purple.

"On the first and last days of the week they were to approach the altar for the communion in the holy Mysteries, and were then to unloose their girdles and throw off their robes of skin. They were to pray twelve times every day and as often during the evening; and they were to offer up the same number of prayers during the night. At the ninth hour they were to pray thrice; and, when about to partake of food, they were to sing a psalm before each prayer.

"The whole community was to be divided into twenty-four classes, each of which was to be distinguished by one of the letters of the Greek alphabet; so that each might have a cognomen fitting to the grade of its conduct and habit. Thus the name of Iota was given to the more simple, and that of Zeta or of Ksi to the difficult or perverse; and the names of the other letters were chosen according as the purpose of the order most fittingly answered the form of the letter.

"These were the laws by which Pachomios ruled his own disciples. He was a man who loved men and was beloved of God. He was vouchsafed the gift of foreknowing future events. He was frequently admitted to intercourse with the holy angels. He resided at Tabenna, in Thebais, and hence the name Tabennesians, which still continues. By adopting these rules for their government, they became very renowned. As time proceeded, they increased so vastly that they reached to the number of seven thousand men. But the community on the island of Tabenna, with which Pachomios lived, consisted of about thirteen hundred; the others resided in the Thebais and the rest of Egypt. They all observed one and the same rule of life; and they possessed everything in common. They regarded the community established in the island of Tabenna as their mother, and the rulers of it as their fathers and their princes." See *The Ecclesiastical History of Sozomen*, Bk. III, Ch. XIV, Nicene and Post-Nicene Fathers, Second Series, II:291, 292. See also Budge, *Paradise*, Vol. I, "The Rule of Pachomius," pp. 144-146.

At one point, the angel commanded that during each day they should repeat twelve sections of the Psalter, and during each evening twelve sections of the Psalter, and during each night twelve sections of the Psalter, and that when they came to eat they should repeat the great psalm. The blessed Pachomios said to the angel, "The sections of the Psalter which thou hast appointed unto us for repetition are far too few." The angel said to him, "The sections of the Psalter which I have appointed are indeed few, so that even the monks who are weak may be able to fulfill the canons and may not be distressed thereby. For unto the perfect no law whatsoever is laid down, because their mind is at all seasons occupied with God; but this law, which I have laid down, is for those who have not a perfect mind. So that although they fulfill only such things as are prescribed by the canons, they still can acquire openness of face."[24]

After the numbers kept growing, Pachomios deputed the material cares of the community to others. To the various monasteries there were annexed infirmaries, hostels, and other indispensable structures.[25] He appointed stewards and attendants, in accordance with the number of brethren. This is because in the first or main monastery there were one thousand three hundred inhabitants, while the others had less. In all the monasteries, those built by Pachomios, there were seven thousand monastics. In this multitude of brethren there were to be found representatives of all the trades. For instance, there were ten calligraphers, fifteen tailors, a proportionate number of gardeners and

---

[24] This paragraph on the recitation of the Psalter is taken from Budge, *Paradise*, Vol. I, "The Rule of Pachomius," pp. 145, 146.

[25] D. J. Chitty notes that "the general plan of the monastery may be reminiscent of the military camps Pachomius would have known as a soldier. There was an enclosing wall (one of the marks of a coenobium), a gate-house and guest-house, a synaxis or assembly hall for worship (not called an 'ecclesia' except in the *Letter of Ammon*); a refectory nearby, with kitchen, bakehouse, etc.; a hospital; and a number of houses (cf. barrack-blocks in a legionary camp), holding between twenty to forty monks each. The plan of a house is never clear, but it must have included a common-room—for prayer and instruction and any other communal activity of the house—storerooms, and originally separate cells for each monk. By Palladius' time, with the increase in numbers, there were three monks to a cell. This is the arrangement found, for instance, in the ruins of Saint Simeon's Monastery at Assuan. In the Pachomian system, however, the monks reclined on chairs of plastered brick or similar material. Each house had its own house-master and second. Some houses were devoted to particular trades or services of the monastery, others to less specialized work. Three houses would undertake in weekly rotation the daily routine of the monastery, which had as its head or father a steward (*oikonomos*) with a second in support. Agriculture was undertaken outside the walls. The dead were buried in the old rock-cut tombs a few miles away, where the valley meets the mountain." *The Desert a City*, p. 22.

cobblers, and craftsmen from each occupation, all of whom were governed by the wise and righteous Pachomios with much discretion.[26] He was wont to teach them that which was profitable to the soul and for their salvation. His words were so sweet and salutary that even speaking but once with him proved not only beneficial for the listener but also difficult for him to depart from Pachomios.

The saint also had a care for other people, secular folk who were shepherds, in the surrounding regions. He desired that they, too, might hear the word of God. On the advice of Bishop Serapion of Nitentori,[27] he built a church. He went with some of the monastic brethren and read to the shepherds on Saturdays and Sundays. Pachomios not only read with much reverence, guarding his mind, eyes, and mouth, but also undertook the expenses for their gatherings, until a priest was finally appointed for the parish. [28]

At that time, the Patriarch of Alexandria, Athanasios the Great,[29] at the beginning of his episcopacy, desired to go to the Upper Thebaid, up to Aswan, that he might comfort the flock of his great see. He needed to go through

---

[26] "There were living in that mountain about seven thousand brethren, and in the monastery in which the blessed Pachomios himself dwelt there were living one thousand three hundred brethren; and besides these there were also other monasteries, each containing about three hundred, or two hundred, or one hundred monks, who lived together. They all toiled with their hands and lived thereby. Each day those whose week of service it was rose up and attended to their work; and others attended to the cooking, and others set out the tables and laid upon them bread, and cheese, and vessels of vinegar and water. And there were some monks who went in to partake of food at the third hour of the day, and others at the sixth hour, and others at the ninth hour, and others in the evening, and others who ate once a day only; and there were some who ate only once a week; and according as each one of them knew the letter which had been laid upon him, so was his work. Some worked in the orchard, and some in the gardens, and some in the blacksmith's shop, and some in the baker's shop, and some in the carpenter's shop, and some in the fuller's shop, and some wove baskets and mats of palm leaves. Accordingly, one was a maker of nets, and one was a maker of sandals, and one was a scribe. Now all these men, as they were performing their work, were repeating the psalms and other Scriptures in order. Moreover, there were there large numbers of virgins who were nuns, and who closely followed this rule of life. They came from the other side of the river and beyond it. There were also married women who came from the other side of the river close by." Budge, *Paradise*, Vol. I, "The Rule of Pachomius," p. 146.

[27] The Coptic name of Nitentori (Gk. Tentyra) is the diocese to which Tabennesi belonged.

[28] "The First Greek Life," ¶ 29, pp. 316, 317.

[29] Saint Athanasios the Great (b. 295, patriarch from 328, after which followed five depositions and exiles, until his repose in 373) is commemorated by the holy Church on the 18th of January and the 2nd of May.

Tabennesi. The brotherhood went forth and greeted the patriarch with joy and the chanting of psalms. It was during this visit that the Bishop of Nitentori, whom we just mentioned, requested of the young patriarch that Pachomios be set over all the monks in his diocese as father and priest. Pachomios learned of his bishop's petition and hid.[30] Pachomios looked from afar upon Athanasios, as the latter traveled by boat, and perceived him to be a slave of God. The patriarch blessed him with the entire brotherhood, marvelling at them all. Pachomios supported the same theology as Athanasios, loathing the blasphemous doctrines of Origen and Arius. He ordered his disciples not to read any of these writings. He so revered the Orthodox bishops that he estranged himself from those who denounced them and right-believing doctrine.[31]

The righteous man had a sister, named Mary.[32] When she heard from many people that her brother was such a very great holy man, she went to see him. He, however, did not wish to set his eyes upon her. He sent word to her by means of a message to the doorkeeper: "Be not grieved that thou hast not seen me. It suffices that thou hast learned that I am well. If thou dost wish to be garbed in this holy Schema, I will gladly build a nearby convent so that other women, as nuns, might come and join thine assembly (*synodia*). I speak thus because the one who in this world does not do any good before death, such a one has no hope of salvation; inasmuch as we shall all be judged after death. Then shall each receive the recompense for one's deeds." He then said to her, "Indeed, one experiences no other satisfaction on earth except that one does good and that which is pleasing to God."[33] When Mary heard these words, she wept and deemed the world hateful. Consequently, Pachomios tonsured her a nun. On her account, then, he built a convent close to his own monastery. By and by, a multitude of women gathered at that convent; and the numbers kept

---

[30] D. J. Chitty notes that "in the early stages, when they needed a Eucharist, Pachomius would call in a priest of one of the neighboring churches. He did not wish any of the brethren to seek ordination—for 'the beginning of the thought of love of command is ordination.'" *The Desert a City*, p. 23.

[31] "The First Greek Life," ¶¶ 30, 31, pp. 317, 318.

In the Orthros Canon for Saint Pachomios, who was of like mind with the great Athanasios, we learn from the hymnographer Saint Theophanes that the most blessed Pachomios possessed an Orthodox mentality, proclaiming a Unity three in number and a Trinity one in essence. He taught the awesome incarnation of the Logos and hymned the Theotokos as the Ever-virgin. [Ode Seven, Mode Two.] He also chants that Pachomios acknowledged the coessentiality and divinity of the Trinity, proclaiming Christ begotten before the ages of the unoriginate Father. [Ode Eight].

[32] The sister's name is given in "The Bohairic Life of Pachomius," ¶ 27, p. 49.

[33] This last line of advice was found in *The Evergetinos*, Volume II of The First Book, "Hypothesis XV," p. 75.

growing.[34] Mary was the hegumene (abbess) over all of them. Pachomios accommodated the nuns by sending forth a venerable priest-monk. He was an old man, reverent and sober, named Peter. He was in the habit of teaching the nuns and elucidating monastic order with all exactness. Pachomios had written down for the sisters the rules of the brothers, which he sent by the old man Peter, that the sisters, too, might govern themselves by the same statutes. Now the convent was also surrounded by a wall. None of the nuns ever exited. No stranger ever gained admittance inside. Whensoever a nun had a visitor—only kinfolk—then the nun would go to the gate accompanied by a superioress or another deputed as her guardian. Only a few words, with great discretion, were exchanged. If the visitor was one of the brothers, who had not yet reached perfection and wished to visit his mother or sister among the nuns, such a brother made arrangements through the old man Peter. Only in the presence of another sister would they be allowed to speak briefly, being mindful to forget at the same time their kinship according to the flesh.

Saint Theodore

In the monastery of Pachomios there were many brethren. No one, however, attained to the virtues of the aforementioned Theodore—the saint's disciple. Let us, also, say a few words about his wonderful and divine accomplishments. His parents were affluent and pious. He showed religious tendencies, fasting and praying, before he reached adolescence. He entered a monastery in the Nome (province) of Latopolis when he was but fourteen years of age. The ancient fathers of his monastery were good models of piety. It was not long before he heard of the great old man, Pachomios, and his shining virtues. Theodore, therefore, repaired to Tabennesi. When Pachomios first saw him, he accepted him into the monastery. Pachomios knew, immediately, by the grace of the All-Holy Spirit, what this youth would later become. The venerable Pachomios kept Theodore close at hand, rejoicing in the lad's progress. Pachomios loved and esteemed him above the others, because he saw how he possessed absolute obedience.

After a time, Theodore's mother heard that her son was directly under Pachomios' supervision. She, out of motherly affection and exceeding love for her son, conceived the desire to see him. She, thereupon, arranged to secure letters from certain bishops. They were addressed to the righteous Pachomios, wherein they requested him to hand over the boy to his mother. The mother, armed with the letters, first went to the convent where she received hospitality. She, thereupon, dispatched her servants to convey the episcopal letters to Pachomios.

---

[34] According to *The Evergetinos*, there came to be four thousand sisters. Volume III of The First Book, "Hypothesis XXVI," p. 53.

The venerable Pachomios read the letters. He gave Theodore permission to meet with his mother, but the young man replied, "O father, shall I become a source of stumbling for the brethren and provoke the Lord to anger for a mother's love? From the moment that I renounced the world, I no longer had a mother or brethren. Instead of them, it is conspicuously fitting to prefer the Master Christ more than anything in the world. So I have neither mother nor anything in this transient world save Christ." Pachomios, hearing these words, both marvelled and praised Theodore. Pachomios then remarked, "Since thou hast preferred, with such knowledge and such prudence, the Master Christ above thy mother, I laud thy saving judgment; inasmuch as our Lord Jesus Christ Himself determined this and said: 'The one who loveth father or mother more than Me is not worthy of Me [Mt. 10:37].' Furthermore, the bishops, the ones who wrote to us, shall also rejoice when they hear thy God-loving opinion." When the mother of Theodore heard that her son would not come out to see her, she no longer returned to her own house. Much rather, she remained with the virgins and said, "I shall abide, then, in this soul-saving convent, so that once in a while I might see my boy. In the meantime, I, the miserable one, might even gain my soul." However, let us, for the present, leave the account of Theodore that we might return to that of the renowned Pachomios.

An Unruly Element

Now before the brotherhood increased to a multitudinous degree and the rules were not as yet enforced, some of the men that joined Pachomios still kept alive the old man[35] and the carnal mind.[36] It became evident that not all the brothers had the fear of God. Despite the many times that Pachomios exhorted and admonished them for their correction, they disobeyed. They kept on their own self-appointed path and grieved the elder. This was no small grief to the man of God. One day, he went apart and prayed privately. He prostrated himself before God and entreated Him regarding these brethren, saying, "O God, Thou hast commanded us to love our neighbor as ourselves.[37] Do Thou look upon these souls and have mercy on them. Inspire them in the fear of Thee and in the proper knowledge of the life of a monk, so that, as the other brethren, they may place their hopes in Thee." After uttering this heartfelt prayer in their behalf, Pachomios still perceived that they did not want to follow him as their elder; instead, they continued to oppose him. Pachomios, therefore, brought to bear upon them the rules of the synaxis (assembly) and the other rules. When those disobedient brethren of his first group of disciples finally realized that Pachomios was not going to let them have their own way,

[35] Col. 3:9.

[36] 1 Cor. 3:1, 3, 9; 9:11.

[37] Lev. 19:18; Mt. 19:19.

they withdrew in fear. Indeed, after their withdrawal, the remaining brethren grew as wheat does when the darnel is rooted up.[38]

Some Miracles of Saint Pachomios

A certain woman, the wife of one of the councillors, who was dwelling in that neighborhood, suffered from a flow of blood. She found no physicians who could cure her of her hemorrhagic episodes. She besought a favor from the steward (*oikonomos*) of the Tentyra, one named Dionysios, who was a confessor and deeply virtuous man. Dionysios was also a genuine friend of Pachomios. She knew this and asked Dionysios to invite Pachomios to the church on the pretext that he, Dionysios, wished to consult with him on some important matter. When Pachomios came to the church and sat down with Dionysios, they began conversing. In the meantime, the infirm woman drew close to Pachomios. With her hand, she gently touched the venerable elder's cowl. Straightway—behold the wonder!—she was completely healed of her disorder, even as she had believed with all her soul.

Hearken at this time, you pious listeners, to another more marvellous miracle. A man had a daughter who was enlisted in the rank of the virgins. Since she was possessed by a demon that dashed against her, the father appealed to the righteous man and begged him to heal his daughter. Pachomios, however, did not engage in conversation with any woman. He said to the father whose daughter was suffering, "Bring here a piece of her clothing that has been washed." The father obeyed and brought back a garment. The righteous man, as he looked at the garment, remarked very sadly, "Thy daughter is only a virgin in name but not truly. Say to her that if she should preserve herself undefiled at least from this time henceforth, then also would the merciful God return her to health." The father then went to his daughter, interrogating her until she divulged her sin. After confessing her error, she promised never to fornicate again. As for the great Pachomios, he sent forth to her some sanctified oil. After she anointed herself, the demon also took flight.

In another instance, a man had a demonized son. He brought the boy to the righteous one, seeking a cure. Pachomios, beholding the sufferer, gave the father blessed bread and said to him, "When thy son is hungry, give him to eat of this bread." The father agreed to do according as he was bidden. But when the boy became hungry and his father offered him the blessed bread, he would not taste it. At other times the father disguised morsels of the bread in other dishes that the boy might partake without realizing it. But he discovered the fragments of bread and isolated them from the rest of the food. The father then left the boy without food for two days. At the end of that period, when the boy was weak, the father prepared a sauce with oil and aromatic spices. He also

[38] "The First Greek Life," ¶ 38, p. 324.

cast in particles from the blessed bread. The boy ate of the dish and—lo, the wonder!—the demon fled from him that very hour. Thus, his health was completely restored.

These and many other miracles were wrought by God through the saint. The blessed Pachomios in no wise was vainglorious. Much rather, he was saying that God worked these wonders to the advantage of His slaves. For this cause, he was diligent about not acting on his own will but that of the Lord. He was even teaching this practise, that is to say, that we ought not to do our own will but that which is commanded by our fathers and teachers. That most wise man was saying that the therapy of the soul is more useful and beneficial than that of the body. He also counseled the following for consideration. Let us say that thou shouldest see someone who is careless, negligent, heedless, and who does not work that which is good, but thou, by thy teaching, shouldest make him eager to perform that which is good. Let us say that thou shouldest bring an idolater to piety, or a pitiless person to a state of compassion, or one who is proud to humility, or a harlot to sobriety. Are such works any less beneficial to them than if they were paralyzed and thou hadst bestowed healing upon the body? Although the Lord performed many acts of healing through the man of God, upon both those living in the monastery and those in the world, still there were times when he prayed for a petitioner's health and the Lord did not grant the request. Pachomios was neither taken unawares nor dismayed. His prayer to the Lord was always prefaced with the very words of the Lord: "May Thy will be done, not mine."[39]

A Monk Seeks a Certain Office

Now the blessed Pachomios was also very long-suffering and meek. He never was irascible or wroth. He never remembered wrongs nor bore grudges. Attend presently to the following account. In one of the Pachomian monasteries there dwelt a certain monk who sought a particular ministration from the hegumen. The abbot believed the task of steward to be above that monk's power and ability, for he knew the weakness of his subordinate. For this reason, he deemed it not prudent to place upon him this ministration. Since the monk was audacious, the hegumen wished to avoid being troubled by him. The hegumen, therefore, told him that it was the venerable Pachomios who did not permit him to be placed in the ministration which he was seeking. That shameless monk took hold of the hegumen, demanding that Pachomios prove what he said against him. The monk dragged the hegumen until they came before the righteous man who, at that moment, was building a wall. The hegumen wondered how this affair would end, since Pachomios knew nothing of the matter. That monk, catching sight of Pachomios, was overcome by

[39] Lk. 22:42; Mt. 6:10; 26:42.

anger. He began shouting up at Pachomios, who was on the wall, saying, "Get down here, thou liar, and tell me why I am not worthy of the steward's office for which I sought. Give me proof of my unworthiness." The venerable elder, however, kept silence. The insolent monk waxed bolder and continued, saying, "Thou canst find nothing in thy defense, canst thou? Thou callest thyself a clairvoyant, yet thou art a liar and blind too!" Pachomios, who knew nothing of what that angry monk was complaining about, gave answer in this fashion: "I have sinned. Do thou forgive me, child. Hast thou never made a mistake?" With these words of self-recrimination, that unreasonable monk's wrongful anger was abated. The elder then left off his work and came down from off the wall. He then privately spoke to the hegumen of the monastery, who, weeping and brokenhearted, disclosed the matter. The hegumen owned that the ministry was beyond the monk's worth. "This brother," the hegumen continued, "does not listen to me, so I used thy name to put him off since we know thou hast the gift of clairvoyance; but I did not expect him to lose his senses and revile thee, O righteous father." Pachomios reflected upon what was said. He gave his opinion to the hegumen, believing it to be the will of God. "Grant that monk the office which he sought," said Pachomios. "Peradventure, he will alter his judgment and become good lest the poor man come to condemnation. For ofttimes, the bad man, when he is the recipient of a benefaction, becomes better. Hence, we shall receive a reward since we saved our brother. This, too, is how God demonstrates love on the undeserving; so let us, also, with long-suffering, bear with one another in love."[40] Indeed, in accordance with the saint's word, this is what happened in reality. The monk who received the steward's office perceived his own foolishness. His evil disposition was conquered with good,[41] and he too admitted as much. With tears in his eyes, he hastened to Pachomios. In gratitude, he fell before his feet and declared, "I thank thee, O man of God, for on account of thy profound magnanimity and kindness, thou hast vanquished my audacity and my rashness. Moreover, if thou hadst punished me, even as I deserved, I, the wretched one, would have turned away from the monastic life."

The Vision of Future Monks

One day, when the brethren went to the island to cut the rushes used for plaiting ropes and mats, Pachomios accompanied them. While they were sailing in a fishing-boat, the elder beheld a vision in a state of ecstasy according to which he beheld monks. Some were surrounded by fire and could not pass through, while others were walking barefooted over thorns that pierced their feet but they found no way out. There were also others who were perched halfway on a sheer cliff. They could neither climb up the steep precipice nor

[40] Cf. Eph. 4:2.

[41] Cf. Rom. 12:21.

dive into the river below that was filled with crocodiles ready to swallow them. Beholding these scenes, the righteous man revealed the vision to all. While he was in this state, the other brethren took notice of his altered countenance. In their concern, they dropped their work and prayed alongside him. Although he spoke of what he had seen, still they waited until they returned to the monastery to ask him to explain the meaning of the vision. This was the venerable elder's answer: "After my repose, I believe that such predicaments will come upon you, since you will not find anyone competent to shepherd you with diligence and self-denial and with the right consolation needed to comfort you in your afflictions." Thus, the brothers wept with great fear.

Conversation Misunderstood

There was an occasion when a certain anchorite came to visit the great Pachomios. As the two were conversing on spiritual matters, Pachomios said to Theodore, "I should like thee to prepare something special to eat for our visiting brother." Theodore then went outside and sat down, for he thought he heard Pachomios tell him, "I should like especially to speak privately to our visiting brother." Since no food was forthcoming, Pachomios espied the steward passing by and asked him for the same thing that he requested of Theodore. But the steward also went his way, thinking the great man wished to be alone with the visiting anchorite. Still no food was brought out for Pachomios' guest. The great old man, watchful in spirit as he was, discerned that some temptation was afoot. Instead of summoning someone else to bring food, Pachomios himself prepared a meal for the anchorite. After the anchorite partook and departed, Pachomios inquired of Theodore, "If thy father according to the flesh were to ask thee for something, wouldest thou ignore him? I think not. So why wouldest thou not prepare food for our visiting brother?" Theodore, surprised at what he was hearing, replied, "Believe me, father, I thought thou didst bid me leave that thou mightest speak privately with thy guest!" Pachomios then asked the steward why he disappeared after being given an order. He, too, said the exact same thing as Theodore. Hearing the separate testimony of these two fathers, Pachomios sighed and remarked, "Verily, an evil spirit created this annoyance in order that we might be vexed before our guest. But blessed be the name of the Lord Who gives patience,[42] prudence, and sufferance!" He then told the others that they, too, from what took place, ought to exercise forbearance when under provocation.[43]

Out of the Mouths of Babes

In those days, the venerable man commanded Theodore to teach the brotherhood. Even though Theodore was a young man, yet according to purpose, thought, judgment, and good sense, he was more sagacious than the

[42] Is. 57:15.

[43] "The First Greek Life," ¶ 72, p. 347.

Christ Flanked by Saint Pachomios On His Right and Saint Theodore on His Left

old timers. The young man, on that command, stood up, though unwillingly, and spoke as the Lord enlightened him. But some of the old men walked out of the synaxis and retired to their cells. As for Pachomios, he stood and listened to every single word. After the talk given by Theodore, the venerable Pachomios questioned those old men why they abandoned the teaching and departed without permission. They answered, "Why dost thou place a child to teach the elders?" The righteous man sighed and said, "Woe to you, the wretched ones! For inside of one hour you have suffered damage to all of your labors by reason of your pride and arrogance, for which Lucifer also fell.[44] Have you not heard the Scriptures wherein it is written that 'the proud in heart is unclean before God [Prov. 16:5]'? Have you not heard these passages which declare 'that which is exalted among men is an abomination before the face of God [Lk. 16:15]' and 'whosoever shall exalt himself shall be humbled [Mt. 23:12]'? So why were you vexed? On account of his age? Did not our Lord say that 'whosoever shall receive one such little child in My name, receiveth Me [Mt. 18:5]'? You have not deserted Theodore, but rather have taken yourselves away from the word of God and have deprived yourselves of the grace of the Holy Spirit. You, therefore, have a great judgment upon you. Did not God so humble Himself, O wretched ones, for us who are useless earth and who exalt ourselves? The One Who is above all and most glorious is able by only His glance to enlighten all the world, but He saved us, who are worms filled with vainglory, by means of His abasement. Did you not see how I remained standing, listening

[44] Is. 14:12.

reverently? Believe me, I did not feign attention when he spoke. I truly was benefitted by his words; but you, as mindless ones, left the congregation.[45] If you do not repent of this transgression, you shall all go to perdition; for 'the Lord is nigh unto them that are of a contrite heart, and He will save the humble of spirit [Ps. 33:18].'"

These and many other admonitions were delivered by the venerable Pachomios who put those elders under a penance. Furthermore, he appointed Theodore steward of the great monastery at Tabennesi. Abba[46] Pachomios stayed in the Great Monastery called Phbow, where the administration of all the coenobia were subject.[47] Theodore, at that time, was thirty-four years of age. Though a young man, he had mortified all the passions of the flesh. While he was assigned to the office of monastery steward, it was as if he had not been. This is because in regard to his own will, it was as if it did not exist. Indeed, the word of God had made Theodore fervent. It strengthened him to such a degree that he minded only those heavenly good things. All of his endeavors and studies and heart were dedicated to divine love and to the salvation of the brethren. Actually there were many other men of merit whose names must be passed over, designedly, for the sake of brevity.[48] They, too, observed every rule and order of the Schema. They were conspicuous, also, for their self-mastery and temperance. Such was the severity of their fasting that whensoever they succumbed to illness, even then they did not dare to drink wine or recline on a bed for some small bodily relief. No, indeed, they abided until their repose, sitting at their benches, as the thrice-blessed strugglers that they were.

The Monk Silvanos

There was among the brethren one named Silvanos. He spent twenty years at the monastery. Formerly, when he was living in the world, he had been a mime. When he became a monk, he was restored to reason and conducted himself with discretion and self-control for a long time. Later,

---

[45] *The Paradise* describes the scene further: "Theodore spake unto them concerning the things which were to be employed as helpers, but made no mention of not stumbling. And some of the aged sages who saw what had taken place did not wish to listen to him, and they said within themselves, 'What he is teaching us is for novices, and we need not listen unto him.' And they left the congregation of the brethren. Departing from that place, they went to their cells." See Budge, *The Paradise of the Fathers*, Vol. I, "The Rule of Pachomius at Tabenna," p. 283, ¶ 1.

[46] Either abba or apa signifies "father" herein.

[47] Ca. 336-337: Theodore becomes steward at Tabennesi and Pachomios settles at Phbow.

[48] Those men of merit included "Cornelios, Psentaesi, Sourous, Psoi, Pecos, another Pachomios, Paul, John, Paphnutios, and many others (Titoue, Jonas). Pachomios saw the life of each and he appointed most of them as leaders and fathers of the monasteries." "The First Greek Life," ¶ 79, p. 351.

however, when he brought to mind his previous art, he lost his hard-won moderation. He began eating unsatiably, telling jokes and jesting, and singing ribald songs he used to hear in the theater. The venerable Pachomios, thereupon, seeing this backsliding, was sorrowed for that brother's loss. Many were the times that Silvanos received blows for his unmonastic behavior, so that he might come to his senses and strive for his salvation.[49] But Pachomios toiled in vain, for Silvanos was in no wise persuaded to correct himself. One day, when the saint was oppressed by him and could hardly bear it, he announced in the presence of all the brotherhood the following: "Did I not tell thee, when thou didst begin as a novice, that the monastic life is heavy and wearisome? Did I not say to thee that thou wast not able to endure? But didst thou not promise before God and man that thou wouldest preserve the order of the Schema? Why, then, dost thou disdain thy soul, O miserable man? Why dost thou not bring to mind the day of the Judgment? Why dost thou prefer everlasting punishment to the heavenly kingdom? Go, therefore, to thy parents and do not dare to return here anymore."

After the blessed man spoke in this manner, he commanded that they strip Silvanos of his monastic garb. He was to be clad in secular clothes and cast out of the monastery. Silvanos, prostrating himself at the venerable elder's feet, besought him with tears and said, "Forgive me, father, and do not chase me away. I promise before God to make such a repentance that thou shalt

---

[49] *The Paradise* describes the scene further: "And the holy man answered and said unto Silvanos, 'Dost thou know how much I have borne from thee, and how many times I have admonished thee, and how many times I have beaten thee? I am a man who has no wish to stretch out my hands in a matter of this kind; because when, of necessity, I was obliged to act thus in respect of thee, my soul suffered far more....I beat thee for the sake of thy salvation in God, so that by that means I might be able to correct thee of thy folly. But since even though I admonished thee and entreated thee and beat thee, thou didst not change thy course of life and didst not follow after spiritual excellence and didst not have fear, how is it possible for me to forgive thee any more?' But when Silvanos multiplied his entreaties, and begged for forgiveness long and earnestly, and promised that he would amend his life henceforward, Pachomios demanded a surety from him." See Budge, *Paradise*, Vol. I, "The Rule of Pachomius at Tabenna: Sylvanus the Actor," p. 285, Ch. II.

The Evergetinos has Pachomios saying, "Thou knowest well how many things I put up with in thee, even to the point, many times, of striking thee—something which I have never done to any other man. Indeed, I have never even reached out my hand to another person. But in thy case, I was compelled to use physical force, which caused more pain to me than it did to thee since we are linked through spiritual compassion. Besides, I used this severe measure for no other reason than for thy salvation, so that at least in this way I might be able to correct thy faults." Volume IV of The First Book, "Hypothesis XLIV," p. 95.

rejoice whensoever thou seest me." Pachomios then remarked, "Thou knowest how many times I, for thy salvation, endured thee and exhorted thee and beat thee in order to correct thine error. And it pained me—as God is my witness—more than thee when I, as thine affectionate spiritual father, was scourging thee. If, then, when admonished, thou art neither set aright nor afraid of the rod, how shall I believe thee on this occasion, O thoughtless one?" Silvanos implored the venerable elder to pardon him for the sake of the mercies of God. He promised never to err again in the future. Pachomios said, "Provide me with a guarantor in order to keep thee."

They, consequently, brought forward a virtuous elder named Petronios.[50] It was he who had elected Silvanos when he became a monk. Petronios became surety for Silvanos then and, again, now, before the venerable Pachomios. In this manner did the man of God retain him in the monastery. Afterward, Pachomios privately advised Petronios and said, "We know that thou hast toiled many years in asceticism. But do thou take this labor upon thyself for the sake of thy spiritual child. Sympathize with him and struggle along with him until he should be saved, because I have the concerns of the many and I cannot find the time." Petronios took charge of Silvanos and worked together with him at the handicraft of making rush-mats. They also fasted and prayed together, as was meet. Henceforth, Silvanos submitted to his elder in all things, so much so that he would not even partake of a vegetable leaf without the determination of the elder. Such was the degree of humility and meekness obtained by Silvanos that he would neither lift his eyes to anyone nor open his mouth to speak. He was constant in keeping vigil, praying, and making prostrations. He slept very little at night and, again, only sitting in the midst of his cell.

But why speak at great length? The marvellous Silvanos became a worthy slave of God and an elect vessel. He rendered, at that time, such a contest for the salvation of his soul that he became for all an example and outline of every virtue and piety. He especially shone forth in humility. Tears were never absent from his eyes after this divine transformation. Moreover, what little food he consumed, the thrice-blessed man soaked with his falling tears. When the brethren cautioned him not to weep before the faces of strangers, he replied, "Believe me, brothers, many times I wished to cease weeping but I was unable." The brethren then began to say, "Brother, when thou art alone in the church or in thy cell or in another place, weep as much as thou art able. But when thou findest thyself with other people, hold back thy tears lest thou shouldest be judged as one vain and a hypocrite. For it is

[50] Psenamon is the name given in "The First Greek Life," ¶ 104, p. 369.

possible for the soul to weep without an outward show of tears. Nevertheless, tell us, during the time that thou art weeping, what art thou reckoning?"

The blessed Silvanos began to say to them, "I see that you holy men minister to me, the fornicator and babbler, who is not even deserving to wash your feet, for which I fear that the earth might open and swallow me up as it once did Dathan and Abiron.[51] Because it seems only yesterday that I vexed you and put myself in danger of being driven out as an apostate of the holy Schema. I am not able to contain my tears because I am thinking about the everlasting fire into which I, the shameless one, shall be condemned if I do not perform deeds of virtue and the analogous repentance according to the lawless acts which I committed." Hearing this deposition of himself, the great Pachomios rejoiced and assured the entire brotherhood with these words: "You should know that there is only one thrice-blessed one found among us who preserves with exactness the monastic conduct of life as it properly should be. For even as white wool is dyed to costly porphyry, and the color can no longer be washed out, thus it is with the soul of our thrice-blessed brother who has been tinctured by the Holy Spirit; for the Spirit's grace is not made away with or obliterated." Among those who heard these words, some thought that the elder was talking about Theodore but others thought Petronios or Orsisios (Horsiesios or Orsiesius).

Theodore and the other notable monks inquired of the saint to reveal the identity of the one whom he praised. Pachomios answered, "I truly know that such a one, worthy as he is by his virtuous deeds, is not about to become vainglorious; but rather, as one who is humble-minded, he will reproach and reprove more so that of which I shall speak. For this reason, I should like you to know his identity that you, too, might imitate his manners and ways. Furthermore, I want you, Theodore and the others, who have struggled in the monastery, to know that though you are his fathers and seniors in years and ascetical contests that still he is greater and surpasses you all in humility and purity of conscience. Indeed, you have fettered the devil as a sparrow and, moreover, you have trampled upon him daily as dust under your feet. But if you are even slightly unmindful, waxing bold that you have vanquished him completely, he will escape from under your feet and rise up and war against you again.

"Now as for Silvanos who is younger," continued the righteous Pachomios, "whom we wanted to expel on account of his unwholesomeness and negligence, he has set at nought the demon by reason of his excessive humble-mindedness. He has so reduced the demon that he can no longer raise up any warfare against Silvanos. Silvanos, with all his soul and mind, believes

---

[51] Num. 16:1 ff.; Deut. 1:6; Ps. 105:18.

himself to be useless, unprofitable, and unfit. This is not a false humility. He is convinced that he is a worthless person and unworthy of all of us. For this cause does he have a ready supply of tears. You, on the one hand, by means of knowledge, patience, and other struggles have thrown over the devil. Silvanos, on the other hand, by means of humble-mindedness, has soared to the heavens. And you will not be able to overtake him, because not one virtue can so debase and lay low the devil as that soul completely possessed with humble-mindedness existing together with knowledge, action, and discretion." It was in this manner, therefore, that the blessed Silvanos, striving for eight years after his marvellous and hallowed transformation, reposed in peace. He treaded the godly path and fought the good fight in the Lord. The great Pachomios testified, in fear of God, that he beheld a numberless multitude of holy angels who took along Silvanos' blessed soul with enormous joy and indescribable chanting. They escorted his soul to God, as a choice sacrifice and fragrant incense.

A Lukewarm Monk's Funeral

At another time, when the great Pachomios was going to another monastery to visit the brethren, there happened to be a funeral. The dead man was being carried on a bier around the monastery, accompanied by chanting. The righteous man, however, ordered them to strip the deceased and to burn his garments. Only one man in a private station was charged to bury the corpse, without any chanting. The heads of the monastery and the relatives of the deceased fell on their knees before the righteous man's feet, begging him for leave to at least chant the hymns. But Pachomios did not wish it. The parents of the dead monk then shouted at the holy man, weeping bitterly and saying, "Why dost thou demonstrate such cruelty, crudeness, and lack of compassion toward one dead man, O compassionate one? What barbarian, seeing his enemy dead and silenced, is not softened in his heart? Would that this our wretched son had never been born into the world rather than have thy holiness come hither today and bequeath unto us such sorrow and shame upon our family name which has ever possessed an untarnished reputation!"

The saint responded calmly and gently, "Believe me, brethren, I have more compassion for him than you, even as an affectionate father providing for his salvation. But, according to his deeds, it is not permitted to bury him with a funeral service. And if they chant hymns for him, his soul shall go down further into punishment; and he shall curse you. Indeed, if you chant for him, he will receive more punishments to account for the psalms; for he departed this life without having with him the power of the psalms. So, if you would add to his everlasting sorrows, continue chanting in his behalf. But I warn you, he will then suffer more pain and curse you. If I bless you to chant psalms, I shall be found before God as a man-pleaser; because in order to gratify you, I did not perform that which was to his soul's advantage. God seeks pretexts which He can seize to pour forth on us the streams of His grace. I entreat you to withhold chanting that his punishment may be lightened. God, Who is good, knows how to release him because of this dishonor inflicted upon him and to call him again to life.[52]

"For the most compassionate God is an unfailing spring of goodness and He seeks from you this small offering, in order to supply the streams of His merciful charity and kindness. For this cause, it is needful that we, the spiritual physicians, prescribe the medicine according to the condition. I, therefore, beseech you to listen to my speech that we might ransom the dead from future punishment. Many a time did I admonish and advise him, but he would not give ear." Thus, they hearkened to the word of the righteous man: they left the dead to be buried without the accompaniment of the chant. This did the most wise Pachomios do not only for the sake of the dead man's salvation but also for the living, that they might come to have the fear of God and conduct their lives in a virtuous manner. Pachomios tarried a few days in that monastery, instructing the brothers for their own good.

The Departure of the Soul of an Ill Monk at Chenovoskion

While Pachomios was at that monastery, a message came. He received word from the Chenovoskion Monastery that one of the brothers was gravely ill. The sufferer desired to receive the blessing of Pachomios. The venerable man, thereupon, moved forth immediately. After he walked some two miles, he heard a divine voice. He gazed intently heavenward and beheld the soul of that brother, the one who invited him to his bedside. But now he was being escorted into the heavens in the company of holy angels chanting. Those who were present and walking with the saint neither saw nor heard anything. They, therefore, were saying to him, "Why hast thou halted, father? Let us make haste that we might overtake him before he departs to the Lord." The righteous

---

[52] This paragraph is borrowed from the "Paralipomena," Ch. 3, ¶ 6, of the *Pachomian Koinonia*, Volume Two, Cistercian Studies Series: Number Forty-Six (Kalamazoo, MI, 1981), p. 27. The "Paralipomena" are the chronicles of events omitted in some books. Together with the Lives of Pachomios, there is in Greek a series of anecdotes known as the "Paralipomena." There are many indirect witnesses to this text. Various Greek Lives have either completely or partly integrated them. Papebroch published the "Paralipomena" in his *Acta Sanctorum* along with "The First Greek Life" from the Florence manuscript. In the *Sancti Pachomii Vitae Graecae*, F. Halkin used the Ambrosian fragments as well. There is also a Syriac translation from the 6th C. found in the *Paradise of the Fathers*. The translation used by Veilleux is based on Halkin's critical edition of the Greek text ["Les Vies Grecques de S. Pacome," *Analecta Bollandiana* 47 (Brussels, 1929), 376-388; and "L'Histoire Lausiaque et les Vies Grecques de S. Pachome," AnBoll 48 (1930), 257-301]. All the Greek Lives, except G1 and G4, have incorporated the "Paralipomena" to a different order and extent.

Pachomios remarked, "That brother has reposed; and I see him now going forth into Paradise. Let us, then, return to the monastery." Then they importuned Pachomios to recount the vision. When they returned to the monastery, they inquired the precise time that the ailing brother fell asleep in the Lord. They discovered that it was the exact time that the righteous one had witnessed the vision.

Heretics Visit Saint Pachomios

Certain travelers entered into the monastery. Saint Pachomios saluted them with the brethren. After they had seen all the brotherhood and had taken a tour round about, Pachomios spoke to them alone in a chamber. While he was in their presence, there came to the elder a strong smell of uncleanness; but he knew not whence came such a rank odor, though he thought that it must arise from them because he was speaking with them face to face. He observed that their speech was fruitful and that they were familiar with the sacred Scriptures. When the ninth hour arrived, the travelers rose up and said they needed to be on their way. Pachomios invited them to partake of some food, but they declined the invitation.

After they departed, Pachomios went to his cell and entreated God that he might learn the reason for the foul stench. He knew, then, that it was the doctrine of wickedness which arose from their souls. That was the cause of the unclean smell. He, therefore, made haste out of his cell and pursued those travelers. When he had overtaken them, he said, "I beg of you to allow me to ask you one question." They encouraged him to continue. He said to them, "Do you call that which is written in the works of Origen heresy?" They answered plainly, "We do not deem his works heretical." Consequently, Pachomios remarked, "Behold! I take you to witness before God that every man who reads and accepts the work of Origen shall certainly come to the fire of Sheol, and his inheritance shall be everlasting darkness. That which I know from God I have made you to be witnesses thereof. I am, therefore, not to be condemned by God on this account; and you yourselves know about it. Lo, I have made you to hear the truth! And if you should believe me and wish to please God, then take all the writings of Origen and cast them into the fire; and never seek to read them again." After Abba Pachomios admonished them in this fashion, he departed from them.[53]

Saint Pachomios' Complaint About the Future State of Monks

Pachomios, at another time, was in church praying from the ninth hour until Orthros. He was entreating God to reveal to him the condition and attitude of future brethren; that is to say, he was desiring to learn the disposition and

---

[53] See Budge, *Paradise*, Vol. I, "The Rule of Pachomius at Tabenna: of the Revelation Which Abba Pachomius Received from God Concerning Certain Heretics Who Happened to Visit Him," pp. 292, 293, Ch. VII.

virtue of the monastics that would come in the future. At the hour of midnight, he beheld a light as brilliant as lightning. He came into a state of ecstasy and heard a voice saying that the number of monasteries would multiply in all the world. The monastics would conduct their lives in piety, but they would not be so virtuous. Upon hearing these revelations, it seemed to the righteous man that he viewed an arid valley, wherein a deep pit held a numberless multitude of monastics. The monastics appeared to be walking quickly, but due to the darkness, they fell one upon the other and did not recognize one another. Some of them were trying to ascend to the top, but they were unable. Even after exercising much labor, they kept falling backward. But there were others, as many as were near the upper part of that gloomy valley, that kept falling down headlong onto the slope. There were even others, though very few, who were exiting that pit with much toil and trouble. When they reached the top, they found the light. They entered inside the light and gave thanks to the Lord.

From this vision did the righteous Pachomios know the state of the monks that would come afterward. He foresaw those times of absolute supineness and the blindness of error. He perceived that those future monastics would be careless in performing good things. They would not make progress and they would not have good shepherds. Their superiors would be unworthy and foolish, not providing for the salvation of their subordinates. Much rather, they would be accumulating monies and properties. They would be satisfying their own bad desires. They would dominate and limit the simpler ones by means of force, in a manner tyrannical. The good and humble-minded would have no license of speech or action whatsoever in the monasteries.[54] The great

---

[54] It was revealed to him that monastics would live in the same way with devotion according to Christ and that there would be the future expansion of the monasteries. "But he saw also a numberless multitude of brothers journeying along a deep, parched valley. Many of them wanted to come up out of the valley, but were unable. Many came face to face with each other because of the great darkness that shrouded them, but they did not recognize each other. Many fell down through exhaustion, and others cried out with a pitiful voice. A few of them were able with much labor to force their way out of that valley. As soon as they came up, they were met by light; and coming to the light, they gave thanks to God heartily. Then did the blessed man know what was going to happen to the brothers in the end and what negligence there would be in those times: the great hardening and error, and the failing of the shepherds which was going to affect them. Those who are the most negligent today shall rule over the good, vanquishing them by their number. These things—the beginnings of which we, who are writing, have gone through—are only an example; for bad men shall rule the brothers and those without knowledge shall have control of the monasteries and shall fight for rank. The just shall be persecuted by the wicked, and the good shall not live in the monasteries with confidence; and, as it is said, divine things shall be changed to

(continued...)

Pachomios was roundly grieved by those revelations, so that he cried out to the Lord and said, "O Lord, Ruler of all, if, in the future, those things that Thou hast revealed to me should come to pass, why hast Thou permitted that there be coenobia? Have I, therefore, toiled in vain and been tormented unseasonably? Remember the travails of the brethren who with all their souls have humbled themselves for Thy name's sake. Do Thou bring to remembrance, O Lord, that Thou hast promised me that my spiritual seed should not fail until the consummation of the age. Thou knowest, O Master, that from the moment that I donned the Schema of the monk, I have not taken my fill of either bread, or water, or any other good thing of the earth."

Upon speaking these words, he heard the Master's voice saying to him, "Art thou boasting, O Pachomios? Seek forgiveness lest this speech be reckoned as swelling or elevation on thy part, because all things have been dispensed by My mercy." Pachomios then fell to the ground, seeking forgiveness and saying, "Send down upon me Thy mercy, O omnipotent Lord!" As he was praying, he beheld two angels standing near him. In the midst of the angels there was a young Man. His countenance and aspect were very wonderful and indescribable. He bore upon His head a crown of thorns.[55] The angels then spoke and said, "This is the only-begotten Son of God, the One sent into the world on account of His boundless love for man; it is He Whom you crucified."

Pachomios then said to the young Man, "I pray Thine immaculate nature, Master: it was not I who crucified Thee." The young Man, relaxing His face a little in a smile, said to Pachomios, "I know that it was not thee but your fathers who crucified Me. Take courage, O Pachomios, for the root of thy spiritual seed shall not ever fail; and thy seed shall be preserved upon the earth until the end of time. Those few men who will want to be saved in the last days shall have a bountiful reward that will be equal to that of the choice ones of thy day. Indeed, those few who are going to be saved from the abundant darkness of those latter times shall be found above those who practise a very great ascesis[56] now. For they have thee as a teacher and a lamp before their eyes, and they practise ascesis, counting on the example of thy light. But if those who shall come after them—even though they dwell in a parched land that has no share in virtue and they have no guidance from anywhere other than their own good intention—depart from the naughtiness of falsehood and come to the truth that they may live virtuously, verily I say to thee: they shall be placed in the

---

[54](...continued)
human." "Paralipomena," Ch. 9, ¶ 17, p. 39.

[55] Mt. 27:29.

[56] Ascesis, literally meaning ascetical exercise, entails rigorous training, self-discipline, and self-restraint.

same class as those who now conduct themselves blamelessly and faultlessly. Hence, they shall receive in return for their little labor a rich reward."[57] After the Lord spoke these words, He ascended into the heavens. The righteous man then abided in a state of astonishment and silence! When the brothers assembled for Orthros, it was after the dismissal that Pachomios gave competent and considerable instruction on how they should give heed with respect to the salvation of their souls. He reminded them that the present life is short lived and cut short, and its toils are temporary; but the life to come is everlasting and its good things are most delightful and inexpressible.

The Monk Who Wished to be a Martyr

In another district there lived a most distinguished and virtuous ascetic. He had heard of the angelic life of Pachomios, so he came to him and besought him to enroll him in the coenobium. The righteous Pachomios accepted him into the brotherhood. After that ascetic sojourned a while with the brethren, he conceived the desire to suffer martyrdom for the Lord's sake. Regarding this issue he often begged the righteous Pachomios to permit it. In those days, it was a time of peace. The Church, by the grace of God, was thriving in serenity. This was during the reign of the blessed and Christ-bearing Constantine the Great. The venerable Pachomios, however, would not give his consent for martyrdom. Pachomios, instead, exhorted the ascetic to exercise prudence as he was experienced. He said, "Brother, inasmuch as there are no idolatrous emperors, but rather the most pious Constantine, what is compelling thee to seek the labor of martyrdom? Be patient and persevere in the struggle of asceticism; and do thou, indefatigably, observe the commandments of the Lord. Thus, thou shalt be numbered with the saints in the kingdom of the heavens." Such was the edifying counsel of the knowledgeable Pachomios. But that senseless ascetic would not be persuaded that he could achieve companionship with the martyrs in the way outlined by the elder. In fact, he daily troubled the righteous man to allow him to pursue his wish. Again, Pachomios kept shutting that man's mouth by saying, "Brother, be on thy guard lest the devil deceive and mislead thee; then, instead of undergoing martyrdom, thou shouldest become a denier of the Christ and fall into destruction and perdition. Be mindful of what we pray daily, I mean those words of the Lord Himself: 'Be praying not to enter into temptation [Lk. 22:40].'"

[57] The "Paralipomena" has: "If they run from the darkness and pursue righteousness with a good mind and on their own accord, with no one to guide them to the truth, verily I say to thee that they shall be found with those who now practise ascesis—greatly and blamelessly—enjoying the same salvation." Ch. 9, ¶ 18, p. 40.

After two days,[58] the righteous man dispatched two monks into the upper parts of the village that they might collect rushes for the mats. Since there were many rushes on the island, the fathers were delayed in returning to the monastery. The holy Pachomios sent the above ascetic, the one desiring martyrdom, to bring them some provisions loaded on a donkey. Before he left, Pachomios spoke to him these prophetic words from Scriptures, which were replete with mystical signification for that monk: "Behold, now is an acceptable time; behold, now is a day of salvation—by not giving even one cause of stumbling in anything, that the ministry might not be blamed [2 Cor. 6:2, 3]."

When that ascetic arrived in the desert, he discovered that some Blemmyes[59] were also in that place. Those barbarians had come down from the mountains in search of water. They caught sight of the ascetic and bound his hands, taking his donkey and goods. Then those savages brought that father to their comrades. They sported with him, saying, "Come, O monk, and worship our gods." But soon their mockery turned to coercion. After they slaughtered some animals and began making libations to their senseless idols, they tried to force him to sacrifice to the demons. He, however, at first resisted. After they finished offering sacrifice, they turned their swords against him. He yielded when they threatened to slay him if he did not offer sacrifice to the idols. He cowered before their threats and a temporal death. He preferred at that moment to fall under divine judgment; and so he poured out the libation and offered the very donkey that he led there. That useless and unprofitable servant, casting aside the Master Christ, then partook of the meat of the sacrificial victim. Following this, since he would not accept remaining with them, they let him go. As he was coming down the mountain, he felt the burden of his iniquity; or rather, he sensed his ungodliness. He, thereupon, rent his cassock. He smote his face and started running back to the monastery, weeping and lamenting.

By divine grace, the venerable Pachomios was informed of the matter. Pachomios went forth, very grieved, in order to meet him. When he who had renounced Christ saw the saint coming, he fell on his face to the ground. He cried out, saying to Pachomios, "Father, I sinned against heaven and before thy

---

[58] The "Paralipomena" records that this episode took place "two years later." Ch. 5, ¶ 9, p. 30. See also "The First Greek Life," ¶ 85, pp. 355, 356.

[59] The Blemmyes, half-naked warriors, rode swift horses and camels. They were a pagan and warlike society, perhaps of Libyan Berber origin. They dwelt in the eastern desert between the Nile and Red Sea in Upper Egypt. Diocletian, in 297, ended their raiding parties, by giving them the territory south of the First Cataract and by fortifying the island of Philae. *The Oxford Dictionary of Byzantium*, s.v. "Blemmyes." For the perils and martyrdoms suffered by the holy fathers at the hands of these tribesmen, see also *The Great Synaxaristes* (in English) for the days of: the 16th of May; the 14th of January; and the 16th and 20th of March.

holiness.[60] I did not hearken to thy good advice!" The righteous elder then said, "O how hast thou been deprived of many good things, O miserable one! How wast thou robbed of the crown of martyrdom? The Master Christ was there, present, with the holy angels. In His right hand was the crown of victory, ready to be placed on thy brow if thou hadst been patient and let the barbarians cut thee up. However, thou wast afraid of death which, in any case, will come to thee tomorrow though thou shouldest be unwilling. But instead, O mindless one, thou hast chosen for the sake of an hour, to renounce the most sweet Master. Thou hast lost, therefore, everlasting life; and thou hast inherited unending punishment. What happened to thy desire, the one which thou hadst, to receive martyrdom?" While the venerable man was speaking in this manner, that wretched denier wept with all his heart and said, "I have sinned, father. I am unable even to lift up my eyes to the heaven.[61] I have lost the hope of my salvation."

After the saint spoke these words among others to him, he urged him to repent. The righteous man then said, "On the one hand, thou, O wretched one, hast become utterly alienated and estranged from God; but, on the other hand, the Lord is very merciful and all-good. He is able to sink our iniquities[62] in the sea of His compassion; for He does not desire the death of the ungodly, but that the ungodly should turn from his way and live.[63] On account of this do not come to despair. For if thou shouldest listen to me, thou shalt have hope of salvation. 'For there is hope for a tree, even if it should be cut down, that it shall blossom again, and its branch shall not fail [Job 14:7].' In like manner, by means of obedience, thou shalt be able to return to thy former state." That weeping penitent, with a great voice, cried out, "In all things will I obey thee, abba, from this very moment; and I promise not to depart any longer from whatsoever thou shouldest command me." Consequently, the venerable father had him withdraw to a quiet cell. He charged him not to hold a conversation with anyone. He partook once every two days of dry bread and water. He was to keep vigil in prayer, as much as he was able. He was assigned to plait two palm-leaf mats per day. He was directed that his eyes should not be dry of tears for even a moment. That brother, therefore, did as he was charged and even more. He doubled his efforts, eating only twice weekly. As for conversation, he spoke to no one save Pachomios and the sanctified Theodore and a few of the other great old men. This was permitted lest he should lose his mind from the isolation. He wept over his transgression every day and kept at his rule, by

[60] Cf. Lk. 15:21.
[61] Cf. Lk. 18:13.
[62] Mic. 7:19.
[63] Ez. 33:11.

the grace of Christ, for twelve years. He, after this time, departed to the Lord with good hopes even as the great Pachomios testified to Theodore.

Pachomios is Taught by a Boy

At another time, while Pachomios was weaving a mat at Tabennesi, a boy who was doing the weekly housekeeping service in the monastery came by. He looked upon the work of Pachomios and said to him, "Do not spin the thread that way. Thou art not doing it properly. Abba Theodore weaves in a different way." The great Pachomios then humbly rose up from his handiwork and said to the boy, "My son, teach me the other way." After learning from the lad another way of weaving, Pachomios sat down and resumed working with great joy. He, indeed, laid low, even in this circumstance, the spirit of pride. For if Pachomios had been dominated by the mind of the flesh, he would not have been persuaded to receive a lesson from a boy; but rather, he would have rebuked the boy for speaking out of turn.[64]

A Phantom in the Monastery

Then, on another occasion, during a night while the righteous Pachomios was walking about with Theodore, they suddenly saw from afar a woman most beautiful. Her comeliness, figure, and entire aspect so disturbed and agitated Theodore that his countenance was altered. The saint, beholding this deceitful apparition, also noticed the change in Theodore. He observed how he became fainthearted and said to him, "Take courage in God, O Theodore, and cease fearing."[65] Then the both of them prayed to God that the apparition might vanish from before their eyes. Even as they continued constant in prayer, that woman drew closer to them. It was observed that countless demons were running before her. As she approached those holy men, she said to them, "Cease toiling for nought. You are not able, for the present, to drive me away. This is because the almighty God gave me authority to harass as many as I should like. I have long sought this." Pachomios then asked, "Who art thou? Whence comest thou? Whom hast thou come to tempt?" The woman answered, "I am the daughter of the devil and all his power; for all the demons render service to me. I have warred against the holy luminaries and brought

---

[64] *The Evergetinos*, Volume IV of The First Book, "Hypothesis XXXVIII," pp. 18, 19; "The First Greek Life," ¶ 86, p. 356.

[65] *The Paradise* records: "No man could tell the beauty, or the form, or the appearance, which belonged to that phantom, and even Theodore, who looked at that phantom, was exceedingly perturbed, and his face changed color. And when the blessed Pachomios saw that Theodore was afraid, he said unto him, 'Be of good cheer in the Lord, O Theodore, and fear not.'" See Budge, *Paradise*, Vol. I, "The Rule of Pachomius at Tabenna: of the Phantom Which They Saw by Night When There Going Through the Monastery," p. 304, Ch. XIV.

down many. I plucked Judas from the band of the apostles.[66] Now I have received authority to war against thee, O Pachomios. No one else has so enfeebled me as thou hast with such a multitude of youths and old men. Thou hast converted the desert into a city. Thou hast so fortified thy disciples with the fear of God that it has become impossible for my minions to entice them. But all these events have occurred to me by reason of the incarnation of the Lord. He has given thee authority to trample upon our power and to mock us."

Pachomios, again, made an inquiry: "Hast thou come to trouble only me or others of my flock?" She answered, "Both thee and Theodore." Pachomios asked, "Theodore as well?" She replied, "Yea, I have received authority over thee and Theodore. But as for thee, I cannot draw nigh at all. I dare not." The fathers then said, "Why is that?" She answered, "If I were to war against thee, Pachomios, thou shouldest have an occasion for greater benefit than injury, since, indeed, thou hast been vouchsafed to see with thy bodily eyes the ineffable glory of God. But after thy death, I shall have license to dance in the midst of thy monks because they shall be negligent, indolent, and easier of temper." The righteous man asked, "How dost thou know that those who will come after us will not be more godly men than we?" She retorted, "But I do know." He rejoined, "Thou liest against thine own unhallowed head. Thou art not able to make any prognostication. How, then, dost thou know future events, that which has not yet come to pass, which God alone knows?" The woman then remarked, "By foreknowledge, I can know nothing; but by my own observations and reflections, coupled with my past experience, I conjecture future happenings. I know, for instance, that every act begins with zest and fervor. But with the passage of time, the zeal and fervor gradually cool for the deed until from negligence and carelessness it falls into contempt."[67]

The righteous man continued his questioning: "If thou hast such power and all the demons are subject to thee, here we are, then, fight us." She gave answer again and said, "I told thee that since the all-mighty power of the Crucified appeared on earth, we are not only broken down but also scorned as

---

[66] Her remark about the luminaries and Judas is borrowed from the "Paralipomena," Ch. 10, ¶ 24, p. 48.

[67] "I know that the beginning of everything finds its support in the earnest desire for things that are sought after with zeal, especially divine planting and heavenly calling. That calling is confirmed by God's will, with wonders, signs, and various powers. These give security to those who pursue it. But when that beginning gets older and older, it ceases growing; and when that occurs, the desire is either consumed by time, or withered by disease, or blunted by negligence." Ibid., Ch. 10, ¶ 25, p. 50.

sparrows by His slaves.[68] We, as ones weak, although we are feeble, still we are not indifferent; nor do we cease warring against you. For our nature is such that we never sleep and we sow our moral badness in the soul of the struggler. If we see that he receives it, we kindle within him an even more vehement desire. If the one under attack defies us and does not accept the visitation with sweetness, we immediately vanish as smoke and dissipate into the air. However, God does not permit us to war against all: but only against those perfect and for their greater recompense. This is due to the fact that, if He gave us license to combat against all, many in thy flock would be deceived who now depend upon thy protection." The blessed Pachomios then blew into her face and rebuked her, saying, "Fie upon thy wickedness that never sleeps!" He commanded her to flee and not to approach his monastery ever again. When morning came, Pachomios assembled all the elders. He announced to them all that he had seen and heard from that destructive and seductive demon. Next, he wrote to the other monasteries, confirming them in the fear of God. He also informed them about the apparition.

The Gift of Tongues

At one time, when the righteous man was touring the cells of the monastery, visiting the brethren, he met a certain man from Rome. He was a high ranking dignitary who was bilingual, speaking Latin and Greek. Since Pachomios was only knowledgeable in the Egyptian tongue, each man had no idea what the other was saying. Pachomios, thereupon, summoned an interpreter. During the translation, the Roman was expressing his desire to make his confession to the saint but he did not want an interpreter present. He said, "I do not wish to reveal the greater defects and errors of my heart before another—except for God and thee, O Pachomios." The venerable elder, wishing to oblige him, dismissed the interpreter. After this took place, Pachomios went aside privately and raised his hands heavenward, beseeching God with faith to grant him the gift of His apostles,[69] that is, to be able to speak all the tongues in order to benefit the souls of those who hastened there. The saint's fervent prayer lasted three hours, during which time he entreated God and said, "Omnipotent Lord, if I cannot help the men whom Thou hast sent to me from the ends of the earth because I do not speak their language, what need is there for them to come? If it is Thy will to save them through me, do Thou grant me, O Lord, knowledge of their languages that I may be able to set aright their souls in the straight path."[70] He then, suddenly, beheld something like unto an epistle written on papyrus. It was dispatched from heaven into Pachomios' right hand. As he read what was written thereon—O the wonder!—he

---

[68] Cf. Job 41:5.

[69] Acts 2:4; 1 Cor. 12:28; 14:18.

[70] "Paralipomena," Ch. 11, ¶ 27, p. 52.

was able to speak all the languages without the least difficulty. Pachomios gave thanks to the Holy Trinity. He, therefore, began conversing, faultlessly, with the Roman in both the Greek and Roman dialects. The Roman greatly marvelled at such fluency, avowing that the righteous Pachomios surpassed all the erudite men and orators. Thus, the venerable elder was able to correct the Roman. Pachomios also supplicated the Lord for the forgiveness of the Roman's sins. After he imposed a suitable penance, he commended him to God and departed.[71]

The Fig Tree and the Monk Jonas

The following day, Pachomios repaired to the Monastery of Hoseos.[72] As he entered, he observed a rather large fig tree in the midst of the courtyard. Those who passed the tree were wont to pluck the figs in a secret manner. When Pachomios gazed at the top of the tree, he saw a demon sitting. He understood that it was the spirit of gluttony that deceived the passersby to take up the figs. Pachomios, consequently, called the gardener, whose name was Jonas, and said to him, "Brother, cut down the fig tree because it is becoming a stumbling block to those who do not have a steady purpose. Besides that, it is inappropriate to find this tree in the middle of the monastery." Jonas, hearing these words, was very much saddened. This is because he had planted the fig tree, as well as all the other trees. He, therefore, remarked to the righteous man, "Do not even think of cutting it down, my father, because it provides plenty of fruit for the brethren." The righteous Pachomios, in order not to grieve the elderly monk, since he knew Jonas' virtuous manner of life, yielded; and so the tree was not cut down. But then, the following day, the fig tree withered to the root, so that not even one leaf remained. Jonas, observing this phenomenon, was exceedingly grieved. The drop in his countenance was not due to the loss of the figs, but because he disobeyed the elder and did not cut it down. Straightway, with the sense that he had quibbled with the elder, he wept for this sin until the end of his blessed life.

A few words merit discussion of Jonas' life. Even though that blessed monk had planted all the fruit trees, he, throughout his eighty-five years as a monk, never partook of the fruit produced at that monastery. He would only give the fruit in abundance to the monastery brethren and visitors. He labored

---

[71] D. J. Chitty notes that "the community soon attracted others from farther afield, and there was a house of Greek-speaking brethren at Faou, under another Theodore from Alexandria, some thirteen years before Pachomius' death. Its first inmates included two Romans and an Armenian, as well as four Alexandrians. Their successors in this house were probably responsible for the Vita Prima of Pachomius and Theodore (in a single work), which, while using Coptic material no longer extant, was itself composed in Greek." *The Desert a City*, p. 27.

[72] The name is recorded as Thmousons in the "Paralipomena," Ch. 12, ¶ 28, p. 53.

in the gardens all through the day until evening. In the evenings, he sat on a stool and plaited ropes. All the while, he prayed until the hour of Orthros when he would strike the semantron, giving the signal for the assembling of the brothers by striking a wooden plank. During these cell activities, he labored in the dark. He never used the light of a lamp, even when plaiting ropes. If he felt drowsy, he would allow himself only a little nap that he might address the absolute need of his corporeal nature. Even while slumbering, he was sitting on his stool with the rope he was plaiting in his hands. Inasmuch as he knew the sacred Scriptures by heart, he would also recite texts while working at his handicraft. After the setting of the sun, he partook of a little uncooked food. As for his fare, it consisted of bread and vinegar with raw vegetables. Despite these meager meals, he never was infirm. His raiment was constructed of three goat skins that covered his body. He never used a blanket. He had one mandyas (mantiya),[73] that is, one long cloak, which he wore only when he received the divine Mysteries. These and a multitude of other praiseworthy excellences adorned the blessed Jonas which, for the sake of brevity, we need to omit here.

It is noteworthy, nonetheless, that when the blessed Jonas reposed, he was still sitting on his stool in the position of plaiting a rope. His death was not sudden. Instead, he fell slightly ill and recognized that he had come to the end of his earthly sojourn. Despite his condition, he did not wish to enter the infirmary lest others should be in a position to serve him. Moreover, he wished neither to partake of the food served therein to the patients nor to take his ease, even for a moment, on his back or a pillow. No, he did not want rest or refreshment in this life, that he might enjoy the everlasting one. Indeed, the thrice-blessed Jonas, for his former toils, now enjoys a rich reward.[74]

Saint Pachomios Builds a Church

At another time, the divine Pachomios built a church for the monastery, applying much study and diligence. The design included pillars of brick which he decorated as well as he could. Afterward, he stepped back and observed their comeliness. He gave thanks and was pleased at the construction of such beauty. He, however, then began considering that such admiration and

[73] The mandyas is part of the monastic habit of both the Small Schema and Great Schema.

[74] This conclusion is given elsewhere: "It is a wonder to hear how we buried him. Since his feet could not be stretched out because they had become stiff as wood, and his hands could not be made to lie alongside his body, and he could not be stripped of that skin garment wherewith he was clothed, we were, therefore, obliged to bury him that way, like a bundle of logs." "Paralipomena," Ch. 12, ¶ 30, p. 55; Budge, *Paradise*, Vol. I, "The Rule of Pachomius at Tabenna: of a Certain Holy Man Whose Name Was Jonah, Who Was the Gardener of One of the Monasteries, and of the Wonderful Thing Which Abba Pachomius Wrought in His Monastery," p. 310, Ch. XV.

happiness regarding the beauty of his work was through demonic energy. He, therefore, tied ropes about the pillars. Following this, he sent up a secret prayer. Next, he told the brothers to slightly pull at the ropes that the pillars might bend and remain crooked. When this was executed, he commented to the brethren: "I pray you, brothers, not to take great efforts to adorn the work of your hands lest your mind be carried away in the praise of the work and lest you establish a door for the demon's entry. This is because we ought not in the least to give heed to the beauty of corruptible things, but rather we ought to think slightly of raiment, food, and comfortable cells. This even includes books that are handsomely bound. The comeliness of the faithful man is the keeping of the commandments of God. For this cause, Joseph the All-comely, who was exceedingly good-looking,[75] paid no attention to his looks—as they were features perishable and fleeting. He had, as his comeliness, prudence and sober-mindedness, for which he reigns even eternally. Amnon (Ammon)[76] and Absalom (Abessalom)[77] and a multitude of others, who delighted in physical beauty and preferred and desired it before all else, were lost by means of a bad death."[78]

Heretic Monks Challenge Saint Pachomios to Walk Upon the Waters

A day came when some heretical monks, after hearing about Pachomios, wished to visit with him. These men wore hair garments when they came visiting. At first, they encountered the monks of the righteous Pachomios. The heretics said to the holy monks, "Our father has sent us to your great man with a message. If the Abba Pachomios is a man of God, as the world testifies, let him cross the river with us, walking on our feet, that it might be made manifest which of us is more virtuous and has more access to God." The brethren, thereupon, went and reported the challenge to the righteous Pachomios. When Pachomios heard their words, he censured his monks and said to them, "Why do you give a hearing to such nonsense? Do you not know that such propositions are foreign to God and altogether alien to our correct Faith? What law of God commands such prodigies? What could be more foolish than abandoning my mourning for my sins and meditating upon how to escape everlasting punishment than to take up such challenges as if I

---

[75] Gen. 39:6.

[76] See 4 Kgs. (2 Sam.) 13:1 ff.

[77] See 4 Kgs. (2 Sam) 14:26.

[78] *The Paradise* records: "Take heed lest ye strive to ornament the work of your hands overmuch, and take ye the greatest possible care that the grace of God and His gift may be in the work of each one of you, so that the mind may not stumble toward the praises of cunning wickedness, and the calumniator (Satan) may not obtain his prey." See Budge, *Paradise*, Vol. I, "The Rule of Pachomius at Tabenna: of How Abba Pachomius Would Not Keep Beautiful Buildings," p. 310, Ch. XVI.

were a boy in my thoughts?"[79] Those monks then said to their holy elder, "How, then, does that monk, the heretic, dare to perform such a marvel?" Pachomios replied, "He traverses the river as on dry land only by God's permission. But it is the devil working with that heretic in order to deceive and mislead those wanting in understanding: first that they might believe in him and, second, that his wicked heresy not be brought to nought. Again, as it has been written: 'To the froward God sends froward ways [Prov. 21:8].' Go, therefore, and say to them that the desire of Pachomios is twofold: that I might not pass through this river on foot but that river, the fiery one, which will violently hale me, a man of many sins, before the divine judgment seat; and that I might find leniency and not be judged according to the letter of the law. For this am I making provision and striving, by the power of God: that before such satanic wiles, with which you would provoke me, I might turn away from them and avoid God's judgment." So spoke the righteous man, exhorting his men not to deem highly whatsoever they might achieve. He charged the brethren that they should never long for visions or revelations.[80] They should not yearn to see either demons or apparitions. He strictly forbade them the following: to think highly of their own integrity; and to lust after the sight of seeing their elder walking across the river and conversing with such persons who pry into matters such as these. He admonished them neither to trouble God nor to tempt God by such unfit and discordant requests, even as it is written in the Scripture: "Thou shalt not tempt the Lord thy God [Deut. 6:16; Mt. 4:7]."

---

[79] Saint Pachomios makes this point that the heretics wished to draw him away from his first work: mourning for his sins and pondering upon how to avoid eternal punishment. He believed that he should become childish in his outlook by considering such propositions as walking upon the water. He did not refuse the challenge because he believed it impossible for him but because he did not wish to make a show in order to be glorified by men and thus have his reward in this life. No, in doing works, his motto was "let not thy left hand know what thy right hand is doing [Mt. 6:3]." See "Paralipomena," Ch. 14, ¶ 33, p. 57. "It is said of Pachomius that 'more than the everlasting torments, he feared to be estranged from the humility and sweetness of the Son of God, our Lord Jesus Christ.'" Chitty, *The Desert a City*, loc. cit.

[80] D. J. Chitty notes that "Pachomius' teaching here is worth quoting: 'After the manifest healings of the body, there are also spiritual healings. For if a man is intellectually blind, in that he does not see the light of God because of idolatry, but afterward is guided by faith in the Lord and gains his sight, in coming to know the only true God, is not this a great healing and salvation?...One of the brethren asked him, "Tell us of a vision seen by thee." And he said to him, "A sinner like me does not ask God that he may see visions: for that is against His will, and is error....Hear all the same about a great vision. If you see a man pure and humble, it is a great vision. For what is greater than such a vision, to see the invisible God in a visible man, His temple?"'" *The Desert a City*, p. 28.

The Hour of Warfare Finds Us Unprepared

A certain brother asked the great Pachomios: "I have observed the times that the demon comes to disturb us. The hour of warfare overtakes us not when we are sound and full of prudence and pursuing and speculating on such subjects as continence, temperance, discretion, self-control, or the other virtues. For then we might be able to master the attacking passion. Nay, the demon comes afterward to us wretched ones in order to vanquish us. I cannot help but wonder why we do not apply that which, earlier, we had been philosophizing upon? For instance, in the hour of anger, why do we not utilize the opposing virtue—patience—and, thereby, defeat anger?" Pachomios responded: "Because we have not yet fully kept pace with that which we contemplate and that which we practise in actuality. We also are not so thoroughly acquainted with all the subtle thoughts of the devils. By means of contemplation, as the sharpest power of the soul, we are able, with God's nod of permission, to drive out the darkening thoughts of shamelessness and wickedness suggested by the one who harasses us. For this cause it is necessary, even every moment, to possess the fear of God as a mercy for the contemplative part of the soul. This fear, which preserves us in the application of divine contemplation, is a light and a guide. It keeps the mind still and unmoved toward anger and the other passions, which bring it into captivity, so that we might be protected as we tread upon 'serpents and scorpions and upon all the power of our contender, the demon.'"[81]

The Monasteries' Manufacture of Mats

Now the monastery had prescribed the following: that each brother fabricate one mat each day. There was one brother among them, nevertheless, who plaited two mats. After he finished his work, he spread the mats outside of his cell that he might be praised by the righteous Pachomios for his industry. It happened that Pachomios was sitting opposite that monk's cell, conversing with other elders. When he saw that the monk made two mats for the sake of display that he might be praised for such assiduity, he sighed greatly and remarked to those sitting with him, "Do you see that brother? It is to the devil that he granted his toil, so that this day he has not labored in the least for his most wretched soul. Why? Because he loved the glory of men above the glory of God.[82] He, consequently, has racked his body badly and to no purpose, while his soul has not benefitted in the least from his toil." Having spoken these words, that brother then received a penance. In order to cure his vanity by humiliations, he was told to stand, as the brotherhood sat and ate at trapeza, in their midst, and hold high the two mats. He also was to say aloud the following statement: "I beseech you, my brothers and fathers, pray to God to have mercy

[81] Cf. Lk. 10:19.
[82] Cf. Jn. 12:43.

on my miserable soul, because I preferred these two straw mats before the everlasting kingdom." This monk obeyed and carried out what was commanded of him. After this, he was confined to his cell for six months,[83] where he dwelt alone. His food was only bread and water. He was charged to plait two mats daily. He was not allowed to speak with anyone, save only the brother assigned to bring him his food.

The Monk Athenodoros the Leper

There was also another brother, named Athenodoros, whose story also deserves recounting. He was sufficiently virtuous. He dwelt in the great monastery. His food consisted of nought but dry bread. He was an anchorite, living in his cell, also fulfilling the quota of one mat per day. For him, however, such handiwork was full of pain and labor so that it was a torment. This is due to the leprosy that attacked his hands, weakening and softening them. When he plaited the mats, the rushes pierced his hands. This left his hands bloodied and filled with wounds, so that even the mats were stained with his blood. This could hardly pass unnoticed, since, despite his infirmity, he attended all the gatherings of the brotherhood and never napped during the day. It was also his habit to recite a pericope from the Scriptures every night before sleep. It happened that one of the brothers passed a comment to him and said, "Certainly thou dost not think that by retiring from this work thou shalt be charged with laziness by God? God knows thine infirmity. No one with such a disease as thou hast engages in this employment. Moreover, the brotherhood feeds so many strangers and poor alike. Thou thyself hast been laboring for years and years, so how much more are we happy to take care of one of our own?" But the ailing Athenodoros replied, "It is not possible for me, brother, to quit working, since the apostle himself commanded that 'if anyone is not willing to work, neither let him eat [2 Thess. 3:10].' So that means that the one who does not work does not eat." The other brother continued, "The Apostle Paul was referring to those who labored neither physically nor spiritually. But the one who is ill or labors at spiritual ministrations does not have that sin. But again, if thou dost not wish to remain unemployed, at least anoint with oil thy hands daily at eventide lest thou shouldest injure them further."

Athenodoros complied with that instruction. But, after a few days of anointing his hands with oil, they became softer and, therefore, more vulnerable to the thorns on the reeds. It was not long before Pachomios learned what was happening. He went and visited Athenodoros, asking him, "Who has compelled thee to work? And why dost thou anoint thy hands with oil?[84] Is not

[83] The number of months is given as five in the "Paralipomena," Ch. 15, ¶ 34, p. 58.

[84] The "Paralipomena" has Pachomios revealing that Athenodoros came to trust in the oil rather than God, by asking, "Dost thou think that the oil is helping thee? Who has (continued...)

the Lord able to heal thee speedily? Indeed, most truly is He able. But for the benefit of thy soul and by His dispensation, He has permitted thee to contract this disease." Then the ever-memorable Athenodoros, as if he had stumbled into a great iniquity, made a prostration and said, "I have sinned, father. I beg thee to entreat the Lord to forgive my sin." Hence, the wondrous Athenodoros, for one year, abided weeping on account of his sin. He also ate only once every other day. This man, we should add, had other excellences. The righteous Pachomios knew this, too. Since his affliction imposed that he live separately from the brethren, Pachomios sent him forth, from time to time, to each monastery that he might be a salutary example to the brethren as one who bore infirmity with thanksgiving and cheerfulness.

Silence is Observed in the Monasteries

There were also other men of virtue. "But if I," comments the biographer, "should mention them by name, then in no wise shall I finish my narration." This is because all the brethren carried on in a God-pleasing manner. If there were even some who were careless or negligent, they were corrected by the example of the others who diligently pursued with exactness the monastic mode of life. In fact, not one of them dared to speak to another during their ministrations unless there was some serious need. The saint frequently made the rounds, visiting and inspecting. Silence was observed in all the monasteries. His arrival time was mostly unexpected. Whomsoever he heard chattering during the execution of their ministrations, such as kneading or making bread in a mould or baking in the oven or whatsoever other service, such monks were punished with a heavy penance. For this reason was silence kept in the saint's monasteries.

Saint Theodore's Headache

Theodore, at one time, suffered from a bad headache.[85] The saint, therefore, went to visit him. Pachomios comforted him and said, "Sickness never comes upon a man without the will of God. Cease grieving, since,

---

[84](...continued)
compelled thee to work, that on pretext of work thou hast put thy hopes for health in the oil rather than in God?" Ch. 16, ¶ 36, p. 60. The *Paradise* records Pachomios speaking to him, calling him Theodore, and saying, "Thinkest thou, O Theodore, that the oil had any beneficial effect upon thee? Who forced thee to work? Didst thou not place thy hope of being healed rather upon the operation of the oil than upon God? Peradventure was not thy God able to heal thee? Yet when He saw that thou wast ordering help for thyself He left thee to fall into this pain." See Budge, *Paradise*, Vol. I, "The Rule of Pachomius at Tabenna: of a Certain Monk Who Belonged to the Monastery," p. 314, Ch. XX.

[85] We are told that Theodore suffered periodically from headaches. "The First Greek Life," ¶ 90, p. 358.

whensoever it is the good pleasure of the Lord, He shall heal thee. For the present, if He is testing thee, do thou give thanks to Him for all even as Job who endured all the sorrows and said, 'Blessed be the name of the Lord [Job 1:21]!' The one who shoulders his cross must speak thus and bear all, whether his sufferings are voluntary or involuntary. Even if one is not suffering for anything in particular, his cross and ascesis should suffice him. Voluntary sufferings are those which we endure willingly, even great labors and pains, such as, fasting, keeping vigil, and other similar rigors. Involuntary sufferings are those such as illness and other sorrows which happen to us without our will. But they are the means by which we cleanse the soul from sins: that is, when a man perseveres under such sufferings and rather gives thanks to God. Then do all these things come to be reckoned as voluntary contests and accomplishments, so that the contestant receives a double crown." The divine Theodore heard these words and was consoled and strengthened.[86]

A Righteous Monk Reposes

The saint, on numerous occasions, sent Theodore to visit the brethren. Pachomios had commended Theodore to the brothers that they would listen to him as they would the elder. He charged them to submit themselves to him, as to their own father, with the fear of God, since Theodore possessed much grace as we said earlier. The kindhearted Theodore, in any event, was a great favorite and the brethren rejoiced whenever he visited.[87] On one occasion, Theodore heard the sound of chanting outside the monastery. It was melodious, delightful, and sweet. Since Pachomios was also present, Theodore asked, "Abba, dost thou hear that very pleasant melody?" Pachomios answered, "The soul of a certain virtuous brother has fallen asleep and the holy angels are escorting his blessed soul into the heavens. Grace has been granted us to hear for this moment the voice of rejoicing and praise as he is being borne aloft to a blessed life."[88]

Possess the Fear of God

On one of the saint's tours, he went to Tabennesi on a serious matter. When he arrived, he greeted the brothers and began teaching them concerning evil thoughts. He said the following things: "It is not sufficient that a monk

---

[86] This anecdote is concluded with these words of Pachomios to Theodore in "The First Greek Life": "But the one who lies sick can be struggling far more than the one in good health in strength of soul and patience. Then such a man has a double crown. It is good for the one who suffers to bear his pain about ten years before speaking of it." ¶ 90, p. 359.

[87] Ibid., ¶ 91, p. 359.

[88] This anecdote is found in "The First Life of Saint Pachomius," ¶ 93, p. 360 and the "The Bohairic Life," ¶ 83, p. 110. The latter says that when Pachomios and Theodore looked up, they saw and knew the one who had been thus visited.

should only practise outwardly bodily asceticism, such as keeping fasts and vigils and watchfulness and other exercises. For it is also necessary for him to combat diverse thoughts that injure and incite us to vainglory, hatred, and other faults. The monk is to dispel such thoughts, as much as he is able, by means of humble-mindedness and entreaty to God. But most especially, the monk should possess within his heart the uninterrupted fear of God. Inasmuch as fire smelts iron ore, thus ridding it of worthless rock and cinder,[89] so the fear of God eliminates from the man who possesses such fear every vice and passion."[90]

Concerning Blasphemous Thoughts

While at Tabennesi, Saint Pachomios also gave the following talk concerning blasphemous thoughts: "You should know that one harangued by such thoughts suggested by the enemy may even be a friend of God and a virtuous struggler. But such a one may not be vigilant or watchful as he ought to be. If he does not consult a man of experience on how to overcome that deceitful suggestion, it can wreck him. Such a one needs, with great humility of heart and confession, to seek someone wise and skilled who can explain to him how to overcome such thoughts; or he should read the writings of a holy father which deal with this temptation. But if one leaves this bad thought to abide long in the heart, this one is in danger of being destroyed by an evil death. Many people, by reason of these thoughts, have come to take their own lives—may God avert this!—either by casting themselves off a cliff while beside themselves and out of their wits or by thrusting a sword in their belly or by contriving some other deadly means. It is a great evil not to confess this temptation quickly to someone with knowledge, before the evil has matured into suicide. Whensoever such a thought should intrude into thy mind, the therapy is this: To turn away from it completely, forasmuch as it is not thine own thought. Much rather it is the seed and offspring of the evil one. Thus, you must counter the demon saying these words: 'This blasphemy is yours, O evil demons! May your trouble, your worst, and your injury turn back on your own heads! You see to it and cut yourselves to pieces, because you blasphemed against God, O you apostates and proud ones! As for me, I bless and worship my Creator and Savior.' When you pronounce these and other similar words,[91]

---

[89] Gangue and slag.

[90] Saint Pachomios' teaching, as given in "The First Greek Life," reads "Just as fire cleanses all rust and burnishes the objects, so the fear of God consumes every evil in man and burnishes him into 'a vessel for honor, which has been sanctified, and made useful to the master, having been prepared for every good work [cf. 2 Tim. 2:21].'" ¶ 96, p. 363.

[91] These other words are found in "The First Greek Life": "Here is the therapy through discernment of spirits that the Lord has taught us: 'If I grieve my neighbor with a word,

(continued...)

also be making the sign of the Cross over yourself. Then shall you scatter the demons; and, as smoke, they shall break up and vanish." He then paused a moment and added, "But then also learn the cause which brought me here: I found an earthenware jar."

The Monk Elias and the Figs

The righteous Pachomios spoke these words about an earthenware jar enigmatically. For he knew, by the Holy Spirit, a certain fault that a brother had fallen into. That brother's name was Elias. He was a simplehearted man, guileless and naive. Elias had gathered some figs and hid them away in a ceramic jar that he might eat them alone after the fast. When he heard the venerable elder speak of an earthenware jar, he straightway convicted himself and went to fetch it. He returned with the jar filled with five figs. Before the entire company, he made a prostration and sought forgiveness. The brethren marvelled at the clairvoyance of the righteous man; not only then but also in many other instances he revealed to them those things that were hidden or secret. Pachomios then addressed the brethren and said: "We, whenever we please, are not able to learn those things which are distant or in secret. Such things are revealed to us, for our own good, when it pleases the providence of God. I, furthermore, with the fear of God, speak the truth to you regarding this small misdemeanor that I neither was shown it nor was informed of it. But that this brother might be rescued from the passion of gluttony, it was uncovered to me by the Lord."[92]

The Nine Pachomian Foundations

Then Pachomios rose, prayed with the brothers, and left without eating; for he was in a hurry to return to Phbow, at one time a deserted village, which was situated down river. When Tabennesi became cramped for lack of room, this foundation was started.[93] Actually there were nine Pachomian monasteries.

---

[91](...continued)
my heart becomes contrite when convinced by the word of God; and, if I do not persuade him quickly, I have no rest. Unclean demons! O you apostates, how shall I join you in a thought of blasphemy against the God Who created me? I will not give in, even if you should pull me to pieces in suggesting these things to me. These thoughts are not mine but yours who are going to be chastised in unquenchable fire forever and ever [Is. 66:24; Mk. 9:44]. As for me I shall not cease blessing, praising, and thanking the One Who created me when I did not exist; and I shall not cease from cursing you; for cursed, indeed, are you apart from the Lord.' When one says these things with faith, the demon vanishes like smoke." ¶ 96, pp. 364, 365.

[92] See also "The First Greek Life," ¶ 97, p. 364, and "The Bohairic Life," ¶ 72, p. 94.

[93] Phbow is modern Faw-el-Kebli (Southern Faw), some two miles downstream from Tabennesi. "The Bohairic Life," ¶ 49, p. 71.

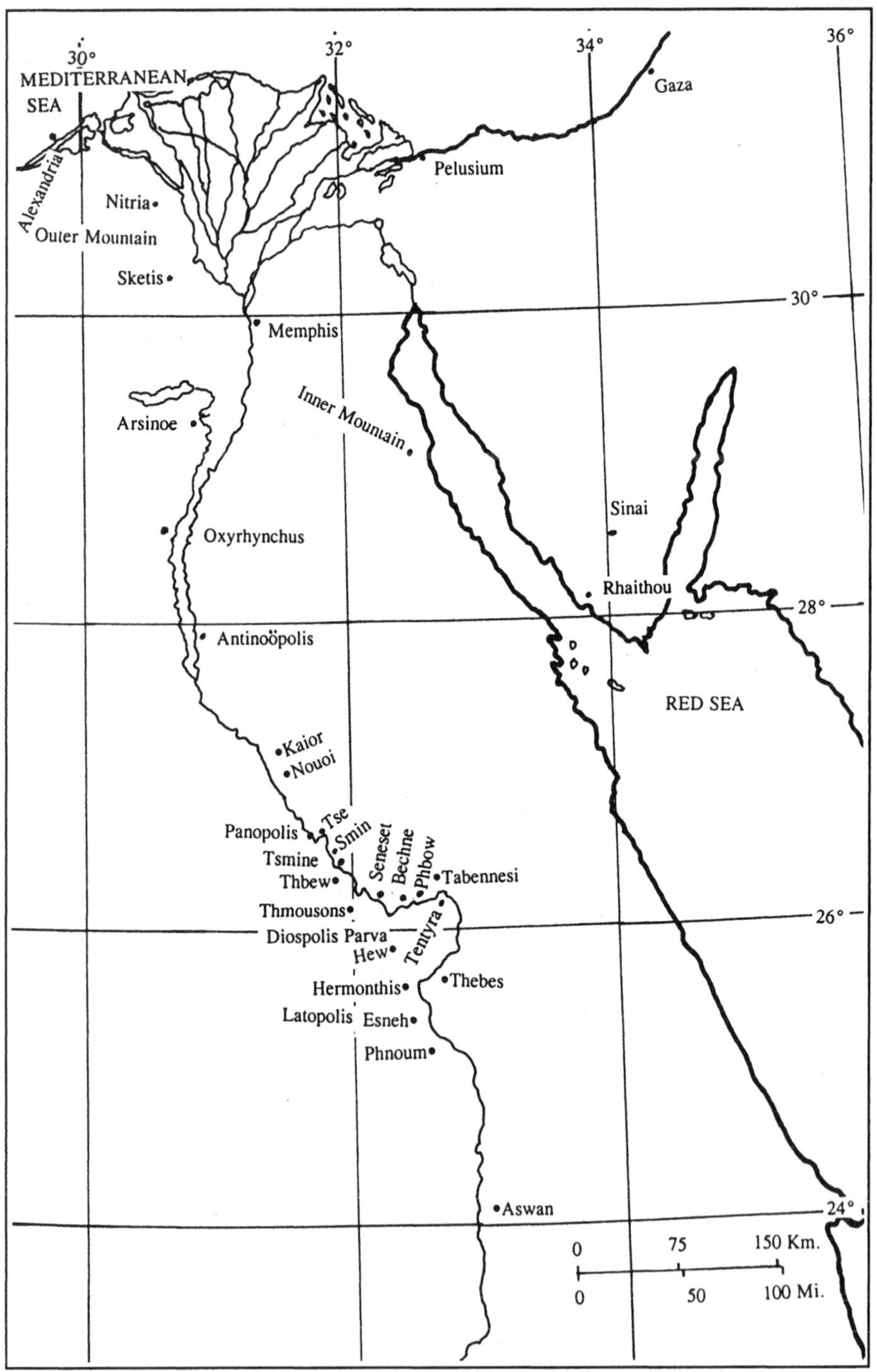

The Pachomian Foundations in Egypt

There was the foundation of Seneset (Gk. Chenovoskion), a community already under Abba Ebonh (Gk. Eponychos), that requested to be placed under Pachomios' jurisdiction.[94] The foundation of Thmousons and annexation of Pmampesterposen, already under Father Jonas, asked to be organized under the Pachomian rules.[95] The foundation of Tse was founded according to a vision given to Saint Pachomios to organize a community in Tkahsmin.[96] The foundation of Smin was founded when the Orthodox Bishop Arios requested Abba Pachomios to organize a monastery at Smin. Pachomios also established the housemasters with their seconds as in the other monasteries.[97] The foundation of Thbew was founded by Petronios on his estate at Coc, in the diocese of Hew. Petronios' father and brother also became monks. Petronios had donated to Abba Pachomios all that he had.[98] The foundation of Tsmine was founded by providence. The brethren went north to the vicinity of the city of Smin where they built a monastery that was named Tsmine. Although some wicked and envious people came and cast down the work done by the fathers, yet God gave Pachomios patience. An angel assured him that the monastery

---

[94] "The Bohairic Life," ¶ 50, p. 72. Also, "The First Greek Life," ¶ 54, pp. 334 f. speaks of the foundations of Phbow, Chenovoskion (Seneset), and Thmousons.

[95] "The Bohairic Life," ¶ 51, p. 72. The first three foundations were near one another on the northeast bank of the river Nile. Thmousons was on the opposite bank, situated somewhere in the plain of Nag'Hammadi, at about a six-hour journey from Phbow. The first four foundations—except Tabennesi in the diocese of Nitentori—were in the diocese of Diospolis Parva (Hiu, Hu, Hut, Hut-Sekhen, 26°01′N 32°17′E). The last five foundations were more distant. Pachomios himself spoke of the nine monasteries altogether at the Latopolis Synod.

[96] "The Bohairic Life," ¶ 52, p. 73. In "The First Greek Life," ¶ 83, p. 354, the account given of the foundations of Tse, Tsmine, and Phnoum is that before the one at Panopolis (Akhmim) in Bishop Arios' city, Pachomios received the monastery called Tse. After Tse, he received those of Panopolis, Thbew, Tsmine, and later on the other one called Phnoum near Latopolis.

[97] "The Bohairic Life," ¶ 54, pp. 73, 74. Smin is Latopolis (modern Isna) of the Greeks. Bishop Arios was a coadjutor appointed to assist Bishop Artemidoros, at the latter's request, on account of his advanced age and illness. It is generally believed that Arios' appointment came at some time between 339 and 343, which helps date the second group of Pachomian foundations. The account given in "The First Greek Life," identifies Arios as the ascetical Bishop of Panopolis (some sixty miles down the Nile). Samuel, a man both cheerful and abstinent, was appointed steward there.

[98] "The Bohairic Life," ¶ 56, p. 77. Thbew was in the same diocese as the first three foundations after Tabennesi, that is, Diospolis Parva. Thbew was situated on the west bank of the Nile, much farther north than Thmousons. Thbew is modern-day Abou-Chouche, twelve miles downstream from Farchout and five miles upstream from Beliana. The story of Petronios and his father Psenthbo is also mentioned in "The First Greek Life," ¶ 80, p. 352.

would be surrounded by a blazing wall. Thus Pachomios and the brothers finished building. Pachomios installed Apa Petronios of Thbew as father, following an inspiration from God.[99] The foundation of Phnoum, founded later by the saint, lies to the south at the mountain of Sne in a place called Phnoum. Even though the bishop and his followers of that place rushed at Pachomios in order to drive him out, the Lord scattered the adversaries. A large monastery was built and Apa Sourous was placed at the head of that brotherhood.[100]

Visits to the Heavens

Let us return now to our narration. Before we speak of the saint's repose, we need to mention his trips to the heavens and the Synod of Latopolis. Saint Pachomios, before his repose, also visited the heavens. Once, when he fell gravely ill, his soul departed his body. As his soul was snatched away and he was approaching the gate of life, an order came from God to bring him back to his body once more. This command grieved him since he did not wish to return to his body again. He perceived that the light of that air was wonderful and of such splendid beauty as to be indescribable. As he was grieving, a man who stood at the gate to guard it turned toward him to look at him. The face of that man shined because of its splendor; and the appearance of his body was all light. That same man said to Pachomios, 'Go, my son, and return to thy body; for thou hast yet to suffer a small martyrdom in the world.' When he heard this word, Pachomios was filled with joy; for he greatly desired to be a martyr for the Lord's name. At that same time, the angels informed him that the one who conversed with him was the Apostle Paul.

As soon as the angels brought Pachomios to the place where his body was lying, the soul considered its body. Behold, the body was dead! It happened that when the soul approached the body, all the members of the body secretly opened up. The soul took up its residence again and the body became alive. After this, Pachomios was carried away to Paradise many other times. In what manner? God knows. So speaks the apostle who said: "Whether in the body I know not, or out of the body I know not, God knoweth—such a one was carried off as far as the third heaven. He was caught up into Paradise and heard unspeakable words, which it is not allowed for a man to speak [2 Cor. 12:2, 4]." But in this place Pachomios beheld the cities of the saints, of which it is not possible to describe the constructions, the monuments, and the good things

---

[99] "The Bohairic Life," ¶ 57, p. 77. Tsmine is the third monastery in the region of Smin. Petronios was entrusted with both Thbew and Tsmine of the same area. Even though Petronios was a newcomer, he was given considerable authority. Some had even singled him out as the probable successor to Pachomios.

[100] Ibid., ¶ 58, p. 78. Phnoum is the last Pachomian foundation. It was built before the autumn of 345, which is the date of the Latopolis Synod. Phnoum was situated some distance away from her sister monasteries, being in the mountain or desert of Sne.

that the Lord has "prepared for those who love Him [1 Cor. 2:9]." Now when Pachomios viewed those cities, he brought to mind what the Lord said in a parable in the Gospel, speaking to the servants whose talents had produced ten and five talents. 'Enter into the joy of thy Lord,'[101] and 'Well done, good slave! Because in a very little thou wast faithful, have authority over ten cities.' And to the second He said, 'Be thou also over five cities.'[102]

Pachomios recounted that the climate of that age was very even and its surface without limits. "A little outside Paradise there were many fruit trees and vineyards unlike those of this world. The fruit trees and the vineyards produced spiritual foods that are incorruptible, while the fruits of the trees of this present age are unworthy and contemptible when compared to the variety of the other. No tree or plant growing in Paradise was ever deprived of fruits emitting an exuberant fragrance. A man, in fact, cannot bear that fragrance without passing out unless the Lord gave such a one the grace to tolerate it. That age is above this earth and outside the firmament. That land is far above the mountains. The lights that are in the firmament and lighten the earth are not those that lighten that age. Nay, it is the Lord Himself that lightens it, as Esaias foretold: 'Thou shalt no more have the sun for a light by day, nor shall the rising of the moon lighten thy night; but the Lord shall be thine everlasting light, and God thy glory. For the sun shall no more set, nor shall the moon be eclipsed; for the Lord shall be thine everlasting light, and the days of thy mourning shall be completed [Is. 60:19, 20].' Hence, there is no day or night in that age; much rather, it is lightened by an abundant and unceasing light. So great are its boundaries that this world is nothing in comparison."[103]

The Synod of Latopolis

Again, as we mentioned earlier, he was at the Synod of Latopolis, which was convened in the autumn of 345, the year before the saint's departure from this life. Since the fame of the saint spread far and wide, accounts of him—both balanced and exaggerated—excited a debate regarding his clairvoyance (the *dioratic* gift). Pachomios was summoned to answer for himself in the church of Latopolis. There had assembled both bishops and monks. Pachomios entered with some of the ancient fathers. He saw his accusers but kept silence. Bishop Philo of Thebes and Bishop Mouei of Latopolis questioned Pachomios and asked him to answer the charge. The man of God responded: "Were you not once monks with me in the monastery before you became bishops?" Pachomios did not wait for an answer, but continued speaking. He reminded them how the grace of God helped other brethren in the monastery, working

---

[101] Cf. Mt. 25:23.

[102] Cf. Lk. 19:17-19.

[103] Saint Pachomios' trips to the heavens are described, in part, in "The Bohairic Life," ¶ 114, pp. 166-168.

Saint Pachomios

through him. The bishops then remarked, "We confess that thou art a man of God. We know that thou hast seen the demons. We know that thou makest war against them to dispel them from troubling other souls. But this issue of clairvoyance is another matter. Clairvoyance is a great gift. Do thou provide some answer regarding that; and we will persuade those who murmur against thee."

Pachomios began by reminding them that he had been of pagan parentage, but that the man-loving God Himself gave him grace to become a Christian. He also spoke of how God wrought through him to bring a great multitude of men, dwelling in nine monasteries. He described how they strived to live in the fear of God and kept their souls without reproach. Pachomios then said, "As you yourselves confess that we have discernment regarding unclean spirits, so too the Lord has given us to recognize, when the Lord wills, who among them is walking aright and who among them is a monk only in appearance. But let the gift of God alone! When those who are wise and sensible according to the world spend a few days in the midst of men, do they not distinguish and recognize each one's disposition? And if the One, Jesus, Who shed His own blood[104] for us, Who is the power and the wisdom of the Father,[105] should see someone trembling with all his heart for the loss of his neighbor, especially of many, will not Jesus give him the means to save them blamelessly, either by the discernment of the Holy Spirit or by an apparition when the Lord wills? For I do not see the realities of our salvation whensoever I will, but when it pleases the Lord, Who governs everything, to show us His confidence; for, 'Man became like unto vanity [Ps. 143:5].' But when he truly submits to God, he is no longer vain. He is become 'a temple of the living God, even as God said, "I will dwell in them [2 Cor. 6:16]."' Now He does not say that He dwells in all but only in the saints—that is, in you and in all and also in Pachomios, if such a one does His will." The bishops and the fathers marvelled at both his confidence in the Lord and in his humility. Then suddenly, someone drew near, a man possessed by the devil.

---

[104] Heb. 9:12.
[105] 1 Cor. 1:24.

He drew his sword, ready to slay Pachomios. But other brethren took hold of the assailant, while a tumult arose in the church. The brethren, in the midst of the uproar, made their escape and went to the monastery called Phnoum, which is in the district of that same city of Latopolis.[106]

Angel of the Lord

The Repose of Saint Pachomios

"Let us now report the repose of Saint Pachomios, that we may bring our account to a close; for if I were to recount all his divine accomplishments, a thousand pages would not suffice." At that time, while they were celebrating the Feast of the Holy Pascha, God permitted a pestilence to visit those parts. All the monasteries were struck. About a hundred and more died in the epidemic of that time. Pachomios himself fell ill of the plague. The symptoms included a high fever which, immediately, altered the sick one's coloring. The eyes of the sufferer also became bloodshot, red as blood. Then it appeared that the victim was suffocating or choking as he gave up the spirit. As such, many ended their lives in this manner, both young and old, including the superiors of the monasteries. Sourous, the father of the monastery at Phnoum reposed, as well as Cornelios of Thmousons, and Paphnutios, who lived at Phbow and was the steward of all the monasteries, and many others.[107] Theodore, meanwhile, tended Pachomios, who lost a lot of weight, as he was ailing for a long while. Even though Pachomios' heart and eyes were burning, as in a flame of fire, from the disease, he summoned the brethren. When the fathers and the abbots of the monastery came, he addressed them and said: "Behold, the Lord wishes to grant me rest! Therefore, choose for yourselves whomsoever is able to govern you." They, however, because of their weeping, could not give him an answer.

Pachomios then called Orsisios from the monastery of Chenovoskion. He said to him, "Go about and learn whom they would have govern them."

---

[106] "The First Greek Life," ¶ 112, pp. 375-377.

[107] Ibid., ¶ 114, p. 378, lists these fathers.

They said, "We know none other than thee, Father Pachomios, since the Lord placed us in thy hands." Pachomios then commented, "It seems to me that Petronios is competent, that is, if he should survive the plague. Therefore, do as you wish." The great man spoke thus because Abba Petronios was also lying abed in his monastery, Tsmine, in the region of Panopolis.[108] The fathers, after paying their respects and asking Pachomios' forgiveness, departed for their own cells. As for the saint, he found it difficult to keep lying on the straw mat where he had been for forty days. His bones began to ache. Those in attendance, thereupon, brought him softer bedding, that which was reserved for guests. When he took his ease on it for a short spell and noticed the difference, he began to fear that perhaps he was sinning by conducting himself in an idiorrhythmic manner, that is, that he was following his own will in an individualized monasticism rather than following the rule of the Koinonia. That this might not happen at the end of his life, he charged them to remove the mattress and replace it with the coenobium-issued one.

When the final hour arrived, Pachomios said to Theodore, "If they should not hide my bones, take them away to another place." Theodore believed he understood. He said that the saint ordered him to transfer his relic to another place, a concealed one. But to be sure that he heard correctly, Theodore repeated the words of instruction. The saint then remarked, "I have not only this concern. But I should also like to speak to thee of another: do not neglect those brethren who are remiss and idle. Keep urging them to keep the law of God that they should observe all His commandments." The venerable Pachomios spoke these words thrice to Theodore.

Theodore then began wondering to himself, "Why such insistence from the elder?" But again, Theodore knew that it was probably out of fear that some people were likely to steal his body and build a *martyrium* for it, even as they do for the holy martyrs. Many a time had Theodore heard Pachomios criticize those who kept such shrines, saying, "The saints have not been pleased with those who do these things, because it results in the commercialization of the saints." Theodore was then suddenly roused from his little reverie. Pachomios seized him by the beard and said again, "Theodore, take care to do quickly what I have told thee. Likewise, if the brothers should become negligent, thou art to stir them up to perform the law of God." Theodore thought inwardly, "What does he mean by stirring up the brethren? Is he saying that after a time the brethren will be entrusted to me? I do not know." And while Theodore was reflecting on these things in his heart, our Father Pachomios answered him, "Do not be hesitant. Do not waver. I am referring not only to what I am saying to thee but to what thou art thinking in thy heart." Weeping, Theodore,

[108] Ibid., ¶ 114, p. 379.

answered him, "It is well."[109] The saint then fell silent for a little while. After making the sign of the Cross thrice, he opened his mouth and gave up his spirit. Pachomios went to the Lord, Whom he desired, on the 15th day of May, in the year 346.

The brethren conducted an all-night vigil, chanting and praying. In the morning, they took up the sacred relics of the saint and went to the mountain for burial. Afterward, secretly, assisted by three trustworthy brethren, Theodore exhumed the body and conveyed it to an unknown place where it remains to this day.[110] As for the brethren, according to the righteous man's word, they proclaimed Petronios as hegumen, but he remained alive for only a few days. Nevertheless, during that short term of office, he governed the brethren with much diligence. When the hour of his falling asleep arrived, he inquired, "Whom have you preferred as your shepherd?" They said to him, "Do thou exercise thy discernment and elect that one." The blessed Petronios, as he was about to breathe his last, chose Orsisios. The latter, with tears in his eyes, desired to decline the leadership and said, "It is beyond my power. I am unworthy." But Petronios had already passed on. His sacred relics[111] were prepared and interred on the mountain, in the company of the brethren's prayers and chanting of psalms.

Our Holy Father Orsisios

Father Orsisios was really very good and meek and guileless. The brethren insisted that he take the office though he, as one most humble in spirit, did not wish it. With the passing of Petronios, however, he was prevailed upon by the brethren. Orsisios made the rounds of the monasteries. He provided for the brethren, exhorting and teaching heedfully the word of God. Much of his instruction was from the sacred Scriptures, as well as from most wise examples, that he might ever be prepared. He did not wish to be careless or negligent regarding their salvation, so he gave his attention to preserving, inviolably, every tradition of the righteous Pachomios.

Orsisios would often repeat the precepts of Pachomios. He remembered that when Pachomios was among the living— that is, while Orsisios was head of Chenovoskion—that the great man told him that even if he had not

---

[109] "The Bohairic Life," ¶ 122, pp. 177, 178.

[110] "With three other brothers, Theodore removed Pachomios from the place where he had been buried. He put him with Apa Paphnutios, the brother of Apa Theodore and accountant of the Koinonia. No one knows to this day where he lies. All the days of his life numbered sixty years. He became a monk when he was twenty-one years old and the other thirty-nine years he spent as a monk." Ibid., ¶ 123, p. 179.

[111] Saint Petronios is commemorated by the holy Church on the 23rd of October. Standing upon the rock of faith, as the namesake of a rock, Petronios was accounted worthy of seeing the Lord before his repose in peace.

received a great knowledge of God, he was to tell the men a parable and God would make that work. So this is what he did, to the great wonder of those who heard his interpretations. One such beautiful example that Orsisios gave is, as follows: "If one neglects a lamp, failing to supply it with oil, it is quenched gradually until it is dark. Furthermore, if a mouse should approach it and nibble at the wick, it can only do so if there is neither the light nor the heat of the fire. Thus, should the mouse snatch the wick, he can even cause the lamp to fall and break, that is, if it is earthenware. If the lamp is brass, the master of the lamp can diligently set it up again. It is the same with the soul. If we neglect the soul, the Holy Spirit withdraws from it. Thus, the soul grows cool and dark. The enemy, meanwhile, enters therein and gnaws at the soul's eagerness and destroys the body through wickedness. But the soul that had grown negligent, if it should still be a little well disposed and eager toward God, it can be ignited again with the man-loving and most compassionate God's fear and the remembrance of everlasting life. Such a soul can be preserved by the grace of God in the future. For this cause that soul must guard itself from being quenched, by means of vigilance, watchfulness, maintaining the fear of God uninterruptedly in the heart, and keeping the commandments of God untiringly." With such examples and soul-edifying teachings did Orsisios prompt the careless and negligent toward the acquisition of virtue.

Visits with Saints Anthony and Athanasios

Now some of the fathers, at one point, wished to travel to Alexandria in order to meet with the most holy Patriarch Athanasios. While they were on their way, they learned that the great Anthony was still alive. They decided to go and see that genuine slave of God in order to receive his blessing.[112] The great Anthony, by then, was of an advanced age. Despite his infirmity, he rose up and greeted the Pachomian fathers. He, consoling the fathers who were still in mourning over the loss of Abba Pachomios, said, "Cease grieving because the great Pachomios has fallen asleep. He has left good disciples and imitators of his virtuous practises, revealing his ministry in gathering together such a

[112] Saint Anthony, ca. 346, ten years before his repose, was ninety-five years of age. When the Pachomian fathers reached the mountain of Tiloc, they asked for Apa Anthony the anchorite. He had been lying ill in his monastery on the Outer Mountain. The saint, after the persecution of Maximinus Daia, had quit his Outer Mountain called Pispir (or Tiloc) that was near the Nile River. He had withdrawn to the Inner Mountain, Mount Kolzin, toward the Red Sea. From time to time, however, Anthony visited his disciples at the Outer Mountain. Evidently, the Pachomian monks caught him on one of these visits. "The Bohairic Life," ¶ 126, p. 182, 287 note; "The First Greek Life," ¶ 120, p. 382.

brotherhood.[113] There was another who wished to take up this ministration, but one must provide wholehearted zeal in order to succeed at such a goal.[114] But concerning your father, I have heard reports of his great achievements. I often desired to see him in the flesh, but perhaps I was unworthy. Nevertheless, in the kingdom of the heavens, by the grace of God, we shall see one another as well as all the holy fathers. But tell me, whom did he leave as his successor?" The fathers replied, "Abba Petronios who, before his repose, chose Orsisios. Abba Petronios said that God appointed Abba Orsisios to the task. Even though the latter finally accepted the office, afterward he said to the brethren that 'the Lord knows that I have not been convinced for a single day that I am the right man for this office. There are others senior to me.'"[115] Anthony remarked, "Call him 'Israelite' and not Orsisios.[116] If you should go to Bishop Athanasios, who is truly worthy of the episcopate, say to him that 'Here is what Anthony says, "Care for the children of the Israelite."'" After Anthony uttered a prayer and blessed them, he prepared an epistle to Athanasios. When the Pachomian fathers arrived in Alexandria, the great Athanasios welcomed them with all his heart—especially because of the word of the great Anthony.

Abba Theodore Assists Abba Orsisios

Abba Orsisios, by reason of his age, was burdened with the leadership and its concerns. He could no longer tend alone to the salvation of so many. After he received a vision that Theodore should help in this office, he gathered the leaders and spoke of Theodore. All the brothers received the great Theodore, since he was much loved, with much joy, though Theodore hesitated giving many excuses. Lest he show himself disobedient and wilful, he fell in with the entreaty of the brethren. As a true child of Pachomios, he showed eagerness in every ministration; and so, he proved to be an excellent lieutenant

---

[113] Saint Pachomios was the first who drew up a monastic rule in writing. Ecclesiastical historian Gennadius (fl. 470), in his *De Viris Illustribus*, writes this summary in his list of authors: "Pachomius the monk, a man endowed with apostolic grace both in teaching and in performing miracles, and founder of the Egyptian monasteries, wrote an order of discipline suited to both classes of monks, which he received by angelic dictation. He wrote letters also to the associated bishops of his district, in an alphabet concealed by mystic sacraments so as to surpass customary human knowledge and only manifest to those of special grace or desert." "List of the Authors Whom Gennadius Added, After the Death of the Blessed Jerome," Ch. VII, Nicene, 2nd Ser., Vol. III (Oak Harbor, WA: Logos Research Systems, Inc., 1997). As for the writings of Saint Pachomios, "Instructions, Letters, and Fragments" are found in *Pachomian Koinonia*, Volume Three, pp. 13-90.

[114] He is identified as Aotas of whom nothing is recorded.

[115] See "The Bohairic Life," ¶ 131, p. 188.

[116] Cf. Jn. 1:47. He is called Israelite, that is, the one who sees God with interior as well as exterior eyes. Ibid., ¶ 133, p. 190.

to Abba Orsisios. Theodore labored day and night, even more than he had before he attained the abbacy. Since the love of rule was eradicated in Theodore, Orsisios commented that "I rule now more than when I was alone." Theodore strived for the salvation of others, as a true and watchful shepherd, with amazing zeal. But he never did anything without the counsel of the Elder Orsisios. Theodore was exceedingly vigilant and attentive in regard to the needs of the brethren and their salvation. He exhorted them in their spiritual struggles, as a proven and experienced physician. All those who saw Theodore commented that they saw him to be a gladsome and cheerful person. He had the ability and patience not only to confirm and strengthen the virtuous by his own example but also to remind the negligent of the fearful punishments and everlasting torments. When seculars from the world visited the Pachomian foundations, bringing their infirm and demon-possessed, the great Theodore would utter a prayer and heal them. Before he accomplished these cures and the dispelling of evil spirits, he would say to the petitioners, "Do not even begin to think that we supplicate God, as we are sinners. But if the merciful God is pleased to relieve His creation, He has the power to do so. He ever demonstrates His goodness toward all." But when the petitioners importuned him for prayers and works of healing, he would act charitably. He entreated that God's will be done and that which was expedient for the sufferer. Indeed, God hearkened to the prayers of Abba Theodore.

At length, Theodore founded two monasteries near Hermopolis: Kaior and Oui (Nouoi). He also founded another monastery further south, near Hermonthis, establishing it after the Pachomian example. This, too, was done, of course, with Abba Orsisios' blessing. Theodore did not swerve from the rule of the Pachomian monasteries. There too, he appointed fathers that were heedful and solicitous for the souls of others. Each monastery, likewise had seconds, housemasters with their seconds, after the manner of the nine other foundations. As Abba Pachomios, Theodore also founded a monastery for virgins in the village of Bechne: one mile from the men's monastery of Phbow. The sisterhood occupied itself with the weaving of garments and blankets and other things, as well as the spinning of raw flax for the tunics. While everything was increasing, Theodore was still always sensible that he lived at a special time and said as much to the brothers: "In our generation, here in Egypt, I see three significant things that flourish by God's grace for the benefit of all those who have understanding: that Bishop Athanasios, the athlete of Christ, contends for the Orthodox Faith to the point of death; that the holy Abba Anthony is the perfect example of the anchoritic life; and that this Koinonia is a model for all those who wish to assemble souls in God and to help them that they might attain perfection."

At about this time, there was another outbreak of plague, so that many of the monastics were reposing daily. Those among the living had the difficult task of going to the mountain two and three times a day for burials. The distance that needed to be traversed was three miles. But, at the same time, the river overflowed and obscured the roads that were softened with mud. This made it difficult for them to convey the dead on foot. The water kept rising and filling fields, but not enough that they could take a boat to the burial ground on the mountain. "What shall we do if another dies?" cried out those assigned to the burial detail. Theodore commented, "According to our faith, God will spare us in this too." Indeed, with that word, the deaths reaped by the plague instantly halted. While the area was inundated, still no one died. All of the brethren marvelled at this miraculous cessation and the boldness that Theodore possessed before God.

One of the brethren, on the occasion of the synaxis of the brotherhood, asked Theodore: "Why is it that when people speak something harsh to me that I, immediately, become angry?" Theodore answered, "The man of virtue may be compared to a vine. Even as in the case of the vine, whenever someone either plucks a cluster of grapes or presses it, there exudes sweet wine. In like manner is it with the virtuous man, whether he is picked at or constrained by an action or a word or distress, he in no wise can produce no other fruit than a good word and blessing and other similar good responses. As for the carnal man, he only offers anger and bitterness which is analogous to his condition. As for myself, to tell you the truth, I fear being deprived of divine grace. This is because the enemy never ceases waging war, even as the prophet remarked, 'Mine enemies have trodden me down all the day long, for many are they that war against me [Ps. 55:2].' Moreover, if angels have fallen and become demons, and if the most wise Solomon among the prophets, and Judas of the Twelve, and some of the disciples of the Apostle Paul, and a crowd of others have become apostates, how should we, the unworthy ones, not tremble? Should we not fear that, perhaps, from either neglect, or indifference, or carelessness, we, too, as they might fall? Whosoever, therefore, should wish to cleanse himself and deliver himself from sin—whether it be anger, greed, arrogance, love of acquisition, fornication, and the other passions—when such a one is reproached or disdained by another, he must endure the insult or slight gladly; otherwise, such a one shall never be delivered from the passions."

The brother then posed another question: "And if someone should revile me twice and thrice and many times, but I continue to endure while the one who upbraids me does not quit, what ought I to do?" Theodore answered, "The commandments of God are 'more to be desired than gold and much precious stone, and sweeter than honey and the honeycomb [Ps. 18:10],' being more honorable and precious. But we, wanting in understanding, do not recognize this, as those with minds of the flesh[117] who are sunk down seeking the ground.

"But let us not be at all fainthearted, neither let us be afraid of men's reproaches. Let us not lose heart if they insult us, for the Lord encourages us: 'Blessed are ye whenever they reproach you and persecute you, and say every evil word against you falsely on account of Me. Be rejoicing and be exceedingly glad, for your reward is great in the heavens [Mt. 5:11, 12].' And again, 'If they persecuted Me, they will also persecute you [Jn. 15:20].' And, 'If the world hate you, ye know that it hath hated Me before it hath hated you [Jn. 15:18].' Remember also the words of our holy Abba Pachomios, who said on this subject that 'the Lord has ordered us to love our enemies, to bless those who curse us, and to do good to those who persecute us.[118] What danger we are in when we hate one another, when we hate our co-members—those one with us—sons of God, branches of the true vine,[119] sheep of the spiritual flock gathered by the true Shepherd[120] Who is the only-begotten Son of God Who offered Himself in sacrifice for us![121] The living Logos underwent manifold sufferings for so great a work. And dost thou, O man, hate it through jealousy, or vainglory, or avarice, or contempt? These vices, by means of which the enemy has ensnared thee, make thee a stranger to God. What defense wilt thou present before Christ? He will say to thee, "Insofar as thou hatest thy brother, it is I Whom thou hatest";[122] and thou shalt go away into everlasting punishment[123] because thou wast inimical toward thy brother. As for thy brother, he will enter into eternal life because, for Jesus, he humbled himself before thee.'[124]

"Hence, my fathers and brothers," continued Theodore, "the devout man is not only patient with those who persecute him but also prays for them.[125] Such a one shall inherit the kingdom. O man, what hast thou done to make thee worthy of becoming an heir of Christ?[126] Wast thou persecuted as our Lord? Wast thou struck as He was? Wast thou put to death as He was? And hast thou been grateful for all these things? The glory of the world is quite sufficient

---

[117] Rom. 8:6.
[118] Cf. Mt. 5:44.
[119] Cf. Jn. 15:5.
[120] Cf. 1 Pe. 2:25; Jn. 10:14.
[121] Cf. Eph. 5:2.
[122] Cf. Mt. 25:45.
[123] Cf. Mt. 25:46.
[124] This text is taken from "The Instructions of Pachomios," ¶ 37, of the *Pachomian Koinonia*, Vol. Three, p. 30.
[125] Mt. 5:11, 44.
[126] Rom. 8:17.

reward for the few pains thou hast endured in this life. And yet, how great is God's goodness toward us! He is like a man who offers gold and silver and precious stones in exchange for the earthenware vessels in thy house. If we do not understand these things now, then this word of Scripture applies to us: 'And man, being in honor, did not understand; he is compared to the mindless cattle, and is become like unto them [Ps. 48:12].' Nevertheless, the Lord, by His grace, is able to restore our senses. May it be given to us to be vigilant to the end by His grace!"[127] With these soul-saving words did the wise Theodore admonish and exhort each of the brothers. He established them and encouraged them in their spiritual contests. He was not only speaking such words but also putting them first into practise. All of his teachings were applied by him in actual demonstration. Therefore, the brethren had Theodore as an archetype to emulate, which is proper to those who are superiors and hold the abbacy.

Saint Athanasios Visits Saint Theodore

The good reputation and virtues of Abba Theodore reached the Patriarch Athanasios at Alexandria. Taking along other hierarchs, the patriarch and his synodia went about visiting all the monasteries. After he spent a few days in the cities of Antinoöpolis and Hermopolis, he also went up to the monasteries of Nouoi and Kahior where he diligently inspected the accommodations of the brethren.[128] He was impressed with the love of the brethren toward him. They entered the church and prayed together. Athanasios took the time to visit everything: where the fathers held their assembly (synaxis), the refectory, and the cells of each house. He even examined their reclining seats where they slept, though many slept on the ground. Athanasios rejoiced and gave thanks to the Lord for all that he saw and heard in Theodore's monasteries. It was evident to Saint Athanasios that the Spirit dwelt in Theodore. The patriarch could not help but notice how Theodore was possessed of eagerness and zeal and resoluteness for things divine. As he praised Theodore and his brotherhood, he said to his fellow hierarchs, "Brothers, dost thou see the manner in which he strives to save their souls? Are we not also fathers? Nevertheless, we do not have such eagerness and fervor for the good. Blessed are these heavenly-minded men who take up the Cross of the Lord, believing that dishonor is glory and that toil is rest, until they should be crowned in the kingdom of the heavens and enjoy a rich recompense from God!" Such was the blessing that the great Athanasios bestowed upon Theodore. He also said to him in particular, "Theodore, verily, it is a great and God-pleasing work which

[127] This anecdote is also in "The First Greek Life," ¶ 142, pp. 399, 400, and "The Bohairic Life," ¶ 186, pp. 227, 228.

[128] More details of Abba Theodore's encounter with the great Athanasios on his tour is found in "The First Greek Life," ¶¶ 143, 144, pp. 400-402, and "The Bohairic Life," ¶¶ 201, 202, pp. 249-252.

thou hast wrought in gathering so many souls and guiding them to everlasting life. May a manifold reward be rendered to thee from the Lord!" He said this and much more, such as: "Thou hast done a great work in obtaining rest for these souls. I have heard especially about thy monastic rules. Everything is very good." Theodore replied humbly, "The grace of God dwells in us through our father, Pachomios. But to see thee, *despota*, is like seeing Christ." The holy Athanasios then departed. Theodore repaired to Orsisios at the monastery at Thmousons, where he was then staying. Although Orsisios preferred to live in solitude, still Theodore was insistent that he come out of retirement and visit the monastery of Phbow.[129] After Theodore's pleading and exhortations, Orsisios went forth. Since they had much love for one another, which was also observed by the brethren, the brethren marvelled at the harmony between their two leaders and were greatly edified by their relationship: for the two were as one man.

Saint Theodore Prays for the Expanding Koinonia

The monasteries and their belongings grew considerably, so that they were burdened by worldly possessions. Theodore observed that many of the brothers were starting to change their manner of life. This alteration grieved him and moved him to fast, partaking of food every other day, keeping vigil with tears, and wearing a hair shirt underneath his tunic at night. It was evident to the others that Theodore was pondering something that was troubling him. In his affliction, he decided to steal away secretly at night and pray at the tombs where the brethren were interred. Now unbeknownst to Theodore, one of the brothers followed him from behind. Theodore went to the tomb of Pachomios and poured out his heart in prayer. The brother who was secretly listening trembled and feared when he heard Theodore's entreaty, which was this: "O Master and Lord, by the intercessions of Thy slave, Pachomios, deign to visit me; for our negligence has multiplied and we do not perform that which is good. However, Lord, do Thou not abandon Thy slaves, but raise up in us Thy fear and empower us to walk in Thy good path. For Thou hast made us, O Lord, Who indeed spared not Thine only-begotten Son but delivered Him up,[130] even to death, for our salvation." After uttering many other prayers in tears, Theodore descended the mountain.

The Repose of Saint Theodore

In those days, one of the brothers, named Eron,[131] had gotten sick and was expected to repose before Pascha. After Eron breathed his last and

---

[129] How Theodore brings Orsisios back to Phbow is spoken of in greater detail in "The First Greek Life," ¶ 145, p. 402.

[130] Cf. Rom. 8:32.

[131] Apa Eron was the second of Theodore the city-man, the housemaster of the Greeks. "The Bohairic Life," ¶ 205, p. 256.

Theodore closed his eyes, Theodore addressed the synaxis of the brethren and said, "This brother who has just reposed is the sign that another among us is about to repose." Theodore spoke in this fashion because he foreknew of his own coming repose, something for which he asked and the Lord hearkened that he might find rest. After the brotherhood kept vigil over the body of Eron and interred him that Sunday, within but a few days, but after Pascha, Theodore, the one great in virtue, became ill. Theodore, knowing that his hour had come that he should pass over from this world[132] to the much-desired Christ, called to his sick bed the brethren that he might receive forgiveness from them all. Orsisios and all the leaders kept watch as they sat about Theodore.[133] They grieved very much at the prospect of losing such a man of God. Consequently, universal supplication was offered up to God that Theodore might be permitted to tarry longer for their benefit. More than the rest did Orsisios lament bitterly, crying out these words, "O Lord, why wilt Thou take this man who pilots us and enlightens us? Take me and leave him that he might correct the brethren, because he has this strength." Thus, the brethren prayed and wept for three days.

As the blessed Theodore was about to surrender his soul, he addressed Orsisios before the whole company that was present and asked, "Well then, have I grieved thee at any time by word or by deed or by transgressing thy commandment?" Orsisios, overwhelmed with tears, was not able to give answer. Theodore then continued and said to the brethren, "I do not know if I grieved any among you. However, in no wise did I disregard the salvation of any of your souls or my own soul. But this is a gift of God and not out of any goodness or kindness on my part.

"Do not trouble yourselves pleading with God in my behalf, for it has been decided that I go to the Lord as my holy fathers before me. Now then, assist our holy Apa Orsisios in all obedience, in all humility, and without any murmuring. For the inheritance is his: I was only his assistant. The Lord knows that it was not my wish to take up this work, for I am more of a sinner than all other men on the earth. Nevertheless, lest I should perish, the grace of God was always with me so that I was never disobedient in anything the Lord made come my way. Now then, give heed! I testify to you that I have not forgotten the sins of my soul for a single day during the whole time I have been living in this world."[134]

Having spoken these words and others, the thrice-blessed Theodore surrendered his blessed soul into the hands of God. He opened his mouth and

---

[132] Cf. Jn. 13:1.

[133] Theodore sent some brothers to bring Apa Orsisios to him. The brothers of the monasteries in the area around Phbow also came. "The Bohairic Life," ¶ 206, p. 258.

[134] This paragraph is taken in part from "The Bohairic Life," ¶ 206, pp. 258, 259.

gave up his spirit very quietly and calmly.[135] Great lamentation for their orphanhood came about in all the monastery, so that the crying brothers could be heard by people on the other side of the river. According to their rule, they conducted an all-night vigil before the sacred relics. In the morning, they went to the mountain and buried the body of Saint Theodore. After they returned to the monastery, some of the leaders secretly interred him together with the sacred relics of the venerable Pachomios[136]—even as Theodore had requested. They were as one soul in two bodies. Their relics, together since then, will not be separated until the general resurrection. In the future kingdom of the heavens, they shall enjoy together one glory and equal rest; for it was together that they performed the same contest and endured hardship.

Some of the brothers, grieving inordinately, believed that God might return his soul. But they came to finally acknowledge that what had happened could not be undone. They, therefore, submitted themselves to Orsisios, as much as they were able. Thus, Abba Orsisios was returned to the sole governance of the brethren in accordance with his capacity. But he really was very good. He loved the brothers and they loved him. God also helped and strengthened him by opening up the meaning of the Scriptures to him. Hence, Orsisios interpreted the Scriptures for the brethren in a most wise manner, instilling willingness in ascetic struggles among the virtuous and the negligent and lazy alike. Thus, Abba Orsisios shepherded the rational flock with wisdom and understanding for a long time.[137]

---

[135] Ca. 368. Saint Theodore is commemorated individually by the holy Church on the 16th of May (see herein). Both accounts record that he gave up the spirit on the second of the month of Pasons, that is, the 27th of April. "The First Greek Life," ¶ 148, p. 405, and "The Bohairic Life," ¶ 206, p. 259.

[136] "Our Father Orsisios took with him three brothers. They went together to the mountain to the grave of our Father Theodore. He removed him from that site and buried him alongside the bones of our righteous Father Pachomios, the father of the Koinonia, in the place where Theodore had buried his brother Paphnutios. They returned to the monastery quietly and no one noticed them." "The Bohairic Life," ¶ 207, p. 260. "The First Greek Life," records that "after they came back to the monastery, an ancient brother, named Naphersaes, went with some others and transferred Theodore near the remains of Abba Pachomios." ¶ 149, p. 405. Veilleux believes the latter is in error. [See his note. Ibid, p. 423.]

[137] Gennadius [op. cit., Ch. IX] writes: "Oresiesis [Orsisios] the monk, the colleague of both Pachomius and Theodorus, was a man learned to perfection in Scripture. He composed a book seasoned with divine salt. It was formed of the essentials of all monastic discipline. And, to speak moderately, it contained almost the whole Old and New Testament set forth in compact dissertations—all, at least, which relates to the special needs of monks. This he gave to his brethren almost on the very day of his (continued...)

When the great Athanasios learned of the repose of Saint Theodore, he was much affected by it. He considered the holy man's brethren and how he might console them. He quickly took up his pen and wrote to the beloved. He counseled them to deem Theodore as one alive, who is now in a haven free from care and grief. He is resting with the fathers. He confirmed that Orsisios now needed to accept the entire care and concern of the brothers. He urged all the brethren of the monasteries to imitate the way of life conducted by Theodore and the other venerable fathers that they, too, might become inheritors with him of that everlasting blessedness. May it be so for all of us by the grace of Christ, through the intercessions of "the lawgiver and guide of ascetics,"[138] Saint Pachomios! Amen.

On the 15th of May, the holy Church commemorates our venerable Father ACHILLIOS, Bishop of Larisa.[139]

137(...continued)
death. He left it as a legacy." For the writings of Saint Horsiesios, see "Instructions, Letters, Fragments, and Testament" found in *Pachomian Koinonia*, Volume Three, Cistercian Studies Series: Number Forty-Seven (Kalamazoo, MI: Cistercian Publications Inc., 1982), pp. 135-224.

Saint Orsisios is commemorated by the holy Church on the 15th of June. He departed in peace, going to the Logos with such a blameless soul that not even slander could find anything with which to reproach him.

138 May 15th, Orthros Canon, Ode Three, Mode Two, by Saint Theophanes.

139 The Life of Saint Achillios (Ἀχίλλιος), the patron of Larisa, as well as his special festal service, was composed by Archbishop Anthony of Larisa (1340-1362). It was published at Venice in 1745. The divine office has a double canon. The first is the work of Archbishop Anthony and the second one is that of Saint Joseph the Hymnographer. It was included in the *Menaia* of a certain publisher, Demetrios Theodosios (Venice, 1761). Following this edition, it appeared in a special text at Larisa in 1882. It was reprinted again at Larisa in 1896. Afterward, it was corrected by G. Makres at Athens, and again at Athens, in 1952, by Metropolitan Dorotheos of Larisa (afterward of Athens). There is another Church service to the saint, the work of the Monk Chariton, which is laid up in the Athonite codices of Kafsokalyvia, from which is taken the doublet found in the *Synaxarion* at the Sixth Ode: "Larisa tells of thine uncommon excellences, having thee in remembrance, O father, even when dead."

Regarding his physical characteristics, we have this description from Athonite Codex I 70, folio 247, at the Great Lavra, which notes as follows: "He was superior not only in virtue and wisdom but also in the fashioning of his bodily members and characteristics. His countenance was very handsome, even beautiful. He had a ruddy complexion and lofty forehead. His aspect was austere and regal. He had a great long beard. His appearance, simply put, was well put together and harmonious." Saint Achillios of Larisa is not to be confused with the ancient Greek hero of Homer's *Iliad*,

(continued...)

Saint Achillios

Achillios, our righteous father, the divine and wondrous, was born during the second half of the third century. His birthplace was far-famed Cappadocia, where the acclaimed pillars of the Church, Basil the Great and Gregory the Theologian, were also to come forth. His parents were noble and wellborn. They were honorable, distinguished, and sufficiently wealthy. Most importantly, and worthy of esteem, was that they were pious Christians. They were deemed good people, affable and approachable, and noted for their alms. The parents, indeed, were full of good works, which they performed daily. They conducted their lives according to Christ and the Gospel. From such a hallowed root sprung Achillios. They bequeathed to their son a heritage of godliness, in both word and deed, until they fell asleep in the Lord.

The example of his parents was more than a memory to the son. Achillios, from childhood, became their imitator in virtue. He also practised ascetical exercises. He did not pamper himself and live softly or luxuriously. He did not indulge himself with the pleasurable things of the body, as youths often do. When his parents departed this life, Achillios gave his inheritance to the poor. He shared much of it with widows and orphans. Thus, for the sake of Christ, the youth became poor and penniless. He chose the narrow gate and the path full of straits that lead to the kingdom of the heavens. He engaged in fasts, vigils, prayers, and other good endeavors. In his struggles he proved to be resolute and eager. By maintaining with earnestness this manner of life, he became a dwelling place and vessel of the All-Holy Spirit and a model of every virtue.

The blessed Achillios attained such a measure of sanctification and desire for Christ that he longed to take himself away from the confusion and turmoil of this life. By this removal both he and others would benefit. He, thereupon, forsook country, kinfolk, and friends. He departed from Cappadocia and directed his steps first toward Jerusalem. Upon his arrival in the holy land, he venerated, with much awe and compunction, the sacred shrines.

---

[139](...continued)
Achilles (Ἀχίλλεὺς) of Thessaly. Well beyond antiquity was that Achilles deemed the ideal warrior (Trojan War), who was also extolled for his medical and musical abilities.

Following this pilgrimage, he conceived the desire to visit celebrated Rome, the great city, that he might reverence the tombs and relics of the saints, especially the chiefs of the apostles, Peter and Paul. His peregrinations were a blessing to him and to others. At Rome, he proclaimed the divine word. Wheresoever he passed through, even as another apostle, he preached to all the Gospel of Christ. He guided and directed a multitude of idolaters to the Christian Faith. Those who were formerly in darkness were baptized and became children of light, that they might become inheritors of the everlasting kingdom of the heavens.

Such were the occupations of the man of God. It was granted to him, as to the apostles, the gift of working wonders. He healed the sick, cleansed the lepers, corrected the spines of hunchbacks, expelled demons, and performed a host of other miracles all wrought in the name of our Lord Jesus Christ. A numberless crowd hastened to this holy man, resulting in countless conversions from the deceit of idol madness to Christianity. Let no one imagine that these divine and apostolic accomplishments of the venerable Achillios were not without toil, temptations, and tribulations. Even as the apostles suffered persecution and expulsion in place after place, so did he. As the disciples underwent hardship and distress, so did he. For Achillios, as the Lord's men, also endured insults, scourges, and a multitude of troubles. But for the love of Christ and for the sake of the Faith and the Gospel teaching of the Lord, he bore with the ungodly who challenged him. Truly, he received all trials that came his way with joy and gladness. For he had but one goal, and his meditation had a single aim: to lead the deceived and wandering to piety. Need anyone wonder if Achillios should be praised as one equal to the apostles and an evangelist? For he, verily, fulfilled the prophetic phrase which reads: "Their sound went forth into all the earth, and their words to the ends of the inhabited world [Rom. 10:18; Ps. 18(19):4]." Such were the achievements and manner of life of the divine Achillios in city after city and country after country that he traversed. When he came into truly happy Greece and progressed through her, he decided to remain in Thessaly.[140] When his fame circulated abroad, throngs of men and women came to him. They longed to enjoy his angelic visage and mellifluous discourses which guided many to the path of the truth. In this manner, for a short time, he drew like a magnet converts who denied idol mania and hastened to the Faith of Christ. Such was his success in Greece that he was established as her second preacher of the Gospel, after the glorious Paul and the other apostles who heralded the Gospel in that ancient land of the so-called gods and goddesses. Therefore, through his labors, the Faith kept growing and being confirmed in Greece. There was much rejoicing in the

[140] Thessaly (Thessalia) is the region of central Greece, south of Macedonia and north of Hellas.

congregations of the Christians who were devoted to Achillios, deeming him their breastplate and apostle.

At length, there took place the repose of the archbishop of the Thessalian capital of Larisa.[141] The widowed see, however, ere long, was not vacant. Without further ado, the citizens and all the surrounding folk of the countryside, both the small and the great, voted to have the righteous Achillios their hierarch and shepherd. But in truth, it was the grace of the Holy Spirit that not only guided Achillios to those parts but also inspired the faithful to choose him. At length, he was consecrated as Archbishop of Larisa. After the venerable man accepted such a lofty and seraphic office, he began by exhibiting unfeigned diligence toward the flock entrusted to him. He also received the veracious assistance of the other bishops under Larisa. They comported themselves as beloved children of Achillios and were obedient to him.

He piloted the poor, helped the widows, fed the orphans, and relieved those who were wronged. He was shown to be a ready helper in every need. As a good teacher and shepherd, he was instructing and exhorting the flock at all times. He, therefore, undertook nourishing hungry souls and building up the Faith. What ensued was that the rational sheep increased daily in the divine grace of the spiritual life. He demonstrated much fortitude among the Larisaeans, possessing the gift of working wonders and miracles. Many among the sick needed only his healing touch and they received cures. The saint's efficacious entreaties rose up mightily to bring down rains during a great drought. There was also no small number of adversaries and barbarians who, as wolves, outraged and injured his flock. But by his supplications to God he, ofttimes, drove these enemies to untrodden mountains and sent them off cliffs. His marvels are multitudinous which, for the sake of brevity, we need to pass over in silence. We should also mention his gift of clairvoyance, by which he not only foresaw and foretold events to come but also revealed hidden thoughts of the mind.

Such were the exploits of the Hierarch Achillios. His fame spread everywhere, so that his excellent reputation came into the ears of the emperor then reigning: the holy Emperor Constantine the Great. The year was 320. The Christ-loving monarch desired to behold the angel-faced man of God and to hear his eloquent speech. This, before long, came to pass with the cooperation of God's divine help in the year 325. Hallowed hierarchs of the inhabited world met together at the First Œcumenical Synod at Nicaea that they might oppose the impious Arius. Among the council members was our sacred Achillios. The great Constantine met with the bishops. He rejoiced and showed no small honor

---

[141] Larisa (Larissa, 39°38′N 22°25′E), the chief city of Thessaly, is on the river Pinios. From 344 B.C. to A.D. 196, the city remained under Macedonia. Afterward, Rome made it capital of the reorganized Thessalian League.

and respect toward Achillios. In the midst of the hierarchs who had assembled, the blessed Achillios appeared like another brilliant sun. He shone forth radiantly by reason of his preeminence in the virtues, together with his sagacity and sobriety. Nearly all those who attended revered and esteemed his presence.

Prior to the opening session of the council, there appeared the ungodly Arius before the emperor and the hierarchs and the notable leaders according to rank. He came forth with his like-minded minions and assistants. He propounded that the Son of God is not coessential (*homoousios*) with the Father, but rather that He is a creature and something built. Much discussion and debate followed. The divine Achillios then appeared in the midst of the assemblage. He raised his hand in a gesture calling for silence. When he had their attention, he lifted up his voice and said, "O Arius and such of you as have the same mind as he: if what you speak is consistent with truth, that the Son of God is a creature and creation of God, command this rock which is before all to gush forth oil. Only then shall we believe in whatsoever you proclaim. For if you would win us over only by your words, then you would be striving in vain." The Arian faction, feeling constrained before the challenge, fell silent for a short time. But then they rallied against Achillios and remonstrated, saying, "Thou hast called upon us to meet this demand that we might make our case. But rather, we say to thee, impose thy words upon thyself and lay claim to the truth." The Arians spoke in this manner, never believing for a moment that Archbishop Achillios was able to extract a drop of oil from the rock. His requirement of them to make their point before the whole company by such a wonderworking seemed to them to be a token of thoughtlessness and recklessness. The possibility that the venerable man was inspired by divine zeal and the Holy Spirit never entered their carnal minds.

The most holy Achillios did not cower or hesitate in the least. He stood before the emperor and the hierarchs in an attitude of prayer, uttering these words: "If the Son and Logos of God is coessential and glorified together with the Father, as we believe, confess, and preach, let oil flow forth from this rock that the factious might believe and be given assurance." Immediately then—O Thy wonders, Christ King!—a torrent of oil gushed down from the rock so that it soaked the ground all around. This miracle was witnessed by the emperor and all the fathers in attendance for the synod meeting. Universal was the astonishment, so that with one voice all the holy fathers honored and praised the saint. As for the Arians, they were roundly put to shame and could not disguise their sorrow and consternation.

In this manner did God, Who wrought wonders through Saint Achillios, extol and exalt the power of the Orthodox Faith. Meanwhile, Arius and those of one mind with him were humiliated and embarrassed. On account of this miracle was God glorified and the truth made clear: it proclaimed to the world at large of the coessentiality of the All-Holy Trinity. The angels were gladdened as men gave glory, for the light of the truth shone more brilliantly than the sun. The heretics of ill-repute, the Arians, were disgraced by this sign and others[142] accomplished by the holy fathers gathered at that first synod. While the synod with a united voice professed the coessential Holy Trinity, still some of the Arians remained obstinate. The holy synod, consequently, banished them.

After these events, Emperor Constantine the Great rejoiced together with the Orthodox hierarchs. The emperor brought them all, including Saint Achillios, from Nicaea[143] to his newly built capital Constantinople[144] that they might confer their blessings upon her. Upon their arrival, they all offered up extended entreaties to God that He confirm the city and make her steadfast. They prayed she might be invincible in war and against her enemies. The Archbishop of Constantinople, the holy Metrophanes, by reason of his advanced years, was not present at the synod. He was represented by the divine Alexander. When the latter heard of the feats of Achillios, he bestowed no small honor upon the archbishop and called him blessed. They conversed for a considerable time, after which Alexander exclaimed, "O champion of the truth Achillios, may it be well with thee! Great is thy reward in the heavens! Depart in peace and may God be with thee!" Without a doubt, Constantine especially held Achillios in honor. Though the emperor gave gifts to all the hierarchs and sent them forth in peace, yet he donated to Achillios gold and silver toward the construction of churches in the Larisaean see and the introduction and bringing together of other good works. Achillios blessed the sovereign and his household. He bid farewell to the other hierarchs and set a course to his own diocese of Larisa, as a victor and trophy-bearer.

Saint Achillios returned to his flock. The faithful, together with priests and monastics, went forth as a multitude to welcome him. Men, women, elders with the younger, from both the city and surrounding parts, went forth *en masse* in order to greet the one whom they looked upon as their father, shepherd, and teacher. They knelt before his holy feet, many kissing the hem of his garment. There then occurred no small disorder and confusion when, out of eager desire, a contest took place among the people as to who among them

---

[142] One brings to mind the signs and miracles accomplished through Saint Spyridon (see the 12th of December) and Saint Nicholas (see the 6th of December).

[143] The large fortified Bithynian city of Nicaea (Iznik), located on major trade and military routes on the shore of a lake close to the Asian coast of the Marmara Sea, became the seat of two œcumenical synods: in 325, to deal with the controversy over Arianism; and in 787, to put an end to Iconoclasm.

[144] Regarding the building of the capital, see, herein, the account of her consecration (11th of May) and the Life of Saint Constantine (21st of May).

should approach first and receive his episcopal blessing. Despite this pious rivalry, the mood of the people was buoyant that day as joy filled their souls and bodies. As all honored the bishop with one voice, they were also chanting hymns and psalms to God. The hallowed Achillios blessed them and uttered a prayer over them. He then took his place on his throne. The first question the multitude wished to have answered concerned the Nicene Synod. When they heard their archbishop's account of its proceedings, the issuance of twenty canons, its Creed or Symbol of the Faith with the first dogmatic definitions, and the synodal letter excommunicating Arius, there was general acclaim and approbation. When the incident of their archbishop and his encounter with the Ariomaniacs was recounted to them, as well as the supernatural occurrence of oil flowing from a moistureless and sapless rock, there was mighty exultation in the ranks of the faithful. God was glorified and the people were confirmed more solidly in right belief of the holy Orthodox Faith. Arius' subordination of the Son to the Father was rejected. The incarnate Logos was defined as coessential or *homoousios* with the Father. The saint explained to them that if Christ were not fully divine, as the Ariomaniacs claimed, then how could mankind hope to share in divinization or salvation? He mentioned to them that the computation for dating the yearly celebration of Pascha was set. He also spoke of the recognition of the jurisdictions of Rome, Alexandria, and Antioch, and that Jerusalem (Aelia) was also honored.[145]

The godly Achillios found that his flock thirsted for the divine word of God. He gave drink to his flock at all times, so that it increased day by day. There was no time or place that he was not proclaiming the divine word, whether he was in the city or in the countryside. As a result of his assiduousness, in but a short time, he brought all of Greece to the knowledge of God. People were coming from all parts. Idol temples were being leveled to the ground. In their places were the buildings of churches, monasteries, hospitals, and asylums and shelters for the poor. The archbishop also participated in ordaining bishops and priests. In accordance with what was decreed at the synod, he promoted no one without due examination and hearing his confession. The candidates had to be men of virtue and piety, full of good works. He did not wish to act contrary to the very canons he helped issue. Thus, he was cautious not to admit or lay his hands upon any who were guilty of lapses or were not irreproachable.[146] Therefore, as we said, the standing of this great Hierarch Achillios in Thessaly was that of an equal to the holy apostles, though he came second in time as a herald of the Gospel and a teacher of the Faith of Christ. His greatness was not confined to theory and synodal meetings. It was

---

[145] Canons VI and VII. The Constantinopolitan Patriarchate was discussed later at the Second Œcumenical Synod.

[146] See Canons IX and X of the First Œcumenical Synod.

also revealed in the mundane affairs of everyday life in his diocese. He was reckoned not only as an evangelist and interpreter of divine laws but also as one strong, who bore the infirmities of the weak and did not live to please himself.[147] With Saint Paul he said, "Who is weak, and I am not weak? Who is made to stumble, and I am not set on fire [2 Cor. 11:29]?" Thus, our holy archbishop was a protector and defender of the poor, a father to orphans, a helper of widows, and a deliverer of those who were wronged. In every need and necessity, he proved to be their benefactor and champion. He was one who could be counted upon to fight in the first rank for the downtrodden.

The divine accomplishments of this holy hierarch and imitator of Christ did not impinge upon his humble-mindedness and moderation, as the following event will demonstrate. There was an occasion when he was invited by a small city under his pastoral direction. A certain necessity had arisen for which he made haste to go there. He learned, only upon his arrival, that the inhabitants had undertaken elaborate arrangements suitable to a hierarch. Suites were made ready, churches were adorned, roads were cleaned, and food was prepared. Before he entered their city, the people came out to greet him. The natives expected to see one of episcopal dignity, elegantly clad and mounted on a steed, with a luxurious train and richly appointed retinue; instead, what they espied from a distance were two clerics who were humbly dressed and on foot. The people of the host city assumed that the two clerics coming toward them were sent out in advance, as scouts, by the archbishop, to bring back information in regard to the preparations for his visit. When the two clerics came before the crowd, they were asked, "Is the archbishop near or far?" One of the walking clerics replied, "I am the unworthy archbishop." But the people, initially, took this as an ironical response. Not much time passed, however, before they ceased asking the same question. After they gauged his humble demeanor, they gave ear to his sweet words as from a honeycomb. Only then were they persuaded of his mind's caliber and that he was truly the archbishop. Their amazement was great as they kneeled before his feet, seeking his blessing. So much honor did they shower upon him that his modesty shunned it. Assuredly, the faithful of that city were benefitted more by his extreme and exalting humility than by any good deed or eloquent speech. After the venerable Achillios sufficiently instructed them in those things needful and salutary, he returned to Larisa.

Such are some of the highlights of the life of the wondrous Achillios. He was as another sun in the firmament, shining with divine gifts of grace and performing wonders too numerous for counting. He shepherded his flock for thirty and five years. When the hour of his departure from this earthly sphere

---

[147] Cf. Rom. 15:1.

arrived that he should go to that life that is ageless, undecaying, and unending, he rejoiced and was glad in spirit. He foreknew the day of his repose, so he set about arranging his grave. After this was done, he called to himself all the nearby clergy and some leading layfolk, for he wished to leave them with admonitions and exhortations. But when they heard that the holy man was going to the Lord, all of his spiritual children hastened to him weeping and lamenting their imminent orphanhood. Then did that good father calm them and speak to them in a meek manner, "Cease weeping, my children, and afflicting my heart! For I am committing you to the true and almighty God, the One Who is and Whom you came to believe in through me. Take heed and be diligent to preserve the Faith pure and undefiled, that you might be vouchsafed the kingdom of the heavens."

Having spoken thus, the saint raised his hands and his eyes heavenward. He uttered a prayer and blessed them all. He, thereupon, surrendered his soul, holy and luminous into the hands of God, thus paying the common debt to nature in the middle of the fourth century. His sacred relics were bequeathed to the Christians, even as a rare and precious stone and as a perpetual and gratuitous treasure. As for the bishops and priests who were then present, as well as the lay people, they took up his holy relics with much reverence. They laid his body in the grave which he himself had made and readied beforehand. Behold what undeniably took place with the interment! The blind recovered their sight, the lame were set right, demons were driven away, and just about every malady was cured for those who touched that hallowed and most honorable hierarchal body.

After the burial of the grace-flowing relic of Saint Achillios, he remained hidden in that tomb for a very long time. In those years, since it was not the custom to exhume the remains of the dead, there was no recovery of the relics. Actually, so much time had passed that not only the relics but even the tomb itself fell into obscurity. For, in fact, three hundred years had elapsed before God intervened. The Almighty, the God Who knows the secret things of men, did not wish to conceal this pearl. He made known this gem of the saint's sacred relics in the following extraordinary manner. This revelation came about in a miraculous fashion, on the 10th day of the month of February, when once again the saint's flock would enjoy his visible presence and patronage. When the revelation resulted in the recovery of the relics, who can describe the boundless wonderworkings wrought through them? This is because all those sick folk who came and venerated his relics received the cure for whatsoever ailed them. Hence, Saint Achillios' tomb of his sacred relics came to be known as "springs of healing." This saint's relics, revered and highly honored by the brilliant city of Larisa, proved to be a rich treasure trove that was inestimable, priceless, and a free gift.

The holy relics of Saint Achillios remained at Larisa, deposited in his majestic church that the inhabitants later raised up from its foundations. It was the seat of the metropolis. The saint was revered and venerated by all. He continued to work miracles. Then, by God's permission, on account of the sins of the people, Larisa was bereaved. She was deprived of her great treasure, which loss befell them in this manner. The Bulgarian Tsar Samuel of the Kometopouloi house ruled the area of Ohrid. He originally reigned in Macedonia but then conquered independent Serbia. He expanded into northern Bulgaria, Albania, and then northern Greece. He desired independence from the Byzantines.[148] As for the Church in Macedonia, she was under the jurisdiction of the Bulgarian Patriarchate founded by Tsar Symeon without the approval of Constantinople. Samuel also wished an independent Church. Samuel decided to launch his attack at a time when the Byzantine Emperor Basil II was sufficiently distracted in his struggles with competing generals, Bardas Skleros and Bardas Phokas, for the throne. Samuel, therefore, seized the opportunity to expand his own kingdom and reestablish the Bulgarian Patriarchate at Ohrid.[149] The year 986 was significant in Samuel's life and for the city of Larisa. Although Samuel failed to take Solun (that is Thessalonike or Salonica), he bore deeply into Byzantine territory. He conquered the region of Thessaly, together with her capital—Larisa. Samuel's successes and the wresting of Macedonia from Byzantine rule, while the Bulgarian Empire collapsed, ushered in ecclesiastical authority independent of Constantinople. The chronicle[150] of 11th-C. historian John Skylitzes records that "Samuel brought the remains of Achillios, the holy Archbishop of Larisa from the time of Constantine,...to Prespa, the place of Samuel's court." Samuel, thus, lorded it over Macedonia, Thessaly, Hellas, and the Peloponnesos. When he came into Larisa, he not only took the relics but also many inhabitants as captives.

While the relics were at Prespa, Samuel also commissioned a stately shrine that was dedicated to the saint. It was to lesser Prespa, on the isle of Achilefs (named after its saintly guest), that Samuel translated the holy relics and built a magnificent three-aisled basilica. The relics of Saint Achillios were

---

[148] The uprising of the Kometopouloi proved deadly for Samuel's two elder brothers, Aaron and Moses. Aaron was slain by Samuel himself. The uprising spread swiftly through both Macedonian lands and throughout the Balkans.

[149] The recorded dioceses, at that time, were the Macedonian towns of Voden, Meglen, Serres, Ohrid, and Skopje. The precise date of Samuel's creation of the autonomous Macedonian archbishopric is unknown. Upon transferring his capital from Prespa to Ohrid, he likewise moved the residence of the archbishopric, known hereafter as the Archbishopric of Ohrid. Samuel and the Macedonians believed that their own archbishopric helped establish their national identity.

[150] John Skylitzes' *Synopsis historiarum* covers the years 811 to 1057.

laid to rest in the diakonicon in a handsomely decorated sarcophagus. An icon was also painted of Saint Achillios. (Today only fragments of the edifice and the frescoes have survived.) Samuel also won a victory over Basil at Trajan's Gate in 986, when the Byzantine army nearly perished in an attack launched from the mountainsides. Basil's warfare, from 991, therefore, was systematic against Samuel. From 1001, the Byzantine offensive was constant as they invaded Serdica, Macedonia, Vidin, Skopje, and Dyrrachion. In 1014, Basil annihilated the Bulgarian army. Fourteen thousand prisoners of war were blinded and returned to Samuel, who died two days later from shock and grief at the sight of the procession of these blind soldiers. As for the relics of Saint Achillios, it was not until 1965 that they were discovered during excavations. The relics of the Archbishop of Larisa were then returned to his see.

While the relics were on the island for centuries, the saint was sincerely reverenced by the natives. The saint did not begrudge them his wonderworkings, but wrought miracles again and again. Hence were the Bulgarians enriched while Greece was deprived of the sacred relics. This, too, in all likelihood, was permitted by God's dispensation since the race of the Bulgarians was newly enlightened and only lately became solid in Orthodoxy. Therefore, it was needful for the sacred relics of Saint Achillios to travel to these parts as a support and bulwark for them. By the grace of Saint Achillios, who continued even in death to work for the Gospel, he performed many miracles for the Christians. Although the holy Larisaean archbishop was absent, still his protection was not completely withdrawn. In 1082/1083, Bohemond I seized the city but failed.[151]

Thereafter, Larisa fell on hard times. After 1204, it became the seat of a Latin archbishop. In the thirteenth century, she belonged to the despotate of Epiros. By 1393 she had fallen to the Turks, remaining under the Ottomans until 1893 or five hundred years. On account of Larisa's arable lands and strategic location, the Muslims flooded in. Larisa became hemmed in by the estate of Turkish feudal lords so that the Greeks left, thereby denuding the Orthodox community. This was amply seen when the city still had twenty-seven mosques at the end of the nineteenth century. On account of this Muslim predominance in the city, an almost unprecedented transfer took place: Larisa's metropolitan seat was transferred to Trikkala! Nearby Pharsala (Tsataltza) was transformed into a Turkish city! Thus, the removal of the relics of Saint Achillios were providentially taken away lest they should be lost or desecrated

[151] In 1081, Alexios I Komnenos became ruler of the Byzantine Empire and challenged the Normans. For more than thirty years Alexios and Bohemond were rivals. Bohemond and his father came close to dismembering the Greek Empire in the west. Although the Norman army won a few victories, yet Alexios drove Bohemond from Larisa in 1083.

under Islamic rule. The departure of the saint's power and protection from his see during this time is brought out in the following history.

In the period just before two notable cities of the Hellenes, Larisa and Thessalonike, were overrun by Islamic hordes, certain godly Christians were walking on the road to Thessalonike. They were going to celebrate the Feast of Saint Demetrios, who is commemorated by the holy Church on the 26th of October. When they reached the royal highway which is at Vardarion, all the pilgrims witnessed with their own eyes one who appeared as a soldier, coming out of Thessalonike. They also observed one who appeared as a hierarch on the road out of Larisa. When the two met, the soldier spoke first, saying to the hierarch, "Rejoice, hierarch of God, Achillios!" The archbishop responded, "And do thou rejoice, O soldier of Christ, Demetrios!" The Christians who were on the road heard the names spoken and stood to one side with fear to see how the meeting would end. The soldier again addressed the hierarch, saying, "From what place comest thou, O hierarch of God, and where art thou going?" Then Saint Achillios wept and answered him, "On account of the sins and the lawlessness of the people, I was commanded by God to depart from Larisa, which I guarded, because it shall be delivered into the hands of the Hagarenes. And behold! I went forth; and I am going where He commands me. And thou, then, from what place comest thou? I beseech thee to tell me!" Then Saint Demetrios wept and said to him, "I, too, suffered the same thing, O Hierarch Achillios. Ofttimes, I helped the Thessalonians and ransomed them from captivity, and from plague, and from sickness. Yet now, because of their sins and lawlessness, God has sent me forth from them. He has commanded me to leave them, that they should be delivered into the hands of the Hagarenes. For this reason, I obeyed His command and, lo, I went forth! I am going where He commands me." When both of them finished speaking, they bowed their heads down to the earth and wept. After a long time, they kissed and bid each other farewell; then, instantly, they both vanished. This miracle was seen by those Christians, who ventured not to go to Thessalonike. Instead, they turned back and reported the wonder. A month had not lapsed thereafter before Thessalonike was plundered and conquered by the Turks, even as was Larisa.

Despite the terrible misfortunes and dreadful circumstances that prevailed at Larisa during these dark years of imperious and inexorable servitude, the city was not totally devoid of the protecting grace and help of the saint. The city's patron was ever present for those who invoked his aid and ever-flowing wonderworkings. He always showed himself to be a ready helper in any circumstance, assisting and delivering faithful suppliants from every need and affliction. Even after their captivity under the Turkish yoke, followed by centuries of enslavement, through the revolution and even now, Saint Achillios never ceased interceding before the Lord for his pious petitioners.

Today Larisa is free of the yoke of the infidels. She is a very important center for the whole of the vast agricultural plain of Thessaly. She is also a bustling university town hosting an important military air base. One may travel by car, bus, or train to the city as there are no flights. By the river area, excavations in front of a medieval castle near Odos Papanastasiou have revealed an early-Christian basilica with mosaics and a painted tomb, most likely that of Saint Achillios. Presently, there is a huge Byzantine church and bell tower to the city's patron. Through the intercessions of the thrice-blessed Hierarch Achillios, may Larisa be delivered from every heresy!

The information herein of the achievements of Saint Achillios has been brief and limited due to the long and ravaging centuries that intervened from his repose in 355. But that which has come down to us is sufficient for us to have some idea of the thrice-blessed Achillios' sanctification, even as one can know a lion by his paws or a garment by its hem. By the salubrious supplications of Saint Achillios, may we be vouchsafed the kingdom of the heavens, by the grace of our holy God to Whom is due glory and dominion to the ages of the ages! Amen.

On the 15th of May, the holy Church commemorates our righteous Father BARBAROS[152] the Myrrh-gusher.[153]

---

[152] *The Great Synaxaristes* (in Greek) suggests that this may be the saint mentioned by Vryennios in his second volume. The righteous Barbaros fell asleep in the Lord on the 23rd of June. However, the 15th of May came to be designated as the day of his commemoration when his relics passed through the village of Potamos of Kerkyra (Corfu). In the Athonite Monastery of the Great Lavra [Codex I 70, folio 244] another biographical description is given, disclosing that he was a former robber who repented in the same neighborhood. A 14th-C. Bulgarian account speaks of a Barbaros of Egyptian origin who, in his twenty-fifth year, joined some pirates and raided the Albanian coast near Durazz. Though he was raised as a Christian, he only remembered his heritage after surviving a shipwreck. He desired, afterward, to live as a hermit in repentance. A hunter, seeing his swarthy looks and failing to comprehend his language, thought him to be Egyptian. A group of local Egyptians, therefore, acted as translators. Elsewhere, Constantine Akropolites (1300) mentions an African saint of the same name. During the reign of Michael II (820-829), he joined the Saracens in their campaign against Ionian waterfronts. When the marauders put in at Nikopolis in Epiros, they suffered defeat at Dragamest. Barbaros survived the battle and went to Neesi (Nys). He converted to Christianity and took up the labors of a hermit atop a mountain. Today's venerable Barbaros, the Myrrh-gusher, as presented in *The Great Synaxaristes* (in Greek), lived during the 16th C. There are, evidently, a number of saints with this name or appellation. Although their lives have some similarities, the dissimilarities merit serious consideration that there was more than one prisoner-hermit

(continued...)

Barbaros, our righteous father, hailed from the parts of Pentapolis.[154] This is testified to in an old manuscript, penned by an important man named Priest-monk Matthew of the august Monastery of the Great-martyr George the Trophy-bearer called Porta. Apart from this reference regarding the provenance of the history, we have no other information concerning the origin of our holy Barbaros. We are told that he had been captured by the Berbers.[155] Barbaros was in bondage to them for twenty-four years. After this period of enslavement, he was delivered by the grace of Christ. From that point to the end of his days, he lived an ascetic life. The arena of his ascetic contests was near the city of Vonitsa,[156] as we shall see as this narrative progresses.

---

[152](...continued)
called Barbaros. The name itself stood for a concept of a world divided between the civilized Rhomaioi and the uncivilized barbarians. It is not incredible that there could be more than one fleeing prisoner who became a recluse in strange parts where he might be subject to the negative stereotyping associated with barbarians from the outside. In any event, the divine office for today's saint was first published at Venice in 1734. A second edition was produced at Kerkyra in 1886.

[153] The record of the saint's Life, as given in *The Great Synaxaristes* (in Greek), does not explain the discovery of streaming myrrh. One account, elsewhere, describes how he received mortal wounds when hunters came upon him at his retreat. All they noticed was a dark creature. Not thinking that it was a man, they fixed their arrows and shot them. Drawing near, the hunters from Nikopolis heard the saint's last words. He asked that the Priest John come. But Barbaros had already reposed before the priest arrived. The body of the saint was then to be transferred to Nikopolis, but it was mysteriously borne away by the Lord. A chapel was erected on that spot from which streamed forth a healing myrrh.

[154] Pentapolis is on the coast of the Djebel Akhdar plateau in northeastern Libya.

[155] The term Berber is derived from the Roman term for barbarians, *barbara*, as is the name Barbary, which formerly denoted the North African coast. The Berbers strenuously resisted the Arab invasion of the 7th C. But they were eventually converted to Islam, many adopting the Arabic language. They participated in the Muslim conquest of Spain in the 8th C. Two distinct confederations of Berber tribes, the Almoravids and Almohads, built Islamic empires in northwestern Africa and Spain during the 11th to the 13th C. In the 12th C., a wave of invading Bedouin Arabs spoiled the Berbers' peasant economy in coastal North Africa. Necessity converted many of the settled tribes into nomads. In subsequent centuries, the Berbers of the mountain and desert regions often remained beyond the control of the coastal states. *Encyclopaedia Britannica*, s.v. "Berbers."

[156] The small town of Vonitsa or Vonditza (38°54′N 20°53′E) is in Vonitsa and Xeromero province of the Aitoloakarnania (Etoloakarnania) prefecture. It sits on the quiet Gulf of Ambracia opposite Lefkada. From Vonitsa one can go to Preveza or Aktio.

It appears that he had been raised by good Christian parents and was staunch in the Orthodox Faith even prior to his captivity. This we surmise because, even though he was taken prisoner by the Muslim Berbers, with whom he spent over two decades, he in no wise waived his Orthodox Faith. Instead, he endured all afflictions and sufferings as adamant. The more he was persecuted, the more he radiated piety. He proved himself to be as gold tried in the furnace. Truly great, O beloved Christians, was his patience and courage, and, to the end, his love for Christ in the midst of tribulations. One can imagine the perils that he was exposed to during those long years in captivity, as well as the injuries he suffered and the threats he received on the part of the tyrants for Christ's sake; yet he underwent and endured everything valiantly. Who can describe the times of implacable hunger and thirst, the unrelenting misery and fetters, together with sleepless nights and a myriad of other ills? In spite of this, he never succumbed to despair; for he had confidence in a certain Helper Who would rescue him one day. Who was this Helper, my Christian listeners? His father or brother or some other kinsman? Indeed, during that long span of time, he did not know where they might be found. In fact, he did not even know if they were alive. Peradventure one of his friends could have effected a rescue? Although friendship among people can be fervent for a time, whensoever friends should be separated, still one may forget the other easily. This is especially true when each has lost contact with the other. To put it more simply, most people show friendship in order to gain a favor. Few are true and real friends, as an early proverb states: "Many who sit at the same table are not friends in truth."

Who was it in Whom our saint based his hope of deliverance? His Helper was none other than the Savior of us all, our Lord Jesus Christ. It is He Who calls brethren all those who perform His will: "For whosoever shall do the will of God, the same is My brother and My sister and My mother [Mk. 3:35; Mt. 12:50]." Christ gave to Saint Barbaros all the strength he needed to remain steadfast in the face of the tyrants, as the Gospel says: "Do not become afraid because of those who kill the body, but are not able to kill the soul; but rather fear the One Who is able to send away both soul and body into Gehenna [Mt. 10:28]." Certainly it was our Lord Who liberated him. But in order to ascertain that it was Christ, listen to the manner in which his deliverance was accomplished.

The Turks had their eye on Kerkyra (Corfu) for some time as a base from which to attack the surrounding Ionian Islands, Italy, and onward to the west. The Ottomans, under Suleyman I the Magnificent (r. 1520-1566), had bought cover for their planned attack in the form of a peace treaty with Venice. Thus, their campaigns would come as a surprise. Suleyman believed that the entire world was his possession as a gift of God. Even though he did not occupy Roman or western lands, he still claimed them as his own. In 1537, the Turkish fleet came to anchor at Igoumenitsa on the mainland of Greece. The pirate Admiral Barbarossa (d. 1546) then landed on the island and besieged it. Both the invaders and the Corfiots suffered heavy losses. The islanders who were not slain were taken to Constantinople and sold as slaves. Suleyman then withdrew his attack on the island.[157] [Now we are not told how Barbaros, also, was caught up in this campaign; but, evidently, his Muslim masters in Africa sold him for service in the sultan's fleet. The Berbers and Ottomans were trading partners.] We next read that when the Turks failed to take the island of Kerkyra and the other islands, Sultan Suleyman returned to Constantinople. His admiral (capitan pasha), with his men and a host of prisoners, marched off to Preveza in order to complete the reconstruction of that city which had begun earlier on the shores of the sea near ancient Nikopolis.[158] As they passed by Vonitsa, they stopped at Neesi in order to take aboard fresh water and firewood. They entrusted this task to their captives, one of whom was our holy Barbaros. He, as the other prisoners, was bound by a chain around his neck, three yards long, and had a great weight attached to his right foot.

Immediately, then, as the blessed Barbaros disembarked from the ship at Neesi, he managed to enter a certain ditch and hide. When night fell, he made away and came to a cave situated near the village called Tryphon. In that cave he established himself, intending to live a monastic life. In this manner, the holy Barbaros eluded the enemy. He managed to do so by divine assistance

---

[157] Although the Turks made subsequent attacks, the island never fell to them. There were two more major attacks on the island in 1571 and 1573. On these occasions they took no prisoners. They burned the towns and massacred the population. Nine-tenths of the island's population was killed in the three major Turkish offenses of the 16th C. In 1576, the Venetians and Corfiots begun to build the Fortezza Nuova and other fortifications that were legendary in their day. When the Turks attacked once again in 1716, they fought unsuccessfully for a month at the gates of the fort. They were finally dispersed by a great storm sent by the island's patron, Saint Spyridon (commemorated the 12th of December).

[158] Nikopolis, Victory City (Paleopreveza) in Epiros (northwest Greece), is situated on the hilly isthmus of a promontory closing the Ambracian Gulf (Gulf of Arta) from the north. The town, sometimes also known as Actia Nikopolis, was founded by Octavian (the future Augustus) in 31 B.C. to celebrate his decisive naval victory over Antony and Cleopatra VII of Egypt off Actium at the entrance to the gulf. Saint Paul also was at Nikopolis, where he decided to winter [Tit. 3:12]. After his visitation, the city became a Christian center. The ruins of Nikopolis, now known as Palaia Preveza (Old Preveza) lie about three miles north of that city, on a small bay of the Gulf of Arta (Sinus Ambracius) at the narrowest part of the isthmus of the peninsula which separates the gulf from the Ionian Sea. One can, with just a short drive from Preveza, visit the ruins of the ancient Nikopolis which was a dominating city in Roman imperial times.

and guidance. For who can deny that if Christ had not brought about his liberation, he could never have escaped thus bound? How could one conceal oneself amid such a great multitude without the protection of God? Could those who had ransacked so many cities and enslaved so many people prove unable to hold one man, and moreover a slave, and a fettered one at that? Though they boasted of conquering so many cities, yet were they vanquished by one soul. The tyrants were defeated by one who was oppressed: the free men by a bondsman, the mighty by a weakling. Behold the power that our faith in God possesses! There is no mightier and more certain assistance than this.

The saint fled. No one was able to pursue him. He concealed himself in neither an aristocratic household nor a walled city; instead, he sojourned in the lonely wilderness, in a featureless and humble cave. In order to avoid the esteem of men, he never appeared to anyone. Even though he was immured to hardship, still he suffered from hunger. He was able to survive by eating shoots and sprouts. He also endured a parched tongue in that desolate place. He searched about and quenched his thirst, but never with wine which ignites the fire of man's heart and intensifies his thirst. He was obedient to the word of Christ, Who said, "Whenever thou art praying, enter into thy chamber, and after thou shuttest thy door, pray to thy Father Who is in secret; and thy Father Who seeth in secret, shall render what is due to thee openly [Mt. 6:6]." He entered the cave and prayed in secret. But our Lord Jesus Christ, Who honors those who honor Him, revealed this saint to the world. This was so that we may be comforted and assured that our hope in Christ saves us from every danger.

Not much time passed before the holy Barbaros was observed by a certain hunter, who brought the news to the village of the discovery of a hermit. Immediately, then, two devout priests made haste to visit the saint. One was named John and the other Demetrios who were in the area. What appeared so extraordinary to the hunter that he declared it everywhere? He marvelled and wondered at the man he observed in chains and naked. But behold the deep piety of the priests! They listened carefully to the awe-inspiring summarization of the hunter. They did not think that the recluse was probably some prisoner or a beggar, whom they might shrug off and say, "There is no need for us to go and see him. If he has need of anything, let him come forward. We shall, then, give him alms." Indeed, many of us speak in this manner, not wishing to get involved, as do those who close their doors to the needy and the poor. Nor did those priests presume to say, "He has need of us, not we of him. Go about thy business, mister hunter. The things thou sayest are not worth hearing!" Nay, no such thing! Rather, they lost no time and hastened to meet the saint. When they gazed upon him, well, that sufficed for them to learn everything they needed to know. They asked him to come into town and rest, but he declined. They tried to persuade him to take the chain from his neck, but he would not consent. Barbaros replied with humility, "This chain is my golden ornament. By it, I subdue the flesh and make it obedient to the spirit. This cave is my splendid palace. Verily, I am not alone in this wilderness. I converse in prayer with my Lord and Savior. Permit me, therefore, to wage my struggle in this place."

As the priests heard his explanation, they did not press him further. They allowed him to continue the course he had set for himself. When they returned to town, they did not forget him. Indeed, they sent him bread every Saturday. Thus, the holy Barbaros remained in the wilderness and contended in that state for eighteen years. He came into town, secretly, only on holy and Great Saturday. It was his custom to enter the sanctuary of the church. Then, after Vespers of the Feast of the Resurrection, he departed and returned again to the cave where he resumed his struggles. He kept the chain around his neck for the rest of his life. No one knew him except the priests, the elders, and Matthew (the spiritual father of the Porta monastery).

How is it possible to remain unmoved when one considers the austerities and the hardships, which the thrice-blessed Barbaros endured for so many years in that desolate spot? If anyone can begin to comprehend his temptations and trials, would not such a one come to reverential fear and awe? Nonetheless, neither spiritual nor physical temptations were able to separate him from the love of Christ.[159] In all conflicts that he confronted, he was victorious and triumphant. He proved to be an emulator of the saints of old. He remained in that cave to the end of his life, until he was translated to the Lord on the 23rd of June. On the same night that our saint rendered up his soul, our Lord Jesus Christ revealed Barbaros' repose to Matthew the spiritual father. The priest was told to assemble the fathers of his monastery at dawn and to go and bury the righteous Barbaros. This vision also was vouchsafed not only to Father Nectarios, hegumen of the Monastery of the Holy Trinity, but also to Father Efthymios, hegumen of the Monastery of Prophet Elias near Dragani.[160] All these abbots assembled their monks and went to pay their last respects to the venerable one.

The sad tidings of the holy one's repose spread to the neighboring towns. A great throng of Christians came thither, young and old. Indeed, a violent struggle ensued while they all tried to pay their last respects, as though he were a king lying in state. All were enthusiastic to venerate the relics. The monastics incited the other monastics, the layfolk other layfolk. Thus, there came men and women, young and old, whether private citizens or those in public life; not one able-bodied person tarried at home. All gathered together and bore up the sacred relics with much honor. Bearing candles and chanting

[159] Cf. Rom. 8:35, 36.

[160] This is possibly Dragani of the Thesprotias prefecture.

psalms, the procession escorted the relics to the village of Tryphon. When they laid them on the ground—lo, the miracle!—a woman, who had been blind for seven years, kissed the holy relics and regained her eyesight.

In this manner does not God glorify those who honor Him by their good acts? Not only does He rescue them from danger but He also grants them strength that they might deliver others. This is the way God glorifies those who honor Him. The natives of that village, seeing the miracle, exalted God Who had given them such a treasure. Others also approached the relics, and they too were healed of their infirmities. Finally, they chanted sacred hymns and interred the holy remains with honor. They removed the chain from the saint's neck, draping it above his tomb. This was shown as proof of his living martyrdom that prevailed for decades. Hence, Saint Barbaros was the boast of the town more than any other precious possession.

In the year 1562,[161] the Italian fleet made an assault on the Turkish armada. The Italians defeated the Turks, by the aid of God, and inflicted severe loses upon them. On their return voyage, fourteen Italian ships landed at Vonitsa, where they imprisoned all of the Turks found therein. One of the Italian ships was captained by a man named Sclavounus, who had fallen grievously ill. In fact, he was bedridden. As he lay asleep, he dreamt that if he did not visit the relics of Saint Barbaros, who was at the village of Tryphon, he would not be able to regain his health.

At dawn, Sclavounus set sail with five ships. He dropped anchor near the village of Tryphon. He took many of his men with him. When he was

---

[161] The year 1562 is given by *The Great Synaxaristes* (in Greek). The closest date that we could find listing such an important event, as the destruction of the Turkish armada, was 1571 at the naval battle at Lepanto. It was fought in the strait between the gulfs of Patrai and Corinth, off Lepanto (Nafpaktos), Greece. It was there that the fleet of the Holy League commanded by John of Austria (d. 1578) opposed the Ottoman armada under Uluc Ali Pasha. The allied fleet consisted mainly of 200 galleys, not counting small vessels. The ships were supplied from Spain and Venice, as well as from the pope and a number of Italian states. The allies carried approximately 30,000 fighting men and was about evenly matched with the Ottoman fleet. The battle ended with the virtual destruction of the Ottoman navy (except 40 galleys, with which Uluc Ali fled). Approximately 15,000 Turks were slain or captured. There were some 10,000 Christian galley slaves who were liberated. Much booty and spoil were taken. The victors, however, lost over 7,000 men.

Lepanto was the first major Ottoman defeat by non-Muslim powers. It certainly ended the myth of Ottoman naval invincibility. It did not, however, affect Ottoman supremacy on the land. Consequently, a new Turkish fleet was speedily built by Sokollu, grand vizier of Selim II. Nevertheless, the battle was decisive in the sense that an Ottoman victory probably would have made that Islamic empire supreme in the Mediterranean. *The Columbia Electronic Encyclopedia*, 6th ed.

brought before the saint, he was immediately cured. As he did not wish to be separated from his healer, he ordered that the relics be removed from the tomb and transferred to the ship. For who would abandon such a protector and treasure in such a remote place? With the bestowal of the captain's health, he was resolved to take along the one who cured him. The removal took place, to Sclavounus' utter jubilation. As for the village of Tryphon, however, its inhabitants lost their benefactor and their strength!

Saint Barbaros

Now why do you suppose that our saint abandoned that location, which he had chosen for his ascetic abode? "I believe, O brethren," comments the biographer, "that he quit that place for no other reason than that he foresaw that the region would once again be overrun by the Turks. This would take place for reasons known only to God, as you will learn with the progress of this narrative. Therefore, lest the holy relics should fall into the unclean hands of the profane, God permitted them to go to another place—a free land. Even though the Lord could have liberated that region near Tryphon by the intercessions of Saint Barbaros, and thereby have kept the holy relics safe, still we see that because of our sins the Almighty permits even sacred things to fall into the hands of the unworthy. For the sins of the Jews, the ark of the covenant repeatedly fell into the hands of the Gentiles. And for the sins of the Christians, many churches have been leveled to the ground and numerous sacred icons have been desecrated. We have as a more recent example the captivity of the unfortunate Peloponnesos."[162] Therefore, so that the holy relics should not fall into the hand of tyrants and ungodly rogues, they were taken away and transported by that captain who, with joy, charted a course to his country of Italy. While sailing past Kerkyra, the ship put in at one of the island's harbors named Potamos.[163] This probably took place so that the saint

[162] Possibly, the biographer is referring to the bloody and devastating Turkish invasions of the Peloponnesos in the mid-15th C., which brought about the destruction of cities and the capture of thousands.

[163] Potamos is a small town, some four kilometers northwest of the capital of the same (continued...)

would become even more famous. Hearken, then, to another one of Saint Barbaros' miracles.

In that place, an elderly man had a son who had been paralyzed for three years. As the Italian ships came into the port, the old man was vouchsafed a dream. It was revealed to him that if he boarded one of the vessels belonging to a certain captain and kneeled before the saint, his son would be cured. At daybreak, the old man did as he was instructed. When he appeared before Captain Sclavounus, the latter received him gladly. The old man proceeded to disclose everything to the captain. Sclavounus then directed the old man to bring his son on board, that he might be cured. Hearing this, the old man hastened home. He had his son conveyed by litter aboard the ship. Then, when the son was brought to the saint—lo, the wonder!—in an instant, his palsied limbs were loosed. He who previously had to be carried by four men now strode about freely, glorifying God and proclaiming Saint Barbaros. The Christians who lived in those parts, witnessing the miracle, begged the captain to bring the relics ashore that everyone might venerate them. Thus, it came to pass.

All the people gathered and venerated the relics of Saint Barbaros. Spiritual joy presided in all, while many ailing people were cured through his intercessions. They also erected on the site a church, in the saint's honor, with a tall belfry.[164] Each year an impressive celebration is held there on the 15th of May, the day that the relics were conveyed to that site. Two days later, the captain took the holy relics and departed from thence. He arrived safely at his home in Italy. News of this joyous event spread far and wide. By direct order of the pope, the sacred relics were transferred to Rome herself and enshrined in a monastery. The shrine drew many pilgrims. Thus wrote the aforementioned Matthew, who obtained his information from many sources. At the village of Tryphon, only the saint's chain remained as a symbol of his presence. Even though the relics have been carried away, the saint's help extends to all places—especially for those who invoke him with faith. But even through the chain, many miracles have been wrought; for numerous infirm people were healed who went there to visit it.

In the year 1688, the Turks reoccupied the Xeromera of the Aitoloakarnania prefecture, and the small town of Katouna and the village of Alevra,[165] as well as the town of Tryphon. During that dreadful captivity, the

---

[163](...continued)
name—Kerkyra.

[164] The church and belfry are still in excellent condition. Saint Barbaros is deemed the patron of Potamos.

[165] The small town of Katouna (38°46′N 22°06′E) of the Medeon municipality, belongs to the province of Vonitsa and Xeromero of the Aitoloakarnania prefecture. The village

(continued...)

chain went missing from its place. It is evident, therefore, that the saint foreknew of the prefecture's captivity. He, therefore, condescended to have his august relics transferred to the west. All of these things were written by the spiritual father of Saint Barbaros, that is, the hegumen of Saint George at Karnania. O God, through the intercessions of Saint Barbaros, have mercy on us and save us!

Saint Andrew

On the 15th of May,
the holy Church commemorates
our venerable Father ANDREW
the Hermit and Wonder-worker.[166]

Andrew, our venerable father, the hermit and wonder-worker, flourished at the time of the pious *despotes* of Epiros, Michael II Komnenos.[167] Andrew hailed from the village of Monodendrion.[168]

Andrew possessed ardent zeal for the ascetical life. He became an emulator of the holy men of old. He forsook the pleasures afforded by plenty of money and fortune. He also left behind a spouse. Having renounced the world and all that is in it, he took up residence in the wilderness. It was there that for the rest of his life he was surrounded by afflictions, tribulations, and straits. He was subjected to all kinds of weather conditions: frost and cold weather and blazing heat. While persevering through the elements, he also struggled against hunger, thirst, and nakedness. He endured for the sake of the Lord's calling: "If anyone is willing to come after Me, let him deny himself, and take up his cross, and keep on following Me [Mt. 16:24]." The blessed man contested well in all contests prescribed for one assuming the

[165](...continued)
of Alevra is probably Alevrada (38°55′N 21°26′E) of the Inachos municipality of the Valtos province of the same prefecture.

[166] The life and divine office were authored by Andreas Hydromenos Hypargios (d. 1847). The text was published at Venice in 1807, of which the biography was incorporated into *The Great Synaxaristes* (in Greek).

[167] Michael II Komnenos Doukas, also called Michael Angelos, was ruler of Epiros and Thessaly from ca. 1230. He was born ca. 1206 and reposed between 1266 and 1268. In 1238, Patriarch Germanos II visited him at Arta. He received the grant of *despotes* by John III Vatatzes after ca. 1249. The title, from the 12th C., was second only to the emperor and co-emperor.

[168] Monodendrion (39°52′N 20°44′E), of the Ioannina prefecture, is at an altitude of 2,824 feet or 860 meters.

bodiless life. After some time, he returned to his homeland. He ascended a mountain nearby his parents. He engaged in all-night standing in prayer. His ascetical practises continued till he was an old man full of years. Thus, in the fullness of years was he translated to the Lord. His departure was revealed by the Lord in the following manner.

When it pleased the Lord God to take unto Himself the soul of the holy Andrew, there appeared lit lamps that emitted a light like lightning. The lamps descended from the sky, signaling where the sacred relics were lying. Afterward, the lights ascended again on high. The manifestation of this sign was not confined to this one place. It was also seen in the surrounding lands and villages. Therefore, not only the inhabitants learned the cause but also those of the royal city. The most pious Empress Theodora and all the Senate hastened forth. The sacred relics were found. There were also trustworthy reports of many wonderworkings, which God wrought through our venerable father, Andrew, which glorified the Almighty. The Christ-loving Theodora commanded the building of a church, honoring Saint Andrew. From that time until this day, his memory is celebrated in a splendid fashion that glorifies the almighty God and His servant, our righteous father, Andrew.

The royal city mentioned above is not Constantinople. The Theodora recorded herein is neither the mother of the autocrat Michael III nor the empress who restored the icons. We are speaking here of another Empress Theodora, who hailed from Arta and who became *despina* of Epiros. The former Theodora Petraliphaina was the spouse of the aforementioned Michael II Komnenos, circa 1230. The despotate of Epiros was one of the independent Greek states established after the fall of Constantinople in 1204. The other two empires which existed along with Epiros were those of Nicaea and Trebizond. The family names used by the despots (*despotai*) of Epiros were Komnenos and Doukas. Theodora and Michael also lived in Akarnania, that is, Epiros, the capital of which was Arta. The blessed Theodora, commemorated by the holy Church on the 11th of March, gave no consequence to imperial privilege. She was humble-minded and ever mindful of how Christ humbled Himself for us. She concerned herself with achieving all the virtues and living a God-pleasing life.

Now the mountain upon which the godly Andrew undertook toils and labors for God is now called Kalana, which is about one-half hour from the village of Chalkiopoulos. There is, at that location, a rather large cave wherein was built the church that is preserved to this day. Outside of the church is found the tomb containing the sacred relics. By command of the empress, the reliquary was thereafter walled all around. In the year 1794, by reason of divine zeal and reverence for the saint, the most reverend Priest John Nicholas Gerodemos of Chalkiopoulos discovered the saint's relics. They consisted of sanctified bones and two pieces from his legs (between the knee and the ankle). He desired to have them encased in silver and set off for Karpenisi.[169]

He arrived in the city and visited the gilder's shop. Since the relics were pure and unravaged, the priest and the silversmith judged that it would not be appropriate to attach any metal. The priest then took counsel with Bishop Dositheos of Litza and Agrapha. Indeed, the priest was prodded by the bishop to divide the relics in two. But during the night, the saint appeared in a dream in order to prevent this action and said, "Straightway, as soon as thou shouldest arise from thy sleep, give the relics to the silversmith. He shall overlay them as he knows how." The godly priest, thus directed, handed over the sacred relics to the silversmith who exercised his craft expertly. But he only proceeded after the priest revealed the vision and the directive he received from the saint himself.

That night the saint appeared to the Priest John and said, "After the completion of the overlaying of the silver, open the tomb and thou shalt find thirty-two parts of the relics. Thou mayest share them with the surrounding monasteries. As for thyself, retain nought except the portions from the leg shanks." This is exactly what he did. He, consequently, invited some holy monastics with whom he accomplished the recovery of the relics. By the time this occurred, however, he did not find thirty-two relics of Saint Andrew; Instead, he uncovered only twenty-eight. As for the missing portions, they were probably snatched, out of piety, by those in and about those parts. Thus, immediately, Father Andrew distributed the relics to the sacred monasteries. The most notable included Boumon, Tatarnas, Aretha, Saint Paraskeve, and Varytadas. He also gave one of the saint's ribs, which was undamaged, to the metropolis of Arta by means of Bishop Makarios Rogos. By Saint Andrew's holy intercessions, O Christ our God, have mercy on us. Amen.

On the 15th of May, the holy Church commemorates Saint ESAIAS the Wonder-worker, Bishop of Rostov (1090).

On the 15th of May, the holy Church commemorates Saint DEMETRI of Moscow, the nine-year-old Tsarevich who was stabbed to death (1591). His relics were found incorrupt (1606) and working healings, in particular, for children.

On the 15th of May, the holy Church commemorates Saint ESAIAS, Wonder-worker of the Lavra of the Kiev Caves (1115).

Through the intercessions of Thy Saints,
O Christ God, have mercy on us. Amen.

---

[169] Karpenisi is a city in central Greece. It is the capital of the Evrytania prefecture.

On the 16th of May, the holy Church commemorates our venerable Father THEODORE the Sanctified.[1]

Theodore, our venerable father, flourished during the reigns of Constantine the Great (r. 306-337) and his sons to Julian the Apostate (361-363). Theodore meditated on the law of God and fully cleansed himself by means of dispassion that he might become a useful vessel of the All-Holy Spirit: "a vessel to honor, which hath been sanctified, and made useful to the Master, having been prepared for every good work [2 Tim. 2:21]." For this reason, by means of the gift of the calling of God,[2] he strived to walk worthily of the calling in which he was called,[3] so that the name of Christ might be glorified in him.[4] He was, therefore, surnamed "Sanctified." He was the spiritually productive and gainful disciple of our righteous father, Pachomios the Great. Elder and spiritual son were of one mind and heart, so that the zealous Theodore showed himself to be his teacher's imitator in virtue. Such

---

[1] The Life of our holy Father Theodore is presented within the biography of Saint Pachomios, commemorated by the holy Church on the 15th of May, who was his elder and fellow ascetic. The edifying and inspiring histories of Saint Theodore, which we have reserved for this day, are not repeated on the 15th of May lest the biography of Saint Pachomios become unduly long for this volume. We extracted from those same sources those anecdotes pertaining to Saint Theodore, so as not to eclipse the accounts given for either saint on the 15th. As on the 15th, the collateral sources, with *The Great Synaxaristes*, include *Pachomian Koinonia* in three volumes from the Cistercian Studies Series, trans. by Armand Veilleux (Kalamazoo, MI), as well as *The Evergetinos* from Center for Traditionalist Orthodox Studies (Etna, CA).

Ecclesiastical historian Gennadius (fl. 470), in his *De Viris Illustribus*, writes this summary in his list of authors: "Theodorus, successor to the grace and the headship of Abbot Pachomius, addressed letters to the Pachomian monasteries. They are written in the language of holy Scripture, in which, nevertheless, he frequently mentions his master and teacher Abba Pachomius and sets forth his doctrine and life as examples. This Pachomius had been taught, he said, by an angel, that he himself might teach again. Theodorus, likewise, exhorts the monks to remain by the purpose of their heart and desire. After the death of the abba, a dissension arose. When some had broken the unity of the Koinonia by separating themselves, he urged the restoration to harmony and unity. Three hortatory epistles of his are extant." "List of the Authors Whom Gennadius Added, After the Death of the Blessed Jerome," Ch. VIII, Nicene, 2nd Ser., Vol. III (Oak Harbor, WA: Logos Research Systems, Inc., 1997). As for the writings of Saint Theodore, "Instructions, Letters, and Fragments," they are found in *Pachomian Koinonia*, Volume Three, Cistercian Studies Series: Number Forty-Seven (Kalamazoo, MI: Cistercian Publications Inc., 1982), pp. 91-134.

[2] Rom. 11:29.

[3] Eph. 4:1.

[4] 2 Thess. 1:12.

deeds were written aforetime, in a state of ecstasy, by Prophet Abbakoum. Since Theodore laid low "the tents of the Ethiopians [Hab. 3:7]"—that is, the gloomy and dark demons, and cut to pieces their heads—he was translated to the Lord. For all those who undertake toils and pains, and who perspire for the sake of supplying virtue in their faith, and knowledge in virtue, and self-control in knowledge, and patience in self-control, and piety in patience, and brotherly affection in piety, and love in brotherly affection, in no wise shall they ever stumble. Neither shall they be barren or unfruitful in the full knowledge of our Lord Jesus Christ. There shall be richly supplied to those who diligently apply themselves the entrance into the eternal kingdom of our Lord and Savior Jesus Christ.[5] Such was the diligence of Saint Theodore the Sanctified, even from boyhood.

Saint Theodore

Saint Theodore's Early Years

Theodore's Christian parents were affluent and pious. We also know that he had a brother, who later became Abba Paphnutios. Now Theodore, even before he reached adolescence, showed religious tendencies—loving to fast and pray. One day, when there was a general holiday for the Christians, Theophany, his family made great preparations for a splendid and luxurious table. All ate and drank, rejoicing. Theodore, still quite young, only felt compunction in his heart. He came to this state by divine grace, so that he began to stipulate to himself, "If thou shouldest enjoy these perishable foods, O Theodore, thou shalt be deprived of everlasting and imperishable benefits." As he uttered these words, he sighed. Afterward, he went and hid in a separate part of the house. Once there, he knelt on the floor. He began praying fervently and tearfully, saying, "O Master, O God, the Knower of all secrets,[6] Thou knowest that I have chosen nothing from the world other than Thy love. It is Thee

[5] 2 Pe. 1:5-11.

[6] Cf. Acts 1:24; 15:8.

Whom I desire with all of my heart. For this reason, I beseech Thee, guide me and enlighten my mind that I might ever keep all Thy commandments." Theodore's mother, in the meantime, was looking about carefully for him. When she discovered him weeping in that place, she asked, "What has embittered thee? Why dost thou not come to the banquet table and eat with thy brethren?" The blessed Theodore, however, gave no answer. In an ingenious manner, he slipped away from her, after he said he was not hungry. He remained the rest of the day alone, spending it prayerfully and in complete abstinence. He did not behave in this manner only once but frequently.

While Theodore was living in the world, he subjected himself to greater hardships than the ascetics of the desert. Theodore had the habit of fasting until evening, ofttimes partaking of food only every other day. When he did eat, he abstained from costly meats and dishes. He was intent on mortifying his flesh and training himself for the ascetical life. His parents, finally realizing the purpose of Theodore's voluntary abstention, gave him permission to join a monastery. He, thus, entered a monastery in the Nome (province) of Latopolis, when he was about fourteen years of age.

Saint Theodore Goes to Tabenna

It was not long before Theodore heard of the great old man, Pachomios, and his shining virtues. Theodore, therefore, repaired to Tabennesi where Pachomios had settled ca. 323. When Pachomios first saw him, he accepted him into the monastery. It was 328, the same year that Saint Athanasios the Great was elected as archbishop at Alexandria.[7] Now Abba

---

[7] "There is a considerable discrepancy among the various documents concerning the chronology of Theodore's life, and especially his age at the time he came to Tabennesi. According to 'The Bohairic Life' [*Pachomian Koinonia*, Volume One, ¶ 31, p. 56], he began to fast in his parents' house at the age of twelve; and he left his home two years later to go and live for six years with a group of anchorites. He arrived at Tabennesi at the age of twenty or, more precisely, in his twentieth year [Ibid., p. 57]. Moreover, in 'Bohairic' [¶ 199, p. 247], Theodore states that he was eighteen years under Pachomius, which means: that he was about thirty when he became Pachomius' assistant; and that he arrived at Tabennesi in 328. The small fragment S14 ['Sahidic'], which gives the same text as 'Bohairic,' also mentions twenty as Theodore's age when he came to Pachomius. But all the other sources are silent about a period of six years with a community of anchorites in Latopolis; and they give fourteen [Gland Av] or thirteen ['Letter of Bishop Ammon'] as his age at that time. 'The Arabic Life' [published by E. Amelineau] adds that it was the fifth year since the foundation of the monastery. That gives us a date of 329. According to 'The First Greek Life' [*Pachomian Koinonia*, Volume One, ¶ 78, p. 351], Theodore was about thirty years old when he was appointed by Pachomius as steward of Tabennesi, around 337, which would give the impossible date of 321 (two years before the foundation of the

(continued...)

Pachomios, immediately, knew, by the grace of the All-Holy Spirit, what this youth would later become. The venerable Pachomios kept Theodore close at hand, rejoicing in the lad's progress. Pachomios loved and esteemed him above the others, because he saw how he possessed absolute obedience.

Saint Theodore's Mother

While Theodore was still young, his mother came searching for him that she might bring him back home. She had heard that he was under obedience to a very holy man, Abba Pachomios. Armed with letters from the bishops that were addressed to the abba, she first went to the convent of the abba's sister, Mary. The nuns offered Theodore's mother hospitality and then sent her letters to Abba Pachomios, which entreated the elder to allow her to see her son.

Pachomios had come to love the young Theodore, esteeming his ready obedience and splendid asceticism in one so young. Pachomios summoned Theodore and said to him, "Child, thy mother has come to the convent. She has letters from the bishops, giving her permission to see thee. Go, then, my son, and comfort her, especially for the sake of the holy bishops who, at her behest, have written these letters." Theodore remarked with all sincerity, "Assure me, my father, that should I see her after all I have learned here in the monastery that the Lord would not require of me some defense at the second coming. I fear that I should become a scandal and stumbling block to a number of the brethren by visiting with her after all this time. For if the sons of Levi, who lived before the period of grace, ignored their parents and their brethren in order to keep the law of God,[8] should I, whom God has vouchsafed such grace, prefer parents or relatives over the love of God? Indeed, the Lord has said, 'The one who loveth father or mother more than Me is not worthy of Me; and the one who loveth son or daughter more than Me is not worthy of Me [Mt.

---

[7](...continued)
monastery) for his coming to Tabennesi. Ammon, according to whom Theodore was thirteen when he came to Pachomius, also states that he was twenty-two when he witnessed a vision of Pachomius that must be identified with the one described in the 'Bohairic Life' [¶ 73, p. 94] and in 'The First Greek Life' [¶ 88, p. 357]. He was then recently appointed steward of Tabennesi, and it was about the year 337—which gives us 328 again as the date of his arrival as in 'The Bohairic Life.' The year 328 (allowing for a certain vagueness in numbers, the difference of one year in 'The Arabic Life' is insignificant), therefore, can be accepted as the date of Theodore's coming to Tabennesi. The convergence of three independent sources ['The First Greek Life,' 'Letter of Bishop Ammon,' and 'The Arabic Life'] in giving thirteen or fourteen as his age at that time militates against Bohairic's figure (twenty) and against the authenticity of Theodore's six-year period as an anchorite in Latopolis prior to his coming to Tabennesi." Note taken from "The Bohairic Life," ¶ 30, pp. 272, 273.

[8] Lev. 21:11; cf. Num. 6:7.

10:37].'" Pachomios responded and said, "If thy conscience assures thee that it is not to thy benefit, I certainly will not constrain thee. The forsaking of kin is the work of those who have utterly renounced the world and themselves. Thus, monastics, at the very least, should avoid worldly contacts which are unprofitable. Those who are members of Christ and serve Him with perfect self-denial, all of these members they should love equally. But if someone resorts to equivocating or quibbling with these precepts, saying, 'My kin are my flesh and I love them,' let such a one be mindful of the apostolic admonition: 'For by whom anyone hath been defeated, by the same hath he been enslaved [2 Pe. 2:19].'"

As a result of this conference, Theodore had no desire to confront his mother. When she was told of her son's deliberate choice, she resigned her claim despite the episcopal letters. She decided to sojourn in the sisterhood of Christ, thinking to herself, "If it is God's will, I shall see my boy sometime with the brothers. Peradventure, by reason of him and my remaining here, I may even save my soul." Thus, by the application of godly strictness, when wrought for the glory of God, benefits accrue to those who endure even though they may suffer distress for a time.[9]

Saint Theodore's Unswerving Obedience

From his youth Theodore demonstrated obedience to the elder as to God. He considered Pachomios as his father and guide. Theodore meditated upon the words of God and was thereby nourished and strengthened in the Spirit. He deemed his elder's admonitions and exhortations to be beyond reproach. If it happened that the elder gave him a charge but then changed it afterward—causing Pachomios to chide Theodore and say, "Why hast thou done this?"—the young man was not offended or piqued. Nor did Theodore attempt to justify himself; instead he kept silence. His confidence in his elder remained unshaken. He rather said to himself, "The man of God had given me that order according to my will, but afterward, inspired by the Holy Spirit, he corrected me. It must be so; for why else would he lay that faulty command to my charge? I have read of a similar circumstance in the book of Jeremias. The Lord spoke to Jeremias and said, 'I spoke not to your fathers, and commanded them not in the day wherein I brought them up out of the land of Egypt, concerning whole-burnt-offerings and sacrifice.'[10] But in fact He had given that

[9] *The Evergetinos*, Volume II of The First Book, "Hypothesis XV: It is essential for those who have abandoned the world not to communicate with their relatives according to the flesh or to nurture the slightest interest in them," pp. 75-77. See also in the *Pachomian Koinonia*, "The First Greek Life of Pachomius," Volume One, ¶ 37, pp. 323, 324.

[10] Jer. 7:22.

precept through Moses. Such being the case, I need to weep until our Savior makes my heart upright and makes me worthy to obey His saints."[11]

Saint Theodore's Brother, Abba Paphnutios

Now Theodore also had a sibling, a brother, named Paphnutios. Theodore had already spent a considerable number of years in the coenobium and had given ample proof of his integrity in keeping his monastic vows. Now Paphnutios, after all this time, came to the monastery, requesting to be made a monk. As for Theodore, who had already "put off the old man with his practises, and had put on the new, that is, being renewed toward full knowledge according to the image of the One Who created him,"[12] did not wish to show any partiality toward his brother after the flesh. While Theodore was reconciled in his mind to act in this fashion yet his brother was not. Paphnutios wept by reason of his distress. Not much time passed before Abba Pachomios was informed of the difficulty that arose. Pachomios could not help but remember the times with his own brother, Father John, who had already died. He called Theodore for a heart to heart talk, saying to him, "My brother, there is no harm in condescending in the beginning with one who has just arrived among us. Even a newly planted tree requires much water and care until it should take root, so it is with those settling down and growing in the ascetical life. When, by God's grace, Paphnutios establishes roots, he will support himself in the Faith." Theodore, as one who always obeyed the counsels of Pachomios, comported himself accordingly. In a sanguine manner, he assisted his brother, Paphnutios, with great understanding.[13]

Saint Theodore Commiserates with a Disgruntled Monk

There was another monk in the monastery who received criticism with difficulty. When Pachomios had reprimanded him for the sake of that monk's salvation, he did not receive the rebuke cheerfully but rather became melancholy. But the monk's sorrow was not in accordance with God, as Saint Paul tells us. He was not sorrowed to repentance, which is in accordance with God and not to be regretted. No, his sorrow was of the world which works out death.[14] Theodore, as one discriminating, recognized the signs, for that monk's dejection made him feel isolated and alienated from the others. In his heart he was planning his departure. Theodore, wishing to comfort him, feigned that he

---

[11] "The First Greek Life," ¶ 50, pp. 331, 332.

[12] Cf. Col. 3:9, 10.

[13] "The First Greek Life," ¶ 65, p. 342; *The Evergetinos*, Volume II of The First Book, "Hypothesis XVI: We must love our relatives in the flesh equally with our other brothers, as long as our relatives lead a similar kind of life; if, however, they conduct themselves in a way discordant with that of our brothers, we mush avoid them as harmful," p. 87.

[14] 2 Cor. 7:9, 10.

too was suffering at the hands of Pachomios and passed this comment to him: "The old man's way of talking to me is abrupt and more than I can stand." The dejected brother, plucking up courage, divulged what was bothering him and said, "So thou hast, in like manner, suffered his style of speech and incivility." Theodore remarked, "Indeed, I have and much more than thou hast. Be that as it may, let us condole together until we might prove him again! If he amends his manners toward us, then let us remain. But if his impoliteness continues, then we will take ourselves away to another place." Hearing Theodore commiserate with him in this manner, the saddened brother received consolation and strength. That same night, Theodore went privately to Pachomios and revealed to the elder how that monk was disquieted with him. Pachomios said, "Very well! Go and bring him here. Both of you offer reproofs and, according to how God shall inspire me, I shall make reparation." Theodore went and said to that brother, "Come, let us be off and face the old man that we might see how he will speak to us." The monk fell in gladly with Theodore's suggestion. Theodore, though he feigned annoyance before Pachomios, took the initiative and began reproaching Abba Pachomios for his abrupt speech and manner. Pachomios replied to the both of them, "I have sinned. Forgive me, my sons. Canst thou not bear with your father, as the good sons that I know you are?" But Theodore showed that he was not satisfied and started again to heap reproaches on the elder. But the other man, discomfited at what was transpiring, gestured to Theodore to have done with it and said, "Enough! It is well. I am satisfied." Thus, through Theodore's good artifice, that brother was comforted and benefitted.[15]

Saint Theodore's Forbearance Toward a Fellow Monk's Attachment

Now at the monastery there was another brother who kept importuning the Elder Pachomios for a blessing to return home and visit his family. After asking many times, he finally threatened the elder that, should he not give him leave to see his kinfolk, he would, in any event, depart and resume secular life. Pachomios told him to wait a few moments and that he would give him a reply. Meanwhile, Pachomios quickly and privately called Theodore. Theodore, beloved by all, readily sympathized with those in distress. Pachomios disclosed how one of the brothers would not be brooked in getting leave to go home for a visit. Pachomios then said to Theodore, "Take charge of this brother and journey with him to his home that he might visit with his parents. Humor him and then escort him back to us. As thou knowest, there is much that is good in this brother. It is well worth the effort and God's will, too, that we humor men until we have delivered their souls from the enemy who would take them captive. Believe me, God will reward thee for thy pains!" Theodore meekly

---

[15] "The First Greek Life," ¶ 66, p. 342; "The Bohairic Life," ¶ 62, pp. 81, 82.

accepted the commission and accompanied that brother. After Theodore and the brother arrived at the parents' house, a meal was prepared for them in a quiet part of the building. Since it was not his custom to eat in the home of seculars, Theodore was loath to take a meal. Theodore's displeasure was immediately spotted by the other monk, whose temper soured and he became sullen. Theodore noticed the effect he had and that he needed to oblige his brother. "Besides," he reasoned to himself, "there are no seculars with us and the fare is entirely monastic. Thus, I had better indulge him lest I return alone to the monastery." Theodore ate, though very little, deeming his concession to be a necessary sacrifice.

Had he not read in the Epistles that we no longer ought to judge one another and put a stumbling block in a brother's way or an occasion of offense? The food itself was not unclean, so why on account of food should he grieve his brother? Then he would no longer be walking according to love. He might even with food destroy one for whom Christ died. He would be serving Christ by eating. Did not the apostle say, "Let us then pursue the things of peace and the things of building up of one another"?[16]

When Theodore and that brother returned to the monastery, Theodore reported all that transpired. Pachomios, hearing Theodore recite his plight, did not censure him. The elder rather said, "Thou didst not eat of thine own will but for the sake of God and for thy brother's salvation."[17]

Saint Theodore Corrects a Monk's Private Interpretation of Scripture

At another time, when Theodore thought that such visits might continue, he took the brother aside and asked him, "How dost thou understand this Gospel passage: 'If anyone come to Me, and hate not his own father, and mother, and wife, and children, and brothers, and sisters, and still, his own life also, he cannot be My disciple [Lk. 14:26].'" The brother replied, "Scripture often puts its words at a lofty level that we might aspire to fulfill some small part of them. For really, how can we hate our parents?" Theodore, pretending to be provoked, remarked, "Is this truly the faith of the Tabennesiots? Does the Gospel pronounce one thing and you, on your own authority, interpret something else? I am not remaining here. I will return to the little monastery from whence I came. At least the old men there do not refute the Gospel!" Thus, Theodore made a pretense of walking out and concealing himself. That brother, guilt-ridden about what he said and how he scandalized another, took the matter to Pachomios. The elder remarked, "Dost thou not know that Theodore is a neophyte? If he should leave here on such grounds, it will not be good for us. Our good reputation will suffer a black eye." The brother, acknowledging what the elder told him, made haste to find Theodore and

[16] Rom. 14:13-20.

[17] "The First Greek Life," ¶ 67, p. 343; "The Bohairic Life," ¶ 63, pp. 82, 83.

prevent his departure. After discovering Theodore's whereabouts, he kept insisting that he not depart the monastery. Theodore, feigning a grave face and indignation, said, "If thou wilt have me remain, promise me before our Lord and the brotherhood that thou shalt uphold the Gospel in all things and not in part." That brother, realizing the absurdity of his private explanation[18] of the Gospel, repented and did as Theodore requested. Thereupon, he never went out again to visit his parents. By Theodore's good artifice, a brother was set on the path of evangelic perfection.[19]

The Spirit of the Fear of God

Abba Theodore had the custom of going to the monastery at Phbow every evening after his labors at Tabennesi. He was punctual in this endeavor, as he enjoyed listening to the words of Scriptures as explained by Abba Pachomios. After Theodore attended, he then repaired to Tabennesi where he recounted to the brethren all that he had heard and learned. This practise was observed by Theodore for quite some time. On one such occasion, when Theodore went to Phbow, Pachomios was not to be found. Theodore climbed up to the roof, where they assembled for the synaxis, that he might recite sections from the sacred Scriptures that he had memorized. As he was reciting, the place where he stood began to shake. Theodore, wondering what was happening, went down into the synaxis area that he might continue reciting by heart. As he entered the place where the synaxes were conducted, he could not abide the place by reason of the fear that filled that place. Theodore shuddered as that Spirit of the fear of God[20] rushed at him. He then leaped out of the door, not knowing what was occurring inside.[21]

Unbeknownst to Theodore, Pachomios was within in the midst of an awesome and terrifying vision. Pachomios was gazing at the east wall of the sanctuary, which became as gold. He beheld a large icon of Christ Who was wearing a crown with images and precious stones. The latter appeared to be the fruits of the Spirit: love, joy, peace, long-suffering, kindness, goodness, faith, meekness, self-control.[22] Two great and august archangels flanked the Lord. They were utterly motionless and contemplating the Lord's image. Pachomios also gazed upon the image, entreating God that the fear of the Lord might descend on the brethren that they might no longer sin against Christ. As he kept repeating this prayer, the archangels remarked, "Thou canst not endure the fear

---

[18] 2 Pe. 1:20.

[19] "The First Greek Life," ¶ 68, p. 343, 344; "The Bohairic Life," ¶ 63, pp. 83, 84. It is the Bohairic anecdote that links this brother, who would visit with his parents, with the preceding account.

[20] Is. 11:3.

[21] "The First Greek Life," ¶ 88, p. 357.

[22] Gal. 5:22, 23.

of the Lord as thou hast requested." Pachomios answered, "Yes, I can, by God's grace." With that word, straightway the ray of fear moved toward Pachomios. When it touched him and penetrated his very members, he collapsed to the ground and began to writhe like a fish. His soul grew sorrowful and nearly fainted away toward death. The angels stood and watched him, while not completely averting their eyes from the Lord. They said, "We forewarned thee that thou couldest not withstand the full shock, did we not?" Pachomios cried aloud, "Have mercy on me, my Lord Jesus Christ!" Immediately, the ray of fear withdrew gradually and mercy moved toward him. He was then comforted and rose to his feet.[23]

After the morning synaxis in the assembly room, Theodore found Pachomios speaking to the ancient fathers. He heard Pachomios say to them, "I nearly surrendered my soul this night! As I was praying where we hold the synaxis, I beheld some awesome apparitions. I was so terrified that it was as if I were no more. I implored the Lord to instill me and the brethren with fear of Him and that we might have it to the end. I then brought to mind how the fathers were with Moses at the foot of Mount Sinai. There was fire and other fearful happenings.[24] Then, in my distress, some bold man came in. But by God's mercy, he went out again immediately." Theodore then interrupted and said, "I am the man." Theodore then explained how, not finding Pachomios, he went up on the roof. When it started to shake, he came down to pray. "But I was unable to do so by reason of the fear in this place. My body was quaking from intense fear, so I fled out the door." The ancient men present marvelled at these coinciding experiences. But they were especially amazed since Pachomios was not in the habit of revealing to them, or anyone for that matter, the hidden things he beheld by the will of the Lord. He only spoke when he thought that such a narration could build up his listeners in the Faith. Indeed, the holy men are always as if in heaven by their thoughts,[25] for they overthrow reasonings and every high thing which lifts itself up against the knowledge of God, and they bring into captivity every thought to the obedience of the Christ.[26]

Saint Theodore's Great Temptation

Theodore was appointed to be, after the man of God Pachomios, a comforter of souls for the brethren. Seven years later, when the elder was

---

[23] "The Bohairic Life," ¶ 73, pp. 95, 96.

[24] There were "voices and lightnings and a dark cloud on Mount Sinai: the voice of the trumpet sounded loud, and all the people in the camp trembled [Ex. 19:16]; and all the people perceived the thundering, and the flashes, and the voice of the trumpet, and the mountain smoking; and all the people feared and stood afar off [Ex. 20:18]."

[25] "The First Greek Life," ¶ 88, pp. 357, 358.

[26] 2 Cor. 10:5.

gravely ill (ca. 344), some of the fathers and monastery superiors were concerned who might succeed the great man. They all deemed Theodore the most fit since he knew best Pachomios' manner of life. They importuned him to promise that he would become Pachomios' successor so that the brethren should not scatter like shepherdless sheep. Although Theodore asked to be excused and would not agree, still they prevailed upon him to give them his word.

As it turned out, Pachomios survived the illness. He was apprised of what had taken place and Theodore's eventual consent. Pachomios summoned the monastery heads, namely, Sourous, Psentaesi, Paphnutios, Cornelios, and Theodore too. When they all assembled before him, he addressed them and said, "Let each man disclose his imperfection. I shall commence: I have been amiss in addressing those brothers who are in turmoil because I have been engaged elsewhere, that is, working in the fields to feed this multitude." (Now the elder was occupied with this labor because there was a famine in the land.) Thus spoke Pachomios. He then turned to Theodore and said, "As for thee, O Theodore, tell us thy shortcoming." Theodore spoke without dissimulation, saying, "These last seven years thou hast dispatched me to make the rounds of the monasteries and handle affairs as thou wouldest. All that time, it never entered into my heart that after thee I would be in charge as the father of this multitude. But now this very thought plagues me, so that I cannot vanquish it." Abba Pachomios remarked, "Well said! No longer hast thou authority over anything concerning the brethren. Take thyself away to some solitary place and beg God to forgive thee."

Theodore, straightway, rose up grief-stricken. He went directly to his cell, where he wept and mourned. He believed that God had turned away His countenance from him because he had grieved the Lord's slave, Pachomios, whom he held to be perfect and invincible. After the passage of two years, Theodore was often visited and encouraged by the brethren. The truth is that most of them did not consider his thought to be a sin. But Pachomios punished him on account of his wish to make Theodore perfect and completely free of ambition for power. The time that Theodore spent weeping and sighing was not over his loss of rank.[27] No, what troubled him the most was that he made room in his heart for such a wicked thought. Pachomios then received a vision to send Theodore to the Monastery of Thmousons that he might visit the brotherhood. Pachomios was told that Theodore would find consolation and refreshment. As Theodore departed, he wept and said, "Lord, do I still have repentance?"

[27] It was ca. 336-337 that Theodore was made steward of Tabennesi.

Now when Theodore reached Seneset, that is, Chenovoskion (Goose-pen), he waited for the ferry to take him westward. He finally boarded and found two old monks in the boat. One of them started praising Theodore, commenting to his companion, "Blessed is this monk!" The other replied, "Why dost thou call this wretched fellow blessed? He has by no means reached the measure of the praise thou art heaping upon him. But when thou seest him grown up to the full measure of the man with the basket,[28] then lay thy praises upon him."[29]

The first one said, "What is its measure?" He began to say, "There was a certain farmer who was so difficult that it was rare for anyone to be able to spend a whole year with him. But someone got up, came to him, and said, 'I will work with thee.' He said to him, 'So be it.' The one who volunteered showed his mettle, by wisely irrigating at night and by intelligently sowing various crops in the field and by sensibly putting the green chaff to good

---

[28] The exact meaning of the word μαϱγώνιον is unclear. The origin of the word, either Arabic or Syriac, is also the subject of long discussions. But whatever the form of the basket in question or the origin of its name, it does not alter the general meaning of the story. Note taken from "The Bohairic Life," ¶ 95, p. 282.

[29] The Prophet Jeremias was also given a sign by baskets—two of them [Jer. 24:1, 5-10]. After Nebuchadnezzar took Jechonias and the captives to Babylon, Prophet Jeremias writes: "The Lord showed me two baskets of figs, lying in front of the temple of the Lord. The one basket was full of very good figs, as the early figs; and the other basket was full of very bad figs, which could not be eaten, for their badness [Jer. 24:1]." The Lord gave the interpretation to the prophet, saying, "As these good figs, so will I acknowledge the Jews that have been carried away captive....And I will fix Mine eyes upon them for good, and I will restore them into this land for good [Jer. 24:5, 6]." The Lord also promised to give them a heart to know Him, and that they shall be to Him a people. So it was in the case of Theodore. If he willingly endured his exile, as did the Prophets Daniel, Ezekiel, and the holy Three Children, he would be as the basket of good figs. But as for the bad and inedible figs, the Lord said this regarding those who refused exile: "I will cause them to be dispersed into all the kingdoms of the earth, and they shall be for a reproach, and a proverb, and an object of hatred, and a curse, in every place whither I have driven them out. And I will send against them famine, and pestilence, and the sword, until they are consumed from off the land which I gave them [Jer. 24:8-10]." The basket of bad figs represents those who fell into pride and rebellion. God looked with favor upon the exiles and indicated that the chastening effect of bondage would be worked to their good; such was the case with Theodore. The bad figs were those who challenged the judgment of God and the message of the prophet. If they had yielded and surrendered to their due and just captivity, they would have been healed. Hence, the two angels, heard by Theodore remonstrating over him, were demonstrating that Theodore could come to either the measure of the good basket or the bad basket. It was his decision.

purpose.[30] Hence, after the farmer had tested the man in all these and found him obedient without questioning, he said to him, 'Thou art no longer to be my hired servant but my son and heir.' Well then, if this one has also measured with the basket, he can deserve to be called blessed."

The other old man said to the first one, "Since thou hast spoken this parable, pray, give its interpretation as well." He said, "The farmer is God; He is difficult since He commands us to bear the cross and not follow the impulses of our hearts. Now, Pachomios, this man's father, by obeying God in all things became well-pleasing in His sight. And if this man is steadfast like Pachomios, then he too will become God's heir." Hearing this explanation, Theodore was strengthened, marvelling at what was said and at those who said it. And stepping off the boat, he saw them no more; for they were angels from God who had appeared to him this way to correct and console him, as Abba Pachomios testified later. After he had come to the monastery and returned to Phbow, Theodore pondered by himself upon what he had heard; and he was comforted. Now it is important to know that Theodore was grieved not because he had been punished, but because he had ever entertained such a thought that "after Pachomios, it will be me." This pain was especially acute to him since he heard Abba Pachomios saying, "Even as a corpse does not say to other corpses, 'I am thy head,' so too I never considered that I am the father of the brothers. God Himself alone is their Father."

Saint Theodore's First Trip to Alexandria with Abba Zacchaeos

After this episode, Abba Zacchaeos, the head of the boatmen, went to Abba Pachomios and said, "The eyes of Theodore have sustained injury by reason of his continual weeping. Dost thou wish that I should take him with me on the boat to Alexandria?" Pachomios approved. Therefore, Theodore went, comporting himself as a newly tonsured monk. With his head bowed, he was like a child arrayed with extreme humility and meekness. He undertook to be

[30] The text here is abridged giving a description of how that man served the farmer and proved himself. It was the same for the exiles. The prophet gave them this word from the Lord: "Build ye houses, and inhabit them, and plant gardens, and eat the fruits thereof; and take ye wives, and beget sons and daughters; and take wives for your sons, and give your daughters to husbands, and be multiplied, and be not diminished. And seek the peace of the land into which I have carried you captive, and ye shall pray to the Lord for the people: for in its peace ye shall have peace....Let not the false prophets that are among you persuade you;...I sent them not. When seventy years shall be on the point of being accomplished at Babylon, I will visit you, and will confirm my words to you, to bring back your people to this place [Jer. 36:5-10 LXX; 29:5-10 KJV]." So it was for Theodore. He did not idle away his time while banished. Thank God he was not away for seventy years but seven!

of service to the boatmen at every possible opportunity, seeing that they ate first or that he jumped out on the bank first to tie the boat to the stake.

Afterward, Abba Pachomios declared that God had granted Theodore a sevenfold increase of his previous progress. Even the great Athanasios, the patriarch, heard of Theodore and wrote Pachomios that he should like to see the man for himself. Pachomios also said to the brethren, "Think not that our Theodore has suffered a diminution before the Lord because he was publicly demoted before the eyes of men. On the contrary, he has progressed far beyond what he had been by reason of the humility in which he endured his penance. Remember: 'Whosoever shall exalt himself shall be humbled; and whosoever shall humble himself shall be exalted [Mt. 23:12].'" So spoke Pachomios in recognition of Theodore.[31]

Dissent in the Church

Some time after this event, in the autumn of 345, the great Pachomios was summoned to a synod at Latopolis. It was there that he was made to offer a defense and explanation of the gift of clairvoyance. Now when Zacchaeos and Theodore came back from Alexandria, they greeted Abba Pachomios and the brethren. Pachomios asked, "How fares the Church?" He made this inquiry since the blaspheming Ariomaniacs wronged the Church and deprived the flock of her chief shepherd, Athanasios. Pachomios remarked, "We believe in the Lord. He has permitted this to happen in order to test the faithful. But punishment will come swiftly and wrath will not tarry long."[32] After this he spoke to them of the events that took place at the Latopolis Synod.

The Leadership at the Koinonia after the Repose of Saint Pachomios

At Pascha of 346, there was an outbreak of plague in the monasteries that claimed the lives of many of the brethren. The great Pachomios also contracted the illness, as well as other monastery heads and stewards. Theodore, by the grace of God, remained immune. He ministered to the greatly emaciated Pachomios. On his deathbed, Pachomios named Petronios as his successor. He was the superior at the Monastery called Tsmine in the region of Panopolis. After the repose of Pachomios, it was Theodore who was entrusted with exhuming the elder's body and concealing the relics elsewhere, even as he was instructed by the great old man. Petronios, however, was also ill, and died soon thereafter. Just as he was about to surrender his spirit into the hands of God, he appointed Abba Orsisios, father of Chenovoskion, for the care of the brethren. Thus, Orsisios became the father of the Koinonia.

---

[31] "The First Greek Life," ¶¶ 107-109, pp. 372, 373; "The Bohairic Life," ¶¶ 94-97, pp. 124-134.

[32] Wis. of Sirach 7:16.

Saint Theodore's Second Trip to Alexandria with Abba Zacchaeos

Later that year, in October, Archbishop Athanasios returned from the imperial court. Zacchaeos and Theodore, for a second trip, went to Alexandria. They first visited with Saint Anthony the Great who was in the Outer Mountain. He welcomed them and blessed them. After he uttered a prayer in their behalf, Zacchaeos and Theodore left for Alexandria that they might visit with the holy Pope Athanasios who welcomed them warmly. It was after this that Abba Orsisios appointed Theodore, for a time, as housemaster of the carpenters at Phbow.

Saint Theodore and the Phnoum Bakery

Now after Pascha in the year 347, a certain Abba Makarios—father of the Monastery of Phnoum, after the passing of Abba Sourous from the plague—asked a blessing of Abba Orsisios to send for Abba Theodore. Makarios asked for Theodore that together they might prepare bread, for Makarios knew that this occupation would be a source of encouragement to Theodore. He also knew that Theodore was experienced in baking. And so, after Pascha, Theodore went with Makarios to Phnoum. While they were yet on the Nile, and Theodore was sitting in the boat, a brother came to him. That brother, newly arrived in the brotherhood and a skilled baker, took a look at Theodore. Observing Theodore's humble and quiet demeanor, he imagined he must be a novice. The brother struck up a conversation with Theodore, asking, "How long hast thou been with the brotherhood?" Theodore replied, "Not very long." The brother continued, "Hast thou acquired experience in baking prior to coming to the monastery?" Theodore answered, "It is scarcely worth mentioning." The monk then said, "When thou findest thyself in the bakery, be not scandalized if thou shouldest see anyone jesting or bickering. It is inevitable that one finds all kinds of people in such a community. Just look to thyself and those who are watchful." Theodore replied, "Very well!" Now after the boat was secured by mooring at the monastery, the brethren came forth to welcome and embrace Theodore; for they remembered Theodore as a comforter of souls when he used to go about the monasteries with Saint Pachomios. As for that brother who offered his unsolicited advice, he was embarrassed and afraid for having presumed to speak as he did before such an honored abba. Nevertheless, as Theodore tarried with them, all were edified at his profound and unstudied humility.[33]

Saint Theodore's Modesty and Humility before Abba Orsisios

After he discharged this duty, Theodore returned to Abba Orsisios who taught the brethren in parables and provided them with interpretations of diverse sayings and passages. On one occasion, the brothers asked Theodore

---

[33] "The First Greek Life," ¶ 121, pp. 383, 384; "The Bohairic Life," ¶¶ 137, 138, pp. 194, 195.

to render an explanation to some spiritual saying or to recount a vision of Abba Pachomios. Theodore deferred, saying, "Here is our Father Orsisios. Let us ask him anything we wish and he shall tell us, for he is our father." While Orsisios was speaking and teaching, Theodore could be seen sitting and listening like a guileless child. Theodore was wont to say within himself, "I know nothing, because I grieved God and our Abba Pachomios by what I did then."

Rebellion at the Thmousons Monastery and Saint Theodore's Elevation

As the brethren increased, so did the properties and goods of the monasteries expand. It was reasoned that fields and materials were needed to sustain such a multitude. A certain Father Apollonios, head of the monastery of Thmousons, contrary to the rule of the Koinonia, desired to purchase some superfluous commodities. Since the head of the Koinonia, Abba Orsisios, told him not to buy certain goods, Apollonios was vexed and threatened to separate his monastery from the community. This and numerous other disturbances were provoked by him. When he finally seceded from the union of the other eight men's monasteries, this ushered in no small temptation. As for the good and kindhearted Orsisios, this division was a deep grief to him; for he feared the dispersion of the souls gathered by God through Saint Pachomios. Since Apollonios refused to have anything to do with the rules of the Koinonia, Orsisios had every reason to fear the dissolution of the Koinonia. With a broken heart and contrite spirit, Orsisios implored God to instruct him how to continue. With copious tears, he wept and said that "many do not listen to us even for the sake of their own salvation. Each follows his own heart. All is in a state of turmoil. I fear for the others lest they take occasion for not desiring any longer the early life of love in concord. O Lord, I am no longer able to do this alone! Reveal to me one who is able to help that I might not become responsible for the loss of so many souls."

Orsisios then was granted a vision. He beheld two beds: one was a beautiful antique while the other was new and strong. As Orsisios looked upon the two beds, he saw a man like unto our Abba Pachomios who spoke to him in confidence, "Cease fearing, Orsisios. The antique bed may rest upon the new one, and thus thou shalt be unburdened." In that state of ecstasy, Orsisios understood that the new and firm bed was Theodore. When he arose in the morning, it was as if he were already relieved of his burden. Indeed, all the more was his mind set at ease since he loved Theodore, as did everyone, for his humility and because Theodore knew how to endure contradiction by sinners.[34] The following morning, Abba Orsisios convened a council of all the ancients,

[34] Heb. 12:3.

with the exception of Theodore. After he explained his plight in governing the brethren and how he was unable to bear all the cares and concerns alone, he asked them to choose one who could help. But they, with one mind and voice, urged him to make the selection. He then gave the following recommendation: "If you are unanimous in your consent that I should decide, then know that the one revealed to me by God, as being capable to shepherd you in all matters, is our own Theodore. Indeed, it is generally known that it was he whom we had as our abba after our Abba Pachomios." Now, as we said, Orsisios excluded Theodore from the meeting; for he knew that by reason of Theodore's profound humility he would protest the distinction given him. As for the venerable fathers that were there, they rose up and went to Theodore. They embraced him with joy and exclaimed, "Our Father Pachomios is indeed living again for us!" Theodore could not hold back his tears, for he refused the appointment offered by Orsisios who had gone to Chenovoskion and remained there. Theodore brought to mind the bondage he had endured when he had listened to other brothers who had once spoken to him about becoming their superior. He had begged the Lord to dispel such thoughts, so that the seven years he had spent since that time might not go for nought.[35] Indeed, the thought of obtaining authority or rule no longer entered his heart.

As a result of this latest council, Theodore spent three days neither eating nor drinking. His nourishment was his tears. When they insisted, he said, "I will in no wise consent to this until I should first meet with the one who named me previously—that is, Abba Orsisios." Thus, all they could do was send for Abba Orsisios at Chenovoskion. When the fathers assembled again, Orsisios and Theodore met face to face. Orsisios said to him, "Was it we ourselves who appointed thee? Nay, it was our father who appointed thee. For he did this ahead of time when, on his deathbed, he took hold of thy beard and said, 'Take care, Theodore, to do quickly what I have told thee, that is, do not leave my bones where they are buried.' Likewise, he said, 'If the brothers should become negligent, thou art to stir them up in the law of God.' This means, therefore, my abba, that the brethren would be entrusted to thee." Hearing these words, especially about the exhumation, Theodore no longer objected. Orsisios commended him to the brethren and went back to Chenovoskion.[36] Thus, it was in 350 that Orsisios went into retirement, leaving our

[35] These seven years comprise the two years of Theodore's great penance and the five years that followed. Since Orsisios' resignation took place less than five years after the repose of Saint Pachomios, this permits us to place the beginning of Theodore's penance a little more than two years before Pachomios' death and his rehabilitation shortly before the founder's repose. "The Bohairic Life," p. 289, note for ¶ 140.

[36] "The First Greek Life," ¶¶ 127-130, pp. 387-389; "The Bohairic Life," ¶¶ 139,

(continued...)

Theodore as acting superior. He instructed the brethren and cared for their souls. He still would do nothing without the counsel of Abba Orsisios and comported himself as his subordinate.

In regard to the rebel Apollonios, Theodore addressed the problem. He embarked on a boat with some of the monks, making the rounds to the monasteries and confirming the brethren. After much exertion and spiritual understanding, Theodore won over Apollonios. The latter finally made peace with the brothers. Hence, the enemy of our salvation, who had tempted both the Thmousonian brotherhood and Apollonios the superior, was put to shame. The sanctified Theodore not only demonstrated his watchfulness over souls in this case but also encouraged each one privately and tended the souls of those who came to him. His zeal and patience were legendary. He was always conscious of having to give an account to our Savior for so many.

Saint Theodore's Orthodoxy and Some of His Visions

Theodore was great among the ascetics, not only in practising abstinence, temperance, and self-restraint, but also in exercising patience, fortitude, and ready obedience. He also upheld the correct Faith, guarding the flock from heresies against the Trinity. As one with a pure mind, who loved divine contemplation, he passed beyond all things visible and communed with the invisible. In a sacred vision, he was lifted up to speak and dwell with God. Even as the God-seer Moses, he yearned to behold the splendor of God. He was deemed worthy to behold the incomprehensible Lord Jesus. Bishop Ammon, a former Pachomian monk at Phbow, entered in 352 under obedience to Abba Theodore. After spending three years at Phbow and many years in Nitria, he became a bishop. He wrote a letter, addressed to Patriarch Theophilos of Alexandria (385-412), outlining some of the visions and miracles of Abba Theodore.

Bishop Ammon describes Theodore's divine vision during the tumultuous time of the Arians. Theodore prayed that God would set men free from the error of Arius. During his prayer, Theodore beheld something like unto three pillars of light that were absolutely identical to one another. Theodore then heard a voice, saying, "Give heed neither to the division of the visible sign nor to its outline, but only to the identity; for there is no sign in creation that can express the Father and the Son and the Holy Spirit."[37]

Abba Theodore had another vision, also during the period when Abba Pachomios was alive, which took place at the monastery of the Tabennesiots. In the midst of his nightly devotions, in order to ward off sleep, he began

---

[36](...continued)
140, 138, pp. 195-197.

[37] In the *Pachomian Koinonia*, Volume Three (Kalamazoo, NI: Cistercian Publications Inc., 1981), see "A Letter of Bishop Ammon," § 11, p. 79.

walking through the monastery and praying. At length, needing to satisfy the relentless demand of nature, he sat down by the door of the monastery church where he dozed. An angel of the Lord awakened him and bade him follow. Theodore rose up and went inside the church. It was diffused with light and overrun with angels in the sanctuary. At such a sight, both fear and awe pervaded him. When he was summoned to draw nigh, he went forth. One of them, who was in much glory, gave Theodore wondrously strange food which he was ordered to eat. As he tasted it and experienced a stupendous taste, the light and the angels in the church began to depart. When he was roused from his slumber, he hastened to disclose what he had seen to Abba Pachomios who declared, "The one who received two talents gained another two talents above them; and the one who received the five talents brought another five talents.[38] Do, thou, therefore, gird up the loins of thy mind,[39] and bear fruit to Him Who has given thee grace." Theodore groaned at these words and said to the elder, "Pray thou to God on my behalf." Now from that day henceforth, Theodore was granted continued revelations from the Lord.[40]

There was also a vision that Pachomios and Theodore shared together. Now there was a monk who was being harassed by a demon. Theodore took the sufferer to Abba Pachomios at Phbow, that the afflicted one might receive the benefit of the elder's prayers. Pachomios espied Theodore from afar. He, thereupon, left off speaking to the brethren and went forth to meet Theodore and the monk whom Theodore had mounted on a donkey in order to transport him. Some of the fathers at Phbow were dismayed with Pachomios' precipitous departure and said as much: "We are elders and Abba Pachomios has left us, indeed, the moment he caught sight of Theodore who is but a young man that he might greet him." These were the same monks who were disgruntled with the elder earlier for having allowed Theodore to give instruction to those who were his seniors. Although Pachomios chided them for their lack of humility, they still bore resentment. Notwithstanding, Pachomios said to Theodore, "I had word of thine arrival by a command of the Lord. Entrust the sick brother to someone else and come with me into the assembly area, where we have the synaxis." Theodore went with Pachomios. They prayed standing from the second to the ninth hour.

Now as they prayed, they both beheld above them, as high as a tower, a great throne. The Lord was seated in glory, but in a form in which He chose to be seen by the abbas. At times, the throne appeared at such a lofty height that it was out of their sight. At other times, the throne descended low enough that they could all but stretch forth their hands and touch it. This ascending and

---

[38] Mt. 25:22, 20.

[39] 1 Pe. 1:13.

[40] "A Letter of Bishop Ammon," § 14, p. 81.

descending of the throne took place for about three hours. When the throne was in the lowered position, Pachomios took hold of Theodore as if he were offering him with his hands to the One seated on the throne. Pachomios was saying, "O Lord, accept this gift from me." Pachomios performed this a number of times, until he heard a voice that said, "I have hearkened to thine entreaty; be manly and brave." After this vision, Abba Pachomios bade Theodore depart in peace and fetch the ailing monk whom he had brought with him. Together, Pachomios and Theodore prayed for the man. He was straightway delivered of being tempted by the demon. Theodore then returned with him, perfectly well, to Tabennesi.

Now when Pachomios was later summoned before a synod at Latopolis to answer charges regarding his clairvoyance, Theodore thought to hide the things he was vouchsafed in visions by the will of God. He perceived that it would be more prudent. Pondering on this, he said to the brothers, "What is greater than to have the Holy Spirit? If the one who has the Orthodox Faith and keeps the commandments of the Lord is accounted worthy to be a temple of God, it is plain that, where God is, there is all power and confidence."[41]

Saint Theodore the Wonder-worker

Abba Theodore, the namesake of "the gift of God," together with his many heavenly gifts and perfections, was also vouchsafed the gift of healing, though he himself suffered from headaches. He wished to be tested like unto Job of old, who endured everything that befell him blessing the name of the Lord.[42] Theodore desired a double crown, that of asceticism and sickness, since his elder, Pachomios, told him that the one who lies sick can be struggling far more than the one in health. Such a man earns a double crown.[43] As for the suffering of others, Theodore maintained a different attitude. Now whether the petitioners, monastics and seculars, were suffering from demonic possession or disease, Theodore would speak in the plural and say, "Do not even begin to think that we supplicate God, as we are sinners. But if the merciful God is pleased to relieve His creation, He has the power to do so. He ever demonstrates His goodness toward all." Theodore, therefore, always prayed that the will of God be done.[44]

Additional Foundations to the Koinonia

Since more seculars were coming to take up the monastic life, Theodore founded two monasteries near Hermopolis, called Kaior and Oui

---

[41] "The First Greek Life," ¶ 135, p. 393.

[42] Job 1:21.

[43] See the 15th of May herein, "The Life of Saint Pachomios," or "The First Greek Life," ¶ 90, pp. 358, 359.

[44] See "A Letter of Bishop Ammon," § 18, pp. 83-85, which describes how Saint Theodore heals a fifteen-year-old girl who was near death.

(Nouoi). He, however, established them only with Abba Orsisios' approval. He also opened up a convent for virgins in the village called Bechne, which was close to the Phbow monastery. These monastic houses were also governed according to the law of the Koinonia. There was no rivalry between Orsisios and Theodore. The brethren of the Koinonia marvelled at the harmony between their two leaders and were greatly edified by their relationship: for the two were as one man.

Saint Theodore and Saint Athanasios Meet

In October of 363, Patriarch Athanasios left Alexandria for Upper Egypt. He was actually fleeing Emperor Julian the Apostate. He came up by boat to the Thebaid and paid a visit to the monasteries in the region of Hermopolis. Abba Theodore took some of the notable fathers and entered a boat. They found the pope just before he reached the Hermopolite Nome. Athanasios was being thronged by bishops, clerics, and monks. Despite the crowds, Athanasios saw the Pachomian fathers from a distance and remarked, "Who are these that fly as clouds, and as doves with young ones to me [Is. 60:8]?" When the delegation from the Pachomian monasteries came up to the pope, Theodore did not embrace him first. Much rather, Theodore had appointed venerable elders to greet him first. But Athanasios recognized Theodore and took him by the hand, saying, "How are the brothers?" Theodore answered, "By thy holy prayers, *despota*, we are well." The brothers then began to chant psalms. There were at least a hundred people there and no one knew his neighbor. But it was Abba Theodore who chose to hold the pope's donkey, as a kind of groom. The abba walked in front of the pope with the brothers who were chanting. There were lamps and torches flanking the pope. Theodore was filled with the Spirit, and the pope perceived this clearly. Theodore's zeal and strength moved him to avoid being in the middle of the press. Meanwhile, the torches nearly burned Theodore. The pope took note of this and remarked to those with him, "Do you see how the father of so many brothers wearies himself? He runs in front of us to secure our passage. It is not we who are fathers, but these monks who have humility and obedience on account of their love and fear of God. Happy are those who do not neglect to carry the Lord's cross to the end, despising the ignominy and toil which to them is glory and refreshment."

Thus, Athanasios visited Antinoöpolis and Hermopolis. He called upon the monasteries and found everything very good, giving praise to Theodore. The pope then wrote to Abba Orsisios, saying: "I have seen thine assistant and the father of the brothers, Theodore; and I have discerned in him the Lord Jesus of thine Abba Pachomios. I rejoiced at seeing the children of the Church, and they delighted us with their presence. Even as Theodore was about to come to thee, Orsisios, he said to me, 'Remember me.' I said to him, 'If I forget thee, O Jerusalem, let my right hand be forgotten. Let my tongue cleave to my throat, if I remember thee not [Ps. 136:6, 7].'"[45]

Saint Theodore's Private Grief

Theodore then, in 367, went to see Abba Orsisios and brought him back to Phbow. By that time, Theodore's sorrow increased with the growing affluence of the monasteries. Since he had grown up under Abba Pachomios, he was not used to leisure since, in those days, they were burdened with many cares. In the time of the great old man, they were vigilant not to be possessed by a spirit of acquisition and collect worldly possessions. But Theodore could see that many were being affected and altering their lives. In his heartfelt distress, he fasted and prayed for guidance. He went to the tomb of our Father Pachomios and complained how negligence multiplied. He begged his holy elder not to forsake his disciples.[46]

Saint Theodore's Repose

Just before Pascha of 368, one of the brothers, named Eron, who was the second of Abba Theodore, known as the City-man, became ill. On Great Saturday of Holy Week, when our holy Father Theodore the Sanctified was in the synaxis with the brethren, he emerged and went to visit the sick man who was in the throes of death. When Eron breathed his last, it was Father Theodore who closed his eyes. Father Theodore then uttered the prophetic remark that "this brother who has just reposed is the sign that another is going to pass away unexpectedly." Theodore, of course, was talking about himself but did not divulge this. God had already revealed to him that the end of his earthly sojourn was drawing nigh. Although far from being old or infirm, for a year prior to his repose, Theodore would say, from time to time, that the Lord would soon be visiting him. Thus, as one who had already died to the world and lived as an angel, he was eager to pass on to the life that never ends.

A few days later, Father Theodore fell ill. Abba Orsisios and all the notable fathers were about his sickbed. After he made his peace with them all and insisted that he had only been Orsisios' assistant and not his successor, he surrendered his soul amid loud lamentation that could be heard on the other side of the Nile. At that moment a great fear and a sweet fragrance came over those who mourned their orphanhood, saying, "It was indeed our righteous Father Pachomios who reposed today. We have become miserable and wretched today, as we recalled Theodore's virtuous conduct, his mild speech, his great humility, and his constant and gentle love toward each one of us."

---

[45] "The First Greek Life," ¶¶ 143, 144, pp. 400-402.

[46] Ibid., ¶ 146, p. 404.

This took place on the 27th of April, in the year 368.[47] Thus, the brethren conducted a service for that whole night. In the morning, his relics were prepared for burial with fine linens. The divine Liturgy was also offered in his behalf. The body was then conveyed to the mountain in the midst of chanting psalms. After the body was interred, Abba Orsisios returned to the monastery. But that night, he took three brothers and went to the grave site. He removed the sanctified Theodore and buried him alongside the holy relics of his spiritual father, Saint Pachomios the Great, and his brother according to the flesh, Abba Paphnutios. The burial party then returned unnoticed. Three days later, Orsisios became ill from grief over the repose of Theodore. But then some ancient brothers urged him to go and speak words of comfort to the brotherhood. He obliged them, though weeping, and consoled the bereaved monks. After they received holy Communion on the third day for Abba Theodore, Orsisios bid the mourners depart in peace. Thereafter, Abba Orsisios resumed sole charge of the Koinonia. The holy Archbishop Athanasios, learning of Theodore's repose, wrote to Abba Orsisios that "blessed is Theodore who walked not in the counsel of the ungodly.[48] Theodore is not dead but asleep in a good repose in the presence of the Lord."[49]

Now Christ does not appear darkly to Theodore. Theodore's divine longing has been fulfilled, for he sees Jesus face to face. Let us emulate Saint Theodore who was wont to say and practise, "Love thy neighbor as thyself; and hold thy tongue." Then we may beg his intercessions to entreat God, Whose power it is, that we might find a little place in heaven.[50]

On the 16th of May, the holy Church commemorates our holy father among the saints, ALEXANDER, Archbishop of Jerusalem.[51]

---

[47] Theodore had written a festal letter to Patriarch Athanasios, dated 367; so he certainly reposed after that date. In "The Bohairic Life" [¶ 199], it says that he had served as the superior of the Koinonia for eighteen years. As Orsisios resigned in 350, less than five years after his appointment in 346, we are left with 368 as the year of Abba Theodore's repose. The date of Pascha fell on the 20th of April. Theodore succumbed to illness three days after he had seen the brothers on their way and reposed some days later, on the 27th of April. The year 369, in which Pascha occurred on the 12th of April would be another possibility, but 368 is generally accepted with very good reason. Note taken from "The Bohairic Life," ¶ 206, p. 294.

[48] Ps. 1:1.

[49] "The Bohairic Life," ¶¶ 207-210, pp. 259-265.

[50] "Fragments from Theodore," ¶ 2, 4, *Pachomian Koinonia*, Volume Three, pp. 133, 134.

[51] See 3rd-C. Hieromartyr Alexander who is commemorated by the holy Church on the (continued...)

On the 16th of May, the holy Church commemorates the holy Hieromartyrs AVDAS and AVDIESOUS (Abd-Jesus), Bishops, and THIRTY-EIGHT MARTYRS with them, that is: SIXTEEN PRESBYTERS; NINE DEACONS; and SIX MONKS and SEVEN VIRGINS.[52]

Avdiesous, the sacred hieromartyr, was bishop of a Persian city named Beth-chasar. He was delivered up by his own nephew to the Persian king, Shāpūr II (309-379), since he refused to be persuaded to accept Persian religious doctrine.[53] On account of his staunch reverence for Christ, Avdiesous was led before the sovereign, together with thirty-eight other Christians, that is: sixteen priests, nine deacons, six monks, and seven nuns. They boldly preached Christ as the true God. They were remanded to the king's brother, Arseeth. After he interrogated the Christians and attempted to convert them, he saw how they rejected his words and persisted in the belief of the Christ. He, therefore, commanded that they be bound with ropes and wooden planks. The ropes held them fast as they were drawn tighter and tighter. As they cut into their bodies, the sound of their bones creaking and breaking could be heard. The blessed martyrs of indomitable will were made to endure this racking torture for seven days.

After this ordeal, they were all cast into prison. The only food passed to them was that which had been offered as sacrifice to the Persian idols. The martyrs gave no heed to the food and would not even turn their eyes to look upon it. The ever-memorable athletes, according to the given command, remained in the prison without eating and drinking. In the meantime, a God-loving woman gained access to the holy prisoners, bearing bread and water. The martyrs partook of the food she brought, giving thanks to God. After a number of days, worn out from mistreatment, they were removed from that prison.

At the same time, the holy Bishop Avdas of the city of Hashar was forewarned in a revelation by God of his pending arrest and martyrdom, by which he would emerge victorious and receive a crown. Both bishops, consequently, Avdas and Avdiesous, and the thirty-eight martyrs were sent by

---

[51](...continued)
12th of December.

[52] See also the 31st of March when the holy Church commemorates Hieromartyr Avdas and others who suffered at Susa under Yazdgird I, the Sasanian king of the Persians (399-420).

[53] Shāpūr II styled himself a Mazdah worshipper and partner of the stars and brother of the sun and the moon. The state religion of the Sasanian Empire was Mazdaism (Zoroastrianism).

the king to the high priest of the Persians, named Mapteen. After all those stalwart Christians professed and upheld the Faith of Jesus Christ, they were first submitted to savage beatings and then beheaded. Bishop Avdiesous was led to the execution site a few days later, at which time he also had his head severed. Thus, they all received the crown of the contest.

On the 16th of May, the holy Church commemorates the holy Martyrs ISAAKIOS, SYMEON, and VACHTHISOËS of Persia, who suffered martyrdom by fire.

On the 16th of May, the holy Church commemorates the holy ABBAS at the Monastery of Saint SAVVAS, who were slain by the sword.[54]

On the 16th of May, the holy Church commemorates the holy Martyr PAPYLINOS, who was slain by the sword.

On the 16th of May, the holy Church commemorates the holy Martyr PETER at Vlachernai, Monk of Petra Monastery, who suffered martyrdom for the sake of the holy icons when he was flogged to death with ox-thongs.[55]

---

[54] Dositheos, in his *Dodekavivlon* [p. 535], records that forty-four fathers were murdered by the Blemmyes. Saint Antiochos, the compiler of the *Pandektes* in his "Epistle to Efstathios" [*P.G.* 89:1422-1428], holds the Bedouins responsible. This massacre took place during the reign of Emperor Herakleios (620-641). These holy fathers are not to be confused with those commemorated on the 20th of March. When Abba Nikomedes, hegumen of the monastery, who had fled with most of the monks to Arabia, returned and beheld the aftermath of the bloodbath, he fell down in a dead faint at the sight of the unburied bodies of the slain. When he finally came to himself, he lamented: "Righteous men are taken away, and no one considers; for the righteous has been removed out of the way of injustice. His burial shall be in peace. He has been removed out of the way [Is. 57:1, 2]." And then Abba Nikomedes cried aloud: "They are in peace. For though they be punished in the sight of men, yet is their hope full of immortality. And having been a little chastised, they shall be greatly rewarded; for God proved them and found them worthy for Himself [Wis. 3:3-5]." Afterward, our holy father, Patriarch Modestos of Jerusalem (632-634), came to the monastery. Upon beholding all the desolate cells of those slain, he could not restrain his tears. He, thereupon, hastened to embrace their precious relics.

[55] Saint Peter lived during the reign of the iconoclast Emperor Constantine V Kopronymos (ca. 761).

On the 16th of May, the holy Church commemorates Saint NICHOLAS the Mystikos, Patriarch of Constantinople, who reposed in peace.[56]

Nicholas was born in Constantinople, in the year 852, of parentage hailing from southern Italy. He was a kinsman and disciple of the Saint Photios the Great, commemorated on the 6th of February, from whom he received an excellent education. When the great Photios fell out of imperial favor and was dismissed as Patriarch of Constantinople in 886, his kinsmen also were persecuted. Since this circle included Nicholas, he repaired to the Saint Tryphon Monastery near Chalcedon where he received the monastic tonsure.

On account of Nicholas' virtue and education, Emperor Leo VI (886-912), a schoolmate of Nicholas, brought him out of the monastery and appointed him as "Mystikos." The term means "secret" or "private," which was the title of a high-ranking functionary who was very close to the emperor. Duties of a Mystikos could involve anything from private imperial correspondence to judging matters. Leo, at length, made Nicholas serve as Patriarch of Constantinople in March 901 to February 907. Nicholas was consecrated on the Sunday of Orthodoxy, which was on the 1st of March that year.

Nicholas and Leo entered into conflict over Leo's fourth marriage to Zoe Karbonopsina, which came to be known as the Tetragamy affair. Leo had three previous marriages—successively with Theophano, Zoe, and Evdokia—that left him a widower thrice and without an heir. But in 905, he fathered a son, the future Constantine VII, by his concubine Zoe Karbonopsina. Leo VI was anxious to legitimize his union and offspring but met resistance from Patriarch Nicholas. The patriarch agreed to baptize the little boy, but he prohibited Leo entry into the church. When Leo went ahead with the wedding, Nicholas declared the marriage null and deposed the celebrant who married them.

In February of 907, Leo deposed Nicholas and exiled him to his own Monastery of Galakrenai[57] near the capital. Leo, that same month, replaced

---

[56] There were two patriarchs of Constantinople named Nicholas: Saint Nicholas I Mystikos who is commemorated today and another patriarch Nicholas on the 16th of December. There has been some confusion identifying their individual dates. A number of *hagiologia* (that is, by Nikodemos the Hagiorite, Sophronios Efstratiades, and others), both old and new, have wrestled with this problem. Chrysoverges erroneously surnamed the Saint Nicholas of the 16th of December with "Mystikos."

[57] Galakrenai, lit. "fountains of milk," is the site of several Byzantine monasteries on the Asiatic shore of the Bosporos near Chalcedon. Its precise location is still unknown. It is believed to have been located where springs of water were made milky by a solution of carbonate of lime. There are three monasteries that have been associated with Galakrenai: (1) the first one founded in 535; (2) the foundation of Patriarch

(continued...)

Nicholas as patriarch with Efthymios, his spiritual father and hegumen of a monastery in the Psamathia quarter of the capital. Since the elevation of Efthymios brought no peace, Nicholas was recalled—most likely before Leo's death. As for Efthymios, he was banished by the new emperor, Alexander (May 912 to June 913), to Agathou on the Bosporos where he died in 917. Alexander certainly agreed with the reinstatement of Nicholas in 912. As for Zoe Karbonopsina, she was expelled from the palace. Despite Nicholas' restoration, there was a fierce struggle within the Church between his supporters and those of Efthymios.

Reconciliation was achieved, albeit after Efthymios' repose, with the Tomos (Tome) of Union which settled the conflict between the partisans of Nicholas and Efthymios. This same Tomos attempted to end the dispute over the fourth marriage of Leo VI and Zoe. What resulted was the banning of a fourth marriage and restricting the third marriage with a penance of four to five years of no Communion. The center of the conflict between partisans, nevertheless, was the validity of episcopal appointments, that is, whether the nominees of Efthymios or Nicholas were rightfully entitled to their sees. Since Patriarch Nicholas had the support of Romanos I Lekapenos, the father-in-law of the emperor, Constantine VII, his partisans succeeded. It was Romanos I, however, who was the actual ruler of the empire.

During his first and second tenures, Nicholas proved to be a relentless preserver of the divine and sacred canons. He was no less soft with himself. His personal life was a model of asceticism and sanctity. He remained patriarch until he was translated to the Lord in the year 925. He was interred in the ancient Monastery of Galakrenai, which he rebuilt and reestablished. It was also the same monastery in which he sojourned between his tenures, that is from 907 to 912.

As for the correspondence of Nicholas I Mystikos, it is considered "a first-rate source for the history of ecclesiastical affairs and of Byzantine relations with southern Italy, with Bulgaria under Symeon of Bulgaria, and with the Caucasus region."[58] There are 162 of his epistles that are extant.[59]

---

[57](...continued)
Nicholas (ca. 900); and, (3) the foundation of John the Rhaiktor (early 10th C.). See *The Oxford Dictionary of Byzantium*, "Galakrenai."

[58] *Oxford*, s.v. "Nicholas I Mystikos."

[59] The saint's works may be found in *Miscellaneous Writings*, trans. by L. G. Westerink (D.C.: Dumbarton Oaks, 1981); "Epistolae 1-163," *P.G.* 111:27; *Letters*, Greek text with English trans. by R.J.H. Jenkins and L.G. Westerink (Dumbarton Oaks, 1973); *De capta Thessalonica* (*Salonike Captured* [by the Arabs], a short homily of A.D. 904), *P.G.* 111:25; also "Sermon on the Capture of Thessalonike," (continued...)

Saint Ephemia

On the 16th of May, the holy Church commemorates Saint EPHEMIA the Great Martyr at the Church of the Holy Power near the shipyard harbor.

On the 16th of May, the holy Church commemorates the holy New-martyr NICHOLAS of Metsovon, who was cast into a fire at Trikkala (1617).[60]

Nicholas, the holy new-martyr and athlete of Christ, had Metsovon[61] as the place

[59](...continued)
Miscellaneous Writings, op. cit.; *De vita monastica*, *P.G.* 111:391; *Responsum canonicum*, *P.G.* 119:825. See Georgios Fatouros' biography, *Nikolaos I Mystikos*, from Biographisch-Bibliographisches Kirchenlexikon, 1993. See also the *Religious and Ethics Encyclopedia* (in Greek), Vol. 9, pp. 519-522.

[60] A number of Greek publications on the Life and divine office to Saint Nicholas of Metsovon, apart from *The Great Synaxaristes* (in Greek), assign the date of this new-martyr's commemoration to the 17th of May. In all likelihood, the day of commemoration may have been transferred to today, the 16th, so as not to eclipse the celebration of the new-martyr with that of the patrons of the Varlaam Monastery (Saints Nectarios and Theophanes) where Saint Nicholas' sacred skull is now treasured.

The Greek biography of the new-martyr, penned by the theologian Symeon G. Katsimpras, entitled *O Hagios Nikolaos o ek Metsovou* (Ioannina, GR: Pnevmatikou Pharou, 1993), was translated into English by Leonidas J. Papadopulos, and edited, revised, and expanded by Dormition Skete and Holy Apostles Convent for incorporation herein. We have chosen this unabridged and engagingly sweet version over the much shorter Greek account written by Metsovite polymath and teacher of the Greek race, Nicholas Kyrkos or Tzertzeles or Tzartzoules (1708-1772), who also composed a divine office to the new-martyr. This latter work was published at Venice in 1767 and 1771. The section on the martyrdom was collected and published by Nikodemos the Hagiorite [*Neon Martyrologion*, 3rd ed., pp. 67-69]. It was later incorporated into *The Great Synaxaristes* (in Greek). The English version of this latter Greek text is found in *New Martyrs of the Turkish Yoke* (Seattle, WA: Saint Nectarios Press, 1985), pp. 185-187, which was used as a collateral source herein. A Supplicatory Canon (in Greek) was composed by Father Gerasimos Mikrayiannanites (Ioannina, GR: G. Douvales-E. Apostolou, Printers, 1987).

[61] A variant name of Metsovon is Metsovo, which is in the Nomos (Department or (continued...)

of his birth.[62] Everyone knows of the famous and picturesque village-city of Metsovon.[63] It was built at the foot of a great cliff on the southern slopes of the Pindos Mountains. It boasts of its magnificent location: for, on one side, there is a deep canyon where the Metsovon river flows; and, on the other side, there are the snow-covered mountains of Katara and Prophet Elias. It has been compared to a beautiful alpine-type village-town. When seen from a distance it looks as if it stretches out in an effort to reach the heavens, so that it might live in the embrace of such natural surroundings, even though for the greater part of the year it is arrayed in a snow-white covering.

The white garment appears to be the characteristic identity of its citizens. They are honest and simple people, radiant souls with sound ideals of country and the Faith. They are people whom one can easily approach and

---

[61](...continued)
Prefecture of) Ioanninon (39°46′N 21°10′E), at an altitude of 3,815 feet or 1,162 meters.

[62] The surname of Saint Nicholas the Metsovite is Basdanes. He was also called Vlachonicholas on account of his Vlach descent. He was also nicknamed Ekseentatriches or "sixty-hairs" because of his scanty beard. See Greek biography of *Hagios Nikolaos, O Neomartyras tou Metsovou*, written by Demetrios G. Kalousios, published at Meteora, by the Holy Varlaam Monastery, in 2000, p. 18, at the behest of this monastery that now possesses the saint's sacred head. According to the *Encyclopaedia Britannica*, s.v. "Greece, History of," the Vlachs of central and southern Thessaly have generally been identified with the indigenous, pre-Slav populations of Dacian and Thracian origin, many of whom migrated into the less-accessible mountainous areas of Greece and the northern Balkan region because of the Germanic and Avar-Slav invasions and immigration of the 5th–7th C.

[63] Metsovon owes its development to the good will of a Turkish governor. In days of old, the Sultans made treaties in order to keep the rebellious mountainous regions under control. The Divan was supposed to keep the Turks out of the villages and the village people were to pay tribute as a show of obedience. Thus, on Pindos, autonomous regions were created: that of Syrakos with 42 Wallachian villages; of Zagoriou with 40 villages; and of Agrapha with 100 villages.

As for Metsovon, there is another reason for its progress. In 1655, Ahmet IV, the grand vizier of the sultan was accused of treason and was sentenced to death. He, however, escaped execution and fled to the inapproachable areas of Metsovon. The mayor of the town, Kyriakos Flokas, had pity on him and gave him hospitality for three years. Meanwhile, the vizier was proven to be innocent and he was reinstalled (to his position) in the government. He, therefore, sought to reward his benefactor. But Mayor Flokas did not wish anything for himself. He only sought rights for Metsovon, which were granted by a firman (a decree, mandate, or order) in 1659. Thus, Metsovon enjoyed peace and prosperity. See the Greek publication of C. P. Zalokostas, "The Garden of God" (Athens, 1944), p. 97.

exchange a warm and sincere greeting. They are noble, courteous, and hospitable.

Saint Nicholas

In that town was Nicholas born, toward the end of the sixteenth century. The day of his birth is unknown. In none of the biographical notes is there any information or reference. One thing that we know for certain is that Nicholas was the fruit of godly and faithful Orthodox parents. Though his parents, in this world, were simple and obscure folks, yet they were known and important before God. In their hearts, their Faith preserved alive love toward God the Father. As for their deeds, they were an expression of that Faith. Indeed, their main concern was to please Him to Whom they owed everything, rendering Him rich fruit in due season.

It is certain that they handed down that treasure of Orthodoxy to their offspring, whom God had given them. There were many times that both father and mother spoke to young Nicholas about the Almighty Who rules the world and mankind. As prime examples of His creation, they pointed to the lofty mountains which stand as champions and their massive size which betokens awesome endurance. "Above all things, my boy," they said, "is God. He is greater than these mountains. He is more pure and radiant than the snow; He is more resolute and firm in virtue than granite and all the proud peaks." Now little Nicholas received the lessons of love toward God from his illiterate but faithful father and his reverent and simple mother. There they sat before the fireplace and an oil lamp with its flickering light. The parents looked upon their son and spoke of "the Light of the world [Jn. 1:9; 3:19; 8:12; 9:5; 12:46]," that is, Christ, "the true Light, which giveth light to every man coming into the world [Jn. 1:9]" and makes his life luminous and successful. They marked the road toward the heights of the true life and led Nicholas toward Him Who is "the way, and the truth, and the life [Jn. 14:6]."

Indeed, how wonderful becomes the training of the child by parents when it is based upon the unique truth! How certain it is that the seeds will yield fruit, and the fruit will hasten to come forth. Satisfaction and joy will follow the toils and the troubles. This act does not become tiresome and joyless. It is joyous and lively. It has a certain and essential meaning, and an inexhaustible freshness. It assumes a nature of creativity and progress. Truly then, the soul of Nicholas received the seed. He, as a receptive soul, allowed the seed to fall on his interior world so that he brought forth fruit: at times he yielded thirtyfold, or sixty, or an hundred.[64] His was a soul that gathered in its treasure-trove not material treasures but spiritual ones which cannot be changed or altered.

First Acquaintance with the World

The boy Nicholas, being reared with eternal truths, blossomed forth. Quickly he became a young man. He was the pride of his parents and the pride of Metsovon. But as he came to know himself, he also became familiar with the world in which he was forced to live. He saw the poverty of his house. He noticed the tyranny of the conqueror who made everyone live as slaves and bondsmen in chains. He understood that he had to work very hard in order to live. He had to toil side by side with his father; and he needed to support and comfort his mother. He never weakened. He never laid down his arms in the difficult struggle of life. He followed his father. When the father went to work, Nicholas went with him. At times, they went into the forest for firewood; and, at other times, they repaired to the slopes as stonemasons in order to fix dry masonry for retainer walls to keep what little soil there was for farming.

Whether it was winter or summer, they worked either in the town or on the mountains. There were days that they were singed by the sun and other days that they were stung and numbed by the chill. Winter meant wind, snow, frost, and stormy weather. All the elements of nature were against them. At times, one would think that they would be wiped off the face of the earth. Yet, in all this, they remained devout and awestruck by the glory of God in all that they beheld. Nicholas endured all these things. There was only one thing that his youthful mind could not digest: the restrictions that the Islamic overlords imposed upon their Christian Faith. When Sunday came, they could not go to church and worship as their hearts wished. They spent the great feast days

[64] Mk. 4:20.

locked up in their homes. Only prayer and the lamp that trembled before their icons bore witness to the fact that they were Christians and believed in the holy religion of Christianity.

Oftentimes, Nicholas would ask his father, "Why are there so many restrictions? In what manner does our Faith and life disrupt the Turks?" And he, with an earnestness of mind, replied to his son, "My boy, they cannot tolerate us because we have the true Faith. We have the true God. They hate us because they are confused as they keep their man-made and false beliefs; which is to say, the false can never withstand what is real and true." Nevertheless, father and son never neglected to open the door of a church which was in the wilderness on their way home from work. At such an opportunity, Nicholas heard his father for the first time recite the Lord's Prayer aloud, kneeling before the icon of the Almighty. Nicholas also bent his head forward and heard his father's heart as he praised God, so that the lips of both recited piously the best hymn of glorification of a laborer with a humble heart. A hymn which was heard by the birds, and they chirped along. The wind bore it on its breath and spread it through all nature. Each time, then, that they passed by the little church, which was hidden in the dark forest precisely at the turn of the road, Nicholas begged his father that they might stop. He wished to visit it so that they might enjoy that inexpressible spiritual beauty, which was the result of their simple and humble prayer. Nicholas' father never disappointed him and granted him this favor. Nicholas asked that he recite the Lord's Prayer, and then he, too, would add a few words of supplication.

Nicholas had no difficulty, no inner conflicts in expressing his devotion. He entered that sacred precinct and would act according to his deepest impulse and intuition. He was wont to recite the Lord's Prayer. He would never forget that prayer. On the contrary, those moments would serve as the guiding light in the future, so that he might stay on the right path in the passage of life. And should he ever lose his way, once more he would find it and return to the path. And lo, what a return he brought about! Thus does the holy Church chant to this saint: "Today thy holy memory has arrived as a spiritual spring refreshing our souls, O holy New-martyr Nicholas! Therefore, we have assembled to honor and extol thy struggles, and with exaltation we cry: 'Rejoice, thou imitator of the ways of the old martyrs. Rejoice, O thou date palm, newly sprouted and laden with fruit, and warm succor of Trikkala! Rejoice, O thou that drivest out the locusts speedily and that destroyest maladies and epidemics! As thou hast boldness before Christ, intercede unceasingly for those who honor thee.' "[65]

---

[65] This Vespers Doxastikon, in Mode Plagal Two, is inserted at this point by the Greek biographer of the saint's Life.

Seeking Employment

Thus passed the years of Nicholas' early youth in Metsovon. Now he knew all his strengths. He realized he could do much more for himself and his parents. The limited environment at Metsovon did not benefit him financially at all. He was ready to open his wings and fly: to seek for work and advancement. For this reason he hearkened to stories told by other young men who had returned from abroad. He listened to how they departed, where they went, and what type of work they did in their place of migration. Some had been successful. They returned with wealth and gave comfort to their elderly parents. Some of them even had made acquaintances and a name for themselves in those distant and strange lands.

Little by little, the thought that he should go to another land had become fixed in his mind. "As others have gone and prospered, so shall I," thought he. "I shall make the sign of the Cross, taking God and His Mother with me, and go forth." Prudent as he was, he did not neglect to tell his father his thoughts. Since he wished his father's opinion and advice, he said, "My father, I, too, shall go away to a strange place that I may work, advance, and be able to give you, my parents, rest." And the father stood there and looked at his son. He could not imagine that so soon he should be separated from his son. Then he drew him close and held his son's hand tightly and said to him, "My child, there are many perils abroad. It will not be easy. Even if thou shouldest find employment and make a living, there are dangers that threaten and easily captivate the souls of young men. My good boy, do not rush into this decision. Tarry a while longer with us. Although we live in poverty here, still thou art more secure and at peace." When he finished talking, there was a deep silence. Father and son were in each other's grasp for a long time. Not a sound was heard. One would think that nature herself respected the sanctity of that moment. The father's sigh interrupted the silence; and a tear could be seen rolling down his cheek. The son plucked up courage and gave answer to his father's request, saying, "I will listen to thee. I shall stay for a time—but not very much longer." He then said to his mother and father, "When everything is ready, then with your blessings shall I go."

Indeed, the moment came soon. Nicholas was to leave with other relatives and villagers for Trikke.[66] He was told that jobs could be found there. It was a big city, situated in the midst of a fertile valley, with a prosperous economy. There he would easily find lodging and employment. When the time arrived for his departure, he took only a few things. He received the blessing of his father and mother, and then he departed with his company. Some

---

[66] Variant names of the city and prefecture of Trikke are Trikka, Trikkala, or Trikala (39°33′N 21°46′E). Trikkala was a suffragan bishopric of Larisa. The Trikkalitans had an abundance of vineyards and gardens in their agrarian center.

traveled on foot, and others on horseback. They started uphill toward the small gorge. They climbed a narrow path which seemed endless. Most of them were young. Some of them had gone away before. Nicholas was the only one who set his first steps in the direction of that distant land. That is why every so often he turned and looked at his village. In fact, one time he fell behind. He could not stop looking at his village as if he were trying to single out his house and parents. His party continued upward toward the gorge. They took the last turn, and the village was lost from their eyes. They were in the midst of the mountain, sometimes ascending and sometimes descending. It was a continuous journey of many hours. Their only companions were the lofty mountains and the murmuring waters that gushed happily and steadily in the streams.

At last they arrived at the great gorge, by the boundaries of Epiros and Thessaly.[67] There, toward the east, the great monoliths of the Meteora were visible to the eye.[68] Toward the west were the ageless peaks of the historical Pindos. "Over there," spoke someone out of the group, "what appears before us, is Meteora." And Nicholas, who had heard stories from his father about the monasteries of Meteora, stretched his ear so that he could hear the speaker's every word. There arose in his heart the desire to visit those towering physical and spiritual pinnacles. How could that young man imagine that one day he would be one of the most valuable ornaments of those historical monasteries!

At Trikke

After a journey of two or three days, they arrived before the colossal monoliths of Meteora. Nicholas gazed at them with awe and amazement, as if

---

[67] Epiros of northwestern Greece is a mountainous area between the Pindos and the Ionian Sea. Epiros was inhabited by Greeks, Slavs, Albanians, and Vlachs. Thessaly is that area of central Greece south of Macedonia and north of Hellas. It is on the west that it is separated from Epiros by the Pindos Mountains. It is characterized by a large central plain formed by the Peneios River and surrounded by high mountains. The main cities are Larisa, Trikkala, Stagoi, Lamia, Neopatras, Demetrias, and Nea Anchialos. The main east-west road ran to Trikkala and thence either north to Grevena and Kastoria or west to the pass of Porta, or in the summer months, over the pass of Metsovo. *Oxford*, s.v. "Epiros," and "Thessaly."

[68] The Monasteries of Meteora (39°43′N 21°38′E) in the prefecture of Trikkala, in the region of Thessaly, rise at the center of Greece. It is situated where the Peneios River emerges from the deep canyons of the Pindos range and surges into the Thessalian plain. These gigantic rocks, etched by time into a variety of shapes, are grey-colored stalagmites rising heavenward. The cliff tops of these formidable pinnacles are crowned with monasteries of wooden galleries and corniced rooftops. The buildings precariously hang over sinister abysses, but breathtaking views, with the Pindos range at their back and the vast plain of woods, gorges, and picturesque villages lying below. In the late Byzantine period and during Ottoman rule, these hermitages became a sanctuary of the persecuted.

they were suspended between the world and God. His traveling party could not fathom the sanctity of the monks whose only preoccupation was vigilance and prayer. The time was not appropriate, however, for a visit. So they headed straight toward the great city of Trikke, that is, modern-day Trikkala of Thessaly. When they approached the city, they stopped before its gates. There were plane-trees and lime trees, which were planted by the banks of the Lethaios River; and they cast a great shadow forming a kind of canopy. They rested there from their long journey. Nicholas recovered from his weariness and began to enjoy the beauty of nature. His eyes, at times, merrily gazed upon the river which divides the great city in two and, at other times, playfully mused upon the large plane-trees and the hill punctuated with mansions that held sway over the commercial section.

He did not forget, however, that he had come to work. He asked for help from certain Christians. After wandering about, he succeeded in taking employment at the bakery of a local Mohammedan.[69] It is unknown where Nicholas lived, and what type of difficulty he encountered in his first steps. One fact that is certain is that he did not know when it was night or day. He became a slave in a strenuous job to an employer who was both cruel and inhuman. Nicholas, however, remained undaunted before the hardship. He had a strong constitution and was vigorous, so that he endured the initial temptations and trials of such a harsh life. He even found a way to escape, more than once, the eye of his employer when he took himself away to a certain place where he stood in prayer and spoke with his God. He found great comfort in these moments. He came back to life and breathed the clean and life-giving air of the Faith in Christ, full of heroes and martyrs.

He sensed a greater joy when he met other Christians or one of his own countrymen who brought him tidings from home or from his relatives. His soul jumped for joy when he heard news about his parents. He glorified God because he received happiness upon learning that his parents were still alive and sound. He was wont to pray this prayer: "When, my Lord, shalt Thou count me deserving to return home and provide them with rest and care?" Sometimes he entered the church, but only after exercising a thousand precautions. When he went for a certain reason, he found the time to stand before Christ and His

---

[69] The organization of guilds was prevalent among the Greeks, even in the metropolis of Trikke. The guilds were loosely controlled by the state. The workshops were clustered together, in accordance with ancient tradition, in a single area of the city or town, a fact which made a particular impression on foreign travelers. Membership in guilds was restricted to the *mastoroi* (masters), that is, the artisans who owned the shops. The master artisan might employ a journeyman assistant (*kalphas*) and an apprentice (*mathitoudi* or *tsiraki*). Apostolos E. Vacalopoulos, *The Greek Nation* 1453-1669 (New Brunswick, NJ: Rutgers University Press), p. 207.

Mother in order to plead for their support, help, and enlightenment. These were among the most refreshing moments of his spiritual life. His Christian soul, which desired the free air of the Faith, found the chance to be joyful under the loving and caring eye of the heavenly Father.

The Temptations

Dark clouds of temptations, however, rolled toward him and gave way to a storm that refused to subside. It was a tempest so violent that it might wash away whatever sacred and holy treasure Nicholas possessed in his heart. Furthermore, with the sweeping away of the treasure of his faith, he, too, might be subject to captivity or enslavement. That robust young man just might be dragged downstream and made to disappear. One might say that a firing squad had been organized, with Nicholas as the chosen target. The goal was the acquisition of Nicholas' youthful, guileless, and pure soul. Nicholas seemed to be surrounded. On one side was Nicholas' employer; on the other side was the little Turk who worked in the adjacent shop; and then there was a Turkish aristocrat, who passed by daily on his horse to buy bread. In the person of Nicholas, the Muslims saw an easy victim. His basic kindness, flexibility, eagerness to work and serve others, coupled with his sincerity, simplicity, and harmlessness of his youthful soul, all caught their attention. The Muslims, consequently, became allies in an effort to draw him into their religion and false Allah.

The Muslim baker was heard to say to the aristocrat, "I cannot bear to see him as a Christian, effendi (sir). I shall change him. I shall do whatever I can to convert him!" Meanwhile, the little Turkish employee worked systematically. He always spoke to Nicholas about Mohammed, saying such things as: "If thou shouldest believe in him, thou wilt become free and do whatsoever thou dost wish. No one shall threaten thee. Everyone, indeed, shall watch out for thee and help thee. Thou wilt make a fortune and wilt be popular and famous." The wealthy aristocrat also spoke to Nicholas, sometimes from atop his horse and at other times inside the bakery, about some great transformation that awaited him. "Thou hast so much to gain. Everyone will love thee. Thou wilt also become an aristocrat just like me. Thou wilt eat the sweetest bread. Thou wilt be liberated from fear and every danger to thy life."

Even if these temptations were momentary and transient, the bakery's proprietor proved to be the greatest temptation and a continual one. Nicholas could not avoid his presence. He was enjoined to listen respectfully to him every day, from sunrise till sunset. He heard his words from the time they awoke in the morning to make dough until the work was completed at night. The employer would say, such things as: "O what a pity, Nicholas, that such a fine boy like thee is an infidel! O for shame that such a lad as thee cannot enjoy liberty and move about freely as he pleases!" Capping off this monologue were these words: "Thou needest to change. Thou oughtest to become a Mohammedan. Thou must convert. To be a Christian is not to thine advantage."

These were hard times for Nicholas. A terrible struggle fomented within him. He was shaken from top to bottom. He was born a Christian and a Greek. He could not comprehend why he had to cast away all these things that identified him. Were the possibilities of prospects opening up for him and chances at success worth such self-renunciation? He could not understand their motives in trying to make him shake off all those things that he considered as treasures and his heritage. In the beginning, he gathered up his strength. He tried to fortify himself lest he cast the precious pearl before the swine. He reacted according to the circumstances. Sometimes he worked with all his might, so that he did not have time to listen to them. Other times he chose a place in the workshop where he would not be able to hear them talk. There were even times that he dared to give answers that were sure to rouse verbal abuse and even beatings from the shop's owner.

Time and again, Nicholas remembered his father who had talked to him about the perils and bitter trials to be found in a faraway place. Nicholas, seeing firsthand what his father meant, thought: "How right was my father! How correct was his advice! Behold, all has come to pass!" As time went by, the more difficult things became. His surroundings posed a terrible strain for his young inner world! He resembled a flower which as soon as it blossomed, a strong wind blew and withered it. It was like a cold north wind, blowing every day in a relentless pursuit to have Nicholas deny his Faith and scatter all his treasure.

The Defeat

The evil was not late in coming. Caught unawares, a change began to take place, even unconsciously, within him. For two long years he sustained their diatribes. For two years, he was struck by the fiery arrows of temptations which chiseled away at his life and standards. He was without any help. The only aid and advice might have come from his parents, but they were far away. They were not there to watch after him, to support him, and to renew his spiritual life. Despite his isolation, he did not cease to be the pure and polite youth who was always eager to help; those characteristics were not tampered with.

However, he listened to his employer who talked with him about his so-called great prophet Mohammed. Nicholas, as before, listened to him without contradiction. He also kept company with the little Turk employee and, eventually, took up his habits and learned his morals. The Muslims around Nicholas spoke about their period of fasting, Ramadan, and their prayers. At length, Nicholas was also standing in an attitude of prayer, as those around him, at the time when the hodja (khodja), a Mohammedan teacher, cried out from the minaret. It was visibly evident that he had accepted the first influence upon his beliefs and life.

His employer observed his conduct and felt personal satisfaction. He viewed it as a triumph, as his own individual accomplishment. He witnessed the aim of his evil scheme coming to fruition. He had changed the belief of the Greek Christian that he might find gratification in the false paradise of the coiner of legends, Mohammed.[70] The proprietor, therefore, did not waste any time in changing his attitude toward Nicholas. He bought him clothes just like his, including shoes and a fez. When the right time came, he sent Nicholas to the mosque. It was his first public appearance like a Turk, an infamous episode that stigmatized him with an embarrassment that he never forgot as long as he lived. But the stigma and the filth were exterior blemishes—that is, his Muslim garb and fez. Within his soul, he retained something yet of his Orthodoxy. He had not lost every trace of Hellenism and the Faith of the Christians. For this cause, there ensued a terrific struggle inside of him.

Whenever he happened to come across a countrymen or a Christian, he was filled with shame; for he recognized and accepted his fault. Many a time did he decide to correct it; but at the same time, he listened to all the congratulations tendered by the enemies of Christ. He was mostly distracted by the sweet words offered by the shop owner, which hindered him from resisting and redressing his grievous folly. Hence, slowly, Nicholas submitted and was enslaved. He became a true little Turk. He surrendered within and conformed without. He, finally, was acknowledged to be a follower of the odious Islamic prophet. Nicholas, subsequently, was living like all the Turks. He was free to live life to his heart's content without limitations and apprehensions.

The one who was most pleased by this conversion was his meddlesome employer, the baker. He vaunted his victory to everyone, especially his customers, as he pointed to the changed Nicholas as a kind of trophy. He

---

[70] During the dark years of Ottoman rule, there were revolts from time to time. In the year 1611, an unsuccessful uprising was staged by Dionysios of Trikke. Many Muslims, afterward, sought to coerce the Orthodox to embrace Islam. Thus, the baker also participated in this Muslim policy at Trikke. See D. G. Kalousios, p. 21. Another biographer, the theologian Michael G. Tritos, in his publication, entitled *O Metsovites Neomartyras Nicholaos* (Ioannina, GR: John E. Routopanes, Pub.), p. 17, informs us that "Nicholas and his parents lived during a period that was both troublesome and tumultuous. The learned Gianniote, Demetrios Salamangas, writes: 'After the unsuccessful revolutionary movements by Dionysios the Philosopher, one in 1600 at Trikke and another in 1611 at Ioannina, these ushered in Muslim persecutors and persuasive proselytizers against the Christian element, causing many, much like Nicholas, to be worn down. However, later, Nicholas repented and openly showed himself to be a Christian, for which the Turks committed him to a death by fire [*O Neomartyras Hagios Georgios Ioanninon* (Athens, 1954), p. 13].'"

invited the hodja to his bake shop in order to acquaint him with the lad. The Muslim teacher praised Nicholas and wished him joy. He told him that he would prosper now that he had the help of Allah. He invited him to go to the mosque in order to pray for whatever help he needed.

Nicholas was not at first sensible to the dire harm in which he placed his soul. For a time, he actually thought that he had gained something. He gave the appearance of being happy, though he was not pleased altogether. In the recesses of his heart, he retained some reservations. It seems that an invisible and mighty hand cautioned him from accepting wholeheartedly that which seemed to be a kind of new treasure for his life.

Acknowledgment of His Error

Thus, a short period of time elapsed. How long? No one knows. It is certain, however, that not more than one year passed by. During that time, Nicholas, who was tested in the struggle of life, tried to justify the advantages obtained by the change. By degrees, he managed to isolate the gains as well as the losses ushered in by the new religion. He met many people, saw many things, and experienced a good deal. He listened to their prayers, and he saw firsthand all the expediencies of Islam. He learned how they celebrated their joys and what kind of future rewards awaited those who faithfully followed their prophet.

The more he learned, the more bewildered he became. As the days passed by, his doubts and hesitations deepened. He was, in fact, never satisfied. His spiritual world was tormented by one abysmal vacuum. He did not find the opportunities the Muslims had promised him. The void within grew as the days passed by. In the beginning of his internal struggle, he brought to mind his old life—though seldom at first but later more often. He remembered his roots, his home, his father and mother, his town, and his occupations and pastimes. Then he recalled those well-known peaks that he had trodden. In his mind's eye, the invisible presence of his father was near him. Nicholas then reminisced about their father-son treks to Prophet Elias and the first recitation of the prayer of "Our Father." He thought of the tears of joy his father shed when, for the first time, he, Nicholas, recited the Lord's Prayer. Nicholas could still sense the hug his father gave him and the accompanying words, "May God, my son, the great God, protect thee from all evil! Take heed, my boy, for thy soul!" These memories, whatever a child's mind could remember, flooded him. These memories lasted not only a single moment but they even endured throughout the day and night. Summoning up these recollections of childhood events brought back vividly into his life the counsels and admonitions of his father and mother.

The beautiful world of the spirit began to awaken within him. A new dawn, the spiritual day, began to appear in the horizon of his soul. Nicholas, furthermore, tasted of this sweetness and it seemed to him that he was in a trance. This change in Nicholas did not go unnoticed for long by his employer, the baker. He perceived that, at times, Nicholas seemed lost and in a distant reverie. He also noticed a certain anxiety and perplexity in him. He perceived that the discussions about the new religion did not impress Nicholas anymore, as in the beginning. Nicholas, now, always found an excuse to avoid them. Thus, the proprietor was puzzled, not knowing exactly what was happening to Nicholas. One day, he asked him, "What is happening with thee? I see that thou art worried. What is wrong? Is there anything that thou needest? Did I not tell thee to let me know, immediately, if thou desirest aught, and I will do whatever I can for thee?" Nicholas did not divulge his soul's anxiety, but he told him of his desire to visit his parents and said, "Here, effendi, I miss my parents and my home. It has been so many years now, and I have not called upon them even once. If thou wilt be so kind as to give me leave for a few days, then I could go and visit them." The baker was angered with the request. He understood not only the reason for the young man's change but also the danger of losing his victim and his great conquest. He, therefore, remarked, "Thou hast no need for such excursions. We have plenty of work here. If thou dost not work, how art thou going to live? Thou hast not the least need to return to Metsovon. Right here, thou hast all thy good things." And after the baker raised his voice a little, he said, "Go now to the marketplace and procure some supplies. Following that, come and pass by the shop. Now I want thee to come back right away. Dost thou hear me?" Nicholas gave no reply. He went out at once and headed toward the marketplace. In his mind's eye, however, he climbed the trails that led to the mountain peaks. His soul longed to flee the many hardships of these past years. With his mind as a vehicle, his spirit was moved to travel to the place that gave him birth, that made him a Christian and a Hellene.

Homeward Bound

Nicholas, gradually, became conscious of his rashness and acknowledged in his heart his grave error. It is not right to abandon the Light and go into darkness. It is not just to call the Light darkness, and the darkness Light. It is a great delusion to be lured from Christianity by the false teachings of such a dealer of myths as Mohammed, who fabricated his own religion. Nicholas, thereupon, did not wish to remain one moment longer in that delusion. He did not play or mince words with what was now patently false to him. Inwardly, he resisted the Islamic precepts and so his soul rebelled. When he was alone at night, immersed in thought, he shed copious tears. His continual sighs of repentance tired his chest. With his every breath, he was resolved to correct his great mistake that his conscience might find rest.

But he had to rediscover himself again, to regain his spiritual powers, and then try to correct himself. In his present location, he could not accomplish anything. The environment was not conducive. He had to change his residence, as well as his spiritual climate. He could not find a better climate than that at his home. Only with the comfort and warmth afforded by his parents and the Christian environment would he be able to experience the dew of the Spirit, in order to soar above every evil which he experienced and allowed to pollute his heart.

Every time he thought of returning to his homeland, he could not wait to leave. He felt a spiritual certainty that this was the best decision for him to make. So he ruminated upon his plan of departure. He would ask permission from his master. But if the baker refused to give him leave, then Nicholas would flee on his own without company. His employer, again, was adverse to the proposal. The baker not only refused his permission but even threatened Nicholas. Nicholas then recalled how the baker treated him in the beginning, when he used to shout at him and abuse him. His master had called him an infidel. Nicholas, nevertheless, did not lose his courage. He had made his decision. He would escape. One night he would make good his flight.

He allowed a few days to pass. When it appeared that all was forgotten, he collected his few garments into a bundle. He, cautiously, fled into the night. He used a narrow alley, which brought him out onto the road that would bring him into his sweet country and into the arms of his father and mother whom he had so missed. In the beginning, he walked rapidly. When he felt more secure, he paused for a while in the cold and dark of that night. He offered up glorification, not to Mohammed but to the Creator of heaven and earth, to the God of his fathers. After he uttered a prayer that he heard in Church, he remarked, "My Lord, what a beautiful doxology that was! How sweet are the words of the psalmist! O God, why did I lose sight of Thy beauty!" After he finished his entreaty, he stood at attention and made a confession of the Orthodox Faith. He did not mind if his act remained unknown in the eyes of men. It meant a lot to him that the eyes of his heavenly Father beheld him, those of God's, Whom he loved so much but had forgotten for a time. Thus, he said, "O Lord, I love Thee! And in order to prove my love, here!" Following this declaration, Nicholas removed the Turkish fez that he wore and tossed it far away. He took off his other garments, those that reminded him of his evil experience and ill fortune, and hurled them at some distance—as far off as he could. He, then, donned other clothes that reminded him of something new, beautiful, and everlasting, so that he would not constantly remember what he had lost. He then hastened into the darkness of that night toward the great peaks, not only those of his country but also those of the true Faith.

At this point, the biographer inserts another hymn to glorify the saint, chanting: "Let us all, who are gathered in the church, honor Nicholas who, as glistening gold, was tested by the fire and shown to be genuine. Let us say to the lover of piety, 'Rejoice, O citizen of heaven, O thou giant of a soul and solid as a diamond! As thou standest before the Trinity, cease not interceding for our souls.'"[71]

Again in Metsovon

Before Nicholas was aware of it, he arrived opposite the hills near his homeland. He did not feel tired in the least. He was light and strong. A sense of optimism and hope circulated through his liberated soul. He stood there on the heights in order to take his ease, that is, before he would follow the narrow path which would soon take him to his village and to his house. He paused to sit down and reminisce. There passed by in his mind all the years that he was absent. He remembered how he had truly passed that narrow path on his way to Trikke. What hopes! What dreams! But even so, his return was necessary. He had made neither a fortune nor a name for himself, albeit, he almost squandered all of the treasure of his Faith. Shuddering at what he committed, he said, "I thank Thee, O Lord, because Thou hast helped me find my way back to this road and to tranquility." He next stood up and made the sign of the Cross. He, then, agilely, dashed down the winding path.

The closer he drew nigh, the quicker his heart beat. The thought that he should soon see his father and his beloved mother made him a volcano, ready to erupt with feelings. Now and again, a warm tear ran down his face; for he thought that, ere long, he should be forced to admit his mistake. His previous imprudence and incautiousness now embittered him, because he knew it would usher in sorrow for his parents. His only consolation was that he had escaped danger and that, presently, he was going to the safety of his family.

As he approached Metsovon on his way up, near the creek that ran by the monastery of Panagia, the all-holy Mother of God, it was afternoon. The villagers, his countrymen, were returning from their farms while drawing along their beasts of burden. Nicholas did not wish to meet anyone at that moment. He passed by quickly, trying to elude their glances. After he made a turn, he noticed the humble church in his neighborhood. He cast a quick glance to the right and to the left. No one could see him, so he made the sign of the Cross. He hurriedly slipped through the gate of the front yard of his house. On the distant mountain he could see a beautiful and serene sunset that spread a quiet and mystical radiance upon his impoverished home.

It was not long before he caught sight of his mother through the window and their eyes met. She went hastily to the door. Opening the doors

---

[71] Doxastikon of the Lity, by Nicholas Kyrkos, Mode Plagal One.

and her arms, she embraced him, kissing him warmly and saying, "Welcome, my child! Thou hast done well, very well, that thou hast come back. I have waited so many years for thee. I thought of thee all the time. Morning and night, my thoughts were always with thee." Nicholas then bowed, took his mother's hand and gave her a pleasant and warm kiss. He felt so secure now, as he held his mother's hand. He did not want to let go. He said almost nothing because, in his attempt to express his joy at finding her well, tears that rolled down from his eyes intervened. Something similar happened again when shortly thereafter his father came home. Now his house seemed very joyous. Only there was something that Nicholas needed to say, but he could not disclose it that night. He did not wish to sadden them. They were elated as they ate together, at which time his father recited a prayer of thanks because they met again after so many years. They all made the sign of the Cross. After they partook of dinner, they laid down to sleep.

Hunger and Poverty Prevail

The next day, Nicholas called his parents near that he might converse with them. With sincerity, he admitted all that had happened. He concealed nothing. "It matters not if I sorrow you, because I owe you the truth. Much rather, you must rejoice. I say this because, like the prodigal son, I have found myself and returned to you and to your love. Here, in Metsovon, I not only will find rest but also will become better than heretofore." His parents listened attentively. They grieved for his misfortune, but they did not underestimate him. They knew that he had found his way again; and they supported him and comforted his soul. They each said something like the following: "My boy, give glory to God that He kept thee sound! Glorify Him, because He guarded thy treasure! Thou oughtest to find a spiritual father and make thy confession that thou mayest receive forgiveness. Cease fearing. Thou shalt start thy life afresh, and God shall bless thee."

The very next day, Nicholas met with a spiritual father. The reverend priest listened in silence. The priest did not tarry long talking about Nicholas' transgression. He persisted in its remedy, encouraging Nicholas to stand firm with his decision. He put him on a program to lead a spiritual life, in order to help him surge forward. "Fear not," said the priest, "for God received a thief. He receives every soul that asks for His mercy and blessing. By the side of thy parents, thou shalt become a new man—a good Christian. Surely God, Who permitted such a trial, will give thee much good in thy life."

Thus, the Metsovite young man, Nicholas, the good Christian and Hellene, rediscovered himself. He became calm. His soul found rest. He started to assist his parents as before. His father's conversation and company gave him rest and consolation. They worked together to make their daily bread. They prayed together. They loved each other as one soul. With great difficulty, however, they met their necessities. They worked for one piece of bread. At times, they went without bread at all. If they ever made wheat bread, that was considered a luxury. Sometimes they lacked even their very *bobota* (corn bread). When they had it, they were glad; and when they went without it, they glorified God because in Him they placed their hopes.

At length, Nicholas needed to look elsewhere to make money. He started to go into the forest. There, with other fellows, they cut pine wood for kindling. They brought it to town and sold it. Some of the men also collected piles of wood, carting them to both bigger and smaller towns. With this occupation, Nicholas began to make money. He took his father along with him. They piled up this resinous wood in their front yard. Then one day, when returning from the forest, Nicholas dared ask permission to go and sell it in the city that he knew well, that is, in the very place where he met his great misfortune. It was only with much difficulty that his father agreed. The father's hesitation was not on account of any uncertainty in Nicholas. He knew that Nicholas would not undergo any ethical danger anymore. During the entire year, he had tested him very well. The father was just uneasy about his son's return to Trikkala where the Turks might recognize him; but he knew he could not stop Nicholas from going.

They readied the firewood and loaded it. The following morning, along with a company of fellow travelers, Nicholas headed in the direction of Trikke. He had no intention of staying there longer than necessary. He thought to go and return at once. He went to do a job which he deemed, with his father's blessing in tow, would be lucrative. He felt he was obliged to make some money to help out his family's finances.

Again at Trikke

The entire company arrived in good time at their destination. In the marketplace of the city, there were many people. Nicholas unloaded his bundles of wood at one end, along with the others. He had no desire to walk around the marketplace, which he knew so well, nor to visit the stores in which so many times he had bought supplies for the bakery. He adhered to his original plan. Meanwhile, merchants and patrons were milling around. They would buy off his load; and when it was exhausted, he would leave immediately. From the outset, it looked as if the plan would go very well. He sold most of his wood. A little more, and his pile would come to the end. He reckoned, "I shall buy a little *bobota* for our home, and whatever else my mother ordered me to purchase; and at once I shall return."

Nicholas stood by the last bundle of wood that remained. He was preparing to sell it to a sixty-year-old Turk from the city. When Nicholas saw the man, he recognized him. He was the barber in the neighborhood where he formerly resided. One time, in fact, Nicholas had his hair cut at his shop.

While Nicholas pretended as if he did not know the barber, yet the latter looked at him curiously. The barber wanted to say something, but he could not immediately place the name and face of Nicholas. It appeared as if his memory was not good. But then, suddenly, the barber stopped checking the wood. Moments later, he addressed Nicholas and said, "Art thou not the little Turk who used to work at the bakery in the neighborhood? So thou hast changed now, hey? H'm, I see thou hast become a Christian. Dost thou not know that what thou hast committed is the biggest insult and blasphemy against our great prophet, Mohammed? How didst thou commit such a dastardly act? Dost thou wish me to publicize thine apostasy? Dost thou wish me to tell everyone, so thou mayest see what punishment awaits thee?"

Nicholas did not expect such a battery of questions. The words of that bedeviled Turk fell upon his head like thunder. He was shaken. He became fearful. Many bad things went through his mind. But he could not bring himself to utter a word. He stood there and looked him in the eye. The barber remarked coolly but in a strong voice, "Why art thou glaring at me? I am not mistaken. It is thee. I remember very well, though thou hast changed. I see that thou art now clad in Christian garments. I also see the company that thou keepest." Nicholas remained calm in the face of this temptation. He reckoned that he must be rid of this dangerous man in any way possible; and then he must disappear from Trikke. In order to be rid of his wood, and at the same time avoid danger, he said to the Turk, "If thou dost wish," he showed him the wood, "take it. I do not want any money." He suggested that he take it for nothing so as to extricate himself from the barber. But the latter would not desist. He tried to extort more from Nicholas, using some degree of subtlety. After the barber got that bundle of wood for free, he wanted to be sure that he would have more in the future. So he said as much to Nicholas: "What thou art giving me to keep quiet is not enough. I am ready to turn thee in to the authorities. I need but shout aloud once and the entire marketplace will pounce upon thee and beat thee. In order to escape such an end, thou must give me thy promise—and thou hadst better keep thy word—otherwise, I will torment thee." Slowly and loudly, the barber said, "Thou must promise that every year thou wilt bring me one load of firewood. Hearest thou? Understandest thou what I want?" Nicholas replied, "Yes, I understand." Without knowing exactly what he said, Nicholas then said to the Turk, "Rest assured, once a year I shall convey to thee one load of pine wood." The Turk, pleased with this response, said, "Fine, we agree. I shall not say anything to anyone." The barber took away the wood and disappeared down the street.

With the Turk moved out of his sight, Nicholas, without any delay, headed on the road back home. His mind was confounded; his thoughts were made turbid. He had trouble ordering his own counsel. He only walked quickly, wanting to get away from the danger which once more he encountered in that city.

The Thought of Martyrdom

In a short while, he found himself outside the city. He began to collect himself again. The sense of security that he felt made him calm once more. His composed state helped him deliberate everything all over again. Then he thought about the promise that he had made to the barber. "Accordingly," he said, "I would have to bring one load of firewood to the infidel every year. That means I would have to toil in the forest, to play with life and death, in order to prepare a load for an infidel with whom I have no ties and no obligation. And why all this? Because he would betray me, saying that I changed my religion and that from a Turk I became a Christian."[72]

Nicholas was shaken up again. He thought to himself, "When in a position such as this, there is no greater accusation that can be made against me than that. Yet I never became a Turk. And if one time I put on the fez and the garb, and passed under the gates of a mosque, yet never did I do that from my heart. Nay, my heart always remained Christian. My blood was always Christian. The candle of the Faith in the true God always burned inside of me. I am living a tragedy. I cannot endure it. I must bring the firewood as a tribute, so that I can believe freely in what I am!" Nicholas stood for a while in the middle of the road. He walked all that distance hurriedly. He was relieved to keep company with mountain air and birds. He could think in such surroundings. He could think a great deal. He could even allow his voice to say whatever he wished, to God Who listens to His own and answers their needs.

He felt he ought not to stand erect if he were to speak with God just at that moment. He went to the side, at the turn of the road, and knelt down. Even though his body was bent downward, his mind and heart bounded heavenward to the throne of God. He took a deep breath and, with a great voice that seemed like that of many people, a plea rose from the depths of his heart: "Thou, O Lord, knowest my heart! Thou knowest all the hearts of men and their reasonings. Thou knowest, therefore, if my heart ever denied Thee. Why should I bear such a shameful stain? Why should I be a prisoner of my careless

[72] *The Great Synaxaristes* (in Greek), the N. Kyrkos version, records that "Nicholas quickly agreed with the barber, and every year he brought wood to the barber. However, Nicholas regretted the pact he had made, and did not wish to give him wood anymore. Instead he made up his mind to give up his life in order to repudiate his previous denial of Christ. Straightway, he went to his spiritual father and disclosed his intention [p. 448]." Nikodemos the Hagiorite, in his *Neon Martyrologion*, with the same version, writes: "Nicholas promised the barber; and every year he went to him with the wood according to that promise [p. 67]." We are not told how many years he agreed to this extortion until he did what was right.

actions as a child? I cannot bear this. O Lord, I wish to be liberated. I wish to prove that I have nothing to do with this matter. I am Thy man, and shall remain Thy man."

How long he stayed on his knees in that spot, he was not aware. But when he stood up, he began to walk with invigorated strength. He felt like a new man, and he noticed something new growing inside of him: one sweet, beautiful, and heavenly feeling. If you asked him to describe it, he could not. He had not the power to enunciate it in words. He would say one thing, "I forgot everything. All had been extinguished within me. Something else was awakened in me, with which I prefer very much to live."

Nicholas continued on his way. He was eager to get to his village before sunset lest he be surrounded by the darkness. But Nicholas was not afraid. He knew all the roads and trails. He sensed a great triumph, as this "other" and "new" perception became more pronounced and stable. In a little while he would be in the village. He passed by the Church of Saint Demetrios. Nicholas, for a moment, hid behind a wall. With precaution, he made the sign of the Cross. And when he tried to say, "Saint Demetrios, guard me and clear my mind," he made a discovery. He conceived something which was pleasant and kept him company throughout the remainder of his trip home. He reasoned that the holy Demetrios became great because he suffered martyrdom for Christ. "Demetrios was a martyr for Christ. That is it!" cried out Nicholas inadvertently. "A martyr for Christ. How beautiful! How grand! No one can frighten thee or threaten thee." He opened the door to his house, and entered its safe haven.

The Great Decision

The decision to undertake martyrdom did not take long to mature. His resolution became as firm as granite. It was with this, and for this, strong desire that Nicholas lived. He persistently supplicated the first Martyr, that is, Christ, to grant him this invaluable gift and honor. For Nicholas, it was the best solution to the dilemma in which he was entangled. He, indeed, desired it with all his heart. He saw in it an unspeakable beauty and grandeur. How could he proceed forward, however, without the opinion of his parents? How could he ignore them? And how could he leave them alone in the world, especially now when their age was advanced and they needed him more than ever? After he had well reasoned on his own that the gigantic decision could not be changed for anything, he decided to tell his parents.

One evening, when his parents walked alone in the dusk under the flickering lights of the lamps, he found the opportunity and told them. "I never ceased to be a Christian. But I fell into misfortune. For years now have I been put to the test by this temptation. It will never be possible for me to tolerate others calling me an infidel. A certain voice inside of me tells me that I must wash away that evil with a courageous public confession of my Faith. I have to go back where it all happened. I must say that I believe in the truth, in the Light, in Christ. And if they should seize me and take my life, as the maniacs that they are, I shall give it. There is no difficulty for me. I wish to give it. I made that decision. And I believe that, with the help of God, I will succeed. I beg of you not to disagree with me."

There was absolute silence on the part of his parents. Not even their breathing was heard. Only the small lamp sent forth its trembling light upon their tired faces and, now and then, a small sound reached their ears from the lantern's wick. The father fixed his gaze upon his son. His mother also looked upon him, but then turned her face downward and leaned against the palms of her hands as she thought. And then the father opened his mouth and spoke with gravity, "It is a great thing, my son, that one should suffer martyrdom for Christ. A great honor for our house. It is not for me to tell thee no. But my heart cannot bear for my lips to say, 'Go forth.' To become a martyr is a gift and a bestowal of heaven. One thing alone I advise thee. Find a spiritual father. Tell him thy thoughts; and he will take the responsibility. He can tell thee what thou shouldest do." Again, his parents fell silent. His mother was immersed in deep thought. And Nicholas dared to ask her, "And thou, mother, what thinkest thou?" There was no answer forthcoming. When he repeated the question, there still was no response. His parents were quiet and deep in thought. When it seemed that that blessed silence must cease, the voice of his mother was heard saying, "My boy, thou hast my blessing; but do as thy father suggests." The lamp was about to go out, and its light became brighter as if it was trying to tell them that it was midnight. They needed time to rest and reflect. They rose and prepared to turn in. Nicholas went to a corner and fell to his knees, praying to God and saying, "I thank Thee, my Lord. It is now easier to draw near to Thee. The road is open. Bring what is expedient very soon, because I am impatient. I must wash away this shame."

The Spiritual Father

Even though Nicholas passed by the obstacle of his parents, yet he might not find such understanding from his spiritual father; for a spiritual father bears responsibility for the souls in his charge. Therefore, before he says something, he ponders upon it. He prays for enlightenment and guidance. Thus, it happened in the case of Nicholas. His spiritual father gave him a patient hearing. He, indeed, listened to him carefully. He asked for many details. He tried to search into the bottom of Nicholas' heart that he might properly weigh Nicholas' resolve and determine his motives. Frightening was the possibility that he might falter and deny the Faith. Even though a significant amount of time had lapsed since his childhood days at the bakery, the danger that he might weaken at the last moment might become a reality.

This was not the first time that the spiritual father heard Nicholas' confession. Then, with a serious voice, he said, "My child, I admire and marvel at thy decision. There is no greater honor for a man than to give his blood for the Faith of Christ. Such a one is revered by the faithful throughout Christendom and is honored for ages. I respect thee, and I am glad because of thy decision. But it is difficult for me to say yes. I am hesitant. I am apprehensive that, at the last moment, thou mightest become fainthearted. I am afraid that thou mightest give in to their demands, that thou mightest cower. There is always the possibility that thou mightest not remain steadfast to the end on the glorious road to martyrdom."

Nicholas was disturbed by these words. He did not allow the spiritual father to proceed. Interrupting, he said, "Nay, father. My decision is sound. I have thought it over many times. I will not bend or be overthrown." The spiritual father then said, "Agreed," as he raised his hand lightly trying to tell him that he should be listening and not talking. "Agreed," he repeated. "Knowest thou not that 'the spirit indeed is willing, but the flesh is weak [Mt. 26:41]'? These words are not my own. It is the very word of God; and 'faithful is the word [1 Tim. 3:1].' It is always true. And that word means: It is easy for one to make a decision, but it is difficult to carry it out. One recognizes with ease what is good and wishes to make it a reality of life. But it is not easily done. It is a hard thing. We are all glued, unfortunately, to this earthly world. Dost thou hear me?" He answered, "Yes, father, I hear. I have listened to everything thou hast said. But I have made my decision. I am not afraid."

The priest continued and said, "Suppose that for a moment thou shouldest weaken. Canst thou imagine the ridicule? Dost thou realize that thou wilt put the name of the true God to shame for a second time?" Nicholas replied, "Yes, father, I realize it. But I am certain that what I have proposed will come to pass. I do not depend on my own strength but in the power of God. He is mighty, and He will help me to win. He will come to my aid that I might overcome my human weaknesses and give my blood to my Christ Who was sacrificed for me on the Cross." The spiritual father added, "When someone relies on the power of God, he is secure." Before the priest finished speaking these words, Nicholas thought that the spiritual father's objection was abating. He, thereupon, fell to his knees. He began to thank the priest and beg him for his blessing, saying, "Bless me, O father! Fear not, I shall not deny my Lord Jesus Christ. I want to die for Him." When the spiritual father saw the desire Nicholas had for martyrdom, he strengthened him with many exhortations and blessings; and then he dismissed him. Indeed, what a holy confession! O Lord, Thou hast made a new-martyr who would shed his blood upon the soil of Epiros and Thessaly! Thou hast fashioned a new-martyr in order to adorn the Church of our Christ.

The Way to Martyrdom

Not many days elapsed before everything was ready for his new trip to Trikkala. It was not the preparation of the wood bundles that concerned Nicholas. His thoughts and cares were focused elsewhere. He pondered upon the burden of sin. The abasement and shame of his denial. More than anything, he wished to shake off that load. He recited the words, "Lift, O Lord, the heavy burden of sin from me; and do Thou accept my repentance as the thief, as the harlot, and the woman with the issue of blood."[73] He pondered upon such thoughts continuously. He always found opportunities to withdraw and communicate with God to seek His help and His encouragement. "Be Thou my helper, O Lord, and forsake me not," he repeated. Nicholas said it loudly, so that his heart and hearing would be content with the thought that God was at his side; for He is everywhere present and fills all things and desires to be a ready helper.

Later, Nicholas went to his knees again. He knelt quietly with a warm faith in the presence of God, the almighty God and Father. There is no greater moment in the life of a man than those moments that he lives in the presence of God and speaks with Him. Nicholas lived those moments vividly. When he was at the zenith of contentment, he released a sigh from the depths of his soul. Who can place a value on these moments of bliss when one lives together with God and witnesses the ineffable beauty of His countenance? Immersed in these thoughts, Nicholas believed, wholeheartedly, in the presence of God. In such times, one does not live in the world. Mountains, forests, animals, voices, and noises seemed to vanish before the mystical union of Nicholas' soul with God. An initiation into the mysteries went on within him. It was a spiritual preparation for the great event that his soul desired.

Then, again, he came to certain harsh realities for his senses. He remembered the hardships that he would encounter. He was mindful of the strict advice of his spiritual father and of the danger that he must necessarily pass through. With humility, he recognized that the road that he must follow was long, uphill, and arduous. At times, he recited the psalms of David. He kept thinking of that passage that says: "Many bullocks encircled me, fat bulls surrounded me [Ps. 21:10]." He completed his conversation with God, saying, "He was to me a helper and protector for salvation: this is my God and I will glorify Him; my father's God, and I will exalt Him [Ex. 15:2]." In this manner did Nicholas close his prayer. As he contemplated the glory of God, he shuddered; to Nicholas, the glory of God was neither something without meaning nor a thing casually thought of by many today. His glory was something incomparable. He desired to become a vessel and temple of the glory

---

[73] Lk. 23:39-43; Lk. 7:37-47; Mt. 9:20-22.

of God. He yearned to offer a spiritual sacrifice, even if he were the whole burnt offering, so as to glorify the name of God. As for the impending testimony he would make through martyrdom, he knew he needed to prepare himself.

For this reason, again, he felt the need for prayer. Thus prepared, he set out at the break of dawn on that day in May. He left before nature was awakened. As yet, neither had the flocks of sheep dispersed on the mountain-side nor had the musical sounds of the nightingales reached the streams. Nicholas set out for his great journey, resolved not to return again. With him he carried two loaves of bread—as well as his sins. His donkeys were laden with the firewood. He thought to himself that the firewood would be given to the people; his sins would be set down at the foot of the Cross of Jesus Christ. He was thinking that if he were called to suffer martyrdom, he would give a good witness. In this manner, he wanted to set a good example for the people. What are the consequences of faults? They should become indicators for finding the road to correction. You must find the path to heaven and follow it at any cost. That is what Nicholas believed. Thus armed, he followed the road to meet the enemy and wrestle with him.

Into the Hands of the Infidels

For the first time, the usual travel difficulties attending that road to Trikke went unnoticed by Nicholas. When from a distance he observed Trikke, it seemed to him that he had just started out from Metsovon. Rested and strong, his disposition was all readiness in every particular. When he entered the city, he was moved in his heart and mind as he remembered those moments when he lived in it: how he came there as a Christian; how he departed; how he returned, and everything—but everything—in detail. Now, though, he felt different. He himself could not describe that which he felt. It was something refreshing, powerful, and protecting, as though an invisible personage stood by his side. When Nicholas attempted to interpret what it was that he was feeling, he stopped himself. "No, it is nought else," he said to himself, "but my God." Thus, his soul found comfort and rest.

He took the road that led to the marketplace. It was already filled with patrons and merchants. On the same spot where other peddlers brought their loads of wood, Nicholas also unloaded. Within him, he called upon the aid of God so that he might finish his work quickly. Then he greeted all those who stood nearby. He thought it odd that he knew not a single one of them. As it turned out, they were all Turks. He recognized them from their attire and their speech. It was an easy day for him. He only needed to sell a little more kindling. If he offered that, too, he would be able to finish his work, that is, purchase a few necessaries and make arrangements to have them sent back with the donkeys to Metsovon. Then moments later, a certain would-be customer approached him. He was ready to buy Nicholas' bundle of wood. Nicholas stooped down in order to tie the bundle, and then he would offer it to him. But at that same moment, he felt a cold hand seizing him by the back of the neck with a tight grip. It was that barber who had forced Nicholas to bring him firewood for free, lest he make it known that Nicholas changed his religion. As he grasped Nicholas, at the same time he growled, "Why didst thou not bring me wood? I am going to strangle thee, thou unbeliever!"

Nicholas did not need to see him. He knew the voice immediately. With his mind's eye, Nicholas discerned that man to be the personification of Satan. The barber was provocative, egotistic, self-serving, and immoral. He took advantage of an incident that involved an immature young man, and he manipulated the circumstances shamelessly and selfishly. Indeed, he was persistent regarding what he wanted. He seized Nicholas' remaining wood. He made religion into a commodity. He used religion for his personal gain and material advantage.

Saint Nicholas Before the Turks

Nicholas was stunned. He stood upright and looked the Turk in the eye. In disdain, Nicholas said, "I have no business with thee. I have not harmed thee at all, so I do not feel guilty. Please do not harass me." Before he finished speaking, that audacious Turk lunged at him and said, "Thou shalt not speak to me in that way," he snarled. "I will turn thee in to the authorities. I will report thee. Dost thou hear me?" The Turk then stretched forth his hands and, again, seized Nicholas by the neck. Now Nicholas did not in the least lose his composure. With readiness and simple words, he repeated, "I owe thee nothing. Understand? I have no obligation to thee. Moreover, that which I did in the past was my mistake. But I never changed my Faith. My heart was always Christian. Only my clothing was involved and was soiled." The Turk descried that something had changed in Nicholas. He now perceived his steadfastness, strength, and courage. It made an impact on him. Why? The Turk was impressed that Nicholas confessed his Orthodox Faith before everybody present. He was not the weak Metsovite that he thought he could take advantage of for a lifetime. He knew that he had lost the wood, his booty. He became enraged instead of being glad. Ignited with rage, he did not hesitate to put into motion his scheme of slander. He thrust himself at Nicholas and, at the same time, shouted aloud vigorously, "Seize him! This fellow changed his faith and insulted Mohammed, the great prophet!"

Suddenly, there was a commotion and clamor in the marketplace. Fanatic Turks, who knew nothing about the matter, created pandemonium. They seized the well-built Metsovite Nicholas and held him in their hands, as if they had caught the chief enemy of their religion. Assailing him and deriding him, they led him to their *cadi* or Muslim judge. As an innocent lamb, Nicholas was silent on his way to the judge. He reckoned that the blessed moment had come. The thought of his father and mother passed through his mind as lightning. He uttered a silent prayer to God, saying, "Lord, give me Thine aid." And then he whispered, "Lord, the blessed moment is come. Give me strength to confess Thy holy name!"

Before the Lawless Tribunal

When they arrived at the house of the judge, which was also the court, they found a crowd of enraged Turks. Many of them heard the bellowing of the barber. But there were also others who did not know what was happening. All they saw was an infidel beset and abused by their coreligionists as he was led to the judge. That was enough for them to spew their poison, which nested in their hearts; and so they also yelled at Nicholas. Finally, they arrived at the house of the judge. The anger of the mob waxed hot, as bloodlusting wolves under pack law they were howling for avengement. As the restless crowd gathered outside the judge's house, the barber kept pulling at Nicholas. It was not because Nicholas resisted and needed to be haled before the judge. On the contrary, Nicholas tread his way to the judge with joy, because he knew that that judgment was the best proof for the next Judgment, the divine one, which will take place at the end of time and which will have the all-knowing God as the Judge. The barber was aggressive, angry, and loud. He had taken the matter personally: the sop was ruined, the buy off was lost. Now the accusation was ready on his lips. What an imputation! What slander! The denouncement was that Nicholas had been a Turk who believed in the great prophet of Islam, but now he had changed and become a Christian. That charge was very compelling for the court. The barber needed no other arguments. The only relief the court could grant was that the accused must renounce Christ and His teachings, and instead profess the faith of Mohammed.

The judge, at the time they came, was unprepared. It was still morning, and he was surrounded by discord and turmoil. He tried to collect himself and ascertain what had taken place. He looked at Nicholas and then at the Turkish barber. He analyzed them both. In the face of Nicholas, he distinguished calm, serenity, and assurance. He saw in Nicholas a well-built lad, in the flower of his youth, who had the characteristics of an honest man. His countenance was covered with beauty and grace. Then the judge cast his eyes upon the Turk, his compatriot. His face was angry. He appeared irritated and excited. There was marked nervousness and impatience. All this was a reflection of the hatred and hostility that controlled the barber's psyche within. The barber could not stand still. He made neurotic motions; he uttered words of abuse. He allowed his inner base nature to become evident.

The judge then understood what was happening. It was not the first time that he had such a case brought before him. He gestured to the Turkish barber to be quiet and control himself. Then he asked Nicholas, "So thou hast denied our prophet?" Before Nicholas could even open his mouth in reply, the judge said, "I want thee to answer with straightforwardness and sincerity. Dost thou hear me?" Nicholas raised his head and looked at him in the eyes. There was a spark in Nicholas' eyes. Nicholas' heart leaped, as his thoughts soared heavenward. He noetically embraced God, pleading with the Lord to put the proper words in his mouth. He entreated God inwardly, saying, "How long, O Lord, have I waited for this hour! Help Thou me, I beg Thee, that I might confess Thy name!" Nicholas then answered the judge and said, "I was never a Turk. I never believed in Mohammed. I was born a Christian. My heart was always Christian. I wish to live as a Christian. Christ is my only love."

The barber, enraged, exploded. He did not allow Nicholas to finish his statement. He made one or two steps toward Nicholas, and stretched out his hand to Nicholas without the judge's permission. The barber yelled, "He was a Turk! He used to go to the mosque. I remember him." Nicholas remained calm and answered this charge, saying, "Yes, there was a time when I was under duress and was swept away. It was a time when my effendi lured me and misled me, which caused me to change my mind. What a disgrace for me, my God! O Christ, forgive me for that! But I was never a Turk. My heart was always Greek and Christian. Yes, I am a Christian. I believe in Christ with all the power of my soul."

Quiet prevailed in the crowd. Nicholas was impressive in pronouncing his confession of the Faith. His manner of speech was strong and convincing, causing everyone to gaze with perplexity at one so eager to dispatch his life. They were all amazed at Nicholas' inner soul. But the Muslims could not admit their defeat. Their spite, malice, and hatred did not allow them to yield. The judge thought for a while and asked Nicholas, while pointing at the barber, "So this man, here, is lying?" Nicholas answered with probity, "Surely he is not telling the truth." Continuing, he firmly added, "The truth is what I have told thee."

The judge did not doubt the verity of Nicholas' statement. But how could he satisfy the Turks? What could he say before the angry mob that waited below? How could he accept the insult to the great prophet of Islam? The Muslims would wonder how he could tolerate the courage and confession of the honest Metsovite. All these things entered into the decision that the judge reached. "Cast him into jail," said the judge. "Once there, he will come to his senses and find himself. Then, when he is made to appear again, we will see if he has the courage to say that he is a Christian." Two muscular officers took hold of Nicholas and pushed him toward the exit. When the crowd saw Nicholas thus, they began jeering and taunting at him and screaming, "Lock up in jail that dog, that infidel!" Some of them followed behind him. They accompanied him to the jail. The rabble did not quiet down until they saw the heavy door close upon the young Greek in the inner parts of the jail.

The Martyr in Jail

It did not take a long time for Nicholas to recollect his thoughts and realize in what type of situation he found himself: the dark environment of the jail, the loneliness, the abandonment, and the disdain. All this made him understand everything that his spiritual father had described to him in such detail. He remembered the advisements of the priest, one by one; and Nicholas tried to put his good counsel into practise accordingly. "When they lock thee in jail," said the priest, "thou shalt be mindful that God created thee a free man, so that thou wilt always live near Him and in His kingdom." And, "When the darkness in the jail envelops thee, then shalt thou bring to mind the light of the kingdom of God. I am speaking of the light that is eternal, that shall never be extinguished; for there is no end to the kingdom of God." Also, "When they abuse thee verbally, do thou pray for those who rail against thee. When they beat thee, thou must remember that also they scourged and crucified Christ. He, however, was sinless and suffered for our sins; whereas, thou shalt suffer for thine own sins. When they leave thee hungry and without nourishment, be not disturbed. Thy mind, then, will live much easier with God."

Nicholas, indeed, recalled all these words and many more, even as he sat on the floor of that gloomy and dark cell. All these things brought to mind the promise that he gave God before his spiritual father. He had said, "I shall not bend. I shall not weaken. I shall stay faithful to Christ. I shall confess His holy name. I shall die for my Savior." Thus, Nicholas began to pray. How long his prayer lasted, he did not know. That which he noticed was an inner and pleasant reassurance that gave comfort to his body and also to his soul. He was very serene. He felt a certainty that everything would go well. He saw himself on a secure path which led to his goal. Therefore, time and again, he said, "Help me, O Lord, to the very end!" Nicholas, at length, grew drowsy. He said with the psalmist: "I laid down and slept; I was awakened, for the Lord Himself will help me [Ps. 3:5]." He then closed his eyes and was overcome by a gentle and light sleep which gave him rest.

"I can picture," comments the biographer, "the soldier of Christ lying down in jail, in the hands of God, overcome by sleep. And I recall that image given by the patriarch, which described Jesus in Juda his son: 'Juda is a lion's whelp; from the tender plant, my son, thou art gone up; having couched, thou liest as a lion and as a whelp; who shall stir him up [Gen. 49:9]?' Such was the courageous offspring of Metsovon. Strong and dauntless as a mountain of his country. He fought the first battle, and now he lies to rest. He rests that he might reawaken and continue the struggle, winning new laurels and victories."

At about midnight, Nicholas was roused. He was alarmed because he needed more time to face harsh reality. "Ah yes!" he said, "I am in jail at Trikkala. I thank Thee, my God, because I am here for Thee." He remained where he was, pondering sometimes on one thing and sometimes another, until a sound sleep closed his eyes again.

The Great Synaxaristes, in Greek, adds here that "since they were unable to compel him, either by flatteries or threats, to comply with their will, they beat the holy martyr with rods for many hours. Afterward, he was flung into a dark prison where he was given neither food nor water but only tortured more. This the martyr patiently endured, not only with a brave mind but even with great joy."[74] Another biographer adds here that "Nicholas' boldness, naturally, led him into tortures that were harsh and full of pain. He suffered many blows, one on top of another, after which he was tossed into a dark and unsanitary dungeon. His only encounter with another was in the person of the severe and bothersome jailor who tortured him a number of days, keeping the prisoner both hungry and thirsty. Nicholas persevered, in an exemplary manner, throughout the scourging and the many terrifying and dread chastisements."[75]

Again Before the Judge

Nicholas, for two days, remained locked in the stony jail. No one thought of him. He was alone, forsaken by people. Even his parents and spiritual father did not know that he made the first step toward his great goal. But abandonment did not enfeeble him. He was comforted by the life-giving presence of God. He remembered and believed the promises of God: "I will not forsake thee nor abandon thee.[76] I will not forget thee.[77] I am the helper of the orphan."[78] His faith made the presence of God very vivid during those dark moments of his life. That is why after his first experience in jail, he was able

---

[74] *The Great Synaxaristes* (in Greek), 5th ed. (Athens, 1978), Vol. V, p. 448. This is the version by Nicholas Kyrkos.

[75] D. G. Kalousios, *Hagios Nikolaos, O Neomartyras tou Metsovou*, p. 29. In this publication, an old icon of martyric scenes is depicted taken from Varlaam Monastery's Codex 280, p. 2. In one scene, Saint Nicholas is show lying prone on the ground with two torturers overhead, holding staves and administering a thrashing from his head to his toes. Kalousios, p. 27.

[76] Cf. Deut. 31:6, 8.

[77] Is. 49:15.

[78] Cf. Ps. 9:34.

to find spiritual tranquility. He felt heavenly consolation in the midst of the viciousness and hatred of the enemies of his Faith. For their cruelty alone would have been more tormenting than the darkness of the jail had he not relied implicitly on Christ's power.

On the second day, he underwent a new trial: hunger. It, too, was added to the list of problems that he had to encounter. In the beginning, it afflicted him severely. But he pondered on one thought: "Nourishment enables the body to live; and the body is the temple of the spirit. It is an instrument of the spirit. When the latter returns to God, it does not need the body. The body will return to the earth as it was and the spirit will return to God Who gave it.[79] Why should I think about my body, when soon I shall surrender my soul to my God, my Father? Take courage, therefore, a little longer! The desire for God must put to rest and extinguish the demands of the body. In but a little while, I shall be neither thirsty nor hungry; for I shall be filled with the heavenly bread, the nourishment of all the world, my Lord and my Savior." There was, nonetheless, one more thing that worried him. He had the fear that the judge might either postpone the trial or dismiss sentencing him altogether. Indeed, the judge might leave him to languish in that gloomy jail. Therefore, Nicholas wished to make haste. He could not wait. He was afire because he wanted to be in the company of Christ. However, he overcame this predicament. He said, "I am ready; and I will remain ready. Whenever God wishes, He shall take me with Him." Then Nicholas rested.

When the third day dawned, he was awakened by a loud noise. There were the approaching footsteps of a multitude and the raised voices of an angry people. Their threats were aimed directly at him. He stood up. He tried to distinguish people's faces through the opening in the door, but it was too late. The characteristic clamor of the bolt was heard at once. The heavy door creaked opened. The servants, still dazed by the sunlight from outside, tried to find the prisoner in that pitch black cell. But then he was directly before them. One of the court officers said to the prisoner, "Come on, we are going to the *cadi*," and he stretched his hand to grasp Nicholas and take him out. Nicholas followed quietly. "Let us see if thou wilt say the same things now," added one voice. It was the barber, the accuser who stood on the wayside. A large group had formed and arrived shortly before the judge.

Two worlds met in that court. The province of the Spirit and the jurisdiction of worldly power; the dominion of Christ and the domain of Mohammed. On the one hand, there was the serene countenance of the defendant, which was visibly calm, sweet, and sympathetic; for one deep hope made beautiful his appearance. On the other hand, there were the plaintiffs who

---

[79] Eccl. 12:7; Gen. 3:19.

were excited, sour-tempered, convulsed, superficial, shallow, and looking to support their false premise. But their case was condemned to be overturned in a short while.

The Second Inquiry

The Turkish judge hoped that Nicholas, now that he had tasted what it was to be liable to a civil action, would relinquish his obstinacy. The judge was thinking that the jail, the abandonment, the torture, the privations, and the hunger must have terrorized Nicholas. The judge, consequently, assumed that his day on the court bench would proceed easily for him. The judge was sure that he would persuade, with ease, the defendant to come to his way of thinking. He thought that this would certainly conclude not only as a judicial victory but also as a personal triumph, which would elevate him in the opinion of his own people. Indeed, the judge was thought not to be far from wrong in his assessment. By Nicholas' outer appearance, he seemed just as the judge imagined. The defendant looked tired and exhausted. Nicholas' clothes were soiled from lying on the slab floor of the jail. He gave the impression by his outward aspect of a broken man. The judge thought, "If he truly has lost his courage and his spiritual orientation, then I shall bend him with little effort." But the judge underestimated Nicholas. The judge had it not in his jurisdiction to examine the depths of Nicholas' heart. If he could, the judge would have discovered the heart of a lion which was determined to proceed unto death. Nicholas was as a lion sitting quietly in a corner. But once provoked, the judge would realize that the lion was neither dead, nor sick, nor indifferent; then one experiences the lion's strength. But what did the Lord say to the apostle? "My power is being made perfect in weakness [2 Cor. 12:9]." Such were the words recorded by the apostle who stood, many times, before judges and courts.

Now the judge attempted to express his sympathy to Nicholas for his apparent condition. But the judge's affectation of pity would result in his understanding that such a state for Nicholas was both an honor and a blessing. "I understand thy suffering," commented the judge, "and I see thy condition. Truly, the jail must have brought thee to thy senses. Admit thy mistake and, immediately, thy life will change. I shall release thee. Thou wilt enjoy thy life. I shall set thee free. Thou canst become once more a man with all thy pride." Nicholas surmised the great trap. He was disturbed by the sugary words of the Turk. They rang familiar to those that he heard in the bakery long ago. He, nevertheless, gathered his strength. His thoughts went to God. He sought the inspiration of the Lord. He closed his ears to the words of the Turkish judge. When the judge finally finished attempting to coax him, Nicholas said loudly and without restraint in a characteristic Metsovite accent: "I desire nought of those things that thou hast promised me and of those enjoyments sought after by the world. I have a treasure. It is my Christ. I shall not exchange that treasure for anything." The judge was vexed. He pounded his fist on his desk and raised his voice, saying, "I have no intention of playing games with thee. Either thou wilt change or I shall light a fire and burn thee alive." Nicholas answered resolutely, "My decision is final. Thou shalt never convince me to commit such a great sin. I believe in Christ. He will help me. He is more powerful than thee. His might is mightier than all the world."

These moments, one would say, were exciting, thrilling, and provoking. At such times, one discerns the power of the spirit and the weakness of matter—especially the weakness of the material-minded of the Ottoman Empire. The physiognomy of Ottoman politics and justice is that of a giant, wielding power and authority, on wooden feet. Such a giant collapses into a heap of relics each time it dares to resist the Spirit of God and His saving and redeeming power. The material-minded have not the Spirit.[80] Their wisdom is earthly and demoniacal.[81] On the one hand, the material-minded man receives not the things of the Spirit of God; for it is foolishness to him, and he is not able to come to know it, because it is spiritually examined. On the other hand, the spiritual man examines all things, yet he himself is examined by no one.[82] Thus, the unarmed and illiterate Nicholas, aflame from the fire of the Spirit, rendered powerless—almost nonexistent—the power of the judge.

For this reason did the judge lose his composure. He knew not what more to say, what more to do, what further arguments he should use. He made an outburst, thundering threats and pounding his fists on the table. He looked to the right and to the left. His heart swelled with hatred and enmity toward the Crucified Who triumphed over the world, so that the judge spat forth abuses and insults. "And Who is that Christ?" he bellowed, "Soon, the court officers shall seize thee and cast thee into the fire. Will Christ take thee out of the flames? Art thou so foolish and wanting in understanding?" He paused and then added contemptuously, "O thou fool, do not forget: Christ died on the Cross as a criminal!" The judge was ready to say other similar things, but Nicholas interrupted him and said, "Christ is the true God. He was sacrificed for us. He will save me. I believe in Him with all my soul." As Nicholas spoke these words, his countenance became radiant from heavenly grace. He appeared in the eyes of all those who watched him to assume a certain beauty that was unknown. It was a phenomenon which they saw for the first time in their lives.

At this juncture, the judge jumped to his feet. He stretched his back and his hands as if to take hold of Nicholas. In this vehement gesture, he tried to win him over and to subdue him. "I will burn thee. Hearest thou me?" Nicholas acknowledged this and said, "I hear. But thy words do not persuade

---

[80] Jude 19.

[81] Jas. 3:15.

[82] 1 Cor. 2:14, 15.

me. Thy voice is filled with falsehood. The truth is one. It is luminous and illumines all the world. Christ is the light of the world. He is the light of my life. I will never exchange the light of Christ for your darkness."

The biographer, at this point, interjects: "O Nicholas, how thou hast taught me with thy confession and with thy boldness! What victory is this, O Nicholas? What refreshment this is for our souls, which have withered from the curse of indifference in our free Orthodox Christian land!"

The judge, seeing that he could not change Nicholas' mind, ordered that a great fire be lit at the center of the marketplace, and that they cast the prisoner in it. The judge left the courtroom. Those Muslims present in the courtroom cheered on account of their fundamentalist fanaticism. In the meantime, the court bailiffs scurried about to light the fire. Others seized the victim, so as to lead him to the place of execution. Thus ended the scene in the courtroom, in order to open soon in the central marketplace of the great city.

(L.) Saint Nicholas Makes His Confession
(R.) The Martyrdom of Saint Nicholas of Metsovon

The Martyrdom

When the great fire was lit in the center of the marketplace, the news circulated everywhere. Rabid Turks, throughout the city, converged upon the site. They all talked loudly and shook their fists. Now and again, one could hear verbal abuses hurled at the martyr. Their feverish hearts were benighted from hatred and religious overzealousness. They looked for an excuse to unsheathe their wrath and fury against the Christians who, without protection, were led to martyrdom.

When those gruff officers brought Nicholas, they brandished their scare tactics to put him to the test. They cried out with stentorian voices, "Into the fire! Quickly! Tarry not! His Christ shall save him!" Thus, those strident officers squawked for a while. If some of the officers had not laid hands on him, the others were ready to pounce on him and to ridicule him and sport with him as a cat with a mouse. Only afterward would they take his life by consigning him to the flames.

As for Nicholas, he saw nothing and he heard nothing. He had shut down the receptacles of his senses. Earthly forms of communication, together with human threats and fears, had no impact on him. Now he saw nothing else but a wall of massive flames. As fire purifies gold and makes it pure throughout, thus he saw in that fire the means by which the love of God would absolve him of the last vestige of dross—of sin. Then, a holy angel would bring him to the bosom of God. That is why the heart of Nicholas jumped for joy at that moment. He concentrated all his powers within his heart, allowing his soul to be ignited by the fire of divine love so that he might pour forth a fervent prayer, saying, "My Lord, I am coming! I am on my way to Thee! Nought separates me save a few footsteps, a few moments. My God, I beseech Thee, accept me!"

Nicholas was no longer on earth. With his entire will and with all his heart, he already lived near God. His face changed. It shone with a brightness that appeared supernatural as the fire was reflected upon his face. With a steady and fixed gait, he came within two meters of the fire. There they untied his hands. And the executioner, a wild Turk, said to him with a harsh voice that resembled that of a beast: "Seest thou the fire? It is going to devour thee. Change thy mind so as to be saved." But Nicholas was already in the heavens. "For me," said Nicholas, "that fire is the greatest benefit. Soon I shall be with my Lord Jesus!" The executioner's anger grew more fierce as he said, "Since thou desirest thine own ruin, it is just as well that thou shouldest be consumed. Thou dost refuse to change thy mind. Go ahead, then, into the fire!" And with some vehemence, that executioner pushed Nicholas into the midst of that great fire.[83] The Turks cheered wildly and shouted aloud exultantly. The few Christians, who watched secretly at a distance, closed their eyes and ears. One saint was added to the myriads of saints. One new-martyr, with all the freshness of his youthful years, joined the hosts of martyrs. One city obtained a new guardian and patron.

Nicholas will no longer be an unknown Metsovite. His renown fills heaven and earth as the holy New-martyr Nicholas of Metsovon, who was martyred in Trikkala of Thessaly by fire during the morning of the 16th day of May, in the year 1617.

After the Martyrdom

The rough and uncouth Turkish mob, after they took revenge in the most inhuman way upon the Christians in the person of Nicholas, started to disperse. They were enormously satisfied over their perceived victory. In reality, it was they who were put to shame before the glory of the kingdom of God, which caused one man to defy death itself. The few Christians present concealed themselves. After such an incident, a relentless uprising against the Christian element was very possible. Passionate tempers that had been inflamed needed to be quieted. Before the sun went down, silence fell over the central square. The fire was extinguished. The body of the saint was covered with ashes. Three or four officers remained behind to guard the holy relics. They conversed quietly, as if they were trying not to disturb the everlasting blessedness of the New-martyr Nicholas.

Then darkness fell. It looked as if the night would bring quiet to the city. Life would continue as if nothing out of the ordinary had happened earlier that day. The officers found a sheltered corner in order to protect themselves from the chill of that May night. That moment, a shadow appeared in a narrow street on the north side. A man carefully approached the fire. He signaled the officers, as if to show them something. He approached closer. The soldiers neither prevented him nor showed any curiosity. The man in the shadows drew nigh and put money into their hands. They understood. Without uttering a word, they showed him the ashes and remains.

---

[83] A 16th-C. manuscript at Meteora's Varlaam Monastery [Codex 109, folio 145β] confirms the martyric death of the Metsovite Vlach in a fire at Trikkala. All hymnographers praise Saint Nicholas for his perseverance, courage, and forgiveness toward his unbelieving executioner. One hymn, given in Kalousios' biography [p. 30], says in melodious words [Doxastikon of Vespers Stichera, Mode Plagal Five, by Nicholas Kyrkos] that "when the fire was lit, thou, O Nicholas did not fear, but rather leaped into the midst of it as a daring lion. Fearlessly and full of joy, thou didst utter, 'Nothing can separate me from Thee, O Lord. Let them burn my body that my soul might be bedewed.'" See also full service (in Greek) given in the M. G. Tritos publication, pp. 44, 45.

The man was a Christian and a potter by profession. He was so moved, for piety's sake and by the martyrdom of the saint, that he wished to take something with him as a keepsake and safeguard against danger and disease. He gave a substantial amount of money to the officers. The potter, all alone, searched and found one relic—a veritable treasure. His eyes caught sight of the sacred skull of the new-martyr. He stooped down, took it up into his hands, and disappeared into the night. He sensed boundless gratitude in his heart toward God with the discovery of that treasure. The greater part of his thankfulness to God was for the opportunity he had to observe, as an eyewitness, the courageous confession of Faith of Saint Nicholas before the Turkish judge and the fiery martyrdom. He also praised God for the blessing and honor of being able to retrieve such a precious relic.

The potter, thereafter, went to his house. He chose not to disturb anyone. Before daybreak, he decided that it was best to safeguard his treasure. He did not need to think very long before he decided to carry out his plan: he dug a hole in the wall of enclosed space in his yard (*mandra*)[84] and enclosed the skull within. He deemed it an unlikely place for anyone to search for the relic. Thus, the sacred head remained close to him both as a blessing and a gift of grace. Concurrently, the presence of the relic afforded him security from destruction or loss. Another biographer adds that the potter noticed that the relic suffered slight damage from the fire to the back of the head. He then writes that the relic was concealed within a wall of the house. The potter made no mention of the hidden treasure to his kinfolk.[85] The bones of the saint, which did not perish in the fire, were scattered except for a few remnants. Regarding these other portions of the relics, we will speak of them later. With regard to the skull, it remained at Trikkala. The relic of the saint's head would be a source of sanctification for the people of God who had to live there in the midst of the fanatical Islamists.

At the Monastery of Varlaam (Barlaam)

Not much time elapsed before the godly potter left this world and went to heavenly blessedness. Meanwhile, his treasure, the sacred skull of the new-martyr, remained concealed in the same place where he had secured it. No one knew of the spot. He had not told any of his relatives. They lived for many years near the treasure, and it kept them from harm, but they did not even

---

[84] A *mandra* is usually a 4-foot wall built of bricks of mud, used as a fence for enclosing the front yard of some homes in Greece.

[85] This information in this paragraph was taken from the publications of D. G. Kalousios [p. 34] and M. G. Tritos [p. 23]. *The Great Synaxaristes* (in Greek) records that the potter "returned to his home and concealed the skull in a place inside the wall for fear of the Turks. Only the members of his household were aware of the secret [loc. cit.]."

know it until the day arrived when things changed. The entire house, along with the courtyard, was sold to someone else. By divine will, the buyer was a Christian and a devout one. His name was Melandros. This, too, was God's plan so that the precious inheritance which was bequeathed by the martyr should remain safe. Melandros knew nothing about the martyrdom that had occurred. He never knew that he would become an instrument of God.

The Finding of the Precious Head

It was the eve of the saint's martyrdom. It seems that Trikke had forgotten the great event, which will never be repeated. The bitter servitude caused the Christian Greeks to sigh under the tyranny of a vulgar, rude, and uncivilized overlord. Melandros decided, that very afternoon, to work in his front yard. He watered the flowers and weeded. Thus, he passed the afternoon. The sun had set and he was tired. Ready to cease whatever he was doing in order to rest from the day's work, he collected his tools. He glanced at the gate, noticing that it was closed, and retired to his little kitchen.

At that time, it seemed to him that he saw a light in the midst of the courtyard wall. He was dumbfounded. He thought he must be mistaken. But behold, it was no mistake! He saw it very clearly. It was a light that shone from the wall in his yard. "My God!" he said, "What is that light! I saw it! It was not an apparition." He tarried a long while gazing at the wall. Melandros, next, closed the door to his house and recited his prayers. Without mentioning the phenomenon to anyone, he reclined and went to sleep. When the sunlight came into his eyes, he said good morning to his Creator and then recalled yesterday's light. He could not remove from his thoughts the sight of that sweet light emanating from his courtyard wall. He thought he was living in a dream; but he still did not disclose what he had seen to anyone. Thus passed that anniversary day in May of the martyrdom of Nicholas of Metsovon.

At night, Melandros performed all his Christian duties. He prayed and gave thanks to God for all His gifts and benefactions. He commended himself to God's providence and lay down to sleep. As he slumbered, once again he saw the light as it appeared to emanate from the wall. How magnificent it was! As he fixed his gaze upon it, the light gave him great and heavenly delight.

Suddenly, that divine scene was interrupted by a young man clad in traditional Metsovite dress. "Melandros," said the young man, "approach the light. The fruit of my martyrdom is hidden within. It is a testimony that I loved the God of our fathers; and, for His love, I offered my life in the flower of my youth." Melandros then heard that sweet voice, again, in the midst of a deep sleep, saying to him, "It is my skull that is hidden therein. It is in thy hands from this moment onward." Melandros jumped up. He opened his eyes. It was midnight. He did not utter a word to anyone. On the one hand, he was elated by the revelation; but, on the other hand, he was sorry that the magnificent appearance of the new-martyr was so short. Melandros, thereupon, set about to pray.

When daylight broke, there he was in the yard. He took his tools and, exercising much caution, began to search on the spot where the light appeared. What amazement he experienced when he saw the sacred skull of the new-martyr buried in the wall! Tears came to his eyes. He did not consider himself worthy of such a treasure. With great reverence, he took it in his hands and kissed it with contrition. Even though chills ran up and down his spine from his astonishment, he placed it securely in his house. He could not rest quietly, however. He knew that the skull of the saint was not in a safe place in his poor and humble abode. He must provide more suitable surroundings. The sacred relic should rest in a holy place. He said, "It ought to be put into hands that could honor and cherish it for the sake of pious and devout Christians who might have recourse to the saint." Now Melandros was in contact with the Monastery of Varlaam at Meteora.[86] It was there that a family member had

---

[86] This monastery, situated at Meteora, within the eparchy of Stagon at Kalambaka, is built on a tall and precipitous geological rock formation. In 1350, an ascetic named Varlaam ascended the precipitous rock, for whom the monastery was named. He built three churches, a small cell, and a reservoir for water. Upon his repose, the rock remained abandoned for about two hundred years. In 1517/1518, the two founders that built up Varlaam, the priest-monks and brothers according to the flesh, Theophanes and Nectarios Apsarades of Ioannina (commemorated the 17th of May), reached the rock. They renovated the little church of the Three Hierarchs and erected the tower. They also built (in 1541/1542) the central church of the monastery (the *katholikon*) dedicated to All Saints. Up to the 16th C., the presence of the monks was constant. From the early part of the 17th C. onward, only a few monks remained. Since then, the decline began. In the time of Saint Nicholas, in order to access the monastery, the ascent was made by a series of wooden ladders, each of which had about 25 rungs. The precarious ladders were hanging from the rock with the help of pegs on the north side of the church and a gap was created between them. The monks often had to jump from one ladder to another risking even their own lives. This difficulty was due to the peculiarity and the morphology of the rocks. There were about four or five ladders consisting of 95 rungs at maximum. In 1517/1518, the founders who built the tower of the monastery reached

(continued...)

become a monk. The monks, therefore, placed the holy skull of Saint Nicholas near the other most valuable relics and treasures.

The Great Synaxaristes (in Greek) records that "Melandros, aware of his unworthiness to possess such a treasure in his domicile, went to the Monastery of Varlaam at Meteora, where his brother was a monk. Melandros offered the precious relic in their parents' memory. There the head of the holy New-martyr Nicholas, which performs countless miracles, may be found to this day."[87] The relic of the skull is housed in a silver *kouvouklion* (canopy-type) reliquary that is octagonal. The outward sides of the reliquary have scenes from the saint's life.[88]

When God deems thee worthy, my dear reader, to visit the Monastery of Varlaam at Meteora, ask that thou mayest venerate the sacred skull or *kara* of Saint Nicholas. Thy soul will be astonished by the fragrance that has emitted therefrom for centuries to those who show reverence. Thus, thou wilt have venerated one of the most important and most sacred ornaments of that monastery and also of our Faith. It is a treasure that remains as a testimony that the Lord our God lives unto all ages.

The Great Synaxaristes (in Greek) reports a few of the saint's many miracles, so that you may believe the others. Once a plague struck Trikkala and

---

[86](...continued)
the rock. Monks and materials were hoisted by hand in a rope net. From the early part of the 19th C., they created steps carved in the rock with a bridge between them, which fabrications have been altered many times. Nowadays, objects are hoisted electrically.

Varlaam contains a lot of relics that give off a sweet smell and delight the faithful. These precious relics are kept, as valuable treasures of Orthodoxy, in the sanctuary of the Church of All Saints. There are the skulls of the holy founders, as well as New-martyr Nicholas from Metsovon and pieces of the relic of Saint John Chrysostom, Saint John the Baptist, Saint Paraskeve, and Saint Anastasia. See http://www.kalampaka.com/en/meteora/monasteries_varlaam.asp.

[87] *The Great Synaxaristes* (in Greek), p. 449.

[88] Within, exactly on the incision and continuing all around, there is inscribed an inscription: "This present box containing the august skull of Saint Nicholas the New of Metsovon was constructed at the expense of the blessed John and his children, Constantine and George, and the rest of the Christians of the village of Deskata, for the succor and salvation of the souls of the most reverend Hieromonk Stephen, Father Christopher, and Father Efthymios of the august Monastery of Varlaam at Meteora...." It then continues with these words: "1819, January 1st, by the hand of Demetrios Misiou," followed by words difficult to decipher. It is suggested that this family from Deskata of the Elasson eparchy offered the reliquary in thanksgiving for a miracle performed by the saint. On the inside of the *kouvouklion* one may read: "The august skull of the holy New-martyr Nicholas of Metsovon. 1819 January 1st. Builders of the Holy Monastery of Varlaam, Meteora, Nectarios and Theophanes." See S. G. Katsimpras, pp. 91-94.

many died each day. Yet by only the relic's presence and consolation, the plague quickly ceased. Similarly, in the village of Distata (present-day Deskata), the inhabitants suffered the same scourge; but they, also, were delivered by Saint Nicholas' holy head. Even those of Kalarrytai who were visited by sickness were immediately saved by its presence. By the grace of the holy skull, locusts, both then and even in modern times, were destroyed throughout the Thessalian countryside and all the fruit preserved unharmed. Both the Christians and the Turks were ecstatic about this miracle, for it occurred not only once or twice but even many times to this day. Not only the above mentioned type of cures took place but also incurable diseases were wondrously healed in every place that the saint was invited. Indeed, this and many more wonder-workings occurred.

Relic of the Precious Head of Saint Nicholas

In recent memory, there was the case of the nun of the Holy Monastery of Saint Stephen at Meteora. She had been suffering from 1963 with a grave illness to her finger joints that had atrophied, despite five painful surgeries, and left her with fingers bent and stiffened by disease. Her pains were terrible, especially when she was feverish. The saint, in Metsovite garb, appeared to the sufferer while she was taking the waters at Smokovou. He offered his help and invited her to his monastery at Meteora, where he was staying. He explained that his monastery neighbored her own. Now prior to this encounter, she never knew of Saint Nicholas. She, nevertheless, readily agreed to accept his help. When she returned to her abbess at the convent, the latter identified the Metsovite as Saint Nicholas. She confirmed that his skull was at the nearby men's Monastery of Varlaam. After the sufferer went to Varlaam and kissed the wall icon of the saint with much piety, she afterward placed her crippled hand on the skull. As soon as she removed her hand, it was perfectly sound with complete movement. Thereafter, that nun no longer required medicines and therapies.[89]

Also in 1966, a damsel from the village of Meelia Metsovou suffered from chronic epilepsy. Her parents brought her to many physicians, but they found no remedy for her seizures and convulsions. Eventually, they made a

[89] S. G. Katsimpras, p. 83; Tritos, pp. 27, 28.

pilgrimage to the Monastery of Varlaam in order to kiss the sacred relic of the New-martyr Nicholas. The abbot, Father Isidore, removed the sacred skull from the holy Table of the Church of the Three Hierarchs. The little girl kissed the relic. From that moment, she no longer experienced any symptoms of that neurological disorder.[90]

Chapel at Metsovon

Other martyric relics of Saint Nicholas are treasured at several locations, one of which is at the Holy Monastery of Eleousa on the little isle at Ioannina, where there is found one-half of the right palm of the saint's hand. Another portion of the same hand is at the Monastery of Saint Paraskeve at Skamneli of Ioannina. In eastern Metsovon, at the Holy Monastery of the Dormition, there is a portion of the new-martyr's relic which is thought to be one of his teeth. In the saint's hometown there is also a very modest chapel, or rather a shrine, on the very spot of the garden of the saint's parental home. Although there is no holy Table within, the divine Liturgy is still performed. The Metsovites erected this shrine in 1919, in honor of their hallowed compatriot.

By Saint Nicholas' efficacious intercessions, may we be delivered from every necessity and affliction. Amen.

On the 16th of May, the holy Church commemorates the Recovery of the Relics of our venerable Father EPHRAIM the Wonder-worker of Perekop of Novgorod.

Through the intercessions of Thy Saints,
O Christ God, have mercy on us. Amen.

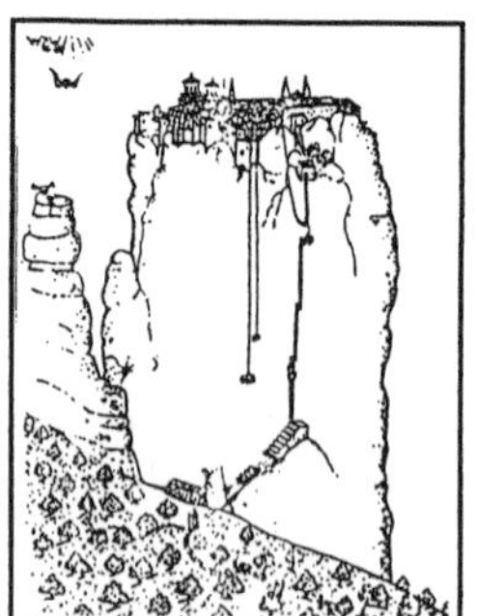
Varlaam Monastery

[90] Tritos, p. 28.

On the 17th of May, the holy Church commemorates the holy Apostles ANDRONIKOS and JUNIA.

Andronikos and Junia, the holy apostles and martyrs of Christ, as winged birds, flew throughout the inhabited world. They uprooted the tentacles of the deceit of idolatry. The most wondrous Junia accompanied the divine Andronikos. They mortified their flesh and were, essentially, dead to the things of the world, living only for Christ. Together they guided many unbelievers to the knowledge of God. Following close upon their cures of incurable diseases, there came the demolition of the idol temples. They taught peoples and tribes past number and brought them to the light of Christ. After shining forth as luminaries before the darkness of the benighted error of paganism, these apostles paid the common debt of nature as they too were mortal. But by means of death they were ushered into everlasting life.

Saint Andronikos

The great Apostle Paul, in his Epistle to the Romans, singles out Andronikos and Junia in his opening salutation: "Greet Andronikos and Junia, my kinfolk and my fellow prisoners, who are notable among the apostles, and who have been in Christ before me [Rom. 16:7]." So we see that the divine Paul addresses both as apostles: "Andronikos and Junia who are notable among the apostles" ('Ανδρόνικον καὶ 'Ιουνίαν οἵτινές εἰσιν ἐπίσημοι ἐν τοῖς ἀποστόλοις). Some are in disagreement over the name Junia, taking it as the masculine Junias. Saint Chrysostom counted the name as that of a woman among the apostles: "Think what an encomium it was to be considered notable among the apostles. They were distinguished by their works and achievements. Bless me, how great the philosophy of this woman to be counted worthy to be addressed also as one of the apostles! But the praise did not stand still here, but again he praises them and says, saying, 'They have been in Christ before me (οἳ πρὸ ἐμοῦ ἐν Χριστῷ).'"[1] Saint Joseph the Hymnographer, in today's divine office, chants: "Those bright and illuminating stars and sacred apostles, let us honor: God-inspired Junia and God-bearing Andronikos."[2]

Saint Andronikos is also commemorated on the 4th of January with the Apostles of the Seventy. He is not on all lists, but Saint Dimitri of Rostov lists him as Bishop of Pannonia, Illyricum. He is also commemorated on the 30th of

[1] Saint John Chrysostom, "Hom. 31 on Romans," *P.G.* 60:747 (cols. 669, 670).

[2] May 17th, Orthros Canon, Ode Five, Mode Plagal Four, by Saint Joseph.

July. It is generally believed that he reposed in peace. He is depicted as a young man, beardless by nature.[3] Some maintain that he was arrested in the year 58 and brought to Rome where he suffered martyrdom. Saint Joseph the Hymnographer, who composed the Orthros Canon to the saint, hints at this when chanting: "Thou wast known as priest and sacrificer, as well as sacrifice, of the One Who for His compassion's sake was made the Sacrifice."[4]

It was during the tenure of Patriarch Thomas I of Constantinople (607-610) that sacred relics were uncovered in the capital, near the gate and tower named Evgenios. During times of persecutions against Christians, holy relics were interred by the faithful in concealed places. With the passage of time, at a particular spot in the Evgenios district of the capital, miracles of healing were taking place. Upon exploring the site and conducting excavations, investigations discovered the precious relics of saints as they lay hidden in the earth. They were straightway removed and transferred to a church with reverence and piety by Patriarch Thomas I. When the patriarch displayed the relics for public veneration, sick folk from all over the city attended and were healed. But, at that time, the names of the saints were unknown. With the passage of many years, a certain cleric, Father Nicholas, who was a calligrapher, received a divine revelation from God in regard to the relics found at Evgenios. Father Nicholas was vouchsafed the identity of the relics of two saints: the holy Apostles Andronikos and Junia. Emperor Andronikos I Komnenos (1183-1185) built a church in Saint Andronikos' honor, in the same place where the relics were venerated.[5] Saint Joseph chants, "Thy house, O apostle, springs forth fountains of healing that wash away spiritual sicknesses."[6] And, "Thou hast received from God divine grace to purge diseases and drive out wicked spirits."[7]

Saint Junia

[3] *The Painter's Manual of Dionysius of Fourna*, trans. by Paul Hetherington (Redondo Beach: Oakwood Pub., 1981), p. 53. This Dionysios (1670-ca. 1745) became a monk at the Athonite Skete of Karyes and was a master iconographer.

[4] May 17th, Orthros Canon, Ode Eight, Mode Plagal Four, by Saint Joseph.

[5] See the finding of the sacred relics of the holy martyrs and apostles at Evgenios in Constantinople, commemorated by the holy Church on the 22nd of February. See note for dating the two occasions for the finding of the relics.

[6] May 17th, Orthros Canon, Ode Six, Mode Plagal Four.

[7] May 17th, Orthros Canon, Ode One, Mode Plagal Four.

On the 17th of May, the holy Church commemorates the holy Martyrs SOLOHONOS, and those with him, PAMPHAMER and PAMPHYLON.

Solohon, Pamphamer, and Pamphylon, the holy martyrs, flourished during the years that Emperor Maximian reigned (286-305). They hailed from Egypt. They were, by profession, soldiers who served with one thousand others under a tribune named Campanus. Their battalion set sail from Egypt bound for Chalcedon,[8] an ancient maritime town on the eastern shore of the Bosporus directly across from Byzantion. The emperor enjoined each commander to have the men under his command offer incense to the idols. Campanus, therefore, planned to execute the decree of the emperor. He did not scruple to use force if needed.

All the soldiers complied except three. Those who resisted were Solohon, Pamphamer, and Pamphylon. They professed themselves to be Christians. They, with much confidence, declared that no matter what torture was employed they would not deny the Christ. Even unto death, they would persist in the Christian religion. The ever-memorable soldiers of Christ were, thereupon, subjected to severe thrashings. Their punishment to the shoulder blades (scapulae) was especially brutal. Bruising and swelling to the tissues and membranes worsened and ruptured, so that each man had a protruding mass that was elevated above the head. Consequently, both Pamphamer and Pamphylon surrendered their souls to God. As for the holy Solohon, he rallied his strength a little and boldly called upon the name of Christ. He accused Campanus of ignorance, since the tribune called insensate idols his gods. Campanus was filled with wrath at this accusation. He commanded the executioners to pry open the martyr's mouth with swords, so that wine offered as sacrifice to the gods could be poured within. Although fettered, still Solohon clenched his teeth so tightly that he broke off part of the sword blade. His bonds were then cut away. Following this, Solohon stood before Campanus. The adamantine soldier of Christ magnified the divinity of Jesus and mocked the evil genius or spirit[9] of the ruler. Suddenly, then, a voice was heard out of heaven, urging him and strengthening him for martyrdom.

After this encounter, the pagan executioners strewed jagged tiles and shards of broken earthenware on the stadium track. Solohon's feet were bound to the back of a chariot as he was dragged, circuiting seven times around the course. The saint's wounds were cleaved and shredded, thereby ushering in the keenest pangs. Following this torturous run, they suspended the martyr by his right hand from a beam. Around his left foot, they tied a heavy rock. They left

---

[8] Chalcedon is modern-day Kadikoy, Turkey. In A.D. 451, it was the site of the Fourth Œcumenical Synod.

[9] Evil genius—κακοδαιμονίαν.

him in that excruciating position from the sixth hour to the tenth hour. Throughout that torture, however, Solohon was not persuaded to denounce Jesus Christ. He, rather, continued to profess Christ as God. The pagans, thereupon, cut the rope with a scythe, causing the martyr to fall down with a thud. Nevertheless, he stood upright and, secure on his own two feet, strode away from that spot.

By nightfall, the brooding Campanus was infuriated. He did not know how to break the Christian's resolve. The tribune took his pen with which he was writing and thrust it into the ear of the saint. He, indeed, forced it to pass through to the inner parts of Solohon's head. Thinking the penetration killed Solohon, who had collapsed, he left him. The tribune then went out to arrange for the soldiers' grain allowance. The Christians of that city took up the saint on a wooden litter. All of Solohon's bodily members, at this point, were either disabled or paralyzed. He was no longer able to walk. The Christians brought him to the house of a certain Christian widow. The saint was able to partake of a little bread. He prayed for the Christians standing by and, afterward, he gazed heavenward and surrendered his blessed soul into the hands of God, receiving the crown of the contest.

On the 17th of May, the holy Church commemorates Saints NECTARIOS and THEOPHANES of Ioannina, Builders of the Varlaam Monastery at Meteora.[10]

Nectarios and Theophanes, our venerable fathers, were the builders of the prodigious Monastery of Varlaam in the rock forest at Meteora. They were brothers according to the flesh, who were born during the second half of the fifteenth century at Ioannina of Epiros.[11] They were the scions of a distin-

[10] Saint Theophanes reposed in 1544. His brother, Saint Nectarios reposed on the 7th of April, in the year 1550. The Church has chosen to celebrate the memory of both brothers on the 17th of May.

[11] Mountainous Epiros was an ancient part of northern Greece which stretched from the Ionian Sea to the Ambracian Gulf and was bounded by Illyria, Macedonia, and Thessaly. After passing through several hands, Epiros became the property of the Turks in 1430. It later formed part of the Turkish Vilayet of Janina (Ioannina, 39°40′N 20°15′E). Greece obtained the part east of the river Arta in 1881. At the close of the Balkan War (1912-1913), Greece added a new province to her territory on her northwest: to this province she gave the name of Epiros. This province, today, is bordered on the north by Albania, on the east by the provinces of Macedonia and Thessaly, and on the south and west by the Gulf of Arta and the Ionian Sea. Its capital, Ioannina (formerly Janina or Jannina; Yanina or Yannina), on Lake Ioannina, is approximately 200 miles northwest of Athens.

guished and prominent family, the Apsarades (Apsaras) of Ioannina,[12] who held positions in Ioannina from Byzantine times.[13] While members of the Apsarades family were noted for their wealth, glory, and power, yet they were also conspicuous for their virtue and sanctity. The parents and three sisters of Nectarios and Theophanes followed the monastic life and dedicated both their lives and wealth to God. Family circumstances, coupled with an upright disposition, were conducive for the excellent Orthodox instruction received by each member. They, thus, abandoned the world and its sweet things to become monks and nuns.

Entering the Monastic Life

A young Nectarios and Theophanes were the first members of the family to renounce the world. This took place in 1495. Due to their wisdom, prudence, and education, they did not embark thoughtlessly upon the monastic life. They chose to submit, with all their soul and thoughts, to the commands of the discreet and holy Elder Savvas who came from a noble family of Ioannina. Their blessed elder, as one most worthy of the angelic life, was graced with the priesthood and taught the brothers all the facets of the monastic life. Nectarios and Theophanes remained as hermits on the island in the midst of Lake Ioannina (also known as Pamvotis), in what is now known as the Isle of Kyra Frosinis. They dwelt and struggled in asceticism with Elder Savvas for ten years until his translation to the Lord in 1505. Later in life, when reflecting upon the repose of their elder, the brothers commented: "We remained as orphans bereft of such a father who was still a relatively young man." Upon his repose, the brothers decided to pursue their ascetic struggles on the Holy Mountain of Athos.

At Mount Athos

Nectarios and Theophanes repaired to the Monastery of Dionysiou, dedicated to Saint John the Baptist. It was built on a narrow and precipitous neck of rock, eighty meters above the sea. At this monastery, they found the

---

[12] The present *Synaxaristes* version of the lives of these saintly brothers, Nectarios and Theophanes, was originally recorded by Metropolitan Matthew of Myra. He partly drew from their autobiographies to be found in the codices of the Monastery of Varlaam [No. 134, folios 5-26; and No. 135, folios 3-8]. A service was also composed by Metropolitan Matthew (Venice: Nicholas Glykys, 1803 and 1815), which was later revised by the Ioanninan Bishop Gabriel of Stagon. See the history of the Varlaam Monastery and the builders, together with the aforementioned divine office to the saints, in Στό Βράχο τῆς' Ισάγγελης Πολιτείας, by Theotekni Monachee (Meteora: Saint Stephen Monastery, 1998).

[13] Members of the old Byzantine family of Apsaras had been either distinguished in the public life of Epiros or endowed with important religious foundations both in Epiros and Thessaly. Miltos Garidis and Athanasios Paliouras, *Monasteries of the Island of Ioannina: Painting* (Ioannina, 1993), p. 323 [see article by Anastasia Tourta].

former Patriarch of Constantinople, Niphon II (1486-1489, 1497-1498).[14] The holy Niphon joyfully welcomed the brothers, after hearing of their difficulties. Nevertheless, he counseled them to return to their philosophical retreat on the island in the midst of Lake Ioannina.

The Lakeside Cave Church of the Forerunner at Ioannina

The holy brothers, as obedient children, returned to their first hermitage. However, during their absence, it was taken over by others. The lay founders were asking payment for the rights of ownership. The two brothers, desiring peace, preferred to forego their rights and build elsewhere. As a result, the brothers thought to avoid further conflict from that direction and move closer toward the interior of the island.

The fathers chose a cave. The site, known as Gouva, was near the shore of the lake and the hermitage of Saint Panteleimon. A small chapel had once been raised up at Gouva.[15] The brothers began clearing and building from 1506/1507. Their difficulties were considerable but not insurmountable. The Turkish authorities, "by the grace of God and through much expense, were made to cease making difficulties; and so we brought the task to completion,"[16] commented the brothers. The *katholikon* for the Forerunner John was built over the cave. This came about after a section of the cave had been cut away and the *katholikon* adapted into the space of the cave. First a part of the cave was cut off and the adjoining lakeside was backfilled with debris, in order to give substance and create a base for the building.[17] Together with the *katholikon* of

---

[14] Saint Niphon is commemorated by the holy Church on the 11th of August. At the Monastery of Dionysiou, in a special crypt in the chancel of the *katholikon* (main church), the relics of Saint Niphon are displayed. They are kept in a silver-plated reliquary in the shape of a church, the gift of the Voivode Neagoe in 1515. After the fall of Constantinople (1453), many Moldo-Wallachian rulers assisted the monastery. Among the listed builders for whom the monastery owes its enlargement and present form are the names of Radoulos and his heir, Neagoe Basarab. See Sotiris Kadas' "The Monastery of Dionysiou," *Mount Athos*, trans. by Louise Turner (Athens: Ekdotike Athenon S.A., 1980), p. 63.

[15] Gouva had formerly been used as a dwelling of hermits. Nectarios and Theophanes found traces "of an old small building that seemed to be an old church." Garidis and Paliouris, *Monasteries: Paintings*, loc. cit.

[16] Ibid.

[17] The architecture of the Church of Saint John the Forerunner is unusual. It is built in stonework interspersed with bricks, with an area of 6.37 meters by 3.76 meters. While it is aisleless, there are two three-sided conches (choirs) in the north and south, with a contemporary narthex to the west. The original narthex on the north side has been demolished. The conch of the sanctuary is inscribed into the body of the east wall. There is an underground crypt with a trapdoor. The roof is a barrel-vault. The current

(continued...)

the Forerunner, Nectarios and Theophanes constructed cells. Concurrently, they also supervised the building of the Monastery of Saint Nicholas in Lepenos. It has been suggested that it had been founded by their father. The ruins of Saint Nicholas have been located at Perama, north of the hill of Goritsa. As we mentioned earlier, the brothers also had three sisters. Nectarios and Theophanes built a cell in the island village for them, so they could pursue monastic struggles as nuns.

After they raised up churches to the Forerunner and Saint Nicholas, a few years had passed. In 1510/1511, the two hieromonks were compelled to leave their Forerunner Monastery. Mounting scandals and stumbling blocks brewed and rose up in that place. Other monks in the neighborhood came into conflict with them. Our fathers chose not to avenge themselves, but gave place to wrath.[18] Since the brothers desired only quietude, they brought to mind the words of Patriarch Niphon who had counseled them aforetime and said, "When the time of trouble comes upon you, do not resist it; flee from that place and go to another place to arrive at peace." Submitting to his admonition, the Apsarades brothers abandoned all their labors

Monastery of the Forerunner (Katholikon from the East)

---

[17](...continued)
frescoes date from 1789. See the English publication of the archaeologist Barbara N. Papadopoulou, *The Monasteries of the Island of Ioannina* (Ioannina: Holy Monastery of Eleousa, 2004), pp. 119, 120. The dimensions are: 6.37 meters in length; 5.60 meters the greatest width and 3.76 meters the smallest width; and 6.75 meters in height. It is a complex building combining elements of two architectural types: the cross-domed roof and the side choirs, semi-hexagonal at their exterior, a characteristic of the Athonite type. The brothers did not seem to have time to adorn the *katholikon* with frescoes, since the continuous polemics prohibited this. Later (1789), Abbot Anastasios, Basil Valkanos, and the Guild of Wine Merchants funded the wall-paintings. Garidis & Paliouras, *Monasteries: Paintings*, loc. cit.

[18] Cf. Rom. 12:19.

upon that island.[19] The year was 1511 when they departed Lake Ioannina and set off for Meteora of Thessaly.

Saints Theophanes (L.) and Nectarios (R.), Founders of Varlaam

At Meteora

When the fathers arrived at the granite pinnacles of Meteora, they found it to be a suitable and peaceful location. With the blessing of the *kathegoumenos* (leader) of the respected and imperial Monastery of the Great Meteoron, they dwelt as eagles perched atop one of the most precipitous rock formations, known as "The Pillar of the Honorable Forerunner." The holy Nectarios and Theophanes strove seven harsh years in that *hesychasterion*,[20] all the while guided by God. They also had received the exhortation and blessing of the Metropolitan of Larisa,[21] whose see included the area known as Stagon (Kalambaka) and Meteora.

The Rock of Varlaam

In October of 1517, the brothers ascended that vertical and nearly inaccessible summit at a height of 373 meters. It was known as "The Rock of Varlaam," which was vacant at the time. Saint Varlaam had been a contemporary of Saint Athanasios of the Great Meteoron (1305-1383).[22] The latter helped his hermit friend when he was attacked by robbers. The venerable

---

[19] Nothing is known what became of the Forerunner Monastery after the brothers took flight. In 1789, the walls of the main church were frescoed under the supervision of Hegumen Anastasios. During the siege of Ali Pasha by the Sultan's men, in 1821-1822, this monastery, as did others, suffered damage. In 1824, the frescoes of the *katholikon* were restored. In 1891, further restorative work was carried out. Today, only the *katholikon* remains of the brothers' labors. Papadopoulou, *The Monasteries of the Island of Ioannina*, pp. 117-119.

[20] A *hesychasterion* is a hermitage proper. It is usually located in some desolate spot, often in a cliff face, as seen also on Athos. Sometimes it is a small hut, but it is more often a cave, scarcely altered. It is to this type of retreat that monks seek and expect the most harsh and austere asceticism.

[21] Larisa, the seat of a Greek archbishopric, is the capital of Thessaly, on the Salambria River, thirty-five miles northwest of Volos.

[22] Saint Athanasios is commemorated by the holy Church on the 20th of April.

Varlaam, who came ca. 1350, was considered the builder and first ascetic of the Holy Monastery of Varlaam. He ascended the rock by a system of successive scaffolds supported on beams wedged into holes in the rocks. This method was imitated by other ascetics throughout the stone forest. The scaffolding system, however, was later replaced by long rope ladders.[23] When Varlaam chose to struggle in the ascetic life on that rock, he built both a small chapel—dedicated to the Three Hierarchs (Saints Basil, Gregory and John Chrysostom)—and a few cells. Upon his repose, the rock remained uninhabited and deserted, though it acquired the name of "The Rock of Varlaam."

The history of the monastery will now commence in the early sixteenth century when the brothers, Nectarios and Theophanes Apsarades, of Ioannina established and organized their coenobium on the summit of this precipitous spire.[24] Nectarios and Theophanes found their new arena for ascetic contests well-aired and suited for hesychasm and prayer. Of the saintly Varlaam's original buildings, there remained only a part of the sanctuary of the Church of the Three Hierarchs and traces of the older *kellia*.[25]

At length, more monks were drawn, as iron is attracted to a magnet, by the virtues of these holy fathers. Thus, their small monastic brotherhood started atop this very high rock. The fathers observed strict fasts and many hours of prayer. By the grace of God, with great effort and considerable expense, the brothers, with two disciples, Benedict and Pachomios, initiated the building of their monastery. It was necessary to reconstruct the Church of the Three Hierarchs.[26] This temple became the first *katholikon*. They also built the tower, the stairs, the cells, and other structures.[27]

---

[23] Those climbers who suffered from vertigo were hauled up in a net. As the winch creaked throughout the ascent, the passenger would usually swing in a circular motion in that aerial void, for about thirty minutes of worry and terror. In 1923, 195 steps were cut in the same rock. Pilgrims and visitors may now ascend easily. The net, however, is still used today to convey foodstuffs and other necessities. Theocharis M. Provatakis, *Meteora* (Athens: Michalis Toubis S.S., 1983), p. 36.

[24] Nikos Nikonanos, *Meteora*, trans. by L. Turner (Athens: George A. Christopoulos, John C. Bastias, Pub.; Ekdotike Athenon S.A., 1987), p. 39.

[25] The *kellion* (pl. *kellia*) or cell can be a spacious monastic dwelling which contains a small chapel. The cell is often manned by three or more monks under deed of trust from the parent monastery.

[26] The small single-aisled and wood-roofed Chapel of the Three Hierarchs, today, terminates in a semi-circular apse at the east end. This simple church is of particular interest for the history of the monastery. The church contains wall paintings (frescoes) executed by the Priest John and his children from Stagi (Kalambaka) from 1627-1637, which survive in perfect condition. N. Nikonanos, p. 47.

[27] Ibid., p. 40.

Now the Elders Nectarios and Theophanes, naturally, desired to construct a larger structure from the ruins of the sanctuary built by the Elder Varlaam. However, a decree of the Turkish sultan ordered the demolition of new Christian churches and of those recently reconstructed. The brothers, therefore, had to restrict their fervor. They used only a small church for the singing of psalms and the chanting of Liturgies.[28]

The righteous brothers were negligent neither in regard to the spiritual progress of the monks nor to the finishing of the coenobium for the sake of those who struggled at Varlaam. By means of donated properties and *metochia* (holdings and dependencies of the monastery), they supported themselves and prospered. During their lifetimes, the brothers provided the monastery with engravings and manuscripts. They endowed it with gardens, vineyards, olive groves, a tower for the windlass, farms, and mills. The holy men also built an infirmary for the sick members of the brotherhood. A geriatric section, in addition, was provided for elderly monks. Simply put, they took loving care to prepare for the needs and requirements of their spiritual children. This is attested to in the codices preserved at their monastery, and also penned by these remarkable brothers. Together with enriching the monastery with all outward and material goods, they laid down the foundations of the exemplary community life for the simple and honest.

Saint Theophanes Offering to God
All-Saints Church at Varlaam

At length, the ranks of monks swelled. Thus, where once not even "a footstep of life" existed, there was now a thriving monastic community. This formerly untrodden rock became a ladder from earth to heaven, conveying toward salvation a colony of men who feared God and lived only for Him.

---

28 By the end of 1627, the Church of the Three Hierarchs arrived at its present form. The visitor may view the three architectural building phases. The most prominent divergence is seen in the sanctuary apse. We know that the foundations are the work of Varlaam. The wall up to the windows marks the rebuilding of the Apsaras brothers in 1517. The upper section of the apse and the rest of the structure belong to the third and last phase in 1627. Ibid., p. 47.

The Church of All Saints

In 1542, when the number of monks had risen to thirty, it was necessary to build a larger and new *katholikon*. Thus, the Church of All Saints was completed in 1544.[29] The church, as one document records, was built in twenty days, though materials had been collected for twenty-two years.[30] The church is of the Athonite type, that is a domed cruciform church, with side apses (the choirs) with a spacious narthex at the west end.[31]

Today, an inscription, in the southern part of the nave of the *katholikon*, may be read: "This sacred and venerable church of the revered Monastery of All Saints was raised from the foundations by the most holy among the monks and brethren, Master Nectarios and Master Theophanes, in

---

[29] The careless walling in limestone, and the cut stones set in thick plaster, and the haphazard layout of the windows, all indicate that the laborers, for all their determination and perseverance, were not skilled artisans. In the conch above the two-lobed window of the sanctuary apse, there is a brick upon which the following is inscribed in capital letters: "NECTARIOS AND THEOPHANES FROM IOANNINA, THE APSARADES." The year shown is 7050=1542. In the corresponding place in the south apse, there is seen on a brick the same inscription and year with the difference that 7026=1517 is shown at the beginning; this refers to the year that the holy brothers first ascended the rock. Ibid., pp. 41, 42.

[30] Provatakis, loc. cit.

[31] The church was smaller than the *katholikon* of the Great Meteoron. The corner spaces behind the piers in the nave are low and covered by vaults which slope from north to south. The eso-narthex roof is a regular four-columned space above which supports a well-lit dome, as high as the dome of the nave.

The narthex was painted in 1566, after the repose of Nectarios and Theophanes, by their relative Antonios Apsarades, Bishop of Vellas. Low in the narthex is the traditional row of full-length saints; among the sacred figures are the two founding brothers on the eastern part of the south wall above their tomb. Wall paintings were carried out in 1548. They were later renovated in 1780.

Low down on the eastern piers of the nave, to the side of the iconostasion, on the left before the Virgin, is depicted Saint Theophanes. Below Christ, we may see Saint Nectarios. The holy brothers are portrayed making an offering of their church, which is pictured in great detail. N. Nikonanos, pp. 42-43.

The building inscription makes no mention of the iconographers who decorated the nave. However, the technique, color, and style are the same as those in the Chapel of Saint Nicholas at the Monastery of Great Lavra (Athos), executed in 1560 by Frangos Katellanos. He was one of the greatest iconographers when the Cretan School reached its zenith, though he, personally, was inspired to draw from Palaiologan models.

In 1566, the brothers, George and Frangos Kontaris of Thebes, also added their hands to the iconography in the narthex. Ibid., pp. 44-46; Konstantine Michalopoulos, *Meteora* (Kalambaka: Kon. Michalopoulos, Pub., n.d.).

the year 1548, and was restored in 1780." Further attestations to the labors of the Apsarades brothers may be seen in two inscriptions: one outside the sanctuary and the second on the window of the niche.[32]

Monastery of Varlaam

The Repose of the Saints

Until the end of their earthly sojourn, the fathers never relented in their labors and struggles; thus, God counted them worthy of many gifts. However, the time of Saint Theophanes' earthly sojourn came to a close when he departed to his much desired Lord on Saturday, the 17th of May, in the year 1544.

A disciple of the holy fathers wrote a description of the saintly brothers. He said that, during their monastic lives, they never tasted oil, wine, fish, cheese, or milk. They partook of fruits, legumes, and vegetables with vinegar. They would sit only with their fellow ascetics, but they never ate with a visiting friend at the same table and, certainly, never with a stranger. Lord Theophanes, during the first week of the Great Fast, and many times, would eat only on Saturday. The remainder of the fast, he ate every other day. For many years, he valiantly restrained the restlessness of the flesh. In addition, the fame of his clear teachings and exhortations spread, though his sweet tongue slightly stammered. He was a man of genius and possessed a good disposition.

A disciple of Saint Theophanes also recorded his glorious finish, writing: "In the year 7052 (7052-5508=1544), on the 17th of May, the most august and beautiful Church of All Saints was completed, together with the narthex above at 'The Rock of Varlaam.' The most holy and reverend fathers and brothers, lords Nectarios and Theophanes, those blessed men, contributed in this building project. Concurrently, for ten months, the blessed Theophanes fell sick. This grave illness ushered in many trials and temptations, which brought him to the threshold of death. However, his cheerfulness and eager desire never waned while raising up this temple, despite his terrible infirmity. When we finished, steadying his gait with a cane, he entered the newly finished holy temple. He raised his hands heavenward and, with much fervor, glorified

---

[32] Provatakis, p. 38.

God and offered thanks to all the saints. In the same manner, he blessed and prayed for all the brethren that built, hewed stone, and laid bricks. Some of the brethren were builders, stonemasons, quarrymen, bricklayers, and cabinet-makers. Afterward, he returned to his cell and made the sign of the precious Cross. He then sat the holy tabernacle of his body upon his bedding, facing east with his honorable feet extended before him. Reclining at those last moments, with his sweet countenance, the elder looked upon us with a joyful and benevolent glance. All the fathers and brethren standing by him were mourning. From their innermost depths, both brother and disciples wept for their teacher. Cutting short their laments, the monks began to chant a compunctious canon over Elder Theophanes. Then—O the wonder!—in the midst of their chanting, a brilliant and shining star appeared over his dwelling, illuminating all. When the sun set in the west, the holy soul of that 'sun' of the monastic life left this realm and entered the heavenly and sublime palaces where the just celebrate with unceasing song. Then, that star also made away."

Saints Theophanes (*L.*) *and Nectarios* (*R.*)

His brother, Saint Nectarios, reposed in Christ on the 7th of April, in the year 1550. These holy fathers are honored by our Mother, the holy Church. It has been determined that the 17th of May should be their joint commemoration. Through their holy intercessions, O Christ God, have mercy on us and save our souls. Amen.

The Monastery after the Founders' Repose

The spacious narthex contains the tombs of the sacred builders, Nectarios and Theophanes. Indeed, the tomb was originally carved out by the proprietors themselves in the Chapel of the Three Hierarchs; later the relics were transferred to the *katholikon*. Upon the repose of Saints Nectarios and

Theophanes, the monastery continued to increase with the addition of properties. A scriptorium was organized and many valuable benefactions from Wallachian rulers were received. The monastery, economically, was secure—though it housed and supported many monks. The monastery was often conspicuous for its spiritual leadership and its genuine participation in national struggles.

Varlaam Monastery

The Monastery Today

The Holy Monastery of Varlaam, atop one of the more spacious rocks of Meteora, rises to a height of 373 meters. Today, the refectory has been converted into an exhibition for the monastery's treasures. The treasures include icons, manuscripts, embroideries, and wood carvings. On the south side are the sacerdotal garments and altar vessels, carved crosses, an abbatial throne with inlaid mother-of-pearl decoration, an *epitaphion*[33] (1609), and several post-Byzantine portable icons, including the icon painted by Emmanuel Tzanes (1668). In the center cases, there is a display of vestments worn by the higher clergy, crucifixes, and illuminated manuscripts (both Byzantine and post-Byzantine).[34] Many of the holy relics are kept in the sanctuary. Among them are the holy skull of Saint Nicholas, new-martyr from Metsovon, commemorated the 16th of May, which emits a wonderful fragrance.[35]

The square kitchen is one of the most beautiful surviving examples of times past. It has a low dome topped by a small cupola, above which stands the chimney in the shape of an octagonal dome. The walls are a plain brick, but the east wall is decorated with an apse.

Along the north side of the infirmary stands the small single-aisled vaulted Chapel of the Unmercenary Healers. There is also a small antechamber which originally was the open stoa of the chapel.

[33] The *epitaphion* is a richly embroidered veil of Christ's burial.

[34] Provatakis, p. 49.

[35] Sister Theotekni, *Meteora: History, Art, Monastic Presence*, trans. by K. Koini-Moraitis (Greece: G. Tsiveriotis Society, 1980), p. 5.

Located behind the *katholikon*, to the north and west, are outbuildings, cells, and the tower for the windlass which is still in use today for very heavy loads. On the south side of the roofed space enclosing the winch is an apse depicting the Deïsis (Entreaty). One may also view an inset brick on which is written: "†Nectarios and Theophanes, founders ͵ζμδ' (7044=1536)." Thus, we have an exact date for the commencement of the building of the tower.[36]

In 1948, a public road brought many to the rock forest of Meteora. Now thousands of pilgrims and tourists of both genders come from all over the world to venerate or visit the churches and icons, though, presently, few monks and nuns dwell in the monasteries of Meteora.

On the 17th of May, the holy Church commemorates Our holy father among the saints, ATHANASIOS the New, Bishop of Christianoupolis,[37] the Wonder-worker.[38]

Athanasios, the most holy Bishop of Christianoupolis, was born at Kerkyra (Corfu) in the year 1665 of pious parents. He was baptized with the name of Anastasios. His father's name was Andrew, and his mother's name was Ephrosyne. Anastasios' father was one of the official leaders in the Venetian administration of the Ionian Islands. In the year 1684, Andrew

---

[36] N. Nikonanos, p. 48.

[37] Christianoupolis, undoubtedly, is in the Peloponnesos. Some identify it with the modern village of Christianou in western Messenia. It is the most important Byzantine church of Messenia, distinguished by its cloisonne masonry. Few fragments of wall paintings, dating from the 12th C., are preserved within this domed and octagonal church dedicated to the Transfiguration. It was the cathedral of the metropolitan bishopric of Christianoupolis, which was established at the end of the 11th C. The building attached to the west side of the church was used as an episcopal residence and possibly as a defensive tower in the late Byzantine period. The monument had been ruined, but later, in 1951, it was restored; it now serves as a parish church. Others also suggest that Christianoupolis is connected with ancient Megalopolis in Arkadia. While Christianoupolis did not seem to exist in antiquity, it was eminent in the 12th C. By the 13th C., the city declined; and in 1222, Pope Honorius III divided her territory between the bishops of Korone and Methone. *The Great Synaxaristes* (in Greek) does not add further material to identify the city. See http://www.culture.gr/2/21/212/21205n/e212en07.html, for Church of the Metamorphosis at Christianoi, as displayed by the Hellenic Ministry of Culture, and also *The Oxford Dictionary of Byzantium*, s.v. "Christianoupolis."

[38] The Life of this Saint Athanasios was authored by the Metropolitan John (Martinos) of Gortyna and Megalopolis (Arkadia). He also added the saint's wonderworkings of his time and composed a divine office. The manuscript was published, as follows: 1st ed. at Hermopolis in 1877; 2nd ed. at Athens in 1886; and the 3rd ed., again at Athens, in 1919.

migrated with his family to Karytaina[39] since he was attached to the newly appointed governor of the Peloponnesos. During that time all of the Peloponnesos and the Ionian Islands were under Venetian rule. Anastasios was not the only son but had three other sons as well. One son was already married and settled at Christianoupolis. Another son, named Anthony, remained at Karytaina, who took to wife the sister of then celebrated Armatolos[40] Athanasios Koulas, generally known as Captain Thanasi. The third son, having an inclination to serve in the military, enlisted in the Venetian Navy.

Now Anastasios demonstrated no small propensity for learning, especially esoteric instruction. He was entrusted to teachers eminent in moral excellence and learning. The child Anastasios was one whom God foreknew and foreordained to be called and distinguished in His service. Anastasios gave himself over quite completely to his Christian studies more so than to his secular subjects. Despite his young years, Anastasios exercised mastery over himself. He demonstrated discipline and temperance. He showed constancy in prayer. He frequently communed the immaculate Mysteries of Christ. His behavior was Christian and affable toward all with whom he came into contact. He maintained humility and shunned every vanity. He endeavored, from moment to moment and from day to day, to add to his soul a new Christian virtue so as to draw closer to God. On account of this, ofttimes, when he

---

[39] Quaint and charming Karytaina (37°28′N 22°02′E), also known as Skorta by the Franks, is situated in the Arkadia prefecture of the Peloponnesos. It is the site of a Byzantine settlement and a Frankish castle (dating from 1245) on a steep rocky outcrop. This historic spot is surrounded by rocky mountains and bushes and a larger mountain to the north. The stone-built houses are about fifty meters lower than the fortress. The plain of Megalopolis is to the southeast. There are forests to the south and in the valleys where the river Alpheos flows southward. The river Loussios flows west of Karytaina.

[40] The Armatoloi were local Greek villagers that functioned as military/police units governing Byzantine lands. They were given weapons by the Ottomans in order to repel Greek brigands known as the Klephts. Their history does not begin in Ottoman times. In fact, the entire military/police organization was based off feudalism under which military/police units maintained their duties in exchange for titles of land. When the Ottomans conquered Greece and numerous islands, they made treaties with the local Armatoloi and allowed them to continue with their military/police functions. Many remnants of Greek Byzantine forces became Klephts, as they migrated into the mountains and resisted the Turks. The Ottomans would mobilize the Armatoloi in order to repel the Klephts, as well as protect mountain passes and maintain order in their territories. The Armatoloi, nevertheless, considered the Klephts as their brothers. As a result, both groups supported each other throughout Ottoman times and during the Greek Revolution. Consequently, it was quite difficult for the Ottomans to distinguish between both groups, so that the terms Armatoloi and Klephts were virtually indiscriminate. See http://www.wiki.phantis.com/index.php/Armatolos.

offered up entreaty, he was saying inwardly these words of the Psalmist David: "Cause me to know, O Lord, the way wherein I should walk; for unto Thee have I lifted up my soul [Ps. 142:10]."

When Anastasios came to a man's estate, his father constrained him to enter into wedlock as this was the conventional route for most men. For parents find this a subject of boasting and joy: to behold sons of sons and daughters of daughters. In reality, it is sweet and pleasing to see sons, daughters, and grandchildren. For this is blessed, even as it is written to see "thy sons as young olive trees round about thy table [Ps. 127:4]." Nevertheless, virginity surpasses these blessings because it is lofty and sublime in dignity and equal in honor to the angels. There are, consequently, few that embrace such a life and few that are being saved by it: "For many are called, but few are chosen [Mt. 20:16]." Anastasios, therefore, having the divine Paul as a model and the rest of the choir of the fathers, hastened to a more exalted degree of perfection. He kept resisting his father's proposal concerning taking a wife. Anastasios, on several occasions, used the pretext that the times were unstable; on other occasions, he gave the excuse that life is surrounded with reversals and that it was needful for him to consider the matter with mature deliberation. But his father was persistent in bringing to reality what he wished his son to pursue. Andrew, thereupon, arranged that Anastasios should become engaged. Though the would-be groom was unwilling, Andrew entered into talks with a certain rich and renowned man of Patras[41] for his maiden daughter. The match was corresponding, of course, with the social rank of his family. When the time arrived for the marriage to take place, Anastasios was sent by his father, two days earlier, to Nafplion, the capital of the Peloponnesos. Such was the custom at that time to obtain the best possible wedding clothes.

Now Anastasios felt pressured on one side by his father and inflamed on the other side by the sacred sentiment within him. Coupled with this was his profound aversion to worldly things. Thus, he had the sensation of being fixed between a hammer and the anvil. Simply put, he was in straits and at a loss how to proceed. Now as he was going to Nafplion, in the middle of the road, he slackened his pace and charged his servants to go on ahead. He, thereupon, turned off slightly from the road. He entered the Church of the Theotokos by the side of Vidoni. He knelt down and began supplicating with tears and a contrite heart, uttering such things as these: "O my Lord Jesus Christ, Who examines the heart and reins, Thou art He that perceivest the hidden things of men. Thou, O Knower of hearts, Who hast helped me from my mother's womb [Ps. 138:12], knowest my heart and my wish. Thou knowest that I desire and love Thee. Thou hast heard how my father compels me. Therefore, 'cause me

[41] The maiden was from Patras, capital of Achaia, the chief port of the Peloponnesos. It was long contested by Venetians and Turks.

to know, O Lord, the way in which I shall conduct myself, for to Thee did I lift up my soul [Ps. 142:10].'"

After Anastasios prayed fervently these words, he went on his way. When he reached Nafplion, he began to make arrangements for the wedding clothes. But he was always under the power of the same thoughts, mentations that were cold and indifferent to all the work at hand. As he was feeling disgust and nausea, he turned away from the required wedding preparations. Instead, more and more, he was beseeching God and the most holy Theotokos for help since his affliction and distress mounted. As he was to leave on the morrow, there appeared in his sleep to him the Theotokos and the Forerunner. She addressed him and said, "Thou shalt become a chosen vessel and servant of my Son, O Athanasios.[42] Send forth, then, the servants with the wedding clothes to thy father; and let the maiden enter into marriage with another man. As for thee, proceed to Constantinople." Anastasios then awoke and began to tremble, as he cried aloud, "Blessed be God, the One Who led me forth out of my tribulation and anxieties! Not my will, but may the Lord's will be done!"

Lovers of God, and those who have been loved by Him and who have been vouchsafed to taste such supernatural and inexplicable appearances, are able to understand to what degree of spiritual delight and joy of soul that God-revering man was found at that moment. He, immediately, composed a letter to his father which he dispatched by means of his servants. His epistle conveyed the following message: "Send forth, O father, to the one who is my betrothed, the wedding clothes and this advice: she should select another man as her spouse. To speak the truth, sir, Anastasios is departing to a faraway place; and perhaps she shall never see him again." Upon writing these words, Anastasios repaired for Constantinople.

It was there that Anastasios became acquainted with Patriarch Gabriel III (1702-1707), former Metropolitan of Chalcedon. In 1702, while at Smyrna, Anastasios declared his aspiration to the patriarch; that is to say, he declared his fiery yearning to embrace the monastic Schema. He asked leave of the patriarch to enter this angelic vocation. Patriarch Gabriel, after proving Anastasios' mettle, discerned the man's understanding and prudence. He also beheld his virtue and holy manner of life. The patriarch, thereupon, tonsured Anastasios and ordained him to the diaconate for the patriarchate. Anastasios' name was then changed in the tonsure to Athanasios. By and by, after a number of years, Father Athanasios was advanced to the rank of presbyter. Now during the early 1700s, there was a preacher of sacred subjects at Kerkyra. He was the eminent Church orator, Elias Meniates (1669-1714). The Venetian governor

[42] The Theotokos addresses Anastasios by his future monastic name—Athanasios.

of the Peloponnesos, at that time, was Angelo Emo.[43] He was a close acquaintance of Meniates, whom he loved exceedingly by reason of the latter's preeminent faculties. Emo, therefore, proposed Meniates to the Great Church as a candidate for the widowed archbishopric of Christianoupolis. Meniates, nevertheless, moved by either humble-mindedness or knowledge that he could better profit his neighbor by remaining where he was—in Kerkyra—declined the position. Quitting that proposed lead, Patriarch Gabriel consecrated our Athanasios for Christianoupolis. He was then forty-six years old.

Athanasios, therefore, having ascended to the great and lofty dignity of the high priesthood, was conscious of the burden he had taken upon his shoulders before God and man. As soon as he arrived among the flock entrusted to him, he first inscribed upon the tablet of his heart these Petrine words: "For to this ye were called, because Christ also suffered for us, leaving behind for you an example, that ye should follow His footsteps [1 Pe. 2:21]." With regard to this, Athanasios was also ever mindful that whosoever shall do and teach the commandments, this one shall be called great in the kingdom of the heavens.[44]

Now the Venetians, it was observed, were employing oblique and treacherous counsels. They attempted to draw away their subjects from the Orthodox religion and Latinize them. One way that they hoped to achieve this goal was to direct them away from literacy by prohibiting the learning of letters. This method of subjugation was not even practised by the wild and fierce Turks. Bishop Athanasios was not going to allow ignorance to prevail in his diocese. He raised up schools in various locations under his jurisdiction so that the sacred letters could be taught. By these important works, the Christians were being taught to remain steadfast and unmoveable in our own holy Faith, which was confirmed by the blood of fourteen million martyrs. Our Faith had

[43] Angelo Emo was Provveditore Generale in Morea (Peloponnesos) from 1705 to 1708. Documentary sources dating from the Venetian occupation of the Peloponnese (1688-1715) confirm a pattern, established by the late 17th C., of Ottoman estates dominating the lowland plain while the majority of Greeks lived in inland villages. The Venetian occupation of the Peloponnesos, or Morea, of 1688-1715, is usually known as the "Second" period of Venetian rule. This appellation is given to distinguish it from periods of Venetian control of the cities of Nafplion, Methone, Korone, and Monemvasia between the 13th and early 16th C. It was only in the 17th C. that Venice acquired sovereignty over the entire peninsula. It was difficult, however, for Venice to sustain the Morea while all of central Greece was under Ottoman control; and the Turks successfully recovered the peninsula in 1715. This last Veneto-Turkish war marked the end of three centuries of rivalry for naval and commercial hegemony in the eastern Mediterranean. The Peloponnesos remained in Ottoman hands until the Greek War of Independence in 1821.

[44] Cf. Mt. 5:19.

already overcome and resisted the violent waves of persecution and atheism for the last eighteen centuries. Athanasios urged the Christians during this period of time to send their children to the schools. The majority of these institutions were supported by the same bishop, as the communities were in dire straits. Thus, the episcopal purse undertook this needful expenditure to advance the learning of the sacred writings as well as Greek letters. In this fashion, piety could be promoted so that the children would be made steadfast in the Orthodox Faith of the holy fathers.

It should also be mentioned that through the saint's teachings and subscription for education, many of the Christian temples in his dioceses were raised. One such church, which is still preserved, was dedicated to the most holy Theotokos at Karytaina. The saint had two metropolises: one cathedral at Christianoupolis, where he wintered, and the other at Karytaina. The man of God was also openhanded with his own substance in regard to the poor. His charities included helping poor maidens and orphans to marry, dressing the naked, offering consolation to the afflicted, admonishing the unruly, reproving the disobedient, retrieving the deceived and misled, and softening the hardhearted. As for those who were arrogant and audacious, he was a censuring scourge that summoned them to repentance. In regard to those who were upright in heart and in a state of repentance, he was soothing, gentle, and meek. He was verily, to the virtuous, an outline and archetype of virtue. With relation to the indolent and negligent, he was the plectrum that spurred them to the path of repentance.

In the matter of his own fare, it was similar to that of the ancient holy hierarchs. He was mindful to fulfill the command of the divine Apostle Paul, who touched on this point and said, "For we brought nothing into the world, and it is manifest that neither are we able to carry anything out; but having sustenance and coverings, we shall be satisfied with these [1 Tim. 6:7, 8]."

Miracles of Saint Athanasios

Now before we commence the narration of the miracles, those wrought by the holy hierarch, we ought to briefly say the following in order to help support those who are inclined to disbelief. This is because many, even among the faithful, when they either hear or read of the exploits wrought by holy men in the martyric accounts and biographies, hesitate at their veracity. While in this dubious state, such persons leave doubts to mount in their minds. Hence, they deliberate within themselves: "Well, then, are such phenomena true? Can what is possessed in the books have happened in real life? Peradventure the chroniclers are exaggerating? Can their accounts be the product of religious minds made mad with an infatuation for such feats?" But when such thoughts assail us, let us pray for faith. For when an event is covered by the passage of time out of mind, and there are no witnesses, then perhaps there could be some skepticism. But here we can provide live eyewitnesses who have seen some of the saint's miracles. So then, should even the slightest incredulity abide? Assuredly, it is not permissible.

From the foundation of the world, men have been organs through whom God executes His counsels and determinations. Through men, His divine providence energizes changes and the aspirations of mankind. These people of grace, the sacred friends of God, imitators of Jesus Christ and followers in His footsteps, are glorified by means of signs and prodigies, both while alive and after death. God's wonders are performed for either the benefit of mankind, or the endorsement of the true Faith of Christ, or the sobering of those who persist in bad deeds. The Faith of Jesus Christ, from the beginning, triumphed not by means of words and human ingenuity but rather by means of signs and wonders. When Jesus Christ sent forth His God-inspired apostles in order to herald the Gospel to all creation, He indicated to those having faith that signs would follow. Hearken to what our Lord uttered: "And these signs shall accompany those who believe: In My name they shall cast out demons; they shall speak in new tongues; they shall take up serpents; and if they should drink anything deadly, in no wise shall it harm them; they shall lay hands on the sick, and they shall be well [Mk. 16:17, 18]." Let us also hear the Gospel of Saint John where Jesus says, "Verily, verily, I say to you, the one who believeth in Me, the works which I do shall that one do also; and greater works than these shall he do, because I go to My Father [Jn. 14:12]." Let us, then, first narrate those miracles which the saint wrought while alive, those preserved by tradition, and afterward those accomplished after his death.

Among the long-standing accounts, kept safe, one discloses that when the saint was conducting the sacred rites, there appeared, many times, a shining and splendid star before his mouth. This was observed when he came forth from the beautiful gate and said aloud during the Liturgy, "Lord, Lord, look down from heaven...." Now those who were pure in heart and, doubtlessly, Christians of moral excellence, were witnessing this appearance. On one such occasion, one of those Christians hastened to the holy man and related what he had seen. The saint, possessed of humble-mindedness, said to him, "Hush, thou hast been beguiled! The light has merely reflected on account of the many lamps in the temple." But that Christian man would not be put off. Thus, the saint reproved him with striking words and then gave him a command to say nothing while he was still in this life.

Now there was in Chistianoupolis a man, named Christos, who was the head of a family. He was a merchant that was God-fearing and acquainted with the holy bishop. Christos' son, Pantelis, led two horses to Patras for a business transaction. While Pantelis was on the road, he was abducted by robbers. They first slew the horses and then fettered Pantelis. He was taken prisoner into the mountains. The kidnappers sent instructions to his parents by a wayfarer, saying that, if within fifteen days they did not send the ransom money, they would kill the captive Pantelis. The sum, however, was far and beyond the family fortune. They became dispirited because they could not meet the demand. Weeping and wailing and woe enveloped the unhappy parents and brethren. The distraught father went to the hierarch, recounting his family's misfortune. The hierarch said to Christos, "My child, I can do nothing regarding the abductors' demand, except send up entreaty to our compassionate God; for He is great and strong." This is exactly what Athanasios did. After a fortnight, at evening, the robbers, were filled with good cheer by drinking overmuch. They threatened their captive that, if by the evening of the next day, the money was not delivered, they would send his head to his parents! The unfortunate Pantelis was seized then with shivering. The brigands clapped him in irons and set him in their midst, after which they succumbed to a heavy sleep.

It was about midnight, as Pantelis dozed from grief, that he beheld in his sleep Hierarch Athanasios who said to him, "Rise up, my child, and take flight quickly, because thy parents are mourning inconsolably!" The distressed Pantelis discovered that he was released miraculously from his bonds. Rising up instantly, he wasted no time in striding over the robbers and escaping. The following day, that is, the fifteenth day and the last day to make the fixed deposit of money, Christos, with his wife and children, went to the hierarch's house. Sobbing and lamenting, they would not be comforted. The saint, filled with sympathetic emotion for their plight, said, "Calm thyself, Christos, and tomorrow at eventide, there comes Pantelis." Behold the mighty intercessions of Athanasios! Pantelis, in truth, arrived home at the designated time. Pantelis went to the saint and wet the bishop's feet with his tears, describing what had been revealed to him while asleep. It is manifest, therefore, that the saint, even while he was among the living, had received from God the spiritual gift of foresight. It is patently evident that God hearkened to his supplications, even as it is written: "The will of them that fear Him shall He do, and their supplication shall He hear [Ps. 144:20]."

At another time, when the man of God was making pastoral visits in his the diocese, he came into Megalopolis[45] and the Church of the Transfiguration. Beside the church there was a great lake which was full of frogs. After Vespers, the saint lodged there with his deacon as he was wont to do during the summer for the sake of peace and quiet. As it happened, throughout the night, those frogs kept croaking in their usual harsh and raucous manner. On account

---

[45] The town of Megalopolis (37°24′N 22°08′E) and its fruit-bearing valley are in the municipality and province of the same name, which belongs to the Arkadia prefecture of the Peloponnesos.

of the multitude of amphibians, their deep and resonant voices made a noisy disturbance. The saint, forcing himself, only closed his eyes for a few moments. In the morning, after divine Liturgy, when the priests and the congregation asked how he spent the night in the open air, he replied, "What can I tell you, my children? Those frogs, may they not have a good year! They made such a din this past night that I hardly slept." After he made this comment about the frogs, the croakers ceased and remained noiseless. But, at that time, no one present gave heed to the sudden silence, since frogs do not croak so much during the day as they do at night. What was worthy of amazement is that the frogs, henceforth, whether by day or by night, kept silence by the lake. This engendered no small wonder and surprise to the natives. Now after the passage of two years, the saint returned again for a pastoral visit. After Vespers, he, too, noted that not one frog made the slightest croaking sound. Upon the completion of the divine Liturgy, he, out of curiosity, inquired of one of the priests of that assembly, "What became of that multitude of frogs that used to be heard in times past?" The priest remarked, "*Despota*, from that time that they would not let thee sleep in peace and thou didst charge them to have a poor year, they have not been heard again." Then the saint, as a smile played about his lips, remarked, "And did they hear me, those blessed creatures?" Even as he finished speaking thus—behold, the wonder!—immediately, all the frogs commenced croaking as if on cue, ushering in a great confusing clamor as aforetime.

While the saint was yet living, an incident took place toward the end of his life. In the village of Soulima there was a woman who was a witch. She lead many astray and delivered up numerous souls to Satan. Athanasios learned of her activities and summoned her that he might rebuke her. He directed her to cease committing sorcerous deeds. He recommended that she go to confession and put herself under the prescribed penance for her lawlessness lest she should find herself in the end outside of the Church. The woman, then, came to her senses and deep compunction. She confided to the hierarch that she repented with all her heart. She expressed her desire that he himself hear her confession. The saint, filled with enthusiasm, took the opportunity to snatch the soul that had long been captive in the devil's nets. She, consequently, made her confession. He consoled her and put upon her a penance analogous to the sins, according to the divine and sacred canons. He then commanded her to return to him when she came to the end of her penance that she might receive absolution and permission to come forward and communicate the immaculate Mysteries. Ere long, to her surprise, she learned that the hierarch was gravely ill and was about to die! She made haste, therefore, to Christianoupolis. But before she arrived, the holy man had already reposed. At that very moment his bier was being conveyed to the tomb, she forcefully cut her way through the crowd. When she came before the sacred relics, she fell prostrate upon them. In her distress, she wailed and lamented. Those bearing the relics came to a halt. The woman then raised her voice plaintively, saying, "O my misfortune! What shall become of me, the wretched one? Why, O saint of God, hast thou left me the hapless one unpardoned? How am I to live the remainder of my life under the ban of penance? Have mercy on me, O saint, and grant me absolution!" So this woman bewailed her sorrow and anguish with profuse tears and wails. The saint, forthwith—O thy great boldness before God, O Athanasios!—raised his hand and blessed her as though he were still alive. Those following the procession, beholding this prodigious wonder, were struck with astonishment and cried out, "Lord, have mercy!"

In the year 1834, King Otto[46] of Greece disbanded the majority of the monasteries of the Greek nation. Among those that were closed was that of Gortyna,[47] the Monastery of the Honorable Forerunner, where many of the relics of Saint Athanasios were kept. Consequently, the administrator of the prefecture, P. Negas of Hydra, directed two of his underlings to go to that particular monastery. They were instructed to collect the moveable property of the monastery and bring it to Demetsana.[48] Those sacrilegious minions went to the monastery. With a lever they forced open the gates. They confiscated many things. Among the sacred spoils were the liturgical vessels and the holy relics. This included the chest that contained most of the relics of our saint, as well as his hallowed head which was in its own special silver chest. After they stuffed the consecrated articles into dirty sacks, they conveyed them to the prefect's house. As for the reliquary chests, they were brought into the basement. The sacks were then emptied onto the wooden boards in one chamber. Horror, truly, ought to take hold of every conscientious person before a spectacle as this! The sanctified vessels were cast on the floor in an offhand manner, hither the holy Chalice and the holy Spoon, and thither the Sponge, and elsewhere the Paten and the Lance. They were strewn about as though they were some useless items of the marketplace! When night fell, about the midnight hour, a terrible

---

[46] Otto (b. 1815-1867) was the first king of modern Greece (1832–1862). He was the son of King Louis I of Bavaria. Otto was chosen king of Greece by the great powers at the conference of London in May of 1832. He was a Roman Catholic who governed an Orthodox country autocratically, that is, until he was forced to become a constitutional monarch in 1843. He was finally deposed in a revolt on the 23rd of October, in the year 1862, and returned to Bavaria.

[47] Gortyna (37°23′N 22°02′E) is part of the Gortynia province in the Arkadia prefecture, as is Karytaina which is one kilometer away toward the northwest.

[48] The village of Demetsana (37°57′N 22°02′E, ancient Teuthis) of northwestern Arkadia, is the seat of the province of Gortynia. Demetsana is at least fifty kilometers from Gortyna.

rattling noise could be heard from the reliquary chests. It sounded as though some great and towering tree was being uprooted. The clashing introduced what felt like an earthquake. This disturbance roused the prefect from his sleep. After a few moments, when it seemed that the commotion had subsided, the prefect came to himself. He then prepared to lie down again. But then a second crash struck that resonated as rumbling thunder. The exceeding shaking of the building compelled him to exit the house. He was trembling as he hastened outside, half-clad, in his night dress.

The prefect, amazed and at a loss as to where to go, made his way to the adjoining house. The resident was Bishop Ignatios, former hierarch at Ardamerio,[49] who, at that time was administrating the diocese of Gortynia. He had learned about Saint Athanasios from Bishop Joseph of Androusis. The prefect, therefore, knocked at the door of the bishop's house. He was still trembling when the door opened and he said, "A terrible thing, my *despota*, has happened to my house. There was a snap, and then a crackling sound, followed by a great crash. I heard these sounds twice emanating from the cellar. Together with the rattling and crashing, there was an earthquake that nearly caused my house to collapse." Ignatios, after listening carefully to his neighbor, remarked, "That is odd, I did not hear any quake." The bishop then went quickly and awakened the deacon. He asked him if he felt any tremors from an earthquake. He, too, answered negatively. The hierarch turned to the prefect and asked, "What dost thou conclude, therefore, Mister Negas, sir?" The prefect disclosed, "Today, my men brought two sacks from a monastery. There were various articles from the Monastery of the Honorable Forerunner. Along with the sacks were two chests: a large wooden one and a small silver one. Those whom I dispatched to carry out the work reported to me that the chests contained relics." The bishop, hearing this, cried aloud, "Perhaps they brought hither the relics of the holy one of Christianoupolis?" Hearing this query put to him so emphatically, the prefect was unable to articulate further. Straightway, the bishop dressed and raced to the prefect's house. As he went down into the cellar, his gaze fell upon the relics of the saint. He recognized them to be those of Saint Athanasios, which relics he had previously visited at that monastery desecrated the previous day. The bishop turned to the prefect and rebuked him sternly. He cast in his teeth that what he committed was sacrilege, by the transfer of the relics to his own house. The prefect swore in God's name that the men who conveyed the relics did so without his knowledge. That evening, the bishop, by means of a manservant, invited the fathers of the monastery of Aimyalo. They were close by, needing only a quarter of an hour in travel time. He bade them take the holy relics. The fathers came the

[49] Titular see of Ardamerio (Ardamerium, Ardameriensis) of Macedonia.

following morning, very early. They arrived in their sacred vestments, accompanied by lanterns and censers. The transfer, that is, their receipt of the relics, took place just slightly outside of the city, for fear of the reaction of the people.

After the restoration of the Monastery of the Honorable Forerunner, the holy relics were transferred again to their former place. Only Saint Athanasios' jawbone was retained by the Aimyalo Monastery. Eyewitnesses included: P. Negas, prefect; Bishop Ignatios, formerly of Ardamerio; Nicholas Kydonakes of Piraeus, a businessman, secretary of the diocesan *oikonomos*; Athanasios Synaniotes of Tripoli,[50] registrar of the prefect; and Bishop Joseph of Androusis. Ignatios, the former Ardamerion bishop, as a member of the synod and under synodal direction, wrote a letter to Bishop Joseph about these events, which text also contained the testimony of P. Negas, given later at Nafplion. Others who were also present were the following: Agapios Economos, hegumen of the monastery; John Kyriakos, Greek teacher; and the reverent Priest John Sakellarios from Stemnitsa.[51] The miracle of the saint, after this translation, spread throughout the prefecture, so that even to this day the elders recount it to the younger.

Verily, it is amazing, even to this day, the miracles energized through those sacred relics of Saint Athanasios! Whenever there is about to occur some calamity or disaster or scourge or epidemic, whether to monastery fields, or to farms, or to the whole prefecture, or to the nation—often interpreted as the wrath of God—the reliquary containing the sacred relics discharges a crackling or grinding sound. The volume of the sound varies—at times it is light and at other times more pronounced. It depends upon the magnitude of the coming misfortune or destruction. By reason of this sign, even those who know nothing about the sacred relics lying in the sacred bema, if they should happen to hear the sound, they are straightway seized with inexplicable terror and trembling. Such a dreadful and grating sound was heard in the year 1769, when the monastery was about to suffer a siege by the Albanians. Many layfolk who had taken refuge in the monastery were saved, as by a miracle. The same sound kept signaling, many times, one year prior to the Greek Revolution of 1821. Theodore Kolokotronis used the Castle of Karytaina as his headquarters during his fight against Ibrahim Pasha. A few years later, the sound, again, caught the

[50] Arkadia has its present-day capital at Tripoli. It forms the largest prefecture on the Peloponnesian peninsula.

[51] The mountainous village of Stemnitsa of Arkadia, slightly south of Demetsana but north of Karytaina, is forty-five kilometers west of Tripoli. Demetsana and Stemnitsa are two representative Arkadian towns, situated at altitudes of 1,000 and 1,100 meters respectively. The houses are beautiful and the views superb. From Stemnitsa, one descends to the Prodromos Monastery.

attention of the fathers, which presaged the dissolution of the monasteries. In the year 1849, after the sound made its forewarning presence known, excessive flooding destroyed the monastery fields, washing away people and animals that quickly drowned. The sound is soft or light whensoever any among the monastery's fathers is about to repose or if the fathers overlooked keeping lit the sanctuary light.

The sacred relics of the saint were brought out of Christianoupolis, by rights of kin, to Karytaina. This was executed by the saint's kinsmen through marriage, the aforementioned Athanasios Koulas. When the latter dug up the grave and broke it open, he found the saint's body half incorrupt and yielding an ineffable fragrance. The relics, afterward, were brought to Karytaina or, more specifically, to the Monastery of the Honorable Forerunner. This took place because that monastery was not sacked and because it pleased divine providence to bring it about thus. Many stories are told regarding the translation of the holy relics and the appearance of signs which, for the sake of brevity, we have designedly passed over. As for the scent that wafts forth from the precious relics, it was so perceptible that it stirred and still stirs the curiosity of many who visit the monastery and declare that they sense a fragrance not of this world.

Behold, O pious readers! In Gortynia, also, there is concealed a great treasure even as there are other treasures and pillars of the Faith: Saint Spyridon at Kerkyra, Saint Dionysios at Zakynthos, and Saint Gerasimos at Kephalonia. Their relics, from time to time, work miracles and thus demonstrate the power of the Orthodox Christian Faith. Indeed, the sacred head of Saint Athanasios is also brought forward to assist against catastrophic circumstances, whether they be grave sicknesses, or pestilential diseases, or droughts, or the appearance of ruinous swarms of locusts, or other such events. In such instances, the relics bring about, speedily, the desired request and result. As many of those who, with faith, invoke the name of the saint, they are forthwith delivered from perils. "I should have liked to recount," says the biographer, "if time had not checked me, the diversified wonderworkings of Saint Athanasios, through whose holy intercessions may God have mercy and save us. Amen."

Through the intercessions of Thy Saints,
O Christ God, have mercy on us. Amen.

On the 18th of May, the holy Church commemorates the holy Martyrs PETER, DIONYSIOS, CHRISTINA the Virgin, ANDREW, PAUL, VENEDIMOS, PAVLINOS, and HERAKLEIOS.

Peter and the holy martyrs, celebrated today with him, originated from different countries. All these courageous contestants of Christ, who appeared before tyrants, were vouchsafed martyric crowns, however, on the same day.

(L.) Saint Peter; (R.) Saints Paul, Andrew, and Dionysios

Peter of Lampsakos,[1] the holy martyr, was made to stand before the tyrant Decius[2] at Abydos.[3] The tyrant commanded Peter to offer sacrifice to Aphrodite (Venus). Being unpersuaded, he confessed Christ before the benighted pagans. Thus, they broke his body by the application of chains, wood, and a wheel designed for torture. He was bound to the wheel and

---

[1] Lampsakos was on the eastern shore of the Hellespont facing Kallipolis (Gallipoli).

[2] Decius was Roman emperor from 249 to 251. He instituted the first organized persecution of Christians throughout the empire. In January of 250, he issued an edict ordering all citizens to perform a religious sacrifice in the presence of his commissioners. Many Christians defied the emperor and lost their earthly lives that they might gain eternal life with Christ the King of all. The violence and suppression perpetrated by the government actually caused public opinion among the majority of the pagans to condemn the imperial edict and applaud the passive resistance of the martyrs. In 251, a few months before Decius' demise, the persecution of Christians ceased.

[3] The *Menaion* records the venue of his martyrdom to be Evridinos. Abydos was a customs post and city on the Hellespont, near present-day Canakkale. Over against Abydos is Sestos, a garrison town on the European side of the Hellespont. The Turks call it Boyaz Hisar. Between these two cities is the narrowest section of the channel.

crushed with instruments of torture, and was beaten without respite.[4] Due to all these torments, the holy Peter, who had set his feet on the rock of faith,[5] surrendered his soul and received the unfading crown of the contest from God.

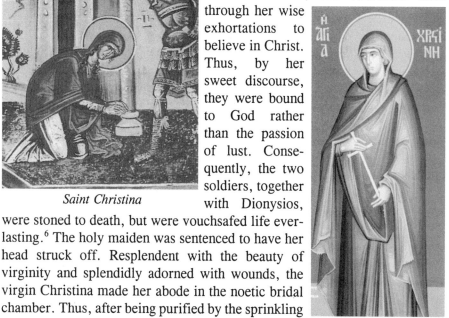

Another two men, Paul and Andrew, from Mesopotamia, were soldiers under the ruler Daknon. When they were dispatched to Athens, they arrested and incarcerated two confessing Christians, Dionysios and Christina. When Paul and Andrew gazed upon the beautiful virgin Christina, who was then of marriageable age, they encouraged her to share in shameful conduct with them. She, however, in no wise would countenance their solicitations. Indeed, instead of them doing violence to her, she converted them through her wise exhortations to believe in Christ. Thus, by her sweet discourse, they were bound to God rather than the passion of lust. Consequently, the two soldiers, together with Dionysios, were stoned to death, but were vouchsafed life everlasting.[6] The holy maiden was sentenced to have her head struck off. Resplendent with the beauty of virginity and splendidly adorned with wounds, the virgin Christina made her abode in the noetic bridal chamber. Thus, after being purified by the sprinkling of their sanctified blood, all four received the unfading crown of martyrdom for their mighty sufferings.

Saint Christina

Saint Christina

Herakleios, Pavlinos, and Venedimos were Athenians. After these holy men preached the Gospel, they exhorted many of the impious idolaters to turn away from the foolishness and deception of idols. The three were arrested for their missionary activities and brought before the magistrate. That tyrant, before any determination was made, ordered that they be subjected to a harsh

[4] May 18th, Orthros Canon, Ode One, Mode Four, by Saint Joseph the Hymnographer.
[5] Cf. Mt. 16:18.
[6] May 18th, Orthros Canon, Ode Four, Mode Four, by Saint Joseph the Hymnographer.

thrashing and a testing with many other punishments. First, the holy confessors were cast into a lit furnace. They remained unharmed by the enveloping flames, being protected by the power of God. Finally, they were beheaded with swords and received their martyric crowns.

On the 18th of May, the holy Church commemorates the holy Martyrs at Ankyra: TEKOUSA, ALEXANDRIA, CLAUDIA, PHAEINEE, EPHRASIA, MATRONA, JULIA, THEODOTE, and THEODOTOS.

Tekousa, the holy virgin and martyr, together with her seven virginal co-contestants,[7] hailed from Ankyra of Galatia.[8] This was also the same city as their fellow athlete, Saint Theodotos. Though Theodotos was a married man and had the concerns of attending to a wife, he did not neglect the spiritual life and the pursuit of virtue. He heeded the words of the Apostle Paul: "Now this I say, brethren, the time hath been shortened henceforth, that even they who have wives be as though they did not have [1 Cor. 7:29]." Since Theodotos was a resourceful man, he purchased uncontaminated wheat and leavened bread, the firstfruits of which he offered to God. As for the remainder of these goods, Theodotos distributed them among the needy. He did this because the profane magistrate of Ankyra, Theoteknos, thinking to defile Christian consumers, ordered the sprinkling and staining of these provisions with the drink-offerings and sacrifices of the idols. In addition to providing food for the poor, the

---

[7] Other accounts of the lives of these holy women, including the record of Bartholomew of the Athonite Monastery of Koutloumousiou, list the names we have given, less that of Saint Theodote. The current *Menaia* also record in the *Synaxarion* at the Sixth Ode of the Orthros Canon that "on this day we commemorate the seven women martyrs at Ankyra of Galatia: Tekousa, Alexandria, Claudia, Phaeinee, Ephrasia, Matrona, and Julia, as well as Martyr Theodotos." However, *The Great Synaxaristes* records all eight names of the virgins. Some have suggested that Tekousa was the mother of the seven maidens, but this is not the case since she is described as a virgin herself. Furthermore, these eight women are not to be confused with the seven women martyrs (Alexandria, Claudia, Ephrasia, Matrona, Juliane, Ephemia, and Theodora) of Amisos on the Black Sea, of similar name, commemorated by the holy Church on the 20th of March during the time of Emperor Maximian (286-305). These latter martyrs suffered beatings, crude mastectomies, disemboweling, and a violent furnace. They finally reposed when cast into the fire, while today's martyrs' earthly lives ended in the waters of a lake. The date for today's present martyrdom is unknown, though 303 has been suggested. The place of their martyrdom is some 125 miles (200 kilometers) south of the Black Sea.

[8] Ankyra, a military base, was the capital of the Galatian province, which is a region in central Asia Minor (modern Turkey). The city was a center of trade and the seat of a pagan landowning aristocracy. The ruling class became Christian only in the 5th C.

blessed Theodotos visited the prisons where the Christians were incarcerated, strengthening them in the Faith of our Lord Jesus Christ. Moreover, he supported other Christians when he harbored them. Ever mindful of the apostolic utterance to the people of Galatia, Theodotos obeyed this exhortation: "So then, as we have opportunity, let us be working that which is good toward all, and most of all toward those of the household of faith [Gal. 6:10]."

Now Tekousa, the aunt of Theodotos, was apprehended and fettered for Christ, together with seven other virgins: Alexandria, Claudia, Phaeinee, Ephrasia, Matrona, Julia, and Theodote. The maidens were then led before the magistrate who desired that they should sacrifice to the idols. The magistrate, in his devilry, delivered up the virgins to his soldiers in order for the maidens to be violated and dishonored. However, by the grace of Christ, all the virgins remained unharmed and undefiled. The idolaters, threatening to usher in the final danger, bound rocks to the feet of these Christians and submerged them into the depths of a nearby lake. Thus, these holy maidens received the crown of the contest.

Saint Claudia

Their august relics were then drawn out by certain Christians, of whom one was the holy Theodotos, and interred honorably. Due to his participation in the burial, Theodotos was informed upon to the Greek idolaters. Learning that he had been reported and was now sought by the authorities, Theodotos, voluntarily, appeared before his accusers. Straightway, he was led before Theoteknos the magistrate. Since Theodotos would only confess Christ as true God, he was raised aloft and made to endure the laceration of his flesh. Afterward, they cast vinegar with salt upon his open wounds and injuries. Bearing all nobly, the holy Theodotos was then beheaded.

In the meantime, the rage of the savage magistrate did not desist with the death of these Christians. He exhumed the relics of the virgin saints from their tombs and burned them. Elsewhere,[9] it is recorded that a priest buried

[9] Bishop Nikolai Velimirović, *The Prologue From Ochrid*, Part 2, trans. by Mother Maria (Birmingham, UK: Lazarica Press, 1985), p. 194.

Saint Ephrasia of Nicaea

Saint Theodotos' relics on a hill, outside the city where a church was later dedicated to him.

On the 18th of May, the holy Church commemorates the holy Martyr EPHRASIA of Nicaea, who was cast into the sea.

On the 18th of May, the holy Church commemorates our holy father among the saints, STEPHEN the New, Patriarch of Constantinople.

Stephen the New, our father among the saints, was Patriarch of Constantinople. He was the son of Emperor Basil the Macedonian (who reigned from 867 to 886), and his second wife Evdokia Ingerina.[10] Stephen was a simple young man with a guileless disposition. Despite his young years, his understanding and maturity were per-

[10] "The path by which Basil I, the founder of the Macedonian Dynasty, reached the throne was murky indeed. At his side was his wife, Evdokia Ingerina, the former mistress of the murdered Michael III (842-867). To safeguard the succession to the throne, he crowned his eldest son Constantine as co-emperor as early as the 6th of January, in the year 869; exactly a year after, Leo, his second son, was also crowned, and then later on his third son, Alexander (about 879, after the premature death of Constantine), while his youngest son, Stephen, entered on an ecclesiastical career and was to become patriarch (886-893) during the reign of his brother, Leo VI (886-912). Constantine, the emperor's firstborn and his favorite, was the issue of a youthful marriage with Maria, a Macedonian. Leo, Alexander, and Stephen were the sons of Evdokia Ingerina, the two younger boys being born only after Basil had become emperor. The question as to whether Leo VI was the legitimate son of Basil I or the illegitimate son of Michael III has been frequently and hotly disputed, but it can now be taken as proved that he was the son of Basil I.... The sources give conflicting information on the ages of Alexander and Stephen. Some believe that Alexander was Basil I's youngest son. The acrostic, BEKLAS, which is attributed to Patriarch Photios (858-867 and 877-886), consists of the initial letters of the names Basil, Evdokia, C(K)onstantine, Leo, Alexander, and Stephen, and in any case it also shows that Stephen was the youngest son of Basil I, and as such he was designated for an ecclesiastical career. In a similar manner had Romanos I dedicated his fourth and youngest son to the Church. Both of them ascended the patriarchal throne at the age of sixteen, for Stephen was born about 871 and became patriarch in December 886." See George Ostrogorsky's *History of the Byzantine State*, p. 207. Elsewhere, the date of Stephen's birth is given as November 867. See *The Oxford Dictionary of Byzantium*, s.v. "Eudokia Ingerina."

fected. By God's good pleasure and judgment, and by reason of the election of both the emperor and the holy synod, he was consecrated Patriarch of Constantinople after the displacement of Photios the Great.

Upon Stephen's ascending the patriarchal throne and assuming all the cares and concerns of the Church of God, he showed himself to be a wakeful and vigilant guardian and a true shepherd of the flock of Christ. His pastoral activities among the rational sheep brought them to the fresh and flourishing meadow of the Orthodox Faith. He showed himself to be the helper of the widows, the protector of the orphans, the balm of the poor, and the deliverer of the wronged from the hands of the mighty. After having pleased God in all his works, he reposed in the flower of manhood and was translated to the Lord. For, "He, being made perfect in a short time, fulfilled a long time. For his soul pleased the Lord. He, therefore, hastened to take him away from among the wicked [Wis. of Solomon 4:8-14]."

On the 18th of May, the holy Church commemorates the holy Martyr JULIAN, who was dragged through a thornbush.

On the 18th of May, the holy Church commemorates the holy Hieromartyr THEODORE, Pope of Rome, who suffered carving and scraping of his flesh.[11]

On the 18th of May, the holy Church commemorates Saint ANASTASO of LEFKADION, who reposed in peace.

On the 18th of May, the holy Church commemorates our venerable Father MARTINIAN of Areovindos in Constantinople.

Through the intercessions of Thy Saints,
O Christ God, have mercy on us. Amen.

---

[11] *The Great Synaxaristes* (in Greek) suggests this might be Theodore I, pope from 642 to 649. He was a Greek from Jerusalem. Throughout his pontificate he struggled against the Monothelites (the One Will Heresy). He had sent an epistle to Emperor Constans II saying that he did not recognize Paul as Patriarch of Constantinople. He exhorted Constans to abolish the *Ekthesis*. When Saint Maximos the Confessor (commemorated the 21st of January) brought to Rome, in 645, the deposed Constantinopolitan Patriarch Pyrrhus, the latter recanted his errors before Theodore—but later he relapsed. This pope was also known for his good works among the poor of Rome. He was also a benefactor of the city's churches. There is no record of a martyric death.

On the 19th of May, the holy Church commemorates the holy Hieromartyr PATRICK and those with him at Prousa: AKAKIOS, MENANDER, and POLYAENOS, the Presbyters.

Patrick (Patrikios), the sacred hieromartyr, and his companions—the holy Martyrs Akakios, Menander, and Polyaenos—were accounted worthy of the crown of martyrdom at Prousa of Asia Minor during the rule of Julian the consular governor.[1] The holy Patrick, during that period, became the Bishop of Prousa by reason of his virtue and wisdom which he possessed from a young age. On account of his espousal of the Christian Faith and his fiery zeal, he was accused before the authorities. He was arrested by Julian, the consular governor. Patrick censured the deception and the vanity of the idols before the consul's face. Julian, in order to persuade the holy Hieromartyr Patrick to deny the Christ, put him to the test with manifold and diverse tortures. All that Julian achieved was further acknowledgment of the bishop's stalwart resolution to persevere for his Faith.

Saint Patrick

Now the city of Prousa had gained renown also by its famous hot springs and baths situated near the temple to Aesculapius[2] and Hygieia.[3] Julian, being at Prousa, visited the famous hot springs.[4] He also offered sacrifice to

[1] The era of the martyrdom of these saints is unknown. The compilers of *The Great Synaxaristes* (in Greek) suggest it took place during the time of Emperor Diocletian (284-305).

[2] Aesculapius (Asclepius, Asklepios) was the pagan god of healing. A snake, and sometimes also dogs, was used to assist in the cures.

[3] Hygieia (Salus) was a pagan goddess who personified health.

[4] To the present, Prousa (Bursa, 40°12′N 29°04′E) has warm mineral-rich springs. It is a thermal springs center. Most of the hotels and *hamam* (Turkish baths) in this province have thermal bath facilities. The Eski Kaplica ("Old Spring" or "Old Thermal Baths") is the oldest in the province, located on the site of sumptuous Byzantine baths built by Justinian. The Karamustafa Pasha Baths are famous and boast the best hot

(continued...)

Aesculapius and Hygieia. Feeling refreshed and invigorated, he imagined himself obligated to the above mentioned pagan deities. He, accordingly, attributed his renewal to these divinities; and, therefore, he thought to keep their favor by bringing Patrick before the idols to offer sacrifice. But first Julian endeavored to have Patrick appreciate the benefit in the cure that he received and that it was due to the beneficence of Aesculapius and Hygieia. Julian began by saying to the bishop, "The hot waters that spring up from the earth are endued with therapeutic qualities by virtue of the gods' providence for the benefit and advantage of mankind. Thou, as one having been misled by foolish legends regarding invoking Christ, must now see the gods' divine care for us. Look at how I have revived after visiting their baths and praying at their shrine! Acknowledge the salutary powers of Aesculapius and offer sacrifice. I insist that thou offerest the prescribed oblation, if only to avoid the penalties that must necessarily follow shouldest thou choose otherwise." Patrick, before a large and mostly pagan audience, remarked to the consul: "Thou hast uttered many wicked things in but a few words." The consul responded: "I have spoken nothing bad in principal or practise. What have I declared other than that which is patently demonstrable? Acts of healing take place daily after sufferers bathe in these mineral-rich thermal springs, even as we have witnessed them and experienced them. Thou must see that it is so; thou art not some transient guest in this city." Patrick answered, "I never said that I disputed the therapeutic virtues of our hot mineral waters."

Then the holy Patrick, enlightened by God, answered, "Indeed, the hot springs have been bestowed for the benefit of mankind. Their creation, however, was not by the providence of the false gods; but rather, they came to be with the power of my Lord Jesus Christ. It was He Who determined two regions: one place is filled with many good things which the righteous shall enjoy in the future, whereas the other place is full of darkness and fire wherein the sinners shall be punished. This is to occur after the resurrection. God granted us fire, not only in all that which is under the firmament but even in the heaven this is evident.[5] It was God Who created the heaven and the earth. It was He Who gave the command, and fire and water were created. Now the waters upon the earth are called a sea, while those below are called an abyss or a great deep.[6] Whensoever the fountains of the abyss are broken up and ascend as a water-spout, this results in the springs and the wells for our consumption

[4](...continued)
waters full of minerals. Cekirge, located in the western part of Bursa, has been known since Roman times for its hot springs rich in minerals. The Romans had started to exploit the many hot springs and their healing waters in the surroundings.

[5] Gen. 1:6-8.

[6] Gen. 7:11.

and use. With regard to fire that is found below the earth,[7] it spouts up warm waters. As for those who are near to the source of the fire, the waters gushing forth are warm; whereas, those who are far off find them cool. This fire, which is in the lower parts of the earth, punishes the ungodly. The water beneath the surface, correspondingly, which is ice, and named Tartarus, is where punishment for eternity awaits both men and demons.[8] The latter are those whom the idol worshippers have made into gods, but there will they join them later."

After Patrick spoke thus, he was being compelled by the tyrant to cease speaking. But Patrick was filled by the grace of God and added these further proofs: "The holy martyred Presbyter Pionios of Smyrna[9] said that he had been walking about Judaea and passing through the parts about the river Jordan when he beheld the land of the Sodomites. He remarked that the place, even to this day, bears testimony to how fearful a thing is God's wrath and anger toward homosexuality and the other iniquities of the Sodomites.[10] He said that he observed smoke rising in a land consumed by fire, and bereft of all vegetation, fruit, and water. Now anyone might be informed regarding this fire even now.

---

[7] Cf. Num. 26:10.

[8] "God spared not angels who sinned, but cast them into Tartarus...[2 Pe. 2:4]." Tartarus was thought by the Greeks to be a subterranean place that was lower than Hades where divine punishment was meted out. It was so regarded by the Jews also [cf. Job 41:24 Rahlfs' LXX; Enoch 20:2; Philo, Exs. 152; Josephus, C.Ap 2, 240]. Saint Hippolytos: "Tartarus is situated in a doleful and dark locality and is not touched by a ray of light." ["On Proverbs," *Fragments*, Ante-Nicene, V:174.] Saint Bede: "Final judgment is still due the apostate angels. Concerning it the Lord says, 'Go from Me, ye who have been cursed, into the fire, the everlasting one, which hath been prepared for the devil and his angels [Mt. 25:41],' although by way of punishment they have already received this lower world, that is, this lower dark atmosphere, as a prison. For insofar as the lower world can be said to be space (comparable) to the height of the sky of the present atmosphere, so also to this extent can be said of the lower world and its depth which lies beneath be understood as land (comparable) in deepness to the same atmosphere." ["2 Peter," *Commentary on the Seven Catholic Epistles*, Cistercian Studies Series: No. 82, pp. 136, 137.]

[9] Saint Pionios is commemorated by the holy Church on the 11th of March. This sacred hieromartyr of Christ was a presbyter of the holy Church of Smyrna during the years of Emperor Decius (249-251). He was a true heir of the spirit of the martyred Bishop Polycarp (commemorated the 23rd of February). The distance between Prousa (Bursa) and Smyrna (Izmir) is 193 miles or 308 kilometers or 3.5 hours of driving time.

[10] The Apostle Jude speaks of their judgment saying that those such "as Sodom and Gomorrah, and the cities around them in like manner to these, having committed fornication and gone away after other flesh, are set forth for an example, undergoing the punishment of everlasting fire [Jude 1: 7]."

"There is, furthermore, the Sicilian volcano at Mount Etna which spews forth fire.[11] It is possible for one to observe this phenomenon and to be fully assured of the accounts thereof. These, therefore, bear testimony that with fire shall God judge all the earth and mete out punishment for the sinner."[12] The saint paused and then related: "I myself saw in Naples of Italy, at about a distance of six miles from the city,[13] a mountain full of chasms and ravines. Such was the intensity of its fire that there issued forth hot mineral water that attained a height of about eighteen hundred feet[14]—well above the mountain's summit. It then descended and burned the place round about it for a distance of

[11] *The Great Synaxaristes* (in Greek) notes that even the great Saint Gregory the Dialogist referred to Etna as "the mouth of Hades," as an indication that fire awaits the ungodly and sinners. It is the highest active volcano in Europe, appropriately named from the Greek Aitne, from αἴθω, "I burn; I blaze." The early pagan Greeks created legends about the volcano, saying that it was the workshop of Hephaestus. Etna covers an area of 600 square miles (1,600 square kilometers); its base has a circumference of about 93 miles (150 kilometers). See the Life of Saint Agatha, commemorated the 5th of February, who is invoked to tame its fury.

[12] "For with the fire of the Lord all the earth shall be judged, and all flesh with His sword: many shall be slain by the Lord....And they shall go forth, and see the carcasses of the men that have transgressed against Me: for their worm shall not die, and their fire shall not be quenched; and they shall be a spectacle to all flesh [Is. 66:16, 24].

"A stream of fire rushed forth before Him. Thousand thousands ministered to Him, and ten thousands of myriads, attended upon Him. The judgment sat, and the books were opened [Dan. 7:10]."

"But the present heavens and the earth, which have been laid up in store by the same word, are being kept for fire until a day of judgment and perdition of ungodly men [2 Pe. 3:7]." And, "What manner of persons ought ye to be in holy modes of life and acts of piety, expecting and earnestly desiring the coming of the day of the Lord, by reason of which the heavens, being set on fire, shall be dissolved, and the elements, being burned with intense heat, shall be melted [2 Pe. 3:11, 12]!"

[13] Undoubtedly, Saint Patrick is speaking of Pozzuoli (Latin Puteoli), a town and episcopal see of the province of Napoli, in southern Italy, lying just west of Naples. It fell into decline when local volcanic and seismic activity caused most of its inhabitants to move to Naples. Intense local volcanicity has given rise to thermal springs and to changes in the level of the land. Inland, to the northeast, is the famous Solfatara, a semiactive volcano that exhales sulfurous vapors and gives vent to liquid mud and hot mineral springs. The famous Solfatara ("sulphur place") of Pozzuoli is made up of approximately forty ancient volcanoes. Renowned volcanic phenomena may be seen, as well as other geological and botanical wonders. See the Life of Saint Januarius, commemorated the 21st of April, for more information in the notes on this geological wonder.

[14] The saint actually said "three hundred *orgyion*" (from ὄργυια), of which one such unit of measurement is the length of outstretched arms—that is, about six feet or one fathom.

six miles. It scorched the earth and even the stones, necessitating the most holy Bishop Stephen to go forth in a procession, with all the people, supplicating God concerning this danger. The bishop succeeded in halting the vehemence of that fire. Thus, from these occurrences, even though they are partial yet they take place in this way that we may comprehend the nature of the whole from the part."

The consul then said, "Earlier thou didst say that thou didst not dispute the therapeutic value of these waters. Well, then, pay homage to the gods." The hierarch said, "That which I am refuting is the statement that your deities created these healing springs when, undeniably, these waters were made by the Logos of God, Jesus Christ." The consul scoffed at these words and said, "Thou then dost assert that thy Christ not only made these waters but also gave them their curative powers?" Patrick answered, "Yes, indeed." The consul uttered a quick rejoinder, saying, "If I should have thee thrown into the hottest water of these springs, as a punishment for thy blatant contempt of the gods, dost thou imagine that thy Christ, Who supposedly called these waters into existence, will preserve thy life?" Patrick answered, "My God is able to rescue me from the hot waters and from thy hands, O consul. But if not, be it known to thee that I will not serve thy gods[15] who are not God. Whether or not I should survive these waters is known perfectly by Him and all will come to pass by His good will and pleasure. He is everywhere present. A little sparrow neither falls on the ground nor is forgotten before the face of God, and so even the hairs of my head are all numbered by Him.[16] But trembling shall seize the ungodly before the devouring fire[17] that will burn both idol and idolater, at the 'revelation of the Lord Jesus from heaven with the angels of His power, in a flaming fire rendering vengeance on those who know not God, and on those who obey not the Gospel of our Lord Jesus Christ. These shall pay the penalty, everlasting destruction from the face of the Lord.'"[18]

Saint Patrick is Cast into the Hot Springs

---

[15] Cf. Dan. 3:17, 18.

[16] Mt. 10:29, 30; Lk. 12:6.

[17] Is. 33:14.

[18] Cf. 2 Thess. 1:7-9. Cf. "For, behold, a day comes burning as an oven, and it shall consume them; and all the aliens, and all that do wickedly, shall be stubble: and the day that is coming shall set them on fire, saith the Lord Almighty, and there shall not be left of them root or branch [Mal. 4:1]." And, "All the powers of the heavens shall melt,

(continued...)

The Martyrdom of Saints Patrick, Akakios, Menander, and Polyaenos

Enraged at these words, the consul charged that Patrick be stripped and cast into the hot waters. As the soldiers carried out the order, the bishop supplicated God, uttering, "Lord Jesus Christ, help Thy servant!" As Patrick was cast inside, several of the soldiers were scalded by the dashing of the waters. As for the holy bishop, he remained unharmed. Who can describe Julian's exasperation and embarrassment? He was vexed that the Jesus Whom he previously railed at, and taunted Patrick to ask for His protection, did in fact protect Patrick who was swimming as if in a comfortable bath. Julian ordered that the bishop be taken from the waters. He sentenced the holy Patrick to have his head severed. After uttering a short prayer, commending his soul to God, the bishop went to his knees. Pursuant to the sentence, he was beheaded. The faithful that were present as witnesses managed to bear away his relics after the execution. He was interred discreetly, after they gave him a modest burial near the high road. Both the Greek and Roman calendars speak of his companions—Saints Akakios, Menander, and Polyaenos, the presbyters[19]—who were also beheaded for the Faith along with him. The blessed ones, therefore, received crowns of the contest. Their synaxis (liturgical gathering) and feast were celebrated in the Church of the Most Holy Theotokos, that was called Kyrou.[20]

---

[18](...continued)
and the sky shall be rolled up like a scroll: and all the stars shall fall like leaves from a vine, and as leaves fall from a fig-tree [Is. 34:4]."

[19] May 19th, both the Vespers Stichera and the Orthros Canon, by Saint Theophanes, identify them as hieromartyrs and priests who laid down their lives with their Bishop Patrick. We learn that Akakios spat upon the error of the idols and that Polyaenos showed himself to be invincible, as they all triumphed over the tyrants' flatteries [Ode Four]. We also learn that all four were dead to the world through ascetical mortification. They endured bitter pangs and scourges [Ode Five]. The hymnographer chants that "the pains of bodily diseases are ended by the steadfast ones with the streams of the hot waters that gush forth automatically from your tombs" [Ode Six, Mode Plagal Four], and that "Christ, through them, causes unintermittent springs of healing as from a fountain for those who hasten to these martyrs" [Ode Nine].

[20] As we said earlier, it does not appear in what persecution their witness took place. Saint Alexander, who is honored with the title of Bishop of Prousa and martyr, is commemorated by the holy Church on the 9th of June in the Greek *Menaia*. He is the

(continued...)

On the 19th of May, the holy Church commemorates our venerable Father MEMNON the Wonder-worker.[21]

On the 19th of May, the holy Church commemorates the holy Martyr AKOLOUTHOS of Egypt.

Saint Theotime

Akolouthos, the holy martyr, flourished during the years of Emperor Maximian who reigned from 286 to 305. Akolouthos hailed from the Thebaid of Egypt and was born at Hermopolis.[22] On account of his confession of the Faith of Christ, he was brought before the governor. Since neither blandishments enticed him nor threats frightened him, the pagans punished him. First they tied a heavy rock to his neck. Next they consigned him to the flames. The ever-memorable one was burned alive, bearing away the crown of martyrdom.

On the 19th of May, the holy Church commemorates the holy Martyr KYRIAKE of Nikomedia, who suffered martyrdom by fire.

On the 19th of May, the holy Church commemorates the holy Martyr THEOTIME of Nikomedia, who was slain by the sword.

Through the intercessions of Thy Saints,
O Christ God, have mercy on us. Amen.

---

[20](...continued)
first bishop of that city whose name has reached us. Saint Patrick is deemed the second bishop of the city. George, who is considered third, attended the Nicene Synod (325). Timothy, who is considered fourth, was crowned with martyrdom under Julian the Apostate in 361. Saint Timothy is commemorated on the 10th of June. The relics of Saint Patrick were preserved at Constantinople in a church which bore his name.

[21] The chief feast day for our venerable Egyptian Father Memnon is the 28th of April.

[22] Hermopolis Magna, present-day al-Ashmunayn, was an ancient town of Upper Egypt located on the Nile River south of al-Minya. It was an episcopal see from the first half of the 3rd C. The pagans worshipped Thoth, deity of learning and patron of scribes. The German Hermopolis expedition (1929–1939) uncovered part of the temple of Thoth, as well as considerable remains of Hellenistic and Roman times. In the necropolis on the west bank at Tunah al-Jabal, an Egyptian University expedition (1930–1939) discovered a labyrinth of underground streets and catacombs connected with cults sacred to Thoth. *Encyclopaedia Britannica*, s.v. "Hermopolis Magna."

On the 20th of May, the holy Church commemorates the holy Martyr THALLELAIOS.[1]

Thallelaios, the great martyr of Christ, was thriving during the time of Emperor Numerian (283-284). He hailed from Phoenicia (Lebanon) of a distinguished lineage. His father, Veroukios, was high priest.[2] His mother's name was Romylia. Thallelaios was instructed and exhorted in the fear of the Lord. He was also educated in the divine and sacred writings. When he arrived at an age of understanding, he desired to study medicine and become a physician. He deemed it the most necessary and philanthropic of all the professions. He found an excellent and God-revering practitioner, Asterios, with whom he studied and assisted. Ere long Thallelaios learned perfectly this art, being by nature dextrous. From his youth, Thallelaios was very pious and God-fearing, so he adorned his soul with all the virtues and with every God-pleasing deed. He had the habit of receiving into the house all those who were handicapped, whether strangers or locals. He administered to them with love, offering them rest and every comfort. His house, consequently, became a hostel for both the poor and rich that were ill. He took on these labors because he loved the virtue of hospitality. He rejoiced to be of service and offer treatment. Adding toil to toil, he abundantly served every need through his kindly bestowed solicitude. It made him happy to help heal the sick in whom he maintained the keenest interest.

Most of his sympathy and compassion were expressed toward the poor and the chronically ill needing great care. He commiserated with them in their pains as if they were his own. Many times, in order to relieve the pain and suffering of the infirm, he conveyed them to his house on his shoulders for more personalized treatment, as he stood before his patients as a slave ready to assist. He preferred to serve others than to perform any other good work. His sympathy and pity were exercised to such degree that he did not wait to be asked for help. As a ready balm to all those who needed his doctoring, he went forth and hastened to find those in need. He did not charge his patients. He rendered all his services and cures free of charge. Together with his loving-kindness and mercy, he chose non-acquisition and poverty. He had no desire to collect money or the things of this world. His humility was such that he,

---

[1] The Life of the holy Martyr Thallelaios was paraphrased from an ancient manuscript and included in the *Neon Eklogion* of Nikodemos the Hagiorite, who also composed a complete service to the unmercenary that was published in western Greece at Mesolonghi of the Etoloakarnania prefecture in 1878. Another full divine office was created by Gregory, which is found in the Athonite Codices at Great Lavra: Δ 36, Δ 45, and Ω 147.

[2] *The Great Synaxaristes* (in Greek) identifies him as a hierarch ('αρχιερέως), which may indicate that he was a widower.

alone, treated and cared for the wounds and lesions of the sick until they were well.

In this manner, therefore, did he conduct his life and was accounted worthy of apostolic gifts. While he boldly proclaimed the name of Christ, he also healed every malady without drugs, surgery, cautery, plasters, or salves. He accomplished miracles through the evocation of Christ's name. He diligently strived to bring all to godliness, by making Christians of those idolaters who received cures at his hands. Mindful of his goal, he made no distinction in his amiable care and treatment between the believers and the unbelievers. Without prejudice or partiality, he cured everyone. All those, therefore, who hastened to him could expect a double healing: that of the soul and that of the body. He exhibited equal fellow feeling, forbearance, and tenderness toward each one. He besought God for the sake of all his patients: those who were Christians, he entreated the Lord in behalf of their repentance and correction of errors; and those who were idolaters, he supplicated the Lord that they might forsake the deception of idolatry and believe in Jesus Christ. For this cause, he even rebuked those who displayed no charity or benevolence toward the unbelievers in their misfortunes and illnesses.

Saint Thallelaios

On one occasion, Thallelaios observed that a certain Christian was angry with an idolater. That same Christian, beholding the bad times that befell that pagan, gloated over the infidel's plight. But Thallelaios was grieved by that Christian's attitude. Thallelaios was mindful of the words of Solomon: "If thine enemy should fall, rejoice not over him, neither be elated at his overthrow [Prov. 24:17]." Thus, he reproved that Christian for his hardness of heart, saying, "Brother, thou oughtest not to rejoice at the mishaps and adversities of thy brother, because calamities and sufferings are common to us all and no one knows what reverses he may suffer in the end." The Christian remarked, "It is better that the ungodly should soon die rather than live, for what benefit is there in their living, since they grow old in impiety and in all sorts of bad ways?" Thallelaios commented, "We, brother, have a commandment from the Lord to love our enemies and pray for those who despitefully use us or persecute us. We are not told to exult and be glad in their setbacks. We are exhorted in this manner that we might become true sons of God; for our Lord continues to bestow benefactions upon the evil and unjust.[3] If with warmth of heart we condole with them and share their sorrows, we might in this way weaken their unbelief and bring them to some reverential regard and, eventually, piety." By these words and many more was he able to soften the harshness of that Christian brother, so that Thallelaios cultivated within him clemency and compassion.

The man of God possessed abundant zeal for piety. He endeavored in different ways to blot out the error and deceit of the idols. He, on this account, went by night and cut down lofty cedars, which the idolaters were wont to fell and make sacrifices to their gods. At the same time, the heathen were defiling themselves with fornication. Many entertainments and women dancing to playing instruments accompanied these pagan devotions. By chopping down and taking away the trees, Thallelaios hoped to cut off their disporting and amusements of pleasure. As it turned out, since he made it more difficult for them to offer sacrifices to their abominable idols, he also hindered their licentious diversions. Gradually, by means of his clinic and medical services, he drew many to himself. By degrees, he led his patients to the true Faith of our Lord Jesus Christ.

There was a case involving a man suffering a bite to the chest by a poisonous serpent. After the fangs penetrated his flesh and secreted their venom, it was speedily absorbed into the victim's circulation. Without antivenin therapy, the toxic effect would soon become lethal. The tissue in the area developed gangrene. The decay soon spread to the sides. He was in danger of dying. The bite victim went to physicians and spent that which he had, but he found neither relief nor remedy. He, therefore, utterly despaired and awaited death. He was found, however, by the good-willed and devoted doctor, the holy Thallelaios who was prepared to undertake his treatment and cure. He told the sufferer that he sought for nought save his coming to believe in the Christ. The man swiftly confessed that he would come to unhesitating belief if Jesus Christ were to cure him. Thallelaios placed his right hand on the patient's chest and traced the sign of the life-giving Cross, which sign yielded a complete cure. So perfect was this curative that there remained neither the least trace of the wound nor the slightest hint of the symptoms. The grateful man wholeheartedly thanked the saint and glorified God for the double therapy which he received, both that of his soul and of his body.

At another time, a certain doctor succumbed to a grave illness which resulted in the loss of his voice. He was unable to speak a word. His kinfolk,

[3] Cf. Mt. 5:44, 45.

losing hope in all conventional physicians and their pharmaceuticals, took refuge in the saint. They brought their kinsman, the ailing doctor, and set him before Thallelaios beseeching him for a cure. The compassionate Thallelaios drew near to the doctor and said to him, "If thou wouldest recover thy health, it is necessary to believe in the Christ; and He shall heal thee forthwith." The mute doctor knelt before the feet of the saint and soaked them with the effusion of his tears. By these actions and other gestures, he expressed his unrestrained willingness to believe with all his soul if Christ were to bring about his cure. Then—behold the wonder!—immediately divine grace came to the man who was unable to speak, so that the string of his tongue was loosed and he articulated clearly as before.

Thereafter, the saint, embracing the evangelic life, took to walking about the entire city. Heedless of his own safety, he kept asking and searching for the poor or the hungry or those engulfed in the darkness of pagan error that he might administer treatment both to the body and to the soul. On one such round, he found a man who was paralyzed and naked. He was sprawled out on the ground and incited much pity within Thallelaios who approached him. Thallelaios asked him about his loss of voluntary movement. The man replied, "One day I was walking on a precipitous path when I stumbled. I was hurled down and shattered my foot. I visited different clinics for a long time, but I was unable to find any therapy for the injury. I am, therefore, as thou seest me, the most forlorn of men: a palsied invalid, in the throes of despair, being deprived of normal function. But I see that thou hast more compassion than any father after the flesh. Have mercy on my mishap! Treat me and heal me!" The saint, with his usual unexampled and sweet-tempered kindness, said, "I shall bind up thy wound with the Faith of the Christ; and thou shalt be healed. All that is asked of thee is that thou shouldest believe in the Christ. He shall speedily grant thee the grace of a cure." The paralytic declared that he believed in the Christ with all his soul. The saint then took hold of the afflicted limb and brought the bones and nerves into place. Instantly, even as Thallelaios touched the foot, motor and sensory paralysis vanished. All atrophy and neurological damage disappeared. The one who had been lame in his foot was now empowered to run to and fro. This is exactly what happened as he gave thanks to the holy physician Thallelaios. But the saint restrained him, saying, "If thou wouldest thank me, then I charge thee not to reveal the wonderworking to anyone." Thallelaios spoke thus for he would shun both glory and praise from men. The former paralytic could not resist expressing his joy. He hastened to the streets and proclaimed to all the cure that he received from the man of God.

It was not long before a certain woman, possessed by a demon, heard these tidings. She quickly scampered off and went to Thallelaios' house. She found him within and recounted her calamity of harassment by a demon. She besought him, sobbing and wailing, to deliver her from the malignant and unclean spirit. But the demon, the one that tormented her, promptly flew into a rage. He dashed her to the ground and convulsed her. The saint, seeing the woman tortured in this manner, was moved to pity. He made the sign of the honorable Cross over her forehead, while calling upon the name of Jesus Christ. Then—lo, the miracle!—on the instant, the demon departed from her and took flight.

After the woman was freed from that foul spirit, she hastened off with profound joy. She kept proclaiming in an uplifted voice the mighty works of God. As she passed through a certain neighborhood, she met an acquaintance who was a blind man. She addressed him exultantly with a raised voice, saying, "Why art thou sitting here to no benefit? Hast thou not heard that there is a wonderful physician in our very own city who heals all the infirm in an extraordinary and mysterious manner? He also expels demons. Indeed, he delivers the bodies of men from maiming and mutilation and from every kind of lesion. In addition, didst thou know that he also introduces the opportunity for all to be saved? He provides all things without remuneration. The blessed man teaches and urges the people to perform good works. As for sick folk, those who have recourse in him, he receives everybody and turns no one away. He provides beds for rest. His home is the scene of genuine care and consolation for all those in sore plight. He is motivated by sincere compassion and charity toward his neighbor for whom he spares nothing. Come, then, and I shall go with thee to him that thou mightest recover thy sight."

So spoke the woman to the blind man, and he hearkened to her advice. She led him forth to the saint. The loss of vision, nonetheless, was not confined solely to his bodily eyes. His soul, also, afflicted with the disease of veneration of the idols, lost its sight. The blind man was hopeful that Thallelaios would cure him. He knelt before the saint's feet and, with waves of tears from his sightless eyes, he began to say, "Until now I was pitiful and wretched; but from henceforth shall I be blessed and fortunate, because I shall have received the light of my eyes from thee." How did the saint respond to this acclamation? He said, "The unsleeping eye of God, O man, sees all the hearts of men and their pursuits and practises. Believe, then, in the Christ, the Creator of nature, and thou shalt receive healing to thine eyes. For if thou wilt believe that He is the Physician of souls and bodies, then He shall heal thee." Hearing these spirit lifting words, the blind man stated solemnly, "I believe with all my soul in the Christ." The blind man then took hold of the saint's thrice-blessed hands and placed them upon his diseased eyes. He, instantly, received his sight. He gave glory to God and remained next to the faithful of the Church.

In view of the fact that the saint healed every illness in a manner contrary to all expectation, he was everywhere extolled. Sick persons from all quarters were hastening to the saint, for whom he was healing both the infirmities of the body and the soul. Divine zeal propelled Thallelaios to walk about from place to place, forsooth for healing—which he wrought—but in actuality to herald the name of Jesus Christ and direct the people to piety. On his tour, he also went to Edessa.[4] By reason of his skill in the medical arts, he drew many and brought them to believe in the Christ. The hater-of-good, the devil, unable to endure the increase of the Faith of Christ, incited some malevolent persons. They went before the man in authority at that place, namely Tiberian, and denounced the holy physician. As we mentioned earlier, Numerian was reigning at the time. He was completely given over to the delusion of idol mania. He instigated a great persecution against the Christians. All petty rulers, subordinate to his sovereignty, were issued terrifying decrees for putting to death the Christians in order to wipe out the name of Christ. Each ruler strived to demonstrate greater obedience to the emperor than his peers. Consequently, when Tiberian learned of the existence and activities of the sacred Thallelaios—that he was preaching the name of Christ—he delayed not in dispatching his solders to bring that Christian before him. Thallelaios was apprehended and, under Tiberian's orders, was administered an excessive beating. Tiberian, perceiving that Thallelaios' firmness of purpose was not altered one bit, thought the physician was out of his mind and despised him as a booby. He, therefore, released him but limited him from walking about the places under Tiberian's jurisdiction.

---

[4] Osrhoene was an ancient kingdom in northwestern Mesopotamia, located between the Euphrates and Tigris Rivers and lying across the modern frontier of Turkey and Syria. Its capital was Edessa (Urhay, Sanliurfa or modern Urfa, Tur., 37°08′N 38°45′E). Seleucus I Nicator, when he refounded the town as a military colony (303 B.C.), mixed Macedonians and Greeks with its eastern population. He called it Edessa, in memory of Edessa (Aigai) the ancient capital of Macedon (later also known as Vodena). The name is also recorded as Callirrhoe. Under Antiochus IV Epiphanes, the town was called "Antiochia on the Callirhoe" by colonists from Syrian Antioch (modern Antakya, Turkey) who had settled there. Its Kurdish name is Riha. From 212 to 214 the kingdom was a Roman province. The literary language of the tribes which had founded this kingdom was Aramaic, whence came the Syriac. Traces of Hellenistic culture were soon overwhelmed in Edessa, whose dynasty employed Syriac legends on their coinage—with the exception of the Roman client-king Abgar IX (179-214); and there is a corresponding lack of Greek public inscriptions. It was later rebuilt by the Emperor Justin and called after him—Justinopolis. Edessa was taken in 609 by the Persians, but was soon retaken by Herakleios who lost to the Arabs in 638. The Byzantines often tried to retake Edessa, especially under Romanos Lekapenos. The latter obtained from the inhabitants the "Holy Mandylion" (the ancient image of Christ) and solemnly transferred it to Constantinople, on the 16th of August, in the year 944.

The saint, thus enjoined, departed from that place and went to those parts in Cilicia. Once again, under the ostensible motive of practising the medical arts, he proclaimed the name of Christ. It was then that some of the idol madmen accused the saint to the man in authority, one named Theodore, at Aegae by the sea.[5] Those detractors of Jesus censured Thallelaios before him, saying that "a certain Galilean, a Christian, practising quackery, is misleading the people. He even boasts that he heals the sick merely by mentioning the name of Jesus the Christ, the One Who was crucified by the Hebrews. He publishes Jesus as the Redeemer and Savior of the world. Furthermore, this follower of that Galilean disdains the gods and does not cease from cutting down the holy trees of Lebanon." Theodore, hearing this complaint lodged against Thallelaios, wasted no time in sending out soldiers to bring him in before his judgment seat. The soldiers discovered the saint concealed inside the trunk of an olive tree at Anazarbos.[6] After they bound him and gave him a thrashing, they brought him to Theodore. Thallelaios came before Theodore the following day, when the ruler sat upon his throne to judge in the temple of Hadrian. The soldiers untied Thallelaios' fetters and then escorted him in a violent manner, as though he were already a condemned criminal. Theodore opened the questioning and asked, "Whence comest thou? State thy name and thine occupation." The saint answered, "My homeland is Phoenicia. I am the son of freeborn parents. My name is Thallelaios. I practise medicine. And I am a Christian and slave of Jesus Christ."

The ruler interrogated further: "How didst thou come into this land?" The saint replied, "I walk about from place to place in order to preach the Faith of Jesus Christ and that I might blot out the error of the idols, because nothing else is more pleasing to God save this work." Theodore, hearing this statement, was angered thereby and ordered the boring through of Thallelaios' joints at the ball of the ankle. He then instructed the executioners to pass a rope through the openings and suspend Thallelaios upside down. But the minds of the soldiers were confounded by divine power. Instead of exercising themselves against the saint, whom they failed to distinguish from a piece of wood, they bored a hole through the wood and hung that—all the while thinking they were handling the saint. Theodore, the ruler, seeing the wood hanging in the place of the prisoner, thought that the soldiers were mocking him. He, therefore, chastised them. He right away summoned forth other soldiers to resume the torture. This

[5] Aegae was an ancient seaside city of Cilicia (Kilikia) built by Greek colonists. It was the seat of a bishopric of whom the first bishop was the sacred Hieromartyr Zenovios, also a trained physician, who is commemorated by the holy Church on the 30th of October.

[6] Anazarbos (Anavarza), from the time of Diocletian, was the metropolis of Cilicia II. It is situated on the eastern plain of Cilicia on a tributary of the Pyramos.

time he bid them flog Thallelaios with a bullwhip. Theodore believed that by employing torments, he could subdue the martyr. The valiant man of Christ remained unvanquished. Although his entire body sustained wounds from those harsh soldiers and their mighty thrashing, still the stalwart doctor stood unswayed. Nay, not in the least was he moved from his devotion to Christ's Faith. He remained firm and unflinching. He abided as one feeling no pain. He endured the stripes and the scourges in a manly fashion, all for the love that he possessed for the man-loving God.

The tyrant, perceiving that the punishments carried out by the soldiers upon the martyr were for nought, could not help but marvel at Thallelaios' courage and perseverance. Theodore began to speak to Thallelaios in a guileful and false manner, festering with evil, saying, "In what way dost thou attend the sick, beloved Thallelaios? Tell me the truth if thou wouldest have my affection. If thou healest with magic, say so that I too may learn. If thou dost effect cures with the power of the gods, I want to believe also that they are able to treat every malady. I do not wish to believe that the healing was wrought by the Christ and, especially, through the Cross, which is the greatest condemnation in the world." These irreverent remarks and other blasphemies against the Master Christ were uttered by that profane ruler. The martyr, hearing his wicked irreligion, was more wounded by his blasphemies than the rawhide lashes and torments that Theodore wielded against him.

Boldly and openly, Thallelaios spoke his mind to the ruler and said, "I am by no means a sorcerer. I am neither applying magic therapies upon patients nor appealing to thy gods, that is, those soulless, deaf, and insensate graven images. The idols, indeed, fall down and break to pieces before the name of Jesus Christ. If thou shouldest like, therefore, to be assured of the truth of this claim of the actual healing of the infirm, examine those who received these cures. They themselves can inform thee that by no other means were they treated other than by the pronouncement of the name of Jesus Christ and the making of the sign of the life-giving Cross—which sign thou dost despise because thou knowest not Him. For He is the Son and Logos of God Who casts out demons, sets aright the paralyzed, gives light to the blind, raises the dead, and cures every weakness and infirmity. These deeds can be affirmed by both witnesses and the recipients of these wonderworkings.

"Jesus, therefore, the only-begotten Son of God, saw that His image, man, the creation of His own hands, had fallen by reason of man's disobedience. When man was exiled from Paradise, man was deprived of all good things. Man was kept in bondage by the devil. By reason of the fall, man succumbed to idolatry and all that was bad. But Jesus had compassion upon man and came down into the world, being born a man, that He might save man by means of His divine teachings and His own example and, hence, lead us to the path of Paradise. The sinless One was crucified on account of His love for us. By means of His immaculate blood, He gave His life a 'ransom for many.'[7] He gave Himself for us that He might ransom us from all lawlessness and might make us zealous of good works.[8] As a ransom for us, He delivered us from slavery to the devil. It was through death that He brought to nought the one who has the power of death, that is, the devil, that He might set free those who through fear of death were all their lifetime subject to bondage.[9] The benefits and good things done for the world by the Son and Logos of God, our Lord Jesus Christ, cannot be numbered. When the kindness and the love of God our Savior toward mankind appeared,[10] there came the healing of paralytics, deaf, blind, dropsical, demonized, and every illness that has befallen us, so that even the dead are raised and all good things are granted to men.

"Our Lord, when He desired to be taken up into the heavens, gave His apostles the promise of His grace. He told them to go into all the world and proclaim the Gospel to the whole creation. As for those who came to believe and were baptized, He said that such signs will accompany those who believe: 'In My name they shall cast out demons; they shall speak in new tongues; they shall take up serpents; and if they should drink anything deadly, in no wise shall it harm them; they shall lay hands on the sick, and they shall be well [Mk. 16:17, 18].' Now to all those who believe in Him and keep His commandments, He offers these bountiful acts of kindness to the race of man according to His will. This gift of grace has He vouchsafed to me, His humble slave, in such wise that, through His holy name and the sign of His honorable Cross, every sickness and infirmity is cured. So then, why dost thou blaspheme against Jesus Christ, the Redeemer and Savior of the world? Much rather, thou oughtest to have believed in Him and abandoned thy dumb idols that thou mightest attain to everlasting life. Hearken to me, O ruler, if thou wouldest have what is for thy good: believe in the Christ, the true God. Then shalt thou know His compassion, His love for man, and His power to heal not only ailments of the body but also maladies of the soul. Owing to the reason that the man-befriending God is merciful, He desires that all men should be saved. Indeed, 'to this end we both toil and are reproached, because we have hoped upon a living God, Who is the Savior of all men, especially of believers [1 Tim. 4:10].' And we are mindful that 'our citizenship exists in the heavens, from where we also patiently await the Savior, the Lord Jesus Christ [Phil. 3:20].'"

---

[7] Mt. 20:28.

[8] Tit. 2:14.

[9] Cf. Heb. 2:14, 15.

[10] Tit. 3:4.

Toward the end of his public statement, as the martyr was speaking these words, the tyrant gazed upon the crowd. It was evident to him that they were avidly listening to every syllable of these words of salvation with great longing. Theodore's wrath was inordinately kindled as he cried out emphatically, "O skilled avenger of the Christ, thou hast succeeded in condemning thyself! I shall now demonstrate how empty thy hope is in thy Christ." With this declaration, Theodore, suddenly, lunged at Thallelaios, in order to discipline him with his own hands. But O Thy wonders, Christ King! In an instant, both of Theodore's hands withered. Thus he remained in his place with useless hands! Nevertheless, this prodigious sign still did not bring to prudence that thrice-accursed man. Instead, he charged the soldiers to take the martyr and torment him with diverse tortures. Immediately then, those savage and inhumane underlings, in accordance with Theodore's command, tortured Thallelaios with the application of iron claws to his flesh. This was followed by bouts with fire and knives and other sorts of horrible martyrdoms. As for the martyr, he received whatever they contrived with sublime courage and even joy. This is because he had with him the Christ Who was lightening and relieving all the chastisements. So while Thallelaios was sustaining numberless wounds throughout his body, that is to say, iron claws shredding his flesh and fire burning his members, he withstood all with a manly attitude and solemn resoluteness in his Faith.

In truth, the saint despised all their tortures, and began to say to the tyrant, "Do not think for a moment that I am afraid either of thy punishments or of death itself with which thou threatenest me. For I will fight thee with greater daring, since I prefer to die for piety's sake than to live in impiety. Moreover, even if thou shouldest shiver to atoms the clay vessel of my flesh, nonetheless, the treasure of my soul thou art unable to seize. And if thou shouldest lead me forth from my tabernacle of the senses, yet thou art unable to deprive me of the noetic tabernacle of the heavenly kingdom. I have praised the victories of other men. But now that I find myself in the midst of the contest, how is it possible that I should cast away the weapons given to me by my Christ that I might emerge as the winner? Christ offers His gifts neither to the cowardly nor to the careless. Nor does He crown those who are fast asleep. For this cause does the consuming of my flesh by thy fire seem to me to be a game, for I am being bedewed by the dew of my Savior. All of thy torments I count as terrifying as a tree leaf; for though we walk in the flesh, we do not war according to the flesh. For the weapons of our warfare are not of the flesh, but mighty through God to the pulling down of strongholds, overthrowing reasonings and every high thing which lifts itself up against the knowledge of

God.[11] My convictions have become hardened and unmoveable, even as rock. I am, therefore, prepared to present my body to Christ as a sheep of slaughter;[12] since I am obliged to sacrifice it for Him even as He sacrificed Himself for my sake."

Theodore scowled at these attestations, so that he made the following public statement: "I, on account of my kindness, gave him leave to speak these words. Though he has not yet attained his eighteenth birthday, still his eloquence exceeds that of the rhetoricians. I myself was thinking that by way of torture I would bring him to my way of thinking, but this fellow does not in the least fear or shift from his aim. Well then, shall I bring him around by promising him wealth? But he cares not a whit for wealth. Perhaps I should employ sweet words of flattery? But he is no wise prevailed upon. So I must needs utilize another method. Here is what I shall do: I shall cast him inside a cockboat and set him adrift in the midst of the sea. Now if he is a godly and good man, divine providence will guard him. But if he is a bad man, divine justice will drown him; and thus he will not be slain by my hands." Theodore, as the judge, spoke aloud his thoughts which immediately were put into effect.

Therefore, the martyr of Christ, Thallelaios, was thrown into a cockboat and, afterward, cut loose in choppy waters. Though Thallelaios was left without provisions and exposed to the harsh elements, yet he remained undaunted. He conducted himself as though he were walking about on dry land. While the waves rolled upon the vessel, he raised his hands heavenward and uttered this prayer: "Unto Thee, O Lord Who dwellest in heaven, have I lifted up my soul. I have, ofttimes, called upon Thy name and Thou hast had pity upon me. Have compassion on me, even now, and lead me to the harbor of salvation lest the deep of the sea should swallow me up and I should be deprived of bearing witness to Thy great name. Do Thou fulfill my desire that I may sacrifice my body unto Thee, my Christ. Do Thou grant me, by means of patient endurance here and now, to be presented boldly before Thy dread judgment seat. For the eyes of my soul hope in Thee, O Lord." Then—lo, the wonder!—straightway the sea curbed her surges and became calm as though she had tenderness for the saint. He was thereafter piloted gently to the shore. He landed in a place contiguous to Aegae, clad in a white garment, so that he was bright and shining with divine light.

Not before long, Theodore, the judge, was apprised of the safe conduct of Thallelaios to their beach. He was beside himself at the unexpected tidings. Although he realized how he was now exposed to contempt, still he composed himself and instructed his men to bring the Christian before him. The soldiers, as fierce wolves, proceeded briskly along the waterfront to carry out his sinister

[11] 2 Cor. 10:3-5.

[12] Rom. 8:36.

command. They apprehended the innocent lamb of Christ and haled him before the judge. Concurrently, the court filled to capacity with idolaters and, yes, many physicians. Why the latter? They bore malice and professional envy toward the young doctor, Thallelaios, for his practises and for the treatments he administered. Those miserable ones, inflamed with passion, kept shouting stridently their accusations against the martyr, hoping to prejudice the unjust judge against the defendant. For they desired Theodore to impose the death penalty upon Thallelaios. The judge then addressed the saint, saying, "What sayest thou, O Thallelaios, regarding all these allegations with which they are charging thee?" The martyr replied, "The God Whom I revere and worship, let Him help me even if the whole world is at war with me. For this reason I must undergo such hardship and distress, without any regard to even the least bodily torment, that I might be accounted worthy to receive death for the sake of the love of my Christ." Then Theodore, who was in charge, in order to silence the shouts and cries of the people and the imminent threat to the martyr, spoke artfully and not with an ounce of truth. After adapting his conversation to the listeners, he came to the object of his address and said to Thallelaios: "Inasmuch as no evil demon drowned thee in the sea, I must needs now put an end to thy life. I, therefore, command that thou be nailed, with four nails, to a plank. Following this, boiling tar is to be poured over thee, from head to toe. Next, thou art to be cast into a stone melting-pot and burned by fire until thou shouldest expire." The blessed face of Thallelaios, after hearing his sentence, began perspiring, even as a wrestler might be imperceptibly moved to tears upon becoming wearied or fatigued by the matches. He, however, was not dismayed before the application of these new torments.

That most ruthless and shameless tyrant, thinking that the man of God became frightened, remarked to those present: "The evil geniuses (genii) have fled from him, and for this reason he cowers before the torments. But I ought to show pity." He then turned quickly toward the saint and said, "If thou wilt make obeisance, O Thallelaios, to the gods, for which thou shalt earn their clemency and indulgence, I promise thee wealth and abundant glory. If, however, thou shouldest disobey, thou shalt forfeit not only these good allowances but also thy life." But the valiant athlete of Christ showed his mettle as a martyr and gave this response: "I scorn what thou callest compassion and gifts. Thy terms would have me oppose godliness and deny my religion. As for thy wealth, I consider it as the dirt of the earth. Nothing can give me greater gain than the pure sacrifice of my body. When the torments commenced I was firm and unshaken in my constancy. At present, I am at the finish line and expect to win. So now dost thou choose to entice me, O most reprehensible man, into changing my mind? Thy torments have I for my joy. Thy stripes have I for my glory. The perils that I have sustained are as a crown. Am I to strip my body of these trophies and begrudge my own salvation that I might be garbed in simple attire? But the paramount loss before all thine endowments would be the disentitlement of my hopes in Christ."

The tyrant, seeing that there were no means left to alter the saint's resolve, was moved to wrath. He muttered to himself, "Many speeches have I given to him. Much compassion have I exhibited to him. Punishment after punishment have I used upon him. It is simply not possible to persuade him. For nought have I applied a multitude of scourges. So many soldiers have toiled to no benefit. This fellow exhibits no reluctance, he rather yearns for slaughter. He would love to die. Why then should I continue to speak into ears that are deaf? The blame falls to his charge. Let me pass down the death sentence and have done with him." Now Theodore no longer could endure the mortifying conferences with the martyr and being publicly put down. He, therefore, gave the order to cast the saint to four ferocious lions in the stadium. The tyrant was sure that the brute beasts would tear him to pieces. But the Lord God of hosts did not leave Thallelaios without help. In an instant, the wild ferocity of the beasts was converted so that they were as gentle lambs. Approaching the martyr, they wagged their tails and fawned at his feet. The tyrant, put to shame, found himself in a quandary. What remained for him to exercise? Ultimately, he decided to put down in writing the decision of death by decapitation. Afterward, he could not repress his rage and disgust, so he threw the warrant down to the ground. He then rose up from his judgment seat, not being able to regulate his conduct, and stormed out.

Saint Thallelaios

The much-tried athlete of Christ, Thallelaios, young in body but perfect in mind, consequently, on the 20th day of the month of May, emerged as victor and received the crown of martyrdom. This virgin-martyr's relics drive away diseases and suffering. The earth that received his precious blood became a fountain of healings.[13] It was then that many others, after beholding

[13] The introductory two-line or couplet verses (*distichon*) provided in the *Synaxaristes* of Nikodemos the Hagiorite provides the following: "God sends herbs to loose every suffering." This means that upon the spot where Saint Thallelaios was beheaded, God caused an herbal plant to sprout that cured every infirmity and suffering. See also the Orthros Canon of this day, Ode Nine, Mode Four, by Saint Joseph the Hymnographer, who chants of the dust of the unmercenary's sanctifying relics and the site of his execution as a spring of healing. Elsewhere, it is reported that our merciful Lord Jesus Christ caused collyrium (eye salve or wash) to rain upon the tomb of the divine Luke

(continued...)

the courage and patience of the martyr, as well as his wonderworkings, came to believe in our Lord Jesus Christ. They, too, after seeing Thallelaios set the goal of emulation, contested by martyrdom without faltering and were slain for the sake of Christ. The following notables distinguished themselves with Thallelaios: Asterios, the saint's teacher of medicine, who also helped Thallelaios carry away the cedar trees; Alexander, a soldier; and Steronas, Philegrios, Timothy, Theodoule, Makaria, and many others, through whose intercessions may we be vouchsafed also the kingdom of the heavens. Amen.

On the 20th of May, the holy Church commemorates the Martyrs ALEXANDER the soldier and ASTERIOS the physician, who were slain by the sword.

On the 20th of May, the holy Church commemorates the holy Martyr ASKLAS of the Thebaid, who was cast into the Nile River.

Asklas, the holy martyr, contested during the years of Emperor Diocletian who reigned from 284 to 305. Asklas hailed from the Thebaid of Egypt. He was denounced before Governor Arrianos for his devotion to Christ's Faith. Upon making a bold and public profession of his belief in the Christ, Asklas was suspended on a wooden pole and subjected to having his sides scraped and flayed with sharp instruments. After this intense punishment, he was cast into prison. As for the governor, he at some point afterward was traversing the river Nile by boat. Meanwhile, the saint was still in his prison cell. Asklas was praying that Arrianos be prevented from disembarking onto dry land. Arrianos' arrival was contingent upon his written confession that Christ is God. Therefore, Arrianos' ship was held fast in a mysterious and unexpected manner. Even as the ship could not sail, as though anchored to that spot, so the saint knew of it in the Spirit while surrounded by the walls of his cell. Asklas, nevertheless, sent an epistle to Arrianos. The message was simple and straightforward. The governor's ship would remain stationary and not reach dry land unless Arrianos wrote in his own hand his acknowledgment of the divinity of Christ. The governor, at that juncture, requested papyrus. He took up a stylus and began writing that "the God of the Christians is great and beside Him there is no other God." Immediately, with his written admission, the ship moved forward and sailed toward the embankment. When Arrianos set foot on the shore, his heart once again hardened even as Pharaoh's of old. Arrianos summoned Asklas to stand before him. Arrianos then commanded that the torture of the saint resume. Asklas' sides were burned with lit torches.

---

[13](...continued)
(commemorated the 18th of October) as a sign that the apostle was a physician.

Following this acutely painful chastisement, Arrianos ordered that a great rock be tied to Asklas. Arrianos then had the martyr cast into the waters of the Nile. Hence, the ever-memorable one clinched the crown of martyrdom.[14]

On the 20th of May, the holy Church commemorates the venerable and God-bearing Fathers NIKETAS, JOHN, and JOSEPH, founders of the Nea Moni Monastery at Chios.[15]

Niketas, John, and Joseph, our very venerable fathers, were born and raised on the far-famed island of Chios. They sprouted up as blossoming roses during the end of the tenth century after Christ. These saints of God had no fondness for human glory and honor, since they possessed that heavenly glory that lives unto the ages. Solomon speaks of this, writing: "The righteous live forevermore; their reward also is with the Lord, and the care of them is with the Most High [Wis. of Sol. 5:15]." And, "The souls of the righteous are in the hand of God, and there shall no torment touch them [Wis. of Sol. 3:1]." Though they did not relish glory and honor, yet their names are recorded in the book of life. We, for this reason, have a necessary obligation to pay homage and write down their lives and achievements to their glorification. We ought to continue praising and blessing them, as they were slaves of God. Nay,

---

[14] See the very interesting account of the conversion of this persecutor of Christians in the Lives of the holy Martyrs Philemon, Apollonios, and those with them, together with Arrianos and the four bodyguards of the Thebaid in Egypt, who are commemorated by the holy Church on the 14th of December.

[15] The biographical account of these venerable and righteous fathers was written by Saint Nikephoros of Chios (1750-1821), who is himself commemorated by the holy Church on the 1st of May. Saint Nikephoros came to be hegumen of Nea Moni in 1802. See his Life herein with more details about Nea Moni, for which he compiled a synopsis and history. He left us records of its iconographic adornments, heirlooms, and treasures. While conducting the inventory, he also found the imperial chrysobulls of the emperors who endowed it. We are indebted to his labors, since all would have been lost to us; because, shortly after the saint's repose, all those treasures were destroyed by fires. The Turks set the monastery on fire in 1822 and again in 1828.

The venerable Nikephoros composed a melodic divine office in a pamphlet, entitled "The Divine and Holy Service of Our Holy and God-inspired Fathers Niketas, John, and Joseph, Founders of the Venerable, Holy, Royal, and Cross-possessing Monastery Named the New, Which is Dedicated to Our All-holy Lady Theotokos and Ever-virgin Mary, and the History of the Monastery and Certain Strange Miracles Performed by the Mother of the Lord" (Venice, 1804). A second edition, by Gregory Photeinos, appeared in *Writings Pertaining to Nea Moni* [*Ta Neamonesia*], Book I (Chios, 1865), pp. 1-33. See also *New Leimonarion* and *New Chian Leimonarion* (pp. 241-246).

rather, they should be described as His genuine friends. Indeed, according to Basil the Great, the honor we accord to our good fellow slaves shows that we have love toward our common Master. When magnanimous slaves of God are not simply holy ones struggling for their own salvation but for our general benefit, we extol them as universal patrons. Such were the fathers we celebrate today. They strived, perspiring much, and contributed everything, for the redemption of the many. We are justified in exalting these doers of good works. In fact, it is incumbent upon us to make encomiums to those who donated their lives for the regeneration and conversion of others.

Brethren, such God-bearing fathers who have befriended and benefitted us are the righteous fathers at Chios—we mean our Niketas, John, and Joseph, whom we commemorate today. We are mindful that they battled for not only their own salvation but that of others as well. They entered into superhuman struggles of asceticism, enduring for long years. They contended and provided for the reformation of many. These ever-memorable ones, whether on land or sea, overworked themselves for the sake of others. They undertook the building of monasteries, for the salvation and rescuing of souls. Many were delivered from the devil's snare and came to repentance by these fathers' sacred and living example of the virtues, as well as by their God-inspired teachings. This is why we feel that it is right to commend them as our benefactors. Their feats proclaimed the glory of God Who is glorified in His saints. It is, therefore, to our advantage to be reading and listening to their hallowed conduct of life and their godly excellences. Now, however, we need to commence this narration in an orderly fashion.

The thrice-blessed fathers and sacred ascetics, as we said, flourished on the East Aegean island of Chios. It was during the times when there reigned at Constantinople Emperor Michael IV Paphlagon (1034-1041) and then Michael V Kalaphates (1041-1042). Following Paphlagon and Kalaphates, there came Emperor Constantine IX Monomachos (b. ca. 1000, r. 1042-1055),[16] who reigned with the elderly royal sisters, his wife Zoe and his sister-in-law Theodora.[17] By this time, our three holy fathers—Niketas, John, and Joseph—had forsaken the world and all that pertained to it. They repaired to a mountain on the island, named Provation ("Little Sheep" Mountain). It was

[16] The family name of Monomachos means "fighting in single combat" or "gladiator," though Constantine himself was a senator and a member of the Byzantine civil aristocracy.

[17] The ever-beautiful Empress Zoe, daughter of Emperor Constantine VIII, now sixty-four years old but still wrinkle-free, was heiress of the Macedonian Dynasty. She embarked upon her third marriage with a man twenty-two years her junior. Her June wedding in 1042 was with the eminent senator Constantine Monomachos, who received the imperial crown the day after his marriage.

there that they took up the labors of asceticism. Initially, the two brothers according to the flesh, Niketas and John, were alone. By and by, they were joined by the blessed Joseph.

We cannot say exactly from what part of the island they hailed. Perhaps they originated from Chora or some other village? But—alas!—as much as we are desirous to know their birthplace and parentage, it remains unknown from where these God-planted trees sprung forth. We are not sure what events might have invigorated their desire to flee the world. There is no record extant to inform us what enlivened them to enroll in the wrestling-school of ascetic toils and contests. Had they dwelt in a monastery and then from a desire for more solitude took up residence in a rough cave on Provation Mountain? It goes without saying that their outdoor life in that rugged wilderness retreat was fraught with difficulties and deprivations. We do know that they persevered courageously, adding and perfecting the virtues by their practises. However, instead of speaking of what has not been left to us, let us recount what we have found written regarding these men of God.

Saints Niketas, Joseph, and John

The righteous and ever-blessed fathers, Niketas, John, and Joseph, had separated themselves from all that was material and carnal. They were diligent and persistent in their ascetical exercises, living only to please God. They patiently and painstakingly adhered to their rule of prayer and continence. They devoted themselves to chanting and prayer. They disdained all that was earthly and temporal. Their gaze was fixed solely on heavenly and everlasting things. The thrice-blessed ones had as their singular desire such endeavors as these: to cleanse their souls of every worldly longing and to exercise themselves in those virtues that were great and lofty. As a result of their pursuits, their ascetical conduct of life became exquisitely refined by a continual progress toward consummate perfection that vied with the divine life of Anthony the Great; for it was the latter whom these fathers held up as the model of what a monk and his works ought to be. In consequence of their austere training and ill-plight, by which they mortified their bodies, they also added the hardship of eating only one time during the week. What was their fare after so many days of fasting? A little bread and a small amount of water for drinking. When they did take their ease for a short spell, they slept on the ground for what seemed moments. They had neither bedding nor blankets. They spent most of their time in standing through all-night vigils and remaining watchful in prayer throughout the day. Do not think that they found any real rest in that desolate place. No, brethren. The site was full-laden with hard work, bodily pain and suffering, and distress. The topography of that mountain, indeed, was heavily punctuated with rocks and was difficult to traverse. As for water, there was no supply close at hand. We should also mention the high altitude of the mountain and its exposure to mighty and violent winds. During the winter, when there was heavy snowfall, the blessed ones had nought but their primitive subterranean cave for shelter.[18]

By these ascetic tournaments in which they entered, they were accounted worthy to see visions. Who can describe what they perceived or what contemplative states they entered while at prayer? Such sublime matters are not known to us, brethren. Those things, however, which are written and are certain give us to understand to what degree these blessed men were holy and God-bearers. Living as they did in perfect sobriety and purity upon that mount, an extraordinary occurrence took place. Many times, by night, they discerned a radiant light peering through the profusion of trees in the forest. They were wishing to know from whence this light emanated. For they distinguished something glowing on the eastern cliffs of the mountain, but it would disappear in the thick bushes and indigenous trees. Prompted by God, they went down into the forest in eager pursuit; for like Moses of old before the burning bush, each man said, "I will go near and see this great sight [Ex. 3:3]." As they were approaching the spot that had been resplendent with light, it was concealing itself so that they could not discover from where it was issuing. Those blessed

[18] The cave on Provation is exactly the same spot where the Hermitage of the Holy Fathers (Hagion Pateron) now lies. It boasts of some important religious wall-paintings. The altitude of the monastery is 660 meters (38°22′N 26°02′E). In 1688, the cave was given to the Monk Jeremias, a Cretan, who constructed the temple and built living quarters. Later, in 1868, the holy Monk Pachomios, from the village of Elata in Chios, asked for the buildings and converted them into the largest monastic center on the island. Religious painting began to flourish in 1900. Presently, four monks live in the cloister. Entrance is forbidden to women after sunset.

hermits were left wondering and marvelling. They, therefore, decided to burn that section of the forest with this idea in mind: "If the light is from God, then the place about it will not be consumed but rather be made manifest." Such was their thinking, which plan they began to put into effect. The result was that they started burning the copse in the thickest and shadiest part.

Miraculous Icon of Virgin at Nea Moni

While the shrubs and bushes in that section of the thicket caught fire, the flames leaped to and fro with no small vehemence devouring the brush and underwood. As the burn progressed, it arrived and halted before one myrtle bush.[19] The fire was then quenched and that evergreen shrub stood unscathed by the conflagration. Behold the wonder! As the burning bush of old abided unconsumed before Moses, so the myrtle tree remained untouched by those fearful flames that found combustible all its neighboring trees in that wood. The fathers observed that the heat of the fire neither incinerated nor withered the dew-laden and lustrous leaves of the myrtle. As the unburnt bush of old was a type of the all-holy Theotokos,[20] in like manner did the myrtle not burn. That shrub

[19] The plant may grow more than 5 meters (about 16.5 feet) high, possessing many small, translucent, oil-bearing glands. There are two species of flowering plants native to southern Europe and north Africa: evergreen shrubs or small trees having leaves about 3 to 5 centimeters in length. The flowers have five petals and sepals, and an amazingly large number of stamens. Petals are usually white, with globose bluish or purplish black many-seeded berries. The flowers are pollinated by insects, and the seeds are dispersed by birds which feed on the berries. Solitary white flowers are borne on short stalks. There are yellow-fruited and white-fruited varieties cultivated for ornament. The plants are grown for myrtle oil, used in perfume manufacture and as a condiment.

[20] The flaming bush that remained unconsumed had disclosed to Moses the secret mystery that would come to pass in the Virgin. As the bush received the fire and fed the flames but was not consumed, so did the Virgin conceive the Son and lend Him flesh. She provided nourishment to the immaterial Fire, and drew incorruptibility in return. These things seen by Moses prefigured her maternity and delivery, so that even

(continued...)

resisted the power of the flame, because it bore within its branches and foliage the sacred type, that is, the holy icon of the all-pure Mother of God and our Lady. This will soon be demonstrated by what follows.

Straightway, the venerable fathers observed how the flame stopped spreading and extinguished itself. This inexplicable phenomenon appeared against its natural course, given the extent of the forest and the combustible material in ready supply. They were, therefore, curious to learn the cause of the fire's remarkable cessation. As they drew closer to get a better look, they were astonished at how the myrtle stood as an impregnable wall before the furious flames and denied any further advance. They investigated the myrtle and found an icon nestled in its branches. There was depicted the Mother of God, Mary, with arms extended, who was portrayed without the Only-begotten and divine Infant, our Lord Jesus Christ. What they had thus far witnessed with their own eyes was real and could not be doubted. But how and for what reason the wonderworking icon was perched upon the boughs of the myrtle, they knew not. They conceived the notion that it was probably hidden away thereon by an iconophile from the time of the iconoclasts. There was also the possibility that some solitary of ancient times sheltered it within the bush. Then again, by divine power, the Theotokos herself might have deposited it in that place, in accordance with her wish that a monastery should be founded at the site—which is precisely what came to pass. Now as the fathers made this discovery of the icon, their joy was abundant. They firmly believed that the light went forth from the Theotokos. They, thereupon, dislodged the icon, exercising profound reverence. They conveyed the sacred image, accompanied by hymns to the Virgin, to their dwelling place, that is, inside their hallowed cave.

What happened after this finding and transfer of the icon? Did the wonder end here? Were they only meant to uncover the icon of the Panagia, the all-holy one, and then continue their lives as before? No, brother Christians, no! For them this was neither their sole function nor their finale in the matter. Much rather another miracle followed upon this miracle. It is a marvel great and worth the telling. Our Lady Theotokos, in a mysterious manner that was unexpected and extraordinary, exhibited ere long to those righteous monks why it pleased her to be found surrounded by that fragrantly aromatic and verdant myrtle. The most holy Theotokos' purpose was this: the location of her icon was the site upon which a majestic church was to be built. It was to become a spiritual fold for the rational sheep of her Son and God. Now the actual building of the sacred monastery, which became a reality, took place in this wise. It was for this cause that the icon discovered by the fathers and brought back to their cave was wont to vanish, by divine power, and situate itself amid

---

[20](...continued)
after childbirth she remained ever-virgin.

the branches of that small myrtle tree. Thus, the icon returned to where it was first found. Now this shuttling took place many times. The venerable fathers came to perceive that the Theotokos had chosen the spot as a habitation for herself. They, therefore, set about building with their own hands, as much as they were able, a small church adjacent to the myrtle. The sacred precinct was dedicated to the Mother of God. Within the church they settled the divine icon. This was done in company with the chanting of psalms and odes of thanksgiving to God's Birthgiver, who elected to reveal her holy icon to them.

It was about that time, when these events occurred on Chios, that Constantine Monomachos was exiled to the East Aegean island of Mytilene (Lesvos), by Emperor Michael Paphlagon.[21] Monomachos sojourned there until the reign was resumed by the Porphyrogennetos or "purple-born" family, that is, the sisters Zoe and Theodora, in 1042.[22] It was during their reign that it pleased God not only to deliver Monomachos from banishment but also to call him to the highest secular office in the realm. The holy fathers, meanwhile, as they were in quietude at Chios, knew the future by divine revelation. They foreknew that Monomachos would be recalled out of exile to the capital. The divinely enlightened fathers, Niketas and Joseph, traveled north by boat to nearby Mytilene and became acquainted with Monomachos. The unhappy Monomachos listened to the fathers. He told the fathers that he hoped for nothing but rather expected the worst. The venerable fathers attempted in every manner to console him that they might curb his grief. They left him, saying that when their words came to pass and he was at the head of the empire at

---

[21] The 11th C. intellectual, historian, philosopher, and Monk Michael Psellos (Psellus) records in his *Chronographia* about the exile and the mistress who followed Monomachos: "Constantine was driven from the city. His punishment was relegation to the island of Mytilene, and there for seven years—the exact length of Michael's reign—he endured his misfortune. Michael Kalaphates, like Paphlagon, inherited the emperor's hatred of the young man....Whatever the reason, Constantine and Sclerina were so much in love with each other that both found separation intolerable, even when they were threatened with misery; for when Constantine went into exile, this woman still remained at his side. With loving care, she tended his wants....*Fourteen Byzantine Rulers*, trans. by E. R. A. Sewter (NY/UK: Penguin Books, 1966), Book Six, pp. 164, 181.

[22] Michael Psellos, an eyewitness, records: "So the empire passed into the hands of the two sisters (Porphyrogennitae princesses), and for the first time in our lives we saw the transformation of the women's quarters (*gynaeconitis*) into an emperor's council chamber. What is more, both the civilian population and the military caste were working in perfect harmony under the empresses, and more obedient to them than to any proud overlord issuing arrogant commands. In fact, I doubt if any other family was ever so favored by God as theirs....For a while the sisters preferred to govern alone." Ibid., p. 155.

Constantinople, he should remember them; that is, those hermits who, divinely enlightened by the Holy Spirit, disclosed his future. Indeed, what the fathers predicted came to pass quickly.

But how did Monomachos receive these tidings? While he was being tempered by banishment and misfortune, perhaps his heart skipped at this unhoped-for elevation? He speculated: was it possible that, one day, as sovereign, he might come to enjoy those great and worldly good things associated with the crown? Though this imagining seemed fanciful to him, nevertheless it was also cheering. He then mused upon how long it would be before it came to pass. Then he gazed upon the fathers. They appeared to him to be plain in dress and speech. But were they prophets? He could not envision himself back in the queen of cities; and he told the fathers as much. He said that what they forecasted was strange and unbelievable. He admitted that he entertained no hopes of being released or rescued from his current misfortune and peril. He said he anticipated that in the end the authorities would hang him. This phobia caused him much perturbation so that he wept profusely. Although the fathers listened to him patiently, still they possessed unshaken trust in the revelations they received. They believed they had been informed of the truth. They opposed and contradicted Monomachos' disquietude. Monomachos believed the fathers to be well-intentioned. He thought to be gracious to the kindness they showed him. Even though he did not believe that he would be freed, yet he promised that should their words come to pass that he would remember them. And since the fathers spoke to him of the miraculous appearance of the icon of the Theotokos, Monomachos added that he would build a grand monastery for the icon should he ever be crowned emperor. The former senator then gave his pledge to the fathers from Chios. He asked that they remember him in their holy prayers. The fathers, truly illumined by the Spirit, thanked him and lightened somewhat his heart's sorrow with these words: "Take courage, O master, and have good hopes, because not before long shall our beneficent God hand over the kingdom to thee. So instead of sorrow, receive great joy. Take comfort from thy sorrow in this prediction which we have declared beforehand; for it was made manifest to us from God."

So then, even though Monomachos thought his succession to the throne high-flown and their prophecy improbable, he was heartened. But by degrees, he began accepting the fathers' clairvoyance. This came about when he noticed that the fathers' second sight was announced to him without the use of any artifice or craftiness, but rather they spoke with simplicity and goodness. At length, he conceived a high opinion of the venerable Niketas and Joseph. He was sure that they were neither deceivers nor tricksters, but rather he was certain that they were God-bearing and holy men who spoke the truth. He allowed himself a reverie about the fulfillment of their words and said to them,

"O honorable fathers in God, if I should succeed and come to reign even as you have predicted and promised me, whatsoever would be in my power to bestow as a benefaction, you will receive it from me."[23] The fathers replied candidly that their poverty and non-possessiveness was their boast, saying also that "we are in need of nothing, O great autocrat, and we are not seeking anything." After this, they piously spoke to him in detail regarding what took place at the myrtle in the forest.

After the fathers recounted all that took place, they put forth a proposal requiring imperial assistance. Hearken to what the fathers said to Monomachos: "With regard to the icon of which we have spoken to thee, there is need for a monastery and spacious temple, one that is lofty and beautiful, constructed and executed skillfully. For such a monastery and church would be an imperial gift to the Mother of God and not a work performed artlessly and in an offhand manner. Since it must needs be the home of this wonderworking icon, let us build a splendid monastery and church." Monomachos then remarked to the righteous fathers, "O most holy fathers, if I were to receive the reins of the empire as you have proclaimed, be assured that you would receive great contributions from me. Moreover, the church of the all-pure Theotokos shall receive befitting attention for a harmonious composition. Indeed, the

---

[23] It appears that the same revelation was also vouchsafed to Saint Lazarus of Mount Galesios near Ephesus (commemorated the 7th of November).

Psellos hints of this knowledge that was either heard already by Monomachos or confirmed after the visit of the Chian fathers. He writes about Constantine Monomachos' mistress, Sclerina, who followed him and attended to all his needs. She was the niece of his late wife of the famous Scleros family. Psellos notes that "Sclerina put at Constantine Monomachos' disposal all her possessions, gave him all manner of comfort, and lightened the bitter load of his affliction at Mytilene. The truth is, she, no less than himself, was sustained by hopes of power; nothing else mattered if only in the future she might share the throne with her husband. I say 'husband' because at that time she was convinced that their marriage would be legally sanctioned, and all her desires fulfilled when Constantine, as emperor, overruled the laws. When one of these ambitions was realized (his elevation to the throne), but circumstances did not permit the realization of the second, because the Empress Zoe seized all power for herself, she despaired altogether not only of her cherished hopes but even of life itself. Nevertheless, the emperor did not forget his beloved, even after his accession. Regardless of the consequences, regardless of Zoe's jealousy, turning a deaf ear to all entreaty, he brushed aside every counsel that would frustrate his wishes." Ibid., p. 181. (Thus, Monomachos kept his mistress. As for Psellos, an eyewitness to many of the improprieties in the royal household, he became disgusted and disappointed; he eventually became a monk.) Now whether Saint Lazarus prophesied before or after the coming of the Chian fathers, we do not know. But it is evident that the couple entertained sanguine hopes of future power and glory.

specifications shall far exceed whatsoever you might hope for it to be." Constantine gave his pledge with all willingness and eagerness. As for our venerable fathers, though they were simplehearted and undesigning and not given to dissembling, yet words alone would not suffice. The God-bearers desired a more palpable guarantee. Without dissimulation they sought his pledge. They, consequently, received his signet ring as a souvenir that sealed his promise. The fathers, thus assured of his sponsorship toward honoring the Theotokos, returned to their homeland—the island of Chios.

Not much time elapsed before the death of the two emperors, that is, Michael IV Paphlagon and his nephew, Michael V Kalaphates, in 1041 and 1042, respectively. Empress Zoe, former wife of Romanos III and Michael IV, had been exiled by Kalaphates. She returned to the capital and took up the scepter of government, as she had no brother or son.[24]

---

[24] Zoe (b. 978, d. 1050), heiress of the Macedonian Dynasty, was the middle sister of the three daughters of Emperor Constantine VIII. Evdokia, the eldest, whose face was disfigured by smallpox, entered a convent. Zoe, at fifty years old, married for the first time the city prefect Romanos Argyros. After his death, she married a younger man, Michael IV, who suffered from epilepsy. His death brought the regime of the Paphlagonian family to an abrupt conclusion. Kalaphates came into power but crammed his brief reign with blunders and excesses. The population, meanwhile, was still loyal to the dynasty of Zoe and Theodora (the youngest sister). Kalaphates was deposed and blinded. The sisters ruled jointly from April of 1042. The younger sister came out of the Petrion Convent. The claim of women to rule in their own right was no longer questioned. Zoe, at sixty-four, took a third husband on the 11th of June that same year: the eminent senator Constantine Monomachos. Among his lavish foundations were the Monastery of Nea Moni on Chios and the Constantinopolitan Monastery of Saint George at Mangana. See George Ostrogorsky's *History of the Byzantine State*, trans. from the German by Joan Hussey (NJ: Rutgers University Press, 1957), pp. 284-289.

But, eventually, according to Psellos, Constantine exhausted the treasury of every obol. Zoe's apartment in the palace was the scene of a laboratory with a host of burning braziers. It was there that she consumed most of her time, developing, improving, and bottling perfumes and unguents. As we said, Constantine kept a mistress, Sclerina, who previously followed him into exile. When Constantine was building the Mangana Monastery and the campus, a grand building endeavor, he used a number of pretexts to see his mistress. He used to tell the royal sisters that he needed to supervise some building detail. He went out several times a month. He tried to keep the intrigue of his assignations a secret, in order to avoid open scandal, but as emperor he could hardly move about the city unnoticed and unescorted. He took certain individuals of Zoe's faction and had Sclerina set a banquet for them. A table, laden with delicacies, was ready for them outside while he was with his mistress. As the meetings increased, the menu to the banquets was chosen by the emperor's escort beforehand. Thus, all their demands were satisfied. Of course, they knew very well the real reason

(continued...)

She did not waste much time sending a ship to fetch Constantine Monomachos to Constantinople.[25] The old empress had already considered a few candidates for marriage. At last, after several fruitless attempts, the empress remembered a former friend, Constantine Monomachos. He was related to her first husband. She remembered that some twelve or thirteen years earlier, Constantine cut an impressive and important figure at court. He was

---

[24](...continued)
for the charade. Some were even indignant at the way that Zoe was being treated, but it did not outweigh their own desires. When Constantine exhibited some shame in seeing his lady-love, these so-called friends helped smooth the path for him, each suggesting a different pretext so as to win his favor. At length, Constantine lost all sense of propriety. He had his mistress move into the palace. He had the royal sisters sign a treaty with Sclerina. His bedchamber was thus flanked by the sisters and Sclerina was across the hall. As for Zoe, as she aged, she lost her capacity for vehement hatred. Sclerina, who had hitherto been only a lover, was now introduced to the private apartments of the palace, and called "milady," and even "empress"—and that officially. While most were greatly distressed at the way in which Zoe had been deceived and neglected and despised, she herself evinced no emotion whatever.

[25] Psellos speaks of his emperor: Regarding Constantine, there was in him no gaucherie in society. He made himself perfectly agreeable to the sisters. When he came to power, honors were conferred indiscriminately on a multitude of persons who had no right to them. Many earned their honors simply because Constantine was amused by their witticisms. So then, the privileges, much coveted in the old days, were now distributed with a generous abandon that knew no limits, with the consequence that the recipients lost distinction. Constantine won everyone's affections by an art that was conscious yet unaffected. In all fairness, in his efforts to charm there was no trace of insincerity. He had a genuine desire to cultivate friendship, by deliberately setting out to please. To him, the exercise of power meant as follows: rest from his labors, fulfilment of desire, and relaxation from strife. Even from the start, he ruled with neither vigor nor discretion. Zoe was openhanded, Constantine generous, and Theodora parsimonious. Constantine forgave his former accusers and sought no retribution.

He, nevertheless, had no clear conception of the nature and responsibility of monarchy. As for the administration of public affairs, and the privilege of dispensing justice, and the superintendence of the armed forces, they were delegated to others. "A healthy animal, with a thoroughly strong constitution, is not altered in a moment at the first symptoms of illness. So with the empire in the reign of Constantine. It was by no means moribund and its breathing was still energetic. The neglect from which it was suffering seemed an insignificant item. For only by slow degrees was the malady growing until, reaching a crisis, the patient was thrown into utter confusion and complete disorder....The emperor, seeking recreation in a multitude of pleasures, was preparing the then healthy body of his empire for a thousand maladies to attack it in the years to come." *Fourteen Byzantine Rulers*, pp. 179, 180.

handsome, elegant, and a good speaker. He also had a talent for amusing her. She was so captivated with him at that time that there was even some gossip about them. Michael IV, the previous emperor, immediately after his accession, took the precaution of exiling this compromising friend. Zoe never really forgot him. She seized the opportunity afforded by the revolution of 1042 to end Constantine's disgrace. She first appointed him governor of Greece. But she was planning to exalt him further.[26]

Christ Enthroned, Flanked by the Autocrats Constantine IX Monomachos and Zoe (*Hagia Sophia*)

The marriage ceremony was duly performed. It was a third marriage for both parties. It was a marriage of high policy. Thus, in 1042, the day after the nuptials, he received imperial authority and was crowned, even as the fathers on Chios had prophesied. He was, indeed, at the helm of the empire. As for those venerable fathers, they learned of the coronation. They boarded a ship bound for the capital. They gained an audience with the emperor, Constantine IX Monomachos. Holding the former senator's signet ring in view, they reminded him of his pledge to build a church to the Queen of all. Monomachos, hearing their words and seeing his ring, was moved and exclaimed joyfully to the fathers, "You have brought to my remembrance, by means of the ring, my promise."

Nea Moni

The emperor, at that point, showed, with all his heart, much respect to the venerable fathers; for their prophesy was fulfilled. He honored his pledge, giving the construction his royal patronage. Monomachos invited the fathers to tour the city and select a church, except Hagia Sophia, to be used as a model for the upcoming building project at Chios. The fathers preferred the Church of Saints Sergius and Bacchus. The church, therefore, at Chios was to be built in an octagonal shape. Monomachos had commissioned an ingenious architect, together with the best craftsmen who would be under the latter's supervision. Shiploads of ornate marble columns, luminous and splendid, together with other porphyry-colored marble that reflected light as a mirror, fitting for an imperial edifice, were also conveyed to Chios. The holy fathers, meanwhile, put out to sea. They came into the harbor of Chios, also named Chios, on the east coast and fourteen kilometers from the building site at nearly the center of

[26] Charles Diehl, "Zoe Porphyrogenita," *Byzantine Portraits* (NY: Alfred A. Knopf, 1927), pp. 257, 258.

the island. The fathers toiled earnestly and untiringly at this great work to erect a most majestic church where beauty, symmetry, and harmony pervaded every part. The building expenditure was afforded by imperial pecuniary aid. After twelve years, an architectural marvel emerged in the midst of the island, so that it could easily have been numbered with the seven wonders of the world.[27]

The Schism of 1054[28]

If we were to pinpoint the final schism between Rome and Constantinople from the last mentioning of a pope in the diptychs of Constantinople, then the date would be 1009. The last recorded pope was John XVIII (1004-1009). Pope John's successor, Pope Sergius IV (1009-1012), had sent his Systatic Letter to Constantinople. With his customary synodical letter on taking possession of the papal throne, his profession of faith contained the *Filioque*.

---

[27] The main advantage of such a design was that there is no need for columns to support the dome. Thus, the faithful have a clear prospect of the iconostasion. The church, dedicated to the Virgin Theotokos for the Monastery of Nea Moni (Nea Mone) or the New Monastery, was spared no expense. Outer and inner narthexes and a low bema form parts of the structure. The inner narthexes and the bema are internally sheathed with local red marble and mosaic. The overall design is of Constantinopolitan origin. The mosaics include an orant Virgin in the apse and eight Great Feasts in the deep squinches of the drum. The inner narthex is guarded by military saints and martyrs. There is also a defense tower and cistern. A steeple was built much later, in 1512. The inner narthex is ten meters long by four meters wide, and is approximately 24 spans in height. The floor was covered with purple pieces of marble, of which only a few remain to this day. The main church is square in shape, with each side about ten meters long. Much of the original church was destroyed with the 1881 earthquake. The miracle-working icon of the Virgin, however, still adorns the iconostasion. The altar is ten meters in length and four meters wide. The eastern side of the altar leads to three semi-circular shells. As for the monastery, cells furnished housing for one thousand monks. The cells formed an inner wall, in the middle of which used to stand the church. The refectory, to the south of the church, is an oblong building. The cistern, for the collection of rainwater, lies on the northwest side of the church and is decorated with ceramics. There are two chapels, one to Saint Panteleimon and one to the Holy Cross. The cemetery and its chapel, dedicated to Saint Luke, was built later. There is also an aqueduct to move drinking water and its nearby fountain. The mosaics are examples of pure Byzantine art. They were made of natural glass or stones. Andreas S. Axiotakis, *The New Monastery (Nea Moni) of Chios*, trans. by Despina Georganopoulou (Chios, 1982).

Monomachos was also careful to create chrysobulls and *sigillia*. There were also charters of later emperors. Nea Moni was also exempted from episcopal jurisdiction. She was granted the right to invite any bishop for the ordination of priests and deacons. *The Oxford Dictionary of Byzantium*, s.v. "Nea Mone."

[28] See "Events Leading to the Schism of 1054," *The Lives of the Pillars of Orthodoxy*, compiled by Holy Apostles Convent (Buena Vista, CO, 2000), pp. 120 ff.

Naturally, Patriarch Sergios of Constantinople (999-1019) excluded the name of Pope Sergius IV from Orthodox diptychs.[29] Henceforward, no pope was ever mentioned in the diptychs again. Not wishing to exaggerate the importance of the 1009 date, of which several may be critical, it still must be remembered that the date of 1054 was a culmination of earlier developments. The lists on the diptychs were incomplete, because for many generations Constantinople received no Systatic Letters from the eastern patriarchates under Moslem domination, despite full communion with them. It was not until the end of the ninth century that the improvement of international communications allowed the hierarchs to keep in regular touch with one another.[30]

In the early eleventh century, in spite of the difference over the Creed as the first symptom of danger likely to arise in the future, there was no feeling that the unity of Christendom had been broken. With the election to the papal throne of Leo IX (1049-1054), the nephew of Emperor Henry III, the Church of Rome extended her activities over southern Italy into Byzantine territory, where were found both Greek and Latin communities. Leo IX also laid claim to Sicily, a territory considered to be Byzantine, although occupied by the Arabs. After the pope convoked a council at Siponto in 1050, where a great number of decrees were voted with a view of furthering reform, some of the decrees were directed against Greek liturgical practises which had been established in Italy. An active campaign to halt this was launched in all of the provinces, including Apulia, a Byzantine area.[31]

When the Normans began to overrun the Lombard principalities and to approach the frontiers of Rome, Pope Leo IX decided that it would be prudent to ally himself with the Byzantine emperor, Constantine IX Monomachos. The emperor agreed to suppress the Normans, realizing that a military and political alliance was necessary to protect Byzantine territory.[32]

Now Constantine IX, despite his wayward private life, made an important and far-reaching decision: he appointed the Orthodox Michael I Keroularios as patriarch (1043-1058). Keroularios had previously been involved in the 1040 plot against Emperor Michael IV Paphlagon. In order to avoid punishment, Keroularios became a monk. Now Keroularios espoused the rigorism of Saint Symeon the Theologian. He was in conflict with liberal intellectuals such as Psellos. It was in the early 1050s that the conflict and chasm between Constantine and Rome widened. The controversy centered

---

[29] Francis Dvornik, *Byzantium and the Roman Primacy* (NY: Fordham University Press, 1966), p. 127; George Ostrogorsky, *History of the Byzantine State*, p. 296.

[30] Steven Runciman, *The Eastern Schism* (London: Oxford University Press, 1956, repr.), p. 39.

[31] Dvornik, p. 131.

[32] Runciman, loc. cit.; Dvornik, p. 132.

around azymes, that is, the Latin use of unleavened bread in the eucharistic sacrifice. When the papal legate, Humbert of Mourmoutiers, Cardinal of Silva Candida, arrived in Constantinople for negotiations, Constantine wished to promote an alliance in order to resist the Norman invasion into southern Italy. Neither Humbert nor Keroularios came to an agreement.

Patriarch Michael, meanwhile, understood that Pope Leo was endeavoring to extend the sway of Rome to Sicily and southern Italy and also campaigned against married priests. Further to this, when Keroularios discovered that the Normans, with the approval of Rome, were forbidding Greek usages in the areas that they now controlled, and that reforming synods throughout Italy were denouncing the various churches that maintained Greek customs, he at once ordered the Latin churches in Constantinople to adopt Greek usages. When the Latins in the capital refused, Patriarch Michael ordered their closing at about the end of the year 1052.[33]

Though the patriarch ignored the legates, they were well received by Emperor Constantine. Humbert opened the discussion at once, entering upon the defense of the Latin Church. He made various accusations against the Eastern Church, indicating that she had her own peculiar discipline and her own peculiar abuses as well as the Western Church. Encouraged by the emperor's cordiality, the Latins published the documents they had brought. Cardinal Humbert took the offensive in handling Keroularios' attitude. In an attempt to depose the patriarch, he published a very long letter—as a sort of pamphlet against the patriarch—that was translated into Greek. For the first time the motives of the legates became clear to the Byzantines from the pamphlets and letters of Humbert. Up until that time they had not realized the changes that had taken place in the mentality of the Church of Rome. The extension of absolute and direct authority of the pope over all the bishops and the faithful was, to the Byzantine mind, nothing less than a complete denial of the tradition which they and their ancestors knew. Such power would lead to the abolition of the autonomy of their churches.

The fact that Humbert leaned upon the spurious document of the "Donation of Constantine" was completely unacceptable to the Byzantines. What Humbert had to say was too novel, and his criticism of Orthodox liturgical usages offended their traditional and even patriotic sentiments. Humbert's behavior was undiplomatic and offensive. He failed to turn the Byzantines against the patriarch. Indeed, the whole of the Byzantine clergy closed ranks around Keroularios.[34] Patriarch Michael knew that it was a forgone conclusion with the emperor to sacrifice the Church to the papacy in order to obtain some aid for his throne. On the other hand, Emperor Constan-

---

[33] Runciman, pp. 40, 41.

[34] Dvornik, pp. 133, 134.

tine feared that Humbert's wrath might imperil the political alliance that he desired.

Cardinal Humbert's patience ran out. Even though he knew that the pope had died on Saturday, the 16th of July (1054), Humbert and his colleagues, in full view of the congregation in attendance for divine Liturgy, stormed into the Church of Hagia Sophia. After loudly complaining of the obstinacy of Patriarch Michael, they laid on the holy altar a bull, excommunicating Michael Keroularios, Leo of Ohrid, Michael Constantine (the patriarchal chancellor), and all their followers. The bull of excommunication read, in part: "Michael and his followers, guilty of errors and insolence,...along with all heretics, together with the devil and his angels...."[35] They then strode out of the church, ceremoniously shaking its dust off their feet. A deacon then ran after them, imploring them to take back the bull. They refused, and he dropped it in the street. It was picked up and eventually brought before the patriarch.

The document was then translated for the patriarch. It is extraordinary that a man of Humbert's learning could have penned so lamentable a manifesto. The document began by refusing to Keroularios, both personally and as Bishop of Constantinople, the title of Patriarch. Patriarch Michael quickly brought a Greek translation of the bull to the emperor. Constantine Monomachos was profoundly shocked because he had just bid the legates a friendly farewell, hoping that his plan for a political alliance had been achieved. Initially, the emperor would not agree to recall them back to the capital. He then relented, agreeing to send a messenger to ask them for the original Latin version of the bull. The messenger, overtaking them at Selymbria, returned with a copy of the text. The emperor indeed found that the patriarch's translation was correct. The emperor then dispatched another message ordering the legates to return to the capital that they might explain the meaning of it before a synod. The legates refused and continued their trip.[36]

Patriarch Michael was actually distressed at the breach, and he was also anxious about the reaction of the imperial court. The friends of the patriarch had caused the contents of the bull to be publicized throughout the city. The average Byzantine, annoyed by the legates' arrogance, resented the emperor's cordiality toward them. Many were convinced of the emperor's connivance. Demonstrations and riots flared up. Emperor Constantine Monomachos, realizing that public opinion backed the Church against him, announced that he would punish the translators who had collaborated with the legates. The emperor then ordered that a copy of the bull be publicly burned. The riots were then stilled.

---

[35] Migne, *P.L.* 143:1004

[36] Runciman, pp. 48, 49.

Then, on Sunday, the 24th of July, a synod was held to respond to the entire matter. The synod declared that irresponsible men from the west had excommunicated the patriarch and all else who refused to conform with the Latin doctrine about the Holy Spirit and Latin practises of shaving and a celibate priesthood. The text of the bull and Emperor Constantine's decree ordering the bull to be burned were given in full. Humbert and his cohorts were then solemnly excommunicated, for they had come to the "God-guarded city like a thunder, or a tempest, or a famine, or, better still, like wild boars, in order to overthrow truth."[37]

However, the record was carefully drawn up so as to involve neither the papacy nor the Western Church in general. Most wished to believe that Humbert acted beyond his legal power or authority.[38] The failure of Humbert and the other legates did not compromise the papacy. A subsequent pope could have repudiated the actions of these legates without any loss of prestige. The situation was not really any worse between the Churches, except for an increase of ill will. The rupture, thus, began, and Keroularios, thereafter, used the title of Œcumenical Patriarch on his seal.

The tradition has arisen that the events of 1054 mark the final breach between Rome and the Eastern Churches. As we mentioned earlier, though no pope had been mentioned in the diptychs of Constantinople since 1009, yet contact between Rome and Constantinople was not entirely broken. At Constantinople, the episode with Humbert was barely noticed except as an internal crisis in which Patriarch Michael won a victory over Emperor Constantine. However, in the west, the incident was taken very seriously. Why is this? At that time, the reform of the papacy meant that events that concerned Rome were followed with avid interest throughout the Western Church. The sudden Byzantine attack on their usages roused hostile publicity more than anything else.

From that time onward Rome and Constantinople were permanently divided. In the eyes of the west, the Greeks were now merely schismatics who were to be distrusted. The western aim now was to achieve the reunion of the Churches on their own terms by either amicable means or compulsion.[39] Patriarch Michael admonished his flock: "O you who are Orthodox, flee the fellowship of those who have accepted the heretical Latins and who regard

---

[37] A. Lebedev, *History of the Separation of the Churches in the Ninth, Tenth and Eleventh Centuries* (in Russian) 2nd ed. (Moscow, 1905), cited in A.A. Vasiliev, *History of the Byzantine Empire*, Vol. 1 (Madison, WI: The University of Wisconsin Press, 1978), p. 338.

[38] Runciman, pp. 49, 50.

[39] Charles Diehl, *Byzantium: Greatness and Decline*, 9th ed., translated from the French by Naomi Walford (New Brunswick, NJ: Rutgers University Press, 1957), p. 216.

them as the first Christians in the catholic and holy Church of God!" For, as he said a little later, "The pope is a heretic." The charge, consequently, was not only schism but also heresy.[40]

Keroularios remained the dominant figure in the state until Emperor Constantine IX died the following January. His successor was Theodora, his sister-in-law, the last of the Macedonian Dynasty, who was immensely popular. In her desire to have Keroularios cease meddling in state business, she once tartly told Keroularios to mind his own concerns and keep to Church affairs. She reigned for only eighteen months and was succeeded by Michael VI Stratiotikos (1056-1057). He proved a weak emperor, and historians believe that Keroularios took part in the political plot to place on the throne the commander-in-chief, Isaac I Komnenos (1057-1059). However, Komnenos was not subservient to Keroularios when the patriarch began to meddle in civil affairs. Keroularios even went so far as to wear the purple buskins that were the symbol of imperial rank. Keroularios' popularity then began to wane in the capital. No one was ready to tolerate a patriarch who saw himself as emperor. Isaac, secure in the support of the army, quietly deposed Keroularios.

Patriarch Michael Keroularios, honored by some and regarded by others as chief architect of the schism, did not long survive the disgrace of the deposition, and reposed a few days later near the end of 1058. He was immediately canonized by popular acclaim. Emperor Isaac was compelled by public opinion to give him an elaborate funeral. The next patriarch, Constantine III Leichoudes (1059-1063), instituted an annual feast in his honor.[41]

The Western Church demanded that the pope's authority over all the Churches of Christendom should be unquestioned and complete. But the idea of the collegiality was an expression of the universality of the Church. From the Byzantine point of view this safeguarded the rights of the *sacerdotium* which the imperium should never infringe. The four oriental patriarchates did not oppose that the Bishop of Rome should be accorded the honor of first among equals. This was only valid, however, as long as the pope professed the true Faith. He lost this honor when he adopted the heresy of the *Filioque*. Nevertheless, to the Latin mentality, the idea of Pentarchy was considered as being very dangerous and even in direct opposition to the primacy of the Church of Rome.[42]

---

[40] Cerularius, *Panoply* 26.1 (Michel 2:244) and 36.2 (Michel 2:254), cited in Jaroslav Pelikan's *The Spirit of Eastern Christendom (600-1700)*, Vol. 2 (Chicago: The University of Chicago Press, 1977), p. 171.

[41] Kenneth Scott Latourette, *A History of Christianity*, Vol. 1 (NY: Harper & Row, 1975), p. 569.

[42] Dvornik, pp. 103, 104.

Patriarch Michael Keroularios was merely the interpreter of the complaints put forward by Eastern Christendom. He never had enough influence to impose his grievance upon the entire Christian East. What made the strength of Saint Photios the Great (b. ca. 810-ca. 895) against the papacy was that all the churches of the east were with him, in spite of political intrigues, imperial influence, papal violence, and the malice of relentless enemies. Patriarch Michael, on the other hand, possessed neither the learning, nor the genius, nor the virtues of Saint Photios, but he spoke in the name of the east, and the east recognized its own position in his protests against the innovations of Rome.[43]

The Death of Emperor Constantine and the Persecution of the Fathers

Emperor Constantine reposed in January of 1055 in what Saint Nikephoros, the biographer of the saints' lives of today, notes was "with a righteous and good end, as also Zoe, his spouse,"[44] who died earlier in 1050 at Constantinople. As we said, the project took twelve years. Zoe and Monomachos did not live to see the mosaics completed. By reason of Monomachos' death, the work on the church was hindered and even halted before it was finished. However, Theodora, the empress' younger sister, took charge of the project for the next two years. She saw to it that all was magnificently wrought and the building completed. She arranged everything necessary for the monastics' welfare of Nea Moni. She, also, did not fail to confer many gifts and all kinds of helps, so that Nea Moni would be handsomely endowed with rich revenues. She issued an imperial chrysobull, confirming those of Constantine, benefitting the new monastery and assuring its freedom from outside encumbrances and interference.

In like manner, *Despina* Zoe and *Despina* Theodora of the Porphyrogennetos house, who offered many donations, were deemed founders of the monastery.[45] They, too, confirmed that the monastery was free and self-ruling

---

[43] Abbe Guettee, *The Papacy* (NY: Minos Publishing, n.d.), p. 352; Runciman, p. 58.

[44] Evidently, according to Saint Nikephoros, the royal pair repented and made their confessions before the end. Zoe's portrait, flanking Christ with an emperor whose inscription has been altered to show the name of Constantine IX, is still extant in Hagia Sophia. Psellos, who was with the emperor, said he genuinely wept for his wife and revered her memory. Now on account of the sufferings Constantine had endured as an exile, he needed complete rest and absolute tranquillity. He bore excruciating pain and paralysis in his limbs. He admitted that, with his illness, the unruly desires of his heart were repressed. But when he recovered somewhat, his desires remained feverish. Monomachos, after Sclerina died, took another mistress—an Alan (Georgian) princess living at court.

[45] Together with the royal sisters, other favors followed with successors to the throne, so that donations and chrysobulls flowed in. Today, only twenty-one of such documents

(continued...)

in accordance with the command of the emperor. The ever-memorable Theodora, who succeeded alone to the imperial power after her brother-in-law Constantine, took an avid interest even in expanding the present project. After everything was brought together and organized at Nea Moni, a foundation for male monastics, she went on to build a dwelling place for nuns. She found a suitable place at some distance from the men's monastery. The goodly fathers of Nea Moni, with regard to all in which it was entitled—dedications, revenues, and wheat—did not hoard everything for themselves. They shared what came to them with the convent. Thus, the two communities were as two beloved siblings. The distribution for the maintenance, protection, and care was based upon the number of inmates in each community. Hence, there was sufficiency for all, which continued diligently and uninterruptedly.

However, the devil, the enemy of man, could not tolerate seeing progress in the Faith of Jesus Christ. The opening of gymnasiums of virtue and monasteries for the salvation of souls was insufferable to that hideous creature. In order, then, for him to prevent the advancement of good, he instigated certain persons from Chios to slander the saints. The calumny was neither paltry nor bearable but rather grave and unbearable. Those fathers who were most pious and Orthodox were accused of impiety and cacodoxy. This affair is mentioned in the chrysobull of Constantine X Doukas (1059-1067). The administrators appointed by Empress Theodora proceeded against the fathers, without her least knowledge. Since they despised her simply because she was a woman, they deemed her gender inexperienced in matters sacred and political. They, therefore, acted independent of her. The unjust and lawless ones ordered a wrongful exile upon the venerable fathers. After all the cares and concerns with the building projects, the fathers had hoped to resume their former monastic struggles without distraction. But now they were banished to what appeared to be beyond hope of return. Matters only turned worse. The administrators, not satisfied with driving out the fathers, now joined with other monasteries in the nearby village. The monasteries dedicated to God were now seized and converted into secular establishments.

The blessed fathers, therefore, spent time in exile during the reigns of Empress Theodora (1055-1056) and Michael VI Stratiotikos.[46] Afterward, with

---

[45](...continued)
are extant, including chrysobulls from: Isaac I Komnenos, Constantine X Doukas, Romanos IV Diogenes, Michael VII Doukas, Nikephoros III Botaneiates, Alexios I Komnenos, Michael VIII Palaiologos, and Andronikos II Palaiologos (that is, up until 1289).

[46] Theodora, as we know, reigned with her sister Zoe. She was sole empress for about one year. She ruled authoritatively. She, also, appointed clerics, deemed a masculine

(continued...)

the reign of Emperor Isaac Komnenos, the holy fathers found the appropriate opportunity to bring forward their case. Upon imperial examination of the matter, it became evident that the fathers had been victimized by false accusation and, consequently, were wrongly condemned. Isaac, in his chrysobull, accuses and holds blameworthy those appointed during Theodora's reign. This memorable emperor stated that the fathers were not guilty of practising deeds against the sacred canons. Thus, he upheld the fathers' innocence. He respected the fathers as God-fearing ascetics. Therefore, as his predecessor, Constantine IX Monomachos, a builder of Nea Moni, honored the fathers with a chrysobull, Isaac also issued such a document. He incorporated articles breaking up the monasteries of the village and rendered up Nea Moni to both God and the holy fathers. Nea Moni was also made immune from further interference from any person. The monastery property and prerogatives were rendered free and not subject to other authorities. Thus, Isaac upheld all the privileges afforded by Constantine IX and *Despina* Theodora. After enduring a bitter and exhausting exile, the happy fathers returned to Nea Moni and took up the labors of asceticism in silence and retirement. They lived out the remainder of their earthly days in peace and quiet, exercising the virtues and taking up their customary ascetic rule. The first among them to repose was the holy Niketas on the 20th of May. Next, but at another time, was the blessed John. Following him was the sacred Joseph. Their precious relics were laid to rest in the narthex of the church, that which is called Phialion. It was in this precise location that a terrifying account and wonderworking took place against intruding barbarians.

Before the Ottoman yoke, but during the period when the barbarians attacked and raided the island of Chios, there came into the monastery a group of Arab marauders who thought to seize whatever they pleased. They entered into the temple, but they were unable to open the interior doors of the *katholikon* (main church). They were being hindered by the fear of the wondrous and majestic icon of the Master Christ Who was depicted in mosaics above the gate. They exhibited all their frenzy and barbarism in the narthex. Regarding the upright marbles against the wall, of excellent fit and craftsmanship, those abominable maniacs destroyed them. As for the marble of porphyry hue, they took them. They then proceeded to the reliquary containing the august relics of our righteous fathers—Niketas, John, and Joseph. It was constructed of purple-colored marble and gold. While two of the Arabs destroyed the marble that was situated close to the reliquary, they naturally

---

[46](...continued)
privilege, aroused the animosity of Patriarch Michael I Keroularios. As she lay dying, she consented to her officials' choice of the pliable Michael VI. *Oxford*, s.v. "Theodora."

thought to open the sacred chest. The dagger in the hands of one of them, used to pry open the reliquary, suddenly fell and made a clattering sound on the floor. For behold the wonder! There suddenly leaped forth a frightening flame that burned those pitiless barbarians. The evidence of this miracle remains to this day [that is, the time of this writing]. The wall still shows signs of scorching. This proof stands as a perpetual memorial to the miracle. The spoil sustained in that sacred precinct and to the iconography by those sacrilegious heathen was corrected afterward. But the spot by the reliquary remained ruined and without icons. This was the way it appeared until the 1822 catastrophe, of which we shall speak later.

After the passage of many years, there came the Priest-monk Jeremias from Crete. He was in search of an appropriate place to live the hesychastic life. The monks whom he found on the island directed him to Provation Mountain, to the sacred cave where our venerable fathers lived in asceticism. Jeremias went and found the environment acceptable and in accordance with his intention. He, therefore, remained in that cave. He revered the cave, as the sacred and holy spot of ascetical struggles conducted by the previous sanctified occupants. After he made modifications, he transformed the cave. He dedicated a church inside of it, in honor of the names of our venerable Fathers Niketas, John, and Joseph. Pursuant to this undertaking, he also built some cells. This was the making of a hermitage, as a dwelling place for ascetics, in the year 1688. Now while Jeremias dwelt in this retreat as a hesychast, he did not know how and from where he contracted a deadly disease; so that he was at death's door. He despaired of every human remedy. He, thereupon, took refuge in the help of our saints: the patrons of his cave-church. With much exertion, he made his way into the temple. He prostrated himself before the icon of the saints and entreated them to visit him. As he had fallen prone to the ground, he succumbed to a slight slumber. Lo, it appeared to him that the three saints were standing above him! They blessed him and dispelled the odious disease.

Father Jeremias shook off that light sleep. Behold! He found himself completely healthy. He gave glory to God and to the saints, his heavenly benefactors. In thanksgiving to the holy fathers and also as a remembrance of their appearance, he painted, with his own hands, an icon of the three saints even as he saw them in the vision. He made one icon that he placed above the door of his cell and another for the sanctuary. He also painted others. Many persons, even at the writing of this account, recall the incident and still speak of it. But these icons and all the work of Father Jeremias were overturned and reduced during the captivity of Chios, so that the hermitage was desolated.

Now afterward, there came, in the year 1868, the Elder Pachomios from Jerusalem or, more particularly, the Monastery of Saint Savvas. He remodeled the cave and expanded it. After installing the iconostasion, he adorned the area with marble. He also erected a more spacious church with a dome. The precinct became a perfect skete with cells and guest quarters. The chief handiwork of the brethren at the Skete of the Holy Fathers was iconography. They also engaged in other handicrafts generally found at monastic foundations.[47]

This, my fellow Christians, is the account of the righteous lives and virtuous conduct of our holy Fathers Niketas, John, and Joseph. By means of their apostolic zeal, as you have heard, these blessed ascetics forsook all earthly things and followed Christ. By reason of their love for Jesus, these God-inspired fathers submitted to hardships and weariness on Provation Mountain. They fasted and prayed unceasingly. They participated in all-night vigils. They subjected themselves to winter cold and broiling summers. Indeed, they were counted worthy of the grace of prophecy. As ones who have boldness with God, the heavenly King, they showed themselves to be fearless before earthly ones. They were wondrously endowed so that they, as Solomon of old, built a splendid temple. They constructed and established monasteries and coenobia, even as the leading desert fathers of old: Efthymios the Great, Savvas the Sanctified, and Theodosios the Coenobiarch. Saints Niketas, John, and Joseph were established as a type and outline of the monastic life for their island, even as was the great Anthony for Egypt and beyond. The proof of their laborious efforts and blessed industry may be seen in the very beautiful temple and monasteries built for our salvation. They have enriched all the island by their virtue and godliness. Their piety blossoms even to this day in Chios. One may visit the Skete of the Holy Fathers and other monasteries that issued forth as a result of their labors. We, my brethren and fellow Christians, therefore, are obliged to love those venerable fathers, who are celebrated

---

[47] From the Monastery of the Holy Fathers, we follow an asphalt road, which is approximately 200 meters in length. We come to a stone paved road of descending levels of steps that form curves that lead to the Nea Moni Monastery. The pedestrian on the trail takes in a breathtaking view of the town of Chios, as well as the shore of Asia Minor on the horizon. On the elevated peaks of the trail, the ground is rocky with sparse plant life. There are also the remains of burnt pine trees, but there is also evidence of reforestation. Towering trees and cliffs create a beautiful view. As you walk downhill, the foliage thickens. As you approach Nea Moni, the landscape is altered. There are olive trees as well as tall cypress trees. Before reaching the monastery, you will pass the small Church of Saint Luke that is part of the monastery's churchyard. Saint Luke contains underground-arched crypts that have been preserved. Within these crypts, you will find bones neatly kept from the time of the Great Massacre of 1822. The graves of the monks of Nea Moni are also scattered across the church grounds. At Nea Moni, there is also the Church of the Holy Cross, containing the bones from the victims of the Massacre of Chios in 1822 that decimated the island's population.

today, and to revere their memory. We are not only mindful of the good things that they have ushered in for us. We are also grateful for their protection and patronage, since they supplicate God uninterruptedly in our behalf.

O honorable fathers, you were raised up as early teachers of virtue and the monastic life for the island of Chios! You had patiently endured ten thousand toils that we might have the benefit of the Theotokos icon that you wondrously plucked from the boughs of the myrtle. You have set up monasteries for the worship and glory of God, while you were also persecuted for His name's sake. Cease not, O fathers, entreating the Trinity—to Whom is due honor, glory, and dominion unto the ages of the ages—for the salvation of our souls that we, too, might be vouchsafed the kingdom of the heavens. Amen.

Present-day Nea Moni

Some Events and Miracles at Nea Moni

From the time of its inception, in the eleventh century, Nea Moni and Chios had hosted many intruders: Venetians, Genoese, and then the Turks in 1556. During an invasion, a Goth soldier shot an arrow at the icon of the Virgin. In the company of others inside the church, he witnessed the arrow fly forward and then turn back. As it flew back over his head and those of others, it struck the icon of the resurrection. This icon still exhibits the puncture of the arrow. During a Saracen raid, the icon was successfully hidden in the village of Pyrgi, some twenty-two kilometers south of the island's capital.

At another time, a Chian ship encountered a storm of great magnitude. The ship's captain, envisioning the icon of the Virgin in his mind's eye, invoked her to save his crew and vessel. He promised the Mother of God that should she save them, he would present a torch as large as the ship's mast to her monastery. He, suddenly, beheld the Virgin through the waves. He discerned that she was holding in her hands a string and piece of wood. She then vanished beneath the waves. Instantly, the tempest abated and the ship was brought safely to land. How surprised was everyone when they disembarked and discovered that a hole that would have sunk their ship had been miraculously patched. The captain distinguished that the repair to the hull was made with the same string and wood that the Virgin had been holding. Consequently, not only the captain but also the crew made a pilgrimage to Nea Moni and offered the promised torch.

During the hegemony of the Turks on the island, a certain Turkish woman desired to visit Nea Moni—though women were barred entry. She went in any event. But as she was going, she was informed that her villa was burning. She, at that very moment, could only think of her jewels. She promised the Virgin that should she rescue her jewelry, she would present her with a golden robe. The Turkish woman hastened to her home and found that her bedchamber and jewels were intact. She, straightway, sent a gold-embroidered dress to the monastery.

In 1732, Priest-monk Makarios of Nea Moni was approached by one of the new monks who asked that he be ordained. Makarios declined, saying he was young and inexperienced. The young monk left and managed to receive ordination elsewhere. When he returned to Nea Moni, he asked for permission to serve. Makarios said that it would be sinful. The young monk ignored the warning and served Vespers. The following morning, he did not appear in church for the divine Liturgy. He was found dead in his cell.

In 1802, during the Turkish occupation, two Muslim sisters, the daughters of the Turkish *archon* (ruler), Mamunis, converted to Orthodoxy. Nea Moni suffered reproach from the father, the Moslem-Turkish ruler of the island. The monastery, consequently, was fined 800,000 piasters. The fathers, rather than betray the two new daughters of Christ, paid the exorbitant sum by selling most of the monastery's lands. Together with this penalty, they also lost their independence and privileges.

In 1822, the island's population was depleted. While women and children hid at Nea Moni, the Turks attacked the monastery. They slew the unarmed civilians, numbering eighteen hundred as well as two hundred monks.[48] The Turks proceeded to loot the holy compound. They set fire to the magnificent church, thus consuming most of the mosaic work. Later that year, seamen of the Turkish fleet also started another fire. Throughout these attacks of arson, the icon of the Virgin remained unscathed. Now there used to be a small reliquary coffin containing the relics of the three hermits, Niketas, John, and Joseph. The reliquary was destroyed in 1822. The sacred bones of one of the hermits survived, but the identity of these relics is not known. The relics of the surviving father are kept in a special showcase inside the main building of the Church.

In 1822, the Turks also plundered a monastery carpet that was a work of art, designed by the celebrated artist Pyrinos Antonios. It had been commissioned in 1742 by Abbot Neophytos. Now the Turks sold it to some

[48] The charnel house, with the skulls and bones of the Orthodox suffering martyrdom during this massacre, is still open for veneration.

Christians, who donated the carpet to the Church of the Holy Sepulcher at Jerusalem. Bishop Peter Misael, who was at Jerusalem, recognized the heirloom of Nea Moni. When two monks, Makarios and Gregory, from that Chian monastery came to the holy city, the bishop gifted them the carpet which they returned to their monastery.

In 1828, the invasion of Chios by the French commander Fevier, brought about a third attack by the Turks. The monastery was set on fire, while the Monk Gregory Photinos took flight with the icon of the Virgin and hid on the roof of the monastery tower.

During the Turkish occupation, the monastery was governed by the *demogerondes*, a group of rich educated citizens. In the beginning, one of the monastery brothers was elected hegumen every five years, and, afterward, every two years. Since there were no emperors, the patriarchs assumed responsibility for Nea Moni, so that it became dependent on the patriarchate. It had been entitled "Stavropegion" until 1859, when the distinction was removed.

In the latter half of the nineteenth century, fire again ravaged the monastery. The icon of the Virgin was later found hanging from the bishop's throne. Again, it remained unharmed.

In 1881, an earthquake struck the area. There was damage to the church and mosaics—since the dome caved in—and to the surrounding structures. This last catastrophe left the monastery forlorn and forgotten.

In 1950, Bishop P. Phostinis established women monastics at Nea Moni. From that time, Nea Moni has been a convent. The same bishop also moved the feast day of the convent from the 15th of August to the 23rd of that same month for the leave-taking of the Feast of the Dormition.[49]

Together with Saint Nikephoros of Chios (d. 1821), who was hegumen of Nea Moni, Saint Nectarios of Aegina (d. 1920) also was tonsured here and ordained to the diaconate.

On the 20th of May, the holy Church commemorates the Recovery and Translation of the sacred Relics of our holy father among the saints, NICHOLAS the Wonder-worker, Bishop of Myra of Lycia.[50]

---

[49] A. Axiotakis, *The New Monastery*, pp. 15-21.

[50] The present account of the transfer of the precious relics of Saint Nicholas was translated from the Slavonic by Nikodemos the Hagiorite. He inserted it into his own *Synaxaristes* from whence we have borrowed it and presented herein, revised and abridged. A record of this translation is found in a 14th-C. manuscript at the Monastery of Grottoferrata (B. s. IV, folio 118). Nikodemos composed a complete service with (continued...)

Nicholas, our righteous father among the saints, Bishop of Myra of Lycia and wonder-worker, is commemorated today in regard to the translation of his holy relics that occurred in 1087. Now during the reign of the pious Emperor Alexios I Komnenos (1081-1118),[51] when Nicholas III Grammatikos

---

[50](...continued)
canon for the event of the translation of the saint's relics. This is preserved in a *kellion* of Saint Nicholas known as Barberados, in the vicinity of Karyes on Mount Athos. Another service exists in a manuscript at Kafsokalyvia, which has been printed several times. Two additional services were composed, also, to commemorate this event: one by Victor Klapazaras, and the other by an anonymous author. In another manuscript, in the Monastery of Grottoferrata (B 6 IV, folio 168), there is a canon written for the precious relics of Saint Nicholas that is composed by Stephen. In the same manuscript (leaf 129), there is also found "A sermon for the *anakomide* (carrying away or recovery) of the relics of our glorious father, Saint Nicholas." Among the Russians and Bulgarians, the event is celebrated on the 9th of May. However, in Greece, it is celebrated on the 20th of May. In Kerkyra (Corfu), they have the tradition that, while en route to Bari, the ships paused at Kerkyra and the relics were venerated by the entire population.

There are at least four documents written shortly after the transfer of the relics to Myra in 1087. Though all four were written independently, three of them borrowed from the first document, a Latin rendition, by Nikephoros [*Istoria della vita di S. Nicolo*, ed. Putignani, 1771]. The latter worked for the aristocrats of Apulia, mostly Greeks, who sponsored the new basilica for the relics within the old Greek palace. The second account, also in Latin, is by Archdeacon John at the request of Archbishop Ursus [*De Probatis Sanctorum Vitis*, ed. Surius, 1618]. The archdeacon, also, borrowed data from the Nikephoros version. The third document, written by an anonymous Greek, is based on the two aforementioned documents. The recorder protests the Latin acquisition of the relics, but remarks that the emperors and patriarchs were relieved that the relics were safe from the hands of the Seljuk Moslems. The fourth document, written in Russian by Ephrem (ca. 1089-1091), relied on the report of Archdeacon John. The Russian report discusses the grim situation in Lycia before the translation of the relics, reproaching the Turks for their scorched earth warfare from Antioch to Jerusalem. The Russian account describes the massacres, plunders, arson, and slavery that resulted from the Muslim invasion. This version confirms not only that Saint Nicholas appeared to an Orthodox priest at Bari, ordering him to bring about the transfer, but also that the Barians cooperated in the evacuation of the relics. This, evidently, is the version used by Nikodemos the Hagiorite. Andreas C. George, *In the Footsteps of Saint Nicholas* (Astoria, NY: Seaburn, 2005), pp. 31, 32. See also the 6th of December for the Life.

[51] During Emperor Alexios' reign, the region of Lycia and its metropolis of Myra were threatened by Saracen invaders and Islamists. Many Muslim invaders had already destroyed cities and villages by fire, slaying the citizens or selling them into slavery. Myra fell to the Saracens in 1036. Pilgrims no longer visited the shrine that was
(continued...)

was Patriarch of Constantinople (1084-1111),[52] an Arab Muslim invasion of the Near East took place, the result of which was to the destruction of the Greek Christians. Many were slain or immolated. Their cities and villages were razed as far as Antioch and Jerusalem. The men, women, and children that escaped the sword were eventually caught, imprisoned, and had their goods seized. Such was the plight of Myra in Lycia in southwestern Asia Minor. It was in Myra that the venerable relics of Saint Nicholas were enshrined.[53] All the death and plundering by the infidel occurred by God's permission, because of the sins we commit thereby estranging ourselves from God and His grace. In the words of the psalmist, "they sinned yet more against Him; they provoked the Most High in the wilderness [Ps.77:17]."

Many times, the sins of people harden their hearts; and the incorrigible abide as reprobates. We have heard that God will not even accept the supplication of His own saints. As the Lord said to the Prophet Jeremias, "Though Moses and Samuel stood before My face, My soul could not be toward them: dismiss this people and let them go forth [Jer. 15:1]." Therefore, the city of Myra was devastated along with other cities and villages. However, the church and diocese survived. At that time, God allowed the holy relics of our great Father Nicholas to be taken up and carried away from that blighted area to the large and populous city of Bari (Paros), Italy.[54]

---

[51](...continued)
maintained by a few remaining Greek monks. The Turks, nevertheless, saw that revenues could be derived from the shrine from the few pilgrims that braved entering Myra. Thus, they left the tomb comparatively unscathed. A. C. George, pp. 28-30.

[52] *The Great Synaxaristes* (in Greek) identifies the patriarch of this time to be Nicholas III Kyrdiniates.

[53] The saint was born at Patara, a major port at the mouth of the Xanthos River (Esen Cayi) until it was silted up and turned into a marsh. Traveling a little eastward on the Mediterranean is the famous Church of Saint Nicholas at Myra (36°17′N 29°58′E), which is west of Demre village between Kas and Finike. It was the port in which Saints Paul, Luke, and Aristarchos changed ships on their way to Rome [Acts 27:5]. The original Myraean church dates from the 3rd C. When it collapsed during an earthquake, it was rebuilt by Justinian. The church was connected to a monastery by a wall built by Emperor Constantine IX Monomachos. In 1862, the Russians began reconstructing the church. Turkish archeologists completed the structure in 1963-1964. The entire east side of the building with three naves and the south side have been unearthed. Presently, the church lies seven meters below ground level. The south side appears to have a fourth nave added later. The west side has two chambers, an outer and inner narthex. The saint was buried within a marble sarcophagus toward the south of the middle nave. The Turks also claim to have a few relics which are kept in the Antalya Museum.

[54] This Paros is not to be mistaken with the island that lies in the Aegean Sea.

The transfer of the relics took place for a number of reasons. The first reason was that the holy relics of the saint might not be without honor among men while his holy soul received heavenly reward. The second reason was that those in need might not be deprived of receiving the benefit of the saint's gift of wonderworking, which is like unto a perpetual spring. The third reason was that since a great number of Orthodox Christians fled to the west to escape the Turks, it was their desire to have the saint's relics in their new area that they might not be bereft of God's beneficence through the intercessions of His Saint Nicholas. Thus, the translation took place in the following manner.

The Appearance of Saint Nicholas

The Repose of Saint Nicholas

A certain pious and respected presbyter lived in Bari. One night, Saint Nicholas appeared to him and said, "Arise and say to this people and to all the clergy of the church to go to Myra of Lycia. Take up my relics and bring them hither to Bari. I can no longer suffer to remain in that desolate place. This is the Lord's will." After the vision, the presbyter arose and went to the church to declare to the clergy all those things that the saint uttered. On hearing these words, all were overjoyed and exclaimed, "Today the Lord has increased His mercy upon us and our city!"[55]

Sailing to Myra of Lycia

Straightway, they equipped three ships and selected the most distinguished and God-fearing men to be sent, together with the priests and deacons, for the translation of the sacred relics. At that time, however, the sea was the domain of pirates. Therefore, they embarked under the guise of merchants. They loaded the vessels with wheat and set sail for Antioch. Arriving safely, they traded their cargo in exchange for goods. It so happened that they heard from certain Venetian merchants, who arrived prior to them, that they too planned to travel to Myra for the very same purpose. The Barians

[55] One of the chroniclers, Nikephoros, notes that the four monk-caretakers at Myra were also previously apprised that the saint appeared in a vision, revealing that the chosen resting place for his relics would change in one year's time. A. C. George, p. 33.

made haste to depart that they might arrive at the port of Lycia before the Venetians. In the event that they might be challenged, the ship also carried arms on board. With the help of God, they found favorable winds and put in at the port before the other contenders. All three ships came into the port of Andriake, about three kilometers from the shrine.[56]

They safely reached the church of the saint and, finding four monks therein, inquired of them, "Where is the tomb of holy Nicholas, that we may venerate him?" The monks showed the Barians the tomb, which was beneath the church grounds. The Barians then proceeded to make an agreement with the monks. Afterward, they dug into the earth and recovered the sacred coffer which encased the holy relics. As the sarcophagus was unearthed, they sensed the fragrance of the precious myrrh that emitted from the holy relics.[57]

---

[56] Forty-seven Barians, bearing arms, dividing into two groups, marched to the shrine. Since they did not meet with any Muslims, they did not need to use their weapons. The church was deserted, save for the four monks acting as caretakers. The rest of the population had fled into the mountains. Ibid. pp. 32, 33.

[57] The Medieval Source Book records that the mariners bowed down with great humility in the church. The monks acting as custodians had thought, initially, that the foreigners were only interested in venerating the relics as pilgrims. When it was evident that they had other designs, the monks sharply asked, "You do not intend to carry off the relics of the holy saint from here, do you? You do not hope to remove them to your own country, do you? If that is your purpose, then let us be clear: we would sooner give up our lives than yield. For we do not fear you and will not allow you to make away with the saint. We are not as Iscariot of old who betrayed his own Savior and Master. Away with the thought! We cannot act treacherously toward our own guardian, protector, champion, and intercessor!" The Barians replied humbly to the monks: "We have come for no other purpose than to rescue the relics of our inspired holy Father Nicholas. We implore your acquiescence in this matter. Let not our efforts be in vain." The monks said, "We do not believe that the saint will allow this removal. He will not consent to have his body touched by you. We suggest that you depart with all haste lest the Myraeans should discover your purpose and put you to death." The Barians then thought it better to alter their strategy and not convey an air of impudence. They informed the monks that they had been commissioned by the pope, archbishops, bishops, and Roman authorities. They claimed that the pope himself received a vision to translate the relics to the west. The Barians then offered what they thought suitable recompense that they might depart in peace and benevolence.

It was apparent to the Barians, nevertheless, that the monks were not interested in money and that tears and pleas did not move them. They, therefore, forced their way into the miraculous sarcophagus. The custodians rent their garb and pulled at their hair and beards. The monks then thought to get help from the Myraeans. The Barians, perceiving this move, set guards at the entrances and exits of the holy church. They overpowered the monks but did not injure them. They then deliberated upon how to

(continued...)

One of the sailors, Matthew, struck the side of the sarcophagus with a hammer. After creating a rectangular aperture, he was able to open it and view the saint. The saint's relics were intact, surrounded by a precious perfumed fluid. He removed the relics and entrusted them to the two priests of the expedition, Lupus and Grimaldus. As for the myrrh, it was stored in containers. Grimaldus bore away the relics of Saint Nicholas on his shoulders, and then entered one of the ships. Some of the Greek populace espied what was taking place and emerged from their hideaways. They confronted the foreign seamen and accused the Greek custodians of treachery. After the visitors reasoned with the disgruntled Myraeans, the natives implored the Barians at least to leave a small portion of the relics for veneration at Myra. The Barians left behind the tomb and the myrrh, together with an icon.[58] Now two of the four monks accompanied them on their return to Bari. This successful operation took placed on the 1st of April.[59] The ships with their precious cargo passed by Kakkavos (Kekova), Castellorizo (Megiste), Patara (the saint's birthplace), Perdika, Telmessos (Turk. Fethiye), Symi, Rhodes, Santorini, Milos, Gerakas, Monemvasia,

Present-day Church of Saint Nicholas at Myra

---

[57](...continued)
remove the relics. One of them, a priest named Lupus, was holding a glass vial filled with the holy prelate's sacred oils. When he saw that his comrades were in distress, he let it fall from his hands. The vial made a crashing sound upon the stones. When he and his companions turned toward the vial and discovered it to be intact, this was taken as a sign of the saint's approval for the recovery of his relics. One of the monks then owned up to a vision that was seen a year ago, saying that Saint Nicholas appeared and foretold that he would be carried off to a foreign land. See *The Translation of Saint Nicholas: An anonymous Greek account of the transfer of the body of Saint Nicholas from Myra of Lycia to Bari in Italy*, trans. by J. McGinley and H. Mursurillo, Bolletino di S, Nicola, N. 10, Studi e testi, Bari: October 1980), 3-17, from the Internet Medieval Source Book at http://www.fordham.edu/halsall/basis/nicholas-bari.html.

[58] The icon is now believed to be in the Antalya Museum in Turkey.

[59] There were, according to the Nikephoros version, seventy seamen on this expedition, of whom sixty-two were from Bari. The names of those Barians who participated in the mission have their names recorded on parchment, preserved to this day, in the archives of the Basilica of Saint Nicholas at Bari. The same seamen and their heirs were later awarded privileges and burial places next to the basilica wall. A. C. George, p. 32.

Methoni, and Sykia (of Corfu). The sailing ships averaged about 1.5 miles per hour. They covered approximately one thousand miles.

Saint Nicholas

The Relics Are Brought to Bari

Sailing with a good wind and calm seas, on Sunday, the 20th of May, at eventide, they arrived in their homeland. They sailed into the harbor of Saint George, about four miles from Bari. News of the arrival of the holy relics spread everywhere. The people of Bari, led by their bishops, priests, monks and all the clergy, hastened to escort the relics with candles and censers, all the while chanting and praising God and extolling the hierarch of Christ. With great honor and joy, the relics were led to the Church of Saint John the Forerunner that is by the sea.[60]

Miraculously, the crippled, blind, deaf, possessed, and those stricken with every sort of infirmity received healing as soon as they touched the grace-filled relics of our holy father, Nicholas the Wonder-worker. After the second day, the number of those healed reached forty-seven, which included both men and women. On the third day, twenty-two more people were cured; and on the fourth, twenty-nine. On the fifth day, a deaf and mute man was cured after suffering five years. Following close upon these events, the saint appeared in a dream to a virtuous monk and revealed: "It is by the will of God that I came to this city on a Sunday, at the ninth hour. And, at the same time, by the grace of God, I healed eleven people." The monk revealed the vision to everyone, to the glory of God and to the honor of His servant. The sacred relics continued to bring about cures to them that had recourse to them with faith. The relics were as an ever-flowing fountain. Thus, the citizens of

---

[60] Since the reign of Emperor Justinian (r. 527-565), Bari was Byzantine except for a thirty-year period (841-871) when the Arabs took the city. Between 1035 and 1062, the archbishops of Bari were Greeks who built two churches near Bari in honor of Saint Nicholas. Between 970 and 1071, Bari was the seat of the Byzantine governor with a very large number of Greeks who settled there. Bari became a bishopric under Byzantine control in the 10th C. It was recognized as a metropolitan see in 1025 by Pope John XIX. Emperor Constantine IX Monomachos (r. 1042-1054) built a church inside the walls of Bari dedicated to Saint Nicholas, staffing it with Greek monks. Ibid., p. 28.

Bari decided to construct a large church, magnificently appointed. They also resolved to prepare a silver coffer to enshrine the holy relics. The coffer was then gilded throughout and adorned with precious stones.

The New Church of Saint Nicholas at Bari

Three years later, the archbishops and bishops of the surrounding cities and towns convened a council. Consequently, the clergy conducted a solemn transfer of the relics of Saint Nicholas from the Church of the Forerunner to the newly erected church on the very same day on which the relics were brought to Bari from Myra.[61] The silver coffer was set in the sanctuary. Then they left a small portion of the relics in the old reliquary which was placed outside the sanctuary for public veneration. On account of the translation of these precious relics, it has become the custom to celebrate this event annually on the 20th of May.

Bari's Basilica di San Nicola

[61] Now the sailors on board had fashioned a beautiful casket for the relics of their honored passenger. (The empty casket, even now, may be viewed in the treasury next to the basilica.) Upon arriving in Bari, the relics were placed in the care of Abbot Elias of Saint Benedict's Church. He was also the same person given charge to build a church to house the relics. While the construction was underway, the relics were kept on the altar of the Church of Saint Eustratius.

The underground church was the first section finished in the new basilica. In October of 1099, Abbot Elias invited Pope Urban II to deposit Saint Nicholas' relics in the new rectangular crypt. The area itself is 30.7 meters by 14.8 meters. The ceiling is supported by twenty-six columns. As for the relics, they are enclosed in blocks of reinforced concrete. It has been noted that some small bones were missing before the relics were finally settled in Bari. The main building of the basilica was completed by 1099, but necessitated the leveling of four small churches that left only the Church of Saint Gregory standing. Though the basilica's structure and stonework were completed by Abbot Elias, yet it was his successor, Eustratius (1115-1125), who finished the sculptures. In 1951, Pope Pius II entrusted the basilica and its affairs to Dominican friars.

During 1953 and 1957, when the basilica was undergoing restorative work, L. Martino of the University of Bari, together with two physicians, examined the sacred bones of the saint. They determined that they were the bones of a male, 1.67 meters in height, who was older than seventy at the time of death. They reported that he possessed a broad forehead and large sunken eyes. The bones were consistent to Mediterranean stock, more likely a Greek of Asia Minor. The saint's bone condition revealed poor nutrition and adverse exposure to living in damp climes. Ibid., pp. 36-39.

However, in Russia and Bulgaria, this event is celebrated with great splendor on the 9th of May. During this period of time, Russia had recently been converted to Christianity, and it became the recipient of innumerable miracles wrought by Saint Nicholas.

The Myrrh-streaming Relics

After the placement of the relics into the sanctuary, several years passed before the saint appeared to a monk in a vision. The saint told him that his relics should be placed beneath the holy Table. This was done in accordance with the saint's request. Then myrrh began to stream forth, healing every sickness, to the glory of God Who is glorified in His saints. At this point, we must add when and in what manner this myrrh flowed from the relics of the saint. This has been transmitted to us by wise men and from reliable sources. Every year, on the day of the saint's commemoration, at the commencement of divine Liturgy, myrrh would begin to flow from the feet of the relics. Myrrh flowed from the heels, not the toes. It was so plenteous that everyone brought containers and vessels for storage.

The divine Liturgy was chanted slowly, lasting three hours. This was done so that the myrrh might stream forth for a longer period of time, thus filling numerous jugs and containers. The aromatic fragrance emitted by the myrrh was so penetrating that the entire church was filled with the scent. Some of the Christians even grew faint from the loveliness of the divine scent. But at the close of Liturgy, the myrrh ceased flowing. The bottled myrrh was then distributed throughout the Italian peninsula and the continent as well. Innumerable miracles were performed for many infirm folk who anointed themselves with faith.[62]

---

[62] A. C. George (p. 40), a recent pilgrim (1999), reports: "The manna or the liquid which forms in the tomb is collected by tilting the concrete block at the base of the tomb. Since 1980, the manna has been formally extracted from the tomb on the evening of the 9th of May, in front of a large crowd. Usually 50 milliliters of manna are recovered from the tomb. When mixed with a large quantity of water, it is distributed to the worshippers. Some drink of it; others sprinkle it on that part of the body that is suffering from any kind of ailment. The consecrated liquid manna mixture is carried by the worshippers in fancy phials designed by local artists depicting episodes from the life of Saint Nicholas. In the treasure room, I observed beautifully decorated phials and containers of different sizes and shapes....Professor Vasili Borski, who visited the basilica on the 28th of July, in the year 1724, found that one could carry the holy manna from the saint's tomb if he or she bought a glass container from two stores near the Church of Saint Nicholas. The money for the purchase of the glass container was used to support and maintain free of charge the hospitality rooms used by the pilgrims....Pilgrims took phials with the holy myrrh to their homes as late as 1940. The manna is like pure water that forms in the tomb. It is not of the same origin or

(continued...)

The Saint is a Proponent of Orthodoxy

The flow of myrrh held true while the Western Church was not yet anathematized and separated from the Eastern Church.[63] As long as the Western Church persisted in her heretical beliefs, she was alienated and excommunicated by the Orthodox; and Saint Nicholas would not accept the Mass of the papists. If a Latin priest served, the myrrh would not flow from the saint's feet. The Latins, as a result, were obliged to bring in an Orthodox priest who kept the doctrines of the true Church to serve the divine Liturgy. As soon as the Orthodox priest would commence the divine Liturgy—behold, the miracle!—the divine myrrh would begin to flow from the heels of the saint.

This is a great miracle indeed, O Christians. It proves that the great Nicholas was a true vessel of the spiritual myrrh of Christ our God Whose name fills the entire universe like myrrh. As it is written in sacred Scripture,

---

[62](...continued)
composition as the oil-based perfumed liquid that flowed from Saint Nicholas' tomb at Myra. The origin of the pure water that forms inside the tomb in Bari is a mystery. However, in 1925 the University of Bari analyzed the liquid and found it to be very pure water. Some people believe that the liquid seeps from the bones of the saint, while others believe its origin to be the marble of the tomb. The use of the manna is a source of hope and health for those who look to God and His servant Saint Nicholas, beseeching his intercession and protection."

[63] In 1098, the pope presided over the pseudo-council of Bari, at which the Greeks of southern Italy and Sicily were persuaded to accept the *Filioque* and other Latin innovations. As we mentioned earlier in the account of the founding fathers of Nea Moni, also commemorated today, it was Emperor Constantine IX Monomachos (r. 1042-1055) who had appointed the rigorist Michael I Keroularios as patriarch, whose tenure was from 1043 to 1058. In the early 1050s, the conflict and chasm between Constantine and Rome widened. The controversy centered around azymes and the *Filioque* and married clergy. The crisis reached the breaking point in the reciprocal excommunications of Humbert and Keroularios on the 16th of July, in the year 1054. The rupture, thus, began. Keroularios, thereafter, used the title of Œcumenical Patriarch on his seal. Nevertheless, the schism was not yet final. The interpretation among the papists that the easterners were schismatics did not become rooted in western minds for more than a century to come. The great mass of the population reacted very calmly to the separation. For some time afterward many remained unaware of the distinction between the teachings of Constantinople and Rome. The break was felt immediately only in official circles, by the clergy and the government. By the 14th C., the Greeks were acknowledging that the schism had taken place from the time of Patriarch Michael. They came to believe that he responded to the attack correctly by the excommunication. They also approved his telling the eastern patriarchs to recognize him in the future as senior patriarch. See "Events Leading to the Schism of 1054," *The Lives of the Pillars of Orthodoxy*, pp. 156, 157.

"Thy name is ointment poured forth [Song of Solomon 1:3]." This awesome miracle should convince all that Saint Nicholas was a champion and teacher of the theology of the Son, declaring, at the First Œcumenical Synod, the dogma of Christ's one essence with the Father. Notwithstanding, even after death, Saint Nicholas is also a proponent of the true theology of the Holy Spirit. Though the saint's relics are silent, yet, by deed, the saint indicates, by the privation of myrrh at the service of the Latins, his displeasure in their foolish doctrine that the Holy Spirit proceeds from both the Father and the Son. Our Savior speaks of this to His disciples at the Mystical Supper: "But whenever the Paraclete should come, Whom I shall send to you from the Father, the Spirit of the truth Who proceedeth from the Father, that One shall bear witness concerning Me [Jn. 15:26]."

Saint Nicholas

Orthodoxy and Heterodox Theological Issues

The holy and apostolic Eastern Church of Christ rightly believes and confesses, "We venerate the one essence of the Divinity in three Persons, or hypostases, and confess the coessential Trinity. Particular to the three Persons are fatherhood, sonship, and procession. Common to Them are essence, nature, divinity, and goodness."[64] The Spirit is manifested by the Son, but does not proceed from the Son. The Father is the unique origin, source, and cause of Godhead. The Cappadocian fathers aver that there is one God because there is one Father. The other two Persons are from the Father and are defined in terms of their relation to Him.

Saint Thalassios correctly preaches: "We regard the Father as unoriginate and as the source: as unoriginate because He is unbegotten, and as the source because He is the begetter of the Son and the sender forth of the Holy Spirit, both of Whom are by essence from Him and in Him from all eternity. Paradoxically, the One moves from Itself into the Three and yet remains One, while the Three return to the One and yet remain Three. Again,

---

[64] See Saint Thalassios, "Second Century," § 98, 99, *The Philokalia*, Volume Two, trans. by G. E. H. Palmer, Philip Sherrard, and Kallistos Ware (London/Boston: Faber and Faber, 1984 repr.), p. 318. Saint Thalassios, the particular friend of Saint Maximos the Confessor, is also commemorated today by the holy Church.

the Son and the Spirit are regarded as not unoriginate, and yet as from all eternity. They are not unoriginate because the Father is their origin and source; but They are eternal in that They coexist with the Father, the one begotten by Him and the other proceeding from Him from all eternity. The single divinity of the Trinity is undivided and the three Persons of the one divinity are unconfused. The individual characteristics of the Father are described as unoriginateness and unbegottenness; of the Son, as co-presence in the source and as being begotten by it; and of the Holy Spirit, as co-presence in the source and as proceeding from it. The origin of the Son and Holy Spirit is not to be regarded as temporal: how could it be? On the contrary, the term 'origin' indicates the source from which Their existence is eternally derived, as light from the sun. For They originate from the source according to Their essence, although They are in no sense inferior or subsequent to it. Each Person preserves His individual characteristics immutably and irremovably; and the common nature of Their essence, that is to say, Their divinity, is indivisible. We confess Unity in Trinity and Trinity in Unity, divided but without division and united but with distinctions. The Father is the sole origin of all things. He is the origin of the Son and the Spirit as Their begetter and source, coeternal, coinfinite, limitless, coessential, and undivided. He is the origin of created things, as the One Who produces, provides for, and judges them through the Son in the Holy Spirit. 'For of Him, and through Him, and to Him, are all things: to Whom be the glory to the ages. Amen [Rom. 11:36].' Again, the Son and the Holy Spirit are said to be coeternal with the Father, but not co-unoriginate with Him. They are coeternal in that They coexist with the Father from eternity; but They are not co-unoriginate in that They are not without source, as has already been said. They are derived from Him as the light from the sun, even though They are not inferior or subsequent to Him. They are also said to be unoriginate in the sense that They do not have an origin in time. If this were not the case, They would be thought of as subject to time, whereas it is from Them that time itself derives. Thus They are unoriginate not with regard to Their source, but with regard to time. For They exist prior to, and transcend, all time and all the ages; and it is from Them that all time and all the ages are derived, together with everything that is in time and in the ages. This is because They are, as we said, coeternal with the Father: to Him, with Them, be glory and power through all the ages. Amen."[65]

Thus, the Roman Catholic heresy of the *Filioque*, the word meaning that addition to the Creed of the words "and the Son" to that article of Faith that says "...the Holy Spirit...Who proceeds from the Father," confuses the Persons (Hypostases) and destroys the proper balance in the Godhead. Indeed,

[65] Ibid., "Fourth Century," §§ 92-100, *The Philokalia*, pp. 331, 332.

as a result of the *Filioque*, the Holy Spirit has become subordinated to the Son. Saint Nicholas would never have countenanced such a blasphemy.[66]

---

[66] The Orthodox Church has remained unchanged from what the Orthodox believed from the first. External alterations (vestment changes, new feast days, canons, translations) do not add or take away the everlasting landmarks [Prov. 22:28]. We have been exhorted to contend for the Orthodox Faith, which was once for all delivered to the saints [Jude 1:3]. Christ admonished the apostles to teach all nations to observe all things whatsoever He commanded them [Mt. 28:20]. Roman Catholicism maintains a development of its doctrine in stages, such as the dogmas of papal infallibility and the immaculate conception. They contend that Christ gave only a deposit or seed that required maturity and cultivation. Orthodoxy uses the sciences and philosophy, taking only the honey from it, to defend and explain her Faith; whereas, Roman Catholicism builds and relies on human reason and wisdom.

Roman Catholicism believes that, in the future age, the essence of God will be seen. The Orthodox believe that it is not possible to see God. God speaks to us through the Son, Who is the effulgence of the glory and impress of His hypostasis [Heb. 1:1-3]. The Orthodox make a distinction between God's essence and His uncreated energies. For the Latins, grace was created by God. For the Orthodox grace is uncreated.

The purpose of the incarnation is also viewed differently. Western theology, generally legalistic, propounds that God became man and died on the Cross that He might satisfy the divine justice that was offended by Adam's transgression. They put forward that Adam's sin displeased the infinite God, a transgression that had infinite consequences. Finite man could not make amends. The sin of Adam, that is, what the papists call "original sin" or "inherited guilt," passed on to all his progeny. Only the God-Man Christ could remit this debt by dying on the Cross. Jesus' death propitiates Adam's sin. Consequently, by Jesus' death, the offended Father is no longer angry with man. Little concern was given by the papacy to the virtue of man's striving for divinization or theosis.

The Orthodox, on the other hand, believe that Christ gave His life a ransom for many [Mt. 20:28], even as He says in the Gospel; but the ransom was paid to deliver us out of the power of Hades and redeem us from death [Hos. 13:14]. For Christ, through death, brought to nought the one who has the power of death, that is, the devil, so that He might set free those who through fear of death were all their lifetime subject to bondage [Heb. 2:14, 15]. Death reigned from Adam, even over those who did not sin in the likeness of Adam's transgression [Rom. 5:14]. The sting of death is sin, and the power of sin is the law [1 Cor. 15:56]. When we were in the flesh, the passions of the sins, which were through the law, were energizing in our members to bear fruit to death [Rom. 7:5]. Saint Paul saw another law in our members, warring against the law of our mind, and taking us captive in the law of sin which is in our members. It was death, for which he asks, "Who shall deliver me from the body of this death?"—to which he replies, "I thank God through Jesus Christ our Lord. So then on the one hand with the mind I myself serve the law of God, but on the other

(continued...)

[66](...continued)
hand with the flesh the law of sin [Rom. 7:23-25]." We then are called upon to mortify our members [Col. 3:5]. Hence, Christ suffered and was buried to conquer the devil and death, not as a vicarious atonement as explained by the west. Christ's was a voluntary death. It was not that we loved God, but that "He Himself loved us, and sent forth His Son to be an expiation for our sins [1 Jn. 4:10; cf. Rom. 3:25; Heb. 2:17; 1 Jn. 2:2]." Death and Hades could not hold Him Who rose on the third day. "The many" for whom Christ died were ransomed from the grave and the devil. Sin reigned in death [Rom. 5:21]. The law of the Spirit of life in Christ Jesus freed us from the law of sin and death [Rom. 8:2]. We now have the possibility to become like God (divinization). The difference in views between the Latins and the Orthodox is seen in the naturalism of Latin statues as opposed to the Orthodox view that the icons depict the saints as transfigured and glorified.

As for the Mystery of Baptism, Roman Catholicism believes that "original sin" is thereby sprinkled away. Orthodoxy does not recognize the idea of "original sin." For the Orthodox, all those who have been baptized in Christ have put on Christ [Gal. 3:27]. We have been baptized into His death, so that even as Christ was raised from the dead, thus also we should walk in newness of life [Rom. 6:3, 4]. We who have been buried with Him in the baptism, were raised with Him through faith in the energy of God, Who raised Him from the dead [Col. 2:12]. But also by one Spirit were we all baptized into one body—whether Jews or Greeks, whether slaves or free—and were all given to drink into one Spirit [1 Cor. 12:13].

With regard to the head of the Church, the Roman Catholics acknowledge the pope as that visible head and Christ's vicar. He speaks for the whole Church (*ex cathedra*). Other bishops, subordinate to him, look to him as their unity. Orthodoxy maintains that the bishops are equal, though there do exist different distinctions between the bishops (patriarch, archbishop, metropolitan, bishop) with regard to Church administration. The Latins assign each local church as part of the universal Church. The head of the local church is then both its bishop and the pope, that is, two heads, with the pope as supreme. The bishop for the Orthodox is the living icon of Christ. His flock constitutes the Church.

Canon law for the west is also in continual change, so as to regulate human relationships and rights. The canons for the Orthodox are not abrogated over time. They were and they are tools for building up the Church of Christ and for bringing about the new man and putting off the old through obedience to them.

Both the Western and the Eastern Churches acknowledge at least seven Sacraments or Mysteries. The eucharist of the Roman Catholics is considered effective by means of the priest who acts in the person of Christ. The Orthodox teach the invocation of the Holy Spirit (*epiklesis*) for the changing of the bread and wine. While the Roman Catholic usually receives only the bread or wafer, the Orthodox receives the immaculate Mysteries, both the body and the blood. The west holds Extreme Unction as the final sacrament, preparing one for death, Purgatory, and the future life. The Orthodox deems the administration of this Holy Oil to be for healing, in concert with Confession and Communion.

(continued...)

The Relics of the Saint

At this point, in *The Great Synaxaristes* (in Greek), it is written that the sacred relics of Saint Nicholas are not present today in the city of Bari. Where they are deposited is not known. This is the allegation of the author Nikodemos of the Holy Mountain (1749-1809). Among the handwritten notes of B. D. Zotos Molossos, it is recorded that because Saint Nicholas would not perform any miracles when a Latin priest served Mass in the church, the pope sold the saint's right hand to Prince Gikas of Wallachia for three thousand florins. The precious relics of the saint's body were then sold to the Russians for ten thousand florins. And now the place of their concealment is known only to our Savior Christ in the depths of His providence and judgment, to Whom be glory, dominion, and worship with the Father and the life-creating Spirit, now and ever, and unto the ages of ages. Amen.[67]

On the 20th of May, the holy Church commemorates our venerable Father THALASSIOS, who reposed in peace.[68]

Thalassios, our venerable father, became a presbyter and hegumen in Libya. He lived during the reign of Emperor Constantine IV Pogonatos (668-685). Thalassios' ascetic conduct of life was concurrent with that of Saint Maximos the Confessor,[69] with whom he maintained a spiritual relationship as a personal friend. Saint Maximos had written to him in what came to be his largest extant work, entitled *To Thalassios: On Various Questions Relating to Holy Scripture*. The work comprises of responses to difficult passages raised by Thalassios. Maximos' *Two Hundred Texts on Theology* are also dedicated to his friend. Maximos is also known to have penned at least five letters to him. Maximos thought very highly of Thalassios and called himself a disciple of

---

[66](...continued)

Purgatory is a condition which the Roman Catholics believe is for the departed awaiting the final judgment. They also acknowledge the accumulated merits and grace of the saints who can grant indulgences and shorten one's stay in Purgatory. The Orthodox do not believe in any new doctrine, such as purgatorial fire which burns away sins. The Orthodox believe that some have a foretaste of the glory to come, whereas others have a foretaste of suffering until the particular Judgment. At Christ's second coming, the soul will be united with the risen body for judgment. The work of each shall become manifest; for the day shall declare it, because it is being revealed in fire; and the fire shall put to the test the work of each, of what sort it is [1 Cor. 3:13]. Some will inherit eternal life, some will inherit eternal damnation.

[67] See images at http://www.stnicholascenter.org/Brix?pageID=462.

[68] For the writings of Abba Thalassios the Libyan (d. 648), see *The Philokalia*, Vol. Two, p. 306 ff. See also Greek text in *P.G.* 91:1427-1470.

[69] Saint Maximos is commemorated by the holy Church on the 21st of January.

Thalassios who was older than he. The Libyan abbot also composed an important spiritual treatise, entitled *On Love, Self-control and Life in Accordance with the Intellect*, which was written for Paul the presbyter. The work is laid out in what is called four centuries. Saint Thalassios, of one mind with Saint Maximos, wrote that "just as we speak of one Christ as being 'from Divinity,' and 'from manhood,' and 'in Divinity' and 'in manhood,' so we speak of Him as being 'from two natures' and 'in two natures.' We confess that in Christ there is a single hypostasis, or subject, in two indivisibly united natures. We glorify the one indivisible hypostasis of Christ and confess the union without confusion of the two natures."[70]

Both Thalassios and Maximos discuss how love is paramount. Saint Thalassios says that "if you wish to overcome impassioned thoughts, acquire self-control and love for your neighbor.[71] Strive to love every man equally, and you will simultaneously expel all the passions."[72] And, "He who loves no human thing loves all men."[73] The one who possesses true love "does not tolerate suspicion or disparagement of others.[74] Without rancor, he prays for those who offend him. As for the unstinting giver, he is set free from rancor.[75] He who patiently endures unsought trials becomes humble, full of hope, and spiritually mature."[76] For, "A saint-like soul helps its neighbor and, when ill-treated by him, is patient and endures what it suffers at his hands."[77]

As for self-love, he writes: "If you want to be freed from all the vices simultaneously renounce self-love, the mother of evils."[78] And, "Self-love—that is, friendship for the body—is the source of evil in the soul."[79] And again, "The three most common forms of desire have their origin in the passion of self-love. These three forms are gluttony, self-esteem, and avarice."[80]

He writes succinctly that "the person advancing in the spiritual life studies three things: the commandments, doctrine, and faith in the Holy Trinity."[81] We should also know that "there are four prevalent passions which

---

[70] Saint Thalassios, "Second Century," § 95-97, *The Philokalia*, Vol. Two.
[71] "First Century," § 14.
[72] "Second Century," § 39.
[73] "First Century," § 70.
[74] Ibid., § 6.
[75] "Third Century," § 49.
[76] Ibid., § 15.
[77] Ibid., § 43.
[78] "Second Century," § 1.
[79] Ibid., § 4.
[80] "Third Century," §§ 87, 88.
[81] Ibid., § 28.

God in His wisdom sets one against the other: distress checks sensual desire; the fear of punishment withers desire."[82]

He also exhorts us with his own observations, saying: "Only those who have reached the extremes of virtue or of evil are not judged by their consciences."[83] And, "The one who applies the laws of virtue to soul and body is truly fit to rule."[84] And, also, that "only spiritual conversation is beneficial; it is better to preserve stillness than to indulge in any other kind."[85]

On the 20th of May, the holy Church commemorates the venerable MARK the Hermit, who reposed in peace.

On the 20th of May, the holy Church commemorates the Finding of the honorable Relics of our holy father among the saints, ALEXIOS the Wonder-worker, Metropolitan of Moscow and of All Russia (14th C.).

Through the intercessions of Thy Saints,
O Christ God, have mercy on us. Amen.

[82] Ibid., §§ 19, 20.
[83] "First Century," § 72.
[84] Ibid., § 79.
[85] Ibid., § 66.

On the 21st of May, the holy Church commemorates the holy and glorious God-crowned emperors and Equals-to-the-apostles CONSTANTINE and HELEN.[1]

Constantine the Great and ever-memorable first emperor of the Christians, the Byzantine autocrat and builder of Constantinople, was born at Naissus, present-day Nis of Dardania in the area that now belongs in today's Serbia and Croatia, ca. A.D. 274. His father, Flavius Constantius, drawn from an Illyrian background,[2] was then a general of the Roman government. Afterward, he was proclaimed Caesar of the westernmost part of the empire, that is, Britannia, Galatia (Gaul), Spain, and other territories. On account of

---

[1] The Lives of these royal saints were recorded in Greek. The text is extant in the Athonite Monastery of Iveron, which manuscript begins, "The fairest of narrations." In the Athonite Monastery of the Great Lavra, the biographies of these saints are taken from various historical selections which manuscript begins with these words: "Of the most blessed and holiest and first...." Sophronios Efstratiades, in his *Hagiologion of the Orthodox Church* (Athens, 1960), p. 267, notes that ecclesiastical compositions to these saints abound. A full divine service, with canon, by the Damascene is found in the Parisian Codex 1566. There is another canon by Kyril the Lavrite in Lavreote Codex Ω 111. Hymns (both *stichera* and *idiomela kathismata*) are found in Parisian Codices 1574 and 1575; Lavreote Codices Δ 5, Θ 32, I 70; as well as in the codices of Athonite Kafsokalyvia. Services for the Equals-to-the-apostles Constantine and Helen were also published by George Vouteres (Athens, 1899 and 1917). A sermon also survives regarding Emperor Constantine and the 318 God-bearing fathers of the First Œcumenical Synod, penned by the Presbyter Gregory the Caesarean of Cappadocia, which is preserved in the Athonite Monastery of Pantocrator. In like manner, the sermon of the *Great Logothete* Constantine the Akropolite is kept in the Great Lavra, as well as in the Athonite Coenobium of Dionysiou and the Monastery of Vatopedi. Constantine and Helen were guardians and caretakers of Orthodoxy. We read in the New Testament: "Thou [Jesus] wast slain and didst redeem us to God in Thy blood out of every tribe and tongue and people and nation, and didst make them kings and priests to our God, and they shall reign on the earth [Rev. 5:9, 10]."

Many latter-day books in English contain inimical criticisms of Saints Constantine, Helen, and Athanasios the Great (who is also part of this great history). Orthodox readers are cautioned to apply circumspection if ever they should peruse such hostile heterodox authors.

[2] Illyricum was a Roman province in the northwestern part of the Balkans. In the 4th C. there were attempts to create an Illyricum prefecture, which included Pannonia, Macedonia, and Dacia. Latin was the language in the western part. Beginning in the 2nd C., Christianity began to grow through the western part. The two metropolitan sees were Salona (Solin, Yugoslavia), a port on the Dalmatian seacoast, and Sirmium (Sremska Mitrovica, Yugoslavia), on the left bank of the Sava (Savus). *The Oxford Dictionary of Byzantium*, s.v. "Illyricum."

Constantius' pale countenance he was surnamed Chlorus. The mother of Saint Constantine was the most pious and holy Empress Helen (Helena) who, together with her son, is commemorated this day. The blessed Helen hailed from Bithynia of Asia Minor. She was born in a city called Drepanum which had the honor to be renamed Helenopolis (Helenoupolis), later, by the great Constantine.[3] On Constantine's mother's side, he was a nephew of Emperor Claudius II (268-270).[4]

Saints Constantine and Helen

Saint Helen

A daughter was born, circa 255, to an innkeeper at Drepanum of Bithynia on the Nikomedian Gulf.[5] Her name was Helen. She was believed to be of humble parentage. She bore her poverty with dignity. Saint Ambrose, in his "Oratio de obitu Theodosii," referred to her as a *stabularia*, or innkeeper. As she grew, the slender, blond lass helped her pagan parents attend to the needs of travelers who halted to find rest and refreshment at their establishment in Naissus. The people spoke Dardanian, with a touch of broken Latin and Greek, so as to communicate with passersby and soldiers. Life was not only difficult and primitive but there was also the threat of an invasion by hordes of Sarmatians and Goths. In June of 271, a twenty-three-year-old military tribune, named Flavius Constantius, entered Naissus. He was tall, thin, well-built, of fair complexion, and grey-blue eyes, with an elegant nose. He cut an impressive figure in uniform. He, too, was from a small village further north. His arrival,

---

[3] Drepanum or Drepana, a village of Nikomedia in Bithynia, is modern-day Hersek.

[4] *The Great Synaxaristes* (in Greek), 5th ed. (Athens, 1977), p. 511.

[5] It was long believed that she was a native of Britain, for which there is no historical justification. The statement had been made by English chroniclers of the Middle Ages, according to which Helen was supposed to have been the daughter of a British prince. The misinterpretation may have arisen from the term used in the fourth chapter of the panegyric on Constantine's marriage with Fausta, that Constantine, *oriendo* (i. e., "by his beginnings," "from the outset") had honored Britain, which was taken as an allusion to his birth, whereas the reference was really to the beginning of his reign. *Catholic Encyclopedia*, s.v. "Helena, Saint."

together with his troops, animated the villagers. The distinguished tribune would stay at the inn for several days. Sixteen-year-old Helen and her parents took care of their guests. Constantius fell in love with the gracious lass and asked for her hand in marriage. Helen soon conceived and bore Constantine. She raised him alone, as Constantius moved up the ranks in the legion commanded by Diocles, another Illyrian. Nine years had passed. Constantius was summoned to the tent of Emperor Carus (282-283), the general the legions had chosen as emperor after the slaying of Emperor Probus (276-282) eight months earlier. Carus appointed Constantius to the governorship of Dalmatia, the Illyrian province along the Adriatic. Helen and little Constantine were brought to Salonae and the governor's mansion. All chroniclers of the time agree that Flavius Constantius did marry Helen, but in a *matrimonium concubinatum*, a form of marriage the law allowed for one of the equestrian class to marry a peasant. Any child from the union was considered legitimate, but the son had limited rights when inheriting from his father. Divorce also was easier in such marriages. What was important to Flavius Constantius was that his son would be regarded as legitimate. Constantius arranged for tutors to teach both mother and son.[6]

The Tetrarchy of the Roman Empire

During that era of the birth of the great Constantine, the Roman Empire was in a most terrible state of chaos. The emperors, one after the other, were murdered. When one came to the throne, he was succeeded in but a short time by another. In the year 284, with the murder of Numerian (283-284), Diocletian of Dalmatia was proclaimed emperor. He was to become a great persecutor of the Christians. Diocletian reigned for twenty years. Now two years after his accession, that is, in 286, he divided the Roman Empire into two. The eastern part included Illyricum, Greece, Asia Minor, and Egypt. The capital was at Nikomedia of Asia Minor, where Diocletian had his residence and spent much of his time. The western part included Rome and Italy, Gaul, Spain, Britannia, and North Africa. The capital was at Milan (Mediolana), where Diocletian established his trusted friend Maximian, surnamed Herculius (Hercules or Herakles), who hailed from Sirmium of Pannonia.

Much later, in 293, Diocletian appointed two others to assist in the exercise of power, who were called Caesars. As for Diocletian and Maximian, they bore the title of Augustus. The Caesars were co-emperors, helpers and successors of the Augusti. Diocletian, in the east, appointed as his Caesar

---

[6] D. G. Kousoulas, "At the Governor's Mansion," *The Life and Times of Constantine the Great* (Danbury, CT: Rutledge Books, 1997), pp. 10-12. Kosoulas notes that there is no written record of Constantine's childhood years. His early beginnings were borrowed by Kousoulas from a manuscript written by a monk centuries later [p. 9, note].

Galerius Maximianus, his son-in-law, who had taken to wife Diocletian's daughter Valeria. Galerius was assigned the governance of Macedonia, mainland Greece, the Peloponnesos, and Crete. His seat was in Sirmium of Pannonia.[7] In the west, the Caesar appointed under Augustus Maximian Herakles was the father of the great Constantine: Constantius Chlorus. The latter was given the charge of the westernmost part of the empire, that is, Britannia, Galatia, and Spain, as we mentioned earlier. Diocletian obliged Constantius to separate from his lawful wife, the blessed Helen, and to wed Theodora, the stepdaughter of Maximian Herakles.[8] Theodora was from Maximian's wife's previous marriage. She was some twenty-six years younger than Constantius. Maximian had a daughter of his own with his wife Eftropia. Her name was Fausta, but the maiden was but two years of age. Fausta's brother, Maxentius, was slightly over five. But sister and brother would enter Constantius' son's life later. Now Diocletian made these arrangements that he might solidify the bonds of loyalty, thinking that, as a kinsman, Constantius would never raise up a war against the others of the tetrarchy. As further security, Diocletian retained, as a hostage, Constantine, the son of Constantius and Helen. Constantine was just entering puberty. As Moses of old, Constantine was reared in the palaces of kings; and when his hour came, he was ready to free his people, the Christians, in like manner as Moses freed his people, the Jews.[9]

The Young Constantine at Court

In this way, the young Constantine was held as a hostage in the court of Diocletian. Constantine, furthermore, was kept in this state under Galerius Maximianus. Hence, Constantine was reared among the impious and tyrants. In his morals, judgment, and practises, however, he in no way resembled them. From his early youth, he was not only handsome of countenance but also had an innocent and a good heart. As he grew in stature and age, so did his

---

[7] Pannonia would be present-day western Hungary and northern Croatia and Slovenia. Sirmium (Mitrovica), a town in Pannonia, is at the point where the river Savus runs into the river Danube (Istrus).

[8] The members of the tetrarchy were bound by ties of marriage. The Augusti, as senior emperors, called each other "brothers" and their Caesars "sons." The Augusti also characterized themselves as Jupiter (Zeus) for Diocletian and Hercules for Maximian, since Jupiter was believed to command and Hercules carried out his orders. The Caesars were incorporated into the system and grouped into Jovian and Herculian Dynasties. *Oxford*, s.v. "Tetrarchy."

[9] Eusebius, Bk. I, Ch. XII. Eusebius (Evsevios) Pamphilus, Bishop of Caesarea, wrote in Greek his work entitled *The Ecclesiastical History*. His major work, entitled "The Life of Constantine," is contained in *Patrologiae Graecae*, ed. by J. P. Migne, Vol. 20, 909-1232. See also English version in Nicene Fathers, *The Life of Constantine*, Vol. I, 2nd edition, revised translation by Ernest Cushing Richardson, Ph.D. (Grand Rapids, MI: Wm. B. Eerdmans Pub., February 1961).

comeliness and goodness increase. But also he was wondrously endowed with strength, so that no one was able to stand in array against him. He remained invincible against all his opponents. The wretched tyrants, taking notice of his talents and gifts, instead of loving him, envied his manliness, courage, and even a prediction that had been made in his behalf. They, as mindless men, consulted the oracle of Apollo, asking what would become of Constantine later. God permitted the diviner to say that in the future: Constantine would be master of the world and proclaim Christ God; and, moreover, that he would usher in the ruin of idol worship. For this cause they hated him so much that they meditated upon putting him to death in a manner both convenient and secret. But the all-good God, Who foreknew the future, preserved him from their machinations and villainies. So we shall see as the story unfolds how these treacherous plotters and jealous designers ended badly and were destroyed.

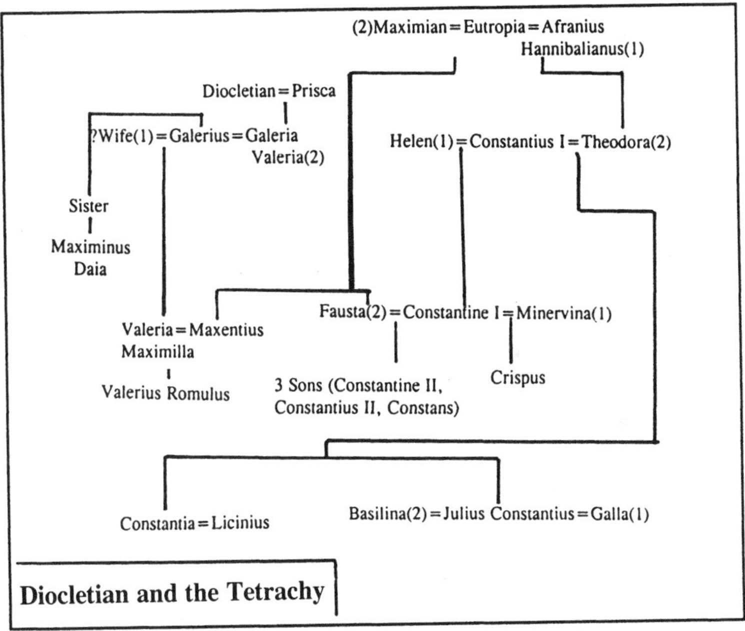

Diocletian and the Tetrachy

Such were affairs until 305. Roman rule held sway in each of four areas under this "rule of four" system of government—at least theoretically. Then, in the year 305, since they came to an earlier agreement, Diocletian and Maximian Herculius resigned. Diocletian retired to his property in Dalmatia, where he lived until 316. As for Maximian Herculius, he remained at Rome. The Augusti, therefore, proclaimed their Caesars as the new Augusti. In the west reigned Constantius, the father of the great Constantine; whereas in the east, there was Galerius Maximianus who was the son-in-law of Diocletian.

Constantine, then, was still kept in Galerius' court. The latter continued to be jealous of Constantine on account of the young man's superior abilities.

Constantine later testified that, in the meantime, the persecution of the Christians originated on account of an oracle of Apollo, that is, the demon that dwelt at the idol's shrine. Thus, Apollo complained he could not give oracles because of "the righteous men." Constantine later wrote: "About that time it is said that Apollo spoke from a deep and gloomy cavern; and, through the medium of no human voice, he declared that the righteous men on earth were a bar to his speaking the truth; and, accordingly, that the oracles from the tripod were fallacious. Hence, it was that Apollo suffered his tresses to droop as a token of grief, and that he mourned the evils which the loss of the oracular spirit would entail on mankind. But let us mark the consequences of this.

"I call now on Thee, most high God, to witness that, when young, I," continues Constantine, "heard him [Diocletian] who at that time was chief among the Roman emperors—unhappy, truly unhappy as he was, and laboring under mental delusion—make earnest enquiry of his attendants as to who might be these 'righteous ones' on earth. Then one of the pagan priests, who was present, replied that they were doubtless the Christians. This answer Diocletian eagerly received, like some honeyed drought. He, therefore, unsheathed the sword which was ordained for the punishment of crime against those whose holiness was beyond reproach. Immediately, therefore, he issued those sanguinary edicts, traced, if I may so express myself, with a sword's point dipped in blood. At the same time, he commanded his judges to tax their ingenuity for the invention of new and more terrible punishments.

"Then, indeed, one might see with what arrogance those venerable worshippers of God were daily exposed. It continued with relentless cruelty, to outrages of the most grievous kind. So did modesty of character, which no enemy had ever treated with disrespect, become the mere sport of their infuriated fellow citizens. Was there any punishment by fire? Were there any tortures or forms of torment which were not applied to all, without distinction of age or sex? Then, it may be truly said, the earth shed tears, the all-encircling compass of heaven mourned because of the pollution of blood; and the very light of day itself was darkened in grief at the spectacle.

"But what is the consequence of this? Why, the barbarians themselves may boast now of the contrast their conduct presents to these cruel deeds. For the barbarian received and kept in gentlest captivity those Christians who then fled from amongst us. These same barbarians secured for the Christians not merely safety from danger but also free exercise of their holy religion. And now the Roman people bear that lasting stain which the Christians, at that time driven from the Roman world and taking refuge with the barbarians, have branded on them."[10]

Now the young Constantine also knew that his father, Constantius, favored the Christians in the face of an empire-wide persecution of them by the tyrannical rulers in the height of its fury. In fact, Constantius his father was reproached for his poverty-stricken treasury by Diocletian. On one occasion Constantius was challenged by the evil and covetous Diocletian, ruler of the empire, to show the contents of his treasury: Diocletian charged that it had better be full or Constantius was to give good reason and just cause as to why it, as he suspected, remained empty. Constantius called upon his richest subjects to voluntarily bestow their largess upon him. They, voluntarily, entrusted their wealth to him until his cup ran over. The treasury was then seen by Diocletian's astonished messengers to be overflowing with riches. It was not maintained in the usual and customary way, that is, it was not kept perpetually filled and under guard in his own palace. It was filled through the willing generosity and gratitude of his subjects, where it was, in Constantius' own words, kept as securely as if it had been under the charge of faithful treasurers. The emperor's ambassadors were overwhelmed. After they had left, Constantius, without covetousness, returned the wealth to its former owners. Such were the blessedness and generosity of Constantine's own father, under whose tutelage the great and future Christian emperor was raised by such an eminent example.[11]

Constantius' son, Prince Constantine, was a superior physical specimen in every way: in natural grace, handsomeness, stature, strength, intelligence, and divinely imparted wisdom, as well as royal education. He surpassed all others to such a degree that his superiors, the other rulers then in power, became inordinately fearful and jealous, and watched perpetually with a jaundiced eye for the chance to disgrace or discredit him somehow. Thereupon, he determined to flee from their presence and plots.[12] But let us describe how the jealous Galerius, for instance, contrived to slay him by means of a ruse.

Now in the east there was a custom, in accordance with the desire of the emperor and his retinue, to engage in various contests and war games. One such amusement was as follows. In the amphitheater, they released one bear and one lion which were first rendered toothless and clawless. Next the emperor would enter the arena and slay the beast with his stave. Simultaneously, thirty men were kept hidden inside the arena. Each held in his hands sponges instead of stones. They would pelt the emperor with these as he would exchange the volley casting actual stones. After the emperor brought them

---

[10] Eusebius, *Life*, Bk. II, Chaps. L-LIII.
[11] Ibid., Bk. I, Chaps. XIII, XIV.
[12] Ibid., Bk. I, Chaps. XIX, XX.

down one by one to the ground, the spectators would acclaim the emperor as the winner. During one such spectacle, the deceitful Galerius Maximianus wished to subtly destroy Constantine by employing the following trick. He commanded the underlings working at the amphitheater to set free one bear and one lion that had not had their teeth extracted. Following this, Galerius feigned illness and commanded Constantine to take his place in the theater. Constantine rose to the occasion bearing in his hand a stave. Constantine proved himself so brave against those creatures that he killed both. Next he cast to the ground all thirty men who, as trusted men of the emperor, were not casting sponges but real stones. Galerius learned what took place. Though filled with wrath at his foiled scheme, he quickly thought of a pretext. He came forward as though he knew nothing of the plan, rebuking the arena workers for their supposed carelessness which nearly cost the life of Constantine. Although Galerius never liked Constantine, he knew that Diocletian did. Thus, he was careful not to show any open animosity toward the young man. Politics changed, however, when Diocletian handed over to Galerius the reins of power.

Constantine Flees Court

Word of this event in the amphitheater came into the ears of Constantius, now the new Augustus of the west, who was resolved to deliver his son. By way of pretext, Constantius contended that he was ill and asked Galerius Maximianus to send his son that he might behold him for the last time. As it happened, Constantius actually did fall ill and needed more than ever to meet with Constantine. Galerius, after procrastinating a few weeks, received a second letter from the ailing Constantius in Gaul. Galerius did not wish to cause a precarious breach with his imperial colleague. Thus, Galerius agreed only because he had in mind to have Constantine murdered by "bandits" on the road. But by the grace of Christ, all the snares of Galerius were frustrated when Constantine took flight earlier than expected. Thus, he arrived before his father safe and sound.[13]

Saint Theophanes, confessor and chronicler,[14] describes Constantine's narrow escape: "While Constantine was in the east and in Palestine espousing

---

[13] Lactantius (240-ca. 320) writes that Constantine was suspicious of Galerius' intentions and hastened his departure. Constantine set off at full speed, killing the horses in each post as he advanced so that Galerius' men would not find fresh mounts. But Zosimas, in his *Historia Nova* (*New History*, Augustus to 410), says he maimed the horses kept in the posts by the public treasury. Most historians agree that Constantine had neither the time nor the inclination to overpower the guards at these posts and then kill or main all the horses. See Kousoulas. "A Hasty Departure," *The Life and Times of Constantine the Great*, pp. 146-148.

[14] Saint Theophanes (d. 845) is commemorated by the holy Church on the 12th of March. His *Ecclesiastical History* is found in *P.G.* 108.

the cause of the Christians, Galerius Maximianus saw how the young man was enhancing his position through his intelligence of mind, strength of body, and aptitude in education. Galerius then learned by divination that this man, Constantine, would put an end to his tyranny and his religion. Galerius, therefore, planned to murder him treacherously. But through divine providence, Constantine, like David of old, learned of the plot and escaped to safety and to the protection of his own father. Both father and son then gave bounteous thanks to Christ Who had delivered Constantine."[15]

Saint Constantine

Constantius rejoiced greatly when he saw that his son came at the appropriate moment that he might appoint him as successor of his throne. Now besides Constantine, Constantius Chlorus also had three other sons by his second wife Theodora, who was the daughter of Maximian Herculius. They were Dalmatius, Hannibalianus, and Julius Constantius II. The latter son would become the father of Julian the Apostate. But it was Constantine who was best loved by his father because he was not only the eldest but also the most prudent and disciplined. Eusebius comments that with divinely ordained timeliness, Constantine, having fled the machinations of the other emperors, arrived at his beloved father's bedside just when the elder was on the point of death.[16]

---

[15] *The Chronicle of Theophanes Confessor*, AM 5793, A.D. 300/301, trans. by C. Mango and R. Scott (Oxford: Clarendon Press, 1997), pp. 12, 13. Constantine served under Galerius during the Persian War and then on the Danube. He accompanied Diocletian through Palestine in the winter of 301/302. Constantine was with him in Nikomedia in March of 303 and March of 305, and presumably in the intervening period, including the journey to Rome [Ibid., p. 13, note 7]. Constantine left Galerius soon after the 1st of May, in the year 305, and met with his father, Constantius, who was on his deathbed. Constantine campaigned successfully with his somewhat recuperating father, north of Hadrian's wall. Constantine remained with his father until the latter's death at York, on the 25th of July, in the year 306 [Ibid., p. 14, note 8].

[16] Eusebius, Bk. IV, Ch. XXI.

Thereupon, as soon as Constantius set his eyes on Constantine, he embraced him. Before all present, Constantius foretold the advancement of the young man and said, "Even as Christ has guarded thee from the assaults of the enemies and has brought thee at the appropriate hour in order to receive the kingdom, as one worthy, so I believe that He will help thee to the end to confirm all in piety."[17] Upon saying this, he selected him as his Augustus. Constantius then said, "Be mindful, child, to love the Christians and to help them if thou dost wish to be glorified in all the world." By these words, it was understood that Constantius Chlorus was a Christian. Constantius had proved he was a virtuous and just judge, merciful and philanthropic at all times. He never hoarded gold or silver. He never spent beyond his needs. He was compassionate to the poor.

Augustus Constantine

While Constantine was with Crocus in the land of the Picts, they installed garrisons that would maintain peace and order. It was there that Constantine received an urgent message from his father's praetorian prefect. Constantine was urged to come to the frontier town of Eboracum (York) without delay. The dying Flavius Constantius asked that Constantine take under his protection his wife Theodora and their six children, since the eldest, Dalmatius, was only twelve years of age. Constantius died on the 25th day of July, in the year 306, at the age of fifty-five. Eusebius tells us that Constantine was forthwith appointed emperor by Constantius, who thereupon breathed his last. He reposed on the imperial couch in the royal palace, giving thanks to God in all things. He was surrounded by a devoted circle of his loving sons and daughters.[18]

Much later, in a letter, Constantine made these remarks about his father and his peers: "The former emperors I have been accustomed to regard as those with whom I could have no sympathy, on account of the savage cruelty of their character. Indeed, my father was the only one who uniformly practised the duties of humanity, and with admirable piety called for the blessing of God the Father on all his actions. But the rest, unsound in mind, were more zealous of cruel than gentle measures; and this disposition they indulged without restraint. Thus, they persecuted the true doctrine during the whole period of their reign. Nay, so violent did their malicious fury become that, in the midst of a profound

---

[17] Father and son, together with the German chieftain Crocus, crossed the Channel (Fretum Gallicum) to lead an expedition against the Picts from the northern part of the British Isles (today's Scotland) who were raiding and pillaging farms and villages in the south. The campaign ended successfully in June, thanks to an ingenious but risky plan of Constantine to surround the Picts and cut them off. Kousoulas, "Constantine Shows His Mettle," *The Life and Times*, pp. 149-152.

[18] Eusebius, loc. cit.

peace, as regards both the religious and ordinary interests of men, they kindled, as it were, the flames of a civil war."[19]

For the launching of great persecutions, Eusebius tells us, had prevailed upon the Christians of the empire, perpetrated by the other rulers, until all the royal palaces in their domains were bereft of God-fearing men. The emperors, too, dispossessed themselves of the prayers of the Christians who were wont to utter such in the rulers' behalf. Thus were those very same evil emperors deprived of the grace and protection of almighty God at their own ill-advised instruction.[20]

It is worth our time to describe one of Constantius Chlorus' episodes with the Christians in his domain. In sage mimicry of his colleague-emperors, Chlorus purported to do the same and put to the test the spiritual loyalties of his subjects, yet with less harsh penalties. State policy was that all idolaters willing to give proof of their beliefs could remain in, or gain, public office, whereas all self-professing Christians were to be banished. The idolaters and the Christians sorted themselves out before Constantius in obedience to this decree. They declared themselves to be in favor of the one or the other spiritual master: either the Christian God or—would to God that they knew it to be so!—the demons. Then they awaited Constantius' verdict. It was not long in coming. For in a contrariwise fashion to his initially declared purpose, Constantius banished the idolaters. He entrusted the Christians with the guardianship of his person and empire. Thus, he surrounded himself with believers in Christ, who enjoyed his protection; and, therefore, was he blessed with a peaceful reign.[21]

Now before Constantius surrendered his soul, he disclosed from his deathbed, in the presence of Crocus and his senior commanders, that he wanted Constantine as his successor. The senior legion cried out, "Hail Flavius Valerius Aurelius Constantinus, Augustus!" Thus, at thirty-two years old, came the call for the elevation of Constantine to Augustus.[22] As for his personal life, Constantine, earlier, at twenty-two, had met Minervina and wedded her

---

[19] Ibid., Bk. II, Ch. XLIX.

[20] Ibid., Bk. IV, Ch. XV.

[21] Ibid., Bk. IV, Ch. XVI, XVII.

[22] The pagan Zosimus (6th C.), in his *Historia Nova*, records that the "legitimate children" of the dead emperor "were not deemed worthy of the imperium." Kousoulas informs us that "actually, they were much too young, and for this reason were they bypassed. The pointed reference to the 'legitimate children' was a sly way of implying that Constantine was not 'legitimate.' On this, the pagan historian allowed his personal feelings to take over. Under Roman law, the marriage of Flavius Constantius to Helena was legitimate and so was their son....But the practise of distorting reality because of political enmity has a long tradition." Kousoulas, "Constantine is Proclaimed Augustus," *The Life and Times*, p. 154.

in 295. He begot a son, but the mother apparently died in childbirth or soon thereafter. The handsome infant with the curly dark hair was left with Helen to raise. Helen called the boy Crispus.

Meanwhile, Constantine, still in Britain, received a report that the Franks violated a peace treaty they had signed with his father. They were ravaging lands in the northeastern part of Gaul. Constantine crossed the Channel and annihilated the Franks. When he left that battlefield for Treves near the Rhine, he encountered his stepmother, Theodora, and his three half-brothers and three half-sisters. Theodora, some five years younger than the thirty-four-year-old Constantine, offered to leave the palace. Constantine graciously remarked that the palace was her home and that, as a soldier, he did not need much space to abide in. Mindful of his promise to his father, he put away any resentment he felt toward his stepmother. She, after all, was commanded by her stepfather, Augustus Maximian, for the sake of imperial expediency, to replace his mother Helen. In governing those under him, Constantine showed himself to be one noble, honorable, and sympathetic.[23]

Prior to the death of Constantine Chlorus, as we said, there took place the voluntary abdication of the old emperors, Diocletian and Maximian Herculius. There followed that the two men to be elected to the dignity of Augustus were Galerius and Constantius. The two new Caesars (junior emperors) were Severus and Maximinus Daia. Caesar Severus was appointed in May of 305 to the Emperor Constantius I Chlorus. Severus was given control of Pannonia, Italy, and Africa. Upon Constantius' death, Severus was made Augustus of the west by the remaining emperor, Galerius, who still controlled the east. Maximian Herculius' son, Maxentius, now twenty-one years of age, was maddened that he was passed over in favor of Severus. The latter was made a Caesar and, then, in 306, an Augustus. Maxentius was equally frustrated when Constantine was made Augustus of the west and then formally declared Caesar under Severus. But Severus became unpopular when he imposed higher taxes on the people of Rome and of Italy. In 306, a revolt broke out in Rome, led by Maxentius, son of the former Emperor Maximian Herculius and son-in-law of Galerius. Maxentius urged his father, who abdicated in 305, to reenter public life. All sources agree that Maximian Herculius was not enamored with his retirement, so he assisted his son Maxentius. The following spring Severus marched upon Rome from Milan, but his troops deserted him and he was forced to take refuge in Ravenna. He surrendered to Maximian Herculius on condition that his life be spared, but

[23] Constantine's half-brother, Hannibalianus, begot two sons, Dalmatius and Hannibalianus. The great Constantine, just before his death, gave his nephews a part in governing: Thrace, Macedonia, and Achaia went to Dalmatius, while Armenia and the Pontos were under Hannibalianus.

shortly afterward he was executed in 307. Also, in 305, Daia was proclaimed Caesar to Galerius. He was assigned to the rule of Syria and Egypt. After Galerius elevated Licinius to the rank of Augustus in 308, Maximinus also claimed and obtained the same title. It was not long before father and son, that is, Maximian Herculius and Maxentius, quarreled. Maximian sought refuge with great Constantine, who had been designated an Augustus by Maximian. Maxentius at first controlled Italy, Spain, and Africa. But in 308, the vicar of Africa, Lucius Domitius Alexander, revolted and proclaimed himself Augustus. Two years later Constantine annexed Spain. Africa was recovered by Maxentius in 311, but he was soon slain at the Battle of the Milvian Bridge in 312. Before this took place, father and son had made an agreement with Constantine that they would remain in Rome; meanwhile, Constantine had the charge of the western provinces which his father Constantius Chlorus ruled.

Building family ties by way of matrimony was important to the tetrarchy for solidifying loyalty. Constantine's father, Flavius Constantius, was forced to divorce Helen and marry Maximian Herculius' stepdaughter, Theodora. She was the offspring of Maximian's wife's previous marriage and she was twenty-six years younger than Constantius. In Constantine's case, he also made a marriage bond with Maximian Herculius' house. The latter had a daughter of his own by his wife Eutropia. The girl's name was Fausta, who was also the sister of Maxentius. The damsel was famed for her beauty, but favored her father in his mischievousness and malignant judgment.[24] The wedding ceremony was held at the palace in Arelate. Constantine showed every indication that he was in love with his young bride. Constantine was no longer a simple Caesar but an Augustus and a legitimate member of the Herculean house, the Dynasty of Maximian Herculius.

Peace was then established for a time, to the joy of all. Constantine set up his capital in the city of Arelate (Arles) in southeastern Gaul, where the Rhone River divides to form its delta, northwest of Marseille. Constantine governed his realm with all justice, for which he was beloved by all the people. Nevertheless, to his enemies he became a terror because he would always emerge victorious. He fought against the Germans over whom he triumphed and subjected to his rule together with those areas in the west.

After the festivities, Maximian Herculius asked his new son-in-law to move against Augustus Galerius Maximianus of the east should he invade Italy. Constantine was not amenable; but he pledged to remain in south Gaul as a

---

[24] Maximian had been father-in-law to Flavius Constantius, Constantine's father, and so Maximian's grandchildren were also Constantine's stepbrothers and sisters. To entangle matters even more, Fausta's stepsister Theodora was now in a way her widowed mother-in-law. Kousoulas, "Galerius Seeks Revenge," *The Life and Times*, p. 173.

deterrent to Galerius. The latter, nevertheless, had a design: he wished to rule in the west and remove Maxentius and Constantine. Galerius, thereupon, amassed a large army and proclaimed his commander Licinius as Caesar. They moved toward Rome, passing through the lands of Illyricum.[25] He came into upper Italy and then moved toward Rome. When Galerius crossed into Italy, Maxentius, his son-in-law, demanded that Galerius and his legions leave Italy. The latter retreated, plundering heavily. Galerius returned to Nikomedia and resumed persecuting the Christians. About that time Maximian Herculius came into conflict with his son Maxentius. The old emperor denounced Maxentius publicly for allowing Galerius to leave behind a scorched earth. Though he stripped his son of the purple, the men and officers still rallied behind Maxentius. Maximus Herculius left Rome humiliated. He, in the spring of 308, returned to his son-in-law, Constantine. The latter received him cheerfully and with all the deference accorded to an emperor. As David of old toward Saul, Constantine showed himself to be an honorable and dutiful son-in-law. Thus, for the time, Maximus Herculius settled for living with his two daughters, Theodora and Fausta. As much as Constantine would have liked his mother to live with him in Arelate, it was not practical. His stepmother Theodora and her children lived at the palace. Thus, Helen remained at Drepanum with her grandson Crispus. But the time was approaching when Maxentius would clash with his brother-in-law, our Constantine.

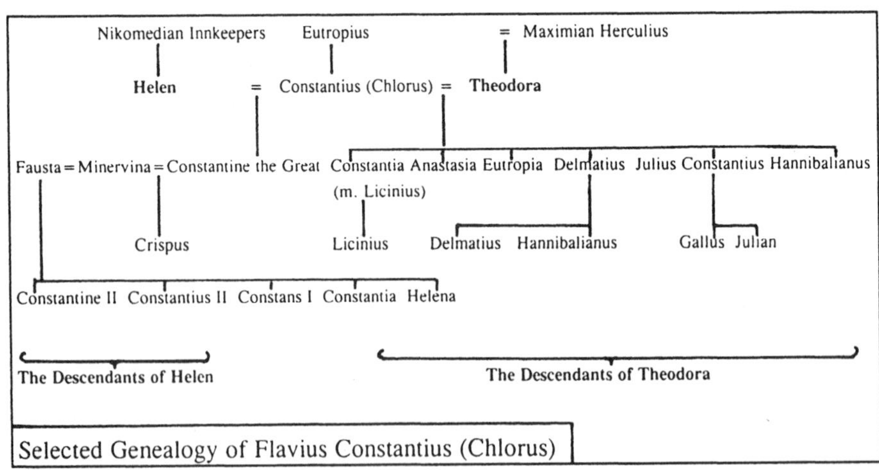

Selected Genealogy of Flavius Constantius (Chlorus)

[25] Galerius crossed into Italy probably in the month of May, not meeting with much resistance. He moved from Aquileia (east of Venice) through the Padus Valley to Ravenna and on to Fanum Fortunae (Fano) on the Adriatic coast. In June, he marched through the Appenine passes. He came to Umbria and then to Interamna (Terni). Ibid., pp. 173, 174.

Maximian Herculius was still indignant with his son, Maxentius. Maximian Herculius wanted his son-in-law, Constantine, to take away the African provinces from Maxentius, in order to deprive him of grain. The old Emperor Maximian Herculius still had followers in the legions stationed in Mauretania and Africa Proconsularis. In the places where the revolt started, Maximian Herculius was not proclaimed Augustus but Domitius Alexander. The old emperor blamed Constantine for their not declaring allegiance to him. Meanwhile, Maxentius bided his time. He feared that should he go to Africa, Constantine might invade Italy. Hence the empire was partitioned five ways under Constantine, Maxentius, Galerius, Maximinus Daia, and Alexander. Galerius, who was suffering from colon cancer, asked the other old emperor, Diocletian, to return and end the fragmentation. Diocletian agreed to meet at Carnuntum, near present-day Vienna, with Galerius and Maximian. When they met, Galerius had a legion commander with him, a man named Licinius. Galerius disclosed how he was bleeding heavily and recommended Licinius to the dignity of Augustus. Maximian wished to resume the purple, but Diocletian reminded him that they gave an oath before Jupiter to surrender the crown. Thus, Licinius was invested with the purple as Augustus; and he left for his new capital at Sirmium. The empire, therefore, had Galerius and Licinius with the rank of Augustus, and Constantine and Maximinus Daia as the two Caesars. Maxentius and Domitius Alexander were denounced as usurpers.[26]

In the spring of 309, Constantine sent for his son Crispus. He came with his tutor Lactantius.[27] The boy's grandmother, Helen, remained in Drepanum. The old emperor Maximian Herculius, suffering from dementia, spread the rumor that Constantine had died. Constantine could scarcely believe that his hospitality to his father-in-law should be thus repaid. He perceived a conspiracy behind the rumor—with Maxentius involved. Since Constantine was quelling a disturbance among Frankish tribes, he needed to return to Arelate quickly. Taking the Rhone (Rodhanus) River was the fastest way. Constantine commandeered as many vessels as he could to transport men and horses. He also improvised by having logs tied together to make crude rafts for the fleet. When Maximian learned that his son-in-law was coming, he stole Constantine's treasure and headed for Massalia. When Constantine followed and appeared at Massalia, Maximian shouted down insults. Constantine, despite his father-in-

[26] Ibid., "The Conference at Carnuntum," *The Life and Times*, pp. 185-187.

[27] Lactantius, a convert to Christianity, wrote in Latin. He accompanied Constantine in the 312 invasion of Italy. His works include *De Mortibus Persecutorum* (*On the Death of the Persecutors*), ed. by Samuel Brant (Leipzig, 1897), which speaks of the horrible ends of the Christian persecutors. His other work, entitled *Divinae Institutiones* (*Divine Institutions*), praises Constantine. The English translation is found in the Ante-Nicene Fathers, Vol. VII.

law's ingratitude, dispatched emissaries offering the old emperor his life. It was only after a few days that the old man went forth and surrendered. Father-in-law and son-in-law rode back home. The whole affair was charged to a misunderstanding. Many believe that Constantine went along with this arrangement to please his wife, but Constantine was not a fool. Furthermore, he understood that his father-in-law was suffering from a deranged mind bent on recovering his lost imperium. Eventually, Maximian Herculius tried to murder his son-in-law. Such treachery ended in the old man's suicide by hanging. Constantine, to set his wife at ease, gave his father-in-law a funeral worthy of an emperor.[28]

Now Constantine also needed to turn his attention to rebellion among the Franks. Fighting was brutal and there were losses on both sides. Constantine overcame them and gave the remaining notables the following opportunities. They could either fight and die or live under Roman protection and have their own chiefs. The latter choice allowed them to continue worshipping as they chose and enjoying the fruits of their labors. The Romans would help them rebuild their villages. Roman garrisons would also remain and keep the peace. Their sons were invited to join the army, and one day even receive citizenship. They agreed to the second offer. Constantine then went to Spain and the Pyrenees, which had been lost. The renegade governors and legion commanders, expecting Constantine by sea, fled when they heard he traversed the mountain range.[29]

Maxentius, hearing of Constantine's success in Spain, turned his attention to the recovery of the African provinces. Italy needed either Spain or Africa for foodstuffs and grain. The siege lasted three days. Domitius Alexander was strangled. While this was taking place, Constantine was still in Spain. Maxentius, pleased with his acquisition of grain-filled lands, resumed his life of banquets and orgies. At twenty-five years of age, he announced that pleasure was his only purpose in life. He was again popular in Rome. Despite the excesses in drunkenness, he was acutely aware of two facts: Constantine and his legions were still in Gaul; and Licinius was with his men in Illyricum and Pannonia. Maxentius was also thinking about his cancer-ridden father-in-law. How much longer could he last? Who would gain the eastern portion of the empire?[30]

Galerius Valerius Maximianus (305-311), the persecutor of the Christians, was struck with an incurable disease in that organ of his in-

---

[28] Kousoulas, "Tragedy in Arelate," *The Life and Times*, pp. 190-195.

[29] Ibid., "Constantine Recovers Spain," *The Life and Times*, pp. 197-201.

[30] Ibid., "The End of the Rebellion in Africa," *The Life and Times*, pp. 202-207.

temperance.[31] A malignant ulcer attacked the area of his genitals, but the tumor continued to grow. The more the surgeons cut, the more it spread. His entrails were decaying and his genitals were rotting. The stench from the abscess was accompanied by swarms of maggots. Such are the descriptions of Eusebius[32] and Lactantius. The former persecutor, after appealing to his gods who had failed him, decided that his unspeakable suffering was punishment for his persecution of the Christians. He issued an edict in the spring of 311 in their favor, not that he joined the Christians but he did ask for their prayers. Galerius, before issuing the edict, dispatched copies to Licinius, Constantine, and Daia for their signatures. Constantine and Licinius agreed to the edict but Daia did not. Galerius then signed the edict at Serdica (modern Sofia of Bulgaria) on the last day of April, and then he died a few days later. The document says in part: "We have issued other edicts to help the Christians return to the ancient institutions and rituals, to which many submitted out of fear. But many more of them resisted and suffered all kinds of death. And since many insist on their foolishness and we see that they refuse proper worship to the celestial gods, we have turned to our clemency and to our constant habit of rendering forgiveness to all men. We have thought it best to extend willingly our forgiveness so that immediately all Christians will be able to congregate in their houses of worship; thus, they will do nothing against the law. In another letter, we shall state to the judicial magistrates what they should do. Therefore, because of our benevolence, the Christians should pray to their God for our salvation, for that of the commonwealth, and for their own, so that the state will be safe and prosperous, and they themselves may dwell in safety in their homes."[33] Who can adequately describe the high emotions seeing the Christian prisoners and living martyrs released from dungeons and mines? Even the pagan populace was relieved that the violence was quelled and that kith and kin were being reunited. Those Christians that had lapsed and agreed to offer sacrifice, in order to avoid torture and death, asked forgiveness of the returning faithful brethren.

When Maximinus Daia, in faraway Antioch, learned that his uncle Galerius was dead, his legions went into action and secured Cilicia, Cappadocia, and then Nikomedia. Daia had added Galerius' territories to his own

[31] Galerius Maximianus was such a fornicator that his subjects sought anxiously to hide their own wives lest the women suffer his debaucheries. He also refrained from tasting anything without the support of divination. He ordered total destruction of the Christians, not so much because of his own ancestral impiety as to plunder their goods and properties. *The Chronicle of Theophanes Confessor*, AM 5797, A.D. 304/305, p. 20.

[32] Eusebius, Bk. I, Ch. LVII.

[33] Kousoulas, "The Death of Galerius," *The Life and Times*, pp. 213, 214.

in a matter of weeks. Licinius, who had been elevated to the rank of Augustus by his friend Galerius, had believed himself to be the legitimate successor since the conference at Carnuntum. Galerius intended for Licinius to rule the west, but since Italy, Africa, and Spain were held by the usurper Maxentius, while Constantine reigned in Gaul and Britain, Licinius resigned himself to the governance of Pannonia. Thus, Licinius took over Galerius' European dominions. By the summer of 311, Licinius marched his legions to the north side of the Bosporos to confront Daia. Licinius sent a delegation to Daia so as to discuss peace. Since Daia had added Galerius' legions to his own, Licinius quickly calculated that he was vastly outnumbered. The two Augusti agreed that the Strait of Bosporos[34] and the Hellespont would mark the boundary between their territories. Daia, therefore, would be left with the lands he seized after Galerius' death, with a pledge that he would supply Licinius with grain. Thus, Licinius, could safeguard his present lands until he could build his army. Meanwhile, Daia, who despised the Christians, issued an edict of official toleration. Even though the fifty-year-old Daia was married to Evdoxia, he made a marriage proposal to Valeria (the daughter of Diocletian and Galerius' widow). He hoped with such a connection to establish himself as senior emperor at Nikomedia in Diocletian's palace, where he was currently living. He looked to bring himself into Diocletian's Jovian family, which name was held in prestige by the pagans in those days. Valeria refused his proposal, thinking it improper for Daia to divorce his faithful wife and marry a widow who was still in her mourning clothes. Daia became spiteful and drove Valeria and her mother Prisca into destitution and exile in Syria. Diocletian was apprised of the abominable treatment of his wife and daughter. He wrote Daia to have them sent to Salonae. Daia ignored the continued letters of Diocletian, who never saw his wife or daughter again.[35]

The Liberation of Italy

In the meantime, Constantine dealt justly with the people in his realm. The rakish and avaricious Maxentius, however, was a continual problem. Constantine, therefore, took pity on the tortured people of Rome and moved with all his army. Constantine, however, needed to be sure that Licinius would stay out of the fighting. Licinius was more than amenable, because he, too, needed Constantine's friendship. In the fall of 311, Constantine sent an emissary to the forty-six-year-old Licinius, suggesting that he marry his sixteen-year-old half-sister, Constantia. Both Daia and Maxentius learned of the proposed match and interpreted it as an alliance that threatened them.

---

[34] The Strait of Bosporos (nineteen miles) is located in southwestern Asia and southeastern Europe. It connects the Black Sea (from the north) and the Sea of Marmara (from the south), and splits northwestern Turkey.

[35] Kousoulas, "Land Grab," *The Life and Times*, pp. 216-221.

In early April of 312, Constantine made his move. Maxentius had 170,000 foot soldiers and 18,000 horsemen under his command. Constantine, even after vigorous recruiting efforts, had no more than 90,000 foot soldiers and 8,000 horsemen, because he had to keep at least three to five legions along the Rhine. Constantine first attacked the garrison town of Segusio with its strong walls. It was situated on the route leading from Gaul to the Padus (Po) Valley. Since the garrison commander refused to surrender, Constantine, with catapults and rams, pounded the walls. After a few days, they crumbled. The garrison still refused to surrender. Constantine's men then burned the city gates. As the fire spread, Constantine ordered his men to save as many houses as they could. Meanwhile, the garrison finally surrendered. Constantine issued strict orders that no looting and raping were to occur. Constantine hoped that the report would spread through Italy of his humanitarian treatment of the people. He came as a liberator against the tyrant Maxentius. With the fall of Segusio, Constantine moved to the next city, Augusta Taurinorum, which was guarded by cavalry fully covered with armored tunics and horses draped with a protective covering with jointed metal clips. These were the *katafraktoi* who could mow down foot soldiers and pierce their bodies with their lances and swords. They were equipped with long spears that could push opposing horsemen off their mounts. Constantine and his men were aware of this terrifying force. Constantine, therefore, had his men train with a tactic that would counter the armored horsemen. Constantine had his men allow the *katafraktoi* to approach. When the armored horsemen drew nigh, they quickly opened their ranks and let the *katafraktoi* gallop through the opening. Before they could turn about their mounts, Constantine's soldiers closed ranks. The horsemen, consequently, could neither maneuver nor avoid one another. Constantine's foot soldiers, with their shields up, pushed in closer and closer. Horses and riders clashed with one another, severing the horses knees and hocks which were not covered with armor. With the tendons thus severed, the horse collapsed and the rider came crashing down. The fallen

Saint Constantine

riders, unable to move properly, were trapped in their suits and easily put to death.

The next day Constantine marched up to the walls of Augusta Taurinorum. The gates were already opened and the city notables were waiting to greet Constantine. They heard of the humane treatment received by their neighbors at Segusio and hoped for the same benevolence. Constantine left one cohort and moved toward Milan with its strong walls. Anticipating a long siege, Constantine found that the Milanese nobles were waiting for him with a large crowd in a festive mood. Constantine rode through Milan as thousands cheered. Although he was pleased at the peaceful surrenders, Constantine was mindful of Maxentius' force in the north under the able legion commander Ruricius Pompeianus. These legions were spread from Verona to the provinces of Venetia and Istria to prevent a possible attack by Licinius. Constantine thought that should he continue further south, Pompeianus would be at his back. He, therefore, decided that before moving south he had to eliminate the force behind him. Constantine stayed in Milan for ten days to rest his troops before they mounted an attack on Pompeianus at Verona, another well-fortified city on the banks of the river Adige.

When Constantine began marching on Verona, Pompeianus dispatched his *katafraktoi* and regular cavalry to Brescia (Brixia) to impede their progress. Constantine's men used the same tactic of having his lines swallow the armored horsemen. Many were slaughtered, but Constantine kept pushing toward Verona. Since Verona was surrounded on three sides by a swift stream with only one approach by land, Constantine wanted to constrain Pompeianus to divide his forces. Constantine sent several cohorts and catapults across the river to the east bank, and then south opposite the city walls. The city was besieged for many days with rams and catapults pounding the walls. Pompeianus realized the walls could not withstand the bombardment and ramming indefinitely. He needed his forces in Venetia and Istria. He, therefore, put on peasants' garb and escaped Verona by boat. A week later, Pompeianus appeared at the head of a strong force. Constantine and Pompeianus met and fought outside the walls of Verona. Constantine fought as an angry torrent. He fought as a common soldier beside his men. When the bloody and ferocious battle ended, Constantine, with blood on his uniform and hands, returned to his tent. His officers, with tears in their eyes, said, "It is unseemly for the emperor to strike down the enemy with his own hands and to sweat with the toil of battle." At the end of the day, Pompeianus was slain. Both officers and soldiers from the dead commander's legions asked to join the legions of Constantine. They were readily accepted into the ranks. Others who did not join were allowed to disband and go their own ways. Once again, Verona, as the other Italian cities, was not subjected to plunder or to rape. As word spread, Aquileia and the other towns in the Venetia and Istria regions peacefully surrendered and opened their gates to Constantine's detachments. The men in those garrisons either joined Constantine's legions or went back to their villages. Constantine's rear guard was now free as Rome lay before him.[36]

Maxentius acted unconcerned, as he continued with plans for his festive fifth anniversary on the 28th of October, which he was planning to observe on the 26th of that same month. He had the notion that his brother-in-law Constantine would not venture close to Rome. Meanwhile, in Arelate, Fausta was torn between love for her husband Constantine and her brother Maxentius. Constantine and his legions left Verona and marched through the Padus Valley, going toward Bologna (Bononia) and then on to Rimini (Ariminium) where the garrisons did not challenge the legions. Afterward, they went through Fanum Fortunae and the mountain passes. Constantine, meeting no opposition, reached Saxa Rubra, nine miles from Rome where he set up camp.

In the meantime, on the 26th of October, in the year 312, the streets of Rome were filled with people awaiting the parade and festivities. All the Romans thought Maxentius would not have proceeded with the anniversary party if war were imminent. At first there was a military parade, followed by acrobatic acts and chariot races. Then in the midst of the races at the Circus Maximus, certain individuals cried out to Maxentius, "Art thou a coward, hiding from Constantine behind the city walls?" Then the multitude shouted, "Art thou a coward?" Maxentius, enraged, left the podium. He was maddened that the Romans could even think of him as one fearful or timid before his brother-in-law, Constantine, whom he despised. He went and consulted the Sibylline books for a prophecy. He received the following reply: "Tomorrow, the enemy of Rome shall perish." Maxentius accepted the omen, interpreting it as it suited him. He, therefore, prepared for battle with Constantine outside the walls.[37]

Constantine heard the prophesy, as well as his soldiers and officers of whom many were pagans and the prophesy from the Sibylline books was a dire augur.[38] Constantine pondered upon the tyrannous rule of Maxentius in Rome, who had defeated other Roman governors' outraged attempts to unseat him. It, therefore, fell to Constantine himself, their junior in age and rule, to overthrow the tyranny. Maxentius was hated and despised. His crude habit of granting favors to husbands in exchange for a night with their wives had turned many

---

[36] Ibid. "Constantine Invades Italy," *The Life and Times*, pp. 222-233.

[37] Ibid., "The March on Rome," *The Life and Times*, pp. 234-238.

[38] "The great Constantine," notes Saint Theophanes, "feared the sorcery of Maxentius, who cut up newborn babes for his lawless divination. While Constantine was in great distress, there appeared to him at the sixth hour of the day the sacred Cross made of light." *The Chronicle of Theophanes Confessor*, AM 5802, A.D. 309/310, p. 23.

men into mortal enemies. His other custom of demanding expensive gifts also multiplied his adversaries.[39] As such, there was much smoldering hatred toward Maxentius. But the prediction was still fearsome to many.

The Appearance of the Cross: the Christogram or Monogram of Christ

Constantine then considered the rich and long-enduring heritage of his fellow countrymen's nationalist paganism, and his own father Constantius' devotion to the strange and new Christian God. He perceived the singular blessedness of his father's life, and the universally ill-fated destiny of his father's compatriots of the ruling class. His heart and soul were stirred to the depths when he meditated upon Christ's sinless life and sacrifice. Thus, he determined to seek Christ as his heavenly standard-bearer in the coming military battle with the undefeated armed forces of Maxentius. Added to this, there was the influence of Hosius of Cordova, the saintly Spanish bishop who spent time at Arelate, even in the palace and at Augusta Treverorum, as the

---

[39] Eusebius tells us that Maxentius, undefeated militarily, sought such victories and conquests in the civilian quarter as brooked no equal in vice, impiety, evil-doing, and wickedness. Counting himself divine and above the law of Rome, Maxentius was in the habit of sending for women both free and slave, and those who were the wives of both common-born and senator alike, and returning them in a dishonored state. Now, the demons had found in Maxentius a man who would physically act out his lewd desires upon every woman within reach, including Christian women. For, urged on by demonic lusts, Maxentius assayed to corrupt Christian women also; but he found himself frustrated in this design, since they chose rather to submit their lives to death than yield their persons to be defiled by him. [Bk. I, Ch. XXXIII.]

Indeed, there was the wife of a senator who was a prefect that was abandoned by her fearful husband to Maxentius' soldiers. She was bidden to come forth and be led away to be ravished by him; but she begged a few moments to prepare herself. And being granted this, she retired to her chamber. There, alone, she sheathed a sword in her own breast. She immediately expired, leaving indeed her dead body to the procurers. But she declared to all mankind, both to present and future generations, by an act which spoke louder than any words, that the chastity for which Christians are famed is the only thing which is invincible and indestructible. Such was the conduct displayed by this woman. [Bk. I, Ch. XXXIV.]

Maxentius' devilry had become monstrous. He ordered countless multitudes of the Roman people to be slain within the city limits under the merest of pretexts, by Roman soldiers expected to protect their lives. Even Roman senators of privileged status were falsely implicated and slain by the soldiers, that Maxentius might seize their properties. [Bk. I, Ch. XXXV.]

Maxentius openly embraced sorcery, ripping up women with child...or searching into the bowels of newborn infants. His harsh rule subverted Rome's established law, reducing its citizens to *de facto* slavery by means of extreme penury and famine. He sought by means of the occult arts to defeat Constantine in battle, or to halt or slay him even before their armies could meet. [Bk. I, Ch. XXXVI.]

guest and confessor of his father's second wife, Theodora. Accordingly, Constantine prayed to the God of his father, Who was the God of the Christians, with fervent supplications. Constantine entreated Him to reveal to him Who He was and to stretch forth His right hand to help him in his present difficulties. While Constantine was yet praying, he beheld a cross of light in the heavens, above the sun, and bearing this inscription: "In this, conquer."[40] Both Constantine and his whole army saw this marvellous sign.[41]

Constantine was a sane man and endowed with reasonable sensibilities. He was not one inclined to flights of fancy. He was so humble-minded as to doubt whether an almighty God would deign to vouchsafe such a miraculous vision to a sinful man like himself. He doubted within himself with an honest self-abnegation, and not in any faithless manner at all. He wondered what this apparition could be. That night during sleep, Christ appeared to him with the same sign of the Cross. He commanded him to raise a standard like unto it, by means of which he could safeguard himself in all his military campaigns and overcome all his enemies. Constantine, arising at dawn, communicated the marvel to his friends. Then, calling together the workers in gold and precious stones, Constantine sat in the midst of them. He began to describe to them the figure of the sign he had seen, bidding them represent it in such materials.[42]

It consisted of a long spear and crossbar in the shape of a cross which was overlaid in gold. On top of it was an upright wreath of gold and precious stones, within the circle of which was the symbol of the Savior's name, two letters signifying His name (the first two letters of Christos): the letter 'X' (Greek Chi) overlaying the letter 'P' (Greek Rho), so that it looked like an 'X' superimposed upon the letter 'P.' The emperor also wore, thereafter, the symbol of these two overlapping letters on his helmet. From the crossbar depended a cloth, a royal piece, covered with a profuse embroidery of most brilliant precious stones, and richly interlaced with gold. This banner was of a square form; and the upright staff, of which the lower section was of great length, bore a golden half-length portrait of the pious emperor and his children on its upper part, beneath the trophy of the cross, and immediately above the embroidered banner. The emperor constantly made use of this sign of salvation

[40] *In this, conquer*, in Latin is *in hoc vinces*; or in Greek *en touto nika*. Saint Theophanes the Confessor notes: "The Lord appeared to Constantine in a vision during the night, saying, 'Use what has been shown to thee and conquer.' Thus, having devised a golden cross, which exists to this day, he ordered it to be carried forward into battle." *The Chronicle of Theophanes Confessor*, AM 5802, A.D. 309/310, loc. cit.

[41] Eusebius, Bk. I, Chaps. XXVI, XXVII, XXVIII.

[42] Ibid., Bk. I, Chaps. XXIX, XXX.

as a safeguard against every adverse and hostile power, and commanded that others similar to it should be carried at the head of all his armies.[43]

Constantine, hence, was so struck with amazement at the extraordinary vision that he was resolved to worship exclusively the Christ Whose symbol had appeared. Constantine sent for men learned in the mysteries of Christ's doctrines. He inquired of the vision he had seen. He wished to learn more of the Christian God. He was given instruction about Christ and His holy Cross, that it was the symbol of immortality and the trophy of that victory over death which Christ had gained in His Passion. He was instructed also in the cause of Jesus' advent, and the true account of His incarnation. Constantine was filled with wonder. Comparing, therefore, the heavenly vision with the interpretation given, he found his judgment confirmed; and, in the persuasion that the knowledge of these things had been imparted to him by divine teaching, he determined thenceforth to devote himself to the reading of the inspired writings. He also retained the Christian priests as his counselors. Thus spiritually fortified, he prepared himself for the impending battle.[44]

The Great Synaxaristes (in Greek) says that Constantine was standing and pondering about the pending battle, being somewhat downcast, when he beheld in the sky at about the hour of noon the sign of the precious Cross. There were letters in Greek which read: "Constantine, in this conquer." As such, Constantine was told not to trust in his own human strength to vanquish the enemy; but in this sight of the cross, he would conquer the enemy in war. That same night, the crucified Christ appeared to him and said, "Rise up and construct a cross, even as the one thou didst behold. Hold it in battle with faith that thou mightest always overcome thine opponents." Constantine then rose up from his sleep. He, again, during the night, saw in the sky above the trophy-bearing symbol. He then believed with all his soul in the true God, our Lord Jesus Christ. When dawn broke, he commanded the construction of a cross made of silver according to the type that was made manifest to him. The men of his army always kept it before them.

Thus, on the 27th of October, according to Lactantius, Constantine caused the heavenly sign to be delineated on the shields of his soldiers and so proceeded to battle. When all was readied, his troops stood to arms. Eusebius adds that Constantine told him that it was around noon, as the day was already moving toward its end. Constantine had seen, with his own eyes, the sign of the Cross in the sky. It was composed of light, appearing over the sun with the attached writing. Thus, the mystical monograph of Chi-Rho was drawn with charcoal on shields and helmets. This divine symbol was believed by

[43] Ibid., Bk. I, Ch. XXXI.
[44] Ibid., Bk. I, Ch. XXXII.

Constantine's soldiers to be more powerful than the fearsome prophesy of their Sibylline books.

Constantine, motivated by love of his fellow man and reverence for God, invoked the name of Christ as his divine patron. With his royal standard to the fore, he marched on Rome. Maxentius barricaded all roads to Rome with divisions of soldiers. He resorted to his vile magic arts as he awaited Constantine's advance. Ever fearless at the head of his army, Constantine led his forces to victory after victory. He advanced undefeated against the first and second and third divisions of the tyrant's forces, vanquishing them all with ease; and thus, he made his way into the very interior of Italy.[45]

At dawn, Maxentius' soldiers emerged from Rome and marched along Via Flaminia in a northerly direction, with the Tiber to their left. Maxentius' Praetorian Prefect Rufius Volusianus designed the following operation. A strong force with the Praetorian Guards at the forefront would cross the Tiber using the Milvian bridge.[46] It was a narrow stone bridge. Another bridge, made of pontoons, would also be used by them. They planned to attack Constantine's forces that were camped north of the river, between and about Via Cassia and Via Flaminia. Another large force, in the meantime, would cross the river using other bridges further south. They, too, would march north and close in to join the battle for the kill. Of course Volusianus depended on the element of surprise. The prefect figured that Constantine would never expect Maxentius' forces to exit the city walls. In addition, the prefect anticipated to find Constantine's men still asleep. The assault would be swift; and then Volusianus and his force would move back across the river. The strategy was that the pontoon bridge was to be used to trap as many as possible of Constantine's soldiers. The pontoon bridge could be cut off midway by engineers. They would be protected while doing this severance by experienced archers inside a tower position on the south bank of the river. Volusian contrived to cut the bridge in half when most of his troopers were safely across with the rear ranks about midway. Constantine's soldiers, thereupon, would be on the northern side of the pontoon bridge. They would be left stranded, while archers rained down arrows upon them. The prefect was partly right. He did catch a number of Constantine's men fast asleep. But the others, at the clamor that was made, were quickly stirred into action. Constantine quickly perceived that the prefect made a bad mistake. Volusianus and his army had the river to their back, so that they could scarcely maneuver.

---

[45] Ibid., Bk. I, Ch. XXXVII.

[46] The Milvian, the present Ponte Molle, is nearly 1.5 miles from the Porta del Popolo (at the Mons Pincius). The walls at that time were the ones built by Aurelian, and are substantially the same as the present ones. The Pons Milvius was first built in 100 B.C.

Constantine directed his commanders by messenger to spread their units along the low hills to the east and the south of Via Cassia. Hence, the enemy forces would be pinned between the hills and the river. The prefect observed this and ordered his men to attack those units. But Constantine, famed for his quickness, charged his archers to break the prefect's advance with a barrage of arrows. At that point, Constantine's horsemen and foot soldiers, moving in battle formation, came in from the side. Clanging swords and cries of men filled the air. Constantine's men kept pushing and pushing, trampling upon bodies, so that they forced many of Maxentius' soldiers to leap into the river. Many were drowned by the weight of their uniforms and armor. Maxentius arrived and beheld the carnage. He commanded his troops to retreat behind the city walls. But in order to reach the city, they needed to cross the Tiber with Constantine's soldiers in hot pursuit. Constantine observed the press of Maxentius' men to cross the river, so he ordered an attack exerting every ounce of energy. At the same time, a shower of arrows fell on the fleeing men. Hundreds of disorderly soldiers descended on the bridges. Many trampled upon one another. Maxentius rode to the Milvian bridge. The pushing throng caused Maxentius to fall off his horse and into the waters below. He attempted to swim to safety, but the strong current and the weight of his mailed tunic brought him down. His drowned body was found the following morning, smeared and encrusted with mud, having become tangled in the weeds.[47]

The battle ended in the middle of the afternoon. Many died, but the heaviest losses were those among Maxentius' men. Countless suffered wounds or drowning. The city learned that Maxentius was dead and that Constantine had won. He was then forty years of age. Eusebius tells us that what had taken place was a most striking and miraculous chain of events. Maxentius, not content with sorcery, ordered a formidable war engine to be brought forward and mounted on a pontoon bridge over the Tiber River. Before Constantine could approach at the head of his army, the pontoon bridge began to sink; and Maxentius, and the soldiers and guards with him, went down into the depths like stone.[48] Thus were fulfilled various and telling types of the Old Testament history and parables of old: Pharaoh's chariots and his host have been cast into the sea, and his chosen chariot-captains have been drowned in the Red Sea.[49] As for Maxentius—even as it is written—"He has opened a pit, and dug it up;

---

[47] Kousoulas, "The Battle," *The Life and Times*, pp. 245-248.

[48] Cf. Ex. 15:5.

[49] Kousoulas, loc. cit. Saint Theophanes the Confessor describes the scene: "Maxentius fled with the survivors, but the bridge collapsed by the power of God. Maxentius was thrown into the river, just as Pharaoh had been long ago with his army; so that the river was filled with horses and their drowning riders." *The Chronicle of Theophanes Confessor*, AM 5896, A.D. 309/310, loc. cit.

and he shall fall into the hole which he himself made. His toil shall return to his own head, and upon his own pate shall his wrongdoing come down [Ps. 7:15, 16]." So, "Let us sing to the Lord, for He is very greatly glorified: horse and rider He has thrown into the sea. Who is like to Thee among the gods, O Lord? Who is like to Thee? Glorified in holiness, marvellous in glories, doing wonders [Ex. 15:1, 11]." Now the wretch Maxentius, with his armed attendants and guards, "sank like lead in the mighty water [Ex. 15:10]" even as the sacred oracles described. Thus, Maxentius was lost, and his sorceries utterly vanquished, in consequence of which his army immediately surrendered.[50]

The citizens of Rome, who had begged Constantine to come to their aid and were now released from the tyranny of the wicked Maxentius, garlanded the city and received with joy the victorious Constantine together with the victory-bringing Cross. The people proclaimed him as their savior.[51] After he gained control of Rome, Constantine ordered, before all else, that the relics of the holy martyrs be collected and handed over for a holy burial. The Romans celebrated a victory festival, honoring the Lord and the life-giving Cross. The festival, exalting Constantine, took place for seven days.[52]

Constantine's men then burned the corpses and carcasses. On the 29th of October, a triumphant parade was made into the city through Porta Aurelia. The head of Maxentius, whose features still wore the savage and threatening look which even death itself had not been able to remove, was carried on the point of a spear behind Constantine amid the jeers and insults of the crowd. A few weeks later, Constantine sent the head to Africa as evidence that Maxentius was truly dead. All thoughts of rebellion were relinquished.

On the 30th of October, Constantine visited and addressed the Senate. The senators wished to be treated with respect and delivered from onerous taxes. Constantine promised these things. The conqueror then proposed to raise the status of the Senate by allowing prominent individuals from other parts of the empire to become members. Constantine promised no retaliation for those who had been friendly to Maxentius. All those who had lost properties when Maxentius or his father, Maximian Herculius, were in power would have them restored. The Praetorian Guard was to be abolished. At the end of the ceremony, the senators proclaimed Constantine "Augustus Maximus," that is Supreme Emperor, superior to Licinius and Maximinus Daia. The Senate then voted to erect a statue and a triumphal arch in Constantine's honor. It stands today near the Coliseum in Rome. The dedication reads: "To the Emperor, Caesar, Flavius Constantinus Maximus, Felix Pious, Augustus: the Senate and

---

[50] Eusebius, Bk. I, Ch. XXXVIII.

[51] *The Chronicle of Theophanes Confessor*, AM 5896, A.D. 309/310, loc. cit.

[52] Ibid., AM 5803, A.D. 310/311, pp. 23, 24.

the people of Rome—because through the inspiration of the Divinity, and the magnificence of his mind and the deployment of his army, he destroyed the tyrant and his faction, with one stroke, and vindicated the Republic—this distinguished triumphal arch we dedicate to thee." Constantine tarried for two months.

Fausta came from Arelate and stayed at the Lateran palace. In regard to Maxentius' widow, Galerius' daughter, she and her three-year-old son were slain. The male line of Maximian Herculius was now extinct. As for Rufus Volusianus, the following year, he was appointed urban prefect and was elected consul the year after. Six years later he was made Praetorian Prefect by Constantine. Before Constantine departed Rome, he called upon the Bishop of Rome, Miltiades (Melchiades, 311-314). He offered him the Lateran palace as his official residence. Within a few weeks, Constantine had the powerful monogram embroidered on a deep red fabric with the Latin words *In Hoc Vinces*. He fashioned the banner which came to be known as the *labarum*.[53]

According to *The Great Synaxaristes* (in Greek), the triumphant Constantine was received with great rejoicing by the people. He mounted the imperial throne and took his place. All paid homage and reverenced him, as was meet. The God-protected emperor issued an edict to set up the life-creating Cross in the chief place of the city. He also commanded the diligent and careful finding of the holy relics of those wondrous martyrs who shed their blood for the sake of the name of the Master Christ. He charged that the martyrs were to be interred with fitting honors and piety. Those Christians who were still imprisoned were released; and those sent into exile were free to return wheresoever they wished.

Thus, the victory of the great Constantine was indeed a victory for Christianity against idolatry. During three hundred years, that is, the era of the holy apostles until the great Constantine, Christianity unceasingly was wrangling with paganism. But now the Faith emerged as victor from the spiritual stadium and cast off the tyrants' yoke. Martyrs' relics were brought forward, to the shame of the tyrants. Those Christians hidden in the catacombs came out in the open to worship the true God. The Cross prevailed and Maxentius was put to nought. How much joy was there among the Christians? It was boundless, unimaginable, and indescribable. It was a justified joy.

Constantine's Early Years

While this was taking place, Maximinus Daia was in Antioch. His campaign against the Christian king of Armenia failed. His area was suffering from plague, killing thousands. He was further vexed that Constantine was proclaimed by the Senate as Augustus Maximus, since he considered himself

[53] Kousoulas, "The Battle," *The Life and Times*, pp. 249-253.

the senior Augustus over Constantine and Licinius. He had been proclaimed Caesar to Galerius, his uncle, and assigned to rule Syria and Egypt. After Galerius elevated Licinius to the rank of Augustus in 308, Maximinus Daia also claimed and obtained the same title. Both in 306 and 308, Daia ordered a general sacrifice to the pagan gods. Those who refused suffered martyrdom or mutilation or hard labor in the mines and quarries. In 311, he grudgingly accepted Galerius' edict of toleration for Christians. He encouraged the *Acts of Pilate*, an anti-Christian forgery, to be taught in the schools.[54] He blamed the Christians for every calamity and pestilence that beset his realm. With the death of Galerius in 311, Daia occupied Asia Minor. In the autumn of 312, Maximinus relaxed his persecutions somewhat; and, shortly before his death in 313, he granted full toleration and the restoration of the confiscated church property. In the same year, he invaded Licinius' dominions in Thrace. He was roundly beaten at Tzurulum and forced to retreat into Asia Minor, where he died of disease.

After Constantine took Rome, Licinius thought Italy should have gone to him, but he was unwilling to face Constantine from the west and Daia from the east. He also thought to himself that Constantine was his brother-in-law. By marrying Constantia, his sister, it was a token of his agreement that Constantine launch the invasion of Italy. In February of 313, the wedding party—consisting of the bride Constantia, Theodora her mother, and Fausta her aunt—left Arelate, with Constantine and three hundred courtiers and squads of officers and soldiers, to meet with the bridegroom, Licinius in Milan.

The wedding was also an occasion for Constantine to speak with Licinius regarding issues facing the empire. In but a few days, they came to a religious policy for the realm. The recognition of Christianity as a valid corporation greatly strengthened recognition of the Faith under Roman law. The new status neither pronounced Christianity as the official state religion nor Christ as the only true God. The Edict of Milan, for the first time, assured freedom of religion by the state. They went on to say that "henceforth, every person who has chosen to observe the religion of the Christians will be free to do so without any hindrance or molestation." Moreover, with the Christian, "a similar right for free and unrestricted observance is granted to all others to practise their own rituals and religion as they wish, in keeping with the tranquillity of our times, so that each has the right to worship any deity they

[54] Galerius, persuaded by the magician Theoteknos, was sacrificing to demons and taking oracles. Theoteknos, crawling into his cave, gave the anxious Galerius an oracle: slay the Christians. Consequently, the *Memoirs of the Savior* were invented. The text was an insult and sent to every quarter, so that even schoolmasters were ordered to include it in the curriculum. The purpose was to ridicule the Christian mystery. *The Chronicle of Theophanes Confessor*, AM 5794, A.D. 301/302, pp. 14, 15.

should like." The blessed Constantine was still concerned with the welfare of the Christians as is evidenced by the following: "In addition, we resolve the following with regard to the Christians. If any persons have purchased from the public treasury or from others the places where in the past the Christians had the custom of congregating,...such places must be returned to the Christians without money and without demand for payment, removing any subterfuge or doubt. And also those who have purchased those places or have acquired them as a gift, if they have any claim on our benevolence, they are to appear before the local magistrate so that we may provide for them in our clemency. All these properties must be delivered without delay to the corporation of the Christians (*corpori Christianorum*)."[55] It was not until the 5th of June, in the year 313, that the edict granting toleration to the Christians and restoring Church property was issued. Although there is no record of a formal edict—and if they issued one the text has been lost—yet we have the text of official letters (rescripts) addressed to specific governors that have been preserved by Lactantius and Eusebius. A great festival was held in Milan, and in all the world, as a result of this edict. As for Licinius, now brother-in-law to Constantine, he was bound to him by ties of marriage and promises.

These and many other benefactions were achieved by the goodly Constantine at the beginning of his reign, as the firstfruits and offering to the munificent and beneficent God Who enlightened and elevated him. Afterward, moved by divine zeal, he also promulgated various laws, to the glory of God, toward the strengthening of our Faith. First, it anyone dared to blaspheme the Christ or harass a Christian, the offender was punished rigorously and all his goods were confiscated. Second, he commanded the enlisting into the army only of Christians; and, only Christians could be eligible candidates for offices or governorships. Furthermore, orders were given for the demolition of the altars of the idolaters. Churches were commissioned to be built in every place to the glory of Christ. Constantine himself undertook the construction of a large church in Rome, dedicated to the Savior God, the design of which was drawn by Constantine himself. He, as one most reverent, was the first to dig the church's foundation. The removal of the rocks in the digging was borne by him on his back and hauled away, that he might have a greater reward from Christ. He even went as far as to declare all work and employment suspended during the two weeks around the holy Pascha, that is, from Saturday of the Righteous Lazarus until the Sunday of the Apostle Thomas, so that all might hasten to the church. All poor folk who were baptized were fed and clothed at the imperial expenditure.

---

[55] Kousoulas, "The Edict of Milan," *The Life and Times*, pp. 261-263.

These and many other God-pleasing customs were put into law by the God-chosen and God-elected emperor. By reason of Constantine's governance, there was great joy and rejoicing throughout the inhabited world. From every quarter and at all times were people without number coming to the Orthodox Faith and being baptized. As for the temples of the idols, they were dashed to the earth and overturned from their foundations. The churches were adorned and endowed by the most pious emperor with rich revenues. The idol madmen, therefore, were put to shame, whereas piety kept increasing and striding in might. This growth was not taking place only in Rome but also in other cities. The Master, Christ God, the pre-eternal One, was being preached. The pious emperor continued appointing Christian governors and rulers. He sent them forth in every direction, commanding them to apply diligence in putting down idolatry, so that it might utterly vanish. He also urged them to confirm the Orthodox Faith as well as they could. These were just some of the enterprises of that thrice-holy emperor while at Rome.

Saint Constantine

Now Constantine knew full well that some of the leaders of Rome abided in their ancestral impiety. Such persons were not eager to leave their bad habits and customs. The emperor, thereupon, called the Senate into session and summoned the wealthy and nobility of the city. He exhorted them with the following words: "You know, my beloved friends, that, on the one hand, the mind of the impure and profane is not able to accept saving counsel; for these unfortunates find themselves submerged in the darkness of ignorance. But, on the other hand, the one who opens the eyes of his mind shall clearly understand the truth, so as not to venerate senseless, unseemly, and useless statues which are crafted by the hands of men. Take my example, and believe in the one true God. Him alone let us all venerate, as the Almighty and the all-good One. And let us not place our hopes in the idols that are unable to render us even one benefit. I do not compel or force anyone to come to piety, but I do advise you, as a friend, for your highest benefit, to practise this as your own deliberate course of action. Because human work ofttimes takes place even by imposition or enforcement, but the all-good God compels no one and coerces no one. He desires voluntary worship with an understanding and prudent mind." Upon uttering such words, all cried out, "One is the true God, the Christ!" In this way, many came to believe and were baptized. Once again, joy and gladness filled the city; and there was a great festivity. The entire realm was lit with lights. The tombs of the saints were adorned. Many good and God-pleasing deeds were taking place. Thus, not only the Romans came to believe in Christ but also all the Hesperian lands, that is, the western lands and western Europe, paid homage.

The Treachery of Licinius and Maximinus Daia

Now Licinius, after the marriage ceremony, and at the end of his talks on policy with Constantine, could not tarry. An alarming report cut short his visit in Milan. Maximinus Daia departed Antioch at the head of a huge force. His mission was to cross the Bosporos and invade the Balkans. He convinced himself that Constantine and Licinius were planning to attack him, so he thought he would make the first move in the midst of the wedding festivities. He ordered a forced march through Cilicia and Cappadocia. In the middle of a winter of heavy snowfall, after losing many men and mounts, he reached Bithynia. It was actually the beginning of March when he arrived, just opposite the garrison town of Byzantion,[56] with an exhausted and depleted army. It took four days for him to cross the Bosporos with 70,000 men and supplies. He made the gross tactical error of attacking the garrison at Byzantion. The time that Daia paused there allowed a message to be dispatched to Licinius in Milan, warning him of the pending attack. Eleven days the valiant garrison fought off Daia's men, but it finally surrendered out of sheer exhaustion.

Licinius moved quickly to Sirmium, leaving behind his bride with her mother and aunt. He needed to amass a force to beat off thirteen legions. His forces were camped in Pannonia and Dacia. It would take more than three weeks to assemble even 30,000 men, that is, six legions. There was no time to recruit and train new men. By the third week, Licinius and his forces reached Hadrianopolis in Thrace. Maximinus had moved on from Byzantion, taking Perinthos.[57] He kept moving northeast, until eighteen miles out of Perinthos he encountered Licinius. The latter sent a delegation to Daia, who had a superior

[56] Byzantion, the name of the Megarian colony at the southern mouth of the Bosporos, was later absorbed into Constantinople.

[57] Perinthos is the ancient name of Herakleia in Thrace and modern-day Marmara Eregli, on the north shore of the Sea of Marmara. It is at the junction of the Via Egnatia and the main Balkan road to Naissus. Perinthos had been renamed Herakleia by Diocletian, who preferred it to be named Herculius in official terminology. It had been the most important city in the province of Europa, but it was replaced by Constantinople. *Oxford*, s.v. "Herakleia."

force. Daia wanted war, so the talks came to nothing. Lactantius then recounts what took place.

Maximinus Daia vowed to Jupiter that should he win the battle, he would exterminate the Christians. The following night, Licinius later said that an angel of the Lord came to him in his sleep and told him to rise up and offer prayer to the supreme God. The emperor had the prayer transcribed and sent copies to the commanders and tribunes to have them teach the prayer to the men under them.[58] Licinius perceived how the mysterious monogram gave Constantine the victory, he hoped that offering up such a prayer would achieve the same result. The prayer, in fact, emboldened the men for battle, believing their victory had been announced from on high. On the last day of April, the two armies met across a barren field. Licinius' men halted and set their shields on the ground. Then they removed their helmets as they prayed the prayer with uplifted hands. The prayer was recited thrice, to the surprise and consternation of the opposing army. At the sound of the trumpets, Licinius' men advanced. As for Maximinus' men, terror filled them so that they could not raise their swords or aim their arrows. The larger force was mowed down by Licinius' men. Maximinus, disguised as a slave, rode off. Half of his men were slaughtered, the other half escaped or surrendered at the ignominious departure of their emperor. Maximinus, so frightened, rode one hundred and sixty miles, arriving in Nikomedia the following day. He took his family and hurried to the Taurus Mountains, hoping to block Licinius with his forces that came from Cappadocia. Licinius arrived in the third week of May at the Taurus Mountains in Cilicia, where Daia had time to construct barriers on the slopes.

Every man who had been a shepherd or a goat tender as a civilian was dispatched to climb up with axes and swords. Licinius' men came up from the rear and surprised Daia's men as they split their skulls. Daia escaped, deserting his men and riding away to Tarsus of Cilicia.[59] He, nevertheless, was visited by God's angels when he was given a beating. He began to hit his head on the wall, resulting in the loss of his eyes and blindness. His entrails seemed to be on fire and worms issued from his neck. He confessed to those around him that he was struck by angels. He, initially, did not wish to acknowledge this: but, lest the miracle abide unspoken of, he was forced against his will. Thus, all

---

[58] "Supreme God, we beseech Thee. Holy God, we pray to Thee. We commit to Thy hands all just cause. To Thee we entrust our salvation, and to Thee we commit our imperium. Through Thee we live and through Thee we gain victory and happiness. Supreme God, holy God, hear our prayer. It is to Thee we raise our arms. Hear us, holy God, supreme God!" Kousoulas, "The End of Maximin Daia," *The Life and Times*, pp. 270, 271.

[59] Ibid., "The End of Maximin Daia," *The Life and Times*, pp. 272, 273.

came to know the truth that divine retribution punishes the evil.[60] Daia, as his uncle Galerius, attempted to reconcile with the God of the Christians by offering freedom of religion and the rebuilding of the churches and oratories. With Maximinus Daia's death, Licinius was now sole master of the eastern half of the empire: from Pannonia to Mesopotamia, to Egypt.

Eusebius describes Maximinus thus: Still another emperor, Maximinus, was outdoing himself in all manner of outrage against the Christians. For he charged Christians to be put to the sword, pierced with nails, exposed to wild beasts, and consigned to the watery deeps. As well, he commanded the putting out of their eyes, not only of men but also of women and children. He ordered the cauterization and mutilation of their feet and limbs, followed by banishment to the mines. Yet, ever so brave from his throne, he found that his courage had mysteriously abandoned him athwart his horse when faced by opposing forces in the field, and—deserting the battle in cowardice—he took refuge as a vagabond in rags in the villages. It was there that God's vengeance unerringly found him. He smote him in the body, ravaging him until his appearance was skeletal and as dry bones. His condition continued to deteriorate until his eyes protruded and fell from their sockets, divinely returning upon the sower that which was sown: an eye for an eye, or in his case, both of his eyes for the eyes of ever so many of his subjects. Thereupon, Maximinus also repented of his evil laws. He rescinded them all. He acknowledged the error of his ways. He begged mercy of the very souls he had persecuted. This, by turns, being observed by the very same Licinius, was of no effect; he continued fearlessly in demonic perversions upon his own God-fearing subjects.[61]

Even though Licinius had signed the Edict of Milan and uttered the prayer that gained him the victory over Daia, he still had not accepted Christianity. Licinius systematically had members of the imperial families murdered, that is, the kinfolk of Daia, Galerius, and Diocletian. While these eliminations were taking place, Constantine was putting down minor incursions in Gaul and from across the Rhine as well as countering pirate raids along the Spanish coast. He also became involved in Church disputes involving the bishops in North Africa. He now had many demands on his time that necessitated appointing a Caesar. Since his son Crispus was only eighteen, he chose Bassianus, a *legatus* in the army and one of the wedding guests at the wedding of Licinius and Constantia. Constantine arranged a marriage with this dashing officer and his young half-sister, Anastasia.

---

[60] See the Life of Saint Menas Kallikelados, commemorated by the holy Church on the 10th of December.

[61] Eusebius, Bk. I, Ch. LVIII.

The perfidious Licinius incited an implacable war against his benefactor, Constantine, altogether heedless of the laws of friendship, the obligation of oaths, the ties of kindred, and already existing treaties. Pretending friendship, he did all by guile and treachery. But God enabled His servant, Constantine, to detect the schemes thus devised in darkness between Bassianus, Licinius, and Bassianus' brother Senecius. Licinius, at length, resorted to fresh frauds and then solemn treaties. But his conniving ways carried him away. He broke his word again and, finally, declared war against Constantine. But he was not content to challenge openly his royal, political, and familial superior, Constantine, to open combat. He also, with the churches and bishops under his rule, dealt treacherously: banning synods, communication, visitation, or councils by members of the clergy. Many other like-minded evil laws did he enact. He banished all Christians from the imperial palaces, and demoted them to positions of menial labor. He threatened to seize the property—on pain of death—of anyone who professed the Savior Christ's name. Above all, he denied that the virtue of chastity and continence existed among men. Licinius also passed a strange law that men and women could not appear together in churches. He forbade women to attend sacred schools of virtue, or receive instruction from bishops; but he allowed that women could be taught by other women. The law was received with general ridicule. He, in retaliation, ordered that congregations could only meet out-of-doors and outside the city gates, under the pretense that it was more suitable for a multitude. Failing, however, to obtain obedience in this respect also, at length he threw off his mask: he ordered all military personnel to sacrifice to demons. Those who refused would be demoted. He also ordered that prisoners should no longer be fed. Anyone found feeding them was to be punished with the same penalties as that assigned to the various prisoners. He also enacted many other equally like-minded, evil, and misguided innovations of law concerning marriage, the inequitable measurement of land, and the unseemly taxation of the estates of the survivors of the dead as if they were living. He found opportune twists of judgment, whereby countless folk from among the commoners and the nobility were imprisoned, thus rendering wives and female relations subject to violation by his underlings. Moreover, he himself violated, at will, wives and virgins. All this took place under the august pomp and ceremony of Roman rule.[62]

Constantine learned of the treachery against his life. He demanded that Licinius deliver up the conspirator, Senecius. Licinius refused and then moved his legions into western Pannonia, closer to Italy. Licinius then ordered the demolition of Constantine's statues at Ljubljana (Emona). Constantine prepared for war. Licinius amassed his forces of infantry and cavalry, totaling 35,000

[62] Ibid., Bk. I, Chaps. LI, LV.

men, according to an ancient secular account,[63] near the town of Civalis[64] in Pannonia. The town, situated on a hill, was nestled between a deep lake and a mountain. Beyond the town was a large plain where Licinius deployed his main force. Constantine strategically spread his men on the mountainside, where he would rely on his cavalry. The battle commenced at dawn and lasted until evening. It only ended when the right wing, led by Constantine himself, won the day. When Licinius' soldiers saw Licinius' attempting to escape on horseback, they, too, turned to flight with him. They fled all together, leaving everything behind, to Sirmium. He then cut off the bridge over the river Savus and moved on. Before he departed, however, he took his wife Constantia and his new son Licinianus. Licinius, after losing nearly 20,000 men, hoped to rebuild his army from the villages in Thrace. Still considering himself an Augustus, Licinius appointed Valens. The latter was his *dux limitis* (the general officer commanding the frontier troops), to the rank of his Caesar. Constantine interpreted this elevation as a pointed insult to himself. Constantine followed Licinius, and he seized Civalis and Sirmium. He also rebuilt the bridge that Licinius had taken apart. In the meantime, Constantine sent out 5,000 of his men to track down Licinius; but they were unable to discover his whereabouts. Constantine did not immediately pursue Licinius into Thrace. He needed to reinforce his army. The time that this took allowed Licinius the chance to bring in fresh troops from his legions in the Orient. But Constantine, now much too far from Gaul, thought it imprudent to leave his army insufficiently supplied. He, finally, marched into Thrace. Licinius was discovered on a plain, where he had set up camp. Constantine, aware that time was of the essence and that Licinius was gaining strength, went to Philippopolis (Plovdiv). He found a delegation from Licinius. Constantine dismissed them, believing it to be a ploy to gain time for Licinius to bring in even more men out of Asiana and Pontica. Constantine dismissed the representatives and marched southeast. Within days, Constantine arrived at night before the valley of the river Hebros (Evros),[65] where Licinius was assembling his forces.

The battle, beginning at dawn, lasted all day with neither side winning. When night fell, Licinius moved his men north toward Verea (Beroea). Constantine went in an easterly direction, toward Hadrianopolis and then on toward the Bosporos. Constantine captured Byzantion, where his scouts were informed that Licinius went north. Licinius then sent another delegation led by

---

[63] Zosimus tells the account with his usual hostile bias against Constantine, in *Historia Nova*, available in a modern translation by Ronald T. Ridley, *New History* (1982). The battle, however, described herein is given with a fairly impartial description.

[64] Civalis (Cibalae; Vincovci).

[65] This river, also known as Marica or Maritsa is in Thrace, flows into the Aegean Sea near Ainos.

one of his highest officials, Mestrianus. At the outset, when Mestrianus announced to Constantine that he was representing the co-emperors Licinius and Valens, Constantine quickly said he only recognized Licinius. Constantine gave the first condition of peace: the removal of Valens, and that Mestrianus would remain as a hostage until the demand was conveyed to Licinius. Constantine, thereupon, received word that Valens had been removed. Licinius, furthermore, had Valens arrested and executed. Constantine was persuaded that Licinius desired reconciliation. After negotiations, Licinius retained all the lands beyond the Strait of Bosporos: Asiana and Pontica, Syria, Mesopotamia, Palestine, Egypt and Libya, and an area of eastern Thrace on the northern side of the strait. Constantine received Pannonia, Illyricum, Moesia, and the Greek peninsula. The agreement between Constantine and Licinius was sealed with oaths by both, as guarantee that both would observe and be faithful to their treaties. Constantine raised to the rank of Caesar both his twenty-year-old son Crispus and his infant son Constantine. Licinius raised to the rank of Caesar his own infant, Licinianus. The principle of succession by birth was now introduced. The agreement between the brothers-in-law was sealed the following year when the Roman Senate appointed both Constantine and Licinius as consuls for the year 315.[66]

Saints Constantine and Helen

Constantine Becomes Involved in Ecclesiastical Affairs

In July of 315, Rome celebrated the *Decennalia*, the tenth anniversary of Constantine since he had been proclaimed Augustus in Eboracum in the British Isles. He had, during the last ten years, lived in Mediolanum, August Treverorum, Arelate, and Sirmium. Constantine went to Rome and accepted all of the honors bestowed upon him, with one important exception. He refused to make the traditional sacrifices to the pagan gods. He, rather, offered prayers of thanksgiving to God, the King of all, as sacrifices without flame and smoke. He did not, however, relinquish his title as Pontifex Maximus, for it gave him control over appointments of pagan priests. In August of that year, he

[66] Kousoulas, "Treason Shatters the Bonds," *The Life and Times*, pp. 278-287.

appointed the aged pagan aristocrat Vettius Rufinius to be prefect of Rome. He also was a high priest of the sun cult and a priest at the temple of Mars on the Palatine Hill. By his appointment, Constantine was following what was written in the Edict of Milan; but he also wished to demonstrate to the patrician pagans that he did not permit religious difference to interfere with affairs of state. He hoped by his example that others would follow suit. Many pagans did not care for Constantine's policy of admitting Christians into the aristocracy, but they could do nothing against such a powerful emperor.[67]

Constantine, for a time, directed his attention to the legitimate and universal religion. He wished for unity among the Christians of the supreme Deity. He was very generous with public funds to support his favorite religion, Christianity.[68] His contribution to the Faith was not only of a financial nature but also of a personal commitment, using imperial authority to maintain the Church's internal stability. This is seen early on in his steps to remedy the feud between bishops in North Africa. Constantine believed and wrote that the prosperity of all depends on offering veneration to the Divinity. In a letter to Anulinus, the proconsul of Africa, he speaks of his anxieties in this regard, writing: "Exempt the Christian clergy from public service lest through some error or sacrilegious mischance they should neglect their duties of worship and, by so doing, displease the supreme Divinity."[69]

It was Constantine's deliberate policy not to divide men but to collect them, to confer with their representatives, and to make them collectively responsible. Constantine respected the fact that the full council of bishops was by a long way the most representative conference the empire could produce. The Church's organization covered the entire empire and was based upon the civil organization; that is, the divisions and subdivisions of the ecclesiastical body almost exactly corresponded to those of the secular state. He not only listened to the bishops but also intervened to preserve the order of the Church. He retained the office of Pontifex Maximus among his imperial powers, in order to possess a legal right to supervise religious questions. The October following the Edict of Milan, Constantine appointed the Bishop of Rome, together with a committee of bishops, to inquire into the Donatist controversy in the African Church.[70] Constantine wrote to Bishop Miltiades of Rome "to investigate and close this matter according to justice." He then concluded with

---

[67] Ibid., "Celebrating the Decannalia," *The Life and Times*, pp. 319-321.

[68] See his letter to Caecilianus, Bishop of Carthage in North Africa, dated 313. A copy is found in Eusebius' *The Ecclesiastical History*, Bk. X, Ch. 6.

[69] Kousoulas, "Embroiled in Church Quarrels," *The Life and Times*, pp. 291-295. See epistle in Eusebius' *The Ecclesiastical History*, Bk. X, Ch. VII(2).

[70] *Concise Oxford Dictionary of the Christian Church*, ed. by E. A. Livingstone, s.v. "Donatism."

these words: "It should not escape thy notice how much respect I render to the legitimate and catholic Church, and that I do not intend to tolerate schisms or dissension anywhere. May the divinity of the great God protect thee for many years, most honorable!"[71]

The body of Donatists was a schismatic entity in the African Church. They had refused to accept Bishop Caecilianus of Carthage, on the ground that one of his three consecrators (Bishop Felix of Aptunga) was a traditor (one who surrendered the Scriptures to heathen inquisitors) in the Diocletianic persecution. The Numidian bishops consecrated Majorinus as a rival to Caecilian. He was succeeded by Donatus, from whom the schism is named. A commission under Bishop Miltiades of Rome investigated the dispute in October of 313, and decided against the Donatists. Miltiades wrote: "Since it is shown that Caecilianus is not accused by those who came with Donatus, as they promised to do, and Donatus has in no way established his charges against Caecilianus, I find that Caecilianus should be maintained in the communion of his Church with all his privileges intact." The Donatists appealed, and Constantine was willing to hear the case. Caecilianus did not return. When the Donatists insisted that they had won by default, they prepared to return to Africa. Caecilianus finally arrived. By then, Constantine incarcerated him and the Donatist bishops. He, in February of 314, sent two Italian bishops to Carthage with orders to consecrate a new, third bishop, to supersede the two rivals. When Constantine learned that riots ensued, he ordered the deputy prefect, Domitius Celsus, to punish the culprits. The victims of these measures were hailed by the Donatists as "martyrs." Finally, Constantine wrote to Domitius Celsus that he was coming to Africa. He said, "There is no higher responsibility for me by virtue of my imperial office than to dispel errors and repress all rash thoughts so as to cause all to offer to the almighty God true religion, honest concord, and proper worship." He, however, did not go to Africa, because he had to deal with his brother-in-law. Meanwhile, the two bishops left Carthage, declaring that Caecilianus was the only legitimate bishop. The emperor was then called away to distant Gaul. Caecilianus and Donatus escaped and returned to Carthage, where the feud continued.[72]

Constantine decided to call another synod in order to end the schism. Before he left for his war with Licinius, who was persecuting Christians, a second synod was readied. The enemies of Caecilianus declared that Pope Miltiades and other bishops had closeted themselves and judged the case according to their own wishes. They wanted another synod, and Constantine planned to have them meet at Arelate (Arles). He wrote to Aelianus, proconsul of Africa that "before the bishops leave their dioceses to come to Arles, they

---

[71] Eusebius, *The Ecclesiastical History*, Bk. X, Ch. V(20).

[72] Kousoulas, "Arbiter of the Faith," *The Life and Times*, pp. 307, 308.

ought to make the necessary arrangements whereby, during their absence, reasonable discipline may be preserved. Hence, with the application of some forethought, no rebellion against the authorities or individual quarrels might take place; because such actions bring the Church into great disgrace." The emperor then added, "For as I am well assured that thou art a worshipper of the supreme God, I confess to thee, excellency, that I consider it by no means lawful for me to ignore disputes and quarrels of such a nature as may incite the supreme Divinity to wrath not only against the human race but against myself personally into whose charge the Divinity by His divine will has committed the governance of all that is on earth. In His just indignation, He might decree some ill against me. I can only feel really and absolutely secure, and hope for an unfailing supply of all the richest blessings that flow from the instant goodness of almighty God, when I shall see all mankind worshipping the most holy God in brotherly unity of worship in the rites of the catholic religion." Hence, by this letter, we see that Constantine not only fears that the Divinity may turn against him but he also speaks of royal authority by the grace of God. He also expresses his desire to bring all of mankind to the all embracing catholic Church. While Constantine wrote this letter, and addressed other personal letters to all the bishops, he wished to attend Arles. He showed remarkable attention to detail, even in the midst of his military campaign.[73]

The Synod of Arles bears the names of thirty-three bishops and lower clergy.[74] The synod, called on the 1st of August, in the year 314, endorsed the verdict of the synod of Rome; so wrote the bishops to the new pope, Silvester I (314-335). Twenty-two canons were written, but the synod failed to put an end to the schism. The Donastists simply refused to quit. They actually asked Constantine to allow another examination into their case. Constantine wrote a letter thanking the bishops at Arles, and then vented his anger at the Donatists' new petition. He wrote: "O truly prevailing is the providence of Christ our Savior, that is solicitous even for those who have deserted and turned their weapons against the truth!...Now they clamor for a judgment from me, who myself await the judgment of Christ. For I say that, as far as the truth is concerned, a judgment delivered by bishops ought to be considered as valid as though Christ Himself were present and delivering judgment. For priests can form no thought and judgment, except what they are told to say by the admonitory voice of Christ. What, then, can these malignant creatures be thinking of, creatures of the devil, as I have truly said?"[75]

---

[73] Ibid., "Thinking of Another Synod," *The Life and Times*, pp. 309-311.

[74] Between forty and fifty sees were represented at the council by bishops or proxies; the Bishops of London, York, and Lincoln were there. Saint Silvester sent legates.

[75] Kousoulas, "A New Petition," *The Life and Times*, pp. 314, 315.

The Donatists still demanded a rehearing. The long-suffering emperor acceded to their request. Incredibly, the case was heard again. Constantine, in November of 316, issued his decision. He once more affirmed the innocence of Caecilianus and condemned his accusers. The letter was followed by an edict prescribing penalties against the schismatics. Three years after the Edict of Milan, Constantine employed the force of state authority to suppress disunity in the Church. Churches and properties were confiscated. The Donatists still did not relinquish their cause. Constantine decided to try gentle persuasion to restore unity to the Church. He wrote: "We must hope, therefore, that almighty God may show pity and gentleness to His people, as this schism is the work of a few. For it is to God that we should look for a remedy....Let there be no paying back injury with injury; for it is only the fool who takes into his usurping hands the vengeance which he ought to reserve for God....If you observe my will, you will speedily find that, thanks to the supreme Power, the designs of the presumptuous standard-bearers of this wretched faction will languish; and thus all men,...by the grace of penitence, may correct their errors and be restored to eternal life."[76]

Constantine, as we said, issued in the year 316, after close investigation and debate, a formal judgment in full consistorium. He did not prevent the Donatist split, but he gave the whole weight of his official support to the side which was undoubtedly in the right. These ecclesiastical conferences were something new. The expenses of the bishops were paid. They were also given official authority to use the government traveling service. The precedent that Constantine set was beyond reckoning. Constantine accepted the existence of great parties and movements, and he controlled their activities. This alone was a revolution. He was not ignorant of partisanship in religious matters. He could be cordial enough to the heterodox, but his actions in all cases were based upon careful inquiry into the facts. Constantine showed his special benevolence toward the Church, an organization that recruited its members from every rank and class without distinction.[77] Meanwhile, Donatist obstinacy continued.[78]

---

[76] Ibid., pp. 315, 316.

[77] G. P. Baker, "The New Empire," *Constantine the Great and the Christian Revolution* (NY, NY: Cooper Square Press, 1992), Ch. VIII(XII), pp. 213-215.

[78] In 321, Constantine relaxed his vigorous measures, having found that they did not produce the peace for which he had hoped. He weakly begged the Orthodox to suffer the Donatists with patience. This was not easy, for the schismatics broke out into violence. At Cirta, with the return of their Donatist Bishop Silvanus (a consecrator of Majorinus), the schismatics seized the basilica which the emperor had built for the Orthodox. They would not give it up, and Constantine found no better expedient than to build another. Throughout Africa, but above all in Numidia, they were numerous.

(continued...)

In the years that followed his tenth anniversary, Constantine spent his time at his favorite occupations: strengthening fortifications, reinforcing city walls, building highways, taking care of the empire, and, from time to time, trying to bring unity to the Church at Carthage. The influence of Saint Hosius' teachings was reflected in a number of laws that Constantine issued during those years. In 319, it was put into law that masters could not kill their slaves. In 320, there was another law that prohibited prison wardens from mistreating prisoners or branding convicts on the face. On the 7th of March, in the year 321, it went into law that Sunday was the official day of rest. While all this was taking place, the relationship and uneasy peace between Licinius and Constantine were tolerable. In 318, the Roman Senate elected Licinius consul for the fifth time. Crispus was elected for the first time. Constantine was elected as consul for the fifth time the following year. Little Licinianus was elected for the first time. But then in 320, while elections took place for Constantine's sixth term, for Crispus' second, and for Constantine's little boy Constantine, no mention was made of Licinius' return. Something was amiss. Constantine had moved the seat of Licinius' administration from Sirmium to Serdica.

The Menace of War

The Goths also were always in more or less force, continuing their border aggressions along the Danube. Constantine's campaign against them was on a front of some three hundred miles. Great battles occurred at Campona, the Margus, and Bononia. Constantine and his men repaired the old bridge at Viminiacum. He advanced indeed into Dacian land. The unconditional surrender of the Goths came after hard fighting, but he chose not to permanently occupy that territory. Constantine needed to be assured that his rear guard was secure before he could take on Licinius. In 320, Constantine invited his eldest son to Serdica that they might celebrate Crispus' fifth anniversary as Caesar. Crispus, during the past five years, had been in Gaul. He distinguished himself as a warrior and administrator. Crispus also met a girl of humble origin with whom he had a son in 322. This delighted Constantine who, to mark the occasion, released prisoners—except those convicted of murder, poisoning, sorcery, and adultery. Naturally, Constantine spoke to his son regarding the looming problem of Licinius' demonic deeds. This was Constantine's life until the summer of 323.

Relations were worsening. The hater-of-good, the enemy of truth, was unable to bear the success of the great Constantine's works. He found, as his

---

[78](...continued)
They taught that in all the rest of the world the Orthodox Church had perished, through having communicated with the traditor Caecilianus. They pronounced that their sect alone was the true Church. *Catholic Encyclopedia*, s.v. "Donatists."

worthy vessel of maliciousness, the vile Licinius whom he entered. Through Licinius he fought against the Christians and Constantine. Licinius did not keep his oaths. He did not bring to remembrance what happened to previous persecutors and tyrants against the Faith. The cruel, unseemly, and ungrateful Licinius put many to death. Reports came through to Constantine, who first wrote many letters to Licinius cautioning him to cease the works of the devil; otherwise he would be condemned to a fitting death. But Licinius gave no heed. Saint Theophanes the Confessor comments that "Constantine ordered Licinius in rescripts to stop this madness, but he did not persuade him. Licinius brought about the death through torture of Vasilefs, Bishop of Amaseia,[79] and, according to some sources, the holy Forty Martyrs of Sebasteia[80] and others."[81]

Eusebius informs us that Licinius rekindled the persecution of the Christians. Though a long-extinguished fire, yet he fanned the unhallowed flame to a fiercer height than any who had gone before him. He dared not at first resist the God-fearing example of Constantine openly. He, therefore, by artifice and secret machinations, pursued the persecution of the bishops and churches of God within his realm. He contrived unheard-of charges against the most eminent. He bound them and consigned them to prison, where he surpassed all former cruelties.[82]

The name of Licinius acquired an evil luster. His name was associated with malignancy, as he continued to execute the most distinguished prelates of the churches. That murderer had their bodies cut piecemeal and fed to the fishes. The churches were closed to worship lest Constantine should receive prayers. Licinius did not really believe that the Christians would utter any prayers in his own vile behalf, since he raised up a general persecution against them. At this time, by God's providence, Constantine ventured to pay a visit to Licinius' realm of darkness. Thus did the emperor from the west shine forth as a brilliant light in the midst of that gloomy night in the east.[83]

As we mentioned earlier, Licinius prevented bishops from meeting in synods. Those who defied him were removed; their property was confiscated. He also kept in force some unusual laws. He continued to prohibit women from attending churches with men, insisting that they be taught by women clerics. Services could not be held in buildings, only in the open air. All Christian officers in his army were discharged. He made changes in the measurement and

---

[79] Saint Vasilefs is commemorated by the holy Church on the 26th of April.

[80] The Forty Martyrs are commemorated by the holy Church on the 9th of March.

[81] *The Chronicle of Theophanes Confessor*, AM 5811, A.D. 318/319, pp. 28, 29.

[82] Eusebius, *Life*, Bk. II, Ch. I.

[83] Ibid., Bk. II, Ch. II.

assessment of land for the purposes of the public treasury, so that the rate of taxation upon land was raised.[84]

Constantine became painfully aware that the advent of his royal personage in that darkened land was a long-overdue event. Venturing no rash decisions, as was his hallmark, he took wise counsel. He tempered the natural clemency of his character with a certain measure of severity, as he hastened to succor those who were thus grievously oppressed. For Constantine rightly judged that it would be deemed a pious and holy task to brook Licinius' rule of evil doings and death, so as to allow the reign of righteous judgement and the fear of God. Constantine perceived that no kind word could sway his brother-in-law's demented behavior or alleviate his subjects' misery and sufferings. Accordingly, Constantine made preparations for battle. His army began to march on Licinius, bearing before them the standard of the holy Cross.[85]

Saints Constantine and Helen

Constantine and Licinius Clash

While on the march, Constantine was accompanied by priests of God; whereas, Licinius kept soothsayers in his entourage. As their two armies marched toward a headlong clash of swords, so too their respective guardians of the spiritual realm accompanied them—with blessings on the former hand, and curses and vile divinations on the latter. Each was informed by his priests that victory was assured. Hence, Constantine prepared himself for war by prayer; Licinius readied himself by the practise of divination.[86]

Licinius had a sizeable fleet, under the command of Avantos, with about 350 triremes. Constantine needed to build up his inventory of fighting ships and transport barges. This came by building, buying, and chartering vessels of all kinds to transport troops and supplies. Much of this work took place in Thessalonike, where he was widening and deepening the harbor. By the summer of 323, Constantine had a fleet of some 230 thirty-oared warships and 2,000 transport barges. Slightly

---

[84] Baker, "The Conquest of the East and the Council of Nicaea," *Constantine the Great and the Christian Revolution*, Ch. IX(I), pp. 216, 217.

[85] Eusebius, *Life*, Bk. II, Ch. III.

[86] Ibid., Bk. II, Ch. IV, V.

before this, in the autumn of 322, King Rausimond of the Sarmatians crossed the Danube into Moesia. He seized villages and captives. The latter he either held for ransom or sold into slavery. Constantine and Crispus pursued the barbarian. When Rausimond was slain, his men surrendered. Although most of the fighting took place in Constantine's realm while he chased after the Sarmatians, both he and his men entered briefly into Licinius' territory. Licinius, afterward, complained that Constantine violated their agreement by entering his territory. Constantine argued his entry was accidental, since it was necessary to rescue civilians from the barbarians. Licinius insisted that Constantine's straying, intentional and calculated, was really probing in advance for a full-scale war. After the Sarmatian invasion, Licinius sent a huge force to Hadrianopolis. Constantine did not take any action against what Licinius protested was a defensive move. Constantine was busy recruiting and training. He even had coins struck for both the Augustus and the young Caesar Crispus with the inscription "Sarmatia Conquered." Constantine also appointed Crispus *Dux* of the Fleet he had built. During the winter months, he brought together a force of 120,000 infantrymen and 10,000 cavalrymen.[87]

In the spring of 323, Crispus left Thessalonike in command of the fleet that was to meet with supply ships. The last week of June, Constantine crossed the frontier on the way to Hadrianopolis. Licinius was waiting with his army in a strong defensive position on a hillside. Constantine's army, with the *labarum* held high by a standard-bearer, went west of the city. They came near the banks of the river Hebros. For a few days, the two armies faced each other without any fighting.

Zosimus tells the story of the decisive battle. Constantine observed that the river Hebros was narrow at one point. Constantine ordered his men to bring logs from the surrounding hills. They constructed rafts with the wood and ropes with which the troops were moved across. Some 5,000 men, including horsemen, were transported and strategically hidden in a thick wood. When more horsemen were conveyed, they unexpectedly encountered enemy troops. While some of Licinius' men were slain, others were so confounded at the sight of Constantine's men that they fled. The story relates how Constantine swam the river himself, having about him only twelve horsemen, though far more followed. Zosimus reckons that 34,000 of Licinius' men died on that day, which was the 3rd of July, in the year 324. The fighting lasted all day. Constantine himself joined the combatants and suffered a spear wound to his thigh. The hit, however, did not dismount him. Licinius also fought, but many of his men were running and deserting.[88] Numerous soldiers of Licinius espied the fearsome sign of the Cross, which filled them with terror and trembling.

---

[87] Kousoulas, "Preparations for War," *The Life and Times*, pp. 331-333.
[88] Ibid., "A Decisive Clash," *The Life and Times*, pp. 334, 335.

They could not bear the light that emitted from that cross. Filled with shame and confusion, they retreated.

That same night, Licinius took those men that remained and marched through Thrace. He needed to reach his navy waiting at the point where the Hellespont meets with the Propontis (Sea of Marmara). As for the men that deserted Licinius, they surrendered to Constantine. Licinius, nonetheless, still had a formidable force and fleet. He was not ready to capitulate. Licinius went to Byzantion, after which Constantine moved his army to lay siege to the town. He ordered Crispus to sail the fleet to the mouth of the Hellespont. Licinius' admiral, Avantos, with his superior triremes, lost the chance to destroy Crispus' vessels. He could have moved out of the strait of the Hellespont into the Aegean, where he would have had room to maneuver his fighting ships. Instead, he kept them idling in the narrow waterways, where he thought he was safe. Crispus took the initiative and chose his best vessels, 80 thirty-oared boats with veteran seamen, and sailed into the strait toward the Propontis and Avantos' two hundred ships. Avantos saw Crispus and Constantine's admirals coming and scoffed at what he thought was a young man's foolhardiness. Each side, thereupon, moved toward one another. Constantine's admirals sailed in an orderly formation, ready to attack. Avantos' vessels moved in a disorderly fashion, so that their ships became entangled. This allowed Crispus to move in for the kill and inflict fatal damage. It was a scene of clashing and sinking ships, with shouting mariners and soldiers being taken down into the depths. By nightfall, it appeared that the naval battle was over. The strait was opened and Byzantion was isolated. Constantine's victorious fleet anchored in the Thracian port of Eleounda. Those remaining among Avantos' men entered the port of Aention, according to Zosimus. But the battle at sea was far from over.

The following day, Crispus, with many ships, moved in the direction of the Sea of Marmara. Avantos wished to come out of port, but he hesitated before the spectacle of the opposing fleet. During the delay to act, suddenly, a strong south wind forced Avantos' ships to founder or capsize with the men on board. He lost, thereupon, 130 ships and 5,000 men. As for Avantos, he managed to escape with four boats. With Licinius' fleet destroyed, Crispus set his course for Byzantion as he sailed through the Sea of Marmara. It was his plan to meet with Constantine's forces, which were besieging the town by land. Even though Licinius was worsted at sea and was losing on land, he still would not surrender. Constantine persisted outside the walls. He directed his men to raise up earthworks to the height of the town's walls. Atop each mound he built wooden towers so that the archers could take better aim at Licinius' men. Constantine also continued with the battering ram at the foot of the walls. Licinius now looked for a way to escape. He left behind a few defenders and took flight with a small number of men to Chrysopolis, which was on the

Asiatic side. He still had ideas about building a new army and coming back. Again, Licinius chose to be intentionally contemptuous of Constantine. He openly declared not only that Constantine was no longer Augustus but also that Licinius' new caesar was his *Magister Officiorum*, Marcus Martinianus, former chief of the civil service.[89]

Licinius imagined that he could still win, but he needed to be sure that Constantine did not cross from the European coast to the Asiatic. Licinius deployed his forces around Chrysopolis and sent Martinianus to Lampsakos, on the south shore of the Hellespont. Constantine, meanwhile, celebrated the victory of young Crispus and gave thanks to God. He then decided to move his many ships toward Chrysopolis. He disembarked a few miles from that city with his men and materiel. Licinius beheld the approach of Constantine, but he obstinately refused to surrender. He called back Martinianus and readied for battle. Licinius gave explicit directions that his men were to be wary of the *labarum* banner of the Cross, and to avoid it as much as possible.

Eusebius, speaking of the decisive battle, which took place on the 18th of September, in the year 324, comments that even while the two contestants prepared for mortal combat with otherworldly supplications—each to his respective Divinity or divinities—an apparition was seen in the cities that were subject to Licinius. Detachments of Constantine's army were supernaturally observed passing through various of Licinius' cities. They appeared to be moving in a victory march. Although, in reality, it was but a vision, yet it foreshadowed what was shortly to occur. After their prayers were concluded, upon meeting in battle, the armies of Constantine and Licinius fought valiantly. Constantine's men overcame their opponents through the battle cry of "God the Supreme Savior!" in the first battle, and again in the second. Wherever the holy standard of the Cross appeared, Constantine's forces prevailed. This being observed repeatedly, they began to employ the tactic of putting forth the salutary trophy in those places where Constantine's forces were hard pressed. Every time they did so, immediate victory ensued. Realizing the importance of the holy standard, Constantine assigned fifty of his bodyguard—those men most distinguished for personal strength, valor, and piety—entrusting them with the sole care and defense of the standard of the Cross.[90]

One of Constantine's men, during the heat of battle, fearing he would be overrun, handed the standard to another. After he turned and fled, he received a dart to the stomach. He, thereupon, perished in his cowardice. As for the man who received the standard, he bore it bravely. He soon observed that, despite the repeated showers of darts which assailed him, he remained unharmed. In fact, the staff of the standard received every weapon. Thus, the

[89] Ibid., "The Final Confrontation," *The Life and Times*, pp. 334-337.

[90] Eusebius, *Life*, Bk. II, Ch. VI-VIII.

standard-bearer was saved from death. Furthermore, none of those engaged in this service ever received a wound.[91]

Licinius' men came to acknowledge that they were unable to resist the emperor's army. They threw down their arms, prostrating themselves at his feet; and thus were they spared. But others, resisting still, turned and fled. These men were overrun by Constantine's army and slain according to the laws of war. Others, nevertheless, fell on each other in the confusion of their flight; and they perished by the swords of their comrades. Licinius observed what was taking place and wished to flee. As he tried to break away from his own men, he forbade any of them to follow him closely. He did not wish to draw attention to himself, that he might stealthily take flight. He managed to secure his own mortal safety—but only for a time. Licinius, again, resorted to the loathsome arts of magic. He, consequently, added crime to crime, and more daring atrocities than before, so that it might well be said of him, as it was of the Egyptian tyrant of old, that God had hardened his heart.[92]

Constantine was also fond of retiring from the heat of battle, but only to prepare himself for the next contest. He had a tabernacle, a tent a little distance from the camp, where he would pass the time in prayers to God. For he was deliberate in his measures—the better to insure safety—and desired in everything to be directed by divine counsel. He, therefore, made earnest supplications to God, for which he was always honored after a little with a manifestation of His presence. As a consequence, all of a sudden, Constantine would rush from his prayers in the tabernacle, and order the call to battle without delay. His men, in response, would always fight vigorously. This was so that, with incredible celerity, they could secure the victory and raise trophies of triumph over their enemies.[93]

Constantine endeavored to do all according to God's will, which he ever sought in fervent prayer. He also, witnessing the excesses of battle and of bloodlust, was unwilling to have any of his enemies slain unnecessarily. In order to insure their safety, Constantine put a bounty of gold upon the head of every enemy soldier spared. Not surprisingly, a great number, even of the barbarians, were thus saved and owed their lives to the emperor's gold.[94]

Constantine exhibited qualities not merely rare among men but scarcely found even among the most wise and gifted of rulers. For, as we said, before battle, he would retire to his beloved tabernacle and give himself over to prayer. More than this, he would abstain from slothful bodily ease or luxury. He resorted to the uncharacteristic rule of kings and took up that of monks with

---

[91] Ibid., Bk. II, Ch. IX.

[92] Ex. 7:13. Eusebius, *Life*, Bk. II, Chaps. X, XI.

[93] Eusebius, *Life*, Bk. II, Ch. XII.

[94] Ibid., Bk. II, Ch. XIII.

fasting and bodily mortification. He would implore our Lord for aid and concurrence of mind that he might be ever ready to do God's will. He obeyed Christ's teachings in ways that few ever obeyed them, as he prayed for his enemies as fervently as for his own subjects. Contrariwise, Licinius seemed to be trying to outdo himself in treachery and idolatry: he resorted to renewed false promises of friendship and fealty to Constantine. Licinius even found himself new false deities, discarding the untrustworthy old ones for having failed him.[95]

Constantine still sought peace, but Licinius was really for war, as their two armies came into full view of one another and prepared to clash. Licinius' standard-bearers carried images of the dead and lifeless statues as their spiritual defense. Licinius also cautioned his men never to direct their attack against Constantine's standard of the Cross. In fact, he warned them not even incautiously to allow their eyes to rove and catch sight of it. He warned them of its terrible power that was especially hostile to him. Thus, they were ordered to avoid it lest any collision with it cost them the victory. Constantine, secure in the armor of godliness, held back, hoping for a truce, and a right-thinking change of heart on the part of Licinius, even on the verge of the contest.[96]

The battle was fierce. Zosimus records that only 30,000 survived. Byzantion and Chalcedon (present-day Kadikoy) opened their gates to Constantine's victors. Licinius, with a few thousand foot soldiers, retreated to Nikomedia, his capital and palace. Licinius returned to Constantia, telling her he would resume the war. She told him that the war was already lost. The Augusta, thereupon, went to see her half-brother. She had always been Constantine's favorite. For her sake, he agreed to her tear-filled pleas not to slay Licinius. Soon thereafter, she invited her husband and half-brother to an imperial dinner. They all sat down together. Licinius, naturally, duly performed the act of submission. He was received with the kiss of peace, and then sat down at table.

Eusebius remarks that Constantine the Great, the mighty, the merciful and benevolent, showed himself to be an even mightier ruler than many a peace-loving king before or after him. Who would have abided so long with one of Licinius' low caliber? He was vile and treacherous on and off the battlefield, thoroughly steeped in the ways of the serpent. But he was allowed to go free. Constantine had heard the passages that Solomon said that "to all things there is a time, and a season for every matter under heaven:...a time to kill, and a time to heal; a time to pull down, and a time to build up;...a time to love, and a time to hate; a time of war, and a time of peace [Eccl. 3:1, 3, 8]." The difference between an ordinary king and a great king was due in part to a

[95] Ibid., Bk. II, Chaps. XIV, XV.

[96] Ibid., Bk. II, Chaps. XVI.

proper and painstaking humility toward God, whereby, such a king might obtain the wisdom to know which of the times of Ecclesiastes might portend for which occasion. And to know this not just once or for the present occasion, but to know as in Constantine's case; for virtually throughout his entire life, he knew. Constantine, the lover of the God of Solomon the author of Ecclesiastes, was given the gift of God to rightly understand Solomon's wise words and those of Christ in the Gospel. He thus knew that the time had come for giving just judgment, as only a proper spiritual descendant of Solomon could declare. For the common man might forgive until seventy-times seven, but the divinely-appointed king of an empire had a greater responsibility to uphold the rule of an entire nation under God.[97]

Saint Theophanes the Confessor remarks that "Constantine had shown his customary humanity....He was a man resplendent in all respects: manly in spirit, sharp in mind, and educated in speech. In meting out justice, he was upright; as a benefactor, he was ready. He was dignified in appearance. He was great in the barbarian wars through acts of courage. He was invincible in civil wars. He was strong and unswerving in his faith. As a result, he gained victory over all his enemies by prayer."[98]

Sole Emperor of the Roman Empire

Constantine appointed Licinius a pension at his Thessalonian residence. As for Martinianus, he was delivered up to death. Licinius was kept under house arrest at Thessalonike. As for Constantia and her son, the young Licinianus, they remained at Nikomedia as members of Constantine's household. Constantine was now sole master of the Roman Empire, from the British Isles to Egypt, from the Balkans to Mauretania. The following year, Licinius, nevertheless, was executed by hanging, in accordance with the laws of war, on a charge of attempted rebellion. He, evidently, was in correspondence with the Goths.[99] Saint Theophanes remarks that "Licinius, having hired some barbarians, would have begun a revolt, had not the gentle Constantine learned of it in advance and ordered his decapitation by the sword."[100]

Following the battle of Chrysopolis, Constantine opened the prisons throughout the east. He set free, according to his command, all who were suffering for the Christian Faith. Eusebius tells us that Constantine's enactment of edicts had a twofold purpose: to undo all of Licinius' evil laws and to right all of Licinius' ungodly actions. He mandated that the churches

---

[97] Ibid., Bk. II, Ch. XVIII.

[98] *The Chronicle of Theophanes Confessor*, AM 5815, A.D. 322/323, p. 33.

[99] Baker, "The Conquest of the East and the Council of Nicaea," *Constantine the Great*, Ch. IX(IV, V), pp. 223-226.

[100] *The Chronicle of Theophanes Confessor*, AM 5815, A.D. 322/323, loc. cit. Other sources say that Licinius was strangled [*Epit. Caes*. 41.7 and Zos. ii 28].

should enjoy special privileges throughout the land. All who had been wronged, he restored to their former dignity and social positions. He freed all who had been made captive for Christ's sake. He determined restitution for anyone so deprived of their goods, their freedom, or their welfare. He made special consideration for martyrs who died for Christ under Licinius, that their estates should be transferred to the next of kin or to the churches. Indeed, such were the blessings bestowed by Constantine. Those of the eastern regions, hearing of these things, requested and received equal blessings from him; thus, they praised God for Constantine's rule. Constantine declared God to be the author of his prosperity. He also declared, in both the Latin and Greek tongues, that it was the God of the Christians, and not himself, Who was the Author of his past victories.[101]

The Roman Empire was now reunited under the head of a single ruler, Constantine, who took for himself the appellation of "Victor." He proclaimed the God of the Christians to be the one and true God.[102] Constantine's injunctions were speedily carried out. He also promoted Christians to offices of government, and forbade pagans in such stations to offer sacrifice. He enacted statutes that no one should erect images, or practise divination and other false and foolish arts, or sacrifice to these in any way. Also he promoted that oratories should be heightened and enlarged in length and breadth. The smaller churches were to be enlarged, and the larger ones were to be enriched, at the expense of the imperial treasury.[103]

"Constantine," writes Saint Theophanes the Confessor, "gave his mind entirely to holy matters, by building churches and enriching them lavishly from public funds. First he legislated that the temples used for idols were to be handed over to persons consecrated to Christ. Constantine's son, Crispus, was cosignatory of this legislation. Many accepted Baptism and broke up their ancestral idols."[104]

The emperor and Maximus Augustus, Victor Constantinus, addressed an epistle to the people of the eastern provinces on the subject of how vengeance overtook those who raised the Great Persecution. "But why need I longer dwell on these lamentable events, and the general sorrow which in consequence pervaded the world? The perpetrators of this dreadful guilt are now no more: they have experienced a miserable end, and are consigned to unceasing punishment in the depths of the lower world. They encountered each other in civil strife, and have left behind neither name nor race. And surely this

[101] Eusebius, *Life*, Bk. II, Chaps. XX-XXIII.

[102] Ibid., Bk. II, Ch. XIX.

[103] Ibid., Bk. II, Chaps. XLIII-XLV.

[104] *The Chronicle of Theophanes Confessor*, AM 5810, A.D. 317/318, p. 37.

calamity would never have befallen them, had not that impious deliverance of the Pythian oracle exercised a delusive power over them.[105]

"And now I beseech Thee, O most mighty God, to be merciful and gracious to Thine eastern nations, to Thy people in these provinces, worn as they are by protracted miseries. Do Thou grant them healing through Thy servant. Not without cause, O holy God, do I prefer this prayer to Thee, the Lord of all. Under Thy guidance have I devised and accomplished measures fraught with blessings. Preceded by Thy sacred sign, I have led Thine armies to victory. And still, on each occasion of public danger, I follow the same symbol of Thy perfections while advancing to meet the foe. Therefore, have I dedicated to Thy service a soul duly softened by love and fear. For Thy name I truly love, while I regard with reverence that power of which Thou hast given abundant proofs, to the confirmation and increase of my faith. I hasten, then, to devote all my powers to the restoration of Thy most holy dwelling place which those profane and impious men have defiled by the contamination of violence.

"My own desire is, for the common good of the world and the advantage of all mankind, that Thy people should enjoy a life of peace and undisturbed concord. Let those, therefore, who still delight in error, be made welcome to the same degree of peace and tranquillity which they have who believe. For it may be that this restoration of equal privileges to all will prevail to lead them into the straight path. Let no one molest another, but let each one do as his soul desires. Only let men of sound judgment be assured of this: that those only can live a life of holiness and purity whom Thou callest to a reliance on Thy holy laws. With regard to those who will hold themselves aloof from us, let them have, if they please, their temples of lies: we have the glorious edifice of Thy truth, which Thou hast given us as our native home. We pray, however, that they too may receive the same blessing; and thus, they may experience that heartfelt joy which unity of sentiment inspires."[106] Constantine then gave glory to God, Who gives light by His Son to those who are in error. He also glorified Him again for His government of the universe.

Since the pious emperor no longer had the concerns of battles, he bound himself to perform God-pleasing works. He built churches and enriched them with imperial revenues. He, as well, adorned them with gold and silver in a majestic manner. This and many other good works were accomplished under his direction. In his thought, judgment, and inclination, he was honorable, generous, and sympathetic. His deeds and words were prudent. In his appearance, he was a comely man and even sweet. Simply put, he possessed all the gifts in his soul and body. For this cause was all the world subject to

[105] Eusebius, *Life*, Bk. II, Ch. LIV.

[106] Ibid., Bk. II, Chaps. LIV-LVI.

him, more so for his good judgment and pursuits as well as his reverential fear of his own power and authority. He was conspicuous for pardoning his enemies and not bearing grudges. Even as David of old, he withheld his hand, no matter what the provocation, from slaying his father-in-law. He was tireless in seeking justice and truth. No detail was too small when it came to the welfare of others, even if it meant putting himself in peril or at risk for them. He bestowed many favors and gifts upon the Christians in all places.

The Vision of the City

It was as early as 316 when Constantine was vouchsafed a divine vision. He was commanded to build a city in the parts of the east, a city which he was to dedicate to the most holy Theotokos. Thus, this holy command was ever with him as he hastened to perform the divine will.

Now Constantine, at that time, went forth to Thessalonike. He began building great and majestic churches, thinking to build the God-commanded city in that place, but he was prevented. After that, he traveled to Chalcedon, directly across the Bosporos, which suffered from the frequent ravages of barbarian raiders. The site of the maritime town pleased the emperor, so he began building in that place. Since that location for a new city was not God's good pleasure, this was made evident when eagles swooped down and snatched the tools of the craftsmen. The birds cast them in Byzantion. The great Constantine, seeing this marvel, departed Chalcedon and went to Byzantion. He looked over the topography and believed it to be appropriate, but he did not know how large to make the new city. During the night, he beheld a vision of an angel who addressed him and said, "In the morning, when it is dawn, be thou following me. And wheresoever I should go, do thou mark the place and there lay the foundations." In the morning, Constantine summoned the chief architect. He commanded him to follow him and to place landmarks wheresoever he passed through. They set off together. The emperor was following the angel, who was walking ahead with a brisk pace. Only the emperor could see the angel. Behind Constantine was the architect, who went about wherever the emperor passed through and marked all the land where God had willed that the new city should be built. Afterward, Constantine began building the city.[107]

The emperor appointed a certain skilled and experienced man, named Efratas, to undertake the study and planning of the city that it might be a work both marvellous and God-pleasing. Constantine handed over to him an abundance of gold for the expenditure. Efratas was capable and careful, so that

[107] Church historian Sozomen (early 5th C.) also records the accounts of Constantine following the angel of the Lord, tracing out the boundaries, and of the eagles bearing aloft the tools to the akropolis of Byzantion. Sozomen wrote his Greek *Ecclesiastical History* [*P.G.* 67] covering the period of 324 until 439, depending on Socrates Scholasticus (ca. 380-450). See also Nicene Fathers, 2nd Ser., Vol. 2.

he constructed and laid out the city beautifully, as was meet and as was borne out in chronographs of the time. The new city was so aptly and serviceably designed that it was similar to Rome in all the buildings. From Old Rome they transported a certain huge stone column of porphyry to the Forum, which may be seen to this day.[108]

Saints Constantine and Helen

Arius

In the midst, however, of newfound peace and tranquility, the empire experienced a series of controversies having to do with one Arius. The problem originated in the Alexandrian Church, spreading throughout Egypt, the Thebaid, Libya, and beyond. The dispute pitted bishop against bishop, and church against church. The scandal that ensued exposed the sacred matters of inspired teaching to the most shameful ridicule in the very theaters of the unbelievers.[109] Schisms resulted as bishops raged against bishops, and people rose up against their neighbors. This caused Constantine deep sorrow of spirit. There was also a long-standing disagreement having to do with the observance of Pascha: whether to follow the Jewish custom or to follow the exact recurrence of the period.[110] Constantine, the peer of the apostles, asked that the First Œcumenical Synod ordain that Pascha be celebrated in all parts of the inhabited earth on one and the same day. He could not bear seeing the Church of Christ divided on account of this festival.[111]

---

[108] The Column of Constantine had marked the center of what was once the Forum of Constantine. It was surrounded by the Senate, a Praetorium, and several churches and temples. Originally, the column had a square pedestal standing on five steps. The relics buried under the column or in the statue itself contain the following: the Palladium of Troy, the hatchet of Noah, the stone from which Moses made water flow, the baskets and remains of the loaves by which Christ fed the multitude, the nails of the Passion, and relics of the true Cross which Constantine received from his mother. See note regarding this famous column in *The Great Synaxaristes* (in English), under the Life of Saint Hypatios, commemorated by the holy Church on the 31st of March.

[109] Eusebius, *Life*, Bk. II, Chaps. LXI, LXII.

[110] Ibid., Bk. III, Chaps. IV, V.

[111] The Quartodecimans, that is, the "Fourteeners," mostly found in Asia Minor, presumably followed a tradition of Saint John the Theologian who celebrated Pascha

(continued...)

The emperor's anxiety over the lack of unity caused him to shed tears and postpone his trip to the east. "Restore to me my quiet days and untroubled nights, that the joy of undimmed light and the delight of a tranquil life may henceforth be my portion; else must I needs mourn with constant tears, for I shall not be able to pass the residue of my days in peace. For while the people of God, whose fellow servant I am, are thus divided amongst themselves by an unreasonable and pernicious spirit of contention, how is it possible that I shall be able to maintain tranquillity of mind? And I will give you a proof how great my sorrow has been in their behalf. Not long after I had visited Nikomedia with the intention of going further east to see you [Bishop Alexander and Presbyter Arius], after I already accomplished the greater part of the distance, that the news of this matter reversed my plan that I might not be compelled to see with my own eyes that which I felt myself scarcely able even to hear. Open then for me, henceforward, by your unity of judgment, that road to the regions of the east which your dissensions have closed against me. Permit me speedily to see yourselves and all other peoples rejoicing together. Render due acknowledgment to God, in the language of praise and thanksgiving for the restoration of general concord and liberty to all." But the controversy continued without

---

[111](...continued)
on the Passover of the Jews, that is, the 14th of Nisan, even if it fell on a weekday. Constantine desired that the Christians celebrate Pascha together. The question before the First Œcumenical Synod was whether Pascha should be celebrated as the Fourteeners wished or on the Sunday after the Passover. The bishops sent a synodal letter to other bishops stating that an agreement concerning Pascha was reached: All the brethren in the east who formerly followed the custom of the Jews were now to celebrate Pascha at the same time with the Romans. Pascha must fall after the Passover. [See "The Synodal Letter," in *The Seven Ecumenical Councils*, Nicene Fathers, Vol. XIV:53-55.]

The difference in calculating Pascha did not disappear after the Nicene Synod. Alexandria and Rome continued to disagree. The Romans used a cycle of eighty-four years and placed the equinox on the 18th of March, whereas the Alexandrians observed the 21st of March. There were also differences in the placement of the new moon. The 343 Sardican Synod attempted to put an end to the misunderstanding, but could not get the parties to compromise on a common day. Emperor Theodosios (ca. 387) asked Bishop Theophilos of Alexandria for an explanation. This response, giving Alexandrian formulas, is not extant. His nephew, Kyril of Alexandria, abridged the paschal table and fixed the time for the ninety-five following Paschas from 436 to 531. Kyril also showed how the Roman calculation was defective. Pope Leo gave preference to the Alexandrian calculation. In 457, Victor of Aquitane, reworked the calculations and eliminated many of the differences between the Latin and Greek renderings. But it was Dionysios the Less who overcame all the differences, by giving to the Latins a paschal table having as its basis the cycle of nineteen years, which corresponded perfectly with that used in Alexandria. [Ibid., pp. 55, 56].

abatement, even after the receipt of this letter. Instead, the acrimony of the contending parties ever worsened. The effects of the mischief extended to all the eastern provinces, aggravated by the finger of the devil and the spirit of jealousy.[112]

The peace and rejoicing of the faithful of the Church stirred up the envy and malice of the devil, the originator of evil. Since all the tyrants were put to shame, he raised up a new antichrist during the reign of the great Constantine. The devil's instrument was Arius, a protopresbyter of Alexandria and a teacher of the school at Alexandria. He began uttering blasphemous words against the Son of God: that Jesus was not true God. He was saying that Christ was not co-essential with the Father. He was preaching Christ as a creation and creature of God, even a tool and organ by means of Whom God the Father made the beginning of the cosmos.

At that time, the Patriarch of Alexandria, the most holy Peter (d. 311), beheld a vision.[113] He beheld standing by him the Master Christ as a comely boy of about twelve years old. He observed the Christ Child clad in a linen tunic, divided into two parts from the neck to the feet. He was holding in His hands the rents of the tunic, putting them over His breast to cover His nakedness. The patriarch was stupefied at this sight and asked, "Lord, who has rent Thy tunic?" He forthwith answered, "Arius has stripped Me. Arius, the deranged, O Peter, says that I am not God. Be taking heed not ever to accept him into communion. Behold, tomorrow they shall come to entreat thee in his behalf! See, therefore, that thou be not persuaded to acquiesce; nay, rather enjoin upon Achillas and Alexander the priests,[114] who after thy translation shall shepherd My Church, not by any means to forgive him and receive him." Now after the repose of Peter, Arius would ask forgiveness of Peter's successor: Achillas (312-313). Despite the warnings of his prelate—nay, of Christ Himself—Achillas restored Arius to his office as deacon, and afterward elevated him to the presbytery. As long as Achillas lived, Arius kept silence. When the hallowed Alexander became Patriarch of Alexandria, Arius again began to preach his original heretical views into which he also drew the following bishops: Evsevios of Nikomedia, Paulinus of Tyre, Theonas, Secundus, and other clergymen. By reason of this spreading heretical infection, Alexander convoked a synod. He assembled one hundred bishops from his

---

[112] Eusebius, *Life*, Bk. II, Chaps. LXXII, LXXIII. This is an extract of Constantine's epistle to Alexander and Arius, beginning in Eusebius' Bk. II, Ch. LXIV.

[113] Saint Peter the Confessor is commemorated by the holy Church on the 24th of November. He had been imprisoned by order of Maximianus Galerius and his son Maximinus. He underwent a glorious martyrdom and was beheaded.

[114] The holy Church commemorates Saint Alexander on the 29th of May.

province. The synod members deposed Arius and his followers. These Arians, consequently, provoked a great deal of confusion and agitation for the Church.

The great and pious Constantine, beholding these sorry events and desiring to usher in peace for Christ's agitated Church, dispatched epistles gathering together from all quarters every bishop of the inhabited world to the great city of Nicaea that the issue might be discussed.

The First Œcumenical Synod

The First Œcumenical Synod

Constantine the Great, as emperor over the Christians, with the help of divine power, closed the temples of the idols so that the Church was in the open to the glory of God. The First Œcumenical Synod was held at Nicaea of Bithynia during his reign, in the year 325.[115] Three hundred and eighteen fathers attended. He offered the attendees the use of public means of conveyance, or afforded horses, for their transport. The bishops responded with

[115] The holy First Œcumenical Synod is commemorated on the seventh Sunday after Pascha, that is, the Sunday of the Holy Fathers.

utmost willingness to hasten thither, as though they would outstrip one another in a race.[116] It was Constantine who decided to assemble the episcopal pastors from the entire civilized world for the first time since the days of Christ and the apostles. He refrained from any misuse of his power, for he took a position at the synod only at the behest of the fathers and, as the *Synaxarion* of the *Triodion* states, "He sat not upon a royal throne, but upon a seat of little note." The major sees of the Eastern Empire were well represented. The anti-Arians included Alexander of Alexandria, Efstathios (Eustathius) of Antioch, Markellos of Ankyra, and Makarios of Jerusalem. The Arian side had Evsevios of Palestinian Caesarea, Theognis of Nicaea, Maris of Chalcedon, and Secundus and Theonas the Libyans. Western bishops included Caecilian of Carthage, Domnus of Pannonia, Nicasius of Gaul, Mark of Calabria, and Hosius of Cordoba. Papal legates were the Priests Vito and Vincent, since Pope Silvester asked to be excused on account of old age and infirmity. From beyond the empire, there came John of Persia and Theophilos of Scythia. These were men adorned with apostolic gifts, as were our Spyridon of Cyprus,[117] Nicholas of Myra,[118] Athanasios[119] (the twenty-five-year-old deacon and secretary of Alexander of Alexandria), and the Priest-monk Alexander who represented Patriarch Metrophanes of Constantinople. There were also present men who survived the sufferings of martyrdom: Paul of Neocaesarea, who lost the use of his hands from torture, and the half-blind Paphnutios of Egypt.

The synod was assembled against Arius, who kept spreading his blasphemy, saying that the Son and Logos of God was not coessential (*homoousios*) with the Father.[120] Thus, Arius was declaring that Jesus is not

---

[116] Eusebius, *Life*, Bk. III, Ch. VI.

[117] See the account of Saint Spyridon's defense and miraculous graphic demonstration with a tile against the Ariomaniacs at the First Synod. He is commemorated by the holy Church on the 12th of December.

[118] See the account of Saint Nicholas at the First Synod who delivered a slap to the vile mouth of Arius, compelling Constantine to follow the law and have the hierarch jailed. He is commemorated by the holy Church on the 6th of December.

[119] See the Life of Saint Athanasios the Great, which provides much background information on the position of the Church against Arianism. He is commemorated by the holy Church on the 18th of January and the 2nd of May.

[120] Many argued that the word *homoousios* "coessential" was not of biblical origin. The reason why this latter term was so precious to the younger contemporaries of the synod is explained through the mouth of Saint Basil the Great. He affirmed that they were ready to offer their souls for this word, and even for one *iota* (the name of the Greek letter ι), as mentioned by the Savior [Mt. 5:18]; for upon this *iota* hung Orthodoxy itself. The fact of the matter is that only a single *iota* in Greek distinguishes *homoousios* 'co-essential' ('of one and the same essence') from *homoiousios* 'of like essence,'

(continued...)

true God but a creature (*ktisma*), a Greek word meaning anything that is built. No account of the synodal proceedings is extant, in either Greek or Latin,[121] except a list of twenty canons issued by the synod, the Symbol of the Faith (Creed), and a synodal letter excommunicating the odious Arius. This synod, rejecting Arius' ontological subordination of the Logos to the Father, defined the incarnate Logos as coessential. This synod also declared the computation of the paschal date, by ordering this feast of feasts to be celebrated on the Sunday after the full moon following the vernal equinox.[122] This synod also

[120](...continued)
which was the term used by the Arians to refer to the Son of God. See "The First Ecumenical Council," by Blessed Metropolitan Anthony (Khrapovitsky), trans. by Timothy Fisher from *Tserkovnya Vedomosti*, No. 9 & 10, (May, 1925), pp. 14-17.

[121] The records of this First Synod are not extant, except whatever historical accounts have been affirmed by Eusebius, Rufinus, Socrates, Sozomen, Theodoret, and Jerome, and, principally, what has been handed down by Gelasios I (Kyzikos) who wrote in the reign of Emperor Zeno (476) and afterward served as Bishop of Caesarea in Palestine (Vol. I, p. 151, *Collection of the Synods*). See *The Rudder*, pp. 155-160.

[122] *The Rudder* [footnote 14 to Canon VII of the 85 Canons of the Apostles] records that Constantine desired that the holy Pascha be celebrated in all parts of the inhabited earth on one and the same day. For the blissful man could not bear seeing the Church of Christ being divided on account of this festival, resulting in the convocation of many synods in various parts and the opposition of the westerners against the Asiatics on account of it. The former followed the custom which had been established before them by their presbyters; whereas the Asiatics followed the bosom disciple John and the rest of the apostles, as Polycrates, the Bishop of Smyrna, wrote to Victor, the Bishop of Rome, according to Eusebius [*The Ecclesiastical History*, Bk. V, Ch. XXIII].

There are four necessary factors to be sought in connection with the date of our Pascha. The first is that Pascha must always be celebrated after the occurrence of the vernal equinox. Second, that it must not be celebrated on the same day as the legal Passover of the Jews. (These two factors are ordained by the present Apostolic Canon VII.) Third, that it is not to be celebrated simply and indefinitely after the vernal equinox, but after the first full moon of March that happens to occur after the equinox. And fourth, that it must not be celebrated on the first Lord's day that comes after the full moon. (These two factors are derived from tradition, and not from any canon.) Hence, in order for these four conditions to be observed equally throughout the inhabited earth, and for Christians to celebrate holy Pascha at the same time and on the same day, and in order to escape from the necessity of consulting astronomers and synods every year, the God-wise and God-learned fathers framed the rule concerning Pascha. Note, however, that on account of the irregularity of the moon's motion, the fourth condition is not always kept, but is sometimes violated, because of the fact that, according to the same Blastaris, every three hundred years, two days after the first full moon, the legal Passover happens to occur on a Sunday. These two days which are left over on account of this anomaly, which when added, sometimes exceed the first Sunday

(continued...)

recognized the jurisdiction of the patriarchates of Rome, Alexandria, and Antioch. Though Hieromonk Alexander and Deacon Athanasios were not adorned with the dignity of the episcopacy, they nevertheless were first in the debates.

These ministers of God were of all ages. Some were distinguished by wisdom and eloquence, some by the gravity of their lives and patient fortitude of character, and some by all of these gifts combined. Constantine furnished ample provision for all during their stay.[123]

On the appointed day for the final solution of the questions in dispute, the bishops gathered in the central building. They were seated according to ecclesial rank, with becoming orderliness and an uncommon silence. Preceding the arrival of Constantine—the tall, aquiline, majestic man in his purple silk and pearled diadem—were three of his immediate family in succession, then friends in the Faith. Then, all rising at the signal, the emperor entered through their midst like some heavenly messenger of God, clothed in raiment which glittered as it were with rays of light, reflecting the glowing radiance of a purple robe, and adorned with the brilliant splendor of gold and precious stones. It was evident he was distinguished by piety and godly fear,...indicated by his downcast eyes, the blush on his countenance, and his gait. For the rest of his personal excellencies, he surpassed all present in height of stature and beauty of form, as well as in majestic dignity of mien, and invincible strength and vigor. All these gifts, united to a suavity of manner, and a serenity becoming his imperial station, declared the excellence of his mental qualities to be above all praise. As soon as he had advanced to the upper end of the seats, at first he remained standing. And when a low chair of wrought gold had

---

[122](...continued)
that happens to occur after the full moon of March, on which Sunday we celebrate Palm Sunday, and observe Pascha on the following Lord's day. This slight violation is not attended by any deviation from piety or any unseemly fault or any danger to the soul. That is why Saint Chrysostom (in his discourse to those fasting the first Paschas) says that the Church of Christ "knows no accuracy of times or observation of days, since as often as she eats this life-giving bread, and drinks this cup, she is proclaiming the death of the Lord and is celebrating Pascha; but inasmuch as the fathers assembled at the First Synod and ordained how the date of Pascha is to be reckoned for its celebration, because the Church honors agreement and union everywhere, she accepted the regulation which they provided." See D. Cummings' *The Rudder*, "The Eighty-Five Canons," Canon VII: "If any bishop, or presbyter, or deacon celebrate the holy day of Pascha before the vernal equinox with the Jews, let him be deposed" and the "Interpretation" thereafter [pp. 9-20].

[123] Eusebius, *Life*, Bk. III, Ch. IX.

been set for him, he waited until the bishops had beckoned to him; and then he sat down, and after him the whole assembly did the same.[124]

The ranking bishop, in the chief place to the right, delivered a concise speech thanking almighty God on behalf of Constantine. Then he sat and, amidst a general silence, all regarded the emperor. He looked serenely round on the assembly with a cheerful aspect and, having collected his thoughts, in a calm and gentle tone gave utterance to the following words.[125] He addressed the synod concerning peace. "It was once my chief desire, dearest friends, to enjoy the spectacle of your united presence; and now that this desire is fulfilled, I feel myself bound to render thanks to God the universal King, because, in addition to all His other benefits, He has granted me a blessing higher than all the rest, in permitting me to see you not only all assembled together but also everyone united in a common harmony of sentiment. I pray, therefore, that no malignant adversary may henceforth interfere to mar our happy state. Now that the impious hostility of the tyrants has been forever removed by the power of God our Savior, I pray that the spirit who delights in evil may devise no other means for exposing the divine law to blasphemous calumny. For, in my judgment, intestinal strife within the Church of God is far more evil and dangerous than any kind of war or conflict. These differences between us appear to me to be more grievous than any outward trouble. Accordingly, when, by the will and with the cooperation of God, I had been victorious over my enemies, I thought that nothing more remained but to render thanks to Him, and sympathize in the joy of those whom He had restored to freedom through my instrumentality. As soon as I heard that intelligence—which I had least expected to receive—I mean the news of your dissension, I judged it to be of no secondary importance. But with the earnest desire that a remedy for this evil also might be found through my means, I immediately sent to require your presence.

"And now I rejoice in beholding your assembly. But I feel that my desires will be most completely fulfilled when I can see you all united in one judgment. I pray that I shall see the common spirit of peace and concord prevailing among you all—which becomes you, as consecrated to the service of God—and commending this spirit to others. Delay not, then, dear friends: delay not, you ministers of God, and faithful servants of Him Who is our common Lord and Savior. Begin from this moment to discard the causes of that disunion which has existed among you. Remove the perplexities of controversy, by embracing the principles of peace. For by such conduct you will at

[124] Ibid., Bk. III, Ch. X.
[125] Ibid., Bk. III, Ch. XI.

the same time be acting in a manner most pleasing to the supreme God, and you will confer an exceeding favor on me who am your fellow servant."[126]

Constantine gave permission for the bishops who presided to give their opinions. At once, a violent controversy arose from the very commencement. Notwithstanding, he gave a patient audience. He received every proposition with steadfast attention. And, by occasionally assisting the argument of each party in turn, he gradually disposed even the most vehement disputants to a reconciliation. By the affability of his address, and use of Greek, he appeared in a truly attractive and amiable light. He persuaded some, convinced others, and praised those who spoke well. He continued to urge all to unity of sentiment, until at last he succeeded in bringing them to one mind and judgment respecting every disputed question. The crisis was settled. The time for celebrating Pascha was also agreed upon and committed to writing, and signed by all. Constantine proceeded to solemnize a triumphal festival in honor of God.[127]

The emperor took his seat on the throne, and one hundred and fifty-nine fathers also took their seats. As we mentioned earlier, the synod had been assembled against Arius, who blasphemed that the Logos of God was not coessential with the Father; that is, that Jesus was not true God, but, on the contrary, a creature and something built. The sessions lasted at least three and one-half years.[128] This synod produced the divine Symbol of the Faith (the Nicene Creed of 325), proclaiming the Son and Logos of God to be true God coessential with the Father, saying: "I believe in one God, the Father almighty, Maker of all things visible and invisible; and in one Lord Jesus Christ, the Son of the God, the Only-begotten, begotten of the Father, that is, of the essence of the Father; God of God; Light of Light; true God of true God; begotten, not made; being of one essence with the Father; by Whom all things were made, including all things in the heaven and all things on the earth; Who for us men, and for our salvation, came down, and became incarnate, and became Man; and He suffered and arose on the third day; and ascended to the heavens and is sitting at the right of the Father; and He is coming again to judge the living and dead; and in the Holy Spirit. As for those who are saying that 'there was a time when He was not,' and 'He was not existent before He was born'; and who are saying that 'He came to be out of non-being,' or assert 'He is out of another hypostasis' or 'essence,' or that 'the Son of God is mutable or alterable,' the

---

[126] Ibid., Bk. III, Ch. XII.

[127] Ibid., Bk. III, Chaps. XIII, XIV.

[128] Saint Photios records six and one-half years *(Anagnosma* 256). *The Great Synaxaristes* (in Greek) records three and one-half years or 325 to 329.

catholic and apostolic Church anathematizes them."[129] Constantine's object was to gain the agreement of as large a majority as possible, so that Church unity could be preserved. The new Creed was read out by Bishop Hermogenes, on the 19th of July. It was indeed signed by the majority of bishops. Constantine was the outside force applying both gentle and far-reaching coercion so the bishops could overcome their differences. Without the unity of will and ideal that Constantine sought, civilization and daily life could never be satisfactory or safe.[130]

"Constantine," notes Saint Theophanes the Confessor, "liberally provided for everyone's needs. This holy and œcumenical synod, with the cooperation of the holy and co-essential Trinity, deposed Arius and his sympathizers, Eusebius of Nikomedia, Theognis of Nicaea, and those with them—except for Eusebius Pamphilus, who for the present accepted the term *homoousios*—and sent them into exile. The all-praiseworthy Emperor Constantine was present at the synod and was an associate in all its actions that were agreeable to God. He ordered that others be ordained to replace those banished. He published a written exposition of the Faith that is today recited in every Orthodox Church."[131]

After the First Synod, Constantine completed the twentieth year of his reign. Public festivals were celebrated, but the emperor feasted with the ministers of God. Troops were also to be seen in attendance with drawn swords, appearing within and without the palace and its entrance like guardian angels, assuring the safety of all. Afterward, the emperor courteously received all of his guests, and presented gifts to each according to rank. He also sent a letter summarizing the proceedings of the synod to each of those who could not attend, written in his own hand.[132]

At the close of the meeting, the great Constantine invited all the holy fathers to a banquet, where he entertained them sumptuously at table. He sat in their midst and accorded the appropriate gift to each one. He greatly revered the holy Paphnutios, a holy confessor of the Faith, and ardently kissed the socket of the eye that had been gouged during the Great Persecution. The emperor kissed his eyeless cheek for a blessing and sanctification, which was

---

[129] This original Nicene Creed was later enlarged in 381 at the Second Œcumenical Synod held in Constantinople, convened by and during the reign of Theodosios. At that time, besides some minor changes in the first two articles, there were added all the clauses after the "Holy Spirit"; the anathema was omitted.

[130] Baker, "The Conquest of the East and the Council of Nicaea," *Constantine the Great*, Ch. IX(XII, XIII), pp. 237-239.

[131] *The Chronicle of Theophanes Confessor*, AM 5816, A.D. 323/324, pp. 35, 36.

[132] Eusebius, *Life*, Bk. III, Chaps. XV, XVI.

an action both significant and symbolic.[133] He urged the bishops to maintain peace, for some wished to examine the condemned Arian bishops. The emperor burned those petitions, pronouncing those memorable words, "Even if I should see a hierarch sinning, I certainly would cover him with my porphyry cloak." He then bade the fathers farewell; and each returned to his diocese.

The emperor then addressed a letter to the Churches, writing: "Having had full proof, in the general prosperity of the empire, how great the favor of God has been toward us, I have judged that it ought to be the first object of my endeavors, that unity of faith, sincerity of love, and community of feeling in regard to the worship of almighty God, might be preserved among the highly favored multitude who compose the catholic Church. And inasmuch as this object could not be effectually and certainly secured unless all, or at least the greater number of the bishops, met together and discussed all particulars relating to our most holy religion, for this reason as numerous an assembly as possible has been convened. I myself was present, as one among yourselves—and far be it from me to deny that which is my greatest joy, that I am your fellow servant. Every question received due and full examination until the judgment of the God, Who sees all things, could give approval. And that which tended to unity and concord regarding the Faith was brought to light, so that no room was left for further discussion or controversy."[134]

The emperor then spoke of Christian unanimity respecting the Feast of Pascha, and against the practise of the delusional Jews. All should unite in desiring that which sound reason appears to demand. All should avoid participation in the perjured conduct of the Jews. Thus, it had been determined by the common judgment of all, that the most holy Feast of Pascha should be kept on one and the same day. The emperor then exhorted the Christians to obey the decrees of the synod. "Receive, then, with all willingness this truly divine injunction, and regard it as in truth the gift of God. For whatever is determined in the holy assemblies of the bishops is to be regarded as indicative of the divine will. As soon, therefore, as you have communicated these proceedings to all our beloved brethren, you are bound from that time forward to adopt this determination for Pascha for yourselves. You are to enjoin on others the arrangement above mentioned and the due observance of this most sacred day. Thus, whensoever I should come into the presence of your love, which I have long desired, I would be able to celebrate the holy feast with you

---

[133] Socrates, *The Ecclesiastical History*, Bk. I, Ch. XI, Nicene, 2nd Ser., Vol. II. Socrates, a Constantinopolitan lawyer, was born ca 380. The Greek text of his *Ecclesiastical History* carries on Eusebius' work to the year 439. He lived only one generation after the repose of Saint Constantine. His work is useful insofar as it quotes original texts.

[134] Eusebius, *Life*, Bk. III, Ch. XVII.

on the same day. I could then behold the cruel power of Satan removed by divine aid through the agency of our endeavors, while your faith, and peace, and concord everywhere flourish. God preserve you, beloved brethren!"[135] The emperor transmitted a faithful copy of his words to every province in the realm, wherein they who read it might discern as in a mirror the pure sincerity of his thoughts and of his piety toward God.

When the synod meeting was on the point of being dismissed, Constantine summoned all the bishops. He addressed them in a farewell speech, in which he recommended them to be diligent in the maintenance of peace and to avoid contentious disputations. He advised them not to be mindful of any whose excellence or gifts were greater or less than their own. He urged them to hasten to forgive offenses and overlook weaknesses that the saving doctrine might be fully honored by all and, in conclusion, to offer diligent supplications to God in his behalf. He then gave them all leave to return. The emperor sent letters to those absent from the council. In observance of the twentieth anniversary of his reign, he bestowed monetary gifts on all the people in the country and cities. The truth be told, the Arian controversy still raged in Egypt. Disturbed but not angered, Constantine entreated the contending parties as fathers—nay rather, as prophets of God—and summoned their presence and mediated their disputes. He then honored them with gifts, and communicated the result of his arbitration by letter. He confirmed and sanctioned the decrees of the synod, and called on them to strive for concord. These injunctions he sent also by a letter in his own hand.[136]

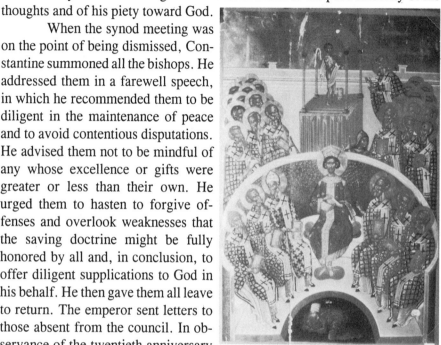

The First Œcumenical Synod

The Tragedy of Crispus and Fausta

Constantine had one singular quality. "Clever as he was in some special ways, rapid in decision, and sure in his instinct for the right course, he nevertheless seems to have possessed some of the ingrained unworldliness which often distinguishes men of special gifts. He does not seem ever to have

[135] Ibid., Bk. III, Ch. XX.

[136] Ibid., Bk. III, Chaps. XXI-XXIII.

been a man of deep and subtle knowledge of human nature. That power of handling the calculus of human nature, which marks other men like Richelieu and Tallyrand, was foreign to Constantine. He remained all his life a little unsophisticated and, outside of his own special milieu, somewhat 'innocent.' He was prone to accept men's own account of themselves. He owed much of his success and power to a capacity for working with all kinds of men—and therefore for bearing with their idiosyncrasies, having had plenty of practise in the military. He was a long way from being a fool. Every now and then he would awake to the consciousness that he was being deceived."[137]

In February of 326, an imperial retinue was bound for Rome, with Constantine, Fausta, and Constantia, Crispus, and young Constantine. Fausta, then thirty-six years of age, was eighteen years younger than her husband, Emperor Constantine. If Fausta considered Crispus a threat to her sons, it is unlikely that Helen would not have noticed. Crispus had been brought up by his grandmother, Helen, who loved the youth immensely. The whole family arrived in Rome by June. At a July secular celebration, Constantine stayed inside the palace. He did not wish to participate in ceremonies which included a sacrifice to Jupiter. The Romans were angry and some pelted Constantine's statue with stones. When the emperor was informed of the misdeed, he remarked as he stroked his face and smiled, "I am not able to see any wound inflicted on my face. Indeed, both the head and countenance appear quite sound." The emperor was conspicuous for his rye humor.[138] Meletios remarks that the ever-memorable Constantine was one who did not remember wrongs. Even though he was urged by his friends to punish the detractors of his image, he would not even consider it.[139]

Neither Eusebius nor Lactantius record the tragic affair that followed. Zosimus claims that Fausta had become enamored with the thirty-one-year-old Crispus and attempted to seduce him. He goes on to record that Crispus rejected the advances of his stepmother. The spurned woman then took her vengeance. Zosimus, who was not an admirer of Constantine, then says that the father, on suspicion of debauching Fausta, put to death his son. "Helen expressed her grief to Constantine for the atrocity, lamenting the death of the young Crispus. Constantine then ordered a bath to be heated to an extremely high temperature: he had Fausta thrown within, and a short time later she was

---

[137] Comment of G. P. Baker, "The Conquest of the East and the Council of Nicaea," *Constantine the Great*, Ch. X(III), p. 246.

[138] Kousoulas, "Three Women" and "A Wrong Start," *The Life and Times*, pp. 375-379.

[139] See Meletios, *Ekklesistikes Historias*, Vol. I, p. 335; and Saint John Chrysostom, who also mentions this incident in his "Sermon 20, On the Statues."

taken out dead." Sextus Aurelius Victor,[140] in his book *De Caesaribus*, knows not why Crispus was dispatched. In the *Epitome*, we read the rumor that "it was on the instigation of Fausta that Constantine ordered his son Crispus to be executed." He adds that "afterward, Constantine had his wife Fausta herself killed in a boiling bath, when his mother Helen accused her for having done her grandson a grave injustice." Two facts are beyond dispute: In late July, in 326, Constantine ordered the arrest of Crispus who was then executed. Then, shortly thereafter, Fausta was cast into a scalding bathtub and suffocated in the steam. The executions were the acts of a sane man who needed to set aside personal feelings and obey the law. He, therefore, felt it incumbent upon himself to reveal that neither family nor he was above the law. The details of what led to this tragedy are not known. It is known that on the 21st of July, Constantine, at a lavish banquet, was on terms of affection with Crispus, where the young man was held in honor. Coins of the time bear the inscription "Augusti." Was Constantine contemplating elevating Crispus to the rank of Augustus? Was Fausta fearful for the lives of her sons who might be deemed by Crispus to be rivals? Was Fausta dreading that if something should happen to her husband, then fifty-four, would Crispus and Helen send her into exile? It was evident to her and everyone else that Constantine loved all his children. Earlier that year he ordered the casting of medals showing together the Caesars Crispus, Constantine II, and even Constans II who was only five or six years old. Obviously, Crispus was the only one old enough to be of assistance to his father in running the government and military.

Sozomen writes that Crispus was "the hope of the Orthodox, the only one, with his father, being their favorite." The incest charges were abominable and against nature. For Constantine to have had Crispus arrested the proof must have been incontrovertible to him. Was there an informer?[141] Was the informer Fausta herself of an attempted seduction? Fausta charged Crispus with having offered to make her his empress. The custom of kings securing a title by marrying the predecessor's wife was not unknown.[142] But who else could accuse Crispus of aspiring to seize the scepter from his father? Constantine knew his son to be better than that. But the charge of Constantine's much younger wife being ravished may have pricked his sensibilities. We do not

---

[140] Sextus Aurelius Victor, who served under Julian the Apostate, is known for his two works, entitled *De Caesaribus* (Augustus to Constantius II) and *Epitome*, both of which were edited by Pichlmayr and Gruendal (Leipzig, 1961).

[141] In October of 325, Constantine had issued an edict inviting informers to report any conspiracies. He gave license to any citizen, with sufficient evidence of abuse or corruption, to make his grievance known to the emperor himself.

[142] Baker, "Rome and Constantinople," *Constantine the Great*, Ch. X(VII), pp. 252, 253.

know if Fausta produced any witnesses, either false or trustworthy ones. The emperor, certainly, would have demanded proof, even for the sake of justifying his judgment to his mother Helen who actually raised Crispus. Not much time passed before Crispus was arrested and taken to Pola, Venetia (near Trieste) and imprisoned. After his execution in 326, we are told by Aurelius Victor that "Helen upbraided Constantine."

Constantine, to his horror and bewilderment, came to be aware that he had been duped. His son's death was irremediable. Nothing could prevent the reign of Fausta's sons, despite her delinquency. The boys were innocent in both their words and actions. Besides, Constantine would never countenance punishing the children for their mother's act. Fausta's tale, so says Baker, could not hold up under Helen's questioning. Helen's arrival was like a fireball or an earthquake to Constantine.[143]

Then again, there is no certainty that Constantine himself signed the death-warrant so soon after Crispus' arrest; but others also, shortly after, were executed under Constantine's orders, so the chroniclers say. Could Fausta, using the imperial seal, have had him dispatched to the next world? Could witnesses that she produced have abused Constantine's signature and seal? Then Fausta, too, was executed under his orders. Ancient writers imply that she was punished because she had unjustly accused Crispus. Even so, the father did not restore Crispus' memory after the son's execution. Ancient sources tell us that shortly after these mysterious events that the names and images of both Fausta and Crispus were eradicated from every place of honor, as well as coins and medallions.[144]

---

[143] Ibid., Ch. X(VIII), pp. 254, 256.

[144] The victory at sea for the young man Crispus, as commander of the fleet, is significant. He vanquished the far superior force of an experienced admiral. In the public eye, this triumph brought Crispus the inestimable esteem of all—save one, Fausta. The Greek compilers of *The Great Synaxaristes* maintain that Crispus' acclaim excited the envy and malice of Constantine's present wife, the "odious" Fausta, who sought to undermine the young man. What was the cause of her jealousy? Constantine, as we know, begot Crispus through a previous marriage with Minervina. Fausta had three sons with Constantine: Constantine II, Constantius II, and Constans I. She also had two daughters, Constantia and Helena. Frenchman Charles LeBeau, in *Historia tou Byzantinou Kratous*, claims there was a third daughter, Constantina, though her existence is doubtful. The latter Helena became the wife of Julian the Apostate who traced his lineage back to Constantius Chlorus' second wife, Theodora. The Greek compilers attribute Fausta's invidiousness to fear that the glory of Crispus might eclipse her sons and even displace them. The compilers of *The Great Synaxaristes* (in Greek) believe that she fell in love with him, but afterward slandered the young man when he rebuffed her advances. They place all culpability on the stepmother, declaring that the

(continued...)

Some speculate that Fausta enticed Crispus in a ploy to implicate him so that she could accuse him of seduction. After these occurrences, Constantine departed Rome, both angry and despondent.[145] He set his energies on

---

[144](...continued)
stepson in no wise wished to commit adultery or slay his father so as to take his wife and throne.

Constantine, basically a man of simple manners and pursuits, learned what took place and came to believe the charges against his son. The weight and gravity of his position and power would not permit him to look askance at the crime and leave the culprit unpunished. It would have been a terrible abuse of his authority and attack on the dignity of the person of the autocrat. The thought that he should appear unjust, that is, to apply the law to others while his own son was granted amnesty, caused a profound pain in his heart. The law at that time demanded the death penalty for infidelity. Blessed Helen, learning that her grandson was executed, lamented greatly at his loss. She exceedingly censured Constantine, so enhancing his affliction that he had the matter reopened. He thoroughly came to believe that it was a case of slander and trickery perpetrated by Fausta. Again, according to the laws of that time, she, too, had to forfeit her life to the same sentence she inflicted on another. These two events—the deaths of his well-loved son and his own wife, the mother of his young children—left him so bereaved that he mourned and lamented for the rest of his life. The compilers mention that Constantine had fashioned a silver statue of Crispus, to the young man's honor and memory, with the inscription: "To my wronged son." [Codinus recorded that Constantine erected a gold statue to Crispus, but this may be a legend.]

This unhappy incident, according to Dositheos of Jerusalem and the fathers of the Eastern Church, took place before the Baptism of the great Constantine. He did not act out of personal interest or disposition, but the demands of his office and the existing law which he upheld in other similar cases demanded his action. Let none be too confounded or harsh at his decisions. Justice meted out by the court system in those years was different than today. All authorities and officials were answerable to the emperor who held the penal law in his hands. How could he be seen by everyone else in his realm as allowing crime to go unpunished in his own house, while subjecting others to undergo executions and prison sentences? He lived at a time when he was expected to be a model and example, and not one who evaded his own laws and customs. The great Constantine is not the only one revered as a saint by our holy Mother Church who slew others. There is also the example of Prophet Elias who slew the priests of Baal 3 Kgs. (1 Kgs.) 18:40. [Taken from note 1, pp. 528-531 of *The Great Synaxaristes* (in Greek), s.v. "May 21st."]

[145] Constantine, as an avid reader of the Scriptures, could not have been unaware of the trials that befell King David in his private life. In the Old Testament, we learn that King David had taken many wives and produced sons and daughters. His daughter Tamar and her brother Absalom were the offspring of one Gentile wife, while David's eldest son, Amnon, was the issue of another wife. David had taken heathenish wives, in disobedience to God's command "neither shall ye contract marriages with them: thou

(continued...)

completing the building of Byzantion and turning the humble garrison town into the queen of cities.[146] As for Bishop Hosius, he left Constantine's court.

Building Constantinople

Constantine, Helen, and Constantia left Rome for Nikomedia. During that journey, he announced that he was going to build a new Rome on the site of the strategically-placed Byzantion. He already had lived there for more than ten years when he was in the service of Diocletian and then Galerius. Constantine's architect already had many of the buildings in place. While Constantine took up again his construction projects and city planning specifications, Helen became more devout in her Christian Faith, especially after the untimely death of her beloved grandson. Although nearly eighty, she felt ready to make a pilgrimage to Jerusalem.

Meanwhile, Constantine had a statue, with a seven-rayed nimbus, brought from Heliopolis of Phyrgia. In the foundation of the column, they

---

[145](...continued)

shalt not give thy daughter to his son, and thou shalt not take his daughter to thy son [Deut. 7:3]." When David learned that his daughter Tamar was humbled by her half-brother Amnon, "he was very angry; but he did not grieve the spirit of his son Amnon, because be loved him, for he was his firstborn [2 Kgs. (2 Sam.) 13:21]." Now Amnon had prevailed against Tamar and lay with her [2 Kgs. (2 Sam.) 13:14]. David, as the chief magistrate in Israel was obliged to see that the law of God was impartially enforced. As head of the nation, it was his duty to punish the incestuous act perpetrated by his son. The law was clear: "Whosoever shall take his sister by his father or by his mother, and shall see her nakedness, and she see his nakedness, it is a reproach: they shall be destroyed before the children of their family; he has uncovered his sister's nakedness, they shall bear their sin [Lev. 20:17]." Although Constantine was not under the same law, we also read: "And if any one should lie with his father's wife, he has uncovered his father's nakedness: let them both die the death, they are guilty [Lev. 20:11]." It is evident that the doting father, David, did not inflict the penalty demanded by the law and his public duty. God, however, dealt with Amnon. Tamar's full brother Absalom, came to hate Amnon for forcing his sister. Absalom took revenge and slew Amnon. Again, David's inordinate leniency with another son, Absalom, led to the latter's open rebellion. Though David did not exercise God's judgment, God does not pervert judgment. As king, David was entrusted with the administration of the public interest, but he preferred natural affection to the discharge of his public and religious duty. The practical warnings against natural inclinations from these incidents are obvious [cf. Col. 3:5]. These admonitions may have been conspicuous to Constantine as well. David's inordinate affection for his sons had two bad effects: it hindered him from acting justly and it caused him to condone grievous crimes. But David's inordinate love ended in inordinate grief. His indulgence to the crimes of his wayward sons led to the murder of Amnon by Absalom and Absalom's insurrection and death. Constantine may have approached his own family dilemma with this knowledge.

[146] Kousoulas, "Intrigue and Violence," *The Life and Times*, pp. 380-386.

placed the twelve baskets. They had been full of the fragments remaining from the five loaves and two fish, which the Lord blessed and broke and gave to the disciples who, in turn, gave to a multitude of more than 5,000.[147] Sacred relics were also deposited in the column toward the protection and sanctification of the city.[148]

The emperor also built many churches for the new city, such as those dedicated to the holy apostles, to the peace of God, to Saint Mochios,[149] and to the Archangel Michael at Anaplous.[150] He donated to these sacred precincts many liturgical vessels and furnishings. He also proclaimed a general edict for that city that the profane altars of the idols were to be torn down and Christian churches were to be built.[151] The city was also endowed with a Senate. Noble Roman families and distinguished leaders were invited to abide in the new city. Constantine built beautiful houses for new residents.

Eusebius tells us that one might see the fountains in the midst of the marketplace graced with figures representing the good Shepherd, and that of Daniel with the lions, forged in brass, with plates of gold. In the principal apartment of the imperial palace, on a vast tablet in the center of its gold-covered paneled ceiling, he caused the symbol of our Savior's Passion—the Cross—to be fixed, composed of a variety of precious stones richly inwrought with gold.[152]

---

[147] Cf. Mt. 14:20.

[148] See the interesting article herein of *The Great Synaxaristes* (in English), on the 11th of May, when the holy Church commemorates the inauguration or consecration of Constantinople. Saint Theophanes writes that "Constantine decreed that, at the founding of Constantinople, it was to be styled 'New Rome,' and ordered it to have a Senate. Constantine set up a porphyry column with a statue of himself on top of it at the place where he began to build the city in the western part, by the gate leading out toward Rome. He decorated the city and brought to it works of art and statues of bronze and marble from every province and city." *The Chronicle of Theophanes Confessor*, AM 5821, A.D. 328/329, p. 46. Note 2 from that source remarks that the statue on the porphyry column was a reworked Apollo from Ilium. Other sources place it in the center of the Forum.

[149] Saint Mochios is commemorated by the holy Church on the 11th of May.

[150] Anaplous or Sosthenion (Istinye) is a small natural bay on the Bosporos, the strait linking the Black Sea with the Propontis, usually called Stenon by the Byzantines.

[151] Saint Theophanes confirms this, saying that "Constantine intensified the destruction of idols and their temples. They were demolished in various places. The revenues from these were bestowed upon the churches of God." *The Chronicle of Theophanes Confessor*, AM 5822, A.D. 329/330, p. 47.

[152] Eusebius, *Life*, Bk. III, Ch. XLIX.

It was also about that time that the Abyssinians were baptized, after being taught by the holy Froumentios of Tyre,[153] with Meropios and Adesios.[154] By God's direction, the courage and piety of Emperor Constantine the Great had become celebrated throughout the civilized world. During his reign, while he was at Byzantion, in 330, the Iberians (Georgians) also embraced Christianity as their state religion.[155] Bishop Theodoretos of Kyros, in his *Ecclesiastical History*,[156] writes about how Iberia was guided into the way of the Gospel truth by a captive, a holy woman of God, who healed the Iberian king of blindness which took hold of him while hunting.[157] She persuaded the king to send an embassy to Constantine, asking for teachers of religion. The king accordingly dispatched an embassy for that purpose. Constantine gladly welcomed the ambassador and selected a bishop endowed with great faith, wisdom, and virtue.

Constantine, also, of his own accord, undertook the protection of the persecuted Christians in Persia. Constantine wrote in earnest to the Persian king, entreating him to embrace the Christian religion as well as to honor its teachers. During that same period, the Armenians also came to Christ. This was the result of the missionary efforts of Hierarch Gregory, the illuminator of Greater Armenia, who reposed ca. 328.[158] Both Gregory and the king, Tiridates, had visited Constantine while he was in Rome. Gregory's successor, the son of Tiridates, named Aristanes, also received epistles of exhortation from Constantine. Saint Theophanes adds that "many races that had earlier overrun Roman territory came forward to be baptized, because of the miracles performed by captive priests who had been taken prisoner during the reign of Emperor Gallienus (253-268). These included Goths, Celts, and the western Galatians. And now, under Constantine the victorious, many races were baptized, hastening to Christ."[159]

---

[153] Saint Froumentios, Archbishop of Ethiopia, is commemorated by the holy Church on the 30th of November.

[154] See *The Church History of Rufinus of Aquileia*, trans. by Philip Amidon (NY: Oxford University Press, 1997), Bk. 10.9, 10.

[155] Ibid., Bk. 10.11.

[156] Theodoret or Theodoretos (ca. 393-ca. 466) was Bishop of Kyros (Cyrrhus) near Antioch. He wrote in Greek. His historical chronicles of the Church and monasticism in the mid-5th C. are of particular interest.

[157] See this account of the "Christian woman" in the narration concerning the Iberians, which is found in *The Great Synaxaristes* (in English), s.v. "October 27th," as well as the history of Saint Nina who is commemorated on the 14th of January.

[158] See, in *The Great Synaxaristes* (in English), the Life of Saint Gregory who is commemorated by the holy Church on the 30th of September.

[159] *The Chronicle of Theophanes Confessor*, AM 5816, A.D. 323/324, loc. cit.

The far-famed buildings of the new city were mostly completed during the emperor's twenty-fourth year, that is, the year 330 or 5838 from the creation of the world. The city, known as New Rome, came to be called Constantinople or Constantine's city, having senators, grandees, dignitaries, and generals. The city was adorned with all magnificence, embellished with columns and statues, so that she should be the queen of cities.[160]

Saint Helen in the Holy Land

It was also at that time that Constantine was vouchsafed a vision. For this reason, he sent his blessed mother Helen to Jerusalem that she might search for the precious Wood of the Cross.[161] It was still buried, or rather hidden away out of malice, in the holy land where our Lord was crucified and buried, by the ungrateful people of the Jews. Socrates and Sozomen mention that the haters of Christ had covered the spot of the crucifixion. By design, they were instrumental in the construction of a temple to Aphrodite (Venus) that they might blot out the memory of Jesus. When the location came to be known to the Augusta, she ordered the temple cast down and the earth removed.[162]

---

[160] "The emperor was turning his back on Rome. He took with him the heritage of civilized mankind, as it had been modified and improved by Rome, rather than the particular local spirit of Rome herself. The Roman Empire was more than a product of Rome. The empire always had been largely Greek. The Italian peasant might have despised them, but the Greeks pulled their weight and were half the team. We must not forget that even the leading Romans were Greek by education. The empire was a Greek empire as much as an Italian one, long before Constantine arose to give its Graecism a local habitation at old Byzantion. If anything, he segregated the Greek element and withdrew it from the west. He concentrated it in the eastern provinces, leaving those in the west once more purely western, de-Hellenized—even, to a certain extent, barbarized: for Hellenism was eight-tenths of human civilization. As for Constantine he was no Greek himself. He used Latin as his familiar language. In it he composed his speeches, which, at necessity, were translated and delivered in Greek by interpreters. He was not a deliberate apostle of things Hellenic, but was following the trend of the day." Baker, *Constantine the Great*, Ch. X(XII), pp. 261-263.

[161] The full account of Saint Helen's exploits in the finding of the Cross may be read in *The Great Synaxaristes* (in English), on the 14th of September, when the holy Church commemorates the Feast of the Exaltation of the Honorable and Life-giving Cross.

[162] Eusebius writes that Constantine then granted money for the Church at Jerusalem, in the holy place of our Savior's resurrection [*Life*, Bk. III, Ch. XXIX]. Now, the holy sepulcher of the Lord, formerly the tomb of Joseph of Arimathea, to which the radiant angel had descended from heaven and rolled away the stone, had been completely buried in dirt and paved over with stone. An edifice of a temple to Venus was erected over the spot. Constantine gave orders, under the guidance of the Holy Spirit, that the place should be excavated down to the original lay of the land and the whole purified. The temple to Venus, its statues, and the whole panoply, were destroyed. The entire

(continued...)

Saint Theophanes tells us that "the emperor ordered Makarios I, Bishop of Jerusalem (314-333), who was present at the First Synod at Nicaea, to search out, on his return, the sites of the holy resurrection and that of Golgotha (Place of a Skull) and the life-giving Wood. In this year he crowned Helen, his God-minded mother, and assigned her as empress the privilege of coinage. She had a vision commissioning her to go to Jerusalem and to bring to light the sacred sites buried by the impious. She begged her son Constantine to fulfill these commands sent to her by God. And he acted in obedience to her will."[163]

Saint Helen

Thus, this episode of great moment began as follows. Saint Helen, of pious mind, took along with her an army and multitude of generals and dignitaries. During her pilgrimage, she distributed much in the way of alms and imperial support of the Church and clergy. "Constantine," adds Saint Theophanes, "sent his mother with money and soldiers. Makarios, Patriarch of Jerusalem, having met the empress with due honor, made the search for the longed-for life-giving Wood along with her, in tranquility, with earnest prayers and fasting. When these things had been done, the site was quickly revealed to Makarios by God in the place where the temple and statue of the impure demon Aphrodite stood. The divinely crowned Helen, using her imperial authority, immediately arranged for a large number of workmen to destroy the temple, which had been lavishly built by Emperor Aelius Hadrian (117-138). She razed it to its foundation, and removed the excavated soil."[164]

Helen came to the site of the Lord's Passion. So she sought out those full of learning, not only Christians but also Jews in order to inform her of the

---

[162](...continued)
mass of earth and stone were removed as far as possible outside of the city. Thereupon, the venerable and hallowed monument of our Savior's resurrection was uncovered. Eusebius, *Life*, Bk. III, Chaps. XXV-XXVIII. The Church of the Holy Sepulcher was officially dedicated in the thirtieth year of Constantine's reign, according to Eusebius [Ibid., Bk. IV, Ch. XLVII].

[163] *The Chronicle of Theophanes Confessor*, AM 5816, A.D. 323/324, p. 37.

[164] Ibid., AM 5817, A.D. 324/325, pp. 41, 42.

precious relic's whereabouts. The Augusta secured the help of a certain Jew named Juda, who was most familiar with the holy land. He, initially, was not cooperative. He was, consequently, cast into a dry well. He was not given any bread or water. Finally, after seven days, Juda could no longer bear the hunger and thirst. He cried out in a great voice, "Release me and I will reveal where the Christ was crucified!" Straightway, he was drawn out of the well. He made manifest the site, but he did not know exactly where the Cross was to be found. The holy Helen offered up prayer to the Lord. Forthwith, there occurred a great earthquake which shook the depths of that place. An ineffable fragrance wafted forth, even as the scent of incense. The empress charged the workers to dig. As the diggers went deeper into the earth, they began to detect a fragrant scent emanating from underground. The Augusta gave orders for the digging to continue.

To general astonishment, but precisely as the empress alone had believed, deep digging opened up cavities in the earth and revealed the secret of the hidden Cross. Helen and all marvelled, as well as Juda. That Jew came to believe in Christ and gave thanks to Him. The earth yielded up three crosses, the placard, and the nails. The custom at that time was to bury the implements of torture close to the site of suffering. The inscription, however, had been wrenched from the true Cross and tossed aside. The Cross of Jesus had been cast aside with the others, without any distinction. Rufinus of Aquileia (b. 345) notes: "The three crosses were jumbled together. But Helen's joy at the discovery was darkened by the fact that the crosses were indistinguishable from each other. There was also found the inscription which Pilate had made with Greek, Latin, and Hebrew letters, but not even it showed clearly enough which was the Lord's gibbet."[165] Saint Theophanes reports that "straightway the holy sepulcher and the Place of a Skull were revealed; and close by, to the east, there were buried three crosses. After searching, they even found the nails. But they were all at a loss to know which cross was the Lord's."[166]

The empress was filled with profound gladness upon the discovery. When Juda was asked, he knew not how to identify which one of the three crosses was the one upon which the Lord was crucified. It so happened, as if by the appointment of God, that a funeral procession was in progress. Juda, moved by a sanguine faith, summoned the mourners to bring the deceased before the empress. The bier of the corpse was carried in and set down. As the body lay there, the first cross was placed on the dead person, but there was no response from the deceased. This took place again with the second cross and, once more, there was no sign. Nothing occurred because these were the crosses of the two thieves. Finally the Cross of our Lord Jesus Christ was placed on the

---

[165] *The Church History of Rufinus of Aquileia*, Bk. 10.7.

[166] *The Chronicle of Theophanes Confessor*, AM 5817, A.D. 324/325, p. 42.

corpse. O Thy wonder, Christ King! The dead man arose. By this miracle was there revealed the power of the honorable Cross. This wonderworking was witnessed by many Jews, who came to believe in the Christ. As for Saint Helen, she was joyous and gave thanks to our Lord Jesus Christ. Following this momentous event, the empress summoned Juda who, in the interim, received holy Baptism and was named Kyriakos.[167] As Kyriakos and others were offering veneration to the Cross, the place was radiant. They dug a little further and discovered the nails.[168]

The Exaltation of the Cross

---

[167] During the reign of Julian the Apostate (360), the holy Kyriakos succeeded Bishop Makarios as Patriarch of Jerusalem (314-333). Kyriakos suffered and was martyred with his mother Anna. Both are commemorated by the holy Church on the 28th of October.

[168] See *The Great Synaxaristes* (in English) for the finding by Saint Helen of the precious nails of the Passion of our Lord Jesus Christ, which is commemorated by the holy Church on the 6th of March.

Saint Theophanes adds another account that further testified to the true Cross. In their attempt to discover the Cross of the Lord, while "Helen was particularly grieved, the well-named Makarios solved the problem by his faith. For by bringing each of the crosses to a distinguished lady who was in despair and near death, he discovered which of them was the Lord's. For barely had its shadow come close to the sick woman when she, though hardly able to breathe or move, suddenly and immediately through God's power leaped up and began glorifying God in a loud voice."[169]

Rufinus also records this story, saying, "There happened to be in the city a woman of high station who was lying near death of a serious illness. When Bishop Makarios perceived the empress' perplexity and of all who were also present, he said, 'Bring here all the crosses which have been found; and God will now disclose to us which one it was that bore God.' Makarios, thereupon, with the empress and the people, went to the ailing woman. The bishop knelt down and poured out the following prayer to God: 'O Lord, Thou hast deigned to bestow salvation upon the human race through Thine only-begotten Son and His suffering of the Cross. Thou hast recently inspired the heart of Thy handmaid to seek the blessed Wood on which our salvation hung. Do Thou show clearly which of these three crosses was foreordained for the Lord's glory and which were made for servile punishment. In so doing, this woman, who lies here half-dead, may be called back to life from the gates of death even as the healing Wood touches her.' Having spoken thus, Makarios first touched her with one of the three, but it did not help. He touched her with the second; and again nothing happened. But when he touched her with the third, she at once opened her eyes and rose up. With renewed strength and far more liveliness than when she possessed health, she began to run about the whole house and glorify the Lord's power. The empress then, having been granted her prayer with such a clear token, poured her royal ambition into the construction of a wonderful temple on the site where she had found the Cross. The four nails too, with which the Lord's body had been fastened, she brought to her son Constantine. He made of some of them a bridle to use in battle; and, with the others, he is said to have equipped himself with a helmet no less useful in battle. As for the healing Wood itself, part of it she presented to her son, and part she put in silver reliquaries at the site; it is still kept there as a memorial with unflagging devotion."[170]

The prophecy of Esaias, also, came to pass in Helen's discovery: "And the glory of Libanus shall come to thee, with the cypress, and pine, and cedar together, to glorify My holy place [Is. 60:13]." For she recognized the three parts of the Cross in the cedar, the pine, and the cypress whereby the suffering

---

[169] *The Chronicle of Theophanes Confessor*, AM 5817, A.D. 324/325, loc. cit.
[170] *The Church History of Rufinus of Aquileia*, Bk. 10.7, 8.

of the Savior was accomplished.[171] Saint Theodore the Stoudite chants: "Let us sing the praises of the Cross, made from three kinds of wood [Is. 60:13] as a figure of the Trinity; and venerating it with fear, let us raise our cry, as we bless, praise, and exalt Christ above all forever."[172] And, "Thou wast crucified, O Son of God, on the pine, the cedar, and the cypress. Sanctify us all, and count us worthy to look upon Thy life-giving Passion."[173] Saint Joseph the Hymnographer also solemnly sings: "Let us venerate the Cross of the Lord, offering the following: our tender affection as the cypress, the sweet fragrance of our faith as the cedar, and our sincere love as the pine. And let us glorify our Deliverer Who was nailed upon it [Is. 60:13]."[174]

Saint Gregory of Tours (538-594) notes that the nails used to transfix the thieves were black and rusted; but the nails of the Lord were radiant and shone forth like lightening. Fifth-century Church historian Sozomen,[175] a native of Palestine, records that "after the venerated Wood had been identified, the greater portion of it was deposited in a silver case; it is still preserved in Jerusalem. Empress Helen gave part of it to her son Constantine, together with the nails by which the body of Christ had been fastened. Of these, it is related, the emperor had a headpiece and bit made for his horse according to the prophecy of holy Zacharias."[176]

Bishop Theodoretos, a native of Antioch, says that "the Augusta had given orders that a portion of the nails should be inserted in the royal helmet, in order that the head of her son might be preserved from the darts of his enemies. The other portion of the nails she ordered to be formed into the bridle of his horse, not only to ensure the safety of the emperor but also to fulfill an ancient prophecy spoken of by Zacharias....She had part of the Cross of our Savior conveyed to the palace. The rest was enclosed in a covering of silver, and committed to the care of the bishop of the city, whom she exhorted to preserve it carefully, in order that it might be transmitted uninjured to posterity. She then sent everywhere for workmen and for materials, and caused the most spacious and most magnificent churches to be erected."[177]

---

[171] May 21st, Orthros Oikos after Ode Four.

[172] Triodion, Tuesday in the Fourth Week, Orthros Canon, Ode Eight, Mode Plagal Four.

[173] Triodion, Friday in the Fourth Week, Orthros Canon, Ode Five, Mode Four.

[174] Triodion, Wednesday in the Fourth Week, Orthros Canon, Ode Seven, Mode Plagal Two.

[175] Sozomen, Salaminus Hermias, *The Ecclesiastical History*, Bk. II, Ch. I, Nicene and Post-Nicene Fathers, 2nd Ser., II:259.

[176] Zach. 14:20.

[177] Theodoret, *The Ecclesiastical History*, Bk. I, Ch. XVII, Nicene, 2nd Ser., III:55.

Greek Church historian Socrates, a lawyer and native of Constantinople, says that the "emperor's mother erected over the place of the sepulcher a magnificent church, and named it New Jerusalem, having built it facing that old and deserted city. There she left a portion of the Cross, enclosed in a silver case, as a memorial to those who might wish to see it. The other part she sent to the emperor. He believed that the city would be perfectly secure where that relic should be preserved. He privately enclosed it in his own statue, which stands on a large column of porphyry in the Forum called Constantine's at Constantinople.[178] I have written this from an intermediary report indeed; but almost all the inhabitants of Constantinople affirm that it is true. Moreover, the nails with which Christ's hands were fastened to the Cross—for his mother Helen, having found these also in the sepulcher, had sent them—Constantine took and had made into bridle-bits and a helmet, which he used in his military expeditions.[179] The emperor supplied all materials for the construction of the churches, and wrote to Bishop Makarios to expedite these edifices. When the emperor's mother had completed the New Jerusalem, she reared another church that was not at all inferior. It was over the cave at Bethlehem, where Christ was born according to the flesh. Nor did Helen stop here, but built a third on the mount of His ascension."[180] Saint Theophanes confirms that "she ordered that churches be built at the holy Sepulcher and at Calvary in the name of her son, where the life-giving Wood was discovered, and also at Bethlehem and on the Mount of Olives."[181]

At Golgotha, Saint Helen was the first to venerate the holy Cross and kiss it. She fully intended to bring the relic of the Cross to the new city, as a gift for her son. Thus she had it sawn vertically, parallel to the front face, thereby retaining the form of the entire front and rear of the Cross. Hence, she

---

[178] The statue of Constantine, with the relic of the nail at the foot of the statue, also contained the curbstone from the well of Patriarch Jacob [Jn. 4:12]. See more on the relics within the Column of Constantine in the Life of the holy Hieromartyr Hypatios, Bishop of Gangra, commemorated by the holy Church on the 31st of March.

[179] Without the upholding predisposition of history, world opinion, or family tradition—beyond the example of his own father—Constantine, far from being ashamed to own the Christian name, cross, and religion, made it manifest to all as his highest honor, glorying in it as the trophy which led him on to victory. He caused it to be painted on a lofty tablet, and set up in the front of the portico of his palace visible to all, the cross above his head, and a flying dragon beneath his own and his children's feet, stricken through with a dart, and cast headlong into the depths of the sea. Eusebius, *Life*, Bk. III, Chaps. II, III.

[180] Socrates Scholasticus, *The Ecclesiastical History*, Bk. I, Ch. XVII, Nicene, II:21, 22.

[181] *The Chronicle of Theophanes Confessor*, AM 5817, A.D. 324/325, loc. cit.

had two Crosses, one of which was left in Jerusalem and the other which was taken, rejoicing, along with her, together with the precious nails, to her son.

She, according to Saint Ambrose, sought the nails with which the Lord was crucified, and found them. "From one nail," says he, "she ordered a bridle to be made; from the other she wove a diadem. She turned the one to an ornamental use, the other to a devotional use. And so the beginning of the faith of the emperors is the holy relic which is upon the bridle, in accordance with the prophecy of Zacharias: 'In that day there shall be upon the bridle of every horse holiness to the Lord almighty [Zach. 14:20].' Therefrom came the faith whereby persecution ended and devotion to God took its place. Wisely did Helen act who placed the Cross on the head of sovereigns, that the Cross of Christ might be adored among kings. That was not a presumption but piety, since honor was given to our holy redemption....On the head, a crown; in the hands, reins. A crown made from the Cross, that faith might shine forth; reins likewise from the Cross, that authority might govern, and that there might be just rule, and not legislation that was unjust. May the princes also consider that this has been granted to them by Christ's generosity, that in imitation of the Lord it may be said of the Roman emperor: 'Thou hast set upon his head a crown of precious stones [Ps. 20:3].'"[182]

Sozomen tells us that "Constantine indeed kept a portion, but most of it was given a silver cover and preserved in the church that was soon erected on the site of its discovery. The emperor, in fact, had a headpiece and bit made for his horse, according to the prophecy of Zacharias who referred to this period."[183] Saint Theophanes agrees and says that "Constantine welcomed his mother with joy. He placed the particle of the life-giving Wood in a gold chest, handing it over to the bishop for safekeeping. Of the nails, Constantine forged some onto his helmet; others he inserted in his horse's bridle, so that the word of the prophet might be fulfilled."[184]

When Constantine learned that his mother was approaching the new city, he went out to meet her. With profound gladness, he venerated the honorable Cross. He handed over to the bishop of the church both the sacred Cross and the chest with the precious nails.

In the two years that she spent in Palestine, Helen built churches. Later, a chapel was dedicated to Helen at the site of the excavations, on the very place of the finding of the true Cross. Constantine adorned his mother's

[182] Saint Ambrose, "Funeral Oration on Theodosius," *Funeral Orations*, The Fathers of the Church, trans. by R. J. DeFerrari, Ph.D., Vol. 22, pp. 328, 329.

[183] *The Ecclesiastical History of Sozomen*, loc. cit.

[184] *The Chronicle of Theophanes Confessor*, AM 5817, A.D. 324/325, loc. cit.

efforts with further splendor of his own.[185] Some accounts have associated her with the construction of the Dormition Church near Gethsemane, Hebron at the Oak of Mambre,[186] and even Mount Sinai. She also spent her time in the holy land helping the poor and needy. The Augusta furnished food, and even served the tables herself, always dressed in simple garb.

Rufinus records that "the venerable empress also left the following mark of her religious spirit. She is said to have invited to lunch the virgins consecrated to God whom she found there in the holy land. She is said to have treated them with such devotion that she thought it unfitting for them to perform the duties of servants. Much rather, she herself, in servant's garb, set out the food with her own hands, offered the cup, and poured water over their hands. Indeed, the empress of the world and mother of the empire appointed herself servant of the servants of Christ. This took place in Jerusalem.

"In the meantime," records Rufinus, "Constantine, trusting in his faith, conquered by force of arms, on their own soil, the Sarmatians, the Goths, and the other barbarian nations, except for those which had already achieved peace by treaties of friendship or self-surrender. The more he submitted to God in a spirit of religion and humility, the more widely God subjected everything to him. He also sent letters to Antony, the first desert-dweller, as to one of the prophets, begging him to beseech the Lord for him and his children.[187] Thus, Constantine longed to make himself acceptable to God, not only by his own merits and his mother's devotion but also through the intercession of the saints."[188]

According to Sozomen, when Helen visited the cities of the east, she bestowed befitting gifts on the churches in every town, enriched those individuals who had been deprived of their possessions, supplied ungrudgingly the necessities of the poor, and restored to liberty those who had been long imprisoned or condemned to exile or to the mines.[189] Eusebius confirms her generosity and beneficent acts, telling us, "In the splendor of imperial authority, she bestowed abundant proofs of her liberality. On her circuit of the eastern provinces, she helped the inhabitants of several cities and individuals who approached her. At the same time, she scattered largesses among the soldiery with a liberal hand. But especially noteworthy were the gifts she bestowed on the naked and unprotected poor. To some she gave money, to others an ample supply of clothing. She liberated some from prison, or from

---

[185] Eusebius, *Life*, Bk. III, Ch. XLIII.

[186] Ibid., Bk. III, Ch. LIII.

[187] Saint Anthony the Great is commemorated by the holy Church on the 17th of January.

[188] *The Church History of Rufinus of Aquileia*, Bk. 10.8.

[189] *The Ecclesiastical History of Sozomen*, Book II, Ch. II, II:259.

the bitter servitude of the mines. Others she delivered from unjust oppression; and others again, she restored from exile....She was also far from neglecting personal piety toward God. She adorned the houses of prayer with splendid offerings, not overlooking the churches of the smallest cities. This admirable woman was to be seen in simple and modest attire, mingling with the crowd of worshippers."[190] The Augusta was immensely popular across the empire. Her enthusiasm for the Faith was responsible for bringing about untold conversions. Her pilgrimage and journey caught the imagination of Christendom, since she is one of the first recorded pilgrims. She began a tradition which has continued to our own day, though little remains of the splendid edifices for which she was responsible. Fires, earthquakes, and invasions have taken their toll over the last seventeen centuries. Yet her vision and energy to preserve and adorn the holy shrines of Orthodoxy were perpetuated.

Upon returning home, she was exhausted from her labors and mourned her slain grandson Crispus. Saint Helen reposed in the arms of her son Constantine at Nikomedia. Eusebius remarks that Helena Augusta, faithful beloved wife of Constantius, and devoted mother of Constantine the Great, spouse of one Christian Roman emperor and the mother of another still greater, unstinting and tireless patroness of the Bride of Christ, the holy Church, an imperial guardianess of the flock no dire wolf ever dared transgress, having attained to her eightieth year, surrendered her spirit and breathed her last. She reposed in the presence of her illustrious son, who was kneeling in attendance by her side, caring for her and holding her hands with utmost reverence and devotion. She was ushered by holy saints and angels of the highest rank and order to be received up into our everlasting Savior's eternal presence. Her body was honored with special tokens of respect. She was escorted to the imperial city by a vast train of escorts and royal honor guards. She was vouchsafed an imperial tomb in the Church of the Holy Apostles. Eusebius comments that Constantine "rendered her through his influence so devout a worshipper of God, though she had not previously been such, that she seemed to have been instructed from the first by the Savior of mankind. Besides this, he had honored her so fully with imperial dignities, that in every province, and in the very ranks of the soldiery, she was spoken of under the titles of Augusta and empress, and her likeness was impressed on golden coins."[191]

---

[190] Eusebius, *Life*, Bk. III, Chaps. XLIV, XLV, I:531.

[191] Ibid., Bk. III, Chaps. XLVI, XLVII.

Some date her repose in 327. It certainly must have occurred before 330, the year that the last known coins bearing her name were struck. Her precious relics were translated to Constantinople and laid to rest in the imperial vault of the Church of the Apostles. It is presumed that her remains were transferred in 849 to the Abbey of Haut-

(continued...)

Constantine wrote to Makarios to hurry with the building. Constantine gave instructions for the construction of a church over the holy Sepulcher of Christ. The emperor sent an officer of works, bearing plenty of money with orders to build the holy places so that there would be nothing so beautiful in the entire inhabited world. He also wrote to the governors of the province to join in the work earnestly from the public account. He told Makarios that he had already given orders to Drakilius, the provincial governor, to provide artisans and laborers and all the necessary building material that the patriarch might require. Constantine followed his words with actual deeds. The emperor in splendid celebration gave thanks to God for having made such good things happen in his time.[192]

Paganism

With regard to paganism and the idol temples and their statues, Constantine used every means to rebuke the superstitious errors of the heathen. He was not content to merely reduce the idols of stone to rubble, or those of metal to molten lumps. With Solomon-like shrewdness and understanding of human nature, he ordered the idols stripped of their most precious adornments of gemstones, precious metals, and lacquer or veneer. He reduced the artistically refined idols, of the most exquisite workmanship, to cheap caricatures of their former images. He ordered them to be removed from their former places of honor in the pagan temples. He had them exposed out-of-doors in all the public places of the imperial city, as common objects of public derision. Furthermore, in a similar fashion, he wisely did not order the outright destruction of pagan temples. Instead, he put their patrons to the test by ordering their front doors and roof tiles removed. He, therefore, permitted the priests and most persistent idolaters to continue their vile, loathsome, and defiled paganistic ceremonies, but only on pain of being exposed to the natural elements: the heat of the sun, the cold of winter, the rains, the dust, the biggest and most intrusive insects, and so on. After this fashion, even the birds were thereby indirectly enabled to roost in the open rafters. Thus, the pagan altars and sanctuaries were transformed into veritable natural receptacles of bird guano. All this took place, in addition to having been forced to give up the

---

[191](...continued)
villers, in the French Archdiocese of Reims, as recorded by the monk Altmann in his *Translatio*. Others record that some of her relics were taken to Rome. Her veneration spread, early in the ninth century, even to western countries. Her feast in the west falls on the 18th of August.

[192] *The Chronicle of Theophanes Confessor*, AM 5817, A.D. 324/325, loc. cit.

ownership of their own statuary formerly regarded as the very sacred gods themselves.[193]

In one instance, Constantine discovered the foul practises of the patrons of a grove and temple at Aphaca, on part of the summit of Mount Lebanon, in Phoenicia. Here men propitiated the demon by effeminate conduct; here too unlawful commerce of women and adulterous intercourse, with other horrible and infamous practises took place. Constantine inspected the site himself. He gave orders that the building and its offerings be utterly destroyed. Its former patrons were threatened with punishment should they resume their former practises after his absence again.[194]

He came to the Temple of Aesculapius at Aegae, a pagan monument to quackery and false cures, and did the same to it as the temple of Venus. He ordered its utter destruction and the forbiddance of a resumption of the practise of its foul demonic ceremonies. Thus, pagans everywhere abandoned idol worship in the wake of Constantine's destruction of the pagan temples; and they turned to the knowledge of Christ. In like fashion, he destroyed the temple of Venus at Heliopolis. In its place, he built a church of great size and magnificence. He also enacted a new statute forbidding the continuance of former licentious practises. He exhorted the people by written letter, that he might instruct all men in the principles of chastity. He also made abundant provision for the poor that they might learn to praise the name of the Savior, in Whose name all these wonderful things were coming to pass.[195]

He also issued an edict against the heretics—Novatians, Valentinians, Marcionites, Paulians, Cataphrygians, and all who devise and support heresies by means of private assemblies—and he deprived them of their meeting places. He wrote: "You are positively deprived of every gathering point for your superstitious meetings, I mean all the houses of prayer—if such be worthy of the name—which belong to heretics. These, without delay, are to be made over to the catholic Church. Any other such places are to be confiscated to the public service, so that no facility whatever should be left for any future gathering. This is so that, from this day forward, none of your unlawful assemblies may presume to appear in any public or private place. Let this edict be made public."[196]

As a result of Constantine's edict, many heretics renounced their false beliefs and took recourse to the holy Church. However, the prelates of the several churches continued to make strict inquiry. They utterly rejected those who attempted an entrance under the specious disguise of false pretenses, while

---

[193] Eusebius, *Life*, Bk. III, Chaps. LIII, LIV.

[194] Ibid., Bk. III, Ch. LV.

[195] Ibid., Bk. III. Chaps. LVI-LVIII.

[196] Ibid., Bk. III, Chaps. LXIV, LXV.

those who came with sincerity of purpose were proved for a time. Then, after sufficient trial, they were numbered with the congregation. Those who were merely led astray, were, after examination, admitted without delay. Others, disguising their sentiments, crept secretly into the Church. Books, those which detailed the practise of evil and forbidden arts and heresies, were destroyed and their owner's properties confiscated. As for the authors of such texts, they were driven from the land. Thus was the holy Church made whole.[197]

Constantine was desirous of conferring and bestowing benefits of every kind. No one's case was too small or insignificant. He aided those unjustly burdened with taxes. In litigations of judicial arbitration, Constantine even went so far as to arrange that the losers might not quit his presence less contented than the victorious litigant. The emperor, therefore, from his own private means, gave recompense: in some cases he bestowed lands and in other cases he gave money awards to the defeated party.[198] Constantine's most impressive administrative changes were the increasing equatability of taxation, the complete separation of the military commands from the civil careers, and the opening of another channel of information to the emperor through the *Magister Officiorum.*[199]

Scythians and Sarmatians

While the former emperors had actually rendered tribute to the Scythians, yet, through the sign of our Savior, Constantine subjugated the Scythian and Sarmatian tribes to Rome. Some he conquered by military might, others he conciliated by wisely conducted embassies. Thus, at length, the Scythians learned to acknowledge subjection to the power of Rome and to the Cross. With respect to the Sarmatians, the following chain of events transpired. The Scythians attacked the Sarmatians. The Sarmatians entrusted their slaves with arms in order to help repel the enemy. The slaves first overcame the Scythians, but then turned and drove the Sarmatians from their native land. The expelled Sarmatians then sought Constantine's protection. They were received by him into the confines of the Roman Empire. Some he incorporated with his own troops, the rest he allotted lands.[200]

---

[197] Ibid., Bk. III, Ch. LXVI.

[198] Ibid., Bk. IV, Chaps. I-IV.

[199] T. G. Elliott, "Gothic wars; Building; Administration," *The Christianity of Constantine The Great*, Ch. XIII, p. 268.

[200] Eusebius, *Life*, Bk. IV, Chaps. V, VI.

More particularly, these incidents took place in 328.[201] Constantine had responded to an appeal by the Sarmatians against the Goths. Constantine received the Gothic king's son, among other hostages, in 332. Shortly afterward, the Sarmatian Limigantes, who having been armed by their masters against the Goth, had revolted and pursued their erstwhile masters out of their lands, provoked an appeal by the free Sarmatians to the emperor. Constantine, in 334, settled about 300,000 on devastated but cultivable land in Italy and the Balkans. In 336, Constantine undertook a campaign north of the Danube, in which he recovered part of Dacia. Constantine's dealings with the Danubian barbarians secured the peace of the Balkans for over thirty years. His treatment of the Goths as human beings went a long way in insuring this success.[202]

Thus, like a second Solomon, virtually all nations—among whom were numbered the Blemmyan tribes, the Indians, and the Ethiopians—came to acclaim the wisdom and greatness of Constantine. They sent him gifts and embassages. They offered him their services and alliances. Constantine, in return, even went so far as to honor the noblest among them with Roman offices of dignity.[203]

King Shāpūr

Constantine Augustus wrote to the Persian king, Shāpūr II (310-381). Constantine had sent him an embassy on behalf of the Christians in the Sasanian realm. After the manner of Solomon and the Queen of Sheba, many magnificent gifts were exchanged as a showing of good will.[204] The letter contained Constantine's truly pious confession of God and Christ: "By keeping the divine Faith," wrote the Augustus, "I am made a partaker of the light of truth. Guided by the light of truth, I advance in the knowledge of the divine Faith. Hence it is that, as my actions themselves evince, I profess the most holy religion. And this worship I declare to be that which teaches me deeper acquaintance with the most holy God....I have aroused each nation of the world in succession to a well-grounded hope of security, so that those who groan in servitude to the most cruel tyrants,...have been restored, through my agency, to a far happier state. This God I confess that I hold in unceasing honor and remembrance. This

---

[201] Constantine claimed victories over the Sarmatians in 323 and again in 334. He claimed victories over the Germans in 307, 308, ca. 314, and 328/329. He also claimed victory over the Dacians in 336. Constantine, after crossing the Danube, built a stone bridge over it and also subdued the Scythians (327/328). The bridge, from Oescus to Sucidava, was a necessary prerequisite for these campaigns. *The Chronicle of Theophanes Confessor*, AM 5818-5819, A.D. 325-328, pp. 44, 45.

[202] T. G. Eliott, "Gothic wars; Building; Administration," *The Christianity of Constantine the Great*, Ch. XIII, pp. 254, 255.

[203] Eusebius, *Life*, Bk. IV, Ch. VII.

[204] 3 Kgs. (1 Kgs.) 10:7; 2 Chr. 9:6.

God I delight to contemplate with pure and guileless thoughts in the height of His glory. This God I invoke with bended knees, and recoil with horror from the blood of sacrifices, from their foul and detestable odors, and from every earthborn magic fire. For these profane and impious superstitions, together with the defiled ceremonies, have cast down and consigned to perdition many, nay, whole nations of the Gentile world. For He Who is Lord of all cannot endure that those blessings which, in His own loving-kindness and consideration of the wants of men, He has revealed for the use of all, should be perverted to serve the lusts of any. His only demand from man is purity of mind and an undefiled spirit. It is by this standard He weighs the actions of virtue and godliness. For His pleasure is in works of moderation and gentleness. He loves the meek, and hates the turbulent spirit. He delights in faith, and chastises unbelief. By Him all presumptuous power is broken down; and He avenges the insolence of the proud. While the arrogant and haughty are utterly overthrown, He requites the humble and forgiving with deserved rewards. He also highly honors and strengthens, with His special help, a kingdom justly governed; and He maintains a prudent king in the tranquillity of peace.

"I cannot, then, my brother, believe that I err in acknowledging this one God, the Author and Parent of all things. It was this one God Whom many of my predecessors in power, led astray by the madness of error, have ventured to deny. But they were all visited with a retribution so terrible and so destructive, that all succeeding generations have held up my predecessors' calamities as the most effectual warning to any who desire to follow in their steps.[205] And it is surely a happy circumstance that the punishment of such persons, as I have described, should have been publicly manifested in our own times. For I myself have witnessed the end of those who, by their impious edicts, lately harassed the worshippers of God. And for their end is there an abundance of giving thanks due to God, that through His excellent providence all men who observe His holy laws are gladdened by the renewed enjoyment of peace. Hence, I am fully persuaded that everything is in the best and safest posture, since God is vouchsafing—through the influence of their pure and faithful religious service, and their unity of judgment respecting His divine character—to gather all men to Himself.

"Imagine, then, with what joy I heard tidings so accordant with my desire, that the fairest districts of Persia are filled with those men in whose behalf alone I am at present speaking, I mean the Christians. I pray, therefore, that both thou and they may enjoy abundant prosperity, and that thy blessings and theirs may be in equal measure. For thus, shalt thou experience the mercy

[205] Constantine mentions here Emperor Valerian (253-260), a persecutor of the Christians, whose expedition against the Persians led to his own captivity. He was then subjected to every kind of insult and cruelty from his conquerors.

and favor of that God Who is the Lord and Father of all. And now, because thy power is great, I commend these persons to thy protection. On account of thy piety being eminent, I commit them to your care. Cherish them with thy wonted humanity and kindness; for by this proof of faith thou shalt secure an immeasurable benefit both to thyself and us."[206]

A New Military

Constantine, cognizant of his position of authority and the greatly enhanced power of example which his life must inevitably have upon others, caused himself to be represented on his coins, and in his portraits, in the attitude of prayer. After the same fashion, as a most powerful treatment and defense against the wiles of the devil, Constantine forbade, by express enactment, the setting up of any resemblance of himself in any idol temple. He became a devout student of the sacred Scriptures. He would offer up regular prayers with all the members of his imperial court. The Roman Empire was being transformed by one man, its emperor, from a bastion of devils to a sanctuary of holiness. Constantine further enjoined all citizens and subjects, by edict and example, to observe the Lord's day as a day of worship and rest.[207] He also caused the observance of commemorative days for the martyrs, and to honor the festal seasons in the churches.[208]

The Roman army, grounded in base weaponry and the last resort of strength of arms, together with toughness of sensibilities, hardness of heart, and unflinching devotion to militaristic duty, Constantine sought to transform and uplift with an edict. His soldiers were to appear on each Lord's day on an open plain near the city, to pray with uplifted hands in proper array and orderly fashion, even as they had formerly fought by rank and file. He admonished them not to trust in spears, armor, or bodily strength, but to acknowledge the supreme God as Giver of every good and of victory itself. He also commanded them to pronounce the following prayer in the Latin tongue: "We acknowledge Thee the only God. We own Thee as our King, and implore Thy succor. By Thy favor have we gotten the victory. Through Thee are we mightier than our enemies. We render thanks for Thy past benefits, and trust Thee for future blessings. Together we pray to Thee, and beseech Thee long to preserve to us, safe and triumphant, our Emperor Constantine and his pious sons." Constantine caused the sign of the Cross to be engraved on his soldiers' shields, and their embattled forces to be preceded in their march, not by golden images, as heretofore, but only by the standard of the Cross.[209]

---

[206] Eusebius, *Life*, Bk. IV, Chaps. IX-XIII.
[207] Ibid., Bk. IV, Chaps. XV-XVIII.
[208] Ibid., Bk. IV, Ch. XXIII.
[209] Ibid., Bk. IV, Chaps. XIX-XXI.

Constantine restructured the military of more than 300,000 men. There were two high-level positions: the Master of Infantry and the Master of Cavalry. The size of the legions was reduced from 5,500 men to 1,000. The army had three branches. There were the *limitanei* or *riparienses* who guarded the frontier. The latter grade referred to those units along the Rhine and Danube. Next there were the highly mobile infantry and cavalry units—the *comitatenses*. Then there were the small garrison units in nearly every town and city. They also assisted the local magistrates in tax collections, catching criminals, and peacekeeping operations. Now that the legions were smaller, Constantine established many new ranks in the chain of command, providing more opportunities for men of ability to move up the ranks.

A New Conduct of Life

Constantine secluded himself daily at a set hour in the innermost chambers of his palace in prayer. His living example was founded with all his heart on that edict that a true ruler leads the way, even as Christ opened the gates of Hades by His heavenly leadership and divine example. Such devotions were redoubled during Holy Week and Pascha. He changed the holy night vigil of that time into an event of wonder and splendor, by causing waxen tapers of great length to be lighted throughout the city, together with torches which diffused their light, so as to impart to this mystic vigil of the night a mystical splendor of brilliance and light. As soon as day returned, he further exemplified Christ's own selfless example and commandment that "freely ye received, freely give [Mt. 10:8]," by lavishing abundant gifts to his subjects of every nation, province, and people.[210]

"On the occasion of his entertaining a company of bishops, he let fall the expression 'that I myself am also a bishop,' addressing them in my [Eusebius'] hearing in the following words." He said, "You are bishops whose jurisdiction is within the Church. I also am a bishop, ordained by God to overlook whatever is external to the Church."[211] At another time, Bishop Eusebius begged permission to pronounce a discourse on the subject of our Savior's sepulcher, to the emperor and a large number of auditors. In response, Constantine stood and listened to the entire lengthy discourse, and refused to sit in spite of being begged to by Eusebius.[212] At yet another time, the modest emperor heard one of the ministers pronounce Constantine as being destined to share the empire of the Son of God in the world to come. Constantine reacted with indignation, and forbade the speaker to hold such language, exhorting him

[210] Ibid., Bk. IV, Ch. XXII.

[211] Ibid., Bk. IV, Ch. XXIV.

[212] Ibid., Bk. IV, Ch. XXXIII.

rather to pray earnestly in the emperor's behalf, that whether in this life or the next, he might be found worthy to be a servant of God.[213]

Constantine was a monarch for all seasons. He continued to bestow lands upon the churches. He neglected not the charge of the apostle[214] to make provision for those less fortunate, as he turned next to the widows, the orphans, and the virgins. For the world, ever antagonistic to those who can offer it nothing or who wilfully turn their backs on it, despised the upkeep of the lowly nuns, the "virgins" so spoken of by Scripture, and those who had no man or woman of the house to care for them, that is, the orphans.[215] The emperor's acts of philanthropy seemed boundless. Constantinople had old-age homes, orphanages, hospitals, and other institutions, together with kitchens and shelters for the poor. He hoped that others would follow the example, especially local magistrates and wealthy Christians throughout the sprawling empire.[216]

Constantine was ever-mindful that a ruler of his own caliber and Christ-loving sentiment came but once in a great while, and that he was breaking virgin ground in the annals of Roman history, which others to follow might never wish to emulate to such a degree as he had done—if at all. Hence, he made every effort to set an enduring example, and to leave a vast and compelling repository of writings from which later rulers and subjects might draw the waters of saving grace. He dug the well of his soul as deep as the well of Jacob, and from it he afforded living waters to all, that in later times of drought the land which Christ had redeemed might not perish.[217]

He passed sleepless nights in study of Scripture. He composed discourses, many of which were delivered by him in public. He sought to appeal to his subjects' intelligence and reason, rather than to their fear. He preferred securing their voluntary and rational obedience to his authority, acting as a father figure as much as a ruler. Constantine also arranged by letter to Eusebius Pamphilus, for the preparation of fifty copies of the holy Scriptures. He commissioned that they were to be written on prepared parchment in

---

[213] Ibid., Bk. IV, Ch. XLVIII.

[214] Jas. 1:27.

[215] Eusebius, *Life*, Bk. IV, Ch. XXVIII.

[216] Kousoulas, "The Role of the Church," *The Life and Times*, p. 419.

[217] The God-inspired emperor was producing an efficacious influence. When the market-town of Gaza embraced Christianity, Constantine was so pleased that he distinguished it with the special honor of raising it to the rank of a city, and giving it the name of his sister, Constantia. In that town of Phoenicia, which received its name from that of the emperor, the inhabitants committed their innumerable idols to the flames and adopted Christianity. Many other cities did likewise. Eusebius, *Life*, Bk. IV, Ch. XXXVIII, XXXIX.

a legible manner, and in a convenient, portable form, by professional transcribers thoroughly practised in their art.[218]

During assemblies convoked by him, on which occasions vast multitudes enthusiastically attended, he would stand erect and touch on sacred subjects with a grave aspect and subdued tone of voice; and thus, he seemed reverently to be initiating his auditors in the mysteries of the divine doctrine. And when they greeted him with shouts of acclamation, he would direct them by his gestures to raise their eyes rather heavenward and to reserve their admiration for the supreme King alone. He usually divided the subjects of his address in orderly fashion. First, he exposed the errors of polytheism and proved the superstitions of the Gentiles to be fraudulent and a cloak for impiety. He would then assert the sovereignty of God and His providence, both general and particular. Like a wise general on the field of intellectual battle, having identified the twain directions of both the demonic foe and the divine Ally, he would proceed next to the dispensation of salvation. He would demonstrate its necessity, and the peril of the coming divine judgment. He would delineate the teachings of Christ that one cannot love both God and mammon, condemning lovers of worldly gain. He convicted and appealed to his listeners' consciences, denouncing rapacity, violence, and avarice. He pointed their minds to the certainty of the coming account to be rendered of their deeds to God. This judgment included himself. Each one would be summoned, in due time, to give account of his actions to the supreme Sovereign of all. Such utterances were his constant testimony, admonition, and instruction.[219] He was in the habit of composing his orations in the Latin tongue, from which they were translated into Greek by specially appointed interpreters.[220]

On one occasion Constantine personally addressed one of his courtiers: "How far, my friend, are we to carry our inordinate desires?" Then, drawing the dimensions of a human figure with a lance which the emperor happened to have in his hand, he continued, "Though thou couldest obtain the whole wealth of this world, yea, the whole world itself, thou wilt carry with thee at the last no more than this little spot [that is, the plot, the grave] which I have marked out, if indeed even that be thine." In fact, the course of events proved Constantine's admonitions to be more like divine prophecies than mere words.[221]

---

[218] Eusebius, *Life*, Bk. IV, Ch. XXXVI; *The Chronicle of Theophanes Confessor*, AM 5817, A.D. 324/325, p. 43.

[219] Eusebius, *Life*, Bk. IV, Ch. XXIX.

[220] Ibid., Bk. IV, Ch. XXXII.

[221] Ibid., Bk. IV, Ch. XXX.

New Laws and Ordinances

Constantine issued successive laws and ordinances, forbidding any to sacrifice to idols, to consult diviners, to erect images, or for gladiators to engage in combat in the cities. He prohibited the licentious worship by effeminate men of the Nile River. Children who lost their parents were no longer subject to forfeiture of their hereditary property, but were allowed to inherit it. Constantine showed himself an exemplary and thoroughgoing emperor; for he also passed a law to the effect that no Christian should remain in servitude to a Jewish master anymore, on the ground that it could not be right that those whom the Savior had ransomed should be subjected to the yoke of slavery by a people who had slain the prophets and the Lord Himself. If any were found hereafter in these circumstances, the slave was to be set at liberty and the master punished by a fine. He also forbade the provincial governors to annul any of the decrees of the bishops passed at their synods.[222]

So beneficent was Constantine's rule that there was neither capital punishment nor crucifixion. None of the provincial governors visited offenses with their proper penalties—according to the harsh historic precedent of ancient Roman law—causing the more faithless to deride his rule because of his excessive clemency.[223]

Meanwhile, the devil raised further contentions amidst the Egyptian churches. Constantine dealt with this as before, by summoning a synod of the bishops of Egypt, Libya, Asia, and Europe, to settle the questions in dispute. He further enjoined the churches in dispute, not to engage in the service of God until their differences were settled. This was due to his law expressly forbidding those who were at variance to offer their gift,[224] that is, until they have first become reconciled and mutually disposed to peace.[225]

After the conclusion of the synod, Constantine's twentieth anniversary (*Vicennalia*) was celebrated with a magnificent banquet at Nikomedia.[226] It was after his twentieth year that Constantine built a strong administration with a complex system of officials who owed their rank, welfare, and promotion to the emperor. The praetorian prefect oversaw four prefectures,[227] which had twelve

---

[222] Ibid., Bk. IV, Ch. XXV-XXVII.

[223] Ibid., Bk. IV, Ch. XXXI.

[224] Mt. 5:23-25.

[225] Eusebius, *Life*, Bk. IV, Ch. XLI.

[226] According to Saint Theophanes, in the year 330/331, "the basilica of Nikomedia, a fine church, was burned by a divine fire." *The Chronicle of Theophanes Confessor*, AM 5823, A.D. 330/331, p. 47.

[227] These prefectures were huge: (1) Gaul, Spain, and the British Isles; (2) Italy and North Africa (but not Egypt); (3) Illyricum, Pannonia, Dacia, Moecia, Macedonia, and (continued...)

dioceses.[228] The prefect had no military authority, but he did have extensive civil functions. During the last years of his reign, Constantine raised his sons and nephews to the rank of Caesar. Each was sent to the major prefectures of the far-flung empire. Constantine was careful to separate military and civilian functions throughout the bureaucratic structure. The people bore heavy taxes which were tolerable if they had a good harvest. The aristocracy was taxed also, as were shopkeepers and moneylenders. Constantine understood that a stable currency made for a stable economy. He established a gold coin, named *solidus*, with the inscription "victories everywhere," the worth of which was established at seventy-two coins to a pound of gold. The coin held a stable value for centuries.

Many more titles and positions, as well, were added in civilian circles that created a new aristocracy. The emperor's court was assisted by an imperial council, praetorian prefects, Masters of Infantry and Cavalry, the *Questor* (general secretary), the *Magister Officorum* (Master of Offices of palace administration and the police of the capital), Grand Chamberlain, two Ministers of Finance, and plenty of subordinate titles that created a vast bureaucracy.

Baker comments that Constantine understood that civilization is based on law. Constantine believed in a reign of law, in which law transcended even the lawgiver. No autocracy, dependent on the arbitrary will of an individual, ever founded a strong political state. But law will found a state. If Constantine founded an empire to endure more than a thousand years, it was because he induced men to believe in the virtue of obeying the moral law of God and the political law of man. The diversity of elements out of which the Roman Empire was made called for a quality of rigidity in its legal framework, to compensate for the lack of it elsewhere.[229]

Patriarch Athanasios of Alexandria

The propaganda of the Arian party continued to grow after the Nicaean Synod. One great victory of theirs was the deposition of Efstathios, the Orthodox Bishop of Antioch.[230] He was falsely charged with insulting the

---

[227](...continued)
the Greek Peninsula; and (4) Asia Minor, Syria, Palestine, Mesopotamia. Egypt was governed by a proconsul since she was the major source of grain for the empire's capital.

[228] The twelve dioceses: (1) Orient; (2) Pontica; (3) Asiana; (4) Thracia; (5) Moesia; (6) Pannonia; (7) Italia; (8) Gallia; (9) Viennensis; (10) Brittania; (11) Hispania; and (12) Africa.

[229] Baker, "The Second Death," *Constantine the Great*, Ch. XIII(V, VI), pp. 327-330.

[230] Eusebius presided over the Synod of Antioch, in 327, which deposed Efstathios. The decision was reviewed and endorsed by Constantine, who examined Efstathios

(continued...)

empress, Helen, and fathering an illegitimate son. Even though there was no proof, still a majority of bishops accepted the charges.[231] The emperor's half-sister, Constantia (the widow of Licinius), had an Arian priest as her spiritual father. On her deathbed, but not prior to her illness, she attempted to recommend him to Constantine. She told her brother that Arius was treated unfairly. Constantine, moved by her last wishes, sent an order to Arius to appear before him. The emperor directed Arius to write out the creed to which he subscribed. Constantine thought that what Arius wrote was correct enough,[232] but he had the prudence to urge Arius to show it to Alexandria's bishop. History records that neither Alexander (313-326) nor Athanasios (326-373) would accept Arius.

Athanasios immediately saw that what was written by Arius omitted the essential points. Athanasios refused to accept Arius. Arius, predictably, appealed to Constantine. The emperor sent the Alexandrian bishop a written request to readmit Arius, to which Athanasios declined.[233] It is likely that Constantine had written this on the advice of Eusebius and Constantia. Athanasios was not in the least perturbed that he refused the emperor, though his banishment was threatened. Athanasios declared that there could be no fellowship between heretics and true believers. Although no imperial embassy was sent to remove or deport Athanasios, the Arians seemed to be gaining on the Orthodox.

---

[230](...continued)
(Eustathius) in person. Saint Theophanes writes that "Eusebius Pamphilus testified to the total orthodoxy of the Creed of the Faith published at Nicaea by the fathers. Athanasios, for his part, in a letter to the Africans, gave evidence that Eusebius Pamphilus had accepted the term *homoousios*. Theodoret, however, says that Eusebius Pamphilus was in agreement with the Arians [*The Ecclesiastical History*, Bk. I, Ch. XXI], such as Eusebius of Nikomedia and his associates, for which reason he lent his support to the deposition of the divine Eustathios of Antioch, and, having joined with them in persuading the emperor that Eustathios was rightly deposed, he caused him to be exiled to Illyricum." *The Chronicle of Theophanes Confessor*, AM 5818, A.D. 325/326, p. 44, 45, and notes 3-5. Note 3 disclosed that Eustathius of Antioch attacked Eusebius Pamphilus over his interpretation of the Nicene Creed, to which Eusebius counter-attacked with a charge of Sabellianism.

[231] Kousoulas, "The Arians Gain More Ground," *The Life and Times*, p. 440. The mother later admitted that the father of her child was another man, Efstathios the coppersmith in Antioch.

[232] *The Church History of Rufinus of Aquileia*, Bk. 10.12.

[233] Saint Theophanes writes that, in 332/333, "Arius was recalled from exile, following a feigned repentance. He was sent to Alexandria, but he was not accepted by Athanasios." *The Chronicle of Theophanes Confessor*, AM 5825, A.D. 332/333, p. 49.

Not much time passed before Constantine saw that the blame placed on Athanasios was false. Constantine did not like being deceived. He ignored his sister's pleas and issued an order for the deposition of Eusebius of Nikomedia and Theognis of Nicaea.[234] He called for a synod of bishops to fill the vacant sees. Some argued that the emperor had no right to remove a bishop. Constantine wrote to the Nikomedians that Eusebius was a traitor to the Orthodox Church. He said that Eusebius and Theognis had been plotting with Egyptian and Libyan dissidents to undermine the Nicene Creed and sow discord in the Alexandrian Church. In the end, Constantine won and new bishops were appointed to Nikomedia and Nicaea.[235] Constantine recommended two other presbyters as candidates for the Antiochene bishopric. He named them since they had been appointed by Alexander of Alexandria; and so he believed both men to be of the true Faith, though this may not have been the case. Half the synod voted for Ephronios, whereas the other half complained of imperial interference and refused to recognize the election. As a result, Athanasios encouraged the anti-Arians to vote for their own man. Thus, the unity Constantine sought to create ended in disunity at Antioch for the next eighty years.[236]

The Arians, meanwhile, not really desirous of disproving Athanasios' doctrinal position, wanted him out of Alexandria. Rufinus points out that the heretics were already well aware that Athanasios was a man of keen intelligence and altogether tireless in the management of the Church. They remembered all too well when he came as a deacon to Bishop Alexander at the Nicene Synod and how he exposed their tricks and deceits. The heretics knew that when Athanasios should be made bishop that their concerns would find no easy way past his vigilance. Since it was their intent to upset the settled articles of Nicaea, they could not ignore Athanasios who was a Nicene leader. They, therefore, cast about everywhere for deceptions to use against him.[237] Hence, the Arians went about accusing Athanasios of breaches of the secular law. They thought they could carry the day in the climate of an emperor whose policy was seen by them to be generally that of pacification and reconciliation.[238]

From the time when a council readmitted Arius in 327, there was an element among the eastern episcopacy that had a complete case against Athanasios. The latter was refusing to comply with the decision of this council. Between the Nicene Synod in 325 and the Antiochene Synod in 328, several

---

234 The record is not clear how anti-Athanasios clerics from Egypt and Libya formed close ties with Eusebius of Nikomedia and Theognis of Nicaea.

235 Kousoulas, "Athanasius is Elected Bishop," *The Life and Times*, p. 436.

236 Ibid., "The Arians Gain More Ground," *The Life and Times*, pp. 441, 442.

237 *The Church History of Rufinus of Aquileia*, Bk. 10.15.

238 Baker, "Problems of the North," *Constantine the Great*, Ch. XI(VII), p. 283.

bishops had been deposed who, as Athanasios, refused to accept the genuineness of the suspects' confession of the Faith. Constantine, in 328, even threatened Athanasios with deposition if he would not readmit Arius. In 330, Constantine wrote to Arius: "Constantine, Victor, Augustus Maximus, to Arius. A long time ago, thy reverence received an invitation to come to me so that thou mightest enjoy my presence. I have been surprised that thou didst not come forthwith. Take now a public carriage and hurry to my court; so that having enjoyed my benevolence, thou mayest return to thy native city. May God keep thee, most dear friend!" Constantine decided to end Arius' exile. Arius responded, avoiding the word *homoousion* (co-essential), but artfully managed to word his response in such a way that he appeared to be accepting the Nicene Creed. He wrote: "Because our faith and our thoughts are those of the Church and of the holy Scriptures, we pray that by exerting thy peace-loving and godly piety thou wilt unite us to our mother Church,...so that we may all pray as one for the peace of thy kingdom and for that of thy family." Arius was free to go. He was conveyed in a state coach from Treves. This also meant that Eusebius and Theognis were free men.[239]

In 331, the Arians joined forces with the supporters of Meletios who established a separate congregation in Upper Egypt. Their goal was to eliminate Athanasios. Since Meletios had already died, his successor, John Arcaph was elected. He, too, hated Athanasios as much as the Arians. Athanasios defended himself, charge after charge. At some time in 333/334, the Meletians attacked Athanasios. They wrote and alleged to the emperor that a priest, Makarios, was acting as an agent of Athanasios. This agent broke the chalice of one Ischyras, who, as it happened, had a questionable ordination.

Saint Theophanes records that "in this year, the *Tricennalia* of the most pious and victorious Constantine, Arius along with Eusebius of Nikomedia and those of like mind were stirred up and offered sworn statements of their orthodoxy to the emperor, who was thirsting for unity among the divided. They persuaded him falsely that they were in agreement with the fathers of Nicaea. Convinced by them, the emperor was annoyed with Athanasios for not accepting back Arius and Euzoios. But the latter two had been deposed by Alexander, Euzoios being then a deacon. Eusebius and his supporters, having finally found a pretext, campaigned against Athanasios."[240]

The following year, Saint Theophanes records: "Thus, an evil opportunity was provided for the supporters of Eusebius of Nikomedia together with the Meletians. They began plotting against Athanasios. First they found fault with his ordination, even though Apollinarios the Syrian gave strong evidence in favor of the said ordination of Athanasios. Second, there was the

---

[239] Kousoulas, "Constantine Pardons Arius," *The Life and Times*, p. 439.

[240] *The Chronicle of Theophanes Confessor*, AM 5826, A.D. 333/334, pp. 49, 50.

accusation that Athanasios illegally imposed a tax, so he could purchase striped linen for the churches. Since that absurd charge was too frivolous, they contrived to add bribery and sacrilege. Third, they alleged falsely that he had sent a great quantity of gold to one named Philoumenos to arrange a plot against the emperor. Constantine, having summoned Athanasios, found that these were all lies. He sent Athanasios back to Alexandria with official letters and much honor."[241]

According to Saint Theophanes, in the same year (334/335), the Arians concocted another plot against Athanasios in Mareotis. "Ischyras, who disguised himself as a priest, traveled about conducting divine offices. Athanasios learned of this imposture and forbade the outrageous behavior, through the Presbyter Makarios. Ischyras then fled to Eusebius of Nikomedia. He accused Athanasios of having cast down the sacred vessels off the altar at the time of the Liturgy, and of having burned the sacred books through the agency of Makarios."[242] What actually happened was that Makarios was sent by Athanasios to the house of Ischyras, where the latter used to play at performing services. Makarios demanded Ischyras to halt. Since Ischyras refused, a scuffle ensued. The wine cup of Ischyras overturned and broke. The Meletians, dismissing the fact that Ischyras was not a priest, so the wine cup could not be deemed a chalice, accused Athanasios of sacrilege since he was responsible for the "priest" Ischyras.

In the spring of 332, Constantine was involved with the deployment of men against the invasion of the Goths under Araric. Athanasios left for Constantinople to appeal his case. He persuaded the emperor. Athanasios dealt with the first charge by producing a document in which Ischyras swore before thirteen priests that he had been intimidated by the Meletians into making the accusations of the overturning of his altar and breaking of his chalice. Constantine threw out the charge. But he wrote to the Censor Dalmatius, his half-brother at Antioch (who was the father of Caesar Dalmatius and King Hannibalianus), to investigate the murder charge. Dalmatius wrote to Athanasios, ordering him to appear and make a defense. On the advice of the Praetorian Prefect, Avlavios, an admirer of Athanasios, the charges were dismissed. Constantine also wrote a letter to the Alexandrians to receive back, peaceably, their archbishop. "You are to avoid disturbances," he wrote, "for I have received your Bishop Athanasios with a large measure of benevolence and have treated him as a man of God." Athanasios returned. But he would not let Arius, freed from exile, resume his work at his parish. Only for the sake of unity, Constantine thought Arius should be allowed to return to his parish. At the same time, the emperor sent a letter to the Patriarch of Alexandria decrying

---

[241] Ibid., AM 5827, A.D. 334/335, pp. 50, 51.

[242] Ibid.

the Arians. Athanasios, consequently, set upon burning heretical writings. Still, the Arians would not surrender; instead, they devised more charges."[243]

In 334, Arcaph, the Meletian bishop, accused the holy Athanasios of complicity in the murder of the Meletian Bishop Arsenios of Hypsele. The plaintiffs, meanwhile, produced an amputated human hand and claimed the limb to be that of Priest Arsenios. The charges only reached Constantine one year later, when he was preparing for his thirtieth anniversary. He was, simultaneously, arranging for the dedication of the Church of the Holy Sepulcher, started by his mother who had not lived to see its completion. He wanted the case closed. Since it involved murder, a crime punishable not only by the Church but also civil laws, he asked his half-brother Dalmatius, then Praetorian Prefect for the Orient, to investigate the case. Constantine also asked the bishops of that area to meet in Caesarea. Some fifty clerics assembled, in 335, at Tyre.[244]

Saint Theophanes writes: "The Arians claimed that Athanasios used the amputated hand for magic. The trial was transferred to Caesarea. Since Athanasios put it off because of Eusebius Pamphilus, he was tried at Tyre by those opponents of the truth (particularly Eusebius of Nikomedia). The Nikomedian bishop had tricked the emperor with his supposed longing to see the holy site that had been built up. Eusebius told Constantine how he longed to be present at the consecration. The emperor sent Eusebius on his way with great honor, ordering that the slanders against Athanasios be dismissed; and thereafter that he, together with Athanasios, should be present at the feast for the consecration in Jerusalem."[245]

And "so when they had gathered in Tyre,...Athanasios entered the assembly of these malignant men and scattered, like cobwebs, the calumnies of his accusers. They shouted so in their rage, 'Remove the man who has silenced everyone by magic!' The Caesar Dalmatius, the emperor's kinsman, and his band of soldiers were scarcely able to save Athanasios from impending death at their hands. It was then that Arsenios arrived in Tyre. When Arsenios finally appeared with his own two hands, the charge against Athanasios was dropped. Athanasios left Tyre. Constantine dissolved the council formed against Athanasios."[246]

---

[243] Ibid.; Kousoulas, "Attacks on Athanasius," *The Life and Times*, pp. 443-446.

[244] Kousoulas, "Athanasius Accused of Murder," *The Life and Times*, pp. 447, 448.

[245] *The Chronicle of Theophanes Confessor*, AM 5827, A.D. 334/335, p. 51.

[246] Elliott, "Constantine and Athanasios to the Council of Tyre in 335," *The Christianity of Constantine The Great*, Ch. 15, pp. 285, 286.

Rufinus gives us more details, saying that "since the council was being held not to judge but to put down Athanasios, a clamor suddenly arose from all sides that

(continued...)

The time arrived for Constantine's *Tricennalia*, the thirtieth year of his reign, held on the Bosporos, since that day in the city of York when the army accepted the son of Constantius. The Arians now charged Athanasios with conspiracy to prevent the grain shipments from Alexandria to Constantinople. Eusebius of Nikomedia, Theognis, Ursacius, and Patrophilos, on reaching Byzantium, were silent about the initial slanders against Athanasios. They produced four men with the rank of bishop as false witnesses. These men dared affirm on oath that they heard Athanasios threatening to prevent the corn supply from Egypt coming to Byzantium. As a result, they moved the Christ-loving emperor to anger. Athanasios protested that he had not contrived to turn back the corn supply. They even drove Constantine to banish the great Athanasios to Treviri in Gaul. This took place in the spring of 336, but it was not because Constantine believed the charge about the grain shipments. Constantine exiled Athanasios to the court of his son Constantine II, as a safe haven. The latter received Athanasios with every courtesy and respect. Constantine sincerely wished to remove Athanasios away from Alexandria. He desired to cut short all arguments. Athanasios was sent to Gaul until further notice. The deposition of Athanasios was suspended. No successor was appointed to the Alexandrian bishopric. Constantine contemplated Athanasios' return, in quieter times, where they could all settle down peaceably. Thus, Constantine neutralized the Arian intrigue against Athanasios. Constantine perceived that the Arians were not really interested in discussing doctrine but in discrediting Athanasios. Constantine set his face for peace and concord. He thought that differences could be remedied in discussion and not by making a victim of Athanasios. Meanwhile, with Athanasios banished, Arius once again began troubling Egypt. On being informed of this, the emperor summoned Arius. The exile for Athanasios turned out to be a blessing. He won over Constantine's young son, Constantine II. Upon the repose of the elder Emperor Constantine, this same son became the strongest supporter and protector of the Alexandrian patriarch and upheld his anti-Arian convictions.[247]

---

[246](...continued)
Athanasios was a sorcerer who was deceiving the eyes of the onlookers. The attendees agreed that such a man should by no means be allowed to live any longer. They rushed at him, ready to tear him apart with their hands. But Archelaos, who with the others was presiding at the council by the emperor's command, snatched him from the hands of his assailants. He led him out by secret ways, and advised him to seek safety by flight—as it was the only way he could attain it." *The Church History of Rufinus of Aquileia*, Bk. 10.18.

[247] Baker, *Constantine the Great*, Ch. X(XI), pp. 289, 290; Kousoulas, "Athanasius Accused of Murder," pp. 451, 452.

Constantine wanted to know from Arius if he accepted the canons of Nicaea. Constantine, therefore, summoned Arius to Constantinople. Arius affixed his signature to the Nicaean declaration. Arius was then asked to take an oath, and he did so. The Nicaeans still had difficulty believing in his sincerity. They were convinced that Arius agreed only with mental reservations and misrepresentations, when the emperor asked, "Dost thou hold to the Faith of the Orthodox Church?" Upon affirming that he did, the emperor said, "If thy faith be impious and thou hast sworn, may God judge thee according to thine oath!" The popular belief was that Arius kept his heretical deed in his armpit as he signed and swore that he believed what he had written, that is, the concealed document. Constantine still accepted Arius' subscription and oath. He directed the Bishop of Constantinople to receive Arius into communion.[248]

As with the majority of heretics, Arius was not simply an erring thinker, he was a cunning and malicious enemy of Christ. Arius strived to spread his false teaching by means of court intrigues and slandering the defenders of the truth. Later, Saint Athanasios the Great of Alexandria was subjected to numerous exiles and Constantine almost fell into heretical error. Athanasios excommunicated Arius. He, evidently, sent a dossier of the transaction to the emperor. Constantine proscribed Arius' writings. He ordered that Arius and like-minded Arians be declared enemies of Christ. Arian books were to be burned. Eusebius concealed the fact that Constantine regarded the Arians as heretics and that the emperor banned Arius' books.[249] But Arius was again declared Orthodox by the Councils of Tyre and Jerusalem in 335. In 336, the right-believing emperor believed that Arius had repented.

Emperor Constantine tried to persuade Patriarch Alexander, disciple of Metrophanes,[250] to receive Arius back into communion with the Church; but the

---

[248] Baker, *Constantine the Great*, Ch. X(XII), pp. 290, 291; Elliott, "Last Years," *The Christianity of Constantine The Great*, Ch. XVI, p. 322.

[249] Elliott, "Constantine, Athanasius, and Arius," *The Christianity of Constantine The Great*, pp. 278-284. The letter shows that Constantine understood Arianism very well. Though he did not use the Greek word *homoousion* in the letter, yet "we should keep in mind how things stood in theology during the years of 325-337 [before the Cappadocian fathers came of age], and not expect Constantine to be fifty years ahead of his time." Ibid., p. 284.

[250] When the Emperor Constantine first set eyes on Metrophanes, he loved him as a father. Since he was a very old man at the time of the First Synod, he was unable to fully participate in the deliberations. He appointed his assistant bishop, Alexander, as his representative. Constantine had Metrophanes raised to the rank of patriarch by the synod. At the close of the synod, the emperor and the holy fathers visited with the ailing patriarch. At the request of the emperor, the saint named a worthy successor to himself, Bishop Alexander. He also revealed to Patriarch Alexander of Alexandria that

(continued...)

Lord prevented this from being realized. On the evening before the intended reception and procession from the imperial palace to the Church of the Apostles, Arius suddenly died in the latrine. Even as Judas, "he fell headlong and burst asunder in the midst [Acts 1:18]."[251] For Arius' daring criminalities, there was a violent relaxation of the bowels. Soon afterward, a faintness came over him. Together with the evacuations, Arius' bowels protruded. This was followed by a copious hemorrhage and the descent of the smaller intestines. Portions of his spleen and liver were discharged in the effusion of blood, so that he almost immediately died in the back of Constantine's Forum. When Constantine learned of Arius' evil demise, he perceived that God punished the man by reason of the false oath he had uttered. Constantine was further confirmed in his mind that Arius was not only a perjurer but also a heretic. The emperor was adamant that the articles pronounced at the Nicaean Synod were correct.

After Constantine's repose in 337, his son, Constantine II, wrote a letter to the people of Alexandria explaining his father's treatment of Saint Athanasios: "Athanasios was sent away into Gaul for a time, with the intent that, as the savageness of his bloodthirsty and inveterate enemies persecuted him to the hazard of his sacred life, he might thus escape suffering some irremediable calamity, through the perverse dealing of those evil men. In order, therefore, to escape this, he was snatched out of the jaws of his assailants; he was ordered to pass some time under my government, and so was supplied abundantly with all the necessaries in this city where he lived....Now seeing that it was the fixed intention of our master Constantine Augustus, my father, to restore the said bishop to his own place, and to your most beloved piety—but my father was taken away by that fare which is common to all men, and went to his rest before he could accomplish his wish—I have thought it proper to fulfill that intention of the emperor of sacred memory which I have inherited from him. When Athanasios comes to present himself before you, you will learn with what reverence he was treated." Dated from Trier, 27th of June.[252]

The Persians

Now there were Jews who bore malice against the multiplying Christians. They incited the Persian king, Shāpūr, against the faithful of that land. In those days, already one hundred Christian clergymen were murdered,

---

[250](...continued)
his successor would be the archdeacon: Saint Athanasios (the Great). Saint Metrophanes reposed in the year 326, at age 117. His relics rest at Constantinople in a church dedicated to him.

[251] Metropolitan Anthony Khrapovitsky, "The First Ecumenical Council," loc. cit.

[252] Robertson's translation, *Apologia contra Arianos* 87, cited in Elliott's "Constantine and Athanasius," *The Christianity of Constantine The Great*, pp. 307, 308.

of whom many were bishops, together with 18,000 Christians. Constantine the Great received intelligence regarding the genocide. He, straightway, sent an official embassy to halt the persecution and slaughter. Shāpūr took no heed. It so happened that when this took place, Constantine's thirtieth anniversary was in progress. He was in the midst of festive celebrations, entertaining grandees and armies. While the perfect host, the emperor was still at work behind the scenes. A huge army was being prepared for a heavy strike against the Persian idolaters in order to address the systematic extermination of Christians.

Saint Theophanes reports the carnage, telling us that "the Jews and Persians, seeing that Christianity was flourishing in Persia, brought an accusation before the Persian king, Shāpūr, against Symeon,[253] Archbishop of Ctesiphon, and against the Bishop of Seleukeia. They were charged with being friends of the Roman emperor and spies of Persian affairs. As a result, a great persecution took place in the realm and a great many people were adorned with martyrdom for Christ's sake. Among these Ousthaxades, Shāpūr's teacher, the Archbishop Symeon, and, in addition to many others, a hundred clerics and bishops were martyred on a single day, as well as countless masses of others. Of these martyrs, 18,000 are conspicuous for the terrifying tortures of an unnatural kind which destroyed them at the hands of the utterly godless Shāpūr. It was then that Bishop Akepsimas, the Presbyter Aeithalas,[254] and Terboulia (sister of Archbishop Symeon), were martyred with a great many women. The most godlike Emperor Constantine advised Shāpūr by means of a letter to spare the Christians. He begged him to cease from this enormous cruelty. The letter, though brilliantly composed and most hallowed, did not persuade Shāpūr."[255]

At about this time, the Persians made trouble again. In the spring of 336, an Armenian delegation hastened to Constantinople. They informed Constantine that a Persian satrap, named Waras, had seized by treachery the Armenian King Tiran. He was conveyed to Persia where his eyes were plucked out. Now Armenia had been largely Christian since 309, when King Tiridates became a Christian.[256] Although Armenia was independent, she had been an ally of the Romans. The delegation was now asking for Constantine's help. While the Armenians were still in Constantinople, the Persian army invaded and conquered Armenia. The treaty of Diocletian and the Persians, now over forty years old, had been violated. Constantine, deliberating upon Shāpūr's seizure of Armenia and the unrest in Mesopotamia, decided to lead the military

---

[253] Saint Symeon is commemorated by the holy Church on the 17th of April.

[254] Saints Akepsimas and Aeithalas are commemorated by the holy Church on the 3rd of November.

[255] *The Chronicle of Theophanes Confessor*, AM 5817, A.D. 324/325, p. 41.

[256] See the Life of Hieromartyr Gregory, Illuminator of Greater Armenia, commemorated by the holy Church on the 30th of September.

expedition himself.[257] By late February of 336, Constantine notified his bishops of the campaign. Constantine judged it right to take with him, as companions, these Orthodox bishops as needful coadjutors in the service of God. They, for their part, cheerfully declared their willingness to follow in his train, disclaiming any desire to leave him. They, too, engaged in the battle by supplicating God in his behalf. Constantine was very gladdened by the bishops willingness to accompany him. He, therefore, unfolded to them his projected line of march. He also caused a tent of great splendor, shaped like a church, to be prepared for his own use in the war, in which he intended to offer, with the bishops, prayers to God for victory.[258]

Saint Theophanes reports that "the Persians, in the year 335/336, declared war on the Romans. The pious Constantine went out to the city of Nikomedia, on his way to fight the Persians, but became ill."[259] When the Persians received word that Constantine was preparing to march on them, they sent an embassy to ask for conditions of peace. He at once accepted, and entered into friendly relations.[260] At this time, it was Pascha; and Constantine, emperor of the Roman Empire, held holy night vigil with the bishops.[261]

The Closing Year

Constantine lived another ten months after his thirtieth anniversary. During those final months, he received an Indian embassy. Ambassadors from India brought gifts: brilliant precious stones and animals of strange species. They acknowledged Constantine's sovereignty even to the Indian Ocean, where they rendered homage to him by paintings and statues. Thus, Constantine's rule extended from thence in the east to Britain in the west, and exceeded—and that, by peaceful means—the sheer expanse of kingdom and length of rule of Alexander the Great.[262] The emperor also finished the building of the Church of the Holy Apostles, where his own tomb awaited him.[263] In the spring, there were rumors of a war with the Persians. At about that time, a Persian embassy arrived, which put matters between the empires more satisfactorily. The

---

[257] Kousoulas, "Trouble with the Persians, Again," *The Life and Times*, pp. 430, 431.

[258] Eusebius, *Life*, Bk. IV, Ch. LVI.

[259] *The Chronicle of Theophanes Confessor*, AM 58277, A.D. 335/326, p. 54.

[260] Cf. Mt. 5:9.

[261] Eusebius, *Life*, Bk. IV, Ch. LVII.

[262] Ibid., Bk. IV, Ch. L.

[263] Within this edifice, the Church of the Apostles at Constantinople, Constantine the Great caused twelve coffins to be set up like sacred pillars in honor and memory of the Twelve Apostles, in the center of which his own was placed, having six of theirs on either side of it. The timing of this move was to prove both stunning and prophetic, for he was soon to fall mortally ill, though none could have anticipated it at the time. Ibid., Bk. IV, Ch. LX.

reception of the Persian mission was the last important public business transacted by Constantine.[264]

Now Constantine not only preached the word of God but also lived it virtuously. He, furthermore, enriched those subject to him with the rich fruits of his devout godliness. His governance was of a principled and liberal nature, uncommonly humanitarian; and, like his Master Christ, his rule was easy and his burden both good and light upon his subjects. He inherited the throne from a pious father, and left it to three royal sons.[265] Constantine took care before his repose to divide his empire between his three sons. To the eldest, Constantine II, he assigned his grandfather's portion; to the second, Constantius II, the empire of the east; to the third, Constans I, the countries between. He had ordered his sons raised under pious tutors; and now he handed over to them the reins of empire. They were taught the best principles of secular learning and of war. They were instructed in political and legal science. To each son, moreover, Constantine granted a royal retinue of infantry, spearmen, and body guards, with every other kind of military force. These were commanded respectively by captains, tribunes, and generals, of whose warlike skill and devotion to his sons the emperor had had previous experience.[266]

At this time, Constantine had been reigning for over thirty years, and had been alive about twice that long. He still possessed a sound and vigorous body, free from all blemish, and of more than youthful vivacity. He was distinguished with a noble mien and strength equal to any exertion. Indeed, he was as active as he had ever been. Constantine's mental qualities had reached the highest point of human perfection. He was distinguished by every excellence of character, but especially by charitable acts. This was a virtue, however, which caused men of vile character, rapacious and unprincipled wolves in sheep's clothing who crept in unawares into the flock of God's churches, to take advantage of Constantine's benevolence and goodness of heart, genuineness of faith, and truthfulness of character. Indeed, he was ofttimes criticized for being too lenient with evildoers in high places of Church authority.[267] These offenders, however, were soon overtaken by divine chastisement. Constantine continued, to the last, to compose discourses on various subjects. He continued delivering frequent orations in public and instructing his hearers in the sacred doctrines. He was also habitually engaged

---

[264] Baker, "The Testament of Constantine," *Constantine the Great*, Ch. XII(VIII), p. 307.

[265] Eusebius, *Life*, Bk. I, Ch. IX.

[266] Ibid., Bk. IV, Ch. LI.

[267] Ibid., Bk. IV, Chaps. LIII, LIV.

in legislating both on political and military matters, or on whatever contributed to the general welfare of the empire.[268]

The Baptism and Repose of Saint Constantine

As Constantine felt illness coming upon him, he took a course of hot baths. He first began treatments in Constantinople and then in Helenopolis. Constantine traveled with Orthodox clergymen, officials, and servants. In the latter city, named after his mother, he visited and prayed at the Church of the Martyrs. But he perceived the hand of God upon Him, calling him from this earthly sphere. With his death imminent, he was thus set upon receiving holy Baptism. He labored under the prevailing custom, especially in the west, that his royal and military functions would be hampered after receiving the Mysteries. Even as the prophet and king, David, Constantine still bore the sword against enemies of the empire. He wished to leave this life after having been cleansed and having been "delivered from blood-guiltiness."[269] This also explains why he was unwilling to remove his baptismal garment after Baptism and don the purple again.[270] Hence, he postponed illumination in the hope of being baptized in the Jordan. At length, he did not think it possible, given his present medical condition, that he could make the journey to the waters of the Jordan for holy Baptism. Constantine, thereupon, abandoned such a pilgrimage and made his confession in that Church of the Martyrs.

Saints Constantine and Helen

[268] Ibid., Bk. IV, Ch. LV.

[269] Cf. Ps. 50:14. Eusebius [Bk. IV, Ch. LXI] says that it would appear that Constantine's tactic—he the master tactician of so many battles—was to delay Baptism until the very end, that this signal event should wash away as many of his prior sins as possible, leaving but comparatively few to confess thereafter on his deathbed. Such is the reasoning proposed by others who can but speculate. But only Constantine and his Maker know the full truth. Perhaps he felt too unworthy and unprepared to seek it sooner. It is sometimes supremely difficult to fathom the depths of humility in such a man as he was, at once both the emperor of the Roman Empire and the humblest of sinners before almighty God.

[270] It was customary in those days for neophytes to wear white garments, which they laid aside on the eighth day from their Baptism.

He then went to Nikomedia, where he requested holy Baptism.[271]

[271] In regard to Saint Silvester's healing and baptism of Constantine, as well as the Donation of Constantine, these are entirely legendary. Several unabridged Lives describe this holy pope officiating at Saint Constantine's baptism in Rome. The compilers of the first edition of *The Great Synaxaristes* (in Greek), referring to Saint Silvester's participation in the baptism, refer to the manuscripts preserved at the Great Lavra and Iveron. Furthermore, the event is also mentioned by Meletios of Athens, in his *Ecclesiastical History* [p. 309], as well as Saint Theophanes [*The Chronicle of Theophanes Confessor*, AM 5814, A.D. 321/322, p. 31], Michael Glykas, and others. But upon those same compilers making a closer study of the *Synaxaria* of the *Menaia* and that of Nikodemos the Hagiorite, they find no mention of the emperor's baptism in the west. While *The Great Synaxaristes* (in Greek) had referred to Pope Silvester's acts in the first edition of the biography, the same compilers decided to excise the account in their later editions. Overwhelming and significant references to the emperor's baptism at Nikomedia are given herein.

When Constantine was in Rome, Pope Silvester visited with the emperor and began teaching him the Mysteries of the Orthodox Faith of the Christ. The blessed Constantine readily believed all that the bishop imparted. He bowed his head and received the saint's blessing. Silvester uttered a prayer over Constantine, making him a catechumen. This is one account, which is frequently found and said to be the earliest of the *Acts* of Silvester. Some of the many who repeat it are Ephraim, Kedrenos, and Zonaras [*Epitome*, ed. by Lindorf (Leipzig, 1875)]. John Malalas [*Chronographia*, *P.G.* 97] was familiar with the account in the 6th C. It is not known when the Latin *Acts* of Silvester, describing his miracles and the baptism of Constantine, was translated into Greek. George Hamartolos (mid-9th C.) used the *Acts*.

The claims of Constantine's baptism by Saint Silvester are handled more fully in the Life of Saint Silvester (2nd of January). There are many varieties of the story and various details as to the baptism, but in general the whole series of stories regarding his baptism at Rome centers in this story, and gratitude for this cure is the supposed occasion of the famous Donation of Constantine—which we said was a forgery.

The Great Synaxaristes (in Greek) maintains that, in accordance with historical sources and the universal glory of the Orthodox Church, Constantine the Great was not baptized in Rome by Saint Silvester but in the suburbs of Nikomedia. This took place at the end of his earthly sojourn. Saint Silvester had catechized Constantine. Though the pope offered to baptize him in Rome, Constantine put off receiving divine illumination in Rome, preferring to be baptized in the Jordan as was Christ. This history regarding Constantine's baptism has fomented great discord in historical accounts. Many stories have attached themselves to the name of Constantine. Another history relates that Constantine was baptized by the heretic Evsevios of Nikomedia. The Greek compilers, examining historical accounts, have proved this false and even ridiculous. They maintain that Constantine was baptized in a Nikomedian suburb by notable Orthodox hierarchs who had accompanied the emperor from Constantinople.

Meletios of Athens rejects the story that the Arian Evsevios officiated, but he

(continued...)

Constantine was conscious of being the first Roman emperor to be publicly received into the Church. He returned to his house in his white baptismal robe. He then lay down upon his bed, which he did not leave. He never again chose to be clad in the imperial purple.

The Great Synaxaristes (in Greek) confirms that Constantine, perceiving that the condition of his health was endangering his life, invited the Orthodox bishops, those who had accompanied him and deliberated with him. He said to them the following memorable words: "This is the time for which I have supported my hopes. And it is with thirst and prayer that I hope to be vouchsafed the long-awaited salvation of God. The hour, moreover, is come for me to enjoy the immortal-making seal and to partake of the saving sealing. I had thought to receive this Mystery in the waters of the river Jordan, in which our Savior, according to the Scriptures, received Baptism for us men. God, however, knows best what is in our interest here and now that we should perform this."

Eusebius concurs with the Nikomedian Baptism, in *The Life of Constantine*, writing: "Constantine, at first, experienced some slight bodily indisposition, which was soon followed by positive disease. In consequence of this he visited the hot baths of his own city. He thence proceeded to that which bore the name of his mother, Helenopolis. Here he passed some time in the Church of the Martyrs, and offered up supplications and prayers to God. Being at length convinced that his life was drawing to a close, he felt the time had come when he should seek purification from the sins of his past career. He firmly believed that whatever errors he had committed as a mortal man, his soul would be purified from them through the efficacy of the mystical words and the salutary waters of Baptism. Impressed with these thoughts, he poured forth his supplications and confessions to God. He kneeled on the pavement in the church itself, in which he also now for the first time received the imposition of hands with prayer. After this he proceeded as far as the suburbs of Nikomedia. Once there, he summoned the bishops to meet him. He addressed them in the following words: 'The time has arrived. It is the moment for which I have long hoped, with an earnest desire and prayer that I might obtain the salvation of God....I had thought to do this in the waters of the river Jordan, wherein our Savior, for our example, is recorded to have been baptized: but

---

[271](...continued)
admits that the holy Silvester catechized and baptized Constantine. He also concurs that, when the emperor emerged from the font, his health was restored [*The Ecclesiastical History*, Vol. 1, p. 309]. Dositheos of Jerusalem [*Dodekavivlos*, p. 30] upholds that Constantine was baptized by neither Saint Silvester nor Evsevios, but received the Mystery in a certain Nikomedian suburb, at the end of his life, with a company of Orthodox bishops present who were wont to accompany him in his entourage.

God, Who knows what is expedient for us, is pleased that I should receive this blessing here. So be it , then, without delay....' After he had thus spoken, the prelates performed the sacred ceremonies in the usual manner, and, having given him the necessary instructions, made him a partaker of the mystic ordinance."[272]

Theodoretos agrees that "the emperor was taken ill at Nikomedia, a city of Bithynia; and, knowing the uncertainty of human life, he received the holy rite of Baptism, which he had intended to have deferred until he could be baptized in the river Jordan."[273] Sozomen records that Constantine "was indisposed and required to have recourse to bathing. He repaired for that purpose to Helenopolis, a city of Bithynia. His malady, however, increased. He went to Nikomedia and was initiated into holy Baptism in one of the suburbs of that city."[274] Socrates Scholasticus also writes: "The emperor, having just entered the sixty-fifth year of his age, was taken with a sickness. He, therefore, left Constantinople. He made a voyage to Helenopolis that he might try the effect of the medicinal hot springs, which are found in the vicinity of that city. Perceiving, however, that this illness progressed, he deferred the use of the baths. He removed from Helenopolis to Nikomedia, where he took up his residence in the suburbs. It was there that he received Christian Baptism."[275]

Now Constantine's officers were admitted to his sick chamber, only a few at a time, to bid farewell to him. In reply to their condoling words, he commented that he had now for the first time begun to live and to experience happiness. In fact, he said he was eager to be gone. Eusebius recounts the scene, saying, "Constantine then lifted his voice and poured forth a strain of thanksgiving to God, after which he added these words. 'Now I know that I am truly blessed. Now I feel assured that I am accounted worthy of immortality, and am made a partaker of divine light.' He further expressed his compassion for those who knew not such blessings. He assured the lamenting and bereaved tribunes and generals that, contrary to their tearful prayers for his recovery, he was now in possession of true life. He assured them that he alone knew the value of the blessings thereof, and that he was anxious rather to hasten than to defer his departure. He then proceeded to complete the needful arrangement of his affairs, bequeathing an annual donation to the Roman inhabitants of his

---

[272] Eusebius, *Life*, Bk. IV, Chaps. LXI, LXII.

[273] Theodoret, *The Ecclesiastical History of Theodoret*, Bk. I, Ch. XXX, Nicene, III:63.

[274] Sozomen, *The Ecclesiastical History of Sozomen*, Bk. II, Ch. XXXIV, Nicene, II:282.

[275] Socrates, *The Ecclesiastical History*, Bk. I, Ch. XXXIX, Nicene, II:35.

imperial city and apportioning the inheritance of the empire among his own children."[276]

Saint Constantine the Great reposed on the Sunday of Pentecost, in the year 337, at about noon, on the 22nd day of May.[277] He had entered upon the threshold of the eighth day.[278] Later, Saint Ambrose comments upon his repose and says, "Constantine not only was freed in his last hours by the grace of Baptism from all sins, but also, as the first of the emperors to believe, was distinguished for leaving a heritage of faith to princes for which he found a place of great merit. In his time, the prophesy of Zacharias had been fulfilled. This was revealed by the great Helen of holy memory, who was inspired by the Spirit of God."[279]

Immediately the assembled spearmen and bodyguards rent their garments in grief. They prostrated themselves on the ground, striking their heads. They uttered lamentations and cries of sorrow, calling on their imperial lord and master, or rather, like true children, on their father. In the meantime, their tribunes and centurions addressed him as their preserver, protector, and benefactor. Satan went out and wept bitterly that he had sustained, at the hands of Constantine, so great a defeat. The people, meanwhile, ran wildly throughout the city. Some expressed the inward sorrow of their hearts with loud cries, whereas others were confounded with grief. Each conducted himself as at a calamity which had befallen him alone.[280]

None of Constantine's sons were present. Messages by express post had been sent, but their father's exit was swift. The body was laid upon a cerecloth[281] of gold, and covered with a purple pall. Candles were placed all about. Constantine, crowned and robed in his full imperial insignia, was lying in state—a new procedure for the time. Guardsmen stood to arms about him. Constantius finally arrived. The body was conveyed to Constantine's city: Constantinople. An impressive procession was formed with the troops setting forth first and the civilians bringing up the rear. On each side of the catafalque[282] paced the guardsmen, with splendid accouterments and glittering spears.[283] Thousands of grieving subjects came out of the towns and villages that lined the way. The procession crossed the Bosporos on barges. The entire capital came out to pay their respects. Before his repose, Constantine had

---

276 Eusebius, *Life*, Bk. IV, Ch. LXIII.
277 Baker, *Constantine the Great*, Ch. XII(IX), p. 309.
278 Eusebius, *Life*, Bk. IV, Ch. LXIV.
279 Saint Ambrose, "Funeral Oration on Theodosius," op. cit., p. 325.
280 Eusebius, *Life*, Bk. IV, Ch. LXV.
281 A cerecloth was a waterproof wax-coated cloth formerly used for wrapping the dead.
282 A catafalque is a decorated bier on which a coffin rests in state during a funeral.
283 Baker, *Constantine the Great*, Ch. XII(X, XI), pp. 309-312.

ordered the distribution of goods and food to the people from his private purse. He was generous to the end—and thereafter. Although the Senate and people of Rome requested his body, they were refused. The body of Constantine was solemnly buried in the Church of the Apostles, where many miracles took place. With the passage of a little time, Constantius II built the imperial mausoleum adjacent to the church and had his father's coffin moved into it.[284]

Afterward, the soldiers laid the body in a golden casket and enveloped it in a purple covering. The body was transported to Constantinople, where it was placed in an elevated position in the principal chamber of the palace, surrounded by burning candles in golden candlesticks. There the body lay, arrayed in symbols of sovereignty: the diadem and purple robe. He was encircled by a numerous retinue of attendants, watching over the body night and day. He received the same honors from dignitaries and other officers as before his death. The military officers of the highest rank and the whole order of magistrates came, as before, at the appointed times when the emperor was among the living, and continued to pay homage. They saluted with bended knee as though he were still alive. After them, the senators and all those distinguished by any honorable office came to render the same homage. These were followed by multitudes of every rank, with their wives and children, to participate and also to witness the spectacle. The soldiers continued to stand guard over the body until his sons should arrive, and take on themselves the conduct of their father's funeral. It was the resolution of the army to confer, thenceforward, the title of Augustus on his sons. For most of the Christ-loving tribunes were mindful of the danger of pagan influences taking advantage of any perceived political weakness or power vacuum in the repose of the emperor. Such was the attitude adopted by the army. Thus, any chance of Satan's usurpation of power in the name of a resumption of old Rome's historic paganism was dashed. These firm resolutions they communicated to each other by letter, so that the unanimous desire of the legions became known throughout the whole extent of the empire.[285] The descendants of Helen came into power rather than those of Theodora.

---

[284] Saint John Chrysostom comments that Saint Constantine the Great was buried in the narthex of the temple of the Holy Apostles, a church which the emperor built. In this manner, the divine Chrysostom remarks, "The son of Constantine the Great, Constantius, considered he should be honoring with great honor his father should he bury him in the porch of the fishermen [Mt. 4:18; Mk. 1:16]. And what gatekeepers and porters are to kings in their palaces, that kings are to fishermen at their tombs. And these, indeed, as lords of the place reside within, while the others, as though but sojourners and neighbors, were glad to have the gate of the porch assigned to them." Saint Chrysostom, "Homily XXVI(5)," *Second Corinthians*.

[285] Eusebius, *Life*, Bk. IV, Chapter LXVI-LXVIII.

In accordance with Constantine's will, his three sons were bequeathed the following lands: Constantine II was given Britain, Gaul, and Spain.[286] Constantius II was originally assigned Oriens, Pontica, Asiana, and Thrace.[287] Constans I was initially given control of Italy, Africa, Pannonia, Dacia, and Macedonia.[288] Saint Theophanes records that "Constantine wrote a will in which he left the empire to his three sons, having carried out his office with piety and mercy. He entrusted his will to a certain Arian presbyter who had been introduced with evil intent by his sister Constantia, enjoining on him to hand it to none other than Constantius, the emperor of the east. Constantine had also ordered Athanasios' return from exile."[289]

What mind is able to comprehend the superiority of the great Constantine? What tongue is able to recount his divine works? What pen has the power to extol sufficiently that God-fearing man? He is, in many respects, shown to be incomparable in the midst of the choir of the saints. For this, he deserves great praise. The holy Scripture records that the Prophet-king David was humble and meek.[290] But Constantine was more so and not one to hold grudges, even as he demonstrated on a number of occasions during his rule over many lands, when he pardoned assaults and plots against himself. While Constantine held sway over a vast empire, David reigned only in Jerusalem. Even though we call David God's forefather, still Constantine became a blessed son of God by grace. Constantine, too, we may call firstborn, in the sense that as the first Christian emperor he reigned first over the inheritance of Christ, even as a paternal inheritance. We all, also, marvel over Solomon's wisdom and knowledge. Constantine was taught by God, enlightened from on high in the divine mystery. He, too, had wisdom and understanding, so that he brought about the disappearance of idolatry and upheld piety, whereas Solomon did not. The latter, in some instances, dallied with the idolatrous beliefs of his many pagan wives. Solomon fell into imbecility by reason of pleasure of the flesh and

---

[286] Constantine II (b. February 317-340), Caesar from 317 and Augustus from the 9th of September, 337, was regarded as the senior emperor. He was against the Arians and returned Saint Athanasios from exile in Gaul, despite the opposition of his brother Constantius II.

[287] Constantius II (b. August 317-361), Caesar from 324 and Augustus from September of 337, was originally assigned Oriens, Pontica, Asiana, and Thrace. He became sole ruler after the overthrow of brother Constans I and the defeat of Magnentius in 353. He was susceptible to moderate Arianism and refused to recall Saint Athanasios, despite the urging of his brothers.

[288] Constans I (b. ca. 323-350), Caesar from 333 and Augustus from September of 337, became master of the west with the death of his brother Constantine II. He opposed the Ariomaniacs and supported Athanasios.

[289] *The Chronicle of Theophanes Confessor*, AM 8528, A.D. 335/336, p. 54.

[290] Ps. 131:1.

caused veneration to the idols.[291] Thus, instead of being a lover of wisdom, even of this world, he raised up the trophy of fornication and estranged himself from God and His angels; but he repented of his follies in the end. The marvellous Constantine, in an all-wise manner, established the Faith and strived to keep it inviolate and his chastity unsullied. We, therefore, ought to prefer him before all others in acclamations to kings. We, furthermore, call Constantine the equal-to-the-apostles. While Peter, chief of the apostles, preached the sacred Gospel, he too won the crown of victory. The thrice-blessed Constantine championed the Gospel throughout the inhabited world, in an effort to utterly efface the graven images and make firm piety. Constantine, as the great Paul, was called from on high, who also suffered at the hands of the impious who would upset individual churches. Constantine diligently exerted all his strength to make firm the entire Orthodox Church, so that neither the gates of Hades nor the mouths of the irreverent should shake her unity. We, therefore, with many entreaties implore the God-crowned Constantine to intercede in our behalf for the cessation of the violent snorting and arrogance of the heretics, so that peace might be granted to the Church of Christ and that the pious might abide without harassment and turmoil.

We now must bring our account to a close. We praise the name of the noble and fair Helen. Attracted neither by the imperial purple nor daunted by old age and hardships, she made a difficult pilgrimage to the holy land. For all time shall she be connected with the discoveries of the Cross, the placard, and the nails of Jesus. She was the first to venerate it upon its finding. She pulled down the abominable temple of Venus and built up sacred shrines at those places sanctified by our Lord's earthly sojourn. She caused the founding of those churches marking the sites of our Lord's nativity, sepulcher, resurrection, and ascension. Putting aside imperial dignity, Augusta Helen gathered the poor and lowly; and clad in simple garb, she herself served them meals. Yea, O Constantine, most reverent king blessed by God, who as an emperor sought to imitate Christ as His genuine slave, we invoke thee in faith and truth! Hearken to thy faithful petitioners and supplicate the merciful Lord to deliver those of thy city in captivity. Strengthen them in right-believing piety! Do thou help those who call on thee whether they are at sea or on land or in the midst of troubles: do thou pilot and console them. Rescue the godly captives and visit those who are sick. As for the Church of the Orthodox Christians that thou didst labor to preserve in peace and keep from harm, do thou preserve her. For

---

[291] Toward the close of Solomon's reign, God chastised him for idolatry because of his toleration of his foreign wives' superstitions; so that the strange women turned away his heart after their gods. His heart was not perfect with the Lord his God, and he built high places to the idol of the Moabites and Astarte of the Sidonians. He reigned forty years and slept with his fathers. See 3 Kgs. (1 Kgs.) 11 ff.

those who keep thine august feast in a God-pleasing manner, do thou protect from enemies seen and unseen and grant their soul-saving requests. Hearken to us, thy humble suppliants, and vouchsafe us, through thine intercessions, that we might approach the Master Christ and be found acceptable and attain to that everlasting blessedness and His kingdom; for to Him is due honor and homage, together with His unoriginate Father and the all-holy and good and co-eternal Spirit, to the ages of the ages. Amen.

Through the intercessions of Thy Saints,
O Christ God, have mercy on us. Amen.

Saint Constantine

On the 22nd of May, the holy Church commemorates the holy Martyr VASILISKOS, a kinsman of the Great-martyr Theodore the Teron (Recruit).[1]

Vasiliskos, the holy martyr, hailed from a certain village, named Houmiala, on the Black Sea by Amaseia (Amasya). He flourished during the reign of Diocletian (284-305) and his successor. At that time, the emperor sent Agrippa, a governor, to inner Anatolia. He was replacing the then governing Asklepiodotos, who owed his office to Emperor Galerius Maximianus (305-311) and his son-in-law Maximinus Daia (ca. 308-ca. 314). Asklepiodotos was notorious and cruel in his heinous punishment and persecution of the Christians. As soon as Agrippa arrived in Comana of Cappadocia,[2] he quickly took up the business of interrogating and chastising the Christians. The holy Vasiliskos, who was a kinsman of the holy Great-martyr Theodore the Teron

---

[1] See additional details on the life and times of the Martyr Vasiliskos (Basiliskos or Basiliscus) within the pages of the recorded martyrdoms of his companions, Saints Eftropios and Kleonikos, who are celebrated all together on the 3rd of March, though the martyrdom of Saint Vasiliskos took place on the 22nd of May. All of these martyrs were believed to have been kinsmen of Saint Theodore the Recruit, commemorated by the holy Church on the 17th of February.

In the account, by Ephraim, given on the 3rd of March, we are told Vasiliskos served in the military as a young man. He is portrayed as a young soldier in an ancient Russian icon, showing the saints commemorated for the month of May. *The Painter's Manual of Dionysius of Fourna* describes Vasiliskos "as a young man" (3rd of March and the 22nd of May). The same description is given and shown in *An Iconographer's Patternbook: The Stroganov Tradition* (22nd of May). A row of images in the same panel of a wall-painting at Meteora, depicting saints from the latter part of May, contains the martyrdom by the stroke of the sword of an older man, named Saint Vasiliskos, with a beard. It is more likely that Saint Vasiliskos is the martyr depicted to the immediate right (as shown herein) of the same wall-painting; the misnamed martyr fits more the description of Saint Hermeias (commemorated the 31st of May). As a young man, Vasiliskos suffered imprisonment with the Martyrs Eftropios and Kleonikos. We are not told how much time he was detained in prison or spent afterward at home before he met his death by martyrdom. In the interim he could have prematurely aged or had an incipient beard. The Orthros Canon of Saint Joseph does not speak of him as either a soldier or a hierarch.

[2] There were two ancient cities of Asia Minor bearing the name of Comana. The one, of upper Cappadocia and another of Cappadocia of the Pontos. The second Comana was a colony of the first. Saints Chrysostom and Vasiliskos reposed in Pontic Comana. Comana of Pontos stood on the river Iris (Tozanli Su or Yeshil Irmak). Pontic Comana, surnamed Hierocaesarea, possessed a temple of Ma-Enyo, a variant of the great west Asian mother goddess, the scene of solemn pagan celebrations. This town is today known as Gomenek, or Gomanak, a village southwest of Neocaesarea (Niksar), in the vilayet of Sivas.

(Recruit), had previously gone forth to the contest of martyrdom and struggled alongside Eftropios and Kleonikos the Cappadocians. They were comrades-in-arms with Vasiliskos' uncle, Saint Theodore. While Eftropios and Kleonikos completed the course of martyrdom, Vasiliskos was shut up in the prison. This saddened him because he was very hot to finish the path of martyrdom. While incarcerated, Vasiliskos was accounted worthy of the appearance of Jesus Christ our God. The Lord commanded him, first, to bid farewell to his kinfolk and, then, to repair to Comana of Cappadocia that he might suffer martyrdom for the sake of piety.

The Beheading of Saint Vasiliskos

The holy Vasiliskos requested the prison guards to let him go to his village that he might bid his kinfolk farewell. Since they esteemed his manner of life of virtue and working miracles, they granted him leave with supervision. Some escorted him to his native place. He greeted his relatives and then bid them good-by. As for all those warders with Vasiliskos, he instructed them in the elements of religion by the word of piety. In the meantime, the governor sought the holy Vasiliskos in the prison. When the governor discovered that Vasiliskos was no longer confined, he was filled with wrath. He charged that, wheresoever Vasiliskos should be found, the soldiers were to take him into custody and bind him with two chains. They soon ascertained his whereabouts, arrested him, and brought him back. The soldiers were told to close Vasiliskos' feet within steel shoes, having nails that projected and penetrated into his soles. With such an acutely painful fitting, they escorted him, forcing him to run, to the governor's judgment seat. Now when those dispatched by the governor first found and seized Vasiliskos, they pushed and pulled him violently. All the while he was drawn along, he was clad in those nail-ridden shoes. The nails that jutted from that footwear bore deep into his feet, so that they struck the bone. Every footstep left behind a trail dyed in blood. When the military escort arrived with Vasiliskos in a village called Daknon, a certain lady of that neighborhood treated them hospitably. Her name was Traiana. Before the soldiers supped and rested, they decided to bind Vasiliskos to a plane tree that was next to her house. While the holy man was left alone outside, he began to pray. Then—behold the wonder!—the withered plane tree blossomed forth verdant leaves. A spring of fresh water also gushed forth miraculously at the root of that tree, which still exists to this day and spouts forth an abundant amount of water.

This wonder was noticed by the inhabitants of the village. Many came running and gathered before the saint. They contended with one another who might touch the garment of the holy man. Traiana also observed the signs that took place outside of her door. She came to believe in the Christ with all those of her household. The villagers, thereupon, brought forward a demonized man. Vasiliskos, by divine grace, not only healed one demoniac but also performed many wonderworkings. As a result, both the soldiers who escorted him and the people of Daknon were inspired to believe in the Christ. As it happened, while the saint was loosed from his chains, these people were bonded to the Faith of the Christ. But the time came for Vasiliskos and the soldiers to leave the village. In all the places that they marched through, the man of God was working miracles. Consequently, many among the nations were turning to the Lord. In one such place that they entered, the soldiers were looking for food. They turned to Vasiliskos and remarked, "Lo! we have eaten many times in the last three days, whilst thou, O slave of God, hast partaken of nought." The saint answered them, saying, "I, my brothers, am sated by imperishable meat and have no appetite for perishable victuals. As for you, the bread nourishes and the wine cheers; but for me, the grace of the Holy Spirit vivifies. You love gold, and I love Christ. You serve a temporal ruler, and I an everlasting One Who will summon us during the day of the judgment to eternal life. He shall say to those on His right, 'Come, ye who are blessed of My Father, inherit the kingdom which hath been prepared for you from the foundation of the world.'"[3] In this manner did the saint address the soldiers and continue in his state of material abstinence.

The following day, they arrived at Comana. The governor had arrived earlier and was apprised that the soldiers were bringing in Vasiliskos. The governor gave orders that, as soon as Vasiliskos arrived, he was to be led immediately to the temple of Apollo. It was Agrippa's intention to have Vasiliskos offer sacrifice to the idols. If he disobeyed, Vasiliskos would be sentenced to death shortly thereafter. Other soldiers were dispatched to bring Vasiliskos to the temple. They counseled him not to offer veneration indiscriminately to Jesus as God; for, as they pointed out to Vasiliskos, Jesus cannot appear. The saint, undaunted, answered, "I do not believe in an undiscriminating fashion in my God, but, rather, by exercising profound judgment do I believe unhesitatingly. Furthermore, I also know that my God is, according to His divinity, invisible. But in my mind do I contemplate Him, as much as I am able, and form a notion of Him Who works great wonders. If you do not

---

[3] Mt. 25:34.

believe me, question the soldiers who conducted me here. Learn the truth from them. As eyewitnesses, they can report the number of signs wrought by the Master Christ in me." Now the troops of the convoy that accompanied Vasiliskos to Comana were standing nearby. They confirmed the martyr's words and confessed, "Truly, awesome powers and extraordinary wonders were seen by us during our journey to Comana."

Following this exchange, the soldiers brought the holy Vasiliskos before the governor. Agrippa opened the interrogation by asking, "Thou art the much talked of Vasiliskos?" The saint answered, "I am the humble Vasiliskos." The governor, not masking his vexation, asked angrily, "Why, then, wilt thou not sacrifice to the gods according to the imperial command?" The saint replied, "Who told thee that I do not offer sacrifice? I sacrifice to God a sacrifice of praise and confession." The governor, hearing these words and thinking he finally concurred, rejoiced very much. He thought that Vasiliskos was referring to sacrifices to the gods. The saint, thereupon, approached the profane altar. Vasiliskos then addressed the temple priests, asking, "How do you call your deity?" They began to say "Apollo," which answer the saint finished by adding, "the significance of whom is derived in the meaning of his name. Apollo is the namesake of destruction for those who believe in him.[4] For as many as revere him, they are utterly destroyed and perish unto the ages." The governor retorted, "And thy God, how is He named?" The saint answered, "He is inexpressible, incomprehensible, and invisible." The governor then asked, "So then, thy God does not have a name?" The saint replied, "He is called Almighty,[5] Lord, King of Sabaoth,[6] I AM,[7] Adonai,[8] Savior,[9] as well as One compassionate, merciful, long-suffering, and plenteous in mercy.[10] It is to Him that I offer a sacrifice of praise."[11] The governor roared, "Sacrifice to whichever god thou dost wish, only do not trouble us with thy philosophy." The saint then raised his hands and eyes heavenward, uttering this prayer: "O God, Ruler of all, the only good and compassionate One, Who ever hearkens to those who put their trust in Thee: show Thy goodness to me, the unworthy one. As Thou didst fashion the man, form and adorn him, and breathe upon his

---

[4] See 1 Cor. 1:18 ("those who are perishing," ἀπολλυμένοις); Rev. 9:11 (Ἀπολλύων).

[5] 2 Cor. 6:18.

[6] Rom. 9:29; Jas. 5:4.

[7] Ex. 3:14; Mt. 14:27; Jn. 4:26; 8:58.

[8] 1 Sam. (1 Kgs.) 1:11.

[9] Acts 5:31; 1 Jn. 4:14; Jude 1:25.

[10] Ex. 34:6; Neh. 9:17; Ps. 85:14; 102:8; 144:8; Joel 2:13; Jon. 4:2.

[11] Heb. 13:15; Ps. 26:7; 49:15, 24; 106:22; 115:8.

face the breath of life[12] and he became a living soul,[13] and after, when Thou didst breathe on Thy disciples, Thou didst say, 'Receive ye the Holy Spirit [Jn. 20:22],' do Thou now give ear to mine entreaty. Stir Thou the deaf and senseless idol: shatter it and scatter the bloodstained sacrifice of the idolaters. Show to them that Thou only art God and blessed to the ages of the ages. Amen." With the pronouncing of this prayer, fire descended out of the sky. It struck and burned the temple, breaking into fragments the idol of the falsely-named god; so that, as sand, its particles were apportioned to the winds. The governor, witnessing the confuting of his god, exited the burning temple; for at this juncture, the entire city was dashed down with fear and terror. The saint was preserved from all injury, as he stood and chanted, "Let God arise and let His enemies be scattered, and let those hating Him flee far from His face [Ps. 67:1]," and the rest of the psalm.

After the governor's fear subsided and he composed himself, he became exceedingly angry with the martyr. Agrippa gnashed his teeth and directed his soldiers to drive Vasiliskos out of the temple. The governor next shouted at the martyr, saying, "Tell me, mindless one and alien to the gods' favor, why dost thou speak one thing and do another? Were they not thine own words that thou wouldest offer sacrifice? But instead thou hast called down fire by thine own sorcerous contrivance, consuming the temple and the god, O shameless and all-daring fellow that thou art! If thou wert not a magician, then thou also most certainly wouldest have been burned by the fire. Indeed, we nearly were devoured by the flames, only narrowly escaping by taking flight. But as for thee, since thou hast confidence in thy sorcerous arts, that is why thou hast remained unmoved. Without the least perturbation, thou didst remain standing in thy place inside the burning temple. I suppose thou wast thinking that 'now am I enabled to escape the governor's hands.' Therefore, I charge thee to confess thy villainies. But only offer sacrifice now and I shall release thee." To these effusions, the saint responded: "I do not pay homage to abominable graven images. I only revere the heavenly God. The signs which thou wast vouchsafed to behold are not magic, as thou fanciest, but the power of my God energizing in these outward manifestations in order to put you to shame. The purpose is to censure and check the deception and error of your vain and empty gods. You, as ones wanting in understanding, who make obeisance to the idols, are going to endless perdition. Think not that our God is capable only of what you witnessed here today. Our God works many more signs and wonders; for with God all things are possible[14] and all things are

[12] Gen. 2:7, 8.
[13] 1 Cor. 15:45.
[14] Mk. 10:27.

possible to His slaves who believe.[15] Since I have declared that I will neither obey these commands nor give any consequence to the imperial decrees, do that which thou hast purposed to do. Tarry not and cease wasting time to no benefit."

The governor, perceiving nothing could impeach Vasiliskos' resoluteness of purpose, remarked, "Thou hast repaid my tolerance with contempt." Lest the prisoner should blight his days any further, he issued the final decision. The executioners took hold of Vasiliskos and marched him outside of the city where they beheaded him. The execution took place immediately upon reaching the site called Dioskoros. They severed the honorable head of the martyr on the 22nd day of the month of May. The lawless tyrant added to his crime: he bade them cast Vasiliskos' precious and august relics in some desolate place. After this vile act was done, a certain lover of Christ, a man named Marinos, bribed the soldiers with much money and took away the holy relics. He built a temple at Comana where the relics were laid to rest honorably. A multitude of manifold miracles took place therein, on account of the intercessions of the holy Martyr Vasiliskos and by the grace of our Lord Jesus Christ, to Whom is due honor and dominion together with the Father and the Holy Spirit, now and ever and to the ages of the ages. Amen.

It was in the Church of Saint Vasiliskos, situated in the neighborhood of Comana, that the divine Saint John Chrysostom was buried alongside the martyr. The repose of Saint John took place on the eve of the 13th toward the 14th of September, in the year 407. When Saint John was sent into exile, the journey of three months on foot was a slow martyrdom to the sickly hierarch. He did not reach his destination, but ended his pilgrimage five or six miles from Comana in Pontos at the Chapel of the Martyr Vasiliskos. It was also there that he last partook of the Mysteries. Vasiliskos appeared to John in a vision and said, "Have courage, brother John; for tomorrow we shall be united." Now even before John stopped there, one day before, Vasiliskos appeared to the church rector and said, "Prepare a place for brother John, because tomorrow he is coming." The following day, when John besought the soldiers to make a stopover at the Church of Saint Vasiliskos, they refused out of obstinacy. They forced him to continue trudging the path they set before themselves. All day they trod across unknown terrain without a person in sight. When evening came, they found themselves again before the Church of Saint Vasiliskos. Behold how God blinded the guards! For this was God's will that the saint should find rest here. That evening, Saint John understood that the hour of his death was at hand. Sozomen, the ecclesiastical historian, says John was afflicted with pain in the head, from the day's march in the heat of the

[15] Mk. 9:23.

sun.[16] After he called the two hieromonks and the deacon, he disclosed his imminent departure. He asked for white clothes and received them. He gave his own garments, except his shoes, to those around him. Then, after receiving holy Communion the following day, the victorious athlete laid down and surrendered his soul to God, saying, "Glory be to God for all things!" At the last "Amen," he signed himself with the Cross and reposed. The body that had struggled so bravely was buried by the side of the coffin of the martyred Vasiliskos,[17] for so the martyr had ordained in a dream.[18]

Upon the noetic basilisk[19] did Vasiliskos tread, for he set his hope in Christ Who delivered him and sheltered him. He cried unto the Lord Who rescued him and glorified him, and showed him His salvation.[20]

On the 22nd of May, the holy Church commemorates the HOLY SECOND ŒCUMENICAL SYNOD, which assembled in 381 at Constantinople, that deposed Archbishop Makedonios of Constantinople who said that the Holy Spirit is not God.

The holy and Second Œcumenical Synod was held during the reign of Theodosios I the Great (379-395). Since it was convened in the capital, it is also referred to as Constantinople I or the First Œcumenical Synod in Constantinople. The most notable of the fathers in attendance included Archbishop Nectarios of Constantinople, Archbishop Timothy of Alexandria, Archbishop Meletios of Antioch, Archbishop Kyril of Jerusalem, as well as Gregory the Theologian and Gregory of Nyssa. Many other eastern bishops made up a total number of 150 fathers. No bishop from the west attended. Pope Damasus of Rome neither attended in person, nor by deputies, nor by the customary synodal letter. Later, however, Pope Damasus and the westerners concurred and acceded to the decrees of the Second Synod, recognizing it as truly œcumenical.

---

[16] *The Ecclesiastical History of Sozomen*, Bk. VIII, Ch. XXVIII.

[17] The sacred relic of Saint John abided with the holy Martyr Vasiliskos until the year 435, when it was transferred to Constantinople. The tomb was preserved empty. In Palladios' biography of the divine Chrysostom, the holy Vasiliskos is described as a hierarch and a hieromartyr, though the *Synaxarion* does not mention that he held such an office. For further information on the relics of Saint Chrysostom, see in *The Great Synaxaristes*: the 13th of November, for the day of his commemoration; and the 24th of January, for the translation of his sacred relic.

[18] *The Ecclesiastical History of Theodoret*, Bk. V, Ch. XXXIV.

[19] The basiliscus is a carnivorous lizard, and a basilisk (meaning "little king") is a reptile or lizard.

[20] Cf. Ps. 90:13-16.

The Second Œcumenical Synod
(Emperor Theodosios I and Patriarch Nectarios to His Left)

The emperor summoned this synod. It commenced on the 9th of May and the sessions lasted until the 9th of July, in the year 381. Earlier, in 380, he had issued an edict declaring Orthodoxy the true Faith. Arianism was condemned the following year at the First Synod of Constantinople. The assembly was held primarily against Makedonios, who had died before 364. He blasphemously declared that the Holy Spirit was a creature, constructed or created by the Son. The Makedonians or Pnevmatomachoi ("Fighters of the Spirit"), therefore, railed against the divinity of the Spirit. They taught that the Spirit was a gift of God and not God Himself. This synod also dealt decisively with other groups: Apollinarians, Evnomians, Evdoxians, Sabellians, Markellians, Photinians, and, in general, anathematized every heresy that had risen during the reigns of Constantius, Julian, Valens, and the emperors thereafter. The fathers at this synod corrected the glorification and adoration of the Holy Trinity which had been altered by the Arians, who used to say, "Glory be to the Father through the Son in the Holy Spirit." Under the presidency of Meletios, Archbishop of Antioch, the First Synod of Constantinople endorsed the full coessentiality and divinity of the Holy Spirit.

The fathers also renewed the doctrine of the earlier Nicene Synod. Hence, in order that it might be made manifest that the Second Œcumenical Synod held in Constantinople professed the same beliefs as the First Œcumenical Synod held in Nicaea, it did not draw up a creed of its own. The fathers at Constantinople, however, simply made a small change in the Creed adopted by the Nicene Synod. They appended the clause "of Whose kingdom there shall be no end." They made this addition on account of the heresy of Apollinaris the millenarian. They also developed the meaning of Article 8 in reference to the Holy Spirit. Furthermore, they supplied that which was wanting in the remaining four articles to the end. It is now the identical Symbol of the Faith or Creed which is recited by all Orthodox Christians. Nevertheless, although this Second Œcumenical Synod made these additions to, and changes in, the Creed adopted by the First Œcumenical Synod held in Nicaea, still the synods held thereafter accepted the Creed of the First and Second Synods as a single Creed—the Nicene Creed. At the same time, to all these articles, the Second Œcumenical Synod likewise adopted and promulgated seven canons pertaining to the organization and discipline of the Church. These canons, afterward, were indefinitely confirmed by Canon I of the Fourth Œcumenical Synod, but definitely by Canon II of the Sixth Œcumenical Synod and Canon I of the Seventh Œcumenical Synod. It should also be mentioned, herein, that Constantinople I proclaimed Constantinople as the second see of Christendom. The foundation for such a canon is stated succinctly: "Let the Bishop of Constantinople have the priorities of honor after the Bishop of Rome, because of its being New Rome [Canon III]."[21]

On the 22nd of May, the holy Church commemorates the holy Martyr MARKELLOS, who was made to imbibe molten molybdenum (lead) which he drank as one would water.

On the 22nd of May, the holy Church commemorates the holy Martyr KODROS, who was dragged by horses.

On the 22nd of May, the holy Church commemorates the holy Martyr SOPHIA, the physician, who was slain by the sword.

On the 22nd of May, the holy Church commemorates Saint JOHN of Vladimir, the Wonder-worker and King of Serbia, who was slain by the sword.[22]

John or Jovan or Ivan, the most holy and glorious king and standard-bearer, who suffered martyrdom in a wondrous manner, originated from a certain Bulgarian village named Vladimir. The village name came to be used as his surname; hence he is often referred to as John Vladimir. *The Great Synaxaristes* (in Greek) records that he was the son of Neheman, the son of the

---

[21] D. Cummings, *The Rudder* (in English), pp. 201, 202, 210.

[22] The Greek account of Saint John's martyrdom is found in the Athonite Monastery of Iveron and in other places. The divine office, composed anonymously, was printed at Venice in 1760, followed by reprints in 1774 and 1858. The service to the crowned martyr and his biography were written, first in Serbian and then in Greek. When the Serbian text was afterward lost, Monks Luke and Parthenios of the Athonite Monastery of Hilandar translated the service and the biography from Greek back into Serbian. Metropolitan Michael of Belgrade included them in the *Serbliak* in 1861.

first king at Achrida (Ochrida, Ohrid)[23] of Bulgaria, Symeon (890-927).[24] His mother was Anna, a princess of the Rhomaioi. Numerous sources override this pedigree and tell us that he was the scion of a princely family from Zahumlje.[25] The genealogy for the dynasty at Zeta[26] lists John's grandfather as Hvalimir II, prince (*knez*) of Zeta (d. 971)[27] and his father as Petrislav II, prince of Zeta (971-990).[28] Pretislav had two sons: Dobroslav I and our John Vladimir I (990-1016). But this is wide to the point when compared to his mode of life. John Vladimir became prince of Duklja and [part of] Trebinje, in Krajina.[29] John flourished at the time of Emperor Basil II the "Bulgar-Slayer," who reigned from 976 to 1025 at Constantinople. Basil fought to destroy the Bulgarian state led by Samuel, tsar of Bulgaria (976-1014),[30] who ruled the area

---

[23] Lychnidus or Achrida.

[24] Tsar Symeon's successor was Tsar Peter I (927-970).

[25] Zahumlje, also known as the Land of Hum, was a medieval principality located in today's Herzegovina (modern-day Bosnia and Herzegovina) and southern Dalmatia (modern-day Republic of Croatia). The Serb prince Caslav Klonimirovic of the House of Vlastimirovic fully incorporated this area into his domain between 927 and 940.

[26] Zeta, part of the Adriatic littoral, is in the hinterland of the Gulf of Kotor. Zeta and its neighboring Raska (roughly modern Kosovo) then provided the territorial nucleus for a succession of Serb kingdoms. It was only under the later Nemanjic rulers that the ecclesiastical allegiance of the Serbs to Constantinople was finally confirmed. Serb disunity coincided tragically with the arrival in the Balkans of the Ottoman armies; and, in 1389, Lazar fell to the forces of Sultan Murad I at the Battle of Kosovo. During the late 15th- C. reign of Djuradj, Zeta came to be more widely known as Montenegro (this Venetian form of the Italian Monte Nero is a translation of the Serbo-Croatian Crna Gora, "Black Mountain").

[27] Hvalimir, Knez of Trebinje.

[28] Petrislav, Knez of Duklja (Dioclea in present-day Montenegro) and [part of] Trebinje after 971.

[29] Duklja roughly encompassed the territories of the Zeta River, Skadar Lake, and the Boka Bay. It bordered with Travunia at Kotor. Duklja was named after Dioclea (from Docleata, the ancient Illyrian tribe). Dioclea, located near present-day Podgorica, was the capital of early Duklja. The relationship between the names of Duklja and Zeta is somewhat unclear, as the two terms overlap. Duklja was mostly referenced as the littoral area between the Bay of Kotor and the Skadar Lake, while Zeta refers to the river located inland. Zeta is thus the more accurate predecessor of the 19th-C. Montenegro, while today's Montenegro encompasses the territory of both. According to another interpretation, Duklja was composed of Zeta and Travunia. The name Duklja went out of use by the end of the Middle Ages.

[30] Samuel, the youngest of the Kometopouloi house, ruled at first with his brother and then alone after 987 or 988. He ruled as *vasilefs* (emperor) after 996 or 997. He had a daughter named Kosara. Samuel died in 1014 after Basil annihilated the Bulgarian army

(continued...)

of Ohrid where he reestablished the patriarchate. Samuel struggled against Byzantium for independence and looked to expand his realm. From the year 991, Basil persevered in waging war against Samuel.

Now the holy John, from his youngest years, shone forth in a splendid array of the virtues and spiritual gifts. He proved himself to be a pure vessel of the Holy Spirit, exhibiting the fear of God, meekness, and humility. No emotion moved him to loquacity. He was indifferent to luxury and covetousness. He was tutored by the marvellous Nicholas, Bishop of Achrida. Slavonic sources[31] tell us that he ascended the Serbian throne in the second half of the tenth century. He ruled in Zeta and other regions of Illyria and Dalmatia. He mastered military science and was esteemed by the armed forces as a competent commander. He fought the Arbanass tribes that menaced the eastern territories. Skadar was subsequently formalized as the political center of Duklja. He was not only an exemplary soldier but also a model of piety to his subjects. He was respected for his broad knowledge of the sacred Scriptures. He was loved as one who was openhanded to the poor. Now according to the Byzantine historian John Skylitzes,[32] Jovan Vladimir was *knez* (prince) of Tribalia and Serbia.

The blessed John, aflame with zeal to bring all his people to right-believing Orthodoxy, arranged that all of his realm enjoy preachers and teachers. He promoted Orthodoxy by sending out these catechists, who instructed and returned many people to the Faith of the Christ. By reason of John's example of moral excellence, he himself brought many of the heretical Bogomils to Orthodoxy.[33] As a sovereign, he was revered by all on account of

---

[30](...continued)
and blinded 14,000 prisoners of war.

[31] See http://www.russia-hc.ru/eng/religion/legend/JohnVlad.cfm.
See http://www.en.wikipedia.org/wiki/Duklja.
See http://www.en.wikipedia.org/wiki/Jovan_Vladimir.
See http://www.en.wikipedia.org/wiki/Chronicle_of_the_Priest_of_Duklja.
See http://www.encyclopedia.thefreedictionary.com/Chronicle+of+the+Priest+of+Dioclea.
See http://www.njegos.org/orthodoxy/hagiog.htm.
See http://www.suc.org/culture/history/Serb_History/Rulers/Jovan_Vladimir. html.

[32] Skylitzes flourished in 1081. His major work, the *Synopsis of Histories*, covers the reigns of the Byzantine emperors from 811 to 1057. His work continues the *Chronicle* of Saint Theophanes Confessor.

[33] Bogomilism (a sect of Manichaean origin) spread rapidly in the Balkans of the 11th C. Strenuous measures were applied against them in Serbia (ca. 1180) and in Bulgaria (1211). They recognized only the New Testament and Psalms. They did not believe that Christ had a human body, save in appearance. They rejected the Mysteries, churches, and relics. Bosnia, in the 13th C. became the center of the movement. Many Bogomils (continued...)

his wisdom and goodness. John undertook the erection of monasteries and churches. He also engaged in construction projects for lodges and inns for strangers, as well as hospitals for his people. He felled trees in woodlands and thick forests, personally building an extraordinary church to the trihypostatic God. The history of this church is as follows.

He, one day, went out on horseback with three grandees of his realm. While hunting, he was being hunted by God. As another Saint Efstathios of old, or rather, better to say as another Constantine, he was led on high. This came about when John caught sight of an eagle, shaped as the sun, from which a most brilliant cross was suspended from its neck. John gave chase to overtake the creature, which brought him deep into that dense forest. The eagle then halted. Then, instead, of a bird, there appeared to John an angel of the Lord. The angelic being was wearing the cross upon his breast. Straightway, the king, together with his grandees, made obeisance before the honorable cross. This event drew John closer to Christ. John, in accordance with the angel's command, built a church on that spot. John went seven times a day to offer up entreaty in that sacred precinct. He was wont to remain there all night, keeping vigil and praying. His reign was not a quiet one. He needed to deal with the internal strife caused by the Bogomils. As for external foes, he faced Tsar Samuel of Bulgaria and Emperor Basil II the Macedonian.

Saint John

John Vladimir entered an alliance with Emperor Basil. This provoked Tsar Samuel of Bulgaria into attacking Duklja in 997 with a large army. During the invasion, John Vladimir, the saintly king, wished to avoid a direct

---

[33](...continued)
fled to Herzegovina from Hungary. When the Turks conquered Bosnia in 1463 and Herzegovina in 1482, many of the Bogomils adopted Mohammedanism with which they found not a few affinities. *The Oxford Dictionary of the Christian Church*, s.v. "Bogomils."

confrontation with Samuel. John took his troops to the lofty summit of Mount Oblik (Kosogor). While they set up camp at that height, the soldiers were bitten by poisonous snakes. John supplicated God for his men, with tears asking for divine assistance. God hearkened to his prayers. Try as he might, Tsar Samuel failed in besieging the Serbs. Then a Judas among the local princes betrayed John Vladimir. When the holy sovereign perceived that the Serbs could not fight the overwhelming number of invaders, he did not wish his men to die in a battle that could not be won. He gathered his men and made a direct appeal, saying, "It is better for me to lay down my life for you and willingly accept death, than for you to die of starvation or the sword." Since he would not suffer their contradiction, he bid farewell to his loyal troops. John Vladimir then surrendered to Tsar Samuel.

John Vladimir was imprisoned in the jail at Presna. He allotted his time wisely to continual prayer. An angel of God was sent to him as a consolation and comfort. The angel strengthened John's spirit. He also foretold that John not only would be released but also would suffer a martyr's death after a time. Now the Slavonic source tells us that Tsar Samuel had a daughter, named Kosara (Theodora). This lady was inclined to spend her time in acts of mercy and kindness. Putting aside her rank, she entered into the dark and unsanitary prisons where she visited the prisoners and gave them provisions. She, in the course of her rounds, visited the Presna prison where she became acquainted with one of its most distinguished inmates—John Vladimir. She fell in love with the young and handsome prisoner. Her father, Samuel, who doted on his daughter, was unwilling to deny her any favor. She pressed the match and succeeded in having her father release John Vladimir that they might enter into marriage. Tsar Samuel agreed to the considered choice of his daughter's heart. During the interim, he had come to know John better and found him to be a genuinely good man of impenetrable probity. As a wedding gift, he had John Vladimir restored to his throne.

After the wedding ceremony, John Vladimir took his bride home. On the way, he suggested to Theodora that they live in chastity. She was willing to be guided by him and consented to the arrangement, after he quoted to her the words of Saint Paul, who said, "Now this I say, brethren, the time hath been shortened henceforth, that even they who have wives be as though they did not have [1 Cor. 7:29]." He, undoubtedly, was mindful of the prophecy: that his life would be shortened by martyrdom. Henceforth, John Vladimir and Theodora lived in love for God as the center of their marriage, ruling their people in the fear of God.[34]

---

[34] The story of John Vladimir and Kosara-Theodora is the subject of one of the most romantic tales of early Serbian literature. It began as an oral tradition reported ca.

(continued...)

While these charitable works became the focus of their lives, significant changes took place in the neighboring Bulgarian kingdom. Tsar Samuel died suddenly after the Bulgarian army was destroyed by the Byzantines and thousands of Bulgarian soldiers suffered blinding. As for John Vladimir, he ruled in peace and managed to evade involvement in that catastrophic conflict in the year 1014. Samuel's son, Gabriel Rodomir, succeeded his father and ruled what remained of Bulgaria. Rodomir, however, was assassinated by his bellicose cousin Jovan Vladislav (1015-1018). Thus, Vladislav murdered the very man who earlier saved his life.[35] Vladislav was not content with his cousin's domain. He also coveted the estates of John Vladimir, Samuel's son-in-law. Greed overcame his scruples. He pondered how to annex the territory with as little trouble as possible.

Jovan Vladislav contrived a scheme wherein he invited John Vladimir to his court that they might negotiate an agreement. As a sign of good will, Tsar Vladislav sent along a gold cross as a gift with the messenger. The saint, with a penetrating glance, remarked to the tsar's messenger, "Our Savior was crucified on the Tree of the Cross. It was neither gold nor silver. If thy master's words are true, let him send me, by means of consecrated men of God, a wooden cross. Then shall I accede to his request and go forth to him in the name of our Orthodox Faith." The messenger reported all to Vladislav, who quickly had a wooden cross delivered by two hierarchs and a hermit. John

---

[34](...continued)
1172-1196 in *The Chronicle of the Priest of Duklja (Dioclea)*, detailing how the tsar's daughter fell in love with the handsome captive. The medieval book by a Roman Catholic cleric is also known as *Slavonic Kingdom* (*Sclavorum Regnum*). This chronicle, built round a core written in Slavonic, was added to by a bishop of Bar intent on demonstrating his diocese's superiority over that of Split, is one of the oldest known written sources; but it has survived only in several late and widely divergent Latin translations from the 16th C. The text is named *Ljetopis popa Dukljanina* in Serbian and Croatian.

The Greek Life of Saint John of Vladimir, from the Iveron manuscript, provides another account and view of Kosara. When John Vladimir came of age, his parents arranged a marriage with Tsar Samuel for his daughter. The thrice-blessed bridegroom desired to remain a virgin and devote his life to good works. Upon the repose of his parents, he was established as king over the Serbs. Kosara was suspicious that he would not share the marital bed with her, presuming he kept a mistress secretly. She stirred up her brother against John Vladimir, so that he should be removed from power and put to death. After John Vladimir successfully countered an attack by Basil the Macedonian, then Kosara's brother took the opportunity to dispatch his brother-in-law. Taken from p. 548, *The Great Synaxaristes* (in Greek), 5th ed., s.v. "May 22nd."

[35] It was at Gabriel Rodomir's request that John Vladislav be spared in the massacre of that branch of the family by Samuel.

was thus persuaded in Vladislav's token of good faith through the men of God—albeit Vladislav made barbarous use of them. Theodora, filled with a bad premonition as to her cousin's true and vile character, was uneasy about letting her husband go forth. John fell into a deep reverie and then bade her farewell. He did not hearken to her justified anxiety and left for Presna with the party sent by Vladislav. As they proceeded, John encountered diverse prearranged traps set by Vladislav. When John arrived safely at Vladislav's court, the latter was astonished to see him alive. Vladislav then decided to take matters into his own hands. The sinister tsar drew his sword and struck hard at John. The blade caused no injury. When Vladislav failed in even delivering a cut to the saint's flesh, John turned to him and said gravely, "Brother, thou wouldest kill me but cannot." Although the tsar's conspiracy was unmasked, he, after a blush of surprise and then some displeasure, acted more brashly.

The Iveron manuscript describes the heavy scene: John then offered Vladislav his own sword, saying, "Take my own sword and by means of it, cut off my head for the sake of Orthodoxy and the truth; because I am ready to die as Abel and to be sacrificed as Isaac of old, for the sake of the Faith and confession of Christ." The beastly Vladislav, benighted and pitiless, took up John's sword and severed his head. One miracle followed another, more mysterious and remarkable. After the holy head was decapitated, the slain King John Vladimir took up his own head into his hands. He hastened out to his horse. The martyr mounted his steed, praising God and saying, "I was glad because of them that said unto me: 'Let us go into the house of the Lord [Ps. 121:1].'" Meanwhile, divine wrath fell upon the saint's murderer. The miserable tsar's features writhed in agony and he began consuming his own flesh. Thus, by his actions that day, he disgraced his man's apparel. As for King John, he rode away to a certain spot. Once there, he uttered, "O Lord, into Thy hands I commend My spirit [Lk. 23:46]." Immediately, thereafter, chanting could be heard from on high. The area was permeated with a spiritual fragrance. It was in that spot that they buried the ever-memorable king's virginal body of many contests. Bishops and priests, people of all ranks and stations of life, bewailed and wept the loss of such a protector and prince. Many who were lame and infirm that embraced his sacred relics were vouchsafed their much-desired health. The beheading took place on the 22nd of May, in the year 1015.

The Iveron account then concludes that, after they buried the holy relics, a wonderful church dedicated to the saint's name was built at the site. When the structure came to be unsound and weak, it was renewed afterward by Karol, a nephew of the then king of Italy. Later, the Christians recovered the relics and installed them in a monastery that Saint John Vladimir had built during his lifetime. It is there that he remained, acting as an odour of sanctity that repels fornicators and lewd persons. As for the faithful that take refuge in him, he has proven to be a guardian in every peril and temptation. Myrrh also flows forth from his relics. Diverse wonderworkings are energized for those who hasten to him with faith and piety.

Slavonic sources add that after the tsar slew John, he learned that a supernatural light could be discerned over the martyr's grave. Vladislav was so terrified at this report that he gave the body to his wife Theodora, so that she could bury him in a place of her choice. The widow took up the relics and deposited them in the Church of the Most Holy Virgin Mary in Krajina. Theodora then became a nun. She spent the rest of her days near her beloved husband's grave site. Upon her repose, she was buried next to him. Soon after his martyrdom, John Vladimir was recognized as a saint and martyr.

As for the beastly Tsar Vladislav, he died during the campaign at the Serbian town of Drach in early 1018. A warrior bearing the likeness of Saint John Vladimir suddenly appeared in front of him. Vladislav was so horrified at the sight, that he took to his heels in terror. It was then that an angel of God struck him down. His wife Maria surrendered Ohrid, herself, and her three sons and six daughters to Emperor Basil. Three others sons were yielded later.

After two hundred years, ca. 1215, the incorrupt relics of Saint John were transferred to Drach and later to Saint John's Monastery at Elbasan in Albania. The saint's right hand still bears the wooden cross sent by his murderer as a token of good will. Countless miracles are wrought by the wonderworker and myrrh-giver. In 1925, a church in honor of the holy Martyr John Vladimir was built in the Monastery of Saint Nahum on Lake Ohrid. In icons, he is often depicted wearing a crown, with a cross in his right hand and his own head in his left hand. Duklja is not mentioned for another twenty years following his repose. It is assumed that it remained a vassal principality of Byzantium.[36]

On the 22nd of May, the holy Church commemorates our glorious and right-victorious venerable New-martyr PAUL of the Peloponnesos (1818).[37]

[36] In the *Synaxaristes* of Nikodemos the Hagiorite, as well as that of Constantine Doukakes, there is placed on this day also the commemoration of the holy New-hieromartyr Zacharias of Prousa. The day of his commemoration, according to the compilers of *The Great Synaxaristes* (in Greek), should be the 28th of May, which Life has been included herein on that day.

[37] The martyrdom of Saint Paul of the Peloponnesos was written by Hieromonk Iakovos Vertsagia of Zakynthos, a monk of Mount Athos, from the Russian coenobium. The service to the new-martyr was composed by the Monk Christopher, the pilgrim of

(continued...)

Paul, shining anew as a righteous martyr of Christ, had as his homeland the famous Peloponnesos. He was born in the village of Sopoto,[38] which is in the province of Kalavryta. He was reared by pious but poor parents who were Orthodox Christians. At holy Baptism, the child was called Panagiotes (Panayiotes). In order to come to know, however, in very truth how from a good and thriving root he sprouted but fell into the snare of denial, hearken to his full history. You will learn how he recovered from such a swoon, and how he came to blossom forth as one righteous and venerable and a martyr of Christ. This was penned by the ever-memorable Priest-monk Iakovos the Hagiorite, from whom we are able to set forth this account.

Most glorified art Thou O Christ our God Who has revealed new martyrs and new luminaries in the firmament of the holy, catholic, Eastern Orthodox Church! They shine forth so that in these latter times we may see how godliness and piety unmasks the folly of godless impiety and the blasphemy of wretched heretics! During our times, our holy Church has suffered the reproach of the heretical Latins who accuse us of a dearth of new saints from the time of the Schism of 1054. But they should be ashamed of themselves! For our Church, the immaculate Bride of the Savior Christ, is splendidly adorned and fittingly crowned. She is arrayed with precious jewels and pearls by reason of her new-martyrs, her new righteous and venerable ones, and her new hierarchs and ascetics. The truth of this statement is demonstrated by the evidence, that is, their incorrupt or fragrant relics through which boundless wonderworkings are wrought.

The papists, meanwhile, fashion statues for their new saints, a work which is contrary to the definition given by the Seventh Œcumenical Synod (Nicaea II, 787).[39] But the statues are not their only novelty. They, meanwhile, have propagated many innovations: papal supremacy and infallibility; altering

---

[37](...continued)
Limnos. This work was published twice at Tripoli in 1858 and 1893.

[38] Sopoto (37°52′N 22°00′E) is present-day Aroania (alt. 940 meters), a village east of Psofida, in the prefecture of Achaia. It is some one hundred kilometers from the prefectural capital of Patras.

[39] Only images produced with paints (or colors), with mosaic, or tessellated, and with any other suitable material—as gold, silver, and other metals—are acceptable as Bishop Theodosios of Amorion says in Act IV of the same synod. The images may be inscribed upon sacred utensils, Gospels, crosses, robes, sheets, cloths, walls, boards, and houses. To this class, also, is assigned images cast in wax, which Saint John Chrysostom himself loved. No word is ever mentioned about the making of statues, sculptured figures or plaster of Paris replicas. Many assert that the reason why the Church rejected the veneration of statues, apart from the legal observation and custom noted herein above, was in order to avoid entirely any likeness to pagan idols which were statues of massive sculpture, capable of being touched on all sides with the hand and fingers.

the Creed with the *Filioque*; sprinkling instead of immersion at Baptism; the host of unleavened wafers; "Words of institution," rather than the Invocation or *Epiklesis* at the consecration of the holy gifts; partial lay participation in communion; Purgatory; the Immaculate Conception; compulsory clerical celibacy; shaved clergy; use of the Gregorian Calendar; misuse of holy Unction with the viaticum; original sin; predestination; stigmata; seated temples; and pope-sanctioned crusades, inquisitions, and genocide. We see since the Schism that the papal claims tell the story of an apostate church that follows the road first traveled by Lucifer, who rose as the bright morning-star.[40] First came pride when Lucifer said, "I will set my throne above the stars of heaven....I will be like the Most High [Is. 14:13, 14]." This pride also manifested itself by the popes saying their throne is supreme, high above all other bishops and the councils. On this account they were not able to believe, because Esaias said again, "He hath blinded their eyes and hardened their heart, that they should not see with their eyes and understand with their heart and should be converted; and I shall heal them [Jn. 12:40; Is. 6:10]."

We need to leave this subject and return to the subject of this narration. We invite lovers of martyrs to hear the life and martyrdom of this saint, which is not inferior to the accounts recorded of martyrs from ancient times. It lacks in neither the contender confessing the Faith boldly before tyrants nor the martyr suffering manifold punishments ending in a martyric death. Indeed, this story covers all these aspects and is equal to those of a bygone age.

Our blessed Panagiotes, when still quite young, left his home and village. He went to Patras[41] of the Achaia prefecture, where he apprenticed himself to learn the trade of sandal making. Panagiotes sojourned in the city for fourteen years. The Bishop of Patras, at that time, was the prominent Greek leader George Germanos. All the time that Panagiotes spent in that city, he was working at his trade. He was an honorable young man and a burden to no one. He supported himself by his own industry, even as urged by Saint Paul who said: "Ye yourselves know that these hands ministered to my needs [Acts 20:34]." At length, Panagiotes returned to his home province of Kalavryta and entered the town of the same name.[42] Panagiotes rented a workplace and set

[40] Is. 14:12.

[41] Patras (38°14′N 21°43′E) is an ancient city and the third largest in Greece. It is a significant commercial and converging point, as it constitutes the western gateway to Greece as well as to the Ionian Islands and Italy. It is 102 nautical miles east via Corinth isthmus to Piraeus, 210 kilometers east of Athens, and 70 kilometers from Kalavryta.

[42] Kalavryta (38°01′N 22°06′E), a town of extraordinary natural beauty, is the capital of the province of Kalavryta. It became the city-symbol of freedom, since it was at (continued...)

himself up in the trade he had learned at Patras. Panagiotes labored and conducted his life and affairs well. He was prompt with payment of the rent. On one occasion, however, the landlord of the store came in and asked for more money than what they had agreed upon. The adversary, that is, the devil, as a roaring lion, was going about and seeking whom he might devour. The devil caught Panagiotes at a time when he was not watchful.[43] Since Panagiotes was adamant in his refusal to pay more than what they had originally agreed upon, he—alas!—became flurried and spoke these fearful and ill-judged words: "I would sooner become a Turk than pay more!" However, afterward, he was compelled to meet the demand of the owner's rent increase.

Saint Paul

After uttering this impulsive and incautious expression, he was pushed further by the evil one who found a foothold in him; for he had wounded him with a powerful shaft. Panagiotes went to Tripoli of the Peloponnesos, a distance away of about eight to ten hours.[44] He was accompanied by two

---

[42](...continued)
Kalavryta, in 1821, that the Greek Revolution commenced against Ottoman domination. The banner of the revolution is kept at the historical monastery of Hagia Lavra. The famous Monastery of the Great Cave lies not far from Kalavryta. This monastery houses the sacred icon of the Theotokos, painted by the Evangelist Luke. Kalavryta is 77 kilometers northwest of Patras.

[43] Cf. 1 Pe. 5:8.

[44] Tripoli (37°30′N 22°22′E) is a city in the central part of the Peloponnesos and the capital of the prefecture of Arkadia and the province of Mantineia which is the most populated province in Arkadia. Tripoli is at a distance of 144 kilometers southeast of Patras and 78 kilometers (old: 120 km.) southeast of Kalavryta. It is 166 kilometers from Athens. In the Middle Ages, the place was known as Drobolitsa. The main section of the city is enclosed with castle walls built during the Ottoman occupation. The city is surrounded by pine trees to the south and west. Mount Mainalo (Maenalus) is one

(continued...)

friends. When they entered those parts, Panagiotes began to say that he was a Turk that he might eat and drink freely. Afterward, when they returned from Tripoli, he came to himself somewhat when he had time to consider in a sober light. He sensed the evil that he had stumbled into. The small voice of conscience told him so. He, therefore, without any sluggishness or delay, betook himself to a spiritual father and confessed his terrible and rash sin. The spiritual father, then, tried to comfort him and encourage him not to despair. Panagiotes could not repress his feelings. He went to another spiritual father who advised him in the same manner. But the blessed penitent could not find rest, as he was being censured by his conscience. After these experiences, his soul was conceiving divine love. He decided to have done with it all. He thought then to find good anchorage at the Holy Mountain of Athos. He went and searched for spiritual and God-bearing fathers to help him overcome the blunder of his lapse which left him in such ruins. Upon arrival, he went straightway to the sacred Lavra of Saint Athanasios. It was there that he discovered a fellow Peloponnesian, a certain monk, named Timothy, who hailed from the village of Rogo.[45] "Now Father Timothy, a short while before he reposed in the Lord," says the author of this account, "arrived at our own Russian coenobium. He was, at that time, in deep old age. It was to me that he recounted the martyrdom of his friend. He, furthermore, gave me a command to commit it to my humble pen lest the martyr's tomb be covered with forgetfulness. He had lived together with the saint for a considerable time. He knew firsthand the saint's struggles since they trained together."

The Monk Timothy said that he had welcomed Panagiotes with much joy. He kept Panagiotes at the monastery where he was assigned kitchen duty, at which Timothy labored alongside him for a year and a half. Father Timothy recounted how the saint described, in detail, what had befallen him and how he was searching to find a remedy. The young man could not acquit his previous conduct. Panagiotes remained at the Great Lavra and, with the passage of time, he became a monk—a Stavrophore—at which time his name was changed to Paul. After this period, Timothy left the Lavra and went to the Russian coenobium—after receiving permission from his spiritual father. The monastery had been organized by the ever-memorable Hieromonk Savvas of the Peloponnesos, who was also the coenobium's hegumen. The construction of the monastery, on the inlet of the Singitic Gulf, was being carried out during the first two decades of the nineteenth century. This came about largely with

---

[44](...continued)
kilometer to the west, while another mountain is five kilometers east with fertile lands elsewhere. Wetlands used to dominate much of the area in the northeast.

[45] Possibly Rogozio (present-day Alifira), a village belonging to the prefecture of Ilia in the western region of the Peloponnesos, is meant.

the help of the ruler of Moldo-Wallachia, Skarlatos Kallimachis (1773-1821), who also built the main church or *katholikon*. The work for the *katholikon* began in 1812. When it was completed in 1821, it was dedicated to the Great-martyr Panteleimon the unmercenary healer. It was built in the style of all the Athonite churches.[46] In 1803, Patriarch Kallinikos (1801-1806, 1808) had confirmed the coenobitic mode of monasticism at the Russian coenobium. He decreed that the monastery should enjoy the title of "the true Coenobium of the Kallimachides."[47] The blessed Father Paul, learning that Father Timothy was there, went to join him at the Russian coenobium. Paul remained there for three years. He practised his trade of making sandals. The blessed Paul underwent many struggles during the time that he lived at that sacred coenobium. He engaged in unbroken fasts, uninterrupted vigils, and countless prostrations.

By reason of these spiritual struggles and exercises, in which the righteous one engaged tirelessly, there was kindled in his heart divine love toward our most sweet Savior. Paul also desired to undergo martyrdom for Jesus' most holy name's sake. Father Timothy and the other fathers attempted to prevent him. Why? Because the outcome was unknown and there was anxiety by reason of his young age. He was then twenty-five years old. For this reason, Paul left the coenobium and went to the Skete of Saint Anna[48] dedicated to the foremother of God. There was a certain spiritual father there, named Ananias, who was a priest-monk. It was to him that Father Paul confessed all that happened to him. He did not neglect to add that he now longed for death on behalf of Christ. Initially, Father Ananias was not in agreement with the young monk's goal of martyrdom. But after they conversed and he perceived Father Paul's desire and steadfast purpose, he exhorted him and put him under the appropriate testing. He had to prove himself that he had the mettle of a martyr. He needed to fast forty days without respite, keep vigil, pray unceasingly, and make numerous prostrations. It was also Father Ananias who tonsured Father Paul to the Angelic Schema. Afterward, with the general disposition and permission of the fathers of the Saint Anna Skete, and with the blessing of the spiritual Father Ananias, Father Paul was sent forth into the stadium to contest in martyrdom. Father Paul made the rounds for the blessings

---

[46] The walls are constructed of dressed stone and support eight domes. Unlike its sister churches on the peninsula, this church possesses the onion-domes that terminate in a gilded cross. The frescoes and iconostasion within are in the Russian style. A decree of 1875 established that the divine offices must be chanted in both Greek and Russian.
[47] The holy Patriarch Gregory V also contributed to the establishment of the monastery.
[48] The Skete of Saint Anna is a dependency of the Great Lavra. It is the oldest and the largest idiorrhythmic skete on the Mountain. The community was organized in 1666. Most of the monks were either woodcarvers or iconographers.

and prayers of the fathers. He then, with gladness, went forth on the path to martyrdom.

It was during those days, when the would-be martyr was traveling to his homeland of the Peloponnesos, that Father Timothy beheld a vision. He found himself at Lavra, before the monastery table opposite the church. He observed the blessed Paul who appeared clad in his *rason* that shone forth as lightning. He noticed that Paul was bearing a cup, brimming with blood. Paul then said to Timothy, "Drink, brother." But Timothy remarked, "I am not able, since it is blood." But the hallowed martyr constrained him to drink, commenting that it was quite sweet. Timothy took the cup into his hands and swallowed a little of its contents. It seemed so sweet to him that his mind was transformed from the indescribable pleasure. Timothy said to Paul, "Indeed, it is deliciously sweet." Paul replied, "Do you sense, my brother, how dulcet it is? Well, then, why art thou hindering me?" Afterward, when Father Timothy awakened, that delectable taste remained in his mouth. Now it was during that time, as we said, that the martyr departed for the Peloponnesos.

Paul arrived at that peninsula and went to the sacred monastery of our Lady Theotokos, the Great Cave,[49] which is situated not far from Kalavryta. He stayed forty days at that unique monastery in which the *katholikon* is dug within the rock of the mountain. When Paul arrived, they were working on the frescoes in the narthex. He continued his ascetical practises in that mountain retreat, fasting and keeping vigil. He besought our Lady the Theotokos to strengthen him in the upcoming contest for a sanctified martyrdom. While he spent time there, he was accounted worthy of a vision. He spoke to the fathers how assurance was given to him by a vision, but he did not reveal what he had seen or heard. After this visitation, Paul summoned all his courage. He had no doubts, no demurs. He left and proceeded gladly and joyfully on the road to martyrdom. He glorified our supremely-hymned Lady, the Theotokos, who did not look askance at his entreaties. He went straight through the parts of Kalavryta and from there to Tripoli. He next went to Nafplion[50] which belongs to the prefecture of Argolida in the Peloponnesos. He went down to this coastal city that he might visit with a cousin who had embraced Islam and lived as a Turk. Father Paul found his cousin and urged and admonished him to return to the Christian Faith. He exhorted his cousin to rise up from his terrible fall caused by his calamitous denial. But the cousin, fearful of the tortures inflicted

---

[49] See the 18th of October regarding the Great Cave (Mega Spelaion), the icon painted by Saint Luke of the Theotokos, and its founders—Saints Symeon, Theodore, and Ephrosyne.

[50] Nafplion (37°33′N 22°48′E) on the Argolic Gulf is an attractive town with elegant Venetian homes and neoclassical mansions, dominated by the towering Venetian Palamidi Fortress (1711-1714). It became the first capital of Greece after independence.

by the tyrants, declined. Afterward, however, the cousin made an about-face and cast off cowardice, when Paul began to say, "Do come with me! Come and see how I will endure the martyric torments with the grace and help of our Lord and Savior, Jesus, by the intercessions of His all-holy Mother."

Thus, Father Paul, with his cousin as his companion, went toward Tripoli, the capital of the picturesque rural prefecture of Arkadia that is encircled by high mountains.[51] When they entered the city, Father Paul, without putting off his purpose or delaying, presented himself to the mufti—that is, a professional jurist who interprets Islamic religious law. Father Paul addressed him and said, "I should desire that thou wouldest provide me with a judgment that is true and just." The mufti promised, "I shall do that." Father Paul continued, "I, when I was a child, had a costly vessel made of gold and adorned with precious stones. But a liar and cheat tricked me, as I was a boy wanting in understanding. He seized it and gave me in its place a vessel that was false. Is it right or no, then, that I should receive again the true vessel?" The mufti answered, "Thou oughtest, in all fairness, to receive it." Paul then declared, "Do thou, then, give me thy written judgment in this matter." This was done, so that Father Paul had in his hand the written decision of the mufti. He went forth, with his cousin accompanying him, and brought the judgment to the court of the governor. Despite the fact that the court was crowded that day, no one prevented Paul from entering or questioned him regarding his business. The reason for his uneventful passage was that a meeting was convened and was underway. Concurrent with his entry, all the eminent men of the Peloponnesos had assembled. There was in that company both high priests and all the notables of the prefectures and villages. The animus for this gathering was that the Turks suspected that a revolution was in the making since they received intelligence to this effect from an informer. Among those present was a kinsman of the Elder Timothy. He heard the words of the venerable athlete Paul and, with his own eyes, watched the splendid martyrdom as it unfolded. It was he who conveyed the details of the martyrdom to Father Timothy on Athos, who afterward went into the Peloponnesos during the time of the Greek Revolution.

The valiant athlete of Christ, as we said, went up to the courthouse. He fearlessly presented himself before the governor. He placed in the governor's hands the mufti's judgment. The governor read the document and then said to Paul, "And who is thine opponent in this suit?" The martyr answered, "It is thou, O governor." The governor remarked, "I have never seen thee prior to this moment." Paul, filled with faith and the Holy Spirit, explained: "Before

[51] Three years later, Tripoli, in 1821, became the scene of a massacre when it was captured by Kolokotronis. Its ten thousand Turkish inhabitants were slain. The Turks retook it three years later and burned it to the ground before withdrawing in 1828.

thou didst assume this office, another held it. It was he who deceived me and seized the deposit which I received as a sacred trust. In its place, he gave me a counterfeit voucher, that of Mohammed the liar, the cheat, the ungodly one, the misleader of the people." The governor, astonished by this declaration, controlled his anger and said firmly, "Have thy wits about thee, man, and confess the religion which thou didst accept without anyone coercing thee, because otherwise I am going to burn thee alive." The intrepid martyr gave his resolute answer and said, "Even if thou wert to render me up to tens of thousands of deaths, never will I deny my true Faith. Thou art morally impure and a profligate person. For what kind of purity do you possess through which you compel us to come to your own impiety and deny the truth which is the immaculate and holy Faith of our Lord Jesus Christ?" So spoke the martyr as he stood before the entire company that was present. He then proclaimed, with exceeding boldness, the divinity of our Lord Jesus Christ and His presence on earth when He became man, through a seedless birth, of the Holy Spirit and the Virgin Mary. He expounded upon the boundless and extraordinary miracles that the most holy Lord performed in His life. He expounded upon the death by the Cross, which Jesus endured for the salvation of the human race. He also proclaimed the glorious resurrection and the taking up of Jesus into the heavens at His ascension.

Now among the bystanders there were Christians. They heard the sacrosanct words of the martyr and they marvelled, because they knew that he was unlettered. One of the spectators commented, "This latter-day martyr, verily, is like unto those of old; for he is filled with the hallowed word of the Lord Who had spoken these words: 'I will give you a mouth and wisdom, which all those who oppose you shall not be able to contradict nor withstand [Lk. 21:15].'" At this point, the Hagarenes, with one accord, rushed at Paul in order to tear to shreds the guileless lamb of the Christ, with their bare nails, if it were possible. They would have stoned him to death as the Jews did the First-martyr Stephen, if they were out of doors. The governor, after this incident, kept trying by various means to break the martyr's resolve. He soon, however, perceived the martyr's immoveable determination. Paul, in no wise, would relinquish his objective. The governor, little disposed to draw out the case, forthwith, handed down his decision to have Paul consigned to the flames. Some of the more inexorable Hagarenes, who were present, objected to this mode of execution lest the Christians remain and take the relics so as to honor him as a saint. The governor was swayed by their request and modified his order by imposing another penalty. The prisoner Paul was to be decapitated by three strokes of the sword, so as to heighten his sufferings.

The bailiffs of the tyrannical governor took hold of the martyr and led him outside of the courthouse, where they smote and scourged him repeatedly until they brought him to the appointed execution site. The stalwart martyr of Christ went to his knees and raised his mind heavenward. He offered up prayer to our one God in Trinity. He then turned to the executioner, emboldening him with these words: "Now I should like to see if thou art courageous as thou claimest." The executioner swelled at the martyr's words. He brought down the sword. With one fell swoop, rather than three strokes as he was charged, he severed the sacred head of the martyr. The ever-memorable Paul received the unfading crown of martyrdom. His blessed soul went away to the One Whom he desired: our Savior and God. The New-martyr Paul now rejoices with the apostle of the same name, as well as with the rest of the righteous and the martyrs. We, therefore, beseech the new-martyr that he intercede for us before the Lord.

The honorable relics remained three days, cast off, at the execution site. The profane tyrant had issued orders that threatened punishment and death if anyone drew near and took any part of the remains; this included the clothing or blood of the deceased. By reason of this order, not one Christian dared to approach. Besides the fear that was instilled by the governor, the relics were being guarded by soldiers lest any Christians should venture to take away any part of them. The Lord, nevertheless, glorifies those who glorify Him; and He glorified His martyr. By night, as the relics were lying on the ground, a light appeared as a flame of fire above the sacred relics of the sanctified martyr. Meanwhile, the minions of the antichrist Mohammed gave a perfunctory and foppish explanation: "Do you see? Since he did not receive our religion, God cast down fire in order to consume him." After the third day, the Muslims heaved the honorable relics onto the rubbish heap at the governor's house. The governor explicitly directed that this be done so that the Christians would not be able to find their Saint Paul. The relics remained on that pile of uncleanness for twenty days. When the Christians learned of the martyr's whereabouts, there was universal sorrow among them. Two bold friends of the saint, however, were not put off. They were contriving a way to remove the sacred relics from that dishonorable and unclean place, that they might bury their sanctified friend in a place that was clean and hallowed.

What did they do? One of them took up a basket that was at the scene. He affected as though he were busy about some chore for his occupation, since he dealt with skins and leathers. He kept hunting for a sign of the relic. He looked hither and thither, until he noticed an opening where a small portion of the saint's foot was poking out from among the debris. He was filled with joy when he discerned his comrade's foot. He thought it prudent to return under the cover of night and extract the precious relic. When it was dark, he came back. He enlarged the small opening that he earlier saw and distinguished a projecting foot. As he extracted the relic, he could not find the sacred head. He feared discovery, so he missed how the head had fallen into a secluded recess. The following day, as the saint's friend was walking and looking about with his companion, they caught sight of the holy head. That night, both friends went out and snatched their sacred comrade's head. They went and washed the honorable relic, burying it in a clean and consecrated place in the holy Monastery of Saint Nicholas at Varses,[52] which had been established in 1030. It is situated fifteen kilometers west of Tripoli or about two hours travel time in that period before the revolution.

We honor Saint Paul, to the glory and adoration of Father, Son, and Holy Spirit of the All-Holy Trinity, the one and only God Who is glorified in His saints and Who glorified His new righteous athlete, Paul, a genuine martyr, through whose acceptable and holy intercessions may we be delivered from unending punishment and be granted the everlasting kingdom of the heavens. Amen.

Through the intercessions of Thy Saints,
O Christ God, have mercy on us. Amen.

The Third Finding of the Honorable Head of the Forerunner (May 25th)

---

[52] Moni Varson, Mantineia, Greece.

On the 23th of May, the holy Church commemorates our venerable father, MICHAEL the Confessor, Bishop of Synnada.[1]

Michael, our venerable father and confessor, Bishop of Synnada, flourished during the years of Emperor Leo V the Armenian (813-820). The gleaming life of the righteous Michael was indeed splendid and lucid, as we shall shortly demonstrate. With all his strength, he applied diligence in practising the virtues that he might be pleasing to God. He, verily, was among those who lived a life according to God. He, as others who possessed this depth of love for God, purified himself by means of asceticism and self-mastery. He strived to become an elect vessel and sacred tabernacle of the Holy Spirit. He followed the words of the Lord and gave alms. Michael, together with the merciful, therefore, enjoys the rewards promised by the Lord. As a friend of Christ, he followed that path of emulation with others who suffered as did our Lord Jesus Christ. Michael, as a confessor of the Faith, professed Jesus' name before emperors and tyrants. Together with other Orthodox confessors for the veneration of the sacred icons, he patiently endured imprisonment, exile, hardships, ill-treatment, threats, scourges, and blows by God-hating rulers and princes, so that he might inherit the kingdom of the heavens. These godly-wise lovers of Christ do not put their trust in princes, in the sons of men, in whom there is no salvation.[2] They count the glory, pleasures, and lusts of this world as deceitful[3] and as rubbish. They disdain the pleasures and good things of this life. They mind not the loss of such things that they might gain Christ.[4]

Michael was among the valiant champions of the Church of Christ as a genuine Orthodox confessor of Christ. The holy Michael, named after the archangel, endured all things for the sake of Christ. He bore in his body the marks of the Lord Jesus.[5] As with the Apostle Paul, who tread the heavens, Michael's boast was in God through our Lord Jesus Christ[6] and in afflictions with patience.[7] It is Michael's life and times which we shall narrate today for

---

[1] Concerning Saint Michael, his final moments are recorded in a correspondence of the venerable Theodore the Stoudite to Peter of Nicaea. See *P.G.* 99:1612, 1613. A divine office was composed for Saint Michael by Chrysanthos the Cypriot, which was published at Venice in 1769. Another service is found in part in an Athonite codex at Kafsokalyvia. The honorable head of this hallowed Michael is kept as a precious treasure in the sacred Athonite Monastery of the Great Lavra.

[2] Ps. 145:2.

[3] Eph. 4:22.

[4] Phil. 3:8.

[5] Gal. 6:17.

[6] Rom. 15:11, 17; 1 Cor. 1:31.

[7] Rom. 5:3.

our beloved listeners. Hearken, then, to his struggles and contests. Give heed to how he sweat and suffered pangs, contending lawfully, for God and the holy icons.[8]

Saint Michael

The homeland of our father, Michael, where he was born and raised and, later, taught and shepherded, was Phrygia of Asia Minor. He hailed from the distinguished and glorious city of Synnada (Synada).[9] His parents were affluent. Before the birth of Michael, however, they were in distress over their childlessness. They entreated God fervently to bestow upon them a child. Both promised that they would dedicate the child to God in the local Church of the Archangel Michael, which was preeminent in their city. Since the will of them that fear the Lord shall God do, and their supplication shall He hear,[10] He granted them a son. They named the child Michael, in honor of the archangel. They, therefore, quickly paid their vow. Now when Michael came of age, he exceedingly loathed childish pastimes. He shunned them, deeming that he could carry away nothing beneficial from participation in them. Quite the opposite was exhibited by him with regard to teaching and instruction. With a solemn bearing and self-control, he took his seat in the schoolroom and gave strict heed to everything the teacher uttered. From school he went to his house, accompanied by prudence and decency. Such was the becoming behavior of the child Michael. In but a short while, he attained a thorough knowledge of the whole curriculum. He was by nature dexterous and smart. All marvelled at the lad's wisdom and were pleased to hear his sensible conversation. At length the chiefs of Synnada made free to summon him, preferring his worthwhile solutions for texts that were obscure

[8] 2 Tim. 2:5.

[9] Synnada (38°31′N 30°29′E) is east of Pergamon and northeast of Laodikeia. Although Synnada was a small city, it was celebrated throughout the empire for its trade in marble that was quarried at neighboring Dacimium. Synnada, under Diocletian, at the time of the creation of Phrygia Pacatiana, was at the intersection of two great roads and became a metropolis. On its coins, the inhabitants identify themselves as Dorians and Ionians. Today it is the city of Schifout Kassaba, situated five hours south of Afoun Kara Hissar, vilayet of Bursa (Prousa).

[10] Cf. Ps. 144:20.

or difficult to understand. He deciphered and resolved all that they required without the least difficulty.

With all these gifts and talents, which would have advanced him far in secular professions, his preference before all occupations was the monastic conduct of life. In fact, he wished to avoid the glory of the world and come into union with God. In order to realize this desire, he forsook his homeland. He betook himself to Constantinople. It was there that he met with the most holy Theophylact, who later became Bishop of Nikomedia.[11] Theophylact, at the time of their acquaintance, was an assistant to Tarasios, the imperial first secretary (*asekretis*) of the imperial archives. Theophylact was privy to many confidential matters of the crown. Tarasios took a liking to Theophylact and provided him with a good education in both religious and secular studies. Tarasios, eventually, was selected as patriarch by the devoted iconophile Empress Irene (b. 752), widow of Leo IV and regent of her son Constantine VI (b. 771). Before the blessed Tarasios took holy orders, he was tonsured a monk. Tarasios made progress in every virtue. Since they do not light a lamp and put it under the bushel but upon the lampstand that it might give light to all those in the house, so was Tarasios elevated to be Patriarch of Constantinople (784-806).[12] Patriarch Tarasios and Empress Irene convoked the Second Synod of Nicaea in 787, which abolished Iconoclasm. Tarasios was as a foundation of Orthodox fullness. He was the boast of those who labored at virtue and piety.

In the intervening time, Michael and Theophylact lodged together. They were united in divine love so that the prophet's expression applied aptly to them: "Behold now, what is so good or so joyous as for brethren to dwell together in unity [Ps. 132:1]?" These two heaven-sent pillars, these two radiant luminaries, these two new apostles of Christ, shone throughout the ecclesiastical firmament for the correctness of their doctrine. Before Patriarch Tarasios' tenure in December of 784, his predecessor, Patriarch Paul the Cypriot (780-784), voluntarily resigned his office when he became gravely ill. He recommended Tarasios, a layman, as his successor. Irene found in her imperial first secretary the pious ally she needed. After Tarasios was consecrated to the office of Archbishop, he established a monastery with the share he received from his father's inheritance. It was located on the left bank, as one sailed upstream, of the Thracian Bosporos. Thus, Tarasios cultivated and nurtured the virtues among that sacred brotherhood. A fair number of the monks from that holy community were elected to the ministry of the priesthood. Since they were adorned with Orthodox belief, they were able to put down heresy. Their labors

---

[11] Theophylact (Theophylaktos) is commemorated by the holy Church on the 8th of March. He had come to Constantinople in about the year 780.

[12] Saint Tarasios is commemorated by the holy Church on the 25th of February.

succeeded under the teaching and example of Tarasios, while they endured many tribulations and afflictions at the hands of the heretics. Early in Tarasios' tenure, both Michael and Theophylact were inclined to keep company with the holy Tarasios. The patriarch asked them what they intended to do with their lives. Were they planning a secular career? Were they contemplating a monastic profession, which would be more beneficial for the soul? Both disciples yearned to live a life according to God. Tarasios, thereupon, sent them to his monastery on the strait of the Black Sea.

These two blessed men, Michael and Theophylact, hastened eagerly to the spiritual arena and vied with one another in all spiritual contests. They advanced in the virtues, keeping the commandments of the Lord day and night. Their manner of life was so austere that they ate once daily—and only after the setting of the sun. They partook of a little dry bread and water. They trained and exercised themselves for every contest and struggle. They contended with hunger, thirst, standing throughout the night in vigil, and studying and contemplating the divine Scriptures. By the weapon of abstinence, they armed themselves with a coat of mail, thereby defying carnal warfare and nurturing continence and temperance. As a special adornment to their labors, they added humble-mindedness. The manly feats of these two men came to be proclaimed in every quarter. But we shall speak later of such exploits, one by one. But for the time being, we can know the lion by his claws.

During the season of harvesting, as the monks were laboring under a torrid noonday sun, they were seized with a fierce thirst. There happened to pass by a man with a jug of refreshing cool water. He twisted open the copper plug and offered them a drink. But neither Michael nor Theophylact would quench his burning thirst. Each preferred to spill the water to the ground rather than partake. Why? They had promised to hold fast and develop self-discipline. They thought that should they be vanquished by thirst, they would be giving place to the will of the flesh. The great Patriarch Tarasios learned of this incident. He perceived the godly progress made within those two disciples and their degree of asceticism. He, consequently, invited them to the Great Church of Hagia Sophia. Upon arriving, he appointed them both to the office of *Skevophylax* or Keeper of the vessels. The duties of this appointment did not distract the blessed ones from their ascetical drills and brilliant fostering of the virtues. As much as they attempted to conceal themselves, they became more conspicuous. The grace of the All-Holy Spirit dwells in such souls as these who attained to ineffable contemplation and to purity of soul.

The divine Tarasios, seeing the two saintly monks faring well on the path of virtue, compelled them onward to the rank of the priesthood. Both utterly declined the offer. Tarasios, ultimately, pressed them and ordained them priests and liturgists of the Most High. After a short period, he pushed them forward to the great dignity of the episcopacy. They did not attain to this by their own request or recompense by money—though this happens now with some degree of regularity. Away with the thought for these two fathers! No sort of simony overshadowed their virtue or character. The evil of securing offices in this guise, so as to overcome and hold down piety, neither establishes shepherds nor hierarchs of the Holy Spirit; nay, rather it introduces fierce wolves clad in sheepskins. Once installed, they outrage the flock of Christ rather than lead it to the saving pastures! But Michael and Theophylact went onward to the loftiness of the eminence of the high priesthood by the decree and approval of the All-Holy Trinity, Whose divine light was indwelling in these men; for they were verily worthy of the grandeur of such a ministration of service to the Church.

On the one hand, the holy Theophylact ascended the archiepiscopal throne of Nikomedia. On the other hand, the sacred Michael succeeded to the glorious Metropolis of Synnada, where he was born and bred. It was then possible for one to behold a true hierarch of God: one vested with righteousness and adorned with holiness; one who followed in the footsteps of His teacher Christ in both action and speech; one who cut in a straight line the word of the truth;[13] and one who kept the Faith inviolate. He embellished his perfections with guilelessness, meekness, forbearance, and philanthropy. He displayed no marks of a hot temper. He did not harbor resentful anger. His most distinguishing characteristics were his reverence, mercy, sympathy, and love of the poor. While it is still possible, we need to mention here with some of his works, that is to say, his projects that included the raising up of sacred churches, monasteries, and other institutions for the salvation, care, and relief of strangers and orphans. He became a protector of widows and strangers. He visited the poor, aided the destitute, and provided raiment for the naked. All these endeavors were undertaken with eagerness and cheerfulness. But again, the enemy of the truth and the adversary of the race of man could not tolerate the building up of the Church. For him, the sight of godliness and piety in action and progressing was insufferable. For this cause, the devil attempted to check the course of the ship of the Church. He tried to cut from below and stop short the labors of the saint. Michael resisted Satan, rebuking and beating back the would-be assailant by putting him to shame through his prayers, vigils, and entreaties to God.

During the year 806, the saintly Patriarch Tarasios, as a mortal man, reposed in the Lord. His relics were conveyed to the strait of the Black Sea on Wednesday of the first week of the Great Fast and buried in the monastery he had built on the European side of the Bosporos. The successor to his throne was

---

[13] 2 Tim. 2:15.

the holy layman, Nikephoros (806-815),[14] who was distinguished as an ardent zealot of the Orthodox Faith of the Christ. Nikephoros governed the holy Church of God well and in a God-loving fashion. He shepherded the flock of Christ in a pious and Orthodox manner. The emperor during his tenure bore the same name, Nikephoros I (802-811). He and his conspirators had deposed Irene (797-802).

Bishop Nikolai in *The Prologue from Ochrid*[15] informs us that, at the wish of Emperor Nikephoros, Michael visited Caliph Harun al-Rashid (786-809) of the Abbasids[16] to conduct peace negotiations. We know that in 803, Emperor Nikephoros campaigned against the Arabs in Asia Minor. In 805, a combined Slav and Arab attack against Patras in the Peloponnesos was repelled. After the repose of Patriarch Tarasios, the former layman Nikephoros was appointed patriarch—despite monastic opposition. It was in 806 that Caliph Harun al-Rashid led Arab forces into Asia Minor, for which Emperor Nikephoros was obliged to increase terms for a truce. Soon thereafter, in 807, Khan Krum and his Bulgars advanced toward Constantinople.

According to Saint Theophanes the Confessor, in his *Chronographia*, regarding Michael's state visit to the Abbasids, he notes the following. Emperor Nikephoros was in his fourth year, while Patriarch Nikephoros was in his first year, that is, 806, when Harun (Aaron), the leader of the Muslim Arabs, invaded the country of the Rhomaioi. "He entered with a great force composed of Mavrophoroi, Syrians, Palestinians, and Libyans—in all 300,000.

---

[14] Saint Nikephoros is commemorated on the 2nd of June.

[15] Bishop Nikolai Velimirović, *The Prologue*.

[16] The Abbasids were the dynasty of caliphs who ruled the Islamic Empire from 750 until the Mongol conquest of the Middle East in 1258. The dynasty takes its name from its ancestor al-Abbas, the uncle of Mohammed. In 750 the Abbasids defeated the Umayyads and transferred the capital of the Caliphate from Damascus to Baghdad, thereby shifting the empire's center from Syria to Iraq. The regime reasserted the theocratic concept of the caliphate and continuity with orthodox Islam as the basis of unity and authority in the empire. The Abbasid "revolution" also made Islam and the fruits of power accessible to non-Arabs. A strong Persian influence persisted in the government and culture of the Abbasid period, and Hellenistic ideas led to the rapid growth of intellectual life. In the period from 750 to 945 the authority of the caliphs gradually declined, while the Turkish military leaders gained increasing influence. The dynasty's power peaked in the reign of Harun al-Rashid. The 8th- and 9th-C. caliphs Harun al-Rashid and his son Abdullah al-Mamun are especially renowned for their encouragement of intellectual pursuits and for the splendor of their courts. During their reigns scholars were invited to the court to debate various topics, and translations were made from Greek, Persian, and Syriac works. Embassies also were exchanged with Charlemagne, emperor in the west. See general information on the Abbasids at http://www.mb-soft.com/believe/txh/abbasid.htm.

Having come to Tyana, he built a house of his blasphemy [that is, a mosque]. After a siege, he captured the fort of Herakles [Herakleia Kibotos], which was very strong, as well as Thebasa, Malakopea [mod. Derinkuyu], Sideropalos, and Andrasos. He sent a raiding contingent of 60,000 which penetrated as far as Ankyra and withdrew after reconnoitering it. Emperor Nikephoros, seized with fright and perplexity, set out also in a state of despair, exhibiting the courage that comes from misfortune. After winning many trophies, he sent an embassy to Harun. The party included Metropolitan Michael of Synnada,[17] Abbot Peter of Goulaion, and Gregory, *oikonomos* of Amastris, to ask for peace. After lengthy negotiations, they concluded peace on the following terms and remittances: that a tribute of 30,000 *nomismata* would be paid to the Arabs each year; and a capitation (poll) tax of three *nomismata* on behalf of the emperor and another three on behalf of his son.[18] On accepting these terms, Harun was pleased and overjoyed, more than he would have been had he received ten thousand talents, because he had subjugated the Rūm, that is, the Roman Empire. They also stipulated that the captured forts should not be rebuilt. When the Arabs had withdrawn, however, Nikephoros immediately rebuilt and fortified the same forts. On being informed of this, Harun sent out a force and, once again, took Thebasa. He also dispatched a fleet to Cyprus, where he destroyed the churches and deported the Cypriots [16,000 to Raqqa]. By causing much devastation, he violated the peace treaty."[19]

Nikephoros, after taking to the field of battle on many occasions against the Bulgarians, was slain. His son, Stavrakios, succeeded briefly for five months in 811. When Stavrakios abdicated, he was succeeded by Nikephoros I's son-in-law, Michael I Rangabe, the husband of his daughter Prokopia. Michael I came into power that October of the same year. Patriarch Nikephoros blessed his elevation, after Michael Rangabe vowed in writing to uphold Orthodox doctrine and to respect the clergy. Since Michael Rangabe was a man of integrity and equitable and loved Christ, he agreed. Michael Rangabe, previously, had joined his father-in-law, Nikephoros I, on the battlefield against the Bulgarians, and survived the encounter with the Bulgarian Khan Krum (ca. 802-814) which took Nikephoros' life and nearly annihilated the Byzantine army. But Michael Rangabe's later failure to keep checks on the Bulgarians caused his defeat at Versinikia, north of Adrianople, where the Byzantines and Bulgarians clashed. He was forced to abdicate that July in favor

[17] Some attest that Saint Michael had been a bishop between 787 and 815, and reposed in 826. Saint Dimitri of Rostov and Bishop Nikolai ascertain 818 as the year of his repose.

[18] The total sum for both father and son was equal to 50,000 dinars.

[19] *The Chronicle of Theophanes Confessor*, AM 6298, A.D. 805/806, trans. by C. Mango and R. Scott (Oxford: Clarendon Press, 1997), pp. 661, 662.

of Leo V the Armenian. Michael Rangabe became a monk, and his sons were castrated. One of his sons, named Niketas, eventually became Patriarch Ignatios. Leo V the Armenian was proclaimed emperor in July of 813, that is, after the June battle of Versinikia, and crowned in Hagia Sophia by Patriarch Nikephoros.

Leo V, for a little while, appeared to be reverent and Orthodox. Not before long, however, he declared his profane purpose and opinion. He raised up a persecution against the holy icons. By imperial decree he prohibited their veneration. He did not only issue these orders but also broke and burned wall-paintings and portable icons. This godless decree was circulated throughout the empire. In the spring of 815, a local council met in Hagia Sophia. This marked the second restoration of Iconoclasm when icons were declared spurious and needed to be destroyed. Patriarch Nikephoros had already been replaced by the iconoclast Patriarch Theodotos I. John Grammatikos prepared an anthology of various writings. He filled it with arguments opposing veneration, based on the findings of a former local council in 754 that condemned both veneration and production of images. The iconoclasts of that former council, under the direction of Constantine V, argued that Christ's icon depicted either His humanity divided from His divinity or His uncircumscribable divinity. They further argued that if the icon separated the human from the divine nature, this was Nestorianism. If the icon confuses the two natures, that is Monophysitism. The iconodules, who reverenced the icons, deemed the anti-iconic attitude as Manichaean (Paulician) and Jewish. The Seventh Œcumenical Synod[20] defined the degree of veneration due to images, by clearly distinguishing between relative veneration (*schetike proskynesis*) of the icon and saints from actual worship (*latreia*). The true object of honor was not the image, but the one who was depicted thereon. Above all, the main justification for the icon was the reality of Jesus' historic incarnation—He did "show Himself upon earth, and conversed with men [Bar. 3:35, 37]." Since He was visible, He was paintable.[21]

While the sinister Leo believed his lack of success in war was due to icon veneration, he ushered in worse times for his subjects by his imperial command to prohibit the sacred images. The Orthodox were severely afflicted, weeping bitter tears and saying, "It is better that we should die in one day than see the holy icon of Christ our God, or even the most holy Theotokos and any of the saints, disdained and trampled upon before our eyes and we are not able to resist."

---

[20] For the commemoration of the Seventh Œcumenical Synod, see the 11th of October.

[21] According to a Serbian source [Bishop Nikolai Velimirović, *The Prologue from Ochrid*, s.v. "May 23rd"], Michael took part in the Seventh Œcumenical Synod in 787.

Before the malice of the impious emperor surged out of control, the most holy Patriarch Nikephoros, moved by zeal, assembled around him the principal hierarchs of Orthodox conviction: Efthymios of Sardis,[22] Emilian of Kyzikos,[23] Joseph of Thessalonike,[24] Evdoxios of Amorion, Theophylact of Nikomedia, Michael of Synnada, and others. In that illustrious company there were also abbots and monks, especially the holy confessor and Hegumen Niketas of Medikion Monastery.[25] Michael, the blessed Bishop of Synnada, stood firmly while he began to say to the assembled fathers: "If the restive emperor wishes to be ill-advised and pull down the sacred icons, we ought to remain in opposition for the sake of the piety of our Orthodox Faith and the sacred images. We must do so even if it means enduring his anger and wrath. On the one hand, how can we remain of one mind for the pure Faith by not resisting him? On the other hand, if we do not contradict him, will it not appear that we validate his position? At all events, the latter course of action will give the impression that we either despise the holy icons or fear the emperor's fury against us." All in attendance, with one mind, agreed with Michael's assessment that hypocrisy and dissembling were unworthy of their offices and vows. Cloaking the emperor's impiety or keeping themselves out of sight, they could not do, they ought not to do. Besides, how might they ignore Leo or avoid his decree? Nay, they needed to be of one mind and heart on this issue, even to the point of shedding their blood for their beliefs. No dissimulation was to be committed by any of them. They said as much in that meeting, declaring, "We are ready and, if need be, will spill our blood for the sake of our Savior's name and the holy icons." All of the above mentioned hierarchs, together with the divine Nikephoros and certain of the righteous fathers, made haste and went forward bravely to have an audience with the emperor. They all took part in speaking before Leo V. During the discussion, the holy fathers brought forth as examples the witness of the divine Scriptures and the writings of the holy fathers. Despite the massive evidence and proofs in defense of the icons and warnings about the soul-destroying heresy and denuding the Church of Christ of her august icons, Leo remained obdurate. The fathers perceived that the emperor gave no heed to the teachings on sound Orthodoxy that were being expounded. Those hallowed fathers were acutely grieved and even wept.

At this juncture, Patriarch Nikephoros dispatched Michael of Synnada to Rome and to the pope.[26] The patriarch deemed him the most experienced and

---

[22] Saint Efthymios is commemorated by the holy Church on the 26th of December.

[23] Saint Emilian is commemorated by the holy Church on the 8th of August.

[24] Saint Joseph is commemorated by the holy Church on the 14th of July.

[25] Saint Niketas is commemorated by the holy Church on the 3rd of April.

[26] *The Great Synaxaristes* (in Greek) gives the pope's name as Adrian or Hadrian I (continued...)

dextrous in such matters. Michael went and stated the position of the Eastern Church in the controversy. The pope convened a council and issued an anathema against Emperor Leo. The holy Michael then returned with documents and letters to Constantinople. Patriarch Nikephoros, with his bishops, went again to speak to Emperor Leo. They reiterated their position on behalf of the icons. Again, Leo, wanting in understanding, remained incorrigible. He remained firmly fixed in the mire of ill-counsel.

It was then that the divine Michael, with daring and courage, addressed the tyrant and said, "Thou oughtest, O emperor, to have been persuaded by the teachings and entreaties of such holy men. But instead, thou dost now persist in thy ruinous opinion that will lead to destruction and everlasting punishment! We honor the holy icons as did the ancients—such as Saint Basil; for the honor paid to the image passes over to its prototype; and whoever venerates the icon, also venerates the hypostasis of the one depicted. By so doing, we maintain the teaching of our holy fathers and the tradition of the universal Church, which has proclaimed the Gospel from one end of the inhabited earth to the other. If someone should dare to treat despitefully thine image, sire, shalt thou not subject him to worse chastisements? Furthermore, if thou, being an earthly and temporal king, art enraged at the one who insulted thine image, how much greater punishments is one deserving who dares to spit upon or mock the icon of the heavenly King and Creator of all the cosmos? Take heed, O emperor, peradventure, seeing that thou art without fear, thou shouldest disdain the boundless long-suffering of God and shouldest be overtaken by some unexpected evil. I revere and venerate the immaculate icon of our Savior Jesus Christ, His holy Mother, and all the saints. As for thy godless doctrine, I spit upon it and give it no consequence whatsoever. Those of like mind with thee, let them be liable to anathema."

The sanctified Michael spoke courageously and resolutely, reckoning neither the imperial authority of the tyrant, nor his punishments, nor his

---

[26](...continued)
(772-795). This is unlikely since, during Emperor Leo V's reign, it was Leo III who was pope from 795 to 816. Patriarch Nikephoros was deposed in March of 815. Roman Catholic sources confirm that Bishop Michael of Synnada had, at some earlier time, carried a synodal document from Saint Tarasios (d. 806) to Pope Leo III in Rome; so it is not incredible that he may have gone more than once on these patriarchal commissions. Saint Tarasios, even earlier, contacted Pope Hadrian I. Tarasios' epistle to him was an anti-Iconoclast profession of the Faith. Tarasios hesitated to take the decisive step in restoring veneration; so he wrote the pope, looking for support, saying that the heretics had been condemned by six previous œcumenical synods. Hadrian wrote back cautiously, urging him to take action; but he also protested the election of a layman to the patriarchal throne. It was Empress Irene who took matters into her own hands and, with her ally, Tarasios, convoked Nicaea II.

threats. As for Leo, after hearing such things spoken in his court, he was filled with rage and shame. His mind became so darkened and discomfited that he was unable to perceive who was present. When he allayed his excitability, he immediately drove out the saints. He banished them far from one another so that one knew not where the other was abiding. His intended purpose in separating them was so that the holy fathers might not unify their efforts in writing and censuring his erroneous and baneful aims. The beastly-named Leo had the patriarch deposed. Nikephoros was taken from the place where he practised hesychasm—so as to take flight from the uproar and irreverence of the tyrant—and exiled to the island of Thasos. Saint Theophylact was consigned to Strovilon in Caria, a fortress by the sea. The ever-memorable Michael was sent to the city of Evdokiada, an Anatolian garrison of Cappadocia. Michael sojourned there for over ten years. He patiently endured every hardship, maltreatment, misery, and distress. He continued to pray for the emperor who banished him,[27] according to the word of our Lord Jesus Christ Who exhorted to "keep on loving your enemies, doing well to those who hate you, blessing those who curse you, and praying for those who act despitefully toward you."[28]

What human tongue is able to recount the struggles and pangs which the saint took upon himself in that exile? Who can narrate the care and concern he exhibited on behalf of the Church and Orthodoxy? The resourceful Michael gave no thought to repining. Even thus banished, who can describe his forethought for the poor, as well as his compassion, teaching, and consoling words to the afflicted? Who can tell of his all-night standing, pouring out supplications to the Lord? What was most worthy of memory is how Michael strengthened and confirmed the faithful in the Orthodox Faith and how he converted the unfaithful to a better acquaintance of God, so that he transplanted into their hearts both piety and full knowledge of the word. Moreover, added to these works among the people, he also performed miracles. Solely by his fervent invocation of the name of the Savior, Michael cured every disease. His salutary prayers proved salubrious not only for human sufferers but for irrational animals as well. The people of that land, the barbarians and the uninstructed, he educated. He wrought a change to their former wild and fierce manners. He transfigured them to the knowledge of God by his mellifluous teachings, exhortations, and advisements. Some he admonished and some he

[27] Leo V died at Constantinople, on the day of our Lord's Nativity, in the year 820, after being assassinated. His successor, Michael II (820-829), founder of the Amorion Dynasty, supported Iconoclasm but forbade public discussion of the controversy. While he restored some iconophiles, he did not bring back Patriarch Nikephoros.

[28] Lk. 6:27, 28; cf. Mt. 5:44.

won over by persuasion, while for others he performed wonders. Many respected him and held him up as a model of emulation.

Now a certain inhabitant of that land happened to be traveling to another place. He planned to sell a load of lead that he was conveying by means of a beast of burden. While he was on the way, by demonic complicity and through inattention on his part, the beast stumbled and shattered one of its feet. The man, saddened and dismayed by this mishap, turned back and sought another animal to bear the load. In the midst of his adversity, he encountered the holy Michael. The saint asked the peddler, "For what reason art thou so agitated, my man?" The peddler, sighing deeply, said, "O holy man of God, do not even make an inquiry, because my present situation is miserable and pitiable. I am so burdened by my affliction that I think that I should prefer to die voluntarily rather than live." The saint remarked, "Wilt thou not entrust thy tribulation to me? Perhaps I might be able to assist thee?" The peddler, then, told the bishop of his unhappy lot. Michael said, "Let us go there and have a look!" They went and found the beast of burden outstretched on the ground, convulsing and sorely distressed by pain. The saint, then, removed his handkerchief and wrapped it about the animal's foot. This was the same handkerchief with which he used to wipe the perspiration from his brow. With his staff, in a crosswise manner, he tapped the beast of burden. O the wonder! Straightway, the animal rose to its four feet, intact and sound. The master of that beast, beholding the wonderworking event, kneeled before the feet of the holy bishop. With tears of joy flowing profusely, he was thanking him and saying, "God, in truth, sent thee here for nought else but for my sake!" Afterward, the peddler, according to the holy Michael's command, did not bind up the load but left it unsecured. The peddler then took to the road rejoicing.

The peddler would not, or rather he could not, restrain himself and remain silent about the miracle. Everywhere he went, he published the fame of the saint. The majority of those who heard him did not believe the story, except when he showed them the animal. Although the load was not tied down on the beast, yet it remained solid and entire. As for the handkerchief on the animal's foot, it was all that was fettered to the creature. Those same people went to the saint and sought his forgiveness, even those who treated him ill in his exile. Michael, as one free of rancor, willingly fulfilled the commandment of the Master Christ. He forgave them and blessed them. He counseled them not to conduct themselves with others as they had toward him. Word of the miracle, meanwhile, spread from mouth to mouth. As is to be expected, word reached the ears of the emperor. He was furious and delayed not in dispatching his men for the saint in that place. Leo issued an edict pertaining to the people of that place, wherein he stated that whosoever dared to receive the bishop into his house would be subject to a grave penalty.

The saint, consequently, was spurned and kicked out. He went from place to place. He came upon a town called Areous (Ares), which had fallen under the wrath of God. Only the hearing of what took place can hatch visions of horror to the listener. Numberless hordes of mice appeared and devoured the crops of the fields and the vineyards. The helpless natives, at a loss how to proceed, found themselves without means or resources. The saint, newly arrived, seeing their profound sorrow, asked them what was the cause of their tribulation. The people responded: "Countless field mice have made inroads into our land. They have ravaged the fruits and crops of our fields. We are in danger this year of total deprivation of food; for this cause we expect to die of hunger." The saint remarked, "God, despite your sins, has shown compassion upon you. He has turned His wrath upon the crops, so that you might come to repentance and return to Him." They answered him, mindful of the miracles which he wrought in every quarter, and said, "Take pity on us, O saint of God, and do not leave us to perish in the end. Only utter a prayer in our behalf before God, and we shall be saved. For we believe that God will grant whatsoever thou shouldest ask of Him." The saint directed them, saying, "Keep a fast for three days and purify yourselves from everything. Do as I say and, perhaps, in this way, the wrath of God might be turned away, as He is compassionate."

After the passing of three days, the saint declared, "Come forth, all of you of every age and station. Come to the fields and to the vineyards, crying aloud with reverence and fear of God, 'Lord, have mercy!'" After the whole crowd converged, they began to cry out, "Lord, have mercy!" The saint went to his knees, raising his hands and eyes heavenward, and uttered, "O Lord Jesus Christ, God and Creator of the cosmos, look down upon Thy people and Thine inheritance, upon those who hope in Thee and fear Thy name: Do not forsake Thy creature to the end, even though he has sinned, O Lord, and has provoked Thy goodness to anger; for from Thee has he not withdrawn.[29] Turn back Thine anger to compassion and mercy on Thy creature, as Thou art good and the Lover of mankind." Upon offering up such a supplication—lo, the miracle!—right away, all of the ground, underneath where they stood, quaked. Intense fear gripped all of the people. The hordes of field mice, instantly, died. The people were thus delivered of that menacing scourge, for which all sent up glory to God. Therefore, they said to the saint, "Even though thou hast come to our place without our will, yet God sent thee forth lest we, the pitiful ones, should be destroyed. If thou hadst not come at the appropriate time, we would have come to utter ruin."

Bishop Michael went from thence, by reason of a new command of the emperor ordering him to go to another place—namely Efrantisia. The people

[29] Evidently, these sinners were at least free of Iconoclasm.

of that location accepted him gladly, for there were certain folk of that land for whom the saint performed a miracle. When they caught sight of the saint approaching, they began to say, "He is the one who eliminated the hordes of field mice from Areous." Hence, the bishop's fame preceded him. Many went forth and greeted him before he entered their neighborhood. They were saying to him, "Thy coming into our presence is good, O saint of God, that thou mightest save us. This is because countless swarms of locusts have invaded our land, consuming the crops of our fields, without leaving anything. They have just now started to destroy our vineyards and fruit trees. On account of this, we are in peril of being deprived of our last hope of yielding any fruit crop. We, therefore, entreat thee, O saint, protect us and make an entreaty for our sake, because thou hast boldness before God. We know this, forasmuch as thy good reputation has gone ahead of thee. We know that if thou shouldest ask God for something that He would grant it to thee." The saint, after discoursing with them on those things needful and customary, said to them, "You are to be ready by tomorrow to meet at the place where the locust has caused damage; and God, the Giver of good things, He shall deliver you of this dreadful spoiler."

During the night, the saint, standing with much compunction, raised his hands and eyes heavenward. He began to utter with tears, "I direct my prayer to Thee, O Lord God, Who by the Logos of God created all things—the things in the heavens and the things upon the earth, the visible and the invisible[30]—and Who, by His hands, formed the man of dust of the earth,[31] and likewise created the angelic host who glorify Thee: Unto man Thou gavest dominion over the fish of the sea, and over the flying creatures of heaven, and over the cattle and all the earth, and over all the reptiles that creep on the earth;[32] and so these creatures fear man. Man, however, disobeyed the true God and partook of the tree which was not permitted. Man was banished from Paradise by reason of Thy righteous judgment. Thus, in the sweat of his face he eats his bread, while the earth brings forth thorns and thistles.[33] Look down, O Lord, now, upon Thy people and Thine inheritance, and forget them not to the end. For though they have sinned, O Lord, yet they have not apostatized from Thee. Do not, O Lord, in Thy wrath chastize them; but deal with them according to Thy mercy. Thou art the One Who said, 'Return to Me, and I will return to you [Mal. 3:7].' Grant, O Lord, aid to those who hope in Thee. Turn away Thine anger from Thy creature. Do Thou drive out the beasts—creeping things and reptiles—that have harmed their fruits and crops. Do Thou bestow

[30] Cf. Col. 1:16.

[31] Gen. 2:7.

[32] Gen. 1: 26, 28.

[33] Gen. 3:18, 19.

Thy help and protection that they might glorify with gladness Thy holy name; for blessed art Thou in Thy saints unto the ages. Amen."

The following day, as the sun rose, all the people emerged and went to the appointed site with the saint. With a great voice they cried out, "Lord, have mercy!" Then—behold the marvel!—all the locusts promptly sprung up and mounted on high into the air. The masses of insects appeared as a dense cloud that overshadowed the people, blocking out the rays of the sun. In a short time they sundered into two distinct swarms. The one group, appearing obscured, inscrutably vanished; but the other group was plainly seen to fall into a nearby lake and drown. The people witnessed this strange and mysterious wonder. They went to their knees before the saint, offering their thanks for delivering them from that terrible scourge.

We see from these few anecdotes how the saint spent his latter years in exile. He struggled through every kind of trial and tribulation, all the while being persecuted by the iconoclasts. He moved about from place to place, working countless wonders and miracles. We have set forth only a brief account of some of the luminary's works, but hopefully it is enough to provide the reader with a good idea regarding the rest. Who should wish to conceal the great gifts and wonderworkings of the confessor and hierarch, Michael of Synnada? But brevity is a factor that we need to consider, for there would be no end to speaking of his perfections. Since we do not wish to appear indifferent or indolent or scornful of his accomplishments, we shall recount another episode in his journey. Hearken to the next incident. After the kindly and compassionate bishop was again chased away by the emperor's minions, he came into another region. He could not help but notice that though vineyards punctuated the countryside, yet the vines were bereft of verdure. Michael longed to learn the etiology of this peculiarity. "Why are the vines bare of foliage?" he inquired of some natives. They answered plaintively, "Caterpillars, which are nestled in the soft bark of the branches, are eating away at the leafage. They are ready to strip the branches the moment there is any budding. Hence, we have been working for nought throughout the year." The saint heard their plight and was moved to pity. By his efficacious prayers that plague of caterpillars was plucked from the land.

Bishop Michael's continual flights from place to place, eventually, took a toll on his toilsome life. Relentless hardships and inexorable enemies were exhausting even for the valiant and indefatigable Michael. Concurrently, he was also getting to be a venerable age. Christ, the Umpire of athletes of piety and virtue, allowed illness to rage against Michael's sacred body not only that we might see the frailty of his physical constitution but more so to reveal undisguised the endurance of that godly soul and his manly resolution. Now he had reached eighty years of age and could no longer walk. He, therefore, was bedridden for some days. Three days before his blessed end, he made a tear-filled entreaty to God: for the emperor, for the peace of the Church and the whole world, and for the abundance of the fruits of the earth. He also spoke such words as these: "O Lord Jesus Christ our God, Thou didst speak to Thy divine and sacred disciples and didst say that those who follow Thee would be hated for Thy name's sake[34] and always persecuted.[35] But, also, Thou didst say that the very hairs of our heads are numbered,[36] and that the one who shall confess in Jesus before men, that Thou also wilt confess in him before Thy Father and the angels.[37] Behold, Lord, for Thy name's sake have I till now undergone so many persecutions! Receive Thou my spirit presently and grant me refreshment in a place of rest. I entreat Thee, O Lord, and Thy tender mercy, that should one invoke my name on dry land or in the sea, that Thou wouldest grant the request. And if one should celebrate my memory and offer incense, let such a one have forgiveness of sins and strength of body that Thy most holy name might be glorified on earth through Thy works; for Thou art the only God Who is wondrous and glorified in Thy saints to the ages. Amen."

Such were his words and supplication, which concluded in his falling asleep in the Lord. His blessed soul ascended into the heavens where he rejoices with the hierarchs as a worthy hierarch and with the martyrs as a great martyr. Now the majority of martyrs struggled for three or four hours or even days, and then there was an end of it. But the life of the divine Michael was crowded with struggles, ill-plights, exiles and, in short, turned out to be one continual martyrdom, apart from spilling his blood as is characteristic of the divine martyrs. Michael was consecrated from his mother's arms and sacrificed his whole life to Christ as a sacrifice of most sweet savor. The august relic of his body was interred in the place where he finished the course of his contest. Through his relic were diseases healed for those who hastened to it. Not only at that time did this take place but also numberless wonders have continued to take place through those sanctified relics, which can be described by neither the hand nor the mouth of man. "I shall set forth one of the many miracles, which I beheld with my own eyes as well as many others. I will make this one last report, which caused wonder and astonishment in my homeland, not to be easily forgotten; and then shall I bring an end to this history."

Divine and great wrath fell upon the island of Skopelos.[38] Plagues—not one but many—struck the island on the scale of those that riddled Egypt of

---

[34] Cf. Mt. 10:22; 24:9; Mk. 13:13; Lk. 21:17.

[35] Cf. Mt. 5:10, 12; Jn. 15:20.

[36] Mt. 10:30; Lk. 12:7.

[37] Mt. 10:32; Lk. 12:8.

[38] Skopelos, of the North Sporades Islands of the prefecture of Magnesia, falls in the region of Thessaly, Greece.

old.[39] The first plague was the caterpillar, which devoured the buds and the leaves of the vines. The second was a disease that attacked the offshoots. The third was a kind of beetle that not only consumed everything that was edible but even shredded clothing. It preferred moist places, so it crawled into water pots. It did not even desist in creeping into the mouths and ears of humans fast asleep at night. The creature even bit its victim on the ear and ushered in all kinds of health problems. The fourth blight was a multitude of field mice. They overran and destroyed vineyards, planting fields, gardens, and whatever else they could find. These horrible infestations brought untold affliction, oppression, and heavy losses. These visitations, moreover, pestered and provoked the islanders for a long time. Now the renown, also, of the sacred relic of the head of Saint Michael for performing wonderworkings spread to Skopelos. This inestimable and precious treasure was kept on the Holy Mountain of Athos at the Great Lavra of Saint Athanasios. Some notables of the island visited the Great Lavra. Armed with letters and accompanied by the bishop and the clergy, they, on behalf of the islanders, fervently sought the sacred relic of Saint Michael's head. The eminent fathers of the Great Lavra read the letters and took note of the tears and sighs of the representatives. Since the islanders' fervid pleas for their lives and their island were sincere, the fathers consented to send the wonderworking head of the confessor and hierarch, Saint Michael. The relic was escorted by the island's embassy, consisting of a virtuous spiritual father, a devout deacon, and a venerable elder.

When the hallowed head arrived on Skopelos, it was April and during the Great Fast. The islanders went forth to the harbor and reverently venerated the relic. This included the godly and dignified Bishop Metrophanes, together with all the priests and the faithful. Before all the men, women, and children, the Service for the Blessing of Holy Water was conducted. A procession was formed that wended its way through the fields and vineyards. The people entreated God with much contrition, as they cried out unrestrainedly, "Lord, have mercy!" O how great and wondrous are Thy works, O Lord Who art glorified in Thy saints! On the return circuit of the procession through the city, all those plagues that harmed man, field, vineyard, and everything that sprouted from the ground, were removed from that stricken land. In a year's time the vineyards yielded abundantly. All those that had contracted infirmities from the plagues were no longer afflicted. The hierarch and all the islanders, beholding the prodigious wonders wrought by the sacred head, showed proper gratitude. They gave glory to God and thanked His saint that they had been released from such terrible woes. On account of this miracle, the people built a church and dedicated it to the name of Saint Michael of Synnada, whose

[39] Cf. Ex. 9:14 ff.

memory they celebrate festively. As for the spiritual father and the others who escorted the sacred head to the island, they fittingly and bountifully made a certain small offering to the Great Lavra, by reason of the holy head of the ever-memorable Michael of Synnada.

This, brethren, is the life and conversation of Saint Michael. Herein, for your love that you might revel in spiritual delight, were presented some of his miracles. This brilliant luminary of the inhabited earth, Michael of Synnada, who unceasingly toiled and strived for the sake of Christ's name and the holy icons, conducted his life in a pure and blameless manner while enduring all manner of temptations, afflictions, exiles, and persecutions. Throughout all these tribulations, the indomitable and tenderhearted Michael prayed for his persecutors according to the unerring command from our Savior's mouth. The Paymaster, God, seeing how His servant endured all with thanksgiving, recompensed him with the gift and the power of working miracles, which have so glorified Michael, that his fame has spread as a loud but melodious trumpet to the four corners of the world.

Let us, therefore, hymn, honor, and glorify, as much as we are able, Saint Michael. Let us keep festival and celebrate his august memory. Let us offer to him chants and odes and all that befits the saints. We have him in this present life as a ready helper and protector. For as many times as we call upon his aid in our critical circumstances, now and in the future, he will act as a go-between and intercessor before the Master Christ that we might be vouchsafed the blessed and endless kingdom of the heavens. Amen.

On the 23th of May, the holy Church commemorates the holy Martyr SALONAS the Roman, who was slain by the sword when he refused to offer libations to the idols.

On the 23th of May, the holy Church commemorates the holy Martyr SELEFKOS (SELEUCUS), who, without a groan, was sawn asunder.

On the 23th of May, the holy Church commemorates the venerable Monk-Martyr MICHAEL of the Lavra of Saint Savvas.[40]

[40] The Life of Saint Michael is given in full within the Life of Saint Theodore of Edessa, commemorated by the holy Church on the 19th of July.

On the 23th of May, the holy Church commemorates the holy Myrrh-bearer MARY, the wife of Cleopas, who reposed in peace.[41]

The Myrrh-bearers Before the Disciples

On the 23th of May, the holy Church commemorates the venerable EPHROSYNE, Abbess of Polotsk (1173).

On the 23th of May, the holy Church commemorates the Finding of the Relics of our holy father, the Hieromartyr LEONTIOS the Wonder-worker, Bishop of Rostov (1077).

Through the intercessions of Thy Saints,
O Christ God, have mercy on us. Amen.

---

[41] Jn. 19:25: "Now there had stood by the Cross of Jesus His Mother, and His Mother's sister, Mary the wife of Cleopas, and Mary Magdalene." Apostle Cleopas of the Seventy is commemorated, individually, on the 30th of October. See also Mt. 27:55; Mk. 15:40, 41; Lk. 23:27, 49, 55, 24:1 ff. regarding those women who followed and ministered to Jesus.

The icon herein shows the myrrh-bearers proclaiming to the hiding disciples what they saw and heard at the Lord's sepulcher. The scene reminds us of what Jesus said to His disciples: "Ye all shall be made to stumble because of Me during this night, for it hath been written: 'I will smite the Shepherd, and the sheep shall be scattered abroad [Mk. 14:27; Mt. 26:31; cf. Zach. 13:7].'" Afterward, the myrrh-bearers "returned from the sepulcher and related all these things to the eleven and to all the rest. And there were Mary Magdalene, and Joanna, and Mary the Mother of Iakovos, and the rest of the women with them, who were telling these things to the apostles [Lk. 24:9-11]."

On the 24th of May, the holy Church commemorates our venerable Father SYMEON at the Wonderful Mountain.[1]

Symeon, our holy father, at the Wonderful Mountain, lived during the reign of the Emperor Justin II (565-578). God was pleased to grant his birth so that there might be not only an intercessor and go-between before God but also a physician of souls and bodies, a model of the eremitical life, and an example of the patristic philosophy. From infancy and through puberty, he followed after that which was virtuous and excellent. Indeed, from his youth until death, he was accounted worthy of divine visions and enjoyed the grace of working miracles. Let us, therefore, who are of little strength to recount his life and accomplishments, call upon our universal Master, Christ, and invoke the intercessions of the venerable Symeon, for help.

A certain man, John, who was young in years, hailed from Edessa of Mesopotamia. He migrated with his parents, makers of myrrh,[2] to Antioch. The parents were desirous that their son should enter into wedlock. They found

---

[1] The Life of this righteous Father Symeon was recorded in Greek. The text is extant in the Athonite Monastery of Iveron and in other places. The manuscript begins, "Blessed is God, for it is worthy to bless...." The text was rendered in simpler Greek by Agapios the Cretan, who published it in his *Kalokairine*, from which it was incorporated into *The Great Synaxaristes* (in Greek). Divine offices to Saint Symeon were composed by Saint Theophanes and Saint Joseph the Hymnographer, which texts are found in Codex B 71 at the Great Lavra. There exist other *stichera*, *idiomela*, *kathismata*, etc., which hymns are found in the codices of Kafsokalyvia and of Lavra (Γ 19 and I 70), as well as in the Parisian Codex 1574. The biographer clearly identifies in his *Kalokairine* edition that today's Saint Symeon Thavmastoreitis (of Wonderful Mountain) or Saint Symeon the Stylite the Younger is not to be confused with his namesake, who is known simply as Saint Symeon the Stylite (commemorated by the holy Church on the 1st of September). They lived in different centuries under different emperors. The September saint was born in 392 and reposed in 461. He flourished during the reign of Leo the Great (457-474). The May saint flourished during the reign of Justin II (565-578). There is still some confusion when the appellation "at Mandra" is added to either saint's name. Mandra was the name of the monastery of today's saint who also had an enclosed space around the pillar to prevent the entry of women. This pen itself was also called Mandra. Nikodemos the Hagiorite, however, also identifies the September saint not only as a "stylite" but also "at Mandra." It should be known, furthermore, that the Saint Symeon at the Mandra, whose name is invoked in the Smaller Blessing of Water, is the May stylite. As it happened, both saints had sainted mothers with the same name—Martha. Saint Martha, commemorated on the 1st of September, is the mother of the September Saint Symeon the Stylite. Saint Martha, commemorated on the 4th of July, is the mother of the May Saint Symeon of the Wonderful Mountain.

[2] Perfumers.

for him a beautiful maiden, named Martha, whom he took to wife. Martha was excessively devout and regularly attended the church of the divine Forerunner. She had this pious custom before she was married, and she retained it afterward. She fasted and besought Christ the Master, through the intercessions of Saint John the Forerunner, to grant her a child. She promised that the child, from birth, would be dedicated to the sacred Forerunner. One evening, as Martha was engaged at prayer, she beheld a vision in which Saint John the Forerunner said, "Take courage, O woman, for thine entreaty has been heard. As a sign, take this fragrant incense. Go and cense my house many times." She, straightway, awakened. She was filled with both joy and fear. She then noticed—O Christ, great is Thy goodness!—that in her right hand she was grasping a lump of extraordinary incense. She, thereupon, went to her knees, tearfully giving thanks to the Lord.

Saint Symeon

As the sun's first light at the dawning of the day found her awake, she placed the incense into a censer. She went to the church and began censing. So exceptional was the fragrance wafting forth from the censer that those present were astonished. They understood that the scent was divine and not of this earth. When only the least fragment of the incense remained, she extinguished it that she might use it again. On the morrow, she went to the church for the same purpose. Lo, the miracle! She found the incense whole and unburnt, as the great Forerunner had presented it to her originally. This phenomenon of the replenishing incense took place for many days. Afterward, she beheld another vision in which the Baptist John visited her and said, "Take thine ease, O woman, for thou shalt give birth to a son whom thou art to name Symeon. Thou shalt nurse him only from thy right breast, for thy child will ever tread the path to the right. He will not incline to any sin, for he shall become a great saint. Feed him, therefore, only with bread, water, salt, and honey. Take heed to guard well this child, before and after birth, for as a vessel of God is he being prepared. When he attains the age of three, bring the lad to my temple that he might receive holy Baptism."

After the hallowed Forerunner uttered these admonitory words, it was but a short time before they came to pass. When the term of her confinement came to an end, Martha was delivered of her prophesied child.[3] The newborn accepted nourishment only from her right breast. But one day, Martha tested to see if the infant might nurse from her left breast. Little Symeon, nevertheless, turned his face away. Since the mother persisted, the infant went without taking the breast all that day. As evening drew nigh—O the mysterious wonder!—Martha's left breast no longer gave milk and ran dry.

After three years, the child was baptized and named Symeon. As the newly-illumined child emerged from the holy font, he exclaimed, "I have a father and I do not have one!" The infant repeated this statement for seven days, signifying his future renunciation of parents and their departure and translation to the heavenly heights. On those days that Martha partook of meat, Symeon abstained and would not take the breast.

Now after five years, an earthquake struck Antioch.[4] Houses were leveled, taking the lives of inhabitants. The house of Symeon also collapsed, burying his father under the debris. At that same hour, Martha was offering up prayer in the Church of the Forerunner. She was preserved. Symeon, however, was in the Church of Saint Stephen. When the quake ceased, Symeon exited. He became confused in the midst of all the destruction. He did not know which direction to take for his home. A woman found the boy and brought him to her home. In the meantime, Martha went about seeking Symeon. Not being able to find him, she sorrowed exceedingly. She, too, came to believe that he was killed in the earthquake and buried under the rubble. One night, however, in her sleep, she beheld the Baptist. It was he who revealed to Martha where Symeon was to be found. With the Baptist's sure instructions, Martha went and found her boy. The discovery ushered in gladness and rejoicing.

After several days, Martha beheld a vision. She saw herself flying into the heavens, holding the child in her hands. She was offering him to God, as an acceptable gift. She later told Symeon, "I desired aforetime, O child, to behold thy divine mounting on high, in order that the Most High might acquit me as one worthy to render to Him the fruit of my womb." Some time after this

[3] Other sources record his birth at Antioch in 521.

[4] The earthquake took place on the 26th day of May, in the year 526.

apparition, Symeon also beheld a vision. He beheld the Master Christ seated upon a lofty throne borne up in the air. The righteous thronged about Him, and the book of life was being opened. Off to the east, there was situated the Paradise of delights; and to the west, there was the lake of fiery torment. Then Symeon heard the Lord's voice saying, "Take heed of this vision, O Symeon: for the Paradise of delight, a promise of everlasting rejoicing, is promised to the radiant and vigorous righteous; and the Gehenna of the fire awaits sinners for perpetual punishment. Therefore, choose what is best. Hasten to be delivered from that which is dreadful. Be diligent in striving for those ineffable good things so as to enjoy and rejoice in them forever." This vision did the divinely inspired one behold. Indeed, from God, Symeon, invisibly and paradoxically, attained knowledge and understanding of hidden and sacred revelations.

After several days, Symeon beheld a man in white raiment who said to him, "Be thou following me!" Straightway, he obeyed. He was led to a land called Tiberine, which was near Seleukeia. Following this, he was brought to a desolate mountain. He ascended and saw the village of Pilasa (Pila) lying below. Symeon remained in that wilderness spot, subsisting on the same food as the wild beasts. His guide, after spending several days instructing him how to conduct himself, departed. Symeon remained there alone, but judged it good to tread deeper into an even more remote area. He walked about for a long while in that lonely and wild place, until he came before a small monastery. The hegumen of that establishment, a virtuous ascetic, named John, had earlier received a vision regarding Symeon's arrival. When John beheld Symeon, he felt a rush of abundant joy. Symeon took up his abode with John. Thus, the youth attached himself to a community of ascetics living within the "Mandra" or enclosure of the pillar-hermit, John. Symeon found rest and quietude in that solitary location, leading a life equal to that of the angels. Symeon partook of food every seven days and, ofttimes, even every ten days. His fare consisted of a few soaked legumes and a little water. As he advanced in age and maturity, so did he progress in his asceticism. The very young and humble Monk Symeon came to possess a handsome countenance, with beautiful eyes, framed by hair the color of gold. He was a young man of few words. When he did converse, it was sensibly and prudently; and so it was that such gifts and grace were from God.

The ecclesiastical historian Evagrios Scholastikos (b. ca. 536), in Coele Syria, recounts an event which took place when Symeon first came, which led to his ascending a pillar as a stylite. He writes: "The occasion on which he was first elevated on the column came about as follows. While still very young, he was roving about, sporting and bounding along the eminences of the mountain. He suddenly met with a panther. Symeon threw his belt around its neck. With a kind of halter, he led forth the creature—beguiled of its ferocity—to the monastery. His preceptor, the Elder John, who himself occupied a column, observing the circumstance, inquired, "What is this?" Symeon replied, "It is a cat." Conjecturing from this occurrence how distinguished the child would become a struggler for virtue, John took him up upon the column."[5] The youth obeyed his elder, as if it had been the voice of God.

The hater-of-good, the devil, envied Symeon and harbored deep malice against him. He prompted a certain guileful monk to slay Symeon, because the blessed one struggled to a greater degree to which he could not equal. When that murderous monk lifted his hand, clenching a dagger, suddenly, by divine energy, his arm withered. This caused him such bitter pangs as to penetrate even to his heart, so that he nearly died. He then betook himself to the hegumen and showed him his paralyzed right hand. The perpetrator, wanting in understanding, was nevertheless too ashamed to divulge the cause. As the days passed, so did his condition worsen. Fearing that he might die, he secretly confessed his lawlessness to the hegumen. John, in turn, disclosed to the righteous Symeon the attempted assault on his life. The hegumen also affirmed that a just retribution was being visited upon this most daring monk. The abbot requested of Symeon, as his genuine son, that he forgive the transgression. He further asked that Symeon entreat God to heal the wayward monk. Immediately, Symeon, bearing no ill will or rancor, obeyed. He bowed his head and knees in prayer. When he arose from that attitude, he made the sign of the Cross over the sufferer's withered hand. Lo, the wonder! The offending hand was restored to its former soundness.

A few days later, while the righteous Symeon was praying, he beheld before him a young Man of very comely aspect. Symeon knew that it was the Master Christ. Summoning his courage, Symeon, even as once did the beloved disciple John, inquired of Christ, "Lord, how did the Jews crucify Thee?" The Master, then, in order to teach Symeon patience amid tribulation and mortification of the flesh, stretched forth His immaculate hands in the same manner when He was suspended upon the Cross and replied, "I was crucified according to My good pleasure. Play the man and endure." Symeon, however, at that moment, did not quite understand the words of the Lord. Nevertheless, he meditated upon these words. He struggled further by adding more toils and austerities to his ascetical exercises. For example, if John recited thirty psalms nightly, Symeon would recite eighty. Many times, Symeon deployed his efforts to reading the entire Psalter and would not sleep that night. His superior attempted to prevent him, saying, "What thou doest, my child, is sufficient.

---

[5] Evagrius, *Ecclesiastical History: A History of the Church from A.D. 431 to A.D. 594*, Bk. VI, Ch. XXIII (London: Samuel Bagster and Sons, 1846), reprinted of late by Kessinger Publishing in the US (May, 2005), p. 311.

Engage not in excessive contests, and do thou govern thy body with a little less rigor. Do not overwork thyself, but strive to do all in moderation. Eat in measure and sleep little, as thou art but a mortal man, so as to keep thy rule; for, according to the Lord, food does not defile the man."[6] Symeon answered, "True, reverend father, but food makes gross the delicate mind. Sleep abducts us from divine contemplation, so that we become lethargic out of indifference; then are we beset by passionate thoughts and our soul's strength is drained. For this reason, we younger monks must strive to overcome the passions."

These early wondrous struggles of Symeon annoyed the demons. They were troubled to such a degree that they beset Symeon with thoughts fraught with fantasies. Thus, there appeared to him such things as gold, precious stones, musical instruments, dances, and pleasurable pastimes, so as to vanquish the invincible monk. But those odious creatures toiled in vain. This is because the righteous Symeon scattered them, making the sign of the Cross. Apart from these demonic manifestations, the just one was deemed worthy of more exalted and perfect visions. He beheld a holy and splendid church effusing glory. Next, a certain patriarch anointed him with sweet-smelling myrrh and declared: "By this myrrh, thou shalt cast out demons; and thou shalt receive divine strength from heaven, whereby thou shalt render their assaults empty and ineffective." Such was the favor that the righteous Symeon attained before God.

On one occasion, a demon-possessed man, in the company of others, came to the monastery. When the demon caught sight of Symeon, that creature wrested his demonized victim from the hands of those who accompanied him. The demon then dragged his victim to the precipice so as to cast him down headlong. The righteous Symeon, calling upon the name of the Lord, then called the possessed man to come to him. He responded, even out of fear. The righteous one, sealing him with the sign of the Cross, rebuked the demon who then fled. Thus, the former demoniac remained in that state of health. However, the demon, so as to intimidate, went and brought many other demons and swarms of reptiles and creeping things. They hissed and whirred for many days, making such a clamor that the monks could find no quiet. The demons did this, attempting to impede his ascetic rule. Nevertheless, the blessed one showed absolutely no fear. He drove them out by reciting those words from David that begin "He that dwelleth in the help of the Most High [Ps. 90:1 ff.]," and the rest of the psalm. Yet, the inexorable demons once more warred against him. At times, they would seize his *koukoulion* (cowl) and *rason* (cassock), or they would stir up howling winds, and thunder and lightning. They even

[6] Cf. Mt. 15:17-20; Mk. 7:15-23.

attempted to cast him down a defile, and committed other similar misdeeds. But the grace of God always guarded the righteous man.

The venerable Symeon exhorted the monks wonderfully with soul-saving words, so much so that they were beside themselves on account of his understanding. The brethren would relate that, at times, they beheld an angel of the Lord. He was bearing in his right hand a honeycomb, from which he was offering honey to the righteous one. At other times, they would see a dove perched upon Symeon's head; and from there it would fly into the heavens. While the brethren related these things, the righteous one was deemed worthy of a loftier vision. Symeon was caught up into heaven and ascended seven ladders. When he asked what place it was, he heard a voice say, "Thou hast ascended the seven heavens; and now do thou behold Paradise." He saw there a palace full of light and a fountain flowing with myrrh. He, however saw no man, save Adam and the thief. When he came to himself, he disclosed the vision to John. The hegumen glorified God Who had bestowed such grace upon His slave, the blessed Symeon.

Saint Symeon

The blessed Symeon possessed the following virtue: Whensoever someone poor came to visit him, Symeon would remove his cassock and give it to the needy man, though he himself was left naked. This, more times than not, occurred during the cold winter months. John, grieving to see Symeon suffer from the elements, would give him another garment. At another time, Symeon was sitting on the ground for an entire year. As a result, his thighs and knees were joined fast in their place. His flesh began to rot and to emit a foetid odor. John deemed it wise to bring in a physician to examine and offer him treatment. But the righteous Symeon smiled and stated, "The Lord my God lives Who shall heal me; for I have been dedicated to Him from my mother's womb! Therefore, let His will be done!" Verily, as he said this–O the wonder!—he became completely well. On account of the righteous one's way of life and prayer, a many-lighted flame descended from heaven just as on the day of the Pentecost. For we read that on that day of Pentecost there appeared to the apostles and others, tongues, as it were of fire, being distributed.[7] They, thus, were enlightened by the Holy Spirit. After this, the holy Symeon began to compose sermons concerning repentance and the future judgment. He could interpret pericopes of the divine Scriptures, those difficult to comprehend, to the astonishment of all. He wrote ascetic works and *troparia*.[8]

When the Samaritans effaced the holy images that were in the churches, Saint Symeon wrote to Emperor Justin in defense of the veneration due to the sacred icons. This letter is quoted by Saint John the Damascene (b. d. 749), and by the Second Synod at Nicaea (787). Saint Symeon of the Wonderful Mountain wrote: "Perhaps some contentious unbeliever might dispute with us, saying that we venerate images in our churches and he had therefore concluded that we pray to lifeless idols. Far be it from us to do this! Christians live by faith and by God, Who does not deceive us and Who has shown mighty signs in our midst. Our images are not merely colored pictures; for when we remember whose representation the painting is, we see the invisible made visible through visible representation and glorify Him Who was made present. For we do not believe in a God Who is absent, but in Him Who is truly present. It is the same for the saints. They have not ceased to exist, but they are present, because they are alive in God; and the spirits of the saints are enabled by the power of God to help those who pray to them."[9]

The blessed Symeon was so replete with divine grace that each day he waxed more fervent in faith. He directed that a pillar be set up, reaching a height of forty feet. When they had constructed it, the Archbishop of Antioch came with the Bishop of Seleukeia. Afterward, they kindled a great fire. They brought Symeon into the sanctuary and celebrated the divine Liturgy, during which divine office they ordained him to the rank of hierodeacon. He next ascended to the top of the pillar with due reverence. He remained there for eight years. He intensified his struggles, for the demons vexed him at night

---

[7] Acts 2:3.

[8] *Bibliotheca Hagiographica Graeca*, ed. F. Halkin (Brussels, 1957), 1689-1691C.

[9] This extract of Saint Symeon's defense of the holy icons is found in Saint John of Damascus' extensive bibliography, found partially in the text entitled *On the Images* (Crestwood, NY: Saint Vladimir's Seminary Press, 1980), p. 104. Saint John attributes the Life of Saint Symeon to Archbishop Arkadios of Constantia (Cyprus), whereas P. van den Ven [*La Vie ancienne de s. Syméon Stylite le Jeune*, 2 vols. (Brussels, 1962-1970), I:101f] rejects this attribution, suggesting the biographer was an anonymous contemporary of the saint. Nikephoros Ouranos (civil functionary, hagiographer, poet, lay guardian of Great Lavra, annihilator of the forces of Samuel of Bulgaria), who died after 1007, also, reworked the Life of Saint Symeon, which is also in several abridged versions [J. Bompaire, *Hellenika* 13 (1954), pp. 71-110] and in Georgian and Arabic translations [J. Nasrallah, *Analecta Bollandiana* 90 (1972) 387-389]. *The Oxford Dictionary of Byzantium*, s.v. "Symeon the Stylite the Younger."

with apparitions. It was there that he beheld a vision. An elder in priestly vestments descended from heaven, bearing a holy chalice. He communed the immaculate Mysteries to Symeon, saying, "Be courageous and may thy heart be strengthened, because the demons shall no longer trouble thee whilst thou slumberest." Now Symeon also foreknew the day of the hegumen's repose. John, imitating Symeon's example, was struggling at the base of the latter's pillar. From atop the pillar, Symeon conveyed to him by gesture that John, after a few days, would be translated to the Lord. Verily, Hegumen John soon reposed. The holy Symeon, whether day or night, kept constant in prayer atop his pillar. He recited the Psalter and the Odes of Moses. He was only coming down from on high to make prostrations for his deceased abbot.

The venerable stylite, however, became the object of fresh assaults by the demons. Symeon, nevertheless, vanquished them roundly. At that time, there appeared to him our Lord Jesus Christ, the Master of all creation. He was flanked by the holy Archangels Michael and Gabriel. Symeon besought Christ to grant him the fruits of virtue and to strengthen him, that he might keep the Lord's divine commandments. God, therefore, Who glorifies those who glorify Him, blessed the righteous man thrice with His most sacred fingers. Christ bestowed upon Symeon the grace of the Holy Spirit to perform miracles. Afterward, in accordance with this vision, many wonderworkings were wrought. As many as hastened to him who were demoniacs, he restored to health and gave glory to God. The holy angels brought tidings to him that he would heal not only the demonized but also those suffering from every kind of malady. These cures were accomplished either by the touch of his hands, or through his mantle, or his coarse *rason*, or his staff. Moreover, these occurred not only in his lifetime but also after his repose. Divine grace was bestowed upon the righteous one, so that the power of God energized wonders daily. We now wish to describe some briefly.

A certain man from Cappadocia was possessed by an unyielding and a hard demon. The man approached the pillar and, standing below, cried up, "Have mercy on me, O servant of God, for I am being put to death by the demon!" The venerable Symeon leaned over and rebuked the demon. He gave the man a swatch of his *rason* and sent him home. Behold the miracle! That man not only regained his health but also gave that patch of cloth to other sick folk. They, too, were cured and were giving glory to God. In yet another case, there was a certain man from Antioch. He had a serious stomach complaint, so that the disease racked him with pain throughout his inward parts. He arrived at such a crisis that he began rolling on the ground and crying out woefully. Saint Symeon cured this man, using a piece of his *rason*. We should add here that a certain young man was restored to life by the prayer of the venerable stylite.

On another occasion, the venerable Symeon beheld another splendid vision of glory. He beheld our Lord Jesus Christ amid the ranks of the angelic hosts. The first group was carrying a precious crown and a cross flashing like lightning. They also bore a porphyry garment. They intended to clothe the righteous one in that garment, but Symeon declined. Then the holy angels said, "By these art thou crowned by God the Father and His only-begotten Son, and, by the purple, the Holy Spirit, with Whom thou shalt reign together with the saints in the everlasting kingdom." Symeon then turned his eyes to the Master and answered, "O Lord and Master, because Thou hast vouchsafed me to reign with Thy saints, I beseech Thy goodness to endue me with the grace no longer to require human nourishment." Upon uttering these words, the Lord answered that He would hearken to his request. Straightway, the holy angels vested Symeon with the porphyry garment, fitting it over his *rason*. Upon his head they set the crown, chanting to Christ God and honoring with praises the righteous Symeon.

After this divine theophany, our venerable father performed new miracles. Many people, who were stricken with disease, after they heard of the renown of the holy Symeon, hastened to him. They sought him out as a mediator to intercede in their behalf for healing before the all-good God. Now, on account of the great multitude that gathered, he gave to his disciples wooden staffs which he blessed. He instructed them to pray, while holding the blessed staffs over the sick. By this method, without climbing down the pillar, he cured the infirm and dispelled evil spirits. Lest his disciples should succumb to the vainglorious idea that they themselves were curing the sick, the saint directed that the staffs be returned after every third person was cured for another blessing. He would again entreat God's healing grace, resulting in cures of every disease. By invoking the name of God, he even saved people from the jaws of brutes. Furthermore, he was vouchsafed the gift of clairvoyance. In one case, he foretold the inroads of the Persians against Antioch.[10] He warned that Chosroes I (531-579), the Persian king, would be permitted to massacre the population because of their sins. By Symeon's supplication, their mountaintop monastery was enveloped by a cloud, so as to conceal it from the eyes of the approaching barbarians. He also cured a blind man who had been struck on the neck with a sword by a barbarian. Behold the wonderworking! In this latter instance, Symeon, taking water and dirt, fashioned a plaster over the wound and caused it to close and heal the gash at the same instant.

As a result of the wonders performed by the righteous man, numberless crowds of people came seeking him. They wanted him to ease their pains. Symeon, therefore, gave thought to leaving those parts in order to flee from the

---

[10] The Persian siege of 540.

commotion and tumult. By a divine vision, he was guided to the mountain that lay to the right side of his column. He summoned the brethren and appointed the most virtuous among them as their superior. After he climbed down from the pillar and uttered a prayer for their sakes, he asked their forgiveness and took leave of them. He set his path for the summit of the mountain that was revealed to him in the vision. At one point, he ascended a rock and prayed. It should be noted that he was thirty years old at that time. Now the very next day, many sick folk had gone to the pillar as had become the custom. However, learning that he had ascended the peak of the mountain, they sought him out there that they might be healed. The saint, at this juncture, was grieved because even there he could find no quietude. Nonetheless, he was moved to pity them. As tears flowed from their eyes, he laid his hands on their heads and cured them by the divine compassion working in him.

On the mountain whereon he was now sojourning, the righteous one worked a great number of miracles. One sick man, who was on his way to visit the saint, was rescued from the mouth of a lion; for Saint Symeon drove the beast from the mountain. He sent his disciple Anastasios to the den of the creature to cry out: "Thus says Symeon, the humble slave of God: 'In the name of the Lord, thou art to depart from this mountain and return hither no more!'" Other miracles of the blessed one include saving Antioch from a persistent plague (542). He also healed a possessed youth who was in peril from a snake bite. Symeon, furthermore, clothed the youth since he was naked. Saint Symeon announced the death of the Lakhmid al-Mundhir in 553.[11] Saint Symeon foretold the coming of a great earthquake at Antioch (557). He was concerned that the elite of Antioch were infected with paganism, Manichaeanism, belief in astrological gazing, and other heresies. He healed a man who was not only blind and paralyzed but also under the influence of three demons. In another case, a maiden was cured who suffered from a gangrenous foot. He restored to health a paralytic, a demonized woman, and a leper, asking nought else than the repentance of their sins and their return to keeping the commandments of God. He predicted that Justin II (November 565 to 578) would succeed his uncle, Justinian I. While he was on his pillar, he also foresaw the elevation of Maurice (582-602) to the empire. Evagrios confirms this about Symeon, saying, "While in the neighborhood of Theopolis (Antioch), Symeon, a most energetic man and distinguished by every divine virtue, both said and did many things which betokened Maurice's succession to the empire."[12]

[11] The pagan al-Mundhir (or Alamundarus, ca. 505-554) raided the Byzantine frontiers for almost half a century, both as a Persian client and as Lakmid king (an Arab dynasty that flourished in Hira on the lower Euphrates).

[12] Evagrius, *Ecclesiastical History*, Bk. V, Ch. XXI, p. 279.

As we said, the region in which the mountain was situated was desolate and arid, situated north of the Orontes. There were no caves in which people might take cover in the winter. Therefore, they built wooden huts for temporary shelter. Now the holy Symeon wore only a small mantle, while he abided on that rock exposed to the elements. Moreover, his visitors were often in extreme distress because of the lack of water and other essentials, as were the brethren who had gathered about him. Thus, the all-merciful God, knowing the needs of His slaves, enlightened the saint. He heard a divine voice saying, "Direct the brothers to build a monastery that they may find a little rest." When the holy Symeon heard this command, he watched an angel of the Lord lay out the plan and dimensions of the monastery and church. He followed the instructions of God and ordered his monks to begin construction. Those people who were benefitted by the saint's cures also remained and assisted in the building of the monastery, each one contributing according to his trade and skill. In fact, many came from Syria and other parts.

By reason of the increased number of visitors, together with the needs of the builders, the construction project required a good deal of water to mix with the unslaked lime. Therefore, the venerable one directed them to gather the white substance at one site. When this was accomplished, he besought God to rain down water. Behold the wonder! Two huge cisterns, constructed by idolaters of old, containing rocks and dirt, were cleaned out when torrential rains fell and filled them. Henceforth, whenever they needed water, abundant rain poured down from the sky; and there was enough to fulfill the needs of all. When they built the hostel, an unclean spirit caused a terrible earthquake. The walls shook and the structures wobbled, so that the stonemasons could not work. Then the saint said to one of the monks, "Strike the foundations with thy staff and repeat these words: 'Thus says Symeon, the slave of God: 'In the name of our Lord Jesus Christ, thou, O defiled spirit, shalt flee from this place!'" Straightway, after the monk executed what he was told to do—lo, the miracle!—the tremors ceased. Construction, straightway, proceeded to completion without further hindrance. They raised up a pillar along the side of the monastery. They also dug another cistern that there might always be an adequate water supply for the monastery.

Another miracle was performed over the Patriarch Ephraim's[13] servant, named Vingillios, who was totally paralyzed. They brought him to the venerable Symeon and begged him to have pity upon him. The righteous one addressed the ailing man and said, "If thou believest that the faith which thou hast in God can save thee, arise and walk!" Vingillios gave answer in a great voice, "O Lord Jesus Christ, I believe that Thou canst perform anything

[13] Patriarch Ephraim of Antioch (526-546).

through Thy slave Symeon!" Behold the miracle! He regained his health and leapt up. Standing upright, he glorified the Lord. The fame of the blessed Symeon reached as far away as Iberia. Many infirm people came to him and were cured. Indeed, some chose to remain in the holy Mandra of Symeon, completing their lives with God-pleasing works.

The sacred temple was also completed and dedicated in the name of the life-creating Holy Trinity, but the columns were in need of the stonecutter's tool. At that time, one of the brothers, named John, went to the righteous man. John knew nothing about hewing in stone, much less carving and dressing it, but said to the venerable elder, "Place thy holy hand upon my heart, O father, that God may endow me with knowledge that I may cut the marble." Then, in the name of the Lord, the righteous one prayed in John's behalf. Indeed—behold!—the word of the saint became deed; for just like another Beseleel in the days of Israel's tabernacle,[14] John worked diligently in the church. (As if this were not enough, Saint Symeon foresaw the repose of this monk.) Now when the columns were completed, at the third hour on the day of the Holy Spirit, that is, the day after Pentecost, the righteous one beheld Jesus Christ. Our Lord was arrayed as a hierarch, descending in the midst of a host of angels. He celebrated the Liturgy, on the column, with bread and wine, according to the order of our Church. After the office of Proskomide, He ascended into the heavens. Witnessing this mystery, Symeon desired all the more to ascend the pillar again. Therefore, he summoned the brethren together and, in all humility, made known the vision to them. He, consequently, ordered that they make that day a splendid holy day and feast. After this was done, the righteous man ascended his second pillar that was planted there on the Wonderful Mountain.[15] Symeon was then forty years of age.

---

[14] Ex. 31:1-5.

[15] Wonderful Mountain (*Thavmaston Oros*), now Saman Dagi in Turkey, was a pilgrimage complex of old that was built between 541 and 591. Wonderful is situated southwest of Antioch, standing prominently above the north bank of the Orontes River—a short distance before it flows into the Mediterranean. The port of Seleukeia (Selefkeia or Seleucia) Pieria lies to the west. The building of the complex took place in spurts, usually from spontaneous gestures of thanksgiving for cures wrought by the resident stylite—our Saint Symeon. The complex included the saint's pillar, the main church, hostels, and service buildings. Pilgrims participated in the construction from 541 to 551. Masons from Isauria also came. Between 551 and 591, a forge and cemetery church were added. The baptistry and circuit walls were built after 591. Some of the structures still remain, including the rock-cut base of the 50-foot column with staircase and its surrounding octagonal court. In the 10th C., the monastery was refounded by Greek and Georgian monks. The mountain was called the Mont Parlier by the Crusaders, who settled nearby at al-Mina at the mouth of the Orontes. The

(continued...)

A few days later, they brought to the holy one a three-year-old child named Epiphanios, who was in pain and in danger of dying from a stomach ailment. Our saint cured the child by the laying on of hands. In another incident, a certain priest named Thomas, who hailed from a village called Paradise, uttered blasphemies while under demonic inspiration. Although he was about to die, his soul would not depart. He lost his power of speech and was tormented for sixty days, unable to close his eyes. He finally acknowledged his sin and, by motioning with his hands, communicated to those around him, "Beg forgiveness in my behalf from the just Symeon, because I once anathematized him; and now I am being justly punished." Thomas' relatives conveyed the message to righteous Symeon who summoned one of his disciples and said to him, "Take one of these blessed loaves and go to Thomas the priest. When he kisses the bread, his sin shall be forgiven." Thus it came to pass; for when the priest kissed the bread, he received God's forgiveness and reposed.

There was another case involving a woman at Oreinee. She had just given birth to a child who was totally blind. The newborn's parents decided to bring their son to the saint in the hope that he might be cured. As they proceeded on their journey, passing through mountainous terrain, they stopped on the way to rest; for they were tired. Suddenly—lo, the miracle!—they observed that the child opened his eyes and had the ability to see. Therefore, they hastened to Saint Symeon and, in tears, related what had occurred. Indeed, the great boldness that he had before God delivered those in need according to the disposition and sincerity of their hearts. Saint Symeon also cured a woman who was possessed and separated from her husband, so that she returned to her spouse. Another woman, who for three years had an issue of blood, merely touched the saint's *rason* with reverence and faith; and she was cured of her hemorrhaging.

An epidemic visited the monks of Mandra Monastery. Many monks fell victim to the disease. Some died, while others languished. Among those who reposed was a certain Conon, whom our saint loved dearly. By his ardent prayer to the all-good God and to the most holy Theotokos, Symeon resurrected Conon by the grace of God. He also expelled the epidemic from the monastery. On another occasion, a certain priest, an Iberian, visited the righteous Symeon. They conversed for a long time, for which the priest was greatly edified. When he returned to his homeland, he constructed a church. On its cross, he placed the hairs of the saint. Numerous miracles were performed as a result, and many gifts were offered to the church. The other Iberian priests became envious of him and slandered him to the bishop, claiming he was a diviner and a deceiver of the people. As a result, the bishop deposed that poor priest. The innocent

[15](...continued)
Mamluks, in 1260, ruined the site. *Oxford,* s.v. "Wondrous Mountain."

priest now suffered a double misfortune. He, therefore, decided to invoke the holy Symeon. A demon then entered into the bishop and tormented him. The bishop perceived the reason and asked forgiveness of the priest. The latter brought the cross which had the righteous one's hairs bound to it, and the bishop was cured. He reinstated the priest to his rank.

So numerous were the miracles performed by the righteous one, that crowds thronged to his monastery just to receive a blessing from his hands. He was due to receive ordination to the priesthood, because he was still a deacon; but, out of humility, the blessed Symeon said that he was unworthy. However, by a divine vision he became convinced that it was the will of God that he receive the dignity of this office (as he was most worthy). The following day, Bishop Dionysios of Seleukeia came to the monastery. He ascended the pillar, greeted the saint, and said to him, "The Lord, Who knew thee from the womb, has ordained that thou shouldest become a presbyter." The holy one acquiesced to the pressure and accepted the ordination, though with great reluctance and humility. They entered the sanctuary. The bishop solemnly ordained to the priesthood one who was sanctified even before becoming a priest. At that time, the righteous one was forty-three years old.[16] The bishop, after he bade

---

[16] In the ancient editions of the long biographies of the righteous Symeon, it is mentioned that he reposed at the age of seventy-five. The Greek compilers of *The Great Synaxaristes* (in Greek) opine that this is an error, mentioning the *Synaxaria* of the *Menaion* and Nikodemos the Hagiorite who put his death at the age of eighty-five. Thus, the Greek compilers of *The Great Synaxaristes* (in Greek) adjusted the saint's age, so that he descended the first pillar at thirty and not twenty, and that he became a priest at forty-three and not thirty-three. This correction also alters the time of life that he ascended the first pillar, the 12-foot one by his elder the Hermit John.

The *Synaxaria* records that he forsook the world at the age of six, and that he spent six years at the monastery, followed by eighteen years on the first pillar. Next, it says that he spent ten years on a dry rock of the Wonderful Mountain. He, thereafter, ascended a pillar where he sojourned another forty-five years. They conclude that he was eighty-five at his repose.

The Greek compilers of the *Synaxaristes* maintain that he was ordained a deacon at twenty-two years of age. They acknowledge that, after he was ordained a deacon, he ascended the pillar for eight years—though they believe that he was living on the pillar prior to his ordination. Following this, they maintain that at thirty years of age, and not at twenty, he came down from his first pillar and went to the summit of the Wonderful Mountain. They agree with the *Synaxaria* that he lived ten years on that arid and roofless rocky outcrop. They believe that with the building of the monastery and a second pillar, he ascended it at the age of forty-three when he was also ordained to the priesthood. Thereafter, they hold that he sojourned atop that second pillar for the remainder of his life, that is, forty-five years, which they believe is close to the time of his death at eighty-five years old. They contend that he reposed in the

(continued...)

everyone peace and farewell, departed with joy. Afterward, the disciples of the righteous one asked the holy Symeon to celebrate the divine Liturgy, that he might bless them as was meet. He, however, possessed such ardent love for his much-desired Lord that he was hesitant to approach the Holies until it was revealed to him from on high in a vision. He was accounted worthy of such a vision wherein he beheld holy angels concelebrating, who said to him, "To whomsoever does not participate in the confession of this Faith, let him be anathema!" Upon being thus informed, he served the Liturgy and blessed everyone.[17]

New miracles were added to the old by the grace of our Lord Jesus Christ. He expelled a serpent from the stomach of a certain drunken Iberian as he slept. A maiden who was mute and paralyzed received, by his intercession, speech and motion. A father who was blind had his eyesight restored, by Symeon's word alone. Women who had no milk to nurse their children were cured. The barren were released from infertility. Those possessed during pregnancy were cured, together with their infant, at the supplication of the righteous one. A paralytic man from Antioch, an idolater, was persuaded to reject the idols and accept the Lord Christ, Son of God, and His ever-virgin Mother the Theotokos, and the doctrine of the Trinity. On yet another occasion, the righteous one washed his hands and, with that same water, anointed another sick man who was completely cured. With the pronouncement of a contrite prayer, he resurrected one who was dead. He continued to drive out demons from the possessed. He healed the deaf, disabled, and paralytics, and those nigh unto death. Innumerable were the miracles, O brethren, which the righteous one performed through the loving-kindness of God. If we attempted to describe them all, time would overtake us. However, we shall relate one more miracle, trusting in your goodness, that you will believe that our righteous Father Symeon of the Wonderful Mountain possessed the gift of foresight.

---

[16](...continued)
year 595.

The Greek compilers of the *Synaxaristes* wrestle with the original text regarding his age. If, as it is written, he descended the first pillar at twenty, after spending eight years as a deacon, he was just entering puberty when he was ordained. They point out, however, that the *Synaxaria* says he spent eighteen years on that first pillar, so he could not have descended it at the age of twenty. It is for this reason that they justify themselves for adjusting his age to thirty instead of keeping twenty as it is written in the original text. Taken from note 1, pp. 587, 588, of *The Great Synaxaristes* (in Greek), 5th ed., s.v. "May 24th."

[17] Elsewhere, we read that Symeon, as a priest, offered the holy sacrifice in memory of his mother. On such occasions his disciples, one after another, climbed up the ladder to receive Communion at his hands. *Catholic Encyclopedia*, loc. cit.

There was a saintly monk who had immured himself in a house at Laodikeia of Syria for many years. He practised silence but wearied of it. He, therefore, sent a message to the righteous Symeon, saying that he wished to visit and venerate him. The holy one knew the monk's condition by foresight. He wrote to him in reply that it was not proper for him to abandon his quietude at Laodikeia in order to pay his respects to a sinful man. Symeon recommended that it would be better to pay homage to God in his own house. The monk practised patience for a little while longer. Not before long, however, he was troubled by his thoughts. He could endure no longer, so he abandoned his cell. Moreover, by demonic complicity, he fell into fornication. Then he went to the righteous Symeon, but he did not confess his sin. He was too ashamed, so he affected sadness because he had scorned his solitude. The saint, however, knew things that were hidden. In order to bring the solitary to repentance and save him—and that Symeon's disciples might receive a lesson and be cautions—he revealed this sin of the monk before all and said, "I do not judge thee, because thou hast torn down the wall of thy cell; for thou canst easily repair it and enclose thyself therein as before. But I do sorrow for thee on account of thy fornication, whereby thou hast demolished the tower of thy soul and hast become—alas!—a captive of the devil!" When the monk heard his secret sin divulged he marvelled and, at the same time, felt shame. He fell to the ground and wept. He confessed his transgression and begged for forgiveness. The holy Symeon armed him with the seal of the Cross, rendering him invulnerable thenceforth against the devil. After he blessed him, he sent him to his cell in Laodikeia.[18]

Now because the Elder Symeon was a mortal man, the time came for him to go to the One Whom he desired. At the time, he was eighty-five years old. He had spent forty-five years atop the second pillar on the Wonderful Mountain, below which the monastery named Mandra was situated. [When the Service for the Lesser Blessing of Holy Water is conducted, he is invoked as "Symeon at the Mandra," elsewhere he is mentioned as "Symeon of the Wonderful Mountain," but of course these both refer to one and the same Symeon.] When it was revealed to him by the Holy Spirit that he had come to the end of his earthly sojourn, he called his disciples to himself and disclosed the matter. Although these doleful tidings saddened them, yet his imminent departure was sweet and most desirable for him. He addressed them as follows:

"Brethren and fathers: Pray ceaselessly. Be humble of heart. Despise avarice and be mindful of the poor as much as possible. He who does not give

---

[18] Evagrius, *Ecclesiastical History* was an eyewitness to many wonderworkings. He, too, assures the reader that he had experienced Symeon's knowledge of the thoughts of others in himself, when he visited him for spiritual advice. He declares that Symeon lived only upon the branches of a shrub that grew near Theopolis.

alms to the poor shall not enter the bridal chamber with the wise virgins, but rather will be shut out with the foolish ones, because his lamp has gone out for lack of oil.[19] He who does not have pity for his brother and does not help him in his need, denies the Son of God. Such a one does not confess the resurrection of the dead, and is like unto the Sadducees, not believing in the future retribution. Guard yourselves also with self-control and temperance, for such will keep reins on the passions and still the conflicts of the flesh, thereby enabling one to attain prudence. If an unclean thought should enter thy mind, cry to the Lord with the bitterest tears, 'O Master Christ, God of many tender and compassionate mercies: Thou wast before all ages and shalt always be. Thou dost not put to shame them that hope in Thee. Do Thou rescue me from the hands of my enemies. Lay hold of my soul and save me in Thy mercy. O my rejoicing, deliver me from them that compass me round about. O Lord, my Lord, the strength of my salvation, overshadow me in the time of war. Have mercy on me, O God, and come unto my aid, O God!' With such utterances and like expressions shall one make when troubled by unclean thoughts. In such a manner, with a contrite heart, shall the one who is harassed by filthy thoughts pray to God. And indeed, the Lord shall rescue him."

This advice and many other admonitions and exhortations were imparted by the righteous Symeon to his disciples. They were desirous to ask him how he acquired such a degree of abstinence; but, out of respect, they hesitated to do so. He, however, knew this thought that plagued them. He revealed the answer to them in his last hour. He did this so as to strengthen them, as would a compassionate father, that they might place their hope in God. He said, "I, my brethren, have received many and great benefactions from my Master; but the greatest gift I have received is the one which I am about to disclose to you. It is many years now that I have besought God to exempt me from having to partake of physical food." He then broke off a moment and gazed heavenward, saying, "Is it possible, O Christ, to describe the mercy and love that Thou hast shown to me, Thine unworthy servant?" He then turned to his disciples and continued: "I beheld a fair Youth, arrayed in priestly vesture, or shall I say garments of light. He was bearing in His hand a sacred vessel, from which He drew forth three types of food with a spoon. What type of food it was, I know not. But, in taste and appearance, it was exceedingly sweet—so much so that I cannot describe it. Every Sunday, after the divine Liturgy, and to this day, He would come and bring this divine ration. It filled my heart to plenitude and sustained me until the following Sunday. In the interim, I was no longer hungry. This, indeed, is the only secret I have withheld from you. You must live virtuously. Continue conducting yourselves

[19] Cf. Mt. 25:1 ff.

in the days to come as though I were present, that each one may receive according to his works." And with such words, the blessed one counseled his disciples to his last breath.

Ten days after this, on the 24th of May (592), the blessed Symeon went forth to Christ, Whom he desired, to enjoy the indescribable good things prepared by Christ for him and for those who love Him, the Fashioner and Master of all. Now when it was learned that Symeon was taken ill, Patriarch Gregory I of Antioch (571-594) was informed. Since the stylite was at the point of death, the patriarch went in all haste to assist at his last moments; but, before he arrived, Saint Symeon had already departed to the Lord. Evagrios mentioned this episode, writing: "At this time, when the sainted Symeon was afflicted with a mortal disease, Gregory, on being informed by me of the circumstance, hastened to salute him for the last time; but he was nevertheless disappointed. This Symeon far surpassed all his contemporaries in virtue, and endured the discipline of a life on the top of a column from his earliest years, since he even cast his teeth in that situation.[20]...And on this column, and on another, towering above the summit of the mountain, he spent sixty-eight years. He, thereby, attained the highest gifts of grace: in respect of the ejection of demons; the healing of every disease and malady; and the foresight of future things as if they were present. He also foretold to Gregory that the latter would not witness his death; Symeon also said that he was ignorant of the events pertaining to Gregory which should follow it.

"On an occasion when I was deeply pondering the cause," continues Evagrios, "on the loss of my children, I was perplexed with this suggestion: Why do not such things befall heathens who had numerous offspring? Although I had not disclosed my thoughts to anyone, still Father Symeon wrote advising me to abandon such notions as being displeasing to God.

"In the case of the wife of one of my amanuenses, when the milk would not flow after childbirth and the infant was in extreme danger, Symeon was consulted. He lay his hand upon the right hand of her husband. Symeon bid him

[20] It is Symeon himself who, in a letter to Thomas (the guardian of the true Cross at Jerusalem), writes that while living upon the pillar (from the age of seven), he lost his first baby teeth. He maintained this kind of life for sixty-eight years. *The Catholic Encyclopaedia*, s.v. "Saint Simeon Stylites the Younger," suggests reading the long Life of Saint Symeon the Younger by Nikephoros of Antioch, as well as the Life of Saint Martha. All these have been printed by the Bollandists, *Acta SS.*, May, V, 296-431; fragments of a biography by Arkadios have been published by Papadopulos Kerameus in *Vivantisky Vremennik* (1894), 141-150 and 601-604. See also Allatius, *De Simeonum scriptis* (Paris, 1864), 17-22; Krumbacher, *Gesch. der Byzant. Litt.* (2nd ed., Munich, 1897), 144-145 and 671; Philotesia P. Kleinert zum 70 Geburtstag (Leipzig, 1907).

place it upon the breasts of his wife. When this was done, immediately the milk flowed, as if from a fountain, so as to saturate her dress.

"Now a child had been forgotten in the dead of night by his fellow travelers. A lion took the child on its back, and conveyed it to the monastery. Then, by the orders of Symeon, the servants went out and brought in the child under the protection of the lion.

"Many other actions were performed by him, surpassing everything that has been recorded. These anecdotes demand of an historian elegance of language, leisure, and a separate treatise....For persons came to visit him from almost every part of the earth, not only Romans but also barbarians. They all obtained the object of their prayers."[21]

Saint Symeon's honorable and venerable relics remained in the Mandra on the Wonderful Mountain, the site of his wonderful struggles. His relics are a repository of unceasing miracles that spring forth not only for the body but also for the soul, in Christ Jesus our Lord to Whom be all glory, honor, and homage to the ages. Amen.

On the 24th of May, the holy Church commemorates the holy Martyr MELETIUS Stratelates (the General) and those with him: Martyrs JOHN, STEPHEN, SERAPION the Egyptian, CALLINICUS the Magician, and the TWELVE TRIBUNES; the holy women Martyrs MARCIANE, PALLADIA, and SOSSANA (SUSANNA); the two children, CYRIACUS and CHRISTIAN; and 11,208 MARTYRS.[22]

Meletius, the glorious general and martyr of Christ, and those with him, hailed from Rome. He contested for Christ during the reign of Emperor Antoninus (138-161), and when Maximus was governor of Rome. His martyrdom took place as follows. Once, the holy general and his handpicked Christian soldiers, having angels as co-workers, went to the temple of the idolaters. By the lever of Meletius' prayer, the temple was toppled and the idols

---

[21] Evagrius, *Ecclesiastical History*, Bk. VI, Ch. XXIII, pp. 312, 313.

[22] The Greek compilers of *The Great Synaxaristes* (in Greek) point out that Nikodemos the Hagiorite lists the martyrdom of Saint Meletius and those with him during the reign of Emperor Anthony the Heliogabalus or Elagabalus (218-222). They are certain, however, that this date is erroneous, and that Emperor Antoninus Pius was meant. Regarding where the martyrdom took place, Sophronios Efstratiades [*Hagiologion tes Orthodoxou Ekklesias* (Athens, 1960), p. 331] records that these saints suffered martyrdom in Rome. However, the latest, in Greek, *Religious and Ethics Encyclopedia* (vol. 8, p. 926), records that they were martyred in Tavium of Galatia.

were rendered into clouds of dust. Governor Maximus was informed of the destruction and sent his men to arrest Meletius and his company. The Christian soldiers were led before the governor who incited them to sacrifice to the idols. Refusing to comply, the Christians suffered a thrashing with dry switches for many hours. Afterward, Christ's soldiers received cruel injuries to their ankles by iron hammers and the nailing of their feet to wood. As this gruesome trial was carried out, the Christian men had their minds only riveted upon the Lord. Thus, they did not feel the pain of their wounds. The executioners then dug into the prisoners' sides with iron hooks and struck their foreheads. Later, from the blows received to their holy foreheads, their wounds formed the sign of the Cross. Now these and many other heinous tortures were administered to these blessed and valiant men, which eventually ushered in their deaths. Hence, 11,208 Christian soldiers wrestled and wounded the invisible hordes of demons, setting up glorious trophies over their foes. The holy martyrs Stephen and John, who were with Meletius, were then beheaded. However, Saint Meletius was finally put to death when they suspended that blessed man from a pine tree.

Saint Meletius

Now a man named Serapion, an Egyptian, witnessed the wondrous martyrdoms of Saint Meletius and his men. Serapion came to believe in Christ and received holy Baptism. By means of a divine angel, he was later ordained to the episcopate.

It also happened that the magician Callinicus came to confess Jesus Christ. Indeed, he previously prepared a fatal concoction for Saint Meletius. However, through his magical arts and poisons, he was unable to slay that holy man of God. When Governor Maximus learned of the sorcerer's conversion, he sentenced both Callinicus and the holy Serapion to have their heads struck off.

Meanwhile, the holy Festus, Faustus, Marcellus, Theodore, another Meletius, Sergius, Marcellinus, Felix, Photinus, Theodoriscus, Mercurios and Didymus—of whom some were commanders, tribunes, and princes—also observed the wonders wrought by Saint Meletius. Hence, they came to believe in Christ. Due to their confession of Faith, there were, at the governor's command, cast into a lit furnace. These ever-memorable ones received their crowns of martyrdom.

Saint Christian

The holy Martyrs Sossana, Marciane, and Palladia were the wives of three of these courageous men. Now the governor ordered the massacre of these women, together with their infant children, by means of wooden instruments of punishment. After the soldiers meted out death-dealing blows to the women—O the wonder!—straightway, the executioners died, receiving an exceedingly evil end.

Following close upon this carnage, the governor questioned two very small children. Cyriacus and Christian were asked, "Who is the greater god, Zeus or Christ?" Then out of the mouths of those grace-filled babes came the godly-wise answer. They declared firmly, "Christ." Forthwith, the governor charged that the two minors be dispatched by decapitation. Thus, Cyriacus and Christian also received crowns of the contest.

The synaxis (liturgical gathering) and feast of these holy martyrs were celebrated in the Church of the Holy Martyr Platon, found in the courtyards of Domninos in Constantinople.

On the 24th of May, the holy Church commemorates our holy Father VINCENT of Lerins (450).

On the 24th of May, the holy Church commemorates the venerable NIKETAS the Stylite and Wonder-worker of Pereyaslavl (12th C.).

Through the intercessions of Thy Saints,
O Christ God, have mercy on us. Amen.

On the 25th of May, the holy Church commemorates the Third Finding of the honorable Head of the glorious prophet, forerunner, and Baptist JOHN.[1]

John, the holy and glorious prophet, precursor, and Baptist, is celebrated today with reference to his honorable head that was cut off by means of a girl's voluptuous dance and a sword. There were other revelations of this precious relic, for which its first and second finding is commemorated by the holy Church on the 24th of February. The third discovery was made at Comana of Cappadocia. The relic was entrusted to the bosom of the earth until there passed the destructive days of the iconoclasts in the eighth century. During that terrible time, some Orthodox Christians took away the sacred head of Saint John the Forerunner from Constantinople. They escaped, with the precious

[1] For the Feast of the Third Finding of the Honorable Head of the Forerunner an encomium was written by Saint Theodore the Stoudite (b. 759-826), the text of which is found at the Athonite monasteries of the Great Lavra and Dionysiou. Within his composition, he refers to the relic that either the entire head or a portion was residing in his Monastery of Stoudios, which was dedicated to Saint John the Baptist. This encomium begins, "A third indication of the Forerunner's memory...." It is extant at the Athonite monasteries of Vatopedi and Iveron. Another elegant work that was penned in honor of this feast was by the sacred teacher and preacher of the Great Church, Makarios Christianopoulos. His manuscript begins: "'Out of the seed of the serpent [Is. 14:29],' says Esaias...." This work was printed by Nicholas Glykeos, being incorporated into the publication *Christopanygyrikon* (Venice, 1783).

relic, to Comana of Cappadocia, where the exiled Saint John Chrysostom had earlier reposed in 407. The precious head of the Forerunner John, after it was reverently housed in a silver vessel, was committed to the ground for safekeeping. It was not found until the reign of Emperor Michael (842-867), son of Theophilos (829-842) and the pious Augusta Theodora (842-856). This was a time when veneration of the icons had been restored by the empress. The relic was miraculously revealed to Patriarch Ignatios (847-858 and 867-877), while he was at his evening prayers. He informed the imperium, which resulted in a delegation dispatched to Comana. It was uncovered by a certain Orthodox priest. Thus was the relic recovered and returned to the imperial city (ca. 850) by the patriarch.

The hymnographer for today's feast, Tarasios, gives us more details of the discovery and triumphal return. He tells us that we draw grace and sanctification from the Forerunner's head, which is brighter than the sun. The head was made known to a priest of the Lord, named Basil, who till then knew nothing of its whereabouts in Comana. Filled with faith and led by grace, he made a diligent search for the head. When it arose from the bowels of the earth, he made its finding known.[2] The gleaming relic poured forth gifts of healing. Its discovery was like gold extracted from a mine, since it flashed forth rays from the earth.[3] The fragrant relic, a wellspring of cures, was met by Basil the priest and the faithful who had gathered to the site.[4]

Thus, from Comana to the queen of cities did the Forerunner travel. The emperor delighted more in the Forerunner's coming than in his porphyry robe; and so he eagerly welcomed him. The divine priest and foremost of shepherds, the namesake of the God-bearer, Patriarch Ignatios, stretched forth his hands and embraced the head to his breast. He, most solemnly, blessed himself and the faithful.[5]

There were reports of ever-flowing gifts that were bestowed by Saint John: bodily pangs and diseases were taken away.[6] Both the Priest Basil and the chief shepherd Ignatios were divinely informed beforehand of the head's discovery.[7] While the head flashed brighter than gold, it was treasured in a silver vessel upon discovery.

The hymnographer says that the emperor, the angel's namesake (Michael), rejoiced and received the Forerunner in his palace. The chief shepherd, bearing the name of the sacred God-bearer (Ignatios), piously and

---

[2] May 25th, Vespers Stichera, Mode Plagal Four; Doxastikon, Mode Plagal Two.
[3] May 25th, Vespers Aposticha, Mode Two.
[4] May 25th, Orthros Canon, Odes Three and Four, Mode Plagal Four, by Tarasios.
[5] May 25th, Orthros Canon, Odes Five and Eight.
[6] May 25th, Orthros Canon, Oikos.
[7] May 25th, Orthros Canon, Ode Seven.

excellently ministered in his service toward the precious head.[8] We, too, revere that hallowed head that not only proclaimed the Lamb of God but also washed in the waters of Jordan the head of Jesus.

The Third Finding of the Honorable Head of the Forerunner

On the 25th of May, the holy Church commemorates the holy Martyr CELESTINE who had his heels pierced with iron.

On the 25th of May, the holy Church commemorates the venerable OLVIANOS who reposed in peace.

Through the intercessions of Thy Saints,
O Christ God, have mercy on us. Amen.

[8] May 25th, Orthros Canon, Ode Nine.

On the 26th of May, the holy Church commemorates the holy and glorious Apostle KARPOS (Carpus).

Saint Karpos

Karpos, the apostle of the Lord, flourished during the reign of Nero (54-68). Karpos is numbered among the apostles and disciples of the Seventy [Lk. 10:1], commemorated on the 4th of January. We read in Saint Paul's epistle to Saint Timothy: "When thou comest bring thou the cloak which I left behind in Troas with Karpos, and the books, especially the parchments [2 Tim. 4:13]."[1] Karpos taught many idolaters and brought them to reverence of Christ. He, afterward, became Bishop of Beroe or Verea (Stara Zagora) of Thrace.[2] He enlightened the benighted minds of the inhabitants by the Holy Spirit. This luminary appeared as a free-lance and never-setting star, rising out of the east and shining throughout the inhabited world with the illumination of his divine teachings and the beams of his words.

Karpos performed great miracles and drove out wicked demons from men. There were many cities and peoples whom he attracted to the Faith of Jesus Christ. By holy Baptism he separated the faithful from the unbelievers. On account of all these missionary activities, he incurred temptations, tribulations, and afflictions at the hands of the heathen. Throughout all his trials, he proved valiant and persevering. He did not shrink before the anger and wrath of the tyrants. Since he glorified God in all his works, God also glorified him. Having borne fruits pleasing to God, Karpos—the namesake of fruit—reposed in the Lord, in that sweet and seemly sleep of the saints. Even

---

[1] Troas, a city of Mysia, is south of ancient Troy and opposite the island of Tenedos. It was the chief port between Macedonia and Asia Minor. This was where Saint Paul saw the vision of the man of Macedonia beseeching, "Pass over into Macedonia and help us [Acts 16:9]."

[2] Nikodemos the Hagiorite, in his *Synaxaristes*, records Varne of Thrace. Verea, also written as Beroe or Beroea, of Thrace, is the present-day Bulgarian city of Stara Zagora.

after death, through his relics, Karpos continues to work wonders in every place and at all times. For those who call upon him in faith, he has dispelled maladies, sufferings, and foul spirits.

On the 26th of May, the holy Church commemorates the holy Apostle ALPHAEOS, who reposed in peace.[3]

On the 26th of May, the holy Church commemorates the holy Martyr AVERKIOS, son of the Apostle Alphaeos, who was stretched out naked in an apiary and stung to death by bees.

On the 26th of May, the holy Church commemorates the holy Martyr HELEN, the sister of Saint Averkios, who was stoned to death.

On the 26th of May, the holy Church commemorates the holy New-martyr ALEXANDER the Thessalonian, a former dervish, who was beheaded at Smyrna (1794).[4]

Alexander, the holy new-martyr, hailed from the great city of Thessalonike. He parents dwelt at Monasterion of Laodegia, which is called Lagodiani. The parents, seeing that Alexander was young and handsome of countenance, thought it impossible that their son could avoid falling into temptation, that is, the snare of carnality. The Hagarenes, according to their usual tyrannical mode of conduct that they exercised over that city, were likely to target their son. Indeed, already, there was a Turk who would do violence to their son and molest him. The parents desired to spare their son from such perversity and depravity. Thus, they were constrained, even as the mother later testified, to take flight. The family repaired to Smyrna,[5] which city they

---

[3] Alphaeos, the apostle of the Lord, is called the Logos' divine mouth in the couplet verses (*distichon*). His identity is not generally known in the Church Militant. Nikodemos the Hagiorite conjectures that he is Iakovos of Alphaeos (see the 9th of October), one of the Twelve, and brother of the Evangelist Matthew. Sophronios Efstratiades [*Hagiologion*, p. 30] represents the three commemorated today—Alphaeos, Averkios, and Helen—as the children of the Apostle Jude (19th of June).

[4] The martyrdom of New-martyr Alexander was taken from Nikodemos the Hagiorite's *Neon Martyrologion*, 3rd ed. (pp. 217-221), and incorporated into *The Great Synaxaristes* (in Greek).

[5] Smyrna, a principal port of the Ottomans, was a prosperous and robust center of international trade on the west coast of Asia Minor. It maintained a large traffic with France and Great Britain, and was considered by many to be the first city, and certainly one of the largest and richest, for commerce in the Levant. Its exports were cottons,

(continued...)

thought to be a safe haven. In reality, however, they fled the serpent and stumbled upon the dragon. Alexander avoided the smaller peril to his virtue only to be cast down headlong from the precipice of utter destruction. This came about when Alexander disowned upon oath the religion of his fathers and became a Muslim. We do not know if his abjuration was the result of force or deceit. They say that Alexander was working for a Turkish agha[6] who guilefully entrapped the youth's simple soul—alas!—into impiety. After a little time, he left that agha and wandered about. He arrived in Mecca, where the tomb of Mohammed was found. We know he went there because he later admitted it before a Turkish judge (mullah),[7] when he scorned and mocked their polluted and bloodstained religion.

After his pilgrimage to Mecca, he passed through cities and lands. He was clad in the dress of a dervish.[8] It seems, however, that he in no wise committed any further wicked practises that could either burden his conscience or befoul his soul. He was, nevertheless, feeling the vivid pangs of rebuke from his holy conscience. Not much time passed before his mind began to conceive the idea of undergoing martyrdom, so that with blood he might wipe away his lawlessness. This thought contained him and afforded him some self-possession, as he walked hither and thither with much pusillanimity and a grave look. While he was thought to be in possession of his faculties, he also feigned

---

[5](...continued)
wools, silks, rugs, tobacco, raisins, figs, and various natural products. Smyrna, from the early 17th C. until 1825, was the chief provincial factory of the British Turkey Company, as well as French, Dutch, and other trading companies. Half the population was Greek.

[6] An agha (aga) was a title of respect for a man in authority. He was also either a military or a civil officer in the Ottoman Empire.

[7] The mullah (mollah) was considered a learned Muslim teacher who expounded upon the religious law and doctrine of Islam.

[8] The dervishes, first established in the 12th C ., were a Muslim fraternity. The main ritual practised by the dervish is the *dhikr*, which involves the repeated recitation of a devotional formula in praise of Allah as a means of attaining an ecstatic experience. The rituals of the Sufi brotherhoods stress the dervishes' attainment of hypnotic states and ecstatic trances through ritual recitation and through such physical exertions as whirling and dancing. A wandering or mendicant dervish is called a *fakir* (*faqir*). A ritual dance was instituted in the Sufi mystical order of the Mawlawiyah (Mevleviyah) in Turkey. The dance performed by dervishes is considered to be a manifestation of mystical ecstasy. *Encyclopaedia Britannica Deluxe Edition 2004 CD-ROM*, s.v. "Dervish." The traditional whirling dervish costume is made up of five pieces. A robe with the "whirling skirt" is the main portion of the outfit. The bottom of the skirt is weighted to produce the spinning effect. A pair of pants is worn under the skirt. There is a matching vest. A belt is worn, as well as a tall hat.

madness. When he was in such a state, he spoke against the Hagarenes. He did not hesitate in reproving them sharply for committing their many wrongs, crimes, and outrages. He charged them with acting as tyrants over a poor slave whom God subjected to them so as to govern and not to degrade him. He accused the Turks of not reckoning all men as creatures of the one God.

Such protestations were voiced by other dervishes as well. But it was Alexander, the future holy new-martyr, who expressed his words with a pronounced and strange boldness before which the Turks were unaccustomed. In fact, ofttimes, his rebukes moved them to wrath against him. At Rashid in Egypt,[9] there were some Muslims (of whom a number were Turks out of Crete), that had become so vexed with him that they plotted to slay him. They agreed among themselves that the dervish could not possibly be a Turk; much rather, they said that "he is a Christian, albeit in disguise." Meanwhile, Alexander learned of their murderous intent and departed from there. Such a swift death he did not adjudge to be congruous—either as a fitting penalty for his past denial or a becoming end as a witness for Christianity. Nay, to his mind, such an end was neither consistent with the profession of the Faith he hoped to make publicly nor adequate punishment for his crime. It was not sufficiently severe to purge his sin and reconcile his conscience. Now the reason they suspected that the dervish was a Christian in sentiment was due to what they witnessed with their own eyes. The dervish frequently met and conversed with Christians. His manner with them was gentle and even sweet. On those occasions when he met privately with Christians, he was wont to say in an enigmatic way that "One is Three, and the Three One." He spoke candidly with them, uttering even more mystifying expressions, in particular to a man named Panagiotes of Zagora. In the latter's mind, he was certain that the dervish was a Christian. By and by, Alexander left Egypt. He was bound for his homeland, Thessalonike, where he was unknown. This took place some ten years before his actual martyrdom. From Thessalonike, he traveled about from place to place for a number of years. He finally arrived on the island of Chios, the year when he would undergo martyrdom. He disembarked from his ship during the Great Fast. He betook himself to a certain church where he offered up prayer. He waited for the divine office to commence. This was later attested to by the parish priest of that church. Then, one day, he again began bitterly convicting

Saint Alexander

[9] Rashid (31°24′N 30°24′E).

the Turks. A certain Christian man of Chios, of the old aristocracy, who happened to be near, took himself far away, as fast as he could, fearing repercussions.

It appears that despite all that he met with and suffered, the blessed Alexander, garbed as a dervish, found a way to teach the Turks moderation, temperance, philanthropy, and every other moral excellence. Though he masqueraded as a dervish for religious Muslim eyes, he was an example to them. He discoursed with them on humility, toleration, non-possessiveness, and other virtues of self-denial. He also had no wish to impose himself and seek money from the wealthy, as was the custom with dervishes. Nay, he rather chose to labor at whatever employment he could secure for his daily bread. He took on the form of a dervish for eighteen years. After this period, he set off from Chios, still wearing his dervish outfit, and went to Smyrna. The would-be new-martyr heard the grace of God speaking mystically from within his gentle heart, revealing to him that the hour had come for him to present himself and finish what he had contemplated for himself many years earlier.

He, undoubtedly, had a spiritual father under whose discerning direction he entered into such a great stadium. It was, therefore, on the Tuesday of the week prior to the Feast of the holy Pentecost that Alexander armed himself well by the power of the honorable Cross; for by the Cross came salvation to the world and us. Alexander went to the city judge and addressed him very boldly, saying, "O mullah, I was a Christian. But from want of understanding, I denied my Faith and became a Turk. I, afterward, perceived that my first Faith, which I lost, is the true light. I understood that your religion, as I have come to know it, is verily darkness. I am come today, therefore, to confess that I erred in forsaking the light and accepting the darkness. So, as I was born a Christian, it is as a Christian that I wish to die. Behold, O mullah, thou hast heard my decision! Now do to me whatsoever thou dost wish, because I am ready to withstand every torment and even to spill my blood for the love of my Jesus Christ Whom I had so badly renounced." After Alexander made these statements openly, he removed the tall dervish hat from his head. He tossed it before the judge and declared, "Behold the sign of your religion!" In its place he fitted, with some deliberateness, the head-covering donned by Christians.

One can well imagine how much malice overwhelmed the boastful and proud heart of that powerful man of rank and influence. In fact, both he and all who were found in the court were beside themselves in their collective wrath and indignation. The unexpected spectacle of seeing a dervish, one of their holy men, professing himself to be a Christian was insufferable. Furthermore, to hear him openly and confidently despising Mohammedanism, and rejecting their baseless beliefs, and turning up his nose at their unholy religion, was beyond their endurance. Nevertheless, since it was compulsory to give an answer, the judge and the others present said with much consternation, "What are these unanticipated effusions? Hast thou lost thy wits? Dost thou, who art a dervish, a member of an Islamic religious fraternity, utter such words to the shame of thy faith and thy high repute?" Christ's witness, nonetheless, answered most wisely: "In truth, I had lost my wits; and it is now that I have come to myself. I confess openly my iniquity. You say, because I am a dervish, why do I speak such things as I do? Verily, I speak the truth. I have gone to Mecca.[10] I have examined Islam. I have found it all hateful and to be a lie and a blasphemy." These words and many others did the martyr assert with much freedom of speech. The bystanders, hearing his annunciations, responded with strong feeling and passion. In their fury they said, "He is drunk; that is why he speaks as he does." At this point, the judge gave orders to have him thrown into jail until the dark cloud of intoxication should pass.

The following day, which was Wednesday, the judge ordered that the detainee be brought forward for a second examination. The martyr, spending the night in jail, summoned all his courage. He confessed before all that Jesus Christ is true God. He, in addition, with even greater daring, sneered and reviled their religion, to the horrified astonishment of all the Muslims present. At first, the Muslims threatened him. After this attack, despite the fact that he nettled the Muslims, they put aside their vexation. With flattery they hoped to alter his resolve. It was not that any of them cared to gain his life. It was more so that they did not relish enduring to the end the shame he heaped upon them. They thought to beguile him when they began to say, "Dost thou not pity thy life, O man? Dost thou not pity thy youth? Only ask for whatsoever thou dost wish, whether it be money or raiment or some other desire—only cease speaking such fooleries." But the blessed Alexander would not give way.

[10] The martyr, according to Nikodemos the Hagiorite, actually said "Kaaba" ("Ka'bah"), signifying he made a pilgrimage to Mecca. In the center of the Great Mosque in Mecca is a cube-shaped stone building, called the Kaaba or the Black Stone of Kaaba since it is made from the granite of the surrounding hills. The Muslims believe that Abraham and his son Ishmael built it. The pilgrimage is part of "The Five Pillars of Islam," that is, (1) *Shahada*—declaration of faith; (2) *Salah*—formal prayer; (3) *Zakat*—almsgiving or charity; (4) *Sawm*—fasting during Ramadan; and, (5) *Hajj*—pilgrimage to Mecca. Pilgrims enter the open-air mosque and walk around the Kaaba seven times in a counter-clockwise direction. Following this, they walk seven times along a corridor in the Great Mosque. This ritual recreates the search for water by Hagar. In the next stage of the *Hajj*, pilgrims leave Mecca for the desert as they travel toward the sprawling tent city of Mina. They throw stones at three pillars, representing the devil. Men shave their heads and women cut locks of their hair. Pilgrims sacrifice animals, or pay people to sacrifice animals for them. Then they make a trip to Mecca for another walk. The pilgrims then return to Mina, stoning the pillars each day, and then return again to Mecca for one last turn.

Neither did their threats frighten him nor did their blandishments make him flaccid or fill him with conceit. He answered them wonderfully and resolutely, saying, "O mindless ones, why do you threaten me with death? For that very reason I am come here, in order to die for the love of my most sweet Jesus Christ. Why, O foolish ones, do you diligently strive to convert my steadfast decision with wily and worthless promises? I believe there is only one true and full happiness for me: to die for the holy Faith, the one which I for ill denied; and to depart from this false life that I might gain the other, the true and everlasting one. I was born a Christian, and I want to die a Christian. This is what I desire; for this I thirst and for this I am come here."

The martyr was again jailed. He remained there until Friday of that same week. As it is known, the Ottomans esteem Friday greatly as a solemn day. For this reason, they have the custom of congregating on Fridays. The aghas and notables meet at the court in each city. From that location, they proceed all together to the mosque. There, either because of such a habit in the Muslim community or because the rumor circulated that a dervish presented himself before the mullah as a Christian—an event which ushered in deep reproach and embarrassment upon the name of Mohammed—on that Friday, all the aghas and eminent men of Smyrna met at the mullah's court. Since the man parading as a dervish gained much notoriety among the Muslims, no small number of common folk converged there upon learning this intelligence. The martyr was then led from the jail and brought to the court for a third examination. This proved to be the third opportunity for Alexander to confess his faith in the Holy Trinity, which belief he previously denied without taking thought. On this third occasion, more than before, Alexander displayed fuller assurance and divine favor for his love of God. They asked him again, "Hast thou come to thy senses from the previous hearing?" The stalwart athlete of Christ answered, "I was in possession of my wits then as I am now, with the grace of my Christ. Moreover, I have told you—and I repeat again and again—that I was born a Christian, and I want to die a Christian. I am not going to exchange the light for the darkness. Indeed, I revere Father, Son, and Holy Spirit: Trinity coessential and undivided." Professing himself in this manner, he made the sign of the honorable Cross over himself. The Hagarenes, at that moment, perceived the immovability of his holy soul. His declarations got short shrift from the Muslims. They utterly despaired of any other method of persuasion. It was the universal opinion among the Muslims that this abuser of Mohammedanism be put to death without delay. Consequently, the judge issued a written order that Alexander be executed by the sword.

Alexander, the brave contestant of Christ, was escorted by the bailiffs to the execution site. His hands were fettered, even as is the custom with the condemned. On his way to the block, the imams[11] and hodjas[12] did not refrain from imposing their last unsolicited counsels. With such attempts, they persisted artfully in their attempts to draw away the martyr to their way of thinking. But the happy Alexander gave their soul-destroying admonitions no consequence. His mind was riveted to Christ and to that blessed end. His response was the same: "A Christian I am; and as a Christian I want to die." So he spoke repeatedly. O blessed voice! O brave endurance! O soul aflame with divine love! There appeared at that extraordinary public execution a numberless crowd of onlookers, not only of Turks but also of Greeks, Franks, and Armenians. In the midst of that multitude there stood the executioner and the martyr. The executioner unsheathed his sword and brandished the shining blade before the eyes of Alexander in order to instill terror. The martyr was undaunted before this ostentatious ploy. He did not evince the slightest discomposure. A Frank who was present, seeing the martyr's fearlessness, remarked that he had never seen a man as the blessed Alexander with such constancy and calmness of spirit.

After this display, the executioner directed the saint to kneel. The martyr went to his knees. Suddenly, there was an interruption. A judicial order arrived for a stay of execution. The judge indicated in his message that his son wished to watch the beheading. The headsman, therefore, postponed carrying out his office for at least an hour or more. Throughout that intermission, the martyr remained kneeling. His head was bowed as he fixed his gaze straight ahead. He prayed unceasingly in his mind and with his lips. It is certain that from on high, the Judge of the contest, Jesus Christ, strengthened His athlete with His all-powerful grace. In the interim, members of the Orthodox community, as well as the heterodox, while they saw the time passing, were conjecturing whether human weakness might prevail. In the end, however, Christ conquered and exalted His holy Faith through this contest. The brilliant martyrdom of the holy New-martyr Alexander took place that day, on the 26th of May, in the year 1794. The pious were gladdened and the angelic host rejoiced. The demons wailed and the servants of error and deception were put to shame. Why? Because they witnessed the death of the valiant and marvellous contestant of our Lord Jesus Christ, Alexander, the former dervish, who died for the sake of Christ, to Whom is due glory and dominion, together with the Father and the Holy Spirit, to the ages of the ages. Amen.

Through the intercessions of Thy Saints,
O Christ God, have mercy on us. Amen.

---

[11] The imam was the leader of a mosque. He was considered an authoritative Muslim scholar.

[12] The hodja (khoja) was considered a Muhammadan teacher.

On the 27th of May, the holy Church commemorates the holy Hieromartyr ELLADIOS.[1]

Saint Elladios

Elladios (Helladius), the sacred hieromartyr, purified of every pollution, became a vessel of the Holy Spirit. By God's good pleasure, he was anointed high priest and assumed the steering-paddle of the ship of the holy Church of Christ. Regrettably, there is no information extant to let us know either to what century he belonged or to which see he was consecrated. Since the divine office for the day mentions that he refused to sacrifice to the idols, we understand that the tyrant was a pagan.[2] The introductory two lines of Greek verse given before his short biography indicate that he was adorned with the oil of the priesthood and that he shed his blood as a martyr. The icon from the 16th-C. wall painting at Meteora depicts him making the sign of the Cross as the executioners brutally administer a thrashing with clubs.

He was a good shepherd to the flock entrusted to him by Christ. He drove away the noetic wolves, that is to say, the heretics and the ungodly, who relish devouring the rational sheep. As a sensible and prudent steersman, he kept watch over the vessel of the Church. He secured the ship and kept her sailing on a straight course against swells and stormy winds.

When the hallowed bishop was led before the tyrant, he shone forth with more splendor. Neither straits nor circumstances brought about by his arrest and hearing caused him to lose the opportunity to enlighten the minds of the faithful. He valiantly and rapidly went forth to the stadium of martyrdom. With exceeding candor and freedom of speech, he proclaimed piety and the coessential divinity of the Trinity. The ungodly, according to the divine office to this saint, offered him a gold diadem of precious stones which he roundly refused.[3] The ever-memorable one was condemned to manifold tortures, which resulted in the merciless laceration of his body. Since his soul received pleasure rather than repugnance from the rack, his countenance appeared like a rose. He, thus, in an aged body struggled in the contest as a ruddy-faced youth. He was returned to the prison, where his face shone as the sun; for the Master Christ appeared to him. Jesus gazed upon him and healed his grievous and open

---

[1] A canon to Hieromartyr Elladios was composed by Theophanes, which manuscript is found in the Parisian Codex 1566, folio 83a.

[2] May 27th, Orthros Canon, Ode Six, Mode Four.

[3] May 27th, Orthros Canon, Ode Four.

wounds. His fetters were rent asunder as though they were a spider's web.[4] This visitation increased Elladios' eagerness and willingness to undergo further torments.

The resilient disposition of the hierarch infuriated the tyrant. He cast the hierarch into the flames in order to dispose of him, but Elladios stood in the midst of the fire and remained, by the grace and cooling dew of God, unburned and untouched. Witnessing this miraculous phenomenon brought shame to some of the ungodly, but many of the unbelievers were attracted to the truth of the Faith of Christ. Afterward, Elladios was subjected to harsher chastisements and blows. But again, he feared neither fire nor sword. Today's hymns tell us that he was dragged upon the ground and endured the excruciating piercing of his heels,[5] spilling much blood. He finally surrendered his soul into the hands of God and, thus, received the crown of martyrdom.

Saint Therapon

On the 27th of May, the holy Church commemorates the holy Hieromartyr THERAPON of Sardis.[6]

Therapon, the sacred hieromartyr, by reason of his excellent and virtuous manner of life, became a priest in the city of Sardis.[7] He was arrested by the ruler, Valerian,[8] since he was

[4] May 27th, Orthros Canon, Ode Five.
[5] May 27th, Orthros Canon, Ode Seven.
[6] There is a complete divine office that includes today's Saint Therapon of Sardis and the holy Bishop Therapon of Cyprus (commemorated the 14th of May), which was composed by Nikodemos the Hagiorite.
[7] Sardis (38°25′N 28°55′E) was situated on the east bank of the Pactolus River, about eighty kilometers (fifty miles) east of Smyrna. Considerably wealthy Sardis was one of the seven churches of the Apocalypse [Rev. 3:1 ff]. It was the civil and ecclesiastical metropolis of Lydia in western Asia Minor. There are, presently, excavations of the city that reveal a busy urban life with classical buildings and rows of shops. It contained the largest synagogue in the ancient world.
[8] Imperator Caesar Valerian (253-260) left Rome for Antioch in 254, and spent the remainder of his reign in the east. He fancied himself the "Restorer of the Orient" and (continued...)

teaching the Christian Faith.[9] The detractors of Jesus bound Therapon and submitted him to torture. After persisting throughout grueling chastisements, he was fettered and remanded to the city of Sinaos (Phrygia). Following this episode, he was sent to Ankyra of Galatia.[10] When he was taken to the river Asteles, the guards cast him prone to the ground and thrashed his with staves. The earth beneath the holy priest was reddened with his precious blood. As a result of his blood watering the earth on that spot, there sprouted forth a great oak tree. The leaves were perpetually verdant and provided cures for every disease. The tree and its cures were still flourishing at the time of the hagiographer of this piece.[11] From the riverbank, the saint was led to the Thrakesian *theme*[12] by the river Hermos just north of Sardis. He was taken to Satala, an episcopal town in the metropolis of Sardis. Once again, the ever-memorable Therapon was put to the test by diverse and dreadful chastisements. He was ultimately beheaded, upon which he received the amaranthine crown of martyrdom.

On the 27th of May, the holy Church commemorates the holy Martyr EVSEVIOTES, who suffered martyrdom by fire.

On the 27th of May, the holy Church commemorates the holy Martyr ALYPIOS, whose head was shattered by a stone.

---

[8](...continued)
"Restorer of the Human Race," but was a noted persecutor of Christians. He issued two edicts in 257 and 258 against Christians and their hierarchy. He was captured by the Persians who humiliated him when Shāpūr used his back to mount his horse. Valerian's skin was flayed and placed in the Persian temple. C. Scarre's *Chronicle of the Roman Emperors*, p. 173.

[9] Bishop Nikolai Velimirović records that Saint Therapon brought many Greek pagans to Christianity. *The Prologue from Ochrid*, s.v. "May 27th."

[10] Ankyra (39°55′N 32°50′E), the civil and ecclesiastical metropolis of Galatia, is situated on the main highway across Anatolia. It was a thriving commercial city with a military base often frequented by the emperors.

[11] Bishop Nikolai Velimirović notes that the pagans bound the priest to four posts and beat him, stripping the flesh from his bones. The four posts, he says, became green and grew into tall trees having healing properties.

[12] The Thrakesian *theme*, or territorial unit for both military and civil power, encompassed both ancient Lydia and Ionia. The hagiographer uses the term *theme*, which was generally a Byzantine designation of districts. The Thrakesion was a later *theme*.

On the 27th of May, the holy Church commemorates our righteous and God-bearing father, JOHN the Russian, the New Confessor and Wonder-worker (1730).[13]

Saint John

John the Russian, our righteous and God-bearing father and new confessor, the tender-loving and bloodless martyr of Christ, calls us together today, the Christ-named complement, to his most sacred temple, for the celebration of his sacred memory of gracious import. By reason of his excessive perseverance, coupled with his unhesitating and godly faith, he was shown to be not only an eminent confessor but also a great wonder-worker. He astonishes all by his supernatural wonderworkings and his exalting humility. Although he stands together with the angels who are around the throne of Majesty, still he comes invisibly among those who honor his holy memory.

On account of his charity, we are obliged to commemorate Saint John with fitting honor and deep piety. This is because he found himself under the yoke of a cruel and harsh master who treated with contumely, so

---

[13] The Life of this righteous one, written in Greek, was authored anonymously, as well as the composition of the divine office. Editions have been printed in special issues, the first one appearing in Athens, twice in the same year of 1849, and then again in 1897. In 1899, it was reprinted in Constantinople with the service composed by Manuel Gedeon; this edition was erroneously registered as the second. Afterward, it was reprinted many times (New York, 1944; Athens, 1960). The last edition at Athens was published by Apostolike Diakonia, commissioned by the Sacred Shrine of the Righteous John the Russian at Neon Prokopion or New Prokopi of Evia (Euboea). This edition contains the Life, Service, and Supplicatory Canon, which was composed by the Monk Daniel. The appendix has a chapter regarding the recovery of the sacred relics from Asia Minor to Evia, via the ship *Vasileios Destounes*, as well as the miracles. This account, herein, is also presented with the saint's miracles. Wall-painting scenes from the Church of Saint John at Prokopi were executed by Sergios Sergiadis.

See other English versions of the Life: Father Ioannis Vernezos' *Life and Recent Miracles of Saint John the Russian*, trans. by A. & E. Vernezos (Prokopi, Euboea, GR, 1999); Monk John Vranos' *The Illustrated Life of Saint John the Russian* (Wildwood, CA: Saint Xenia Skete, 1983); and, Photios Kontoglu, "The Life of Saint John the Russian," *The Orthodox Word*, Vol. 3, No. 3(14) (June-July, 1967): 73-86.

that he endured insults and abuses in every place and moment. Why? Because that violent Muslim exploiter sought to compel John to relinquish his Orthodox Faith. But John, though he found himself in the midst of such torments and dangers, not only abided invincible and immovable but also succeeded in achieving perfection in virtue. Today, then, for the love of our Christ-loving listeners, we shall narrate the life and divine accomplishments of Saint John the Russian.

The namesake of grace, John, hailed from a village of Little Russia. His parents were godly Orthodox Christians who named their son John at holy Baptism. From an early age, the lad was reared in piety and was diligently taught our blameless Faith. He studied at all times to improve his spiritual life, by avoiding base company and evil and worthless conversations. He possessed excessive love for the Creator of all, God. He was both anxious and careful to preserve with exactness all of the Lord's commands. When he came of age, the tall, handsome, and fair-haired youth enlisted in the military and remained in the service until the breakout of the great Turkish War during the reign of the Russian Czar Peter I (1672-1725).[14] Indeed, the valiant John, together

---

[14] The Turkish War (1710–1713). The Turkish Grand Vizier Mehemed Baltadshi marched out of Constantinople on the 6th of March, in the year 1711, leading an army of perhaps 80,000 soldiers. Swedish King Charles XII, in exile in Bendery (in the present republic of Moldova, then part of the Ottoman Empire), was greatly relieved. His representatives at the court of Sultan Ahmed III had been working hard for a follow up of the Ottoman declaration of war in November of 1710 against Russia. It had been the main reason for his stay in the northern outskirts of the Ottoman Empire. Czar Peter had defeated the Swedish-Ukrainian armies at Poltava in June of 1709. The policy of Charles XII and his successor was to find Turkish aid against Russia. The Swedish mission in Constantinople worked hard to persuade Sultan Ahmed III (1703-1730) to take military action against Czar Peter. The goal was a formal Swedish-Ukrainian-Turkish-Crimean Tartar alliance.

In 1710, the Russians managed to conclude a peace treaty with Turkey. As a result Charles tried to find ways to topple the grand vizier. The grand vizier was later sacked and replaced with a pro-Swedish successor. The Ukrainians also took part in the grand strategy game when Charles XII promised them help who were under Muscovite rule. When the Turks, in the spring of 1711, marched toward Ukraine from the southwest, Ismail Pasha had been detailed by the grand vizier to attack the Russian strongholds of Taganrog and Azov on the eastern shore of the Black Sea. Then 5,000 Ukrainians, 4,000 Poles, and 1,000 Swedes joined the Turkish forces.

Meanwhile, in late spring of the same year, 40,000 Crimean Tartars led by the son of the Crimean khan, with Swedish military adviser Major Sven Lagerberg, moved northward into Ukraine to join the Turkish forces advancing from the southwest. Czar Peter's 38,000 Russian troops now faced 170,000 alliance troops. In July of 1711, Czar Peter marched against the Turks through Bessarabia into Moldavia. But he was

(continued...)

with his comrades-in-arms, was part of an expeditionary force. They were overtaken and vanquished by Tartars who took them as prisoners of war.[15] The Tartars, thereupon, sold John to a certain Ottoman, a cavalry commander.[16] He

---

[14](...continued)
surrounded with all his forces on the Prut River. Peter's men were suffering from hunger and disease. Provisions were low. The horses were unfed. Peter marched down the right bank of the Prut, thinking the grand vizier's army was far away; but the Ottoman army was already advancing up the left bank to meet him. Ten thousand Crimean Tartars had brushed aside an advance guard which attempted to prevent them crossing. Very soon, the entire Russian army found itself held up between the Prut and a marsh. Ottoman guns on the opposite side prevented any soldier from approaching the river. After two days of desperate fighting, the Russians were unable to break the Turkish encirclement. Peter was trapped and obliged to sue for peace. He was fortunate to obtain very light terms from the inept Turkish negotiators, who allowed him to retire with no greater sacrifice than the ceding back of Azov. This greatly maddened the Swedish king who arrived a little later—after the negotiations.

Charles continued the attempts to persuade Turkey to start hostilities once again during the second half of 1711 and 1712. Once more, Turkey declared war on Russia. A Turkish army was to march northward in the spring of 1713, but a peace treaty was signed with Moscow in 1713 and with Warsaw in April of 1714. The grand alliance to contain Russia sought by Charles had collapsed. From that time, Peter's military effort was concentrated on winning his war against Sweden. See "Sequel to Poltava: Diplomacy to Contain Russia 1709-1714," by Bertil Haggman, Member, Swedish Authors Association at http://www.euronet.nl/users/sota/haggman.html. See also Jason Goodwin's *Lords of the Horizons* (NY: Picador, 1998), p. 242.

For the record, it should be known that the grand vizier also had insufficient supplies. He was uncertain whether the Tartars would remain loyal or whether the Russians were waiting for replacements from the north. Anxious to get negotiations underway, the Russians were made to surrender their cannons but not their arms for talks. The final Treaty of Prut (23rd of July, in the year 1711) provided that the Russians return all conquered areas to the Ottomans. They had to destroy all their frontier forts and promise to abstain from further intervention in Ottoman internal affairs. The sultan in return agreed to free trade in his dominions for Russian merchants and to attempt mediation for peace between Russia and Sweden. Stanford J. Shaw's *History of the Ottoman Empire and Modern Turkey*, Vol. 1 (NY: Cambridge University Press, 1998), p. 230.

[15] We also remember another Orthodox Christian taken as captive by the Tartars, Saint Pachomios, who suffered martyrdom at Ousaki of Philadelphia, on the 7th of May, in the year 1730.

[16] "For slaving wholesale, there were none like the Tartars of the Crimea. They became the slave-runners of southern Russia 'as jackal to the Turkish lion'—with heads half-shaved, terrible mustachios flying in the wind, and making raids into Poland and the Ukraine." Goodwin, pp. 106, 107.

brought John back to his homeland in Asia Minor, to the Cappadocian village-town of Prokopion (Urgup) some twelve-hours distant from Caesarea.[17]

According to the preserved tradition, many of the holy John's fellow captives were enticed by earthly good things and delights that were offered by their captors who had become their masters. Many of the Russians—alas!—submitted, either before undergoing bitter and harsh tortures or during severe punishments, adjuring that they would foreswear the holy Faith of their fathers. But the calm and undisturbed athlete of Christ, John, when he was offered such earthly delights and pleasures gave them not the least consequence, having his

---

[17] One of the most important centers in Cappadocia is Urgup, twenty kilometers to the east of Nevsehir. The famous site of Goreme is ten kilometers from Nevsehir. The nearest airport to Urgup is Kayseri Erkilet Airport, seventy-five kilometers away, or the new Nevsehir Airport, near the village of Tuzkoy, with twice-weekly flights from Istanbul. Urgup also had different names in history: Osian (Assiana); Hagios Prokopios (Byzantine); Bashisar (Seljuk); Burgat Kaalesi or Burgat Castle (Ottoman); and finally Urgup (shortly after the founding of the Turkish Republic). During the Byzantine period, it was a bishopric of the rock-cut churches and monasteries found in the villages, towns, and valleys. Urgup became a part of the Ottoman Empire in 1515. By 1888, Urgup contained seventy mosques, five churches, and eleven libraries. With a geological structure of volcanic formations, Urgup was established within the region which had been sculpted by erosions from water and wind. Shapes resulted in fantastic forms known as "Fairy Chimneys." They were formed as floodwater poured down the sides of the valleys, combined with strong winds which tore away the softer volcanic rocks, resulting in this unique landscape. The erosion of the tufa (porous rock) layer, was sculpted by wind and floodwater, running down on the slopes of the valleys. The chimneys have a conical shaped body and a boulder on top of it. The cone is constructed from tufa and volcanic ash, while the cap is of hard, more resistant rock such as lahar (a mudflow of volcanic debris) or ignimbrite (compact volcanic pyroclastic rock). Another characteristic feature of the area is the sweeping curves and patterns on the sides of the valleys, formed by rainwater. These lines of sedimentation, exposed by erosion, display a range of hues. The array of color seen on some of the valleys is due to the difference in heat of the lava layers. From season to season, the climate is quite extreme. Summers are hot and dry, with warm nights. Winters are cold and it can even snow, while spring and autumn are mild. It has many hotels and guest-houses, and one may see the old Greek houses from before the population exchange of 1923, and an atmosphere which has remained attached to its tradition despite a modernizing tourist industry. It is a good base to explore the nearby Goreme Valley. In the Urgup Museum, which opened in 1971, there are exhibits from various periods: Prehistorical, Ancient Bronze Age, Hittite, Frig, Persian, Hellenistic, Roman, Byzantine, and Ottoman pieces of arts (as well as fossil samples from Urgup and its environs). There is also an ethnographic section for regional clothes, furniture, and guns within the museum. Ruins of Urgup Museum are: Mustafapasa (Sinasos); Saint Basil Church; Monastery Valley Churches; Yesiloz (Saint Theodore) Church; and Pancarlik Church. See Internet under "Urgup."

mind fastened on the crucified Savior of the cosmos. Thus, John, with largeness of soul, bore the chastisements. He resisted his earthly master, citing those apostolic words to him: "Who shall separate us from the love of Christ? Shall affliction, or distress, or persecution, or famine, or nakedness, or danger, or sword [Rom. 8:35]?"

Continuing in this stream of thought, John would say aloud, "Thou art master of my body, but in no wise art thou of my soul. And if thou shouldest freely allow me to perform the duties of my religion, I would eagerly obey all thy commands. If, however, thou shouldest wish to sever me from the affectionate bosom of my Faith, by means of threats or guileful promises of wealth, glory, and pleasure, know this, not one of these things is able to bait me and shake my faith toward my Savior Christ. Moreover, I have ever before my eyes Christ, my 'Prince and Savior [Acts 5:31],' so that I will gladly sleep in a dark corner of thy stable where thou hast condemned me to sojourn. I, indeed, regard it as an imperial couch; for my Savior also had but a manger at His birth in Bethlehem. I, too, am mindful of the reed used by the soldiers who smote His undefiled and pure head;[18] and so I willingly receive thy blows with the rod. I also always bring to remembrance the crown of thorns put upon His head by His crucifiers;[19] so that I am prepared to endure bravely this instrument of torture, this iron head-covering. I know that thou hast heated it red-hot. I know that thou hast the custom, ofttimes, to fit it on the heads of those who refuse to submit to thy wishes. Finally, know that, no matter how many ways thou wouldest attempt to break me and bring me to Islam, I will, with Christ helping me, withstand the greatest and the worst of tortures; however, my Christ I will never renounce."

With the utterance of these righteous and ardent words by the saint of the Christian Faith, it showed him to be fearless yet calm before his earthly lord. John's humble demeanor, together with his prudent behavior, suddenly converted the ungentle and hard heart of his master; and so he was rendered compassionate. Thereafter, the Ottoman master ceased tyrannizing and coercing him to deny his Orthodox Faith. He only imposed the following living arrangements: John was to take up his abode in the corner of the stable. His duties entailed the care of the Ottoman's beloved horses. Whensoever the master went on horseback into the village, John was to follow along as his groom—which duty is expected of slaves in his position. These stipulations were accepted with great thanks by the saint. He continued to glorify, in the innermost part of his heart, the Lord Who delivered him invisibly from an enormous temptation, that is, of denial of the Faith. The Lord also rendered the heart of his master to be sympathetic toward John's plight. John, consequently,

---

[18] Mt. 27:30.

[19] Mt. 27:29; Mk. 15:17; Jn. 19:2, 5.

resided in that dark and rocky stable, giving attention with all his powers to his master's horses.

Who is able to narrate in detail his harsh struggles and asceticism? Who can describe the hunger and thirst, which the ever-memorable one endured, as well as the all-night prostrations and prayers on his little dung-heap as the blessed Job?[20] He was naked and barefoot, even in winter weather, as he tirelessly attended to his master's horses. As a horse groom, he was responsible for the day-to-day care of his masters' horses—maintaining clean stalls (mucking), feeding the horses the correct feed mix at the right time and in the proper amounts, and keeping them hydrated. With the grooming, feeding, mucking out, turning out and bringing in, tack cleaning, and exercising, he also checked their general health and treated minor injuries being somewhat aware of equine first aid. There was also involved general yard duties, such as sweeping, checking fences, and much more. In like manner, who can recount how he patiently bore the insults, abuses, and scoffing of his fellow servants while ministering to them in every possible way? There were also his practises of all-night standing and keeping vigil at prayer in the narthex of the nearby sacred church of the glorious Great-martyr George. It was necessary that he do this secretly, that is, take refuge there by night that he might offer up entreaty, even as Saint Alexis the man of God,[21] and communicate the immaculate Mysteries of Christ every Saturday. This deed and all others were observed by the unsleeping eye of God, the Most High God, Who glorifies those who glorify Him unceasingly.

What then did the Lord dispense in his œconomy? Hearken. We remember how the Lord acted through Prophet Elias in the case of the righteous widow of Sarepta (Zarephath),[22] when the pitcher of meal did not fail and the cruse of oil did not diminish; and we also recall how, through Joseph the All-comely, the Lord blessed the Egyptian Potiphar's house, possessions, and fields for His servant's sake.[23] In like manner did God bless the master of the blessed John, enriching him and making him notable among fellow citizens. Now the Ottoman, even though he was of another religion, perceived, nevertheless, that his enhanced wealth and success were coming to pass for him by reason of the prayers to God by the captive John. Moreover, the Muslim was not embarrassed to speak of this before others. Then, for that Ottoman lord, there occurred the following event: one that was mysterious, exceptional, and unexpected, which he proclaimed everywhere. Give ear to the following account.

---

[20] Job 2:8.

[21] Saint Alexis (Alexios) is commemorated by the holy Church on the 17th of March.

[22] 3 Kgs. (1 Kgs.) 17:9 ff.

[23] Gen. 39:5.

The master of John noted the unanticipated increase of his substance flowing in daily. As he pondered upon how lucky and cheerful days had come upon him, he thought it his religious duty to make a pilgrimage to Mecca.[24] After the passage of a few months, the Ottoman lord departed from Prokopion with a grand procession and retinue. He arrived in Mecca, only after undergoing abundant toils and exhaustion that such a journey entails. Not many weeks went by before the Ottoman's wife and lady of the house, who stayed behind in Prokopion, invited both kinfolk and friends to her house. She prepared a table that they might rejoice together and pray for her husband's favorable and prosperous return. The holy John, as a slave, was waiting at table, ministering readily and with much modesty. He also was serving a food which was a favorite of his absent master. The hostess, remembering how much her husband loved pilaf, pointed to the dish in John's hand and openly remarked, "How pleased and happy would his lord be if he were here, eating among us and enjoying his well-loved dish!"

Saint John Makes an Entreaty on Behalf of His Master

The holy John, hearing the desire of his mistress, had faith in our God Who is wondrous in His saints; and so he prayed noetically. He then asked permission from his mistress to prepare a full platter of pilaf for the master and send it to him in Mecca. Everyone at the table laughed at John, deriding and scorning his suggestion as impossible. But the lady gave orders to the cook that he be given a platter, even one from the

[24] Mecca of western Saudi Arabia is deemed the holiest of Muslim cities. Mohammed was born in Mecca, and it is toward this place that Muslims turn in prayer five times daily. All devout Muslims attempt a pilgrimage, or *hajj*, to Mecca at least once in their lifetime. Since the Muslims deem it a sacred city, only Muslims are allowed entry. The black stone of Mecca, a Muslim object of veneration built into the wall of the Ka'bah or Kaaba (a small shrine within the Great Mosque), according to popular Islamic legend, was given to Adam on his fall from Paradise. The stone was originally white but has become black by absorbing the sins of the thousands of pilgrims who have kissed and touched it. It now consists of three large pieces and some fragments, surrounded by a stone ring and held together with a silver band. *Encyclopaedia Britannica, Deluxe Edition 2004 CD-ROM*, s.v. "Mecca" and "Black Stone."

ceramic dinnerware bearing the family crest. She presumed he would either eat the pilaf himself or send it to someone in need. The latter, that is, giving away food to the poor, she knew he was wont to do. Meanwhile, the guests, jesting, said, "The prisoner of war is hungry and that is why he seeks a platter of pilaf, using the excuse that it is for his master. But when he is alone he will eat the food at his leisure." The saint remained silent before the accusation and went forth from the dining area. He took the platter and shut himself in the dark stable. He prayed fervently to the all-good God. He brought to mind how the Lord, once, in days of old, sent Prophet Abbakoum into Babylon from Judea that he might bring dinner to the Prophet Daniel in the lions' den.[25] John, too, entreated God that the platter be sent. He asked that God send it, as He knew best, from his hands in the stable to his master's table in Mecca. Then, indeed, in a mysterious and extraordinary manner, the platter of food, still hot from the cook's stove, vanished before John's eyes.

The man of God then returned to the dining hall. When asked what became of the platter, he reported to his mistress that the food was taken to his lord. This excited general laughter around the table, as the guests charged John with speaking falsely and eating the food himself. The matter was then dropped. The truth would only be learned with the return of John's master. Then the appearance at Mecca and the discovery of the family platter would be made known. When the Ottoman master finally came home, all were surprised at the unpacking of the platter by the master. John, however, was not surprised. The returning Ottoman, candidly and openly, described to them all the particulars regarding the platter. He then told them the day that he found the platter. It was the same day that his wife held a banquet in their home. The listeners were then further surprised when the master commented, "It was in the afternoon," and then he gave the time. It was self-evident to the others that this was the exact hour that John requested that the food be dispatched. "I had been in the sacred precinct of the shrine," continued the Ottoman, "and returned to my lodgings that I might rest. The door to my chamber was locked securely and there was no evidence of any forced entry. I suddenly found, to my great surprise and satisfaction, a covered platter on the table. I removed the cover and found steaming hot food. I was astonished and wondered how my favorite pilaf arrived. Again, the door was locked securely and there was no evidence of any tampering with the latch. Whoever brought the platter must have done so seconds earlier. I then looked carefully and was startled to note my own family emblem decorating the porcelain platter. Although I was bewildered, yet I saw no reason not to enjoy the much-desired nourishment. I

---

[25] Bel 1:33-37.

sat down and ate. I have kept the platter with me from that time. And I tell you, honestly, I have no idea how this came about."

This communication of the cavalry commander amazed everyone. He, consequently, seeing their reaction to his story, enjoined his wife and the others to confess the truth. The Ottoman lady recapitulated how she gave a dinner party that day and what transpired. She also disclosed how, at that very hour he had received the steaming platter of pilaf, she had expressed how she wished he were present to partake thereof. She then said, "John offered to prepare a full platter of food for thee and send it to Mecca. I had the platter prepared and gave it to him, though all of us just stared at him knowing the impossibility of achieving what he proposed; and so we mocked him. But now we see that he truly kept his word and did as he said, which deed could only have been performed by divine power." Then the Muslims present shouted aloud, "Allah! Allah!" As a result of this miraculous occurrence, the holy John was no longer treated scornfully or despitefully. In fact, they dealt with him as a saint or righteous man, honoring him excessively. His masters offered him a special room outside of the stable, leaving him free. But the saint, after thanking them, wished to avoid human glory. He preferred rather to remain in that dark corner of the stable, where he took up greater struggles and glorified God.[26]

Saint John Receives Holy Communion from a Hollowed-out Apple

Thus, after these events, the saint lived a God-pleasing life and engaged in ascetic contests. After the passage of some years, he became ill. He foreknew that his end was near. He, thereupon, besought one of the priests of the village-town to bring him the immaculate Mysteries that he might receive Communion. The priest, fearing to bring the divine Mysteries into the house

---

[26] One of the priests serving at the Church of Saint John in New Prokopi of Evia received the platter in a miraculous fashion, when it was discovered among the baggage of the refugees leaving Asia Minor. The saint visited the daughter of one such refugee and informed her of what she had no idea: that the platter was in her basement and that she bring it to the saint's church in Evia where it was needed. Vernezos, *Life and Recent Miracles*, pp. 58, 59.

of the cavalry commander, was made wise by divine grace. The priest hollowed out an apple, lining the cavity with beeswax, and put the Mysteries within. He went to see the saint and offered to him the specially prepared apple. The goodly priest thought of this arrangement, so that he might avoid any unnecessary peril. The blessed John received the immaculate Mysteries of Christ, glorifying God with all his heart. Not long after, he surrendered his soul. He was, therefore, conveyed from temporal captivity and difficult hardships to the heavenly freedom and everlasting gladness, on the 27th of May, in the year 1730. When the Ottoman lord learned that his slave John had reposed, he summoned all the distinguished Christians of the village-town and the priests as well. He permitted them, without charge, to take the body. The man of God was then given the customary Christian burial. The Ottoman lord, wishing to show the love he bore John, brought a costly carpet and laid it upon the saint's coffin. The priests with all the Christians of the village-town went forth with much piety and compunction, bearing lamps and incense. They reverently gave burial to his much-tried and much-toiling body in the burial ground of the Christians.

Three and one-half years after the righteous John's departure to the Lord and the committal of his body to the earth, the elderly priest was vouchsafed a dream wherein he was urged by the saint to recover his relics. The priest, however, doubted the truth of the vision since the Christians had not as yet pronounced John as a saint. But when a heavenly light, as a fiery column, descended repeatedly around the midnight hour over the holy man's tomb, this compelled the devout priest to take action. With other Christians, all together they went down diligently and brought up the redolent coffin. It was then that they acknowledged that the phenomenon of the heavenly light over the saint's tomb was an undoubtable sign of his sanctity. They opened the tomb and found—behold the wonder!—that the saint's body was completely unravaged and incorrupt. Thus, with all spiritual good cheer and reverence, they took up the saint's body, accompanied by psalms and hymns and incense, and transferred him to the stone hewn church of the glorious martyr, the Church of Saint George, that was nearby the house of the saint's former earthly master. This was the same church in which the former captive John hastened to keep vigil. Therefore, his reliquary was placed beneath the holy table. Straightway, the good fame of his sanctity was spread abroad. Christians from all places were coming to Prokopion that they might venerate the sacred relics. Those suffering from infirmities came for the healing of soul and body. In the midst of these pilgrimages, there came about a host of wonderworkings performed by the righteous one through the holy relics. We shall narrate some of the miracles which took place, to the glory of God and to the honor of Saint John the Russian.

Some Miracles of Saint John

In the year 1832, the Turkish armies under Osman Pasha (the delegate of the Sultan) were passing straight through Prokopion in order to put down an Egyptian revolt that broke out.[27] Osman intended to pass the night at Prokopion. Since, at that time, a multitude of Ottomans resided in Prokopion, many of whom were Janissaries[28] that hated the sultan, they agreed together not to welcome Osman Pasha into either their village-town or their borders. In vain did the unfortunate Christians, fellow citizens of Prokopion, attempt to change the minds of the Janissaries. The Christians, seeing that they could not persuade them in the least, took refuge by night with their women and children in the outskirts of the village-town, on Christian fields, that they might preserve them. Elderly men and women, alone, were left behind.

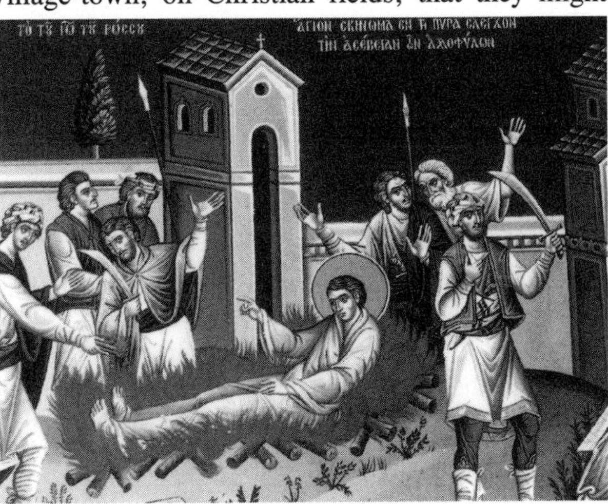

The Holy Relic of Saint John in the Fire Censures the Impious Infidels

The following day, Osman Pasha and his army approached Prokopion and began immediately slaughtering and plundering, committing many acts of violence. The soldiers seized whatsoever valuables they had chanced upon. They finally came to the sacred Church of the Great-martyr George and burst inside, first pillaging and carrying off as booty the sacred vessels and lamps. Then, afterward, they opened the reliquary containing the sacred relics of Saint John. They thought to find hidden treasure within. When their hopes

[27] It would be in Syria that Ibrahim Pasha and his French chief of staff won military fame. In 1831/1832, after a disagreement between Muhammad Ali, viceroy and pasha of Egypt, and the Ottoman Sultan Mahmud II (r. 1808-1839), Ibrahim led an Egyptian army through Palestine and defeated an Ottoman army at Homs. He then forced the Bailan Pass and crossed the Taurus, gaining a final victory at Konya in December of 1832. By the Convention of Kutahya, signed in May of 1833, Syria and Adana were ceded to Egypt, and Ibrahim became governor-general of the two provinces. *Encyclopaedia Britannica*, s.v. "Ibrahim Pasha."

[28] The Turks would abduct the sons of Christians and raise them as fanatical Moslem soldiers. Prokopion was an army-camp of these Janissaries, for whom, in Saint John's lifetime, he had become a target of their jeering and derision.

were dashed at not discovering either gold or silver, they were filled with wrath. They decided to burn that sacred body in order to mock and deride the Christians as revenge for their own failure of finding more booty. They, thereupon, took the relics outside of the sacred temple and the courtyard. They went about fetching twigs and branches. After they collected a considerable heap of burnable materials, they lit a great fire. Those unholy and sacrilegious ones then cast the body of the saint upon the roaring flames. The sacred relics, nevertheless, by indwelling grace, not only remained unharmed but also unburnt in the least.[29] When those who perpetrated this crime later recounted their impious act to their coreligionists, they affirmed that the saint appeared alive; for he suddenly arose and threatened them, vehemently casting them out of the courtyard. The Muslims, half-dead with terror and trembling, abandoned everything and fled to their tents. Afterward, the elder Christians took up the sacred relics of the saint and returned them to the reliquary.

By the year 1845, another church was built in Prokopion. The new edifice was dedicated to the name of our holy father among the saints, Basil the Great. It was the desire of the Christians of that village-town to convey the relics of Saint John from the old church, dedicated to the Great-martyr George, to the new one. Unbeknownst to them, the saint, as it will soon be shown, did not wish this transfer. During the night, the saint within his reliquary was transferred, in a manner mysterious and extraordinary, back to the old church, that is, to the one in which he struggled to keep the Faith while alive. The Christians, though seeing what had transpired, did not understand it properly. They, again, took up the sacred reliquary and returned it to the Church of Saint Basil. Now this change of venue took place two and three times. Whenever the reliquary was deposited in the Church of Saint Basil, the following morning it was restored to the Church of Saint George.[30] While the wonderworking saint made known his preference, still the parishioners, after much entreaty and supplication, finally won the consent of the saint. His relics and reliquary were moved again to the Church of Saint Basil, where they were honored and venerated by all.

In the year 1862, on a Saturday, while it was still morning and the divine Liturgy was being conducted, a certain pious woman began to narrate that the evening before she beheld Saint John in a night vision. She described how he emerged from his reliquary and hastened to the Greek School, which structure he supported with both hands as it was about to collapse. As she was speaking these words, there suddenly occurred a loud rattling and crackling which ended in a crash. The noise dinned the ears of all present so that they

[29] The relics, remaining whole, although blackened by the smoke still remained pliant and fragrant. Vernezos, p. 37.

[30] The fissure-ridden cave-Church of Saint George soon thereafter fell into ruin.

filed out of the church, only to see that the roof of the school adjacent had fallen. All made haste, weeping and wailing, pushing and lifting debris out of their path. It was a heavy roof that fell upon twenty students within. But instead of being buried alive or injured or killed, all the pupils—lo, the wonder!—survived, safe and sound. The children were asked how they managed to remain unscathed. They answered, "Suddenly, we heard a violent grating and grinding from the roof beams. We saw that we were in imminent danger. Then, as if on signal and as if an invisible hand guided us, in a moment's time, we, though frightened and trembling, found ourselves underneath our desks. There was a loud snapping sound when the roof caved in, crashing down over our rickety desks. Though we were beyond all human remedy, yet were we preserved unharmed." Thus, by the grace of God and the invisible watchfulness of our righteous Father John, so many innocent creatures survived.

In the year 1874, the eighteen-year-old daughter of the offspring begotten by that Ottoman cavalry commander, the former master of the saint, had suddenly gone missing. Her distraught parents, looking everywhere for her, in no wise knew where to find her. They, finally, took refuge in the saint, entreating him to uncover the whereabouts of their daughter. The saint, appearing in a dream to the mother of the missing lass, made the following revelation. He revealed that a pauper woman, whom Saint John named, of the same nation, invited the daughter the previous evening to her dwelling. She coaxed the lass to give her the gold earrings and other expensive jewelry that she was wearing. But afterward, the wicked woman choked to death the lass and buried the body in the chimney of her house. The mother, stirred from her bed, made haste to report the homicide to her husband and the rest of the household even as it had been made manifest to her. They went to that house and discovered their daughter's corpse in the previously indicated place. The murderess was arrested and punished by the authorities.

Another descendant of the Ottoman cavalry commander was Esset Agha. He explained to the Christians his grief of having lost a number of children in infancy. His wife, finally, took refuge in the relics of the family's former slave, John the Russian. She begged for a child that would thrive, either a boy or a girl, as long as it lived to adulthood. She did not go empty-handed to the tomb. Not that the saint required anything of her, but she wished to show her sincerity. She, therefore, made an offering of beeswax and other gifts to the church's lamplighter, beseeching him to pray for her plight. She vowed that should the child live, she would call the infant "the child of John." The saint hearkened to her request and granted a son. She kept her promise. She named the boy Kole Giuvan Ogul, meaning in their language, "Son of the slave John." Esset Agha, then an old man, affirmed that his boy flourished and was proud of his name. Now many other miracles and wonders were wrought by the saint for the Orthodox, but by these two we see that the saint harbored no remembrance of wrongs.

A certain Athonite monk, Andrew, in 1878, came to Prokopion on a pilgrimage in order to venerate the relics of the righteous John. On his return to his monastery, he went in the company of six other coaches that happened to be journeying to Constantinople. As they traveled and came to a narrow pass with rough terrain, five of the coaches separated from the other two. Of the latter, one was carrying Andrew. All the drivers agreed to meet again on the road ahead. As Andrew's coach approached a hill, a young man, mounted on a red stallion, having the looks of Saint John, waved and told the monk to go back and proceed in another direction. The young man, after warning the monk that robbers had captured the five other coaches, then vanished. Andrew's coach and the other with him, then, went back. The robbers, catching sight of the two coaches, fired their pistols but missed. The monk entered the nearby village. Before continuing his journey in the company of some Turkish soldiers, he met his former traveling companions in the other five coaches. They were Turkish merchants of Anatolia. They told Father Andrew that the robbers took their money and clothing. The monk then informed them how he had been forewarned by a young man, who resembled Saint John. They all glorified the saint who protected the pilgrim monk. Thus, he was preserved safe by the intervention of the saint from the inroads of robbers.[31]

Now some tiny portions of the saint's relics were filched, from time to time, for the purpose of veneration and sanctification. Saint John, with a displeased countenance, would visit those who took pieces and reprove them. He told them to return them. The holy Athonite Monastery of Saint Panteleimon had no intention of furtively stealing the relics. In a wonderful manner were the inhabitants of the village-town of Prokopion persuaded to part with the right hand from the sacred tabernacle of the saint, that it might be taken to the Russian Monastery of the Great-martyr Panteleimon on the Holy Mountain. The brotherhood, in 1881, through their envoy, Priest-monk Dionysios, made the first request for the saint's hand as a blessing for the sacred monastery. But the request, having become the cause of offense and friction to the natives, was denied. The brotherhood was not put off. The fathers' persistent and ardent pleas were fulfilled when the saint moved the hearts of the Prokopions. The people also reasoned that it was only right that the Russians should have a relic, that the name of their compatriot might also be known and venerated among them. Father Dionysios, together with a committee of distinguished Prokopions, escorted the relic back to Mount Athos. The laymen visited for one month as guests of the monastery. At their departure, the brotherhood made a

[31] See also Vranos, *The Illustrated Life*, op. cit., p. 32.

donation to the faithful of Prokopion toward the construction of a chapel over the saint's grave. The Prokopions indeed commenced its construction; but instead of a chapel they laid the foundations of a large church.[32]

In 1924, during the population exchange between Greece and Turkey,[33] there took place the translation of the sacred relics from Prokopion of Caesarea in Cappadocia to Neon Prokopion (New Prokopi, formerly the village of Ahmet-Aga) on the island of Evia. The ship *Vasileios Destounes* that October, which took as passengers some of the inhabitants of Prokopion to Evia, also transported the august tabernacle of the righteous one.[34] While at sea, they sailed to Rhodes. However, the ship would neither proceed nor turn around. The pilot then remarked, "Children, either good or bad has found us!" One of the stewards, Panagiotes Prodromos Papadopoulos, gave the following explanation of the phenomenon to the ship's captain: "Within the ship's hold there is found the precious relics of one saint, the righteous John the Russian." The pilot sought to remedy the unintentional impertinence shown to the saint. He ordered that the saint's tabernacle be moved. It was conveyed to that section used by the crew as an oratory, where also an oil lamp was kept lit. As this was carried out forthwith, only then did the ship miraculously move. When the vessel put in at the landing-stage of Chalkida (Halkida), capital of Evia, it was met by Metropolitan Gregory of Chalkida, as well as by the prefect and other leaders of the city. They deposited the relics, temporarily, in the holy cemetery Church of Saint John at Chalkida. Afterward, the relics were transported to Neon Prokopion of northern Evia, some fifty-two kilometers from Chalkida. The village had been the place where the refugees of Prokopion of Asia Minor

---

[32] The Church of Saint John, after the Asia Minor Catastrophe (at Smyrna in 1922), was used as a granary and was then destroyed by the Muslims in the 1950s.

[33] "The 1923 Exchange of Populations between Greece and Turkey refers to the first large scale population exchange, or agreed mutual expulsion in the 20th C. It involved some two million persons, most forcibly made refugees and *de jure* denaturalized from homelands of centuries or millennia, in a treaty promoted and overseen by the international community as part of the Treaty of Lausanne. Following these models, as part of the Treaty of Lausanne, almost all Greeks, about 1.5 million, from Turkish Anatolia and Turkish Thrace were expelled or formally denaturalized, and about 500,000 Turks were expelled from Greece. The Greeks of Istanbul, Gokceada (Imbros in Greek) and Bozcaada (Tenedos), as well as the Turks and other Muslims of Western (Greek) Thrace were exempted from this transfer. In Greece this was called the 'Asia Minor Catastrophe' as it involved the expulsion of about one third of the Greek population from millennia-old homelands." See www.http://en.wikipedia.org/wiki/Exchange_of_populations_between_Greece_and_Turkey.

[34] In order to elude Turkish authorities, the fleeing Orthodox clad the incorrupt relic of Saint John as an old woman. Two elderly women, with covered heads bent down, took him from under the arms and walked him on board the ship.

had settled. The relics, thereupon, were placed in the village church, dedicated to the names of Saints Constantine and Helen. In 1930, the foundation of a church for the holy relics was commenced. The raising of that majestic church was finally completed in 1951, when the sacred relics were translated from the Church of Saints Constantine and Helen to the new church in honor of Saint John the Russian. In 1962, after an agreement between the Church and the state, the Saint John Church functions as a place of worship and a charitable foundation. The wonderworking relics wrought cures of every kind. Multitudes were drawn to the church, especially on the saint's feast day. Two comfortable guest houses were built: one offering free lodging and the other maintaining low rates. The monies are used for the philanthropic endeavors of the Foundation, which include two orphanages, two old age homes, and a students' hostel. There is also a children's summer camp.

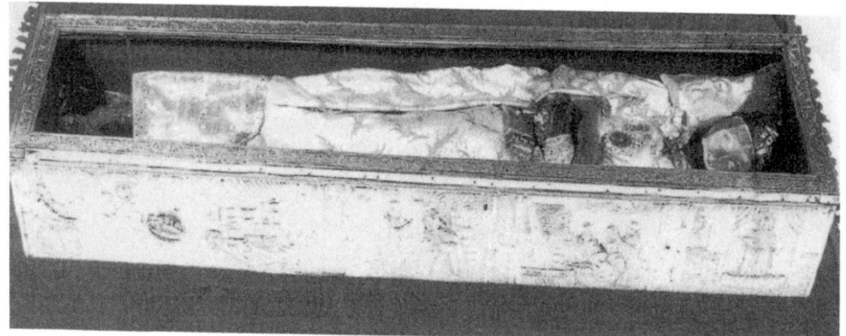

Present-day Reliquary of Incorrupt Relics of Saint John the Russian

While the saint's precious relics are a wellspring of divine grace, apt to dry every tear and heal every infirmity, the saint often personally visits and identifies himself. He is seen as a tall and handsome soldier, sometimes on horseback. He is known to help even when not asked. The miraculous cures listed below are a few that took place in Cyprus, France, Greece, and the United States of America from 1964 to 1988. Recorded works of healing, from the time that Saint John came to New Prokopi, include infirmities also documented by medical science and previous medical records, blood work, tests, and x-rays: abnormally elongated tongue impeding speech; acromegaly; arrested development of limbs; cancer and cancer of the large intestine; congenital deformities; coma; humpback (kyphosis); infertility; leukemia; lung tumor; neurological complaints; nosebleeds (epistaxis); paralysis; sickle-cell anemia; strokes from intracerebral hemorrhage or cerebral thrombosis; and thromboses. Heterodox physicians in New York declared that the disappearance of a lung tumor, the size of an apple, was "a cure of great scientific interest." But an Orthodox doctor in Greece said, "Over and above science is the Almighty and His saints." The saint has also been invoked for averting shipwrecks, settling court cases, rescue from assault and battery, deliverance from drug addiction, dispelling of demonic possession, and finding missing persons. Furthermore, during the 1947 Civil War with the communists in Greece, the saint kept his people at Prokopi safe and free of bloodshed. Every time guerilla firing-squads were sent out, as they approached the hills surrounding Prokopi, they felt dizzy and their legs became paralyzed so that they needed to desist.[35]

A model of holiness, humility, meekness, and the virtuous life, worthy of our emulation, is our blessed Saint John the Russian, Cappadocia's boast. By undergoing much hardship and grief while suffering captivity and tyranny, he persevered in unceasing God-pleasing prayer and vigilance, so that he became a glorious champion and contestant for Orthodoxy. Let us, in like manner, conduct ourselves for piety's sake that we may have lasting confidence and boldness that not only may we pass this temporal life with peace in our hearts but also might be accounted worthy of the heavenly kingdom, through the intercession of this Saint John, in our Lord Christ Jesus, to Whom is due all glory, honor, and veneration, together with His beginningless Father and the good and life-creating, and All-Holy Spirit, now and ever and to the ages of the ages. Amen.

Saint John

Through the intercessions of Thy Saints,
O Christ God, have mercy on us. Amen.

[35] See Vernezos, pp. 45-93, for details. Another book of more recent miracles is also being prepared.

Saints Eftychous, Bishop of Melitene; Andrew, the Fool for Christ; and Demetrios, New-martyr

On the 28th of May,
the holy Church commemorates
the holy Hieromartyr
EFTYCHOUS (EFTYCHIOS),
Bishop of Melitene.[1]

Eftychous (Eftychios), acting out of his free will, went before the tyrants and proclaimed that our Lord Jesus Christ is true God. He also sneered and spat at the idols. He underwent a myriad of punishments and hardships, having withstood all by the grace of Christ. He finally was plunged into the sea, where the blessed one drowned and received his much-desired end.[2]

Saint Joseph the Hymnographer (ca. 812-886) confirms that the blessed Eftychous met his end by drowning. He further records that the relics were retrieved and became a font of every gift of healing. From the divine office to the saint, it appears that he converted to Christianity. He received the seed of the Spirit upon hearing the sowers of the Logos. He remained with the godly Christians and was living a saintly life. Saint Joseph describes the martyr's end before he was delivered to the briny deep. He kept preaching the word of salvation, even as his hands were being bound and he was enclosed in a leather sack.[3] By his wrestlings, he proved to be an earthly angel and a heavenly man. He is invoked for deliverance from captivity to godless barbarians and all manner of straits.[4]

---

[1] Concerning this saint, not even a footnote has survived; therefore, our knowledge of him is limited. In various *Menaia* for this day, he is called either Eftyches or Eftychios (Eutychius). The divine office composed by Joseph the Hymnographer (d. ca. 886), addresses him as Eftychios. Within his melodic hymns, he portrays him as a martyr who suffered drowning; but no verse mentions that he is a bishop. Participating in this perplexing dilemma of identification and iconic representation is Hetherington's description [*The Painter's Manual of Dionysius of Fourna* (p. 79)]: "28th of May: The martyr-priest Eutychius dies by the sword; a young man with a wide beard."

[2] This succinct biographical paragraph is quoted in *The Great Synaxaristes* (in Greek). The original is found in Lavreote Codices Δ 5 and I 70, folio 279. The Great Lavra text gives the rendering of his name as Eftychios.

[3] May 28th, Odes Five and Six, Mode Four, Saint Joseph the Hymnographer.

[4] May 28th, Ode Nine.

On the 28th of May, the holy Church commemorates the holy Virgin-martyr ELIKONIS (HELICONIS) of Thessalonike.

Saint Elikonis

Elikonis (Heliconis), the holy martyr, flourished during the years of Emperors Gordian III (238-244) and Philip the Arab (244-249). Elikonis, a maiden hailing from Thessalonike, was a stunning beauty. Since she was a Christian and exhorted the pagans, she was arrested and led before the military commander (*doux*) of Corinth. His name was Perinios. At first, he was attracted to her and did not wish to mar such an exquisite picture of perfection. Since she did not stoop to making an offering to the idols, but instead courageously proclaimed the Christ as true God, he did his worst. As a result of her confession, her feet were bound with leather thongs to a pair of oxen. She was then dragged over rough terrain. Following this battering punishment, the pagans prepared a cauldron of corrosives for her, comprising of molten lead, bitumen, and pitch. The holy virgin was cast within that thick and stinking deadly mixture, but she remained unscathed. Since they were put to shame, they thought to humiliate her. They shaved her rich tresses so that she was rendered bald. Nonetheless, she now had the look of another world. Next, they took fiery torches that they might quench her resolve by burning her entire body. The power of fire, however, was quenched and extinguished. Following this nullification, they brought her within the idol temple so as to subvert her piety by offering her the title of priestess. By her prayers, she overturned and demolished the idols of Athena, Dios (Zeus), and Aesculapius.[5] Maddened by the damage to their gods, the barbarous pagans thought of another mutilation to impose upon her whom they deemed to be a sorceress. They carved into her chest wall and cut away her breasts.

Now the successor of Perinios was the Proconsul Justin. The holy Martyr Elikonis was made to stand before him. Once again, she refused to be persuaded to make a drink-offering and sacrifice to the idols. The pagans conspired to snuff out the maiden in a fiery furnace. The flame, in no wise, touched the virgin. Justin then devised another method of torture to obliterate the Christian maiden. Elikonis was stretched out upon a bronze bier that had been fired until it was flame-red. As her flesh began to dissolve from the heat, there appeared the Archangels Michael and Gabriel to the holy maiden. They healed her and undid the bier, that is, they broke it into little pieces which they cast to the ground. This torment, therefore, left no trace upon her flesh. The maddened pagans, unwilling to surrender, intended to make mincemeat of her,

[5] Minerva, Jupiter, and Asklepius.

giving her up as prey to wild animals in the arena. The lions, nevertheless, did not touch Elikonis. The hungry brutes, much rather, ran after and pounced upon the proconsul's officers. Thus, they slaughtered and swallowed one hundred and twenty men. Justin, as this juncture, wished to make an end of it. He thought to do away with Elikonis by having her head struck off. As she proceeded to the block, a voice from on high was heard inviting her to the heavenly abodes. The blessed Elikonis was beheaded here by Justin; but she was crowned there, in the heavens, by Jesus.

On the 28th of May, the holy Church commemorates the holy Martyrs CRESCENS, PAUL, and DIOSCORIDES of Rome.

Crescens, Paul, and Dioscorides, the holy martyrs, spent their lives in Old Rome. They prudently allotted their time to preaching the Gospel message to unbelievers. Since the seed of their teaching did not fall on stony ground, they offered many converts to Christ. Intransigent pagans had the holy trio arrested. Those heathen next administered a strenuous thrashing. Afterward, the three were cast into a fiery furnace. Hence, these ever-memorable Romans received their laurels of martyrdom.

On the 28th of May, the holy Church commemorates the gloriously triumphant and new Hieromartyr ZACHARIAS of Prousa (1802).[6]

Zacharias, the valiant hieromartyr of Christ, hailed from the renowned city of Prousa.[7] He was born in the second half of the eighteenth century. His parents were of Christian lineage. They were noble and honorable stock.

---

[6] The martyrdom of Saint Zacharias was published in the Greek work entitled *Neon Leimonarion*, from which it was borrowed and revised for incorporation into *The Great Synaxaristes* (in Greek).

[7] Prousa (Bursa, 40° 12′N 29°04′E) of northwestern Turkey, was formerly of Bithynia. It is situated on the northern foothills of Ulu Dag (the ancient Mysian Olympos of monastics and iconodule stronghold). The city first fell to the Seljuk Turks at the end of the 11th C. During the First Crusade in 1096, it changed hands several times. The Ottomans took it in 1326, after a decade of harassment and a hard siege which left the city streets strewn with corpses. The Turks made it their first great capital. Tamerlane sacked the city in 1402. When the Ottomans recovered their territory, they relocated their capital: first to Edirne (Adrianople) in 1413, and, later, to Constantinople in 1458. Bursa, nevertheless, expanded and prospered under Ottoman rule. Its silk industry has a long heritage. The city lies among orchards, watered by plentiful mountain streams. It is a city of multicolored houses and winding streets filled with fountains. Prousa was a suffragan bishopric of Nikomedia.

Zacharias was nurtured in the instruction and admonition of the Lord.[8] From his childhood years, he was reared in the virtues. As he matured, he demonstrated a conduct of life in accordance with moral excellence. On account of his godly manner of life, he was vouchsafed the grace of the priesthood. Now why and how such an individual, who exhibited upright behavior from his youth, stumbled into the calamity and ruin of recanting his Orthodox Faith is about to be described. Hearken.

The hallowed Apostle Paul tells us that "every creature of God is good, and nothing is to be cast away, if it is received with giving of thanks [1 Tim. 4:4]." Prior to Paul, the God-inspired account of Genesis assures the truth of the foregoing statement in this passage: "And God saw all the things that He had made, and, behold, they were very good [Gen. 1:31]." But O the misfortune of man! All those good things, those very good things made by God for man's benefit, through misuse or ill use of these things, became for man ruinous and fatal. Wine, for instance, is confessedly one of the good things of God's creating—not only that it makes glad the heart of man[9] but also that it preserves him.[10] But excessive consumption leads to transgression, dishonor, violence, and illness of both body and soul. The narration of the life of the holy Hieromartyr Zacharias will fully inform us of what can happen to those who tarry long and entangle themselves in banquets of wine and drink.

The monk and New-martyr Zacharias was a priest at Prousa, in the parish called Kagiabasi. The intemperate use of wine over the years led to lamentable results: one who was once noble became ignoble; one who was honorable became dishonorable. Zacharias' uncurbed drinking habit caused the priest to desert his post and his Christianity. He denied Christ. But God—Who wills that all men be saved,[11] on account of His goodness and all-wise providence—did not sever Zacharias and leave him in the depths of desperation and despair lest accursed intoxication should submerge him in everlasting and unending punishment. But how did the denial of a priest come to pass? On one occasion when Zacharias, by reason of his self-indulgence, was in an inebriated state, he became delirious. He was beside himself with thoughts swimming in his mind, so that he was as one deranged. Blind drunk was he, as they say, and knew neither his mind nor his whereabouts. Alas! Having lost his bearings, he, with a little prodding, dared to renounce his Creator and Savior Jesus Christ. He accepted the error and impiety of the deceived Hagarenes. The great Basil says that just as smoke dispels honeybees, so does the befuddlement of

---

[8] Cf. Eph. 6:4.
[9] Ps. 103:16.
[10] "Give strong drink to those that are in sorrow, and the wine to drink to those in pain [Prov. 31:6]."
[11] 1 Tim. 2:4.

winebibbing push aside spiritual gifts. Desolating himself of divine grace, the wretched Zacharias fell into dissipation and disorderliness. The truth be told, he was drinking with some Turks who took advantage of him in their desire to take such a prize as Father Zacharias for Islam. While drunk, they pressed him to accept their religion. They had him repeat what they recited. It was a declaration in favor of Mohammed as the prophet, which Zacharias mumbled through. With malignant joy, those Turks garbed him as a Muslim and paraded their drunken conquest through the streets of Prousa, to the alarm and horror of Zacharias' parishioners. Meanwhile, those Turks kept giving him more and more to drink, but they could not keep him perpetually drunk. When they tired of their sport, they cast him off and abandoned him.

The blessed man-befriending God did not wish the death of this sinner. The mania for wine and insobriety gave the man-hating devil the weapons he needed to hold mastery over Zacharias, whose bouts ultimately brought him to apostasy. Yea, an Orthodox priest forsook piety and the Orthodox Faith. Though he made himself a slave of the demon of wine, Bacchus, who soaked his brains, Christ saved Zacharias from swilling himself with the wine of apostasy. He would take Zacharias not as His own slave but as a friend and splendid martyr of His divinity and an heir of His kingdom. Indeed, God remembered Zacharias whose name signifies "remembrance of God" or "God remembered" in the Hebrew tongue.[12] O martyr-loving brethren, listen to the way in which this was accomplished! As we said, after giving free rein to indulgence, Zacharias wallowed in wine and accepted the antichrist religion of the Muslim Turks. The year was 1801.

Immediately after the passing of his drunken stupor, he recognized the mishap which rent his heart. He wept bitterly as did the blessed Peter long ago.[13] Zacharias repented of his heedlessness and recklessness. But even before he was fully aware of his wanton foolhardiness, he felt the pangs of remorse in his secret recesses. Although he repented before God, still it gave the disconsolate man no satisfaction; for his tyrannical conscience seared him unceasingly. Rather than endure the accusations of that inner voice, he desired to make a public profession. He wanted, once again, to confess his holy Orthodox belief. He believed it necessary to wash away the sin of denial with the streams of his blood. At the same time, he also thought to glorify God by means of his martyric death.

---

[12] The name of the Prophet Zacharias, from the tribe of Levi, is interpreted by Blessed Jerome as *memoria Domini* "remembrance of God"; by others, it is interpreted as "he whom God remembers" or "God remembered." Saint Jerome, "Letter LIII, to Bishop Paulinus of Nola (A.D. 394)," Nicene and Post-Nicene Fathers, 2nd Ser., Vol. VI:101.

[13] Mt. 26:75; Lk. 22:62.

But once again his compulsion to drink returned. Having imbibed to excess once again, he staggered to the house of a certain widow. He asked her for payment of money that he had lent to her earlier. When she told him that she could not remit the sum, he lost his temper. He then quickly ran straight to the judge in order to bring her into account for the amount owed. One of the judge's law clerks, seeing Zacharias reeling, went over to him. Zacharias' sodden mind caused him to muddle through his words with slurred speech. The clerk, catching a whiff of his wine-laden breath, comprehended his condition immediately. The Muslim, raising his voice, spoke openly so that anyone could hear him and declared: "Why listen to such a fellow? He is faithless and thinks slightly of our religion, because he is always drunk."[14] In this way did that fanatical Muslim berate Zacharias. As for Zacharias—O Thine unspeakable love and care for man, O Christ most merciful!—when he heard that devotee of Islam speak in such a taunting manner, he came to his senses in an instant. He was in his right mind and sober. Verily, it is better to say that his heavenly-granted lucidity made him godly-wise and God-inspired. In fact, it is certain that this transformation came about from the right hand of the Most High. Zacharias came to file a complaint against the widow, but providence outmaneuvered him! Lo, even on his way to persecute the Church, as Saul of old on the road to Damascus,[15] so was he illumined! Zacharias answered the clerk without cowing, "Indeed, unfaithful am I in regard to your faith, and disdainful of your abominable religion. With respect to my Faith, however, I am not faithless. Much rather, I believe in my Lord Jesus Christ as true God and the Creator of the cosmos." Zacharias then cast down to the floor his Muslim fez and said, "Behold the sign of your error! I trample upon it and I am ready to receive the harshest death for my Faith, for the love of my Christ."

The onlookers were shocked at such a strange and abrupt change in the drunk man. They remained in wonderment how to proceed. Finally, they put away the blessed one into the prison—perhaps on the charge of drunkenness, at least for the time being—until they could decide how to win him over and not take his life. It was then the 25th of May. The holy and consecrated Zacharias, by divine energy was completely changed and became better and better. While he was in that prison, he wept bitterly. He mourned for his sins and prayed unceasingly with his head uncovered. Do not think he was alone heaving deep sighs and sobbing and supplicating God. The message went abroad, to the churches in Prousa, to chant supplicatory prayers. The entreaty of the Orthodox

---

[14] According to the Koran [5:90, 91], "intoxicants and games of chance" were called "abominations of Satan's handiwork," intended to turn people away from Allah and forget about prayer. Thus, Muslims were ordered to abstain.

[15] Acts 9 ff.

was unified: grant to Zacharias strength that he might worthily and in a God-pleasing manner finish his martyric contest.

Such were the events of the first day. The aghas, the following day, converged at the courthouse where the martyr was also made to appear. The Muslims began employing sweet words of exhortation and flattery upon Zacharias, hoping to cajole and coax him. Then they asked him, "For what reason or under what compulsion didst thou speak as thou didst yesterday those unbecoming statements? Perhaps thou art in need of money? Do not discompose thyself, we shall give thee whatsoever thou needest and whatsoever else thou shouldest ask. Or perhaps thou dost wish to marry? Calm thyself. We shall give thee as a wife the most beautiful daughter of the richest among us." Now these words seemed like errant nonsense to Zacharias. The godly-minded man refused staunchly, "I do not want either wealth, or a rich spouse, or a part in your useless and false religion. In fact, I abjure Islam with all my soul and heart. I anathematize your religion as a demonic imposture. I believe in my Lord Jesus Christ as true God. I profess, in addition, that I am a Christian even as I was earlier. Do not even begin to entertain vain hopes that you can convert me. Indeed, though you were to apply however many torments you could contrive and were to condemn me to ten thousand deaths, still you could not separate me from the love of my Christ."[16]

The Muslims, seeing that they were not able to achieve anything, even with their blandishments and promises, tried to scare him with their threats. But they saw that their terrifying intimidations also failed with him. He remained firm and unmoved. They, therefore, threw him back into the prison. Zacharias, giving no thought to repining, took up his abode in that prison as one glad and rejoicing in a palace. Divine grace dwelt in him. Courage and manliness mounted in his heart. Desire and love for Christ lighted upon his soul, so that he longed to undergo death for Jesus. As for the Hagarenes, they were reconsidering their tactics. They decided to submit Zacharias first to a cudgeling of the soles of his feet, that is, a bastinadoing. The act of contusing the bottoms of his feet was carried out. Following this grinding punishment, they took a steel tripod, which they heated by firing, and placed it on his head. This brought about the burning of the holy martyr's scalp and manifold pangs. However, at the same time, there kindled the flame of Christ's love which set his heart on fire. It was by divine power that Zacharias valiantly withstood this acute torture, as it was beyond the natural endurance of man. The intrepid martyr, in no wise dismayed, boldly proclaimed Orthodox piety. He sharply and roundly censured the ungodliness and deceit of those misguided Hagarenes.

[16] Cf. Rom. 8:35, 39.

The impious Muslims, nonplused by his reaction, what did they cruelly devise against him? Another torture, similarly racking and pungent, took the form of red-hot copper sheathing that fit as a hood over his head. The lofty minded and ever-memorable Zacharias, with great manliness and bravery and a gladsome soul, bore this agonizing punishment. But since neither thrashing, nor burns to his head, nor a dark dungeon, nor chains, nor hunger, nor thirst, nor the most excruciating tortures proved equal to alter his resolve, those blood-dripping executioners and barbarians invented other tortures, more afflictive and harrowing. They, with much violence and savagery, fixed sharp reeds and splints under his fingernails and toenails. After the flow of much blood and resultant swelling, they then uprooted and pulled out the holy martyr's nails. This was done both to his hands and to his feet. Next they twisted his fingers. Zacharias remained shut up in the accursed house of the judge all the time that they were torturing him. The Muslims did not allow any Christian access to him. Only the guards entered therein, and they had only one concern: how to severely torture the insulter of their religion.

It should also be mentioned that no one in that house treated his wounds and hemorrhaging. As for the blessed Zacharias, he was happy with the thought that he was in some measure partaking of the Master Christ's sufferings. One anxiety alone plagued him: that he might die without having made his confession and without having received holy Communion of the Lord's body and blood. But God, Who does the will of those who fear Him,[17] hearkened to Zacharias' entreaty. He dispensed in His œconomy that the holy martyr should find a way to send a message to the *protosynkellos*[18] of the Metropolitan of Prousa. On the one hand, there was fear that perhaps Zacharias was not firm; on the other hand, there was no way to get near him. The matter was referred to the *demogerontia*, the municipal elders of the Orthodox community. The elders found a way to fulfill Zacharias' wish. A spiritual father was secretly brought to him. He made his confession and partook of the immaculate Mysteries. The blessed Zacharias arranged with that spiritual father to distribute all of his money, even as much as three thousand silver coins, as alms. The hallowed Zacharias, thus, contested well on behalf of Christ and conducted himself commendably in all things. His adversaries then summoned him for a final examination. The judge, before all present, asked him, "Of what persuasion art thou? Hast thou come to thy senses and repented?" The martyr gave answer: "It is well with me. I am come to the decision to die a Christian, believing in the trihypostatic God: Father, Son, and Holy Spirit, in the name of Whom I was baptized."

---

[17] Ps. 144:20.

[18] The *protosynkellos* in this case was the metropolitan's secretary.

The Hagarenes, hearing his statements, were amazed at his pluck and his freedom from dread in the face of death. However, what did they begin to do? They scoffed at him and treated him scornfully, saying, "Who is thy God and thy Christ for Whose love thou seekest death?" Zacharias spoke many things regarding the Trinity and the dispensation of the incarnation. He boldly addressed his mockers, who could not bear to hear him. Since they interrupted him, he brought his discourse unabashedly to a conclusion and said, "You are hardened, blinded, and led astray. You wretched ones do not even know what you believe. Believe, therefore, in the Christ that He might enlighten you to know your error." The Muslims, hearing these reproaches, answered him by raining down blows upon the martyr. They pushed him outside where he received a written decision, sentencing him to death by decapitation. Yea, even at this point, the Muslims entertained the notion that he might shrink back upon hearing the mode of execution! He was, after all, only thirty-eight years old. So they thought it to their advantage to leave him languishing in their prison for another day, thinking he might have a change of heart. The following day, they led the martyr to the judgment seat at the court. For the last time they offered him a great number of recoveries and dignities if, of course, he would deny his Orthodoxy. The martyr lifted up his voice and exclaimed, "O blind and unbelieving ones, in vain do you toil! For nothing is able to separate me from my most sweet Christ."

After this, they abused him and called him faithless and deserving of death. They directed the executioner to take charge of him and conduct him to the execution site. Similarly, the public herald was summoned and ordered to walk ahead and announce that the condemned man was faithless. The herald, before he began to blazon about the charge, approached the martyr. He, with an air of sympathy, started to say, "Why not come to thyself? Dost thou not pity thy life?" The martyr replied to him, "Go, go forth, and bruit about what they have commanded thee and have not a care for me." With this response, Zacharias' inner joy of soul was seen in his aspect. His countenance was made glad and joyous. With a modest and blessed chuckle, he sped to the execution site that he might receive, for the sake of Christ, the ever-blessed death that ushers in everlasting and endless life. Wheresoever he chanced upon Orthodox Christians, he shouted aloud, "Forgive me, brethren, and may God forgive you!" As he strode to the site, not too far off, he caught sight of the Church of Saint John the Theologian. Since it was necessary to pass by that church, Zacharias asked his escorts if he might go in and offer homage. The bailiffs allowed him this last request. After he set foot into the church and offered veneration, they pressed on into the neighborhood where Zacharias had his *kellion* (hermitage). Following this, he went to his knees and offered up prayer to God. He then waited upon the executioner to carry out his orders. The executioner unsheathed his sword. He brandished it before Zacharias in a threatening manner, having a mind to incite the prisoner to pity himself and to repent. But he was unable to sway him from his purpose. He wielded the sword and severed that sacred head with two blows.

Such was the end of the Hieromartyr Zacharias, who glorified God in his good contest and martyric death. There was joy in the heavens and earth—except for the patron of darkness, the devil, who sighed heavily, and his Hagarene minions. The beheading took place on the 28th day of May, in the year 1802. Zacharias' kinfolk assured us that he was thirty-eight years old. In order to view the holy martyr, there closed in upon that site not only Christians but also everyone found at Prousa. The Christians, enthusiastically but reverently, rushed forward to see the precious relics. They began sponging and wiping up the blood, taking even the ground that was touched by the holy relics. They collected these sacred souvenirs for their own sanctification.

It was then decided by the judge and the officers that the body was to be left for three days and nights at the execution site. But what happened? A divine light from on high, during the first night, shone down directly upon the martyric body, to the wonder and awe of the Hagarenes in the neighborhood. Fear came upon them so that sleep was seized from their eyes. In the morning, they went straightaway to the judge and recounted the night's frightening incident. They asked for permission to take away the dead man from that place. The judge would not condescend to their plea. The second night came and the same phenomenon took place. In the morning, the Hagarenes returned to their judge. This time they were raging mad and shouted at the judge, protesting, "Either give permission to remove the dead man from the site or we shall light a bonfire and burn thee!" The judge could neither convince them otherwise nor take on all of them. They were too filled with wrath to hear anything other than what they wanted to hear. The judge, thereupon, in order to avoid a fracas, gave orders to have the body removed that second day. The Christians gave the Hagarenes money, five hundred *grosia* (piasters)—a significant sum—in exchange for the relics. The Christians took the saint's body and buried him outside of the city.

Now it was heard that a mute child of one of the Armenians had touched the sacred relics and was immediately vouchsafed a clear speaking voice without the least impediment. This event was made known by the Orthodox to their metropolitan, Anthimos of Prousa. The obvious peril that could ensue from such a report caused him to take quick action. In his capacity as hierarch, and one full of praiseworthy zeal, he wrote to the church warden of the metropolis of the former Bishop Ignatios Lititzes and secretly had the relics transferred and buried in the Church of the Archangels at Demir Kapu. The Christians of Prousa, unaware that the original grave was evacuated of its sanctified occupant, still kept coming to honor the martyr. Bearing candles and incense, they chanted supplicatory hymns over the empty grave and entreated his help, for which they received healing of their infirmities. Indeed, brethren, the grace of the Spirit dwells in the saints, according to the divine Gregory of Thessalonike, and also does not depart from their relics and graves and churches and icons. Through the intercessions of the saints, may we, who are sinners, be vouchsafed the divine grace of the Holy Spirit that we, too, might be accounted worthy of the heavenly kingdom. Amen.

On the 28th of May, the holy Church commemorates Saint ANDREW, the Fool for Christ.[19]

Andrew, our righteous father, the one being called a fool for the sake of Christ, was of Scythian descent.[20] He shone forth in Constantinople during

---

[19] According to the unabridged Life of our venerable Father Andrew, the fool for the sake of Christ, the author is the Priest Nikephoros of the Great Church of God's Holy Wisdom (Hagia Sophia). Variant texts are found in different codices. Sophronios Efstratiades [*Hagiologion tes Orthodoxou Ekklesias* (Athens, 1960), p. 39] notes that there are three such versions in Hagiorite codices: Vatopedi 85 folio 1, 211 folio 15, 96 folio 1, 767; and, Lavreote Λ 15 folio 79, Ι 108 folio 2, Θ 17 folio 1. In like manner, there are different Sinaite codices. This text is printed in editions of the Greek *Patrologia Graeca*, Vol. 111, pp. 625-888. Testimonies are also contained within the *Leimonarion* [*P.G.* 87:2932-2936]. A special edition was printed with the service to the saint by Augustine the Jordanite (Jerusalem, 1912), which was taken from the 17th-C. Sinaite Codex under number 543 folios 1α-186α. This title was reprinted for a second time by the memorable Hagiorite, Hieromonk Evgenios Lemones (Athens, 1933). The Life, alone, some one hundred pages, was printed by Soterios Schoinas (Volos, 1961), which was taken from Codices 230 and 259 of the Athonite Monastery of Dionysiou. The compilers of *The Great Synaxaristes* (in Greek), on account of the length of the Life, have revised, edited, and abridged this version for incorporation into the May volume. The English version was enhanced as indicated within, using these collateral Greek sources: "S. Andreae Sali" in *P.G.* 111:627-888, also applying most of the subtitles; and *Osios Andreas o dia Christon Salos*, 10th ed., published by the Holy Paraclete Monastery (Oropos, Attike, 1995), with introduction by the monastery's prohegumen, Archimandrite Ignatios. The Paraclete publication is based on a number of sources: *P.G.* 111:627-888; and a Schoinas edition (Volos, 1976), which borrows from the Dionysiou codex of the 17th C. and two Sinaite codices of the 18th and 19th C. from Monk Augustine (Jerusalem, 1912).

[20] The Scythians were nomadical tribal groups of the Eurasian steppe, who were forced out of their habitat north of the Black Sea. They temporarily retained Dobrudja: this Roman province was officially called Scythia Minor and the interior of Crimea. Byzantines used the term Scythians as an archaism denoting all nomadic peoples. *The Oxford Dictionary of Byzantium*, s.v. "Scythians."

the reign of the Christ-loving and great Leo.[21] Under what kind of circumstances Andrew found himself in Constantinople is unknown. However, we do know this: that as a child he was in service to a certain dignitary of Constantinople. His master, Theognostos, was pious and God-fearing. To such a degree were Theognostos' prudence and discipline that his virtues came to the attention of the emperor, who honored him by raising him to the rank of *protospatharios*[22] and general of the east.

Theognostos, therefore, as one noble and wealthy, had significant substance and plenty of slaves. One of those who was in service to him was the blessed Andrew, who was still very young when his master bought him. The lad had a handsome countenance. Seeing his comely features, Andrew's master rejoiced and favored him above the others. Andrew alone was entrusted by him with those matters that required the utmost integrity, so that Andrew served as a courier. Theognostos, perceiving the youth's progress, enrolled him in school that Andrew might learn letters. The youth possessed such a fertile mind that even his teacher marvelled. Such was his genius, by reason of his advancement and knowledge in scholarship, that none could recognize that he was a Scythian. It was Theognostos' wish that Andrew should have more honor and recognition than the rest, because he saw that he was faithful and trustworthy. He, therefore, had Andrew clad in his own garb. As for the blessed Andrew, he nurtured a great love for reading the divine Scriptures and, especially, for the martyrdoms of the holy martyrs and the books of the God-bearing fathers.

---

[21] The phrase of Nikephoros "Leo the Christ-loving and great," has been interpreted variously: Some refer the description to Leo I the Butcher (457-474), in order to distinguish him from his grandson, Leo II the Little. Both Leo I and his wife Verina were conspicuous for their piety to the Virgin and ordering a reliquary for her *maphorion*. Others identify the sovereign to be Leo VI the Wise or Philosopher (886-912). He is the emperor depicted over the central door of Hagia Sophia. He had deposed Saint Photios and ushered in a controversy over his fourth royal marriage. Between the two emperors it is not possible to declare with absolute certainly one over the other. Most agree, however, that it was Leo I for the following reasons: (1) Saint Andrew speaks of meeting and praying with Saint Daniel the Stylite, who reposed in 493; (2) the saint mentions visiting the original Church of the Holy Apostles, which had been burnt during the Nika Revolt (January of 532), and afterward splendidly rebuilt by Justinian (r. 527-565), which new construction he beheld in a vision; and, (3) just before his repose, the saint foretold of his joining Saint Symeon, another fool for the sake of Christ in the east, who lived at the time of Emperor Justin I (518-527).

[22] *Protospatharios* or the chief *spatharios* was a dignity of the imperial hierarchy. It was a title which usually conferred membership in the Senate. The first reliable evidence is dated from 718. Up to the 10th C., it was a high title granted mostly to commanders of *themes*. In the 10th C., the dignity had two groups: the bearded and the eunuchs. *Oxford*, s.v. "Protospatharios."

He received, on the one hand, such delight upon hearing of the saints' feats; but, on the other hand, he was filled with compunction upon learning of their torments and tribulations. As a result, divine zeal was kindled in his heart. Let us now commence narrating how Andrew began a virtuous conduct of life and how he finished his course.

Concerning the Vision

The blessed Andrew, at every opportunity, was reading the martyric accounts of the saints, as we said earlier, which incited him to emulate their good conduct of life. He, thereupon, during the night, would rise up from his bed and recite prayers. The malicious devil, by God's permission, would not leave him untroubled. But as Andrew commenced to pray—behold!—the all-wicked creature fomented no common disturbance and struck the door. The blessed one, being a youth and still unlearned in such warfare, became frightened. He left off praying and immediately slipped into his bed and hid under the covers. Satan, beholding how Andrew became frightened and ceased praying, was happy and said to his fellow demons, "Behold, saliva is still dribbling from the mouth of this babe, yet he would arm for war against us!" After speaking thus, he became invisible. Andrew then slumbered and beheld in his sleep that he was at the city theater. On the one hand, in a certain section he observed many white-clad and luminous men; but, on the other hand, he beheld an innumerable horde of those creatures as dark as night like Ethiopians or Arabs. The two sides were seeking to enter into a wrestling match. The dusky creatures had in their midst one who was larger than the rest. He had a thousand under his command (*chiliarch*). The dark ones began speaking in the direction of those arrayed in white, saying, "Whosoever among you wishes to enter the lists, let him come forth and wrestle with this one."

The saint, hearing these words, looked and—behold!—there descended from the heaven a certain young and very comely Man Whose countenance was brighter than the sun. He bore in His hands three wondrous crowns. One crown was adorned with pearls. The second was embellished with precious stones. The third was decorated with lilies and flowers of Paradise. It was an amaranthine garland of such fragrance that the blessed Andrew marvelled and desired, if it were possible, to receive one of those crowns. Andrew, then, approached Him and said, "In the name of my Christ, for what sum wilt thou sell those crowns? Speak to me that I may know. Even though I am not able to purchase them, nevertheless, I shall go with haste and inform my master to come and obtain at least one of them; and he will give Thee as much money as Thou requirest." The young Man, just made manifest, Who was Christ Himself, appeared to smile slightly and said to Andrew, "Believe me, beloved, even if thou shouldest bring Me all the gold in this world, I would not give thee even one flower from among these, nor would I give one blossom to the one whom thou callest thy master. For these come not from this vain world, as thou dost imagine, but rather from the heavenly treasuries. With these are crowned as many as vanquish those blackened creatures. If, therefore, thou shouldest desire any of these, wrestle with that disgusting and swarthy creature; and, if thou shouldest overcome him, I shall give thee not only of these but also as many others as thou dost wish."

Saint Andrew

The blessed Andrew, hearing these things, plucked up courage and said to Him, "Master, receive me into the lists for the fight, only with what technique should I use to throw him over?" The Lord replied to Andrew, "Know, beloved, that these dark creatures are solely audacious, but they have no power at all. Cease fearing, then, this seemingly strapping fellow, because as a head of foul cabbage is he putrid and weak." Since He gave Andrew courage, Christ took hold of Andrew from the middle and showed him how to fight the bogey, commanding him with these words: "When the dark one grapples with thee, do not become afraid, but rather enfold him in a cross-like manner and thou shalt behold the power of God." Then did Andrew go forth to the middle of the arena and said with a great voice, "Make haste and come forth, O thou revolting, abject, and useless one! Let the two of us wrestle." Lo, there emerged that dusky creature, the commander of a thousand, who was challenged by Andrew! He lunged quickly, huffing and puffing and neighing. The creature attempted to instill terror in Andrew with his glance. He then seized Andrew for what seemed like an unbearably long time. Meanwhile, his fellow dusky creatures were filled with malignant joy and clapped while the white-clad men sighed. For Andrew was now pinned to the ground and felt as though his eyes would burst. Andrew then turned round and clutched at his opponent. Holding him in a cross-like brace, Andrew cast him to the ground. In this manner was Andrew's antagonist rendered speechless for a long while.[23] Those in white raiment, thereupon, filled with great joy, straightway, ran and took hold of Andrew. They embraced and kissed him, anointing him with divine myrrh. As for those creatures, black as the night, they fled in their profound shame. Forthwith, then, that illustrious young Man gave the crowns to the blessed Andrew and kissed him, saying, "From today, thou art My particular friend and sweet brother. Be fighting the good fight, stripping thyself for the race. Fix thy thoughts and think slightly of the things of this world. Become a fool for My sake, and I shall count thee worthy of many good things in My kingdom."

The blessed one, after hearing these things, was awakened and deliberated upon the vision he had seen. "When dawn broke, Andrew came to me, the unworthy one (Nikephoros), and told me of the vision. As I was listening to him recount it, I was beside myself because a marvellous fragrance wafted forth from him as the scent of costly myrrh. The two of us thus decided to feign imbecility, even as fools, in accordance with the utterance of the Lord, 'Become a fool for My sake that I should count thee worthy of many good things in My kingdom.' In fact, there was no other way possible for Andrew to be released from his present earthly master. During the following night, at the hour of midnight, Andrew rose up to pray. At the close of his prayer, he took up a dagger. He went to the mouth of the well and began cutting into little pieces his garments. Affecting as though he were a lunatic, he muddled and confused his words,[24] shouting loudly in imitation of those afflicted with madness. From his many outcries, he stirred up the cook who thought dawn broke. The cook hurried to the well to fill his jar. When the situation became clear to him, he left the jar and sped to the house. He shouted aloud, 'Come and see! Andrew is possessed by a demon!' The master, meanwhile, was chanting his morning prayers.[25] When the master heard such tidings, he was grieved. He called his wife and the others of his household. They hastened to Andrew and, as soon as they caught sight of him, they began to weep. Indeed, they truly lamented and acknowledged that he was possessed. The master of the house, with profound sorrow, commanded that Andrew be brought to the Church of the Great-martyr Anastasia. Theognostos directed that iron chains be put on Andrew's feet. He also sent money along to the warden of that temple for the care and treatment of Andrew."

---

[23] *P.G.* 111:636BC.

[24] *P.G.* 111:637B.

[25] *P.G.* 111:637C.

The blessed Andrew, thereupon, spent the entire day babbling, as one out of his wits and beside himself. When night fell, Andrew was praying with tears. He besought Saint Anastasia to reveal in his sleep if endeavoring upon such behavior were pleasing to God. When he rested a little from his prayer and lamentations, he saw—lo!—an elder, replete with glory, coming. Five women accompanied him and were going around to the sick folk in the temple. After they visited all who were there, they advanced toward Andrew. The elder, pretending that he knew nothing, turned toward one of those very radiant women and said, "Lady Anastasia, why dost thou not also heal this one?" The holy woman remarked, "His Teacher has already told him, 'Become a fool for the sake of My love and I will make thee an heir of all the good things in My kingdom.' The Teacher has healed him and so he no longer requires healing. But he shall be an elect vessel of the Lord, and sanctified and beloved in the Holy Spirit." The elder then commented, "I, too, knew it, my lady, I knew it." Having spoken these words, the holy women bid farewell to the elder and entered into the church where they became invisible. Andrew wondered at all he had seen and he gave glory to God and His Great-martyr Anastasia, who came quickly when invoked for help.

Andrew spent the entire day in chains and put nothing in his mouth. The coming night, at the hour of midnight, as he was standing and entreating the Lord in his thoughts, he supplicated Saint Anastasia to assist him that he might finish the work which he had undertaken. Then the devil appeared before his eyes. He appeared as a black Arab and with him came many demons. Some were toting axes; others were armed with swords and spears; and still others were carrying ropes. That accursed Arab-like creature, bearing an axe, gnashed his teeth and rushed upon Andrew to cut him. In like manner followed the others who were with him. The blessed Andrew stretched forth his hand to God. With tears, he cried out loudly, "O Lord, deliver not unto beasts the soul that does confess Thee."[26] After that, he added, "O Saint John, apostle and theologian, help me!" Straightway, with the word—O the wonder!—there occurred a thunderclap from on high, and a sound as it were from a multitude. There appeared a large-eyed elder, a little bald on the forehead, whose countenance was more brilliant than the sun.[27] Many others accompanied him. The elder made the sign of the Cross in the air. He then turned to the others who were with him, saying, "Run quickly and make fast the temple doors lest any should flee!" Forthwith, they ran and closed the doors. The demons shrieked loudly and were saying one to the other, "Woe to us! It was a bad hour that we came here. For John is strict and will torment us terribly."

---

[26] Ps. 73:20.

[27] *P.G.* 111:641BC.

The Apostle John—for it was he who appeared—ordered the removal of Andrew's chain, which was coiled about his neck, and that it be brought to him. This took place as directed. The apostle then folded the chain in three and stood outside the door, saying, "Bring to me here, one by one, those black beings." The first one was brought whom they stretched out on the ground. The holy apostle scourged him mercilessly, by means of Andrew's threefold chain, with one hundred lashes. Then the other creatures were brought forth, one after the other, who were flogged by the apostle in the same manner. Not one was left unpunished. The blessed Andrew heard the noise that the demons were making. He began to laugh and say, "Of a truth they received such scourges that no other nature could have endured." Those who beat them were saying as they did so, "Go and teach these things to thy father, Satan, and see if he likes it."[28] After the demons vanished, that honorable elder went to the slave of God, Andrew, and again placed the chain about his neck, saying, "Dost thou see how I came instantly and helped thee? I have much concern and love for thee, only be patient until thou art proven in all things. Not many days will pass before I shall loose thee from the irons that thou mayest walk about according to thine own will and good pleasure." After the Apostle John spoke thus, the blessed Andrew asked, "And who art thou, milord?" He answered, "I am John, the one who leaned on the immaculate and life-creating breast of the Christ." After that disclosure, he vanished from before the eyes of Andrew. The blessed Andrew remained and glorified God Who delivered him from such temptations, so that he began to say, "O Lord Jesus Christ, great is Thy might that Thou hast had mercy on me, the sinner. Guard me in Thy truth and vouchsafe me to find grace by Thee, O Master most merciful!"

Such were the words of the saint's prayer as he passed that day. When night came, he slumbered a little. As he rested, he beheld in his sleep that he was in a royal palace. The King summoned him and said, "Wilt thou serve Me with all thy heart that I might make thee one of the glorious ones of My palace?" The blessed Andrew said, "And who is that one, Lord, who loves not what is good for him? I very much love that which Thou hast determined." Then the King said, "Therefore, since thou hast love, receive introspection of My kingdom." With that word, He gave Andrew something to eat which was like unto snow. Andrew took it and ate it. He found it so sweet that the mind of man is unable to form a notion of it. As he ate it, he asked to be given another taste; because even as the blessed one was saying that when he partook of it, he thought it was divine myrrh. Andrew, consequently, was given another. But this one resembled quince, and the Lord said, "Take and eat." Andrew then partook. This mouthful was sour and bitter as wormwood. From

[28] *P.G.* 111:644A.

the bitterness, Andrew shook his head a little and forgot the sweetness of the first food. When the King observed that Andrew was affected harshly, He said to him, "Behold how thou dost not endure the bitter taste! I have given thee a taste of My perfect service, because this is the narrow and straitened pathway that leads to life."[29] The blessed man said, "Bitter is this thing, Master, and who is able to eat of these and to serve Thee?"[30]

The King continued, "What sayest thou? The bitter only hast thou known? Did I not give thee first the dulcet and afterward the bitter?" Andrew answered, "Yea, Master, but is it only the bitter, concerning which Thou didst say it is like unto the narrow pathway, that will be given?" The King replied, "In no wise! May it not be! But between the bitter and the sweet is the narrow pathway. On the one hand, the bitter comprises the contests and pangs. On the other hand, the sweetness is the dew of My Spirit and the consolation of as many as have suffered temptations for My love. It is, therefore, not one pattern of bitterness throughout; nor, again, is it one sweet direction. But sometimes the way is sweet, and at other times it is bitter; each episode is being succeeded by the other experience. If, then, thou wouldest serve Me, even as thou hast spoken, declare it to Me that I may attend to it."[31] The blessed man said, "Grant me to eat of it for one other time, and then shall I say yea or nay." He, once more, gave him from the bitter and it affected him very harshly; and so he commented, "I am not able to eat from this and to serve Thee." It then seemed that the King smiled somewhat. He drew out of His breast something of a fiery constitution to contemplate. After the fashion of many flowers was it most fragrant and colorful. He then said to Andrew, "Take and eat that thou mayest forget everything thou hast seen and heard." Andrew took it and ate from that most sweet food. He came to be beside himself, from the delight and boundless joy. This happened for a long while. He had never before experienced that in himself, that is, to be as one in ecstasy[32] from some great sweet

---

[29] Cf. Mt. 7:14.

[30] *P.G.* 111:645A.

[31] *P.G.* 111:645B (ἐπίσταμαι as an old med. form of ἐφίστημι).

[32] Saint Chrysostom: "What does this expression *ekstasis* mean? A spiritual contemplation or view happened to him—the soul was caused to stand outside of the body." ["Hom. 22 on Acts 10:10," *P.G.* 60:178 (col. 172).] Saint Gregory Palamas: "Although God makes those who pray sincerely go out of themselves, rendering them transcendent to their natures and mysteriously ravished away to heaven, yet even in such cases, since they are concentrated within themselves, it is through the mediation of their souls and body that God effects things supernatural, mysterious, and incomprehensible to the wise of this world." ["The Hesychast Method of Prayer, and the Transformation of the Body," *The Triads*, II.ii.5(14), The Classics of Western Spirituality (New York, NY: Paulist Press, 1983).]

savor and glory and delightful contentedness.[33] When he came to himself, he fell at the feet of the King and said to Him, "Have mercy on me, O good Master, and, henceforth deprive me not of service to Thee! For I know it is truly sweet." The King said, "Believe, beloved, that of the good things that I possess, this is the smallest. However, if thou wilt enter with thy heart into service to Me, My things shall be thine and I shall make thee an heir of My kingdom." The blessed Andrew then awakened. He kept all these things in his heart.

After the passage of four months at the church, the clergy observed that Andrew was not being healed; much rather, he suffered worse symptoms of one stark mad. They went and informed his master. Theognostos, after he heard this evaluation, decided to register Andrew in the rolls of the mentally disturbed as one out of his wits and demonized. Theognostos then ordered that Andrew be loosed from his chains and released to go wheresoever he wished. After he was freed from his bonds, Andrew ran into the streets and squares of the city where he played throughout the day and danced. "When evening fell, he came to me, the unworthy one, that is to say, his spiritual father.[34] He found me alone in my cell. He smiled slightly and then tears began to drench his countenance. I, as soon as I caught sight of him, straightway, rose up and embraced him for a while as we greeted one another. We then sat down. I asked him how he was delivered from his bonds. He, then, began to recount to me, meekly, the whole truth from beginning to end. For it was only with me that he spoke frankly and correctly, without playing a part. To everyone else, however, he talked as one delirious or not at all."[35]

Concerning the Abusive Youths

Then, "at the crack of dawn, Andrew embraced me and departed for his spiritual labor. He found his way to the bakeries, where certain young men noticed how he spoke crazily. They took Andrew by the hand and went to a tavern and bought wine. The young men sat down and drank. When intoxication began to overtake them, they struck Andrew, as on object of derision, on the back of his neck. They wished to use him for their own entertainment and to exalt themselves upon his debasement. They would let Andrew neither leave, nor drink, nor eat. In a state of abstinence he only stood there before them, as they laughed him to scorn. The righteous one, seeing how ill-disposed were the young men, was thinking how he might most fittingly requite them. As Andrew observed that one of them placed on the table his cup full of the best wine, he seized the wine and drank it. Andrew took the cup, broke it over that young man's head, and then took to his heels. They gave chase and caught him. They

---

[33] *P.G.* 111:645C.

[34] Father Nikephoros, the biographer, is speaking here.

[35] *P.G.* 111:648B.

swooped upon him and gave him a beating. Following this, they brought him back to the tavern. Once again, the youths sat down and drank. As for the blessed Andrew, they gave him nothing except for cuffs on the back of the neck which made them laugh. When night fell, they rose up and exited the tavern. Andrew then said to them, 'Imbeciles and madmen, now what will I answer when I meet with the night sentries and they bind me?' The righteous man spoke, thus, in his own person, but actually it foretold what he knew was about to befall the young men. They, nevertheless, left him behind and departed. Andrew went forth and came upon a corner of the marketplace where he went to sleep. In the meanwhile, the young louts, after they roistered about and fulfilled their evil desires in a house of prostitution with unseemly women, remained there until the second watch of the night, destroying the beauty of their souls. Afterward, they went toward their houses. On the way, they encountered the city patrol on their night rounds. They arrested the youths and bound them. They passed by the place where the saint had been taking his ease. At that site, the patrolmen rained down blows on the wayward youths. Andrew witnessed this and, with tears, besought God that the young men not be sent to prison. By the intervention of their kinfolk and Andrew's prayers, the young men were released and returned to their homes. One of them acknowledged that Andrew truly predicted what would befall them by speaking of them in his own person. He also admitted to one of his fellows that they ought not to have beaten Andrew so piteously. The youth just scoffed, saying Andrew was not only a fool and demonized but also one for whom God had no care to requite any wrongs done to him."[36]

In the morning, the blessed Andrew arose and walked about in the midst of the marketplace. He was not only hungry and thirsty but also treated despitefully by others throughout the day. He did not sit down even once. When night came, he went to a corner of the city and chased away the dogs from the spot where they had been resting. Andrew, instead, took their place. He was naked and destitute. When dawn arrived, he began to say to himself, "Behold, O wretched Andrew, as a dog thou hast spent the night with the dogs! Let us be off to work, for—woe to thee!—death is imminent. Let not thy thoughts mislead thee that thou shalt have someone to help thee in the hour of thy death. For each person, at the time of death, shall eat of the fruits of his labors and pains. Hasten, then, with toil. Moreover, let us undergo insults and let us suffer persecution in this world, that we might receive glory and honor from the heavenly King: our Lord Jesus Christ, the Son of God." And so Andrew sped onward, in accordance with the words of the Apostle Paul: he

[36] *P.G.* 111:648C-649C.

stretched forth to those things which are before.[37] When Andrew came into the view of others, they were saying that he was one of the newly demonized. Others were saying that Andrew's ways were not those of a fool. There were some who had compassion upon him, but there were others who boxed his ears or spat upon him. Andrew bore with all these indignities. Now the blessed man was engaged at secret prayer in the treasury of the heart, so that his whispering lips were heard from afar even as one hears a boiling kettle seething. Those who saw the vapor from his mouth imagined something else and remarked, "See how, from the evil spirit's violent irritation to his heart, he produces vapor!" This was how his unceasing and God-pleasing prayer was made manifest.[38]

Concerning Meretricious Conduct

One day, as the saint was walking in the district where there were houses of fornication and harlots, he was playing the fool and laughing, as was his custom. One of the courtesans, seeing him disport in this fashion, thought him a madman. She ran and grabbed hold of him, taking him to her house of sin. The steadfast Andrew, of adamantine will and the true mocker of the devil, did not oppose her. He followed her straightway. The other courtesans, when they caught sight of Andrew, ran over and surrounded him. They began laughing, even as they were accustomed, and pertly questioned him in a saucy manner. "Hapless one, how has this happened to thee?" The righteous one only released a half-amused laugh and did not respond. Those indecent women then slapped him on the neck. Some brazen ones attempted to draw him into sin. The righteous one saw that the devil of fornication was standing in the midst of the women. He was swarthy as an Ethiopian, black as midnight. He had no hair on his head but dung mingled with ashes. His eyes were like those of a fox. He held at his shoulder a filthy rag which smelled strong of three malodorous scents: rot, sewage, and dung. From the rank odors, the blessed man felt nauseous. He kept spitting on the ground. The demon, seeing that he was repulsive to Andrew, began to say, "The people hold me in their hearts to be as sweet as honey, and does this fellow, who mocks the world, loathe me with spittle?" The blessed Andrew beheld the creature with his senses. The harlots, though they saw nothing yet they heard him. The blessed one derided the demon for his obscene behavior and foul smell. Andrew became angry with him and cast him out. The harlots said, "See how he converses in a ridiculing manner with his demon." The harlots then observed, "What a fine garment he has! Come and let us take it and sell it that we might drink wine this day." They removed his tunic and left him naked. One of the harlots then made a suggestion: "Let us dress him in a straw mat." They, therefore, cut an opening

---

[37] Phil. 3:13.

[38] *P.G.* 111:652A-C.

in a straw mat that Andrew's head might pass through. As it hung from his neck, he departed from that place. Whoever caught sight of him, with that old straw mat wrapped about him, snickered and said, "That is a good pack-saddle that thy donkey is wearing, thou fool!" Andrew said, "Indeed, O silly ones, it is a good and large cloak, for the Master made me a patrician."[39] Now not everyone acted disagreeably toward the saint. Some Christ-lovers gave alms, though he asked for nought. He received from such twenty or thirty *lepta*,[40] which he distributed among the poor. First he would visit those haunts where the indigent collected. Andrew would mock them and stir them up. If anyone attempted to seize him, Andrew pushed him off. The other paupers, thereupon, would rise up and strike him with staves. Using this as a cause to flee, Andrew would scatter the obols[41] which the paupers snatched up as their own.[42]

Concerning the Prediction for the Child Epiphanios

The blessed one, as was his custom, went about the bakeries. On one such occasion, he encountered three fair-haired youths who were comely in both body and soul. They were extremely virtuous and God-fearing. The eldest was the leader in their practise of good works. He was the first among those youths who, in the Spirit, recognized the true things about the blessed Andrew; so that he remarked to his comrades, "Believe me, beloved ones, when I say that, as I understand it, that fool is verily a slave of God!" The other youth said, "I beseech thee, make a way so we might take him privately to a secret place that he might explain himself to us." The first one answered, "If thou dost wish it now, I will bring him to you." Immediately, the first one hastened and went before the blessed Andrew. He addressed him and said, "Brother, lovest thou me? Come and sit down with us, for my companions and I very much love thee." The blessed Andrew smiled and said, "Art thou my friend, Epiphanios, my child?" The blessed one then prophesied in the Holy Spirit and said, "Know this, my child, that in the future thou shalt become patriarch of this city."[43] They took one another's hand and went to the other two youths.

---

[39] *P.G.* 111:652C-656A. *The Great Synaxaristes* (in Greek), as well as *Osios Andreas* of Paraclete Monastery [p. 39] have the phrase "the emperor made me a patrician," whereas the *Patrologia Graeca* [111:656A] has "the Master made me a patrician."

[40] The *lepton* (pl. *lepta*) was a small copper coin.

[41] Obols were small coins.

[42] *P.G.* 111:656AB.

[43] This is, possibly, Epiphanios, Patriarch of Constantinople (520-535), who is commemorated by the holy Church on the 25th of August. Some sources assume the youth was later Patriarch Polyefktos (956-970), commemorated on the 5th of February [see note in "The Life of Saint Andrew, Fool for Christ of Constantinople," *The Orthodox Word*, Vol. 15, No. 3(86) (May-June 1979): 129, translated from the Slavonic of the October Volume (Moscow, 1904), pp. 52-74].

Epiphanios divulged how the blessed Andrew addressed him by name and then called him friend, though an earlier acquaintance never existed between them.[44]

The desire and faith of those goodly youths, upon hearing such a report, increased. Thus, they went to a tavern and sat down in a place hidden from general view. The three young men bought bread and fish, placing it before Andrew. The venerable man, seeing their good disposition, rejoiced greatly. He uttered a prayer in his inward thoughts, offering thanks to God. He partook of something, but he also gave them of the food from his own hands. However, true and faithful is the word. Faithful is the saying and worthy of all acceptance[45] that Andrew partook of only half of a biscuit in an entire day. Even at table, then, with the three young men, he again left more on his plate than he consumed. With regard to wine, it was the same. Whenever someone offered him a cup, he drank. When he was alone, however, he never drank. Ofttimes, he spent three and four days, and even a week, when he put nothing in his mouth. This happened when Satan hardened the heart of most and, thus, they would not give him anything. As for Andrew, he would never constrain anyone to give him anything lest he should become a burden.[46]

"Let us come to the order of the narration. As he was sitting in the tavern with those three honorable young men, I, the least of all, also happened to pass by. Since I heard his voice, I took a seat in a concealed spot and observed carefully what was transpiring. The youths bid Andrew farewell, rose up, and departed. The tavern-keeper, as well, also stepped away from his shop for some errand, thus leaving Andrew alone. Since he saw no one else and believed he was alone, Andrew raised his hands heavenward and made an entreaty on behalf of those youths. As God is my witness, beloved, I beheld him, when he was praying, that he was lifted from the floor. He was suspended in the air. And as I witnessed this, I became afraid. After he completed his prayer, he made the sign of the Cross. Feet on the ground once more, he again resumed his work as a fool for Christ. He went forth to the crowd of people and performed his usual antics."[47]

Concerning the Violence of a Winter Storm

There was at one time a great winter storm with heavy snowfall that covered the city. It was so cold that many were found dead from hunger and cold. Some trees snapped and others were uprooted. Birds perished from the dearth of food. "I was exceedingly grieved for the slave of God. First, I was aware that he was totally in need; second, I knew not where he might be. So I only made this remark: 'By now, wheresoever he may be, he shall have died.'

[44] *P.G.* 111:657AB.
[45] 1 Tim. 1:15; 4:9.
[46] *P.G.* 111:657C.
[47] *P.G.* 111:660B.

That bitter winter weather held out for two weeks. Just as the winds abated—behold!—there appeared the blessed man. He came to me in the deep of night. When I clapped my eyes on him, my soul was amazed. Straightway, I embraced him and greeted him with a holy kiss. After much time passed, keeping silent from excessive joy, I said to the righteous one, 'Let us be seated, my beloved, for I have something to tell thee.' As he ceased weeping, he said to me very pleasantly, 'Set a table that we may eat.'[48]

"When I heard him speak thus, I was very happy. As I provided that the manservant should prepare the table, Andrew said to me, 'Why wast thou sorrowing so much for me, father, thinking that I too died from the cold as my brethren and fellow indigents? Dost thou not know that the One Who said to me that if I should serve with all my heart that He would make me an inheritor of His kingdom, that He is with me and guards me? And dost thou not know that for all those who hope in God with all their heart, they have great joy both now and in the age to come?' Hearing him speak in this manner, it entered my mind that some miracle for him came to pass. I began to question him with supplicating words to disclose what befell him. The blessed man said to me, 'Dost thou not know, my brother, that I was in the streets and squares doing what I always do? However, my friend, thy yearning and love very much compels me to declare the truth. But I adjure thee, that for as long as I am living and am in this world, not to publish anything out of thy mouth of those things that I am about to reveal to thee.' I then promised not to speak a word to anyone.

"Since I promised to keep his secret, he said to me, 'As thou knowest, beloved, great need overtook me in that storm; for I was naked, uncovered, and barefoot. I did not think I could endure, so I went to some needy folk like unto me that I might sit with them for a little while. They would not have me; but rather, as a dog, they drove me off with their staves and said, "Depart from here, thou dog!" I had no place to rest, so that I despaired of my life. I began to say, "Blessed art Thou my God! For if I should die from the cold, yet it would be reckoned as a martyrdom for me." Upon such things was I deliberating as I went to a certain corner where a dog was sleeping. I thought to lay down next to the creature, for it came into my mind that I might find a little warmth near him. That creature, nonetheless, as it glanced at me, rose up and dashed off. I then mulled over what took place and said to myself, "Wretched one, seest thou what a sinner thou art, so that even the dogs flee from thee? Men turn away from me as they would from a wicked demon. My fellow poor folk chase me away. What recourse, then, hast thou? What wilt thou do? Die, profligate, die! For thou hast no other deliverance." Shivering and trembling

---

[48] *P.G.* 111:660CD.

from that acute cold spell, in dire pain I came to compunction and wept. All my members were frozen when I fixed the gaze of my inward eyes on God alone, thinking that I should soon be expiring from this present sphere.'"[49]

Concerning the Seizure into the Heavens

Andrew continued: "'As I was ruminating in this manner, there suddenly came to me a warmth. I then opened my eyes and beheld an exceedingly beautiful youth, whose lightning flash countenance was radiant like the sun. He was holding in his hand a golden branch intertwined with dewy lilies and roses. They were not like unto the roses of this world. Away with the thought! They were rather of diverse colors of another nature and appearance. He brushed my face with that florid bough, saying, "Andrew, where art thou?" I said, "In darkness and in a shadow of death." He again brushed my face with that beauteous flower-bearing branch and said to me, "Receive life unmastered by thy body." Immediately with that phrase, the fragrance of those flowers entered into my heart; and like lightning, life came to me again. I, once more, heard a voice saying, "Take him away for a consolation, till two weeks pass, and then send him back; for I say that he must needs be struggling a while longer in the earth." Furthermore, together with that word, a heavy sleep came over me. And what happened I know not. Although it seemed that I slept all night and awakened in the morning, yet actually two weeks had gone by which the counsel of the all-good God commanded.[50]

"'I beheld that most pleasant, wondrous, and grace-filled Paradise of variegated flowers and scents. My soul was in an ecstatic spiritual state and I was going over in my mind, "What then was that which happened to me? My dwelling place is Constantinople, so how do I find myself here?" Wondering at the event, I was unable to comprehend it. I then began to say to myself, "Behold how I truly am mad! For while I ought to give thanks and to glorify God, Who has wrought so much good for me, yet I sit here and make inquiries about such a great and admirable wonder." I felt within myself that I was without flesh, because it seemed to me that I was utterly bereft of flesh.[51] I,

---

[49] *P.G.* 111:664A.

[50] *P.G.* 111:664BC.

[51] Saint Symeon the New Theologian: "He who is united to God by faith and recognizes Him by action is indeed enabled to see Him by contemplation. He sees things of which I am not able to write. His mind sees strange visions and is wholly illuminated and becomes like light, yet he is unable to conceive of them or describe them. His mind is itself light and sees all things as light, and the light has life and imparts light to him who sees it. He sees himself wholly united to the light; and, as he sees, he concentrates on the vision and is as he was. He perceives the light in his soul and is in ecstasy. In his ecstasy he sees it from afar, but as he returns to himself he finds himself again in the (continued...)

rather, was covered with a white garment, which glistened like snow, and was studded with precious stones. When I looked upon it, I rejoiced on account of its great beauty. My head was encircled with a shimmering crown of gold, plaited with every kind of flower. My feet, so it seemed to me, were shod with sandals. A belt girded me that was deep scarlet. The air of Paradise gleamed with ineffable light, redolent from the diverse blooming flowers beaming in every hue. Exotic scents entered my nostrils which filled me with gladness.' He then paused—but believe me, my hair stood on end!—as my mind and thought shuddered from all that he uttered. He then said that he felt as though he were a king in the house of God. 'Seeing what I saw for myself,' he added, 'I greatly rejoiced within myself.'[52]

"He then said that 'God made to rise up in that place every specie of tree. But they were not as those of this world. Certainly not! They were ever-green and ever-blooming. They were of a different nature, flowing with honey and lofty foliage. They were bending their boughs and swaying toward one another. They emitted a delightful fragrance into the atmosphere and assumed a form like unto a rainbow.[53] The blessed share in these things and are bedewed with joy and gladness, whereby the sight thereof and the delight fill the soul. What is most uniquely marvellous is the appearance of some. There are those that are strangely altered or entwined and those that are comely and majestic. Some possessed perennial and unwithering blossoms, whereas others He commands to be adorned with leaves and fruits. Still others bore blossoms and leaves, showing a delightful aspect. The sight was alien to this world. The precious fruits were resplendent and beyond anything with which I could make a comparison. There were also these great wonders. On the towering branches

---

[51](...continued)
midst of the light." *The Discourses*, Ch. II, § 12, Classics of Western Spirituality Series (NY: Paulist Press, 1980), p. 56.

"I conversed with this light. The light itself knows it. It scattered whatever mist there was in my soul and cast out every earthly care. It expelled from me all material denseness and bodily heaviness that made my members to be sluggish and numb. What an awesome marvel! It so invigorated and strengthened my limbs and muscles, which had been faint through great weariness, that it seemed to me as though I was stripping myself of the garment of corruption. Besides all this, there was poured into my soul, in unutterable fashion, a great spiritual joy and perception and a sweetness surpassing every taste of visible objects, together with a freedom and forgetfulness of all thoughts pertaining to this life. In a marvellous way there was granted to me and revealed to me the manner of the departure from this present life. Thus, all the perceptions of my mind and soul were wholly concentrated on the ineffable joy of that light." Ibid., Ch. XVI, § 3, pp. 200, 201.

[52] *P.G.* 111:664C-665A.

[53] *Osios Andreas*, Paraclete, p. 49.

were flying creatures, and sparrows, and winged insects,[54] and other creatures with their own beautiful names, with wings that were gold and snow-white. Some were perched among the leaves of the trees and were chirping and twittering. The sound of their sweet melody, harmonious and pleasing, seemed to me to be heard to the height of the heaven. As I conjectured on those sparrows, trying to understand them, my mind was seized as in a state of ecstasy. Because as a rose or as a lily or as some other kind of flower, which I do not know how to classify, were those sparrows, since they were exceedingly strange and poised on high as in midair. Again, after I was astonished at the exquisiteness of the first bird, I contemplated another bird having the gilding and color of another glory and appearance. Once more, I found another creature, most singular, taking great joy in its unceasing and cheering melody. Who, however, can narrate of the foreign character and disquieting beauty which appeared in that place? All those beautiful trees standing in due proportion and harmony, placed side by side, arrayed in order. O the blessed hand that planted these![55]

"'But again, I went to the inner parts of Paradise, so that I thought I should never again behold the darkness of this world. For it seemed to me that all things of this world were comparatively dark in relation to those there. As I was walking about, there was, in the middle of the Paradise, a great river that watered all those trees gently entering their root systems. Those well-favored sparrows were coming and drinking from those waters, continuing their harmonious melodies. Encroaching the river there was a spreading vine, adorned with leaves glistening like gold. The luminosity of its goodly branches was like unto light and a precious stone, even as it has been written: "I am the vine,"[56] and "Behold, I lay for the foundations of Sion a costly stone, a choice, a cornerstone, a precious stone, for its foundations."[57] Now this vine unfolded over the garden, laden with clusters of enormous and eye-filling grapes. Its tendrils coiled and enmeshed themselves, crowning and embellishing all the plants and trees which were there. As I observed all these things, my heart rejoiced within me, as I was conveyed from awe to wonder and from wonder to ecstasy in my soul. For a considerable time I just stood there and marvelled. I then heard a wind out of the east, wafting forth an indescribable fragrance.

---

[54] Τέττιγες (τέττιξ), that is, *cicala*, *Cicada plebeia* or allied species, a winged insect fond of basking on trees. The chirping and clicking sound made by them is frequently used as a simile for sweet sounds. Liddell & Scott, *Greek-English Lexicon*, 9th ed. (1968, repr.). These winged creatures, seen by Saint Andrew, are a genus by themselves.

[55] *P.G.* 111:665B-668A.

[56] Jn. 15:1.

[57] Is. 28:16; Eph. 2:20.

The blowing wind met the trees and rustled them. The scent was such that I had the notion that angels were offering incense in the heavens before God.[58]

"'With the abating of that wind, which brought forth that unexampled scent which I thought to be the angels' incense before God, I then thought that I heard the sound of another wind. It came from the west, bearing a sweet scent that filled me with delight. When this wind blew, it emitted a vapor like unto snow. The sight and stateliness of the trees effused a unique scent, surpassing all earthly fragrances, so that I forgot those notable wonders which I earlier enjoyed. As for those melodic sparrows, I was beside myself at the harmonious flow of music. Now those sparrows, whether they were or were not angels only God knows. Again, there came forth a third wind out of the north that was more magnificent, fiery, emitting rays like unto the iris of the sun. When that north wind blew it was very gentle as it undulated those glittering plants and trees. As it passed, it stirred up a rosy scent among the trees, so that for a long while I was ecstatic from that most sweetened air. Feeling both awe and happiness, it left me greatly marvelling at this paradoxical phenomenon of lovely sweetness and how I should come to enjoy such gladness. Thereupon, that third wind grew still and there came to be a great silence. I walked a short space that I might pass through the river. As I advanced to the wide plain of the garden of God, I further reflected on the ineffable wealth of the almighty God which He has laid up in store and which the mouth of man cannot recount.[59]

"'Therefore, as I was proceeding toward the broad plain of the garden and considered carefully the Holy of the holies—behold!—again, a fourth wind blew, as the north, bearing a scent as that of roses and lilies, possessing a porphyry color like unto violets. The trees, as they quivered, yielded an odor superior to that of myrrh and musk, which entered the inner recesses of my heart. I was thinking then whether I possessed such eyes of the body or those of the spirit. The Master knows. To me it seemed that my body was that with which we shall have after the resurrection or, rather, with this body of mine I was walking around in that place. I, however, was feeling neither weight, nor desire, nor anything else in regard to my body. So much so did my thoughts refute me that I thought that I was without my body, clinging to the things that were there. I do not know what to tell thee. God, Who knows the hearts, knew.[60] Now as those plants and trees were fluttering back and forth from the

---

[58] *P.G.* 111:668AB.

[59] *P.G.* 111:668B-669B.

[60] "Although the vision of God through the power of the Cross and the resurrection is beyond the senses and reason and mind, it includes them all, senses and reason and mind, because the entire man is granted *theosis*, that is, the entire man becomes god by grace, seeing the Father through Christ in the Spirit." John Romanides, *An Outline of*

(continued...)

breeze of that fourth wind, I heard the sweetest sound as gusts of that astonishing fragrance, again, entered into my nostrils. Speechlessness befell me as I stood there. However, I was sensing an inexpressible dazzling radiance in my mind. I felt great gladness and cheer, so that my heart shouted aloud and my spirit rejoiced. Then the fourth wind fell still. I then discovered a wonder both awesome and contrary to expectation. Although so much time had elapsed, still there was not the least appearance of night. But rather what I saw there was uninterrupted light, as well as joy and life, splendor and much gladness.[61]

"'After these things, I came into a state of ecstasy. I, thereupon, thought that I was standing above the firmament of the heaven and that a certain youth, wrapped in a cloak, went before me, whose countenance shone like the sun. I was thinking that he was the same one who had caressed my face with that flowering branch when I was perishing from the cold. He charged his subordinates to raise me up. As he was guiding me—behold!—I saw a great cross, terrifying and of remarkable beauty. It appeared in the form of a rainbow in the cloud. There were four veils round about, methinks, like a brilliant cloud of light. Two of the veils, fiery red, shone forth like lightning; the other two, however, were as white as snow. Encircling the cross there stood melodists, tall and handsome, and as white as the light. Their eyes shone as lightning with fiery rays. They were chanting a certain marvellous melody concerning the One Who was crucified—Christ. The young man, my guide with the mantle, went straight to the cross, and kissed it with ardor. He then beckoned to me to do likewise. I followed suit, venerating and kissing the cross. As I kissed that fiery precious wood, I was filled with a spirit, honey sweet, and a scent greater than any I had smelled even in Paradise.'[62]

"'I lifted my eyes and saw—behold!—there was below the abyss of the sea. I was seized with trembling and fear, so that I cried out to my guide and said to him, "Milord, guide me. Behold, it is as if I am walking on a cloud! And I am fearful that, perhaps, I should stumble and fall into the waters that lie below us." Then he said to me, "Cease fearing, for we are going up higher." And, forthwith, he took me by the hand. We found ourselves above the second firmament, which appeared to be as white as snow. I saw there, also, two crosses which were the same as the earlier one. An awesome service was being conducted, even as had been chanted before the cross below. The air was fiery, which was restful and refreshing to the beautiful youths. We, thereupon, kissed the two crosses with love and divine longing, even as we had the first cross. The fragrance of the two crosses was as the fragrance of God, inexplicable

---

[60](...continued)
Orthodox Patristic Dogmatics, p. 115.

[61] *P.G.* 111:669B-D.

[62] *P.G.* 111:669D-672B.

beyond compare to the gladness of heart, delights, and pleasures that we know below. And again I looked, and—behold!—everything was aflame. Frightened again, I called out for help to my guide. He took me by the hand and said, "We must yet ascend higher." Straightway, we found ourselves above the third heaven. Now this place did not look like here, in this world, but something else. Instead of a solid or firm ground beneath us, a glen or gully spread before us, as a kind of golden petal. We again found ourselves before three crosses, bright as lightning. These three crosses were larger and more terrible than the previous two, and surpassed that of the first. My guide then, with much boldness, led me into the midst of the fire, so that we should reverence the three crosses. As for me, I was not so strong; so I went and venerated them at some distance.[63]

"'After we walked a short distance, we came to the second veil. I then observed a kind of lightning unfold in the air, we went up higher and passed through. Inside the veil there was a multitude of heavenly ranks, praising and glorifying God. We passed by those celestial scenes. And—behold!—again, another veil, made of fine linen and porphyry beyond description. We came into a place most glorious, where there was a fearful veil, very splendid, as of electrum, that was exceedingly pure. There then appeared a fiery hand that drew back the veil, and made it ready for us to pass. There was within a countless multitude of noetic beings—young, beautiful, fiery, with countenances more lustrous than the sun. They were standing, according to rank at that dreadful height in midair courts, holding in their hands terrible scepters. There were legions hither, and legions thither, without number. Then my guide said to me, "Behold, after this veil is drawn aside, thou shalt behold the Son of God sitting at the right of the Father![64] And so prostrate thyself and pay homage to Him; every contemplation of thy mind, do thou strain and lift up to Him. And do thou hearken to what shall be spoken by Him to thee." After informing me thus, I was considering the fine appearance of the veil. And behold! A huge dove flew down over the veil. The head of the creature appeared as gold. The breast was as porphyry. The wings were glowing as a flame, and the feet, too, were far-shining. And from the eyes, there went forth rays of light. As I was considering such a goodly appearance, the dove immediately rose up on high.[65]

"'I, consequently, gazed upon that lofty height which struck my mind with amazement. I beheld a terrible and fiery throne, borne aloft, as though suspended in air. There came forth from the throne a fire, but not as the common fire; for it appeared whiter than snow. And there was sitting upon the

---

[63] *P.G.* 111:672B-D.

[64] Cf. Acts 7:55; Rom. 8:34; Eph. 1:20; Col. 3:1; Heb. 1:3; 8:1; 10:12; 12:21; 1 Pe. 3:22.

[65] *P.G.* 111:673AB.

throne our Lord Jesus Christ,[66] clad in porphyry and linen, flashing as with lightning. He, however, constrained His splendor, by reason of my worthlessness, so that I might be able to direct my eyes upon Him. I beheld the God-Man, in His majesty and beauty, in the manner in which the sun rises in the east and joyfully appears with its beams. After this occurrence, I was no longer able to see clearly.[67] When the veil was raised, I fell down and made three

---

[66] Saint Gregory Palamas: "God lets Himself be seen face to face, and not through enigmas....He unites Himself to them to the extent of coming to dwell in His entirety in their entireties; so that, on their side, they dwell completely in Him and, through the Son, the Spirit is poured out richly on them [Tit. 3:6]....You do not, however, consider that God lets Himself be seen in His superessential essence, but according to the divinizing gift and according to His energy, according to the grace of adoption, uncreated divinization, and the direct hypostasized (hypostatized) glory." [*Triads* III, I, 29; cf. Tr. II, 3, 26, 37, in J. Meyendorff's *A Study of Gregory Palamas* (London, UK: The Faith Press, 1964), pp. 213, 214.]

Saint Maximos the Confessor: "God made us so that we might become 'partakers of the divine nature' and sharers in His eternity, and so that we might come to be like Him [1 Jn. 3:2] through divinization by grace. It is through divinization that all things are reconstituted and achieve their permanence; and it is for its sake that what is not is brought into being and given existence." ["First Century on Various Texts," ¶ 42, *The Philokalia, the Complete Text*, Vol. II:173.]

Saint Gregory Palamas: "Those who have pleased God and reach that for which they came into being, namely, theosis (divinization, that is, participation in the uncreated energies, not the essence which the word 'deification' connotes)—for they say it was for this cause that God made us, in order that we be made partakers of His own divinity—even such as these are in God, as they are divinized by Him and He is in them since He is divinizing them. These also participate in the divine energy, though in another manner, but they do not participate in the essence of God. Therefore, also, the theologians state that divinity is a name for the divine energy." [*The One Hundred and Fifty Chapters*, Ch. 105, p. 201.]

The distinction made between the essence and the energies makes it possible to preserve the true meaning of the Apostle Peter's words "partakers of the divine nature [2 Pe. 1:4]."

[67] Saint Hilary of Poitiers: "Paul, the apostle, who was chosen not of men nor through man, but through Jesus Christ, to be the teacher of the Gentiles, expounds in language, as expressive as he can command, the secrets of the heavenly dispensations. He who had been caught up into the third heaven and had heard unspeakable words, reveals to the perception of human understanding as much as human nature can receive. But he does not forget that there are things which cannot be understood in the moment of hearing. The infirmity of man needs time to review, before the true and perfect tribunal of the mind, that which is poured indiscriminately into the ears. Comprehension follows the spoken words more slowly than hearing, for it is the ear which hears, but the reason which understands, though it is God Who reveals the inner meaning to those

(continued...)

prostrations. I, again, tried to rise up that I might survey His comeliness, but, as I said before, I was gripped by fear and joy and awe. I, therefore, was not able to look steadily at the fiery effulgence of the infinite power of His divinity. Then there came forth a voice out of that light, which echoed loudly, so that the wondrous air should have been shattered. But that voice, nevertheless, was sweet as dropped honey; and it was meek and mellifluous. He spoke three divine words and I understood them. My soul was thus given knowledge as I never before had. After a little while, He uttered another three words. When I heard and received those, my heart was filled with divine joy. Again, a third time, He spoke to me three awesome words, so that, suddenly, a great cry was heard as the hallowed hosts of holy angels sent up glorification.[68] It was, I think, that extraordinary melody, "Holy, Holy, Holy."[69] Upon hearing those divine and ineffable words, I instantly returned.

"'I went back even as I had ascended. I was altogether in myself, standing in the place where I was earlier seized. I kept pondering deeply upon all that had occurred to me: where I was and where I was found. I wondered and was beside myself as to how I traversed the breadth of that divine garden. I then went over in my mind all that belonged to that place. I then reasoned

---

[67](...continued)
who seek it....But God's gift of understanding is the reward of faith; for through faith the infirmity of sense is recompensed with the gift of revelation." *On the Trinity*, Bk. XI(23) in *Nicene*, 2nd Ser., IX:210.

Saint Gregory Palamas: "When the mind is totally separated from all being through pure prayer, this ecstasy (*ek-stasis*, a standing apart) is incomparably higher than negative theology; for it belongs only to those who have attained impassibility....God's revelation ravishes such a one to the contemplation of the light....This is why the great Paul, after his extraordinary rapture, declared himself ignorant of what it was. Nevertheless, he saw himself. How? By sense perception, by the reason, or by the spiritual intellect. But in his rapture he had transcended these faculties. He therefore saw himself by the Spirit, Who had brought about the rapture. But what was he himself since he was inaccessible to every natural power, or rather deprived of all such power? He was that to which he was united, by which he knew himself, and for which he had detached himself from all else. Such, then, was his union with the light. Even the angels could not attain to this state, at least not without transcending themselves by unifying grace. Paul therefore was light and spirit, to which he was united, by which he had received the capacity of union, having gone out from all beings, and become light by grace, and non-being by transcendence, that is by exceeding created things....But in attaining this condition, the divine Paul could not participate absolutely in the divine essence, for the essence of God goes beyond even non-being by reason of transcendence, since it is also 'more than God.'" "Deification in Christ," *Triads*, II.iii.8(35-37).

[68] *P.G.* 111:673C-676A.

[69] Cf. Is. 6:1-3.

within myself and said inwardly, "Well then, is there another here or am I alone?" As I was conjecturing upon these things—behold!—I saw a level area in the midst. There were no garden plants or trees on that plain. However, it was an exceedingly beautiful plain, covered with verdure, as well as violets, lilies, roses, and a variety of other flowers that were thick with abundant blossoms. There were also fountains in that place which, little by little, gushed forth milk and honey, so that they flowed to the height of one cubit. These things permeated the air with a tremendous fragrance and sweetness. Taking in the prospect of that pleasant land and its green luster, which was refreshing and relaxing, I was quite at a loss considering the marvels of God, changing from glory to glory.[70]

"'I then caught sight of a man, radiant as lightning. He was garbed in a garment like a bright and lucent cloud. He was holding a cross. He drew nigh to me and said, "The crucifixion of our Lord Jesus Christ be with thee! For blessed are the foolish, for they have much in the way of prudence![71] For God has appointed thee to be here; but thou shalt come whensoever thou shouldest be called. Now, do thou go to the temptations of the world and to the goads and stings where there are prickly plants, threshing machines, and caltrops, as well as vipers, and serpents, and dragons. Nevertheless, even this which I tell thee is a strange wonder. For no one else, wearing flesh, has migrated here, save

---

[70] *P.G.* 111:676BC.

[71] "God chose for Himself the foolish things of the world, that He may put to shame the wise [1 Cor. 1:27; cf. Mt. 11:25]." The apostles were also considered fools for Christ's sake: "For I think that God showed forth us the apostles last, as condemned to death; for we became a spectacle to the world, both to angels and to men. We are fools for Christ's sake,...we are dishonored...until the present hour, we both hunger and thirst, and are naked, and are being buffeted, and never at rest...being reviled, we bless; being persecuted, we bear up...being evilly spoken of...we became as the filth of the world, the off-scouring of all until now....Therefore, I beseech you, keep on becoming imitators of me [1 Cor. 4:9-16]." Acts of foolishness for Christ's sake occurred also in the Old Testament Church. Did not the holy Prophet Ezekiel lie before a depiction of Jerusalem on his left side continually for one hundred and fifty days, and then on his right side for another forty days in the presence of Israel to instruct them [Ez. 4:4, 5]? Did not the holy Prophet Jeremias bear an ox's yoke and place ropes about his neck to foretell the future captivity of the Jews [Jer. 34:2]? Did not the holy Prophet Esaias go naked and barefoot for three years to prophesy the future to the children of Israel [Is. 20:1-4]? The humble Andrew obeyed God and was given grace not only to behold hidden and spiritual realities but also to discern the deep secrets in the hearts of men. This saint's life is an example that censures many of us who fear to confess Christ and are even ashamed of making the sign of the Cross in public places or when entering a motor vehicle.

that one who toiled more abundantly than any other in the Gospel[72] and thyself who has taken in hand the horn of extreme humility. But that thou mayest understand how this came about, it was on account of thine abundant poverty and humility that were made manifest by means of those words, 'Depart from here, thou dog'; and also because thou, who art naked, young, and foolish, hast entered into the stadium of the ruler of this world. Thou hast engaged in a duel with him, turning him upside-down, to the shame of his degraded throne. Thou hast seen many awesome and shuddering things here. Thou hast come to understand the true delight and recompense of the righteous. Thou hast known the Paradise of the Christ, hast thou not? For I know that thou hast seen and hast shivered and hast been inspired with reverential awe. How then is the vain world to be reckoned by thee? What sayest thou? Hast thou beheld glory? Verily. Hast thou seen majesty? Yea. Beholdest thou, O humble one, what kind of joy the sinners have voluntarily turned away from. See how they are minded to deprive themselves of these good things just now glimpsed at." So spoke that light-bearing man to me. He looked upon me and was gladdened.

"'He then resumed speaking, again addressing me and saying, "The Lady and Queen, surpassing in splendor, of the heavenly hosts, knowest thou whither she has gone about? She encompasses the vain world, going around and visiting as a succor and help to those who invoke her only-begotten Son and Logos of God and her most holy name. It would have been appropriate for me to show thee her exceedingly bright habitation, which is indescribable, my friend, but we cannot take the time. For thou art obliged to depart from here and go forth, as the Master has commanded." This was how he spoke to me, and I returned as to a sweet slumber, as though I had slept from the evening until the morning. I awakened and found myself here, as thou seest me. Therefore, my beloved brother, rejoice in the Lord, and let us struggle

---

[72] Saint Paul: "But by the grace of God I am what I am, and His grace which was toward me did not become void; but I toiled more abundantly than all of them, yet not I, but the grace of God which was with me [1 Cor. 15:10]." Elsewhere, the apostle wrote: "I know a man in Christ who fourteen years ago—whether in the body I know not, or out of the body I know not, God knoweth—such a one was carried off as far as the third heaven. And I know such a man—whether in the body or out of the body I know not, God knoweth—that he was caught up into Paradise and heard unspeakable words, which it is not allowed for a man to speak [2 Cor. 12:2-4]."

Saint Chrysostom: "Great indeed was this revelation....Was it the mind that was caught up and the soul, whilst the body remained dead? Or was the body caught up? It is impossible to tell. For if Paul who was caught up and whom so many and great unspeakable things had happened to him, and he was in ignorance, much more we. For, indeed, that he was in Paradise he knew, and that he was in the third heaven he was not ignorant, but the manner he knew not clearly." "Hom. 26 on 2 Cor. 12:4," *P.G.* 61:618, 619 (cols. 575, 576).

diligently to be saved and to be found thither in possession of everlasting things.'[73]

"While the blessed Andrew was recounting these events to me, my soul was led into an ecstatic state of mind. As he was speaking to me, he was a fearful and extraordinary sight to behold. For even as the scent of flowers, that is, of lilies and roses suffused the air, so did he exhale such vapors. Indeed, I had the notion that holy angels came by and were invisibly offering incense in the presence of his divine conversation. Long did I supplicate him to recite one word spoken to him by our Lord Jesus Christ, but he could not be persuaded. I do not know for what reason, but it pertained to the Lord and Andrew's blessed soul.[74] We, therefore, rejoiced in the good things of the Lord throughout that night. In the morning, he departed. He walked about the avenues and boulevards carrying out his affectations and antics. He struggled in this manner of foolishness and as one being tried in the midst of the fire. There were times that he played the drunk, even pushing others and being pushed away because he was a hindrance to passersby. There were some who kicked him and others who gave him blows. Some, even though they were Christians, who had no fear of God, cast him to the ground and dragged him with ropes through the streets and in the marketplace. Indeed, this even took place during feast days. The righteous man endured all, by reason of the hope that was laid up in store for the righteous."[75]

Concerning the Transformation of the Devil

The wicked demon, burning from his malice and envy toward Andrew, knew not what to do until he assumed the form of an old crone. She sat by the roadside wailing and saying, "Woe is me, the impoverished and old woman! How much evil did that trickster perpetrate against me, so that I have no rest from him? What can I, one penniless and a stranger, do?" When some people saw her in such a state, they came over to her and inquired, "What ails thee?" She then began to say, "Andrew, who lives in this city, took hold of me by my hair and dragged me to this spot. He tore hair out of my head, and kicked me, and broke these old teeth of mine." Meanwhile, the venerable Andrew, who was nearby, performing his usual pranks, distinguished in the hag the artifice of the demon. He rose up and went to that site. Andrew fixed his eyes on her with a stern gaze and said, "Wail and lament, thou raving mad and benighted old woman! O thou piece of dung from the multitude of thy transgressions of trickery and conjuring! For from of old, O thou alien of God and of the saints, by thy magical arts, enchantments, drugs, potions, and spells hast thou been greedily drawing souls." Andrew then took up a handful of mud and fashioned

[73] *P.G.* 111:676C-677B.

[74] *P.G.* 111:677BC; Paraclete, p. 57.

[75] *P.G.* 111:677C-680A.

a ball. He threw it at her face. When it struck and splattered, the remnants left marks that formed a cross. The old hag was immediately changed from her human form to a large serpent which disappeared. The blessed Andrew, thereupon, went on his way, conducting himself in his usual manner.[76]

Concerning Epiphanios' Encounter with the Devil

On Andrew's return, he encountered the goodly youth Epiphanios, of whom we spoke earlier in the narration. He was in a state of terror from a troublesome demon. The saint embraced the youth. He then led him by the hand to a place that was quiet and solitary that they might sit and converse. While they were walking, the righteous one said to Epiphanios, "Behold the changeableness of the perverse demon! At one time, he is seen as an old woman; and, at another time, he is dressed in black as a Hagarene that he might meet with my beloved child so as to rebuke and threaten him." Epiphanios, hearing Andrew speak first, marvelled at what he heard. For indeed, prior to meeting with the blessed Andrew on the road, Epiphanios had been confronted by an Ishmaelite who frightened him. The Ishmaelite had seen the virtuous conduct of Epiphanios' life. For the eighteen-year-old young man, indeed, maintained a God-pleasing and God-befitting manner of life. Epiphanios strived to oppose the pleasures of the flesh and to keep vigil and to remain continent from all the passions. He possessed a sharp mind and eloquence of speech. And yet he was also meek and gentle, and sweet in his regard for others. He also was fluent in the divine Scriptures, so that when speaking with philosophers they were amazed at his knowledge and his responses.[77]

They found a quiet place and sat down. Epiphanios then began to describe the Hagarene, saying, "He was an old man with a white beard, having a wild and fierce glance. He was clothed in a black cloak. His boots were made of tan leather. He said to me, 'Thou art, art thou not, Epiphanios, the son of John, regarding whom the people say that thou hast trampled upon the devil? Hypocrite! Since thou hast made war against me, I will entwine thee in my net. I will dig a pit and cast thee within. Then I have a cauldron in which to cook thee, if thou shouldest challenge me.' Such were his nonsensical words, so that I wondered at his threats and why this had befallen me. I knew not who had filled me with dread; for prior to this, I had neither made his acquaintance nor seen him. I kept turning over the scene in my mind, but I was at a loss what all this meant. In fact, I was driven to confusion and intolerable turmoil. But then I came upon thy holiness, and thou hast made manifest all things to me in an unfeigned manner."[78]

---

[76] *P.G.* 111:680D-681B; Paraclete, p. 59.

[77] *P.G.* 111:681BC.

[78] *P.G.* 111:688B.

The venerable man then said to him, "That Hagarene, who appeared to thee, my child, is a centurion of the demons. He is appointed to war against those who struggle on behalf of God, so that he might cast their souls into sins of licentiousness, wanton violence, and shameless desires. I beseech thee, therefore, child, guard thyself, for thou art not ignorant of his devices. The evil one, seeing thee advancing in things spiritual, gnashes his teeth against thee. He diligently strives to put thee in the way of a myriad of temptations, for he bears exceeding ill-will toward thy moral excellence, understanding, and meekness. He wrings his hands before thy purity and wisdom. He resents that, with all thy heart, thou lovest God and His saints who have shed their blood for Christ that they might attain to everlasting life and perpetual blessedness.[79] With much care take heed, therefore, walking with the fear of God and with truth: subdue the body and the impulses of the flesh with fasts. Put on for thyself, as a garment, humble-mindedness; and, in thy prayers, be glad of countenance and rejoice. Keep all thy bodily senses undefiled: thy vision, hearing, smell, taste, and touch. For the most wicked one desires to debauch thy heart and make thee a slave of uncleanness that thou mightest be condemned to the Gehenna of the fire. For the one who commits sin is a slave of sin.[80] For there are two rulers: the Lord of righteousness and the devil exercising sin. Therefore, my beloved child, be a well-disposed worker of righteousness; and the Lord Most High shall protect and preserve thee; and His help shall encompass thee; and He shall enjoin His angels concerning thee, to keep thee in all thy ways."[81] After the saint finished exhorting him, they exchanged a holy kiss in Christ. The righteous one went forth to mock the world, whereas Epiphanios passed over to his house.[82]

Concerning Epiphanios' Father

One day, while Epiphanios was sitting outside the house of his parents, the blessed Andrew was passing by exercising his usual capers. The man of God appeared as one needy and naked, having only a rag to cover his loins.[83] Epiphanios, as one compassionate, espying him from a distance, desired to invite him into his home. Epiphanios did not wish to reveal to his father the previous acquaintance he made with Andrew. Feigning ignorance, therefore, he remarked to his father, "Milord father, seest thou that man how he walks about ill-clad? I am imagining that he is suffering under the influence of a demon. But I beseech thee, father, sir, of our goodly things granted to us by God, do thou give me permission to set a table unto the salvation of our souls

---

[79] *P.G.* 111:688BC.

[80] Jn. 8:34.

[81] Ps. 90:11; Lk. 4:10.

[82] *P.G.* 111:688D-689B.

[83] *P.G.* 111:693D.

and that we might attain to the kingdom of the heavens." His father, moved by God, was filled with joy. He embraced his son and said, "O myrrh of my soul and light of my eyes, needest thou question me about this slight matter? Do as thou dost wish." Epiphanios made haste and caught up to Andrew who had shortly passed by. Epiphanios took Andrew by the hand and led him to the porch where his father had previously been sitting. The father, in the interim, had already gone inside. Andrew would not enter the gate, so he stood without. Meanwhile, some passersby, seeing him naked and assuming that he was cursed by Satan, offered him an obol or some wine. He declined their charity and sat down.[84]

Concerning the Licentious Eunuch

There happened to come by that very gate a eunuch who was a companion of Epiphanios. Since Epiphanios and the eunuch were friendly, they greeted one another. The eunuch then asked Epiphanios about the identity of Andrew and why the latter went about with scarcely any covering in such wintry weather. Epiphanios simply said that he did not understand the matter entirely, but that the poor man's thoughts were in captivity and that he walked about in such a state as one out of his wits. The eunuch, feeling pity, offered to Andrew all that he had with him, that is, thirty dates. The eunuch even offered to bring him some necessities. The righteous Andrew, with the noetic eyes that he possessed, perceived the works of the eunuch. With an austere expression, Andrew commented, "The fools do not eat of the gift of colon-foulers." Not understanding the word properly, the eunuch said, "Truly thou art mad, for seeing dates, thou thinkest them to be cauliflowers?"[85]

The blessed one remarked, "Begone, O guileful one, to the bed-chamber of thy master, working there with him the sickly work of the Sodomites, that thou mightest be recompensed more dates! Thou seest neither the rays of the kingdom of the heavens nor the bitter ferocity of Gehenna. But art thou not ashamed before the angel who attends thee, since thou art a Christian? What must befall thee, O unclean one, who goes off into corners and works that which neither dogs, nor reptiles, nor serpents, nor swine practise? Where, O accursed one, hast thou learned to work such unnaturalness? Woe to thy youth, which Satan has perverted and brought down to the dreadful depths of Hades! Take heed and see that thou shouldest go not further lest the just fire should destroy thee and seize thy youth before the hour, so that from one fire

---

[84] *P.G.* 111:696C.

[85] *P.G.* 111:697AB; Paraclete, p. 71; Liddell & Scott, *Greek-English Lexicon*. Saint Andrew said *colofonias* (κωλοφονίας), literally meaning colon-killer. The eunuch, not bringing to mind the anatomical term "colon," (κωλόν), thought that Andrew pronounced the similar sounding word *colofonion* (κολοφώνιον), which is a kind of vegetable.

thou shouldest tumble into another, the baneful Gehenna of the fire, and be utterly burned." The eunuch, hearing such language, was aghast. In his shame, he flushed cherry-red as he remarked, "Woe is me, the wretched one!" Epiphanios then asked the eunuch, "What has happened to thee, milord and genuine friend, that thou hast reddened and become embarrassed? Did I not tell thee that he speaks like one mad? In any case, as to those things which thou hast heard and which have censured thy conscience, make provision to correct thyself and do not deem his words odious. Thou art young and Satan is terrible. He goads us to commit sins for nought else than that he should have some consolation in the flame of Gehenna." Hearing this counsel, the eunuch went his way.[86]

The honorable Epiphanios then escorted the righteous Andrew into his chamber. They found the table prepared, at which they ate and rejoiced in the gifts of the Savior. After the repast, Epiphanios made this inquiry: "Why, my great sir, didst thou speak so abruptly to my beloved friend?" Andrew answered, "Because he is cordial with thee and dear to thee. It is for that reason I spoke to him as I did; for if he were not thy friend, he would not have listened to one single word of mine. For it is not my aim to censure and rebuke sinners. But rather, my intent is to run the straight path that leads to the better part." Epiphanios said, "I know, O slave of God. I also know that the youth is a household servant and that he is compelled to act according to his master's bidding. What is he to do?" The righteous one remarked, "I know that he is a manservant, and have not forgotten this. The servant is obliged to minister to the physical needs of the one who purchased him. Nevertheless, his ministrations should not comprise the works of the devil and deeds of dishonor. He ought not to commit such accursed and beastly unnaturalness, which even the senseless brutes do not do. For what man is there that does not run away when he smells the foul odor of dung?" Epiphanios said, "If his master should summon him for some bodily service, one that is sinful, or some intellectual or psychical activity that is unwholesome, and he, as a slave, does not obey, I think thou knowest how many things he must suffer: insults, blows, threats, and other unpleasant consequences." The venerable man answered, "This is the testimony of Jesus Christ, of which He hinted at in this saying: 'Blessed are they who have been persecuted on account of righteousness, for theirs is the kingdom of the heavens.'[87] Furthermore, if household servants do not submit to their masters in regard to the loathsome and filthy desire of the Sodomites,

[86] *P.G.* 111:697B-700A; Paraclete, 72.
[87] Mt. 5:10.

blessed are they, and thrice-blessed; for by means of the tortures that thou didst list, they are to be accounted among the martyrs."[88]

Concerning Epiphanios' Manservant

Now while they were having this conversation, one of the menservants of Epiphanios, the moment he set eyes on Andrew, perceived the manner of the righteous one's labor of foolishness for God. The lad sat at the feet of the saint, beseeching him with tears to entreat God that he, too, might take upon such a work as his. The righteous Andrew, knowing with the gift of clairvoyance what the manservant was asking, wished to speak to him privately regarding it. Andrew, thereupon, by the power of the Holy Spirit, converted their tongue into that of the Syrians. Thus, both Andrew and that manservant were speaking Syriac. The servant then began asking, "Supplicate the Lord that I might become even as thou art." The venerable man responded: "Thou art not able to endure the profuse perspiration and the toils of such a virtue. For narrow and afflicted is the path which leads to the kingdom of the heavens. But it is better for thee to remain as thou art, abiding here in piety, that thou mightest be taught by thy master piety and all that is needful for thy salvation." Epiphanios, seeing and hearing how that manservant had instantly changed his language and spoke in a tongue which he had never even heard, marvelled and exclaimed, "O the wonder! Wondrous is God in His saints!"[89]

Saint Andrew

The blessed Andrew prayed to God concerning that manservant that He might reveal to him what to do in the matter. A voice then came and said, "It is not to his advantage, but show him how it is with thee lest he should think thee without strength." Straightway, then, the blessed Andrew said to the angel who was guarding him, "Fill the cup of glad-heartedness, when the grace of my gift blossomed forth." The angel did so and gave the young man to drink in an invisible manner. That slave, too, also began to show characteristics in his behavior similar to those of the blessed Andrew. When the God-bearing

[88] *P.G.* 111:700BC.

[89] Ps. 67:35.

father observed this, he rejoiced and smiled. Epiphanios, witnessing the phenomenon, was disturbed. By reason of the probable event that his father should become indignant at the alteration in the household servant, Epiphanios said to Andrew, "I beseech thee, O slave of God, do not start this thing in my father's manservant lest my father, thinking himself to be an object of contempt, should drive out thee and the young man. Then instead of ushering in a good word and example, an unintended blasphemy would be uttered. I, too, would incur my father's anger and be despised by him." The saint, persuaded by these words, straightway bade the angel bring the manservant back to his first state. That slave, as he beheld himself stripped of the grace, sorrowed very much. He kept imploring the venerable man to bestow it anew. The saint said, "It is not the will of God."[90]

Following this episode, the man of God was enjoined to stay the night at Epiphanios' house. When Epiphanios' servants gathered round their master, the holy Andrew, with the gift vouchsafed him by the Spirit, perceived the spiritual state of all the servants. He, thereupon, began telling a tale, describing the sins of each without naming the sinner; for each servant knew in his heart who was spoken of when his turn came. Some said he was a saint, others claimed that he divined by astrology. When Andrew retired that night, he left his bed and went to rest on the dung heap outside.

In the morning, Epiphanios escorted the saint who went forth to spiritual contests yet to be entered into. When Epiphanios returned to his house, he called forth that manservant with whom the saint spoke Syriac. Epiphanios asked him, "How were those mysteries wrought in thee?" The young manservant, having confidence in Epiphanios, did not conceal anything. He revealed all that he underwent, saying, "Master, when I entered thy chamber, I was suddenly struck dumb. The lightning-flash countenance of the saint was more fulgent than the sun. I stood there amazed, hearing a voice saying to me, 'Dost thou see how much grace is received when one becomes a fool for the sake of Christ's love?' Then one of the small beams separated from the saint's radiance and came to my face. Straightway, I, too, had the manners of the saint which thou didst see with thine own eyes. Afterward, when the grace was withdrawn from me, I resumed what I was formerly in the world. Behold, milord, from this day do thou become the administrator of my salvation!" Epiphanios then said to him, "From this day I shall deem thee as my friend and spiritual brother."[91]

Concerning Various Trials

Meanwhile, the servant of God, Andrew, went his way, enduring chill and frost. He could be seen smeared with dung or charcoal. People of all ages

[90] *P.G.* 111:700D-701C.

[91] *P.G.* 111:705C.

and genders struck him and thrashed him with staves and sticks. He was pulled and dragged through public places. Some kind and Christ-loving folks, seeing him suffer such vile treatment, would give him a coin or some food or ask him how he was faring. Once, when the hallowed fool for Christ was relieving a natural need in public, he was savagely beaten with rods and sticks.[92] The saint felt bitter pain as he collapsed to the ground. He then kissed the feet of one of his assailants, praying for him. At another time, while the God-protected holy fool slumbered in a narrow street, an intoxicated wagoner rode over the saint with his oxen and load. Again, God shielded him from harm though eyewitnesses thought a demon kept him unharmed. In another instance, Andrew pretended to be drunk. He went to a hot place, where he rested in the street since he was hungry and thirsty. Some would kick him as they passed by, while others struck him. Finally, some dragged him to the other side of the street.

Concerning the Opening of the Gates

Now the blessed Andrew had the custom of going to the forecourts of the churches where he would pray. On one such night, he went to the temple of the all-hymned Theotokos, which is to the left side of the portico of the Forum of Constantine. At that time, a slave boy was on an errand for his master. The slave boy was going in the direction of that same church, though it was after the hours when it was left open to the public. As the saint went toward the church, the slave, who had a quicker gait, caught up to the venerable man. By the dispensation of God, Andrew did not perceive that the boy was right behind him. When the saint reached the locked doors of the church, he raised his right hand and traced the sign of the precious Cross over the doors. Straightway, the doors opened of themselves to Andrew. Following this action, he entered the temple and offered up prayer, not realizing that someone was following his every move. The slave boy recognized Andrew, who was known throughout the city as one possessed and mad. When he observed the doors open automatically, he was astonished and wondered within himself. Seized with dizziness and trembling, he reasoned within himself and said, "Behold what kind of slave of God is this fellow! But truly they are fools who name him fool. Where now are those mindless ones who beat him without mercy? O how many concealed slaves has God and none understands or knows the things of them!"[93]

Such were his conjectures as he stood outside the front doors of the church. He then went closer in order to see what the saint was about. He was amazed when he beheld him suspended in the air before the ambo engaged in

---

[92] *P.G.* 111:708D.

[93] *P.G.* 111:712B-D.

prayer.[94] Around the holy Andrew there went forth a flame of fire, as wafts of an incomparable fragrance came as far as the gates of the temple. Then that slave boy, out of fear, exited the church and went hurriedly to fulfill his master's command. The righteous Andrew, at the same time, finished his prayer. He departed as he entered that sacred precinct, making the sign of the honorable Cross over the doors which locked of themselves. As he left, Andrew recognized the slave boy. He also came to understand in the Spirit that the boy had seen what had transpired. This very much sorrowed Andrew, who dreaded that perhaps the boy would speak to his master. Consequently, when the slave boy returned to his ministrations, the righteous Andrew appeared before him and said, "Guard thyself, child, and tell no one anything of what thou hast seen in the church; and God shall have mercy on thee. If thou shouldest divulge even a word about the slightest thing of that which thou hast seen, I shall command an unclean spirit to hold thee up to ridicule throughout the city. I shall, however, by Jesus, charge thine angel, the one who guards thee, lest a word should escape thee, to assume this care over thee that I might have no further concern regarding it." The slave boy, looking upon the saint, answered fearfully, "No, milord, I will not speak to anyone." The boy then returned to his master, saying to himself, "I have witnessed a wonder of wonders. Behold how great a saint he is! And we, ignorant ones, are fools in truth. Bless me, what a mystery! How many hidden slaves has the Lord, who maintain a good conduct of life and conscience! Indeed what we have heard in the lives of the holy saints, we have seen with our own eyes." He then recalled the command of the blessed one. But, at length, the boy forgot the promise he made to be keeping silence. When he attempted to open his mouth and speak, a youth, who appeared to him as lightning, said, "Halt, abject one, lest thou art taken up by a wicked demon and become the plaything of demons!" The boy was filled with trembling. In his fear, he wished to cry out, but that fiery being placed his right palm over the slave boy's mouth to close it, and said, "Hush, child!" The angel then instantly vanished. The slave boy, filled with dread at that vision, marvelled at that extraordinary wonder. Each time he brought the episode to mind, he felt dazed. At length, he held his tongue and did not utter a word of the righteous man's feats.[95]

Concerning the Figs

During the harvest, when the vendors set up their produce, there were certain ill-disposed folk who wasted their time making farces. They took Andrew and brought him to the fig stand, where the dealer was fast asleep. They said to Andrew, "Eat fool, and fill thy belly, since in but a short time

---

[94] The ambo, a large pulpit, once stood in the middle of the church. Today it is opposite the holy doors of the iconostasion from where the Gospel is read.

[95] *P.G.* 111:713A-C.

there will not be any!" Andrew fell in with their suggestion, eating as many as he could. Those instigators, meanwhile, stirred up the fig dealer who began raining down blows upon Andrew and driving him away with kicks. The same slave boy, who had followed the blessed one to church, noticed what took place. He helped up the bruised saint, kissing his hands and face. Andrew chided himself aloud and said, "These bruises, my child, came about on account of my voracious gullet. I, the wretched one, was enticed by some paltry figs, which led to my bruising by rods. How shall God deal with those who commit the uttermost hedonistic deeds and repent not?" The saint then paused and asked the boy, "Why didst thou so quickly forget the command I gave thee? If that splendid youth had not prevented thy mouth by his fiery hand, thou shouldest now be among the demoniacs." Stunned at hearing these words, the slave boy quaked at the thought. Andrew then drew him along, leading him by the hand.[96]

Concerning the Encounter with the Devil

When the demon observed that the righteous man was attentive toward the boy and spoke to him of the previous wonders, he shook with malice. The demon took along impure Satan, even as Andrew and the slave boy were walking along a dark colonnade. The evil spirits accosted them with these words: "O mocker of the world, what is this mania to keep seizing! Was it not enough that thou hast cleansed of sin the house of Epiphanios and brought the inmates therein to God? Now wilt thou cleanse this one, too, and bring him to repentance?" He immediately then began to recount the sins of the slave boy. The righteous man interposed, cutting him off and saying, "What has taken place through my unworthiness was through God's help. And thou, most defiled one, what has this to do with thee? I would lay my soul down for this one. Thou shalt have no portion in his soul."[97] These words of the righteous man maddened the demon and Satan, the agitators of cities and instigators of sin. Though they wished to carry the boy away for their own shameless works,

---

[96] *P.G.* 111:716AB; Paraclete, 85, 86.

[97] Moses said, "And now if Thou wilt forgive their sin, forgive it; and if not, blot me out of Thy book which Thou hast written [Ex. 32:32]." Thus, Moses showed his great love for the brethren. Saint Paul, also, demonstrated selfless and perfect love: "I say the truth in Christ, I lie not, my conscience bearing witness with me in the Holy Spirit, that my grief is great and unceasing pain is in my heart. For I could wish to be an anathema from the Christ on behalf of my brethren [Rom. 9:3]." Christ Himself tells us: "This is My commandment, that ye be loving one another, even as I loved you. Greater love hath no one than this, that one should lay down his life for his friends [Jn. 15:12, 13]." The love of one, such as that possessed by Saint Andrew, who is in *theosis*, seeks not his own profit but is crucified for his neighbor.

Andrew picked up a stone and cast it at them. They vanished into the air, squealing like pigs.[98]

Concerning the Adolescent Thief

Andrew went with the slave to a tavern, where the boy ordered bread and wine. They sat down together and ate. Another boy, with an incipient beard, entered the establishment in the company of a companion. They sat down and ate next to Andrew and the little slave. The venerable man perceived their sins that kept them in thrall. Andrew began his routine of foolishness, which amused the other customers. Andrew, wishing to bring to repentance those at the table next to him, stretched forth his hand and snatched a biscuit from one of those lads. The lad became indignant at the righteous fool and called him a madman. But the blessed man brought forth the lad's crime in his robbery of one named Symeon. With those words, Andrew gave him a mighty slap; so that the lad's ear was ringing for one-half hour. The lad, recognizing his transgression, was amazed that Andrew knew of this secret crime. Andrew then slapped the lad's companion, and asked, "And thou, art thou not ashamed of eating stolen food?" The blessed man then said, "Believe me, if thou shouldest continue to steal, thou shalt be mastered by a demon." Then Andrew turned about, and spoke to one not seen, saying, "If he should steal one more time, put him under examination." Speaking thus, Andrew departed with the slave boy.[99] As for the young thief, he returned to his life of crime and became worse. Andrew knew of it and saw that his long-suffering was not to the thief's benefit. The lad was given over to a demon to harass him that he might confess and repent. While in that state, the lad remembered the blow to his face by Andrew. He repaired to the Church of the most holy Theotokos, known also as Myrelaion because of a miraculous gushing forth of myrrh as oil.[100] He anointed his whole body and took refuge therein with the Theotokos.[101]

With fervent tears he entreated the protectress of our race, and he came into a state of ecstasy. He beheld a Woman standing before the gates of the holy sanctuary. She was dressed in linen and porphyry. Her countenance was more splendorous than the sun. Appearing angry, she looked askance at the demon and remarked, "Art thou still about, thou black knave? Come out of the creation of my Son, O thou accursed one, for the youth has taken refuge in me." The demon, using the lad as his instrument, replied, "The one who com-

---

[98] *P.G.* 111:716C-717A; Paraclete, 86, 87.

[99] *P.G.* 111:717BC; Paraclete, 87, 88.

[100] The all-brick Myrelaion Monastery (Bodrum Camii), a cross-in-square structure, is located west of the Forum Tauri in Constantinople. It received its name from an icon of the Theotokos that exuded myrrh. Romanos I Lekapenos added a church, ca. 920-922. It is now a mosque. *Oxford*, s.v. "Myrelaion, Monastery of."

[101] *P.G.* 111:720D-721A.

mits pranks for thy Son's sake, Andrew, handed him over to me for examination." But she answered him, "Come forth, and cease babbling; for otherwise I will have my Son sentence thee." The demon, in terror, went out of the lad. It then seemed that she entered into the sanctuary. As for the lad, he came to himself and understood that he had been delivered of the evil spirit. He glorified the man-loving God and offered profound thanks to the all-holy Theotokos. He affirmed that he would never steal again, nor would he commit fornication, nor keep company again with buffoons and sinners. He pledged himself thus before her august icon. He then returned home and amended his ways, so that he came to the summit of virtue. Those who knew of his past and saw his reformation were amazed. Whensoever the lad chanced upon the holy fool, our Andrew, he approached him and said, "By the Lord Jesus do I declare that thou art a hard man, O righteous one!" The lad then offered his heartfelt thanks, for he acknowledged Andrew as the cause of his salvation.[102]

More on the Encounter with the Devil

Now let us return to the departure of Andrew and the slave boy from the tavern. As they were walking along, the devil, with a crowd of demons, encountered them with a loud clamor. Andrew rebuked them in the name of Jesus. They complained that Andrew had wronged them. The devil then threatened to prove him as he once did Job.[103] The blessed one declared, "O accursed one, in what manner wouldest thou have the Lord prove me? O thy nonsensical talk, most evil one! On what account should the Lord wish me tested as thou wouldest have it? Because of the gold which I do not possess? Because of the silver which does not exist? Because of my holdings in the suburbs? Because of my household and all those of mine who live within? Go ahead and have no pity: destroy my belongings, houses, and estates in an attempt to make me blaspheme the Lord. Art thou not envious of my raiment or my polished sandals? What of my hut? Thou canst do nothing against me, thou filthy dog." Andrew then removed his tattered tunic and cast it in the devil's face. The boy, beholding what took place, clothed him. Andrew kissed the boy and sent him on his way, admonishing him to avoid that which was harmful to the soul. Andrew then went his way and, in the midst of all the noise in the streets and byways, took up his spiritual struggles, that is, of fasting, keeping vigil, daily enduring pangs and toils, being insulted, abused, struck, and spat upon.[104]

Concerning the Vision at the Rich Man's Funeral

On one of those days of his spiritual struggle, Andrew met with a large funeral procession of a grandee. A multitude surrounded the bier, as the

---

[102] *P.G.* 111:721BD-724A.

[103] Job 1:6 ff.

[104] *P.G.* 111:717D-720D.

chanters were loudly singing the service. There was a sea of candles and incense, while the relatives mourned and lamented. The servant of God observed the procession for a considerable time. He then perceived candlesticks borne aloft and a multitude of black demons who were crying out above the chanters' voices, "Woe!" The incense was like unto dung in odor. It seemed to Andrew that the demons had wineskins from which they were drawing out ashes and sprinkling them. They were laughing shamelessly, in the manner of immodest women and harlots. At times they growled like dogs or squealed like swine. They were clearly delighted and in good cheer at what was taking place. Some of the demons sprinkled the deceased's face with mire, sewage, and filthy water. Some befouled his face from the air, so that the stench was as when one empties out a pit in the ground of waste matter. Some of the demons followed from behind, singing indecent songs and dancing wildly as they laughed. Others applauded or stamped their feet. They were mocking the chanters and yelling, "May God not let any of you vain Christians see the light! For though you are singing for him 'with the saints give rest,' and calling him 'a slave of God,' yet in his lifetime he was a participant in every evil."[105]

This hideous vision was observed by the blessed man. Then, at that same moment, there appeared the ruler of the demons. His eyes were savagely intractable, which provoked trembling and nauseousness. He was holding fire in his hand, as well as pitch and brimstone. He hastened to the tomb of that wretched dead man that he might blacken the body after the burial. Then the venerable man noticed a handsome youth who was following along at the very end of the procession. He was excessively grieved and downcast, making great lamentation. Andrew was struck by the depth of his mourning, as though he had forgotten God's work. Andrew held out his hand to comfort the youth and asked, "In God's name, why dost thou weep and wail in this manner? I beseech thee, do thou explain to me why." Andrew spoke thus because he never had seen anyone weep so. That youth, the dead man's guardian angel, said to Andrew, "I mourn for the man because the devil has inherited him and because I lost him; it is for that reason I lament." Andrew remarked, "Now I understand who thou art. Tell me, then, what were this man's sins." The angel answered, "I will tell thee, Andrew, thou elect of God, for thou art radiant as pure gold. Just now, when I caught sight of thee, I had some relief from my grief. Hearken then: This fellow was one of the grandees of the emperor, but exceedingly sinful, perverse, and twisted. He was a fornicator, adulterer, homosexual, and miser. He lacked compassion. He was pretentious and proud. Furthermore, he was a liar, misanthrope, and remembered wrongs. He took bribes and broke oaths. He subjected his slaves to hunger, thirst, scourges, and

[105] *P.G.* 111:724A-C; Paraclete, 92, 93.

nakedness. Some of his slaves were left ill-clad and unshod in the winter; some he slew with a club and buried them with the bones of his dead horses. He was also given over to the abominable and fire-burning practise of laying with those of his own sex. In this licentiousness and God-hating lust that bloodsucker corrupted boys and eunuchs, totaling three hundred. Well, beloved of the Lord, the day of reaping arrived for him. Death found him unrepentant. His defiled and vile body, deserving dishonor, was abducted by the devil; he is not even being vouchsafed his own tomb. And so, thou holy and God-loving soul, for this cause am I distressed, because he became the plaything of the demons and the dirty habitation of their stench."[106]

The blessed Andrew then said to the angel, "I beseech thee, O thou of fiery form, be consoled and mourn no longer; for he received an end to such a life. But thou, O fiery and great one, who art filled with gladness, in the name of the Lord Sabaoth and God Almighty, by the same rule, thou shalt dwell among good things from now and unto the ages." While they were speaking, the angel became invisible. Now only Andrew could be seen standing and talking alone, for which some people, unworthy of viewing an angel, commented, "Look at the addled one and how he busies himself conversing with an insensate wall!" Some persons pushed Andrew and chased him off, saying, "What art thou saying, thou madman?" But the venerable man gave their words no consequence. He smiled and mocked them, and then withdrew from those ignorant ones. Andrew then betook himself to a secret place in the city, where he might rest and reflect. He brought to mind the entire pitiful funeral which caused him to weep bitterly and profusely, so that his eyes became puffy. He then was moved to make intercession for the deceased.[107]

Saint Andrew then prayed this prayer: "O God, the uncircumscribed One and terrible, Creator and Lord, the initiator of the endless ages, the fount of wisdom and knowledge, the incomparable begotten One, the majesty of the glory of the holiness, Thou art of one and the same nature with the Father and Thy lovable and all-ruling Spirit, all equal in honor. O Thou Who wast begotten of the Great One, before the beginning, and coexisting, and Who art ever in the glory and bosom of the Begetter: Do Thou rescue the all-wretched body of that suffering man from being made an example of in the pitch and the brimstone! Incline Thy compassion and mercy to the entreaty of Thy worthless servant in regard to that most profane soul who departed from Thee and whom death has locked up. I pray, beseeching and supplicating, let his tabernacle be kept from such an indignity, that the accursed dragon of the pit may not completely rejoice over him, swallowing his soul together with the body." And when the righteous man uttered this prayer, there came to be a divine

---

[106] *P.G.* 111:724D-725C; Paraclete, 94, 95.
[107] *P.G.* 111:725D-728A; Paraclete, 95.

illumination to him, so that he came to be in a state of ecstasy. Behold, an angel of the Lord descended as a bolt of lightning, bearing a fiery rod in his hand! The just man then found himself in the dead man's sepulcher, as the angel dispelled the unclean spirits therein. Hence, the body of the man ceased to be in burning pitch and brimstone. When the righteous one beheld these things, he gave thanks for the speedy reply to his prayer. When Andrew came to himself from this divine vision, it was already eventide. He made the sign of the honorable Cross and departed from that place, after which he passed the entire night in prayer.[108]

Concerning the Vision During Orthros

At another time, the saint went at the hour of Orthros to the Church of the Most Holy Theotokos (the same temple attended by Epiphanios). The latter was at the front door of the church, when his spiritual eyes were opened. Epiphanios beheld the righteous Andrew who appeared to him as a flame of fire; then Andrew appeared as white as snow, and his face glowed red as fire. When Epiphanios observed these manifestations, he marvelled. He drew near to the saint, casting his glance hither and thither lest anyone else be present, and kneeled before his feet and said, "Give the blessing, father, to thy spiritual child!" But then the saint knelt before Epiphanios and remarked, "Supplicate, *despota*, the Lord in my behalf. Because rather thou shouldest give the blessing, since today I beheld what would come to pass for thee. Only one hour earlier, I was standing in the Great Church of God where I saw that thy countenance was most resplendent. Thou wast clad in episcopal vestments and an *omophorion* (pallium). They were bestowed from heaven by the hand of the Lord, the Ruler of all. Then I noticed two very handsome youths. They took the vestments and garbed thee, as they smiled and said among themselves, 'By the Master Christ, how majestic he appears in this *omophorion*! For understanding, prudence, and eloquence adorn his soul.'[109] Then one of the youths made the sign of the Cross on thy forehead, and gave thee a kiss. The other one sealed all thy members and then kissed thine eyes. These things, though thou knewest not that they were taking place, O most sweet Epiphanios, yet were they done to thee. I am persuaded that God will entrust thee with the steering of His Church, and thou shalt shepherd His people who have been procured with His own blood. For this reason, do thou bless me and pray on behalf of thy beloved Andrew."[110]

---

[108] *P.G.* 111:728BC; Paraclete, 96.

[109] Some sources have "understanding and eloquence" [*P.G.* 111:729B]; others have "understanding and prudence" [*The Great Synaxaristes* (in Greek)] or "understanding and knowledge" [Paraclete, 97].

[110] *P.G.* 111:728D-729B.

After the venerable Andrew uttered these prophetic words regarding the future episcopacy, they exchanged a holy kiss and went to sit down in the church narthex. They were in a concealed place as the blessed Andrew began instructing Epiphanios regarding his ecclesiastical situation, saying, "I know well, my child, how thou art upright in the commandments and always struggling to save thy soul. However, I beseech thee, receive my exhortation. From today, my child, increase thy tears toward the cleansing of thy soul that thou mightest become a lover of good things in righteousness. Add meekness that thou mayest become pure in heart, even as the blessed Paul has bidden the elect vessel should be holy, guileless, and undefiled.[111] Yea, I beseech thee, my sweet joy, diligently strive to obtain for thy life a better condition, that is more wonderful: understanding, modesty, goodness, knowledge, unceasing prayer, courage, love unfeigned, prudence, sobriety, and moderation. Become sympathetic and love the poor. Be also a lover of God and of virtue and of the monastics. Exercise thyself to achieve silence and perseverance, as well as patience in afflictions. Neither babble, nor rail, nor revile. Strive to attain freedom from wrath, vainglory, and pride, so that the Lord may magnify thee before the angels, saints, and numberless powers. Be struggling, as much as thou art able, in doing good works for the love of God, that He might exalt thee and glorify thee." Now after the righteous one had spoken with Epiphanios, he entered into the church. People noticed him and began to say, "How is it that the madman has entered herein?" Some thought he probably found some respite within the church from the demon that troubled him. But others said that he mistakenly entered by the side door, thinking the church was a private house.[112]

As for the righteous man, he beheld the demon of despondency within that sacred precinct. He saw the demon tempting some to leave before the dismissal of the divine office. The demon reminded some of the urgency of their labors that awaited them, and so those Christians departed early; for they had forgotten how the Lord cried out that we should cease being anxious about what we shall eat and what we shall drink and what we shall put on our body, but rather we ought to be seeking first the kingdom of God,[113] and the rest of what the Lord uttered. Andrew then saw two other demons. One was the demon provoking yawning and drowsiness and the other appeared to be his helper who was carrying dirty spools on his shoulder and striking those attending the divine readings that they might slumber. The saint, maddened by the demon's machinations, rebuked him and called upon the Lord Jesus Christ of the heavenly hosts. And suddenly, a flame of fire exited the sanctuary and

[111] Heb. 7:26.
[112] *P.G.* 111:729C-732B.
[113] Mt. 6:25, 33.

burned the demons. Those who had been under the influence of their demonic energy were quickly roused and hearkened to the readings.[114]

As for Epiphanios, he was greatly edified by their discussion and returned home. While alone, he thought to himself, "Bless me! Our queen city has a luminary in her midst and knows it not! For in truth did our Lord say that seeing ye shall see, and in no wise shall perceive.[115] For even as when Christ spent time on earth and there came to pass signs and wonders,[116] so I detect such things accomplished by the servant of God."[117]

Concerning the Vision of the Saint's Place in Paradise

That night, Epiphanios besought God to reveal to him certain things regarding the righteous Andrew. He desired to know how God regarded Andrew's virtues. He also wished to learn what sort of place would Andrew attain to in the kingdom of the heavens. Epiphanios was vouchsafed a vision when he fell asleep. He found himself on a plain which was filled with trees and plants that were unsearchable to know. Some were withered and burned, and others had no fruit but thorns. Some had luscious fruit, while others bore that which was bitter and foul-smelling. There were those with healthy leaves and those with rotten ones. But then he observed in their midst a certain fruit-laden tree, beautiful to behold. Captivated by it, the young man drew closer to gaze upon it. He felt giddy but was awestricken. He saw an august swallow sitting on one of the branches of the tree. On the one hand it appeared to be a swallow from its head to the breast; but on the other hand—strange is the telling of the wonder!—its face was that of a nightingale; so that, paradoxically, at times it sounded like a swallow and at times like a nightingale. Epiphanios, from his joy, wept. He then beheld an elder, majestically clad in white, who was coming toward him. The elder asked, "Who brought thee here, young man, without my ordering it?" After a pause, the elder repeated, "I am asking thee." Epiphanios replied, "Reverend elder, I will answer thee. But hearken to me with leniency. I was passing by and noted this beautiful tree. I had only wished to better enjoy its marvellous harmony and the variety of its fruits. Its beauty has captivated me. The sweet voice of the bird has enchanted me. Pardon me, the pitiful one. But come and search, that is, if thou hast a sense of touch, to see if I have stolen any fruit." The elder remarked, "Ingrate, thou makest as though thou knowest nothing. Did I not see thee cut and eat from this fruit until thou didst sate thyself?" Epiphanios avowed that he refrained from not only touching the fruit in the least but even rubbing off any shavings. The elder then said, "Cease telling falsehoods, young man, for I do not throw any

---

[114] *P.G.* 111:732D-733A.

[115] Mt. 13:14.

[116] Cf. Jn. 14:12.

[117] *P.G.* 111:733AB; Paraclete, 100.

blame on thee that thou didst come and eat. For I am delighted that someone has eaten and rejoices. Come along with me, and I shall show to thee something strange and new."[118]

As they went, Epiphanios noted that the elder was holding a Gospel in his right hand and a volume in his left. They passed through gardens until they came to a forecourt filled with light. Within were majestic palaces built by sun rays and filled with gladsomeness. They entered without anyone's leave. Epiphanios began to feel both fright and wonder before the strange chambers filled with extraordinary mysteries. There were also terrifying fiery thrones that shone as lightning. Upon one of those thrones, shimmering like the sun and at a fearful height, Epiphanios saw the King sitting, with spheres of fire proceeding from His countenance; so that His immense glory and splendor and dazzling radiance illuminated the air. There stood around Him ten thousands of ten thousands and thousands of thousands of ranks and hosts of both cherubim and seraphim and the powers. They rose up to a prodigious height as forests on mountains. Both the elder and Epiphanios then fell down and paid homage. Epiphanios was filled with fear and trembling as he lay prone, unable to lift his eyes to such a sight. His guide, however, rose up and stood straight, which gave Epiphanios courage. The King, thereupon, asked the venerable elder, "Is this the youth who besought us to reveal to him the things of our ever-memorable and beloved friend Andrew?" The elder answered and said, "It is he, O Master."[119] Then the King said to Epiphanios, "Behold, the tree which thou didst see bearing every kind of fruit is an icon of the body of My servant! For such is Andrew's conduct of life in his love for Me, even as thou didst see in the beauty of the tree. The bird, appearing as a swallow and nightingale, is that soul of My beloved Andrew that chants to me unceasing doxologies and fitting hymns; so that the bodiless angels of my armies recline and rest on him. Though thou hast said that thou didst not eat of the fruit thereof, yet rather thou hast partaken to excess. This has come to pass since the day that thou didst first give heed to Andrew." The King then said to the guide, "Since he desires to know exactly what is Andrew's place in the kingdom of the heavens, take him and bring him into the splendor of the saints. Show him all things according to the order of the saints."[120]

The elder then brought the youth into a chamber that was like lightning. Behold! There exited, as an icon, the ever-memorable Andrew. He possessed a countenance similar in likeness to that imperial and awesome One; for Andrew's face was diffusing splendor as the sun. His hands were a kind of electrum. His feet were clad in sandals with gold thongs. His garments were

---

[118] *P.G.* 111:733B-736AB; Paraclete, 101, 102.
[119] *P.G.* 111:736C-737A; Paraclete, 102, 103.
[120] *P.G.* 111:737AB.

diverse, as if they were constructed of sunbeams and lightning. Underneath he wore a garment that appeared to be a vivid snowy white, so that it caught the eye as does a flower with its sweet pleasantness. Over that garment was another, something like a wine color but not porphyry, yet with no ornament. A third garment was like a kind of cloak, most beautiful; and the glory of the Lord appeared shooting forth. A crown was on his head, adorned with precious stones and pearls looking as the stars of the heavens. Now there was a cross on the royal diadem that was above his forehead. He had a scepter in his left hand, upon which were letters. The words verily inscribed read: "Holy, Holy, Holy." And he had a cross in his right hand.[121]

Epiphanios, seeing all these marvels, was beside himself. The elder remarked, "Dost thou wonder at what thou hast seen in a dream? What shalt thou do when thou seest it in reality? Well, then, thou hast beheld the splendor of the slave of God. Thy desire has been fulfilled. Be thou struggling now lest thou shouldest be deprived of the kingdom of God." With those words, he was roused from his sleep. Meanwhile, the divine office being conducted at the church was at the midpoint of the Orthros Canon. Epiphanios rose up and hastened to the service. He was thinking of the divine condescension that vouchsafed a vision of the almighty Lord Jesus to one sinful and impure as he. After church, he returned to his home and bedchamber where he wept.[122]

Concerning the Holy Apostles

On a certain night, as the blessed Andrew was walking about, striving in his customary spiritual labors, he happened to find himself nearby the Church of the Holy Apostles, the one built by the first Christian emperor.[123] Due to the deep darkness of that night, Andrew could not see where he was going. By God's permission, he found he had fallen into a pit in the middle of the road. For Satan took the guise of an Ethiopian and pushed Andrew into the miry pit. Out of that hole in the earth, Andrew cried out, "O holy apostles, who enlightened the ends of the inhabited earth, help me, your base slave, and lead

---

[121] *P.G.* 111:737BD.

[122] *P.G.* 111:740A; Paraclete, 104.

[123] The magnificent and glorious Church of the Holy Apostles in Constantinople was first built by the first Christian emperor, Saint Constantine the Great (d. 337). It treasured the sacred relics of the holy Apostles Andrew, Luke, Timothy, and Matthew. Constantine, as well as other autocrats, were committed therein. Holy patriarchs were also laid to rest in that sacred precinct, including John Chrysostom, Gregory the Theologian, Methodios the Confessor, Flavian, and others. The original church was burnt during the Nika Revolt (January of 532), and afterward splendidly rebuilt by Justinian (r. 527-565). The newer building was deemed the most distinguished church of Constantinople after the Great Church (Hagia Sophia). Shortly after the captivity of the city, the edifice was cast down to the ground by Mohammed the Kataktetos, who raised up on that very spot a mosque (Mehmedie Tzami).

me out of this pit!" Straightway, then, there appeared a shiny cross coming forth from the church. It remained suspended in the air over the pit. It appeared white as marble, and was fiery, so that it illumined the murky hole below. Andrew, even as he beheld the cross, cried out, "Sign the light of Thy countenance, O Lord, upon us."[124] Concurrently, two exceedingly comely men appeared in the air. Most likely, they were the holy Apostles Peter and Paul who were standing on either side of the cross. One of them extended his right hand toward Andrew below, while the other stretched out his left hand; thus they extracted him from the pit and set him on the direct road, since he had been knee-deep in the mud. They, thereupon, immediately disappeared. As for that luminous cross, it proceeded in the air before Andrew and lit the walkway for him until he reached the colonnade.[125]

The saint turned his eyes to see the cross. He observed that it attained a great height over the city. As it ascended, it emitted flame-colored rays into the air. When the cross disappeared, Andrew was standing in the middle of the road under the colonnade. Then—lo!—the oratory of the holy apostles was transformed architecturally so that it appeared to Andrew with five domes, far more beautiful and greater than the original building. And—behold!—in the midst of the church, sitting upon a throne, Andrew gazed upon the Lord Who was encircled by the cherubim and seraphim and all the hosts of the heavenly powers who were round about with fear and much trembling. As the venerable man looked intently at the Lord, Andrew stretched forth his hands to the Lord and said to Him, "Remember me, O Lord, in Thy kingdom."[126] Forthwith, Andrew came to be in an ecstasy so that he foretold what would become of that temple, saying that in the future a pious emperor would rebuild and enlarge the church in the form which he had been vouchsafed to see.[127]

Concerning the Petition to Halt the Plague

During that time there struck a deadly plague upon the queen of cities. The blessed Andrew poured forth great lamentation for the citizens, begging the man-befriending God to forgive the sins of the people and stay the epidemic. The Lord inclined to his entreaty, so that Andrew came to be in a state of ecstasy. Andrew found himself with the slave of God and stylite, Daniel, at Anaplous.[128] In a vision, Daniel also saw Andrew and exclaimed, "Come, O excellent runner and modest leader of the stadium, who in the midst

---

[124] Ps. 4:7.

[125] *P.G.* 111:740B-741A.

[126] Lk. 23:42.

[127] *P.G.* 111:741AB.

[128] Anaplous or Sosthenion (Istinye) is a small natural bay on the Bosporos. The saint's pillar was one mile inland. Saint Daniel, who reposed in 493, was well into his eighties. He is commemorated by the holy Church on the 11th of December.

of the clamor art a lightning flash more refulgent than the sun, let us entreat the Lord Who is long-suffering and plenteous in mercy that He might rescue the queen of cities from the destroyer!" As both holy fathers prayed, straightway, fire out of heaven apprehended a certain creature, black as ebony, whose hands were full of blood. The fire continued devouring the air, driving out the pestilence from the queen of cities.[129]

Concerning the Clothes-stealer

After those days, there occurred the death of the daughter of a high-ranking court official (*primikerios*). The modest maiden, earlier, had adjured her father to bury her body on one of their properties that had an oratory in a vineyard. He obeyed her last wishes. Now there was also at that time a man who plundered graves, stripping the dead of whatever was buried with them. He stood from a safe distance that he might observe where the maiden's body would be laid to rest. Concurrently, the blessed Andrew was passing by that place, working at his labors for Christ's sake. Seeing with noetic eyes, he perceived in the Spirit what depraved act that scoundrel was about to commit. Andrew wished to dissuade him from his intent, for he foresaw the punishment that awaited him who intruded upon the abode of the dead. Andrew said to him with a dour look, "Thus says the Holy Spirit to the one who pillages the graveclothes of those laid to rest. No longer shalt thou see the sun or the form of mankind. For the gates of thy house shall be shut and shall no longer open to thee; and the day shall be dark and never shine light unto the age." The sacrilegious one heard the words of the righteous man but gave them no further thought. The thief went on his way, but Andrew called after him and said, "Come back, thief, O vain one! By Jesus, thou shalt nevermore see the sun if thou shouldest commit this heinous deed!" He answered Andrew this time, saying, "Indeed, thou half-wit, thy words are dark and confusing, rivaling the demons! I am going forth, and I shall see if thy words will actually come to reality." The venerable one then went his way. That evening, the thief rolled away the stone before the sepulcher and entered. He first removed the winding-sheet and the veil that covered the dead maiden's head and shoulders. He then had the thought to turn around and leave. The man-hating demon, however, suggested that he snatch not only her raiment but her linen undergarments as well, thus leaving the body naked. This is what he did. But then—O inexpressible narration!—at God's beckoning, the virgin, with her right hand, delivered such a slap that the thief was blinded in both eyes. In abject terror, his fear was such that his knees shook and his chattering jaw ground down his teeth.

The maiden then opened her mouth and spoke to him, saying, "Wretched and miserable one! Fearest thou neither God nor His angels? As a

[129] *P.G.* 111:741B-744B; Paraclete, 107.

human being wast thou not embarrassed to gaze upon a naked female body? Wast thou not satisfied with that which thou didst first grasp? Couldest thou not grant me this mean covering for my body? But since thou wast merciless, savage, rude, and crude, wanting to make me a laughingstock to all the holy virgins at the second coming—lo!—I will demonstrate to thee how not to steal anymore. Hence, thou mightest come to know that the living God and true One is the Christ, and that there is a judgment and a recompense, and that those who love God live and rejoice after death." After the virgin spoke in this manner, she took up her vesture, as well as the winding-sheet and veil, and dressed herself, uttering, "In peace in the same place I shall lay me down and sleep. For Thou, O Lord, alone hast made me to dwell in hope."[130]

As for that vain graverobber, he just barely groped his way to the vineyard fence. He stumbled out onto the public road, running his fingers over wall after wall until he came to the city gate. To those who asked him the cause of his sudden blindness, he gave diverse pretexts. At last, coming to compunction, he recounted the whole truth. Henceforth, he begged for his daily bread. He was wont to sit and complain aloud, "Be thou accursed, O insatiable gullet! For on account of thee and the enjoyment of my belly, I am blind!" And again he was heard to say, "For the delights of the belly and thievery, I am thus made a fine show!" He, in fact, became an example so that many at that time, being informed of the matter, renounced Satan's hold over themselves and amended their habits and customs. As for the blind man, he often brought to mind the venerable Andrew's prediction of how he would be called into account for his sins. This filled him with astonishment, for which he glorified God.[131]

Concerning the Parsimonious Monk

On another occasion, Andrew came to the Stavrion.[132] He found there a certain monk, reputed for his piety. While this fellow performed the labors of a monk in a God-pleasing manner, he had one fault: he pursued niggardly practises and avarice. Some who came and made their confession also gave him, for the salvation of their souls, considerable sums of money. But since he was overcome by the passion of greed, he gave none of it to the poor; instead he kept it as *corban*,[133] that is, as a kind of gift or votive offering for his services, which he stored away in his private treasury. The blessed Andrew, with the gift of clairvoyant eyes, passed by and perceived that a terrible three-headed serpent was coiled about that monk's neck. Its tail was hanging down

---

[130] Ps. 4:9, 10.

[131] *P.G.* 111:744C-748B; Paraclete, p. 110.

[132] The Stavrion was a column close to the Church of the Holy Forty Martyrs of Sebasteia. It is one of three columns, with crosses, set up by the great Constantine. Paraclete, 112.

[133] Cf. Mk. 7:11.

to the monk's feet. The three heads were these: one of avarice, another of mad desire (mania), and another of lack of sympathy. Andrew, wishing to take a closer look, drew nigh to the monk. He understood the significance of the dragon and the form it had assumed. Now the monk thought that Andrew approached to ask for alms, for which he said, "God, have mercy on thee!" The blessed Andrew, hearing this, drew back from him. Andrew next began to write in the air, in a circle about the monk, so that dark letters became visible that read: "The dragon of avarice, it is said, is the root of all lawlessness."[134]

Andrew then looked behind him. He noticed two beings, who had the appearance of eunuchs. They seemed to be attempting to determine what would become of the monk. The one eunuch was blackened and his eyes were darksome. The other eunuch, undoubtedly a heavenly creature, was white as snow. The dusky-colored one said to the one full of light, "In vain dost thou stay and guard this one. He is mine, because he does my will. He is hard-hearted and a lover of money, and has no portion with God. His avarice is a secondary idolatry.[135] Since he obeys me, to me he belongs." But the other began to say, "Nay, but to me does he belong since he fasts and prays. Moreover, he is simple, meek, humble, and peaceable." But the dispute ensued between the two of them. The dark one then retorted, "What says the Judge of all? Does He say, 'Come ye avaricious, miserly, heartless, and ill-disposed'? Or does He invite the almsgivers, the sympathetic, the compassionate, and others like unto them?"[136] But the angel answered, "And what says the Lord, 'To whom will I have respect, but to the humble and meek, and the man that trembles at My words?'[137] And, also, 'Blessed are the poor in spirit; blessed are the meek; and blessed are the pure in heart, and the rest.'"[138] The creature that was black as pitch then countered, "What a sight he is, quivering, when he hears these verses: 'Blessed are the merciful, for they shall find mercy'[139] or 'Keep on becoming compassionate, even as your Father also is compassionate.'[140] And again, elsewhere, when he hears, 'I wish mercy, and not sacrifice,'[141] and 'Break thy bread to the hungry'[142] he is in trepidation. There are many other commandments of God, which for me to plead is

[134] Cf. 1 Tim. 6:10.
[135] Cf. Col. 3:5.
[136] Cf. Mt. 25:34.
[137] Is. 66:2.
[138] Mt. 5:3, 5, 8.
[139] Mt. 5:7.
[140] Lk. 6:36.
[141] Mt. 9:13; Hos. 6:7.
[142] Is. 58:7.

abhorrent since they oppose me. So then, how does he belong to thee?" That being of light responded: "A great judgment, today, is between us; and I will not leave it unsettled if we do not make inquiry of the Judge of the truth."

The benighted being, hearing these things, was annoyed and said to the radiant being, "Since the One Who loves mankind is the beginning and the end of philanthropy and goodness, for this cause thou dost play the knave and take refuge in God. And I know that the decision will not be in my favor." The angel of the Lord countered this, saying, "Guileful one and rogue, the Lawgiver of the sons of men neither favors the poor in judgment nor gives respect to the person of the mighty; for He is the standard and measure of wisdom and justice. So how, even by reason of thy perfect vileness, can He be incited to judge unrighteously? Come then with me, and either I shall or thou shalt be persuaded of the judgment of God." These words emboldened that dark creature that the judgment of God was straight; and so he nodded his approval. Turning toward the east, the radiant youth inquired of the Lord regarding the matter. Now while the foul demon turned to the east, he forthwith spun around and faced the west. As the angel of the Lord made the inquiry, a voice came forth from out of the heavens and declared, "I commanded My apostles, saying, 'Receive ye the Holy Spirit: if ye forgive the sins of any, they are forgiven to them; if ye retain the sins of any, they are retained.'[143] Inasmuch as I did not say to My friends, 'Receive ye gold for the Holy Spirit, and then pardon men their transgressions,' this monk has no part in thee; for the kingdom of the heavens is a rest and a habitation of the merciful." This having been spoken by that voice, the angel of the Lord transferred those firstfruits of the monk to that gloomy and dark creature. The angel then made obeisance to the Lord and proceeded away from that monk.

The blessed Andrew witnessed these things and was beside himself. From the agitation of his mind, he felt flustered and dizzy; for that wicked demon persuaded the angel of light by that which was in holy Writ. Andrew then said to himself, "O that odious and evil counsel! We have armed him with our own weapons. Moreover, that mischievous corrupter and thief is acquainted with the writings." Andrew ruminated upon these things and hastened to the road where he knew the monk would be passing. When he saw the monk coming and that he was alone, Andrew was happily relieved; for he had prayed for this opportunity. Andrew sallied forth in his direction to meet with him. The devil, surmising that Andrew was about to correct the monk, cried out against him, "Again, Andrew, art thou countering me? Despite all that has been said, thou art here to do me no good. Begone now and tyrannize me no longer! The abba is neither thy friend nor thy kinsman. In fact, thou dost not

[143] Jn. 20:23.

even know him. He does not need thine instruction. So away with thee and do not wrong me!" While the demon was sounding loudly and talking nonsensically, the venerable one kept constant in prayer with tears. As the monk came closer, Andrew took hold of him by his right hand. Bringing the monk to a halt, he said to him, "I entreat thee, abba, bear with me and hear me, thy servant. Be thou graciously disposed to receive my simple words. For I am in affliction on thine account and cannot endure the pain. For what reason hast thou, once being God's friend, made thyself into an underling of the devil? In what way, having the wings as the seraphim, didst thou permit Satan to clip them? How, as one resplendent with lightning-like form, didst thou become as one unsightly and dark in form? Woe is me! For having had eyes like the many-eyed cherubim (*polyommata*), thou hast been blinded by the dragon. And being like the rising sun, thou hast set as nightfall. For what reason hast thou put to death thy soul? Why hast thou taken as thy friend the dragon of avarice? Dost thou not understand what is the profession of a monk? Why shouldest thou want money, brother? For what purpose is it hoarded? In what manner didst thou gain it that thou shouldest suffer thine own destruction? What to thee is gold which, after thy death, will go either to those whom thou wouldest not or to thine enemies as thine inheritors? Tell me, please, why thou dost pile it up? Was the money acquired from thy toil or digging with a pick or earning wages? Was it from a parental inheritance? Dost thou keep it to have it buried with thee or to nourish thy children? Others are hungering, and thirsting, and shivering to death, and thou dost watch thy money grow and rejoice? Are these the signs of repentance? Is this the order of the monastic life and non-acquisition and flight from this vain world? In this manner wouldest thou imitate the Lord? In this fashion hast thou renounced the world? Is this how thou hast crucified thyself to the world and to desires? Thou hast turned aside for gain[144] and amassing wealth. For this greed of filthy lucre hast thou alienated thyself from thy siblings and all the vain and chaff-like things of this life? Hast thou not heard the words of the Lord? 'Do not begin to procure for yourselves gold, nor silver, nor money in your belts, nor two tunics.'[145]

"I am amazed at the way thou hast forgotten these commandments! Indeed, today or tomorrow we shall be informed of thy departure from this life, and then to whom shall go all these things which thou hast readied? Seest thou not the devil who is standing here, possessing the firstfruits of thy soul? And seest thou not that thy guardian angel is standing at a distance and wailing? My friend, behold! Seest thou not the wicked serpent of avarice? It is wrapped about thy neck. And even if thou dost not see it, the creature has found plenty of rest in thee. I, thy humble servant, being led here, heard the voice of the

[144] 1 Kgs. (1 Sam.) 8:3.
[145] Cf. Mt. 10:9, 10.

Lord God setting thee aside. For He spoke, saying: 'My kingdom belongs to the merciful. But as for that one, such as he is, My soul has hated.' But I beseech thee, hear me, and disperse thy monies to those in need: widows, orphans, strangers, and those who have no place to lay their head. And be thou struggling, by means of non-possessiveness, to become a friend of God as thou hast with thine other virtues. For this is the monastic profession: to collect nothing of the things of this life. Cease fearing that thou mightest be lacking in bread or any other necessity, for thou art in the Lord's service. For if He refreshes unbelievers and harlots and adulterers and the ungrateful, and other sorts who hate Him and are well-disposed to sin, how much more will He fill with good things those that slave for Him? See that thou dost not disobey my words. For, in the first place, I have besought thee that thou shouldest have no excuse. But by Jesus and Christ's kingdom! Seest thou the devil? If thou shouldest disobey me, I would deliver thee to him for punishment."[146]

The inward eyes of that monk were then opened. He saw the devil in the guise of an Ethiopian, black as pitch, who was hairy, bristling, and burly. That creature stood at some distance, nevertheless, out of fear of the saint, and said to the blessed Andrew, "I see, O slave of God, that thou dost wish to set in order that which pertains to the salvation of a soul." The slave of God then spoke again to the monk, saying earnestly, "Take heed that thou dost not disobey me; for to him shall I send thee forth to trouble thee greatly. Indeed, the shame of thy countenance shall be noised not only here in this queen of cities but also abroad to the four extremities of the inhabited earth. See to it that thou dost not forget for a moment; but do even as I have enjoined thee." The monk, hearing these things, shuddered and was beside himself in spirit. All the words out of the blessed man's mouth, he collected so that Andrew's bidding should be his command. The monk, therefore, so settled it in his heart. The righteous one, meanwhile, beheld a spirit, bearing a bolt of lightning, rise out of the east. Igniting the dragon, he spent its strength. The dragon, thereupon, that was coiled like a serpent about the monk's neck, changed itself in the guise of a crow and disappeared. Behold, another swarthy creature, the companion of the one that was burned, also vanished! Forthwith, the angel of God accumulated the firstfruits of the man.

The monk then was about to depart from him, when the venerable Andrew commanded him and said, "Take care that thou neither make known any discoveries regarding me nor speak nought of what I have said to thee. And if thou wilt guard these things, believe me that, even though I am a sinner and pitiful, I will remember thee in my prayers day and night so that the Lord Jesus Christ might prosper the way to that which is good." Listening to these things,

---

[146] Cf. 1 Cor. 5:5; 1 Tim. 1:20.

the abba kept them and guarded them with diligence. He then kissed the righteous man and departed. As for all his gold that he had amassed, he gave it to the poor and needy in a wonderful manner. He, thereafter, was vouchsafed great glory from God. An abundance of gold was offered to him for distribution among the poor, of which he kept only a couple of coins for his own expenses. But as for the rest of the monies, he delegated that those who made the offering ought to disperse it with their own hands. This is because he brought to mind the words of the blessed Andrew who said, "What benefit is it to me that I should become a steward for the thorns of others?" For he thought within himself, "I observe that in taking what I do not need and giving it to the poor that a conceit comes over me that the reward is mine and not that of the donor." Thus, the monk conducted his life in an upright and godly manner befitting a monk. He was accounted worthy of beholding the slave of God, Andrew, in a dream. The saint was smiling at him as he showed him a splendid tree planted on a plain covered with flowers. The tree was laden with the sweetest fruit. Andrew said to him, "The tree, this delightful one before thine eyes, really symbolizes the condition of thy soul from the day thou didst encounter me and distribute thy gold." The monk was then awakened and further strengthened toward advancement in spiritual work, for which he offered up thanks daily both to God and His servant Andrew.[147]

Concerning the Wayward Youth

Now Epiphanios had an acquaintance who chose to keep company with the godly youth, since Epiphanios enjoyed a good and honorable reputation. The acquaintance, nevertheless, did not emulate Epiphanios' manner of life. Andrew perceived the waywardness of that youth, and so he slapped him. This action enraged that vainglorious youth. In his maddened state, he rushed forward to seize the saint by his hair, but Andrew had already taken himself away. Epiphanios stopped the young man and rebuked him, saying, "Hast thou never read 'not to render evil for evil'[148] and that 'whosoever shall strike thee on the right cheek, turn to him the other also'?[149] If thou wilt be my companion, desist. Keep thyself from requiting evil for evil and thus avoid strife, wrath, and malice. Much rather, be poor in spirit and contrite of heart. Mourn and grieve for thine own transgressions. Exercise restraint, moderation, and love. Flee indolence, stupid tricks, self-conceit, pride, high-mindedness, adultery, lusting after men, masturbation, gluttony, and intoxication. By means of these sins the wrath of God comes upon the sons of disobedience."[150] Epiphanios, therefore, urged him to struggle; but the devil hardened that youth's heart. The

---

[147] *P.G.* 111:749B-760B; Paraclete, p. 116-119.

[148] 1 Pe. 3:9.

[149] Mt. 5:39.

[150] Col. 3:6.

young man, therefore, said that he would enjoy himself now and relinquish his bad pastimes later. Thus, he no longer kept company with Epiphanios. That profligate fell into penury and tribulation and terrible temptations. When Epiphanios asked Andrew about this former acquaintance and also entreated Andrew to pray for him, the saint remarked, "Nay, child, but continue being sympathetic toward his soul while his body suffers in this life. Leave him for now, for that which has befallen him is fitting for now. But with the passage of time, the Lord will look upon the lowliness of his misery and recall him to his former state." Epiphanios asked, "I beseech thee, O slave of God, canst thou tell me the cause?" Andrew answered, "The Lord was wroth with him by reason of his swearing falsely, lying, audaciousness, and pride. Indeed, he had worse carnal sins, but not so much was he punished for these as for the former things. For this reason has he been left for his own good. As food which is not cooked in the pot has neither savor nor sweetness, so we sinners and lowly ones, unless we are broiled by many afflictions and temptations, we shall not enter into the kingdom of the heavens." Epiphanios then said, "If this is to the benefit of his soul's salvation, I shall no longer speak concerning him. Only I should like to see him exercising courageous patience and having good hopes, with the help of the Lord, walking on the path leading to His courts."[151]

Concerning the Profligate John

Epiphanios had another friend, named John, a profligate who lusted after women. It was a passion for which he blamed God, saying that the Lord was the cause since He made woman. Epiphanios asked him did God bring knives, ropes, and staves into our lives so that we might slay, hang, and accost one another? Epiphanios, therefore, urged his friend to find a virtuous woman and marry, but not for the sake of carnality and pleasure. He warned him against fornication, adultery, and sodomy; for those who commit such loathsome acts are compared to blind and irrational brutes or even worse. Although John called his friend and the words he spoke blessed, still he said he could not fast and pray and comport himself as Epiphanios. He said he was compelled by the demon, and even his own nature, when he allowed himself to succumb to fits of anger and to talk ill of others. Epiphanios called these pretexts, and he urged him to struggle in order to save himself. The blessed Andrew, at that moment, passed by. Epiphanios left John and went to greet his beloved friend. Andrew warned him that his depraved friend was deaf to his salutary counsels. The saint then prophesied that John, a fornicator, adulterer, and Sodomite, would perish soon. Andrew disclosed to Epiphanios that John would have died earlier had not his guardian angel prayed for more time and received a temporary reprieve. But since the extension was expiring with no

[151] *P.G.* 111:760B-764C; Paraclete, 123.

sign of reformation, disease would soon overtake John and dispatch him to Hades.

In but a short time, the voluptuary John was consumed by disease and still remained in an unrepentant state. Epiphanios was vouchsafed a vision of Hades. The venerable Andrew was with Epiphanios as they traversed through rough places that were very gloomy and difficult to distinguish. Epiphanios took a candle into that place of no light. It seemed to him that such phenomena existed beneath the earth. There were guards and dungeons filled with plenty of mice, cats, and foxes. There were other prison cells with serpents, asses, vipers, asps, crows, ravens, and birds—unclean and malodorous. There were beasts and dogs, more than the stars of the heaven. Epiphanios asked the blessed Andrew what they were doing in such a place. Andrew explained that he would see how the works of sinners transform them. The saint then pointed to letters on a dark tablet in midair. Epiphanios, when he was told to read them, discerned: "The everlasting abode and violent punishment of John, son of Celestine." Now Celestine was the name of John's father. Epiphanios exclaimed, "Woe is me, the sinner! I should not wish to see my worst enemy among these! What are these pieces of dung?" Andrew explained that they were the labors of the soul. Souls were kept in chains, having their fill of that stench, until the resurrection of their bodies at which time they would be given up entirely to the fire.[152] Epiphanios then asked about the mice, dogs, wild animals, asses, mules, and reptiles kept secured in that place. The righteous man remarked, "These are the souls of the lawless and sinners and profligates." Epiphanios commented, "Woe! Milord, the souls of men, do they have such appearances and forms?" Andrew answered, "No, most beloved child, but for our sakes has God prepared them to be shown to us; for each one represents a conduct of life and a shameless practise committed in the world."[153]

Continuing, Andrew explained, "God has shown them thus in this vision: for He regards murderers as scorpions; idolaters as dross; adulterers as those who have lost their minds; magicians and users of drugs and potions as snakes; those who commit bestiality and homosexuality as the mouse or rat and as the worm-eaten dog thrown onto a dung heap; fornicators as pigs; thieves as wolves; the guileful as foxes; the avaricious as cats; those prone to anger as wild beasts; those who remember wrongs as vipers; liars as the serpent; gluttons as horses; drunkards as demonized; heretics as dung; and brothel-keepers as asses. As for pimps who—with oaths and lies arrange assignations between men and women for illicit relations—make others temples of the devil and habitations of dung, these He reckons like the coming Antichrist. He deems the abusers and revilers as crows, and the babblers and slanderers as ravens. As

[152] Cf. 1 Cor. 3:13-15.

[153] *P.G.* 111:764D-772D.

for those who insensibly judge the faults of others, He takes to be as mad dogs that bite the flesh of men. He views singers as frogs, instrument players as the devils' instruments, dancing women as herons,[154] harlots as goats. He looks at youths involved in their games, and laughter, and mimicry, and in drunkenness and corruption of boys, as the unclean reptiles of the earth, and as brutes, and as the generation of the vipers."[155]

After the venerable Andrew uttered these words to Epiphanios, the latter was roused from his vision and awoke, being amazed at what had been shown to him. He then received tidings that his friend John contracted the plague. Epiphanios went straightway to see him. John acknowledged that the words of the blessed Andrew came to pass for him. Daily, John's flesh failed until he was brought down into Hades. John asked Epiphanios to pray for him that God might spare him. Epiphanios said to him, "Brother, the Lord knows what is needful, for He knows those things which are profitable. I cannot benefit thee now. Supplicate God and He, in His goodness, shall work what is to His glory." Meanwhile, John deteriorated daily. Those who beheld him cried out, "Lord, have mercy!" The wretched one suffered painfully to the end of his life until his bones were scattered nigh unto Hades.[156] Afterward, Epiphanios met with the God-bearing Andrew in the central square. They discussed the vision, and Andrew reminded him of that harsh tablet with John's name. Epiphanios expressed his horror and how he was seized with terror, saying, "Fear and trembling came upon me, and darkness has covered me.[157] I am very fearful that the prince of darkness should take me in the embrace of sinful pleasures and pull me down." The blessed man said, "This is why I showed it to thee, my child, that thou mightest be afraid. Keep struggling with eagerness, that thou mightest inherit the heavenly kingdom. Keep fighting the good fight of continence, that I might see spiritual progress in thy soul and rejoice with thee in spirit." After speaking in this manner, some people began approaching them. Andrew then saluted Epiphanios and departed.[158]

Concerning the Vision of the Prophet-King David

One day, at the fulfillment of the forty-day Great Fast, when multitudes in the queen of cities were celebrating Palm Sunday, the blessed Andrew was in Hagia Sophia. He beheld a very handsome man with white hair in the midst of a multitude bearing palms and crosses, scintillating forth as translucent lightning, as they chanted a melodious and sweet and saving hymn. One by

---

[154] The Greek word ἐρωδιοὺς or *herodious* is given, meaning the common heron or egret.

[155] *P.G.* 111:773AB; Paraclete, 130.

[156] Ps. 140:8.

[157] Ps. 54:5.

[158] *P.G.* 111:773C-776D; Paraclete, 131, 132.

one, each of those beautiful faces ascended the ambo and entered the holy bema.[159] The comely elder was plucking strings on a harp, in accompaniment to those who were chanting. Andrew heard these things and, as his heart leaped, he rejoiced and said, "'Remember, O Lord, David and all his meekness!'[160] Behold, we have heard the Lady and Lord's ambassadress who intercedes with Him in our behalf, and we have found her even like the delectable Wisdom!"[161] Now some standing by overheard the blessed man and called him into account as a fool, saying, "Does the Psalter have any verse that pertains to the Lady?" The venerable man said, "'House' and 'Habitation'[162] and 'God's rest'[163] refer to her, as well as 'at Thy right hand stood the Queen.'[164]" But those people, out of ignorance, laughed at Andrew. Now Andrew spoke thus after beholding a vision of David, whom he deemed both glorious among the prophets and as one who exerted much influence. "For behold!" said Andrew, "David, in ancient times, was saying that 'until I find a place for the Lord, a habitation for the God of Jacob'[165] he would rest neither his eyes nor his temples. God first made His dwelling place and rest in the great Mistress (the Theotokos), and then in this Great Church (Hagia Sophia). This very hour such was the melody heard from the noetic harps." The saint then departed and went on chanting softly, with whispering lips.[166]

Concerning the Righteous and Sinners

When it was the Feast of the Resurrection of Christ, the blessed Andrew went to the Great Church in order to pray. He stood at the entrance of the Horologion,[167] where he observed those entering and exiting. Then did the Lord wish to reveal how each one passed the Great Fast. Some had countenances as white as snow, and others more dazzling than the sun. Their heads were anointed with oil and myrrh, and crowns of precious stones encircled their brows. The sweet fragrance of violets and roses filled the air. They wore royal robes of linen and purple. They were reverenced by handsome youths who honored and glorified them. These were the faithful who completed the Great

---

[159] The bema or sanctuary has the altar located in the center.

[160] Ps. 131:1.

[161] *P.G.* 111:788D-789A; Paraclete, 142, 143.

[162] Ps. 131:14.

[163] Ps. 131:15.

[164] Ps. 44:8.

[165] Ps. 131:5.

[166] *P.G.* 111:789B; Paraclete, 143.

[167] The *horologion* in Byzantine times signified either a sundial or a waterclock, used for the scheduling of religious services. At Hagia Sophia, it was a magnificent structure with twenty-four doors that opened and shut according to the hours of the day. *Oxford*, s.v. "Horologion."

Fast well, with fasts and prayers. Andrew rejoiced in his soul and glorified God upon beholding their progress.

Again, he beheld others, like the first, who were snow white and with faces beaming as the sun. The Holy Spirit rested upon them, as they were pure and virtuous. They lived far from fornication, adultery, vindictiveness, and all types of foolish talking and babbling. Moreover, they communed the life-giving Mysteries daily.

Others were clad in gold robes, radiant and majestic. Above their heads were white doves dripping oil upon their robes. There wafted forth from them a cloud of myrrh and the fragrance of incense, from before those noetic doves that were angels of God. These were the faithful who shared their bread with the poor, who avoided company with wrongdoers and criminals, who paid the debts of strangers, and who supplied the poor with clothing and coverings. Such persons retreated before adultery and fornication. They participated in the divine offices for the saints, and they were humble. They, according to the blessed Paul, were those who were "in need, afflicted, ill-treated."[168]

There were others also in magnificent garments with grace-filled countenances, clad in costly raiment who walked with a happy gait. With them there was an exceedingly beautiful maiden, wearing a crown of olive branches. She was the eldest daughter of the King. She anointed with oil the faces of those who accompanied her. These were the ones who visited those in prison,[169] who loved quietude,[170] and never were absent from Church services. They ate their bread with thanksgiving, and uttered no blasphemies or slanders or gossip.

Now the saint also beheld those whose faces were blackened with soot and uncleanness. Cats and small dogs lay in wait and played at their feet. Snakes hung from their bodily members and sucked uncleanness. The people did not drive them away but rather helped them carefully. Upon their feet there were frogs, together with other reptiles which symbolized their passions, so that they were pitiable spectacles. They embittered the Lord and caused Him to turn His face from them. The angels that guarded them also were grieved and unhappy. These were persons that engaged in profligate deeds, homosexuality, adultery, masturbation, and miserliness. Even as swine, they wallowed in their sins. They feared neither God nor angelkind. They felt no pity for their own souls, and they gave no consequence to the days of the holy fast. In fact, they hated such days and found them a burden. So they continued to steal and overeat. Having no fear of the Judge, they continued giving over their members to the devil to work that which was unseemly. Demons of centurion rank,

[168] Heb. 11:37.

[169] Mt. 25:36.

[170] 2 Thess. 3:12; 1 Thess. 4:11; 1 Pe. 3:4.

together with their minions, abided among them. The snakes and asps are nothing other than manifestations of the demons, who rejoice whenever one falls into fornication or adultery or the most abominable homosexuality. There were not only men but women as well. The sin of adultery being only second after murder, in accordance with the divine law.[171]

Now there were some who were naked, dusky, and with eyes quite red-hued. Their faces resembled burned biscuits, so blackened were they. Some fierce creatures, deep black as Ethiopians, were dragging them as though they were mules. Those coal-black beings were holding sharp daggers, as they pulled at the ropes around the necks of these people. There were others, dark as night, holding fiery staves, beating others to make them hasten their pace. Over them there was an inscription that read: "Magicians, drug and potion users, and sorcerers." The sight ushered in both fear and grief to the righteous man. He went to a place apart and wept.

He then observed other naked people, appearing dark and benighted. They were holding bloodied two-edged swords. On the tops of their heads were vipers, all of wrath and anger. They roused to anger each one until they satisfied their desire. These people conducted themselves as though they were wanting in sense and mind. They appeared to be in much tribulation and agitation. They were provoked by the noetic beast, the viper, and did not come to repentance for homicide, robbery, and licentiousness.

The saint also noted others who were clad with rags, together with many women. Their bodies were filled with thorns and thistles. Around them went revolting reptiles, frogs, mice, tortoises, and other worse creatures. These people were those who were irascible, fierce, wicked, bitter, and who inhumanely scourged their slaves and left them to starve. There were others covered with smoke. Their faces were bristly, all noxious, and blackened like demons. Vipers and asps blocked off their ears and eyes lest they should see and hear the writings of the sacred temples. Above them were written these words: "Remembrance of wrongs, the first daughter of the devil." From their nostrils there came forth poisonous asps, scorpions, and reptiles that filled the air and the souls of men with bitterness. Such people also subjected other people to perils and deaths: the vindictive, the proud, the foulmouthed, the revilers, the calumniators, and all those who fostered enmity. There were also those who judged and condemned others of sins, as though they were strangers to such things, but which crimes they themselves had committed. The blessed man then rose up and left the crowd behind. He prayed, for he was in a state of turmoil. The moment he finished his prayer, he heard a divine voice, saying, "Why art thou dismayed, Andrew, and sullen of countenance at the little that thou hast

[171] See Canon VII of Saint Basil; Canon XXVIII of Saint Nikephoros of Constantinople.

seen? I behold these things, and worse, all the days of their lives. I, however, endure and await their repentance." The venerable man marvelled and remarked, "Well hast Thou spoken, O Lord, by Thy forefather: 'Man, being in honor, did not understand; he is compared to the mindless cattle, and is become like unto them.'"[172] Andrew then departed from that place.[173]

Concerning Marital Relations on the Lord's Day

At another time, on a Sunday morning, Andrew and Epiphanios were talking when a nobleman was on his way to the imperial palace. The moment Andrew laid eyes on him, he perceived the sin he committed on that holy Lord's day. Andrew then addressed the nobleman and said, "See here, O absurd one who defiles the holy Lord's day, wilt thou also defile the palace?" The man, hearing these words directed at him, was profoundly amazed. He smiled a little and passed on. But when he encountered some friends, he gave utterance to his astonishment. He told them how he met "the fool" who told him what he had done secretly. Some of his friends marvelled, but others did not believe it; and yet others said that the revelation was made by a demon. In the meantime, Epiphanios wondered at the foreknowledge of the righteous man and inquired, "What, O father, didst thou mean by those words spoken to the nobleman?" The blessed one answered, "This night I beheld a woman, a queen, arrayed with her crown of pearls and precious stones. It was she who condemned the passing nobleman, saying, 'How darest thou defile the Lord's day, O wretched one? Hast thou not howled enough in filling thy desire, O insatiate one, all throughout the week, that even on my day, the holy one, thou dost enter heedlessly? By my Bridegroom Christ, if thou shouldest do it a second time, there would not be a third!' I heard her speak in this manner, so I was incited to put him on his guard. After seeing this, my child, I lamented for him in my heart. It is for this reason that I rebuked him, hoping to bring him to a sound mind. For she said that should he do it a second time that there would be no third time—that is to say, 'I shall request that a sickle harvest thee.' Inasmuch as when a man dies neither does he sin nor does he do good deeds; for when the soul is loosed from the body, death puts an end to all activity."[174]

Concerning the Vision of Barbara

The venerable Andrew, at another time, was walking about in the public Forum. He was near the porphyry Column of Constantine, which that emperor of blessed memory had erected in his reign. Constantine had the vault of the base filled with relics, among which were the precious nails that pierced the life-giving body of Christ. They were meant to be a protection and guard

---

172 Ps. 48:21.

173 Paraclete, 144-148.

174 *P.G.* 111:800C-801A; Paraclete, 158, 159.

for the imperial city. Now—behold!—there was a certain woman, named Barbara, who was made bright by the Holy Spirit. She came to be in a state of ecstasy, so that her spiritual eyes were opened. She discerned that the blessed Andrew walked in the midst of the multitude as a shining pillar of fire, discharging fiery missiles into the air. Now some imbeciles gave Andrew a box on the ear, while others smote his neck. There were others who looked at him and said, "Good Lord! If we had an enemy, we should not want what has befallen this fellow to come upon him." As they were speaking thus, some gloomy and dusky demons came. They followed behind those that were walking and remarked, "Indeed, may God hear your prayers and may He not raise up ever such a one as this upon the earth! For no one has consumed our hearts, as this tireless one! Not wishing to labor for his master, Theognostos, he plays the idiot and mocks the world." Now as those dark demons were conversing, Barbara observed that they were keeping track and marking those who ill-treated Andrew, saying among themselves, "For this we shall have a consolation in the judgment; for they sinned by wrongfully striking Andrew. At the hour of each one's death, we shall condemn them for unjustly striking an elect one of God." The blessed Andrew, by the divine Spirit, heard them speaking. Desiring to dissolve their villainies, he condemned them saying, "It is not permitted for you to keep track of these things. For I besought my dread Master, Jesus, for their sake that striking me not be a sin put to the account of any one of them. Their ignorance will be used as a ground for their defense."

Now Barbara, also, heard Andrew speaking to those dark beings. She then looked up—and behold!—even as a gate of heaven was opening, she saw a multitude of delightful swallows. In the midst of that flock, she saw a dove, like unto snow, that was exceedingly large. It flew together with the swallows over the blessed Andrew. The dove had in its beak an olive twig of sparkling gold. A human voice addressed the blessed Andrew and announced: "Receive this twig. This is a token from Paradise, sent to thee by the almighty Father and the Lord Sabaoth. For thou hast manifested mercy and philanthropy in the same manner as God Who is merciful and compassionate. For—behold!—the Lord will glorify thee, again and again, and exalt His holy name upon thee, since thou hast not adjudged it as sin those who smote thee daily." As these words were being pronounced, the dove sat upon Andrew's head. She was all of a pale color of gold and silver. Her eyes were as precious pearls. Her feet were dyed in the imperial hue. A cross, fashioned of flowers, adorned her head. The flock of swallows was singing beautifully as they encircled her.

When Barbara, that God-fearing woman, viewed all these things, she was exceedingly astonished. She was unable to say ought except, "Bless me! The goodness of God has wrought such luminaries upon the earth, but the people understood it not." She, ofttimes, wanted to recount to him the vision, but a divine power, immediately, hindered her so that she began to tremble; and thus, she involuntarily was silenced. But then one day the righteous man met her and said, "Be guarding my secret for now, Barbara, and tell no one of me until 'I shall go to the place of the wondrous tabernacle, even to the house of God.'"[175] Barbara answered, "Even if I did desire to speak, I could not. For should I wish to recount it to anyone, I am unable, O honorable luminary and elect of the Lord, O most wonderful! For I am hindered by an invisible power, so that trembling enters into my bones and my strength fails me."[176]

Concerning the Vision of the Panagia at Vlachernai

During another night, when an all-night vigil was being conducted at the Chapel of the Holy Soros, found at the Church of Vlachernai, there came a vision to Saint Andrew[177] that revealed the holy protection of the Theotokos. The chapel contained a reliquary with the precious sash of the Theotokos.[178] Epiphanios was also present with one of his menservants. Epiphanios had the custom of standing until midnight or until dawn. It was the blessed Andrew's custom to offer up doxologies. Then—behold!—at about the fourth hour of the night, the holy Andrew saw with his own eyes the most holy Theotokos coming out from the beautiful gate toward the narthex. She then appeared to be at a lofty height, as high as were the heavens, with a train of awesome and terrifying ranks of holy angels. In the midst were the honorable Forerunner and

---

[175] Ps. 41:4.

[176] *P.G.* 111:837C-841A; Paraclete, 189, 190.

[177] The Feast of the Protection of the Mother of God is celebrated with special solemnity by the holy Church on the 1st of October—an ancient date. The icon of the Protection also depicts Saint Andrew and his disciple Epiphanios, in the lower right, beholding the sublime vision. The feast, in modern Greek times (1960), was moved to the 28th of October, making it also civil holiday, in memory of the saving of the Greek people from the 1940 inroads of the Italians.

[178] Vlachernai, comprising of a church and palace, is an area in the northwestern corner of Constantinople where there is a spring. The basilica is believed to have been built by Empress Pulcheria (ca. 450). It was Leo I who added a circular reliquary chapel (Hagia Soros, meaning reliquary casket) where the honorable robe of the Theotokos was brought, the feast day of which is the 2nd of July. The imperial palace, set up on higher ground, was built ca. 500. On the south side of the Vlachernai temple there was the Chapel of the Holy Soros wherein was kept the Virgin's mantle (*esthes*). The belt (*zonee*) of the Virgin was placed in the Chalkoprateia Church by Emperor Arkadios. By the time of Justin II, the belt was installed in an architectural *soros* of its own: the translation of which is commemorated by the holy Church on the 31st of August. It is unclear whether the *maphorion* (a veil that covers head and shoulders) of the Virgin is the same article of clothing as the Virgin's robe or mantle (*esthes*). *Oxford*, s.v. "Blachernai, Church and Palace of"; "Maphorion"; "Soros."

the son of thunder, the Theologian John, who escorted by hand the Queen of the angels. The holy angels went on ahead with others clad in white. They were chanting spiritual songs very sweetly, which only Andrew and Epiphanios could discern. The Theotokos came to the center of the church where, of old, was situated the sacred ambo. The Lady Theotokos stood in the middle of the soleas[179] and then went to her knees. She then offered up prayer, entreating her only-begotten Son on behalf of the salvation of the believers, so that for a long while she remained with tears streaming down that godlike countenance. Andrew then went and said to Epiphanios, "Seest, child, the Lady and Mistress of the cosmos?" Epiphanios said, "Yea, honorable father, I see, by thy holy prayers, the Lady."

The Holy Protection of the Theotokos

After the Theotokos offered up considerable prayer, she rose up and went within the holy bema, removing her *maphorion* or *esthes*, which had been contained in the holy Soros. She then came to the royal gates of the bema. She placed the veil upon her most immaculate head, unwinding it beautifully in a modest but august manner. Following this, she took it into her immaculate hands. The article was large and terrifying. She spread it over the people, as many as were there. The blessed Andrew and Epiphanios witnessed these actions. The Theotokos held the *maphorion* for a considerable time and unfolded it over the people. It gave forth a lightning-like radiance, shining as electrum. As long as the Lady Theotokos stood there, in that attitude, providing her holy protection, the rutilant *maphorion* was manifest. When the Lady Theotokos began to ascend into the heavens, little by little, the *maphorion* was no longer visible; for

[179] Soleas or solea is the platform outside the iconostasion.

though she had taken it, yet the grace of her divine protection abided. The relic of her *maphorion* was still kept there in the sacred Church of Vlachernai, the grace of which overshadows the faithful. These events were seen by the hallowed Andrew and his initiate in the mysteries, Epiphanios, by the mediation of our divine Father Andrew. For he was richly endowed with the gift of lofty contemplation of supernatural revelations, for which he graciously interceded with God that Epiphanios might participate in them with him.[180]

Concerning the Most Wicked Grandee

Again, at another time, when the blessed man was playing his usual games at the Hippodrome, some of the people, seeing his nonconformable behavior as much too unconventional, were grieved. Some even cast curses at him and repulsed him as one troubled by a bitter demon. Then, as it happened, a certain grandee also passed by. He, too, abominated Andrew and spat upon him! The servant of Christ, for a long while, watched him and came to understand those privy things about him. Andrew then said to the grandee, "Guileful one, thou adulterer, thou mocker of the Church! Thou dost use as a pretext participation in the Church service. Satan has thee rise up early, after the midnight hour, that thou mightest do his work. Behold! The hour is come that thou shalt pay in accordance with thy practises. Didst thou think that thou wouldest escape from the terrible eye of the One Who searches out the hearts and reins?"[181] Hearing this reprimand, the grandee struck his heel into his horse and raced off. Now he was the *chartoularios*, that is, an officer having fiscal and archival duties, regarding the shipping industry for the city of Amastris.[182]

After a few days, that grandee contracted a dreadful disease that progressed. Those with him conveyed him from church to church and from physician to physician, but these visits were without any positive results. One night, when the saint was near the grandee's dwelling, he observed an angel of the Lord who arrived through the air from the west. He was a fiery being, having a fiery countenance and fierce eyes. He was bearing in his hand a flaming rod. He went to that pitiful man and threatened to uproot his house, even to the foundations. When that angel approached the sick grandee, Andrew heard a voice from on high that said, "Strike the mocker, the Sodomite, the adulterer, the fornicator, the impious, and wretch who merits divine vengeance! As thou givest him a thrashing, thus speak: 'Dost thou commit fornication and adultery? Dost thou rise early for the devil? Art thou again about the licentiousness of the Sodomites?'" And so the angel administered the blows. The falling rod came down with a mighty sound. The grandee's cries could be heard by all. Whether or not he wanted to confess, by the stress of

[180] *P.G.* 111:848C-849A, Paraclete, 195-197.

[181] Ps. 7:9.

[182] Amastris (present-day Amasra) is on the Black Sea coast of Anatolia.

circumstances, he did confess and say: "I will not ever commit fornication, only have mercy on me!" In this manner was he tortured for three nights and days, as he kept saying, "I will not commit fornication." Thus was his pitiful soul cast into everlasting punishment.[183]

"I," interposes the biographer Nikephoros, "have written these things concerning the blessed Andrew, O friends, for the benefit of your souls and to put the fear of God in them, so that we may know how to labor and walk in this world. Nothing is hidden from God and His saints. Now when I asked the righteous man, 'In what manner had this man sinned?' he answered, 'He had two eunuchs with whom he engaged in sin. Moreover, he would dispatch those eunuchs to bring him unmarried women, and, if none were available, harlots and adulteresses. His fornications were beyond counting. He had taken care that, before the cock crowed, he would engage in these depravities that were catastrophic for his soul. Frequently, his wife questioned where he was going at such an hour. He would say, "To church." First he went and performed the work of the devil, and then he would arrive in the church reeking from foul stains and defilement. Now those who saw him attending church with such regularity, remarked, "Behold that holy man!" But all along he was a secret devil. Furthermore, although he knew himself to be such a sinner, still he fell into vainglory over the praise heaped upon him by others. But God abominated all these practises; and so he came to the end I have earlier described. These particulars, O friends, had been narrated to me by the luminary himself.'"[184]

Concerning Some Prophesies

Epiphanios invited the saint to his home, where they discussed the times to come with regard to Constantinople and the latter days. Now Saint Andrew prophesied future events, which are not possible to reproduce in their entirety herein.[185] Saint Andrew foretells periods of prosperity and hardship for the city of Constantinople. He speaks of peace and of war: attacks by the Hagarenes; and those whose name begins with the eighteenth letter of the alphabet (*rho*), most likely the Rus, and tells how the city sustains these attacks.[186] He predicts the coming of the God-hated religion (Islam of the Muslims), as well as the sodomy practises of the Hagarenes which provoke the

---

[183] *P.G.* 111:849B-852A; Paraclete, 197, 198.

[184] *P.G.* 111:852BC; Paraclete, 199.

[185] *P.G.* 111:852C.

[186] See the various examples in which the city's patroness, the Theotokos, defends and protects her flock, given herein on the 11th of May, when the holy Church commemorates the consecration of Constantinople. Saint Andrew also speaks of her protection in saving the city [*P.G.* 111:853B].

Lord to wrath.[187] He also tells of a time of incestuous relationships, many of them enjoined by law. He speaks of internal problems within the empire when monks and nuns would be forced to live with one another,[188] which did occur during the periods of Iconoclasm. He forecasts lightning and thunders, famines and deaths, and great wrath along with other disasters, though he mentions a few places where the blessed shall dwell in peace.[189] He announces how an emperor will read the books of the pagan Greeks and espouse their religion. He will, thereafter, fight both the saints and Christ's Church, as well as destroy sacred vessels. At that time there will be domestic wars within families, relatives putting one another to death. He also speaks of the appearance of fire in the sky, as from burning carbon or cinder that covers and threatens with the speed of lightning all the earth. This will create confusion so that birds will fall upon one another. The earth will be filled with snakes that will bite unrepentant sinners. This will be the beginning of the pangs. He then warns about the end of the kingdom of the Rhomaioi. An angel of the Lord shall descend and take the precious Cross and diadem as well as the soul of the emperor. He calls those blessed who will flee from that city and find refuge in wilderness places and caves.[190]

He then speaks of how the Jews will once again acquire Jerusalem just before the end. "The Lord will permit them to possess what they had held earlier. He does this in order to overturn their pretext that their loss and destruction are owing to their dispersion among the nations. Hence, on the day of judgment they cannot say the following to Christ: 'If we had been gathered together in Jerusalem and Thou wouldest have given again to us all that we had, then we would have believed in Thee; for then there would not have been any reason for us to envy the nations who, to our detriment, were so preferred to us.' But He will allow them to gather together and obtain again what they had, though they will abide in the same unbelief. Then how will they be saved? Instead, in the same era of their restoration, Antichrist will come among them and they all will believe in him, in accordance with the prophecy of the Lord.[191] Thus with their restoration there will be no pretext. The Apostle Paul, saying that they will be saved, does not mean that they will be rescued from everlasting punishment, but delivered from their wanderings of so many years in foreign parts, and from the reproach of the other peoples, and from shameful humiliation. They will assemble in their homeland and will be saved from the slavery and the yoke and the jeering which they underwent for years. Since

[187] Paraclete, 201.

[188] *P.G.* 111:852C-857A; Paraclete, 202.

[189] *P.G.* 111:857B; Paraclete, 203.

[190] *P.G.* 111:857C-860B; Paraclete, 205.

[191] Jn. 5:43.

they were not persuaded to believe in the Christ through affliction and tribulation, how will they be persuaded in this supposed happiness?"[192]

Saint Andrew

Epiphanios then asked about Hagia Sophia, if she would still be standing. The saint indicated that the city would be submerged, "So how could the church survive? Who could enter and offer veneration?" He told Epiphanios that God does not dwell in handmade temples. What would remain would be the precious nails within the column in the marketplace. He said that ships would tie their ropes to it, and that they will mourn the seven-hilled Babylon, saying, "Woe to us! The great and ancient city is sunk. Here we successfully transacted business and were enriched." He then says, "The period of mourning will be forty days. By reason of the affliction of those days, the realm (or kingdom) shall be given to Rome, as well as to Sylaio and Thessalonike. This will occur when the consummation draws nigh, when the condition of the world shall worsen, when pangs and misfortunes shall be multiplied."[193]

The saint then speaks of an abominable nation that will persecute the churches or what he calls islands.[194] He speaks of the coming of Enoch who lived before the law and of Elias who lived during the law, and how they will preach in the end times.[195] They will work wonders and have great authority against Antichrist, but shall be slain.[196] Their bodies will be left for three whole days in the square. "On the fourth day," he says, "a radiant dove will descend from the heaven as lightning. The dove shall alight upon them and they shall be given life. They shall walk, to the

[192] *P.G.* 111:865B-868A; Paraclete, 210, 211.

[193] *P.G.* 111:868BC; Paraclete, 211, 212.

[194] *P.G.* 111:868CD. See Is. 24:15; 42:10-12, 15, where the churches are spoken of as islands.

[195] Paraclete, 214.

[196] Rev. 11:5-10.

terror of many; but a cloud shall take them up and set them in Paradise."[197] Although the saint calls all martyrs blessed, he calls thrice-blessed those that shall suffer martyrdom in the times of Antichrist, for whom much glory and rejoicing await.[198]

Concerning Incense

At yet another time, in the morning, Andrew and Epiphanios were sitting together and discussing spiritual matters. As a book of Saint Basil the Great was lying nearby, the venerable man urged Epiphanios to take it into his hands and read aloud. As he was reading on holy Baptism, there came into his nostrils the sweet smell of aromatic spices. The blessed man also observed Epiphanios inhaling the perfumed scent. When Epiphanios finished reading, no longer did the fragrance waft forth. He then inquired, "I beseech thee, my great sir, whence came forth that fragrance?" The blessed one answered, "How sweet to my palate are Thy sayings! More sweet than honey to my mouth."[199] Epiphanios interrupted him and said, "Leave off speaking thus, father, and tell me what thou hast contemplated; for I know this came about by means of thine entreaty." The blessed man replied, "What wouldest thou have me say, my beloved? For a considerable number of the angels of the Lord were present as thou didst read. One among them, glorifying the words of the Holy Spirit, offered incense in a befitting manner and rejoiced." Epiphanios continued, "And where are the angels of the Savior? Where is the censer and the coals, which are not of matter and not to be confused with it." The blessed man gazed on Epiphanios and, stretching forth his hand toward him, commented, "Thou speakest wonderfully, my man. For who told thee that the angels possess censers, felt with fingers of sense-perception, or that they need incense and coal of this world? For the spiritual beings have spiritual things, and the material beings possess material objects. Angels, when desirous to offer incense before the Most High or the throne of the One Who transcends every mind, offer nothing else than the sweet fragrance that comes forth from the awesome and unapproachable Divinity. The angels stand before the dread throne of the Almighty, receiving the fragrant lightnings therefrom and, afterward, are unceasingly scented with the ineffable fragrance of the Divinity. Another means of being scented is by the flowers of Paradise, which they do collect. With an invisible presence they then fill the nostrils of man. Now there are three situations in which the holy angels do incense. First, whenever the sacred books are being read, they invisibly circle round about, wishing to hear the godly sweet words of the All-Holy Spirit. Second, whenever one is praying and conversing with God. Third, whenever one, for the sake of God, is amid toil

---

[197] Rev. 11:9-13.

[198] *P.G.* 111:869C; Paraclete, 215.

[199] Ps. 118:103.

and pain and persevering in scourges; for then they continually anoint and perfume the struggler to make such a one more eager to struggle on behalf of piety."[200]

Now as they spoke of these things and others, the Priest Nikephoros was present at their spiritual teachings. "Epiphanios was advanced," said the priest, "but not as the blessed Andrew. For by the Holy Spirit he interpreted foreign tongues and the secret things of Scriptures unerringly. For indeed, he attained to the pinnacle of learning. Andrew was also pure, chaste, eloquent, and possessed of knowledge not to be guessed. He knew, from awesome and dread contemplation of the Holy Spirit, the elements of the twenty-four letters and of those things noetic and of sense-perception. Now only to me and to Epiphanios did he converse on lofty matters of Scriptures but not to any other person."[201]

Concerning the Judgment and the Second Coming

At another time, when they were speaking of the incomprehensibility of God, Epiphanios asked about the second coming. "How," he inquired, "shall the people be judged at the second coming?" Andrew answered, "Hast thou not heard the apostolic utterance? 'For as many as did sin without law shall also perish without law; and as many as did sin in the law shall be judged by the law.'[202] The Jews who lived in the epoch from Moses to Christ shall be resurrected and judged on the basis of the law of Moses. The rest, however, who were from the epoch of our Lord Jesus Christ until the consummation, they shall be judged on the basis of the Gospel. Blessed is the one who has kept the law and the Gospel. Blessed are those who sinned and repented thereof. Blessed shall be each nation that lived in accordance with the natural law in a God-pleasing manner. But woe to the heretics and all the sinners! The Lord God shall resurrect all the nations. Then shall there stand up Abel, Seth, Enoch, Noah, Abraham, Isaac, and Jacob, and the wondrous and glorious Joseph, and they shall pass sentence upon all those men who had the benefit of the law but did not keep it, as well as those sinners who were not vouchsafed to know it. All the prophets and apostles shall rise up and pass sentence upon the twelve tribes of Israel. All the teachers of the Church shall rise, that is, the great Basil, the Theologian Gregory, and the golden-mouthed John, and they shall pass sentence on all those who heard their teachings and remained incorrigible. Then there shall stand at the judgment seat the heretics, but every heresy separately, with their heresiarchs. The Judge will cast a glance of disdain at them and say, 'Where have the catechisms of your shepherds brought

---

[200] *P.G.* 111:873B-876D; Paraclete, 217.
[201] *P.G.* 111:881B; Paraclete, 222, 223.
[202] Rom. 2:12.

you? Verily I say to you, I know you not.'[203] Then shall He say also to those on the left, 'Go from Me, ye who have been cursed, into the fire, the everlasting one, which hath been prepared for the devil and his angels.'"[204]

Epiphanios then put forth another query. "How shall God gather up, from the ends of the earth and in the twinkling of an eye, all these people and resurrect them? It should be a fearsome sight to see all the generations and tribes of man 'in the vale of weeping, in the place which He hath appointed.'"[205] The venerable man corrected him and said, "Darest thou to think that anything is impossible for God? One legion of angels dispatched by the Lord can not only collect all of the people in one place but also expedite it in the twinkling of an eye."

Epiphanios then pursued another question. "After the judgment and the recompense, what shall become of the heaven and the earth, the sea, the sun, and the moon? Will they abide as they do now, so that there will exist night and day and the orderly arrangement of matter and the animal kingdom? I beseech thee, if thou wilt, do me the favor and discourse on these things." The righteous Andrew gave reply: "Whensoever that terrifying hour of the second coming of our Lord should come, then four chief commanders (*archistrategoi*) with their hosts shall go, each one, unto one of the farthest corners of the earth. They shall stand and await the terrible order. When the Most High shall give the nod, each host shall lay hold of the respective extremity of the heavens and begin to roll up all of it; and then shall they depart. The prophet speaks in part, saying, 'In the beginning, O Lord, Thou didst lay the foundation of the earth, and the heavens are the works of Thy hands. They shall perish, but Thou abidest; and all like a garment shall grow old, and as a vesture shalt Thou fold them, and they shall be changed.'[206] This means, therefore, that the heavens and the earth shall be changed: the old shall become new, and the corruptible incorruptible. This is mentioned in the sacred Scriptures: 'And I saw a great white throne and the One sitting on it, from Whose face the earth and the heaven fled.'[207] Without a doubt shall all indeed be changed. The same essence will be raised up, but restored and transformed with incorruptibility and immortality.[208] When God,

[203] Mt. 25:12; 7:23.

[204] Mt. 25:41.

[205] Ps. 83:6.

[206] Ps. 101:25-27.

[207] Rev. 20:11.

[208] 1 Cor. 15:53. Saint John Chrysostom: "It is the same, and not the same: the same, because the essence is the same; but not the same, because this is more excellent, the essence remaining the same, but its beauty becoming greater, and the same body rising up new." ["Hom. 41 on 1 Cor. 15:37," *P.G.* 61:388 (col. 357).] Again, "It is not that

(continued...)

thereupon, shall resurrect the bodies of men, incorruptible and whole, from the epoch of Adam unto the consummation, then shall He make a new heaven and a new earth. There shall be nothing corruptible in them. All shall be incorruptible, wondrous, and extraordinary. No human mouth is able to provide a description. There will be no wild beasts, creeping things, and birds. There will only be creations enjoyable, beneficial, and scented as myrrh. Then there will be no night. All other lights shall be exhausted; and there will be one illumination, one light, myriads of times more splendid. The Lord God shall grant something to the saints that is wondrous: He shall vouchsafe them to see the angels as they are in their essence and to contemplate the beauty of the unapproachable glory of His divinity; and they shall rejoice."[209]

Concerning the Devil's Admission

As the two of them sat there discussing these last things, there appeared Satan whom only the saint could discern. He was readying a snare for Epiphanios. Andrew ordered him, "Begone from here, thou wicked and unclean creature!" Satan retorted, "A more good-for-nothing fellow and mocker than thyself does not exist in this city. And if thou wouldest have me speak the truth, the time will come that I shall lose my craft, because men will become more knavish and base than the demons, so that small children will be more wicked and malicious than their elders. We, then, shall stop warring against men, since men will know of themselves that which is evil." The venerable Andrew then

---

[208](...continued)

one essence is raised up instead of another, but that it is improved, that it is more splendid....Do not suppose because grain is sown and all come up ears of corn that therefore there is equality of honor in the resurrection. First and above all neither indeed in seeds is there only one rank: some, on the one hand, are more honorable; but, on the other hand, others are inferior." ["Hom. 41 on 1 Cor. 15:38," *P.G.* 61:388, 389 (col. 357).] For, "It is sown an animal body, it is raised a spiritual body. There is an animal body, and there is a spiritual body [1 Cor. 15:44]."

Saint Symeon the New Theologian: "However renewed, creation will not return to what it was created in the beginning. God forbid! Rather, just as it is sown an 'animal body,' so it is raised a body. It is not like the first man's before the transgression—that is, material, perceptible, and mutable, requiring moreover physical food—but instead a body wholly spiritual and immutable; such a body as that of our Master and God after His resurrection, the body of the second Adam, Who is our firstborn from the dead [cf. Col. 1:18]. As His body was a far different thing than the old Adam's, so shall the whole creation, in the same way and at God's command, not become what it was before—material and perceptible—but shall be transformed in the rebirth into an immaterial, spiritual dwelling place, beyond any perception of the senses." ["The Church and the Last Things," *On the Mystical Life: The Ethical Discourses*, Vol. I, First Discourse, V:38, 39.]

[209] Paraclete, 226-229.

asked, "Where didst thou learn such things?" The demon answered, "Our father is most experienced. He sits in Hades and divines all things. Then he teaches us, because our nature knows nothing." The blessed one then inquired, "With what kind of iniquities do you, the demons, most rejoice?" He answered, "We rejoice over idolatry, magic, and the use of drugs and potions and spells; but chiefly we exult over envy, jealousy, vindictiveness, and remembrance of wrongs which become the causes of all that is bad—and also in the sins of sodomy and adultery." The saint then responded: "If one renounces your demonic passions and comes in repentance to the Lord, how do you feel?" The demon answered, "Well, didst thou not know that it provokes disgust and annoyance in us? We, however, maintain hopes that such a one will return again and do our will; because many, even though they renounce and betray us, do return close to us and we still win." When the saint heard these words, he blew at him. Straightway, that vile creature disappeared.[210]

Concerning the Saint's Repose

These and many similar terrifying and extraordinary occurrences and discussions took place, which, for the sake of brevity and the space within this volume, we cannot report all herein. The saint's God-pleasing but strange conduct of life arrived at its blessed end. When he foreknew his end, he went early in the morning to the house of Epiphanios. Andrew sat down and wept. Then he rose up and, for a long time, being in a state of ecstasy, he gazed heavenward contemplating the loving-kindness of the Master and the inexpressible good things of Paradise. "My reverend father and spiritual teacher," said the young Epiphanios, "for what cause dost thou weep and stand so long in an ecstatic state?" Andrew answered, "My child, since thou dost ask, I shall announce tidings that have something to do with me. There has come, therefore, the end of my life. The time for us to be separated in these mortal bodies, one from the other, has arrived. Be not disheartened, however! I am going from this perishable world." Epiphanios, nevertheless, became sad of countenance at these words. Andrew countered, "Why art thou sullen, my child, upon hearing of the translation of thy beloved? It is a great blessing to depart from this life. What connection do we have with this vain world? We were not fashioned to live here always, but only to struggle and return to our place. Here, we have nought of our own. This world is bitter, since it is full of malevolent demons who, as they mingle with men, draw away many and cast them into everlasting punishment. The other world, however, to which I long to go, has the cherubim and the seraphim. In that place there is eternal light, but here there is darkness. There is the glory of the Holy Trinity, shining with an incomparable light and splendor. But here there is only a glory that is vain

[210] Paraclete, 230, 231.

and false, which accompanies lawlessness in a manner beguiling and treacherous."[211]

The saint then said, "Behold, my most sweet child, this is my final discourse with thee! For thou shalt see me no longer, living or dead, except in the Spirit. Hearken to me and I shall tell thee all that will come to pass that thou mayest remember what I have said. For when thy father reposes, thou shalt be garbed in the monastic Schema. Thou shalt distinguish thyself and do well, in the mercy and grace of the only-begotten Son of God. Thy fame shall spread, although thou shalt change thy name in the Schema. When this holy Church is widowed, the Lord shall raise up an experienced luminary and guide and shepherd of this wandering and erring flock. In future, the time will come when thou shalt confess the name of Christ and thy lot shall be with the saints. Now, child, have the fear of God in thy soul and love Him with all thy soul. Moreover, be taking heed with many tears. Remember me always in thy sacred *anaphoras*[212] when thou standest with reverence and humble-mindedness before the Lord in the Liturgies. Behold, the Lord God on high shall protect thee in every circumstance! The most blessed and glorified Birthgiver of God shall pilot and succor thee.[213]

"I adjure thee by the Holy Trinity and our immaculate Lady, Mary Theotokos: when what I have spoken should come to pass, do not think to raise a church or memorial to my memory. If thou shouldest disobey my command, believe me, thou wilt fall into temptation. This is because I have besought God that neither should I be glorified on earth nor should I acquire anything in this life. Even my remains, thou wilt never see. This is because the merciful Lord has pardoned my transgressions and will place my body together with the blessed Symeon, who lived a little earlier than I.[214] Be mindful to communicate the Mysteries on the feast days of the saints and to pray for all people, whether they be friends or foes. Remember also those who are in captivity and for the brethren being tempted by diverse afflictions and misfortunes. And I, should I find boldness before the Christ, I shall be with thy spirit unceasingly. And when God intends to take thee from this life, I shall come earlier and reveal the day that God has appointed. In that way, the two of us will be in glory and joy eternally, even as the Lord revealed to me."[215]

Saint Andrew also offered this discerning advice: "Be careful, my child, each time thou wouldest ordain someone. Be not thinking to ordain to

---

[211] Paraclete, 235, 236.

[212] By *anaphoras*, he means offering up the eucharistic prayer.

[213] *P.G.* 111:884D-885A.

[214] Saint Symeon of Emessa of Mesopotamia (b. 522-ca. 590) is commemorated by the holy Church on the 21st of July.

[215] Paraclete, 236, 237.

gain friendship or for the sake of a gift or as a respecter of persons. Place hands on no one by reason of either the supplications of acquaintances, or the comely outer appearance, or the show of wisdom. Nay child, to none of these things give consequence, but rather examine the virtue of the man; and then ordain men who will struggle for righteousness, the Faith, and the truth. Ever have before thine eyes God 'Who will render to each according to his works.'[216] Again, each time thou shalt liturgize, commemorate me; for no other sacrifice or supplication inclines the mercy and loving-kindness of God to have sympathy upon the sinners as this sacrifice. Yea, my child, inscribe my words upon the tablet of thy heart. Furthermore, make provision, as much as thou art able, to protect and provide for the poor, the widow, and the orphan. Collect the stranger at thy table. Aid and visit the sick and those in prison. Take heed to all these things, and the Theotokos shall become thy helper and protectress. And may the love of the Father and of the Son and of the Holy Spirit be with thee![217]

"And now child, come and let us bend our knees before the Lord God." The saint then uttered this prayer. "O Father, Son, and Holy Spirit, the life-creating and undivided Trinity, coessential and of one throne, we beggars and strangers and paupers and naked have no place to lay our head. For Thy name's sake, we bow the knee of our soul and body and heart and spirit. And we entreat Thee, O God, Whose awesome name is Sabaoth, incline Thine ear O good One and holy Master, Fashioner, Creator, Almighty. And do Thou receive with good will our supplicatory and humble prayer, and vouchsafe us to be sanctified in Thy power and Thy name, O compassionate One, benevolent, long-suffering, and most merciful Lord. Come, O Father, Son, and Holy Spirit. Come, terrible lightning of the Divinity. Come, O name above every other, O Father, Son, and Holy Spirit, and show Thy clemency upon the transgressions which we commit, either in word, or deed, or desire, or thought. We beseech Thee, O compassionate One, Who from Thy superabundant love is moved by pity to grant the prayers of those who love Thee, put us not to shame and cast us not aside from Thy countenance. I implore Thee, O Master—even for the sake of my spiritual child who has bent the knee behind me, the unworthy one—enlighten his eyes with the lightning flash of Thy Divinity. Do Thou sanctify his noetic senses with Thy Holy Spirit. Make joyous the thoughts of his soul with the ineffable fragrance of Thine ever-living grace. Inspire him with the Spirit of wisdom, the Spirit of might, the Spirit of understanding, the Spirit of love, the Spirit of peace, the Spirit of meekness,

---

[216] Rom. 2:6.

[217] Paraclete, 237, 238.

the Spirit of flowing tears,[218] in order that being prospered and piloted by Thine ineffable right hand, he may do all things pleasing to Thee, in Thy strength being saved.[219] To Thee, O Christ, is due all glory, honor, and veneration, together with the Father and the Holy Spirit, now and ever and to the ages of the ages. Amen."

After the venerable Andrew prayed in this manner, he rose up. A light like lightning flashed before them, emitting an indescribable fragrance. It was so overwhelming that Epiphanios fell to the floor. The saint, raising him up, made the sign of the Cross on his forehead. Andrew uttered a prayer in Epiphanios' behalf, saying, "May the great name of the invisible Light overshadow us! May the God of the cherubim be our helper! May the prayers of the seraphim, the thrones, the dominions, the principalities, and the authorities[220] accompany us! May the mediation of myriads upon myriads of bodiless powers protect us! May the entreaty of thousands upon thousands of angels of the unutterable Divinity support the slave of God, Epiphanios! May the prayers of the apostles, martyrs, preachers, evangelists, confessors, and masters of self-control, together with the supplications of the hierarchs, venerable, and righteous, and also the prayers of all those living God-pleasing lives on the mountains, in the caves, and in the holes of the earth,[221] may they all help thee! And I beg Thee, my God: do Thou save my spiritual child, Epiphanios. Keep him in Thy sanctification and Thy power, and Thy love, and Thy will, so that having lived his life virtuously, he shall arrive in peace at the front door of Thy kingdom."[222]

Andrew kissed Epiphanios on his eyes, his face, his breast, and his hands.[223] He peaceably gave orders that Epiphanios, who was lamenting bitterly, enter his bedchamber. He then departed and made his way toward the theater of the hippodrome, in the stoas which are under the colonnades. The hot atmosphere was heavy. He went through that district where the harlots dwelt. It was there that he stood and prayed with raised hands throughout that night for all those in peril, tribulation, necessity, and captivity, and for the whole world. He then took his rest on the ground. Looking up with a gladsome countenance, he beheld the angels and the saints, who were like friends. They, rejoicing, drew nigh to him and then he surrendered his soul. Immediately, the place was filled with the scent of myrrh and incense. They escorted Andrew into the heavens with great boldness and chanting. While this took place there

---

[218] Cf. Is. 11:2.
[219] *P.G.* 111:885B-D; Paraclete, 238, 239.
[220] Cf. Col. 1:16.
[221] Heb. 11:38.
[222] Paraclete, 239, 240.
[223] *P.G.* 111:885D; Paraclete, 240.

was nearby a certain pauper woman who dwelt in a hut. That incomparable and intoxicating fragrance came into her nostrils. She rose up quickly and, looking for some light, lit a lamp. She followed the scent to that spot where the saint was lying on the ground in what appeared to be a sweet sleep. She, however, observed that he had reposed and that a heavy and divine fragrance wafted forth from his relics. She also detected that myrrh gushed forth, in an extraordinary manner, as a river, from his relics. She made haste, thereupon, to announce the wondrous discovery to some people, even calling upon God as her witness in an oath. Many ran together. As they approached the spot, they saw no one there any longer. They discerned the scent of the myrrh and incense, as well as the light that rose up therefrom, which astounded them. They did not manage to uncover the whereabouts of the righteous man's relics. The Lord, Who saw Andrew's hidden accomplishments, translated him for reasons known to Him.[224]

Now after the night in which the blessed one reposed, it was dawn when Epiphanios found himself in the drying-yard for clothes that was situated to the east of his bedchamber. He, thereupon, beheld the soul of the venerable man, much more luminous than the sun, gleaming sevenfold with divine radiance while ascending into the heights of the heaven. Angels went before and after, accompanying the soul with a sweet melody which sounded like a symphony of musical instruments. This caused Epiphanios to fall into a state of ecstasy. When he came to himself, he raised his hands heavenward and said, "Remember me, O saint of God, in the kingdom having been made ready for thee; for today I beheld mysterious and extraordinary signs that surpass human logic."[225]

Saint Andrew, the hidden sun and heaven-high pillar of fire, who, for the Lord's sake, was indigent, a stranger, held in contempt, and set at nought by all, but now, by grace, is a son of God and an heir of the kingdom of the heavens, finished his mystical and good struggle, as an excellent contestant according to God, on the 28th day of May, at sixty-six years of age. "And I, Nikephoros, by the mercy of almighty God, a priest in the queen of cities at the Great Church, also known as God's Wisdom, have written down this much-spoken-of and wondrous biography of our venerable father among the saints, Andrew. With regard to the biographical data, apart from myself as an eyewitness, the other information was provided by the ever-memorable Epiphanios who afterward became archbishop. But verily have I written by the grace and love for man of our Lord Jesus Christ, to Whom be glory with the

[224] *P.G.* 111:888AB; Paraclete, 240, 241.
[225] Paraclete, 241.

Father and the Holy Spirit both now and ever and unto the ages of ages. Amen."[226]

On the 28th of May, the holy Church commemorates the holy New-martyr DEMETRIOS (or MEETROS) of the Peloponnesos (1794).[227]

Demetrios, the newly-revealed martyr of Christ, was a native of the Peloponnesos. He was the son of devout parents. Just before puberty, at the age of eleven, he was deceived by the Turks. Out of childish innocence—alas!—he denied Christ and became a Turk, that is, a Moslem. As he increased in age, he began attaching himself to various pashas. After the passage of some time, he came to be promoted to diverse offices. In the end, he succeeded to the rank of prefect, through which privileged position he also acquired many slaves, riches, and other possessions.

But what followed upon all this worldly success and approbation? The goodly Demetrios came to his senses. He reckoned all these material attainments and dignities as contemptuous as dung. He brought to mind his ancestral Faith and the piety that he had once possessed. He understood that he had fallen victim to deception and plummeted into the false religion of the Hagarenes. As a result of these reflections, he sighed from the depths of his heart. With tears, he said to himself, "Woe to thine ignorance, O unfortunate one! Woe to thy mishap, O wretched Demetrios! How many years am I now found in this inexorable darkness? How was I tricked into denying my Lord? But I shall return to the holy Faith of my Christ, which is the true one. Indeed, I shall renounce the unholy and abominable superstition of the Hagarenes." This was the decision he made within himself as he was strengthened by the grace and power of the Holy Spirit. He then ventured to Tripoli, in the central part of the Peloponnesian peninsula in the prefecture of Arkadia, where he sold all his belongings. He, afterward, visited his kinfolk, confessed his sin to a spiritual father, and repented deeply for the great evil he brought upon himself. After weeping bitterly, he fulfilled the proper penance ascribed by the sacred order of the Church. He lived, henceforward, as a devout and God-fearing Christian for a period of ten whole years.

One day, he was on his way to perform an errand at Mystra in the Lakedemona province of the Peloponnesian prefecture of Lakonia. He was recognized by some of his former Moslem acquaintances. They seized him and

---

[226] *P.G.* 111:888CD; Paraclete, 241, 242.

[227] The martyrdom of this New-martyr Demetrios was written by Saint Makarios Notaras, the former Bishop of Corinth (commemorated by the holy Church on the 17th of April). The biography was published in the *Neon Leimonarion*, whence it was borrowed and incorporated in *The Great Synaxaristes* (in Greek).

brought him back to Tripoli, haling him before the governor. They kept shouting and bearing testimony against him. They asserted that he had denied Christ and accepted Islam, but he afterward espoused Christianity anew. The governor inquired of him, "Why hast thou changed thy former conviction? Why hast thou denied our faith? Why hast thou, again, become a Christian?" The martyr of Christ answered with a resounding voice, "I was a Christian but, due to my naiveness, I was deceived by you and became a Moslem. Later, I realized that my former Faith possesses light and that I had lost it, while yours is darkness as I have known it. Therefore, I confess before all of you that I have erred gravely in departing from the light and, in its stead, accepting darkness. I was born a Christian and I want to die a Christian. I believe in the Father, the Son, and the Holy Spirit: Trinity, one in essence and undivided. I am prepared to face every torture for my Faith and to shed my blood for the love of Jesus Christ, my Savior." These and other similar things the blessed one confessed with gallant courage and great boldness.

One of the aghas, who was present, addressed him by his Turkish name and said, "Where is thy beard,[228] O prefect?" He answered, "I am not a prefect. My true name is Demetrios, and I am baptized in the name of the Holy Trinity. In regard to the beard that thou hast asked me about, I was wearing it in bondage for many years. Furthermore, I observed not the least progress or benefit whatsoever from it. I, therefore, shaved it, as it was useless, and I gave it back to the master whom I flattered vainly for so many years." Then the governor said to him, "If thou wilt come back within our fold, we would bestow upon thee great honors. We would give thee important dignities and gifts." They hoped by these means to lure, capture, and lead the blessed Demetrios to perdition. However the courageous and heavenly-minded man abhorred all these petty things as rubbish, and said to them, "I told you that I am a Christian and that I believe in Jesus Christ, the true God. Keep those things you have promised me for yourselves. I do not need them." Then they put him in jail. Subsequently, they summoned together a number of imams and hodjas. They sent them into the prison to teach him the distorted doctrines of their superstition and to attempt in every way to divert him and bring him about to their own way of believing. Even so, that blessed one paid no attention to their harmful words and commenced to ridicule their prophet, their Islamic laws, and their despised religion. The Moslem teachers, having failed to make any impression on him, left in shame. Therefore, the governor, seeing that Demetrios was irretrievable, ordered that he be put to the sword as a defamer of Mohammedanism.

---

[228] At that time in Tripoli the Moslems wore beards, which were forbidden to the Christians.

The valiant contestant of Christ was then taken by the underlings of the governor to the place of execution, fettered in the manner of those who are condemned. As the executioner was about to sever Demetrios' martyric head, he said to the martyr, "O unfortunate fellow, profess thy former confession now, even if it is the final hour, and Allah, the merciful, shall have mercy upon thy soul." When the martyr heard this last remark, he not only laughed at their false religion but also spat at the swordsman. Demetrios began to anathematize Islam and those who believed in it. Again he confessed that the Holy Trinity is true God and that he based his hope of salvation in Christ. Then he said to the Christian bystanders, "I am one of you. Demetrios is my name. Therefore, entreat the Lord in my behalf." Finally, after he prayed briefly, they beheaded him on the 28th of May. It was the Sunday of Pentecost in the year 1794. Thus, the blessed one received the crown of martyrdom from the Prize-bestower, Christ our God.

The following day, the Christians received the sacred relics of the saint by permission of the authorities. They buried the relics with honor and reverence in the Church of the Holy Great Martyr Demetrios the Myrrh-streamer. However, Demetrios' right arm remained stiff so that it could not be bent; his three fingers were poised to make the sign of the Cross. Those that buried the relics labored in every way to bend it, since it was protruding outside the coffin, but were unable to bend it. So they decided to break it with an axe, but—lo, the wonder!—the arm that was stiff and immovable immediately flexed and fell automatically on the sacred body of the gloriously triumphant New-martyr Demetrios, by whose intercessions may we be vouchsafed the kingdom of the heavens. Amen.

On the 28th of May, the holy Church commemorates our holy father among the saints, IGNATIOS the Wonder-worker, Bishop of Rostov (1288).

Through the intercessions of Thy Saints,
O Christ God, have mercy on us. Amen.

On the 29th of May, the holy Church commemorates the holy Virgin-martyr THEODOSIA of Tyre.[1]

Saint Theodosia of Tyre

Theodosia, a venerable and all-holy virgin, hailed from Tyre of Phoenicia. She lived at a time of persecution aimed at the Christians by the Roman Empire. At the time when our story opens, she was a faithful Orthodox Christian at Caesarea in Palestine which was under the subjugation of idol worshippers. Not quite eighteen years of age, she was conspicuous for her great reserve and staidness. This serious maiden, on the very Lord's day of our Savior's resurrection, made bold and went to see the Christian brethren who were taken into custody. Certain of the prisoners who were before the judgment seat of the pagans had just confessed Christ and His heavenly kingdom. Theodosia saluted them before the entire company. She was arrested moments later and cast into prison. Since she had asked the prisoners to pray for her when they were in Christ's kingdom, she was charged with committing a public act of profanity and impiety against the emperor's majesty and the gods.

When her turn came for trial, the judge and pagan rulers sat on the tribunal. With uniform regularity, they passed sentences condemning Christians who were confessors of the Faith of Christ. Among the confessors was Theodosia. She had been brought forward, bound, by the soldiers. She stood before the governor, Urbanus, who commanded her to sacrifice to the idols. Since the sacred maiden flatly refused, the brutal governor was as a man possessed. In the manner of a wild beast, he inflicted dreadful wounds to her ribs. The inhuman tyrant harrowed her to her very bones and entrails. The holy maiden, thereupon, suffered all these punishments with extreme courage and utter silence. Still breathing, she possessed a radiant and glowing countenance.

Theodosia was again interrogated. Urbanus urged her to be obedient, instead of obstinate and disagreeable. "Consent," said he, "and offer the prescribed sacrifice to the deities." However, the saint looked at him warily.

[1] Evsevios, in his *Martyrs of Palestine* (Ch. VII), records her martyrdom to have taken place "when the persecution had continued to the fifth year, on the second day of the month Xanthicus, which is the fourth before the Nones of April."

With a smile that revealed both her amusement and her scorn at his words, she said, "Deceive not thyself, O governor. Know this: thou hast vouchsafed me to be in the company of Jesus' holy martyrs." Therefore, the governor, considering the maiden's words a pointed insult and mockery, had her tortured in excess of her prior injuries. Then Urbanus commanded that she be committed to the ocean deep. It was there that the virgin's blessed soul was surrendered into the hands of God; and, thus, she obtained an undying crown from Him. As for the others who stood with her at Urbanus' judgment seat, they were condemned to the copper mines in Phaeno of Palestine.

Saint Theodosia of Tyre

On the 29th of May, the holy Church commemorates the venerable Martyr THEODOSIA of Constantinople.[2]

Theodosia, our holy mother and martyr, lived during the reign of Theodosios III the Adramyttinos (715-717). Before Theodosia's birth, her pious and noble parents lived in Constantinople. After praying for a child, the holy Martyr Anastasia appeared to Theodosia's mother. The saint told her that she would give birth to a child. The mother promised to dedicate the child, whether girl or boy, to the Lord. Thereupon, she conceived and gave birth to a female infant. She received the name Theodosia, an appellation signifying either "given by God" or "gift to God." On the fortieth day after her birth, the churching took place in the Church of Saint Anastasia. The mother promised to consecrate her child to monasticism when she came of age. At an early age, little Theodosia was taught to read. Her earliest readings were from holy books. At seven years of age, Theodosia's father reposed. The young Theodosia was consecrated by her mother to a Constantinopolitan convent, where she was tonsured a nun. Later, after three years, Theodosia's mother reposed and left her daughter a considerable fortune. From this inheritance, the blessed Nun Theodosia ordered from a goldsmith three gold and silver holy

[2] The martyrdom of Saint Theodosia was put into written form, in the 14th C., by Constantine Akropolites. He drew upon early written records and oral tradition. He dwelt in a house at Constantinople near the nun-martyr's tomb, and was one of her chief votaries. Her biography was then published by Abbé Migne [*P.G.* 140:893-935]. An encomium to this saint was composed by John Stavrakios the Archivist (*Chartophylax*) of Thessalonike, which manuscript begins: "The pillar of Orthodoxy, Theodosia, the good martyr...." The text is extant in the Athonite Monasteries of the Great Lavra, Dionysiou, and Iveron.

icons of Christ, the Theotokos, and the holy Martyr Anastasia. Each icon was three cubits in height. The remainder of her inheritance she distributed among the poor.

Emperor Leo, the Isaurian, and Imperial Support of Iconoclasm

While Emperor Theodosios was on the throne, it came to pass that, after two years, the iconoclast, Leo III the Isaurian (717-741), claimed the throne. Leo's real name was Conon. Nevertheless, the childhood nickname of "Leo," bestowed upon him for his lion-like courage, was made the emperor's official name. He was given the epithet "Isaurian," though he was not an Isaurian. By birth he was from northern Syria and, as a lad, his family moved to the province of Thrace. When the Arabs besieged the city by land and sea, Leo triumphed over their siege lest they should ever again come so near to capturing the capital.[3]

A few years later, Emperor Leo enforced his new policy of the destruction of the sacred images. Unable to persuade Patriarch Germanos (715-730) to concur with the impiety of his dogmas and to set at nought the veneration of the holy images, the emperor drove out the most holy and great patriarch with a sword and club. Emperor Leo then replaced the legitimate Patriarch Germanos with Anastasios, the chancellor of the holy Germanos. Anastasios, however, proved to be another Judas who collaborated with the emperor to supplant his spiritual father, Germanos.[4]

The wretched Emperor Leo not only committed this heinous deed, but, in his bestiality, even attempted to pull down and burn to ashes the holy image of our Lord and God Jesus Christ. The icon stood over the gilded bronze portals of the city gates of Constantinople, known as Chalke. Therefore, one of the emperor's guards took a ladder and began to ascend it. His mission was to hurl the Master Christ's image to the earth. Though the vast majority of Byzantines were Orthodox iconodules, that is, veneraters of the images, it was the blessed Nun Theodosia, with a contingent of other devout women, including Mary the patrician, who took hold of the ladder and overturned it. This caused the guard to topple to his death. A number of men, including the holy Monks Julian, Marcian, John, Iakovos, Alexios, Demetrios, Photios, Peter, and Leontios also took part in removing the ladder.[5]

---

[3] Constance Head, "Leo III, the Iconoclast," *Imperial Byzantine Portraits* (New Rochelle, NY: Caratzas Bros., Pub., 1982), p. 56.

[4] This event is recorded by Patriarch Dositheos II of Jerusalem (1669-1707), in his *Dodekavivlos* or *Twelve Books* (Thessalonike: Regopoulos, 1983), p. 626. The tenure of Anastasios was from 730 to 753.

[5] Saint Theophanes the Confessor mentions that a significant crowd assembled, "for the populace of the imperial city was much distressed by the novel doctrine and, thus, they (continued...)

Later, when Emperor Leo learned of the event, under his orders, a multitude suffered execution by decapitation. The aforementioned nine monks were arrested, cruelly lashed, and cast into prison. Afterward, they received a thrashing of fifty stripes by rods. They were to endure this brutal treatment for eight months. Theodosia, meanwhile, leading many of the modest and honorable women of Constantinople to the patriarchate, took up rocks and clubs. Finding the usurper and pseudo-Patriarch Anastasios, they called him a mercenary, a traitor, and a Judas.[6] The women then stoned Anastasios, the impious iconomach. For this action, many of the women were beheaded. Theodosia, of noble birth, was deemed a ringleader. She was flogged, receiving one hundred lashes. She was, consequently, tortured for seven days. On the eighth day, Emperor Leo charged that she be dragged through the city and beaten publicly. Among the soldiers that escorted the venerable Theodosia, one of them was not looking where he was walking. He stepped on a ram's horn which penetrated his foot. In a fit of anger, that cruel and inhuman soldier, upon arrival at a place called Voös (Forum of the Ox),[7] took the ram's horn and, in a rage, thrust it into the nun's

Saint Theodosia of Constantinople

---

[5](...continued)
meditated an assault upon him (Leo)." [*The Chronicle of Theophanes Confessor*, AM 6218, A.D. 725/726, trans. by C. Mango and R. Scott (Oxford: Clarendon Press, 1997), p. 559.]

Stephen the Deacon, in his Life of Saint Stephen the Younger, also notes that the dissenters were "honorable women." Pope Gregory II, in an epistle to Emperor Leo III, refers to the demonstrators as "the zealous women" as the ones who defied the imperial order. Although the accuracy of who attended and how many were present varies, yet the emphasis is placed on the role of women in opposing the iconoclasts. See *Byzantine Defenders of Images*, ed. by Alice-Mary Talbot (Washington, D.C.: Dumbarton Oaks Research Library and Collection), pp. 1, 2.

[6] The women called him a conspirator or "fatriarch" instead of "patriarch," thus making a pun between the Greek word *fatria*, meaning conspiracy, and his title.

[7] The Forum of the Ox (Forum Bovis) was situated on Constantinople's Mese, a main thoroughfare between the Arkadian and Taurian (or Theodosian) Forums. It is some

(continued...)

throat. Thus, the blessed woman received a martyr's crown in the year 730. The much-tried body of the athlete of Christ was collected by Christians and buried.

In the meantime, Leo, thwarted by the steadfastness of the nine aforementioned monks, ordered the preparation of red-hot iron forks to sear their martyric faces. Afterward, at a place called Kynegesion, they were to have their heads struck off together with Mary the patrician woman. Their sacred relics were then cast into the open sea.[8]

The Relics of our Venerable Mother Theodosia

The sacred relics of the holy nun-martyr were deposited in the Monastery of Saint Ephemia, situated in the Petrion quarter, east of the Phanar, in the proximity of the Golden Horn, at a location called Dexiokrates. Her grace-filled relics wrought numerous miracles for those that sought her intercession.[9] For this reason, the monastery was quickly named Saint Theodosia, which celebrates its feast day on the 29th of May.[10]

After the Fall of Constantinople, which took place on a Tuesday, the 29th day of May, in the year 1453, the monastery church was converted into a mosque during the reign of Salim II (1566-1574). The name was also changed,

---

[7](...continued)
two kilometers from the Chalke Gate. Voös had a large antique monument in its forum of an ox's head from Pergamon.

[8] The holy Mary the Patrician and this group of monks are commemorated by the holy Church on the 9th of August.

[9] John Bryennios (1350-ca. 1437), the teacher of Saint Mark of Ephesus, refers to the miracles of Saint Theodosia in his treatise concerning the Cypriots [vol. ii]. In the year 1200, Russian pilgrim Anthony of Novgorod noted in his journal that he beheld the relics of Saint Theodosia, which were on view for veneration at a nunnery in the capital. He said that the relics were carried in procession periodically and that miracles were wrought [Majeska, *Russian Travelers*, p. 349]. Historian Pachymeres records, in 1306, that the saint healed a deaf and dumb lad at her shrine. Other Russian pilgrims gave testimony that her relics were carried aloft in procession twice weekly. Multitudes of pilgrims converged at her church seeking her intercession [Talbot, *Byzantine Defenders*, p. 3]. The Great Logothete Constantine (13th C.) also recorded miracles. Among those cited was the case of a Phrygian youth who lost the use of both legs. He was brought to the martyr's tomb and received healing. Another youth, who was thrown from his mount, suffered a brain contusion that altered his reason. After he was anointed with the oil from the saint's oil lamp, he too was cured. The chronicler himself, that is, Constantine, says that both his legs were diseased. The physicians lost hope of any remedy. It was only Saint Theodosia who helped him and completely restored his legs to health [*May Menology* of Saint Dimitri of Rostov].

[10] By the year 1301, the holy Church was commemorating her feast day on the 29th of May, evidently as the result of conflation with her homonym, Saint Theodosia, the virgin-martyr of Tyre.

being called "Hasan Pasha" or "Giul-Tzami," meaning the "Mosque of Roses," which survives to this day. It is said that the name "Mosque of Roses" remained, since, during the sack of the capital, while the Monastery of Saint Theodosia was celebrating its matronal feast, it was adorned with an abundance of roses. Multitudes, lamenting and wishing to escape Turkish captivity, sought refuge within the monastery's walls; but God permitted otherwise.[11]

On the 29th of May, the holy Church commemorates our venerable Father ALEXANDER, Pope of Alexandria.

Alexander, Archbishop of Alexandria from 313, was born at Alexandria ca. 250. He served as a priest under Bishop Peter of Alexandria.[12] The latter suffered martyrdom under Maximinus (308-314). After the repose of Saint Peter, the Priest Achillas was installed in the episcopal office (312-313). Soon thereafter, Alexander succeeded him (313). He is described as a man held in the highest honor by the clergy and layfolk. He was dignified, eloquent, and just. He was a lover of God and man. He was devoted to the poor, and good and sweet to all. Even as a prelate he never broke the hour of his rule of fasting, while the sun was in the heaven.

As the new archbishop or pope of the Alexandrian see, Alexander first dealt with the Meletian Schism. The Meletian Schism, sometimes called the First Meletian Schism, was incited by Meletios, Bishop of Lykopolis in Upper Egypt. During the persecution of 306, Bishop Meletios condemned those Christians who hid from the pagan authorities. Meletios gave no care or thought for the above mentioned Archbishop Peter. Meletios, for that matter, gave no consequence to Christ Who was in the person of Peter. After Archbishop Peter suffered martyrdom, Bishop Meletios founded his schismatic church with clergy of his own ordination. He excluded those who had lapsed or fallen during the persecution and had yielded before the persecutors. By his moral authority, his schism thrived. By the year 325, twenty-eight bishops supported him. He challenged one of the successors, Archbishop Alexander. The struggle against Arianism constrained Alexander to a policy of reconciliation with the Meletians.

Now Arius had begun to teach his heresy in 300 when Archbishop Peter, by whom he was excommunicated, was pope. Arius had been reinstated by Achillas, the successor of Peter, and made a priest. Arius, almost immediately, began to scheme to be made a bishop. When Achillas died, Alexander

---

[11] *P.G.* 157:1108. On the day that the city fell, the saint's church was celebrating her memory. The historian Michael Doukas [*Byzantina Historia*, ed. I. Bekker (Bonn, 1834), pp. 293, 294] notes that thousands congregated at the martyr's church. Thousands were slaughtered by Turkish troops.

[12] Saint Peter is commemorated by the holy Church on the 24th of November.

was elected. It was at that point that Arius threw off all disguise of his envy and jealousy. When Alexander came to the see, Arius was still tolerated for a time.

The Dispute of Arius with His Bishop Alexander

Now Alexander "in the fearless exercise of his functions for the instruction and government of the Church, attempted one day in the presence of the presbytery and the rest of his clergy, to explain that great theological mystery—the unity of the Holy Trinity. A certain one of the presbyters under his jurisdiction, whose name was Arius, possessed of no inconsiderable logical acumen, imagined that the bishop was subtly teaching the same view of this subject as Sabellius (fl. ca. 217-ca. 220). Arius, out of love of controversy, took the opposite opinion. Arius responded to what was said by the bishop, saying, 'If,' said he, 'the Father begat the Son, He that was begotten had a beginning of existence: and from this it is evident, that there was a time when the Son was not. It therefore necessarily follows, that He had His substance (hypostasis) from nothing.'"[13]

The Excommunication of Arius and His Adherents

A division began in the Church. From a little spark there was a conflagration in the Alexandrian Church that spread throughout Egypt and the rest of the provinces and cities. Many adopted Arius' opinion, including Evsevios, Bishop of Nikomedia in Bithynia. "When Alexander became conscious of these things, both from his own observation and from report, being exasperated to the highest degree, he convened a synod of many prelates. Arius and the abettors of his heresy were excommunicated. At the same time, Bishop Alexander wrote to the bishops constituted in the several cities.

"Know that there have recently arisen in our diocese lawless and anti-Christian men, teaching apostasy such as one may justly consider and denominate the forerunner of Antichrist....Those who have become apostates are: Arius, Achillas, Aithales, and Carpones, another Arius, Sarmates, Euzoius, Lucius Julian, Menas, Helladis, and Gaius; with these also must be reckoned Secundus and Theonas, who once were called bishops. The dogmas they have invented and assert, contrary to the Scriptures, are these: that God was not always the Father, but that there was a period when He was not the Father; that the Word (Logos) of God was not from eternity, but that He was made out of nothing; and that the ever-existing God ('the I AM'—the eternal One) made Him, Who did not previously exist, out of nothing. There was, then, a time when He did not exist, inasmuch as the Son is a creature and a work. Therefore, He is not like the Father as it regards His essence. He is not by nature either the Father's true Word or the Father's true Wisdom. But indeed, He is one of His works and creatures, being erroneously called Word

[13] Socrates Scholasticus, "Rise of Arian Heresy," *Ecclesiastical History*, Bk. I, Ch. V, Nicene Fathers, 2nd Ser., II:3.

and Wisdom, since He was Himself made of God's own Word and the Wisdom which is in God, whereby God both made all things and Him also. Therefore, He is as to His nature mutable and susceptible of change, as are all other rational creatures. Hence, the Word is alien to, and other than, the essence of God; and the Father is inexplicable by the Son, and invisible to Him, for neither does the Word perfectly and accurately know the Father, neither can He distinctly see Him. The Son knows not the nature of His own essence: for He was made on our account, in order that God might create us by Him, as by an instrument; nor would He ever have existed, unless God had wished to create us....

"We then, with the bishops of Egypt and Libya, being assembled together to the number of nearly a hundred, have anathematized Arius for his shameless avowal of these heresies, together with all such as have countenanced them. Yet the partisans of Evsevios have received them; endeavoring to blend falsehood with truth, and that which is impious with what is sacred....

"Who that hears John saying, 'In the beginning was the Logos (Word) [Jn. 1:1],' does not condemn those that say, 'There was a period when the Word was not'? or who, hearing in the Gospel of 'the only-begotten Son [Jn. 1:18],' and that 'all things came into being through Him [Jn. 1:3],' will not abhor those that pronounce the Son to be one of the things made? How can He be one of the things which were made by Himself? Or how can He be the Only-begotten, if He is reckoned among created things? And how could He have had His existence from nonentities, since the Father has said that 'from the womb before the morning star have I begotten Thee [Ps. 109:4]'? Or how is He unlike the Father's essence, Who is 'the image of the invisible God [Col. 1:15],' and 'the effulgence of the glory and impress of His hypostasis [Heb. 1:3],' and says that 'the one who hath seen Me hath seen the Father [Jn. 14:9]'? Again, how if the Son is the Word and Wisdom of God, was there a period when He did not exist? For that is equivalent to their saying that God was once destitute both of Word and Wisdom. How can He be mutable and susceptible of change, Who says of Himself that 'I am in the Father, and the Father is in Me [Jn. 14:10],' and 'I and the Father are one [Jn. 10:30],' and again by the prophet that 'I am the Lord your God, and I am not changed [Mal. 3:6]'? But if anyone may also apply the expression to the Father Himself, yet would it now be even more fitly said of the Word; because He was not changed by having become man, but as the apostle says, 'Jesus Christ, the same yesterday and today and to the ages [Heb. 13:8].' But what could persuade them to say that He was made on our account, when Paul has expressly declared that because of Him 'are all things and by means of Him are all things [Heb. 2:10]'?...

"Many heresies have arisen before these, which exceeding all bounds in daring, have lapsed into complete infatuation: but these persons, by attempting in all their discourses to subvert the divinity of the Logos, as having made a nearer approach to Antichrist, have comparatively lessened the odium of former ones. They, therefore, have been publicly repudiated by the Church, and anathematized. We are indeed grieved on account of the perdition of these persons, and especially so because, after having been previously instructed in the doctrines of the Church, they have now apostatized from them. Nevertheless we are not greatly surprised at this, for Hymenaeos and Philetos[14] fell in like manner; and before them Judas, who had been a follower of the Savior, but afterward deserted Him and became His betrayer....And Paul wrote that 'in latter times some shall apostatize from the faith, giving heed to deceiving spirits and teachings of demons [1 Tim. 4:1],' who pervert the truth....

Saint Alexander

"Seeing then that our Lord and Savior Jesus Christ has Himself warned us—'Be taking heed lest ye be led astray; for many shall come in My name, saying, "I am the Christ," and "The time hath drawn near." Do not then begin to go after them [Lk. 21:8]'—as well as the apostle, and we ourselves have heard their impiety, we have in consequence anathematized them. We have declared them to be alienated from the catholic Church and Faith....For it is incumbent on us who are Christians to turn away from all those who speak or entertain a thought against Christ, as from those who are resisting God and are destroyers of the souls of men. Neither does it become us even to say 'fare-thee-well, for the one who saith to him fare-thee-well partaketh in his evil

[14] 2 Tim. 2:17.

works [2 Jn. 10, 11].'" And so these words of Bishop Alexander exposed and declared the cancer.[15]

In this state of things among them, the discussion in relation to Arius arose. Meletios with his adherents took part with Arius, entering into a conspiracy with him against the archbishop. Meanwhile, Evsevios of Nikomedia and his partisans, with such as favored the sentiments of Arius, demanded by letter the following: that the sentence of excommunication which had been pronounced against Arius should be rescinded; and that those who had been excluded should be readmitted into the Church, as they held no unsound doctrine. Thus, letters from the opposite parties were sent to Alexander. As for Arius he made a collection of those which were favorable to himself, while Alexander did the same with those which were adverse. Needless to say, Emperor Constantine the Great was sorely grieved at the disturbance in the Churches. He dispatched Hosius the Spaniard (ca. 257-357) to Alexandria, exhorting Alexander and Arius to reconciliation and unity.

Pope Alexander Writes to Patriarch Alexander

Alexander also wrote an epistle to the Patriarch of Constantinople, who bore the same name, Alexander (315-325), to put him on his guard. He mentioned Presbyter Arius and Deacon Achillas, by name, and others who make a trade of Christ for lucre. He wrote: "They revile every godly apostolical doctrine. Moreover, in Jewish fashion have they organized a gang to fight against Christ, denying His divinity and declaring Him to be on a level with other men. They pick out every passage which refers to the dispensation of salvation, and to Jesus' condescension for our sake. They endeavor to collect from these passages their own impious assertion, while they evade all those which declare Jesus' eternal divinity and the unceasing glory that He possesses with the Father....

"Now we unanimously ejected them from the Church that reveres the divinity of Christ. They then ran hither and thither to form cabals against us, even addressing themselves to our fellow ministers who were of one mind with us, under the pretense of seeking peace and unity with them. But in truth endeavoring by means of fair words to sweep some among them away into their own disease....

"It is on this account that without delay I have stirred myself up to let it be known the unbelief of certain persons that say that 'there was a time when the Son of God was not' and 'He Who previously had no existence subsequently came into existence; and when at some time He came into existence He became such as every other man is.' God, they say, created all things out of that which was non-existent, and they include in the number of creatures, both

[15] Socrates, *Ecclesiastical History*, Bk. I, Ch. VI, Nicene, 2nd Ser., II:3-5.

rational and irrational, even the Son of God....But we agree with the Evangelist John who said that 'the only-begotten Son is in the bosom of the Father.'[16] Thus, there was never a time in which Christ was not. This divine teacher desired to show that the Father and the Son are inseparable; and, therefore, he said that 'the Son is in the bosom of the Father.' Moreover, the same John affirms that the Word of God is not classed among things created out of the non-existent; for, he says that all things were made by Him.[17] So how is it that He Who thus bestowed existence on all, could at any period have had no existence Himself?...

"The interval during which they say the Son was still unbegotten of the Father was, according to their opinion, prior to the Wisdom of God, by Whom all things were created. They thus contradict the Scripture which declares Him to be 'the firstborn of all creation [Col. 1:15].' In consonance with this doctrine, Paul with his usual mighty voice cries concerning Him: 'For in Him were all things created, the things in the heavens and the things upon the earth, the visible and the invisible, whether thrones, or dominions, or principalities, or authorities. All things through Him and to Him have been created. And He is before all things, and in Him all things have come into existence [Col. 1:16, 17].' Since the hypothesis implied in the phrase 'out of the non-existent' is manifestly impious, it follows that the Father is always Father. And He is Father from the continual presence of the Son, on account of Whom He is called Father. And the Son being ever present with Him, the Father is ever perfect, wanting in no good thing, for He did not beget His only Son in time, or in any interval of time, nor out of that which had no previous existence....To assert that the 'effulgence of the glory [Heb. 1:3]' of the Father once did not exist destroys also the original light of which it is the brightness. Furthermore, if there ever was a time in which the image of God was not, it is plain that He Whose image He is, is not always. Nay, by the non-existence of the express image of God's Person, He also is taken away of Whom this is ever the express image. Hence it may be seen, that the sonship of our Savior has not even anything in common with the sonship of men. For just as it has been shown that the nature of His existence cannot be expressed by language, and infinitely surpasses in excellence all things to which He has given being, so His sonship, naturally partaking in His paternal divinity, is unspeakably different from the sonship of those who, by His appointment, have been adopted as sons. He is by nature immutable, perfect, and all-sufficient, whereas men are liable to change and need His help.

"His true, peculiar, natural, and special sonship was declared by Paul, who, speaking of God, says, that 'He spared not His own Son, but delivered

[16] Cf. Jn. 1:18.

[17] Jn. 1:1, 3.

Him up for us all,'[18] who are not by nature His sons. It was to distinguish Him from those who are not 'His own,' that He called Him 'His own Son.' It is also written in the Gospel: 'This is My Son, the Beloved, in Whom I am well pleased [Mt. 3:17]'; and in the Psalms the Savior says, 'The Lord said unto Me: "Thou art My Son, this day have I begotten Thee [Ps. 2:7]."' By proclaiming natural sonship He shows that there are no other natural sons besides Himself. And do not these words, 'From the womb before the morning star have I begotten Thee [Ps. 109:4],' plainly show the natural sonship of the paternal birth of One Whose lot it is, not from diligence of conduct, or exercise in moral progress, but by individuality of nature? Hence, it ensues that the filiation of the only-begotten Son of the Father is incapable of fall; while the adoption of reasonable beings who are not His sons by nature, but merely on account of fitness of character, and by the bounty of God, may fall away....

"These rogues also bring forward passages to disprove Christ's eternal existence and divinity, while they forget the passage 'I and the Father are one [Jn. 10:30].' In these words the Lord does not proclaim Himself to be the Father, neither does He represent two natures as one; but that the essence of the Son of the Father preserves accurately the likeness of the Father, His nature taking off the impress of likeness to Him in all things, being the exact image of the Father and the express stamp of the prototype. When, therefore, Philip, desirous of seeing the Father, said to Him, 'Lord, show us the Father [Jn. 14:8],' the Lord with abundant plainness said to him, 'The one who hath seen Me hath seen the Father [Jn. 14:9],' as though the Father were beheld in the spotless and living mirror of His image....It is on this account that 'the one who honoreth not the Son honoreth not the Father Who sent Him [Jn. 5:23].' And rightly, for every impious word which men dare to utter against the Son is spoken also against the Father.

"These inventors of silly tales assert that we, who reject their impious and unscriptural blasphemy concerning the creation of Christ from the non-existent, teach that there are two unbegotten Beings. In their ignorance and want of practise in theology they do not realize that the only-begotten nature of Him Who is the Logos of God, by Whom the Father created the universe out of the non-existent, was begotten of the self-existent Father....

"Arius and Achillas, together with their fellow foes, have been expelled from the Church, because they have become aliens from our pious doctrine. Thus, according to the blessed Paul, 'If anyone preach a gospel to you besides what ye received, let such a one be anathema [Gal. 1:9],' even though he should pretend to be an angel from heaven,[19] and, 'If anyone teach differently and draw not near to sound words—those of our Lord Jesus Christ,

[18] Cf. Rom. 8:32.

[19] Cf. Gal. 1:8.

and the teaching according to piety—he hath been puffed up with pride, knowing nothing [1 Tim. 3, 4],' and so forth."[20] It should be known that Pope Alexander was very patient with the Arians. His leniency even aggravated many of the zealots. Nevertheless, he admitted to Patriarch Alexander at Constantinople that "many kindly attempts have been made by me to gain back those who have been led astray, but no remedy has proved more efficacious in restoring the laity who have been deceived by them and leading them to repentance than the manifestation of the union of our fellow ministers."[21]

As we said earlier, after the repose of Archbishop Peter, Arius was disappointed at the election of Alexander to the see of Alexandria. His ill will reached a climax when he opposed Alexander's Orthodox teachings. Archbishop Alexander was at first conciliatory, and agreed to give Arius a patient hearing. Arius was intractable. By the concoctions of the enemy of our salvation, Satan, the ideas of Arius were widely accepted. All of this necessitated a synod meeting at Alexandria. As we mentioned, under Archbishop Alexander, a synod condemned Arius. In September of 324, Emperor Constantine sent Saint Hosius the Confessor, as his acting ecclesiastical advisor, to Alexandria. He investigated the dispute between Alexander and Arius. He reported his findings—which strongly favored Alexander—to the emperor, who decided to convene an œcumenical synod.

The First Œcumenical Synod

In 325, the emperor summoned the bishops of the empire by a letter of invitation, putting at their service the public conveyances, and liberally defraying from the public treasury the expenses of their residence in Nicaea and of their return trip. The clergy were to meet in Nicaea of Bithynia from the end of May until the 25th of August. Each bishop was entitled to bring with him two presbyters and three servants. A young deacon, named Athanasios,[22] the disciple of Pope Alexander, was acting as the representative of the Patriarch of Alexandria who was feeling ill.

Among the prominent men at the meeting was Evsevios of Caesarea, noted for his historical writings. The Orthodox party held firmly to the deity of Jesus Christ. At first they were in the minority, but in talent and impact they were certainly the more weighty. At the head of the party stood Archbishop Alexander of Alexandria, Efstathios of Antioch, Makarios of Jerusalem, Markellos of Ankyra, Hosius of Cordova (the court bishop), and above all our Alexandrian archdeacon, Athanasios. According to then current practise, he was not admissible to a voice or a seat in the synod meeting; yet he exhibited

[20] Theodoret, *Ecclesiastical History*, Bk. I, Ch. III, Nicene Fathers, 2nd Ser., III:35-40.
[21] Ibid., Bk. I, Ch. III, Nicene, 2nd Ser., III:40.
[22] Saint Athanasios the Great is commemorated by the holy Church on the 18th of January and the 2nd of May.

more exuberance and insight than all others. He showed promise already of being the future head of the Orthodox party.

The Arians or Evsevians numbered some twenty bishops, under the head of the influential Evsevios, Bishop of Nikomedia (later of Constantinople). He was allied with the imperial family (not Constantine the Great), and the presbyter Arius, who was commanded by the emperor to attend, so that he might explain his views. Also in that ill-famed group were Theognos of Nicaea, Maris of Chalcedon, and Menophantos of Ephesus. Evsevios of Caesarea took a middle ground. The Arians first proposed a creed, which was rejected and torn to shreds.

A middle-of-the-road confession was introduced but avoided the term *homoousios* (*omo-ousios*, of the same essence). The Arians hated the word *homoousios*, declaring it unscriptural. Hosius of Cordova then announced that a confession was prepared. He declared that Deacon Hermogenes of Caesarea, the secretary of the synod, would read it aloud. It was in substance what came to be the well-known Nicene Creed or Symbol of the Faith, with some additions and omissions. Almost all subscribed to the Creed—Hosius at the head, and then the two Roman Presbyters Vito and Vincentius as delegates of the aged Pope Silvester I (314-335). Evsevios of Caesarea signed after a day's deliberation. Evsevios of Nikomedia and Theognos of Nicaea signed without the condemnatory formula of the Arian heresy. Only the two Egyptian bishops, Theonas and Secundas, refused to sign. They were banished with Arius to Illyria.

As for the Meletian schismatics, their case was also discussed at the council. It was decided that Meletian clerics would be allowed to continue in their offices, but they were to be under Archbishop Alexander. In 328, when Athanasios the Great came to the Alexandrian throne, he took a harder stand against the Meletian dissidents.

The Repose of Saint Alexander

Saint Athanasios was always on hand as Saint Alexander's assistant. He behaved toward him as a son would to his own father. On his deathbed, Alexander summoned Athanasios. With God's help, he believed the succession was to devolve upon Athanasios. When Saint Alexander was at the point of death, he wished to entrust Athanasios with shepherding the Church. He called upon Athanasios, who was then out of town. It was believed he fled to escape the proposed honor. At the time, however, there happened to be another deacon of that same name who answered the summons. When that other Athanasios entered the sickroom of Saint Alexander, the latter kept silent since he was not summoning that man. Again Alexander called out for the absent Athanasios, while the one present kept still. At length, the blessed Alexander then made a prophetic utterance, "O Athanasios, thou thinkest to escape, but thou shalt not escape! It cannot be." The meaning of these words was that Athanasios would be called to the conflict. Not much time later, by the help of God, Saint Athanasios was discovered in the place of his concealment. Bishop Alexander of Alexandria reposed in 328. Only three epistles are extant from his voluminous correspondence.[23]

On the 29th of May, the holy Church commemorates TWO MARTYRS, husband and wife, whose bones were broken with clubs.

On the 29th of May, the holy Church commemorates the holy Hieromartyr OLVIAN, Bishop of Anaia, and his disciples.

Olvian, the sacred hieromartyr, bore fruit during the years of Emperor Maximian, who reigned from 286 to 305, at the time of the consulate of Alexander and Maximus, when Julius Sextus and Ailianus were governing Asia. A decree contrary to the Christian members of the populace was promulgated and dispatched to the aforementioned governors. All Christians were enjoined to offer sacrifice to the false goddess Rhea (Hera). Christians complying with this order were to make the prescribed offerings before the idolatrous priests, namely, Agrippinus and Clement.

Olvian, the Bishop of Anaia in Asia Minor,[24] with many dialectical proofs, exalted and magnified the Faith of Christ. As for the religion of the idols, he disparaged and prosecuted it. Since he rallied the Christians, he was taken by the pagans and subjected to torture. They applied red-hot spits to his body, burning his back and inward parts. Next, since they could not persuade him to make a sacrifice to the sun in the sky, the governors reported his disobedience to the proconsul. He, therefore, commanded that the Christian

[23] Saint Alexander of Alexandria's extant works include: (1) "Epistle Addressed to Alexander of Constantinople on the Arian Heresy and the Deposition of Arius," *P.G.* 18:548; (2) "Epistle to the Beloved and Honorable Coliturgists in All Places of the Catholic Church," *P.G.* 18:572; (3) "Deposition of Arius and Those with Him, by Alexander of Alexandria," *P.G.* 18:581; and, (4) "Sermon on the Soul and Body, and on the Passion of Our Lord," *P.G.* 18:585 (in Latin and Syriac only).

[24] Ephesus or Kusadasi, the Aegean port in western Asia Minor, was one of the important centers of trade during Roman period (1st C. B.C.-A.D. 4th C.). Kusadasi had two major ports namely, Phygela and Anaia. Anaia was protected against probable attacks from sea by a castle, today known as "Kadi Kalesi." Anaia was a settlement north of Phygela, a port, and the center of an episcopacy during the Byzantium period until 11th C. The Byzantines, according to a later treaty, gave the city to the Genoese in the 13th C. "Scala Nuova" was the city of present-day Kusadasi. The city was also called "New Harbor," since Ephesus was destroyed by serious earthquakes and route changes of the Caystros River. The Ottomans conquered Kusadasi in 1413-1414.

bishop receive a thrashing with staves after they first stripped him of his garb. Following this, the servants of deception and error lit a great bonfire. They cast inside the roaring flames the athlete of Christ and his disciples—Saints Makedonios, Symphoros, and Kallistos. Hence, these martyrs completed their struggle by means of fire and received the crown of the contest from the Lord. Many wonderworkings were performed by Bishop Olvian in his lifetime. After his martyric repose, prodigious miracles were energized through his honorable and precious relics for those who hastened to him with faith. Thus Saint Olvian, the namesake of "happy" and "blest," has wrought such responses in his petitioners.

On the 29th of May, the holy Church commemorates the holy New-martyr JOHN (commonly called NANNOS) of Thessalonike who was slain by the sword at Smyrna (1802).[25]

John, the namesake of grace and latter-day martyr of Christ, was commonly known as Nannos.[26] The nickname was an affectionate diminutive of John, the same name as his father. He, therefore, was little John to differentiate him from his father. The name of Nannos' mother was Thomais. Today's saint, John, was born at Thessalonike. The saint's father originated from the village of Gynaikokastron, which was renamed by the Turks as Abret-Hisar. It was situated in the valley of the Azios River, some thirty-five kilometers from Thessalonike. The saint's mother hailed from Kolovi, which is near Polygyro of Chalkidike. Both of his parents, however, grew up in Thessalonike. It was there that they met and married. They had two children. The eldest was Theodore. John Junior, who was born on the eve of the Feast of the Nativity of the Honorable Forerunner, was named by his parents after the Baptist. After a time, since his father could not earn an adequate livelihood from his trade of shoemaker at Thessalonike, he left that city and went to Smyrna. The family remained behind in Thessalonike. The father opened a shop in bustling Smyrna and was able to send money back to Thessalonike for his family's maintenance. He also, periodically, returned for short durations to Thessalonike and visited with his family. He then returned to Smyrna and resumed his occupation. When his eldest son, Theodore, came of age, he took him back with him to Smyrna. The son, thereupon, learned his father's trade. When little John, who is the protagonist of our account, came of age, the father employed him also that he might learn how to be a cobbler.

---

[25] The martyrdom of New-martyr John was recorded by the venerable Nikephoros of Chios (commemorated by the holy Church on the 1st of May). The biography was published in the *Neon Leimonarion* (Venice, 1819), which text was borrowed and revised for incorporation into *The Great Synaxaristes* (in Greek).

[26] Nannos signifies tiny, shrimp, or undersized, though he was normal for his age.

The eldest brother, Theodore, knew letters. Since Theodore was both religious and warmhearted, whenever he had time, he had the habit of reading the lives of the saints and soul-benefitting books to his brother. His blessed younger brother, John, though he was unlettered, loved to hear Theodore read aloud. He especially favored hearing the lives of the saints. With much liveliness, he often expressed the desire to imitate those excellent feats that he heard spoken of in the martyric accounts. This salutary pastime of the brothers became part of their everyday routine. As for little John, his love and practise of virtue grew daily. The youth, therefore, exhibited from an early age, as one filled with grace, a propensity for the virtuous life. He was serious about adorning his own life with the virtues that characterized and distinguished the people of God. From his brother's readings, he gleaned much deserving of emulation. He understood that humble-mindedness was highly praised. He also came to love prudence and temperance as desirable acquisitions. He did not just hear the words and then forget about them. Throughout his waking hours, he pondered and meditated upon the various personalities and their struggles described in the readings. Their lives were more real to him than the mundane affairs he took part in to help the family. As it happened, little John had a powerful memory. He remembered everything that was spoken. His mind and soul were enriched by divine thoughts, which were engendered by the readings he heard, which gave him real satisfaction. He perceived a growing sense of unreality and insufficiency in this world's mode of life. The readings nourished him and created a sanctuary for him. The saints and their exploits became the scene of his real life and mental activities. There were no boundaries between him and the other world. In the kingdom of his heart, the invisible reality coexisted with the visible present. He emulated his heroes as best he could, given his young age. He strived to keep his life blameless and irreproachable in both his soul and body. With regard to his physical appearance, he was handsome of countenance and of an average height for his age. He had a pleasing aspect and physique, with all features fitted together for a harmonious and pleasing look. Such were the physical gifts of John. Most importantly, however, was that within this body there dwelt a soul that was virtuous and pious. Thus, beauty of soul and dignity of form were wonderfully fused.

Saint John

The blessed John, from the perspective of spiritual excellences, was in no wise deficient. He was humble, prudent, disciplined, an avid listener of divine words, and a lover of good works. Now it was only out of necessity that he was enjoined to enter the marketplace and deal with various merchants and tradesmen. Nevertheless, he kept himself undefiled and pure. Divine love, which warmed his heart, caused him to hate that which was inimical to God. The belief systems of the heterodox and those of other creeds, especially Islam of the Hagarenes,[27] filled him with perfect hatred. So spoke the Psalmist David: "With perfect hatred have I hated them; they are reckoned enemies with me [Ps. 138:21]." For this reason, during the Church feast days, when the Orthodox community was not engaged in business, John remained at home. He devoted the entire day either to listening to the divine words being spoken or to meditating upon what he heard. In this manner, then, did the goodly John spend his youthful days well and in a godly fashion. In accordance with the testimony of others, both his father and his elder brother were also upright Orthodox Christians.

Such were the lives of the men of this family, at least until the 3rd of May, a Saturday in the year 1802.[28] The father sent his youngest son with shoes to the workshop of the marketplace herald. On that particular day, John went to this establishment two or, perhaps, three times. What was significant was that he never came back from that errand. Now on that same day, when the father and elder brother, as well as some cousins, saw that John was long overdue in returning, they suspected something was amiss. They began to think that the tax collector of the poll-tax arrested him and put him in prison. They hastened, therefore, to the prison, but he was not incarcerated therein. The kinsmen could not imagine where the lad might be found. Since they knew not where to look, they began to surmise all kinds of situations that could have occurred. Later that evening, they received the most shocking of tidings. Alas! John became a Turk without a backward glance. This newly arrived intelligence wounded the hearts of John's kinfolk. They lamented upon hearing this unexpected calamity. The father bewailed his son. The brother mourned for his brother. The cousins wept for their cousin. All those who were acquaintances and friends of the members of that family condoled and sympathized with them, but the kinsmen did not yet utterly despair.

They found it difficult to persuade themselves that a youth of such unimpeachable character and moral excellence, who, with deep fervor loved

[27] Hagar was Abraham's (Abram's) Egyptian bondwoman and concubine, who gave birth to Ishmael who took a wife out of Egypt. The appellation was used in Christian literature and Byzantine chronicles for Arabs. Following this, it was applied to the Islamic forces, known collectively as Saracens. During the height of the Ottoman Empire, writers of the lives of the new-martyrs applied the term to describe either the followers or the descendants of Hagar. The name is used interchangeably with Ishmaelites, which came also to mean any Muslim.

[28] This is obviously the traditional Church calendar date when there was a 12-day difference between the Julian and Gregorian calendars. Pascha in 1802 took place almost three weeks earlier, on 13/25 April.

God and was a fiery zealot of piety and a deadly opponent of the ungodliness of Islam, should all of a sudden renounce his God and embrace the perdition of the barbarian. It was so out of character and beyond his nature. They wondered how could they have been so mistaken in assessing his temperament and disposition. How did the Muslims impose themselves upon him? The family made haste and went all together to the Turkish workshop, the one in which they learned he was employed. Indeed, they actually saw him there, but they were not permitted to approach him. John's relatives were told that enemies of Islam could not enter. The Muslims heaped reproaches upon those Orthodox men, as they held wooden clubs in their hands and threatened the kinsmen if they did not take themselves away. Thus, the kinsmen were driven off the premises with the Turks shouting, "He is ours now! He has nothing to do with you anymore!" The words fell chillingly on the distraught father. He could say nothing more about his son's denial. He could not disguise his misery and mortification. In his grief, the only thing he could think to ask, that was outside of the burning issue between them, was about the work order: "What became of the shoes that I gave him to deliver?" When he learned where they left the shoes, the father departed with tears in his eyes. He was sighing heavily as his lips trembled. The pain in his heart was relentless. O Christian brethren, who would not be saddened by the father's inexorable anguish of soul? Who would not sorrow at hearing of this youth's destruction? Who would not commiserate with the family over such a misfortune? How is it possible not to be moved? Where now is the lad who daily clamored for the divine readings that ushered in unceasing and pious reveries? Where now is that zeal for Orthodoxy? Where now is that love for Christ? O Christians, do you not wonder at such a conversion that is contrary to, and past, expectation? Do you not suspect such an abrupt and startling reversal of character?

But take courage! Do not let any outlandish thought pass through your mind regarding John. John still continued to be John, the namesake of grace, because divine grace was dwelling in him and in no wise departed from him. Behold the fruit of divine thoughts! Behold his love for his Savior! The love of Christ was kindled in his heart. He desired to offer himself as a sacrifice by means of a martyric death. Since there was no other way that he could bring this about, he pretended that he wanted to be a Turk. He needed a pretext: as a kind of fool for Christ he found it in playacting a part. He thought of the words of the sacred Paul who said, "To the Jews I became as a Jew, that I might gain Jews [1 Cor. 9:20]." With the same thought in mind, so did John conduct himself. To the Hagarenes he became as a Hagarene. He did not do it, however, that he might gain Hagarenes, but that he might gain Christ. Therefore, in his case, there were neither tears of repentance, nor expiration of heavy sighs, nor appearances of a downcast face. The reason why there was no salving of his conscience was because he was not convicted by his conscience. He recognized the divine thoughts that dwelt in his heart. By his performance, he was striving to be like the martyrs of old. In how many instances did the ancient heroes promise tyrants that they would enter their idol temples? Those confessors had no intention of worshipping the idolaters' graven images, but the tyrants assumed otherwise. Afterward, when the martyrs of old entered those abominable precincts, their prayers razed to the ground their temples and idols.

The case with John, as we just told it, is the absolute truth. In his desire to undergo martyrdom for Christ, he contrived to use those means available to him. His calculated lip service of a denial of Christ before the Turks was a ruse. With this premeditated pretext that he became a Turk, he would soon snub the Muslims and spurn their religion. This writing is not a retrospective whitewash for one who lapsed from Orthodoxy for fear of death or for desire of worldly attainments. His previous conduct and mode of life bear witness to his pure intention. He, indeed, put himself in the way of a dangerous temptation, but God would overlook the ostensible misdeed of his denial on account of his youthful simplicity and guilelessness. This manner of entering the arena of martyrdom is not advocated. Most would deprecate the choice of such a method. In John's case, his intent would soon be revealed. His concealed devotion and God-loving purpose would be made manifest in but a few days. His predetermined recantation in order to undergo martyrdom would soon find him deserving of a martyr's crown. Do not judge his plan as strange, O Christians. He was a mere youth—simple, plain, and uneducated—who just of late apprenticed as a shoemaker. He dared to commit such a reprehensible action, but it was an expedient. It was the bait used for a greater good, that is, to suffer a martyric death. If one is looking for a precedent of this instance, one need look no further than the life of the holy Apostle Auxibius.[29]

Now eight days passed since John was physically separated from his father. "Note," writes the biographer, "how I have said 'physically' and not 'spiritually separated.'" As for the father, John, he wept as another Jacob of old who mourned for his son Joseph.[30] In the meantime, little John or Nannos was ruminating upon martyric crowns and those ineffable good things of heavenly blessedness. He was happy and rejoicing in his heart. On the eighth day, after he left home, Nannos, in the ordinary course of the day, happened to meet with one of his cousins. The name of the cousin was Harizanees. Now Harizanees saw little John from a distance and averted his eyes. He feigned that he did not see his little cousin. He, therefore, did not greet him, for Harizanees

---

[29] See the Life of Saint Auxibius, Bishop of Soloi in Cyprus, who is commemorated by the holy Church on the 17th of February.

[30] Gen. 37:34.

was mute with grief. Harizanees' downcast and sullen look bespoke his heart's sorrow. As for John, at the sight of his cousin, he was all gladness and exclaimed, "Dost thou mean to no longer greet me, O cousin?" Harizanees replied, "Thou art a Turk. I am a Christian. What kind of salutation could we possibly exchange?" Any liaison was now repugnant to Harizanees. What did the supposed new recruit of the Turks answer? He, in fact, took this opportunity to disclose his secret and spoke frankly: "Fifteen days will not have passed before thou shalt see what kind of Turk I am!" Now by reckoning a fortnight and a day, what did the holy John signify? Did he mean fifteen days from the time he left his father's house? No, he intimated that fifteen days will not have elapsed from that moment. At length, eleven days had come and gone. When it was the 22nd of May, a Thursday, John was seen on the road by fellow Thessalonians who were also cobblers. They thought to tease John. They began sporting with him and saying, "So thou becamest a Turk, and yet thou hast not changed thine apparel? Where are thy good clothes that they had made for thee? Art thou still in the shoes fashioned by thy father?" John remarked, "I put in an order that they make me clothing, as well as gold weapons. But come Sunday, I should have them that I might wear them in the marketplace of Soan." Now it should be noted that the place mentioned so mysteriously by John was where executions were carried out.

After they went on their way, John went to see another compatriot. His name was Demetrios. John asked him, "Hast thou a cross to give me?" Since Demetrios did not know John's reason for making such a request, he was not keen on presenting him with one. Undaunted, John went to see him two and three times. Despite John's fervent entreaty for a cross, Demetrios gave him nothing and expelled him. After the last visit, Demetrios went straight to the father, the elder John, and the other relations of Nannos. He reported what had been taking place. They were consoled and heartened by these tidings concerning Nannos. When Harizanees brought up before the whole company the enigmatic words of Nannos, that they would see what kind of Turk he was in fifteen days' time, they remembered another encounter. For the comment that Nannos made to some fellow artisans, the Thessalonians, was equally puzzling. For Nannos claimed to have some clothes on order, which he was planning to wear at the marketplace of Soan. They put together these three individually intriguing pieces of the puzzle, which gave evidence of a promising sign: the youth was intending to undergo martyrdom. Now was the father wakened to his son's true character. The father then declared to Demetrios, "Go and tell him that should he repent, with a view to martyrdom, he need not go looking for a cross; much rather, tell him he ought to be seeking the power of the Cross. Let him invoke the name of God for help. Then he will not be needing anything else."

On the 25th of May, which fell on a Sunday, little John went again to see Demetrios. Once more, John asked him for a cross. Demetrios then recited the advice proffered by the youth's father and whatsoever else the family bade him do. The blessed John, hearing the paternal admonitory counsel spoken especially for him, was extremely happy. He said to Demetrios, "Is that what my father uttered? May it be well with him!" Immediately, John turned around and went to the workshop of his agha. The agha dispatched him to his house with the customary prepared food. John removed his Turkish garb and put on his former Christian attire. He then made straight for the courthouse.[31] He went inside, still in his clothing marking him as a Christian but with the added Muslim accessory of a turban on his head. Well then, what he spoke against that antichrist religion, Islam, as he held fast to the holy Faith of Jesus Christ, we do not know. When he made his public profession of the Christian Faith, there was no Christian present in the court who heard him so as to recount it to us. One statement has certainly been left to us. It was one he repeated over and over again: "I do not want to be called Mehmet but John." The judge ordered the jailing of the child. News of this electrifying development quickly spread throughout Smyrna. It was said that a youth was going to martyrdom. The Christians, verily, exulted in these tidings, while the Hagarenes were saddened and confounded.

On the third day, a meeting convened at the administration building. Together with the administrator, there were two false witnesses in league, and all the aghas and notables of Smyrna. It was as though some major imperial decree had convoked the conference. The martyr, even in his rayless dungeon, learned of the lawless meeting. He sought divine help from on high. In the meantime, his father, through Hatzi Stavrinos, got a message to a guard in the prison that was passed on to his son. John Senior gave his blessing to John Junior. That blessed father greatly desired to see his boy. His paternal longings were inflamed. He wished one last time to bid farewell to his youngest son, and to give him the final kiss, but he was afraid. With tears of compunction in his eyes, he commissioned Hatzi Stavrinos with the following communication for his son: "May he have the blessing of Christ and the Panagia and of me, the sinner! May the grace of the All-Holy Spirit empower him to receive that for which he yearns! Tell him, however, that when he is under examination, lest

---

[31] John went over to the Turks on Saturday, the 3rd of May. Eight days later, on the 11th of May, he came upon his cousin, Harizanees. On Thursday, the 22nd of May, he met fellow Thessalonians on the road. He saw his compatriot Demetrios that day and a couple of times thereafter. On Sunday, the 25th of May, he went to see Demetrios again. That same evening, John went before the Muslims at the courthouse. Thus, from the 11th of May—when he disclosed to Harizanees that before fifteen days he would reveal what kind of Turk he was—to the 25th of May, fourteen days had passed.

there should follow some trial or tribulation or other evil upon the family, he ought not to make mention of either father, or brother, or any relative."

In the meantime, the sinister council of Hagarenes held discussions. A preliminary examination was held for the prisoner. The martyr was taken out of prison again, for a second examination, and presented before the council. The martyr, under interrogation, boldly confessed before all present the holy Faith of Christ. He fearlessly denounced Islam before them. Distinguished men among the Hagarenes began truckling, with servile humility, the shoemaker John. With their usual unvarying flatteries and promises of ten thousand good things, one pledged him a new wardrobe and another a considerable sum of money. Indeed, a representative of a Frank, who was a Thessalonian, adulated John. He effusively praised him, making a point that they were familiars and compatriots. In the kaleidoscope of promises, they even went as far as pledging to make him an agha, a titled man of authority. Others expressed their sympathy and sorrow that one so young, with his life stretching before him, was going to be put to death because he refused to hearken to their older and wiser counsel. How were their salvos of praises and promises countered? What was the response of the godly-disposed and heavenly-minded John?

He, in no wise, gave any consequence to their blandishments. His mind was not dwelling on worldly and perishable promises. He turned his thoughts from the terrestrial to the heavenly and inviolate good things awaiting to be enjoyed. He, therefore, stood silently before them as Saint Mardarios of old,[32] who simply answered the tyrant's questions with "I am a Christian." The same approach was taken by our John who uttered nothing. When he was compelled to answer, he spoke nought but this declaration: "I am a Christian. I believe in my original Faith. I want to be called John and not Mehmet." His unshakeable resolve was evident to them. Each gave his opinion on how to deal with the youth. The administrator, the Agha Souleiman, stood in their midst. He certainly was inspired by the devil when he addressed them with these words: "I should tell you that these Hellenes are a stubborn lot. When they make up their minds to do something, they first decide their own deaths; and then they put their hand to the work. We, therefore, are laboring in vain. But you know what we should do? I shall tell you. There is a ship ready to depart for Algeria. Let us put him on board. There will be three hundred Turks with him. So whether he wants to or not, he will remain a Turk. After all, what can he do in Algeria?" Such were the foetid words vomited through that satanic mouth so as to impeach the martyr's purpose. All the Muslims at that session agreed to the plan, so that they even praised Souleiman's "wonderful" counsel.

---

[32] Saint Mardarios is commemorated by the holy Church on the 13th of December.

When John heard these words and their decision, then he became apprehensive. He sensed a sudden dejection of mind. The devil tried to check every endeavor of his. He feared that his hope to contend as a martyr would be thwarted. In order to avoid hazarding the loss of such a struggle, the pious John imitated the blessed Auxibius. John addressed the assembly and said, "Allow me some time to consider what I should do." This device was contrived by John to secure a delay. The Lord, for His part, stupefied the listeners as they imagined that reflection could show him the madness of his conduct. Their minds were made insipid so that they rejoiced at his proposal, granting him two days to bethink himself. In their want of judgment, God permitted that they should forget what was just mentioned, that is, the ship was ready to depart for Algeria. They were incogitant of the consequences should he refuse to comply with their wishes after two days. For by then the ship would have sailed and they would have lost the opportunity to pack him off to Algeria. Such temporary vacuousness on the part of men who were always machinating was certainly from God. With minds diverted by God, not one of them anticipated such an outcome. Meanwhile, the nearly two days that John spent in prison, he was not troubled by them in the least.

The martyr went back into the prison where he was allowed to speak a little while with a certain Christian, a servant in the commissioner's office. John asked him, "Brother, I beseech thee to do me a favor. Go and check well the port schedule that thou mightest learn when the ship departs with the Barbaresi." That Christian servant, not knowing the aim of the martyr, commented, "Thou dost not recognize the misfortune that has befallen thee? Yet thou wouldest learn only when the Barbaresi set sail?" The martyr answered, "Brother, I am a Christian. For the sake of Christ, grant me this benefaction. For I fear that they will set me on board this vessel and send me to lands of gross impiety. If that should happen, I would lose my hope. For the present I have asked for a little time, supposedly that I might reconsider what is in my best interest. It is for this reason that I am asking thee to go down to the harbor and learn exactly when the ship will get under way. Then come back and tell me. Because if the ship is still lying at anchor, then I will stall by renewing my petition for time until it weighs anchor." The Christian servant agreed to do it. He returned that evening and related his gladsome news: the ship had put out to sea. Hence, the so-called wonderful counsel of Souleiman came to nought.

That same evening (Wednesday), the military governor put in prison a certain sailor. He was a foreigner and a poor man. He was charged with wearing red shoes. Our martyr asked the sailor, "For what reason have they put thee in prison?" The sailor politely but sardonically answered, "The governor is hoping to receive a bribe from me. That is why I have been locked in here. But I am being charged with wearing red shoes. The poor fellow is unaware of two facts: he is not going to receive a sop from me; and, he is going to be enjoined to feed me for as long as they hold me in here. I have no money. I have been continually serving on ships, where red shoes were all that could be had. If I possessed any extra money, I would have bought a new pair of shoes." After the sailor narrated his case, he asked the martyr, "But thou, O brother, how hast thou come to be imprisoned?" The martyr then unraveled his sentiments and set forth the entire matter. The sailor's cynicism vanished, to be replaced with awe and amazement. He began to say to John, "Brother, thy proposed action is great and thy work is formidable." The martyr then handed over his pouch to the sailor. There were seven *grosia* (piasters) inside his wallet. John urged the sailor, saying, "Take it, brother, so that thou mightest have a few days' worth of necessities while thou art detained herein. Take, also, this handkerchief, that thou mightest remember me." The sailor exclaimed, "What art thou doing? Thou art a poor man also, and yet thou wouldest give me thy small savings? I do not need them." The martyr replied, "Take it, seeing that, tomorrow, I am leaving thee in health." John then spent that night in prayer and making prostrations.

On Thursday, two hours before noon, a great meeting was convoked in the courthouse. All attendees had good hopes that the young witness for Christ had repented and that they would regain him for Islam. John, therefore, was brought forward for a third examination. Straightaway, John stated that he had reasoned well. He went on to say that he did not judge it blessed to be anything other than a Christian and to be named John. These words cast a pall over the deeply afflicted hearts of his Muslim audience. Immediately, they all had gloomy countenances. As for the judge, knowing that words were empty in this case, he began to go to work. Behold his zeal and earnestness! He quickly counted out five hundred gold florins. The others present followed his example and added money to the pile. The superstitious Muslims then had a costly Barbaresi-type garment that was all gold added to the collection. Although these artifices were gross and palpable, let each one deliberate upon how much was placed on the table to incite the youth to recant. Added to this, they were fulsome in praise and flattery to win him over. The martyr remained silent. His mind was fixed in the heavens, so that he was not following their conversation. He then directed a penetrating gaze upon them and commented, "Woe to you who have now so much glory, authority, and wealth, which in the next life shall condemn you to everlasting punishment! As for me, I desire nought save that I am a Christian and that I am named with the Christian name of John."

Manifold and diverse were the machinations and artifices of the chief mischief-maker and adversary, the devil. The Muslims, blazing with indignation, did not allow these words to agitate them, which normally would have wounded them to the quick. Instead, they appeared meek and peaceful, speaking in a voice of forced calmness, "See here! Just emerge from here as Mehmet. Then go wheresoever it pleases thee. Use whatever name thou dost prefer. No one will hinder thee." This, too, was a wicked and deceitful ploy of the enemy in order to prevent the martyrdom. But John would not mock his scruples and leave with a stricken conscience. At the same time, the employees of the judge began to say, "Pity thy life and thy youth. Leave from here and go where thou wilt. Become whatever pleases thee, only thou must depart from this examination as Mehmet lest thou shouldest suffer death." The stalwart John responded to their proposition by saying, "Nay! I want to exit, both in name and reality, as John." What he proclaimed is certain. There is no doubt. It was neither a relative, nor a friend of the martyr, nor an Orthodox Christian who retold what took place. It was a heretic, an enemy of the Faith, a papist. He, too, admired the virtue and mettle of his opponent. He happened to be present, acting as interpreter for a Moscovite.

When they finally perceived that what John had determined for himself was immutable, they became indignant. After flashing a malevolent glance, the judge erupted and said tartly, "Do not even begin to think that we shall help speed thy release from this world that thou mightest be delivered of us. Oh no! We are going to submit thee to such torments until thou shouldest die under torture." With this pronouncement, the judge drew his yataghan (saber). Next, with mad vehemence, he pushed John who was brought down to the prison to be subjected to punishments. But just as he quitted the chamber and went toward the prison area, they brought him back to the court. Concurrently, the Muslim sent forth officers to bring in John's father. They planned to use the father to exact obedience from John. They would have the father persuade him to do as they wished for that hour and, afterward, the youth could go his own way. The bailiffs found the father. He was so frightened that he did not wish to accompany them. It was beyond his courage. The officers, with frenzied wrath, grabbed him and began taking him to the courthouse. Now some Turkish neighbors witnessed how he was apprehended and interceded in his behalf. The officers let him go and returned. They stated that the father disassociated himself from this business. They claimed that he said he had not the least connection with the prisoner and that he no longer considered him his son. This brought down a swift sentence for John: beheading.

The Hagarenes, thereupon, took John and tied his hands behind his back. Following this, they escorted him to the execution site. As they proceeded, the town crier kept vociferously shouting aloud: "Behold how one who denied our faith is punished!" John, as he was being dragged from behind, cried out, "Forgive me, O Christians, and may God forgive you!" Thus, the invincible martyr, who excelled in valor, ran to gain the highest prize of distinction. He hastened to Soan, the bazaar and market, in order to set up the final trophy of victory against the visible and invisible enemies, which was his original aim and desire. The place to which he was heading was very broad and spacious. By reason of the locale, it was filled to capacity with those who converged to see this extraordinary and strange drama. On the one hand, while the Hagarenes were filled with crazed fervor, they thought that they were offering worship to God by spilling the blood of the martyr. We read about this mania similarly in the Scripture, wherein Jesus says: "These things I have spoken to you, in order that ye should not be made to stumble. They shall put you out of the synagogues; yea moreover, there cometh an hour that everyone who killeth you should think that he offereth God a service. And these things they will do, because they know not the Father nor Me [Jn. 16:1-3]." Furthermore, the Hagarenes, in their delirium, closed in upon that place that they might exult in the spectacle of seeing vengeance committed upon a defamer of their religion. On the other hand, the Christians ran together to that spot to behold the power of the Cross. They poured in to witness the triumph of our divine Faith which, according to the disciple who rested on Jesus' breast, "is the victory, the victory having overcome the world—our Faith [1 Jn. 5:4]." Smyrna, a great commercial and cosmopolitan port, had all kinds of people living there. Consequently, among the multitudes in attendance, there were to be found Franks and Armenians and many other peoples. The press of the crowd was so great that the executioners struck the throngs of people with clubs. As for the blessed John, it was only with difficulty that the execution party wedged their way through the masses to bring John to the site.

Now the Hagarenes went there with their leaders in order to turn back the onrush of the multitude. Next, the execution squad told the martyr to go to his knees. He, joyfully, with gladness exhibited broad across his face, quickly kneeled. The Christians had tears in their eyes as they secretly prayed, "Lord, have mercy." The Turks, with profound wonder, observed the sublimity, elevation of spirit, and fearlessness of the martyr. The executioner, attempting to instill terror in the youth, drew his yataghan. He brandished it thrice in front of the martyr. He touched the martyr's throat with its cold sharp blade, at which John laughed. The executioner then stooped over the lad and half-whispered three times into his ear. The martyr, with an upward motion of his head, indicated that the content of the secret whisperings was not acceptable. The executioner then took out a kerchief that he might bind it over the martyr's eyes. Immediately, a certain coffeehouse keeper, a Turk, sallied forth and crouched next to the martyr. That accursed man, making a show of compassion and sympathy, began to say, "Come to thy right mind. Take pity on thy life and on thy youth. Only say the word that thou art a Turk, and save thyself!" The martyr, again, threw his head back in token of his flat refusal. He once more said, "Nay." Then the executioner covered the martyr's eyes with the kerchief and tied it. The Martyr John then uttered, "Remember me, O Lord, when Thou comest in Thy kingdom [Lk. 23:42]." He said it three times, after which his head was struck off. Thus, he ascended bearing his crown into the heavenly kingdom. The divine John, the namesake of one shown grace, glorified God and was glorified by Him on the 29th day of May, a Thursday, in the year 1802.[33]

While the struggle of the martyr ended here, another one, however, opened up for the Christians. Nearly all who had congregated to witness the execution rushed forward to glimpse at the holy relics. Many attempted to secure a martyric relic for their sanctification. There was an abundance of money that flowed in order to obtain some of his blood, or strands of his hairs, or a piece of his garment. There were some who wished to have the rope that bound his hands. These acquisitions continued into the next day. After all those sanctified objects were sold off, the Turks began to cut away at the martyr's fingers and sold them. Such was the ardor of the Christians to obtain a holy keepsake of the martyr, that the Turkish tyrants brokered for themselves over three thousand *grosia*. Then there remained his sacred head. The sale of this precious relic was promised for Saturday night. The Turks, meanwhile, cut away at his fingers and feet secretly, and sold those relics to some Christians.

This dismemberment was learned of by a devout lover of martyrs, a certain Moscovite Christian. His name was Panagiotes Panagiotopoulos. He was of the opinion that it was not good to cut to pieces the martyric relics so newly reposed. Since he maintained a close acquaintance with the judge and his retinue of men, he conjectured that a way could be found for him to take charge of the whole body and provide it with a proper burial. It came to pass, even as he desired, in the following manner. Panagiotes visited the administrator with whom, as we said, he had a close friendship. As a start, he went to discuss certain other matters. After they concluded the business they had between them, Panagiotes then said, "Since thou art my particular friend, I do not mind telling thee that I have an idiosyncrasy. It happens to do with decapitations. Whensoever it should happen that I see a man lose his head, then I am not able to take my ease whether it is night or day. I lose my sleep. My appetite is cut. I cannot tolerate any food. My life, roughly speaking, is in peril. In order to remedy this eccentric malady, I do whatever I can to bury that dead man. It is of no consequence to me what religion he may have followed. I am only interested in providing a proper interment, so that I might be able to find rest. Now it has come to pass that I saw the recent execution. I am, consequently, suffering from sleeplessness and loss of appetite in the worst way. I request, therefore—that is, if thou lovest me which I am sure that thou dost—that thou

[33] Saint Nikephoros, the biographer, incorrectly records Wednesday.

givest me help in securing the remains for burial. Coinciding with this, of course, I should like to reciprocate by making thee a splendid gift for friendship's sake."

The Hagarene, hearing his friend's overtures, found himself hard pressed in either case, and said as much, "Thy plight has put me between two opposing forces." On the one hand, he did not wish to fret their friendship. Then there was the added attraction of the promised gift which, knowing his openhanded friend, would undoubtedly be generous. But on the other hand, the Muslim knew that it would be no easy matter to hand over the remains to his friend. Panagiotes, seeing the hesitation of the administrator, volunteered, "Do not distress thyself. I can show thee how this can be done in an expeditious manner to everyone's advantage. Visit the prefect and tell him that a Moscovite entered into a transaction, wherein he gave four hundred *grosia* for the beheaded man's remains that he might bury them. When the prefect hears about this business, he will ask for a kickback. Pay the secret rebate he wishes to exact, and I will reimburse thee. After that, go to the judge and tell him how the prefect received payment and granted permission for the beheaded one's burial. Then, when he also asks for money, tell him, 'Thou shalt not be ill-rewarded by our mutual friend Panagiotopoulos. He will handsomely compensate thee—only grant this favor.'" Working in this manner with the Ottoman authorities and their legal system, a parody of justice, Panagiotopoulos was thus issued the pertinent written documents. He received one license from the judge and another from the prefect, permitting him to bury the relics with all propriety.

Thereafter, with the passage of much time, the martyr's account excited reverence and respect, not only from the Orthodox but also from the Franks and Armenians. He became the theme of great admiration. Furthermore, even the Turks, when talking among themselves about the youth, remarked, "He pitied not his youth. He had no fear of death. By all means was he a holy man, because he died for his religion." Thus, all acknowledged the youth's steadiness, manliness of bearing, and self-command to the end.

Hearken to a miracle, worthy of mention, which was energized during those days of the Christ's Martyr John. A certain youth took some cotton and dipped it in the martyr's blood, for which attainment he was overjoyed. With much piety, he guarded the sacred swatch as a heavenly treasure. His sister begged him many times to give her a portion of the blood-soaked cotton, but he would in no wise consent. Since she importuned him so many times, he finally relented and gave her half. Upon receiving the much-desired keepsake, she reverenced it and kissed it. She then went to her icon corner and hanged it thereon. She kept speaking of it to those living in the houses around her. She said, "May God be glorified Who vouchsafed even me to receive the martyr's blood! What I have been granted is truly great." But then an old woman said to her, "It is a pity, my girl, for thee to render it such devotion. So thou deemest him to be a saint? Thou art deceived." Now the young woman believed the evil counsel of the cantankerous hag. Straightway, the young woman's fervor cooled toward the martyr. She cast off her former warm esteem which she possessed. She went to her icon corner and took down the cotton swatch in order to burn it. This she did.

But, behold the wonder! Instantly, in that same hour, her hands and feet began to grow numb. The debilitation increased so that only with force could she move her limbs. Concurrently, her conscience was censuring her. She sensed that she was suffering under divine wrath, because she committed to the flames the cotton cloth with the martyr's blood. Now she attempted to hold her infant in her arms to breast-feed the babe. But she was unable to proceed, since following the paralysis there was the onset of pain. The limbs swelled and she was confined to her bed. Her family summoned the doctor. The young mother, nevertheless, knew that what she was suffering did not require a doctor but a priest who could chant the Service for the Blessing of Water. As a result of her insistence, a priest came and conducted the office. When the priest learned from her what took place previously, he recommended that her kinfolk ask about for the blood of the martyr so that she might be anointed. "Perhaps," said he, "the new-martyr will pardon her and heal her." This is exactly what took place—and in a manner most curious. As soon as the young woman's mother came in with the other half of the bloodstained cotton swatch kept by her son, she made the sign of the Cross with it over her sick daughter. The others who were present began weeping and asking for her cure from the martyr. Indeed, wondrous is God in His saints![34] Forthwith, her pangs ceased. She speedily sensed that she received strength in her extremities and became completely well.

Listen to another wonderworking. A father with a small eighteen-month-old child had seen that it was impossible for the child to raise its head. Hear how the saint wrought a miracle for the child. The father made the sign of the Cross with a cotton swab with blood that he had of the Martyr John. The father then dipped the cotton in water. After taking it out, he gave the mixture to the child to drink. Lo, the wonder! Immediately, the child was cured from that incurable neurological disorder. The grace of the glorious New-martyr John delivered the infant. Through Saint John's intercessions, may we be delivered from spiritual and bodily calamities and misfortunes, and may we be vouchsafed the kingdom of the heavens with all those who throughout the ages pleased God. Amen.

---

[34] Ps. 67:35.

On the 29th of May, the holy Church commemorates the holy New-martyr ANDREW ARGENTES of Chios, who suffered at Constantinople (1465).[35]

The Orthodox Church regards as new-martyrs those men and women who were put to death for the true Faith of our Lord, from the days of the Fall of Constantinople to the time of the Greek Revolution. The Church was unable to declare all the victims of Moslem extremism and to list them in the *Martyrologion*, because either they were so numerous or many of them met martyrdom in distant lands and in obscurity.

One of these new-martyrs whom we wish to honor today is Andrew Argentes. This virtuous soldier of Christ was born on the island of Chios in 1438. He came from a devout, well-to-do, and aristocratic Argentes family. Endowed by God with nobility of soul, he also received a Christian upbringing and spiritual training. When Andrew was twenty-seven, he was stricken with a serious illness. The chief symptom, a high fever, nearly cost him his life. In this precarious state, the devout young man prayed to the Queen of heaven, the holy Virgin Mary, to intercede with her Son, the Savior of the world, to cure him. Andrew, for his part, promised to maintain virginity and purity throughout his life. Lo, the miracle! The holy Virgin hearkened to his plea and he was cured, returning to a state of health. Andrew, in order that he remember the promise made and the debt owed, clad himself in white garb. At the same time, his heart burned with the desire for martyrdom. He wished to offer himself as a sacrifice for the name of the Founder of our Faith, Jesus Christ.

This divine desire caused him to leave Chios for Constantinople. He went neither to marvel at the sites of the queen of cities nor to become a merchant in the silk trade and build a fortune as did his relatives and countrymen, the Chiotes. Nay, he went forth in order to receive the crown of martyrdom. When he arrived in Constantinople, he was accused of being an apostate by a group of merchants from Syria. They contended that, when in Alexandria, he denied Christ, stepped upon the honored Cross, and became a Muslim. Hence, as a Muslim, they further charged him with consorting with

---

[35] A few years after the martyrdom of New-martyr Andrew, George of Trebizond sailed to Constantinople and was in danger of drowning. He vowed that if, by the grace of Saint Andrew, he were to be rescued, he would record his vita. George was preserved. On his return to Italy, he wrote this brief account in Latin. This, therefore, is one of the first martyrdoms of the Greek new-martyrs after the Fall of Constantinople. We have borrowed from the vita earlier published by the learned Emily K. Saros in 1935. The text of the martyrdom of Saint Andrew is found in Sophronios Efstratiades, *Hagiologion* (Athens, 1960), pp. 40, 41; Stylianos N. Kementzetzis, *Synaxaristes Neomartyron* (Thessalonike, 1984), p. 563; and *Enkyklopaedia* 2, Col. 61. English translation from the Greek is by Leonidas J. Papadopoulos.

Christians and even attending their churches. Andrew appeared before the judges and denied all the accusations which were hurled at him regarding a conversion to Islam. He assured them that he never traveled to Alexandria. He stated that he neither knew his accusers nor thought of committing such a sin. In his defense, he, furthermore, added that there was no sign of circumcision on him. He even produced witnesses to testify that he never left his country, and that his journey to Constantinople was his first voyage.

None of these efforts, however, were fruitful. For his voice was as that of a man directed at deaf ears. The plaintiffs and their witnesses were far more numerous. The Moslem judges would no longer listen to the defendant. Andrew was chained and cast into prison where he was treated as the other prisoners. He who committed no crime was punished as a criminal. The reason why they ill-treated him was not due to his committing any crime, but because he was a Christian and believed in Christ. When Sultan Mohammed II was informed that Andrew was a youth of noble background, educated, and tall in stature, he made an offer: if he espoused Islam, he would be classed among his good, dutiful, and brave subjects. In order to convince him to deny Christ, Mohammed ordered that they promise him positions of authority and posts of honor; otherwise, they should most certainly put him to death.

The next day they ushered Andrew inside the courtroom. The judge, with his assistants, encouraged and coaxed him to accept their religion. They promised to recompense him with handsome rewards, positions, benefits, and gold and silver. To all this cajolery, the true soldier of Christ responded, "I have no desire for all these things you offer me. I only have one purpose in mind: not to lose eternal life for the sake of material goods." To this the Turks answered, "If thou wert to live well in this life, we promise thee that thou shalt live well in the next one too!" Andrew was adamant in the Faith of our Lord and answered, "This cannot be so! For if one leads a life of pleasure here, he cannot find Paradise. Know this once and for all, O Turks: I shall withstand your every torture, and even death itself, rather than hearken to your words and meet your demands!"

We praise thy courage, O valiant athlete of Christ! We laud thy fearlessness, which is deserving of celestial honors. In thee were fulfilled the words of the wise Solomon, who wrote: "The righteous is confident as a lion [Prov. 28:1]." David, also, wrote in the Psalms: "And I was speaking in respect of Thy testimonies before kings, and I was not being put to shame [Ps. 118:46]." Andrew's bold tongue so enraged the Turks that they cast him back in jail and, on the third day, led him to the eastern sector of the city where there was a large concentration of people. After they stripped him of his clothes, they thrashed him harshly—cruel as they were. His bones were shattered; he shook violently and crossed his hands, begging the Mother of God with the words, "O

Virgin Mary, assist me!" And—lo! the miracle—he drew courage, gained his senses, and stood upright, intrepid and strong, and viewed the sun as it beamed its last rays for that day.

Now in that sector, there was a high tower. Imprisoned within was a Christian from Trebizond. He was charged in like manner as Andrew. As that Christian beheld from the height of the tower how courageously and without fear Andrew answered the Turks, he raised his voice and said, "O blessed Christian! Joy to that land that raised thee, and joy to the parents who brought thee into the world! If only it were the will of God for me to share a portion of thy pains and even of thy rewards!"

The guards led our martyr back to jail. They let him sleep. They anointed his sores with expensive ointments, so that he should recover quickly. They gave him water to drink into which they had poured gold dust. The infidels did not do this out of pity or sympathy or courtesy. They had two reasons: first, they did not wish for him to die immediately but that he should survive and undergo more torture; and second, because they feared it might be told that he was cured by a miracle. On the 21st of May, they took him out of jail and cut him at the shoulders, which they previously covered only a few days earlier with blows. For a moment, it seemed that the victorious soldier of Christ had given up the spirit, but then he pronounced the words, "O Virgin Mary, help me!" At once, he came to his senses and stood on his feet. With courage and joy, he withstood the inhuman and merciless tortures of the infidels.

At night, they began to attend to him again. They nursed his wounds and gave him water with gold dust in order to show that these things had the power to heal him, not the divine might. The following day, the 22nd of May, he was completely healed; but the infidels were unable to shake him from the Orthodox Faith. Therefore, they brought him back, to the spot of martyrdom, where they beat him to such a degree that his bones would have been exposed had it not been for his skin. At that time, Andrew called upon the name of the Mother of God, and cried out, "O Virgin Mary, come to my aid!" And—lo, Thine unspeakable philanthropy, O Christ merciful!—blessed Andrew recovered and regained new vigor, even though the executioners had lost their composure. At that moment, the prisoner from Trebizond, who was confined in the tower, shouted aloud in joy and triumph for the victory of the martyr. The executioners, meanwhile, again used balsams and water with gold.

On another day, they led Andrew to the place of martyrdom. With their knives, they cleaved the flesh on his shoulders. On the following day, they cut away the flesh of his buttocks and behind the calves. But when he called upon the name of the Virgin Mother of God, Mary, he felt relief and strength while they tortured him.

By the 27th of May, the executioners knew not what to do. They perceived that they were toiling in vain. They, therefore, lashed him as harshly as they could in order to vanquish his miraculous persistence. But he never succumbed to their wishes despite the pain, as he was unshakeable in the Faith of our Lord. Then they cut one of his cheeks, casting it on the ground. The Christians took it immediately, and brought it to the Church of the Directress Theotokos at Galata. There, it was encased in a gold chest, whence it emitted a divine fragrance for a long time and was a miracle-working shrine for all Christians. In spite of all the harsh tortures they applied, when they led him to the place of martyrdom on the 29th of May, he was found safe and unharmed throughout his body.

Even though the Turks taunted him, the saint spoke of death as if it were life. He insisted that his miraculous healing was the result of God's power. His froward tormentors were outraged. They were resolved to cut off his honored head. Having carried out his beheading, Andrew Argentes' soul flew with the angels to the bosom of the Creator. The holy relics would have been deprived of burial, because the infidels were inclined to cast them to the fowls of the air or the fish of the sea. But the Christians of Constantinople opposed this, because the body of Andrew, a man very near to God, was worthy of honor. In spite of the attempts and intrigues made by the infidels to dissuade Sultan Mohammed II, even he recognized the martyrdom of the saint. He turned the body over to the Christians, praising his steadfastness and judging him worthy of an honorable burial.

Following this decision made by the sultan, upwards of ten thousand spectators, including Greeks, Latins, and many Turks, converged from all parts of the city. They received the most sacred relics of the blessed new-martyr. Saint Andrew's relics were transferred amid psalms and mourning to the Church of the Mother of God at Galata, also named Kataphatiane. The relics were interred in an underground vault at that end of the church which is near the waterfront.[36] Let us, therefore, O Christians, emulate the conviction of Saint Andrew by living a God-pleasing life, so that by his intercessions we may be deemed worthy of the kingdom of the heavens. Amen.

---

[36] The example of the New-martyr Andrew Argentes was later imitated by family descendants: Efstratios Argentes the Younger, and Anthimos Argentes the hieromonk and abbot of the Monastery of Saint John of Moudon at Chios. The first refuted and berated two emissaries of the pope in Alexandria, who were sent to Egypt to give unleavened bread to the Christians of the east. With his eloquence and erudition, he put them to shame. The second was a grandson of the first. He was strangled along with the renowned champion of the rebirth of Greece, Rigas Phedeos, whose body was thrown into the waters of the Istros River (Danube). A third was slain during the horrid days of the 1822 massacre in Chios.

On the 29th of May, the holy Church commemorates the holy and blessed JOHN of Ustiug, the Fool for Christ and Wonder-worker.

On the 29th of May, the holy Church remembers THE FALL OF CONSTANTINOPLE, the Queen of Cities, into the hands of the antichrist Hagarenes in 1453.[37]

The Byzantine Empire, founded by Flavius Valerius Constantine I (306-337) the Great, after more than eleven hundred years, ended with Constantine XI Palaiologos (d. 1453). The Greeks attributed the fall of their glorious empire to their sins and apostasy.[38]

Sultan Mehmet II (1432-1481) coveted the Byzantine capital, and said to himself, "If I conquer this city (Constantinople), I shall surpass the glory of all my ancestors who tried to capture her so many times but failed miserably." By June of 1452, at thirty years old, Sultan Mehmet II and his troops invaded the suburbs of Constantinople, enslaving all inhabitants outside the walls. By August of 1452, the sultan erected his castle, known as Rumeli Hisari, by the European side of the strait in the district of Asomatee. Mehmet did not ask permission to build, though the district was technically in Byzantine territory. He had assembled a thousand masons and two thousand laborers, who worked day and night to construct the castle. The structure was in the orthographical form of the name "Mohammed." Material for its construction was collected from churches and monasteries in the immediate vicinity. The purpose of erecting the tower was twofold: to deny passage to all vessels sailing from the Black Sea toward the Constantinopolitan harbor; and to provide easy passage from Asia Minor to Thrace for his troops.[39]

---

[37] See "The Fall of Constantinople," *The Lives of the Pillars of Orthodoxy*, 3rd ed. (Buena Vista, CO: Holy Apostles Convent, November 2000), pp. 501-527.

[38] Concerning the common notion that their sins brought about their downfall, an exhaustive analysis of this theory and its exploitation by the Turks is discussed in the book of Apostolos E. Vacalopoulos, *Origins of the Greek Nation: The Byzantine Period, 1204-1461*, Ch. 7; for the persistence of this attitude after the Fall of 1453, see Georgios T. Zoras, *Concerning the Fall of Constantinople* (Athens: Spoudasterion Byzantines kai Neoellenikes Philologias tou Panepistemiou Athenon, 1959), Ch. 1.

[39] Makarios Melissenos (Melissourgos), "The Chronicle of the Siege of Constantinople," *The Fall of the Byzantine Empire*, p. 99, 160; Michael Doukas, *Decline and Fall of Byzantium to the Ottoman Turks*, Ch. 34, 7 ff. and p. 304, n. 234. For the Turkish account of the construction, see, Beg Tursun, *The History of Mehmed the Conqueror.* Also, Franz Babinger, *Mehmed the Conqueror and His Time*, p. 75 ff. Also, Kemal Cig, "Rumeli Hisari," Istanbul (Istanbul: Net Turizim ve Ticaret, n.d.).

Ambassadors sent by Constantine XI Dragases Palaiologos (1449-1453) to speak to Mehmet about the breach of treaty were disdained and some were decapitated.[40] Mehmet retorted proudly: "My father, prevented by the Byzantines from passing through the Hellespont during the campaign of Varna, swore to build a fortress at this point of the Bosporos. I am only executing his wish. Tell your emperor that I do not resemble my ancestors, who were too weak, because my abilities reach a height to which they could not aspire."[41]

Meanwhile, in the capital, Emperor Constantine had consented to have the name of Pope Nicholas V (1447-1455) commemorated in the services, from whom he hoped to receive some aid. In the Church of Hagia Sophia, any willing priest would pronounce the commemoration of the pope. Those that refused to commemorate the pope's name, however, incurred no blame. Papal commemorative services commenced on the 12th of November, in 1452. On the 12th of December, the union of the two Churches was solemnly commemorated in the Church of Hagia Sophia. Nevertheless, Greek monastics and most of the Greek inhabitants of Constantinople were opposed to the union. Two political parties had formed: the unionists, headed by the Palaiologoi, and the anti-unionists, headed by Grand Duke Loukas Notaras and George Kourtesis Scholarios (the Monk Gennadios).[42]

---

[40] Steven Runciman, *The Fall of Constantinople 1453* (NY: Cambridge University Press, 1988, repr.), pp. 65, 66.

[41] Cig, op. cit.

[42] **Anti-union Sentiments:** By the middle of the 13th C., the Eastern and Western Churches were consciously separated. The disapproval of the Eastern Church to the odious insertion of a word into the Creed was genuine. Considering the divergent customs, interests, and ideas, a schism in Christendom was inevitable, together with the crisis caused by an extraordinary coincidence in the 11th and 12th C. of political events. A more serious aspect of the addition to the Creed was that it raised questions of the pope's right to be absolute arbiter of Christian doctrine. If the western churches tampered unilaterally with the Creed of the synods, thereby questioning the authority and inspiration of the fathers of the Church, they must thereby automatically lapse into heresy, despite any pronouncement by the pope. The east saw in the dispute a direct attack on its whole understanding of Church government and doctrine.

In 1095, when Pope Urban II (1088-1099) preached his great sermon at Clermont, launching the First Crusade, the Turks were threatening the Bosporos. Thus, in the east, the emperors were particularly anxious to preserve good relations with the west. The Second and Third Crusades increased the antipathy between the average Byzantine citizen and the ordinary soldier and pilgrim in the crusading armies. To the ordinary Byzantine citizen, it was horrifying to watch great armies from the west marching through their land, apparently on the orders of the pope, pillaging as they went. Moreover, the Byzantines were deeply shocked by the armed and fighting priests in the Crusader armies, for Apostolic Canon Law deposes any bishop, priest, or deacon

(continued...)

[42](...continued)
for striking a believer or unbeliever [Apostolic Canon XXVII]. Until the 12th C., the ordinary Byzantine believed the ordinary westerner to be a genuine fellow Christian, however deplorable his habits might be. Nevertheless, in time, dislike and distrust increased. Conferences and debates between the Churches only worsened matters, emphasizing the differences not only in political outlook and interests but also in religious practise and theology. [Steven Runciman, *The Great Church in Captivity*, p. 83; see also his work, entitled *The Eastern Schism*, p. 124-144.]

Contemporary with the Crusades and partly affected by them was the growth and commercial aggression and power of the Italian maritime republics, especially Venice, in the 11th and 12th C. The whole of international commerce of Byzantium was passing into Latin hands. Furthermore, the Latins brought their own chaplains and were permitted to erect Latin churches, thus increasing public anger. [Idem, *The Byzantine Theocracy*, pp. 132, 133; Idem, *The Eastern Schism*, p. 167.]

Foreign commanders and mercenaries fought in the emperor's army, comprised of Lombards, Frenchmen, Englishmen, and Germans. In administration and diplomacy also, the Latins held important positions. Such blatant favoritism displeased the Greeks. The great tragedy of the Crusades is not that they failed in their mission, but that they succeeded in destroying Byzantium. The horror of the sack of Constantinople on the 13th of April, in the year 1204, produced an intensity of hatred that could not be forgotten. The westerners took advantage of an especially inept government in Constantinople. The weak emperors of the House of Angeli (1185-1204) were powerless to halt the hostility. The Fourth Crusade was the logical outcome of religious antipathy, political ambition, economic greed, and incurable antagonism between two peoples and two worlds. The Latin overthrow of the Byzantine capital, with the tacit connivance of the papacy and the universal applause of Western Christendom, together with the dismembering of the realm for the benefit of the Venetians, dealt a blow to Byzantium from which it never fully recovered. [Charles Diehl, *Byzantium: Greatness and Decline*, pp. 220, 221.]

They pillaged for three days, robbing, raping, and taking particular delight in the torturing of Orthodox priests. Priceless treasures were squandered among the conquerors, and many were destroyed in sheer barbarism. The French historian of the Fourth Crusade, Villehardouin commented, "Since the creation of the world such a vast amount of booty had never been taken from one city." [Villehardouin, *La conquete de Constantinople*, ed. E. Faral, t. II (1939), cited in George Ostrogorsky, *History of the Byzantine State*, p. 370.] The Byzantine writer, Niketas Choniates, commented, "Even the Saracens are merciful and kind" in comparison to these creatures "who bear the Cross of Christ upon their shoulders." [Nic. Choniates, *History*, pp. 761, 762; Ostrogorsky, loc. cit.] They come from the west to fight the infidel Turk, but diverted to plunder the greatest of Christian cities. How ironic that the army of Crusaders, who had begun their campaign with the avowed goal of saving the holy places from the infidel, should now desecrate Constantinople which was dedicated to the Virgin Theotokos. The Latins, after storming and sacking the great city, proceeded to establish a

(continued...)

[42](...continued)
Latin Empire under a Frankish emperor, with a Venetian viceroy to share his power. The tragic evolution of the 1204 massacre was crowned by the installation of a Venetian patriarch in Constantinople, Thomas Morosini (1204-1211). Many of the Greek clergy had been dispossessed of their ecclesiastical properties, and the people were forced to accept the supremacy of the Church of Rome.

In particular, the Greeks were required to recite the Creed with the *Filioque*, and the divine Liturgy was to be celebrated with unleavened bread. At the start of the conquest, Pope Innocent III (1198-1216) directed that the Greeks be permitted to retain their rites; but this was not observed. In fact, the Greeks of southern Italy, in 1284, were enjoined by Pope Martin IV (1281-1285) to chant the Creed with the *Filioque*, under pain of excommunication. Certain feudal practises, characteristic of the Latin Church, were also imposed on the Greek clergy, such as the taking of a compulsory personal oath recognizing papal authority through the clasping of one's hands with those of a Latin superior. A vast number of Orthodox clergy remained true to the Faith and did not submit to these practises. Eloquent testimony of deep Orthodox resentment toward the papal overlords is provided by a Latin canon of the Fourth Lateran Council in Rome (1215), which referred to the Orthodox custom of purifying their altars following each use by the Latins, and to baptize their children after the performance of the same Latin rite. [Hefele-Leclercq, *Histoire des Conciles*, V, pt. 2, 1333.] It was only after the partial Latin conquest of their empire that the Byzantines fully understood the development that had taken place with respect to papal primacy. Nevertheless, what the Greeks resented most was a loss of their national identity—in other words, the beginnings of Latinization of the Greek Church and people.

Under Latin rule, Constantinople, the queen of cities, was steadily depopulated by poverty and famine. Byzantium survived in three parts. In the east a branch of the Komnenian Dynasty set itself up in Trebizond. In the west a branch of the last dynasty of the Angeli set itself up in Epiros. Nearer to the center, Theodore I Laskaris, a son-in-law of the last emperor, established a government in the ancient and holy city of Nicaea. Frankish lordships in Greece itself and in the islands lasted for some two centuries. The Venetians also acquired some islands and ports of strategic and commercial value. [*The Great Church*, p. 12]. Baldwin II (1217-1273) was the last Latin emperor of Constantinople. Thus, after more than fifty years in exile at Nicaea, the imperial authorities re-entered the capital, and the Latin Empire collapsed. However, the empire restored by Michael Palaiologos was no longer the dominant power in the Christian east. [Idem, *The Fall of Constantinople 1453*, p. 3.]

Hard though it may be to believe, yet almost every emperor after the recapture of Constantinople tried to keep the door for ecclesiastical reunion open—even though the majority of Byzantine subjects would never countenance a compromise with the papacy. The masses remained implacable in their loathing and mistrust of foreigners. Together with them was the Orthodox Church, especially among the lower ranks of clergy, which were always disturbed by papal ambitions. It seemed that wherever the Latins established themselves, they installed a Latin upper hierarchy which attempted

(continued...)

In his soul, Emperor Constantine was troubled. Many Greeks blamed him for his support and consent for the union of the Churches in 1452. By early spring of 1453, the sultan began the blockade of the city. With Mehmet's newly built fleet, he brought in artillery, siege engines, and similar devices, which had been constructed earlier. Mehmet realized the immense potential of artillery and gunpowder, and transported giant cannons in great quantities. In fact, some pieces of artillery could only be moved by the combined efforts of forty or fifty pairs of oxen and 2,000 men.[43] On the 2nd of April, in the year 1453, the sultan, with his multitude of cavalry and infantry, reached the city walls. The same day there appeared about thirty triremes and forty warships, as well as 130 ships with single oarbanks, small boats, and vessels. With all these forces, the sultan was able to cover eighteen miles of territory.[44]

---

[42](...continued)
to enjoin Latin practises and doctrines upon Orthodox congregations.

Attempts at union by several theological debates revealed that Eastern and Western Christendom thought differently about the Faith. While the debaters were busy hurling texts at one another, several Greek manuscripts that had been rendered into Latin were often misquoted and mistranslated. Linguistic problems added to the difference in thought. The west was unable to follow the terminology, the grammatical formulation, and the way of thinking of the Greeks. The Greeks, as a result, complained of the poverty of Latin to convey profound theological terminology. The westerners were more interested in the formal and technical aspects of the validity of the sacraments. The real meaning of the Eucharist was obscured in the midst of rubrical prescriptions, measured movements, drops of water, of countless rubrical commentaries. This may have resulted in a worship that was technically accurate to them, but internally it was dead. The west evolved toward a type of analytical knowledge which, in sum, is rational; it needs to define the exact shape of things, to see them independently of one another. The east followed the road of tradition. Thus, the Latin theologians, inured to Scholasticism, have often been baffled at seeing the Greeks take refuge in the realm of patristic texts and conciliar canons, and refusing to yield to their arguments of reason. Papal demands were backed by the aggressive public opinion of the west insisting on the subjection of the east. However, when public opinion in the Orthodox East remembered the Crusades and the Latin Empire, they perceived in papal supremacy a savage form of alien domination—then no amount of compromise over the procession of the Holy Spirit or the bread of the Sacrament would be of avail. The easterners had no wish to submit to the west—but the west would accept nothing less than submission. [See "Causes for Anti-Union Feelings Among the Byzantines," *The Pillars of Orthodoxy*, pp. 161-176.]

[43] To learn more about Mehmet's artillery that pounded the city, see Doukas, op. cit., Ch. 38.

[44] Melissenos, pp. 100, 101. The estimate of forces, both defenders and besiegers, varies greatly from author to author. A summary of this problem may be found in (continued...)

The Greeks counted only 4,773 defenders, as well as the foreigners, numbering about 2,000. They faced an attacking force of 250,000 men (regular and irregular troops). The effective force of Mehmet's army probably amounted to no more than 80,000 men, the rest being ill-equipped irregulars. The Byzantines secured the entrance into the harbor with a heavy boom of iron links. The city's naval forces, positioned behind the harbor, consisted of three ships from Genoa, one from Spanish Castile, one owned by a Frenchman from Provence, and three from Crete; they were all well equipped for battle. There were also three Venetian merchantmen with their escorts, certain fast triremes, in the harbor. This was the naval defense of the city. On the land side, the enemy positioned their biggest piece of artillery, having a nine-inch diameter, together with other cannons, so they could concentrate their bombardment on fourteen spots along the city's defenses. Cannons, catapults, crossbows, and similar devices contributed to heavy casualties on both sides. Onslaughts, attacks, bombardment and general warfare were continuous, throughout the day and night. The sultan would allow no respite, for he hoped that the few defenders of the city would become exhausted by uninterrupted stress. However, the sultan's cannons exploded into many fragments from the constant firing and impure metal, dealing death and wounds to many. Though extremely upset, the sultan ordered that a more powerful cannon be made to replace the damaged one. On the 15th of April, in the year 1453, the sultan's fleet arrived, amounting to 300 vessels, in addition to 320 long ships transporting archers and soldiers.[45]

There was a Genoese nobleman named Giovanni Giustiniani Longo in the city. He had arrived in the city with 700 Italian soldiers on the 29th of January, in the year 1453. Giustiniani, as one expert in all matters, was made general and tribune by Emperor Constantine. He was given charge of 300 men and entrusted with the supervision and management of the city's defenses. Thus, together with the emperor, Giustiniani formed the nucleus of the defense.[46]

Repairs were made to the sultan's damaged cannon. He once more directed a violent bombardment against the walls, day and night. After experiencing the sultan's war engines, the city's soldiers became accustomed to them and displayed neither fear nor cowardice. They even improvised their own engines and new machines, which caused extensive damage to the enemy.

---

[44](...continued)
Doukas, p. 309, n. 263. A compromise figure would be defenders totaling 8,000 Greeks and 2,000 foreigners that faced an attacking force of 250,000 men (regular and irregular troops). Vacalopoulos, pp. 193, 194.

[45] Melissenos, pp. 102, 103.

[46] Doukas, p. 309, n. 262.

Nevertheless, they could not hold up for long, due to the lack of materials and inadequate time for their construction.

The towers of the middle and inner walls—192 in all—were staggered in alignment. The invaders were first faced with a moat some sixty-feet wide and twenty-two-feet deep that was normally dry, but flooded by pipes in time of war. Behind the moat was a low wall to shield a line of archers. The second wall was twenty-seven-feet high, which sheltered more troops. The third and strongest bulwark, with its towers, some seventy-feet high, housed more archers and missile throwers. Only the force of gunpowder could bring the walls down.

However, when several strategic points along the wall were demolished, the sultan decided to have the moat and ditches filled with soil, branches and similar material. He ordered his men to carry out his new plan, so they might cross the moat and obtain access through the gaps in the demolished wall. Through all this, however, the sultan's men suffered casualties, falling victim to the city's artillery, arrows, and heavy rocks flung from the walls. Mehmet then decided to bring his artillery close to the moat and ditches. Both sides performed valiantly. The defenders fought with relentless courage and superhuman strength, even though most were inexperienced in warfare. Nevertheless, by God's grace, it was considered a miraculous event that the Byzantines carried the day. Though the enemy would fill the moat by day, still the city's inhabitants would work all night and clear out the material, dragging away soil, material, and timber. By night were repairs made to the damaged towers with supports. Thus, they were able to shame the sultan who was despised because of the continuous failure of his plans.[47]

The sultan then resorted to another tactic. He decided to dig passages underneath the city walls and defenses, thus providing easy access into the city. The foreigner, John Grant,[48] a military engineer on the side of the Byzantines, was expert in the construction of war engines and in the production of the secret weapon of liquid fire or Greek fire.[49] Greek fire, first used in the naval battle of 673, was a chemical mixture that ignited and burned furiously when it came in contact with water. It even burned under water. Though the ingredients were a secret, it probably contained sulfur, resin, oil, pitch and either calcium phosphide or quicklime. Later it was changed to include naphtha, saltpeter, and turpentine. By the 1200s, it may have resembled

---

[47] Melissenos, pp. 103, 104.

[48] John Grant or Grande or Grando is described as being of either German or Scottish descent; see, Runciman, *The Fall of Constantinople 1453*, pp. 84, 217, n. 1.

[49] On the composition of Greek fire, see J. Haldon and M. Byrne, "A Possible Solution to the Problem of Greek Fire," *Byzantinische Zeitschrift* 70 (1977): 91-99.

gunpowder, then unknown.[50] Grant surmised the sultan's plans and had a countermine tunneled, which was expertly flooded with liquid fire, thereby frustrating and incinerating many Turks. Once again the sultan failed.[51]

The next device of the sultan was the use of a broad and tall tower erected on a platform, with many thick wooden wheels. The forms of so many machines could not have been imagined in earlier periods. No emperor would have ever believed that so many engines could be constructed to storm a citadel. When the horrible tower was brought near the walls, a savage attack followed near the Gate of Saint Romanos. However, the enemy tower was immediately pushed over the breach. The city's defenders resisted the enemy nobly until the first hour of the night, when the sultan's men decided that they had enough of toil and blood. They planned to come back the following morning and utilize their tower. Their expectations were not to be fulfilled. Emperor Constantine, with considerable reinforcements, arrived on the spot to aid Giustiniani, and kept urging his soldiers throughout the night to empty the filled ditches and restore the city's fallen wall. The defenders were also able to destroy the enemy's bizarre tower by burning it to the ground. When the enemy arrived to find their tower in ashes, the sultan was put to shame and extremely wroth. He then expressed admiration for the defenders' skill and exclaimed, "Even if the 37,000 prophets had predicted that our impious enemies (the Byzantines) were about to complete this task in a single night, I would have doubted them!" Mehmet also made the observation that the defenders displayed no sign of fear or cowardice. This attitude confounded both Mehmet and his council, so they again began deliberations.[52]

While the siege was proceeding, three Genoese ships set sail for Constantinople. On the way, they were joined by an imperial vessel, captained by Phlantanelas, transporting grain from Sicily. As they approached the city by night, they were spotted early in the day by the sultan's patrol boats. The Turks, advancing to the sound of their horns and drums, assaulted the imperial ship with missiles. The defenders, in return, gave the Turks a nasty greeting with a shower of missiles, arrows, and rocks. The Turks reached the lower parts of the vessel's prow, but the Greek sailors, on their high decks, poured down onto the enemies liquid fire and rocks, causing great casualties. From the city walls, the inhabitants observed the battle, all the while praying to God to have mercy on their sailors and on themselves. Phlantanelas urged his men on while he was running the whole length of the deck. As the struggle increased,

[50] Harold C. Kinne, Jr. "Greek Fire," Vol. 8, *The World Book Encyclopedia* (Chicago, IL; Field Enterprises Education Corp., 1976).
[51] Melissenos, p. 104.
[52] Ibid., pp. 105, 106.

two enemy triremes were set on fire and many enemy sailors were slain or wounded.

When Mehmet understood that his enormous fleet could accomplish nothing, but, in fact, was taking a terrible beating, he flew into a rage. The sultan shouted, gnashed his teeth and heaped insults upon his seamen. With his horse, Mehmet galloped into the water, followed by his cavalry officers. When the sailors beheld their sultan's disgust and heard his curses, they were ashamed and attacked the Byzantine vessel with more vehemence. However, they could not inflict the slightest damage on any of the defenders' vessels. In fact, after suffering heavy losses and damage, they were not even able to retreat. More than 12,000 infidels perished in that conflict alone! With the approach of night, the enemy floated slowly away while the defenders' ships sailed into the harbor. The defenders suffered no loss of life, save a few sailors that were wounded, and two or three that died some days later. The sultan once again became depressed and kicked the ground in desperation and bit his own hand like a dog. He could not understand how 150 triremes, biremes, and vessels with single oarbanks failed to capture four ships. Moreover, the casualties to his naval forces made him fume.

The sultan now had a new idea. He would haul his ships overland from the Bosporos into the Golden Horn. This had never been done before on ground, where all the ridges were at least 200 feet about sea level. Nonetheless, Mehmet was determined, especially since he had ample manpower and material at his command. It took several weeks to lay more than a mile of roadway between the Bosporos and the Horn. On the 21st of April, the work took on a frantic pace as thousands of laborers were drafted into the final preparations. To divert the attention of the city's defenders, the sultan's cannons fired continuous volleys at the entrance of the Horn and the black smoke billowed up the Bosporos, concealing Turkish activities. At dawn the following day, the procession of more than seventy Turkish ships, tied to wheeled cradles, were dragged ashore. Teams of oxen were harnessed to the bows of the ships and squads of men helped push and pull along the sides. Slowly the ships creaked up over the ridges, to the eerie accompaniment of fifes and drums. In each galley the sails were fully hoisted, ready for sea, and the oarsmen sat at their places and pulled their oars through the air to a beat given by officers who paced alongside. The sight of this monstrous flotilla lumbering down the slopes and slithering into the Golden Horn shocked the city's defenders.[53] As a result of this Turkish maneuver, the defenders' forces were thinned out. Now they

[53] Philip Sherrard and Editors of Time-Life Books, *Byzantium*, Great Ages of Man Series (NY: Time Inc., 1966), pp. 168, 169.

had to maintain a close watch over the sea walls, previously closed off to enemy ships by the floating boom.[54]

Many talented Italians were entrusted with key positions throughout the city. In addition to the Italians, Cardinal Isidore of Russia guarded the district of Kynegesion with 200 archers paid by the pope. The Grand Duke Loukas Notaras took charge of the Petrion district. Notaras, as an anti-unionist, however, came into conflict with Giustiniani regarding strategy. Some churchmen protested the union with Rome and demanded that the emperor dismiss the papal legate, Cardinal Isidore; but the emperor avoided their complaints.

The remainder of the citizenry was arranged and stationed appropriately, fulfilling various tasks. Orders were issued to monks, priests, clerics, and other servants of the church to distribute themselves throughout the city and to conduct services unceasingly for the salvation of the city.[55] Since the imperial treasury was empty, salaries for the soldiers were provided when the emperor requisitioned Church holy vessels and dedicatory offerings to God. They were melted down for coins.

The defenders then put into action their plan of igniting enemy ships with Greek fire. They would have been successful if the traitorous Faiuzo, a Genoese, had not made known the secret plan to the Turks. The sultan, therefore, captured about forty young Greek and Italian sailors and executed them. The emperor, out of sadness, ordered the execution by hanging of 260 Turkish prisoners. This naval disaster touched off riots and fighting between the Genoese and the Venetians in the city. One group blamed the other for incompetence. It was necessary for Emperor Constantine to intervene and put a stop to the quarrel.[56]

Mehmet was not in the least convinced that the Genoese ships were merely merchant ships. He shot at the houses so he might continue, unobstructed, to bombard the vessels. It was a miracle that even after more than 130 missiles, no other vessel was hit and no one on board was killed. The houses

---

[54] Doukas, Ch. 38, 5 ff. A marginal note in the diary of the Venetian Nicolo Barbaro [*Diary of the Siege of Constantinople 1453*, trans. by J. R. Jones (NY: Exposition Press, Inc., 1969), p. 56] states that a Christian engineer was responsible for the ingenious plan. For a Turkish description of the operation, see Tursun Beg, op. cit., p. 35.

[55] Melissenos, pp. 110, 111. The Byzantine historian, courtier and diplomat, George Sphrantzes (1401-1477), recorded this chapter of history in his work, entitled "A Chronicle, 1401-1477" ("Chronicon Minus") in *The Fall of the Byzantine Empire*, trans. from the Greek by Marios Philippides, p. 142, n. 26.

[56] Melissenos, pp. 112, 113.

in the city were destroyed, but no one was killed, except one woman who was felled by a loose stone from the walls.[57]

It was the 24th of May, in the year 1453, when whispers circulated that the sultan was preparing his most serious attack, by land and sea for the 29th of May. The fortifications were repaired in countless ways. A rumor then went about the enemy camp that the Italian fleet and the cavalry and infantry of the Hungarian Governor Janos Hunyadi were on the way to aid the city and her defenders.[58] Mehmet and his men feared the worst. Fear gripped them, and they lost their confidence. They could not understand how their vast army, having command over land and sea, had accomplished nothing after so many days. After numerous attacks to the walls with their diverse engines, forces, and ladders, they were still thrust back and suffered heavy casualties.

Then, there were many portents at that time. A poor forecast was seen in a thick cloud that covered the capital. This was interpreted to mean that God was abandoning the city. With spirits very lowered in the capital, a last appeal was made to the Theotokos. Her holiest icon was carried on the shoulders of the faithful round the streets of the city. Everyone who could be spared from the walls would join in the procession. As the procession slowly moved, the icon suddenly slipped off the platform on which it was borne aloft and fell to the ground. When men rushed to raise it up, it seemed as though it were made of lead. Only with extreme difficulty did they manage to lift it. After this, the procession continued until a thunderstorm burst on the city. It was almost impossible for the participants to stand outside against the hail. Torrential rains fell so that whole streets were flooded and children were nearly swept away. By necessity the procession was abandoned.[59] Divine displeasure was also seen when unusual thunderstorms, heavy showers, and hail descended upon the city, further lowering the morale of the defenders.[60] Makarios Melissenos records that every night a fire descended from the sky, stood over the city, and enveloped her with light all night long. Some interpreted this sign as God's wrath upon the city, while others interpreted it as a sign of God's protection. The sultan, however, construed it as a bad sign for his men. They even decided upon lifting the siege and departing. On the 25th of May, the sultan made a proposal for peace. He would spare the city on condition that an annual tribute

[57] Ibid., p. 113.

[58] Doukas [Ch. 38, 13] believes that Hunyadi had wished the destruction of the Byzantine Empire.

[59] Runciman, *The Fall of Constantinople 1453*, p. 121; Donald M. Nicol, *The Last Centuries of Byzantium 1261-1453* (NY: St. Martin's Press, 1972), p. 406.

[60] Vacalopoulos, p. 197.

be paid; alternatively, the citizens could have free passage to safety if they gave up their city. Both offers of Mehmet were rejected.[61]

On the night before their scheduled departure, the heavenly sign descended in its customary manner but did not envelop the city. The light appeared to be distant, and then it scattered quickly and vanished at once. This filled the sultan and his court with malignant joy. They interpreted the sign, saying, "Allah has now abandoned the Christians forever!" Mehmet then ordered his men to wash seven times, so that purified they could pray to Allah for victory. Mehmet then addressed his men. Among many things, he said, "Recall the promises of our prophet concerning fallen warriors in the Koran: the man who dies in combat shall be transported bodily to Paradise and shall dine with Mohammed in the presence of women, handsome boys, and virgins." He then promised that, if the city fell, he would double their salaries. He also assured them that, for three days, he would permit them to loot and keep all the garments and the gold and silver vessels. He pledged that he would allow the enslavement of men and women of all ages. The men then shouted, *La ilaha; Muhammad rasulullah*, meaning, "There is only one Allah and Mohammed is his prophet." The roar could be heard clear into the city, but no one within knew what was happening.[62]

The handful of defenders held out with desperate courage to stave off what now appeared to them to be the inevitable end. Their faith was renewed by services at night in the churches and Emperor Constantine's unquenchable resolve in battle, setting an example to his subjects. Though many severe attacks were beaten back, after seven weeks of ceaseless bombardment, the walls of the beleaguered city showed serious breaches. The defenders worked to repair shattered defenses of the great city, with its fourteen-mile wall, wide moat, and numerous towers.

The end was near. It was Monday, the 28th of May. With the knowledge that the crisis was upon them, soldiers and citizens overlooked their quarrels. While men were on the walls to repair the shattered defenses, Emperor Constantine ordered the priests, high clerics, monks, and women and children, to enter a procession and exhibit the holy and revered icons. Though the Turkish camp was quiet, the bells of the city rang, while wooden gongs sounded as icons and relics were brought out upon the shoulders of the faithful. As they carried them through the streets and along the length of the walls, they paused to bless, with the icons' presence, those spots of greatest damage. A

[61] Sherrard, p. 169.

[62] Melissenos, pp. 117-120.

throng of Greeks and Italians followed, and they sang hymns and repeated, "Lord, have mercy." The emperor joined the procession.[63]

Evening was fast approaching and crowds were hastening toward the Church of Hagia Sophia. During the services of the past five months, no pious Greek Orthodox Christian stepped through that church's portals, defiled by Latins and renegades. However, on the eve of the commemoration of Saint Theodosia (the 29th of May), on the last night of the city's freedom, clergy and congregation, whatever they might feel about union, came together for a final liturgical office in Hagia Sophia, realizing that the Florentine Union had saved neither them nor Byzantium. Having put aside all bitterness, barely a citizen, except those watching the walls, stayed away from this desperate service of intercession. Those priests who maintained that union with Rome was a grave sin now came to the altar to serve with unionists. The cardinal was there, and beside him were bishops who would never acknowledge his authority. All came to confession, so they might take communion, not caring whether Orthodox or Papist administered it. As the golden mosaics glimmered in the light of a thousand lamps and candles, and the priests in their splendid vestments moved in solemn rhythm, it was at this moment in time that there was a pitiful and ignominious union in the Church of Hagia Sophia.[64]

All these weeks after countless assaults by the Turks, the defenders, by God's mercy, held the city, to the point where the sultan had decided to abandon the project. The last few days, however, marked a turning point for the anti-unionist defenders. After the majority succumbed to union, they betrayed Orthodoxy and God's protection. The Monk Gennadios (George Scholarios, the future patriarch that year), took no part in the ceremonies, for when the Turks were at the gates, Gennadios fled toward Adrianople. Then, every man of fighting age returned to his post. Women, nuns among them, also hastened to the walls. They helped bring up stones and beams to strengthen the defenses, and pails of water to refresh the other defenders.

Before the early morning light, the Turks mounted their assault. On the land side, the Turkish plan of operation was to divide the sultan's forces into three sections. The first, designed to wear the defenders down, consisted of ill-equipped Turkish irregulars, including Slavs, Greeks, and Hungarians. The second consisted of Mehmet's Anatolian regiments commanded by Ishak Pasha. The third section was the nucleus of the enemy army, the Janissary regiments.[65] The defenders resisted bravely and pushed the enemies from the

[63] Runciman, *The Fall of Constantinople 1453*, p. 130.

[64] Ibid., p. 131; Sherrard, *Byzantium*, loc. cit.

[65] The Janissary regiments had the reputation of being one of the best army in the field, skilled in the use of the lance, the dagger, and the curved sword. The word in Turkish, (continued...)

walls; they, also, destroyed some war engines and equipment. The assault by land and sea lasted for two hours, yet somehow the defenders prevailed. Rocks and heavy boulders were thrown from the city walls, killing many of the sons of Hagar. Some were burned with the liquid fire, others were dispersed with catapults and arrows. Many of the sultan's men wished to fall back, but the sultan's military police beat them back with iron clubs and whips. Who can narrate the voices, the cries of the wounded, and the lamentation on both sides? The shouts and din went beyond the boundaries of heaven.[66] The emperor, mounted on his horse, encouraged and exhorted the people to fight.

Constantine Palaiologos

The Janissaries of Mehmet II finally broke through the fortifications of Constantinople. The Janissary Hasan led thirty of his cohorts toward the walls, joined by many others. When the infidel forces were on the walls, the defenders were put to flight. They abandoned the outer walls and retreated to the inside ones through the gate, trampling over one another. The emperor kept fighting bravely, and many followed his example. After the Turks scaled the walls, they dispersed the defenders within the inner walls with missiles, bolts, arrows, and stones. Many of the Christians fought to the end. Refusing enslavement, they deemed death preferable to life. Emperor Constantine XI, at forty-nine years old, fought on to the end. He was slain fighting, just as he desired.[67] The city of Constantinople was taken on Tuesday, the 29th day of May, in the year 1453, about two and a half hours after dawn. The Byzantines could hardly believe that their God-guarded city had fallen into the hands of the infidel. The Turks were now everywhere. The

---

[65](...continued)
yeni ceri, means "new army." They were recruited from an early age as a levy of male children from Christian families. Converted to Islam, the children lived a rigid military life. By the 15th C., the Janissary regiments comprised the only regular army of the Ottoman Turks.

[66] Melissenos, p. 126.

[67] A detailed account of Constantine XI's final moments is not known. What is certain is that he perished near the Gate of Saint Romanos; see Doukas, p. 314, n. 289. The Turks claim that the emperor, while fleeing to the Golden Horn, was decapitated by their militiamen; see Tursun Beg's account, pp. 36, 37.

defenders of the Golden Horn fled—first Cardinal Isidore, disguised as a beggar, and, finally, the Venetian commanders.[68]

For three days and nights, the sultan allowed his men to plunder the city. The Turks seized and enslaved every person who came their way, and those that resisted were put to death. The ground was covered with heaps of corpses. There were all sorts of lamentations emanating from rows of enslaved noble ladies, virgins, and nuns. Many had been dragged by the Turks—by either their headgear, or hair, or braids—out of the shelter of churches. Children could be heard crying. By mid-morning the slaughter ceased: live prisoners were a profitable commodity.

Property of priceless value, works of art, precious manuscripts, holy icons and ecclesiastical treasures were destroyed. The Turks did not shudder to trample over the holy Mysteries, which poured all over the ground. Precious vessels were passed from hand to hand, while some were broken. Sacred icons that were decorated with gold, silver, and precious stones were stripped, cast to the earth, and then kicked. Wooden decorations in the churches were pulled down and turned into couches and tables. The enemy then arrayed their horses with priestly garments of silk embroidered with golden threads. Some vestments were used as tablecloths. Holy vessels were stripped of their precious pearls. Sacred relics were strewn about.

The Church of Hagia Sophia was crowded with people seeking sanctuary, and praying for a miracle. It was not long before the doors were battered down, trapping the worshippers. The old and infirm were killed on the spot, but most were tied or chained together. Veils and scarves were torn off women, serving as ropes. Many beautiful maidens and youths were nearly torn apart as their captors quarreled over them. A long procession was then made of tightly bound people being dragged off to the solders' bivouacs, there to be fought over again. The priests, however, continued chanting at the altar, until they were apprehended. The Turks then made the famous holy church a place of feasting. The inner sanctum was converted into a dining area. The holy altar supported food and wine. There also the heathen were employed in the enactment of their perversions with Constantinopolitan women, virgins, and children.

Lamentation and weeping could be heard in every house. There was screaming in the crossroads and sorrow in all churches, with the groaning of men and the shrieking of women. There was unprecedented looting, enslavement, separation, and rape. No place remained unsearched and untouched. Even gardens and houses were probed and excavated to yield any possible

---

[68] Jean DeFrasne, *Stories of the Byzantines*, p. 176.

hidden wealth. Mehmet II then made his solemn entry into the city, and it became the capital of the Ottoman Empire.

During the centuries that followed under Turkish rule, the Greeks, Bulgarians, and Serbians regarded their Orthodoxy as the expression of their spiritual and national individuality. Orthodoxy is what preserved them from being engulfed by the Turkish deluge. It became a time of martyrdom. The beauty of the Church did not perish before a sultan's sword. The earthly empire fell, but the spiritual empire endures. Saint Nectarios, Bishop of Pentapolis (1846-1920), writes: "Orthodoxy is our treasure, our priceless pearl....Orthodoxy is our light that guides us. If we were ever to lose this treasure, this light, then we would be scattered to the ends of the earth like dust."

The Ark

Through the intercessions of Thy Saints,
O Christ God, have mercy on us. Amen.

On the 30th of May, the holy Church commemorates our venerable Father ISAAKIOS or ISAKIOS the Confessor, Hegumen of the Monastery of the Dalmatons.[1]

Isaakios, our holy father, was a Syrian by birth. He flourished during the reign of Emperor Valens (364-378)[2] and afterward. At the time of Valens, the Arian heresy prevailed everywhere. The churches of the Orthodox had been closed, to the lamentation and mourning of all the faithful. In the year 376, Valens arranged for a large number of Visigoths, wishing to escape the Huns, to settle in Thrace. The operation to settle multitudes of Visigoths was seriously bungled with the lack of food supplies. Some unscrupulous Roman officials, left in charge of the population transfer of the Visigoths, took advantage of the situation to their own profit. The Visigoths, hungry and disappointed, began pillaging the Thracian countryside. Valens swiftly left Antioch in order to engage them in battle. During the final year of Valens' life (378), a powerful army of barbarian Goths had massed on the Danube River. They were poised to strike Constantinople. Valens gathered his army and marched against them.

At that time, Saint Isaakios was living in the east. He was informed of all that occurred. He came to Constantinople, where he preserved his ascetic regime and lived as a solitary. He met the emperor, even as the latter was marching off to war. Isaakios addressed him, saying, "O emperor, whither goest thou? Shalt thou fight against God or take Him as thine ally? It is God Himself Who has permitted these barbarians to rise up against thee. Thou needest not look far or long for the reason. Thou hast stirred many tongues to blaspheme Him. Thou hast driven out His worshippers from their sacred precincts. Cease this campaigning and there shall be an end to the war. Give back to the rational flocks of Christ their excellent shepherds. Then shalt thou see how thou canst gain a victory without trouble. If thou shouldest do otherwise and continue persecuting Jesus, thou shalt learn by experience how

---

[1] That which is known about Saint Isaakios is left to us by Theodoretos of Kyros in his work, entitled *Ecclesiastical History*, at the end of his fourth book, which the present *Synaxarion* has borrowed and revised. A special service was composed (which is still unpublished) by an anonymous author. It is extant in the codices of Kafsokalyvia on Mount Athos, as well as two other texts, according to the notes of Sophronios Efstratiades [*Hagiologion*, p. 225]: the Parisian Codices 1566 (by George) and 1574 (by Germanos). The memory of Saint Isaakios is also commemorated by the holy Church on the 3rd of August, together with Dalmatios and Faustus.

[2] Valens of Pannonia had been a low-ranking army officer during the reigns of Julian and Jovian. He campaigned against the Persians, causing him to spend much time in Antioch. He had been a Christian but, possibly, had been swayed toward Arianism by his wife. This persuasion instigated a persecution against the Orthodox. He was not popular and was scorned for his poor education and scanty knowledge of Greek.

hard it is for thee to kick against the goads![3] It shall come to pass that thou shalt never again see thy city and that thou shalt bring thine army to destruction." Valens, hearing these reproofs, was in a passion when he rejoined, "I shall come back; and I will kill thee, and so exact punishment for thy lying prophecy." But Isaakios was not dismayed by the threat. He rather said, "If what I utter should prove false, then slay me." The emperor remained stubborn. He refused to listen further, considering the saint's words as nonsense.

Saint Isaakios

Isaakios did not withdraw. He returned the following day. He, again, urged Valens that the churches of the Christians ought to be reopened. "If thou

---

[3] Acts 26:14.

wilt do this," he said to Valens, "thou shalt emerge victorious against the enemy." But again the emperor scorned the saint and continued with his preparations for war. On the third day, the saint appeared for a third time before Valens. On this occasion, the holy monk held the emperor's horse by the reins. He varied his manner of speech: at times, he spoke in an admonishing tone and at other times in an imploring voice. As Isaakios addressed the emperor, they came upon a deep precipice that was overspread with sharp thorns. Valens ordered his men to cast the holy man into those prickly bushes.

As the saint fell on the thorns, he thought he had fallen on bedding made of soft feathers. For this deliverance, he gave thanks to the Lord. Behold, there had appeared two beautiful men garbed in white raiment![4] It was they who bore aloft the saint. Isaakios emerged from that chasm unscathed. They delivered him, in the twinkling of an eye, and transported him before the emperor who was galloping hard into the marketplace. When the emperor clapped his eyes on Isaakios, he was astonished and exclaimed to his companions, "Is not he the one whom we cast into that fearful precipice further back?" Isaakios said to the emperor, "Open the churches, I beseech thee. If thou shouldest do this, thou wilt return triumphant from the war. If thou shouldest act contrariwise, know this: that when the war is waged against the barbarians, thou wilt flee with thy companions and hide, lying on straw and chaff from the threshing floor, where thou wilt be burned alive by the barbarians." Admittedly, the superstitious emperor was appalled and terrified by this prediction, yet he did not disdain the saint any less. Valens was foolish and impetuous. He had Isaakios seized and handed over to two soldiers, named Satornicus and Victor. Valens charged them to carefully guard the monk until his return from the war, at which time he boasted that he would repay the compliment by subjecting Isaakios to a death by fire. The saint remarked, "If thou wert to return from the war safe and sound, then it was not God Who had spoken to me."

Theodoretos adds that another, besides Saint Isaakios, also forewarned the emperor. A zealous hierarch of all the cities of Scythia, named Vrettanio, also admonished Valens. Vrettanio was distinguished by various virtues. This bishop's soul was fired with enthusiasm. He protested against the corruption of doctrines, and the emperor's lawless attacks upon the saints. As the Prophet David, he cried, "And I spoke of Thy testimonies before kings, and I was not ashamed [Ps. 118:46]."

Valens, however, spurned these excellent counselors. He deployed his troops to join the battle, while he himself sat waiting in a hamlet for the victory. His troops could not withstand the onslaught of the barbarians' charge.

---

[4] They were probably the Archangels Michael and Gabriel, as they appeared to others in the same manner.

They turned tail and were slain one after another as they fled. What a spectacle, indeed, to see Romans fleeing at full speed and the barbarians chasing them with all their might! When Valens learned of his army's defeat, he hid away in the village where he lay. But even there, the barbarians came and set the place afire. Together with that village, they burned the enemy of piety who concealed himself in a barn for chaff. Thus, in this present life, Valens was made to remit the penalty of his errors.

This took place on the 9th day of August, in the year 378. It would be a day long and fatally memorable in the annals of the empire. Valens' legions had sallied forth from their entrenched camp under the walls of Adrianople. After an eight-mile march under a hot August sun, they came in sight of the barbarian vanguard behind a wall of wagons. The line of wagons encircled the host of Goths. The Roman soldiers—hot, thirsty, and weary—only half understood that negotiations were ended and the battle had begun. Though they fought at a terrible disadvantage, yet they did not fight ill. The infantry on the left wing appeared to have pushed back the Goths and penetrated their wall of wagons. But the Roman infantry, for reasons not known, did not receive the customary cover of cavalry. Thus, that Roman wing was crowded into a very narrow patch of earth. They could not properly use their spears to any advantage. Instead, they proved an easy mark for Gothic bowmen. The Romans fell in dense masses under Gothic arrows. Then the whole weight of the Goths shifted against the Roman center and right. Evening was then drawing near. The utterly routed Romans were rushing in disorderly flight from the fatal battlefield. The night, dark and moonless, may have protected some, but more met their death rushing blindly over a rugged and unknown country.[5]

In the meantime, Valens had sought shelter with some of his soldiers from two regiments, the Lancearii and Mattiarii. They appeared unmoved in the midst of the ruin. Not before long, their ranks, also, were broken. Some of their bravest officers had fallen around Valens. The emperor, consequently, joined the common soldiers in their headlong flight. Valens was suddenly struck by a Gothic arrow. He collapsed to the ground, but was carried off by some of the eunuchs and bodyguards who still accompanied him. They brought

[5] It is also said that when Valens had accused General Trajan of being defeated by the Goths because of cowardice, he boldly replied, "I was not defeated, O emperor, but thou hast forfeited the victory by opposing God, and by provoking Him to side with the barbarians; for as He was persecuted by thee, He joined their ranks. It is God Who decides victory, and it is granted to those who are led by God. Is this not so?" He then added, "Which of the churches didst thou not persecute? Into whose hands didst thou entrust them?" Aritheus and Victor, the two generals, concurred with his testimony. Taken from note 1, p. 679, of *The Great Synaxaristes*, 5th ed., s.v. "May 30th."

him to a nearby peasant's barn and cottage. The Goths, ignorant of his identity, but eager to strip the gaily-clothed guardsmen, surrounded the structure and attempted in vain to burst in the doors. The Goths clambered to the rooftop, attempting to smoke out the trapped inmates. They, instead, set fire to the building. The emperor, eunuchs, and guardsmen perished in the flames. Only one of the bodyguards survived by climbing through one of the blazing windows and falling into the hands of the barbarians. He told them, when it was too late, what a prize they had missed in their cruel eagerness—nothing less than the emperor of Rome.[6]

The remainder of the emperor's forces returned from the war. They attempted to mock and frighten the man of God, our holy Father Isaakios, declaring, "Prepare to defend thyself against the emperor, who comes to carry out all that he said about thee." The saint answered, "It is now seven days that my nostrils have been filled with the odor of the stench of his bones, which were completely consumed by the fire."[7] As the soldiers heard this, they were aghast at his clairvoyance. None but God could have divulged all that had happened. Those Roman soldiers went to their knees before the holy man, beseeching him to remain permanently in Constantinople. The saint answered, "Permit me the space of seven days to entreat God if this is His will."

Isaakios besought God in order to learn His will. He was divinely informed to remain in Constantinople. He relayed this to the ones who begged him to sojourn among them. Thereafter, the citizens competed with each other to erect a monastery for the saint's habitation. One Constantinopolitan, named Satornilos, was more eager than the rest to build a monastery. He carried out the endeavor, in a location that was stately and suitable, outside the Constantinian walls in the eastern part of the Psamathia quarter. The Dalmatou or Dalmatiou Monastery was thus founded in 382.[8] The saint took up his abode

---

[6] Ecclesiastical historians for generations were keen on pointing out the moral of the story of Valens: he who had seduced the whole Gothic nation into the heresy of Arius, and thus caused them to suffer the punishment of everlasting fire, was himself by those very Goths burned alive on that terrible day—the 9th of August. See Thomas Hodgkin's *The Dynasty of Theodosius*, p. 97. See also Roberts, Alexander and Donaldson, James, in Nicene and Post-Nicene Fathers, 2nd Ser., Vol. III (Oak Harbor, WA: Logos Research Systems, Inc.) 1997.

[7] The demise of Valens caused his nephew, Gratian, the western Roman emperor (367-383), to perceive God's judgment upon the Arians. Under the influence of Saint Ambrose of Milan (commemorated the 7th of December), Gratian came to be an avid supporter of Orthodoxy. He appointed Theodosios I as ruler in the east (379). He opened all the churches of Christ.

[8] Now after Saint Isaakios' repose, ca. 406, he was succeeded by his disciple Dalmatos (Dalmatios), a former officer of the imperial guard, after whom the monastery came (continued...)

therein and glorified God. Those who had pleaded with the saint donated victuals and large tracts of land to the new monastery. Numerous Christians gathered at that bastion of Orthodoxy and became monastics. All of Father Isaakios' disciples studied to be cultivated by this teacher and led by this shepherd in working the commandments of God. His incorporeal mode of life made him the cherished guide and rule for monks. Isaakios was often visited by Emperor Theodosios, who took counsel with him. Other monasteries, under his influence, were also founded. He was renowned for his care of the poor, from whom he provided the necessities of life through his connections with affluent faithful in the city.

Now, on the 26th day of February, in the year 398, Saint John Chrysostom became Archbishop of Constantinople (398-404).[9] At that time there was at least one monastery, that of Abbot Isaakios, and one convent, that of Abbess Olympia.[10] There were many monks and virgins not living in communities, but alone or in family dwellings inside the city. Saint John did not approve of monks who were idle and unemployed. He wished them to stay off the city streets, unless they had good reason to be out of their monastery. Saint John did not want to see reproach brought upon the angelic life and that honorable vocation brought into disrepute. Many monks were disturbed at this censure, while others approved. Many monastics were accustomed to roaming the streets and visiting friends in private houses. Those who protested took their complaint to the holy Isaakios the Syrian and hermit, previously of the Syrian desert. He, as we know, was an acclaimed confessor of the Faith who fought the Arians and suffered imprisonment. At first he did not complain about Saint John's restrictions upon the monks' freedom, but later he made an open complaint at the Synod of the Oak instigated by Pope Theophilos of Alexandria. The two saints, John and Isaakios, did clash over the issue, though not much mention is made of it. Theophilos knew how to manipulate and insinuate. Thus, he managed to lure both Isaakios and other monastics to his cause against Saint John. Afterward, when Patriarch John was recalled from exile, his return brought joy to some and terror to others. When Theophilos learned that Chrysostom still maintained his demand for a new synod to judge between him and his accusers, under the cover of night he raced to the harbor and embarked on a ship bound for Alexandria. As for Saint Isaakios, he withdrew from public life and Church affairs.

---

[8](...continued)
to be named. Dalmatos was distinguished in his fight against the Nestorians. Dalmatou Monastery later became a stronghold for the iconodules, for which it was persecuted.

[9] Saint John is commemorated by the holy Church on the 13th of November.

[10] Saint Olympia the deaconess is commemorated by the holy Church on the 25th of July.

Saint Isaakios' repose was foretold to him by God. In the year 406, while anticipating his departure to the Lord, he gathered all the brethren and catechized them. Then he chose one of them, named Dalmatos, and assigned him as abbot in his stead. Thus, Saint Isaakios was translated to the Lord. Emperor Theodosios and the whole city mourned his departure. One of the spiritual children of the saint, a courtier named Aurelian, seized the body on the way to burial at the Monastery of the Dalmatons. Instead, the relics were interred in the crypt of the church, built by Aurelian, dedicated to Saint Stephen. The Dalmatons were dismayed but could not remonstrate with the courtier and his many soldiers. The superiors of Dalmatou Monastery, thereafter, received the title of archimandrite or exarch, which entitled the bearer of the title the supervision of the other monasteries in the city. Those who hastened to the saint's relics or prayed to him were freed from perils and diseases and demons, as an abundant flow of miracles were wrought by him.

On the 30th of May, the holy Church commemorates the holy Martyr NATALIOS, who was slain by the sword.

On the 30th of May, the holy Church commemorates the venerable BARLAAM (VARLAAM), who reposed in peace.[11]

On the 30th of May, the holy Church commemorates the holy Martyrs ROMANOS and TELETIOS, who were slain by the sword.

On the 30th of May, the holy Church commemorates the holy Martyr EFPLOS, who was wrapped in cowhide and burned under the sun.

On the 30th of May, the holy Church commemorates JOHN, King of the Persians, who was slain with knives in the hippodrome.[12]

Through the intercessions of Thy Saints,
O Christ God, have mercy on us. Amen.

---

[11] The Greek compilers of *The Great Synaxaristes* (in Greek) note that perhaps this is the same Barlaam who catechized Saint Ioasaph, King of India, who is commemorated by the holy Church on the 26th of August.

[12] The Life of Saint John is given in full within the Life of Saint Theodore of Edessa, commemorated by the holy Church on the 19th of July.

On the 31st of May, the holy Church commemorates the holy Martyr HERMEIAS the soldier of Comana in Cappadocia.[1]

Hermeias, the holy martyr, made his mark during the years of Antoninus Pius (138-161) and Marcus Aurelius (161-180).[2] Hermeias had served as a soldier for many years,[3] until he was elderly and white-haired. He was comely not only in the flesh but also in the spirit as he put away worldly things. While in the city of Comana of Cappadocia,[4] he was arrested upon

---

[1] A full divine office to Saint Hermeias, unpublished, is found in the Athonite Great Lavra under Codices Γ 19 and Θ 87.

[2] Slavic sources assign him to Antoninus' reign as does the Greek *Synaxarion*.

[3] It is unclear when and if he had been discharged from the army. The Greek compilers of *The Great Synaxaristes* (in Greek) question whether he served under the reign of Antoninus or his adoptive son and heir Aurelius, though the latter's full name was Imperator Caesar Marcus Aurelius Antoninus Augustus. During the reign of Antoninus, there were no major wars, but there was continuous fighting and unrest. In the first part of his reign, the decision was made to conquer southern Scotland. Hadrian's Wall was abandoned, and a new frontier defense was constructed forty miles to the north: the Antonine Wall. There were troubles, elsewhere, however, in Mauritania, then in Germany, and rebellions in Egypt, Judaea, and Greece. Later in his reign, there was combat with Dacians and Alans who threatened Danube provinces. During the reign of Marcus Aurelius, there were many campaigns on the Danube with Germanic invaders. There was fierce fighting on both the northern and eastern frontiers. The Parthian War was over control of Armenia. Roman soldiers brought back the plague with them. See C. Scarre's *Chronicle of the Roman Emperors*. Thus, whichever emperor he was under while in the military, Saint Hermeias certainly saw active service throughout his career.

[4] Comana of Cappadocia was surnamed Aurea or Chryse ("Golden"). The site lies at Shahr, a village in the Anti-Taurus on the upper course of the Sarus (Sihun), mainly Armenian, but surrounded by new settlements of Avshar Turkomans and Circassians. It was also important for its position on the road from Caesarea Cappadociae (Kayseri) to Melitene (Malatya), converted by the Emperor Septimius Severus (146-211) into the chief military road to the empire's eastern frontier. The extant remains at Shahr include a theater on the left bank of the river, a fine Roman doorway, and many inscriptions. The site of the great temple has not been satisfactorily identified. There are many traces of Severus' road, including a bridge at Kemer, and an immense number of milestones, some in their original positions, others in cemeteries. Another surname in epigraphy is Hieropolis, owing to a famous temple of the cult of Ma-Enyo. The latter was a variant of the great west Asian mother goddess, where celebrations included orgiastic rites. There was a sumptuous temple serviced by as many as six thousand temple servants of whom a considerable number were of the Persian race. Later, Comana was a suffragan of Melitene, the metropolis of Armenia Secunda. The ruins of Comana are visible ten miles northwest of Guksun (Cocussus), in the vilayet of Adana.

(continued...)

professing Jesus and upholding his belief in the Christian Faith. Hermeias was brought before Governor Sebastian. Since the old soldier laid aside earthly soldiery, he refused to offer sacrifice to the idols. With his denial of the pagan gods of perdition, the application of harsh tortures was the penalty for the soldier of Christ.

The first punishment involved the breaking of his jaw upon a face that was generally deemed fair. Close upon this brutal act, they flayed his facial flesh. This was followed by the uprooting of his teeth. Afterward, they lit a furnace into which the saint was cast. He was bedewed with the grace of the Spirit so that, after three days, the gallant martyr was still standing in the flames until he exited unharmed. Next, they contrived to put him to death by having him drink a deadly potion. The concoction was mixed by a magician, named Marus. The saint partook of the poisonous draft and suffered no ill effects. A second drink, more toxic, was prepared. This also failed to kill Hermeias. In the sequel, he not only survived the noxious goblet but also drew to the Faith of the Christ the very magician who formulated the lethal mixture. The magician also publicly confessed Jesus Christ, for which declaration he was swiftly beheaded. In this manner, he received the crown of martyrdom.

As for Hermeias, he was to suffer subsequent torments. He endured all the vehement pain and rending of his body as though someone else were suffering. With the use of rakes and combs, they severed and shivered his sinews and muscles. After a while, a cauldron of boiling oil was prepared. The martyr was thrown into that bubbling unction, but he emerged unscathed. From that moment, they began the operation of plucking out his eyes. During the gouging, he spoke calmly to Sebastian and said, "Thou mayest take the eyes of the flesh that used to look upon this world's vanity. But the eyes of my heart remain, clearly fixed upon the true light."

As if this excruciating torture were not enough, there ensued another punishment: he was suspended upside down for three days. In this position,

---

[4](...continued)

Another Comana, of the ancient city of Pontus, is said to have been colonized from Comana in Cappadocia. It stood on the river Iris (Tozanli Su or Yeshil Irmak). From its central position, it was a favorite emporium of Armenian and other merchants. It, too, had a temple of Ma and was surnamed Hierocaesarea. This town is today Gomenek, or Gomanak, a village southwest of Neocaesarea (Niksar), in the vilayet of Sivas. Saint Vasiliskos (commemorated the 22nd of May) was put to death at Comana and was buried there; Saint John Chrysostom (13th of November) was exiled and reposed there.

There is another Comana in Pamphylia Prima, suffragan of Side. Its true name is Conana, present-day Gunen, in the vilayet of Adana. *Encyclopaedia Britannica Deluxe Edition 2004 CD-ROM*, s.v. "Comana"; *Catholic Encyclopedia*, s.v. "Comana."

too, the martyr triumphed as he fixed his mind's eye heavenward upon God. When men were sent to confirm whether Hermeias had survived his wounds and hemorrhaging, they were blinded from terror at seeing him alive. The blind appealed to the martyr for help. He invited them to approach and then healed them in the name of our Savior. Since he continued to refuse worship to the pagan deities, the idolaters could no longer bear his heroic exploits and wonders. The governor, losing command of himself, with his own sword, dispatched Hermeias to the next life. The honorable head of Christ's warrior, Hermeias, was severed but crowned in the heavens. Christians secured his relics and gave him an honorable burial. His relics were known to work wonders.

Saint Hermeias

On the 31st of May, the holy Church commemorates the holy Martyr MARUS at Comana, the former magician in the time of Saint Hermeias, who was slain by the sword.

On the 31st of May, the holy Church commemorates the holy FIVE MEN MARTYRS of ASKALON, who were slain when dragged along the ground.

On the 31st of May, the holy Church commemorates the holy Martyrs EVSEVIOS and HARALAMBOS, who suffered martyrdom by fire.

Through the intercessions of Thy Saints,
O Christ God, have mercy on us. Amen.

May Bibliography

Non-English or Greek Sources

῾Ο Μέγας Συναξαριστὴς τῆς ᾽Ορθοδόξου ᾽Εκκλησίας (*The Great Synaxaristes of the Orthodox Church*). 5th ed. Volume 5. Athens, GR: Archimandrite Matthew Langes, Publisher, 1977.

Μηναῖον τοῦ Μαΐου (*Menaion of May*). S. Michael Saliveros A.E. Amarousion, GR.

Migne, J. P. *Patrologia Graeca*. Athens, GR: Kentron Paterikon Ekdoseon. Facsimile of the 1859 Paris edition.
———*P.G.* 26, *Saint Athanasios*, 1999.
———*P.G.* 59, *Saint John Chrysostom*, 1996.
———*P.G.* 60, *Saint John Chrysostom*, 1996.
———*P.G.* 61, *Saint John Chrysostom*, 1997.
———*P.G.* 73, *Saint Kyril of Alexandria*, 1993.
———*P.G.* 111, *Life of Saint Andrew, Fool for Christ*, 2001.

Νέον Μαρτυρολόγιον (*New Martyrologion*). Nikodemos the Hagiorite (1749-1809). 3rd ed. Athens, GR: Aster Publishing, Al. & E. Papademetriou, 1961.

\+ + +

Michalopoulos, Konstantine. *Meteora*. Kalambaka, GR: Kon. Michalopoulos, Pub.

῾Ο ῞Αγιος Νεομάρτυς Νικόλαος ὁ ἐκ Μετσόβου (The Holy New-martyr Nicholas of Metsovon). Compiled by Symeon G. Katsimpras. Ioannina, GR: Pnevmatikou Pharou, 1993.

῞Οσιος ᾽Ανδρέας ὁ διά Χριστόν Σαλός (*Saint Andrew, Fool for Christ*). 10th ed. Oropos, Attike, GR: Holy Monastery of the Paraclete, 1995.

The Septuagint Version. Greek and English. London: Samuel Bagster and Sons Ltd.

English Sources

A Greek-English Lexicon. Compiled by Henry George Liddell and Robert Scott. 9th ed. Oxford at the Clarendon Press, 1977.

Alexander, Archimandrite. "Saint Nilos' Posthumous Discourses." *The Orthodox Word*. Volume 4, Number 4(21). July-August 1968.

Andrew Simonopetritis (Haralampos Theophilopoulos), Hagiorite. *Holy Mountain: Bulwark of Orthodoxy and of the Greek Nation*. Translated by John-Electros Boumis. Athens, GR: Eptalofos Co., Ltd., 1967.

An Iconographer's Patternbook: The Stroganov Tradition. Translated and edited by Father Christopher P. Kelley from the original 1869 Moscow Edition. Torrance, CA: Oakwood Publications, 1992.

A Patristic Greek Lexicon. 12th ed. Edited by G. W. H. Lampe. Oxford at the Clarendon Press, 1995.

Axiotakis, Andreas S. *The New Monastery (Nea Moni) of Chios*. Translated by Despina Georganopoulou. Chios, 1982.

Babinger, Franz. *Mehmed the Conqueror and His Time*. Translated from the German by Ralph Manheim. Edited by William C. Hickman. Bollinger Series 96. Princeton: Princeton University Press, 1978.

Baker, G. P. *Constantine the Great and the Christian Revolution*. NY, NY: Cooper Square Press, 1992.

Brewer, David. *The Greek War of Independence*. Woodstock & NY: The Overlook Press, 2001.

Bury, J. B. *The Invasion of Europe by the Barbarians*. NY and London: W. W. Norton & Company, 2000.

Byzantium. Great Ages of Man Series. Philip Sherrard and Editors of Time-Life Books. NY: Time Inc., 1966.

Butler's Lives of the Saints. 4 Volumes. Edited, revised, and supplemented by Herbert J. Thurston and Donald Attwater. Westminster, MD: Christian Classics, 1981, repr.

Cavarnos, Constantine. *Saint Nikephoros of Chios*. Modern Orthodox Saints Series. Volume 4. Belmont, MA: Institute for Byzantine and Modern Greek Studies, 1976.

Christou, Pan. C. and Tom. M. Provatakis. *Athos*. Thessalonike, GR: Patriarchal Institute for Patristic Studies, 1970.

Cig, Kemal. "Rumeli Hisari." Istanbul: Net Turizim ve Ticaret, n.d.

Concise Oxford Dictionary of the Christian Church. Edited by E. A. Livingstone. Oxford/NY: Oxford University Press, 2000.

Craigie, Peter C., Page H. Kelley and Joel F. Drinkard, Jr. *Jeremiah 1-25*. Word Biblical Commentary. Volume 26. Waco, TX: Word Books, Pub., 1991.

Cummings, D. *The Rudder*. Chicago, IL: The Orthodox Christian Educational Society, 1957.

Day, Peter D. *The Liturgical Dictionary of Eastern Christianity*. Collegeville, MN: Michael Glazier Book, Liturgical Press, 1993.

DeFrasne, Jean. *Stories of the Byzantines*. Translated by Patricia Crampton NY: The World Publishing Company, 1966.

de Voragine, Jacobus. *The Golden Legend*. 4th ed. Two Volumes. Translated by William Granger Ryan. Princeton, NJ: Princeton University Press, 1995.

Diehl, Charles. *Byzantium: Greatness and Decline*. 9th ed. Translated from the French by Naomi Walford. New Brunswick, NJ: Rutgers University Press, 1957.
——*Byzantine Portraits*. Translated by Harold Bell. NY: Alfred A. Knopf, 1927.

Dionysius of Fourna. *The Painter's Manual*. Translated by Paul Hetherington. Redondo Beach, CA: Oakwood Publications, 1981, repr.

Doukas, Michael. *Decline and Fall of Byzantium to the Ottoman Turks*. Annotated and translated by H. J. Magoulias. Detroit, MI: Wayne State University Press, 1975.

Dvornik, Francis. *Byzantium and the Roman Primacy*. NY: Fordham University Press, 1966.

Elliott, Thomas George. *The Christianity of Constantine The Great*. Scranton, PA: University of Scranton Press, 1996.

Encyclopaedia Britannica. 1965 Edition and the 2004 Deluxe Edition CD-ROM.

Eusebius. *The Church History*. The Nicene and Post-Nicene Fathers of the Christian Church. Second Series. Volume I. 2nd edition. Translated by the Rev. Arthur Cushman McGiffert, Ph.D. Grand Rapids, MI: Wm. B. Eerdmans Pub., February 1961, repr.
——*The Life of Constantine*. Vol. I. 2nd edition. Revised translation by Ernest Cushing Richardson, Ph.D. Grand Rapids, MI: Wm. B. Eerdmans Pub., February 1961, repr.

Evagrius. *Ecclesiastical History: A History of the Church from A.D. 431 to A.D. 594*. London: Samuel Bagster and Sons, 1846, reprinted of late by Kessinger Publishing in the US (May 2005).

Garidis, Miltos, and Athanasios Paliouras. *Monasteries of the Island of Ioannina: Painting*. Ioannina, 1993.

George, Andreas C. *In the Footsteps of Saint Nicholas*. Astoria, NY: Seaburn, 2005.

Goodwin, Jason. *Lords of the Horizons*. NY: Picador, 1998.

Guettee, Abbe. *The Papacy*. NY: Minos Publishing, n.d.

Haldon, John. *Warfare, State and Society in the Byzantine World 565-1204*. NY and London: Routledge, 1999.

Kadas, Sotiris. *Mount Athos*. Translated by Louise Turner Athens: Ekdotike Athenon S.A., 1980.

Karpodini-Dimitriadi, E. *The Greek Islands*. Athens: Ekdotike Athenon S.A., 1987.

Keil, C. F., and F. Delitzsch. *Jeremiah, Lamentations*. Commentary on the Old Testament. 1st ed. Volume 8. Translated by David Patrick. Peabody, MA: Hendrickson Publishers, 1989.

Kittredge, George Lyman, and Frank Edgar Farley. *An Advanced English Grammar*. Boston, MA: Ginn and Company, The Athenaeum Press, 1913.

Kousoulas, Dimitrios G. *The Life and Times of Constantine the Great*. Danbury, CT: Rutledge Books, Inc., 1997.

Lang, David Marshall. *The Georgians*. Volume 51 of Ancient Peoples and Places Series. Bristol, UK: Thames and Hudson, 1966.

Latourette, Kenneth Scott. *A History of Christianity*. Volume 1. NY: Harper & Row, 1975.

Lockyer, Dr. Herbert. *All the Parables of the Bible*. Grand Rapids, MI: Zondervan Publishing House, 1963.

Logos Electronic Edition of The Writings of the Early Church Fathers, extracted from the 38-volumes of the Eerdman's Reprint of the Edinburgh edition. Bellingham, WA: Logos Research Systems, Inc., 1997.

Mango, Cyril. *The Homilies of Photius, Patriarch of Constantinople*. Cambridge, MA: Harvard University Press, Dumbarton Oaks Studies Three, 1958.

Maurice's Strategikon: Handbook of Byzantine Military Strategy. Translated by George T. Dennis. Philadelphia, PA: University of Pennsylvania Press, 1984.

Melissenos (Melissourgos), Makarios. *The Fall of the Byzantine Empire*. Translated by Marios Philippides. Amherst, MA: The University of Massachusetts Press, 1980.

Meyendorff, John. *A Study of Gregory Palamas*. Translated by George Lawrence. London, UK: The Faith Press, 1964.

Nicol, Donald M. *The Last Centuries of Byzantium 1261-1453*. NY: Saint Martin's Press, 1972.

Nikolau, Timothy. "Great-martyr Christopher." *Orthodox Life*. Vol. 42, No. 3. Translated from the Spanish. May-June 1992.

Nikonanos, Nikos. *Meteora: A Complete Guide to the Monasteries and Their History*. Translated by L. Turner. Athens, GR: George A. Christopoulos, John C. Bastias, Pub.; Ekdotike Athenon S.A., 1987.

Obolensky, Dimitri. *Six Byzantine Portraits*. NY: Oxford University Press, 1988.

Ostrogorsky, George. *History of the Byzantine State*. New Brunswick, NJ: Rutgers University Press, 1957.

Palladius: Dialogue on the Life of Saint John Chrysostom. Ancient Christian Writers. Number 45. Translated and edited by Robert T. Meyer. NY, NY: Newman Press, n.d.

Papadopoulou, Barbara N. *The Monasteries of the Island of Ioannina*. Ioannina: Holy Monastery of Eleousa, 2004.

Provatakis, Theocharis. *Mount Athos*. Translated by Paul Markouisos. Thessalonike, GR: John Rekos and Co. Pub. House, n.d.

Provatakis, Theocharis M. *Meteora: History of Monasticism at Meteora*. Athens, GR: Michalis Toubis S.S., 1983.

Psellus, Michael. *Fourteen Byzantine Rulers*. Translated by E. R. A. Sewter. NY/UK: Penguin Books, 1966.

Romanides, Protopresbyter John. *An Outline of Orthodox Patristic Dogmatics*. Rollinsford, NH: Orthodox Research Institute.

Rufinus of Aquileia. *The Church History of Rufinus of Aquileia*. Translated by Philip Amidon. NY: Oxford University Press, 1997.

Runciman, Steven. *The Byzantine Theocracy*. NY: Cambridge University Press, 1977.
——*The Eastern Schism*. London: Oxford University Press, 1956, repr.
——*The Fall of Constantinople 1453*. NY: Cambridge University Press, 1988, repr.
——*The Great Church in Captivity*. NY: Cambridge University Press, 1968.

Saints Kyril and Methody, Evangelizers of the Slavs. Juneau, AK: Saints Kyril and Methody Society.

Scarre, Chris. *Chronicle of the Roman Emperors*. NY/London: Thames & Hudson, 2001, repr.

Shaw, Stanford J. *History of the Ottoman Empire and Modern Turkey*. Volume 1. NY: Cambridge University Press, 1998.

Socrates Scholasticus. *The Ecclesiastical History*. The Nicene and Post-Nicene Fathers. Volume II. Edited by Philip Schaff, D.D., LL.D., and Henry Wace, D.D. Grand Rapids, MI: Wm. B. Eerdmans Publishing Co., November 1983, repr.

Sozomen, Salaminus Hermias. *The Ecclesiastical History*. The Nicene and Post-Nicene Fathers of the Christian Church. Second Series. Volume II. Revised by Chester D. Hartranft. Edited by Philip Schaff, D.D., LL.D. and Henry Wace, D.D. Grand Rapids, MI: Wm. B. Eerdmans Publishing Co., November 1983, repr.

Tachiaos, Anthony-Emil. N. *Cyril and Methodius of Thessalonica*. Crestwood, NY: Saint Vladimir's Seminary Press, 2001.

The Catholic Encyclopedia. New Advent CD-ROM. Kevin Knight, 2003.

The Chronicle of Theophanes. An English translation of *anni mundi* 6095-6305 (A.D. 602-813). Translated by Harry Turtledove. Philadelphia, PA: University of Pennsylvania Press, 1982.

The Chronicle of Theophanes Confessor. Translated by Cyril Mango and Roger Scott. Oxford, UK: Clarendon Press, 1997.

"The Dormition of Our Most Holy Lady." *The Orthodox Teachings of the Mother of God*. Moundsville, WV: Fr. Demetrios Serfes Publications.

The Epistle of Barnabas. The Apostolic Fathers, The Ante-Nicene Fathers. Volume I. Edited by the Rev. Alexander Roberts, D.D. and James Donaldson, LL.D. Grand Rapids, MI: Eerdmans Pub. Co., May 1987, repr.

The Evergetinos: A Complete Text. Translated and edited by Hieromonk Patapios, Bishop Auxentios, Constantine Kokenes, John V. Petropoulos, Rev. Gregory Telepneff. Volume II of The First Book (1991); Volume III of The First Book (1998); Volume IV of The First Book (1999). Etna, CA: Center for Traditionalist Orthodox Studies.

The Expositors Bible Commentary. Frank E. Goebelein, Gen. Ed. Grand Rapids, MI: Zondervan Publishing House, 1986.

The Life of the Virgin Mary, the Theotokos. 6th ed. Compilation and translation by Holy Apostles Convent. Buena Vista, CO: Holy Apostles Convent, December 2000.

The Lives of the Holy Apostles. 4th ed. Translated by Holy Apostles Convent and Reader Isaac E. Lambertsen. Buena Vista, CO: Holy Apostles Convent, 2001.

The Lives of the Holy Prophets. Compiled and translated by Holy Apostles Convent. Buena Vista, CO: Holy Apostles Convent, 1998.

The Lives of the Pillars of Orthodoxy. 3rd ed. Compilation and translation by Holy Apostles Convent. Buena Vista, CO: Holy Apostles Convent, November 2000.

Theodoret. *The Ecclesiastical History*. The Nicene and Post-Nicene Fathers. Second Series. Volume III. Edited by Philip Schaff, D.D., LL.D., and Henry Wace, D.D. Grand Rapids, MI: Wm. B. Eerdmans Publishing Co., February 1979, repr.

The Old Testament Pseudepigrapha. Volume 2. Edited by James H. Charlesworth. NY: Doubleday, 1985).

The Orthodox New Testament. 5th ed. Translated by Holy Apostles Convent and Dormition Skete. Buena Vista, CO: Holy Apostles Convent, 2005.

Theotekni, Sister. *Meteora: History, Art, Monastic Presence*. Translated by K. Koini-Moraitis. Athens, GR: G. Tsiveriotis Society, 1980.

The Oxford Dictionary of Byzantium. Alexander P. Kazhdan, Editor in Chief. NY and Oxford: Oxford University Press, 1991.

The Oxford Dictionary of the Christian Church. Edited by F. L. Cross and E. A. Livingstone. Oxford/NY: Oxford University Press, 1989, repr.

The Paradise of the Fathers. Translated by Ernest A. Wallis Budge. Two Volumes. Seattle, WA: Saint Nectarios Press, 1978, repr.

The Philokalia: The Complete Text. Translated from the Greek and edited by G.E.H. Palmer, Philip Sherrard, and Kallistos Ware. Vol. II. London: Faber and Faber, 1984 repr.

The Orthodox Psalter. Translated by Holy Apostles Convent from the Greek of *The Psalterion of the Prophet and King David*, of Apostolike Diakonia of the Church of Greece (1st ed., 1968; 3rd ed., 1981; and 11th ed., 2009). Buena Vista, CO, 2nd ed., 2012.

The Seven Ecumenical Councils. The Nicene and Post-Nicene Fathers of the Christian Church, Second Series. Volume XIV. Translated by Henry R. Percival, M.A., D.D. Edited by Philip Schaff, D.D., LL.D., and Henry Wace, D.D. Grand Rapids, MI: Wm. B. Eerdmans Pub. Co., November 1979, repr.

Toal, M. D., D.D. *The Sunday Sermons of the Great Fathers*. 3rd edition. Volume I. Chicago: Henry Regnery Co., 1964.

Tsougarakis, Dimitris. *The Life of Leontios Patriarch of Jerusalem: Text, Translation, Commentary*. The Medieval Mediterranean: Peoples, Economies and Cultures, 400-1453. Leiden/NY/Koln: E. J. Brill Academic Publishers, August 1993.

Tursan, Beg. *The History of Mehmed the Conqueror*. Text published in facsimile with English translation by H. Inalcik and R. Murphey. MN and Chicago: Bibliotheca Islamica I, 1978.

Vacalopoulos, Apostolos E. *The Greek Nation 1453-1669*. Translated from the Greek by Ian and Phania Moles. NJ: Rutgers University Press, 1976.

Velimirović, Bishop Nikolai. *The Prologue from Ochrid*. Translated by Mother Maria. Birmingham: Lazarica Press, 1986.

Vernezos, Ioannis. *Life and Recent Miracles of Saint John the Russian*. Translated by Anthoussa and Emmeleia Vernezos. Prokopi, Euboea, GR, 1999.

Vranos, Monk John. *The Illustrated Life of Saint John the Russian*. Wildwood, CA: Saint Xenia Skete, 1983.

Webster's Third New International Dictionary Unabridged. Springfield, MA: G. & C. Merriam Co., 1967.

Writings of the Holy Fathers in English

Saint Ambrose. *Concerning Repentance*; *Concerning Widows*; *Duties of the Clergy*; *Of the Christian Faith*; *On Belief in the Resurrection*. The Nicene and Post-Nicene Fathers. Second Series. Volume X. Translated by Rev. H. DeRomestin, M.A. Edited by Philip Schaff D.D., LL.D. and Henry Wace, D.D. Grand Rapids, MI: Wm. B. Eerdmans Pub. Co., August 1979, repr.

——*Letters*. The Fathers of the Church. Volume 26. Translated by Sister Mary Melchior Beyenka, O.P. Washington, D.C.: Catholic University Press of America (CUA), 1987, repr.

——*Hexameron*. The Fathers of the Church. Volume 42. Translated by John J. Savage. Washington, D.C.: CUA Press, 1985, repr.

——*Theological and Dogmatic Works*: *The Holy Spirit*; *The Mysteries*. The Fathers of the Church. Volume 44. Translated by Roy J. Deferrari, Ph.D. Washington, D.C.: CUA Press, 1987, repr.

——*Seven Exegetical Works: Joseph*; *The Patriarchs*; *The Flight from the World*; *Isaac, or the Soul*; *Prayer of Job and David*. The Fathers of the Church. Volume 65. Translated by Michael P. McHugh. Washington, D.C.: CUA Press, 1985, repr.

Saint Aphrahat. *Select Demonstrations*. The Nicene and Post-Nicene Fathers of the Christian Church. Second Series. Volume XIII. Translated by Rev. A. Edward Johnston, B.D. Edited by Philip Schaff, D.D., LL.D., and Henry Wace, D.D. Grand Rapids, MI: Wm. B. Eerdmans Pub., May 1976, repr.

Saint Athanasios. *Select Works and Letters*: *Four Discourses Against the Arians*; *On the Incarnation of the Word*; *Statement of Faith*; *To The Bishops of Egypt*; *Defence of the Nicene Definition*; *History of the Arians*; *On the Councils of Ariminum and Seleucia*. The Nicene and Post-Nicene Fathers. Second Series. Volume IV. Edited by

Philip Schaff D.D., LL.D. and Henry Wace. Grand Rapids, MI: Eerdmans, August 1975, repr.

Saint Basil. *Letters and Select Works*: *On the Spirit*; *The Hexaemeron*. The Nicene and Post-Nicene Fathers. Second Series. Volume VIII. Translated by Rev. Blomfield Jackson, M.A. Grand Rapids, MI: Eerdmans, June 1975, repr.
——*Ascetical Works: Give Heed to Thyself*; *On Detachment from Worldly Goods and Concerning the Conflagration Which Occurred in the Environs of the Church*; *On Renunciation of the World*; *The Long Rules*. The Fathers of the Church. 3rd ed. Volume 9. Translated by Sister S. Monica Wagner, C.S.C. Washington, D.C.: CUA, 1970.
——*Exegetic Homilies*. The Fathers of the Church. 2nd ed. Volume 46. Translated by Sister Agnes Clare Way, C.P.D. Washington, D.C.: CUA Press, 1981.

Saint Bede the Venerable. *Homilies on the Gospels*. Book One: Advent to Lent. Translated by Lawrence T. Martin & David Hurst OSB. Cistercian Studies Series: No. 110. Kalamazoo, MI: Cistercian Publications, 1991. Translated from *Corpus Christianorum*, 122. Turnhout: Brepols, 1955.
——*Homilies on the Gospels*. Book Two: Lent to the Dedication of the Church. Translated by Lawrence T. Martin & David Hurst OSB. Cistercian Studies Series: No. 111. Kalamazoo, MI: Cistercian Publications, 1991. Translated from *Corpus Christianorum*, 122. Turnhout: Brepols, 1955.
——*Commentary on the Seven Catholic Epistles*. Cistercian Studies Series: No. 82. Translated by Monk David Hurst. Kalamazoo, MI: Cistercian Publications, 1985.

Saint Cyprian. *The Epistles of Cyprian*; *The Treatises of Cyprian*. The Ante-Nicene Fathers, Fathers of the Third Century. Volume V. Translated by Rev. Ernest Wallis, Ph.D., and Rev. Alexander Roberts, D.D. and James Donaldson, LL.D., Editors. Grand Rapids, MI: Wm. B. Eerdmans Pub. Co., December 1986, repr.
——*Letters 1-81*. The Fathers of the Church. 2nd ed. Volume 51. Translated by Sister Rose Bernard Donna, C.S.J. Washington, D.C.: CUA Press, 1981.

Saint Cyril (Kyril) of Alexandria. *Commentary on the Gospel of Saint Luke*. Translated by R. Payne Smith. New York: Studion Publishers, 1983.

Saint Cyril (Kyril) of Jerusalem. *Catechetical Lectures*. The Nicene and Post-Nicene Fathers. Second Series. Volume VII. Revised translation by Edwin Hamilton Gifford, D.D. Edited by Philip Schaff D.D., LL.D. and Henry Wace, D.D. Grand Rapids, MI: Eerdmans, August 1974, repr.
——*The Works of Saint Cyril of Jerusalem: Catechesis, Volume 1*. The Fathers of the Church. Volume 61. Translated by Leo P. McCauley, S.J. and Anthony A. Stephenson. Washington, D.C.: CUA, n.d.
——*The Works of Saint Cyril of Jerusalem: Catechesis, Volume 2*. The Fathers of the Church. Volume 64. Translated by Leo P. McCauley, S.J. and Anthony A. Stephenson. Washington, D.C.: The CUA Press, n.d.
——*Letters 1-50*. The Fathers of the Church. Volume 76. Translated by John I. McEnerney. Washington, D.C.: The CUA Press, 1987.

Saint Dionysios the Areopagite. *The Mystical Theology and the Celestial Hierarchies of Dionysius the Areopagite*. Translated by the Editors of The Shrine of Wisdom. Surrey, England: The Shrine of Wisdom, 1965.
——*The Complete Works: The Ecclesiastical Hierarchy*. Translated by Colm Luibheid with Paul Rorem. New York, NY: Paulist Press, 1987.

Saint Dorotheos of Gaza. *Discourses and Sayings*. Cistercian Studies Series. Number 33. Translated by Eric P. Wheeler. Kalamazoo, MI: Cistercian Publications, 1977.

Saint Ephraim Syrus. *Hymns and Homilies*. The Nicene and Post-Nicene Fathers of the Christian Church. Second Series. Volume XIII. Translated by Rev. J. B. Morris, M.A. Grand Rapids, MI: Wm. B. Eerdmans Pub. Co., 1976.
——*Commentary on Tatian's Diatessaron*. Journal of Semitic Studies Supplement 2, an English translation of Chester Beatty, Syriac MS 709 with introduction and notes by Carmel McCarthy. Cary, NC: Oxford University Press, 1993.
——*The Luminous Eye: The Medicine of Life*. Cistercian Studies Series: Number One-Hundred Twenty-Four. Translated by Sebastian Brock. Kalamazoo, MI: Cistercian Publications, 1992.

Saint Epiphanios. *The Panarion of Saint Epiphanius, Bishop of Salamis: Selected Passages*. Translated and edited by Philip R. Amidon, S.J. NY/Oxford: Oxford University Press, 1990.

Saint Gregory Nazianzen [actually, the Theologian]. *Epistles* and *Orations*. The Nicene and Post-Nicene Fathers of the Christian Church. Second Series. Volume VII. Translated by Charles Gordon Browne, M.A., and James Edward Swallow, M.A. Edited by Philip Schaff, D.D., LL.D., and Henry Wace, D.D. Grand Rapids, MI: Wm. B. Eerdmans Pub. Co., August 1974, repr.

Saint Gregory of Nyssa. *Against Eunomius*; *Ascetic and Moral, On Virginity*; *Oratorical, On the Baptism of Christ*. The Nicene & Post-Nicene Fathers. Second Series. Volume V. Translated by Wm. Moore, M.A. and H. A. Wilson, M.A. Edited by Philip Schaff, D.D., LL.D and Henry Wace, D.D. Grand Rapids, MI: Wm. B. Eerdmans Pub., n.d.
——*Commentary on the Song of Songs*. Translated by Casimir McCambley OCSO. Brookline, MA: Hellenic College Press, 1987.

Saint Gregory Palamas. *The One Hundred and Fifty Chapters*. Pontifical Institute of Mediaeval Studies and Texts 83. Translated and edited by Robert E. Sinkewicz. Toronto, Ontario, Canada: Pontifical Institute of Mediaeval Studies, 1988.
——*The Triads*. The Classics of Western Spirituality. Translated by Nicholas Gendle. New York, NY: Paulist Press, 1983.

Saint Gregory the Great. *The Book of Pastoral Rule*; *Selected Epistles*. The Nicene and Post-Nicene Fathers of the Christian Church. Second Series. Volume XII. Translated

by Rev. James Barmby, D.D. Edited by Philip Schaff, D.D., LL.D., and Henry Wace, D.D. Grand Rapids, MI: Wm. B. Eerdmans Pub. Co., September 1979, repr.
——*Selected Epistles*. The Nicene and Post-Nicene Fathers of the Christian Church, Second Series. Volume XIII. Translated by Rev. James Barmby, D.D. Edited by Philip Schaff, D.D., LL.D., and Henry Wace, D.D. Grand Rapids, MI: Wm. B. Eerdmans Pub. Co., May 1976, repr.
——*The Homilies of Saint Gregory the Great On the Book of the Prophet Ezekiel*. Translated by T. Gray. Edited by J. Cownie. Etna, CA: Center for Traditionalist Orthodox Studies, 1990.
——*Forty Gospel Homilies*. Cistercian Studies Series: One Hundred Twenty-Three. Translated from the Latin by Dom David Hurst. Kalamazoo, MI: Cistercian Publications, 1990.
——*Dialogues*. The Fathers of the Church. 2nd ed. Volume 39. Translated by Odo John Zimmerman, O.S.B. Washington, D.C.: CUA Press, 1983.

Saint Hilary of Poitiers. *On the Councils*; *On the Trinity*. The Nicene and Post-Nicene Fathers of the Christian Church. Second Series. Volume IX. Translated by Rev. E. W. Watson, M.A., Rev. L. Pullan, M.A. Edited by Rev. W. Sanday, D.D., LL.D. Grand Rapids, MI: Eerdmans, August 1976, repr.

Saint Hippolytus. *Against the Heresy of One Noetus*; *The Extant Works and Fragments of Hippolytus*; *Treatise on Christ and Antichrist*. Fathers of the Third Century, The Ante-Nicene Fathers. Volume V. Translated by the Rev. S.D.F. Salmond. Edited by Rev. Alexander Roberts, D.D. and James Donaldson, LL.D. Grand Rapids, MI: Eerdmans Pub. Co., December 1986, repr.

Saint Ignatius. *Epistles*. The Apostolic Fathers, The Ante-Nicene Fathers, The Writings of the Fathers down to A.D. 325. Volume I. Edited by Rev. Alexander Roberts, D.D. and James Donaldson, LL.D. Grand Rapids, MI: Eerdmans, May 1987, repr.

Saint Irenaeos. *Against Heresies*. The Apostolic Fathers. The Ante-Nicene Fathers: The Writings of the Fathers down to A.D. 325. Volume I. Edited by Rev. Alexander Roberts, D.D. and James Donaldson, LL.D., and notes in American edition by A. Cleveland Coxe, D.D. Grand Rapids, MI: Wm. B. Eerdmans Publishing Co., May 1987, repr.
——*Proof of the Apostolic Preaching*. Ancient Christian Writers. Volume 16. Translated and annotated by Joseph P. Smith, S.J. NY: Newman Press, n.d.

Saint Isaac the Syrian. *Mystical Treatises by Isaac of Nineveh*. Translated from Bedjan's Syriac text, by Arent Jan Wensinck. Volume One and Volume Two.

Saint Jerome. *Letters and Select Works*. The Nicene and Post-Nicene Fathers. Second Series. Volume VI. Translated by the Hon. W. H. Fremantle, M.A., Rev. G. Lewis, M.A., and Rev. W.G. Martley. M.A. Grand Rapids, MI: Eerdmans, October 1983, repr.

——*1-59 On The Psalms, Volume 1*. The Fathers of the Church. 2nd ed. Volume 48. Translated by Sister Marie Liguori Ewald, I.H.M. Washington, D.C.: CUA Press, 1981, repr.
——*60-96 On The Psalms, Volume 2*. The Fathers of the Church. 2nd ed. Volume 57. Translated by Sister Marie Liguori Ewald, I.H.M. Washington, D.C.: CUA Press, n.d.
——*Dogmatic and Polemical Works*. The Fathers of the Church. Volume 53. Translated by John N. Hritzu, Ph.D. Washington, D.C.: CUA Press, n.d.

Saint John Cassian. The Works of John Cassian: *Conferences* and *Institutes*. The Nicene and Post-Nicene Fathers of the Christian Church, Second Series. Volume XI. Translated by Edgar C. S. Gibson, M.A. Edited by Philip Schaff, D.D., LL.D. and Henry Wace, D.D. Grand Rapids, MI: Wm. B. Eerdmans Publishing Co., June 1978, repr.

Saint John Chrysostom. *Baptismal Instructions*. Ancient Christian Writers. Number 31. Translated by Paul W. Harkins, Ph.D., LL.D. NY/NJ: Newman Press, n.d.
——*Discourses Against Judaizing Christians*. The Fathers of the Church. Volume 68. Translated by Paul W. Harkins. Washington, D.C.: CUA Press, 1979.
——*On the Incomprehensible Nature of God*. The Fathers of the Church. Volume 72. Translated by Paul W. Harkins. Washington, D.C.: CUA Press, 1988, repr.
——*Apologist: Demonstration Against the Pagans that Christ is God*. The Fathers of the Church. Volume 73. Translated by Margaret A. Schatkin and Paul W. Harkins. Washington, D.C.: CUA Press, 1985.
——*Homilies on Genesis*. The Fathers of the Church. Volume 74. Translated by Robert C. Hill. Washington, D.C.: CUA Press, 1986.
——*Old Testament Homilies: Homilies on Isaiah and Jeremiah*. Translated by Robert Charles Hill. Brookline, MA: Holy Cross Orthodox Press, 2003.
——*Instructions to Catechumens*; *Letters to the Fallen Theodore*; *An Exhortation to Theodore After His Fall; On the Statues*. The Nicene and Post-Nicene Fathers of the Christian Church. First Series. Volume IX. Translated by Rev. W. R. W. Stephens, M.A. Edited by Philip Schaff, D.D., LL.D. Grand Rapids, MI: Wm. B. Eerdmans Publishing Co, June 1975, repr.
——*Homilies on the Gospel of Matthew*. The Nicene and Post-Nicene Fathers of the Christian Church. First Series. Volume X. Translated by Rev. Sir George Prevost, Baronet, M.A., Philip Schaff, D.D., LL.D. Edited and revised, with notes by Rev. M. B. Riddle D.D. Grand Rapids, MI: Eerdmans Pub., Co., 1975.
——*Homilies on Acts and Romans*. The Nicene and Post-Nicene Fathers of the Christian Church. First Series. Volume XI. Edited by Philip Schaff, D.D., LL.D. Grand Rapids, MI: Wm. B. Eerdmans Publishing Co., June 1975, repr.
——*Homilies on First and Second Corinthians*. The Nicene and Post-Nicene Fathers of the Christian Church, First Series. Volume XII. Edited by Philip Schaff, D.D., LL.D. Grand Rapids, MI: Wm. B. Eerdmans Pub. Co. July 1969, repr.
——*Homilies on Galatians, Ephesians, Philippians, Colossians, Thessalonians, Timothy, Titus, and Philemon*. The Nicene and Post-Nicene Fathers. First Series.

Volume XIII. Edited by Philip Schaff, D.D., LL.D. Grand Rapids, MI: Eerdmans, May 1976, repr.
——*Homilies on the Gospel of Saint John and the Epistle to the Hebrews*. The Nicene and Post-Nicene Fathers of the Christian Church. First Series. Volume XIV. Edited by Philip Schaff, D.D., LL.D. Grand Rapids, MI: Wm. B. Eerdmans Pub. Co., August 1975, repr.

Saint John of Damascus. *Exposition of the Orthodox Faith*. The Nicene and Post-Nicene Fathers of the Christian Church. Second Series. Volume IX. Translated S.D.F. Salmond, D.D., F.E.I.S. Grand Rapids, MI: Wm. B. Eerdmans Pub. Co., August 1976, repr.
——*On the Images*. Translated by David Anderson. Crestwood, NY: Saint Vladimir's Seminary Press, 1980.

Saint Justin. *Dialogue with Trypho*; *Hortatory Address to the Greeks*; *On the Resurrection*; *The First Apology*. The Ante-Nicene Fathers, The Apostolic Fathers. Volume I. Rev. Alexander Roberts, D.D. and James Donaldson, LL.D., Editors, and notes in American edition by A. Cleveland Coxe, D.D. Grand Rapids, MI: Wm. B. Eerdmans Publishing Co., May 1987, repr.
——*Writings of Saint Justin Martyr: Dialogue with Trypho*. The Fathers of the Church. 3rd ed. Volume 6. Translated by Thomas B. Falls, D.D., Ph.D. Washington, D.C.: CUA Press, 1977.

Saint Leo the Great. *Select Letters and Sermons*. The Nicene and Post-Nicene Fathers. Second Series. Volume XII. Translated by Rev. Charles Lett Feltoe, M.A. Edited by Philip Schaff, D.D., LL.D and Henry Wace, D.D. Grand Rapids, MI: Eerdmans, September 1979, repr.

Saint Makarios (Macarius) the Great. *Fifty Spiritual Homilies*. Translated by A. J. Mason. Willits, CA: Eastern Orthodox Books, 1974.

Saint Maximus the Confessor. *Selected Writings: The Four Hundred Chapters on Love*. The Classics of Western Spirituality. Translated by George C. Berthold. New York/Mahwah/Toronto: Paulist Press, 1985.

Saint Paulinus. *The Poems of Saint Paulinus of Nola*. Ancient Christian Writers. Number 40. Translated and annotated by P. G. Walsh. NY, NY: Newman Press, n.d.
——*Letters of Saint Paulinus of Nola: Letters 1-22, Volume 1*. Ancient Christian Writers. Number 35. Translated and annotated by P. G. Walsh. NY, NY: Newman Press, n.d.
——*Letters of Saint Paulinus of Nola: Letters 23-51, Volume 2*. Ancient Christian Writers. Number 36. Translated and annotated by P. G. Walsh. NY, NY: Newman Press, n.d.

Saint Photios. *On the Mystagogy of the Holy Spirit*. Translated by Ronald Wertz. NY: Studion Publishers, 1983.

Saint Romanos the Melodist. *Kontakia of Romanos, Byzantine Melodist*. Volume I. Translated and annotated by Marjorie Carpenter. MO: University of Missouri Press, 1970.

Saint Symeon the New Theologian. *The Discourses*. The Classics of Western Spirituality Series. Translated by C. J. deCatanzaro. NY: Paulist Press, 1980.
——*On the Mystical Life: The Ethical Discourses*. Volume 1. Translated by Alexander Golitzin. Crestwood, NY: Saint Vladimir's Seminary Press, 1995.

Saint Thalassios the Libyan. *The Philokalia*. Volume Two. Translated by G. E. H. Palmer, Philip Sherrard, and Kallistos Ware. London/Boston: Faber and Faber, 1984, repr.

Saint Glykeria
(May 13th)

ALPHABETICAL INDEX OF MAY SYNAXARISTES

All the Saints Entering into Paradise

For Ordering: HOLY APOSTLES CONVENT, 29001 County Road 187, P.O. Box 3118, Buena Vista, Colorado 81211. Telephone 719-395-8898; Facsimile 719-395-9422. Http://www.HolyApostlesConvent.org. The Greek fonts in this work are available from https://www.linguistsoftware.com/lgku.htm.